SOCIAL SECURITY LEGISLATION 2024/25

VOLUME II: UNIVERSAL CREDIT, STATE PENSION CREDIT AND THE SOCIAL FUND

SOCIAL SECURITY LEGISLATION 2024/25

General Editor
Nick Wikeley, M.A. (Cantab)

VOLUME II: UNIVERSAL CREDIT, STATE PENSION CREDIT AND THE SOCIAL FUND

Commentary By

John Mesher, B.A., B.C.L. (Oxon), LL.M. (Yale)
Retired Judge of the Upper Tribunal
Emeritus Professor of Law,
University of Sheffield

Tom Royston, M.A. (Cantab)
Barrister

Nick Wikeley, M.A. (Cantab)
Judge of the Upper Tribunal,
Emeritus Professor of Law,
University of Southampton

Consultant Editor
Child Poverty Action Group

Sweet & Maxwell

Published in 2024 by Thomson Reuters, trading as Sweet & Maxwell.
Thomson Reuters is registered in England & Wales, Company
No.1679046. Registered Office and address for service: 5 Canada Square,
Canary Wharf, London, E14 5AQ.

For further information on our products and services, visit
http://www.sweetandmaxwell.co.uk

Typeset by Cheshire Typesetting Ltd, Stockport, Cheshire
Printed and bound by CPI Group (UK) Ltd, Croydon, CR0 4YY

A CIP catalogue record for this book is available
from the British Library

ISBN (print): 978-0-414-121508
ISBN (e-book): 978-0-414-121522
ISBN (print and e-book): 978-0-414-121515

For orders and enquiries,
go to: *http://www.tr.com/uki-legal-contact*; Tel: 0345 600 9355.

CHILD POVERTY ACTION GROUP

The Child Poverty Action Group ("CPAG") is a charity, founded in 1965, which campaigns for the relief of poverty in the UK. It has a particular reputation in the field of welfare benefits law derived from its legal work, publications, training and parliamentary and policy work, and is widely recognised as the leading organisation for taking test cases on social security law.

CPAG is therefore ideally placed to act as Consultant Editor to this five-volume work—**Social Security Legislation**. CPAG is not responsible for the detail of what is contained in each volume, and the authors' views are not necessarily those of CPAG. The Consultant Editor's role is to act in an advisory capacity on the overall structure, focus and direction of the work.

For more information about CPAG, its rights and policy publications or training courses, its address is 30 Micawber Street, London, N1 7TB (telephone: 020 7837 7979—website: *http://www.cpag.org.uk*).

FOREWORD

These volumes of *Social Security Legislation* are an indispensable resource for the judiciary of the First-tier Tribunal (Social Entitlement Chamber) and all those involved in social security proceedings. Along with expert commentaries, they provide comprehensive, up-to-date and learned coverage of this vast and complex field of law. Given the scale and complexity of the legislation and the continuing development of the jurisprudence by the Upper Tribunal and appellate courts, the subject matter would be practically inaccessible without these books. As ever, I am grateful to the authors and to Sweet and Maxwell for their continued commitment to producing them each year.

Judge Kate Markus KC
Chamber President of the First-tier Tribunal,
Social Entitlement Chamber

PREFACE

Universal Credit, State Pension Credit and the Social Fund is Volume II of *Social Security Legislation 2024/25*. The companion volumes are Volume I: *Non-Means Tested Benefits*; Volume III: *Administration, Adjudication and the European Dimension*; Volume IV: *HMRC-administered Social Security Benefits and Scotland*; and (from 2021/22) *Volume V: Income Support and the Legacy Benefits*. The "year" in the title of the works relates to the tax/contribution year, and conveys the period the books (and the mid-year Supplement) are designed to cover.

The present volume covers the three current Department for Work and Pensions means-tested benefits: universal credit, state pension credit and social fund payments for maternity and funeral expenses and for cold weather and winter fuel. The primary legislation relevant to all those benefits is in Part I and the regulations are in Parts II (universal credit), III (state pension credit) and IV (social fund). Part V covers the current provisions on persons subject to immigration control as relevant to those benefits. The relevant provisions on claims and payments and on decisions and appeals are now to be found in Volume III of this series, *Administration, Adjudication and the European Dimension*, as for other benefits. The operative Commencement Orders for the Welfare Reform Act 2012 are to be found in Volume V of this series, *Income Support and the Legacy Benefits 2021/22*, as up-dated in the Cumulative Supplements to be found at the end of the present volume and in mid-year Supplements. Those Orders now have primary relevance to the abolition of legacy benefits for new claims and to savings provisions. Provisions restricted to those living in Scotland and administered by the Scottish Ministers are covered in Volume IV of this series. Housing benefit, as administered by local authorities, is not covered by this series: see *CPAG's Housing Benefit and Council Benefit Legislation*.

Three years ago we began the process of restructuring the series to reflect the fact that universal credit (UC) has now become the default means-tested benefit in the social security system. That resulted in some re-ordering of material across the Volumes to provide readers with a clear and coherent explanation (at least so far as we can) of the various social security benefits (see further the Note on Restructuring the Social Security Legislation Series at p.xi of last year's edition of this volume).

Each of the volumes in the series provides the text of benefits legislation in Great Britain, clearly showing the form and date of amendments, and is up to date to April 11, 2024. There have been scarcely any changes to primary legislation within the scope of Volume II this year (a special gold star to any reader who spots where they are). However, this edition includes the usual miscellany of detailed amendments made by secondary legislation beyond the annual up-rating of benefit rates, in particular to take account of developments in the provision of devolved benefits in Scottish legislation and in the proliferating range of compensation schemes, as well as changes in administrative arrangements. Perhaps the amendments closest to the core purposes of the UC scheme have been the increases to the level of earnings known as the administrative earnings threshold (AET) bringing many thousands more claimants who are in work within the scope of full conditionality and subjection to all work-related requirements. The commentary provides extensive and in-depth analysis of such developments. Where possible, the commentary includes references to some later case law since April 11, 2024, and there is discussion of the botched implementation of further increases to the AET in May 2024.

There has been a steady, though slow, flow of UC decisions from the Upper Tribunal, including two decisions finding aspects of the regulations on transitional protection where a claimant "migrates" from a legacy benefit to UC to breach the Human Rights Act 1998 as discriminatory and therefore not to be applied: *FL v Secretary of State for Work and Pensions (UC)* [2024] UKUT 6 (AAC) and *Secretary of State for Work and Pensions v JA (UC)* [2024] UKUT 52 (AAC). As the pace of migration increases, as it is forecast to do, such problems are likely to become more significant. This edition also considers the implications of the refusal of permission to appeal to the Supreme Court from the decision in *Secretary of State for Work and Pensions v AT* [2023] EWCA Civ 1307 on the right to reside rules.

As always, revising and updating the legislative text and commentary has required considerable flexibility on the part of the publisher and a great deal of help from a number of sources, including CPAG as advisory editor to the series. We remain grateful for this assistance in our task of providing an authoritative reflection on the current state of the law.

Users of the series, and its predecessor works, have over the years contributed to their effectiveness by providing valuable comments on our commentary, as well as pointing out where the text of some provision has been omitted in error, or become garbled, or not been brought fully up to date. In some cases, this has drawn attention to an error which might otherwise have gone unnoticed for many years. In providing such feedback, users of the work have helped to shape the content and ensure the accuracy of our material. We hope that users of the work will continue to provide such helpful input and feedback. This is all the more important given the major restructuring of the series that has taken place. Please write to the General Editor of the series, Emeritus Professor Nick Wikeley, c/o School of Law, University of Southampton, Highfield, Southampton SO17 1BJ, e-mail njw@soton.ac.uk, and he will pass on any comments received to the appropriate commentator.

Our gratitude also goes to the Chamber President of the Social Entitlement Chamber of the First-tier Tribunal and her colleagues there for continuing the now long tradition of help and encouragement in our endeavours.

Last, but by no means least, we wish to recognise that the 2023/24 main edition of Volume III in this series was the last for which Mark Rowland had a direct responsibility (although much of what he has written will undoubtedly continue to feature in the book for many editions to come). The current editors of all the volumes would like to take this opportunity to pay tribute to Mark's tremendous contribution to the series as a whole since 1993, when he first produced the volume on *Medical and Disability Appeal Tribunals* that went into three editions before the restructuring of the series in 2000. In that restructuring, he took on joint responsibility with Robin White for Volume III, *Administration, Adjudication and the European*

Dimension. Thus, for more than 20 years Mark has brought his formidable knowledge and experience of social security law and adjudication, from his work as an advocate, as a part-time chair of appeal tribunals and then as a Social Security Commissioner and later Upper Tribunal Judge to bear on the often opaque legislative material on administration, decision-making and appeals. As readers will know, his gift for clarity of exposition enabled his commentary both to bring out matters of principle and to provide practical guidance to tribunals and users with an appreciation of the way problems actually arise. More behind the scenes, Mark's contribution to the way in which the series as a whole has developed, from wise advice about the needs of readers to knowledge of why choices were or were not made over the years, cannot be overstated. The current editors will greatly miss having that wisdom and experience on tap.

August 2024

John Mesher
Tom Royston
Nick Wikeley

CONTENTS

PART IIB
TRANSITIONAL AND SAVINGS PROVISIONS

PART III
STATE PENSION CREDIT REGULATIONS

PART IV
THE SOCIAL FUND

PART V
PERSONS SUBJECT TO IMMIGRATION CONTROL

SUPPLEMENT MATERIAL TO VOLUME V

USING THIS BOOK: AN INTRODUCTION TO LEGISLATION AND CASE LAW

Introduction

This book is not a general introduction to, or general textbook on, the law relating to social security but it is nonetheless concerned with both of the principal sources of social security law—*legislation* (both primary and secondary) and *case law*. It sets out the text of the most important legislation, as currently in force, and then there is added commentary that refers to the relevant case law. Lawyers will be familiar with this style of publication, which inevitably follows the structure of the legislation.

This note is designed primarily to assist readers who are not lawyers to find their way around the legislation and to understand the references to case law, but information it contains about how to find social security case law is intended to be of assistance to lawyers too.

Primary legislation

Primary legislation of the United Kingdom Parliament consists of *Acts of Parliament* (also known as *Statutes*). They will have been introduced to Parliament as *Bills*. There are opportunities for Members of Parliament and peers to debate individual clauses and to vote on amendments before a Bill is passed and becomes an Act (at which point the clauses become sections). No tribunal or court has the power to disapply, or hold to be invalid, an Act of Parliament, although, until December 31, 2020, that could be done if it was inconsistent with European Union law.

An Act is known by its "short title", which incorporates the year in which it was passed (e.g. the Social Security Contributions and Benefits Act 1992), and is given a chapter number (abbreviated as, for instance, "c.4" indicating that the Act was the fourth passed in that year). It is seldom necessary to refer to the chapter number but it appears in the running headers in this book.

Each *section* (abbreviated as "s." or, in the plural, "ss.") of an Act is numbered and may be divided into *subsections* (abbreviated as "subs." and represented by a number in brackets), which in turn may be divided into *paragraphs* (abbreviated as "para." and represented by a lower case letter in brackets) and *subparagraphs* (abbreviated as "subpara." and represented by a small roman numeral in brackets). Subparagraph (ii) of para.(a) of subs.(1) of s.72 will usually be referred to simply as "s.72(1)(a)(ii)". Upper case letters may be used where additional sections or subsections are inserted by amendment and additional lower case letters may be used where new paragraphs and subparagraphs are inserted. This accounts for the rather ungainly s.109B(2A)(aa) of the Social Security Administration Act 1992.

Sections of a large Act may be grouped into a numbered *Part*, which may even be divided into *Chapters*. It is not usual to refer to a Part or a Chapter unless referring to the whole Part or Chapter.

Where a section would otherwise become unwieldy because it is necessary to include a list or complicated technical provisions, the section may simply refer to a *Schedule* at the end of the Act. A Schedule (abbreviated as "Sch.") may be divided into paragraphs and subparagraphs and further divided into heads and subheads. Again, it is usual to refer simply to, say, "para.23(3)(b)(ii) of Sch.3". Whereas it is conventional to speak of a section *of* an Act, it is usual to speak of a Schedule *to* an Act.

Secondary legislation

Secondary legislation (also known as *subordinate legislation* or *delegated legislation)* is made by *statutory instrument* in the form of a set of *Regulations* or a set of *Rules* or an *Order*. The power to make such legislation is conferred on ministers and other persons or bodies by Acts of Parliament. To the extent that a statutory instrument is made beyond the powers (in Latin, *ultra vires*) conferred by primary legislation, it may be held by a tribunal or court to be invalid and ineffective. Secondary legislation must be laid before Parliament. However, most secondary legislation is not debated in Parliament and, even when it is, it cannot be amended although an entire statutory instrument may be rejected.

A set of Regulations or Rules or an Order has a name indicating its scope and the year it was made and also a number, as in the Social Security (Disability Living Allowance) Regulations 1991 (SI 1991/2890) (the 2890th statutory instrument issued in 1991). Because there are over a thousand statutory instruments each year, the number of a particular statutory instrument is important as a means of identification and it should usually be cited the first time reference is made to that statutory instrument.

Sets of Regulations or Rules are made up of individual *regulations* (abbreviated as "reg.") or *rules* (abbreviated as "r." or, in the plural, "rr."). An Order is made up of *articles* (abbreviated as "art."). Regulations, rules and articles may be divided into paragraphs, subparagraphs and heads. As in Acts, a set of Regulations or Rules or an Order may have one or more Schedules attached to it. The style of numbering used in statutory instruments is the same as in sections of, and Schedules to, Acts of Parliament. As in Acts, a large statutory instrument may have regulations or rules grouped into Parts and, occasionally, Chapters. Statutory instruments may be amended in the same sort of way as Acts.

Scottish legislation

Most of the social security legislation passed by the United Kingdom Parliament applies throughout Great Britain, i.e. in England, Wales and Scotland, but a separate Scottish social security system is gradually being developed and relevant legislation is included in Volume IV in this series. Acts of the Scottish Parliament are similar to Acts of the United Kingdom Parliament and Scottish Statutory Instruments are also similar to their United Kingdom counterparts. One minor difference is that "schedule" usually has a lower case "s" and references are to a schedule *of* an Act, rather than *to* an Act.

Northern Ireland legislation

Most of the legislation set out in this series applies only in Great Britain, social security not generally being an excepted or reserved matter in relation to Northern Ireland. However, Northern Irish legislation—both primary legislation, most relevantly in the form of *Orders in Council* (which, although statutory instruments, had the effect of primary legislation in Northern Ireland while there was direct rule from Westminster and still do when made under the Northern Ireland (Welfare Reform) Act 2015) and *Acts of the Northern Ireland Assembly*, and subordinate legislation, in the form of *statutory rules*—largely replicates legislation in Great Britain so that much of the commentary in this book will be applicable to equivalent provisions in Northern Ireland legislation. Although there has latterly been a greater reluctance in Northern Ireland to maintain parity with Great Britain, one example of which led to some delay in enacting legislation equivalent to the Welfare Reform Act 2012, this is usually resolved politically by, for instance, the allocation of funds to allow the effects of some of the changes to be mitigated in Northern Ireland while the broad legislative structure remains similar.

European Union legislation

European Union primary legislation is in the form of the *Treaties* agreed by the Member States. Relevant subordinate legislation is in the form of *Regulations*, adopted to give effect to the provisions of the Treaties, and *Directives*, addressed to Member States and requiring them to incorporate certain provisions into their domestic laws. Directives are relevant because, where a person brings proceedings against an organ of the State, as is invariably the case where social security is concerned, that person may rely on the Directive as having direct effect if the Member State has failed to comply with it. Treaties, Regulations and Directives are divided into *Articles* (abbreviated as "Art.").

While the United Kingdom was a Member State of the European Union, United Kingdom legislation that was inconsistent with European Union legislation had to be disapplied. The United Kingdom ceased to be a Member State on January 31, 2020, but the effect of the European Union (Withdrawal Act) 2018, as amended in 2020, is that, with very limited exceptions, European Union law continued to apply in the United Kingdom during the implementation period ending on December 31, 2020. After that date, European Union law remains relevant only to the extent that United Kingdom legislation so provides. For instance, the 2018 Act, as amended, provides for the enforcement of the Withdrawal Agreement, under which rights acquired by individuals before the end of the implementation period may be retained.

Finding legislation in this book

If you know the name of the piece of legislation for which you are looking, use the list of contents at the beginning of each volume of this series which lists the pieces of legislation contained in the volume. That will give you the paragraph reference to enable you to find the beginning of the piece of legislation. Then, it is easy to find the relevant section, regulation, rule, article or Schedule by using the running headers on the right hand pages. If you do not know the name of the piece of legislation, you will probably need to use the index at the end of the volume in order to find the relevant paragraph number but will then be taken straight to a particular provision.

The legislation is set out as amended, the amendments being indicated by numbered sets of square brackets. The numbers refer to the numbered entries under the heading "AMENDMENTS" at the end of the relevant section, regulation, rule, article or Schedule, which identify the amending statute or statutory instrument. Where an Act has been consolidated, there is a list of "DERIVATIONS" identifying the provisions of earlier legislation from which the section or Schedule has been derived.

As regards the European Union, United Kingdom legislation concerned with the consequences of the United Kingdom's withdrawal is set out in Part V of Volume III in this series, together with relevant extracts from the Withdrawal Agreement and the Social Security Protocol to the Trade and Cooperation Agreement. Following the extracts from the Withdrawal Agreement is up-dating commentary on the European Union legislation that is set out in Part III of the 2020-21 edition of Volume III. Readers are encouraged to retain that volume so as to be able to find the main text of relevant European Union legislation there.

Finding other legislation

United Kingdom legislation and legislation made by the legislatures in Scotland, Wales and Northern Ireland may now be found on *http://www.legislation.gov.uk* in both its original form and (usually) its amended form. Northern Ireland social security legislation may also be found at *https://www.communities-ni.gov.uk/services/law-relating-social-security-northern-ireland-blue-volumes*. European Union legislation may be found at *https://eur-lex.europa.eu/homepage.html*.

Interpreting legislation

Legislation is written in English (or, at least, there is an official English version) and generally means what it says. However, languages being complicated, more than one interpretation is often possible. Most legislation itself contains definitions. Sometimes these are in the particular provision in which a word occurs but, where a word is used in more than one place, any definition will appear with others. In an Act, an interpretation section is usually to be found towards the end of the Act or of the relevant Part of the Act. In a statutory instrument, an interpretation provision usually appears near the beginning of the statutory instrument or the relevant Part of it. In the more important pieces of legislation in this series, there is included after every section, regulation, rule, article or Schedule a list of "DEFINITIONS", showing where definitions of words used in the provision are to be found.

However, not all words are statutorily defined and there is in any event more to interpreting legislation than merely defining its terms (see the note to s.3(1) of the Tribunals, Courts and Enforcement Act 2007 in Part III of Volume III of this series). Decision-makers and tribunals need to know how to apply the law in different types of situations. That is where case law comes in.

Case law and the commentary in this book

In deciding individual cases, courts and tribunals interpret the relevant law and incidentally establish legal principles. Decisions on questions of legal principle of the superior courts and appellate tribunals are said to be binding on decision-makers and the First-tier Tribunal, which means that decision-makers and the First-tier Tribunal must apply those principles. Thus the judicial decisions of the superior courts and appellate tribunals form part of the law. The commentary to the legislation in this series, under the heading "GENERAL NOTE" after a section, regulation, rule, article or Schedule, refers to this *case law.*

Most case law regarding social security benefits is in the form of decisions of the Upper Tribunal (Administrative Appeals Chamber), to which the functions of the former Social Security Commissioners and Child Support Commissioners in Great Britain were transferred on November 3, 2008. However, decisions of those Commissioners remain relevant, as are decisions of the Commissioners who still sit in Northern Ireland.

The commentary in this series is not itself binding on any decision-maker or tribunal because it is merely the opinion of the author. It is what is actually said in the legislation or in the judicial decision that is important. The legislation is set out in this series, but it will generally be necessary to look elsewhere for the precise words used in judicial decisions. The way that decisions are cited in the commentary enables that to be done.

The reporting of decisions of the Upper Tribunal and Commissioners

A few of the most important decisions of the Administrative Appeals Chamber of the Upper Tribunal are selected to be "reported" each year in the Administrative Appeals Chamber Reports (AACR), using the same criteria as were formerly used for reporting Commissioners' decisions in Great Britain. The selection is made by an editorial board of judges and decisions are selected for reporting only if they are of general importance and command the assent of at least a majority of the relevant judges. The term "reported" simply means that they are published in printed form as well as on the Internet (see *Finding case law*, below) with headnotes (i.e. summaries) and indexes, but reported decisions also have a greater precedential status than ordinary decisions (see *Judicial precedent* below).

A handful of Northern Ireland Commissioners' decisions are also selected for reporting in the Administrative Appeals Chamber Reports each year, the selection being made by the Chief Social Security Commissioner in Northern Ireland.

Citing case law

As has been mentioned, much social security case law is still to be found in decisions of Social Security Commissioners and Child Support Commissioners, even though the Commissioners have now effectively been abolished in Great Britain.

Reported decisions of Commissioners were known merely by a number or, more accurately, a series of letters and numbers beginning with an "R". The type of benefit in issue was indicated by letters in brackets (e.g. "IS" was income support, "P" was retirement pension, and so on) and the year in which the decision was selected for reporting or, from 2000, the year in which it was published as a reported decision, was indicated by the last two digits, as in *R(IS) 2/08.* In Northern Ireland there was a similar system until 2009, save that the type of benefit was identified by letters in brackets after the number, as in *R 1/07 (DLA).*

Unreported decisions of the Commissioners in Great Britain were known simply by their file numbers, which began with a "C", as in *CIS/2287/2008*. The letters following the "C" indicated the type of benefit in issue in the case. Scottish and, at one time, Welsh cases were indicated by a "S" or "W" immediately after the "C", as in *CSIS/467/2007*. The last four digits indicated the calendar year in which the case was registered, rather than the year it was decided. A similar system operated in Northern Ireland until 2009, save that the letters indicating the type of benefit appeared in brackets after the numbers and, from April 1999, the financial year rather than the calendar year was identified, as in *C 10/06-07 (IS)*.

Decisions of the Upper Tribunal, of courts and, since 2010, of the Northern Ireland Commissioners are generally known by the names of the parties (or just two of them in multi-party cases). In social security and some other types of cases, individuals are anonymised through the use of initials in the names of decisions of the Upper Tribunal and the Northern Ireland Commissioners. Anonymity is much rarer in the names of decisions of courts. In this series, the names of official bodies are also abbreviated in the names of decisions of the Upper Tribunal and the Northern Ireland Commissioners (e.g. "SSWP" for the Secretary of State for Work and Pensions, "HMRC" for Her/His Majesty's Revenue and Customs, "CMEC" for the Child Maintenance and Enforcement Commission, "DSD" for the Department for Social Development in Northern Ireland and "DC" for the Department for Communities in Northern Ireland). Since 2010, such decisions have also been given a "flag" in brackets to indicate the subject matter of the decision, which in social security cases indicates the principal benefit in issue in the case. Thus, the name of one universal credit case is *SSWP v AJ (UC)*.

Any decision of the Upper Tribunal, of a court since 2001 or of a Northern Ireland Commissioner since 2010 that has been intended for publication has also given a neutral citation number which enables the decision to be more precisely identified. This indicates, in square brackets, the year the decision was made (although in relation to decisions of the courts it sometimes merely indicates the year the number was issued) and also indicates the court or tribunal that made the decision (e.g. "UKUT" for the Upper Tribunal (which sits in Great Britain for social security purposes but throughout the United Kingdom for some others), "UT" for the separate Upper Tribunal for Scotland, "NICom" for a Northern Ireland Commissioner, "EWCA Civ" for the Civil Division of the Court of Appeal in England and Wales, "NICA" for the Court of Appeal in Northern Ireland, "CSIH" for the Inner House of the Court of Session (in Scotland), "UKSC" for the Supreme Court and so on). A number is added so that the reference is unique and finally, in the case of the Upper Tribunal or the High Court in England and Wales, the relevant chamber of the Upper Tribunal or the relevant division or other part of the High Court is identified (e.g."(AAC)" for the Administrative Appeals Chamber, "(Admin)" for the Administrative Court and so on). Examples of decisions of the Upper Tribunal and a Northern Ireland Commissioner with their neutral citation numbers are *SSWP v AJ (UC)* [2020] UKUT 48 (AAC) and *AR v DSD (IB)* [2010] NICom 6.

If the case is reported in the Administrative Appeals Chamber Reports or another series of law reports, a reference to the report usually follows the neutral citation number. Conventionally, this includes either the year the case was decided (in round brackets) or the year in which it was reported (in square brackets), followed by the volume number (if any), the name of the series of reports (in abbreviated form, so see the Table of Abbreviations at the beginning of each volume of this series) and either the page number or the case number. However, before 2010, cases reported in the Administrative Appeals Chamber Reports or with Commissioners' decisions were numbered in the same way as reported Commissioners' decisions. *Abdirahman v Secretary of State for Work and Pensions* [2007] EWCA Civ 657; [2008] 1 W.L.R. 254 (also reported as *R(IS) 8/07*) is a Court of Appeal decision, decided in 2007 but reported in 2008 in volume 1 of the Weekly Law Reports at page 254 and also in the 2007 volume of reported Commissioners' decisions. *NT v SSWP* [2009] UKUT 37 (AAC); *R(DLA) 1/09* is an Upper Tribunal case decided in 2009 and reported in the Administrative Appeals Chamber Reports in the same year. *Martin v Secretary of State for Work and Pensions* [2009] EWCA Civ 1289; [2010] AACR 9 is a decision of the Court of Appeal that was decided in 2009 and was the ninth decision reported in the Administrative Appeals Chamber Reports in 2010.

It is usually necessary to include the neutral citation number or a reference to a series of reports only the first time a decision is cited in any document. After that, the name of the case is usually sufficient.

All decisions of the Upper Tribunal that are on their website have neutral citation numbers. If you wish to refer a tribunal or decision-maker to a decision of the Upper Tribunal that does not have a neutral citation number, contact the office of the Administrative Appeals Chamber (*adminappeals@justice.gov.uk*) who will provide a number and add the decision to the website.

Decision-makers and claimants are entitled to assume that judges of both the First-tier Tribunal and the Upper Tribunal have immediate access to reported decisions of Commissioners or the Upper Tribunal and they need not provide copies, although it may sometimes be helpful to do so. However, where either a decision-maker or a claimant intends to rely on an unreported decision, it will be necessary to provide a copy of the decision to the judge and other members of the tribunal. A copy of the decision should also be provided to the other party before the hearing because otherwise it may be necessary for there to be an adjournment to enable that party to take advice on the significance of the decision.

Finding case law

The extensive references described above are used so as to enable people easily to find the full text of a decision. Most decisions of any significance since the late 1990s can be found on the Internet.

Decisions of the Upper Tribunal may be found at *https://www.gov.uk/administrative-appeals-tribunal-decisions*. The link from that page to "decisions made in 2015 or earlier" leads also to decisions of the Commissioners in Great Britain. This includes reported decisions since 1991 and other decisions considered likely to be of interest to tribunals and tribunal users since about 2000, together with a few older decisions. Decisions of Commissioners in Northern Ireland may be found on *https://iaccess.communities-ni.gov.uk/NIDOC*.

The Administrative Appeals Chamber Reports are also published by the Stationery Office in bound volumes which follow on from the bound volumes of Commissioners' decisions published from 1948.

Copies of decisions of the Administrative Appeals Chamber of the Upper Tribunal or of Commissioners that are otherwise unavailable may be obtained from the offices of the Upper Tribunal (Administrative Appeals Chamber) or, in Northern Ireland, from the Office of the Social Security and Child Support Commissioners.

Decisions of a wide variety of courts and tribunals in the United Kingdom may be found on the free website of the British and Irish Legal Information Institute, *http://www.bailii.org*. It includes all decisions of the Supreme Court and provides fairly comprehensive coverage of decisions given since about 1996 by the House of Lords and Privy Council and most of the higher courts in England and Wales, decisions given since 1998 by the Court of Session and decisions given since 2000 by the Court of Appeal and High Court in Northern Ireland. Some earlier decisions have been included, so it is always worth looking and, indeed, those decisions dating from 1873 or earlier and reported in the English Reports may be found through a link to *http://www.commonlii.org/uk/cases/EngR/*. Since 2022, decisions of the Upper Tribunal, the Employment Appeal Tribunal and most courts that sit in England and Wales are also to be found on The National Archives' website at *caselaw.nationalarchives.gov.uk/structured_search*. However, courts and tribunals that sit only in Wales, Scotland or Northern Ireland are not included there. Decisions of the Upper Tribunal for Scotland and of Scottish courts can be found at *https://www.scotcourts.gov.uk*.

Decisions of the Court of Justice of the European Union are all to be found at *https://curia.europa.eu*.

Decisions of the European Court of Human Rights are available at *https://www.echr.coe.int*.

Most decisions of the courts in social security cases, including decisions of the Court of Justice of the European Union on cases referred by United Kingdom courts and tribunals, are reported in the Administrative Appeals Chamber Reports or with the reported decisions of Commissioners and may therefore be found on the same websites and in the same printed series of reported decisions. So, for example, *R(I) 1/00* contains Commissioner's decision *CSI/12/1998*, the decision of the Court of Session upholding the Commissioner's decision and the decision of the House of Lords in *Chief Adjudication Officer v Faulds*, reversing the decision of the Court of Session. The most important decisions of the courts can also be found in the various series of law reports familiar to lawyers (in particular, in the *Law Reports*, the *Weekly Law Reports*, the *All England Law Reports*, the *Public and Third Sector Law Reports*, the *Industrial Cases Reports* and the *Family Law Reports*) but these are not widely available outside academic or other law libraries, or subscription-based websites. See the Table of Cases at the beginning of each volume of this series for all the places where a decision mentioned in that volume is reported.

If you know the name or number of a decision and wish to know where in a volume of this series there is a reference to it, use the Table of Cases or the Table of Commissioners' Decisions 1948–2009 in the relevant volume to find the paragraph(s) where the decision is mentioned.

Judicial precedent

As already mentioned, decisions of the Upper Tribunal, the Commissioners and the higher courts in Great Britain become case law because they set binding precedents which must be followed by decision-makers and the First-tier Tribunal in Great Britain. This means that, where the Upper Tribunal, Commissioner or court has decided a point of legal principle, decision-makers and appeal tribunals must make their decisions in conformity with the decision of the Upper Tribunal, Commissioner or court, applying the same principle and accepting the interpretation of the law contained in the decision. So a decision of the Upper Tribunal, a Commissioner or a superior court explaining what a term in a particular regulation means, lays down the definition of that term in much the same way as if the term had been defined in the regulations themselves. The decision may also help in deciding what the same term means when it is used in a different set of regulations, provided that the term appears to have been used in a similar context.

Only decisions on points of law set precedents that are binding and, strictly speaking, only decisions on points of law that were necessary to the overall conclusion reached by the Upper Tribunal, Commissioner or court are binding. Other parts of a decision (which used to be known as obiter dicta) may be regarded as helpful guidance but need not be followed if a decision-maker or the First-tier Tribunal is persuaded that there is a better approach. It is particularly important to bear this in mind in relation to older decisions of Social Security Commissioners because, until 1987, most rights of appeal to a Commissioner were not confined to points of law.

Where there is a conflict between precedents, a decision-maker or the First-tier Tribunal is generally free to choose between decisions of equal status. For these purposes, most decisions of the Upper Tribunal and decisions of Commissioners are of equal status. However, a decision-maker or First-tier Tribunal should generally prefer a reported decision to an unreported one unless the unreported decision was the later decision and the Commissioner or Upper Tribunal expressly decided not to follow the earlier reported decision. This is simply because the fact that a decision has been reported shows that at least half of the relevant judges of the Upper Tribunal or the Commissioners agreed with it at the time. A decision of a Tribunal of Commissioners (i.e. three Commissioners sitting together) or a decision of a three-judge panel of the Upper Tribunal must be preferred to a decision of a single Commissioner or a single judge of the Upper Tribunal.

A single judge of the Upper Tribunal will normally follow a decision of a single Commissioner or another judge of the Upper Tribunal, but is not bound to do so. A three-judge panel of the Upper Tribunal will generally follow a decision of another such panel or of a Tribunal of Commissioners, but similarly is not bound to do so, whereas a single judge of the Upper Tribunal will always follow such a decision.

Strictly speaking, the Northern Ireland Commissioners do not set binding precedent that must be followed in Great Britain but their decisions are relevant, due to the similarity of the legislation in Northern Ireland, and are usually regarded as highly persuasive with the result that, in practice, they are generally given as much weight as decisions of the Great Britain Commissioners. The same approach is taken in Northern Ireland to decisions of the Upper Tribunal on social security matters and to decisions of the Great Britain Commissioners. Similarly, the Upper Tribunal and the Upper Tribunal for Scotland are likely to find each other's decisions persuasive where the issues are the same, or similar.

Decisions of the superior courts in Great Britain and Northern Ireland on questions of legal principle are almost invariably followed by decision-makers, tribunals and the Upper Tribunal, even when they are not strictly binding because the relevant court was in a different part of the United Kingdom or exercised a parallel – but not superior – jurisdiction.

Decisions of the Court of Justice of the European Union come in two parts: the Opinion of the Advocate General and the decision of the Court. It is the decision of the Court which is binding. The Court is assisted by hearing the Opinion of the Advocate General before itself coming to a conclusion on the issue before it. The Court does not always follow its Advocate General. Where it does, the Opinion of the Advocate General often elaborates the arguments in greater detail than the single collegiate judgment of the Court. Within the European Union, courts and tribunals must apply decisions of the Court of Justice of the European Union, where relevant to cases before them, in preference to other authorities binding on them. This is no longer so in the United Kingdom, but it will still be necessary for courts and tribunals in the United Kingdom to take account of such decisions when issues of European Union law are relevant, and they are arguably bound by a decision of the Court of Justice on the interpretation of the Citizens' Rights provisions of the Withdrawal Agreement.

The European Court of Human Rights in Strasbourg is quite separate from the Court of Justice of the European Union in Luxembourg and serves a different purpose: interpreting and applying the European Convention on Human Rights, which is incorporated into United Kingdom law by the Human Rights Act 1998. Since October 2, 2000, public authorities in the United Kingdom, including courts, Commissioners, tribunals and decision-makers have been required to act in accordance with the incorporated provisions of the Convention, unless statute prevents this. They must take into account the Strasbourg case law and are required to interpret domestic legislation, so far as it is possible to do so, to give effect to the incorporated Convention rights. Any court or tribunal may declare secondary legislation incompatible with those rights and, in certain circumstances, invalidate it. Only the higher courts can declare a provision of primary legislation to be incompatible with those rights, but no court, tribunal or Upper Tribunal can invalidate primary legislation. The work of the Strasbourg Court and the impact of the Human Rights Act 1998 on social security are discussed in the commentary in Part IV of Volume III of this series.

See the note to s.3(2) of the Tribunals, Courts and Enforcement Act 2007 in Part III of Volume III of this series for a more detailed and technical consideration of the rules of precedent.

Other sources of information and commentary on social security law

For a comprehensive overview of the social security system in Great Britain, CPAG's *Welfare Benefits and Tax Credits Handbook*, published annually each spring, is unrivalled as a practical introduction from the claimant's viewpoint.

From a different perspective, the Department for Work and Pensions publishes the 14-volume *Decision Makers' Guide* and the newer *Advice for Decision Making*, which covers personal independence payment, universal credit and the "new" versions of Jobseeker's Allowance and Employment and Support Allowance (search for the relevant guide by name at *https://www.gov.uk* under the topic "Welfare"). Similarly, His Majesty's Revenue and Customs publish manuals relating to tax credits, child benefit and guardian's allowance, which they administer, see *https://www.gov.uk/government/collections/hmrc-manuals*. (Note that the *Child Benefit Technical Manual* also covers guardian's allowance.) These guides and manuals are extremely useful but their interpretation of the law is not binding on tribunals and the courts, being merely internal guidance for the use of decision-makers.

There are a number of other sources of valuable information or commentary on social security case law: see in particular publications such as the *Journal of Social Security Law*, CPAG's *Welfare Rights Bulletin*, *Legal Action* and the *Adviser*. As far as online resources go there is little to beat *Rightsnet* (*https://www.rightsnet.org.uk*). This site contains a wealth of resources for people working in the welfare benefits field but of special relevance in this context are Commissioners'/Upper Tribunal Decisions section of the "Toolkit" area and also the "Briefcase" area which contains summaries of the decisions (with links to the full decisions). Sweet and Maxwell's online subscription service *Westlaw* is another valuable source (*https://legalsolutions.thomsonreuters.co.uk/en/products-services/westlaw-uk.html*), as is LexisNexis *Lexis* (*https://www.lexisnexis.co.uk*).

Conclusion

The internet provides a vast resource but a search needs to be focused. Social security schemes are essentially statutory and so in Great Britain the legislation which is set out in this series forms the basic structure of social security law. However, the case law shows how the legislation should be interpreted and applied. The commentary in this series should point the way to the case law relevant to each provision and the Internet can then be used to find it where that is necessary.

CHANGE OF NAME FROM DEPARTMENT OF SOCIAL SECURITY TO DEPARTMENT FOR WORK AND PENSIONS

The Secretaries of State for Education and Skills and for Work and Pensions Order 2002 (SI 2002/1397) makes provision for the change of name from the Department of Social Security to Department for Work and Pensions. Article 9(5) provides:

"(5) Subject to article 12 [which makes specific amendments], any enactment or instrument passed or made before the coming into force of this Order shall have effect, so far as may be necessary for the purposes of or in consequence of the entrusting to the Secretary of State for Work and Pensions of the social security functions, as if any reference to the Secretary of State for Social Security, to the Department of Social Security or to an officer of the Secretary of State for Social Security (including any reference which is to be construed as such as reference) were a reference to the Secretary of State for Work and Pensions, to the Department for Work and Pensions or, as the case may be, to an officer of the Secretary of State for Work and Pensions."

CHANGES IN TERMINOLOGY CONSEQUENT UPON THE ENTRY INTO FORCE OF THE TREATY OF LISBON

The Treaty of Lisbon (Changes in Terminology) Order 2011 (SI 2011/1043) (which came into force on April 22, 2011) makes a number of changes to terminology used in primary and secondary legislation as a consequence of the entry into force of the Treaty of Lisbon on December 1, 2009. The Order accomplishes this by requiring certain terms in primary and secondary legislation to be read in accordance with the requirements of the Order. No substantive changes to the law are involved.

The changes are somewhat complex because of the different ways in which the term "Community" is used, and the abbreviations "EC" or "EEC" are used. References to the "European Community", "European Communities", "European Coal and Steel Communities", "the Community", "the EC" and "the EEC" are generally to be read as references to the "European Union".

The following table shows the more common usages involving the word "Community" in the first column which are now to be read in thc form sct out in the second column:

Original term	**To be read as**
Community treaties	EU treaties
Community institution	EU institution
Community instrument	EU instrument
Community obligation	EU obligation
Enforceable Community right	Enforceable EU right
Community law, or European Community law	EU law
Community legislation, or European Community legislation	EU legislation
Community provision, or European Community provision	EU provision

Provision is also made for changes to certain legislation relating to Wales in the Welsh language.

Relevant extracts from the Order can be found in Volume III, *Administration, Adjudication and the European Dimension*.

THE MARRIAGE (SAME SEX COUPLES) ACT 2013

The Marriage (Same Sex Couples) Act 2013 (c.30) provides in s.3 and Schs 3 and 4 that the terms "marriage", "married couple" and being "married" in existing and future legislation in England and Wales are to be read as references to a marriage between persons of the same sex. The same approach is taken to any legislation about couples living together as if married. This is subject to certain specified exclusions contained in Sch.4, and in any Order providing for a contrary approach to be taken.

Schedule 2 to The Marriage (Same Sex Couples) Act 2013 (Consequential and Contrary Provisions and Scotland) Order 2014 (SI 2014/560) contains a substantial list of contrary provisions to s.11(1) and (2) and paras 1 to 3 of Sch.3 to the 2013 Act. Most of these relate to specific enactments, but note that Pt 2 of the Schedule provides that s.11(1) and (2) do not apply to "EU instruments". This term is defined in Sch.1 to the European Communities Act 1972 (as amended) as "any instrument issued by an EU institution". It refers mainly to regulations, directives, decisions, recommendations and opinions issued by the institutions.

TABLE OF CASES

TABLE OF SOCIAL SECURITY COMMISSIONERS' DECISIONS

C1/01–02(SF) **4.74**, **4.83**
C10/06–07(IS) 2.256
CCS/7967/1995 .... 2.224
CCS/4912/1998 .... 2.225
CCS/4056/2004 .... 2.224
CCS/2533/2014 .... 2.209
CDLA/708/2007 .... **5.8**
CFC/10/1989 .... 2.543
CFC/21/1989 .... 2.163
CFC/26/1989 .... 2.301
CG/30/1990 .... 4.45
CH/393/2002 .... 2.542
CH/3393/2003 .... 2.256
CH/3801/2004 .... 3.8
CH/117/2005 .... **2.542**, 3.179
CH/1561/2005 .... 2.255, 2.546
CH/264/2006 .... 2.185
CH/715/2006 .... 2.162
CH/4429/2006 .... **2.278**
CH/377/2007 .... 2.542
CH/1672/2007 .... 1.64, **2.256**
CH/1076/2008 .... 2.256
CIS/25/1989 .... 2.256
CIS/40/1989 .... 2.177
CIS/212/1989 .... 2.256
CIS/264/1989 .... 2.185
CIS/124/1990 .... 2.184
CIS/494/1990 .... 2.165, 2.177
CIS/93/1991 .... 2.225
CIS/231/1991 .... 3.100
CIS/553/1991 .... 2.162, 2.177
CIS/563/1991 .... **2.256**
CIS/621/1991 .... 2.186
CIS/807/1991 .... 2.163
CIS/12403/1991 .... 2.182
CIS/307/1992 .... 2.186
CIS/391/1992 .... 2.173
CIS/417/1992 .... 2.173
CIS/422/1992 .... 2.225
CIS/634/1992 .... **2.160**, **2.182**
CIS/14/1993 .... 3.134
CIS/30/1993 .... 2.184, **2.542**
CIS/127/1993 .... 2.173
CIS/147/1993 .... 2.225
CIS/242/1993 .... **2.185**
CIS/368/1993 .... 2.162, 2.165, **2.180**
CIS/109/1994 .... **2.186**
CIS/112/1994 .... **2.186**
CIS/166/1994 .... 2.249
CIS/191/1994 .... 2.173
CIS/295/1994 .... 2.256
CIS/701/1994 .... 2.225
CIS/185/1995 .... 3.117
CIS/1459/1995 .... 3.138
CIS/2059/1995 .... **4.71**
CIS/5185/1995 .... **2.163**
CIS/6818/1995 .... **4.88**
CIS/7097/1995 .... 2.162, **2.172**
CIS/7127/1995 .... 2.160, 2.166
CIS/8485/1995 .... 4.85
CIS/1459/1996 .... 2.39
CIS/12344/1996 .... **4.74**
CIS/12703/1996 .... 2.34
CIS/13120/1996 .... **4.76**
CIS/14409/1996 .... 2.213
CIS/14657/1996 .... 3.139
CIS/16097/1996 .... 2.39
CIS/16957/1996 .... 4.90
CIS/1304/1997 .... 2.35, 2.36
CIS/1586/1997 .... 2.182
CIS/2916/1997 .... 2.225
CIS/3108/1997 .... 5.2
CIS/5119/1997 .... 4.83
CIS/5479/1997 .... **2.256**
CIS/1218/1998 .... **4.82**
CIS/2288/1998 .... 4.82
CIS/5321/1998 .... 4.83, 4.84
CIS/1678/1999 .... 3.139
CIS/2474/1999 .... 5.4
CIS/3150/1999 .... 4.77
CIS/3280/2001 .... 4.71
CIS/3508/2001 .... **5.5**
CIS/4498/2001 .... **4.83**
CIS/4769/2001 .... 4.77
CIS/5119/2001 .... 3.139
CIS/47/2002 .... 5.4
CIS/376/2002 .... 2.35, **2.36**
CIS/667/2002 .... 3.138
CIS/982/2002 .... 2.162, 2.179
CIS/984/2002 .... 2.162, 2.165, **2.180**
CIS/1722/2002 .... 4.71
CIS/2497/2002 .... **4.31**
CIS/2816/2002 .... 5.4
CIS/4843/2002 .... 2.542
CIS/426/2003 .... 5.4
CIS/788/2003 .... **4.76**, 4.82
CIS/1189/2003 .... **2.160**
CIS/1972/2003 .... **2.37**
CIS/2031/2003 .... 4.53
CIS/2208/2003 .... 2.177
CIS/2467/2003 .... 2.199, **2.543**
CIS/2532/2003 .... 3.117
CIS/2607/2003 .... 4.91
CIS/2651/2003 .... 4.91

TABLE OF ABBREVIATIONS USED IN THIS SERIES

1975 Act	Social Security Act 1975
1977 Act	Marriage (Scotland) Act 1977
1979 Act	Pneumoconiosis (Workers' Compensation) Act 1979
1986 Act	Social Security Act 1986
1996 Act	Employment Rights Act 1996
1998 Act	Social Security Act 1998
2002 Act	Tax Credits Act 2002
2004 Act	Gender Recognition Act 2004
2006 Act	Armed Forces Act 2006
2008 Act	Child Maintenance and Other Payments Act 2008
2013 Act	Marriage (Same Sex Couples) Act 2013
2014 Act	Marriage and Civil Partnership (Scotland) Act 2014
A1P1	Art.1 of Protocol 1 to the European Convention on Human Rights
AA	Attendance Allowance
AA 1992	Attendance Allowance Act 1992
AAC	Administrative Appeals Chamber
AACR	Administrative Appeals Chamber Reports
A.C.	Law Reports, Appeal Cases
A.C.D.	Administrative Court Digest
Admin	Administrative Court
Admin L.R.	Administrative Law Reports
Administration Act	Social Security Administration Act 1992
Administration Regulations	Statutory Paternity Pay and Statutory Adoption Pay (Administration) Regulations 2002
AIP	assessed income period
All E.R.	All England Reports
All E.R. (E.C.)	All England Reports (European Cases)
AMA	Adjudicating Medical Authorities
AO	Adjudication Officer
AOG	*Adjudication Officers Guide*
art.	article
Art.	Article
ASD	Autistic Spectrum Disorder
ASPP	Additional Statutory Paternity Pay

Table of Abbreviations used in this Series

ASVG	Allgemeines Sozialversicherungsgesetz (General Social Security Act)
A.T.C.	Annotated Tax Cases
Attendance Allowance Regulations	Social Security (Attendance Allowance) Regulations 1991
AWT	All Work Test
BA	Benefits Agency
Benefits Act	Social Security Contributions and Benefits Act 1992
B.H.R.C.	Butterworths Human Rights Cases
B.L.G.R.	Butterworths Local Government Reports
Blue Books	*The Law Relating to Social Security*, Vols 1–11
B.P.I.R.	Bankruptcy and Personal Insolvency Reports
BSVG	Bauern-Sozialversicherungsgesetz (Social Security Act for Farmers)
B.T.C.	British Tax Cases
BTEC	Business and Technology Education Council
B.V.C.	British Value Added Tax Reporter
B.W.C.C.	Butterworths Workmen's Compensation Cases
c.	chapter
C	Commissioner's decision
C&BA 1992	Social Security Contributions and Benefits Act 1992
CAA 2001	Capital Allowances Act 2001
CAB	Citizens Advice Bureau
CAO	Chief Adjudication Officer
CB	Child Benefit
CBA 1975	Child Benefit Act 1975
CBJSA	Contribution-Based Jobseeker's Allowance
C.C.L. Rep.	Community Care Law Reports
CCM	HMRC *New Tax Credits Claimant Compliance Manual*
C.E.C.	European Community Cases
CERA	cortical evoked response audiogram
CESA	Contribution-based Employment and Support Allowance
CFS	chronic fatigue syndrome
Ch.	Chancery Division Law Reports; Chapter
Citizenship Directive	Directive 2004/38/EC of the European Parliament and of the Council of April 29, 2004
CJEC	Court of Justice of the European Communities
CJEU	Court of Justice of the European Union
Claims and Payments Regulations	Social Security (Claims and Payments) Regulations 1987
Claims and Payments Regulations 1979	Social Security (Claims and Payments) Regulations 1979

Claims and Payments Regulations 2013	Universal Credit, Personal Independence Payment, Jobseeker's Allowance and Employment and Support Allowance (Claims and Payments) Regulations 2013
CM	Case Manager
CMA	Chief Medical Adviser
CMEC	Child Maintenance and Enforcement Commission
C.M.L.R.	Common Market Law Reports
C.O.D.	Crown Office Digest
COLL	*Collective Investment Schemes Sourcebook*
Community, The	European Community
Computation of Earnings Regulations	Social Security Benefit (Computation of Earnings) Regulations 1978
Computation of Earnings Regulations 1996	Social Security Benefit (Computation of Earnings) Regulations 1996
Consequential Provisions Act	Social Security (Consequential Provisions) Act 1992
Contributions and Benefits Act	Social Security Contributions and Benefits Act 1992
Contributions Regulations	Social Security (Contributions) Regulations 2001
COPD	chronic obstructive pulmonary disease
CP	Carer Premium; Chamber President
CPAG	Child Poverty Action Group
CPR	Civil Procedure Rules
Cr. App. R.	Criminal Appeal Reports
CRCA 2005	Commissioners for Revenue and Customs Act 2005
Credits Regulations 1974	Social Security (Credits) Regulations 1974
Credits Regulations 1975	Social Security (Credits) Regulations 1975
Crim. L.R.	Criminal Law Review
CRU	Compensation Recovery Unit
CSA 1995	Children (Scotland) Act 1995
CSIH	Inner House of the Court of Session (Scotland)
CSM	Child Support Maintenance
CS(NI)O 1995	Child Support (Northern Ireland) Order 1995
CSOH	Outer House of the Court of Session (Scotland)
CSPSSA 2000	Child Support, Pensions and Social Security Act 2000
CTA	Common Travel Area
CTA 2009	Corporation Tax Act 2009
CTA 2010	Corporation Tax Act 2010
CTB	Council Tax Benefit
CTC	Child Tax Credit
CTC Regulations	Child Tax Credit Regulations 2002
CTF	child trust fund

CTS	Carpal Tunnel Syndrome
DAC	Directive 2011/16/ EU (Directive on administrative co-operation in the field of taxation)
DAT	Disability Appeal Tribunal
dB	decibels
DCA	Department for Constitutional Affairs
DCP	Disabled Child Premium
Decisions and Appeals Regulations 1999	Social Security Contributions (Decisions and Appeals) Regulations 1999
Dependency Regulations	Social Security Benefit (Dependency) Regulations 1977
DfEE	Department for Education and Employment
DHSS	Department of Health and Social Security
Disability Living Allowance Regulations	Social Security (Disability Living Allowance) Regulations
DIY	do it yourself
DLA	Disability Living Allowance
DLA Regs 1991	Social Security (Disability Living Allowance) Regulations 1991
DLAAB	Disability Living Allowance Advisory Board
DLADWAA 1991	Disability Living Allowance and Disability Working Allowance Act 1991
DM	Decision Maker
DMA	Decision-making and Appeals
DMG	*Decision Makers' Guide*
DMP	Delegated Medical Practitioner
DP	Disability Premium
DPP	Director of Public Prosecutions
DPT	diffuse pleural thickening
DPTC	Disabled Person's Tax Credit
DRO	Debt Relief Order
DSD	Department for Social Development (Northern Ireland)
DSM IV; DSM-5	Diagnostic and Statistical Manual of Mental Disorders of the American Psychiatric Association
DSS	Department of Social Security
DTI	Department of Trade and Industry
DWA	Disability Working Allowance
DWP	Department for Work and Pensions
DWPMS	Department for Work and Pensions Medical Service
EAA	Extrinsic Allergic Alveolitis
EAT	Employment Appeal Tribunal
EC	European Community
ECHR	European Convention on Human Rights

ECJ	European Court of Justice
E.C.R.	European Court Reports
ECSC	European Coal and Steel Community
ECSMA	European Convention on Social and Medical Assistance
EEA	European Economic Area
EEC	European Economic Community
EESSI	Electronic Exchange of Social Security Information
E.G.	Estates Gazette
E.G.L.R.	Estates Gazette Law Reports
EHC plan	education, health and care plan
EHIC	European Health Insurance Card
EHRC	European Human Rights Commission
E.H.R.R.	European Human Rights Reports
EL	employers' liability
E.L.R	Education Law Reports
EMA	Education Maintenance Allowance
EMP	Examining Medical Practitioner
Employment and Support Allowance	Employment and Support Allowance
Regulations	Regulations 2008
EPS	extended period of sickness
Eq. L.R.	Equality Law Reports
ERA	evoked response audiometry
ERA scheme	Employment, Retention and Advancement scheme
ES	Employment Service
ESA	Employment and Support Allowance
ESA Regs 2013	Employment and Support Allowance Regulations 2013
ESA Regulations	Employment and Support Allowance Regulations 2008
ESA WCAt	Employment and Support Allowance Work Capability Assessment
ESC	employer supported childcare
ESE Scheme	Employment, Skills and Enterprise Scheme
ESE Regulations	Jobseeker's Allowance (Employment, Skills and Enterprise Scheme) Regulations 2011
ESES Regulations	Jobseeker's Allowance (Employment, Skills and Enterprise Scheme) Regulations 2011
ETA 1973	Employment and Training Act 1973
ETA(NI) 1950	Employment and Training Act (Northern Ireland) 1950
ETS	European Treaty Series
EU	European Union
Eu.L.R.	European Law Reports

Table of Abbreviations used in this Series

EWCA Civ	Civil Division of the Court of Appeal (England and Wales)
EWHC Admin	Administrative Court Division of the High Court (England and Wales)
FA 1993	Finance Act 1993
FA 1996	Finance Act 1996
FA 2004	Finance Act 2004
Fam. Law	Family Law
FAS	Financial Assistance Scheme
FCDO	Foreign, Commonwealth and Development Office
F.C.R.	Family Court Reporter
FEV	forced expiratory volume
FIS	Family Income Supplement
FISMA 2000	Financial Services and Markets Act 2000
F.L.R.	Family Law Reports
FME	further medical evidence
F(No.2)A 2005	Finance (No.2) Act 2005
FOTRA	Free of Tax to Residents Abroad
FRAA	flat rate accrual amount
FRS Act 2004	Fire and Rescue Services Act 2004
FSCS	Financial Services Compensation Scheme
FTT	First-tier Tribunal
General Benefit Regulations 1982	Social Security (General Benefit) Regulations 1982
General Regulations	Statutory Shared Parental Pay (General) Regulations 2014
GMC	Group Medical Coverage
GMCA	Greater Manchester Combined Authority
GMFRA	Greater Manchester Fire and Rescue Authority
GMP	Guaranteed Minimum Pension
GMWDA	Greater Manchester Waste Disposal Authority
GNVQ	General National Vocational Qualification
GP	General Practitioner
GRA	Gender Recognition Act 2004
GRB	Graduated Retirement Benefit
GRP	Graduated Retirement Pension
GSVG	Gewerbliches Sozialversicherungsgesetz (Federal Act on Social Insurance for Persons engaged in Trade and Commerce)
HB	Housing Benefit
HB (WSP) R (NI) 2017	Housing Benefit (Welfare Social Payment) Regulations (Northern Ireland) 2017
HBRB	Housing Benefit Review Board
HCA	Homes and Communities Agency
HCD	House of Commons Debates

HCP	healthcare professional
HCV	Hepatitis C virus
Health Service Act	National Health Service Act 2006
Health Service (Wales) Act	National Health Service (Wales) Act 2006
HIV	Human Immunodeficiency Virus
HL	House of Lords
H.L.R.	Housing Law Reports
HMIT	His Majesty's Inspector of Taxes
HMRC	His Majesty's Revenue and Customs
HMSO	His Majesty's Stationery Office
Hospital In-Patients Regulations 1975	Social Security (Hospital In-Patients) Regulations 1975
HP	Health Professional
HPP	Higher Pensioner Premium
HRA 1998	Human Rights Act 1998
H.R.L.R.	Human Rights Law Reports
HRP	Home Responsibilities Protection
HSE	Health and Safety Executive
IAC	Immigration and Asylum Chamber
IAP	Intensive Activity Period
IB	Incapacity Benefit
IB PCA	Incapacity Benefit Personal Capability Assessment
IB Regs	Social Security (Incapacity Benefit) Regulations 1994
IB Regulations	Social Security (Incapacity Benefit) Regulations 1994
IB/IS/SDA	Incapacity Benefits Regime
IBJSA	Income-Based Jobseeker's Allowance
IBS	Irritable Bowel Syndrome
ICA	Invalid Care Allowance
I.C.R.	Industrial Cases Reports
ICTA 1988	Income and Corporation Taxes Act 1988
IFW Regulations	Incapacity for Work (General) Regulations 1995
IH	Inner House of the Court of Session
I.I.	Industrial Injuries
IIAC	Industrial Injuries Advisory Council
IIDB	Industrial Injuries Disablement Benefit
ILO	International Labour Organization
Imm. A.R.	Immigration Appeal Reports
Incapacity for Work Regulations	Social Security (Incapacity for Work) (General) Regulations 1995
Income Support General Regulations	Income Support (General) Regulations 1987
IND	Immigration and Nationality Directorate of the Home Office

I.N.L.R.	Immigration and Nationality Law Reports
I.O.	Insurance Officer
IPPR	Institute of Public Policy Research
IRESA	Income-Related Employment and Support Allowance
I.R.L.R.	Industrial Relations Law Reports
IS	Income Support
IS Regs	Income Support Regulations
IS Regulations	Income Support (General) Regulations 1987
ISA	Individual Savings Account
ISBN	International Standard Book Number
ITA 2007	Income Tax Act 2007
ITEPA 2003	Income Tax, Earnings and Pensions Act 2003
I.T.L. Rep.	International Tax Law Reports
I.T.R.	Industrial Tribunals Reports
ITS	Independent Tribunal Service
ITTOIA 2005	Income Tax (Trading and Other Income) Act 2005
IVB	Invalidity Benefit
IW (General) Regs	Social Security (Incapacity for Work) (General) Regulations 1995
IW (Transitional) Regs	Incapacity for Work (Transitional) Regulations
Jobseeker's Allowance Regulations	Jobseeker's Allowance Regulations 1996
Jobseeker's Regulations 1996	Jobseeker's Allowance Regulations 1996
JSA	Jobseeker's Allowance
JSA 1995	Jobseekers Act 1995
JSA (NI) Regulations	Jobseeker's Allowance (Northern Ireland) Regulations 1996
JSA (Transitional) Regulations	Jobseeker's Allowance (Transitional) Regulations 1996
JSA Regs 1996	Jobseeker's Allowance Regulations 1996
JSA Regs 2013	Jobseeker's Allowance Regulations 2013
JS(NI)O 1995	Jobseekers (Northern Ireland) Order 1995
J.S.S.L.	Journal of Social Security Law
J.S.W.L.	Journal of Social Welfare Law
K.B.	Law Reports, King's Bench
L.& T.R.	Landlord and Tenant Reports
LCW	limited capability for work
LCWA	Limited Capability for Work Assessment
LCWRA	limited capability for work-related activity
LDEDC Act 2009	Local Democracy, Economic Development and Construction Act 2009
LEA	local education authority
LEL	Lower Earnings Limit
LET	low earnings threshold
L.G. Rev.	Local Government Review

L.G.L.R.	Local Government Reports
L.J.R.	Law Journal Reports
LRP	liable relative payment
L.S.G.	Law Society Gazette
Luxembourg Court	Court of Justice of the European Union (also referred to as CJEC and ECJ)
MA	Maternity Allowance
MAF	Medical Assessment Framework
Maternity Allowance Regulations	Social Security (Maternity Allowance) Regulations 1987
MDC	Mayoral development corporation
ME	myalgic encephalomyelitis
Medical Evidence Regulations	Social Security (Medical Evidence) Regulations 1976
MEN	Mandatory Employment Notification
Mesher and Wood	*Income Support, the Social Fund and Family Credit: the Legislation* (1996)
M.H.L.R.	Mental Health Law Reports
MHP	mental health problems
MIF	minimum income floor
MIG	minimum income guarantee
Migration Regulations	Employment and Support Allowance (Transitional Provisions, Housing Benefit and Council Tax Benefit (Existing Awards) (No.2) Regulations 2010
MP	Member of Parliament
MRSA	methicillin-resistant Staphylococcus aureus
MS	Medical Services
MWA Regulations	Jobseeker's Allowance (Mandatory Work Activity Scheme) Regulations 2011
MWAS Regulations	Jobseeker's Allowance (Mandatory Work Activity Scheme) Regulations 2011
NCB	National Coal Board
NDPD	Notes on the Diagnosis of Prescribed Diseases
NHS	National Health Service
NI	National Insurance
N.I..	Northern Ireland Law Reports
NICA	Northern Ireland Court of Appeal
NICom	Northern Ireland Commissioner
NICs	National Insurance Contributions
NINO	National Insurance Number
NIRS 2	National Insurance Recording System
N.L.J.	New Law Journal
NMC	Nursing and Midwifery Council
Northern Ireland Contributions and Benefits Act	Social Security Contributions and Benefits (Northern Ireland) Act 1992

N.P.C.	New Property Cases
NRCGT	non-resident capital gains tax
NTC Manual	Clerical procedures manual on tax credits
NUM	National Union of Mineworkers
NUS	National Union of Students
OCD	obsessive compulsive disorder
Ogus, Barendt and Wikeley	A. Ogus, E. Barendt and N. Wikeley, *The Law of Social Security* (1995)
Old Cases Act	Industrial Injuries and Diseases (Old Cases) Act 1975
OPB	One Parent Benefit
O.P.L.R.	Occupational Pensions Law Reports
OPSSAT	Office of the President of Social Security Appeal Tribunals
Overlapping Benefits Regulations	Social Security (Overlapping Benefits) Regulations 1975
P	retirement pension case
P. & C.R.	Property and Compensation Reports
para.	paragraph
Pay Regulations	Statutory Paternity Pay and Statutory Adoption Pay (General) Regulations 2002; Statutory Shared Parental Pay (General) Regulations 2014
PAYE	Pay As You Earn
PC	Privy Council
PCA	Personal Capability Assessment
PCC	Police and Crime Commissioner
PD	Practice Direction; prescribed disease
Pens. L.R.	Pensions Law Reports
Pensions Act	Pension Schemes Act 1993
PEP	Personal Equity Plan
Persons Abroad Regulations	Social Security Benefit (Persons Abroad) Regulations 1975
Persons Residing Together Regulations	Social Security Benefit (Persons Residing Together) Regulations 1977
PIE	Period of Interruption of Employment
PILON	pay in lieu of notice
Pilot Scheme Regulations	Universal Credit (Work-Related Requirements) In Work Pilot Scheme and Amendment Regulations 2015
PIP	Personal Independence Payment
P.I.Q.R.	Personal Injuries and Quantum Reports
Polygamous Marriages Regulations	Social Security and Family Allowances (Polygamous Marriages) Regulations 1975
PPF	Pension Protection Fund
Prescribed Diseases Regulations	Social Security (Industrial Injuries) (Prescribed Diseases) Regulations 1985
PSCS	Pension Service Computer System

Pt	Part
PTA	pure tone audiometry
P.T.S.R.	Public and Third Sector Law Reports
PTWR 2000	Part-time Workers (Prevention of Less Favourable Treatment) Regulations 2000
PVS	private and voluntary sectors
Q.B.	Queen's Bench Law Reports
QBD	Queen's Bench Division
QCS Board	Quality Contract Scheme Board
QEF	qualifying earnings factor
QYP	qualifying young person
r.	rule
R	Reported Decision
R.C.	Rules of the Court of Session
REA	Reduced Earnings Allowance
reg.	regulation
REULRRA	Retained EU Law (Revocation and Reform) Act 2023
RIPA	Regulation of Investigatory Powers Act 2000
RMO	Responsible Medical Officer
rr.	rules
RR	reference rate
RSI	repetitive strain injury
RTI	Real Time Information
R.V.R.	Rating & Valuation Reporter
s.	section
S	Scottish Decision
SAP	Statutory Adoption Pay
SAPOE Regulations	Jobseeker's Allowance (Schemes for Assisting Persons to Obtain Employment) Regulations 2013
SAWS	Seasonal Agricultural Work Scheme
SAYE	Save As You Earn
SB	Supplementary Benefit
SBAT	Supplementary Benefit Appeal Tribunal
SBC	Supplementary Benefits Commission
S.C.	Session Cases
S.C. (H.L.)	Session Cases (House of Lords)
S.C. (P.C.)	Session Cases (Privy Council)
S.C.C.R.	Scottish Criminal Case Reports
S.C.L.R.	Scottish Civil Law Reports
Sch.	Schedule
SDA	Severe Disablement Allowance
SDP	Severe Disability Premium
SEC	Social Entitlement Chamber

SEN	special educational needs
SERPS	State Earnings Related Pension Scheme
ShPP	statutory shared parental pay
ShPP Regulations	Statutory Shared Parental Pay (General) Regulations 2014
SI	Statutory Instrument
SIP	Share Incentive Plan
S.J.	Solicitors Journal
S.J.L.B.	Solicitors Journal Law Brief
SLAN	statement like an award notice
S.L.T.	Scots Law Times
SMP	Statutory Maternity Pay
SMP (General) Regulations 1986	Statutory Maternity Pay (General) Regulations 1986
SPC	State Pension Credit
SPC Regulations	State Pension Credit Regulations 2002
SPCA 2002	State Pension Credit Act 2002
SPL Regulations	Shared Parental Leave Regulations 2014
SPP	Statutory Paternity Pay
ss.	sections
SS (No.2) A 1980	Social Security (No.2) Act 1980
SSA 1975	Social Security Act 1975
SSA 1977	Social Security Act 1977
SSA 1978	Social Security Act 1978
SSA 1979	Social Security Act 1979
SSA 1981	Social Security Act 1981
SSA 1986	Social Security Act 1986
SSA 1988	Social Security Act 1988
SSA 1989	Social Security Act 1989
SSA 1990	Social Security Act 1990
SSA 1998	Social Security Act 1998
SSAA 1992	Social Security Administration Act 1992
SSAC	Social Security Advisory Committee
SSAT	Social Security Appeal Tribunal
SSCBA 1992	Social Security Contributions and Benefits Act 1992
SSCB(NI)A 1992	Social Security Contributions and Benefits (Northern Ireland) Act 1992
SSCPA 1992	Social Security (Consequential Provisions) Act 1992
SSD	Secretary of State for Defence
SSHBA 1982	Social Security and Housing Benefits Act 1982
SSHD	Secretary of State for the Home Department
SSI	Scottish Statutory Instrument
SS(MP)A 1977	Social Security (Miscellaneous Provisions) Act 1977

SSP	Statutory Sick Pay
SSP (General) Regulations	Statutory Sick Pay (General) Regulations 1982
SSPA 1975	Social Security Pensions Act 1975
SSPP	statutory shared parental pay
SSWP	Secretary of State for Work and Pensions
State Pension Credit Regulations	State Pension Credit Regulations 2002
S.T.C.	Simon's Tax Cases
S.T.C. (S.C.D.)	Simon's Tax Cases: Special Commissioners' Decisions
S.T.I.	Simon's Tax Intelligence
STIB	Short-Term Incapacity Benefit
subpara.	subparagraph
subs.	subsection
T	Tribunal of Commissioners' Decision
T.C.	Tax Cases
TCA 1999	Tax Credits Act 1999
TCA 2002	Tax Credits Act 2002
TCC	Technology and Construction Court
TCEA 2007	Tribunals, Courts and Enforcement Act 2007
TCGA 1992	Taxation of Chargeable Gains Act 2002
TCTM	*Tax Credits Technical Manual*
TEC	Treaty Establishing the European Community
TENS	transcutaneous electrical nerve stimulation
TEU	Treaty on European Union
TFC	tax-free childcare
TFEU	Treaty on the Functioning of the European Union
TIOPA 2010	Taxation (International and Other Provisions) Act 2010
TMA 1970	Taxes Management Act 1970
T.R.	Taxation Reports
Transfer of Functions Act	Social Security Contributions (Transfer of Functions etc.) Act 1999
Tribunal Procedure Rules	Tribunal Procedure (First-tier Tribunal)(Social Entitlement Chamber) Rules 2008
UB	Unemployment Benefit
UC	Universal Credit
UC Regs 2013	Universal Credit Regulations 2013
UCITS	Undertakings for Collective Investments in Transferable Securities
UKAIT	UK Asylum and Immigration Tribunal
UKBA	UK Border Agency of the Home Office
UKCC	United Kingdom Central Council for Nursing, Midwifery and Health Visiting
UKFTT	United Kingdom First-tier Tribunal Tax Chamber

UKHL	United Kingdom House of Lords
U.K.H.R.R.	United Kingdom Human Rights Reports
UKSC	United Kingdom Supreme Court
UKUT	United Kingdom Upper Tribunal
UN	United Nations
Universal Credit Regulations	Universal Credit Regulations 2013
URL	uniform resource locator
USI Regs	Social Security (Unemployment, Sickness and Invalidity Benefit) Regulations 1983
USI Regulations	Social Security (Unemployment, Sickness and Invalidity Benefit) Regulations 1983
UT	Upper Tribunal
VAT	Value Added Tax
VCM	vinyl chloride monomer
Vol.	Volume
VWF	Vibration White Finger
W	Welsh Decision
WCA	Work Capability Assessment
WCAt	limited capability for work assessment
WFHRAt	Work-Focused Health-Related Assessment
WFI	work-focused interview
WFTC	Working Families Tax Credit
Wikeley, Annotations	N. Wikeley, "Annotations to Jobseekers Act 1995 (c.18)" in *Current Law Statutes Annotated* (1995)
Wikeley, Ogus and Barendt	Wikeley, Ogus and Barendt, *The Law of Social Security* (2002)
W.L.R.	Weekly Law Reports
WLUK	Westlaw UK
Workmen's Compensation Acts	Workmen's Compensation Acts 1925 to 1945
WP	Widow's Pension
WPS	War Pensions Scheme
WRA 2007	Welfare Reform Act 2007
WRA 2009	Welfare Reform Act 2009
WRA 2012	Welfare Reform Act 2012
W-RA Regulations	Employment and Support Allowance (Work-Related Activity) Regulations 2011
WRAAt	Work-Related Activity Assessment
WRPA 1999	Welfare Reform and Pensions Act 1999
WRP(NI)O 1999	Welfare Reform and Pensions (Northern Ireland) Order 1999
WRWA 2016	Welfare Reform and Work Act 2016
WSP (LCP) R (NI) 2016	Welfare Supplementary Payment (Loss of Carer Payments) Regulations (Northern Ireland) 2016
WSP (LDRP) R (NI) 2016	Welfare Supplementary Payment (Loss of Disability-Related Premiums) Regulations (Northern Ireland) 2016

WSPR (NI) 2016	Welfare Supplementary Payment Regulations (Northern Ireland) 2016
WTC	Working Tax Credit
WTC Regulations	Working Tax Credit (Entitlement and Maximum Rate) Regulations 2002

PART I

STATUTES

Social Security Contributions and Benefits Act 1992

(1992 c.4)

SECTIONS REPRODUCED

PART VIII

THE SOCIAL FUND

138. Payments out of the social fund. 1.1

Payments out of the social fund

[[1]**138.**—(1) There may be made out of the social fund, in accordance with this Part of this Act—

(a) Payments of prescribed amounts, whether in respect of prescribed items or otherwise, to meet, in prescribed circumstances, maternity expenses and funeral expenses; and

(b) . . . *[Omitted as relating solely to the discretionary social fund.]*]

(2) Payments may also be made out of that fund, in accordance with this Part of this Act, of a prescribed amount or a number of prescribed amounts to prescribed descriptions of persons, in prescribed circumstances, to meet expenses for heating, which appear to the Secretary of State to have been or to be likely to be incurred in cold weather.

(3) . . . *[Omitted as relating solely to the discretionary social fund.]*

(4) In this section "prescribed" means specified in or determined in accordance with regulations.

[[2](4A) This section has effect in or as regards Scotland as if—

(a) references in subsections (1)(a) and (2) to the making of payments out of the social fund were to the making of payments by the Scottish Ministers,

(b) the reference in subsection (2) to the Secretary of State were to the Scottish Ministers, and

(c) the reference in subsection (4) to regulations were to regulations made by the Scottish Ministers.

(4B) Where regulations are made by the Scottish Ministers under this section—

(a) sections 175(2) and (7) and 176 do not apply, and

(b) the regulations are subject to the negative procedure (see section 28 of the Interpretation and Legislative Reform (Scotland) Act 2010).

(4C) The power to make an Order in Council under section 30(3) of the Scotland Act 1998 is exercisable for the purposes of this section as it is exercisable for the purposes of that Act.]

(5) . . . *[Omitted as relating solely to the discretionary social fund.]*

AMENDMENTS

1. Social Security Act 1998 s.70 (April 5, 1999).

2. Scotland Act 2016 s.23(5) (May 17, 2017 for the purpose of making regulations: see SI 2017/455 reg.2(b)(iii); April 1, 2024 for all other purposes: see SI 2017/455 reg.3.

GENERAL NOTE

Subsection (1)(a)

1.2 Subsection (1)(a) is re-enacted by s.70(1)(a) of the SSA 1998 with effect from April 5, 1999. This part of the social fund scheme was originally brought into operation in April 1987 to enable payments to be made for maternity and funeral expenses. These are made under the ordinary system of adjudication and under regulations required to be made by subs.(1)(a). They are not subject to any budget. See the Social Fund Maternity and Funeral Expenses (General) Regulations 2005. The death grant and the maternity grant, formerly payable under the Social Security Act 1975, were abolished (1986 Act ss.38 and 41) and the provisions for maternity and funeral expenses under the supplementary benefit regulations were removed in April 1987 (General Regulations regs 13–15).

Subsection (1)(a) does little more than provide the framework for the detailed entitlement set out in the General Regulations. See s.78(4) of the SSAA 1992 on the recovery of funeral payments from the estate of the deceased.

New restrictions on payments for funeral expenses were introduced on June 5, 1995 and there was further clarification and tightening-up of the rules on April 7, 1997 (see regs 7 and 7A of the General Regulations and the notes to those regulations). Note also the changes introduced on November 17, 1997.

Subsection (2)

1.3 Although the predecessor of this subsection was in force from April 1988, the regulations it required were not in place until November 7, 1988 (Social Fund Cold Weather Payments (General) Regulations 1988). The form of the scheme, as embodied in the 1988 Regulations, has been amended several times. The current form does not require a separate claim to be made for a severe weather payment. As for maternity and funeral expenses, the decisions are made by decision-makers, with appeals to a tribunal, and are not subject to any budget.

See also the notes to the Social Fund Winter Fuel Payment Regulations 2000.

Subsections (4A)–(4C)

1.4 These subsections make provision for the operation of the social fund in Scotland. They were, pursuant to the Scotland Act 2016 (Commencement No. 5) Regulations 2017/455 reg.3, initially anticipated to come into full force on April 1, 2020 but that date was repeatedly pushed back, most recently to April 1, 2024 by the Scotland Act 2016 (Commencement No. 5) (Amendment) Regulations 2023/395 reg.2 (March 27, 2023).

Immigration and Asylum Act 1999

(1999 c.33)

SECTION REPRODUCED

PART VI

SUPPORT FOR ASYLUM-SEEKERS

Exclusions

Exclusion from benefits

115.—(1) No person is entitled [10 to universal credit under Part 1 of the Welfare Reform Act 2012 or] to income-based jobseeker's allowance under the Jobseekers Act 1995 [4 or to state pension credit under the State Pension Credit Act 2002] [6 or to income-related allowance under Part 1 of the Welfare Reform Act 2007 (employment and support allowance)] [9 or to personal independence payment] or to— 1.6

(a) attendance allowance,
(b) severe disablement allowance,
(c) [1carer's allowance],
(d) disability living allowance,
(e) income support,
(f) [2. . .]
(g) [2. . .]
(h) a social fund payment,
[7 (ha) health in pregnancy grant;]
(i) child benefit,
(j) housing benefit, [8 . . .]
(k) [8 . . .]

under the Social Security Contributions and Benefits Act 1992 while he is a person to whom this section applies.

(2) [*Omitted as relating solely to Northern Ireland*]

(3) This section applies to a person subject to immigration control unless he falls within such category or description, or satisfies such conditions, as may be prescribed.

(4) Regulations under subsection (3) may provide for a person to be treated for prescribed purposes only as not being a person to whom this section applies.

(5) In relation to [7 health in pregnancy grant or] [3 child benefit], "prescribed" means prescribed by regulations made by the Treasury.

(6) In relation to the matters mentioned in subsection (2) (except so far as it relates to [7 health in pregnancy grant or] [3 child benefit]), "prescribed" means prescribed by regulations made by the Department.

(7) Section 175(3) to (5) of the Social Security Contributions and Benefits Act 1992 (supplemental powers in relation to regulations) applies to regulations made by the Secretary of State or the Treasury under subsection (3) as it applies to regulations made under that Act.

(8) Sections 133(2), 171(2) and 172(4) of the Social Security Contributions and Benefits (Northern Ireland) Act 1992 apply to regulations made by the Department under subsection (3) as they apply to regulations made by the Department under that Act.

(9) "A person subject to immigration control" means a person [[11] . . .] who—

(a) requires leave to enter or remain in the United Kingdom but does not have it;

(b) has leave to enter or remain in the United Kingdom which is subject to a condition that he does not have recourse to public funds;

(c) has leave to enter or remain in the United Kingdom given as a result of a maintenance undertaking; or

(d) has leave to enter or remain in the United Kingdom only as a result of paragraph 17 of Schedule 4.

(10) "Maintenance undertaking", in relation to any person, means a written undertaking given by another person in pursuance of the immigration rules to be responsible for that person's maintenance and accommodation.

AMENDMENTS

1. Regulatory Reform (Carer's Allowance) Order 2002 (SI 2002/1457) art.2(1) and Sch. para.3(c) (April 1, 2003).

2. Tax Credits Act 2002 s.60 and Sch.6 (April 8, 2003).

3. Tax Credits Act 2002 s.51 and Sch.4 paras 20–21 (February 26, 2003).

4. State Pension Credit Act 2002 s.4(2) (October 6, 2003).

5. State Pension Credit Act (Northern Ireland) 2002 s.4(2) (October 6, 2003).

6. Welfare Reform Act 2007 Sch.3 para.19 (October 27, 2008).

7. Health and Social Care Act 2008 s.138 (January 1, 2009).

8. Welfare Reform Act 2012 s.147 and Sch.1 Pt 1 (April 1, 2013).

9. Welfare Reform Act 2012 s.91 and Sch.9 para.44 (April 8, 2013).

10. Welfare Reform Act 2012 s.31 and Sch.2 para.54 (April 29, 2013).

11. Immigration and Social Security Co-ordination (EU Withdrawal) Act 2020 (Consequential, Saving, Transitional and Transitory Provisions) (EU Exit) Regulations 2020 (SI 2020/1309) reg.12(1) and (7) (December 31, 2020 at 11.00pm) (subject to the saving provided for by regs 3(4), 4(5) and 12(1)(i) of the Citizens' Rights (Application Deadline and Temporary Protection) (EU Exit) Regulations 2020 (SI 2020/1209): see Vol.V).

GENERAL NOTE

1.7 See the notes to the Social Security (Immigration and Asylum) Consequential Amendments Regulations 2000 (Part V below).

Paragraph 17 of Sch.4 to the Act was repealed on April 1, 2003 by Sch.9 para.1 of the Nationality, Immigration and Asylum Act 2002 but the reference to the repealed provision in s.115(9)(d) has not itself been repealed. *EE v City of Cardiff (HB)* [2018] UKUT 418 (AAC) holds that by virtue of s.17(2) of the Interpretation Act 1978, that reference should now be construed as a reference to ss.3C(1) and (2)(b) of the Immigration Act 1971 which was inserted into that Act by the 2002 Act (but not as a reference to the former s.3D of that Act). However, while *EE* appears to bind first-tier tribunals, query whether it is correctly decided: s.3C of the Immigration Act 1971 is not identically worded to para.17 of Sch.4 and it is questionable whether it really can be treated as a "re-enactment" such as to engage s.17(2) of the Interpretation Act 1978. If *EE* were wrong, a person with s.3C leave would continue to be eligible for benefit if they had been eligible before their non-s.3C leave expired.

Health in Pregnancy Grants were abolished for women who reached the 25th week of their pregnancy on or after January 1, 2011: see s.3(2) of the Savings Accounts and Health in Pregnancy Grant Act 2010. However, s.115(1)(ha) has not been repealed to reflect that circumstance.

State Pension Credit Act 2002

(2002 c.16)

SECTIONS REPRODUCED

State pension credit: entitlement and amount

1. Entitlement. **1.8**
2. Guarantee credit.
3. Savings credit.
3ZA. Power to limit savings credit for certain mixed-age couples
3A. Housing credit (not in force)
4. Exclusions.

Aggregation

5. Income and capital of claimant, spouse, etc.

Retirement provision

6. Duty to specify assessed income period for pre-6 April 2016 awards.
7. Fixing of claimant's retirement provision for assessed income period.
8. Fresh determinations increasing claimant's entitlement.
9. Duration of assessed income period.
10. Effect of variations under s.7(4).

Miscellaneous and supplementary

11. Administration.
12. Polygamous marriages.
13. Transitional provisions.
14. Minor and consequential amendments.

Interpretation of state pension credit provisions

15. Income and capital.
16. Retirement pension income.
17. Other interpretation provisions.

Effect of guaranteed minimum pension on social security benefits

18. Equal treatment for widows and widowers *[Omitted]*.
18A. Pilot schemes.

Final provisions

19. Regulations and orders.
20. Financial provisions.

21. Enactments repealed.
22. Short title, commencement and extent.

SCHEDULES

Schedules 1–3 [*omitted.*]

INTRODUCTION AND GENERAL NOTE

1.9 The prime purpose of this Act, embodied in ss.1–17, was to set the framework for the state pension credit that has been available to people aged 60 and over as from October 6, 2003. The Labour Government elected in 1997 set out its initial proposals in *A New Contract for Welfare: Partnership in Pensions* (Cm.4179, 1998). This led to the introduction of stakeholder pensions under Pt I of the Welfare Reform and Pensions Act 1999, with effect from April 2001, as a new option for private pension provision for those on moderate incomes.

So far as the poorest pensioners were concerned, the Government at that time resisted demands from its own backbenchers and supporters to restore the link between the state retirement pension and increases in average earnings. Instead, the value of income support for pensioners was dramatically increased and that benefit relabelled as the minimum income guarantee (or "MIG") for that client group. This had the effect of increasing the gap between the (higher) MIG entitlement and the (lower) basic state retirement pension respectively for a single pensioner. The disparity increased from £5.75 in April 1998 (when the basic pension represented 92 per cent of the MIG rate) to £22.65 by April 2002 (by which time the basic pension had fallen to 77 per cent of the MIG level). This exacerbated the longstanding problem that pensioners with small amounts of private incomes on top of their state retirement pension saw no benefit from such thrift as any such income is deducted pound-for-pound under income support rules.

The proposal for a pension credit was first canvassed in a DSS consultation paper in November 2000 (DSS, *The Pension Credit: a consultation paper,* Cm.4900), which was followed by the publication of a further paper entitled *The Pension Credit: the government's proposals* (DWP, 2001). The pension credit both continues the previous income support arrangements (or MIG) for pensioners in a modified form and provides some reward for those with small private incomes. Thus the state pension credit comprises two quite distinct elements. The first is the "guarantee credit", which is intended to provide a minimum level of income to those aged 60 or over. This replaces the MIG, the marketing name for income support for pensioners. The second is the "savings credit", which is designed to provide an additional form of income for pensioners from the age of 65 who have low or modest private incomes (e.g. an occupational pension and/or income from savings) in addition to the basic state retirement pension.

1.10 Section 1 specifies the common conditions for access to the pension credit, whilst ss.2 and 3 respectively stipulate the extra conditions which must be satisfied in order to qualify for either or both of the guarantee credit and the savings credit. The common conditions for state pension credit in s.1 are that the claimant is in Great Britain and has reached the qualifying age (set at the pensionable age for women). Note also that in *EC v Secretary of State for Work and Pensions* [2010] UKUT 93 (AAC); [2010] AACR 39 it was held that state pension credit is a special non-contributory benefit within art.10a of Regulation 1408/71 (see now art.70 of Regulation 883/2004) and so is payable only to those living in Great Britain. In addition, s.4 includes a number of exclusions from entitlement to the pension credit and s.5 confirms that a claimant's resources must be aggregated with those of their partner.

The calculation of the guarantee credit entitlement under s.2 essentially works in the same way as the income support scheme. There are, however, two important differences in the substantive rules of entitlement to the guarantee credit when contrasted with those that apply to income support. Income support is not available to those who work for 16 hours or more a week and is subject to an upper capital limit. Neither rule applies to state pension credit.

The savings credit under s.3, comprising the second potential element in the state pension credit, is an entirely novel form of benefit. It works in the opposite way to the traditional means-test which applies for the purposes of income support. Previously a pensioner who had a small private income over and above the state retirement pension saw their MIG or income support reduced pound-for-pound by any such income. In contrast, the savings credit provides a small weekly supplement to reward those with modest savings or private incomes. Section 3 sets out the two extra criteria for the award of the savings credit (in addition to the common rules contained in s.1 for the pension credit as a whole).

As originally enacted in the 2002 Act, the first of these was simply that the claimant (or their partner) was at least 65. This condition was radically altered by the Pensions Act 2014. As from the start date for the new state pension (April 6, 2016), s.3 as amended now provides that the savings credit element of state pension credit is only payable (from the savings credit qualifying age) to those who had already reached pensionable age before that date.

The second is effectively a complicated mathematical formula which is translated into text form. This can only really be understood by following the example provided in the annotation to s.3. Its effect is to provide a small savings credit of up to £17.01 a week at 2024/25 rates for a single pensioner for those with incomes which are just above the MIG level. 1.11

The other important difference from the previous arrangements, at least as the state pension credit scheme was originally enacted, concerns the duration of awards of any pension credit (of either type) and the effects of change in circumstances. Income support is a weekly benefit and any changes in circumstances (e.g. in the amount of an occupational pension) must be reported to the DWP. Where the pension credit is awarded, the Secretary of State had to specify an "assessed income period" (s.6), which will typically be for five years (s.9). The statutory assumption under s.7(4) is that the claimant's income will then remain constant throughout this period, subject to any deemed increases of a foreseeable and regular nature, such as the arrangements for indexation of any occupational or other private pension (e.g. in line with the Retail Price Index); see also s.10. The remarkable effect of these provisions was that where the claimant received a windfall increase during the period of the award, any such increases were disregarded (s.7(5)) and accordingly did not give rise to any obligation to report such a change to the Department. In the event that the pensioner's income fell, a fresh assessment could be applied for (s.8).

However, in the 2013 Spending Round the Government announced the abolition of the assessed income period in state pension credit cases from April 2016, a change effected by the Pensions Act 2014 (ss.28, 29 and Sch.12 paras 88–91). As a result, in future any change in retirement income will need to be reported to the Department when it occurs, triggering a review and a change in benefit award where appropriate.

The remaining provisions of the Act which relate to the state pension credit are of a supplementary nature. Section 11 introduces Sch.1, which applies the social security claims, decisions and appeals procedures to the state pension credit. Section 12 makes special provision for the few polygamous marriages that may fall within the ambit of the new scheme whilst s.13 enables the Secretary of State to make regulations governing transitional arrangements. Section 14 introduces Sch.2, which makes minor and consequential amendments. Sections 15–17 provide definitions of a number of key terms, such as "income" (s.15) and "retirement pension income" (s.16), as well as other general expressions (s.17), but also grant the Secretary of State extensive regulation-making powers to provide further definitions of certain terms. The relevant regulations, also in this volume (see paras 3.1, et seq.), are the State Pension Credit Regulations 2002 (SI 2002/1792), as amended. 1.12

The final point to note about the state pension credit is a matter of nomenclature. Throughout the 2002 Act the new benefit is referred to as the *state* pension credit. This formula is required because s.29 of the Welfare Reform and Pensions Act 1999 makes provision for the creation of "pension credits" as a mechanism for effecting pension sharing on divorce. This Act, therefore, could not describe the benefit simply as the pension credit. However, the benefit is known as the *state* pension credit purely for the purposes of statutory drafting. The Department's publicity material describes the benefit as pension credit *simpliciter.* For the reasons explained in the General Note to s.3, the "savings credit", one of the constituent elements in the pension credit, is itself something of a misnomer, as it is not merely a credit on savings. State pension credit has nothing whatsoever to do with the working tax credit and the child tax credit which were introduced in April 2003 by the Tax Credits Act 2002 (see Vol. IV in this series). Those *tax* credits are administered by HRMC; the state pension credit remains firmly in the province of the DWP and its Pension, Disability and Carers Service, the Department's operational arm which now has responsibility for all pensions matters. See further N. Wikeley, "State Pension Credit: completing the pensions jigsaw?" (2004) 11 *Journal of Social Security Law* 12.

The independent Pensions Commission pointed out that maintaining existing indexation rules for pension credit and the basic state retirement pension respectively would lead to a steady extension of means-testing of pensioners over time. It estimated that by 2050 over 70 per cent of all pensioners would be subject to means-tested withdrawal of either the state second pension or their private pension income: *Pensions Commission, A New Pension Settlement for the Twenty-First Century – The Second Report of the Pensions Commission* (November 2005), p.142.

1.13 Major changes to the state pension regime were made by the Pensions Act 2014, coming into force with effect from April 6, 2016. Pensioners who had already reached state pension age as at that date will continue to be entitled to the state pension under the previous rules. However, 'new' pensioners will now qualify for the new single tier state pension. One of the main principles of the reform was that the new state pension is to be set above the basic level of means-tested support. Thus whereas the standard minimum guarantee under the state pension credit scheme is £218.15 in 2024/25, the starting rate for the new state pension is £221.20.

See also s.142 of the Pensions Act 2008, which enables the Secretary of State to make regulations to supply social security information about state pension credit recipients to energy suppliers (or persons providing services to the energy suppliers or the Secretary of State). These provisions also authorise energy suppliers to share their customer information with the Secretary of State or a service provider, so as to enable either the Secretary of State or a third party to match DWP and energy supplier data to identify the relevant state pension credit recipients. The intention is to identify those persons who are eligible for financial assistance towards their electricity bill in accordance with a support scheme established under arrangements made between the Secretary of State and electricity suppliers. See further the Disclosure of State Pension Credit Information (Warm Home Discount) Regulations 2011 (SI 2011/1830) as amended by the Warm Home Discount (Miscellaneous Amendments) Regulations 2021 (SI 2021/667), the Warm Home Discount (England and Wales) Regulations 2022 (SI 2022/772) and the Warm Home Discount (Scotland) Regulations 2022 (SI 2022/1073).

Note that the State Pension Credit (Coronavirus) (Electronic Claims) (Amendment) Regulations 2020 (SI 2020/456) amended the Claims and Payments Regulations, with effect from May 4, 2020, so as to allow electronic claims to be made for pension credit. Owing to the impact of the Covid-19 outbreak in Great Britain, an online digital platform was developed to provide claimants with an additional route for claiming (and thereby to ease the operational impacts of the pandemic, given the pressure on the DWP's telephony system). Regulation 2 of the 2020 Regulations accordingly amended reg.4ZC of, and para.2 of Sch.9ZC to, the Claims and Payments Regulations to permit the use of an electronic communication in connection with a claim for pension credit. The use of an electronic communication by claimants must be in accordance with a direction of the Secretary of State. These directions are available online at: *https://www.gov.uk/government/publications/the-social-security-electronic-communications-directions* [Accessed 1 April 2023].

Commencement

The Act received the Royal Assent on June 25, 2002. Sections 19, 20 and 22 came into effect on that date (s.22(2)). Other provisions come into effect as the Secretary of State may order (s.22(3)). The State Pension Credit Act 2002 (Commencement No.1) Order 2002 (SI 2002/1691 (c.51)) provided that July 2, 2002 was the day appointed for the coming into force of the regulation making powers under ss.1 to 7, 9 and 11–17 (except for certain provisions in s.14). The relevant regulations are the State Pension Credit Regulations 2002 (SI 2002/1792, as amended), which came into force on October 6, 2003. **1.14**

The final Commencement Order was the State Pension Credit Act 2002 (Commencement No.5) and Appointed Day Order 2003 (SI 2003/1766 (c.75)). This brought into force on October 6, 2003 all those provisions of the Act which were not already in force and appointed that day as the "appointed day" for the purposes of s.13 of the Act (transitional provisions).

Note also that s.34 and Sch.4 of the Welfare Reform Act 2012 have prospectively amended the 2002 Act to create a new credit within state pension credit to cover housing costs. This is intended to provide support for people who have reached the qualifying age for state pension credit (or for couples where both members have reached the qualifying age) once housing benefit is no longer available following the full introduction of universal credit. In particular, the new s.3A (inserted by Welfare Reform Act 2012 s.34 and Sch.4 paras 1 and 4 as amended by s.20(8) of the Welfare Reform and Work Act 2016), sets out the conditions of entitlement to the new housing credit and provides the powers to set out the structure of the housing credit in regulations. There are also a number of consequential amendments. However, s.3A and these other amendments introduced by the Welfare Reform Act 2012 have yet to be brought into force, and so are not included in this edition.

State pension credit: entitlement and amount

Entitlement

1.—(1) A social security benefit to be known as state pension credit shall be payable in accordance with the following provisions of this Act. **1.15**

(2) A claimant is entitled to state pension credit if—

(a) he is in Great Britain;

(b) he has attained the qualifying age; and

(c) he satisfies—

(i) the condition in section 2(1) (guarantee credit); or

(ii) the conditions in section 3(1) and (2) (savings credit).

(3) A claimant who is entitled to state pension credit is entitled—

(a) to a guarantee credit, calculated in accordance with section 2, if he satisfies the condition in subsection (1) of that section, or

(b) to a savings credit, calculated in accordance with section 3, if he satisfies the conditions in subsections (1) and (2) of that section,

(or to both, if he satisfies both the condition mentioned in paragraph (a) and the conditions mentioned in paragraph (b)).

(4) Subsections (2) and (3) are subject to the following provisions of this Act.

(5) Regulations may make provision for the purposes of this Act—

(a) as to circumstances in which a person is to be treated as being or not being in Great Britain; or

(b) continuing a person's entitlement to state pension credit during periods of temporary absence from Great Britain.

(6) In this Act "the qualifying age" means—
(a) in the case of a woman, pensionable age; or
(b) in the case of a man, the age which is pensionable age in the case of a woman born on the same day as the man.

DEFINITIONS

"claimant"—see s.17(1).
"entitled"—*ibid.*
"guarantee credit"—*ibid.*
"pensionable age"—*ibid.*
"the qualifying age"—see subs.(6).
"regulations"—see s.17(1).
"savings credit"—*ibid.*

GENERAL NOTE

1.16 This section sets out the entitlement criteria for the state pension credit. The conditions laid down by this section are the common entitlement rules. These are that the claimant is in Great Britain (subs.(2)(a); see further subs.(5)) and has reached the qualifying age (subs.(2)(b), as defined by subs.(6)). Note also *EC v Secretary of State for Work and Pensions* [2010] UKUT 93 (AAC); [2010] AACR 39, where it was held that state pension credit is a special non-contributory benefit within art.10a of Regulation 1408/71 (now art.70 of Regulation 883/2004) which is payable only to those living in Great Britain. In addition, a claimant must satisfy either or both of the additional rules relating to eligibility for the guarantee credit (s.2) and the savings credit (s.3) (see subs.(2)(c)). The guarantee credit replaced the MIG (or, in other words, income support) for the pensioner population. The calculation of the guarantee credit itself works in the same way as the MIG and is designed to bring a pensioner's income up to a minimum threshold, which for 2024/25 is £218.15 for a single claimant and £332.95 for a couple. The savings credit, which may be payable additionally to or independently of the guarantee credit, seeks to provide a reward for those pensioner claimants who have a modest private income over and above the basic state retirement pension. A claimant's entitlement thus comprises either or both such components, depending on which conditions are met (subs.(3)). These requirements are obviously subject to the remaining provisions of the Act (subs.(4)).

Subsection (2)(a)

1.17 In *NB v Secretary of State for Work and Pensions (SPC)* [2013] UKUT 266 (AAC), an overpayment appeal, Judge Wright held that living on a British registered boat outside UK territorial waters was not being "in Great Britain" for the purpose of s.1(2)(a) (following *R(IS) 8/06*). However, the claimant will have been in Great Britain for any period that he was either on land in the UK or on his boat when in UK waters, and the tribunal erred in law in not enquiring into this aspect. Remitting the appeal to a new tribunal, the Judge directed it to consider whether the temporary absence rule applied for any period (which provides that a claimant will continue to be entitled to SPC for 13 weeks while not in Great Britain if the period of absence is unlikely to exceed 52 weeks and he continues to satisfy the other conditions of entitlement; see reg.3).

For detailed discussion of the position of persons subject to immigration control, see Part V of this Volume.

Subsection (5)

1.18 This power enables regulations to make further provision in respect to the residence requirement. See further State Pension Credit Regulations 2002 (SI 2002/1792) regs 2 and 3, requiring pension credit claimants to be habitually resident, although they may retain their entitlement for up to 13 weeks during a period of temporary absence abroad.

Subsection (6)

This definition of "qualifying age" must be read together with the definition of "pensionable age" in s.17(1). Its effect is that the qualifying age for both men and women is the pensionable age for women. From the 1940s until 2010 the state pension age was 65 for men and 60 for women. The Pensions Act 1995 (s.126 and Sch.4) originally provided for the increase from 60 to 65 in the state pension age for women to be phased in over the period from April 2010 to 2020. However, the Coalition Government brought forward the Pensions Act 2011 (see s.1) to accelerate the latter part of this timetable, so that the pensionable age for women reached 65 in November 2018. The reason for this change was the overall increase in life expectancy since the timetable was last revised. It had also initially been intended that the equalised pensionable age for men and women would then rise to 66 by April 2020. However, because of concerns expressed about the impact on women born in March 1954, who would see their pensionable age increase by as much as two years as a result, it decided that this should happen over a slightly longer period, with the uniform state pension age reaching 66 in October 2020. See further the report by the House of Commons Work and Pensions Committee, *Communication of state pension age changes*, Seventh Report of 2015/16, HC 899). Note that the Pensions Act 2014 also includes provision to bring forward the increase in the common state pension age to 67 to between 2026 and 2028. 1.19

The basic requirement under subs.(2)(a) is that a pension credit claimant must have reached this qualifying age; this is also sufficient for entitlement to the guarantee credit under s.2. However, a claimant must actually be 65 (or their partner must be) in order to claim the savings credit (s.3(1)). The Government's justification for this distinction was that "the age of 65 is the first point at which we judge that the savings credit can be fairly and equally paid to ensure that we are not open to legal challenge in respect of gender equality" (Ms M. Eagle MP, Parliamentary Under-Secretary for Work and Pensions, Standing Committee A, col.104). Thus retired single women aged between 60 and 64 may claim the guarantee credit but not the savings credit, even though they may have a small private income. Women of this age who are members of a married or unmarried couple may claim the savings credit if their partner is aged 65 or over, and so may see some benefit from private savings.

In a number of recent decisions the Upper Tribunal has dealt with some of the difficult evidential issues associated with proof of age. In the first, *LS v SSWP (SPC)* [2014] UKUT 249 (AAC), the issue was whether the claimant, the wife of a Gurkha, was born on January 1, 1951 or some other date in 1951. Judge Williams in the Upper Tribunal held that the tribunal had failed to apply the correct standard of proof (balance of probabilities) and to consider all the relevant evidence. Similar issues arose in *SW v SSWP (SPC)* [2016] UKUT 163 (AAC), where the claimant, who had originally obtained an Ethiopian passport showing her date of birth to be January 1, 1963, subsequently became a naturalized British citizen, her UK passport again showing her date of birth to be January 1, 1963. She later claimed pension credit, stating that her true date of birth was May 23, 1950. The DWP decision-maker and the First-tier Tribunal decided the passport(s) showed the correct date of birth and concluded the claimant was not eligible for pension credit on age grounds. The claimant's explanation, amongst other matters, was that she had obtained her Ethiopian passport at a time when she was travelling to Qatar for domestic work, and had been advised that she would not find employment if she was aged over 30, and so a false date had been used. Judge Hemingway allowed the claimant's appeal and, tasking into account all the evidence, re-made the decision, holding that the claimant had indeed reached the qualifying age. In doing so, Judge Hemingway made the following more general observations:

> "41. ... There is the question of whether the documents are forgeries, the original tribunal of course thought they were, and I am quite prepared to accept that it is possible to obtain fraudulent documents in Ethiopia just as, of course, it is possible to obtain fraudulent documents, in the right circumstances, I imagine

in pretty much every country in the world. There may, of course, be significant variations in the ease with which fraudulent but apparently genuine documents might be obtained. It seems to me that where an allegation of fraud is being made by a party then it will be necessary for the asserting party to prove it to the requisite standard which, here, is a balance of probabilities. Here, though, I cannot see that the respondent did actually submit to the tribunal that the documents were forged. It also seems to me that it will seldom be necessary for a tribunal to reach a definitive view as to whether a document is forged or not. Rather, the inquiry should be directed more as to whether any weight can be attached to the documents provided by a claimant having regard to the evidence as a whole and a claimant's general credibility. There may also be other reasons, irrespective of the veracity of any allegation as to forgery, as to why documents cannot be accorded weight. In this case I have decided, whilst I do not on balance find the appellant to be dishonest, that the documents cannot be accorded weight because of the lack of any evidence and information concerning the existence of or accuracy of record keeping on the part of the church or the relevant government department responsible for issuing birth certificates. So, as it turns out, the documents assist neither the appellant nor the respondent."

Guarantee credit

1.20 **2.**—(1) The condition mentioned in section 1(2)(c)(i) is that the claimant—

(a) has no income; or

(b) has income which does not exceed the appropriate minimum guarantee.

(2) Where the claimant is entitled to a guarantee credit, then—

(a) if he has no income, the guarantee credit shall be the appropriate minimum guarantee; and

(b) if he has income, the guarantee credit shall be the difference between the appropriate minimum guarantee and his income.

(3) The appropriate minimum guarantee shall be the total of—

(a) the standard minimum guarantee; and

(b) such prescribed additional amounts as may be applicable.

(4) The standard minimum guarantee shall be a prescribed amount.

(5) The standard minimum guarantee shall be—

(a) a uniform single amount in the case of every claimant who is a member of a [1 couple]; and

(b) a lower uniform single amount in the case of every claimant who is not a member of [1 a couple].

(6) Regulations may provide that, in prescribed cases, subsection (3) shall have effect with the substitution for the reference in paragraph (a) to the standard minimum guarantee of a reference to a prescribed amount.

(7) Where the claimant is severely disabled, there shall be included among the additional amounts prescribed under subsection (3)(b) an amount in respect of that circumstance.

(8) Where—

(a) the claimant is entitled to an allowance under section 70 of the Contributions and Benefits Act [2 or carer support payment], or

(b) if the claimant is a member of a [2 couple], the other member of the couple is entitled to such an allowance [2 or payment],

there shall be included among the additional amounts prescribed under subsection (3)(b) an amount in respect of that circumstance.

(9) Except for the amount of the standard minimum guarantee, the powers conferred by this section to prescribe amounts include power to prescribe nil as an amount.

AMENDMENTS

1. Civil Partnership Act 2004 s.254 and Sch.24 paras 140 and 141 (December 5, 2005).
2. Carer's Assistance (Carer Support Payment) (Scotland) Regulations 2023 (Consequential Modifications) Order 2023 (SI 2023/1214) art.5(2) (November 16, 2023).

DEFINITIONS

"appropriate minimum guarantee"—see subs.(3) and s.17(1).
"claimant"—see s.17(1).
"Contributions and Benefits Act"—*ibid.*
"couple"—*ibid.*
"entitled"—*ibid.*
"guarantee credit"—*ibid.*
"income"—*ibid.*
"prescribed"—*ibid.*
"regulations"—*ibid.*
"standard minimum guarantee"—see subss.(4) and (5) and s.17(1).

GENERAL NOTE

This section sets out the extra condition (further to the common conditions in s.1) which a pension credit claimant must satisfy in order to be entitled to the guarantee credit (which replaced the MIG, or income support, for pensioners). The extra condition is that the claimant either has no income or has an income which does not exceed the "appropriate minimum guarantee" (subs.(1)). "Income" is defined in accordance with ss.15 and 16 (and see State Pension Credit Regulations 2002 (SI 2002/1792 Pt III)); but note also that the claimant's income is to be aggregated with that of any partner (s.5). The "appropriate minimum guarantee" is equivalent to the applicable amount in the income support scheme. It therefore comprises the "standard minimum guarantee" and other prescribed amounts (subs.(3)). The former is a standard prescribed amount (subss.(4) and (5)) which for 2024/25 is £218.15 for a single person and £332.95 for a couple (State Pension Credit Regulations 2002 (SI 2002/1792) reg.6(1)). The other prescribed amounts mirror the premiums in the income support scheme. Specific provision is made for two particular types of extra prescribed amounts under subs.(3)(b), namely for those who are severely disabled (subs.(7); this is based on SSCBA 1992 s.135(5)) and for those who are entitled to a carer's allowance under SSCBA 1992 s.70 (subs.(8)). The extra amounts under subs.(3)(b) also include other elements, e.g. prescribed sums for owner-occupiers as regards their housing costs (see generally State Pension Credit Regulations 2002 (SI 2002/1792) Schs I and II). 1.21

The Secretary of State also has the power to substitute a prescribed amount for the uniform standard minimum guarantee (subs.(6)). This only has effect for the purpose of calculating the appropriate minimum guarantee for that person under subs.(3)(a), which is then based on the prescribed amount plus any other prescribed additional amounts. It does not, therefore, affect the standard minimum guarantee for other purposes in the Act, most notably the assessment of the maximum savings credit under s.3(7). This power has been inserted to enable a different rate to be applied where the claimant (or their partner) remains in hospital for more than 52 weeks. The previous regime provided for "hospital downrating" to apply after six weeks in hospital, but the Government initially increased this period to 13 weeks and then subsequently to 52 weeks by the Social Security (Hospital In-Patients and Miscellaneous Amendments) Regulations 2003 (SI 2003/1195); see now State Pension Credit Regulations 2002 (SI 2002/1792) Sch.III para.2.

The Secretary of State also has the power, taking subss. (6) and (9) together, to prescribe nil as the amount of the standard minimum guarantee in subs.(3)(a). The wording of subs.(9) is not entirely clear, but its import (when read with subs.(6)) appears to be that nil can be prescribed as the amount of the standard minimum guarantee under subs.(3)(a) but not as the rate of the normal standard minimum guarantee under subss.(4) and (5). This enables a nil amount to be specified for prisoners and members of religious orders who are fully maintained by their orders (both being groups who are currently excluded from income support; see now State Pension Credit Regulations 2002 (SI 2002/1792) reg.6(2) and (3) and *Scott v Secretary of State for Work and Pensions* [2011] EWCA Civ 103; [2011] AACR 23).

Three important differences with the rules governing entitlement to income support should be noted. First, there is no provision in the Act for a "16-hour rule" in the state pension credit scheme. Thus, unlike those of working age who claim income support or jobseeker's allowance, pensioners are not disentitled if they work 16 hours or more a week. Secondly, there is no upper capital limit for the pension credit (see further s.15); moreover the deemed rate of return by virtue of the tariff income rule is halved (State Pension Credit Regulations 2002 (SI 2002/1792) reg.15(6)). Finally, the traditional weekly means-test for income support was not originally replicated in the arrangements for the pension credit; instead the typical award was made for an "assessed income period" of five years (see further s.7). However, assessed income periods were abolished by the Pensions Act 2014 with effect from April 2016.

Savings credit

1.22 **3.**—[1 (1) The first of the conditions mentioned in section 1(2)(c)(ii) is that the claimant—

(a) has attained pensionable age before 6 April 2016 and has attained the age of 65 (before, on or after that date), or

(b) is a member of a couple, the other member of which falls within paragraph (a).]

(2) The second of the conditions mentioned in section 1(2)(c)(ii) is that—

(a) the claimant's qualifying income exceeds the savings credit threshold; and

(b) the claimant's income is such that, for the purposes of subsection (3), amount A exceeds amount B.

(3) Where the claimant is entitled to a savings credit, the amount of the savings credit shall be the amount by which amount A exceeds amount B.

(4) For the purposes of subsection (3)—

"amount A" is the smaller of—

(a) the maximum savings credit; and

(b) a prescribed percentage of the amount by which the claimant's qualifying income exceeds the savings credit threshold; and

"amount B" is—

(a) a prescribed percentage of the amount (if any) by which the claimant's income exceeds the appropriate minimum guarantee; or

(b) if there is no such excess, nil.

(5) Where, by virtue of regulations under section 2(6), the claimant's appropriate minimum guarantee does not include the standard minimum guarantee, regulations may provide that the definition of "amount B" in

subsection (4) shall have effect with the substitution for the reference in paragraph (a) to the appropriate minimum guarantee of a reference to a prescribed higher amount.

(6) Regulations may make provision as to income which is, and income which is not, to be treated as qualifying income for the purposes of this section.

(7) For the purposes of this section—

"the savings credit threshold" is such amount as may be prescribed;

"the maximum savings credit" is a prescribed percentage of the difference between—

(a) the standard minimum guarantee; and

(b) the savings credit threshold.

(8) Regulations may prescribe descriptions of persons in whose case the maximum savings credit shall be taken to be nil.

AMENDMENT

1. Pensions Act 2014 s.23 and Sch.12 Pt 3 para.89 (April 6, 2016).

DEFINITIONS

"appropriate minimum guarantee"—see ss.2(3) and 17(1).
"claimant"—see s.17(1).
"couple"—*ibid.*
"entitled"—*ibid.*
"income"—*ibid.*
"maximum savings credit"—see subs.(7).
"prescribed"—see s.17(1).
"regulations"—*ibid.*
"savings credit"—*ibid.*
"savings credit threshold"—see subs.(7).
"standard minimum guarantee"—ss.2(4) and (5) and 17(1).

GENERAL NOTE

This section sets out the extra conditions (further to the common conditions in s.1) which a pension credit claimant must satisfy in order to be entitled to the savings credit. A claimant may be entitled to the savings credit even if he or she is not entitled to the guarantee credit (s.1(3)). In order to qualify for a savings credit there are two additional requirements that must be satisfied. **1.23**

The first, as originally enacted, was that the claimant (or their partner) was at least 65. This stood in contrast to the eligibility conditions for guarantee credit, for which the qualifying age was (and remains) the pensionable age for women as specified in the common criteria for pension credit (ss.1(2)(a) and (6)). However, as a result of amendments made by the Pensions Act 2014 (fully in force from April 6, 2016), there is no longer access to the savings credit element for those claimants reaching state pension age on or after that date *unless* they are a member of a couple where the other member reached state pension age before April 6, 2016 (known as "a mixed-age couple"; see further s.3ZA). The policy justification for this change is that whereas the previous basic state pension was set below the level of the standard minimum guarantee in pension credit, the new state pension is set at a level above that threshold, so removing the problem that the savings credit was designed to address. See further the State Pension Credit Regulations 2002 (SI 2002/1792) reg.7A. The policy was first announced in the new state pension green and white papers (DWP, "A State Pension for the 21st Century", Cm 8053, April 2011, Ch.3 and "The single-tier pension: a simple foundation for saving", Cm 8528, January 2013, Ch.4).

The second additional condition is more complex. The claimant's "qualifying income" (including that of their partner: see further ss.5, 15 and 16 and State Pension Credit Regulations 2002 (SI 2002/1792) reg.9) must exceed the "savings credit threshold" and must be such that "amount A exceeds Amount B" (subs.(2)), the difference being the amount of savings credit entitlement (subs.(3)). The complexity is the inevitable consequence of the draftsman's attempt to reduce an arithmetical calculation into comprehensible prose. The good news is that this formula does not require the same skills in advanced algebra as did the original child support scheme.

1.24 The term "savings credit" is itself something of a misnomer, as will be seen from the examples discussed below. The savings credit is not a credit that is payable simply because a pensioner has savings, e.g. in a bank account. Rather, it is a supplement that is payable to pensioners who have small amounts of private income, whether in the form of an occupational or other private pension or indeed by way of income which is generated from savings.

Note, however, that now the Pensions Act 2014 (Sch.12 para.89) is in force the savings credit element of pension credit will in future only be payable to those who have reached state pension age before April 6, 2016 (however, a younger individual may still qualify in future if they are a member of a couple and their partner qualifies).

Subsection (1)

1.25 See further the annotation to s.1(6). Note also that the words "the age of 65" in subs.(1) will be replaced by the expression "pensionable age" but that this amendment will only take effect from April 6, 2024 (Pensions Act 2007 s.13 and Sch.8 para.44).

Subsections (2)–(4)

1.26 The additional condition in subs.(2) can be understood better if it is broken down into its four constituent terms: qualifying income, the savings credit threshold and amounts A and B respectively, although the component parts of these terms also require further definition.

Qualifying income

1.27 The expression "qualifying income" is further defined by regulations (subs.(6): see State Pension Credit Regulations 2002 (SI 2002/1792) regs 15–18). The claimant's qualifying income includes those elements of their income which arise from contributions to the National Insurance scheme (e.g. the basic state retirement pension and any additional pension such as SERPS) and from their own private provision (e.g. an occupational pension or income from capital). After considerable debate, the government announced that income from work is to be treated in the same way as income from an occupational pension or savings. The term "income" is further defined by ss.15 and 16, and such income must be aggregated with that of any partner (s.5).

Savings credit threshold

1.28 The "savings credit threshold" is "such amount as may be prescribed" (subs.(7)). This threshold for 2024/25 is £189.80 for a single claimant and £301.22 for a couple (State Pension Credit Regulations 2002 (SI 2002/1792) reg.7(2)). This means that pensioners whose qualifying income is less than this level, even though they have, e.g. a small occupational pension or income from savings, are unable to claim the savings credit. This is likely to be the case with those women who are not entitled to a full retirement pension because of gaps in their contributions records. Thus these women pensioners may claim the guarantee credit to bring their income up to the appropriate minimum guarantee under s.2, but see no extra benefit for their thrift as their combined income from other sources does not exceed the basic retirement pension.

Furthermore, Government policy since the April 2012 uprating has been to increase the pension credit minimum guarantee and to fund this increase for the very poorest pensioners by restricting eligibility to the savings credit. In April 2011 the maximum weekly award of savings credit was £20.52 for a single person and

£27.09 for a couple. However, raising the savings credit threshold has the effect of both reducing the numbers of pensioners eligible for the savings credit and reducing the maximum weekly savings credit payable. As a result the maximum savings credit, available to the slightly better off pensioners, has been squeezed further to £17.01 for a single person and £19.04 for a couple for 2024/25.

Amount A

"Amount A" is the *smaller* of the "maximum savings credit" and "a prescribed percentage of the amount by which the claimant's qualifying income exceeds the savings credit threshold" (subs.(4)). The "maximum savings credit" is a prescribed percentage (60 per cent: State Pension Credit Regulations 2002 (SI 2002/1792) reg.7(1)(a)) of the difference between the standard minimum guarantee and the savings credit threshold (subs.(7)). By this stage (if not before) the reader of these annotations might appreciate a simple algebraic notation. An example may therefore assist. **1.29**

For 2024/25 the maximum savings credit is 60 per cent of the difference between the standard minimum guarantee (£218.15 for a single person, £332.95 for a couple) and the savings credit threshold (£189.80 for a single person and £301.22 for a couple). The difference for a single person is thus £28.35, of which 60 per cent is £17.01. For a couple the difference is £31.73, of which 60 per cent is £19.04. The maximum savings credit is accordingly £17.01 for single claimants and £9.04 for couples.

This figure must then be compared with a second figure representing "a prescribed percentage of the amount by which the claimant's qualifying income exceeds the savings credit threshold". In this context the prescribed percentage is also 60 per cent (State Pension Credit Regulations 2002 (SI 2002/1792) reg.7(1)(b)). The savings credit threshold, which used to be aligned with the basic Category A state retirement pension, is now higher and for 2024/25 is £189.80 for a single person and £301.22 for a couple. The "qualifying income" is to be calculated in accordance with ss.15 and 16 and with regulations under subs.(6) (see also above). If a single claimant's qualifying weekly income is £199.80, comprising the basic state retirement pension and a small occupational pension, then this second figure is £6 (being 60 per cent of the difference between £199.80 and £189.80). As £6 is less than £17.01 in this scenario, Amount A is the former, i.e. £6.

Amount B

Amount B is "a prescribed percentage of the amount (if any) by which the claimant's income exceeds the appropriate minimum guarantee" or, if there is no such excess, nil (subs.(4)). The prescribed percentage in this calculation is 40 per cent in this instance, not 60 per cent (State Pension Credit Regulations 2002 (SI 2002/1792) reg.7(1)(c)). It is also important to note that in this calculation the reference is to the claimant's income, not their qualifying income (which may be a lower figure). The appropriate minimum guarantee is defined by s.2(3) and represents the previous minimum income guarantee for pensioners. Let us assume that in the scenario under discussion the claimant's appropriate minimum guarantee consists of the standard minimum guarantee (i.e. there are no extra sums equivalent to further premiums) and is £218.15 in 2024/25. In this example the claimant's income (£199.80) is clearly less than the appropriate minimum guarantee (£218.15) and so amount B must be nil. **1.30**

In the hypothetical case set out above, amount A is £6 and amount B is nil. We have already established that the claimant's qualifying income (£199.80) exceeds the savings credit threshold (£189.80) and so subs.(2)(a) is met. As amount A exceeds amount B, the requirement in subs.(2)(b) is also satisfied. Assuming that the claimant (or partner) is over 65, this means that both conditions for the award of the savings credit are fulfilled. The amount of the savings credit in such a case is the amount by which amount A exceeds amount B, namely £6 (subs.(3)).

If, however, a single pensioner's total income and qualifying income in 2024/25 is say £218.15, e.g. comprising the state retirement pension and an occupational pension, then amount A is £17.01. This figure is both the maximum savings credit, i.e. a figure which is both 60 per cent of the difference between the standard minimum guarantee and the savings credit threshold and 60 per cent of the amount by which this individual's qualifying income exceeds the savings credit threshold. In such a scenario the claimant's income is the same as the appropriate minimum guarantee and so amount B is nil. The excess of amount A over amount B is therefore £17.01 and this sum is payable by way of a savings credit under subs.(3). The pensioner's income is thus £235.16 (retirement pension and occupational pension together with £17.01 savings credit), whereas under the previous arrangements there would have been no entitlement to income support, leaving such a pensioner in the same position as a pensioner claimant whose sole income was the state retirement pension.

Once a pensioner's income starts to exceed the appropriate minimum guarantee, then the way in which amounts A and B are defined is such that the claimant's entitlement to the savings credit is gradually withdrawn as their income increases. A further simple example will suffice. Assume that a single pensioner's total weekly income is £227.80, comprising the state retirement pension and an occupational pension. On these facts amount A is the smaller of the maximum savings credit (£17.01) and 60 per cent of the amount by which the claimant's income (£227.80) exceeds the savings credit threshold (£189.80). The latter figure is £22.80 (60 per cent of the difference, being £38.00). As this obviously is more than £17.01, amount A will be £17.01. Amount B is 40 per cent of the amount by which the claimant's income (and again, for the purposes of exposition, we assume that income and qualifying income are identical) exceeds the appropriate minimum guarantee (i.e. £218.15). The difference between those two figures in this example is £9.65, of which 40 per cent is £3.86. Both the conditions set out in subs.(2) are therefore satisfied, and so the claimant's savings credit is the amount by which amount A (£17.01) exceeds amount B (£3.86), namely £13.15. The claimant, on this scenario, thus has a final income of £240.95; that is, £227.80 by way of retirement pension and occupational pension topped up by £13.15 savings credit). Thus, the value of the savings credit will gradually diminish as the claimant's combined income from other sources rises.

Subsection (5)

1.31 Section 2(6) enables the Secretary of State to provide for a different rate for the guarantee credit to be applied in place of the standard minimum guarantee where the claimant (or their partner) remains in hospital for more than 52 weeks. If this same principle were to be carried over into the calculation of the savings credit, the effect would be that amount B would be much higher and might well exceed amount A, which would extinguish any entitlement to the savings credit by virtue of subs.(3). This provision allows regulations to be made to provide for a higher figure to be stipulated in place of the reference to the appropriate minimum guarantee in the definition of amount B. This will reduce amount B and accordingly increase the likelihood that amount A will exceed amount B and so result in the savings credit being payable (State Pension Credit Regulations 2002 (SI 2002/1792) Sch.III para.2).

Subsection (8)

1.32 This power enables a nil amount to be specified as the maximum savings credit for prisoners and members of religious orders who are fully maintained by their orders. This mirrors the power under s.2(9) and reflects the fact that both groups who are currently excluded from income support (see State Pension Credit Regulations 2002 (SI 2002/1792) reg.7(3)).

[1 Power to limit savings credit for certain mixed-age couples

1.33 **3ZA.**—(1) Regulations may provide that, in prescribed cases, a person who is a member of a mixed-age couple is not entitled to a savings credit.

(2) For example, the regulations could provide that a member of a mixed-age couple is not entitled to a savings credit unless—

(a) the person has been awarded a savings credit with effect from a day before 6 April 2016 and was entitled to a savings credit immediately before that date, and

(b) the person remained entitled to state pension credit at all times since the beginning of 6 April 2016.

(3) In this section "mixed-age couple" means a couple (whenever formed) one member of which had attained pensionable age before 6 April 2016 and the other had not.]

AMENDMENT

1. Pensions Act 2014 s.23 and Sch.12 Pt 3 para.90 (July 7, 2015).

DEFINITIONS

"mixed-age couple"—subs.(3).
"couple"—see s.17(1).
"entitled"—*ibid.*
"pensionable age"—*ibid.*
"prescribed"—*ibid.*
"savings credit—*ibid.*

GENERAL NOTE

The first requirement for entitlement to the savings credit element of pension credit, as originally enacted, was that the claimant (or their partner) was at least 65 (s.3(1)). However, as a result of amendments made by the Pensions Act 2014, there is no longer access to the savings credit element for those claimants reaching state pension age on or after April 6, 2016 unless they are a member of a couple where the other member reached state pension age *before* that date (known as "a mixed-age couple"). This section provides for entitlement to the savings credit to be so restricted and defines what is meant by a "mixed-age couple". The policy justification for this change is that whereas the previous basic state pension was set below the level of the standard minimum guarantee in pension credit, the new state pension is set at a level (just) above that threshold, so removing the problem that the savings credit was designed to address. See further the State Pension Credit Regulations 2002 (SI 2002/1792) reg.7A. 1.34

Exclusions

4.—(1) A claimant is not entitled to state pension credit if he is a member of a [1 couple] the other member of which is entitled to state pension credit. 1.35

[2(1A) A claimant is not entitled to state pension credit if he is a member of a couple the other member of which has not attained the qualifying age.]

(2) In section 115(1) of the Immigration and Asylum Act 1999 (c.33) (exclusion of certain persons from benefits) in the words preceding paragraph (a), after "Jobseekers Act 1995" insert "or to state pension credit under the State Pension Credit Act 2002".

(3) Where the amount payable by way of state pension credit would (apart from this subsection) be less than a prescribed amount, it shall not be payable except in prescribed circumstances.

AMENDMENTS

1. Civil Partnership Act 2004 s.254 and Sch.24 para.140 (December 5, 2005).
2. Welfare Reform Act 2012 s.31 and Sch.2 para.64 (May 15, 2019).

DEFINITIONS

"claimant"—see s.17(1).
"couple"—*ibid.*
"entitled"—*ibid.*
"prescribed"—*ibid.*

GENERAL NOTE

Subsection (1)

1.36 Only one member of a married or unmarried couple is entitled to the pension credit, so preventing double provision from public funds (subs.(1), modelled on SSCBA 1992 s.134(2)).

Subsection (1A)

1.37 As from May 15, 2019, a claimant is not entitled to pension credit (or to pension age housing benefit) if they are a member of the couple and their partner has not reached the qualifying age. Such a couple is known as a "mixed-age couple" (but this term has a different definition to that which continues to apply for the purpose of the savings credit—on which see ss.3(1) and 3ZA). A mixed age couple for the purpose of subs.(1A) may be eligible to claim universal credit instead. However, if the younger partner was entitled to income support, income-based JSA or income-related ESA, then they may be able to keep that entitlement with the other person as their partner. Alternatively, the younger member may assume responsibility for an income-based JSA joint-claim for both of them. Note also that the normal rules on the three-month time limit for claiming pension credit apply (Claims and Payments Regulations, reg.19(2) (and (3)(i)). As a result, claims that were made on or before August 13, 2019 can be backdated to before the rule change so long as the claimant meets the entitlement conditions as they stood on the earlier date. Conversely, advance claims could be made for up to four months before a person reaches the qualifying age, but subject to the changes effective from May 15, 2019 (Claims and Payments Regulations, reg.13D(1)).

There are savings provisions in art.4 of the Welfare Reform Act 2012 (Commencement No. 31 and Savings and Transitional Provisions and Commencement No. 21 and 23 and Transitional and Transitory Provisions (Amendment)) Order 2019 (SI 2019/37)—see Part I above and also Vol.V in this series. The savings provisions mean that the exclusion of mixed-age couples from pension credit entitlement does not apply. So, their effect is that a member of a mixed-age couple who was entitled to pension credit (or housing benefit or both benefits) on May 14, 2019 continues to be so entitled on or after May 15, 2019 (art.4(1)). However, the savings provisions cease to apply on or after May 15, 2019 to a member of a mixed-age couple when that person is not entitled to pension credit (or pension age housing benefit) as part of the same mixed-age couple (art.4(2)). At that point, the usual alternative benefit will be universal credit.

The High Court has ruled that the exclusion of mixed-age couples from pension credit is neither discriminatory nor in breach of the public sector equality duty (PSED): see *R. (on the application of Prichard) v SSWP* [2020] EWHC 1495 (Admin), where the claimant was due to reach state pension age on July 6, 2020, but his wife would not do so for a further six years. As a result of the changes outlined above, the couple would have to continue to claim working-age benefits until 2026 and would be £65,000 worse off than they would have been had the changes not been made. Both the claimant and his wife had serious illnesses and were in receipt of disability benefits. The couple would be classed as a "no-conditionality mixed-age couple" as the claimant was over pension age and his wife received carer's allowance (and so she would not be subject to any work-related requirements). On the application for judicial review, Laing J held that the Secretary of State had had appropriate regard to the relevant equality needs under the PSED (see further Equality Act

2010, s.149). She further held that the policy in question, in its application to no-conditionality mixed-age couples, was not manifestly without reasonable foundation. It followed that "the differential treatment of which the claimant complains is not a breach of article 14 (whether read with article 8 or with A1P1), and, therefore, that the 2019 Order, which provides for the commencement of paragraph 64 of the 2012 Act (and by that route, of section 4(1A) of the SPCA) is not incompatible with the claimant's Convention rights" (at [136]).

Subsection (2)

The general exclusion of persons who are "subject to immigration control" from access to the benefits system is extended to the pension credit scheme (subs.(2); for the limited exceptions to the rule in s.115 of the Immigration and Asylum Act 1999, see the Social Security (Immigration and Asylum) Consequential Amendments Regulations 2000 (SI 2000/636)). On the meaning of "residence" in that context see *CPC/1035/2005.* Commissioner Jacobs held there that "in its ordinary meaning a person does not have to be physically present at a place in order to be resident there. Whether a person is or is not resident in a particular place during a period of physical absence depends on a calculus consisting of the duration and circumstances of the absence" (para.14). On the facts of that case it was held that three prolonged periods of absence in Pakistan— each period being for more than one year—meant that the claimant had not remained "resident" in the UK. **1.38**

The concept of a 'person subject to immigration control' may require careful analysis of the basis upon which a person is lawfully in the UK. In *SJ v SSWP (SPC)* [2016] AACR 17 the claimant had originally entered the UK as a sponsored visitor, subject to a maintenance undertaking. She then applied for indefinite leave to remain ("ILR") in the UK as a dependant of her adult daughter, who was settled here. The Home Office ("HO") refused the application. The First-tier Tribunal (Immigration and Asylum Chamber) allowed her appeal under both the Immigration Rules (para.317) and under art.8 ECHR human rights grounds. The HO then granted the claimant ILR. The DWP refused the claimant's subsequent pension credit claim on the basis that she was still in the UK within five years of the original maintenance undertaking. The Upper Tribunal, distinguishing *R(PC) 1/09*, rejected the Appellant's argument that she had ILR on art.8 grounds, free of the maintenance undertaking given under the Rules. It followed she was a person subject to immigration control and not entitled to pension credit.

Note that all British citizens have a right of abode under the Immigration Act 1971. As a result, British citizens cannot be regarded as sponsored immigrants or be barred for that reason from access to public funds such as state pension credit (*R(PC) 2/07*).

Subsection (3)

Provision is also made to set a minimum threshold for payment of the pension credit. Entitlement of less than 10 pence a week is not payable, unless it can be combined with another benefit (subs.(3)), modelled on SSCBA 1992 s.134(4); see State Pension Credit Regulations 2002 (SI 2002/1792) reg.13). **1.39**

Aggregation

Income and capital of claimant, spouse, etc.

5.—Where the claimant is a member of a [1 couple], the income and capital of the other member of the couple shall, except in prescribed circumstances, be treated for the purposes of this Act as income and capital of the claimant. **1.40**

AMENDMENT

1. Civil Partnership Act 2004 s.254 and Sch.24 para.140 (December 5, 2005).

DEFINITIONS

"capital"—see s.17(1).
"claimant"—*ibid.*
"couple"—*ibid.*
"income"—*ibid.*
"prescribed"—*ibid.*

GENERAL NOTE

1.41 This section provides for the aggregation of the income and capital resources of the claimant and his or her partner, irrespective of marital status or sexual orientation. This is in line with standard means-tested benefit principles. Indeed, this provision is closely modelled on SSCBA 1992 s.136(1). The definition requires that the partners are living in the same household. For special cases where persons are treated as either being or not being members of the same household, see State Pension Credit Regulations 2002 (SI 2002/1792) reg.5).

Retirement provision

Duty to specify assessed income period [2 for pre-6 April 2016 awards]

1.42 **6.**—(1) In any case falling within subsection (3) or (4) [2 where the relevant decision takes effect before 6 April 2016], the Secretary of State shall, on the making of the relevant decision, specify a period as the assessed income period, unless prevented by subsection (2).

(2) The Secretary of State is prevented from specifying a period as the assessed income period under subsection (1)—

(a) if the relevant decision takes effect at a time when an assessed income period is in force in the case of the claimant by virtue of a previous application of this section; or
(b) in such other circumstances as may be prescribed.

(3) The first case is where—

(a) the Secretary of State determines the amount of a claimant's income for the purposes of a decision relating to state pension credit;
(b) the decision is a decision under section 8(1), 9 or 10 of the Social Security Act 1998 (c.14) (decisions on claims etc, and decisions revising or superseding decisions);
(c) the decision takes effect on or after—
  (i) the day on which the claimant attains the age of 65; or
  (ii) if earlier, in a case where the claimant is a member of a [1 couple], the day on which the other member of the couple attains that age; and
(d) the decision is not to the effect that the claimant is not entitled to state pension credit.

(4) The second case is where—

(a) the amount of the claimant's income is determined on, or for the purposes of, an appeal against a decision that the claimant is not entitled to state pension credit;

(b) on the appeal, it is decided that the claimant is entitled to state pension credit; and
(c) the decision takes effect as mentioned in subsection (3)(c).
(5) In this section "the relevant decision" means—
(a) so far as relating to the first case, the decision mentioned in subsection (3)(a);
(b) so far as relating to the second case, the decision on appeal mentioned in subsection (4)(b).
(6) This section is subject to section 9.
(7) This section and sections 7 to 10 shall be construed as one.

AMENDMENTS

1. Civil Partnership Act 2004 s.254 and Sch.24 para.140 (December 5, 2005).
2. Pensions Act 2014 s.28(1) (April 6, 2016).

DEFINITIONS

"assessed income period"—see s.17(1).
"claimant"—*ibid.*
"couple"—*ibid.*
"entitled"—*ibid.*
"income"—*ibid.*
"prescribed"—*ibid.*
"the relevant decision"—see subs.(5).

GENERAL NOTE

When making a decision before April 2016 that a person is entitled to the pension credit, the Secretary of State was required to specify an "assessed income period" in relation to the claimant (subs.(1)). Such a decision could be made in the first instance by the Secretary of State (subs.(3)) or following an appeal (subs.(4)). The Secretary of State was prevented from so doing where an assessed income period was currently in force (subs.(2)(a)). For circumstances prescribed under subs.(2)(b), see State Pension Credit Regulations 2002 (SI 2002/1792) reg.10(1). The significance of the "assessed income period" was that it was used as the basis for a long-term award of the pension credit (see s.7). It should also be noted that this section was subject to s.9 (see subs.(6)), which specifies that the "assessed income period" was normally five years, and that ss.7–10 "shall be construed as one" (subs (7)). 1.43

Note, however, that now s.28 of the Pensions Act 2014 is in force assessed income periods are being phased out as from April 2016. As a result, any change in retirement income will in future need to be reported to the Department when it occurs, triggering a review and change in benefit award where appropriate. Thus s.28(3) expressly provides that "Regulations under section 9(5) of the State Pension Credit Act 2002 may in particular be made for the purpose of phasing out, on or after 6 April 2016, any remaining assessed income period that is 5 years or shorter than 5 years". See now the amendments to reg.12 of the State Pension Credit Regulations 2002 (SI 2002/1792).

Fixing of claimant's retirement provision for assessed income period

7.—(1) This section applies where, pursuant to section 6(1), the Secretary of State on the making of the relevant decision specifies a period as the assessed income period. 1.44

(2) This section has effect for the purpose of determining, as at any time in the assessed income period—

(a) the claimant's entitlement to state pension credit; or

(b) the amount of state pension credit to which the claimant is entitled.

(3) Where the claimant's income, as determined for the purposes of the relevant decision, includes an amount (the "assessed amount") in respect of an element of the claimant's retirement provision, the amount of that element as at any time in the assessed income period shall be taken to be the assessed amount as for the time being varied in accordance with regulations under subsection (4).

(4) The assessed amount shall be deemed, except in prescribed circumstances—

(a) to increase, or

(b) in the case of income from capital, to increase or decrease,

on such date or dates and by such amounts as may be prescribed.

(5) Where it is determined for the purposes of the relevant decision that the claimant's income does not include any, or any further, elements of retirement provision, the claimant's income throughout the assessed income period shall be taken not to include those elements.

(6) For the purposes of this Act "retirement provision" means income of any of the following descriptions—

(a) retirement pension income, other than benefit under [[2] Part 1 of the Pensions Act 2014 or] the Contributions and Benefits Act;

(b) income from annuity contracts (other than retirement pension income);

(c) income from capital;

and an "element" of a person's retirement provision is income of any of those descriptions from a particular source;

[[1] (d) PPF periodic payments.]

(7) For the purposes of this section, regulations may make provision—

(a) for treating income of any particular description as income of another description; or

(b) for treating income from different sources as income from the same source.

(8) Nothing in subsections (3) to (5) prevents the revision under section 9 of the Social Security Act 1998 (c.14) of the relevant decision or of any earlier or later decision under section 10 of that Act.

(9) This section is subject to section 8.

AMENDMENTS

1. Pensions Act 2004 (PPF Payments and FAS Payments) (Consequential Provisions) Order 2006 (SI 2006/343) art.3(1) (February 14, 2006).

2. Pensions Act 2014 s.23 and Sch.12 Pt 1 paras 42 and 43 (April 6, 2016).

DEFINITIONS

"assessed amount"—see subs.(3).
"assessed income period"—see s.17(1).
"capital"—*ibid.*
"claimant"—*ibid.*
"Contributions and Benefits Act"—*ibid.*
"element"—see subs.(6) and s.17(1).
"entitled"—see s.17(1).
"income"—*ibid.*

"regulations"—*ibid.*
"relevant decision"—see s.6(5).
"retirement pension income"—see ss.16 and 17(1).
"retirement provision"—see s.7(6) and s.17(1).

GENERAL NOTE

This provision is the key to understanding how the pension credit scheme fundamentally differs from other means-tested benefits in terms of the usual requirement to report changes in income during the period of an award. Once the Secretary of State has specified the "assessed income period" under s.6 (which is typically five years: s.9(1)), this has the effect of fixing the "assessed amount" derived from the claimant's "retirement provision" (effectively their income: see subs.(6)) for the duration of that period (subs.(3)). This assessed amount is subject to deemed increases or decreases (reflecting, e.g. the terms of a claimant's pension arrangements, such as a cost-of-living increase) (subs.(4); for further detail on this, see State Pension Credit Regulations 2002 (SI 2002/1792) reg.10(2)–(7)). Any further elements of retirement provision which are acquired at some later date within the assessed income period are then disregarded (subs.(5)). Such changes accordingly need not be reported during the lifetime of the award. Even if the changes deemed under subs.(4) work in favour of the claimant (i.e. their actual increase is more than the deemed increase), the effect of subs.(3) is that there is no overpayment and no need to report the change. **1.45**

The implications of this radical change were spelt out by Mr Ian McCartney MP, the then Minster for Pensions:

> "Let us be clear about this: if a pensioner wins the lottery in the second week of his or her assessed income period, the increase in capital, be it £10 or £1 million, will not be reflected in the pension credit entitlement until the end of the assessed income period—in four years and 50 weeks' time . . . We can live with ignoring a few individuals' good fortune for the sake of simplification for the overwhelming majority of pensioners". (Standing Committee A, cols 166 and 184.)

But if the claimant actually loses out, in that the deemed increase is more than their actual increase, a new decision can be sought (s.8(1)). The normal powers to effect a revision of an initial decision under s.9 of the SSA 1998 remain in place (subs.(8)).

The Minister's statement to the Standing Committee about the lottery winner was considered by Commissioner Levenson in *CPC/0206/2005*. The claimant disclosed in her claim that she was moving into sheltered accommodation and her house was on the market. An official decided that its value should be disregarded for the time being, but noted that this decision would change in the event of sale. However, the Secretary of State then awarded pension credit for a five-year assessed income period. Later the claimant reported that her house had been sold. Commissioner Levenson observed that the Minister's statement did not cover a case such as this, where the issue was "what the Secretary of State should do if it is known that a large amount of capital is likely to be on its way" (para.10). The Commissioner held that the original decision should be revised for official error and replaced with an award which did not specify an assessed income period ("AIP"). That decision was then subject to supersession for the change of circumstances in the receipt of the proceeds of sale. According to the Commissioner: **1.46**

> "23. It seems to me that the concept of 'error' involves more than merely taking a decision that another decision maker with the same information would not take, but is not limited to (although it includes, subject to the statutory exceptions) a public law or any other error of law. Other than that it is not helpful (and could be misleading) to go beyond the words of the regulation. On the facts of the present case, though, I take the view that no Secretary of State or decision maker acting reasonably could have imposed a 5 year AIP. It was already known that number 8 was up for sale and that it would realise a sum of several tens of thousands of

pounds (even if the exact amount was not known) and a view had already been taken that the progress of the sale should be monitored. In these respects the position was very different from that of a lottery winner who, at the time of the decision on the claim, had done no more than buy a ticket."

See also the decision of Commissioner Rowland in *CPC/1928/2005*, discussed in the note to s.9, below.

Fresh determinations increasing claimant's entitlement

1.47 **8.**—(1) Subsections (3) to (5) of section 7 do not prevent the making of fresh determinations as to the elements, or any of the elements, or the amount of any of the elements, of the claimant's retirement provision as at any time during the assessed income period, if—

(a) the fresh determinations are for the purpose of making a decision under section 10 of the Social Security Act 1998 (c.14) ("the new decision");
(b) the new decision increases the amount of state pension credit to which the claimant is entitled; and
(c) the increase is in whole or in part the result of the fresh determinations (taken as a whole).

(2) The conditions in paragraphs (b) and (c) of subsection (1) shall be taken to be satisfied if—

(a) the new decision reduces the amount of state pension credit to which the claimant is entitled; but
(b) the reduction is less than it would have been apart from the fresh determinations (taken as a whole).

(3) Where a fresh determination is made by virtue of subsection (1), then, as respects the part of the assessed income period that begins with the day on which the new decision takes effect, subsections (3) to (5) of section 7 shall have effect in accordance with the fresh determination, instead of the determination which it replaces, but as if—

(a) the fresh determination were (and the determination which it replaces were not) a determination for the purposes of the relevant decision;
(b) any assessed amount resulting from the fresh determination were not subject to variation under subsection (4) of that section at any time before the day on which the new decision takes effect; and
(c) the claimant's income, as determined for the purposes of the relevant decision, were constituted accordingly.

DEFINITIONS

"assessed income period"—see ss.9(1) and 17(1).
"claimant"—see s.17(1).
"element"—*ibid.*
"entitled"—*ibid.*
"income"—*ibid.*
"retirement provision"—see ss.7(6) and 17(1).

GENERAL NOTE

1.48 The presumption under s.7 is that the assessment of the claimant's "retirement provision" will remain unchanged during the typical five-year award of pension credit, subject to the usual uprating. However, a fresh determination can be made by way of a supersession decision within the assessed income period to increase the claimant's entitlement. This will not affect the assessed income period (subs.(1)). The assessed income period can also continue where the effect of the supersession decision is to reduce entitlement to the pension credit, but the reduction is less than it would otherwise have been because of the recalculation of some other element of the claimant's income (subs.(2)). Where a supersession decision is made, the remaining elements of the retirement provision are treated as unchanged for the rest of the assessed income period (subs.(3)). See also State Pension Credit Regulations 2002 (SI 2002/1792) reg.11.

Duration of assessed income period

9.—[2 (1) An assessed income period shall (subject to the following subsections) be— **1.49**

(a) in the case of a claimant who is under the age of 75 on the day on which the relevant decision takes effect, the period of 5 years beginning with that day;

(b) in the case of a claimant who is aged 75 or over on that day, an indefinite period beginning with that day.]

(2) If the Secretary of State considers that the particulars of the claimant's retirement provision as determined for the purposes of the relevant decision are not likely, after taking account of any assumed variations under subsection (3), to be typical of the claimant's retirement provision throughout the period of 12 months beginning with the day on which that decision takes effect—

(a) he need not specify a period under section 6(1); and

(b) if he does so, [2 shall specify a period that is shorter than 5 years] (but beginning as mentioned in subsection (1)).

(3) It shall be assumed for the purposes of subsection (2) that the same variations fall to be made in relation to the amount of an element of the claimant's retirement provision as determined for the purposes of the relevant decision as would fall to be made under section 7(4) if an assessed income period were to be specified in accordance with subsection (1).

(4) An assessed income period shall, except in prescribed circumstances, end at any time at which—

(a) the claimant becomes a member of a [1 couple];

(b) the claimant ceases to be a member of a [1 couple];

(c) the claimant attains the age of 65; or

(d) in a case where the claimant is a member of a [1 couple], the other member of the couple attains the age of 65.

(5) Regulations may prescribe further times at which, or circumstances in which, an assessed income period shall end.

[2 (6) Where—

(a) an assessed income period is brought to an end [3, on or after 6 April 2009 but before 6 April 2014,] by the expiry of a period of 5 years or more, and

(b) the claimant is aged 80 or over at that time,

the assessed income period shall be treated as not ending at that time but, subject to subsection (4) and provision made under subsection (5), as continuing indefinitely.]

AMENDMENTS

1. Civil Partnership Act 2004 s.254 and Sch.24 para.140 (December 5, 2005).
2. Pensions Act 2008 s.105 (April 6, 2009).
3. Pensions Act 2014, s.29(2)(b) (May 14, 2014).

DEFINITIONS

"assessed income period"—see subs.(1) and s.17(1).
"claimant"—see s.17(1).
"couple"—*ibid.*
"element"—*ibid.*
"prescribed"—*ibid.*
"regulations"—see s.17(1).
"relevant decision"—see s.6(5).
"retirement provision"—see ss.7(6) and 17(1).

GENERAL NOTE

1.50 The normal rule is that the "assessed income period" for the purposes of an award of the pension credit is five years (subs.(1)). Throughout this period the claimant's "retirement provision" (see s.7), i.e. their standard income during retirement, is treated as remaining the same, subject only to uprating in line with inflation. This is in contrast to the requirement that claimants of other means-tested benefits report any changes in income which affect their benefit entitlement. However, if the Secretary of State takes the view that the claimant's retirement provision as assessed is not likely to be typical of their actual income over the next 12 months, a period shorter than five years may be specified (subs.(2)). Foreseeable increases in income on retirement (e.g. in line with inflation) are not treated as making the assessment atypical (subs.(3)). Whatever its initial duration, an assessed income period terminates if the claimant becomes a member of a couple, separates from their partner or reaches 65 (or any partner does so) (subs.(4)). Further circumstances which will result in the termination of an assessed income period, as prescribed under subs.(5), are specified in the State Pension Credit Regulations 2002 (SI 2002/1792) reg.12.

In *CPC/1928/2005* the claimant applied for pension credit, having moved into rented property with her husband and having put their house up for sale. Pension credit was awarded with a seven-year assessed income period and without taking account of the capital value of the house. On April 22, 2004 the claimant's husband moved permanently to a care home. On May 19, 2004 the couple received the proceeds of sale in respect of their former home. The Secretary of State became aware of these facts later made a supersession decision on the basis that the claimant should be treated as a single person from April 22, 2004 and should be regarded as having additional capital representing half the proceeds of sale as from May 19, 2004. The tribunal disallowed the claimant's appeal. Commissioner Rowland, dismissing the claimant's further appeal, held that the tribunal had reached the correct conclusion, albeit for the wrong reasons. On these facts, with sale to be anticipated within a few months, no assessed income period should have been set. Moreover, "Where a substantial sum is expected on an uncertain date, not setting an assessed income period will generally be preferable to setting a short one, in the absence of other considerations such as likely minor variations of other income that the decision-maker considers should be ignored" (para.11). See also the decision of Commissioner Levenson in *CPC/0206/2005*, discussed in the note to s.7, above.

Subsection (5)

1.51 Note that now s.28(3) of the Pensions Act 2014 provides that regulations made under this provision "may in particular be made for the purpose of phasing out, on or after 6 April 2016, any remaining assessed income period that is 5 years or shorter than 5 years."

Subsection (6)

1.52 Subsection (6) was a transitional provision and was originally thought to be necessary only until April 6, 2014. It was therefore repealed from that date by the Pensions Act 2008 (ss.105(6) and 149(2)(c) and (4)). That repeal left some doubt about whether existing assessed income periods under subs.(6) would remain in place after April 6, 2014. Section 29 of the Pensions Act 2014 was therefore enacted to remove the doubt by ensuring that existing indefinite assessed income periods governed by s.9(6) remained in place on or after that date. Section 29(2)(a) accordingly repealed s.105(6) of the Pensions Act 2008 and treated it as never having had effect while s.29(2)(b) amended the restored version of subs.(6) in the terms indicated in the statutory text above.

Effect of variations under section 7(4)

10.—(1) This section applies where— 1.53

(a) an assessed income period is in force; and

(b) there is an alteration in an element of the claimant's retirement provision which affects the computation of the amount of state pension credit to which the claimant is entitled.

(2) Where, as a result of the alteration, the amount of state pension credit to which the claimant is entitled is increased or reduced, then, as from the commencing date, the amount of state pension credit payable in the case of the claimant shall be the increased or reduced amount, without any further decision of the Secretary of State (and the award of state pension credit shall have effect accordingly).

(3) Where, notwithstanding the alteration, the claimant continues on and after the commencing date to be entitled to the same amount of state pension credit as before, the award shall continue in force accordingly.

(4) In this section—

"alteration" means a variation in the amount of an element of the claimant's retirement provision in accordance with regulations under section 7(4);

"commencing date", in relation to an alteration, means the date on which the alteration comes into force.

DEFINITIONS

"alteration"—see subs.(4).
"assessed income period"—see s.17(1).
"claimant"—*ibid.*
"commencing date"—see subs.(4).
"element"—see s.17(1).
"entitled"—*ibid.*
"regulations"—*ibid.*
"retirement provision"—*ibid.*

GENERAL NOTE

Section 7(4) provides for the assessed amount of a claimant's retirement provision to be increased or decreased during the assessed income period. This provision deals with the consequences of such a change (subs.(1)). Subsection (2) allows the amount of the pension credit payable to be increased or decreased accordingly without the need for a further decision by the Secretary of State. If the level of the award remains the same, the award continues in force unaffected (subs.(3)). See also State Pension Credit Regulations 2002 (SI 2002/1792) reg.11. 1.54

Miscellaneous and supplementary

Administration

11.—Schedule 1 shall have effect and in that Schedule— 1.55

Part 1 makes amendments to Part 1 of the Administration Act (claims for, and payments and general administration of, benefit);
Part 2 makes amendments to Part 1 of the Social Security Act 1998 (c.14) (decisions and appeals); and
Part 3 makes miscellaneous and supplementary provision.

DEFINITION

"the Administration Act"—see s.17(1).

GENERAL NOTE

1.56 This section introduces Sch.1 to the Act. This makes amendments to the SSAA 1992 and the SSA 1998 which are designed to apply the normal social security rules for claims, decisions and appeals to the state pension credit scheme.

Polygamous marriages

1.57 **12.**—(1) This section applies to any case where—

(a) a person ("the person in question") is a husband or wife by virtue of a marriage entered into under a law which permits polygamy;
(b) either party to the marriage has for the time being any spouse additional to the other party; and
(c) the person in question, the other party to the marriage and the additional spouse are members of the same household.

(2) Regulations under this section may make provision—

(a) as to the entitlement of the person in question to state pension credit;
(b) as to any guarantee credit or savings credit to which that person is entitled;
(c) for prescribing a different amount as the standard minimum guarantee in the case of the person in question;
(d) in a case where the person in question is the claimant, for treating the income and capital of the other party and of the additional spouse as income and capital of the person in question.

(3) Any such regulations may provide—

(a) that prescribed provisions shall apply instead of prescribed provisions of this Act; or
(b) that prescribed provisions of this Act shall not apply or shall apply subject to prescribed modifications or adaptations.

(4) Except in relation to the amount of the standard minimum guarantee, any power to prescribe amounts by virtue of this section includes power to prescribe nil as an amount.

DEFINITIONS

"capital"—see s.17(1).
"claimant"—*ibid.*
"entitled"—*ibid.*
"guarantee credit"—*ibid.*
"income"—*ibid.*
"prescribed"—*ibid.*
"regulations"—*ibid.*
"savings credit"—*ibid.*
"standard minimum guarantee"—*ibid.*

General Note

This section makes special provision for claimants who are parties to polygamous marriages. See also State Pension Credit Regulations 2002 (SI 2002/1792) reg.8 and Sch.III para.1. 1.58

Transitional provisions

13.—(1) The Secretary of State may by regulations make such transitional provision, consequential provision or savings as he considers necessary or expedient for the purposes of, or in connection with— 1.59

(a) the coming into force of any of the state pension credit provisions of this Act; or

(b) the operation of any enactment repealed or amended by any of those provisions during any period when the repeal or amendment is not wholly in force.

(2) The provision that may be made by regulations under this section includes in particular—

(a) provision for a person who attains or has attained the qualifying age on or before the appointed day and who immediately before that day is entitled to income support—

(i) to be treated as having been awarded on, and with effect as from, that day state pension credit of an amount specified in or determined in accordance with the regulations; or

(ii) to be treated as having made a claim for state pension credit; and

(b) provision for an assessed income period under section 6 of such length as may be specified in or determined in accordance with the regulations (which may be longer than the maximum period provided for by section 9(1)) to have effect in the case of a person who attains or has attained the qualifying age on or before the appointed day.

(3) In this section—

"the appointed day" means such day as the Secretary of State may by order appoint;

"the state pension credit provisions of this Act" means this Act other than section 18.

Definitions

"the appointed day"—see subs.(3).
"the qualifying age"—see s.1(6).
"regulations"—see s.17(1).
"the state pension credit provisions of this Act"—see subs.(3).

General Note

This section enables regulations to be made governing the transitional arrangements for the introduction of the pension credit. The scheme came into force on October 6, 2003 (the "appointed day": see State Pension Credit Act 2002 (Commencement No.5) and Appointed Day Order 2003 (SI 2003/1766 (c.75)) and all claims made before October 2004 were backdated to October 2003 (see State Pension Credit (Consequential, Transitional and Miscellaneous Provisions) Regulations 2002 (SI 2002/3019 reg.38(4)). 1.60

For the text of regs 36–38 and full commentary on reg.38, see the 2012/13 edition of this Volume, paras 4.170–4.173.

Minor and consequential amendments

1.61 **14.**—Schedule 2 (which makes minor and consequential amendments relating to state pension credit) shall have effect.

GENERAL NOTE

1.62 This section introduces Sch.2 to the Act, which makes a series of minor and consequential amendments to the SSCBA 1992, the SSAA 1992 and other statutes.

Interpretation of state pension credit provisions

Income and capital

1.63 **15.**—(1) In this Act "income" means income of any of the following descriptions—

(a) earnings;
(b) working tax credit;
(c) retirement pension income;
(d) income from annuity contracts (other than retirement pension income);
(e) prescribed social security benefits (other than retirement pension income and state pension credit);
(f) foreign social security benefits of any prescribed description;
(g) a war disablement pension or war widow's or widower's pension;
(h) a foreign war disablement pension or foreign war widow's or widower's pension;
(i) income from capital;
(j) income of any prescribed description.

(2) Regulations may provide that a person's capital shall be deemed to yield him income at a prescribed rate.

(3) Income and capital shall be calculated or estimated in such manner as may be prescribed.

(4) A person's income in respect of any period shall be calculated in accordance with prescribed rules.

(5) The rules may provide for the calculation to be made by reference to an average over a period (which need not consist of or include the whole or any part of the period concerned).

(6) Circumstances may be prescribed in which—

(a) a person is treated as possessing capital or income which he does not possess;
(b) capital or income which a person does possess is to be disregarded;
(c) income is to be treated as capital; or
(d) capital is to be treated as income.

(7) Subsections (2) to (6) have effect for the purposes of this Act.

DEFINITIONS

"capital"—see s.17(1).
"earnings"—*ibid.*
"foreign social security benefits"—*ibid.*
"foreign war disablement pension"—*ibid.*
"foreign war widow's or widower's pension"—*ibid.*
"income"—see subs.(1).

"prescribed"—see s.17(1).
"regulations"—*ibid.*
"retirement pension income"—see s.16(1).
"social security benefits"—see s.17(1).
"war disablement pension"—*ibid.*
"war widow's or widower's pension"—*ibid.*
"working tax credit"—*ibid.*

GENERAL NOTE

The term "income" is given a very broad definition in subs.(1) for the purposes of the pension credit scheme. In particular, the Secretary of State has the power under subs.(1)(e) to specify which social security benefits count as income (see State Pension Credit Regulations 2002 (SI 2002/1792) reg.15(1), (3) and (4); and for foreign social security benefits see ibid., reg.15(2)). The Secretary of State may also extend the definition of income to include "income of any prescribed description" (subs.(1)(j)). This latter power has been used to include less commonly found forms of income that some pensioners have (e.g. maintenance payments); see State Pension Credit Regulations 2002 (SI 2002/1792 reg.15(5)). However, neither s.15 nor reg.15 seem to include as assessable income for state pension credit purposes regular payments of income from a benevolent institution (e.g. the Royal British Legion) or from a family member: see *AMS v SSWP (PC) (final decision)* [2017] UKUT 381 (AAC); [2018] AACR 27 at para.13. In *R(PC)3/08* the Commissioner ruled that the 2002 Act adopts the ordinary meanings of income and capital. **1.64**

Relevant authorities on the meaning of income (*Leeves v Chief Adjudication Officer (R(IS) 5/99)*, *R(IS) 4/01*, *Chandler v Secretary of State for Work and Pensions* [2007] EWCA Civ 1211 and *CH/1672/2007* were analysed by Judge Farbey QC in *BL v SSWP (SPC)* [2018] UKUT 4 (AAC), where she drew the following conclusions:

> "30. From these authorities, the following propositions may be derived. The term 'income' in sections 15 and 16 of the State Pension Credit Act 2002 should be given its natural and ordinary meaning. Any qualification of, or restriction on, the ordinary meaning may be justified only by reference to the particular statutory context. The meaning is not to be determined by reference to other welfare benefits in other legislative contexts. Case law relating to other benefits may not, therefore, provide the correct approach.
> 31. Income includes not only money paid to a recipient but also money paid to a person's order or instruction. There is no principled reason to distinguish between money paid directly by A to C at B's instruction and money paid by A to B which B then forwards to C. In each case, B is in control of the money and directs or chooses where it goes.
> 32. It will generally be useful to consider not only whether a claimant has taken possession of funds but also whether he has practical power to treat the funds as his income. Following *Leeves*, above, money which is subject to a certain and immediate obligation of repayment will not count as income.
> 33. Cases will be fact sensitive: the tribunal must consider all relevant evidence relating to the funds in question and the precise nature of the payment or transaction in question. If the tribunal has applied the meaning of income in its ordinary sense and based its decision on relevant evidence, its decision is not likely to be impugned by the Upper Tribunal whose jurisdiction is limited to errors of law."

In *BL v SSWP (SPC)* itself the appeal related to money which the claimant had paid to his wife from his Standard Life pension. The couple had separated in 1991. Under a written separation agreement drawn up by lawyers, the claimant had undertaken to make monthly maintenance payments to his wife. From 2001 he directed monthly payments to her from the Standard Life pension. Judge Farbey QC upheld the FTT's finding that the payments remained the claimant's income within s.15(1) as they were under his control.

1.65 There is, however, no upper capital limit for the purposes of entitlement to the pension credit. Instead, capital is deemed, by regulations made under subs.(2), to have an assumed rate of return for the purposes of assessing entitlement to both forms of the pension credit. This rate is set at £1 for every £500 (or part thereof) in excess of the threshold of £10,000: see State Pension Credit Regulations 2002 (SI 2002/1792) reg.15(6)–(8). Any capital below this threshold is disregarded. The net result is that pensioners are treated markedly more favourably than those persons of working age in receipt of means-tested benefits, who are subject both to the capital rule and to a harsher tariff income rule on capital below that threshold.

Note that for the purposes of claiming housing benefit, pension credit claimants receiving the guarantee credit have the whole of their capital and income disregarded (see the Housing Benefit (Persons who have attained the qualifying age for state pension credit) Regulations 2006 (SI 2006/214) reg.26). For claimants receiving solely the savings credit, the local authority is required to use the DWP's calculations for claimants' capital and income, see *ibid.*, reg.27. For these reasons it is important that a tribunal reaching a decision on the amount of capital or income in a pension credit case should specify the amount of such capital or income in the Decision Notice.

The extensive powers contained in subss.(3)–(6) replicate those which apply to means-tested benefits by virtue of SSCBA 1992 ss.136(3)–(5). In *R(PC)3/08* the Commissioner observed that the powers in subs.(6) indicate "that income and capital are separate and mutually exclusive categories (even if the boundary line might sometimes be fuzzy)" (para.21).

Retirement pension income

1.66 **16.**—(1) In this Act "retirement pension income" means any of the following—

[6 (za) a state pension under Part 1 of the Pensions Act 2014 or under any provision in Northern Ireland which corresponds to that Part;]

(a) a Category A or Category B retirement pension payable under sections 43 to 55 of—
  (i) the Contributions and Benefits Act; or
  (ii) the Social Security Contributions and Benefits (Northern Ireland) Act 1992 (c.7);

[7 (b) a shared additional pension payable under—
  (i) section 55A of either of those Acts, or
  (ii) section 55AA of the Contributions and Benefits Act or any corresponding provision under the law of Northern Ireland;]

(c) graduated retirement benefit payable under section 62 of either of those Acts;

(d) a Category C or Category D retirement pension payable under section 78 of either of those Acts;

(e) age addition payable under section 79 of either of those Acts;

(f) income from an occupational pension scheme or a personal pension scheme;

(g) income from an overseas arrangement;

(h) income from a retirement annuity contract;

(i) income from annuities or insurance policies purchased or transferred for the purpose of giving effect to rights under a personal pension scheme or an overseas arrangement;

(j) income from annuities purchased or entered into for the purpose of discharging liability under—
  (i) section 29(1)(b) of the Welfare Reform and Pensions Act 1999 (c.30) (pension credits on divorce); or

(ii) Article 26(1)(b) of the Welfare Reform and Pensions (Northern Ireland) Order 1999 (SI 1999/3147 (NI 11)) (corresponding provision for Northern Ireland).

[1 [5 (k) any sum payable by way of pension under section 5 of the Civil List Act 1837 or section 7 of the Civil List Act 1952;]

[2 (l) any payment, other than a payment ordered by a court or made in settlement of a claim, made by or on behalf of a former employer of a person on account of the early retirement of that person on grounds of ill-health or disability];

[3 (m) any payment made at regular intervals under an equity release scheme];

[4 (n) any payment made under the Financial Assistance Scheme Regulations 2005].

(2) The Secretary of State may by regulations amend subsection (1); and any such regulations may—

(a) add to or vary the descriptions of income for the time being listed in that subsection; or

(b) remove any such description from that subsection.

(3) In this section—

"overseas arrangement" has the meaning given by section 181(1) of the Pension Schemes Act 1993 (c.48);

"retirement annuity contract" means a contract or scheme approved under Chapter 3 of Part 14 of the Income and Corporation Taxes Act 1988 (c.1).

AMENDMENTS

1. State Pension Credit Regulations 2002 (SI 2002/1792) reg.16 (October 6, 2003).
2. State Pension Credit (Consequential, Transitional and Miscellaneous Provisions) (No.2) Regulations 2002 (SI 2002/3197) reg.2 and Sch. para.3 (October 6, 2003).
3. Social Security (Housing Benefit, Council Tax Benefit, State Pension Credit and Miscellaneous Amendments) Regulations 2004 (SI 2004/2327) reg.7(4) (October 4, 2004).
4. State Pension Credit (Amendment) Regulations 2005 (SI 2005/3205) reg.2(3) (December 18, 2005).
5. Sovereign Grant Act 2011 s.14 and Sch.1 para.32 (April 1, 2012).
6. Pensions Act 2014 s.23 and Sch.12 Pt 1 paras.42 and 44 (April 6, 2016).
7. Pensions Act 2014 s.15 and Sch.11 para.15 (April 6, 2016).

DEFINITIONS

"the Contribution and Benefits Act"—see s.17(1).
"occupational pension scheme"—*ibid.*
"overseas arrangement"—see subs.(3).
"personal pension scheme"—*ibid.*
"regulations"—see s.17(1).
"retirement annuity contract"—see subs.(3).

GENERAL NOTE

This section provides a comprehensive definition of the term "retirement pension income" for the purposes of this Act (subs.(1)). The extensive list includes both social security benefits paid to pensioners as well as various forms of private income received by pensioners. The Secretary of State may by regulations add to, vary or remove any of the descriptions so listed (subs.(2); see further State **1.67**

Pension Credit Regulations 2002 (SI 2002/1792) reg.16). This power provides the necessary flexibility to accommodate other social security benefits or private financial products for pensioners that may become available in the future. But it also includes the power to remove matters listed in subs.(1).

Judge Williams analysed the definition of "overseas arrangement" in subs.(3) in *SSWP v JK* [2009] UKUT 55 (AAC) and rejected the Secretary of State's argument that all foreign state pensions should necessarily be taken into account for the purposes of the assessed income period. On the facts, the claimant's Irish state pension was an "overseas arrangement" and had therefore to be left out of account. The remedy for the Secretary of State to deal with any perceived unfairness was to set either no assessed income period or a short one. However, reg.6 of the Social Security (Miscellaneous Amendments) (No.2) Regulations 2010 (SI 2010/641) amended the relevant regulations with effect from April 13, 2010 with the intention of reversing the effect of *SSWP v JK*.

Other interpretation provisions

1.68 **17.**—(1) In this Act—

"the Administration Act" means the Social Security Administration Act 1992 (c.5);

"assessed income period" shall be construed in accordance with sections 6 and 9;

"appropriate minimum guarantee" shall be construed in accordance with section 2(3);

"capital" shall be construed in accordance with section 15;

[7"carer support payment" means carer's assistance given in accordance with the Carer's Assistance (Carer Support Payment) (Scotland) Regulations 2023;]

"claimant" means a claimant for state pension credit;

"the Contributions and Benefits Act" means the Social Security Contributions and Benefits Act 1992 (c.4);

[5 "couple" means—

(a) two people who are married to, or civil partners of, each other and are members of the same household; or

(b) two people who are not married to, or civil partners of, each other but are living together [6 as if they were a married couple or civil partners] otherwise than in prescribed circumstances;]

"earnings" has the same meaning as in Parts 1 to 5 of the Contributions and Benefits Act (see sections 3(1) and 112, and the definition of "employment" in section 122, of that Act);

"element", in relation to the claimant's retirement provision, shall be construed in accordance with section 7(6);

"entitled", in relation to state pension credit, shall be construed in accordance with—

(a) this Act,

(b) section 1 of the Administration Act (entitlement to be dependent on making of claim, etc.), and

(c) section 27 of the Social Security Act 1998 (c.14) (restrictions on entitlement to benefit in certain cases of error),

(and, in relation to any other benefit within the meaning of section 1 of the Administration Act or section 27 of the Social Security Act 1998, in accordance with that section or (as the case may be) both of those sections in addition to any other conditions relating to that benefit);

"foreign social security benefit" means any benefit, allowance or other payment which is paid under the law of a country outside the United Kingdom and is in the nature of social security;

"foreign war disablement pension" means any retired pay, pension, allowance or similar payment granted by the government of a country outside the United Kingdom—

(a) in respect of disablement arising from forces' service or war injury; or

(b) corresponding in nature to any retired pay or pension to which [1section 641 of the Income Tax (Earnings and Pensions) Act 2003] applies;

"foreign war widow's or widower's pension" means any pension, allowance or similar payment granted to a [2 widow, widower or surviving civil partner] by the government of a country outside the United Kingdom—

(a) in respect of a death due to forces' service or war injury; or

(b) corresponding in nature to a pension or allowance for a [2 widow, widower or surviving civil partner] under any scheme mentioned in [1section 641(1)(e) or (f) of the Income Tax (Earnings and Pensions) Act 2003];

"guarantee credit" shall be construed in accordance with sections 1 and 2;

"income" shall be construed in accordance with section 15;

[2 . . .]

"occupational pension scheme" has the meaning given by section 1 of the Pension Schemes Act 1993 (c.48);

"pensionable age" has the meaning given by the rules in paragraph 1 of Schedule 4 to the Pensions Act 1995 (c.26) (equalisation of pensionable ages for men and women);

"personal pension scheme" means a personal pension scheme—

(a) as defined in section 1 of the Pension Schemes Act 1993; or

(b) as defined in section 1 of the Pension Schemes (Northern Ireland) Act 1993 (c.49);

[4 "PPF periodic payments" means—

(a) any periodic compensation payments made in relation to a person, payable under the pension compensation provisions as specified in section 162(2) of the Pensions Act 2004 or Article 146(2) of the Pensions (Northern Ireland) Order 2005 (the pension compensation provisions); or

(b) any periodic payments made in relation to a person, payable under section 166 of the Pensions Act 2004 or Article 150 of the Pensions (Northern Ireland) Order 2005 (duty to pay scheme benefits unpaid at assessment date etc.);]

"prescribed" means specified in, or determined in accordance with regulations;

"the qualifying age" has the meaning given by section 1(6);

"regulations" means regulations made by the Secretary of State;

"retirement pension income" shall be construed in accordance with section 16;

"retirement provision" shall be construed in accordance with section 7(6);

"savings credit" shall be construed in accordance with sections 1 and 3;

"social security benefits" means benefits payable under the enactments relating to social security in any part of the United Kingdom;

"standard minimum guarantee" shall be construed in accordance with section 2(3) to (5) and (9);

[2 . . .]

"war disablement pension" means—

(a) any retired pay, pension or allowance granted in respect of disablement under powers conferred by or under—

(i) the Air Force (Constitution) Act 1917 (c.51);

(ii) the Personal Injuries (Emergency Provisions) Act 1939 (c.82);

(iii) the Pensions (Navy, Army, Air Force and Mercantile Marine) Act 1939 (c.83);

(iv) the Polish Resettlement Act 1947 (c.19); or

(v) Part 7 or section 151 of the Reserve Forces Act 1980 (c.9); or

(b) without prejudice to paragraph (a), any retired pay or pension to which [1 any of paragraphs (a) to (f) of section 641(1) of the Income Tax (Earnings and Pensions) Act 2003] applies;

"war widow's or widower's pension" means—

(a) [2 any widow's, widower's or surviving civil partner's] pension or allowance granted in respect of a death due to service or war injury and payable by virtue of any enactment mentioned in paragraph (a) of the definition of "war disablement pension"; or

(b) a pension or allowance for a [2 widow, widower or surviving civil partner] granted under any scheme mentioned in [1section 641(1)(e) or (f) of the Income Tax (Earnings and Pensions) Act 2003];

"working tax credit" means a working tax credit under the Tax Credits Act 2002 to which a person is entitled whether alone or jointly with another.

[3(1A) [5 . . .]

(2) Regulations may make provision for the purposes of this Act—

(a) as to circumstances in which persons are to be treated as being or not being members of the same household;

(b) as to circumstances in which persons are to be treated as being or not being severely disabled.

(3) The following provisions of the Contributions and Benefits Act, namely—

(a) section 172 (references to Great Britain or United Kingdom to include reference to adjacent territorial waters, etc.), and

(b) section 173 (meaning of attaining an age, etc.), shall apply for the purposes of this Act as they apply for the purposes of that Act.

AMENDMENTS

1. Income Tax (Earnings and Pensions) Act 2003 Sch.6 para.263 (October 6, 2003).

2. Civil Partnership Act 2004 s.254 and Sch.24 para.142 (December 5, 2005).

3. Civil Partnership Act 2004 s.254 and Sch.24 para.143 (December 5, 2005).

4. Pensions Act 2004 (PPF Payments and FAS Payments) (Consequential Provisions) Order 2006 (SI 2006/343) art.3(2) (February 14, 2006).

5. Marriage (Same Sex Couples) Act 2013 (Consequential and Contrary Provisions and Scotland) Order 2014 (SI 214/560) art.2 and Sch.1 para.28 (March 13, 2014).

6. Civil Partnership (Opposite-sex Couples) Regulations 2019 (SI 2019/1458) reg.41(a) and para.22 of Sch.3, Part 1 (December 2, 2019).

7. Carer's Assistance (Carer Support Payment) (Scotland) Regulations 2023 (Consequential Modifications) Order 2023 (SI 2023/1214) art.5(3) (November 16, 2023).

GENERAL NOTE

This is the general definition section for the Act. For definitions of "income" and "retirement pension income", see ss.15 and 16 respectively. **1.69**

In *CPC/3891/2004* Commissioner Mesher followed his earlier decision in *CIS/1720/2004* and confirmed that a decision simply that a claimant is "living together as husband and wife" is not in itself a decision which gives rise to a right of appeal. Such a decision is merely a "building block" for an outcome decision which would affect entitlement to benefit and so be capable of appeal under Social Security Act 1998 s.12(1). Accordingly a tribunal has no jurisdiction to make a substantive decision on such a "building block" decision as there is no appeal properly before it.

18.—*[Omitted.]*

[[1] Pilot schemes

18A.— **1.70**

(1) Any regulations to which this subsection applies may be made so as to have effect for a specified period not exceeding 12 months.

(2) Subject to subsection (3), subsection (1) applies to—

(a) regulations made under this Act, and

(b) regulations made under section 1 or 5 of the Administration Act.

(3) Subsection (1) only applies to regulations if they are made with a view to ascertaining whether their provisions will—

(a) make it more likely that persons who are entitled to claim state pension credit will do so;

(b) make it more likely that persons who are entitled to claim state pension credit will receive it.

(4) Regulations which, by virtue of subsection (1), are to have effect for a limited period are referred to in this section as a "pilot scheme".

(5) A pilot scheme may, in particular—

(a) provide for a relevant provision not to apply, or to apply with modifications, for the purposes of the pilot scheme, and

(b) make different provision for different cases or circumstances.

(6) For the purposes of subsection (5)(a), a "relevant provision" is—

(a) any provision of this Act, and

(b) section 1 of the Administration Act.

(7) A pilot scheme may provide that no account is to be taken of any payment made under the pilot scheme in considering a person's—

(a) liability to tax,

(b) entitlement to benefit under an enactment relating to social security (irrespective of the name or nature of the benefit), or

(c) entitlement to a tax credit.

(8) A pilot scheme may provide that its provisions are to apply only in relation to—

(a) one or more specified areas or localities;

(b) one or more specified classes of person;

(c) persons selected—

(i) by reference to prescribed criteria, or

(ii) on a sampling basis.

(9) A pilot scheme may make consequential or transitional provision with respect to the cessation of the scheme on the expiry of the specified period.

(10) A pilot scheme may be replaced by a further pilot scheme making the same or similar provision.

(11) The power of the Secretary of State to make regulations which, by virtue of this section, are to have effect for a limited period is exercisable only with the consent of the Treasury.]

AMENDMENT

1. Welfare Reform Act 2009 s.27(2) (November 12, 2009).

GENERAL NOTE

1.71 This section makes provision for a pilot scheme to test ways in which state pension credit entitlement may be calculated and paid in order to increase the number of eligible persons receiving the credit. See also s.142 of the Pensions Act 2008, which permits data sharing between the Secretary of State and energy suppliers (and see further the Disclosure of State Pension Credit Information (Warm Home Discount) Regulations 2011 (SI 2011/1830)). The pilot scheme was extended until March 31, 2018 and then for a further three years until March 31, 2021 (see Warm Home Discount (Miscellaneous Amendments) Regulations 2018 (SI 2018/909)). It was then extended for a further year until March 31, 2022 (see Warm Home Discount (Miscellaneous Amendments) Regulations 2021 (SI 2021/667)). The scheme has now been extended until March 31, 2026—see the Warm Home Discount (England and Wales) Regulations 2022 (SI 2022/772) and to similar effect the Warm Home Discount (Scotland) Regulations 2022 (SI 2022/1073).

Regulations and orders

1.72 **19.**—(1) Subject to the following provisions of this section, subsections (1), (2) to (5) and (10) of section 175 of the Contributions and Benefits Act (regulations and orders etc) shall apply in relation to any power conferred on the Secretary of State by any provision of this Act to make regulations or an order as they apply in relation to any power conferred on him by that Act to make regulations or an order, but as if for references to that Act (other than references to specific provisions of it) there were substituted references to this Act.

(2) A statutory instrument containing (whether alone or with other provisions) the first regulations under—

(a) section 2(3)(b), (4) or (6),
(b) section 3(4), (5), (6), (7) or (8),
(c) section 4(3),
(d) section 12, or
(e) section 15(1)(e), (f) or (j), (2), (3), (4) or (6),

shall not be made unless a draft of the instrument has been laid before, and approved by a resolution of, each House of Parliament.

[1 (2A) A statutory instrument containing regulations which, by virtue of section 18A, are to have effect for a limited period shall not be made unless a draft of the instrument has been laid before, and approved by a resolution of, each House of Parliament.]

(3) A statutory instrument—

(a) which contains regulations under this Act (whether alone or with other provisions), and

(b) which is not subject to any requirement that a draft of the instrument be laid before, and approved by a resolution of, each House of Parliament,

shall be subject to annulment in pursuance of a resolution of either House of Parliament.

AMENDMENT

1. Welfare Reform Act 2009 s.27(3) (November 12, 2009).

DEFINITIONS

"the Contribution and Benefits Act"—see s.17(1).
"regulations"—*ibid.*

GENERAL NOTE

This section applies the usual regulation-making powers for social security benefits under SSCBA 1992 s.175 to the pension credit scheme (subs.(1)). The first regulations made under the various powers listed in subs.(2) were subject to the affirmative procedure. Other regulations remain subject to the usual negative resolution procedure (subs.(3)). **1.73**

Financial provisions

20.—(1) There shall be paid out of money provided by Parliament— **1.74**

(a) any sums payable by way of state pension credit;
(b) any expenditure incurred by the Secretary of State or other government department under or by virtue of this Act; and
(c) any increase attributable to this Act in the sums payable out of money so provided under any other Act.

(2) There shall be paid into the Consolidated Fund any increase attributable to this Act in the sums which under any other Act are payable into that Fund.

Enactments repealed

21.—The enactments specified in Schedule 3 to this Act are repealed to the extent there specified. **1.75**

GENERAL NOTE

Schedule 3 to the Act made a small number of minor repeals to existing social security legislation which appeared to be unconnected with the introduction of the pension credit. **1.76**

Short title, commencement and extent

22.—(1) This Act may be cited as the State Pension Credit Act 2002. **1.77**

(2) This section and sections 19 and 20 come into force on the passing of this Act.

(3) Except as provided by subsection (2), this Act shall come into force on such day as the Secretary of State may by order appoint; and different days may be so appointed for different purposes.

(4) Any order under this section may make such transitional provision as appears to the Secretary of State to be necessary or expedient in connection with the provisions brought into force by the order.

(5) Any amendment or repeal made by this Act has the same extent as the enactment to which it relates (unless otherwise provided).

(6) Subject to that, this Act extends to England and Wales and Scotland only.

GENERAL NOTE

1.78 For the reasons explained in the Introduction and General Note, although this Act is to be known as the State Pension Credit Act 2002 (subs.(1)), the credit itself is described in official literature as the pension credit. This section (along with ss.19 and 20) came into force on Royal Assent (June 25, 2002) (subs.(2)).

SCHEDULES

1.79 **Sch.1. to Sch.3.** *[Omitted.]*

Welfare Reform Act 2012

(2012 C.5)

ARRANGEMENT OF SECTIONS

PART 1

UNIVERSAL CREDIT

CHAPTER 1

ENTITLEMENT AND AWARDS

Introductory

Entitlement

Awards

Elements of an award

Chapter 2

Claimant Responsibilities

Introductory

Work-related requirements

Application of work-related requirements

Work-related requirements: supplementary

Reduction of benefit

Administration

Chapter 3

Supplementary and General

Supplementary and consequential

Universal credit and other benefits

General

Regulations

PART 5

SOCIAL SECURITY: GENERAL

Benefit cap

PART 7

FINAL

SCHEDULES

An Act to make provision for universal credit and personal independence payment; to make other provision about social security and tax credits; to make provision about the functions of the registration service, child support maintenance and the use of jobcentres; to establish the Social Mobility and Child Poverty Commission and otherwise amend the Child Poverty Act 2010; and for connected purposes.

[8th March 2012]

General Note

Part 1 of the Welfare Reform Act 2012 ("WRA 2012") and the associated schedules to that Act establish a social security benefit known as universal credit, set out the underlying structure of that benefit and confer regulation-making powers that allow the Secretary of State for Work and Pensions to make more detailed rules. **1.84**

The (ongoing) introduction of universal credit is the biggest change to the social security system since the abolition of supplementary benefit and its replacement with income support ("IS") by the Social Security Act 1986. It replaces four social security benefits (IS, housing benefit ("HB"), income-based jobseeker's allowance ("JSA(IB)"), and income-related employment and support allowance ("ESA(IR)")) and two tax credits (child tax credit ("CTC") and working tax credit ("WTC")). (The Department for Work and Pensions ("DWP") often refers to the benefits and tax credits that are to be replaced as the "legacy benefits", but this volume sometimes describes them as "existing benefits"). When the transfer to universal credit is complete it will technically be the *only* means-tested, non-contributory benefit for people of working age (albeit that its conceptual elegance, as well as the practical simplicity for claimants, is spoiled by the fact that child benefit, technically non-means-tested, is in substance means-tested; and that council tax reduction, technically not a benefit, is in substance a benefit).

To understand why it has been felt necessary to make such complete overhaul of the benefits system, it is necessary to set out in greater detail what the problems with the existing benefits were perceived to be and how universal credit was intended to solve them. After that, this note will discuss the slow introduction of the new benefit (and the extent to which the delay may have made matters worse rather than better) and conclude with a summary of how universal credit is structured.

The problem: complexity and disincentives to work

Before the introduction of universal credit began, people of working age who needed to claim benefit because they were not working (or, though working, were not earning enough to meet their basic needs) had to choose from a complex array of benefits some of which complemented each other and others of which were mutually exclusive. **1.85**

Those who were able to work, but could not find a job, generally had to claim JSA, entitlement to which was either "contribution-based", or "income-based" which was a euphemism for "means-tested". Those who could not work because they were prevented from doing so by illness or disability claimed ESA, which again could be contributory or "income-related". Those who could not be expected to work for other reasons (e.g., because they were caring for a young child or for a disabled person) could claim IS, entitlement to which was based on a means-test and had no contributory component.

The three benefits listed above were administered by the DWP and included elements to help meet a claimant's housing costs if (broadly speaking) the claimant was an owner-occupier. However, for claimants who rented their homes, help for housing costs was provided by a fourth benefit, housing benefit ("HB") which was administered by local authorities.

Moreover, ESA(IR) and—except in a limited class of transitional cases—JSA(IB) and IS were "adults only" benefits. For claimants whose families included children or "qualifying young persons" (people aged between 16 and 20 who are in education or training) state help for the cost of feeding, clothing and bringing up the child or qualifying young person was provided by HM Revenue & Customs ("HMRC") through two further benefits, child benefit and CTC.

Finally, people working more than 16 hours a week were excluded from IS, JSA(IB) and ESA(IR). However, they could sometimes claim WTC, which was not open to anyone working fewer than 16 hours a week. HB had no hours rule (although, of course, the more hours a person worked, the more likely their claim might fail on income grounds).

The complexity of that system, in which a claimant with children living in rented property might have to claim four different benefits from three different agencies was further aggravated by the fact entitlement to tax credits was normally calculated with respect to, and paid over, an entire tax year whereas entitlement to IS, JSA(IB), ESA(IR) and HB was calculated weekly and usually paid fortnightly or, in the case of HB, four-weekly or monthly. It was often difficult to ensure that the two different calculation and payment systems meshed together properly, not least because the mechanisms for sharing information between the DWP, HMRC and local authorities were less than perfect. The whole system operated against the background that a mistake, whether by the claimant or the administering authority, could result in an overpayment, leaving the claimant in debt, often for hundreds or thousands of pounds.

The old system had the further effect of providing financial disincentives to work at certain levels of income. Under the means-tests for IS, JSA(IB) and ESA(IR) only relatively small amounts of earnings were ignored. Claimants whose earnings exceeded those "disregards" had their benefits reduced penny for penny by the amount of the excess and therefore derived no further benefit from their earnings until they earned enough to lose entitlement to benefit altogether.

This is not the place for a detailed discussion of the poverty trap. An example should suffice to make the point.

> During 2024/25, a single claimant, call her Jane, aged over 25 on the basic rate of JSA(IB) receives £90.50 per week. Jane's weekly earnings disregard is £5.00. Suppose she does one hour's work a week at the national minimum wage of £11.44 per hour. The first £5 of those earnings is disregarded but her JSA(IB) is reduced by £6.44 (the amount by which £11.44 exceeds £5) to £84.06. Jane's total weekly income is thus £95.50 (£11.44 in earnings plus JSA(IB) of £84.06). Now, suppose Jane increases her working hours to eight per week. Her weekly earnings are now £91.52 (£11.44 × 8) but her earnings disregard is still £5. Therefore, her weekly entitlement to JSA(IB) is reduced by £86.52 (£91.52 – £5.00) from £90.50 to £3.98, giving her a total weekly income of £95.50 (£91.52 in earnings plus £3.98 in JSA(IB)). In short, Jane's income remains exactly the same whether she works one hour per week or eight. It is only once she works nine hours a week, taking her earnings to £102.96 and losing entitlement to JSA(IB) altogether, that Jane begins to be better off. And at that stage, if she is in rented accommodation, she is likely to lose 65 pence in HB for each additional pound that she earns. She will also lose entitlement to "passported" advantages such as automatic free prescriptions, which will provide a further disincentive to work.

The solution: universal credit

1.86 Universal credit is designed to get rid of both the problems outlined above by simplifying the social security system and ensuring that claimants will always be better off in work.

Simplification

1.87 The simplification of the system is to be achieved by abolishing IS, JSA(IB), ESA(IR) HB, CTC and WTC and replacing them with universal credit. As universal credit is administered and paid by the DWP, the effect will be to end the role of local authorities in the administration of cash working-age social security benefits and to restrict the role of HMRC to the administration of child benefit and guardian's allowance.

However, the simultaneous decision to replace council tax benefit with local council tax reduction schemes means that local authorities do still have an important role in social security adjudication, but now under a host of local schemes rather than a single national structure. Further, local authorities have come to play increasingly significant role in administering discretionary support, such as discretionary housing payments, for claimants whose needs are not adequately met by benefits available by right.

In the new system, as noted above, child benefit continues unaffected and two new benefits, confusingly called "jobseeker's allowance" and "employment and support allowance"—and referred to as "new style" JSA and ESA to distinguish them from the older, identically-named, "old style" benefits—are paid without any means-test, but for limited periods, to those who meet the contribution conditions.

Nevertheless, the new structure is undoubtedly simpler than the system it replaces.

The aim of simplification has, however, been frustrated by the decision to phase universal credit in over a period of many years. That decision is entirely understandable, given the new benefit's reliance on information technology. It would have been a recipe for disaster for universal credit to be introduced on a general basis before it had been established in pilot areas that it could be properly administered.

However, the effect of a phased introduction is that the two systems continue to co-exist, so that what has been achieved is not a simplification of the benefits system but a significant complication. During the transition, universal credit is not a *replacement* benefit but an *additional* benefit.

Moreover, it is inherent in the design of universal credit that it overlaps with each of the older benefits it is eventually intended to replace. That overlap means that, in addition to the complication of the old and new systems existing side-by-side (including having two different and mutually exclusive benefits both called JSA and two called ESA), it is also necessary to have legislation defining which set of rules applies to any particular claimant at any given time. That legislation is now to be found first, in the Universal Credit (Transitional Provisions) Regulations 2014 ("the 2014 Regulations") and, second, in a series of Commencement Orders that, even by the high standards set by past social security legislation, are bewilderingly complex.

If that were not enough, the procedures by which universal credit was introduced meant that, at least in relation to some issues, the benefit existed for a period in two forms with different substantive rules: see *Introduction of universal credit* below.

As a final complication, the need to devote departmental resources to the introduction of universal credit appears to have delayed the extension of the housing costs element of state pension credit (SPC) to cover rent and other payments made by those who are not owner-occupiers. Further, even claimants who have become subject to the universal credit rules may still claim HB if they live in "exempt accommodation" (see the definition in Sch.1, para.1 to the Universal Credit Regulations, below). The effect is that local authorities will need to retain their benefits departments—and incur the associated costs and overheads that might otherwise have been saved—to deal with claims for HB from those who are above working age and those in exempt accommodation.

Challenges of transition

All of that might not matter if the transition from the old system to the new had been relatively swift. It had originally been envisaged that all households would have **1.88**
moved to UC by the end of 2017: DWP, *Iain Duncan Smith sets out next steps for moving claimants onto Universal Credit* (November 1, 2011). However, that has not transpired. The DWP's report *Completing the move to Universal Credit: Learning from the Discovery Phase* (January 10, 2023), published almost a decade after UC was introduced, noted that there were still 2.5 million households receiving legacy benefit. (In comparison there were about 4.9 million households receiving UC: DWP, *Universal Credit statistics: 29 April 2013 to 12 January 2023* (February 14, 2023), para.5.)

The Secretary of State intends, ultimately, to move all legacy benefit recipients onto universal credit by a process known as "managed migration". But most UC claims so far have been either (i) brand new benefit claims; or (ii) the result of claimants' own decisions to end legacy benefits to claim UC; or (iii) the consequence of existing claimants undergoing a change of circumstances which ends their existing award (sometimes known as "natural migration").

The Universal Credit (Managed Migration Pilot and Miscellaneous Amendments) Regulations 2019 (SI 2019/1152) allowed for up to 10,000 people to experimentally undergo "managed moves" onto universal credit from legacy benefit. The managed migration legislation itself is in Pt 4 of the Universal Credit (Transitional Provisions) Regulations 2014; the 10,000 person limitation was imposed by reg.2 of SI 2019/1152.

A pilot scheme began in Harrogate in July 2019, but as of January 2020, only 13 people had actually moved to universal credit [HC Deb (January 27, 2020), vol.670 col.521], and operation of the scheme was suspended altogether upon the outbreak of coronavirus.

On November 8, 2021, the Secretary of State announced that the Harrogate scheme would not be resumed, and that a plan was "still in preparation, on resuming the managed move to universal credit" [HC Deb (November 8, 2021), vol.703 col.8]. The Secretary of State subsequently removed the 10,000 limit on managed moves, through reg.10 of the Universal Credit (Transitional Provisions) Amendment Regulations 2022 (SI 2022/752), so can in principle now complete the process without further legislative change. The policy which will underpin that process continues to develop.

In 2023–24 DWP migrated most tax credits claimants. Its plans for 2024-25 are to complete 'the remaining moves of those on tax credits (including those on both Employment and Support Allowance and tax credits), all cases on Income Support and Jobseeker's Allowance (Income Based) and all Housing Benefit only cases': DWP, *Completing the Move to Universal Credit: learning from initial Tax Credit migrations* (15 August 2023).

Once that is done, the main remaining group will be people on ESA who are not receiving tax credit. Until April 2024, DWP's plan was that the group's migration would not be completed until 2028/29: *Autumn Statement 2022* (CP 751, November 2022), para.5.15. However, in April 2024 a post on X/Twitter by the Senior Responsible Owner (SRO) for Universal Credit, Neil Couling, stated that this would instead be done by the end of 2025: see the Public Accounts Committee letter, *Announcement in relation to Progress implementing Universal Credit and the ongoing Public Accounts Committee inquiry* (26 April 2024).

Finally, there have been no announcements whatsoever about plans for claimants receiving housing benefit for temporary or supported accommodation, who are in a strange position currently, receiving UC for adult and child subsistence, but HB for housing costs.

All that can currently be said with confidence is that when the move to UC finishes, the process will have taken a lot longer than the four years originally expected (2013–17).

The slow pace of the transition so far means that, for un-migrated existing working age claimants, the benefits system continues to be as described in the opening paragraphs of this introduction: they will continue to deal with up to three different authorities and to be subject to disincentives to work from the poverty trap.

The slow pace of the transition is also significant because it means that "natural migration" from legacy benefits to UC has become a much more significant part of the process than originally anticipated. And the Secretary of State has experienced a number of court defeats about the treatment of certain sub-groups in that category, in which some claimants can be substantially worse off on UC than on their previous benefits: *R. (TP, AR & SXC) v Secretary of State for Work and Pensions* [2020] EWCA Civ 37; [2020] P.T.S.R. 1785; *R. (TD) v Secretary of State for Work and Pensions* [2020] EWCA Civ 618; *R. (TP) v Secretary of State for Work and Pensions* [2022] EWHC 123 (Admin). In all three cases the courts decided that there was unlawfully discriminatory treatment of affected groups, contrary to s.6 of the Human Rights

Act 1998. A more recent transitional protection case, *Secretary of State for Work and Pensions v JA* [2024] UKUT 52 (AAC) (19 February 2024), also rules against the government, in the context of problems arising from the retention of housing benefit for supported and temporary accommodation. *JA* holds that universal credit claimants leaving supported or temporary accommodation have been unlawfully losing transitional protection due to the discriminatory effect of the Universal Credit (Transitional Provisions) Regulations 2014. It also holds that affected claimants can obtain a remedy for that discrimination through tribunal appeals.

Incentivising work

Although the universal credit scheme embodies political judgments about what claimants should be required to do in return for their benefit with which it is possible to disagree, progress has been made towards eliminating the poverty trap. 1.89

If we return to the example given above and suppose that, instead of claiming JSA, Jane had been eligible to claim universal credit, then her basic entitlement to universal credit (ignoring housing costs as we did implicitly in the JSA example) would be her "maximum amount" which would consist of the modified standard allowance (see the commentary to reg.36 of the Universal Credit Regulations) for a single person aged at least 25, namely £393.45 per month. That equates to £90.80 per week (£393.45 × 12 ÷ 52). Jane then begins to work one hour a week at the minimum wage of £11.44 per hour. In an average month she would earn £49.57 (£11.44 × 52 ÷ 12). From April 2016, Jane no is longer entitled to a work allowance (i.e. because she does not have responsibility for a child or qualifying young person and does not have limited capability for work). There would therefore be no equivalent of the £5 weekly disregard in the JSA calculation. However, under universal credit, from November 2021, only 55% of Jane's earnings will be deducted from the maximum amount, not the full amount of her (undisregarded) earnings as in JSA. In cash terms, the deduction is £27.26 (£49.57 × 55%) giving a monthly universal credit award of £366.19 (£393.45 –£27.26), equivalent to £84.50 per week (£366.19 × 12 ÷ 52). Jane's equivalent weekly income is therefore £95.94 (£84.50 in universal credit + £11.44 in earnings). Jane is therefore £5.14 (£95.94 – £90.80) per week better off as a result of working one hour a week. At that very low level of work, she is no better off than she would be on JSA. However, not many people work for just 1 hour a week and the more work Jane does, the more the universal credit rules begin to operate in her favour. If Jane works eight hours a week (at which level, it will be remembered, her combined weekly earnings and benefit under JSA would still have been £95.50, the same as if she had worked for just one hour), the equivalent weekly income from universal credit and earnings is £131.98 ((£90.80 – (£11.44 × 8 × 0.55)) + £11.44 × 8).

In addition to the different earned income rules, simple and effective support with childcare costs was also intended to play a significant role in UC incentivising work. However, as the Spring Budget 2023 recorded, "Currently, only around 13% of households eligible for the childcare element in Universal Credit claim it. The current offer means parents on Universal Credit in work [are] paid in monthly arrears. This presents an issue for many low-income families who struggle to find the funds to pay for their childcare upfront." That budget announced plans to "make sure [claimants] have support with childcare costs upfront when they need it rather than in arrears" and also to increase the Universal Credit childcare cost maximum amounts after some years of stagnation *Spring Budget 2023* (HC 1183, March 15, 2023), paras 3.53–3.55. (With effect from 28 June 2023, those policy changes have now been given effect by the Universal Credit (Childcare) (Amendment) Regulations 2023 (SI 593/2023), reg.2. See also ADM Memo 12/23.

Introduction of universal credit

1.90 Universal credit raises two transitional issues. The first is whether a person making a fresh claim for benefit is free to claim IS/HB/JSA/ESA or whether he or she must now claim universal credit. The second is in what circumstances existing recipients of IS/HB/JSA/ESA will be moved from those benefits to universal credit.

Fresh claims

1.91 The process of introducing universal credit was begun by the Universal Credit (Transitional Provisions) Regulations 2013 ("the 2013 Regulations"). The text of those Regulations (which have now been revoked) is set out on pp.305-354 of Vol.V of the 2013/14 edition. In summary, they provided that claimants may (and must) claim universal credit rather than IS/JSA/ESA if, at the time their claim was made or treated as made, they resided in one of the "relevant districts" and were either in the Pathfinder Group or had formerly been jointly entitled to universal credit as a member of a former couple. The relevant districts were postcode areas linked to particular Jobcentres and specified in the various Commencement Orders (see Pt IV below). The extension of universal credit proceeded by issuing further Commencement Orders that widened the geographical scope of the rules by adding further "relevant districts".

Membership of the Pathfinder Group was governed by regs 4-12 of the 2013 Regulations (pp.312-323 of Vol.V of the 2013/14 edition). The criteria for membership of the Pathfinder Group were so narrowly drawn that it, in summary, it only included single, adult, British citizens who would otherwise have had to claim JSA. The issues that were likely to give rise to disputes were narrower still because any claimant whose circumstances were likely to give rise to complications had been excluded from the Pathfinder Group and therefore had to continue to claim IS/JSA/ESA. Unsurprisingly in those circumstances, the initial experience of the Social Entitlement Chamber of the First-tier Tribunal was that universal credit appeals were overwhelmingly about backdating and the imposition of sanctions.

The 2013 Regulations were revoked by the 2014 Regulations with effect from June 16, 2014. Nothing equivalent to the former Pathfinder conditions appeared in the 2014 Regulations. Instead, a policy decision was taken that new "Gateway conditions" would be specified in Commencement Orders. This approach gave the government flexibility to vary those conditions for different areas, or to include no Gateway conditions at all.

That flexibility was used to establish two different models for the implementation of universal credit. From November 11, 2014, the No.20 Commencement Order (see Vol.V) allowed (and required) claimants who lived in a small area of the SM5 postcode in the London Borough of Sutton to claim universal credit without having to satisfy the Gateway conditions. On the same day, the Universal Credit (Digital Service) Amendment Regulations 2014 (SI 2014/2887) came into force and made substantive changes to the Universal Credit Regulations, that only apply in what are described as "digital service" areas. At that time, the SM5 2 postcode area was the only such area. However, subsequent Commencement Orders have expanded the areas covered by the digital service and further statutory instruments (SI 2014/3225 and SI 2015/1647) have introduced additional amendments to the Universal Credit Regulations that only apply in such areas.

In keeping with its long-standing institutional reluctance to call anything by its correct statutory name, the DWP referred to digital service areas as "full service" areas and distinguished them from the areas in which the Gateway conditions still applied by referring to the latter as "live service" areas.

The distinction reflected the fact that, during this period, universal credit was administered using two separate and incompatible IT systems, depending on whether the claimant lived in a full/digital service area or a live service area.

Once the rules for universal credit were in force on at least a live service basis (i.e., for claimants who satisfied the Gateway Conditions) throughout Great Britain, the further roll-out of universal credit consisted of a process of "de-gatewayfication": instead of Commencement Orders extending universal credit to new geographical areas by prescribing additional relevant districts, they converted existing live service areas to full/digital service areas by revoking the Gateway conditions in those areas. That process ended on December 12, 2018, since when, it is not normally possible to make a fresh claim for a "legacy benefit". The significant remaining exception is the continuing availability of housing benefit to people over pension age, and to people in "specified" or "temporary" accommodation. The exception is made by reg.6A of the Universal Credit (Transitional Provisions) Regulations 2014 SI 2014/1230. For the definitions of "specified" and "temporary" accommodation see Sch.1 paras 3A–3B of the Universal Credit Regulations. (In summary, "specified" accommodation refers to "supported living" type arrangements, while "temporary" accommodation is what gets provided at the interim stage of discharge of a homelessness duty under the Housing Act 1996.)

Existing claimants

The legal basis for managed migration can currently be found in Part 4 of the Universal Credit (Transitional Provisions) Regulations 2014 (SI 2014/1230) as substituted with effect from July 24, 2019 by reg.3(7) of the Universal Credit (Managed Migration Pilot and Miscellaneous Amendments) Regulations 2019 (SI 2019/1152) and further amended with effect from July 25, 2022 by the Universal Credit (Transitional Provisions) Amendment Regulations 2022 (SI 2022/752). Migration is commenced by the Secretary of State issuing a "migration notice" under the substituted reg.44 to a person who is entitled to an award of an existing benefit. The notice must inform that person that all awards of any existing benefits to which they are entitled are to terminate and that they will need to make a claim for universal credit. It must also specify a day ("the deadline day") by which a claim for universal credit must be made. If no universal credit claim is made by the deadline day (which the Secretary of State can change to a later day: see reg.45) then all awards of any existing benefits to which the person is entitled terminate on the deadline day (except for awards of housing benefit, which terminate two weeks later: see reg.46). Under reg.46(3) and (4), a claimant who does not claim universal credit by the deadline day can retrieve the situation by claiming before "the final deadline", which is the day that would be the last day of the first assessment period in relation to an award commencing on the deadline day. **1.92**

Unlike "natural migration", managed migration gives entitlement to transitional protection, so that claimants should not receive less in benefit immediately after the move to universal credit than they were receiving immediately before. Substituted regs 48-57 of the Transitional Provisions Regulations 2014 contain detailed rules on how the transitional protection operates.

The structure of Universal Credit

Almost any general proposition about social security law will be subject to qualifications and exceptions. Failing to note those qualifications and exceptions risks giving an unhelpfully approximate explanation of how the structure is meant to work. However, dealing with them in full risks obscuring the view of the wood by concentrating on the trees. The purpose of this Note is to give the big picture. **1.93**

There is never any substitute for looking at the actual words of the legislative text. Until they have checked both that text and the commentary to it, readers should assume that everything in this introduction is subject to unstated exceptions, particularly when such exceptions are implied by the use of words such as "normally" and "usually".

The legal structure of the universal credit scheme is as follows. As already noted, the benefit is established by Pt 1 of the Welfare Reform Act 2012 ("WRA 2012" or "the Act") and by the Schedules to that Act that are given effect by provisions in Pt 1. The Act has subsequently been amended by the Welfare Reform and Work Act 2016 ("WR&WA 2016"). As is common in social security law, the Act sets out the structure of the scheme and confers extensive powers on the Secretary of State to make regulations prescribing matters of detail. The main regulations are the Universal Credit Regulations 2013 ("the Universal Credit Regulations" or "the Regulations"), but there are others including the 2014 Regulations and regulations dealing with claims and payments, and decisions and appeals, for universal credit, personal independence payment ("PIP"), new style JSA and new style ESA.

Universal credit is a non-contributory, means-tested, working age, social security benefit. That means that it is not "universal". With very limited exceptions, people who are not of working age are excluded from entitlement, as are (with no exceptions) those who do not satisfy the means-test. Moreover, as is the case with all non-contributory benefits, the rules contain residence and presence conditions (including a right to reside test) which exclude those who are felt not to have a legitimate connection with Great Britain or who have been absent from the UK for an extended period.

In addition, the fact that universal credit is a social security benefit means that it is not "credit" in the sense in which that word is used in ordinary speech. As with the child tax credit and working tax credit which preceded it, universal credit is a *payment*, made as a matter of legal right to those who meet the conditions of entitlement, not a *loan* to tide claimants over a period of reduced income. With the sole exception of the hardship payments made to those who have been sanctioned, universal credit that has been correctly paid does not have to be repaid.

Couples

1.94 One of the basic principles of universal credit is that it cannot usually be claimed by one member of a couple: WRA 2012 s.2(1) provides that a claim for universal credit may only be made a single person or by members of a couple jointly. It is implicit that any award of universal credit made on a joint claim will be a joint award to both members of the couple.

The basic conditions

1.95 Entitlement to universal credit depends upon satisfying both the "basic conditions" and the "financial conditions" set out in the Act (WRA 2012, s.3(1)). Where a joint claim is made, those conditions must usually be satisfied by both members of the couple (WRA 2012, s.3(2)).

The basic conditions are set out in s.4(1) of the Act. They are that the claimant:

- must be at least 18 years old;
- must not have reached the qualifying age for SPC (which is now pensionable age);
- is in Great Britain;
- is not receiving education; and
- has accepted a claimant commitment.

The last three of those conditions are further defined, or partially defined, in regulations. For example, a person who does not have a right to reside in the UK is treated as not being habitually resident here and hence as not being "in Great Britain": see reg.9 of the Universal Credit Regulations. All of those conditions are subject to exceptions which are specified in regulations. In addition, a person who meets the basic conditions cannot acquire entitlement to universal credit if he or she falls within the restrictions specified in s.6 of the Act and reg.19 of the Regulations.

It should be noted that it is not a condition of entitlement to universal credit that any claimant should be, or should not be, in remunerative work. The only way in which work affects universal credit is through the income that is earned from undertaking it.

The financial conditions

The financial conditions are set out in s.5 of the Act. They are that **1.96**

- the claimant's capital (or, for couples, joint capital) is not greater than a prescribed amount (fixed at £16,000 ever since 2013 by reg.18 of the Regulations); and that
- the claimant's income (or, for couples, joint income) is "such that, if the claimant were entitled to universal credit, the amount payable would not be less than any prescribed minimum" (currently fixed at one penny by reg.17 of the Regulations).

As is discussed above and below, entitlement to universal credit reduces as a claimant's income increases. The effect of the convoluted wording quoted in the second bullet point above is that if, as a result of that reduction, the amount of universal credit payable would be less than one penny (i.e., nil), the financial conditions are not satisfied. In other words, one cannot be entitled to universal credit at a nil rate.

As would be expected, the calculation of a claimant's income and capital are the subject of detailed provisions in the Regulations.

Assessment periods

Universal credit is a monthly benefit. Entitlement is normally assessed by reference to the claimant's circumstances during an "assessment period", which is defined by WRA 2012 s.7(2) and reg.21(1) of the Regulations as "a period of one month beginning with the first date of entitlement and each subsequent period of one month during which entitlement subsists". That entitlement is then normally paid monthly in arrears after the end of the assessment period to which the payment relates (see reg.47 of the Universal Credit, Personal Independence Payment, Jobseeker's Allowance and Employment and Support Allowance (Claims and Payments) Regulations 2013). **1.97**

Advances

The potential hardship which could result from a long wait between claim and payment is in principle mitigated by large-scale availability of advance payments on account under reg.5 of the Social Security (Payments on Account of Benefit) Regulations 2013 (SI 2013/383). About 60% of UC claimants receive an advance payment on account, generally within a matter of days of making their claim, on the basis that it is "likely" they will be entitled to UC: NAO, *Rolling Out Universal Credit* (HC 1123, June 2018), para.2.8. The Secretary of State had taken the position that certain claimants are in principle ineligible as a class for advances (in particular, those without a national insurance number) on the basis that it can not ever in such cases be said that it was "likely" they would ultimately be entitled; but in *Bui v Secretary of State for Work and Pensions* [2023] EWCA Civ 566 (May 25, 2023) the Court of Appeal decides that approach to be unlawful; any claimant is entitled to an individual decision on whether they are "likely" to qualify; any claimant can in principle be eligible for an advance. The Secretary of State was refused permission to appeal by the Supreme Court on October 18, 2023. From April 1, 2024, the *Bui* principle is legislatively reversed, in relation to claimants without national insurance numbers, by Social Security and Universal Credit (Migration of Tax Credit Claimants and Miscellaneous Amendments) Regulations 2024 (SI 2024/341), reg.6. *Bui* may nevertheless have continued relevance, for example in relation to claimants not yet determined to have a right of residence.

Calculation of entitlement to universal credit

1.98 Under s.8(1) of the Act, the amount of an award of universal credit is the balance of the "maximum amount" less "the amounts to be deducted".

Note that both the "maximum amount" and the "amounts to be deducted" can be affected by the "transitional protection" rules. See the commentary to Pt 4 of the Universal Credit (Transitional Provisions) Regulations 2014 (SI 2014/1230).

The amount so calculated will normally be reduced by the "benefit cap" (see below) if the claimant's total entitlement to specified social security benefits would otherwise exceed the amount of the cap.

The maximum amount

1.99 The maximum amount is a monthly amount. It is conceptually equivalent to the weekly "applicable amount" used in the calculation of entitlement to IS, JSA(IB) and ESA(IR). It is the total of the standard allowance (equivalent to the personal allowances for IS/JSA/ESA) established by WRA 2012, s.9 and reg.36 of the Regulations, and any of the following amounts to which the claimant is (or the joint claimants are) entitled:

- the child element

  Under WRA 2012, s.10 and regs.24 & 36 of the Regulations, an amount is allowed for each child or qualifying young person for whom a claimant is responsible, up to (subject to exceptions and transitional savings) a maximum of two children or qualifying young persons. A challenge to the compatibility with Convention rights of the two-child limit was rejected by the Supreme Court in *R. (SC, CB and 8 children) v Secretary of State for Work and Pensions* [2021] UKSC 26; [2022] A.C. 223.

  An additional amount is allowed for each child or qualifying young person who is entitled to disability living allowance ("DLA") or PIP. The amount is higher if entitlement is to the highest rate of the care component of DLA or the enhanced rate of the daily living component of PIP or if the child or qualifying young person is registered blind.

- the housing costs element

  The housing costs element is payable under WRA 2012, s.11 and regs 25 & 26 of, and Schs 1-5 to the Regulations. The rules are summarised below.

- the LCWRA element

  This is payable where the claimant has limited capability for work-related activity. It is equivalent to, but paid at a considerably higher rate than, the support component of ESA (see WRA 2012, s.12 and regs 27(1)(b) & 36 of the Regulations). The former LCW element (equivalent to the former work-related activity component of ESA) was abolished with effect from April 3, 2017 and is now only payable to claimants with transitional protection.

- the carer element

  This is equivalent to, and is paid at approximately the same rate as, the carer premium for IS/JSA/ESA (see WRA 2012, s.12 and regs 29 & 36 of the Regulations). To qualify, a claimant must satisfy the conditions of entitlement to carer's allowance other than having earnings below the prescribed limit and making a claim for that benefit (see regs 30(1) & (2) of the Regulations).

- the childcare costs element

  The childcare costs element is 85% of the charges incurred by a claimant for relevant childcare (defined in reg.35 of the Regulations) subject to a prescribed maximum (regs 34(1) and 36) and also to anti-abuse rules in reg.34(2). To qualify, a claimant must satisfy both the work condition (reg. 32) and the childcare costs condition (reg.33).

The childcare costs element is not subject to the benefits cap (reg. 81(1)(b) and (2)).

The amounts of the standard allowance and the various elements are specified in a table that forms part of reg.36 of the Regulations.

The amounts to be deducted

Once the maximum amount has been ascertained, it is necessary to calculate the amounts to be deducted from it. By WRA 2012, s.8(3) & reg.22 of the Universal Credit Regulations, those amounts are: **1.100**

- All the claimant's, or the claimants' combined, *unearned* income;
- Either (where the claimant does not have responsibility for a child or qualifying young person and does not have limited capability for work) 55% of his or her *earned* income; or
- (where the claimant has responsibility for a child or qualifying young person or has limited capability for work) 55% of the amount by which the claimant's, or the claimants' combined, *earned* income exceeds the work allowance.

The "work allowance" is what is described in IS/HB/JSA/ESA as an "earnings disregard". There are two rates, which are specified in a table that forms part of reg.22. The higher work allowance is applicable if the award of universal credit does not include the housing costs element: otherwise the lower work allowance applies.

Until April 2016, all claimants with earned income had work allowances, but, as indicated above, work allowances are now only available when the claimant (or at least one joint claimant) has responsibility for a child or qualifying young person or has limited capability for work. In addition, some of the pre-April 2016 allowances were higher than is now the case. For some claimants who have responsibility for a child, the reduction in the work allowances were at least partially offset by the April 2016 increases in the maximum rates of the childcare costs elements (reg.36 of the Regulations) and the percentage of relevant childcare charges that is eligible to be met by universal credit (reg.34). The maximum increase in the child care costs element was £114.06 per month for one child and £192.54 for two or more children, By contrast, the higher work allowance for a single person with children was cut by £337 from £734 to £397 (now £673 in 2024/25).

In fairness, the cuts in the lower work allowance are considerably less than in the higher allowance (and it is likely that many claimants who have responsibility for a child or qualifying young person will have housing costs and so only be eligible for the lower allowance). So the combined effect of the cut in the work allowance and the increase in the childcare costs element will often be a modest increase in entitlement to universal credit.

Those adjustments were made at the cost of a swingeing reduction in work incentives for able-bodied, childless claimants.

Calculation of income

Earned income

Employees

1.101 The treatment of the earned income of employees is another new feature of the universal credit scheme and one of the areas in which the benefit depends heavily upon the efficient operation of information technology. Most employers are now obliged to submit their PAYE returns to HMRC online and on a monthly basis under the "Real-Time Information" system. The idea is that that PAYE information should then be used to calculate the claimant's entitlement to universal credit for that month. If the system works, it has the advantage that claimants need not report fluctuations in their earnings (and therefore need not fear having to repay overpayments if they omit to do so). The possibility of treating earned income in this way was the main reason for establishing universal credit as a monthly, rather than weekly, benefit and for providing that payment should be in arrears after the end of the assessment period.

For those advantages to accrue, the way in which earnings from employment are calculated are different from those for IS/HB/JSA/ESA. First, earnings are to be based on the actual amount received by the claimant during the assessment period (see reg.54(1)). Then, reg.55 defines "earned income" by reference to the income tax definition. Finally reg.61 provides that where the claimant's employer is a "Real Time Information employer", the information on which the Secretary of State bases his calculation of earned income is to be the information reported by that employer through the PAYE system and the claimant is normally treated as having received those earnings in the same assessment period as the Secretary of State received the information: see *Secretary of State for Work and Pensions v Johnson* [2020] EWCA Civ 778; [2020] P.T.S.R. 1872.

As was recognised in *Johnson*, the rigidity of that rule can lead to unintuitive outcomes where—whether because of what the Court in *Johnson* referred to as "the non-banking day salary shift", or because the claimant is paid four weekly rather than monthly—a claimant receives two payments of salary in the same assessment period. The rules for the non-banking day salary shift (in which a monthly payment due on a weekend or Bank Holiday is paid early), that were declared to be irrational in *Johnson*, were changed prospectively from November 16, 2020 by the substitution of a new regulation 61 which allows the reallocation of payments from one assessment period to another where the claimant is paid monthly. In another case, *Pantellerisco*, the High Court had also found to be irrational the way in which the incomes of claimants paid four weekly are calculated (for the purposes of reg.82). But in *Secretary of State for Work and Pensions v Pantellerisco* [2021] EWCA Civ 1454; [2021] P.T.S.R. 1922 the Court of Appeal reversed that decision. Further, in *Secretary of State for Work and Pensions v LM* [2023] UKUT 72 (AAC) the Upper Tribunal decides that the logic of the *Pantellerisco* decision applies also to fortnightly-paid claimants. The fluctuations produced by the Regulations in calculating the earned income of non-monthly paid claimants may indeed sometimes be unintuitive, and may individually produce hard results, but the regulations are not in that respect irrational.

With effect from April 11, 2018 the new reg.54 introduces the rule that if a claimant's earned income (whether as an employee or as a self-employed person) is more than sufficient to wipe out entitlement to UC for an assessment period, the amount of the excess ("surplus earnings") is to be taken into account on any new claims within the following six months. There are complex provisions, with a potential to confuse claimants, for the erosion of surplus earnings within that six months by the making of claims that do not result in any entitlement. However, the practical effect of those provisions has hitherto been very considerably reduced by an annual Determination of the Secretary of State every year since then to "temporarily" make the threshold for surplus earnings £2,500 per month rather than £300. The most recent Determination was dated February 22, 2024 and extends that position to April 2025.

The self-employed

The principle in reg.54(1) of the Universal Credit Regulations that earnings are to be taken as the actual amount received by the claimant during the assessment period also applies to self-employed earnings. Under reg.57(2), a person's self-employed earnings in respect of an assessment period are to be calculated by taking that person's "gross profits" (defined by reg.57(3) as "the actual receipts in [the assessment] period less any deductions for expenses allowed under regulation 58 or 59") and then deducting any payments of income tax and Class 2 and 4 national insurance contributions actually made to HMRC in that period and any "relievable pension contributions made" (as defined in s.188 of the Finance Act 2004, i.e., contributions to a registered pension scheme for which tax relief is available). Regs 58 & 59 establish an exhaustive list of the expenses that can be deducted. In particular, reg.59 provides for flat rate deductions for business mileage and the use of the claimant's home for business purposes. **1.102**

Where a claimant would otherwise be subject to all work-related requirements—or is only exempt from all work-related requirements because their earnings exceed the earnings threshold (see below)—self-employed earnings are subject to a "minimum income floor" (see regs 62-64). The minimum income floor is usually an amount representing the person's "individual threshold" (see below) converted to a monthly figure and subjected to a notional deduction to reflect the tax and national insurance contributions payable on that level of self-employed earnings. Except during a start-up period (reg.63) self-employed claimants whose earnings in any assessment period are less than their minimum income floor are treated as having earnings equal to that floor.

The operation of the minimum income floor is affected from April 2018 by the "surplus earnings" rule (see above). That, and the general calculations, is also affected from the same date by the new provision (reg.57A and amendments to reg.57) for "unused losses" in past (but not pre-April 2018) assessment periods to be set against profits in the current assessment period.

Unearned income

Unearned income is deducted from the maximum amount without any disregard or taper. However, in contrast to the rules for IS/JSA/ESA and working-age HB, not all types of unearned income fall within the definition. Those that do are set out in reg.66 of the Universal Credit Regulations and include: **1.103**

- retirement pension income;
- certain social security benefits (including "new style" JSA and ESA);
- spousal maintenance payments;
- student income (e.g., student loans and grants: see reg.68);
- payments under permanent health insurance policies and certain mortgage protection policies;
- income from (non-retirement) annuities and from trusts unless disregarded as compensation for personal injury (regs 75 & 76);
- income treated as the yield from capital under reg.72 (see below);
- miscellaneous income that is taxable under Part 5 of Income Tax (Trading and Other Income) Act 2005;

Unearned income is calculated as a monthly amount but—in contrast to earned income—does not necessarily represent the amount actually received by the claimant in the assessment period for which the award is made. Regulation 73 contains detailed rules for converting unearned income (other than student income) received in respect of periods other than a month into a monthly equivalent. Student income has its own detailed rules, which are set out in regs 69-71.

Treatment of capital

1.104 Capital is relevant to universal credit entitlement in two ways. First, there is a maximum capital limit of £16,000 for both single and joint claimants (see reg.18 of the Universal Credit Regulations). Claimants who have capital in excess of that limit do not satisfy the first financial condition (see WRA 2012 s.5) and are therefore not entitled to benefit. Second, claimants with capital of more than £6,000 but less than £16,000 are treated as receiving an amount of unearned income equal to an "assumed yield" on that income. Reg.72 of the Universal Credit Regulations provides that that assumed yield is to be £4.35 per assessment period for each £250 (or part thereof). Readers who are familiar with IS/HB/JSA/ESA will recognise the "tariff income" rule under a different name.

The calculation of capital is governed by regs.45-50. By reg.46(1) and (2), the whole of a claimant's capital (other than his or her personal possessions) is to be taken into account unless it is treated as income under regs 46(3) and (4) or disregarded under reg. 48 and Sch.10. The valuation rules closely follow those for IS/HB/JSA/ESA and reg.50 contains a notional capital rule which is similar, though not identical, to that for the older working age benefits.

The benefit cap

1.105 Awards of universal credit are subject to the "benefit cap" established by ss.96-97 of the Act and regs 78-83 of the Universal Credit Regulations. This means that, subject to limited exceptions, if an award of universal credit would lead to the claimant's total entitlement to social security benefits exceeding the level of the cap then the amount of universal credit that the claimant would otherwise be awarded for the assessment period is reduced by the amount of the excess.

Until 2023 the benefit cap rates had not been changed, or even reviewed, since its rates were inserted into s.96 of the Act in 2016. But in April 2023 they were uprated in line with the level of annual increase to other benefit levels. In April 2024 they were frozen again.

The cap is fixed at four different levels. If the claimant is (or joint claimants are) resident in Greater London, the cap is £25,323 per annum—equivalent to £486.98 per week—for joint claimants or those responsible for a child or qualifying young person and £16,967 per annum—£326.29 per week—for other claimants. If the claimant is (or joint claimants are) not resident in Greater London, the equivalent levels are £22,020 per annum and £14,753 per annum (£423.46 per week and £283.71 per week). The higher levels in Greater London are intended to reflect the higher cost of accommodation in the capital. The childcare costs element of universal credit is not subject to the cap and the cap does not apply at all if the universal credit award contains the LCWRA element; if a claimant is receiving certain other benefits including new style ESA with the support component, industrial injuries disablement benefit and attendance allowance; or if any member of the household is receiving DLA or PIP.

Housing costs

1.106 Section 8(2)(c) of the Act provides that the maximum amount is to include "any amount included under s.11 (housing costs)". Section 11(1) says that an award of universal credit must include "an amount in respect of any liability of a claimant to make payments in respect of the accommodation they occupy as their home". By s.11(2), the accommodation must be in Great Britain and must be residential accommodation but need not be self-contained. The remainder of s.11 confers powers for the Secretary of State to make regulations, which have been used to make regs 25 and 26 of, and Schs 1-5 to, the Universal Credit Regulations.

Regulation 25 establishes three conditions for eligibility, the "payment condition", the "liability condition" and the "occupation condition"(see reg.25(5)(b)).

The payment condition (reg.25(1)(a) and (2) is that payments must be rent payments (as defined in Sch.1, paras.2 and 3), owner-occupier payments (Sch.1, paras.4-6) or service charges payments (Sch.1, para.7). Until April 5, 2018, owner-occupiers were, in some circumstances, entitled to an amount of housing costs in respect of the interest on their mortgages or on loans taken out for repairs and improvements. However, from April 6, 2016 such housing costs have been replaced with loans under the Loans for Mortgage Interest Regulations 2017 (SI 2017/725): see below. As a result the only UC housing costs still payable to owner-occupiers are those in respect of service charges.

The inclusion of rent payments was a major change. Previously help with rent was given through HB which was administered by local authorities rather than the DWP. Many—but not all—of the rules about rental payments are similar to those for HB.

The liability condition (reg.25(1)(b) and (3)) is that the claimant (or either joint claimant) must either be liable to make the payments on a commercial basis, or treated as liable to make the payments (Pt 1 of Sch.2) and must not be treated as not liable to make the payments (Pt 2 of Sch.2).

The occupation condition (reg.25(1)(c) and (4)) is that the claimant must normally be treated as occupying the accommodation as his or her home (Pt 1 of Sch.3) and not be treated as not occupying it (Pt 2 of Sch.3)

The rules for the calculation of the housing costs element are set out in Schs 4 (for renters) and 5 (for the residual housing costs payable to owner occupiers).

Claimant responsibilities and the claimant commitment

The claimant commitment

Under s.4(1)(e) of the Act, it is a basic condition of entitlement to universal credit that the claimant "has accepted a claimant commitment". By s.14, a claimant commitment is "a record of a claimant's responsibilities in relation to an award of universal credit" and is to include a record of the requirements with which the claimant must comply, any prescribed information, and any other information the Secretary of State considers it appropriate to include. However, the claimant commitment does not itself impose requirements on the claimant and the condition that the clamant should accept it appears to have been included so that there is no doubt about what requirements have, in fact, been imposed. Any failure to comply with a requirement is dealt with by a sanction rather than by ending entitlement to benefit. **1.107**

Claimant responsibilities

Work-related requirements

Section 13(1) of the Act empowers the Secretary of State "to impose work-related requirements with which claimants must comply". There are four different types of work-related requirement: **1.108**

- the work-focused interview requirement (WRA 2012 s.15)

  As its name suggests, this is a "requirement that a claimant participate in one or more work-focused interviews as specified by the Secretary of State".

- the work preparation requirement (WRA 2012 s.16)

  This is a "requirement that a claimant take particular action specified by the Secretary of State for the purpose of making it more likely in the opinion of the Secretary of State that the claimant will obtain paid work (or more paid work or better-paid work)". Section 16(3) gives the following examples of actions that the Secretary of State may specify:
  - o attending a skills assessment;
  - o improving personal presentation;
  - o participating in training;
  - o participating in an employment programme;
  - o undertaking work experience or a work placement;
  - o developing a business plan;
  - o any prescribed action.

In addition any claimant with limited capability for work may also be required to participate in a work-focused health-related assessment.

- work search requirements (WRA 2012 s.17 and reg.95)

  There are two of these. The first is that a claimant must take all reasonable action for the purpose of obtaining paid work (or more paid work or better-paid work). The second is that he or she must also take any particular action specified by the Secretary of State for that purpose. Section 17(3) gives the following examples of actions that the Secretary of State may specify

  - o carrying out work searches;
  - o making applications;
  - o creating and maintaining an online profile;
  - o registering with an employment agency;
  - o seeking references;
  - o any prescribed action.

  Under reg.95, claimants are treated as not having complied with the first work search requirement unless they have spent at least the "expected number of hours each week minus any relevant deductions" taking action to obtain paid work unless the Secretary of State is satisfied that the claimant has taken all reasonable action for that purpose despite having spent fewer hours taking action.

  Reg.88 provides that the expected number of hours is 35 per week unless the claimant has caring responsibilities or is physically or mentally impaired and the Secretary of State agrees to a lesser number of hours. Reg.95(2) specifies that relevant deductions means the total of any time agreed by the Secretary of State for the claimant to carry out paid work, voluntary work, a work preparation requirement, or voluntary work preparation in that week or to deal with temporary childcare responsibilities, a domestic emergency, funeral arrangements or other temporary circumstances.

- work availability requirements (WRA 2012 s.18 and reg.96)

  This is a requirement that the claimant be available for work which is defined as "able and willing immediately to take up paid work (or more paid work or better-paid work)".

The work-related requirements which may be imposed on a claimant depend on which of the following groups the claimant falls into—

- Claimants subject to no work-related requirements (WRA 2012 s.19 and regs 89-90);

  These include claimants with limited capability for work and work-related activity, claimants with regular and substantial caring responsibilities for a severely disabled person, and claimants who are the responsible carer for a child under the age of 1, claimants who have reached the qualifying age for state pension credit; pregnant women within 11 weeks of the expected date of confinement and new mothers within 15 weeks of the birth, recent adopters, certain claimants in education and foster parents of children under 1.

  Claimants also fall within this group if they are in work and their earnings equal or exceed the threshold that applies to them. For most people that threshold will be the amount they would earn if they worked for their expected number of hours (usually 35 per week) at the minimum wage converted to a monthly figure. Because the minimum wage rate is lower for those aged under 21, and lower for apprentices, lower thresholds apply to people aged 20 or less who would otherwise be subject to the work-focused interview requirement only, or the work preparation requirement only, and to apprentices. Couples have a joint threshold that applies to their combined weekly earnings.

- Claimants subject to the work-focused interview requirement only (WRA 2012 s.20 and reg.91);

  This group comprises the responsible carers of children who are aged 1 and certain foster parents and others caring for children.

- Claimants subject to the work-focused interview and work preparation requirements only (WRA 2012 s.21);

  This group comprises claimants who have limited capability for work, but do not also have limited capability for work-related activity, or are responsible carers of children aged 2.

- Claimants subject to all work-related requirements (WRA 2012 s.22 and reg.92).

  This group comprises every claimant who is not in any of the other groups. The Secretary of State *must* save in prescribed cases (see below), impose the work search requirement and the work availability requirement on everyone in this group and *may* also impose the work-focused interview requirement and a work preparation requirement.

- A Claimant can be exempted from the work search requirements and work availability requirements while in a variety of circumstances prescribed by reg.99 of the 2013 Regulations. The most important of those is reg.99(6) (the "administrative earnings threshold"), which exempts a person earning more than a prescribed amount. Until September 2022 this was set only just above legacy benefit personal allowance levels, but from that point it has increased repeatedly and since May 2024 has exempted only those single claimants with earnings equivalent to NMW work for at least 18 hours per week, and those in couples where the combined earnings equal at least 29 hours per week.

- Reg.98 establishes special rules for the recent victims of domestic violence, providing for exemption from work-related requirements for 13 weeks, or 26 weeks where victims are caring for children.

Connected requirements

Under s.23 of the Act, the Secretary of State may also impose a "connected requirement". There are three of these. First, claimants may be required to participate in an interview in connection with a work-related requirement. Second, they may be required to provide evidence to verify that they have complied with work-related requirements that have been imposed on them. Finally, they may be required to report specified changes in their circumstances which are relevant to work-related requirements. 1.109

Sanctions

It is not a condition of entitlement to universal credit that claimants should comply with requirements imposed by the Secretary of State under the provisions summarised above. Instead, compliance is enforced by the imposition of sanctions under which the amount of universal credit payable is reduced. Under regs 110-111 of the Universal Credit Regulations, the maximum reduction is the amount of the standard allowance applicable to the award of universal credit for the assessment period that is being considered or, where the sanction has only been imposed on one of two joint claimants, half the amount of that standard allowance. 1.110

There are four levels of sanction.

Higher-level sanctions are imposed under s.26 of the Act, which specifies that various actions or omissions by the claimant are to be "sanctionable failures". The definition of each of those failures is technical but, in broad terms, higher-level sanctions apply where, for no good reason, a claimant fails to undertake a work placement or apply for a vacancy when required to do so; fails to take up an offer of paid work; ceases work or loses pay voluntarily or through misconduct (whether before or after claiming universal credit). The sanction period is fixed by reg.102 of the Universal Credit Regulations. Again the rules are technical but for adults who commit a sanctionable failure during the currency of a claim, the length of the sanction period depends upon whether there has been a previous sanctionable failure within the previous 365 days (including the date of the failure that led to the imposition of the current sanction). If not, then the sanction period is 91 days. If there was one previous sanctionable failure within the period, it is 182 days. The sanction period for a third or subsequent sanctionable failure within the 365 day period was originally 1095 days (3 years) but was reduced to 182 days with effect from November 27, 2019. Shorter periods apply if the claimant was under 18 when the sanctionable failure occurred or in the case of a failure that occurred before the claim for universal credit. Reg.102 is subject to reg.113 which specifies a number of circumstances in which a sanctionable failure does not result in a reduction of universal credit.

Medium-level sanctions, *low-level sanctions* and *lowest-level sanctions* are imposed under s.27 of the Act. That section provides that it is to be a sanctionable failure for a claimant to fail, for no good reason, to comply with a work-related requirement or a connected requirement unless that failure would also be a sanctionable failure under s.26, in which case the higher-level sanction applies. The level of sanction that such a failure attracts is prescribed in regs.103-105. The regulations themselves do not say so but it is important to remember that, by virtue of s.27, each of the failures discussed below is only sanctionable if it occurred for no good reason. Moreover, regs.103-105 are subject to reg.113 which specifies a number of circumstances in which a sanctionable failure does not result in a reduction of universal credit.

A failure to take all reasonable action to obtain paid work in breach of a work search requirement under s.17(1)(a) or a failure to comply with a work availability requirement attracts a medium-level sanction under reg.103. The sanction period is 28 days for the first such failure in any 365 day period and 91 days for a second or subsequent failure in that period.

Reg.104 provides that low-level sanctions apply to claimants who are subject to the work preparation requirement or to all work-related requirements and who have failed to comply with a work-focused interview requirement, a work preparation requirement, or a connected requirement, or failed to take a particular action specified by the Secretary of State to obtain work in breach of a work search requirement. The sanction lasts until 7, 14 or 28 days (depending on the number of previous such failures in the preceding 65 days) after the claimant complies with the requirement, or has a change of circumstances so that he or she is not longer subject to any work-related requirements, or the requirement is withdrawn, or the award of universal credit ends. Again, the period for 16 and 17 year-olds is shorter.

Lowest-level sanctions are governed by reg.105. They apply to claimants who are subject to the work-focused interview requirement only (i.e., under WRA 2012, s.20) and who fail to comply with that requirement. The sanction continues until the claimant complies with the requirement, or has a change of circumstances so that he or she is no longer subject to any work-related requirements, or the award of universal credit ends.

When deciding whether there has been a previous sanctionable failure within the 365 day period, failures occurring in the 14 days immediately preceding the failure in question are disregarded (reg.101(4)).

The total of all outstanding sanction periods in relation to a particular claimant, cannot exceed 1095 days (reg.101(3)).

Under reg.109, a sanction terminates (irrespective of the length of the unexpired sanction period) if, since the most recent sanction was imposed, the claimant has been in paid work for six months (not necessarily consecutively) and during each of those months his or her earnings were equal to or exceeded the applicable threshold (see above).

Regulations provide for the date on which the sanction period is to begin. Where a claimant is subject to more than one sanction, they run consecutively (reg.101(2)).

Where a 100% sanction has been imposed (but not where there has been a 40% reduction), the Secretary of State must make a hardship payment under WRA 2012, s.28 in the (very limited) circumstances prescribed by regs 115-118. Under reg.119, hardship payments are usually recoverable in accordance with s.71ZH of the Social Security Administration Act 1992. However, any hardship payment ceases to be recoverable if, since the last date on which the award of universal credit was subject to a sanction, the claimant (or the joint claimants) has (or have) been in paid work for six months (not necessarily consecutively) and during each of those months his or her earnings (or their joint earnings) were equal to or exceeded the applicable threshold (see above).

PART 1

UNIVERSAL CREDIT

CHAPTER 1

ENTITLEMENT AND AWARDS

Introductory

Universal credit 1.111

1.—(1) A benefit known as universal credit is payable in accordance with this Part.

(2) Universal credit may, subject as follows, be awarded to—

(a) an individual who is not a member of a couple (a "single person"), or
(b) members of a couple jointly.

(3) An award of universal credit is, subject as follows, calculated by reference to—

(a) a standard allowance;
(b) an amount for responsibility for children or young persons;
(c) an amount for housing; and
(d) amounts for other particular needs or circumstances.

DEFINITIONS

"child"—see s.40.
"couple"—see ss.39 and 40.

GENERAL NOTE

Part 1 of the Welfare Reform Act 2012 ("WRA 2012") contains the provisions and confers regulation-making powers in relation to universal credit. Universal credit is to be the new means-tested, non-contributory benefit for people of working age. It replaces income support, income-based jobseeker's allowance (JSA), income-related employment and support allowance (ESA), housing benefit, working tax credit and child tax credit. Thus it will be paid to people both in and out of work. State pension credit will continue for people who are over the qualifying age for state pension credit—see s.4(4), which applies the definition of "the qualifying age" for state pension credit in s.1(6) of the State Pension Credit Act 2002 (see Vol.II in this series) for the purposes of universal credit. ESA and JSA will also continue but as contributory benefits only. 1.112

Note that "a person who is subject to immigration control" is not entitled to universal credit (Immigration and Asylum Act 1999, s.115, as amended by WRA 2012, Sch.2, para.54 with effect from April 29, 2013).

Initially universal credit was introduced only for people in the "pathfinder group" and only on an extremely limited geographical basis. See the Introduction and the General Note at the beginning of Part IV of this Volume for a summary of the process by which universal credit has been "rolled out" on a national basis.

As usual, Part 1 creates the legislative framework and the detail is to be found in the Universal Credit Regulations 2013 (SI 2013/376)—on which see Pt III of this Volume.

Subsection (2)

1.113 This provides that in the case of a couple awards are to be made to the couple jointly. Note the definition of "claimant" in s.40, which states that "claimant" in Pt 1 of the Act means "a single claimant or each of joint claimants".

Subsection (3)

1.114 Depending on the claimant's (or claimants') circumstances, an award of universal credit will include a standard allowance (see s.9 and reg.36 of the Universal Credit Regulations), an amount for children and young persons for whom the claimant is responsible (see s.10 and regs 24 and 36 of the Universal Credit Regulations), housing costs (see s.11 and regs 25–26 of, and Schs 1–5 to, the Universal Credit Regulations) and an amount for "other particular needs or circumstances" (see s.12 and regs 23(2) and 27–35 of, and Schs 6-9 to, the Universal Credit Regulations). Note that although subs.(3)(b) refers to an amount for children and young persons, in the case of the latter, s.10 restricts this to "qualifying young persons". For who counts as a "qualifying young person" see s.40 and reg.5 of the Universal Credit Regulations.

Claims

1.115 **2.**—(1) A claim may be made for universal credit by—

(a) a single person; or

(b) members of a couple jointly.

(2) Regulations may specify circumstances in which a member of a couple may make a claim as a single person.

DEFINITIONS

"claim"—see s.40.
"couple"—see ss.39 and 40.
"single person"—see s.40.

GENERAL NOTE

1.116 In the case of a couple, claims for universal credit are to be made jointly. This does not apply in prescribed circumstances (subs.(2)). On subs.(2), see reg.3(3) of the Universal Credit Regulations and note reg.3(4)-(6).

For the rules for claims for universal credit see the Universal Credit, Personal Independence Payment, Jobseeker's Allowance and Employment and Support Allowance (Claims and Payments) Regulations 2013 (SI 2013/380) in Vol.III. Generally a claim for universal credit has to be made online. Note reg.6 (claims not required for entitlement to universal credit in certain cases).

Entitlement

Entitlement

1.117 **3.**—(1) A single claimant is entitled to universal credit if the claimant meets—

(a) the basic conditions; and

(b) the financial conditions for a single claimant.

(2) Joint claimants are jointly entitled to universal credit if—

(a) each of them meets the basic conditions; and

(b) they meet the financial conditions for joint claimants.

DEFINITIONS

"claim"—see s.40.
"claimant"—*ibid.*
"joint claimants"—*ibid.*
"single claimant"—*ibid.*

GENERAL NOTE

This sets out the general conditions of entitlement to universal credit. A single claimant has to meet all of the basic conditions (see s.4) and the financial conditions (i.e., the means-test) (see s.5). In the case of joint claimants, both of them have to meet all of the basic and the financial conditions. Note, however, s.4(2) which allows for regulations to provide for exceptions from any of these conditions, either in the case of a single claimant, or one or both joint claimants. **1.118**

Basic conditions

4.—(1) For the purposes of section 3, a person meets the basic conditions who— **1.119**

(a) is at least 18 years old;
(b) has not reached the qualifying age for state pension credit;
(c) is in Great Britain;
(d) is not receiving education; and
(e) has accepted a claimant commitment.

(2) Regulations may provide for exceptions to the requirement to meet any of the basic conditions (and, for joint claimants, may provide for an exception for one or both).

(3) For the basic condition in subsection (1)(a) regulations may specify a different minimum age for prescribed cases.

(4) For the basic condition in subsection (1)(b), the qualifying age for state pension credit is that referred to in section 1(6) of the State Pension Credit Act 2002.

(5) For the basic condition in subsection (1)(c) regulations may—

(a) specify circumstances in which a person is to be treated as being or not being in Great Britain;
(b) specify circumstances in which temporary absence from Great Britain is disregarded.
(c) modify the application of this Part in relation to a person not in Great Britain who is by virtue of paragraph (b) entitled to universal credit.

(6) For the basic condition in subsection (1)(d) regulations may—

(a) specify what "receiving education" means;
(b) specify circumstances in which a person is to be treated as receiving or not receiving education.

(7) For the basic condition in subsection (1)(e) regulations may specify circumstances in which a person is to be treated as having accepted or not accepted a claimant commitment.

DEFINITIONS

"claim"—see s.40.
"claimant"—*ibid.*
"joint claimants"—*ibid.*

General Note

1.120 Subsection (1) lists the basic conditions that have to be satisfied for entitlement to universal credit. Subsection (2) allows for regulations to provide for exceptions from any of these conditions, either in the case of a single claimant, or one or both joint claimants.

Subsection (1)(a)

1.121 The minimum age for entitlement to universal credit is generally 18. However, under subs.(3) regulations can provide for a lower age in certain cases. See reg.8 of the Universal Credit Regulations for the cases where the minimum age is 16.

Subsection (1)(b)

1.122 This subsection excludes the possibility that a person could be entitled to both state pension credit and universal credit by providing that no person who has reached "the qualifying age for state pension credit" will meet the basic conditions for universal credit. But note subs.(2) and see reg.3(2) of the Universal Credit Regulations. The effect of reg.3(2) is that a couple may still be entitled to universal credit even if one member is over the qualifying age for state pension credit, provided that the other member of the couple is under that age.

Subsection (4) applies the definition of "the qualifying age" for state pension credit in s.1(6) of the State Pension Credit Act 2002 (see Part I of this volume) for the purposes of universal credit. The effect of that definition is that the qualifying age for state pension credit for both men and women is the pensionable age for women.

Subsection (1)(c)

1.123 It is a basic condition of entitlement to universal credit that the person is in Great Britain. Note subs.(5) under which regulations may treat a person as being or not being in Great Britain (see reg.9 of the Universal Credit Regulations for when a person is treated as not being in Great Britain, and reg.10 on Crown servants and armed forces) and may provide for the circumstances in which temporary absence from Great Britain is ignored (see reg.11).

Subsection (1)(d)

1.124 A person must not be "receiving education" to be eligible for universal credit. For the regulations made under subs.(6) see regs 12–14 of the Universal Credit Regulations.

Subsection (1)(e)

1.125 The concept of a claimant commitment as a condition of receiving benefit is an important part of the underlying policy behind the Government's social security reforms. See s.14 below and the notes to that section. Note that the condition is met merely by having accepted the most up-to-date version of the claimant commitment. Further, in *FO v SSWP* (UC) [2022] UKUT 56 (AAC) at paras 14 and 15, Judge Wikeley expressed no disagreement with the Secretary of State's assertion that where a UC award is in place and the Secretary of State wants to update the claimant commitment, a claimant's failure to engage, while potentially sanctionable, is not a basis for ending the award because the existing claimant commitment will remain in force (but see the notes to reg.15 of the Universal Credit Regulations, at 2.55).

A failure to comply with the claimant commitment does not entail any breach of subs.(1)(e), nor is that in itself any ground for a sanction, although sanctions may be imposed for failures to comply with work-related and connected requirements that are recorded in the claimant commitment and other legal consequences may follow from failures to carry out other obligations. Under subs.(7) regulations may specify the circumstances in which a person can be treated as having accepted or not accepted a claimant commitment—see reg.15 of the Universal Credit Regulations. In addition, subs.(2) allows regulations to provide exceptions to the requirement to meet any basic condition.

That power has been exercised in relation to the condition of having accepted a claimant commitment in reg.16, which may have been of particular importance during the 2020 coronavirus outbreak, when "conditionality" was suspended for three months from March 30, 2020. Since there was no new legislation to lift the operation of s.4(1)(e) during that period, in contrast to the position on the work search and work availability requirements, allowing entitlement on new claims without s.4(1)(e) being met appears to have been the key to not imposing those requirements. Regulation 16(b) (exceptional circumstances make it unreasonable to expect the claimant to accept a claimant commitment) could clearly have been applied (see further in the notes to reg.16). For existing claimants, who had already accepted a commitment, the work search and work availability requirements were expressly lifted. For other requirements, there were to be no sanctions imposed for failing to comply and/or a flexibility in reviewing requirements over the telephone.

On July 1, 2020 it was announced in Parliament (Under-Secretary of State, Mims Davies, WQ 62431) that from that date the requirement for universal credit claimants (among others) to accept a claimant commitment was being reintroduced. The commitments of existing claimants would be reviewed and up-dated as capacity allowed. It appears that the reintroduction for new claimants was also to be phased in.

Note that the new style Jobseekers Act 1995 (Vol.I of this series) does not allow regulations to provide exceptions to the requirement to meet the conditions of entitlement in s.1(2), including that of having accepted a claimant commitment (s.1(2)(b)), so that reg.8 of the JSA Regulations 2013 appears not to have been validly made. Nor does the new style Welfare Reform Act 2007 (on new style ESA) in relation to the conditions of entitlement in s.1(3), including that of having accepted a claimant commitment (s.1(3)(aa)), so that reg.45 of the ESA Regulations 2013 appears not to have been validly made.

Subsection (5)

It is worthy of note that this superficially innocuous provision is relied on in regulations to authorise many of the practical restrictions on migrants' access to universal credit, under reg.9 of the Universal Credit Regulations. "Persons subject to immigration control" are separately excluded by s.115(9) of the Immigration and Asylum Act 1999. But there are many migrants—especially EU nationals with pre-settled status—who have a grant of leave to be in the UK, and are not excluded from access to public funds under the terms of their leave. There does not appear to be any case law analysing whether a power to "specify circumstances in which a person is to be treated as ... not being in Great Britain" can authorise indefinitely excluding a person who is in fact here and has a positive right to be here. **1.126**

Financial conditions

5.—(1) For the purposes of section 3, the financial conditions for a single claimant are that— **1.127**

(a) the claimant's capital, or a prescribed part of it, is not greater than a prescribed amount, and
(b) the claimant's income is such that, if the claimant were entitled to universal credit, the amount payable would not be less than any prescribed minimum.

(2) For those purposes, the financial conditions for joint claimants are that—

(a) their combined capital, or a prescribed part of it, is not greater than a prescribed amount, and
(b) their combined income is such that, if they were entitled to universal credit, the amount payable would not be less than any prescribed minimum.

DEFINITIONS

"claim"—see s.40.
"claimant"—*ibid.*
"joint claimants"—*ibid.*
"prescribed"—*ibid.*
"single claimant"—*ibid.*

GENERAL NOTE

1.128 This section contains the means-test for universal credit. Both the capital and the income condition have to be met. For joint claimants it is their combined capital and their combined income that counts (subs.(2)).

Capital

1.129 The capital limit for universal credit for both a single claimant and joint claimants is £16,000 (see reg.18(1) of the Universal Credit Regulations). The limit has not altered since the inception of the universal credit scheme, or indeed since 2006 for other means-tested benefits (see the notes to reg.18). Note that where a claimant who is a member of a couple makes a claim as a single person (see reg.3(3) of the Universal Credit Regulations for the circumstances in which this may occur) the capital of the other member of the couple counts as the claimant's (reg.18(2)).

Thus the capital limit for universal credit is the same as for income support, income-based JSA, income-related ESA and housing benefit. There is no capital limit for working tax credit and child tax credit.

Since having capital not exceeding the prescribed limit is a condition of entitlement under s.3(1)(b) it must be the case that the burden of showing that that is so rests on the claimant. That principle had been accepted for other income-related benefits where there was more of an argument that the capital limit operated as an exclusion and so might be for the Secretary of State to show (see the notes to s.134(1) of the SSCBA 1992 in Vol.V of this series, 2021/22 edition, as up-dated in Cumulative Supplements included in this volume and in mid-year Supplements). That would be in accord with the principle in *Kerr v Department for Social Development* [2004] UKHL 23; [2004] 1 W.L.R. 1372, also reported as *R 1/04 (SF)*, in which Baroness Hale emphasised that the process of adjudication for social security benefits is a co-operative one in which both the Department and the claimant should play their part, according to who is likely to have the necessary information available, and that normally it ought not to be necessary to resort to more formal concepts such as the burden of proof. So, in *MB v Royal Borough of Kensington and Chelsea (HB)* [2011] UKUT 321 (AAC), the answer to the claimant's argument that it was for the Council to show that she had a beneficial interest in the capital at issue was that it was she who had exclusive knowledge about the purchase of the property in question and the mortgage payments and thus it was her responsibility to marshal what evidence she could to show that, although she was the legal owner, she was not the sole beneficial owner of the property. Similarly, once it is accepted that a claimant possessed or received an asset, the burden is on them to show that they no longer possess it (*R(SB) 38/85* and see the notes to reg.50(1) of the Universal Credit Regulations).

The amount of a claimant's capital is quite likely to vary during the course of an assessment period. What if it exceeds £16,000 (or some lower figure relevant to the assumed yield from capital rule in reg.72 of the Universal Credit Regulations) at the beginning of the period, but has fallen below the limit by the end of the period, or vice versa? It is generally assumed that, since the basic rule on the date on which a supersession on the ground of change of circumstances takes effect is that it is the first day of the assessment period in which the change occurred (Decisions and Appeals Regulations 2013 Sch.1 para.20), whatever is the case at the end of the assessment period is to be taken as having been so since the first day of the period and thus governs the outcome. That, however, seems a fragile basis for what would seem to be a fundamental step in the calculation of entitlement.

For the rules on calculating capital see regs 45–50 and 75–77 of, and Sch 10 to, the Universal Credit Regulations.

Income

The effect of subs.(1)(b) in the case of a single claimant and subs.(2)(b) in the case of joint claimants is that there will be no entitlement to universal credit if the amount payable is less than the minimum amount. The minimum amount is 1p (see reg.17 of the Universal Credit Regulations and note reg.6(1) on rounding). Thus it is possible for a person to be entitled to universal credit of 1p. **1.130**

In *Ipswich BC v TD and SSWP (HB)* [2024] UKUT 118 (AAC), Judge Wright has confirmed that a decision that the amount payable to the claimant is less than the minimum amount, by reason of the amount of income, is a decision that they are not entitled to universal credit. That followed inexorably from s.3(1)(b) and (2)(b) and s.5(1)(b) and (2)(b), regardless of the claimants having received notifications of an amount of £0 being payable in the first affected assessment period and of there being DWP screen prints showing current awards as £0. In the particular case, the First-tier Tribunal had erred in law in concluding for housing benefit purposes that in the affected assessment periods the claimants were "on universal credit". The judge was prepared to accept, though there appeared to be no decisions mentioning any exercise of a power of supersession, that, in the light of the decision for the first affected assessment period that the amount payable was nil, the Secretary of State had superseded the awarding decision on the basis of a relevant change of circumstances. Further, decisions issued in relation to subsequent assessment periods must have been made on deemed claims under either reg.6 or 32A of the Claims and Payments Regulations 2013. The notion of "nil awards" encapsulating some kind of continuing entitlement has thus been firmly rejected, with pointed criticism of inaccurate, confusing and misleading language in DWP communications. It is submitted that the reference to reg.6 was misguided, as that provision was revoked in November 2014, and that the decisions on subsequent assessment periods could only have been made on deemed claims under reg.32A.

Note that where a claimant who is a member of a couple makes a claim as a single person (see reg.3(3) of the Universal Credit Regulations for the circumstances in which this may occur) the combined income of the couple is taken into account when calculating an award (reg.22(3)(a)).

Any income of a child is not taken into account.

See also the regulation-making powers as regards the calculation of capital and income in para.4 of Sch.1.

Restrictions on entitlement

6.—(1) Entitlement to universal credit does not arise— **1.131**

(a) in prescribed circumstances (even though the requirements in section 3 are met);

(b) if the requirements in section 3 are met for a period shorter than a prescribed period.

(c) for a prescribed period at the beginning of a period during which those requirements are met.

(2) A period prescribed under subsection (1)(b) or (c) may not exceed seven days.

(3) Regulations may provide for exceptions to subsection (1)(b) or (c).

Definition

"prescribed"—see s.40.

General Note

1.132 This enables regulations to be made which provide that a person will not be entitled to universal credit: (i) even though they meet the basic and financial conditions (subs.(1)(a)); (ii) if they meet those conditions for seven days or less (subs.(1)(b) and subs.(2)); or (iii) for a period of seven days or less at the beginning of a period during which those conditions are met (subs.(1)(c) and subs.(2)).

The power conferred by subs.(1)(a) has been exercised to make reg.19 of the Universal Credit Regulations and that conferred by subs.(1)(c) to make reg.19A. No regulations have yet been made under subs.(1)(b).

Awards

Basis of awards

1.133 **7.**—(1) Universal credit is payable in respect of each complete assessment period within a period of entitlement.

(2) In this Part an "assessment period" is a period of a prescribed duration.

(3) Regulations may make provision—

(a) about when an assessment period is to start;

(b) for universal credit to be payable in respect of a period shorter than an assessment period;

(c) about the amount payable in respect of a period shorter than an assessment period.

(4) In subsection (1) "period of entitlement" means a period during which entitlement to universal credit subsists.

General note

1.134 See the commentary to reg.21 of the Universal Credit Regulations.

Calculation of awards

1.135 **8.**—(1) The amount of an award of universal credit is to be the balance of—

(a) the maximum amount (see subsection (2)), less

(b) the amounts to be deducted (see subsection (3)).

(2) The maximum amount is the total of—

(a) any amount included under section 9 (standard allowance);

(b) any amount included under section 10 (responsibility for children and young persons);

(c) any amount included under section 11 (housing costs), and

(d) any amount included under section 12 (other particular needs or circumstances).

(3) The amounts to be deducted are—

(a) an amount in respect of earned income calculated in the prescribed manner (which may include multiplying some or all earned income by a prescribed percentage), and

(b) an amount in respect of unearned income calculated in the prescribed manner (which may include multiplying some or all unearned income by a prescribed percentage).

(4) In subsection (3)(a) and (b) the references to income are—

(a) in the case of a single claimant, to income of the claimant, and

(b) in the case of joint claimants, to combined income of the claimants.

DEFINITIONS

"claim"—see s.40.
"claimant"—*ibid.*
"joint claimants"—*ibid.*
"prescribed"—*ibid.*
"single claimant"—*ibid.*

GENERAL NOTE

See the commentary to reg.22 of the Universal Credit Regulations. 1.136

Elements of an award

Standard allowance

9.—(1) The calculation of an award of universal credit is to include an amount by way of an allowance for— 1.137
(a) a single claimant, or
(b) joint claimants.
(2) Regulations are to specify the amount to be included under subsection (1).
(3) Regulations may provide for exceptions to subsection (1).

DEFINITIONS

"claim"—see s.40.
"claimant"—*ibid.*

GENERAL NOTE

See the commentary to regs 23 and 36 of the Universal Credit Regulations. 1.138

Responsibility for children and young persons

10.—(1) The calculation of an award of universal credit is to include an amount for each child or qualifying young person for whom a claimant is responsible. 1.139

[[1] (1A) But the amount mentioned in subsection (1) is to be available in respect of a maximum of two persons who are either children or qualifying young persons for whom a claimant is responsible.]

(2) Regulations may make provision for the inclusion of an additional amount [[1] for each] child or qualifying young person [[1] for whom a claimant is responsible who] is disabled.

(3) Regulations are to specify, or provide for the calculation of, amounts to be included under subsection (1) or (2).

(4) Regulations may provide for exceptions to subsection (1) [[1] or (1A)].

(5) In this Part, "qualifying young person" means a person of a prescribed description.

AMENDMENT

1. Welfare Reform and Work Act 2016 s.14(1)-(4) (April 6, 2017).

DEFINITIONS

"child"—see s.40.
"disabled"—*ibid.*

General note

1.140 See the commentary to regs 24 and 36 of the Universal Credit Regulations.

Housing costs

1.141 **11.**—(1) The calculation of an award of universal credit is to include an amount in respect of any liability of a claimant to make payments in respect of the accommodation they occupy as their home.

(2) For the purposes of subsection (1)—

(a) the accommodation must be in Great Britain;

(b) the accommodation must be residential accommodation;

(c) it is immaterial whether the accommodation consists of the whole or part of a building and whether or not it comprises separate and self-contained premises.

(3) Regulations may make provision as to—

(a) what is meant by payments in respect of accommodation for the purposes of this section [1 ...];

(b) circumstances in which a claimant is to be treated as liable or not liable to make such payments;

(c) circumstances in which a claimant is to be treated as occupying or not occupying accommodation as their home (and, in particular, for temporary absences to be disregarded);

(d) circumstances in which land used for the purposes of any accommodation is to be treated as included in the accommodation.

(4) Regulations are to provide for the determination or calculation of any amount to be included under this section.

(5) Regulations may—

(a) provide for exceptions to subsection (1);

(b) provide for inclusion of an amount under this section in the calculation of an award of universal credit—

(i) to end at a prescribed time, or

(ii) not to start until a prescribed time.

Amendment

1. Welfare Reform and Work Act 2016 s.20(9) (April 6, 2018).

Definitions

"claim"—see s.40.
"claimant"—*ibid.*
"prescribed"—*ibid.*

General Note

1.142 This provides for an award of universal credit to include an amount in respect of the claimant's (or claimants') liability to make payments in respect of the accommodation they occupy as their home. It could cover payments both by people who are renting their homes and by owner occupiers (as well as service charges), though in fact universal credit provides support only with rent and service charges. Owner occupier payments are addressed through a separate loans scheme (see ss.18–21 of the Welfare Reform and Work Act 2016, and the Loans for Mortgage Interest Regulations 2017 in Pt IIA of this volume).

Under subs.(2), the accommodation must be residential accommodation and must be in Great Britain. It can be the whole or part of a building and need not comprise separate and self-contained premises.

For the rules relating to housing costs see regs 25–26 of, and Schs 1–5 to, the Universal Credit Regulations.

Other particular needs or circumstances

12.—(1) The calculation of an award of universal credit is to include amounts in respect of such particular needs or circumstances of a claimant as may be prescribed. **1.143**

(2) The needs or circumstances prescribed under subsection (1) may include—

(a) [[1] . . .]

(b) the fact that a claimant has limited capability for work and work-related activity;

(c) the fact that a claimant has regular and substantial caring responsibilities for a severely disabled person.

(3) Regulations are to specify, or provide for the determination or calculation of, any amount to be included under subsection (1).

(4) Regulations may—

(a) provide for inclusion of an amount under this section in the calculation of an award of universal credit—

(i) to end at a prescribed time, or

(ii) not to start until a prescribed time;

(b) provide for the manner in which a claimant's needs or circumstances are to be determined.

AMENDMENT

1. Welfare Reform and Work Act 2016 s.16 (April 3, 2017).

DEFINITIONS

"claim"—see s.40.
"claimant"—*ibid.*
"limited capability for work"—*ibid.*
"prescribed"—*ibid.*
"work"—*ibid.*

GENERAL NOTE

Section 12(2)(a) identified having limited capability for work as one of the needs or circumstances which "may" be prescribed. It was repealed when the LCW element was removed from the Universal Credit Regulations. **1.144**

Section 12(2)(b) is carried into the regulations as one of the prescribed needs or circumstances (regs 27–28 of the Universal Credit Regulations), as is s.12(2)(c) (regs 29–30). The only prescribed need or circumstance not specifically foreshadowed in s.12 is childcare costs provision (regs 31–35).

See further the commentary to regs 27–36 of the Universal Credit Regulations.

CHAPTER 2

CLAIMANT RESPONSIBILITIES

Introductory

Work-related requirements: introductory

1.145 **13.**—(1) This Chapter provides for the Secretary of State to impose work-related requirements with which claimants must comply for the purposes of this Part.

(2) In this Part "work-related requirement" means—

(a) a work-focused interview requirement (see section 15);
(b) a work preparation requirement (see section 16);
(c) a work search requirement (see section 17);
(d) a work availability requirement (see section 18).

(3) The work-related requirements which may be imposed on a claimant depend on which of the following groups the claimant falls into—

(a) no work-related requirements (see section 19);
(b) work-focused interview requirement only (see section 20);
(c) work-focused interview and work preparation requirements only (see section 21);
(d) all work-related requirements (see section 22).

GENERAL NOTE

1.146 The remaining sections of this Chapter of the WRA 2012 in the main set out what sort of work-related requirements can be imposed on which universal credit claimants, as well as the system for imposing sanctions (reductions in benefit) on claimants for failure to comply with those requirements. Although s.13(1) refers only to work-related requirements as defined in ss.15–18, s.23 allows the Secretary of State to require a claimant to participate in an interview for various related purposes and to provide information and evidence. A failure to comply with a requirement under s.23 can lead to a sanction under s.27(2)(b) in the same way as can a failure to comply with any work-related requirement under s.27(2)(a). Section 14 contains rules about the "claimant commitment", acceptance of which is a condition of entitlement under s.4(1)(e).

There is a handy summary of the sanctions framework in Chapter 47 of CPAG's *Welfare Benefits and Tax Credits Handbook* 26th, 2024/2025, edn.

It was noted in paras 17 and 18 of *S v SSWP (UC)* [2017] UKUT 477 (AAC) that s.13(1) means that a work-related requirement can only come into being when it has been *imposed* by the Secretary of State (under the duty in s.22). See the discussion in the notes to s.14 for the important implications for the effect in law of the standard terms of claimant commitments.

Note that if a claimant is entitled to both universal credit and new style JSA, reg.5 of the JSA Regulations 2013 provides that no work-related requirements can be imposed under the new style JSA regime (ss.6B-6G of the new style Jobseekers Act 1995) and that the provisions for reduction of JSA on sanctions under ss.6J and 6K of that Act do not apply. See the annotations to reg.5 in Vol.I of this series for discussion of the consequences and of a proposal for change in the indefinite future, and the notes to reg.111 of and Sch.11 to the Universal Credit Regulations. There is an equivalent provision in reg.42 of the ESA Regulations 2013 in relation to new style ESA.

Claimant commitment

14.—(1) A claimant commitment is a record of a claimant's responsibilities in relation to an award of universal credit. 1.147

(2) A claimant commitment is to be prepared by the Secretary of State and may be reviewed and updated as the Secretary of State thinks fit.

(3) A claimant commitment is to be in such form as the Secretary of State thinks fit.

(4) A claimant commitment is to include—

(a) a record of the requirements that the claimant must comply with under this Part (or such of them as the Secretary of State considers it appropriate to include),

(b) any prescribed information, and

(c) any other information the Secretary of State considers it appropriate to include.

(5) For the purposes of this Part a claimant accepts a claimant commitment if, and only if, the claimant accepts the most up-to-date version of it in such manner as may be prescribed.

Definitions

"claimant"—see s.40.
"prescribed"—*ibid.*

General Note

Under s.4(1)(e) the final basic condition of entitlement is that the claimant has accepted a claimant commitment. Section 14 defines the nature of a claimant commitment and there are further provisions in regs 15 and 16 of the Universal Credit Regulations. Where a claim has to be made jointly by both members of a couple, both are claimants and subject to this condition, as illustrated by *FO v SSWP (UC)* [2022] UKUT 56 (AAC) (see the notes to reg.15). 1.148

See the notes to s.4(1)(e) and reg.16 for the position during the 2020/21 coronavirus outbreak, as well as the notes on the work search and work availability requirements. It appears that at least for the period from March 30, 2020 to June 30, 2020 the power to award entitlement without having met the basic condition of having accepted a claimant commitment was invoked. On July 1, 2020 it was announced in Parliament (Under-Secretary of State, Mims Davies, WQ 62431) that from that date the requirement for universal credit claimants (among others) to accept a claimant commitment was being reintroduced. The commitments of existing claimants would be reviewed and up-dated as capacity allowed. It appears that the reintroduction for new claimants was also to be phased in. The answer stressed that claimant commitments agreed or reviewed from July 1, 2020 would have to be reasonable for the "new normal" after the coronavirus pandemic and acknowledge the reality of a person's local jobs market and personal circumstances.

Note that the condition is met merely by having accepted the most up-to-date version of the claimant commitment, as discussed below. A failure to comply with the claimant commitment does not entail any breach of s.4(1)(e), nor is that in itself any ground for a sanction, although sanctions may be imposed for failures to comply with work-related and connected requirements that are recorded in the claimant commitment and other legal consequences may follow from failures to carry out other obligations.

It is an important element of the universal credit scheme, in contrast to the schemes that it has replaced, that the acceptance of the claimant commitment is a condition of entitlement for all categories of claimant, not merely those who would previously have been within the ambit of old style JSA. However, for those other categories the commitment can only be a much more generalised statement of responsibilities (see below), since the application of "conditionality" in the full sense to the claimant's personal circumstances will not be in issue.

Subsections (1) and (2) define a claimant commitment as a record prepared by the Secretary of State (in such form as he thinks fit: subs.(3)) of a claimant's responsibilities in relation to an award of universal credit. In particular, by subs.(4)(a), the record is to include the requirements that the particular claimant must comply with under the WRA 2012. These will in the main be work-related and connected requirements (see ss.15-25). However, in relation to those with limited capability for work or work-related activity the requirements will include those to provide information or evidence and to submit to a medical examination (s.37(5)-(7) and regs 43 and 44 of the Universal Credit Regulations). Work-related requirements can sometimes be to take specific action (e.g. to participate in a particular interview under s.15 or to take particular action to improve prospects of paid work under s.16 or to obtain paid work under s.17), although often the specification of such action by the Secretary of State will take place outside the claimant commitment (see the discussion in *JB v SSWP (UC)* [2018] UKUT 360 (AAC), detailed near the end of the notes to s.14). Nonetheless, the document will need to be detailed and closely related to the claimant's circumstances as they are from time to time. As such, it may be subject to frequent change, although there is a discretion in subs.(4)(a) to omit requirements if appropriate. The process of review and updating under subs.(2) appears to be completely informal, in stark contrast to the process for variation of a jobseeker's agreement under s.10 of the old style Jobseekers Act 1995, so can accommodate that. Each updating will trigger a new requirement to accept the most up-to-date version. Subsection (4)(b) requires the record to contain any prescribed information. Regulations have not as yet prescribed any such information. Subsection (4)(c) requires the record to contain any other information (note, information, not a further requirement) that the Secretary of State considers appropriate. For the claimant commitment to serve the basic purpose discussed below, that information must at least include information about the potential consequences under the Act of receiving a sanction for failure to carry out a requirement.

Since subs.(4) is, though, not an exhaustive statement of what a claimant commitment can contain, merely a statement of elements that it must contain, there is no reason why other responsibilities in relation to an award of universal credit cannot also be recorded, along with any appropriate accompanying information, although the perceived need to include subs.(4)(c) could be argued to cast doubt on that conclusion. For instance, the general obligations under regs 38 and 44 of the Claims and Payments Regulations 2013 to supply information and evidence in connection with an award and to notify changes of circumstances should probably be recorded, as it is in the example mentioned below.

Very limited exceptions from the application of the basic condition in s.4(1)(e) are set out in reg.16 of the Universal Credit Regulations. The WRA 2012 does not seek to define what is meant by acceptance of a claimant commitment beyond the provision in subs.(5) that it must be the most up-to-date version that has been accepted in such manner as prescribed in regulations. Regulation 15 of the Universal Credit Regulations provides for the time within which and the manner in which the claimant commitment must be accepted, but says nothing about what accepting the commitment entails in substance. In practice, the normal method specified under reg.15 is via a "To Do" action placed on the claimant's electronic journal, where a button must be clicked to indicate acceptance (Williams, Lack of commitment?, *Welfare Rights Bulletin 274* (February 2020) p.4).

1.149 Since the commitment is the record of the particular claimant's responsibilities as imposed by or under the legislation itself it does not seem that acceptance can mean much more than an acknowledgement of its receipt or possibly also that the claimant understands the implications of the requirements set out. There can be no question of a claimant having to express any agreement with the justice or reasonableness of the requirements, let alone of the policy behind universal credit. Nor does acceptance seem to involve any personal commitment to carrying out the stated requirements, despite the language used in the example mentioned below. A failure to comply with any requirement imposed by the Secretary of State is a matter for a potential sanction under ss.26 or 27, not for a conclusion that the basic condition of entitlement in s.4(1)(e) is no longer met. There is no direct sanction for a failure to comply with a requirement just because it is included in the claimant commitment, nor does such a failure show that the claimant commitment has ceased to be accepted in the sense suggested above.

However, this distinction may be of little significance in practice, since inclusion in the claimant commitment appears to be a sufficient means of notifying a claimant of the imposition of a requirement (see s.24(4) below) and a failure for no good reason to comply with any work-related requirement attracts a sanction under s.27(2) at the least. For instance, if the Secretary of State acting under s.17(2)(b) (work search requirement) specifies in the claimant commitment an impossibly large or internally inconsistent number of actions per week, then a failure to carry out the actions is at least prima facie a sanctionable failure and the question of whether what was specified was unreasonable would appear to be relevant only to "good reason" (though see the further discussion in the notes to ss.26 and 27). It is not like the actively seeking employment condition in old style JSA where, whatever was set out in a jobseeker's agreement, the fundamental test was whether claimants had in any week taken such steps as they could reasonably have been expected to have done to have the best prospects of securing employment.

Despite the incontrovertible nature of the legal framework, official sources continue to describe an essential feature of the claimant commitment as being that it and its conditionality requirements have been agreed by the claimant. See the DWP's statement of the aim of conditionality and sanctions set out in para.10 of the House of Commons Work and Pensions Committee's report of November 6, 2018 on *Benefit Sanctions* (HC 995 2017-19) and the Committee's own description of the claimant commitment as recording "the actions a [...] claimant has agreed to undertake as a condition of receiving their benefit". Even the Social Security Advisory Committee's March 19, 2019 call for evidence on the operation of the claimant commitment in universal credit for those subject to all work-related requirements talked of the commitment setting out what a claimant has agreed to do to prepare for work, or to increase their earnings if they are already working, and what will happen if a claimant fails to meet the agreed responsibilities. It might not matter much if such terminology is restricted to policy discussions. No doubt, for the sort of reasons mentioned below, it will always be better if the requirements set out in the claimant commitment have been worked out after a full and co-operative discussion with the work coach and the claimant agrees that the requirements are realistic and achievable. But there is evidence that the approach has infected the standard terms of claimant commitments, with consequent problems in ascertaining whether the legal requirements for the imposition of sanctions have been made out (see the discussion below of the standard terms and of the decision in *JB v SSWP (UC)* [2018] UKUT 360 (AAC)).

Chapter J1 of *Advice for Decision Making* says that the claimant commitment is generated as the result of a conversation with the claimant (para.J1010) and that claimants who fall into the all work-related requirements group or the work preparation group will need to have a discussion with a work coach before a claimant commitment can be drawn up and accepted. Claimant commitments for claimants not in either of those groups may be accepted as part of the normal claims process (para.J1011). The meaning of that last phrase is not entirely clear, but may refer to those groups of claimants on whom it is clear from the outset that no personalised requirements will be imposed. There is a recognition that claimants may well not feel able to accept on the spot at a first interview with an adviser (now called a work coach) the full range of requirements set out in the claimant commitment, so that if the claimant declines to accept the document then, a "cooling-off period" of a maximum of seven days must be allowed for reconsideration (para. J1010). The legislative basis for this is under reg.15(1) of the Universal Credit Regulations, which provides that s.4(1)(e) is to be treated as satisfied from the outset when the claimant commitment is accepted within such period after the making of the claim as the Secretary of State specifies. It must in law be open to a work coach, depending on the particular circumstances, to specify a longer period or to alter the period initially specified. See the notes to reg.15 for further discussion of the dates on which claimant commitments are deemed to be accepted and of the point at which a claimant commitment is formally presented to a claimant for acceptance.

1.150 Work requirements are supposed to be set through a one-to-one relationship between work coach and claimant, enabling the development of a good understanding of the claimant's circumstances, so that the work coach can best help the claimant find work (see the DWP's evidence to the Work and Pensions Committee in para.87 of the report above). However, the Committee received evidence that many claimant commitments were "generic" in nature, failing to take account of individual circumstances, and that "easements" (i.e. circumstances in which in accordance with regulations the requirement in question could be lifted or modified) were insufficiently used. Taking the view that it was unrealistic for claimants to know the rules about when easements could apply or for them to pour out the details of their personal lives at each meeting, the Committee recommended that the DWP develop a standard set of questions that work coaches routinely ask claimants when developing their claimant commitments, as well as improve the information available to claimants on easements. The DWP's response (House of Commons Work and Pensions Committee, *Benefit Sanctions: Government Response* (HC 1949 2017-19, February 11, 2019, paras 55-65) was that current training, guidance and monitoring of work coaches involved standard key questions to identify things like caring responsibilities, health conditions and other complex circumstances that could impact ability to meet requirements. Additional easements were said to be more specific and sensitive, so should not be presented as if they would apply to the majority of claimants. Instead, a new information package on easements to be provided at the start of the claim was to become available in Spring 2019.

Thus, when it was announced (Parliamentary answer, Under-Secretary of State, Mims Davies, WQ 62431) that from July 1, 2020 the requirement for universal credit claimants (among others) to accept a claimant commitment was being reintroduced, it was stressed that claimant commitments agreed or reviewed from that date would have to be reasonable for the "new normal" after the coronavirus pandemic and acknowledge the reality of a person's local jobs market and personal circumstances. That must entail an increased focus on "easements", but doubts have been expressed about the practicality of that when the length of meetings was being restricted, at least initially, to 30 minutes (now increased to 50 minutes a week: see the notes to reg.97(4) and (5) of the Universal Credit Regulations). Paragraph 4.31 of the September 2022 *Growth Plan 2022* (CP 743) said that the Government would be strengthening the universal credit sanctions regime to set clear expectations, including applying for jobs, attending interviews or increasing hours, but it was left unclear exactly what that was to entail or whether any legislative change was envisaged. It is not known whether the plan, such as it was, has survived the change of administration.

The Social Security Advisory Committee's (SSAC's) September 2019 study on *The effectiveness of the claimant commitment in Universal Credit* (Occasional Paper No.21) contains much interesting information on policy and the practical operation of the claimant commitment, without addressing the mismatch suggested above with the legal framework. It puts forward, within the overarching principle that the process of developing a commitment for a particular claimant should be reasonable and based on evidence of what works to help people move into sustained employment, five principles for the effectiveness of a commitment for a claimant in the intensive work search regime. It should be accessible, clear, tailored to the needs of each claimant, accepted by both parties and the claimant should have the right information. The SSAC identified many examples of good practice by work coaches, but also examples of failure to meet those principles, especially on the tailoring to individual needs and circumstances.

The notion of the claimant commitment is in many ways at the heart of what "conditionality" is meant to achieve under universal credit. It looks on its face to be an expression of what Charles Reich in his classic essay *The New Property* (1964) 73 Yale Law Journal 733 called "the New Feudalism". The universal credit claimant not only has, as the price of securing entitlement to the benefit, to accept a defined status that involves the giving up of some rights normally enjoyed by ordinary citizens, but appears to have to undertake some kind of oath of fealty by accepting a commitment to the feudal duties of that status. However, in reality the claimant commitment is a much more prosaic, and more sensible, thing. In its interesting paper *Universal Credit and Conditionality* (Social Security Advisory Committee Occasional Paper No. 9, 2012) the SSAC reported research findings that many claimants of current benefits subject to a sanctions regime did not understand what conduct could lead to a sanction, how the sanctions system worked (some not even realising that they had been sanctioned) and in particular what the consequences of a sanction would be on current and future entitlement. Paragraph 3.12 of the paper states:

> "The lessons to be learned from the research ought to be relatively straightforward to implement, although providing the appropriate training for a large number of Personal Advisers may present a considerable challenge:
>
> - claimants need to have the link between conditionality and the application of sanctions fully explained at the start of any claim
> - clear and unambiguous communication about the sanctions regime between advisers and claimants is vital at the start of any claim and must form a key element in the Claimant Commitment
> - claimants need to know when they are in danger of receiving a sanction and to be told when a sanction has been imposed, the amount and the duration
> - claimants need to know what actions they have to take to reverse a sanction—the process and consequences of re-compliance."

If one of the main aims of conditionality, of encouraging claimants to avoid behaviour that would impede a possible return to or entry into work and thus reducing the incidence of the imposition of sanctions or of more severe sanctions, is to be furthered, it therefore makes sense to build into the system a requirement to set out each claimant's responsibilities and the consequences of not meeting them in understandable terms. However, as the SSAC suggests, the nature of the personal interaction between personal advisers, now known as work coaches, and claimants may be much more important than a formal written document in getting over the realities of the situation and in encouraging claimants to take steps to avoid or reduce dependence on benefit.

A similar line of thought seems to be behind what was set out in paras 65 and 66 of the joint judgment of Lords Neuberger and Toulson in *R (on the application of Reilly and Wilson) v Secretary of State for Work and Pensions* [2013] UKSC 68; [2014] 1 A.C. 453, in relation to the JSA regime, after noting the serious consequence of imposing a requirement to engage in unpaid work on a claimant on pain of discontinuance of benefits: **1.151**

> "65. Fairness therefore requires that a claimant should have access to such information about the scheme as he or she may need in order to make informed and meaningful representations to the decision-maker before a decision is made. Such claimants are likely to vary considerably in their levels of education and ability to express themselves in an interview at a Jobcentre at a time when they may be under considerable stress. The principle does not depend on the categorisation of the Secretary of State's decision to introduce a particular scheme under

statutory powers as a policy: it arises as a matter of fairness from the Secretary of State's proposal to invoke a statutory power in a way which will or may involve a requirement to perform work and which may have serious consequences on a claimant's ability to meet his or her living needs.

66. Properly informed claimants, with knowledge not merely of the schemes available, but also of the criteria for being placed on such schemes, should be able to explain what would, in their view, be the most reasonable and appropriate scheme for them, in a way which would be unlikely to be possible without such information. Some claimants may have access to information downloadable from a government website, if they knew what to look for, but many will not. For many of those dependent on benefits, voluntary agencies such as Citizens Advice Bureaus play an important role in informing and assisting them in relation to benefits to which they may be entitled, how they should apply, and what matters they should draw to the attention of their Jobcentre adviser."

These principles were discussed by the Court of Appeal in *SSWP v Reilly and Hewstone* and *SSWP v Jeffrey and Bevan* [2016] EWCA Civ 413; [2017] Q.B. 657; [2017] AACR 14 in relation to Mr Bevan's cross-appeal against the decision of the three-judge panel of the Upper Tribunal in *SSWP v TJ (JSA)* [2015] UKUT 56 (AAC). There was a detailed description and discussion of the decision in *TJ* in the 2015/16 edition of what was then Vol.II of this series (notes to the Jobseekers (Back to Work Schemes) Act 2013), which need not be repeated here in the light of the Court of Appeal's decision. The Upper Tribunal had concluded, in the terms of its own summary in para.13(vi), that in the case of schemes which were mandatory both at the stages of referral onto them and once on them, no basis could be identified on which *meaningful* representations could be made prior to the decision to refer, in the sense of those representations being able to affect the decision to refer. In the 2015/16 edition of Vol.II there was some criticism of the Upper Tribunal's use of the word "mandatory" in this context.

The Court of Appeal first held that the Upper Tribunal had been right on the particular facts of Mr Bevan's case (where his complaint was that he could not afford the bus fare to attend the appointment given, so needed payment in advance rather than a refund) to find that it would have made no difference to what he would have said to the provider about the fares if he had known about what *The Work Programme Provider Guidance* issued by the DWP said about ability to use transportation.

So far as the Upper Tribunal's general guidance is concerned, the Court said this in para.172 about the submission that the Upper Tribunal had erred in saying that there was no scope for making representations in connection with a decision to refer a claimant to the Work Programme since referral was mandatory:

> "We do not believe that that is a fair reading of what the Tribunal said; and if it is properly understood there does not seem to be any dispute of principle between the parties. The Tribunal was not laying down any absolute rule. The Secretary of State's policy, embodied in the guidance, is that referral to the Programme should be automatic (ignoring the specified exceptions) if the criteria are met. All that the Tribunal was doing was to point out that, that being so, any representations would have to address the question why he should depart from the policy; and that it was not easy to see what such representations might be. That seems to us an obvious common sense observation, particularly since referral to the Work Programme does not as such involve any specific obligation: see para.151 above. But it does not mean that there could never be such cases, and indeed para.224 is expressly addressed to that possibility. The Tribunal did not depart from anything that the Supreme Court said in [*Reilly and Wilson*]. It was simply considering its application in the particular circumstances of referral to the Work Programme."

The Court considered that in the real world application of the prior information duty was unlikely to be important at the point of initial referral to the Work Programme under the old style JSA legislation, as claimants were unlikely to object at that stage, before any specific requirements were imposed. Problems were likely to emerge when particular requirements were imposed on claimants that they considered unreasonable or inappropriate. The Upper Tribunal had appeared to say in para.249 of its decision that there was little or no scope for the operation of the duty at that stage. The Court of Appeal says this in paras 177 and 178:

> "177. Mr de la Mare [counsel for Mr Bevan] submitted that that is wrong. If it is indeed what the Tribunal meant, we agree. So also does Ms Leventhal [counsel for the Secretary of State], who explicitly accepted in her written submissions that 'the requirements of fairness continue to apply after referral'. In principle, JSA claimants who are required, or who it is proposed should be required, under the Work Programme to participate in a particular activity should have sufficient information to enable them to make meaningful representations about the requirement – for example, that the activity in question is unsuitable for them or that there are practical obstacles to their participation. The fact that participation is mandatory if the requirement is made is beside the point: the whole purpose of the representations, and thus of the claimant having the relevant information to be able to make them, is so that the provider may be persuaded that the requirement should not be made, or should be withdrawn or modified.
>
> 178. However we should emphasise that the foregoing is concerned with the position in principle. It is quite another matter whether the Work Programme as operated in fact fails to give claimants such information. The Secretary of State's evidence before the Tribunal was that the relevant guidance in fact provides for them to be very fully informed. We have already referred to the Tribunal's findings about the information given at the referral interview. But it was also the evidence that at the initial interview with the provider post-referral, which is designed to find out how the claimant can be best supported, and in the subsequent inter-actions between claimant and provider claimants are supposed to be given both information and the opportunity to make representations. Whether in any particular case there has nevertheless been a failure to give information necessary to enable the claimant to make meaningful representations will have to be judged on the facts of the particular case. Tribunals will no doubt bear in mind the point made in [*Reilly and Wilson*] that it is important not to be prescriptive about how any necessary information is provided: see para.74 of the judgment of Lord Neuberger and Lord Toulson."

It is understood that Mr Bevan, who had been represented by CPAG, abandoned the possibility of applying for permission to appeal to the Supreme Court against the Court of Appeal's decision, having been unable to obtain legal aid. The Supreme Court refused Mr Hewstone's application for permission to appeal on the ground that it did not raise a point of law that deserved consideration at that point, as the outcome would not have affected the position of the parties to the case. That was because the claimants had succeeded on the point on art.6 of the ECHR and had only been seeking a declaration of incompatibility with the ECHR. The judges did indicate, though, that the issue whether the 2013 Act breached art.1 of Protocol 1 of the ECHR might deserve consideration in another case in which its resolution could affect the outcome.

A remedial Order, the Jobseekers (Back to Work Schemes Act 2013) (Remedial) Order 2020 (SI 2020/1085), was eventually approved by Parliament, after many convolutions described in the notes to the 2020/21 edition, to come into effect on October 3, 2020. The Order inserts new ss.1A and 1B into the 2013 Act, designed to resolve the limited incompatibility with art.6 of the ECHR held by the Court of Appeal in the restricted number of old style JSA cases affected. See the notes to the 2013 Act in Vol.V of this series, 2021/22 edition as updated in Cumulative Supplements included in this volume and in mid-year Supplements.

In relation to the universal credit scheme, there might well be scope therefore for the application of the general principle of fairness at the stage of the application of a work-related or connected requirement and at the stage of specification of particular actions or activities. However, the process of discussion leading to the drawing up of a claimant commitment and its notification of the requirements imposed, as described above, certainly gives full opportunity for the provision of sufficient information to enable claimants to make meaningful representations about the content of the claimant commitment and to decide whether or not to accept initially and to make meaningful representations and decisions about taking particular specified actions further down the line. But the crucial questions in any appeals will most likely be, as suggested in para.178 of *Jeffrey and Bevan*, how the process was actually carried out in the particular case in question.

In *NM v SSWP (JSA)* [2016] UKUT 351 (AAC) Judge Wright held, as eventually conceded by the Secretary of State, that the inability to show that relevant DWP guidance had been considered before the claimant was given notice to participate in a Mandatory Work Activity scheme meant either that the claimant should not have been referred to the scheme (because the officer either would have followed the guidance or could have been persuaded to do so on representations from the claimant) or that he had good reason for not participating in the scheme. The appeal related to a sanction for failing to participate, through behaviour on the scheme. The guidance, in something called *Mandatory Work Activity Guidance* or *Operational Instructions– Procedural Guidance–Mandatory Work Activity–January 2012*, was relevant because at the time it instructed that claimants should not be considered for referral to Mandatory Work Activity if, among other circumstances, they were currently working (paid or voluntary). The claimant had been volunteering in a Sue Ryder shop, which he had to give up to attend the required scheme as a volunteer in a Salvation Army shop. The Secretary of State submitted that the guidance had since been changed to introduce an element of discretion about referral of claimants doing voluntary work. Judge Wright held that this would not excuse a failure by an officer of the Secretary of State to consider his own guidance or, on any appeal, a failure to provide the guidance to a First-tier Tribunal in accordance with the principles of natural justice.

Judge Wright has since emphasised some important elements of the application of the prior information duty, that should serve to rein in an over-enthusiastic use of the principle in some First-tier Tribunals, but only when properly placed in context. In *SSWP v SD (JSA)* [2020] UKUT 39 (AAC) he stressed, by reference both to the Supreme Court in *Reilly and Wilson* and the Court of Appeal in *Reilly and Hewstone* and *Jeffrey and Bevan*, that even if there has been a breach of the duty at the stage of initial referral to the Work Programme the notice of referral would only be invalidated if the breach was material. In the particular case, the claimant had never objected to his referral and his appeal against a sanction for failing to participate by non-attendance at a notified appointment was solely based on the ground that he had previously been told not to attend by his work coach. The tribunal, which had raised and sought evidence on the prior information point on its own initiative, failed to explain why it considered any breach of the duty material. In substituting a decision the judge rejected any unfairness in the referral to the Work Programme and rejected on the evidence the claimant's contention about the appointment.

In *SSWP v CN (JSA)* [2020] UKUT 26 (AAC), the claimant's sole ground of appeal against a sanction for failing to participate in the Work Programme by not attending an appointment was that she had never failed to keep an appointment (i.e. implicitly that she could not have received the notice of the appointment and/or had good cause under the regulations then in force). The tribunal allowed her appeal on the ground that the bundle did not contain a copy of the notice referring her to the Work Programme (i.e. the WP05) so that it was not satisfied that she had properly been notified of the requirement to participate. The tribunal appeared to think that

that issue was one "raised by the appeal" within s.12(8)(a) of the SSA 1998, which it manifestly was not as the Secretary of State's submission in the bundle was that there was no dispute that the claimant was referred to the Work Programme. Nor did it give any explanation, if it had exercised its discretion under s.12(8)(a) to consider the issue, as to why it did so and how it was clearly apparent from the evidence so as to be capable of being dealt with under that discretion. Even if those hurdles had been overcome, the Secretary of State had not been given a fair opportunity to deal with the point. It is not necessary for the Secretary of State in all sanctions cases to provide evidence in the appeal bundle that *all* preconditions for the imposition of the sanction are satisfied. It depends what issues have been put in dispute in the appeal. Having therefore set the tribunal's decision aside, the judge substituted a decision finding on the evidence that the claimant had received the letter notifying her of the appointment in question.

The judge's statement that the Secretary of State need not in all sanctions cases provide evidence in the appeal bundle to support the satisfaction of all the preconditions to imposing a sanction must be read in the light of the approach in *SSWP v DC (JSA)* [2017] UKUT 464 (AAC), reported as [2018] AACR 16, and *PO'R v DFC (JSA)* [2018] NI Com 1. There it was said that the Secretary of State should in all cases involving a failure to participate in some scheme or interview where notice of certain details of the scheme etc. was required to be given, as well as notice of date, time and place, include in the appeal bundle a copy of the appointment letter, whether the claimant had raised any issue as to the terms of the letter or not. That was on the basis that unrepresented claimants could not be expected to identify technical issues about the validity of notices and it could not be predicted what particular issues might arise in the course of an appeal. If the letter was not included in the initial bundle, the decisions approved the action of tribunals in directing its production as a proper exercise of their inquisitorial jurisdiction. That exercise must rest on a use of the discretion in s.12(8)(a) to consider issues not raised by the appeal. The resolution of the approaches is no doubt that whenever a tribunal exercises that discretion it must do so consciously and explain why it has done so in any statement of reasons, and give the Secretary of State a fair opportunity to produce the document(s). It may be that an adequate explanation is to be found more readily when it is a notice of a specific appointment is in issue rather than an initial reference to a scheme.

A probably now rather out-dated sample claimant commitment has been produced by the DWP in response to a freedom of information request (available at *https://www.gov.uk/government/publications/foi-query-universal-credit-claimant-commitment-example* (accessed January 27, 2014), or through a link in the universal credit part of the discussion forum on the Rightsnet website). The document puts things in terms of what the claimant says he or she will do. It is suggested above that that is not quite what the legislation requires, but there is obviously a tension with an attempt to use everyday and simple language. Nevertheless, the document is long and complicated. In the sample, there is no attempt to specify the precise length of the sanction that would be imposed for a failure for no good reason (the document says "without good reason") to comply with a requirement, but the maximum possible duration is included, plus the words "up to". It is arguable that this information is insufficiently precise.

No more recent sample claimant commitment has become publicly available. However, examples that have emerged in tribunal documents display the same fundamental defects and, it is submitted, a misunderstanding of the DWP's own legislation. There is also a Child Poverty Action Group mock-up of an automated and a tailored claimant commitment at pp.58–9 of Mears & Howes, *You reap what you code: Universal credit, digitalisation and the rule of law* (CPAG June 2023). The emphasis is on what claimants commit themselves to doing, in terms of finding and taking work and the actions and activities involved, rather than making any record of the requirements imposed on them under the legislation. Examples would be "I will be available to attend a job interview immediately [and to] start work immediately",

"I will normally spend 35 hours per week looking and preparing for work" and "I will also attend and take part in appointments with my adviser when required". Thus, it appears that claimant commitments in themselves may fail to carry out the duty in s.14(3)(a) to record "the requirements that the claimant must comply with" under Part I of the WRA 2012. As noted in paras 17 and 28 of *S v SSWP (UC)* [2017] UKUT 477 (AAC) (see the introductory part of the note to s.26), s.13(1) means that a work-related requirement only comes into being when imposed by the Secretary of State and s.22(2) requires the Secretary of State to impose a work search requirement and a work availability requirement on claimants who are not exempted from those requirements (with a discretion to impose a work-focused interview requirement and/or a work preparation requirement on non-exempt claimants). Requirements must be *imposed*, with notification required by s.24(4), not merely undertaken by claimants.

In *JB v SSWP (UC)* [2018] UKUT 360 (AAC) the claimant was made subject to a sanction under s.27(2)(a) of the WRA 2012 for failing for no good reason to comply with a work-related requirement under s.15 (work-focused interview requirement). He had failed to attend an appointment with an adviser on January 12, 2017, saying later that he had thought that the appointment was for the next day and later still that he did not attend because of health issues.

The First-tier Tribunal found that the claimant had signed and agreed a claimant commitment on October 27, 2016 that included a requirement to attend and take part in appointments with advisers when required and had been notified at a previous appointment of the requirement to attend on January 12, 2017. In fact the provision before the tribunal was "I will attend and take part in appointments with my adviser when required". The tribunal rejected his argument that he had had good reason for failing to attend. However, the claimant commitment supplied in evidence by the SSWP was not signed or dated and contained a provision for action to be taken by September 20, 2016. It was therefore improbable that the document in the papers had been notified to the claimant on October 27, 2016 and the SSWP had not supplied any other evidence of what claimant commitment had been accepted and what requirements might have been notified in it. Accordingly, although the unrepresented claimant had not raised the issue of whether he had been properly notified of the requirement to attend the particular appointment, the tribunal went wrong in law by proceeding on the basis that a claimant commitment agreed by the claimant on October 27, 2016 imposed a work-related requirement to attend a work-focused interview. Nor had the SSWP put forward coherent evidence of what had been said at an earlier appointment. The written submission relied on an attendance on June 1, 2016, which did not work because the universal credit claim began on September 7, 2016. The appointment history showed a "work-focused review" on December 21, 2016, but there was no evidence of any notification then of a future appointment. There could be no reliance on any presumption of regularity because there was no evidence of a general practice or "script" of what claimants are told at appointments about the need to attend work-focused interviews. Although it was implicit in the claimant's position that he knew of the appointment on January 12, 2017, a sanction could only be imposed if there had been proper notification of the requirement in question and the SSWP had failed to show that. The case was remitted to a new tribunal for rehearing, as it was fair (the issue not having been raised until an Upper Tribunal judge gave permission to appeal), to allow the SSWP an opportunity to produce further evidence.

Judge Poole QC therefore did not need to decide whether the terms of the claimant commitment in the papers were capable of constituting a notification of a requirement to participate in work-focused interviews when notified of appointments. However, she did make interesting observations on that and other wider issues. The SSWP had submitted that the standard terms of claimant commitments were prepared so that claimants could understand them, but were clear and imperative, and that in the context of a system including sanctions claimants and advisers knew that when they were requested to attend interviews it was obligatory to turn up.

Judge Poole did not in so many words either accept or reject that submission, but her observations indicate that it could only be accepted subject to heavy qualifications.

In her introductory discussion of the legal principles, the judge stressed that while the universal credit legislation gave the SSWP considerable flexibility, the flip side of that was that in sanctions cases the SSWP had to be able to evidence the imposition of the requirement in question. The more informal the means of communication to a claimant the more efficient its recording systems will have to be, so that copies can be produced in cases of appeal. Her opinions on the wider issues were set out as follows in para.29:

> "29.1 The UC legislation is deliberately drafted to leave a degree of flexibility for the SSWP, and permits multiple methods of communication to claimants (paragraphs 16 and 17 above). There is a flexibility in the manner and means of notification. Given this legislative intention, it would be inappropriate for the Upper Tribunal to set out particular requirements for wording of notifications, or the means by which this is done.
>
> 29.2 In cases where the issue arises, the key matter for tribunals to consider is whether fair notice has been given, having regard to all the communications between the SSWP and the claimant (paragraphs 18 – 20 above). What tribunals need to do is look at the evidence produced by the SSWP, in the context in which it arises, together with any evidence taken from the claimant, and ask the question: does the evidence show that the substance of the relevant requirement and consequences of non-compliance were notified to the claimant? The answer to this question will turn on the particular circumstances of a case.
>
> 29.3 There is a virtue in plain English, and in couching notifications about what a claimant has to do in terms that claimants can readily understand. The Upper Tribunal Judge who granted permission raised the issue of whether requirements should be spelled out expressly and not left to implication. In my view it is not necessary that there is reproduction of statutory wording or reference to particular section or regulation numbers, or indeed any prescribed form of wording. *What is important is the substance. In this case the question was whether it could fairly be said, on the totality of the evidence, that the claimant had been notified of an obligation to attend a work-focused interview and the consequences of non-compliance.* [emphasis added by editor]
>
> 29.4 Unless the only evidence bearing on the imposition of a requirement in a sanctions case is the claimant commitment, it is artificial to focus on the sufficiency of the precise terms of the claimant commitment. This is because requirements can be imposed in various ways, including by a combination of documents (paragraph 20 above). Indeed, in this case the SSWP does not maintain that the wording in the claimant commitment of itself imposed a work-related requirement to attend a work-focused interview on 12 January 2017. Where a claimant commitment is part of the evidence, general reference to 'appointments' in the claimant commitment seems to me to be a sensible shorthand way of conveying a need to attend meetings but leaving flexibility to impose requirements at a later stage under either Section 15 or Section 23 of the 2012 Act. I also consider the passages set out in paragraph 26 above about sanctions for not meeting requirements, giving detail of how payments are cut, and sanctions for not meeting requirements. So where the claimant commitment has been notified, then those requirements have to be considered in conjunction with other evidence before the tribunal bearing on communication to the claimant of requirements and consequences of non-compliance. This can include, for example, later appointment cards, texts about appointments, and verbal communications at interview. It seems to me that when considering the efficacy of verbal communication, although the SSWP's record keeping will be key, it is permissible to take into account a regular pattern of interviews. For example, a claimant may have been asked at interview to come back for the same sort of interview two weeks later. The claimant's experience from earlier interviews may be relevant to whether

they have been informed of the substance of a requirement and consequences of non-compliance. Further, while intimation of date, time and place of appointment is a necessary component of intimation, that will be insufficient of itself unless linked in some way to notification to a claimant of a requirement to attend and consequences of non-compliance. The overall point is that tribunals have to consider not only the wording of the claimant commitment, but of all the evidence bearing on whether the substance of the relevant requirement and consequences of non-compliance were notified to the claimant.

29.5 [Deals with some of the consequences of the differences between the powers in s.15 and s.23 of the WRA 2012]."

That overall approach may not be too difficult to apply if the DWP takes on board at all levels the lessons of *JB* and routinely maintains and provides to tribunals clear and consistent records of the requirements imposed on claimants. However, if the familiar lazy assumptions exemplified in *JB* continue (or appear in older cases from before a hoped-for change of practice), a sharper focus may be necessary on how to resolve the tensions between some of the principles canvassed in para.29 in the circumstances of individual cases. For instance, at a broad level it might continue wrongly to be assumed that, if what is done (e.g. in the drafting of the standard form of terms in claimant commitments) is sensible in policy terms, the actual terms of the relevant legislation have been complied with. At a more grassroots level, there might well continue to be a failure to realise the need to provide tribunals with copies of all the evidence beyond the claimant commitment necessary to show the imposition of the requirement in question and the consequences of non-compliance. In either case, it might become necessary to address directly the effect of the standard form of terms in the claimant commitment. As well as the provision about appointments in issue in *JB*, drafted in terms of what the claimant said he would do rather than in terms of the imposition of a requirement, other standard provisions take the same form (see the examples given above from the sample claimant commitment). It is submitted that the principle expressed at the end of para.29.3 (and in earlier paragraphs) of *JB* that the test is whether the evidence shows that the claimant has been notified of an obligation becomes primary and that there is a fundamental difference between a commitment being undertaken by a claimant and a requirement being imposed by the SSWP.

In para.34 of *JB*, Judge Poole mentions two documents produced to the Upper Tribunal by the SSWP, of potential relevance in the rehearing. One was a computer printout recording the signing, acceptance and issue of a claimant commitment on September 13, 2016, together with something called a "claimant pack". The other was a standard form document headed "Your meeting plan" with spaces for entering dates, times and contacts of next meeting, with a warning on the back that missing meetings without rearranging in advance risks a sanction. According to the SSWP, the meeting plan document is issued with the "commitment pack", which the judge noted might or might not be the same thing as the "claimant pack". Such documents, in particular a complete copy of the claimant or commitment pack, might well be relevant in future cases, but only if properly put into evidence before tribunals. It is also understood that a leaflet "About Sanctions" is routinely uploaded to a claimant's electronic journal early in the course of an award.

Quite rigorous guidance has been issued to decision-makers in the universal credit context in Memo ADM 5/19. It in general emphasises the necessity for the SSWP to be able, in order to show that any failure to comply with a requirement is sanctionable, to evidence that the requirement has been imposed and that the claimant has been properly been informed of the substance of the requirement and the consequences of non-compliance. The Memo accepts that evidence other than the claimant commitment will be crucial and that copies of all relevant communications will need to be included in any appeal papers to found a notification by a combination of means. Paragraph 7 states that:

"it is expected that the SSWP will produce to a tribunal, as a minimum, copies of

1. the claimant commitment
2. any appointment letters ((for example, standard notification letters used for referring to employment programmes such as sbwa [sector based work academy], WHP [Work and Health Programme] etc)
3. records of telephone or electronic communications (for example, a copy of the relevant 'to-do' or journal notes)
4. internal electronic records (for example, a copy of the sanctions information screen)
5. any other relevant documents (for example a copy of the relevant ALP [Action List Prompt]) that shows the imposition of any work-related requirement and the consequences of non-compliance to the claimant."

Paragraph 14 says rather oddly that the ordinary meaning of "substance" is "to specify the intended purpose or subject matter". The meaning surely is not so restricted, but the Memo emphasises that where interviews are concerned the claimant must be told the purpose of the interview and the reason for it. There is now more comprehensive guidance in the section on Public Law Principles of Fairness in Ch.K1 of the ADM.

In para.29 of *S v SSWP (UC)* [2017] UKUT 477 (AAC), the judge accepted that if the Secretary of State failed to carry out the s.22(2) duty, the claimant should not bear the consequences of that (which must entail that the requirement(s) in question had not been imposed and there could be no sanction for failing to comply).

In *S*, it was said that the imposition of the work search requirement was not in issue, but the evidence to support that conclusion was not spelled out. The decision should not therefore be taken as any endorsement of a view that terms of a claimant commitment like that in *S* would be sufficient in themselves to impose work-related requirements on a claimant. Nor should the language used by Judge Jacobs in *SP v SSWP (UC)* [2018] UKUT 227 (AAC), where he talked of a claimant having to make a commitment, in that case about attendance at work-focused interviews, and about the standard term in the claimant commitment not becoming effective until made specific by a notification of the date, time and place of a particular interview by the Secretary of State. The issue in the case was whether the claimant had received the letter notifying him of the interview. Nothing in the decision undermines the principle that work-related requirements must be *imposed* and that on any sanction appeal the Secretary of State must provide evidence of such an imposition (compare the approach in *SSWP v DC (JSA)* [2017] UKUT 464 (AAC), reported as [2018] AACR 16, to the need for evidence of appointment letters to attend schemes under s.17A of the old style Jobseekers Act 1995 and in *MB v SSWP (PIP)* [2018] UKUT 213 (AAC) to the need for evidence of a requirement to attend and participate in a consultation under regulation 9 of the Social Security (Personal Independence Payment) Regulations 2013).

There is some difficulty in working out what remedies a claimant would have who disagrees with the imposition of a requirement included in the claimant commitment. If the claimant declines to accept the Secretary of State's form of the record, at the outset of the claim or as later reviewed and up-dated, then any initial disallowance of the claim or subsequent supersession of an awarding decision would be appealable. However, it is not clear whether such an appeal could succeed on the basis that a requirement in fact included in the claimant commitment should not have been imposed under the conditions in ss.19–24. If the requirement was one whose imposition was prohibited by the legislation and the claimant was prepared to accept everything else in the document, it is submitted that it could properly be concluded that the condition in s.4(1)(e) had been satisfied (compare the approach of Judge Rowland in *CJSA/1080/2002* and *GM v SSWP (JSA)* [2014] UKUT 57 (AAC) in holding that a claimant was to be accepted as satisfying a condition of attendance at a Jobcentre when he had in fact not attended after being informed that he was not entitled to JSA so that attendance was pointless:

see further the notes to reg.23 of the JSA Regulations 1996 in Vol.V of this series, 2021/22 edition as updated in Cumulative Supplements included in this volume and in mid-year Supplements). If it was a matter of the Secretary of State's discretion under s.22(3), the result might be different. A claimant who accepts a claimant commitment under protest about some requirement may no doubt request the Secretary of State not to impose the challenged requirement and in consequence to review the claimant commitment. However, it appears that the claimant cannot appeal directly either against the imposition of the requirement or the content of the claimant commitment or against a refusal by the Secretary of State to remove a requirement and to review the claimant commitment. See the discussion in the note to s.24 below, which would apply equally to any of the kinds of decision mentioned. None of them are "outcome" decisions.

Work-related requirements

Work-focused interview requirement

1.152 **15.**—(1) In this Part a "work-focused interview requirement" is a requirement that a claimant participate in one or more work-focused interviews as specified by the Secretary of State.

(2) A work-focused interview is an interview for prescribed purposes relating to work or work preparation.

(3) The purposes which may be prescribed under subsection (2) include in particular that of making it more likely in the opinion of the Secretary of State that the claimant will obtain paid work (or more paid work or better-paid work).

(4) The Secretary of State may specify how, when and where a work-focused interview is to take place.

DEFINITION

"claimant"—see s.40.

GENERAL NOTE

1.153 This section defines what a "work-focused interview" is and makes the related requirement "participation" in the interview. This is for the purposes of ss.20–22, and in particular s.20, which applies the requirement to participate in such an interview to the great majority of claimants within the general work-seeking ambit, although on a discretionary basis. Note the circumstances specified in and under s.19 in which no work-related requirement may be imposed.

Under subss.(2) and (3) regulations must prescribe the purposes, relating to work or work preparation, for which an interview may be required. The prescription, in very wide terms, is in reg.93 of the Universal Credit Regulations. "Paid work" is not defined in the Act, but when that phrase is used in reg.93 the definition in reg.2 will apply (see the note to reg.93). The Secretary of State is allowed under subss.(1) and (4) to specify how, when and where the interview is to take place, so that there is no straightforward limit on the number or frequency of the interviews that may be specified, or on the persons who may conduct the interview. The interviews must of course properly be for one of the purposes prescribed in reg.93. The requirement to participate in an interview cannot be used for punitive purposes or simply as a means of control of a claimant. No doubt it is also to be implied that only rational requirements may be imposed, so that a specification of two interviews in different places at the same time or so that they could not practicably be coordinated could be disregarded (see the approach of Judge Rowland in *GM v SSWP (JSA)* [2014] UKUT 57 (AAC): notes to s.14 above). Rationality would also require that what was specified should not be incompatible with other requirements, in particular the work search and work availability requirements where there is no discretion under s.22(2) about their imposition. Thus a claimant could not validly be required to attend so many interviews that it made it impossible to take work search actions for the hours specified under s.17, unless there was a corresponding reduction in the s.17 requirements. These are rather extreme examples, which it is hoped would not arise in practice. Because, as discussed in the notes to s.24, there is no right of appeal against an imposition of a work-related or connected requirement as such, the issues will normally arise in the course of challenges to or appeals against removal of entitlement for failing to accept a claimant commitment containing the requirement(s) in questions or against reductions in benefit following a sanction for non-compliance. The main focus in the latter case may be on whether the claimant had a good reason for not complying with the requirement, but sight should not be lost of whether there had been non-compliance with the requirement as properly interpreted (see below).

However, there may also often be questions whether a requirement has in fact been imposed. There appear to be two stages. The Secretary of State may indicate in general that a claimant will be required to participate in interviews (although see the notes to s.14 for serious doubts whether the current standard form of claimant commitment achieves that result). But the requirement under subs.(1) appears not to arise, in the sense of a requirement that the claimant can comply with or fail to comply with for sanctions purposes, until the Secretary of State has specified the particular interview or interviews under subs.(4) and probably (although subs.(1) is not entirely clear) that the claimant participate. See the notes to s.14 for extensive discussion of the decision in *JB v SSWP (UC)* [2018] UKUT 360 (AAC) on the evidence that the SSWP needs to produce to show that a requirement to participate in a s.15 interview has been imposed and the guidance given to decision-makers in Memo ADM 5/19. Paragraph 6 of *JB* states that it is a condition precedent of imposing any sanction under s.27(2)(a) that the claimant was subject to the work-related requirement in issue, thus confirming the approach in para.29 of *S v SSWP (UC)* [2017] UKUT 477 (AAC) that if a specific requirement has not been imposed by the SSWP, no sanction can follow.

SP v SSWP (UC) [2018] UKUT 227 (AAC) is consistent with such a two-stage approach, but see the discussion in the notes to s.14 for how the language used should not be taken as contrary to the argument made there about evidence of the imposition of a requirement.

JB was endorsed and applied in *KG v SSWP (UC)* [2020] UKUT 307 (AAC). Before the Upper Tribunal the Secretary of State accepted that the available evidence did not show that the claimant had been properly notified of the requirement to take part in the particular telephone interview with his work coach, so that no sanction could be applied under s.27. The documents were ambiguous as to whether the interview was under s.15 or s.23 (connected requirements) and what issues the claimant was told were to be investigated, and left it unclear whether he had been adequately informed of the consequences of non-compliance.

Specification must necessarily imply communication to the claimant in time to attend the interview.

There is no requirement that the specification under subs.(4) of how, when and where an interview is to take place should be in writing or in other permanent form. However, good practice, plus the potential need for acceptable evidence of the existence and terms of the specification in the light of the principle that the claimant should in sanctions cases be given the benefit of any doubt that might reasonably arise (*DL v SSWP (JSA)* [2013] UKUT 295 (AAC)), must surely point to the need for written or computer records to be kept and to be available to the claimant for reference. Arguably, the "prior information duty" (see the notes to s.14 for detailed discussion) would require that information about the purpose of the particular interview be given in the specification. Arguably also, in accordance with the approach in *SSWP v DC (JSA)* [2017] UKUT 464 (AAC), reported as [2018] AACR 16, and *PO'R v DFC (JSA)*

[2018] NI Com 1, a copy of the appointment letter should be included in the Secretary of State's submission on any appeal against a sanction for failing to comply with a requirement to participate in the interview. There it was said that the Secretary of State should in all cases involving a failure to participate in some scheme or interview where notice of certain details of the scheme etc was required to be given, as well as notice of date, time and place, include in the appeal bundle a copy of the appointment letter, whether the claimant had raised any issue as to the terms of the letter or not. That was on the basis that unrepresented claimants could not be expected to identify technical issues about the validity of notices and it could not be predicted what particular issues might arise in the course of an appeal. If the letter was not included in the initial bundle, the decisions approved the action of tribunals in directing its production as a proper exercise of their inquisitorial jurisdiction. That exercise must, if the claimant has not taken the point, rest on a use of the discretion in s.12(8)(a) of the SSA 1998 to consider issues not raised by the appeal. The resolution with the approach in *SSWP v SD (JSA)* [2020] UKUT 39 (AAC) and *SSWP v CN (JSA)* [2020] UKUT 26 (AAC) (see the notes to s.14) is no doubt that whenever a tribunal exercises that discretion it must do so consciously and explain why it has done so in any statement of reasons, and give the Secretary of State a fair opportunity to produce the document(s). It may be that an adequate explanation is to be found more readily when it is a notice of a specific appointment that is in issue rather than an initial reference to a scheme.

Note that the requirement, as now for both old style and new style JSA, is not attendance at an interview at the specified time and date, but participation in it. This would appear to mean that a claimant can be required to participate in an interview over the telephone, providing that that manner of conducting it has been specified under subs.(4). In an ambiguous (so far as JSA is concerned) Parliamentary answer on 24 November 2015 (UIN 17005), the Minister of State Priti Patel said:

> "Under JSA, claimants are not sanctioned for failing to answer their telephone. In Universal Credit, claimants who have a prearranged telephone interview with their Work Coach, and who fail to participate without good reason, can be referred for a sanction decision."

There is no further provision about what participating in a work-focused interview entails. It must at least entail turning up at the place and time specified, although the decision of Judge Knowles in *SA v SSWP (JSA)* [2015] UKUT 454 (AAC) (see the notes to s.27 for full discussion) would indicate that tribunals should consider, in cases where the claimant arrives not very late, whether it is proportionate to the nature of all the circumstances to regard that as a failure to participate in an interview. There were all sorts of mitigating circumstances in *SA*, that may well not be present in other cases. See *SN v SSWP (JSA)* [2018] UKUT 279 (AAC), detailed in the notes to s.26(2)(a) and 27(2)(a), for discussion of what might amount to a failure to participate (in that case in a mandatory work activity scheme and involving conduct before the scheme started) and the expression in para.45 of some doubt about the result in *SA*.

The requirement to participate must also extend to making some meaningful contribution to the interview, but the limits will probably not be established until there have been some more sanctions appeals in JSA or universal credit that reach the Upper Tribunal. Behaviour that leads to the premature termination of the interview may well amount to a failure to participate (see the facts of *DM v SSWP (JSA)* [2015] UKUT 67 (AAC) in the notes to s.27(2)(b)). There may, though, in cases of uncooperative claimants or heavy-handed officials or a combination, be difficult questions about when an interview has ceased to exist, so that subsequent behaviour cannot be relevant to whether there has been a failure to participate (see *PH v SSWP (ESA)* [2016] UKUT 119 (AAC) on failing to submit to a medical examination).

It was recognised in *CS v SSWP (JSA)* [2019] UKUT 218 (AAC), detailed in the notes to s.26(2)(a), that it was legitimate for a scheme provider to require a person attending to verify their identity before starting a scheme, so that a refusal to do so would usually amount to a failure to participate in the scheme. The same principle could apply to an interview, but the particular issues that arose in *CS*, to do with a scheme provider external to the DWP, are unlikely to arise if it is an interview with a work coach or other adviser that has been notified.

A failure for no good reason to comply with any work-related requirement is sanctionable under s.27(2)(a). That is the context in which what amounts to a failure to comply will be identified, as well as what might amount to a good reason for non-compliance. For instance, there appear to be no provisions prescribing the length of notice of an interview to be given or how far a claimant can be required to travel, but there could plainly be a good reason for failing to comply with unreasonable requirements, especially if the claimant had attempted in advance to draw any problem with attendance to the Secretary of State's attention. Claimants who are found not in fact to have been aware of an interview must have a good reason for failing to comply, whether or not the requirement is said to have been imposed in such circumstances (*SP v SSWP (UC)* [2018] UKUT 227 (AAC)).

Note that under s.23(1) the Secretary of State is empowered to require a claimant to attend an interview relating to the imposition of a work-related requirement on the claimant or assisting the claimant to comply with a requirement.

Work preparation requirement

16.—(1) In this Part a "work preparation requirement" is a requirement that a claimant take particular action specified by the Secretary of State for the purpose of making it more likely in the opinion of the Secretary of State that the claimant will obtain paid work (or more paid work or better-paid work). 1.154

(2) The Secretary of State may under subsection (1) specify the time to be devoted to any particular action.

(3) Action which may be specified under subsection (1) includes in particular—

(a) attending a skills assessment;
(b) improving personal presentation;
(c) participating in training;
(d) participating in an employment programme;
(e) undertaking work experience or a work placement;
(f) developing a business plan;
(g) any action prescribed for the purpose in subsection (1).

(4) In the case of a person with limited capability for work, the action which may be specified under subsection (1) includes taking part in a work-focused health-related assessment.

(5) In subsection (4) "work-focused health-related assessment" means an assessment by a health care professional approved by the Secretary of State which is carried out for the purpose of assessing—

(a) the extent to which the person's capability for work may be improved by taking steps in relation to their physical or mental condition, and
(b) such other matters relating to their physical or mental condition and the likelihood of their obtaining or remaining in work or being able to do so as may be prescribed.

(6) In subsection (5) "health care professional" means—

(a) a registered medical practitioner,
(b) a registered nurse,

(c) an occupational therapist or physiotherapist registered with a regulatory body established by an Order in Council under section 60 of the Health Act 1999, or
(d) a member of such other profession regulated by a body mentioned in section 25(3) of the National Health Service Reform and Health Care Professions Act 2002 as may be prescribed.

DEFINITIONS

"claimant"—see s.40.
"limited capability for work"—*ibid.*

GENERAL NOTE

1.155 This section defines "work preparation requirement" for the particular purposes of ss.21 and 22. The requirement is to take particular action specified by the Secretary of State for the purpose of making it more likely that the claimant will obtain paid work or obtain more or better-paid such work. If a specific requirement has not been imposed, then no sanction can follow (*S v SSWP (UC)* [2017] UKUT 477 (AAC) para.29). See the notes to s.14 for extensive discussion of the decision in *JB v SSWP (UC)* [2018] UKUT 360 (AAC) on the evidence that the SSWP needs to produce to show that a requirement (in that case to participate in a s.15 interview) has been imposed and the guidance given to decision-makers in Memo ADM 5/19. Paragraph 6 of *JB* states that it is a condition precedent of imposing any sanction under s.27(2)(a) that the claimant was subject to the work-related requirement in issue, thus confirming the approach in para.29 of *S*.

Subsection (3) gives a non-exhaustive list of actions that may be specified, including under para.(g) any action prescribed in regulations. No regulations have as yet been made under para.(g). The list is in fairly broad terms, not further defined in the legislation, even "employment programme". The sorts of activities required do not themselves have to be paid, so long as they can legitimately be related to the purpose of improving prospects of obtaining paid work or more or better paid work (see below and the notes to s.26(2)(a)). So unpaid work experience or placements (e.g. as an intern) or voluntary work can be made mandatory. See the notes to s.15 above for the need for the co-ordination with the practical application of other work-related or connected requirements for the specification of any particular work preparation requirement to be rational.

The Secretary of State has a discretion under ss.21 and 22(3) whether to impose a work preparation requirement in any particular case. It appears that the requirement therefore cannot arise until the Secretary of State has specified the particular action, so that general statements in a claimant commitment about normally spending 35 hours a week looking and preparing for work (even if they could be regarded as *imposed* by the Secretary of State: see the notes to s.14) would not be enough in themselves. Also note the circumstances specified in and under s.19 in which no work-related requirement may be imposed.

The Secretary of State may under subs.(2) specify the time to be devoted to any particular action, but in practice this is likely to be less controversial than the similar power in s.17(2) in relation to a work search requirement. However, the DWP appears to use a default maximum of 16 expected hours per week, subject to "tailoring" for the claimant's individual circumstances, for someone subject only to the work preparation regime (Guidance on expected hours deposited in House of Commons Library: collected on the Rightsnet website). Subsections (4)–(6) allow the application of a particular requirement to take part in a work-focused health-related assessment to claimants with limited capability for work (only claimants who also have limited capability for work-related activity being exempted from all work-related requirements under s.19(2)(a)). Paragraph 15 of *JS v SSWP (ESA)*; [2013] UKUT 635 (AAC) suggests that if a claimant is patently not going to be able to obtain work at any stage or is already in a suitable apprenticeship or placement no action could make it more likely that work or more work would be obtained, so that no action could be legitimately specified.

There is no requirement that the specification under subss.(1) and (2) of the particular action to be taken and the time to be devoted to it should be in writing or in other permanent form. However, good practice, plus the potential need for acceptable evidence of the existence and terms of the specification in the light of the principle that the claimant should in sanctions cases be given the benefit of any doubt that might reasonably arise (*DL v SSWP (JSA)* [2013] UKUT 295 (AAC)), must surely point to the need for written or computer records to be kept and to be available to the claimant for reference. See *NM v SSWP (JSA)* [2016] UKUT 351 (AAC), discussed in para.1.151 above, for circumstances in which failure to consider relevant DWP guidance about the circumstances in which there should or should not be referral to a scheme, with sufficient information to the claimant to allow the making of meaningful representations, undermines the applicability of any sanction for failure to comply with a requirement. The principles of natural justice require that the terms of the relevant guidance be provided to a tribunal on any appeal.

Arguably, the "prior information duty" (see the notes to s.14 for detailed discussion) would require that information about the purpose of the particular course, programme, placement etc. be given in the specification. Arguably also, in accordance with the approach in *SSWP v DC (JSA)* [2017] UKUT 464 (AAC), reported as [2018] AACR 16, and *PO'R v DFC (JSA)* [2018] NI Com 1, a copy of the appointment letter should be included in the Secretary of State's submission on any appeal against a sanction for failing to comply with a requirement under s.16. There it was said that the Secretary of State should in all cases involving a failure to participate in some scheme or interview where notice of certain details of the scheme etc. was required to be given, as well as notice of date, time and place, include in the appeal bundle a copy of the appointment letter, whether the claimant had raised any issue as to the terms of the letter or not. That was on the basis that unrepresented claimants could not be expected to identify technical issues about the validity of notices and it could not be predicted what particular issues might arise in the course of an appeal. If the letter was not included in the initial bundle, the decisions approved the action of tribunals in directing its production as a proper exercise of their inquisitorial jurisdiction. That exercise must, if the claimant has not taken the point, rest on a use of the discretion in s.12(8)(a) of the SSA 1998 to consider issues not raised by the appeal. The resolution with the approach in *SSWP v SD (JSA)* [2020] UKUT 39 (AAC) and *SSWP v CN (JSA)* [2020] UKUT 26 (AAC) (see the notes to s.14) is no doubt that whenever a tribunal exercises that discretion it must do so consciously and explain why it has done so in any statement of reasons, and give the Secretary of State a fair opportunity to produce the document(s). It may be that an adequate explanation is to be found more readily when it is a notice of a specific appointment that is in issue rather than an initial reference to a scheme.

A failure for no good reason by a claimant subject to all work-related requirements to comply with a requirement under this heading to undertake a work placement of a prescribed description (i.e. the Mandatory Work Activity Scheme: reg.114 of the Universal Credit Regulations) is sanctionable under s.26(2)(a) (higher-level sanctions). The scheme has not operated after April 2016. Outside that limited category, failure for no good reason to comply with any work-related requirement is sanctionable under s.27(2)(a). That is the main context in which there will be exploration of what action can be said to make it more likely that the claimant will obtain paid work or more or better-paid work, since the addition of the Secretary of State's opinion in subs.(1) will not be allowed to take away the power of tribunals to reach their own conclusions on that matter. What amounts to a failure to comply will also be identified, as well as what might amount to a good reason for non-compliance.

The issue may also arise in challenges to the removal of entitlement following a failure to accept a claimant commitment containing a disputed work preparation requirement (see the notes to s.14).

Note that under s.23(1) the Secretary of State is empowered to require a claimant to participate in an interview relating to the imposition of a work-related requirement on the claimant or assisting the claimant to comply with a requirement. Under s.23(3) he can require the provision of information and evidence for the purpose of verifying compliance and that the claimant confirm compliance in any manner.

Work search requirement

1.156 **17.**—(1) In this Part a "work search requirement" is a requirement that a claimant take—

(a) all reasonable action, and
(b) any particular action specified by the Secretary of State,

for the purpose of obtaining paid work (or more paid work or better-paid work).

(2) The Secretary of State may under subsection (1)(b) specify the time to be devoted to any particular action.

(3) Action which may be specified under subsection (1)(b) includes in particular—

(a) carrying out work searches;
(b) making applications;
(c) creating and maintaining an online profile;
(d) registering with an employment agency;
(e) seeking references;
(f) any action prescribed for the purpose in subsection (1).

(4) Regulations may impose limitations on a work search requirement by reference to the work to which it relates; and the Secretary of State may in any particular case specify further such limitations on such a requirement.

(5) A limitation under subsection (4) may in particular be by reference to—

(a) work of a particular nature,
(b) work with a particular level of remuneration,
(c) work in particular locations, or
(d) work available for a certain number of hours per week or at particular times,

and may be indefinite or for a particular period.

DEFINITION

"claimant"—see s.40.

GENERAL NOTE

Temporary Coronavirus Provisions

1.157 The last of the temporary coronavirus provisions relevant to the work search requirement expired on November 12, 2020. See previous editions of this volume for the details.

1.158 This section defines "work search requirement" for the particular purpose of s.22, under which the requirement must be imposed on all claimants except those exempted by s.19, 20 or 21. See the notes to s.14 for discussion of whether the current standard terms of claimant commitments are sufficient in themselves to *impose* such a requirement. It is a requirement that a claimant take both all reasonable action (subs.(1)(a)) and any particular action specified by the Secretary of State (subs.(1)(b)) for the purpose of obtaining paid work or more or better-paid work. "Paid work" is not defined in the Act, nor is it defined in regulations for the specific purpose of ss.17 and 22. However, under the power in s.25, regs 94 and 95 of the Universal Credit Regulations deem the work search requirement not to have been complied with in certain circumstances and make references to "paid work". For those purposes, the definition in reg.2 will apply, i.e. work done for payment or in expectation of payment, excluding work for a charity or voluntary organisation, or as a volunteer, in return for expenses only. Regulation 87 adds nothing to the terms of s.17 itself. Thus it appears that both self-employment and employment can be considered both under the reg.2 definition and under the ordinary meaning of the phrase "paid work" and that voluntary work or unpaid internships or work placements are excluded. According to the then Minister of State Esther McVey (House of Commons written answers April 2, 2014 and September 1, 2014) guidance to Jobcentre Plus staff is that, in contrast to the position for JSA, universal credit claimants can be mandated to apply for vacancies for zero hours contracts. At the time it appeared not to matter whether there was an exclusivity clause in the contract or not, but such clauses were made unenforceable from May 26, 2015 by the new s.27A of the Employment Rights Act 1996. There will be a question in challenges to and appeals against sanctions decisions whether claimants have a good reason for not complying with a requirement to search for zero hours contracts.

Subsections (4) and (5) allow regulations to impose limitations on the kind of work search which can be required and also allow the Secretary of State to specify further limitations. Regulation 97 contains the prescribed limitations, in terms of hours of work for carers and those with a disability, of the maximum time for travel to and from work and of the type of work recently undertaken. See the notes to reg.97. There appears to be no limitation on the number of hours a week that work could involve while still falling for consideration, apart from in the cases of the particular categories of claimant identified in reg.97(2). Note also that reg.99 exempts claimants from the work search requirement in a variety of individual circumstances that would make the carrying out of any work search impracticable. See the notes to reg.99 for the details. The circumstances include several to do with care of children, the carrying out of various worthwhile activities, unfitness for work for short and (subject to conditions) more extended periods and, particularly important to the structure of universal credit, where earnings are at a defined level. Regulation 98 exempts recent victims of domestic violence for a fixed period.

What is "all reasonable action" under subs.(1)(a) for the purpose of obtaining paid work within any applicable limitations is obviously in general a matter of judgment. That includes a judgment about what counts as "action" and about the significance of any potential action that has not been taken. The actions mentioned in subs.(3) might be a starting point, but other things could plainly count, such as carrying out research into the job market or potential for self-employment. No doubt just sitting and thinking falls the other side of the line, but can often form an essential element of the hours devoted to some more active action. Subsection (3) does not include in its list accepting an offer of suitable work. However, it could certainly be argued that a claimant who failed to accept such an offer had failed to take all reasonable action for the purpose of obtaining paid work. A medium-level sanction could then follow under s.27(2)(a) if the failure was for no good reason unless the case fell within s.26(2)(c) (failing for no good reason to comply with a work availability requirement by taking up an offer of paid work). There is a certain artificiality to the s.26(2)(c) sanction (see the notes to that section) but no doubt in practice decision-makers will prefer to use that provision first in a case where an offer of work has not been taken up. If for any reason that provision does not apply, it can be argued that s.27(2)(a) and s.17(1)(a) should be considered in addition. It seems very unlikely that in practice the Secretary of State would ever be in a position to specify under sub.(1) that a claimant should accept a particular offer of paid work.

Regulation 95 of the Universal Credit Regulations deems a claimant not to have complied with the requirement unless quite stringent conditions about the weekly hours devoted to work search are satisfied. See the notes to reg.95 and remember that the sanctions in s.26(4)(a), in relation to having, before claiming universal credit, failed to take up an offer of paid work, and s.27(2)(a) can only be imposed when there was no good reason for the failure to comply. But note that the two alternative conditions in reg.95(1)(a) of spending at least the "expected hours" under reg.88 (starting point, 35) per week or of taking all reasonable action though for fewer than the expected hours are logically of equal status. A rigid approach that claimants are in general expected to devote 35 hours a week to work search is likely to lead into error. It is also arguable that if a claimant shows, say, that they have spent 35 hours on work search action in a week, they should only be regarded as not having taken all reasonable action in that week if that action does not give them the best prospects of obtaining work (reg.95(1)(b)). Paragraph 15 of *JS v SSWP (ESA)* [2013] UKUT 635 (AAC) suggests that if a claimant is patently not going to be able to obtain work at any stage or is already in a suitable apprenticeship or placement no action could make it more likely that work or more work would be obtained, so that no action could be legitimately specified.

1.159 The particular action that can be specified by Secretary of State under subs.(1)(b) can, by subs.(3), include a number of actions, including those prescribed in regulations. No relevant regulation has yet been made. The list includes, at (c), creating and maintaining an online profile. That was relied on by the DWP to support requiring claimants to create a public profile and a public CV in Universal Jobmatch. There is helpful guidance on this in Memo ADM 15/16 of June 2016, which recognised that claimants could not be mandated to do that or create an email account from day one of their claim, merely encouraged, and that mandation was not to follow until the claimant had had an initial work search interview with a work coach. The requirement was not to be imposed unless the benefits of Universal Jobmatch had been explained, its use was reasonable in the claimant's individual circumstances (including health, learning problems, whether English was a second language, lack of appropriate literacy and numeracy skills), the claimant had access to the internet (including at a Jobcentre) and the cookies fact sheet had been issued. From May 14, 2018 Universal Jobmatch has been replaced by the Find a job service, run by Adzuna. Paragraphs K5171 – K5209 of the ADM apply effectively the same approach to Find a job. Paragraphs K5174 and K5175 explain the differences between Universal Jobmatch and the new service.

Particular vacancies could also be notified to a claimant within Universal Jobmatch and a requirement to apply notified through the claimant commitment. A failure for no good reason to comply with such a requirement leads to a higher-level sanction under s.26(2)(b). Memo ADM 15/16 suggests that if a claimant subject to such a sanction has also failed to take all reasonable action for the purposes of obtaining paid work by not applying for enough notified vacancies, there can also be a medium-level sanction under s.27(2)(a). However, it is arguable that an imposition of the medium-level sanction in those circumstances would contravene s.27(3) (no s.27 sanction if failure is also a s.26 sanctionable failure).

Where a claimant has been required to apply for a particular vacancy, reg.94 of the Universal Credit Regulations deems the work search requirement not to have been complied with where the claimant fails to participate in an interview offered in connection with the vacancy.

There is no requirement that the specification under subss.(1)(b), (2) and (3) of the particular actions to be taken and the time to be devoted to them should be in writing or in other permanent form. However, good practice, plus the potential need for acceptable evidence of the existence and terms of the specification in the light of the principle that the claimant should in sanctions cases be given the benefit of any doubt that might reasonably arise (*DL v SSWP (JSA)* [2013] UKUT 295 (AAC)), must surely point to the need for written or computer records to be kept and to be available to the claimant for reference. See the notes to ss.14 and 16 for the potential application of the "prior information duty" in requiring the claimant to be given an opportunity to make informed and meaningful representations about the actions proposed to be specified before they are imposed.

Note that under s.23(1) the Secretary of State is empowered to require a claimant to participate in an interview relating to the imposition of a work-related requirement on the claimant or assisting the claimant to comply with a requirement. Under s.23(3) he can require the provision of information and evidence for the purpose of verifying compliance and that the claimant confirm compliance in any manner. A failure for no good reason to comply with any of those connected requirements is also sanctionable under s.27(2)(b).

Work availability requirement

18.—(1) In this Part a "work availability requirement" is a requirement that a claimant be available for work. 1.160

(2) For the purposes of this section "available for work" means able and willing immediately to take up paid work (or more paid work or better-paid work).

(3) Regulations may impose limitations on a work availability requirement by reference to the work to which it relates; and the Secretary of State may in any particular case specify further such limitations on such a requirement.

(4) A limitation under subsection (3) may in particular be by reference to—

(a) work of a particular nature,
(b) work with a particular level of remuneration,
(c) work in particular locations, or
(d) work available for a certain number of hours per week or at particular times,

and may be indefinite or for a particular period.

(5) Regulations may for the purposes of subsection (2) define what is meant by a person being able and willing immediately to take up work.

DEFINITION

"claimant"—see s.40.

GENERAL NOTE

Temporary Coronavirus Provisions

The last of the temporary coronavirus provisions relevant to the work availability requirement expired on November 12, 2020. See previous editions of this volume for the details. 1.161

This section defines "work availability requirement" for the particular purpose of s.22, under which the requirement must be imposed on all claimants except those exempted by s.19, 20 or 21. See the notes to s.14 for discussion of whether the current standard terms of claimant commitments are sufficient in themselves to *impose* such a requirement. It imposes the apparently extremely stringent requirement that a claimant be able and willing immediately to take up paid work, or more or better-paid work. "Paid work" is not defined in the Act, nor is it defined in regulations for the specific purpose of ss.18 and 22. However, under the power in s.25, reg.96 of the Universal Credit Regulations deems the work availability requirement not to have been complied with in certain circumstances and to have been satisfied in other circumstances and makes references to "paid work". For those purposes, the definition in reg.2 will apply, i.e. work done for payment or in expectation of payment, excluding work for a charity or voluntary organisation, or as a volunteer, in return for expenses only. Regulation 87 adds nothing to the terms of s.18 itself. Thus it appears that willingness to take up both self-employment and employment can be considered. Under the ordinary meaning of the phrase "paid work" it would seem that voluntary work or unpaid internship or work placements are excluded (but see s.16 on work preparation).

Note that reg.96(1) in effect extends the requirement to be able and willing immediately to take up paid work to ability and willingness immediately to attend an interview in connection with obtaining paid work. There is no specification of who the interview can be with.

It is notable, by contrast with the position that will be familiar to many readers from old style JSA and, before it, unemployment benefit, that being available for work is not a condition of entitlement to universal credit, failure to satisfy which means that there can be no entitlement to benefit at all, although it is a condition of entitlement under s.4(1)(e) to accept a claimant commitment that should record the requirement. Instead, a failure to comply with the work availability requirement, if imposed on a claimant, is merely a potential basis for a sanction under ss.26 or 27. Under s.26(2)(c) a higher-level sanction can be imposed if a claimant fails for no good reason to comply by not taking up an offer of paid work, though that can only operate through the mechanism of that being evidence that the claimant was either unable or unwilling immediately to take up the work offered. Section 27(2)(a) allows the imposition of a medium-level sanction for a failure for no good reason to comply with any work-related requirement.

The general formulation of the obligation under s.18 is in many ways the same as that imposed statutorily for old style JSA (on which see Vol.V of this series, 2021/22 edition as up-dated in Cumulative Supplements included in this volume and in mid-year Supplements) and developed in the case law on unemployment benefit. However, the structure of the universal credit legislation is not the same. In some ways what was apparently intended as simplification has left holes that make the route to a coherent or even rational position troublesome. ADM para.J3112 continues to rely on *R(U) 5/80* for the proposition that availability implies being available in an active, positive sense and taking steps to draw attention to that availability. However, as convincingly demonstrated by Judge Lane in paras 22–25 of *RL v SSWP (JSA)* [2018] UKUT 177 (AAC), the separate existence for old style JSA of the actively seeking employment condition meant that that proposition was no longer relevant. The same must apply for universal credit and questions of whether claimants are taking sufficient active steps should be considered under s.17 on the work search requirement.

The rest of this note first sets out how the Universal Credit Regulations, made under subss (3)–(6) and ss.24 and 25, provide some specific rules that avoid the need to grapple with the implications of the general s.18 obligation and then discusses some problem areas relevant to that obligation. The relevant provisions are regs 96, 97, and 99. Note also that reg.98 prevents the imposition of any work-related requirement on recent victims of domestic violence.

Regulation 96. Section 25(a) of the WRA 2012 allows regulations to specify circumstances in which a claimant is to be treated as having complied or not complied with a requirement. Regulation 96(2) provides that a claimant is to be treated as having complied with a work availability requirement, despite not being able immediately to take up employment (or presumably, by necessary implication, not being willing), where para.(3), (4) or (5) applies. Paragraph (3) applies to responsible carers or relevant carers who need a longer period of up to a month to take up work or 48 hours to attend an interview and are able and willing to take up the work or attend the interview on being given notice of the period. Under s.19(6), a responsible carer is a single person or the nominated member of a couple who is responsible for a child (under 16) as determined under reg.4. Under reg.85, a relevant carer is anyone else who has caring responsibilities (not further defined) for the child or for someone who has a physical or mental impairment. That is therefore an important protection from the "immediately" test, remembering also that ss.19 and 20 prevent the work availability requirement being imposed at all on responsible carers of children under three or those with regular and substantial caring responsibilities for a severely disabled person. Paragraph (4) provides an equivalent rule for claimants carrying out voluntary work and para.(5) for claimants employed under a contract of service who have to give notice to terminate the contract.

Regulation 97. Subsections (3) and (4) allow regulations to impose limitations on the kind of work for which a claimant can be required to be available and also allow the Secretary of State to specify further limitations. Regulation 97 contains the prescribed limitations, in terms of hours of work for responsible and relevant carers and those with a disability (to be limited to the "expected hours" under reg.88), of the maximum time for travel to and from work and of the nature of work, either recently undertaken or within the ability of claimants with a physical or mental impairment. See the notes to reg.97 for detailed discussion. Presumably as well as some claimants not being required to be willing to take up work that involves more than the expected hours, they are not to be expected to take up work immediately at a time affected by circumstances relevant to reg.88. There appears to be no specific limitation on the number of hours a week that work could involve while still falling for consideration or the times in the week at which a claimant was expected to take up work, apart from in the cases of the particular categories of claimant identified in reg.97, but the Secretary of State could use their power in subs.(3) to specify further limitations in particular cases. See the further discussion below under *Type of work* and *Immediately*. Where a limitation under reg.97 or s.18(3) applies, there may also be a deemed compliance under reg.96 or a further qualification to the meaning of the availability requirement under reg.99.

Regulation 99. Subsection (5) allows regulations to define what is meant in subs.(2) by being able and willing immediately to take up work. It is that power that reg.99, so far as it concerns availability, exercises. Thus, the effect if any of the prescribed circumstances exists is similar to the effect of reg.96, but through a different mechanism. Regulation 99(1)(b) provides in relation to the work availability requirement that claimants in any of the circumstances set out in reg.99(3), (4), (4A) or (6) are regarded as being available for work if able and willing to take up paid work or attend an interview immediately after the relevant circumstance ceases to apply. Paragraph (3) applies to a variety of circumstances where the claimant is prevented from being available by something outside their control or is subject to some particularly testing experience, usually of a temporary nature. Paragraph (4), with (4ZA) and (4ZB), applies where the claimant is unfit for work for up to 14 days. Paragraph (4A), with (4B) and (4C), applies where the death of a specified person or an incident of violence or abuse has caused significant disruption to a responsible carer's normal childcare responsibilities. Paragraph (6) applies where the claimant is "working enough", i.e. has earnings at least equal to the "administrative earnings threshold". Regulation 99(2B) with (5A) and reg.99(2C) with (5B) applies the equivalent of the para.(1) rule, subject to an extra test of reasonableness, where the claimant is carrying out a work preparation requirement or voluntary work preparation, subject to temporary circumstances or unfit for work outside the limits of para.(4).

Able and willing

There was a body of case law under the old unemployment benefit regime on inability to take up employment that may possibly be relevant to universal credit, although many particular issues have now been overtaken by specific rules. Examples are where immigration law precludes the claimant working (*Shaukat Ali v CAO*, Appendix to *R(U) 1/85*), but now see s.115 of the Immigration and Asylum Act 1999 and Part V of this volume; where the claimant is about to go abroad (*R(U)2/90*—dealing with the position of wives of servicemen about to join their husbands for a posting abroad); or is contractually bound to another employer (*R(U)11/51*), for example, to be on call each working day, but now see reg.96(5). Thus, it would seem 1.162

that a person subject to a zero hours contract who is given no hours of work could be available for work. Even if the contract contained an exclusivity clause (not made ineffective until the coming into force of s.153 of the Small Business, Enterprise and Employment Act 2015 on May 26, 2015), the claimant might be deemed to have complied with the availability requirement if all the conditions of reg.96(5) are met. By the same token, it is arguable that a person "furloughed" under the Coronavirus Job Retention Scheme, which by its initial terms only prohibited employment by the furloughing employer, was available for alternative employment unless the contract of employment prohibited that. The issue of possible inability to take up work while away on holiday is discussed under *Immediately* below.

What claimants are willing and not willing to do can, of course, most obviously be judged from their professions of willingness in interviews that then form the basis for the content of a work search requirement. But it can also be inferred from conduct (see *R(U)4/53*). There the claimant had shown by his long practice of not taking up the option of working voluntary shifts on Saturdays that he was not available for work on Saturdays. See *Type of work* below for how far claimants can restrict the kind of work they are willing to do.

Type of work

1.163 Section 19(3) with subs.(4)(a) and (d) allows regulations to impose limitations on the work availability requirement by reference to work of a particular nature and to work available for a certain number of hours per week or at particular times. That power has only been exercised in reg.97(4) and (5), to now quite a limited effect where a claimant has previously carried out work of a particular nature and level of remuneration, and in reg.97(6), where the claimant has a physical or mental impairment, in relation to the nature and location of employment. Otherwise, there is nothing specific in the legislation about how far claimants can restrict the types of work or the hours of work they are willing to undertake and still meet the work availability requirement. The rule is not in terms of being available for suitable work. However, reg.97 applies both to the work search requirement under reg.17 and the work availability requirement. It appears that, for consistency, the question of the nature of work or number of hours or level of remuneration that a claimant is prepared to accept must be assessed primarily by reference to the content of the s.17 requirement, since s.18 contains no further conditions on those matters. Since the fundamental requirement in s.17 is to take all reasonable action for the purpose of obtaining paid work or more or better-paid work, with the requirement to take any particular action specified by the Secretary of State necessarily restricted to actions that are reasonable, the same standard must be applied in so far as s.18 involves asking what kind of work and/or hours and what level of remuneration the claimant can be required to be prepared to accept. That seems to be acknowledged in the current DWP guidance document on availability for work deposited in the House of Commons Library (collected in the Resources section of the Rightsnet website), where it is said that "any agreed restriction on hours of availability will determine a claimant's 'expected hours' of work search". The reverse would seem to be equally valid. The guidance also contains a general section about the tailoring of work search requirements to individual claimants. The Child Poverty Action Group mock-up of a tailored claimant commitment in Mears & Howes, *You reap what you code: Universal credit, digitalisation and the rule of law* (CPAG June 2023), lumps work search and availability together under a heading of "Work I can do" and restricts the contents of the "My availability" box to the issue of immediate availability for interviews or to take up work. Such tailoring of the work availability requirement must rest on the use of the power in s.18(3) for the Secretary of State to specify further limitations than those provided by reg.97.

There may well be scope for differences of opinion between claimants and work coaches about how far it is reasonable for them to restrict their work search and availability to their usual kind of work or the kind of work for which they are particularly suited or trained, rather than merely excluding the kind of work of which are simply not capable. A current impetus, as exemplified in the justification for the February 2022 amendment to reg.97(5) (permitted period reduced to four weeks), is towards encouraging claimants into any work that they can do, as more beneficial to them and to the economy, rather than waiting around for the ideal opportunity. Claimants might legitimately argue for more time before expanding their search, especially if their particular prospects of finding work of a particular kind are good, but no doubt policy arguments about the general economic good are outside the remit of work coaches. However any arguments are resolved, there should be clarity in the requirement that is in the end imposed on behalf of the Secretary of State about the scope of work the claimant must be willing and able to take up.

Claimants may have religious or other conscientious objections to particular kinds of work, such as vegetarians or vegans to working in a meat pie or sausage factory, even perhaps in the office. Readers can no doubt think of many other examples. Such restrictions can be accommodated by work coaches specifying a suitable limitation under s.18(3). If such a limitation is not accepted, then if a case gets to the stage of a sanction being imposed for failure to comply with the availability for work requirement, the question of whether the claimant had no good reason for the failure would come to the fore.

So far as hours of work are concerned, the default position, outside the cases specifically dealt with by reg.97, appears to be that claimants should be able and willing to take up full-time work or additional work to take the weekly hours up to the reg.88 expected hours (starting point, 35 hours). Thus, where those expected hours are reduced from 35, affecting in particular responsible carers and relevant carers of children and claimants with a physical or mental impairment, there is a knock-on effect on the availability for work requirement. The default position would also be that the hours could be distributed over any days of the week. However, as specifically recognised in the DWP guidance document deposited in the House of Commons Library, the effect of sincerely held religious beliefs against working on repeated days (like Saturdays or Sundays) or on specific festival days should be accepted. The same document notes that a pattern of availability may be agreed with a claimant so long as they have reasonable prospects of finding work within that pattern. It is submitted that it would in general not be reasonable to require claimants to be willing to work seven days a week. Especially for those with any caring responsibilities for school age children and young persons working at weekends might be problematic.

Immediately

The condition of being able and willing immediately to take up paid work or attend an interview is on its face an oppressive one. It apparently requires a claimant to be willing immediately, on a moment's notice, to take up an offer of work in the middle of the night, seven days a week (say, for shelf-stacking in a supermarket). Although the general formulation of the rule can be traced back at least as far as the 1930s, under unemployment benefit there was arguably some restriction to opportunities brought to the claimant's notice during normal business hours and under old style JSA there was an explicit link between the "immediate" obligation and a statutorily recognised pattern of availability (see *R(JSA) 2/07*). Modern conditions, with an extension of the 24-hour economy, have made the issues more pointed. 1.164

The dangers for claimants, along with some suggestions as to a common sense approach to "immediately", in the specific context of reg.7 of the JSA Regulations 1996 on old style JSA, were pointed out by Simon Brown LJ in *Secretary of State for Social Security v David*, reported in *R(JSA) 3/01*, at paras 25 and 26:

> "That 'immediately' means within a very short space of time indeed is clear not only from the word itself but also from regulation 5 which provides for exceptions to this requirement in the case of those with caring responsibilities or engaged in voluntary work (who need only be willing and able to take up employment on

> 48 hours' notice) and certain others engaged in providing a service (who get 24 hours' notice). No doubt the requirement for immediate availability allows the claimant time to wash, dress and have his breakfast, but strictly it would seem inconsistent with, say, a claimant's stay overnight with a friend or relative, or attendance at a weekend cricket match, or even an evening at the cinema (unless perhaps he had left a contact number and had not travelled far).
> 26. In these circumstances, claimants ought clearly to be wary of entering into an agreement which offers unrestricted availability throughout the entire week, day and night, weekdays and weekends."

Some claimants will escape the full rigour of the "immediate" requirement through reg.96 or 99 or by way of limitations under s.18(3). It must also be the case that, if a pattern of availability has been accepted, that will also control the days on which the claimant is required to be willing immediately to take up employment. Thus, it would seem always to be in the interests of a claimant to get such a pattern into the claimant commitment. The DWP guidance document deposited in the House of Commons Library says that claimants must be as ready and flexible as possible to attend interviews and start work and that if they have regular commitments they must consider how they can be rearranged so they can take up interviews or start work. That seems in itself an unobjectionable approach and it may be that, from the absence of examples of oppressive requirements, some sensible flexibility is allowed in practice. Nevertheless, the formula apparently used in claimant commitments without a pattern of availability is in peremptory terms ("I will be available to attend a job interview immediately. I will be available to start work immediately", repeated in essence in the CPAG mock-up mentioned above). If it were just a matter of that wording in the claimant commitment, it could perhaps be rejected as so unduly oppressive as to be irrational. But if all the documents and information made available to the claimant, including the claimant commitment, are sufficient to impose the availability for work requirement (on which see the notes to s.14), then it is the requirement as defined in s.18(2) that is imposed, including the reference to being able and willing immediately to take up paid work (or attend an interview: reg.96(1)). Can that be interpreted in a non-oppressive way without some express basis in the legislation for doing so? It seems wrong that a claimant commitment should contain a requirement in terms that no-one could be expected actually to follow, even if there would almost automatically be good reason for any failure to comply in the context of a middle of the night summons to a job if a case got to the stage of a sanction.

It is notable, by contrast with the position that will be familiar to many readers from old style JSA and, before it, unemployment benefit, that being available for work is not a condition of entitlement to universal credit, failure to satisfy which means that there can be no entitlement to benefit at all, although it is a condition of entitlement under s.4(1)(e) to accept a claimant commitment that should record the requirement. Instead, a failure to comply with the work availability requirement, if imposed on a claimant, is merely a potential basis for a sanction under ss.26 or 27. Under s.26(2)(c) a higher-level sanction can be imposed if a claimant fails for no good reason to comply by not taking up an offer of paid work, though that can only be by showing a failure to meet the general availability requirement. Section 27(2)(a) allows the imposition of a medium-level sanction for a failure for no good reason to comply with any work-related requirement.

Note that under s.23(1) the Secretary of State is empowered to require a claimant to participate in an interview relating to the imposition of a work-related requirement on the claimant or assisting the claimant to comply with a requirement. Under s.23(3) he can require the provision of information and evidence for the purpose of verifying compliance and that the claimant confirm compliance in any manner. A failure for no good reason to comply with any of those connected requirements is also sanctionable under s.27(2)(b).

Application of work-related requirements

Claimants subject to no work-related requirements

19.—(1) The Secretary of State may not impose any work-related requirement on a claimant falling within this section. 1.165

(2) A claimant falls within this section if—

(a) the claimant has limited capability for work and work-related activity,

(b) the claimant has regular and substantial caring responsibilities for a severely disabled person,

(c) the claimant is the responsible carer for a child under the age of 1, or

(d) the claimant is of a prescribed description.

(3) Regulations under subsection (2)(d) may in particular make provision by reference to one or more of the following—

(a) hours worked;

(b) earnings or income;

(c) the amount of universal credit payable.

(4) Regulations under subsection (3) may—

(a) in the case of a claimant who is a member of the couple, make provision by reference to the claimant alone or by reference to the members of the couple together;

(b) make provision for estimating or calculating any matter for the purpose of the regulations.

(5) Where a claimant falls within this section, any work-related requirement previously applying to the claimant ceases to have effect.

(6) In this Part "responsible carer", in relation to a child means—

(a) a single person who is responsible for the child, or

(b) a person who is a member of a couple where—

(i) the person or the other member of the couple is responsible for the child, and

(ii) the person has been nominated by the couple jointly as responsible for the child.

Definitions

"child"—see s.40.
"claimant"—*ibid.*
"limited capability for work"—*ibid.*
"limited capability for work-related activity"—*ibid.*
"regular and substantial caring responsibilities"—*ibid.*
"severely disabled"—*ibid.*
"work-related requirement"—see ss.40 and 13(2).

General Note

The default position in s.22 is that a claimant is, unless falling within ss.19–21, to be subject to all work-related requirements, i.e. the work search and work availability requirements, with the optional additions of a work-focused interview and/or a work preparation requirement. Section 19 defines the circumstances in which no work-related requirement at all may be imposed. Under reg.98 of the Universal Credit Regulations, made under s.24(5) below, recent victims of domestic violence must be free of any work-related requirement for a period of 13 weeks, subject to an extension for a further 13 weeks in relation to the work search and work availability requirements for responsible carers of children (reg.98(1A)). Where a claim has 1.166

to be made jointly by both members of a couple, both are claimants and it must be asked separately whether work-related requirements can be imposed on each. Note that a claimant who cannot, by virtue of s.19, have any work-related requirement imposed may nevertheless be required by the Secretary of State under s.23(1)(a) to participate in an interview relating to the possible imposition of any such requirement.

Subsection (2)

1.167 Three categories are specifically identified in subs.(2)(a)–(c). Others can, and have been, prescribed in regulations (subss.(2)(d) and (3)–(4)):

(a) Claimants who have limited capability for work and for work-related activity cannot have any work-related requirement imposed. Once claimants who currently qualify for employment and support allowance (ESA) fall within the ambit of universal credit, limited capability will be tested in essentially the same way as for ESA. Note that claimants who do not fall within s.19(2)(a) are exempted from the application of the work search and work availability requirements if they have limited capability for work, but not limited capability for work-related activity (s.21(1)(a)). Under reg.99 of the Universal Credit Regulations claimants who are unfit for work (not further defined) and provide prescribed evidence cannot have the work search requirement imposed and have the work availability requirement modified, for limited periods. See the notes to reg.99 for the details of the various permutations of circumstances covered.

(b) Claimants who have regular and substantial caring responsibilities for a severely disabled person cannot have any work-related requirement imposed. Although s.40 allows the meaning of "regular and substantial caring responsibilities" and "severely disabled" to be prescribed separately in regulations, reg.30 of the Universal Credit Regulations defines the two phrases in combination in terms of meeting the conditions of entitlement to carer's allowance, disregarding the earnings conditions, or, from November 19, 2023, being entitled to Scottish carer support payment. There seems no reason why that should not be valid. The test where the conditions of entitlement to carer's allowance are in issue (the claimant not being resident in Scotland or being resident outside Great Britain not having a genuine and sufficient link to Scotland: reg.30(1)(a)(ii)) is therefore, in brief, that the person cared for is entitled to attendance allowance, at least the middle rate of the care component of disability living allowance or Scottish child disability payment, the standard or enhanced rate of the daily living component of personal independence payment or Scottish adult disability payment, or armed forces independence payment and that the carer devotes at least 35 hours per week to caring for such a person. For Scottish residents or those resident outside Great Britain with a genuine and sufficient link the test in reg.30(1)(b) is actual entitlement to carer support payment under the Carer's Assistance (Carer Support Payment) (Scotland) Regulations 2023 (see Vol.IV of this series). But note that by virtue of reg.30(3) anyone who derives any earnings from the caring is excluded from the definition. See the extension in reg.89(1)(b) of the Universal Credit Regulations, under para. (d) below.

(c) Claimants who are the responsible carer for a child under the age of one cannot have any work-related requirement imposed. By subs.(6) a responsible carer is a person who is responsible for a child or, for couples, either partner nominated jointly provided one is responsible for the child. Regulation 4 of the Universal Credit Regulations, made under para.5 of Sch.1 to the WRA 2012, sets out how responsibility is to be determined. See the notes to reg.4. See ss.20(1)(a) and 21(1)(aa) for children aged one and two respectively.

(d) Regulations 89 and 90 of the Universal Credit Regulations set out the additional categories of claimant who cannot have any work-related requirement imposed. Regulation 90 covers the special rules needed by virtue of the special characteristic of universal credit as both an in-work and an out-of-work benefit. It thus exempts claimants whose earnings are of an amount at least equal to a threshold figure, calculated by reference to the national minimum wage and differing weekly hours for different groups of claimants. That in most cases produces a relatively high figure. For claimants with earnings below that threshold, see the effect of reg.99 on the work search and work availability requirements.

Regulation 89 covers more general categories. Regulation 89(1)(b) allows in some claimants who do not quite meet the conditions of subs.(2)(b). Regulation 89(1)(d) and (f) allow in some claimants who do not quite meet the conditions of subs.(2)(c). Regulation 89(1)(a) applies to claimants who have reached the qualifying age for state pension credit, i.e. state pension age. Regulation 89(1)(c) brings in women for shortish periods before and after confinement. Regulation 89(1)(e) brings in some claimants in education.

Claimants subject to work-focused interview requirement only

20.—(1) A claimant falls within this section if— 1.168

(a) the claimant is the responsible carer for a child who is aged [[1]1], or

(b) the claimant is of a prescribed description.

(2) The Secretary of State may, subject to this Part, impose a work-focused interview requirement on a claimant falling within this section.

(3) The Secretary of State may not impose any other work-related requirement on a claimant falling within this section (and, where a claimant falls within this section, any other work-related requirement previously applying to the claimant ceases to have effect).

AMENDMENT

1. Welfare Reform and Work Act 2016 s.17(1)(a) (April 3, 2017).

DEFINITIONS

"claimant"—see s.40.
"responsible carer"—see ss.40 and 19(6).
"work-focused interview requirement"—see ss.40 and 15(1).
"work-related requirement"—see ss.40 and 13(2).

GENERAL NOTE

The default position in s.22 is that a claimant is, unless falling within ss.19–21, to be subject to all work-related requirements, i.e. the work search and work availability requirements, with the optional additions of a work-focused interview and/or a work preparation requirement. Section 20 defines the circumstances in which a claimant who does not fall within s.19 (no work-related requirements), that condition applying because the discretion in para.(2) is subject to the rest of Pt I of the Act, can have a work-focused interview requirement, but not any other requirement, imposed. Regulation 93 of the Universal Credit Regulations specifies the permissible purposes of such an interview. They are in very wide terms but do not include discussion of the drawing up or revision of a claimant commitment as such, although discussion of matters listed may be relevant to what is to be included in the commitment. If the conditions of s.20(1) are met, there is a discretion whether actually to impose the work-focused interview requirement (subs.(2): *may*) and there is no statutory limit on the frequency of interviews that can be required. Where a claim 1.169

has to be made jointly by both members of a couple, both are claimants and it must be asked separately whether work-related requirements can be imposed on each. Note that under s.23 the Secretary of State may require a claimant to participate in an interview for purposes relating to the imposition of any work-related requirement, verifying compliance with any work-related requirement or assisting the claimant's compliance with any work-related requirement. They may also require the reporting of relevant changes of circumstances.

Note that a claimant falls within s.19 (no work-related requirements) if any of the provisions of reg.89 or 90 of the Universal Credit Regulations apply (s.19(2)(d)), e.g. where the conditionality earnings threshold in reg.90 is met, so that the s.20 requirement cannot then be imposed. Though do not forget the power in s.23(1) to require a claimant to participate in an interview for certain specified purposes, which is not a work-related requirement. A claimant whose employed earnings (combined such earnings for couples) do not meet that threshold but equal or exceed the "administrative earnings threshold" under the "light touch regime" of reg.99(6) remain potentially subject to the imposition of the work-focused interview requirement, but in practice are apparently only required to attend work search interviews in the first and eighth weeks on the regime.

See s.24 for the process of imposing a requirement.

The most important category covered by s.20 and subject to the discretion to impose a work-focused interview requirement is of "responsible carers" (defined in s.19(6)) of a child aged one. Responsible carers of a child under one are exempt from all work-related requirements under s.19(2)(c), with slight extensions under s.19(2)(d) (and see s.21 for responsible carers of a child aged two and the notes to s.22 and regs 88 and 97 of the Universal Credit Regulations for the position where the youngest child reaches three). It was announced in a press release of July 24, 2023 that (as presaged in general terms in the Spring Budget 2023) from that date responsible carers of a child aged one would be required to meet a work coach, presumably for an interview with a purpose specified in reg.93 (but just possibly for a s.23 interview if so indicated), every three months, instead of every six months as previously.

The scope of the protection given by s.20 to limit the permissible work-related requirements that can be imposed on a claimant has been narrowed considerably since April 2013. Initially, in combination with reg.91(1), subs.(1)(a) applied where the child in question was aged less than five. In April 2014, the crucial age was reduced to three, but with some further protection under s.21(1)(b) in combination with a new reg.91A for responsible carers of children aged three or four, who could not have any work-related requirements other than the work-focused interview or work preparation requirement imposed. The April 2017 amendments limit subs.(1)(a) to responsible carers of a child aged one (not under or over that age) and take away the power to prescribe any different age in regulations. As a result, reg.91(1), which had carried out the prescription previously required by subs.(1)(a), has been revoked. The further protection under s.21(1) has been limited to responsible carers of children aged two (subs.(1)(aa)) and reg.91A has been revoked.

Under s.20(1)(b), reg.91(2) continues to extend the effect of the provision to responsible foster carers of any child aged from one to 15 and to certain categories of foster parents and "friend and family carers". It seems anomalous that "ordinary" responsible carers should be treated less favourably then those groups, but no challenge under the Human Rights Act 1998 on the ground of discrimination could lead to any finding that the amendments were invalid, since they were all carried out by primary legislation.

The nature of the requirement and the purposes of the interview are defined in s.15 and reg.93 of the Universal Credit Regulations.

Claimants subject to work preparation requirement

1.170 **21.**—(1) A claimant falls within this section if the claimant does not fall within section 19 or 20 and—

(a) the claimant has limited capability for work,
[1 (aa) the claimant is the responsible carer for a child who is aged 2,] or
(b) the claimant is of a prescribed description.

(2) The Secretary of State may, subject to this Part, impose a work preparation requirement on a claimant falling within this section.

(3) The Secretary of State may also, subject to this Part, impose a work-focused interview requirement on a claimant falling within this section.

(4) The Secretary of State may not impose any other work-related requirement on a claimant falling within this section (and, where a claimant falls within this section, any other work-related requirement previously applying to the claimant ceases to have effect).

(5) [1 . . .]

AMENDMENT

1. Welfare Reform and Work Act 2016 s.17(1) (April 3, 2017).

DEFINITIONS

"claimant"—see s.40.
"limited capability for work"—see ss.40 and 37(1).
"prescribed"—see s.40.
"responsible carer"—see ss.40 and 19(6).
"work preparation requirement"—see ss.40 and 16(1).
"work-focused interview requirement"—see ss.40 and 15(1).
"work-related requirement"—see ss.40 and 13(2).

GENERAL NOTE

The default position in s.22 is that a claimant is, unless falling within ss.19–21, to be subject to all work-related requirements, i.e. the work search and work availability requirements, with the optional additions of a work-focused interview and/or a work preparation requirement. Section 21 defines the circumstances in which a claimant who does not fall within ss.19 or 20 (no work-related requirements or work-focused interview requirement only) can have a work preparation requirement and, under subs.(3), a work-focused interview requirement, but not any other requirement, imposed. Under s.23(1) the Secretary of State is empowered to require a claimant to attend an interview relating to the imposition of a work-related requirement, verifying compliance with any work-related requirement or assisting the claimant's compliance with any work-related requirement. He may also require the reporting of relevant changes of circumstances. Where a claim has to be made jointly by both members of a couple, both are claimants and it must be asked separately whether work-related requirements can be imposed on each. 1.171

Note that a claimant falls within s.19 (no work-related requirements) if any of the provisions of reg.89 or 90 of the Universal Credit Regulations apply (s.19(2)(d)), e.g. where the conditionality earnings threshold in reg.90 is met, so that no requirement of either kind can then be imposed under s.21. A claimant whose employed earnings (combined such earnings for couples) do not meet that threshold but equal or exceed the "administrative earnings threshold" under the "light touch regime" of reg.99(6) remain potentially subject to the imposition of the work-focused interview and work preparation requirement, but in practice are apparently only required to attend work search interviews in the first and eighth weeks on the regime.

See s.24 for the process of imposing a requirement. Note that there is a discretion ("may") to impose the requirement if the conditions are met.

The first main category of claimants covered by s.21 is, under subs.(1)(a), of those who have limited capability for work (but not also limited capability for work-related activity, which would exempt from all work-related requirements under s.19(2)(a)). The former phrase is to be construed in accordance with s.37(1), which refers to a claimant's capability for work being limited by their physical or mental condition such that it is not reasonable to require them to work. But those tests are not be applied in their ordinary meanings because s.37(3) provides that the question of whether they are met is to be determined in accordance with regulations, which means through the application of the points-based "work capability assessment" under regs 38–44 of and Schs 6 and 8 to the Universal Credit Regulations, in the same way as for ESA.

The second main category, under subs.(1)(aa), is of responsible carers (defined in s.19(6)) of a child aged two. Responsible carers of a child under one are exempt from all work-related requirements under s.19(2)(c), with slight extensions under s.19(2)(d), and responsible carers of a child of one can under s.20 only have a work-focused interview requirement imposed (and see the notes to s.22 and regs 88 and 97 of the Universal Credit Regulations for the position where the youngest child reaches three). It was announced in a press release of July 24, 2023 that (as presaged in general terms in the Spring Budget 2023) from that date responsible carers of a child aged two would be required to meet a work coach, presumably for an interview with a purpose specified in reg.93 (but just possibly for a s.23 interview if so indicated), every month, instead of every three months as previously. In relation to the discretion to impose a work preparation requirement under s.16, the current guidance document deposited in the House of Commons Library suggests that the "default maximum expected hours" for action under such a requirement, to be specified under s.16(2), would be 16. That would, just as in cases where reg.88 applies and as recognised in the guidance, be subject to the constraints of the claimant's individual circumstances, including health conditions and caring responsibilities, and external realities, such as the actual availability and affordability of childcare.

Initially, s.21 only covered limited capability for work, no regulations having been made under subs.(1)(b). The duty in subs.(5) to make regulations did not arise in practice because any claimant who was the responsible carer for a child aged three or four fell within s.20(1)(b) by virtue of reg.91(1) of the Universal Credit Regulations as they stood at the time. In the period from April 6, 2014, when the crucial age under s.20(1)(a) was reduced to three, a prescription became necessary, which produced a new reg.91A. With effect from April 3, 2017 and the restriction of the effect of s.20(1)(a) to children aged one (and not under or over that age), the protection of s.21 has been limited to responsible carers of a child aged two (and not under or over that age). The former duty in subs.(5) to make regulations in certain circumstances has been removed and reg.91A has been revoked.

The nature of the work preparation requirement is defined in s.16.

Claimants subject to all work-related requirements

1.172 **22.**—(1) A claimant not falling within any of sections 19 to 21 falls within this section.

(2) The Secretary of State must, except in prescribed circumstances, impose on a claimant falling within this section—

(a) a work search requirement, and
(b) a work availability requirement.

(3) The Secretary of State may, subject to this Part, impose either or both of the following on a claimant falling within this section—

(a) a work-focused interview requirement;
(b) a work preparation requirement.

DEFINITIONS

"claimant"—see s.40.
"prescribed"—*ibid.*

"work availability requirement"—see ss.40 and 18(1).
"work preparation requirement"—see ss.40 and 16(1).
"work search requirement"—see ss.40 and 17(1).
"work-focused interview requirement"—see ss.40 and 15(1).

GENERAL NOTE

Temporary Coronavirus Provisions

The last of the temporary coronavirus provisions relevant to the imposition of work-related requirements expired on November 12, 2020. See previous editions of this volume for the details. 1.173

This section sets out the default position that a claimant of universal credit is, unless falling within ss.19–21, to be subject to all work-related requirements, i.e. the work search and work availability requirements, with the optional additions of a work-focused interview and/or a work preparation requirement. Note that a claimant falls within s.19 (no work-related requirements) if any of the provisions of reg.89 or 90 of the Universal Credit Regulations apply (s.19(2)(d)), e.g. where the earnings threshold in reg.90 is met, so that no work-related requirement of kind can then be imposed under s.22. Under s.23(1) the Secretary of State is empowered to require a claimant to attend an interview relating to the imposition of a work-related requirement, to the verification of compliance or to assisting the claimant to comply with a requirement. By contrast with other provisions, where this section applies the work search and work availability requirements *must*, subject to the exceptions prescribed in regs 98 and 99 of the Universal Credit Regulations, be imposed (subs.(2)), but there is a discretion about the other requirements (subs.(3)). See the notes to ss.19–21 for the circumstances in which either no or only some work-related requirements may be imposed. The content of the requirements is set out in ss.15–18 and associated regulations. Where a claim has to be made jointly by both members of a couple, and both are claimants it must be asked separately whether work-related requirements can be imposed on each. See s.24 for the process of imposing a requirement.

Since April 2017 healthy responsible carers of children aged three and above have in principle been subject to the Secretary of State's duty under s.22(2) to impose work search and work availability requirements (though note the potential exemptions under regs 89, 90 (conditionality earnings threshold) and 91 (some foster parents and friend or family carers) of the Universal Credit Regulations). That is subject to the rule in reg.97(2) that those requirements must be limited to the claimant's expected number of hours a week under reg.88. With effect from October 25, 2023, the administrative guidance on the maximum hours to be considered under reg.88 introduced a significant increase, according to the press release of that date to give such claimants more support to get back to work. However, the legal structure for identifying the proper level of expected hours under reg.88 has not changed. See the notes to reg.88 for the details.

See the notes to s.14 for discussion of *JB v SSWP (UC)* [2018] UKUT 360 (AAC) and the question whether the current standard terms of claimant commitments (e.g. in the form of provisions like "I will also attend and take part in appointments with my adviser when required", "I will be available to attend a job interview immediately [and to] start work immediately" or "I will normally spend 35 hours per week looking and preparing for work") are sufficient in themselves to carry out the duty in s.22(1) and the power in s.22(2) to impose the specified work-related requirements. The judge considered that that question would rarely arise in practice and that what was important was whether consideration of all the evidence produced by the SSWP of communications to the claimant showed that the substance of the requirement in issue and the consequences of non-compliance had been properly notified to the claimant. In para.29 of *S v SSWP (UC)* [2017] UKUT 477 (AAC), the judge accepted that, if the SSWP failed to carry out the s.22(1) duty, the claimant should not bear the consequences of that (which must entail that the requirement(s) in question had not been imposed and there could be no sanction for failing to comply). That approach has in effect been confirmed in para.6 of *JB*, where it was said to be a condition precedent of the imposition of a sanction under s.27(2)(a) that the claimant was subject to the work-related requirement in question. See also the notes to ss.13, 14 and 24.

Work-related requirements: supplementary

Connected requirements

1.174 **23.**—(1) The Secretary of State may require a claimant to participate in an interview for any purpose relating to—

(a) the imposition of a work-related requirement on the claimant;
(b) verifying the claimant's compliance with a work-related requirement;
(c) assisting the claimant to comply with a work-related requirement.

(2) The Secretary of State may specify how, when and where such an interview is to take place.

(3) The Secretary of State may, for the purpose of verifying the claimant's compliance with a work-related requirement, require a claimant to—

(a) provide to the Secretary of State information and evidence specified by the Secretary of State in a manner so specified;
(b) confirm compliance in a manner so specified.

(4) The Secretary of State may require a claimant to report to the Secretary of State any specified changes in their circumstances which are relevant to—

(a) the imposition of work-related requirements on the claimant;
(b) the claimant's compliance with a work-related requirement.

DEFINITIONS

"claimant"—see s.40.
"work-related requirement"—see ss.40 and 13(2).

GENERAL NOTE

1.175 This section gives the Secretary of State power to require a claimant to do various things related to the imposition of work-related requirements, verifying compliance and assisting claimants to comply: to participate in an interview (subss.(1) and (2)); for the purpose of verifying compliance, to provide specified information and evidence or to confirm compliance (subs.(3)); or to report specified changes in a claimant's circumstances relevant to the imposition of or compliance with requirements (subs.(4)). Note that the permitted purposes of an interview under subs.(1) do not include discussion of the drawing up or review of a claimant commitment as such. However, discussion of whether a work-related requirement should be imposed and what its content should be, which would then be recorded in a claimant commitment, would be included.

The requirements under s.23 do not fall within the meaning of "work-related requirement", but there is a separate ground of sanction under s.27(2)(b) for failing for no good reason to comply with them, but only as a low-level sanction for claimants subject to all work-related requirements or to the work preparation requirement (see reg.104(1) of the Universal Credit Regulations in conjunction with regs 102, 103 and 105). The Secretary of State is allowed under subs.(2) to specify how, when and where any interview under subs.(1) is to take place, so that there is no straightforward limit on the number or frequency of the interviews that may be specified, or on the persons who may conduct the interview. The interviews must of course properly be for one of the purposes specified in subs.(1). The requirement to participate in an interview cannot be used for punitive purposes or simply as a means of control of a claimant. The requirement, as now for new style JSA, is not attendance at an interview at the specified time and date, but participation in it. This would appear to mean that a claimant can be required to participate in an interview over the telephone, providing that that manner of conducting it has been specified under subs.(2). In an ambiguous (so far as JSA is concerned) Parliamentary answer on 24 November 2015 (UIN 17005), the Minister of State Priti Patel said:

> "Under JSA, claimants are not sanctioned for failing to answer their telephone. In Universal Credit, claimants who have a prearranged telephone interview with their Work Coach, and who fail to participate without good reason, can be referred for a sanction decision."

JB v SSWP (UC) [2018] UKUT 360 (AAC) (see the notes to ss.14 and 15) was endorsed and applied in *KG v SSWP (UC)* [2020] UKUT 307 (AAC). Before the Upper Tribunal the Secretary of State accepted that the available evidence did not show that the claimant had been properly notified of the requirement to take part in the particular telephone interview with his work coach, so that no sanction could be applied under s.27. The documents were ambiguous as to whether the interview was under s.15 (work-focused interview requirement) or s.23 and what issues the claimant was told were to be investigated, and left it unclear whether he had been adequately informed of the consequences of non-compliance.

There is no further provision about what participating in an interview entails. It must at least entail turning up at the place and time specified, although the decision of Judge Knowles in *SA v SSWP (JSA)* [2015] UKUT 454 (AAC) (see the notes to s.27 for full discussion) would indicate that tribunals should consider, in cases where the claimant arrives not very late, whether it is proportionate to the nature of all the circumstances to regard that as a failure to participate in an interview. There were all sorts of mitigating circumstances in *SA*, that may well not be present in other cases. See *SN v SSWP (JSA)* [2018] UKUT 279 (AAC), detailed in the notes to ss.26(2)(a) and 27(2)(a), for discussion of what might amount to a failure to participate (in that case in a mandatory work activity scheme) and the expression in para.45 of some doubt about the result in *SA*.

The requirement to participate must also extend to making some meaningful contribution to the interview, but the limits will probably not be established until some more sanctions appeals in JSA or universal credit reach the Upper Tribunal. Behaviour that leads to the premature termination of the interview may well amount to a failure to participate (see the facts of *DM v SSWP (JSA)* [2015] UKUT 67 (AAC) in the notes to s.27(2)(b)). There may, though, in cases of uncooperative claimants or heavy-handed officials or a combination, be difficult questions about when an interview has ceased to exist, so that subsequent behaviour cannot be relevant to whether there has been a failure to participate (see *PH v SSWP (ESA)* [2016] UKUT 119 (AAC) on failing to submit to a medical examination).

It was recognised in *CS v SSWP (JSA)* [2019] UKUT 218 (AAC), detailed in the notes to s.26(2)(a), that it was legitimate for a scheme provider to require an attender to verify their identity before starting a scheme, so that a refusal to do so would usually amount to a failure to participate in the scheme. The same principle could apply to an interview, but the particular issues that arose in *CS*, to do with a scheme provider external to the DWP, are unlikely to arise if it is an interview with a work coach or other adviser that has been notified.

The compulsory imposition of a sanction for failure for no good reason to report specified changes in circumstances, to provide specified information and evidence or to confirm compliance with a work-related requirement is a new departure.

See s.24 for the process of imposing a requirement.

Imposition of requirements

1.176 **24.**—(1) Regulations may make provision—

(a) where the Secretary of State may impose a requirement under this Part, as to when the requirement must or must not be imposed;

(b) where the Secretary of State may specify any action to be taken in relation to a requirement under this Part, as to what action must or must not be specified;

(c) where the Secretary of State may specify any other matter in relation to a requirement under this Part, as to what must or must not be specified in respect of that matter.

(2) Where the Secretary of State may impose a work-focused interview requirement, or specify a particular action under section 16(1) or 17(1)(b), the Secretary of State must have regard to such matters as may be prescribed.

(3) Where the Secretary of State may impose a requirement under this Part, or specify any action to be taken in relation to such a requirement, the Secretary of State may revoke or change what has been imposed or specified.

(4) Notification of a requirement imposed under this Part (or any change to or revocation of such a requirement) is, if not included in the claimant commitment, to be in such manner as the Secretary of State may determine.

(5) Regulations must make provision to secure that, in prescribed circumstances, where a claimant has recently been a victim of domestic violence—

(a) a requirement imposed on that claimant under this Part ceases to have effect for a period of 13 weeks, and

(b) the Secretary of State may not impose any other requirement under this Part on that claimant during that period.

(6) For the purposes of subsection (5)—

(a) "domestic violence" has such meaning as may be prescribed;

(b) "victim of domestic violence" means a person on or against whom domestic violence is inflicted or threatened (and regulations under subsection (5) may prescribe circumstances in which a person is to be treated as being or not being a victim of domestic violence);

(c) a person has recently been a victim of domestic violence if a prescribed period has not expired since the violence was inflicted or threatened.

DEFINITIONS

"claimant"—see s.40.

"work-focused interview requirement"—see ss.40 and 15(1).

GENERAL NOTE

1.177 This section contains a variety of powers and duties in relation to the imposition by the Secretary of State of either a work-related requirement or a connected requirement under s.23. It makes the imposition of a requirement and the notification to the claimant a moderately formal process, which raises the question of whether the decision of the Secretary of State to impose a requirement is a decision that is appealable to a First-tier Tribunal under s.12(1) of the SSA 1998, either as a decision on a claim or award or one which falls to be made under the WRA 2012 as a "relevant enactment" (s.8(1)(a) and (c) of the SSA 1998). However, if it is a decision not made on a claim or award, it is not covered in Sch.3 to the SSA 1998 (or in Sch.2 to the Decisions and Appeals Regulations 2013 (see Vol.III of this series)), so could not be appealable under that heading. The discussion in the note to s.12(1) of the SSA 1998 in Vol.III would indicate that, since the imposition of a requirement is not an "outcome" decision determining entitlement or payability of universal credit or the amount payable, it is not appealable under s.12(1)(a) as a decision on a claim or award or as a decision on another basis.

Thus, it appears that a direct challenge to the imposition of any particular requirement, including any element specified by the Secretary of State, and/or its inclusion in a claimant commitment under s.14 of this Act, can only be made by way of judicial review in the High Court, with the possibility of a discretionary transfer to the Upper Tribunal. Otherwise, a challenge by way of appeal appears not be possible unless and until a reduction of benefit for a sanctionable failure is imposed on the claimant for a failure to comply with a requirement or entitlement is ended for failing to accept a claimant commitment containing the requirement. It must therefore be arguable that in any such appeal the claimant can challenge whether the conditions for the imposition of the requirement in question were met, with the result that, if that challenge is successful, the sanction must be removed. That appears to have been the assumption of the Supreme Court in *R. (on the application of Reilly and Wilson) v Secretary of State for Work and Pensions* [2013] UKSC 68; [2014] 1 A.C. 453. In para.29 of their judgment, Lords Neuberger and Toulson mentioned without any adverse comment Foskett J's holding at first instance that a consequence of a breach of a regulation requiring a claimant to be given notice of a requirement to participate in a scheme was that no sanctions could lawfully be imposed on the claimants for failure to participate in the scheme. Paragraph 6 of *JB v SSWP (UC)* [2018] UKUT 360 (AAC) states that it is a condition precedent of imposing any sanction under s.27(2)(a) that the claimant was subject to the work-related requirement in issue, thus confirming the approach in para.29 of *S v SSWP (UC)* [2017] UKUT 477 (AAC) that if a specific requirement has not been imposed by the SSWP no sanction can follow.

Subsection (1)

Regulation 99 of the Universal Credit Regulations is made in part under para.(a), **1.178**
reg.98 on domestic violence falling more specifically under subss.(5) and (6). No regulations appear to have been made under paras (b) and (c).

Subsection (2)

No regulations appear to have been made under this provision. **1.179**

Subsection (3)

The inclusion of this express power to revoke or change any requirement, or any **1.180**
specification of action, is an indication of the formality entailed in the imposition of a requirement. However, there appears to be no restriction on the circumstances in which the Secretary of State may carry out such a revocation or change, subject of course to the legislative conditions being met for whatever the new position is. A mere change of mind without any change in circumstances or mistake or error as to the existing circumstances will do.

Subsection (4)

There is serious doubt whether the standard terms currently used in universal **1.181**
credit claimant commitments are sufficient in themselves to impose any work-related requirements (see the notes to s.14 for extensive discussion of the effect of the decision in *JB v SSWP (UC)* [2018] UKUT 360 (AAC)). If they are not, the necessity for notification by some other means, as allowed by subs.(4), becomes more important. It is necessarily implied in subs.(4) in conjunction with ss.13(1) and 22 that claimants are not subject to a work-related requirement if the Secretary

of State has not notified them of its imposition: see para.29 of *S v SSWP (UC)* [2017] UKUT 477 (AAC), *SP v SSWP (UC)* [2018] UKUT 227 (AAC) and now para.6 of *JB* (above)). Careful consideration will need to be given by tribunals to what evidence of imposition by the Secretary of State and notification to the claimant has been put before them.

JB was endorsed and applied in *KG v SSWP (UC)* [2020] UKUT 307 (AAC). Before the Upper Tribunal the Secretary of State accepted that the available evidence did not show that the claimant had been properly notified of the requirement to take part in the particular telephone interview with his work coach, so that no sanction could be applied under s.27. The documents were ambiguous as to whether the interview was under s.15 (work-focused interview requirement) or s.23 (connected requirements) and what issues the claimant was told were to be investigated, and left it unclear whether he had been adequately informed of the consequences of non-compliance.

It is plainly arguable that no work-related or connected requirement can be imposed unless the claimant has received sufficient information about the requirement to enable them to make meaningful representations about whether the requirement should be imposed or not (the "prior information duty"). That duty stems from principles stated by the Supreme Court in *Reilly and Wilson* (above) and elaborated by the Court of Appeal in *Secretary of State for Work and Pensions v Reilly and Hewstone* and *Secretary of State for Work and Pensions v Jeffrey and Bevan* [2016] EWCA Civ 413; [2017] Q.B. 657; [2017] AACR 14. See the discussion in the notes to s.14, especially for points about when any breach of the duty might be material and when issues about the duty arise on appeals. If the process for the production of claimant commitments as described in the notes to s.14 is followed, there should be ample opportunity for the giving of sufficient information, although what happened in practice in individual cases will be what matters.

This provision allows the Secretary of State to notify the claimant of the imposition of any requirement, if not included in a claimant commitment under s.14, in any manner. Thus, it may be done orally (or presumably even through the medium of mime), but it is a necessary implication that a requirement must be notified to the claimant. That in turn implies that, whatever the manner of notification, the content must be such as is reasonably capable of being understood by the particular claimant with the characteristics known to the officer of the Secretary of State (so perhaps the medium of mime will not do after all). Less flippantly, this principle may be important for claimants with sensory problems, e.g. hearing or vision difficulties. The expectation of course is that the requirements imposed under the Act will be included in the claimant commitment, one of whose aims is to ensure that claimants know and understand what is being required of them and the potential consequences of failing to comply. That expectation may not in practice have been fulfilled. However, it is clear in law that the validity of a requirement is not dependent on inclusion in the claimant commitment. There is no such express condition and under s.14(4)(a) the Secretary of State is only under a duty to record in the claimant commitment such of the requirements under the Act as he considers it appropriate to include. It may be that the fact that a requirement is not recorded in the claimant commitment could be put forward as part of an argument for there having been a good reason for failing to comply with the requirement.

Subsections (5) and (6)

1.182 The duty to make regulations providing that no work-related requirement or connected requirement under s.23 may be imposed for a period of 13 weeks on a claimant who has recently been a victim of domestic violence is partially carried out in reg.98 of the Universal Credit Regulations. Most of the meat is in the regulation, including the definition of "domestic violence", which has been amended since April 2013. See the note to reg.98 for the details. However, subs.(6)(b) does define "victim" to include not just those on whom domestic violence is inflicted but also those against whom it is threatened.

Regulation 98 appears to be defective in that it applies only to work-related requirements, which in accordance with the definition in s.13(2) do not include connected requirements under s.23. Thus the duty in subs.(5) in relation to any requirement under Part 1 of the Act has not been fulfilled in relation to connected requirements. That defect cannot affect the application of reg.98 to work-related requirements.

Compliance with requirements

25. Regulations may make provision as to circumstances in which a claimant is to be treated as having— **1.183**

(a) complied with or not complied with any requirement imposed under this Part or any aspect of such a requirement, or

(b) taken or not taken any particular action specified by the Secretary of State in relation to such a requirement.

General Note

Under subs.(a) regulations may deem a claimant either to have or not to have complied with any work-related requirement or connected requirement under s.23 in particular circumstances. Regulations 94–97 of the Universal Credit Regulations make use of this power, mainly in treating claimants as not having complied. No regulations appear to have been made as yet under subs.(b). **1.184**

Reduction of benefit

Higher-level sanctions

26.—(1) The amount of an award of universal credit is to be reduced in accordance with this section in the event of a failure by a claimant which is sanctionable under this section. **1.185**

(2) It is a failure sanctionable under this section if a claimant falling within section 22—

(a) fails for no good reason to comply with a requirement imposed by the Secretary of State under a work preparation requirement to undertake a work placement of a prescribed description;

(b) fails for no good reason to comply with a requirement imposed by the Secretary of State under a work search requirement to apply for a particular vacancy for paid work;

(c) fails for no good reason to comply with a work availability requirement by not taking up an offer of paid work;

(d) by reason of misconduct, or voluntarily and for no good reason, ceases paid work or loses pay.

(3) It is a failure sanctionable under this section if by reason of misconduct, or voluntarily and for no good reason, a claimant falling within section 19 by virtue of subsection (3) of that section ceases paid work or loses pay so as to cease to fall within that section and to fall within section 22 instead.

(4) It is a failure sanctionable under this section if, at any time before making the claim by reference to which the award is made, the claimant—

(a) for no good reason failed to take up an offer of paid work, or

(b) by reason of misconduct, or voluntarily and for no good reason, ceased paid work or lost pay,

and at the time the award is made the claimant falls within section 22.

(5) For the purposes of subsections (2) to (4) regulations may provide—

(a) for circumstances in which ceasing to work or losing pay is to be treated as occurring or not occurring by reason of misconduct or voluntarily;
(b) for loss of pay below a prescribed level to be disregarded.
(6) Regulations are to provide for—
(a) the amount of a reduction under this section;
(b) the period for which such a reduction has effect, not exceeding three years in relation to any failure sanctionable under this section.
(7) Regulations under subsection (6)(b) may in particular provide for the period of a reduction to depend on either or both of the following—
(a) the number of failures by the claimant sanctionable under this section;
(b) the period between such failures.
(8) Regulations may provide—
(a) for cases in which no reduction is to be made under this section;
(b) for a reduction under this section made in relation to an award that is terminated to be applied to any new award made within a prescribed period of the termination;
(c) for the termination or suspension of a reduction under this section.

DEFINITIONS

"claimant"—see s.40.
"prescribed"—*ibid.*
"work availability requirement"—see ss.40 and 18(1).
"work preparation requirement"—see ss.40 and 16(1).
"work search requirement"—see ss.40 and 17(1).

GENERAL NOTE

1.186 Sections 26–28 set up a very similar structure of sanctions leading to reductions in the amount of universal credit to that already imposed in the new ss.19–20 of the old style Jobseekers Act 1995 substituted by the WRA 2012 and in operation from October 22, 2012 (see Vol.V of this series, 2021/22 edition as updated in Cumulative Supplements included in this volume and in mid-year Supplements). The similarity is in the creation of higher-level sanctions, here under s.26, and of medium, low and lowest-level sanctions, here under s.27, and in the stringency of the periods and the amount of reductions to be imposed, in particular for higher-level sanctions. See the discussion in the notes to s.19 of the old style Jobseekers Act 1995 in Vol.V. There are even more similarities to the structure of sanctions in ss.6J and 6K of the new style Jobseekers Act 1995, also introduced by the WRA 2012 and only in operation in relation to claimants to whom the universal credit provisions have started to apply. In all three places the maximum length of a higher-level sanction was initially three years, a very considerable increase on the previous position. On May 9, 2019, following a report of November 6, 2018 by the House of Commons Work and Pensions Committee on *Benefit Sanctions* (HC 995 2017–19), the Secretary of State (Amber Rudd) made a written statement to Parliament (HCWS1545) including the following:

> "I have reviewed my Department's internal data, which shows that a six-month sanction already provides a significant incentive for claimants to engage with the labour market regime. I agree with the Work and Pensions Select Committee that a three-year sanction is unnecessarily long and I feel that the additional incentive provided by a three-year sanction can be outweighed by the unintended impacts to the claimant due to the additional duration. For these reasons, I have now decided to remove three year sanctions and reduce the maximum sanction length to six months by the end of the year."

That decision was implemented, subject to qualification, in relation to universal credit by the amendment to reg.102 of the Universal Credit Regulations with effect from November 27, 2019 (see below).

Paragraph 4.31 of the September 2022 *Growth Plan 2022* (CP 743) said that the government would be strengthening the universal credit sanctions regime to set clear expectations, including applying for jobs, attending interviews or increasing hours, but it was left unclear exactly what that was to entail or whether any legislative change was envisaged. It is not known whether the plan, such as it was, has survived the change of administration. Paragraph 4.148 of the *Spring Budget 2023* (HC 1183) stated that the government would strengthen the way that the universal credit sanctions regime was applied by automating part of the process, to reduce error rates, and provide additional training to work coaches to enable them to apply sanctions more effectively, including for claimants who do not look for or take up employment. It has since been clarified (Written answer of March 28, 2023 by Guy Opperman, Minister for Employment) that the automation is only to be of the initial creation of referral forms for work coaches when a mandatory appointment is missed, not of decision-making or the application of the sanctions regime.

For a summary of past government reactions to official reports and studies on the effectiveness or fairness of sanctions regimes see pp.210–11 of the 2021/22 edition of Vol.V of this series, as updated in Cumulative Supplements included in this volume and in mid-year Supplements. More recently, a letter dated June 15, 2022 from the Chair of the House of Commons Work and Pensions Committee, Sir Stephen Timms, to the then Secretary of State, noted that the Committee's 2018 report on *Benefit Sanctions* had recommended that the Department "urgently evaluate the effectiveness of reforms to welfare conditionality" and that the government had accepted the recommendation, saying that it would focus its evaluation on "whether the sanctions regime within Universal Credit is effective at supporting claimants to search for work". Some research was carried out, but the DWP after initial equivocation declined to publish a report, saying that it did not adequately cover the deterrent effect of the sanctions regime. The draft report on the *Impact of Benefit Sanctions on Employment Outcomes* was eventually published on April 6, 2023 after a ruling by the Information Commissioner's Office.

The Public Law Project published a distinctly critical report, *Benefit Sanctions: A Presumption of Guilt*, on July 20, 2022.

There are some differences in the wording of otherwise similar provisions made by different parts of the WRA 2012, which will be noted below. The sanctions framework is limited to the operation of work-related and connected requirements, so that universal credit claimants who fall outside that ambit cannot be sanctioned (although other consequences might follow failure to comply with some requirements). That result is secured through the general restriction of the application of s.26 to claimants who are subject to all work-related requirements under s.22 (except under subs.(3)) and through the scope of s.27 being limited to failures to comply with work-related or connected requirements.

The test of being subject to all work-related requirements is applied at the date of the sanctionable failure (or award of universal credit for pre-claim failures) and it does not in general affect the continuing operation of the sanction if the claimant ceases to be so subject. The reduction rate drops from 100% of the standard allowance to nil if the claimant begins to have limited capability for work and work-related activity (Universal Credit Regulations, reg.111(3)). The reduction rate drops to 40% if the claimant comes within s.19 (no work-related requirements) because of certain caring responsibilities for children under one (reg.111(2)). The DWP rejected the Work and Pensions Committee's recommendation in its report on *Benefit Sanctions* (above) that sanctions be cancelled when a claimant ceased to be subject to the requirement that led to the sanction (House of Commons Work and Pensions Committee, *Benefit Sanctions: Government Response* (HC 1949 2017-19, February 11, 2019, paras 49-51). It was said that that would undermine the incentive effect of the sanctions and that the mitigations in reg.111 were adequate. Note also the termination of a reduction when the claimant has been in paid work at at least a weekly rate of 35 times the hourly national minimum wage for 26 weeks (reg.109).

Note the important provision in reg.5 of the JSA Regulations 2013 that, if a claimant is entitled to both universal credit and new style JSA, no work-related requirements can be imposed under the new style JSA regime (ss.6B-6G of the new style Jobseekers Act 1995) and that the provisions for reduction of JSA on sanctions under ss.6J and 6K of that Act do not apply. See the annotations to reg.5 in Vol. I of this series for discussion of the consequences. That note shows that the issues arising from the rule have been raised with the DWP by the Social Security Advisory Committee, but that it is currently unlikely that any changes will be made in the near future, as the DWP has higher priorities for legislative amendments. The equivalent provision for new style ESA purposes is reg.42 of the ESA Regulations 2013.

The central concept under these provisions is of a "sanctionable failure", which under s.26(1) (subject to reg.113 of the Universal Credit Regulations), and s.27(1), is to lead to a reduction in the amount of an award of universal credit. For higher-level sanctions under s.26, the reduction for most adult claimants initially was in brief of 100 per cent of the claimant's individual standard allowance for 91 days for a first higher-level failure, 182 days for a second such failure (or a new style ESA or JSA failure) within a year and 1095 days for a third or subsequent such failure within a year. However, the amendment with effect from November 27, 2019 has changed the period in the third category to 182 days. That is in fulfilment of Amber Rudd's undertaking noted above. Regulation 5(3) of the amending Regulations made the transitional provision that, where an award of universal credit was subject to a 1095-day reduction under s.26 as at November 27, 2019, that reduction was to be terminated where the award had been reduced for at least 182 days.

It must, though, be noted that there has been no amendment to reg.101(3) of the Universal Credit Regulations, which imposes a 1095-day limit on the total outstanding reduction period that is allowed. Because by virtue of reg.101(2) reduction periods under universal credit (as for new style JSA, but not old style JSA) run consecutively, the result is still that a claimant subject to a series of higher-level sanctions, each individually limited to 182 days, may be subject to a continuous reduction of benefit for up to 1095 days. The precise words of Amber Rudd's pledge set out above may thus have been carried out, but the effect is not as comprehensive as may have been thought.

There is no discretion under either ss.26 or 27 as to whether or not to apply a reduction if the conditions are met and no discretion under the regulations as to the amount and period of the reduction as calculated under the complicated formulae there. Regulation 113 of the Universal Credit Regulations, made under ss.26(8)(a) and 27(9)(a), sets out circumstances in which no reduction is to be made for a sanctionable failure. There is also provision for hardship payments under s.28.

As a matter of principle, a claimant has to be able, in any appeal against a reduction in benefit on the imposition of a sanction, to challenge whether the conditions for the imposition of sanction were met. See the note to s.24.

It has recently been stated that the Secretary of State need not in all sanctions cases provide evidence in the appeal bundle to support the satisfaction of all the preconditions to imposing a sanction, but that principle must be properly understood in context. In *SSWP v CN (JSA)* [2020] UKUT 26 (AAC), the claimant's sole ground of appeal against a sanction for failing to participate in the Work Programme by not attending an appointment was that she had never failed to keep an appointment (i.e. implicitly that she could not have received the notice of the appointment and/or had good cause under the regulations then in force). The tribunal allowed her appeal on the ground that the bundle did not contain a copy of the notice referring her to the Work Programme (i.e. the WP05) so that it was not satisfied that she had properly been notified of the requirement to participate. The tribunal appeared to think that that issue was one "raised by the appeal" within s.12(8)(a) of the SSA 1998, which it manifestly was not as the Secretary of State's submission in the bundle, not challenged by the claimant, was that there was no dispute that the claimant was referred to the Work Programme. Nor did it give any explanation, if it had exercised its discretion under s.12(8)(a) to consider the issue nonetheless, as to why it did so and how it was clearly apparent from the evidence so as to be capable of being dealt with under that discretion. Even if those hurdles had been overcome, the Secretary of State had not been given a fair opportunity to deal with the point. What evidence it was necessary for the Secretary of State to provide in the appeal bundle depended what issues have been put in dispute in the appeal. Having therefore set the tribunal's decision aside, Judge Wright substituted a decision finding on the evidence that the claimant had received the letter notifying her of the appointment in question.

The same approach was applied in *SSWP v SD (JSA)* [2020] UKUT 39 (AAC). There, the tribunal had raised and sought evidence on its own initiative on the issue whether the "prior information duty" (on which see the notes to s.14) had been satisfied at the stage of initial referral to the Work Programme, which the claimant had never challenged. As well as the s.12(8)(a) problem, the tribunal had failed to explain why, even if there was a breach of the duty at that stage, the breach was material. In substituting a decision the judge rejected any unfairness in the referral to the Work Programme and rejected on the evidence the claimant's contention about the appointment.

That view of what evidence must be provided in the appeal bundle as to satisfaction of the preconditions to imposing a sanction must be read in the light of the approach in *SSWP v DC (JSA)* [2017] UKUT 464 (AAC), reported as [2018] AACR 16, and *PO'R v DFC (JSA)* [2018] NI Com 1. There it was said that the Secretary of State should in all cases involving a failure to participate in some scheme or interview where notice of certain details of the scheme etc was required to be given, as well as notice of date, time and place, include in the appeal bundle a copy of the appointment letter, whether the claimant had raised any issue as to the terms of the letter or not. That was on the basis that unrepresented claimants could not be expected to identify technical issues about the validity of notices and it could not be predicted what particular issues might arise in the course of an appeal. If the letter was not included in the initial bundle, the decisions approved the action of tribunals in directing its production as a proper exercise of their inquisitorial jurisdiction. That exercise must rest on a use of the discretion in s.12(8)(a) to consider issues not raised by the appeal. The resolution of the approaches is no doubt that whenever a tribunal exercises that discretion it must do so consciously and explain why it has done so in any statement of reasons, and give the Secretary of State a fair opportunity to produce the document(s). It may be that an adequate explanation is to be found more readily when it is a notice of a specific appointment is in issue rather than an initial reference to a scheme. See also para.6 of *JB v SSWP (UC)* [2018] UKUT 360 (AAC), detailed in the notes to s.14.

Another important concept is that of a "good reason" for the conduct or failure to comply with a requirement under the WRA 2012. Most of the definitions of sanctionable failures in ss.26 and 27 incorporate the condition that the failure was "for no good reason". Paragraph 8 of Sch.1 to the Act allows regulations to prescribe circumstances in which a claimant is to be treated as having or as not having a good reason for an act or omission and to prescribe matters that are or are not to be taken into account in determining whether a claimant has a good reason. No regulations have been made under this power. There is no equivalent to reg.72 of the JSA Regulations 1996 (but the problem dealt with there is covered for universal credit by the allowance of limitations on work search and work availability requirements). The House of Commons Work and Pensions Committee (in para.111 of its report on *Benefit Sanctions*, above) recommended that regulations be introduced containing a non-exhaustive list of circumstances that could constitute good reason. The DWP (paras 66-69 of *Benefit Sanctions: Government Response*, above) rejected that recommendation as undermining flexibility, while noting that a list of good reasons is available in the DMG and on GOV.uk (the link provided in the response is to chapter K2 of the ADM for universal credit).

1.187 Thus, the concept of "good reason" remains an open-ended one, no doubt requiring consideration of all relevant circumstances but also containing a large element of judgment according to the individual facts of particular cases. The amount and quality of information provided to the claimant in the claimant commitment or otherwise about responsibilities under the WRA 2012 and the consequences of a failure to comply will no doubt be relevant, especially in the light of the approach of the Supreme Court in paras 65 and 66 of *R (on the application of Reilly and Wilson) v Secretary of State for Work and Pensions* [2013] UKSC 68; [2014] 1 A.C. 453 and of the Court of Appeal in *SSWP v Reilly and Hewstone* and *SSWP v Jeffrey and Bevan* [2016] EWCA Civ 413; [2017] Q.B. 657; [2017] AACR 14 (see the notes to s.14 above). Probably, in addition, as in the previously familiar concept of "just cause", a balancing is required between the interests of the claimant and those of the community whose contributions and taxes finance the benefit in question. See the discussion below in relation to subs.(4) and voluntarily and for no good reason ceasing paid work or losing pay.

In *SA v SSWP (JSA)* [2015] UKUT 454 (AAC), a decision on s.19A(2)(c) of the old style Jobseekers Act 1995 and failing to carry out a jobseeker's direction, Judge Knowles accepted the Secretary of State's submission that in determining whether a good reason had been shown for the failure all the circumstances should be considered and that the question was whether those circumstances would have caused a reasonable person (with the characteristics of the claimant in question) to act as the claimant did. Expressing the approach in such terms tends to point away from the notion of a balance.

However, there is a potentially significant difference in wording. In ss.26 and 27 and in ss.6J and 6K of the new style Jobseekers Act 1995 the condition is that the claimant fails "for no good reason", not that the claimant acts or omits to act "without a good reason". It may eventually be established that these two phrases have the same meaning, but in the ordinary use of language the phrase "for no good reason" carries a suggestion that something has been done or not done capriciously or arbitrarily, without any real thought or application of reason. It could therefore be argued that it is easier for a claimant to show that they did not act for no good reason and on that basis that the balancing of interests mentioned above could not be applicable. It would be enough that the claimant acted or failed to act rationally in the light of his or her own interests. It can of course be objected that such an argument fails to give the proper weight to the identification of what is a good reason and that it would seem contrary to the overall policy of the legislation if it was much easier to escape a universal credit sanction than an old style JSA sanction. On the other hand, it can be asked why Parliament chose to use a different phrase for the purposes of universal credit sanctions than "without a good reason" when the latter phrase could have fitted happily into ss.26 and 27. It is to be hoped that the ambiguity will eventually be resolved in decisions of the Upper Tribunal or the courts.

One of the points raised when permission to appeal to the Upper Tribunal was given in *S v SSWP (UC)* [2017] UKUT 477 (AAC) was whether "for no good reason" has any different meaning from "without a good reason". In para.54 Judge Mitchell expresses the view that there is no material difference and that both phrases refer to the absence of a good reason. However, the point made in the previous paragraph about a possible difference in meaning may not yet have been conclusively rejected, as it is not clear that in the particular circumstances of *S* it would have mattered which was adopted.

The case actually decides only a relatively short point about the meaning of "for no good reason" in ss.26 and 27 of the WRA 2012. The First-tier Tribunal had said that the claimant's professed ignorance of the effect of work (including part-time work) on his universal credit entitlement could not amount to a good reason for failing to undertake all reasonable work search action because ignorance of the law was no defence. On the claimant's appeal to the Upper Tribunal the Secretary of State accepted that, by analogy with the well-established case law on good cause for a delay in claiming, ignorance of the law was capable of constituting a good reason. The judge agreed that the tribunal had erred in law, but concluded that the error was not material because the only proper conclusion on the evidence was that the claimant could reasonably have been expected to raise with his work coach or other DWP official any concerns or confusions over the financial implications on his universal credit award of taking any of the sorts of work he had agreed to search for. Thus, even on the correct approach the claimant did not have a good reason for what the tribunal had concluded was a failure under s.27(2)(a).

It may also be that the analogy with good cause (indeed in para.57 the judge said that "good reason" expressed the same concept as "good cause" but in more modern language) is misleading or at least incomplete. That is because when considering good cause for a delay in claiming there is no difficulty in adopting the general meaning approved in *R(SB) 6/83* of some fact that, having regard to all the circumstances (including a claimant's state of health and the information that he had or might have obtained), would probably have caused a reasonable person of the same age and experience to act or fail to act as the claimant had done. It was in that context that the principle that a reasonable ignorance or mistaken belief as to rights could constitute good cause was established. But the question there is what a reasonable person could be expected to do to secure an advantage to them in the form of the benefit claimed late. In the context of universal credit sanctions, the notion of reasonableness carries a distinctly different force. So where the work search requirement under s.17(1)(a) to take all reasonable action to obtain paid work is concerned, reasonableness must be based on what level of activity the community that funds universal credit is entitled to expect from a claimant as a condition of receipt of the benefit. Similar, although not necessarily identical, factors are present in relation to the other work-related requirements and the sanctions for voluntarily and for no good reason ceasing work or losing pay. Although all personal circumstances are relevant, the notion of a balance between those circumstances and the claimant's proper responsibilities is not captured by the traditional concept of "good cause". The better analogy would seem to be with "just cause" as used in unemployment benefit and in old style JSA before the 2012 amendments. The adoption of the "good cause" approach in relation to claimed ignorance of rights in *S* cannot be taken as excluding such an approach. The full meaning of "for no good reason" remains to be worked out.

Subsections (2)–(4) set out what can be a sanctionable failure for the purposes of s.26 and higher-level sanctions. All except subs.(3) are restricted to claimants who are at the time of the sanctionable failure or the imposition of the sanction subject to all work-related requirements under s.22. Thus, claimants excused from all work-related requirements under s.19 (e.g. those with limited capability for work and work-related activity or with specified caring responsibilities) or from some element of such requirements under s.20 or 21 cannot be subject to higher level sanctions. They can be subject to s.27 sanctions. Subsections (5)–(8) give regulation-making powers.

Subsection (2)

(a) It is a higher-level sanctionable failure for a claimant subject to all work- **1.188**
related requirements to fail for no good reason (on which see the note above) to comply with a work preparation requirement under s.16 to undertake a work placement of a description prescribed in regulations. Regulation 114(1) of the Universal Credit Regulations prescribes Mandatory Work Activity as a work placement for the purposes of this provision (although the scheme has ceased to operate after April 2016) and reg.114(2) in its substituted form gives sufficient details of the scheme to satisfy the requirement in subs.(2)(a) to give a description and not just a label (the problem identified by the Court of Appeal in relation to the then state of the JSA legislation in *R (on the application of Reilly and Wilson) v Secretary of State for Work and Pensions* [2013] EWCA Civ 66; [2013] 1 W.L.R. 2239), as approved by the Supreme Court ([2013] UKSC 68; [2014] 1 A.C.453). That was decided in relation to s.17A(1) of the old style Jobseekers Act 1995 and reg.2 of

the Jobseeker's Allowance (Mandatory Work Activity Scheme) Regulations 2011 (where the description of the scheme is in substance the same as in reg.114) by Hickinbottom J in *R (Smith) v Secretary of State for Work and Pensions* [2014] EWHC 843 (Admin). That conclusion and the judge's reasoning was in essence endorsed by the Court of Appeal on the claimant's appeal ([2015] EWCA Civ 229).

Before undertaking a Mandatory Work Activity scheme could have become a work preparation requirement it must have been specified for the claimant in question by or on behalf of the Secretary of State and meet the condition of improving the particular claimant's work prospects. As the particular scheme and the potential application of subs.(2)(a) has been defunct for some years, cases on such specification and what amounts to a failure to participate in a scheme or a good reason for such a failure are discussed elsewhere in these notes.

(b) It is a higher-level sanctionable failure for a claimant subject to all work-related requirements to fail for no good reason (on which see the note above) to comply with a work search requirement under s.17 to apply for a particular vacancy for paid work. It would seem that for there to have been a requirement to apply for a particular vacancy the taking of that action must have been specified by or on behalf of the Secretary of State under s.17(1)(b). It appears that scheme providers can be authorised persons under s.29 to act on behalf of the Secretary of State to "mandate" claimants to apply for a particular vacancy or to accept it if offered (see note 3 to ADM para.K3051), though failing to accept the offer cannot lead to a sanction under subs.(2)(b), only under subs.(2)(c) by showing a failure to be available for work. See the note to s.17 for discussion of the meaning of "paid work", the notification of vacancies through Universal Jobmatch or the Find a job service and requirements to apply for vacancies in the claimant commitment. It appears in the nature of the word "vacancy" that it is for employment as an employed earner, or possibly some form of self-employment that is closely analogous to such employment, e.g. through an agency.

In *MT v SSWP (JSA)* [2016] UKUT 72 (AAC) doubts were expressed whether failure to register with an employment agency could fall within the equivalent provision for old style JSA (s.19(2)(c) of the old style Jobseekers Act 1995), at least without evidence of some specific vacancy. It is not entirely clear whether a vacancy has actually to exist at the time that the Secretary of State specifies that the claimant is to apply for it or whether it is enough that a vacancy is about to arise at that point (compare the terms of s.19(2)(c)). It may be that it is enough that the requirement is conditional on the post becoming open for applications before the next meeting with the work coach, but the "failure" cannot take place until applications are possible. And the claimant must have been given sufficient information about the vacancy in order to have been able to make meaningful representations at the time about whether the requirement should be imposed (see notes to s.14 for discussion of the "prior information duty"). Some doubt was expressed in *CJSA/4179/1997* whether the offer of a "trial" as a part-time car washer properly fell within s.19(2)(c). It was suggested that if it did not, the case should have been considered under s.19(2)(d) (neglect to avail oneself of a reasonable opportunity of employment), to which there is no direct equivalent in the universal credit legislation (see the notes to para.(c) below). But if applying for or accepting the offer of the trial had been specified by the Secretary of State as a work search action under s.17, failure to comply for no good reason would be a sanctionable failure under s.27(2)(a) of the WRA 2012.

There is no express provision that the vacancy is for work that is suitable for the claimant in question. However, plainly the question of suitability would be relevant to the issue of whether a claimant had no good reason for failing to apply for the vacancy, even in the absence of the decisions in *PL v DSD (JSA)* [2015] NI Com 72 (followed and applied in *PO'R v DFC (JSA)* [2018] NI Com 1). There, the Chief Commissioner for Northern Ireland approved and applied the obiter suggestion of Judge Ward in *PL v SSWP (JSA)* [2013] UKUT 227 (AAC) (on the pre-October 2012 form of the Great Britain legislation) that, in deciding whether claimants had good cause for failing to avail themselves of a reasonable opportunity of a place on a training scheme or employment programme, a tribunal erred in law, where the circumstances raised the issue, in failing to consider the appropriateness of the particular scheme or programme to the particular claimant in the light of their skills and experience and previous attendance on any placements. Judge Ward's suggestion had been that the test was whether the claimant had reasonably considered that what was provided would not help him. It seems likely that a similar general approach will be taken to the issue of "good reason" under s.26(2)(b) and the appropriateness of the vacancy in question, as also suggested in *MT* (above). It may though still need to be sorted out how far the issue turns on the claimant's subjective view, within the bounds of reasonableness, in the light of the information provided at the time, as against a tribunal's view of the appropriateness of the situation in employment. The Chief Commissioner made no comment in *PL* on the treatment of the claimant's refusal to complete and sign forms with information about criminal convictions and health, that the First-tier Tribunal had found were reasonably required by the training provider as part of its application process for the scheme, as a failure by the claimant to avail himself of a reasonable opportunity of a place on the training scheme. Regulation 113(1)(a) of the Universal Credit Regulations prevents any reduction in benefit being made when the vacancy was because of a strike arising from a trade dispute. According to the then Minister of State Esther McVey (House of Commons written answers April 2, 2014 and September 1, 2014) the instruction to Jobcentre Plus staff not to mandate claimants to apply for zero hours contracts applies only to JSA, not universal credit. However, again, and even though exclusivity clauses have been made unenforceable from May 26, 2015 by the new s.27A of the Employment Rights Act 1996, the suitability of such a contract for the particular claimant will certainly be relevant to the issue of no good reason.

Failure to apply for a vacancy no doubt encompasses an outright refusal to apply and also behaviour that is "tantamount to inviting a refusal by the employer to engage [the claimant]" (*R(U) 28/55*, para.7). In that case the claimant had presented himself for an interview for a job as a parcel porter in what the employer had described as a dirty and unshaven state, as a result of which he was not engaged. The Commissioner accepted that on the employer's evidence the claimant had neglected to avail himself of a reasonable opportunity of suitable employment. There is no reason why that general approach should not also apply in the present context.

It has long been accepted that a refusal or failure to complete an unobjectionable application form can amount to a failure to apply (see *R(U) 32/52* and *CJSA/2692/1999*). As Commissioner Howell noted in para.5 of *CJSA/4665/2001* there will be cases:

> "where the way a claimant completes or spoils a job application will be unsatisfactory and unfit to put in front of any employer so as to prevent it counting as a genuine application at all, so that he or she will have 'failed to apply': it is all a question of fact."

In *CJSA/4665/2001* itself, though, the Employment Service had refused to pass on otherwise properly completed application forms because the claimant had included criticisms of the Service and of government training initiatives. The Commissioner held that in the absence of any evidence that employers had been or would have been put off from considering the claimant by his comments or of any evidence of an intention to spoil his chances it had not been shown that he had failed to apply for the vacancies. A similar approach has been taken by Commissioner Rowland in a case in which the claimant disputed the necessity of including a photograph with the application form (*CJSA/2082/2002* and *CJSA/5415/2002*). As the employment officer did not have clear information from the employer contrary to the claimant's contention and had not tested the matter by submitting a form without a photograph, the sanction should not have been applied.

See the notes to para.(a) above for further discussion of good reason. Apart from the suitability and location of the work, personal, domestic and financial circumstances might be relevant. No doubt, as in the past, conscientious or religious objections would need particularly careful consideration. For instance, in *R(U) 2/77* (on neglect to avail) the claimant's sincerely held objection on what he described as moral grounds to joining a trade union were held to make to make an opportunity of employment unsuitable and unreasonable (and see *R(U) 5/71* for a case where a more intellectual conviction against joining a teachers' registration scheme did not have that effect). For a further example on its own facts (and no more than that) of a potential good reason for not applying for a vacancy, see *GR v SSWP (JSA)* [2013] UKUT 645 (AAC), where it was held that a claimant with a genuine fear that prevented him going to the town where a course was to take place had good cause (under reg.7 of the Jobseeker's Allowance (Employment, Skills and Enterprise Scheme) Regulations 2011) for failing to participate in the scheme.

In *KB v SSWP (UC)* [2019] UKUT 408 (AAC) the claimant failed to apply for a vacancy (as a barista) as she had agreed with her work coach to do. She said that she had later concluded that there was no point in applying, as she was temperamentally unsuited to the employer's requirements (she did not have "a passion for coffee" and was an introvert). The judge suggests that, in the absence of any further consultation with the work coach about the matter, there could not be a good reason for the failure. Although there was a misguided emphasis by the Secretary of State and the First-tier Tribunal on what the claimant agreed to do in her claimant commitment, there was no dispute that the Secretary of State had, through the work coach, "required" her to take the specified action of applying for the vacancy by, after discussion, saving the details to her Universal Jobmatch account.

Regulation 94 of the Universal Credit Regulations deems a claimant not to have complied with a requirement to apply for a particular vacancy for paid work where the claimant fails to participate in an interview offered in connection with the vacancy. Participation must at least entail turning up at the place and time for the interview, although the decision of Judge Knowles in *SA v SSWP (JSA)* [2015] UKUT 454 (AAC) (see the notes to s.27 for full discussion) would indicate that tribunals should consider, in cases where the claimant arrives not very late, whether it is proportionate to the nature of all the circumstances to regard that as a failure to participate in an interview. There were all sorts of mitigating circumstances in *SA*, that may well not be present in other cases. Participation must also extend to making some meaningful contribution to the interview, but the limits will probably not be established until there have been some more sanctions appeals to the Upper Tribunal. Behaviour that leads to the premature termination of the interview may well amount to a failure to participate (see the facts of *DM v SSWP (JSA)* [2015] UKUT 67 (AAC) in the notes to s.27(2)(b)). There may, though, in cases of uncooperative claimants or heavy-handed officials or a combination, be difficult questions about when an interview has ceased to exist, so that subsequent behaviour cannot be relevant to whether there has been a failure to participate (see *PH v SSWP (ESA)* [2016] UKUT 119 (AAC) on failing to submit to a medical examination).

See *SN v SSWP (JSA)* [2018] UKUT 279 (AAC) and *CS v SSWP (JSA)* [2019] UKUT 218 (AAC), detailed in the notes to s.27(2)(a), for further helpful discussion of what might amount to a failure to participate (in those cases in a mandatory work activity scheme and a work programme scheme) and the expression in para.45 of *SN* of some doubt about the result in *SA*.

Where non-compliance with the requirement to apply for a vacancy is constituted by failure to participate in an interview, good reason must extend to good reason for that failure to participate. There appear to be no provisions prescribing the length of notice of an interview to be given or how far a claimant can be required to travel, but there could plainly be a good reason for failing to comply with unreasonable requirements, especially if the claimant had attempted in advance to draw any problem with attendance to the attention of the Secretary of State or the potential employer.

(c) It is a higher-level sanctionable failure for a claimant subject to all work-related requirements to fail for no good reason (on which see the note above) to comply with a work availability requirement under s.18 by not taking up an offer of paid work. See the note to s.17 for discussion of the meaning of "paid work". Since the requirement under s.18 is in the very general terms of being able and willing immediately to take up paid work, the relevance of not taking up an offer can only be in revealing an absence of such ability or willingness. Therefore, both any limitations under reg.97 of the Universal Credit Regulations on the kinds of paid work that a claimant must be able and willing to take up immediately and the provisions of reg.96(2)–(5) on when a claimant is deemed to have complied with the requirement despite not being able to satisfy the "immediately" condition must be taken into account in determining whether a claimant has failed to comply with the requirement.

There is case law on what might amount to refusing or failing to accept a situation in employment that is vacant or about to become vacant (under s.19(2)(c) of the old style Jobseekers Act 1995) that may still be relevant, subject to possible differences between that test and not taking up an offer of paid work. Accepting an offer but then telling lies which caused the employer to withdraw it was treated as refusal in a Northern Ireland decision (*R 6/50 (UB)*). In *CSU/7/1995* the claimant accepted the offer of a job of a lampshade maker at a wage of £79 per week, having been informed of the vacancy by the Employment Service. But she changed her mind and did not start the job because the wage was too low to meet her commitments. The tribunal decided that since she did accept the offer of employment, the equivalent of s.19(2)(c) did not operate to disqualify her from receiving unemployment benefit. However, the Commissioner held that although, normally, acceptance of an offer of a situation would be tantamount to accepting the situation it could not have been intended that it would be possible to defeat the operation of the legislation by an acceptance in theory but a repudiation in practice. The claimant had not "accepted the situation" within the meaning of the legislation.

See also *CJSA/4179/1997* in which the claimant was offered a "trial" as a part-time car washer. The tribunal dealt with the case under s.19(2)(c) of the old style Jobseekers Act 1995, but the Commissioner expressed doubt as to whether the "trial" was an offer of a "situation in any employment". The tribunal should have investigated what the trial involved. If that provision did not apply, the equivalent of s.19(2)(d) (neglect to avail oneself of a reasonable opportunity of employment) should then have been considered. There is no equivalent of s.19(2)(d) in s.26. However, it may be that even a "trial", if remunerated, is an offer of paid work.

Presumably a claimant escapes a sanction under this head by showing either a good reason for not accepting the particular offer, if that offer is compatible with the availability requirements currently imposed by the Secretary of State, or a good reason why those requirements should have been different in some way. See the notes to para.(b) above and the cases mentioned there for discussion of the relevance of the suitability of the work in question for the particular claimant. See also reg.113(1)(a) of the Universal Credit Regulations excluding reductions in benefit on consideration of vacancies due to strikes arising from trade disputes.

(d) It is a higher-level sanctionable failure for a claimant subject to all work-related requirements to cease paid work or lose pay by reason of misconduct or voluntarily and for no good reason (on which see the notes above). Since by definition the claimant must, if already subject to s.22, have an award of universal credit, this sanction can only apply to those claimants who are entitled to the benefit while in work. See the note to s.17 for discussion of the meaning of "paid work". See the note to subs.(4) below for discussion of the meanings of "misconduct" and "voluntarily and for no good reason", as well as of the implications of fixed and severe sanctions for losing pay apparently no matter what the amount of loss, subject to the exception from reductions in benefit in reg.113(1)(g) of the Universal Credit Regulations (earnings have not fallen below the level set in reg.99(6)). See the further exceptions in reg.113(1)(b) (trial periods in work where the claimant attempts hours additional to a limitation under ss.17(4) or 18(3)); (c) (voluntarily ceasing paid work or losing pay because of a strike); (d) (voluntarily ceasing paid work or losing pay as a member of the regular or reserve forces); and (f) (volunteering for redundancy or lay-off or short-time).

Subsection (3)

1.189 This provision applies to claimants with an award of universal credit who are subject to no work-related requirements under s.19(2)(d) because reg.90 of the Universal Credit Regulations, made under the specific powers in s.19(3), applies s.19 where the claimant's earnings equal or exceed the individual threshold, called by the DWP the conditionality earnings threshold. If the claimant ceases the paid work from which those earnings are derived or loses pay so that the earnings are then below the individual threshold, either by reason of misconduct or voluntarily and for no good reason (on which see the note above), and does not fall within either s.20 or 21, a higher-level sanction is to be imposed. See the note to subs.(4) below for discussion of the meanings of "misconduct" and "voluntarily and for no good reason". The exception in reg.113(1)(g) of the Universal Credit Regulations (earnings have not fallen below the level set in reg.99(6)) cannot by definition apply if this provision applies. If reg.99(6) (monthly earnings equal or exceed the (lower) administrative earnings threshold calculated by reference to specified hours at national minimum wage level) applies to the new level of earnings, no work search requirement can be imposed and the claimant therefore does not fall within s.22 (subject to all work-related requirements). In that case, subs.(3) cannot apply under its own terms and no exception is needed. If, as part of the ongoing process of working out an acceptable approach to in-work conditionality by subjecting claimants to pilot schemes under the Universal Credit (Work-Related Requirements) In Work Pilot Scheme and Amendment Regulations 2015 (see the notes to reg.99(6) and (6A) of the Universal Credit Regulations for discussion), entitlement is to be determined on the basis that reg.99(6) does not exist, then the terms of the exception in reg.113(1)(g) cannot apply either. A very slight decrease in earnings could, in a marginal case, have the effect identified in subs.(3), yet (no regulations having been made under subs.(5)(b)) the full force of the higher-level sanction must be imposed. It may be that in such circumstances it will be correspondingly easier for a claimant to show that a voluntary loss of pay was not "for no good reason". These issues will have to be worked out during the operation of the in-work conditionality pilot schemes mentioned above, which apparently expose claimants subject to them to very severe sanctions rules, although the DWP has stated that sanctions will be applied for failures to comply with in-work requirements under a pilot scheme "in the last resort" (see the notes to reg.99(6) and (6A)). See also the further exceptions in reg.113(1)(c) (voluntarily ceasing paid work or losing pay because of a strike); (d) (voluntarily ceasing paid work or losing pay as a member of the regular or reserve forces); and (f) (volunteering for redundancy or applying for a redundancy payment after lay-off or short-time).

Subsection (4)

1.190 Where a claimant has an award of universal credit and is subject to all work-related requirements under s.22 it is a higher-level sanctionable failure if before making the claim relevant to the award the claimant for no good reason failed to take up an offer of paid work (para.(a)) or by reason of misconduct or voluntarily and for no good reason ceased paid work or lost pay (para.(b)). A practical limit to how far back before the date of claim such action or inaction can be to lead to a reduction of benefit is set by regs 102(4) and 113(1)(e) of the Universal Credit Regulations. If the gap between the action or inaction and the date of claim is longer than or equal to the period of the reduction that would otherwise be imposed, there is to be no reduction. Thus a lot depends on whether it is a first, second or subsequent "offence" within a year. These two grounds of sanction are the most similar to the familiar JSA grounds now in s.19(2)(a), (b) and (c) of the old style Jobseekers Act 1995.

Under para.(a), see the discussion in the note to subs.(2)(c), but note that this sanction applies to any offer of paid work. Therefore, all questions of whether the work is suitable for the claimant and whether or not it was reasonable for the claimant not to take it up will have to be considered under the "no good reason" condition. See the introductory part of the note to this section for the meaning of that phrase as compared with "without a good reason".

Under para.(b), it would appear that misconduct and voluntarily ceasing work will have the same general meaning as misconduct and leaving employment voluntarily for the purposes of old style JSA and, before it, unemployment benefit, on which see the extensive discussion below. The scope of the sanction has to be wider to take account of the nature of universal credit. Ceasing paid work certainly has a significantly wider meaning than losing employment as an employed earner if it encompasses self-employment in addition, as suggested in the note to s.17. The notion of ceasing paid work seems in itself wider than that of losing employment and to avoid difficulties over whether suspension from work without dismissal and particular ways of bringing a contract of employment to an end are covered. But remember that under reg.113(1)(f) of the Universal Credit Regulations a reduction cannot be applied on the ground of voluntarily ceasing work where the claimant has volunteered for redundancy or has claimed a redundancy payment after being subject to lay-off or short-time working, although the action remains a sanctionable failure. See also the exceptions for voluntarily ceasing paid work or losing pay because of a strike arising from a trade dispute or as a member of the regular or reserve forces (reg.113(1)(c) and (d)).

The other particularly significant widening of the scope of the sanction as compared with those in old style JSA is in the application of this and the similar sanctions under previous subsections to losing pay as well as to ceasing paid work. This is necessary, both in relation to circumstances before the date of claim and later, because it is possible for a claimant to be entitled to universal credit while still in paid work. If the earnings from the work are below the amount of the claimant's work allowance (if and as applicable according to circumstances) they are disregarded in the calculation of any award (see reg.22(1)(b) of the Universal Credit Regulations). If they exceed that amount, 55 per cent of the excess is taken into account as income to be set against the maximum amount of universal credit. If a claimant does not have a work allowance, 55 per cent of earnings are taken into account. 1.191

There are also the rules, under s.19(2)(d) and (3), in reg.90 of the Universal Credit Regulations making a claimant subject to no work-related conditions if earnings are at least equal to an individual threshold (in the standard case the National Minimum Wage for 35 hours per week, with lesser hours used in defined circumstances), the conditionality earnings threshold. The sanction regime under subs.(4) can only apply when at the time of the award in question the claimant is subject to all work-related requirements under s.22 and so cannot be receiving earnings at or above that individual threshold. Subsection (3) above deals with the situation where during the course of an award of universal credit a claimant moves from having earnings at least equal to the individual threshold to a situation where the earnings are lower than that threshold. For loss of pay, short of the ceasing of work, prior to the date of claim to trigger the application of the sanction under subs.(3) it must be within a fairly narrow limit. To bring the claimant within the scope of s.22 the loss of pay must leave earnings below the individual threshold and also below the (lower) administrative earnings threshold in reg.99(6), which exempts claimants from the work search requirement.

Old style JSA authority on losing employment through misconduct and universal credit

As explained above, the authority built up in unemployment benefit and old style JSA remains highly relevant to universal credit sanctions for ceasing paid work or losing pay by reason of misconduct. Possible points of difference will be noted below. 1.192

"*Loses employment as an employed earner*". This concept was not confined to dismissal, but could also embrace persons claiming benefit while suspended from 1.193

work for misconduct (*R(U) 10/71*) and the person who accepts the chance to resign rather than be dismissed as a result of their misconduct (*R(U) 2/76*, where the claimant used a company car without permission to give driving lessons and was found at home in the bath when he should have been out selling). In *CU/56/1989*, Commissioner Heggs, dealing with a situation in which the claimant had been allowed to resign rather than be dismissed, noted in para.7:

> "In Decision *R(U) 17/64* it was held that 'loss of employment' is a more comprehensive phrase than 'leaving voluntarily' because loss of employment may result either from voluntarily leaving or from dismissal. In considering whether employment has been lost through misconduct, therefore, it is not always necessary to determine categorically whether the claimant left voluntarily or was dismissed. In the present case the tribunal, in my view, correctly concluded that the claimant lost his employment through misconduct."

The claimant had been allowed to resign rather than be dismissed after he had been caught eating company products (pies) at his workplace in violation of a general prohibition on eating company products in the production area. He had previously violated this rule and been warned about his conduct. He had also received a final written warning that future misconduct would result in his summary dismissal. Unfortunately, the SSAT decision was erroneous in law because it contained no explanation of why the claimant's admitted conduct constituted misconduct.

The notion of ceasing paid work in s.26 cannot be any narrower than that of losing employment, if not wider in encompassing any route to ceasing work, quite apart from the addition of the category of losing pay as a result of misconduct. That seems to open up the possibility of a sanction for someone in part-time work who remains in that employment, but is disciplined and subjected to deductions from earnings or given reduced hours of work by reason of misconduct. There is definitely a wider application through the use of the term "paid work", which would apply to self-employment as well as employment and avoids some of the other problems about the meaning of "employment" in old style JSA (see the notes to s.19(2)(a) of the old style Jobseekers Act 1995 in Vol.V of this series, 2021/22 edition as updated in Cumulative Supplements included in this volume and in mid-year Supplements).

1.194 "*Through misconduct*". The term in s.26 is "by reason of", but there is nothing to indicate that any difference of substance was intended. The old style JSA principle was that the loss of employment must be brought about because of the claimant's misconduct, not anyone else's. Any contrary reading would be absurd and unjust and contrary to the aim of penalising "voluntary unemployment".

Where there were several reasons for the loss of employment, the claimant's misconduct did not need to be the sole cause of the loss of employment so long as it was a contributory cause, a necessary element in bringing about the loss (*R(U) 1/57*; *R(U) 14/57*; *CU/34/92*). Suggestions that it had to be the main cause in order to ground disqualification read too much into *R(U) 20/59*, where the Commissioner's statement that misconduct (trouble with the police) was there the main cause seems to be no more than a finding of fact in that particular case in which the multiple cause point was not really an issue.

1.195 *The meaning and scope of misconduct*. "Misconduct" has never been statutorily defined. Case law offers such definition as there is. The term has to be interpreted in a common-sense manner and applied with due regard to the circumstances of each case (*R(U) 24/56*; *R(U) 8/57*, para.6). It is narrower than unsatisfactory conduct (*R 124/51 (UB)*). Misconduct is "conduct which is causally but not necessarily directly connected with the employment, and having regard to the relationship of employer and employee and the rights and duties of both, can fairly be described as blameworthy, reprehensible and wrong" (*R(U) 2/77*, para.15). The Commissioner, in para.6, saw nothing wrong with a tribunal's description of it as an indictment of the claimant's character as an employee. A useful test, particularly where the conduct in question occurred away from work, would be: was the claimant's blameworthy, reprehensible or wrong conduct such as would cause a reasonable employer to dispense with their services on the ground that, having regard to this conduct they were not a fit person to hold that appointment (*R(U) 7/57*, para.6).

The act or omission alleged to constitute misconduct need not have been deliberate or intentional, although such might often be the case. Misconduct can consist in carelessness or negligence, but there it is necessary to discriminate between that type and degree of carelessness which may have to be put up with in human affairs, and the more deliberate or serious type of carelessness which justifies withholding benefit because the claimant has lost their employment through their own avoidable fault. In *R(U) 8/57* the claimant, a manager of a branch pharmacy, was dismissed for "negligence in the discharge of responsible duties" when a number of cash shortages were discovered over a period of weeks. Serious carelessness could legitimately be inferred and his disqualification was upheld, notwithstanding his acquittal on a charge of embezzlement arising out of the same situation. A claimant who acts on a genuine misunderstanding cannot properly be said to be guilty of misconduct; the behaviour cannot there be described as "blameworthy, reprehensible and wrong" (*CU/122/92*, para.6, citing *R(U) 14/56*).

Where the conduct grounding the loss of employment might be regarded as whistleblowing (public interest disclosure) the public interest disclosure provisions in the Employment Rights Act 1996 (ss.43A–43L, 47B and 103) should be considered, since the question of whether the disclosure was a protected one is relevant to the question of whether the conduct was blameworthy, reprehensible and wrong. Judge Mesher so held in *AA v SSWP (JSA)* [2012] UKUT 100 (AAC), reported as [2012] AACR 42 (see especially paras 10–15). There it had been appropriate for the claimant School Manager to refer concerns about the head teacher's expenses claim to the appropriate LEA officer and probably to the school governors. However, the misconduct found by the disciplinary panel and grounding the dismissal (the "loss of employment") was his disclosure to several other employees to whom, under the legislation, it was not reasonable to disclose the matter. So that, while the tribunal had erred in law by not considering the public interest disclosure provisions, that error was not material. Note that with effect from June 25, 2013, s.43B(1) of the Employment Rights Act has been amended to add the specific condition that the worker reasonably believes that the disclosure is made in the public interest (see *Chesterton Global Ltd v Nurmohamed* [2017] EWCA Civ 979; [2018] I.C.R. 731). In *Kilraine v Wandsworth LBC* [2018] EWCA Civ 1436; [2018] I.C.R. 1850 it is clarified that, to qualify, a disclosure must in its context have sufficient factual content to count as a disclosure of "information".

Misconduct which occurred before the claimant took up the employment, the loss of which by reason of the misconduct is under consideration, cannot ground a sanction: see *R(U) 26/56*, where an accountant was dismissed when his employers learned of a conviction for fraud which occurred before he commenced employment with them. There, both the conduct and its consequences (the criminal conviction) occurred before the employment was taken up. *R(U) 1/58* applied the same principle where the conduct occurred before the taking-up of the employment, but the consequences came after its commencement. There a civil engineer and buyer was awaiting trial for certain acts committed before he entered the employment. By agreement with his employer he ceased work pending the result of the trial. On conviction, he simply did not return to the employment. Nor, however, was he pressed to do so. The Commissioner held that "acts or omissions occurring before the commencement of the employment do not constitute 'misconduct'" (at para.4), citing *R(U) 26/56*, so the only matter remaining was the issue of voluntary leaving without just cause. The leaving was not voluntary: "he merely anticipated a decision by his employers to dispense with his services; he was not altogether a free agent when deciding or agreeing not to attend further at his place of business" (at paras 5 and 6). So, to refer to a case of interest notified to the authors, an SSAT was correct in holding that a van driver, dismissed after conviction of a drink-driving offence and disqualification from driving, could not be disqualified from benefit because the conduct constituting the offence had taken place before he took up the employment in question, even though the conviction came after he had done so.

It may perhaps be arguable that the authority discussed in the previous paragraph depended to an extent on an adoption (whether explicit or implicit) of the "causal theory" of unemployment benefit disqualifications, that the primary object was not to penalise the claimant, but more to discourage avoidable claims against the fund from which benefit was paid. As it was put in *R(U) 20/64*, the "basic purpose of unemployment benefit is to provide against the misfortune of unemployment happening against a person's will". Thus there was a responsibility on a claimant to do what was reasonable to avoid becoming a burden on the fund that could only arise once the claimant became employed. The causal theory was in the past bolstered by the limitation of the period of disqualification to a maximum of six weeks, after which time it was said that the primary cause of continued unemployment was the state of the labour market, rather than the claimant's act of misconduct or leaving employment voluntarily or whatever. Now that the sanctions regime gives every appearance of imposing penalties, with more extensive periods of exclusion from benefit possible (even though now reduced from their peak), it might be argued that it is irrelevant to whether such penalties are deserved or not that the misconduct occurred before the claimant started the employment that was later lost. However, it is submitted that to constitute misconduct an act still has to be "blameworthy" in the context of the employment relationship and that there cannot be blameworthiness in that sense if the person has not yet taken up the employment in question.

Note, however, that instances of dishonesty during employment or in the application or appointment process about matters occurring before the employment starts can properly be regarded as misconduct. Examples might be knowingly answering inaccurately questions on an application form about previous convictions or matters that might embarrass the prospective employer. There might even be some special categories of office or employment where there can be said to be an ongoing duty to disclose information, so that merely continuing to keep quiet about a matter, even though not specifically asked about it, would be misconduct during the office or employment (see *R. (on the application of the Chief Constable of Thames Valley Police) v Legally Qualified Chair* [2024] EWHC 1454 (Admin) in the very particular police context).

The causal connection with the employment need not be direct (*R(U) 2/77*, para.15), though there the refusal to join a union in a closed shop was found not to be misconduct. The conduct need not have taken place at work or in working hours, though cases where it did will be common. In *R(U) 1/71* the Chief Commissioner upheld the disqualification of a local authority parks' gardener dismissed for an act of gross indecency with another man, away from work and out of working hours (although apparently not in private within the meaning of s.1 of the Sexual Offences Act 1967), but reduced the period of disqualification to one week (an option not available under the current legislation). The Commissioner said in para.10:

> "If a person loses his employment by reason of misconduct which has a sufficient connection with the employment it may not matter that it was committed outside the employment. Common examples are those of the man employed as a motor vehicle driver who loses his licence as a result of his driving outside his employment and is disqualified from driving: there is an obvious link between the misconduct and the work. [See, e.g. *R(U) 7/57* and *R(U) 24/64*.] Similarly a person who commits offences of dishonesty outside his work may be disqualified . . ., since most employers regard a thief as unsuitable to have about their premises. [See, e.g. *R(U) 10/53*.]" (Case references added by annotator)

Sexual offences outside the employment were said by the Commissioner in para.11 to present considerable difficulty but could rank as misconduct in special circumstances where they could be said to have something to do with the employment:

"The commercial traveller's case [*CU/381/51*] is a good instance. The employers may well have thought that there was a real danger that when visiting houses trying to sell ribbons, probably to women who might often be alone in the house, the claimant might attempt some sort of liberties. Further, there are some employments where the employer has a legitimate interest in the conduct of employees even outside the employment. One example may be that of a person who holds a special position, e.g. a school teacher. Another may be that of an employee of a government department or a local authority, who rightly feel that their employees should maintain a high standard of conduct at all times."

In *R(U) 1/71* itself, even though the claimant did not work in public parks, the Commissioner, in a case he thought close to the line, was not prepared to overturn the tribunal's view that the claimant had lost his employment through misconduct, though substantially reducing the period of disqualification. Modern sensibilities might make the assessment of such circumstances more complex. On the one hand, there is a widespread feeling that no opprobrium should attach to the acts involved in the offence concerned. On the other, there is perhaps a more widespread feeling than in the past that actions and opinions outside employment are relevant to whether that employment should continue.

Examples of misconduct. Apart from those already noted, instances have been: 1.196
persistent absenteeism without permission (*R(U) 22/52*, *R(U) 8/61*); unauthorised absence through ill health and/or domestic circumstances when coupled with failure to notify the employer (*R(U) 23/58*; *R(U) 11/59*); repeated unauthorised absence to seek work more suited to the claimant's state of health in circumstances in which the claimant gave the employer no reasons for his absences and he had received previous warnings about his conduct (*R(U) 8/61*); overstaying a holiday without permission (*R(U) 2/74*; *R(U) 11/59*). Theft from fellow workers at a works' social function has been held to be misconduct (*R(U) 10/53*). So has offensive behaviour to fellow employees, consisting of obscene language and an element of what would now be termed sexual harassment (suggestive remarks to and, in their presence, about female colleagues) (*R(U) 12/56*). By analogy, one would today expect many other types of abuse and discrimination to be capable of constituting misconduct. Recklessly or knowingly making false allegations about superiors or colleagues can be misconduct, and where a false criminal charge is so laid it would plainly be misconduct (*R(U) 24/55*, para.13), but it was not enough to prove misconduct to show that the employee's charge of assault by his supervisor had been dismissed in the magistrates' court (*ibid*). Refusal to obey a reasonable instruction in line with the claimant's contract of employment (e.g. a refusal to work overtime) has been held to be misconduct (*R(U) 38/58*), even where obeying the instruction would conflict with trade union policies (*R(U) 41/53*). However, disobedience of such an order due to a genuine misunderstanding has been held not to constitute misconduct (*R(U) 14/56*), and not every breach of every trivial rule would suffice (*R(U) 24/56*). And, of course, the claimant can legitimately refuse to obey instructions not contractually stipulated for without its constituting misconduct (*R(U) 9/59*; *R 9/60 (UB)*). Where an employee was dismissed for refusing to join a trade union as part of a closed-shop arrangement negotiated after his employment commenced, he did not lose his job through misconduct *(R(U) 2/77)*.

Establishing misconduct, matters of proof and the duties of the statutory authorities; 1.197
decision-makers, First-tier Tribunals and the Upper Tribunal. The Secretary of State (decision-maker) bears the onus of proof of establishing misconduct, and it must be clearly proved by the best available evidence. As a general rule, of course, hearsay evidence can be accepted by the statutory authorities, but particularly where a claimant is charged with misconduct and disputes the facts that are alleged to constitute it, "it is desirable that the most direct evidence of those facts should be adduced, so that the allegations may be properly tested" (*R(U) 2/60*, para.7).

Officers of the Secretary of State now have extensive powers to require employers to provide information (see, e.g. ss.109A and 109B of the SSAA 1992) and First-tier

Tribunals have power to summons witnesses and/or require them to produce documents and answer questions (reg.16 of the Tribunal Procedure (First-tier Tribunal) (Social Entitlement Chamber) Rules 2008: Vol.III of this series). Nevertheless, the use of such powers is often considered out of proportion if, say, an employer is reluctant to supply much detail on request and it may be difficult to get to the truth of the matter. In some cases the statutory authorities may be able to have regard to what has happened in other legal or disciplinary proceedings arising out of the same situation now said to show misconduct. Where such proceedings are pending one option in difficult cases where the available evidence about the relevant conduct conflicts would be to postpone a decision on the "sanctionable failure" issue until the outcome of such proceedings as are pending is known. There is no obligation to await their outcome (*R(U) 10/54* and see *AA v SSWP (JSA)* [2012] AACR 42, above), and one must always keep in view the relationship between those proceedings and the precise issues before new style JSA tribunals.

Another option would be to try to resolve the matter by weighing and comparing the evidence available (e.g. does the tribunal believe the direct evidence given by a claimant it has seen and questioned and how does that compare with the indirect and/or hearsay evidence in any written material from the employer or others which is relied on by the decision-maker) and ultimately, where doubts persist, allow the matter to be settled by application of the rules on onus of proof. It would presumably be open to the decision-maker to revise or supersede the tribunal's decision if new material facts came to light in the course of those other proceedings. The other legal proceedings could be criminal proceedings, court proceedings for breach of contract, or complaints of unfair dismissal heard in employment tribunals. Disciplinary proceedings may take place before a much wider variety of bodies. An important issue is what is the relationship to the decision-making task of the JSA decision-makers and tribunals, of decisions given by these other bodies on a matter relevant to the claimant's case?

While in varying degrees decisions given by such bodies certainly can constitute relevant evidence for the statutory authorities, they are not, legally speaking, conclusive of the outcome before the universal credit authorities, who are duty bound to make up their own minds as to what constitutes misconduct grounding reduction of benefit, irrespective of the conclusions reached by employers, the courts or other tribunals or disciplinary bodies (*R(U) 10/54*, para.6; *R(U) 2/74*, para.15). The other proceedings do not deal with the exact issue dealt with by the universal credit decision-makers and tribunals. For example, a motoring conviction as a private motorist which did not attract a ban from driving would not necessarily constitute misconduct warranting the disqualification of a lorry-driver who had been sacked by their employer as a result. It would depend on the nature of the conduct constituting the offence: the claimant might be able to show that notwithstanding the conviction their conduct was not "blameworthy" (*R(U) 22/64*, para.6). It must be remembered too that the standard of proof of guilt in criminal cases is proof beyond reasonable doubt, a higher standard than that applicable here—proof on the balance of probabilities. So an acquittal on a criminal charge arising out of the conduct now said to constitute misconduct does not necessarily preclude a finding of misconduct. Thus in *R(U) 8/57*, where the manager of the branch pharmacy was acquitted of embezzlement in relation to the cash shortages, he nonetheless lost his employment through misconduct since his inadequate supervision of staff amounted to serious carelessness.

Similarly, there are important differences between proceedings before First-tier Tribunals on the one hand, and unfair dismissal proceedings in the employment tribunal on the other. In unfair dismissal, while the employee's conduct is relevant, the main issue before the employment tribunal concerns the employer's behaviour in consequence. Before the tribunals dealing with universal credit, in contrast, the emphasis is more on the employee's conduct, although that of the employer is also relevant. The issues of losing employment through misconduct and of ceasing paid work by reason of misconduct entail consideration of what is fair between claimant and the other contributors to the insurance fund and not simply what is fair as between employer and employee. Commissioners stressed that social security tribunals when dealing with misconduct cases should not express their decisions in such terms as fair or unfair dismissal or proper or improper dismissal. The onus of proof in employment tribunal proceedings may not be the same on relevant issues as it is in proceedings before those universal credit tribunals. Equally, while the issue before universal credit tribunals is one of substance, the employment tribunal can find a dismissal unfair on procedural grounds. Hence, while the decision of the employment tribunal is conclusive of the matters it had to decide, it does not conclude anything in proceedings before universal credit decision-makers and tribunals, and its findings of fact are not binding on them, even where some of the facts before the employment tribunals are identical with facts relevant to the universal credit proceedings:

> "There will, therefore, be cases where a claimant succeeds before an [employment] tribunal on the unfair dismissal question, but the relevant adjudicating authority has decided that disqualification [from benefit] must be imposed by reason of misconduct, and vice versa." (per Commissioner Rice in *CU/90/1988*, para.4)

The findings of fact in the employment tribunal are, however, cogent evidence on which universal credit decision-makers and tribunals can act (*CU/17/1993*), since it may well be that with both employer and employee present and examined by the employment tribunal, a judicial authority presided over by a lawyer, reaching its deliberate findings of fact after due inquiry, it is better placed than the universal credit decision-makers and tribunals to fully investigate the facts of the matter. But the universal credit decision-makers and tribunals are not bound to decide the facts in the same way as the employment tribunal (*R(U) 2/74*, paras 14 and 15 and see generally on the relationship between the two sets of proceedings: *R(U) 4/78* and *R(U) 3/79*).

For similar reasons of ability to obtain and to probe evidence, decisions of the criminal courts on matters relevant to the case before universal credit decision-makers and tribunals are entitled to great respect. Thus, where it is clear that a criminal court has decided the identical issue which the claimant needs to reopen before the judicial authorities (First-tier or Upper Tribunal) in order to succeed in their appeal, the decision of that court is likely in practice to have considerable weight before those authorities. The approach in *R(U) 24/55* that in such circumstances the benefit authorities must, save in exceptional cases, treat a conviction by a criminal court as conclusive proof that the act or omission constituting the offence did occur seems now to have been generally rejected. Even that approach would not have prevented a claimant from seeking to explain or give further information on the circumstances of the offence and, in any event, allowed for a more direct challenge in exceptional cases. Nor would it prevent argument on the legal inferences to be drawn in the misconduct context from the fact of the criminal act or omission. A more flexible approach was taken in *R(S) 2/80*, where the Commissioner held that the fact of a conviction would have a bearing in benefit appeals, once it had been shown to be relevant to the benefit issue in question, because of the burden of proof in criminal cases, but that the burden would then in the benefit appeal shift to the claimant to show that they were nonetheless entitled to the benefit in question. In *AM v SSWP (DLA)* [2013] UKUT 94 (AAC) Judge Mark considered that *R(S) 2/80* was wrongly decided if it was intended to refer to the legal burden of proof rather than the evidential burden. In that case, as well as in *Newcastle City Council v LW (HB)* [2013] UKUT 123 (AAC) and *KL v SSWP (DLA)* [2015] UKUT 222 (AAC), the same judge appears to endorse even more flexibility. The criminal conviction is not conclusive as res judicata before the benefit authorities. Then it would depend on whether it was an abuse of process for the claimant to attempt to re-argue an issue of fact that was a necessary part of the criminal conviction. But in sanctions appeal cases claimants would not be caught by the principle that it is an abuse of process for a person to use civil proceedings to attack a criminal conviction, because they are not in a position analogous to a plaintiff, but are defending themselves against the imposition of a penalty by the Secretary of State. Then in considering whether the administration of justice would be brought into disrepute it would all depend on the circumstances, including if new or convincing evidence has come to light, whether the claimant pleaded guilty in the criminal proceedings (and if so, why) and whether the particular expertise of the specialist tribunal leads to a re-evaluation of the legal findings and inferences. See para.1.96 of Vol.III of this series and Buchanan-Smith, *Bound or Unrestrained: Social Security Tribunals, Res Judicata and Abuse of Process* (2022) 29 J.S.S.L. 129, where it is suggested, with some justice, that this area is ripe for some authoritative resolution by the Upper Tribunal of the confusing case law.

It has always been for the person relying on it to prove the fact of a conviction, and it is preferably done through official certification (*R(U) 24/64*).

Where the decisions of disciplinary bodies (which may well examine a wide range of witnesses) are concerned, it appears that although never binding on universal credit decision-makers and tribunals, they are entitled to an increasing degree of respect the more their proceedings approximate to proceedings in a court of law. Thus a finding by a chief constable after police disciplinary proceedings was cogent evidence that the claimant had committed particular acts (*R(U) 10/63*), but a decision by a hospital management committee, the precise reasons for which were not disclosed to the Commissioner, was not so regarded (*R(U) 7/61*).

Whether the concern is with decisions of the courts, of employment tribunals or disciplinary proceedings, it is submitted that crucial questions for universal credit decision-makers and tribunals will be: what was the decision; by what sort of body, how, by what process, and on what sort(s) of evidence was the decision made; and how closely does the matter involved in that decision relate to that before the universal credit decision-makers and tribunals? But where the other decision is from a prima facie cogent source and is properly proved by one party, a tribunal need not go behind that decision unless the other party comes forward with sufficient evidential or legal argument. See also the discussion in the notes to s.3 of the Tribunals, Courts and Enforcement Act 2007 under the heading Relying on decisions of other bodies in Vol.III of this series.

1.198 *Old style JSA authority on leaving voluntarily without just cause and voluntarily and for no good reason ceasing paid work or losing pay*

As explained above, the authority built up in unemployment benefit and old style JSA remains highly relevant to universal credit sanctions for voluntarily and with no good reason ceasing paid work or losing pay. Possible points of difference will be noted below.

Note at the outset the protections given by reg.113 of the Universal Credit Regulations (made under s.26(8)(a)) from reductions in benefit when there has been a sanctionable failure under s.26. Those particularly relevant to voluntarily and for no good reason ceasing paid work or losing pay are as follows. Regulation 113(1)(b) protects current claimants, in relation to s.26(2)(d) only, not s.26(4), whose work search and availability requirements are limited to a certain number of weekly hours and who take up paid work for extra hours for a trial period. There is to be no reduction of benefit if they voluntarily cease that paid work or lose pay. There is no protection when such ceasing is a pre-claim failure, but there might always be, as also in cases covered by reg.113(1)(b), good reason for ending a trial period of employment so that there is not in fact a sanctionable failure (see further below). Regulation 113(1)(c) protects anyone voluntarily ceasing paid work or losing pay because of a strike arising from a trade dispute. Regulation 113(1)(d) protects anyone voluntarily ceasing work as a member of the regular or reserve forces. Regulation 113(1)(f) protects anyone who has voluntarily ceased paid work either (i) because of redundancy after volunteering or agreeing to be dismissed; or (ii) on an agreed date without being dismissed following an agreement on voluntary redundancy or under this head or (iii) when laid off or kept on short time. See the notes to reg.113 for more details.

Section 26(2)(d), (3) and (4)(b) refers to voluntarily ceasing any paid work, so that there is now no need to consider the possible limitations in the meaning of "employment" in s.19(2)(b) of the old style Jobseekers Act 1995. It would appear that self-employment as well as any form of employment is covered. Paragraph K3274 of the ADM says that a claimant cannot be subject to a sanction for voluntarily and for no good reason ceasing paid work or misconduct if the work was under a zero hours contract if the contract contains an exclusivity clause (that the person cannot work for another employer). Such clauses were made ineffective with effect from May 26, 2015 (Employment Rights Act 1996, s.27A). Paragraph K3275 says that from then on the application of sanctions is not excluded. It is hard to see the legal basis for the pre-May 2015 guidance. Ceasing any employment would appear to bring the legislation into play, although the terms of the contract might contribute to a good reason for ceasing the work.

In *CJSA/3304/1999*, Commissioner Levenson considered the case of someone who had left employment A for unspecified reasons, then found employment with employer B, from which he was dismissed, and only then claimed JSA. The tribunal allowed the claimant's appeal against preclusion of payment founded on his having voluntarily left employment A without just cause. The Commissioner upheld the tribunal, saying that payment could only be precluded where a claim for benefit had been made and only "in respect of the employment immediately preceding the claim" (at para.16). Insofar as *R(U) 13/64* might be thought to say otherwise, the Commissioner, drawing support from Commissioner Goodman in para.9 of *CU/64/1994*, declined to follow it. The issue does not really arise under s.26(2)(d), but in relation to s.26(4)(b) on pre-claim failures it may be arguable that the reference to "at any time before making the claim" reverses the effect of *CJSA/3304/1999*. However, as noted above, regs 102(4) and 113(1)(e) of the Universal Credit Regulations set a practical limit to how far back a voluntary ceasing of work can be relevant.

The extension of the sanction to voluntarily losing pay is necessary because of the possibility of entitlement while doing a substantial amount of paid work. It theoretically opens a wide range of potential sanctions. The extension applies equally to potential pre-claim circumstances as to those arising during the course of an award. There will be a great many situations in which a claimant (pre-claim or during an award) loses pay in a way that could be regarded as voluntary (e.g. a person on a zero hours contract opting for fewer hours of work in one week than previously). The power in s.26(5)(b) to make regulations providing for the disregard of loss of pay below a prescribed level has not been exercised. Nor is there any discretion to shorten the prescribed periods for reduction of benefit (minimum, 91 days) in proportion to the gravity of the "offence" if the conditions for application of a s.26 higher-level sanction are met. In those circumstances, it must be arguable that trivial or disproportionately small losses of pay are to be ignored (compare *SA v SSWP (JSA)* [2015] UKUT 454 (AAC) on turning up late for a course). Even so, a great deal of weight will be put on what is a "good reason" for losing pay and also on common sense in not referring trivial situations to a decision-maker for determination.

In the discussion below references to ceasing paid work should be taken to include losing pay unless there is some specific point of difference that needs to be identified.

Onus of proof. Those who assert that the claimant left employment or ceased paid 1.199
work and did so voluntarily must prove it. Once done, it was clear that under the "without just cause" test the onus passed to the claimant to prove on the balance of probabilities that they had just cause for so leaving (*R(U) 20/64(T)*). The use of the formula "voluntarily and for no good reason" could be argued to make showing the absence of good reason part of what the Secretary of State has to prove. However, there is no evidence of an intention to make such a radical change. And it would be contrary to the approach in principle demanded by *Kerr v Department for Social Development* [2004] UKHL 23; [2004] 1 W.L.R. 1372; *R 1/04 (SF)*, putting emphasis on who is in a better position to supply information on any particular issue in

a co-operative process, rather than formal concepts of onus of proof. The claimant will in the great majority of cases be the person best placed to come forward with an explanation of their reasons for ceasing paid work. It is assumed below that the onus of showing, on the balance of probabilities, that they had a good reason lies on the claimant. See the detailed discussion of good reason below.

1.200 "*Voluntarily leaves*". The commonest case of voluntarily leaving was when the claimant of their own accord handed in their notice or otherwise terminated their contract of employment. Indeed, in many cases there would be no dispute about this aspect of the case; the real issue was that of "just cause" or "good reason". The same will apply to voluntarily ceasing paid work. But voluntarily leaving also embraced other means by which employment was lost. So the actors who threatened to leave unless certain demands were met and were then treated by their employers as having given notice left voluntarily (*R(U) 33/51*). It was still voluntarily leaving where the employment ended because the employer refused to accept the claimant's withdrawal of notice (*R(U) 27/59*). It could also embrace in limited instances cases where the loss of employment took the form of a dismissal brought about by conduct of the claimant which would inevitably lead to termination of the employment (*R(U) 16/52*; *R(U) 2/54*, *R(U) 9/59*, *R(U) 7/74*), but such situations had to be looked at with caution and restraint (*R(U) 2/77*). Thus, in *R(U) 16/52* the claimant's appointment was conditional on her completing a satisfactory medical. She refused to undergo X-ray examination and was given notice. The Commissioner stated as a general rule of unemployment insurance law that if a person deliberately and knowingly acts in a way that makes it necessary for his employer to dismiss him, he may be regarded as having left his employment voluntarily. But another Commissioner later made clear in *R(U) 7/74* that "this would normally require a finding that the employee had acted, or was threatening to act, in a manner involving a deliberate repudiation of his contract of employment". So in that case an employee whose written terms of employment made no reference to a requirement to work overtime, did not leave voluntarily when he was dismissed for refusing to work overtime (cf. *R(U) 9/59*). Similarly, dismissal of an existing employee for refusal to join a trade union when a closed shop agreement was negotiated was not voluntary leaving (*R(U) 2/77*). Nor was dismissal for refusing for good reason to pay a trade union subscription (*R(U) 4/51*). Leaving was not voluntary where the claimant who departed had no effective choice but to quit, e.g. because dismissal appeared inevitable (*R(U) 1/58*: cf. *R(U) 2/76*). That appears to be in line with the employment law principle of "constructive dismissal", though perhaps with a wider scope because of the focus on the voluntariness of the ceasing of work rather than on whether the claimant was dismissed or not. It is submitted that the "general rule of unemployment insurance law" invoked in *R(U) 16/52* should be taken, with the qualifications mentioned above, to apply the question of whether a claimant has voluntarily ceased paid work even when it was the employer who terminated the contract of employment.

In *R(U) 1/96*, Commissioner Goodman considered the case of a female nursery assistant who gave her employer four weeks' notice, was prepared to work out those weeks, but whose employer, after an unsuccessful attempt to persuade her to stay on, told her to leave after two days. The Commissioner considered and applied *CU/155/50* and *R(U) 2/54* so as to reject the argument that the claimant had not left voluntarily but had been dismissed (and could therefore only be disqualified if misconduct could be proved). He regarded *British Midland Airways v Lewis* [1978] I.C.R. 782 (a decision of the Employment Appeal Tribunal in the context of dismissal under labour legislation) as not laying down "any categorical proposition of law" but as merely being a decision on the facts of that case, and continued:

> "In my view the ruling in *CU/155/50* and *R(U) 2/54* that there is a voluntary leaving applies equally, whether it is a case of an employer not allowing an employee to work out his or her notice or whether it is a case of actual notice to leave given first by the employee, followed by a notice of termination given during the currency

of the employee's notice by the employer. In the latter case, once the employee has given in his notice to leave it is a unilateral termination of the employment contract and cannot be withdrawn without the consent of the employer (*Riordan v War Office* [1959] 1 W.L.R. 1046). It follows that in the present case, when the claimant gave her four weeks notice in on Wednesday December 9, 1992 she had herself terminated the employment and thereby left it voluntarily. Even if what the employer did on Friday December 11, 1992 can be construed as giving in a counter-notice requiring her to leave on that day and not to work out her four weeks notice, that does not, in my view, alter the fact that the effective termination of the employment was a voluntary leaving by the claimant." (at para.12)

Taking early retirement could constitute voluntarily leaving (*R(U) 26/51, R(U) 20/64, R(U) 4/70, R(U) 1/81*). Even where a schoolteacher retired three years early in response to the generalised encouragement to take early retirement offered to teachers in his position by his local education authority, which further certified that his retirement was in the interests of the efficient discharge of the education authority's functions, it was still voluntarily leaving (*Crewe v Social Security Commissioner* [1982] 2 All E.R. 745 CA, Appendix to *R(U) 3/81*). However, in *R(U) 1/83* the Commissioner distinguished *Crewe* and held that a civil servant who acceded to his employer's specific request that he retire early should not be regarded as having left his employment voluntarily. Now, for universal credit, reg.113(1)(f) prevents there being any reduction in benefit whenever a claimant is dismissed for redundancy after volunteering or agreeing to be dismissed or ceases work on an agreed date in pursuance of a voluntary redundancy agreement. That would appear to exempt claimants on the *Crewe* side of the line. The voluntary ceasing of work, if for no good reason, would remain a sanctionable failure, but, importantly for purposes of calculating the period of reduction for future sanctionable failures, not a "sanctionable failure giving rise to a higher-level sanction" (reg.102(2) of the Universal Credit Regulations). For early retirement cases not saved by reg.113, the fine distinction between the *Crewe* type of case and those of the type considered in *R(U) 1/83* may still be important. In *CSU/22/94*, Commissioner Mitchell applied *R(U) 1/83* in favour of a claimant (a principal teacher) who had been pressured by his employers to accept an early retirement package, in a context in which his only alternative was to accept a lower status position, albeit one without loss of income (being placed on a long-term supply teacher basis). That alternative was one which "a teacher of the claimant's experience and standing could not reasonably be expected to accept" (at para.5). The decision thus stresses the need for tribunals carefully to consider whether the claimant can be said to have left voluntarily before moving on to the "for no good reason" aspect.

"*For no good reason*". There is no definition of "good reason" in the WRA 2012, **1.201** just as there was none of "just cause" or "good cause" in previous legislation dealing with disqualification from benefit or preclusion of payment of JSA and none of "good reason" in the old style JSA amendments to put the test in terms of "without a good reason" from October 2012. When those amendments were introduced there was some expression of an intention that "good reason" would be applied in the same way as the predecessor terms. See the beginning of this note on s.26 as a whole for discussion of the possible (just) difference between "without a good reason" and "for no good reason", of whether, despite the views expressed in *S v SSWP UC)* [2017] UKUT 477 (AAC), the proper analogy in the context of voluntarily ceasing work is with "just cause" as explained below, rather than with "good cause", and for the government's rejection of proposals for regulations to set out a non-exhaustive list of circumstances that could constitute good reasons. It is therefore still necessary to examine the case law authority on "just cause" when that was the test for unemployment benefit and old style JSA before considering the "no good reason" test.

That case law avoided laying down hard and fast rules for all circumstances, but most significantly "just cause" was regarded as requiring a balancing of the interests of the claimant with those of the community of fellow contributors to the National Insurance Fund. It was not a matter simply of what was in the best interests of the claimant, or of what was just as between employee and employer, or of what was in the public interest generally. To establish that they did not leave without just cause (that phraseology giving the proper emphasis) claimants had to show that in leaving they acted reasonably in circumstances that made it just that the burden of their unemployment should be cast on the National Insurance Fund (*Crewe v Social Security Commissioner* [1982] 2 All E.R. 745 per Slade LJ at 752; per Donaldson LJ at 750–751, explaining *R(U) 20/64(T)*, para.8; per Lord Denning MR at 749). Was what the claimant did right and reasonable in the context of the risk of unemployment? Was the voluntary leaving such as to create an unreasonable risk of unemployment, bearing in mind that there may be circumstances that leave a person no reasonable alternative but to leave employment (per Donaldson LJ at 750)? Establishing just cause may well be a heavier burden than showing "good cause" (per Slade LJ at 751). In *R(U) 4/87*, Commissioner Monroe stated that "the analogy with insurance seems now the paramount criterion of just cause" (para.8). His examination of decisions on the matter led him "to think that in general it is only where circumstances are such that a person has virtually no alternative to leaving voluntarily that he will be found to have had just cause for doing so, rather as a person who throws his baggage overboard to make room in the lifeboat can claim on his baggage insurance" (para.9).

There is therefore a faint suggestion in the earlier authority that there may be some difference in the ordinary use of language between "good cause" and "just cause". It may also be arguable that the formula "with no good reason" shifts the focus away from the notion of a balance between the interests of the claimant and those of the community of contributors to the fund from which benefit is paid towards more emphasis on the interests of the claimant. That would make it easier for a claimant to avoid the imposition of a sanction. In *SA v SSWP (JSA)* [2015] UKUT 454 (AAC), a decision on s.19A(2)(c) of the old style Jobseekers Act 1995 and failing to carry out a jobseeker's direction, Judge Knowles accepted the Secretary of State's submission that in determining whether a good reason had been shown for the failure all the circumstances should be considered and that the question was whether those circumstances would have caused a reasonable person (with the characteristics of the claimant in question) to act as the claimant did. Expressing the approach in such terms tends to point away from the notion of a balance.

In *S v SSWP (UC)* [2017] UKUT 477 (AAC), however, a similar approach was taken. The First-tier Tribunal had said that the claimant's professed ignorance of the effect of work (including part-time work) on his universal credit entitlement could not amount to a good reason for failing to undertake all reasonable work search action (thus leading to a sanction under s.27(2)(a)) because ignorance of the law was no defence. On the claimant's appeal to the Upper Tribunal the Secretary of State accepted that, by analogy with the well-established case law on good cause for a delay in claiming, ignorance of the law was capable of constituting a good reason. There was reference to the general meaning approved in *R(SB) 6/83* of some fact that, having regard to all the circumstances (including a claimant's state of health and the information that he had or might have obtained), would probably have caused a reasonable person of the same age and experience to act or fail to act as the claimant had done. Judge Mitchell agreed that the tribunal had erred in law, but concluded that the error was not material because the only proper conclusion on the evidence was that the claimant could reasonably have been expected to raise with his work coach or other DWP official any concerns or confusions over the financial implications on his universal credit award of taking any of the sorts of work he had agreed to search for. Thus, even on the correct approach the claimant did not have a good reason for what the tribunal had concluded was a failure under s.27(2)(a). The statements discussed below about the analogy of "good reason" with "good cause" were thus not necessary to the decision.

It is submitted that the analogy with good cause in *S* and in *SA* (indeed in para.57 of *S* the judge said that "good reason" expressed the same concept as "good cause" but in more modern language) is misleading in the present context or at least incomplete. That is because when considering good cause for a delay in claiming there is no difficulty in adopting the general meaning approved in *R(SB) 6/83*. It was in that context that the principle that a reasonable ignorance or mistaken belief as to rights could constitute good cause was established. But the question there is what a reasonable person could be expected to do to secure an advantage to them in the form of the benefit claimed late. In the context of universal credit and JSA sanctions, the notion of reasonableness carries a distinctly different force. So when considering what circumstances could justify a voluntary ceasing of work, it is submitted that the notion of a good reason must still be based on whether it is reasonable to place the burden of the claimant's unemployment on the community that funds universal credit and new style JSA. Although many personal circumstances will be relevant, the notion of a balance between those circumstances and the claimant's proper responsibilities is not captured by the traditional concept of "good cause" in the context of delay in claiming. The better analogy would seem to be with "just cause" as used in unemployment benefit and in old style JSA before the 2012 amendments (or with "good cause" as used in some of those provisions). The adoption of the "good cause" approach in relation to claimed ignorance of rights in S cannot be taken as excluding such an approach to s.26(2)(d) and (4)(b). The full meaning of "for no good reason" in this context remains to be worked out.

Accordingly, reference to authority based on the notion of a balance and reasonableness in the sense adopted above remains valuable.

Whether the claimant succeeds in discharging the burden of showing a good reason depends essentially on all the circumstances of the case, including the reasons for leaving and such matters as whether they had another job to go to, whether before they left they had made reasonable inquiries about other work or its prospects, or whether there were in their case good prospects of finding other work. Such elements should not be considered in water-tight compartments (*R(U) 20/64(T)*), para.9). The previous claims record is not directly relevant (*R(U) 20/64(T)*) para.18). In *R(U) 4/87* Commissioner Monroe, following para.10 of *R(U) 3/81* (approved in *Crewe*), ruled as remote from and irrelevant to the just cause issue long-term considerations prayed in aid by the claimant who had "urged that his leaving had in the long run actually benefited the national insurance fund, in that he had made available a vacancy for someone who would otherwise have continued unemployed, and that he was now earning more so that he was paying higher contributions" (at para.10). Such factors had nothing to do with the issue of being forced to leave.

In *CU/048/90*, Commissioner Sanders considered the appeal of a claimant who had, as a result of his employer's attitude, become dissatisfied with his employment and had sought alternative employment by circulating his curriculum vitae to 30 companies. During interviews with Barclays Bank he was given the impression that his application for a particular post would be successful, and he resigned from his employment. In the event he was not offered the post. Commissioner Sanders considered the correct approach to "just cause" to be that set out in *R(U) 4/87* (para.9). He thought that the "circumstances have to be very demanding before a claimant can establish just cause for leaving" (para.3). It seemed to the Commissioner "that in the circumstances of the case the claimant had reason to leave because he thought he was not progressing in his career" but took the view "that the circumstances were not so pressing as to justify his leaving, from an unemployment benefit point of view, before he had secured the job with Barclays Bank even though he had been led to believe that his application for that job would be successful". He agreed with the SSAT that the claimant did not have just cause for leaving voluntarily and had to be disqualified.

In some cases, probably rare in practice, an actual promise of immediate suitable new employment (which then falls through after the employment was left or the start of which is delayed) might afford just cause in the absence of any other justificatory circumstances (*R(U) 20/64(T)*, para.17; *Crewe* per Donaldson LJ, para.750). However, there was no rule of law saying that just cause cannot be established where the claimant leaves without another job to go to. Indeed, in *R(U) 20/64(T)* a Tribunal of Commissioners suggested that there could be circumstances in the claimant's personal or domestic life which become so pressing that they justify leaving employment "without regard to the question of other employment" (para.12) and they cited as illustrations *R(U) 14/52*, *R(U) 19/52* and *R(U) 31/59*, all noted below. Equally, it was clearly established that some feature of the claimant's existing employment may justify leaving it immediately without any regard to the question of other employment (para.11) and here the Commissioners quoted as instances *CU 248/49*, *R(U) 15/53*, *R(U) 38/53* and *R(U) 18/57*, also considered below. But there had to be some urgency in the matter and, as regards the latter class of case, the circumstances had to be so pressing that it would not be reasonable to expect the claimant to take such steps before leaving as were open to them to resolve the grievance connected with work through the proper channels of existing grievance procedures. *CU/106/1987* made it clear that a tribunal could not merely rely on the Secretary of State's (decision-maker's) suggestion that there would be such a grievance procedure in the circumstances of the claimant's employment. It was wrong in law to take account of a suggested grievance procedure to reject the claimant's appeal without having proper findings of fact as to its actual existence. One would equally have thought that a tribunal should also consider whether any procedure found to exist could cover the claimant's complaint and whether it was reasonable in the circumstances to expect the claimant to have resort to it.

A simple desire to change jobs was not usually enough to warrant putting the burden of one's unemployment on the Fund. Nor did moving house without more constitute just cause; it depended on the reasons for the move (*R(U) 20/64(T)*, para.15). Rather than approaching the just cause issue from the angle of considering it necessary for the claimant to be assured of suitable alternative employment, unless there were circumstances justifying them in leaving without it (the approach in *R(U) 14/52*), the Commissioners in *R(U) 20/64(T)* preferred a different perspective. They preferred to look: (1) at whether the reasons for leaving themselves amounted to just cause (i.e. leaving aside the matter of alternative employment or its prospects); and (2) where the reasons did not of themselves establish just cause to then consider whether the "promises or prospects of other employment may be effective as an additional factor which may help the claimant establish just cause. For example, where a man almost establishes just cause [in relation to, e.g. pressing personal or domestic circumstances] the fact that he has a promise or prospects of other employment may serve to tip the scale in his favour . . . In considering these matters of course the strength of his chances of employment and the gap, if any, likely to occur between the two employments must be taken into account" (para.17). The Commissioners stated:

> "that it is impossible to lay down any period of time representing a gap between employments, or any degree of probability of fresh employment which will give an automatic answer to the question whether the claimant has shown just cause for leaving. We think that there is a distinction between on the one hand, having suitable employment to go to, as where there is an actual promise of employment, and having only prospects of employment on the other. It may be reasonable to expect a claimant who has only prospects to take some steps before leaving, such as communicating with the employment exchange to see whether his prospects cannot be made more certain."

A number of cases concerning, on the one hand, grievances about existing employment and, on the other, personal or domestic circumstances, can usefully be quoted as instances in which just cause was established, and it may be useful to note in contrast a number of examples in each category where it was not, subject to the importance of looking to the precise circumstances of each and every case and not regarding factual decisions as legal precedents.

1.202 *(i) Grievances about work.* In *R(U) 15/53* a piece-worker who lost his job when he refused to accept a substantial reduction in earnings thrust on him by his employer had just cause for leaving. In *R(U) 38/53* the claimant left after subjection to pressure to join a trade union and was able to establish just cause; it would have been intolerable if he had to remain. In *R(U) 18/57* an apprentice ordered to do work clearly outside the scope of his apprenticeship had only the options of doing as he was told or leaving immediately. In choosing the latter he had just cause. It may be now that working under a zero hours contract, especially when it was still legally possible for an exclusivity clause to be enforceable, could contribute towards a good reason for ceasing the employment (and see the guidance mentioned above under "such employment"). But mere failure to get on with colleagues (*R(U) 17/54*) or strained relations with one's employer (*R(U) 8/74*) has been held not enough. Not feeling oneself capable of the work, where one's employer was satisfied, was unlikely to be enough without clear medical evidence of that fact (*R(U) 13/52*), but leaving employment during a probationary period because the claimant considered himself unsuited to the work and that it was unfair to his employer to continue training him was more generously treated in *R(U) 3/73*.

Indeed, in *CU/43/87* Commissioner Davenport said that "a person who is experimenting in trying a new line of work should not lightly be penalised if that experiment fails". People should be encouraged to try new types of employment where work in their usual field is not available:

> "It must be recognised that in such circumstances a person may find that he cannot stay in his employment and it may be that he is reasonable in leaving that employment, whereas a person who had more experience in the field in question would not be held to have acted reasonably if he gave up the employment. Not everyone finds that new and unfamiliar employment is such that she or he can reasonably stay in it." (At para.7)

CU/90/91 further illustrates that claimants who left employment as unsuitable after a trial period could have just cause for doing so and be protected from preclusion of payment without having to rely on the time-limited "trial period" concept found in the old style JSA legislation. Commissioner Hallett stated:

> "It is clear from the evidence, which I accept, that the claimant took the job with Fords (which would have been permanent) on trial, conditionally on his being able to obtain accommodation in the area. It is well-settled in social security unemployment law that claimants should be encouraged to take jobs on trial and that if, after trial, the job proves unsuitable, they do have just cause for leaving. It is in the interests of the national insurance fund, and of public policy, to encourage persons to obtain employment and not penalise them if, after fair trial, the job proves unsuitable." (At para.10)

The claimant had just cause for leaving. There is no such well-settled principle applying to leaving a job taken, not on trial, but as a "stop-gap" pending something better turning up (*R(U) 40/53*; *CJSA/63/2007*, para.15).

(ii) Personal or domestic circumstances. In *R(U) 14/52* the claimant had just cause **1.203**
for leaving his job in order to be with his elderly and sick wife who lived alone. It was not possible for her to move to live with him so as to be near enough to his work. He also thought his chances of employment would be good in his wife's area, but there was little evidence in the case of searching inquiries about those prospects. In *R(U) 19/52* the claimant, who left her job to move with her service-man husband to a new posting, likely to be more than short-term, had just cause. Had the posting been short-term, however, she would have had to make inquiries about job prospects in the new area before leaving. See further *R(U) 4/87* and *CU/110/1987*. In *CU/110/1987* the claimant's service-man husband received telephone notice of posting to Germany on February 14, 1986. He went there on March 1, 1986. On February 14, the claimant gave the one week's notice required under her contract of employment and ceased work on February 21, claiming benefit the next day. She had to be available to vacate the married quarters in Aldershot from March 1.

However, she did not join her husband in Germany until March 25, since repairs were needed to the married quarters there. Commissioner Monroe held that in those circumstances she had just cause for leaving when she did, rather than later. That, rather than whether she should have left at all, was the real issue in the case, since in the Commissioner's view it could hardly be said that she did not have just cause to leave (whenever she could) to join her husband in Germany. She was not to be disqualified from benefit. Actual entitlement to benefit, however, would turn on the unresolved matter of her availability for work. On the issue of availability in that context, see *R(U) 2/90(T)*. In *R(U) 31/59* the reason for leaving was the move to a new home, too far from the job, because the existing home (two small attic rooms) was wholly unsuitable for the claimant's family. By contrast, in *R(U) 6/53* the 21-year-old woman who left her job to move with her rather strict parents to a new area did not have just cause; it was reasonable to expect her to live alone, at least until she could find work in the new area. In *CJSA/2507/2005*, Commissioner Williams applied Commissioner Monroe's statement at para.9 of *R(U) 4/87*, quoted in 1.201 above, to dismiss the 28-year-old claimant's appeal against a tribunal-imposed three week disqualification for voluntary leaving (the decision-maker had imposed eight weeks). He had left to join his fiancée and get married, but had no job to go to. The three-week disqualification represented the period up to the marriage. The Commissioner also noted the need to treat with some caution decisions on this area which are 50 years' old, reflecting a very different job market and attitudes to married women, and given when appeal to the Commissioners covered fact and law.

Leaving for a financial advantage, e.g. to draw a marriage gratuity only payable on resignation (*R(U) 14/55*), or to take early retirement, even where this was encouraged by the employer and might be said to be in the public interest in terms of opening the way for younger teachers and promoting the efficiency of the education service, has been held not to rank as just cause (*Crewe v Social Security Commissioner* [1982] 2 All E.R. 745; *R(U) 26/51*; *R(U) 23/59*; *R(U) 20/64(T)*; *R(U) 4/70*; *R(U) 1/81*). However, if "good reason" has different nuances of meaning from "just cause", as discussed above, that might justify more emphasis on what was reasonable in the claimant's own interests. Further, it may be that a different approach is justified where a claimant leaves a job to avoid hardship rather than to pursue extra money (as suggested in *CJSA/1737/2014*, where one of the claimant's arguments was that the cost of travel to and from work was prohibitive).

Note the significant assistance, discussed above, that may be provided by reg.113(1)(f) of the Universal Credit Regulations in cases of voluntary redundancy, although that provision only prevents a reduction in benefit rather than making the voluntary ceasing of paid work not a sanctionable failure.

Subsection (5)

1.204 Regulations may deem ceasing work or losing pay not to be by reason of misconduct or voluntarily in certain circumstances and may provide that loss of pay below a prescribed level is to be disregarded. No such regulations have been made. Regulation 113 of the Universal Credit Regulations is made under the powers in subs.(8)(a) and only affects whether a reduction in benefit is to be imposed, not whether there is or is not a sanctionable failure.

Subsections (6) and (7)

1.205 See regs 101 and 106—111 of the Universal Credit Regulations for the amount and period of the reduction in benefit under a higher-level sanction. The three-year limit is imposed in subs.(6)(b) and cannot be extended in regulations.

Subsection (8)

1.206 Under para.(a), see reg.113 of the Universal Credit Regulations. Under para.(b), see reg.107. Under para.(c), see regs 108 and 109.

Other sanctions

27.—(1) The amount of an award of universal credit is to be reduced in accordance with this section in the event of a failure by a claimant which is sanctionable under this section. 1.207

(2) It is a failure sanctionable under this section if a claimant—

(a) fails for no good reason to comply with a work-related requirement;

(b) fails for no good reason to comply with a requirement under section 23.

(3) But a failure by a claimant is not sanctionable under this section if it is also a failure sanctionable under section 26.

(4) Regulations are to provide for—

(a) the amount of a reduction under this section, and

(b) the period for which such a reduction has effect.

(5) Regulations under subsection (4)(b) may provide that a reduction under this section in relation to any failure is to have effect for—

(a) a period continuing until the claimant meets a compliance condition specified by the Secretary of State,

(b) a fixed period not exceeding 26 weeks which is—

(i) specified in the regulations, or

(ii) determined in any case by the Secretary of State, or

(c) a combination of both.

(6) In subsection (5)(a) "compliance condition" means—

(a) a condition that the failure ceases, or

(b) a condition relating to future compliance with a work-related requirement or a requirement under section 23.

(7) A compliance condition specified under subsection (5)(a) may be—

(a) revoked or varied by the Secretary of State;

(b) notified to the claimant in such manner as the Secretary of State may determine.

(8) A period fixed under subsection (5)(b) may in particular depend on either or both the following—

(a) the number of failures by the claimant sanctionable under this section;

(b) the period between such failures.

(9) Regulations may provide—

(a) for cases in which no reduction is to be made under this section;

(b) for a reduction under this section made in relation to an award that is terminated to be applied to any new award made within a prescribed period of the termination;

(c) for the termination or suspension of a reduction under this section.

Definitions

"claimant"—see s.40.

"work-related requirement"—see ss.40 and 13(2).

General Note

See the introductory part of the note to s.26 for the general nature of the universal credit sanctions regime under ss.26 and 27 and for discussion of the meaning of "for no good reason". Section 27(1) and (2) requires there to be a reduction, of the amount and period set out in regulations, wherever the claimant has failed for no good reason to comply with any work-related requirement or a connected requirement under s.23. 1.208

There is no general discretion whether or not to apply the prescribed deduction, but that is subject first to the rule in subs.(3) that if a failure is sanctionable under s.26 (and therefore subject to the higher-level regime) it is not to be sanctionable under s.27 and to the rules in reg.113 of the Universal Credit Regulations about when a reduction is not to be applied although there is a sanctionable failure (none of which currently apply to s.27). While the power and duty under subs.(4) for regulations to provide for the amount and period of the reduction to be imposed is in fact more open-ended than that in s.26(6), because it does not have the three-year limit, subss. (5)–(7) introduce the specific power (that does not of course have to be used) for regulations to provide for the period of the reduction for a particular sanctionable failure to continue until the claimant meets a "compliance condition" (subs.(6)) or for a fixed period not exceeding 26 weeks specified in regulations or determined by the Secretary of State or a combination of both. The 26-week limit in subs.(5)(b) appears not to have any decisive effect because a longer period could always be prescribed under subs.(4)(b), unless "may" is to be construed as meaning "may only".

In practice, the powers have been used in the Universal Credit Regulations to set up a structure of medium-level (reg.103), low-level (reg.104) and lowest-level (reg.105) sanctions. See the notes to those regulations for the details.

The medium-level sanction applies only to failures to comply with a work search requirement under s.17(1)(a) to take all reasonable action to obtain paid work etc. or to comply with a work availability requirement under s.18(1). A failure to comply with a work search requirement under s.17(1)(b) to apply for a particular vacancy attracts a higher-level sanction under s.26(2)(b) if the claimant is subject to all work-related requirements. The reduction period under reg.103 is 28 days for a first "offence" and 91 days for a second "offence" or subsequent offence within a year of the previous failure (7 and 14 days for under-18s).

1.209 The low-level sanction under reg.104 applies where the claimant is subject either to all work-related requirements under s.22 or to the work preparation requirement under s.21 and fails to comply with a work-focused interview requirement under s.15(1), a work preparation requirement under s.16(1), a work search requirement under s.17(1)(b) to take any action specified by the Secretary of State or a connected requirement in s.23(1), (3) or (4). Note that this is the sanction that applies to a failure for no good reason to report specified changes in circumstances (s.23(4)) or to provide specified information and evidence (s.23(3)) as well as to failure to participate in an interview. The reduction period under reg.104 lasts until the claimant complies with the requirement in question, comes within s.19 (no work-related requirements), a work preparation requirement to take particular action is no longer imposed or the award terminates, plus seven days for a first "offence", 14 days for a second "offence" within a year of the previous failure and 28 days for a third or subsequent "offence" within a year (plus seven days in all those circumstances for under-18s).

The lowest-level sanction under reg.105 applies where a claimant is subject to s.20 and fails to comply with a work-focused interview requirement. The reduction period under reg.105 lasts until the claimant complies with the requirement, comes within s.19 (no work-related requirements), a work preparation requirement to take particular action is no longer imposed or the award terminates.

For the purposes of regs 104 and 105, "compliance condition" is defined in subs.(6) to mean either a condition that the failure to comply ceases or a condition relating to future compliance. A compliance condition may be revoked or varied by the Secretary of State, apparently at will, and may be (not must be) notified to the claimant in such manner as the Secretary of State might determine (subs. (7)). But under regs 104 and 105 a compliance condition has to be "specified" by the Secretary of State. On the one hand, it is difficult to envisage it being decided that the Secretary of State can specify such a condition to himself, rather than to the claimant. On the other hand, it is difficult to envisage it being decided that a claimant who has in fact complied with a requirement has not met a compliance condition merely because the Secretary of State failed to give proper notice of the condition. It appears that during the 2020 coronavirus outbreak any contact by the claimant with the DWP was treated as compliance with any condition, thus bringing that part of the reduction period to an end.

The test of being subject to the work-related requirement in question is applied at the date of the sanctionable failure and it does not in general affect the continuing operation of the sanction if the claimant ceases to be so subject. The reduction rate drops from 100% of the standard allowance to nil if the claimant begins to have limited capability for work and work-related activity (Universal Credit Regulations, reg.111(3)). The reduction rate drops to 40% if the claimant comes within s.19 (no work-related requirements) because of certain caring responsibilities for children under one (reg.111(2)). The DWP rejected the House of Commons Work and Pensions Committee's recommendation in its report of November 6, 2018 on *Benefit Sanctions* (HC 995 2017-19) that sanctions be cancelled when a claimant ceased to be subject to the requirement that led to the sanction (House of Commons Work and Pensions Committee, *Benefit Sanctions: Government Response* (HC 1949 2017-19, February 11, 2019, paras 49 - 51). It was said that that would undermine the incentive effect of the sanctions and that the mitigations in reg.111 were adequate. Note also the termination of a reduction when the claimant has been in paid work at a weekly rate of 35 times the hourly national minimum wage for 26 weeks (reg.109).

Regulation 113 of the Universal Credit Regulations, made in part under subs.(9) **1.210**
(a), prescribes circumstances in which no reduction is to be made for a sanctionable failure under s.27 as well as s.26, but none of the circumstances covered seem relevant to s.27.

Under para.(b) of subs.(9), see reg.107. Under para.(c), see regs 108 and 109.

One of the most common grounds of sanction under s.27(2)(a), given the demise of the Mandatory Work Activity Scheme covered by s.26(2)(a), is the failure to comply with a work-related requirement to participate in an interview under s.15 (work-focused interview requirement) or s.17 and reg.94 of the Universal Credit Regulations (work search requirement: applying for particular vacancies and interviews). There is a separate power in s.23 to require a claimant to participate in an interview for any purpose relating to the imposition of a work-related requirement on a claimant, verification of compliance with work-related requirements or assisting a claimant to comply. Failure to comply attracts a sanction under s.27(2)(b). Many work preparation requirements (s.16) and other work-related requirements involve attendance and/or participation in various courses, assessments, training programmes etc, often provided by third parties contracted to the DWP. All of those areas raise similar questions about whether the requirement and the specification of what the claimant is to do has been properly notified, about what is involved in "participation" and about what could amount to a good reason for failure to comply. Similar issues were raised in relation to requirements to participate in various schemes under s.17A of the old style Jobseekers Act 1995.

For a sanction to be applied, the relevant work requirement must have been imposed in accordance with the legislation and been made enforceable where necessary by specification of a particular appointment and an obligation to attend and participate. See the notes to s.14 for the general principles, in particular the general guidance and application to the specific facts in *JB v SSWP (UC)* [2018] UKUT 360 (AAC), and to s.15 for other points on interviews. This will often involve a two-stage process, although in the case of s.15 or s.23 (connected requirements) interviews, it would appear, as pointed out by Judge Jacobs in *SP v SSWP (UC)* [2018] UKUT 227 (AAC), that even if a general obligation to attend interviews is mentioned in the claimant commitment the requirement does not become enforceable until a particular interview has been specified. Thus in *JB*, the evidence that the DWP produced to the First-tier Tribunal did not show notification of the specific interview in which it was said that the claimant had failed to participate. But Judge Poole QC stressed in para.29 the flexibility given by the legislation in permitting multiple methods of communication with claimants, such that it would be inappropriate for the Upper Tribunal to set out particular requirements for the wording of notifications or for methods used. She stated in para.29.3:

> "What is important is the substance. In this case the question was whether it could fairly be said, on the totality of the evidence, that the claimant had been notified of an obligation to attend a work-focused interview and the consequences of non-compliance."

In *SP* Judge Jacobs also suggested that it is inherent in the nature of notification that it cannot be effective unless and until it is received. However, he did not have to rely on that proposition in dealing with a case where the claimant's evidence was that an appointment letter was not delivered until after the time of the appointment. That was because, even if notification were regarded as having been given, there was necessarily a good reason for not participating in an interview when the claimant was not aware of the appointment.

Sometimes the question of satisfaction of those legislative requirements becomes entangled with the question of whether the public law duty of fairness, often described as the "prior information duty" in the current context, has been fulfilled. Thus, in *KG v SSWP (UC)* [2020] UKUT 360 (AAC) not only did the documents in evidence fail to show whether the interview in question was required under the equivalent of s.15 or s.23, but they failed to show that the claimant had been informed what issues were to be investigated in the interview and of the consequences of non-compliance. And in *JB* the importance of notifying the claimant of the consequences of non-compliance seemed to stem from the duty of fairness rather than from the legislative obligation to go beyond mere notification of date, time and place of appointment to communicate a requirement to attend and participate. The prior information duty is considered in detail in the notes to s.14.

See also the decision in *NM v SSWP (JSA)* [2016] UKUT 351 (AAC), where Judge Wright held, as eventually conceded by the Secretary of State, that the inability to show that relevant DWP guidance had been considered before the claimant was given notice to participate in a Mandatory Work Activity scheme meant either that the claimant should not have been referred to the scheme (because the officer either would have followed the guidance or could have been persuaded to do so on representations from the claimant) or that he had good reason for not participating in the scheme. The appeal related to a sanction for failing to participate, through behaviour on the scheme. The guidance, in something called Mandatory Work Activity Guidance or Operational Instructions–Procedural Guidance–Mandatory Work Activity–January 2012, was relevant because at the time it instructed that claimants should not be considered for referral to Mandatory Work Activity if, among other circumstances, they were currently working (paid or voluntary). The claimant had been volunteering in a Sue Ryder shop, which he had to give up to attend the required scheme as a volunteer in a Salvation Army shop. The Secretary of State submitted that the guidance had since been changed to introduce an element of discretion about referral of claimants doing voluntary work. Judge Wright held that this would not excuse a failure by an officer of the Secretary of State to consider his own guidance or, on any appeal, a failure to provide the guidance to a First-tier Tribunal in accordance with the principles of natural justice.

The necessity for a sufficiently specific requirement to have been imposed does not necessarily mean that the DWP in the case of an appeal must, either in the response to the appeal in the bundle of documents or at a hearing, produce a full paper-trail. It all depends on what issues have been raised by the appeal or have been legitimately raised by the tribunal.

In *SSWP v CN (JSA)* [2020] UKUT 26 (AAC), the claimant's sole ground of appeal against a sanction for failing to participate in the Work Programme by not attending an appointment was that she had never failed to keep an appointment (i.e. implicitly that she could not have received the notice of the appointment and/or had good cause under the regulations then in force). The tribunal allowed her appeal on the ground that the bundle did not contain a copy of the notice referring her to the Work Programme (i.e. the WP05) so that it was not satisfied that she had properly been notified of the requirement to participate. The tribunal appeared to think that that issue was one raised by the appeal within s.12(8)(a) of the SSA 1998, which it manifestly was not as the Secretary of State's submission in the bundle, unchallenged by the claimant, was that there was no dispute that the claimant was referred to the Work Programme. Nor did it give any explanation, if it had exercised its discretion under s.12(8)(a) to consider the issue, of why it did so and how it was clearly apparent from the evidence so as to be capable of being dealt with under that discretion. Even if those hurdles had been overcome, the Secretary of State had not been given a fair opportunity to deal with the point. It is not necessary for the Secretary of State in all sanctions cases to provide evidence in the appeal bundle that all preconditions for the imposition of the sanction are satisfied. It depends what issues have been put in dispute in the appeal. Having therefore set the tribunal's decision aside, Judge Wright substituted a decision finding on the evidence that the claimant had received the letter notifying her of the appointment in question.

The judge's statement that the Secretary of State need not in all sanctions cases provide evidence in the appeal bundle to support the satisfaction of all the preconditions to imposing a sanction must, though, be read in the light of the approach in *SSWP v DC (JSA)* [2017] UKUT 464 (AAC), reported as [2018] AACR 16, and *PO'R v DFC (JSA)* [2018] NI Com 1.There it was said that the Secretary of State should in all cases involving a failure to participate in some scheme or interview where notice of certain details of the scheme etc. was required to be given, as well as notice of date, time and place, include in the appeal bundle a copy of the appointment letter, whether the claimant had raised any issue as to the terms of the letter or not. That was on the basis that unrepresented claimants could not be expected to identify technical issues about the validity of notices and it could not be predicted what particular issues might arise in the course of an appeal. If the letter was not included in the initial bundle, the decisions approved the action of tribunals in directing its production as a proper exercise of their inquisitorial jurisdiction. That exercise must rest on a use of the discretion in s.12(8)(a) to consider issues not raised by the appeal. The resolution of the approaches is no doubt that whenever a tribunal exercises that discretion it must do so consciously and explain why it has done so in any statement of reasons, and give the Secretary of State a fair opportunity to produce the document(s). It may be that an adequate explanation is to be found more readily when it is a notice of a specific appointment that is in issue rather than an initial reference to a scheme.

DC concerned two sanctions imposed in August 2013 for failures, without good cause, to participate in a Scheme as required under reg.4 of the Jobseekers Allowance (Employment, Skills and Enterprise Schemes) Regulations 2011 (SI 2011/917) in June and August 2012. By August 2013, the Regulations had been revoked, but continued to apply in relation to failures to participate that occurred while they were in force. For the same reason, the sanctions provisions in reg.8 (revoked with effect from October 22, 2012) applied in *DC*, rather than s.19A of the old style Jobseekers Act 1995.

The first appeal (in relation to August 2012) raised the issue of the effect of the Secretary of State's being unable to provide to the First-tier Tribunal, as directed, a copy of the appointment letter known as a Mandatory Activity Notification (MAN) sent or handed to the claimant in respect of the appointment that he failed to attend. The tribunal had allowed the claimant's appeal on the basis that the Secretary of State had failed to show that the claimant had been properly notified in accordance with the conditions in reg.4(2). In concluding that there was no error of law in that, Judge Rowland held that this was not a matter of the drawing of adverse inferences, but of the Secretary of State simply having failed to come forward with evidence on a matter on which the burden of proof was on him. Although there was evidence before the tribunal that the claimant had been given an appointment letter, that evidence did not go beyond showing the date and time of the appointment. It did not show where the claimant was to attend or what other information was provided and how it was expressed. The judge rejected the Secretary of State's submission relying on the presumption of regularity and the "inherent probabilities". Although the tribunal could, using its specialist experience, properly have concluded that the letter had contained enough information to make it effective, it was not bound to do so, given that it is not unknown for documents to be issued in an unapproved form or to use language that is not intelligible to an uninitiated recipient. The judge agreed with the tribunal that a copy of the appointment letter should have been in the tribunal bundle: a decision-maker might be able to rely on the presumption of regularity, but on an appeal (where it is not known what issues may eventually emerge) a copy of the letter should be provided. Much the same approach was taken by the Chief Commissioner in Northern Ireland in *PO'R*, where it was said that the tribunal there should not have decided against the claimant without having adjourned to obtain a copy of the appointment letter.

If a copy of the appointment letter was not in the bundle, then Judge Rowland's view was that a tribunal could, using its inquisitorial jurisdiction in an area where unrepresented claimants in particular could not be expected to identify such technical points, properly exercise its discretion under s.12(8)(a) of the SSA 1998 to direct that a copy be provided. It would not be fair to decide the case against the Secretary of State without giving that opportunity to provide the evidence. But where, as in *DC*, the evidence directed was not provided, the tribunal could properly conclude that the Secretary of State had failed to come forward with evidence on a matter on which the burden of proof was on him. There is therefore no formal incompatibility with the decision of Judge Wright in *CN*, although there was less emphasis there on the inquisitorial role of the tribunal. If there were any incompatibility, the fact that *DC* is a reported decision would point to its being preferred.

Judge Rowland accepted that the tribunal in *DC* had erred in law in deciding against the Secretary of State on the authorisation point (discussed below) without giving him an opportunity to provide relevant evidence, but that error was not material as, even if there was evidence that the provider was authorised to issue reg.4 notices, the tribunal would have been entitled to allow the claimant's appeal on the basis of the lack of necessary evidence that an effective notice had been given.

The second appeal (in relation to June 2012) raised the issue of whether the tribunal had been entitled to conclude that the Secretary of State had not shown that the Scheme provider in question had been authorised under reg.18 of the ESES Regulations to give reg.4 notices when he was unable to produce a copy of a letter of authorisation. Judge Rowland held that the tribunal had gone wrong in law. Regulation 18 did not specify the form in which authorisation had to be given (nor does s.29 of the WRA 2012 or s.6L of the new style Jobseekers Act 1995 on delegation and contracting out), so that it was a matter of fact and degree. Authority could be found to exist in evidence as to the conduct of those concerned, including what they have said and written over a period. The tribunal did not consider that possibility, raised by the provider acting as though authorised and the Secretary of State asserting that authority had been given. The judge went on to re-make the decision on the appeal. It had emerged that, by an administrative mistake, no formal letter of authority had ever been issued, but the existence of a contract between the Secretary of State and the main contractor for the sub-contractor to act in the area in question and a draft authorisation letter was sufficient to satisfy reg.18. He found that the claimant had been properly notified and had not shown good cause for his failure to participate, so that a sanction was to be imposed. On close analysis of reg.8 the sanction was to be for four weeks, rather than the 26 that had originally been imposed.

Even though the literal legislative requirements of notification have been satisfied, it may be that the claimant has not been "properly" notified because of a material breach of the public law duty of fairness or more specifically the prior information duty. See the extensive discussion of that in the notes to s.14.

Many of the requirements that can give rise to sanctions under s.27 involve undertaking or participating in interviews, courses, assessments, programmes etc that that have a specified start time. Participation must in general involve at least turning up at the right time and place and also making some meaningful contribution to whatever is involved. Behaviour that leads to the premature termination of the interview or course may well amount to a failure to participate (see the facts of *DM v SSWP (JSA)* [2015] UKUT 67 (AAC) where the claimant was asked to leave a session that he was said to be disrupting by asking questions and heckling (but see the discussion below about good reasons for failing to comply with requirements and the suitability of courses etc). There may, though, in cases of uncooperative claimants or heavy-handed officials or a combination, be difficult questions whether an interview or course has ceased to exist. Behaviour after the interview or course has ceased to exist cannot be evidence of a failure to participate, in contrast to behaviour before it starts (see *SN* below).

In *SA v SSWP (JSA)* [2015] UKUT 454 (AAC) the claimant, who had hearing difficulties and wore a hearing aid in one ear, was directed by an employment officer to attend and complete a CV writing course with Learn Direct two days later from 11.15 a.m. to 12.15 p.m. He was given a letter to confirm the time and date. The claimant arrived at 11.25 a.m. and was told that he was too late and so had been deemed to have missed his appointment. He immediately went to the Jobcentre Plus office to rebook an appointment for the course and explained that he had misheard the time for the appointment as 11.50, the time that he normally signed on. A fixed four-week sanction for failing, without a good reason, to carry out a reasonable jobseeker's direction was imposed. On appeal the claimant said that at the meeting with the employment officer he had not been wearing his hearing aid and that he had not thought to check the time of the appointment on the letter as he genuinely thought that it was the same as his two previous appointments. The First-tier Tribunal regarded it as clear that the direction had been reasonable and that the claimant had failed to comply with it, so that the sole question was whether he had had a good reason for the failure. On that question, the tribunal concluded that, although the error was genuine, that did not in itself give him a good reason and that he had failed to take reasonable steps to confirm the time of the appointment and dismissed his appeal. In setting aside the tribunal's decision and substituting her own decision reversing the imposition of the sanction (as had been suggested by the Secretary of State), Judge Knowles held that the tribunal had erred in law by failing to consider the question of whether the claimant had failed to comply with the direction. In the substituted decision, she concluded that, the claimant not having refused to carry out the direction and taking into account that his error was genuine and that he took immediate steps to rebook, it was disproportionate to treat his late arrival in isolation as amounting to a failure to comply with the direction. That can only be regarded as a determination on the particular facts that does not constitute any sort of precedent to be applied as a matter of law in other cases. The outcome may have reflected an understandable desire in a deserving case to get around the absence of any scope for varying the fixed period of four weeks for a sanction under s.19A of the old style Jobseekers Act 1995 for a "first offence". However, there could have been nothing unreasonable about a conclusion that arriving 10 minutes after the beginning of a course that only lasted for an hour amounted to a failure to comply with a direction to attend and complete the course, no matter how genuine the error that led to the late arrival.

SN v SSWP (JSA) [2018] UKUT 279 (AAC) discusses, from para.42 onwards, what can amount to a failure to participate in a scheme (at a time when the consequent sanction was under reg.8 of the MWAS Regulations, rather than s.19(2)(e) of the old style Jobseekers Act 1995). It confirms that conduct of the claimant related to the ordinary requirements of the work activity in question leading to the termination of their placement can amount to a failure to participate. In particular, it is held in paras 59-62 that actions before the start of the scheme can be relevant. In *SN* the claimant was required to work for four weeks as a retail assistant in a charity shop. As found by Upper Tribunal Judge Wright in substituting a decision on the appeal, the claimant visited the shop about a week before the placement was due to start, to find out what would be entailed. During the visit he used offensive language to one member of staff and about the nature of the work involved, that were unreasonable in any work setting. He attended at the shop at the specified time for the start of the placement, but, as the representative of the programme provider was not to arrive for about 20 minutes, retired to a changing cubicle to sit down, took off his shoes and appeared to go to sleep. When the representative arrived, the deputy manager of the shop told him that the claimant would not be allowed to work there in view of his earlier offensive conduct. The judge concludes that the combination of the claimant's behaviour on the earlier visit and his attitude of antagonism and lack of interest on the first day of the placement meant that he had failed to meet the notified requirements for participation in the scheme. There was no good cause for the failure to participate. Some doubt is expressed in para.45 about the result in *SA*.

In *CS v SSWP (JSA)* [2019] UKUT 218 (AAC) Judge Hemingway accepted that it was legitimate for a scheme provider to require an attender to verify their identity before starting the scheme, so that a refusal to do so would usually amount to a failure to participate in the scheme. However, in the particular case the claimant had declined to verify various items of information about him appearing on a computer screen, largely because of misguided views about the effect of the Data Protection Act 1998, but also because of concerns about the security of social security information held by scheme providers. The judge held that the tribunal had erred in law by failing to make findings of fact about whether the claimant had been offered the opportunity to verify his identity by other means, e.g. by producing a passport or driving licence or other document in addition to the appointment letter that he had already produced. In the absence of such findings the tribunal had not been entitled to conclude that the claimant had refused to confirm his identity rather than merely refused to confirm it by the method initially put forward by the scheme provider. It might in other cases be relevant to enquire what the appointment letter or other documents do or do not say about confirming identity.

Claimants who are found not in fact to have been aware of an interview must have a good reason for failing to comply, whether or not the requirement is said to have been imposed in such circumstances (*SP v SSWP (UC)* [2018] UKUT 227 (AAC)).

See the notes to s.26 for general discussion of what might be a good reason and in particular for the suggestion that in the present context, if any analogy is to be drawn with previous authority, it should not be with the concept of "good cause" for a late claim, but with "just cause" for leaving employment voluntarily or with "good cause" under the pre-2012 form of s.19 of the old style Jobseekers Act 1995. It would seem that on any appeal, if the Secretary of State has proved on the balance of probabilities that there had been a failure to comply with a work-related or connected requirement, the practical burden would fall on the claimant of showing on the balance of probabilities that they have a good reason for the failure. That would be in accord with the principle demanded by *Kerr v Department for Social Development* [2004] UKHL 23; [2004] 1 W.L.R. 1372; *R 1/04 (SF)*, putting emphasis on who is in a better position to supply information on any particular issue in a co-operative process, rather than formal concepts of onus of proof. The claimant will in the great majority of cases be the person best placed to come forward with an explanation of their reasons for failing to comply with the requirement in question.

It appears to be accepted that the suitability of whatever it is that the claimant has been required to do is relevant to whether there is a good reason for not complying with the requirement. In *PL v DSD (JSA)* [2015] NI Com 72 (followed and applied in *PO'R v DFC (JSA)* [2018] NI Com 1), the Chief Commissioner for Northern Ireland has approved and applied the obiter suggestion of Judge Ward in *PL v SSWP (JSA)* [2013] UKUT 227 (AAC) (on the pre-October 2012 form of the Great Britain legislation) that, in deciding whether claimants have good cause for failing to avail themselves of a reasonable opportunity of a place on a training scheme or employment programme, a tribunal erred in law, where the circumstances raised the issue, in failing to consider the appropriateness of the particular scheme or programme to the particular claimant in the light of their skills and experience and previous attendance on any placements. Judge Ward's suggestion had been that the test was whether the claimant had reasonably considered that what was provided would not help him. It seems likely that a similar general approach will be taken to the issue of "good reason" under s.27(2) and the appropriateness of the activity in question. It may though still need to be sorted out how far the issue turns on the claimant's subjective view, within the bounds of reasonableness, in the light of the information provided at the time, as against a tribunal's view of the appropriateness of the activity. There may also be difficult questions in circumstances where what has been required seems quite reasonable and suitable and fairly imposed, but what is provided when the claimant attends turns out to be something different and of no assistance in the claimant's particular case, as in *DM v SSWP (JSA)* [2015] UKUT 67 (AAC) below. In such circumstances, does the claimant have a good reason for not participating in the activity at all, perhaps after raising queries with the provider, or are they, to escape sanction, obliged to sit through to the end?

DM was a case on jobseekers directions under s.19A(2)(c) of the old style Jobseekers Act 1995, but with insights relevant to universal credit. The claimant was directed to attend and participate in a group information session for work programme returnees that it was said would enable him to improve his chances of employment in several ways. Judge Rowley apparently accepted the claimant's evidence that the course turned out to be about the sanctions regime. After he was asked to leave before the end because he was said to be disrupting the course by asking questions and heckling, he was sanctioned for failing to carry out a reasonable jobseeker's direction by not fully participating in the session. The judge was able to dispose of the case on the basis that the direction was not reasonable in the absence of any evidence of how the group information session would have assisted the particular claimant to find employment or have improved his prospects of becoming employed and in the absence of evidence that the administrative guidance that directions should be personalised and appropriate to the individual claimant had been applied. Thus she did not have to grapple with the question of whether the claimant had had a good reason for failing to comply with the direction. That question may well arise in cases where the imposition of the requirement in question and a failure to comply cannot be challenged.

In *DH v SSWP (JSA)* [2016] UKUT 355 (AAC), a case about the Jobseeker's Allowance (Schemes for Assisting Persons to Obtain Employment) Regulations 2013 SI 2013/3196 (see Vol.V of this series, 2021/22 edition as updated in Cumulative Supplements included in this volume and in mid-year Supplements), it was held that the First-tier Tribunal erred in law in apparently dismissing the claimant's objections to attending a Work Programme run by a particular provider (on the grounds that staff of the company concerned had lied in a police statement and in court about whether travel expenses had been refunded to him and had bullied him) as, even if true, irrelevant to whether he had a good reason for failing to comply with requirements to participate. The tribunal had said that the claimant's remedies were to contact the police and to use appropriate complaints procedures, not to refuse to attend interviews or courses. The judge asked the rhetorical question in para.20 of what could amount to good reason if such matters did not. The circumstances are to be distinguished from those in *R(JSA) 7/03*, not mentioned in *DH*, where the claimant's objection was a generalised, though principled, one to the involvement of private companies in the provision of such schemes, rather than to specific aspects of the particular provider. The Commissioner held that that was not a "conscientious" objection under special provisions then in reg.73 of the JSA Regulations 1996 and did not amount to good cause for failing to carry out a direction to enroll in a Jobplan workshop, because his state of mind did not exist as a fact independently of his refusal to attend the workshop. It was not like having a particular fear of carrying out some activity that would be involved in the course or being in the location involved (on which see *GR v SSWP (JSA)* [2013] UKUT 645 (AAC) in the notes to s.26).

Hardship payments

1.211 **28.**—(1) Regulations may make provision for the making of additional payments by way of universal credit to a claimant ("hardship payments") where—

(a) the amount of the claimant's award is reduced under section 26 or 27, and

(b) the claimant is or will be in hardship.

(2) Regulations under this section may in particular make provision as to—

(a) circumstances in which a claimant is to be treated as being or not being in hardship;

(b) matters to be taken into account in determining whether a claimant is or will be in hardship;

(c) requirements or conditions to be met by a claimant in order to receive hardship payments;

(d) the amount or rate of hardship payments;

(e) the period for which hardship payments may be made;

(f) whether hardship payments are recoverable.

DEFINITION

"claimant"—see s.40.

GENERAL NOTE

1.212 The provision of hardship payments is an important part of the sanctions regime for universal credit. The payments are to be made by way of universal credit. However, it will be seen that s.28, first, does not require the making of provision for hardship payments in regulations and, second, gives almost complete freedom in how any regulations define the conditions for and amounts of payments. The provisions made are in regs 115–119 of the Universal Credit Regulations, which contain stringent conditions and a restricted definition of "hardship", which nevertheless retains a number of subjective elements. Payments are generally recoverable, subject to exceptions. See the notes to those regulations for the details and the relevant parts of Ch.52 of CPAG's *Welfare benefits and tax credits handbook 2024/2025* for helpful explanations and examples. There seems to be no reason why a decision of the Secretary of State to make or not to make hardship payments on an application under reg.116(1)(c) should not be appealable to a First-tier Tribunal.

Administration

Delegation and contracting out

1.213 **29.**—(1) The functions of the Secretary of State under sections 13 to 25 may be exercised by, or by the employees of, such persons as the Secretary of State may authorise for the purpose (an "authorised person").

(2) An authorisation given by virtue of this section may authorise the exercise of a function—

(a) wholly or to a limited extent;

(b) generally or in particular cases or areas;

(c) unconditionally or subject to conditions.

(3) An authorisation under this section—

(a) may specify its duration;

(b) may be varied or revoked at any time by the Secretary of State;

(c) does not prevent the Secretary of State or another person from exercising the function to which the authorisation related.

(4) Anything done or omitted to be done by or in relation to an authorised person (or an employee of that person) in, or in connection with, the exercise or purported exercise of the function concerned is to be treated for all purposes as done or omitted to be done by or in relation to the Secretary of State or (as the case may be) an officer of the Secretary of State.

(5) Subsection (4) does not apply—

(a) for the purposes of so much of any contract made between the authorised person and the Secretary of State as relates to the exercise of the function, or

(b) for the purposes of any criminal proceedings brought in respect of anything done or omitted to be done by the authorised person (or an employee of that person).

(6) Where—

(a) the authorisation of an authorised person is revoked, and

(b) at the time of the revocation so much of any contract made between the authorised person and the Secretary of State as relates to the exercise of the function is subsisting,

the authorised person is entitled to treat the contract as repudiated by the Secretary of State (and not as frustrated by reason of that revocation).

DEFINITION

"person"—see Interpretation Act 1978, Sch.1.

GENERAL NOTE

This section allows the Secretary of State to authorise other persons (which word in accordance with the Interpretation Act 1978 includes corporate and unincorporated associations, such as companies) and their employees to carry out any of his functions under ss.13–25. Any such authorisation will not in practice cover the making of regulations, but may well (depending on the extent of the authorisations given) extend to specifying various matters under those sections. The involvement of private sector organisations, operating for profit, in running various schemes within the scope of the benefit system is something that claimants sometimes object to. Such a generalised objection, even if on principled grounds, is unlikely to amount in itself to a good reason for failing to engage with a scheme in question (although see the discussion in the note to s.26 on whether "for no good reason" has a restricted meaning). An objection based on previous experience with the organisation concerned or the nature of the course may raise more difficult issues. See also the discussion in *R(JSA) 7/03* plus *CSJSA/495/2007* and *CSJSA/505/2007*. 1.214

In *DH v SSWP (JSA)* [2016] UKUT 355 (AAC), an old style JSA case under the Jobseeker's Allowance (Schemes for Assisting Persons to Obtain Employment) Regulations 2013, it was held that the First-tier Tribunal erred in law in apparently dismissing the claimant's objections to attending a Work Programme run by a particular provider (on the grounds that staff of the company concerned had lied in a police statement and in court about whether travel expenses had been refunded to him and had bullied him) as, even if true, irrelevant to whether he had a good reason for failing to comply with requirements to attend. The tribunal had said that the claimant's remedies were to contact the police and to use appropriate complaints procedures, not to refuse to attend interviews or courses. The judge asked the rhetorical question in para.20 what could amount to good reason if such matters did not. The circumstances are to be distinguished from those in *R(JSA) 7/03*, not mentioned in *DH*, where the claimant's objection was a generalised one to the involvement of private companies in the provision of such schemes.

Chapter 3

Supplementary and General

Supplementary and consequential

Supplementary regulation-making powers

1.215 **30.** Schedule 1 contains supplementary regulation-making powers.

Supplementary and consequential amendments

1.216 **31.** Schedule 2 contains supplementary and consequential amendments.

Power to make supplementary and consequential provision etc.

1.217 **32.**—(1) The appropriate authority may by regulations make such consequential, supplementary, incidental or transitional provision in relation to any provision of this Part as the authority considers appropriate.

(2) The appropriate authority is the Secretary of State, subject to subsection (3).

(3) The appropriate authority is the Welsh Ministers for—

(a) provision which would be within the legislative competence of the National Assembly for Wales were it contained in an Act of the Assembly;

(b) provision which could be made by the Welsh Ministers under any other power conferred on them.

(4) Regulations under this section may amend, repeal or revoke any primary or secondary legislation (whenever passed or made).

Universal credit and other benefits

Abolition of benefits

1.218 **33.**—(1) The following benefits are abolished—

(a) income-based jobseeker's allowance under the Jobseekers Act 1995;

(b) income-related employment and support allowance under Part 1 of the Welfare Reform Act 2007;

(c) income support under section 124 of the Social Security Contributions and Benefits Act 1992;

(d) housing benefit under section 130 of that Act;

(e) council tax benefit under section 131 of that Act;

(f) child tax credit and working tax credit under the Tax Credits Act 2002.

(2) In subsection (1)—

(a) "income-based jobseeker's allowance" has the same meaning as in the Jobseekers Act 1995;

(b) "income-related employment and support allowance" means an employment and support allowance entitlement to which is based on section 1(2)(b) of the Welfare Reform Act 2007.

(3) Schedule 3 contains consequential amendments.

Definitions

"income-related employment and support allowance"—see subs(2)(b).
"income-based jobseeker's allowance"—see subs.(2)(a).

GENERAL NOTE

Subsection (1)

The purpose of this provision is simple enough. Sub-section (1) provides for the abolition of income-based JSA, income-related ESA, income support, housing benefit, council tax benefit, child tax credit and working tax credit. The implementation of this section is much less straightforward. Council tax benefit was abolished in favour of localised schemes from April 2013. As a general rule abolition of the other benefits will only happen when all claimants have been transferred to universal credit. See now the Welfare Reform Act 2012 (Commencement No.34 and Commencement No.9, 21, 23, 31 and 32 and Transitional and Transitory Provisions (Amendment)) Order 2022 (SI 2022/302). **1.219**

This sub-section is modelled on the drafting of s.1(3) of the Tax Credits Act (TCA) 2002, which provided for the abolition of e.g. the personal allowances for children in the income support and income-based JSA schemes. Section 1(3) of the TCA 2002 has never been fully implemented. The fate of subs.(1) here remains to be seen.

Subsection (3)

This introduces Sch.3, which makes consequential amendments relating to the abolition of these benefits. Those changes remove references in other legislation to contributory ESA or JSA, as these will be unnecessary once ESA and JSA are contributory benefits only, and update references to other legislation which has been amended. **1.220**

Universal credit and state pension credit

34. Schedule 4 provides for a housing element of state pension credit in consequence of the abolition of housing benefit by section 33. **1.221**

GENERAL NOTE

This section, which is not yet in force, provides for a new housing credit element of state pension credit to replace housing benefit for claimants above the qualifying age for state pension credit. In its original form under the SPCA 2002, state pension credit was made up of two elements: the guarantee credit (performing the same function as income support used to) and the savings credit (providing a small top-up for those claimants with modest savings). Schedule 4 amends the SPCA 2002 to create a new third credit to cover housing costs. This will provide support for people who have reached the qualifying age for state pension credit (or for couples where both members have reached the qualifying age) once housing benefit is no longer available following the introduction of universal credit. **1.222**

Universal credit and working-age benefits

35. Schedule 5 makes further provision relating to universal credit, jobseeker's allowance and employment and support allowance. **1.223**

GENERAL NOTE

This section (and Sch.5) deals with the inter-relationship between universal credit, JSA and ESA. After the introduction of universal credit, ESA and JSA will continue to be available but only as contributory benefits. **1.224**

Migration to universal credit

36. Schedule 6 contains provision about the replacement of benefits by universal credit. **1.225**

GENERAL NOTE

This section gives effect to Sch.6, which makes provision relating to the replacement of the benefits that will be abolished under s.33, as well as any other prescribed benefits, and the consequential migration (or transfer) of claimants to universal credit. **1.226**

General

Capability for work or work-related activity

1.227 37.—(1) For the purposes of this Part a claimant has limited capability for work if—

(a) the claimant's capability for work is limited by their physical or mental condition, and

(b) the limitation is such that it is not reasonable to require the claimant to work.

(2) For the purposes of this Part a claimant has limited capability for work-related activity if—

(a) the claimant's capability for work-related activity is limited by their physical or mental condition, and

(b) the limitation is such that it is not reasonable to require the claimant to undertake work-related activity.

(3) The question whether a claimant has limited capability for work or work-related activity for the purposes of this Part is to be determined in accordance with regulations.

(4) Regulations under this section must, subject as follows, provide for determination of that question on the basis of an assessment (or repeated assessments) of the claimant.

(5) Regulations under this section may for the purposes of an assessment—

(a) require a claimant to provide information or evidence (and may require it to be provided in a prescribed manner or form);

(b) require a claimant to attend and submit to a medical examination at a place, date and time determined under the regulations.

(6) Regulations under this section may make provision for a claimant to be treated as having or not having limited capability for work or work-related activity.

(7) Regulations under subsection (6) may provide for a claimant who fails to comply with a requirement imposed under subsection (5) without a good reason to be treated as not having limited capability for work or work-related activity.

(8) Regulations under subsection (6) may provide for a claimant to be treated as having limited capability for work until—

(a) it has been determined whether or not that is the case, or

(b) the claimant is under any other provision of regulations under subsection (6) treated as not having it.

(9) Regulations under this section may provide for determination of the question of whether a claimant has limited capability for work or work-related activity even where the claimant is for the time being treated under regulations under subsection (6) as having limited capability for work or work-related activity.

DEFINITIONS

"claim"—see s.40.
"claimant"—*ibid.*
"limited capability for work"—*ibid.*
"prescribed"—*ibid.*
"work search requirement"—*ibid.*

General Note

If a person has limited capability for work (LCW) or LCW and limited capability for work-related activity (LCWRA), this is relevant to universal credit in three ways. First, at least so far as LCWRA is concerned, it affects the amount of the award of universal credit (see ss.1(3)(d) and 12(2)(a) and (b) and regs 27–28 and 36 of the Universal Credit Regulations). Secondly, it determines the work-related requirements that can be imposed. Under s.19(1) and (2)(a) no work-related requirements can be imposed on a claimant who has limited capability for work and work-related activity and under s.21(1)(a) a claimant who has limited capability for work (and who does not fall within s.19 or 20) is only subject to the work preparation requirement. Thirdly, it enables the application of the appropriate work allowance (see s. 8(3)(a) and reg. 22 of the Universal Credit Regulations). 1.228

This section contains provisions that are broadly equivalent to those in ss.1(4), 2(5), 8 and 9 of the Welfare Reform Act 2007. Thus the question of whether a person has limited capability for work or limited capability for work and work-related activity, is determined in the same way as for ESA.

In relation to subs.(7), note also the regulation-making power in para.8 of Sch.1.

Information

38. Information supplied under Chapter 2 of this Part or section 37 is to be taken for all purposes to be information relating to social security. 1.229

Couples

39.—[1 2 (1) In this Part "couple" means— 1.230

(a) two people who are married to, or civil partners of, each other and are members of the same household; or

(b) two people who are not married to, or civil partners of, each other but are living together [3 as if they were a married couple or civil partners].]

(2) [1 2 . . .]

(3) For the purposes of this section regulations may prescribe—

(a) circumstances in which the fact that two persons are [1 2 married] or are civil partners is to be disregarded;

(b) circumstances in which [1 2 two people are to be treated as living together [3 as if they were a married couple or civil partners]];

(c) circumstances in which people are to be treated as being or not being members of the same household.

Amendments

1. Marriage (Same Sex Couples) Act 2013 (Consequential and Contrary Provisions and Scotland) Order 2014 (SI 2014/560) art.2 and Sch.1, para.36 (March 13, 2014). This amendment extended to England and Wales only.

2. Marriage and Civil Partnership (Scotland) Act 2014 and Civil Partnership Act 2004 (Consequential Provisions and Modifications) Order 2014 (SI 2014/3229) art.29 and Sch.5, para.20 (December 16, 2014). This amendment extended to Scotland only. However, as it was in the same terms as the amendment made in England and Wales by SI 2014/560 (see above), the effect is that the law is now the same throughout Great Britain.

3. Civil Partnership (Opposite-sex Couples) Regulations 2019 (SI 2019/1458) reg.41(a) and Sch.3 Pt 1 para.35 (December 2, 2019).

General Note

See the commentary to reg.3 of the Universal Credit Regulations. 1.231

Interpretation of Part 1

1.232 **40.** In this Part—

"assessment period" has the meaning given by section 7(2);

"child" means a person under the age of 16;

"claim" means claim for universal credit;

"claimant" means a single claimant or each of joint claimants;

"couple" has the meaning given by section 39;

"disabled" has such meaning as may be prescribed;

"joint claimants" means members of a couple who jointly make a claim or in relation to whom an award of universal credit is made;

"limited capability for work" and "limited capability for work-related activity" are to be construed in accordance with section 37(1) and (2);

"prescribed" means specified or provided for in regulations;

"primary legislation" means an Act, Act of the Scottish Parliament or Act or Measure of the National Assembly for Wales;

"qualifying young person" has the meaning given in section 10(5);

"regular and substantial caring responsibilities" has such meaning as may be prescribed;

"responsible carer", in relation to a child, has the meaning given in section 19(6);

"secondary legislation" means an instrument made under primary legislation";

"severely disabled" has such meaning as may be prescribed;

"single claimant" means a single person who makes a claim for universal credit or in relation to whom an award of universal credit is made as a single person;

"single person" is to be construed in accordance with section 1(2)(a);

"work" has such meaning as may be prescribed;

"work availability requirement" has the meaning given by section 18(1);

"work preparation requirement" has the meaning given by section 16(1);

"work search requirement" has the meaning given by section 17(1);

"work-focused interview requirement" has the meaning given by section 15(1);

"work-related activity", in relation to a person, means activity which makes it more likely that the person will obtain or remain in work or be able to do so;

"work-related requirement" has the meaning given by section 13(2).

Regulations

Pilot schemes

1.233 **41.**—(1) Any power to make—

(a) regulations under this Part,

(b) regulations under the Social Security Administration Act 1992 relating to universal credit, or

(c) regulations under the Social Security Act 1998 relating to universal credit, may be exercised so as to make provision for piloting purposes.

(2) In subsection (1), "piloting purposes", in relation to any provision, means the purposes of testing—

(a) the extent to which the provision is likely to make universal credit simpler to understand or to administer,

(b) the extent to which the provision is likely to promote—

(i) people remaining in work, or

(ii) people obtaining or being able to obtain work (or more work or better-paid work), or

(c) the extent to which, and how, the provision is likely to affect the conduct of claimants or other people in any other way.

(3) Regulations made by virtue of this section are in the remainder of this section referred to as a "pilot scheme".

(4) A pilot scheme may be limited in its application to—

(a) one or more areas;

(b) one or more classes of person;

(c) persons selected—

(i) by reference to prescribed criteria, or

(ii) on a sampling basis.

(5) A pilot scheme may not have effect for a period exceeding three years, but—

(a) the Secretary of State may by order made by statutory instrument provide that the pilot scheme is to continue to have effect after the time when it would otherwise expire for a period not exceeding twelve months (and may make more than one such order);

(b) a pilot scheme may be replaced by a further pilot scheme making the same or similar provision.

(6) A pilot scheme may include consequential or transitional provision in relation to its expiry.

GENERAL NOTE

This section was brought into force for all purposes on September 15, 2014 by art.6 of the Welfare Reform Act 2012 (Commencement No. 19 and Transitional and Transitory Provisions and Commencement No. 9 and Transitional and Transitory Provisions (Amendment)) Order 2014 (SI 2014/2321). 1.234

This important provision is similar to that in s.29 of the Jobseekers Act 1995. It contains the power to pilot changes in regulations across particular geographical areas and/or specified categories of claimants for up to three years, although this period can be extended, or the pilot scheme can be replaced by a different pilot scheme making the same or similar provision (subs.(5)). The power can only be exercised in relation to the types of regulation listed in subs.(1) and with a view to assessing whether the proposed changes are likely to make universal credit simpler to understand or administer, to encourage people to find or remain in work (or more or better-paid work) or "to affect the conduct of claimants or other people in any other way" (subs.(2)). Regulations made under this section are subject to the affirmative resolution procedure (s.43(4)).

Regulations: general

42.—(1) Regulations under this Part are to be made by the Secretary of State, unless otherwise provided. 1.235

(2) A power to make regulations under this Part may be exercised—

(a) so as to make different provision for different cases or purposes;

(b) in relation to all or only some of the cases or purposes for which it may be exercised.

(3) Such a power includes—

(a) power to make incidental, supplementary, consequential or transitional provision or savings;

(b) power to provide for a person to exercise a discretion in dealing with any matter.

(4) Each power conferred by this Part is without prejudice to the others.

(5) Where regulations under this Part provide for an amount, the amount may be zero.

(6) Where regulations under this Part provide for an amount for the purposes of an award (or a reduction from an award), the amount may be different in relation to different descriptions of person, and in particular may depend on—

(a) whether the person is a single person or a member of couple.

(b) the age of the person.

(7) Regulations under section 11(4) or 12(3) which provide for the determination or calculation of an amount may make different provision for different areas.

DEFINITIONS

"couple"—see ss.39 and 40.
"single person"—see s.40.
"work"—*ibid.*

Regulations: procedure

1.236 **43.**—(1) Regulations under this Part are to be made by statutory instrument.

(2) A statutory instrument containing regulations made by the Secretary of State under this Part is subject to the negative resolution procedure, subject as follows.

(3) A statutory instrument containing the first regulations made by the Secretary of State under any of the following, alone or with other regulations, is subject to the affirmative resolution procedure—

(a) section 4(7) (acceptance of claimant commitment);

(b) section 5(1)(a) and (2)(a) (capital limits);

(c) section 8(3) (income to be deducted in award calculation);

(d) section 9(2) and (3) (standard allowance);

(e) section 10(3) and (4) (children and young persons element);

(f) section 11 (housing costs element);

(g) section 12 (other needs and circumstances element);

(h) section 18(3) and (5) (work availability requirement);

(i) section 19(2)(d) (claimants subject to no work-related requirements);

(j) sections 26 and 27 (sanctions);

(k) section 28 (hardship payments);

(l) paragraph 4 of Schedule 1 (calculation of capital and income);

(m) paragraph 1(1) of Schedule 6 (migration), where making provision under paragraphs 4, 5 and 6 of that Schedule.

(4) A statutory instrument containing regulations made by the Secretary of State by virtue of section 41 (pilot schemes), alone or with other regulations, is subject to the affirmative resolution procedure.

(5) A statutory instrument containing regulations made by the Secretary of State under this Part is subject to the affirmative resolution procedure if—

(a) it also contains regulations under another enactment, and
(b) an instrument containing those regulations would apart from this section be subject to the affirmative resolution procedure.

(6) For the purposes of subsections (2) to (5)—

(a) a statutory instrument subject to the "negative resolution procedure" is subject to annulment in pursuance of a resolution of either House of Parliament;
(b) a statutory instrument subject to the "affirmative resolution procedure" may not be made unless a draft of the instrument has been laid before, and approved by resolution of, each House of Parliament.

(7) A statutory instrument containing regulations made by the Welsh Ministers under section 32 may not be made unless a draft of the instrument has been laid before, and approved by resolution of, the National Assembly for Wales.

DEFINITIONS

"child"—see s.40.
"claim"—*ibid.*
"claimant"—*ibid.*
"work"—*ibid.*
"work availability requirement"—*ibid.*

PART 5

SOCIAL SECURITY: GENERAL

Benefit cap

Benefit cap

96.—(1) Regulations may provide for a benefit cap to be applied to the welfare benefits to which a single person or couple is entitled. 1.237

(2) For the purposes of this section, applying a benefit cap to welfare benefits means securing that, where a single person's or couple's total entitlement to welfare benefits in respect of the reference period exceeds the relevant amount, their entitlement to welfare benefits in respect of any period of the same duration as the reference period is reduced by an amount up to or equalling the excess.

(3) In subsection (2) the "reference period" means a period of a prescribed duration.

(4) Regulations under this section may in particular—

(a) make provision as to the manner in which total entitlement to welfare benefits for any period, or the amount of any reduction, is to be determined;
(b) make provision as to the welfare benefit or benefits from which a reduction is to be made;
(c) provide for exceptions to the application of the benefit cap;

(d) make provision as to the intervals at which the benefit cap is to be applied;
(e) make provision as to the relationship between application of the benefit cap and any other reduction in respect of a welfare benefit;
(f) provide that where in consequence of a change in the relevant amount, entitlement to a welfare benefit increases or decreases, that increase or decrease has effect without any further decision of the Secretary of State;
(g) make supplementary and consequential provision.

[1 (5) Regulations under this section may make provision for determining the "relevant amount" for the reference period applicable in the case of a single person or couple by reference to the annual limit applicable in the case of that single person or couple.

(5A) For the purposes of this section the "annual limit" is—
(a) [2 £25,323 or £16,967], for persons resident in Greater London;
(b) [2 £22,020 or £14,753], for other persons.

(5B) Regulations under subsection (5) may—
(a) specify which annual limit applies in the case of—
  (i) different prescribed descriptions of single person;
  (ii) different prescribed descriptions of couple;
(b) define "resident" for the purposes of this section;
(c) provide for the rounding up or down of an amount produced by dividing the amount of the annual limit by the number of periods of a duration equal to the reference period in a year.]

(6) [1 . . .]
(7) [1 . . .]
(8) [1 . . .]

(9) Regulations under this section may not provide for any reduction to be made from a welfare benefit—
(a) provision for which is within the legislative competence of the Scottish Parliament;
(b) provision for which is within the legislative competence of the National Assembly for Wales;
(c) provision for which is made by the Welsh Ministers, the First Minister for Wales or the Counsel General to the Welsh Assembly Government.

(10) In this section—
"couple" means two persons of a prescribed description;
"prescribed" means prescribed in regulations;
"regulations" means regulations made by the Secretary of State;
"single person" means a person who is not a member of a couple;
"welfare benefit" [1 means—
(a) bereavement allowance (see section 39B of the Social Security Contributions and Benefits Act 1992),
(b) child benefit (see section 141 of the Social Security Contributions and Benefits Act 1992),
(c) child tax credit (see section 1(1)(a) of the Tax Credits Act 2002),
(d) employment and support allowance (see section 1 of the Welfare Reform Act 2007), including income-related employment and support allowance (as defined in section 1(7) of the Welfare Reform Act 2007),

(e) housing benefit (see section 130 of the Social Security Contributions and Benefits Act 1992),
(f) incapacity benefit (see section 30A of the Social Security Contributions and Benefits Act 1992),
(g) income support (see section 124 of the Social Security Contributions and Benefits Act 1992),
(h) jobseeker's allowance (see section 1 of the Jobseekers Act 1995), including income-based jobseeker's allowance (as defined in section 1(4) of the Jobseekers Act 1995),
(i) maternity allowance under section 35 or 35B of the Social Security Contributions and Benefits Act 1992,
(j) severe disablement allowance (see section 68 of the Social Security Contributions and Benefits Act 1992),
(k) universal credit,
(l) widow's pension (see section 38 of the Social Security Contributions and Benefits Act 1992),
(m) widowed mother's allowance (see section 37 of the Social Security Contributions and Benefits Act 1992), or
(n) widowed parent's allowance (see section 39A of the Social Security Contributions and Benefits Act 1992).

(11) [1 . . .]

AMENDMENTS

1. Welfare Reform and Work Act 2016 s.8(1)-(5) (assessment periods beginning on or after November 7, 2016: see SI 2016/910).
2. Benefit Cap (Annual Limit) (Amendment) Regulations 2023 (SI 2023/335) reg.2 (assessment periods beginning on or after April 10, 2023).

GENERAL NOTE

See the commentary to regs 78–83 of the Universal Credit Regulations. **1.238**

[1 Benefit cap: review

96A.—(1) The Secretary of State must at least once [2 every five years] review the sums specified in section 96(5A) to determine whether it is appropriate to increase or decrease any one or more of those sums. **1.239**

(2) The Secretary of State may, at any other time the Secretary of State considers appropriate, review the sums specified in section 96(5A) to determine whether it is appropriate to increase or decrease any one or more of those sums.

(3) In carrying out a review, the Secretary of State must take into account—
(a) the national economic situation, and
(b) any other matters that the Secretary of State considers relevant.

(4) After carrying out a review, the Secretary of State may, if the Secretary of State considers it appropriate, by regulations amend section 96(5A) so as to increase or decrease any one or more of the sums specified in section 96(5A).

(5) Regulations under subsection (4) may provide for amendments of section 96(5A) to come into force—
(a) on different days for different areas;

(b) on different days for different cases or purposes.

(6) Regulations under subsection (4) may make such transitional or transitory provision or savings as the Secretary of State considers necessary or expedient in connection with the coming into force of any amendment made by regulations under subsection (4).

(7) Regulations under subsection (6) may in particular—

(a) provide for section 96(5A) to have effect as if the amendments made by regulations under subsection (4) had not been made, in relation to such persons or descriptions of persons as are specified in the regulations or generally, until a time or times specified in a notice issued by the Secretary of State;

(b) provide for the Secretary of State to issue notices under paragraph (a) specifying different times for different persons or descriptions of person;

(c) make provision about the issuing of notices under paragraph (a), including provision for the Secretary of State to issue notices to authorities administering housing benefit that have effect in relation to persons specified, or persons of a description specified, in the notices.

(8) Section 176 of the Social Security Administration Act 1992 (consultation with representative organisations) does not apply in relation to regulations under subsection (4).

(9) [2 . . .]

AMENDMENT

1. Welfare Reform and Work Act 2016 (c.7) s.9(1) (November 7, 2016).

2. Dissolution and Calling of Parliament Act 2022 (c.11) Sch.1 para.21(b) (March 24, 2022).

GENERAL NOTE

1.240 A difficulty with s.96A(1)–(2) is that the provisions are not accompanied by any obligation to publish the outcome of a review unless it results in a change to the cap levels. That omission obstructs the ability of an external observer to know whether the requirement to conduct five-yearly reviews is being complied with. In July 2022 a minister informed Parliament that there had not ever been a review of benefit cap levels under s.96A(1): PQ UIN 27503, July 4, 2022. Then, in November 2022 the Government announced that it had decided to raise the cap levels in 2023 (implying that it had at some point after July 2022 conducted a review): Autumn Statement 2022 (CP 751, November 2022), para.2.47. It follows that the s.96A(1) duty will next require a review at some point between July and November 2027—unless the Secretary of State meanwhile chooses to conduct a review, which would restart the clock.

Benefit cap: supplementary

1.241 **97.**—(1) Regulations under section 96 [3 or 96A] may make different provision for different purposes or cases.

(2) Regulations under section 96 [3 or 96A] must be made by statutory instrument.

(3) [2 . . .]

(4) A statutory instrument containing [2 . . .] regulations under section 96 is subject to annulment in pursuance of a resolution of either House of Parliament.

[3 (4A) A statutory instrument containing regulations under section 96A may not be made unless a draft of the instrument has been laid before, and approved by a resolution of, each House of Parliament.]

(5) [1 . . .]

(6) In Schedule 2 to the Social Security Act 1998 (decisions against which no appeal lies) after paragraph 8 there is inserted—

"*Reduction on application of benefit cap*

8A A decision to apply the benefit cap in accordance with regulations under section 96 of the Welfare Reform Act 2012."

AMENDMENTS

1. Welfare Reform and Work Act 2016 s.9(6) (March 16, 2016).

2. Welfare Reform and Work Act 2016 s.8(6) (assessment periods beginning on or after November 7, 2016: see SI 2016/910).

3. Welfare Reform and Work Act 2016 s.9(2)-(5) (November 7, 2016).

GENERAL NOTE

See the commentary to regs 78–83 of the Universal Credit Regulations. **1.242**

PART 7

FINAL

Repeals

147. *[Omitted]* **1.243**

Financial provision

148. There shall be paid out of money provided by Parliament— **1.244**

(a) sums paid by the Secretary of State by way of universal credit or personal independence payment;
(b) any other expenditure incurred in consequence of this Act by a Minister of the Crown or the Commissioners for Her Majesty's Revenue and Customs;
(c) any increase attributable to this Act in the sums payable under any other Act out of money so provided.

Extent

149.—(1) This Act extends to England and Wales and Scotland only, subject as follows. **1.245**

(2) The following provisions extend to England and Wales, Scotland and Northern Ireland—

(a) section 32 (power to make consequential and supplementary provision: universal credit);
(b) section 33 (abolition of benefits);
(c)–(f) *[Omitted]*

(g) this Part, excluding Schedule 14 (repeals).

(3) *[Omitted]*

(4) Any amendment or repeal made by this Act has the same extent as the enactment to which it relates.

Commencement

1.246 **150.**—(1) The following provisions of this Act come into force on the day on which it is passed—

(a)–(e) *[Omitted]*

(f) this Part, excluding Schedule 14 (repeals).

(2) *[Omitted]*

(3) The remaining provisions of this Act come into force on such day as the Secretary of State may by order made by statutory instrument appoint.

(4) An order under subsection (3) may—

(a) appoint different days for different purposes;

(b) appoint different days for different areas in relation to—

(i) any provision of Part 1 (universal credit) or of Part 1 of Schedule 14;

(ii)–(iii) *[Omitted]*

(iv) section 102 (consideration of revision before appeal);

(c) make such transitory or transitional provision, or savings, as the Secretary of State considers necessary or expedient.

Short title

1.247 **151.** This Act may be cited as the Welfare Reform Act 2012.

SCHEDULES

Section 30

SCHEDULE 1

UNIVERSAL CREDIT: SUPPLEMENTARY REGULATION-MAKING POWERS

Entitlement of joint claimants

1.248 **1.** Regulations may provide for circumstances in which joint claimants may be entitled to universal credit without each of them meeting all the basic conditions referred to in section 4.

Linking periods

2. Regulations may provide for periods of entitlement to universal credit which are separated by no more than a prescribed number of days to be treated as a single period.

Couples

3.—(1) Regulations may provide—

(a) for a claim made by members of a couple jointly to be treated as a claim made by one member of the couple as a single person (or as claims made by both members as single persons);

(b) for claims made by members of a couple as single persons to be treated as a claim made jointly by the couple.

(2) Regulations may provide—

(a) where an award is made to joint claimants who cease to be entitled to universal credit as such by ceasing to be a couple, for the making of an award (without a claim) to either or each one of them—

(i) as a single person, or
(ii) jointly with another person;

(b) where an award is made to a single claimant who ceases to be entitled to universal credit as such by becoming a member of a couple, for the making of an award (without a claim) to the members of the couple jointly;
(c) for the procedure to be followed, and information or evidence to be supplied, in relation to the making of an award under this paragraph.

Calculation of capital and income

4.—(1) Regulations may for any purpose of this Part provide for the calculation or estimation of—
(a) a person's capital,
(b) a person's earned and unearned income, and
(c) a person's earned and unearned income in respect of an assessment period.

(2) Regulations under sub-paragraph (1)(c) may include provision for the calculation to be made by reference to an average over a period, which need not include the assessment period concerned.

(3) Regulations under sub-paragraph (1) may—
(a) specify circumstances in which a person is to be treated as having or not having capital or earned or unearned income;
(b) specify circumstances in which income is to be treated as capital or capital as earned income or unearned income;
(c) specify circumstances in which unearned income is to be treated as earned, or earned income as unearned;
(d) provide that a person's capital is to be treated as yielding income at a prescribed rate;
(e) provide that the capital or income of one member of a couple is to be treated as that of the other member.

(4) Regulations under sub-paragraph (3)(a) may in particular provide that persons of a prescribed description are to be treated as having a prescribed minimum level of earned income.

(5) In the case of joint claimants the income and capital of the joint claimants includes (subject to sub-paragraph (6)) the separate income and capital of each of them.

(6) Regulations may specify circumstances in which capital and income of either of joint claimants is to be disregarded in calculating their joint capital and income.

Responsibility for children etc

5.—(1) Regulations may for any purpose of this Part specify circumstances in which a person is or is not responsible for a child or qualifying young person. 1.249

(2) Regulations may for any purpose of this Part make provision about nominations of the responsible carer for a child (see section 19(6)(b)(ii)).

Vouchers

6.—(1) This paragraph applies in relation to an award of universal credit where the calculation of the amount of the award includes, by virtue of any provision of this Part, an amount in respect of particular costs which a claimant may incur.

(2) Regulations may provide for liability to pay all or part of the award to be discharged by means of provision of a voucher.

(3) But the amount paid by means of a voucher may not in any case exceed the total of the amounts referred to in sub-paragraph (1) which are included in the calculation of the amount of the award.

(4) For these purposes a voucher is a means other than cash by which a claimant may to any extent meet costs referred to in sub-paragraph (1) of a particular description.

(5) A voucher may for these purposes—
(a) be limited as regards the person or persons who will accept it;
(b) be valid only for a limited time.

Work-related requirements

7.—Regulations may provide that a claimant who—
(a) has a right to reside in the United Kingdom under the EU Treaties, and
(b) would otherwise fall within section 19, 20 or 21,is to be treated as not falling within that section.

Good reason

8.—Regulations may for any purpose of this Part provide for— 1.250

(a) circumstances in which a person is to be treated as having or not having a good reason for an act or omission;
(b) matters which are or are not to be taken into account in determining whether a person has a good reason for an act or omission.

DEFINITIONS

"assessment period"—see s.40 and s.7(2).
"child"—see s.40.
"claim"—*ibid.*
"claimant"—*ibid.*
"couple"—see ss.39 and 40.
"joint claimants"—see s.40.
"prescribed"—*ibid.*
"single claimant"—*ibid.*
"single person"—*ibid.*

Section 31

SCHEDULE 2

UNIVERSAL CREDIT: AMENDMENTS

[Omitted]

Section 33

SCHEDULE 3

ABOLITION OF BENEFITS: CONSEQUENTIAL AMENDMENTS

Social Security Contributions and Benefits Act 1992 (c.4)

1.251 *1. The Social Security Contributions and Benefits Act 1992 is amended as follows.*

2. In section 22 (earnings factors), in subsections (2)(a) and (5), for "a contributory" there is substituted "an".

3. In section 150 (interpretation of Part 10), in subsection (2), in the definition of "qualifying employment and support allowance", for "a contributory allowance" there is substituted "an employment and support allowance".

Social Security Administration Act 1992 (c.5)

1.252 4. The Social Security Administration Act 1992 is amended as follows.

5. In section 7 (relationship between benefits), in subsection (3), for "subsections (1) and (2)" there is substituted "subsection (1)".

6. In section 73 (overlapping benefits), in subsections (1) and (4)(c), for "a contributory" there is substituted "an".

7. In section 159B (effect of alterations affecting state pension credit), for "a contributory", wherever occurring, there is substituted "an".

8. In section 159D (as inserted by Schedule 2 to this Act) (effect of alterations affecting universal credit), for "a contributory", wherever occurring, there is substituted "an".

Immigration and Asylum Act 1999 (c.33)

1.253 *9. In the Immigration and Asylum Act 1999, in section 115 (exclusion from benefits of persons subject to immigration control)—*

(a) in subsection (1), after paragraph (ha) there is inserted "or";
(b) in subsection (2)(b) for "(a) to (j)" substitute "(a) to (i)".

Child Support, Pensions and Social Security Act 2000 (c.19)

1.254 *10. The Child Support, Pensions and Social Security Act 2000 is amended as follows.*

11. (1) Section 69 (discretionary financial assistance with housing) is amended as follows.

(2) In subsection (1)—

(a) for "relevant authorities" there is substituted "local authorities";

(b) in paragraph (a), the words from "housing benefit" to "both," are repealed.

(3) In subsection (2)—

(a) in paragraph (b), for "relevant authority" there is substituted "local authority";

(b) in paragraph (e), for "relevant authorities" there is substituted "local authorities";

(c) in paragraphs (f), (g) and (h), for "relevant authority" there is substituted "local authority".

(4) In subsection (5), for "relevant authorities" there is substituted "local authorities".

(5) In subsection (7), for the definition of "relevant authority" there is substituted—

""local authority" has the meaning given by section 191 of the Social Security Administration Act 1992."

12. (1) Section 70 (grants towards cost of discretionary housing payments) is amended as follows.

(2) In subsection (1), after "payments" there is inserted "("grants")".

(3) For subsection (2) there is substituted—

"(2) The amount of a grant under this section shall be determined in accordance with an order made by the Secretary of State with the consent of the Treasury."

(4) In subsection (8)—

(a) for the definition of "relevant authority" there is substituted—

""local authority" has the same meaning as in section 69;";

(b) the definition of "subsidy" is repealed.

13. After section 70 there is inserted—

"70A. Payment of grant

(1) A grant under section 70 shall be made by the Secretary of State in such instalments, at such times, in such manner and subject to such conditions as to claims, records, certificates, audit or otherwise as may be provided by order of the Secretary of State with the consent of the Treasury. **1.255**

(2) The order may provide that if a local authority has not complied with the conditions specified in it within such period as may be specified in it, the Secretary of State may estimate the amount of grant under section 70 payable to the authority and employ for that purpose such criteria as he considers relevant.

(3) Where a grant under section 70 has been paid to a local authority and it appears to the Secretary of State that—

(a) the grant has been overpaid, or

(b) there has been a breach of any condition specified in an order under this section, he may recover from the authority the whole or such part of the payment as he may determine.

(4) Without prejudice to the other methods of recovery, a sum recoverable under this section may be recovered by withholding or reducing subsidy.

(5) An order under this section may be made before, during or after the end of the period to which it relates.

(6) In this section "local authority" has the same meaning as in section 69.

(7) Section 70(5) to (7) applies to orders under this section."

14. [1 ...] **1.256**

Social Security Fraud Act 2001 (c.11)

15. The Social Security Fraud Act 2001 is amended as follows. **1.257**

16. In section 6B (loss of benefit for conviction etc), in subsection (5), for "to (10)" there is substituted "and (8)".

17. In section 7 (loss of benefit for repeated conviction etc), in subsection (2), for "to (5)" there is substituted "and (4A)".

18. In section 11 (regulations), in subsection (3)(c), for the words from "section" to the end there is substituted "section 6B(5A) or (8), 7(2A) or (4A) or 9(2A) or (4A)".

Commissioners for Revenue and Customs Act 2005 (c.11)

19. The Commissioners for Revenue and Customs Act 2005 is amended as follows. **1.258**

20. In section 5 (initial functions), in subsection (1), after paragraph (a) there is inserted "and".

21. In section 44 (payment into Consolidated Fund), in subsection (3), after paragraph (b) there is inserted "and".

Welfare Reform Act 2007 (c. 5)

1.259 22. The Welfare Reform Act 2007 is amended as follows.

23. In section 1 (employment and support allowance), in subsection (3)(d), at the end there is inserted "and".

24. In section 2 (amount of contributory allowance), in subsection (1), for "In the case of a contributory allowance, the amount payable" there is substituted "The amount payable by way of an employment and support allowance".

25.(1) Section 27 (financial provisions) is amended as follows.

(2) In subsection (1), for the words from "so much of" to the end there is substituted "any sums payable by way of employment and support allowance".

(3) In subsection (3), for "contributory" there is substituted "employment and support".

26. In each of the following provisions, for "a contributory allowance" there is substituted "an employment and support allowance"

(a) section 1A(1), (3), (4), (5) and (6) (as inserted by section 51 of this Act);
(b) section 1B(1) (as inserted by section 52 of this Act);
(c) section 3(2)(d);
(d) section 18(4);
(e) section 20(2), (3)(a), (b) and (c), (4), (5)(a), (b) and (c), (6), (7)(a), (b) and (c);
(f) in Schedule 1, paragraphs 1(5)(d) and 3(2)(a);
(g) in Schedule 2, paragraphs 6 and 7(2)(d).

Corporation Tax Act 2009 (c. 4)

1.260 *27. The Corporation Tax Act 2009 is amended as follows.*

28. In section 1059 (relief relating to SME R&D: total amount of company's PAYE and NICs liabilities), in subsection (5) after "sick pay" there is inserted "or".

29. In section 1108 (relief relating to vaccine research etc: total amount of company's PAYE and NICs liabilities), in subsection (5) after "sick pay" there is inserted "or".

AMENDMENT

1.261 1. Finance Act 2019, s.33(2)(c)(viii)(a) (April 1, 2020).

GENERAL NOTE

1.262 The amendments contained in this Schedule to other primary legislation fall into two main categories (italicised text indicates amendments that are not yet in force).

First, and for the most part, the amendments are consequential upon the abolition of income support, housing benefit, council tax benefit, child tax credit, working tax credit and the income-based forms of ESA and JSA. So, for example, references in other Acts to "a contributory employment and support allowance" are changed to "an employment and support allowance". This is because, after the full implementation of universal credit, the only form of ESA which will be available will be a contributory allowance.

The second category of amendments concerns those made to the Child Support, Pensions and Social Security Act 2000. These amend the provisions relating to discretionary housing payments and are consequential on the abolition of council tax benefit and housing benefit.

Section 34

SCHEDULE 4

HOUSING CREDIT ELEMENT OF STATE PENSION CREDIT

PART 1

AMENDMENTS TO STATE PENSION CREDIT ACT 2002

State Pension Credit Act 2002 (c.16)

1.263 *1. The State Pension Credit Act 2002 is amended as follows.*

2. In section 1 (entitlement), in subsection (2)(c), at the end there is inserted "or (iii) the conditions in section 3A(1) and (2) (housing credit)."

3. In that section, in subsection (3)—

(a) after paragraph (b) there is inserted "or

(c) to a housing credit, calculated in accordance with section 3A, if he satisfies the conditions in subsections (1) and (2) of that section,";

(b) for the words from "(or to both)" to the end there is substituted "(or to more than one of them, if he satisfies the relevant conditions)".

4. After section 3 there is inserted—

"3A. Housing credit

(1) The first of the conditions mentioned in section 1(2)(c)(iii) is that the claimant is liable to make payments in respect of the accommodation he occupies as his home. **1.264**

(2) The second of the conditions mentioned in section 1(2)(c)(iii) is that the claimant's capital and income are such that the amount of the housing credit payable (if he were entitled to it) would not be less than a prescribed amount.

(3) Where the claimant is entitled to a housing credit, the amount of the housing credit shall be an amount calculated in or determined under regulations (which may be zero).

(4) For the purposes of subsection (1)—

(a) the accommodation must be in Great Britain;

(b) the accommodation must be residential accommodation;

(c) it is immaterial whether the accommodation consists of the whole or part of a building and whether or not it comprises separate and self-contained premises.

(5) Regulations may make provision as to—

(a) the meaning of "payments in respect of accommodation" for the purposes of this section (and, in particular, as to the extent to which such payments include mortgage payments);

(b) circumstances in which a claimant is to be treated as liable or not liable to make such payments;

(c) circumstances in which a claimant is to be treated as occupying or not occupying accommodation as his home (and, in particular, for temporary absences to be disregarded);

(d) circumstances in which land used for the purposes of any accommodation is to be treated as included in the accommodation.

(6) Regulations under this section may make different provision for different areas."

5. In section 7 (fixing of retirement provision for assessed income period), at the end there is inserted—

"(10) Regulations may prescribe circumstances in which subsection (3) does not apply for the purposes of determining the amount of a housing credit to which the claimant is entitled."

6. In section 12 (polygamous marriages), in subsection (2)(b), after "savings credit" there is inserted "or housing credit".

7. In section 17 (interpretation), in subsection (1), after the definition of "guarantee credit" there is inserted—""housing credit" shall be construed in accordance with sections 1 and 3A;".

8. In Schedule 2 (consequential amendments etc), paragraph 9(5)(a) is repealed.

PART 2

AMENDMENTS TO OTHER ACTS

Social Security Administration Act 1992 (c.5)

9. The Social Security Administration Act 1992 is amended as follows. **1.265**

10. In section 5 (regulations about claims and payments) in subsection (6), before "subsection" there is inserted "or housing credit (within the meaning of the State Pension Credit Act 2002)".

11. [1 ...].

12. (1) Section 122F (supply by rent officers of information) is amended as follows.

(2) In subsection (3)(a) at the end of the words in brackets there is inserted "or housing credit".

(3) In subsection (4) at the end there is inserted "or housing credit".

(4) After that subsection there is inserted—

"(5) In this section "housing credit" has the same meaning as in the State Pension Credit Act 2002".

Housing Act 1996 (c.52)

13. (1) Section 122 of the Housing Act 1996 (rent officers) is amended as follows. **1.266**

(2) In the heading, at the end there is inserted "and housing credit".

(3) In subsection (1), at the end there is inserted "or housing credit (within the meaning of the State Pension Credit Act 2002)".

Child Support, Pensions and Social Security Act 2000 (c.19)

1.267 *14. In section 69 of the Child Support, Pensions and Social Security Act 2000 (discretionary financial assistance with housing), in subsection (1)(a), after "universal credit" there is inserted "or housing credit (within the meaning of the State Pension Credit Act 2002)".*

AMENDMENT

1. Welfare Reform and Work Act 2016 s.20(11)(f)(ii) (April 6, 2018).

GENERAL NOTE

1.268 Schedule 4 (which at the time of writing is still not yet in force) amends the State Pension Credit Act 2002 to create a new type of credit within state pension credit to cover housing costs. This will provide support for people who qualify for state pension credit once housing benefit is no longer available. In November 2022, the Government announced that the movement of pensioners from housing benefit to housing credit (and therefore the commencement of Sch.4) would be delayed to 2028/29: Autumn Statement 2022 (CP 751, November 2022), para.5.14.

The key provision is para.4, which inserts a new s.3A into the SPCA 2002. This provision sets out the conditions of entitlement to the housing credit (subss.(1) and (2)); it also provides the power to set out the manner in which the housing credit is to be calculated or determined in regulations (subs.(3)). The policy intention is that claimants will be entitled to broadly the same amount of support under the housing credit as they would previously have been entitled to by way of housing benefit. Subsection (5) of new s.3A simply adds detail to the power in subs.(3) by listing a number of specific matters in respect of which regulations may be made. Subsection (6) provides that regulations may make different provision for different areas. The underlying aim is to ensure that persons in different but abutting areas may be treated in a different manner depending on the circumstances obtaining in that area (e.g. to reflect different local taxation applied by different local authorities).

The other provision of note is para.5, which inserts a new s.7(10) into the SPCA 2002. Section 7 provides for assessed income periods in state pension credit, during which a person's retirement provision as assessed at the start of the period is taken to be the same throughout the period. The power exists in s.6(2)(b) to prescribe circumstances in which an assessed income period may not be set. The new s.7(10) provides that regulations may prescribe circumstances in which a person's retirement provision is not taken to be the same throughout the assessed income period for the purposes of determining the amount of housing credit to which a person is entitled. This power is inserted in order to replicate the current position in respect of housing benefit, which does not operate a system based on assessed income periods.

Section 35

SCHEDULE 5

UNIVERSAL CREDIT AND OTHER WORKING-AGE BENEFITS

General

1.269 1.(1) In this Schedule "relevant benefit" means—

(a) jobseeker's allowance, or

(b) employment and support allowance.

(2) In this Schedule "work-related requirement" means—

(a) a work-related requirement within the meaning of this Part,

(b) a work-related requirement within the meaning of the Jobseekers Act 1995, or
(c) a work-related requirement within the meaning of Part 1 of the Welfare Reform Act 2007.

(3) In this Schedule "sanction" means a reduction of benefit under—
(a) section 26 or 27,
(b) section 6J or 6K of the Jobseekers Act 1995, or
(c) section 11J of the Welfare Reform Act 2007.

Dual entitlement

2. (1) Regulations may make provision as to the amount payable by way of a relevant benefit where a person is entitled to that benefit and universal credit. **1.270**

(2) Regulations under sub-paragraph (1) may in particular provide for no amount to be payable by way of a relevant benefit.

(3) Regulations may, where a person is entitled to a relevant benefit and universal credit—
(a) make provision as to the application of work-related requirements;
(b) make provision as to the application of sanctions.

(4) Provision under sub-paragraph (3)(a) includes in particular—
(a) provision securing that compliance with a work-related requirement for a relevant benefit is to be treated as compliance with a work-related requirement for universal credit;
(b) provision disapplying any requirement on the Secretary of State to impose, or a person to comply with, a work-related requirement for a relevant benefit or universal credit.

(5) Provision under sub-paragraph (3)(b) includes in particular—
(a) provision for the order in which sanctions are to be applied to awards of relevant benefit and universal credit;
(b) provision to secure that the application of a sanction to an award of a relevant benefit does not result in an increase of the amount of an award of universal credit.

Movement between working-age benefits

3. Regulations may provide— **1.271**
(a) in a case where a person ceases to be entitled to universal credit and becomes entitled to a relevant benefit, for a sanction relating to the award of universal credit to be applied to the award of the relevant benefit;
(b) in a case where a person ceases to be entitled to a relevant benefit and becomes entitled to universal credit, for a sanction relating to the award of the relevant benefit to be applied to the award of universal credit;
(c) in a case where a person ceases to be entitled to one relevant benefit and becomes entitled to the other, for a sanction relating to the award of the former to apply to the award of the latter.

Hardship payments

4. Regulations under section 28 (hardship payments) may be made in relation to a person whose award of universal credit is reduced by virtue of regulations under paragraph 2(3)(b) or 3(b) as in relation to a person whose award is reduced under section 26 or 27. **1.272**

Earnings tapers

5. In section 4 of the Jobseekers Act 1995 (amount payable by way of a jobseeker's allowance), in subsection (1)(b)— **1.273**
(a) after "making" there is inserted—
"(i) deductions in respect of earnings calculated in the prescribed manner (which may include multiplying some or all earnings by a prescribed percentage), and
(b) "earnings," (before "pension payments") is repealed.

6. (1) Section 2 of the Welfare Reform Act 2007 (amount of contributory allowance) is amended as follows.

(2) In subsection (1)(c), after "making" there is inserted—
"(i) deductions in respect of earnings calculated in the prescribed manner (which may include multiplying some or all earnings by a prescribed percentage), and

(3) At the end there is inserted—

"(6) In subsection (1)(c)(i) the reference to earnings is to be construed in accordance with sections 3, 4 and 112 of the Social Security Contributions and Benefits Act 1992."

DEFINITIONS

"relevant benefit"—para.1(1)
"sanction"—para.1(3)
"work-related requirement"—para.1(2)

GENERAL NOTE

1.274 Schedule 5 makes provision to allow the Secretary of State to prescribe details of the relationship between universal credit on the one hand and ESA and JSA on the other. At the time of writing only paras 1-3 inclusive are in force; paras 4-6 are yet to be brought into force.

Paragraph 2

1.275 In certain circumstances claimants may meet the conditions of entitlement to both universal credit and JSA or ESA (as contributory benefits only). Paragraph 2 enables the Secretary of State to make provision as to the amount of contributory benefit payable where a person is entitled to both a contributory benefit and universal credit. According to the Department, Memorandum from the Department for Work and Pensions, *Welfare Reform Bill, as brought from the House of Commons on 16 June 2011*, House of Lords Select Committee on Delegated Powers and Regulatory Reform (at para.166):

> "It is intended that the power will in particular be used to:
> a) specify whether, in cases where the claimant might be entitled to both universal credit and either ESA or JSA, the claimant will be paid to only universal credit, or only the contributory benefit, or to both.
> b) make provision in relation to cases where a claimant might be able to choose which benefit to claim, in the event of them being potentially entitled to both.
> c) provide for exceptions, if appropriate, from the general rule.
> d) prescribe how work-related requirements are to apply in such cases.
> e) set out, if sanctions are applicable, which benefit is to be reduced first (in a case where a claimant is receiving both), what limitations any reductions are subject to, and to provide, if appropriate, that the application of a sanction to one benefit does not increase payment of the other."

Paragraph 3

1.276 Paragraph 3(a) and (b) allows for regulations to provide that where a person is entitled to universal credit and has their award reduced by a sanction, and then becomes entitled to JSA or ESA, the sanction can be applied to the new JSA or ESA award. This is obviously designed to ensure that claimants cannot avoid a sanction simply because they move between universal credit and JSA or ESA. Paragraph 3(c) makes similar provision for regulations to provide that sanctions imposed on claimants entitled to JSA or ESA can be applied to a subsequent award of the other benefit.

Paragraph 4

1.277 This allows for regulations made under s.28 (hardship payments) to apply to a person whose universal credit award is reduced by virtue of either para.2(3)(b) or 3(b) above. Section 28 only allows for universal credit hardship payments to be made to claimants who have their universal credit award reduced under ss.26 or 27, and so para.4 allows for claimants whose awards are reduced under other provisions to also be eligible for universal credit hardship payments.

Paragraph 5

This amendment to s.4 of the Jobseekers Act 1995 creates a power which allows the Secretary of State to deduct earnings which have been calculated in a prescribed manner, which may include multiplying some or all of the earnings by a prescribed percentage. The intention is to make provision for the amount of benefit payable to be tapered as earnings increase and to allow for some earnings to be disregarded before the taper is applied. **1.278**

Paragraph 6

This amends s.2 of the Welfare Reform Act 2007, and has similar effect on provision for the calculation of earnings in ESA as does para.(5) in relation to JSA. **1.279**

Section 36

SCHEDULE 6

MIGRATION TO UNIVERSAL CREDIT

General

1.(1) Regulations may make provision for the purposes of, or in connection with, replacing existing benefits with universal credit. **1.280**

(2) In this Schedule "existing benefit" means—

(a) a benefit abolished under section 33(1);

(b) any other prescribed benefit.

(3) In this Schedule "appointed day" means the day appointed for the coming into force of section 1.

Claims before the appointed day

2. (1) The provision referred to in paragraph 1(1) includes— **1.281**

(a) provision for a claim for universal credit to be made before the appointed day for a period beginning on or after that day;

(b) provision for a claim for universal credit made before the appointed day to be treated to any extent as a claim for an existing benefit;

(c) provision for a claim for an existing benefit made before the appointed day to be treated to any extent as a claim for universal credit.

(2) The provision referred to in paragraph 1(1) includes provision, where a claim for universal credit is made (or is treated as made) before the appointed day, for an award on the claim to be made in respect of a period before the appointed day (including provision as to the conditions of entitlement for, and amount of, such an award).

Claims after the appointed day

3. (1) The provision referred to in paragraph 1(1) includes— **1.282**

(a) provision permanently or temporarily excluding the making of a claim for universal credit after the appointed day by—

(i) a person to whom an existing benefit is awarded, or

(ii) a person who would be entitled to an existing benefit on making a claim for it;

(b) provision temporarily excluding the making of a claim for universal credit after the appointed day by any other person;

(c) provision excluding entitlement to universal credit temporarily or for a particular period;

(d) provision for a claim for universal credit made after the appointed day to be treated to any extent as a claim for an existing benefit;

(e) provision for a claim for an existing benefit made after the appointed day to be treated to any extent as a claim for universal credit.

(2) The provision referred to in paragraph 1(1) includes provision, where a claim for universal credit is made (or is treated as made) after the appointed day, for an award on the claim to be made in respect of a period before the appointed day (including provision as to the conditions of entitlement for, and amount of, such an award).

Awards

1.283 4.(1) The provision referred to in paragraph 1(1) includes—

(a) provision for terminating an award of an existing benefit;

(b) provision for making an award of universal credit, with or without application, to a person whose award of existing benefit is terminated.

(2) The provision referred to in sub-paragraph (1)(b) includes—

(a) provision imposing requirements as to the procedure to be followed, information to be supplied or assessments to be undergone in relation to an award by virtue of that sub-paragraph or an application for such an award;

(b) provision as to the consequences of failure to comply with any such requirement;

(c) provision as to the terms on which, and conditions subject to which, such an award is made, including—

(i) provision temporarily or permanently disapplying, or otherwise modifying, conditions of entitlement to universal credit in relation to the award;

(ii) provision temporarily or permanently disapplying, or otherwise modifying, any requirement under this Part for a person to be assessed in respect of capability for work or work-related activity;

(d) provision as to the amount of such an award;

(e) provision that fulfilment of any condition relevant to entitlement to an award of an existing benefit, or relevant to the amount of such an award, is to be treated as fulfilment of an equivalent condition in relation to universal credit.

(3) Provision under sub-paragraph (2)(d) may secure that where an award of universal credit is made by virtue of sub-paragraph (1)(b)—

(a) the amount of the award is not less than the amount to which the person would have been entitled under the terminated award, or is not less than that amount by more than a prescribed amount;

(b) if the person to whom it is made ceases to be entitled to universal credit for not more than a prescribed period, the gap in entitlement is disregarded in calculating the amount of any new award of universal credit.

Work-related requirements and sanctions

1.284 5.(1) The provision referred to in paragraph 1(1) includes—

(a) provision relating to the application of work-related requirements for relevant benefits;

(b) provision relating to the application of sanctions.

(2) The provision referred to in sub-paragraph (1)(a) includes—

(a) provision that a claimant commitment for a relevant benefit is to be treated as a claimant commitment for universal credit;

(b) provision that a work-related requirement for a relevant benefit is treated as a work-related requirement for universal credit;

(c) provision for anything done which is relevant to compliance with a work-related requirement for a relevant benefit to be treated as done for the purposes of compliance with a work-related requirement for universal credit;

(d) provision temporarily disapplying any provision of this Part in relation to work-related requirements for universal credit.

(3) The provision referred to in sub-paragraph (1)(b) includes—

(a) provision for a sanction relevant to an award of a relevant benefit to be applied to an award of universal credit;

(b) provision for anything done which is relevant to the application of a sanction for a relevant benefit to be treated as done for the purposes of the application of a sanction for universal credit;

(c) provision temporarily disapplying any provision of this Part in relation to the application of sanctions.

(4) In this paragraph—

"relevant benefit" means—

(a) jobseeker's allowance,

(b) employment and support allowance, and

(c) income support;

"work-related requirement" means—

(a) for universal credit, a work-related requirement within the meaning of this Part;

(b) for jobseeker's allowance, a requirement imposed—

(i) by virtue of regulations under section 8 or 17A of the Jobseekers Act 1995,

(ii) by a jobseeker's direction (within the meaning of section 19A of that Act),
(iii) by virtue of regulations under section 2A, 2AA or 2D of the Social Security Administration Act 1992, or
(iv) by a direction under section 2F of that Act;

(c) for employment and support allowance, a requirement imposed—
(i) by virtue of regulations under section 8, 9, 11, 12 or 13 of the Welfare Reform Act 2007,
(ii) by a direction under section 15 of that Act,
(iii) by virtue of regulations under section 2A, 2AA or 2D of the Social Security Administration Act 1992, or
(iv) by a direction under section 2F of that Act;

(d) for income support, a requirement imposed—
(i) by virtue of regulations under section 2A, 2AA or 2D of the Social Security Administration Act 1992, or
(ii) by a direction under section 2F of that Act;

"sanction" means a reduction of benefit under—
(a) section 26 or 27 above,
(b) section 19, 19A or 19B of the Jobseekers Act 1995,
(c) section 11, 12 or 13 of the Welfare Reform Act 2007, or
(d) section 2A, 2AA or 2D of the Social Security Administration Act 1992.

Tax credits

6. In relation to the replacement of working tax credit and child tax credit with universal credit, the provision referred to in paragraph 1(1) includes— **1.285**
(a) provision modifying the application of the Tax Credits Act 2002 (or of any provision made under it);
(b) provision for the purposes of recovery of overpayments of working tax credit or child tax credit (including in particular provision for treating overpayments of working tax credit or child tax credit as if they were overpayments of universal credit).

Supplementary

7. Regulations under paragraph 1(1) may secure the result that any gap in entitlement to an existing benefit (or what would, but for the provisions of this Part, be a gap in entitlement to an existing benefit) is to be disregarded for the purposes of provision under such regulations. **1.286**

DEFINITIONS

"appointed day"—see para.1(3).
"existing benefit"—see para.1(2).
"relevant benefit"—see para.5(4).
"sanction"—*ibid.*
"work-related requirement"—*ibid.*

GENERAL NOTE

Schedule 6 contains regulation-making powers to make provision in connection with replacing the existing means-tested benefits system with universal credit, and more particularly with the "migration" of claimants from one benefit to the other. Regulations made under this Schedule were subject to the affirmative resolution procedure where the power in para.1(1) was used in a way described in paras.4, 5 or 6 for the first time. This Schedule is fully in force (and has been since July 18, 2019: Welfare Reform Act 2012 (Commencement No.33) Order 2019 (SI 2019/1135), art.2). **1.287**

Paragraph 1

The principal such regulations are the Transitional Provisions Regulations 2014. **1.288**

Paragraph 2

Regulations may specify when a claim can be treated as a claim for an existing benefit and when a claim can be treated as a claim for universal credit. For example, **1.289** regulations may provide that a claim for an existing benefit made before the day that universal credit comes into effect, but for a period beginning after universal credit is introduced, (i.e. people making advance claims), can be treated as a claim for universal credit.

Paragraph 3

1.290 Regulations may provide that after the appointed day (i.e. the day universal credit is introduced), existing benefits cannot be claimed (see Transitional Provisions Regulations 2014 regs 5 and 6). Regulations can also provide for a claim to universal credit to be treated as a claim for existing benefit. This might be used where e.g. a claimant's benefit is backdated to a period before universal credit was introduced. Regulations may also provide that these cases may be awarded universal credit on terms, which match wholly or partly, the existing benefit.

Paragraph 4

1.291 Regulations may make provision for the "migration" of existing claimants onto universal credit. Such migration may be voluntary or mandatory. Regulations can prescribe the timing, conditions, kind and amount of any such entitlement to universal credit which was previously an award for an existing benefit. As regards para.4(1), see further the Transitional Provisions Regulations 2014.

Paragraph 5

1.292 This makes provision for the continuity of both work-related requirements and sanctions; see further especially regs 30–34 of the Transitional Provisions Regulations 2014 as regards sanctions.

Paragraph 6

1.293 The Secretary of State may, through regulations, modify any provision of the Tax Credits Act 2002 (or regulations) as necessary for the purposes of transferring people from working tax credit and child tax credit to universal credit. This power may be used to align certain tax credit rules more closely with universal credit to facilitate the transition process (para.(a)). Paragraph 6 also makes it clear that overpayments of tax credits can, through the transitional regulations, be treated as overpayments of universal credit (para.(b)). See further regs 11-12A of the Transitional Provisions Regulations 2014.

Welfare Reform and Work Act 2016

(2016 c.7)

SECTIONS REPRODUCED

Welfare benefits

1.294 8 Benefit cap
14 Changes to child element of universal credit

Loans for mortgage interest etc

18 Loans for mortgage interest etc
19 Section 18: further provision
21 Transitional provision

Final

34 Power to make consequential provision

An Act to make provision about reports on progress towards full employment and the apprenticeships target; to make provision about reports on the effect of certain support for troubled families; to make provision about life chances; to make provision about the benefit cap; to make provision about social security and tax credits; to make provision for loans for mortgage interest and other liabilities; and to make provision about social housing rents.
[March 16, 2016]

General Note

Sections 8-21 of, and Schedule 1 to, this Act are of potential relevance to entitlement to social security benefits and tax credits. They have been reproduced below to the extent that they are in force, do not make amendments that have been reproduced in the text of other legislation in this work, and have not been reproduced in other volumes. **1.295**

Sections 1-7 concern social policy, section 22 governs an aspect of social security administration that cannot give rise to an appeal and sections 23-33 make provision about social housing rents. They are therefore beyond the scope of this work.

Welfare benefits

Benefit cap

8.—(1)-(7) *[Omitted]* **1.296**

(8) Regulations made by the Secretary of State may make such transitional or transitory provision or savings as the Secretary of State considers necessary or expedient in connection with the coming into force of subsections (1) to (6).

(9) Regulations under subsection (8) may in particular—

(a) provide for section 96 to have effect as if the amendments made by subsections (2) to (5) and (7) had not been made, in relation to such persons or descriptions of persons as are specified in the regulations or generally, until a time or times specified in a notice issued by the Secretary of State;

(b) provide for the Secretary of State to issue notices under paragraph (a) specifying different times for different persons or descriptions of person;

(c) make provision about the issuing of notices under paragraph (a), including provision for the Secretary of State to issue notices to authorities administering housing benefit that have effect in relation to persons specified, or persons of a description specified, in the notices.

(10) Section 176 of the Social Security Administration Act 1992 (consultation with representative organisations) does not apply in relation to regulations under subsection (8).

(11) Regulations under subsection (8) must be made by statutory instrument.

(12) A statutory instrument containing regulations under subsection (8) is subject to annulment in pursuance of a resolution of either House of Parliament.

GENERAL NOTE

1.297 Section 8 was brought into force on March 16, 2016 for the purpose of making regulations (s.36(3)(a)), and on November 7, 2016 for all purposes (SI 2016/910, reg.2(1)). It extends to England, Wales and Scotland (s.35(3)). Subss.(1)-(6) amend WRA 2012 ss.96 and 97 (above) and subs.(7) revokes Pensions Act 2014 Sch.12 para.52. The regulation-making powers conferred by subs.(8)-(12) have been exercised to make the Benefit Cap (Housing Benefit and Universal Credit) (Amendment) Regulations 2016 (SI 2016/909).

Changes to child element of universal credit

1.298 **14.**—(1)-(5) *[Omitted]*

(6) The Secretary of State may by regulations make such transitional or transitory provision or savings as the Secretary of State considers necessary or expedient in connection with the coming into force of this section.

(7) Regulations under subsection (6) must be made by statutory instrument.

(8) A statutory instrument containing regulations under subsection (6) is subject to annulment in pursuance of a resolution of either House of Parliament.

GENERAL NOTE

1.299 Subss.(1)-(5), which amend Welfare Reform Act 2012 s.10 and Universal Credit Regulations, reg.24 came into force on April 6, 2017 (see SI 2017/111 reg.4). The other sub-sections came into force on February 8, 2017 (see SI 2017/111 reg.2(a)). The section as a whole extends to England and Wales and Scotland (s.35(3)(c)).

The regulation-making powers in subss.(6)-(8) have been used to make the Social Security (Restrictions on Amounts for Children and Qualifying Young Persons) Amendment Regulations 2017 (SI 2017/376) which amend Universal Credit Regulations, regs 2 and 24 and introduce new regs 24A and 24B and a new Sch.12 into those Regulations: see the commentary to regs 24-24B below.

Loans for mortgage interest etc

Loans for mortgage interest etc

1.300 **18.**—(1) The Secretary of State may by regulations provide for loans to be made in respect of a person's liability to make owner-occupier payments in respect of accommodation occupied by the person as the person's home.

(2) The regulations may make provision about eligibility to receive a loan under the regulations.

(3) Regulations under subsection (2) may in particular require that a person—

(a) is entitled to receive income support, income-based jobseeker's allowance, income-related employment and support allowance, state pension credit or universal credit;

(b) has received such a benefit for a period prescribed by the regulations.

(4) The regulations may make provision about the liabilities in respect of which a loan under the regulations may be made.

(5) Regulations under subsection (4) may in particular provide that a loan under the regulations may only be made if, and to the extent that, a person's liability to make owner-occupier payments was incurred for purposes prescribed by the regulations.

(6) Regulations under subsection (4) may in particular make provision about—

(a) determining or calculating the amount of a person's liabilities;

(b) the maximum amount of a person's liabilities in respect of which a loan under the regulations may be made.

(7) The regulations may—

(a) make provision about determining or calculating the amount that may be paid by way of loan under the regulations;

(b) require that a loan under the regulations be secured by a mortgage of or charge over a legal or beneficial interest in land or, in Scotland, by a heritable security.

(8) The regulations may define "owner-occupier payment".

(9) Regulations under this section may make different provision for different purposes.

(10) Regulations under this section must be made by statutory instrument.

(11) A statutory instrument containing regulations under this section is subject to annulment in pursuance of a resolution of either House of Parliament.

General Note

This section (and ss.19 & 21 below) came into force on April 3, 2017 (SI 2017/111 reg.3(d)-(f)). Section 20, which repeals and amends primary legislation governing mortgage interest support for IS, income-based JSA, SPC, income-related ESA and universal credit, came into force on July 27, 2018 (sub-ss (2)-(7) and (10): see SI 2017/802) and April 6, 2018 (sub-ss (1), (8)-(9) and (11): see SI 2018/438). All four sections extend to England and Wales and Scotland (s.35(3)(g)). 1.301

Taken together, ss.18, 19 and 21 confer powers on the Secretary of State to make regulations which replace the housing costs element for owner-occupiers under Universal Credit Regulations, reg.25(2) and Sch.5 (and the equivalent payments under IS Regulations, Sch.3; Jobseeker's Allowance Regulations 1996, Sch.2; SPC Regulations, Sch.2; and ESA Regulations, Sch.6) with repayable loans.

The Loans for Mortgage Interest Regulations 2017 (SI 2017/725) were made on July 5, 2017. They were fully in force, subject to limited transitional provision, by April 6, 2018. They make repayable loans available to eligible persons, and amend reg.25 of and Sch.1 to the Universal Credit Regulations 2013 (SI 2013/376), as well as regulations relating to various legacy benefits, to remove provision for owner-occupier housing costs payments. Significant amendments were made with effect from April 3, 2023 by the Loans for Mortgage Interest (Amendment) Regulations 2023 (SI 2023/226) (see Part IIA below). The key changes are a reduction in the waiting period from nine to three months, and abolition of the rule preventing claimants with earned income from obtaining these loans.

Section 18: further provision

19.—(1) This section makes further provision about regulations under section 18. 1.302

(2) The regulations may make provision about—

(a) circumstances in which a person is to be treated as liable or not liable to make owner-occupier payments;

(b) circumstances in which a person is to be treated as occupying or not occupying particular accommodation as a home.

(3) The regulations may include—

(a) provision about applying for a loan;

(b) provision requiring a person to satisfy requirements prescribed by the regulations before a loan may be made under the regulations, including requirements about receiving financial advice;

(c) provision about entering into an agreement (which may contain such terms and conditions as the Secretary of State thinks fit, subject to what may be provided in the regulations);

(d) provision about the time when, and manner in which, a loan must be repaid;

(e) provision about other terms upon which a loan is made;

(f) provision about the payment of interest, including provision prescribing or providing for the determination of the rate of interest;

(g) provision enabling administrative costs to be charged;

(h) provision about adding administrative costs to the amount of a loan;

(i) provision about accepting substituted security.

(4) The regulations may make provision—

(a) requiring that, in circumstances prescribed by the regulations, money lent in respect of a person's liability to make owner-occupier payments—

(i) is paid directly to the qualifying lender;

(ii) is applied by the qualifying lender towards discharging the person's liability to make owner-occupier payments;

(b) for the costs of administering the making of payments to qualifying lenders to be defrayed, in whole or in part, at the expense of the qualifying lenders, whether by requiring them to pay fees prescribed by the regulations, by deducting and retaining such part as may be prescribed by the regulations of the amounts that would otherwise be paid to them or otherwise;

(c) for requiring a qualifying lender, in a case where by virtue of paragraph (b) the amount paid to the lender is less than it would otherwise have been, to credit against the liability in relation to which the amount is paid the amount of the difference (in addition to the payment actually made);

(d) for enabling a body which, or person who, would otherwise be a qualifying lender to elect not to be regarded as a qualifying lender for the purposes of this section (other than this paragraph);

(e) for the recovery from any body or person—

(i) of any sums paid to that body or person by way of payment under the regulations that ought not to have been so paid;

(ii) of any fees or other sums due from that body or person by virtue of paragraph (b);

(f) for cases where the same person is liable to make owner-occupier payments under more than one agreement to make such payments.

(5) The regulations may provide for the Secretary of State to make arrangements with another person for the exercise of functions under the regulations.

(6) The regulations may include—

(a) provision requiring information and documents to be provided;
(b) provision authorising the disclosure of information.

(7) The bodies and persons who are "qualifying lenders" for the purposes of this section are—

(a) a deposit taker;
(b) an insurer;
(c) a county council, a county borough council, a district council, a London Borough Council, the Common Council of the City of London or the Council of the Isles of Scilly;
(d) a council constituted under section 2 of the Local Government etc. (Scotland) Act 1994;
(e) a new town corporation;
(f) other bodies or persons prescribed by regulations under section 18.

(8) In this section—

"deposit taker" means—

(a) a person who has permission under Part 4A of the Financial Services and Markets Act 2000 to accept deposits, or
(b) an EEA firm of the kind mentioned in paragraph 5(b) of Schedule 3 to that Act which has permission under paragraph 15 of that Schedule (as a result of qualifying for authorisation under paragraph 12 of that Schedule) to accept deposits;

"insurer" means—

(a) a person who has permission under Part 4A of the Financial Services and Markets Act 2000 to effect and carry out contracts of insurance, or
(b) an EEA firm of the kind mentioned in paragraph 5(d) of Schedule 3 to that Act which has permission under paragraph 15 of that Schedule (as a result of qualifying for authorisation under paragraph 12 of that Schedule) to effect and carry out contracts of insurance.

(9) The definitions of "deposit taker" and 'insurer" in this section must be read with—

(a) section 22 of the Financial Services and Markets Act 2000;
(b) any relevant order under that section;
(c) Schedule 2 to that Act.

General Note

See the General note to s.18 above. **1.303**

Consequential amendments

20. *[Not reproduced]* **1.304**

General Note

The amendments made by s.20 have been reproduced at the appropriate places in the text of this, and the other volumes. **1.305**

Transitional provision

21.—(1) Regulations made by the Secretary of State may make such transitional or transitory provision or savings as the Secretary of State considers necessary or expedient in connection with the coming into force of sections 18 to 20. **1.306**

(2) The regulations may include provision for temporarily excluding the making of a loan under regulations under section 18 after the coming into force of sections 18 to 20.

(3) Regulations under subsection (2) may in particular—

(a) provide for a temporary exclusion to continue until a time or times specified in a notice issued by the Secretary of State;

(b) enable the Secretary of State to issue notices under paragraph (a) specifying different times for different persons or descriptions of person.

(4) The regulations may include provision for enabling assistance with payments in respect of accommodation occupied as a home to be given by means of a qualifying benefit after the coming into force of sections 18 to 20 (including where the making of loans is temporarily excluded).

(5) Regulations under subsection (4) may in particular—

(a) provide for legislation that has been repealed or revoked to be treated as having effect;

(b) provide for assistance by means of a qualifying benefit to continue until a time or times specified in a notice issued by the Secretary of State;

(c) enable the Secretary of State to issue notices under paragraph (b) specifying different times for different persons or descriptions of person.

(6) In this section "qualifying benefit" means income support, income-based jobseeker's allowance, income-related employment and support allowance, state pension credit or universal credit.

(7) Regulations under this section may make different provision for different areas, cases or purposes.

(8) Regulations under this section must be made by statutory instrument.

(9) A statutory instrument containing regulations under this section is subject to annulment in pursuance of a resolution of either House of Parliament.

General Note

1.307 See the General note to s.18 above.

Final

Power to make consequential provision

1.308 **34.**—(1) The Secretary of State may by regulations make such amendments and revocations of subordinate legislation (whenever made) as appear to the Secretary of State to be necessary or expedient in consequence of any provision of this Act.

(2) In this section "subordinate legislation" has the same meaning as in the Interpretation Act 1978.

(3) Regulations under this section must be made by statutory instrument.

(4) A statutory instrument containing regulations under this section is subject to annulment in pursuance of a resolution of either House of Parliament.

The Social Security (Additional Payments) Act 2022

(2022 c.38)

An Act to make provision about additional payments to recipients of means-tested benefits, tax credits and disability benefits.

[June 28, 2022]

ARRANGEMENT OF SECTIONS 1.309

GENERAL NOTE

This Act implements part of the package of measures announced by the Chancellor of the Exchequer on May 26, 2022 in response to the increasing cost of living crisis. The package included (i) an expansion of the Energy Bills Support Scheme, providing £400 to every household, without repayments; (ii) a one-off cost of living payment of £300, paid through the Winter Fuel Payment scheme; (iii) additional funding for the Household Support Fund, administered by local authorities; (iv) extra support for those on certain means-tested benefits in the form of a one-off cost of living payment of £650, payable in two instalments; and (v) a further £150 disability cost of living payment paid to those in receipt of eligible disability benefits. The Act makes provision for the latter two measures ((iv) and (v)). The Act was introduced in the House of Commons on June 15, 2022 on a fast-track procedure and received Royal Assent less than a fortnight later on June 28, 2022. 1.310

See also, on the same model, the Social Security (Additional Payments) Act 2023, which implements part of the package of further measures announced on November 17, 2022.

Means-tested additional payments: main payments

1.—(1) The Secretary of State must secure that— 1.311

(a) a single payment of £326 is made to any person who has a qualifying entitlement to a social security benefit in respect of 25 May 2022 (the first "qualifying day"), and

(b) a single payment of £324 is made to any person who has a qualifying entitlement to a social security benefit in respect of the second qualifying day.

(2) HMRC must secure that—

(a) a single payment of £326 is made to any person who has a qualifying entitlement to child tax credit or working tax credit, but not to a social security benefit, in respect of 25 May 2022, and

(b) a single payment of £324 is made to any person who has a qualifying entitlement to child tax credit or working tax credit, but not to a social security benefit, in respect of the second qualifying day.

(3) The social security benefits are—

(a) universal credit under the Welfare Reform Act 2012 or the Welfare Reform (Northern Ireland) Order 2015 (S.I. 2015/2006 (N.I. 1));
(b) state pension credit under the State Pension Credit Act 2002 or the State Pension Credit Act (Northern Ireland) 2002;
(c) an income-based jobseeker's allowance under the Jobseekers Act 1995 or the Jobseekers (Northern Ireland) Order 1995 (S.I. 1995/2705 (N.I. 15));
(d) an income-related employment and support allowance under Part 1 of the Welfare Reform Act 2007 or Part 1 of the Welfare Reform Act (Northern Ireland) 2007;
(e) income support under section 124 of the Social Security Contributions and Benefits Act 1992 or section 123 of the Social Security Contributions and Benefits (Northern Ireland) Act 1992.

(4) The second qualifying day is such day, not later than 31 October 2022, as may be specified by the Secretary of State in regulations.

(5) Regulations under subsection (4) may specify a day before the regulations come into force.

(6) In this section, and in sections 2 to 4, references to a "person" are to an individual or to a couple (but not to each member of a couple separately).

DEFINITIONS

"person"—see subs.(6).
"HMRC"—see s.9(1).
"a qualifying day"—see s.9(2).
"the second qualifying day"—see s.9(1).
"social security benefit"—see s.9(1).

GENERAL NOTE

1.312 This section provides for means-tested additional payments to be paid to eligible persons in two tranches. These additional payments are the "main payments" (see the heading to the regulation) to distinguish them from the "disability additional payments" made under section 5. The payments are not mutually exclusive. Subsection (1) deals with payments by the Secretary of State to social security claimants while subsection (2) makes parallel provision for payments by HMRC to recipients of tax credits. The Act does not in terms give all such claimants a direct entitlement to an additional payment (nor does it provide for claims for such payments to be made). Instead, a duty is imposed on the Secretary of State (and HMRC) to make such payments to those claimants who have a "qualifying entitlement", i.e. a right to at least one of the specified means-tested social security benefits or tax credits (see subs.(3) and s.2).

Subs.(1)

1.313 This subsection requires the Secretary of State to make two means-tested additional payments of £326 and £324 respectively to an eligible person (but see subs.(6) on what is meant by a "person", which stipulates that a "person" is an individual or a couple but not each member of a couple separately). Eligibility depends on having a "qualifying entitlement" (on which see s.2) to a "social security benefit" (as listed in subs.(3)) in respect of either one or both of two dates, being the "first qualifying day" and the "second qualifying day" in turn. The "first qualifying day" is May 25, 2022 (see subs.(1)(a)) while the "second qualifying day" has since been fixed by regulations as September 25, 2022 (see subs.(4)).

The one-off payment of £650 was split into two payments with two eligibility windows to ensure that people who became claimants of relevant means-tested benefits by autumn 2022 will receive assistance even if they did not qualify for the first instalment earlier in the year. The qualifying days were both announced after they had passed (and so a claimant's eligibility or not was already determined) to limit the risk of fraud. Thus, the first qualifying day was fixed as the day before the cost of living package was announced. The slightly uneven split of the total £650 payment was also an anti-fraud measure.

Subs. (2)

This subsection makes parallel provision to subs.(1) for working tax credit and child tax credit claimants, with the duty to make means-tested additional payments at the two dates being imposed on HMRC. But see also s.4 below. **1.314**

Subs. (3)

This subsection lists the relevant social security benefits that can generate a "qualifying entitlement" for the purposes of subs.(1). In short, they are universal credit, state pension credit and the means-tested legacy benefits, albeit with the exception of housing benefit. The thinking is that those on means-tested income-replacement benefits are most likely to struggle with the sharply rising cost of living. Claimants who only receive housing benefit have been excluded because of the difficulty (or impossibility) of the DWP and HMRC identifying such individuals, as local authorities deal with housing benefit claims. Some of these individuals may benefit from the discretionary Household Support Fund administered by local authorities. Claimants who qualify only for contributory benefits are likewise excluded. Note that state pension credit is a relevant social security benefit irrespective of whether it comprises the guarantee element or the savings credit or both variants of state pension credit. **1.315**

Subss. (4) and (5)

The second qualifying day was September 25, 2022 (see Social Security Additional Payments (Second Qualifying Day) Regulations 2022 (SI 2022/1011) reg.2). **1.316**

Qualifying entitlements

2.—(1) A person has a qualifying entitlement to a social security benefit in respect of a qualifying day if— **1.317**

(a) in respect of universal credit, the person is entitled to a payment of at least 1p in respect of an assessment period ending during the period of one month ending with the qualifying day;

(b) in respect of state pension credit, an income-based jobseeker's allowance, an income-related employment and support allowance or income support, the person is entitled to a payment of at least 1p in respect of any day during the period of one month ending with the qualifying day.

(2) A person has a qualifying entitlement to child tax credit or working tax credit in respect of a qualifying day if—

(a) where the qualifying day is 25 May 2022, the person receives a payment or has an award of the credit in question in the period beginning with 26 April 2022 and ending with 25 May 2022;

(b) where the qualifying day is the second qualifying day, the person receives a payment or has an award of the credit in question in the period of one month ending with the second qualifying day, and, in either case, the payment or award of the credit in question is of at least £26 or HMRC expects the person to receive total payments or have an award of the credit in question of at least £26 in respect of the tax year 2022-23.

(3) References in this section to a person receiving a payment or having an award do not include payments received or awards made as a result of fraud.

DEFINITIONS

"HMRC"—see s.9(1).
"a qualifying day"—see s.9(2).
"the second qualifying day"—see s.9(1).
"social security benefit"—see s.9(1).
"tax year 2022-2023"—see s.9(1).

GENERAL NOTE

1.318 This section defines what is meant by a "qualifying entitlement" to a relevant social security benefit (subs.(1)) or tax credit (subs.(2)) by reference to a qualifying day. These definitions reflect the minimum amounts of benefits and tax credits payable – see e.g. Universal Credit Regulations 2013 (SI 2013/376) reg.17 and Tax Credits (Income Thresholds and Determination of Rates) Regulations 2002 (SI 2002/2008) reg. 9. Payments received or awards made as a result of fraud do not count for the purposes of a "qualifying entitlement" (subs.(3)).

Subs. (1)

1.319 The definition of a "qualifying entitlement" differs depending on whether universal credit or one of the other social security benefits is involved. This reflects the different structures of universal credit and other benefits respectively. Thus, for universal credit the test is whether "the person is entitled to a payment of at least 1p in respect of an assessment period ending during the period of one month ending with the qualifying day" (subs.(1)(a)). It follows that a claimant with an assessment period running from the 30th of one month to the 29th of the next month would have to have been entitled in the assessment period ending on April 29, 2022. Entitlement in the assessment period ending on May 29, 2022 would not qualify as that assessment period does not end "during the period of one month ending with the qualifying day" (May 25, 2022). This is so even though that assessment period would have covered the great majority of days in the month ending on May 25, 2022. More straightforwardly, claimants of other relevant social security benefits must just have an entitlement of at least 1p. in the month preceding the relevant qualifying day (subs.(1)(b)).

Subs. (2)

1.320 Tax credit recipients must have had an entitlement in respect of one day in the month before the relevant qualifying day and have a payment or an award for the tax year 2022/23 of at least £26.

Applicable benefits or tax credits

1.321 **3.**—(1) Where a person has a qualifying entitlement to universal credit and to another social security benefit in respect of a qualifying day, the benefit by reference to which the means-tested additional payment in respect of the qualifying day is to be made is universal credit (if the payment is made under section 1(1)).

(2) Where a person has a qualifying entitlement to child tax credit and to working tax credit in respect of a qualifying day, the tax credit by reference to which the means-tested additional payment in respect of the qualifying day is to be paid is child tax credit (if the payment is made under section 1(2)).

DEFINITIONS

"means-tested additional payment"—see s.9(1).
"a qualifying day"—see s.9(2).
"social security benefit"—see s.9(1).

GENERAL NOTE

Claimants may have a qualifying entitlement to both universal credit and another social security benefit in respect of the period of a month ending with the same qualifying day (e.g. where they move from one benefit to universal credit). In such a case the means-tested additional payment is paid by reference to the universal credit entitlement, which takes precedence (subs.(1)). In the same way, where both child tax credit (CTC) and working tax credit (WTC) are in payment, the child tax credit entitlement takes priority (subs.(2)). So, for example if CTC and WTC are paid to different members of the same couple, the additional payment will be made to the CTC recipient. **1.322**

Means-tested additional payments: final payments

4.—(1) HMRC must secure that a single payment of £326 is made to any person who— **1.323**

(a) receives a payment or has an award of child tax credit or working tax credit in respect of the period beginning with 26 April 2022 and ending with 25 May 2022,
(b) is not entitled to a payment under section 1(1)(a) or (2)(a), and
(c) receives total payments or has an award of the credit in question of at least £26 in respect of the tax year 2022-23.

(2) HMRC must secure that a single payment of £324 is made to any person who—

(a) receives a payment or has an award of child tax credit or working tax credit in respect of the period of one month ending with the second qualifying day,
(b) is not entitled to a payment under section 1(1)(b) or (2)(b), and
(c) receives total payments or has an award of the credit in question of at least £26 in respect of the tax year 2022-23.

(3) Where a person is entitled to a payment under this section by reference to child tax credit and working tax credit, the tax credit by reference to which the payment is to be made is child tax credit.

(4) References in this section to a person receiving a payment or having an award do not include payments received or awards made as a result of fraud.

DEFINITIONS

"HMRC"—see s.9(1).
"the second qualifying day"—see s.9(1).
"tax year 2022–2023"—see s.9(1).

General Note

1.324 This is a fall-back provision for tax credits claimants who did not qualify for an additional payment under s.1(1) or s.1(2) above. It applies to claimants who have an award or payments of tax credits of at least £26 for the 2022/23 tax year and who have an award or payments of CTC or WTC for the month from April 26, 2022 to May 25, 2022. HMRC must pay them the first additional payment if they have not already otherwise received it (subs.(1)). The same principle applies with the necessary modification for the dates involved for the second additional payment (subs.(2)). The second qualifying day was September 25, 2022 (see Social Security Additional Payments (Second Qualifying Day) Regulations 2022 (SI 2022/1011) reg.2). Where both CTC and WTC are in payment, CTC takes precedence as under s.3(2) (see subs.(3)). As with s.2(3), payments made because of fraud do not count (subs.(4)).

Disability additional payments

1.325 **5.**—(1) The Secretary of State must secure that a single payment of £150 (a "disability additional payment") is made to each individual who is entitled to a payment of a disability benefit that is payable in respect of 25 May 2022.

(2) The disability benefits are—

(a) a disability living allowance under section 71 of the Social Security Contributions and Benefits Act 1992 or section 71 of the Social Security Contributions and Benefits (Northern Ireland) Act 1992;

(b) a personal independence payment under the Welfare Reform Act 2012 or Part 5 of the Welfare Reform (Northern Ireland) Order 2015;

(c) an attendance allowance under section 64 of the Social Security Contributions and Benefits Act 1992 or section 64 of the Social Security Contributions and Benefits (Northern Ireland) Act 1992;

(d) a constant attendance allowance under section 104 of the Social Security Contributions and Benefits Act 1992 or section 104 of the Social Security Contributions and Benefits (Northern Ireland) Act 1992;

(e) an adult disability payment under the Disability Assistance for Working Age People (Scotland) Regulations 2022 (S.S.I. 2022/54);

(f) a child disability payment under the Disability Assistance for Children and Young People (Scotland) Regulations 2021 (S.S.I. 2021/174);

(g) an armed forces independence payment under article 24A of the Armed Forces and Reserve Forces (Compensation Scheme) Order 2011 (S.I. 2011/517);

(h) a constant attendance allowance under—

(i) article 14 or 43 of the Personal Injuries (Civilians) Scheme 1983 (S.I. 1983/686);

(ii) article 8 of the Naval, Military and Air Forces etc. (Disablement and Death) Service Pensions Order 2006 (S.I. 2006/606);

(i) a mobility supplement under—

(i) article 25A or 48A of the Personal Injuries (Civilians) Scheme 1983;

(ii) article 20 of the Naval, Military and Air Forces etc. (Disablement and Death) Service Pensions Order 2006.

(3) Where an individual is entitled to a payment of more than one disability benefit that is payable in respect of 25 May 2022, the benefit by reference to which the disability additional payment is to be made is the first benefit in the list in subsection (2) to which the individual is entitled.

DEFINITIONS

"disability additional payment"—see subs.(1) and s.9(1).
"disability benefit"—see s.9(1).

GENERAL NOTE

The one or two means-tested additional payments may be supplemented by a single disability additional payment made under this section, amounting to £150. The Secretary of State must make such payments to claimants who were entitled to a qualifying payment of a prescribed disability benefit in respect of May 25, 2022 (subs.(1)). The relevant disability benefits are those listed in subs.(2). Those listed in subs.(2)(a)–(d) are the responsibility of the DWP or its Northern Ireland equivalent. Those in subs.(2)(e)–(f) are paid by the Scottish government, while the benefits in subs.(g)–(i) are administered by the Secretary of State for Defence (or on his behalf by the Veterans UK). Given these disparate responsibilities, the Act makes provision for data-sharing (see s.7). 1.326

Administration of additional payments

6.—(1) For all purposes relating to the administration of an additional payment, any provision applying in relation to a social security benefit, child tax credit, working tax credit or disability benefit by reference to which that payment is made is to apply in relation to that payment as if that payment were a payment or award of the social security benefit, child tax credit, working tax credit or disability benefit in question. 1.327

(2) The provision applied by subsection (1)—

(a) includes provision relating to overpayments and recovery, and appeals relating to overpayments and recovery (but not provision relating to appeals or reviews about entitlement to the social security benefit, tax credit or disability benefit in question), and

(b) is subject to any necessary modifications.

(3) Subsection (1) has effect in relation to a payment made in purported compliance with a duty under section 1 [[1],4 or 5] as if that payment were the additional payment which it purported to be.

(4) Subsection (1) (including as it has effect as a result of subsection (3)) is subject to regulations made by the Secretary of State, the Treasury or HMRC under subsection (5).

(5) The Secretary of State, the Treasury or HMRC may by regulations make provision, in relation to additional payments or payments purporting to be additional payments, applying or disapplying, with or without modifications, any provision applying in relation to a social security benefit, child tax credit, working tax credit or a disability benefit.

(6) The regulations may make provision having effect from the day on which this Act comes into force.

AMENDMENT

1. Social Security (Additional Payments) Act 2003 s.9 (1) and (2) (June 28, 2022).

DEFINITIONS

"additional payment"—see s.9(1).
"disability benefit"—see s.9(1).
"HMRC"—see s.9(1).

GENERAL NOTE

1.328 Note that there is no provision in the Act for anyone to make a claim for a means-tested additional payment. As a result, there is also no provision for the Secretary of State to make a decision under s.8(1)(a) of the Social Security Act 1998. In the same way it follows that the usual mechanism of revisions, supersessions and appeals does not apply. Instead, s.1 simply imposes a duty on the Secretary of State and HMRC to make payments to eligible individuals.

Subs. (1)

1.329 This provision applies the relevant administrative provisions relating to the qualifying benefit to the new additional payment. This method has been adopted so that the additional payments can be administered in the same manner and subject to the same rules as those which apply to a claimant's existing benefit entitlement (e.g. by payment to the same bank account as the qualifying benefit).

Subs. (2)

1.330 The provision made under subs.(1) includes provision relating to overpayment and benefit recovery procedures. This reflects the fact that different rules govern overpayment and benefit recovery procedures for different social security benefits and tax credits. This does not include provisions relating to appeals or reviews, there being no decision as such on entitlement to an additional payment to be appealed. See further the Tax Credits Act 2002 (Additional Payments Modification and Disapplication) Regulations 2022 (SI 2022/1208).

Cooperation etc between the Secretary of State and HMRC

1.331 **7.**—(1) The Secretary of State and HMRC must cooperate in exercising their functions in relation to additional payments.

(2) Section 3 of the Social Security Act 1998 (use of information) has effect—

(a) in relation to HMRC as it has effect in relation to the Secretary of State, and
(b) as if, in subsection (1A), the reference to social security included additional payments.

(3) Section 127 of the Welfare Reform Act 2012 (information-sharing between Secretary of State and HMRC) has effect as if—

(a) functions of HMRC conferred by or under this Act were HMRC functions within the meaning of that section, and
(b) functions of the Secretary of State conferred by or under this Act were departmental functions within the meaning of that section.

(4) Section 34 of the Scotland Act 2016 (information-sharing between the Secretary of State and the Scottish Ministers) has effect as if, in subsection (7), the reference to social security in the definition of "social security function" included additional payments.

(5) Subsection (6) applies where—

(a) the Secretary of State or HMRC make a payment to a person in purported compliance with a duty in section 1 or 4,

(b) the person was entitled to receive an additional payment of an amount equal to that payment under a different duty in section 1 or 4 ("the applicable duty"), and
(c) the person does not receive the additional payment to which they are entitled under the applicable duty.

(6) The payment made in purported compliance with a duty in section 1 or 4 is to be treated as if it had been made in accordance with the applicable duty (and, accordingly, the payment is not recoverable on the grounds that it was not made in compliance with a duty in section 1 or 4).

DEFINITIONS

"additional payment"—see s.9(1).
"the applicable duty"—subs.(5)(b).
"HMRC"—see s.9(1).

GENERAL NOTE

This section provides for data-sharing between the DWP, HMRC and the Secretary of State for Defence (given his role in administering the benefits itemised at s.5(2)(g)–(i)) along with the relevant authorities in Northern Ireland and Scotland. 1.332

Payments to be disregarded for the purposes of tax and social security

8.—No account is to be taken of an additional payment in considering a person's— 1.333
(a) liability to tax,
(b) entitlement to benefit under an enactment relating to social security (irrespective of the name or nature of the benefit), or
(c) entitlement to a tax credit.

DEFINITION

"additional payment"—see s.9(1).

GENERAL NOTE

Additional payments under this Act are disregarded for the purposes of liability to income tax (para.(a)) and entitlement to social security benefits (para.(b)) and tax credits (para.(c)). So far as entitlement to social security benefits is concerned, the usual drafting technique to provide for a disregard for such forms of capital or income other than earnings is by way of a regulation (see e.g. Universal Credit Regulations 2013 (SI 2013/376) reg.76) or Schedule (see e.g. Income Support (General) Regulations 1987 (SI 1987/1967), Sch.9). However, the fact that entitlement to additional payments is directly governed by primary legislation has allowed a different and all purposes route to a statutory disregard to be adopted. 1.334

Interpretation

9.—(1) In this Act— 1.335
"additional payment" means a means-tested additional payment or a disability additional payment;
"disability additional payment" has the meaning given by section 5(1);
"disability benefit" means a benefit listed in section 5(2);

"HMRC" means the Commissioners for Her Majesty's Revenue and Customs;
"means-tested additional payment" means a payment under section 1 or 4;
"the second qualifying day" means the day specified in regulations under section 1(4);
"social security benefit" means a benefit listed in section 1(3);
"the tax year 2022–23" means the period beginning with 6 April 2022 and ending with 5 April 2023.

(2) In this Act—

(a) references to "a qualifying day" are to—

(i) 25 May 2022, or

(ii) the day specified in regulations under section 1(4);

(b) references to child tax credit or working tax credit are to child tax credit or working tax credit under the Tax Credits Act 2002.

Regulations

1.336 **10.**—(1) A power to make regulations under any provision of this Act includes power to make—

(a) consequential, supplementary, incidental, transitional or saving provision;

(b) different provision for different purposes.

(2) Regulations under this Act are to be made by statutory instrument.

(3) A statutory instrument containing regulations under this Act is subject to annulment in pursuance of a resolution of either House of Parliament.

Extent, commencement and short title

1.337 **11.**—(1) This Act extends to England and Wales, Scotland and Northern Ireland.

(2) This Act comes into force on the day on which it is passed.

(3) This Act may be cited as the Social Security (Additional Payments) Act 2022.

General Note

1.338 The Act received Royal Assent on June 28, 2022.

The Social Security (Additional Payments) Act 2023

(2023 Ch.7)

An Act to make provision about additional payments to recipients of means-tested benefits, tax credits and disability benefits.

[March 23, 2023]

Arrangement of Sections

General Note

This Act is modelled on the Social Security (Additional Payments) Act 2022 and implements part of the package of further measures announced on November 17, 2022 to assist in tackling the cost of living crisis. The 2023 Act provides for payments of up to £900 (in three instalments) to households in receipt of eligible means-tested social security benefits or tax credits at a total cost to the Exchequer of around £7.5 billion in 2023/24. The Government estimates that some 8 million benefit units (defined as a single adult or a married or cohabiting couple and any dependent children) are expected to receive the first £301 cost of living payment. The 2023 Act also makes provision for disability additional payments of £150. 1.340

Means-tested additional payments

Means-tested additional payments: main payments

1.—(1) The Secretary of State must secure that— 1.341

(a) a single payment of £301 is made to any person who has a qualifying entitlement to a social security benefit in respect of the first qualifying day,

(b) a single payment of £300 is made to any person who has a qualifying entitlement to a social security benefit in respect of the second qualifying day, and

(c) a single payment of £299 is made to any person who has a qualifying entitlement to a social security benefit in respect of the third qualifying day.

(2) HMRC must secure that—

(a) a single payment of £301 is made to any person who has a qualifying entitlement to child tax credit or working tax credit, but not to a social security benefit, in respect of the first qualifying day,

(b) a single payment of £300 is made to any person who has a qualifying entitlement to child tax credit or working tax credit, but not to a social security benefit, in respect of the second qualifying day, and

(c) a single payment of £299 is made to any person who has a qualifying entitlement to child tax credit or working tax credit, but not to a social security benefit, in respect of the third qualifying day.

(3) The social security benefits are—

(a) universal credit under the Welfare Reform Act 2012 or the Welfare Reform (Northern Ireland) Order 2015 (S.I. 2015/2006 (N.I. 1));

(b) state pension credit under the State Pension Credit Act 2002 or the State Pension Credit Act (Northern Ireland) 2002;

(c) an income-based jobseeker's allowance under the Jobseekers Act 1995 or the Jobseekers (Northern Ireland) Order 1995 (S.I. 1995/2705 (N.I. 15));
(d) an income-related employment and support allowance under Part 1 of the Welfare Reform Act 2007 or Part 1 of the Welfare Reform Act (Northern Ireland) 2007;
(e) income support under section 124 of the Social Security Contributions and Benefits Act 1992 or section 123 of the Social Security Contributions and Benefits (Northern Ireland) Act 1992.

(4) The first qualifying day is such day, not later than 30 April 2023, as may be specified by the Secretary of State in regulations.

(5) Regulations under subsection (4) may specify a day before this Act or the regulations are in force.

(6) The second qualifying day is such day, not later than 31 October 2023, as may be specified by the Secretary of State in regulations.

(7) The third qualifying day is such day, not later than 29 February 2024, as may be specified by the Secretary of State in regulations.

(8) Regulations under subsections (6) and (7) may specify a day before the regulations are in force.

(9) In this section, and in sections 2 to 4, references to a "person" are to an individual or to a couple (but not to each member of a couple separately).

GENERAL NOTE

1.342 This section is modelled on s.1 of the 2022 Act. The first qualifying day (see subs.(4)) is February 25, 2023: see the Social Security Additional Payments (First Qualifying Day) Regulations 2023 (SI 2023/361). The second qualifying day was September 17, 2023: see the Social Security Additional Payments (Second Qualifying Day) Regulations 2023 (SI 2023/1017).

Qualifying entitlements: social security benefits

1.343 **2.**—(1) A person has a qualifying entitlement to a social security benefit in respect of a qualifying day if—
(a) in respect of universal credit, the person is entitled to a payment of at least 1p in respect of an assessment period ending during the period of one month ending with the qualifying day;
(b) in respect of state pension credit, an income-based jobseeker's allowance, an income-related employment and support allowance or income support, the person is entitled to a payment of at least 1p in respect of any day during the period of one month ending with the qualifying day.

(2) For the purposes of subsection (1)(b), a person is considered to be entitled to a payment irrespective of whether that payment is not payable as a result of—
(a) regulation 13 of the State Pension Credit Regulations 2002 (S.I. 2002/1792);
(b) regulation 13 of the State Pension Credit Regulations (Northern Ireland) 2003 (S.R. (N.I.) 2003 No.28);
(c) regulation 87A of the Jobseeker's Allowance Regulations 1996 (S.I. 1996/207);

(d) regulation 87A of the Jobseeker's Allowance Regulations (Northern Ireland) 1996 (S.R. (N.I.) 1996 No.198);
(e) regulation 26(4) or 26C(6) of the Social Security (Claims and Payments) Regulations 1987 (S.I. 1987/1968);
(f) regulation 26(4) or 26C(6) of the Social Security (Claims and Payments) Regulations (Northern Ireland) 1987 (S.R. (N.I.) 1987 No.465).

GENERAL NOTE

Section 2(1) mirrors s.2(1) of the 2022 Act. Section 2(2) ensures entitlement to additional payments is retained even where payment of the relevant means-tested benefit is withheld because of the de minimis rule. **1.344**

Qualifying entitlements: tax credits

3.—(1) A person has a qualifying entitlement to child tax credit or working tax credit in respect of a qualifying day if HMRC makes a payment to the person of the credit in question in respect of a day falling within the period of one month ending with that qualifying day (the "qualifying period"). **1.345**

(2) References in this section to HMRC making a payment do not include—
(a) a payment made under regulation 10 of the Tax Credits (Payments by the Commissioners) Regulations 2002 (S.I. 2002/2173), where the person to whom HMRC has made the payment would not be entitled to that payment if their entitlement were assessed on any day during the qualifying period, or
(b) a payment made as a result of fraud.

Applicable benefits or tax credits

4.—(1) Where a person has a qualifying entitlement to more than one social security benefit in respect of a qualifying day, the benefit by reference to which the means-tested additional payment in respect of the qualifying day is to be paid is the first benefit in the list in section 1(3) to which the person has a qualifying entitlement (if the payment is made under section 1(1)). **1.346**

(2) Where a person has a qualifying entitlement to child tax credit and to working tax credit in respect of a qualifying day, the tax credit by reference to which the means-tested additional payment in respect of the qualifying day is to be paid is child tax credit (if the payment is made under section 1(2)).

GENERAL NOTE

See the General Note to s.3 of the 2022 Act. **1.347**

Disability additional payments

Disability additional payments

5.—(1) The Secretary of State must secure that a single payment of £150 (a "disability additional payment") is made to each individual who is **1.348**

entitled to a payment of a disability benefit that is payable in respect of the disability additional payment day.

(2) The disability benefits are—

(a) a disability living allowance under section 71 of the Social Security Contributions and Benefits Act 1992 or section 71 of the Social Security Contributions and Benefits (Northern Ireland) Act 1992;

(b) a personal independence payment under the Welfare Reform Act 2012 or Part 5 of the Welfare Reform (Northern Ireland) Order 2015 (S.I. 2015/2006 (N.I. 1));

(c) an attendance allowance under section 64 of the Social Security Contributions and Benefits Act 1992 or section 64 of the Social Security Contributions and Benefits (Northern Ireland) Act 1992;

(d) a constant attendance allowance under section 104 of the Social Security Contributions and Benefits Act 1992 or section 104 of the Social Security Contributions and Benefits (Northern Ireland) Act 1992;

(e) an adult disability payment under the Disability Assistance for Working Age People (Scotland) Regulations 2022 (S.S.I. 2022/54) or the Disability Assistance for Working Age People (Transitional Provisions and Miscellaneous Amendment) (Scotland) Regulations 2022 (S.S.I. 2022/217);

(f) a child disability payment under the Disability Assistance for Children and Young People (Scotland) Regulations 2021 (S.S.I. 2021/174);

(g) an armed forces independence payment under article 24A of the Armed Forces and Reserve Forces (Compensation Scheme) Order 2011 (S.I. 2011/517);

(h) a constant attendance allowance under—

(i) article 14 or 43 of the Personal Injuries (Civilians) Scheme 1983 (S.I. 1983/686);

(ii) article 8 of the Naval, Military and Air Forces etc. (Disablement and Death) Service Pensions Order 2006 (S.I. 2006/606);

(i) a mobility supplement under—

(i) article 25A or 48A of the Personal Injuries (Civilians) Scheme 1983;

(ii) article 20 of the Naval, Military and Air Forces etc. (Disablement and Death) Service Pensions Order 2006 (S.I. 2006/606).

(3) The disability additional payment day is such day, not later than 30 June 2023, as may be specified by the Secretary of State in regulations.

(4) Regulations under subsection (3) may specify a day before the regulations are in force.

(5) Where an individual is entitled to a payment of more than one disability benefit that is payable in respect of the disability additional payment day, the benefit by reference to which the disability additional payment is to be made is the first benefit in the list in subsection (2) to which the individual is entitled.

GENERAL NOTE

1.349 This is in essentially the same terms as s.5 of the 2022 Act.

Administration of additional payments

6.—(1) For all purposes relating to the administration of an additional payment, any provision applying in relation to a social security benefit, child tax credit, working tax credit or disability benefit by reference to which that payment is made is to apply in relation to that payment as if that payment were a payment of the social security benefit, child tax credit, working tax credit or disability benefit in question. **1.350**

(2) The provision applied by subsection (1)—

- (a) includes provision relating to overpayments and recovery, and appeals relating to overpayments and recovery (but not provision relating to appeals or reviews about entitlement to the social security benefit, tax credit or disability benefit in question), and
- (b) is subject to any necessary modifications.

(3) Subsection (1) has effect in relation to a payment made in purported compliance with a duty in section 1 or 5 as if that payment were the additional payment which it purported to be.

(4) Subsection (1) (including as it has effect as a result of subsection (3)) is subject to regulations made by the Secretary of State, the Treasury or HMRC under subsection (5).

(5) The Secretary of State, the Treasury or HMRC may by regulations make provision, in relation to additional payments or payments purporting to be additional payments, applying or disapplying, with or without modifications, any provision applying in relation to a social security benefit, child tax credit, working tax credit or disability benefit.

(6) The regulations may make provision having effect from the day on which this Act comes into force.

General Note

See the commentary to s.6 of the 2022 Act. **1.351**

Cooperation etc between the Secretary of State and HMRC

7.—(1) The Secretary of State and HMRC must cooperate in exercising their functions in relation to additional payments. **1.352**

(2) Section 3 of the Social Security Act 1998 (use of information) has effect—

- (a) in relation to HMRC as it has effect in relation to the Secretary of State, and
- (b) as if, in subsection (1A), the reference to social security included additional payments.

(3) Section 127 of the Welfare Reform Act 2012 (information-sharing between Secretary of State and HMRC) has effect as if—

- (a) functions of HMRC conferred by or under this Act were HMRC functions within the meaning of that section, and
- (b) functions of the Secretary of State conferred by or under this Act were departmental functions within the meaning of that section.

(4) Section 34 of the Scotland Act 2016 (information-sharing between the Secretary of State and the Scottish Ministers) has effect as if, in subsection (7), the reference to social security in the definition of "social security function" included additional payments.

(5) Subsection (6) applies where—

(a) the Secretary of State or HMRC make a payment to a person in purported compliance with a duty in section 1,

(b) the person was entitled to receive an additional payment of an amount equal to that payment under a different duty in section 1 ("the applicable duty"), and

(c) the person does not receive the additional payment to which they are entitled under the applicable duty.

(6) The payment made in purported compliance with a duty in section 1 is to be treated as if it had been made in accordance with the applicable duty (and, accordingly, the payment is not recoverable on the grounds that it was not made in compliance with a duty in section 1).

GENERAL NOTE

1.353 This mirrors s.7 of the 2022 Act.

Payments to be disregarded for the purposes of tax and social security

1.354 **8.**—No account is to be taken of an additional payment in considering a person's—

(a) liability to tax,

(b) entitlement to a benefit under an enactment relating to social security (irrespective of the name or nature of the benefit), or

(c) entitlement to a tax credit.

GENERAL NOTE

1.355 This provision is in the same terms as s.8 of the 2022 Act.

Amendments to other legislation

1.356 **9.**—(1) In the Social Security (Additional Payments) Act 2022, in section 6(3), for "or 4" substitute ", 4 or 5".

(2) The amendment made by subsection (1) is to be treated as having come into force on 28 June 2022.

(3) The Tax Credits Act 2002 (Additional Payments Modification and Disapplication) Regulations 2022 (S.I. 2022/1208) are amended in accordance with subsections (4) and (5).

(4) In paragraph (2) of regulation 1—

(a) for "payments" substitute "a payment";

(b) at the end insert "or section 1(2) of the Social Security (Additional Payments) Act 2023."

(5) In regulation 6, after "2022" insert ", a payment made under section 1(2) of the Social Security (Additional Payments) Act 2023,".

(6) The amendments made by subsections (4) and (5) are to be treated as if they had been made by regulations made under sections 6(5) and (6) and 11(1) of this Act.

Final provisions

Interpretation

10.—(1) In this Act— 1.357

"additional payment" means a means-tested additional payment or a disability additional payment;

"disability additional payment" has the meaning given by section 5(1);

"the disability additional payment day" means the day specified in regulations under section 5(3);

"disability benefit" means a benefit listed in section 5(2);

"the first qualifying day" means the day specified in regulations under section 1(4);

"HMRC" means the Commissioners for His Majesty's Revenue and Customs;

"means-tested additional payment" means a payment under section 1;

"the second qualifying day" means the day specified in regulations under section 1(6);

"social security benefit" means a benefit listed in section 1(3);

"the third qualifying day" means the day specified in regulations under section 1(7).

(2) In this Act—

(a) references to "a qualifying day" are to—

(i) the first qualifying day specified in regulations under section 1(4),

(ii) the second qualifying day specified in regulations under section 1(6),

(iii) the third qualifying day specified in regulations under section 1(7);

(b) references to child tax credit or working tax credit are to child tax credit or working tax credit under the Tax Credits Act 2002.

Regulations

11.—(1) A power to make regulations under any provision of this Act includes power to make— 1.358

(a) consequential, supplementary, incidental, transitional or saving provision;

(b) different provision for different purposes.

(2) Regulations under this Act are to be made by statutory instrument.

(3) A statutory instrument containing regulations under this Act is subject to annulment in pursuance of a resolution of either House of Parliament.

Extent, commencement and short title

12.—(1) This Act extends to England and Wales, Scotland and Northern Ireland. 1.359

(2) This Act comes into force on the day on which it is passed.

(3) This Act may be cited as the Social Security (Additional Payments) Act 2023.

General Note

The Act received Royal Assent on March 23, 2023. 1.360

PART II

UNIVERSAL CREDIT: REGULATIONS

PART IIA

UNIVERSAL CREDIT REGULATIONS

The Universal Credit Regulations 2013

(SI 2013/376)

Made on February 25, 2013 by the Secretary of State for Work and Pensions in exercise of the powers conferred by sections 2(2), 4(2), (3), (5), (6) and (7), 5, 6(1)(a) and (3), 7(2) and (3), 8(3), 9(2) and (3), 10(2) to (5), 11(3) to (5), 12(1), (3) and (4), 14(5), 15(2), 17(3) and (4), 18(3) and (5), 19(2)(d), (3) and (4), 20(1), 22(2), 24(1), (5) and (6), 25, 26(2)(a), (6) and (8), 27(4), (5), (9), 28, 32(1), 37(3) to (7), 39(3)(a), 40, 96 and 97 of, and paragraphs 1, 4, 5 and 7 of Schedule 1 and paragraphs 2 and 3 of Schedule 5 to, the Welfare Reform Act 2012; a draft having been laid before Parliament in accordance with section 43(3) of the Welfare Reform Act 2012 and approved by a resolution of each House of Parliament; and without the instrument having been referred to the Social Security Advisory Committee because it contains only regulations made by virtue of or consequential on Part 1 and sections 96 and 97 of, and Schedules 1 and 5 to, the Welfare Reform Act 2012 and is made before the end of the period of 6 months beginning with the coming into force of those provisions. 2.1

[April 29, 2013, but see the introductory General Note to WRA 2012]

Arrangement of Regulations

Part 1

Introduction

Part 2

Entitlement

PART 3

AWARDS

PART 4

ELEMENTS OF AN AWARD

PART 5

CAPABILITY FOR WORK OR WORK-RELATED ACTIVITY

PART 6

CALCULATION OF CAPITAL AND INCOME

CHAPTER 1

CAPITAL

CHAPTER 2

EARNED INCOME

CHAPTER 3

UNEARNED INCOME

CHAPTER 4

MISCELLANEOUS

PART 7

THE BENEFIT CAP

PART 8

CLAIMANT RESPONSIBILITIES

CHAPTER 1

WORK-RELATED REQUIREMENTS

CHAPTER 2

SANCTIONS

106. Start of the reduction
107. Reduction period to continue where award terminates
108. Suspension of a reduction where fraud penalty applies
109. When a reduction is to be terminated
110. Amount of reduction for each assessment period
111. Daily reduction rate
112. Application of ESA or JSA sanctions to universal credit
113. Failures for which no reduction is applied
114. Sanctionable failures under section 26—work placements

Chapter 3

Hardship

115. Introduction
116. Conditions for hardship payments
117. The period of hardship payments
118. The amount of hardship payments
119. Recoverability of hardship payments

Schedules

1. Meaning of payments in respect of accommodation **2.3**
2. Claimant treated as liable or not liable to make payments
   - Part 1 Treated as liable to make payments
   - Part 2 Treated as not liable to make payments
3. Claimant treated as occupying or not occupying accommodation
   - Part 1 Treated as occupying accommodation
   - Part 2 Treated as not occupying accommodation
4. Housing costs element for renters
   - Part 1 General
   - Part 2 Exception to inclusion of housing costs element
   - Part 3 General provisions about calculation of amount of housing costs element for renters
   - Part 4 Private rented sector
   - Part 5 Social rented sector
5. Housing costs element for owner-occupiers
   - Part 1 General
   - Part 2 Exception to inclusion of housing costs element
   - Part 3 No housing costs element for qualifying period
   - Part 4 Calculation of amount of housing costs element for owner-occupiers
6. Assessment of whether a claimant has limited capability for work
   - Part 1 Physical Disabilities
   - Part 2 Mental, cognitive and intellectual function assessment
7. Assessment of whether a claimant has limited capability for work and work-related activity
8. Circumstances in which a claimant is to be treated as having limited capability for work
9. Circumstances in which a claimant is to be treated as having limited capability for work and work-related activity
10. Capital to be disregarded
11. Application of ESA or JSA sanctions to universal credit
12. Order of children and qualifying young persons

PART 1

INTRODUCTION

Citation and commencement

2.4 **1.**—These Regulations may be cited as the Universal Credit Regulations 2013 and come into force on 29th April 2013.

GENERAL NOTE

2.5 Although the Regulations come into force on April 29, 2013, they do not apply to all claimants. See further the Universal Credit (Transitional Provisions) Regulations 2014, the commencement orders in Pt V of Vol.V of this series and the introductory General Note to the WRA 2012 in Pt I of this volume.

Interpretation

2.6 **2.**—In these Regulations—

"the Act" means the Welfare Reform Act 2012;

[8 . . .]

[2 "adopter" has the meaning in regulation 89(3)(a);]

[18 "adult disability payment" has the meaning given in regulation 2 of the Disability Assistance for Working Age People (Scotland) Regulations 2022;]

"attendance allowance" means—

(a) an attendance allowance under section 64 of the Contributions and Benefits Act;

(b) an increase of disablement pension under section 104 or 105 of that Act (increases where constant attendance needed and for exceptionally severe disablement);

(c) [3 . . .]

(d) a payment by virtue of article 14, 15, 16, 43 or 44 of the Personal Injuries (Civilians) Scheme 1983 or any analogous payment;

(e) any payment based on the need for attendance which is paid as an addition to a war disablement pension;

[1(f) armed forces independence payment under the Armed Forces and Reserve Forces (Compensation Scheme) Order 2011;]

"bereavement allowance" means an allowance under section 39B of the Contributions and Benefits Act;

[6 "blind" means certified as severely sight impaired or blind by a consultant ophthalmologist;]

"care leaver" has the meaning in regulation 8;

"carer's allowance" means a carer's allowance under section 70 of the Contributions and Benefits Act;

"carer element" has the meaning in regulation 29;

[17 "child disability payment" has the meaning given in regulation 2 of the DACYP Regulations;]

[21 "carer support payment" means carer's assistance given in accordance with the Carer's Assistance (Carer Support Payment) (Scotland) Regulations 2023;]

"childcare costs element" has the meaning in regulation 31;

"child element" has the meaning in regulation 24;

"close relative", in relation to a person, means—
(a) a parent, parent-in-law, son, son-in-law, daughter, daughter-in-law, step-parent, step-son, step-daughter, brother or sister; and
(b) if any of the above is a member of a couple, the other member of the couple;

"confinement" has the meaning in regulation 8;

"Contributions and Benefits Act" means the Social Security Contributions and Benefits Act 1992;

"course of advanced education" has the meaning in regulation 12;

[[17] "the DACYP Regulations" means the Disability Assistance for Children and Young People (Scotland) Regulations 2021;]

"disability living allowance" means an allowance under section 71 of the Contributions and Benefits Act;

"earned income" has the meaning in Chapter 2 of Part 6;

"EEA Regulations" means the [[14] Immigration (European Economic Area) Regulations 2016] [[16] and references to the EEA Regulations are to be read with Schedule 4 to the Immigration and Social Security Co-ordination (EU Withdrawal) Act 2020 (Consequential, Saving, Transitional and Transitory Provisions) Regulations 2020.]

"employment and support allowance" means an allowance under Part 1 of the Welfare Reform Act 2007 as amended by Schedule 3 and Part 1 of Schedule 14 to the Welfare Reform Act 2012 (removing references to an income-related allowance);

[[4] "enactment" includes an enactment comprised in, or an instrument made under, an Act of the Scottish Parliament or the National Assembly of Wales;]

"ESA Regulations" means the Employment and Support Allowance Regulations 2013;

"expected number of hours per week" has the meaning in regulation 88;

"foster parent" means—
(a) in relation to England, a person with whom a child is placed under [[22] the Care Planning, Placement and Case Review (England) Regulations 2010];
(b) in relation to Wales, a person with whom a child is placed under [[22] the Care Planning, Placement and Case Review (Wales) Regulations 2015];
(c) in relation to Scotland, a foster carer or kinship carer with whom a child is placed under the Looked After Children (Scotland) Regulations 2009;

"grant" has the meaning in regulation 68;

"health care professional" means (except in regulation 98)—
(a) a registered medical practitioner;
(b) a registered nurse; or
(c) an occupational therapist or physiotherapist registered with a regulatory body established by Order in Council under section 60 of the Health Act 1999;

"housing costs element" has the meaning in regulation 25;

"individual threshold" has the meaning in regulation 90(2);

"industrial injuries benefit" means a benefit under Part 5 of the Contributions and Benefits Act;

"ITEPA" means the Income Tax (Earnings and Pensions) Act 2003;

"jobseeker's allowance" means an allowance under the Jobseekers Act 1995 as amended by Part 1 of Schedule 14 to the Act (removing references to an income-based allowance);

"local authority" means—

(a) in relation to England, a county council, a district council, a parish council, a London borough council, the Common Council of the City of London or the Council of the Isles of Scilly;

(b) in relation to Wales, a county council, a county borough council or a community council;

(c) in relation to Scotland, a council constituted under section 2 of the Local Government etc. (Scotland) Act 1994;

[[20] "local welfare provision" means occasional financial or other assistance given by a local authority, the Scottish Ministers or the Welsh Ministers, or a person authorised to exercise any function of, or provide a service to, them, to or in respect of individuals for the purpose of—

(a) meeting, or helping to meet, an immediate short term need—

(i) arising out of an exceptional event, or exceptional circumstances; and

(ii) that requires to be met in order to avoid a risk to the well-being of an individual; or

(b) enabling individuals to establish or maintain a settled home, where those individuals have been or, without the assistance, might otherwise be—

(i) in prison, hospital, a residential care establishment or other institution; or

(ii) homeless or otherwise living an unsettled way of life;]

[[12] "LCWRA element" has the meaning in regulation 27;]

"looked after by a local authority" in relation to a child or young person means a child or young person who is looked after by a local authority within the meaning of section 22 of the Children Act 1989 [[10], section 17(6) of the Children (Scotland) Act 1995 or section 74 of the Social Services and Well-being (Wales) Act 2014];

"maternity allowance" means a maternity allowance under section 35 [[5] or 35B] of the Contributions and Benefits Act;

"Medical Evidence Regulations" means the Social Security (Medical Evidence) Regulations 1976;

[[9] "monthly earnings" has the meaning in regulation 90(6);]

"national insurance contribution" means a contribution under Part 1 of the Contributions and Benefits Act;

[[11] "National Minimum Wage Regulations" means the National Minimum Wage Regulations 2015;]

"[[8] ...] statutory paternity pay" means [[8] ...] statutory paternity pay under Part 12ZA of the Contributions and Benefits Act;

"paid work" means work done for payment or in expectation of payment and does not include being engaged by a charitable or voluntary organisation, or as a volunteer, in circumstances in which the payment received by or due to be paid to the person is in respect of expenses;

"partner" means (except in regulation 77) the other member of a couple;

"personal independence payment" means an allowance under Part 4 of the Welfare Reform Act 2012;

"prisoner" means—

(a) a person who is detained in custody pending trial or sentence upon conviction or under a sentence imposed by a court; or

(b) is on temporary release in accordance with the provisions of the Prison Act 1952 or the Prisons (Scotland) Act 1989,

other than a person who is detained in hospital under the provisions of the Mental Health Act 1983 or, in Scotland, under the provisions of the Mental Health (Care and Treatment) (Scotland) Act 2003 or the Criminal Procedure (Scotland) Act 1995;

"qualifying young person" has the meaning in regulation 5;

"redundancy" has the meaning in section 139(1) of the Employment Rights Act 1996;

[6 . . .]

"regular and substantial caring responsibilities for a severely disabled person" has the meaning in regulation 30;

"relevant childcare" has the meaning in regulation 35;

"responsible for a child or qualifying young person" has the meaning in regulation 4;

"statutory adoption pay" means a payment under Part 12ZB of the Contributions Benefits Act;

"statutory maternity pay" means a payment under Part 12 of the Contributions and Benefits Act;

[15 "statutory parental bereavement pay" means statutory parental bereavement pay payable in accordance with Part 12ZD of the Contributions and Benefits Act;]

[7 "statutory shared parental pay" means statutory shared parental pay payable in accordance with Part 12ZC of the Contributions and Benefits Act;]

"statutory sick pay" means a payment under Part 11 of the Contributions and Benefits Act;

[13 "step-parent", in relation to a child or qualifying young person ("A"), means a person who is not A's parent but—

(a) is a member of a couple, the other member of which is a parent of A, where both are responsible for A; or

(b) was previously a member of a couple, the other member of which was a parent of A, where immediately prior to ceasing to be a member of that couple the person was, and has since continued to be, responsible for A.]

"student loan" has the meaning in regulation 68;

"terminally ill" means suffering from a progressive disease where death in consequence of that disease can reasonably be expected within [19 12 months];

"total outstanding reduction period" has the meaning in regulation 101(5);

"trade dispute" has the meaning in section 244 of the Trade Union and Labour Relations (Consolidation) Act 1992;

"unearned income" has the meaning in Chapter 3 of Part 6;

"war disablement pension" means any retired pay, pension or allowance payable in respect of disablement under an instrument specified in section 639(2) of ITEPA;

[1 . . .]

"widowed mother's allowance" means an allowance under section 37 of the Contributions and Benefits Act;

"widowed parent's allowance" means an allowance under section 39A of the Contributions and Benefits Act;

"widow's pension" means a pension under section 39 of the Contributions and Benefits Act.

AMENDMENTS

1. Armed Forces and Reserve Forces Compensation Scheme (Consequential Provisions: Subordinate Legislation) Order 2013 (SI 2013/591) art.7 and Sch., para.54 (April 8, 2013).

2. Universal Credit (Miscellaneous Amendments) Regulations 2013 (SI 2013/803) reg.2(1) and (2) (April 29, 2013).

3. Social Security (Miscellaneous Amendments) (No.2) Regulations 2013 (SI 2013/1508) reg.3(1) and (2) (October 29, 2013).

4. Universal Credit and Miscellaneous Amendments Regulations 2014 (SI 2014/597) reg.2(1) and (2) (April 28, 2014).

5. Social Security (Maternity Allowance) (Miscellaneous Amendments) Regulations 2014 (SI 2014/884) reg.6(1) (May 18, 2014).

6. Universal Credit and Miscellaneous Amendments (No.2) Regulations 2014 (SI 2014/2888) reg.3(1)(a) (Assessment periods beginning on or after November 26, 2014).

7. Shared Parental Leave and Statutory Shared Parental Pay (Consequential Amendments to Subordinate Legislation) Order 2014 (SI 2014/3255) art.28(1) and (2)(c) (December 31, 2014).

8. Shared Parental Leave and Statutory Shared Parental Pay (Consequential Amendments to Subordinate Legislation) Order 2014 (SI 2014/3255) art.28(1) and (2)(a) and (b) (April 5, 2015). The amendments are subject to the transitional provision in art.35 (see below).

9. Universal Credit and Miscellaneous Amendments Regulations 2015 (SI 2015/1754) reg.2 (Assessment periods beginning on or after November 4, 2015).

10. Universal Credit (Care Leavers and Looked After Children) Amendment Regulations 2016 (SI 2016/543) reg.2(1) and (2) (May 26, 2016).

11. Social Security (Jobseeker's Allowance, Employment and Support Allowance and Universal Credit) (Amendment) Regulations 2016 (SI 2016/678) reg.5(1) and (2) (July 25, 2016).

12. Employment and Support Allowance and Universal Credit (Miscellaneous Amendments and Transitional and Savings Provisions) Regulations 2017 (SI 2017/204) reg. 4(1) and (2) (April 3, 2017).

13. Social Security (Restrictions on Amounts for Children and Qualifying Young Persons) Amendment Regulations 2017 (SI 2017/376) reg.2(1) and (2) (April 6, 2017).

14. Social Security (Income-related Benefits) (Updating and Amendment) (EU Exit) Regulations 2019 (SI 2019/872) reg.8(1) and (2) (May 7, 2019).

15. Parental Bereavement Leave and Pay (Consequential Amendments to Subordinate Legislation) Regulations 2020 (SI 2020/354) reg.28(1) and (2) (April 6, 2020).

16. Immigration and Social Security Co-ordination (EU Withdrawal) Act 2020 (Consequential, Saving, Transitional and Transitory Provisions) (EU Exit) Regulations 2020 (SI 2020/1309) reg.75(1) and (2) (December 31, 2020 at 11.00 pm).

17. Social Security (Scotland) Act 2018 (Disability Assistance for Children and Young People) (Consequential Modifications) Order 2021 (SI 2021/786) Sch.11 para.2 (July 26, 2021).

18. Social Security (Disability Assistance for Working Age People) (Consequential Amendments) Order 2022 (SI 2022/177) reg.13(2) (March 21, 2022).

19. Universal Credit and Employment and Support Allowance (Terminal Illness) (Amendment) Regulations 2022 (SI 2022/460) reg.2(1) (April 4, 2022).

20. Universal Credit (Local Welfare Provision Disregard) (Amendment) Regulations 2022 (SI 2022/448) reg.2 (May 4, 2022).

21. Carer's Assistance (Carer Support Payment) (Scotland) Regulations 2023 (Consequential Amendments) Order 2023 (SI 2023/1218) art.23 (November 19, 2023).

22. Social Security and Universal Credit (Migration of Tax Credit Claimants and Miscellaneous Amendments) Regulations 2024 (SI 2024/341) reg.7(2) (April 1, 2024).

Definitions

"child"—see WRA 2012 s.40.
"couple"—see WRA 2012 ss.39 and 40.
"disabled"—see WRA 2012 s.40.
"qualifying young person"—see WRA 2012 ss.40 and 10(5).
"work"—see WRA 2012 s.40.

General Note

Most of these definitions are either self-explanatory, or references to definitions in other regulations, or discussed in the commentary to the regulations where the defined terms are used. A number are similar to terms defined for the purposes of IS, JSA and ESA: see further the commentary to reg.2(1) of the ESA Regulations 2008 and to reg.2(1) of the IS Regulations and reg.1(2) of the JSA Regulations 1996 in Vol.V. **2.7**

The Benefit Unit

Couples

3.—(1) This regulation makes provision in relation to couples, including cases where both members of a couple may be entitled to universal credit jointly without each of them meeting all the basic conditions referred to in section 4 of the Act (see paragraph (2)) and cases where a person whose partner does not meet all the basic conditions [1 or is otherwise excluded from entitlement to universal credit] may make a claim as a single person (see paragraph (3)). **2.8**

(2) A couple may be entitled to universal credit as joint claimants where—

(a) one member does not meet the basic condition in section 4(1)(b) (under the qualifying age for state pension credit) if the other member does meet that condition; or
(b) one member does not meet the basic condition in section 4(1)(d) (not receiving education) and is not excepted from that condition if the other member does meet that condition or is excepted from it.

(3) A person who is a member of a couple may make a claim as a single person if the other member of the couple—

(a) does not meet the basic condition in section 4(1)(a) (at least 18 years old) and is not a person in respect of whom the minimum age specified in regulation 8 applies;
(b) does not meet the basic condition in section 4(1)(c) (in Great Britain);
(c) is a prisoner; [1 . . .]
(d) is a person other than a prisoner in respect of whom entitlement does not arise by virtue of regulation 19 (restrictions on entitlement) [; or
(e) is a person to whom section 115 of the Immigration and Asylum Act 1999 (exclusion from benefits) applies,]

and regulations 18 (capital limit), 36 (amount of elements) and 22 (deduction of income and work allowance) provide for the calculation of the award in such cases.

(4) Where two people are parties to a polygamous marriage, the fact that they are husband and wife is to be disregarded if—

(a) one of them is a party to an earlier marriage that still subsists; and

(b) the other party to that earlier marriage is living in the same household,

and, accordingly, the person who is not a party to the earlier marriage may make a claim for universal credit as a single person.

(5) In paragraph (4) "polygamous marriage" means a marriage during which a party to it is married to more than one person and which took place under the laws of a country which permits polygamy.

(6) Where the claimant is a member of a couple, and the other member is temporarily absent from the claimant's household, they cease to be treated as a couple if that absence is expected to exceed, or does exceed, 6 months.

DEFINITIONS

"claim"—see WRA 2012 s.40.
"claimant"—*ibid.*
"prisoner"—see reg.2 as modified by SI 2020/409.
"single person"—see WRA 2012 ss.40 and 1(2)(a).
"couple"—see WRA 2012 ss.39 and 40.

AMENDMENT

1. Universal Credit (Consequential, Supplementary, Incidental and Miscellaneous Provisions) Regulations 2013 (SI 2013/630) reg.8(1) and (2) (April 29, 2013).

GENERAL NOTE

2.9 This regulation is the first of four under the sub-heading, "The Benefit Unit". That phrase is used extensively in departmental guidance (e.g., Chapter E2 of ADM) but is not defined anywhere in WRA 2012 or these Regulations. The Department intends the phrase to mean all the people in a given household who may, or must, be included in a claim for universal credit. That is consistent with these Regulations because identifying those people is also the subject-matter of regs 3–5 inclusive, which appear under the sub-heading.

It is not generally possible for a person who is a member of a couple to claim, or be awarded, universal credit as a single person. By s.2(1) WRA 2012, members of a couple must claim jointly and by s.1(2) any award of benefit is made jointly to both members of the couple. Further, under s.3(2)(a), the basic conditions of entitlement must be met by both members of the couple and, by ss.3(2)(b) and 5(2), whether or not they satisfy the financial conditions is assessed by reference to their combined income and capital.

It is therefore important for claimants to know whether or not they are members of a couple. The word is defined by s.39(1) and (2) WRA 2012 in terms which follow the standard definition for income-related benefits (e.g., in s.137 SSCBA 1992). It covers:

- two people who are married to each other (whether they are of different sexes or the same sex), or are civil partners of each other, and are members of the same household; and

- two people who are not married to, or civil partners of, each other but are living together as a married couple

see further the commentary to reg.2(1) of the IS Regulations in Vol.V. Note also the commentary to para.(6) below as regards temporary absence.

Paragraph (2)

Under s.4(2) WRA 2012, the Secretary of State has a general power to make regulations which provide for exceptions to the requirement to meet any of the basic conditions for universal credit. In the case of joint claimants, that power can be used to make an exception for one or both of them. Similarly, WRA 2012 Sch.1, para.1 empowers the Secretary of State to make regulations providing for circumstances in which joint claimants may be entitled to universal credit without each of them meeting all the basic conditions referred to in s.4. Those powers have been exercised to make para.(2) (among other regulations). 2.10

Under s.4(1)(b) it is a basic condition for universal credit that a person should not have reached the qualifying age for SPC (as defined in s.4(4) and s.1(6) SPCA 2002). However, under para.2(a) a couple may be jointly entitled to universal credit if one member is over that age, as long as the other member is under it. Until 15 May 2019 a couple where one member was over SPC age and the other under SPC age (a `mixed age couple') could elect whether to claim UC or SPC. That was ended by the Welfare Reform Act 2012 (Commencement No. 31 and Savings and Transitional Provisions and Commencement No. 21 and 23 and Transitional and Transitory Provisions (Amendment)) Order 2019 (SI 2019/37), art.3, which commenced s.4(1A) SPCA 2002. Since that time a mixed age couple can only claim UC, and are excluded from claiming SPC (though art.4 of the 2019 Order gives transitional protection to couples who were entitled to SPC before 15 May 2019, enabling those existing awards to continue).

Under s.4(1)(d), it is a basic condition for universal credit that a person should not be "receiving education". For the definition of that phrase, see regs 12 and 13. Note also that by s.4(2) and reg.14 some people are exempt from the condition imposed by s.4(1)(b). The effect of para.(2)(b) is that a couple may be jointly entitled to universal credit even though one member is receiving education (and does not fall within reg.14) as long as the other member is not receiving education (or does fall within reg.14).

Note that couples who fall within para.(2) must still claim universal credit jointly. The exceptions are from the requirement that both should meet the basic conditions, not the requirement for a joint claim.

Paragraph (3)

By contrast, a member of a couple who falls within para.(3) may claim universal credit as a single person. 2.11

The paragraph is made under s.3(2) WRA 2012 which empowers the Secretary of State to make regulations that "specify circumstances in which a member of a couple may make a claim as a single person". There is no express power to make regulations which disapply the requirement in s.1(2) that universal credit must be awarded jointly where the claimants are members of a couple. However, it is implicit that a member of a couple who may lawfully *claim* universal credit as a single person may also lawfully be *awarded* benefit in that capacity.

Under para.(3) a member of a couple may claim universal credit as a single person if the other member:

- is aged less than 18 (and is not a person who is entitled to claim universal credit from the age of 16 under reg.8): para.(3)(a);
- is not in Great Britain for the purposes of s.4(1)(c) WRA 2012 (see reg.9): para.(3)(b);
- is a prisoner (as defined in reg.2 as modified by SI 2020/409): para.(3)(c).

  (Note that, under reg.19(2), certain prisoners retain entitlement to the housing costs element of universal credit during the first six months of their sentence. However, para.(3)(c) applies whenever the other member of the couple is a prisoner. There is no additional requirement, as there is under para.(3)(d)—which also covers people who fall within reg.19—that the other member of the couple should be excluded from entitlement by that regulation. The implication is that the member of the couple who is not in prison can immediately make a claim as a single person.)

- is a member of a religious order or serving a sentence of imprisonment detained in hospital and excluded from entitlement to universal credit by reg.19: para.(3)(d); or
- is a person subject to immigration control who is excluded from entitlement to benefit under s.115 Immigration and Asylum Act 1999 (see above: para.(3)(e)).

There are special rules for calculating entitlement under claims made by virtue of para.(3). Under reg.36(3) the claimant's maximum amount is calculated using the standard allowance for a single claimant. However, under reg.22(3) the couple's combined income is taken into account when calculating the income to be deducted from that amount. and, under reg.18(2), the claimant's capital is treated as including the capital of the other member of the couple.

Note that the restricted standard allowance under reg.36(3) only applies to a member of a couple who claims as a single person under para.(3). It does *not* affect claims by those who are able to make a joint claim by virtue of para.(2).

Under reg.9(1) of the Claims and Payments Regulations 2013, if a person who is a member of a couple but is entitled to claim as a single person under para.(3), instead makes a joint claim, that claim is treated as made by that person as a single person.

Paragraphs (4) and (5)

2.12 Paragraphs (4) and (5) apply to those in a polygamous marriage. "Polygamous marriage" is defined by para.(5) as "a marriage during which a party to it is married to more than one person and which took place under the laws of a country which permits polygamy". That definition could clearer. A possible interpretation is that once a party to the marriage has been married to more than one person, the marriage is to be treated as polygamous for as long as it lasts (i.e., because it is a marriage "during which" there were, at least for a period, more than two members). However, it is suggested that in the context of the regulation of the whole, that interpretation is not correct. The use of the present tense ("is married") and the provisions made by para.(4)—which can only apply if the marriage has more than two members—indicate that the head (a) of the definition is to be read as meaning that a marriage is polygamous *during any period in which* a party to it is married to more than one person. In other words, the definition preserves the distinction, which applies elsewhere in social security law, between a marriage that is actually polygamous and one that is only potentially polygamous, so that where neither party is actually married to more than one person, the marriage is not polygamous for universal credit purposes.

For the definition to apply, the party who is married to more than one person must be legally married to them under the law of England and Wales or the law of Scotland (as the case may be). This can raise complex issues of private international law: see further the commentary to the Social Security and Family Allowances (Polygamous Marriages) Regulations 1975 (SI 1975/561) in Vol.I and s.4 of Ch.17 of Dicey, Morris & Collins *The Conflict of Laws* 16th edn (Sweet & Maxwell, London, 2022).

The effect of para.(4) is that where a marriage is actually polygamous, and at least three members of that marriage live in the same household, the parties to the earlier or earliest marriage are treated as a couple and all other members of the marriage may make a claim for universal credit as a single person. Where such member of the marriage actually makes a joint claim with another member, that claim is treated as a claim made by that member as a single person (reg.9(2) and (3) of the Claims and Payments Regulations 2013).

Paragraph (6)

At first sight, the drafting of para.6 is puzzling. It seems to draw a distinction between the member of the couple who is "the claimant" who, it is implied, is the head of "the claimant's household" and that person's partner who is "the other member", when, as noted above, the structure of universal credit is that if a claim is to be made by a member of a couple, *both* parties must normally be *joint* claimants. However, WRA 2012, s.40, defines "claimant" as including "each of joint claimants". Therefore, the effect of para.(6) is that when either member of the couple is temporarily absent from the household, they cease to be treated as a couple if the absence is expected to last, or actually lasts, for more than six months. 2.13

Relationship formation and breakdown

TCA 2002 s.3, which requires couples to make a joint claim for tax credits, contains an express provision (s.3(4)), that entitlement to tax credits ceases if the claim was made by a couple and the members of that couple split up ("could no longer make a joint claim") or if, in the case of a single claim, the claimant becomes a member of a couple ("could no longer make a single claim"). By contrast, WRA 2012 does not include any such provision relating to universal credit. Various provisions in these Regulations and of the Claims and Payments Regulations 2013 *assume* that a joint award comes to an end when a couple separate and that an award to a single claimant ends if the claimant becomes a member of a couple. However, it is not permissible to interpret primary legislation on the basis of assumptions made in the secondary legislation made under it. It is more persuasive that the same assumption is made by WRA 2012, Sch.1, para.3(2), but even that paragraph empowers the Secretary of State to make regulations about what happens *if* an award of universal credit comes to an end because of a relationship change, rather than saying that is automatically the case. 2.14

One can argue that it is inherent in the concept of a joint award to a couple, that it should come to an end if that couple no longer exists. But if that is the case, why was it felt necessary to make express provision for the situation in TCA 2002? And, when one thinks about it further, it becomes less and less clear why—in the absence of any provision equivalent to s.3(4) TCA 2002—ceasing to be a couple, or becoming one, should not be treated like any other change of circumstances, like a change of address, or a change in the amount of income or capital, rather than as a change which brings the award of benefit to an end irrespective of the circumstances of the claimants after that change. The rules in reg.9(6)-(8) and (10) of the Claims and Payments Regulations (which dispense with the need for a fresh claim where people who have been awarded universal credit become, or cease to be, members of a couple) and reg.21(3)-(3B) (under which new awards of universal credit in such cases adopt the assessment periods of the old awards) mean that, in practice, that will often be the effect of relationship formation and breakdown, even though, formally, the regulations assume that a previous entitlement to universal credit comes to an end in such circumstances.

When a person is responsible for a child or qualifying young person

4.—(1) Whether a person is responsible for a child or qualifying young person for the purposes of Pt 1 of the Act and these Regulations is determined as follows. 2.15

(2) A person is responsible for a child or qualifying young person who normally lives with them.

(3) But a person is not responsible for a qualifying young person if the two of them are living as a couple.

(4) Where a child or qualifying young person normally lives with two or more persons who are not a couple, only one of them is to be treated as responsible and that is the person who has the main responsibility.

(5) The persons mentioned in paragraph (4) may jointly nominate which of them has the main responsibility but the Secretary of State may determine that question—

(a) in default of agreement; or

(b) if a nomination or change of nomination does not, in the opinion of the Secretary of State, reflect the arrangements between those persons.

(6) [1 Subject to regulation 4A,] a child or qualifying young person is to be treated as not being the responsibility of any person during any period when the child or qualifying young person is—

(a) looked after by a local authority; or

(b) a prisoner,

[1 . . .]

(7) Where a child or qualifying young person is temporarily absent from a person's household the person ceases to be responsible for the child or qualifying young person if—

(a) the absence is expected to exceed, or does exceed, 6 months; or

(b) the absence is from Great Britain and is expected to exceed, or does exceed, one month unless it is in circumstances where an absence of a person for longer than one month would be disregarded for the purposes of regulation 11(2) or (3) (medical treatment or convalescence or death of close relative etc.).

DEFINITIONS

"the Act"—see reg.2.

"child"—see WRA 2012 s.40.

"couple"—see WRA 2012 ss.39 and 40.

"looked after by a local authority"—see reg.2.

"qualifying young person"—see WRA 2012 s.40 and 10(5) and regs 2 and 5.

AMENDMENT

1. Social Security (Miscellaneous Amendments) (No.2) Regulations 2013 (SI 2013/1508) reg.3(1) and (3) (July 29, 2013).

GENERAL NOTE

2.16 Whether or not a claimant is responsible for a child or qualifying young person is relevant to their maximum amount under Pt 4, to the level of any work allowance under reg.22 and to the imposition of work-related requirements under Pt 8.

Paragraphs (1)–(5)

2.17 The general rule is that a person is responsible for a child or qualifying young person who normally lives with them (para.(2)) unless (in the case of a qualifying young person) the two of them are living together as a couple (para.(3)).

Where a child or qualifying young person normally lives with two people who are a couple, both members of the couple are responsible for him or her (because that is the effect of para.(2) and no other rule applies).

However, where he or she lives with two or more persons who are not a couple, only one of them is to be treated as responsible and that is the person who has the main responsibility for him or her (para.(4)). In those circumstances, the people with whom the child or qualifying young person lives may agree which of them has the main responsibility. However, the Secretary of State may overrule that agreement, if in his opinion, it does not reflect the arrangements those people have made (i.e., for the care of the child or qualifying young person) (para.(5)(b)). The Secretary of State may also decide who has main responsibility if the people with whom the child or qualifying young person lives do not agree who has the main responsibility (para.(5)(a)).

The application of para.(4) was considered by the Upper Tribunal (Judge Wikeley) in *MC v SSWP (UC)* [2018] UKUT 44 (AAC). In that case, the claimant was the father of a daughter who—to put the matter neutrally—stayed overnight and took her meals at her godparent's home for 12 days a fortnight. She did so to facilitate her attendance at a college near the godparent's house. However, the daughter spent every other weekend with the claimant and he contributed the cost of her keep and was responsible for all other aspects of her upbringing. Judge Wikeley rejected Departmental guidance to the effect that "a child or qualifying young person normally lives with a person where they spend more time with that person than anyone else" in favour of a "more holistic approach" in which the proportion of time spent living with an adult was a factor to be taken into consideration but was not necessarily determinative. Paras (2) and (4) established a two-stage test for first identifying who the child or young person normally lives with, and then ascribing main responsibility if more than one adult is involved. On the facts of *MC*, Judge Wikeley decided that the daughter was "normally living" with both her father and her godparent but that her father had main responsibility for her. As far as the "normally lives with" limb of the two-stage test is concerned, it should be applied with a focus on the *quality* rather than *quantification* of the normality. As regards main responsibility, Judge Wikeley took the view that the guidance at paragraph F1065 of *Advice for decision makers* is "a good starting point". That guidance is in the following terms:

> "If the DM [decision maker] is required to determine who has main responsibility they should note that main responsibility is not defined in regulations and should be given the meaning of the person who is normally answerable for, or called to account for the child or young person. In determining who has the main responsibility for a child or young person consideration should be given to:
>
> 1. Who the child normally lives with
> 2. Who makes day to day decisions about the child's welfare including, for example, arranging and taking them to visits to the doctor or dentist or enrolling and taking the child to and from school?
> 3. Who provides the child with clothing, shoes, toiletries and other items needed for daily use?
> 4. Who is the main contact for the child's school, doctor and dentist?
> 5. Who cares for the child when the child is ill?
>
> This list should not be considered exhaustive."

Judge Wikeley also endorsed the approach recommended by Judge Jacobs in *PG v HMRC and NG (TC)* [2016] UKUT 216 (AAC); [2016] AACR 45. That decision relates to child tax credit. However, the statutory test is similar.

Paragraph (6)

Children or qualifying young persons who are being looked after by a local authority or are prisoners (as defined in reg.2) are treated as not being the responsibility of any person. The effect is that the child or qualifying young person is disregarded for the purposes of reg.22, Pt 4 and Pt 8 even if he or she normally lives with the claimant or claimants. **2.18**

However, para.(6) is subject to reg.4A, so that the child or qualifying young person is not treated as not being the responsibility of any person during any period in which he or she is being looked after by a local authority and either:

- his or her absence is "in the nature of a planned short term break, or is one of a series of such breaks, for the purpose of providing respite for the person who normally cares for" him or her; or

- (though being formally looked after by a local authority) the child or qualifying young person is placed with, or continues to live with, their parent or a person who has parental responsibility for them. For the definition of parental responsibility, see reg.4A(2).

Paragraph (7)

2.19 Paragraph 7 deals with the temporary absence of a child or qualifying young person from a claimant's (or the claimants') household. In those circumstances, the person who was previously responsible for the child or qualifying young person ceases to be so as soon as the absence is expected to exceed six months or if, unexpectedly, it actually exceeds six months (para.7(a)). That period is reduced to one month if the child or qualifying young person is also absent from Great Britain unless that absence would be disregarded under reg.11(1) by virtue of reg.11(2) or (3).

[1 Responsibility for children looked after by a local authority

2.20 **4A.**—(1) There is excluded from regulation 4(6)(a)—

(a) any period which is in the nature of a planned short term break, or is one of a series of such breaks, for the purpose of providing respite for the person who normally cares for the child or qualifying young person;

(b) any period during which the child or qualifying young person is placed with, or continues to live with, their parent or a person who has parental responsibility for them [2 ...;

(c) any period during which the child or qualifying young person is placed for adoption under the Adoption and Children Act 2002(17) or the Adoption and Children (Scotland) Act 2007.]

(2) For the purposes of this regulation, a person has parental responsibility if they are not a foster parent and—

(a) in England and Wales, they have parental responsibility within the meaning of section 3 of the Children Act 1989; or

(b) in Scotland, they have any or all of the legal responsibilities or rights described in sections 1 or 2 of the Children (Scotland) Act 1995.]

AMENDMENTS

1. Social Security (Miscellaneous Amendments) (No.2) Regulations 2013 (SI 2013/1508) reg.3(1) and (4) (July 29, 2013).
2. Social Security and Universal Credit (Migration of Tax Credit Claimants and Miscellaneous Amendments) Regulations 2024 (SI 2024/341) reg.7(3) (April 1, 2024).

DEFINITIONS

"child"—see WRA 2012 s.40.
"qualifying young person"—see WRA 2012 ss.40 and 10(5) and regs 2 and 5.
"looked after by a local authority"—see reg.2.
"local authority"—*ibid.*

GENERAL NOTE

2.21 See the general note to reg.4(6) above.

Meaning of "qualifying young person"

2.22 **5.**—(1) A person who has reached the age of 16 but not the age of 20 is a qualifying young person for the purposes of Part 1 of the Act and these Regulations—

(a) up to, but not including, the 1st September following their 16th birthday; and

(b) up to, but not including, the 1st September following their 19th birthday, if they are enrolled on, or accepted for, approved training or a course of education—

(i) which is not a course of advanced education,

(ii) which is provided at a school or college or provided elsewhere but approved by the Secretary of State, and

(iii) where the average time spent during term time in receiving tuition, engaging in practical work or supervised study or taking examinations exceeds 12 hours per week.

(2) Where the young person is aged 19, they must have started the education or training or been enrolled on or accepted for it before reaching that age.

(3) The education or training referred to in paragraph (1) does not include education or training provided by means of a contract of employment.

(4) "Approved training" means training in pursuance of arrangements made under section 2(1) of the Employment and Training Act 1973 or section 2(3) of the Enterprise and New Towns (Scotland) Act 1990 which is approved by the Secretary of State for the purposes of this regulation.

(5) A person who is receiving universal credit, an employment and support allowance or a jobseeker's allowance is not a qualifying young person.

Modification

With effect from June 16, 2014, reg. 5 is modified by reg. 28 of the Universal Credit (Transitional Provisions) Regulations 2014 (SI 2014/1230) (see Pt IV of this book). The modification applies where a person who would otherwise be a "qualifying young person" within the meaning of reg. 5 is entitled to an "existing benefit" (namely income-based JSA, income-related ESA, income support, housing benefit, child tax credit or working tax credit: see reg.2(1) of SI 2014/1230). The modifications are (i) that such a person is not a qualifying young person for the purposes of the Universal Credit Regulations, and (ii) that reg. 5(5) applies as if, after "a person who is receiving" there were inserted "an existing benefit (within the meaning of the Universal Credit (Transitional Provisions) Regulations 2014),".

Definitions

"employment and support allowance"—see reg.2.
"jobseeker's allowance"—*ibid.*

General Note

Under s.8(2)(b) and s.10(1) WRA 2012 the calculation of an award of universal credit includes an amount for a qualifying young person for whom the claimant is responsible. Regulation 5 defines who is a qualifying young person. The definition is similar to that which applies for the purposes of child benefit (see by way of comparison regs 3, 7 and 8 of the Child Benefit (General) Regulations 2006 in Vol.IV of this series) but not quite. In particular, the concept of "terminal date" has gone. **2.23**

Under reg.5, a person who is aged 16 or over but under 20 counts as a qualifying young person:

(i) up to (but not including) the 1st September following their 16th birthday if they are aged 16; or

(ii) up to (but not including) the 1st September following their 19th birthday if they are aged 16–19 and has been accepted for (or has enrolled on) approved training (defined in para.(4)) or non-advanced education at a school or college (or elsewhere as approved by the Secretary of State; note that in the case of education provided other than at a school or college there is no requirement that the qualifying young person must have been receiving such education before they became 16, as there is for child benefit (see reg.3(3) of the 2006 Regulations in Vol.IV of this series and *JH v HMRC (CHB)* [2015] UKUT 479 (AAC)). In the case of a course of education at least 12 hours on average a week must be spent on tuition, practical work, supervised study or examinations. Meal breaks and unsupervised study are not included. *R(F) 1/93* held that "supervised study" (in reg.5 of the Child Benefit Regulations 1976) "would normally be understood to import the presence or close proximity of a teacher or tutor". If the person is aged 19, they must have started (or been accepted for or enrolled on) the education or training before reaching 19. The education or training must not be provided as part of a contract of employment.

But note that if a person is receiving universal credit, new style ESA or new style JSA in their own right, they cannot be a qualifying young person (para.(5)). Note also the modification to para.(5) in reg. 28 of SI 2014/1230 referred to above, which has the effect that if the person is receiving income-based JSA, income-related ESA, income support, housing benefit, child tax credit or working tax credit they are not a qualifying young person.

See also reg.12(1) which provides that if a person is a qualifying young person they are regarded as receiving education and so will not meet the basic condition in s.4(1)(d) WRA 2012 (unless they come within one of the exceptions to this requirement in reg.14).

Rounding

2.24 **6.**—(1) Where the calculation of an amount for the purposes of these Regulations results in a fraction of a penny, that fraction is to be disregarded if it is less than half a penny and otherwise it is to be treated as a penny.

[1 (1A) Where the calculation of an amount for the purposes of the following [3 provisions] results in a fraction of a pound, that fraction is to be disregarded—

[2 (za) regulation 82(1)(a) (exceptions – earnings);]

(a) regulation 90 (claimants subject to no work-related requirements – the earnings thresholds); and

(b) regulation 99(6) (circumstances in which requirements must not be imposed) [3[4 . . .] and

(c) [4 . . .].]

(2) This regulation does not apply to the calculation in regulation 111 (daily rate for a reduction under section 26 or 27 of the Act).

AMENDMENTS

1. Universal Credit and Miscellaneous Amendments Regulations 2015 (SI 2015/1754), reg.4 (November 4, 2015, or in the case of existing awards, the first assessment period beginning on or after November 4, 2015).

2. Universal Credit (Benefit Cap Earnings Exception) Amendment Regulations 2017 (SI 2017/138) reg.2(2) (April 1, 2017).

3. Universal Credit (Housing Costs Element for claimants aged 18 to 21) (Amendment) Regulations 2017 (SI 2017/252) reg.2(2) (April 1, 2017).

4. Universal Credit and Jobseeker's Allowance (Miscellaneous Amendments) Regulations 2018 (SI 2018/1129) reg.3(2) (December 31, 2018).

DEFINITION

"the Act"—see reg.2.

PART 2

ENTITLEMENT

Introduction

7. This Part contains provisions about— 2.25

(a) the requirement to meet the basic conditions in section 4 of the Act, including exceptions from that requirement;

(b) the maximum amount of capital and the minimum amount of universal credit for the financial conditions in section 5 of the Act; and

(c) cases where no entitlement to universal credit arises even if the basic conditions and the financial conditions are met.

DEFINITION

"the Act"—see reg.2.

Minimum age

Cases where the minimum age is 16

8.—(1) For the basic condition in section 4(1)(a) of the Act (at least 18 2.26
years old), the minimum age is 16 years old where a person—

(a) has limited capability for work;

(b) is awaiting an assessment under Part 5 to determine whether the person has limited capability for work and has a statement given [2...] in accordance with the Medical Evidence Regulations which provides that the person is not fit for work;

(c) has regular and substantial caring responsibilities for a severely disabled person;

(d) is responsible for a child;

(e) is a member of a couple the other member of which is responsible for a child or a qualifying young person (but only where the other member meets the basic conditions in section 4 of the Act);

(f) is pregnant, and it is 11 weeks or less before her expected week of confinement, or was pregnant and it is 15 weeks or less since the date of her confinement; or

(g) is without parental support (see paragraph (3)).

(2) Sub-paragraphs (c), (f) and (g) of paragraph (1) do not include any person who is a care leaver.

(3) For the purposes of paragraph (1)(g) a young person is without parental support where that person is not being looked after by a local authority and—

(a) has no parent;

(b) cannot live with their parents because—

(i) the person is estranged from them, or

(ii) there is a serious risk to the person's physical or mental health, or that the person would suffer significant harm if the person lived with them; or

(c) is living away from their parents, and neither parent is able to support the person financially because that parent—
  (i) has a physical or mental impairment,
  (ii) is detained in custody pending trial or sentence upon conviction or under a sentence imposed by a court, or
  (iii) is prohibited from entering or re-entering Great Britain.

(4) In this regulation—

"parent" includes any person acting in the place of a parent;

"care leaver" means—

(a) in relation to England [1 . . .], an eligible child for the purposes of paragraph 19B of Schedule 2 to the Children Act 1989 or a relevant child for the purposes of section 23A of that Act;

[1 (b) in relation to Scotland, a person under the age of 18 who—
  (i) is looked after by a local authority; or
  (ii) has ceased to be looked after by a local authority but is a person to whom a local authority in Scotland is obliged to provide advice and assistance in terms of section 29(1) of the Children (Scotland) Act 1995 or a person who is being provided with continuing care under section 26A of that Act,

 and who, since reaching the age of 14 has been looked after by a local authority for a period of, or periods totalling, 3 months or more (excluding any period where the person has been placed with a member of their family);

(c) in relation to Wales, a category 1 young person or category 2 young person within the meaning of section 104(2) of the Social Services and Well-being (Wales) Act 2014.]

"confinement" means—

(a) labour resulting in the birth of a living child; or

(b) labour after 24 weeks of pregnancy resulting in the birth of a child whether alive or dead,

and where a woman's labour begun on one day results in the birth of a child on another day she is to be taken to be confined on the date of the birth.

AMENDMENTS

1. Universal Credit (Care Leavers and Looked After Children) Amendment Regulations 2016 (SI 2016/543) reg.2(3) (May 26, 2016).

2. Social Security (Medical Evidence) and Statutory Sick Pay (Medical Evidence) (Amendment) (No.2) Regulations 2022 (SI 2022/630) reg.4(3)(a) (July 1, 2022).

DEFINITIONS

"the Act"—see reg.2.
"child"—see WRA 2012, s.40.
"limited capability for work"—see WRA 2012, ss.40 and 37(1).
"local authority"—see reg.2.
"looked after by a local authority"—*ibid.*
"Medical Evidence Regulations"— *ibid.*
"qualifying young person"—see regs 2 and 5.
"regular and substantial caring responsibilities"—see WRA 2012, s.40 and reg.30.
"responsible for a child or qualifying young person"—see reg.4.

General Note

One of the basic conditions for entitlement to universal credit is that the claimant must be at least 18 years old (s.4(1)(a) WRA 2012). Regulation 8 provides for the exceptions to that rule. 2.27

Under para.(1) a person aged 16 or 17 (who satisfies the other basic conditions) can qualify for universal credit if they:

(a) have limited capability for work; or
(b) are waiting for a work capability assessment and have submitted a medical certificate stating that they are not fit for work; or
(c) have "regular and substantial caring responsibilities for a severely disabled person" (see reg.30), but not if they are a "care leaver" (defined in para. (4)); or
(d) are responsible for a child (see reg.4 for when a person is responsible for a child); or
(e) are a member of a couple and the other member satisfies the basic conditions and is responsible for a child or a qualifying young person (see reg.5 for who counts as a qualifying young person); or
(f) are pregnant and it is 11 weeks or less before their expected week of confinement (defined in para.(4)), or was pregnant and it is 15 weeks or less since the date of confinement, but not if they are a care leaver; or
(g) are "without parental support" (defined in para.(3)), but not if they are a care leaver.

In relation to the definition of "care leaver", for who is an "eligible child" for the purposes of para.19B of Sch.2 to the Children Act 1989 or a "relevant child" for the purposes of s.23A of that Act, or a "category 1 young person" or "category 2 young person" within the meaning of s.104(2) of the Social Services and Well-being (Wales) Act 2014, see the Children (Leaving Care) Act 2000 and the notes to that Act in Vol.V of this series.

A care leaver who is aged 16 or 17 is not entitled to a housing costs element for rent payments (see Sch.4, para.4) But note that a person aged 18-21, who was a care leaver before they became 18, is exempt from the "shared accommodation rate" for renters (see para.29(2) of Sch.4). 2.28

On para.(1)(g), a young person is "without parental support" if they are not being looked after by a local authority and come within one of the categories listed in para.(3). These categories are similar to those in reg.13(2)(c), (d) and (e) of the Income Support Regulations (see the notes to those provisions in Vol.V of this series). Note the definition of "parent" in para.(4). On para.(3)(b)(ii), para.E1055 of ADM gives examples of "serious risk" as: (i) having a brother or sister who is a drug addict, which poses a risk to the young person who is exposed to the drugs at the parental home; (ii) having a history of mental illness which is made worse by the parent's attitude; or (iii) suffering from chronic bronchitis, which is made worse by the damp conditions of the parent's home.

Note that under reg.3(3)(a) a person who is a member of a couple (and is either 18 or over or falls within para.(1)) but whose partner is under 18 and does not fall within para.(1) can claim universal credit as a single person.

A person is not normally eligible for universal credit if they are receiving education (see s.4(1)(d) WRA 2012). However, see reg.14 for the exceptions.

In Great Britain

Persons treated as not being in Great Britain

9.—(1) For the purposes of determining whether a person meets the basic condition to be in Great Britain, except where a person falls within paragraph (4), a person is to be treated as not being in Great Britain if the person is not habitually resident in the United Kingdom, the Channel Islands, the Isle of Man or the Republic of Ireland. 2.29

(2) A person must not be treated as habitually resident in the United Kingdom, the Channel Islands, the Isle of Man or the Republic of Ireland unless the person has a right to reside in one of those places.

(3) For the purposes of paragraph (2), a right to reside does not include a right which exists by virtue of, or in accordance with—

(a) regulation 13 of the EEA Regulations [5 . . .]; [2 . . .]

[2 (aa) regulation 14 of the EEA Regulations(3), but only in cases where the right exists under that regulation because the person is–

(i) a qualified person for the purposes of regulation 6(1) of those Regulations as a jobseeker; or

(ii) a family member (within the meaning of regulation 7 of those Regulations) of such a jobseeker; [3 . . .]]

(b) [3 regulation 16] of the EEA Regulations, but only in cases where the right exists under that regulation because [3 the person] satisfies the criteria in [3 regulation 16(5)] of those Regulations [5 . . .][3; or]

[3 (c) a person having been granted limited leave to enter, or remain in, the United Kingdom under the Immigration Act 1971 by virtue of—

(i) Appendix EU to the immigration rules made under section 3(2) of that Act; or [6 . . .]

(ii) being a person with a Zambrano right to reside as defined in Annex 1 of Appendix EU to the immigration rules made under section 3(2) of that Act]; [6; or]

[6 (iii) having arrived in the United Kingdom with an entry clearance that was granted under Appendix EU (Family Permit) to the immigration rules made under section 3(2) of that Act.]

[4 (3A) Paragraph (3)(c)(i) does not apply to a person who—

(a) has a right to reside granted by virtue of being a family member of a relevant person of Northern Ireland; and

(b) would have a right to reside under the EEA Regulations if the relevant person of Northern Ireland were an EEA national, provided that the right to reside does not fall within paragraph (3)(a) or (b)]

(4) A person falls within this paragraph if the person is—

[7 (za) a person granted leave in accordance with the immigration rules made under section 3(2) of the Immigration Act 1971, where such leave is granted by virtue of—

(i) the Afghan Relocations and Assistance Policy; or

(ii) the previous scheme for locally-employed staff in Afghanistan (sometimes referred to as the ex-gratia scheme);

(zb) a person in Great Britain not coming within sub-paragraph (za) or (e)[8 ...] who left Afghanistan in connection with the collapse of the Afghan government that took place on 15th August 2021;]

[8 (zc) a person in Great Britain who was residing in Ukraine immediately before 1st January 2022, left Ukraine in connection with the Russian invasion which took place on 24th February 2022 and—

(i) has been granted leave in accordance with immigration rules made under section 3(2) of the Immigration Act 1971; [9 ...]

(ii) has a right of abode in the United Kingdom within the meaning given in section 2 of that Act;] [9 or

(iii) does not require leave to enter or remain in the United Kingdom in accordance with section 3ZA of that Act;]]

(a) a qualified person for the purposes of regulation 6 of the EEA Regulations as a worker or a self-employed person;

(b) a family member of a person referred to in sub-paragraph (a) [4 . . .];

(c) a person who has a right to reside permanently in the United Kingdom by virtue of regulation 15(1)(c), (d) or (e) of the EEA Regulations;

[10 (zd) a person who was residing in Sudan before 15th April 2023, left Sudan in connection with the violence which rapidly escalated on 15th April 2023 in Khartoum and across Sudan and—

(i) has been granted leave in accordance with immigration rules made under section 3(2) of the Immigration Act 1971;

(ii) has a right of abode in the United Kingdom within the meaning given in section 2 of that Act; or

(iii) does not require leave to enter or remain in the United Kingdom in accordance with section 3ZA of that Act;]

[11 (ze) a person who was residing in Israel, the West Bank, the Gaza Strip, East Jerusalem, the Golan Heights or Lebanon immediately before 7th October 2023, who left Israel, the West Bank, the Gaza Strip, East Jerusalem, the Golan Heights or Lebanon in connection with the Hamas terrorist attack in Israel on 7th October 2023 or the violence which rapidly escalated in the region following the attack and—

(i) has been granted leave in accordance with immigration rules made under section 3(2) of the Immigration Act 1971;

(ii) has a right of abode in the United Kingdom within the meaning given in section 2 of that Act; or

(iii) does not require leave to enter or remain in the United Kingdom in accordance with section 3ZA of that Act;]

[4 (ca) a family member of a relevant person of Northern Ireland, with a right to reside which falls within paragraph (3)(c)(i), provided that the relevant person of Northern Ireland falls within paragraph (4)(a), or would do so but for the fact that they are not an EEA national;]

[5 (cb) a frontier worker within the meaning of regulation 3 of the Citizens' Rights (Frontier Workers) (EU Exit) Regulations 2020;

(cc) a family member of a person referred to in sub-paragraph (cb), who has been granted limited leave to enter, or remain in, the United Kingdom by virtue of Appendix EU to the immigration rules made under section 3(2) of the Immigration Act 1971;]

(d) a refugee within the definition in Article 1 of the Convention relating to the Status of Refugees done at Geneva on 28th July 1951, as extended by Article 1(2) of the Protocol relating to the Status of Refugees done at New York on 31st January 1967;

[1(e) a person who has been granted, or who is deemed to have been granted, leave outside the rules made under section 3(2) of the Immigration Act 1971 [8 . . .]

(f) a person who has humanitarian protection granted under those rules; or

(g) a person who is not a person subject to immigration control within the meaning of section 115(9) of the Immigration and Asylum Act 1999 and who is in the United Kingdom as a result of their deportation, expulsion or other removal by compulsion of law from another country to the United Kingdom.

[4 (5) In this regulation—

"EEA national" has the meaning given in regulation 2(1) of the EEA Regulations;

"family member" has the meaning given in regulation 7(1)(a), (b) or (c) of the EEA Regulations, except that regulation 7(4) of the EEA Regulations does not apply for the purposes of paragraphs (3A) and (4)(ca);

"relevant person of Northern Ireland" has the meaning given in Annex 1 of Appendix EU to the immigration rules made under section 3(2) of the Immigration Act 1971.]

AMENDMENTS

1. Social Security (Miscellaneous Amendments) (No.2) Regulations 2013 (SI 2013/1508) reg.3(1) and (5) (October 29, 2013).

2. Universal Credit (EEA Jobseekers) Amendment Regulations 2015 (SI 2015/546) reg.2 (June 10, 2015).

3. Social Security (Income-related Benefits) (Updating and Amendment) (EU Exit) Regulations 2019 (SI 2019/872) reg.8(1) and (3) (May 7, 2019).

4. Social Security (Income-Related Benefits) (Persons of Northern Ireland—Family Members) (Amendment) Regulations 2020 (SI 2020/683), reg.8 (August 24, 2020).

5. Immigration and Social Security Co-ordination (EU Withdrawal) Act 2020 (Consequential, Saving, Transitional and Transitory Provisions) (EU Exit) Regulations 2020 (SI 2020/1309) reg.75(1) and (3) (December 31, 2020 at 11.00 pm).

6. Immigration (Citizens' Rights etc.) (EU Exit) Regulations 2020 (SI 2020/1372) reg.25 (immediately after December 31, 2020 at 11.00 pm).

7. Social Security (Habitual Residence and Past Presence) (Amendment) Regulations 2021 (SI 2021/1034) reg.3 (September 15, 2021).

8. Social Security (Habitual Residence and Past Presence) (Amendment) Regulations 2022 (SI 2022/344) reg.3 (March 22, 2022).

9. Social Security (Habitual Residence and Past Presence) (Amendment) (No.2) Regulations 2022 (SI 2022/990), reg.2 (October 18, 2022).

10. Social Security (Habitual Residence and Past Presence) (Amendment) Regulations 2023 (SI 2023/532) reg.3 (May 15, 2023).

11. Social Security (Habitual Residence and Past Presence, and Capital Disregards) (Amendment) Regulations 2023 (SI 2023/1144) reg.2 (October 27, 2023).

DEFINITION

"EEA Regulations"—see reg.2.

GENERAL NOTE

2.30 Under s.4(1)(c) WRA 2012, it is a basic condition of entitlement to universal credit that the claimant is "in Great Britain" and s.4(5)(a) empowers the Secretary of State to make regulations specifying "circumstances in which a person is to be treated as being, or not being, in Great Britain". Regulation 9 is made under that power. The general rule (para.(1)) is that to be "in Great Britain" a person must be habitually resident in the United Kingdom, the Channel Islands, the Isle of Man or the Republic of Ireland. Apart from people who fall within para.(4), everyone who is not so habitually resident is treated as not being in Great Britain.

Right to reside – general

2.31 The habitual residence test in para.(1) is supplemented by para.(2) which establishes an ancillary right to reside test: no-one may be treated as habitually resident in the United Kingdom, the Channel Islands, the Isle of Man or the Republic of Ireland for universal credit purposes unless the person has a right to reside in one of those places, other than a right to reside specified in para.(3).

Following the UK's exit from the EU, the right to reside test only affects people with "pre-settled" status under the EU Settlement Scheme (EUSS) in Appendix EU to the Immigration Rules. Affected persons (mainly EEA nationals) who wish to continue to live in the UK after December 31, 2020 (technically at 11.00 pm on that date) had to apply under the EUSS by June 30, 2021 (subject to limited provision for late applications) or lose their former rights under EU law.

Applicants who can satisfy the Home Office that they meet the criteria in paras EU11 or EU12 of the Appendix, and that they should not be refused on grounds of suitability (paras EU15 and EU16), will be given indefinite leave to remain (also known in this context as "settled status"). Those who have been granted settled status have a right to reside in the UK that counts for the purposes of all income-related benefits: para.(3)(c) does not affect them (because they have not been granted *limited* leave to enter or remain, within that paragraph).

Applicants who do not qualify for settled status (and who are not refused altogether) will be given limited leave to remain for five years (also known as "pre-settled status") if they meet the criteria in para.EU14. Those with pre-settled status may apply for settled status as soon as they meet the criteria in paras EU11 or EU12. That right of residence counts for immigration purposes, but the effect of para.(3)(c)(i) is that it does not count for the purposes of the right to reside test (unless they fall within para.(3A). However, some of the rights of those with pre-settled status under the former Immigration (European Economic Area) Regulations 2016 are preserved and modified by SI 2020/1309: see under the heading, *The United Kingdom's withdrawal from the European Union*, in the General Note to those Regulations in Part VII of Vol.V. Those modified rights of residence do potentially count for the purposes of the right to reside test, unless they fall within the other provisions of para.(3). Therefore people with pre-settled status who can show that they are engaged in the activities previously covered by the 2016 Regulations (e.g. as a worker, or a person who has retained worker status), may be able to access UC.

In *R. (Fratila) v Secretary of State for Work and Pensions* [2021] UKSC 53; [2022] P.T.S.R. 448, the Supreme Court allowed the appeal by the Secretary of State against a decision of the Court of Appeal which had found reg.9(3)(c)(i) unlawfully discriminatory contrary to art.18 of the TFEU for treating EU nationals with pre-settled status differently to UK nationals. The judgment of the Court of Appeal had become unsustainable following the decision of the CJEU, in *CG v Department for Communities* (C-709/20, July 15, 2021) [2021] 1 W.L.R. 5919, that such a provision is not contrary to art.18 of the TFEU, or Directive 2004/38.

However, what the Supreme Court elected not to address (since it was a new point, which would have required new evidence) was the implications for the domestic Regulations of what had also been said in *CG* about the Charter of Fundamental Rights of the European Union (the Charter). The Court of Justice had stated:

> "[93] … [Where] a Union citizen resides legally, on the basis of national law, in the territory of a Member State other than that of which he or she is a national, the national authorities empowered to grant social assistance are required to check that a refusal to grant such benefits based on that legislation does not expose that citizen, and the children for which he or she is responsible, to an actual and current risk of violation of their fundamental rights, as enshrined in Articles 1, 7 and 24 of the Charter. Where that citizen does not have any resources to provide for his or her own needs and those of his or her children and is isolated, those authorities must ensure that, in the event of a refusal to grant social assistance, that citizen may nevertheless live with his or her children in dignified conditions. In the context of that examination, those authorities may take into account all means of assistance provided for by national law, from which the citizen concerned and her children are actually entitled to benefit."

'Right to reside – Withdrawal Agreement'

Important unanswered questions arising from *CG* were: 2.32

- whether the Charter has any ongoing application, since the end of the transition period in December 2020, for EU nationals resident in the UK on the basis of pre-settled status; and

- what if any substantive or procedural requirements are imposed on the Secretary of State by the obligation to "check" that Charter rights will not be breached.

In *SSWP v AT (UC)* [2022] UKUT 330 (AAC), in response to the first issue, a three-judge panel of the UT decided that the Charter does continue to confer enforceable rights on individuals. In response to the second question, it held that in order for reg.9(3)(c)(i) of the Universal Credit Regulations 2013 to be compatible with the UK's enforceable Withdrawal Agreement obligations, the Secretary of State had to be satisfied in individual cases that a claimant's right to reside in dignity was not breached. In AT's own case, her dignity right was breached by a period of time living on very meagre resources in a hostel with her small child, having fled domestic violence, dependent on charity, the local authority having declined to give significant support. As a result, reg.9(3)(c)(i) had to be disapplied in her case, with the effect that she was entitled to UC.

The Secretary of State made a second appeal to the Court of Appeal; the Court of Appeal unanimously dismissed it: [2023] EWCA Civ 1307 (November 8, 2023). On February 7, 2024, the Supreme Court refused the Secretary of State permission to appeal any further.

Several further questions about the operation of reg.9(3)(c)(i) still await definitive judicial determination.

First, is reg.9(3)(c)(i) unlawful (or at least subject to disapplication in individual cases) on the basis that:

- there is a right to equal treatment under art.23 Withdrawal Agreement for all those with pre-settled status, given the way that the UK implemented art.18 WA? The argument runs that grants of pre-settled status constitute 'residence on the basis of this agreement' within the meaning of art.23, which triggers an equal treatment right and distinguishes the position from pre-WA cases given that claimants such as Fratila and CG were not residing 'on the basis of' Directive 2004/38/EC, and as such had no equal treatment right. In a homelessness eligibility context, this argument has been accepted at county court level in one case, *Hynek v Islington* K40CL206 (HHJ Saunders, 24 May 2024), and rejected (obiter) in another, *C v Oldham* [2024] EWCC 1 (22 May 2024). It has been rejected by the High Court in *Fertre v Vale of White Horse District Council* [2024] EWHC 1754 (KB) (8 July 2024). No application for permission to appeal was made in either County Court case; a PTA application is pending with the Court of Appeal in *Fertre*.
- it discriminates unlawfully against EEA nationals in comparison with third country nationals, contrary to art.14 ECHR and s.3 HRA 1998?
- it is ultra vires s.4(5) WRA 2012?

Those arguments were raised in *AT* at the Upper Tribunal stage, but never required determination, because of AT's success on her 'dignity' point.

Second, what kind of residence is necessary to be within the scope of art.10 WA? Neither the decided *AT* 'dignity' basis for disapplying reg.9(3)(c)(i) in individual cases, nor the potential 'equal treatment' argument for setting reg.9(3)(c)(i) aside altogether, could apply where a person is outside the scope of the Citizens Rights part of the WA. Relatedly, is a grant of EUSS leave conclusive evidence that a person is in the scope of the WA, or does there exist a category of persons granted PSS or SS who have domestic law rights only?

Art.10(1)(a) applies to 'Union citizens who exercised their right to reside in the United Kingdom in accordance with Union law before the end of the transition period and continue to reside there thereafter'. It might be suggested that the requirement to 'continue to reside there thereafter' requires residence in accordance with EU law (i.e. exercising a positive EU law right of residence) at least until, and perhaps even beyond, the end of the transition period. See *Secretary of State for the Home Department v Abdullah* [2024] UKUT 66 (IAC), e.g. [68]. However, the contrary—and, it is suggested, better—argument is that once there has been a pre-transition period of residence, continuous factual residence thereafter is sufficient. The 'continuous residence in accordance with EU law' position would be textually strained, and hard to reconcile with analysis of analogous wording in *Secretary of State for Work and Pensions v Gubeladze* [2019] UKSC 31, [2019] AC 885, [76]–[92]. It would also generate great uncertainty: it would mean that there was indeed a class of persons with PSS or SS who have domestic law rights only, but nobody would know who they were until a dispute arose about their rights, potentially years or even decades later.

Third, can people with leave under the EUSS who are neither EU citizens nor their family members (i.e. EFTA state members) rely on the *AT* principle of protection against a breach of the right to dignity?

Note the special rules for family members of a "relevant person of Northern Ireland" in paras.(3A) and (4)(ca). That phrase is defined by Annex 1 of Appendix EU to the Immigration Rules as:

"a person who:

(a) is:
   (i) a British citizen; or
   (ii) an Irish citizen; or
   (iii) a British citizen and an Irish citizen; and

(b) was born in Northern Ireland and, at the time of the person's birth, at least one of their parents was:
   (i) a British citizen; or
   (ii) an Irish citizen; or
   (iii) a British citizen and an Irish citizen; or
   (iv) otherwise entitled to reside in Northern Ireland without any restriction on their period of residence"

For the "Zambrano right to reside" referred to in para.(3)(c)(ii), see under the heading, *Carers of British citizens*, in the General Note to reg.16 of the former Immigration (European Economic Area) Regulations 2016 in Part VII of Vol.V of this series.

Habitual residence

The requirement to be habitually resident only applies to the claimant, not to a partner or dependant. 2.33

"Habitual residence" is not defined in the regulation but case law since 1994 has established that, except in cases where EU citizens are exercising their transitional rights (see Vol.V), to be habitually resident in the CTA, a claimant must:

- have a settled intention to reside here; and
- have been "[resident] in fact for a period that shows that the residence has become 'habitual' and . . . will or is likely to continue to be habitual"

see *Nessa v Chief Adjudication Officer* [1999] 1 W.L.R. 1937; [1999] 4 All E.R. 677, HL (also reported as *R(IS) 2/00*). Whether that legal test is satisfied so that a person is habitually resident is a question of fact to be decided by reference to all the circumstances in each case (*Re J*).

The period of residence that is necessary is usually referred to as the "appreciable period" in accordance with the use of that phrase by Lord Bridge of Harwich in *Re J (A Minor) (Abduction: Custody Rights)* [1990] 2 A.C. 562; [1990] 2 All E.R. 961 HL:

> "In considering this issue it seems to me to be helpful to deal first with a number of preliminary points. The first point is that the expression 'habitually resident' . . . is nowhere defined. It follows, I think, that the expression is not to be treated as a term of art with some special meaning, but is rather to be understood according to the ordinary and natural meaning of the two words which it contains. The second point is that the question whether a person is or is not habitually resident

in a specified country is a question of fact to be decided by reference to all the circumstances of any particular case. The third point is that there is a significant difference between a person ceasing to be habitually resident in country A, and his subsequently becoming habitually resident in country B. A person may cease to be habitually resident in country A in a single day if he or she leaves it with a settled intention not to return to it but to take up long-term residence in country B instead. Such a person cannot, however, become habitually resident in country B in a single day. An appreciable period of time and a settled intention will be necessary to enable him or her to become so. During that appreciable period of time the person will have ceased to be habitually resident in country A but not yet have become habitually resident in country B. The fourth point is that, where a child of J.'s age is in the sole lawful custody of the mother, his situation with regard to habitual residence will necessarily be the same as hers."

Habitual residence is not the same as domicile (*R(U)8/88*). It is possible to be habitually resident in more than one country although it is unusual (*R(IS) 2/00*, para.20); it is also possible to be habitually resident in none. Habitual residence can continue during absences of long or short duration.

The test dates from 1994, when it was the primary immigration-related gateway to benefit entitlement. That is no longer the case. Partly that is due to s.115 Immigration and Asylum Act 1999, which excludes "persons subject to immigration control" from entitlement to most benefits. Partly it is due to the rigours (since 2004) of the "right to reside" test, textually incorporated into the habitual residence test, but operating conceptually distinctly.

It might be questioned whether the requirement to have actual "habitual residence" in itself continues to serve its originally intended purpose. It was a measure to combat "benefit tourism", but very few foreign nationals making a temporary trip to the UK are now likely to enter with a right of residence conferring entitlement to receive public funds. The increasing complexity of reg.9(4) chronicles the legislator's Sisyphean attempts to avoid the hardships which would be caused by a blanket application of the habitual residence test.

"Settled intention" and "appreciable period of time"

2.34 The two limbs of the habitual residence test, a settled intention and an appreciable period of time, are difficult to analyse separately. This is because the two are closely linked: the overall question is whether "in all the circumstances, including the settledness of the person's intentions as to residence, the residence has continued for a sufficient period for it to be said to be habitual" (*R(IS) 2/00*). So, if there is a doubt about the claimant's intention to reside in the UK, it may require a longer period of residence to resolve that doubt. Similarly, where a person's circumstances are such that s/he clearly intends to make a home in the UK, it may be possible to say that s/he has become habitually resident after a relatively short period of time. There is thus no minimum "appreciable period": the length of the period required will depend upon all the circumstances of the individual case.

The intention to reside here does not need to be permanent or indefinite. It can be for a limited period. To be resident a person had to be seen to be making a "genuine home for the time being" here but it need not be his only home or a permanent one (*R(IS) 6/96*). (Actual residence in two places is perfectly possible: *R(IS) 9/99*.) Some of the relevant factors in judging intention will include the reason for coming (or returning) here, the location of his/her possessions and family, where s/he has previously worked, the length and purpose of any absence from the UK, etc.

If the claimant's intention is conditional, e.g. on benefit being awarded, this is not a settled intention to stay (*CIS/12703/1996*).

The leading case on the requirement for an appreciable period is the decision of the House of Lords in *Nessa* [1999] 1 W.L.R. 1937. Mrs Nessa came to the UK in August 1994, aged 55. She had previously lived all her life in Bangladesh. Her father-in-law, in whose house she had been living, had died and she had come to the UK for the emotional support of her late husband's brother and his family. Her husband had lived and worked in the UK until his death in 1975 and she had a right of abode here. She claimed income support in September 1994.

The Commissioner (*R(IS) 2/00*) and a majority of the Court of Appeal followed *Re J* and held that in order to establish habitual residence it was necessary for a claimant not only to have been in the UK voluntarily, and for settled purposes, but also to have fulfilled those conditions for an appreciable period of time. However, the Court of Appeal considered that the appreciable period need not be particularly long. The dissenting judge (Thorpe LJ) considered that Lord Brandon's comments in *Re J* were clearly obiter and that an appreciable period was not an essential ingredient of habitual residence. In his view the adjective "habitual" ensured that "the connection [to the country] is not transitory or temporary but enduring and the necessary durability can be judged prospectively in exceptional cases".

Mrs Nessa appealed again to the House of Lords which unanimously upheld the majority in the Court of Appeal. Lord Slynn of Hadley, with whom all the other judges agreed, reviewed the authorities discussed above and stated:

> "With the guidance of these cases it seems to me plain that as a matter of ordinary language a person is not habitually resident in any country unless he has taken up residence and lived there for a period. . . . If Parliament had intended that a person seeking to enter the United Kingdom or such a person declaring his intention to settle here is to have income support on arrival, it could have said so. It seems to me impossible to accept the argument at one time advanced that a person who has never been here before who says on landing, 'I intend to settle in the United Kingdom' and who is fully believed is automatically a person who is habitually resident here. Nor is it enough to say I am going to live at X or with Y. He must show residence in fact for a period which shows that the residence has become 'habitual' and, as I see it, will or is likely to continue to be habitual."

Lord Slynn did accept that there might be "special cases where the person concerned is not coming here for the first time, but is resuming an habitual residence previously had . . . On such facts the Adjudication Officer may or of course may not be satisfied that the previous habitual residence has been resumed. This position is quite different from that of someone coming to the United Kingdom for the first time." Although *Swaddling* (see below) was cited by Lord Slynn as one example of this type of case the exception seems to be considerably narrower than the principle of Community law established by that case, namely that the length of residence in a Member State could not be regarded as an intrinsic element of the concept of habitual residence where a claimant comes within Regulation 1408/71. Lord Slynn appears to be saying no more than that in some cases it will be possible to say on the facts that a returning resident is merely resuming a habitual residence which has already been established. The reference to the possibility that the AO (now decision-maker) "may not be satisfied" clearly indicates that this will not always be the case and that some returning residents will need to re-establish habitual residence by living in the CTA for a period of time.

How long is the appreciable period?

Lord Slynn's opinion also contains interesting observations on how long the appreciable period of time should be. Whilst recognising that the period is not fixed and "may be longer where there are doubts", he also stated that "it may be short" and quoted with approval the statement of Butler Sloss LJ in *Re F (A Minor) (Child Abduction)* [1994] F.L.R. 548, at 555 that "A month can be . . . an appreciable period of time". He also agreed with the Commissioner that there were factors which indicated that habitual residence had been established in Mrs Nessa's case, "even by the date of the tribunal hearing *or as I see it, even earlier*" (emphasis added). 2.35

At the date of her tribunal hearing on December 6, 1994, Mrs Nessa had been in the UK for 15 weeks.

It must be stressed that the House of Lords clearly regarded this issue as one to be determined by tribunals on the facts of individual cases; however the view of the Commissioner in *R(IS) 6/96* that the establishment of habitual residence would normally require residence of at least some months must now be read in the light of Lord Slynn's comments.

As the issue of what is an "appreciable period" is one of fact and degree, and the decisions highlighted by Commissioners for wider circulation normally concern issues of law, there are few public examples of how the Commissioners approach that issue when exercising their discretion under s.14(8)(a) of SSA 1998. However, post-*Nessa* examples can be found in *CIS/1304/1997* and *CJSA/5394/1998* and in *CIS/376/2002*, all of which involved returning residents.

2.36 In the former decision, guidance was given that in a typical case tribunals should conduct a three-stage enquiry into: (i) the circumstances in which the claimant's earlier habitual residence was lost; (ii) the links between the claimant and the UK while abroad; and (iii) the circumstances of his return to the UK. So, for example, if the claimant's departure from the UK was temporary (albeit long-term) or conditional or if habitual residence was lost only as a result of events which occurred after the claimant's departure, those would be factors favouring a resumption of habitual residence immediately on return. On the facts of those appeals, the Commissioner held that the claimants, both British nationals who—as was accepted—had previously been habitually resident here, but had lost that habitual residence during an extended period of absence abroad, nevertheless resumed their previous habitual residence on the very day of their return to Britain. The relevant extracts from *CIS/1304/1997* and *CJSA/5394/1998* were reissued as an Appendix to *CIS/4474/2003* (see below).

By contrast the claimant in *CIS/376/2002*, a naturalised British citizen who had worked in Britain for many years but had spent no more than 11 months here in the five years before the claims for benefit which were under consideration, was held not to have become habitually resident immediately. Commissioner Howell Q.C. accepted the tribunal's finding that although the claimant had been habitually resident in the past he had ceased to be so over that five-year period, but rejected the tribunal's doubts about whether he had a settled intention to remain here. On that basis, the Commissioner held that the claimant had not been resident for an appreciable period of time when his claim for IS was made (some three days after his arrival) but had become habitually resident by the date of the decision on that claim approximately five weeks later. In reaching his decision the Commissioner denied the possibility that a claimant who had lost his or her habitual residence could resume it immediately without first being present for an appreciable period of time. He stated (at para.12):

> "Everything therefore depends on what counts as an 'appreciable period' of resumed residence in this context so that his residence in the United Kingdom can be said to have become established as habitual . . . As has been said many times in the cases where judges from the House of Lords down to more humble levels have had to struggle with the meaning of this expression, this is ultimately a question of fact and degree, depending on the individual circumstances of each case, and there are no hard and fast rules to apply. For a returning citizen of this country coming back to live here again after a period of residence overseas . . . the period may be short: as little as a month or so. But it is not zero or minimal, since even a returning expatriate may change his plans again and there is therefore at least some space of time after actual arrival when one simply has to wait and see."

The issue of the length of the appreciable period was also considered by the Commissioner in *CIS/4474/2003*. The Commissioner also noted that the approach taken by Commissioners to that issue had developed since *R(IS) 6/96* and gave the following guidance:

"19. What is an appreciable period depends on the circumstances of the particular case. But I agree with the Secretary of State that in the general run of cases the period will lie between one and three months. *I would certainly require cogent reasons from a tribunal to support a decision that a significantly longer period was required*" (emphasis added).

In *R(IS) 7/06*, the Commissioner indicated his broad agreement with *CIS/ 4474/2003*: **2.37**

"I am content to accept that, where a claimant is likely to remain in the United Kingdom permanently or for a substantial period of time, the conventional period that must have elapsed between his arrival and his establishing habitual residence is between one month and three months. However, those are not rigid limits. In an exceptional case, a person with a right of abode in the United Kingdom who, although not falling within the scope of regulation 21(3)(d), has been forced to flee another country and is nonetheless able to show a settled intention to remain in the United Kingdom might be accepted as habitually resident after less than a month of residence. Perhaps less exceptionally, a person with no ties to the United Kingdom and making no effort to become established here despite a vague intention to remain might be found not to be habitually resident in the United Kingdom until considerably longer than three months had elapsed."

However, disagreement with that approach was expressed in *CIS/1972/2003* (at para.14):

"I comment only that I have seen tribunals decide on shorter periods than a month and longer periods than three months without being appealed, or appealed successfully. Too much should not be read into the facts of individual decisions or, I suggest, trends in the small number of—usually difficult—cases that Commissioners come to decide on the facts. It does not help when Commissioners' decisions are used to play a forensic game (for it is no more than that) of finding the longest, or the shortest, period endorsed by a Commissioner and then claiming some general rule from it. Parliament could have set a specific time limit. It did not. Advisors cannot seek certainty where it does not exist."

That disagreement was echoed by the Tribunal of Commissioners in *CIS/2559/2005*. The Commissioners stated that:

"The relevant period of residence required to support evidence of intention is not, in our view, something which can be reduced to a tariff. In so far as the decision of Mr Commissioner Jacobs in *CIS/4474/2003* can be interpreted to the contrary, we take a different view."

It is suggested that the approach in *CIS/4474/2003* and *R(IS) 7/06* (a reported decision that was subsequently upheld by the Court of Appeal) is to be preferred. Although it is accepted that no two cases are identical and that the decision must always be one of fact and degree in an individual case, justice as between claimants in similar situations requires that there should be some consistency in decision-making: that the appreciable periods of time required by different decision makers, tribunals and Commissioners should at least be "in the same ball park". In the early days of the test, the periods chosen varied wildly from case to case: at that time, many decision-makers—and some tribunals—would have required an appreciable period of at least a year and sometimes more on the facts of *Nessa*, whereas the Commissioner and Lord Slynn considered that Mrs Nessa had become habitually resident in approximately three months or less. In such circumstances, recognising the existence of a conventional period does not involve the imposition of a tariff as long as the period is applied flexibly in each individual case. As Commissioner Jacobs has subsequently said (in *CJSA/1223/2006* and *CJSA/1224/2006*): **2.38**

"I respectfully agree with the Tribunal of Commissioners in *CIS/2559/2005* . . . that: 'The relevant period of residence required to support evidence of intention is not, in our view, something which can be reduced to a tariff.' I do not understand why the Tribunal thought that my comments might be interpreted as setting a tariff and counsel could not suggest how they might have been so understood. I remain of the view that for most cases an appreciable period is likely to be between one and three months. [Counsel for the Secretary of State] told me that that was the experience of decision-makers and he was not instructed to argue otherwise".

It is suggested that Commissioner Jacobs was surely correct to express the point in *CIS/4474/2003* as being about reasoning: a tribunal may be justified in giving a decision that is outside the normal range of decisions given by tribunals generally, but if so, it should be prepared to explain why.

For an analysis of the process involved in fixing an appreciable period, see *CJSA/1223/2006* and *CJSA/1224/2006*. That decision emphasises the importance of looking at the steps taken by the claimant to integrate him- or herself into the UK during that period.

Viability

2.39 Another issue that has vexed the application of the habitual residence test over the years is that of viability. The starting point is *R(IS) 6/96*, the first Commissioner's decision on the habitual residence test. The Commissioner in that case held that the "appreciable period of time" should be a period which showed "a settled and viable pattern of living here as a resident". Thus the practicality of a person's arrangements for residence had to be considered. In determining whether the plans were viable, the possibility of claiming income support had to be left out of account (although this did not mean that there must be no conceivable circumstances in which a person might need to resort to income support). In reliance on that decision, some decision-makers and tribunals took the view that many people from abroad could never become habitually resident because the mere fact that they had claimed income support showed that their residence was not viable in the sense required by the Commissioner. The requirement of viability certainly contributed towards the phenomenon of very long appreciable periods in the early days of the test that has been referred to above.

However, the law has developed since *R(IS) 6/96*. The Commissioner in *Nessa* (*R(IS) 2/00*) disagreed with *R(IS) 6/96* to the extent that the viability of a person's residence in the UK, either generally or with or without assistance from public funds, was only one relevant factor among others, to be given the appropriate weight according to the circumstances. In his view *R(IS) 6/96* should not be read as imposing an additional condition that only residence without resort to IS or public assistance was relevant to the *Re J* test.

The approach that whether the claimant's residence in the UK is viable without recourse to public funds is only one factor and not by itself decisive was followed in *CIS/1459/1996* and *CIS/16097/1996*. And in *CIS/4474/2003*, the Commissioner warns against the danger of overemphasising viability as a factor:

> "16. The danger of overemphasising viability is this. A claimant needs to establish habitual residence in order to claim an income-related benefit. A claim would not be necessary if the claimant has a guaranteed source of funds sufficient for survival. The danger is that the only claimants who can establish habitual residence will be those who have sufficient access to funds not to need it. That cannot be right. Habitual residence is a test of entitlement, not a bar to entitlement. It must be applied in a way that allows for the possibility of a claimant establishing both habitual residence and an entitlement to income support."

Crown servants and members of Her Majesty's forces posted overseas

10.—(1) The following persons do not have to meet the basic condition to be in Great Britain— 2.40

(a) a Crown servant or member of Her Majesty's forces posted overseas;

(b) in the case of joint claimants, the partner of a person mentioned in sub-paragraph (a) while they are accompanying the person on that posting.

(2) A person mentioned in paragraph (1)(a) is posted overseas if the person is performing overseas the duties of a Crown servant or member of Her Majesty's forces and was, immediately before their posting or the first of consecutive postings, habitually resident in the United Kingdom.

(3) In this regulation—

"Crown servant" means a person holding an office or employment under the Crown; and

"Her Majesty's forces" has the meaning in the Armed Forces Act 2006.

DEFINITIONS

"joint claimants"—see WRA 2012 s.40.
"partner"—see reg.2.

GENERAL NOTE

Under s.4(1)(c) WRA 2012, it is a basic condition of entitlement to universal credit that the claimant is "in Great Britain". However s.4(2) empowers the Secretary of State to make regulations that "provide for exceptions to the requirement to meet any of the basic conditions". Regulation 10 is made under that power. 2.41

Crown Servants and members of Her Majesty's forces who are posted overseas (as defined in para.(2)) do not have to meet the basic condition to be in Great Britain.

Neither does the partner of such a Crown Servant or member of Her Majesty's forces, if a joint claim for universal credit is made. However, as it seems probable that a Crown Servant or member of Her Majesty's forces who has been posted overseas will be in full-time work, many such joint claims seem likely to fail on the basis that the financial conditions are not met.

By para.(3), the phrase "Her Majesty's forces" has the meaning in the Armed Forces Act 2006. However, that phrase is not defined in that Act except to the extent that ""Her Majesty's forces" . . . do not include any Commonwealth force" (see s.374). "Commonwealth force" is defined by the same section as meaning "a force of a Commonwealth country".

Temporary absence from Great Britain

11.—(1) A person's temporary absence from Great Britain is disregarded in determining whether they meet the basic condition to be in Great Britain if— 2.42

(a) the person is entitled to universal credit immediately before the beginning of the period of temporary absence; and

(b) either—

(i) the absence is not expected to exceed, and does not exceed, one month, or

(ii) paragraph (3) or (4) applies.

(2) The period of one month in paragraph (1)(b) may be extended by up to a further month if the temporary absence is in connection with the death of—

(a) the person's partner or a child or qualifying young person for whom the person was responsible; or

(b) a close relative of the person, or of their partner or of a child or qualifying young person for whom the person or their partner was responsible,

and the Secretary of State considers that it would be unreasonable to expect the person to return to Great Britain within the first month.

(3) This paragraph applies where the absence is not expected to exceed, and does not exceed, 6 months and is solely in connection with—

(a) the person undergoing—

(i) treatment for an illness or physical or mental impairment by, or under the supervision of, a qualified practitioner, or

(ii) medically approved convalescence or care as a result of treatment for an illness or physical or mental impairment, where the person had that illness or impairment before leaving Great Britain; or

(b) the person accompanying their partner or a child or qualifying young person for whom they are responsible for treatment or convalescence or care as mentioned in sub-paragraph (a).

(4) This paragraph applies where the absence is not expected to exceed, and does not exceed, 6 months and the person is—

(a) a mariner; or

(b) a continental shelf worker who is in a designated area or a prescribed area.

(5) In this regulation—

"continental shelf worker" means a person who is employed, whether under a contract of service or not, in a designated area or a prescribed area in connection with any activity mentioned in section 11(2) of the Petroleum Act 1998;

"designated area" means any area which may from time to time be designated by Order in Council under the Continental Shelf Act 1964 as an area within which the rights of the United Kingdom with respect to the seabed and subsoil and their natural resources may be exercised;

"mariner" means a person who is employed under a contract of service either as a master or member of the crew of any ship or vessel, or in any other capacity on board any ship or vessel where—

(a) the employment in that other capacity is for the purposes of that ship or vessel or its crew or any passengers or cargo or mails carried by the ship or vessel; and

(b) the contract is entered into in the United Kingdom with a view to its performance (in whole or in part) while the ship or vessel is on its voyage;

"medically approved" means certified by a registered medical practitioner;

"prescribed area" means any area over which Norway or any member State [1 ...] exercises sovereign rights for the purpose of exploring the seabed and subsoil and exploiting their natural resources, being an area outside the territorial seas of Norway or such member State, or any other area which is from time to time specified under section 10(8) of the Petroleum Act 1998;

"qualified practitioner" means a person qualified to provide medical treatment, physiotherapy or a form of treatment which is similar to, or related to, either of those forms of treatment.

AMENDMENT

1. Social Security (Amendment) (EU Exit) Regulations 2019 (SI 2019/128) reg.4 and Sch, para.11 (December 31, 2020 at 11.00 pm).

DEFINITIONS

"child"—see WRA 2012 s.40.
"close relative"—see reg.2.
"partner"—*ibid.*
"prescribed"—see WRA 2012 s.40.
"responsible for a child or qualifying young person"—see regs 2, 4 and 4A.
"qualifying young person"—see WRA 2012 s.40 and 10(5) and regs 2 and 5.

GENERAL NOTE

Under s.4(1)(c) WRA 2012, it is a basic condition of entitlement to universal credit that the claimant is "in Great Britain". However s.4(5)(b) and (c) empowers the Secretary of State to make regulations that specify circumstances in which temporary absence from Great Britain is disregarded (subs.(5)(b)) and modify the application of WRA 2012 in relation to a person who is not in Great Britain but who is entitled to universal credit by virtue of subs.(5)(b) (subs.(5)(c)). Regulation 11 is made under the former power. 2.43

Paragraphs (1) and (2)

The general rule is that a person who is entitled to universal credit retains that entitlement during a temporary absence—for whatever reason—that is not expected to exceed one month and does not in fact exceed that period (para.(1)(b)(i)). By para.(1)(a), there must be an existing entitlement to universal credit for the rule to apply. It might therefore have been thought that it is not possible to claim universal credit for the first time while temporarily absent abroad. However, note that the Secretary of State's guidance for decision makers, *Going Abroad* (*<https://data.parliament.uk/DepositedPapers/Files/DEP2023-0365/070_Going_Abroad_V8-0.pdf>*) states at p.2:

> "If the claimant is abroad when they make a claim for Universal Credit but return within the first assessment period, they will be awarded Universal Credit from the date of declaration..."

The one-month period in para.(1)(b)(i) can be extended by up to a further month in the circumstances set out in para.(2)(a) and (b) if the Secretary of State considers it would be unreasonable to expect the person to return home during the first month.

Paragraphs (3) and (4)

The one-month period in para.(1)(b)(i) is also extended to six months if either para.(3) or para.(4) applies. Those paragraphs are not subject to the condition that the Secretary of State should consider that it would be unreasonable to expect the person to return home sooner. 2.44

Paragraph (3) permits an extended temporary absence for medical treatment, physiotherapy, or a treatment that is similar to either of those forms of treatment, or medically approved convalescence in the circumstances set out in para.(3)(a) and (b). Note the definitions of "medically approved" and "qualified practitioner" in para.(5). The phrase, "registered medical practitioner" is further defined by para.1 of Sch.1 Interpretation Act 1978 as meaning "a fully registered person within the meaning of the Medical Act 1983 who holds a licence to practise under that Act."

Paragraph (4) permits an extended temporary absence for a "mariner" and a "continental shelf worker" who is in a "designated area" or a "prescribed area". All four of those terms are defined in para.(5). The definition of "mariner" is self-explanatory. The definition of "continental shelf worker" is more technical but, to summarise, it means a person working on an oil or gas rig in a specified area. Readers are referred to the Continental Shelf Act 1964, the Petroleum Act 1998 and the Orders in Council made under those Acts for further details of the areas concerned.

2.45 Note that paras (2) and (3) are also relevant to the question whether a person remains responsible for a child or qualifying young person during the temporary absence of that child or qualifying young person: see the commentary to reg.4(7) above.

Receiving education

Meaning of "receiving education"

2.46 **12.**—[1 (1) This regulation applies for the basic condition in section 4(1)(d) of the Act (not receiving education).

(1A) A qualifying young person is to be treated as receiving education, unless the person is participating in a [2 relevant training scheme]

(1B) In paragraph (1A) [2 "relevant training scheme" means—

(a) a traineeship, or

(b) a course or scheme which—

(i) comprises education or training designed to assist a claimant to gain the skills needed to obtain paid work (or more paid work or better-paid work);

(ii) is attended by a claimant falling within section 22 of the Act as a work preparation requirement or as voluntary work preparation, and

(iii) the claimant has been referred to by the Secretary of State;]

"traineeship" means a course which—

(a) is funded (in whole or in part) by, or under arrangements made by, the—

(i) Secretary of State under section 14 of the Education Act 2002, or

(ii) Chief Executive of [2 Education and Skills Funding];

(b) lasts no more than 6 months;

(c) includes training to help prepare the participant for work and a work experience placement; and

(d) is open to persons who on the first day of the course have reached the age of 16 but not 25;]

(2) [1 Except in circumstances where paragraph (1A) applies] "receiving education" means—

(a) undertaking a full-time course of advanced education; or

(b) undertaking any other full-time course of study or training at an educational establishment for which a student loan or grant is provided for the person's maintenance.

(3) In paragraph (2)(a) "course of advanced education" means—

(a) a course of study leading to—

(i) a postgraduate degree or comparable qualification,

(ii) a first degree or comparable qualification,

(iii) a diploma of higher education,

(iv) a higher national diploma; or

(b) any other course of study which is of a standard above advanced GNVQ or equivalent, including a course which is of a standard above a general certificate of education (advanced level), or above a Scottish national qualification (higher or advanced higher).

(4) A claimant who is not a qualifying young person and is not undertaking a course described in paragraph (2) is nevertheless to be treated as receiving education if the claimant is undertaking a course of study or training that is not compatible with any work-related requirement imposed on the claimant by the Secretary of State.

AMENDMENTS

1. Social Security (Traineeships and Qualifying Young Persons) Amendment Regulations 2015 (SI 2015/336) reg.4 (March 27, 2015).
2. Social Security (Qualifying Young Persons Participating in Relevant Training Schemes) (Amendment) Regulations 2017 (SI 2017/987) reg.4 (November 6, 2017).

DEFINITIONS

"claimant"—see WRA 2012 s.40.
"qualifying young person"—see WRA 2012 ss.40 and 10(5) and regs 2 and 5.

GENERAL NOTE

It is a condition of entitlement to universal credit that the person is not receiving education (s.4(1)(d) WRA 2012) (but see reg.14 for the exceptions to this rule). 2.47

Note that a couple may be entitled to universal credit as joint claimants even where one member of the couple is receiving education (and does not come within reg.14), provided that the other member is not receiving education, or comes within reg.14 (see reg.3(2)(b)).

Regulation 12 defines who counts as receiving education. Firstly, a qualifying young person (see reg.5 for who is a qualifying young person) is deemed to be receiving education, unless they are participating in a relevant training scheme (para.(1A)). "Relevant training scheme" is defined in para.(1B) as either a traineeship (further defined in para.(1B)) or certain courses or schemes as defined therein. Where someone is participating in a relevant training scheme as so defined they will not count as receiving education for the purposes of s.4(1)(d).

If para.(1A) does not apply, receiving education means being on a full-time course of advanced education (defined in para.(3)) or on another full-time course of study or training at an educational establishment for which a student loan or grant is provided for the person's maintenance (para.(2)). But in addition a claimant will also be treated as receiving education if they are on a course of study or training that is not compatible with the work-related requirements imposed on them (para.(4)).

Paragraph (2)(a)

The meaning of "undertaking a full-time course of advanced education" under reg.12(2)(a) was in issue in *BK v SSWP (UC)* [2022] UKUT 73 (AAC), where Upper Tribunal Judge Rowley ruled as follows: 2.48

"19. The following propositions may be gleaned from the jurisprudence:

a. Whether or not a person is undertaking a full-time course is a question of fact for the tribunal having regard to the circumstances in each particular case (*R/SB 40/83* at [13]; *R(SB) 41/83* at [12]). Parameters have been set, as appear below:
b. The words 'full-time' relate to the course and not to the student. Specifically, they do not permit the matter to be determined by reference to the amount of time which the student happens to dedicate to their studies (*R/SB 40/83* at [14,15]; *R(SB) 2/91* at [7]; *R(SB) 41/83* at [11]).
c. Evidence from the educational establishment as to whether or not the course is full-time is not necessarily conclusive, but it ought to be accepted as such unless it is inconclusive on its face, or is challenged by relevant evidence which at least raises the possibility that it ought to be rejected (*R/SB 40/83* at [18]), and any evidence adduced in rebuttal should be weighty in content (*R/SB 41/83* at [12]). See also *Flemming v Secretary of State for Work and Pensions* [2002] EWCA Civ 641, [2002] 1 WLR 2322 at [21]–[22] and [38];

and *Deane v Secretary of State for Work and Pensions* [2010] EWCA Civ 699, [2011] 1 WLR 743 where the Court of Appeal repeated an earlier statement in *Flemming* that:

> '38 ... A tribunal of fact should, I think be very slow to accept that a person expects or intends to devote – or does, in fact, devote – significantly less time to the course than those who have conduct of the course expect of him, and very slow to hold that a person who is attending a course considered by the educational establishment to be a part-time course is to be treated as receiving full-time education because he devotes significantly more time than that which is expected of him...'

d. If the course is offered as full-time course, the presumption is that the recipient is in full-time education. There may be exceptions to the rule, such where a student is granted exemptions from part of the course: *Deane* [51]."

Paragraph (3)

2.49 The definition of "course of advanced education" in reg.12(3) is the same as the definition in reg.61(1) of the Income Support Regulations (see Vol.V in this series). "Full-time" is not defined.

See reg.13 for when a person is regarded as being on a course.

Meaning of "undertaking a course"

2.50 **13.**—(1) For the purposes of these Regulations a person is to be regarded as undertaking a course of education [1, study] or training—

(a) throughout the period beginning on the date on which the person starts undertaking the course and ending on the last day of the course or on such earlier date (if any) as the person finally abandons it or is dismissed from it; or

(b) where a person is undertaking a part of a modular course, for the period beginning on the day on which that part of the course starts and ending—

  (i) on the last day on which the person is registered as undertaking that part, or

  (ii) on such earlier date (if any) as the person finally abandons the course or is dismissed from it.

(2) The period referred to in paragraph (1)(b) includes—

(a) where a person has failed examinations or has failed to complete successfully a module relating to a period when the person was undertaking a part of the course, any period in respect of which the person undertakes the course for the purpose of retaking those examinations or completing that module; and

(b) any period of vacation within the period specified in paragraph (1)(b) or immediately following that period except where the person has registered to attend or undertake the final module in the course and the vacation immediately follows the last day on which the person is to attend or undertake the course.

(3) In this regulation "modular course" means a course which consists of two or more modules, the successful completion of a specified number of which is required before a person is considered by the educational establishment to have completed the course.

(4) A person is not to be regarded as undertaking a course for any part of the period mentioned in paragraph (1) during which the following conditions are met—

(a) the person has, with the consent of the relevant educational establishment, ceased to attend or undertake the course because they are ill or caring for another person;
(b) the person has recovered from that illness or ceased caring for that person within the past year, but not yet resumed the course; and
(c) the person is not eligible for a grant or student loan.

AMENDMENT

1. Universal Credit (Consequential, Supplementary, Incidental and Miscellaneous Provisions) Regulations 2013 (SI 2013/630) reg.38(3) (April 29, 2013).

DEFINITIONS

"grant"—see regs 2 and 68(7).
"student loan"—*ibid.*

GENERAL NOTE

2.51 Paragraphs (1) to (3) of reg.13 reproduce the rules in reg.61(2) to (4) of the Income Support Regulations. See the notes to reg.61 in Vol.V of this series.

Paragraph (4) is similar to the provision in reg.1(3D) and (3E) of the JSA Regulations 1996 (see Vol.V in this series). The person must have recovered from the illness or their caring responsibilities must have ended within the past year for para.(4) to apply (see para.(4)(b)). See further *RVS v SSWP (ESA)* [2019] UKUT 102 (AAC), a decision on a similar provision in reg.17 of the ESA Regulations 2008; however, note that the ESA Regulations 2008 do not have a provision equivalent to para. (4).

Exceptions to the requirement not to be receiving education

2.52 **14.**—[1(1)] A person does not have to meet the basic condition in s.4(1)(d) of the Act (not receiving education) if—
(a) the person—
(i) is undertaking a full- time course of study or training which is not a course of advanced education,
(ii) is under the age of 21, or is 21 and reached that age whilst undertaking the course, and
(iii) is without parental support (as defined in regulation 8(3));
[1[2 (b) the person is entitled to attendance allowance, disability living allowance, child disability payment [3, adult disability payment] or personal independence payment and, on a date before the date on which the person starts receiving education—
(i) it has been determined that the person has limited capability for work or limited capability for work and work-related activity on the basis of an assessment under Part 5 or under Part 4 or 5 of the ESA Regulations; or
(ii) the person is treated as having limited capability for work under Schedule 8 or limited capability for work and work-related activity under Schedule 9;]
(c) the person is responsible for a child or a qualifying young person;
(d) the person is a single person and a foster parent with whom a child is placed;
(e) the person is a member of a couple, both of whom are receiving education, and the other member is—
(i) responsible for a child or qualifying young person, or
(ii) a foster parent with whom a child is placed; or

(f) the person—
   (i) has reached the qualifying age for state pension credit, and
   (ii) is a member of a couple the other member of which has not reached that age.

[1(2) [2 ...]]

AMENDMENTS

1. Universal Credit (Exceptions to the Requirement not to be receiving education) (Amendment) Regulations 2020 (SI 2020/827) reg.2 (August 5, 2020).

2. Universal Credit (Exceptions to the Requirement not to be receiving Education) (Amendment) Regulations 2021 (SI 2021/1224) reg.2 (December 15, 2021).

3. Social Security (Disability Assistance for Working Age People) (Consequential Amendments) Order 2022 (SI 2022/177) Part 2 art.13(3) (March 21, 2022).

DEFINITIONS

"the Act"—see reg.2.
"adult disability payment"—*ibid.*
"attendance allowance"—*ibid.*
"child"—see WRA 2012 s.30.
"child disability payment"—see reg.2.
"couple"—see WRA 2012 ss.39 and 40.
"course of advanced education"—see regs 2 and12.
"disability living allowance"—see reg.2.
"foster parent"—*ibid.*
"personal independence payment"—*ibid.*
"qualifying young person"—see WRA 2012 ss.40 and 10(5) and regs 2 and 5.
"qualifying age for state pension credit"—see WRA 2012 s.4(4), SPCA 2002 s.1(6).

GENERAL NOTE

2.53 This regulation sets out the exceptions to the rule in s.4(1)(d) WRA 2012 that a person must not be receiving education. Note that most student funding will count as income—see regs 68–71. If a person who comes within reg.14 has student income in relation to the course that they are undertaking which is taken into account in the calculation of their universal credit award, they will not have any work requirements (see reg.89(1)(e)(ii)).

The following are exempt from the condition in s.4(1)(d):

- a person who is on a course which is not a course of advanced education (see reg.12(3) for what counts as a course of advanced education) and who is under 21 (or is 21 and reached that age while on the course) and who is "without parental support" (see reg.8(3) for who counts as without parental support) (para.(a)). Such a person will have no work requirements (see reg.89(1)(e)(i));
- a person who has limited capability for work (see reg.39(1)) and who is entitled to disability living allowance, personal independence payment, child disability payment, adult disability payment, attendance allowance or armed forces independence payment (see the definition of "attendance allowance" in reg.2 which includes armed forces independence payment) (para.(b));
- a person who is responsible for a child or qualifying young person (para.(c));
- a single person who is a foster parent with whom a child is placed (para.(d));

- a member of a couple, both of whom are receiving education, whose partner is responsible for a child or qualifying young person or is a foster parent with whom a child is placed (para.(e)); or
- a member of a couple who has reached the qualifying age for state pension credit but whose partner is below that age (para.(f)). Note that a person who falls within reg.13(4) is not regarded as undertaking a course and so is not treated as receiving education (see reg.12(2)). Note also that a couple may be entitled to universal credit as joint claimants even where one member of the couple is receiving education (and does not come within this regulation), provided that the other member is not receiving education, or comes within this regulation (see reg.3(2)(b)).

This regulation has been subject to both case law and substantial amendment. The original amendments made by the Universal Credit (Exceptions to the Requirement not to be receiving education) (Amendment) Regulations 2020 (SI 2020/827) were a response to the litigation in *R. (Kauser and JL) v Secretary of State for Work and Pensions* CO/987/2020. In those proceedings, the High Court (Fordham J) issued a declaration that under the previous law the Secretary of State had breached (what was then) reg.14(b) when read with regs 38 and 39(1)(a), in failing to determine whether the claimants had limited capability for work; and in failing to conduct a work capability assessment *before* deciding the claimants' entitlement to universal credit. The Order making the declaration in *R. (Kauser and JL) v SSWP* is available on Rightsnet at *https://www.rightsnet.org.uk/pdfs/CO_987_2020.pdf.*

A challenge to the amended reg.14(1)(b), as inserted by the 2020 amending regulations, and requiring a student to have an assessment of limited capability for work and work-related activity before making an application for universal credit, was unsuccessful in *R. (Kays) v Secretary of State for Work and Pensions* [2022] EWHC 167 (Admin). Furthermore, the Court of Appeal dismissed an appeal by the claimant against the decision of Swift J. The unsuccessful grounds of appeal were that (1) the decision to make the 2020 Regulations without consultation was irrational; (2) the 2020 Regulations achieved their purpose in an irrational and arbitrary way; (3) the purpose of those regulations was irrational and discriminatory; and (4) the respondent had not had due regard to the public sector equality duty: see *R. (Kays) v Secretary of State for Work and Pensions* [2022] EWCA Civ 1593. On May 23, 2023, the Supreme Court refused permission to appeal from that decision.

Meanwhile reg.14(1)(b) was amended for a second time by the 2021 amending regulations. This latter amendment was designed to put beyond doubt that a person who is entitled to one of the designated disability benefits must have been determined to have limited capability for work (LCW) *before* the person starts undertaking a course of education. This amendment was intended to close off a "workaround" whereby an existing disabled student, who does not have a pre-existing LCW determination, could make a claim to new-style (contributory) employment and support allowance in order to be referred for a work capability assessment so that, if the person is subsequently determined to have LCW, they could then claim and be entitled to universal credit—an outcome contrary to the policy intent.

Accepting a claimant commitment

Claimant commitment—date and method of acceptance

15.—(1) For the basic condition in section 4(1)(e) of the Act, a person who has accepted a claimant commitment within such period after making a claim as the Secretary of State specifies is to be treated as having accepted that claimant commitment on the first day of the period in respect of which the claim is made. 2.54

(2) In a case where an award may be made without a claim, a person who accepts a claimant commitment within such period as the Secretary of State specifies is to be treated as having accepted a claimant commitment on the day that would be the first day of the first assessment period in relation to the award in accordance with regulation 21(3) [[1]or (3A)].

(3) The Secretary of State may extend the period within which a person is required to accept a claimant commitment or an updated claimant commitment where the person requests that the Secretary of State review—

(a) any action proposed as a work search requirement or a work availability requirement; or

(b) whether any limitation should apply to those requirements,

and the Secretary of State considers that the request is reasonable.

(4) A person must accept a claimant commitment by one of the following methods, as specified by the Secretary of State—

(a) electronically;

(b) by telephone; or

(c) in writing.

AMENDMENT

1. Income Support (Digital Service) Amendment Regulations 2014 (SI 2014/2887) reg.3(1)(a) (November 26, 2014).

DEFINITIONS

"claimant commitment"—see WRA 2012 s.14(1)

"work availability requirement"—see WRA 2012 ss.40 and 18(1)

"work search requirement"—see WRA 2012 ss.40 and 17(1)

GENERAL NOTE

2.55 By virtue of s.4(1)(e) of the WRA 2012 it is one of the basic conditions for making an award of universal credit that a claimant, including each of joint claimants, has accepted a claimant commitment, the meaning of which is then set out in s.14. See that provision and its annotations for the nature of a claimant commitment (i.e. a record of the claimant's responsibilities under the WRA 2012) and what is entailed in accepting such a record. There are exceptions from the basic condition in reg.16 below. Regulation 15 deals with the time within which and the method by which a claimant commitment must be accepted. The relevant regulation-making powers for reg.15 are in s.14(5) of the WRA 2012, which requires the most up-to-date version of a claimant commitment to be accepted "in such manner as may be prescribed", and in s.4(7), which allows regulations to specify circumstances in which a person is to be treated as having or as not having accepted a claimant commitment.

Note that, before there can be a question of acceptance, a claimant commitment must have been prepared on behalf of the Secretary of State and offered for acceptance. A claimant should not be found to have failed to satisfy the basic condition in s.4(1)(e) merely by failing to attend and participate in what is called a commitments interview with a work coach.

However, the effect of such a failure is difficult to work out, especially if the interview is on a new claim. In general, such a failure to participate, for no good reason, whether in relation to an interview under s.15 of the WRA 2012 (work-focused interview requirement) or under s.23(1) (connected requirements), is a matter for a sanction under s.27(2), not for a decision that there is no entitlement to universal credit. But a claimant cannot be allowed to stymie the process of drawing up a claimant commitment into a form in which it can be accepted or not accepted by refusing to take part in that process. It would not appear proper in such circumstances for the work coach to prepare a generic commitment recording work requirements that had not been identified through consideration of the claimant's individual circumstances and present that formally to the claimant for acceptance or otherwise. However, it is suggested that, once the question of any good reason for failing to participate in the interview has been explored, possibly after a second appointment has been offered, a decision could properly be made that the claimant is not entitled to universal credit from the outset by reason of failing to satisfy the basic condition in s.4(1)(e). The claimant will not have accepted a claimant commitment and on a new claim it is as a matter of principle for the claimant to show satisfaction of the basic conditions. Chapter J1 of *Advice for decision making* does not seem to deal with this scenario.

By contrast, that chapter does deal in some detail with the situation where a claimant has accepted a claimant commitment, so has an award of universal credit, and there is a question of review of some work-related requirement recorded in that current version. J1031 says that a requirement to accept the most up-to-date version of the claimant commitment (see s.14(5) of the WRA 2012) does not necessarily require participation in an interview to discuss, review and ask the claimant to accept the revised commitment, but that the public law principles of fairness must be met when notifying the claimant of the requirement to accept any new commitments and of the consequences of failing to do so. If the claimant attends the interview and the work coach draws up a revised commitment, the claimant can accept then or be given a "cooling-off period", usually of seven days, in which to do so (during which entitlement continues by virtue of the acceptance of the existing version). If the claimant does not attend the interview or participate in substance, this guidance is currently given in J1034 and J1036:

> J1034 Taking part in an interview can be set as a requirement for the claimant even if taking part in an interview is not included on the current claimant commitment. The claimant **must** be separately and correctly informed of the date, time and place of the appointment, the reasons for the interview and the consequences of failing to take part in that appointment.
>
> "J1036 If the claimant
>
> 1. fails to attend the interview the DM will consider a sanction (see Note 1) or
> 2. takes part in the interview but fails or refuses to accept the new commitments at the end of the cooling off period the DM will end the award of UC (see Note 2).
>
> Note 1: There is no legal basis to consider ending the award of UC for not having a new claimant commitment since the previous claimant commitment still applies, but requirements can be set outside of the claimant commitment to take part in an interview, if it is reasonable to do so. Any failure to comply with a requirement to participate in a commitments review for no good reason, i.e. they fail to attend the interview, is a sanctionable failure and not reason to suspend or terminate the award of UC. The guidance on low-level sanctions in ADM Chapter K5 will apply.
> Note 2: Only if the claimant attends the interview as required but refuses or fails to accept the new commitments can the DM consider terminating the award of UC after a cooling off period."

This guidance has been hardened up from the previous version (see the 2022/23 edition of this volume), but in what is submitted is the wrong direction. It can be accepted that as at the point that a claimant fails to attend or properly participate in a "commitments review interview" that failure does not in itself justify terminating the award of universal credit for failing to satisfy the basic condition in s.4(1)(e) of the WRA 2012. There could be a sanction under s.27(2), as explained above, although note that neither s.15, with reg.93, nor s.23(1) allow participation in an interview to be required for the sole purpose of reviewing or discussing the claimant commitment. Under s.15 and reg.93 the purpose must be related to wider matters relating to work prospects, opportunities or activities and under s.23(1) must be related to the imposition or compliance with a work-related requirement. However, for similar reasons as discussed above, it would be wrong to allow a claimant to stymie the process of review by refusing to participate in interviews, even though the first sanction might continue until the claimant met the compliance condition of participating in an interview. The claimant's loss of benefit might not be total, especially if there was concurrent entitlement to new style JSA, so that under reg.5 of the JSA Regulations 2013 (discussed in the notes to reg.111) payment of that benefit could not be affected by the sanction, only the universal credit element topping up the amount of new style JSA. It is submitted that a point would come where a revised claimant commitment could be put formally to a claimant for acceptance within a reasonable time, despite there having been no interview, so that a failure to accept that most up-to-date version would constitute a failure to satisfy s.4(1)(e).

The confusion that can result from a misunderstanding of the ADM guidance is well illustrated in *FO v SSWP (UC)* [2022] UKUT 56 (AAC). There, according to the DWP, the appellant claimant's partner (therefore also a claimant) had been set an online "To-do" on her universal credit account on March 23, 2020 to accept her claimant commitments (sic) by March 29, 2020 (later extended to April 14, 2020). In the absence of such acceptance, the couple's "claim" was "closed" on April 14, 2020. The appeal against that decision was disallowed by the First-tier Tribunal. Judge Wikeley had no difficulty in allowing the further appeal because the documentary evidence submitted to the First-tier Tribunal was hopelessly inadequate and substituting a decision that the universal credit award should not have been terminated on April 14, 2020. There was no copy of the claimant commitment document said not have been accepted or of the "To-do", let alone of any existing document or evidence of prior discussions, so that the DWP's submission relied almost entirely on mere assertion about what had happened. Even before the Upper Tribunal, the Secretary of State's representative was unable to provide any of that material or explain why, given the suspension of work search and availability requirements from March 30, 2020 due to the coronavirus pandemic, the matter was pursued after that date.

However, in the course of the Upper Tribunal proceedings, the Secretary of State's representative made a submission that the First-tier Tribunal erred in law in finding that entitlement would automatically end where a claimant failed to accept a claimant commitment in circumstances where there was an award already in place, repeating the substance of the guidance in ADM J1034. The difficulty with that submission is that it would seem that if a "To-do" of the form described above has been placed on a claimant's account a revised claimant commitment must have been prepared that has become the most up-to-date version. Although the condition, through the combination of ss.4(1)(e) and 14(5) of the WRA 2012, of having accepted the most up-to-date version of the claimant commitment could not be said to have ceased to be satisfied until after the expiry of the time given for acceptance, after that point the existence of the previous claimant commitment would not seem to be an obstacle to the termination of the couple's award. The submission also noted that the representative had been unable to find any documentary evidence of any discussion (or, it seems, any appointment for one) about the contents of the revised claimant commitment before the "To-do" of March 23, 2020. Such a breach of the duty of fairness or the "prior information duty" (see the notes to s.14 of the WRA 2012) could undermine the validity of a revised claimant commitment on appeal against the termination of an award, if the claimant or the subsisting evidence raised an issue as to a lack of a fair opportunity to make meaningful representations about the contents of the revised claimant commitment. The judge's substituted decision in *FO* that the award of universal credit should not have been terminated on April 14, 2020 might be better supported on that basis (or on the judge's alternative reasoning that by April 14, 2020 there were exceptional circumstances absolving the partner under what is now reg.16(1)(b) from the condition of having accepted a claimant commitment), rather than on the apparent basis of the Secretary of State's submission.

But if in other cases the lack of opportunity was created by a claimant's own unreasonable failure to participate in an interview there can hardly be said to have been any unfairness.

FO also illustrates that where there are joint claimants a failure by one to satisfy the basic conditions in s.4(1) of the WRA 2012 means, subject to some exceptions in reg.3, that neither has any entitlement to universal credit (s.3(2)(a)).

Paragraph (1)

On a new claim, if the claimant commitment is accepted within the time specified by the Secretary of State (as extended under para.(3) if applicable), and by a method prescribed in para.(4), the basic condition is deemed to be satisfied from the first day of the period claimed for. Otherwise, the condition would only be met from the date on which the acceptance by a prescribed method actually took place. Paragraph (1) must therefore be made under s.4(7) of the WRA 2012. Under s.14(2) of the WRA 2012, the Secretary of State may review and up-date a claimant commitment as he thinks fit and under s.14(5) a claimant has to accept the most-up-date version. Such circumstances do not seem to fall within either paras (1) or (2), although para.(3) refers to a period within which a claimant is required to accept an up-dated claimant commitment and its possible extension. There is doubt whether an acceptance under such circumstances strictly takes effect only from its actual date or from the date of the preparation of the up-dated version, but the point may not arise in practice because prior to the expiry of the period given for acceptance of the most up-to-date version the condition in s.4(1)(e) would be satisfied by the acceptance of the existing version (see the discussion of *FO* above). 2.56

Paragraph (2)

Where no claim is required to be made (see reg.9(6), (7) and (10) of the Claims and Payments Regulations 2013), effectively the same rule is applied as in para.(1) with effect from the first day of the award. 2.57

Paragraph (3)

This paragraph allows the Secretary of State, in defined circumstances, to extend the period within which a person is required (which is only in the sense of required in order to take advantage of giving a retrospective effect to the acceptance) to accept a claimant commitment or an up-dated version. It is arguable that no such authorisation is needed to allow the Secretary of State to extend any period as first specified under paras (1) or (2), so that the form of the restrictions in sub-paras (a) and (b) may not matter too much. Those provisions purport to apply when a claimant has requested that the Secretary of State review any action proposed as a work search or work availability requirement (see ss.17(1)(b) and 18 of the WRA 2012) or whether any limitation should apply to those requirements (see reg.97 below). The main difficulty with them, apart from the fact that s.18 contains no power for the Secretary of State to specify particular action in relation to a work availability requirement, is that the legislation contains no formal process of review of the "proposals" mentioned. The reference must presumably be to the power under s.24(3) of the WRA 2012 for the Secretary of State to revoke or change any requirement imposed under the Act or any specification of action to be taken and to a request to exercise that power in relation to action specified under ss.17 or 18. Those difficulties perhaps reinforce the argument for the Secretary of State being able to extend the period for acceptance of the claimant whenever it appears reasonable to do so, although that would involve giving no effective force to para.(3). See the notes to s.14 of the WRA 2012 for the administrative guidance on "cooling-off periods". 2.58

Paragraph (4)

This paragraph, as allowed by s.14(5) of the WRA 2012, requires that any acceptance of a claimant commitment that can count for the purposes of s.4(1)(e) be done electronically, by telephone or in writing, with the Secretary of State able to specify which in any particular case. "Electronically" will no doubt cover a range 2.59

of methods, but in practice the method specified is via a "To Do" action placed on the claimant's electronic journal where a button must be clicked to indicate acceptance. It seems bizarre that acceptance orally or otherwise face-to-face is not allowed, although the telephone is covered. Both methods are capable of being recorded in some permanent form. But the standard method is in keeping with the imperative towards on-line administration, even though claimants who think that everything was agreed in the meeting with their work coach may easily get confused. In so far as no account is taken of the circumstances of claimants with disabilities and the problem cannot be taken care of under reg.16 this provision must be vulnerable to a challenge under the Human Rights Act 1998 for discrimination contrary to art.14 of the European Convention on Human Rights.

Claimant commitment—exceptions

2.60 **16.**—[[1](1)] A person does not have to meet the basic condition to have accepted a claimant commitment if the Secretary of State considers that—

(a) the person cannot accept a claimant commitment because they lack the capacity to do so; or

(b) there are exceptional circumstances in which it would be unreasonable to expect the person to accept a claimant commitment.

[[1](2) A person does not have to meet the basic condition to have accepted a claimant commitment if the person is terminally ill.]

DEFINITIONS

"claimant commitment"—see WRA 2012 s.14(1)

"terminally ill" —see reg.2.

AMENDMENT

1. Universal Credit and Employment and Support Allowance (Claimant Commitment Exceptions) (Amendment) Regulations 2022 (SI 2022/60) reg.2 (February 15, 2022).

GENERAL NOTE

2.61 As authorised by s.4(2), the basic condition in s.4(1)(e) of the WRA 2012 does not have to be met where the claimant either lacks the capacity to accept a claimant commitment (para.(1)(a)) or there are exceptional circumstances in which it would be unreasonable to expect the claimant to accept a claimant commitment (para.(1)(b)), plus now, from February 15, 2022, where the claimant is terminally ill (para.(2)). Both parts of para.(1), but especially sub-para.(b), contain elements of judgment. If "accepting" a claimant commitment has the restricted meaning suggested in the notes to s.14 of the WRA 2012, that will affect when it might be unreasonable to expect a claimant to do so. If a claimant would be unable or experience undue difficulty in accepting a claimant commitment by one of the methods required by reg.15(4), that would suggest that it would be unreasonable to expect the claimant to take those steps to accept the claimant commitment. See Williams, Lack of commitment?, *Welfare Rights Bulletin 274* (February 2020) p.4 for some suggestions of arguments that might possibly be made relying on what is now reg.16(1)(b), e.g. where a claimant genuinely believed that there was no need to do more to accept a commitment after agreement at an interview with the work coach or where the claimant commitment contained unlawful conditions (but note the corrections on some technical matters in the online version of this article).

The introduction with effect from February 15, 2022 of the specific rule in para.(2) that a person who is terminally ill is not required to accept a claimant commitment was intended to avoid the risk that for some terminally ill claimants it might have been found under para.(1)(b) that the circumstances were not exceptional or did not make it unreasonable to accept a commitment (Explanatory Memorandum to SI 2022/60 para.7.2). A claimant who is terminally ill must be treated as having limited capability for work and work-related activity (Sch.9, para.1), so if properly identified as such cannot have any work-related requirements imposed (WRA 2012, s.19(2)(a)). Any claimant commitment sought to be put to a claimant for acceptance in such circumstances could therefore have only very limited content, but the existence of para.(2) may make the avoidance of that process more straightforward. At the time of the amendment, the definition of "terminally ill" in reg.2 was in terms of death in consequence of a progressive disease being reasonably expected within six months, as referred to in the Explanatory Note and the Explanatory Memorandum to SI 2022/60. Since then the definition has been amended by SI 2022/260 with effect from April 4, 2022 to substitute 12 months for six months.

The effect of para.(2) is somewhat limited by the restriction of the definition of "terminally ill" to those who are suffering from a progressive disease. There will be others with an equal claim that having to accept a claimant commitment is unreasonable, such as those who have suffered some severe personal injury which they are unlikely to survive for long, who fall outside para.(2).

The rule in what was then reg.16(b) may have been of particular importance during the 2020 coronavirus outbreak, when "conditionality" was suspended for three months from March 30, 2020 and was applied in that context in *FO v SSWP (UC)* [2022] UKUT 56 (AAC) (see the notes to reg.15). Since there was no new legislation to lift the operation of s.4(1)(e) during that period, in contrast to the position on the work search and work availability requirements, allowing entitlement on new claims without s.4(1)(e) being met appears to have been the key to not imposing those requirements. The terms of reg.16(b) on exceptional circumstances and unreasonableness would plainly have been met. So an award of universal credit could then have been made without needing to consider what work-related requirements might be imposed and need to be included in the claimant commitment. That would then have allowed the condition in reg.6(1) of the Social Security (Coronavirus) (Further Measures) Regulations 2020 (SI 2020/371) that a new claimant has an award of universal credit to be met, so that sub-paras (a) and (c) could be applied to lift the work search requirement and suspend the work availability requirement. Although para.11 of Memo ADM 04/20, purporting to explain the effect of reg.6, gave no clue that those provisions were linked (presumably because the Further Measures Regulations did not need to amend reg.16 at all), it is submitted that such a mechanism must have been envisaged. For existing claimants as at March 30, 2020, who had already accepted a commitment, the work search and work availability requirements were expressly lifted by reg.6(1)(b). For other requirements, there were to be no sanctions for failing to comply and/or a flexibility in reviewing requirements over the telephone.

The period of application of reg.6 of the Further Measures Regulations expired at the end of June 30, 2020, the power to extend the three-month period not having been exercised. On July 1, 2020 it was announced in Parliament (Under-Secretary of State, Mims Davies, WQ 62431) that from that date the requirement for universal credit claimants (among others) to accept a claimant commitment was being reintroduced. The commitments of existing claimants would be reviewed and up-dated as capacity allowed. It appears that the reintroduction for new claimants was also to be phased in.

It is unclear whether, in a case in which a claimant is entitled to both universal credit and new style JSA (so that in accordance with reg.5 of the JSA Regulations 2013 no work-related or connected requirements can be imposed in relation to JSA), the claimant would still be required to accept a claimant commitment to retain entitlement to JSA. Even if the claimant is so required, the effect of reg.5 would be that it was the universal credit claimant commitment that was the controlling document.

Financial conditions

Minimum amount

2.62 **17.** For the purposes of section 5(1)(b) and (2)(b) of the Act (financial conditions: amount payable not less than any prescribed minimum) the minimum is one penny.

DEFINITION

"the Act"—see reg.2.

Capital limit

2.63 **18.**—(1) For the purposes of section 5(1)(a) and (2)(a) of the Act (financial conditions: capital limit)—

(a) the prescribed amount for a single claimant is £16,000; and
(b) the prescribed amount for joint claimants is £16,000.

(2) In a case where the claimant is a member of a couple, but makes a claim as a single person, the claimant's capital is to be treated as including the capital of the other member of the couple.

DEFINITIONS

"claimant"—see WRA 2012 s.40.
"couple"—see WRA 2012 ss.39 and 40.
"joint claimants"—see WRA 2012 s. 40.
"prescribed"—*ibid.*
"single claimant"—*ibid.*
"single person"—see WRA 2012 ss.40 and 1(2)(a).

GENERAL NOTE

2.64 This provides that the capital limit for universal credit for both a single claimant and joint claimants is £16,000. Thus the capital limit for universal credit is the same as for income support, income-based JSA, income-related ESA and housing benefit (there is no capital limit for working tax credit and child tax credit). The £16,000 limit has not altered since 2006. In the Institute for Government and the SSAC's 2021 joint report *Jobs and benefits: The Covid-19 challenge* it was noted that if the limit had risen in line with prices since 2006 it would be close to £23,500 (or £25,000: different figures are given) and recommended that the limit should be increased to £25,000 and subsequently automatically indexed to maintain its real value (pp.22 and 31). That recommendation was summarily rejected in the Government's response of March 22, 2022.

See the notes to s.5 of the WRA 2012, the provision actually imposing the limit, for why the burden of showing that the value of capital does not exceed £16,000 falls on the claimant.

Under para.(2), where a claimant who is a member of a couple makes a claim as a single person (see reg.3(3) for the circumstances in which this may occur) the capital of the other member of the couple counts as the claimant's.

For the rules on calculating capital, including important disregards, see regs 45–50 and 75–77 and Sch.10.

With effect from July 24, 2019, reg.51 of the Transitional Provisions Regulations 2014, as inserted by reg.3 of the Universal Credit (Managed Migration Pilot and Miscellaneous Amendments) Regulations 2019 (SI 2019/1152), supplies a transitional capital disregard to claimants who (i) were previously entitled to a tax credit and had capital exceeding £16,000; (ii) are given a migration notice that existing benefits are to terminate; and (iii) claim universal credit within the deadline. The disregard is of any capital exceeding £16,000. The disregard can apply only for 12 assessment periods and ceases (without the possibility of revival) following any assessment period in which the amount of capital the claimant has falls below £16,000. See regs 56 and 57 of the Transitional Provisions Regulations for further provisions on termination of the protection. The £16,000 non-disregarded capital that the claimant by definition possesses will produce an assumed yield as income of £174 per month under reg.72. Paragraph 7 of Sch.2 to the Transitional Provisions Regulations, inserted by the same Regulations, contains a disregard as capital of any amount paid as a lump sum by way of a "transitional SDP amount" under that Schedule.

Restrictions on entitlement

Restrictions on entitlement—prisoners etc.

19.—(1) Entitlement to universal credit does not arise where a person is— 2.65

(a) a member of a religious order who is fully maintained by their order;

(b) a prisoner; or

(c) serving a sentence of imprisonment detained in hospital.

(2) Paragraph (1)(b) does not apply during the first 6 months when the person is a prisoner where—

(a) the person was entitled to universal credit [1 as a single person] immediately before becoming a prisoner, and the calculation of their award included an amount for the housing costs element; and

(b) the person has not been sentenced to a term in custody that is expected to extend beyond that 6 months.

(3) In the case of a prisoner to whom paragraph (2) applies, an award of universal credit is not to include any element other than the housing costs element.

(4) In paragraph (1)(c) a person serving a sentence of imprisonment detained in hospital is a person who is—

(a) being detained—

(i) under section 45A or 47 of the Mental Health Act 1983 (power of higher courts to direct hospital admission; removal to hospital of persons serving sentence of imprisonment etc), and

(ii) before the day which the Secretary of State certifies to be that person's release date within the meaning of section 50(3) of that Act (in any case where there is such a release date); or

(b) being detained under—

(i) section 59A of the Criminal Procedure (Scotland) Act 1995 (hospital direction), or

(ii) section 136 of the Mental Health (Care and Treatment) (Scotland) Act 2003 (transfer of prisoners for treatment of mental disorder).

AMENDMENT

1. Universal Credit (Consequential, Supplementary, Incidental and Miscellaneous Provisions) Regulations 2013 (SI 2013/630) reg.38 (April 29, 2013).

DEFINITIONS

"housing costs element"—see regs 2 and 25.
"prisoner"—see reg.2 as modified by SI 2020/409.

General Note

2.66 WRA 2012, s.6(1)(a) provides that "entitlement to universal credit does not arise . . . in prescribed circumstances even though the requirements of section 3 [i.e., the requirements to satisfy the basic conditions and the financial conditions] are met". Regulation 19 is made under that power. Its effect is that, where a person's circumstances fall within para.(1), entitlement to universal credit "does not arise" even though that person otherwise meets all the conditions of entitlement. Those circumstances as that the claimant is a fully maintained member of a religious order, a prisoner (subject to para.(2)), or serving a sentence of imprisonment in a hospital (as defined in para.(4)).

The wording "entitlement . . . does not arise" in both s.6 and reg.19 creates problems. It would have been more natural to say that a person whose circumstances fall within para.(1) "is not entitled to Universal Credit" even if he or she satisfies s.3.

One possibility is that the wording may have been chosen to forestall any suggestion that the rules in reg.19 amount to conditions of disentitlement or disqualification (in which case, subject to the principles enunciated by the House of Lords in *Kerr v Department of Social Development*, [2004] UKHL 23 (also reported as *R 1/04 (SF)*), the burden would be on the Secretary of State to show that affected claimants were not entitled to universal credit, rather than for the claimants to prove that they were). However, this seems unlikely. Whether or not a person is a fully maintained member of a religious order, a prisoner, or serving a sentence of imprisonment in a hospital are not questions that would normally raise difficult issues of proof. And if this was the intention, it is not entirely clear that s.6 and reg.19 achieve it.

2.67 Whatever the reason for the wording, the problem it creates is that (to use prisoners as an example) although departmental policy is that prisoners should generally have no entitlement to universal credit other than under reg.19(2) (see ADM E3030 and E3040), that is not what s.6 and reg.19 say. They only say that entitlement does not arise where a person is a prisoner. But that does not cover the position in which entitlement has already arisen but the claimant subsequently becomes a prisoner. If s.6 and reg.19 contained a clear statement that a person who is a prisoner "is not entitled" to universal credit (except where reg.19(2) applies), then imprisonment would be a relevant change of circumstances and a ground for superseding the decision awarding universal credit. As it is, the effect of reg.19 appears to be limited to cases in which a new claim is made by a person who is already a prisoner because it is only in such cases that there is any issue about whether entitlement has "arisen". This view is reinforced by s.6(1)(b) and (c) and (2) which provide that entitlement to universal credit does not arise if the basic conditions or the financial conditions are met for a period shorter than a prescribed period or for up to seven days at the beginning of a period during which those conditions are met. In those provisions the "entitlement . . . does not arise" wording is being applied to circumstances where there is no existing entitlement, as is apt.

Paragraphs (2)and (3)

2.68 The above analysis, creates some difficulties in the interpretation of para.(2). This says that para.(1)(b) "does not apply" during the first six months when the person is a prisoner where that person was entitled to universal credit immediately before becoming a prisoner, and certain other circumstances exist. If what is said above is correct, then para.(1)(b) does not apply at all in such a case, irrespective of the other circumstances. (That is not an objection to the analysis. The "entitlement . . . does not arise" wording is in primary legislation and the way in which the Secretary of State has interpreted that wording when making secondary legislation is not a guide to what it actually means).

The policy which para.(2) seeks to implement is that where someone with an existing award of universal credit that includes the housing costs element is sentenced to a term in custody that is not expected to extend beyond that 6 months, entitlement to universal credit is retained but the award may not include any element other than the housing costs element.

See also the commentary under the headings *Members of religious orders* and *Person serving a sentence of imprisonment in hospital* in the General Note to reg.21 of the IS Regulations in Vol.V.

[1 Waiting Days

19A. [4 . . .]] 2.69

AMENDMENTS

1. Universal Credit (Waiting Days) (Amendment) Regulations 2015 (SI 2015/1362) reg.2(1)(a) (August 3, 2015).

2. Universal Credit and Miscellaneous Amendments Regulations 2015 (SI 2015/1754) reg.2(3) (Assessment periods beginning on or after November 4, 2015).

3. Universal Credit and Miscellaneous Amendments Regulations 2015 (SI 2015/1754) reg.5 (Assessment periods beginning on or after November 4, 2015).

4. Universal Credit (Miscellaneous Amendments, Saving and Transitional Provision) Regulations 2018 (SI 2018/65) reg.3(3) (February 14, 2018).

DEFINITIONS

"terminally ill"—*ibid.*
"weekly earnings"—*ibid.*
"work-related requirements"—see WRA 2012 s.13.

GENERAL NOTE

WRA 2012 s.6(1)(c) provides that "entitlement to universal credit does not arise . . . for a prescribed period at the beginning of a period during which" the claimant satisfies the basic and financial conditions for universal credit (i.e., as required by WRA 2012 s.3). By s.6(2), the period for which there is no entitlement may not exceed seven days. 2.70

Regulation 19A was made under the power conferred by s.6(1)(c) and provided that with effect from August 3, 2015, entitlement to universal credit was normally deferred for seven "waiting days". The regulation was revoked with effect from February 4, 2018. See the commentary on p.161 of the 2017/18 edition Vol. V for details of how the regulation operated when it was in force.

PART 3

AWARDS

Introduction

20. This Part contains provisions for the purposes of sections 7 and 8 of the Act about assessment periods and about the calculation of the amount of an award of universal credit. 2.71

DEFINITIONS

"the Act"—see reg.2.
"assessment period"—see WRA 2012 ss.40 and 7(2).

General Note

2.72 Part 3 is made under powers conferred by ss.7 to 12 WRA 2012 and is concerned with the calculation of an award of universal credit. There are two underlying principles. The first is that an award is made by reference to an "assessment period" (s.7 and reg.21). The second is that the amount of the award is calculated by ascertaining the claimant's (or claimants') "maximum amount" and then deducting "the amounts to be deducted", namely all unearned income and some earned income (s.8 and reg.22).

[1 Awards

2.73 **20A.** [2 . . .]]

Amendments

1. Universal Credit (Waiting Days) (Amendment) Regulations 2015 (SI 2015/1362) reg.2(1)(b) (August 3, 2015).
2. Universal Credit (Miscellaneous Amendments, Saving and Transitional Provision) Regulations 2018 (SI 2018/65) reg.3(4) (February 14, 2018).

General Note

2.74 When it was in force between August 3, 2015 and February 14, 2018, reg.20A clarified that where entitlement to another benefit is conditional on a person "having an award of universal credit" a person does not have such an award on any day when they are not entitled to universal credit (e.g., on waiting days). The intention was to prevent the reasoning of the Upper Tribunal in *SSWP v SJ (IS)* [2015] UKUT 0127 (AAC) (see the commentary to reg.7(3) and (4) of the Social Fund Maternity and Funeral Expenses (General) Regulations 2005) from being extended to universal credit. Following the abolition of waiting days by the revocation of reg.19A with effect from February 14, 2018, reg.20A would no longer have served any purpose and it has therefore been revoked too.

Assessment periods

2.75 **21.**—(1) An assessment period is [4 . . .] a period of one month beginning with the first date of entitlement and each subsequent period of one month during which entitlement subsists.

[2(1A) [3 . . .]]

(2) Each assessment period begins on the same day of each month except as follows—

(a) if the first date of entitlement falls on the 31st day of a month, each assessment period begins on the last day of the month; and

(b) if the first date of entitlement falls on the 29th or 30th day of a month, each assessment period begins on the 29th or 30th day of the month (as above) except in February when it begins on the 27th day or, in a leap year, the 28th day.

[4 (2A) But paragraphs (1) and (2) are subject to regulation 21A (assessment period cycle to remain the same following change in the first date of entitlement).]

[1 (3) Where a new award is made to a single person without a claim by virtue of regulation 9(6)(a) or (10) of the Claims and Payments Regulations (old award has ended when the claimant ceased to be a member of a couple) each assessment period for the new award begins on the same day of each month as the assessment period for the old award.

(3A) Where a new award is made to members of a couple jointly without claim by virtue of regulation 9(6)(b) or (7) of the Claims and Payments Regulations (two previous awards have ended when the claimants formed a couple) each assessment period for the new award begins on the same day of each month as the assessment period for whichever of the old awards ended earlier.

(3B) Where a claim is treated as made by virtue of regulation 9(8) of the Claims and Payments Regulations (old award ended when a claimant formed a couple with a person not entitled to universal credit), each assessment period in relation to the new award begins on the same day of each month as the assessment period for the old award.

(3C) Where a claim is made by a single person or members of a couple jointly and the claimant (or either joint claimant) meets the following conditions—

(a) the claimant was previously entitled to an award of universal credit the last day of which fell within the 6 months preceding the date on which the claim is made; and

(b) during that 6 months—

(i) the claimant has continued to meet the basic conditions in section 4 of the Act (disregarding the requirement to have accepted a claimant commitment and any temporary period of absence from Great Britain that would be disregarded during a period of entitlement to universal credit); and

(ii) the claimant was not excluded from entitlement by regulation 19 (restrictions on entitlement – prisoners etc.),

each assessment period for the new award begins on the same day of each month as the assessment period for the old award or, if there was an old award in respect of each joint claimant, the assessment period that ends earlier in relation to the date on which the claim is made.

(3D) For the purposes of this regulation it does not matter if, at the beginning of the first assessment period of the new award, the following persons do not meet the basic conditions in section 4(1)(a) and (c) of the Act (at least 18 years old and in Great Britain) or if they are excluded from entitlement under regulation 19 (restrictions on entitlement – prisoners etc.) provided they meet those conditions (and are not so excluded) at the end of that assessment period—

(a) in a case to which paragraph (3B) applies, the member of the couple who was not entitled to universal credit; or

(b) in a case to which paragraph (3C) applies, the member of the couple who does not meet the conditions mentioned in that paragraph.

(3E) In this regulation "the Claims and Payments Regulations" means the Universal Credit, Personal Independence Payment, Jobseeker's Allowance and Employment and Support Allowance (Claims and Payments) Regulations 2013.]

(5) [[1] . . .]

(6) [[1] . . .]

AMENDMENTS

1. Universal Credit (Digital Service) Amendment Regulations 2014 (SI 2014/2887) reg.3(1) (November 26, 2014). The amendment is subject to the saving provision in reg.5 of SI 2014/2887 (see pp.799–800 of the 2020/21 edition of Vol.V of this series).

2. Universal Credit (Waiting Days) (Amendment) Regulations 2015 (SI 2015/1362) reg.2(1)(c) (August 3, 2015).
3. Universal Credit (Miscellaneous Amendments, Saving and Transitional Provision) Regulations 2018 (SI 2018/65) reg.3(5) (February 14, 2018).
4. Universal Credit (Miscellaneous Amendments, Saving and Transitional Provision) Regulations 2018 (SI 2018/65) reg.3(5) (April 11, 2018).

DEFINITIONS

"assessment period"—see WRA 2012 ss.40 and 7(2).
"claim"—see WRA 2012 s.40.
"couple"—see WRA 2012 ss.39 and 40.
"jobseeker's allowance"—see reg.2.
"personal independence payment"—*ibid*.

GENERAL NOTE

2.76 WRA 2012, s.7(1) provides that universal credit "is payable in respect of each complete assessment period within a period of entitlement". "Assessment period" is defined by s.7(2) as a "period of prescribed duration" and "period of entitlement" is defined by s.7(4) as a "period during which entitlement to universal credit subsists". Section 7(3) empowers the Secretary of State to make regulations about when an assessment period is to start, for universal credit to be payable in respect of a period shorter than an assessment period and for the amount payable in respect of a period shorter than an assessment period. Regulation 21 is made under the powers conferred by s.7(2) and (3).

2.77 *Paragraph (1)* provides that an assessment period is a period of one month beginning with the first date of entitlement and each subsequent period of one month during which entitlement subsists.

2.78 *Paragraph (1A)* clarifies that where the waiting days rule applies (see the General Note to reg.19A), the first day of entitlement (and therefore the first day of the assessment period) is the day after the expiry of the seven waiting days.

2.79 *Paragraph (2)* makes provision to avoid the administrative problems that would otherwise occur in shorter months. The general rule is that each assessment period begins on the same day of each month. But that is not always possible when the first assessment period began on the 29th, 30th or 31st of a month because not all months have more than 28 days. Therefore:

- if the first date of entitlement falls on the 31st day of a month, each subsequent assessment period begins on the last day of the month (para.(2)(a)); or
- if the first date of entitlement falls on the 29th or 30th day of a month, each subsequent assessment period begins on the 29th or 30th day of the month except in February when it begins on the 27th day or, in a leap year, the 28th day.

2.80 *Paragraphs (3)–(3B)*: Reg.9(6)–(8) and (10) of the Claims and Payments Regulations 2013 (see the definition in para.(3E)) specify circumstances in which it is possible to become entitled to universal credit without making a claim for it. All of those circumstances involve there having been a previous award of universal credit. Paras (3)–(3B) govern the day on which the first assessment period begins under the new award:

- *Paragraph (3)* applies where an award is made to a single person who had previously been awarded universal credit as one of two joint claimants, but who has ceased to be a member of a couple, either through relationship breakdown (reg.9(6)(a) of the Claims and Payments Regulations 2013) or through death (reg.9(10)). In such circumstances, each assessment period for the new award begins on the same period of each month as the assessment period for the old award.

- *Paragraph (3A)* applies either (1) where a joint award of universal credit ends because one former joint claimant has formed a new couple with a third person who is already entitled to universal credit (reg.9(6)(b)) or (2) where two single claimants who are already entitled to universal credit form a couple. In those cases, the dates on which the assessment periods began under the previous awards will not necessarily be the same, so para.(3A) provides that the assessment periods for the new award will begin on the same day of each month as the assessment period for whichever of the two old awards ended earlier.
- *Paragraph (3B)* applies if a joint award of universal credit ends because one former joint claimant has formed a new couple with a third person who was not previously entitled to universal credit (reg.9(8)), and provides that each assessment period for the new award begins on the same period of each month as the assessment period for the old award. This rule applies even if—at the beginning of the first assessment period under the new award—one member of the new couple was under 18, or was not in Great Britain, or was excluded from entitlement under reg.19,as long as they were 18 or over, in Great Brittan, and not excluded from entitlement at the end of that assessment period (para.(3D)).

Paragraph (3C) is not—or, at any rate, not necessarily—concerned with relationship formation or breakdown, but rather with repeat claims. It applies if a new claim for universal credit is made and the claimant (or either or both joint claimants) was (or were) entitled to universal credit within the previous six months and, during the period between the old award and the new claim, the claimant (or both claimants): **2.81**

- were at least 18 years old, below state pension credit age, in Great Britain (other than for periods of temporary absence that would have been disregarded under reg.11 if there had been an award of universal credit at the time) and were not receiving education; and
- were not excluded from entitlement to universal credit by reg.19 as a member of a religious order, as a prisoner, or as a person serving a sentence of imprisonment detained in hospital.

If the new claim is made by a couple, and—at the beginning of the first assessment period under the new award—one member was under 18, or was not in Great Britain, or was excluded from entitlement under reg.19, the conditions in the two bullet points above are treated as having been met provided was 18 or over, in Great Britain and not excluded from entitlement at the end of that assessment period (para.(3D)).

Where para.(3C) applies, each assessment period for the new award begins on the same day of the month as each assessment period of the old award or, if there were two old assessment periods (*i.e.,* because two people who were previously single claimants have formed a couple between the end of the old award and the new claim), on the same day of the month as whichever assessment period of the old award ended earlier.

Under reg.26(5) of the Claims and Payments Regulations 2013, a claim must be made before the end of the assessment period in respect of which it is made in order to benefit from para.(3C).

This will normally be more favourable to claimants that the rules for initial claims. The claims process for repeat claimants is intended to be simpler. In addition, the fact that the first assessment period of the new award will normally begin before the date of the new claim (*i.e.,* unless that date happens to coincide with the start of an assessment period) means that the claimant(s) will be entitled to universal credit before that date (although any income earned during the assessment period from a previous employment will be brought into account). However, where any claimant is not in work at the date of the new claim and has ceased being in paid work since the old award ended, the amount of universal credit paid for the first assessment period is reduced (technically, "apportioned") unless the new claim is made within seven days of the date on which work ceased: see reg.22A, below.

[1Assessment period cycle to remain the same following change in the first date of entitlement

2.82 **21A.**—(1) This regulation applies where—

(a) the first date of entitlement has been determined;

(b) it is subsequently determined that the first date of entitlement falls on a different date (the "start date"); and

(c) applying regulation 21(1) and (2) following that subsequent determination (and thereby changing the beginning of each assessment period) would, in the opinion of the Secretary of State, cause unnecessary disruption to the administration of the claim.

(2) Where this regulation applies—

(a) the first assessment period is to be a period of a length determined by the Secretary of State beginning with the start date;

(b) the amount payable in respect of that first assessment period is to be calculated as follows—

$$N \times \left(\frac{A \times 12}{365} \right)$$

where—

N is the number of days in the period; and

A is the amount calculated in relation to that period as if it were an assessment period of one month; and

(c) regulation 21(1) and (2) apply to the second and subsequent assessment periods as if the day after the end of the first assessment period were the first date of entitlement.]

AMENDMENT

1. Universal Credit (Miscellaneous Amendments, Saving and Transitional Provision) Regulations 2018 (SI 2018/65) reg.3(6) (April 11, 2018).

Deduction of income and work allowance

2.83 **22.**—(1) The amounts to be deducted from the maximum amount in accordance with section 8(3) of the Act to determine the amount of an award of universal credit are—

(a) all of the claimant's unearned income (or in the case of joint claimants all of their combined unearned income) in respect of the assessment period; and

[1 (b) the following amount of the claimant's earned income (or, in the case of joint claimants, their combined earned income) in respect of the assessment period—

(i) in a case where no work allowance is specified in the table below (that is where a single claimant does not have, or neither of joint claimants has, responsibility for a child or qualifying young person or limited capability for work), [2 55%] of that earned income; or

(ii) in any other case, [2 55%] of the amount by which that earned income exceeds the work allowance specified in the table.]

(2) The amount of the work allowance is—

(a) if the award contains no amount for the housing costs element, the applicable amount of the higher work allowance specified in the table below; and

(b) if the award does contain an amount for the housing costs element, the applicable amount of the lower work allowance specified in that table.

[1 (3) In the case of an award where the claimant is a member of a couple, but makes a claim as a single person, the amount to be deducted from the maximum amount in accordance with section 8(3) of the Act is the same as the amount that would be deducted in accordance with paragraph (1) if the couple were joint claimants.]

[1 Higher work allowance	
Single claimant—	
responsible for one or more children or qualifying young persons and/or has limited capability for work	[3 £673]
Joint claimants	
responsible for one or more children or qualifying young persons and/or where one or both have limited capability for work	[3 £673]
Lower work allowance	
Single claimant—	
responsible for one or more children or qualifying young persons and/or has limited capability for work	[3 £404]
Joint claimants—	
responsible for one or more children or qualifying young persons and/or where one or both have limited capability for work]	[3 £404]

AMENDMENTS

1. Universal Credit (Work Allowance) Amendment Regulations 2015 (SI 2015/1649) reg.2 (Assessment periods beginning on or after April 11, 2016).

2. Universal Credit (Work Allowance and Taper) (Amendment) Regulations 2021 (SI 2021/1283) reg.2(1) (Assessment periods beginning on or November 24, 2021).

3. Social Security Benefits Up-rating Order 2024 (SI 2024/242) art.32 (Assessment periods beginning on or after April 8, 2024).

DEFINITIONS

"the Act"—see reg.2.
"assessment period"—see WRA 2012, ss.40 and 7(2).
"child"—see WRA 2012, s.40.
"claimant"—*ibid.*
"couple"—see WRA 2012, ss.39 and 40.
"earned income"—see reg.2.
"housing costs element"—see regs 2 and 25.
"joint claimants"—see WRA 2012, s.40.
"limited capability for work"—see WRA 2012, ss.40 and 37(1).
"qualifying young person"—see WRA 2012, ss.40 and 10(5) and regs 2 and 5.
"responsible for a child or qualifying young person"—see regs 2, 4 and 4A.
"single claimant"—see WRA 2012, s.40.

"unearned income"—see reg.2.
"work"—see WRA 2012, s.40.

General Note

2.84 Under s.8(1) WRA 2012, the amount of an award of universal credit is the balance of the maximum amount less the amounts to be deducted which, by s.8(3), are to be two prescribed amounts, one in respect of earned income and the other in respect of unearned income. Regulation 22 is made under s.8(3) and specifies how those prescribed amounts are to be determined.

2.85 *Paragraph (1)* contains the three general principles. First, the claimant's (or the claimants' combined) *unearned* income (i.e., as calculated in accordance with regs 65-74) is deducted in full (para.(1)(a)). Second, where no claimant has either responsibility for a child or qualifying young person or limited capability for work, 55% of *earned* income (i.e., as calculated in accordance with regs 51-64) is deducted. Third, where any claimant has responsibility for a child or qualifying young person or limited capability for work, the deduction is 55% of the amount by which the claimant's (or the claimant's combined) earned income exceeds the "work allowance" specified in the table to the regulation (para.(1)(b)(ii)).

2.86 *Paragraph (3)* modifies those principles where a member of a couple is claiming as a single claimant under reg.3(3): the couple's combined income is take into account when calculation earned and unearned income, even though the circumstances of the other member of the couple will be excluded when calculating his or her maximum amount (see reg.36(3)).

Paragraph (1)(b) is—or, at any rate, was until April 11, 2016 see below—the main mechanism by which the policy that, under universal credit, claimants will always be better off in work is achieved. The "work allowance" is what would previously have been described as an earnings disregard: an amount deducted from a claimant's earnings before any means-test is carried out. But, even at the lowest rate, it is a more generous disregard than applied for the purposes of IS, income-based JSA and income-related ESA. Even where there is no responsibility for a child or qualifying young person—and therefore no work allowance—the 55% "taper" means that the claimant keeps 45 pence in every additional pound he or she earns, whereas under IS, income-based JSA and income-related ESA, benefit was reduced pound for pound so that, once a claimant's earnings exceeded the earnings disregard (and ignoring any potential entitlement to WTC), there was no financial incentive to work unless he or she could earn enough to come off income-related benefits altogether.

Before April 11, 2016, the work allowances specified in most cases were higher than those that now appear above. In addition, work allowances were also specified for claimants who were not responsible for a child or qualifying young person, For a more detailed discussion of the effects of the reduction and removal of work allowances in those cases, see *Universal Credit—An Introduction* above.

Paragraph (2)

2.87 The amount of the work allowance to be deducted from earned income in cases where a claimant has responsibility for a child or qualifying young person is specified in para.(2) and the table at the end of the regulation. The higher work allowance is applicable when the award of universal credit does not contain the housing costs element and the lower work allowance when it does. Very few universal credit claimants will not have to pay anything towards housing costs. The most likely recipients of the higher work allowance are, those living as non-dependants in another person's household, owner-occupiers whose earnings exclude them from entitlement to housing costs under Sch.5, para.4 and those renters treated as not liable to make payments under Sch.2, paras 5 to 10.

[1 Apportionment where re-claim delayed after loss of employment

22A.—(1) This regulation applies where— 2.88

(a) a new award is made in a case to which regulation 21(3C) (new claim within 6 months of a previous award) applies; and

(b) the claimant (or either joint claimant) is not in paid work and has ceased being in paid work since the previous award ended, other than in the 7 days ending with the date on which the claim is made.

(2) In calculating the amount of the award for the first assessment period in accordance with section 8 of the Act—

(a) the amount of each element that is to be included in the maximum amount; and

(b) the amount of earned and unearned income that is to be deducted from the maximum amount,

are each to be reduced to an amount produced by the following formula—

$$N \times \left(\frac{A \times 12}{365} \right)$$

Where—

N is the number of days in the period beginning with the date on which the claim is made and ending with the last day of the assessment period; and

A is the amount of the element that would otherwise be payable for that assessment period or, as the case may be, the amount of earned and unearned income that would otherwise be deducted for that assessment period.

(3) The period of 7 days in paragraph (1)(b) may be extended if the Secretary of State considers there is good reason for the delay in making the claim.

Amendment

1. Universal Credit (Digital Service) Amendment Regulations 2014 (SI 2014/2887) reg.3(1)(d) (November 26, 2014). The amendment is subject to the saving provision in reg.5 of SI 2014/2887 (see pp.799–800 of the 2020/21 edition of Vol.V of this series).

Definitions

"assessment period"—see WRA 2012 ss.40 and 7(2) and reg.21.
"claim"—see WRA 2012 s.40.
"claimant"—*ibid.*
"earned income"—see reg.2 and regs 51-64.
"joint claimants"—see WRA 2012 s.40.
"maximum amount"—see WRA 2012 s.8(2).
"unearned income"—see reg.2 and regs 65-74.

General Note

The effect of the saving provision in reg.5 of SI 2014/2887 is that the new reg.22A only applies in "Full Service" (or "Digital Service") areas (see *Universal Credit—An Introduction*, above). It does not affect claims that are subject to the "Live Service" rules (as to which see the commentary to reg.6 of the Claims and Payments Regulations 2013 (below) and pp.432-3 of the 2013/14 edition). 2.89

Until November 25, 2014, it was unnecessary in some circumstances to re-claim universal credit if there had been a gap in entitlement of no more than six months. However, in Full Service cases only, and from November 26, 2014, a claim is now necessary but such repeat claims are subject to more favourable rules (see reg.21(3C) above). In particular, the assessment period from the old award of universal credit is adopted, with the effect that the claimant will normally become entitled to universal credit before the date of his or her claim.

However, in cases where the new claim is made more than seven days after any claimant ceased paid work, reg.22A removes the benefit of that more favourable rule. The monthly amounts of each element included in the maximum amount for the assessment period and of the earned and unearned income received in the assessment period are apportioned by multiplying by 12 and dividing by 365 to give a daily rate and then multiplying by the number of days between the date of claim and the end of the assessment period. Note that the apportioned result is likely to less favourable to the claimant than simply starting a new assessment period on the date of claim would have been. Under the apportionment, income earned during the assessment period in the claimant's former employment is taken into account, albeit at a reduced rate. If the assessment period had started at the date of claim, that income would have been received before it started and would not be taken into account.

According to the explanatory memorandum to SI 2014/2887 reg.22A was introduced "... to encourage claimants to re-claim universal credit as quickly as possible. Evidence has shown that where claimants enter a conditionality regime within two weeks of losing a job it significantly decreases their time between periods of employment".

Under para.(3), the seven day time limit for re-claiming may be extended if the Secretary of State (and, on appeal, the First-tier Tribunal or Upper Tribunal) considers there is good reason for the delay in making the claim.

PART 4

ELEMENTS OF AN AWARD

Introduction

2.90 **23.**—(1) This Part contains provisions about the amounts ("the elements") under—

(a) section 9 (the standard allowance);
(b) section 10 (responsibility for children and young persons);
(c) section 11 (housing costs); and
(d) section 12 (particular needs and circumstances),

of the Act that make up the maximum amount of an award of universal credit, as provided in section 8(2) of the Act.

(2) The elements to be included in an award under section 12 of the Act in respect of particular needs or circumstances are—

(a) [[1] . . .] the LCWRA element
(b) the carer element (see regulations 29 and 30); and
(c) the childcare costs element (see regulations 31 to 35).

AMENDMENT

1. Employment and Support Allowance and Universal Credit (Miscellaneous Amendments and Transitional and Savings Provisions) Regulations 2017 (SI 2017/204) reg. 4(1) and (3) (April 3, 2017).

DEFINITION

"the Act"—see reg.2.

General Note

The maximum amount for the purposes of s.8 WRA is the total of: 2.91

- the standard allowance: WRA 2012, s.9 and reg.36;
- an amount for each child or young person for whom a claimant is responsible ("the child element") WRA 2012,s.10 and reg.24;
- any amount included in respect of any liability of the claimant to make payments in respect of the accommodation they occupy as their home ("the housing costs element"): WRA 2012, s.11 and regs 25 and 26; or
- any amount included in respect of "other particular needs and circumstances": WRA 2012, s.12 and regs.27 to 35.

The amounts to be included in respect of other particular needs and circumstances are the LCWRA element (regs 27 and 28), the carer element (see regs 29 and 30) and the childcare costs element (regs 31–35). The former LCW element was abolished with effect from April 3, 2017 by the Employment and Support Allowance and Universal Credit (Miscellaneous Amendments and Transitional and Savings Provisions) Regulations 2017 (SI 2017/204) subject to the transitional and savings provisions in Sch.2, Pt 2 to those Regulations (see below).

Responsibility for children or young persons

The child element

24.—(1) The amount to be included in an award of universal credit for each child or qualifying young person for whom a claimant is responsible [2 and in respect of whom an amount may be included under section 10] ("the child element") is given in the table in regulation 36. 2.92

(2) An additional amount as shown in that table is to be included in respect of each child or qualifying young person who is disabled and that amount is—

(a) the lower rate, where the child or qualifying young person is entitled to disability living allowance [3, child disability payment] [4, adult disability payment] or personal independence payment (unless sub-paragraph (b) applies); or

(b) the higher rate where the child or qualifying young person is—

(i) entitled to the care component of disability living allowance at the highest rate [3, the care component of child disability payment at the highest rate in accordance with regulation 11(5) of the DACYP Regulations][4, the daily living component of adult disability payment at the enhanced rate in accordance with regulation 5(3) of the Disability Assistance for Working Age People (Scotland) Regulations 2022] or the daily living component of personal independence payment at the enhanced rate, or

(ii) [1 . . .] blind.

Amendments

1. Universal Credit and Miscellaneous Amendments (No.2) Regulations 2014 (SI 2014/2888) reg.3(1)(b) (Assessment periods beginning on or after November 26, 2014).

2. Welfare Reform and Work Act 2016 (c.7) s.14(5)(a) (April 6, 2017).

3. Social Security (Scotland) Act 2018 (Disability Assistance for Children and Young People) (Consequential Modifications) Order 2021 (SI 2021/786) Sch.11 para.4 (July 26, 2021).

4. Social Security (Disability Assistance for Working Age People) (Consequential Amendments) Order 2022 (SI 2022/177) reg.13(4) (March 21, 2022).

DEFINITIONS

"adult disability payment"—see reg.2.
"blind"—*ibid.*
"child"—see WRA 2012, s.40.
"child disability payment"—see reg.2.
"child element"—*ibid.*
"the DACYP Regulations"—*ibid.*
"disability living allowance"—*ibid.*
"disabled"—see WRA 2012, s.40.
"personal independence payment"—see reg.2.
"responsible for a child or qualifying young person"—see regs 2, 4 and 4A.
"qualifying young person"—see WRA 2012, s.40 and 10(5) and regs 2 and 5.

GENERAL NOTE

2.93 The child element includes two amounts, which are specified in reg.36. The first, which is included for each child or qualifying young person for whom a claimant is responsible, is £269.58 per assessment period subject to a maximum of two children: see regs 24A and 24B and Sch.12.

Before April 6, 2017 the rate of the child element was higher for the first child or qualifying young person for whom the claimant was responsible. Under reg.43 of the Transitional Provisions Regulations 2014, the higher rate continues to apply where the claimant is responsible for a child or qualifying young person born before April 6, 2017. The transitionally protected higher rate was £277.08 from 2017/18–2019/20, £281.20 in 2020/21, £282.50 in 2021/2022, £290.00 in 2022/23, and is £315.00 in 2023/24: see art.33(2) of, and Sch.13, to SI 2023/316.

An additional amount is included for each child or qualifying young person who is entitled to disability living allowance or personal independence payment or a Scottish equivalent or is registered as blind. The higher amount of £456.89 per assessment period is included where the child or qualifying young person is blind or entitled to the highest rate of the care component of disability living allowance or the enhanced rate of personal independence payment or a Scottish equivalent; the lower amount of £146.31 is included in any other case.

In *R. (SC, CB and 8 children) v Secretary of State for Work and Pensions*, two mothers and their children challenged the two-child limit on two grounds. The first was that the limit was incompatible with their Convention Rights to respect for their private and family lives (i.e. under art.8 ECHR) and to marry and to found a family (art.12). The second was that the limit discriminated against them unlawfully contrary to art.14 taken together with art.8 and art.1 of the First Protocol. However, that challenge was rejected by the High Court (Ouseley J) [2018] EWHC 864 (Admin); [2018] 1 W.L.R. 5425; the Court of Appeal (Patten, Leggatt and Nicola Davies LJJ) [2019] EWCA Civ 615; [2019] 1 W.L.R. 5687; and the Supreme Court (Lords Reed and Hodge, Lady Black, and Lords Lloyd-Jones, Kitchin, Sales and Stephens) [2021] UKSC 26; [2022] A.C. 223. The challenge in *SC* was to the two-child limit as it applied to CTC, but the reasoning of the Supreme Court applies equally to the other benefits to which the limit applies, including universal credit.

An application has subsequently been made (by different claimants) to the ECtHR, on the grounds which failed in *SC*.

In *SSWP v MS (UC)* [2023] UKUT 44 (AAC) (February 15, 2023) the Upper Tribunal decides that the child element of universal credit is not a social security family benefit under Regulation (EC) 883/2004. In this respect the UC child element is therefore differently classified from child tax credit. So the UC child element is not payable in respect of a child who: is living abroad and therefore deemed not to be a child for whom the claimant is "responsible" within the meaning of reg.4 of the Universal Credit Regulations, even if the child is a member of the claimant's family within the meaning of arts1 and 67 of Regulations (EC) 883/2004. The UT holds that the UC child element is not severable from the other parts of UC, and that even if it were severable, it would remain social assistance, outside the scope of art.67.

[1 Availability of the child element where maximum exceeded

24A.—(1) Where a claimant is responsible for more than two children or qualifying young persons, the amount mentioned in section 10(1) of the Act is to be available in respect of— 2.94

[2 (za) any child or qualifying young person in relation to whom an exception applies in the circumstances set out in—

(i) paragraph 3 (adoptions) or paragraph 4 (non-parental caring arrangements) of Schedule 12; or

(ii) paragraph 6 of Schedule 12 by virtue of an exception under paragraph 3 of that Schedule having applied in relation to a previous award;]

(a) the first and second children or qualifying young persons in the claimant's household; and

(b) the third and any subsequent child or qualifying young person in the claimant's household if—

(i) the child or qualifying young person is transitionally protected; or

(ii) an exception applies in relation to that child or qualifying young person [2 in the circumstances set out in paragraph 2 (multiple births), paragraph 5 (non-consensual conception) or, except where sub-paragraph (za)(ii) applies, paragraph 6 (continuation of existing exception in a subsequent award) of Schedule 12].

(2) A reference in paragraph (1) to a child or qualifying young person being the first, second, third or subsequent child or qualifying young person in the claimant's household is a reference to the position of that child or qualifying young person in the order determined in accordance with regulation 24B.

(3) A child or qualifying young person is transitionally protected [3 if the child or qualifying young person was born before 6th April 2017.]

(4) [2 ...]]

AMENDMENT

1. Social Security (Restrictions on Amounts for Children and Qualifying Young Persons) Amendment Regulations 2017 (SI 2017/376) reg.2(1) and (3) (April 6, 2017).

2. Universal Credit and Jobseeker's Allowance (Miscellaneous Amendments) Regulations 2018 (SI 2018/1129) reg.3(1) and (3) (November 28, 2018).

3. Universal Credit (Restriction on Amounts for Children and Qualifying Young Persons) (Transitional Provisions) Amendment Regulations 2019 (SI 2019/27) reg.3 (February 1, 2019).

General Note

2.95 From April 6, 2017 until October 31, 2018, the rules described in this Note applied to existing universal credit claimants only (including those who claimed after April 6, 2017 and subsequently became responsible for two or more children or qualifying young persons). During that interim period, a person who was responsible for two or more children or qualifying young persons could not make a new claim for universal credit—and therefore needed to claim IS/JSA/ESA and CTC (and, where relevant, HB) instead—unless the claim was made within six months of a previous award terminating under reg.21(3C) or was made by a single person within one month of an award of universal credit terminating because that person ceased to be a member of a couple. See generally, reg.39 of the Transitional Provisions Regulations 2014.

From April 6, 2017 s.10(1A) of the WRA 2012 (as inserted by WR&WA 2016, s.14(1)-(4)) provides that the child element of universal credit established by s.10(1) "is to be available in respect of a maximum of two persons who are either children or qualifying young persons for whom a claimant is responsible." However, s.10(4) provides that "[r]egulations may provide for exceptions to subsection (1) or (1A). Regulations 24A and 24B are made under that power. Reg.24A and Sch.12 create exceptions to the "two-child limit".

In the interests of brevity, the rest of this note will refer to "child" and "children" as if those words included qualifying young persons.

2.96 *Paragraph (1)* provides that where a claimant is responsible for two or more children, the child element is to be available in respect of:

- any child to whom the exceptions (see below) for adoptions or non-parental caring arrangements in paras 3 and 4 of Sched 12 (including any extension of an adoption exception under para. 6 of Sch.12) apply: see subpara.(za).

  Children into whom these exceptions apply are excluded when determining the order of children under reg.24B: see reg.24B(2A);

- the first and second children (as determined in accordance with reg.24B): see subpara.(a) and para.(2); and

- any additional child:

  - who was born before 6 April 2017 and is therefore transitionally protected: see subpara.(b)(i) and para.(3); or
  - to whom the exceptions for multiple births or non-consensual conception in paras 2 and 5 of Sch.12: see subpara (b)(ii); or
  - who have the benefit of any continuing exception under para.6 of Sch.12 except for a continuing exception for adoption (which is already covered by subpara.(za)(ii)): see, again, subpara.(b)(ii).

2.97 Children to whom these exceptions apply are not excluded when determining the order of children under reg.24B. The exceptions therefore only apply to third and subsequent children because if a first or second child fell within the exception s/he would be eligible for a child element in any event under sub-para.(a).

Exceptions

2.98 These are set out in Sch.12. They apply in certain cases where there has been:

- a multiple birth (para.2);

- an adoption (para.3);
- a "non-parental caring arrangement" (para.4);
- non-consensual conception (para.5); or
- a previous exception where the claimant is a step-parent of the child.

In *R. (SC, CB and 8 children) v Secretary of State for Work and Pensions* [2018] EWHC 864 (Admin); [2018] 1 W.L.R. 5425, as well as the main, unsuccessful, challenge to the two-child limit, a successful challenge was made to the rationality of restricting the two-child limit exemptions to children born in a particular order, such that where a third child was born to a family which already had an adoptive child or a "non-parental caring arrangement" child, the third child would not be eligible for benefit. The Secretary of State did not seek to appeal against Ouseley J's finding that this was irrational, and remedied the position with reg.3 of the Universal Credit and Jobseeker's Allowance (Miscellaneous Amendments) Regulations 2018 (SI 2018/1129). However, that litigation, and the amending regulations, did not address the situation of households whose first or second child is the result of non-consensual conception or multiple birth. Those households benefit from exceptions only where the relevant child is the third or subsequent child, a situation which is capable of generating striking results. For example, a childless woman who was raped and consequently gave birth to twins would not receive benefit for any voluntarily conceived children she might subsequently bear.

In *AT v Secretary of State for Work and Pensions* [2023] UKUT 148 (AAC), the Upper Tribunal rejected a claim that this situation breached the Convention rights of a woman who had conceived two children non-consensually, followed by a third consensually. But it cited this commentary, and commented (at §30) that [a] 'judicial review challenge, alleging irrationality in the terms of the ordering provision, might well have a more promising prospect of success', but went on to state (at §31) 'these are not judicial review proceedings and the Upper Tribunal's jurisdiction is in any event limited in that regard'.

Multiple births

The child element is available for the third or subsequent child in a household where that child was one of two or more children born as the result of the same pregnancy, the claimant is the child's (non-adoptive) parent and is responsible for at least two of the children born as a result of that pregnancy and the child is not the first in order (*i.e.*, under reg.24B) of the children born as a result of that pregnancy (see Sch.12, para.2). 2.99

In plain English what this means is that the childcare element is included for all children born as a result of a multiple birth as long as the household did not already include two or more older children.

Adoption

The child element is available for an adoptive child (irrespective of how many other children the household already includes) except where, the claimant (or their partner) was the child's step parent immediately before the adoption or is the child's (non-adoptive) parent (see Sch.12, para.3). There are also exceptions in certain cases where the child has been adopted in or from another country. 2.100

Non-parental caring arrangements

The child element is available for the third or subsequent child in a household where the child's parent is herself (or himself) a child (not, in this case, a qualifying young person) and the claimant (or either joint claimant) is responsible for the child's parent: see para.4(1)(b). 2.101

There is a further exception where the claimant (or either joint claimant) is a "friend or family carer" as defined in para.4(2): see para.4(1)(a). That definition covers people who are responsible for a child but who are not (and whose partner, if any, is not) a parent or step parent of the child and have care of the child under a variety of different statutes, or who are entitled to guardian's allowance for the child or who have undertaken the care of the child in circumstances where it is likely that the child would otherwise be looked after by a local authority.

Non-consensual conception

2.102 This exception applies where the claimant is the child's parent and the Secretary of State (or, on appeal, a Tribunal) accepts that the child "is likely to have been conceived as a result of sexual intercourse to which the claimant did not agree by choice or did not have the freedom and capacity to agree by choice": see para.5(1)(a) and (b). It is also a condition that the claimant "is not living at the same address as the other party to the intercourse". The use of the present tense ("is not living") suggests that the exception can apply if the claimant lived with the other party at the time of the non-consensual conception but no longer does so. That is implicitly confirmed by para.5(5)(b) (see below).

There is a partial definition of the circumstances in which the claimant is to be treated as not having the freedom or capacity to agree by choice to sexual intercourse in para.5(2). They include (but are not limited to) circumstances in which (at the time of conception) the two parties were "personally connected", the other party was "repeatedly or continuously engaging in behaviour towards [the claimant] that was controlling or coercive" and that behaviour had a "serious effect" on the claimant.

Under para.5(5), the claimant and other party are "personally connected" if, at or around the time of the conception, the were in an intimate personal relationship with each other, or were living together as members of the same family having previously been in an intimate personal relationship with each other.

Under para.5(6), behaviour is to be regarded as having a "serious effect" on the claimant if it caused her to fear, on at least two occasions, that violence would be used against her or caused her serious alarm or distress which had a substantial adverse effect on her day-to-day activities.

The Secretary of State may accept the claimant's unsupported word that she is not living at the same address as the other party (para.5(4)). However, under para.5(3), he may only determine that the child is likely to have been conceived as a result of sexual intercourse to which the claimant did not agree by choice or did not have the freedom and capacity to agree by choice in two sets of circumstances.

The first set of circumstances apply if:

- there has been a conviction for rape or controlling or coercive behaviour in an intimate family relationship, or an analogous offence under the law of a country outside Great Britain; or
- an award of compensation has been made has been made under the Criminal Injuries Compensation Scheme in respect of a "relevant criminal injury" (as defined in para.5(7)); and

where the offence was committed, or the criminal injury caused, by the other party and resulted in the conception or diminished the claimant's freedom or capacity to agree by choice to the sexual intercourse that resulted in the conception (see para5(3)(b)).

The second set of circumstances apply if the claimant provides evidence from an "approved person" which demonstrates that the claimant has had contact with that, or another, approved person and her circumstances "are consistent with those of a person to whom" paras 5(1)(a) and (1)(b)(i) apply. "Approved person" is defined by para.5(7) as "a person of a description specified on a list approved by the Secretary of State ... and acting in their capacity as such". That list can be found in Form NCC1, *Support for a child conceived without your consent (England, Scotland and Wales)*, which those claiming to have conceived a child non-consensually must complete. The list reads:

- a healthcare professional in a Sexual Assault Referral Centre, or
- other healthcare professionals, such as a doctor, midwife, nurse or health visitor
- a registered social worker
- a specialist support worker from an approved organisation as listed on http://www.gov.uk/government/publications/support-for-a-child-conceived-without-your-consent

At the time of going to press, that website lists:

- members of The Survivors Trust;
- members of Rape Crisis England and Wales;
- Refuge;
- certain member organisations of Women's Aid Federation Northern Ireland and Women's Aid Federation of England.

Note that there is no restriction on when the claimant must have had contact with the approved person.

Under reg. 42 of the Transitional Provisions Regulations 2013, the Secretary of State may treat the requirement for evidence from an approved person as satisfied where the claimant has previously provided such evidence to HMRC for the purposes of the corresponding exception in relation to CTC.

Continuation of an existing exception for step-parents

Para.5 of Sch.12 applies where the claimant is the step-parent of a child ("A"); has previously had the benefit of an exception in a joint award of universal credit with one of A's parents; in that award the claimant was also responsible for one or more children born as a result of the same pregnancy as A; A is not the first in order (*i.e.*, under reg.24B) of the children born as a result of that pregnancy; and that award ended because the step-parent and parent ceased to be a couple, or in any other circumstances in which the assessment periods for a later award begin and end on the same day of each month as an earlier award under reg.21. 2.103

In those circumstances, if the step-parent continues to be responsible for A, under the new award, the childcare element continues to be available for A, even if they are the third or subsequent child in a household.

Finally, under reg.41 of the Transitional Provisions Regulations 2014, a similar exception applies where, within 6 months before the step-parent became entitled to universal credit, they had an award of CTC, IS or old style JSA in which an exception corresponding with one of those set out above applied in respect of A.

[1 Order of children and qualifying young persons

24B.—(1) Subject to to [2 paragraphs (2) and (2A)], the order of children or qualifying young persons in a claimant's household is to be determined by reference to [2 the date of birth of each child or qualifying young person for whom the claimant is responsible, taking the earliest date first.] 2.104

(2) In a case where—

(a) the date in relation to two or more children or qualifying young persons for whom the claimant is responsible (as determined under paragraph (1)) is the same date; [2 . . .]

(b) [2 . . .]

the order of those children or qualifying young persons (as between themselves only) in the claimant's household is the order determined by the Secretary of State that ensures that the amount mentioned in section 10(1) of the Act is available in respect of the greatest number of children or qualifying young persons.

[2 (2A) Any child or qualifying young person to whom regulation 24A(1)(za) applies is to be disregarded when determining the order of children and qualifying young persons under this regulation.]

(3) In this regulation and Schedule 12, "claimant" means a single claimant or either of joint claimants.]

AMENDMENTS

1. Social Security (Restrictions on Amounts for Children and Qualifying Young Persons) Amendment Regulations 2017 (SI 2017/376) reg.2(1) and (3) (April 6, 2017).

2. Universal Credit and Jobseeker's Allowance (Miscellaneous Amendments) Regulations 2018 (SI 2018/1129) reg.3(1) and (4) (November 28, 2018).

GENERAL NOTE

2.105 This regulation establishes the rules for determining the order of children and qualifying young persons ("children" as in the General Note to reg.24A) in a household for the purposes of the "two-child limit" in s.10(1A) WRA 2012 (see the General Note to reg.24A above) by allocating a date to each child for whom the claimant is responsible. The child with the earliest date is first in the order and so on.

The general rule in *para. (1)* is that where the claimant (or either joint claimant) is the child's parent or step-parent (other than by adoption) the date is the child's date of birth. Otherwise, the date is the date on which the claimant became responsible for the child or, if two joint claimants became responsible on different dates, the earlier of those dates.

2.106 *Paragraph (2)* establishes a qualification and an exception to that general rule. The qualification applies where the para.(1) rule determines the same date for two or more children. The exception applies where a claimant gives birth to a child less than 10 months after becoming responsible for another child as a result of a "non-parental caring arrangement" (see Sch.12, para.4). In either case, the Secretary of State must determine the order of those children so as to maximise the number of children for whom the child element is available.

Paragraph (2A) provides that children and young persons who fall within reg.24A(1)(za)—*i.e.*, those to whom the exceptions for adoptions or non-parental caring arrangements in paras 3 and 4 of Sched 12 (including any extension of an adoption exception under para.6 of Sch.12) apply.

Housing costs

The housing costs element

2.107 **25.**—(1) Paragraphs (2) to (4) specify for the purposes of section 11 of the Act (award of universal credit to include an amount in respect of any liability of a claimant to make payments in respect of the accommodation they occupy as their home)—

(a) what is meant by payments in respect of accommodation (see paragraph (2));
(b) the circumstances in which a claimant is to be treated as liable or not liable to make such payments (see paragraph (3));
(c) the circumstances in which a claimant is to be treated as occupying or not occupying accommodation and in which land used for the purposes of any accommodation is to be treated as included in the accommodation (see paragraph (4)).

(2) The payments in respect of accommodation must be—
(a) payments within the meaning of paragraph 2 of Schedule 1 ("rent payments");
(b) [1 . . .];
(c) payments within the meaning of paragraph 7 of that Schedule ("service charge payments").

(3) The circumstances of the liability to make the payments must be such that—
(a) the claimant (or either joint claimant)—
 (i) has a liability to make the payments which is on a commercial basis, or
 (ii) is treated under Part 1 of Schedule 2 as having a liability to make the payments; and
(b) none of the provisions in Part 2 of that Schedule applies to treat the claimant (or either joint claimant) as not being liable to make the payments.

(4) The circumstances in which the accommodation is occupied must be such that—
(a) the claimant is treated under Part 1 of Schedule 3 as occupying the accommodation as their home (including any land used for the purposes of the accommodation which is treated under that Part as included in the accommodation); and
(b) none of the provisions in Part 2 of that Schedule applies to treat the claimant as not occupying that accommodation.

(5) References in these Regulations—
(a) to the housing costs element are to the amount to be included in a claimant's award under section 11 of the Act;
(b) to a claimant who meets the payment condition, the liability condition or the occupation condition are, respectively, to any claimant in whose case the requirements of paragraph (2), (3) or (4) are met (and any reference to a claimant who meets all of the conditions specified in this regulation is to be read accordingly).

AMENDMENT

1. Loans for Mortgage Interest Regulations 2017 (SI 2017/725) reg.18 and Sch.5 para.5(a) (April 6, 2018).

DEFINITIONS

"the Act"—see reg.2.
"claimant"—see WRA 2012, s.40.

General Note

2.108 Section 11 of the WRA 2012 allows for universal credit to include "an amount in respect of any liability of a claimant to make payments in respect of the accommodation they occupy as their home". It also provides that the accommodation must be residential accommodation and must be in Great Britain, and that the accommodation can be the whole or part of a building and need not comprise separate and self-contained premises. All the other detailed rules relating to the housing costs element are in this regulation and reg.26 and in Schs 1–5 to these Regulations (made under the powers in s.11).

Paragraphs (2) to (4) contain the three basic conditions for the payment of a housing costs element: the payment condition (para.(2)), the liability condition (para.(3)) and the occupation condition (para.(4)).

Under para.(2) and Sch.1 the payments in respect of the accommodation must be "rent payments", or "service charges" (referred to hereafter as "eligible payments"). See the notes to Sch.1 for further discussion. Owner-occupier payments are not eligible, pursuant to the Loans for Mortgage Interest Regulations 2017 (SI 2017/725), but note that those Regulations make provision for such persons to claim loans instead.

Under para.(3) and Sch.2 the claimant (or either joint claimant) must be liable to make the eligible payments on a commercial basis, or be treated as liable to make them, and must not be treated as not liable to make them. See the notes to Sch.2.

Under para.(4) and Sch.3 the claimant (or each claimant in the case of joint claimants: s.40 of the WRA 2012) must be treated as occupying the accommodation as their home, and not be treated as not occupying it. See the notes to Sch.3.

Note:

- Paragraph 4 of Sch.4 which excludes any 16 or 17 year old who is a care leaver (defined in reg.8(4)) from entitlement to a housing costs element.
- The lower work allowance applies if an award includes a housing costs element (reg.22(2)(b)).
- People who live in "specified accommodation" (see Sch.1, paras 3(h) and 3A, together with the definition of "exempt accommodation" in para.1 of Sch.1) do not receive help with housing costs through universal credit but for the time being at least this will continue to be provided by way of housing benefit.

Amount of the housing costs element—renters and owner-occupiers

2.109 **26.**—(1) This regulation provides for the amount to be included in an award in respect of an assessment period in which the claimant meets all the conditions specified in regulation 25.

(2) Schedule 4 has effect in relation to any claimant where—

(a) the claimant meets all of those conditions; and

(b) the payments for which the claimant is liable are rent payments (whether or not service charge payments are also payable).

(3) Schedule 5 has effect in relation to any claimant where—

(a) the claimant meets all of those conditions; and

(b) the payments for which the claimant is liable are—

(i) [1 . . .]

(ii) service charge payments [1 . . .].

(4) Where both paragraphs (2) and (3) apply in relation to a claimant who occupies accommodation under a shared ownership tenancy—

(a) an amount is to be calculated under each of Schedules 4 and 5; and
(b) the amount of the claimant's housing cost element is the aggregate of those amounts.

(5) But where, in a case to which paragraph (4) applies, there is a liability for service charge payments, the amount in respect of those payments is to be calculated under Schedule 4.

(6) "Shared ownership tenancy" means—
(a) in England and Wales, a lease granted on payment of a premium calculated by reference to a percentage of the value of accommodation or the cost of providing it;
(b) in Scotland, an agreement by virtue of which the tenant of accommodation of which the tenant and landlord are joint owners is the tenant in respect of the landlord's interest in the accommodation or by virtue of which the tenant has the right to purchase the accommodation or the whole or part of the landlord's interest in it.

AMENDMENT

1. Loans for Mortgage Interest Regulations 2017 (SI 2017/725) reg.18 and Sch.5, para.5(b) and (c) (April 6, 2018).

DEFINITION

"claimant"—see WRA 2012 s.40.

GENERAL NOTE

This provides that the amount of the housing costs element for renters (whether or not service charges are also payable) is to be calculated in accordance with Sch.4 (para.(2)). The amount for owner-occupiers (whether or not service charges are also payable) is calculated in accordance with Sch.5 (para.(3)(a) and (b)(i)). Schedule 5 also applies if only service charges are payable (para.(3)(b)(ii)). If the claimant occupies the accommodation under a shared ownership tenancy (defined in para.(6)), the amount of the claimant's (or claimants') housing costs element is the aggregate of the amount calculated under Schs 4 and 5 (para.(4)); in the case of shared ownership any amount for service charges is calculated under Sch.4 (para.(5)). 2.110

Note reg.39(4) of the Decisions and Appeals Regulations 2013 which provides that if the Secretary of State considers that he does not have all the relevant information or evidence to decide what housing costs element to award, the decision will be made on the basis of the housing costs element that can immediately be awarded.

Particular needs or circumstances—capability for work

Award to include [1 LCWRA element]

27.—[1 (1) An award of universal credit is to include an amount in respect of the fact that a claimant has limited capability for work and work-related activity ("the LCWRA element").] 2.111

(2) The [1 amount of that element is] given in the table in regulation 36.

(3) Whether a claimant has limited capability for [1 . . .] work and work-related activity is determined in accordance with Part 5.

[1 (4) In the case of joint claimants, where each of them has limited capability for work and work-related activity, the award is only to include one LCWRA element.]

AMENDMENT

1. Employment and Support Allowance and Universal Credit (Miscellaneous Amendments and Transitional and Savings Provisions) Regulations 2017 (SI 2017/204) reg.4(1) and (4) (April 3, 2017).

DEFINITIONS

"claimant"—see WRA 2012 s.40.
"limited capability for work"—see WRA 2012 ss.40 and 37(1).
"limited capability for work-related activity"—see WRA 2012 ss.40 and 37(2).
"work-related activity"— see WRA 2012 s.40.

GENERAL NOTE

2.112 Section 12(2)(a) and (b) WRA 2012 allows for an award of universal credit to include an additional element if the claimant (or each claimant in the case of joint claimants: s.40 WRA 2012) has limited capability for work and work-related activity ("LCWRA"). Paras (1) and (2) establish that element at a rate (in 2023/24) of £390.06. See reg.29(4) where the claimant also qualifies for the carer element (note if it is the other member of the couple that qualifies for the carer element reg.29(4) will not apply).

If both joint claimants have LCWRA, only one additional element will be included (para.(4)).

See reg.36 for the amount of the LCWRA element and reg.28 for when it will be included.

The former LCW element was abolished with effect from April 3, 2017 by the Employment and Support Allowance and Universal Credit (Miscellaneous Amendments and Transitional and Savings Provisions) Regulations 2017 (SI 2017/204) subject to the transitional and savings provisions in Sch.2, Pt 2 to those Regulations (see below). In 2023/24, the transitional rate of the LCW element is £146.31: see art.32(2) of, and Sch.13 to, SI 2023/316. See pp.166-167 of the 2016/17 edition of Vol.V for the rules that apply if Sch.2. Pt 2 applies and both joint claimants are entitled to the LCW or LCWRA elements or one is entitled to the LCW element and the other is entitled to the LCWRA element.

LCW and LCWRA are assessed in accordance with Part 5 of these Regulations. Under reg.39(1) a claimant will have LCW if it has been decided on the basis of an assessment under these Regulations or Part 4 of the ESA Regulations 2013 that they have LCW, or if they are treated as having LCW because any of the circumstances in Sch.8 apply (see reg.39(6)). Similarly, under reg.40(1), a claimant will have LCWRA if it has been decided on the basis of an assessment under these Regulations that they have LCW and LCWRA or under Part 5 of the ESA Regulations 2013 that they have LCWRA, or if they are treated as having LCW and LCWRA because any of the circumstances in Sch.9 apply (see reg.40(5)).

See reg.41 as to when an assessment may be carried out.

Note regs 19 to 27 of the Universal Credit (Transitional Provisions) Regulations 2014 (see Pt IV of this Volume) which concern the transition from old style ESA, income support on the ground of incapacity for work or disability and other incapacity benefits to universal credit.

In relation to the effect of a determination of LCW (or not), see reg.40(1) and (2) of the Decisions and Appeals Regulations 2013 which is the equivalent of reg.10 of the Social Security and Child Support (Decisions and Appeals) Regulations 1999. See the notes to reg.10 in Vol.III of this series.

Period for which the [2 . . .] LCWRA element is not to be included

28.—(1) An award of universal credit is not to include the [2 . . .] LCWRA element until the beginning of the assessment period that follows the assessment period in which the relevant period ends. 2.113

(2) The relevant period is the period of three months beginning with—

(a) if regulation 41(2) applies (claimant with [1 monthly] earnings equal to or above the relevant threshold) the date on which the award of universal credit commences or, if later, the date on which the claimant applies for the [2 . . .] LCWRA element to be included in the award; or

(b) in any other case, the first day on which the claimant provides evidence of their having limited capability for work in accordance with the Medical Evidence Regulations.

(3) But where, in the circumstances referred to in paragraph (4), there has been a previous award of universal credit—

(a) if the previous award included the [2 . . .] LCWRA element, paragraph (1) does not apply; and

(b) if the relevant period in relation to that award has begun but not ended, the relevant period ends on the date it would have ended in relation to the previous award.

(4) The circumstances are where—

(a) immediately before the award commences, the previous award has ceased because the claimant ceased to be a member of a couple or became a member of a couple; or

(b) within the six months before the award commences, the previous award has ceased because the financial condition in section 5(1)(b) (or, if it was a joint claim, section 5(2)(b)) of the Act was not met.

(5) Paragraph (1) also does not apply if—

(a) the claimant is terminally ill; or

(b) the claimant—

(i) is entitled to an employment and support allowance that includes the support component [2 . . .], or

(ii) was so entitled on the day before the award of universal credit commenced and has ceased to be so entitled by virtue of section 1A of the Welfare Reform Act 2007 (duration of contributory allowance).

(6) [2 ...] [3 Paragraph (1) does not apply where a claimant has limited capability for work and it is subsequently determined that they have limited capability for work and work-related activity.]

(7) Where, by virtue of this regulation, the condition in section 5(1)(b) or 5(2)(b) of the Act is not met, the amount of the claimant's income (or, in the case of joint claimants, their combined income) is to be treated during the relevant period as such that the amount payable is the prescribed minimum (see regulation 17).

AMENDMENTS

1. Universal Credit and Miscellaneous Amendments Regulations 2015 (SI 2015/1754), reg.2(3) (November 4, 2015, or in the case of existing awards, the first assessment period beginning on or after November 4, 2015).

2. Employment and Support Allowance and Universal Credit (Miscellaneous Amendments and Transitional and Savings Provisions) Regulations 2017 (SI 2017/204) reg.4(1) and (5) (April 3, 2017).

3. Social Security and Universal Credit (Miscellaneous Amendments) Regulations 2023 (SI 2023/543) reg.4 (June 29, 2023).

Definitions

"the Act"—see reg.2.
"assessment period"—see WRA 2012 ss.40 and 7(2) and reg.21.
"claim"—see WRA 2012 s.40.
"claimant"—*ibid.*
"couple"—see WRA 2012 ss.39 and 40.
"employment and support allowance"—see reg.2.
"joint claimants"—see WRA 2012 s.40.
"LCW element"—see regs.2 and 27.
"LCWRA element"—*ibid.*
"limited capability for work"—see WRA 2012 ss.40 and 37(1).
"limited capability for work-related activity"—see WRA 2012 ss.40 and 37(2).
"Medical Evidence Regulations"—see reg.2.
"monthly earnings"—see regs 2 and 90(6).
"work-related activity"—see WRA 2012 s.40.

General Note

2.114 The LCWRA element will not normally be included until the beginning of the assessment period following the assessment period in which the "relevant period" ends (para.(1)), but see the exceptions below.

The "relevant period" is a three months waiting period, starting on the first day on which the claimant submits a medical certificate, or if reg.41(2) applies because the claimant has monthly earnings equal to or above the "relevant threshold" (16 × the national minimum national wage, converted to a monthly amount by multiplying by 52 and dividing by 12), the date on which the claimant's universal credit award starts, or the date the claimant applies for the LCWRA element to be included, if later (para.(2)).

A claimant does not have to serve the three months waiting period if they:

- were previously entitled to universal credit including the LCWRA element, or the three months waiting period for the LCWRA element in relation to the previous award had started but not ended, and the previous award ended immediately before the current award started because the claimant had stopped being or become a couple, or ended in the six months before the current award started because the income condition was not met (and note para.(7)). If the three month waiting period in the previous award had not been completed, the claimant will have to serve the remainder of it (paras.(3) and (4));
- are terminally ill (para.(5)(a)); or
- are entitled to ESA that includes the support component, or was so entitled on the day before the universal credit award started but the ESA ended because of the 52 week limit on entitlement to contributory ESA (para.(5)(b)).

A person who had been claiming ESA, but upon reaching pension age has to claim UC as part of a mixed-age couple, is not prima facie excepted under reg.28 from the three-month waiting period. But in *PR v Secretary of State Work and Pensions* [2023] UKUT 290 (AAC), the Upper Tribunal finds that omission to be unlawfully discriminatory, and decides that for such persons, s.3 of the Human Rights Act 1998 requires the waiting period to be disapplied.

In *JW v SSWP (UC)* [2022] UKUT 117 (AAC), the Upper Tribunal decides that a claimant who had been entitled to an award of ESA including the support component, and then claims UC, can avoid the three month waiting period even if there is a gap between receipt of the two benefits, provided the ending of ESA entitlement was not due to the claimant ceasing to meet the support component criteria:

> "[14] … the various exceptional circumstances set out in regulation 28(3)–(5) do not represent a complete code of exemptions from the normal three-month rule. Indeed, there is a common thread between the apparently disparate exceptions provided for by paragraphs (3)–(5) inclusive. None of these exceptions deals with the situation in which a claimant was previously entitled to a legacy benefit (i.e. one of those means-tested social security benefits that is in the process of being phased out by the introduction of Universal Credit). The situation of claimants entitled to legacy benefits (and to national insurance credits in default of such entitlement) is governed by the Universal Credit (Transitional Provisions) Regulations 2014."

With effect from June 29, 2023 reg.4 of the Social Security and Universal Credit (Miscellaneous Amendments) Regulations 2023 (SI 2023/543) inserts a new para.6:

> "(6) Paragraph (1) does not apply where a claimant has limited capability for work and it is subsequently determined that they have limited capability for work and work-related activity."

Particular needs or circumstances–carers

Award to include the carer element

29.–(1) An award of universal credit is to include an amount ("the carer element") specified in the table in regulation 36 where a claimant has regular and substantial caring responsibilities for a severely disabled person, but subject to [3 paragraphs (2) to (6)] [1 and [3 section 70] of the Contributions and Benefits Act (entitlement by different persons to the carer element and to carer's allowance [3 or carer support payment] in respect of the same severely disabled person]. 2.115

(2) In the case of joint claimants, an award is to include the carer element for both joint claimants if they both qualify for it, but only if they are not caring for the same severely disabled person.

(3) Where two or more persons have regular and substantial caring responsibilities for the same severely disabled person, an award of universal credit may only include the carer element in respect of one them and that is the one they jointly elect or, in default of election, the one the Secretary of State determines.

[2 (4) Where an amount would, apart from this paragraph, be included in an award in relation to a claimant by virtue of paragraphs (1) to (3), and the claimant has limited capability for work and work-related activity (and, in the case of joint claimants, the LCWRA element has not been included in respect of the other claimant), only the LCWRA element may be included in respect of the claimant.]

[3 (5) Paragraph (6) applies where—

(a) a person (A)—

  (i) has, or would have but for regulation 5(3) of the Carer's Assistance (Carer Support Payment) (Scotland) Regulations 2023, an entitlement to carer support payment; or

  (ii) has, or would have but for section 70 of the Contributions and Benefits Act, an entitlement to carer's allowance in respect of which the Scottish Ministers have the power to make decisions; and

(b) another person (B) has, or would have but for this regulation, an entitlement to the carer element of universal credit for the same day in respect of the same severely disabled person; and

(c) section 70 of the Contributions and Benefits Act does not apply to the decision in respect of B's entitlement to universal credit.

(6) The universal credit award of B shall not include a carer element unless—

(a) A and B jointly elect that B shall have entitlement to the carer element and that A shall not have an entitlement mentioned in paragraph (5)(a) for that day in respect of that severely disabled person; or

(b) in default of such an election, the Secretary of State is satisfied, following consultation with the Scottish Ministers, that—

(i) Scottish Ministers have decided, or will decide, that A shall not have an entitlement mentioned in paragraph (5)(a); and

(ii) B shall have a carer element included in their award of universal credit, for that day in respect of that severely disabled person.]

AMENDMENTS

1. Universal Credit and Miscellaneous Amendments Regulations 2015 (SI 2015/1754), reg.13 (November 4, 2015).

2. Employment and Support Allowance and Universal Credit (Miscellaneous Amendments and Transitional and Savings Provisions) Regulations 2017 (SI 2017/204) reg.4(1) and (6) (April 3, 2017).

3. Carer's Assistance (Carer Support Payment) (Scotland) Regulations 2023 (Consequential Amendments) Order 2023 (SI 2023/1218) art.23 (November 19, 2023).

DEFINITIONS

"carer element"—see reg.2.
"claimant"—see WRA 2012 s.40.
"disabled"—*ibid.*
"joint claimants"—see WRA 2012 s.40.
"LCW element"—see regs 2 and 27.
"LCWRA element"—*ibid.*
"limited capability for work"—see WRA 2012 ss.40 and 37(1).
"limited capability for work-related activity"—see WRA 2012 ss.40 and 37(2).
"regular and substantial caring responsibilities for a severely disabled person"—see regs 2 and 30.
"severely disabled"—*ibid.*
"work"—*ibid.*
"work-related activity"—*ibid.*

GENERAL NOTE

2.116 The carer element (£185.86 per assessment period: see reg.36) is included in the maximum amount if a claimant has "regular and substantial caring responsibilities for a severely disabled person" (as defined in reg.30): para.(1). Where there is a joint claim, and both parties have regular and substantial caring responsibilities for a severely disabled person, the amount is included twice, as long as they are caring for different severely disabled people: para.(2). However, if awards would also include the LCWRA element (see regs 27 and 28) as well as the carer element, then only the LCWRA element is included, unless (in the case of a joint claim), the LCWRA element has been included in respect of the other member of the couple (see reg.27(4)). This reflects the fact that, at £185.86 per assessment period, the carer element is not as high as the LCWRA element at £390.06.

Paragraph (3) governs the situation where two or more people have regular and substantial caring responsibilities for the same person. Only one of those carers can have the carer element included in an award of universal credit. They can agree between them which it is to be but, if they do not do so, the Secretary of State will decide. Under reg.50(2) and Sch.3, para.4 of the Decisions and Appeals Regulations 2013, there is no right of appeal against the Secretary of State's decision on that point.

Meaning of "regular and substantial caring responsibilities for a severely disabled person"

30.—[1 (1) For the purposes of Part 1 of the Act and these Regulations, a person has regular and substantial caring responsibilities for a severely disabled person if— 2.117

(a) they satisfy the conditions for entitlement to a carer's allowance or would do so but for the fact that—
 (i) their earnings have exceeded the limit prescribed for the purposes of that allowance; or
 (ii) they are—
  (aa) resident, or treated as resident, in Scotland; or
  (bb) resident outside of Great Britain and have a genuine and sufficient link to Scotland; or

(b) they are entitled to carer support payment.]

(2) [1 Paragraph (1)(a)] applies whether or not the person has made a claim for a carer's allowance.

(3) But a person does not have regular and substantial caring responsibilities for a severely disabled person if the person derives earned income from those caring responsibilities.

[1 (4) For the purposes of paragraph (1), "sufficient" has the meaning given in paragraph 3 of Schedule 1 to the Carer's Assistance (Carer Support Payment) (Scotland) Regulations 2023.]

AMENDMENT

1. Carer's Assistance (Carer Support Payment) (Scotland) Regulations 2023 (Consequential Amendments) Order 2023 (SI 2023/1218) art.23 (November 19, 2023).

DEFINITIONS

"carer's allowance"—see reg.2.
"disabled"—see WRA 2012 s.40.
"prescribed"—see WRA 2012 s.40.
"severely disabled"—see WRA 2012 s.40.

GENERAL NOTE

A claimant has regular and substantial caring responsibilities for a severely disabled person if he or she satisfies the conditions of entitlement to carer's allowance apart from the general earnings limit (see Vol.I) as long as he or she does not have earned income from those responsibilities. It is not necessary for the claimant to have claimed carer's allowance (para.(2)): it is enough that they would meet the conditions of entitlement if they did. 2.118

Particular needs or circumstances—childcare costs

Award to include childcare costs element

31. An award of universal credit is to include an amount in respect of childcare costs ("the childcare costs element") in respect of an assessment period in which the claimant meets both— 2.119

(a) the work condition (see regulation 32); and
(b) the childcare costs condition (see regulation 33).

DEFINITION

"childcare costs element"—see reg.2.

General Note

2.120 The childcare costs element is included in the maximum amount if a claimant satisfies both the work condition (reg.32) and the childcare costs condition (reg.33). By reg.34, the amount of the element is 85 per cent of the charges incurred by the claimant for "relevant childcare" up to a maximum of £646.35 per assessment period for a single child (£951 from June 28, 2023) or £1,108.04 for two or more children (£1,630 from June 28, 2023) (reg.36). The childcare costs element is not reduced under the benefit cap: see reg.81(1) and (2).

The work condition

2.121 **32.**—(1) The work condition is met in respect of an assessment period if—

(a) the claimant is in paid work or has an offer of paid work that is due to start before the end of the next assessment period; and

(b) if the claimant is a member of a couple (whether claiming jointly or as a single person), the other member is either in paid work or is unable to provide childcare because that person—

(i) has limited capability for work,

(ii) has regular and substantial caring responsibilities for a severely disabled person, or

(iii) is temporarily absent from the claimant's household.

(2) For the purposes of meeting the work condition in relation to an assessment period a claimant is to be treated as being in paid work if—

(a) the claimant has ceased paid work—

(i) in that assessment period,

(ii) in the previous assessment period, or

(iii) if the assessment period in question is the first or second assessment period in relation to an award, in that assessment period or in the month immediately preceding the commencement of the award; or

(b) the claimant is receiving statutory sick pay, statutory maternity pay, [2 . . .] statutory paternity pay, [2 . . .] statutory adoption pay [1, statutory shared parental pay] [3, statutory parental bereavement pay] or a maternity allowance.

Amendments

1. Shared Parental Leave and Statutory Shared Parental Pay (Consequential Amendments to Subordinate Legislation) Order 2014 (SI 2014/3255) art.28(1) and (3)(c) (December 31, 2014).

2. Shared Parental Leave and Statutory Shared Parental Pay (Consequential Amendments to Subordinate Legislation) Order 2014 (SI 2014/3255) art.28(1) and (3)(a) and (b) (April 5, 2015). The amendments are subject to the transitional provision in art.35 (see below).

3. Parental Bereavement Leave and Pay (Consequential Amendments to Subordinate Legislation) Regulations 2020 (SI 2020/354) reg.28(1) and (3) (April 6, 2020).

Definitions

"assessment period"—see WRA 2012, ss.40 and 7(2).
"claimant"—see WRA 2012, s.40.
"maternity allowance"—see reg.2.
"paid work"—ibid.

"single person"—see WRA 2012, ss.40 and 1(2)(a).
"statutory adoption pay"—see reg.2.
"statutory maternity pay"—*ibid.*
"statutory paternity pay"—*ibid.*
"statutory shared parental pay"—*ibid.*
"statutory sick pay"—*ibid.*
"work"—see WRA 2012, s.40.

General Note

A claimant satisfies the work condition if she or he is in paid work or has an offer of paid work that is due to start before the end of the next assessment period: para.(1)(a). For joint claims (or in cases where by a member of a couple claims as a single person under reg.3(3)) there is an additional condition that the other member is either in paid work or is unable to provide childcare for one of the reasons set out in heads (i)–(iii). Claimants are treated as if they were still in paid work if they have stopped work within the periods set out in para.(2)(a) or if they are receiving statutory sick pay, statutory maternity pay, statutory paternity pay, statutory shared parental pay, statutory adoption pay (see Vol.IV) or a maternity allowance (see Vol.I). 2.122

The childcare costs condition

33.—(1) The childcare costs condition is met in respect of an assessment period if— 2.123

[1 (za) the claimant has paid charges for relevant childcare that are attributable to that assessment period (see regulation 34A) and those charges have been reported to the Secretary of State [2 before the end of the assessment period that follows the assessment period in which they were paid];]

(a) [1 the charges are in respect of]—
  (i) a child, or
  (ii) a qualifying young person who has not reached the 1st September following their 16th birthday,

for whom the claimant is responsible; and

(b) the charges are for childcare arrangements—
  (i) that are to enable the claimant to take up paid work or to continue in paid work, or
  (ii) where the claimant is treated as being in paid work by virtue of regulation 32(2), that are to enable the claimant to maintain childcare arrangements that were in place when the claimant ceased paid work or began to receive those benefits.

[1 (2) The late reporting of charges for relevant childcare may be accepted in the same circumstances as late notification of a change of circumstances may be accepted under regulation 36 of the Universal Credit, Personal Independence Payment, Jobseeker's Allowance and Employment and Support Allowance (Decisions and Appeals) Regulations 2013 and, in such cases, subject to regulation 34A below, all or part of any such charges may be taken into account in any assessment period to which they relate.]

[2 (3) For the purposes of paragraph (2), "the relevant notification period" in regulation 36 of the Universal Credit, Personal Independence Payment, Jobseeker's Allowance and Employment and Support Allowance (Decisions and Appeals) Regulations 2013 means a period of time ending on the last day of the assessment period that follows the assessment period in which the charges for relevant childcare were paid.]

AMENDMENT

1. Universal Credit (Digital Service) Amendment Regulations 2014 (SI 2014/2887) reg.2(1) and (2) (November 26, 2014). The amendment is subject to the saving provision in reg.5 of SI 2014/2887 (see pp.799–800 of the 2020/21 edition of Vol.V of this series).

2. Universal Credit (Childcare Costs and Minimum Income Floor) (Amendment) Regulations 2019 (SI 2019/1249) reg.2 (October 3, 2019).

DEFINITIONS

"assessment period"—see WRA 2012, ss.40 and 7(2).
"claimant"—see WRA 2012, s.40.
"paid work"—see reg.2.
"relevant childcare"—see reg.35.
"responsible for a child or qualifying young person"—see regs 2, 4 and 4A.

GENERAL NOTE

2.124 A claimant satisfies the childcare costs condition in the circumstances set out in para.(1)(za), (a) and (b). Those paragraphs are cumulative. All three must apply before the childcare costs condition is satisfied.

Paragraph (1)(za) applies if a claimant has paid charges for relevant childcare (as defined in reg.35) that are attributable to the assessment period under consideration and, subject to para.(2), have been reported to the Secretary of State before the end of that period. Reg.34A governs the assessment period to which charges are attributable.

In *Secretary of State for Work and Pensions v Salvato* [2021] EWCA Civ 1482; [2022] P.T.S.R. 366, the Court of Appeal allowed an appeal from a decision of the High Court ([2021] EWHC 102 (Admin); [2021] P.T.S.R. 1067 (Chamberlain J)) that the reg.33(1)(za) "Proof of Payment rule" (i.e. the requirement that the claimant should actually have paid childcare costs, as opposed to merely incurring a liability to do so, before the childcare costs element can be paid) was irrational and unlawfully discriminatory contrary to art.14, taken together with art.8 of, and with art.1 of the First Protocol to, the European Convention on Human Rights. The Court of Appeal decided that the "Proof of Payment rule" was rational and justified.

2.125 *Paragraph (1)(a)* applies if the charges are in respect of a child or a qualifying young person for whom she the claimant is responsible. A qualifying young person ceases to count for these purposes on September 1st following his or her 16th birthday.

2.126 *Paragraph (1)(b)* applies if the charges are for childcare arrangements to enable the claimant to work or to maintain childcare arrangements that were in place before a period when she or he is not in paid work but is treated by reg.32(2) as if she or he were.

Under para.(2) the Secretary of State may accept childcare charges that are reported after the end of the assessment period after the end of the assessment period to which they are attributable, in the same circumstances as any late notification of a change of circumstances may be accepted under reg.36 of the Decisions and Appeals Regulations 2013 (see Vol.III of this series).

Amount of childcare costs element

2.127 **34.**—(1) The amount of the childcare costs element for an assessment period is the lesser of—

[1 (a) [2 85%] of the charges paid for relevant childcare that are attributable to that assessment period; or]

(b) the maximum amount specified in the table in regulation 36.

(2) In determining the amount of charges paid for relevant childcare, there is to be left out of account any amount—

(a) that the Secretary of State considers excessive having regard to the extent to which the claimant (or, if the claimant is a member of a couple, the other member) is engaged in paid work; or

(b) that is met or reimbursed by an employer or some other person or is covered by other relevant support.

[1 (3) "Other relevant support" means payments out of funds provided by the Secretary of State or by Scottish or Welsh Ministers in connection with the claimant's participation in work-related activity or training but does not include payments made by the Secretary of State where—

(a) the claimant—

(i) has taken up, or is due to take up, paid work; or

(ii) has increased, or is due to increase, their hours of paid work;

(b) the claimant is required to pay the charges for relevant childcare before they receive a payment of universal credit that reflects the increase in the claimant's earned income as a result of sub-paragraph (a); and

(c) if the payment is not taken into account in determining the charges paid by the claimant for childcare the claimant will be less likely to continue in paid work or maintain the increase in hours of paid work.]

AMENDMENT

1. Universal Credit (Digital Service) Amendment Regulations 2014 (SI 2014/2887) reg.2(1) and (3) (November 26, 2014). The amendment is subject to the saving provision in reg.5 of SI 2014/2887 (see pp.799–800 of the 2020/21 edition of Vol.V of this series).

2. Universal Credit and Miscellaneous Amendments Regulations 2015 (SI 2015/1754) reg.6 (Assessment periods beginning on or after April 11, 2016).

3. Universal Credit (Childcare) (Amendment) Regulations 2023 (SI 2023/593) reg.2 (June 28, 2023).

DEFINITIONS

"childcare costs element"—see reg.2.
"claimant"—see WRA 2012, s.40.
"couple"—see WRA 2012, ss.39 and 40.
"relevant childcare"—see reg.2 and reg.35.
"work"—see WRA 2012, s.40.

GENERAL NOTE

Paragraph (1): See the note to reg.31. 2.128

The effect of the saving provision in reg.5 of SI 2014/2887 is that the amendment to para.(1) with effect from November 26, 2014 (but not the increase in the rate at which childcare costs are met from 70% to 85% with effect from April 11, 2016) only applies in "Full Service" (or "Digital Service") cases (see *Universal Credit—An Introduction* above). For the text of para.(1) as it continues to apply in "Live Service" cases (except for the change from 70% to 85%), see p.150 of the 2013/14 edition.

Paragraphs (2) and (3): Charges for relevant childcare are not taken into account to the extent that the Secretary of State considers them excessive; if they are reimbursed by the claimant's employer or some other person; or if they are covered by 2.129

"other relevant support" (as defined in para.(3)) paid to claimants participating in work-related activity or training.

[1 Charges attributable to an assessment period

2.130 **34A.**—(1) Charges paid for relevant childcare are attributable to an assessment period where—

(a) those charges are paid in that assessment period for relevant childcare in respect of that assessment period; or
(b) those charges are paid in that assessment period for relevant childcare in respect of a previous assessment period; or
(c) those charges were paid in either of the two previous assessment periods for relevant childcare in respect of that assessment period.

(2) For the purposes of paragraph (1)(c), where a claimant pays charges for relevant childcare in advance, the amount which they have paid in respect of any assessment period is to be calculated as follows:

Step 1

Take the total amount of the advance payment (leaving out of account any amount referred to in regulation 34(2)).

Step 2

Apply the formula—

$$\left(\frac{PA}{D}\right) \times AP$$

Where—

PA is the amount resulting from step 1;

D is the total number of days covered by the payment referred to in step 1, and

AP is the number of days covered by the payment which also fall within the assessment period in question.

(3) In this regulation, a reference to an assessment period in which charges are paid, or in respect of which charges are paid, includes any month preceding the commencement of the award that begins on the same day as each assessment period in relation to a claimant's current award.

AMENDMENT

1. Universal Credit (Digital Service) Amendment Regulations 2014 (SI 2014/2887) reg.2(1) and (4) (November 26, 2014). The amendment is subject to the saving provision in reg.5 of SI 2014/2887 (see pp.799–800 of the 2020/21 edition of Vol.V of this series).

DEFINITIONS

"assessment period"—see WRA 2012 ss.40 and 7(2) and reg.21.
"claimant"—see WRA 2012 s.40.
"relevant childcare"—see reg.2 and reg.35.

GENERAL NOTE

2.131 Reg.34A governs when childcare charges are attributable to an assessment period for the purposes of reg.33(1)(za).

Para.(1) provides that charges are attributable either:

- to the assessment period in which they are paid if they are for relevant childcare in that period or (in arrears) for relevant childcare in a previous assessment period (sub-paras (a) and (b)) including, in the latter case, periods before the start of the award of universal credit (para.(3)); or

- to the assessment period in which the relevant childcare is provided if they were paid in advance in one of the two previous assessment periods (sub-para.(1)(c)). In practice, this means that childcare charges can be paid at least two months, and sometimes up to three months, in advance. Again, the previous periods can be before the start of the award of universal credit (para.(3)).

Para.(2) sets out the formula for deciding the amount of childcare charges paid in advance under para.(1)(c) that is to be attributed to an assessment period. The full amount of the advance payment (other than sums that are to be left out of account under reg.34(2) because they are excessive or are met or reimbursed by another person) is divided it by the number of days to which it relates, to produce a daily rate, and then multiplied by the number of days in the assessment period.

Meaning of "relevant childcare"

35.—(1) "Relevant childcare" means any of the care described in paragraphs (2) to (5) other than care excluded by paragraph (7) or (8). 2.132

(2) Care provided in England for a child—

(a) by a person registered under Part 3 of the Childcare Act 2006; or

[1(b) by or under the direction of the proprietor of a school as part of the school's activities—

(i) out of school hours, where a child has reached compulsory school age, or

(ii) at any time, where a child has not yet reached compulsory school age; or]

[1(c) by a domiciliary care provider registered with the Care Quality Commission in accordance with the requirements of the Health and Social Care Act 2008.]

(3) Care provided in Scotland for a child—

(a) by a person in circumstances in which the care service provided by the person consists of child minding or of day care of children within the meaning of [1 schedule 12 to the Public Services Reform (Scotland) Act 2010 and is registered under Part 5 of that Act; or]

(b) by a childcare agency where the care service consists of or includes supplying, or introducing to persons who use the service, childcarers within the meaning of [1 paragraph 5 of schedule 12 to the Public Services Reform (Scotland) Act 2010; or]

(c) by a local authority in circumstances in which the care service provided by the local authority consists of child minding or of day care of children within the meaning of [1 schedule 12 to the Public Services Reform (Scotland) Act 2010 and is registered under Part 5 of that Act].

(4) Care provided in Wales for a child—

(a) by a person registered under Part 2 of the Children and Families (Wales) Measure 2010;

(b) in circumstances in which, but for articles 11, 12 or 14 of the Child Minding and Day Care Exceptions (Wales) Order 2010, the care would be day care for the purposes of Part 2 of the Children and Families (Wales) Measure 2010;

(c) by a childcare provider approved in accordance with a scheme made by the National Assembly for Wales under section 12(5) of the Tax Act 2002 [3 or made by the Welsh Ministers under section 60 (promotion etc. of well-being) of the Government of Wales Act 2006];

[1(d) out of school hours, by a school on school premises or by a local authority;]

[1 (e) by a person who is employed, or engaged under a contract for services, to provide care and support by the provider of a domiciliary support service within the meaning of Part 1 of the Regulation and Inspection of Social Care (Wales) Act 2016; or]

(f) by a foster parent in relation to the child (other than one whom the foster parent is fostering) in circumstances in which the care would be child minding or day care for the purposes of Part 2 of the Children and Families (Wales) Measure 2010 but for the fact that the child is over the age of the children to whom that Measure applies.

(5) Care provided anywhere outside Great Britain by a childcare provider approved by an organisation accredited by the Secretary of State.

[1 (5A) In paragraph (2)(b), "school" means a school that Her Majesty's Chief Inspector of Education, Children's Services and Skills is, or may be, required to inspect.]

(6) In paragraphs (2)(b) and (4)(d)—

(a) "proprietor", in relation to a school, means—

(i) the governing body incorporated under section 19 of the Education Act 2002, or

(ii) if there is no such governing body, the person or body of persons responsible for the management of the school; and

(b) "school premises" means premises that may be inspected as part of an inspection of the school.

(7) The following are not relevant childcare—

(a) care provided for a child by a close relative of the child, wholly or mainly in the child's home; and

(b) care provided by a person who is a foster parent of the child.

(8) Care is not within paragraph (2)(a) if it is provided in breach of a requirement to register under Part 3 of the Childcare Act 2006.

(9) In this regulation "child" includes a qualifying young person mentioned in regulation 33(1)(a)(ii).

AMENDMENT

1. Social Security (Miscellaneous Amendments) (No.2) Regulations 2013 (SI 2013/1508) reg.3(1) and (6) (July 29, 2013).

2. Social Security and Child Support (Regulation and Inspection of Social Care (Wales) Act 2016) (Consequential Provision) Regulations 2018 (SI 2018/228) reg.14 (April 2, 2018).

3. Universal Credit (Childcare in Wales) (Amendment) Regulations 2021 (SI 2021/228) reg.2 (March 25, 2021).

DEFINITIONS

"child"—see WRA 2012 s.40 and para.(9).

"foster parent"—see reg.2.

"local authority"—ibid.

"qualifying young person"—see WRA 2012 s.40 and 10(5) and regs 2 and 5.

GENERAL NOTE

Under reg.33(1)(a), charges only count for the purposes of the childcare costs condition if they are paid for "relevant childcare". Regulation 35 defines that phrase. By para.(1) care is "relevant childcare" if it falls within paras (2) to (5) unless it is excluded by paras (7) or (8). 2.133

Paragraphs (2)–(5): The details differ as between England, Scotland and Wales but the rule may be summarised as being that to qualify as relevant childcare, the care must be provided by a person authorised or approved by an organ of the state to do so. In England and Wales, it can also be provided by the "proprietor" of a "school" on "school premises". The words and phrase in quotation marks are defined in paras (5A) and (6). 2.134

Paragraphs (7) and (8): Care is not relevant childcare if it is provided by an unregistered childminder (para.(8)), by a foster parent (para.(7)(b) or by a close relative of the child (or qualifying young person: see para.(9)) wholly or mainly in the child's own home (para.(7)(a)). 2.135

General

Table showing amounts of elements

36.—(1) The amounts of the standard allowance, the child element, the [3 LCWRA element] and the carer element (which are all fixed amounts) and the maximum amounts of the childcare costs element are given in the following table. 2.136

(2) The amount of the housing costs element is dealt with in regulation 26.

(3) In the case of an award where the claimant is a member of a couple, but claims as a single person, the amounts are those shown in the table for a single claimant.

Element	Amount for each assessment period
Standard allowance—	
single claimant aged under 25	[5 £311.68]
single claimant aged 25 or over	[5 £393.45]
joint claimants both aged under 25	[5 £489.23]
joint claimants where either is aged 25 or over	[5 £617.60]
Child element—	
[5 . . .]	[5 . . .]
[5 each] child or qualifying young person	[5 £287.92]
Additional amount for disabled child or qualifying young person—	
lower rate	[5 £156.11]
higher rate	[5 £487.58]

[3 LCWRA element]—	
[3...]	[3 . . .]
limited capability for work and work-related activity	[5 £416.19]
Carer element	[5 £198.31]
Childcare costs element—	
maximum amount for one child	[5 £1,014.68]
maximum amount for two or more children	[5 £1,734.39]

AMENDMENTS

1. Welfare Benefits Up-rating Order 2015 (SI 2015/30) art.13 and Sch. 5 (Assessment periods beginning on or after April 6, 2015).

2. Universal Credit and Miscellaneous Amendments Regulations 2015 (SI 2015/1754) reg.6 (Assessment periods beginning on or after April 11, 2016).

3. Employment and Support Allowance and Universal Credit (Miscellaneous Amendments and Transitional and Savings Provisions) Regulations 2017 (SI 2017/204) reg.4(1) and (7) (April 3, 2017).

4. Welfare Reform and Work Act 2016 s.14(5)(b) (April 6, 2017).

5. Social Security Benefits Up-rating Order 2024 (SI 2024/242) art.32(3) and Sch.13 (assessment periods beginning on or after April 8, 2024).

DEFINITIONS

"assessment period"—see WRA 2012, ss.40 and 7(2).
"carer element"—see reg.2.
"child element"—*ibid.*
"childcare costs element"—see reg.2.
"claimant"—see WRA 2012, s.40.
"disabled"—*ibid.*
"housing costs element"—see regs 2 and 25.
"joint claimants"—see WRA 2012, s.40.
"LCWRA element"—see regs 2 and 27.
"limited capability for work"—see WRA 2012, ss.40 and 37(1).
"limited capability for work-related activity"—see WRA 2012, ss.40 and 37(2).
"qualifying young person"—see WRA 2012, s.40 and 10(5) and regs 2 and 5.
"single claimant"—see WRA 2012, s.40.

GENERAL NOTE

2.137 The amount of each element in the universal credit calculation is prescribed by the table (other than the housing costs element, the amount of which is prescribed by reg.26(2)). Para.(3) provides that where a member of a couple claims as a single person (i.e., under reg.3(3)), it is the amounts for a single person that apply.

For the rules about entitlement to each of the elements, see the notes to the earlier regulations in Pt 4.

The amounts in the table have been up-rated multiple times since the first edition of this volume. The current amounts are as set out above and, with two exceptions, apply from April 8, 2024.

To obtain a precise history of uprating in Universal Credit, consult previous volumes of this commentary and the mid-year supplements. However, in broad terms note that there have been two major departures from the principle of annual uprating.

First, on March 16, 2016, s.11 and Sch.1 of the Welfare Reform and Work Act 2016 came into force. As a result the following amounts were frozen at their 2015/16 levels for four tax years and were not up-rated again until April 6, 2020:

- all the rates of the standard allowance (para.1(j) of Sch.1 to the 2016 Act);
- the lower rate of the additional amount for a disabled child or qualifying young person (para.1(k)); and
- the LCW element (para.1(l)).

Second, the original 2013/14 childcare costs element rates of £532.29 and £912.50 were not increased until April 11, 2016; they were not increased again until April 9, 2018; and then were not increased again until June 28, 2023 (but then, they were increased at the same time as the other rates from April 8, 2024).

The amounts for the child element, the higher rate of the additional amount for a disabled child or qualifying young person, the LCWRA element, the carer element, the childcare costs element, and the housing costs element were not subject to the four-year freeze. However, they were not up-rated for 2016/17 as the Secretary of State decided that those amounts had maintained their value in relation to prices as measured by the Consumer Prices Index over the 12 month period ending September 2015 (which had showed negative inflation of 0.1%): see para.4.2 of the Explanatory Memorandum to SI 2016/230.

Before April 6, 2017 the rate of the child element was higher for the first child or qualifying young person for whom the claimant was responsible. Under reg.43 of the Transitional Provisions Regulations 2014, the higher rate continues to apply where the claimant is responsible for a child or qualifying young person born before April 6, 2017. In 2024/25, the transitionally protected higher rate is £333.33.

Run-on after a death

37. In calculating the maximum amount of an award where any of the following persons has died— 2.138

(a) in the case of a joint award, one member of the couple;

(b) a child or qualifying young person for whom a claimant was responsible; [1 . . .]

(c) in the case of a claimant who had regular and substantial caring responsibilities for a severely disabled person, that person [1; or

(d) a person who was a non-dependant within the meaning of paragraph 9(2) of Schedule 4,]

the award is to continue to be calculated as if the person had not died for the assessment period in which the death occurs and the following two assessment periods.

AMENDMENT

1. Universal Credit and Miscellaneous Amendments Regulations 2014 (SI 2014/597) reg.2(1) and (3) (April 28, 2014).

DEFINITIONS

"assessment period"—see WRA 2012, ss.40 and 7(2).
"claimant"—see WRA 2012, s.40.
"couple"—see WRA 2012, ss.39 and 40.
"regular and substantial caring responsibilities for a severely disabled person"—see regs 2 and 30.

"responsible for a child or qualifying young person"—see regs 2, 4 and 4A.
"severely disabled"—see WRA 2012, s.40.

GENERAL NOTE

2.139 Where a joint claimant, a child or qualifying young person for whom a claimant is responsible, a severely disabled person for whom a claimant had regular and substantial caring responsibilities or, from April 28, 2014, a non-dependant dies, the award of universal credit runs-on (i.e., it continues as if that person had not died) for the assessment period in which the death occurred and the following two assessment periods.

PART 5

CAPABILITY FOR WORK OR WORK-RELATED ACTIVITY

Introduction

2.140 **38.** The question whether a claimant has limited capability for work, or for work and work-related activity, is to be determined for the purposes of the Act and these Regulations in accordance with this Part.

DEFINITIONS

"the Act"—see reg.2.
"work-related activity"—see WRA 2012, s.40.

GENERAL NOTE

2.141 The question of whether a person has limited capability for work ("LCW") or limited capability for work and work-related activity ("LCWRA") is relevant for three reasons. Firstly, if a person has LCW or LCWRA, it affects the work requirements that can or cannot be imposed on him/her (see ss.19(2)(a) and 21(1)(a) WRA 2012). Secondly, it will entitle him/her to an additional element as part of their universal credit (see regs 27–28), although note reg.29(4) where the claimant is also eligible for the carer element. Thirdly, it determines which level of the lower or higher work allowance (if applicable) applies (see reg. 22).

Note also that the minimum age for claiming universal credit is 16 (not 18) if a person has LCW or is waiting for a work capability assessment and has submitted a medical certificate stating that they are not fit for work (see reg.8(1)(a) and (b)). In addition, if a claimant's universal credit award includes the LCWRA element, or the claimant (or either or both joint claimants) is receiving new style ESA that includes the support component, the benefit cap does not apply (see reg.83(1)(a)).

Limited capability for work

2.142 **39.**—(1) A claimant has limited capability for work if—

(a) it has been determined that the claimant has limited capability for work on the basis of an assessment under this Part or under Part 4 of the ESA Regulations; or

(b) the claimant is to be treated as having limited capability for work (see paragraph (6)).

(2) An assessment under this Part is an assessment as to the extent to which a claimant who has some specific disease or bodily or mental disablement is capable of performing the activities prescribed in Schedule 6 or is incapable by reason of such disease or bodily or mental disablement of performing those activities.

(3) A claimant has limited capability for work on the basis of an assessment under this Part if, by adding the points listed in column (3) of Schedule 6 against each descriptor listed in column (2) of that Schedule that applies in the claimant's case, the claimant obtains a total score of at least—

(a) 15 points whether singly or by a combination of descriptors specified in Part 1 of that Schedule;

(b) 15 points whether singly or by a combination of descriptors specified in Part 2 of that Schedule; or

(c) 15 points by a combination of descriptors specified in Parts 1 and 2 of that Schedule.

(4) In assessing the extent of a claimant's capability to perform any activity listed in Schedule 6, it is a condition that the claimant's incapability to perform the activity arises—

(a) in respect of any descriptor listed in Part 1 of Schedule 6, from a specific bodily disease or disablement;

(b) in respect of any descriptor listed in Part 2 of Schedule 6, from a specific mental illness or disablement; or

(c) in respect of any descriptor or descriptors listed in—

(i) Part 1 of Schedule 6, as a direct result of treatment provided by a registered medical practitioner for a specific physical disease or disablement, or

(ii) Part 2 of Schedule 6, as a direct result of treatment provided by a registered medical practitioner for a specific mental illness or disablement.

(5) Where more than one descriptor specified for an activity applies to a claimant, only the descriptor with the highest score in respect of each activity which applies is to be counted.

(6) [1 Subject to paragraph (7),] A claimant is to be treated as having limited capability for work if any of the circumstances set out in Schedule 8 applies.

[1 (7) Where the circumstances set out in paragraph 4 or 5 of Schedule 8 apply, a claimant may only be treated as having limited capability for work if the claimant does not have limited capability for work as determined in accordance with an assessment under this Part.]

AMENDMENT

1. Universal Credit and Miscellaneous Amendments Regulations 2014 (SI 2014/597) reg. 2(4) (April 28, 2014).

DEFINITIONS

"the Act"—see reg.2.
"claimant"—see WRA 2012 s.40.
"ESA Regulations"—see reg.2.
"limited capability for work"—see WRA 2012 ss.40 and 37(1).

General Note

2.143 A claimant will have LCW if it has been decided on the basis of an assessment under these Regulations or Part 4 of the ESA Regulations 2013 that they have LCW, or if they are treated as having LCW because any of the circumstances in Sch.8 apply (paras (1) and (6)). The effect of para.(7) is that a claimant can only be treated as having LCW under para.4 of Sch.8 (substantial risk to their health or that of someone else) or para.5 of Sch.8 (life threatening disease) once a work capability assessment has been carried out and they have been assessed as not having LCW.

Note that if a claimant has reached the qualifying age for state pension credit (the qualifying age for state pension credit for both men and women is the pensionable age for women (s.4(4) WRA 2012 and s.1(6) State Pension Credit Act 2012)—since April 2010 this has been increasing from 60 and will reach 65 in November 2018) and is entitled to disability living allowance or personal independence payment, they are treated as having LCW (para.6 of Sch.8).

See Sch.6 for the activities and descriptors for assessing LCW. They are the same as the activities and descriptors in Sch.2 to the ESA Regulations 2008 and Sch.2 to the ESA Regulations 2013 for assessing LCW.

Limited capability for work and work-related activity

2.144 **40.**—(1) A claimant has limited capability for work and work-related activity if—

(a) it has been determined that—
 (i) the claimant has limited capability for work and work-related activity on the basis of an assessment under this Part, or
 (ii) the claimant has limited capability for work related activity on the basis of an assessment under Part 5 of ESA Regulations; or
(b) the claimant is to be treated as having limited capability for work and work-related activity (see paragraph (5)).

(2) A claimant has limited capability for work and work-related activity on the basis of an assessment under this Part if, by reason of the claimant's physical or mental condition—

(a) at least one of the descriptors set out in Schedule 7 applies to the claimant;
(b) the claimant's capability for work and work-related activity is limited; and
(c) the limitation is such that it is not reasonable to require that claimant to undertake such activity.

(3) In assessing the extent of a claimant's capability to perform any activity listed in Schedule 7, it is a condition that the claimant's incapability to perform the activity arises—

(a) in respect of descriptors 1 to 8, 15(a), 15(b), 16(a) and 16(b)—
 (i) from a specific bodily disease or disablement; or
 (ii) as a direct result of treatment provided by a registered medical practitioner for a specific physical disease or disablement; or
(b) in respect of descriptors 9 to 14, 15(c), 15(d), 16(c) and 16(d)—
 (i) from a specific mental illness or disablement; or
 (ii) as a direct result of treatment provided by a registered medical practitioner for a specific mental illness or disablement.

(4) A descriptor applies to a claimant if that descriptor applies to the claimant for the majority of the time or, as the case may be, on the majority

of the occasions on which the claimant undertakes or attempts to undertake the activity described by that descriptor.

(5) [1 Subject to paragraph (6),] A claimant is to be treated as having limited capability for work and work-related activity if any of the circumstances set out in Schedule 9 applies.

[1 (6) Where the circumstances set out in paragraph 4 of Schedule 9 apply, a claimant may only be treated as having limited capability for work and work-related activity if the claimant does not have limited capability for work and work-related activity as determined in accordance with an assessment under this Part.]

AMENDMENT

1. Universal Credit and Miscellaneous Amendments Regulations 2014 (SI 2014/597) reg.2(5) (April 28, 2014).

DEFINITIONS

"the Act"—see reg.2.
"claimant"—see WRA 2012 s.40.
"ESA Regulations"—see reg.2.
"limited capability for work"—see WRA 2012 ss.40 and 37(1).
"limited capability for work-related activity"—see WRA 2012 ss.40 and 37(2).

GENERAL NOTE

A claimant will have LCW and LCWRA if it has been decided on the basis of an assessment under these Regulations that they have LCW and LCWRA or under Part 5 of the ESA Regulations 2013 that they have LCWRA, or if they are treated as having LCW and LCWRA because any of the circumstances in Sch.9 apply (see paras (1) and (5)). The effect of para.(6) is that a claimant can only be treated as having LCW and LCWRA under para.4 of Sch.9 (substantial risk to their health or that of someone else) once a work capability assessment has been carried out and they have been assessed as not having LCW and LCWRA. 2.145

Note that if a claimant has reached the qualifying age for state pension credit (the qualifying age for state pension credit for both men and women is the pensionable age for women (s.4(4) WRA 2012 and s.1(6) State Pension Credit Act 2012)—since April 2010 this has been increasing from 60 and will reach 65 in November 2018) and is entitled to the highest rate of the care component of disability living allowance, the enhanced rate of the daily living component of personal independence payment, attendance allowance or armed forces independence payment (see the definition of "attendance allowance" in reg.2 which includes armed forces independence payment) they are treated as having LCW and LCWRA (para.5 of Sch.9).

See Sch.7 for the activities and descriptors for assessing LCW and LCWRA. They are the same as the activities and descriptors in Sch.3 to the ESA Regulations 2008 and in Sch.3 to the ESA Regulations 2013.

Work Capability Assessment

When an assessment may be carried out

41.—(1) The Secretary of State may carry out an assessment under this Part where— 2.146

(a) it falls to be determined for the first time whether a claimant has limited capability for work or for work and work-related activity; or

(b) there has been a previous determination and the Secretary of State wishes to determine whether there has been a relevant change of circumstances in relation to the claimant's physical or mental condition or whether that determination was made in ignorance of, or was based on a mistake as to, some material fact,

but subject to paragraphs (2) to (4).

(2) If the claimant has [1 monthly] earnings that are equal to or exceed the relevant threshold, the Secretary of State may not carry out an assessment under this Part unless—

(a) the claimant is entitled to attendance allowance, disability living allowance [3, child disability payment] [4, adult disability payment] or personal independence payment; or

(b) the assessment is for the purposes of reviewing a previous determination that a claimant has limited capability for work or for work and work-related activity that was made on the basis of an assessment under this Part or under Part 4 or 5 of the ESA Regulations,

and, in a case where no assessment may be carried out by virtue of this paragraph, the claimant is to be treated as not having limited capability for work unless they are treated as having limited capability for work or for work and work-related activity by virtue of regulation 39(6) or 40(5).

(3) The relevant threshold for the purposes of paragraph (2) is the amount that a person would be paid at the hourly rate set out in [2 regulation 4 of the National Minimum Wage Regulations] for 16 hours a week [1, converted to a monthly amount by multiplying by 52 and dividing by 12].

(4) If it has previously been determined on the basis of an assessment under this Part or under Part 4 or 5 of the ESA Regulations that the claimant does not have limited capability for work, no further assessment is to be carried out unless there is evidence to suggest that—

(a) the determination was made in ignorance of, or was based on a mistake as to, some material fact; or

(b) there has been a relevant change of circumstances in relation to the claimant's physical or mental condition.

AMENDMENTS

1. Universal Credit and Miscellaneous Amendments Regulations 2015 (SI 2015/1754), reg.2(4) (November 4, 2015, or in the case of existing awards, the first assessment period beginning on or after November 4, 2015).

2. Social Security (Jobseeker's Allowance, Employment and Support Allowance and Universal Credit) (Amendment) Regulations 2016 (SI 2016/678), reg.5(3) (July 25, 2016).

3. Social Security (Scotland) Act 2018 (Disability Assistance for Children and Young People) (Consequential Modifications) Order 2021 (SI 2021/786) Sch.11 para.5 (July 26, 2021).

4. Social Security (Disability Assistance for Working Age People) (Consequential Amendments) Order 2022 (SI 2022/177) art.13(5) (March 21, 2022).

DEFINITIONS

"adult disability payment"—see reg.2.
"attendance allowance"—*ibid.*
"child disability payment"—*ibid.*
"claimant"—see WRA 2012 s.40.

"disability living allowance"—see reg.2.
"ESA Regulations"—*ibid.*
"limited capability for work"—see WRA 2012 ss.40 and 37(1).
"limited capability for work-related activity"—see WRA 2012 ss.40 and 37(2).
"monthly earnings"—see regs 2 and 90(6).
"National Minimum Wage Regulations" – see reg. 2.
"personal independence payment"—*ibid.*
"work-related activity"—see WRA 2012 s.40.

GENERAL NOTE

Paragraph (1) **2.147**

This provides when a work capability assessment can be carried out but it is subject to paras (2)–(4).

Paragraphs (2) and (3) **2.148**

The effect of these two paragraphs is that a claimant who has monthly earnings that are equal to or above the "relevant threshold" (16 × the national minimum national wage, which is £10.42 per hour from April 1, 2023, converted to a monthly amount by multiplying by 52 and dividing by 12) is treated as not having LCW (unless they are deemed to have LCW under reg.39(6) and Sch.8 or LCW and LCWRA under reg.40(5) and Sch.9) and no assessment may be carried out. But this rule does not apply if the claimant:

- is entitled to disability living allowance, personal independence payment, attendance allowance, Scottish child or adult disability payment or armed forces independence payment (see the definition of "attendance allowance" in reg.2 which includes armed forces independence payment); or
- has already been assessed as having LCW or LCW and LCWRA under these Regulations or Pt 4 or 5 of the ESA Regulations 2013 and the purpose of the assessment is to review that determination.

Paragraphs (2) and (3) thus contain what could be viewed as a rump of a "permitted work rule" (somewhat oddly placed in a regulation that is also concerned with when an assessment may be carried out). But the effect of para.(2)(b) is that a claimant will only be treated as not having LCW under para.(2) if their weekly earnings are equal to or above the relevant threshold (see para.(3)) *and* they have not yet been assessed under the work capability assessment. If the claimant has already been assessed as having LCW or LCW and LCWRA, para.(2) will not apply, although the work capability assessment may well be re-applied in these circumstances. Until it is determined that the claimant does not have LCW or LCW and LCWRA, the claimant's universal credit award will continue to include the LCW or LCWRA element (as appropriate) (confirmed in para.G1035 ADM).

Note reg.40(1) and (2) of the Decisions and Appeals Regulations 2013 which provides that a determination that a person has, or does not have, LCW, or is to be treated as having, or not having, LCW, that has been made for the purposes of new style ESA or universal credit is conclusive for the purpose of any further decision relating to that benefit.

Paragraph (4) **2.149**

If it has been decided that the claimant does not have LCW either under these Regulations or the ESA Regulations 2013, no further assessment will be carried out for the purposes of universal credit unless the evidence suggests that the decision was made in ignorance of or mistake as to a material fact or that there has been a relevant change in the claimant's physical or mental condition (para.(4)). Note that this provision applies without time limit.

Assessment—supplementary

2.150 **42.**—(1) The following provisions apply to an assessment under this Part.

(2) The claimant is to be assessed as if the claimant were fitted with or wearing any prosthesis with which the claimant is normally fitted or normally wears or, as the case may be, wearing or using any aid or appliance which is normally, or could reasonably be expected to be, worn or used.

(3) If a descriptor applies in the case of the claimant as a direct result of treatment provided by a registered medical practitioner for a specific disease, illness or disablement, it is to be treated as applying by reason of the disease, illness or disablement.

DEFINITION

"claimant"—see WRA 2012 s.40.

Information requirement

2.151 **43.**—(1) The information required to determine whether a claimant has limited capability for work or for work and work-related activity is—

(a) any information relating to the descriptors specified in Schedule 6 or 7 requested by the Secretary of State in the form of a questionnaire; and

(b) any additional information that may be requested by the Secretary of State.

(2) But where the Secretary of State is satisfied that there is enough information to make the determination without the information mentioned in paragraph (1)(a), that information is not required.

(3) Where a claimant fails without a good reason to comply with a request under paragraph (1), the claimant is to be treated as not having limited capability for work or, as the case may be, for work and work- related activity.

(4) But paragraph (3) does not apply unless the claimant was sent a further request to provide the information at least 3 weeks after the date of the first request and at least 1 week has passed since the further request was sent.

DEFINITIONS

"claimant"—see WRA 2012 s.40.

"limited capability for work"—see WRA 2012 ss.40 and 37(1).

"limited capability for work-related activity"—see WRA 2012 ss.40 and 37(2).

"work-related activity"—see WRA 2012 s.40.

GENERAL NOTE

2.152 On paras (3) and (4), see regs 22 and 37 of the ESA Regulations 2008 and the notes to those regulations in Vol.V of this series.

Medical examinations

2.153 **44.**—(1) Where it falls to be determined whether a claimant has limited capability for work or for work and work-related activity, the claimant may be called by or on behalf of a health care professional approved by the Secretary of State to attend a medical examination.

(2) Where a claimant who is called by or on behalf of such a health care professional to attend a medical examination [1 in person, by telephone or by video] fails without a good reason to attend or submit to the examination, the claimant is to be treated as not having limited capability for work or, as the case may be, for work and work-related activity.

(3) But paragraph (2) does not apply unless—

(a) notice of the date, time and place of the examination was given to the claimant at least 7 days in advance; or

(b) notice was given less than 7 days in advance and the claimant agreed to accept it.

Amendment

1. Social Security (Claims and Payments, Employment and Support Allowance, Personal Independence Payment and Universal Credit) (Telephone and Video Assessment) (Amendment) Regulations 2021 (SI 2021/230), reg.4 (March 25, 2021).

Definitions

"claimant"—see WRA 2012 s.40.
"health care professional"—see reg.2.
"limited capability for work"—see WRA 2012 ss.40 and 37(1).
"limited capability for work-related activity"—see WRA 2012 ss.40 and 37(2).
"work-related activity"—see WRA 2012 s.40.

General Note

See regs 23 and 38 of the ESA Regulations 2008 and the notes to those regulations in Vol.V of this series. But note that unlike regs 23 and 38, the notice under reg.44 does not have to be in writing (see para.(3)). 2.154

Part 6

Calculation of Capital and Income

Chapter 1

Capital

Introduction

45. This Chapter provides for the calculation of a person's capital for the purpose of section 5 of the Act (financial conditions) and section 8 of the Act (calculation of awards). 2.155

Definition

"the Act"—see reg.2.

General Note

It has been said for many years in the predecessors to this volume that "resources are to be either capital or income. There is nothing in between". That statement was cited with approval in *R(IS) 3/93* and without disapproval in *R(IS) 9/08*. On the 2.156

distinction between capital and income, see the notes to reg.66(1) (unearned income), where there is some limited discussion of the general principles. Those general principles are not explored here, because the approach to income other than earnings to be taken into account in universal credit is different from that in income support, earnings have their own special definitions and deemings and, as noted below, there is a simpler approach to capital. There are particularly important disregards and deemings of capital to be income in reg.46. There will be reference back to the general principles at the appropriate places.

Compared with income support, income-based JSA, income-related ESA and housing benefit, the rules for the treatment of capital under universal credit are refreshingly concise. For example, there are still, after amendments, only 26 paragraphs in Sch.10 (capital to be disregarded), whereas Sch.10 to the Income Support Regulations has over 70 (although a few have been omitted over the years).

The capital limit for universal credit for both a single claimant and joint claimants is £16,000 (see reg.18(1)). Note that where a claimant who is a member of a couple makes a claim as a single person (see reg.3(3) for the circumstances in which this may occur) the capital of the other member of the couple counts as the claimant's (reg.18(2)).

With effect from July 24, 2019, reg.51 of the Transitional Provisions Regulations 2014, as inserted by reg.3 of the Universal Credit (Managed Migration Pilot and Miscellaneous Amendments) Regulations 2019 (SI 2019/1152), supplies a transitional capital disregard to claimants who (i) were previously entitled to a tax credit and had capital exceeding £16,000; (ii) are given a migration notice that existing benefits are to terminate; and (iii) claim universal credit within the deadline. The disregard is of any capital exceeding £16,000. The disregard can apply only for 12 assessment periods and ceases (without the possibility of revival) following any assessment period in which the amount of capital the claimant has falls below £16,000. See regs 56 and 57 of the Transitional Provisions Regulations for further provisions on termination of the protection. The £16,000 non-disregarded capital that the claimant by definition possesses will produce an assumed yield as income of £174 per month under reg.72. Paragraph 7 of Sch.2 to the Transitional Provisions Regulations, inserted by the same Regulations, contains a disregard as capital of any amount paid as a lump sum by way of a "transitional SDP amount" under that Schedule.

What is included in capital?

2.157 **46.**—(1) The whole of a person's capital is to be taken into account unless—

(a) it is to be treated as income (see paragraphs (3) and (4)); or

(b) it is to be disregarded (see regulation 48).

(2) A person's personal possessions are not to be treated as capital.

(3) Subject to paragraph (4), any sums that are paid regularly and by reference to a period, for example payments under an annuity, are to be treated as income even if they would, apart from this provision, be regarded as capital or as having a capital element.

(4) Where capital is payable by instalments, each payment of an instalment is to be treated as income if the amount outstanding, combined with any other capital of the person (and, if the person is a member of a couple, the other member), exceeds £16,000, but otherwise such payments are to be treated as capital.

General Note

2.158 The whole of a claimant's capital, both actual and notional (see reg.50), counts towards the £16,000 limit under reg.18(1), except if it is treated as income under paras (3) and (4), or is ignored under Sch.10 or regs 75 and 76 (para.(1)). There is also the important provision in para.(2) that personal possessions, however acquired, are not to be treated as capital and so cannot count towards the capital limits (see the detailed notes below). In the case of joint claimants, it is their combined capital that counts towards the £16,000 limit (s.5(2)(a) WRA 2012). A child's capital is not taken into account.

See the notes to s.5 of the WRA 2012 for why the burden of proving that capital does not exceed £16,000 lies on the claimant.

Note reg.49 which maintains the rule that applies for income support, old style JSA, old style ESA and housing benefit that it is only if a debt is secured on a capital asset that it can be deducted.

There is a great deal of case law, both in the context of other social security benefits and more generally, that will be equally applicable in the context of universal credit. See also the notes to reg.66(1) (unearned income) on the distinction between income and capital.

Although there is no definition of capital in the legislation, the general principle would appear, by necessary implication especially from the rules on calculation and valuation in reg.49, to be that anything that is not in its nature income and is not expressly to be treated as not being capital or to be disregarded is to count if it is capable of being sold or being converted into value in the claimant's hands (e.g. by withdrawing money from an account, surrendering an insurance policy or raising money by borrowing on the strength of possession of an asset or interest). The discussion in the rest of this note (see in particular the section on *Choses in action*) illustrates the range of things that can fall within that principle. That range will change as social and economic developments happen. For instance, at some point, the valuation of digital assets, such as non-fungible tokens, cryptocurrency etc., may have to be addressed, including how they fit into the notions of capital and of personal possessions. There is extensive discussion of the existing legal framework in the Law Commission's *Digital Assets: Consultation Paper* (Law Com No.256, July 28, 2022). Now see *Digital Assets: Final report* (Law Com. No.412, June 27, 2023). The DWP guidance on the treatment of capital deposited in the House of Commons library (as collected in the Resources section of the Rightsnet website) suggests that cryptoassets, including cryptocurrency, be treated as investments, with a 10% deduction from valuation for expenses of sale. If cryptocurrency were to be treated like any other money, reg.49(3) on commission or banking charges for conversion into sterling would need consideration.

Note the discussion in the notes to reg.49 of the question of the date within an assessment period as at which the value of capital is to be taken for the purposes of the various limits and the calculation of "tariff" income. The unstated underlying principle, by analogy with rules on when a supersession on the ground of change of circumstances takes effect, appears to be that it is the position as at the end of each assessment period that matters, including the possible attribution of notional capital consequent on disposals during the assessment period. That position then applies for the whole of that assessment period.

Distinguishing between actual and notional capital

AB v SSWP and Canterbury CC (IS and HB) [2014] UKUT 212 (AAC) empha- **2.159**
sises the importance of decision-makers and tribunals making a clear distinction in their findings of fact as to whether the claimant has actual or notional capital. If it is found that the claimant has actual capital over £16,000, there will usually be no entitlement to universal credit. If the claimant shows that they possess capital of less than £16,000, because some of it has been spent or otherwise disposed of, it is usually necessary to consider whether they should be treated as possessing notional capital (see reg.50(1) and the notes to that regulation). In this case the claimant's wife had received an inheritance. On the DWP's discovery of this, supersession of the claimant's income support and housing benefit was sought. The burden therefore shifted to the claimant to show that his wife no longer possessed that capital. See *R(SB) 38/85* where Commissioner Hallett held at para.18:

"The claimant says that he expended this sum of £18,700 in repaying loans. It is for him to prove that this is so. Failing a satisfactory account of the way in which the money has been disposed of, it will be open to the tribunal, and a natural conclusion, to find that the claimant still has, in some form or other, that resource and consequently to conclude that his actual resources are above the prescribed limit."

The tribunal's statement of reasons in *AB* concluded that the claimant "should be deemed to still have, through his partner, capital in excess of £16,000". Judge Wikeley held that the ambiguity inherent in the use of the word "deemed" (or "treated") meant that it was not sufficiently clear whether the tribunal had found that the claimant, through his wife, still had the capital from the inheritance in some form or whether he had deprived himself of it for the purpose of obtaining benefit such as to be fixed with notional capital. In addition, the tribunal had failed to adequately explain why it did not accept the claimant's wife's explanation. In relation to this issue Judge Wikeley emphasises the importance of having a sound evidential basis for an adverse credibility finding against a claimant.

MS v DfC (JSA) [2020] NICom 42 holds that where a tribunal is not satisfied by a claimant's assertion that they have disposed of money, so that the amount remains part of their actual capital, it is not necessary for the tribunal to make a positive finding of fact about where the money was actually held. Submissions to the contrary were based on a misreading of remarks in *DMcC v DSD (IS)* [2012] NICom 326. That is different from a situation like that in *WR v SSWP (IS)* [2012] UKUT 127 (AAC), where the tribunal was not satisfied by the claimant's explanation of why she had made payments to each of her parents. That dissatisfaction did not justify a conclusion that the money involved remained part of her actual capital.

Actual capital

2.160 There is a good deal of law on actual capital.

The first condition is of course that the capital resource is the claimant's or their partner's. This is not as simple as it sounds.

In *CIS/634/1992* the claimant was made bankrupt on November 29, 1990. However, his trustee in bankruptcy was not appointed until April 1991. Between November 29 and December 28, 1990, when he claimed income support, the claimant divested himself of most of his capital. Under the Insolvency Act 1986 (subject to certain exceptions) a bankrupt's property does not vest in their trustee in bankruptcy on the making of a bankruptcy order, but only when the trustee is appointed. The appointment does not have retrospective effect. It is held that since he had failed to give a satisfactory account of how he had disposed of his capital he was to be treated as still possessing it (*R(SB) 38/85* referred to in the notes to reg.50). Thus the claimant was not entitled to income support prior to the appointment of the trustee in bankruptcy because until then he possessed actual capital over the income support limit.

KS v SSWP (JSA) [2009] UKUT 122 (AAC), reported as [2010] AACR 3, however, disagrees with *CIS/634/1992*. Judge Mark points out that a person cannot realise or use any part of their capital after a bankruptcy order has been made and that, subject to any order of the court, it will vest in his trustee in due course. Whether the capital remained the claimant's with a nil value or whether it ceased to be his capital at all (on which Judge Mark did not reach any firm conclusion), the result was that the claimant had no capital, or no capital of any value, after the bankruptcy order had been made.

In *SH v SSWP* [2008] UKUT 21 (AAC) Judge Turnbull also does not reach a final conclusion as to whether money in a bank account or other property that is subject to a restraint order under s.77 of the Criminal Justice Act 1988 (now the Proceeds of Crime Act 2002) or a freezing order ceases to be the claimant's capital. He was inclined to think that such assets remained the claimant's capital. However, their market value would be nil since the claimant was prohibited by court order from disposing of them. *CS v Chelmsford BC (HB)* [2014] UKUT 518 (AAC) takes the same view as *SH* but again without reaching a final conclusion on the point. In *CS*, which concerned assets subject to a restraint order under the Proceeds of Crime Act 2002, Judge Markus points out that not only is a restraint order under the Proceeds of Crime Act 2002 not expressed to deprive people of their interest in the property but also the terminology of the Act consistently presupposes that they retain their interest in property that is subject to a restraint order. Its market value, however, would be nil.

R(IS) 9/04 confirms that assets being administered on a patient's behalf either at the Court of Protection or by their receiver remain the patient's assets which have to be valued at their current market value (see reg.49) (following *CIS/7127/1995*). Such assets are held under a "bare trust" with the entire beneficial ownership remaining with the patient. The fact that the Court had discretionary powers of control over the management of the patient's property for their benefit did not mean that the patient's beneficial ownership had ceased.

However, capital that a claimant is under a "certain and immediate liability" to repay at the moment of its receipt by, or attribution to, the claimant, will not count as their capital (*CIS/2287/2008*). In *CIS/2287/2008* the Commissioner decides that the principle in *Chief Adjudication Officer v Leeves*, reported as *R(IS) 5/99*, does apply to capital as well as income. However, it only applies at the moment of receipt or attribution and is relevant only to the issue of whether money or an asset should be classified as the claimant's capital. *Leeves* does not apply if the liability to repay arises after something has become capital in the claimant's hands. That issue continues to be governed by the principle in *R(SB) 2/83* that, in calculating capital, liabilities are not to be deducted, except those expressly provided for in the legislation. *SSWP v GF (ESA)* [2017] UKUT 333 (AAC), discussed later in this note under the heading *Deduction of liabilities*, is a recent application of the principle of *R(SB) 2/83*. See also *JH v SSWP* [2009] UKUT 1 (AAC) which explains that *Leeves* only operates where, outside trust relationships, there is a certain obligation of immediate repayment or return of the asset to the transferor. It does not bite where the claimant is under some liability to a third party.

Interests under a will or intestacy when someone has died

The ADM (paras H1169–1178) contains guidance adopting in para.H1174 the general principle that a beneficiary under a will or intestacy has no legal or equitable interest in any specific property while the estate remains unadministered. The personal representative in those circumstances has full ownership of the assets of the estate. That principle was applied by the Tribunal of Commissioners in *R(SB) 5/85*, relying on the foundational Privy Council decision in *Commissioner of Stamp Duties (Queensland) v Livingston* [1965] A.C. 694. 2.161

However, there are two important qualifications. The first is that, even where the *Livingston* principle applies, the beneficiary has a right to have the deceased's estate properly administered. That is a chose in action that has a market value. It can be transferred and can be borrowed against. Depending on the particular circumstances, the market value can be considerable and not far off the value that would be put on the asset(s) in question if owned outright. That point was made clearly by Commissioner Howell in para.28 of his decision in *R(IS) 1/01* and nothing to the contrary was said in the Court of Appeal in *Wilkinson v Chief Adjudication Officer*, reported as part of *R(IS) 1/01*, in upholding the Commissioner's decision. Nor is *R(SB) 5/85* to the contrary: the Commissioners there expressly noted that the claimant had a chose in action (para.7). It is submitted that that is the basis on which the later decision of Commissioner Howell in *CIS/1189/2003* is to be supported. The claimant there was the sole residuary beneficiary under her mother's will and the estate, whose main asset was a property that the claimant did not live in, remained unadministered for several years, so that the property had not actually vested in the claimant. In para.11, the Commissioner said that the claimant was beneficially entitled to the property from the date of her mother's death subject only to the formalities needed to perfect her title, so that for all practical purposes she had an entitlement equivalent to full beneficial ownership. That proposition can easily be misinterpreted, but in para.12 the Commissioner noted that as the claimant was the sole *residuary* beneficiary, it was para.28 of *R(IS) 1/01* that was applicable. So the valuation was of the claimant's chose in action, but in the circumstances the difference in value from that of full beneficial ownership was negligible.

The second qualification is that the position may be different where there has been a specific gift of some asset, as was the case in *R(IS) 1/01*, where the will of the claimant's mother gave the claimant and her brother equal shares in some income bonds and other money in a bank account and in a property. The matter was put very strongly by Commissioner Howell in para.27 of his decision, where he said that the *Livingston* principle had:

> "never had any application to property specifically devised or bequeathed by a will. Such property becomes in equity the property of the legatee as soon as the testator dies, subject only to the right of the personal representative to resort to it for payment of debts if the remainder of the estate is insufficient for this purpose [citations omitted]."

No specific comment on that proposition was made in the judgments of the Court of Appeal in *Wilkinson*, but Mummery LJ did note generally that the evidence did not suggest that there was any question of the executors needing to have recourse to the property for payment of debts or that there was any other legal obstacle to the immediate completion of the administration of the estate and to an assent by the executors vesting the property in the names of the claimant and her brother as joint owners. That strongly suggests that what was being considered was a valuation of the claimant's chose in action, rather than of some equitable interest. It is submitted that that is the proper approach. The valuation would therefore be sensitive to the possibilities mentioned by Mummery LJ in the particular case, as well as to the value of the underlying asset. That approach would hold also for personal property or money, although there it should be noted that the process of the personal representative giving an assent, i.e. an indication that a certain asset is not required for administration purposes and may pass under the will or (possibly) an intestacy into the ownership of the beneficiary, does not need to be in writing and may be implied from conduct.

Beneficial ownership

2.162 The mere fact that an asset or a bank or building society account is in the claimant's sole name does not mean that it belongs to the claimant. It is the "beneficial ownership" which matters. It is only such an interest that has a market value. The claimant may hold the asset under a trust which means that they cannot simply treat the asset as theirs, but must treat it as if it belonged to the beneficiary or beneficiaries under the trust. It is they who are "beneficially entitled." A trustee may also be a beneficiary, in which case the rule in reg.47 may come into play, or may have no beneficial interest at all (see further below under *Claimant holding as trustee*).

The basic principle was confirmed, as might have been thought unnecessary, by Judge Poynter in *SSWP v LB of Tower Hamlets and CT* (IS & HB) [2018] UKUT 25 (AAC) (see the notes under *Claimant holding as a trustee* for the details). However, it appeared that local authorities had routinely been submitting in housing benefit cases, wrongly taking a single sentence from the same judge's earlier decision in *CH/715/2006* out of context, that only legal interests were relevant.

These issues often arise in the context of attributing the beneficial ownership of former matrimonial assets. One example is *R(IS) 2/93*. The claimant had a building society account in her sole name, which she had had since before her marriage. Her husband deposited the bulk of the money in it, including his salary. On their separation, the AO and the SSAT treated the entire amount in the account as part of the claimant's capital. The Commissioner holds that she was not solely beneficially entitled to the money so that the equivalent of reg.47 on jointly held capital had to operate (although that operation would not now be accepted as following in such circumstances: see the notes to reg.47). There is helpful guidance on the limited circumstances in which the "presumption of advancement" (i.e. that when a husband puts an asset into his wife's name he intends to make an outright gift of it) will operate in modern circumstances. (Note that the presumption of advancement was due to be abolished by s.199 of the Equality Act 2010 but this section has not yet been brought into force.) And see *CIS/982/2002* on the valuation of a share in a frozen joint bank account. Note also *R(IS) 10/99* below. In *CIS/553/1991*, where a house was in the husband's sole name, it was held that its valuation should take into account the wife's statutory right of occupation under the Matrimonial Homes Act 1967. See also *R(IS) 1/97*, where the claimant, who separated from his wife, agreed that she could live in the former matrimonial home, which was in his sole name, for her lifetime, which the Commissioner considered created a constructive trust.

In most cases of spouses or civil partners, in whoever's name the asset is, there will be some degree of joint ownership. But if an asset is in the sole name of one, the other should not be treated as having a half share as a beneficial tenant in common under reg.47 until it has been established that they do own at least part of it. On this, see *R(IS) 1/03*, which holds that a person's right to seek a lump sum payment or property transfer order under the Matrimonial Causes Act 1973 is not a capital asset. Moreover, *CIS/984/2002* should also be noted in this context. This holds that money held by the claimant's solicitor pending quantification of the statutory charge to the Legal Services Commission under s.10(7) of the Access to Justice Act 1999 was not part of the claimant's capital. Until that quantification had been carried out, it was not possible to identify any particular amount as the claimant's capital. Another way of looking at it was to treat the statutory charge as an incumbrance for the purpose of the equivalent of reg.49(1)(b) (see *CIS/368/1993*). Nor was any part of the money available to the claimant on application for the purposes of reg.51(2) of the Income Support Regulations. See also *CIS/7097/1995*, discussed in the notes to reg.47.

In *LC v Bournemouth Borough Council (HB)* [2016] UKUT 175 (AAC), the proceeds of sale of a former matrimonial home were being held in a solicitors' client account until the claimant's partner and his ex-wife agreed how the sum was to be split or the issue was resolved by a court order after a Financial Dispute Resolution hearing. In the judge's view the value of the capital prior to agreement or an order of the court would be minimal. The local authority had jumped the gun by treating the claimant as having capital in excess of £16,000 from the date the proceeds were placed in the client account.

Claimant holding as trustee

It would take many whole books to explore all the circumstances in which a trust relationship arises such that a person who holds the legal ownership of assets is subject to trust duties towards other people and so is a trustee and either has no beneficial interest in the assets or only a partial interest. The notes that follow concentrate on the social security case law, but only the barest outline of the general law can be given. In novel or complex cases there may need to be reference to specialist trust books. Sometimes the social security cases refer helpfully to the more general authorities. See, for recent examples, *SSWP v LB of Tower Hamlets and CT (IS & HB)* [2018] UKUT 25 (AAC) on resulting trusts and *VMcC v SSWP (IS)* [2018] UKUT 63 (AAC) on the *Quistclose* principle, both discussed further below. **2.163**

The following notes first deal briefly with express trusts, where the existence and terms of the trust are stated or accepted, then with circumstances in which trusts arise by some form of implication, i.e implied, resulting or constructive trusts.

A trust can be created by declaration when assets are acquired (e.g. the familiar transfer of a house to a couple as beneficial joint tenants or tenants in common) or over assets already owned. In relation to assets other than land, no particular formality is required, although there must be certainty as to the assets covered by the trust and the beneficiaries as well as on the intention to create a trust. However, note that in such cases the burden of proving an intention to create a trust is the balance of probabilities, not any higher standard, as confirmed in *Gill v Thind* [2023] EWCA Civ 1276; [2024] 1 W.L.R. 2837 (Arnold LJ at para.58, with some more general helpful discussion at paras 55–59). There may therefore be difficult questions in particular cases over whether there is sufficient persuasive evidence of the existence of a trust (as exemplified in several cases discussed below). It is in general for a claimant who has been shown to be the legal owner of an asset to show that they are not a beneficial owner (*MB v Royal Borough of Kensington and Chelsea (HB)* [2011] UKUT 321 (AAC) and *CT*, above).

In relation to trusts of land, *SB v SSWP (IS)* [2012] UKUT 252 (AAC) is a useful reminder that s.53(1)(b) of the Law of Property Act 1925 only requires a trust relating to land to be evidenced in writing. Absence of writing makes the trust unenforceable but not void. The tribunal had found that there was no trust of the property in question because there was no trust deed. That error of law had led the tribunal to fail to investigate and make findings on whether there had been a declaration of trust, whether the scope of the trust was certain, the subject matter of the trust, the objects/persons intended to benefit from any such trust and (in the absence of any documentation) whether the surrounding circumstances were consistent with the existence of a trust. It follows from the principle that the trust is merely unenforceable that the existence of later evidence in writing satisfies s.53(1) from the date of the original declaration. It is also said that the statute cannot be used as an instrument of fraud, so that a person who has taken the property knowing of the trust cannot be heard to deny the trust, despite there being no evidence in writing. Note also that s.53(1) does not apply to implied, resulting or constructive trusts.

In *R(IS) 1/90*, the claimant established a building society account in his own name which was to be used solely to finance his son's medical education. He executed no documents about the account. It was argued that there was sufficient evidence of a declaration of trust over the account, but the Commissioner held that the claimant had not unequivocally renounced his beneficial interest in the sum in the account. Although he had earmarked the money for the son's education, the situation was like an uncompleted gift and there was insufficient evidence of a declaration of trust.

For the position under Scots law see *R(IS) 10/99*. The claimant agreed that he would pay his former wife (from whom he was separated) £22,250, representing a share of his pension. When he claimed income support, the claimant had £15,500 in his bank account that he said he was holding for his wife. The Commissioner decides that the £15,500 was not subject to a trust. That was because there had been no delivery of the subject of the trust, nor any satisfactory equivalent to delivery, "so as to achieve irrevocable divestiture of the truster [the equivalent of the settlor in English law] and investiture of the trustee in the trust estate", as required by Scots law (see *Clark Taylor & Co Ltd v Quality Site Development (Edinburgh) Ltd* 1981 S.C. 11). There was no separate bank account and there had been no clear indication to the claimant's wife that the money was held on trust for her. In addition, as the truster would have been the sole trustee, the Requirements of Writing (Scotland) Act 1995 required the trust to be proved in writing. That had not been done. Nor was there an "incumbrance" within the meaning of the equivalent of reg.49(1)(b) preventing the claimant disposing of the money. The consequence was that the £15,500 counted as the claimant's capital. No doubt the result would have been the same if the principles of trust law in England and Wales had been applied. Mere mental earmarking of an asset for a particular purpose is not enough to show the existence of a trust.

For a further case which considered whether a trust had been validly constituted for the purposes of Scots law, see *CSIS/639/2006*.

One particular instance of a resulting trust is where a person gives or loans some amount to another to be used for a particular purpose. In *R(SB) 53/83* the claimant's son had paid him £2,850 to be used for a holiday in India. The claimant died without taking the holiday or declaring the existence of the money to the DHSS. The Commissioner, applying the principle of *Barclays Bank Ltd v Quistclose Investments Ltd* [1970] A.C. 567, held that there was a trust to return the money to the son if the primary purpose of the loan was not carried out. Since the Commissioner held that there had been no overpayment while the claimant was alive, this must mean that the claimant held the money on trust to use it for the specified purpose or to return it (a result most recently confirmed by the decision of the Privy Council in the *Prickly Bay* case: see further below). It was not part of the claimant's resources. This is an important decision, which overtakes some of the reasoning of *R(SB) 14/81* (see the notes to reg.49). The actual decision in *R(SB) 53/83* was reversed (by consent) by the Court of Appeal, because the Commissioner had differed from the appeal tribunal on a point of pure fact. *R(SB) 1/85* holds that this does not affect its authority on the issue of principle. In *R(SB) 1/85*, the claimant's mother-in-law had some years previously provided the money for the purchase of the lease of a holiday chalet for the use of the claimant's mentally handicapped son, Keith. The lease was in the claimant's name and its current value was probably about £5,000. The AO's initial statement of the facts was that the mother-in-law had bought the chalet in the claimant's name. The Commissioner held that this would give rise to a presumption of a resulting trust in her favour, so that the claimant would have no beneficial interest in the chalet—nothing he could sell. The presumption could be rebutted if in fact the mother-in-law had made an outright gift to the claimant, or to Keith. In the second case the claimant again would have no beneficial interest. In the first, he would be caught, for even if he had said that he intended to use the chalet purely for Keith, there was not the necessary written evidence of the trust (Law of Property Act 1925 s.53). Another possibility was that the mother-in-law had made a gift to the claimant subject to an express (but unwritten) trust in favour of Keith, when again the claimant clearly would not be the beneficial owner, as that would be a fraud. This is a very instructive decision, which will give valuable guidance in sorting out many family-type arrangements.

The dangers and difficulties of *Quistclose* were pointed out in *CSB/1137/1985*, particularly where family transactions are concerned. There, the claimant had received loans of £1,000 and £500, to fund a trip to India, from friends originally from the same village, who both later provided letters to say that, as the trip had not been taken, they had asked for, and received, their money back. Commissioner Rice held that the tribunal had gone wrong in law in concluding, following *R(SB) 53/83*, that the claimant did not have any beneficial interest in the funds, because the relationship between the lenders and the claimant indicated that nothing as sophisticated as the imposition of a trust had been intended. Rather, it had not been shown that there was any restriction on the claimant's use of the money.

Judge Wikeley in *VMcC v SSWP (IS)* [2018] UKUT 63 (AAC) has recently helpfully summarised the test required for the imposition of a *Quistclose* trust as set out in recent authority (in particular *Twinsectra Ltd v Yardley* [2002] 2 A.C. 164 and *Bellis v Challenor* [2015] EWCA Civ 59) and also discussed the distinction between *R(SB) 53/83* and *CSB/1137/1985*. The summary in para.42 is this:

> "The funds must be transferred on terms, typically for a stated purpose, which do not leave them at the free disposal of the transferee;
> There must be an intention to create what is, viewed objectively, a trust;
> A person creates a trust by their words or conduct, not their innermost thoughts;
> If such a trust is created, then the beneficial interest in the property remains in the transferor unless and until the purposes for which it has been transferred have been fulfilled;
> If such a trust is not created, then the ordinary consequence is that the money becomes the property of the transferee, who is free to apply it as they choose."

In addition, *Twinsectra* established that if there is a lack of clarity in identifying the stated purpose such that the funds cannot be applied the transferor's beneficial interest continues. Judge Wikeley acknowledged that there appeared to be a very thin line between the circumstances in *R(SB) 53/83* and *CSB/1137/1985*, but suggested in para.48 that, as well as the purpose being more specific, it might have been significant that the funds in *R(SB) 53/83* had been transferred, while the transaction in *CSB/1137/1985* was described in terms of a loan. With respect, it is hard to see why the transaction being a loan should point towards the claimant in *CSB/1137/1985* being subject to no trust obligations. It might be thought that the distinction, fine though it may be, was more in there not having been the necessary words or conduct, rather than innermost thoughts.

The Privy Council in *Prickly Bay Waterside Ltd v British American Insurance Co Ltd* [2022] UKPC 8; [2022] 1 W.L.R. 2087, while accepting the value of summaries of principles, in particular of those established by the judgment of Lord Millett in *Twinsectra*, warned against not going back to the "core analysis" in that judgment. It was emphasised again that it is not enough that money is provided for a particular purpose. The question is whether the parties intended that the money should be at the free disposition of the recipient. An intention that it should not be need not be mutual, in the sense of being shared or reciprocated, but could be imposed by one party and acquiesced in by the other. A *Quistclose* trust is a default trust, so can be excluded or moulded by the terms of the parties' express agreements. In the particular case, involving complex commercial transactions in which a sum was loaned to a bank that contracted to guarantee payment of the purchase price of a property on future completion, it was significant to the outcome that a *Quistclose* trust had not been established that there had been no requirement that the sum be segregated by the bank from its other funds. It is submitted that in other contexts, such as family or other relatively informal arrangements more likely to be encountered in the social security context, a lack of segregation, say into a separate account, would not carry nearly such weight.

Cases in which *Quistclose* has been applied include the following. In *R(SB) 12/86*, £2,000 was lent to the claimant on condition that she did not touch the capital amount, but only took the interest, and repaid the £2,000 on demand. The £2,000 was not part of her capital, never having been at her disposal. The Commissioner in *CSB/975/1985* was prepared to apply the principle to a loan on mortgage from a Building Society for property renovation. But it would have to be found that the loan was made for no other purpose and was to be recoverable by the Building Society if for any reason the renovations could not be carried out. The furthest extension so far of the *Quistclose* principle is in *CFC/21/1989*. The claimant's father paid her each month an amount to meet her mortgage obligation to a building society. The Commissioner accepts that the money was impressed with a trust that it should be used only for that purpose and did not form part of her capital. The extension is that the purpose was to meet expenditure on an item that could be covered by income support.

The facts in *VMcC* were very unusual. The claimant, who was a member of the Traveller community, had two accounts with TSB and Nationwide opened in her own name when she was a child (probably when she was about seven) for members of her family to put money in for her future education. When she became pregnant at the age of 19 she was disowned by her family and claimed income support in April 2015, disclosing two bank accounts, but not the TSB and Nationwide accounts. She said she only became aware of those accounts at a compliance interview in July 2015 and in August produced evidence that both accounts had been closed. She said that all the amounts in the accounts (some £13,000) had been returned to the family members by her mother, save for £2,000 that she was allowed to keep for her baby. The decision-maker treated all the amounts as the claimant's, generating a tariff income, and that was upheld on appeal. The tribunal found that as the claimant had opened the accounts she would have known of them and concluded that she could have used the money as she pleased. If her mother or the family had wanted to set aside money for her education they could have opened a trustee account. Judge Wikeley set the tribunal's decision aside because there was not evidence to support the finding that the claimant had opened the TSB and Nationwide accounts and gave some guidance to a new tribunal on rehearing. In para.44 he cited what had been said in the commentary in Vol.II of this series, that there may well be evidential difficulties in establishing the components of a *Quistclose* trust in the context of family arrangements, not least because there is often no contemporary documentation, but stressed that the absence of a paper trail is not necessarily determinative. In principle a *Quistclose* trust can be created informally and by word of mouth, although very careful fact-finding is necessary. After comparing the outcomes of *R(SB) 53/83* and *CSB/1137/1995* (see above), he mentioned in para.47 two particular factors to be considered in family-type cases:

> "The first is that in practice it is unusual for informal family arrangements to be contemporaneously evidenced in writing (whether within the Traveller community or elsewhere). The second is that if the Appellant's account about being cast out by the community is accepted, that in itself may explain the failure of witnesses to attend an oral hearing to support her."

The question was not what was objectively reasonable (or what a High Street solicitor would have advised) but whether the claimant's account could be accepted in the light of what was customary in the particular community (para.61). It should also be noted that the Secretary of State accepted that an account may contain funds subject to a trust mixed with funds that are not so subject (para.51).

Cases in which *Quistclose* has not been applied include the following, many of which illustrate the thinness of the line between an outright gift or loan and one subject to an implied trust. *R(IS) 5/98* reached a similar outcome without any mention of *Quistclose*. The claimant had transferred her flat to her daughter partly on the condition that her daughter looked after her. It was held that the gift failed when this condition was not fulfilled and the daughter held the flat on trust for her mother. An appeal against this decision was dismissed by the Court of Appeal (*Ellis v Chief Adjudication Officer*, reported as part of *R(IS) 5/98*). The claimant had argued that the condition was void for uncertainty but this was rejected by the Court (and in accordance with the principles summarised in *VMcC* that would have led to the beneficial interest remaining with the mother from the outset).

In *YH v SSWP (IS)* [2015] UKUT 85 (AAC) the claimant raised a loan on his property and gave the money to his sons to establish a business. The sons used the money to set up the business and made the repayments on the loan. The *Quistclose* principle did not apply because there was no evidence to suggest that the lender had advanced the money on the condition that it was only to be used to establish the sons' business. A borrower does not create a trust in favour of the lender simply by having their own clear intention as to the application of the money. There was no separation between legal and beneficial interest so far as the sons were concerned, so that there was a question of whether the claimant had notional capital on the deprivation under the equivalent of reg.50(1).

A further example occurred in *CIS/5185/1995*, which held that *Quistclose* did not apply to a student grant which the claimant became liable to repay to the education authority when he left his course early. The grant could not be disregarded under the *Quistclose* principle because the education authority retained no beneficial interest in the grant. The authority merely reserved the right to demand repayment of a sum calculated according to the unexpired balance of the relevant term when the person ceased to be a student. In *Chief Adjudication Officer v Leeves*, reported as *R(IS) 5/99*, it was conceded on behalf of the claimant that there was no constructive trust in these circumstances, since no proprietary right had been retained by the education authority, nor had any fiduciary obligation been created.

In *MW v SSWP (JSA)* [2016] UKUT 469 (AAC), reported as [2017] AACR 15, a Scottish case, it was held that circumstances which would in England and Wales have given rise to a *Quistclose* trust did not do so as a matter of Scots law, because Scots law did not recognise a trust where the sole beneficiary was a trustee. The claimant had been lent money by his mother in order to buy his house. If it was not used for that purpose it was to be returned. Judge Gamble held that nevertheless the claimant was subject to a personal obligation to his mother to use the money only for the specified purpose, which in Scots law had a similar effect to a *Quistclose* trust, so that for the period in question the money lent did not form part of his capital. It is perhaps unclear to a non-Scots lawyer just why a trust could not be recognised (would not the mother also be a beneficiary?), but that appears not to matter as the essence of the decision is in the effect of the personal obligation identified by the judge.

So far as resulting trusts in general are concerned, the most authoritative statement is that of Lord Browne-Wilkinson, speaking for the majority of the House of Lords, in *Westdeutsche Landesbank Girozentrale v Islington LBC* [1996] A.C. 669 at 708:

> "Under existing law a resulting trust arises in two sets of circumstances: (A) where A makes a voluntary payment to B or pays (wholly or in part) for the purchase of property which is vested either in B alone or in the joint names of A and B, there is a presumption that A did not intend to make a gift to B: the money or property is held on trust for A (if he is the sole provider of the money) or in the case of a joint purchase by A and B in shares proportionate to their contributions. It is important to stress that this is only a presumption, which presumption is easily rebutted either by the counter-presumption of advancement or by direct evidence of A's intention to make an outright transfer .... (B) [*Quistclose* cases]."

That statement was cited in para.48 of *SSWP v LB of Tower Hamlets and CT (IS & HB)* [2018] UKUT 25 (AAC), where it was also noted that in *R(SB) 49/83* Commissioner Hallett stated that "the principle that purchase of land in the name of another gives rise to a resulting trust for the true purchaser has been settled for centuries". The principle rests on giving effect to the common intention of the parties.

In *R(SB) 49/83* the claimant had bought a house, but said that this was on behalf of his son, who had not been able to obtain a loan in his own name but was paying off the loan. The Commissioner held that if this could be established, the claimant would hold the house on a resulting trust for his son. However, he stressed that the credibility of the claimant's evidence, in the light of any further documents that came forward, needed to be carefully tested. For instance why did the house have to be transferred into the claimant's name, rather than him guaranteeing a loan to his son?

In *CT* the claimant bought a house in her sole name with a buy-to-let mortgage, intending that the mortgage interest would be met by the rental income. The purchase price and expenses came to £377,728.09. The mortgage loan was for £310,215. The claimant only had £250 capital to contribute, so agreed with a friend, Mr G, for him to contribute the remaining £67,263.09. They could reach no agreement at the time about what interest that gave him in the property. On claims for income support and housing benefit the claimant was initially treated as having capital of the value of the house less the amount of the incumbrance of the mortgage and 10% for expenses of sale. A tribunal held that she held the property on a resulting trust for Mr G. That decision was upheld by the Upper Tribunal on the basis that the claimant's beneficial interest was only 0.04% of the value (£250 as against £67,362.09). That result would follow from the plain application of the general resulting trust principles, in that the payments of mortgage had no effect on the beneficial interests, as while the house was let they came out of the rent (to which the two would have been entitled in proportion to their beneficial interests). That was not affected by a period in which the claimant was forced to live in the house while her own home was uninhabitable and she paid the mortgage interest. That was equivalent to her paying an occupation rent.

The main submission made by the Secretary of State on the appeal to the Upper Tribunal was that the tribunal's approach was incompatible with that of the Supreme Court in *Jones v Kernott* [2011] UKSC 53; [2012] 1 A.C. 776, under which what was fair in the light of the whole course of dealings between the parties was determinative. Judge Poynter provides a helpful analysis of the effect of the decisions in *Stack v Dowden* [2007] UKHL 17; [2007] 2 A.C. 432 and *Jones v Kernott* in "family home" type cases. The principles applicable in such cases were summarised as follows in para.51 of the joint judgment of Lady Hale and Lord Walker in *Jones v*

Kernott (the words in square brackets in sub-para.(1) were added by Judge Poynter when citing this passage in *CT*):

> "*Conclusion*
>
> 51. In summary, therefore, the following are the principles applicable in a case such as this, where a family home is bought in the joint names of a cohabiting couple who are both responsible for any mortgage, but without any express declaration of their beneficial interests.
>
> (1) The starting point is that equity follows the law and they are joint tenants both in law and in equity. [As this decision will be read by people who are not legally qualified, I should explain that the phrase "joint tenants" in this context has a technical legal meaning and is not a generic reference to any co-owner. To summarise, the distinction being drawn by the Supreme Court is between "joint tenants", who always own a property equally, and "tenants in common" who may own a property in equal shares but do not necessarily do so.]
>
> (2) That presumption can be displaced by showing (a) that the parties had a different common intention at the time when they acquired the home, or (b) that they later formed the common intention that their respective shares would change.
>
> (3) Their common intention is to be deduced objectively from their conduct:
>
>> "the relevant intention of each party is the intention which was reasonably understood by the other party to be manifested by that party's words and conduct notwithstanding that he did not consciously formulate that intention in his own mind or even acted with some different intention which he did not communicate to the other party" (Lord Diplock in *Gissing v Gissing* [1971] A.C. 886, 906).
>
> Examples of the sort of evidence which might be relevant to drawing such inferences are given in *Stack v Dowden*, at para 69.
>
> (4) In those cases where it is clear either (a) that the parties did not intend joint tenancy at the outset, or (b) had changed their original intention, but it is not possible to ascertain by direct evidence or by inference what their actual intention was as to the shares in which they would own the property, "the answer is that each is entitled to that share which the court considers fair having regard to the whole course of dealing between them in relation to the property": Chadwick LJ in *Oxley v Hiscock* [2005] Fam 211, para.69. In our judgment, "the whole course of dealing ... in relation to the property" should be given a broad meaning, enabling a similar range of factors to be taken into account as may be relevant to ascertaining the parties' actual intentions.
>
> (5) Each case will turn on its own facts. Financial contributions are relevant but there are many other factors which may enable the court to decide what shares were either intended (as in case (3)) or fair (as in case (4))."

Judge Poynter took the view that, while the "family home" category has been expanded to some extent beyond the confines of cohabiting couples, it could not apply in *CT*, where the purchase of the house was intended as an investment, with no intention of the claimant and Mr G living together there or anywhere else. Therefore the traditional resulting trust approach was correct.

However, the important, but somewhat inconclusive, Privy Council case of *Marr v Collie* [2017] UKPC 17, [2018] A.C. 631 shows that things are not as simple as that, while not throwing doubt on the actual result in *CT*.

Mr Marr, a banker, and Mr Collie, a building contractor, were in a personal relationship in the Bahamas from 1991 to 2008. During that time a number of properties were acquired, not for them to live in, that were conveyed into their joint names. Mr Marr provided the purchase price and paid the mortgage instalments. According to Mr Marr, Mr Collie repeatedly assured him that he would make an equal contribution to the costs, but never did. According to Mr Collie, he was to carry out renovations and works on the properties, some of which he did. There were also purchases of a truck and a boat that were registered in joint names. After the relationship broke down Mr Marr brought proceedings claiming that he was entitled to full beneficial ownership of those properties and the truck and boat. At first instance, the judge, relying on *Laskar v Laskar* [2008] EWCA Civ 347, [2008] 1 W.L.R. 2695, held that the *Stack v Dowden* presumption that a conveyance into joint names indicated a legal and beneficial joint tenancy unless the contrary was proved applied only in the "domestic consumer context". So, as the properties were intended primarily as investments, that presumption did not apply even though there was a personal relationship between the parties and there was a presumption that there was a resulting trust in favour of Mr Marr unless Mr Collie could demonstrate that a gift to him had been intended, which the judge concluded he had failed to do. On appeal, the Court of Appeal of the Bahamas found that there was cogent evidence of Mr Marr having intended that the beneficial interest in the properties be shared equally, so that the presumption of a resulting trust was rebutted. However, that was in large part in reliance on a 2005 email from Mr Marr that he had not been given the opportunity to comment on. For that reason and because the Court of Appeal's conclusions on the common intention of the parties failed to address a number of factual findings by the first instance judge, the Privy Council allowed Mr Marr's appeal, but was unable to substitute a decision in view of the absence of a proper examination of the parties' intentions. Thus the discussion of the general principles noted below was not anchored in a concrete application to specific findings of fact.

Lord Kerr, giving the judgment of a Board that included both Lady Hale and Lord Neuburger, opined in para.40 that by stating in para.58 of *Stack v Dowden* that the starting point, at least in the domestic consumer context, was that conveyance into joint names indicates both legal and beneficial joint tenancy, unless and until the contrary is proved, Lady Hale did not intend that the principle be confined to the purely domestic setting. Nor was *Laskar,* a case of the purchase of the claimant's council house, for letting out, effectively funded by the claimant's daughter, to be regarded as an authority to the contrary. Thus where a property was bought in the joint names of a cohabiting couple, even if that was as an investment, the "resulting trust solution" did not provide the inevitable answer on beneficial ownership (para.49). However, "save perhaps where there is no evidence from which the parties' intentions can be identified", the answer was not to be provided by the triumph of one presumption over another (Lady Hale's starting point as against the resulting trust solution). Rather, the context of the parties' common intention, or lack of it, was crucial (para.54) and apparently (it is not entirely clear) it was accepted that that common intention could alter after the initial acquisition of the property (para.55).

Most recently, the Court of Appeal (*Williams v Williams* [2024] EWCA Civ 42; [2024] 4 W.L.R. 10) has applied what it described as the "long-standing principle of equity that property acquired in joint names for business purposes would be presumed to be held beneficially as tenants in common rather than as joint tenants with the accidents of survivorship". There was nothing in *Stack v Dowden* or *Jones v Kermott* relied on in the domestic context to suggest that that principle had been undermined or affected in any way.

Applying those principles to the facts of *CT*, it would seem that there was a lack of any common intention both at the time of acquisition of the property and subsequently about what beneficial interest the claimant and Mr G should have. Accordingly, either the case was one where the resulting trust solution should apply for that reason (most probable) or it was one where the lack of common intention in the context of an investment property was sufficient to displace the starting point of the beneficial interests following the legal ownership.

The main lesson to be taken from *Marr v Collie* is perhaps that great care needs to be taken in making findings of fact about the parties' intentions, common or otherwise, both at the time of acquisition of the property in question and subsequently. In addition it is noteworthy that the Privy Council apparently accepted that the same approach applied to the acquisition of chattels, in the form of the truck and boat, as to the acquisition of real property. What in particular is left unclear, even though the notion of a clash of presumptions was rejected, is on which party does the burden fall of showing that the common intention works in their favour. Or is the common intention to be identified on an objective analysis of the evidence, including the evaluation of credibility, without resort to propositions about burden of proof?

The same principle can apply to cases where a claimant has an account into which someone else's money is put either solely or mixed with the claimant's own money. In *R(IS) 9/08* payments of a boarding-out allowance which the foster parent had saved up over the years were not held on trust for the children in her care. However, *MC v SSWP (IS)* [2015] UKUT 600 (AAC) reaches the opposite conclusion where the claimant had saved up her daughters' disability living allowance in an account in the claimant's name. A tribunal accepted that in relation to an earlier period the claimant was holding the money on trust for her daughters. However, when she used a substantial part of the money to meet rent arrears, the tribunal considered that this suggested that what was previously held on trust had been subsequently "converted" into the claimant's capital by her actions. Judge Wikeley holds, however, that this was wrong in law. First, as the claimant had been made an appointee by DWP to act on behalf of her daughters in benefit matters, she was acting as a de facto trustee. Second, this was an obvious example of an informal trust over money, created without any legal formalities. Third, paying off rent arrears helped to keep a roof over the daughters' heads and was a perfectly reasonable use of their savings, consistent with the purposes of the trust. See also *DL v Southampton CC (CTB)* [2010] UKUT 453 (AAC) for a case where the tribunal failed to make adequate findings of fact about the circumstances in which the claimant's daughter had transferred funds into the claimant's savings account, so as to be able to decide whether there was a resulting trust or not.

JK v SSWP (JSA) [2010] UKUT 437 (AAC), reported as [2011] AACR 26, holds that by asking whether there was a trust the tribunal had posed the wrong question in relation to Scots law. It should have considered whether the presumption of ownership had been rebutted under Scots law. The claimant had contended that some of the money in his and his wife's joint account belonged to his mother-in-law. Applying the principle in *Cairns v Davidson* 1913 S.C. 1053, the tribunal should have considered, by way of such written or oral evidence available to it that it accepted, whether the presumption in favour of all the money in the joint account belonging to the claimant and his wife had been rebutted, so as to establish whether or not some of it belonged to his mother-in law.

It will sometimes be the case that the claimant's explanation as to why they are holding capital for someone else may involve some unlawful purpose, e.g. in order to conceal assets from the HMRC. In *MC v SSWP* [2010] UKUT 29 (AAC) the claimant had purchased a house for £26,000 in her own name. The money had come from her bank account. She asserted that £14,000 of the £26,000 had been paid into her account by her husband by way of a gift for their son and that the remaining £12,000 was her son's money which had been paid into her bank account because he had no bank account of his own. The tribunal found that the only explanation for her son providing the £12,000 was to "deny monies obtained illicitly to the revenue or that the sums were obtained from some illegal sources" and that as a consequence her son was estopped from denying that the capital belonged to the claimant. Judge Turnbull points out, however, that this was wrong in law. As the House of Lords held in *Tinsley v Milligan* [1994] 1 A.C. 340, the principle that prevents a person putting forward evidence of his own wrongdoing in order to establish a resulting trust in his favour only applies where the person needs to put forward that evidence in order to rebut the presumption of advancement or of resulting trust. It does not apply where the person does not need to assert the illegality and only needs to show that he paid or contributed to the purchase price. In this case the claimant's son would be able to rely on the presumption of resulting trust without asserting any illegality. The question therefore was, in so far as it was accepted that the money was provided by her son, whether there was a resulting trust in his favour or whether he had intended to make a gift to the claimant.

DF v SSWP (ESA) [2015] UKUT 611 (AAC) concerns the question of whether the claimant could argue that he was not the beneficial owner of the funds in an

Individual Savings Account (ISA) that was in his name. One of the conditions for an ISA account is that money invested in the account is in the beneficial ownership of the account holder (see reg.4(6) of the Individual Savings Account Regulations 1998 (SI 1998/1870) (ISA Regulations 1998)). The claimant maintained that the money in his ISA account really belonged to his daughter. His daughter confirmed this, stating that the ISA was designed to keep her money away from an unreliable partner. The Secretary of State argued that a person in whose name an ISA is held has to be regarded as the beneficial owner of the money in the account, relying on the decision in *CIS/2836/2006*. While that decision concerned the Personal Equity Plan Regulations 1989 (SI 1989/469), the ISA Regulations 1998 were said to be identical.

Judge Mitchell, however, concludes that *CIS/2836/2006* is restricted to "presumption of advancement" cases, i.e. cases in which the money is given by someone standing in loco parentis to a child, or by a husband to a wife, where there is a presumption that a gift was intended (note that the presumption of advancement was due to be abolished by s.199 of the Equality Act 2010 but this section has not yet been brought into force). To the extent that *CIS/2836/2006* could be read as going further, in his view it was not consistent with the decision in *Tinsley v Milligan* (above). He also holds that *CIS/2836/2006* did not decide that ISA-type legislation operates to extinguish beneficial interests of third parties in ISA deposits. Neither the ISA Regulations 1998 nor the enabling power under which they were made (Income and Corporation Taxes Act 1988 s.333(2)) had the effect of altering existing rights in relation to property. The legislation was only concerned with creating a special account with special tax advantages.

Judge Mitchell then goes on to reject the Secretary of State's argument that the law of illegality meant that, as a matter of public policy, the claimant could not rely on a beneficial interest that he had previously denied. This was inconsistent with the Supreme Court's decision in *Hounga v Allen* [2014] UKSC 47; [2014] 1 W.L.R. 2889 and the Court of Appeal's decision in *R. (Best) v Secretary of State for Justice (Rev 1)* [2015] EWCA Civ 17. In his view it was better for a First-tier Tribunal in an ISA case to ignore the role that may or may not be played by the law of illegality and simply focus on whether it accepted that the beneficial interest in the funds lay elsewhere. He does, however, point out the risks that a claimant runs in arguing that a third party has a beneficial interest in the sums deposited in an ISA, namely conceding that any ISA tax reliefs were improperly awarded and the possibility of criminal proceedings for a tax offence under s.106A of the Taxes Management Act 1970 (see para.17 of the decision).

An illustration of a constructive trust, which does not operate on the basis of a common intention but on it being unconscionable for the person with the legal interest to deny the beneficial interest of another, is *R(SB) 23/85*. The claimant's wife in a home-made and legally ineffective deed of gift purported to give an uninhabitable property to her son. He, as intended, carried out the works to make it habitable. The Commissioner held that, although a court will not normally "complete" such an "uncompleted gift" in favour of someone who has not given valuable consideration, one of the situations in which a transfer of the property will be ordered is where the intended recipient is induced to believe that he has or will have an interest in the property and acts on that belief to his detriment. Thus in the meantime the claimant's wife held the property merely as a "bare trustee" and could not lawfully transfer it to anyone but the son. There is discussion of what kind of action might give rise to the right to complete the gift in *R(SB) 7/87*, where there was evidence of the claimant's intention to give a flat to her two sons, but all that one son had done in reliance was to redecorate the flat prior to its sale. See also *CIS/807/1991* on proprietary estoppel.

However, similar circumstances should probably now be approached from the standpoint of the principles adopted in the decision of the Supreme Court in *Guest v Guest* [2022] UKSC 27, [2022] 3 W.L.R. 911 on proprietary estoppel and the nature of the remedies available in equity. Lord Briggs, giving the majority judgment (two justices dissented), conducted an exhaustive survey of the English and Australian case law, as well as academic debate, and rejected the theory that the aim of the remedy was to compensate the person given a promise or assurance about the acquisition of property for the detriment suffered in reliance on the promise or assurance, rather than primarily to hold the person who had given the promise or assurance to the promise or assurance, which would usually prevent the unconscionability inherent in the repudiation of the promise or assurance that had been detrimentally relied on (paras 71 and 61). However, the remedy was a flexible one dependent on the circumstances. Lord Briggs summarised the principles as follows:

> "74. I consider that, in principle, the court's normal approach should be as follows. The first stage (which is not in issue in this case) is to determine whether the promisor's repudiation of his promise is, in the light of the promisee's detrimental reliance upon it, unconscionable at all. It usually will be, but there may be circumstances (such as the promisor falling on hard times and needing to sell the property to pay his creditors, or to pay for expensive medical treatment or social care for himself or his wife) when it may not be. Or the promisor may have announced or carried out only a partial repudiation of the promise, which may or may not have been unconscionable, depending on the circumstances.
>
> 75. The second (remedy) stage will normally start with the assumption (not presumption) that the simplest way to remedy the unconscionability constituted by the repudiation is to hold the promisor to the promise. The promisee cannot (and probably would not) complain, for example, that his detrimental reliance had cost him more than the value of the promise, were it to be fully performed. But the court may have to listen to many other reasons from the promisor (or his executors) why something less than full performance will negate the unconscionability and therefore satisfy the equity. They may be based on one or more of the real-life problems already outlined. The court may be invited by the promisor to consider one or more proxies for performance of the promise, such as the transfer of less property than promised or the provision of a monetary equivalent in place of it, or a combination of the two.
>
> 76. If the promisor asserts and proves, the burden being on him for this purpose, that specific enforcement of the full promise, or monetary equivalent, would be out of all proportion to the cost of the detriment to the promisee, then the court may be constrained to limit the extent of the remedy. This does not mean that the court will be seeking precisely to compensate for the detriment as its primary task, but simply to put right a disproportionality which is so large as to stand in the way of a full specific enforcement doing justice between the parties. It will be a very rare case where the detriment is equivalent in value to the expectation, and there is nothing in principle unjust in a full enforcement of the promise being worth more than the cost of the detriment, any more than there is in giving specific performance of a contract for the sale of land merely because it is worth more than the price paid for it. An example of a remedy out of all proportion to the detriment would be the full enforcement of a promise by an elderly lady to leave her carer a particular piece of jewellery if she stayed on at very low wages, which turned out on valuation by her executors to be a Faberge worth millions. Another would be a promise to leave a generous inheritance if the promisee cared for the promisor for the rest of her life, but where she unexpectedly died two months later."

Winter v Winter [2024] EWCA Civ 699, in another farm case, has explored the requirement of detriment in some detail, in particular holding that when deciding whether a claimant has suffered detriment as a result of reliance on an assurance, the court must weigh any non-financial disadvantage against any financial benefit even where the disadvantage is not susceptible to quantification, and even though it is a difficult exercise.

Thus, in circumstances where proprietary estoppel might be in play (as would probably now be the case on similar facts to *R(SB) 23/85* and *R(SB) 7/87*), great care would be needed in establishing the primary facts and, outside the clearest cases, in a deeper investigation of the principles of law governing the nature of any remedy available. And would a repudiation of a promise when the promisor would otherwise be forced to rely on a means-tested benefit be unconscionable? However, even if it were to be concluded that the claimant did not hold the property in question on trust for someone else, the possibility of a claim in equity, e.g. for some monetary compensation, might well affect the valuation of the property.

Note also the doctrine of secret trusts, under which a person who receives property under an intestacy when the deceased refrained from making a will in reliance on that person's promise to carry out their expressed intentions, holds the property on trust to carry out those intentions (*CSB/989/1985*). The doctrine also applies to property left by will where on the face of the will the property has been left to A but this is on the understanding that A is merely a trustee of it in favour of B.

For an example of where there may have been a secret trust, see *GK v SSWP (JSA)* [2012] UKUT 115 (AAC). In that case the claimant had inherited money from her aunt which she understood from conversations with her aunt was to be shared between her five children and herself. She used the money to purchase some land, which, although in her sole name, she regarded as belonging to all six of them. Judge Mark held that the tribunal had erred in not considering whether there was a secret trust.

CIS/213/2004 and *CIS/214/2004* concerned the applicability of French law. A property in France had been purchased in the name of the claimant but the purchase price and renovation costs had been met by Ms V. Ms V was not the claimant's partner but they had a son and the purpose of putting the property in the claimant's name was so that their son and not Ms V's other children would inherit it (under French law all five of Ms V's children would otherwise have been entitled to an interest in the property). On the same day that the property was purchased the claimant executed a holograph will bequeathing a "usufruct" (the French equivalent of a life interest) in the property to Ms V. Applying the Recognition of Trusts Act 1987, which implements the Hague Convention of 1986 on the law applicable to trusts and their recognition, the Commissioner concludes that French law was the applicable law. But since French law does not recognise the concept of a trust, it followed that there was no resulting or constructive trust in favour of Ms V (although in the Commissioner's view if English law had been applicable the facts would have given rise to such a trust). The Commissioner directed the Secretary of State to obtain a further opinion as to the remedies available under French law to Ms V if the claimant decided to treat the property as his own, but after receiving this concluded that there was no reason under French law or otherwise why the value of the property should not be included in the claimant's capital. The claimant appealed against this decision to the Court of Appeal but the appeal was dismissed (*Martin v Secretary of State for Work and Pensions* [2009] EWCA Civ 1289; [2010] AACR 9).

It will be an error of law if a tribunal fails to consider the question of the applicable law in relation to property abroad (*MB v Royal Borough of Kensington & Chelsea (HB)* [2011] UKUT 321 (AAC)). The claimant in *MB* was an Irish national, who had, while domiciled and resident in Ireland, bought a property in Ireland with the assistance of a mortgage from an Irish bank. In those circumstances it was difficult to see how the applicable law could be other than Irish law, but the tribunal had not referred to this issue at all, nor had it sought any evidence as to the nature and content of Irish law and the Irish law of trusts (foreign law is a question of fact (see *R(G) 2/00,* at para.20)).

Choses in action

2.164 There is also a remarkable range of interests in property which do have a present market value and so are actual capital resources. These are usually things in action (or choses in action), rights to sue for something. See the earlier section of this note on *Interests under a will or intestacy when someone has died* for specific discussion of the importance of considering the existence of choses in action. Debts, even where they are not due to be paid for some time, are things in action which can be sold. A good example is *R(SB) 31/83* where the claimant in selling a house allowed the purchaser a mortgage of £4,000, to be redeemed in six months. The debt conferred a right to sue and had to be valued at what could be obtained on the open market. In *CJSA/204/2002* the claimant had lent her son £8,500 for the deposit on a flat. The Commissioner holds that the legal debt owed by the son to the claimant had to be valued in order to decide whether the claimant had actual capital in excess of £8,000 (which was then the prescribed limit). The terms of the loan, including the rate of any interest and whether there was any security for the loan, as well as the terms of repayment, were clearly relevant to this valuation. Once the value of the loan had been determined, the question of deprivation of capital then had to be considered. To the extent that the value of the loan was less than £8,500, to that extent the claimant had deprived herself of capital. However, on the facts the Commissioner found that the claimant had not deprived herself of the capital for the purpose of securing entitlement to, or increasing the amount of, jobseeker's allowance (see further the note to reg.50(1)). See also *JC v SSWP* [2009] UKUT 22 (AAC) which points out that the value of the loan will depend on whether it is likely to be recoverable. If the claimant had lent the money with no expectation of getting it back, he had in effect reduced the value of the chose in action to nil. The issue of deprivation of capital then arose. *R 2/09(IS)*, a Northern Ireland decision, gives further guidance on the approach to choses in action and their value.

In *GS v DSD (IS)* [2012] NI Com 284 (another Northern Ireland decision) the claimant agreed in June 2004 to buy a house (not yet built) from Mr McK in return for the transfer of ownership of the claimant's present house, plus £33,000. The £33,000 was paid by cheque in August 2006. However, the building work was delayed due to the illness of Mr McK's brother and the house was only eventually built during 2009. But by March 2010 (the date of the decision under appeal) the agreement still had not been fulfilled due to difficulties with Mr McK's title to the land. Mr McK accepted that the £33,000 deposit would be returned if these difficulties could not be resolved. Commissioner Stockman points out that a chose in action can only arise upon breach of contract, or possibly frustration of contract; the mere existence of the contract did not give rise to the right to sue for return of the deposit. The difficulty was determining whether there had been a breach of contract and in identifying when that occurred. In the circumstances of this case, where there was no date for the completion of the contract and the delay in completing the building work had been waived by the claimant because of the personal friendship between Mr McK and himself, the claimant would not have had a strong case for breach of contract for unreasonable delay. This would have a resultant effect on the value of the chose in action, for which there was unlikely to be a ready market. The Commissioner decides that the value of the chose in action was nil from August 2006 and £3,000 from November 2008 up to March 2010.

An action for breach of fiduciary duty against an attorney appointed under the Enduring Powers of Attorney Act 1985 who had used the claimant's capital to repay her own debts also constitutes actual capital; so too would a claim against the attorney for misapplication of capital on the ground that she had made gifts outside the circumstances sanctioned by s.3(5) of the 1985 Act (this allows an attorney to make gifts (to herself or others) "provided that the value of each such gift is not unreasonable having regard to all the circumstances and in particular the size of the donor's estate") (*R(IS) 17/98*).

Bank or building society accounts

A more direct way of holding capital is in a bank or building society account. In *CSB/296/1985* the claimant's solicitor received £12,000 damages on behalf of the claimant and placed the money on deposit, presumably in the solicitor's client account. The Commissioner held that the £12,000 was an actual resource of the claimant, on the basis that there was no difference in principle between monies being held by a solicitor on behalf of a client and monies held by a bank or building society on behalf of a customer. This decision was upheld by the Court of Appeal in *Thomas v Chief Adjudication Officer*, reported as *R(SB) 17/87*. Russell LJ says "the possession of this money by the solicitors as the agent for the claimant was, in every sense of the term, possession by the claimant." 2.165

However, note *CIS/984/2002* which holds that money held by the claimant's solicitor pending quantification of the statutory charge to the Legal Services Commission under s.10(7) of the Access to Justice Act 1999 was not part of the claimant's capital. Until that quantification had been carried out, it was not possible to identify any particular amount as the claimant's capital. Another way of looking at it was to treat the statutory charge as an incumbrance for the purpose of the equivalent of reg.49(1) (b) (see *CIS/368/1993*).

See also *LC v Bournemouth Borough Council (HB)* [2016] UKUT 175 (AAC), where the proceeds of sale of a former matrimonial home were being held in a solicitors' client account until the claimant's partner and his ex-wife could agree how the sum was to be split or the issue was resolved by a court order after a Financial Dispute Resolution hearing. In Judge White's view the value of the capital prior to agreement or an order of the court would be minimal.

The approach taken in *Thomas* seems to involve valuing the amount of money directly, not as a technical chose in action. However, the importance of the legal relationship between a bank and a customer being one of debtor and creditor was revealed in *CSB/598/1987*. A large cheque was paid into the claimant's wife's bank account on October 9, 1987. The amount was credited to her account on that date, but the cheque was not cleared until October 15. The bank's paying-in slips reserved the bank's right to "postpone payment of cheques drawn against uncleared effects which may have been credited to the account." The effect was that the bank did not accept the relationship of debtor and creditor on the mere paying in of a cheque. Thus the amount did not become part of the claimant's actual resources until October 15. A person who deliberately refrains from paying in a cheque may be fixed with notional capital under reg.50(1).

CIS/255/2005 concerned the effect on capital of the issue of a cheque. The Commissioner holds that the claimant's capital was reduced from the date that the cheque was issued (this would not apply if the cheque was postdated). After that time she could not honestly withdraw money from her bank account so as to leave insufficient funds to meet the cheque.

In *R(IS) 15/96* the Commissioner confirms that money in a building society or bank (or solicitor's client) account is an actual resource in the form of a chose in action. It is not, as the SSAT had decided, held in trust. If the money is in an account from which it can be withdrawn at any time, its value is the credit balance (less any penalties for early withdrawal, etc.). But if the money cannot be withdrawn for a specified term the value will be less (although the notional capital rules may come into play in respect of the difference in value: *CIS/494/1990*; see also *R(1S) 8/04*.

Interests in trusts

2.166 The nature of interests in capital under trusts gives rise to several problems. It is clear that a person may have an absolute vested interest under a trust, although payment is deferred, e.g. until the age of 21. This was the case in *R(SB) 26/86*, where the resource was held to be the person's share of the fund. However, an interest may be contingent on reaching a particular age. This appears to have been one of the assumptions on which the Court of Appeal decided the unsatisfactory case of *Peters v Chief Adjudication Officer*, reported as *R(SB) 3/89*. It was conceded that sums were held on trust to be paid over to each of three sisters on attaining the age of 18, with the power to advance up to 50 per cent of the capital before then. In the end, the Court of Appeal accepted the valuation of half of the full value for each sister under 18. The precise finding may depend on the supplementary benefit rule on discretionary trusts, which was not translated into the income support or universal credit legislation. But some statements about the general market value of such interests are made. May LJ says "in an appropriate market a discretionary entitlement of up to 50 per cent now and at least 50 per cent in, say, six months in a given case, or three to four years in another, could well be said to have a value greater than 50 per cent of the capital value of the trust." This clearly supports the view that a contingent interest has a market value and so is actual capital. See also *CTC 4713/2002* which concerned a similar trust in favour of the claimant's son to that in *Peters* (although in this case the trustees had power to advance the whole of the fund). The Commissioner notes that in *Peters* the Court of Appeal had accepted the valuation agreed by the parties without argument. He acknowledged that each case must turn on its facts and that valuation of different interests would differ depending on such factors as the nature of the underlying investments (there was evidence in this case that due to lack of investor confidence the market value of the fund was much diminished); in addition in this case, unlike *Peters*, the whole of the fund could be advanced. However, he concluded that the Court of Appeal's approach in *Peters* led to a valuation of the claimant's son's equitable interest as being more or less equal to the whole net value of the trust fund (less 10 per cent for the expenses of sale).

A life interest in a trust fund or the right to receive income under a liferent in Scots law is a present asset which can be sold and has a market value (*R(SB) 2/84, R(SB) 43/84, R(SB) 15/86* and *R(SB) 13/87*). The practical effect is reversed for income support by para.13 of Sch.10 to the Income Support Regulations, but no such disregard is included in Sch.10 to the present Regulations.

All interests which can be sold or borrowed against will need to be considered. However, in the case of an interest under a discretionary trust, the DWP will normally only take payments of capital (or income) into account when they are actually made.

In *R(IS) 9/04* it was argued that funds held by the Court of Protection were analogous to those held by a discretionary trustee. Since neither the claimant nor her receiver could insist on the Court releasing any part of the funds it was contended that the market value of the claimant's actual interest was so small as to be negligible. However, the Commissioner followed *CIS/7127/1995* in holding that the entire beneficial interest in the funds administered by the Court remained with the claimant to whom alone they belonged. The fact the Court had discretionary powers of control over the management of a patient's property for his or her benefit did not mean that the patient's beneficial ownership had ceased. The funds therefore had to be valued at their current market value, less any appropriate allowance for sale expenses, in the normal way (see reg.49).

Realisation of assets

R (SB) 18/83 stresses that there are more ways of realising assets than sale. In particular, assets can be charged to secure a loan which can be used to meet requirements. In that case the asset was a minority shareholding in a family company. The Commissioner says that only a person prepared to lend money without security would do so in such circumstances. The articles of association of the company provided that if a shareholder wanted to sell shares they were to be offered to the existing shareholders at the fair value fixed by the auditors. The Commissioner holds that the regulations do not require assets to be valued at a figure higher than anything the person would realise on them, i.e. the auditor's fair value. This is in line with the purpose of the capital cut-off that a claimant can draw on resources until they fall below the limit. **2.167**

This approach to valuation can usefully deal with unrealisable assets. See the notes to reg.49. However, it is no part of the definition of capital that it should be immediately realisable, although its market value may be affected by such factors. It remains possible for claimants to be fixed with large amounts of actual capital that are not immediately available to them by everyday means, but may have a value in some specialised market.

Deduction of liabilities

The general rule is that the whole of a capital resource is to be taken into account. Liabilities are not to be deducted from the value (*R(SB) 2/83*). In general, the "remedy" if the capital limits are in issue, is for the claimant to discharge the liability, the amount of which cannot, by virtue of reg.50(2) constitute notional capital under the deprivation rule. **2.168**

SSWP v GF (ESA) [2017] UKUT 333 (AAC) is an illustration of the application of the principle. For one part of the period in issue the claimant's brother-in-law had paid a costs order of some £48,000 made against the claimant in the expectation at least that he would be repaid once the 120-day notice period for withdrawal of funds in the claimant's building society bond with a balance of £75,000 had expired. On the evidence available the judge rightly concluded that there was no implied, resulting or constructive trust and that the claimant's debt did not change the beneficial ownership of the funds in the bond. However, there could in other similar cases be evidence of discussions or arrangements before the brother-in-law made his payment that could lead to a conclusion either that the debt had been secured on the claimant's rights in the bond or that the claimant had made a declaration of trust. In *GF* itself no such argument could have helped the claimant because even if he had not been the beneficial owner of £48,000 of the balance in the bond, the value of the remainder (even subject to the 120-day notice provision) would no doubt have exceeded £16,000.

Otherwise, it is only if a debt is secured on the capital asset that it can be deducted, at the stage specifically required by reg.49 (*R(IS) 21/93*). See the notes to reg.49 and note *JRL v SSWP (JSA)* [2011] UKUT 63 (AAC), reported as [2011] AACR 30. There, the claimant had three accounts with the same bank, of which one was in credit, one was overdrawn, and one had a nil balance. The three-judge panel pointed out that this meant that the claimant was both a creditor and a debtor of the same body. Under the bank's terms and conditions, the bank had a contractual right to debit at any time any of a customer's accounts which were in credit with sums sufficient to clear the customer's indebtedness to the bank. This created what was effectively a charge on the customer's credit balance(s). The market value of the account that was in credit was therefore its net value after deduction of the amount of the claimant's overdraft on his other account.

Personal possessions

2.169 Note that personal possessions are not treated as capital (para.(2)). There is no equivalent to the rule for income support, old style JSA, old style ESA and housing benefit that personal possessions are taken into account if they have been acquired with the intention of reducing capital in order to secure, or increase, entitlement to benefit (see, e.g., para.10 of Sch.10 to the Income Support Regulations in Vol.V of this series, 2021/22 edition as updated in Cumulative Supplements included in this volume and in mid-year Supplements). However, in such circumstances claimants may be found to have notional capital under reg.50(1) and (2), by reason of having deprived themselves of capital through the mechanism of acquisition of personal possessions. For reg.50(1) to operate, the deprivation must have been for the purpose of securing entitlement to or increasing the amount of universal credit (rather than any other benefit), which may significantly limit its effect in relation to acquisitions some way in the past. In addition, reg.50(2), in a provision not replicated in relation to any other benefits (except state pension credit), prevents claimants being treated as having deprived themselves of capital if they have purchased goods or services and the expenditure was reasonable in the circumstances (see further in the notes to that provision).

R(H) 7/08 was a case about whether a moveable but static caravan, attached to mains services on a non-residential site, was a "personal possession" for the purposes of the disregard in the housing benefit legislation. A tribunal had decided that it was not, so that its value counted as capital. The Commissioner held that it erred in law in doing so. After a discursive discussion of the legislative background and the scant authority, he said this in para.53:

> "My conclusion is that 'personal possessions' mean any physical assets other than land and assets used for business purposes. . . . [This] avoids uncertainty of scope and difficulties of application. It is consistent with the legislative history of the disregard and the more humane approach to resource-related benefits that has

increasingly been shown over the period of the welfare state. It recognises the increased emphasis that has been given over recent decades to ways of assisting claimants off welfare by not requiring particular categories of possessions to be disposed of for what may be a relatively short period on benefit."

That approach would seem to require that the actual value of items acquired mainly, or even solely, as investments be disregarded, but there will sometimes be very difficult lines to be drawn in particular circumstances even if that basis were accepted. At what point might coins, say, or gold bars cease to be regarded as personal possessions and be regarded as a way of holding capital in the same way as everyday cash?

Might it still be argued that, as Commissioner Jacobs was not directly concerned in *R(H) 7/08* with any line between personal possessions and investments, the decision does not exclude a conclusion that the adjective "personal" is an indication that something has to be used at least partly for personal or domestic or household purposes, not solely for investment? Prior to its amendment in October 2014 by s.3(1) of the Inheritance and Trustees' Powers Act 2014, the definition of "personal chattels" in s.55(1)(x) of the Administration of Estates Act 1925 (for the purposes of identifying how an estate is to be distributed on intestacy), as well as setting out a long list of specific items, included "articles of household or personal use or ornament". The courts, bearing in mind the test in terms of the use made of the article at the time of death, took quite a generous approach to when that use had a personal element. In one case, *Re Reynolds' Will Trusts* [1966] 1 W.L.R. 19, the aptly named Stamp J, having held the intestate's valuable stamp collection, built up since childhood as his main hobby, to be part of his personal chattels, suggested that if he had gone into a shop and bought a similar collection that he then installed in his flat it could hardly be said that that was an article of personal use. Regulation 46(2) makes no express reference to the use made of any possession, but it may be arguable that the word "personal" entails the exclusion of items with no element of personal enjoyment or cherishing (such as collections of jewellery, art work, stamps etc locked away in a safe or bank vault and never inspected). However, such an approach would again involve the drawing of difficult lines after careful investigation that it may be thought that the legislation was intended to avoid. It would have been helpful if matters had been made plainer on the face of the legislation.

No doubt, whatever the general answer, the more evidence there is that an item was acquired by a person for investment, the stronger the argument would be for its cost having been a deprivation of capital under reg.50(1), subject to the working out of the scope of the exception in reg.50(2)(b) for purchasing goods and services where the expenditure was reasonable.

Capital treated as income

Under paras (3) and (4), certain payments that might otherwise be capital are treated as income (and therefore do not count as capital). **2.170**

Paragraph (4) deals with capital payable by instalments. If the amount outstanding plus the claimant's (including, in the case of couples, the other member of the couple's) other capital is more than £16,000, each instalment when paid is treated as income. Otherwise the payment counts as capital. That position follows inevitably from the nature of capital payable by instalments, but was confirmed to operate in the circumstances of the purchase price of a house being paid in monthly instalments over ten years in *Lillystone v Supplementary Benefits Commission* [1982] 3 F.L.R. 52. If para.(4) applies to treat the instalment as income, then reg.66(1)(l) includes the income as unearned income that is to be taken into account in full. See the notes to reg.66(1) for difficulties about how such income is to be attributed to particular assessment periods.

There may be some conundrums in working out the application of para.(4) in particular cases. Presumably the value of the claimant's other capital is tested as at the date that each instalment is received. Then in taking the value of "other capital", presumably the capital value of the right to continue receiving the instalments must be excluded, otherwise there would be unfair double counting with the amount outstanding (even though the market value would no doubt be less than the amount outstanding). That capital value is not disregarded for universal credit purposes, as it is for income support and other benefits (Income Support Regulations Sch.10 para.16: Vol.V of this series, 2021/22 edition as updated in Cumulative Supplements included in this volume and in mid-year Supplements). Thus, it is theoretically possible for the £16,000 limit under para.(4) to be breached while the value of the claimant's capital in accordance with reg.49, including the value of the right to continue receiving the instalments, does not exceed £16,000, so that entitlement to universal credit would not be removed entirely under the capital rule.

Weekly sums that the claimant was allowed to withdraw for living expenses from his bank account which was subject to a restraint order under s.77 of the Criminal Justice Act 1988 did not constitute capital payable by instalments (*SH v SSWP* [2008] UKUT 21 (AAC)). The old style JSA equivalent of para.(4) only applied if there was a contractual or other obligation on the part of some other person to pay a capital sum to the claimant by instalments.

Paragraph (3) applies to sums (other than capital payable by instalments) that are paid regularly and by reference to a period, such as payments under an annuity. They are treated as income, even if they would otherwise be regarded as capital or as having a capital element. This is wider than the previous rule in, e.g., reg.41(2) of the Income Support Regulations (which only applies to payments under an annuity) and would seem to be an attempt to draw more of a line between capital and income. Although para.(3) thus has an important effect in drawing that line for the purposes of the Regulations as a whole, it is submitted that its operation must be limited to treating the payments concerned as income in the general sense or to circumstances where they would otherwise constitute capital. That is because capital treated as income under para.(3) or (4) counts as unearned income under reg.66(1)(l), to be taken into account as full. If reg.66(1)(l) were to be taken to apply to every sum paid regularly and by reference to a period, that would subvert the express limitation imposed by the other parts of reg.66(1). For instance, the great majority of social security benefits, both within the UK and abroad, are paid regularly and by reference to a period. If they then fell within reg.66(1)(l), that would render nugatory the careful specification in reg.66(1)(a), (b), (c) and (da) of the benefits that are to be taken into account (with the necessary result that any not specified are not to be taken into account). That cannot possibly have been intended. See the notes to reg.66(1)(l) for how it is suggested that provision must be interpreted.

Note the "assumed yield from capital" rule in reg.72(1) (the equivalent to the "tariff income rule" for income support, old style JSA, old style ESA and housing benefit). That rule does not apply to capital that is disregarded or produces income that is taken into account under reg.66(1)(i) (annuities) or (j) (trusts) (reg.72(2)). If the rule produces any assumed income, actual income from capital is treated as capital from the day that it is due to be paid (reg.72(3)).

Jointly held capital

2.171 **47.** Where a person and one or more other persons have a beneficial interest in a capital asset, those persons are to be treated, in the absence of evidence to the contrary, as if they were each entitled to an equal share of the whole of that beneficial interest.

General Note

2.172 This provision is much the same in structure as the income support and income-based JSA equivalents (reg.52 of the Income Support Regulations and reg.115 of the JSA Regulations 1996), with the addition of the apparently significant words "in the absence of evidence to the contrary". However, close analysis suggests that those words are ineffective for the vast majority of practical purposes and that reg.47, like its equivalents, achieves only limited results of substance.

That conclusion follows from the decision of the Court of Appeal in *Hourigan v Secretary of State for Work and Pensions* [2002] EWCA Civ 1890, reported as *R(IS) 4/03*. There the claimant bought her council house with a contribution of five-sixths of the purchase price from her son. The legal estate was transferred to her in her sole name, but it was accepted that in those circumstances she held the legal estate on trust for herself and her son as tenants in common in the proportions of their contributions to the purchase price. The Secretary of State argued that reg.52 of the Income Support Regulations applied because the claimant and her son were beneficially entitled to the capital asset of the equitable interest in the house and that as a result she had to be treated as having a half share in the equitable interest, although her actual share was one-sixth. It was argued that it was that deemed half share that had to be valued as capital, in which case the claimant was not entitled to income support because the capital limit was breached. Brooke LJ held that it would be a misuse of language to say that the claimant and her son were both beneficially entitled to a capital asset in the form of the house because the beneficial interest of each as a tenant in common was a separately disposable asset. To interpret reg.52 in the way contended for by the Secretary of State would require very much clearer words. Not only was it unfair to the claimant to treat her as possessing more capital than she could actually realise, but the Secretary of State's argument could also work unfairly in favour of claimants (e.g. if it had been a claimant who had a five-sixths share who was deemed to have only a half-share). Thus it was only the claimant's actual one-sixth share as tenant in common that fell to be valued as capital.

Brooke LJ accepted that the language of reg.52 could apply to circumstances in which the claimant and one or more persons were jointly entitled to the equitable interest in the same capital asset. In that situation the effect of reg.52 was to treat the joint tenancy as severed and to deem the claimant to have an equal share (with the other joint tenants), with there being a tenancy in common as between the claimant and the other joint tenant(s).

That appears correct, but the limit of the effect of reg.47 (just as for reg.52 of the Income Support Regulations) would appear to be in deeming that there has been a severance of the joint tenancy of the beneficial interest (as can be carried out by a joint tenant at any time or by selling or otherwise alienating or attempting to alienate the interest as a joint tenant). The limit is because there is no need for any regulation to deem that the claimant's share on severance is proportionate to the number of former joint tenants (i.e. a half share if there were previously two, a third share if there were previously three etc). That consequence follows from the nature of a joint tenancy, where there is only one interest (the so-called unity of interest), so that the interest of each tenant must be the same in extent, nature and duration. *Goodman v Gallant* [1985] EWCA Civ 15, [1986] Fam. 106 establishes that the sole exception could be where the terms of the trust establishing the joint tenancy expressly provided that on any severance the shares were not to be equal (which would be a vanishingly rare circumstance). There is no room at the stage of severance (or deemed severance) for going back to, say, the amount of contribution to the purchase price, to justify anything other than an equal share. (But do not forget that tenancies in common created in other ways can, and often do, have unequal shares). Thus, if the claimant in *Hourigan* had expressly had the council house conveyed to her to hold in trust for herself and her son as joint tenants, there could have been no escape, regardless of any regulations, from the consequence on a severance (actual or deemed) of the joint tenancy in the beneficial interest that her share as tenant in common was one-half. It could make no difference that the son had contributed five-sixths of the purchase price. It is a common elementary student error to think otherwise, one into which it appears that Auld LJ fell in *Hourigan*.

The upshot is that, once it is determined that reg.47 is restricted to joint tenancies, the reference to the absence of evidence to the contrary becomes redundant. The purported relevance of the phrase "in the absence of evidence to the contrary" to the deeming in reg.47 can only be to the shares in which the beneficial interest is to be held under the tenancy in common (the phrase "in equal shares" having long been accepted as indicating a tenancy in common). Evidence to the contrary cannot prevent the deeming of a tenancy in common because in all circumstances where there was still actually a joint tenancy there would be evidence to the contrary, i.e. whatever the evidence was that produced that actual result, and the regulation could then never apply at all. However, no evidence to the contrary could influence the shares under the deemed tenancy in common, because the equal shares follow from the nature of a joint tenancy, subject to the rare exception where the express terms of a trust indicate a different share on severance (see above).

In cases, like the above, involving real property, there will usually be no difficulty in identifying the property subject to a joint tenancy. It may not be so easy when the joint interest is in some other asset or in a bank or building society account. That is shown by *CIS/7097/1995*. There, the claimant's husband went to live permanently in a nursing home. To help finance the cost of that accommodation, £7,000 of the husband's National Savings certificates were cashed in and the proceeds paid into the couple's joint bank account, so that the nursing home could be paid regularly by direct debit. There was evidence that the intention had not been that the sum should form part of the joint money in the account. The £7,000 had been declared as the husband's own money in an application to the local authority for financial assistance with the fees and a separate tally was kept of the use of that money. The AO treated the claimant's capital as including half of the balance in the joint account, including the proceeds of the husband's National Savings certificates, which took her over the limit, so that she was not entitled to income support. The Commissioner reversed that decision. There was clear evidence that the normal presumption of joint beneficial ownership between a husband and wife operating a joint bank account did not apply in relation to the £7,000. It was obviously intended that the proceeds of the husband's National Savings certificates were to remain his sole property and had been paid into the joint account merely for convenience. They did not form part of the claimant's capital. The Commissioner also analysed the nature of joint beneficial ownership and ownership in equal shares in a way consistent with what is said above.

A similar approach was taken in the Scottish case of *JK v SSWP (JSA)* [2010] UKUT 437 (AAC), reported as [2011] AACR 26. The claimant contended that some of the money in his and his wife's joint bank account belonged to his mother-in-law. It was held that the First-tier Tribunal, instead of asking whether there was a trust in favour of the mother-in-law, should have considered, by reference to such oral or written evidence available to it that it accepted, whether under Scots law (see *Cairns v Davidson* 1913 S.C. 1053) the presumption in favour of all the money in the joint account belonging to the claimant and his wife had been rebutted, so as to establish whether or not some of it belonged to the mother-in-law.

Valuation under regulation 47

2.173 It is the deemed equal share that has to be valued, not the proportionate share of the overall value (see the Court of Appeal's decision in *Chief Adjudication Officer v Palfrey*, reported as part of *R(IS) 26/95*, which had upheld the Tribunal of Commissioners' decisions in *CIS/391/1992* and *CIS/417/1992* (reported as part of *R(IS) 26/95*). The Tribunal of Commissioners gave detailed guidance as to the basis of a proper valuation of such a share (*CIS 391/1992*, paras 53 and 54), which is still relevant as a foundation for later decisions. In both *CIS/391/1992* and *CIS/417/1992* ownership was shared with relatives who were unable or unwilling to sell the property or buy the claimant's interest. The Commissioners recognised, as did the Court of Appeal, that the market value in such cases may well be nil, although as discussed below all will depend on the circumstances of particular cases.

In *Palfrey* the Tribunal of Commissioners state that the SSAT should have exercised its inquisitorial jurisdiction to call for the documents under which the property was acquired in order to sort out the beneficial ownership, but that may not be necessary where there is no dispute about the actual conveyancing history (*CIS/127/1993*).

The current guidance to decision makers in Ch.H1 of the ADM (in particular paras H1638 – H1642) suggests that they should obtain an expert opinion on the market value of a deemed share in land/premises. It gives quite rigorous and detailed guidance, in the main firmly based on the case law discussed below fleshing out what is entailed by the principle laid down in *Palfrey*, on the criteria for a valuation to be acceptable. For instance, the guidance states that where the other owners will not buy the share or agree to a sale of the asset as a whole, the expert should not simply assume that a court would order a sale but must consider the particular circumstances and take into account legal costs, length of time to obtain possession, etc. The guidance also says that the expert would need to explain whether on the facts of the case there was any market for the deemed share, explain what assumptions, if any, have been made, whether and, if so what, comparables have been considered and indicate how the value of the deemed share had been calculated. The expert should also indicate their experience and/or knowledge of the market for shared interests in real property. Slightly oddly, it is said in para.H1641 that in working out the reg.49(1) value of the premises, only 10 per cent for expenses of sale should be deducted and not anything for encumbrances, because they will already have been taken into account in the expert's valuation. That may work out if the expert has had full information about the nature and amount of the encumbrances, but that may need to be checked before the process as set out in reg.49(1) is short-circuited.

If that guidance was carefully followed, there would little problem in the production of acceptable evidence on behalf of the Secretary of State, although of course there would always be room for differences of opinion as a matter of judgment. However, experience over the years shows continuing difficulties in the production of valuations that properly adopt the principles of *Palfrey*. There have also been some differences of expression in the cases that have created some uncertainties, although it is submitted below that the basic principles have not been subverted.

R(IS) 3/96 contains a useful discussion as to whether the District Valuer's opinion supplied in that case met the requirements of *CIS/391/1992*. *R(JSA) 1/02* was concerned with valuing the claimant's interest in his former matrimonial home. His wife, from whom he was separated and who was in ill-health, continued to live there with their daughter, who had learning difficulties. The valuation obtained by the Jobcentre on a standard form (A64A/LA1) gave the open market value as £30,000 and the claimant's deemed undivided share as £9,200. No reasons were given for that conclusion. The property was leasehold but there was no evidence as to the remaining term of the lease, or as to the condition of the property. There was also no evidence as to the age of the daughter and no consideration as to whether a court would order a sale (which seemed very unlikely, given the purpose for which the property had been acquired and the purpose for which it was being used). The Commissioner, referring to *CIS/191/1994*, holds that there was no evidence that the claimant's capital exceeded the then prescribed limit of £8,000. He stated that everything depended on the facts and the evidence before the tribunal. In this case the valuation evidence was so unsatisfactory as to be worthless. He set out the following guidance on valuation:

> "13. Proper valuation evidence should include details of the valuer's expertise, the basis on which he or she holds him or herself out as able to give expert evidence in relation to the property in question. Where it is the sale of a share in a property which is in issue, the evidence should deal with the valuer's experience in relation to such shares, and their sale. The property, and any leasehold interest, should be described in sufficient detail, including details of the length of any lease, of any special terms in it, and of the location, size and condition of the property, to show that the factors relevant to its value have been taken into account, and the reasons for the conclusion as to the value should be given. A similar approach should be applied to a share of a property, and an explanation should be given of the factors identified as relevant to the valuation, and how they affect it. The expert should also give evidence of any comparables identified, or of other

reasons why it is concluded that the share could be sold at any particular price. If there is no evidence of actual sales of such interests, an acceptable explanation of the absence of such evidence should be given.

14. I appreciate that, in cases of this kind, this will on occasions be a counsel of perfection which cannot be realised. Where a valuer does not have relevant information, and proceeds upon assumptions, the report should state what is missing, and should also state the assumptions upon which it is based. This will normally give the claimant the opportunity to correct any mistaken assumptions or other errors of fact in the report."

See also *JC-W v Wirral Metropolitan BC (HB)* [2011] UKUT 501 (AAC), paras 13–18, for Judge Mark's critical comments in relation to the District Valuer's valuation in that case, and *MN v LB Hillingdon (HB)* [2014] UKUT 427 (AAC) and *PE v SSWP (SPC)* [2014] UKUT 387 (AAC) noted below.

It will not always be the case that a deemed equal share in a property will be of minimal value, even if the other co-owners are unwilling to sell. As *Wilkinson v Chief Adjudication Officer*, CA, March 24, 2000, reported as *R(IS) 1/01*, illustrates, the purposes for which the joint ownership was established will need to be scrutinised in order to assess whether a court would order a sale. In *Wilkinson* the claimant's mother had died, leaving her home to the claimant and her brother jointly "to do with as they wish". It was accepted that the mother had expressed the hope that the claimant's brother would live in the house with his son when his divorce proceedings in Australia were resolved (although there was nothing in the will to that effect). The claimant contended that the capital value of her half-share in the property was of a nominal value only, because her brother was unwilling to leave the property and unwilling to sell his share in it. She maintained that a court would not order a sale under s.30 of the Law of Property Act 1925 (repealed with effect from January 1, 1998 and replaced by ss.14 and 15 of the Trusts of Land and Appointment of Trustees Act 1996). But the Court of Appeal, by a majority (Mummery and Potter LJJ), disagreed. This was not a case like *Palfrey* where property had been acquired by joint owners for a collateral purpose (e.g. for them to live in as long as they wished) and that purpose would be defeated by ordering a sale. On the contrary, this was a case where an order for sale would enable the claimant's mother's wishes, as expressed in her will, to be carried out. Her brother's unwillingness to sell or pay the claimant for the value of her share was in fact having the effect of defeating that testamentary purpose. Potter LJ said that the proper starting point for valuation of the claimant's half-share was half the market value of the house with vacant possession, with a discount for any factors materially affecting her ability to market the house on that basis. The tribunal's conclusion that in the circumstances the value of her half-share was half of the market value of the house less 10% for expenses of sale and a charge to the testatrix's former husband was upheld. Evans LJ, however, took the opposite view. He considered that the claimant's share should be valued on the basis that a sale would not be ordered because this would defeat the mother's wish that her son and grandson be allowed to live in the property. As this case illustrates, much will depend on the circumstances in a particular case (and the view that is taken of those circumstances).

On very similar facts (a mother leaving a property to the claimant and his two sisters in equal shares, with no restriction or superadded purpose expressed in the will) the approach in *Wilkinson* was applied to the same effect in *JM v Eastleigh Borough Council (HB)* [2016] UKUT 464 (AAC).

Those cases were ones where there was no obstacle to the sale of the property with vacant possession, even though there might have been some normal delay in the process during which the disregard in para.6 of Sch.10 could come into play. The approach of starting with the market value of the property as a whole and then dividing by the number of joint owners, but not ignoring other factors, does not undermine the fundamental principle that under reg.47 it is the claimant's deemed severed share (i.e. as a deemed tenant in common) that must be valued.

The following decisions illustrate some of problems of valuation in the more complicated cases where there is real doubt whether a court would order a sale if other joint owners were unwilling to agree.

In *CIS/3197/2003* the claimant owned a house with her daughter, who had a two-thirds share. (As we now know as a result of *Hourigan*, such circumstances do not fall within reg.47, but the approach to valuation is still relevant). The claimant went into a nursing home, leaving the house in the occupation of her daughter and the daughter's disabled child. The daughter would not agree to a sale of the house nor was she willing to buy out the claimant's share. It seemed unlikely that a court would order a sale. In view of the Secretary of State's failure to provide proper evidence of the value of the claimant's share the Commissioner found that the value of the claimant's interest was nil. However, he added that tribunals should not approach the matter in this way. If the evidence was incomplete, they should adjourn with directions as to the ways in which the evidence should be supplemented and should not decide the case on the burden of proof. Clearly where there has been no attempt to obtain any valuation evidence this should apply. However, if such attempts have been made and the evidence remains inadequate, it is suggested that the burden of proof may need to come into play (and indeed this was the approach taken in both *R(IS) 3/96* and, in effect, *R(JSA) 1/02*). For example, in *R(IS) 3/96* it was held that grounds for revising the claimant's award had not been shown in the light of the deficiencies in the District Valuer's report and in *R(JSA) 1/02* the Commissioner substituted his own decision on the existing evidence despite such deficiencies.

Despite the above case law, examples have continued to crop up of a claimant's share in a property being wrongly valued simply as a proportion of the whole, rather than the claimant's actual or deemed share being properly valued, taking into account all the relevant circumstances. See, for instance, *R(IS) 5/07* and *AM v SSWP (SPC)* [2010] UKUT 134 (AAC).

Examples of inadequate valuation evidence from the District Valuer, where a tribunal erred in law by relying on it, also continue to arise, such as *MN v London Borough of Hillingdon (HB)* [2014] UKUT 427 (AAC). The claimant there had been living in the jointly-owned matrimonial home with his wife, who had serious mental health problems, and their severely disabled son. However, it became necessary for the claimant and his son to leave, due to deterioration in his wife's health. Judge Ovey, after noting that the District Valuer appeared to have arrived at her valuation by halving the total value of the property and deducting just under 1 per cent, despite having been given details of the circumstances of the case, stated:

> "32. . . . As a matter of common sense, it seems unlikely in the extreme that a purchaser would pay just under half the vacant possession value of a property for a half interest which would not enable him to occupy the property without first obtaining some form of court order against a defendant suffering from paranoid schizophrenia who was in occupation of a former matrimonial home, bought for the purpose of being a home, and who might be entitled to a property adjustment order. . . ."

See also *PE v SSWP (SPC)* [2014] UKUT 387 (AAC) which concerned the value of the claimant's interest in his former home, which remained occupied by his wife, son and step-son (the step-son had mental health problems). The District Valuer's valuation was based on an assumption that there had been a hypothetical application under the Trusts of Land and Appointment of Trustees Act 1996. The Secretary of State argued that in the circumstances of the case the District Valuer's assumption was unrealistic. Although no divorce proceedings were in place at the time, any application under the 1996 Act would be likely to generate such proceedings by the other party who was likely to obtain a more favourable outcome under the Matrimonial Causes Act 1973. Judge Jacobs accepted that the evidence relied on by the tribunal as to valuation was therefore flawed and decided, with the consent of the Secretary of State, that there were no grounds to supersede the decision awarding state pension credit.

There is a difficult balance between what might be a counsel of perfection (as in *R(JSA) 1/02*) and a realistic approach to what assumptions are acceptable in the inevitably imprecise exercise of valuing hypothetical interests. *Reigate and Banstead BC v GB (HB)* [2018] UKUT 225 (AAC) shows that tribunals should not go overboard in picking holes in a District Valuer's report. On the assumption (quite possibly inaccurate) that the claimant and his daughter were beneficial joint tenants and that there had not already been a severance, the tribunal went wrong in the reasons it relied on to find that the District Valuer had not properly valued the claimant's deemed equal share as a tenant in common and had not taken into account the possible need for an application to the court, as the property was occupied by the daughter and her son. In particular, the District Valuer did not need to provide evidence of a local market for an interest of the kind the claimant was deemed to have. There is undoubtedly a market for actual interests of the kind deemed to exist by reg.47 (see the many cases discussed above), often in specialist auctions, although that is no doubt not well-known to claimants. But there remains a question how much detail a District Valuer needs to give of the existence of such a market and of the prices fetched for comparable interests to validly underpin the valuation.

Capital disregarded

2.174 **48.**—(1) Any capital specified in Schedule 10 is to be disregarded from the calculation of a person's capital (see also regulations 75 to 77).

(2) Where a period of 6 months is specified in that Schedule, that period may be extended by the Secretary of State where it is reasonable to do so in the circumstances of the case.

General Note

2.175 The number of disregards in Sch.10 is considerably reduced from those that apply for income support, old style JSA, old style ESA and housing benefit but they cover many of the same items, such as premises, business assets, rights in pension schemes, earmarked assets, etc. But note that some of the disregards that are in Schedules for the purposes of those benefits are to be found elsewhere in these Regulations, e.g., in regs 46(2), 49(3), 75 and 76. See also reg.77 in relation to companies in which the person is like a sole trader or partner. And note that with effect from May 21, 2020 there is a disregard as capital (for 12 months from the date of receipt) for the self-employed of any payment in respect of a furloughed employee under the Coronavirus Job Retention Scheme or "by way of a grant or loan to meet the expenses or losses of the trade, profession or vocation in relation to the outbreak of coronavirus disease" (Universal Credit (Coronavirus) (Self-employed Claimants and Reclaims) (Amendment) Regulations 2020 (SI 2020/522) reg.2(2)) (see discussion in the note to para.7 of Sch.10 and the general note for other disregards stemming from provisions outside the Universal Credit Regulations).

Note the general extension on the grounds of reasonableness that can be applied to the six months' period in any of the provisions in Sch.10 (para.(2)).

With effect from July 24, 2019, reg.51 of the Transitional Provisions Regulations 2014, as inserted by reg.3 of the Universal Credit (Managed Migration Pilot and Miscellaneous Amendments) Regulations 2019 (SI 2019/1152), supplies a transitional capital disregard to claimants who (i) were previously entitled to a tax credit and had capital exceeding £16,000; (ii) are given a migration notice that existing benefits are to terminate; and (iii) claim universal credit within the deadline. The disregard is of any capital exceeding £16,000. The disregard can apply only for 12 assessment periods and ceases (without the possibility of revival) following any assessment period in which the amount of capital the claimant has falls below £16,000. See regs 56 and 57 of the Transitional Provisions Regulations for further provisions on termination of the protection. The £16,000 non-disregarded capital that the claimant by definition possesses will produce an assumed yield as income of £174 per month under reg.72. Paragraph 7 of Sch.2 to the Transitional Provisions Regulations, inserted by the same

Regulations, contains a disregard as capital of any amount paid as a lump sum by way of a "transitional SDP amount" under that Schedule. See the notes to Sch.10 for other disregards outside the terms of Sch.10.

Valuation of capital

49.—(1) Capital is to be calculated at its current market value or surrender value less— 2.176

(a) where there would be expenses attributable to sale, 10 per cent; and

(b) the amount of any encumbrances secured on it.

(2) The market value of a capital asset possessed by a person in a country outside the United Kingdom is—

(a) if there is no prohibition in that country against the transfer of an amount equal to the value of that asset to the United Kingdom, the market value in that country; or

(b) if there is such a prohibition, the amount it would raise if sold in the United Kingdom to a willing buyer.

(3) Where capital is held in currency other than sterling, it is to be calculated after the deduction of any banking charge or commission payable in converting that capital into sterling.

GENERAL NOTE

The rules for the valuation of capital are the same as for income support, old style ESA and JSA and housing benefit. Paragraph (1) is the equivalent of reg.49 of the Income Support Regulations. Paragraph (2) on assets outside the UK is the equivalent of reg.50. Paragraph (3) on capital held in foreign currency previously took the form of a disregard (para.21 of Sch.10 to the Income Support Regulations). 2.177

The general rule under para.(1) is that the market value of the asset is to be taken. The surrender value will be taken if appropriate (the disregard in para.9 of Sch.10 of the value of life insurance policies must refer to whichever value has been chosen). The value at this stage does not take account of any encumbrances (always spelt with an "i" in the former legislation) secured on the assets, since those come in under sub-para.(b) (*R(IS) 21/93*). There is no definitive requirement that there be a local market (*Reigate and Banstead BC v GB (HB)* [2018] UKUT 225 (AAC)), but the way in which markets work in practice in whatever asset is in question must be taken into account.

In *R(SB) 57/83* and *R(SB) 6/84* the test taken is the price that would be commanded between a willing buyer and a willing seller at a particular date. In *R(SB) 6/84* it is stressed that in the case of a house it is vital to know the nature and extent of the interest being valued. Also, since what is required is a current market value, the Commissioner holds that an estate agent's figure for a quick sale was closer to the proper approach than the District Valuer's figure for a sale within three months. All the circumstances must be taken into account in making the valuation. Arguments have been raised that during the 2020 coronavirus outbreak, in the period when estate agents' offices were closed and most viewings impossible, there was no market in existence for domestic properties. In *CIS/553/1991* it is held that in valuing a former matrimonial home the wife's statutory right of occupation under the Matrimonial Homes Act 1967 has to be taken into account. See further the decisions discussed under *Valuation under reg.47* in the notes to reg.47.

Reigate and Banstead BC v GB (above, and in detail in the notes to reg.47) is a helpful example of valuation of an interest as a tenant in common, in that case a deemed such interest, and of an acceptable District Valuer's report.

RM v Sefton Council (HB) [2016] UKUT 357 (AAC), reported as [2017] AACR 5, provides a good practical example of the valuation of a property with sitting shorthold tenants.

Similarly, if chattels are being valued, it is what they could be sold for that counts, not simply what was paid for them (*CIS/494/1990, CIS/2208/2003*). See also *JJ v SSWP (IS)* [2012] UKUT 253 (AAC) which points out that where a sale of a chattel is by auction there are buyer's premiums added as well as seller's commission and that this could result in the seller being treated as having much more capital than he would realise on a sale. In the judge's view this was not the object of the regulations and the valuation had to be based on the standard test of what the claimant could expect to realise on a transaction between a willing seller and a willing buyer. Despite the disregard in universal credit of the value of personal possessions (reg.46(2)) and of business assets (paras 7 and 8 of Sch.10), it may occasionally be necessary to take the value of chattels, e.g. if a claimant retains former business assets beyond the limits of para.8 of Sch.10 or if investment assets are found to fall outside the meaning of "personal possessions" (see the notes to re.46(2)).

Sometimes a detailed valuation is not necessary, such as where the value of an asset is on any basis clearly over the prescribed limit of £16,000) (*CIS/40/1989*). That, however, has the undesirable result that no baseline has been established for assessing the effects of future disposals of the assets.

Shares

2.178 It is accepted that the test of the willing buyer and the willing seller is the starting point for the valuation of shares (*R(SB) 57/83*, *R(SB) 12/89* and *R(IS) 2/90*). The latter case emphasises that in the income support context, as would also be the case for universal credit, the value must be determined on the basis of a very quick sale, so that the hypothetical willing seller would be at a corresponding disadvantage. In the case of private companies there is often a provision in the articles of association that a shareholder wishing to sell must first offer the shares to other shareholders at a "fair value" fixed by the auditors (this was the case in *R(SB) 18/83* and *R(IS) 2/90*). Then the value of the shares ought not to be higher than the fair value, but for benefit purposes may well be less. The possible complications are set out in *CSB/488/1982* (quoted with approval in *R(SB) 12/89* and *R(IS) 2/90*). In *R(IS) 8/92* it is suggested that the market value is what a purchaser would pay for the shares subject to the same restriction. Whether the shareholding gives a minority, equal or controlling interest is particularly significant. All the circumstances of the share structure of the company must be considered. For instance, in *R(SB) 12/89* shares could only be sold with the consent of the directors, which it was indicated would not be forthcoming. It seems to be agreed that valuation according to Revenue methods is not appropriate (*R(SB) 18/83* and *R(IS) 2/90*), although it is suggested in *R(SB) 12/89* that the Revenue Shares Valuation Division might be able to assist tribunals. It is not known if this is so. What is absolutely clear is that the total value of the company's shareholding cannot simply be divided in proportion to the claimant's holding (*R(SB) 18/83*).

However, in para.14 of *P v SSWP and P (CSM)* [2018] UKUT 60 (AAC) it was said, in a passage not necessary to the decision, that the tribunal in that child support case:

> "was correct in basing the value of the shares on the book value of the company's net assets, without making any discount to reflect the difficulty in selling part of the shareholding in a private company. In *Ebrahimi v Westbourne Galleries Limited* [1973] A.C. 360 it was held that in some circumstances a limited company could co-exist with a 'quasi-partnership' between those involved in the company, for example, if the shareholders were bound by personal relationships involving mutual confidence, if the shareholders were in practice involved in the conduct of the business, and if the transfer of the shares was restricted. In *re Bird Precision Bellows Ltd.* [1986] Ch. 658 Oliver LJ held [674A] that in a 'quasi-partnership' case it was appropriate that: 'the shares of the company should be valued as a whole and that the petitioners should then simply be paid the proportionate part of that value which was represented by their shareholding, without there being made a discount for the fact that this was a minority shareholding'."

It is not though clear how far that approach should be translated to means-tested benefits and how far it turns on the particular context of the child support variation provisions with their stress on a parent's control in practice over a company (see para.15 of *P*). But the application of reg.77 (company analogous to a partnership or one-person business) would have to be considered in such circumstances. If that provision applies, reg.77(2) expressly requires that the actual value of the claimant's shareholding be disregarded and the claimant be treated as owning the capital of the company, or the appropriate proportion of it (see the notes to reg.77 for further discussion).

In the case of shares in companies quoted on the London Stock Exchange the Revenue method of valuation should be used (*R(IS) 18/95*). This involves looking at all the transactions relating to the relevant share during the previous day, taking the lowest figure and adding to this a quarter of the difference between the lowest and the highest figure. The Commissioner considered that decision-makers could use the valuation quoted in newspapers (which is the mean between the best bid and best offer price at the close of business the previous day) to obtain approximate valuations. However, where a completely accurate valuation was essential, the Revenue method would need to be adopted. See also *DW v SSWP (JSA)* [2012] UKUT 478 (AAC).

Valuation affected by difficulties in realisation

The proper approach to valuation can usefully deal with unrealisable assets. 2.179
Sometimes their market value will be nil (e.g. a potential interest under a discretionary trust: *R(SB) 25/83*; assets that are subject to a restraint or freezing order: *SH v SSWP* [2008] UKUT 21 (AAC); *CS v Chelmsford BC (HB)* [2014] UKUT 518 (AAC)); sometimes it will be very heavily discounted. However, if the asset will be realisable after a time, it may have a current value. The claimant may be able to sell an option to purchase the asset in the future (see *R(IS) 8/92*) or borrow, using the asset as security. But the valuation must reflect the fact that the asset is not immediately realisable. In *R(IS) 4/96* the claimant had on his divorce transferred his interest in the former matrimonial home to his wife in return for a charge on the property which could only be enforced if she died, remarried or cohabited for more than six months. The claimant's former wife was 46 and in good health. A discount had to be applied to the present day value of the charge to reflect the fact that it might not be realisable for as long as 40 years or more; consequently it was unlikely to be worth more than £3,000. See also *CIS/982/2002* in which the Commissioner sets out a number of detailed questions that had to be considered when valuing the claimant's share (if any) in a joint bank account that had been frozen following the claimant's separation from her husband. And note *LC v Bournemouth Borough Council (HB)* [2016] UKUT 175 (AAC), discussed in the notes to reg.46.

In *JC-W v Wirral MBC (HB)* [2011] UKUT 501 (AAC) Judge Mark concluded that nobody would be willing to purchase (for more than a nominal amount) the claimant's beneficial interest pending divorce in two heavily mortgaged properties, one of which was only partly built, in respect of which the claimant's parents-in-law claimed an interest in the proceeds of sale, and which the claimant's husband was unwilling to sell.

As the Tribunal of Commissioners in *R(SB) 45/83* point out, the market value (in that case of an interest in an entire trust fund) must reflect the outlay the purchaser would expect to incur in obtaining transfer of the assets and the profit they would expect as an inducement to purchase. If there might be some legal difficulty in obtaining the underlying asset (as there might have been in *R(SB) 21/83* and in *R(IS) 13/95*, where shares were held in the names of the claimant's children) this must be taken into account.

See also *MB v Wychavon DC (HB)* [2013] UKUT 67 (AAC) which concerned the valuation of the claimant's beneficial interest under a declaration of trust made by his mother in relation to a property held in the mother's name. The claimant had contributed 10 per cent towards the purchase price. In the absence of a family member willing to purchase the claimant's share, Judge Mark finds that the market value of the claimant's interest was substantially less than the amount of his contribution to the purchase price (he decided it was less than half that amount). However, it was possible that there would be no market at all for the claimant's share, in which case its value would be nil.

Where the property is jointly owned, see the decisions discussed under *Valuation under reg.47* in the notes to reg.47.

Deductions from market value

2.180 The general rule is that the whole of a capital resource is to be taken into account. Liabilities are not to be deducted from the value (*R(SB) 2/83* and *SSWP v GF (ESA)* [2017] UKUT 333 (AAC)). The "remedy" in such a case is for the claimant to discharge the liability, which does not give rise to notional capital under the deprivation rule (see reg.50(2)(a)). It is only where a debt is secured on the capital asset that it is deducted under reg.49(1)(b).

In this connection, note *JRL v SSWP (JSA)* [2011] UKUT 63 (AAC), reported as [2011] AACR 30. The claimant had three accounts with the same bank, of which one was in credit, one was overdrawn and one had a nil balance. The Three-Judge Panel pointed out that this meant that the claimant was both a creditor and a debtor of the same body. Under the bank's terms and conditions, the bank had a contractual right to debit at any time any of a customer's accounts which were in credit with sums sufficient to clear the customer's indebtedness to the bank. This created what was effectively a charge on the customer's credit balance(s). The market value of the account that was in credit was therefore its net value after deduction of the amount of the claimant's overdraft on his other account.

The first deduction to be made is a standard 10 per cent if there would be any expenses attributable to sale, as there almost always will be. The second is the amount of any encumbrance secured on the asset. There is particularly full and helpful guidance on the nature of incumbrances on real property and the evidence which should be examined in *R(IS) 21/93*, and see below. In *R(IS) 10/99* the Commissioner points out that the word "encumbrance" is unknown to the law of Scotland, but goes on to interpret the equivalent of sub-para.(b) as meaning that there must be something attached to the capital in question that prevents the claimant from disposing of it.

The standard case of a debt being secured on a capital asset is a house that is mortgaged. The amount of capital outstanding will be deducted from the market value of the house. In *R(SB) 14/81* the claimant had been lent £5,000 for work on his bungalow, which was mortgaged to secure the debt. He had £3,430 left. Although he was obliged to make monthly repayments this liability could not be deducted from the £3,430, for the debt was not secured on the money. However, the principle of *R(SB) 53/83* (see the notes to reg.46) would make the money not part of the claimant's resources. In *JH v SSWP* [2009] UKUT 1 (AAC) the site owner's commission payable on the sale of a beach hut was not "an incumbrance secured on" the hut but a personal contractual obligation on the seller which could not be enforced against the asset itself.

In *R(SB) 18/83* the Commissioner says that personal property such as shares (or money) can be charged by a contract for valuable consideration (e.g. a loan) without any writing or the handing over of any title documents. But this is not the case in Scots law (*R(SB) 5/88*). In *R(IS) 18/95* the claimant's brokers had a lien on his shares for the cost of acquisition and their commission which fell to be offset against the value of the shares. *CIS/368/1993* concerned money held under a solicitor's undertaking. £40,000 of the proceeds of sale of the claimant's house was retained by his solicitors in pursuance of an undertaking to his bank given because of a previous charge on the property. The Commissioner decides that the undertaking was an incumbrance within the equivalent of sub-para.(b). It was the equivalent of a pledge or lien and was secured on the proceeds of sale. Thus the £40,000 did not count as part of the claimant's resources. See also *CIS/984/2002* which concerned money held by the claimant's solicitor pending quantification of the statutory charge to the Legal Services Commission under s.10(7) of the Access to Justice Act 1999. The Commissioner holds that this was not part of the claimant's capital until the charge had been quantified, as until then it was not possible to identify any particular amount as the claimant's capital. He added that another way of looking at it was to treat the statutory charge as an incumbrance for the purpose of the equivalent of sub-para.(b).

In *R(IS) 5/98* the claimant transferred her flat to her daughter on the understanding that the daughter would care for her in the flat and pay off the mortgage. The daughter complied with the second condition, but evicted her mother from the flat. The Commissioner decides that the gift of the flat to the daughter had been subject to the condition that she looked after her mother. As that condition had not been fulfilled, the gift failed and the daughter held the property on trust for the claimant. In valuing the claimant's interest, the mortgage was to be deducted because the daughter was to be treated as subrogated to the rights of the mortgagee. In addition, the costs of the litigation to recover the property from the daughter also fell to be deducted. The claimant appealed against this decision to the Court of Appeal but her appeal was dismissed (*Ellis v Chief Adjudication Officer*, reported as part of *R(IS) 5/98*).

Notional capital

50.—(1) A person is to be treated as possessing capital of which the person has deprived themselves for the purpose of securing entitlement to universal credit or to an increased amount of universal credit. 2.181

(2) A person is not to be treated as depriving themselves of capital if the person disposes of it for the purposes of—

(a) reducing or paying a debt owed by the person; or

(b) purchasing goods or services if the expenditure was reasonable in the circumstances of the person's case.

(3) Where a person is treated as possessing capital in accordance with this regulation, then for each subsequent assessment period (or, in a case where the award has terminated, each subsequent month) the amount of capital the person is treated as possessing ("the notional capital") reduces—

(a) in a case where the notional capital exceeds £16,000, by the amount which the Secretary of State considers would be the amount of an award of universal credit that would be made to the person (assuming they met the conditions in section 4 and 5 of the Act) if it were not for the notional capital; or

(b) in a case where the notional capital exceeds £6,000 but not £16,000 (including where the notional capital has reduced to an amount equal to or less than £16,000 in accordance with sub-paragraph (a)) by the amount of unearned income that the notional capital is treated as yielding under regulation 72.

DEFINITION

"unearned income"—see reg.2.

GENERAL NOTE

Paragraph (1)

Under universal credit the only circumstance in which someone will be treated as having notional capital is where they have deprived themselves of it for the purpose of securing, or increasing, entitlement to universal credit (although note also reg.77(2) in relation to companies in which the person is like a sole trader or partner). 2.182

Deprivation

There is a considerable amount of case law on the "deprivation rule"—see the extensive notes to reg.51(1) of the Income Support Regulations in Vol.V of this series, 2021/22 edition as updated in Cumulative Supplements included in this volume and in mid-year Supplements. That will be referred to below, but note that some of the case law will need to be read in the light of para.(2). The very important exceptions there for reducing or paying a debt or purchasing reasonable goods and services take a lot of formerly contentious areas out of consideration for universal credit.

In particular, the principle laid down in *R(SB) 38/85* will no doubt be relevant, that once it is shown that a person did possess, or received, a capital asset, the burden shifts to that person to show that it has ceased to be part of their actual capital, apparently whether on an initial claim or on revision or supersession by the Secretary of State (*LP v SSWP (ESA)* [2018] UKUT 389 (AAC), at para.13). If the person fails to show that, the proper conclusion is then that the asset remains part of their actual capital, rather than to invoke any notional capital rule (see *R(SB) 40/85*). Tribunals should therefore in such circumstances avoid vague formulations such as 'the claimant is treated as having capital of £x' and make it clear whether the conclusion is that the person has actual or notional capital of that amount (see *AB v SSWP and Canterbury CC (IS and HB)* [2014] UKUT 212 (AAC)). One consequence of the difference is that, if a person is found to have actual capital as a consequence of not having shown that some asset or assets have been disposed of, there is no statutory diminishing capital rule to be applied. Normally where a claimant is not entitled to benefit because the amount of capital exceeds the £16,000 limit (or the amount of assumed tariff income from capital over £6,000 precludes entitlement) the 'remedy' is to dip into the capital to meet living and/or other reasonable expenses or pay off some debt and to claim again when the amount of capital has reduced to the level that allows entitlement. However, a claimant may be in difficulty in making such an argument while maintaining that the assets in question had been disposed of.

MS v DfC (JSA) [2020] NICom 42 holds that where a tribunal is not satisfied by a claimant's assertion that they have disposed of money, so that the amount remains part of their actual capital, it is not necessary for the tribunal to make a positive finding of fact about where the money was actually held. Submissions to the contrary were based on a misreading of remarks in *DMcC v DSD (IS)* [2012] NICom 326. That is different from a situation like that in *WR v SSWP (IS)* [2012] UKUT 127 (AAC), where the tribunal was not satisfied by the claimant's explanation of why she had made payments to each of her parents. That dissatisfaction did not justify a conclusion that the money involved remained part of her actual capital.

In *CIS 634/1992* the claimant was made bankrupt on November 29, 1990. Between November 29 and December 28, 1990, when he claimed income support, he divested himself of most of his capital. His trustee in bankruptcy was not appointed until April 1991. Under s.284 of the Insolvency Act 1986 any disposal of property or payment by a bankrupt between the presentation of a bankruptcy petition and the vesting of their estate in their trustee is void (except with the consent or later ratification of the court). The claimant could not therefore in law deprive himself of any resources from November 29, onwards and the equivalent of para.(1) could not apply. However, since the claimant had failed to give a satisfactory account of how he had disposed of his capital, the Commissioner held he was to be treated as still possessing it in accordance with *R(SB) 38/85*. Thus he was held not to be entitled to income support prior to the appointment of the trustee in bankruptcy because until then he possessed actual capital over the income support limit. However, in *KS v SSWP (JSA)* [2009] UKUT 122 (AAC), reported as [2010] AACR 3, Judge Mark agreed that the effect of s.284 of the Insolvency Act was that the deprivation rule could not apply, but disagreed that a bankrupt's capital remains their capital until the appointment of the trustee in bankruptcy. He pointed out that a bankrupt cannot realise or use any part of their capital after a bankruptcy order has been made and that, subject to any order of the court, it will vest in their trustee in due course. Whether the capital remains their capital with a nil value or whether it ceases to be their capital at all (on which the judge did not reach any firm conclusion), the result was that the claimant in that case had no capital, or no capital of any value, after the bankruptcy order had been made. As a reported decision, *KS* is to be given more weight on this issue.

It is suggested that *R(SB) 38/85* should not be taken as sanctifying the Department's common practice of requiring claimants to produce receipts to substantiate their expenditure and of automatically treating them as still having the balance of their capital not covered by receipts. As the Commissioner in *CIS/515/2006* pointed out, it is inherently improbable that a claimant will be able to produce receipts for day to day expenditure, particularly in relation to a period sometimes several years in the past. Claimants should be asked to produce what records they do have and can be asked to explain any large or unusual payments. But to demand actual receipts for all expenditure, however small, particularly over a lengthy period is not reasonable. General conclusions should be drawn on the basis of the claimant's oral evidence and the documentary evidence that is available. See also *KW v SSWP (IS)* [2012] UKUT 350 (AAC) in which lack of receipts for the claimant's alleged expenditure on sexual services was understandable, given the nature of that expenditure. The question as to whether this expenditure took place, and if so, how much, therefore came down to a question of credibility.

It is arguable that someone cannot deprive themselves of something which they have never possessed, but it may be that a deliberate failure to acquire an asset is also a deprivation. In *CSB/598/1987* it was suggested that a deliberate failure to pay a cheque into a bank account could be a deprivation. See also *CIS/1586/1997* which stated that a sale at a known undervalue and the release of a debtor from a debt were capable of amounting to deprivation. However, someone does not deprive themselves of an asset by failing to seek a lump sum payment or property transfer order under the Matrimonial Causes Act 1973, since the right to make an application under the Act is not a capital asset (*R(IS) 1/03*). Moreover, even if this had constituted deprivation, the claimant's reasons for not bringing proceedings (which included, inter alia, fear of her abusive husband) clearly indicated that her purpose had not been to secure entitlement to income support.

R(IS) 7/07 decides that the rule can apply to deprivations made by someone who only later becomes the claimant's partner. About a year before she became the claimant's partner, Ms H, who was unemployed and who had been in receipt of JSA, sold her house. She used the proceeds of sale to, among other things, repay her daughter's debts of £30,000 and to take her family on holiday. The tribunal found that in disposing of her capital Ms H had acted with the purpose of securing entitlement to income support. Commissioner Jacobs considered that this conclusion was one that was open to the tribunal to make on the evidence before it. He then went on to decide that the claimant was caught by the rule in para.(1) even though Ms H was not his partner at the time of the deprivation. In his view the combined effect of s.134(1) of the SSCBA 1992 and the enabling provision in s.136(5)(a) was to treat a partner's deprivation of capital as a deprivation by the claimant, even though they were not a couple at the time. The focus of the deprivation rule was on the purpose of a past disposal but it operated at the time when entitlement was in issue, so that the reference to the claimant (which by virtue of reg.23(1) of the Income Support Regulations included a reference to the claimant's partner) related to the person's status at that time. The Commissioner stated:

> "Both in aggregating the capital of the members of a family and in taking account of notional capital, the legislation fulfils an anti-avoidance function. If notional capital were not aggregated, a future partner could dispose of capital before coming to live with the claimant or couples could separate in order to dispose of capital before reuniting ... The notional capital rule will only apply to a future

partner where there has been conduct that is related to future entitlement to benefit either for the person alone or as a member of a family. That will limit the circumstances in which the rule applies and restrict it to those cases in which a course of conduct has been directed at future benefit entitlement."

In relation to universal credit s.5(1)(a) of the WRA 2012 is the equivalent of s.134(1) of the SSCBA 1992, but s.5(2)(a) expressly provides in the case of joint claimants for the £16,000 capital limit to be applied to their combined capital (and see para.4(5) of Sch.1 to the WRA 2012). Paragraph 4(2)(e) of Sch.1 is more explicit than s.136(5)(a) of the SSCBA 1992, but would only be needed in cases where a claimant who is a member of a couple claims as a single claimant (reg.3), when reg.18(2) provides for the capital of the other member of the couple to be included in the claimant's, apparently for all purposes under the Regulations. Thus there seems no obstacle to applying the reasoning in *R(IS) 7/07* to universal credit.

Although it is not made absolutely explicit in *R(IS) 7/07*, it would seem that the Commissioner (and the tribunal) must have taken the view that Ms H was at least contemplating becoming the claimant's partner at the time of the disposals because otherwise there was no basis for the finding that Ms H had deprived herself of capital for the purpose of securing entitlement to income support (there is no indication that as a single person she would qualify for income support since before she received the proceeds of sale of her house she had been in receipt of JSA). Under reg.50(1) the deprivation has to be for the purpose of securing entitlement to universal credit or an increased amount of it (see further below). It is suggested that the decision should therefore be limited to such circumstances, that is where the parties may become a couple in the future. Moreover, this would seem to be in line with the Commissioner's view of when the rule will apply to a future partner (see above).

The decision in *R(IS) 7/07* was a refusal of leave to appeal by the Commissioner. The claimant applied for judicial review of the Commissioner's decision but his application was dismissed (*R. (on the application of Hook) v Social Security Commissioner and Secretary of State for Work and Pensions* [2007] EWHC 1705 (Admin), reported as part of *R(IS) 7/07*).

If the claimant's attorney appointed under the Enduring Powers of Attorney Act 1985 repays a loan or makes gifts of the claimant's capital this may amount to deprivation by the claimant, since the attorney is the agent of the claimant (*CIS/12403/1991*). In that case there was a question as to whether the loan was the responsibility of the claimant or the attorney and whether the gifts were allowable under s.3(5) of the 1985 Act, which permitted the making of gifts "provided that the value of each such gift is not unreasonable having regard to all the circumstances and in particular the size of the donor's estate". The Commissioner states that the new tribunal would have to consider whether the payments were properly made; if not, there would be a claim against the attorney which would constitute actual capital; if they were properly made, the question of deprivation would have to be considered. Under the Mental Capacity Act 2005, enduring powers of attorney have from October 1, 2007 been replaced by lasting powers of attorney, but existing powers continue in effect. Section 12(2) of the 2005 Act is in similar terms to s.3(5) of the 1985 Act.

It should also be remembered that another result of *R(SB) 38/85* and *R(SB) 40/85* is that there is a deprivation of capital whenever a person ceases by their own act to possess some asset, even though some other asset is received in return. Otherwise it would be possible to convert capital that counts towards the limits into a form in which it is disregarded without falling foul of the notional capital rule. However, para.(2) of the present regulation sets out important limitations on the effect of that principle, which are not present in the income support or old style ESA or JSA legislation (see below).

There is no equivalent in reg.50 (or in reg.75) to reg.51(1)(a) of the Income Support Regulations (reg.115(1)(a) of the ESA Regulations 2008 and reg.113(1)(a) of the JSA Regulations 1996) excluding the operation of the deprivation rule where the capital disposed of is derived from a payment made in consequence of a personal injury and is placed on trust. If the sum was initially paid without restriction and that action, or the purchase of an annuity, was not taken, then after the expiry of the 12 months allowed for a reg.75 disregard by reg.75(6) there would be no applicable disregard. Therefore, depending on the amounts involved and the other circumstances, it could appear on the face of it that such a transfer of the capital either before or after the expiry of the 12 months was for the purpose of securing entitlement to universal credit or increasing its amount. The person would then have to be treated (as there is no discretion) as still possessing the amount disposed of. However, it is suggested that the policy behind reg.75 is so clear that where funds deriving from a personal injury are held in the ways specified in paras.(2) – (5) of reg.75 there should be no effect on universal credit entitlement, that the notional capital rule should not be applied in these circumstances.

Purpose

There is a great deal of case law on when there has been a deprivation of capital for the purpose of securing entitlement to or increasing the amount of benefit. See the very full discussion in the notes to reg.51(1) of the Income Support Regulations in Vol.V of this series, 2021/22 edition as updated in Cumulative Supplements included in this volume and in mid-year Supplements. The issues are simplified to quite an extent for universal credit by the exclusions from the application of the notional capital rule in para.(2): where the disposal is for the purposes of reducing or paying a debt and where it is for the purposes of purchasing good or services if the expenditure was reasonable in the circumstances. That has removed some of the most difficult questions, although there are still problems (see the notes to para.(2) below). The main remaining potential ways of disposing of capital are transferring it to other people and converting it into a source of income or a different form of capital which is either disregarded or would have a lesser value for universal credit purposes. The general principles established through the cases remain relevant to universal credit, though. **2.183**

(i) Knowledge of the capital limit

CIS/124/1990 held that it must be proved that the person actually knew of the capital limit rule, otherwise the necessary deliberate intention to obtain benefit could not have been present. It is not enough that the person ought to have known of the rule. The crunch comes, and the resolution with the approach in *R(SB) 40/85* (where it was suggested that the existence of some limit might be said to be common knowledge), in the assessment of the evidence about the person's knowledge. The Commissioner stressed that the person's whole background must be considered, including experience of the social security system and advice which is likely to have been received from the family and elsewhere. The burden of proof is on the Secretary of State, but in some circumstances a person's assertion that they did not know of the rule will not be credible. In *CIS/124/1990* itself the claimant was illiterate and spoke and understood only Gujerati. The Commissioner said that this should put her in no better or worse situation than a literate claimant whose mother tongue was English, but that the possibility of misunderstandings in interpretation should be considered. *CIS/124/1990* was followed in *R(SB) 12/91*, where the necessity of a positive finding of fact, based on sufficient evidence, that the person knew of the capital limit was stressed. Evidence that the person had been in receipt of supplementary benefit or income support for some years was not in itself enough. But information that the person has received, together with their educational standing and other factors, will be material in deciding whether actual knowledge exists or not. *CIS/30/1993* similarly held that it is not possible to infer actual knowledge of the capital limit simply from the claimant signing a claim form which contained that information. The claimant there was partially sighted and had not completed the **2.184** claim form herself but merely signed it. It was necessary for the tribunal to indicate what evidence satisfied it that the claimant did know of the capital limit.

Where a claimant had not previously claimed a means-tested benefit, nor made any inquiry about the conditions of entitlement, nor had any dealings with benefits, a specific finding that they knew of the capital limit was required (*Waltham Forest LBC v TM* [2009] UKUT 96 (AAC)).

However, in *RB v SSWP (ESA)* [2016] UKUT 384 (AAC), Judge Markus, while accepting that normally a precise finding has to be made, said that there are some cases where there is no potentially credible alternative explanation for the payments made by the claimant and where the facts speak for themselves on both purpose and knowledge. So in the particular case the tribunal's statement that, after rejecting the claimant's explanations, it was left with only one conclusion that he had deprived himself of capital to continue to obtain old style ESA encompassed his knowledge of the effect of having the capital. It was also relevant that the claimant had never suggested at any stage of the case that he did not know of the capital limit. It is submitted, though, that when what is in issue is not whether the notional capital is above the £16,000 limit, but whether it would give rise to an assumed yield of income by exceeding £6,000, be necessary to consider whether the claimant knew of that rule, which is not as well-known as the £16,000 limit. That point was unfortunately not explored in *RB*, although it potentially arose on the facts found by the tribunal (see the discussion in para.2.185 below).

See also the discussion below of the effect of advice having been given by an officer of the DWP

(ii) The test for "purpose"

2.185 The decision-maker has to show that the person's purpose is one of those mentioned in para.(1). That approach was applied in *LP v SSWP (ESA)* [2018] UKUT 389 (AAC) at para.13, but see the discussion of *RB v SSWP (ESA)* [2016] UKUT 384 (AAC) below. There is unlikely to be direct contemporaneous evidence of purpose (although there might be letters or documents), so that primary facts must be found from which an inference as to purpose can be drawn (*CSB/200/1985*, *R(SB) 40/85*). And of course what the claimant says or writes to a tribunal is evidence that must be properly assessed. See further discussion below.

Although in *R(SB) 38/85*, where a "predominant purpose" test was rejected, there was a faint suggestion that it was enough that a subsidiary purpose was to obtain the benefit in question, the test in *R(SB) 40/85* has been accepted. There, Commissioner Monroe said that obtaining the benefit or an increased amount must be a "significant operative purpose". If the obtaining of benefit was a foreseeable consequence of the transaction then, in the absence of other evidence, it could be concluded that that was the person's purpose. That would exclude some cases caught by the width of the approach to deprivation, e.g. where a resource is converted into another form in which it is still taken into account. For then there would be no effect on eligibility for benefit. But beyond that situation there remain great difficulties. The Commissioners mention a number of relevant factors, e.g. whether the deprivation was a gift or in return for a service, the personal circumstances of the person (e.g. age, state of health, employment prospects, needs), whether a creditor was pressing for repayment of a loan. It must be an issue of fact when these other factors indicate that the reasonably foreseeable consequence of obtaining benefit was not a significant operative factor. A tribunal is not entitled to infer that the claimant had the relevant purpose simply from rash and excessive expenditure with some knowledge of some sort of capital limit—it has to go further and consider whether on its assessment of the claimant's character and thinking that is what happened (*CH/264/2006*, a case on the equivalent housing benefit provision). As *R(H) 1/06* (another case on the equivalent housing benefit provision) confirms, the test is a subjective one, which depends upon the evidence about the particular claimant in question (the claimant in that case was a schizophrenic whose mental state was such that he was unlikely to fully appreciate the implications of his behaviour and had limited capacity to plan for the future). See also *KW v SSWP (IS)* [2012] UKUT 350 (AAC) in which the claimant spent £40 to £100 a day of his inheritance on "one or two females out of four doing some fetish things for me". The claimant had a personality disorder and may not have appreciated the potential implications of his behaviour.

R(H) 1/06 was followed in *CIS/218/2005*, where the claimant had made large gifts to her children from the proceeds of the sale of her former matrimonial home. The Commissioner stated that whether a gift is reasonable or prudent, although relevant, does not answer the question of whether it was made for the purpose of securing or increasing entitlement to income support. The test is not one of reasonableness or prudence but what has to be considered is the claimant's purpose. On the other hand, in *CJSA/1425/2004* the fact that it was reasonable for the claimant to pay his credit card debts in order to avoid further liability for interest led to the conclusion that this had not been done for the purpose of obtaining or increasing entitlement to income-based JSA. The payment of debts, reasonably or not is now taken out of consideration for universal credit purposes by para.(2)(a), but reasonableness will have to be considered under para.(2)(b) if assets have been spent on goods or services. The length of time between the disposal of the capital and the claiming of benefit may also be relevant (*CIS/264/1989*).

A number of decisions have firmed up the general principles and given helpful examples, sometimes using different language to express the same essentials. The Commissioner in *R(SB) 9/91* stressed that a positive intention to obtain benefit must be shown to be a significant operative purpose. It was not enough for the adjudication officer merely to prove that the obtaining of benefit was a natural consequence of the transaction in question. The claimant had transferred her former home to her two daughters. Evidence was given that her sole intention was to make a gift to her daughters, as she intended to leave the property to them in her will and it was no longer of any use to her (she being permanently in need of residential nursing care). Commissioner Rice noted that that did not explain why the transfer was made when it was, why the proceeds of sale of the property would not have been of use to the claimant and what she thought she would live on if she gave the property away. She had been in receipt of supplementary benefit for several years. On the evidence the obtaining of benefit was a significant operative purpose. The decision thus endorsed the attribution of a purpose to a claimant by implication from all the circumstances, but the conclusion must be in terms of the claimant's purpose, not in terms of the natural consequences of the transaction in question. *R(H) 1/06*, referred to above, reiterated that it is necessary for a tribunal to determine the claimant's actual (i.e. subjective) intention. In effect, the question whether the person would have carried out the transaction at the same time if there had been no effect on eligibility for benefit is a useful one.

In some circumstances the principles of *Kerr v Department for Social Development* [2004] UKHL 23; [2004] 1 W.L.R. 1372; *R 1/04 (SF)* may be relevant, even though the burden of showing a prohibited purpose lies on the Secretary of State, in that a failure by a claimant to come forward with evidence within their knowledge to support their explanations for the making of payments may support an inference that the purpose was to obtain benefit. That was the case in *RB v SSWP (ESA)* [2016] UKUT 384 (AAC). The claimant, who had been in receipt of income-related ESA since January 2013, received some £26,000 from a divorce settlement on March 7, 2014. On March 26, 2014, he made two payments of £6,000 each to his parents, which he said was to repay loans. On April 9, 2014, he paid £5,760 to his landlord by way of a year's rent in advance. The claimant supplied bank statements showing a number of cash withdrawals from his mother's account totalling £8,980 between June 2012 and April 2014, but no statements for his father's bank account. The tribunal confirmed the initial decision that all three payments had been made to reduce his capital below £16,000 and secure entitlement to ESA, so that the equivalent of reg.50(1) applied and entitlement to ESA ceased. It stated that it could not be "sure to the required standard" that the withdrawals from the mother's account, in the light of the pattern of amounts, were not merely to meet her own living expenses and that, with the absence of any contemporaneous evidence of the loans and of bank statements from the father's account, the claimant had not established that he had borrowed £12,000 from his parents. The advance payment of rent was said to be ridiculous in the absence of evidence that it was required by his tenancy agreement, so that it had to be concluded that it had been made to deprive himself of capital. Judge Markus held that the tribunal had not erred in law in its approach to the burden and standard of proof. She took perhaps a generous view in reading the tribunal's statement of reasons as a whole, which in parts had given the appearance of requiring the claimant to disprove, to a level of sureness, that the payments were not made for the purpose of securing entitlement to ESA. Applying the *Kerr* principle that the claimant should supply as much information as he reasonably could, the state of the evidence was such that, the tribunal having rejected the claimant's credibility in general, there could have been no doubt that the finding as to the purpose of the payments was properly established.

It is unfortunate that the following conundrum was not addressed in *RB*. There was no mention of the claimant having other capital assets. On that basis, by the time that he paid the year's rent in advance his actual capital had been reduced below £16,000 by the two payments to his parents. Could it then be said that his purpose was to secure entitlement to ESA? If he had sufficient knowledge of the capital rules for the regulation to apply in the first place, it is plainly arguable that it could not. It would be odd to draw a line between claimants who knew that there was a capital rule, but not of the amount of the limit, and claimants who knew of the significance of the amount of £16,000. However, the question would then have to be asked whether the advance payment of rent was made for the purpose of increasing the amount of ESA, by reducing the amount of tariff income treated as produced by capital exceeding £6,000. In those circumstances, it might then be argued that a specific finding needed to be made as to the claimant's knowledge of the rules on tariff income from capital below £16,000.

In *CIS/242/1993*, another case where the claimant had gone into residential care, the Commissioner reached the opposite conclusion on the facts to that in *R(SB) 9/91*. The claimant's son had cared for his mother for 15 years. When she went into a residential care home, she gave her share of the proceeds of sale of their jointly owned home to her son to be used towards the purchase of his flat. The Commissioner accepted that she had relinquished her share in gratitude to her son and not to secure income support.

2.186 In *R(IS) 13/94* the claimant's capital was in excess of the statutory limit when he purchased his council house. The deposit used up enough of his capital to bring him below the limit. It was necessary to consider whether para.(1) applied to this use of the capital since the claimant was apparently dependent on income support to meet the mortgage interest. But in *R(IS) 15/96* using a criminal injuries compensation award to pay off part of a mortgage was not caught by para.(1) (now see para.(2)(a)). The SSAT had found that the claimant's purpose had been to secure his future and to reduce the burden on the DSS for his mortgage payments. That was a matter for the judgment of the tribunal.

A further example is *CJSA/204/2002*. The claimant had agreed to provide the deposit for a flat that she and her son would buy. In the event the claimant did not move into the new flat with her son and his girlfriend because of a disagreement but she still lent her son the deposit. The claimant did correspond with her solicitor about obtaining security for the loan but no formal agreement or legal charge was entered into. The Commissioner held that the claimant clearly had reasons for keeping her promise to lend the deposit (for example, so as not to let her son down or sour relations further) and in his view there had been no deprivation within the rule. See also *R(IS) 1/03* above, under *Deprivation*. It may often be pertinent in similar cases to pose the *R(SB) 9/91* question of what the claimant thought they would live on if the asset in question was disposed of.

In *CIS/109/1994* and *CIS/112/1994* the claimants had used their capital to purchase an annuity and a life insurance policy respectively. In *CIS/109/1994* the claimant was both physically and mentally frail and lived in a nursing home. The tribunal found that at the material time she had no knowledge of the income support capital and deprivation of capital rules, and entered into the transaction on her son's advice, who considered that this was the best use of her capital to enable her to stay in the nursing home. The Commissioner held that the tribunal had not erred in concluding that she had not purchased the annuity in order to obtain income support. In *CIS/112/1994* the Commissioner decided that para.(1) did apply, but that para.15 of Sch.10 to the Income Support Regulations applied to disregard the value of the life policy. Thus what the Commissioner considered would have been an unfair "double counting" of notional and actual capital was avoided. See also *R(IS) 7/98* where capital had been used to purchase an "investment bond". The Commissioner decided that the bond fell within the definition of "policy of life insurance" in reg.2(1) and so could be disregarded under para.15 of Sch.10. But the claimant's intention at the time of the investment had to be considered to see whether para.(1) applied. The value of any policy of life insurance is disregarded as capital by para.9 of Sch.10 to the Universal Credit Regulations, but the value of an annuity is not. There may therefore be "double counting" issues resulting from the lack of any discretion in the application of reg.50(1), which may not be resolved through the diminishing notional capital rule in para.(3) (see below).

Where a transaction has no effect on the claimant's entitlement, as in *CJSA/3937/2002* where the property transferred was the house in which the claimant was living (which was therefore disregarded under para.1 of Sch.8 to the JSA Regulations 1996), an intention to secure entitlement to income-based JSA was not shown.

In many cases of alleged deprivation of capital there will have been a course of spending, often on various items, and sometimes over a considerable period of time. In *R(H) 1/06*, the Commissioner emphasised the need to go through all the various items of expenditure, taking account of any explanations put forward by the claimant, and to reach a specific determination as to: (i) what amounts (if any) represent deprivation of capital in excess of a reasonable level of general expenditure in the claimant's circumstances; and (ii) what had been the claimant's purpose at the time and whether this included an intention to obtain benefit. The tribunal had erred in simply expressing its decision in generalised terms without attempting to analyse the movements on the claimant's account during the relevant period. *CIS/1775/2007* makes the same point. The tribunal had been wrong to treat all payments as having been made with the same motivation but should have considered each type of expenditure separately when applying the significant operative purpose test.

It has been held that where the claimant had been accurately warned about the consequences of a transaction by the local DSS office (i.e. that the equivalent of reg.50(1) would be applied) and still went ahead, this showed that he could not have had as any part of his purpose securing of entitlement, or continued entitlement, to income support (*CIS 621/1991*). But there must be limits to generalising from this decision. Can claimants, in cases not involving specific Departmental advice, be heard to say that because of their existing knowledge of the capital limits and the notional capital rules they anticipated that depriving themselves of some capital asset would not affect entitlement to benefit because they would be treated as having notional capital as a result, and thereby secure the very opposite result on the basis that their purpose could not have been to secure or increase entitlement? To admit the validity of such an argument would seem to involve internal contradictions in identifying claimants' purposes, not to mention ludicrous outcomes. That argument cannot be right.

An even more misguided suggestion, extraordinarily made on behalf of the Secretary of State, was rejected in *LP v SSWP (ESA)* [2018] UKUT 389 (AAC) at paras 8–11. This was that, since at the time of the deprivation (of amounts received as lump sums from a personal pension scheme) the claimant was in receipt of the maximum amount of income-related ESA she could aspire to, she could not have thought that spending the money could increase the amount of that benefit and securing or increasing benefit could not have been an operative purpose. The fundamental mistake in that suggestion was to ignore the potential purpose of securing entitlement for the weeks following the receipt of the capital if the DWP were informed or found out about the receipt. That could have been in her thoughts.

The effect of DWP advice on the claimant's intention was further considered in *LH v SSWP (IS)* [2014] UKUT 60 (AAC), although somewhat inconclusively because in the end the judge decided on the evidence that the operative purpose of the deprivation was the paying off of debts, regardless of the advice given. The claimant received £54,000 from an endowment policy. She did not inform the DWP at the time because she thought that since the policy had been set up to pay a mortgage the proceeds did not count as capital, but should not be used for ordinary living expenses. However, she did not need to use the money to pay off her mortgage and used part of it to pay other debts that charged a higher rate of interest. When she was later visited by a DWP officer, she sought advice from him about the impact on her income support entitlement of using the proceeds from the policy to pay off her debts before meeting her mortgage liability. He informed her that it was reasonable and acceptable to pay off outstanding loans and debts before using the remainder to pay off part of the mortgage, as long as she did not spend the money on, for example, exotic holidays. The officer did not advise the claimant that she would be able to secure entitlement to income support if she used the remaining excess capital in the way she was doing, nor was this the advice sought by the claimant. After the visit she continued to use the proceeds of the policy to pay her debts before paying off part of the mortgage.

Judge Wright rightly emphasised that the effect of the advice depends on precisely what advice is sought, and given, and its context. He disagreed with the obiter remarks made in *CIS/307/1992* that advice given that a proposed disposal would in no way affect entitlement would of itself nullify any finding of adverse intention under para.(1) and thus insulate a claimant from being caught by para.(1). In his view (again obiter), if a claimant sought advice from the DWP in relation to disposal of capital, e.g. an inheritance, and was wrongly advised that that would not affect their entitlement, arguably securing or retaining entitlement to income support would still have been the significant operative purpose behind the disposal of the capital. That was the object desired. On the other hand, if the claimant was being taken to court over debts, the advice given would not change the position that staying on benefit was not a "significant operative purpose", the main motivation being to pay the debts.

It is submitted that the first view mentioned in the previous paragraph is of dubious validity. Surely, if a claimant is advised in the particular terms mentioned, even though the consequence of the disposal might be that the claimant's entitlement continues (not being excluded by the capital rule) or can quickly be re-established, it can be argued that their operative purpose is to do whatever the disposal achieves and that consequence on entitlement is not operative. But the precise terms of any advice will be crucial.

Effect of bankruptcy on the notional capital rule

2.187 In *Waltham Forest LBC v TM* [2009] UKUT 96 (AAC) the claimant used the proceeds of sale of a property to repay loans to three family members three months before he was made bankrupt. The issue was whether any resulting notional capital that the claimant was found to have for the purposes of his housing benefit claim was part of his estate as a bankrupt. It was held that since by definition the claimant does not possess the capital but is only deemed to do so for the purposes of entitlement to benefit, notional capital is not part of a bankrupt's estate as defined in the Insolvency Act 1986. Thus the application of the notional capital rule was not affected by the claimant's bankruptcy. *KS v SSWP (JSA)* [2009] UKUT 122

(AAC), reported as [2010] AACR 3, agreed with *TM* where the deprivation occurs before a bankruptcy order is made. After the making of the order, however, claimants cannot deprive themselves of capital for the purposes of para.(1) (see under *Deprivation* at the beginning of this note). Judge Mark went on to suggest that if a claimant presents a petition, or possibly fails to resist a petition presented by a creditor, and is declared bankrupt as a result, they may be found to have deprived themselves of capital if they have taken this step (or not opposed the petition) for the purpose of securing entitlement to benefit. The capital they would have deprived themselves of would be the capital they were entitled to after taking into account what they would have to pay to avoid bankruptcy. This is unlikely to be much in most circumstances.

The operation of para.(1) is restricted to circumstances where the person's purpose is related to entitlement to universal credit. That is in contrast to the terms of reg.113(1) of the JSA Regulations 1996 (which covers purposes related to both old style JSA and income support) and of reg.115(1) of the ESA Regulations 2008 (which covers purposes related to all of old style ESA and JSA and income support), but not to the terms of reg.51(1) of the Income Support Regulations (which is restricted to income support). *R(IS) 14/93* was concerned with a similar problem on the transfer to income support from the corresponding supplementary benefit provisions in 1988. That was whether claimants who deprived themselves of capital under the supplementary benefit regime, before income support existed, could be said to have done so for the purpose of securing entitlement to income support so as to be caught by reg.51(1) once the income support legislation had come into force. The decisions on the point do not now need to be examined in detail. *R(IS) 14/93* held that the words "income support" in reg.51(1) could not be taken to refer to means-tested benefits that previously went under the name of supplementary benefit. Thus, if a deprivation of capital occurs while a person is receiving, or contemplating a claim for, income support or old style JSA or ESA, it may be arguable, depending on the exact circumstances, that if there is later a claim for universal credit the purpose of the deprivation was not to secure entitlement to universal credit. It may also be slightly more onerous to establish the person's knowledge of the capital rules in universal credit, as a new and not yet familiar benefit, especially if previous entitlement had been to tax credits, where the amount of capital did not affect entitlement.

The reasoning behind that outcome is supported by the decision of the Northern Ireland Commissioner in *DB v DfC (JSA)* [2021] NICom 43 on the scope of the Northern Ireland equivalent (in identical terms) of reg.113(1) of the JSA Regulations 1996. The claimant had been entitled to old style ESA. On November 25, 2016, the decision was given that she was not entitled from August 2015, apparently on the basis that, although she asserted that she had disposed of some £40,000 of capital that she said did not belong to her, it was her capital and she had not shown that she had disposed of it. She claimed old style JSA on September 14, 2017. On October 16, 2017, it was decided that she was not entitled, on the basis that her actual capital exceeded £16,000, despite her further assertions of having depleted bank accounts. A revision of that decision and submissions made on appeal were hopelessly confused as between actual and notional capital, but the decision of October 16, 2017, was never formally changed. The appeal tribunal found that the claimant had deprived herself of more than £40,000 in 2016 for the principal purpose of bringing her capital below the limits to obtain benefits including JSA, so that she was treated as having notional income over £16,000 after the application of the diminishing notional capital rule (reg.114). The Chief Commissioner held, as had been submitted by the DfC, that because reg.113(1) could only bite when the claimant's purpose was securing entitlement to or increasing the amount of old style JSA or income support, the appeal tribunal had failed to make the necessary findings of fact or show that it had applied the legally correct approach. It was inherently improbable that when depriving herself of capital while in receipt of ESA, more than a year before she claimed JSA, the claimant had possible entitlement to JSA in mind.

The decision also illustrates that on a new claim neither the decision-maker nor a tribunal on appeal is bound by the findings of fact on capital that have underpinned a decision of non-entitlement on capital grounds. The basis of the ESA decision, that the claimant as at that date still had actual capital of more than £40,000, did not have to be adopted on the JSA claim.

Paragraph (2)

2.188 Paragraph (2)(a) provides that someone will not be treated as having deprived themselves of capital if they have used it to repay or reduce a debt. This provision avoids a lot of difficult issues under the notional capital rules for other benefits about the exact circumstances in which paying off debts in whole or part might indicate that securing entitlement to or increasing the amount of benefit was not a significant operative purpose of the deprivation. It appears to have a very wide application. There is no requirement that the debt is legally enforceable, or even that it is due to be repaid, or any restriction as to the type of debt involved. It should therefore apply to the repayment of loans from family or friends (subject to possible issues about when there is sufficient evidence to establish the existence of the debt on the balance of probabilities) and to the repayment of overdrafts or credit card balances as well as mortgages, personal loans etc. Although para.(2)(a) expressly refers to debts owed by the person who carries out the deprivation, it is submitted that where the person is a member of a couple (whose capital would be aggregated under reg.18(2) or s.5(2) of the WRA 2012) payment of a debt owed by the other member of the couple would be covered.

Under para.(2)(b) the deprivation rule is not to apply if the deprivation takes the form of purchase of goods or services and the expenditure was reasonable in the circumstances of the person concerned. It is not at all clear what might be covered by the word "goods". Regulation 46(2) provides that personal possessions are not to be treated as capital. In the notes to that provision the approach in *R(H) 7/08* is mentioned, that personal possessions mean any physical assets other than land and assets used for business purposes, with no distinctions to be drawn, say to exclude assets acquired for investment. However, a question is raised there whether the use of the adjective "personal" could be taken to exclude items used solely as investments. It could be argued here that "goods" should not have any narrower meaning than whatever is the correct meaning of personal possessions in reg.46(2). Indeed, it would seem that in the absence of the adjective "personal" the meaning should include things used for business purposes. On the other hand, it could be argued that the word "goods" suggests items used in the course of daily living, even though they might be regarded as capital purchases, so that it would not cover items acquired for investment or something like a classic car. The practical importance of such uncertainties may be lessened by the condition of reasonableness. That test must depend on reasonableness as at the date of the potential deprivation, rather than as assessed later with the benefit of hindsight. Although the relevant circumstances will include the person's financial situation and prospects at the time, including the likelihood of having to claim a means-tested benefit and how much the person actually knew about the capital limits for such benefits, it is submitted that the assessment of benefit must balance the principle that in general people are free to spend their own money on whatever they like against what is reasonable in relation to the community of taxpayers who fund universal credit.

If the deprivation is by way of buying goods and the expenditure is found not to have been reasonable, the claimant on the face of it would be fixed with the amount of the expenditure as notional capital and also actual capital in the form of the market value of the goods bought. Under reg.51(1) of the Income Support Regulations and equivalents there had to be a process of treating the deprivation of capital as restricted to the difference between the former and the latter. There will be no such problem in relation to universal credit if the meaning of "personal possessions" (which are not to be treated as capital under reg.46(2)) encompasses everything that could be classified as goods under para.(2)(b).

Note that if neither of the two situations in para.(2) apply, it remains necessary to consider whether the person did deprive themselves of the capital for the purpose of securing, or increasing, entitlement to universal credit. That will have to be considered, for instance, where a claimant buys some interest in property, e.g. in the home.

Paragraph (3)

This paragraph contains the diminishing notional capital rule for universal credit. If the notional capital is more than £16,000, it is reduced in each subsequent assessment period, or each subsequent month if the universal credit award has ceased, by the amount of universal credit that the person would have received but for the notional capital. In the case of a person who has notional capital of between £6,000 and £16,000, the notional capital reduces by the amount of income deemed to be generated by that amount of capital under the "assumed yield from capital" rule in reg.72(1). **2.189**

This diminishing notional capital rule is different from that in income support (reg.51A of the Income Support Regulations), old style ESA (reg.116 of the ESA Regulations 2008) or old style JSA (reg.114 of the JSA Regulations 2006). Those provisions apply whenever taking the notional capital into account has either taken the claimant out of entitlement or resulted in a reduction in the amount of benefit received. Then the amount of notional capital is reduced week by week by the amount of benefit in question that would otherwise have been paid for that week. Thus the rule can apply regardless of the initial amount of the notional capital. What matters is whether the combination of actual capital (if any) and notional capital takes the claimant over a relevant limit.

By contrast, para.(3) on its face applies only where the amount of notional capital alone exceeds either £16,000 or £6,000. If a claimant has actual capital of £15,000 and is then fixed with £2,000 of notional capital, so that there can no longer be entitlement to universal credit, the terms of para.(3) are not met and there apparently can be no reduction in the £2,000 of notional capital. If the claimant had no actual capital and was fixed with £17,000 of notional capital para.(3) could apply. That difference in treatment within universal credit and between different means-tested benefits seems inequitable. However, it may be that there is unjustified double counting in the other benefits in favour of claimants who have actual capital. In the example quoted of £15,000 actual capital and £2,000 notional capital, the claimant would need to dip into actual capital to meet essential living expenses in the absence of the previous benefit payments, and that expenditure on goods and services would no doubt be accepted as reasonable under para.(2)(b). So once the actual capital had reduced below £14,000, there could be entitlement again. The difference is that a universal credit claimant cannot take advantage of a reduction in the amount of notional capital in addition to that reduction in actual capital, whereas it appears that income support, old style ESA and old style JSA claimants can. There are similar problems where it is a combination of actual and notional capital that takes the claimant over the £6,000 limit for an assumed yield under reg.72(1). It may be that the problems and inequities are so great that the references to notional capital exceeding £6,000 or £16,000 must be interpreted as references to the amount of notional capital taking the claimant over one or other of those limits, whether on its own or in combination with actual capital.

There may, despite the application of para.(3), be difficult issues of apparently unfair double counting. Say that a universal credit recipient receives some lump sum of over £16,000 and with the plain purposes of retaining entitlement uses it to buy an annuity. Not only will the claimant be fixed under para.(1) with the amount disposed of as notional capital, but the capital value of annuity is not disregarded under Sch.10 and the payments of income under the annuity count in full as unearned income under reg.66(1)(i). It is not obvious that reducing the amount of notional capital assessment period by period by the amount of universal credit that would have been paid if the claimant did not have the notional capital is adequate compensation.

Presumably a person's notional capital will be calculated in the same way as if it were actual capital, that is, by applying any relevant disregard, although neither reg.50 nor reg.48 specifically states this. This is assumed in para.H1885 ADM.

CHAPTER 2

EARNED INCOME

Introduction

2.190 **51.** This Chapter provides for the calculation or estimation of a person's earned income for the purposes of section 8 of the Act (calculation of awards).

DEFINITIONS

"the Act"—see reg.2.
"earned income"—see reg.52.

GENERAL NOTE

2.191 In the case of joint claimants their income is aggregated (see s.8(4)(b) of the WRA 2012). If a member of a couple is claiming as a single person (see reg.3(3) for the circumstances in which this can happen) the income of the other member of the couple is taken into account when calculating the universal credit award (see reg.22(3)).

Any income of a child is ignored.

In calculating universal credit, 55 per cent of the claimant's, or the claimants' combined earned income, or, where a work allowance is applicable, 55 per cent of the excess over the amount of the allowance is taken into account (see s.8(3) WRA 2012 and reg.22). Immediately prior to November 24, 2021 the taper rate was 63 per cent.

Regulations 52–64 deal with the calculation of earned income and regs 65–74 with unearned income. Regulations 75–77 contain a number of additional rules in relation to treatment of a person's capital and income.

Meaning of "earned income"

2.192 **52.** "Earned income" means—

(a) the remuneration or profits derived from—
   (i) employment under a contract of service or in an office, including elective office,
   (ii) a trade, profession or vocation, or
   (iii) any other paid work; or
(b) any income treated as earned income in accordance with this Chapter.

DEFINITION

"paid work"—see reg.2.

GENERAL NOTE

2.193 Paragraph (a) spells out what counts as earned income. It comprises earnings as an employee, as an office-holder, including a holder of elective office, such as a local councillor, self-employed earnings, and remuneration or profits from any other paid work (for the definition of "paid work" see reg.2).

Note first that sub-para.(ii) uses the term "trade, profession or vocation", which is then labelled as "self-employed earnings" in reg.57. The term is that used in the

Income Tax (Trading and Other Income) Act 2005 (ITTOIA) in the Part to do with the taxation of trading income, but there is no direct adoption of the tax rules as there is for employed earnings in reg.55. Thus, the term would, in principle, be given its own meaning, especially as the meaning of "self-employed earner" in s.2(1)(b) of the SSCBA 1992 has not been incorporated either, but the recent approach of the courts has been that the definitions should be applied uniformly across the tax and benefits systems. That was the line strongly taken by the Court of Appeal in the child support context in *Hakki v Secretary of State for Work and Pensions* [2014] EWCA Civ 530 and *French v Secretary of State for Work and Pensions* [2018] EWCA Civ 470; [2018] AACR 25 in cases of "professional" poker players, even though there was a coherent case to be made that the policy arguments against treating the profits of gambling as taxable (that that would enable gambling losses to be set off against all profits from any self-employment) did not apply in the light of specific child support legislation preventing that. It was held that gambling winnings are only earnings from self-employment where they are an adjunct to a trade or profession (e.g. where someone was paid fees for appearing on TV programmes advising the public how to play poker and had incidental winnings from other participants).

In *SSWP v MA (ESA)* [2024] UKUT 131 (AAC), Judge Wikeley indicates, referring to the tax case law, that a trade does not cease to be a trade because it is being carried on illegally. In the particular case, the claimant bought and sold stolen bikes on an industrial scale, which was as much a trade as if he had run a legitimate business in second-hand bikes. His activity was held to constitute "work" for the purposes of ESA and his income to be earnings from self-employment.

One particular potential consequence of the restriction of the category of self-employed earnings to remuneration or profit derived from a trade etc., as opposed to the approach in s.2(1) of SSCBA of covering any gainful employment that is not employed earner's employment, is in the treatment of income derived from property. See the notes to reg.77(1) (2.299) for discussion of the tax case law suggesting that "trade" is a narrower concept than "business" and that there is a difference between the exploitation of an interest in property (as by letting it out) and trading (as in running a hotel or bed and breakfast establishment). Thus, in the present context, decisions on whether and when the duties involved in the letting out of a single tenanted property could constitute a business or self-employment in the s.2(1) of SSCBA sense (e.g. *R(FC) 2/92* and *RM v Sefton Council (HB)* [2016] UKUT 357 (AAC), reported as [2017] AACR 5) may not be on point, although *RM* contains extensive helpful citations from the general case law. But could the duties involved in, say, maintaining and cleaning the common parts of a house of rooms let out to students be "paid work" within para.(a)(iii)? It is suggested that the answer is no, because the work cannot be regarded as done for payment or in expectation of payment, as required by the definition in reg.2, because the rent is paid fundamentally for the occupation of the property or part of it and only tangentially for any specific work done in support of the letting. Rent or other payments for the occupation of premises are not unearned income as they are not listed in reg.66(1) (see in particular the note to reg.66(1)(m)). If the capital value of the premises is not disregarded (e.g. as the claimant's home or as an asset used for the purposes of a trade etc.) and is not high enough to exclude entitlement altogether, it would give rise to an assumed yield as income under reg.72(1) and any actual income derived from that capital, specifically including rent is treated as capital from the day it is due to be paid (reg.72(2)).

The DWP regards shared lives carers (who receive fees from the NHS or local authorities for looking after adults with care needs) as self-employed, whereas foster-carers are regarded as not self-employed and not even engaged in work, because what they provide is a service, not work. The result for the latter would be that none of their income as foster-carers counts for universal credit purposes, because it is not listed in reg.66. That distinction in treatment seems hard to justify (see further below). If, as seems to be the case, shared lives carers are properly treated as self-employed, why should that conclusion not also apply to foster-carers, who not uncommonly make an organised "career" of fostering. In either case, there might then be difficult questions whether rent or contributions to accommodation costs and household expenses paid out of benefits received by the looked-after person could be regarded as income other than earnings, and so not to count as not listed in reg.66, or as part of the actual receipts of the trade, profession or vocation being carried on. If there is a self-employment being carried on, such a separation out of expenses and receipts seems artificial.

What might fall within sub-para.(iii) as paid work that does not already fall within sub-para.(i) (contract of employment or office) or (ii) (self-employment) and how income derived from it should be treated is left inexcusably obscure in the Regulations, despite the nature of the modern labour market and economy having rendered the category more important since 2013. Indeed, especially when full consideration is given to the terms of reg.66(1)(m) on unearned income, the whole question is deeply problematic. No clues are given in the chapters of the ADM (H3 and H4) on earned income—employed earnings and earned income—self-employed earnings.

Some exclusions are established by the definition of "paid work" in reg.2. The general meaning is work done for payment or in expectation of payment. Thus, activity carried out for recreation or mainly as a hobby does not count even if products are occasionally sold (e.g. a hobby painter or art collector or allotment holder who occasionally sells paintings or produce). That would not be "work" or done "for" payment. Nor would activities done in the course of being trained (in the absence of a contract of employment), although that conclusion might also be based on any payment made not being in return for the carrying out of the activities (see *R(FIS) 1/83* and *Smith v Chief Adjudication Officer*, reported as *R(IS) 21/95*, on the enterprise allowance). No doubt, some activities done within a family setting, out of natural love and affection, would also not be regarded as work, even if the beneficiary of the service agreed to make some payment going beyond expenses and the activity would be regarded as work if done by some unconnected person (though then query the attribution of notional earned income under reg.60(3) where services are provided at less than the going rate). However, the boundaries are very hard to establish. There is some old case law from family credit (where claimants wanted to be classified as in remunerative work to qualify). In *R(FC) 2/90*, the claimants were full-time officers of the Salvation Army, whose relationship with the organisation was expressly agreed to be spiritual and not contractual, but received free accommodation and living allowances. Commissioner Goodman held that the onerous duties of a Salvation Army officer were work and that the payments were in return for that work, so that the claimants were engaged in remunerative work.

The work must then be done for payment or in expectation (not mere hope) of payment. That seems to entail that payment must have been arranged in advance of the work or been reasonably expected from a course of dealing or was a motive for undertaking some preparatory activity. Thus a gift received after the carrying out of some task for which no payment had been arranged or expected would not be derived from paid work. There is a somewhat wider exclusion in the definition where the person is a volunteer (not further defined) or engaged by a charitable or voluntary organisation (also not further defined) and the payment received is for expenses. That seems to entail, if no charitable or voluntary organisation is involved, asking whether the person would be regarded as a volunteer if the payments for expenses were ignored. Thus, the unemployed painter and decorator who agrees to paint a elderly neighbour's house in return for being reimbursed for the cost of the paint would appear not to be engaged in paid work within sub-para.(iii). Regulation 60(3) on notional earned income would not automatically be excluded from application, because reg.60(4)(a) only supplies an exemption from its operation where a person is engaged to provide services by a charitable or voluntary organisation. But the neighbour's means to pay would be relevant under reg.60(3).

There nonetheless remains quite a wide category of people carrying out activities for or in expectation of payment who do not become employees each time that they are engaged and do not operate with sufficient regularity or organisation to be said to be trading. So the unemployed painter and decorator who agrees as a one-off to paint the elderly neighbour's house for so much a day, not related to the cost of materials, would be engaged in paid work when doing so. Readers can no doubt envisage many other examples of other sorts of activities, like babysitting or occasional buying and selling of items on websites. An increasingly important category would be those working in the gig economy, in the sense of using an online platform to offer services like giving rides, making deliveries, running errands etc, but whose activity is not sufficiently regular or organised to amount to a trade.

The difficulty then is to work out how the payments for the service in question are to be taken into account. Regulations 54 and 54A apply to all forms of earned income, so that the calculation in any assessment period would be based on the actual amount received in that period, with the possibility of the surplus earnings rule applying. However, regs.55 (including the deduction of income tax etc paid) and 56 only apply to "employed earnings" (i.e. within reg.52(a)(i)) and regs 57 to 59 and 62 to 64 only apply to "self-employed earnings" (i.e. within reg.52(a)(ii)). Regulation 60 on notional earned income applies to all forms. So does reg.61, but the only part that is not restricted to employed earnings is the obligation in para.(1) to provide such information as the Secretary of State requires. Thus there is nothing in the legislation to say how much of any reg.52(a)(iii) payment is to be taken into account as earned income in any assessment period. In that circumstance, the principle of *Parsons v Hogg* [1985] 2 All E.R. 897, appendix to *R(FIS) 4/85*, can be invoked, so that the income to be taken into account is not the gross amount received, but the receipts after the payment of expenses wholly and necessarily incurred in the course of winning those receipts. That principle would not, though, allow the deduction of any income tax, social security contributions or pension contributions paid in the assessment period in question. In the great majority of cases within the scope of universal credit there will probably be no liability to income tax or social security contributions (bearing in mind that the income tax £1,000 trading allowance applies to miscellaneous income, including casual earnings, as well as to trading income). However, it is possible that someone could receive substantial amounts through a portfolio of activities on which income tax would be payable under s.687 of ITTOIA.

That point exposes a more serious internal contradiction within the 2013 Regulations. Regulation 66(1)(m) lists income that is taxable under Part 5 of ITTOIA as a category of unearned income, that is therefore to be taken into account for universal credit purposes. Part 5 of ITTOIA includes s.687, which charges income tax on income from any source that is not charged to income tax under any other provision of ITTOIA or any other Act, and is the provision under which casual earnings, not derived from employment or self-employment, are taxed. Although this has not previously been noted by your commentator in past editions, and is not mentioned in the part of the ADM dealing with reg.66(1)(m), that appears to produce the result that income derived from paid work within reg.52(a)(iii) is simultaneously earned income and unearned income. Such a result cannot of course be allowed. The counting twice of the same amount as income cannot be allowed, but the way out is not clear. It is submitted in the more detailed notes to reg.66(1)(m) that payments that fall within the meaning of earned income in reg.52 cannot be made subject to the operation of reg.66(1).

It appears that para.(a) establishes an overarching condition that payments that would fall to be calculated as employed earnings or self-employed earnings be remuneration or profit derived from the sources specified. That would cover the provisions in reg.55 for adopting income tax principles as a matter of calculation and in regs 57–59 on self-employed earnings. See the notes to reg.55 for some of the income tax case law on the "from the employment" test.

On para.(b), see regs 55(4) and (4A), 62 (minimum income floor) and 77(3) (person standing in a position analogous to that of a sole owner or partner in relation to a company carrying on a trade). Note also reg.60 on notional earned income.

Meaning of other terms relating to earned income

53.—(1) In this Chapter—

2.194 "car" has the meaning in section 268A of the Capital Allowances Act 2001;

"employed earnings" has the meaning in regulation 55;

"gainful self-employment" has the meaning in regulation 64;

"HMRC" means Her Majesty's Revenue and Customs;

"motor cycle" has the meaning in section 268A of the Capital Allowances Act 2001;

"PAYE Regulations" means the Income Tax (Pay As You Earn) Regulations 2003;

"relievable pension contributions" has the meaning in section 188 of the Finance Act 2004;

"self-employed earnings" has the meaning in regulation 57; and

"start-up period" has the meaning in regulation 63.

(2) References in this Chapter to a person participating as a service user are to—

(a) a person who is being consulted by or on behalf of—

(i) a body which has a statutory duty to provide services in the field of health, social care or social housing; or

(ii) a body which conducts research or undertakes monitoring for the purpose of planning or improving such services,

in their capacity as a user, potential user, carer of a user or person otherwise affected by the provision of those services; or

[1 (ab) a person who is being consulted by or on behalf of—

(i) the Secretary of State in relation to any of the Secretary of State's functions in the field of social security or child support or under section 2 of the Employment and Training Act 1973; or

(ii) a body which conducts research or undertakes monitoring for the purpose of planning or improving such functions,

in their capacity as a person affected or potentially affected by the exercise of those functions or the carer of such a person;]

(b) the carer of a person consulted under [1 sub-paragraphs (a) or (ab)].

AMENDMENT

1. Social Security (Miscellaneous Amendments) Regulations 2015 (SI 2015/67) reg.2(1)(g) and (2) (February 23, 2015).

DEFINITION

"Her Majesty's Revenue and Customs"—see Interpretation Act 1978 Sch.1.

Calculation of earned income—general principles

2.195 **54.**—(1) The calculation of a person's earned income in respect of an assessment period is, unless otherwise provided in this Chapter, to be based on the actual amounts received in that period.

(2) Where the Secretary of State—

(a) makes a determination as to whether the financial conditions in section 5 of the Act are met before the expiry of the first assessment period in relation to a claim for universal credit; or

(b) makes a determination as to the amount of a person's earned income in relation to an assessment period where a person has failed to report information in relation to that earned income, that determination may be based on an estimate of the amounts received or expected to be received in that assessment period.

DEFINITIONS

"the Act"—see reg.2.
"assessment period"—see WRA 2012 ss.40 and 7(2) and reg.21.
"claim"—see WRA 2012 s.40.
"earned income"—see reg.52.

GENERAL NOTE

Under para.(1), the normal rule is that a person's earned income (as defined in reg.52 and so covering both employed earnings and self-employed earnings as well as remuneration or profit derived from other paid work, whatever that is) is to be based on the actual amount received during an assessment period. 2.196

In *PT v SSWP (UC)* [2015] UKUT 696 (AAC) the claimant claimed universal credit on January 6, 2015 and received his final wages from his previous job on January 16, 2015. These were taken into account in calculating his entitlement to universal credit in the first assessment period. The claimant contended that they should not have been taken into account as his job had ended. Judge Jacobs raises the question of how there can be an assessment period before a decision has been made that the claimant is entitled to universal credit. He accepts the Secretary of State's explanation that the answer lies in s.5(1)(b) of the WRA 2012. The assessment period is fixed by reference to the first date of entitlement (reg.21(1)). Until the decision is made on entitlement, s.5(1)(b) provides for income to be calculated on the assumption that an award will be made. The earnings were received during the first assessment period and so fell to be taken into account under para.(1). It did not matter that the employment had ceased to exist by the time the wages were paid. Nor can it matter that the wages were earned in respect of weeks prior to the first assessment period. It is the time of receipt that is crucial.

However, para.(2) allows an estimate to be made (i) where the calculation is made before the expiry of the first assessment period or (ii) where there has been a failure to report information about earned income in an assessment period.

The principle exemplified in *PT* has been affirmed many times since, although many cases in the end turn on the application of reg.61 on employed earnings reported to HMRC and then to the DWP through Real Time Information (RTI). A new and significantly changed reg.61 was introduced with effect from November 16, 2020. See the notes to reg.61 for detailed discussion of the interpretation of those new provisions. It is though necessary to explore the authorities developed on the validity or otherwise of the terms of the regulations before that amendment, both because some cases from before November 16, 2020 could still be working their way through the system and to help understand the structure of the current provisions.

Johnson, Pantellerisco and the pre-November 16, 2020 law

A judicial review challenge to the inflexibility of the structure of assessment periods and the attribution of earned income actually received in each period (or information received from HMRC under the real time information provisions of reg.61), which, as operated by the DWP, could easily lead to two regular monthly payments being counted in one assessment period and none in another, was first heard in November 2018. However, the Divisional Court (*R. (Johnson) v Secretary of State for Work and Pensions* [2019] EWHC 23 (Admin), Singh LJ and Lewis J) decided that it did not need to address the issues of irrationality, breach of art.14 (discrimination) of the ECHR and breach of the Equality Act 2010 that had been raised originally. That was because it concluded that the DWP had been interpreting regs 54 and 61 wrongly and that the correct interpretation removed the claimants' problems. That conclusion was overturned by the Court of Appeal on the Secretary of State's appeal in *Secretary of State for Work and Pensions v Johnson* [2020] EWCA 2.197

Civ 778; [2020] P.T.S.R. 1872. The regulations were to be interpreted in the way put forward by the DWP, but the court rejected the Secretary of State's appeal because the claimants' case succeeded on the ground that there was irrationality in the failure, when the regulations were drafted and subsequently, to make an express adjustment to avoid the adverse consequences for those in the claimants' circumstances of applying the basic reg.54 rule of using the date of receipt of earned income to decide in which assessment period it counted. There was then no need to consider the alternative ground of discrimination.

The court did not in either of the judgments suggest that any part of reg.54 or 61 was invalid or say what the consequences of its conclusions on irrationality were on the entitlement decisions challenged by the four claimants. However, as discussed below, the declaration contained in the order dated June 30, 2020, presumably accepted on behalf of the Secretary of State as consistent with the judgments, appears to go further. On June 25, 2020, the Under-Secretary of State, Will Quince, confirmed in Parliament that the DWP did not intend to appeal against the judgment (HC Hansard, Vol.677, col.1456).

The four *Johnson* claimants were all single claimants of youngish children, so qualifying for the work allowance, and in monthly paid employment. All of their employers were Real Time Information (RTI) employers. Ms Johnson was paid on the last working day of each month, unless (according to Rose LJ) that was a non-banking day, in which case she was paid earlier. Ms Barrett was paid on the 28th of each month, unless that was a non-banking day, in which case she was paid on the last working day before the 28th. Ms Woods was paid on the last working day of each month (presumably with a similar dispensation if that was a non-banking day). Ms Stewart was paid on the 28th of each month (again presumably with a similar dispensation) Ms Johnson's assessment period ran from the last day of each month to the penultimate day of the following month. Ms Barrett's and Ms Stewart's assessment periods ran from the 28th of each month to the 27th of the following month. Ms Woods' assessment period ran from the 30th of each month to the 29th of the following month. The problems arose when the attribution of payments to a particular assessment period was affected by what Rose LJ called "the non-banking day salary shift".

To take the facts of Ms Johnson's case as an example, she was paid her salary for November 2017 on November 30, 2017 and her salary for December 2017 on December 29, 2017, since December 30 and 31, 2017 were a Saturday and Sunday. (Note that it is accordingly not entirely clear whether that represented payment on the contractual pay-day, Saturday and Sunday not being working days, rather than being a precise example of non-banking day salary shift, but that term might have been intended not to exclude situations where there was in fact no shift from the contractual pay-day). It appears that her employer reported the payments through the RTI system to HMRC on the dates of payment and the information transmitted to the DWP on the same date. A decision-maker took the view that, since the information about both payments was received within the assessment period running from November 30, 2017 to December 30, 2017, reg.61 required them both to be taken into account in that assessment period. The result was that 63% of the excess of the amount of the two payments (after the deductions required by reg.55(5)) over her work allowance of £192 was deducted from the maximum amount of universal credit for that period. It was the decision to that effect on January 6, 2018 that Ms Johnson challenged in her judicial review application. It was accepted that, on that basis, her earnings in the assessment period running from December 31, 2017 to January 30, 2018 would be nil (payment of the January 2018 salary being due on Wednesday January 31, 2018). There would then be no deduction at all for earnings from the maximum amount of universal credit for that assessment period, resulting in a much higher amount of universal credit than in a one-payment assessment period, but Ms Johnson would have been "deprived" of the ability to use £192 worth of work allowance against each separate payment of salary (see further below for discussion of the amount of net losses involved). Ms Woods' challenge was in essence the same, to a decision on January 3, 2018 taking both November and

December salary payments into account in the assessment period running from November 30, 2017 to December 29, 2017.

Ms Barrett and Ms Stewart were more definite examples of non-banking day salary shift. If their pay-day of the 28th of the month was a Saturday or Sunday or a bank holiday, they would be paid at least a day earlier, the payment apparently to be taken into account in the assessment period ending on the 27th of that month (see below for why the employers' RTI returns should in accordance with HMRC guidance/instructions nevertheless have designated payment as made on the 28th).

The Divisional Court concluded that in both reg.54(1) and 61, but with the emphasis on the former, the use of the formula that the amount of earned income "in respect of" an assessment period is to be "based on" the actual amounts received in that period, or the HMRC information received by the Secretary of State in that period, meant that there was "intended to be some other factor, not the mere mechanical addition of monies received in a particular period, which the calculation has to address" (para.51). That other factor was said to be the period in respect of which the earned income was earned, so that there might need to be an adjustment where it was clear that the amounts received in an assessment period did not, in fact, reflect the amounts received in respect of the period of time included within that assessment period. There was a direction that claimants' earned income was to be calculated in accordance with that principle. It is not now necessary to go into more detail on the Divisional Court's reasoning or into the criticisms made of it in the 2019/20 edition of this volume (at 2.164), because its conclusion has been shortly rejected by the Court of Appeal as a matter of construction.

Rose LJ, giving the lead judgment, held that the terms "to be based on" and "in respect of" did not have to be given the meaning given by the Divisional Court to have some substantial content. Looking at the use of different phrases throughout the legislation, "in respect of" meant no more than "in" or "for". The formula of "to be based on" made sense in support of the DWP's approach because of the need to take account of provisions like reg.55(3) on the disregard of certain categories of receipts, which entailed not using the full amount of actual receipts. The Divisional Court's approach also left open many questions about other circumstances in which an adjustment might be made, that reg.54 was intended to avoid, in particular because the universal credit system was designed to be automated, so that decisions could be made by computer without the need for a manual intervention. Another important factor was that "earned income" as defined in reg.52 covered a very wide range of payments, including many where the pattern of payment might well be genuinely irregular. The general principle in reg.54 had to apply to all such payments and in general it made sense for the amount actually received in the assessment period to be not only the starting point but also the finishing point. It was then not possible to give the phrase "is to be based on" in reg.61(2)(a) any different meaning from that in reg.54.

The Secretary of State's challenge to the Divisional Court's reasoning was thus found to be soundly based, but her appeal was nonetheless dismissed because the claimants' arguments on irrationality were accepted. Despite the challenge to specific decisions, Rose LJ described the irrationality arguments, on the basis of her acceptance of the general good sense of the reg.54 rule, as directed at "the initial and ongoing failure of the SSWP to include in the Regulations a further express adjustment to avoid the consequence of the combination of the non-banking day salary shift and the application of regulation 54 for claimants in the position of the Respondents" (para.47).

Counsel for the Secretary of State had accepted that the result of reg.54 for the claimants was arbitrary and that there was no policy reason why they should be faced with the difficulties involved, but submitted that no solution to their difficulties had been found that was not outweighed by other factors. Rose LJ agreed with the Divisional Court that the way that reg.54, as construed in the way she accepted, applied to the claimants was "odd in the extreme". She accepted that there was a wide and frequent oscillation in the amounts of universal credit payable and the total income available to the claimants assessment period to assessment period, leading to budgeting difficulties, the expense of taking out loans or going into overdraft, the effect on entitlement to other advantages (e.g. council tax reduction) and associated stress and anxiety. She also accepted that, through the loss of the benefit of the work allowance in assessment periods when no earned income was received, the claimants suffered an overall loss of income compared with a claimant whose assessment period was dated in a way that required each regular payment of monthly salary to be taken into account in its own assessment period. (Despite that acceptance, it appears in fact very difficult to work out whether any individual claimant would be worse or better off by sometimes having two monthly salaries counted in one assessment period and sometimes none: the calculations are too complicated to explore here). There could also possibly be an effect on other aspects of the universal credit scheme, such as the earnings exemption from the benefit cap, but that did not affect any of the claimants involved.

Rose LJ rejected the Secretary of State's submission that the oscillation was a reflection of a central feature of the scheme in responding immediately to changes in claimants' circumstances as they move in and out of work. Rather, there was no change here in the claimants' circumstances or irregularity in the pattern of their receipt of monthly payments. The oscillation was a response only to whether the regular monthly pay date coincided with the end date of the assessment period. There was no practical way for the claimants to alter the dates of their assessment periods once they were set at the date of claim (having received no warning of the potential consequences) or to alter their contractual pay-day, but there was evidence that the consequences cut across the overall policy of the scheme by creating perverse employment incentives for the claimants to change or turn down employment on the basis of payment patterns.

The Secretary of State had put forward three reasons for not resolving the problems of non-banking day salary shift either initially or once the scheme was in operation, linked it seems by the argument that to do so would undermine the coherence of the universal credit scheme as a whole. The first was that the suggested irrationality was based on the misconception of aligning an assessment period with a calendar month or that the problem arose from the irregularity of payment set against the intended regular and fixed pattern of assessment periods. Rose LJ rejected that characterisation of the origin of the difficulty. The second reason was the need for "bright lines" in the rules for the attribution of receipts of earned income, that would inevitably lead to some hard cases falling just on the wrong side. Rose LJ accepted the need for bright lines in many circumstances, but noted that the regulations contained several exceptions to such lines where the policy imperative overrode the need for simplicity and that, as the claimants submitted, flexibility was allowed when it was in the Secretary of State's interests. Careful and detailed drafting had been adopted to address specific issues. It could not be impossible to draft an exception to cover the particular problem highlighted in *Johnson*, which involved significant and predictable, but arbitrary, effects, and it was not a valid argument against doing so that there might be other groups of claimants for whom such a solution could not be found. The third reason was the need for a rule that would allow the calculation of the amount of a universal credit award to take place in an automated way without the need for manual intervention. Such automation was said to have many advantages for claimants and the cost of rebuilding the calculator in the computer system was said to be substantial. Rose LJ could not accept that the computer programme could not be altered to recognise cases where the end of a claimant's assessment period coincided with the salary pay date, so that action might be needed to prevent two payments counting in one assessment period when there was a non-banking day salary shift.

Rose LJ also took into account the potential size of the cohort affected, suggesting (without adjudicating between the competing figures put forward by the parties) that many tens of thousand were likely to be involved. That was because 75% of working people are paid monthly, the most common pay-day being the last working day of the month followed by the 28th, and many claims are made towards the end of the month when jobs come to an end. She also considered it significant that there was no practical way for the claimants to get themselves out of the situation, that the problem was arbitrary in nature and without prior warning to the claimant (increasing stress) and in particular involved inconsistency with the policy of incentivising work. Thus there were serious personal consequences for those affected and results that ran counter to some fundamental features of the universal credit scheme.

Although the threshold for establishing irrationality was very high, here the refusal to put in place a solution to the very specific problem was an outcome that no reasonable Secretary of State would have adopted. There was to be a direction (to be agreed by counsel) focusing on that specific problem, that would leave it to the Secretary of State to consider the best way to solve the problem (para.110). Underhill LJ agreed, saying that there was nothing to justify a conclusion that no solution could be devised without causing unacceptable cost or problems elsewhere in the system, but also that the case turned on its own particular circumstances. He added, at para.116, that the case turned on its own very particular circumstances and had no impact on the lawfulness of the universal credit system more generally.

The court's discussion of the construction of reg.54 was rather limited and it is arguable that a proper basis had not been established for regarding the need for automated calculation (not mentioned anywhere in the legislation) as a significant factor in identifying the purpose that the provision was intended to achieve. However, since the closer textual analysis, especially in the relationship with reg.61(2)(b), set out in para.2.164 of the 2019/20 edition of what was then Vol.V of this series, supports the same construction, that may not matter. As there was no further appeal to the Supreme Court, the issue appears settled unless it is raised again in some other case that reaches the Court of Appeal at least.

It is also arguable that the Court of Appeal here, perhaps because of the way that the court below had approached the issues, gave insufficient attention in general to reg.61 as in force at the relevant time and the various specific provisions within it, since all the employers concerned were RTI employers. Those specific provisions could possibly have qualified the general principle in reg.54 and it was accepted that reg.61(2) applied. Rose LJ said two interesting things, possibly inconsistent, about reg.61. In para.44 she rejected the submission for the claimants that they could rely on reg.61(3), on the ground that there was nothing inaccurate or untimely in the information the employers were providing to HMRC and the DWP, so that there was nothing incorrect in a way specified in reg.61(3). In para.86 she referred to HMRC guidance/instructions that employers should report payment on the contracted pay date in the RTI feed even if payment was made earlier. She cited guidance dealing with Easter 2019 and information on behalf of the claimants that such general guidance had been in place since at least 2018. The guidance may, therefore, not have been in place at the time of the particular decisions challenged by the four claimants, but surely should have played a much more prominent part in the discussion of the ongoing rationality. If an employer in a non-banking day salary shift case where payment is made early enters the date of actual payment in the relevant field (43) of the Full Payment Submission instead of the contractual date, surely it is arguable on the pre-November 16, 2020 form of reg.61 that the information received from HMRC is incorrect in a material respect within s.61(3)(b)(ii), so that the general rule in reg.61(2) need not apply. Regulation 54 would then apply, but with the power to treat a payment of employed earnings received in one assessment period as received in a later period (reg.61(5)(a)). As Rose LJ notes, the following of the HMRC guidance would have obviated the problems for claimants paid on the last day of the month (and, it would seem, for most of those paid on a fixed day of the month, such as the 28th), but not for those paid on the last working day of the month (like Ms Johnson and Ms Woods). That would be because the "early" date of actual payment would still be the contractual or usual pay date. The following of the HMRC guidance/instruction by employers and the use of reg.61(3)(b)(ii) when it was not followed would greatly decrease the size of the cohort subject to extremely odd outcomes. See the notes to reg.61 for further details of the HMRC guidance/instructions.

It is not at all clear how the Court of Appeal's decision on irrationality left the four claimants concerned in practical terms or affected other monthly-paid claimants whose usual pay day is close to the end of their assessment period. The nature of the irrationality accepted and para.110 of Rose LJ's judgment seems to envisage that the terms of the applicable provisions would only be changed through amendment once the Secretary of State, as directed, had come up with a solution to the specific problem. That would have raised difficult questions about whether the Secretary of State would have been required to make any such amendment retrospective, so as to affect the amount of universal credit that should have been awarded (under the terms of the amendment) in the decisions specifically challenged by the four claimants in *Johnson* and in the cases of other claimants. However, the declaration made in the order of June 30, 2020 is as follows:

> "It is declared that the earned income calculation method in Chapter 2 of Part 6 of the Universal Credit Regulations 2013 is irrational and unlawful as employees paid monthly salary, whose universal credit claim began on or around their normal pay date, are treated as having variable earned income in different assessment periods when pay dates for two (consecutive) months fall in the same assessment period in the way described in the judgment."

Thus, rather than a focus on the process of legislating a solution to the specific problem in *Johnson*, the declaration appears to bite on the substance of the legislation and to declare the outcome of the application of regs 54 and 61 for claimants affected by that problem to be "irrational and unlawful". That would in principle be so from the date that those provisions first came into effect. While such a declaration does not directly invalidate any part of those provisions, the inevitable effect must be that the four *Johnson* claimants cannot now, in relation to the decisions challenged, have an irrational and unlawful outcome applied.

That is consistent with the approach of Rose LJ in para.108 of *Johnson*, where she said that the claimants' argument of discrimination under the ECHR did not arise for consideration because of the success of their case on irrationality. It is submitted that the judge, and thus the Court, could only have taken that view if she thought that the four *Johnson* claimants had, by that success, achieved all that they could have achieved by success in the discrimination argument. Since the judicial reviews were directed against the decisions made in particular assessment periods in 2017 or 2018, the Court must by necessary implication from that part of the judgment have accepted that those decisions had to be re-made without applying the method of calculation found to be unlawful, even though the apparent mismatch between the nature of irrationality accepted and that result was unaddressed in the judgments. A mere redrafting of the regulations with effect from a subsequent date would not achieve that result. There is thus strong support, not just in the terms of the declaration, but also in Rose LJ's judgment, that *Johnson* means that the earned income calculation method in the pre-November 16, 2020 form of the regulations has been unlawful from the outset.

The above argument was referred to by Judge Wright in his much more detailed decision in *JN v SSWP (UC)* [2023] UKUT 49 (AAC), reported as [2023] AACR 7. The claimant was an employee paid on the last Wednesday of each month. It was accepted by the Secretary of State that her circumstances were on all fours with those in *Johnson*. She appealed against four decisions that she was not entitled to universal credit in assessment periods in which two monthly payments were reported. (Incidentally, the last decision under appeal was dated November 28, 2020 and might therefore have related to the assessment period ending on November 27, 2020, but it was rightly agreed that the new reg.61 did not take effect in her case until the next assessment period: Decisions and Appeals Regulations 2013 Sch.1 para.32). The First-tier Tribunal dismissed the appeal on the basis that it had to apply the regulations in force at the relevant times. On the further appeal, the Secretary of State submitted that that had been right and that the declaration in *Johnson* had no effect until the unlawfulness exposed in that decision was removed by the November 16, 2020 amendment, which was not retrospective. The judge comprehensively demolishes that submission. First, he shows with copious authority that a declaration is a binding statement by the court upon the existence of a legal state of affairs and that the Secretary of State, as a Minister of HM Government, was required by a core principle of the rule of law to act in conformity with it (para.33). Thus, the declaration in *Johnson* was a binding statement that the earned income calculation method in the regulations was irrational and unlawful. The crucial question of when that binding effect bit then turned on the terms of the declaration, which had no express temporal qualification. There were conflicting indications in the judgments in *Johnson*, but Judge Wright concludes (para.56) that the Court of Appeal intended it to bite at least from the date of the decisions under appeal in that case in 2017 or 2018, well before the assessment periods in issue in *JN*. He therefore did not need to consider any argument that the effect should extend back to the start of the universal credit scheme.

In substituting a decision on the claimant's appeals, the judge, while clear that the Secretary of State's initial decisions had to be set aside as they applied legislation that was irrational and unlawful, could find no obvious basis on which he could lawfully re-make those decisions. Accordingly, he left it to the Secretary of State to redecide on a lawful basis the claimant's entitlement to universal credit in the assessment periods in question, while noting that a way had apparently been found to make payments to the *Johnson* claimants by manual adjustments to the system. In past editions, suggestions have been made about what approaches could be taken in providing a remedy in similar cases, but it may well be that in cases before tribunals there is no alternative to requiring the Secretary of State to redecide the matter of entitlement. There would no doubt be a right of appeal against whatever was decided, if the claimant was dissatisfied. An "automated fix" for *Johnson* lookalike cases was said to have been put in place from August 2021.

The same questions apply to other claimants in the same situation who either have appeals or mandatory reconsideration applications already lodged or are awaiting decisions that had been deferred under the Secretary of State's powers in s.25 of the SSA 1998 and reg.53 of the Decisions and Appeals Regulations 2013. For claimants who now wish to challenge past decisions there are the hurdles of being in time for a valid challenge and of decisions made before *Johnson* not having arisen for "official error" because the error was only revealed by the Court of Appeal's decision. They may, though, wish to try the discrimination argument on which the court expressed no opinion to argue for invalidity of the regulations in so far as they have the outcome found irrational by the Court of Appeal.

But note again the suggestion made above that the problems for those paid on the last day of the month or on a fixed day of the month could be obviated by employers properly following HMRC instructions, where payment is made earlier because the contractual or usual pay day is a non-banking day, to report payment as made on the contractual or usual day. Then, if an employer fails to follow that instruction and reports the actual payment date, which circumstance is drawn to the DWP's attention, it is suggested that payment can be treated as made in another assessment period because the information received from HMRC is incorrect in a material respect (reg.61(3)(b)(ii), (4) and (5)(a) in their pre-November 16, 2020 form: see the notes to reg.61 for the significant differences in the new form and *DfC v OS (UC)* [2022] NICom 29).

Similar problems can arise for claimants who are paid four-weekly, bi-weekly or weekly, regardless of whether the normal pay day is a non-banking day or not. For instance, the pattern of four-weekly payment, being out of sync with the pattern of monthly assessment periods, will inevitably lead to two payments being counted in one assessment period in a year, causing a severe fluctuation in income (and potentially more severe problems in the other assessment periods in relation to the benefit cap: see below). The Secretary of State appears to have taken the view, based in particular on Underhill LJ's statements in *Johnson* and Rose LJ's acceptance at para.47 that in the great majority of circumstances the use of actual receipts was sensible and right, that the decision meant that the effect of the regulations could not be found irrational for any pay patterns other than monthly and that to do so would reintroduce the uncertainty for which the Court of Appeal had criticised the Divisional Court's approach. That seems to have been the central submission to the Administrative Court in *R. (Pantellerisco) v Secretary of State for Work and Pensions* [2020] EWHC 1944 (Admin); [2020] P.T.S.R. 2289, a case of four-weekly earnings, decided shortly after *Johnson* with the parties given the opportunity of comment on that decision and the direction given. Garnham J rightly rejected that submission. The only reasonable inference that could be drawn from the Court of Appeal's necessary restriction of its reasoning to the facts and evidence before it and from its observations that its conclusions did not undermine the whole structure of universal credit, or even the general structure of earnings calculation, is that there was no intention to exclude the possible application of a similar logic to other specific categories of case.

The context of *Pantellerisco* was the earnings exemption from the benefit cap under reg.82(1) (see further in the notes to reg.82) where a claimant's earnings in an assessment period equal or exceed the amount of the national minimum wage per hour times 16, converted to a monthly figure. The claimant was employed for 16 hours a week at the national minimum wage and was paid four-weekly. Because in 11 assessment periods out of 12 only one four-weekly payment was received and the monthly conversion then came out below the crucial level she had the benefit cap applied to her in those 11 assessment periods. If she had been paid at the same rate on a monthly basis, she would not have had the benefit cap applied at all and would have received perhaps £400 per month more. The judge carefully went through the same factors as identified in *Johnson* and came to the same conclusion that, the outcome of the balance being obvious and irresistible, no reasonable Secretary of State could have struck the balance in the way done in the regulations.

However, on the Secretary of State's appeal the Court of Appeal in *Pantellerisco v Secretary of State for Work and Pensions* [2021] EWCA Civ 1454; [2021] P.T.S.R. 1922 overturned the decision of Garnham J. Since the claimant's judicial review challenge was directed specifically against the operation of the earnings-related exception to the operation of the benefit cap for claimants paid four-weekly and working for 16 hours a work at national minimum wage level, see the general notes to Pt 7 on the benefit cap for a full discussion of that issue. In the closely reasoned judgment of Underhill LJ, the Court concluded that it was not irrational for the Secretary of State not to have introduced some solution to the problem that, compared with a claimant in identical circumstances who was paid monthly, Ms Pantellerisco was some £500 a year worse off because she was excepted from the benefit cap in only one assessment period in the year, not all 12. Any suggested solution would involve deeming (at least for benefit cap purposes) some earnings accrued in an assessment period, but not actually received, as having been received. That, in the judges' view, would do unacceptable damage to the system of calculating earnings by reference to receipts in assessment periods of calendar months and seriously undermine the reliability and workability of the assessment of entitlement, because all elements of the system had to fit together. The confirmation by Lord Reed in para.146 of *R. (SC) v Secretary of State for Work and Pensions* [2021] UKSC 26; [2022] A.C. 223 that in the context of social and economic policy, covering social security benefits, the test of unreasonableness should be applied with considerable care and caution, especially where a statutory instrument had been reviewed by Parliament, also appears to have been influential.

Thus, Ms Pantellerisco's application to the Supreme Court for permission to appeal having been refused, so far as the ordinary operation of regs 54 and 61, without the complication of the benefit cap exception, to claimants paid four-weekly or at any other weekly interval is concerned, there now appears no possibility of any conclusion of irrationality or unreasonableness. The effect of a downward fluctuation in universal credit entitlement in the one assessment period in a year (for the four-weekly paid) in which two payments are received is vastly less than that of the benefit cap rule, and might not arise, depending on the accident of how long a claimant was in receipt of universal credit and whether that period included a two-payment assessment period.

That approach was applied to a claimant paid fortnightly in *SSWP v LM (UC)* [2023] UKUT 73 (AAC). It had also been presaged to some extent in *LG v SSWP*

(UC) [2021] UKUT 121 (AAC). There, the claimant was paid four-weekly and was not subject to the benefit cap. In the assessment period running from July 11, 2019 to August 10, 2019, she received two sets of four weeks' pay, on July 12 and August 9. As a result, the amount of universal credit to which she was entitled in that period was considerably reduced, if not completely wiped out (it is not clear which) by comparison with a period in which only one payment was received. The First-tier Tribunal disallowed the claimant's appeal, that had explicitly relied on *Johnson* and on Garnham J's decision in *Pantellerisco*, pointing out that she was advantaged in 11 months of the year by having only four weeks' pay taken into account against a month's universal credit allowance and disadvantaged only in one month. Judge May QC dismissed the further appeal, making clear his view that that level of disadvantage fell a very long way short of showing irrationality in the application of reg.54. Indeed, his view was that taking one of the payments out of attribution to the assessment period in question would unfairly advantage the claimant, if it resulted in only 12 payments, rather than 13, being taken into account over a year. Her representatives had not made any suggestion about how, if one payment were to be taken out of an assessment period in which two payments were actually received, it could be attributed across any other assessment periods.

One thing that did emerge from the evidence discussed by the Court of Appeal in *Pantellerisco* was that, following the report of March 12, 2019 by the House of Commons Work and Pensions Committee, the DWP was apparently considering whether some reform should be made to the rules on pay cycles, although nothing has yet emerged into the public domain.

An assessment period is normally a period of one month beginning with the first day of entitlement to universal credit and each subsequent month while entitlement continues (see reg.21(1)). See regs 57–59 below (with the addition of the new reg.54A on surplus earnings and reg.57A on unused losses, plus reg.62 on the minimum income floor) for the provisions on the calculation of self-employed earnings, including some inroads into the focus on actual receipts and expenditure in a particular assessment period. See regs.54A–56 and 61 for the provisions on the calculation of employed earnings involving slightly fewer inroads. The notes to reg.55 discuss the question of identifying the amount to be regarded as received. See the discussion of *SSWP v RW (rule 17) (UC)* [2017] UKUT 347 (AAC) and of *Johnson* in the notes to reg.61 below for circumstances in which the rules in that provision for taking account of real time information reported by an employer to HMRC and received by the Secretary of State in a particular assessment period must give way to the ordinary rule in reg.54 depending on date of receipt by the claimant.

Also see the notes to reg.61 for discussion of whether any alterations of existing awards resulting from increases or reductions in the amount of earned income are appealable.

[[1]Surplus earnings 2.198

54A.—(1) This regulation applies in relation to a claim for universal credit where—

(a) the claimant, or either of joint claimants, had an award of universal credit (the "old award") that terminated within the 6 months ending on the first day in respect of which the claim is made;

(b) the claimant has not, or neither of joint claimants has, been entitled to universal credit since the old award terminated; and

(c) the total earned income in the month that would have been the final assessment period for the old award, had it not terminated, exceeded the relevant threshold.

(2) Where this regulation applies in relation to a claim, any surplus earnings determined in accordance with paragraph (3) are to be treated as earned

income for the purposes of determining whether there is entitlement to a new award and, if there is entitlement, calculating the amount of the award.

(3) Surplus earnings are—

(a) if the claim in question is the first since the termination of the old award, the amount of the excess referred to in paragraph (1)(c) ("the original surplus");

(b) if the claim in question is the second since the termination of the old award, the amount, if any, by which—

(i) the original surplus, plus

(ii) the total earned income in the month that would have been the first assessment period in relation to the first claim,

exceeded the relevant threshold ("the adjusted surplus");

(c) if the claim in question is the third since the termination of the old award, the amount, if any, by which—

(i) the adjusted surplus from the second claim, plus

(ii) the total earned income in the month that would have been the first assessment period in relation to the second claim,

exceeded the relevant threshold;

(d) if the claim in question is the fourth or fifth since the termination of the old award, an amount calculated in the same manner as for the third claim (that is by taking the adjusted surplus from the previous claim).

(4) For the purposes of paragraph (3)—

(a) if the claim in question is the first joint claim by members of a couple, each of whom had an old award (because each was previously entitled to universal credit as a single person or as a member of a different couple), the amounts of any surplus earnings from the old award or from a previous claim that would have been treated as earned income if they had each claimed as a single person are to be aggregated; and

(b) if the claim in question is—

(i) a single claim where the claimant had an old award, or made a subsequent claim, as a joint claimant, or

(ii) a joint claim where either claimant had an old award, or made a subsequent claim, as a member of a different couple,

the original surplus, or any adjusted surplus, in relation to the old award is to be apportioned in the manner determined by the Secretary of State.

(5) No amount of surplus earnings is to be taken into account in respect of a claimant who has, or had at the time the old award terminated, recently been a victim of domestic violence (within the meaning given by regulation 98).

(6) In this regulation—

"total earned income" is the earned income of the claimant or, if the claimant is a member of a couple, the couple's combined earned income, but does not include any amount a claimant would be treated as having by virtue of regulation 62 (the minimum income floor);

"the nil UC threshold" is the amount of total earned income above which there would be no entitlement to universal credit, expressed by the following formula—

[3(M – U) / 55 × 100 + WA]

where—

M is the maximum amount of an award of universal credit;

U is unearned income;
WA is the work allowance; and
"the relevant threshold" is the nil UC threshold plus £300 [[2]£2,500].]

Amendments

1. Universal Credit (Surpluses and Self-employed Losses) (Digital Service) Amendment Regulations 2015 (SI 2015/345) reg.2(2), as amended by Universal Credit (Miscellaneous Amendments, Saving and Transitional Provision) Regulations 2018 (SI 2018/65) reg.7(3) (April 11, 2018).

2. Universal Credit (Surpluses and Self-employed Losses) (Digital Service) Amendment Regulations 2015 (SI 2015/345) reg.5, as inserted by Universal Credit (Miscellaneous Amendments, Saving and Transitional Provision) Regulations 2018 (SI 2018/65) reg.7(6) (modification effective from April 11, 2018 to March 31, 2019 as extended by the Secretary of State to March 31, 2023).

3. Universal Credit (Work Allowance and Taper) (Amendment) Regulations 2021 (SI 2021/1283) reg.2(2) (November 24, 2021, or, for existing claimants, any assessment period ending on or after November 24, 2021).

Definitions

"assessment period"—see WRA 2012 ss.40 and 7(2) and reg.21.
"claim"—see WRA 2012 s.40.
"claimant"—*ibid.*
"couple"—see WRA 2012 ss.40 and 39.
"earned income"—see reg.52.
"joint claimants"—see WRA 2012 s.40.
"maximum amount of an award of universal credit"—see WRA s.8(2).
"unearned income"—see regs 2 and 65 - 74.
"victim of domestic violence"—see WRA 2012 s.24(6)(b).
"work allowance"—see reg.22.

General Note

The general purpose of reg.54A is described as follows in the Explanatory Memorandum attached to SI 2018/65: **2.199**

> "7.7 This instrument makes a number of changes to the Universal Credit (Surpluses and Self-employed Losses) (Digital Service) Amendment Regulations 2015 which make provision to smooth the peaks and troughs of losses and earnings so that a fairer assessment as to Universal Credit entitlement is made over a period of time, longer than one month. This has, however, proved difficult to operate and simplification is required.
> 7.8 The current provision provides that the carrying forward of surplus earnings will apply to both employed and self-employed claimants. Where there is an increase in earnings that means Universal Credit is lost, the amount of that increase over the "relevant threshold" (which includes a de minimis of £300, but see below) will be taken into account and applied to future Universal Credit awards, for a maximum of 6 assessment periods. This ensures that those with fluctuating earning patterns are not unduly penalised or unfairly rewarded by receiving less or more Universal Credit than they would if they earned the same amount but were paid monthly. It also reduces the risk of claimants manipulating payment patterns to receive bigger payments of Universal Credit.
> 7.9 This instrument will also change the way that surplus earnings are applied when people reclaim Universal Credit within 6 months. Instead of taking account of earnings over the whole period of Universal Credit, only the earnings in the month where people make a claim will be counted. Where couples separate there will be more scope for flexibility in the way the surplus is apportioned. These changes will also increase the de minimis from £300 to £2500 for one year

(which may be extended by the Secretary of State). This will assist the smooth implementation by the reducing the numbers affected in the early stages."

It seems odd to refer to sums like £2,500 or £300 as "de minimis" and that term is not used in the regulation itself. It could more accurately be described as an effective disregard of those amounts in determining whether the claimant has surplus earnings in any months. The initial use of the sum of £2,500 has restricted the effect of the regulation in the first six years from April 2018 (see the extensions noted below, with the possibility of further extensions) to fairly extreme upward variations in earned income and exclude the more routine fluctuations that might be covered by the unmodified form. Potential problems may therefore be to some extent masked during this period, although on the other hand there may also be the opportunity for further amendment before the provision begins to bite more routinely. The modification of the definition of "relevant threshold" in para.(6) and the identification of the "temporary de minimis period" for which it has effect is to be found in reg.5 of the Universal Credit (Surpluses and Self-employed Losses) (Digital Service) Amendment Regulations 2015 (SI 2015/345), as set out at the end of this Part. That provision first applied the modification to £2,500 for one year down to March 31, 2019, but on February 5, 2019 it was announced that the Secretary of State had made a determination to extend the period to March 31, 2020, as allowed by reg.5(2). There have been further annual extensions (by virtue of determinations dated March 5, 2020, March 23, 2021, March 3, 2022, March 20, 2023 and February 22, 2024) taking the operation of the modification down to March 31, 2025. The latest extension is included in the DWP's Guidance on regulations under the Welfare Reform Act 2012 on *gov.uk*.

The Social Security Advisory Committee (SSAC) expressed a number of serious misgivings about the proposals as amended by SI 2018/65 (set out in the letter of January 19, 2018 from the Chairman to the Secretary of State in their Report of January 2018 and response by the Secretary of State). They will be mentioned at appropriate points below.

Regulation 54A appears to be validly made in terms of the powers in para.4(1) and (3)(a) of Sch.1 to the WRA 2012 in the light of the decision of the Court of Appeal in *Owen v Chief Adjudication Officer*, April 29, 1999, dismissing an argument that shifting income from the period in which it was received to a different period was neither "calculation" nor "estimation" (see the notes to reg.35(2) of the Income Support Regulations in Vol.V of this series, 2021/22 edition as updated in Cumulative Supplements included in this volume and in mid-year Supplements). But see the note to para.(2) below for an argument on irrationality. The provision initially applied only in digital service (full service) cases (see the saving provision in reg.4(1) of SI 2015/345), but is now of general application.

See the notes to reg.61 for discussion of whether any alterations of existing awards resulting from increases or reductions in the amount of earned income to be taken into account are appealable.

Regulation 54A entails the attribution of surplus earnings to assessment periods subsequent to the period in which the amount over the threshold was received. Since, by definition that receipt will have precluded entitlement in that period on income grounds, there is no need to enquire about the immediate effect on the claimant's capital. However, in relation to subsequent assessment periods for which a claim is made or treated as made, there is a question whether any funds actually still possessed by the claimant constitute capital if surplus earnings are to be treated under reg.54A as existing in that period. On general principle (see *R(IS) 3/93* and *R(IS) 9/08*) income, and in particular earnings, does not metamorphose into capital until after the end of the period to which it is attributed under the relevant legislation. Although matters are not so clear in universal credit as in income support and similar benefits, that principle would seem to hold because of the irrationality of treating the same amount as both income and capital at the same time.

The principle could arguably extend to assessment periods in which surplus earnings are treated as possessed, so that any actual funds retained from the initial receipt are treated as earnings and not capital to the extent of the amount of surplus earnings taken into account in the period in question. Another way of looking at the situation might be to invoke the further principle in *R(SB) 2/83* that income does not metamorphose into capital until relevant liabilities, including tax liabilities, have been deducted. It could be argued that the operation of the surplus earnings rule on later claims is a relevant liability that should therefore lead to a corresponding reduction in the amount of capital to be taken into account. In income support and similar benefits the metamorphosis principle cannot apply to self-employed earnings, because of the method of calculating such earnings (*CIS/2467/2003*). However, since for universal credit both self-employed and employed earnings are calculated by reference to receipts and expenditure in particular assessment periods, the metamorphosis principle can be applied just as much to one as the other. One difference, though, is that in so far as the self-employed have capital in the form of sums deriving from payments that have caused surplus earnings, the disregards of business assets in paras 7 and 8 of Sch.10 can apply. And note that with effect from May 21, 2020 there is a disregard as capital (for 12 months from the date of receipt) for the self-employed of any payment in respect of a furloughed employee under the Coronavirus Job Retention Scheme or "by way of a grant or loan to meet the expenses or losses of the trade, profession or vocation in relation to the outbreak of coronavirus disease" (Universal Credit (Coronavirus) (Self-employed Claimants and Reclaims) (Amendment) Regulations 2020 (SI 2020/522) reg.2(2)).

Paragraph (1) sets out the basic conditions for the application of the regulation, which are subject to the exclusion in para.(5) of claimants who have recently been the victims of domestic violence. Paragraph (2) sets out the rule as to treating surplus earnings in one assessment period as earned income in certain later assessment periods. Paragraph (3) says what surplus earnings are and how they may be reduced or extinguished. Paragraph (4) deals with circumstances where surplus earnings were received when a couple had a joint claim, but later claim as single or as part of a different couple. Paragraph (6) supplies important definitions.

Paragraph (1)

The issue of surplus earnings arises on a claim for universal credit when the claimant or either of joint claimants had previously had an award of universal credit ("the old award") that had terminated within the six months before the first day of the period claimed for (sub-para.(a)). It does not matter by what method the award terminated, by virtue of a decision of the Secretary of State on revision or supersession or by the claimant withdrawing the claim. But the six months establishes the outer limit of how far back surplus earnings can be relevant on a new claim. The claimant or either joint claimant must not have been entitled to universal credit since that termination (remembering that there can be entitlement while nothing is payable) (sub-para.(b)). Then the final condition is that in the month that would have been the final assessment period for the old award if it had not terminated, total earned income in that month exceeded the "relevant threshold" (sub-para.(c)). It is that excess that is the starting point for calculating surplus earnings under para.(3). The relevant threshold is defined by way of a complicated formula in para.(6). The starting point is basically the amount of earned income that, after taking account of any unearned income (which counts in full), the appropriate work allowance, if any, and the 55% taper applied to earned income, would lead to there being no entitlement to universal credit. That is the "nil UC threshold". Immediately prior to November 24, 2021, the taper rate was 63%, that had been applicable since April 2017. 2.200

In the simplest case of a single claimant of 25 or over with no work allowance, no unearned income and no housing costs (so that the "maximum amount of an award of universal credit" would be limited to the standard allowance), that threshold would on April 2024 rates be £715.36 (the amount of which the standard allowance under reg.36(3) of £393.45 is 55%). Then the amount of £2,500 (currently, to decrease to £300 after March 31, 2025 unless there are further extensions to the substitution of the higher amount) is added to make the "relevant threshold". See pp.133–4 of CPAG's *Welfare Benefits and Tax Credits Handbook 2024/2025* for further examples.

Paragraph (1) thus applies to any form of earned income (defined in reg.52): employed earnings; self-employed earnings; and remuneration from any other paid work (for which see the discussion in the notes to reg.52), as well as notional earned income. The latter category will cover amounts treated as possessed under regs 60 and 77(3), but any amount the claimant is treated as possessing under reg.62 (minimum income floor) is expressly excluded from the definition of "total earned income" in para.(6). The existence of surplus earnings need not have been the reason for the termination of the old award. That could have been, for instance, failing to accept a new claimant commitment or the withdrawal of the claim by the claimant. All that is necessary under sub-para.(c) is that in what would have been the final assessment period of the old award there were surplus earnings. Thus, claimants cannot avoid the operation of reg.54A by, once they know that the earned income received or to be received in a current assessment period will exceed the relevant threshold, quickly withdrawing their claim for that assessment period. That assessment period would seem still to be caught by sub-para.(c). The use of the words "final … had it not terminated" is not problem-free. They cannot mean that the termination is to be ignored completely, because then the award might have continued into the future and it cannot be said what might have been the final assessment period. To make any sense, the words must be taken as referring to the month following the last actual assessment period under the old award, that would have been an assessment period if entitlement had not ceased after the last day of the last actual assessment period. However, that does seem to mean that if a claimant can predict in advance that a particularly large one-off receipt of earnings is to arrive at a particular time it might be worth withdrawing the universal credit claim for the assessment period immediately preceding the period in which the receipt is expected. That period would not then be caught by sub-para.(c) and a new claim for universal credit after the end of that period would not attract any surplus earnings, so that entitlement would be assessed on actual earned income receipts in the new assessment period. However, it would require very careful calculation whether the loss of two months' universal credit would outweigh the benefit of future freedom from the surplus earnings rule.

See the notes to reg.57 for the distinction between income receipts and capital receipts for the self-employed. Only income receipts go into the calculation of what is to be taken into account as self-employed earnings in any assessment period and is therefore capable of contributing to surplus earnings.

Paragraph (2)

2.201 Paragraph (2) provides that, where the conditions in para.(1) are met, surplus earnings as worked out under para.(3) are to be treated as earned income in determining entitlement under the new claim and calculating the amount of any award. Paragraph (3) deals with the consequences on the erosion of the amount of surplus earnings where the taking into account of the surplus earnings results in there not being entitlement on the first claim after the termination of the old claim and so on for further unsuccessful claims (see below for the details).

This process marks the clearest difference from the original 2015 form of the amending regulations, which spread the surplus earnings and thus their erosion over the six months following the assessment period in which the surplus earnings were received, regardless of whether a claim for universal credit was made in those months or not. The rule that the amount of surplus earnings will only be eroded, before the expiry of the six-month limit, for any month in which a claim is made, was one of the main causes of disquiet in the SSAC.

However, para.(3) says nothing about the consequences if the taking into account of surplus earnings on that first or a subsequent claim results in an award of universal credit, but of a lower amount than would have been calculated if they were not taken into account. That works in relation to the first assessment period under the new claim and award, but there is nothing in reg.54A to prevent the same amount of surplus earnings being taken into account for future assessment periods within the same period of entitlement under the award. Paragraph (2) is expressly in terms of an award and the amount of the award, not a particular assessment period. Paragraph (3) only provides for the erosion of the surplus earnings on a new or subsequent *claim*. Once a claim has been successful and an award has been made there can be no further claim during the period of entitlement and no scope for the mechanism of para.(3) to apply. Nor could even the six-month limit apply to stop that continuing effect, because under para.(1)(a) that applies by reference to the first day of the period for which the new claim is made, not each successive assessment period. The result on the face of it is that in such circumstances the claimant is fixed for ever (or at least within the same continuing period of entitlement) with the remaining amount of surplus earnings taken into account in the first assessment period under the new award. Indeed, that seemed to be the assumption in some of the examples given in Memo ADM 11/18 (although several of the original examples contained misleading or incomplete calculations). The examples now given in para. H3311 of the ADM and in Appendix 2 to chap.H3 include claimants who start off with a level of entitlement based on regular earnings and end up after the para.(3) process with a lower level of entitlement when an award is eventually made and the advice says that "surplus earnings have been eroded and no longer apply". But there is no explanation of how in the terms of reg.54A the surplus earnings that have been taken into account in the first assessment period under the new award cease to be taken into account in subsequent assessment periods.

It may well have been thought that para.(1)(b) (claimant has not been entitled to universal credit since the old award terminated) has the effect of preventing the attribution of surplus earnings beyond the first assessment period of some entitlement to universal credit. However, that does not work, because para.(1) contains the conditions for application of the surplus earnings rule in relation to a *claim*, not to an award. In the circumstances described above (and worked through in the example in the notes to para.(3) below), once some entitlement has been awarded for one assessment period there can be no new claim for the following assessment period. The award made for the first assessment period of entitlement continues into the next and subsequent assessment periods on the basis of the claim made for the first assessment period of entitlement. In relation to that claim, the condition in para. (1)(b) was satisfied because *at the date of that claim* the claimant will not have been entitled to universal credit since the old award terminated. It might in some circumstances be possible, in order to produce an equitable result, to interpret the word "claim" as extending to an award and a continuing award. However, that does not seem possible in the context of reg.54A, which so carefully distinguishes between claims and awards throughout.

That result is so obviously unfair, both in fixing claimants with deemed earnings that total more than the surplus earnings involved and in treating different claimants differently by the pure chance of the amount of surplus earnings, large or small, that is left at the end of the last para.(3) calculation that allows an award to be made (see the end of the example worked through in the note to para.(3) below), that it cannot be allowed to stand. However, it is difficult, if not impossible, to identify a technical means of interpretation by which the result can be avoided. Is the unfairness so intractable that the amending provisions can be regarded as irrational and ultra vires on that ground?

This problem would not have arisen on the original 2015 form of the amending regulations, where the erosion of surplus earnings would simply have followed month by month until eroded completely or six months was reached.

Paragraph (3)

Once an old award has terminated when there is an excess of total earned income over the relevant threshold, as identified in para.(1)(c), that "original surplus" (see para.(3)(a)) sits there waiting potentially to come into play once a new claim is made. But the amount of the original surplus remains the same if no claim is made until the six months in para.(1)(a) expires. The only way in the terms of reg.54A that 2.202

the amount of the original surplus can reduce is by the making of new claims. That may involve a claimant in making multiple new claims that will be bound not to lead to entitlement in order to reduce the amount of surplus earnings to a level that will allow satisfaction of the financial condition in s.5(1)(b) or 5(2)(b) of the WRA 2012.

Regulation 3 of the Universal Credit (Coronavirus) (Self-employed Claimants and Reclaims) (Amendment) Regulations 2020 (SI 2020/522) introduced with effect from May 21, 2020 a new reg.32A of the Claims and Payments Regulations 2013 allowing the Secretary of State, subject to any appropriate conditions, to treat a claimant as making a new universal credit claim on the first day of each of five subsequent potential assessment periods after non-entitlement because income is too high. That provision is quite general (as expressed in the guidance in Memo ADM 10/20), but the primary intention expressed in para.7.10 of the Explanatory Memorandum to the Regulations is to use the power where it is earnings received by a furloughed employee supported through the Coronavirus Job Retention Scheme or a grant from the Self-Employed Income Support Scheme (SEISS) that prevents the claimant from satisfying the financial conditions in s.5 of the WRA 2012. That is said to be to make it easier to bring claimants back into universal credit entitlement if actual earnings reduce in those subsequent periods and the surplus earnings are exhausted. There can be circumstances in which a claimant is, depending on the pattern of actual earnings and household circumstances, better off by not making a new universal credit claim for a particular period. It is not clear how the administrative arrangements for deemed claims in cases affected by coronavirus schemes might be able to take that into account or whether claimants might be able to assert that they should not be treated as making a claim. The problem of surplus earnings in this context is most likely to arise for actual (or deemed under reg.77) self-employed claimants. It is not known whether the Secretary of State is still exercising the discretion under reg.32A on the same basis. A condition normally applied is that the DWP has sufficient information to determine the deemed claim.

One of the most serious misgivings of the SSAC was whether claimants would sufficiently understand the need to make multiple unsuccessful claims so as to take the most beneficial action, especially as there are some circumstances (e.g. where a claimant's earnings do not immediately return to the regular level after a peak assessment period, but continue at a higher than regular, but not as high as the peak, level) when it will be more beneficial not to make new claims. As it was put in the chairman's letter of January 19, 2018:

> "One of our main concerns about these proposals is the assumption that claimants will have a detailed understanding of this complex policy, when in reality it seems likely most will not. Many may be disadvantaged simply due to that lack of detailed understanding of the complex rules underpinning this policy.
>
> For example, the only way that claimants can successfully erode surplus earnings that have taken them off Universal Credit is to make repeated monthly claims. But these are destined to fail until the surplus is eroded and entitlement resumes. Requiring claims to be made where it is known that they will be unsuccessful is, at best, counterintuitive and risks damaging the credibility of both this policy and Universal Credit more widely.
>
> …
>
> There is also an assumption that it will be obvious to claimants making a repeat claim whether or not their circumstances have changed in a way that is likely to affect their Universal Credit entitlement. This may be the case where the only change is an increase or decrease in the claimant's earnings. But some changes of circumstances have less predictable outcomes, and multiple changes within a single assessment period are likely to create uncertainty. This might arise, for example, in situations where both members of a couple are in some form of paid work, one member's earnings can go up whilst the other member's goes down, or there may be changes in the household composition."

The Secretary of State's response to that concern was this:

> "The re-claim process in Universal Credit is a simplified one, intentionally designed as a simple and swift process for claimants. For claimants whose only change is the level of earnings, the average time to complete a re-claim could be just eight minutes. The need for affected claimants to re-claim each month does not differ significantly from the current situation. Currently, where the level of earnings causes the UC entitlement to reduce to NIL and the claim to close, claimants need to re-claim if there is a change to their circumstances or level of earnings.
>
> This is also the case with surplus earnings, the claimant has the same need to re-claim as there are no re-awards in Full Service. Notification from DWP on claim closure would advise the claimant of the need to re-claim if their circumstances change.
>
> In addition, the Department will ensure that messaging and guidance, both for those claimants impacted by surplus earnings and for work coaches helping claimants, reinforces this message so that the claimant's responsibilities are clear and they are kept well-informed."

That response, apart from the objectionable nature of much of the terminology (e.g. "claim closure" etc), might be thought almost wilfully to ignore the difference between realising the need to make a claim when the circumstances suggest that entitlement is a real possibility and realising a need when the circumstances point against such a possibility. There was also no answer to the point that had been raised by the SSAC, about circumstances in which claiming would not be beneficial. Overall it is very hard to have any confidence in the ability of the information given at the time of the termination of the old award or in assistance to be given by work coaches to guide claimants through the labyrinth when the experienced experts drafting the DWP's advice to decision-makers could not get even simple examples of the operation of the rules right. And will claimants whose earnings have returned to what they regard as normal appreciate that there has been a change of circumstances?

The technical operation of para.(3) is this. On the first claim (within six months) since the termination of the old award the amount of the original surplus (paras (1)(c) and (3)(a)) is simply added into the calculation for the first assessment period under the claim along with the actual earned and unearned income in that period. If that, after applying the 55% taper to the earned income, leaves the claimant's income below the appropriate maximum amount of universal credit there is entitlement at that reduced level for that assessment period, with the uncertain consequences for future assessment periods under the award as discussed in the note to para.(2) above. If that leaves the claimant's income above the maximum amount there is no entitlement for the month that would have been an assessment period if there had been entitlement. On the next (second) claim, which cannot be made for any period starting earlier than the month for which no entitlement has been determined, surplus earnings will have to be considered under para.(3)(b). For that purpose one has to consider how far in the calculation on the first claim the original surplus plus any actual earned income in that month exceeded the relevant threshold. If there is no excess (i.e. the sum exactly equalled the relevant amount in the previous month), there are no longer any surplus earnings to be carried forward to the second claim. If there is an excess, that is the "adjusted surplus" to be taken into account in determining the second claim. The process then continues under sub-paras (c) and (d), but on these claims taking forward the adjusted surplus from the previous period rather than the original surplus, until there is no longer a surplus to be carried forward or entitlement arises or the six months expires.

That is all fairly impenetrable as an abstract explanation. Trying to work through an example may help the explanation (with caution in view of the criticisms above of the initial official guidance).

Imagine a single universal credit claimant with no children who is also a contributor as a self-employed earner to an annual book of social security legislation and has no other source of income. The claimant is paid an annual fee of £10,500 on May 10, 2024, in the middle of the assessment period running from May 1 to May 30, and no income tax or national insurance contribution is paid in that period. Entitlement will therefore terminate after the end of the previous assessment period as 55% of the self-employed earnings exceeds the maximum amount of universal credit at that date (£393.45 standard allowance with no work allowance as at May 2024).

On an immediate claim for the period from June 1, 2024, in which there will be no actual earned income, surplus earnings from the previous month must be considered under para.(3)(a). The nil UC threshold is £715.36 (the amount of which £393.45 is 55%) and the relevant threshold is £3,215.36 (£715.36 + £2,500). The claimant's earned income of £10,500 in the assessment period to May 30, 2024 exceeded that relevant threshold, so the excess (£7,284.64) is surplus earnings (the original surplus) to be taken into account on this first new claim. The result is that there is no entitlement on that claim, as 55% of that amount (£4,006.55) exceeds the maximum amount of universal credit.

On the second new claim for the period from July 1, 2024, surplus earnings from the previous month must be considered under sub-para.(b). There is no actual earned income. The original surplus is £7,284.64 and the relevant threshold is £3,215.36, so that the excess is £4,069.28. That again is clearly enough to prevent entitlement after the 55% taper. But £4,069.28 then becomes the adjusted surplus to be carried forward to the next claim.

On the third new claim for the period from August 1, 2024, surplus earnings must be considered under sub-para.(c). The adjusted surplus of £4,069.28 from the previous month still exceeds the relevant threshold of £3,215.36, so that the excess of £853.92 is to be taken into account as surplus earnings. The amount after the 55% taper (£469.66) exceeds the maximum amount of universal credit, so there is no entitlement. But £853.92 becomes the adjusted surplus to be carried forward to the next claim.

On the fourth new claim for the period from September 1, 2024, surplus earnings must be considered under sub-para.(d). The adjusted surplus of £853.92 from the previous month does not exceed the relevant threshold of £3,215.36, so that no surplus earnings can be taken into account and the claimant becomes entitled to universal credit of the maximum amount (ignoring for the moment any possible issues under the minimum income floor (reg.62)).

If the fee had been £9,000 the claimant would have become entitled to the maximum amount on the third new claim (calculations as above but reducing the original surplus by £1,500).

If the fee had been £10,000, the claimant would have become entitled to universal credit, but at less than the maximum amount, on the third new claim, because the excess of the adjusted surplus from the second claim (£3,569.28) over the relevant threshold would have been £353.92, 55% of which is £194.66, less than the maximum amount of £393.45. So, the award would have been £198.75 for the assessment period beginning on August 1, 2024. There would then be no surplus earnings to carry forward to a new claim, but no new claim would be possible as the claimant already had an award. Common sense and fairness dictate that in such circumstances the claimant should not be treated as having earned income of £353.92 (before the taper) for the assessment period beginning on September 1, 2024 and subsequent assessment periods, but as discussed in the notes to para.(2), the plain words of subs.(2) seem to require that result.

Remember always that surplus earnings cannot be applied on any *claim* more than six months after the termination of the old award (para.(1)(a)).

Paragraph (4)

2.203 Since the effect of a significant increase in the amount of earned income can under reg.54A affect claims up to six months in the future, claimants may well move in to and out of partnerships with others in that period. Paragraph (4) deals with those circumstances.

Sub-paragraph (a) covers new claims following the termination that are the first joint claim by a couple, both of whom have surplus earnings from an old award or claim when they were either single or members of a different couple that would have been taken into account if they had each claimed as a single person. In those circumstances the surplus earnings that would have counted if they had claimed as single persons are aggregated. That is straightforward if the previous awards or claims were as single persons. If they were as joint claimants, then that seems to bring in the rule in sub-para.(b) about apportionment.

Sub-paragraph (b) covers two alternatives. One is where the relevant claim is as a single person and the claimant had an old award or made a subsequent claim as a joint claimant. The other is where one or other member of a couple (or both) making a joint claim has an old award or made a subsequent claim as a member of a different couple. In both those cases the surplus, original or adjusted, is to be apportioned in the manner determined by the Secretary of State. There is thus a completely open-ended discretion, that of course must be exercised by reference to all the relevant circumstances and the aims of the legislation, as to the share of the surplus to be attributed to the claimant in question, a discretion that on any appeal is to be exercised by the tribunal on its own judgment of the circumstances. However, the guidance in para.H3313 of the ADM is that the proportion between the joint claimants is to be 50% unless there are any exceptional circumstances. Such guidance is inconsistent with the terms of para.(4)(b), under which to adopt any starting point (in effect a default position) that could be differed from only in exceptional circumstances would be placing an unlawful fetter on the discretion given.

The letter of January 19, 2018 from the chairman of the SSAC to the Secretary of State contained the following under the heading "Equality impact":

> "The Committee noted that an equality impact had shown that there were no adverse effects on anyone with a protected characteristic. However it is clear that having, by default, a simple 50/50 apportionment of surplus earnings in the event that a couple separate would adversely affect any non-working partner, or the partner earning a lower amount relative to the current situation of allocating the surplus in proportion to the earnings of each individual of a couple. Some of the non-working partners, or partners on lower wages, are likely to have a protected characteristic (for example gender or those with a mental health condition), therefore we were surprised by the Department's assertion. Although, as was made clear to us, the legislation would give discretion for a different apportionment to be applied, the default position would be 50/50 and it would fall to individual claimants to make a request for it to be changed. Some individuals adversely affected might lack the understanding to request a revision of that decision; others may be put under some pressure from their former partner to accept the Department's decision."

The Secretary of State's response was as follows:

> "The Department has changed the apportionment rules to provide greater clarity to claimants in understanding how a surplus is recovered. The apportionment rules would only come into force in the event a couple separating at the same time a surplus is outstanding also re-claimed within 6 months of the original surplus being created.
>
> It is reasonable that a couple and their household would equally benefit from household income such as a one off bonus. As such, the surplus should be equally apportioned unless there are grounds that this is unreasonable.
>
> Additionally, the regulations allow for a decision maker acting on behalf of the Secretary of State to consider the reasonableness of an individual's circumstances when looking at a decision on apportionment, allowing discretion to ensure claimants are adequately protected.
>
> [Reference to the recent domestic violence exception to remove any financial disincentive from leaving an abusive relationship]."

Apart from it being laughable to suggest that greater clarity had been provided for claimants, either that response demonstrates a complete misunderstanding of the effect of para.(4)(b) or a change was made in its terms before SI 2018/65 was made. As it is, the guidance in the ADM appears to reflect the view set out in that response rather than the requirements of the legislation.

2.204 *Paragraph (5)*

This exclusion of the effect of reg.54A for recent victims of domestic violence can operate if the claimant has that status either at the time the old award terminated or at the time of the new claim being considered. Paragraph (5) refers on to reg.98, which contains the very wide definition of "domestic violence", what counts as recent and some conditions about having reported the domestic violence and notified the Secretary of State. Section 24(6)(b) of the WRA 2012 says when a person is to be regarded as a "victim" of domestic violence.

Employed earnings

2.205 **55.**—(1) This regulation applies for the purposes of calculating earned income from employment under a contract of service or in an office, including elective office ("employed earnings").

(2) Employed earnings comprise any amounts that are general earnings, as defined in section 7(3) of ITEPA, but excluding—

(a) amounts that are treated as earnings under Chapters 2 to 11 of Part 3 of ITEPA (the benefits code); and

(b) amounts that are exempt from income tax under Part 4 of ITEPA.

(3) In the calculation of employed earnings the following are to be disregarded—

(a) expenses that are allowed to be deducted under Chapter 2 of Part 5 of ITEPA; and

(b) expenses arising from participation as a service user (see regulation 53(2)).

(4) The following benefits are to be treated as employed earnings—

(a) statutory sick pay;

(b) statutory maternity pay;

(c) [3 . . .] statutory paternity pay;

(d) [3 . . .]

(e) statutory adoption pay [2; [4...]]

[2(f) statutory shared parental pay;] [4and

(g) statutory parental bereavement pay.]

[1 (4A) A repayment of income tax or national insurance contributions received by a person from HMRC in respect of a tax year in which the person was in paid work is to be treated as employed earnings unless it is taken into account as self-employed earnings under regulation 57(4).]

(5) In calculating the amount of a person's employed earnings in respect of an assessment period, there are to be deducted from the amount of general earnings or benefits specified in paragraphs (2) to (4)—

(a) any relievable pension contributions made by the person in that period;

(b) any amounts paid by the person in that period in respect of the employment by way of income tax or primary Class 1 contributions under section 6(1) of the Contributions and Benefits Act; and

(c) any sums withheld as donations to an approved scheme under Part 12 of ITEPA (payroll giving) by a person required to make deductions or repayments of income tax under the PAYE Regulations.

AMENDMENTS

1. Universal Credit and Miscellaneous Amendments (No.2) Regulations 2014 (SI 2014/2888) reg.4(2) (November 26, 2014, or in the case of existing awards, the first assessment period beginning on or after November 26, 2014).

2. Shared Parental Leave and Statutory Shared Parental Pay (Consequential Amendments to Subordinate Legislation) Order 2014 (SI 2014/3255) art.28(4)(c) and (d) (December 31, 2014).

3. Shared Parental Leave and Statutory Shared Parental Pay (Consequential Amendments to Subordinate Legislation) Order 2014 (SI 2014/3255) art.28(4)(a) and (b) (April 5, 2015). The amendments are subject to the transitional provision in art.35 (see Pt IV of this book).

4. Parental Bereavement Leave and Pay (Consequential Amendments to Subordinate Legislation) Regulations 2020 (SI 2020/354) reg.28 (April 6, 2020).

DEFINITIONS

"Contributions and Benefits Act"—see reg.2.
"earned income"—see reg.52.
"ITEPA"—see reg.2.
"relievable pension contributions" —see reg.53(1).
"PAYE Regulations" —*ibid.*
"statutory adoption pay"—see reg.2.
"statutory maternity pay"—*ibid.*
"statutory parental bereavement pay"—*ibid.*
"statutory shared parental pay"—*ibid.*
"statutory sick pay"—*ibid.*

GENERAL NOTE

This regulation applies to employed earnings (i.e., under a contract of service or as an office holder) (para.(1)). By reason of the overarching definition of "earned income" in reg.52, payments must be derived from such employment. See regs 57-59 for the calculation of self-employed earnings. 2.206

Unlike income support, old style JSA, old style ESA and housing benefit, what counts as employed earnings for the purposes of universal credit is in general defined in terms of the income tax rules (paras (2) and (3)(a)). However, not all amounts that HMRC treats as earnings count for universal credit purposes (see para.(2)(a)). Under para.(2))(a) benefits in kind, for example living accommodation provided by reason of the employment, are excluded. See paras (4) and (4A) for categories of payments deemed to be employed earnings.

The meaning of "general earnings" in s.7(3) of ITEPA (the Income Tax (Earnings and Pensions) Act 2003), which the beginning of para.(2) makes the starting point for calculating earned income, is earnings within Chap.1 of Part 3 of ITEPA or any amount treated as earnings, excluding exempt earnings. Section 62 of ITEPA, which constitutes Chap.1 of Part 3, provides in subs.(2) that earnings means:

"(a) any salary, wages or fee;
(b) any gratuity or other profit or incidental benefit of any kind obtained by the employee if it is money or money's worth; and
(c) anything else that constitutes an emolument of the employment."

That meaning is thus very broad, and there are many categories deemed to be general earnings (see s.7(5) of ITEPA), but the meaning is immediately narrowed for universal credit purposes by para.(2)(a) of reg.55 in the exclusion of amounts treated as earnings in Chaps 2–11 of Pt 3 of ITEPA. Those items covers matters like expenses, vouchers, provision of living accommodation, cars, vans and related benefits and loans. The exclusion by para.(2)(b) of amounts exempt from income tax under Pt 4 of ITEPA would have followed in any event under the terms of ss.7(3) and 8 of ITEPA. The exemptions in Pt 4 of ITEPA, as specifically referred to in s.8, include mileage or transport allowances, travel and subsistence allowances, benefits for training and learning, recreational benefits and a variety of other amounts, including in particular statutory redundancy payments (s.309). Section 8 also refers to exemptions elsewhere in ITEPA. There is some discussion of this in para.36 of *RMcE v DfC (UC)* [2021] NICom 59. The Northern Ireland Commissioner, though not having had submissions on the issue, must have been right in his tentative conclusion that the reference in reg.55(2) to general earnings as defined in s.7(3) of ITEPA must be read in the light of s.8 and the meaning given there to "exempt income". That follows from the specific exclusion in s.7(3) of exempt income. Thus, although reg.55(2)(b) refers only to amounts exempt from income tax under Pt 4 of ITEPA, the incorporation of the s.7(3) definition brings in other ITEPA exemptions. See the further discussion in the separate section below on payments on cessation of employment, including the effect of the amendments to ITEPA with effect from April 6, 2018 by virtue of the Finance (No.2) Act 2017.

As a matter of general principle, any payment, whether of an income or capital nature, can be a profit or emolument within s.62(2) of ITEPA, providing that it is a reward for past services or an incentive to enter into employment and provide future services. See *AH v HMRC (TC)* [2019] UKUT 5 (AAC), where Judge Wikeley discusses the relevant income tax case law, and *Minter v Kingston upon Hull CC* and *Potter v Secretary of State for Work and Pensions* [2011] EWCA Civ 1155; [2012] AACR 21, where Thomas LJ in para.29 emphasised the width of the phrase "any remuneration or profit derived from employment" in reg.35(1) of the Income Support Regulations, such that the essential issue was whether any payment was made in consideration of the employee's services, so as to be derived from the employment, whether it was on general principle to be regarded as capital or income. It would appear that if it is necessary for that effect of reg.55 to be authorised by para.4(3)(b) of Sch.1 to the WRA 2012 (regulations may specify circumstances in which income is to be treated as capital or capital is to be treated as income) the words are clear enough to come within that power.

DfC v RM (UC) [2021] NICom 36 confirms that basic principle in the context of a gross sum of £5,228.42 received in December 2018 by the claimant in settlement, after conciliation, of Industrial Tribunal proceedings against his employer for non-payment of wages or of holiday pay entitlement. The employer described the payment as a gesture of goodwill rather than in fulfilment of a contractual liability, but the payment was apparently calculated to cover 1.5 hours of work a week over a period from 2005 to 2012. The DfC treated the net payment, after deduction of income tax and national insurance, and including regular monthly salary, of £5,221.45 notified by HMRC in the particular assessment period through the real time information system (see reg.61) as employed earnings in respect of that period. The appeal tribunal allowed the claimant's appeal, finding under the equivalent of reg.61(3)(b)(ii) as in force at the time that the information received from HMRC did not reflect the definition of employed earnings in reg.55, so that the amount attributable to the settlement was not to be taken into account in the assessment period in question. On further appeal by the DfC, the Northern Ireland Commissioner rightly rejected its argument that the tribunal must have regarded the payment as capital, contrary to the principles set out in *Minter* and *Potter* (for full details of those decisions see the 2021/22 edition ofVol.V of this series at 2.204–06). Those decisions were not in point because the essential question under reg.55 is how the payment would be treated under s.62(2) of ITEPA, not a general categorisation as income or capital. The Commissioner then declined to hold the tribunal in error of law for failing to deal with the question of what the outcome would be under s.62(2). See the further discussion in the separate section below on compensation payments.

It is a necessary consequence of the centrality of determining what the outcome would be under s.62(2) of ITEPA that in any appeals on these issues the Secretary of State must provide explanatory material, legislation and case law relating to income tax if tribunals are to be able to perform their role properly (stressed in para.34 of *RMcE v DfC (UC)* [2021] NICom 59).

Note the decision of the Court of Appeal in *Commissioners for HMRC v Murphy* [2022] EWCA Civ 1112; [2023] 1 W.L.R. 51 on the meaning of "profit" in s.62(2)(b) of ITEPA. In a complex settlement of police officers' group claims for compensation for underpayment of overtime and certain allowances, the principal sum agreed to be paid by the Metropolitan Police Service ("the Met") covered only some of the claimants' costs. It did not include the amount of their solicitors' and counsel's "success fee" under a "damages-based agreement" or the amount of the premium paid on a policy insuring them against the risk of having to pay the Met's costs. But those amounts were deducted from the principal sum to be paid and only the balance was paid to the individual claimants. Mr Murphy had succeeded before the Upper Tribunal (Tax and Chancery Chamber) ("UTTCC") in an argument that his proportionate share of those amounts should be deducted from his share of the whole principal sum in calculating the "profit" within s.62(2)(b), as they were necessarily incurred in order to obtain the sum derived from his employment. The Court of Appeal held that to have been an error of law. In the context of the statutory scheme, all earnings from employment are taxable, subject only to the deductions allowed under the legislation. In s.62(2)(b) "profit" is used in the sense of "a material benefit derived from a property, position etc; income, revenue", one of the definitions in the *Oxford English Dictionary*. The expenditure not being allowable deductions nor having been incurred in the performance of Mr Murphy's duties, the sole question was whether the profit was "from" employment as a reward for services, as it clearly was, since the principal settlement sum related to amounts alleged to be due under the claimants' contracts of employment. It did not matter that they were left to meet some of their own costs.

Commissioners for HMRC v E.ON UK plc [2023] EWCA Civ 1383 also concerned the "from" test in s.9(2) of ITEPA, for universal credit purposes applied by reg.52(a). E.ON made a one-off payment, called a facilitation payment, to employees who were members of its final salary pension scheme, in which prospective changes adverse to members were being made. The UTTCC ([2022] UKUT 196 (TCC)) overturned the FtT's decision upholding HMRC's view that the payment was taxable as earnings from employment. The Court of Appeal restored the FtT's decision. The judgment of Nugee LJ provides a remarkably accessible exposition of the general principles to be applied. He concludes that the UTTCC created a false dichotomy between the payment being in return for employees' consent to adverse prospective changes in the final salary pension scheme and it being an inducement to provide future services on changed terms and that it was such an inducement (so taxable), the relevant change being that to the pension scheme. His view was that the previous case law, analysed in detail by Falk LJ, did not stand in the way of that straightforward conclusion.

It is difficult to say how the principle adopted in *R(TC) 2/03* (a case on the meaning of "earnings" in reg.19(1) of the Family Credit Regulations) might apply to the identification of the "amount" that is to be taken into account under reg.55, and regarded as "received" under reg.54. In *R(TC) 2/03* the claimant's partner's employer made deductions from his current salary in order to recover an earlier overpayment of salary. His payslips showed the "gross for tax" figure as £76 less than his usual salary. The Commissioner held that his gross salary for the relevant months was the reduced figure, most probably on the basis that there had been a consensual variation of the contract of employment, so that the lower figure was the remuneration or profit derived from employment in the relevant months. In *MH v SSWP and Rotherham MBC (HB)* [2017] UKUT 401 (AAC) Judge Wikeley adopted and applied the analysis in *R(TC) 2/03*. The claimant received a redundancy payment of nearly £15,000 in March 2016, which was used to pay off debts and make home improvements. In May 2016 he was offered his old job back on condition that he repaid the employer the amount of the redundancy payment by monthly deductions from salary within the 2016/17 tax year. The claimant accepted those terms. On his monthly payslips his basic salary was stated as £2,719.04 before overtime with deductions including income tax and national insurance and the sum of £1,222.22 described as "BS loan". On his claim for housing benefit the local authority (and the First-tier Tribunal) decided that under the equivalent of regs 35 and 36 of the Income Support Regulations the gross earnings had to be taken into account and there was nothing to allow the deduction or disregard of the £1,222.22 repayment. The judge held that the proper analysis was that the claimant's contract of employment had been varied by agreement so that he was only entitled to receive a salary reduced by the amount of the repayment and that that amount was his gross earnings. In fact, the case appears stronger than that of *R(TC) 2/03* because the initial terms on which the claimant was re-engaged incorporated the repayments of the redundancy payment.

It is not clear in *MH* what amount was regarded as subject to PAYE income tax. If it was the reduced figure, as in *R(TC) 2/03*, then that would appear to be the amount to taken into account under reg.55 and regarded as received under reg.54. The receipt would presumably also be reflected in the real time information provided by HMRC to the DWP under reg.61. If the employer had regarded the higher figure as subject to PAYE income tax then it seems arguable that the amount to be treated as remuneration or profit derived from the employment (reg.52) and received under reg.54 is the lower figure. If the real time information reflected the higher figure, then it would have to be argued that reg.61(2) did not apply because the information was incorrect or failed to reflect the definition in reg.55 in some material respect (reg.61(3)(b)(ii)).

Under para.(3)(a) expenses that are deductible under ITEPA, Pt 5, Ch.2, are disregarded in calculating employed earnings—this includes, for example, expenses that are "wholly, exclusively and necessarily" incurred in the course of the claimant's employment (see s.336(1) of ITEPA). In addition, expenses from participation as a service user (defined in reg.53(2)) are ignored (para.(3)(b)), although payments for attendance at meetings, etc., will count as earnings.

Note that employed earnings are to be treated as also including statutory sick pay, statutory maternity pay, statutory paternity pay, statutory adoption pay and statutory shared parental pay (para.(4)).

Paragraph (4A), inserted with effect from November 26, 2014, treats a repayment of income tax or NI contributions received from HMRC in respect of a tax year in which the person was in paid work as employed earnings, unless it is taken into account as self-employed earnings. According to DWP (see ADM H3022), this can include repayments of income tax that relate to other sources, such as unearned income, as long as the claimant was in paid work in the tax year to which the repayment relates. ADM H3022 gives as an example a case in which a claimant receives a cheque for £200 from HMRC, which relates to an overpayment of £600 income tax in the tax year 2011/12 in which the claimant was in paid work and an underpayment of £400 in the following year. The amount that counts as employed earnings is £200, which is the repayment that the claimant received.

The proper, restricted, operation of para.(4A) has been very helpfully elucidated in *SK and DK v SSWP (UC)* [2023] UKUT 21 (AAC), reported as [2023] AACR 5. There the claimant, who was on unpaid sick leave from his employer, received a bonus of £20,000 on May 20, 2020, within the assessment period running from April 29, 2020 to May 28, 2020 (AP 1). Under the PAYE system the employer deducted the amount of £6,893.60 for income tax before making the payment, which was reported to HMRC through the Real Time Information scheme. That was on the basis of a code issued by HMRC that was appropriate to a person regularly earning £20,000 a month over the whole tax year. Since that was not the case, on the claimant not receiving any further remuneration from his employer in subsequent months, under the PAYE system he received from the employer a "refund" of overpaid income tax of £2.144.60 in the assessment period running from May 29, 2020 to June 28, 2020 (AP 2) and further refunds in subsequent months. There was no dispute that the receipt of the net amount of the bonus in AP 1 resulted in a nil entitlement to universal credit, but the claimant appealed against the nil entitlement in AP 2 resulting from the taking into account of the £2,144.60. Among his arguments was that a repayment of income tax could only be treated as employed earnings under the conditions of para.(4A), which were not met as he was not in paid work in the tax year 2020/21. The First-tier Tribunal disallowed the appeal. On the further appeal Judge Ovey rejected the tribunal's reasoning but substituted her own decision to the same effect.

The judge's central point was that para.(4A) is restricted to cases where the repayment of income tax or national insurance contributions is received from HMRC, whereas in *SK*, if there could be said to have been a repayment on May 20, 2020 (see paras 47 and 48, set out in the notes to reg.61(2)), it was received from the employer, not HMRC. She shows convincingly from an analysis of the PAYE system that HMRC does not itself make any in-year repayments of overpaid income tax. Instead, they are either sorted out by in-year amendments of the PAYE code governing the amounts to be deducted by the employer or by a direct payment from HMRC after the end of the tax year in question. Similarly, repayments of other sorts of income tax are not made in-year, but by HMRC after the end of the tax year. Paragraph (4A) was concerned with such repayments made after the end of the tax year, as was confirmed by the terms of the Explanatory Memorandum to SI 2014/2888 and of the DWP's description of the amendment to the Social Security Advisory Committee (Annex B to the minutes of the meeting of September 3, 2014).

The judge went on to make suggestions, not necessary to the decision, about how para.(4A) might have been interpreted if it had been relevant, for example about how to work out the tax year in respect of which a bonus was paid, when the entitlement to a bonus arose and whether the claimant was "in paid work" in a tax year while on sick leave. While the claimant was in employment it did not matter that, by agreement with the employer, he did not do any work in that tax year.

In calculating a person's employed earnings in an assessment period the following are deducted: any income tax and Class 1 contributions paid in that assessment period, together with any contributions to a registered pension scheme and any charity payments under a payroll giving scheme made in that period (para.(5)). Since the definition of "relievable pension contributions" in reg.53(1) is by reference only to s.188 of the Finance Act 2004 it is arguable that the annual and lifetime limits imposed in other sections of that Act are not incorporated for universal credit purposes.

Information on a person's employed earnings and deductions made will normally be taken from what is recorded on PAYE records. See further the note to reg.61.

Payments on cessation of employment

There are no special provisions for the treatment of final earnings under universal credit. A claimant's final earnings will be taken into account in the assessment period in which they are paid under the general rule in reg.54(1), subject to the operation of reg.61 on real time information. See in particular *PT v SSWP (UC)* [2015] UKUT 696 (AAC), discussed in the notes to reg.54 and *SSWO v RW (rule 17) (UC)* [2017] UKUT 347 (AAC), discussed in the notes to reg.61. In *Secretary of State for Work and Pensions v Johnson* [2020] EWCA Civ 778; [2020] P.T.S.R. 1872 the Court of Appeal rejected the approach of the Divisional Court below to the interpretation of regs 54 and 61 and its reliance on the phrase "in respect of" in those provisions to introduce other factors than date of receipt into the identification of the assessment period to which a payment is attributed. In para.41 Rose LJ says that the phrase usually means nothing different from "for" or "in". That seems to have put paid to any argument that, say, final payments of earnings should be attributed to the relevant period of employment rather than to the assessment period in which the payment is received. 2.207

The same would apply to items like week-in-hand payments, bonuses due for past work or holiday pay accrued under contractual or statutory entitlements for past periods.

Some payments made on termination of employment and not linked to past periods are "general earnings" under ss.7(3)(a) and 62 of ITEPA, in particular payments that are made by virtue of a contractual obligation (though see the post-April 2018 provisions discussed below), but some fall outside that meaning and so are liable to income tax only under the regime in ss.401–16 and do not come within reg.55. There is general guidance in HMRC's *Employment Income Manual* from para.12850 onwards. The dividing line in principle between payments that are general earnings and payments that fall within s.401 of ITEPA as made in connection with the termination of employment, and so not within s.62, is this. If the payment (including a part of a payment) is in satisfaction of a right to remuneration under the contract of employment it falls within s.62. If it is compensation for a breach of the contract of employment it falls within s.401. So, employment tribunal awards for unfair dismissal, damages for breach of contract and redundancy payments (statutory and contractual) will not count as they are only taxable under s.401 of ITEPA and so do not come within s.7(3) (see *Employment Income Manual*, paras 12960, 12970, 12978, 13005 and 13750). For other employment tribunal awards which do count as earnings see para.02550 of the *Employment Income Manual* and the section below on payments of compensation.

There have been amendments to s.7 of ITEPA and new ss.402A-402E added by the Finance (No.2) Act 2017, that apply to certain payments made on or after April 6, 2018 on the termination of employment that would otherwise fall within s.401. To be a "relevant" termination award the payment must not be a redundancy payment (statutory or contractual). Then so much of the payment as counts as post-employment notice pay (PENP) is taxable as general earnings. That is secured by the addition of new para.(ca) to s.7(5), which lists amounts that are to be treated as earnings under s.7(3)(b). PENP is in essence the amount of basic pay to which the employee would have been entitled after the date of termination of the contract if full statutory notice had been given, less the amount of any contractual payment in lieu of notice that was made. That appears to mean that if an employer makes some sort of global payment on termination, without it being broken down into particular elements, the PENP is to be taken into account as employed earnings for universal credit purposes.

The Northern Ireland Commissioner was therefore right to say in para.36 of *RMcE v DfC (UC)* [2021] NICom 59 that a payment that constituted PENP would count as employed earnings under the equivalent of reg.55. However, that was not relevant to the circumstances of the case, where the payment in issue was received before the amendments to ITEPA creating the new regime came into force.

The policy and legislative background to the amendments has been comprehensively described in House of Commons Library Briefing Paper No.8084 (May 8, 2018), *Taxation of termination payments*. That paper reproduces as an appendix a helpful statement of the legal background produced in 2013 by the amusingly named Office of Tax Simplification. There was on the existing law a distinction between a payment in lieu of notice on termination of the contract on less than the contractual notice that was provided for in the contract of employment (within s.62) and a payment made where there was no such provision or where the employer chose to terminate the contract without making a contractual payment in lieu of notice but made a payment for breach of the contract of employment instead (not within s.62). That distinction was considered not only to be very difficult to draw in particular cases but also to be unjustified.

Payments of compensation

2.208 This section is concerned with payments that are not clearly linked to the termination of employment, but contain an element that is linked to making up some shortfall in what was paid to the employee in the past. Such awards or payments in settlement may be made during the course of the employment or after it has ended. Because they come as a lump sum, their classification as capital or income has caused difficulties in other contexts, as mentioned above. In the present context, of course, the proper question is rather whether the award contains any amount that is "general earnings" as defined in s.7(3) of ITEPA.

As mentioned above, Commissioner Stockman in Northern Ireland has most recently confirmed that basic principle in *DfC v RM (UC)* [2021] NICom 36. The claimant received a gross sum of £5,228.42 received in December 2018 in settlement, after conciliation, of Industrial Tribunal proceedings against his employer for non-payment of wages or of holiday pay entitlement. The employer described the payment as a gesture of goodwill rather than in fulfilment of a contractual liability, but the payment was apparently calculated to cover 1.5 hours of work a week over a period from 2005 to 2012. The DfC treated the net payment, after deduction of income tax and national insurance, and including regular monthly salary, of £5,221.45 notified by HMRC in the particular assessment period through the real time information system (see reg.61) as employed earnings in respect of that period. The appeal tribunal allowed the claimant's appeal, finding under the equivalent of reg.61(3)(b)(ii) as in force at the time that the information received from HMRC did not reflect the definition of employed earnings in reg.55, so that the amount attributable to the settlement was not to be taken into account in the assessment period in question. The Commissioner rejected the DfC's misguided challenge on the ground that the tribunal must, wrongly, have considered that the payment was capital as asking the wrong question. However, he then considered that the inquisitorial duty of the tribunal, and the Commissioner, could not extend to the exploration of income tax law, rather than the familiar social security issues, in the absence of structured submissions (and apparently his view that there was at least a good argument that the payment was made in consideration of the abandonment of the proceedings, rather than in return for the claimant's service in the period from 2005 to 2012). The onus was thus firmly on the DfC to establish its case to the tribunal and the Commissioner. It had not done so, because it had not referred the tribunal or the Commissioner to any case law relevant to the taxation of compensation settlement payments.

It is submitted that that decision is based on too limited a view of the scope of the proper inquisitorial approach of appeal tribunals, and in particular of the Commissioner and, in Great Britain, the Upper Tribunal. It is not as if direct reference to ITEPA was a new feature for universal credit. That is the technique used for working tax credit (see the definition of "earnings" in reg.2 of the Tax Credits (Definition and Calculation of Income) Regulations 2002 in Vol.IV of this series, which also sets out most of the relevant provisions of ITEPA). And there is the instructive decision in *AH v HMRC (TC)* [2019] UKUT 5 (AAC) on that definition, mentioned briefly above (and dealt with in detail in Vol.IV at 2.222), where Judge Wikeley discussed and applied the income tax cases on the meaning of "emolument of employment" in s.62(2) of ITEPA. In those circumstances and when the adoption of the ITEPA test is an express part of the legislation to be applied, it appears wrong for the Commissioner not to have addressed the issue, possibly after obtaining further submissions. As it is, the decision in *RM* gives no guidance as to how future cases should be decided in substance (although of course it would as a Northern Ireland decision technically have had only persuasive authority in Great Britain).

In *AH*, the claimant had reached a draft settlement agreement on his claim against his NHS employer that it had made unlawful deductions from salary, in the sum of £16,000. However, because the parties wanted to avoid HM Treasury restrictions on compensation payments of more than £10,000, payment was made in two lump sums of £3,000 in August 2016 and March 2017 and by way of giving the claimant a 20-month fixed term contract of employment at £500 per month. In the event, before end of the fixed term the employer offered to pay the claimant the balance of his salary entitlement in a lump sum and the contract was terminated by mutual consent. HMRC took all the payments into account as employment income on the WTC claim. In the Upper Tribunal Judge Wikeley agreed. His analysis of the income tax authorities included that older cases decided when the formula of "emolument from employment" was in effect were still instructive although s.62(2) refers to "emolument of the employment". In addition, *Kuehne and Nagel Drinks Logistics Ltd v Commissioner for HMRC* [2012] EWCA Civ 34; [2012] S.T.C. 840 showed that where a payment was made for a reason other than being or becoming an employee (there to compensate for loss of future pension rights on the transfer of a business) and for a reason that was so related (there to encourage the heading off of strike action), it was enough to make the payment "from the employment" that the latter reason was sufficiently substantial, despite the existence of some other substantial reason. The claimant could only escape the conclusion that the payments made to reimburse him for non-payment of salary were emoluments of his employment if the arrangements, especially the fixed-term contract, were a sham, which the judge rejected.

The current HMRC guidance in its *Employment Income Manual* (EIM 12965, updated in respect of that paragraph on January 27, 2020) applies the principle that compensation should derive its character from the nature of the payment it replaces. That principle is of course familiar in the related, but different, social security context of income or capital (see *Minter* and *Potter above*). The guidance relies specifically on the decision in *Pettigrew v Commissioners for HMRC* [2018] UKFTT 240 (TC). Although as a First-tier decision it can have no precedential authority, it is based on an exhaustive survey of the case-law and a detailed analysis of the application of the principles to the facts.

Mr Pettigrew was a part-time fee-paid chairman of Industrial Tribunals and then an Employment Judge from 1996 to 2016. He lodged a claim against the Ministry of Justice (MoJ) for underpayments of fees for training, sitting and other days of service on the basis of discrimination by comparison with salaried office-holders. The MoJ offered him £55,045.42, including interest, in full and final settlement of his claim, which he accepted. When the payment was made, some £22,000 was deducted under PAYE. When submitting his 2014–15 self-assessment tax return Mr Pettigrew challenged that deduction on the basis that the payment was not arrears of wages or salary, but compensation for breach of the Part-Time Workers Regulations. That challenge was rejected by HMRC and by the FtT on appeal. After a comprehensive review of the authorities (which incidentally confirmed the relevance of the pre-ITEPA authority, as had been accepted by Lord Hodge in *RFC 2012 Plc (in liquidation) (formerly the Rangers Football Club Plc) v Advocate General for Scotland* [2017] UKSC 45; [2017] 1 W.L.R. 2767 at para.35), the judge distilled five principles (paras 75–79). Three in particular were (1) that a payment of compensation for loss of rights directly connected with an employment will generally be an emolument of that employment (para.76); (2) that the character for tax purposes of a payment of compensation for failure to make a payment due should be the same as that of the payment if it had been paid (para.78); and (3) that where there is more than one reason for the payment then the employment must be a sufficiently substantial reason for the payment to characterise it as an emolument of the employment (para.79). Applying those principles to the facts found, the lump sum payment, apart from the interest element, plainly constituted an emolument of Mr Pettigrew's employment, particularly as a result of principle (2). Although, as he had submitted, the prompt for the making of the payment was the settlement of the litigation of which he was part, the methodology and quantification of the payment was to remedy the underpayments under the contract of employment, so that the test in *Kuehne and Nagel* (principle (3)) was met.

Applying those principles to the facts of *RM* would seem to lead equally inevitably to the conclusion that the settlement payment constituted general earnings within s.62(2) of ITEPA and so employed earnings within reg.55.

Dividends

The overriding principle set out in reg.52(a) that earned income from employment under a contract of service or in an office must be remuneration or profit derived from that employment or office suggests that payments of dividends on shares cannot be earned income. They are derived from the ownership of the shares. However, sometimes payments that are described as dividends are not properly to be treated as such. The formal company law and accounting processes for declaring a dividend may not have been gone through or the whole transaction may be a sham. There may be other situations in which, although the payments are properly to be regarded as dividends they are derived from employment or an office, so are taxable as general earnings. See the discussion in *H v SSWP and C (CSM)* [2015] UKUT 621 (AAC), citing extensively from the decision in *CCS 2533/2014* (not currently on the AAC website), which itself relied on the decision (described as instructive) of the Court of Appeal in the tax case of *HMRC v PA Holdings Ltd* [2011] EWCA Civ 1414. The overall approach adopted by the Court of Appeal is to look at the substance, or reality, not the form. There, contractual bonuses were structured so as to be paid out as dividends from a company separate from the employing personal service company and were held to be taxable as general earnings. Such highly artificial arrangements are perhaps unlikely to be encountered in universal credit. In more routine cases, there may be little reason to dispute a division between the taking of earnings as an employee or director and taking of dividends as a shareholder. 2.209

Dividends are chargeable to income tax under Part 4 of the Income Tax (Trading and Other Income) Act 2005 (ITTOIA), whether they would otherwise be regarded as capital or income, so cannot as such fall within the definition of general earnings in s.7(3) of ITEPA. Nor, if income, can they be unearned income, since they do not feature in the list in reg.66(1). They do not fall within reg.66(1)(m) because they are not taxable under Pt 5 of ITTOIA. However, if in substance the payments constitute remuneration derived from employment or an office they do fall within that definition. As a matter of principle, a decision-maker or tribunal would not be bound by HMRC having accepted payments as in substance of dividends taxable only under ITTOIA, but would have to come to an independent judgment on all the evidence available about whether payments were general earnings. However, how HMRC treated the payments would of course be a relevant factor to be considered., with the weight to be given to that treatment depending on how far it was based on a mere acceptance of statements on a tax return or on any further consideration of the particular circumstances.

See reg.77 for deemed capital and self-employed earnings where the claimant is like a sole trader or partner in relation to a company carrying on a trade. Dividends cannot be treated as part of self-employed earnings under that provision, because the calculation is in terms of the *company's* income, i.e. receipts less allowable expenses as under reg.57. If the dividend payment is properly to be regarded as a payment of capital, as would often be the case, it would immediately form part of the claimant's capital. But the present context is one in which an argument that it is income, for instance where the person has been taking regular periodic payments as interim dividends, can be made, in which case there would not be a metamorphosis into capital until, presumably, after the end of the assessment period in which it is received. However, note that reg.72(3) assumes that dividends are a form of income from capital in providing that where capital is treated as yielding (notional) income, i.e. the amount is over £6,000 but below £16,000, the actual income is to be treated as part of the claimant's capital from the day it is due to be paid.

Employee involved in trade dispute

56. A person who has had employed earnings and has withdrawn their labour in furtherance of a trade dispute is, unless their contract of service has been terminated, to be assumed to have employed earnings at the same level as they would have had were it not for the trade dispute. 2.210

Definitions

"employed earnings"—see regs 53(1) and 55.
"trade dispute"—see reg.2.

General Note

2.211 There is no general disentitlement of claimants involved in a trade dispute for the purposes of universal credit, as there is for new style JSA (see s.14 of the new style Jobseekers Act 1995 in Vol.I of this series) and as there was for old style JSA, for both contributory and income-based JSA (see ss.14 and 15 of the old style Jobseekers Act 1995 in Vol.V of this series, 2021/22 edition as updated in Cumulative Supplements included in this volume and in mid-year Supplements). Instead, reg.56 operates by deeming affected claimants to have employed earnings of the amount they would have had but for the trade dispute and applying that rule only in considerably more restricted circumstances than for the purposes of JSA, in essence in circumstances covered by s.14(2), but not those covered by s.14(1) of both forms of the Jobseekers Act 1995. Thus a person who becomes entitled to both universal credit and new style JSA on being without employment when affected by a stoppage of work due to a trade dispute at their place of work, without having withdrawn their labour, could be disentitled to new style JSA under s.14(1) of the new style Jobseekers Act 1995, yet not be affected by reg.56. The JSA could then no longer be taken into account as unearned income in the calculation of the universal credit.

The universal credit rule applies in roughly the same circumstances as s.14(2) of both forms of the Jobseekers Act 1995, but since the equivalent of that provision only entered the preceding unemployment benefit legislation in 1986 no case law authority has built up on the interpretation of its terms. There has to be some speculation about that.

To be caught by the rule a universal credit claimant must have had employed earnings, i.e. earned income derived from employment under a contract of service or in an office (reg.55(1)), thus excluding the self-employed from the scope of the rule. It is not clear how far in the past the employed earnings could have been received, but the reference to the withdrawing of labour would suggest that whatever the occupation was from which the labour had been withdrawn would have to be one from the claimant had, immediately before the withdrawal, derived employed earnings.

Then, the rule can only be applied to claimants who have withdrawn their labour. That would cover straightforward strikes or refusals to carry out some significant part of contractual duties, even if the latter led to the employer sending the employees home completely. On the other hand, refusals to work voluntary overtime or works-to-rule would not be covered. And if an employer has initiated a lock-out before the occurrence of anything that would otherwise count as a withdrawal of labour it would seem that the employees could not be regarded as a having withdrawn their labour. A withdrawal must involve a voluntary choice not to work. Much more troublesome would be cases where employees decline to cross picket lines. Being physically prevented from entering work premises or being subjected to threats of violence against self or others would no doubt negate the necessary element of voluntary choice. At the other end of the spectrum, agreeing to polite and reasoned requests not to cross a picket line would also no doubt be regarded as a withdrawal of labour. But there will be many circumstances in the middle where the question will be very difficult to answer. If there are many pickets, with shouted insults and imprecations or more, when do spirited attempts at persuasion turn into intimidation?

The rule also requires that the individual's withdrawal of labour is in furtherance of a trade dispute. Regulation 2 incorporates the definition of "trade dispute" in s.244 of the Trade Union and Labour Relations (Consolidation) Act 1992, which is set out in full in the notes to reg.113. That definition is different from that in the new style Jobseekers Act 1995. It covers only disputes between workers and their employer, not disputes between employees and employees or, for that matter, employers and employers, but the subject-matter of the dispute is widely defined. There is no requirement that the dispute has led to any stoppages of work or similar, nor that the claimant potentially caught by reg.56 has any material interest in the outcome of the dispute. Presumably a trade dispute has to be in existence before a withdrawal of labour can be in furtherance of it. In para.6 of *R(U) 21/59* the Commissioner indicated that a dispute between an employer and an employee must have reached "a certain stage of contention before it may properly be termed a [trade] dispute". He was clearly satisfied that evidence that the workforce had met to consider their response to their employer's rejection of their claims concerning their terms of employment amounted to a trade dispute and suggested that one may well have existed some time before the meeting took place. However, in the unemployment benefit and JSA context such problems have tended to be short-circuited by the question of whether there had been a stoppage of work as a result of any trade dispute. That question does not arise in the universal credit context.

"Furtherance" presumably points towards whatever subjective intention behind the withdrawal of labour can properly be attributed to the claimant, rather than whether the withdrawal is likely to have any practical influence on the outcome of the trade dispute. That would be consistent with the inherent principle that a solo withdrawal of labour can trigger the application of reg.56. It is not necessary for the claimant to have acted in concert with others, provided that the withdrawal of labour was in furtherance of a trade dispute.

Some assistance might possibly be gained from the case law about the meaning of "furtherance" in the context of the legality of industrial action (see most recently *Warrington BC v Unite the Union* [2023] EWHC 3093 (KB); [2024] I.C.R. 599). It is accepted in that context, where the actions of unions are in issue, that the union need not be acting exclusively in furtherance of a trade dispute.

Note that the rule in reg.56 cannot apply, or continue to apply, if the claimant's contract of employment (presumably that relevant to the labour that has been withdrawn) has been terminated. It does not matter, in contrast to the position under s.14 of the new style Jobseekers Act 1995, that the termination of the contract is or was a move in the trade dispute. Nor does it appear to matter who terminates the contract.

Perhaps the most problematic part of reg.56, though, is the way that its effect is described if all the conditions for its application are met. It does not, as might have been expected, provide that claimants be assumed to have the employed earnings they would have received were it not for the withdrawal of their labour. It provides that they be assumed to have the employed earnings they would have received were it not for the trade dispute. Even if the trade dispute is between the claimant's own employer and workers, it is hard to see how the dispute as such, rather than actions taken in furtherance of the dispute, could have any effect on the claimant's earnings. If the meaning is to be taken as simply assuming that usual earnings continue unless the contract of employment is terminated, there will still be difficulties in identifying what is usual. For instance, if fluctuating hours of overtime are worked or fluctuating hours worked under a zero-hours contract, what hours are assumed to have been worked?

An argument might be raised, though, that other provisions render much of the above discussion academic. Claimants who withdraw their labour, either before claiming universal credit or during an award would prima facie be subject to a higher-level sanction under s.26(2)(d) or (4)(b). That withdrawal would not only be a ceasing of paid work and a losing of pay, but would be a breach of the contract of employment, even if there was no intention of permanently severing relations. Thus, it is arguable that the ceasing/losing was by reason of misconduct or, if not, was voluntarily and for no good reason. For the purposes of new style JSA there has not needed to be any debate of the difficult question whether decision-makers and tribunals could adjudicate on such issues without reaching a judgment on the merits of the trade dispute, something that the legislation has traditionally tried to avoid. That is first because the effect of s.14(2) of the new style Jobseekers Act 1995 would be to remove entitlement, so that while it applied there would be nothing for a sanction to bite on. In addition, reg.28(1)(d) of the JSA Regulations 2013 prohibits a reduction of benefit being applied where the sanctionable failure is that a claimant voluntarily ceases work or loses pay because of a strike (a "concerted stoppage of work") arising from a trade dispute. However, for universal credit there is no automatic disentitlement if the conditions of reg.56 are met, merely the deeming of usual earnings. But reg.113(1)(c) of the UC Regulations provides protection in the same terms as reg.28(1)(d) of the JSA Regulations 2013, but without the definition of "strike". In relation to both provisions there is a question whether they refer only to the particular sanction for ceasing paid work or losing pay voluntarily and for no good reason or whether they also cover the sanction for doing so by reason of misconduct, constituted by such voluntary action. The second alternative, on a purposive view and taking into account the policy of state neutrality in trade disputes, is more attractive. If so, then reg.56 does play the central role in trade dispute cases and the problems of its interpretation will need to be addressed sooner or later.

Self-employed earnings

2.212 **57.**—(1) This regulation applies for the purpose of calculating earned income that is not employed earnings and is derived from carrying on a trade, profession or vocation ("self-employed earnings").

[[2](2) A person's self-employed earnings in respect of an assessment period are to be calculated as follows.

Step 1

Calculate the amount of the person's profit or loss in respect of each trade, profession or vocation carried on by the person by—

(a) taking the actual receipts in that assessment period; and

(b) deducting any amounts allowed as expenses under regulation 58 or 59.

Where a trade, profession or vocation is carried on in a partnership, take the amount of the profit or loss attributable to the person's share in the partnership.

Step 2

If the person has carried on more than one trade, profession or vocation in the assessment period, add together the amounts resulting from step 1 in respect of each trade, profession or vocation.

Step 3

Deduct from the amount resulting from step 1 or (if applicable) step 2 any payment made by the person to HMRC in the assessment period [[3]by way of national insurance contributions or income tax in respect of any trade, profession or vocation carried on by the person.]

If the amount resulting from steps 1 to 3 is nil or a negative amount, the amount of the person's self-employed earnings in respect of the assessment period is nil (and ignore the following steps).

Step 4

If the amount resulting from step 3 is greater than nil, deduct from that amount any relievable pension contributions made by the person in the assessment period (unless a deduction has been made in respect of those contributions in calculating the person's employed earnings).

If the amount resulting from this step is nil or a negative amount, the person's self-employed earnings in respect of the assessment period are nil (and ignore the following step).

Step 5

If the amount resulting from step 4 is greater than nil, deduct from that amount any unused losses (see regulation 57A), taking the oldest first.

If the amount resulting from this step is greater than nil, that is the amount of the person's self-employed earnings for the assessment period.

If the amount resulting from this step is nil or a negative amount, the amount of the person's self-employed earnings in respect of the assessment period is nil.]

(3) [2...]

(4) The receipts referred to in [3paragraph (2)] include receipts in kind and any refund or repayment of income tax, value added tax or national insurance contributions relating to the trade, profession or vocation.

[1(5) Where the purchase of an asset has been deducted as an expense in any assessment period and, in a subsequent assessment period, the asset is sold or ceases to be used for the purposes of a trade, profession or vocation carried on by the person, the proceeds of sale (or, as the case may be, the amount that would be received for the asset if it were sold at its current market value) are to be treated as a receipt in that subsequent assessment period].

AMENDMENTS

1. Universal Credit and Miscellaneous Amendments (No.2) Regulations 2014 (SI 2014/2888) reg.4(3) (November 26, 2014, or in the case of existing awards, the first assessment period beginning on or after November 26, 2014).

2. Universal Credit (Surpluses and Self-employed Losses) (Digital Service) Amendment Regulations 2015 (SI 2015/345) reg.3(2) (April 11, 2018).

3. Universal Credit (Surpluses and Self-employed Losses) (Digital Service) Amendment Regulations 2015 (SI 2015/345) reg.3(3) (April 11, 2018).

4. Universal Credit (Miscellaneous Amendments, Saving and Transitional Provision) Regulations 2018 (SI 2018/65) reg.7(4)(a), (April 11, 2018, text to be inserted by SI 2015/345 amended with effect from February 14, 2018).

DEFINITIONS

"assessment period"—see WRA 2012, ss.40 and 7(2) and reg.21.

"Contributions and Benefits Act"—see reg.2.

"earned income"—see reg.52.

"employed earnings"—see regs 53(1) and 55.

"HMRC"—see reg.53(1).

"relievable pension contributions"—see reg.53(1).

GENERAL NOTE

This regulation, now from April 2018 supplemented by reg.57A on unused losses, applies for the purpose of calculating self-employed earnings. As with employed earnings, it is the actual amount received during the assessment period that is taken into account. Thus those who are self-employed will need to report their earnings every month. 2.213

Self-employed earnings are earnings that are not employed earnings and are derived from carrying on a trade, profession or vocation (para.(1)). On the tests for deciding whether a person is an employed earner or in self-employment, see, for example, *CJSA/4721/2001*. Guidance on what amounts to a trade can also be taken from the cases on what is a business for the purposes of the disregard of the assets of a business (Sch.10 para.7), such as *R(FC) 2/92* and *RM v Sefton Council (HB)* [2016] UKUT 357 (AAC), reported as [2017] AACR 5, on the question of when the ownership of a tenanted house is a business. But note that for universal credit the test is in terms of trade, a narrower concept than business (see the discussion, particularly in the context of rented property, in the notes to regs 52 and 77(1) (2.299)). Whether particular earnings are self-employed earnings for the purposes of universal credit is not determined by how they have been treated for other purposes, e.g. contribution purposes (see *CIS/14409/1996* and para.H4017 ADM).

Thus the first question is whether the person is engaged in self-employment. The issue will have to be determined according to the facts. Paragraph H4013 ADM quotes as examples someone who sells their two classic cars after losing their job because they can no longer afford their upkeep (who is not engaged in a trade) and someone who buys 10,000 toilet rolls from a wholesaler with the intention of selling them for a profit (who is so engaged). If it is decided that the person is engaged in self-employment, the question of whether they are in "gainful self-employment" will also need to be considered for the purpose of applying the minimum income floor rule (see the note to reg.62). If the person is not in gainful self-employment, no minimum income floor will apply and the person's actual self-employed earnings will be taken into account for the purposes of calculating their universal credit award.

This is not the place for any extensive discussion of how to distinguish between employed earners (i.e. those employed under a contract of service (employees) or office-holders) and self-employed earners. In most cases there will be no difficulty in identifying a claimant who falls within reg.57 as opposed to reg.55. There is a still helpful, although now dated, summary of the traditional factors in pp.98–103 of Wikeley, Ogus & Barendt, *The Law of Social Security* (5th edn). See also *CJSA/4721/2001*. There is perhaps a recent tendency to give particular significance to who takes the financial risk of operations as between the person doing the work and the employer/customer. Someone who sets up a limited company of which they are the sole or main employee and who controls the company through being the sole or majority shareholder is an employee, but reg.77 supplies a special regime in which they are treated as self-employed and the income of the company is to be calculated under reg.57.

In *SSWP v MA (ESA)* [2024] UKUT 131 (AAC), Judge Wikeley indicates, referring to the tax case law, that a trade does not cease to be a trade because it is being carried on illegally. In the particular case, the claimant bought and sold stolen bikes on an industrial scale, which was as much a trade as if he had run a legitimate business in second-hand bikes. His activity was held to constitute "work" for the purposes of ESA and his income to be earnings from self-employment.

There may be circumstances that fall outside both categories, in which case the category of "other paid work" in reg.52(a)(iii) would have to be considered. See the decision of the Court of Appeal in the child support case *Hakki v Secretary of State for Work and Pensions* [2014] EWCA Civ 530 in which a "professional" poker player was held not to be a self-employed earner on the ground that his activities lacked the necessary degree of organisation to amount to a trade, profession or vocation. The reasoning has been somewhat uncritically endorsed in the further child support case of *French v SSWP and another* [2018] EWCA Civ 470; [2018] AACR 25.

There are no specific rules excluding certain payments from being self-employed earnings (contrast, for example, reg.37(2) of the Income Support Regulations in Vol.V of this series, 2021/22 edition as updated in Cumulative Supplements included in this volume and in mid-year Supplements).

The April 2018 re-casting of paras (2) and (3) into para.(2) does not change the basic substance of the method of calculation of self-employed earnings, apart from new rules on the treatment of losses including the incorporation of the operation of reg.57A on unused losses, but now expressly specifies a series of steps. The whole provision is directed to the calculation for a particular assessment period. The amendment operated only in relation to digital service (full service) cases by a detailed prescription of categories of claimant (see reg.4(1) of the Universal Credit (Surpluses and Self-employed Losses) (Digital Service) Amendment Regulations 2015 (SI 2015/345), as amended), but is now of general application. See previous editions for the previous form of reg.57(2) and (3), which has been subject to slight amendment in its application in live service cases (now extinct).

Note that the guidance on the *gov.uk* website entitled *Report business income and expenses to Universal Credit if you are self-employed*, as updated on May 23, 2023, initially contained a number of very significant errors that displayed a basic misunderstanding of the method of calculation under reg.57, as well as of the process when that method is applied by virtue of reg.77 (company analogous to a partnership or one person business). Corrections were made in an update on June 21, 2023. The current version is updated to April 9, 2024.

Step 1

Now the starting point in step 1 is the actual receipts in the particular assessment period, regardless of when the work to earn those receipts was done, with the deduction of any allowable expenses under reg.58 or 59 (which apply to amounts paid in a particular assessment period, by necessary implication the same assessment period as for the actual receipts). Thus, it is not necessary that a claimant be engaged in self-employment in the assessment period in question, merely that there are actual receipts or allowable expenses incurred in that period that are derived from self-employment. **2.214**

It is important that step 1 requires the calculation not just of a profit but also of a loss for each self-employment. Where the trade etc is carried on by a partnership, the claimant's share, which will depend on the terms of the partnership agreement, is taken. Note that drawings from a partnership or from a trade carried on as a self-employed person are not earnings from self-employment (*AR v Bradford Metropolitan DC* [2008] UKUT 30 (AAC), reported as *R(H) 6/09*), nor can they be regarded as unearned income. They are irrelevant to the method of calculation under reg.57 and, even if they did not fall outside the categories of unearned income in reg.66, to regard them as unearned income would entail an unfair double counting. Under para.(4) receipts include receipts in kind and any refund or repayment of income tax, VAT or national insurance contributions for the self-employed. See the notes on para.(5) below for sale of stock and other assets. This method of calculating self-employed earnings is based on HMRC's "cash basis and simplified expenses accounting system" (the cash basis model, or "cash in/cash out"). According to para.H4141 of ADM, self-employed claimants will be asked to report monthly between seven days before and 14 days after the end date of each assessment period details of actual income receipts and actual expenditure on allowable expenses during the assessment period that has just come to an end. The work of compiling the necessary information and getting through to report it will be quite burdensome. If there is a failure to report on time, an estimate can be made under reg.54(2)(b).

There is a rather difficult issue about what might be called "start-up" costs, expenditure that would fall within the meaning of reg.58 but is incurred before the claimant starts offering or making available the services in question. Can the expenditure be regarded as wholly and exclusively incurred for the purposes of a trade, profession or vocation if it is incurred to enable the trade etc. to start operating in the future? In the absence of reg.57A, the answer would in a sense not matter, because unless the claimant had some receipts to go into step 1 of the calculation there would be no profit, so that expenditure could not reduce the level of earned income below nil. However, reg.57A requires the carrying forward into future assessment periods of "unused losses". Although quite substantial expenses might reasonably be incurred in such circumstances, it seems that they probably cannot be regarded as giving rise to unused losses under reg.57A. That is partly by analogy with the income tax rules, which do not allow the deduction of expenses incurred before the taxpayer starts trading in the sense above. Perhaps more pertinently, reg.57(1) refers to its purpose being the calculation of earned income derived from "carrying on" a trade, profession or vocation. The reference back to the reg.57 calculation in reg.57A in identifying an unused loss seems therefore by implication to impose a similar restriction, that only expenses incurred in the carrying on of a trade etc. can be taken into account, not expenses incurred merely in preparing to carry on the trade etc.

It must be the case that, as accepted in para.H4190 of ADM, capital receipts do not form part of actual receipts for the purposes of reg.57. Examples would be loans, grants, capital introduced into the business by the claimant or others or the proceeds of the sale of capital assets (where such a sale is not part of the business itself). The basic reasoning in *R(FC) 1/97* (and see the other cases mentioned in the notes to reg.37(1) of the Income Support Regulations in Vol.V of this series, 2021/22 edition as updated in Cumulative Supplements included in this volume and in mid-year Supplements) would seem to apply, although there are some differences between the family credit legislation considered there and the provisions in these Regulations. However, it is plain that the object of reg.57 is to calculate the amount of earned *income* as defined in reg.52, as was important in *R(FC) 1/97*, in addition to the principle that the power to treat capital as earned income (in the terms of para.4(3)(b) of Sch.1 to the WRA 2012) can only be exercised by the use of express words in the regulation.

It is no longer necessary to consider how various coronavirus payments available to the self-employed in 2020 and 2021 should have been regarded in carrying out Step 1. See the full discussion on pp.379–381 of the 2023/24 edition of this volume and earlier editions for the details.

Step 2

2.215 Step 2 applies only where the person carries on more than one trade, profession or vocation in the assessment period in question and requires the adding together of the respective results under step 1. Thus a loss in one trade etc goes to offset a profit in another.

Step 3

Step 3 requires the deduction from the figure produced by step 1 (and 2, if applied) of any payment actually made in the assessment period in question to HMRC by way of self-employed national insurance contributions or income tax. Many self-employed people do not pay national insurance contributions and income tax regularly, but they can arrange with HMRC to make such payments monthly. It will obviously be to their advantage for universal credit purposes (to minimise fluctuations in the amounts of earned income to be taken into account) to do so. The process of calculation may stop at the end of step 3. If the resulting figure is nil or a negative amount, then the self-employed earnings for the assessment period are nil. If there is a negative amount there will then be an "unused loss" as defined in reg.57A(1) that can be taken into account in subsequent assessment periods if the process then gets to step 5.

Step 4

Step 4 applies if step 3 results in a positive amount. Then the amount of any relievable pension contributions made in the assessment period in question is deducted, unless already deducted in calculating employed earnings (under reg.55(5)—presumably if not all of the amount was needed to reduce employed earnings to nil, the remainder can be deducted under step 4). See the notes to reg.55 for discussion of "relievable pension contributions". If the resulting figure is nil or a negative amount, then the self-employed earnings for the assessment period are nil. If there is a negative amount at this stage there is not an "unused loss" under reg.57A(1).

Step 5

Step 5 applies if step 4 results in a positive amount. Then at that final stage any unused losses from past assessment periods that have not been extinguished under reg.57A are to be deducted. If the resulting figure is positive, that is the amount of self-employed earnings for the assessment period in question. If the resulting figure is nil or a negative amount, the self-employed earnings are nil. The oldest unused losses are to be looked at first. Although it would have been better if the process had been spelled out, for the structure of regs 57 and 57A to be workable it must be assumed that once deducting a particular unused loss produces a nil result or a negative figure, no more recent unused losses are to be deducted. See the notes to reg.57A for how that affects the amount of unused losses available in subsequent assessment periods.

Note in particular the effect of the saving provision in reg.4(4) of the Universal Credit (Surpluses and Self-employed Losses) (Digital Service) Amendment Regulations 2015, as amended, which provides that there is to be no unused loss under reg.57A from any assessment period that began before April 11, 2018.

Under para.(5), where the purchase of an asset has been deducted as an expense in any assessment period, and in a subsequent assessment period the asset is sold, or ceases to be used for the purpose of the claimant's self-employment, the proceeds of sale, or the amount that would have been received if the asset had been sold at its current market value, will be treated as a receipt in that subsequent period. Paragraph H4181 of the ADM advises decision makers that the full amount of the proceeds of sale (or deemed proceeds of sale) is to be taken into account, even if only a proportion of the purchase price was deducted as a expense in the assessment period in which the asset was purchased because the claimant's self-employed earnings in that assessment period were less than the price of the asset. This provision would seem to embody a somewhat rigid approach which does not take into account the realities of self-employment which usually needs to be viewed over a much longer period than an assessment period (i.e., a month). To quote an example given in the ADM, if a claimant pays £400 for display material in an assessment period in which their earnings are only £100, so that only £100 of the expense is taken into account as this reduces their earnings to nil, it does not seem fair that the whole of the sale price (or deemed sale price) should count as a receipt in a subsequent assessment period, rather than the equivalent of the expenses reduction they were allowed. But now the unused loss in the assessment period in which the display material was purchased can be taken into account under step 5 and reg.57A in subsequent assessment periods, so that the unfairness is diminished. The guidance accepts that if an asset was only to be used partially for business purposes, only that proportion of the proceeds of sale is to be taken into account as a receipt.

This method of calculation, even on the assumption that claimants will be able to supply accurate information month by month, might be expected in many cases to produce considerable fluctuations between assessment periods depending on the chance of when receipts come in and when expenses are incurred. In the case of fluctuations downwards, reg.62 on the minimum income floor may come into play. If a self-employed person is in gainful self-employment as defined in reg.64, would apart from the operation of reg.62 or 90 be subject to all work-related requirements and their actual earned income in an assessment period is below the minimum income floor (usually the hourly national minimum wage times 35), their earned income is deemed to be equal to that threshold. However, the test for gainful self-employment is quite strict. The person must be carrying on a trade, profession or vocation as their main employment and derive self-employed earnings from that. In addition, the trade, profession or vocation must be "organised, developed, regular and carried on in the expectation of profit". Those last conditions, and also the exclusion of the 12-month start-up period under reg.63, will exclude many claimants with fluctuating or more casual operations. See the notes to reg.64 for further discussion. If reg.62 does not apply, the actual level of self-employed earnings as calculated under the present regulation must be taken. Even if reg.62 does apply to some assessment periods, it supplies no mechanism for evening out fluctuations to a higher level for other assessment periods. If earned income exceeds the minimum income floor in any assessment period, the actual level must be taken.

The April 2018 provisions on taking account of losses will give some mitigation in evening out fluctuations in the level of self-employed earnings, but may also lead to an increased application of the minimum income floor. In addition, the new provisions on surplus earnings in reg.54A will add to the unpredictability of outcomes when, as is likely to be the case for any self-employed person, there are continual fluctuations month by month in actual receipts and in expenditure. There are still likely to be differences in total annual income between those universal credit claimants whose earnings are of a regular monthly amount and those (many of whom will be self-employed) who earn the same amount over the year but subject to fluctuations. See the House of Commons Work and Pensions Committee's May 2018 report *Universal Credit: supporting self-employment* (HC 997).

See also reg.77 for the special rules that apply to those whose control of a company is such that they are like a sole trader or a partner. In those circumstances, amongst other things, the company's income or the person's share of it is to be treated as the person's income and calculated under reg.57 as if it were self-employed earnings. It is, though, far from clear how that notional conversion is to take place. Under reg.57, in the case of actual self-employed earnings, the calculation is based on actual receipts in any assessment period less permitted deductions for expenses under regs 58 and 59. Presumably therefore, "the income of the company" does not mean the net income of the company as might be calculated for corporation tax purposes or under ordinary accounting principles. Presumably it means the actual receipts of the company in the assessment period in question less the deductions for expenses under regs 58 and 59, looking at expenditure on behalf of the company rather than by the person in question. It is difficult to say whether in practice information will be available as to such receipts and expenditure in a current assessment period of a month. A further problem is how to calculate the deductions from gross profits under step 3 of para. (2) for national insurance contributions and income tax paid to HMRC in the assessment period and relievable pension contributions made in that period, when the person's actual tax and national insurance status will not have been as a self-employed earner. But some difficulties may be avoided by the provision in reg.77(3)(c) that if the person's activities in the course of the company's trade are their main employment reg.62 (minimum income floor) is to be applied.

See the notes to reg.61 for discussion of whether any alterations of existing awards resulting from increases or reductions in the amount of earned income, including self-employed earnings, are appealable.

[[1]Unused losses

2.216 **57A.**—(1) For the purposes of regulation 57(2), a person has an unused loss if—

(a) in calculating the person's self-employed earnings for any of the previous [[2]...] assessment periods, the amount resulting from steps 1 to 3 in regulation 57(2) was a negative amount (a "loss"); and

(b) the loss has not been extinguished in a subsequent assessment period.

(2) For the purposes of paragraph (1)(b) a loss is extinguished if no amount of that loss remains after it has been deducted at step 5 in regulation 57(2).

(3) Where a person was entitled to a previous award of universal credit and the last day of entitlement in respect of that award fell within the 6 months preceding the first day of entitlement in respect of the new award,

the Secretary of State may, for the purposes of this regulation (provided the person provides such information as the Secretary of State requires), [[2]treat—

(a) the assessment periods under the previous award; and

(b) any months between that award and the current award in respect of which a claim has been made,

as assessment periods under the current award.]]

AMENDMENTS

1. Universal Credit (Surpluses and Self-employed Losses) (Digital Service) Amendment Regulations 2015 (SI 2015/345) reg.3(4) (April 11, 2018).

2. Universal Credit (Miscellaneous Amendments, Saving and Transitional Provision) Regulations 2018 (SI 2018/65) reg.7(4)(b) (text to be inserted by SI 2015/345 amended with effect from February 14, 2018) (April 11, 2018).

DEFINITIONS

"assessment period"—see WRA 2012 ss.40 and 7(2) and reg.21.

"self-employed earnings"—see regs 53(1) and 57.

GENERAL NOTE

Although reg.57A came into force on April 11, 2018, the saving provision in reg.4(4) of the Universal Credit (Surpluses and Self-employed Losses) (Digital Service) Amendment Regulations 2015 (SI 2015/345), as amended, secures that no unused loss is to be produced from any assessment period that began before that date. It will therefore take some months at least for practical consequences to build up. 2.217

An "unused loss" arises in any previous assessment period under reg.57A(1) when the result after step 3 of the calculation of self-employed earnings in reg.57(2) produces a negative figure. That requires calculating profit or loss (i.e. actual receipts in the assessment period less allowable expenses incurred in the same period) for each trade, profession or vocation, combining the figures if more than one trade etc is carried on, and deducting income tax and national insurance payments made to HMRC in that period. Note that the reg.57A test is applied without taking any account of the deduction of the amount of relievable pension contributions under step 4 in reg.57(2). The loss in the form of the negative amount is then "unused" in the sense that the amount of self-employed earnings taken into account in the assessment period in question can never be less than nil.

On the face of it, when such an unused loss is to be taken into account in a subsequent assessment period under reg.57(2), where it comes in at step 5, there is no time limit on how far in the past the relevant assessment period was (subject to the saving that only assessment periods beginning on or after April 11, 2018 can count). The limit to 11 previous assessment periods that existed in previous forms of the amending regulation was removed in the final form. However, the DWP's view is that the rule only operates for assessment periods within the same continuous period of entitlement to universal credit as under the current award, subject to the linking rule in para.(3) of reg.57A, so that a break in entitlement prevents the taking into account of unused losses in pre-break assessment periods. That view must be based on the definition of assessment period in reg.21(1) as "a period of one month beginning with the first date of entitlement and each subsequent period of one month *during which entitlement subsists*" (emphasis added), as well as on the perceived need for para.(3). There may be some doubt about the validity of the emphasised part of reg.21(1) under the powers given in s.7(2) of the WRA 2012 and elsewhere. But leaving that aside and assuming that a month only amounts to an "assessment period" when within a period of universal credit entitlement, that seems to supply no reason why what were undoubtedly assessment periods during the pre-break period of entitlement are not "previous assessment periods" under para.(1)(a). It is suggested that some specific words would have been needed in reg.57A to produce the result that only assessment periods in the current period of entitlement could count and that the existence of para.(3) is insufficient to produce a necessary implication that the plain words of para.(1)(a) do not mean what they say. Thus it is arguable that a break in entitlement does not break the ability to go back to previous assessment periods for unused losses.

If that argument does not work, then para.(3) allows the Secretary of State, where the break in entitlement is of less than six months, to treat the assessment periods in the pre-break period of entitlement and the months in the break as assessment periods under the current award. If that is done, the unused losses in the pre-break period of entitlement and in the deemed assessment periods during the break can then be taken into account if necessary under reg.57(2). There is a discretion ("may") as to whether the deeming should be done, subject to the condition that the claimant provides any required information (presumably mainly as to receipts and expenses in months in the break which were not actually assessment periods). It is not clear what sort of factors might indicate that the basic rule should not be applied. On any appeal a tribunal can make its own judgment as to the exercise of the discretion.

Unused losses are only to be taken into account in step 5 in reg.57(2) if they have not been extinguished (reg.57A(1)(b)). Paragraph (2) links that matter to such use in step 5, but in slightly peculiar terms. It is clear enough that, if the process suggested in the notes to reg.57(2) is followed and only the unused losses, starting with the oldest, that are needed to reduce the final figure to nil or a negative amount are deducted under step 5, the losses that have not needed to be deducted at all are not extinguished. The peculiarity is in relation to the final or sole loss used. Say, for instance, that the figure remaining at the end of step 4 is £300 and the oldest or sole unextinguished unused loss is £500. That produces a negative amount of £200 in step 5 and the amount of self-employed earnings to be taken into account is nil. But to what extent is the unused loss of £500 extinguished by that operation? One would expect it to have been extinguished to the extent of £300. However, para.(2) seems to assume that a loss is either extinguished in its entirety or not extinguished in its entirety and states that a loss is extinguished if "no amount of that loss remains" after it has been deducted in step 5. That test is not clear. In one sense the whole of the £500 unused loss in the example was deducted, producing a negative figure and an amount of self-employed earnings of nil. What does it mean to ask if no amount of the loss "remains"? It seems that, to make any sense, it must mean that in the example £200 remained, because that amount was not needed to reduce the final figure to nil. That then is hard to reconcile with the apparent effect of the plain words of para.(2) that the whole of the £500 unused loss remains unextinguished, because it cannot be said that no amount of that loss remains. That is not the approach taken in the examples given in para.H4503 of the ADM, which are consistent with the carrying forward in the example above of only £200 of unused loss. That would involve interpreting "loss" in para.(2) as meaning something like the whole or part of the original unused loss as identified in para.(1), in so far as not already used up in step 5 of a reg.57 calculation.

Remember of course that if the result of bringing in unused losses results in a low or nil amount of self-employed earnings, the minimum income floor under reg.62 may well come into play.

Permitted expenses

2.218 **58.**—(1) The deductions allowed in the calculation of self-employed earnings are amounts paid in the assessment period in respect of—

(a) expenses that have been wholly and exclusively incurred for purposes of the trade, profession or vocation; or

(b) in the case of expenses that have been incurred for more than one purpose, an identifiable part or proportion that has been wholly and exclusively incurred for the purposes of the trade, profession or vocation,

excluding any expenses that were incurred unreasonably.

(2) Payments deducted under paragraph (1) may include value added tax.

(3) No deduction may be made for payments in respect of—

(a) expenditure on non-depreciating assets (including property, shares or other assets held for investment purposes);

(b) [[2] . . .]

(c) repayment of capital [[1] . . .] in relation to a loan taken out for the purposes of the trade, profession or vocation;

(d) expenses for business entertainment.

[[1](3A) A deduction for a payment of interest in relation to a loan taken out for the purposes of the trade, profession or vocation may not exceed £41.]

(4) This regulation is subject to regulation 59.

AMENDMENTS

1. Social Security (Miscellaneous Amendments) (No.2) Regulations 2013 (SI 2013/1508) reg.3(7) (July 29, 2013).

2. Universal Credit (Surpluses and Self-employed Losses) (Digital Service) Amendment Regulations 2015 (SI 2015/345) reg.3(5) (April 11, 2018).

DEFINITIONS

"assessment period"—see WRA 2012, ss.40 and 7(2) and reg.21.

"self-employed earnings"—see reg 53(1) and 57.

GENERAL NOTE

This regulation, and reg.59, provide for the deductions that can be made from self-employed earnings. Only these deductions can be made in addition to those under steps 3 and 4 of reg.57(2) for national insurance contributions and income tax paid to HMRC and relievable pension contributions. 2.219

The amount of the deduction will normally be the actual amount of the permitted expenses paid in the assessment period, but note para.(4). The effect of para.(4) is that the alternative deductions under reg.59 in respect of the expenses referred to in paras (2)–(4) of that regulation may be made instead. However, note that in the case of a car, the actual costs involved in acquiring or using it are not allowable and the only deduction that can be made is a flat rate deduction for mileage under reg.59(2). Regulation 53(1) gives "car' the same meaning as in s.268A(1) of the Capital Allowances Act 2001. That provision excludes motorcycles, vehicles of a construction primarily suited for the conveyance of goods or some other burden and vehicles of a type not commonly used as a private vehicle and unsuitable for such use. The ADM (paras H4231 and H4234) accepts that black cabs or hackney carriages are not cars, because they are specially adapted for business use, in contrast to minicabs or taxis of that kind.

To be deductible, the expenses must have been paid in the assessment period, be reasonable and have been "wholly and exclusively" incurred for the purposes of the self-employment (para.(1)), but note para.(1)(b). See para.H4214 ADM for examples of allowable expenses. Permitted expenses include value added tax (para.(2)).

Paragraph (1)(b) specifically provides for the apportionment of expenses that have been incurred for more than one purpose (e.g., for business and private purposes). In such a case, a deduction will be made for the proportion of the expenses that can be identified as wholly and exclusively incurred for the purposes of the self-employment. See *R(FC) 1/91* and *R(IS) 13/91* which hold that any apportionment already agreed by HMRC should normally be accepted. But note the alternative flat-rate deductions for expenses if someone uses their home for business purposes in reg.59(3). See also reg.59(4) which provides for flat-rate deductions from expenses if business premises are also used for personal use.

No deduction can be made for the payments listed in para.(3). The limitation of sub-para.(a) to non-depreciating assets confirms that reasonable capital expenditure on depreciating assets or stock-in-trade is to be deducted. Sub-paragraph (b) formerly excluded the deduction of losses from previous assessment periods, but has now been overtaken by the new form of reg.57(2) and reg.57A.

Repayments of capital on a loan taken out for the purposes of the self-employment are not deductible (para.(3)(c)) but deductions can be made for interest paid on such a loan up to a limit of £41 per assessment period (para.(3A)). Paragraph (3A) was introduced to bring universal credit into line with the tax rules which now allow a deduction of up to £500 annually for interest payments made on loans taken out for the purposes of a business. This will include interest on credit cards and overdraft charges if the original expense related to the business. According to para.H4217 ADM only £41 can be deducted in any assessment period, regardless of the number of relevant loans a person has and for what purposes. It might just be arguable that the terms of para.(3A) are sufficient to rebut the normal presumption under s.6(c) of the Interpretation Act 1978 that the singular includes the plural, especially if the person carries on more than one trade etc.

Flat rate deductions for mileage and use of home and adjustment for personal use of business premises

2.220 **59.**—(1) This regulation provides for alternatives to the deductions that would otherwise be allowed under regulation 58.

(2) Instead of a deduction in respect of the actual expenses incurred in relation to the acquisition or use of a motor vehicle, the following deductions are allowed according to the mileage covered on journeys undertaken in the assessment period for the purposes of the trade, profession or vocation—

(a) in a car, van or other motor vehicle (apart from a motorcycle), 45 pence per mile for the first 833 miles and 25 pence per mile thereafter; and

(b) on a motorcycle, 24 pence per mile,

and, if the motor vehicle is a car [1 . . .], the only deduction allowed for the acquisition or use of that vehicle is a deduction under this paragraph.

(3) Where a person carrying on a trade, profession or vocation incurs expenses in relation to the use of accommodation occupied as their home, instead of a deduction in respect of the actual expenses, a deduction is allowed according to the number of hours spent in the assessment period on income generating activities related to the trade, profession or vocation as follows—

(a) at least 25 hours but no more than 50 hours, £10;

(b) more than 50 hours but no more than 100 hours, £18;

(c) more than 100 hours, £26.

(4) Where premises which are used by a person mainly for the purposes of a trade, profession or vocation are also occupied by that person for their personal use, whether alone or with other persons, the deduction allowed for expenses in relation to those premises is the amount that would be allowed under regulation 58(1) if the premises were used wholly and exclusively for purposes of the trade, profession or vocation, but reduced by the following amount according to the number of persons occupying the premises for their personal use—

(a) £350 for one person;
(b) £500 for two persons;
(c) £650 for three or more persons.

Amendment

1. Social Security (Miscellaneous Amendments) (No.2) Regulations 2013 (SI 2013/1508) reg.3(8) (July 29, 2013).

Definitions

"the Act"—see reg.2.
"assessment period"—see WRA 2012 ss.40 and 7(2) and reg.21.
"car"—see reg.53(1).
"motor cycle"—*ibid.*

General Note

This regulation provides for alternative deductions to those that would otherwise be permitted under reg.58 to be chosen (para.(1)). However, note that in the case of a car, there is no choice: only a flat rate deduction for mileage is allowed and no deduction can be made for the actual cost of buying or using the car (para.(2)). This does not apply to other motor vehicles. See the notes to reg.58 for the meaning of "car". **2.221**

Under para.(2), a deduction for mileage on journeys undertaken for the purposes of the business in the assessment period:

- on a motorcycle, of 24 pence per mile; or
- in a car, van or other motor vehicle (other than a motorcycle), of 45 pence per mile for the first 833 miles and 25 pence per mile after that,

can be made instead of the actual cost of buying or using the motor vehicle (in the case of a car this is the only permitted deduction).

If someone uses their own home for the purposes of their self-employment, a flat-rate deduction of:

- £10 for at least 25 hours but no more than 50 hours;
- £18 for more than 50 hours but no more than 100 hours; or
- £26 for more than 100 hours,

of "income generating activities" related to the self-employment in an assessment period can be made instead of the actual expenses incurred in the use of the home (para.(3)). The guidance in paras H4241–H4242 ADM suggests that "income generating activities" include providing services to customers, general administration of the business (e.g. filing and record-keeping) and action to secure business (e.g. sales and marketing) but do not include being on call (e.g. a taxi driver waiting for customers to ring), the use of the home for storage or time spent on completing tax returns (presumably on this basis DWP would also discount any time spent collating evidence of actual receipts and expenses for the purposes of the person's universal credit claim).

For the alternative provision for apportionment of expenses, see reg.58(1)(b).

Paragraph (4) provides that if the person lives in premises that are mainly used for business purposes, the expenses that would be allowed if the premises were used wholly and exclusively for the purposes of the person's self-employment are to be reduced by a set amount depending on the number of people living in the premises. The reduction is £350 for one person, £500 for two and £650 for three or more people in each assessment period. It is not entirely clear but the reduction under this paragraph appears to be a set rule, rather than an alternative to an apportionment under reg.58(1)(b).

Notional earned income

2.222 **60.**—(1) A person who has deprived themselves of earned income, or whose employer has arranged for them to be so deprived, for the purpose of securing entitlement to universal credit or to an increased amount of universal credit is to be treated as possessing that earned income.

(2) Such a purpose is to be treated as existing if, in fact, entitlement or higher entitlement to universal credit did result and, in the opinion of the Secretary of State, this was a foreseeable and intended consequence of the deprivation.

(3) If a person provides services for another person and—

(a) the other person makes no payment for those services or pays less than would be paid for comparable services in the same location; and
(b) the means of the other person were sufficient to pay for, or pay more for, those services,

the person who provides the services is to be treated as having received the remuneration that would be reasonable for the provision of those services.

(4) Paragraph (3) does not apply where—

(a) the person is engaged to provide the services by a charitable or voluntary organisation and the Secretary of State is satisfied that it is reasonable to provide the services free of charge or at less than the rate that would be paid for comparable services in the same location;
(b) the services are provided by a person who is participating as a service user (see regulation 53(2)); or
(c) the services are provided under or in connection with a person's participation in an employment or training programme approved by the Secretary of State.

DEFINITIONS

"earned income"—see reg.52.
"a person who is participating as a service user"—see reg.53(2).

GENERAL NOTE

2.223 This regulation treats a person as having employed or self-employed earnings or earned income from other paid work in two situations. For the rules relating to notional unearned income, see reg.74.

Paragraphs (1)–(2)

2.224 This contains the deprivation of earnings rule for universal credit. It applies if someone has deprived themselves of earned income, for the purpose of securing entitlement to, or increasing the amount of, universal credit. It also applies if the person's employer has "arranged for" the deprivation. Presumably this will only apply if the person's purpose was to secure, or increase, entitlement to universal credit by way of the arrangement and the employer's purpose is not relevant.

See the notes to reg.50(1) on deprivation of capital for discussion of the general notion of deprivation and, in particular, when the purpose is to be said to be to secure entitlement to universal credit or to an increased amount. No doubt, as for capital, the basic test is whether that was a significant operative purpose. See below for discussion of whether the deeming of the existence of a prohibited purpose in para.(2), where the result was a foreseeable and intended result of the deprivation, makes any real difference. There is some authority from the child support jurisdiction that a refusal to take up an offer of employment would not be a deprivation of income (*CCS/7967/1995*), although leaving a job may be depending on the circumstances (*CCS/4056/2004*). In the latter circumstance, note the existence of higher-level sanctions under s.26(2)(d) and (4)(b) for voluntarily and for no good reason ceasing paid work or losing pay. Ceasing paid work for the purpose of securing universal credit or an increased amount would certainly not be a good reason. Cutting back on availability as a self-employed person and reducing hours or days of availability under a zero hours contract or a part-time arrangement could presumably also count as deprivations.

The operation of para.(1) is restricted to circumstances where the person's purpose is related to entitlement to universal credit. That is in contrast to the terms of reg.105(1) of the JSA Regulations 1996 (which covers purposes relating to both old style JSA and income support) and of reg.106(1) of the ESA Regulations 2008 and reg.42(1) of the Income Support Regulations (which both cover purposes relating to all of old style ESA and JSA and income support). *R(IS) 14/93* was concerned with a similar problem on the transfer to income support from the corresponding supplementary benefit provisions in 1988 in relation to the notional capital. That was whether claimants who deprived themselves of capital under the supplementary benefit regime, before income support existed, could be said to have done so for the purpose of securing entitlement to income support so as to be caught by reg.51(1) of the Income Support Regulations once the income support legislation had come into force. The Commissioner holds that the words "income support" in reg.51(1) cannot be taken to refer to means-tested benefits that previously went under the name of supplementary benefit. Thus, if a deprivation of earned income occurs while a person is receiving, or contemplating a claim for, income support or old style JSA or ESA, it may be arguable, depending on the exact circumstances, that if there is later a claim for universal credit the purpose of the deprivation was not to secure entitlement to universal credit. But there might in such circumstances be a continuing deprivation for that purpose if there was not an earlier permanent deprivation.

Note, however, para.(2). The effect of para.(2) is that the person will be deemed to have the necessary purpose if they did obtain universal credit, or more universal credit, and in the opinion of the Secretary of State, this was "a foreseeable and intended consequence" of the deprivation. To some extent para.(2) represents a codification of the case law on the "purpose" part of the traditional deprivation rule. However, it seems likely that much will continue to depend on the view taken by the Secretary of State (and on appeal a tribunal) of the person's intention. It is far from clear what difference there is meant to be between *an* "intended consequence" in para.(2) and "purpose" (interpreted as meaning significant operative purpose) in para.(1). If there is no difference there would be no point in including the deeming in para.(2). It may have been thought that the conditions in para.(2) are easier to determine one way or the other, but it is submitted that a consequence is not intended as well as foreseeable just because a person realises that it will result from the deprivation.

There is a rather difficult question for how long following the deprivation the notional earned income is to be attributed. Presumably, the prima facie answer is for as long as the earned income could reasonably have been expected to continue if the deprivation had not taken place. But if the act of deprivation or something else has the effect that the source of the earned income cannot be reconnected (e.g. because a former employer would not take the claimant back or change arrangements again), can there be any justification for applying the rule in para.(1)?

Regulation 52(b) includes notional earned income as within the meaning of "earned income", but none of regs 54 (on earned income), 55 (on employed earnings) or 57 (on self-employed earnings) say anything about how notional earned income is to be integrated into their calculations. Presumably, at the least the definitions and deductions included in and under those provisions must be applied as if the notional earned income had actually been received.

Paragraphs (3)–(4)

If the two conditions in para.(3)(a) and (b) are met (of the claimant having provided a service for which no payment or less than the going rate is made and the person who received the service having the means to pay or pay more) there is no 2.225

discretion whether or not to apply the rule, unless the claimant comes within one of the exceptions in para.(4). However, the application of both the rule and the exception in para.(4)(a) involve a number of value judgments (e.g. in relation to "comparable services", what remuneration (if any) it is "reasonable" to treat the claimant as having received and whether it is "reasonable" for the claimant to provide the service free of charge or at less than the going rate if they are working for a charitable or voluntary organisation).

The first overriding condition is that the claimant provides services for another person. In the previous income support and equivalent provision (reg.42(6) of the Income Support Regulations: Vol.V of this series, 2021/22 edition as updated in Cumulative Supplements included in this volume and in mid-year Supplements) the condition was of performing "a service". It is suggested that no difference of substance can have been intended, so that the authority on those provisions is still relevant.

In *CIS/2916/1997* the claimant was spending time in her mother's shop to keep her mother company following recent bereavements. The Commissioner said that whether this amounted to a "service" was a question of fact and degree, having regard, inter alia, to the effort and time put in (see *Clear v Smith* [1981] 1 W.L.R. 399 on whether there could be "work" without remuneration) but in particular to the advantage derived by the mother. If the help given was substantial, the claimant was providing a service.

In *R(SB) 3/92* the Commissioner held that the rule applied where a mother provided services to her disabled adult son out of love and affection. On appeal in *Sharrock v Chief Adjudication Officer* (March 26, 1991; Appendix to *R(SB) 3/92*) the Court of Appeal agreed that such relationships came within the supplementary benefit provision, providing that the service provided was of a character for which an employer would be prepared to pay. In *CIS/93/1991* the Commissioner held that the principle of *Sharrock* applies to reg.42(6) of the Income Support Regulations, which thus covered services provided within informal family relationships without any contract. In *CIS/422/1992* (which again concerned Mrs Sharrock), the Commissioner held that she was a volunteer and that it was reasonable for her to provide her services free (which provided an exception under reg.42(6A)). The evidence was that her son made a substantial contribution to the household expenses. If she were to charge for her services the whole basis of the arrangement between them would have to change, which could have a deleterious effect on their relationship. However, note that there is no exception for a mere volunteer in para.(4)(a), only for someone engaged by a voluntary or charitable organisation.

Under para.(3)(a) the "employer" must either make no payment or pay less than is paid for comparable services in the same location. Since the amount of notional earned income is set according to what is reasonable for comparable services, it seems that provision of some comparable services on a remunerated basis must be shown to exist in all cases. It is not clear how restricted "the same location" is. Regulation 42(6) of the Income Support Regulations refers to "the area".

Some of the points made in *R(SB) 13/86* on the previous supplementary benefit provision seem also to apply to para.(3). It is necessary to identify the "employer" for whom the services were provided. "Person" includes a company or other corporate employer (Interpretation Act 1978 Sch.1). Thus in *R(IS) 5/95* where the claimant, who was an employee and director of a small company, was working unpaid because of the company's financial difficulties, and *CSJSA/23/2006* which concerned the sole director and majority shareholder of an unlimited company who was not paid for his part-time work for the company, it was necessary to consider whether the notional income rule applied. See also *CCS/4912/1998* which held that a similar child support rule applied where a person provided his services through a personal service company that he had set up himself and which was paying him a very low hourly rate and *R(CS) 9/08* where it was held that application of that rule had to be considered in the case of a salary sacrifice arrangement whereby an employer made contributions to an occupational pension scheme of the amount contractually agreed to be foregone by the employee.

Particulars of the services provided and any payments made must be ascertained. See *CIS/701/1994* on the factors to consider when assessing comparable employment (the claimant in that case was again a carer) and the amount of notional earnings. In *CJSA/23/2006* the tribunal had erred in simply adopting the decision-maker's use of the national minimum wage as the appropriate comparator for deciding the amount of the claimant's notional earnings. The test was what was paid for a comparable employment in the area and so relevant findings of fact needed to be made to establish local comparable earnings. In addition, in a case where there was no actual or implied contract, the period over which the earnings were payable and when they were due to be paid also had to be established in accordance with what were the likely terms of employment in a similar job in the area.

R(IS) 2/98 decided that a suggestion that, although earnings in kind did not count as income in calculating entitlement to income support (see reg.55(2)(a) for the same result for universal credit), they should be taken into account in deciding whether a payment of earnings had been made under reg.42(6) of the Income Support Regulations was incorrect. The claimant's wife worked as a shop assistant for 12 hours a week for which she was paid £5 in cash and took goods to the value of £36 from the shelves. The Commissioner held that since earnings in kind were ignored when considering whether any payment at all of earnings had been made, that had also to be the case when deciding whether a person was paid less than the rate for comparable employment. Thus in considering whether the claimant's wife was paid less than the rate for comparable employment, the £36 that she received in goods was to be left out of account. But to avoid unfair double counting it was necessary to deduct any cash payments in the calculation of her notional earnings under reg.42(6). That was permissible because reg.42(6) allowed the amount of earnings which would be paid for comparable employment to be adjusted where circumstances made it reasonable. However, it would not be "reasonable" to deduct the earnings in kind because that did not involve a double counting as the actual value of the earnings in kind was disregarded. The same would seem to apply for para.(3).

Under para.(3)(b) the Secretary of State must show that the person to whom the services were provided had sufficient means to pay, or pay more, for the services. For income support and equivalents it is for the claimant to show the "employer's" means were insufficient. That is something could well cause difficulties for claimants reluctant to make embarrassing enquiries or if the "employer" is reluctant to provide information. So the change in the burden is welcome, but there the public interest in preventing employers from economising at the expense of the social security budget means that intrusive enquiries may have to be made on behalf of the Secretary of State. The Court of Appeal in *Sharrock v Chief Adjudication Officer* suggests that "means" refers simply to monetary resources and is a matter of broad judgment. No automatic test of ignoring certain benefits or regarding an income above income support (or now universal credit) level as available should be adopted. In *CIS/93/1991*, the claimant looked after his elderly and severely disabled father, but declined to give any information about the father's means. The Commissioner confirms that in such circumstances the basic rule of para.(6) must be applied, but subject to the exception for volunteers. Now the consequence if information could not be obtained from the father would be that para.(3) could not be applied.

Paragraph (4) specifies three situations in which the rule in para.(3) will not apply. First, under sub-para.(a) those engaged by charities or voluntary organisations are not to have any notional earned income if it is reasonable for them to provide their services free of charge or at less than the going rate. The Commissioner in *CIS/93/1991* held that the means of the "employer" is a factor in assessing reasonableness here, but other factors are relevant too. In *CIS/701/1994* the Commissioner expressed the view that if a person had substantial resources that were genuinely surplus to requirements, that would be different from the situation, for example, of a person saving towards the costs of future residential care. It should be noted that the test is whether it is reasonable to provide the services free of charge or at less than the going rate, rather than whether it is reasonable for payment not to be made for the service, although this is a factor (*CIS/147/1993*). If the claimant was receiving training while, or by doing, the work, that may be relevant (*R(IS) 12/92*).

In *CIS/93/1991* the Commissioner pointed out that the aim of the rule is clearly to prevent an employer who has the means to pay the going rate profiting at the expense of the public purse. If, therefore, an organisation arranges to undertake painting work (as in *CIS147/1993*, although it was an individual claimant volunteer), which otherwise would have remained undone, there is no element of financial profit to the employer in the claimant doing the work. If, however, the employer would have paid if the organisation had not offered to have it done for nothing or a small amount, it may be concluded that it was not reasonable for the services to be provided free of charge or at less than the going rate.

The absence of an individual volunteer from this exception removes a number of difficult issues for determination, as compared with the income support and equivalent rules. But that means that when services are being provided without charge within family settings or to one-person companies or similar by an employee or director it is much more likely that notional earned income will have to be attributed. Perhaps it can be regarded as something of a quid pro quo that it is for the Secretary of State to show under para.(3)(b) that the means of the "employer" are sufficient to pay, or pay more.

Secondly, para.(4)(b) covers services provided by someone participating as a service user, as defined in reg.53(2). There is no further condition as to whether it is reasonable to provide the services free of charge or at less than the going rate.

Thirdly, para.(4)(c) covers the situation where a person is on an approved employment programme or training scheme (not further defined), with no further condition.

[1Information for calculating earned income - real time information etc.

2.226 **61.**—(1) Unless paragraph (2) applies, a person must provide such information for the purposes of calculating their earned income at such times as the Secretary of State may require.

Real time information

(2) Where a person is, or has been, engaged in an employment in respect of which their employer is a Real Time Information employer—

(a) the amount of the person's employed earnings from that employment for each assessment period is to be based on the information reported to HMRC under the PAYE Regulations and received by the Secretary of State from HMRC in that assessment period; and

(b) for an assessment period in which no information is received from HMRC, the amount of employed earnings in relation to that employment is to be taken to be nil.

Exceptions to use of Real Time Information

(3) Paragraph (2) does not apply where—

(a) in relation to a particular employment the Secretary of State considers that the employer is unlikely to report information to HMRC in a sufficiently accurate or timely manner;

(b) it appears to the Secretary of State that the amount of a payment reported to HMRC is incorrect, or fails to reflect the definition of employed earnings in regulation 55 (employed earnings), in some material respect; or

(c) no information is received from HMRC in an assessment period and the Secretary of State considers that this is likely to be because of a failure to report information (which includes the failure of a computer system operated by HMRC, the employer or any other person).

(4) Where paragraph (2) does not apply by virtue of any of the exceptions in paragraph (3) the [Secretary] of State must determine the amount of employed earnings for the assessment period in question (or, where the exception in paragraph (3)(a) applies, for each assessment period in which the person is engaged in that employment) in accordance with regulation 55 (employed earnings) using such information or evidence as the Secretary of State thinks fit.

Reallocation of reported payments

(5) Where it appears to the Secretary of State that a payment of employed earnings has been reported late, or otherwise reported in the wrong assessment period, the Secretary of State may determine that the payment is to be treated as employed earnings in the assessment period in which it was received.

(6) Where a person is engaged in an employment where they are paid on a regular monthly basis and more than one payment in relation to that employment is reported in the same assessment period, the Secretary of State may, for the purposes of maintaining a regular pattern, determine that one of those payments is to be treated as employed earnings in respect of a different assessment period.

Consequential adjustments

(7) Where the Secretary of State makes a determination under any of paragraphs (4) to (6), the Secretary of State may make such other adjustment to the calculation of the person's employed earnings as may be necessary to avoid duplication or to maintain a regular payment pattern.

(8) In this regulation "Real Time Information Employer" has the meaning in regulation 2A(1) of the PAYE Regulations.]

AMENDMENT

1. Universal Credit (Earned Income) Amendment Regulations 2020 (SI 2020/1138) reg.2 (November 16, 2020).

DEFINITIONS

"assessment period"—see WRA 2012, ss.40 and 7(2) and reg.21.
"earned income"—see reg.52.
"employed earnings"—see regs 53(1) and 55.
"HMRC"—see reg.53(1).
"PAYE Regulations"—*ibid.*

GENERAL NOTE

The form of reg.61 set out above is that substituted by the amending regulations with effect from November 16, 2020. For the form in force immediately before that date, and some of the earlier history, readers must consult the 2020/21 edition of what was then Vol.V of this series, *Universal Credit*. The pre-November 2020 form of reg.61 will be discussed below in noting the changes made. To understand those changes, and also because there will still be appeals coming through to do with period before November 16, 2020, it is still necessary to consider the effects of the decision of the Court of Appeal in *Secretary of State for Work and Pensions v Johnson* [2020] EWCA Civ 778; [2020] P.T.S.R. 1872. See the notes to reg.54 for a full description of that decision. 2.227

The explanatory memorandum to the amending regulations (SI 2020/1138) recited that in *Johnson* the Court of Appeal decided that the lack of adjustment in the drafting of regs 54 and 61 for those who have two calendar monthly salary payments taken into account in one assessment period due to a "non-banking day salary shift" was not rational and continued:

> "7.4 These regulations therefore provide a solution to that Judgment. The policy intent is to ensure that ordinarily no more than one set of calendar monthly salary payments from a single employer are taken into account in each assessment period. This will also enable certain claimants to benefit from any applicable work allowance in each assessment period. This change in regulations will allow DWP to reallocate a payment reported via real time information (RTI) to a different assessment period, either because it was reported in the wrong assessment period, or (in the case of monthly paid employee) it is necessary to maintain a regular payment cycle. This issue applies to less than 1% of the people who are working and receiving Universal Credit."

The new reg.61 was thus presented as if it were not just "a solution", but the complete solution to the irrationality identified by the Court of Appeal, as explained in the notes to reg.54, and necessarily operative only prospectively from that date. That assumption also seems to have underlaid the DWP's presentation to the Social Security Advisory Committee on October 7, 2020 (SSAC Minutes October 2020), following which the SSAC agreed not to take the proposed regulations on formal reference. Such an assumption fails to grapple with the consequences of the terms of the declaration agreed by the parties (set out in the notes to reg.54 and exhaustively explored in *JN v SSWP (UC)* [2023] UKUT 49 (AAC)), which declares the earned income calculation method in the regulations to be irrational and unlawful as applied to the monthly paid employees identified. An important consequence appears to be that neither the four *Johnson* claimants nor any others who are able to bring an effective challenge to any past decisions can have that unlawful method applied to them in relation to periods before November 16, 2020. That is supported by the approach of Rose LJ in para.108 of *Johnson*, where she said that the claimants' argument of discrimination under the ECHR did not arise for consideration because of the success of their case on irrationality. It is submitted that the judge, and thus the Court, could only have taken that view if she thought that the four *Johnson* claimants had, by that success, achieved all that they could have achieved by success in the discrimination argument. Since the judicial reviews were directed against the decisions made in particular assessment periods in 2017 or 2018, the Court must by necessary implication from that part of its judgment have accepted that those decisions had to be re-made without applying the method of calculation found to be unlawful, even though the apparent mismatch between the nature of irrationality accepted and that result was unaddressed in the judgments. A mere redrafting of the regulations with effect from a subsequent date does not achieve that result.

It is still submitted that *Johnson* means that the earned income calculation method in the pre-November 16, 2020 form of the regulations has been unlawful from the outset. Although in *JN v SSWP (UC)* [2023] UKUT 49 (AAC), reported as [2023] AACR 7, Judge Wright analysed the effect of the declaration in *Johnson*, which had no express temporal qualification, by reference to somewhat inconsistent statements in the judgments as biting from the date of the Secretary of State's decisions that were under appeal in *Johnson* (i.e. some dates in 2017 and 2018), he did not need to consider any argument that the effect should go back to the start of the scheme. See the notes to reg.54 for the details of *JN*, including the judge's conclusion in remaking the decisions on the claimant's appeals against the Secretary of State's decisions relating to four assessment periods, having set aside those decisions as applying legislation that was irrational and unlawful, that he had no basis on which he could substitute a lawful decision. He therefore left the decisions to be remade on a lawful basis by the Secretary of State, noting that a way had apparently been found to do that for the *Johnson* claimants by manual adjustments to the system. An "automated fix" was said to have been put into operation from August 2021.

However, as from November 16, 2020 (probably in relation to assessment periods beginning on or after that date: see para.32 of Sch.1 to the Decisions and Appeals Regulations 2013 for the rule on supersessions where there is an existing award) the new form of reg.61 must be applied (subject to arguments that other categories of claimant might succeed in irrationality or discrimination arguments, although such arguments seem ruled out of success by the Court of Appeal's decision in *Pantellerisco v Secretary of State for Work and Pensions* [2021] EWCA Civ 1454; [2021] P.T.S.R. 1922, at least for those paid four-weekly or at similar intervals, as discussed in the notes to reg.54). The main difference from the previous form of reg.61 is in the substitution of the new paras (5) to (7), giving various discretionary powers, for the previous para.(5) and in the omission of the previous para.(6) (see detailed discussion below). There have also been several changes to the drafting of paras (1) to (4), some of which are merely cosmetic or clarificatory, such as the helpful introduction of some sub-headings, but some of which potentially introduce changes of substance. The integration of the changes into the structure of reg.61 has not been entirely coherent. The administrative guidance in Memo ADM 27/20 did little more than paraphrase the terms of the regulation and does not seem to have been incorporated into the text of Ch.H3 of the ADM.

The SSAC, despite considering the new regulation to be sufficiently helpful to claimants that a formal reference of the proposal was not necessary, remained "concerned that the new arrangements will be overly reliant on claimants to notify the Department when they have received two monthly payments in a single assessment period and that as a result a significant number could still fail to benefit from a work allowance every month as they should" (letter of October 23, 2020 from the Chair to the Secretary of State). Therefore, they recommended that the Department should closely monitor the impact of the change. The DWP had accepted that their manual process would depend on claimants coming forward with information, but said that it intended to ask employed claimants about the interval at which they are paid at the start of the claim, so as to flag up cases that might encounter problems in the future.

Note that the new powers in reg.61 are not restricted to cases where the work allowance is in play, as it was for the four *Johnson* claimants. The discretions may thus sometimes be very difficult to exercise, especially where claimants would be better off overall (apart from difficulties caused by fluctuations in total income) by having two monthly payments taken into account in the same assessment period and none in another period. That may be problematic if the DWP develops changes to its computer systems to attempt to apply the terms of the new reg.61 automatically without having to rely on claimants coming forward with information.

The regulation as a whole is concerned with the provision of information on earned income. It is one of the most distinctive features of universal credit that it was designed so that normally PAYE information would be used in a way that could be dealt with by an automated computer system to calculate a person's employed earnings and that direct reporting of employed earnings by a claimant ("self-reporting") would only be a fall-back position. That was a significant factor in universal credit assessment being on a monthly basis, with payment made in arrears after the end of each assessment period.

Paragraph (1)

Paragraph (1), unchanged from the old form, contains a general rule that a claimant must provide the information that the Secretary of State requires for the purposes of calculating their earned income (note that earned income includes not only employed earnings, including earnings as an office-holder, but also self-employed earnings, remuneration from any other paid work and income treated as earned income: see reg.52). Thus, self-employed claimants come within this self-reporting rule. However, para.(1) is subject to para.(2), which applies only to those with employed earnings. 2.228

Paragraph (2)

2.229 The new para.(2) is in substance the same as the previous para.(2), except that the rules are said to be "in respect of" particular assessment periods rather than "for" them. There has thus been no change to the unequivocal rule in para.(2)(b) that the amount of employed earnings "is to be taken to be nil" for any assessment period in which no information is received from HMRC. However, it would appear that, as discussed further below, in order to allow the new provisions to bite on the mischief identified in the explanatory memorandum, para.(2) must be read as subject to paras (5) to (7) as well as to the exceptions expressly made in para.(3). Otherwise the reallocation of a payment to an assessment period in which no information was received from HMRC, necessary to those provisions, would be impossible.

Under para.(2), if the claimant's employer is a "Real Time Information employer" (defined in para.(7)), the calculation of the claimant's employed earnings in respect of each assessment period is to be based on the information that is reported to HMRC through the PAYE system and received by the Secretary of State from HMRC in that period (sub-para.(a)). If no information is received from HMRC in an assessment period, the claimant's earnings from that employment are to be taken to be nil (sub-para.(b)). It should especially be noted that the language of sub-para.(b) is different from that of sub-para.(a) ("is to be taken" as opposed to "is to be based on").

Since October 6, 2013 most employers have been Real Time Information employers (see reg.2A(1)(d) of the Income Tax (Pay As You Earn) Regulations 2003 (SI 2003/2682) ("the PAYE Regulations"). Under reg.67B of the PAYE Regulations a Real Time Information employer is required to deliver specified information to HMRC before or at the time of making payments to an employee. The instructions to employers on reporting are to record amounts on the normal payment date. HMRC's October 2019 (Issue 80) Employer Bulletin contains a clarification of the rules about the date on which pay should be reported in a Real Time Information Full Payment Submission as having been made when the normal payment date falls on a non-banking day. Whether the payment is made before or after the normal payment date it should be reported as having been made on the normal date. The Bulletin also contains guidance relating to early payments around Christmas 2019, applying the same rule. What was described as a temporary "easement" for Christmas 2018 has been made permanent. The same should apply when a payment is not made on the normal payment date for any other reason. Those instructions have been repeated with general application in s.1.8 of HMRC *Guidance 2020 to 2021: Employer further guide to PAYE and National Insurance contributions* (CWG2, as updated on May 14, 2020 and available on the internet). What perhaps started as mere guidance has been firmed up into what are now very precise instructions.

Initially, it was considered that para.(2) established a rigid rule of attribution to the assessment period in which the HMRC information was received, that could only be displaced under the conditions in para.(3). That certainly was the assumption in *SSWP v RW (rule 17) (UC)* [2017] UKUT 347 (AAC), discussed below in relation to para.(3). The decision of the Divisional Court in *R. (Johnson and others) v Secretary of State for Work and Pensions* [2019] EWHC 23 (Admin) cast doubt on that assumption by rejecting the Secretary of State's interpretation of regs 54 and 61, relying on a mistaken interpretation of the phrase "on the basis of" (see the notes to reg.54). That doubt was removed by the Court of Appeal's decision to the contrary on appeal. However, the Secretary of State's appeal was not allowed, because the court found that it had been irrational for her not to have included some provision in the legislation to avoid the problems arising for the four monthly-paid claimants from the extremely odd results of applying the accepted interpretation to them. See the notes to reg.54 for a full discussion of the Court of Appeal's decision and the unanswered questions arising about its effect.

Thus, in the new para.(2), sub-para.(a) has the same meaning as above and the meaning of sub-para.(b) is plain and apparently absolute: if no information is received from HMRC in an assessment period the claimant's employed earnings are to be nil. However, although para.(2) is not expressly made subject to the rest of reg.61, in order to give the rest of the provision some practical operation, it must be regarded as subject not only to the exceptions in paras (3) and (4), but also to the discretionary powers in paras (5) to (7). Those powers must be able to treat a claimant as having employed earnings in an assessment period in which no information was received from HMRC.

NM v SSWP (UC) [2021] UKUT 46 (AAC) supplies a practical example of the operation of the basic rule in para.(2), on the pre-November 16, 2020 form of reg.61. The claimant ceased employment in September 2017 and claimed universal credit. In two assessment periods following the first under his award he received, after negotiation and conciliation, payments representing unpaid wages and holiday pay (the return of a deposit on his uniform did not count as earned income: see the notes to para.(3)(b) below). The employer reported the payments through the RTI system, apparently at the correct time. Judge Jacobs confirmed that there was no basis in any arguments of fairness to disapply the basic rule to the wages and holiday pay. Paragraph (3)(a) as it stood at the time could not apply because there was nothing to indicate that information from the employer was unlikely to be sufficiently accurate or timely. Paragraph (3)(b)(ii) as it then stood could not apply because the information received from HMRC was not incorrect. The information was correct as to the payments made, even though they should have been made earlier. The judge's statement in para.14 that "matters relating to the timing of the payment" were irrelevant to para.(3)(b)(ii) must not be taken out of context. It does not detract from the argument (see the notes to that provision in the 2020/21 edition of what was then Vol.V of this series, *Universal Credit* and to para.(3)(b) below) that if an employer reports a payment as having been made on a date that is not in accordance with HMRC guidance/instructions that renders the information received from HMRC incorrect (but contrast the words of the new para.(3)(b)).

The most recent example is *SK and DK v SSWP (UC)* [2023] UKUT 21 (AAC), reported as [2023] AACR 5, (see the notes to reg.55(4A) for the full details). There the claimant, who was on unpaid sick leave from his employer, received a bonus of £20,000 on May 20, 2020, within the assessment period running from April 29, 2020 to May 28, 2020 (AP 1). Under the PAYE system the employer deducted the amount of £6,893.60 for income tax before making the payment, which was reported to HMRC through the Real Time Information scheme. That was on the basis of a code issued by HMRC that was appropriate to a person regularly earning £20,000 a month over the whole tax year. Since that was not the case, on the claimant not receiving any further remuneration from his employer in subsequent months, under the PAYE system he received from the employer a "refund" of overpaid income tax of £2.144.60 in the assessment period running from May 29, 2020 to June 28, 2020 (AP 2) and further refunds in subsequent months. There was no dispute that the receipt of the net amount of the bonus in AP 1 resulted in a nil entitlement to universal credit, but the claimant appealed against the nil entitlement in AP 2 resulting from the taking into account of the £2,144.60. Among his arguments was that a repayment of income tax could only be treated as employed earnings under the conditions of reg.55(4A), which were not met as he was not in paid work in the tax year 2020/21. The First-tier Tribunal disallowed the appeal. On the further appeal Judge Ovey rejected the tribunal's reasoning but substituted her own decision to the same effect.

Having shown that reg.55(4) only applies to repayments of income tax made directly by HMRC to the taxpayer, not to in-year adjustments to tax to be deducted under PAYE, the judge convincingly shows that there was no alternative to taking the two payments into account as employed earnings under reg.61(2) in the assessment periods in which they were reported, giving this explanation:

> "47. For completeness, I add also that although it is convenient to speak in terms of a tax repayment or refund under the PAYE Regulations, there is a sense in

which that is not strictly what happens. In broad terms, the mechanism of the PAYE Regulations involves the payment by the employer to HMRC each month (or each quarter, in some cases) of the global amount payable for income tax by all its employees determined in accordance with their various tax codes. Tax codes may, however, be adjusted from time to time, with the result that the deduction made in respect of some employees may have been too high and the deduction made in respect of other employees may have been too low. The amount payable to HMRC in any month may reflect any adjustments which may be required to give effect to past over-deductions or under-deductions. Any repayment or refund is therefore likely to be achieved not by any payment by HMRC but by a set-off against the next month's liability.

48. It follows that when a claimant receives a tax refund through PAYE it may fairly be said that what is being received is a part of the remuneration earned which was held back for the purpose of meeting a tax liability but which is now being released. It is clearly entirely appropriate to treat such a payment as employed earnings..."

Paragraphs (3) and (4)

2.230 The new para.(3), establishing three exceptions from the para.(2) rules, is made non-discretionary. Then the first exception in the new sub-para.(a) is in substance the same as in the previous sub-para.(a) with some rejigging of language. The second exception in the new sub-para.(b) is the replacement of the previous sub-para.(b)(ii), but with significant changes. The exception now only applies if the amount of a payment reported to HMRC is incorrect or fails to reflect the definition of employed earnings in reg.55. Previously, the reference was to the information received from HMRC. The new sub-para.(c) is in substance the same as the previous sub-para.(b)(i), again with some slight rejigging of language.

Where one of the conditions in para.(3) is met the Secretary of State must determine the amount of employed earnings in accordance with reg.55 (on what count as employed earnings) and such information or evidence as the Secretary of State thinks fit (para.(4). The same must apply to a tribunal on appeal. The power granted by para.(4), although restricted to circumstances where one of the para.(3) exceptions applies and to the particular assessment period(s) affected by the exception, appears very open. It attracts the power in para.(7) to make such other adjustments as may be necessary to avoid duplication or to maintain a regular payment pattern. That would seem to entail a power to reallocate employed earnings to assessment periods other than those affected by the exception. But it is not clear whether such a power of reallocation was intended only to arise under paras (5) and (6), or whether the restrictions in those paragraphs can be sidestepped by the use of paras (3) and (4).

Sub-paragraph (a) applies where, in relation to a particular employment, the Secretary of State considers that the employer is unlikely to report information to HMRC in a sufficiently accurate or timely manner. The effect may thus operate over more than one assessment period. *NM* (above) confirms that the fact that the employer was making payments later than it should did not trigger the form of this exception then in force. It was the reporting of the information about payments that had to be unlikely to be inaccurate or timely. That point is made even clearer by the wording of the new form in sub-para.(a).

The conditions of the Northern Ireland equivalent of sub-para.(a) were found to be satisfied in *AF v DfC (UC)* [2023] NICom 18. The claimant was paid monthly, the due date apparently being the 24th of the month. Her assessment period ran from the 28th of one month to the 27th of the next. She was paid on July 24, 2020, but there was a delay in issuing a payslip until July 31, 2020 and that was the date on which the RTI report was made to HMRC and on to the DfC. Her August salary was paid on August 24, 2020 and reported on that date. The DfC, having apparently calculated the claimant's entitlement to UC for the assessment period ending on July 27, 2020 on the basis that no earned income was to be taken into account, calculated her entitlement for the assessment period ending on August 27, 2020 on the basis that the two payments were to be taken into account as earned income. The claimant's appeal against the decision on that assessment period was disallowed by the appeal tribunal without any reference in its statement of reasons to the equivalent of reg.61. Commissioner Stockman found that plainly to be an error of law, especially as there was evidence before the tribunal of the claimant having informed the DfC that the issue with a delayed payslip had occurred previously. On that evidence he substituted a decision applying the equivalent of sub-para.(a), finding that the information from the employer was manifestly not accurate or timely, and recalculating the claimant's entitlement for the assessment period ending on August 27, 2020 on the basis of actual receipt in that period only of the payment made on August 24, 2020. He did though note there would need to be an adjustment of entitlement for the assessment period ending on July 27, 2020, but the claimant would have the benefit of the work allowance in that period, that she would otherwise have lost. The Commissioner did not identify the power under which that adjustment could be made, but it would apparently lie in the power to revise for official error (GB Decisions and Appeals Regulations 2013, reg.9).

It is submitted that it was crucial to this decision that the issue had occurred before, so that a judgment could be made about the particular employment, not merely the particular assessment period. If the issue had arisen for the first time in relation to the payment due on July 24, 2020, it is submitted that there would have had to be consideration of para.(3)(b) in its pre-November 16, 2020 form. Your commentator's view is that that provision could have applied, but Commissioner Stockman has in other cases rejected that outcome (see below).

Sub-paragraph (b) applies where it appears to the Secretary of State that the amount of a payment reported to HMRC (by the employer) is incorrect or fails to reflect the definition of employed earnings in reg.55 in some material respect. By contrast, the old para.(3)(b)(ii) applied where the information received from HMRC was incorrect, or failed to reflect the definition of employed earnings, in some material respect. That appears to be a significant change.

It was argued in the notes to reg.61 in the 2020/21 edition of what was then Vol.V of this series, *Universal Credit*, that if an employer reported a payment as made on the actual date it was made instead of the date specified in HMRC guidance/instructions (i.e. the usual pay day) the information received from HMRC was incorrect in a material effect, so that a departure from the para.(2) rules was authorised. That argument seems no longer to hold, because the new sub-para.(b) only operates if the *amount* of the payment reported to HMRC is incorrect etc, not if the date reported is incorrect (but see new para.(5) below on reporting in the "wrong" assessment period).

It is still submitted that that argument has considerable force in relation to the pre-November 16, 2020 regulation, but it should be noted that it has attracted no judicial support. It was not mentioned in *SSWP v RW (rule 17) (UC)* [2017] UKUT 347 (AAC) (discussed below in relation to sub-para.(c)), where it could have been relevant, as suggested in the 2020/21 edition. Moreover, in *Johnson* in the Court of Appeal at para.44, Rose LJ rejected the claimants' argument that they could rely on reg.61(3), apparently in the form of sub-para.(b)(ii) as then in force.

Further, the argument was explicitly rejected by Commissioner Stockman in the Northern Ireland case of *DfC v OS (UC)* [2022] NICom 29. There, the claimant's last day of work was November 9, 2018. He claimed universal credit on November 19, 2018. In the assessment period ending on December 18, 2018 he received payments relating to his work down to November 9. Although the DfC appeared not to have identified the amounts accurately in its initial decision, it was agreed before the Commissioner that the relevant payments were a payment of £404.34 in final wages on November 23 and a payment of £225.52 in accrued holiday pay on November 30. Those amounts were apparently reported by the employer through RTI on those dates. The appeal tribunal erroneously applied the post-November 16, 2020 form of the equivalent of reg.61 (which of course was not in force at the relevant time) in holding that no payments fell to be attributed to the assessment period ending on December 18, because the payments were not *for* that assessment period. It was agreed on the DfC's appeal that the tribunal's decision should be set aside for applying the wrong legislation and that the Commissioner should substitute a decision on the underlying appeal. The argument made for the claimant was that he had been entitled to be made the two payments on November 16 (presumably as the next normal or contractual pay-day) and that in accordance with the PAYE legislation and HMRC guidance pay should be recorded on the date on which the employee is entitled to be paid. Therefore, the information provided by HMRC (presumably) on November 23 and/or 30 was incorrect in a material respect because the payment date should have been November 16.

The Commissioner rejected that argument, though finding some force in it. He considered that the key word in issue was "incorrect" and continued in para.35:

> "The term 'incorrect', when applied to information, it appears to me, has the meaning of being inaccurate or being wrong. I can find no authority for construing the expression 'the information received from HMRC is incorrect … in some material respect' to encompass the situation where otherwise accurate information is not recorded on the correct date. There may well be a legitimate expectation that information should be provided on a particular date under legislation and guidance. A failure to do so may well be an incorrect application of the relevant PAYE rules. However, in the absence of persuasive authority, I cannot hold that this procedural failing renders the information 'incorrect' when it amounts to accurate information being provided at the wrong date."

It is submitted that "incorrect" was not the sole key word, but that the word "information" was of equal significance and that the payment date included in the RTI information received from HMRC could be regarded as inaccurate or wrong if the identification of the date did not follow HMRC instructions. Nor is it clear how the absence of existing persuasive authority was relevant to construing the meaning of the relevant provision. In other cases, even under the current form of reg.61, there may be difficult issues following the ending of employment about when particular payments are due to be made and how that fits in with PAYE and RTI reporting obligations.

In *Johnson*, Ms Barrett and Ms Stewart were usually paid on the 28th of each month). Their assessment periods ran from the 28th of one month to the 27th of the next. When the 28th was a non-banking day (Saturday, Sunday or bank holiday) they were paid on last working day before the 28th and their employers reported the date of actual payment on their Full Payment Submission. Rose LJ said that there was nothing inaccurate or untimely in the information provided by the employers to HMRC and the DWP. However, as she noted at para.86, HMRC guidance/instructions (or what was called an "easement" in relation to Easter 2019) had been from at least 2018 to report payment on the usual pay day. There is therefore some doubt whether those instructions were in effect at the date of the decisions challenged in *Johnson* and, if so, how strong the instructions/guidance was. However, the court was considering a continuing failure to make legislative provision for the specific problem of monthly-paid claimants with assessment periods ending near the end of the month and it was clear from the limited evidence it had that HMRC were from 2018 or 2019 telling employers that that was how they were to report payment dates. Rose LJ then failed to connect up that evidence with her conclusion in para.44 in a way that must undermine the force of that conclusion. Surely, doing no more than applying the everyday meaning of "incorrect", it must be arguable that where the employer has failed to follow HMRC instructions the information passed on to the DWP is incorrect in a material respect under old sub-para.(b)(ii). That would, as explained in more detail below, have allowed the Secretary of State or a tribunal on appeal to treat earnings actually received on one date as received on the usual pay day, if that resulted in it counting in a later assessment period (para.(5) of the old reg.61).

A practical problem would have been whether the DWP was able to identify that information was incorrect in the sense above from what was sent to it from HMRC or whether claimants would need to alert the DWP to the occurrence of a shift.

Note that the argument above would appear not to have been of assistance to claimants who, like Ms Johnson and Ms Woods, are usually paid on the last working day of the month. That is because, if the "non-banking day salary shift" occurs, it would merely identify what is the last working day of the month and the date of actual payment would be correctly reported by the employer as the usual pay day. It could possibly help some claimants like those in *Pantellerisco v Secretary of State for Work and Pensions* [2021] EWCA Civ 1454; [2021] P.T.S.R. 1922 (see the notes to reg.54 for the details) who are paid four-weekly, but only in very occasional circumstances (say where payment on a Thursday instead of a bank holiday Friday would take a payment into a different assessment period).

NM v SSWP (UC) [2021] UKUT 46 (AAC) supplies an example of information not reflecting the definition of employed earnings in reg.55. The employer's report to HMRC included the amount of a deposit paid by the claimant for his uniform as a security guard that was returned to him after his employment ended. That was not employed earnings within s.62 of ITEPA, so not within reg.55. Therefore, the information did not reflect the definition and the amount was not to be included under reg.61.

Sub-paragraph (c) applies where no information is received from HMRC in an assessment period and it is likely that that is because of a failure to report information (to HMRC), including failures of computer systems, including those of HMRC. This is a rather specialised provision. Presumably, the "failure" refers mainly to an employer's non-fulfilment of the duty under reg.67B of the PAYE Regulations, mentioned above, and does not require any fault, merely an absence of that duty having been carried out. Thus the inclusion of a failure of HMRC's own computer systems seems to be an extension.

In *SSWP v RW (rule 17) (UC)* [2017] UKUT 347 (AAC), the Secretary of State's submission to the Upper Tribunal supported the application of the equivalent of sub-para.(c) (para.(3)(b)(i) of the old reg.61) in a way that appears wrong. HMRC's real time earnings feed showed notification on two dates in February 2016 (February 1, 2016 and February 29, 2016) of the claimant having received earnings. Her assessment period ran from the first of each calendar month to the last day of that month. Both receipts were taken into account in relation to February 2016, resulting in a much reduced universal credit entitlement. The claimant's case on appeal was that her January 2016 earnings were received on Sunday January 31, 2016, but not reported by her employer until the next day (as apparently confirmed in HMRC documents). She had no control over when the earnings information was reported. The First-tier Tribunal, in allowing the appeal and altering the assessment of entitlement for the February 2016 assessment period by removing the payment actually made on January 31, rejected the Secretary of State's argument at that stage that para.(3) did not justify any departure from the basic rule in para.(2)(a). The tribunal relied on two alternative reasons that the Secretary of State challenged on appeal to the Upper Tribunal. On receipt of detailed directions from Judge Wright, the Secretary of State applied to withdraw the appeal, saying that it had been concluded that the case could be brought within para.(3)(b)(i) of the old reg.61 on the basis that reporting a payment by an employer after the date on which it was actually made can be considered a failure by the employer. In the light of that explanation, Judge Wright consented to the withdrawal of the appeal. He directed that his decision recording that withdrawal, although it determined none of the issues involved, go onto the AAC website as the Secretary of State's reasoning might be relevant in other cases.

However, the reliance on para.(3)(b)(i) of the old reg.61 in relation to the January 2016 assessment period, even if justified, appears to have been a red herring. Paragraph (3)(b) applied in respect of a particular assessment period. If no information was received from HMRC because of a failure by the employer that could only have affected entitlement in the January 2016 assessment period and not entitlement in the February 2016 assessment period. It appears that the tribunal altered the amount of entitlement for the February 2016 assessment period and it is not clear what, if any, adjustment was made in relation to the January 2016 assessment period. Further, it appears a more natural reading of para.(3)(b)(i) that it applied only where no information had been received from HMRC by the date on which a decision is made about a particular assessment period, not where information has been received by that date but it involved some late recording of receipts. Thus the reason for the Secretary of State's support of the tribunal's decision in relation to the February 2016 assessment period appears flawed.

The result might possibly have been different under the new form of reg.61. Sub-paragraph (c) now makes it clearer that it applies when no information has been received from HMRC "in an assessment period", making the crucial time the end of each assessment period. So, "in" the January 2016 assessment period, no information was received from HMRC. That would release the power in para.(4) to adjust the amount of employed earnings to be attributed to that assessment period by adding the payment made on January 31, 2016, despite the existence of para.(2)(b) (see the notes to paras (2) and (5)). But crucially, the new power in para.(7) to make consequential adjustments would allow the removal of that payment from the assessment for the February 2016 assessment period. That would "avoid duplication". And even if sub-para.(c) did not apply, the situation in *RW* would appear to fall within the new para.(5), the January 31, 2016 payment having been reported to HMRC late, or possibly in the wrong assessment period (see below). That would specifically allow that payment to be treated as employed earnings in the assessment period in which it was received.

Paragraph (5)

2.231 The new para.(5) is the first major departure from the previous structure, although it seems to have limited effect. It gives the Secretary of State (and thus a tribunal on appeal) discretion, where a payment has been reported late or in the wrong assessment period, to treat the payment as employed earnings in the assessment period in which it was received. In the context, "reported" must mean reported to HMRC under the RTI system. Paragraph (5) applies whatever the usual pay interval; it is not restricted to those, like the *Johnson* claimants, who are paid monthly. However, it cannot solve the systemic problem identified in *Pantellerisco* (above) for those paid four-weekly of there inevitably being one assessment period each year containing two usual pay-days, which was left unadjusted by that litigation.

The power given by para.(5) is limited to treating a payment as part of employed earnings in the assessment period in which it was received. That would assist in equivalent circumstances to those *RW* (see immediately above). Paragraph (5) does not in itself authorise any more extensive reallocation. For instance, take a claimant with an assessment period running from the 28th of one month to the 27th of the next, who is usually paid on the 28th of the month and is paid their December salary on December 23. If the employer, say because office systems were down over the period, did not report the payment through the RTI system until January 3, that would appear to fall within the "late report" category. But para.(5) would only allow the payment to be allocated to the assessment period including December 23, i.e. the same assessment period to which the payment received as usual on November 28 would have been allocated. For the payment to be allocated to the assessment period beginning on December 28, to avoid the *Johnson* irrationality, there would apparently have to be recourse to para.(6), with its limitation to those paid on a regular monthly basis. But the operation of para.(5) brings in the general power to make any "other adjustments" in new para.(7), which might open up the possibility of reallocation to an assessment period other than that of receipt and of application to claimants paid otherwise than monthly. But what then would have been the point of the restriction in effect in para.(5)?

Presumably, para.(5) is not made expressly subject to para.(6) because both provisions are discretionary, thus allowing the Secretary of State and tribunals to apply whichever is more appropriate, as the justice of the case requires. But para.(6) only applies to claimants who are paid on a regular monthly basis, not to claimants paid at any other intervals. Although para.(2)(b), requiring the taking of employed earnings to be nil in respect of any assessment period in which no information is received by the DWP from HMRC, has not been made expressly subject to paras (5) to (7), that result must presumably follow in order to allow those provisions to operate (see the notes to para.(2) above).

It is no doubt easy enough to identify when a report to HMRC is made late, but what is meant by a report being made "in the wrong assessment period" remains obscure. Presumably, it covers only an assessment period other than that in which the report ought to have been made in accordance with HMRC guidance/instructions, rather than wrongness in any wider sense. But if the report is made after the "right" assessment period, the case would appear already to be covered by the lateness provision. Possibly, there could be some independent operation if the report was made before the "right" assessment period, but there would still be the limitation as to the date to which the payment can be allocated, subject to the possible application of para.(7). There is no guidance as to the meaning of "the wrong assessment period" or example of the application of the rule in Memo ADM 27/20.

Paragraph (6)

The new para.(6) is the main provision designed to deal with the problem identified by the Court of Appeal in *Johnson*. It is restricted to employees paid on a regular monthly (calendar monthly: Interpretation Act 1978 Sch.1) basis. That formula, including the word "basis", must entail that the scope is not restricted to those usually paid on the same day each month, so long as their pay is calculated per month and they are paid a month at a time. Then, if more than one payment is reported (to HMRC) in any one assessment period, the Secretary of State and a tribunal on appeal may, for the purposes of maintaining a regular pattern, allocate one (but only one) of those payments to a different assessment period, either earlier or later. The discretion, particularly in conjunction with the general power in new para.(7) to make any other adjustments, is fairly open, so long as a purpose (main purpose?) is to maintain a regular pattern (of allocation of monthly payments). Although para.(2)(b), requiring the taking of employed earnings to be nil in respect of any assessment period in which no information is received by the DWP from HMRC, has not been made expressly subject to paras (5) and (6), that result must presumably follow in order to allow those provisions to operate (see the notes to para.(2) above). 2.232

See the note to para.(5) above for an example of how para.(6) might be applied. Note that it is not necessary for a report to have been made to HMRC on any wrong date or that there has been a "non-banking day salary shift" in the strictest sense. All that is necessary is that more than one payment has been reported for a monthly-paid claimant in the same assessment period. If the pattern of usual payment on the last working day of the month produces that result, reporting on the two usual pay-days will have been in accordance with HMRC guidance/instructions and there will not have been a "shift" in the sense of a departure from the usual pay-day, but para.(6) can be applied. It might just be that payments other than monthly salary could trigger the potential application of para.(6), for instance if a claimant received a bonus or a reimbursement of non-allowable expenses on a different date from the usual monthly pay-day. But in such a case, there would be no need to exercise the discretion to reallocate such a payment.

Paragraph (7)

The effect of the power in the new para.(7) to make other adjustments in the calculation of employed earnings has been discussed in the notes to paras (4)–(6) above. 2.233

Right of appeal

2.234 The previous para.(6), apparently giving a power to make adjustments where decisions are made under reg.41(3) of the Decisions and Appeals Regulations 2013, arguably unnecessarily, has not been reproduced in the new form of reg.61, but a footnote to the preamble to SI 2020/1138 does refer to reg.41(1) and to s.159D(1)(b)(vi) of the SSAA 1992 (effect of alterations affecting universal credit). Under the latter provision (for which see Vol.III of this series) an alteration (i.e., an increase or decrease) in the amount of a claimant's employed earnings as a result of information provided to the Secretary of State by HMRC takes effect without any further decision by the Secretary of State. However, if the claimant disputes the figure used in accordance with reg.55 to calculate their employed earnings in any assessment period, they can ask the Secretary of State to give a decision in relation to that assessment period (which must be given within 14 days of the request, or as soon as practicable thereafter).

The point of that provision might appear to be to give the claimant a right of appeal, but there are obstacles to such a conclusion in the unnecessary obscurities in the chain of legislation involved. Paragraph 6(b)(v) of Sch.2 to the SSA 1998 (Pt I of this volume) provides that no appeal lies against a decision as to the amount of benefit to which a person is entitled where the amount is determined by an alteration of a kind referred to in s.159D(1)(b) of the SSAA. Thus, even though the alteration is given effect through a Secretary of State's decision, rather than without such a decision as in the general application of s.159D, at first sight there can be no appeal against the decision. It would appear that para.6(b)(v) applies as much to a decision removing entitlement entirely as well as to one reducing the amount of entitlement. The claimant would then be restricted to applying for revision on the "any time" ground in reg.10(a) of the Decisions and Appeals Regulations 2013 (with consequently no right of appeal if unsuccessful) or to an application for judicial review.

However, that effect would arguably be inconsistent with art.6 of the ECHR (fair trial) under the Human Rights Act 1998, on the basis that revision or judicial review would not be adequate alternatives to a right to appeal. There would then be an obligation under s.3 to interpret legislation in a way compatible with ECHR rights. It is possible to interpret the phrase "an alteration of a kind referred to" in s.159D(1)(b) of the SSAA 1992 as used in para.6(b) of Sch.2 to the SSA 1998 as only applying to an alteration that is not merely referred to in s.159D(1)(b) but is not subject to any exception or condition that requires a decision to be given by the Secretary of State. Subsection (1) of s.159D makes its effect subject to such exceptions and conditions as may be prescribed. Regulation 41(3) of the Decisions and Appeals Regulations 2013 may legitimately be regarded as such an exception or condition. Thus, if the process under reg.41(3) leads to the giving of a decision by the Secretary of State, para.6(b) can be interpreted as not standing in the way of there being a right of appeal in the normal way.

That interpretation of para.6(b) of Sch.2 to the SSA 1998 could also lessen, but not completely remove, the adverse consequences of the wider effect of s.159D(1)(b) of the SSAA 1992. Section 159D(1)(b) on alterations to existing awards of universal credit applies to a much wider range of circumstances than the equivalent provisions for other benefits. In addition to alterations in the statutory rates of universal credit or of new style ESA or JSA or other benefit income, head (iii) applies to an alteration in any amount to be deducted in respect of earned income under s.8(3)(a) of the WRA 2012. "Earned income", in accordance with reg.52, covers not just employed earnings, but also remuneration or profit derived from a trade, profit or vocation (i.e. self-employed earnings) or from any other paid work. Thus the prohibition in para.6(b)(v) of Sch.2 would appear to have applied to the circumstances covered by reg.41 even if those circumstances had not been prescribed for the purposes of s.159D(1)(b)(vi). Further, and more seriously, the prohibition on its face extends to any decision on an existing award turning on an alteration for any reason in the amount of any kind of earned income (all of which fall to be deducted from the maximum amount of universal credit under s.8(3)(a)). There is some doubt whether reg.41(3) of the Decisions and Appeals Regulations, establishing the exception from or condition relating to s.159D(1)(b) applies only in relation to cases where there is a dispute under reg.61(6) about the information provided by HMRC and not to other disputes about the amount of employed earnings. Does reg.41(3) only operate as a qualification to reg.41(1) on s.159D(b)(vi) cases or does it have a stand-alone operation on its own terms, which could then apply to any dispute about the amount of employed earnings? The obligation under s.3 of the Human Rights Act 1998 to interpret legislation so as to be compatible with ECHR rights would probably lead to the second alternative being adopted, protecting the right of appeal in those cases. However, can the terms of reg.41(3), with the express reference to reg.55 of the Universal Credit Regulations and employed earnings, possibly be interpreted as also applying to the other forms of earned income that count under s.8(3)(a) of the WRA 2012, i.e. self-employed earnings, other paid work and, it appears, notional earned income (see reg.52)? That would arguably entail the addition or substitution of too many words changing the substance of the provision to be considered part of any legitimate process of interpretation. If reg.41(3) is thus restricted to employed earnings, there is nothing to prevent the operation of s.159D(1)(b)(iii) and para.6(b) in requiring alterations in amounts of self-employed earnings, other paid work and notional earned incomes to take effect without any Secretary of State decision and therefore without anything to appeal against. If that outcome would be considered to entail an inconsistency with art.6 (fair trial) of the ECHR, then the argument at the level of the First-tier or Upper Tribunal would probably have to be that the terms of the secondary legislation cannot be allowed to stand in the way of the provision of a fair trial in any individual case, without seeking to say how the defect in the legislation should be remedied generally.

See also para.22 of Sch.1 to the Decisions and Appeals Regulations 2013 which provides that a supersession decision made where a claimant's employed earnings have reduced and they have provided the information for the purpose of calculating those earnings at the times required by the Secretary of State takes effect from the first day of the assessment period in which that change occurred.

Gainful self-employment

[[1]Minimum income floor

62.—(1) This regulation applies to a claimant who— 2.235

(a) is in gainful self-employment (see regulation 64); and

(b) would, apart from this regulation [[4]or regulation 90], fall within section 22 of the Act (claimants subject to all work-related requirements).

(2) Where this regulation applies to a single claimant, for any assessment period in respect of which the claimant's earned income is less than their individual threshold, the claimant is to be treated as having earned income equal to that threshold.

(3) Where this regulation applies to a claimant who is a member of a couple, for any assessment period in respect of which—

(a) the claimant's earned income is less than their individual threshold; and

(b) the couple's combined earned income is less than the couple threshold,

the claimant is to be treated as having earned income equal to their individual threshold minus any amount by which that amount of earned income combined with their partner's earned income would exceed the couple threshold.

(4) In this regulation, references to the claimant's individual threshold and to the couple threshold are to the amounts set out in regulation 90(2) and 90(3) respectively, converted to net [2 . . .] amounts by—

(a) [2 . . .]

(b) deducting such amount for income tax and national insurance contributions as the Secretary of State considers appropriate.

[3(4A) Where this regulation applies in respect of an assessment period in which surplus earnings are treated as an amount of earned income under regulation 54A (surplus earnings), that amount is to be added to the claimant's earned income before this regulation is applied and, in the case of joint claimants, it is to be added to the earned income of either member of the couple so as to produce the lowest possible amount of combined earned income after this regulation is applied.]

(5) An assessment period referred to in this regulation does not include an assessment period which falls wholly within a start-up period or begins or ends in a start-up period.]

AMENDMENTS

1. Universal Credit and Miscellaneous Amendments (No.2) Regulations 2014 (SI 2014/2888) reg.4(5) (November 26, 2014, or in the case of existing awards, the first assessment period beginning on or after November 26, 2014).

2. Universal Credit and Miscellaneous Amendments Regulations 2015 (SI 2015/1754) reg.2(5) (November 4, 2015, or in the case of existing awards, the first assessment period beginning on or after November 4, 2015).

3. Universal Credit (Surpluses and Self-employed Losses) (Digital Service) Amendment Regulations 2015 (SI 2015/345) reg.2(3) (April 11, 2018).

4. Universal Credit (Childcare Costs and Minimum Income Floor) (Amendment) Regulations 2019 (SI 2019/1249) reg.3 (October 3, 2019).

DEFINITIONS

"assessment period"—see WRA 2012, ss.40 and 7(2) and reg.21.
"claimant"—see WRA 2012, s.40.
"couple"—see WRA 2012, ss.39 and 40.
"earned income"—see reg.52.
"gainful self-employment"—see regs 53(1) and 64.
"individual threshold"—see regs 2 and 90(2).
"joint claimants"—see WRA 2012 s.40.
"national insurance contribution"—see reg.2.
"start-up period"—see regs 53(1) and 63.
"work-related requirement"—see WRA 2012, ss.40 and 13(2).

GENERAL NOTE

Temporary coronavirus provisions

2.236 The last of the temporary coronavirus provisions relevant to the minimum income floor expired on July 31, 2022. See previous editions of this volume for the details.

2.237 This regulation, authorised by para.4(1), (3)(a) and (4) of Sch.1 to the WRA 2012, provides for the "minimum income floor" which applies to certain self-employed claimants and deems them to be receiving that level of income although their actual earnings from self-employment, plus other earned income, if any, are lower. It is an anti-abuse provision which was presumably introduced partly because of the difficulties of checking the hours of work and takings of the self-employed and partly to provide an incentive against sitting back in unproductive self-employment while relying on universal credit to make up income. The operation of the rule has been considerably affected from April 2018 by the operation of the provisions in reg.54A for spreading surplus earnings and in regs 57(2) and 57A on unused losses in self-employment.

A judicial review challenge to the general operation of reg.62, based on alleged differences in treatment of the self-employed and employed earners was rejected by the Administrative Court (Laing J) in *R. (on the application of Parkin) v Secretary of State for Work and Pensions* [2019] EWHC 2356 (Admin).

Ms Parkin had worked in the theatre as a self-employed person for some years before she claimed universal credit in 2017. Her profits in the 2017/18 tax year were £2,306 and in 2018/19 £2,842.24. She also had some earnings as an employee. A minimum income floor (MIF) of £861.11 per month was applied to her on the basis that she was in gainful self-employment within the meaning of reg.64. Her appeal against that on the ground that she was not in gainful self-employment was refused by a First-tier Tribunal in May 2019. Over the 20 months of her universal credit award down to June 2019 she received £5,318.65 less in universal credit for herself and the one child included in the award than if she had been employed with equivalent earnings and £610.86 less than if she had not been employed at all.

The first ground of Ms Parkin's judicial review challenge to the effect of reg.62 was that there was a breach of art.14 of the ECHR. Laing J accepted that art.8 (respect for family life) and probably art.1 of Protocol 1 (protection of property) was engaged and that there was a difference in treatment between self-employed and employed earners. However, she held that the self-employed and employed earners were not in relevantly analogous circumstances and that, even if that was wrong, the difference in treatment was not manifestly without reasonable foundation and so was justified. The essence of her reasoning appears in paras 103, 107 and 108 of the judgment:

> "103. It is clear that one of the intentions of the statutory scheme is to make work pay, and to encourage claimants to do more productive activities in order to encourage them, over time, to reduce their reliance on benefits. The practical effects of the legal distinctions between the two groups mean that a work requirement imposed on an employee has an immediate, predictable and measurable effect. There is no directly effective practical equivalent in the case of a self-employed claimant. If Parliament and the executive wanted to achieve the aims I have described in the case of self-employed claimants, a different mechanism had to be designed in order to influence their behaviour. I therefore consider that employed and self-employed claimants are not in relevantly analogous situations for the purposes of this scheme. I also consider, for that reason, that I can, and should, conclude at this stage of the analysis that this part of the claim fails.
>
> 107. The question then is whether the MIF, in particular, because it applies to [gainfully self-employed] claimants and not to employed or unemployed claimants, is [manifestly without reasonable foundation]. As I have said in paragraph 103, above, a work requirement and an [individual threshold] amount to a practical and objective tool for influencing the behaviour of employed claimants. Their combined effects are visible and can be measured. The differences between claimants which flow from their decisions to be employed or self-employed mean that a work requirement and an [individual threshold] cannot produce the same effects for self-employed claimants. The imposition of a work requirement on a self-employed claimant would not necessarily make his business more profitable, which is what is at issue.
>
> 108. The MIF, however, is such a mechanism. Its effect coheres with the aims I have described, because it encourages self-employed claimants who are in [gainful self-employment] and who wish to claim UC, but whose enterprises consistently generate low profits, to think carefully about whether they should continue to

be in [gainful self-employment]. The MIF encourages such thought because its effect is to treat a self-employed claimant as generating profits equivalent to what he would earn from employment at the [national minimum wage], whether or not he in fact generates such profits. It encourages a rational claimant in that position to ask whether continuing in [gainful self-employment] is in his own best interests, and whether he should take up employment instead, or change the balance of his activities between self-employment and employment so that, while continuing to be self-employed, self-employment is no longer his main employment, with the result that he would cease to be in [gainful self-employment] for the purposes of the scheme, and be subject to work requirements instead."

The same reasoning supported the rejection of the argument that the MIF regulations were irrational at common law. There had also been compliance with s.149 of the Equality Act 2010 by reference to the impact of the universal credit scheme as a whole.

It may be arguable that the judge's suggestions about how a claimant could alter the balance between employment and self-employment, so that self-employment would no longer be the main employment and therefore fall outside the meaning of gainful self-employment (see further in the notes to reg.64) and the reach of the MIF, are not entirely realistic. However, that would probably not be enough to undermine the reasoning completely. Note that self-employment falls outside the meaning of gainful self-employment if there is not an expectation of profit.

A new form of reg.62 was introduced on November 26, 2014 in order to make "clearer provision about the calculation of the MIF [minimum income floor] when a self-employed person is a member of a couple (or when both members of a couple are self-employed)" (see the Explanatory Memorandum which accompanies SI 2014/2888). It is a distinct improvement on the previous form of reg.62. However, some confusion still remains, partly because the phrase "individual threshold" as used in reg.62 does not have quite the same meaning as that phrase in reg.90, even though reg.62(4) cross-refers to reg.90. This is because under para.(4)(b) of this regulation "appropriate" deductions for income tax and NI contributions may be made when calculating a claimant's individual threshold, which is not the case under reg.90 (see below).

There was a further amendment, said to implement the original policy intention, with effect from October 3, 2019. In the condition in para.(1)(b) for the application of the MIF that the claimant would be subject to all work-related requirements, not only is the effect of reg.62 itself to be ignored but also the effect of reg.90 on earnings thresholds. See the notes below on *Would be subject to all work-related requirements*.

Regulation 62 will only apply if in any assessment period a claimant

- is in "gainful self-employment" (as defined in reg.64) (para.(1)(a)); *and*
- is not in a "start-up period" (see reg.63) (para. (5)); *and*
- would, apart from this regulation, fall within s.22 WRA 2012 (claimant subject to all work-related requirements) (para.(1)(b)); *and*
- in the case of a single claimant, their self-employed earnings, together with any other earned income (as defined in reg.52), are below their individual threshold (para.(2)); *or*

  in the case of a couple, their self-employed earnings, together with any other earned income, are below their individual threshold, and the couple's combined earned income is below the couple threshold (para.(3)).

If all four of those conditions are met then claimants are deemed to have earned income equal to the threshold even though their actual earned income is lower.

Gainful self-employment

For what might or might not count as gainful self-employment, see the notes to reg.64. The conditions in reg.64 go a good way beyond the simple issue of whether the activity is carried on in the expectation of gain and must be carefully considered. In particular, the trade, profession or vocation must be the claimant's main employment and must be organised, developed and regular. 2.238

Not in start-up period

See the notes to reg.63 for what is a start-up period and how long it can last. In brief, following the September 26, 2020 amendment to reg.63, it can start where a claimant who is in gainful self-employment has not previously been subject to the MIF in relation to the trade, profession or vocation that is now the main employment and is taking active steps to increase the earnings from that self-employment to the level of the individual threshold. Then the period lasts for 12 months starting with that assessment period unless the claimant ceases to be in gainful self-employment or ceases to take the active steps to increase earnings. 2.239

Would be subject to all work-related requirements

The requirement that the claimant would, apart from the operation of the MIF or reg.90, fall within s.22 of the WRA 2012 and thus not be exempted from the imposition of any work-related requirement adds an important limitation, that must not be overlooked in a focus on the level of earned income in the particular assessment period (see further below). The final condition is that the claimant or claimants' earned income is below the reg.62 individual or couple threshold as appropriate. 2.240

It must, because of the third condition (in para.(1)(b)), be asked in all cases whether some provision in or under ss.19—22 exempts the claimant from one or more work-related requirements. For example, if a claimant is found to have limited capability for work and work-related activity (WRA, s.19(2)(a)) or limited capability for work (s.21(1)(a)) or is unfit for work within the conditions contained in reg.99, the MIF cannot apply. Further, prior to October 3, 2019 the operation of reg.90 needed to be considered. As discussed below, this provision exempts claimants from all work-related requirements if their monthly earnings before any deduction for income tax, national insurance contributions or relievable pension contributions (reg.90(6)(a)) at least equal their individual threshold under reg.90(2), called the conditionality earnings threshold. In the great majority of cases anyone with earnings at that level would not fall within the scope of reg.62, but it should be noted that reg.90(6)(b) requires, in cases where earned income fluctuates or is likely to fluctuate, a monthly averaging over any identifiable cycle or otherwise over three months or such other period as may enable the average to be determined more accurately. That can apply to earnings from employment or other paid work as well as to earnings from self-employment. However, it is in the nature of self-employment in particular that earned income (i.e. actual receipts less allowable expenses in each assessment period) will fluctuate month by month, even in businesses that are well established and large scale. Thus if in a particular assessment period the amount of a claimant's earned income fell below the reg.62 individual threshold it could not immediately be assumed that the MIF would apply. The monthly average could at least equal the reg.90 individual threshold (the conditionality earnings threshold) so that the claimant remained exempted from all work-related requirements.

The position changed with the October 2019 amendment so that if a claimant is only exempted from work-related requirements through the operation of reg.90 that does not prevent the application of the MIF. The change was said by the DWP to restore the original policy intention and was explained in the Explanatory Memorandum as follows:

> "7.9 [The amendment is] to make clear that a reference to a claimant in the All Work Related Requirements conditionality group includes those who are exempt from the requirement to look for work only because their earnings exceed the Conditionality Earnings Threshold.

> 7.10 The Conditionality Earnings Threshold is only relevant to employed claimants and, as such, has no role in the application of the Minimum Income Floor. For example, a claimant could meet the Conditionality Earnings Threshold as a result of average earnings over a period of time if they are an employed earner. However, self-employed universal credit claimants are expected to plan for fluctuations in income in the same way as all other self-employed people must do and which is part of running a sustainable business. Gainfully self-employed claimants are expected to earn at or above the set assumed level in each assessment period and, where earnings fall short of this, the Minimum Income Floor is applied."

If the Explanatory Memorandum intended to suggest that reg.90 only applies to employed earners, that is incorrect. "Earned income" is plainly defined in reg.52 to cover both earnings derived from a contract of service or office and earnings derived from self-employment. So the suggestion must have been more that the mechanism of reg.90 was inadequate in itself to apply the appropriate pressure to self-employed claimants either to abandon unproductive self-employment or to make it more productive. That may be debateable, but what is clear is that the amendment has from October 2019 onwards rendered redundant the discussion above of whether the averaging provision in reg.90(6) might prevent the application of the MIF in an assessment period in which earnings fell below the MIF.

The reference in para.(1)(b) to "apart from this regulation" is necessary because of reg.90(5), which exempts any claimant who is treated by reg.62 as having earned income from all work-related requirements (by putting them within s.19 of the WRA 2012). If it were not for that qualification there would be an endless loop by which application of the MIF led to the conditions for its application not being met. The effect of reg.90(5) should not, though, be forgotten while the MIF is in operation.

Actual earned income below individual or couple's threshold

2.241 Although "earned income" is defined in reg.52(a) merely in terms of the remuneration or profits derived from employment, self-employment or other paid work, it would seem that paras (2) and (3) must be taken as referring to the amount of earned income to be taken into account for universal credit purposes, thus requiring the deduction of income tax, national insurance contributions and relievable pension contributions (employed earnings: reg.55(5) (plus payroll giving); self-employed earnings: reg.57(2)). But note that under para.(4)(b) there is no power to deduct relievable pension contributions or payroll giving from the individual or couple threshold. Claimants who made large pension contributions might therefore have particular need of the possibility that the MIF does not apply because they are exempted from all work-related requirement under reg.90. Although the MIF cannot apply unless the self-employment is the claimant's main employment, employed earnings or income from other paid work may come into the calculation, especially in the case of joint claimants.

Paragraph (4A), in effect from April 2018, confirms that where surplus earnings calculated under reg.54A are to be applied in any assessment period they are to be taken into account as part of claimants' earned income for reg.62 purposes. If the surplus earnings are sufficient on their own to wipe out entitlement to universal credit that consequence does not matter. If the surplus earnings on their own do not have that effect, then they may, depending on their level, help lift earned income up to the individual or couple threshold, so that MIF does not apply and actual earnings plus surplus earnings are taken against the maximum amount of universal credit. Income deemed to exist by reg.62 does not count in the calculation of surplus earnings under reg.54A (reg.54A(5)). The April 2018 provision on unused losses for the self-employed (reg.57A) may work in the opposite direction. Unused losses (unused in the sense that a claimant's self-employed earnings to be counted against the maximum amount in the assessment period in which received cannot be less than nil) from any past assessment period can now operate to reduce the amount of self-employed earnings as calculated under reg.57(2). That could have the effect of taking the amount of earned income in the current assessment period below the individual or couple threshold and triggering the application of the MIF when it would not be triggered on the current earnings. The fairness entailed in the operation of reg.57A on its own would be impaired by that. Fluctuations in earnings, and in particular the new taking into account of fluctuations in terms of past losses by the self-employed, are likely to have unpredictable, and sometimes harsh effects, on the application of the MIF.

Some claimants might think of forming limited companies of which they are the sole or main employee and director in order to pursue the business that would otherwise have been the trade, profession or vocation followed as a self-employed person, aiming not to be self-employed at all and so free of the MIF rules. In most cases, that does not work because of the effect of reg.77(3)(b) and (c). Where a person stands in a position analogous to that of a sole trader or partner in relation to a company carrying on a trade or a property business the company's income or the claimant's share of it is to be treated as the claimant's income and calculated under reg.57 as if it were self-employed earnings and, if the claimant's activities in the course of the trade are their main employment, reg.62 is to apply. See the notes to regs 57 and 77 for some complications and the limited exceptions in reg.77(5).

For a claimant's individual threshold for the purposes of reg.62, the starting point is reg.90(2). This provides that a claimant's individual threshold, known administratively as the conditionality earnings threshold, is the hourly rate of the national minimum wage for a claimant of that age multiplied by, in the case of a claimant who would otherwise be subject to all work-related requirements under s.22 of the WRA 2012, the expected number of hours per week (starting point 35, see reg.88). In the case of a claimant who would otherwise fall within ss.20 or 21, the multiplier is 16. That can be relevant when one of joint claimants is subject to all work-related requirements, but their partner is not (see below for couples). This amount is then multiplied by 52 and divided by 12 (to make it monthly), from which is deducted "such amount for income tax and national insurance contributions as the Secretary of State considers appropriate" (para.(4)). Presumably this will normally be the amount for income tax and NI contributions that would be payable if the claimant's actual earned income was at this level but para.(4)(b) does not actually say that.

It is necessary to give careful consideration to the circumstances in which the expected hours under reg.88 can be less than 35. Apart from cases of caring responsibilities, that number is to be reduced where the claimant has a physical or mental impairment, to whatever is reasonable in the light of the impairment (reg.88(2)(c)). However, it would appear that that provision would not apply to short-term or transient illnesses, but only where something is of a sufficiently long-term nature to amount to an "impairment". A large element of judgment is involved.

If the claimant's earned income is less than this figure (the minimum income floor) they will be treated as having earned income equal to this figure (para.(2)). If it equals or exceeds this figure reg.62 does not apply and the claimant's actual earnings will be taken into account in the normal way.

As and when the administrative changes announced on October 24, 2023 to the calculation of expected hours under reg.88 for responsible carers of children aged three to 12 begin to work through into an increased number of hours (see the notes to reg.88 for discussion of the relationship of those changes with the terms of reg.88, which have not been amended), there will be an effect on the calculation of the level of earnings to constitute the MIF under reg.62(2) and (3) for those in gainful self-employment. That effect was announced as a specific measure in para.5.34 of the *Autumn Statement 2023* (CP977, November 22, 2023), according to the Correction Note issued on December 1, 2023 to operate from January 2024. The effect appears to be an inevitable knock-on effect of the October 2023 administrative changes, but in practice might not have started to operate until actual improvements in the availability and affordability of child care emerged. Responsible carers of children under three cannot have the MIF applied to them because they are not subject to all work-related requirements under s.22 (reg.62(1)(b)), but their circumstances can be relevant to the calculation of the MIF of a partner (as in *Example 2* below).

Example 1

2.242 Michael is single, aged 25 and a self-employed plumber. He declares earnings of £800 (£1,100 less permitted expenses of £300) for the current assessment period. He also has employed earnings of £200 a month as he works in a hardware store on Saturday mornings. His minimum income floor is £1,529.00 a month (35 hours a week x £11.44 x 52 ÷ 12, rounded down, less £206.00 for notional income tax and NI contributions). As his self-employed earnings and employed earnings added together amount to £1,000, this is less than his minimum income floor and so he is treated as having earnings of £1,529.00 and his universal credit is assessed on that basis.

In the case of a couple, the position is more complicated. Under para.(3), in addition to the condition that the claimant's earned income is less than their individual threshold (as calculated under para.(4)), the couple's combined earned income must also be less than the couple threshold (as calculated under para.(4)) for reg.62 to apply. The starting point for calculating the couple threshold under para.(4) is reg.90(3). This provides that in the case of joint claimants their individual thresholds are added together (see reg.90(3)(b) for how the threshold is calculated in the case of a person who is a member of a couple but claims as a single person by virtue of reg.3(3)). This amount is then multiplied by 52 and divided by 12 (to make it monthly), from which is deducted "such amount for income tax and national insurance contributions as the Secretary of State considers appropriate" (para.(4)(b)).

If these two conditions are met, the claimant will be treated as having earned income equal to their individual threshold, less any amount by which that deemed earned income combined with their partner's earned income exceeds the couple threshold (para.(3)).

Example 2

Rafiq and Maggie are a couple (both over 25) and they have one child, Charlie, who is aged two. Rafiq has a photography business and Maggie works in a pub in the evenings. Maggie's earnings are £800 and Rafiq's are £1,000 in the current assessment period.

Maggie has been accepted as the "responsible carer" for Charlie and so falls within s.21(1)(aa) of the WRA 2012. Her individual threshold is therefore £793 (16 hours a week x £11.44 x 52 ÷ 12, rounded down, = £793, with no income tax or NI contribution deductions at this level of earnings).

Rafiq's individual threshold is £1,529 a month (35 hours a week x £11.44 x 52 ÷ 12, rounded down, less £206 for notional income tax and NI contributions).

Rafiq and Maggie's actual combined earnings are £1,800 (£1,000 + £800). That is below their joint earnings threshold of £2,322 (£1,529 for Rafiq + £793 for Maggie).

However, adding Rafiq's minimum income floor to Maggie's actual earnings gives £2,329 (£1,529 + £800). That is £7 above their joint earnings threshold of £2,322, so Rafiq is treated as having earnings of £1,522 (£1,529 less £7). Their universal credit is assessed on the basis of earned income of £2,322 (Rafiq's deemed earnings of £1,522 plus Maggie's actual earnings of £800). If Maggie's earnings had been £700, their universal credit would have been assessed on the basis of earned income of £2,229 (Rafiq's unreduced deemed earnings of £1,529 plus Maggie's actual earnings of £700).

Note that if reg.62 does apply in an assessment period, a claimant will not be subject to work-related requirements in that assessment period (see reg.90(1) and (5)).

Note also that income a claimant is deemed to have by virtue of reg.62 does not count as earned income for the purpose of the benefit cap (see reg.82(4)).

See the notes to reg.61 for discussion of whether any alterations of existing awards resulting from increases or reductions in the amount of earned income apart from employed earnings, which could include such changes resulting from the application of the MIF, are appealable.

Start-up period

63.—(1) A "start-up period" is a period of 12 months and applies from the beginning of the assessment period in which the Secretary of State determines that a claimant is in gainful self-employment where— 2.243

[[1](a) regulation 62 (minimum income floor) has not previously applied to the claimant in relation to the trade, profession or vocation which is currently the claimant's main employment (whether in relation to the current award or a previous award); and]

(b) the claimant is taking active steps to increase their earnings from that employment to the level of the claimant's individual threshold (see regulation 90).

(2) But no start-up period may apply in relation to a claimant where a start-up period has previously applied in relation to that claimant, whether in relation to the current award or any previous award of universal credit, unless that previous start-up period—

(a) began more than 5 years before the beginning of assessment period referred to in paragraph (1); and

(b) applied in relation to a different trade, profession or vocation which the claimant has ceased to carry on.

(3) The Secretary of State may terminate a start-up period at any time if the person is no longer in gainful self-employment or is no longer taking the steps referred to in paragraph (1)(b).

AMENDMENT

1. Universal Credit (Managed Migration Pilot and Miscellaneous Amendments) Regulations 2019 (SI 2019/1152) reg.6(1) (September 26, 2020).

DEFINITIONS

"assessment period"—see WRA 2012 ss.40 and 7(2) and reg.21.
"claimant"—see WRA 2012 s.40.
"gainful self-employment"—see regs 53(1) and 64.
"individual threshold"—see regs 2 and 90(2).

GENERAL NOTE

Temporary coronavirus provisions

The last of the temporary coronavirus provisions relevant to the minimum income floor expired on July 31, 2022. See previous editions of this volume for the details. 2.244

If the claimant is in a "start-up period", the minimum income floor does not apply even if they are in gainful self-employment (as defined in reg.64) (see reg.62(5)). 2.245

A start-up period is a period of 12 months starting from the beginning of the assessment period in which the Secretary of State decides that the claimant is in gainful self-employment, provided that the claimant (i) had not previously been subject to the MIF in relation to the trade, profession or vocation that is now their main employment (on which see the notes to reg.64 on gainful self-employment); and (ii) is taking active steps to increase their earnings from that self-employment to the level of their individual threshold under reg.90, i.e., the level at which they will no longer have to meet work-related requirements (para.(1)).

See the notes in the 2020/21 edition of what was then Vol.V of this series for the position before the introduction of the present form of para.(1)(a) on September 26, 2020. It was then a condition that the relevant trade, profession or vocation had been begun in the previous 12 months, thus excluding from the protection of the start-up period claimants whose self-employment was long-standing, even though they had not claimed universal credit in the past. The amendment appears to dilute the encouragement not to continue with self-employment in some disorganised or irregular way, so avoiding the application of the MIF by not being in "gainful self-employment", that the old rule had supplied. That encouragement now resides in the condition of taking active steps to increase earnings under para.(1)(b) and the power in para.(3) to terminate a start-up period if that condition is no longer met (see the further discussion below). The new form of para.(1)(a) has also rendered redundant the special rule applied in "managed migration" cases by reg.59 of the Transitional Provisions Regulations 2014 and that provision has been revoked from the same date.

The new form of para.(1)(a) has also affected the practical scope of application of para.(2) by directly excluding from the protection of the start-up period anyone who has ever previously been subject to the MIF in relation to the current trade, profession or vocation. Para.(2) provides that there cannot be a start-up period if a start-up period has previously applied to the claimant unless that previous period *both* began more than five years before the assessment period of the Secretary of State's determination of gainful self-employment *and* applied in relation to a different trade, profession or vocation from the current one. If any previous start-up period in relation to the same trade, profession or vocation was followed by an application of the MIF, no matter how far in the past, the condition in para.(1)(a) would already have been failed. So para.(2) can only bite in relation to the same trade, profession or vocation if for some reason (such as ceasing to claim or ceasing to being gainfully employed) there was no application of the MIF, but a start-up period had begun to run. If the current main employment is different from the previous trade, profession or vocation (a test that might be very difficult to apply in practice if there have been changes in some, but not all, elements of the business in question), then the condition in para.(1)(a) is met, but para.(2) would still prevent the initiation of a current start-up period if a previous start-up period began within the five years before the assessment period of the Secretary of State's current determination of gainful self-employment.

But it must always be remembered that if a claimant is making a first claim for universal credit para.(2) cannot have any operation and the new para.(1)(a) must by definition also be satisfied.

Although it is often said that the start-up period only protects the first 12 months of self-employment from the operation of the MIF, in fact the combination of the conditions in para.(1) can extend much longer from the start of the particular self-employment in issue. First, any period of self-employment before the start of entitlement to universal credit is irrelevant. Then, the forward 12 months only starts to run with the assessment period in which the Secretary of State recognises that the claimant is in gainful self-employment as defined in reg.64. Before that date the claimant needs no protection from the MIF because regulation 62 will not apply (reg.62(1)(a)), although of course any profits from the self-employment will count as earned income.

If the claimant is no longer in gainful self-employment, or is not taking active steps to increase their earnings as required by para.(1)(b), the Secretary of State can end the start-up period (para.(3)).

In the first case, the MIF could no longer be applied, as would also be so if the claimant ceased to be subject to all work-related requirements. It is not quite clear what consequences should follow if the Secretary of State chooses not to exercise the discretion to terminate the start-up period. Presumably, the period, being defined in para.(1) simply as the period of 12 months from the beginning of the relevant assessment period, continues to run despite the non-application of the MIF or even the ending of entitlement to universal credit (see ADM para.H4102, example 2). That position is supported by the perceived need for the power in para.(3) to terminate a start-up period if the claimant is no longer taking active steps to increase earnings in accordance with para.(1)(b). Then, if the other conditions for the application of the MIF became satisfied again within that 12 months, the claimant would be able to benefit from the protection of the start-up period rule for the remainder of the 12 months. If the Secretary of State chooses to terminate the start-up period, which power is restricted to circumstances where the claimant is no longer in gainful employment, not extending to ceasing to be subject to all work-related requirements or to be entitled to universal credit at all, then on a successful reclaim within a year, the protection of the start-up period rule would be excluded by para.(2)(a). Any specific challenge to any such choice by the Secretary of State to terminate a start-up period on that ground would probably, because the determination would not affect the claimant's entitlement to universal credit or its amount, have to be by way of judicial review.

In the second case, providing that the circumstances do not point to a ceasing to be in gainful self-employment (which would lead to the non-application of the whole MIF rule and the choices discussed above), the power to terminate the start-up period would appear to be the only sanction to enforce the condition in para.(1)(b) of taking active steps to increase earnings up to the level of the individual threshold in reg.90, known as the conditionality earnings threshold (see the notes to reg.90). The ADM gives no guidance as to what might or might not be regarded as "active steps". The steps must be rationally directed to moving the level of earnings to that level at least, in general that of the national minimum wage for the weekly numbers of hours expected of the claimant under reg.88. Presumably, for the para.(3) power to be exercised the claimant must no longer be taking any active steps to that end, rather than merely taking less than the work coach considers reasonable.

Meaning of "gainful self-employment"

64. A claimant is in gainful self-employment for the purposes of regulations 62 and 63 where the Secretary of State has determined that— 2.246

(a) the claimant is carrying on a trade, profession or vocation as their main employment;

(b) their earnings from that trade, profession or vocation are self-employed earnings; and

(c) the trade, profession or vocation is organised, developed, regular and carried on in expectation of profit.

DEFINITIONS

"claimant"—see WRA 2012, s.40.

"self-employed earnings"—see regs 53(1) and 57.

GENERAL NOTE

Temporary coronavirus provisions

The last of the temporary coronavirus provisions relevant to the minimum income floor expired on July 31, 2022. See previous editions of this volume for the details. 2.247

This defines when a claimant is in "gainful self-employment". This is important because it determines whether the "minimum income floor" (see reg.62) applies to the claimant's earned income. Although the regulation does not expressly say that a claimant is *only* in gainful self-employment when its conditions are met, it appears to be a necessary implication that a claimant is not in gainful self-employment when the conditions are not met. 2.248

Claimants are in gainful self-employment if they are carrying on a trade, profession or vocation as their main employment, the earnings from which are self-employed earnings, and the trade, profession or vocation is "organised, developed, regular and carried on in expectation of profit". The mere hope of profit is not enough. There must be a realistic expectation not just of bringing money in, but of profit. If any of these conditions are not met, the claimant will not be in gainful self-employment. It appears that if the claimant's earnings are from "other paid work" (reg.52(a)(iii)) reg.64 cannot apply, but it is not at all clear what sort of work can fall into that category.

In order to decide whether claimants are in gainful self-employment, they will be asked to attend a Gateway interview soon after making a claim for universal credit or after declaring that they are in self-employment.

There is lengthy guidance on the gainful self-employment test at paras H4020–4058 ADM.

Carrying on a trade etc.

2.249 The guidance gives little attention to the question of whether and when a claimant is carrying on a trade etc under para.(b), treating that as mainly subsumed in the issue of regularity under para.(c). However, it appears that there is a prior condition that the claimant is both carrying on a trade etc and doing so as their main employment. There may be difficult questions whether a claimant is currently carrying on a trade etc, for instance where there are seasonal periods of non-activity or some circumstances intervene to interrupt activity and in which the future of the trade cannot be predicted. In *KD v SSWP (UC)* [2020] UKUT 18 (AAC), a case where there was apparently just a slackening off in gardening work in the winter rather than a period of complete inactivity, the judge did not think that authorities on the rules for other benefits were of any help in deciding how the minimum income floor (MIF) rules were to apply. But there may be some guidance in the cases on whether a person is engaged in remunerative work under reg.5 of the Income Support Regulations (and equivalents) or has ceased to be employed as a self-employed earner for the purposes of para.3 of Sch.8 (disregard of earnings). See the notes to those provisions in Vol.V of this series, 2021/22 edition as updated in Cumulative Supplements included in this volume and in mid-year Supplements, for full discussion.

In *R(JSA) 1/09* Judge Rowland took the view that there is a distinction between whether a person is employed as a self-employed earner, which he took to mean trading, and whether the person, if so employed, is engaged in remunerative work or part-time work as a self-employed earner (in particular for the purposes of the condition of entitlement of not being engaged in remunerative work). That distinction has sometimes been summarised as the difference between being in work and being at work (see para.18 of *R(JSA) 1/07*, in the context of employed earners). He also took the view that a person ceased to be so employed on no longer being employed in the former sense. Although some of the reasoning in that case has been doubted in subsequent decisions, it is submitted that the basic distinction remains. The notion of carrying on a trade etc in reg.64 appears to be equivalent to the question of whether a person is employed, in the above sense of trading, rather than to being engaged in self-employment.

Paragraph 27020 of the DMG (repeated in substance in para.H4055 of ADM) suggests nine factors potentially relevant to whether a person is no longer trading, rather than there merely being an interruption in the person's activities in a continuing employment. The substance of that approach (although then directed to whether the claimant was in gainful employment within the definition of self-employment) was approved in *CIS/166/1994*, although in some other cases reservations have been expressed. The nine factors overlap somewhat and it is recognised that not all will be relevant in a particular case, but represent a sensible approach. In summary, they are whether the person has reasonable prospects of work in the near future; whether the business is a going concern and regarded as such by others; whether the person is genuinely available for and seeking alternative work; whether the person hopes or intends to resume work when conditions improve; whether the person is undertaking any activities in connection with the self-employment; whether there is any work in the pipeline; whether the person is regarded as self-employed by HMRC; whether the person is making it known that the business can take on work; and whether the interruption is part of the normal pattern of the business.

It has though been made clear in some recent decisions that neither an intention to resume self-employment in the future nor the existence of a past seasonal pattern of activity and non-activity in itself requires a conclusion for income support and equivalent purposes that the person is still trading and is still employed in self-employment. The old style JSA claimant in *Saunderson v Secretary of State for Work and Pensions* [2012] CSIH 102; [2013] AACR 16 had worked as a self-employed golf caddie in St Andrews in the spring and summer months for several years. The claim was after the end of the summer season, when his authorisation to act as a caddie had been withdrawn and there was no commitment that he would be able to work in the next or subsequent years. The question was whether entitlement was excluded by reason of the claimant being treated as engaged in remunerative work in periods in which he carried out no activities. The Inner House of the Court of Session held that such a deeming could only operate when the claimant was "in work" in the ordinary meaning of the word. That seems to involve essentially the same factors as the question of whether the person is carrying on trade. The court remitted the question to a new tribunal for decision but said this in para.20 (the language being coloured by arguments that the self-employed had to be treated differently from employees):

> "Plainly there may be many self-employed trading or professional activities in which it is not difficult to say that the professional or trading activity continues notwithstanding an idle period. An example might be the arable farmer who, having ploughed and sowed the winter wheat in the autumn, has relatively little to do until the arrival of the spring. In some respects, one might draw an analogy with a schoolteacher whom one would readily say was in work albeit that his teaching duties are punctuated by school holidays in which he has little by way of professional activity to perform. But conversely, there will be seasonally pursued activities which, while treated in their exercise for contractual or fiscal reasons as a 'self-employed' activity, are in their substance little different from employment. Typically (but not exclusively), such *quasi* employed activities might be those in which the individual has no significant commercial capital invested and the temporal limit on his exercise of that technically self-employed activity is dictated by seasonal factors affecting demand for the person's services."

A Northern Ireland Commissioner followed *Saunderson* in *TC v DSD (JSA)* [2013] NI Com 65. He held that the claimant had ceased self-employment as an eel-fisherman when he made his claim in September 2011 although he hoped to resume fishing in May 2012. For the months of January to April statutory rules prohibited fishing and it was not economically worthwhile to fish from October to December. In the particular year the gearbox of his engine broke in early August and he could not afford a repair or source a replacement in time to resume fishing that season. Some further discussion of the weighing-up of the factors considered relevant would have been helpful. In particular, the steps that the claimant was taking and intended to take in the months before May 2012, to get his boat in a condition to resume fishing, and possibly to recruit helpers, could have been said to point to his continuing to be in work. But the uncertainty of the outcome of such steps as at the date of decision perhaps outweighed that factor in the context of the length of the break and the test not requiring a permanent cessation of employment. What was clear was that the mere fact that the claimant had fished during the restricted season for several years did not automatically lead to a conclusion that the self-employment had not ceased in August 2011.

Main employment

The ADM guidance suggests that the question of whether the self-employment is the claimant's main employment will depend on a number of factors, such as the hours spent undertaking it each week, whether this is a significant proportion of the claimant's expected hours per week, how many hours (if any) the claimant spends on employed activity, the amount of income received, whether the claimant receives a greater proportion of their income from self-employed or employed activity, and whether self-employment is the claimant's main aim. The ordinary use of language would suggest that if the self-employed activity in question, however slight **2.250** or unprofitable, beyond a de minimis level, is all that the claimant does by way of employment, then that has to be their main employment. However, that is not the view taken in para.H4023 of the ADM, where it is said that in such circumstances, if the activity is for only a few hours a week or is on a low-paid basis, it should not be regarded as the main employment. There are various elaborate examples given where either of those factors on their own are said to have that effect, so as to avoid the need to examine the criteria laid down in para.(c).

Organised, developed, regular and expectation of profit

2.251 In order to decide whether the self-employment is "organised, developed, regular and carried on in expectation of profit", the guidance suggests that factors such as whether the work is undertaken for financial gain, the number of hours worked each week, whether there is a business plan, the steps being taken to increase the income from the work, whether the business is being actively marketed or advertised, how much work is in the pipeline and whether HMRC regard the activity as self-employment may be relevant. None of those factors seem related specifically to regularity, which will have to be determined in accordance with the overall pattern of activity. Difficult questions may arise where the nature of the trade etc carried on creates seasonal fluctuations or even seasonal periods of non-activity.

JF v HMRC (TC) [2017] UKUT 334 (AAC) concerned the definition of "self-employed" in reg.2(1) of the Working Tax Credit (Entitlement and Maximum Rate) Regulations 2002 as in force with effect from April 6, 2015 (see Vol.IV of this series), which includes a condition that the trade, profession or vocation be "organised and regular". Judge Wikeley gave guidance that, in assessing organisation and regularity for the purposes of WTC, HMRC should "get real" and adjust expectations about the documentary support to be expected for the modest enterprises often involved. Nor should the facts that a claimant did not have an accountant or a business plan necessarily mean that the condition was not met. However, by contrast with the position in WTC, self-employed universal credit claimants will no doubt often be arguing that their business is not organised, developed and regular, so as to avoid the operation of the minimum income floor under reg.62, rather than the other way round, to qualify for WTC.

In *KD v SSWP (UC)* [2020] UKUT 18 (AAC), the gardener's case mentioned above, the judge did not wish, having not had argument on both sides, to express a definitive conclusion on whether regular meant having a constant frequency or merely according to a standard pattern over some period, so that the trade would continue to be regular through a predictable shortage of work. However, he considered that it would be going too far to say that almost constant frequency was required and was not prepared to overturn the tribunal's conclusion that the claimant was in gainful self-employment although the level of his work and income fell off in the winter months. Again, there may be a testing of the matter in the context of the 2020/21 coronavirus outbreak, especially once the person starts to undertake some activities, such as preparation in adapting premises or procedures for being able to start earning money again. Could such activity be said to be "regular" in that special context?

Clearly if the claimant's business is an established one that has been operating for some time and is still receiving income, it may be relatively straightforward to decide that the claimant is in gainful self-employment. If, however, the business is receiving little or no income, it may be that the self-employment is no longer "organised", "regular" or "carried on in expectation of profit". All the circumstances will need to be considered, including future prospects and whether this is part of the normal pattern of the claimant's work. A claimant may still be in gainful employment while unable to work through illness but in that situation should consider submitting medical certificates with a view to no longer being subject to all work-related requirements and thus the minimum income floor not applying. And at some point it would be said that the claimant had ceased to carry on the business.

If the claimant is not in gainful self-employment, the minimum income floor will not apply and the claimant's actual self-employed earnings will be taken into account.

CHAPTER 3

UNEARNED INCOME

Introduction

65. This Chapter provides for the calculation of a person's unearned income for the purposes of section 8 of the Act (calculation of awards). 2.252

DEFINITION

"the Act"—see reg.2.

What is included in unearned income?

66.—(1) A person's unearned income is any of their income, including income the person is treated as having by virtue of regulation 74 (notional unearned income), falling within the following descriptions— 2.253

(a) retirement pension income (see regulation 67) [2 to which the person is entitled, subject to any adjustment to the amount payable in accordance with regulations under section 73 of the Social Security Administration Act 1992 (overlapping benefits)];

(b) any of the following benefits to which the person is entitled, subject to any adjustment to the amount payable in accordance with regulations under section 73 of the Social Security Administration Act 1992 (overlapping benefits)—

(i) jobseeker's allowance,

(ii) employment and support allowance,

(iii) carer's allowance,

[4(iiia) carer support payment but only up to a maximum of the amount a claimant would receive if they had an entitlement to carer's allowance,]

(iv) [1 . . .],

(v) widowed mother's allowance,

(vi) widowed parent's allowance,

(vii) widow's pension,

(viii) maternity allowance, or

(ix) industrial injuries benefit, excluding any increase in that benefit under section 104 or 105 of the Contributions and Benefits Act (increases where constant attendance needed and for exceptionally severe disablement);

(c) any benefit, allowance, or other payment which is paid under the law of a country outside the United Kingdom and is analogous to a benefit mentioned in sub-paragraph (b);

(d) payments made towards the maintenance of the person by their spouse, civil partner, former spouse or former civil partner under a court order or an agreement for maintenance;

[3(da) foreign state retirement pension;]

(e) student income (see regulation 68);

(f) a payment made under section 2 of the Employment and Training Act 1973 or section 2 of the Enterprise and New Towns (Scotland) Act 1990 which is a substitute for universal credit or is for a person's living expenses;

(g) a payment made by one of the Sports Councils named in section 23(2) of the National Lottery etc. Act 1993 out of sums allocated to it for distribution where the payment is for the person's living expenses;

(h) a payment received under an insurance policy to insure against—
   (i) the risk of losing income due to illness, accident or redundancy, or
   (ii) [2...]

(i) income from an annuity (other than retirement pension income), unless disregarded under regulation 75 (compensation for personal injury);

(j) income from a trust, unless disregarded under regulation 75 (compensation for personal injury) or 76 (special schemes for compensation);

(k) income that is treated as the yield from a person's capital by virtue of regulation 72;

(l) capital that is treated as income by virtue of regulation 46(3) or (4);

[3(la) PPF periodic payments;]

(m) income that does not fall within sub-paragraphs [2(a) to (la)] and is taxable under Part 5 of the Income Tax (Trading and Other Income) Act 2005(miscellaneous income).

[2(2) In this regulation—

(a) in paragraph (1)(da) "foreign state retirement pension" means any pension which is paid under the law of a country outside the United Kingdom and is in the nature of social security;

(b) in paragraph (1)(f) and (g) a person's "living expenses" are the cost of—
   (i) food;
   (ii) ordinary clothing or footwear;
   (iii) household fuel, rent or other housing costs (including council tax),

for the person, their partner and any child or qualifying young person for whom the person is responsible;

(c) in paragraph (1)(la) "PPF periodic payments" has the meaning given in section 17(1) of the State Pension Credit Act 2002.]

AMENDMENTS

1. Pensions Act 2014 (Consequential, Supplementary and Incidental Amendments) Order 2017 (SI 2017/422) art.43(3) (April 6, 2017, subject to arts 2 and 3).

2. Loans for Mortgage Interest Regulations 2017 (SI 2017/725) Sch.5, para.5(d) (April 6, 2018).

3. Universal Credit (Miscellaneous Amendments, Saving and Transitional Provision) Regulations 2018 (SI 2018/65) reg.3(9) (April 11, 2018).

4. Carer's Assistance (Carer Support Payment) (Scotland) Regulations 2023 (Consequential Amendments) Order 2023 (SI 2023/1218) art.23(5) (November 19, 2023).

DEFINITIONS

"bereavement allowance"—see reg.2.
"carer's allowance" —*ibid.*
"carer support payment"—*ibid.*
"child" —see WRA 2012 s.40
"employment and support allowance" —see reg.2.

"industrial injuries benefit" —*ibid.*
"jobseeker's allowance" —*ibid.*
"maternity allowance" —*ibid.*
"partner"—*ibid.*
"qualifying young person" —see WRA 2012 ss.40 and 10(5) and regs 2 and 5.
"retirement pension income"—see reg.67.
"widowed mother's allowance" —see reg.2.
"widowed parent's allowance" —*ibid.*
"widow's pension"—*ibid.*

MODIFICATION

With effect from June 16, 2014, reg.66 is modified by reg.25 of the Universal Credit (Transitional Provisions) Regulations 2014 (SI 2014/1230) (see Pt IV of this Volume). The modification applies where an award of universal credit is made to a claimant who is entitled to incapacity benefit or severe disablement allowance, in which case reg.66 applies as if incapacity benefit or, as the case may be, severe disablement allowance were added to the list of benefits in reg.66(1)(b).

GENERAL NOTE 2.254

Paragraph (1)

Universal credit adopts the general approach taken in state pension credit of specifying what is to be included as unearned income. If a type of income is not listed as included, it is ignored and does not affect the claimant's (or claimants') award. Accordingly, there is no need for any general provisions disregarding specified kinds of unearned income (but see regs 75 and 76, expressly mentioned in para. (1)(i) and (j)). However, note that rather than, as for state pension credit, providing in regulations that all social security benefits count as unearned income except those specified as excluded, reg.66 lists the benefits that do count. That leaves occasional difficulty in deciding whether certain payments count as within the wide meaning given to "retirement pension income".

It follows from that approach that reg.26(1)(a) of the Victims' Payments Regulations 2020 (SI 2020/103) was unnecessary in relation to universal credit in providing that a victims' payment or a lump sum under those Regulations was to be disregarded as income in addition to as capital (on which see the notes to reg.76 and Sch.10). It is enough that such payments of compensation are not listed in reg.66(1). Similarly, it was merely necessary to do nothing to amend reg.66(1) to secure that various coronavirus payments were not to be taken into account as unearned income. The main example is the taxable £500 payment, administered by local authorities, made to those in England entitled to a qualifying income-related benefit (including universal credit) who were required by NHS Test and Trace on or after September 28, 2020 (down to at least summer 2021) to self-isolate for 14 (or ten) days, were unable to work from home and would lose income from employment or self-employment as a result. Nor was the discretionary payment available to those not entitled to a qualifying benefit listed in reg.66(1). Nor were payments under the very similar, but not identical, schemes available in Wales, Scotland and Northern Ireland. See the notes to reg.54A for discussion of the question whether any amount left out of the £500 after the end of the isolation period, or possibly after the assessment period of receipt, is to be taken into account as capital. Another example would be payments by local authorities to assist vulnerable households and families with children with essential needs under the 2020 Covid Winter Grants scheme, continued under the name Covid Local Support Grants until September 30, 2021 and then under the name of the Household Support Fund. By the same token, the £350 per month "thank you" payments under the Homes for Ukraine scheme will not count as unearned income.

Similarly, the one-off non-taxable £500 payment made to working tax credit ("WTC") recipients in April 2021, to provide extra support when the temporary coronavirus uplift to WTC ended on April 5, 2021, would not have constituted unearned income if the claimant had claimed universal credit by the time of receipt even if it had been a payment of WTC (which the HMRC guidance on the scheme stresses it is not), as WTC is not listed in reg.66(1)(b). But the payment appears to be of a capital nature, for which there is no disregard in Sch.10, and, even if it were income, it is arguable that an unspent amount of the £500 constitutes capital. See the notes to reg.45 and Sch.10. The HMRC guidance says that benefits will not be affected by receipt of the payment.

There cannot be a definitive list of kinds of income that cannot be taken into account as unearned income, but a few categories can be mentioned. Payments of dividends do not count, but see the notes to regs 55 (employed earnings) and 77(4) on when they may be treated as earned income in substance. Interest on bank or building society accounts and other investments does not count, nor does rental income or payments from people occupying the claimant's home (see the note below on income taxable under Pt 5 of ITTOIA for why), although if the letting is part of a trade or business it will go towards the calculation of earnings from self-employment: see the notes to reg.57. All of those propositions are subject to the rule in reg.72(3) that if the claimant's capital is assumed to yield monthly "tariff" income under reg.72(1), where the value of the capital exceeds £6,000, any actual income derived from capital ("for example rental, interest or dividends") is to be treated as part of the claimant's capital. In addition, the amount of the income, if not spent by the claimant, will become part of their capital, probably after the end of the assessment period in which the income was received.

Thus payments from relatives (except those caught by para.(1)(d)) or friends or charities (see the view expressed in para.13 of *AMS v SSWP (PC) (final decision)* [2017] UKUT 381 (AAC), [2018] AACR 27 on the comparable state pension credit structure) or local authorities fall outside the scope of unearned income, as do drawings from a partnership or a self-employed business or from, say, a director's loan account within a company structure (though see reg.57 on self-employed earnings and reg.77 on companies analogous to a partnership or a one-person business).

See the notes to para.(1)(b) below for some of the social security benefits that are not taken into account.

In calculating universal credit, all of the claimant's, or the claimants' combined, unearned income that counts is taken into account in full (see s.8(3) of the WRA 2012 and reg.22). There are also some circumstances in which income not listed in reg.66 will affect the application of particular provisions, e.g. the amount of charges allowed in the childcare costs element under reg.34 is reduced to the extent that they are met or reimbursed by some other person or by other relevant support (i.e. in connection with participation in work-related activity or training).

What is income

2.255 The first requirement for unearned income to be taken into account, before examining the list in para.(1), is that the amount concerned is income rather than capital. That is covered in the present section. It is also a requirement, it is suggested, that the amount is income that the claimant "has". That is covered in the following section.

It has been said for many years in the predecessors to this volume that "resources are to be either capital or income. There is nothing in between". That statement was cited with approval in *R(IS) 3/93* and without disapproval in *R(IS) 9/08*. The distinction between income and capital has given rise to many problems in the context of means-tested benefits, as well as in other legal contexts. There is very extensive discussion of the general principles in the notes to reg.23 of the Income Support Regulations in Vol.V of this series, 2021/22 edition as updated in Cumulative Supplements included in this volume and in mid-year Supplements. Not all of that discussion needs to be repeated here. That is mainly because of the important deemings in reg.46(3) and (4) and the fact that the structure of reg.66 means that even if something is income it may fall outside the exhaustive list of categories in para.(1).

Regulation 46(3) provides that, subject to reg.46(4), any sums paid regularly and by reference to a period are to be treated as income even if they would otherwise be regarded as capital. Regulation 46(4) deals with capital payable by instalments, deeming such instalments sometimes to be income, depending on the level of overall capital. Then reg.66(1)(l) lists capital treated as income by virtue of reg.46(3) or (4) as unearned income. Although reg.46(3) builds on the traditional approach that the "essential feature of receipts by way of income is that they display an element of periodic recurrence. Income cannot include ad hoc receipts" (Bridge J in *R. v Supplementary Benefits Commission Ex p. Singer* [1973] 1 W.L.R. 713), it makes the rule more positive. Ad hoc receipts, like the one-off £15 loan to a striking miner by a local authority to meet hire purchase arrears in *R(SB) 29/85*, would still be excluded. But any arguments that loans could never constitute income (already in substance disposed of by *Chief Adjudication Officer v Leeves* (CA), reported as *R(IS) 5/99*, and *Morrell v Secretary of State for Work and Pensions* [2003] EWCA Civ 536, reported as *R(IS) 6/03*)) cannot stand. If the sums are paid regularly and by reference to a period they must be treated as income, subject to reg.46(4) and to the potential argument, based on *Leeves*, that sums have not become income in the claimant's hands (on which, see the following section).

But there is then a problem with the inclusion of capital treated as income by virtue of reg.46(3) or (4) in para.(1)(l). As suggested in the notes to reg.46, that could not possibly have been intended to have the effect that any payment made regularly and by reference to a period must be taken into account as unearned income. That would include, for example, many social security benefits carefully not listed in para.(1)(b), rental payments, regular payments from relatives or friends (whether gifts or loans) and other categories mentioned above as excluded, all of which are plainly acknowledged as intended not to be taken into account. However, it is submitted that it is significant that para.(1)(l) does not apply to every payment treated as income by virtue of reg.46(3) or (4), but only to *capital* treated as income by virtue of those provisions. Thus, it appears that payments that are in their nature income cannot fall within para.(1)(l) and only count for universal credit purposes if listed in some other part of para.(1). On that basis, para.(1)(l) covers only capital payments that are paid either regularly and by reference to a period (reg.46(3)) or by instalments (reg.46(4)).

There is no deeming for payments that are not paid regularly (and the test in reg.46(3) seems to be of the pattern of actual payment, rather than due dates) or have no relation to a period (e.g. they are to help with sporadically arising needs). There might therefore be difficult questions arising in theory about whether the payments were income, rather than capital. Then the other traditional criterion of "the true characteristic of the payment in the hands of the recipient" (see *R. v National Insurance Commissioner Ex p. Stratton* [1979] I.C.R. 209, Appendix II to *R(U) 1/79*, and *Minter v Kingston upon Hull CC* and *Potter v Secretary of State for Work and Pensions* [2011] EWCA Civ 1155; [2012] AACR 21) might come into play. See *R(H) 8/08* for a case where the tribunal gave inadequate consideration to whether the payment by the claimant's accountant of his rent on 20–25 occasions over 33 months constituted income. But in practice, the questions would not have to be answered if the payment would fall outside the para.(1) list anyway. There could of course be an impact on the capital limit rules if the payment was regarded as capital and the value of the claimant's other capital was close to a significant level, but the difference would be slight in reality, because unspent income would relatively quickly metamorphose into capital.

Payments of capital by instalments will usually be easily identified, such as the payment of the purchase price of a house by monthly instalments in *Lillystone v Supplementary Benefits Commission* [1982] 3 F.L.R. 52, where each instalment was on the common law test capital. Now, for universal credit, that would still be the case if the claimant's other capital and the amount of the instalments outstanding did not exceed £16,000. If those amounts did exceed £16,000, reg.46(4) deems each instalment to be income, to be taken into account under para.(1)(l).

A particular area that has given rise to difficulty is where a claimant receives a lump sum, such as of compensation for personal injury or for unfair dismissal or for breach of equal pay or similar legislation. Other examples would be payments of lump sums of arrears of some entitlement or advance payments. The area of personal injury and payments from compensation funds is dealt with by regs 75 and 76. The other compensation cases, on which *Minter* and *Potter* make clear that the central question is whether the compensation was for loss of income or for loss of a capital asset, are to do with earnings. So far as unearned income is concerned, the area of concern is with lump sum payments of arrears or possibly advance payments in commutation of income, exemplified by payments of arrears of social security benefits.

In principle, payments of benefits that would have had the character of income if paid on their due date retain that character when paid in arrears as a lump sum (*R(SB) 4/89* and *CH/1561/2005*). That is entirely consistent with the principle behind the Court of Appeal's decision in *Minter* and *Potter* (above) on lump sum payments of compensation in settlement of equal pay claims. So the same should apply to payments that were not benefit as such, but compensation for the non-payment of benefit over some past period. There seems no reason why that principle should not apply for universal credit purposes, if the income falls within a para.(1) category. In *R(SB) 4/89*, the Commissioner, relying on the principle in *McCorquodale v Chief Adjudication Officer*, reported as *R(SB) 1/88*, held that the income should be taken into account in the periods for which it would have been taken into account if paid on the due dates. There is no equivalent clear rule on due dates for unearned income in the universal credit scheme. There are thus particularly difficult issues about how to take such lump sum payments of unearned income into account, discussed below under the heading *Attribution of unearned income to assessment periods*.

When is income the claimant's

2.256 Regulation 66(1) starts with the assumption that it is concerned with income that is a person's. Paragraph 4(3)(a) of Sch.1 to the WRA 2012 authorises the making of regulations specifying the circumstances in which a person is to be treated as "having or not having capital or earned or unearned income". Thus, it appears necessary, before the list of categories in para.(1) is reached, to be satisfied that the claimant "has" the income concerned. That must entail, except in the category of notional income in reg.74 and assumed yield from capital in regs 66(1)(k) and 72, that the income has actually been received by the claimant or become at their disposal. See the section below on *Attribution of unearned income to assessment periods* for discussion of how those provisions affect that issue.

One founding proposition was established by the Court of Appeal in *Chief Adjudication Officer v Leeves*, reported as *R(IS) 5/99*. The claimant there had been a full-time student in receipt of a local authority grant, the instalment for each term being paid in advance. He abandoned his course shortly after receiving an instalment and having spent all the money on paying off mortgage arrears and other debts. About a month later the local authority wrote to him formally terminating his grant from the date of abandonment, informing him that he had been overpaid by a specified amount and requesting that repayment be made as soon as possible. The adjudication officer decided that the amount of the grant had to be taken into account in calculating the claimant's income support until the end of the term. The grant was income and had been received and under the ordinary non-student provisions was to be taken into account from the due date of payment for the period in respect of which it was payable. It did not matter that the money had all been spent. Potter LJ, with whom the other judges agreed, took the view that "income" was to be given its natural and ordinary meaning. He accepted that the decision would have been right for grants that were not repayable, but that moneys received, or required to be treated as received, "under a certain obligation of immediate repayment" did not have the character of income. Prior to his receipt of the letter from the local authority, the claimant was not in that position, because there was no "certain and immediate" obligation to repay, his undertaking on accepting the grant having merely been to repay such sum as might be determined if he abandoned the course. His liability had not yet crystalised. However, on receipt of the demand from the local authority he came under an immediate obligation in relation to an ascertained sum and from that date the remainder of the grant was not income.

That principle was affirmed in *Morrell* (above). There the regular payments by way of loan from the claimant's mother were income despite there being a repayment obligation. But the basis of the arrangement was that the claimant would repay when her problems decreased or she found work, so that there was no certain obligation of immediate repayment. In *R(JSA) 4/04* there was no such obligation in relation to a student loan at the dates in question, because under the legislation in force repayment could only start in the April following the academic year for which the loan was made. Nor did it matter that the loan might have been made wrongly unless and until the Secretary of State took action to determine that there had been an overpayment. By contrast, in *R(H) 5/05* the Commissioner held that drawing on an agreed overdraft facility is borrowing, as is the honouring of a cheque taking an overdraft over an agreed limit. Those loans could be capable of constituting income, were it not for the fact that the standard terms of bank overdrafts were that they were repayable on demand, although a demand might not be made while the overdraft stayed within agreed limits. The Commissioner considered that there was a certain obligation of immediate repayment, because the amount overdrawn could be identified day by day, and the obligation was immediate even though the bank chose not to enforce it. That brought the *Leeves* principle into operation. The Commissioner considered that that was also in accord with the ordinary and natural meaning of "income", as one would not naturally speak of someone having income by incurring expenditure and running up an overdraft. *R(H) 5/05* did not refer to the decision of the Court of Appeal in *R. v West Dorset DC Ex p. Poupard* (1998) 20 H.L.R. 295 that borrowings by way of a bank overdraft secured on capital and used for living expenses was income for the purposes of the housing benefit scheme as it was at the time. However, *R(H) 8/08*, at para.26, and *AR v Bradford MDC* [2008] UKUT 30 (AAC), reported as *R(H) 6/09*, at paras 16–21, plainly indicate that that decision is no longer relevant in the light of changes in the nature of the governing legislation and of *Leeves*.

The Commissioner in *R(H) 5/05* did not have to decide whether the use of a credit card with no immediate liability to repay beyond the minimum amount each month created a funding facility for regularly recurring expenses to be taken into account as income. He cast some doubt on *CH/3393/2003*, in which it was held that it did. That decision was more strongly disapproved in *R(H) 8/08*, at para.27, and *AR* (above), at para.22.

There is also a line of cases where the circumstances seem to be stronger than in *Leeves*, in that there is not merely a certain obligation of immediate repayment, but a legal mechanism has been applied to effect repayment.

In *R(IS) 4/01* the Commissioner decided, applying *Leeves* on the natural and ordinary meaning of "income", that the part of the claimant's occupational pension that was being paid to his former wife under an attachment of earnings order did not count as his income for the purposes of income support. He concluded that, in the absence of a statutory definition, income meant "money paid regularly to the recipient or to his order but not money which is being paid and which he cannot prevent from being paid directly to a third party instead of him". In *CH/1672/2007* the half of the claimant's pension that he was required to pay to his wife under the terms of a court order following a judicial separation did not count as his income. However, income subject to a direction that could be revoked at any time (in that case a pension signed over by a nun to a religious order under a deed of trust) remained the claimant's income (*C10/06–07(IS)*, a Northern Ireland decision). So did the half of his annuities that the claimant in *CH/1076/2008* voluntarily paid to his wife from whom he was separated. In that case the Commissioner drew attention to the "further problem" that would need to be considered if the annuities were retirement annuity pensions in connection with a former employment, namely the conditions in s.91 of the Pension Schemes Act 1995 for assignment of such an annuity.

In addition, see *CIS/5479/1997* in which an overpayment of an occupational pension was being recovered by the Italian authorities by withholding the complete amount of the monthly payments of the pension. Only the net amount actually received by the claimant was his income. The same result would follow for a UK benefit where there has been not only a decision that past benefit has been overpaid and is legally recoverable, but also a decision that deductions are to be made from current benefit to effect repayment. Then, in the absence of any express provision to the contrary, the gross amount of the current benefit would be subject to the legally imposed deduction and only the net amount would be the claimant's income. The Commissioner may well, though, have gone too far in referring to *Leeves* as confirming his own view that in the general context of the income support scheme income to be taken into account was income that was actually paid to a claimant. He stated that if a claimant who had not actually received income was to be treated as having that income, that had to be achieved by a specific provision in the legislation, but *BL v SSWP (SPC)* [2018] UKUT 4 (AAC) (below) shows that that is an over-generalisation, while not doubting the outcome of *CIS/5479/1997*.

In *R(IS) 4/02* the same Commissioner applied that approach to conclude, contrary to the view taken in *CIS/212/1989*, para.9 (and followed with some hesitation in *CIS/295/1994*), that payments of the claimant's husband's annuity which had vested in his trustee in bankruptcy under s.306 of the Insolvency Act 1986 were not part of his income (and thus not part of the claimant's income) for the purposes of income support. See also *R(IS) 2/03*, which agreed with *R(IS) 4/02* (on the basis of the principle in *Re Landau* [1998] Ch. 223, affirmed in *Krasner v Dennison* [2001] Ch. 76) that *CIS/212/1989* should no longer be followed. Thus the payments under the claimant's self-employed pension annuity that were being applied entirely for the benefit of his creditors were not his actual income (see the note to reg.74 for the position in relation to notional income). Note that the law has now changed so as to exclude pension rights from a bankrupt's estate (Welfare Reform and Pensions Act 1999 s.11 and 12), but only for bankruptcy orders made on or after May 29, 2000. The general principle of the meaning of "income", however, will remain of significance.

BL v SSWP (SPC) [2018] UKUT 4 (AAC) provides a very helpful illustration of the general principles (see the extract set out at para.1.64 of this volume). Payments of the claimant's personal pension to his ex-wife were his income because they were made at his order and he retained practical control over the money. Under a deed of separation he had undertaken to make maintenance payments of a specified amount. Once he started to draw the personal pension he directed the provider to pay those amounts to his ex-wife. It did not matter that the claimant never actually received those amounts from the pension provider. He was still free to deal with that money as he wished and retained not just legal, but also practical, control over it. The statement in *CIS/5479/1997* noted above about claimants who have not actually received income was distinguished as based on different facts. It is submitted that that statement should not be taken out of its context of a withholding of social security payments to recover a debt owed to the social security institution making the payments.

SH v SSWP [2008] UKUT 21 (AAC) concerned the weekly sums which the claimant was allowed to withdraw for living expenses from his bank account which was subject to a restraint order under s.77 of the Criminal Justice Act 1988. It was held that these sums were not income at the time of withdrawal but remained capital. Furthermore there was nothing in the JSA Regulations 1996 which treated those payments of capital as income. They were not capital payable by instalments within the meaning of reg.104(1) of the JSA Regulations 1996 (the equivalent of reg.46(4)) as that provision only applied if there was a contractual or other obligation on the part of some other person to pay a capital sum to the claimant by instalments.

Drawings from a partnership (or a business) are not income other than earnings, nor are they earnings from self-employment (*AR v Bradford MDC* [2008] UKUT 30 (AAC), reported as *R(H) 6/09*). Nor are drawing from a director's loan account within a company structure. They are movements of the claimant's capital from one place to another, as in *SH* (above).

CIS/25/1989 held that, applying the principle of *Parsons v Hogg* [1985] 2 All E.R. 897, Appendix to *R(FIS) 4/85*, from the context of earnings, expenditure necessary to produce income is to be deducted to produce a figure of gross income, as was the term in the relevant legislation. The claimant was entitled to £21.60 per month sickness benefit from the Ideal Benefit Society only while he continued to make a £60 annual payment to the Society. The monthly equivalent (£5) was to be deducted from the £21.60. There have since been conflicting views about the correctness of that decision in the context of the income support legislation on income other than earnings. It was rejected in *CIS 563/1991*. In *R(IS) 13/01* the Commissioner thought that arguably the principle in *Parsons v Hogg* should apply to income other than earnings, but decided that he ought to follow *CIS/563/1991* rather than *CIS/25/1989* on the basis that the former decision had fully considered and rejected the reasoning in *CIS/25/1989*. However, that approach to the issue of precedent where there are two conflicting decisions of equal status has now been overtaken, so that the merits of the decisions should be considered (see *R(IS) 9/08*). More important, the context of the universal credit legislation is significantly different. First, the relevant phrase is not "gross income", but "income" and it was the use of the word "gross" that led to the Commissioner's view in *CIS/563/1991*. Secondly, there is nothing in the universal credit legislation, apart from the provisions on student income, to say how much of any payment of income is to be taken into account or positively providing any deductions or disregards. The perceived need to provide in para.(1)(a) and (b) for taking account of any adjustment in the amount of a benefit under the Overlapping Benefits Regulations suggests that the gross amount would otherwise have been used in s.8(3) of the WRA 2012, but it is arguable that too much should not be inferred from that rule outside sub-paras (a) and (b). In those circumstances, it is submitted that the elementary considerations of fairness behind the approach in *CIS/25/1989* should be applied and that where expenditure has to be incurred in order to produce any unearned income, the amount of that expenditure should be deducted before the income is taken into account. It is the case, though, that it is hard to envisage the practical application of that approach to most of the categories listed in para.(1) (possibly under sub-para.(h) if there was an obligation to continue paying premiums to receive benefits under the insurance policy or under sub-para.(m) for some types of income taxable under Pt 5 of ITTOIA).

Similar questions can be raised about whether, where the type of unearned income concerned is subject to income tax, the amount of income tax due should be deducted in calculating the amount of income to be taken into account. That would apply to most kinds of retirement pension income, including state retirement pension (para.(1)(a) and (la)), some social benefits (British and non-UK—para.(1) (b) and (c)), some income from trusts (para.(1)(j)) and income taxable under Pt 5 of ITTOIA (para.(1)(m)). One starting point of principle must be that, in general, the ordinary and natural meaning of "income" entails that the existence of liabilities that the claimant has or incurs to persons other than the payer of the income does not affect the amount of income to be taken into account. That is consistent with *BL v SSWP (SPC)*, discussed above, and with *Leeves* (where crucially it was a certain obligation of immediate repayment, i.e. to the payer of the grant, that took the sum subject to repayment out of the meaning of income). So a mere liability to account to HMRC for the income tax due on a receipt of unearned income would not prevent the gross amount of the receipt being taken into account, in the absence of any express provision in the regulations requiring a deduction. But what if income tax has been deducted by the payer as required by legislation and HMRC practice, to be remitted to HMRC, before paying the net amount to the claimant? Surely then an argument can be made by analogy with the cases discussed above where the claimant cannot prevent an amount being paid to some third party by virtue of a legal process, so that only the amount actually received by the claimant should be taken into account. The alternative would require the amount of universal credit to be reduced by income that was never available to the claimant as the result of a legal process, a result that is to be avoided if at all possible. See 2.257 for the argument that there are special factors relevant to retirement pension income.

Retirement pension income

2.257 On para.(1)(a) (retirement pension income), see the note to reg.67, in particular on the meanings of occupational pension. In so far as retirement pension income consists of elements of the state retirement pension (all of which are covered in reg.67), the April 2018 amendment confirms that the amount to be taken into account is the figure after any adjustment under the Overlapping Benefits Regulations. The new para.(1)(da) includes a foreign state retirement pension (defined in para.(2)(a)). That definition appears very wide ("pension ... in the nature of social security") when the term "pension" is often used to refer to any periodical social security payments. However, it must be arguable that this is a case where the definition takes on meaning from the nature of term defined, so that para.(1)(d) is restricted to benefits paid on retirement.

Note that the notional unearned income rule in reg.74 has a particular application to retirement pension income. A person who has reached the qualifying age for state pension credit is to be treated as possessing any such income they might expect to be entitled to if a claim were made, even if no application has been made (reg.74(3) and (4)). So a person who defers taking their UK retirement pension or an occupational or personal pension beyond state retirement age will be treated as if they had taken the pension at that age. See the notes to reg.74 for more detail and discussion about how far reg.74(4) qualifies reg.74(3). Regulation 74(3) applies only to retirement pension, so not to a foreign state retirement pension under para.(1)(da), but that would apparently fall under reg.74(1).

Note also that there is a particular issue about the treatment of payments of retirement income when a claimant reaches the qualifying age for state pension credit, now that (from November 25, 2020) entitlement to universal credit does not end until the first day of the assessment period following that in which that age is reached (para.26 of Sch.1 to the Decisions and Appeals Regulations 2013). A further issue has emerged where decisions on claims for retirement pension or the putting of entitlement into payment has been delayed. See below under the heading of *Attribution of unearned income to assessment periods*.

See the end of para.2.256 for discussion of whether the amount of income within reg.66(1) to be taken into account should be net of any income tax deducted at source. ADM H5014 positively asserts that that is not so for retirement pension income because there is nothing in the universal credit legislation equivalent to reg.17(10) of the SPC Regulations (Pt III of this volume), which specifically provides for the deduction of tax and national insurance contributions. That does not in itself seem a compelling basis for that interpretation, but the language of reg.66(1)(a), referring to the retirement pension income to which a person is *entitled*, could be argued also to point in that direction.

Benefits

2.258 Not all benefit income is taken into account—see para.(1)(b) for the benefits that do count in addition to those within the meaning of retirement pension income (note that this will also include incapacity benefit or severe disablement allowance if the claimant is entitled to either of these benefits: see the modification made to para.(1)(b) by reg.25 of SI 2014/1230 referred to above). Thus, for example, child benefit is ignored, as is disability living allowance, attendance allowance and personal independence payment. War disablement pension and war widows', widowers' or surviving civil partners' pensions are also ignored (for income support, old style JSA, old style ESA and housing benefit there is only a £10 disregard). Bereavement allowance, which has been abolished prospectively for deaths on or after April 6, 2017 has been taken out of the list of benefits in para.(1)(b), but remains in the list in relation to awards of the allowance made before April 6, 2017 or to awards made in relation to deaths before that date (see arts 2 and 3 of the amending Order, SI 2017/422). The monthly payments of the new bereavement support payment have not been put into the list, so will not count as income for universal credit purposes, whether paid on time or in arrears. In so far as any payment of arrears is to be treated as capital it is disregarded as such under para.18(1)(c) of Sch.10 (plus, in the case of arrears under the Bereavement Payments (Remedial) Order 2013, para.20(2)). The initial one-off lump sum payment appears to have the character of capital and is disregarded as such under para.20(2) of Sch.10.

Note that the benefits listed are all, except for Scottish carer support payment (sub-para.(b)(iiia), defined in reg.2 specifically by reference to British legislation. Thus the equivalent benefits under Northern Ireland legislation are not covered. Because sub-para.(c) on analogous benefits is restricted to those paid under the law of a country outside the UK, which includes Northern Ireland, it appears that Northern Ireland equivalent benefits cannot count as unearned income. Similarly, benefits payable under Scottish legislation that might look as though they fall within sub-para.(b), like carer's allowance supplement (see Vol.IV of this series), do not do so and cannot fall within sub-para.(c) as analogous. The exception is Scottish carer support payment (CSP) in sub-para.(b)(iiia), defined in reg.2 with effect from November 19, 2023 by reference to the Scottish legislation. Its roll-out started in a few selected areas, with an expansion starting in spring 2024 planned to extend to the whole of Scotland by autumn 2024. Note that, in so far as the amount of CSP exceeds what would have been payable in carer's allowance for a resident of England and Wales, the excess does not count as unearned income under reg.66(1)(b), nor can it be regarded as part of an analogous benefit under reg.66(1)(c) for the reason given above. That is in accordance with the Fiscal Agreement governing the provision of devolved benefits in Scotland (see para.6.9 of the Explanatory Memorandum to SI 2023/1218). Initially, CSP is to be paid at the same rate as carer's allowance.

The definitions of JSA and ESA (listed in heads (i) and (ii)) in reg.2 are in terms restricting the meaning to new style JSA and new style ESA. Thus when a claimant previously entitled to a legacy benefit is entitled to the two-week run-on of housing benefit, extended to income support, IBJSA and IRESA from July 22, 2020, none of those receipts count as unearned income under reg.66(1). None of those benefits is listed in sub-para.(b). However, the effect of reg.8B(b) of the Transitional Provisions Regulations 2014, as inserted with effect from July 22, 2020 by reg.4(4) of the Universal Credit (Managed Migration Pilot and Miscellaneous Amendments) Regulations 2019 (SI 2019/1152), is that, where a claimant has become entitled to new style JSA or ESA on the termination of an award of IBJSA or IRESA, unearned income is to be calculated as if the claimant had been entitled to the new style award from the first day of their universal credit award.

By virtue of reg.10 of the Universal Credit (Transitional Provisions) Regulations 2014 (see the notes to that provision in Pt IIIA), any payment of an "existing benefit" (IBJSA, IRESA, income support or housing benefit, but excluding for these purposes joint claim JSA and any tax credits) made to a claimant who is not entitled to it in respect of a period that falls within a universal credit assessment period is to fall within reg.66(1)(b) as unearned income. The overpayment involved is not then recoverable in the ordinary way. It will in effect be recovered through the deduction in the calculation of universal credit.

In *R. (on the application of Moore) v Secretary of State for Work and Pensions* [2020] EWHC 2827 (Admin); [2021] P.T.S.R. 495, Swift J, while finding two of the grounds of judicial review arguable (discrimination under art.14 of the ECHR read with art.8 and/or art.1 of Protocol 1 and common law irrationality), rejected the case for the claimants against the inclusion of maternity allowance in the list of social security benefits to count in full as unearned income, although statutory maternity pay (SMP) counts as earned income with the advantage of the 55% taper and the work allowance. The claimant did not qualify for SMP because she had not worked for her employer for long enough when she started her maternity pay, so had to claim maternity allowance. Permission to apply for judicial review on the ground of breach of the public sector equality duty (s.149 of the Equality Act 2010) was refused. The Court of Appeal refused the claimant permission to appeal in a reasoned judgment following a short hearing (*Moore v Secretary of State for Work and Pensions* [2021] EWCA Civ 970).

The decision in *Moore* has been followed and applied after detailed consideration by the Northern Ireland High Court in *In the Matter of an Application by 'RK' for Judicial Review* [2022] NIQB 29.

Special provision is made in the annual social security benefit up-rating orders for the assessment period in which the up-rated amount is to be taken into account. Thus art.1(4) of the Social Security Benefits Up-rating Order 2024 (SI 2024/242), in conjunction with art.1(3)(n), ensures that in the case of a beneficiary who has an award of universal credit the provision up-rating the social security benefit comes into force for the purpose of calculating entitlement to universal credit on the first day of the first assessment period to commence on or after April 8, 2024.

Non-UK benefits

2.259 Under sub-para.(c) payments of benefit under the law of a country outside the UK that is analogous to a benefit listed in sub-para.(b) count as unearned income. Because the UK includes Northern Ireland and the benefits in sub-para.(b) are carefully defined in reg.2 by reference to the specific Great Britain or Scottish legislation, this seems to have the anomalous effect that benefits paid under Northern Ireland social security legislation do not count as unearned income for universal credit purposes. See below for the opposite outcome in relation to benefits that are included within retirement pension income.

Benefits payable under Scottish legislation that are in the nature of income (e.g. carer's allowance supplement) likewise cannot fall within sub-para.(b) or (c), apart from carer support payment to the extent specifically included by sub-para.(b)(iii).

See *LR v SSWP (UC)* [2022] UKUT 65 (AAC) on the question of analogy. The claimant came into receipt of an Irish widow's contributory pension following the death of her husband in 2018. Entitlement to that pension depended on a claimant's spouse or civil partner having died and having made sufficient qualifying contributions and on the claimant being under pensionable age for state pension and not having remarried or otherwise become part of a couple. It was payable indefinitely, although on reaching the age of 66 it would be necessary to reapply because, if the claimant qualified for state pension there could be a transfer. Judge West accepted in para.64 that to be "analogous" the foreign benefit must be similar or comparable in relevant respects, but does not have to be identical. The essential question was whether the two benefits are similar in terms of their nature and purpose. In *LR*, the Irish pension was on that test analogous to widow's pension under sub-para.(b)(vii), i.e. a pension under s.38 of the SSCBA 1992 (reg.2, on the assumption that the reference there to s.39 is a correctable mistake). The pensions produced a weekly income for life and the conditions for entitlement were very similar, except that widow's pension did not extend to widowers or civil partners and was payable only to widows aged at least 45 when their husband died, which differences did not undermine the analogy. It did not matter, despite the reference in sub-para.(b) to benefits to which a person was entitled, that the claimant could not have been entitled to British widow's pension, because that was restricted to deaths before April 8, 2001, and was entitled to bereavement support payment, which is not in the sub-para.(b) list.

Under sub-para.(da), with the definition in para.(2)(a), foreign state retirement pension is listed. The definition appears very wide ("pension ... in the nature of social security") when the term "pension" is often used to refer to any periodical social security payments. But perhaps this is a case where the definition takes on meaning from the nature of the term defined, so that sub-para.(da) is restricted to benefits paid on retirement or at least linked to old age. The definition is restricted to pensions paid under the law of a country outside the UK, so that pensions paid under Northern Ireland legislation are not covered. However, the meaning of retirement pension income in sub-para.(a) is, through the reference on to the state pension credit legislation in reg.67, extended to the Northern Ireland legislation corresponding to the British legislation listed.

Payments towards maintenance

Under para.(1)(d) payments "towards the maintenance of a person" from their spouse, or former spouse, or civil partner, or former civil partner, under a court order or maintenance agreement count. Thus maintenance payments that are not made pursuant to an agreement (e.g., ad hoc voluntary payments) will be ignored. There is also no provision for treating such payments as unearned income if they are made directly to a third party. Maintenance for a child is ignored. Note first that para.(1)(d) only applies to current or ex-spouses or civil partners, not to someone who had been living with the claimant as if married or a civil partner. Note also that payments from any other member of the family apart from spouses/civil partners, e.g. parents, for maintenance are not included. **2.260**

The list in reg.66 does not include charitable or voluntary payments and so these will be ignored. On the meaning of charitable and voluntary payments, see the notes to para.15 of Sch.9 to the Income Support Regulations in Vol.V of this series, 2021/22 edition as updated in Cumulative Supplements included in this volume and in mid-year Supplements.

Student income

Here "student income" does not mean any income that someone who is a student has, but the particular forms of income that a person undertaking a course of education, study or training is to be treated as having under reg.68. Any other forms of income, apart from earnings, can only be taken into account in so far as they fall within some other category in para.(1), e.g. training allowances (para. (1)(f) and reg.68(6)). The forms of income covered by reg.68 are student loans, i.e. loans towards maintenance under specified legislation, including loans that have not been taken out but could be acquired by reasonable steps, and grants to under-21s for non-advanced education. See the notes to regs.68 and 69–71 for further details and for how the amounts are to be attributed to particular assessment periods. Although it is a condition of entitlement to universal credit not to be receiving education (s.4(1)(d) of the WRA 2012) there are exceptions to that condition in reg.14 and a claimant with a partner who receives education may be entitled. **2.261**

Training allowances

Payments from employment and training programmes under s.2 of the Employment and Training Act 1973 or s.2 of the Enterprise and New Towns (Scotland) Act 1990 are only taken into account in so far as they are a substitute for universal credit (e.g., a training allowance) or for a person's living expenses (para. (1)(f)). See para.(2)(b) for what counts as "living expenses". **2.262**

Income protection insurance

Under para.(1)(h) payments under an insurance policy count but only if the policy was to insure against the contingencies in heads (i) and (ii). Under head (ii) payments under a mortgage (or other loan) protection policy will only be taken into account if the payment is to pay interest on a mortgage or loan secured on the person's home or to meet "alternative finance payments" (see the notes to paras 4–6 of Sch.1) *and* if the person's universal credit award includes a housing costs element under para.4 of Sch.1. Thus insurance policy payments to meet, e.g., capital repayments or policy premiums, will be ignored. **2.263**

It is arguable that if, for instance, a claimant is obliged to continue paying premiums under the insurance policy to receive the payments, the amount of the premium payable in each assessment period should be deducted applying the principle of *Parsons v Hogg* [1985] 2 All E.R. 897, appendix to *R(FIS) 4/85* (see the end of the section *When is income the claimant's* above).

Annuities

2.264 Income from an annuity (other than retirement pension income) counts unless it was purchased with personal injury compensation (reg.75) as does income from a trust (unless it is disregarded under regs 75 or 76) (para.(1)(i) and (j)).

Note that if income is being taken into account under this provision, there can be no assumed yield under reg.72 from any capital exceeding £6,000 in value associated with the annuity (reg.72(2)). In most cases such capital could only consist of the right to continue to receive the annuity for the remainder of its term, which could have a market value, on the principle explained in *R(SB) 43/84*.

Income from trusts

2.265 The general rule is that any payment from a trust that is income, rather than capital, counts as unearned income. Exceptions are payments from sums of personal injury compensation held on trust (reg.76(4)) and payments from certain compensation schemes (reg.77). It may sometimes be difficult to say as a matter of general principle whether a payment from a trust is of capital or income, but reg.46(3) deems any sums paid regularly and by reference to a period to be income. Further, reg.46(4) deems each instalment of capital payable by instalments to be income if the amount of capital outstanding (aggregated with any other capital that the claimant has or is treated as having) exceeds £16,000. If the amount of aggregated capital does not exceed £16,000, the payment is to be treated as capital. Note that interests under trusts may well have a capital value (see the notes to reg.46 under the heading *Interests in trusts*) and that there is nothing in Sch.10 to disregard such capital (but see regs 76 and 77)

It was pointed out in *Q v SSWP (JSA)* [2020] UKUT 49 (AAC) that many everyday forms of holding assets jointly involve trusts, such as, in that case, funds belonging to the claimant held in a building society account in joint names. The same would apply where the beneficial interest in the funds, whoever put them in, is expressly or by implication to be held under a joint tenancy. The legal interest in the debt owed by the building society or bank would still be held jointly by those named on the account in trust for themselves as joint tenants. The same would also apply to other assets, including real property, held jointly (see the extensive discussion in the notes to reg.46). Thus, if the trust assets yield income, e.g. in the form of interest, dividends or rental payments, that would appear to be income from a trust under para.(1)(j), to be taken into account in full as unearned income. However, it is rather difficult to see why such a result would have been intended when such income, if received without the intervention of a trust, would not count as unearned income at all under reg.66(1), except through the mechanism of reg.72 and para.(1)(k) if the value of capital including that producing the income exceeded £6,000. But maybe the exclusion of the operation of reg.72 in trust and annuity cases (reg.72(2)) is regarded as establishing a balance.

Assumed income from capital

2.266 On para.(1)(k), "assumed yield from capital" (the equivalent to the "tariff income rule" for income support, old style JSA, old style ESA and housing benefit), see the note to reg.72. That applies where the claimant has capital (thus excluding any disregarded capital) in excess of £6,000, when an income of £4.35 per month for each £250 of excess is assumed. If any such income is assumed, reg.72(3) provides that any actual income derived from that capital ("for example rental, interest or dividends") is to be treated as part of the person's capital from the day it is due to be paid. That produces some strange consequences where a claimant is in receipt of rent or some payment for occupation of premises, where not trading in lettings as a self-employed person (see the notes to reg.57). The plain assumption in reg.72(3) is that such income is to be treated as derived from capital in the sense of the value of whatever interest the claimant has in the premises. But neither actual income derived from capital nor rental payments, nor contributions towards household expenses is included in the list of what counts as unearned income. There can only be the assumed income where the value of capital is over £6,000, with the consequence of adding the actual income to the amount of capital, which will go towards keeping it over the £6,000. Regulation 72 can never apply where the income is from letting out some part of the claimant's home, because the capital value of the home is disregarded, so that no yield can be assumed from it.

Capital treated as income

2.267 Paragraph (1)(l) includes as income capital that is treated as income under reg.46(3) (regular payments by reference to a period) or (4) (capital payable by instalments in certain circumstances)—see the note to reg.46. See also the notes above under the heading *What is income* for the proposition that para.(1)(l) does not apply to every payment treated as income by virtue of reg.46(3) or (4), but only to *capital* treated as income by virtue of those provisions. That is in particular because of the use of the word "capital" in para.(1)(l). Thus, it appears that payments that are in their nature income cannot fall within para.(1)(l) and only count for universal credit purposes if listed in some other part of para.(1). On that basis, para.(1)(l) covers only payments that are in their nature capital that are paid either regularly and by reference to a period (reg.46(3)) or by instalments (reg.46(4)). If that is correct, it is unfortunate that the relationship of para.(1)(l) with reg.46(3) and (4) was not made more explicit.

PPF periodic payments

2.268 By virtue of para.(7) the definition in s.17(1) of the State Pension Credit Act 2002 (Pt I of this volume) is incorporated. The Pension Protection Fund ("PPF") was set up under the Pensions Act 2004 in order to provide protection for members of defined benefit (i.e. normally final salary) occupational pension schemes and in relation to the defined elements of hybrid pension schemes that were wound up from April 6, 2005 onwards because of the employer's insolvency. For the complex provisions see Pt 2 of the Pensions Act 2004 and the equivalent Northern Ireland provisions. PPF periodic payments do not fall within the meaning of "retirement pension income" in para.(1)(a). By contrast, payments under the Financial Assistance Scheme Regulations 2005, intended to cover defined benefit occupational pension schemes that wound up between January 1997 and April 2005 because of employer insolvency, are included in the meaning of retirement pension income (s.16(1)(n) of the State Pension Credit Act 2002) and so fall within para.(1)(a).

Other income taxable under Pt 5 of ITTOIA

2.269 Paragraph (1)(m) covers other income that does not fall within sub-paras (a)–(la) and is taxable under Pt 5 of the Income Tax (Trading and Other Income) Act 2005 (ITTOIA). The types of income liable to income tax under Pt 5 include receipts from intellectual property, like royalty payments, income from films and sound recordings, income received as a settlor of a trust and income from estates in administration. Those are the categories mentioned in para.H5111 of the ADM and might therefore not be expected to crop up commonly (except perhaps income from estates in administration).

However, what the ADM does not mention, and your commentator has overlooked in previous editions, is that Pt 5 of ITTOIA also contains s.687 (see Vol.IV of this series) making taxable any income not charged to income tax under any provision in ITTOIA or any other Act. In particular, that is the provision under which casual earnings, not derived from employment under a contract of employment or office or from a trade, profession or vocation are taxed. That appears to produce the result that income derived from other paid work within reg.52(a)(iii) is simultaneously earned income and unearned income within sub-para.(m) (see the extensive discussion in the notes to reg.52 for the wide range of activities that in the present-day labour market might give rise to such earnings). Such a result cannot of course be allowed. The counting twice of the same amount as income cannot be allowed, but the way out is not clear. It is submitted that, although the introductory words of reg.66(1) state that a person's unearned income is any of their income falling within the descriptions that follow or reg.74, thus appearing to apply to any income listed whether it would otherwise be regarded as earned income or not, the application of sub-paras (a)–(m) must be coloured by the overall restriction of the scope of Ch.3 of the Regulations to the calculation of unearned income. It is true that para.4(3)(c) of Sch.1 to the WRA 2012 gives the power to make regulations specifying circumstances in which earned income is to be treated as unearned, but that does not authorise such treatment unless the income ceases to be treated as earned. Thus, it is submitted that the words of sub-para.(m) (and probably the whole of para.(1)) must be interpreted as not applying to any income that has already been specifically included as earned income by some other provision of the Regulations.

The question might well be asked whether income from letting property, not as part of a trade, is taxable under s.687 of ITTOIA and so within sub-para.(m). The answer seems to be that it is not, because the profits of a property business are taxable under Pt 4 of ITTOIA. The notion of a business would on the face of it exclude activities like letting out a room in the home or letting out a single property, but the definitions of a person's "property business" in ss.264 and 265 of ITTOIA cover not only businesses carried on for generating income from land, but also every transaction that a person enters into for that purpose otherwise than in the course of such a business (ss.264(b) and 265(b)). Thus, such income, not being listed in reg.66(1) and not being earned income does not count for universal credit purposes unless and until it metamorphoses into capital.

See the end of the separate section *When is income the claimant's* above for how liability to income tax on the income received is or is not taken into account. It is suggested there that if income tax has been deducted by the payer for remission to HMRC it is only the net amount actually received by the claimant that is to be taken into account. It might also be arguable that expenditure necessary to produce the income is to be deducted applying the principle of *Parsons v Hogg* [1985] 2 All E.R. 897, appendix to *R(FIS) 4/85*, also discussed in that section.

Attribution of unearned income to assessment periods

2.270 Unearned income is calculated monthly in accordance with reg.73, except in the case of student income which is calculated in accordance with reg.71. Regulations 68 and 71 in combination also contain the rules for what amount of student income is to be attributed to what assessment period.

What neither reg.66 nor any other provision on unearned income does is to provide any general rule at to how to decide to which assessment periods particular receipts are to be attributed. Regulation 68 does provide a rule for student income, but otherwise the Regulations are silent, as is Chapter H5 of the ADM. There is no equivalent of reg.31 of the Income Support Regulations (Vol.V of this series, 2021/22 edition as updated in Cumulative Supplements included in this volume and in mid-year Supplements) with a general rule that income other than earnings is to be treated as paid on the date it is due to be paid. Nor is there any equivalent of the final part of reg.29(2), that the period to which income other than earnings is attributed begins with the date on which the payment is treated as made under reg.31.

In most cases, where a regular amount of income is received monthly or more frequently, there will be no practical problem. However, a couple of examples can be taken to indicate the problem. First, (A) suppose that a claimant receives income from a trust (para.(1)(j)) or instalments of capital that are treated as income (para. (1)(l)) on a quarterly basis in arrears, that the most recent receipt was on April 1 and that the first assessment period in the universal credit claim begins on May 1. Is the monthly equivalent to be taken into account immediately and, if not, how is the next payment on July 1 to be treated? Secondly, (B) suppose that either before or during an existing universal credit award the claimant receives a lump sum payment (less than £5,000) of arrears of a social security benefit falling within para.(1)(a) or (b) that relates to a period before the beginning of entitlement to universal credit. Although such a payment would not be disregarded as capital under para.18 of Sch.10 or reg.10A of the Universal Credit (Transitional Provisions) Regulations 2014, the better view (see above under *What is income*) is that benefit that would have been income if paid on the due date retains its character as income even though paid as a lump sum as arrears (see also the notes to para.18 of Sch.10). Is the lump sum to be taken into account forward from the date of receipt or ignored as unearned income as not relating to an assessment period within the award period?

It is submitted that the principle to be applied is that the monthly equivalent of such payments is to be attributed to the assessment period to which it relates. However, that conclusion unfortunately does not rest on clear statements in the legislation, but on inferences from scattered provisions and its overall structure.

First, it appears clear that the general rule for earnings, of taking each payment into account in the assessment period in which it is received, does not apply to unearned income. That rule only applies to earnings by virtue of the specific provisions in regs 54, 57 and 61. There are no such specific provisions for unearned income. And the requirement in reg.73(1) for unearned income to be calculated as a monthly amount is inconsistent with a rule like the earnings rule.

Second, para.4(3)(a) of Sch.1 to the WRA 2012 authorises the making of regulations specifying circumstances in which a person is to be treated as "having or not having" unearned income, which perhaps points towards a test of having such income, as do the terms of the deeming of having such income in regs 68 (student income) and 74(1) (notional income). But that in itself does not tell us in what assessment period any amount of unearned income is to be taken into account. Paragraph 4(3)(a) would seem to authorise regulations like reg.66(1) defining what sort of income is to be treated as the claimant's and thus that the claimant has, but go no further.

Third, although s.8(3)(b), providing in relation to each assessment period for the deduction of an amount "in respect of unearned income calculated in the prescribed manner" in calculating entitlement, does not in itself take matters further forward, the authorisation in para.4(1)(c) of Sch.1 of regulations providing for the calculation or estimation of unearned income in respect of an assessment period begins to suggest the way forward. That is taken on by reg.22(1)(a), providing that the amounts to be deducted include all of the claimant's unearned income (or combined unearned income for joint claimants) "in respect of the assessment period" in question. That suggests that the test is of what unearned income is to be regarded as "in respect of" of each assessment period. But is that merely a reflection of the terms of s.8(3)(b) or a rule requiring the finding of a connection of substance between an amount and the assessment period?

Fourth, other regulations are consistent with the second of those alternatives. In particular, reg.73(2A) operates on the assumption that it is the period in respect of which the payment was made that matters, not the period for which the payment is available to be used as income. It applies when the period in respect of which income is paid begins or ends during an assessment period and then supplies a method of calculation of the amount to be taken into account in that period to reflect the number of days in respect of which the unearned income was paid that fall within that period. That provision can only make sense on the basis that "in respect of" identifies the days that the payment of income was for, or in other words the days to which the payment of income relates.

If that is correct, how do the two examples above work out? On example (A), regular quarterly payments in arrears from a trust or in instalments of capital treated as income, reg.73(2)(c) tells us that the monthly equivalent is to be calculated by multiplying by four and dividing by 12. The monthly equivalent of the payment received on April 1 could not be treated as unearned income in the assessment periods beginning on May 1 and June 1, because it related entirely to, was "in respect of" the three months prior to April 1. It would not, on that basis, matter that the income was available for the claimant to use in the three months forward from

April 1. The amount received would, though, so far as not spent or legitimately disposed of, probably count as part of the claimant's capital. But what should be taken into account in the assessment period beginning on May 1 and June 1 in respect of the payment due on July 1? That payment would be in respect of the previous three months, but could that be used as the basis for taking the monthly equivalent into account for those two assessment periods before the payment had actually been made? Even assuming that full information had been given by the claimant, there might possibly be a change in the amount that the claimant would not know about in advance (such as an increase for inflation or as the result of an alteration in exchange rates). Possibly the answer is that if the amount does not fluctuate, the amount of the April 1 payment can be used to calculate the monthly equivalent for the May and June assessment periods, but that if there is fluctuation then, in the absence of an identifiable cycle, an average can be taken over three months or some other period, presumably prior to the assessment period in question (reg.73(3)). However, that is somewhat speculative unless and until there is some authoritative elucidation.

On example (B), a lump sum payment of arrears of a benefit listed in para.(1)(a) or (b) for a period before the start of universal credit entitlement, the answer is clear on the approach suggested above. The payment is to be treated as income and was paid in respect of a period entirely prior to any assessment period and so could not be taken into account as unearned income, even though the money would be available to spend during the period of entitlement. It would therefore presumably metamorphose into capital immediately on receipt and would, so far as not spent or legitimately disposed of, not be disregarded (Sch.10 para.18). Any continuing award of the benefit concerned would of course count as unearned income. If the period covered by the arrears included the date of the start of universal credit entitlement, the awarding decision would fall to be revised under reg.12 of the Decisions and Appeals Regulations 2013.

It is very unfortunate that there should have to be such speculation about matters that would have been expected to be settled clearly by straightforward regulations.

There is a further problem of attribution that arises when a claimant (or the younger of joint claimants) reaches the qualifying age for state pension credit (i.e. state retirement age), so that the condition of entitlement in s.4(1)(b) of the WRA 2012 is no longer met. With effect from November 25, 2020 the new form of para.26 of Sch.1 to the Decisions and Appeals Regulations 2013 provides that any consequential universal credit supersession takes effect from the beginning of the assessment period following the assessment period in which the person reaches the crucial age. That raises the possibility that the claimant might become entitled to retirement pension or state pension or state pension credit relating to the period from the crucial birthday, which period could begin during the last assessment period of entitlement. So far as state pension credit is concerned, that does not matter as that benefit is not listed in reg.66(1). For retirement pension or state pension, there would be a calculation under reg.73(2A) of the appropriate proportion of the monthly amount of the income to cover the days in respect of which the pension was paid. That will work smoothly if the pension is paid on time, so that the calculation can be done shortly after the end of the last assessment period of universal credit entitlement. What is not entirely clear is what should happen if for some reason the first pension payment is delayed beyond the end of that assessment period (except where no claim for pension has been made, when notional income will be deemed under reg.74(3)). There have been reports of the DWP ignoring such a payment and reports to the contrary. As it has been submitted above that the test for attribution is whether the income is related to ("in respect of") any days in the assessment period in question, that later payment of income would be relevant. But how long could a decision-maker legitimately wait to make a decision on the final assessment period? Just possibly, universal credit could be awarded without taking into account any pension as unearned income, followed immediately by a supersession on the ground that it is expected that a relevant change of circumstances (the award of retirement pension or state pension) will occur (reg.23(1)(b) of the Decisions and Appeals Regulations 2013).

Those speculative problems became concrete following the delays in 2021 in making decisions on claims for retirement pension and putting payment into place. Until payment is put into place no actual unearned income (for an under-pension-age claimant's partner) from that source exists to be taken into account as retirement pension income for universal credit purposes under reg.66(1)(a) and there can be no notional unearned income under reg.74 because an "application" has been made for retirement pension. Universal credit awards were then apparently made taking no retirement income from that source into account. When payment of retirement pension is put into place there may be a large payment of arrears due. Following the principles put forward above, that payment constitutes unearned income and is to be attributed to the assessment periods covered by the weeks to which the arrears relate. That circumstance will, depending on the date from which universal credit had been awarded, constitute a ground of revision of the original award of universal credit from the outset, under reg.12 of the Decisions and Appeals Regulations 1999 and s.9(3) of the SSA 1998, or of supersession on the ground of relevant change of circumstances from the first day of the assessment period in which the entitlement to retirement pension arose, under reg.23(1) of the Decisions and Appeals Regulations 1999 and para.31(2)(a)(i) of Sch.1 to the SSA 1998. That will give rise to an overpayment of universal credit that is recoverable under s.71ZB of the SSAA 1992, possibly by deduction from the arrears of retirement pension otherwise payable. Whether there has been such a deduction or not, the amount of arrears actually remaining in the claimant's possession after the end of the assessment periods to which it has been attributed can then metamorphose into capital, whose value would not fall to be disregarded under para.18 of Sch.10 to the Universal Credit Regulations (see para.18(1)(c)). However, if a universal credit overpayment recoverability decision has been made, but there has been no direct deduction from the arrears and repayment has not yet occurred, it is arguable that to the extent of the amount determined to be recoverable the arrears have not metamorphosed into capital because that amount constitutes a "relevant liability" to be taken into account *(R(SB) 2/83* and see the discussion at para.3.197 in relation to the surplus earnings rule in reg.54A) even though different benefits are involved.

Note that special provision is made in the annual social security benefit up-rating orders for the assessment period in which the up-rated amount of a benefit that counts as unearned income is to be taken into account. Thus art.1(4) of the Social Security Benefits Up-rating Order 2023 (SI 2023/316), in conjunction with art.1(3)(p), ensures that in the case of a beneficiary who has an award of universal credit the provision up-rating the social security benefit comes into force for the purpose of calculating entitlement to universal credit on the first day of the first assessment period to commence on or after April 10, 2023.

Meaning of "retirement pension income"

67.—(1) Subject to paragraph (2), in regulation 66(1)(a) "retirement pension income" has the same meaning as in section 16 of the State Pension Credit Act 2002 as extended by regulation 16 of the State Pension Credit Regulations 2002. 2.271

(2) Retirement pension income includes any increase in a Category A or Category B retirement pension mentioned in section 16(1)(a) of the State Pension Credit Act 2002 which is payable under Part 4 of the Contributions and Benefits Act in respect of a person's partner.

DEFINITIONS

"Contributions and Benefits Act"—see reg.2.
"partner"—*ibid.*

GENERAL NOTE

2.272 "Retirement pension income" has the same meaning for the purposes of universal credit as it does for state pension credit. See the notes to s.16 of the State Pension Credit Act 2002 and reg.16 of the State Pension Credit Regulations 2002 in Pts I and III of this volume. The definition covers most kinds of UK state retirement pension provision, thus including the equivalent Northern Ireland provisions to British provisions and occupational or personal pension payments, including from overseas arrangements. Presumably para.(2) is felt to be necessary because s.16(1) (a) of the 2002 Act does not refer to such increases (although in the case of a couple it is their combined income that counts (s.8(4)(b) of the WRA 2012)).

In relation to occupational and personal pension schemes it is necessary to follow a longer chain of references, through s.17(1) of the 2002 Act to s.1 of the Pension Schemes Act 1993. Personal pension schemes are relatively easily identified, but there are sometimes difficulties in differentiating occupational pension schemes, income from which does count in universal credit, and other sorts of schemes income from which does not. The definition in s.1 of the 1993 Act has been amended over the years. The reference for purposes of the Universal Credit Regulations is presumably to the current form, rather than the form in force at the time when the 2002 Regulations were laid. In summary, s.1(1) gives the meaning as "a pension scheme" established for the purpose of providing benefits to, or in respect of, people with service in employment, or to, or in respect of, other people by an employer, employee or some representative body. That on its face seems rather circular, but s.1(5) provides that "pension scheme" means a scheme or other arrangement comprised in one or more instruments or arrangements, having or capable of having effect so as to provide benefits to or in respect of people (a) on retirement; (b) on having reached a particular age; or (c) on termination of employment. That can cover schemes that include death in service benefits to partners, children or dependants of employees and benefits on early retirement or termination of employment for medical reasons. It can then be difficult to work out whether employers' schemes for benefits payable on disablement or death come within that definition. For instance, although various Armed Forces Pension Schemes are clearly within the definition, what about the various pre-2005 War Pensions Schemes and similar and the Armed Forces Compensation Scheme? It is submitted that the latter are not occupational pension schemes. A possible test (no more than that) might be that if a scheme does not provide any benefits on retirement, reaching a particular age or termination of employment independent of incapacity, disablement or death of the employee, it is not an occupational pension scheme. A note to ADM para.H5010 advises that a non-taxable attributable Service Invalidity Pension (SIP) or a Service Attributable Pension (SAP) is a pension awarded to members of the armed forces who are discharged on medical grounds as a result of illness or injury attributed to service. SAPs and non-taxable attributable SIPs are not occupational pensions and are not taken into account.

Chief Constable of Derbyshire Constabulary v Clark [2023] EAT 135 contains a lengthy discussion of the legal background in answering the question whether a police disablement gratuity under reg.12 of the Police Injury Benefit Regulations 2006 falls within the definition of "occupational pension scheme" in s.1 of the Pension Schemes Act 1993, as amended. The gratuity was payable to officers injured in the execution of their duty who had ceased to be a member of a police force and who became totally and permanently disabled as a result of the injury, within 12 months of the injury. The two claimants were refused gratuities because more than 12 months had elapsed between the injury and the disablement. They wished to challenge that ground of refusal in an employment tribunal (ET) as demonstrating disability discrimination. It was thought that the ET would only have jurisdiction if the gratuity formed part of an occupational pension scheme as defined in s.1. The scheme of injury benefits was separated from the arrangements for police pensions. The President of the EAT, Eady J, held that the gratuity did not fall within the Pension Schemes Act definition because, although it was a condition of payment that the officer had ceased to be a member of a police force, entitlement could only be established at the point where the officer was deemed to be totally and permanently disabled. The regulation did not require any causative link between the ceasing of employment and the injury or disablement. Thus, the benefit was not provided on retirement or termination of service. On the claimants' appeal, the Court of Appeal confirmed that analysis, while ruling that the ET had jurisdiction for another reason (*Clark v Chief Constable of Derbyshire* [2024] EWCA Civ 676).

There is not the space here to mention most of the further categories listed in s.16 of the 2002 Act as extended by reg.16 of the 2002 Regulations. Income from retirement annuity contracts and from annuities bought with the proceeds of personal pension schemes are covered, as are regular payments under an equity release scheme. Payments from a former employer, i.e. not from an occupational scheme as such, on early retirement for ill-health or disability are also covered.

Note the category of notional unearned income in reg.74(3) and (4), where a person has failed to apply for retirement pension income that is available or has deferred taking an annuity or income drawdown that is available from a scheme.

Person treated as having student income

68.—(1) A person who is undertaking a course [[1]of education, study or training] (see regulation 13) and has a student loan[[2], a postgraduate [[3] . . .] loan] or a grant in respect of that course, is to be treated as having student income in respect of— 2.273

(a) an assessment period in which the course begins;

(b) in the case of a course which lasts for two or more years, an assessment period in which the second or subsequent year begins;

(c) any other assessment period in which, or in any part of which, the person is undertaking the course, excluding—

(i) an assessment period in which the long vacation begins or which falls within the long vacation, or

(ii) an assessment period in which the course ends.

(2) Where a person has a student loan [[2] or a postgraduate [[3] . . .] loan], their student income for any assessment period referred to in paragraph (1) is to be based on the amount of that loan.

(3) Where paragraph (2) applies, any grant in relation to the period to which the loan applies is to be disregarded except for—

(a) any specific amount included in the grant to cover payments which are rent payments in respect of which an amount is included in an award of universal credit for the housing costs element;

(b) any amount intended for the maintenance of another person in respect of whom an amount is included in the award.

(4) Where paragraph (2) does not apply, the person's student income for any assessment period in which they are treated as having that income is to be based on the amount of their grant.

(5) A person is to be treated as having a student loan [[2] or a postgraduate [[3] . . .] loan] where the person could acquire [[2] a student loan or a postgraduate [[3] . . .] loan] by taking reasonable steps to do so.

(6) Student income does not include any payment referred to in regulation 66(1)(f) (training allowances).

(7) In this regulation and regulations 69 to 71—

"grant" means any kind of educational grant or award, excluding a student loan or a payment made under a scheme to enable persons under the age of 21 to complete courses of education or training that are not advanced education;

"the long vacation" is a period of no less than one month which, in the opinion of the Secretary of State, is the longest vacation during a course which is intended to last for two or more years;

[3 "postgraduate loan" means a loan to a student undertaking a postgraduate master's degree course or a postgraduate doctoral degree course pursuant to regulations made under section 22 of the Teaching and Higher Education Act 1998;]

"student loan" means a loan towards a student's maintenance pursuant to any regulations made under section 22 of the Teaching and Higher Education Act 1998, section 73 of the Education (Scotland) Act 1980 or Article 3 of the Education (Student Support) (Northern Ireland) Order 1998 [4...].

AMENDMENTS

1. Universal Credit (Consequential, Supplementary, Incidental and Miscellaneous Provisions) Regulations 2013 (SI 2013/630) reg. 38(5) (April 29, 2013).

2. Social Security (Treatment of Postgraduate Master's Degree Loans and Special Support Loans) (Amendment) Regulations 2016 (SI 2016/743) reg. 6(2) (August 4, 2016).

3. Social Security (Income and Capital) (Miscellaneous Amendments) Regulations 2020 (SI 2020/618) reg.8(2) (July 15, 2020).

4. Social Security and Universal Credit (Migration of Tax Credit Claimants and Miscellaneous Amendments) Regulations 2024 (SI 2024/341) reg.7(4) (April 1, 2024).

DEFINITIONS

"assessment period"—see WRA 2012, ss.40 and 7(2) and reg.21.
"housing costs element"—see regs 2 and 25.

GENERAL NOTE

2.274 See the notes to reg.13 for when a person is regarded as undertaking a course of education, study or training. If someone who is exempt from the requirement not to be receiving education under reg.14 has student income that is taken into account in calculating their universal credit award, they will not have any work requirements (see reg.89(1)(e)(ii) and reg.89(1)(da) for couples where only one partner is a student). If the person leaves their course, student income is taken into account up to the end of the assessment period before the one in which they leave the course. That is because the person is no longer undertaking the course and so para.(1) of this regulation does not apply (the change of circumstance will take effect from the first day of the assessment period in which it occurs—para.20 of Sch.1 to the Decisions and Appeals Regulations 2013). In addition, the terms of reg.68(1)(c)(ii) prevent a person being treated as having student income in the assessment period in which the course ends. As any student income that is left over at the end of a course or when a person finally abandons or is dismissed from it does not fall within any other paragraph in reg.66(1), it will be ignored.

Paragraph (1)

2.275 This provides for the assessment periods (i.e. months) in which student income will be taken into account. These are any assessment periods during which, or during part of which, the person is undertaking the course of education, study or training, including the assessment period in which the course begins, or any subsequent year of the course begins. But student income will be ignored in the assessment period in which the course ends, in the assessment period in which the long vacation (defined in para.(7)) starts and in any assessment periods that fall wholly within the long vacation.

Paragraphs (2)–(7)

These paragraphs define what counts as student income. It does not include training allowances and payment for living expenses taken into account under reg.66(1)(f) (para.(6)). 2.276

If a person has a student loan or a postgraduate loan (both defined in para.(7)), or is treated as having a student loan or a postgraduate loan under para.(5) (see the notes to reg.69 for discussion of the test of "could acquire by taking reasonable steps"), the amount of that loan counts as income and any grant (defined in para.(7)) paid for the same period as the loan is ignored. But any specific amount included in the grant for rent payments which are being met by universal credit, or any amount intended for the maintenance of another person included in the person's universal credit award, will count as income (paras (2) and (3)).

SSWP v AD (UC) [2023] UKUT 272 (AAC) confirms that under regs 68(5) and 69(1) it is irrelevant to the amount of a student loan (i.e. a loan towards maintenance under the relevant student support regulations) that is to be taken into account that the claimant had to use £9,250 of the loan to pay fees (not having qualified for a fees loan because of earlier periods of study). The definition in reg.68(7) is based on objective criteria relating to the source of the funds and their characterisation under the student support regulations, rather than how the particular student intends to use or actually uses the funds. The First-tier Tribunal went wrong in applying the exclusion in reg.70(a) of payments intended to meet tuition fees or examination fees, because reg.70 applies only to grants, not loans.

With effect from July 2020 postgraduate doctoral degree loans have been brought within the general definition of "postgraduate loan", so that they are subject to the same rules as previously applied only to master's degree loans. Doctoral degree loans were introduced in 2018, at the same annual rate as for master's degree loans (i.e. £11,836 for courses starting on or after August 1, 2022 and £12,167 for courses starting on or after August 1, 2023, with an overall cap of, for 2022/23, £27,892 and, for 2023/24, £28,673. It would seem that prior to July 2020 postgraduate doctoral degree loans would have fallen within the definition of "student loan", since the relevant English regulations were made under s.22 of the Teaching and Higher Education Act 1998, meaning that the 30% rule in reg.69(1A) would not have applied, but only a loan going towards maintenance would have counted. It is not known if the 30% rule was applied in practice before the July 2020 amendments.

If the person does not have, and is not treated under para.(5) as having, a student loan or a postgraduate loan, grant income is taken into account (para.4)).

Note the exclusion from the definition of "grant" of payments made to enable people under 21 to complete courses of non-advanced education or training. This means that payments from the 16–19 Bursary Fund and educational maintenance allowances (in so far as they still exist) do not count as student income (they are fully disregarded for the purposes of income support, old style JSA, old style ESA and housing benefit). Paragraph H6008 ADM also states that grant income does not include any payment derived from Access Funds (although the basis for this is not clear).

"Student loan" for the purposes of regs 68–71 only includes a loan towards the student's maintenance (see para.(7)). So, for instance, the special support element (intended to contribute to the costs of books, childcare, travel and equipment) of any special support maintenance loan is not included. With effect from April 1, 2024, a reference to a young student bursary in Scotland has been removed because, according to para.7.7 of the Explanatory Memorandum to the amending regulations, such bursaries are no longer payable under the specific legislation formerly mentioned. Instead, the bursaries should be treated as grants.

See regs 69–71 for the calculation of student income. There is a disregard for student income of £110 per assessment period (reg.71).

Calculation of student income—student loans [1 and postgraduate [2...] loans]

2.277 **69.**—(1) Where, in accordance with regulation 68(2), a person's student income is to be based on the amount of a student loan for a year, the amount to be taken into account is the maximum student loan (including any increases for additional weeks) that the person would be able to acquire in respect of that year by taking reasonable steps to do so.

[1 (1A) Where, in accordance with regulation 68(2), a person's student income is to be based on the amount of a postgraduate [2...] loan for a year, the amount to be taken into account is 30 per cent. of the maximum postgraduate [2...] loan that the person would be able to acquire by taking reasonable steps to do so.]

(2) For the purposes of calculating the maximum student loan in paragraph (1) [1 or the maximum postgraduate [2...] loan in paragraph (1A)] it is to be assumed no reduction has been made on account of—

(a) the person's means or the means of their partner, parent or any other person; or

(b) any grant made to the person.

Amendments

1. Social Security (Treatment of Postgraduate Master's Degree Loans and Special Support Loans) (Amendment) Regulations 2016 (SI 2016/743) reg. 6(3) (August 4, 2016).

2. Social Security (Income and Capital) (Miscellaneous Amendments) Regulations 2020 (SI 2020/618) reg.8(3) (July 15, 2020).

Definitions

"grant"—see reg.68(7).

"partner"—see reg.2.

"postgraduate loan—see reg.68(7).

"student loan"—see regs 2 and 68(7).

General Note

2.278 The amount of a student loan that is taken into account is the maximum amount (including any increases for additional weeks) that the person could obtain for that year if they took reasonable steps to do so (para.(1)), bearing in mind the amounts, not being towards the student's maintenance, that are excluded from the definition in reg.68(7). In the case of a postgraduate loan, it is 30 per cent of the maximum postgraduate loan that the person could obtain for that year if they took reasonable steps to do so (para.(1A)). No reduction is made for any assessed contribution from a parent or partner (or any other person) or for any grant which may have reduced the loan.

In *IB v Gravesham BC and SSWP* (HB) [2023] UKUT 193 (AAC) Judge Poynter has declined to follow *CH/4429/2006*, mentioned in previous editions, on the housing benefit equivalent of the rule in regs 68(5) and 69(1). There, Commissioner Powell had held that "reasonable" qualified only the mechanical steps that had to be taken to acquire a loan and was not concerned with matters such as the motives or religious beliefs of the claimant. The facts of *IB* were on all fours with those of *CH/4429/2006*, in that the claimant was a devout and observant Muslim, who did not take out student loans otherwise available to him because that would have involved the paying of interest, which he conscientiously believed was forbidden by his religion. Nonetheless, the local authority treated him as possessing income from the loans, so that he failed the housing benefit means test. That decision was upheld by the First-tier Tribunal, considering itself bound by *CH/4429/2006*. The Upper

Tribunal substituted the decision that on the particular facts the claimant's entitlement to housing benefit was to be recalculated on the basis that he did not possess any income from the loans that he had not applied for.

The judge's view was that the reasoning in *CH/4429/2006* proceeded on a false basis and contained additional errors of logic. The Commissioner had stated in para.4 that the practical effect of the provision was that a student who was "entitled to a student loan", the use of which words was said to be deliberate, was to suffer a diminution in the amount of housing benefit. That was the apparent basis for the conclusion about the meaning of reasonable steps in para.11 of his decision. The judge points out that those words do not appear anywhere in the applicable Regulations, and that the test actually set out is in terms of what could be acquired by taking reasonable steps and does not assume the making of an application. A straightforward analysis of the steps that would be necessary to acquire a student loan would include scrutinising the terms on which the loan was offered, deciding whether to accept those terms and, if so, completing and submitting the application form and finally signing an agreement accepting the paying of interest. The judge concludes that the steps to be considered under the regulation therefore cannot be restricted to the "mechanical", the particular question of whether to accept the terms being one that would involve issues of judgment for anyone (e.g. about whether to accept the future burden of debt and interest payments). Moreover, while the Commissioner had noted that it was difficult to see how the necessary steps to acquire a loan could in themselves be said to be unreasonable except in the most exceptional cases, Judge Poynter suggests that, if personal circumstances were to be ignored, it would be inconceivable that the mechanics of applying for a student loan could ever require students to take steps that were unreasonable. In order for the words "reasonable steps" to be given some practical application, as must be assumed to have been intended, the interpretation adopted in *CH/4429/2006* could not be correct. For those and other subsidiary reasons, the judge declined to follow that decision.

Judge Poynter formulated the correct test to be applied, without the *CH/4429/2006* limitation and in line with the established approach in other areas of social security law, as follows:

> "139. I therefore conclude that "reasonable steps" means steps that are reasonable in all the circumstances including all the personal characteristics of the individual who was eligible to have applied for the student loan. That includes strong conscientious religious or other objections to the payment of interest.
> 140. I would, however, add that all the circumstances includes the interests of the wider public as represented by the Secretary of State and that assessing reasonableness will need to give those interests weight (see paras 190–191 below). Without being prescriptive, I suggest that an omission to acquire a loan that is based on purely financial considerations is unlikely to outweigh those interests."

He rejected the Secretary of State's submission that that approach would involve direct discrimination against claimants who did not share IB's particular religious views. That was because (para.142):

> "[t]he line drawn by my interpretation is not between Muslims and non-Muslims nor even between people who have conscientious objections to taking out a student loan and those who don't. Rather it is between, on the one hand, any student whose personal circumstances as a whole are such that—for whatever reason—he cannot take reasonable steps to acquire a student loan and, on the other, all students who are not so circumstanced. Those two groups are not in analogous situations. The latter could reasonably acquire the loan that [the regulation] takes into account as their income. The former cannot."

The judge also rejected the submission that his interpretation would make the housing benefit scheme unworkable and invite numerous, possibly opportunistic, claims, pointing out the limited scope for students to qualify for housing benefit (as for other means-tested benefits, including universal credit), the fact that to benefit from the rule the claimant would have to turn down the advantages of actually receiving the loan on offer and the difficulties that claimants might have in showing a genuine conscientious religious or other objection to the payment of interest. The latter point might easily be tested by seeing if the particular claimant had any interest-bearing bank or building society accounts, a credit card or a non-Sharia mortgage. Finally, there was the limiting factor of the need to take into account when judging reasonableness the interests of the wider public, in the form of the government policy that the costs of education are usually to be funded from the education budget rather than the social security benefit.

However, in substituting his own decision in *IB* Judge Poynter had no doubt that the claimant's personal circumstances, in particular his sincere and strongly held religious conviction that it would be a major sin to pay interest, outweighed any loss to public funds or dent in the government's general policy.

The result is that at the moment there are two conflicting decisions of equal authority. A First-tier Tribunal may therefore choose to follow the decision whose reasoning it finds more convincing. In doing so it can give weight to the fact that *IB* contains a detailed review of the reasoning in *CH/4429/2006*.

See reg.71 for how the amount of student income to be taken into account in an assessment period is calculated (note the disregard of £110).

Calculation of student income—grants

2.279 **70.** Where, in accordance with regulation 68(4), a person's student income is to be based on the amount of a grant, the amount to be taken into account is the whole of the grant excluding any payment—

(a) intended to meet tuition fees or examination fees;
(b) in respect of the person's disability;
(c) intended to meet additional expenditure connected with term time residential study away from the person's educational establishment;
(d) intended to meet the cost of the person maintaining a home at a place other than that at which they reside during their course, except where an award of universal credit includes an amount for the housing costs element in respect of those costs;
(e) intended for the maintenance of another person, but only if an award of universal credit does not include any amount in respect of that person;
(f) intended to meet the cost of books and equipment;
(g) intended to meet travel expenses incurred as a result of the person's attendance on the course; or
(h) intended to meet childcare costs.

Definition

"grant"—see regs 2 and 68(7).

General Note

2.280 If a grant counts as student income (on which see reg.68 and the note to that regulation), the whole of the grant is taken into account, subject to the disregards in paras (a)–(h). The disregards in paras (d) and (e) do not apply if the person's universal credit award includes an amount in respect of housing costs (para.(d)) or for the maintenance of another person (para.(e)) (see also reg.68(3)). It is important not to forget that satisfaction of the conditions for application of all of the disregards, including the proportion of the overall grant to be attributed to the category in question, depends on the intention of whatever body makes the grant. Although para.(b) does not use the word "intended", it would seem that a payment can only be "in respect of" a person's disability if so identified by the grant-making body.

See reg.71 for how the amount of student income to be taken into account in an assessment period is calculated (note the disregard of £110).

Calculation of student income—amount for an assessment period

71. The amount of a person's student income in relation to each assessment period in which the person is to be treated as having student income in accordance with regulation 68(1) is calculated as follows. 2.281

Step 1

Determine whichever of the following amounts is applicable—

(a) [1 in so far as regulation 68(2) applies to a person with a student loan,] the amount of the loan (and, if applicable, the amount of any grant) in relation to the year of the course in which the assessment period falls; [1 . . .]

[1 (aa) in so far as regulation 68(2) applies to a person with a postgraduate [2 ...] loan, 30 per cent. of the amount of the loan in relation to the year of the course in which the assessment period falls; or]

(b) if regulation 68(4) applies (person with a grant but no student loan [1 or postgraduate [2 ...] loan]) the amount of the grant in relation to the year of the course in which the assessment period falls.

But if the period of the course is less than a year determine the amount of the grant or loan in relation to the course.

Step 2

Determine in relation to—

(a) the year of the course in which the assessment period falls; or

(b) if the period of the course is less than a year, the period of the course, the number of assessment periods for which the person is to be treated as having student income under regulation 68(1).

[3 But where the first day of the person's universal credit award is on a date later than the first day of the year of the course, or period of the course, in question, each period of one month beginning on the same day as the assessment periods for, and preceding the commencement of, that award is to be treated as an assessment period when determining the number of assessment periods for which the person is to be treated as having student income.]

Step 3

Divide the amount produced by step 1 by the number of assessment periods produced by step 2.

Step 4

Deduct £110.

AMENDMENTS

1. Social Security (Treatment of Postgraduate Master's Degree Loans and Special Support Loans) (Amendment) Regulations 2016 (SI 2016/743) reg. 6(4) (August 4, 2016).

2. Social Security (Income and Capital) (Miscellaneous Amendments) Regulations 2020 (SI 2020/618) reg.8(4) (July 15, 2020).

3. Social Security and Universal Credit (Migration of Tax Credit Claimants and Miscellaneous Amendments) Regulations 2024 (SI 2024/341) reg.7(5) (April 1, 2024).

DEFINITIONS

"assessment period"—see WRA 2012 ss.40 and 7(2) and reg.21.
"grant"—see regs 2 and 68(7).
"postgraduate loan"—see reg.68(7).
"student loan"—see regs 2 and 68(7).

GENERAL NOTE

2.282 The amount of a person's student income, of any form within the meaning of reg.68(1), that is to be taken into account in each assessment period (i.e. month) is worked out as follows:

Step 1:

(a) if the person is treated as having student income in the form of a student loan (but not a postgraduate loan), calculate the annual amount of the loan, plus, if applicable, the annual amount of any grant that is to be taken into account (see reg.68(3)), for the year of the course in which the assessment period falls; or

(aa) if the person is treated as having student income in the form of a postgraduate loan, calculate 30 per cent of the annual amount of the loan for the year of the course in which the assessment period falls; or

(b) if the person's student income is under reg.68(4) to be based on the amount of a grant (i.e. where reg.68(2) does not apply because have neither a student loan nor a postgraduate loam), calculate the annual amount of the grant for the year of the course in which the assessment period falls.

(c) if the course lasts for less than a year, take the amount of the loan or grant for the course.

Step 2: calculate the number of assessment periods for which the person is to be treated as having student income in that year of the course, or if the course lasts for less than a year, during the course, in accordance with reg.68(1). Regulation 68(1) points to periods in which the person is undertaking a course of education, study or training. Prior to the April 2024 amendment, it was suggested that the number of assessment periods to count would include such periods even if the person had not made a claim for universal credit at that time (ADM H6140–H6144, example 2). That outcome has now been confirmed by the April 2024 addition to Step 2, which is said always to have been the policy intent.

Step 3: divide the amount in Step 1 by the number of assessments periods in Step 2.

Step 4: deduct £110, as £110 of student income is ignored in each assessment period.

General

Assumed yield from capital

72.—(1) A person's capital is to be treated as yielding a monthly income of £4.35 for each £250 in excess of £6,000 and £4.35 for any excess which is not a complete £250. **2.283**

(2) Paragraph (1) does not apply where the capital is disregarded or the actual income from that capital is taken into account under regulation 66(1)(i) (income from an annuity) or (j) (income from a trust).

(3) Where a person's capital is treated as yielding income, any actual income derived from that capital, for example rental, interest or dividends, is to be treated as part of the person's capital from the day it is due to be paid to the person.

General Note

This contains the universal credit equivalent of the tariff income rule that applies for income support, old style JSA, old style ESA and housing benefit. Under universal credit it is referred to as "assumed yield from capital", which is then taken into account in full under reg.66(1)(k). **2.284**

If a person has capital above £6,000 but below £16,000, it is treated as producing £4.35 per month for each complete £250 above £6,000 and £4.35 per month for any odd amount left over (para.(1)). But this does not apply if the capital is disregarded (see Sch.10 and regs 75 and 76), or if the actual income is taken into account under reg.66(1)(i) (income from an annuity) or (j) (income from a trust) (para.(2)). And remember the deductions that must be made under reg.49 in reaching the value of capital.

If the assumed yield from capital rule does apply, actual income from the capital counts as part of the person's capital from the day it is due to be paid (para.(3)). This rule could produce some tricky conundrums if the amount of the claimant's capital is very close to the £6,000 boundary or to a boundary between different amounts of assumed yield. Say that a claimant with an assessment period from the first to last day of the calendar month and with no other capital owns a heavily mortgaged second property whose capital value for universal credit purposes is £5,900 and which is rented out for £500 a month, payable on the 21st. Prima facie, when the rent is received it does not count as actual unearned income as it is not listed in reg.66(1), nor is it to be added to the claimant's capital because the capital is not treated under para.(1) as yielding an income. If the claimant retained the amount of the rent into the next assessment period, their capital would increase to £6,400, but if the £500 had immediately been spent on mortgage interest, that would not happen. However, if the capital value of the property was £6,100, what would happen? Would the £500 be treated as capital because at the date it was due to be paid income was being assumed and, if so, would the assumed income for that assessment period be based on £6,100 or £6,600? Or should the calculation not be made until the end of the assessment period? If by that date the claimant had used the £500 for the mortgage interest and so no longer had that capital, should the assumed yield be based on £6,100? Readers can no doubt think up more complicated scenarios.

Note that para.(3) assumes that dividends are a form of income from capital in providing that where para.(1) applies the actual income is to be treated as part of the claimant's capital. It is not at all clear that that is necessarily the case under the general law, rather than being a distribution of capital, except in particular circumstances (see the notes to reg.55 at 2.209). There is little assistance from tax law as dividends are chargeable to income tax under Part 4 of the Income Tax (Trading and Other Income) Act 2005 (ITTOIA) regardless of whether they are capital or income. At some point, it will have to be decided on appeal whether para.(3) applies to all dividends or only to those properly characterised as payments of income.

Unearned income calculated monthly

2.285 **73.**—(1) A person's unearned income is to be calculated as a monthly amount.

(2) Where the period in respect of which a payment of income is made is not a month, an amount is to be calculated as the monthly equivalent, so for example—

(a) weekly payments are multiplied by 52 and divided by 12;
(b) four weekly payments are multiplied by 13 and divided 12;
(c) three monthly payments are multiplied by 4 and divided by 12; and
(d) annual payments are divided by 12.

[[1](2A) Where the period in respect of which unearned income is paid begins or ends during an assessment period the amount of unearned income for that assessment period is to be calculated as follows—

$$N \times \left(\frac{M \times 12}{365} \right)$$

where N is the number of days in respect of which unearned income is paid that fall within the assessment period and M is the monthly amount referred to in paragraph (1) or, as the case may be, the monthly equivalent referred to in paragraph (2).]

(3) Where the amount of a person's unearned income fluctuates, the monthly equivalent is to be calculated—

(a) where there is an identifiable cycle, over the duration of one such cycle; or
(b) where there is no identifiable cycle, over three months or such other period as may, in the particular case, enable the monthly equivalent of the person's income to be determined more accurately.

(4) This regulation does not apply to student income.

AMENDMENT

1. Universal Credit (Digital Service) Amendment Regulations 2014 (SI 2014/2887) reg.4 (November 26, 2014). The amendment is subject to the saving provision in reg.5 of SI 2014/2887 (see 2020/21 edition of Vol.V of this series).

DEFINITIONS

"assessment period"—see WRA 2012 ss.40 and 7(2) and reg.21.
"student income"—see reg.68.

GENERAL NOTE

Paragraphs (1) and (2)

2.286 Unearned income is calculated as a monthly amount (paras (1) and (2)). But unlike earned income the amount taken into account in an assessment period (i.e. month) is not necessarily the amount actually received in that month. If the amount of the unearned income varies, the monthly equivalent is calculated in accordance with para.(3)).

See the notes to reg.66 under the heading *Attribution of unearned income to assessment periods* for discussion of how payments of unearned income are to be attributed to particular assessment periods in the absence of specific provisions providing a general rule.

Paragraph (2A)

This paragraph provides an exception to the general rule that unearned income is calculated as a monthly amount. For assessment periods (i.e. months) during which unearned income starts and/or finishes, only an amount based on the actual days in respect of which the income is paid will be taken into account. That is likely mainly to affect benefit payments and pensions. **2.287**

Note that the amendment which inserted para.(2A) is subject to a saving provision–see reg. 5 of the Universal Credit (Digital Service) Amendment Regulations 2014. The effect is that para.(2A) only applies to awards in relation to claims from people living in areas where the "digital service" (also referred to by DWP as the "full service") is in operation or from such persons who subsequently form a new couple or who separate after being part of a couple. Its operation is now general.

Paragraph (3)

This provides that if there is an identifiable cycle, the amount of unearned income received during that cycle is converted into a monthly amount (para.(3)(a)). If there is no cycle, the amount taken into account is averaged over three months, or over another period if this produces a more accurate monthly equivalent (para.(3)(b)). See the notes to reg.5(2)–(3A) of the Income Support Regulations in Vol.V of this series, 2021/22 edition as updated in Cumulative Supplements included in this volume and in mid-year Supplements for discussion of when there is a recognisable cycle, making the necessary allowances for the present regulation applying only to unearned income. There is no equivalent here to paras (3)–(3A) of reg.5. "Identifiable" cannot mean anything different from "recognisable". **2.288**

Paragraph (4)

This regulation does not apply to the calculation of student income. See reg.71 for the amount of a person's student income that is to be taken into account in each assessment period. **2.289**

Notional unearned income

74.—(1) If unearned income would be available to a person upon the making of an application for it, the person is to be treated as having that unearned income. **2.290**

(2) Paragraph (1) does not apply to the benefits listed in regulation 66(1)(b).

(3) A person who has reached the qualifying age for state pension credit is to be treated as possessing the amount of any retirement pension income for which no application has been made and to which the person might expect to be entitled if a claim were made.

(4) The circumstances in which a person is to be treated as possessing retirement pension income for the purposes of universal credit are the same as the circumstances set out in regulation 18 of the State Pension Credit Regulations 2002 in which a person is treated as receiving retirement pension income for the purposes of state pension credit.

Definition

"retirement pension income"—see reg.67.

GENERAL NOTE

Paragraphs (1) and (2)

2.291 A person is treated as having unearned income if "it would be available to [them] upon the making of an application for it". But that does not apply to the benefits listed in reg.66(1)(b).

A person should only be treated as having unearned income under para.(1) if it is clear that it would be paid if an application for it was made. Thus, for example, para. (1) would not apply to payments from a trust that are within the discretion of the trustees. A decision-making process by the trustees would have to be followed before a payment could be made, so that the income could not be said to be available upon making an application for it.

It is commonly said that no rule similar to those applied under paras (3) and (4) below can be applied to a person who has not attained the qualifying age for state pension credit. However, it is not clear why para.(1) should not apply to retirement pension income that a claimant could access before reaching that age. Members of both occupational and personal pension schemes can usually choose to take some or all of their entitlements under the scheme from the age of 55 and that may create income by the buying of an annuity or by drawdown from the funds in the scheme. Since those are options that are freely available and that the scheme administrators are bound to implement, the terms of para.(1) would seem to apply. "Retirement pension income" is defined in s.16 of the State Pension Credit Act 2002, to which reg.67 refers, simply in terms including income from an occupational pension scheme or a personal pension scheme (subs.(1)(f)) with no condition about the age at which the income is taken. The contrary argument would presumably be that the specific provisions in paras (3) and (4) linked to qualifying age for state pension credit are sufficient to indicate that they constitute the complete rules for retirement pension income, to the exclusion of para.(1). But para.(1) is not made subject to paras (3) and (4).

Paragraphs (3) and (4)

2.292 A person who has reached the qualifying age for state pension credit will be treated as having retirement pension income (defined in reg.67), first, under para.(3), of income that the person might expect to be entitled to if a claim were made for it, where no application has been made. Second, under para.(4), a person who has reached that age is to be treated as possessing retirement pension income in the same circumstances as set out in reg.18 of the State Pension Credit Regulations 2002 (Pt III of this volume). Only paras (1)–(1CB) of reg.18 specifically refer to retirement pension income, but presumably paras (1D)–(5), which refer to income from occupational pension schemes and money purchase benefits, which are within the meaning of retirement pension income in s.16 of the State Pension Credit Act 2002, are also intended to be incorporated. If so, paras (3) and (4) of reg.74 appear to cover much of the same ground. Paragraph (3) is in very general terms, but para.(4) may cover some circumstances that do not fall within the notion of not applying for income to which a person might expect to be entitled. See the notes to reg.18 of the SPC Regulations in Pt III of this volume and in particular to reg.42(2ZA) – (2C) of the Income Support Regulations in Vol.V of this series, 2021/22 edition as updated in Cumulative Supplements included in this volume and in mid-year Supplements, for more detailed consideration. A summary of the effect is given below.

Very much in general, the following are covered. A person who defers taking their state pension is treated as having the amount applicable if the pension had been taken at the qualifying age. A person who defers taking benefits from an occupational pension scheme beyond the scheme's retirement age, where the scheme allows that, is treated as having the amount of pension that would have been received if benefits had started at the normal age. A person in a defined contribution occupational pension scheme who does not buy an annuity or take advantage of income drawdown after state pensionable age is treated as having the amount of the annuity that could have been bought with the fund. The qualifying age for state pension credit was 60 but since April 2010 it has gradually risen in line with the staged increase in pensionable age for women and reached 65 in November 2018; thereafter state pension age for both men and women started to rise from 65 in December 2018, to reach 66 by October 2020. Although it is a condition of entitlement to universal credit that a person is below the qualifying age for state pension credit (see s.4(1)(b) of the WRA 2012), a couple may still be entitled if one member of the couple is under that age (see reg.3(2)) and the other is not.

If a person below the qualifying age for state pension credit chooses not to apply for retirement pension income, he or she will not be caught by paras (3) and (4), but see the notes to paras (1) and (2) for the possible application of those provisions.

For the rules relating to notional earned income, see reg.60.

Chapter 4

Miscellaneous

Compensation for personal injury

75.—(1) This regulation applies where a sum has been awarded to a person, or has been agreed by or behalf of a person, in consequence of a personal injury to that person. 2.293

(2) If, in accordance with an order of the court or an agreement, the person receives all or part of that sum by way of regular payments, those payments are to be disregarded in the calculation of the person's unearned income.

(3) If the sum has been used to purchase an annuity, payments under the annuity are to be disregarded in the calculation of the person's unearned income.

(4) If the sum is held in trust, any capital of the trust derived from that sum is to be disregarded in the calculation of the person's capital and any income from the trust is to be disregarded in the calculation of the person's unearned income.

(5) If the sum is administered by the court on behalf of the person or can only be disposed of by direction of the court, it is to be disregarded in the calculation of the person's capital and any regular payments from that amount are to be disregarded in the calculation of the person's unearned income.

(6) If the sum is not held in trust or has not been used to purchase an annuity or otherwise disposed of, but has been paid to the person within the past 12 months, that sum is to be disregarded in the calculation of the person's capital.

General Note

This regulation provides for an extensive disregard of compensation for personal injury, both as capital and income. 2.294

Firstly, the compensation is ignored for 12 months from the date it is paid to the person (para.(6)). Thus if it is spent during that 12 months or reduces to £6,000 or less, it will not have any effect on universal credit.

Secondly, if the compensation is held in trust, it will be disregarded as capital indefinitely and any income from the trust will be disregarded in the calculation of the person's unearned income (para.(4) and reg.66(1)(j)). It is often assumed if the amount is held in trust that will guarantee that the funds are at the least in some account separate from the claimant's other assets, if not held in some specifically created personal injury or other form of trust. However, that does not take into account the decision in *Q v SSWP (JSA)* [2020] UKUT 49 (AAC) that funds held in a joint bank or building society account with someone else are subject to a trust. There, funds derived a payment to the claimant of personal injury compensation were paid into joint accounts with one or other of her parents. Judge Poynter held that since there was no suggestion of any intention to make a gift of any of the funds to her parents, there would be a resulting trust under which the claimant and the parent held the chose in action (the right to payment of the moneys in the account) jointly on trust for the benefit of the claimant. For the purposes of the disregard as capital of the value of the trust fund where the funds of the trust are derived from a payment in consequence of a personal injury to the claimant in para.17 of Sch.8 to the JSA Regulations 1996, the form of the trust did not matter, so that para.17 applied. Although the wording of the disregard in para.(4) is different from that being considered in *Q*, the words "in trust" are not a term of art that has some special or technical meaning. Giving them their ordinary and natural meaning would mean that para.(4) should apply whenever the sum derived from personal injury compensation is subject to a trust, so that, as in *Q*, the form of the trust should not matter. Similarly, if the compensation payment is administered by a court, or can only be disposed of by direction of a court, its capital value is ignored and any regular payments from it are ignored in the calculation of the person's unearned income (para.(5)).

Thirdly, if the compensation is used to purchase an annuity, payments under the annuity are disregarded as unearned income (para.(3) and reg.66(1)(i)).

Fourthly, if, in accordance with a court order or agreement, the person receives all or part of the compensation by way of regular payments, these are ignored as unearned income (see para.(2)).

Although paras (3)–(5) refer to "the sum" awarded or agreed, in contrast to para.(2), which refers to all or part of that sum, it is submitted that in the overall context, "the sum" in paras (3)–(5) must be interpreted to include part of that sum and amounts derived from the original award or agreement.

The discussion at a meeting of the Social Security Advisory Committee (SSAC) on December 8, 2021 in relation to the Social Security (Income and Capital Disregards) (Amendment) Regulations 2021 (SI 2021/1405) (see the notes to reg.76) revealed some conceptual problems in the relationship of capital disregards to the calculation of the amount of capital possessed at a particular date. The essence of the problem put to DWP officials was what would happen if a claimant received a compensation payment within the disregard introduced by those regulations, acquired further non-disregarded capital and then spent a substantial amount of capital: how would it be known what pot of capital the expenditure came out of (SSAC minutes December 8, 2021, para.2.2(f))? The answer given in the letter dated January 12, 2022 from the Minister for Welfare Delivery, David Rutley, (Annex C to the minutes) was that:

> "the Department does not attempt to distinguish the capital derived from a compensation payment from other capital (with the exception of personal injury compensation that has been placed in trust). Wherever a claimant has received a payment of capital which is disregarded, whether indefinitely or for a prescribed period, their capital threshold is effectively increased by the amount of the original payment for the duration of that period. This is regardless of whether it was simply paid into a bank account with other funds or held or invested elsewhere."

That reply leaves it rather unclear what view is taken where a sum derived from compensation for personal injury to the claimant is held in trust, apparently being based on the mistaken view (see above) that that necessarily involves the sum being held in a segregated account. If the sum is so held, whether in a specially created trust or in a joint account of the kind in issue in *Q v SSWP (JSA)* [2020] UKUT 49 if it is used only for money from that source, there should be little difficulty in identifying when payments have been made out of that account, so that the payments out will not serve to reduce the amount of any other capital held by the claimant. The difficulty arises if the sum is held for the benefit of the claimant in a joint account which also contains funds of the claimant from other sources (or is not held in trust at all). The Minister's reply would then suggest that a payment out of the fund would leave the amount disregarded under reg.75(4) or (6) unaffected. That outcome might be justifiable in general (see the notes to Sch.10), but it is far from clear how that approach should hold if, say, the payment out is for a purpose specifically covered by the compensation payment, e.g. providing disability adaptations to a home.

There appears to be no problem with the relationship with reg.50(1) on notional capital (deprivation for the purpose of securing entitlement to or increasing the amount of universal credit) if the court order or agreement directly requires the making of regular payments (para.(2)) or the holding of the compensation payment on trust (para.(4)) or control by a court (para.(5)). However, an apparent problem could arise in cases in which the payment has initially been paid to the person concerned and later some or all of the amount is placed into a trust or is used to purchase an annuity. If that action had not been taken, the disregard under para.(6) could not have lasted for longer than 12 months. Therefore, depending on the amounts involved and other circumstances, it could appear on the face of it that the transfer of the capital was for the purpose of securing entitlement to universal credit or increasing its amount after the running out of that 12 months, so that the person would be treated as still possessing the amount disposed of. There is no equivalent in reg.50 to reg.51(1)(a) of the Income Support Regulations (reg.113(1)(a) of the JSA Regulations 1996 and reg.115(1)(a) of the ESA Regulations 2008) excluding its operation where the capital disposed of is derived from a payment made in consequence of a personal injury and is placed on trust. However, as suggested in the notes to reg.50(1) above, the intention of reg.75 is so clearly that the holding of funds in the ways set out in paras (3)–(5) should not affect entitlement to universal credit that it is submitted that the notional capital rule cannot be applied in those circumstances. The only penalty for continuing to hold funds as capital with no restrictions after the expiry of 12 months from the date of initial payment should be the loss of the para.(6) disregard for so long as the funds remain held in that way.

"Personal injury" is not given any definition in the WRA 2012 or these Regulations. The phrase must therefore be given its ordinary meaning, which in *R(SB) 2/89* was held to include a disease and any injuries suffered as a result of a disease (e.g. amputation of both legs following meningitis and septicaemia), as well as any accidental or criminal injury.

Compensation for personal injury includes all heads of an award for personal injury (*Peters v East Midlands Strategic Health Authority* [2009] EWCA Civ 145; [2010] Q.B. 48, a decision on the meaning of "an award of damages for a personal injury" in para.44(2)(a) of Sch.10 to the Income Support Regulations (see Vol.V of this series, 2021/22 edition as updated in Cumulative Supplements included in this volume and in mid-year Supplements) but the same reasoning will apply). In particular, it is not restricted to general damages for pain, suffering and loss of amenity, but can include other heads of loss, such as loss of earnings and any sum awarded by a court in respect of the cost of providing accommodation and care. See also *R(IS) 15/96* (para.18), applying that approach to criminal injuries compensation.

KQ v SSWP (IS) [2011] UKUT 102 (AAC), reported as [2011] AACR 43, holds that a compensation payment received from negligent solicitors, which purely related to what should have been claimed from a negligent surgeon responsible for damage to the claimant, was in consequence of the personal injury to the claimant. Judge Levenson accepts that the chain of causation does not go on for ever and so damages for the stress caused by the negligent solicitors or an element of punitive damages might not come within the disregards in para.12 or 12A of Sch.10. But there was no such element in the compensation in this case.

The disregards in reg.75 are in terms of compensation paid to a "person" in consequence of personal injury "to that person". Thus, where both members of a couple are claimants under s.2(1)(b) of the WRA 2012 it does not matter which of them is the recipient of the compensation, providing that it was in consequence of a personal injury to that person. However, they do not apply where the personal injury is to someone else, such as where an award is made under the Fatal Accidents Act 1976 (*CP v SSWP (IS)* [2011] UKUT 157 (AAC)). There, the claimant, who had Down's syndrome, received substantial compensation under the 1976 Act after her mother (and primary carer) was killed in a road traffic accident. Paragraph 12 of Sch.10 did not bite on such an award where the personal injury (or rather the fatality) was suffered by the claimant's mother, not the claimant. Nor would reg.75.

Special schemes for compensation etc.

2.295 **76.**—(1) This regulation applies where a person receives a payment from a scheme established or approved by the Secretary of State or from a trust established with funds provided by the Secretary of State for the purpose of—

(a) providing compensation [1or support] in respect of [3any of the following]—

(i) a person having been diagnosed with variant Creutzfeldt-Jacob disease or infected from contaminated blood products,

(ii) the bombings in London on 7th July 2005,

(iii) persons who have been interned or suffered forced labour, injury, property loss or loss of a child during the Second World War; [1 ...]

[1(iv) the terrorist attacks in London on 22nd March 2017 or 3rd June 2017,

(v) the bombing in Manchester on 22nd May 2017], [2 ...]

[4...]

[3(vii) historic institutional child abuse in the United Kingdom;]

(b) supporting persons with a disability to live independently in their accommodation.

[2(1A) This regulation also applies where a person receives a payment from—

(a) the National Emergencies Trust, registered charity number 1182809;

(b) the Child Migrants Trust, registered charity number 1171479, under the scheme for former British child migrants; or

[4 ...]]

[3(d) the scheme established by the Windrush Compensation Scheme (Expenditure) Act 2020.]

[4(e) the Post Office or the Secretary of State for the purpose of providing compensation or support which is—

(i) in connection with the failings of the Horizon system; or

(ii) otherwise payable following the judgment in *Bates and Others v Post Office Ltd* ((No. 3) "Common Issues") [6; or]]

[6(f) the Victims of Overseas Terrorism Compensation Scheme established by the Ministry of Justice in 2012 under section 47 of the Crime and Security Act 2010.]

(1B) This regulation also applies where a person receives a payment made for the purpose of providing compensation or support in respect of the fire on 14th June 2017 at Grenfell Tower.

(1C) This regulation also applies where a person—

(a) receives a vaccine damage payment or is a person for whose benefit a vaccine damage payment is made;

(b) is the partner of a person referred to in sub-paragraph (a) and receives a payment by or on behalf of that person which is derived from a vaccine damage payment;

(c) was the partner of a person referred to in sub-paragraph (a) immediately before the latter's death and receives a payment from their estate which is derived from a vaccine damage payment;

(d) in a case where a vaccine damage payment is made to the personal representative of a person who was severely disabled as a result of vaccination ("P"), was P's partner immediately before P's death and receives a payment from P's estate which is derived from a vaccine damage payment.]

(2) Any such payment, if it is capital, is to be disregarded in the calculation of the person's capital and, if it is income, is to be disregarded in the calculation of the person's income.

[[5](3) In relation to a claim for universal credit made by a person other than the diagnosed or infected person referred to in paragraph (1)(a)(i), a payment received from the scheme or trust, or which derives from a payment received from the scheme or trust, is to be disregarded if it would be disregarded in relation to an award of state pension credit by virtue of paragraph 13 or 15 of Schedule 5 to the State Pension Credit Regulations 2002.]

[[4](4) In this regulation—

"the Horizon system" means any version of the computer system used by the Post Office known as Horizon, Horizon Legacy, Horizon Online or HNG-X;

"the Post Office" means Post Office Limited (registered number 02154540);

"vaccine damage payment" means a payment made under the Vaccine Damage Payments Act 1979.]

AMENDMENTS

1. Social Security (Emergency Funds) (Amendment) Regulations 2017 (SI 2017/689) reg.9 (June 19, 2017).

2. Social Security (Income and Capital) (Miscellaneous Amendments) Regulations 2020 (SI 2020/618) reg.8(5) (July 15, 2020).

3. Social Security (Income and Capital Disregards) (Amendment) Regulations 2021 (SI 2021/1405) reg.8 (January 1, 2022).

4. Social Security (Income and Capital Disregards) (Amendment) Regulations 2023 (SI 2023/640) reg.8 (July 9, 2023).

5. Social Security (Infected Blood Capital Disregard) (Amendment) Regulations 2023 (SI 2023/894) reg.3 (August 30, 2023).

6. Social Security (Habitual Residence and Past Presence, and Capital Disregards) (Amendment) Regulations 2023 (SI 2023/1144) reg.9 (October 27, 2023).

DEFINITIONS

"claim"—see WRA 2012 s.40.

"partner"—see reg.2.

GENERAL NOTE

This regulation disregards payments from various compensation and support schemes and schemes to support people with a disability to live independently set up or approved by the Government. Any payment from these schemes or trusts is ignored as capital if it is capital, and as income if it is income (para.(2) 2.296

and reg.66(1)(j)). There is a degree of overlap with reg.75 on compensation for personal injury. However, that provision only applies where the compensation goes to the person who has suffered the personal injury and, so far as capital sums are concerned, only for 12 months unless held in trust. Where the conditions of reg.76 are met, the disregard is without limit of time, most categories apply to support as well as compensation and some extend to other family members. As a matter of principle, a person should be given the benefit of whatever provision is the most advantageous.

There have been extensions in the course of 2023 to the categories covered, with some restructuring and re-arrangement, leaving no very obvious reason for the order of appearance. So, in a particular case, all the categories covered will need to be looked at carefully before concluding that any payment falls outside the reg.76 disregard. Paragraphs (1) – (1C) now set out the categories of payment that attract the para.(2) disregard, with a specific extension for one category in para.(3) and some definitions in para.(4). Paragraph (1) covers various schemes established or approved by the Secretary of State or with funds provided by the Secretary of State (now excluding those linked to the Grenfell Tower fire, shifted to para.(1B)). Paragraph (1A) covers a number of other categories without any general condition related to the Secretary of State, but with some specific conditions. Paragraph (1B) covers any payments for compensation or support in respect of the Grenfell Tower fire. Paragraph (1C) covers vaccine damage payments under the Vaccine Damage Payments Act 1979. Each paragraph will be considered in turn below, followed by brief mention of a conceptual problem about the operation of the capital disregards dealt with more fully in the notes to reg.75.

An associated problem arises from the fact that all the conditions for the reg.76 disregard to operate are put in the form "where a person receives a payment" of a specified kind, using the present tense. This would not be a particular problem if the provision bringing the specified kind of payment within the scope of those conditions was always brought into effect before payments of the particular kind started to be made. However, recently there have been a number of instances of the relevant provision not being made and brought into effect until after payments started (e.g. paras (1)(a)(vii) (historic institutional child abuse), (1A)(d) (Windrush Compensation Scheme) and (1A)(f) (Victims of Overseas Terrorism Compensation Scheme)). There can be no doubt that in relation to payments received before the effective date there could be no reg.76 disregard for any period prior to that date (though there might be a reg.75 disregard), so that other unusual administrative measures have had to be taken to apply the disregard in practice in that period (see the notes to paras (1)(a)(vii) and (1A)(d) below). But what if the person retains some or all of the money received before the effective date beyond that time? It could be argued that there would still be no disregard under the strict terms of reg.76 because the payment was received before the effective date. That would be an unfortunate outcome and contrary to the assumption in the Explanatory Memorandum to SI 2021/1405, in the Secretary of State's letter of December 3, 2021 to the Permanent Secretary of the DWP (see the notes to para.(1)(a)(vii)) and in ADM Memo 17/23 on the Victims of Overseas Terrorism Compensation Scheme (VOTCS) and a statement given to the Social Security Advisory Committee (see the notes to para.(1A)(f)). It may be that the letter of December 3, 2021 and the extra-statutory arrangements in relation to the Windrush Compensation Scheme can be interpreted as covering that situation, if it were to be held that the operative provision did not apply to the payment in question, but there do not appear to be any such arrangements in relation to the VOTCS. It is, though, likely that the strict legal position will never be resolved. If decision makers follow the assumptions mentioned above, affected claimants will not complain and the issue will not get to an appeal.

Paragraph (1)

The general condition in para.(1) is that the payment is from a scheme established or approved by the Secretary of State or from a trust with funds provided by the Secretary of State and is for one of the purposes specified in sub-paras (a) and (b). Sub-paragraph (a) specifies a number of schemes providing compensation or support and sub-para.(b) covers the rather general purpose of supporting those with a disability to live independently in their accommodation. The general disregard in para.(2) is then from the income or capital of the person who received the payment (but see para.(3) on sub-para.(a)(i)).

The specific schemes or trust listed in sub-para.(a), apart from (vii), are carefully defined and need little further comment. Note that for cases where a person has been diagnosed with variant Creutzfeldt-Jacob disease or been infected from a contaminated blood product (sub-para.(a)(i) for payments to such a person) there is an extension to payments from the person's estate to their children (see para.(3) below).

Sub-paragraph (a)(vii) (historic institutional child abuse in the UK) is in very general terms, so that the general condition of approval by the Secretary of State is important. The Explanatory Memorandum to SI 2021/1405 reveals that four child abuse compensation schemes had been approved by the Secretary of State as at January 1, 2022: under the Historical Institutional Abuse (Northern Ireland) Act 2019; the Redress for Survivors (Historical Child Abuse in Care) (Scotland) Act 2021; the London Borough of Lambeth Redress Scheme and the London Borough of Islington's proposed support payment scheme (also listed in Memo ADM 21/21 with the date of approval: December 10, 2021). All provide one-off capital payments. No further schemes appear to have been approved since. On May 22, 2023, the Government announced that a redress scheme covering England and Wales was to be launched, following on the recommendations of the Independent Inquiry into Child Sexual Abuse. On January 10, 2024, the current Home Secretary, James Cleverley, said in a written statement to Parliament that the Government had been engaging extensively with experts to scope potential options and costs and would continue the work, but with no indication of any timescale for the production of an actual scheme or for any public consultation. The Church of England is also developing a national redress scheme, not limited to child victims, which appears unlikely to start operation before 2025.

The Explanatory Memorandum also reveals that payments under the Northern Ireland and Lambeth schemes could have been made prior to January 1, 2022. The application of the disregards provided under SI 2021/1405 to the period before that date was authorised by a ministerial direction from the Secretary of State, acting under "common law powers", whatever they are, (see the letters of December 3, 2021 between the Permanent Secretary of the DWP and the Secretary of State, published on the internet). Those arrangements raise questions as to what a tribunal on appeal should do if it has evidence of receipt prior to January 1, 2022 of a payment that would have been disregarded under the amendments if it had been received on or after that date. The legislation that a tribunal is bound to apply would not allow a disregard of such a payment before January 1, 2022 (and just possibly from that date: see the introductory note above) unless it fell within the existing "personal injury" disregard in reg.75 (possible for some historic institutional child abuse payments, though not for payments to next of kin or those who had merely been in "harm's way"). However, if an express submission from the DWP recorded the practical result of the application of the disregard on the basis of the ministerial direction, it would appear that the issue of the treatment of the payment would not arise on the appeal (see s.12(8)(a) of SSA 1998) and it is submitted that it would then be irrational for the tribunal to exercise its discretion to consider the issue nonetheless. If evidence of a payment that had not been taken into account as capital emerged in the course of an appeal, but there was no express DWP submission to explain the above outcome, it is submitted that a tribunal with knowledge of the matters mentioned above could still legitimately conclude that the issue did not arise on the appeal and decline to exercise its discretion under s.12(8)(a). Neither Memo ADM 21/21 on the effect of the amendment to reg.76 nor chapter H2 of the online ADM says anything about these questions.

The terms of sub-para.(b) are very general. They look very much as if intended to cover the operation of the old UK Independent Living Fund, a trust providing discretionary assistance out of funds provided by the DWP, that was permanently closed on June 30, 2015. In so far as any replacement support is provided by the Scottish or Welsh Ministers or local authorities, and thus without the connection to the Secretary of State necessary for sub-para.(b), capital payments can only be disregarded if falling within para.18A of Sch.10 ("local welfare provision", defined in reg.2). Payments of an income nature would not come within any categories of unearned income in reg.66(1). It is doubtful whether any scheme has since existed that is established, approved or funded by the Secretary of State that meets the conditions of sub-para.(b).

Paragraph (1A)

This paragraph now, Grenfell Tower payments having been moved to their own place in para.(1B), lumps together payments from the two charities specified in sub-paras (a) and (b) with payments under the statutory Windrush Compensation Scheme (sub-para.(d)), payments from the Post Office or the Secretary of State for compensation or support of the victims of the Horizon computer scandal (sub-para.(e)) and payments under the Victims of Overseas Terrorism Compensation Scheme (sub-para.(f)).

The Windrush provision (sub-para.(d)) was added to reg.76(1A) with effect from January 1, 2022, but some payments had been made under the Scheme before that date. The correspondence of December 3, 2021 between the Permanent Secretary of the DWP and Secretary of State referred to in the notes to para.(1) states that extra-statutory arrangements with HM Treasury provided for the disregard in practice of such payments in means-tested benefits from the outset. The same problems as discussed in the notes to para.(1) could arise if on appeal a tribunal were faced with a payment of compensation received before January 1, 2022 and, it is submitted, could be solved in the same way as suggested there by a tribunal with knowledge of the extra-statutory arrangement. It might be thought that the delay in putting the disregard of payments from the Scheme on a proper statutory basis is symptomatic of the way in which the victims of the Windrush general scandal have been treated.

The new sub-para.(e) provides disregards for any payments for compensation or support from the Post Office or the Secretary of State in connection with the failings of the Horizon computer accounting system (defined in para.(4)) or the decision in the named test case on the Post Office's liability to the now famous group of 555 postmasters within the Group Litigation Order (GLO). The neutral citation number of the decision, as set out in a footnote to the amending regulation, is [2019] EWHC 606 (QB). Following on that and a consequent decision (the Horizon Issues judgment) a settlement was agreed, but the claimants actually received only a small proportion of the overall figure, the remainder being taken up by funding costs. Paragraph 7.3 of the Explanatory Memorandum describes the compensation schemes in being as at July 2023:

> "Government has announced funding to enable the Post Office to deliver compensation schemes and arrangements for various cohorts of postmasters, including the Historical Shortfall Scheme, compensation arrangements for postmasters whose convictions were overturned and a compensation scheme for postmasters who did not receive remuneration during a suspension period, to address issues expressly identified by the parties during the court proceedings or flowing from the Common Issues and Horizon Issues judgments. In March 2022, the Government agreed to provide funding to ensure that the claimants received compensation on a similar basis to other postmasters. A Department for Business and Trade scheme to deliver that outcome opened for applications in March 2023."

No doubt any compensation paid following the proposals announced in February 2024 for the automatic quashing of a much wider range of convictions than hitherto will fall within the condition of being "in connection with the failings of the Horizon system".

The Victims of Overseas Terrorism Compensation Scheme (sub-para.(f)) is administered by the Criminal Injuries Compensation Authority and, as indicated by the date of its establishment, has been making payments for some years. It enables compensation to be paid to persons injured and to partners or close family members of persons killed, where the injury or death is directly attributable to a designated incident. Payments for personal injury would be disregarded as capital under reg.75 (indefinitely only if held on trust, otherwise for 52 weeks), but will now if necessary be disregarded indefinitely under sub-para.(f), along with payments to family members (not covered by reg.75). The amending regulations, in effect from October 27, 2023, were made under urgency procedures following the UK's designation of some aspects of the violence in Israel from October 7, 2023 as incidents of terrorism. Many other previous, and a couple of subsequent, incidents have been designated (as listed on the scheme's website). Any payments received prior to October 27, 2023 could only have been disregarded in that period if the conditions of reg.75 were met. See the introductory part of the note to reg.76 for the question whether capital retained from October 27, 2023 onwards out of a payment received before that date can be disregarded under the new provision. So far as your commentator can ascertain, there have been no formal administrative steps to extend the practical effect of the new provision on an extra-statutory basis. However, the note to para.16 of ADM Memo 17/23 assumes that capital retained from payments received before October 27, 2023 will be covered by the terms of the new provision as from that date:

> "While the classification of the Hamas attack on Israel on 7.10.23 has raised the need to disregard payments under the Victims of Overseas Terrorism Compensation scheme as capital, the regulations will cover any and all payments made under the scheme. There is no intention to differentiate between compensation payments made to victims of different terrorism attacks which are recognised under the compensation scheme."

The same view was expressed in a statement made to the Social Security Advisory Committee (see footnote 2 to para.1.6 of the minutes of the meeting of December 16, 2023). As suggested in the introductory part of this note, the issue may never arise in an appeal if decision makers operate on this assumption in practice.

Paragraph (1B)

Prior to July 9, 2023, the disregards relating to the fire at Grenfell Tower on June 14, 2017 were split between para.(1)(a)(vi) (payments of compensation or support from schemes established or approved by the Secretary of State or from trusts with funds provided by the Secretary of State) and para.(1A)(c) (payments from the Royal Borough of Kensington and Chelsea or a charity to a person, or their personal representative, who had been affected by the fire). Now there is a general disregard through para.(1B) for any payment made to anyone to provide compensation or support in respect of the fire, regardless of the source. That is because other sources of compensation had come to light, including in particular settlements of civil litigation.

Paragraph (1C)

One-off payments under the Vaccine Damage Payments Act 1979, which now covers Covid-19 vaccinations, are already partially dealt with by reg.75 (compensation for personal injury), but only where the payment is awarded to the person who has suffered the personal injury in the form of severe disability. That case is now expressly covered by para.(1C)(a), but the rest of para.(1C) extends the disregard to payments received by the partner of the severely disabled person, either during that person's life or after their death.

Paragraph (2)

This paragraph supplies the disregard, as capital if the payment is capital, and as income if it is income, of any payment specified in paras (1)–(1C). Many of those payments in practice only take the form of capital and most income payments would not be taken into account as unearned income by reason of not being listed in reg.66(1). So far as income payments from trusts are concerned, reg.66(1)(j) expressly excludes any income disregarded under reg.76, as well as any disregarded under reg.75.

Paragraph (3)

Prior to August 30, 2023, para.(3), by its link to para.13 or 15 of Sch.5 (in fact, V) to the SPC Regulations (Part III of this volume), extended the disregard under para.(1)(a)(i) of payments to a person diagnosed with variant Creutzfeldt-Jacob disease or infected from contaminated blood products to payments from the scheme or trust to the partner, parent, son or daughter of the person or payments to such family members (necessarily reading partner to include former partner) from the person's estate. The substituted form of para.(3) extends its scope to anyone other than the diagnosed or infected person who receives a payment from a scheme or trust or out of the person's estate, provided they are covered by the terms of the SPC disregard. Those terms have also been amended with effect from August 30, 2023 by the addition of sub-para.(5A) to para.15 of Sch.V, disregarding payments deriving from payments from a scheme as a result of the recommendation for interim payments of £100,000 made by the Infected Blood Inquiry on July 29, 2022, from the estate of the person to a son, daughter, step-son or step-daughter. See the minutes of the July 19, 2023 meeting of the Social Security Advisory Committee for further details and in particular Annex B, setting out the significant changes in the drafting of the amending regulations as compared with the draft form presented to the SSAC.

The discussion at a meeting of the Social Security Advisory Committee (SSAC) on December 8, 2021 in relation to SI 2021/1405 revealed some conceptual problems in the relationship of capital disregards to the calculation of the amount of capital possessed at a particular date (see further discussion in the notes to Sch.10). The essence of the problem put to DWP officials was what would happen if a claimant received a compensation payment within the disregard introduced by those regulations, acquired further non-disregarded capital and then spent a substantial amount of capital: how would it be known what pot of capital the expenditure came out of (SSAC minutes December 8, 2021, para.2.2(f))? The answer given in the letter dated January 12, 2022 from the Minister for Welfare Delivery, David Rutley, (Annex C to the minutes) was that:

> "the Department does not attempt to distinguish the capital derived from a compensation payment from other capital (with the exception of personal injury compensation that has been placed in trust). Wherever a claimant has received a payment of capital which is disregarded, whether indefinitely or for a prescribed period, their capital threshold is effectively increased by the amount of the original payment for the duration of that period. This is regardless of whether it was simply paid into a bank account with other funds or held or invested elsewhere."

There must be a question whether that approach is justified if the compensation covers certain specific purposes and the expenditure was for one of those purposes.

Company analogous to a partnership or one person business

77.—(1) Where a person stands in a position analogous to that of a sole owner or partner in relation to a company which is carrying on a trade or a property business, the person is to be treated, for the purposes of this Part, as the sole owner or partner. 2.297

(2) Where paragraph (1) applies, the person is to be treated, subject to paragraph (3)(a), as possessing an amount of capital equal to the value, or the person's share of the value, of the capital of the company and the value of the person's holding in the company is to be disregarded.

(3) Where paragraph (1) applies in relation to a company which is carrying on a trade—

(a) any assets of the company that are used wholly and exclusively for the purposes of the trade are to be disregarded from the person's capital while they are engaged in activities in the course of that trade;

(b) the income of the company or the person's share of that income is to be treated as the person's income and calculated in the manner set out in regulation 57 as if it were self-employed earnings; and

(c) where the person's activities in the course of the trade are their main employment, the person is to be treated as if they were in gainful self-employment and, accordingly, regulation 62 (minimum income floor) applies [[1] . . .].

(4) Any self-employed earnings which the person is treated as having by virtue of paragraph (3)(b) are in addition to any employed earnings the person receives as a director or employee of the company.

(5) This regulation does not apply where the person derives income from the company that is employed earnings by virtue of Chapter 8 (workers under arrangements made by intermediaries)[[2], Chapter 9 (managed service companies) or Chapter 10 (workers' services provided through intermediaries) of Part 2 of ITEPA and that income is derived from activities that are the person's main employment].

(6) In paragraph (1) "property business" has the meaning in section 204 of the Corporation Tax Act 2009.

AMENDMENTS

1. Universal Credit and Miscellaneous Amendments (No.2) Regulations 2014 (SI 2014/2888) reg.4(6) (November 26, 2014, or in the case of existing awards, the first assessment period beginning on or after November 26, 2014).

2. Universal Credit and Jobseeker's Allowance (Miscellaneous Amendments) Regulations 2018 (SI 2018/1129) reg.3(5) (November 5, 2018).

DEFINITIONS

"employed earnings"—see regs 53(1) and 55.
"ITEPA"—see reg.2.
"self-employed earnings"—see regs 53(1) and 57.

GENERAL NOTE

If a person's control of a company, which is carrying on a trade or a property business (defined in para.(6)), is such that they are like a sole trader or a partner, the value of the person's shareholding is disregarded and they are treated as having a proportionate share of the capital of the company (para.(2)) and a proportionate share of the company's income as if that was self-employed earnings (para.(3)(b)). 2.298

However, the general rule in para.(3)(a) in cases where the company is carrying on a trade is that so long as the person is engaged in activities in the course of the company's trade the company's assets are disregarded as capital. Those rules are similar to those in reg.51(4) and (5) of the Income Support Regulations, reg.115(6) and (7) of the ESA Regulations 2008 and reg.113(4) and (5) of the JSA Regulations 1996 (Vol.V of this series, 2021/22 edition as updated in Cumulative Supplements included in this volume and in mid-year Supplements), but by no means identical, in particular in the provision for the special category of property businesses. The rules are easily overlooked, as they were in relation to the discretionary housing benefit rule in *CA v Hastings BC (HB)* [2022] UKUT 57 (AAC), especially if the claimant has initially been vague about the exact nature of the legal relationships. Some unpacking and identification of potential problems is necessary.

Note that the heading to reg.77, with its reference to one-person businesses, can easily mislead, as can the tendency in social security case law and discussion to regard trades and businesses as more or less the same. That may have infected the commentary in past editions. The precise terms of the regulation must be considered. Thus, as developed further in the notes to para.(1) below, that provision only applies where a company is carrying on a either a trade, not merely a business, or a property business, the definition of which includes any transaction entered into for the purpose of generating income from land whether the operation would ordinarily be regarded as a business or not. Outside of those categories, the general principles of company law apply, as summarised below.

The basic legal position is that if there is a company, the shareholders' assets are the value of the shares, not the value of the company's assets (*R(SB) 57/83*). But under para.(1), if claimants are in a position analogous to a sole owner or partner in the business of the company (on which, see *R(IS) 8/92* for helpful guidance in paras 8 and 9), the value of their shareholding is disregarded, and they are treated as possessing a proportionate share of the value of the capital of the company, as specified in para.(2). There is usually little difficulty if the analogy is with a sole owner. If it is with a partner, the line between such a person and someone who is merely a shareholder or investor in the company is whether the person is in a position to exercise significant influence over the way the business is conducted *(R(IS) 8/92*, applied in *CA*, above). The value is the net worth of the company's total assets taken together (*R(IS) 13/93*). The value of one particular asset within the total is not relevant in itself. However, as long as the claimant undertakes activities in the course of the the company's trade (but not where there is merely a property business), the amount produced by para.(2) is disregarded (para.(3)(a)). Temporary interruptions in activity (e.g. holidays, short-term sickness) ought not to prevent para.(3)(a) from applying. It was accepted in *R(IS) 13/93* that any activities which are more than de minimis satisfy para.(3)(a). See also *R(IS) 14/98* discussed in the note to para.(3). In addition, under para.(3)(b), if para.(1) applies, the claimant's share of the income of the company is to be treated as their earnings from self-employment under reg.57.

First, note that under para.(5) the regulation as a whole does not apply where the person concerned receives employed earnings from the company that are chargeable to income tax under Chapter 8 (workers under arrangements made by intermediaries), 9 (managed service companies) or, from November 5, 2018, 10 (workers' services provided through intermediaries) of Part 2 of the Income Tax (Earnings and Pensions) Act 2003 (ITEPA). The November 2018 amendment also introduced the important condition for the application of the exception in para.(5) that the activities producing those earnings are the person's main employment. There is no such exclusion in the income support and old style ESA and JSA rules. Chapter 8 of Part 2 of ITEPA is concerned with what are known as IR35 or "off-payroll" arrangements, under which a person provides services to a client who would be an employer except that the arrangements are made by a third party to whom the client makes the payments in return for the services. Then, subject to conditions, the payments to the third party are treated as employed earnings of the person concerned and chargeable to income tax. Chapter 9 applies to similar effect where the intermediary is a managed service company, i.e. one under the control of the service provider(s). Chapter 10 has, from April 6, 2017, applied special rules to cases where the client is a public authority.

Paragraph (1)

The general operation of para.(1) is described above. Before it can operate it must be established that the company that actually owns the capital in question is carrying on either a trade or a property business. "Trade" is given no special definition and there are many disputed and grey areas in the meaning given in other legal contexts. Given the overall approach of the Regulations in adopting tax law concepts and the express adoption of a tax meaning of "property business" in para.(6), that context may supply some pointers. It is clear in that context that "trade" is a narrower concept than "business" (see *American Leaf Blending Co Sdn. Bhd v Director-General of Inland Revenue* [1979] A.C. 676 (PC) and *Griffiths v Jackson* (1982) T.C. 583, both referred to in many other cases including *Ramsay v HMRC* [2013] UKUT 226 (TC), long extracts from which are set out in *RM v Sefton Council (HB)* [2016] UKUT 357 (AAC) reported as [2017] AACR 5). Distinctions are drawn between investing in some asset that yields a return and the trading in such assets and between the exploitation of an interest in property (as by letting it out) and trading. Thus in *Griffiths*, Vinelott J held that the letting out of specially converted student flats was the exploitation of interests in property, not a trade. But by contrast, a person or company running a hotel or a bed and breakfast establishment would be carrying on a trade. 2.299

Some companies not carrying on a trade may be carrying on a "property business", also within para.(1), but not within the para.(3) rules. But remember that some companies carrying on a property business may get within the meaning of carrying on a trade. The definition in s.204 of the Corporation Tax Act 2009, as incorporated by para.(6), does not in itself take matters forward, merely saying that the term includes both UK and overseas property businesses. One has to go on to ss.205–207 to find provisions that a property business consists of (a) every business that the company carries on for generating income from land in the UK and outside, as the case may be, and (b) every transaction that the company enters into for that purpose otherwise than in the course of such a business. It is also provided that generating income from land means exploiting it as a source of rents or other receipts. Schedule 1 to the Interpretation Act 1978 defines "land" to include "building and other structures, land covered with water, and any estate, interest, easement, servitude or right in or over land". Thus, the definition appears to cover, not just companies that are carrying on a business, in the ordinary meaning of the word, for the purposes of generating income from land, but also any transaction entered into by a company for that purpose, whether that is part of the company's business or not or whether the company is carrying on any business at all, in the ordinary meaning of the word, or not. Paragraph H4365 of the ADM refers to the paying of tax on the profits of the business as a condition, but it is not at all clear that the provision in s.204(2) of the 2009 Act that references in that Act to a property business are to such a business in so far as any profits of the business are chargeable to tax under Ch.3 of the Part of the Act containing s.204, affects the "meaning" of property business in s.204. Such uncertainty is another penalty of the highly unhelpful method of legislation by reference, instead of setting out directly the kinds of company intended to be covered by reg.77.

If the definition of property business is in issue in an appeal, the comments of Commissioner Stockman in para.34 of *RMcE v DfC (UC)* [2021] NICom 59 in relation to reg.55 would be equally pertinent. For appeal tribunals to be able to perform their role properly the Secretary of State must provide explanatory material, legislation and case law relating to the relevant tax provisions.

Questions have been raised about the position where a claimant has put their own money into the company, so that that amount is owed to them, possibly through a director's loan account, by a separate legal person (the company). That debt would be a chose in action with a capital value. While the claimant is engaged in the company's trade there is no problem with the amount of the money held by the company being disregarded as capital under para.(3)(a). But what is the status of the claimant's personal chose in action in the right to repayment of the debt? Does that still count as the claimant's capital, since there is no specific disregard of its value? It is (tentatively) suggested that giving effect to para.(1) requires one to translate the claimant's relationship with the company into the relationship that would obtain if the claimant was carrying on the trade as a sole owner or partner. In such a case the money would have been regarded as moved from the claimant's personal assets into funds risked in the trade. As a sole trader is able freely to transfer funds between personal and trade assets (see *R(SB) 4/85* and the notes to para.7 of Sch.10), there would be no question of the creation of a chose in action in the form of a debt from one person to another. If that is correct, the deeming under para.(1) extends to deeming the actual chose in action not to exist. Although things might be more complicated in the case of deemed partners, it would be anomalous if the same result did not follow.

Paragraph (2)

2.300 The approach adopted in *R(IS) 13/93* to the income support rule must also apply to para.(2) in that the value of the company's capital (by reference to which the amount of the person's notional capital is assumed) means the net total value after liabilities have been taken into account. The fact that the company owns some particularly valuable asset or assets does not on its own mean that the claimant's notional capital must be over the limit. The net worth must be identified, no doubt by looking at accounts and using standard accounting practices. It would seem that liabilities could include the amount of any debt owed to the deemed owner. Where the person's position is not analogous to that of a sole owner, but to a partner, the identification of the proportionate share may raise difficult issues of judgment. In *R(IS) 13/93* the Commissioner seemed prepared to adopt the proportionate shareholding as the criterion. There should then be no difficulty in the disregarding under para.(2) of the actual value of the person's shareholding in the company.

Paragraph (3)

2.301 There are further departures from the income support and old style ESA and JSA position in para.(3), in deeming the person's proportionate share of the company's income to be self-employed earnings (sub-para.(b)) and in applying the minimum income floor where the person's activities in the trade are their main employment (sub-para.(c)), as well as the disregard of assets in sub-para.(a). It is important to note that the whole of para.(3) applies only to companies carrying on a trade and not to companies merely carrying on a property business. That distinction has been queried in past editions, but it is now submitted that in view of the particular meanings to be given to "trade" and "property business" (see above) it makes sense. A person who has property that is rented out, the income from which is not unearned income under reg.66(1), should not be able to escape having its value taken into account as capital by acquiring the property through a company that they control, or by transferring it to such a company, unless the company is genuinely carrying on a trade.

Under para.(3)(b) the income of the company or a proportionate share is to be treated as income of the person concerned and calculated under reg.57 as if it were self-employed earnings. That appears to be so even if the person concerned undertakes no activities in the course of the business. It is far from clear how the notional conversion is to take place. Under reg.57, in the case of actual self-employed earnings, the calculation is based on actual receipts in any assessment period less permitted deductions for expenses under regs 58 and 59. Presumably, therefore "the income of the company" does not mean the net income of the company as might be calculated for corporation tax purposes or under ordinary accounting principles. Presumably it means the actual receipts of the company in the assessment period in question less the deductions for expenses under regs 58 and 59, looking at expenditure on behalf of the company rather than by the person in question. It is difficult to say whether in practice information will be available as to such receipts and expenditure in a current assessment period of a month. Even if that is so, there might well be large fluctuations month by month. A further problem is how to calculate the deductions from gross profits under steps 3 and 4 of reg.57(2) for national insurance contributions and income tax paid to HMRC in the assessment period and relievable pension contributions made in that period, when the person's actual tax and national insurance status will not have been as a self-employed earner.

See para.(4) for the effect of the person having employed earnings. Note that normally any remuneration paid by the company to the claimant as a director or an employee will be deducted as an expense at step 1(b) of the reg.57 calculation. Any dividends received by the claimant will simply not figure in the reg.77 operation because they are not either a receipt of the company or an allowable expense under regs 57 and 58. Nor will they normally count as employed earnings and they do not constitute unearned income. They will of course, once received, form part of the recipient's overall capital. If properly to be regarded as payments of capital, as would normally be the case, that would take effect immediately. If properly to be regarded as payments as income, as possibly would be the case if they form part of regular periodic payments, there presumably would not in general be a metamorphosis into capital until after the end of the assessment period of receipt. However, note that reg.72(3) assumes that dividends are a form of income from capital in providing that where capital is treated as yielding (notional) income, i.e. the amount is over £6,000 but below £16,000, the actual income is to be treated as part of the claimant's capital from the day it is due to be paid.

It is no longer necessary to discuss the effect of receipt of payments under the Coronavirus Job Retention Scheme. See the notes at p.458 of the 2023/24 edition of this volume, and earlier editions, for details.

In the light of the difficulties with para.(3)(b), the effect of para.(3)(c) may be particularly important. Where the person's activities in the course of the company's trade are their main employment they are deemed to be in gainful self-employment, so that reg.62 on the minimum income floor applies. For any assessment period in which reg.62 applies (see the notes to that provision) and the claimant's earned income is less than their individual threshold, the earned income is deemed to be equal to that amount. The weekly amount is effectively the hourly national minimum wage multiplied by the expected number of hours under reg.88. That level of income exempts the claimant from all work-related requirements (reg.90(1) and (5) and s.19 of the WRA 2012), but the deemed amount would be taken into account in calculating the amount of benefit payable.

The other element of para.(3) is the disregard of assets of the company that would otherwise be deemed to be part of the claimant's capital by reason of the person's deemed status as sole owner or partner in the business (sub-para.(a)). There are two conditions. The person must be engaged in activities in the course of the company's trade. In reg.51(4) and (5) of the Income Support Regulations, reg.115(6) and (7) of the ESA Regulations 2008 and reg.113(4) and (5) of the JSA Regulations 1996 the condition is that the person undertakes activities in the course of the business of the company. On that form of words the Commissioner in *R(IS) 13/93* was satisfied that the claimant's wife, who took telephone messages and received mail for the company, as well as being a director, was taking part in the company's business. He also said that although the activities were low key, he was far from certain that they were de minimis. It is not entirely clear that he was intending to lay down a rule that any activity beyond something that was de minimis (i.e. so trivial as to be equivalent to nothing) would do, rather than merely describing the circumstances of the particular case, but a principle that anything of substance would do appears right. Does a test in the terms of being engaged in activities in the course of the company's trade require a different approach? In *Chief Adjudication Officer v Knight*, reported as part of *R(IS) 14/98*, the Court of Appeal was concerned with the disregard of the assets of a business in which a person was engaged as a self-employed earner. The claimant was described as a sleeping partner in a farming business with her son and his wife. The court held that that the risking of her assets in the business and her right to a share of profits did not constitute a sufficient positive involvement to conclude that she was engaged in the business. But it was recognised that each case would have to be decided individually. That does not suggest any plain difference in approach, and it is submitted that the word "engaged" does not in its ordinary meaning require anything more extensive than "undertaking activities".

It should be noted that para.(3)(a) applies only while the person is actually engaged in activities. No doubt short breaks, such as for weekends or longer holidays, are to be ignored. But there is no provision in it, as there is in para.6 of Sch.10 to the Income Support Regulations and in para.8 of Sch.10 to the present Regulations (business assets) for an extension where the person has ceased to carry on a trade, business or vocation within the previous six months (extendable) in certain circumstances such as incapacity being thought not to be permanent. It may be arguable that the disregard in para.8 of Sch.10 can apply to the notional capital to be possessed under para.(2) if its conditions would have applied if the person had actually previously been carrying on the business as a self-employed person.

The second condition for the disregard under para.(3)(a) is that the assets are used wholly and exclusively for the purposes of the company's trade. That is not a condition in reg.51(5) of the Income Support Regulations, reg.115(7) of the ESA Regulations 2008 or reg.113(5) of the JSA Regulations 1996, under which the whole of the person's deemed capital under the equivalent of para.(2) is disregarded. Does the phrase "wholly and exclusively" exclude the disregarding of the value of assets that have a dual use? An obvious example would be a vehicle used for both business and personal purposes. In relation to the deduction of expenses in the calculation of the net profits of self-employed earners under reg.38(3)(a) of the Income Support Regulations (reg.98(3)(a) of the ESA Regulations 2008 and reg.101(4)(a) of the JSA Regulations 1996), where it is a condition that the expenses were wholly and exclusively defrayed for the purposes of the employment, it has been held that apportionment can extend not only to items where specific different uses can be identified (e.g. telephone calls or petrol costs) but also to items where there can be an apportionment on a time basis (e.g. vehicle insurance): *R(FC) 1/91*, *CFC/26/1989* and *R(IS) 13/91*. However, there are still some expenses that are not capable of apportionment, such as the cost of clothing or lunches. Where the use of an asset is in issue, there will be less room for apportionment. To take the example of a vehicle to be used equally for business and for personal purposes, for example, although the expenditure on vehicle tax, insurance and maintenance costs could be apportioned just as much as fuel costs, when looked at as a single asset to be valued it is hard to see how it could be said to be wholly and exclusively used for the purposes of the company's trade if it was used for any non-trivial non-trade purpose. Nonetheless, there might possibly be some things, like money in a bank account or a stock of stationery that could be regarded as made up of some assets used wholly and exclusively for the purposes of the company's trade and some not so used. Nor is it necessarily fatal to a conclusion that the asset is used wholly and exclusively for the purposes of the company's trade that a person derives some private advantage from it (e.g. a particularly comfortable office chair or one adapted to a person's disability or physiology).

The second condition seems unfairly restrictive compared to the position in income support and old style ESA and JSA and also compared to the treatment under universal credit of those actually in self-employment. There, para.7 of Sch.10 requires the disregard of assets used "wholly or mainly" for the purposes of the trade, business or vocation being carried on. In view of the express condition in para.(3)(a), it appears that a person could not rely on the wider disregard in para.7 of Sch.10 in relation to their deemed notional capital, on the same basis as suggested above in relation to para.8 of Sch.10. Indeed, that may cast doubt on the validity of the argument about para.8.

Paragraph (4)

2.302 If someone treated as having self-employed earnings under para.(3)(b) also has employed earnings from the company, either as an employee or in the office of director, the two sources of income are both to be taken into account. Dividends are not normally employed earnings, being derived from the ownership of the shares on which they are paid. But sometimes the label of dividend cannot properly be applied to the payments made or dividends properly so called can constitute remuneration derived from a contract of employment or in an office. Dividends cannot constitute unearned income because they do not appear in the exhaustive list in reg.66(1). They are not remuneration or profit derived from employment under a contract of employment or in an office (reg.52(a)(i)). Nor are they general earnings as defined in s.7(3) of ITEPA, being chargeable to income tax under Chapters 3–5 of Part 4 of the Income Tax (Trading and Other Income) 2005 (ITTOIA). It is different if the labelling as dividends is a sham or, taking the broader approach of recent authority, the payments are in substance or reality earnings. See the further discussion in the notes to reg.55 under the heading *Dividends*.

Do not forget that although the claimant's employed earnings from the company count as part of their income, the expense of paying those earnings will be deducted from the receipts of the company under the deemed application of reg.57.

PART 7

THE BENEFIT CAP

GENERAL NOTE

Introduction

Regulations 78–83 are made under ss.96–97 of the WRA 2012. They establish a "benefit cap" under which affected claimants can receive no more in social security benefits than £25,323 pa or £16,967 pa in Greater London and £22,020 pa or £14,753 pa elsewhere. In both cases, the higher of those limits applies to joint claimants or those responsible for a child or qualifying young person and the lower to single claimants who are not responsible a child or a qualifying young person. The higher rates apply irrespective of how many people are in the benefit unit: families consisting of a couple with six children are capped at the same rate as a single parent with one. 2.303

How the benefit cap works

Under reg.79, the benefit cap applies where the total amount of the "welfare benefits" (as defined in WRA 2012 s.96(10)) exceed whichever "relevant amount" applies: see reg.80A. The amount of universal credit that the claimant would otherwise be awarded for the assessment period is reduced by the amount of the excess: reg.81. 2.304

Calculation of entitlement to welfare benefits

Regulation 80 deals with how the amount of the claimant's (or claimants') entitlement to "welfare benefits" is calculated. The rule is that the total entitlement to all specified benefits during the assessment period is taken into account except where that entitlement is not payable because of the overlapping benefit rules: reg.80(1). Under reg.66, many of the benefits listed in WRA 2012 s.96(10) are taken into account as unearned income when calculating entitlement to universal credit. Regulation 80(4) provides that they are to be taken into account for benefit cap purposes at the same rate as they are taken into account under reg.66. Universal credit itself is (obviously) taken into account at the rate to which the claimant(s) would be entitled if the benefit cap did not apply: reg.80(2). Regulation 80(3) provides (presumably for the avoidance of doubt) that where a claimant is disqualified from receiving (new-style) ESA by virtue of reg.93 ESA Regulations 2013, that benefit is not taken into account. Finally, reg.80(5) provides that where a "welfare benefit" is awarded in respect of a period other than a month (which will 2.305

always be the case, except for universal credit itself) the monthly equivalent is to be calculated in the same way as for other unearned income under reg.73.

Exceptions

2.306 There are a number of exceptions, where the benefit cap does not apply, or the reduction is less than the full amount of the excess. The benefit cap does not apply in any assessment period:

- where the award of universal credit includes the LCWRA element, or the carer element, or a claimant (including one or more joint claimants) is receiving "new-style" ESA at a rate that includes the support component: reg.83(1)(a) and (j);
- during which a claimant or a qualifying young person for whom they are responsible is receiving carer's allowance or a claimant is receiving industrial injuries benefit, attendance allowance, disability living allowance or personal independence payment, or guardian's allowance: reg.83(1)(b), (c), (f), (g), (i) and (k) and note that—for obvious reasons—those benefits are not "welfare benefits" as defined in WRA 2012 s.96(10);
- a child or qualifying young person for whom a claimant is responsible is receiving disability living allowance or personal independence payment: reg.83(1)(f) and (g); and
- a claimant is receiving a war pension (as defined in reg.83(2))or certain payments under the Armed Forces and Reserve Forces Compensation Scheme: reg.83(1)(d) and (c).

Where a claimant (or a child or qualifying young person) is entitled to attendance allowance, disability living allowance, personal independence payment—or a war pension or a relevant payment under the Armed Forces Compensation Scheme—but is not receiving it because he or she is in a hospital or a care home, the benefit cap does not apply by virtue of reg.83(1)(h).

Under reg.82(1), the benefit cap does not apply if the claimant's earned income (or the claimants' combined earned income) in the assessment exceeds "the amount of earnings that a person would be paid at the hourly rate set out in regulation 4 of the National Minimum Wage Regulations for 16 hours per week, converted to a monthly amount by multiplying by 52 and dividing by 12" or during the nine month "grace period" as defined in reg.82(2). The rules on the "minimum income floor" in reg.62 (which, in this instance, would be advantageous for the claimant(s)) do not apply to the calculation of earned income in this context.

Finally, where the award of universal credit includes the childcare costs element, the amount of that element is deducted from the amount of the reduction under reg.81. If that amount exceeds the excess of the total entitlement to welfare benefits over the relevant amount, then no reduction is made: reg.81(1) and (2).

Legal challenges

2.307 On March 18, 2015, in *R (SG and others (previously JS and others) v Secretary of State for Work and Pensions* [2015] UKSC 16; [2015] 1 W.L.R. 1449, the Supreme Court (Lords Reed, Carnwath and Hughes, Lady Hale and Lord Kerr dissenting) rejected a legal challenge to the benefit cap on the grounds that it unlawfully discriminated against women in breach of art.14 of, read with art.1 of the First Protocol to, ECHR; and infringed art.3(1) of the United Nations Convention on the Rights of the Child.

On November 26, 2015, in *Hurley v Secretary of State for Work And Pensions* [2015] EWHC 3382 (Admin); [2016] P.T.S.R. 636, Collins J held that the failure to exempt individual family carers caring for adult family members from the benefit cap constituted unlawful discrimination contrary to contrary to Art.14

of—taken together with Art.1 of the First Protocol to, or Art.8 of—the ECHR. The government responded to the judgment by removing carer's allowance from the list of "welfare benefits" in WRA 2012 s.96(10) (see WR&WA 2016 s.8(4)) and by adding exceptions to reg.83 where the claimant (or a qualifying young person for whom they are responsible) is entitled to carer's allowance; or where the carer element is included in the ward of universal credit; or where the claimant is entitled to guardian's allowance.

On June 22, 2017 in *R (DA and Others) v Secretary of State for Work and Pensions* [2017] EWHC 1446 (Admin); [2017] P.T.S.R. 1266, Collins J ruled that the application of the benefit cap (under the equivalent provisions of the Housing Benefit Regulations 2006) to lone parents of children under two infringed their Convention Rights under arts 8 and 14 ECHR taken together. In particular, the applicants were unable to work for 16 hours a week (i.e., so as to take advantage of the earnings exception: see reg.82) because of their caring responsibilities and the cost of childcare. However, on March 15, 2018, the Court of Appeal (Leveson P and Sir Patrick Elias, McCombe LJ dissenting) allowed the Secretary of State's appeal against Collins J's decision ([2018] EWCA Civ 504); [2018] P.T.S.R. 1606, and on May 15, 2019, the Supreme Court (Lords Reed, Wilson, Carnwath, Hughes and Hodge, Lady Hale and Lord Kerr dissenting) dismissed a further appeal together with another appeal backed by CPAG: see further, *R (DA and others and DS and others) v Secretary of State for Work and Pensions* [2019] UKSC 21; [2019] 1 W.L.R. 3289.

On July 20, 2020, the High Court (Garnham J) allowed a challenge to the benefit cap as it affects UC claimants who are paid four-weekly: see *R (Pantellerisco) v Secretary of State for Work and Pensions* [2020] EWHC 1944 (Admin); [2020] P.T.S.R. 2289. As there are 13 four-week periods in each year and only 12 assessment periods, the Regulations treated the claimant as earning 1/13 of her annual salary in 11 of those assessment periods and 2/13 in one of them. By regulation 82(1)(a) the benefits cap does not apply to assessment periods in which the claimant's earned income is equal to or exceeds the amount of earnings that a person would be paid for 16 hours work at the national minimum wage, converted to a monthly amount by multiplying by 52 and dividing by 12. As the claimant actually did work 16 hours a week at the national minimum wage, she would have been exempt from the benefit cap for the whole year if she had been treated as earning 1/12 of her annual salary in each assessment period. However, in 11 out of 12 assessment periods, the universal credit earned income calculation treated her as if she had only worked for 28 days with the result that she was not exempt from the cap. In the claimant's case, that left her approximately £463 worse off in each of the 11 assessment periods in respect of which her benefit was capped. The judge described this issue as the "lunar month problem". It is similar to the "non-banking day salary shift" problem: see the discussion of *Secretary of State for Work and Pensions v Johnson and others* [2020] EWCA Civ 778; [2020] P.T.S.R. 1872 in the General Note to reg.54. Following the Court of Appeal's reasoning in *Johnson*, the judge allowed the application for judicial review and declared that "the calculation required by regulation 82(1)(a) read together with regulation 54 of the Universal Credit Regulations 2013 is irrational and unlawful in so far as employees who are paid on a four weekly basis (as opposed to a calendar monthly basis) are treated as having earned income of only 28 days' earnings in 11 out of 12 assessment periods a year." However, the Court of Appeal allowed an appeal from that decision by the Secretary of State and dismissed the claim ([2021] EWCA Civ 1454; [2021] P.T.S.R. 1922).

Introduction

78.—(1) This Part makes provision for a benefit cap under section 96 of the Act which, if applicable, reduces the amount of an award of universal credit. 2.308

(2) In this Part "couple" means—

(a) joint claimants; or

(b) a single claimant who is a member of a couple within the meaning of section 39 of the Act and the other member of that couple,

and references to a couple include each member of that couple individually.

DEFINITION

"the Act"—see reg.2.

Circumstances where the benefit cap applies

2.309 **79.**—(1) Unless regulation 82 or 83 applies, the benefit cap applies where the welfare benefits to which a single person or couple is entitled during the reference period exceed the relevant amount [1 determined under regulation 80A (relevant amount)].

(2) The reference period for the purposes of the benefit cap is the assessment period for an award of universal credit.

(3) [1...]

(4) [1...]

AMENDMENT

1. Benefit Cap (Housing Benefit and Universal Credit) (Amendment) Regulations 2016 (SI 2016/909) reg.3(1) and (2) (assessment periods beginning on or after November 7, 2016).

DEFINITIONS

"assessment period"—see WRA 2012 ss.40 and 7(2).
"bereavement allowance"—see reg.2.
"carer's allowance"—*ibid.*
"child"—see WRA 2012 s.40.
"claimant"—*ibid.*
"Contributions and Benefits Act"—see reg.2.
"couple"—see reg.78(2).
"employment and support allowance"—see reg.2.
"jobseeker's allowance"—*ibid.*
"joint claimants"—see WRA 2012 s.40.
"maternity allowance"—see reg.2.
"qualifying young person"—see WRA 2012 s.40 and 10(5) and regs 2 and 5.
"responsible for a child or qualifying young person"—see regs 2, 4 and 4A.
"single claimant"—see WRA 2012 s.40.
"single person"—see WRA 2012 ss.40 and 1(2)(a).
"welfare benefit"—see WRA 2012 s.96(10).
"widowed mother's allowance"—see reg.2.
"widowed parent's allowance"—*ibid.*
"widow's pension"—*ibid.*

GENERAL NOTE

2.310 Although "couple" is defined by reg.78(2) as including a member of a couple who is permitted to claim as a single person under reg.3(3), the higher "relevant amount" in reg.79(3)(a) is only available to "joint claimants" and those responsible for a child or a qualifying young person. A member of a couple claiming as a single person who is not responsible for a child or a qualifying young person, will therefore be capped at the lower rate.

The welfare benefits to which reg.79 applies are defined by WRA 2012 s.96(10) as bereavement allowance, child benefit, child tax credit, ESA, housing benefit, incapacity benefit, IS, JSA, maternity allowance, severe disablement allowance, universal credit, widow's pension, widowed mother's allowance and widowed parent's allowance.

Manner of determining total entitlement to welfare benefits

80.—(1) Subject to the following provisions of this regulation, the amount of a welfare benefit to be used when determining total entitlement to welfare benefits is the amount to which the single person or couple is entitled during the reference period subject to any adjustment to the amount payable in accordance with regulations under section 73 of the Social Security Administration Act 1992 (overlapping benefits). 2.311

(2) Where the welfare benefit is universal credit, the amount to be used is the amount to which the claimant is entitled before any reduction under regulation 81 or under section 26 or 27 of the Act.

[1 (2A) Where the welfare benefit is housing benefit under section 130 of the Contributions and Benefits Act, the amount to be used is nil.]

(3) Where a person is disqualified for receiving an employment and support allowance by virtue of section 18 of the Welfare Reform Act 2007, it is disregarded as a welfare benefit.

(4) Where an amount of a welfare benefit is taken into account in assessing a single person's or a couple's unearned income for the purposes of an award of universal credit the amount to be used is the amount taken into account as unearned income in accordance with regulation 66.

(5) Where a welfare benefit is awarded in respect of a period that is not a month, the amount is to be calculated as the monthly equivalent as set out in regulation 73 (unearned income calculated monthly).

AMENDMENT

1. Benefit Cap (Housing Benefit and Universal Credit) (Amendment) Regulations 2016 (SI 2016/909) reg.3(1) and (3) (assessment periods beginning on or after November 7, 2016).

DEFINITIONS

"couple"—see reg.78(2).
"earned income"—see reg.2.
"single person"—see WRA 2012 ss.40 and 1(2)(a).
"unearned income"—see reg.2.

[1 Relevant amount

80A.—(1) The relevant amount is determined by dividing the applicable annual limit by 12. 2.312

(2) The applicable annual limit is—

(a) [2 £16,967] for a single claimant resident in Greater London who is not responsible for a child or qualifying young person;

(b) [2 £25,323] for—

(i) joint claimants where either joint claimant is resident in Greater London;

(ii) a single claimant resident in Greater London who is responsible for a child or qualifying young person;

(c) [2 £14,753] for a single claimant not resident in Greater London who is not responsible for a child or qualifying young person;

(d) [2 £22,020] for—

(i) joint claimants not resident in Greater London;
(ii) a single claimant not resident in Greater London who is responsible for a child or qualifying young person.

(3) For the purposes of section 96 of the Act (benefit cap) and this regulation a claimant is resident in Greater London if—

(a) where the housing costs element is included in the claimant's award of universal credit—
 (i) accommodation in respect of which the claimant meets the occupation condition is in Greater London; or
 (ii) the claimant is in receipt of housing benefit in respect of a dwelling (which has the meaning given in section 137 of the Contributions and Benefits Act) in Greater London;
(b) where the housing costs element is not included in the claimant's award of universal credit—
 (i) accommodation that the claimant normally occupies as their home is in Greater London; or
 (ii) where there is no accommodation that the claimant normally occupies as their home, the Jobcentre Plus office to which the Secretary of State has allocated their claim is in Greater London.]

AMENDMENTS

1. Benefit Cap (Housing Benefit and Universal Credit) (Amendment) Regulations 2016 (SI 2016/909) reg.3(1) and (4) (assessment periods beginning on or after November 7, 2016).

2. Benefit Cap (Annual Limit) (Amendment) Regulations 2023 (SI 2023/335) reg.3 (assessment periods beginning on or after April 10, 2023).

Reduction of universal credit

2.313 **81.**—(1) Where the benefit cap applies in relation to an assessment period for an award of universal credit, the amount of the award for that period is to be reduced by—

(a) the excess; minus
(b) any amount included in the award for the childcare costs element in relation to that assessment period.

(2) But no reduction is to be applied where the amount of the childcare costs element is greater than the excess.

(3) The excess is the total amount of welfare benefits that the single person or the couple are entitled to in the reference period, minus the relevant amount [1 determined under regulation 80A].

AMENDMENT

1. Benefit Cap (Housing Benefit and Universal Credit) (Amendment) Regulations 2016 (SI 2016/909) reg.3(1) and (5) (assessment periods beginning on or after November 7, 2016).

DEFINITIONS

"childcare costs element"—see reg.2.
"assessment period"—see WRA 2012 ss.40 and 7(2).

Exceptions—earnings

82.—(1) The benefit cap does not apply to an award of universal credit in relation to an assessment period where— 2.314

(a) the claimant's earned income or, if the claimant is a member of a couple, the couple's combined earned income, is equal to or exceeds [1 the amount of earnings that a person would be paid at the hourly rate set out in regulation 4 of the National Minimum Wage Regulations for 16 hours per week, converted to a monthly amount by multiplying by 52 and dividing by 12]; or

(b) the assessment period falls within a grace period or is an assessment period in which a grace period begins or ends.

(2) A grace period is a period of 9 consecutive months that begins on the most recent of the following days in respect of which the condition in paragraph (3) is met—

(a) a day falling within the current period of entitlement to universal credit which is the first day of an assessment period in which the claimant's earned income (or, if the claimant is a member of a couple, the couple's combined earned income is [1 less than—

(i) [2 ...]

(ii) [2 ...] the amount calculated in accordance with paragraph (1)(a)];

(b) a day falling before the current period of entitlement to universal credit which is the day after a day on which the claimant has ceased paid work.

(3) The condition is that, in each of the 12 months immediately preceding that day, the claimant's earned income or, if the claimant was a member of a couple, the couple's combined earned income was equal to or [1 exceeded—

(a) [2 ...]

(b) [2 ...] the amount calculated in accordance with paragraph (1)(a)].

(4) "Earned income" for the purposes of this regulation does not include income a person is treated as having by virtue of regulation 62 (minimum income floor).

[2(5) For the purposes of paragraphs (2)(a) and (3), when calculating the amount in accordance with paragraph (1)(a) the reference to regulation 4 of the National Minimum Wage Regulations is a reference to regulation 4 as in force at the beginning of the assessment period or month for which the amount is calculated.]

AMENDMENTS

1. Universal Credit (Benefit Cap Earnings Exception) Amendment Regulations 2017 (SI 2017/138) reg.2(1) and (3) (Assessment periods beginning on or after April 1, 2017).

2. Universal Credit (Miscellaneous Amendments) Regulations 2020 (SI 2020/611), reg.2 (July 13, 2020).

DEFINITIONS

"assessment period"—see WRA 2012 ss.40 and 7(2).
"claimant"—see WRA 2012 s.40.
"couple"—see reg.78(2).
"earned income"—see reg.2 and para.(4).

GENERAL NOTE

See the discussion of *R (Pantellerisco) v Secretary of State for Work and Pensions* [2021] EWCA Civ 1454 in the General Note to Part 7 (above).

Exceptions—entitlement or receipt of certain benefits

2.315 **83.**—(1) The benefit cap does not apply in relation to any assessment period where—

(a) the LCWRA element is included in the award of universal credit or the claimant is receiving an employment and support allowance that includes the support component;

(b) a claimant is receiving industrial injuries benefit;

(c) a claimant is receiving attendance allowance;

(d) a claimant is receiving a war pension;

(e) a claimant is receiving a payment under article 15(1)(c) or article 29(1)(a) of the Armed Forces and Reserve Forces (Compensation Scheme) Order 2011;

(f) a claimant, or a child or qualifying young person for whom a claimant is responsible, is receiving disability living allowance;

(g) a claimant, or a qualifying young person for whom a claimant is responsible, is receiving personal independence payment;

(h) a claimant, or a child or qualifying young person for whom a claimant is responsible, is entitled to a payment listed in [1 sub-paragraphs (b) to (g)] [4, (ha) or (hb)] but—

(i) is not receiving it by virtue of regulation 6 (hospitalisation) or regulation 7 (persons in care homes) of the Social Security (Attendance Allowance) Regulations 1991,

(ii) it is being withheld by virtue of article 53 of the Naval, Military and Air Forces etc (Disablement and Death) Service Pensions Order 2006 (maintenance in hospital or an institution),

(iii) is not receiving it by virtue of regulation 8 (hospitalisation) or regulation 9 (persons in care homes) of the Social Security (Disability Living Allowance) Regulations 1991, [4 . . .]

(iv) in the case of personal independence payment, is not receiving it by virtue of regulations under section 85 (care home residents) or 86 (hospital in-patients) of the Act.

[4 (iva) in the case of adult disability payment, is not receiving it by virtue of regulation 27 (effect of admission to a care home on ongoing entitlement to daily living component) or 28 (effect of admission to hospital on ongoing entitlement to Adult Disability Payment) of the Disability Assistance for Working Age People (Scotland) Regulations 2022, or]

[3 (v) is not receiving it by virtue of regulation 17 (effect of admission to a care home on ongoing entitlement to care component) of the DACYP Regulations;]

[2 (ha) a claimant, or a child or qualifying young person for whom a claimant is responsible, is receiving child disability payment;]

[4 (hb) a claimant, or qualifying young person for whom a claimant is responsible, is receiving adult disability payment;]

[1 (i) a claimant, or a qualifying young person for whom a claimant is responsible, is entitled to carer's allowance;

[5 (ia) a claimant, or a qualifying young person for whom a claimant is responsible, is entitled to carer support payment;]

(j) the carer element is included in the award of universal credit;

(k) a claimant is entitled to guardian's allowance under section 77 of the Contributions and Benefits Act.]

(2) For the purposes of this regulation, "war pension" means—

(a) any pension or allowance payable under any of the instruments listed in section 639(2) of ITEPA—
  (i) to a widow, widower or a surviving civil partner, or
  (ii) in respect of disablement;

(b) a pension payable to a person as a widow, widower or surviving civil partner under any power of Her Majesty otherwise than under an enactment to make provision about pensions for or in respect of persons who have been disabled or have died in consequence of service as members of the armed forces of the Crown;

(c) a payment which is made under any of—
  (i) the Order in Council of 19th December 1881,
  (ii) the Royal Warrant of 27th October 1884, or
  (iii) the Order by His Majesty of 14th January 1922,

to a widow, widower or surviving civil partner of a person whose death was attributable to service in a capacity analogous to service as a member of the armed forces of the Crown and whose service in such capacity terminated before 31st March 1973;

(d) a pension paid by the government of a country outside the United Kingdom which is analogous to any of the pensions, allowances or payments mentioned in paragraphs (a) to (c).

AMENDMENT

1. Benefit Cap (Housing Benefit and Universal Credit) (Amendment) Regulations 2016 (SI 2016/909) reg.3(1) and (6) (assessment periods beginning on or after November 7, 2016).

2. Social Security (Scotland) Act 2018 (Disability Assistance for Children and Young People) (Consequential Modifications) Order 2021 (SI 2021/786) Sch.11 para.6 (July 26, 2021).

3. Social Security (Scotland) Act 2018 (Information-Sharing and Disability Assistance) (Consequential Provision and Modifications) Order 2021 (SI 2021/1188) art.12(2) (November 22, 2021).

4. Social Security (Disability Assistance for Working Age People) (Consequential Amendments) Order 2022 (SI 2022/177) art.13(6) (March 21, 2022).

5. Carer's Assistance (Carer Support Payment) (Scotland) Regulations 2023 (Consequential Amendments) Order 2023 (SI 2023/1218) art.23 (November 19, 2023).

DEFINITIONS

"the Act"—see reg.2.
"adult disability payment"—*ibid.*
"attendance allowance"—*ibid.*
"child"—see WRA 2012, s.40.
"child disability payment"—see reg.2.
"claimant"—see WRA 2012 s.40.
"the DACYP Regulations"—see reg.2.
"disability living allowance"—*ibid.*
"employment and support allowance"—*ibid.*
"industrial injuries benefit"—*ibid.*
"ITEPA"—*ibid.*
"partner"—*ibid.*
"personal independence payment"—*ibid.*

"responsible for a child or qualifying young person"—see regs 2, 4 and 4A.
"qualifying young person"—see WRA 2012, s.40 and 10(5) and regs 2 and 5.

PART 8

CLAIMANT RESPONSIBILITIES

CHAPTER 1

WORK-RELATED REQUIREMENTS

Introductory

Introduction

2.316 **84.** This Chapter contains provisions about the work-related requirements under sections 15 to 25 of the Act, including the persons to whom they are to be applied, the limitations on those requirements and other related matters.

DEFINITION

"work-related requirement"—see WRA 2012 ss.40 and 13(2)

Meaning of terms relating to carers

2.317 **85.** In this Chapter—
"relevant carer" means—
(a) a parent of a child who is not the responsible carer, but has caring responsibilities for the child; or
(b) a person who has caring responsibilities for a person who has a physical or mental impairment; and
"responsible foster parent" in relation to a child means a person who is the only foster parent in relation to that child or, in the case of a couple both members of which are foster parents in relation to that child, the member who is nominated by them in accordance with regulation 86.

DEFINITIONS

"child"—see WRA 2012 s.40
"couple"—see WRA 2012 ss.40 and 39
"foster parent"—see reg.2
"responsible carer"—see WRA 2012 ss.40 and 19(6)

GENERAL NOTE

2.318 The definitions of "relevant carer" and "responsible foster parent" are relevant for the purposes of regs 86, 88, 89(1)(f), 91(2), 96(3) and 97(2). A child is a person under the age of 16. Responsibility for a child is to be determined in accordance with the rules in regs 4 and 4A, under which the basic test is whether the child normally lives with the person in question. The definition of "relevant carer" allows the inclusion into that category of people who do not count as responsible under the reg.4 rules but nevertheless have caring responsibilities (not further defined) for the child in question or have caring responsibilities for a person of any age who has a physical or mental impairment (not further defined). If a child has only one foster parent, that person is the "responsible foster parent". If both members of a couple are foster parents of the child, there must be a nomination of one of them under reg.86.

Nomination of responsible carer and responsible foster parent

86.—(1) This regulation makes provision for the nomination of the responsible carer or the responsible foster parent in relation to a child. 2.319

(2) Only one of joint claimants may be nominated as a responsible carer or a responsible foster parent.

(3) The nomination applies to all the children, where there is more than one, for whom either of the joint claimants is responsible.

(4) Joint claimants may change which member is nominated—

(a) once in a 12 month period, starting from the date of the previous nomination; or

(b) on any occasion where the Secretary of State considers that there has been a change of circumstances which is relevant to the nomination.

DEFINITIONS

"child"—see WRA 2012 s.40
"joint claimant"—*ibid.*
"responsible carer"—see WRA 2012 ss.40 and 19(6)
"responsible foster parent"—see reg.85

GENERAL NOTE

This regulation provides, for the purposes of s.19(6) of the WRA 2012 and reg.85, for the nomination by a couple of which one of them is to be the "responsible carer" or "responsible foster parent". Under s.19(6) the nomination has to be made jointly. Presumably that is implied where the nomination is of the responsible foster parent under reg.85. Where more than one child is involved, the same nomination must cover all of them. The nomination can be changed once within 12 months from the date of the previous nomination or when there has been a relevant change of circumstances 2.320

References to paid work

87. References in this Chapter to obtaining paid work include obtaining more paid work or [[1]better-paid work]. 2.321

AMENDMENT

1. Social Security (Qualifying Young Persons Participating in Relevant Training Schemes) (Amendment) Regulations 2017 (SI 2017/987) reg.4(5) (November 6, 2017, in full service areas only).

DEFINITION

"paid work"—see reg.2

GENERAL NOTE

2.322 References to obtaining paid work, which appears to include self-employment as well as employment, includes obtaining more or better-paid work. This provision does not appear to add anything to the conditions of most of the provisions to which obtaining paid work is relevant. The amendment adding the hyphen between "better" and "paid" applied only for digital service (full service) cases. Its application is now general.

Expected hours

2.323 **88.**—(1) The "expected number of hours per week" in relation to a claimant for the purposes of determining their individual threshold in regulation 90 or for the purposes of regulation 95 or 97 is 35 unless some lesser number of hours applies under paragraph (2).

(2) The lesser number of hours is—

(a) where—

(i) the claimant is a relevant carer, a responsible carer [1(subject to the following sub-paragraphs)] or a responsible foster parent, and

(ii) the Secretary of State is satisfied that the claimant has reasonable prospects of obtaining paid work,

the number of hours that the Secretary of State considers is compatible with those caring responsibilities;

[1(aa) where the claimant is a responsible carer of a child who has not yet reached compulsory school age, the number of hours that the Secretary of State considers is compatible with those caring responsibilities;]

(b) where the claimant is a responsible carer for a child [1who has reached compulsory school age but who is] under the age of 13, the number of hours that the Secretary of State considers is compatible with the child's normal school hours (including the normal time it takes the child to travel to and from school); or

(c) where the claimant has a physical or mental impairment, the number of hours that the Secretary of State considers is reasonable in light of the impairment.

AMENDMENT

1. Employment and Support Allowance and Universal Credit (Miscellaneous and Transitional and Savings Provisions) Regulations 2017 (SI 2017/204) reg.6 (April 3, 2017).

DEFINITIONS

"child"—see WRA 2012 s.40.
"claimant"—*ibid.*
"relevant carer"—see reg.85.
"responsible carer"—see WRA 2012 ss.40 and 19(6).
"responsible foster parent"—see reg.85.

GENERAL NOTE

2.324 Regulation 90 calculates the amount of earnings that will take a claimant out of being subject to all work-related requirements under s.22 of the WRA 2012 by reference to the "expected number of hours per week" and the national minimum wage. Regulation 95 uses the same number as one of the tests for the time that a claimant has to spend in action aimed at obtaining paid work to avoid being deemed not to have complied with the work search requirement under s.17 of the WRA 2012. Regulation 97(2) allows certain claimants to limit the work for which they must be available and for which they must search to work for the expected number of hours per week. The expected number of hours is also relevant to the calculation of the minimum income floor for those in gainful self-employment under reg.62, through the adoption in reg.62(4) of the individual and couple thresholds in reg.90(2) and (3). Regulation 88 defines the expected number of hours for all these purposes.

The number under para.(1) is 35, unless some lesser number is applicable under para.(2). Can the number be reduced to zero? Why not? Zero is a number and it is less than 35. There are four alternative categories in para.(2).

Sub-paragraph (a) applies where the claimant is a relevant carer, a responsible carer (for a child (under 16) or anyone else, unless already covered by one of sub-paras (aa)-(c)) or a responsible foster parent (see s.19(6) of the WRA 2012 and reg.85 above), and so has some substantial caring responsibility. Then, if the claimant nonetheless has reasonable prospects of obtaining paid work (including obtaining more or better-paid work), the expected hours are what is compatible with those caring responsibilities.

Sub-paragraph (aa) applies where the claimant is the responsible carer (as defined in s.19(6) of the WRA 2012 simply in terms of responsibility for the child, on which see reg.4) of a child under compulsory school age, where the number of hours is to be reduced to what is compatible with those caring responsibilities, without any condition of having reasonable prospects of obtaining paid work. Compulsory school age is reached at the beginning of the school terms following 1 January, 1 April or 1 September, according to which date first follows the child's fifth birthday.

Sub-paragraph (b) applies where the claimant is a responsible carer (as defined in s.19(6) of the WRA 2012) for a child under the age of 13, when the expected hours are those compatible with the child's normal school and travel hours. How should this apply in home-schooling cases?

Sub-paragraph (c) applies where the claimant has a physical or mental impairment (not further defined), when the expected hours are those reasonable in the light of the impairment. This is an important rule in the structure of the application of work-related requirements in a benefit not restricted to jobseekers, and one where the argument that the expected hours under reg.88 can be zero is particularly relevant.

It was announced in a press release of October 25, 2023 that (as presaged in general terms in the Spring Budget 2023) from that date healthy carers of children aged three to 12, but not those who were self-employed, would be "supported to increase their chances of getting a job or up their work hours", i.e. "will agree with their Work Coach to spend more time in work or applying for jobs, up to a maximum of 30 hours a week. Commitments will be tailored to parents' personal circumstances, including the availability of childcare." Previously, the "default maximum expected hours" were 16 per week for carers of three and four-year-olds and 25 for five to 12-year-olds. There has been no change to any existing legislation, so the mechanism for giving effect to the change can only be the identification of the expected hours in reg.88, which sets the limit to required hours of work search (including paid or voluntary work and work preparation: reg.95(1)(a)(i) and (2)) and work availability under reg.97(2), and in particular the circumstances in which a number of hours less than 35 must identified (para.(2)(a) to (c)). Sub-paras (a) and (aa) of para.(2) depend on the number of hours compatible with the relevant caring responsibilities and sub-para.(b) (where the child is of compulsory school age, but under 13) depends on the number of hours compatible with the child's normal school hours. On the face of it, at least for existing claimants coming within para.(2), the conclusion on what is so compatible could not be altered merely by an administrative alteration in the "default maximum expected hours" (there has been no alteration for para.(2)(a), where the default number of 35 under para.(1) applies subject to the conditions of para.(2)(a)). However, one unexpressed argument must be, because of the specific mention of this factor in the press release, that the increases in the amounts that universal credit claimants can claim for childcare from June 28, 2023 and the improvements in the meeting of upfront costs has made it possible for more hours than previously to be compatible with caring responsibilities or normal school hours. It might additionally be argued that previously more hours of work search, preparation and work had actually been compatible, but that work coaches had been constrained by the lower administratively set default maximum expected hours (even though those default hours could not be legally binding), so that there is scope for an increase.

Everything will (or ought to) depend on the particular circumstances of individual cases, including the actual availability of childcare in the locality concerned and the claimant's personal circumstances, including of course the effects of any physical or mental impairment of the claimant (para.(2)(c)). Although the press release says that claimants "will agree" to spend more time in work search etc., any approach that the expected hours for the affected groups should automatically be increased unless the claimant shows some special reason why not would be improper. The test in law remains that of compatibility in individual circumstances, without any initial presumptions about what the expected hours should be.

The press release says nothing about how often affected claimants will be expected to meet their work coach, but since the frequency for claimants subject to the work preparation requirement has been increased to once a month (see the notes to s.21 of the WRA 2012), the expectation for the present group of claimants would presumably be no less.

Note that the application of the deeming of non-compliance with the work search requirement under reg.95(1) if the expected hours of action are not taken is subject to deductions of hours under reg.95(2), including for temporary circumstances. Also note regs 96–99 on circumstances in which the work availability and work search requirements cannot be imposed or are moderated, particularly reg.96(4) (voluntary work), reg.96(5) (existing employment), reg.97(2) (physical or mental impairment) and reg.99(4) and (5)(c) (unfitness for work for short periods).

Work-related groups

Claimants subject to no work-related requirements

2.325 **89.**—(1) A claimant falls within section 19 of the Act (claimants subject to no work-related requirements) if—

(a) the claimant has reached the qualifying age for state pension credit;

(b) the claimant has caring responsibilities for one or more severely disabled persons for at least 35 hours a week but does not meet the conditions for entitlement to a carer's allowance[[4], or have entitlement to carer support payment,] and the Secretary of State is satisfied that it would be unreasonable to require the claimant to comply with a work search requirement and a work availability requirement, including if such a requirement were limited in accordance with section 17(4) or 18(3) of the Act;

(c) the claimant is pregnant and it is 11 weeks or less before her expected week of confinement, or was pregnant and it is 15 weeks or less since the date of her confinement;

(d) the claimant is an adopter and it is 12 months or less since—

(i) the date that the child was placed with the claimant, or

(ii) if the claimant requested that the 12 months should run from a date within 14 days before the child was expected to be placed, that date;

[2(da) the claimant is a member of a couple entitled to universal credit by virtue of regulation 3(2)(b) and has student income in relation to the course they are undertaking which is taken into account in the calculation of the award;]

(e) the claimant does not have to meet the condition in section 4(1)(d) of the Act (not receiving education) by virtue of regulation 14 and—
  (i) is a person referred to in paragraph (a) of that regulation (under 21, in non-advanced education and without parental support), or
  (ii) has student income in relation to the course they are undertaking which is taken into account in the calculation of the award; or

(f) the claimant is the responsible foster parent of a child under the age of 1.

(2) In paragraph (1)(b) "severely disabled" has the meaning in section 70 of the Contributions and Benefits Act.

(3) In paragraph (1)(d)—

(a) "adopter" means a person who has been matched with a child for adoption and who is, or is intended to be, the responsible carer for the child, but excluding a person who is a foster parent or close relative of the child; and

(b) a person is matched with a child for adoption when it is decided by an adoption agency that the person would be a suitable adoptive parent for the child.

[1(4) For the purposes of paragraph (1)(e)(ii), a claimant is not to be treated as having student income where—

(a) that income is a postgraduate [3 ...] loan; and

(b) the course in respect of which the loan is paid is not a full-time course.

(5) In paragraph (4), "postgraduate [3 ...] loan" has the meaning given in regulation 68(7).]

AMENDMENTS

1. Social Security (Treatment of Postgraduate Master's Degree Loans and Special Support Loans) (Amendment) Regulations 2016 (SI 2016/743) reg.6(5) (August 4, 2016).

2. Universal Credit (Miscellaneous Amendments, Saving and Transitional Provision) Regulations 2018 (SI 2018/65) reg.3(10) (April 11, 2018).

3. Social Security (Income and Capital) (Miscellaneous Amendments) Regulations 2020 (SI 2020/618) reg.8(6) (July 15, 2020).

4. Carer's Assistance (Carer Support Payment) (Scotland) Regulations 2023 (Consequential Amendments) Order 2023 (SI 2023/1218) art.23(7) (November 19, 2023).

DEFINITIONS

"carer support payment"—see reg.2.
"child"—see WRA 2012 s.40.
"claimant"—*ibid.*
"close relative"—see reg.2.
"Contributions and Benefits Act"—*ibid.*
"postgraduate loan"—see para.(5) and reg.68(7).
"responsible carer"—see WRA 2012 ss.40 and 19(6).
"responsible foster parent"—see reg.85.

General Note

Temporary Coronavirus Provisions

2.326 The last of the temporary coronavirus provisions relevant to the imposition of work-related requirements expired on November 12, 2020. See previous editions of this volume for the details.

2.327 Section 19(2) of the WRA 2012 sets out in paras (a), (b) and (c) three categories of claimants who can be subject to no work-related requirements: (a) those who have limited capability for work and work-related activity; (b) those who meet the definition of having regular and substantial caring responsibilities for a severely disabled person (i.e. satisfy the conditions, apart from level of earnings and claiming, for carer's allowance, but gain no earned income from the caring: reg.30); and (c) those who are the responsible carer for a child under the age of one. Paragraph (d) of s.19(2) includes claimants of a description prescribed in regulations. Regulation 89(1) sets out categories prescribed for this purpose, as noted below. Regulation 90 prescribes another category, dependent on earnings. See also reg.98 on recent victims of domestic violence.

The categories prescribed for the purpose of s.19(2)(d) are as follows:

(a) Claimants who have reached the qualifying age for state pension credit. The qualifying age for men is the same as for a woman born on the same day and for women depends on the date of birth in accordance with a complicated formula. See p.776 of and Appendix 11 to CPAG's *Welfare benefits and tax credits handbook* (2019/2020 edition) for the details. For anyone born before April 6, 1950 the age is 60. For those born on or after that date there is a sliding scale that rose to 65 in November 2018, reaching 66 by October 2020 and 67 by some date from 2026. Although single claimants who have reached the qualifying age for state pension credit cannot be entitled to universal credit (WRA 2012 s.4(1)(b)), someone of that age can be a joint claimant with a partner under that age (a "mixed age couple").

(b) Claimants who do not meet the conditions of entitlement for carer's allowance or Scottish carer support payment, but have caring responsibilities for at least 35 hours per week for a severely disabled person (defined in the same way as for carer's allowance: para.(2)), where it would be unreasonable to expect the claimant to comply with a work search and a work availability requirement, even with limitations. Some claimants who fall within this category will already be covered by s.19(2)(b) and it is not easy to work out who could benefit from the extension. Perhaps the main category would be those who are paid for the caring, who are expressly excluded from the scope of s.19(2)(b) by the definition in reg.30 above. There may be more scope for the operation of para.(b) in relation to the new Scottish carer support payment (CSP), because in such cases s.19(2)(b) only applies, by virtue of the amendment to the meaning of "regular and substantial caring responsibilities for a severely disabled person" in reg.30, where a claimant is actually entitled to CSP.

(c) Claimants who are pregnant in the period from 11 weeks before the expected date of confinement and 15 weeks after the date of confinement.

(d) Claimants who are "adopters" (i.e. who have been matched with a particular child for adoption under the complicated conditions in para.(3)) within 12 months or so of placement. It does not matter how old the child is, so long as below the age of 16. Any person who is actually the responsible carer of a child under the age of one is already covered by s.19(2)(c). It appears that para.(d) can continue to apply after the child has actually been adopted, for the 12 months following placement. See para.(f) for foster parents.

(da) Claimants who are part of a joint claim couple where one claimant fails to meet the basic condition in s.4(1)(d) of the WRA 2012 not to be receiving education, but the other meets that condition or is excepted from it, but only where student income (with the qualification in para.(4)) for the course being attended has been taken into account in the calculation of the award of universal credit. Regulation 3(2)(b) allows such a couple to be entitled to universal credit. See regs 68–71 for student income and how it is taken into account. The aim of this addition in April 2018 was to provide uniformity for couples with the treatment of single claimants in education under sub-para.(e).

(e) Claimants who, by virtue of reg.14(1)(a), do not have to meet the basic condition in s.4(1)(d) of the WRA 2012 of not receiving education or who have student income (see regs 68–71) that is taken into account in the award of universal credit.

(f) Claimants who are the responsible foster parent (there can only be one under reg.85) of a child under the age of one. It appears that such a person cannot get within s.19(2)(c) because reg.4(6)(a) prevents their being treated as responsible for the child while the child is "looked after" by a local authority under s.22 of the Children Act 1989 or s.17(6) of the Children (Scotland) Act 1995.

Claimants subject to no work-related requirements—the earnings thresholds

90.—(1) A claimant falls within section 19 of the Act (claimants subject to no work-related requirements) if the claimant's [2monthly] earnings are equal to or exceed the claimant's individual threshold. 2.328

(2) A claimant's individual threshold is the amount that a person of the same age as the claimant would be paid at the hourly rate applicable under [3regulation 4 or regulation 4A(1)(a) to (c)] of the National Minimum Wage Regulations for—

(a) 16 hours per week, in the case of a claimant who would otherwise fall within section 20 (claimants subject to work-focused interview requirement only) or section 21 (claimants subject to work-preparation requirement) of the Act; or

(b) the expected number of hours per week in the case of a claimant who would otherwise fall within section 22 of the Act (claimants subject to all work-related requirements) [2,

converted to a monthly amount by multiplying by 52 and dividing by 12].

(3) A claimant who is a member of a couple falls within section 19 of the Act if the couple's combined [2monthly] earnings are equal to or exceed whichever of the following amounts is applicable—

(a) in the case of joint claimants, the sum of their individual thresholds; or

(b) in the case of a claimant who claims universal credit as a single person by virtue of regulation 3(3), the sum of—

(i) the claimant's individual threshold, and

(ii) the amount a person would be paid for 35 hours per week at the hourly rate specified in [3regulation 4] of the National Minimum Wage Regulations [2,

converted to a monthly amount by multiplying by 52 and dividing by 12].

(4) A claimant falls within section 19 of the Act if the claimant is employed under a contract of apprenticeship and has [2monthly] earnings that are equal to or exceed the amount they would be paid for—

(a) 30 hours a week; or

(b) if less, the expected number of hours per week for that claimant,

at the rate specified in [3 regulation 4A(1)(d)] of the National Minimum Wage Regulations [2, converted to a monthly amount by multiplying by 52 and dividing by 12].

[1(5) A claimant falls within section 19 of the Act if they are treated as having earned income in accordance with regulation 62 (minimum income floor).]

(6) [2 A person's monthly earnings are]—

(a) [2 the person's] earned income calculated or estimated in relation to the current assessment period before any deduction for income tax, national insurance contributions or relievable pension contributions; or

(b) in a case where the person's earned income fluctuates (or is likely to fluctuate) the amount of that income[2, calculated or estimated before any deduction for income tax, national insurance contributions or relievable pension contributions, taken as a monthly average]—

(i) where there is an identifiable cycle, over the duration of one such cycle, or

(ii) where there is no identifiable cycle, over three months or such other period as may, in the particular case, enable the [2monthly] average to be determined more accurately,

[2and the Secretary of State may, in order to enable monthly earnings to be determined more accurately, disregard earned income received in respect of an employment which has ceased.]

(7) [3...]

Amendments

1. Universal Credit and Miscellaneous Amendments (No.2) Regulations 2014 (SI 2014/2888) reg.4(7) (November 16, 2014).

2. Universal Credit and Miscellaneous Amendments Regulations 2015 (SI 2015/1754) reg.2(6) (November 4, 2015).

3. Social Security (Jobseeker's Allowance, Employment and Support Allowance and Universal Credit) (Amendment) Regulations 2016 (SI 2016/678) reg.5(4) (July 25, 2016).

Definitions

"the Act"—see reg.2.
"assessment period"—see WRA 2012 ss.40 and 7(2), and reg.21.
"claimant"—see WRA 2012 s.40(1).
"couple"—see WRA 2012 ss.40 and 39.
"earned income"—see regs 2 and 52.
"joint claimants"—see WRA 2012 s.40.
"National Minimum Wage Regulations"—see reg.2.
"single person"—see WRA 2012 ss.40 and 1(2)(a).

General Note

2.329 Regulation 90 prescribes additional circumstances, beyond those prescribed by reg.89, in which a claimant falls within s.19(2)(d) of the WRA 2012 and therefore can be subject to no work-related requirements. Thus, if a single claimant or a couple falls within reg.90 no requirement can be imposed under s.20 (work-focused interview) or 21 (work preparation) although the conditions in s.20(1) or 21(1)(a)–(b) are met (see the notes to those provisions for why their express words forbid such an exercise, that has apparently sometimes been operated in practice). That prohibition is even clearer if s.22 (all work-related requirements) appears to be in play, e.g. where a claimant is "merely" the responsible carer of a child aged three or over. The basic test under para.(1) is that the claimant's monthly earnings are at least equal to their "individual threshold", known administratively as the conditionality earnings threshold. This provision is necessary because universal credit, in contrast to the terms of pre-existing benefits, can be payable while a claimant is in work. The policy is that if a claimant is already earning above a minimum level there is no need to require them to do anything to seek further paid work. Entitlement then depends on the income calculation under s.8 of the WRA 2012. See further the notes to reg.99.

Note that reg.6(1A)(a) requires the rounding down to the nearest pound of any amounts produced by reg.90 calculations.

Paragraph (3) applies the para.(1) test to couples. For joint claimants their individual thresholds are added together, as are their monthly earnings. The threshold is calculated under para.(2) by multiplying the hourly rate of national minimum wage by, in the case of a claimant who would otherwise be subject to all work-related requirements under s.22 of the WRA 2012, the expected number of hours per week (see reg.88, starting point 35). In the case of a claimant who would otherwise fall within s.20 or 21, the multiplier is 16.

Under para.(6) monthly earnings are earned income as calculated under Chapter 2 of Part 6 of the Universal Credit Regulations (i.e. regs 51–64) in each monthly assessment period but without deductions for income tax, national insurance contributions or pension contributions, subject to an averaging provision in sub-para. (b) where earned income fluctuates or is likely to fluctuate. The ordinary calculation in regs 51–64 involves the use of "real time" information. In the case of both employment and self-employment the calculation of earned income in respect of any assessment period (i.e. month) is to be based on amounts received in that assessment period (regs 54, 55, 57 and 57A), as now confirmed as a matter of construction by the Court of Appeal in *Secretary of State for Work and Pensions v Johnson* [2020] EWCA Civ 778; [2020] P.T.S.R. 1872 and *Pantellerisco v Secretary of State for Work and Pensions* [2021] EWCA Civ 1454; [2021] P.T.S.R. 1922 discussed in detail in the notes to regs 54 and 61. *Johnson* found that the outcome, especially the fluctuations in the amounts of earnings taken into account in different assessment periods when the general pattern of earnings was regular, was irrational and unlawful for claimants in the very particular categories involved. It is yet to be seen what method of calculation might be accepted as rational prior to the substitution of the November 2020 form of reg.61, but for most claimants the general rule in regs 54 and 61 is to be applied. In those cases, it may be proper for the amount of universal credit to fluctuate month by month or for the claimant to fall in and out of entitlement on the means test. However, if entitlement continues there are plainly arguments against a claimant drifting in and out of exemption from all work-related requirements on the basis of the amount of earned income. That is presumably the thinking behind para.(6)(b). The reference to fluctuation of earned income must be to fluctuation over more than one assessment period, because fluctuation within each assessment period does not affect the total for that month. Under sub-para.(i) it is not clear whether the identifiable cycle refers merely to the pattern of receipts or to the pattern of the employment or self-employment or other paid work that produces the income. There is no reference to a cycle "of work", as there is in reg.42(2) (b) of the JSA Regulations 2013, so that the stricture in *KN v DfC (JSA)* [2022] NICom 21 against conflating a cycle of payment with a cycle of work does not apply. In the overall context of universal credit, with the emphasis in regs 54 and 61 on receipts in a particular assessment period, it may be that it is a cycle of payment that is more important. It would appear that there cannot be an identifiable cycle until it has started and come to an end, which is by definition the start of the next cycle, at least once. Given the difficulties that the notion of a recognisable cycle has given in other contexts it may be that most cases will be dealt with by sub-para.(ii), which requires the taking of an average over the previous three months or such other period as in the particular case enables the weekly average to be determined more accurately. That gives a very wide discretion.

Note also the important power at the end of para.(6) to disregard earned income from an employment that has ceased.

In relation to self-employment some of the problems mentioned above will be avoided by the application of the reg.62 minimum income floor (para.(5)). Providing that a person meets the quite stringent conditions in reg.64 for being in gainful self-employment and is not in a 12-month start-up period (reg.63), earned income below the individual threshold is deemed to be at that level. In those circumstances the claimant is exempted from all work-related requirements by para.(5).

Prior to October 3, 2019, in the converse situation where a person was exempted from all work-related requirements through the operation of reg.90 apart from para.(5), the provisions of reg.62 on the MIF could not apply (reg.62(1)(b) in its original form). See the notes to reg.62 for how that, and in particular the averaging process under reg.90(6), could then affect the MIF. According to the Explanatory Memorandum to the Universal Credit (Childcare Costs and Minimum Income Floor) (Amendment) Regulations 2019 (SI 2019/1249), that did not reflect the policy intention. Regulation 3 of those Regulations inserts into reg.62(1)(b), with effect from October 3, 2019, the rule that for the MIF to apply the claimant must be subject to all work-related requirements not only apart from the effect of reg.62, but also apart from the effect of reg.90. It remains the case that, if a claimant in exempted from any work-related requirement under any provision apart from reg.62 or 90, the MIF cannot apply.

Claimants subject to work-focused interview requirement only

2.330 **91.**—(1) [1 . . .].

(2) A claimant falls within section 20 of the Act if—

(a) the claimant is the responsible foster parent in relation to a child aged at least 1;

(b) the claimant is the responsible foster parent in relation to a qualifying young person, and the Secretary of State is satisfied that the qualifying young person has care needs which would make it unreasonable to require the claimant to comply with a work search requirement or a work availability requirement, including if such a requirement were limited in accordance with section 17(4) or 18(3) of the Act;

(c) the claimant is a foster parent, but not the responsible foster parent, in relation to a child or qualifying young person, and the Secretary of State is satisfied that the child or qualifying young person has care needs which would make it unreasonable to require the claimant to comply with a work search requirement or a work availability requirement, including if such a requirement were limited in accordance with section 17(4) or 18(3) of the Act;

(d) the claimant has fallen within paragraph (a), (b) or (c) within the past 8 weeks and has no child or qualifying young person currently placed with them, but expects to resume being a foster parent; or

(e) the claimant has become a friend or family carer in relation to a child within the past 12 months and is also the responsible carer in relation to that child.

(3) In paragraph (2)(e) "friend or family carer" means a person who is responsible for a child, but is not the child's parent or step-parent, and has undertaken the care of the child in the following circumstances—

(a) the child has no parent or has parents who are unable to care for the child; or

(b) it is likely that the child would otherwise be looked after by a local authority because of concerns in relation to the child's welfare.

AMENDMENT

1. Welfare Reform and Work Act 2016 s.17(2)(a) (April 3, 2017).

DEFINITIONS

"the Act"—see reg.2.
"child"—see WRA 2012 s.40.
"claimant"—*ibid.*
"foster parent"—see reg.2.
"qualifying young person"—see regs 2 and 5.
"responsible carer"—see WRA 2012 ss.40 and 19(6).
"responsible foster parent"—see reg.85.
"work availability requirement"—see WRA 2012 ss.40 and 18(1).
"work search requirement"—see WRA 2012 ss.40 and 17(1).

GENERAL NOTE

Paragraph (1)

Paragraph (1) had formerly prescribed the relevant maximum age of a child for the purposes of s.20(1)(a) of the WRA 2012 to enable a responsible carer to be exempted from all work-related requirements except the work-focused interview requirement (initially five and then, from April 2014, three). From April 3, 2017 the operation of s.20(1)(a) has by its terms been restricted to responsible carers of a child aged one (responsible carers of a child under one being exempted from all work-related requirements under s.19(1)(c)). There is no longer any power to prescribe an age in regulations. 2.331

Paragraph (2)

This provision prescribes the categories of claimant who are subject only to the work-focused interview requirement under s.20(1)(b) and any connected requirements under s.23. They cover mainly foster parents. 2.332

Under sub-para.(a) responsible foster parents of children of any age from one to 15 are covered. Responsible foster parents of children under one are exempted from all work-related requirements under reg.89(1)(f).

That is extended to young persons in education up to the age of 19 if it would be unreasonable to subject the claimant to other work-related requirements (sub-para.(b)).

Sub-paragraph (c) extends the scope of sub-paras (a) and (b) to foster parents who do not meet the condition of being "responsible" if the child or qualifying young person has care needs that make it unreasonable to subject the claimant to other work-related requirements.

Sub-paragraph (d) allows the effect of sub-paras (a)–(c) to continue for eight weeks after the claimant ceases to have any child or qualifying young person placed with them, if a new placement is expected.

Sub-paragraph (e) applies to claimants who are responsible carers of a child of any age up to 15 if they fall within the meaning of "friend or family carer" in para.(3).

[[1]Claimants subject to work preparation requirement

91A. [[2] . . .].] 2.333

AMENDMENTS

1. Income Support (Work-Related Activity) Miscellaneous Amendments Regulations 2014 (SI 2014/1097) reg.16(3) (April 28, 2014).

2. Welfare Reform and Work Act 2016 s.17(2)(b) (April 3, 2017).

General Note

2.334 See the notes to s.21 of the WRA 2012. The operation of that section in so far as it exempts responsible carers of a child from all work-related requirements except the work-focused interview and work preparation requirement has from April 3, 2017 been directly controlled by the terms of s.21 (the child must be aged two and no less or more). There is thus no need for a prescription of conditions including an age in regulations and the former duty in s.21(5) so to do has also been removed.

Claimants subject to all work-related requirements—EEA jobseekers

2.335 **92.** [[1] . . .]

Amendment

1. Universal Credit (EEA Jobseekers) Amendment Regulations 2015 (SI 2015/546) reg.3 (June 10, 2015).

General Note

2.336 For the discriminatory effect of this provision on the entitlement of certain EEA claimants with a right to reside before its revocation in June 2015 see the notes to the 2013/14 edition of what was then Vol.V of this series. Now see reg.9 above, as extensively amended.

The work-related requirements

Purposes of a work-focused interview

2.337 **93.** The purposes of a work-focused interview are any or all of the following—

(a) assessing the claimant's prospects for remaining in or obtaining paid work;
(b) assisting or encouraging the claimant to remain in or obtain paid work;
(c) identifying activities that the claimant may undertake that will make remaining in or obtaining paid work more likely;
(d) identifying training, educational or rehabilitation opportunities for the claimant which may make it more likely that the claimant will remain in or obtain paid work or be able to do so;
(e) identifying current or future work opportunities for the claimant that are relevant to the claimant's needs and abilities;
(f) ascertaining whether a claimant is in gainful self-employment or meets the conditions in regulation 63 (start-up period).

Definitions

"claimant"—see WRA 2012 s.40.
"obtaining paid work"—see reg.87.
"paid work"—see reg.2.

General Note

2.338 This provision prescribes the purposes of a work-focused interview under the definition in s.15(2) of the WRA 2012. The purposes could probably not be set out more widely, especially given that obtaining paid work includes obtaining more or better paid work and that s.15 covers work preparation as well as work. Arguably, even if there is no realistic prospect of a claimant obtaining any kind of paid work, the purpose of assessing those prospects or lack of prospects in an interview could still be fulfilled.

Note that the prescribed purposes do not include the discussion of the drawing up or revision of a claimant commitment as such, but the matters prescribed may be relevant to what requirements are to be included in a claimant commitment.

Work search requirement—interviews

94. A claimant is to be treated as not having complied with a work search requirement to apply for a particular vacancy for paid work where the claimant fails to participate in an interview offered to the claimant in connection with the vacancy. 2.339

DEFINITIONS

"claimant"—see WRA 2012, s.40.
"paid work"—see reg.2.
"work search requirement"—see WRA 2012 ss.40 and 17(1).

GENERAL NOTE

This provision, made under s.25(a) of the WRA 2012, applies when the Secretary of State has required under s.17(1)(b) that the claimant take the particular action of applying for a specified vacancy for paid work. If the claimant fails to participate in an interview offered in connection with the vacancy the work search requirement is deemed not to have been complied with. See the notes to s.17, and the notes to ss.15 and 27 for "participation" in an interview. 2.340

Work search requirement—all reasonable action

95.—(1) A claimant is to be treated as not having complied with a work search requirement to take all reasonable action for the purpose of obtaining paid work in any week unless— 2.341

(a) either—

(i) the time which the claimant spends taking action for the purpose of obtaining paid work is at least the claimant's expected number of hours per week minus any relevant deductions, or

(ii) the Secretary of State is satisfied that the claimant has taken all reasonable action for the purpose of obtaining paid work despite the number of hours that the claimant spends taking such action being lower than the expected number of hours per week; and

(b) that action gives the claimant the best prospects of obtaining work.

(2) In this regulation "relevant deductions" means the total of any time agreed by the Secretary of State—

(a) for the claimant to carry out paid work, voluntary work, a work preparation requirement, or voluntary work preparation in that week; or

(b) for the claimant to deal with temporary childcare responsibilities, a domestic emergency, funeral arrangements or other temporary circumstances.

(3) For the purpose of paragraph (2)(a) the time agreed by the Secretary of State for the claimant to carry out voluntary work must not exceed 50% of the claimant's expected number of hours per week.

(4) "Voluntary work preparation" means particular action taken by a claimant and agreed by the Secretary of State for the purpose of making it more likely that the claimant will obtain paid work, but which is not

specified by the Secretary of State as a work preparation requirement under section 16 of the Act.

DEFINITIONS

"claimant"—see WRA 2012 s.40.
"expected number of hours"—see regs 2 and 88.
"obtaining paid work"—see reg.87.
"paid work"—see reg.2.
"work preparation requirement"—see WRA 2012 ss.40 and 16(1).
"work search requirement"—see WRA 2012 ss.40 and 17(1).

GENERAL NOTE

Temporary Coronavirus Provisions

2.342 The last of the temporary coronavirus provisions relevant to the work search requirement expired on November 12, 2020. See previous editions of this volume for the details.

2.343 This regulation, made under s.25(a) of the WRA 2012, deems certain claimants not to have complied with a work search requirement under s.17(1)(a) of the WRA 2012 to take all reasonable action for the purpose of obtaining paid work (including more or better paid work). Although in form meeting the conditions in reg.95 merely lifts the deeming of non-compliance if its conditions are met, there would seem to be little point in making such detailed provision if claimants were not to be positively treated as having complied if the conditions are met. See the notes to s.17 and see reg.97 for limitations on the kind of work that needs to be searched for. A failure for no good reason to comply with the requirement under s.17(1)(a) can lead to a medium-level sanction under s.27(2)(a) of the WRA 2012 and reg.103(1)(a).

To avoid the deeming a claimant must get within *both* sub-paras.(a) *and* (b) of para.(1).

There are two alternative routes to getting within sub-para.(a). Although the route in head (i), relating to spending the "expected hours" (starting point under reg.88, 35), has been described as the "primary" rule in some previous editions, it is now submitted that that is misleading. Although head (ii), with the route of having taken all reasonable action in the week in question, applies only if the claimant spent less than the expected hours, logically the two routes are of equal status. One of the routes had to appear before the other in sub-para.(a) and the two routes could with the same effect have been put in the opposite order. The effect of reading the two provisions together is that there is no rigid rule that claimants be held to spending the expected hours in work search week after week, even though that may be the easiest point to start the enquiry. The ultimate test is what is reasonable. The sentence in the middle of para.32 of *S v SSWP (UC)* [2017] UKUT 477 (AAC) (see the notes to s.14 of the WRA 2012 for the details) saying that if "a claimant spends less than 35 hours, or the quality of the work search is disputed, he will need to rely on section 27(2) [i.e. the "for no good reason" rule] if he seeks to avoid a sanction" is not to be taken to indicate the contrary. That sentence is immediately followed by an acknowledgement of the effect of head (ii).

The para.(1)(a)(i) route requires that the claimant must spend at least the "expected number of hours per week" (reg.88), less deductions for work, voluntary work or work preparation or various emergency, urgent or other temporary difficulties (para.(2), subject to the further rules in paras (3) and (4)), in taking action for the purpose of obtaining paid work. Note that the starting point of expected hours under reg.88 may be reduced from 35 (arguably to nil, if appropriate) to take account of responsibility for certain categories of young children, of certain other regular caring responsibilities and physical or mental impairments. The time to count as a deduction under para.(2) must be agreed by the Secretary of State. The words might suggest that the agreement must come in advance of the activity that might qualify. However, it would seem unrealistic for claimants to predict, say, the future occurrence of domestic emergencies so as to seek the Secretary of State's agreement in advance. Thus, it would seem, and would be in line with the normal pattern of claimants making a declaration that they have been seeking work in the assessment period that is ending, that a subsequent agreement will do (although no doubt it would be sensible for claimants to raise potential issues in advance where possible). It must be the case that, while the Secretary of State appears to have an open-ended discretion whether or not to agree to any particular hours being deducted under para.(2), on appeal against any sanction for failure to comply with the work search requirement under s.17(1)(a) of the WRA 2012 a tribunal is allowed to substitute its own judgment about what should have been agreed. Even if it were to be held that whatever had or had not been agreed by the Secretary of State has to control whether there had been a sanctionable failure, the reasonableness or otherwise of the Secretary of State's view would be relevant to whether a failure to comply was "for no good reason". The deductions for hours spent in paid work and voluntary work are important, as is that for work preparation requirements in securing a rational co-ordination among the various work-related requirements. Would para.(2)(b) allow the Secretary of State to allow short "holidays" from work search responsibilities, under the heading of temporary circumstances or temporary child care responsibilities (cf. reg.19(1)(p) and (2) of the JSA Regulations 1996)? Or would such an allowance fall more naturally under reg.99(5)(b) (work search requirement not to be imposed where it would be unreasonable to do so because of temporary child care responsibilities or temporary circumstances)?

If the claimant does not meet the expected hours condition, which for the majority of claimants will be 35 hours per week, sub-para.(a) can nevertheless be satisfied through head (ii) if the claimant has taken all reasonable action in the week in question for the purpose of obtaining paid work. This is an important provision which, if properly applied, would go a good way to meeting the commonly expressed criticism that in the real world it is impossible for many claimants to fill 35 hours week after week with meaningful work search action.

In *RR v SSWP (UC)* [2017] UKUT 459 (AAC), the First-tier Tribunal, in upholding two medium-level sanctions on the basis that the claimant had not taken work-search action for the 35 expected hours in two weeks, failed to consider whether there should be deductions from 35 hours under reg.95(2)(b) when there was evidence of circumstances (having to deal with the fall-out from divorce or other family proceedings) that could have amounted to a domestic emergency or other temporary circumstances. The tribunal appeared to think that the 35 hours were immutable, which was plainly an error of law. Alternatively, the claimant could have been taken to satisfy the condition in s.17(1)(a) through reg.95(1)(a)(ii), which applies even though the expected hours, less deductions, are not met. The decision-maker and the tribunal put some emphasis on the claimant having agreed in her claimant commitment to prepare and look for work for 35 hours a week. Judge Wikeley pointed out that the claimant commitment was only in terms of "normally" spending 35 hours a week, but in fact the number of hours specified in a claimant commitment cannot be directly relevant unless they establish a lesser number of hours under reg.88(2) or an agreement to a deduction of hours under reg.95(2). The test is in terms of the expected hours less deductions, which the claimant commitment merely records, or "all reasonable action" under reg.95(1)(a)(ii). It is worth noting that the claimant commitment in *RR* (following what appears to be a standard form) specified 35 hours normally for a combination of work preparation (s.16(1) of the WRA 2012) *and* work search, so did incorporate an unquantified deduction under reg.95(2)(a).

The judge, in re-making the decision in the claimant's favour, did not expressly consider the condition that a deduction under para.(2) be agreed by the Secretary of State. He must either have regarded that condition as one on which a First-tier Tribunal was entitled to substitute its own agreement or have regarded the Secretary of State's support of the appeal in the Upper Tribunal and of the substitution of a decision as necessarily involving agreement to a deduction. He also suggested that an alternative way of looking at the case could have been to consider whether reg.99(5)(b) applied (domestic emergency or temporary circumstances), so that no work search requirement could be imposed for the weeks in question. See the notes to reg.99.

Under (b), the action under (a) must give the claimant the best prospects of obtaining work. Taken at face value that condition imposes an almost impossibly high standard, because there will nearly always be something extra that the claimant could do to improve prospects of obtaining work. The condition must therefore be interpreted in a way that leaves some work for condition (a) to do and with some degree of common sense, taking account of all the circumstances, especially any factors that have led to a reduction in the expected hours below 35 or a deduction under para.(1)(a)(i) and (2), as well as matters such as the state of the local labour market, what the claimant has done in previous weeks and how successful or otherwise those actions were (compare reg.18(3) of the JSA Regulations 1996). The work search requirement in s.17(1)(a) of the WRA 2012 is only to take all reasonable action. The reference here in secondary legislation to the best prospects of obtaining work cannot be allowed to make the test as set out in the primary legislation stricter than that. There will of course be considerable difficulty in checking on the precise number of hours spent in taking relevant action, depending on what might count as action (see the notes to s.17), and in what might be required from claimants in the way of record keeping. It may be that it will be much easier to define non-compliance with the requirement in s.17(1)(b) to take particular action specified by the Secretary of State, although such a failure will only attract a low-level sanction under s.27(2)(a) and reg.104(1)(b)(iii).

In the Upper Tribunal's substituted decision in *RR* (above) there was no express consideration of the overriding condition in sub-para.(b). That must be regarded as having been satisfied in the absence of it having been raised on behalf of the Secretary of State in the support of the appeal to the Upper Tribunal.

In *S v SSWP (UC)* [2017] UKUT 477 (AAC) (see the notes to s.14 of the WRA 2012 for the details), the basis on which the First-tier Tribunal seemed to have accepted that the claimant had failed to take all reasonable action for the purpose of obtaining paid work in the various weeks in question was that he had failed to apply for vacancies outside the healthcare sector that the DWP said were suitable. The claimant's evidence was somewhat inconsistent and unconvincing, but he appears to have said that, although he did not apply for any vacancies, he had spent 35 hours in each week checking jobs websites and local newspapers. If that had been accepted, it could have been argued (see the beginning of this note) that, subject to the operation of para.(2)(b), the claimant not only escaped the deeming of non-compliance in para.(1) but fell to be treated as having complied with the s.17(1)(a) requirement. That point was not addressed in the Upper Tribunal's substituted decision dismissing the claimant's appeal (on the issue of "no good reason"). There was certainly evidence on which it could have been concluded that the action taken by the claimant, even if taking up 35 hours each week, had not given him the best prospects of obtaining work. It would have been better if it had been spelled out just where the inadequacy of the claimant's job search fitted into the legislative structure. Did the claimant fail the expected hours test in para.(2)(a)(i) without being rescued by para.(2)(a)(ii) or did he get within para.(2)(a)(i), but fail the para.(2)(b) test?

Work availability requirement—able and willing immediately to take up paid work

2.344 **96.**—(1) Subject to paragraph (2) a claimant is to be treated as not having complied with a work availability requirement if the claimant is not able and willing immediately to attend an interview offered to the claimant in connection with obtaining paid work.

(2) But a claimant is to be treated as having complied with a work availability requirement despite not being able immediately to take up paid work, if paragraph (3), (4) or (5) applies.

(3) This paragraph applies where—

(a) a claimant is a responsible carer or a relevant carer;

(b) the Secretary of State is satisfied that, as a consequence the claimant needs a longer period of up to 1 month to take up paid work, or up to 48 hours to attend an interview in connection with obtaining work, taking into account alternative care arrangements; and

(c) the claimant is able and willing to take up paid work, or attend an interview, on being given notice for that period.

(4) This paragraph applies where—

(a) a claimant is carrying out voluntary work;

(b) the Secretary of State is satisfied that, as a consequence, the claimant needs a longer period of up to 1 week to take up paid work, or up to 48 hours to attend an interview in connection with obtaining work; and

(c) the claimant is able and willing to take up paid work, or attend an interview, on being given notice for that period.

(5) This paragraph applies where a claimant—

(a) is employed under a contract of service;

(b) is required by section 86 of the Employment Rights Act 1996, or by the contract of service, to give notice to terminate the contract;

(c) is able and willing to take up paid work once the notice period has expired; and

(d) is able and willing to attend an interview on being given 48 hours notice.

Definitions

"claimant"—see WRA 2012 s.40.
"obtaining paid work"—see reg.87.
"paid work"—see reg.2.
"relevant carer"—see reg.85.
"responsible carer"—see WRA 2012 ss.40 and 19(6).
"work availability requirement"—see WRA 2012 ss.40 and 18(1).

General Note

Temporary Coronavirus Provisions

The last of the temporary coronavirus provisions relevant to the work availability requirement expired on November 12, 2020. See previous editions of this volume for the details. **2.345**

This regulation is made under s.25 of the WRA 2012 and relates to the work availability requirement under s.18(1) and (2) of being able and willing immediately to take up paid work or more or better paid work. See reg.97 for limitations on the kind of work for which a claimant must be available and reg.99, and in particular para. (5), for other situations in which the ordinary test of being able and willing immediately to take up work or attend an interview is modified. **2.346**

Paragraph (1)

Paragraph (1) simply confirms that the requirement of being able and willing immediately to take up paid work extends to being able and willing immediately to attend an interview in connection with obtaining paid work, subject to the exemptions in paras (3)-(5), through the operation of para.(2). **2.347**

Paragraphs (2) to (5)

2.348 A claimant who falls within paras (3), (4) or (5) is to be treated as complying with the work availability requirement, including as extended by para.(1). Paragraph (3) applies to those with child-care or other caring responsibilities who would need to take up to one month to take up paid work or up to 48 hours to attend an interview and are able and willing to do so if given that length of notice. Can para.(3)(b) allow claimants with caring responsibilities (noting that such claimants do not need to have sole or main responsibility) to have a holiday without needing to arrange some means of taking up work offers or interviews immediately? Or would such an allowance fall more naturally under reg.99(5A) or (5B) with (5)(b) (no need to be available immediately where work search requirement not to be imposed because it would be unreasonable to do so because of temporary child care responsibilities or temporary circumstances)? Paragraph (4) applies to claimants doing voluntary work (not further defined), subject to the same conditions. Paragraph (5) applies to claimants in employment who are required to give notice to terminate their contract of employment and who are able and willing to take up paid work once that notice has expired and to attend an interview on 48 hours' notice.

Work search requirement and work availability requirement—limitations

2.349 **97.**—(1) Paragraphs (2) to (5) set out the limitations on a work search requirement and a work availability requirement.

(2) In the case of a claimant who is a relevant carer or a responsible carer or who has a physical or mental impairment, a work search and work availability requirement must be limited to the number of hours that is determined to be the claimant's expected number of hours per week in accordance with regulation 88.

(3) A work search and work availability requirement must be limited to work that is in a location which would normally take the claimant—

(a) a maximum of 90 minutes to travel from home to the location; and

(b) a maximum of 90 minutes to travel from the location to home.

(4) Where a claimant has previously carried out work of a particular nature, or at a particular level of remuneration, a work search requirement and a work availability requirement must be limited to work of a similar nature, or level of remuneration, for such period as the Secretary of State considers appropriate, but only if the Secretary of State is satisfied that the claimant will have reasonable prospects of obtaining paid work in spite of such limitation.

(5) The limitation in paragraph (4) is to apply for no more than [[1]4 weeks] beginning with—

(a) the date of claim; or

(b) if later, the date on which the claimant ceases paid work after falling within section 19 of the Act by virtue of regulation 90 (claimants subject to no work-related requirements- the earnings thresholds).

(6) Where a claimant has a physical or mental impairment that has a substantial adverse effect on the claimant's ability to carry out work of a particular nature, or in particular locations, a work search or work availability requirement must not relate to work of such a nature or in such locations.

AMENDMENT

1. Universal Credit and Jobseeker's Allowance (Work Search and Work Availability Requirements—limitations) (Amendment) Regulations 2022 (SI 2022/108) reg.2 (February 8, 2022).

DEFINITIONS

"claimant"—see WRA 2012 s.40.
"expected number of hours per week"—see regs 2 and 88.
"relevant carer"—see reg.85.
"responsible carer"—see WRA 2012 ss.40 and 19(6).
"work availability requirement"—see WRA 2012 ss.40 and 18(1).
"work search requirement"—see WRA 2012 ss.40 and 17(1).

GENERAL NOTE

This regulation is made under ss.17(4) and (5) (work search requirement) and 18(3) and (4) (work availability requirement) of the WRA 2012. It sets out limitations on the kind of work that a claimant can be required to search for or be able and willing immediately to take up. See reg.99 for other situations in which the ordinary tests for those requirements are modified. 2.350

Paragraph (2)

This paragraph establishes an important limitation on the kind of work that can be considered, but only for the particular categories of claimant identified: those with child care responsibilities and the disabled (anyone with a physical or mental impairment). Those categories of claimant can only be required to search for or be able and willing to take up work for no more than the number of hours per week compatible with those circumstances, as worked out under reg.88 (which could, it is suggested in the notes to reg.88, be zero). Note the administrative changes made with effect from October 25, 2023 to the "default maximum expected hours" for healthy carers of children aged three to 12, as discussed in the notes to reg.88. So, as far as the work search requirement is concerned, this limitation appears to apply as much to the sort of work in relation to which the Secretary of State may specify particular action under s.17(1)(b) of the WRA 2012 as to the requirement under s.17(1)(a) to take all reasonable action for the purpose of obtaining paid work or more or better paid work. Although the drafting of para.(2) appears to limit the hours for which either requirement is applicable, it can only, in view of the terms of the regulation-making powers in ss.17(4) and 18(3), relate to the hours of work to which the relevant requirement can be attached. See para.(6) for permissible limitations relating to the location and nature of employment for those with a physical or mental impairment. 2.351

Note that under s.19(1) and (2)(a) no work-related requirements can imposed on a claimant who has limited capability for work and work-related activity, nor can any be imposed on a claimant with regular and substantial caring responsibilities for a severely disabled person (s.19(2)(b)) or who is the responsible carer for a child under the age of one (s.19(2)(c)). Note the other categories prescribed in reg.89. Other groups of claimants with caring responsibilities are free of the work search and work availability requirements under ss.20 and 21 of the WRA 2012. Claimants with limited capability for work fall into that category by reason of s.21(1)(a).

Paragraph (3)

A work search or availability requirement cannot relate to work in a location where the claimant's normal travel time either from home to work or from work to home would exceed 90 minutes, subject to a possible further limitation in para.(6) for some disabled claimants. Travel times below that limit could be relevant in relation to a sanction for non-compliance with a requirement, on the question of whether the claimant had no good reason for the failure to comply. On that question all circumstances could be considered, including the effect of any physical or mental impairment not serious enough to count under para.(6), whereas under this provision time is the conclusive factor unless the location is completely excluded under para.(6). 2.352

Paragraphs (4) and (5)

A claimant who has previously carried out work of a particular nature or at a particular level of remuneration is to have the kind of work to be considered limited to 2.353

similar conditions for so long as considered appropriate up to four weeks from the date of claim or ceasing to fall within s.19 of the WRA 2012 by virtue of the level of earnings (para.(5)). Presumably in the case of level of remuneration the similarity must be in real terms, taking account of inflation. But the rule only applies if and so long as the claimant will have reasonable prospects of work subject to that limitation.

The February 2022 amendment to para.(5) purportedly to reduce the maximum period for which para.(4) can apply from three months to four weeks, subject to the transitional provision in reg.4 of the amending regulations, is of very doubtful validity. Even if valid, it has attracted serious criticism from various sources for a failure to follow proper Parliamentary procedures. To understand that and the doubt as to validity it is necessary to unpack in some detail what had hitherto been a relatively inoffensive and uncontroversial provision, promoting a limited protection of job skills and avoiding a need to make difficult decisions about the proper scope of work search when the period out of work might be short.

Note first that the central part of the provision in para.(4), building on similar rules that applied to old style JSA and in the past to unemployment benefit, contains considerable flexibility. Although, once its conditions are met, the limitations as to work search and availability must be applied, there are quite complicated hurdles to be jumped before that stage is reached. The claimant must first have previously carried out work of a particular nature or at a particular level of remuneration. That work could have been self-employment. There is no limit as to how far in the past the work could have been carried out, but the further in the past the more likely it is that one of the following two conditions might not be met. The second condition in para.(4) is that the claimant has reasonable prospects of obtaining paid work subject to the limitations about nature of work and/or level of remuneration. There could be many circumstances, such as the claimant having moved to a different area or suffered some significant deterioration in physical or mental capacity or the lapse of time having rendered the claimant's previous experience redundant, where no such reasonable prospects exist. The third condition is that the compulsory application of the limitations is to last only for such period as is considered appropriate (subject to the time-limit in para.(5)). Similar factors to those relevant to the second condition might also be relevant here, avoiding difficult judgments about when prospects of obtaining work are reasonable or not. But the nature of the job skills up for protection, as well as other wider considerations, such as the state of the national and local job market and economy, might also be relevant. The length of the appropriate period could be less than the maximum or possibly no period could be appropriate. Thus, although in practice many claimants with recent work experience might, prior to February 2022, have been allowed three months with limited work search and availability without too much investigation, that was by no means inevitable.

It should also be noted that after the expiry of the maximum period under para.(5) the protection of job skills does not become completely irrelevant. Outside the special circumstances catered for in regs 95, 96, 98 and 99, the general work search requirement is only to take all reasonable action for the purpose of obtaining paid work (WRA 2012, s.17(1)(a)) and particular actions specified by the Secretary of State under s.17(1)(b) must as a matter of principle also be reasonable. Although s.18 on the work availability requirement makes no explicit reference to the nature of the work for which the claimant has to be available, it is suggested that by necessary implication, especially considering the power in s.18(3) for the Secretary of State to specify limitations on the work availability requirement beyond those in regulations, that requirement must be in line with the proper work search requirement. It is plainly arguable that it is reasonable for claimants with specific and recent job skills and who have reasonable prospects of obtaining paid work of that kind and/or level of remuneration to limit their work search for a period beyond the para.(5) maximum, at least until a point where the reasonableness of the prospects is undermined. Such an approach might also produce more enduring beneficial results for the economy as a whole. As it was well put by the Institute for Government and the Social Security Advisory Committee (SSAC) at p.33 of their 2021 joint report Jobs and benefits: *The Covid-19 challenge*, a "constructive relationship between work coaches and claimants in finding not just any job but suitable jobs is likely to yield better enduring results for both individuals and the economy than merely enforcing work search conditions".

The impetus for the 2022 amendments, as set out in the Explanatory Memorandum to SI 2022/108, was the adoption of the "Way to Work" campaign, to enable 500,000 people currently out of work into jobs by the end of June 2022. However, that Memorandum gave no other information about the nature of that campaign except that it was launched on January 26, 2022. The thinking behind the campaign was perhaps revealed in paras 7.3 and 7.4:

> "7.3 Claimants with skills and experience for a specific type of role will be permitted up to four weeks to secure employment in that sector from their date of claim. After this period, they will be expected to widen their job search into other suitable sectors where they may find employment that can support them whilst they consider their longer-term career options. This will be part of their work-related requirements for receiving their benefit payment.
> 7.4 This change will enable jobcentres to promote wider employment opportunities for claimants, working with employers to fill local vacancies, supporting people back into work more quickly. This could reduce the time claimants spend out of work, thus preventing them from moving further away from the labour market—a factor that makes it increasingly difficult to get a job."

The Secretary of State had written to the SSAC on February 3, 2022 informing it that she was not going to refer the proposal to make the regulations to it in advance, by reason of urgency, and was also dispensing with the "21-day rule" (i.e. that in general there should be at least a 21-day gap between the making of regulations and their coming into force, to allow Parliamentary scrutiny and to give those affected a chance to react to the provisions). Paragraph 3.2 of the Explanatory Memorandum says that "the regulations could not have been made and laid sooner as the policy was only formulated very recently, and they had to come into effect as quickly as possible in order to achieve the target of getting 500,000 people into work by the end of June". Some more information was given at a scrutiny session of the House of Lords Secondary Legislation Scrutiny Committee on March 8, 2022 and in later correspondence, including that there were currently 1.2 million job vacancies nationally (although higher figures were given at some points). According to para.19 of the Committee's highly critical report (33rd Report):

> "At the oral evidence session, we were told that the *Way to Work* campaign also included a national team and local employer teams that were focused on producing more vacancies. We also discovered that during the pandemic period DWP had doubled its number of work coaches and opened 200 new jobcentres around the country, and, in consequence, is now in a position to devote 50 minutes a week to each claimant's needs so as to encourage them back into work. Given the current high number of vacancies, DWP takes the view that claimants should broaden their job search at a much earlier stage than previously: the change made by these Regulations provides the ability to enforce that where necessary."

The Committee considered that the 500,000 June 2022 target, and the resulting urgency, was self-imposed and arbitrary and did not justify the avoidance of normal procedures. The Explanatory Memorandum was misleading in several ways, especially in not explaining how the specific amendment would contribute to achieving that target, as opposed to all the other elements of the campaign. The Committee therefore drew the regulations specially to the attention of Parliament.

The Joint Committee on Statutory Instruments, in its 30th Report for the session 2021–22 (HL 189, HC 56-xxx), also drew the special attention of both Houses to the regulations on the ground of failure to comply with proper legislative practice in respect of the 21-day rule. There was apparently a debate in the House of Commons Delegated Legislation Committee on April 20, 2022, but a motion to prevent the instrument becoming law lapsed on the ending of the Parliamentary session on April 28, 2002. Following further scrutiny at its meeting of March 28, 2022, the SSAC decided on a fine balance not to take the regulations on formal reference.

On June 23, 2022 (published on the internet on July 6, 2022), the Chair of the SSAC wrote to the Secretary of State to say that after careful consideration the Committee had decided not to take the regulations shortening the "permitted period" on formal reference, but wished to record a number of concerns and make some advisory recommendations. It is worth quoting the statement of concerns relating to the role of the regulatory changes in enhancing the overall policy intent verbatim (footnotes have been omitted):

> **"Scale of the challenge**
>
> In order to assess whether the regulation change could deliver and was proportionate to the policy intent, we were keen to understand the relative size of the role of the regulatory change in combination with the other measures as part of the Way to Work scheme, and the scale of the increase in off-flow into work that would be expected to be required to achieve the 500k target. Officials were unable to provide an estimate of the overall scale of the change from the combined programme or of the expected contribution of the regulatory change. We appreciate that this is difficult to do, but whether this goal involves an increase in off-flow rates of 10%, 50% or 100% compared to an expected counterfactual has a material impact on the proportionality of the policy response.
>
> Given that the off-flow from benefits into employment for the month of February (which would be unlikely to have yet been significantly affected by the programme's components) had been estimated at around 114K – so that on average only 96.5K per month needed to be achieved over the remaining four months to meet the target – it seems as if the required impact could be at the lower end of the scale, and more aligned to avoiding a drop in off-flow rates rather than appreciably boosting them.
>
> We also sought to understand the number of jobseekers whose search expectations would be changed by these regulations for the duration of the scheme. Unfortunately, officials were not in a position to provide an estimate of the scale of the change.
>
> **Evidence base**
>
> We were informed that the rationale for the reduction in the duration of the permitted period was that there was a unique moment in the labour market as, post-COVID, there were significantly higher than normal levels of sectoral shift and high levels of vacancies – which meant there would be greater benefit from jobseekers expanding their search into new sectors at an earlier point.
>
> We have sought access to evidence that could underpin the basis of the decision to shorten the permitted period. We understand that the choice of four weeks as the new duration was a judgment informed by feedback from work coaches. However, no data or explanation has been made available to indicate what the impact would be of making the change. In fact, the evidence offered indicated that there was no noticeable increase in the historic off-flow rate after the 13-week point, suggesting that the extant pattern of broadening of the work-search expectations, at least at this point, did not have a discernible impact.
>
> Our concerns are compounded by the lack of a clear positive outcome expected as a result of the reduction in the permitted period. We are told that no estimate is available of what a positive outcome would be either in terms of the number claiming the benefits, or the fiscal impact though presumably these

have been incorporated in the latest forecasts produced by the Office for Budget Responsibility and adopted by the Government in the Spring Statement.

We asked your officials for an assessment of the baseline (historic) patterns of off-flow, and how these might have been expected to evolve in coming months absent these change in these regulations, alongside any early indication of patterns in the early months of the programme (see Appendix for details). Unfortunately, this information has not been shared with the Committee.

Potential negative impact

At the time of our scrutiny, no assessment had been made of the risk of individuals entering roles that were inconsistent with their qualifications/experience, or simply wrong for them in terms of their career path and ambitions, nor of the risk that increased competition from more highly qualified people would make it more difficult for longer-term unemployed people to find work. Similarly, no consideration had been made of the impact on those with part-time, or other flexible, job-search expectations for whom the four-week cut-off could be disproportionate and one that will certainly vary by protected characteristics, most obviously sex and disability.

There was some acknowledgement that there may be negative consequences from these changes, for example increased cycling on and off benefits, and job mismatches leading to more churn for employers and to claimants potentially having career paths hindered. However, there was no analysis of how to mitigate against negative effects, particularly where those with protected characteristics might be disproportionately impacted.

Evaluating the effectiveness of the permitted period change

These regulations were brought in to deal with a unique moment in the economy as it reopened from COVID restrictions, resulting in a very high number of labour market vacancies. However, the regulations do not have a sunset clause and the Committee would be concerned that, without a proper review of the impact of these regulations, they may be left on the statute book, despite the labour market situation having substantially changed. Therefore, the Committee very much welcomes that in your letter to me of 3 February, you committed to undertake such an evaluation of the regulations at the end of June to assess their effectiveness and whether they should be retained.

The way in which the regulations would be reviewed in terms of (a) by what criteria they would be deemed a success, and (b) how such criteria would be evaluated is in need of detailed thought. It will also be important to differentiate the criteria on which the regulations are evaluated with respect to the current unique point in time and the assessment whether they should be retained for what should then be much more normal times ahead. However, when we asked officials how they plan to undertake this, it was clear that such thinking had not yet matured.

Urgency

The regulations had been laid under the urgency provision before being presented to this Committee for scrutiny. I have previously written to you seeking a better understanding of the nature of the urgency in this instance. As you know, this Committee is supportive of the use of "urgency" where legislation is being brought forward as a direct consequence of either an external factor or a fiscal event. Indeed we welcomed the use of urgency, and expedited our own statutory scrutiny process, to ensure that essential support could be introduced quickly in response to recent crises in Afghanistan and Ukraine. However, a compelling argument for urgency in this specific case remains unclear to us.

We were informed that the regulations had to bypass the scrutiny of the Committee before coming into force, as "every day" was essential in ensuring that the Government can meet its own target. However, there was no explanation of what impact there might be in waiting a few weeks for the Committee to complete its statutory scrutiny – either on the specific issue of the target or in terms of the broader proposals.

Similarly, it is not clear why the target could not simply have been put back a short period, or why the rest of the Way to Work programme could not proceed whilst the permitted period proposals were considered by the Committee."

Despite that politely devastating analysis, success of the Way to Work campaign was declared on June 30, 2022 by way of a tweet and a press release asserting that over half a million people had been helped into work thanks to the campaign in five months (later quoted in the House of Commons by the then Prime Minister on July 6, 2022). That declaration was apparently based on an answer to a Parliamentary Question on June 30, 2022 revealing an estimate using management information that as of June 29, 2022 at least 505,400 unemployed universal credit and JSA claimants had moved into work during the campaign. That use of the figures was castigated by the Director General for Regulation in the Office for Statistics Regulation in his letter of July 29, 2022 to the Permanent Secretary of the DWP. He concluded that it was difficult to attribute and quantify the impact of the campaign in the absence of a clearly defined and published target and details of how it would be measured and reported, so that the way that the DWP had communicated information did not uphold the principles of being trustworthy, of high quality and offering public value. A more targeted point might have been to note the speciousness of using evidence of the numbers who moved into work *during* the campaign to support the assertion that all those claimants had been helped into work *by* the campaign. A further written answer to a Parliamentary Question on September 5, 2022 revealed that no estimate had been made of the number of unemployed universal credit and JSA claimants who would have moved into work between January and June 2022 in the absence of the Way to Work campaign.

Overall, it is hard to avoid the conclusion that this whole shabby episode was little more than a small-scale exercise in grandiose posturing with every appearance of having been foisted on the DWP with no time for thought or preparation. However, the episode is not over. There has been no public sign of the promised evaluation of the effectiveness of the amending regulations and of whether they should be retained (the September 2022 written answer suggests that there has been no attempt at any real evaluation or at meeting the concerns of the SSAC or the Office for Statistics Regulations). But the amendments are unlikely to be reversed while a high level of job vacancies continues, even though that state of affairs is likely to produce a high level of off-flow from benefit independently of the amendments' effect. A letter of May 23, 2023 from the Minister for Employment, Guy Opperman, to the Chair of the House of Commons Work and Pensions Select Committee gives the appearance of attempting to rewrite history by saying that the DWP had achieved its ambition to see at least 500,000 people move into work from universal credit and JSA *during* the campaign (emphasis added by commentator). The letter did say that assurances had been given to the Office for Statistics Regulation about future adherence to its principles.

A close examination of the way in which reg.14(3) of the JSA Regulations 2013 and reg.97(4) and (5) work, as set out above (but not carried out by the Parliamentary committees), would also have fatally undermined any case for urgency. Given the existing power to set an appropriate period for the operation of the provisions at less than 13 weeks, even where a claimant might have reasonable prospects of obtaining paid work subject to the limitations, there was no reason why work coaches should not, immediately on the implementation of the campaign, have taken into account the number of job vacancies nationally and locally, the state of the national and local economy and other measures being undertaken as part of the Way to Work campaign in determining that the "permitted" period should be something less than 13 weeks, say four weeks. What they could not have properly done, in the absence of the February 2022 amendment, would have been to adopt a rigid or blanket view that the permitted period should be no more than four weeks in all cases. The particular circumstances of individual claimants would have had to be considered. But that is what work coaches are supposed to do in producing a personally tailored set of work requirements to be recorded in the claimant commitment, especially with the additional time made available, and would anyway be necessary outside the permitted period (see further below). The substance of the campaign could have been started immediately without the need for any urgent amendment.

That is important, not merely as a criticism of the processes adopted, but because it raises serious doubts about the validity of the amendments. *Howker v Secretary of State for Work and Pensions* [2002] EWCA Civ 1623; [2003] I.C.R. 405, also reported as *R(IB) 3/03* (see Vol.III of this series at para.1.250), established that a failure to follow the mandatory provisions in s.172 of SSAA 1992 for reference to the SSAC of proposals to make regulations led to the invalidity of the regulations and that the then Social Security Commissioners had jurisdiction to decide that that was so. That no doubt now applies to the Upper Tribunal and presumably to the First-tier Tribunal. *Howker* was a case where the SSAC was misled by incorrect information from DWP officials into agreeing under s.173(1)(b) to there being no reference to it. *IC v Glasgow City Council and SSWP (HB)* [2016] UKUT 321 (AAC), reported as [2017] AACR 1, was specifically concerned with the exemption for urgency in s.173(1)(a). Although the three-judge panel of the Upper Tribunal rejected the argument that the Secretary of State had failed to show a need for urgency on the facts of the case, its decision operated on the basis that if that argument had been accepted it would mean that the regulations in question were invalid. In the case of SI 2022/108 it appears that on any objective analysis urgency could not be shown.

Note also that the Explanatory Memorandum to SI 2022/108, in para.2.2 as well as in para.7.2 quoted above, contains misleading statements about the effect of the amendments. The former says that the amendment will require claimants to search more widely for available jobs beyond those of a similar nature or level of remuneration to that of previous work following the fourth week of their claim. The suggestion that that will be an automatic expectation is repeated in para.7.2. That is misleading because, as explained above, where para.(4) has ceased to apply the reasonableness of restricting job search and availability to a similarly limited scope must be considered in the individual circumstances of each particular claimant in asking what is all reasonable action to obtain paid work under s.17(1).

There is a transitional provision in reg.4 of the amending regulations (see para.2.726 below). If on February 8, 2022, a claimant had a work search or availability requirement limited under para.(4), the limitation is to extend for the length of the existing permitted period or until March 7, 2022 if earlier.

Note that there was no equivalent amendment to regs 16 and 20 of the JSA Regulations 1996 on old style JSA.

Paragraph (6)

A claimant who has a physical or mental impairment which has a substantial adverse effect on their ability to carry out work of a particular nature or in particular locations (a significant additional condition over and above that of impairment on its own) is to have the kind of work to be considered under the work search and work availability requirements limited to avoid such work. 2.354

Victims of domestic violence

98.—(1) Where a claimant has recently been a victim of domestic violence, and the circumstances set out in paragraph (3) apply— 2.355

(a) a work-related requirement imposed on that claimant ceases to have effect for a period of 13 consecutive weeks starting on the date of the notification referred to in paragraph (3)(a); and

(b) the Secretary of State must not impose any other work-related requirement on that claimant during that period.

[[2](1A) Where a claimant referred to in paragraph (1) is a person who falls within section 22 of the Act (claimants subject to all work-related requirements) and is the responsible carer of a child, the Secretary of State must not impose a work search requirement or a work availability requirement on that claimant for a further period of 13 consecutive weeks beginning on the day after the period in paragraph (1)(a) expires.]

(2) A person has recently been a victim of domestic violence if a period of 6 months has not expired since the violence was inflicted or threatened.

(3) The circumstances are that—

(a) the claimant notifies the Secretary of State, in such manner as the Secretary of State specifies, that domestic violence has been inflicted on or threatened against the claimant by the claimant's partner or former partner or by a family member during the period of 6 months ending on the date of the notification;

(b) this regulation has not applied to the claimant for a period of 12 months before the date of the notification;

(c) on the date of the notification the claimant is not living at the same address as the person who inflicted or threatened the domestic violence; and

(d) as soon as possible, and no later than 1 month, after the date of the notification the claimant provides evidence from a person acting in an official capacity which demonstrates that—

(i) the claimant's circumstances are consistent with those of a person who has had domestic violence inflicted or threatened against them during the period of 6 months ending on the date of the notification, and

(ii) the claimant has made contact with the person acting in an official capacity in relation to such an incident, which occurred during that period.

(4) In this regulation—

[[1]"coercive behaviour" means an act of assault, humiliation or intimidation or other abuse that is used to harm, punish or frighten the victim;

"controlling behaviour" means an act designed to make a person subordinate or dependent by isolating them from sources of support, exploiting their resources and capacities for personal gain, depriving them of the means needed for independence, resistance or escape or regulating their everyday behaviour;

"domestic violence" means any incident, or pattern of incidents, of controlling behaviour, coercive behaviour, violence or abuse, including but not limited to—

(a) psychological abuse;

(b) physical abuse;

(c) sexual abuse;

(d) emotional abuse;

(e) financial abuse,

regardless of the gender or sexuality of the victim;]

"family member", in relation to a claimant, means the claimant's grandparent, grandchild, parent, step-parent, parent-in-law, son, step-son, son-in-law, daughter, step-daughter, daughter-in-law, brother, step-brother, brother-in-law, sister, step-sister, sister-in law and, if any of those persons is member of a couple, the other member of the couple;
"health care professional" means a person who is a member of a profession regulated by a body mentioned in section 25(3) of the National Health Service Reform and Health Care Professions Act 2002;
"person acting in an official capacity" means a health care professional, a police officer, a registered social worker, the claimant's employer, a representative of the claimant's trade union, or any public, voluntary or charitable body which has had direct contact with the claimant in connection with domestic violence;
"registered social worker" means a person registered as a social worker in a register maintained by—

[[4](a) Social Work England;]
[[3](b) Social Care Wales;]
(c) The Scottish Social Services Council; or
(d) The Northern Ireland Social Care Council.

AMENDMENTS

1. Social Security (Miscellaneous Amendments) (No.2) Regulations 2013 (SI 2013/1508) reg.3(1) (October 29, 2013).
2. Universal Credit and Miscellaneous Amendments (No.2) Regulations 2014 (SI 2014/2888) reg.8(2) (November 26, 2014).
3. Social Security (Social Care Wales) (Amendment) Regulations 2017 (SI 2017/291) reg.2 (April 1, 2017).
4. Children and Social Work Act 2017 (Consequential Amendments) (Social Workers) Regulations 2019 (SI 2019/1094) reg.2(c) and Sch.3 para.30 (July 9, 2019).

DEFINITIONS

"claimant"—see WRA 2012 s.40.
"partner"—see reg.2.
"victim of domestic violence"—see WRA 2012 s.24(6)(b).
"work-related requirement"—see WRA 2012 ss.40 and 13(2).

GENERAL NOTE

This regulation, made as required by s.24(5) and (6) of the WRA 2012, exempts recent victims of domestic violence from the imposition of any work-related requirements for a period of 13 weeks from the date of notification to the Secretary of State under para.(3)(a) and lifts the effect of any existing imposition for the same period. The regulation appears to be defective to the extent that it makes no provision for exemption from the imposition of a connected requirement under s.23 of the WRA 2012, which is not a "work-related requirement" as defined in s.13(2). Thus the duty in s.24(5) to exempt recent victims of domestic violence from any requirement under Part 1 of the Act has not been fully carried out, but that would not seem to affect the validity of what has been provided in reg.98. 2.356

Paragraph (1A), in effect from November 26, 2014, requires the extension of the normal 13-week suspension under para.(1) for a further 13 weeks where the claimant is the responsible carer (see ss.19(6) and 40 of the WRA 2012 and reg.4) of a child.

For these purposes, para.(4) now provides a comprehensive definition of "domestic violence", instead of the former reference to a particular page of a difficult to find Department of Health document. It uses the terms of the government's official approach to the meaning of domestic violence across departments, which had not previously been used as a statutory definition. Note that the new criminal offence of controlling or coercive behaviour in intimate or familial relationships under s.76 of the Serious Crime Act 2015, while using the terms of controlling and coercive behaviour (the meaning of which is discussed in Home Office Statutory Guidance of December 2015) contains conditions that are different from those in reg.98. While the definition here expressly includes coercive behaviour and controlling behaviour (both given their own definition in para.(4)), any other incident of abuse of any kind can come within the ambit of domestic violence. Thus, although the specific definition of "coercive behaviour" requires the act or abuse to be used to harm, punish or frighten the victim and the specific definition of "controlling behaviour" is restricted to acts designed to make the victim subordinate or dependant by particular means (as taken to extremes by the vile Rob Titchener in *The Archers*), abuse of similar kinds where that specific form of intention or purpose is not present or is difficult to prove can nonetheless be domestic violence. The width of that makes the specific conditions in para.(3) for the application of reg.98 particularly important.

Section 24(6)(b) of the WRA 2012 defines a victim of domestic violence as a person on or against whom domestic violence (as defined above) is inflicted or threatened. Under s.24(6)(c) and para.(2) a person is to be treated as having recently been a victim of domestic violence if no more than six months has expired since the infliction or threat.

Paragraph (3)

2.357 This paragraph lays down four quite restrictive conditions that must all be satisfied for reg.98 to apply. Under sub-para.(a) the claimant must have notified the Secretary of State of the infliction or threatening of domestic violence by a partner, former partner or family member (as defined in para.(4)) within the previous six months. Under sub-para.(b), reg.98 must not have applied within the 12 months before the notification. Under sub-para.(c), the claimant must not on the date of the notification have been living at the same address as the person named as the assailant. Under sub-para.(d), the claimant must also provide, as soon as possible and no more than one month after the notification, evidence from a person acting in an official capacity (defined quite widely in para.(4)) both that the claimant's circumstances are consistent with having had domestic violence inflicted or threatened in the six months before notification and that the claimant had made contact (apparently not necessarily within the six months) with the person in relation to an incident of infliction or threat of domestic violence that occurred during the six months before notification.

Circumstances in which requirements must not be imposed

2.358 **99.**—(1) Where paragraph (3), (4)[2, (4A)] [1 . . .] or (6) applies—

(a) the Secretary of State must not impose a work search requirement on a claimant; and

(b) "able and willing immediately to take up work" under a work availability requirement means able and willing to take up paid work, or attend an interview, immediately once the circumstances set out in paragraph (3), (4)[2, (4A)] [1 . . .] or (6) no longer apply.

(2) A work search requirement previously applying to the claimant ceases to have effect from the date on which the circumstances set out in paragraph (3), (4)[2, (4A)] [1 . . .] or (6) begin to apply.

[1(2A) Where paragraph (5) applies—

(a) the Secretary of State must not impose a work search requirement on a claimant; and

(b) a work search requirement previously applying to the claimant ceases to have effect from the date on which the circumstances set out in paragraph (5) begin to apply.

(2B) Where paragraph (5A) applies "able and willing to take up work" under a work availability requirement means able and willing to take up paid work, or to attend an interview, immediately once the circumstances set out in paragraph (5A) no longer apply.

(2C) Where paragraph (5B) applies, "able and willing to take up work" under a work availability requirement means—

(a) able and willing to take up paid work immediately once the circumstances set out in paragraph (5B) no longer apply; and

(b) able and willing to attend an interview before those circumstances no longer apply.]

(3) This paragraph applies where—

(a) the claimant is attending a court or tribunal as a party to any proceedings or as a witness;

(b) the claimant is a prisoner;

(c) regulation 11(3) (temporary absence from Great Britain for treatment or convalescence) applies to the claimant;

(d) any of the following persons has died within the past 6 months—

(i) where the claimant was a member of a couple, the other member,

(ii) a child or qualifying young person for whom the claimant or, where the claimant is a member of a couple, the other member, was responsible, or

(iii) a child, where the claimant was the child's parent;

(e) the claimant is, and has been for no more than 6 months, receiving and participating in a structured recovery-orientated course of alcohol or drug dependency treatment;

(f) the claimant is, and has been for no more than 3 months, a person for whom arrangements have been made by a protection provider under section 82 of the Serious Organised Crime and Police Act 2005; or

(g) the claimant is engaged in an activity of a kind approved by the Secretary of State as being in the nature of a public duty.

(4) [4Subject to paragraph (4ZA), this paragraph] applies where the claimant—

(a) is unfit for work—

(i) for a period of no more than 14 consecutive days after the date that the evidence referred to in sub-paragraph (b) is provided, and

(ii) for no more than 2 such periods in any period of 12 months; and

(b) provides to the Secretary of State the following evidence—

(i) for the first 7 days when they are unfit for work, a declaration made by the claimant in such manner and form as the Secretary of State approves that the claimant is unfit for work, and

(ii) for any further days when they are unfit for work, if requested by the Secretary of State, a statement given [5 . . .] in accordance with the rules set out in Part 1 of Schedule 1 to the Medical Evidence Regulations which provides that the person is not fit for work.

[4(4ZA) Where paragraph (4ZB) applies, paragraph (4) will only apply to a claimant if the Secretary of State makes a decision to carry out an assessment under regulation 41(1)(b).

(4ZB) This paragraph applies where—

(a) (i) it has previously been determined on the basis of an assessment under Part 5 of these Regulations or under Part 4 or 5 of the ESA Regulations that the claimant does not have limited capability for work; or

(ii) the claimant has previously been treated as not having limited capability for work or, as the case may be, for work and work-related activity under regulation 43(3) or 44(2); and

(b) the condition specified in the evidence provided by the claimant in accordance with paragraph (4)(b) is in the opinion of the Secretary of State the same, or substantially the same, as the condition specified in the evidence provided by the claimant before the date—

(i) of the determination that the claimant does not have limited capability for work; or

(ii) that the claimant was treated as not having limited capability for work or, as the case may be, for work and work-related activity.]

[2(4A) This paragraph applies for one or more periods of one month, as provided for in paragraphs (4B) and (4C), where the claimant is the responsible carer of a child and an event referred to in sub-paragraph (a) or (b) has taken place in the last 24 months and has resulted in significant disruption to the claimant's normal childcare responsibilities—

(a) any of the following persons has died—

(i) a person who was previously the responsible carer of that child;

(ii) a parent of that child;

(iii) a brother or sister of that child; or

(iv) any other person who, at the time of their death, normally lived in the same accommodation as that child and was not a person who was liable to make payments on a commercial basis in respect that accommodation; or

(b) the child has been the victim of, or witness to, an incident of violence or abuse and the claimant is not the perpetrator of that violence or abuse.

(4B) Paragraph (4A) is not to apply for more than one period of one month in each of the 4 consecutive periods of 6 months following the event (and, if regulation 98 or paragraph (3)(d) of this regulation applies in respect of the same event, that month is to run concurrently with any period for which that regulation or paragraph applies).

(4C) Each period of one month begins on the date specified by the Secretary of State after the claimant has notified the Secretary of State of the circumstances in paragraph (4A) provided that the Secretary of State is satisfied that the circumstances apply.]

(5) This paragraph applies where the Secretary of State is satisfied that it would be unreasonable to require the claimant to comply with a work search requirement [1 . . .], including if such a requirement were limited in accordance with section 17(4) [1 . . .] of the Act, because [4 . . .]

(a) [4the claimant] is carrying out a work preparation requirement or voluntary work preparation (as defined in regulation 95(4));

(b) [4the claimant] has temporary child care responsibilities or is dealing with a domestic emergency, funeral arrangements or other temporary circumstances; [4 . . .]

(c) [4the claimant] has been unfit for work for longer than the period of 14 days specified in paragraph (4)(a) or for more than 2 such periods in any period of 12 months and, where requested by the Secretary of State, provides the evidence mentioned in paragraph (4)(b)(ii). [4; or

(d) paragraph (4) would apply to the claimant but for paragraph (4ZA).]

[1(5A) This paragraph applies where the Secretary of State is satisfied that it would be unreasonable to require the claimant to comply with a work availability requirement to be able and willing to—

(a) take up paid work; and

(b) attend an interview,

(including if such a requirement were limited in accordance with section 18(3) of the Act) because the claimant falls within [5sub-paragraph (a), (b), (c) or (d)] of paragraph (5).

(5B) This paragraph applies where the Secretary of State is satisfied that it would be—

(a) unreasonable to require the claimant to comply with a work availability requirement to be able and willing to take up paid work because the claimant falls within [4 sub-paragraph (a), (b), (c) or (d)] of paragraph (5); and

(b) reasonable to require the claimant to comply with a work availability requirement to attend an interview,

including if such a requirement were limited in accordance with section 18(3) of the Act.]

[3[6(6) This paragraph applies where—

(a) the claimant has monthly earnings (excluding any that are not employed earnings) that are equal to, or more than, the amount that a person would be paid at the hourly rate set out in regulation 4 of the National Minimum Wage Regulations for [715] hours per week, converted to a monthly amount by multiplying by 52 and dividing by 12; or

(b) the claimant is a member of a couple whose combined monthly earnings (excluding any that are not employed earnings) are equal to, or more than, the amount that a person would be paid at the hourly rate set out in regulation 4 of the National Minimum Wage Regulations for [724] hours per week, converted to a monthly amount by multiplying by 52 and dividing by 12.]

(6A) In paragraph (6) "employed earnings" has the meaning in regulation 55.]

(7) In this regulation "tribunal" means any tribunal listed in Schedule 1 to the Tribunals and Inquiries Act 1992.

AMENDMENTS

1. Universal Credit and Miscellaneous Amendments Regulations 2014 (SI 2014/597) reg.2(7) (April 28, 2014).

2. Universal Credit and Miscellaneous Amendments) (No. 2) Regulations 2014 (SI 2014/2888) reg.8(3) (November 26, 2014).

3. Universal Credit (Work-Related Requirements) In Work Pilot Scheme and Amendment Regulations 2015 (SI 2015/89) reg.3 (February 19, 2015).

4. Universal Credit (Miscellaneous Amendments, Saving and Transitional Provision) Regulations 2018 (SI 2018/65) reg.3(11) (April 11, 2018).

5. Social Security (Medical Evidence) and Statutory Sick Pay (Medical Evidence) (Amendment) (No.2) Regulations 2022 (SI 2022/630) reg.4(3)(b) (July 1, 2022).

6. Universal Credit (Administrative Earnings Threshold) (Amendment) Regulations 2022 (SI 2022/886) reg.2 (September 26, 2022).
7. Universal Credit (Administrative Earnings Threshold) (Amendment) Regulations 2023 (SI 2023/7) reg.2 (January 30, 2023).

Definitions

"child"—see WRA 2012 s.40.
"claimant"—*ibid.*
"couple"—see WRA 2012, ss.40 and 39.
"ESA Regulations"—see reg.2.
"Medical Evidence Regulations"—*ibid.*
"monthly earnings"—*ibid.*
"National Minimum Wage Regulations"—*ibid.*
"paid work"—*ibid.*
"prisoner"—*ibid.*
"qualifying young person"—see WRA 2012 ss.40 and 10(5).
"responsible carer"—see WRA 2012 ss.40 and 19(6).
"voluntary work preparation"—see reg.95(4).
"work availability requirement"—see WRA 2012 ss.40 and 18(1).
"work preparation requirement"—see WRA 2012 ss.40 and 16(1).
"work search requirement"—see WRA 2012 ss.40 and 17(1).

General Note

Temporary Coronavirus Provisions

2.359 The last of the temporary coronavirus provisions relevant to reg.99 expired on August 31, 2021. See previous editions of this volume for the details.

2.360 This regulation is made under ss.22(2) and 24(1)(a) of the WRA 2012 in respect of the work search and availability requirements and under s.18(5) in respect of the work availability requirement. Its structure was revised in 2014 to make its operation somewhat clearer, although at the cost of a more complicated interaction of various paragraphs. Some requirements were tightened and some relaxed, also.

The central rule is under paras (1) and (2) and operates where any of paras (3), (4), (4A) (incorporating (4B) and (4C)) or (6) applies. Under para.(1)(a) no work search requirement can be imposed in those circumstances (and any already imposed requirement lapses: para.(2)) and under para.(1)(b) the work availability requirement is adjusted to require only that the claimant be willing and able to take up paid work or attend an interview immediately once the circumstances in question cease to apply. Paragraphs (3), (4), (4A) and (6) cover fairly specifically defined circumstances, dealt with separately below.

Paragraph (2A) operates where para.(5) applies, to the same effect as under paras (1)(a) and (2) on the work search requirement in relation to the circumstances in para.(5). Paragraph (5) also covers fairly specifically defined circumstances, but with the additional condition that it be unreasonable to require compliance with the work search requirement, and is dealt with separately below.

Paragraph (2B) operates where para.(5A) applies, to the same effect as under para.(1)(b) in relation to the circumstances in para.(5A). Paragraph (5A) involves a judgment that it would be unreasonable to require the claimant to be able and willing to take up paid work and attend an interview (see further below).

Paragraph (2C) operates where para.(5B) applies, but only so as to lift the requirement to be willing and able to take up an offer of paid work, not to lift the requirement to be willing and able to attend an interview. The judgment required under para.(5B) is thus that it would be unreasonable to require the claimant to be able and willing to take up paid work, but reasonable to require willingness and ability to attend an interview (see further below).

Paragraph (3)

Paragraph (3) lists a number of categories of claimant where the circumstances mean that the claimant could not be expected to look for or take up work or attend an interview, generally of a temporary nature: **2.361**

(a) Attending a court or tribunal (defined in para.(7)) as a party to proceedings or as a witness, apparently so long as the hearing continues for a party and so long as attendance is required for a witness.
(b) A prisoner, under the reg.2 definition covering those detained in custody pending trial or sentence on conviction or under sentence or on temporary release, but excluding anyone detained in hospital under mental health legislation.
(c) Temporary absence from Great Britain in connection with medical treatment for illness etc or convalescence, or accompanying a partner or child or qualifying young person undergoing such treatment or convalescence, under the conditions in reg.11(3). See the notes to that provision.
(d) The claimant's then partner, a child or qualifying young person for whom the claimant or partner was responsible or a child of the claimant has died within the previous six months. See para.(4A)(a) for circumstances in which the operation of paras (1) and (2) can be triggered by the death within the previous 24 months of various people connected with a child.
(e) Attending a structured recovery-oriented course of alcohol or drug dependency treatment, for no more than six months.
(f) Having protection arrangements made under s.82 of the Serious Organised Crime and Police Act 2005 (protection of persons involved in investigations or proceedings whose safety is considered to be at risk), for no more than three months. Arrangements for protection are made by protection providers (e.g. Chief Constables and any of the Commissioners for HMRC).
(g) Any other activity of a kind approved by the Secretary of State as being in the nature of a public duty, apparently for as long as the activity and approval lasts. It is therefore unclear whether on any appeal against a sanction where the application of this paragraph is in issue a First-tier Tribunal is required to accept non-approval of an activity by the Secretary of State or can substitute its own judgment.

Paragraphs (4)–(4ZB)

A claimant who is unfit for work (not further defined) and provides a self-certificate for the first seven days and, if requested, a statement under the Medical Evidence Regulations (see Vol.I of this series) for any further days falls within the basic rules in para.(1) on both the work search and the work availability requirement. But the benefit of para.(4) is limited to a period of no more than 14 days after the evidence is provided and to no more than two such periods in any 12 months. There is a possible extension of those restrictions under para.(5)(c) in relation to the work search requirement or under para.(5A) or (5B) in relation to the work availability requirement. **2.362**

There appears on the original form of para.(4) no reason why a claimant should not take the benefit of its provisions from the first day of entitlement to universal credit. But from April 2018 an additional limitation on the operation of para.(4) has been created by the new paras (4ZA) and (4ZB), designed to deal with the common circumstances where a claimant's entitlement to new style ESA has been terminated by reason of a determination following an assessment that they do not have limited capability for work or such a determination has been made under the universal credit provisions, so that the claimant no longer has an automatic exemption from the work search and work availability requirements under s.21(1)(a), or the claimant has previously been deemed not to have limited capability for work or work-related activity for failing to comply with an information requirement or failing to attend or submit to a medical examination (regs 43(3) and 44(2)). Such a universal credit determination would result in a decision removing the limited capability for work or limited capability for work and work-related activity element which would be appealable, but there is no provision for deeming capability and qualification for the appropriate element while the appeal is pending. If the claimant has appealed against the new style ESA decision after the mandatory reconsideration process, the circumstances in which limited capability for work will be deemed for those purposes has been severely restricted. If that deeming does operate, it appears not to translate into universal credit. The effect under regs 39(1)(a) and 40(1)(a)(ii) only follows a new style ESA determination that a claimant does have limited capability for work or for work-related activity.

In the circumstances described above, as prescribed in para.(4ZB)(a), a claimant can only take unrestricted advantage of para.(4) if the condition specified in the medical evidence provided under para.(4)(b) is not the same or substantially the same as the condition specified in the evidence provided by the claimant before the determination of not having limited capability for work (para.(4ZB)(b)). Paragraph (4ZA), which applies the conditions in para.(4ZB), then restricts a claimant who cannot satisfy that test from taking advantage of para.(4) except where the Secretary of State decides to carry out an assessment under reg.41(1)(b) (see the discussion below for the limited circumstances covered). Thus, the claimant is not in general permitted for these purposes to undermine the judgment on capability for work embodied in the adverse new style ESA or universal credit determination. However, paras (5)(d) and (5A) and (5B) allow the application of para.(4) where it would be unreasonable to require a claimant who would otherwise be caught by para.(4ZA) to comply with a work search or availability requirement.

The Explanatory Memorandum for SI 2018/65 describes the effect of these amendments as follows in paras 7.14 and 7.15:

> "7.14 This instrument amends regulation 99 of the Universal Credit Regulations (and makes equivalent amendments to regulation 16 of the Jobseeker's Allowance Regulations 2013) to prevent work search and work availability requirements being automatically switched off for illness in certain circumstances. The amendments apply to claimants who have undergone a work capability assessment and been found not to have limited capability for work, and to claimants who have failed to attend a medical examination or comply with a request for information and are treated as not having limited capability for work. In other words, claimants who are, or are treated as being, fit for work. Where such claimants produce evidence that they are unfit for work and the condition mentioned in the evidence is the same, or substantially the same, as the condition for which they were assessed in the work capability assessment, work search and work availability requirements will only be switched off if they have been referred for another assessment as to their capability for work.
>
> 7.15 If such a claimant has not been referred for another assessment, regulations will continue to allow for work search and work availability requirements to be switched off if it would be unreasonable for a claimant to comply with such requirements."

That seems accurate so far as universal credit is concerned, but not for new style JSA (see the notes to reg.16 of the JSA Regulations 2013 in Vol.I of this series).

A number of points need brief mention. Note first that paras (4ZA) and (4ZB) only apply where the previous assessment and determination of no limited capability for work or deeming was for the purposes of new style ESA or universal credit. It does not apply if it was for the purposes of old style ESA. Then on its face it applies whenever in the past the adverse determination was made. It may need to be decided whether in order to operate in a rational and fair way the provisions should be limited to the most recent determination of no limited capability for work under new style ESA or universal credit. Third, the comparison to be made in para.(4ZB)(b) is between the condition(s) specified in the evidence provided by the claimant before the previous adverse determination or deeming and the condition(s) specified in the evidence put forward by the claimant in support of the application of para.(4).

The evidence provided by the claimant before the adverse determination will presumably cover primarily a medical certificate, but also any questionnaire completed by the claimant and any other evidence, from medical professionals or otherwise, put forward (and, it would seem, the claimant's oral evidence to any tribunal and any further evidence put forward there). It will not cover the opinions of any approved health care professional who has carried out a medical examination, even though it is usually on the basis of those opinions that adverse determinations are made, because that evidence was not provided by the claimant. The evidence to be provided under para.(4)(b) is a self-certificate for the first week and then a medical certificate. Difficulties can be anticipated in making a comparison between what may be a fairly informal and short specification in a self-certificate and the previous evidence. And is it enough to trigger para.(4ZB)(b) that, say, the sole condition specified in the new self-certificate or medical certificate is substantially the same as one, but only one, out of several that were specified before the adverse determination? The reference to "the condition specified" seems to require that a mere worsening in the condition(s) previously specified, even a substantial worsening, does not result in a condition that is not the same. But what if, say, a condition affecting one part of the body starts to affect another part? Is that the same condition?

The rule in para.(4ZA) allowing the lifting of the work search and work availability requirements on the ordinary para.(4) basis, despite the previous determination or deeming, only where the Secretary of State makes a decision to carry out an assessment under reg.41(1)(b) has much more limited scope than first appears. An assessment is not the medical examination (if any) under reg.44, but the assessment by a decision-maker on behalf of the Secretary of State of the extent to which a claimant is or is not capable of carrying out the activities prescribed in Sch.6 (i.e. the points-scoring exercise) (reg.39(2)). There may well be doubt about the exact point when the Secretary of State makes a decision to carry out an assessment, but no doubt it can be accepted that one has been made if the Secretary of State starts the evidence-gathering process by sending a questionnaire to the claimant and/or referring the case to the organisation running medical examinations by health care professionals. However, the Secretary of State's powers to carry out an assessment are circumscribed. Paragraph (4ZA) operates only where the power under reg.41(1)(a) is used, which is limited to cases where the Secretary of State wishes to determine whether since a previous limited capability for work determination there has been a relevant change of circumstances in relation to the claimant's physical or mental condition or whether the previous determination was made in ignorance of or was based on a mistake as to some material fact. Those are terms that relate primarily to the exercise of powers of supersession or revision. It might be thought that if the Secretary of State is merely considering what determination to make under paras (4)–(4ZB) as the result of a claimant's producing medical evidence under para.(4)(b) she does not need to determine any of the things mentioned. However, the further restriction in reg.41(4), to which reg.41(1) is expressly subject, prohibits the carrying out of a further assessment where there has been a previous new style ESA or universal credit determination adverse to the claimant unless there is evidence to suggest ignorance or mistake of material fact or a relevant change of circumstances. Thus, a mere assertion by the claimant that the previous determination was wrong will probably not do, but otherwise the regulations appear to leave a great deal of discretion to the Secretary of State as to when to carry out an assessment following a previous adverse determination.

Remember the provision in paras (2A) and (5)(d), in effect disapplying the effect of paras (4ZA) and (4ZB) when it is unreasonable to require the claimant to comply with any work search requirement and that in paras (2B) and (2C) and (5A) - (5C) modifying the work availability requirement on similar conditions. See the notes to para.(5)(c) below for the suggestion that it allows, where reasonable, the lifting of the requirements from those unfit for work for longer periods than allowed under para.(4) regardless of the existence of any previous determination or deeming.

Paragraphs (4A)–(4C)

2.363 Paragraph (4A) supplies a number of further circumstances, all related to children, in which paras (1) and (2) operate to lift the work search requirement and modify the work availability requirement. The claimant must be the responsible carer of a child (as defined in s.19(6) of the WRA 2012 and see regs 4 and 4A for how responsibility is determined) and reg.26 on nomination by joint claimants. Then one of the events specified in sub-paras (a) and (b) must have occurred in the 24 months prior to the week in question and have resulted in significant disruption to the claimant's normal childcare responsibilities. Although it is not entirely clear, it seems to be necessary that the event is continuing to result in significant disruption in the week in question, not just at or shortly after the time of the event. "Normal childcare responsibilities" should be given its ordinary everyday meaning.

Sub-paragraph (a) applies when one of the persons listed (i.e. a parent or responsible carer or brother or sister of the child or someone else who lived in the same accommodation other than a commercial lodger) has died. Sub-paragraph (b) applies where the child has been the victim of or has witnessed an incident of violence or abuse not perpetrated by the claimant.

Paragraphs (4B) and (4C) limit each application of para.(4A) to a period of one month and to no more than one such application in each of the four periods of six months following the incident in question. Note the possibility of the application of para.(5)(b) without those limits in some circumstances that could have fallen within para.(4A).

Note also that under s.19(2)(c) of the WRA 2012 no work-related requirements may be imposed on the responsible carer of a child under the age of one, that under s.20(1)(a) only the work-focused interview requirement may be imposed on a claimant who is the responsible carer of a child aged one and that under s.21(1)(b) only the work-focused interview and work preparation requirements may be imposed on a claimant who is the responsible carer of a child aged two.

Paragraph (5)

2.364 The direct operation of para.(5) has since April 28, 2014 been limited to the work search requirement. See paras (5A) and (5B) for the effect on the work availability requirement where one of the conditions in para.(5)(a)–(d) is satisfied.

In four sorts of circumstances the imposition of a work search requirement, even as limited under reg.97, is prohibited where it would be unreasonable for the claimant to comply.

Sub-paragraph (a) applies if the claimant is carrying out a work preparation requirement (s.16(1) of the WRA 2012) or voluntary work preparation (reg.95(4)). It appears that voluntary work preparation could include the doing of voluntary work if agreed by the Secretary of State (see the definition in reg.95(4)).

Sub-paragraph (b) applies if the claimant has temporary child care responsibilities (for any child) or is dealing with a domestic emergency, funeral arrangements (for a claimant who is already covered by para.(3)(d)) or with other temporary circumstances. In *RR v SSWP (UC)* [2017] UKUT 459 (AAC) (see the notes to reg.95), Judge Wikeley suggested that another way of looking at the case, rather than exploring deductions from 35 as the expected number of hours under reg.95(2), was to consider whether a work search requirement could not be imposed for the weeks in question on the basis that the claimant was dealing with a domestic emergency or other temporary circumstances (reg.99(5)(b)). His suggestion that reg.99(2A) and (5) apply only when the circumstances are such that it is unreasonable to require the claimant to comply with any work search requirement at all, rather than merely to undertake more than reduced hours of work search action under reg.95, appears right. The evidence in *RR* probably did not support such a conclusion.

Sub-paragraph (c) applies where the claimant is unfit for work and produces a medical certificate if required and the restrictions in para.(4) have been exceeded. This is an important extension to the provision in para.(4) but subject to the overriding condition that it is unreasonable to require the claimant to undertake any work search activities. It must surely be the case, especially in view of the insertion of sub-para.(d) in April 2018, that sub-para.(c) applies regardless of the existence of any previous determination or deeming that the claimant does not have limited capability for work or work-related activity. It is enough, subject to the reasonableness and evidence conditions, that the claimant has been unfit for work for more than 14 days or has exceeded the two periods limit.

Sub-paragraph (d) mitigates the rigour of the paras (4ZA) and (4ZB) rules by in effect disapplying them when it would be unreasonable to require the claimant to comply with any work search requirement.

Would para.(5)(b) allow the Secretary of State to allow short "holidays" from work search responsibilities (and a modification of work availability requirements under para.(5A) or (5B)), under the heading of temporary circumstances or temporary child care responsibilities if satisfied that it would be reasonable to do so (cf. reg.19(1)(p) and (2) of the JSA Regulations 1996)? It is a feature of the universal credit scheme that it will apply to claimants in substantial work, who will have statutory holiday entitlements, as will family members of claimants not themselves in work. If so allowed, there would then be no need to consider the possible application of reg.95(2)(b) or 96(3)(b).

Paragraphs (5A) and (5B)

Where it would be unreasonable, because of the satisfaction of any of the conditions in para.(5)(a)–(d), for the claimant to be required to be able and willing immediately either to take up paid work or attend an interview, the work availability requirement is adjusted to require the claimant to be willing and able to do so immediately the condition ceases to be satisfied (paras (5A) and (1)(b)). Paragraph (5B) produces the equivalent effect where it would be unreasonable to require the claimant to be willing and able immediately to take up paid work, but reasonable to require willingness and ability to attend an interview. 2.365

Paragraphs (6) and (6A)

Where a claimant or joint claimants are not already free of all work-related requirements by reason of having earnings of at least the individual earnings threshold or the combined thresholds, the "conditionality earnings threshold" (reg.90), the work search and availability requirements are not to be imposed if the monthly amount of employed earnings, as defined in reg.55, converted to a weekly equivalent, at least equals the level set by para.(6). That level is called by the DWP the administrative earnings threshold (AET) and the level of conditionality to be applied when those modifications operate is called the "light touch regime", by contrast with the "intensive work search regime" where all work-related requirements are imposed. Para.(6) has used a number of different formulae over the years, for details of which see the previous editions of this volume. This section of the note concentrates on the formula in force from September 23, 2022 onwards, when a new form of para.(6) was substituted, down to April 11, 2024. A separate section below briefly discusses the position as from May 6, 2024. There has also, from February 2015 to the present been provision for pilot schemes to operate by which qualifying claimants are randomly selected to be treated as though para.(6) was not in existence. See the separate section of this note below. 2.366

Regulation 4 of the National Minimum Wage Regulations 2015 (see the definition in reg.2), as amended, sets the hourly rate (£9.50 as from April 2022; £10.42 as from April 2023, £11.44 as from April 2024) for employees aged at least 23 (21 from April 1, 2024), what the government calls the national living wage. Thus, as confirmed in the Explanatory Memorandum to SI 2022/886, the monthly rates prescribed under the new para.(6) with effect from September 26, 2022 were £494 (sub-para.(a) for individual claimants) and £782 (sub-para.(b) for couples). That was the result of multiplying £9.50 by 12 for a single claimant or 19 for a couple, performing the translation to a monthly figure and applying the rounding rule under reg.6(1A)((b). The figures under the previous form of para.(6) were £355 and £567 respectively. If employed earnings (n.b. not self-employed earnings or income from other paid work under reg.52(a)(iii)) equal or exceed the relevant figure, work search and work availability requirements may not be imposed so long as the employed earnings do not fall below the AET, unless the claimant falls within one of the pilot schemes and is to be treated as if para.(6) does not exist.

The rationale for the September 2022 increase in the threshold, exposing more claimants to the more rigorous parts of the conditionality and sanctions regime, was set out as follows in the revised Explanatory Memorandum (the original version was found to be inadequate by the House of Lords Secondary Legislation Scrutiny Committee: *13th Report of Session 2022–23*, HL Paper 68, October 13, 2022):

> "7.1 The current AET is equivalent to an individual claimant working 8.62 hours per week earning the National Living Wage (NLW). The current AET for couples is equivalent to them working 13.77 hrs per week between them earning the National Living Wage (NLW).
>
> 7.2 When Universal Credit (UC) claimants earn more than their Conditionality Earnings Threshold (CET) they move into the Working Enough conditionality group, where no conditionality requirements are applied, and the claimants do not regularly interact with a work coach. The CET is a flexible threshold which is calculated based on the number of hours an individual claimant can reasonably be expected to undertake work or work-related activities based on their circumstances. In most cases, it is set at the rate equivalent to working 35 hours at the NLW, but this can be adjusted to take account of health conditions or caring responsibilities.
>
> 7.3 Where a UC claimant is subject to all work-related requirements, the Administrative Earnings Threshold (AET) is used to determine which conditionality regime the claimant is allocated to. UC claimants are placed in the Intensive Work Search (IWS) regime if they are earning less than their AET, or placed in the Light Touch regime if they are earning at or above their AET but below their CET. Those in the IWS regime are required to accept a Claimant Commitment agreeing work search requirements and work availability requirements as well as work preparation and work-focused interview requirements. Whereas those in Light Touch are not required to comply with work search requirements or work availability requirements.
>
> 7.4 This instrument will support UC claimants to progress in work by extending work coach support to more UC claimants on low incomes. Work coaches provide regular on-going tailored support, and claimants will be able to access a comprehensive range of training and skills provision based on their needs.
>
> 7.5 Departmental analysts have estimated that this change to the AET will bring in an estimated additional 114,000 claimants into the IWS regime from the Light Touch regime (16.5% of Light Touch claimants). This change will require impacted claimants to review and agree a new Claimant Commitment with a work coach, agreeing appropriate work search requirements which will be revised and updated regularly.
>
> 7.6 The policy intent is to support those who find themselves in low income to help them access opportunities to increase their earnings. This might be by increasing their hours, progressing in their current role/sector, or switching careers."

Paragraph 7.4 might be thought somewhat disingenuous in that there seems nothing to have prevented more extensive work coach support being provided to claimants in the light touch regime through the operation of the work-focused interview and work preparation requirements. Nor did the Memorandum explain what was wrong with the previous method of calculating the AET. That was done more explicitly in the DWP's presentation to the SSAC. Paragraph 3.3 of the revised minutes of the SSAC meeting of January 26, 2022 (publication of the minutes of this item having been delayed until SI 2022/886 was laid) contained the explanation that the effect was to return the AET to the real level set in 2015, which had been eroded since because wages had risen faster than benefit levels, which had featured in the previous method of calculation.

With effect from January 30, 2023, the threshold was increased by making the multiple of hours 15 for a single claimant and 24 for a couple, on the 2022/23 level of the NMW resulting in a significant increase in the threshold to £617 and £988 per month respectively. From April 2023 those figures were £677 and £1,083. From April 2024, for the short period until the May 2024 amendments come into force (see below) the figures are £744 and £1,190. It was estimated that about 130,000 additional claimants would be moved into the intensive work search regime (para.7.4 of the Explanatory Memorandum to SI 2023/7), which it was said would enable regular contact with a work coach that had not in practice happened previously. It appears that in practice those in the light touch regime, and thus potentially subject to the work-focused interview and work preparation requirements, were only required to attend interviews in the first and eighth weeks on the regime, although they could volunteer for meetings with a work coach. The House of Lords Secondary Legislation Scrutiny Committee (*27th Report of Session 2022–23*, HL Paper 143) expressed disappointment that the DWP had made no reference in the Explanatory Memorandum to the outcome of the September 2022 increase and how it had contributed to its overarching policy objective, then expressed as helping low-paid claimants increase their income. The Minister for Employment, Guy Opperman, stated in a letter of January 23, 2023, that the DWP had robust evidence, that it planned to publish shortly, that the Intensive Work Search regime could support the lowest earning claimants to boost their earnings, but the Committee considered that without evaluation the January 2023 increase was premature. It emerged in relation to the May 2024 increase (see below) that the evidence referred to had not yet been published.

There are a number of obscurities in the practical application of the AET rules. First, it may have been the case that under the pre-September 2022 form of para.(6) the couple's AET only applied if both joint claimants had employed earnings. The new form of para.(6) no longer contains the condition that "the couple has combined earnings". Instead, para.(6)(b) talks of a claimant who is a member of a couple whose combined monthly earnings exceed the relevant figure. The natural meaning could arguably extend to a couple where one couple is in employment and one is not. Their combined earnings could be said to be whatever the first claimant earns plus nil from the second claimant.

The identification of the "monthly earnings" to be set against the AET in any particular assessment period is also not free from difficulty. The definition of that phrase in reg.2 gives it the meaning in reg.90(6), part of the regulation dealing with the conditionality earnings threshold. See the notes to reg.90(6), subject to the point that while that provision applies to all forms of earned income under reg.52, reg.99(6) expressly excludes anything that is not employed earnings. The main elements of the general definition are that it applies to the earnings calculated or estimated in relation to a particular assessment period, but without any deduction for income tax, national insurance contributions or pension contributions (reg.90(6)(a)) and that where the earnings fluctuate or are likely to fluctuate there can be an averaging process (reg.90(6)(b)). There is also a discretion to disregard earnings in respect of an employment that has ceased. The starting point, in the light of regs.54 and 61, must be on the gross amounts received in a particular assessment period, but the averaging provision must not be forgotten in cases where there is a gap in regular receipts, perhaps because of the way a pattern of payment falls or because of a pattern involving periods of non-working or reduced working, e.g. outside school terms or due to seasonal factors. There is a lot of judgment involved in determining whether there is an identifiable cycle (probably of payment, rather than merely work), which could in some cases extend over a year or, if there is no identifiable cycle, choosing a period over which to determine the amount of monthly earnings accurately. There is also an overall practical problem that the actual receipts in an assessment period cannot be finally calculated until after the end of that period, yet are meant to control what work requirements are to be imposed on the claimant, and what the claimant should have been doing, during that past period. It may be that that is only a real problem where a claimant starts work or extra work and that during a period of employment either the use of an estimate under reg.90(6)(a) or averaging under reg.90(6)(b) can avoid an unprofitable churning into and out of work requirements.

The May 2024 amendments

With effect from May 6, 2024 (see further below for why that is the correct date and why there are two sets of regulations making identical amendments), there have been amendments to further increase the level of the administrative earnings threshold (AET). The weekly multiple of the NMW to be used in sub-para.(a) for claimants not in a couple is increased to 18 from 15 and the multiple to be used in sub-para.(b) for couples is increased to 29 from 24. That has the effect, on the current 21+ NMW hourly rate of £11.44, of raising the AET for an individual claimant to £892 per month and for a couple to £1,437 per month, estimated to bring an additional 180,000 claimants within the Intensive Work Search (IWS) regime of applicability of all work-related requirements. The proposal to make the amending regulations was referred to the Social Security Advisory Committee (SSAC), which subjected it to a searching scrutiny, making 12 recommendations (in particular, in the absence of proper evaluation of the effect of the earlier increases, for a pause in full implementation and a pilot of a phased approach to claimants in a low-risk category and for various measures to deal with complex circumstances) (*Report dated 28 March 2024 on the Draft Universal Credit (Administrative Earnings Threshold) (Amendment) Regulations 2024, with the Secretary of State's Statement in response*, most easily accessed on the SSAC website). The Secretary of State accepted some elements of the recommendations, but not that for any pause in implementation. Unusually, the preambles to both sets of amending regulations only mention the reference to the SSAC, not its report or the Secretary of State's response. Those matters are only mentioned in the Explanatory Memorandums. Presumably that, and the statement on the title page of the report that it had been presented to Parliament under s.174(2) of the SSAA 1992, is good enough to meet the requirement in s.174(2) for laying before Parliament. The SSAC report also noted that "the stated policy intent has evolved from the initial ambition to get more claimants in to higher-paid work, to a reframing of the social contract between claimants and the Department to better balance the responsibilities that are asked of claimants in return for their benefits". That point was taken up by the House of Lords Secondary Legislation Scrutiny Committee (*23rd Report of Session 2023–24*, HL Paper 107) in its critical report drawing the special attention of the House to the second set of regulations, SI 2024/536, on the ground that the explanatory material provided insufficient information to enable a clear understanding of the policy objective and intended application. It was also noted that para.5.24 of the Explanatory Memorandum stated that evaluation of the previous increases was currently ongoing, the "robust evidence" referred to as currently existing in the letter of January 23, 2013 from the Minister for Employment, Guy Opperman, apparently never having been published. The Committee found the lack of data "inexplicable", agreeing with the SSAC that in the current state of the evidence provided the increases were premature.

The Universal Credit (Administrative Earnings Threshold) (Amendment) Regulations 2024 (SI 2024/529) amending reg.99(6) as described above were made on April 12, 2024, to come into force on May 6, 2024, but not laid before Parliament until April 19, 2024, according to para.11.1 of the Explanatory Memorandum to SI 2024/536 because of unfolding events in the Middle East. It appears to have been realised on April 19, 2024 that that would involve a breach of the "21 day" rule or understanding that Parliament should have that time for consideration before secondary legislation came into force. So the Universal Credit (Administrative Earnings Threshold) (Amendment) (No.2) Regulations 2024 (SI 2024/536), coming into force on May 13, 2024, making the same amendments to reg.99(6) and revoking SI 2024/529, were hurriedly made and laid before Parliament on the same day. Unfortunately, nothing was done in the drafting to take the revocation of SI 2024/529 out of the general provision for commencement on May 13, 2024. The result, as recognised by the House of Lords Committee and therefore one might have thought accepted by the DWP, is that the amendments made by SI 2024/529 remained in force from May 6, 2024 until May 12. 2024, being replaced with effect from May 13, 2024 by the identical amendments made by SI 2024/536. That somewhat shambolic state of affairs may not matter in practice if the DWP only operated the new thresholds from May 13, 2024, as it had meant to do. The press release issued on May 13, 2024 seems to confirm that position, although still stubbornly asserting that the amendments were brought into force on that date. In a very apologetic Voluntary Memorandum dated May 2, 2024 to the Joint Committee on Statutory Instruments (22nd Report of Session 2023-24, May 22, 2024, HL 122, HC 36-xxii, Appendix 7), the DWP accepted the points about the operative dates of the two sets of regulations and gave a new explanation of the delay in laying SI 2024/529 (the need to await a speech by the Prime Minister on social security).

The *Spring Budget 2023* (para.4.146) promised a future change in an abandonment of the higher threshold for couples, with each joint claimant to be subject to the individual AET. It had been suggested that that change might come in after those eventually made in May 2024, but no date is currently under public discussion and the controversy around the evidence base for the May 2024 changes indicates that any concrete proposal for further change would come under close scrutiny.

The Pilot Scheme exceptions

According to para.7.14 of the Explanatory Memorandum to the Universal Credit (Work-Related Requirements) In Work Pilot Scheme and Amendment Regulations 2015, reg.99(6) was initially put in a discretionary form because it had not then been worked out what form of intervention in the way of conditionality would be most effective where the claimant was in work. But it was envisaged that para.(6) would later be revoked when it was known how the work availability and work search requirements could be operated in an appropriate way for all those in work. The 2015 Regulations therefore represent an interim position, which has endured for some considerable time during the slow development of policy.

The Pilot Scheme Regulations (see later in this volume) allow the Secretary of State to select on a random basis certain "qualifying claimants" who would otherwise benefit from para.(6), i.e. who would otherwise be subject to light touch conditionality, to be treated on the basis that para.(6) does not exist. The other conditions under reg.7 of those Regulations for being a "qualifying claimant" are falling within s.22 of the WRA 2012 (subject to all work-related requirements), not falling within reg.98 (victims of domestic violence) and not falling within reg.99(3) (except sub-para.(a) or (g)) or (5)(c). The effect of the Regulations was to expire after three years from February 19, 2015, but that period has been extended, as allowed by s.41(5) of the WRA 2012, for a further seven years so far (Universal Credit (Work-Related Requirements) In Work Pilot Scheme (Extension) Order 2018 (SI 2018/168), as supplemented by the 2019, 2020, 2021, 2022, 2023 and 2024 Universal Credit (Work-Related Requirements) In Work Pilot Scheme (Extension) Orders (SIs 2019/249, 2020/152, 2021/147, 2022/139, 2023/157 and 2024/159) and may well, in view of the slow development of policy described below, be extended further.

This is a very important provision, allowing experiments ("test and learn") to take place on how to apply the principle of conditionality to those in more than merely subsidiary work, a question apparently not worked out when the scheme to which in-work conditionality was central was legislated for or in the several years since. The claimants selected for the experiments will bear the brunt of any unfairness or rough justice or impracticability revealed in the experiments. Although the large trial described below has finished, so that the terms of para.(6) will apply unaffected in most cases, smaller-scale research and testing will continue.

See the House of Commons Work and Pensions Committee's report on *In-work progression in Universal Credit* (Tenth Report of Session 2010-16, May 2016, HC 549) for a critical but supportive description of the pilot scheme. The government's response to the report was published as HC 585 on July 21, 2016, in which it was anticipated that the necessary 15,000 participants would have been identified by early autumn 2016, to be randomly allocated into groups receiving either frequent, moderate or minimal support. This was known as the randomised controlled trial (RCT). The DWP's evidence to the Committee was that sanctions would be applied for failures to meet in-work requirements without good reason "as a last resort" (para.47 of HC 549), a phrase repeated in para.27 of HC 585. It is not clear how this can operate in practice, as a decision-maker has no discretion not to impose a sanction or to modify its effects if the statutory conditions for imposition are met. Presumably, the intention is that work coaches or other officers will only refer cases to a decision-maker for a sanction as a last resort. On March 23, 2017 the DWP published *In-Work Progression Trial Progress Update: April 2015 to October 2016*. This revealed that 15,455 people had been on the trial and that during the update period 319 sanctions had been imposed, mainly at the low level for failing to participate in meetings or telephone calls.

The Social Security Advisory Committee published an interesting paper, *In-work progression and Universal Credit* (Occasional Paper No.19) in November 2017. The paper welcomed the DWP's adoption of a cautious test and learn approach and the current RCT, but recommended that the DWP should test a wider range of interventions and quickly develop a wider understanding of the variety of circumstances of working claimants who will fall within the ambit of universal credit. It also recommended tackling operational complexities that can be an obstacle to in-work progression and clarifying policy in a number of areas, such as where claimants are working part-time in order to study, re-train or pursue other interests. The government's response in the policy paper *DWP response to SSAC report on In-work progression and Universal Credit: government response* (March 6, 2018) was to welcome the report, but to stress that the DWP considered itself as still at a relatively early stage in understanding what works and that developments would be informed by a "multi-faceted suite of tests and trials" over the following four years. Clarification of policy and the appropriate guidance to and training of work coaches would emerge from that process.

The Work and Pensions Committee returned to the topic in its report of November 6, 2018 on *Benefit Sanctions* (HC 995 2017-19). The DWP's September 2018 report on the completion of the RCT had found a positive impact on behaviours and increased earnings 52 weeks on (an effect subsequently confirmed at 78 weeks: DWP Ad hoc Report 75, October 2019) for those in the more supported groups. However, the important thing was the tailoring of the support to individual needs rather than frequency. Experience of being sanctioned had no apparent effect on outcomes. The Committee recommended that conditionality and sanctions should not be applied to in-work claimants until universal credit had been fully rolled out and then only on the basis of robust evidence of effectiveness. The DWP (House of Commons Work and Pensions Committee, *Benefit Sanctions: Government Response* (HC 1949 2017-19, February 11, 2019), partially accepted that recommendation, but only to the extent of agreeing that the development of policy should be evidence-based and committing to a cautious approach, involving further research and testing of a range of interventions and a better understanding of structural barriers to progression for in-work claimants.

Chapter 2

Sanctions

Introduction

2.367 **100.**—(1) This Chapter contains provisions about the reduction in the amount of an award of universal credit in the event of a failure by a claimant which is sanctionable under section 26 or 27 of the Act ("a sanctionable failure").

[[1](1A) In this Chapter references to a "current sanctionable failure" are to a sanctionable failure in relation to which the Secretary of State has not yet determined whether the amount of an award of universal credit is to be reduced under section 26 or 27 of the Act.]

(2) How the period of the reduction for each sanctionable failure is to be determined is dealt with in regulations 101 to 105.

(3) When the reduction begins or ceases to have effect is dealt with in regulations 106 to 109.

(4) How the amount of a reduction is calculated for an assessment period in which the reduction has effect is set out in regulations 110 and 111.

(5) Regulations 112 to 114 provide for some miscellaneous matters (movement of sanctions from a jobseeker's allowance or an employment and support allowance, cases in which no reduction is made for a sanctionable failure and prescription of work placement scheme for the purposes of section 26(2)(a) of the Act).

AMENDMENT

1. Social Security (Jobseeker's Allowance, Employment and Support Allowance and Universal Credit) (Amendment) Regulations 2016 (SI 2016/678) reg.5(5) (July 25, 2016).

DEFINITIONS

"the Act"—see reg.2.
"assessment period"—see WRA 2012 ss.40 and 7(2) and reg.21.
"claimant"—see WRA 2012 s.40.
"employment and support allowance"—see reg.2.
"jobseeker's allowance"—*ibid.*

Reduction periods

General principles for calculating reduction periods

101.—(1) The number of days for which a reduction in the amount of an award is to have effect ("the reduction period") is to be determined in relation to each sanctionable failure in accordance with regulations 102 to 105, but subject to paragraphs (3) and (4). **2.368**

(2) Reduction periods are to run consecutively.

(3) If the reduction period calculated in relation to a sanctionable failure in accordance with regulations 102 to 105 would result in the total outstanding reduction period exceeding 1095 days, the reduction period in relation to that failure is to be adjusted so that the total outstanding reduction period does not exceed 1095 days.

(4) [[1]...]

(5) In paragraph (3) "the total outstanding reduction period" is the total number of days for which no reduction in an award under section 26 or 27 of the Act has yet been applied.

AMENDMENT

1. Social Security (Jobseeker's Allowance, Employment and Support Allowance and Universal Credit) (Amendment) Regulations 2016 (SI 2016/678) reg.5(6) (July 25, 2016).

DEFINITIONS

"the Act"—see reg.2.
"sanctionable failure"—see reg.100(1).

GENERAL NOTE

2.369 Under reg.100 and this provision the way in which a sanction bites is through a reduction in the amount of an award of universal credit for a period determined under regs 101–105 (the "reduction period": para.(1)) for each sanctionable failure. A sanctionable failure is a failure which is sanctionable under s.26 or 27 of the WRA 2012. This regulation contains some general rules on sanctions.

Under para.(2) reduction periods for separate sanctionable failures run consecutively. That is subject to the general overall three-year limit in paras (3) and (5). The drafting is fairly impenetrable, but the upshot seems to be that if adding a new reduction period to the end of an existing period or, more likely, chain of reduction periods would take the total days in the periods over 1095 days the new reduction period is to be adjusted to make the total 1095 days exactly. Now that the rule previously in para.(4), about previous sanctionable failures in the 13 days before another sanctionable failure not counting, has been incorporated into the specific provisions in regs 102 – 104 and tidied up, there can be no question of that rule qualifying the effect of para.(3) to allow a total outstanding reduction period to exceed 1095 days, as had been suggested in the 2013/14 edition of this Volume.

Note also the circumstances prescribed in reg.109 (earnings over the individual threshold for 26 weeks) in which a reduction is to be terminated and the circumstances prescribed in reg.113 where there is to be no reduction despite the existence of a sanctionable failure. Under reg.111(3) the amount of the reduction is nil in an assessment period at the end of which the claimant is subject to no work-related requirements because of having limited capability for work and work-related activity under s.19 of the WRA 2012.

On May 9, 2019, following a report of November 6, 2018 by the House of Commons Work and Pensions Committee on *Benefit Sanctions* (HC 995 2017-19), the Secretary of State (Amber Rudd) made a written statement to Parliament (HCWS1545) including the following:

> "I have reviewed my Department's internal data, which shows that a six-month sanction already provides a significant incentive for claimants to engage with the labour market regime. I agree with the Work and Pensions Select Committee that a three-year sanction is unnecessarily long and I feel that the additional incentive provided by a three-year sanction can be outweighed by the unintended impacts to the claimant due to the additional duration. For these reasons, I have now decided to remove three year sanctions and reduce the maximum sanction length to six months by the end of the year."

That decision was implemented (perhaps not fully in spirit) in the November 2019 amendment to reg.102. Note in particular that there was no amendment to reg.101(3), so that in combination with the rule in para.(2) on reduction periods running consecutively it is still possible for a claimant subject to multiple reduction periods to have a total outstanding reduction period of 1095 days.

Higher-level sanction

2.370 **102.**—(1) This regulation specifies the reduction period for a sanctionable failure under section 26 of the Act ("higher level sanction").

[[1](2) Where the sanctionable failure is not a pre-claim failure, the reduction in the circumstances described in the first column of the following table is the period set out in—

(a) the second column, where the claimant is aged 18 or over on the date of the sanctionable failure;
(b) the third column, where the claimant is aged 16 or 17 on the date of the sanctionable failure.

Circumstances in which reduction period applies	*Reduction period where claimant aged 18 or over*	*Reduction period where claimant aged 16 or 17*
Where there has been no previous sanctionable failure by the claimant giving rise to a higher-level sanction	91 days	14 days
Where there have been one or more previous sanctionable failures by the claimant giving rise to a higher-level sanction and the date of the most recent previous sanctionable failure is not within 365 days beginning with the date of the current sanctionable failure	91 days	14 days
Where there have been one or more previous sanctionable failures by the claimant giving rise to a higher-level sanction and the date of the most recent previous sanctionable failure is within 365 days, but not within 14 days, beginning with the date of the current sanctionable failure and the reduction period applicable to the most recent previous sanctionable failure is— (a) 14 days (b) 28 days (c) 91 days (d) 182 days [2...]	 – – 182 days [2182 days]	 28 days 28 days – –
Where there have been one or more previous sanctionable failures by the claimant giving rise to a higher-level sanction and the date of the most recent previous sanctionable failure is within 14 days beginning with the date of the current sanctionable failure and the reduction period applicable to the most recent previous sanctionable failure is— (a) 14 days (b) 28 days (c) 91 days (d) 182 days [2...]	 – – 91 days 182 days	 14 days 28 days – – –.]

(3) But where the other sanctionable failure referred to in paragraph (2) was a pre-claim failure it is disregarded in determining the reduction period in accordance with that paragraph.

(4) Where the sanctionable failure for which a reduction period is to be determined is a pre-claim failure, the period is the lesser of—

(a) the period that would be applicable to the claimant under paragraph (2) if it were not a pre-claim failure; or

(b) where the sanctionable failure relates to paid work that was due to last for a limited period, the period beginning with the day after the date of the sanctionable failure and ending with the date on which the limited period would have ended,

minus the number of days beginning with the day after the date of the sanctionable failure and ending on the day before the date of claim.

[1(5) In this regulation—

"higher-level sanction" means a sanction under section 26 of the Act;

"pre-claim failure" means a failure sanctionable under section 26(4) of the Act.]

AMENDMENTS

1. Social Security (Jobseeker's Allowance, Employment and Support Allowance and Universal Credit) (Amendment) Regulations 2016 (SI 2016/678) reg.5(7) (July 25, 2016).

2. Jobseeker's Allowance and Universal Credit (Higher-Level Sanctions) (Amendment) Regulations 2019 (SI 2019/1357) reg.3 (November 27, 2019).

DEFINITIONS

"the Act"—see reg.2.

"claimant"—see WRA 2012 s.40.

"current sanctionable failure"—see reg.100(1A).

"reduction period"—see reg.101(1).

"sanctionable failure"—see reg.100(1).

GENERAL NOTE

2.371 Higher-level sanctions are applicable to failures under s.26 of the WRA 2012. Such failures fall outside the scope of regs 103–105 and no failures under s.27 can come within the present regulation. Note the effect of reg.113 in specifying circumstances in which no reduction is to be applied although there has been a sanctionable failure. There is a distinction between "pre-claim failures", i.e. a failure under s.26(4) (before the relevant claim failing for no good reason to take up an offer of paid work or ceasing paid work or losing pay by reason of misconduct or voluntarily and for no good reason), and other failures.

The form of para.(2), specifying the length of sanctions reduction periods for non-pre-claim failures, was re-cast with effect from July 25, 2016 to spell out more precisely much the same effect as previously. It is unhelpful that the individual entries in the table are not numbered. Boxes have been added by the publishers to aid clarity. The rules for 16 and 17-year-olds are no longer separated out from those for claimants aged at least 18, but now appear in column 3 of the table. None of the rules set out below may take the overall length of a total outstanding reduction period (reduction periods run consecutively) over 1095 days (reg.101(2) and (3)).

The general rule for adults in the first entry in column 2 is that the reduction period is 91 days if there have been no other higher-level UC sanctionable failures (or equivalent new style ESA or JSA failures if the claimant moved to universal credit with some days of an ESA or JSA reduction period outstanding: reg.112 and Sch.11 para.3) within the previous 365 days (counting the day of the current sanctionable failure). Contrary to what was said in the note to reg.113 in the 2013/14 edition of what was then Vol.V of this series, it appears that if no reduction of benefit was imposed in relation to a previous sanctionable failure, by reason of reg.113, that failure has not "given rise to" a higher-level sanction so as to count for the purposes of the table. However, if a reduction has been terminated under reg.109, the failure would appear to count because it has given rise to a sanction, even though the period of the reduction has not lasted as long as originally set. It might be argued, for the purposes of the later parts of the table, that the relevant period of reduction was no longer applicable, but the definition of "reduction period" in reg.101(1) is in terms of the initial fixing of the period, with no reference to the effect of reg.109. However, para.(3) secures that pre-claim sanctionable failures (only failures under s.26(4) of the WRA 2012: para.(5)) do not count in this process.

Matters become more complicated when there has been a previous relevant failure within the 365 days. But the amendment with effect from November 27, 2019 has led to a considerable simplification through the removal of the category requiring a reduction period of 1095 days. To start at the end of the table, if the sole or most recent previous sanctionable failure was within the 13 days immediately preceding the date of the current failure, the period of reduction for the current failure is of equal length (either 91 or 182 days) to that for the previous failure. But note that the result of reg.101(2) and (3) is that the new period is to be added on to the end of the previous period, subject to the overall 1095-day limit. If the most recent previous sanctionable failure falls outside that 13-day period but within the 364 days immediately preceding the date of the current failure, the period of reduction for the current failure is 182 days. But note again the effect of reg.101(2) and (3).

The November 2019 amendment is in strict fulfilment of the decision announced by the then Secretary of State, Amber Rudd (written statement to Parliament, HCWS1545, May 9, 2019), set out in the notes to reg.101, to remove three-year sanctions for third or subsequent failures and to reduce the maximum sanction length to six months by the end of the year. However, as explained above and in the notes to reg.101, in universal credit and new style JSA, by contrast with the position for old style JSA (see reg.70(2) of the JSA Regulations 1996), the effect of the rules that reduction periods run consecutively, which has not been amended, is that if there have been multiple sanctionable failures within a year a claimant may have a total outstanding reduction period of up to 1095 days imposed. Thus, the precise terms of the decision have been carried out, but it may be said that the spirit of the reasoning behind it has not been adopted for universal credit and new style JSA.

Regulation 5(3) of the amending regulation made the transitional provision that, where an award of universal credit was subject to a 1095-day reduction under s.26 (or such a reduction was treated as falling under s.26) as at November 27, 2019, that reduction was to be terminated where the award had been reduced for at least 182 days. That appears to apply whether the 182 days expired before, on or after November 27, 2019, provided that the award was subject to the 1095-day reduction on that date. It then appears that, once the 1095-day reduction had been terminated the reduction period "applicable" to the previous sanctionable failure became 182 days, so that the case would fall within the new form of para.(d) of the third part of the table.

There is a similar structure for 16 and 17-year-olds, with only two levels of reduction period, at 14 and 28 days.

For pre-claim sanctionable failures, under para.(4) the number of days between the date of the failure and the date of the relevant claim is deducted from the number of days in the reduction period calculated as under para.(2). That is subject to the further rule that if the sanctionable failure relates to paid work that was due to last only for a limited period, the period down to the date when the work was due to end is substituted for the para.(2) period in the calculation. Presumably that is to give an incentive to people to take such work. See also reg.113(1)(e).

Medium-level sanction

2.372 **103.**—(1) This regulation specifies the reduction period for a sanctionable failure under section 27 of the Act (other sanctions) where it is a failure by the claimant to comply with—

(a) a work search requirement under section 17(1)(a) (to take all reasonable action to obtain paid work etc.); or

(b) a work availability requirement under section 18(1).

[[1](2) The reduction in the circumstances described in the first column of the following table is the period set out in—

(a) the second column, where the claimant is aged 18 or over on the date of the sanctionable failure;

(b) the third column, where the claimant is aged 16 or 17 on the date of the sanctionable failure.

Circumstances in which reduction period applies	*Reduction period where claimant aged 18 or over*	*Reduction period where claimant aged 16 or 17*
Where there has been no previous sanctionable failure by the claimant that falls within paragraph (1)	28 days	7 days
Where there have been one or more previous sanctionable failures by the claimant that fall within paragraph (1) and the date of the most recent previous sanctionable failure is not within 365 days beginning with the date of the current sanctionable failure	28 days	7 days
Where there have been one or more previous sanctionable failures by the claimant that fall within paragraph (1) and the date of the most recent previous sanctionable failure is within 365 days, but not within 14 days, beginning with the date of the current sanctionable failure and the reduction period applicable to the most recent previous sanctionable failure is—		
(a) 7 days	–	14 days
(b) 14 days	–	14 days
(c) 28 days	91 days	–
(d) 91 days	91 days	–
Where there have been one or more previous sanctionable failures by the claimant that fall within paragraph (1) and the date of the most recent previous sanctionable failure is within 14 days beginning with the date of the current sanctionable failure and the reduction period applicable to the most recent previous sanctionable failure is—		

Circumstances in which reduction period applies	*Reduction period where claimant aged 18 or over*	*Reduction period where claimant aged 16 or 17*
(a) 7 days	–	7 days
(b) 14 days	–	14 days
(c) 28 days	28 days	–
(d) 91 days	91 days	–.]

AMENDMENT

1. Social Security (Jobseeker's Allowance, Employment and Support Allowance and Universal Credit) (Amendment) Regulations 2016 (SI 2016/678) reg.5(8) (July 25, 2016).

DEFINITIONS

"the Act"—see reg.2.
"claimant"—see WRA 2012 s.40.
"current sanctionable failure"—see reg.100(1A).
"reduction period"—see reg.101(1).
"sanctionable failure"—see reg.100(1).

GENERAL NOTE

This regulation applies to failures for no good reason to comply with two particular work-related requirements to which the claimant in question is subject: the requirement under s.17(1)(a) of the WRA 2012 to take all reasonable action to obtain paid work (but note, not the requirement under s.17(1)(b) to take particular action specified by the Secretary of State, where only some failures to comply fall under s.26 and the higher-level sanctions regime) and the work availability requirement in s.18(1). Note that none of the circumstances specified in reg.113 (no reduction to be applied though sanctionable failure) are relevant to medium-level sanctions under s.27. **2.373**

The form of para.(2), specifying the length of the sanction reduction period, has been re-cast with effect from July 25, 2016 to spell out more precisely much the same effect as previously. It is unhelpful that the individual entries in the table are not numbered. Boxes have been added by the publishers to aid clarity. The rules for 16 and 17-year-olds are no longer separated out from those for claimants aged at least 18, but now appear in column 3 of the table. None of the rules set out below may take the overall length of a total outstanding reduction period (reduction periods run consecutively) over 1095 days (reg.101(2) and (3)).

The general rule for adults in the first entry in column 2 is that the reduction period is 28 days if there have been no other medium-level UC sanctionable failures (or equivalent new style ESA or JSA failures if the claimant moved to universal credit with some days of an ESA or JSA reduction period outstanding: reg.112 and Sch.11 para.3) within the previous 365 days (counting the day of the current sanctionable failure). Arguably, the effect of there having been no reduction of benefit in relation to a previous sanctionable failure, by reason of reg.113, is not quite the same as under reg.102, because here there is no reference to the previous failure having "given rise to" a medium-level sanction. If reg.113 applies there is still a sanctionable failure, although no reduction of benefit is to be applied. However, for the purposes of the later parts of the table, a reduction period applicable to the previous sanctionable failure must be identified. If reg.113 has been applied to that failure there can be no reduction period applicable. Consequently it must be arguable that for the purposes of the table as a whole previous sanctionable failures to which reg.113 has been applied do not count. See the notes to reg.102 for the opposite effect where a reduction period has been terminated under reg.109.

The reduction period under para.(1) as from July 25, 2016 is 28 days if there have been no other medium-level sanctionable failures (or equivalent new style ESA or JSA sanctionable failures) at all or only outside the past period of 365 days including the date of the current sanctionable failure. If the most recent relevant sanctionable failure was in the past period of 14 days including the date of the current sanctionable failure, the length of the reduction period is equal to that for the most recent failure. Where the most recent relevant failure was further in the past but still within the 365 days, the length of the reduction period is 91 days. That is in substance the same result as under the previous form of reg.20 and reg.101(4).

There is a similar structure for 16 and 17-year-olds, with only two levels of reduction period, at seven and 14 days.

Low-level sanction

2.374 **104.**—(1) This regulation specifies the reduction period for a sanctionable failure under section 27 of the Act (other sanctions) where—

(a) the claimant falls within section 21 (claimants subject to work preparation requirement) or 22 (claimants subject to all work-related requirements) of the Act on the date of that failure; and

(b) it is a failure to comply with—

(i) a work-focused interview requirement under section 15(1),

(ii) a work preparation requirement under section 16(1),

(iii) a work search requirement under section 17(1)(b) (to take any particular action specified by the Secretary of State to obtain work etc.), or

(iv) a requirement under section 23(1), (3) or (4) (connected requirements: interviews and verification of compliance).

(2) Where the claimant is aged 18 or over on the date of the sanctionable failure, the reduction period is the total of—

(a) the number of days beginning with the date of the sanctionable failure and ending with—

(i) the day before the date on which the claimant meets a compliance condition specified by the Secretary of State,

(ii) the day before the date on which the claimant falls within section 19 of the Act (claimant subject to no work-related requirements),

(iii) the day before the date on which the claimant is no longer required to take a particular action specified as a work preparation requirement by the Secretary of State under section 16, or

(iv) the date on which the award terminates (other than by reason of the claimant ceasing to be, or becoming, a member of a couple),

whichever is soonest; and

[1(b) in the circumstances described in the first column of the following table, the number of days in the second column.

Circumstances applicable to claimant's case	*Number of days*
Where there has been no previous sanctionable failure by the claimant that falls within paragraph (1)	7 days
Where there have been one or more previous sanctionable failures by the claimant that fall within paragraph (1) and the date of the most recent previous sanctionable failure is not within 365 days beginning with the date of the current sanctionable failure	7 days
Where there have been one or more previous sanctionable failures by the claimant that fall within paragraph (1) and the date of the most recent previous sanctionable failure is within 365 days, but not within 14 days, beginning with the date of the current sanctionable failure and the reduction period applicable to the most recent previous sanctionable failure is—	
(a) 7 days (b) 14 days (c) 28 days	14 days 28 days 28 days
Where there have been one or more previous sanctionable failures by the claimant that fall within paragraph (1) and the date of the most recent previous sanctionable failure is within 14 days beginning with the date of the current sanctionable failure and the reduction period applicable to the most recent previous sanctionable failure is— (a) 7 days (b) 14 days (c) 28 days	7 days 14 days 28 days]

(3) Where the claimant is aged 16 or 17 years on the date of the sanctionable failure, the reduction period is—

(a) the number of days beginning with the date of the sanctionable failure and ending with—

(i) the day before the date on which the claimant meets a compliance condition specified by the Secretary of State,

(ii) the day before the date on which the claimant falls within section 19 of the Act (claimant subject to no work-related requirements),

(iii) the day before the date on which the claimant is no longer required to take a particular action specified as a work preparation requirement by the Secretary of State under section 16, or

(iv) date on which the award terminates (other than by reason of the claimant ceasing to be, or becoming, a member of a couple),

whichever is soonest; and

[[1](b) if there was another sanctionable failure of a kind mentioned in paragraph (1) within 365 days, but not within 14 days, beginning with the date of the current sanctionable failure, 7 days.]

AMENDMENT

1. Social Security (Jobseeker's Allowance, Employment and Support Allowance and Universal Credit) (Amendment) Regulations 2016 (SI 2016/678) reg.5(9) (July 25, 2016).

DEFINITIONS

"the Act"—see reg.2.
"claimant"—see WRA 2012 s.40.
"compliance condition"—see WRA 2012 s.27(6).
"current sanctionable failure"—see reg.100(1A).
"reduction period"—see reg.101(1).
"sanctionable failure"—see reg.100(1).

GENERAL NOTE

2.375 This regulation applies only to claimants who are subject to all work-related requirements under s.22 of the WRA 2012 or to the work preparation requirement under s.21 at the time of the sanctionable failure. Then a low-level sanction is attracted by a failure for no good reason to comply with a work-focused interview requirement under s.15(1), a work preparation requirement under s.16(1), a work search requirement under s.17(1)(b) to take particular action specified by the Secretary of State (see reg.103—medium-level sanction—for failures to comply with the requirement to take all reasonable action to obtain paid work under s.17(1)(a)) or one of the extensive connected requirements under s.23.

The calculation of the reduction period under para.(2) is more complicated than that for higher and medium-level sanctions. It is made up of a period of flexible length depending on the ongoing circumstances under sub-para.(a) plus a fixed period of days under sub-para.(b) to be added to the sub-para.(a) period. Note that none of the circumstances specified in reg.113 (no reduction to be applied though sanctionable failure) are relevant to low-level sanctions under s.27.

The basic rule in sub-para.(a) is that the period runs until any compliance condition specified by the Secretary of State is met. See the notes to s.27(5) of the WRA 2012 for the authorisation for this provision. A compliance condition is either that the failure to comply ceases to exist (e.g. the claimant attends a work-focused interview) or a condition as to future compliance. The condition must in accordance with s.27(5)(a) and sub-para.(a)(i) be specified by the Secretary of State. Although s.27(7) allows the Secretary of State to notify a claimant of a compliance condition in such manner as he determines, the approach of the Supreme Court in *R (on the application of Reilly and Wilson) v Secretary of State for Work and Pensions* [2013] UKSC 68; [2014] 1 A.C. 453 and of the Court of Appeal in *SSWP v Reilly and Hewstone* and *SSWP v Jeffrey and Bevan* [2016] EWCA Civ 413; [2017] 3 Q.B. 657; [2017] AACR 14 to the "prior information duty" and the requirements of fairness might possibly be relevant to the substance of what must be specified (and see the further discussion in the notes to s.27(5)). The sub-para.(a) period will also end if the claimant becomes subject to no work-related requirements for any reason under s.19 of the WRA 2012, is no longer required to take a specific action as a work preparation requirement or the award of universal credit terminates.

It is understood that during the 2020 coronavirus outbreak any contact by the claimant with the DWP was treated as meeting a compliance condition.

Under sub-para.(b) the additional number of days is seven if there have been no other low-level sanctionable failures (or equivalent new style ESA or JSA failures if the claimant moved to universal credit with some days of an ESA or JSA reduction period outstanding: reg.112 and Sch.11 para.3) in the previous 365 days (counting the day of the current sanctionable failure). Arguably, the effect of there having been no reduction of benefit in relation to a previous sanctionable failure, by reason of reg.113, is not quite the same as under reg.102, because here there is no reference to the previous failure having "given rise to" a low-level sanction. If reg.113 applies there is still a sanctionable failure, although no reduction of benefit is to be applied. However, for the purposes of the later parts of the table, a reduction period applicable to the previous sanctionable failure must be identified. If reg.113 has been applied to that failure there can be no reduction period applicable. Consequently it must be arguable that for the purposes of the table as a whole previous sanctionable failures to which reg.113 has been applied do not count. See the notes to reg.102 for the opposite effect where a reduction period has been terminated under reg.109.

The second general rule, where there has been at least one previous low-level sanctionable failure in the 365 day period, is that the para.(b) reduction period is 14 days, where the reduction period for the most recent sanctionable failure was seven days and 28 days in all other cases (subject to the possible application of reg.101(3)). The exception to that general rule is where the most recent sanctionable failure occurred within 14 days before the current sanctionable failure, including the day of that failure. In that case, the reduction period is to be of the same length as that applicable to the previous sanctionable failure.

Under para.(3) for claimants aged under 18, the same rules as in para.(2)(a) apply, plus an additional seven days if there has been one or more low-level sanctionable failures in the previous 365 days (excluding the most recent 14 days).

Lowest-level sanction

105.—(1) This regulation specifies the reduction period for a sanctionable failure under section 27 of the Act (other sanctions) where it is a failure by a claimant who falls within section 20 of the Act (claimants subject to work-focused interview requirement only) to comply with a requirement under that section. 2.376

(2) The reduction period is the number of days beginning with the date of the sanctionable failure and ending with—

(a) the day before the date on which the claimant meets a compliance condition specified by the Secretary of State;

(b) the day before the date on which the claimant falls within section 19 of the Act (claimant subject to no work-related requirements); or

(c) the day on which the award terminates (other than by reason of the claimant ceasing to be, or becoming, a member of a couple),

whichever is soonest.

DEFINITIONS

"the Act"—see reg.2.
"claimant"—see WRA 2012 s.40.
"compliance condition"—see WRA 2012 s.27(6).
"reduction period"—see reg.101(1).
"sanctionable failure"—see reg.100(1).

GENERAL NOTE

This regulation applies only to claimants who are subject only to the work-focused interview requirement under s.20 of the WRA 2012. The reduction period for a sanctionable failure to comply with that requirement runs until the claimant meets a compliance condition specified by the Secretary of State (see notes to reg.104), becomes subject to no work-related requirements for any reason under s.19 or the award of universal credit terminates. 2.377

When reduction to have effect

Start of the reduction

2.378 **106.** A reduction period determined in relation to a sanctionable failure takes effect from—

(a) the first day of the assessment period in which the Secretary of State determines that the amount of the award is to be reduced under section 26 or 27 of the Act (but see also regulation 107(2));

(b) if the amount of the award of universal credit for the assessment period referred to in paragraph (a) is not reduced in that period, the first day of the next assessment period; or

(c) if the amount of the award for the assessment period referred to in paragraph (a) or (b) is already subject to a reduction because of a previous sanctionable failure, the first day in respect of which the amount of the award is no longer subject to that reduction.

DEFINITIONS

"the Act"—see reg.2.
"assessment period"—see WRA 2012 ss.40 and 7(2) and reg.21.
"claimant"—see WRA 2012 s.40.
"reduction period"—see reg.101(1).
"sanctionable failure"—see reg.100(1).

GENERAL NOTE

2.379 These rules for the start of the reduction period follow fairly logically from the structure of the sanctions regime. Where no other reduction period is running the reduction period starts either in the assessment period (month) in which the decision to make the reduction is made or in the following assessment period (paras. (a) and (b)). If there is already a reduction applied in that assessment period, then, unless affected by the overall limit in reg.101(3) and (5), the new period starts on the expiry of the existing one.

Reduction period to continue where award terminates

2.380 **107.**—(1) If an award of universal credit terminates while there is an outstanding reduction period, the period continues to run as if a daily reduction were being applied and if the claimant becomes entitled to a new award (whether as single or joint claimant) before that period expires, that award is subject to a reduction for the remainder of the total outstanding reduction period.

(2) If an award of universal credit terminates before the Secretary of State determines that the amount of the award is to be reduced under section 26 or 27 of the Act in relation to a sanctionable failure and that determination is made after the claimant becomes entitled to a new award the reduction period in relation to that failure is to have effect for the purposes of paragraph (1) as if that determination had been made on the day before the previous award terminated.

DEFINITIONS

"the Act"—see reg.2.
"claimant"—see WRA 2012 s.40.

"joint claimants"—*ibid.*
"reduction period"—see reg.101(1).
"sanctionable failure"—see reg.100(1).
"single claimant"—see WRA 2012 s.40.

General Note

If an award of universal credit terminates while there is an outstanding reduction period, subsequent days count as if an actual reduction of benefit were being applied, so that on any further claim for universal credit the claimant is subject to the reduction only for the remainder of the period (para.(1)). If an award of universal credit terminates before the Secretary of State has made a decision about a reduction for a sanctionable failure, but a new award is in place by the time the decision is made (so that under reg.106 the reduction period would otherwise take effect in the current assessment period), the reduction period starts as if the decision had been made on the day before the previous award terminated. **2.381**

Note that if on or after the termination of entitlement to universal credit the claimant is entitled to new style JSA, the reduction of benefit under the universal credit sanction for its unexpired period transfers to the award of JSA (JSA Regulations 2013 reg.30)

Suspension of a reduction where fraud penalty applies

108.—(1) A reduction in the amount of an award under section 26 or 27 of the Act is to be suspended for any period during which the provisions of section 6B, 7 or 9 of the Social Security Fraud Act 2001 apply to the award. **2.382**

(2) The reduction ceases to have effect on the day on which that period begins and begins again on the day after that period ends.

Definition

"the Act"—see reg.2.

When a reduction is to be terminated

109.—(1) A reduction in the amount of an award under section 26 or 27 of the Act is to be terminated where— **2.383**

(a) since the date of the most recent sanctionable failure which gave rise to a reduction, the claimant has been in paid work for a period of, or for periods amounting in total to, at least [1six months]; and
(b) the claimant's [1monthly] earnings during that period or those periods were equal to or exceeded—
 (i) the claimant's individual threshold, [2...]
 [2(ia) where the claimant has no individual threshold, the amount that a person would be paid at the hourly rate specified in regulation 4 or regulation 4A(1)(a) to (c) of the National Minimum Wage Regulations for 16 hours per week, converted to a monthly amount by multiplying by 52 and dividing by 12, or]
 (ii) if paragraph (4) of regulation 90 applies (threshold for an apprentice) the amount applicable under that paragraph.

(2) The termination of the reduction has effect—
(a) where the date on which paragraph (1) is satisfied falls within a period of entitlement to universal credit, from the beginning of the assessment period in which that date falls; or
(b) where that date falls outside a period of entitlement to universal credit, from the beginning of the first assessment period in relation to any subsequent award.

(3) A claimant who is treated as having earned income in accordance with regulation 62 (minimum income floor) in respect of an assessment period is to be taken to have [1 monthly] earnings equal to their individual threshold in respect of [1 . . .] that assessment period.

AMENDMENTS

1. Universal Credit and Miscellaneous Amendments Regulations 2015 (SI 2015/1754) reg.2(8) (November 4, 2015).

2. Social Security (Jobseeker's Allowance, Employment and Support Allowance and Universal Credit) (Amendment) Regulations 2016 (SI 2016/678) reg.5(10) (July 25, 2016).

DEFINITIONS

"the Act"—see reg.2.
"assessment period"—see WRA 2012, ss.40 and 7(2) and reg.21.
"claimant"—see WRA 2012, s.40.
"individual threshold"—see regs 2 and 90(2).
"sanctionable failure"—see reg.100(1).
"National Minimum Wage Regulations"—see reg.2.

GENERAL NOTE

2.384 Any reduction for any level of sanction or sanctions terminates where since the date of the most recent sanctionable failure the claimant has been in paid work with earnings at least equal to the appropriate individual threshold for at least six months, not necessarily consecutive. It does not matter what the total outstanding reduction period is. The claimant could have had a reduction period of 1095 days imposed, yet after six months' work at minimum wage level (which will have reduced the outstanding period accordingly) the basis for the entire reduction disappears, just as much as if the outstanding period was much shorter. Paragraph (2) confirms that the termination takes effect immediately if the condition in para.(1) is met while the claimant is entitled to universal credit. If the claimant is not then entitled to universal credit the termination takes effect from the beginning of the first assessment period under any new award. Note that this regulation does not take away the status of any sanctionable failure(s) on which the terminated reduction period was based. Thus for the purpose of asking in the future whether there have been other sanctionable failures within 364 days of a new sanctionable failure all such sanctionable failures must be counted.

See also reg.119(3) below, under which any hardship payments made under the conditions in reg.116 cease to be recoverable where the claimant has had earnings of the same level as specified in reg.109 for six months after the last day on which a reduction was applied.

There was a technical difficulty in the operation of reg.109(1)(b) in that under the definition of "individual threshold" in reg.90(2) only claimants who would otherwise (if it were not for the effect of reg.90(1) and s.19 of the WRA 2012) be subject to some work-related requirement could have an individual threshold and so take advantage of the provision in para.(1). That gap has been filled by the new para.(1)(b)(ia), specifying an amount of earnings in terms of the national minimum wage hourly rate and 16 hours per week for claimants without an individual threshold as such.

Amount of reduction

Amount of reduction for each assessment period

2.385 **110.** Where it has been determined that an award of universal credit is to be reduced under section 26 or 27 of the Act, the amount of the reduction for each assessment period in respect of which a reduction has effect is to be calculated as follows.

Step 1

Take the number of days—

(a) in the assessment period; or

(b) if lower, the total outstanding reduction period,

and deduct any days in that assessment period for which the reduction is suspended in accordance with regulation 108.

Step 2

Multiply the number of days produced by step 1 by the daily reduction rate (see regulation 111).

Step 3

If necessary, adjust the amount produced by step 2 so that it does not exceed—

(a) the amount of the standard allowance applicable to the award; or

(b) in the case of a joint claim where a determination under section 26 or 27 of the Act applies only in relation to one claimant, half the amount of that standard allowance.

Step 4

Deduct the amount produced by steps 2 and 3 from the amount of the award for the assessment period after any deduction has been made in accordance with Part 7 (the benefit cap).

DEFINITIONS

"the Act"—see reg.2.
"assessment period"—see WRA 2012 ss.40 and 7(2) and reg.21.
"claimant"—see WRA 2012, s.40.
"standard allowance"—see WRA 2012, s.9.

GENERAL NOTE

This apparently complex calculation will work out easily enough in practice. Its main point is to translate the daily rate of reduction under reg.111 into the appropriate amount for an assessment period, depending on the number of days in the period affected by a reduction. There is a rule of substance concealed in step 3, in that the reduction can never exceed the amount of the claimant's standard allowance, or half of a couple's standard allowance. **2.386**

However, see the notes to reg.111 below for discussion of the capricious results that can follow from the way in which the daily reduction rate is calculated under reg.111 and from the principle that in accordance with ss.26 and 27 of the WRA 2012 the reduction is to be applied to the overall award of universal credit, however that is made up.

See those notes and the notes to reg.5 of the JSA Regulations 2013 in Vol.I of this series and to paras 1 and 2 of Sch.11 to the present Regulations for further discussion of the anomalous results where a universal credit recipient is also entitled to another social security benefit (in particular new style ESA or JSA) and for the non-use of regulation-making powers that could have avoided them.

Daily reduction rate

2.387 **111.**—(1) The daily reduction rate for the purposes of regulation 110 is, unless paragraph (2), or (3) applies, an amount equal to the amount of the standard allowance that is applicable to the award multiplied by 12 and divided by 365.

(2) The daily reduction rate is 40 per cent of the rate set out in paragraph (1) if, at the end of the assessment period—

(a) the claimant is aged 16 or 17;

(b) the claimant falls within section 19 of the Act (claimant subject to no work-related requirements) by virtue of—

(i) subsection (2)(c) of that section (responsible carer for a child under the age of 1), or

(ii) regulation 89(1)(c),(d) or (f) (adopter, claimant within 11 weeks before or 15 weeks after confinement or responsible foster parent of a child under the age of 1); or

(c) the claimant falls within section 20 (claimant subject to work-focused interview only).

(3) The daily reduction rate is nil if, at the end of the assessment period, the claimant falls within section 19 of the Act by virtue of having limited capability for work and work-related activity.

(4) The amount of the rate in [[1]paragraphs (1) and (2)] is to be rounded down to the nearest 10 pence.

(5) In the case of joint claimants—

(a) each joint claimant is considered individually for the purpose of determining the rate applicable under paragraphs (1) to (3); and

(b) half of any applicable rate is applied to each joint claimant accordingly.

AMENDMENT

1. Universal Credit (Consequential, Supplementary, Incidental and Miscellaneous Provisions) Regulations 2013 (SI 2013/630) reg.38(7) (April 29, 2013).

DEFINITIONS

"the Act"—see reg.2.
"assessment period"—see WRA 2012 ss.40 and 7(2) and reg.21.
"claimant"—see WRA 2012, s.40.
"joint claimants"—*ibid.*
"limited capability for work and work-related activity"—see WRA 2012, ss.40 and 37(1) and (2).
"single claimant"—see WRA 2012, s.40.
"standard allowance"—see WRA 2012, s.9.

GENERAL NOTE

2.388 The basic rule under para.(1) is that the reduction for the purposes of the calculation in reg.110 is by the whole amount equal to that of the claimant's standard allowance under s.9 of the WRA 2012. There is on the face of it no reduction to the elements that can make up the maximum amount of universal credit for responsibility for children and young persons (s.10), housing costs (s.11) or particular needs and circumstances (s.12). In the case of joint claimants, under para.(5) each claimant is considered separately for the purposes of calculating the reduction and treated as having half of the standard allowance applicable to them as joint claimants.

Under para.(2) the reduction is by 40 per cent of the standard allowance, rather than 100 per cent, for claimants under 18, claimants subject to no work-related requirements under s.19 of the WRA 2012 by virtue of s.19(2)(c) (responsible carer of a child under one) or reg.89(1)(c), (d) or (f) and claimants subject to the work-focused interview requirement only under s.20.

Despite the apparent simplicity of these rules, there are a number of complicating elements that create a degree of uncertainty. First, the effect of the rounding down under para.(4) to the nearest 10p in producing the daily rate of reduction from the amount of the standard allowance, which is expressed in reg.36 as a monthly amount, i.e. for each assessment period, is fairly clear. When the daily rate is multiplied by the number of days affected by the sanction in each assessment period in step 2 of reg.110 the result will often be less than the exactly proportionate share of the actual standard allowance. If a claimant's universal credit award was made up only of the standard allowance, then even a 100% reduction could leave some small amount still payable.

Second, the specification of the reduction rate in terms of the amount of the standard allowance, rather than the amount of the claimant's award of universal credit, creates problems in certain circumstances. In particular, this is so where the claimant has income to be deducted from the "maximum amount" (the appropriate standard allowance plus any additional elements for children, childcare costs, housing costs etc). Take a simple example of a single universal credit claimant of 25 doing no work who is also entitled to new style JSA of, from April 2023, £84.80 per week through satisfaction of the contribution conditions. The standard allowance is as at April 2023, £368.74 per month, which is also the maximum amount. That would appear to produce a universal credit award of £0.27 per month. If the claimant were then made subject to a 100% sanction for a 30-day assessment period, multiplying the daily reduction rate of £12.00 by 30 would produce a figure of £360. But the concept of a reduction cannot allow the amount of universal credit otherwise payable to go below zero, so that the actual reduction could be no more than £0.27 per month. It must not then be forgotten that reg.5 of the JSA Regulations 2013 prevents any reduction being applied to the claimant's new style JSA entitlement when there is also entitlement to universal credit, even though there may have been a sanctionable failure under the new style JSA legislation. Regulation 42 of the ESA Regulations 2013 does the same in relation to new style ESA. See the notes to reg.5 of the JSA Regulations 2013 in Vol.I of this series for the history of a proposal to alter the effect of reg.5 and of reg.42 of the ESA Regulations 2013 that currently appears unlikely to be implemented in the near future.

However, things would become much more complicated if the claimant had a housing costs and/or a children element included in the universal credit maximum amount, so that the amount payable was higher. The basic calculation of the amount of the reduction under reg.110 by reference to the standard allowance would stay the same. But, since ss.26 and 27 of the WRA 2012 and reg.110 provide simply for the reduction of the amount of an award of universal credit by the amount calculated under reg.110, there appears to be nothing to prevent the reduction in this second case biting into potentially the whole of universal credit award, subject only to the limit under step 3 of reg.110 of the amount of the standard allowance. These results appear arbitrary and unrelated to the merits of cases, but equally appear to follow inexorably from the structure of the universal credit legislation. In the example used, the claimant will still have the £84.80 per week of new style JSA intact (or some other source of income in other cases), which can be used to meet essential expenses.

Those simple examples do no more than scratch the surface of other complexities that may arise. They make the existence of the provision for hardship payments, now restricted to 100% reduction cases, in regs 115-119 even more important, although the conditions for payment are extremely restrictive.

Under para.(3) a nil reduction is to be applied, apparently for a whole assessment period, if at the end of that period the claimant is subject to no work-related requirements under s.19 by virtue of having limited capability for work and work-related activity (see s.19(2)(a)). The effect of applying a daily reduction, but making the rate nil, appears to be that any assessment periods falling within para. (3) count as part of the period of reduction under the sanction in question.

See reg.113 for circumstances in which no reduction is to be applied despite the existence of a sanctionable failure that would otherwise trigger a reduction and reg.109 for the termination of all outstanding reductions if a claimant has earnings equal to the individual threshold (see reg.90(2)) for 26 weeks.

Miscellaneous

Application of ESA or JSA sanctions to universal credit

2.389 **112.** Schedule 11 has effect in relation to persons who are, or have been, entitled to an employment and support allowance or a jobseeker's allowance and who are, or become, entitled to universal credit.

DEFINITIONS

"employment and support allowance"—see reg.2.
"jobseeker's allowance"—*ibid.*

GENERAL NOTE

2.390 The general effect of Sch.11 is that if a claimant moves from new style ESA or JSA to universal credit with some days of an ESA or JSA reduction period outstanding, the reduction for those days translates to the universal credit awards. The failures giving rise to those reductions count as previous sanctionable failures at the equivalent level for the purpose of calculating the length of the reduction period for higher, medium and low-level sanctions under regs 102–104.

Failures for which no reduction is applied

2.391 **113.**—(1) No reduction is to be made under section 26 or 27 of the Act for a sanctionable failure where—

(a) the sanctionable failure is listed in section 26(2)(b) or (c) (failure to apply for a particular vacancy for paid work, or failure to take up an offer of paid work) and the vacancy is because of a strike arising from a trade dispute;

(b) the sanctionable failure is listed in section 26(2)(d) (claimant ceases paid work or loses pay), and the following circumstances apply—

(i) the claimant's work search and work availability requirements are subject to limitations imposed under section 17(4) and 18(3) in respect of work available for a certain number of hours,

(ii) the claimant takes up paid work, or is in paid work and takes up more paid work that is for a greater number of hours, and

(iii) the claimant voluntarily ceases that paid work, or more paid work, or loses pay,

within a trial period;

(c) the sanctionable failure is that the claimant voluntarily ceases paid work, or loses pay, because of a strike arising from a trade dispute;

(d) the sanctionable failure is that the claimant voluntarily ceases paid work as a member of the regular or reserve forces, or loses pay in that capacity;

(e) the sanctionable failure is listed in section 26(4) (failure to take up an offer of paid work, or to cease paid work or lose pay before making a claim), and the period of the reduction that would otherwise apply under regulation 102(4) is the same as, or shorter than, the number of days beginning with the day after the date of the sanctionable failure and ending with the date of claim;

(f) the sanctionable failure is that the claimant voluntarily ceases paid work in one of the following circumstances—

(i) the claimant has been dismissed because of redundancy after volunteering or agreeing to be dismissed,

(ii) the claimant has ceased work on an agreed date without being dismissed in pursuance of an agreement relating to voluntary redundancy, or

(iii) the claimant has been laid-off or kept on short-time to the extent specified in section 148 of the Employment Rights Act 1996, and has complied with the requirements of that section; or

(g) the sanctionable failure is that the claimant by reason of misconduct, or voluntarily and for no good reason, ceases paid work or loses pay, but the claimant's [1 monthly] earnings (or, if the claimant is a member of a couple, their joint [1 monthly] earnings) have not fallen below [1the amount specified in] regulation 99(6) (circumstances in which requirements must not be imposed).

(2) In this regulation "regular or reserve forces" has the same meaning as in section 374 of the Armed Forces Act 2006.

AMENDMENT

1. Universal Credit and Miscellaneous Amendments Regulations 2015 (SI 2015/1754) reg.2(9) (November 4, 2015).

DEFINITIONS

"the Act"—see reg.2.
"claimant"—see WRA 2012 s.40.
"couple"—see WRA 2012 ss.40 and 39.
"paid work"—see reg.2.
"redundancy"—*ibid.*
"sanctionable failure"—see reg.100(1).
"trade dispute"—see reg.2.
"work availability requirement"—see WRA 2012 ss.40 and 18(1).
"work search requirement"—see WRA 2012 ss.40 and 17(1).

GENERAL NOTE

This is an important provision in prescribing, under ss.26(8)(a) and 27(9)(a) of the WRA 2012, cases of sanctionable failure for which no reduction of benefit can be imposed. However, none of the circumstances specified are relevant to medium, low or lowest-level sanctions arising under s.27. Note that if a case comes within this regulation that does not affect the status of the sanctionable failure in question. It can still count if in relation to a future sanctionable failure 2.392

it has to be asked whether there have been any sanctionable failures at the equivalent level in the previous 365 days. See the notes to regs 103 and 104 for further discussion. It will be different if, as under reg.102, the question to be asked is whether there has been a previous sanctionable failure giving rise to a sanction. If reg.113 has applied, the failure would appear not have given rise to a sanction. There remains scope for argument that in some of the circumstances listed there is a good reason for the particular claimant's failure to comply with the requirement in question, so that there is not in fact a sanctionable failure.

The cases are as follows:

(a) Where the sanctionable failure is failing for no good reason to apply for a particular vacancy for paid work or to take up an offer of paid work (WRA 2012, s.26(2)(b) or (c)), no reduction is to be imposed if the vacancy arose because of a strike arising from a trade dispute. "Trade dispute" is defined in reg.2 by adopting the rather long definition in s.244 of the Trade Union and Labour Relations (Consolidation) Act 1992:

> "(1) In this Part a "trade dispute" means a dispute between workers and their employer which relates wholly or mainly to one or more of the following—
> (a) terms and conditions of employment, or the physical conditions in which any workers are required to work;
> (b) engagement or non-engagement, or termination or suspension of employment or the duties of employment, of one or more workers;
> (c) allocation of work or the duties of employment between workers or groups of workers;
> (d) matters of discipline;
> (e) a worker's membership or non-membership of a trade union;
> (f) facilities for officials of trade unions; and
> (g) machinery for negotiation or consultation, and other procedures, relating to any of the above matters, including the recognition by employers or employers' associations of the right of a trade union to represent workers in such negotiation or consultation or in the carrying out of such procedures.
>
> (2) A dispute between a Minister of the Crown and any workers shall, notwithstanding that he is not the employer of those workers, be treated as a dispute between those workers and their employer if the dispute relates to matters which—
> (a) have been referred for consideration by a joint body on which, by virtue of provision made by or under any enactment, he is represented, or
> (b) cannot be settled without him exercising a power conferred on him by or under an enactment.
>
> (3) There is a trade dispute even though it relates to matters occurring outside the United Kingdom, so long as the person or persons whose actions in the United Kingdom are said to be in contemplation or furtherance of a trade dispute relating to matters occurring outside the United Kingdom are likely to be affected in respect of one or more of the matters specified in subsection (1) by the outcome of the dispute.
>
> (4) An act, threat or demand done or made by one person or organisation against another which, if resisted, would have led to a trade dispute with that other, shall be treated as being done or made in contemplation of a trade dispute with that other, notwithstanding that because that other submits to the act or threat or accedes to the demand no dispute arises.
>
> (5) In this section—
> "employment" includes any relationship whereby one person personally does work or performs services for another; and
> "worker", in relation to a dispute with an employer, means—
> (a) a worker employed by that employer; or

(b) a person who has ceased to be so employed if his employment was terminated in connection with the dispute or if the termination of his employment was one of the circumstances giving rise to the dispute."

That is a fairly comprehensive definition, although as compared with s.35(1) of the Jobseekers Act 1995 it does not cover disputes between employees and employees. "Strike" is not defined. It is possible that vacancies could arise because of industrial action short of a strike. There seems no good reason why claimants who on principle are not prepared to apply for such vacancies or accept offers should not also be protected. Perhaps it is arguable that in any event they have a good reason for failing to comply with the requirement in question, so that there is no sanctionable failure.

(b) This provision protects claimants who take up work for a trial period, but only current universal credit claimants who are required only to search for and be available for work subject to limitations as to hours of work under reg.97, made under ss.17(4) and 18(3) of the WRA 2012, or under those subsections. Then if such a claimant takes up work, or more work, for more than the hours of limitation for a trial period, but then voluntarily gives up that work or extra work or loses pay within the trial period, there is to be no reduction. As above, it would be arguable there was good reason for such action, so no sanctionable failure.

(c) This provision provides the same protection as under sub-para.(a) for voluntarily ceasing paid work or losing pay because of a strike arising from a trade dispute. See the notes to reg.56 for discussion of whether this provision protects all who are caught by reg.56 by having withdrawn their labour in furtherance of a trade dispute.

(d) Members of the armed forces, both regular and reserve forces, who voluntarily cease paid work as such or lose pay, cannot suffer a reduction on that ground, whatever the circumstances.

(e) Where there is a pre-claim sanctionable failure and the reduction period normally applicable would expire on or before the date of the relevant universal credit claim, there is to be no reduction. It may be that the same result is achieved by reg.102(4).

(f) This provides protection in the same circumstances as prescribed in reg.71 of the JSA Regulations 1996 (Vol.V of this series, 2021/22 edition as updated in Cumulative Supplements included in this volume and in mid-year Supplements) and reg.28(1)(f) of the JSA Regulations 2013 (Vol.I of this series), except that there the claimant is deemed not to have left employment voluntarily and so not subject to any sanction. Here the claimant is merely protected from having a reduction of benefit imposed, subject to any argument that there was a good reason under general principles for voluntarily ceasing work, so no sanctionable failure.

Sub-paragraph (f) provides protection in the context of a sanctionable failure in the form of voluntarily ceasing paid work in three situations. First, it protects claimants who have been dismissed by their employer because of redundancy after volunteering or agreeing to be dismissed. The reference to "dismissal" might be thought unfortunate if it were to perpetuate or risk reopening old controversies on its precise meaning. Were it the sole protective limb, *R(U) 3/91* ought probably to be followed to give it a wide meaning. But taking a narrower meaning might not now matter much, since head (ii) protects claimants who have left their employment on a date agreed with their employer without being dismissed, in pursuance of an agreement relating to voluntary redundancy. "Redundancy", rather than dismissal, is thus the key limiting factor. It presumably means one of the facts set out in s.139(1) of the Employment Rights Act 1996, i.e. (a) the fact that the employer has ceased, or intends to cease, to carry on the business in the place where the employee [the UC claimant] was employed; and (b) the fact that the requirements of that business for employees to carry out work of a particular kind, or for employees to carry out work of a particular kind in the place where [the claimant] was employed, have ceased or diminished or are expected to cease or diminish. The third situation of protection covers claimants who have been laid off or kept on short-time to the extent specified in s.148 of the Employment Rights Act 1996 and have complied with the requirements of that section, thus protecting claimants like the one in *CU/71/1994*. Section 148 of the 1996 Act enables those laid off or kept on short time to claim a redundancy payment if they serve on their employer written notice of their intention to do so. They must have been laid off or kept on short time either for four or more consecutive weeks or for a series of six or more weeks within a period of 13 weeks prior to service of the notice. To get the s.148 payment, the employee must terminate the contract of employment and not be dismissed by the employer.

(g) Under reg.99(6) it may be determined that a claimant's or joint claimants' earnings are at a level where a work search or work availability requirement is not to be imposed, although the earnings are below the individual threshold or combined individual thresholds that has to be reached to make the claimant(s) subject to no work-related requirements under s.19 of the WRA 2012 and reg.90. If that decision is made after a claimant by reason of misconduct or voluntarily and for no good reasons ceases paid work or loses pay, no reduction of benefit is to be imposed.

Sanctionable failures under section 26—work placements

2.393 [[1]**114.**—(1) A placement on the Mandatory Work Activity Scheme is a prescribed placement for the purpose of section 26(2)(a) of the Act (sanctionable failure not to comply with a work placement).

(2) In paragraph (1) "the Mandatory Work Activity Scheme" means a scheme provided pursuant to arrangements made by the Secretary of State and known by that name that is designed to provide work or work-related activity for up to 30 hours per week over a period of 4 consecutive weeks with a view to assisting claimants to improve their prospects of obtaining employment.]

AMENDMENT

1. Universal Credit (Consequential, Supplementary, Incidental and Miscellaneous Provisions) Regulations 2013 (SI 2013/630) reg.38(8) (April 29, 2013).

DEFINITIONS

"the Act"—see reg.2.
"claimant"—see WRA 2012 s.40.
"paid work"—see reg.2.
"work-related activity"—see WRA 2012 s.40.

GENERAL NOTE

2.394 See the notes to s.26(2)(a) of the WRA 2012 for the validity of this provision in giving sufficient detail of the nature of the Mandatory Work Activity Scheme to constitute a description of the scheme, as required by s.26(2)(a), not just a label, and for the circumstances in which failure to comply with a requirement to undertake a placement could give rise to a sanction. Note that the scheme need not be designed to provide work that is paid and that prospects of employment (not further defined) can in their ordinary meaning include prospects of self-employment. The scheme has ceased to operate after April 2016.

Chapter 3

Hardship

Introduction

115. This Chapter contains provisions under section 28 of the Act for the making of hardship payments where the amount of an award is reduced under section 26 or 27 of the Act. 2.395

DEFINITION

"the Act"—see reg.2.

Conditions for hardship payments

116.—(1) The Secretary of State must make a hardship payment to a single claimant or to joint claimants only where— 2.396

(a) the claimant in respect of whose sanctionable failure the award has been reduced under section 26 or 27 of the Act is aged 18 or over;

(b) the single claimant or each joint claimant has met any compliance condition specified by the Secretary of State under regulation 104(2)(a)(i);

(c) the single claimant or either joint claimant completes and submits an application—

 (i) approved for the purpose by the Secretary of State, or in such other form as the Secretary of State accepts as sufficient, and

 (ii) in such manner as the Secretary of State determines;

(d) the single claimant or either joint claimant furnishes such information or evidence as the Secretary of State may require, in such manner as the Secretary of State determines:

(e) the single claimant or each joint claimant accepts that any hardship payments that are paid are recoverable;

(f) the Secretary of State is satisfied that the single claimant or each joint claimant has complied with all the work-related requirements that they were required to comply with in the 7 days proceeding the day on which the claimant or joint claimants submitted an application in accordance with sub-paragraph (c); [1 . . .]

(g) the Secretary of State is satisfied that the single claimant or each joint claimant is in hardship; [1and

(h) the daily reduction rate in regulation 111(1) applies for the purposes of the reduction in respect of the claimant under section 26 or 27 of the Act.]

(2) For the purposes of paragraph (1)(g) a single claimant or joint claimants must be considered as being in hardship only where—

(a) they cannot meet their immediate and most basic and essential needs, specified in paragraph (3), or the immediate and most basic and essential needs of a child or qualifying young person for whom the single claimant or either of joint claimants is responsible, only because the amount of their award has been reduced—

 (i) under section 26 or 27 of the Act, by the daily reduction rate set out in [1regulation 111(1)], or

(ii) by the daily reduction rate prescribed in regulations made under section 6B(5A), 7(2A) or 9(2A) of the Social Security Fraud Act 2001 which is equivalent to the rate referred to in paragraph (i);

(b) they have made every effort to access alternative sources of support to meet, or partially meet, such needs; and

(c) they have made every effort to cease to incur any expenditure which does not relate to such needs.

(3) The needs referred to in paragraph (2) are—

(a) accommodation;

(b) heating;

(c) food;

(d) hygiene.

AMENDMENT

1. Universal Credit and Miscellaneous Amendments Regulations 2014 (SI 2014/597) reg.2(12) (April 28, 2014).

DEFINITIONS

"the Act"—see reg.2.
"claimant"—see WRA 2012 s.40.
"joint claimants"—*ibid.*
"sanctionable failure"—see reg.100(1).
"single claimant"—see WRA 2012 s.40.
"work-related requirement"—see WRA 2012 ss.40 and 13(2).

GENERAL NOTE

2.397 This regulation is made under s.28 of the WRA 2012 and sets out the very stringent conditions for the making of hardship payments to claimants to whom a sanction has been applied under s.26 or 27, that limitation being imposed by reg.115 and s.28(1)(a). The amount and period of any payment is dealt with in regs 117 and 118. Paragraph (1) of reg.116 lays down seven conditions, all of which must be satisfied. Paragraphs (2) and (3) provide a further exhaustive definition of when claimants can be considered to be in hardship for the purpose of condition (g) in para.(1). No payment can be made under reg.117 for any period prior to the date on which all the conditions in para.(1) are met.

The opening words of para.(1), by providing that the Secretary of State *must* make a hardship payment only where all its conditions are met, appear to open the door to the Secretary of State making payments on a discretionary basis where the conditions are not met. However, that is not the case, because s.28 only allows additional payments of universal credit to be made in hardship cases when regulations so provide. It must remain open to the Secretary of State to make payments, not of universal credit, on an extra-statutory basis, but no doubt the circumstances would have to be truly exceptional to persuade them to do so.

Paragraph (1)

2.398 The seven conditions are as follows:

(a) The claimant to whom the sanction has been applied must be aged at least 18. Under-18s can be sanctioned, but will not have the amount of benefit reduced to nil, as for most over-18s (see reg.111(1) and (2)).

(b) Under reg.104(2)(a) reduction periods for low-level sanctions last unless and until the claimant satisfies a compliance condition specified by the Secretary of State, i.e. the failure to comply with the work-related requirement in question has come to an end or a condition about future compliance is met (WRA 2012, s.27(6)), plus a fixed period on top. If such a compliance condition has been specified, a hardship payment can only be made after it has been met. The result is that in these cases a hardship payment can only be made during the final fixed period.

(c) The claimant or one of joint claimants must make an application for a hardship payment. The Secretary of State may accept an application in any sufficient form, but it is not clear what could also be required by the additional condition of the submission of the application being in such manner as determined by the Secretary of State. Condition (f) below can make the timing of an application important, but there seems nothing to stop multiple applications being made day by day.

(d) The claimant must have supplied any information or evidence required by the Secretary of State.

(e) The claimant or both joint claimants must accept that any hardship payments are recoverable. Since the recoverability is imposed by reg.119 and s.71ZH of the Administration Act, independent of any advance agreement by the claimant, it is not clear quite what level or manner of acceptance will satisfy this condition. The claimant in a sense has no option but to submit to what the law requires, no matter how vehemently dislike of the result is expressed.

(f) The claimant or both joint claimants must have complied with all work-related requirements imposed in the seven days preceding, presumably immediately preceding, the day of submission of the application under condition (c).

(g) The most fundamental condition is that the claimant or both joint claimants are in hardship, presumably as at the date of making the payment or possibly as at the date of the application in question. Because of the use of the present tense, it is arguable that it is not a necessary condition that the claimant or claimants are expected to be in hardship for the duration of the period covered by the payment. Paragraphs (2) and (3) define when a claimant can be accepted as in hardship.

(h) The effect of this provision, operative from April 2014, is to prevent any entitlement to a hardship payment arising for a claimant whose reduction in benefit under the sanction is only by 40% under reg.111(2), rather than by 100% under reg.111(1).

Paragraphs (2) and (3)

The use of the word "only" means that claimants can only be accepted as in hardship if they meet all three of the following conditions: 2.399

(a) The claimant or both joint claimants must be unable to meet their most immediate and basic and essential needs, or those of children or young person for whom they are responsible, only by reason of the reduction in benefit due to a sanction or of a reduction for a benefit offence under the Social Security Fraud Act 2001. The only needs to be considered are accommodation, heating, food and hygiene (para.(3)) and then this condition limits consideration to immediate, basic and essential needs of those kinds. That plainly involves a large element of judgment, but the highly restrictive intention is made clear. There is no specific category of need relating to children no matter how young, e.g. for bedding, clothing or education.

(b) The claimant or both joint claimants must have made every effort to access alternative sources of support to at least go towards meeting needs within condition (a). Some limitations must necessarily be implied either in terms of what efforts can be required or in terms of what alternative sources of support can be considered. The alternative source must at least be lawful. But presumably claimants are not to be required to beg on the streets. Are they to be required to go to back street or payday lenders? How far are they required to explore sources from which there is no practical possibility of support?

(c) The claimant or both joint claimants must have made every effort to cease to incur expenditure not related to condition (a) needs. Given the restrictive scope of those needs, the range of expenditure to be considered is wide. But again some notions of reasonableness and practicability must necessarily be implied, especially if avoiding immediate expenditure in the short term might lead to disproportionate financial penalties or burdens in the longer term.

The period of hardship payments

2.400 [1 **117.**—(1) A hardship payment is to be made in respect of a period which—

(a) begins with the date on which all the conditions in regulation 116(1) are met; and

(b) unless paragraph (2) applies, ends with the day before the normal payment date for the assessment period in which those conditions are met.

(2) If the period calculated in accordance with paragraph (1) would be 7 days or less, it does not end on the date referred to in paragraph (1)(b) but instead ends on the normal payment date for the following assessment period or, if earlier, the last day on which the award is to be reduced under section 26 or 27 of the Act or under section 6B(5A), 7(2A) or 9(3A) of the Social Security Fraud Act 2001.

(3) In this regulation "the normal payment date" for an assessment period is the date on which the Secretary of State would normally expect to make a regular payment of universal credit in respect of an assessment period in a case where payments of universal credit are made monthly in arrears.]

AMENDMENT

1. Universal Credit (Consequential, Supplementary, Incidental and Miscellaneous Provisions) Regulations 2013 (SI 2013/630) reg.38(9) (April 29, 2013).

DEFINITIONS

"assessment period"—see WRA 2012 ss.40 and 7(2) and reg.21.
"joint claimants"—see WRA 2012 s.40.
"single claimant"—*ibid.*

GENERAL NOTE

2.401 The substituted form of reg.117 (in operation from the outset of the universal credit scheme) represents a simplification and clarification of the original form. Each hardship payment is made for a limited period. Once each period expires a new application must be made. Under para.(1)(a) the period of a payment starts when all the conditions in reg.116(1) are met. For that to be so the claimant must, amongst other things, have completed and submitted an application either on the approved form or in some other manner accepted by the Secretary of State (reg.116(1)(c)). The period ends under the general rule in para.(1)(b) on the day before the normal payment day for the assessment period in which the application was made, following which a new application has to be made for the next period. Under para.(2), if the application of para.(1)(b) would result in a period of hardship payment of less than eight days the period extends to the day before the normal payment day for the next assessment period.

The amount of hardship payments

2.402 **118.** The amount of a hardship payment for each day in respect of which such a payment is to be made is to be determined in accordance with the formula—

$$60\% \text{ of } \left(\frac{(A \times 12)}{365}\right)$$

where A is equal to the amount of the reduction in the single claimant's or joint claimants' award calculated under regulation 110 for the assessment period preceding the assessment period in which an application is submitted under regulation 116(1)(c).

DEFINITIONS

"assessment period"—see WRA 2012, ss.40 and 7(2), and reg.21.
"joint claimants"—see WRA 2012, s.40.
"single claimant"—*ibid.*

GENERAL NOTE

The amount of any hardship payment payable per day is effectively 60 per cent of the reduction in the amount of benefit in the assessment period before that in which the application is made. See reg.111 for the daily reduction rate for different categories of claimant. **2.403**

Recoverability of hardship payments

119.—(1) Subject to paragraphs (2) and (3), hardship payments are recoverable in accordance with section 71ZH of the Social Security Administration Act 1992. **2.404**

[1(2) Paragraph (1) does not apply in relation to any assessment period in which—

(a) the single claimant, or each joint claimant, falls within section 19 of the Act by virtue of regulation 90 (claimants subject to no work-related requirements – the earnings threshold);

(b) where regulation 90 applies to one of the joint claimants only, the joint claimants' combined monthly earnings are equal to or exceed the amount of the individual threshold; or

(c) where regulation 90 does not apply to the single claimant or to either of the joint claimants, that claimant or the joint claimants' combined monthly earnings are equal to or exceed the amount that a person of the same age as the claimant, or the youngest of the joint claimants, would be paid at the hourly rate specified in regulation 4 or regulation 4A(1)(a) to (c) of the National Minimum Wage Regulations for 16 hours per week, converted to a monthly amount by multiplying by 52 and dividing by 12,

(3) Paragraph (1) ceases to apply where, since the last day on which the claimant's or the joint claimants' award was subject to a reduction under section 26 or 27 of the Act—

(a) the single claimant, or each joint claimant, has fallen within section 19 of the Act by virtue of regulation 90 (claimants subject to no work-related requirements – the earnings threshold);

(b) where regulation 90 applied to one of the joint claimants only, the joint claimants' have had combined monthly earnings that are equal to or exceed the amount of the individual threshold; or

(c) where regulation 90 did not apply to the single claimant or to either of the joint claimants, that claimant or the joint claimants' have had combined monthly earnings that are equal to or exceed the amount that a person of the same age as the claimant, or the youngest of the joint claimants, would be paid at the hourly rate specified in regulation 4 or regulation 4A(1)(a) to (c) of the National Minimum Wage Regulations for 16 hours per week, converted to a monthly amount by multiplying by 52 and dividing by 12,

for a period of, or more than one period where the total of those periods amounts to, at least 6 months.]

AMENDMENT

1. Social Security (Jobseeker's Allowance, Employment and Support Allowance and Universal Credit) (Amendment) Regulations 2016 (SI 2016/678) reg.5(11) (July 25, 2016).

DEFINITIONS

"the Act"—see reg.2.
"claimant"—see WRA 2012 s.40.
"individual threshold"—see regs 2 and 90(2).
"joint claimants"—see WRA 2012 s.40.
"National Minimum Wage Regulations"—see reg.2
"single claimant"—see WRA 2012 s.40.

GENERAL NOTE

2.405 The basic rule is that any hardship payment is recoverable from the person to whom it was paid (Administration Act, s.71ZH(2)(a)), by the means provided in ss.71ZC to 71ZF. A payment made to one of joint claimants is treated as also paid to the other (s.71ZH(4)). The amount is not recoverable during any assessment period in which the claimant or both joint claimants are subject to no work-related requirements by reason of having earnings of at least the individual threshold(s) under reg.90 (para.(2)(a) and (b)). The same applies under the new provision in para.(2)(c) to claimants who do not have an individual threshold as defined in reg.90(2) because they would not otherwise have been subject to any work-related requirement who meet the test of earnings at the rate of 16 times the national minimum wage hourly rate. It appears from the contrast with the terms of para.(3) that once the reason for freedom from any work-related requirements ceases, the payment becomes recoverable again. Under para.(3) recoverability ceases if since the end of the sanction period the claimant or both joint claimants have had earnings of at least the para.(2) level for a period or periods amounting to six months.

The maximum rate of recovery from payments of universal credit is 40% of the standard allowance (Social Security (Overpayments and Recovery) Regulations 2013 (Vol.III of this series) reg.11(2)(a) and (3)(b)). The report of November 6, 2018 by the House of Commons Work and Pensions Committee on *Benefit Sanctions* (HC 995 2017-19), para.132, recommended that the rate should be no higher than what was affordable by the claimant, with a default rate of 5% of the standard allowance. The DWP (House of Commons Work and Pensions Committee, *Benefit Sanctions: Government Response* (HC 1949 2017-19, February 11, 2019, paras 90-93) rejected the 5% suggestion as unacceptably diluting the effect of sanctions. It stated that it had announced in November 2018 that to assist those in debt it had reduced the normal maximum rate of deduction to 30% of the standard allowance. Where other higher priority deductions are in place there is a corresponding adjustment to the rate of recovery of hardship payments.

Regulation 25(2)

SCHEDULE 1

MEANING OF PAYMENTS IN RESPECT OF ACCOMMODATION

General

Interpretation

1. In this Schedule— 2.406

"approved premises" means premises approved by the Secretary of State under section 13 of the Offender Management Act 2007 (which contains provision for the approval etc. of premises providing accommodation for persons granted bail in criminal proceedings or for or in connection with the supervision or rehabilitation of persons convicted of offences);

"care home"—

(a) in England [4 ...], means a care home within the meaning of section 3 of the Care Standards Act 2000;

[(aa) in Wales, means a place at which a care home service within the meaning of Part 1 of the Regulation and Inspection of Social Care (Wales) Act 2016 is provided wholly or mainly to persons aged 18 or over;]

(b) in Scotland, means a care home service within the meaning of paragraph 2 of Schedule 12 to the Public Services Reform (Scotland) Act 2010; and

(c) in [4 any of the above cases], includes an independent hospital;

[1 "exempt accommodation" has the meaning given in paragraph 4(10) of Schedule 3 to the Housing Benefit and Council Tax Benefit (Consequential Provisions) Regulations 2006;]

"housing association" has the meaning given by section 1(1) of the Housing Associations Act 1985;

"independent hospital"—

(a) in England, means a hospital as defined by section 275 of the National Health Service Act 2006 that is not a health service hospital as defined by that section;

(b) in Wales, has the meaning assigned to it by section 2 of the Care Standards Act 2000;

(c) in Scotland, means an independent health care service as defined in section 10F(1)(a) and (b) of the National Health Service (Scotland) Act 1978;

"registered charity" means a charity entered in the register of charities maintained under Part 4 of the Charities Act 2011 or a body entered on the register of charities maintained under the Charities and Trustee Investment (Scotland) Act 2005;

"shared ownership tenancy" has the meaning given in regulation 26(6);

"tent" means a moveable structure that is designed or adapted (solely or mainly) for the purpose of sleeping in a place for any period and that is not a caravan, a mobile home or a houseboat;

[1 . . .]

"voluntary organisation" means a body (other than a public or local authority) whose activities are carried on otherwise than for profit.

Rent payments

Rent payments

2. "Rent payments" are such of the following as are not excluded by paragraph 3— 2.407

(a) payments of rent;

(b) payments for a licence or other permission to occupy accommodation;

(c) mooring charges payable for a houseboat;

(d) in relation to accommodation which is a caravan or mobile home, payments in respect of the site on which the accommodation stands;

(e) contributions by residents towards maintaining almshouses (and essential services in them) provided by a housing association which is—

(i) a registered charity, or

(ii) an exempt charity within Schedule 3 to the Charities Act 2011.

Payments excluded from being rent payments

3. The following are excluded from being "rent payments"— 2.408

(a) payments of ground rent;

(b) payments in respect of a tent or the site on which a tent stands;

(c) payments in respect of approved premises;
(d) payments in respect of a care home;
(e) [1 . . .]
(f) payments which are owner-occupier payments [2 within the meaning of Schedule 1 of the Loans for Mortgage Regulations 2017];
(g) payments which are service charge payments within the meaning of paragraph 7.
[1 (h) payments in respect of accommodation specified in paragraph 3A] [3;
(i) payments in respect of accommodation specified in paragraph 3B.]

[1 Specified accommodation

2.409 **3A.**—(1) The accommodation referred to in paragraph 3(h) is accommodation to which one or more of the following sub-paragraphs applies.

(2) This sub-paragraph applies to accommodation which is exempt accommodation.

(3) This sub-paragraph applies to accommodation—
(a) which is provided by a relevant body;
(b) into which the claimant has been admitted in order to meet a need for care, support or supervision; and
(c) where the claimant receives care, support or supervision.

(4) This sub-paragraph applies to accommodation which—
(a) is provided by a local authority or a relevant body to the claimant because the claimant has left the home as a result of domestic violence; and
(b) consists of a building, or part of a building, which is used wholly or mainly for the non-permanent accommodation of persons who have left their homes as a result of domestic violence.

(5) This sub-paragraph applies to accommodation—
(a) which would be a hostel within the meaning of paragraph 29(10) (renters excepted form shared accommodation) of Schedule 4 (housing costs element for renters) but for it being owned or managed by a local authority; and
(b) where the claimant receives care, support or supervision.

(6) In this paragraph—
"domestic violence" has the meaning given in regulation 98 (victims of domestic violence);
"relevant body" means a—
(a) council for a county in England for each part of which there is a district council;
(b) housing association;
(c) registered charity; or
(d) voluntary organisation].

[1 Temporary Accommodation

2.410 **3B.**—(1) The accommodation referred to in paragraph (3)(i) is accommodation which falls within Case 1 or Case 2.

(2) Case 1 is where—
(a) rent payments are payable to a local authority;
(b) the local authority makes the accommodation available to the renter—
(i) to discharge any of the local authority's functions under Part II of the Housing (Scotland) Act 1987, Part VII of the Housing Act 1996 or Part 2 of the Housing (Wales) Act 2014, or
(ii) to prevent the person being or becoming homeless within the meaning of Part II of the Housing (Scotland) Act 1987, Part VII of the Housing Act 1996 or Part 2 of the Housing (Wales) Act 2014; and
(c) the accommodation is not exempt accommodation.

(3) Case 2 is where—
(a) rent payments are payable to a provider of social housing other than a local authority;
(b) that provider makes the accommodation available to the renter in pursuance of arrangements made with it by a local authority—
(i) to discharge any of the local authority's functions under Part II of the Housing (Scotland) Act 1987, Part VII of the Housing Act 1996 or Part 2 of the Housing (Wales) Act 2014, or
(ii) to prevent the person being or becoming homeless within the meaning of Part II of the Housing (Scotland) Act 1987, Part VII of the Housing Act 1996 or Part 2 of the Housing (Wales) Act 2014; and
(c) the accommodation is not exempt accommodation.

(4) Sub-paragraph (1) applies irrespective of whether the renter is also liable to make service charge payments.

(5) In sub-paragraph (3), "provider of social housing" has the meaning given in paragraph 2 of Schedule 4.]

Owner-occupier payments

Owner-occupier payments

4.—[2 . . .] 2.411

Meaning of "loan interest payments"

5. [2 . . .] 2.412

Meaning of "alternative finance payments"

6.—[2 . . .] 2.413

Service charge payments

Service charge payments

7.—(1) "Service charge payments" are payments which— 2.414

(a) fall within sub-paragraph (2);

(b) are not excluded by sub-paragraph (3); and

(c) in any case to which paragraph 8 applies, meet all of the conditions set out in that paragraph.

(2) The payments falling within this sub-paragraph are payments of amounts which are, in whole or in part—

(a) payments of, or towards, the costs of or charges for providing services or facilities for the use or benefit of persons occupying accommodation; or

(b) fairly attributable to the costs of or charges for providing such services or facilities connected with accommodation as are available for the use or benefit of persons occupying accommodation.

(3) Payments are excluded by this sub-paragraph where—

(a) [2 a qualifying loan within the meaning of regulation 2 of the Loans for Mortgage Interest Regulations 2017] was taken out for the purposes of making the payments; or

(b) the services or facilities to which the payments relate are provided for the use or benefit of any person occupying—

(i) a tent,

(ii) approved premises,

(iii) a care home, or

(iv) exempt accommodation.

(4) It is irrelevant for the purposes of sub-paragraph (2)—

(a) whether or not the payments are separately identified as relating to the costs or charges referred to in sub-paragraph (2);

(b) whether they are made in addition to or as part of any other payment (including a payment that would otherwise be regarded as a rent payment within the meaning of paragraph 2);

(c) whether they are made under the same or a different agreement as that under which the accommodation is occupied.

Additional conditions: social rented sector renters and owner-occupiers

8.—(1) This paragraph applies for the purposes of calculating the amount of housing costs element to be included in a claimant's award of universal credit but only as regards calculations made under— 2.415

(a) Part 5 of Schedule 4 (social rented sector [3 ...]); or

(b) Schedule 5 (housing costs element for owner-occupiers).

(2) The following are the conditions referred to in paragraph 7(1)(c).

(3) The first condition is that making the payments is a condition on which the right to occupy the accommodation depends.

(4) The second condition is that the payments fall within one or more of the following categories:

Category A—Payments to maintain the general standard of the accommodation

Payments within this category are for—

(a) the external cleaning of windows, but only in relation to upper floors of a multi-storey building;

(b) other internal or external maintenance or repair of the accommodation, but only where the payments are separately identifiable as relating to such maintenance or repair and payable by—
   (i) a claimant who occupies accommodation under a shared ownership tenancy, or
   (ii) a claimant in whose case any amount of housing costs element to be included in their award in respect of those payments would fall to be calculated under Schedule 5.

Category B—Payments for the general upkeep of areas of communal use

Payments within this category are for ongoing maintenance or cleaning of, and the supply of water, fuel or any other commodity relating to the common use of, internal or external areas, including areas for reasonable facilities (such as laundry rooms or children's play areas).

Category C—Payments in respect of basic communal services

Payments within this category are for provision, ongoing maintenance, cleaning or repair in connection with basic services generally available to all persons living in the accommodation (such as refuse collection, communal lifts, secure building access or wireless or television aerials to receive a service free of charge).

Category D—Accommodation-specific charges

Payments within this category are specific to the particular accommodation occupied by a claimant but are limited to payments for the use of essential items contained in it (such as furniture or domestic appliances).

(5) The third condition is that the costs and charges to which the payments relate are of a reasonable amount and relate to services or facilities of such description as it is reasonable to provide.

(6) The fourth condition is that the payments are none of the following—
(a) payments to the extent that they relate to the costs of or charges for providing services or facilities in respect of which payments out of public funds might otherwise be made (irrespective of whether the claimant has any entitlement to payments so made);
(b) payments in connection with the use of an asset which result in the transfer of the asset or any interest in it;
(c) payments to the extent that they relate to the costs of or charges for providing food, medical services or personal services (including personal care) of any description.

(7) Payments that are not service charge payments within the meaning of paragraph 7 by reason only that they fail to meet any of the conditions set out in sub-paragraphs (3) to (6) are nevertheless to be treated as if they were such service charge payments for the purposes of paragraphs 3(g) and 4(2).

AMENDMENTS

1. Housing Benefit and Universal Credit (Supported Accommodation) (Amendment) Regulations 2014 (SI 2014/771) reg.2(2) (November 3, 2014).

2. Loans for Mortgage Interest Regulations 2017 (SI 2017/725) reg.18 and Sch.5, para.5(e) (April 6, 2018).

3. Universal Credit (Miscellaneous Amendments, Saving and Transitional Provision) Regulations 2018 (SI 2018/65) reg.3(12) (April 11, 2018).

4. Social Security and Child Support (Regulation and Inspection of Social Care (Wales) Act 2016) (Consequential Provision) Regulations 2018 (SI 2018/228) reg.14(1) and (2) (April 2, 2018).

DEFINITION

"claimant"—see WRA 2012 s.40.

GENERAL NOTE

In order to be eligible for a housing costs element, the claimant (or claimants) must meet the three basic conditions in reg.25(2) to (4): the payment condition, the liability condition, and the occupation condition. This Schedule is concerned with the payment condition. **2.416**

Under reg.25(2) there are two types of payments that can be met: rent payments and service charge payments.

Paragraphs 2, 3 and 3A

Paragraph 2 lists the payments that are eligible as rent payments and para.3 the payments that are not eligible. Note that the amount of the housing costs element may be restricted under Sch.4 if the rent is higher than allowed (private tenants and temporary accommodation) or the accommodation is larger than allowed (social rented sector). **2.417**

The payments listed in para.2 include most of the payments that can be met by housing benefit but not all, e.g. payments by way of mesne profits (or, in Scotland, violent profits) are not included.

Under para.3 payments in respect of ground rent and in respect of a tent and the site on which it stands are excluded (para.3(a) and (b)). These qualify as "other housing costs" for income support, old style JSA and old style ESA but there seems to be no provision for such payments under universal credit.

Payments by Crown tenants no longer seem to be excluded (as they are for housing benefit).

Paragraph 3(h), together with para.3A, inserted with effect from November 3, 2014, excludes payments in respect of "specified accommodation". There are four categories of "specified accommodation", the first of which, exempt accommodation, was previously excluded under para. 3(e) (now omitted).

The four categories are: (i) "exempt accommodation" (as defined in para.1–this is accommodation which is a "resettlement place" or accommodation provided by a non-metropolitan county council, a housing association, a registered charity or a voluntary organisation, where care, support or supervision is provided to the claimant by that body or a person acting on its behalf); (ii) accommodation provided by a "relevant body" (as defined in para. 3A(6)) into which the claimant has been admitted because of a need for care, support or supervision, which they receive; (iii) temporary accommodation provided by a local authority or a relevant body for people who have left home because of domestic violence, e.g., a women's refuge (note the definition of "domestic violence" in reg. 98(4), which is quite wide); and (iv) hostels owned or managed by a local authority where the claimant receives care, support or supervision. Note that in the case of categories (ii) and (iv) the care, support or supervision does not have to be provided by the relevant body or on its behalf, or by the local authority or on its behalf, as it does in the case of exempt accommodation.

Claimants living in specified accommodation are eligible for housing benefit. Corresponding amendments have been made to the Housing Benefit Regulations 2006 (SI 2006/213), the effect of which is to exclude housing benefit paid to claimants living in specified accommodation from the HB benefit cap for housing benefit purposes (see regs 75C(2)(a) and 75H of those Regulations–the exemption previously only applied to claimants living in exempt accommodation). Housing benefit is not included in the list of welfare benefits in reg. 79(4) to which the universal credit benefit cap applies.

Paragraphs 7 and 8

Service charge payments are eligible payments if they fall within para.7(2) and are not excluded under para.7(3). They do not have to be separately identified, nor does it matter if they are paid in addition to, or as part of, any other payment (including a rent payment within the meaning of para.2), or if they are paid under the same or a different agreement than that under which the accommodation is occupied (para.7(4)). **2.418**

Note the additional conditions in para.8 that have to be met in the case of service charge payments by social sector renters (other those in temporary accommodation). This does not apply to private renters.

According to para.F2074 ADM, where service charges are for the provision of an eligible service, the relevant proportion of staffing costs of a person (e.g. a concierge, groundskeeper or caretaker) employed to provide the eligible service can be included, as can the relevant proportion of the costs of managing and administering eligible services, if the claimant is liable for these costs.

Regulation 25(3)

SCHEDULE 2

CLAIMANT TREATED AS LIABLE OR NOT LIABLE TO MAKE PAYMENTS

PART I

TREATED AS LIABLE TO MAKE PAYMENTS

Certain other persons liable to make payments

2.419 **1.**—(1) A claimant is to be treated as liable to make payments where the person who is liable to make the payments is—

(a) any child or qualifying young person for whom the claimant (or if the claimant is a member of a couple, either member) is responsible; or

(b) in the case of a claimant who is a member of a couple claiming as a single person, the other member of the couple.

(2) Sub-paragraph (1)(b) does not apply to a person who is claiming as a single person by virtue of regulation 3(4).

Failure to pay by the person who is liable

2.420 **2.**—(1) A claimant is to be treated as liable to make payments where all of the conditions specified in sub-paragraph (2) are met.

(2) These are the conditions—

(a) the person who is liable to make the payments is not doing so;

(b) the claimant has to make the payments in order to continue occupation of the accommodation;

(c) the claimant's circumstances are such that it would be unreasonable to expect them to make other arrangements;

(d) it is otherwise reasonable in all the circumstances to treat the claimant as liable to make the payments.

(3) In determining what is reasonable for the purposes of sub-paragraph (2)(d) in the case of owner-occupier payments, regard may be had to the fact that continuing to make the payments may benefit the person with the liability to make the payments.

Payments waived in return for repair work

2.421 **3.** A claimant is to be treated as liable to make payments where—

(a) the liability to make payments is waived by the person ("P") to whom the liability is owed; and

(b) the waiver of that liability is by way of reasonable compensation for reasonable repair or re-decoration works carried out by the claimant to the accommodation which P would otherwise have carried out or been required to carry out.

Rent free periods

2.422 **4.**—(1) Where the arrangements under which the claimant occupies the accommodation provide for rent free periods, the claimant is to be treated as liable to make rent payments and service charge payments in respect of accommodation for the whole of any rent free period.

(2) In paragraph (1), "rent free period" has the meaning given in paragraph 7(4) of Schedule 4.

PART 2

TREATED AS NOT LIABLE TO MAKE PAYMENTS

Liability to make rent and other payments to close relative

5.—(1) A claimant is to be treated as not liable to make rent payments where the liability to make them is owed to a person who lives in the accommodation and who is— 2.423

(a) if the claimant is a member of a couple, the other member; or

(b) a child or qualifying young person for whom—

(i) the claimant is responsible, or

(ii) if the claimant is a member of a couple, the other member is responsible; or

(c) a close relative of—

(i) the claimant, or

(ii) if the claimant is a member of a couple, the other member, or

(iii) any child or qualifying young person who falls within paragraph (b).

(2) A claimant who is treated under sub-paragraph (1) as not liable to make rent payments to any person is also to be treated as not liable to make service charge payments where the liability to make the service charge payments is to the same person.

Liability to make rent and other payments to company

6.—(1) A claimant is to be treated as not liable to make rent payments where the liability to make them is owed to a company and the owners or directors of the company include— 2.424

(a) the claimant;

(b) if the claimant is a member of a couple, the other member;

(c) a qualifying young person for whom a person who falls within paragraph (a) or (b) is responsible; or

(d) a close relative of any of the above who lives in the accommodation with the claimant.

(2) A claimant who is treated under sub-paragraph (1) as not liable to make rent payments to the company is also to be treated as not liable to make service charge payments where the liability to make the service charge payments is to—

(a) the same company; or

(b) another company of which the owners or directors include any of the persons listed in sub-paragraph (1)(a) to (d).

(3) In this paragraph, "owner", in relation to a company ("C"), means a person ("A") who has a material interest in C.

(4) For the purposes of sub-paragraph (3), A has a material interest in C if A—

(a) holds at least 10% of the shares in C; or

(b) is able to exercise a significant influence over the management of C by virtue of A's shareholding in C; or

(c) holds at least 10% of the shares in a parent undertaking ("P") of C; or

(d) is able to exercise a significant influence over the management of P by virtue of A's shareholding in P; or

(e) is entitled to exercise, or control the exercise of, voting power in C which, if it consists of voting rights, constitutes at least 10% of the voting rights in C; or

(f) is able to exercise a significant influence over the management of C by virtue of A's entitlement to exercise, or control the exercise of, voting rights in C; or

(g) is entitled to exercise, or control the exercise of, voting power in P which, if it consists of voting rights, constitutes at least 10% of the voting rights in P; or

(h) is able to exercise a significant influence over the management of P by virtue of A's entitlement to exercise, or control the exercise of, voting rights in P.

(5) For the purposes of sub-paragraph (4), references to "A" are to—

(a) the person; or

(b) any of the person's associates; or

(c) the person and any of the person's associates taken together.

(6) For the purposes of sub-paragraph (5), "associate", in relation to a person ("A") holding shares in an undertaking ("X") or entitled to exercise or control the exercise of voting power in relation to another undertaking ("Y"), means—

(a) the spouse or civil partner of A;

(b) a child or step-child of A (if under 18);

(c) the trustee of any settlement under which A has a life interest in possession (in Scotland a life interest);

(d) an undertaking of which A is a director;

(e) a person who is an employee or partner of A;

(f) if A has with any other person an agreement or arrangement with respect to the acquisition, holding or disposal of shares or other interests in X or Y, that other person;

(g) if A has with any other person an agreement or arrangement under which they undertake to act together in exercising their voting power in relation to X or Y, that other person.

(7) In sub-paragraph (6)(c), "settlement" means any disposition or arrangement under which property is held on trust (or subject to comparable obligations).

(8) For the purposes of this paragraph—

"parent undertaking" has the same meaning as in the Financial Services and Markets Act 2000 (see section 420 of that Act);

"shares" means—

(a) in relation to an undertaking with shares, allotted shares (within the meaning of Part 17 of the Companies Act 2006);

(b) in relation to an undertaking with capital but no share capital, rights to share in the capital of the body;

(c) in relation to an undertaking without capital, interests—

(i) conferring any right to share in the profits, or liability to contribute to the losses, of the body, or

(ii) giving rise to an obligation to contribute to the debts or expenses of the undertaking in the event of a winding up;

"voting power", in relation to an undertaking which does not have general meetings at which matters are decided by the exercise of voting rights, means the rights under the constitution of the undertaking to direct the overall policy of the undertaking or alter the terms of its constitution.

Liability to make rent and other payments to a trust

2.425 **7.**—(1) A claimant is to be treated as not liable to make rent payments where the liability to make them is owed to a trustee of a trust and the trustees or beneficiaries of the trust include—

(a) the claimant;

(b) if the claimant is a member of a couple, the other member;

(c) a child or qualifying young person for whom a person who falls within paragraph (a) or (b) is responsible; or

(d) a close relative of any of the above who lives in the accommodation with the claimant.

(2) A claimant who is treated under sub-paragraph (1) as not liable to make rent payments to the trustee of a trust is also to be treated as not liable to make service charge payments where the liability to make the service charge payments is to—

(a) a trustee of the same trust; or

(b) a trustee of another trust of which the trustees or beneficiaries include any of the persons listed in sub-paragraph (1)(a) to (d).

Liability to make owner-occupier and other payments to member of same household

2.426 **8.**—(1) A claimant is to be treated as not liable to make owner-occupier payments where the liability to make the payments is owed to a person who lives in the claimant's household.

(2) A claimant who is treated under sub-paragraph (1) as not liable to make owner-occupier payments to any person is also to be treated as not liable to make service charge payments where the liability to make the service charge payments is to the same person.

(3) A claimant is to be treated as not liable to make service charge payments where—

(a) there is no liability to make rent payments or owner-occupier payments; but

(b) the liability to make service charge payments is to a person who lives in the claimant's household.

Arrears of payments

2.427 **9.**—(1) A claimant is to be treated as not liable to make payments in respect of any amount which—

(a) represents an increase in the sum that would be otherwise payable; and

(b) is the result of—

(i) outstanding arrears of any payment or charge in respect of the accommodation,

(ii) outstanding arrears of any payment or charge in respect of other accommodation, previously occupied by the claimant, or

(iii) any other unpaid liability to make a payment or charge.

(2) Sub-paragraph (1) does not apply if the claimant is treated as not liable to make the payments under any of the preceding provisions of this Part of this Schedule.

Contrived liability

10.—(1) A claimant is to be treated as not liable to make payments where the Secretary of State is satisfied that the liability to make the payments was contrived in order to secure the inclusion of the housing costs element in an award of universal credit or to increase the amount of that element. 2.428

(2) Sub-paragraph (1) does not apply if the claimant is treated as not liable to make the payments under any of the preceding provisions of this Part of this Schedule.

DEFINITIONS

"child"—see WRA 2012 s.40.
"claimant"—*ibid.*
"close relative"—see reg.2.
"couple"—see WRA 2012 ss.39 and 40.
"partner"—see reg.2.
"qualifying young person"—see WRA 2012 ss.40 and 10(5) and regs 2 and 5.
"rent free period"—see Sch.4, para.7(4).
"single person"—see WRA 2012 ss.40 and 1(2)(a).

GENERAL NOTE

In order to be eligible for a housing costs element, the claimant (or claimants) must meet the three basic conditions in reg.25(2) to (4): the payment condition, the liability condition, and the occupation condition. This Schedule is concerned with the liability condition. 2.429

Note that the Loans for Mortgage Interest Regulations 2017 (SI 2017/725) mean that from April 6, 2018, UC no longer enables a claimant to meet the liability condition through liability for "owner-occupier payments". However, Sch.2 has not yet been amended to remove references to that category.

Under reg.25(3) the claimant (or either joint claimant) must be liable to make rent payments or service charge payments on a commercial basis, or be treated as liable to make them, and must not be treated as not liable to make them. "Liable" is not defined but presumably requires a legal (as opposed to a moral) liability (see *R v Rugby BC HBRB ex parte Harrison* [1996] 28 HLR 36 and the discussion on the meaning of "liability" in the notes to reg. 8 of the Housing Benefit Regulations in *CPAG's Housing Benefit and Council Tax Reduction Legislation*; it is also the view taken in para.F2081 ADM).

For the meaning of "on a commercial basis", see the notes to "*Board and lodging accommodation*" in reg.2 of the Income Support Regulations in Vol.V of this series and the notes to reg.9(1)(a) of the Housing Benefit Regulations in *CPAG's Housing Benefit and Council Tax Reduction Legislation.*

Paragraphs 1–4

Under para.1 a claimant is treated as liable to make payments if the person who is liable is (i) a child or qualifying young person for whom the claimant (or the other member of the couple in the case of a couple) is responsible (sub-para.(1)(a)); or (ii) the other member of the couple, if the claimant is a member of a couple but claiming as a single person (see reg.3(3) for the circumstances in which this can apply) (sub-para.(1)(b)); note that sub-para.(1)(b) does not apply in the case of polygamous marriages (sub-para.(2)). 2.430

A claimant is also treated as liable to make payments if the payments have been waived by the person to whom they were due (e.g. a landlord) as reasonable compensation for the claimant carrying out reasonable repair or redecoration works which the person would otherwise have had to carry out (para.3), or, in the case of rent and service charge payments, during rent free periods (para.4).

Paragraph 2 applies where the person who is liable to make the payments is not doing so. The claimant will be treated as liable if the claimant has to make the payments in order to continue to occupy the accommodation, it would be unreasonable to expect the claimant to make other arrangements and it is reasonable to treat the claimant as liable. These conditions are similar to those in, e.g., reg.8(1)(c) of the Housing Benefit Regulations and para.2(1)(b) of Sch.3 to the Income Support Regulations (see the notes to para.2 of Sch.3 in Vol.V of this series), except for the added condition that it would be unreasonable to expect the claimant to make other arrangements.

Paragraphs 5–10

2.431 These paragraphs deal with when the claimant will be treated as not liable to make payments in respect of their home. Note that some of the exclusions only apply to some types of eligible payments. The situations in which this rule applies to rent payments are reduced compared with housing benefit (see reg.9 of the Housing Benefit Regulations). Note that the "on a commercial basis" requirement applies to any liability to make payments in respect of accommodation under universal credit (see reg.25(3)(a)(i)).

Paragraphs 5–7

2.432 A claimant is treated as not liable to make rent payments and service charges payments if the liability is to the following:

- Someone who also lives in the accommodation, and who is (i) the other member of the couple if the claimant is a member of a couple; (ii) a child or qualifying young person for whom the claimant or other member of the couple is responsible (see reg.4); or (iii) a close relative (defined in reg.2) of the claimant, the other member of the couple or the child or qualifying person (para.5).

  "Lives in the accommodation" probably means the same as "resides in the dwelling" in reg.9(1)(b) of the Housing Benefit Regulations (see the notes to reg.9(1)(b) in *CPAG's Housing Benefit and Council Tax Reduction Legislation*).

- A company, and the owners or directors of the company include (i) the claimant; (ii) the other member of the couple if the claimant is a member of a couple; (iii) a qualifying young person for whom the claimant or other member of the couple is responsible; or (iv) a close relative of the claimant, other member of the couple or qualifying young person (in the case of a close relative, they must live in the accommodation with the claimant) (para.6(1) and (2)).

  Note that the claimant will also be treated as not liable to pay the service charges if the liability for them is to another company whose owners or directors include any of the people listed in para.6(1) (para.6(2)(b)).

  An owner of a company for the purposes of para.6 is a person who has a "material interest" in it (para.6(3)). See para.6(4)–(8) for the detail.

- A trustee of a trust, and the trustees or beneficiaries of the trust include (i) the claimant; (ii) the other member of the couple if the claimant is a member of a couple; (iii) a child or qualifying young person for whom the claimant or other member of the couple is responsible; or (iv) a close relative of the claimant, other member of the couple or child or qualifying young person (in the case of a close relative, they must live in the accommodation with the claimant) (para.7(1) and (2)).

  Note that the claimant will also be treated as not liable to pay the service charges if the liability for them is to a trustee of another trust whose trustees or beneficiaries include any of the people listed in para.7(1) (para.7(2)(b)).

  See the notes to reg.9(1)(e) and (f) of the Housing Benefit Regulations in *CPAG's Housing Benefit and Council Tax Reduction Legislation*.

Paragraph 8

Paragraph 8(1) and (2) are concerned with owner-occupier payments and service charges payments. They treat a claimant as not liable to make owner-occupier payments and service charges payments if the liability is to a person who is lives in the claimant's household. Clearly this is different from "lives in the accommodation" under paras 5 to 8. On the meaning of "household", see the notes to "*couple*" (under the heading "*Spouses and civil partners*") in reg.2 of the Income Support Regulations in Vol.V of this series. **2.433**

Under para.8(3) a claimant is treated as not liable to make service charges payments if they are not liable for rent payments or owner-occupier payments and the liability for the service charges is to someone who is a member of the claimant's household.

Paragraph 9

This paragraph only applies if paras 5–8 do not apply (sub-para.(2)). It applies to all types of eligible payments. **2.434**

It treats a claimant as not liable to pay any increase in the amount that they would otherwise be liable to pay, if that increase is the result of outstanding arrears of any payment or charge in respect of their current or previous accommodation. This also applies in respect of "any other unpaid liability to make a payment or charge" (see sub-para.(1)(b)(iii)) but only if that results in an increase in the amount the claimant is liable to pay.

An example of a payment that would come within para.9 is where a tenant has agreed to pay off arrears of rent by paying an increased amount of rent each month. They will be treated under para.9 as not liable to pay the extra amount above the rent that was originally agreed.

Paragraph 10

This paragraph only applies if paras 5–8 do not apply (sub-para.(2)). It applies to all types of eligible payments. **2.435**

It contains a similar rule to the contrived tenancy provision in housing benefit (see reg.9(1)(l) of the Housing Benefit Regulations). See the notes to reg.9(1)(l) in *CPAG's Housing Benefit and Council Tax Reduction Legislation*. But note that reg.9(1)(l) refers to the liability being "created to take advantage of the housing benefit scheme", whereas the test under para.10 is that the liability "was contrived in order to secure the inclusion of the housing costs element". There may be a distinction between "created" and "contrived".

Regulation 25(4)

SCHEDULE 3

CLAIMANT TREATED AS OCCUPYING OR NOT OCCUPYING ACCOMMODATION

PART I

TREATED AS OCCUPYING ACCOMMODATION

The occupation condition: the general rule

1.—(1) The general rule is that a claimant is to be treated as occupying as their home the accommodation which the claimant normally occupies as their home. **2.436**

(2) Subject to the following provisions of this Part, no claimant is to be treated as occupying accommodation which comprises more than one dwelling.

(3) Where none of those provisions applies and the claimant occupies more than one dwelling, regard is to be had to all the circumstances in determining which dwelling the claimant normally occupies as their home, including (among other things) any persons with whom the claimant occupies each dwelling.

(4) "Dwelling"—

(a) in England and Wales, means a dwelling within the meaning of Part 1 of the Local Government Finance Act 1992;

(b) in Scotland, means a dwelling within the meaning of Part 2 of that Act.

Croft land included in accommodation

2.437 **2.**—(1) Where accommodation which a claimant normally occupies as their home is situated on or pertains to a croft, croft land used for the purposes of the accommodation is to be treated as included in the accommodation.

(2) "Croft" means a croft within the meaning of section 3(1) of the Crofters (Scotland) Act 1993.

Claimant living in other accommodation during essential repairs

2.438 **3.**—(1) Where a claimant—

(a) is required to move into accommodation ("the other accommodation") on account of essential repairs being carried out to the accommodation the claimant normally occupies as their home;

(b) intends to return to the accommodation which is under repair; and

(c) meets the payment condition and the liability condition in respect of either the other accommodation or the accommodation which they normally occupy as their home (but not both),

the claimant is to be treated as normally occupying as their home the accommodation in respect of which those conditions are met.

(2) A claimant is subject to the general rule in paragraph 1 where—

(a) sub-paragraph (1)(a) and (b) apply to the claimant; but

(b) the claimant meets the payment condition and the liability condition in respect of both the other accommodation and the accommodation which they normally occupy as their home.

Claimant housed in two dwellings by provider of social housing

2.439 **4.**—(1) In sub-paragraph (2), "relevant claimant" means a claimant who meets all of the following conditions—

(a) the first condition is that the claimant has been housed in two dwellings ("accommodation A" and "accommodation B") by a provider of social housing on account of the number of children and qualifying young persons living with the claimant;

(b) the second condition is that the claimant normally occupies both accommodation A and accommodation B with children or qualifying young persons for whom the claimant is responsible;

(c) the third condition is that the claimant meets the payment condition and the liability condition in respect of both accommodation A and accommodation B (and for these purposes it is irrelevant whether the claimant's liability is to the same or a different person).

(2) In the case of a relevant claimant, both accommodation A and accommodation B are to be treated as the single accommodation which the relevant claimant normally occupies as their home.

(3) In sub-paragraph (1), "provider of social housing" has the meaning given in paragraph 2 of Schedule 4.

Moving home: adaptations to new home for disabled person

2.440 **5.**—(1) Sub-paragraph (2) applies where—

(a) the claimant has moved into accommodation ("the new accommodation") and, immediately before the move, met the payment condition and liability condition in respect of the new accommodation; and

(b) there was a delay in moving in that was necessary to enable the new accommodation to be adapted to meet the disablement needs of a person specified in sub-paragraph (3).

(2) The claimant is to be treated as occupying both the new accommodation and the accommodation from which the move was made ("the old accommodation") if—

(a) immediately before the move, the claimant was entitled to the inclusion of the housing costs element in an award of universal credit in respect of the old accommodation; and

(b) the delay in moving into the new accommodation was reasonable.

(3) A person is specified in this sub-paragraph if the person is—

(a) a claimant or any child or qualifying young person for whom a claimant is responsible; and

(b) in receipt of—

(i) the care component of disability living allowance at the middle or highest rate, [1 (ia) the care component of child disability payment at the middle or highest rate in accordance with regulation 11(5) of the DACYP Regulations,]

(ii) attendance allowance, [2 . . .]

(iii) the daily living component of personal independence payment [2, or]

[2 (iv) the daily living component of adult disability payment at the standard or enhanced rate.]

(4) No claimant may be treated as occupying both the old accommodation and the new accommodation under this paragraph for more than one month.

Claimant living in other accommodation because of reasonable fear of violence

6.—(1) This paragraph applies where— 2.441

(a) a claimant is occupying accommodation ("the other accommodation") other than the accommodation which they normally occupy as their home ("the home accommodation"); and

(b) it is unreasonable to expect the claimant to return to the home accommodation on account of the claimant's reasonable fear of violence in the home, or by a former partner, against the claimant or any child or qualifying young person for whom the claimant is responsible; but

(c) the claimant intends to return to the home accommodation.

(2) The claimant is to be treated as normally occupying both the home accommodation and the other accommodation as their home if—

(a) the claimant meets the payment condition and the liability condition in respect of both the home accommodation and other accommodation; and

(b) it is reasonable to include an amount in the housing costs element for the payments in respect of both the home accommodation and the other accommodation.

(3) Where the claimant meets the payment condition and the liability condition in respect of one accommodation only, the claimant is to be treated as normally occupying that accommodation as their home but only if it is reasonable to include an amount in the housing costs element for the payments in respect of that accommodation.

(4) No claimant may be treated as occupying both the home accommodation and the other accommodation under sub-paragraph (2) for more than 12 months.

Moving in delayed by adaptations to accommodation to meet disablement needs

7.—(1) The claimant is to be treated as having occupied accommodation before they moved into it where— 2.442

(a) the claimant has since moved in and, immediately before the move, met the payment condition and the liability condition in respect of the accommodation;

(b) there was a delay in moving in that was necessary to enable the accommodation to be adapted to meet the disablement needs of a relevant person; and

(c) it was reasonable to delay moving in.

(2) "Relevant person" means a person specified in paragraph 5(3).

(3) No claimant may be treated as occupying accommodation under this paragraph for more than one month.

Moving into accommodation following stay in hospital or care home

8.—(1) The claimant is to be treated as having occupied accommodation before they moved into it where— 2.443

(a) the claimant has since moved in and, immediately before the move, met the payment condition and the liability condition in respect of that accommodation; and

(b) the liability to make the payments arose while the claimant was a patient or accommodated in a care home (or, in the case of a joint claim, while both joint claimants were patients or were accommodated in a care home).

(2) No claimant may be treated as occupying the accommodation under this paragraph for more than one month.

(3) In this paragraph—

"care home" has the meaning given in paragraph 1 of Schedule 1;

"patient" means a person who is undergoing medical or other treatment as an in-patient in any hospital or similar institution.

PART 2

TREATED AS NOT OCCUPYING ACCOMMODATION

Periods of temporary absence exceeding 6 months

2.444 **9.**—(1) Subject to sub-paragraphs (2) and (3), a claimant is to be treated as no longer occupying accommodation from which they are temporarily absent where the absence exceeds, or is expected to exceed, 6 months.

(2) Sub-paragraph (1) does not apply to a claimant who falls within paragraph 3.

(3) Where a claimant who falls within paragraph 6 is temporarily absent from the accommodation which they normally occupy as their home, the claimant is to be treated as no longer occupying that accommodation where the absence exceeds, or is expected to exceed, 12 months.

AMENDMENTS

1. Social Security (Scotland) Act 2018 (Disability Assistance for Children and Young People) (Consequential Modifications) Order 2021 (SI 2021/786) Sch.11 para.7 (July 26, 2021).

2. Social Security (Disability Assistance for Working Age People) (Consequential Amendments) Order 2022 (SI 2022/177) art.13(7) (March 21, 2022).

DEFINITIONS

"adult disability payment"—see reg.2.
"attendance allowance"—*ibid.*
"care home"—see Sch.1, para.1.
"child"—see WRA 2012 s.40.
"child disability payment"—see reg.2.
"claimant"—see WRA 2012 s.40.
"the DACYP Regulations"—see reg.2.
"disability living allowance"—*ibid.*
"partner"—*ibid.*
"personal independence payment"—*ibid.*
"provider of social housing"—see Sch.4, para.2.
"qualifying young person"—see WRA 2012 ss.40 and 10(5) and regs 2 and 5.

GENERAL NOTE

2.445 In order to be eligible for a housing costs element, the claimant (or claimants) must meet the three basic conditions in reg.25(2) to (4): the payment condition, the liability condition, and the occupation condition. This Schedule is concerned with the occupation condition.

Under reg.25(4) the claimant (or each claimant in the case of joint claimants: s.40 WRA 2012) must be treated as occupying the accommodation as his/her home and not be treated as not occupying it. Croft land is included (see para.2).

Paragraph 1

2.446 This contains the general rule that the claimant must be normally occupying the accommodation as their home (sub-para(1)). On the meaning of "normally occupying", see the notes to "dwelling occupied as the home" in reg.2 of the Income Support Regulations in Vol.V of this series.

In addition, the claimant cannot usually be treated as occupying accommodation which comprises more than one dwelling (sub-para.(2)). However, there are exceptions to these rules (see below). Where these exceptions do not apply, and the claimant (or claimants: s.40 WRA 2012) occupies more than one dwelling, to decide which is the dwelling normally occupied as the home, all the circumstances, including the people who live with the claimant (or claimants) in each dwelling, are to be taken into account (sub-para.(3)).

On the question of whether in certain circumstances two physically separate buildings can constitute one "dwelling", see the notes to reg.2 of the Income Support Regulations in Vol.V of this series. Where a claimant is housed in two dwellings by a "provider of social housing" (defined in Sch.4, para.2), see para.4 below.

Paragraph 3

If the claimant has to move into temporary accommodation because essential repairs (see *R(SB) 10/81)* are being carried out to their normal home, intends to return to that home, and satisfies the payment and liability conditions for either the temporary accommodation or their normal home (but not both), they are treated as occupying as their home the accommodation in respect of which the payment and liability conditions are met (sub-para.(1)). If the claimant satisfies the payment and liability conditions for both the temporary accommodation and their normal home, they are treated as occupying the accommodation that they normally occupy as their home (sub-para.(2)). This may not necessarily be the accommodation that was their normal home. **2.447**

There is no time limit in para.3 itself as to how long it can apply.

Paragraph 4

This allows a housing costs element to be paid for two dwellings in the following circumstances. If the claimant (or claimants: s.40 WRA 2012) has been housed in two dwellings by a "provider of social housing" (defined in para.2 of Sch.4) due to the number of children and qualifying young persons living with them, the claimant normally occupies both dwellings with children or qualifying young persons (see reg.5) for whom they are responsible (see reg.4) and the claimant meets the payment and liability conditions in respect of both dwellings, the claimant will be treated as normally occupying both dwellings as their home. **2.448**

This paragraph can apply without time limit.

See para.17 of Sch.4 as to how the housing costs element is calculated under para.4. A single calculation is made for both dwellings together. This will be carried out under Pt 5 of Sch.4 if the rent is paid to a social sector landlord for both dwellings and neither is temporary accommodation (see para.21 of Sch.4 for the meaning of "temporary accommodation"). Otherwise, the calculation is made under Pt 4 of Sch.4, including applying the four bedroom limit. Note that under para.25(3)–(4) of Sch.4, if the cap rent for the two dwellings is different (e.g. because they are in different areas), the cap rent that is lower at the time the housing costs element is first calculated is the cap rent that applies. The calculation of the renter's housing costs element will continue to be based on that cap rent for as long as the renter is housed in those two homes.

Paragraphs 5 and 7

Under para.5 a claimant (or claimants) can be treated as occupying two homes for up to one month if the claimant: **2.449**

(i) has moved into their new home;
(ii) met the payment and liability conditions for that home immediately before they moved in,
(iii) was entitled to a housing costs element in respect of their old home immediately before the move; and
(iv) the delay in moving in was reasonable and was necessary to enable the new home to be adapted to the disablement needs (not defined) of the claimant (or claimants: s.40 WRA 2012) or any child or qualifying young person for whom the claimant (or claimants) is responsible. The person with the disablement needs must be in receipt of the middle or highest rate of the care component of disability living allowance, the daily living component of personal independence payment (either rate), attendance allowance or armed forces independence payment (note that the

definition of "attendance allowance" in reg.2 includes armed forces independence payment).

If the above circumstances apply but the claimant was not receiving a housing costs element in respect of their old home immediately before they moved in, para.7 will apply to treat the claimant as occupying their home for up to one month before they move in.

On the meaning of "moving in" see *R(H) 9/05* and on "adapting the accommodation to meet disablement needs" see the notes to para.3(7)(c)(i) of Sch.3 to the Income Support Regulations in Vol.V of this series.

See para.18 of Sch.4 as to how the housing costs element is calculated under para.5. Note that any housing cost contributions for non-dependants are only deducted from the housing costs element for the old home.

Paragraph 6

2.450 If the claimant is living in accommodation other than the accommodation they normally occupy as their home because of a reasonable fear of violence in the home, or from a former partner against them or any child or qualifying young person (see reg.5) for whom they are responsible (see reg.4), and they intend to return to the accommodation they normally occupy as their home, they can be treated as occupying both for up to 12 months. This applies if they meet the payment and liability conditions in respect of both the accommodation they normally occupy as their home and the other accommodation, provided that it is reasonable to pay a housing costs element for both. If the claimant only satisfies the payment and liability conditions in respect of one accommodation, they will be treated as occupying that accommodation as their home but only if it is reasonable to pay a housing costs element for that accommodation.

If a claimant in these circumstances is living in a refuge, it is unlikely that they will meet the payment condition for that accommodation (see para.3(h), together with para.3A, of Sch.1, under which payments in respect of "specified accommodation" do not count as rent payments. "Specified accommodation" includes temporary accommodation provided by a local authority or a "relevant body" (defined in para.3A(6)) for people who have left home because of domestic violence (defined in reg.98(4)) (para.3A(4))). However, if they are living in "specified accommodation", they can claim housing benefit for that accommodation.

Note para.9(3) which provides that such a claimant can no longer be treated as temporarily absent from the accommodation which they normally occupy as their home if the absence lasts, or is expected to last, more than 12 months.

See para.19 of Sch.4 as to how the housing costs element is calculated under para.6 where the claimant is entitled to a housing costs element for both homes. This will be calculated for each home under Pt 4 of Sch.4 or under Pt 5 of Sch.4, as the case may be. Note that any housing cost contributions for non-dependants are only deducted from the housing costs element for the home that the claimant is normally occupying.

Paragraph 8

2.451 Under this paragraph a claimant can be treated as occupying their home for up to one month before they move in if they met the payment and liability conditions immediately before moving in and they became liable to make the payments while they were a patient (defined in sub-para.(3)) or in a care home (defined in para.1 of Sch.1), or in the case of joint claimants, while both of them were patients or in a care home.

Paragraph 9

2.452 Unless the absence is due to essential repairs (see para.3) or a fear of violence (see para.6), if a claimant is temporarily absent from the accommodation, they will be treated as no longer occupying it if the absence has lasted, or is expected to last, more than six months.

This is a considerably simplified provision compared with the rules for temporary absence that apply for the purposes of housing benefit and income support, old style JSA and old style ESA housing costs.

If at any time during the six months it becomes clear that the absence is likely to exceed six months, the claimant will be treated as no longer occupying the accommodation from that point (this could apply from the start if the absence was expected to last more than six months from the beginning). However, if the claimant returns to the accommodation for a period, even a very short period, the six months should restart. See *R v Penrith DC Housing Benefit Review Board ex p. Burt* (1990) 22 H.L.R. 292, where Simon Brown J. accepted (dealing with the equivalent provisions relating to housing benefit) that "any period of return, however short, within the...period is sufficient of itself to end the period of temporary absence", and that absence would be unbroken only if it was "literally continuous". As pointed out in *Burt*, the relevance of a return being very brief is that it may make it easier for a decision maker to conclude that in all the circumstances the property is no longer accommodation which, as a matter of fact, the claimant "normally occupies as their home". But that is a separate question, arising under para.1 not para.9. See further the notes to paras 3(8)–(12) of Sch.3 to the Income Support Regulations in Vol.V of this series.

Note that if a person was entitled to universal credit which included a housing costs element immediately before becoming a prisoner (defined in reg.2 as modified by SI 2020/409), and they have not been sentenced to a term in custody which is expected to last more than six months, they will be entitled to universal credit consisting of a housing costs element only during their first six months' absence as a prisoner (see reg.19(2) and (3)).

Regulation 26(2)

Schedule 4

Housing Costs Element for Renters

Part I

General

Introduction

1.—(1) This Schedule contains provisions about claimants to whom regulation 26(2) applies. 2.453

(2) Claimants who fall within sub-paragraph (1) are referred to in this Schedule as "renters" (and references to "joint renters" are to joint claimants to whom regulation 26(2) applies).

(3) Part 2 of this Schedule sets out [[12] [[16] an exception]] to section 11(1) of the Act for certain renters in whose case an award of universal credit is not to include an amount of housing costs element calculated under this Schedule.

(4) The following Parts of this Schedule provide for the calculation of the amount of housing costs element to be included under regulation 26(2) in a renter's award of universal credit—

- (a) Part 3 contains general provisions that apply to all calculations, whether under Part 4 or Part 5;
- (b) Part 4 applies in relation to renters who occupy accommodation in the private rented sector [[14] ...]; and
- (c) Part 5 applies in relation to renters who occupy accommodation in the social rented sector [[14] ...].

Interpretation

2. In this Schedule— 2.454

[[22] "domestic violence" has the meaning given by regulation 98(4);]

[8 "exempt accommodation" has the meaning given in paragraph 4(10) of Schedule 3 to the Housing Benefit and Council Tax Benefit (Consequential Provisions) Regulations 2006;]

"extended benefit unit" has the meaning given in paragraph 9;

"Housing Act functions" means functions under section 122 of the Housing Act 1996 (functions of rent officers in connection with universal credit, housing benefit and rent allowance subsidy and housing credit);

"housing cost contribution" has the meaning given in paragraph 13;

"joint renter" has the meaning given in paragraph 1(2);

"listed persons", in relation to a renter, means—

(a) the renter;

(b) where the renter is a member of a couple, the other member of the couple; and

(c) any child or qualifying young person for whom the renter (or either joint renter) is responsible;

[1 "member of the armed forces" means a member of the regular forces or the reserve forces within the meaning of section 374 of the Armed Forces Act 2006;]

"non-dependant" has the meaning given in paragraph 9(2);

"provider of social housing" means—

(a) a local authority;

(b) a non-profit registered provider of social housing;

(c) in relation to accommodation which is social housing, a profit-making registered provider of social housing;

(d) a registered social landlord;

"registered social landlord" means—

(a) a body which is registered in the register maintained by the Welsh Ministers under Chapter 1 of Part 1 of the Housing Act 1996;

(b) a body which is registered in the register maintained by the Scottish Housing Regulator under section 20(1) of the Housing (Scotland) Act 2010;

[22 "relative" has the meaning given by section 63(1) of the Family Law Act 1996;]

"relevant payments" has the meaning given in paragraph 3;

"the Rent Officers Order 2013" means the Rent Officers (Universal Credit Functions) Order 2013;

"renter" means a single renter within the meaning of paragraph 1(2) or each of joint renters;

"renter who requires overnight care" is to be understood in accordance with paragraph 12(3) to (5);

"shared accommodation" has the meaning given in paragraph 27;

"social housing" has the meaning given in sections 68 to 77 of the Housing and Regeneration Act 2008.

"Relevant payments" for purposes of this Schedule

2.455 **3.**—(1) "Relevant payments" means one or more payments of any of the following descriptions—

(a) rent payments;

(b) service charge payments.

(2) "Rent payments", in relation to any calculation under Part 4 or 5 of this Schedule, has the meaning given in paragraph 2 of Schedule 1.

(3) "Service charge payments"—

(a) for the purposes of calculations under Part 4 of this Schedule, has the meaning given in paragraph 7 of Schedule 1;

(b) for the purposes of calculations under Part 5 of this Schedule, is to be understood in accordance with paragraphs 7 and 8 of Schedule 1.

Part 2

[12 [16 Exception]] to Inclusion of Housing Costs Element

No housing costs element for 16 or 17 year old care leavers

2.456 **4.** Section 11(1) of the Act (housing costs) does not apply to any renter who is 16 or 17 years old and is a care leaver.

[12 No housing costs element for certain renters aged at least 18 but under 22

2.457 **4A.** [16 ...]

Persons to whom paragraph 4A does not apply – general

4B. [16 ...] 2.458

Persons to whom paragraph 4A does not apply – periods of work

4C. [16 ...]] 2.459

PART 3

GENERAL PROVISIONS ABOUT CALCULATION OF AMOUNT OF HOUSING COSTS ELEMENT FOR RENTERS

Application of Part 3

5. This Part contains provisions of general application in calculating the amount of a renter's housing costs element under Part 4 or 5 of this Schedule. 2.460

Payments taken into account

Relevant payments to be taken into account

6.—(1) Where a renter meets the payment condition, liability condition and occupation condition in respect of one or more descriptions of relevant payment, each such description is to be taken into account for the purposes of the calculation under Part 4 or 5 of this Schedule. 2.461

(2) No account is to be taken of any amount of a relevant payment to the extent that all of the conditions referred to in sub-paragraph (1) are not met in respect of that amount.

(3) Any particular payment for which a renter is liable is not to be brought into account more than once, whether in relation to the same or a different renter (but this does not prevent different payments of the same description being brought into account in respect of an assessment period).

Relevant payments calculated monthly

7.—(1) Where any relevant payment is to be taken into account under paragraph 6, the amount of that payment is to be calculated as a monthly amount. 2.462

(2) Where the period in respect of which a renter is liable to make a relevant payment is not a month, an amount is to be calculated as the monthly equivalent, so for example—

(a) weekly payments are multiplied by 52 and divided by 12;

[7 (aa) two-weekly payments are multiplied by 26 and divided by 12;]

(b) four-weekly payments are multiplied by 13 and divided by 12;

(c) three-monthly payments are multiplied by 4 and divided by 12; and

(d) annual payments are divided by 12.

(3) Where a renter is liable for relevant payments under arrangements that provide for one or more rent free periods, [7 subject to sub-paragraph (3A),] the monthly equivalent is to be calculated over 12 months by reference to the total number of relevant payments which the renter is liable to make in that 12 month period.

[7 (3A) Where sub-paragraph (3) applies and the relevant payments in question are—

(a) weekly payments, the total number of weekly payments which the renter is liable to make in any 12 month period shall be calculated by reference to the formula—

$$52 - RFP;$$

(b) two-weekly payments, the total number of two-weekly payments which the renter is liable to make in any 12 month period shall be calculated by reference to the formula—

$$26 - RFP;$$

(c) four-weekly payments, the total number of four-weekly payments which the renter is liable to make in any 12 month period shall be calculated by reference to the formula—

$$13 - RFP;$$

where "RFP" is the number of rent free periods in the 12 month period in question.].

(4) "Rent free period" means any period in respect of which the renter has no liability to make one or more of the relevant payments which are to be taken into account under paragraph 6.

Room allocation

Size criteria applicable to the extended benefit unit of all renters

2.463 **8.**—(1) In calculating the amount of the renter's housing costs element under Part 4 or 5 of this Schedule, a determination is to be made in accordance with the provisions referred to in sub-paragraph (2) as to the category of accommodation which it is reasonable for the renter to occupy, having regard to the number of persons who are members of the renter's extended benefit unit (see paragraph 9).

(2) The provisions referred to in this sub-paragraph are the following provisions of this Schedule—

(a) in respect of a calculation under Part 4, paragraphs 9 to 12 and 26 to 29;

(b) in respect of a calculation under Part 5, paragraphs 9 to 12.

Extended benefit unit of a renter for purposes of this Schedule

2.464 **9.**—(1) For the purposes of this Schedule, the members of a renter's extended benefit unit are—

(a) the renter (or joint renters);

(b) any child or qualifying young person for whom the renter or either joint renter is responsible; and

(c) any person who is a non-dependant.

(2) A person is a non-dependant if the person [6 normally] lives in the accommodation with the renter (or joint renters) and is none of the following—

(a) a person within sub-paragraph (1)(a) or (b);

(b) where the renter is a member of a couple claiming as a single person, the other member of the couple;

(c) a foster child;

(d) a person who is liable to make payments on a commercial basis in respect of the person's occupation of the accommodation (whether to the renter, joint renters or another person);

(e) a person to whom the liability to make relevant payments is owed or a member of their household;

(f) a person who has already been treated as a non-dependant in relation to a claim for universal credit by another person liable to make relevant payments in respect of the accommodation occupied by the renter.

[6 (g) a child or qualifying young person for whom no-one in the renter's extended benefit unit is responsible.]

(3) "Foster child" means a child in relation to whom the renter (or either joint renter) is a foster parent.

Number of bedrooms to which a renter is entitled

2.465 **10.**—(1) A renter is entitled to one bedroom for each of the following categories of persons in their extended benefit unit—

(a) the renter (or joint renters);

(b) a qualifying young person for whom the renter or either joint renter is responsible;

(c) a non-dependant who is not a child;

(d) two children who are under 10 years old;

(e) two children of the same sex;

(f) any other child.

(2) A member of the extended benefit unit to whom two or more of the descriptions in sub-paragraph (1) apply is to be allotted to whichever description results in the renter being entitled to the fewest bedrooms.

(3) In determining the number of bedrooms to which a renter is entitled, the following must also be taken into account—

(a) the provisions of paragraph 11 as to treatment of periods of temporary absence of members of the renter's extended benefit unit;

(b) any entitlement to an additional bedroom in accordance with paragraph 12;

(c) for the purpose of any calculation under Part 4 of this Schedule, the additional requirements in paragraphs 26 to 29.

Temporary absence of member of renter's extended benefit unit

2.466 **11.**—(1) A member of the renter's extended benefit unit who is temporarily absent from the accommodation occupied by the renter is to be included in a determination of the number of bedrooms to which the renter is entitled ("relevant determination") in the circumstances specified in sub-paragraphs (2) to (4).

(2) In the case of a child or qualifying young person, the circumstances specified in this sub-paragraph are that the relevant determination relates to any time—

(a) during the first 6 months of the absence of a child or qualifying young person for whom the renter is treated as not being responsible in accordance with regulation 4(6)(a) (child or qualifying young person looked after by local authority) where, immediately before the local authority started looking after them, the child or qualifying young person was included in the renter's extended benefit unit and the renter's award included the housing costs element;

(b) during the first 6 months of the absence of a child or qualifying young person for whom the renter is treated as not being responsible in accordance with regulation 4(6)(b) (child or qualifying young person is a prisoner) where—

(i) immediately before becoming a prisoner, the child or qualifying young person was included in the renter's extended benefit unit and the renter's award included the housing costs element, and

(ii) the child or qualifying young person has not been sentenced to a term in custody that is expected to extend beyond that 6 months; or

(c) before the renter or joint renter ceases to be responsible for a temporarily absent child or qualifying young person in accordance with regulation 4(7) (absence exceeding specified duration).

(3) In the case of a renter, the circumstances specified in this sub-paragraph are that the relevant determination relates to any time when—

(a) the temporary absence from Great Britain of the renter is disregarded in accordance with regulation 11(1) or (2); or

(b) the renter is a prisoner to whom regulation 19(2) (existing award includes housing costs when person becomes a prisoner) applies.

(4) In the case of a non-dependant, the circumstances specified in this sub-paragraph are that—

(a) the relevant determination relates to any time during a period specified in sub-paragraph (5); and

(b) immediately before the start of that period, the non-dependant was included in the renter's extended benefit unit and [2, in the circumstances specified in sub-paragraph (5)(a) to (c),] the renter's award included the housing costs element.

(5) The specified periods are—

(a) the first month of the non-dependant's temporary absence from Great Britain and, if the circumstances of the non-dependant are such as would be disregarded for the purposes of regulation 11(2) (death of a close relative), a further one month;

(b) the first 6 months of the non-dependant's temporary absence from Great Britain in the circumstances described in regulation 11(3)(a) (absence solely in connection with treatment for illness or physical or mental impairment);

(c) the first 6 months that the non-dependant is a prisoner where the non-dependant has not been sentenced to a term in custody that is expected to extend beyond that 6 months.

[3 (d) any period during which a non-dependant who is the son, daughter, step-son or step-daughter of a renter or joint renters is a member of the armed forces away on operations.]

(6) Any non-dependant who is temporarily absent from the accommodation occupied by the renter in circumstances other than those specified in sub-paragraphs (4) and (5) is not to be treated as being a member of the renter's extended benefit unit if that absence exceeds, or is expected to exceed, 6 months.

[6 **Additional room**

12.—[11 (A1) A renter is entitled to an additional bedroom if one or more of the following persons satisfies the overnight care condition (see sub-paragraph (3))— **2.467**

(a) the renter;

(b) a person in the renter's extended benefit unit;

(c) a child in respect of whom the renter satisfies the foster parent condition (see sub-paragraphs (4) and (5)).]

(1) A renter is entitled to an additional bedroom if they satisfy any of the following conditions—

(a) [11 . . .]

(b) the foster parent condition [11 . . .]; or

(c) the disabled child condition (see sub-paragraph (6)) [11;

(d) the disabled person condition (see sub-paragraph (6A))].

[11 (2) Sub-paragraphs (A1) and (1) apply subject to sub-paragraphs (8) and (9).]

(3) [11 A person satisfies] the overnight care condition if—

(a) they are in receipt of—

(i) the care component of disability living allowance at the middle or highest rate;

[18 (ia) the care component of child disability payment at the middle or highest rate in accordance with regulation 11(5) of the DACYP Regulations;]

(ii) attendance allowance; [20 ...]

(iii) the daily living component of personal independence payment; [20 or]

[20 (iv) the daily living component of adult disability payment at the standard or enhanced rate;]

(b) one or more persons who do not live in the renter's accommodation are engaged to provide overnight [11 care for the person] and to stay overnight in the accommodation on a regular basis; and

(c) overnight care is provided under arrangements entered into for that purpose.

(4) A renter satisfies the foster parent condition if the renter is—

(a) a foster parent; or

(b) an adopter with whom a child has been placed for adoption.

(5) For the purposes of sub-paragraph (4) "foster parent" includes a person who would be a foster parent, but for the fact that they do not currently have any child placed with them, provided that any period since the date when their last placement ended (or, if they have not yet had a child placed with them, since the date when they were approved to be a foster parent) does not exceed 12 months.

(6) A renter satisfies the disabled child condition if they or another member of their extended benefit unit are responsible for a child who would (but for the provisions of this paragraph) be expected to share a bedroom and that child is—

(a) in receipt of the care component of disability living allowance at the middle or highest rate; and

[18 (aa) in receipt of the care component of child disability payment at the middle or highest rate in accordance with regulation 11(5) of the DACYP Regulations;]

(b) by virtue of their disability, not reasonably able to share a room with another child.

[11 (6A) A renter satisfies the disabled person condition if they would (but for the provisions of this paragraph) be expected to share a bedroom with a joint renter and—

(a) the renter is in receipt of—

(i) the care component of disability living allowance at the middle or highest rate;

[18 (ia) the care component of child disability payment at the middle or highest rate in accordance with regulation 11(5) of the DACYP Regulations;]

(ii) attendance allowance at the higher rate;

(iii) the daily living component of personal independence payment; [20 . . .]

[20 (iv) the daily living component of adult disability payment at the standard or enhanced rate; and]

(b) the renter is, by virtue of their disability, not reasonably able to share a bedroom with the joint renter.]

(7) [11 . . .]

(8) Where a renter, or one or both of joint renters, satisfy the disabled child condition in relation to one or more children, they are entitled to as many additional bedrooms as are necessary to ensure that each such child has their own bedroom.

[11 (9) The renter is, or joint renters are, entitled to one additional bedroom for each of the following that apply—

(a) one or more persons satisfy the overnight care condition;

(b) the renter, or one or both of joint renters, satisfies the foster parent condition;

(c) the renter, or one or both of joint renters, satisfies the disabled child condition; or

(d) the renter, or one or both of joint renters, satisfies the disabled person condition.]]

Housing cost contributions

Housing cost contributions

2.468 **13.**—(1) In calculating the amount of the housing costs element under Part 4 or 5 of this Schedule, a deduction is to be made in respect of each non-dependant who is a member of the renter's extended benefit unit.

(2) Paragraph (1) is subject to paragraphs 15 and 16.

(3) Any amount to be deducted under sub-paragraph (1) is referred to in this Schedule as a "housing cost contribution".

Amount of housing cost contributions

14.—(1) The amount of each housing cost contribution to be deducted under paragraph 13 is [24 £291.47]. **2.469**

(2) Deductions are not to be made until the amount has been determined which results from all other steps in the calculation required in relation to the renter under Parts 4 and 5 of this Schedule.

(3) Where the sum of all the housing cost contributions to be deducted in the renter's case exceeds the amount referred to in sub-paragraph (2)—

(a) the amount determined under this Schedule is to be reduced to nil; but
(b) no further reduction in respect of housing cost contributions is to be made from the renter's award.

Exempt renters

15.—(1) No deduction is to be made under paragraph 13 in the case of— **2.470**

(a) any renter who is a single person to whom sub-paragraph (2) applies; or
(b) any joint renter where at least one joint renter is a person to whom sub-paragraph (2) applies.

(2) This sub-paragraph applies to—

(a) a person who is [9 . . .] blind;
(b) a person in receipt of the care component of disability living allowance at the middle or highest rate;
[18 (ba) a person in receipt of the care component of child disability payment at the middle or highest rate in accordance with regulation 11(5) of the DACYP Regulations;]
(c) a person in receipt of attendance allowance;
(d) a person in receipt of the daily living component of personal independence payment;
[20 (da) a person in receipt of the daily living component of adult disability payment at the standard or enhanced rate;]
(e) a person who is entitled to a payment within paragraph (b), (c) [20, (d) or (da)] but is not receiving it under, as the case may be—
(i) regulation 8 of the Social Security (Disability Living Allowance) Regulations 1991,
(ii) regulation 6 of the Social Security (Attendance Allowance) Regulations 1991,
(iii) regulation 21 of the Social Security (General Benefit) Regulations 1982 [20 . . .]
(iv) regulations under section 86 of the Act (payment of personal independence payment while a person is a hospital in-patient) [20; or]
[20 (v) regulation 28 (effect of admission to hospital on ongoing entitlement to Adult Disability Payment) of the Disability Assistance for Working Age People (Scotland) Regulations 2022].

No deduction for housing cost contributions in respect of certain non-dependants

16.—(1) No deduction is to be made under paragraph 13 in respect of any non-dependant who is a member of the renter's extended benefit unit to whom sub-paragraph (2) applies. **2.471**

(2) This sub-paragraph applies to—

(a) a person who is under 21 years old;
(b) a person in receipt of state pension credit;
(c) a person in receipt of the care component of disability living allowance at the middle or highest rate;
(d) a person in receipt of attendance allowance;
(e) a person in receipt of the daily living component of personal independence payment;
[20 (ea) a person in receipt of the daily living component of adult disability payment at the standard or enhanced rate;]
(f) a person who is entitled to a payment within paragraph (c), (d) [20, (e) or (ea)] but is not receiving it under, as the case may be—
(i) regulation 8 of the Social Security (Disability Living Allowance) Regulations 1991,
(ii) regulation 6 of the Social Security (Attendance Allowance) Regulations 1991,
(iii) regulation 21 of the Social Security (General Benefit) Regulations 1982 [20 . . .]
(iv) regulations under section 86 of the Act (payment of personal independence payment while a person is a hospital in-patient) [20; or]
[20 (v) regulation 28 (effect of admission to hospital on ongoing entitlement to Adult Disability Payment) of the Disability Assistance for Working Age People (Scotland) Regulations 2022].

(g) a person in receipt of carer's allowance; [23 (ga) a person in receipt of carer support payment;]
(h) a person who is a prisoner;
(i) a person who is responsible for a child under 5 years old.
[4 (j) a person who is a member of the armed forces away on operations who—
(i) is the son, daughter, step-son or step-daughter of a renter or joint renters, and
(ii) resided with the renter or joint renters immediately before leaving to go on operations and intends to return to reside with the renter or joint renters at the end of the operations.]

Calculations involving more than one accommodation

Single calculation for renter treated as occupying single accommodation

2.472 **17.**—(1) This paragraph applies to any renter where, under paragraph 4 of Schedule 3 (claimant housed in two dwellings by provider of social housing), two dwellings ("accommodation A" and "accommodation B") occupied by a renter are treated as the single accommodation in respect of which the renter meets the occupation condition.

(2) The amount of the renter's housing costs element is to be determined by a single calculation in respect of accommodation A and accommodation B as if they were one, taking account of—
(a) all relevant payments in respect of accommodation A and all relevant payments in respect of accommodation B; and
(b) the total number of bedrooms in accommodation A and accommodation B taken together.

[14 (3) The single calculation is to be made under Part 5 of this Schedule in any case where the renter's liability to make rent payments in respect of accommodation A and accommodation B is to a provider of social housing.]

(4) In any other case, the single calculation is to be made under Part 4 of this Schedule.

Calculation where move to new accommodation delayed for adaptations for disabled person

2.473 **18.**—(1) Sub-paragraph (2) applies to any renter where, under paragraph 5 of Schedule 3 (moving home: adaptations to new home for disabled person), the renter meets the occupation condition in respect of both the new accommodation and the old accommodation.

(2) The amount of the renter's housing costs element under this Schedule is to be calculated as follows.

Step 1

Calculate an amount in accordance with Part 4 or Part 5 of this Schedule (as the case may be) in respect of both—
(a) the new accommodation; and
(b) the old accommodation.

Step 2

Add together the amounts determined in step 1.

Step 3

If a deduction was made for housing cost contributions in respect of both the new accommodation and the old accommodation, take the amount of the housing costs contributions deducted in respect of the new accommodation and add that to the amount resulting from step 2.

(3) In this paragraph, references to "the new accommodation" and "the old accommodation" are to be understood in accordance with paragraph 5 of Schedule 3.

Calculation where renter moves out because of reasonable fear of violence

2.474 **19.**—(1) Sub-paragraph (2) applies to any renter where, under paragraph 6(2) of Schedule 3 (claimant living in other accommodation because of reasonable fear of violence), the renter meets the occupation condition in respect of both the home accommodation and the other accommodation.

(2) The amount of the renter's housing costs element under this Schedule is to be calculated as follows:

Step 1

Calculate an amount in accordance with Part 4 or Part 5 of this Schedule (as the case may be) in respect of—

(a) the home accommodation; and
(b) the other accommodation.

Step 2

Add together the amounts determined in step 1.

Step 3

If a deduction was made for housing cost contributions in respect of both the home accommodation and the other accommodation—

(c) determine which accommodation the renter normally occupies as their home; and
(d) take the amount of the housing costs contributions deducted in respect of the accommodation not so occupied and add that to the amount resulting from step 2.

(3) In this paragraph, references to "the home accommodation" and "the other accommodation" are to be understood in accordance with paragraph 6 of Schedule 3.

PART 4

PRIVATE RENTED SECTOR [14 ...]

Application of Part 4

20.—[14 (1) This Part applies to renters who are liable to make rent payments to a person other than a provider of social housing.] **2.475**

(2) Sub-paragraph (1) applies irrespective of whether renters are also liable to make service charge payments.

Meaning of "temporary accommodation"

21. [14 . . .] **2.476**

The calculation of the housing costs element under this Part

The amount of housing costs element under this Part

22. The amount of the renter's housing costs element under this Part is to be calculated as follows: **2.477**

Step 1

Determine—

(a) the amount of the renter's core rent; and
(b) the amount of the renter's cap rent,

and identify which is the lower amount (if both amounts are the same, that is the identified amount).

Step 2

Deduct the sum of the housing cost contributions (if any) under paragraph 13 from the amount identified in step 1.

The result is the amount of the renter's housing costs element calculated under this Part.

Core rent

23. Except where paragraph 24 applies, the renter's core rent is to be determined as follows: **2.478**

Step 1

Determine the amount of each relevant payment to be taken into account under paragraph 6.

Step 2

Determine the period in respect of which each relevant payment is payable and, in accordance with paragraph 7, determine the amount of the payment in respect of a month.

Step 3

If there is more than one relevant payment, add together the amounts determined in step 2 in relation to all relevant payments.

The result is the renter's core rent.

Core rent for joint tenants

2.479 **24.**—(1) This paragraph applies where, in respect of the accommodation occupied by the renter, one or more persons other than the renter are liable to make relevant payments which are of the same description as those for which the renter is liable and which are to be taken into account under paragraph 6.

(2) The following steps are to be taken in order to determine the renter's core rent.

Step 1

Determine the total of all relevant payments referred to in sub-paragraph (1) for which the renter and others are liable in respect of the accommodation taken as a whole.

Step 2

Determine the period in respect of which each relevant payment is payable and, in accordance with paragraph 7, determine the amount of the payment in respect of a month.

Step 3

Add together all of the amounts determined in step 2 in relation to all relevant payments.

Step 4

Find the allocated amount in accordance with whichever of sub-paragraphs (3) to (5) applies in the renter's case.

The result is the renter's core rent.

(3) Where the only persons liable to make relevant payments are listed persons, the allocated amount is the amount resulting from step 3 in sub-paragraph (2).

(4) Where the persons liable for the relevant payments are one or more listed persons and one or more other persons, the allocated amount is to be found by the applying the formula—

$$\left(\frac{A}{B}\right) \times C$$

where—

"A" is the amount resulting from step 3 in sub-paragraph (2),

"B" is the total number of all persons (including listed persons) liable to make the relevant payments, and

"C" is the number of listed persons [5 liable to make relevant payments].

(5) If the Secretary of State is satisfied that it would be unreasonable to allocate the amount resulting from step 3 in sub-paragraph (2) in accordance with sub-paragraph (4), that amount is to be allocated in such manner as the Secretary of State considers appropriate in all the circumstances, having regard (among other things) to the number of persons liable and the proportion of the relevant payments for which each of them is liable.

Cap rent

2.480 **25.**—(1) The renter's cap rent is to be determined as follows.

Step 1

Determine the category of accommodation to which the renter is entitled under paragraphs 8 to 12 and 26 to 29.

Step 2

Having regard to the determination at step 1, determine the maximum allowable amount for the renter under sub-paragraph (2) or (4) (as the case may be).

The result is the renter's cap rent.

(2) The maximum allowable amount to be used in relation to the renter is the local housing allowance which applies at the relevant time to—

(a) the broad rental market area in which the renter's accommodation is situated; and

(b) the category of accommodation determined at step 1 as that to which the renter is entitled.

(3) But the maximum allowable amount in relation to the renter is to be determined under sub-paragraph (4) in any case where—

(a) paragraph 4 of Schedule 3 (claimant housed in two dwellings by provider of social housing) applies to the renter; and

(b) the maximum allowable amount determined under sub-paragraph (2) for the renter in relation to accommodation A and the amount so determined in relation to accommodation B are different (references to accommodation A and accommodation B are to be understood in accordance with paragraph 4 of Schedule 3); and

(c) a single calculation is to be made in relation to the renter under paragraph 17 (renter treated as occupying single accommodation).

(4) In any such case, the maximum allowable amount to be used in making the single calculation required by paragraph 17—

(a) is to be determined by reference to the accommodation for which the amount referred to in sub-paragraph (3)(b) is lower when the calculation is first made; and

(b) is to continue to be determined by reference to that accommodation for so long as paragraph 4 of Schedule 3 applies to the renter in respect of the same accommodation A and the same accommodation B; and

(c) is to be re-determined in accordance with paragraphs (a) and (b) on each occasion when the renter is re-housed in any other accommodation, provided that paragraph 4 of Schedule 3 continues to apply to the renter.

(5) In this paragraph—

"broad rental market area" means the broad rental market area determined under article 3 of the Rent Officers Order 2013;

"local housing allowance", in relation to a broad rental market area, means the amount determined by a rent officer for that area under article 4 of the Rent Officers Order 2013;

"relevant time" means the time at which the amount of the renter's housing costs element is calculated under paragraph 22.

Further provisions about size criteria for cases to which this Part applies

Four bedroom limit

26. In calculating the amount of a renter's housing costs element under paragraph 22, no renter is entitled to more than 4 bedrooms. **2.481**

Specified renters entitled to shared accommodation only

27.—(1) In calculating the amount of a renter's housing costs element under paragraph 22, any specified renter (within the meaning of paragraph 28) is entitled to shared accommodation only. **2.482**

(2) "Shared accommodation" means the category of accommodation specified in paragraph 1(a) of Schedule 1 to the Rent Officers Order 2013.

Meaning of "specified renters"

28.—(1) For the purposes of paragraph 27, "specified renter" means a renter in respect of whom all of the following conditions are met. **2.483**

(2) The first condition is that the renter is a single person (or a member of a couple claiming as a single person) who—

(a) is under 35 years old; and

(b) is not an excepted person under paragraph 29.

(3) The second condition is that the renter is not responsible for any children or qualifying young persons.

(4) The third condition is that no person is a non-dependant in relation to the renter.

Renters excepted from shared accommodation

29.—(1) "Excepted person" means any renter ("E") who falls within any of sub-paragraphs (2) to [[22] (9C)]. **2.484**

[[10] (2) E is at least 18 but under [[17] 25] years old and was a care leaver (within the meaning of regulation 8) before reaching the age of 18.]

(3) [[10] . . .]

(4) E is at least [[17] 16] but under 35 years old and—

(a) has, for a total of at least 3 months (whether or not continuously), lived in one or more hostels for homeless people; and

(b) whilst E was living in such a hostel, was offered and has accepted services which the Secretary of State considers are intended to assist E to be rehabilitated or resettled within the community.

(5) E is under 35 years old and is in receipt of—

(a) the care component of disability living allowance at the middle or highest rate;

[18 (aa) the care component of child disability payment at the middle or highest rate in accordance with regulation 11(5) of the DACYP Regulations;]

(b) attendance allowance; [20 . . .]

(c) the daily living component of personal independence payment[20; or]

[20 (d) the daily living component of adult disability payment at the standard or enhanced rate].

(6) In relation to England and Wales, E is under 35 years old and is the subject of active multi-agency management pursuant to arrangements established by a responsible authority under section 325(2) of the Criminal Justice Act 2003 (arrangements for assessing etc. risks posed by certain offenders).

(7) In relation to Scotland, E is under 35 years old and is the subject of active multi-agency risk management pursuant to arrangements established by the responsible authorities under section 10(1) of the 2005 Act (arrangements for assessing and managing risks posed by certain offenders).

(8) In relation to Scotland, E is under 35 years old and—

(a) section 10(1) of the 2005 Act does not apply to E by reason only of the fact that section 10(1)(b) or (d) has not been brought fully into force; and

(b) E is considered by the Secretary of State to be a person who may cause serious harm to the public at large.

(9) In relation to Scotland, E is under 35 years old and—

(a) section 10(1) of the 2005 Act does not apply to E by reason only of the fact that section 10(1)(e) has not been brought fully into force; and

(b) by reason of an offence of which E has been convicted, E is considered by the Secretary of State to be a person who may cause serious harm to the public at large.

[15 (9A) E is under 35 years old and satisfies the foster parent condition (within the meaning of paragraph 12(4)).]

[22 (9B) E is under 35 years old and—

(a) after attaining the age of 16 had domestic violence inflicted upon or threatened against them ("the victim") by their partner or former partner, or by a relative; and

(b) provides evidence from a person acting in an official capacity which demonstrates that—

(i) the victim's circumstances are consistent with their having had domestic violence inflicted upon or threatened against them; and

(ii) the victim has contacted a person acting in an official capacity in relation to such an incident.

(9C) E is under 35 years old and has been the subject of a positive conclusive grounds determination relating to modern slavery.]

(10) In this paragraph—

"the 2005 Act" means the Management of Offenders etc. (Scotland) Act 2005;

"care home", "registered charity" and "voluntary organisation" have the meaning given in Schedule 1;

[22 "competent authority" means a person who is a competent authority within the meaning of the Trafficking Convention;

"compulsory labour", "forced labour", "servitude" and "slavery" have the same meaning as in Article 4 of the Convention for the Protection of Human Rights and Fundamental Freedoms, agreed by the Council of Europe at Rome on 4th November 1950 as it has effect for the time being in relation to the United Kingdom;]

"hostel" means a building—

(a) in which there is provided, for persons generally or for a class of persons, domestic accommodation, otherwise than in separate and self-contained premises, and either board or facilities for the preparation of food adequate to the needs of those persons, or both; and

(b) which—

(i) is managed or owned by a provider of social housing other than a local authority, or

(ii) is operated other than on a commercial basis and in respect of which funds are provided wholly or in part by a government department or agency or a local authority, or

(iii) is managed by a voluntary organisation or a registered charity and provides care, support or supervision with a view to assisting those persons to be rehabilitated or resettled within the community; and

(c) which is not a care home;

"hostel for homeless people" means a hostel the main purpose of which is to provide accommodation together with care, support or supervision for homeless people with a view to assisting such persons to be rehabilitated or resettled within the community.

[22 "person acting in an official capacity" means a health care professional (within the meaning given by regulation 98(4)), a police officer, a registered social worker (within the meaning given by regulation 98(4)), the victim's employer, or any public, voluntary, or charitable body which has had direct contact with the victim in connection with domestic violence;

"positive conclusive grounds determination relating to modern slavery" means a determination made by a competent authority that an individual is a victim of trafficking in human beings, slavery, servitude or forced or compulsory labour;

"the Trafficking Convention" means the Council of Europe Convention on Action against Trafficking in Human Beings (done at Warsaw on 16th May 2005);

"trafficking in human beings" has the same meaning as in the Trafficking Convention.]

PART 5

SOCIAL RENTED SECTOR [14 ...]

Application of Part 5

30.—[14 (1)This Part applies to renters who are liable to make rent payments to a provider of social housing.] 2.485

(2) Sub-paragraph (1) applies irrespective of whether renters are also liable to make service charge payments.

[13 Amount taken into account as the relevant payment]

Deduction from relevant payments of amounts relating to use of particular accommodation

31. In determining the amount of any relevant payment to be taken into account under paragraph 6, a deduction is to be made for any amount which the Secretary of State is satisfied— 2.486

(a) is included in the relevant payment; but

(b) relates to the supply to the accommodation of a commodity (such as water or fuel) for use by any member of the renter's extended benefit unit.

Power to apply to rent officer if relevant payments excessive

32.—(1) Sub-paragraph (2) applies where it appears to the Secretary of State that the amount of any relevant payment for which the renter is liable in respect of accommodation occupied by the renter is greater than it is reasonable to meet by way of the housing costs element under this Part. 2.487

(2) The Secretary of State may apply to a rent officer for a determination to be made as to the amount of the relevant payment by the officer in exercise of the officer's Housing Act functions.

(3) Sub-paragraph (4) applies in any case where a rent officer determines that a landlord might, at the time of the application under sub-paragraph (2), reasonably have expected to obtain a lower amount of the description of relevant payment referred to the rent officer.

(4) The lower amount determined by the rent officer is to be used in making the calculation under this Part, instead of the amount of the relevant payment for which the renter is liable, unless the Secretary of State is satisfied that it is not appropriate to use that lower amount.

[13 Reduction under tenant incentive scheme 2.488

32A.—(1) Where a reduction in the rent or service charge payments for which a renter would otherwise have been liable is applied by a provider of social housing under an approved tenant incentive scheme, the amount of any relevant payment to be taken into account under paragraph 6 is to be determined as if no such reduction had been applied.

(2) In paragraph (1) "approved tenant incentive scheme" means a scheme which is—

(a) operated by a provider of social housing and designed to avoid rent arrears by allowing reductions in rent or service charges or other advantages in return for meeting specified conditions; and

(b) approved by the Secretary of State.]

The calculation of the housing costs element under this Part

The amount of housing costs element

33. The amount of the renter's housing costs element under this Part is to be calculated by reference to the formula— 2.489

$S - HCC$

where—
"S" is the amount resulting from whichever of paragraph 34 or 35 applies in the renter's case, and
"HCC" is the sum of the housing cost contributions (if any) under paragraph 13.

Determining the amount from which HCC deductions are to be made

2.490 **34.** Except where paragraph 35 applies, amount S referred to in paragraph 33 is to be found as follows:

Step 1

Determine which relevant payments are to be taken into account under paragraph 6 and determine the amount of each of them (applying paragraphs 31 and 32(3) and (4) as necessary).

Step 2

Determine the period in respect of which each relevant payment is payable and, in accordance with paragraph 7, determine the amount of the payment in respect of a month.

Step 3

If there is more than one relevant payment, add together the amounts determined in step 2 in relation to all relevant payments.

Step 4

Determine under paragraph 36(1) whether an under-occupation deduction is to be made and, if one is to be made, determine the amount of the deduction under paragraph 36(2) and deduct it from the amount resulting from step 2 or 3 (as the case may be).

The result is amount S from which the sum of the housing costs contributions are to be deducted under paragraph 33.

Determining the amount from which HCC deductions are to be made: joint tenants

2.491 **35.**—(1) This paragraph applies where, in respect of the accommodation occupied by the renter, one or more persons other than the renter is liable to make relevant payments which are of the same description as those for which the renter is liable and which are to be taken into account under paragraph 6.

(2) Amount S referred to in paragraph 33 is to be found as follows:

Step 1

Determine the total of all relevant payments referred to in sub-paragraph (1) for which the renter and others are liable in respect of the accommodation taken as a whole (applying paragraphs 31 and 32(3) and (4) as necessary).

Step 2

Determine the period in respect of which each relevant payment is payable and, in accordance with paragraph 7, determine the amount of the payment in respect of a month.

Step 3

Add together all of the amounts determined in step 2 in relation to all relevant payments.

Step 4

Find amount S in accordance with whichever of sub-paragraphs (3) to (5) applies in the renter's case.

The result is amount S from which the sum of the housing costs contributions are to be deducted under paragraph 33.

(3) Where the only persons liable to make relevant payments are listed persons, amount S is the amount resulting from step 3 in sub-paragraph (2) less the amount of the under-occupation deduction (if any) required by paragraph 36.

(4) Where the persons liable for the relevant payments are one or more listed persons and one or more other persons, amount S is to be found by the applying the formula—

$$\left(\frac{A}{B}\right) \times C$$

where—
"A" is the amount resulting from step 3 in sub-paragraph (2),
"B" is the total number of all persons (including listed persons) liable to make the relevant payments, and
"C" is the number of listed persons [5 liable to make relevant payments].

(5) If the Secretary of State is satisfied that it would be unreasonable to determine amount S in accordance with sub-paragraph (4), amount S is to be determined in such manner as the Secretary of State considers appropriate in all the circumstances, having regard (among other things) to the number of persons liable and the proportion of the relevant payments for which each of them is liable.

Under-occupancy deduction

36.—(1) A deduction for under-occupancy is to be made under this paragraph where the number of bedrooms in the accommodation exceeds the number of bedrooms to which the renter is entitled under paragraphs 8 to 12. **2.492**

(2) Where a deduction is to be made, the amount of the deduction is to be determined by the formula—

$$A \times B$$

where—
"A"—
(a) in relation to any deduction under paragraph 34, is the amount resulting from step 2 or 3 in that paragraph (as the case may be), or
(b) in relation to any deduction under paragraph 35(3), is the amount resulting from step 3 in paragraph 35(2);
"B" is the relevant percentage.

(3) The relevant percentage is 14% in the case of one excess bedroom.

(4) The relevant percentage is 25% in the case of two or more excess bedrooms.

(5) No deduction for under-occupation is to be made in calculating the amount of the renter's housing costs element under this Part in any case to which regulation 26(4) to (6) (shared ownership) applies.

[19 (6) No deduction for under occupation is to be made in calculating the amount of a renter's housing cost element under this part where—

(i) domestic violence has been inflicted upon or threatened against the claimant or a member of the claimant's extended benefit unit ("the victim") by that person's partner or former partner, or by a relative;
(ii) the victim is not living at the same address as the person who inflicted or threatened the domestic violence, except where that person is a qualifying young person and is a dependant of a member of the claimant's extended benefit unit; and
(iii) the claimant provides evidence from a person acting in an official capacity which demonstrates that the claimant is living in a property adapted under a sanctuary scheme and—
   (aa) the victim's circumstances are consistent with those of a person who has had domestic violence inflicted upon or threatened against them; and
   (bb) the victim has made contact with the person acting in an official capacity in relation to such an incident;
   (b) in this paragraph—
   [22 "person acting in an official capacity" has the meaning given to it in regulation 98(4) of these Regulations;]
   [22 ...]
   "sanctuary scheme" means a scheme operated by a provider of social housing enabling victims of domestic violence to remain in their homes through the installation of additional security to the property or the perimeter of the property at which the victim resides.]

AMENDMENTS

1. Universal Credit (Miscellaneous Amendments) Regulations 2013 (SI 2013/803), reg.2(3)(a) (April 29, 2013).

2. Universal Credit (Miscellaneous Amendments) Regulations 2013 (SI 2013/803), reg.2(3)(b)(i) (April 29, 2013).

3. Universal Credit (Miscellaneous Amendments) Regulations 2013 (SI 2013/803), reg.2(3)(b)(ii) (April 29, 2013).

4. Universal Credit (Miscellaneous Amendments) Regulations 2013 (SI 2013/803), reg.2(3)(e) (April 29, 2013).

5. Social Security (Miscellaneous Amendments) (No.2) Regulations 2013 (SI 2013/1508), reg.3(10) (July 29, 2013).

6. Housing Benefit and Universal Credit (Size Criteria) (Miscellaneous Amendments) Regulations 2013 (SI 2013/2828), reg.4 (December 4, 2013).

7. Universal Credit and Miscellaneous Amendments Regulations 2014 (SI 2014/597) reg.2(13) (April 28, 2014).

8. Housing Benefit and Universal Credit (Supported Accommodation) (Amendment) Regulations 2014 (SI 2014/771) reg.2(3) (November 3, 2014).

9. Universal Credit and Miscellaneous Amendments (No.2) Regulations 2014 (SI 2014/2888) reg.3(1)(c) (November 26, 2014, or in the case of existing awards, the first assessment period beginning on or after November 26, 2014).

10. Universal Credit (Care Leavers and Looked After Children) Amendment Regulations 2016 (SI 2016/543) reg.3 (May 26, 2016).

11. Housing Benefit and Universal Credit (Size Criteria) (Miscellaneous Amendments) Regulations 2017 (SI 2017/213) reg.6 (Assessment periods beginning on or after April 1, 2017).

12. Universal Credit (Housing Costs Element for claimants aged 18 to 21) (Amendment) Regulations 2017 (SI 2017/652) reg.2(1) and (3) (April 1, 2017).

13. Universal Credit (Tenant Incentive Scheme) Amendment Regulations 2017 (SI 2017/427) reg.2 (April 30, 2017).

14. Universal Credit (Miscellaneous Amendments, Saving and Transitional Provision) Regulations 2018 (SI 2018/65) reg.3(13) (April 11, 2018).

15. Universal Credit and Jobseeker's Allowance (Miscellaneous Amendments) Regulations 2018 (SI 2018/1129) reg.3(1) and (6)(d) (November 28, 2018).

16. Universal Credit and Jobseeker's Allowance (Miscellaneous Amendments) Regulations 2018 (SI 2018/1129) reg.3(1) and (6)(a)-(c) (December 31, 2018).

17. Social Security Benefits Up-rating Order 2021 (SI 2021/162) art.33(3) (assessment periods beginning on or after April 12, 2021.

18. Housing Benefit and Universal Credit (Care Leavers and Homeless) (Amendment) Regulations 2021 (SI 2021/546) reg.3 (May 31, 2021).

19. Social Security (Scotland) Act 2018 (Disability Assistance for Children and Young People) (Consequential Modifications) Order 2021 (SI 2021/786) Sch.11 para.8 (July 26, 2021).

20. Domestic Abuse Support (Relevant Accommodation and Housing Benefit and Universal Credit Sanctuary Schemes) (Amendment) Regulations 2021 (SI 2021/991) reg.4 (Assessment periods beginning on or after October 1, 2021).

21. Social Security (Disability Assistance for Working Age People) (Consequential Amendments) Order 2022 (SI 2022/177) art.13(8) (March 21, 2022).

22. Housing Benefit and Universal Credit (Victims of Domestic Abuse and Victims of Modern Slavery) (Amendment) Regulations 2022 (SI 2022/942) reg.3 (October 1, 2022).

23. Carer's Assistance (Carer Support Payment) (Scotland) Regulations 2023 (Consequential Amendments) Order 2023 (SI 2023/1218) art.23 (November 19, 2023).

24. Social Security Benefits Up-rating Order 2024 (SI 2024/242) art.32(3) (Assessment periods beginning on or after April 8, 2024).

DEFINITIONS

"the Act"—see reg.2.
"adult disability payment"—*ibid.*
"assessment period"—see WRA 2012 ss.40 and 7(2) and reg.21.
"attendance allowance"—see reg.2.
"blind"—*ibid.*
"care leaver"—see regs 2 and 8.
"carer's allowance"—see reg.2.
"child"—see WRA 2012 s.40.
"child disability payment"—see reg.2.
"claim"—see WRA 2012 s.40.
"claimant"—*ibid.*
"couple"—see WRA 2012 ss.39 and 40.
"the DACYP Regulations"—see reg.2.
"disability living allowance"—*ibid.*
"disabled"—see WRA 2012 s.40.
"foster parent"—see reg.2.
"joint claimants"—see WRA 2012 s.40.
"local authority"—see reg.2.
"personal independence payment"—*ibid.*
"prisoner"—see reg.2 as modified by SI 2020/409.
"qualifying young person"—see WRA 2012 ss.40 and 10(5) and regs 2 and 5.
"registered as blind"—see reg.2.
"single person"—see WRA 2012 ss.40 and 1(2)(a).

GENERAL NOTE

Paragraphs 1–7 **2.493**

This Schedule concerns the calculation of the housing costs element for "renters" (see para.1(2)). For the definition of "renter" see para.2. References to "joint renters" are to joint claimants who are renters (para.1(2)).

For a renter (or joint renters) to be entitled to a housing costs element under this Schedule, they must meet the payment, liability and occupation conditions in respect of one or more "relevant payments" (para.6(1) and (2)).

"Relevant payments" for the purpose of Sch.4 mean rent payments (for the meaning of rent payments see para.2 of Sch.1 and note the exclusions in para.3) and service charges (on which see para. 7 of Sch.1 in relation to service charge payments calculated under Pt 4 of this Schedule and paras 7 and 8 of Sch.1 in relation to service charge payments calculated under Pt 5 of this Schedule (para.3)). Relevant payments are calculated as a monthly amount (see para.7). Where a renter has the benefit of rent and/or service charge free periods (see the definition of "rent free period" in para.7(4)), the conversion to a monthly figure is based on a standard 52 week year (see para. 7(3) and the formula in para.7(3A)). In *R. (Caine) v Secretary of State for Work and Pensions* [2020] EWHC 2482 (Admin), the High Court (Julian Knowles J) rejected a challenge to the formulae for converting weekly to monthly amounts.

Para 4 establishes an exception: no housing costs element is to be included in the universal credit award of any 16 or 17 year old renter who is a care leaver as defined in reg.8(4)). The former exclusion of certain 18-21 year olds from entitlement to hosuing costs (as to which see pp.359-360 and 388-389 of the 2018-19 edition of this volume) was revoked with effect from December 31, 2018 by SI 2018/1129.

Part 3 of this Schedule contains general provisions, which apply to all calculations under the Schedule. The rules in Pt 4 apply to renters in the private sector or who occupy temporary accommodation. Part 5 applies to renters in the social rented sector.

A housing costs element for renters is normally paid to the claimant as part of their universal credit award. However, it can be paid to another person (e.g. the claimant's landlord) if this appears to the Secretary of State to be necessary to protect the interest of the claimant, their partner, a child or qualifying young person for whom the claimant or their partner is responsible or a severely disabled person in respect of whom the claimant receives a carer element (see reg.58(1) of the Claims and Payments Regulations 2013).

Note also reg.39(4) of the Decisions and Appeals Regulations 2013 which provides that if the Secretary of State considers that he does not have all the relevant information or evidence to decide what housing costs element to award, the decision will be made on the basis of the housing costs element that can immediately be awarded.

Paragraphs 8–12 and 26–29

2.494 In order to calculate the amount of a renter's housing costs element, it is first necessary to decide the number of "bedrooms"—a word that is not defined—that they are allowed under "the size criteria" (para.8). This depends on who counts as a member of the renter's "extended benefit unit".

The extended benefit unit comprises the renter, or joint renters, any child or qualifying young person (see reg.5) for whom the renter or either joint renter is responsible (see reg.4), and any non-dependant (para.9(1)).

A non-dependant is a person who normally lives in the renter's (or joint renters') accommodation and who is not excluded under para.9(2). There is no definition of "normally lives in the accommodation" but see the notes to reg.3(1) of the Income Support Regulations in Vol.V of this series on the general meaning of "residing with".

See paras 10–12 for the number of bedrooms allowed. Para.12 has been amended with effect from April 1, 2017 by SI 2017/213 to reflect the judgment of the Supreme Court in *R (Carmichael and Rourke) (formerly known as MA and Others) v Secretary of State for Work and Pensions* [2016] UKSC 58; [2016] 1 W.L.R. 4550 that the previous law discriminated unlawfully against adult couples who cannot share a bedroom because of the disabilities of at least one member of the couple and renters who need an extra room to accommodate an overnight carer for a disabled child.

The effect of the *Carmichael* decision was that, as they related to those groups, the restrictions in paras 10-12 had been unlawful since they came into force (and that the equivalent restrictions in the housing benefit schemes had been unlawful since April 1, 2013, when they came into force). As the legislation was only amended to remove the discrimination with effect from April 1, 2017, the question arose what the First-tier Tribunal and Upper Tribunal should do in appeals relating to the intervening period. In *Secretary of State for Work and Pensions v Carmichael and Sefton Council* [2018] EWCA Civ 548; [2018] 1 W.L.R. 3429, the Court of Appeal decided by a majority—and contrary to the previously orthodox view of the law—that courts and tribunals have no power to disapply either primary or secondary legislation that infringes Convention Rights. However, in *RR v Secretary of State for Work and Pensions* [2019] UKSC 52; [2019] 1 W.L.R. 6430, the Supreme Court allowed the claimant's appeal: see further the discussion in Vol.III.

Note that in the case of renters in the private sector or who occupy temporary accommodation (see para.21 for the meaning of "temporary accommodation") the maximum number of bedrooms allowed is four (see para.26). There is no limit for renters in the social rented sector. In addition, in the case of private sector renters and those in temporary accommodation, the housing costs element for single claimants (including a member of a couple who is claiming as a single person: see reg.3(3)) aged under 35, with no children or qualifying young persons for whom they are responsible and no non-dependants, is restricted to the local housing allowance rate for one bedroom shared accommodation, unless they are exempt from this restriction (see paras 27–29).

Under para.10, a renter is allowed one bedroom for each of the categories of people in their extended benefit unit listed in sub-para.(1). If a person falls into more than one category, they are treated as in the category that results in the renter being allowed the lowest number of bedrooms (see sub-para.(2)). Paragraph F3112 ADM gives the following example of when sub-para.(2) might apply. A couple have four children, two boys aged 15 and 6 and two girls aged 12 and 8. The two boys could be allocated one room and the two girls one room under sub-para.(1)(e). Alternatively, having allocated the two girls one room under sub-para.(1)(e), the boys could be allocated one room each under sub-para.(1)(f). But as the first alternative results in a fewer number of bedrooms, that will be the number of bedrooms (two) that is allocated.

Note that joint renters (i.e. joint claimants: see para.1(2)) are allowed one bedroom but a non-dependant couple will be allocated one bedroom each (although a housing cost contribution (see paras 13–16) may be made in respect of each of them).

Under para.12, a renter is allowed additional bedrooms for each of the following conditions that they meet: (i) the overnight care condition (for the test for this see sub-para.(3)); (ii) the foster parent condition (see sub-paras (4) and (5) for the test); (iii) the disabled child condition (see sub-para.(6) for the test). If the renter satisfies two or more of the conditions, the number of additional bedrooms allowed will be the total for both or all conditions (sub-para.(9)). But where multiple occupants satisfy an individual condition, the household will be allowed only one additional bedroom in that category (sub-para (9)).

In *SM v Secretary of State for Work and Pensions (UHC)* [2023] UKUT 176 (AAC) the Upper Tribunal decided that in the context of the Sch.4 para.12(3) "overnight care condition", "regular" care means care that is provided "sufficiently often". The FTT had not correctly understood the meaning of "regular" and the findings of fact it made were therefore insufficient: [28]-[30]. In principle even relatively infrequent and unpredictable overnight care could qualify a claimant for an extra room, albeit that frequency would be a relevant factor in deciding whether care was regular. However, that conclusion did not assist SM: it is implicit in the para.12(3) "overnight care condition" that care must be required, and the FTT had been entitled to find that the care being given was not required [31].

Example

Amy and Nick are foster parents to two children. Nick also meets the overnight care condition. They are allowed two additional bedrooms. One for satisfying the overnight care condition and one for satisfying the foster parent condition. 2.495

If the disabled child condition is met, one additional bedroom will be allowed for each disabled child (see sub-para.(8)).

Note that the disabled child condition applies if it is the renter (or joint renters) *or* a member of the renter's extended benefit unit (i.e. including a non-dependant) who is responsible for the disabled child. The requirement under sub-para.(6)(b) that the child is "not reasonably able to share a room with another child" will be a matter of judgment, depending on the circumstances.

See para.11 for the circumstances in which a renter, a child or qualifying young person or a non-dependant will continue to count for the purpose of deciding the number of bedrooms allowed, despite being temporarily absent. Note also the temporary absence rule for a claimant (or claimants) in para.9 of Sch.3.

See also reg.37 (run-on after a death). Under this provision if a joint claimant, a child or qualifying young person (see reg.5) for whom a claimant was responsible (see reg.4), a severely disabled person for whom a claimant had regular and substantial caring responsibilities (see reg.30) or a non-dependant who was a member of the claimant's extended benefit unit (para.9(1)(c) and (2)) dies the claimant's universal credit award continues to be calculated as if the person had not died for the assessment period in which the death occurred and the following two assessment periods. Thus if such a death affects the number of bedrooms a renter is allowed, it will not do so for that run-on period.

Paragraphs 13–16

2.496 After the calculation of the renter's (or joint renters') housing costs element has been carried out under Pt 4 or 5 of this Schedule, a deduction (referred to as a "housing cost contribution") is made for non-dependants, unless they, or the renter, or joint renters, are exempt. The deduction has been £73.89 since April 8, 2019 for each non-dependant who is a member of the renter's extended benefit unit.

Paragraphs 17–19

2.497 See the notes to paras 4, 5 and 6 of Sch.3.

Paragraphs 20–25

2.498 The housing costs element for private sector renters and those in temporary accommodation (as defined in para.21) is calculated by taking the lower of the renter's core rent and their cap rent and deducting from that amount any housing cost contributions (para.22).

Core rent

2.499 If the renter is solely liable to make the relevant payments, their core rent is the total of the monthly equivalents of the rent payments (as defined in para.2 of Sch.1) and service charges (see para.7 of Sch.1) that they are liable (or treated as liable) to pay (para.23).

If the renter is jointly liable with another person or persons to make the relevant payments, their core rent is worked out by taking the total of the monthly equivalents of the rent payments and service charges for which they and the other person(s) are liable for the whole accommodation and applying the following rules.

If the only people who are jointly liable are "listed persons" (as defined in para.2) (i.e. the renter, their partner and any child or qualifying young person for whom either of them is responsible), the renter's core rent is that total amount (para.24(3)). If the liability is with one or more people who are not listed persons, the total amount is divided by the number of people who are liable and multiplied by the number of listed persons who are liable to make the relevant payments (para.24(4)). This is the renter's core rent. If, however, the Secretary of State (and on appeal a tribunal) is satisfied that it would be unreasonable to apportion the liability in this way, it is to be apportioned in a way that is appropriate in the circumstances (para.24(5)). Paragraph F3197 ADM gives the following example of where such an adjustment might be appropriate. Two brothers are joint tenants of a three bedroom property. One brother has his daughter living with him and pays two thirds of the rent. The decision maker considers that this is reasonable and that the appropriate core rent for that brother is two thirds (not half) of the rent payable.

Cap rent

2.500 A renter's cap rent depends on the category of dwelling, i.e. how many bedrooms they are allowed under the size criteria, subject to the four bedroom limit (see paras 8–12 and 26–29). Their cap rent is the local housing allowance that applies at the time their housing costs element is calculated for that category of dwelling in the area in which they live (para.25(1) and (2)). For how the cap rent is calculated if para.4 of Sch.3 (claimant housed in two dwellings by provider of social housing) applies, see the note to para.4 of Sch.3.

Paragraphs 30–36

2.501 The housing costs element for social sector renters (other than those in temporary accommodation, as defined in para.21) is calculated as follows. First, a deduction is made from any relevant payments (as defined in para.6) of any amount that is for the supply of a commodity (e.g. water or fuel) to the accommodation for use by the renter or any member of their extended benefit unit (para.31). Secondly, if, on the application of the Secretary of State, a rent officer has determined that a landlord might reasonably expect to get a lower amount than the amount of the relevant payment the renter pays, that lower figure will be used in the calculation of the renter's housing costs element, unless the Secretary of State (or on appeal a tribunal) considers that it is not appropriate to use that lower amount (para.32). An example might be where the rent is higher because it includes payment for modifications made to enable a disabled person to live in the property (see para.F3253 ADM) but the wording of para.32(4) is quite wide and is not restricted to this type of situation. Note, however, that (like housing benefit) there is no right of appeal against "so much of a decision as adopts a decision of a rent officer . . ." (para.6 of Sch.3 to the Decisions and Appeals Regulations 2013).

Thirdly, if the number of bedrooms in the accommodation is more than the number the renter is allowed under paras 8–12, an "under-occupation deduction" will be made. The reduction is 14 per cent in the case of one excess bedroom and 25 per cent in the case of two or more excess bedrooms (see para.36).

If a renter is solely liable to make the relevant payments, this deduction will be made from the monthly equivalent of the total of the rent payments and service charges that they are liable (or treated as liable) to pay, as reduced in accordance with paras 31 and 32(3) and (4), if applicable (para.34, step 4).

If the renter is jointly liable with another person or persons to make the relevant payments, an under-occupancy deduction will only be made if the only people who are jointly liable are "listed persons" (as defined in para.2) (i.e. the renter, their partner and any child or qualifying young person for whom either of them is responsible) (para.35(3)). If the joint liability is with one or more people who are not listed persons, no under-occupancy deduction will be made (there is no reference to such a deduction in para.35(4)).

Note also that no under-occupancy deduction is made in the case of a shared ownership tenancy (see para.36(5)).

Under para.35(3)-(5) the rules for working out the amount of the renter's housing costs element if they are jointly liable with another person or persons to make the relevant payments are the same that apply for the purpose of working out a renter's core rent under Part 4 of this Schedule (see above).

A deduction will be made for any housing cost contribution (para.33).

The new para.36(6) is made to remedy the legislative incompatibility with Convention rights identified by the First Section of the ECtHR in *JD & A v United Kingdom* (Apps 32949/17 and 34614/17) [2019] ECHR 753. A victim of domestic violence living in "sanctuary scheme" accommodation was discriminated against, contrary to art.14 of the ECHR read with art.1 of Protocol 1, by having an under-occupation deduction made from her benefit. The effect on her was disproportionately prejudicial (see [91] and [103]–[105]): a major aim of the under-occupation deduction policy was encouraging tenants to move to smaller accommodation, but sanctuary schemes existed to allow tenants to stay where they were, and the UK provided no weighty reasons to justify prioritising the former aim over the latter.

The decision of the ECtHR conflicts directly with the decision of the Supreme Court in *R. (Carmichael) v Secretary of State for Work and Pensions* [2016] UKSC 58; [2016] 1 W.L.R. 4550, where the same argument from the same litigant (*A*) was rejected by a majority of the Court (Hale DPSC and Carnwath JSC dissenting). The UK's request for the case to be referred to the Grand Chamber was rejected, so the ECtHR decision is final.

Regulation 26(3)

SCHEDULE 5

HOUSING COSTS ELEMENT FOR OWNER-OCCUPIERS

PART I

GENERAL

Introduction

2.502 **1.**—(1) This Schedule contains provisions about claimants to whom regulation 26(3) applies.

(2) Claimants who fall within sub-paragraph (1) are referred to in this Schedule as "owner-occupiers" (and references to "joint owner-occupiers" are to joint claimants to whom regulation 26(3) applies).

(3) Part 2 of this Schedule sets out an exception to section 11(1) of the Act for certain owner-occupiers in whose case an award of universal credit is not to include an amount of housing costs element calculated under this Schedule.

(4) Part 3 of this Schedule provides for a qualifying period that is to elapse before an amount of housing costs element calculated under this Schedule may be included in an owner-occupier's award of universal credit.

(5) Part 4 provides for the calculation of the amount of housing costs element to be included under this Schedule in an owner-occupier's award of universal credit.

Interpretation

2.503 **2.** In this Schedule—

[1[7 . . .]]

[7. . .]

"joint owner-occupier" has the meaning given in paragraph 1;

[7 ...]

"owner-occupier" means a single owner-occupier within the meaning of paragraph 1(2) or each of joint owner-occupiers;

"qualifying period" has the meaning given in paragraph 5;

[1 "relevant date" means, in relation to an owner-occupier, the date on which an amount of housing costs element calculated under this Schedule is first included in the owner-occupier's award;]

"relevant payments" has the meaning given in paragraph 3;

[7. . .]

"Relevant payments" for purposes of this Schedule

2.504 **3.**—[7 (1) "Relevant payments" means one or more payments which are service charge payments.]

(2) [7 ...]

(3) "Service charge payments" is to be understood in accordance with paragraphs 7 and 8 of that Schedule.

PART 2

EXCEPTION TO INCLUSION OF HOUSING COSTS ELEMENT

No housing costs element where owner-occupier has any earned income

2.505 **4.**—(1) Section 11(1) of the Act (housing costs) does not apply to any owner-occupier in relation to an assessment period where—

(a) the owner-occupier has any earned income; or

(b) if the owner-occupier is a member of a couple, either member of the couple has any earned income.

(2) Sub-paragraph (1) applies irrespective of the nature of the work engaged in, its duration or the amount of the earned income.

(3) Nothing in this paragraph prevents an amount calculated under Schedule 4 from being included in the award of any claimant who falls within regulation 26(4) to (6) (shared ownership).

PART 3

NO HOUSING COSTS ELEMENT FOR QUALIFYING PERIOD

No housing costs element under this Schedule for qualifying period

5.—(1) An owner-occupier's award of universal credit is not to include any amount of housing costs element calculated under this Schedule until the beginning of the assessment period that follows the assessment period in which the qualifying period ends. 2.506

(2) "Qualifying period" means a period of—

(a) in the case of a new award, [6 9] consecutive assessment periods in relation to which—

(i) the owner-occupier has been receiving universal credit, and

(ii) would otherwise qualify for the inclusion of an amount calculated under this Schedule in their award;

(b) in any case where an amount calculated under this Schedule has for any reason ceased to be included in the award, [6 9] consecutive assessment periods in relation to which the owner-occupier would otherwise qualify for the inclusion of an amount calculated under this Schedule in their award.

(3) Where, before the end of a qualifying period, an owner-occupier for any reason ceases to qualify for the inclusion of an amount calculated under this Schedule—

(a) that qualifying period stops running; and

(b) a new qualifying period starts only when the owner-occupier again meets the requirements of sub-paragraph (2)(a) or (b).

Application of paragraph 5: receipt of JSA and ESA

6.—(1) This paragraph applies to any owner-occupier who immediately before the commencement of an award of universal credit is entitled to— 2.507

(a) a jobseeker's allowance; or

(b) an employment and support allowance.

(2) In determining when the qualifying period in paragraph 5 ends in relation to the owner-occupier, any period that comprises only days on which the owner-occupier was receiving a benefit referred to in sub-paragraph (1) may be treated as if it were the whole or part of one or more assessment periods, as determined by the number of days on which any such benefit was received.

Application of paragraph 5: joint owner-occupiers ceasing to be a couple

7.—(1) This paragraph applies where— 2.508

(a) an award of universal credit to joint owner-occupiers is terminated because they cease to be a couple;

(b) a further award is made to one of them (or to each of them); and

(c) in relation to the further award (or in relation to each further award), the occupation condition is met in respect of the same accommodation as that occupied by the joint owner-occupiers as their home.

(2) In determining when the qualifying period in paragraph 5 ends in relation to the further award (or each further award), the whole or part of any assessment period which would have counted in relation to the award that is terminated is to be carried forward and taken into account in relation to the further award (or each further award).

(3) But where, immediately before the joint owner-occupiers' award was terminated, an amount of housing costs element calculated under this Schedule was already included in the award, no qualifying period under paragraph 5 applies to the owner-occupier in relation to the commencement of the further award (or each further award).

(4) For the purposes of sub-paragraph (1)(b), it is irrelevant whether the further award—

(a) is made on a claim; or

(b) by virtue of regulation 9(6) of the Universal Credit, Personal Independence Payment, Jobseeker's Allowance and Employment and Support Allowance (Claims and Payments) Regulations 2013 is made without a claim.

PART 4

CALCULATION OF AMOUNT OF HOUSING COSTS ELEMENT FOR OWNER-OCCUPIERS

Payments to be taken into account

2.509 **8.**—(1) Where an owner-occupier meets the payment condition, liability condition and occupation condition in respect of one or more relevant payments and the qualifying period has ended, each of the relevant payments is to be taken into account for the purposes of the calculation under this Part.

(2) No account is to be taken of any amount of a relevant payment to the extent that the conditions referred to in sub-paragraph (1) are not met in respect of that amount.

(3) Any particular payment for which an owner-occupier is liable is not to be brought into account more than once, whether in relation to the same or a different owner-occupier (but this does not prevent different payments of the same description being brought into account in respect of an assessment period).

The amount of housing costs element

2.510 **9.** The amount of the owner-occupier's housing costs element under this Schedule is [7 the amount resulting from paragraph 13] in respect of all relevant payments which are to be taken into account under paragraph 8.

Amount in respect of interest on loans

2.511 **10.** [7...]

Amount in respect of alternative finance arrangements

2.512 **11.**—[7...]

Standard rate to be applied under paragraphs 10 and 11

2.513 **12.**—[7...]

Amount in respect of service charge payments

2.514 **13.**—(1) This paragraph provides for the calculation of the amount to be included in the owner-occupier's housing costs element under this Schedule in respect of relevant payments which are service charge payments.

(2) The amount in respect of the service charge payments is to be calculated as follows.

Step 1

Determine the amount of each service charge payment.

Step 2

Determine the period in respect of which each service charge payment is payable and determine the amount of the payment in respect of a month (see sub-paragraphs (3) and (4)).

Step 3

If there is more than one service charge payment, add together the amounts determined in step 2.

The result is the amount to be included under this Schedule in respect of service charge payments.

(3) Where the period in respect of which an owner-occupier is liable to make a service charge payment is not a month, an amount is to be calculated as the monthly equivalent, so for example—

(a) weekly payments are multiplied by 52 and divided by 12;

[5 (aa) two-weekly payments are multiplied by 26 and divided by 12;]

(b) four-weekly payments are multiplied by 13 and divided by 12;

(c) three-monthly payments are multiplied by 4 and divided by 12; and

(d) annual payments are divided by 12.

(4) Where an owner-occupier is liable for service charge payments under arrangements that provide for one or more service charge free periods, [5 subject to sub-paragraph (4A),] the monthly equivalent is to be calculated over 12 months by reference to the total number of service charge payments which the owner-occupier is liable to make in that 12 month period.

[5 (4A) Where sub-paragraph (4) applies and the service charge payments in question are—

(a) weekly payments, the total number of weekly service charge payments which the owner-occupier is liable to make in any 12 month period shall be calculated by reference to the formula—

$$52 - SCFP;$$

(b) two-weekly payments, the total number of two-weekly service charge payments which the owner-occupier is liable to make in any 12 month period shall be calculated by reference to the formula—

$$26 - SCFP;$$

(c) four weekly payments, the total number of four-weekly service charge payments which the owner-occupier is liable to make in any 12 month period shall be calculated by reference to the formula—

$$13 - SCFP;$$

where "SCFP" is the number of service charge free periods in the 12 month period in question.]

(5) "Service charge free period" means any period in respect of which the owner-occupier has no liability to make one or more of the service charge payments which are to be taken into account under paragraph 8.

AMENDMENTS

1. Universal Credit and Miscellaneous Amendments Regulations 2014 (SI 2014/597) reg.2(14)(a) (April 28, 2014).

2. Universal Credit and Miscellaneous Amendments Regulations 2014 (SI 2014/597) reg.2(14)(b) (April 28, 2014).

3. Universal Credit and Miscellaneous Amendments Regulations 2014 (SI 2014/597) reg.2(14)(c) (April 28, 2014).

4. Universal Credit and Miscellaneous Amendments Regulations 2014 (SI 2014/597) reg.2(14)(d) (April 28, 2014).

5. Universal Credit and Miscellaneous Amendments Regulations 2014 (SI 2014/597) reg.2(14)(e) (April 28, 2014).

6. Social Security (Housing Costs Amendments) Regulations 2015 (SI 2015/1647) reg.5(2) (April 1, 2016). The amendment is subject to the saving provision in reg.8 of SI 2015/1647 (see Pt IV).

7. Loans for Mortgage Interest Regulations 2017 (SI 2017/725) reg.18 and Sch.5 para.5(f) (April 6, 2018).

DEFINITIONS

"the Act"—see reg.2.
"assessment period"—see WRA 2012, ss.40 and 7(2) and reg.21.
"claim"—see WRA 2012, s.40.
"claimant"—*ibid.*
"couple"—see WRA 2012, ss.39 and 40.
"earned income"—see reg.2.
"employment and support allowance"—*ibid.*
"jobseeker's allowance"—*ibid.*
"personal independence payment"—*ibid.*

GENERAL NOTE

Paragraphs 1–4 2.515

This Schedule concerns the calculation of the housing costs element for "owner-occupiers" (see para.1(2)). For the definition of "owner-occupier" see para.2. References to "joint owner-occupiers" are to joint claimants who are owner-occupiers (para.1(2)).

For an owner-occupier (or joint owner-occupier) to be entitled to a housing costs element under this Schedule, they must meet the payment, liability and occupation conditions in respect of one or more "relevant payments" (as defined in para.3) and the qualifying period (see paras 5–7) must have ended.

"Relevant payments" for the purposes of Sch.5 are service charges (on which see paras 7 and 8 of Sch.1). If the claimant (or claimants) is only liable for service charges payments, these will be calculated under this Schedule (see reg.26(3)). But if the claimant has a shared ownership tenancy, any service charges are calculated in accordance with Sch.4 (reg.26(5)).

Note the significant exclusion in para.4 from entitlement to a housing costs element under Sch.5. If an owner-occupier, or if they are a member of a couple, either member of the couple, has *any* earned income in an assessment period (i.e. month), they will not be entitled to a housing costs element in that assessment period. However, in the case of a shared ownership tenancy, rent payments and service charges can still be met (para.4(3)).

Paragraphs 5–7

2.516 There is a waiting period (referred to as "a qualifying period") for owner-occupier and service charges payments. In the case of a new award of universal credit, a housing costs element cannot be included until there have been nine consecutive assessment periods (i.e. months) during which the owner-occupier has been receiving universal credit *and* would otherwise have qualified for a housing costs element under Sch.5 (para.5(2)(a)). A housing costs element is included from the start of the next assessment period. If, once awarded, there is a break in entitlement to a housing costs element under Sch.5 (e.g. because of earnings), the owner-occupier has to serve a further nine consecutive months during which they would otherwise qualify for a housing costs element before they can be awarded a housing costs element under Sch.5 again (para.5(2)(b)). This applies even if the owner-occupier continues to be entitled to universal credit during the break in entitlement to a housing costs element under Sch.5. If during a waiting period an owner-occupier ceases to qualify for a housing costs element under Sch.5, that waiting period ends and a new waiting period will have to be served (para.5(3)).

Note that before April 1, 2016 the waiting period under para.5(2)(a) and (b) was only three consecutive assessment periods. The amendment which increased the waiting period to nine months is subject to a saving provision (see reg.8 of the Social Security (Housing Costs Amendments) Regulations 2015 in Pt IV of this Volume). The effect of the saving provision in relation to universal credit is that for those claimants who are entitled, or treated as entitled, to one or more relevant benefits (i.e., income support, old style JSA, old style ESA or universal credit) for a continuous period which includes March 31, 2016, the form of reg.5(2)(a) and (b) and of reg. 29 of the Universal Credit (Transitional) Regulations 2014 that were in force before the April 1, 2016 amendments continues to have effect. So for claimants who are in a waiting period on March 31, 2016 the waiting period for a housing costs element remains three consecutive assessment periods.

Paragraphs 6 and 7 contain exceptions to the rule in para.5.

If immediately before the owner-occupier's award of universal credit began, s/he was entitled to new style JSA or new style ESA, the days that s/he was only receiving one of these benefits can count towards the waiting period (para.6).

Under para.7, if a universal credit award made to joint owner-occupiers comes to an end because they have ceased to be a couple, and a further award is made to one of them who continues to occupy the same accommodation as they did when they were a couple, the further award will include a housing costs element under Sch.5 without a waiting period if a housing costs element was included in the joint award. If a housing costs element was not yet included in the joint award, any assessment period, or part of an assessment period, which counted towards the waiting period under the joint award counts towards the waiting period for the new award. If both members of the former couple remain in the same accommodation and both claim and are awarded universal credit again, this provision will apply to both of them.

The waiting period may also be extinguished or reduced under reg.29 of the Transitional Provisions Regulations 2014, which applies where in the one month before the claim for universal credit was made, or treated as made, the owner occupier, or his/her partner or former partner, was entitled to income support, old style JSA or old style ESA that included help with housing costs or did not yet do so only because a waiting period was being served.

Paras 8, 9 and 13

The amount for service charges that can be included in an owner-occupier's housing costs element is the monthly equivalent of the actual service charge payment or payments (see para.13). Where the owner-occupier has the benefit of service charge free periods (defined in para.13(5)), the conversion to a monthly figure is based on a standard 52 week year (see para. 13(4) and the formula in para.13(4A)). 2.517

Note:

- No "housing cost contribution" for a non-dependant is made in the case of amounts awarded under Sch.5 (this is to be contrasted with the position under income support, old style JSA and old style ESA).
- Under reg.39(4) of the Decisions and Appeals Regulations 2013, if the Secretary of State considers that he does not have all the relevant information or evidence to decide what housing costs element to award, the decision will be made on the basis of the housing costs element that can immediately be awarded.

Regulation 39(2) and(3)

SCHEDULE 6

ASSESSMENT OF WHETHER A CLAIMANT HAS LIMITED CAPABILITY FOR WORK

PART I

PHYSICAL DISABILITIES 2.518

(1)	(2)	(3)
Activity	Descriptors	Points
1. Mobilising unaided by another person with or without a walking stick, manual wheelchair or other aid if such aid is normally or could reasonably be worn or used.	1 (a) Cannot, unaided by another person, either: (i) mobilise more than 50 metres on level ground without stopping in order to avoid significant discomfort or exhaustion; or (ii) repeatedly mobilise 50 metres within a reasonable timescale because of significant discomfort or exhaustion.	15
	(b) Cannot, unaided by another person, mount or descend two steps even with the support of a handrail.	9
	(c) Cannot, unaided by another person, either: (i) mobilise more than 100 metres on level ground without stopping in order to avoid significant discomfort or exhaustion; or	9

(1)	(2)	(3)
Activity	Descriptors	Points
	(ii) repeatedly mobilise 100 metres within a reasonable timescale because of significant discomfort or exhaustion.	
	(d) Cannot, unaided by another person, either: (i) mobilise more than 200 metres on level ground without stopping in order to avoid significant discomfort or exhaustion; or (ii) repeatedly mobilise 200 metres within a reasonable timescale because of significant discomfort or exhaustion.	6
	(e) None of the above applies.	0
2. Standing and sitting.	2 (a) Cannot move between one seated position and another seated position which are located next to one another without receiving physical assistance from another person.	15
	(b) Cannot, for the majority of the time, remain at a work station: (i) standing unassisted by another person (even if free to move around); (ii) sitting (even in an adjustable chair); or (iii) a combination of paragraphs (i) and (ii), for more than 30 minutes, before needing to move away in order to avoid significant discomfort or exhaustion.	9
	(c) Cannot, for the majority of the time, remain at a work station: (i) standing unassisted by another person (even if free to move around); (ii) sitting (even in an adjustable chair); or (iii) a combination of paragraphs (i) and (ii), for more than an hour before needing to move away in order to avoid significant discomfort or exhaustion.	6
	(d) None of the above applies.	
3. Reaching.	3 (a) Cannot raise either arm as if to put something in the top pocket of a coat or jacket.	15
	(b) Cannot raise either arm to top of head as if to put on a hat.	9
	(c) Cannot raise either arm above head height as if to reach for something.	6
	(d) None of the above applies.	0
4. Picking up and moving or transferring by the use of the upper body and arms.	4 (a) Cannot pick up and move a 0.5 litre carton full of liquid.	15
	(b) Cannot pick up and move a one litre carton full of liquid.	9
	(c) Cannot transfer a light but bulky object such as an empty cardboard box.	6
	(d) None of the above applies.	0

(1)	(2)	(3)
Activity	Descriptors	Points
5. Manual dexterity.	5 (a) Cannot press a button (such as a telephone keypad) with either hand or cannot turn the pages of a book with either hand.	15
	(b) Cannot pick up a £1 coin or equivalent with either hand.	15
	(c) Cannot use a pen or pencil to make a meaningful mark with either hand.	9
	(d) Cannot single-handedly use a suitable keyboard or mouse.	9
	(e) None of the above applies.	0
6. Making self understood through speaking, writing, typing, or other means which are normally or could reasonably be used, unaided by another person.	6 (a) Cannot convey a simple message, such as the presence of a hazard.	15
	(b) Has significant difficulty conveying a simple message to strangers.	15
	(c) Has some difficulty conveying a simple message to strangers.	6
	(d) None of the above applies.	0
7. Understanding communication by: (i) verbal means (such as hearing or lip reading) alone; (ii) non-verbal means (such as reading 16 point	7 (a) Cannot understand a simple message, such as the location of a fire escape, due to sensory impairment.	15
	(b) Has significant difficulty understanding a simple message from a stranger due to sensory impairment.	15
print or Braille) alone; or print or Braille) alone; or (iii) a combination of sub-paragraphs (i) and (ii), using any aid that is normally or could reasonably be used, unaided by another person.	(c) Has some difficulty understanding a simple message from a stranger due to sensory impairment.	6
	(d) None of the above applies.	0
8. Navigation and maintaining safety using a guide dog or other aid if either or both are normally used or could reasonably be used.	8 (a) Unable to navigate around familiar surroundings, without being accompanied by another person, due to sensory impairment.	15
	(b) Cannot safely complete a potentially hazardous task such as crossing the road, without being accompanied by another person, due to sensory impairment.	15
	(c) Unable to navigate around unfamiliar surroundings, without being accompanied by another person, due to sensory impairment.	9
	(d) None of the above applies.	0

(1)	(2)	(3)
Activity	Descriptors	Points
9. Absence or loss of control whilst conscious leading to extensive evacuation of the bowel and/or bladder, other than enuresis (bed-wetting), despite the wearing or use of any aids or adaptations which are normally or could reasonably be worn or used.	9 (a) At least once a month experiences: (i) loss of control leading to extensive evacuation of the bowel and/or voiding of the bladder; or (ii) substantial leakage of the contents of a collecting device, sufficient to require cleaning and a change in clothing.	15
	(b) The majority of the time is at risk of loss of control leading to extensive evacuation of the bowel and/or voiding of the bladder, sufficient to require cleaning and a change in clothing, if not able to reach a toilet quickly.	6
	(c) Neither of the above applies.	0
10. Consciousness during waking moments.	10 (a) At least once a week, has an involuntary episode of lost or altered consciousness resulting in significantly disrupted awareness or concentration.	15
	(b) At least once a month, has an involuntary episode of lost or altered consciousness resulting in significantly disrupted awareness or concentration.	6
	(c) Neither of the above applies.	0

PART 2

MENTAL, COGNITIVE AND INTELLECTUAL FUNCTION ASSESSMENT

(1)	(2)	(3)
Activity	Descriptors	Points
11. Learning tasks.	11 (a) Cannot learn how to complete a simple task, such as setting an alarm clock.	15
	(b) Cannot learn anything beyond a simple task, such as setting an alarm clock.	9
	(c) Cannot learn anything beyond a moderately complex task, such as the steps involved in operating a washing machine to clean clothes.	6
	(d) None of the above applies.	0
12. Awareness of everyday hazards (such as boiling water or sharp objects).	12 (a) Reduced awareness of everyday hazards leads to a significant risk of: (i) injury to self or others; or (ii) damage to property or possessions, such that the claimant requires supervision for the majority of the time to maintain safety.	15
	(b) Reduced awareness of everyday hazards leads to a significant risk of: (i) injury to self or others; or (ii) damage to property or possessions, such that the claimant frequently requires supervision to maintain safety.	9
	(c) Reduced awareness of everyday hazards leads to a significant risk of: (i) injury to self or others; or	6

(1)	(2)	(3)
Activity	Descriptors	Points
	(ii) damage to property or possessions, such that the claimant occasionally requires supervision to maintain safety.	
	(d) None of the above applies.	0
13. Initiating and completing personal action (which means planning, organisation, problem solving, prioritising or switching tasks).	13 (a) Cannot, due to impaired mental function, reliably initiate or complete at least two sequential personal actions.	15
	(b) Cannot, due to impaired mental function, reliably initiate or complete at least two sequential personal actions for the majority of the time.	9
	(c) Frequently cannot, due to impaired mental function, reliably initiate or complete at least two sequential personal actions.	6
	(d) None of the above applies.	0
14. Coping with change.	14 (a) Cannot cope with any change to the extent that day to day life cannot be managed.	15
	(b) Cannot cope with minor planned change (such as a pre-arranged change to the routine time scheduled for a lunch break), to the extent that, overall, day to day life is made significantly more difficult.	9
	(c) Cannot cope with minor unplanned change (such as the timing of an appointment on the day it is due to occur), to the extent that, overall, day to day life is made significantly more difficult.	6
	(d) None of the above applies.	0
15. Getting about.	15 (a) Cannot get to any place outside the claimant's home with which the claimant is familiar.	15
	(b) Is unable to get to a specified place with which the claimant is familiar, without being accompanied by another person.	9
	(c) Is unable to get to a specified place with which the claimant is unfamiliar without being accompanied by another person.	6
	(d) None of the above applies.	0
16. Coping with social engagement due to cognitive impairment or mental disorder.	16 (a) Engagement in social contact is always precluded due to difficulty relating to others or significant distress experienced by the claimant.	15
	(b) Engagement in social contact with someone unfamiliar to the claimant is always precluded due to difficulty relating to others or significant distress experienced by the claimant.	9
	(c) Engagement in social contact with someone unfamiliar to the claimant is not possible for the majority of the time due to difficulty relating to others or significant distress experienced by the claimant.	6
	(d) None of the above applies.	0

(1)	(2)	(3)
Activity	Descriptors	Points
17. Appropriateness of behaviour with other people, due to cognitive impairment or mental disorder.	17 (a) Has, on a daily basis, uncontrollable episodes of aggressive or disinhibited behaviour that would be unreasonable in any workplace.	15
	(b) Frequently has uncontrollable episodes of aggressive or disinhibited behaviour that would be unreasonable in any workplace.	15
	(c) Occasionally has uncontrollable episodes of aggressive or disinhibited behaviour that would be unreasonable in any workplace.	9
	(d) None of the above applies.	0

2.519 DEFINITIONS

"claimant"—see WRA 2012 s.40.

"limited capability for work"—see WRA 2012 ss.40 and 37(1).

GENERAL NOTE

2.520 The activities and descriptors for assessing whether a claimant has LCW are the same as the activities and descriptors in Sch.2 to the ESA Regulations 2008. See the notes to Sch.2 to the 2008 Regulations in Vol.I of this series. They are also the same as the activities and descriptors in Sch.2 to the ESA Regulations 2013.

Regulation 40(2) and (3)

2.521 SCHEDULE 7

ASSESSMENT OF WHETHER A CLAIMANT HAS LIMITED CAPABILITY FOR WORK AND WORK-RELATED ACTIVITY

Activity	Descriptors
1. Mobilising unaided by another person with or without a walking stick, manual wheelchair or other aid if such aid is normally or could reasonably be worn or used.	1 Cannot either: (a) mobilise more than 50 metres on level ground without stopping in order to avoid significant discomfort or exhaustion; or (b) repeatedly mobilise 50 metres within a reasonable timescale because of significant discomfort or exhaustion.
2. Transferring from one seated position to another.	2. Cannot move between one seated position and another seated position located next to one another without receiving physical assistance from another person.
3. Reaching.	3 Cannot raise either arm as if to put something in the top pocket of a coat or jacket.
4. Picking up and moving or transferring by the use of the upper body and arms (excluding standing, sitting, bending or kneeling and all other activities specified in this Schedule).	4 Cannot pick up and move a 0.5 litre carton full of liquid.

5. Manual dexterity.	5 Cannot press a button (such as a telephone keypad) with either hand or cannot turn the pages of a book with either hand.
6. Making self understood through speaking, writing, typing, or other means which are normally, or could reasonably be, used unaided by another person.	6 Cannot convey a simple message, such as the presence of a hazard.
7. Understanding communication by: (i) verbal means (such as hearing or lip reading) alone; (ii) non-verbal means (such as reading 16 point print or Braille) alone; or (iii) a combination of sub-paragraphs (i) and (ii), using any aid that is normally, or could reasonably, be used unaided by another person.	7 Cannot understand a simple message, such as the location of a fire escape, due to sensory impairment.
8. Absence or loss of control whilst conscious leading to extensive evacuation of the bowel and/or voiding of the bladder, other than enuresis (bed-wetting), despite the wearing or use of any aids or adaptations which are normally or could reasonably be worn or used.	8 At least once a week experiences: (a) loss of control leading to extensive evacuation of the bowel and/or voiding of the bladder; or (b) substantial leakage of the contents of a collecting device sufficient to require the individual to clean themselves and change clothing.
9. Learning tasks.	9 Cannot learn how to complete a simple task, such as setting an alarm clock, due to cognitive impairment or mental disorder.
10. Awareness of hazard.	10 Reduced awareness of everyday hazards, due to cognitive impairment or mental disorder, leads to a significant risk of: (a) injury to self or others; or (b) damage to property or possessions, such that the claimant requires supervision for the majority of the time to maintain safety.
11. Initiating and completing personal action (which means planning, organisation, problem solving, prioritising or switching tasks).	11 Cannot, due to impaired mental function, reliably initiate or complete at least two sequential personal actions.
12. Coping with change.	12 Cannot cope with any change, due to cognitive impairment or mental disorder, to the extent that day to day life cannot be managed.
13. Coping with social engagement, due to cognitive impairment or mental disorder.	13 Engagement in social contact is always precluded due to difficulty relating to others or significant distress experienced by the claimant.
14. Appropriateness of behaviour with other people, due to cognitive impairment or mental disorder.	14 Has, on a daily basis, uncontrollable episodes of aggressive or disinhibited behaviour that would be unreasonable in any workplace.

15. Conveying food or drink to the mouth.	15 (a) Cannot convey food or drink to the claimant's own mouth without receiving physical assistance from someone else; (b) Cannot convey food or drink to the claimant's own mouth without repeatedly stopping or experiencing breathlessness or severe discomfort; (c) Cannot convey food or drink to the claimant's own mouth without receiving regular prompting given by someone else in the claimant's presence; or (d) Owing to a severe disorder of mood or behaviour, fails to convey food or drink to the claimant's own mouth without receiving: (i) physical assistance from someone else; or (ii) regular prompting given by someone else in the claimant's presence.
16. Chewing or swallowing food or drink.	16 (a) Cannot chew or swallow food or drink; (b) Cannot chew or swallow food or drink without repeatedly stopping or experiencing breathlessness or severe discomfort; (c) Cannot chew or swallow food or drink without repeatedly receiving regular prompting given by someone else in the claimant's presence; or (d) Owing to a severe disorder of mood or behaviour, fails to: (i) chew or swallow food or drink; or (ii) chew or swallow food or drink without regular prompting given by someone else in the claimant's presence.

DEFINITIONS

"claimant"—see WRA 2012 s.40.
"limited capability for work"—see WRA 2012 ss.40 and 37(1).
"limited capability for work-related activity"—see WRA 2012 ss.40 and 37(2).

GENERAL NOTE

2.522 The activities and descriptors for assessing whether a claimant has LCW and LCWRA are the same as the activities and descriptors in Sch.3 to the ESA Regulations 2008 for assessing whether a claimant has LCWRA. See the notes to Sch.3 to the 2008 Regulations in Vol.I of this series. They are also the same as the activities and descriptors in Sch.3 to the ESA Regulations 2013.

Regulation 39(6)

SCHEDULE 8

CIRCUMSTANCES IN WHICH A CLAIMANT IS TO BE TREATED AS HAVING LIMITED CAPABILITY FOR WORK

Receiving certain treatments

2.523 **1.** The claimant is receiving—

(a) regular weekly treatment by way of haemodialysis for chronic renal failure;
(b) treatment by way of plasmapheresis; or
(c) regular weekly treatment by way of total parenteral nutrition for gross impairment of enteric function,

or is recovering from any of those forms of treatment in circumstances in which the Secretary of State is satisfied that the claimant should be treated as having limited capability for work.

In hospital

2.—(1) The claimant is— 2.524

(a) undergoing medical or other treatment as [1 a patient] in a hospital or similar institution; or

(b) recovering from such treatment in circumstances in which the Secretary of State is satisfied that the claimant should be treated as having limited capability for work.

(2) The circumstances in which a claimant is to be regarded as undergoing treatment falling within sub-paragraph (1)(a) include where the claimant is attending a residential programme of rehabilitation for the treatment of drug or alcohol dependency.

(3) For the purposes of this paragraph, a claimant is to be regarded as undergoing treatment as a patient in a hospital or similar institution only if that claimant has been advised by a health care professional to stay [2 for a period of 24 hours or longer] following medical or other treatment.

Prevented from working by law

3.—(1) The claimant— 2.525

(a) is excluded or abstains from work pursuant to a request or notice in writing lawfully made or given under an enactment; or

(b) is otherwise prevented from working pursuant to an enactment,

by reason of it being known or reasonably suspected that the claimant is infected or contaminated by, or has been in contact with a case of, a relevant infection or contamination.

(2) In sub-paragraph (1) "relevant infection or contamination" means—

(a) in England and Wales—

(i) any incidence or spread of infection or contamination, within the meaning of section 45A(3) of the Public Health (Control of Disease) Act 1984 in respect of which regulations are made under Part 2A of that Act (public health protection) for the purpose of preventing, protecting against, controlling or providing a public health response to, such incidence or spread, or

(ii) tuberculosis or any infectious disease to which regulation 9 of the Public Health (Aircraft) Regulations 1979 (powers in respect of persons leaving aircraft) applies or to which regulation 10 of the Public Health (Ships) Regulations 1979 (powers in respect of certain persons on ships) applies; and

(b) in Scotland any—

(i) infectious disease within the meaning of section 1(5) of the Public Health etc (Scotland) Act 2008, or exposure to an organism causing that disease; or

(ii) contamination within the meaning of section 1(5) of that Act, or exposure to a contaminant,

to which sections 56 to 58 of that Act (compensation) apply.

Risk to self or others

4.—(1) The claimant is suffering from a specific illness, disease or disablement by reason of which there would be a substantial risk to the physical or mental health of any person were the claimant found not to have limited capability for work. 2.526

(2) This paragraph does not apply where the risk could be reduced by a significant amount by—

(a) reasonable adjustments being made in the claimant's workplace; or

(b) the claimant taking medication to manage their condition where such medication has been prescribed for the claimant by a registered medical practitioner treating the claimant.

Life threatening disease

5. The claimant is suffering from a life threatening disease in relation to which— 2.527

(a) there is medical evidence that the disease is uncontrollable, or uncontrolled, by a recognised therapeutic procedure; and

(b) in the case of a disease that is uncontrolled, there is a reasonable cause for it not to be controlled by a recognised therapeutic procedure.

Disabled and over the age for state pension credit

6. The claimant has reached the qualifying age for state pension credit and is entitled to disability living allowance [3, personal independence payment or adult disability payment]. 2.528

AMENDMENTS

1. Universal Credit (Consequential, Supplementary, Incidental and Miscellaneous Provisions) Regulations 2013 (SI 2013/630), reg.38(10) (April 29, 2013).

2. Social Security (Miscellaneous Amendments) (No.2) Regulations 2013 (SI 2013/1508), reg.3(11) (July 29, 2013).

3. Social Security (Disability Assistance for Working Age People) (Consequential Amendments) Order 2022 (SI 2022/177) art.13(9) (March 21, 2022).

DEFINITIONS

"adult disability payment"—see reg.2.
"claimant"—see WRA 2012 s.40.
"disability living allowance"—see reg.2.
"health care professional"–*ibid.*
"limited capability for work"—see WRA 2012 ss.40 and 37(1).
"personal independence payment"—see reg.2.

GENERAL NOTE

2.529 Paragraph 1 is similar, though not identical, to reg.26 of the ESA Regulations 2008; para. 2 is similar, though not identical, to reg.25 of those Regulations; and para. 3 is the same as reg.20(1)(c) and (2) of the 2008 Regulations. See the notes to regs 20, 25 and 26 of the 2008 Regulations in Vol.I of this series.

Note that Sch.8 does not contain provisions for treating a claimant who is (i) terminally ill; (ii) a pregnant woman whose health, or whose unborn child's health, is at serious risk of damage: or (iii) receiving treatment for cancer as having limited capability for work. Such a claimant will be treated as having LCW and LCWRA under paras 1 to 3 respectively of Sch.9 (see below).

There is no equivalent of para.6 in the ESA Regulations 2008.

Paragraphs 4 and 5 together contain very similar provisions to those in reg. 29 of the 2008 Regulations (see the notes to reg.29 in Vol.1 of this series). Note the amendment to reg. 39 made on April 28, 2014, the effect of which is that a claimant can only be treated as having LCW under paras 4 or 5 if they have been assessed as not having LCW. Regulation 29 of the 2008 Regulations already contains such a provision.

Regulation 40(5)

SCHEDULE 9

CIRCUMSTANCES IN WHICH A CLAIMANT IS TO BE TREATED AS HAVING LIMITED CAPABILITY FOR WORK AND WORK-RELATED ACTIVITY

Terminal illness

2.530 **1.** The claimant is terminally ill.

Pregnancy

2.531 **2.** The claimant is a pregnant woman and there is a serious risk of damage to her health or to the health of her unborn child if she does not refrain from work and work-related activity.

Receiving treatment for cancer

2.532 **3.** The claimant is—

(a) receiving treatment for cancer by way of chemotherapy or radiotherapy;
(b) likely to receive such treatment within 6 months after the date of the determination of capability for work and work-related activity; or
(c) recovering from such treatment,

and the Secretary of State is satisfied that the claimant should be treated as having limited capability for work and work-related activity.

Risk to self or others

4. The claimant is suffering from a specific illness, disease or disablement by reason of which there would be a substantial risk to the physical or mental health of any person were the claimant found not to have limited capability for work and work-related activity. 2.533

Disabled and over the age for state pension credit

5. The claimant has reached the qualifying age for state pension credit and is entitled to attendance allowance, the care component of disability living allowance at the highest rate or the daily living component of personal independence payment at the enhanced rate [1 or the daily living component of adult disability payment at the enhanced rate in accordance with regulation 5(3) of the Disability Assistance for Working Age People (Scotland) Regulations 2022]. 2.534

AMENDMENT

1. Social Security (Disability Assistance for Working Age People) (Consequential Amendments) Order 2022 (SI 2022/177) art.13(10) (March 21, 2022).

DEFINITIONS

"adult disability payment"—see reg.2.
"attendance allowance"—*ibid.*
"child"—see WRA 2012, s.40.
"claimant"—*ibid.*
"limited capability for work"—see WRA 2012, ss.40 and 37(1).
"limited capability for work-related activity"—see WRA 2012, ss.40 and 37(2).
"personal independence payment"—see reg.2.

GENERAL NOTE

For the equivalent of (i) para.1, see regs 20(1)(a) and 35(1)(a) of the ESA Regulations 2008; (ii) para.2, see regs 20(1)(d) and 35(1)(c) of those Regulations; and (iii) para.3, see regs 20(1)(b) and 35(1)(b) of the 2008 Regulations. See the notes to regs 20 and 35 of the 2008 Regulations in Vol.I of this series. 2.535

There is no equivalent of para.5 in the ESA Regulations 2008.

Paragraph 4 contains very similar provisions to those in regs 29(2)(b) and 35(2) of the 2008 Regulations (see the notes to regs 29 and 35 in Vol.1 of this series). Note the amendment to reg. 40 made on April 28, 2014, the effect of which is that a claimant can only be treated as having LCW and LCWRA under para.4 if they have been assessed as not having LCW and LCWRA. Regulations 29 and 35 of the 2008 Regulations already contain such a provision.

Regulation 48

SCHEDULE 10

CAPITAL TO BE DISREGARDED

Premises

1.—(1) Premises occupied by a person as their home. 2.536

(2) For the purposes of this paragraph and paragraphs 2 to 5, only one set of premises may be treated as a person's home.

2. Premises occupied by a close relative of a person as their home where that close relative has limited capability for work or has reached the qualifying age for state pension credit.

3. Premises occupied by a person's former partner as their home where the person and their former partner are not estranged, but living apart by force of circumstances, for example where the person is in residential care.

4.—(1) Premises that a person intends to occupy as their home where—

(a) the person has acquired the premises within the past 6 months but not yet taken up occupation;
(b) the person is taking steps to obtain possession and has commenced those steps within the past 6 months; or
(c) the person is carrying out essential repairs or alterations required to render the premises fit for occupation and these have been commenced within the past 6 months.

(2) A person is to be taken to have commenced steps to obtain possession of premises on the date that legal advice is first sought or proceedings are commenced, whichever is earlier.

5. Premises that a person has ceased to occupy as their home following an estrangement from their former partner where—
(a) the person has ceased to occupy the premises within the past 6 months; or
(b) the person's former partner is a lone parent and occupies the premises as their home.

6. Premises that a person is taking reasonable steps to dispose of where those steps have been commenced within the past 6 months.

Business assets

2.537 **7.** Assets which are used wholly or mainly for the purposes of a trade, profession or vocation which the person is carrying on.

8. Assets which were used wholly or mainly for a trade, profession or vocation that the person has ceased to carry on within the past 6 months if—
(a) the person is taking reasonable steps to dispose of those assets; or
(b) the person ceased to be engaged in carrying on the trade, profession or vocation because of incapacity and can reasonably expect to be reengaged on recovery.

Rights in pensions schemes etc.

9. The value of any policy of life insurance.

2.538 **10.**—(1) The value of any right to receive a pension under an occupational or personal pension scheme or any other pension scheme registered under section 153 of the Finance Act 2004.

(2) "Occupational pension scheme" and "personal pension scheme" have the meaning in section 1 of the Pension Schemes Act 1993.

11.—(1) The value of a funeral plan contract.

(2) "Funeral plan contract" means a contract under which the person makes payments to a person to secure the provision of a funeral and where the sole purpose of the plan is the provision of a funeral.

Amounts earmarked for special purposes

2.539 **12.** An amount deposited with a housing association as a condition of the person occupying premises as their home.

13. An amount received within the past 6 months which is to be used for the purchase of premises that the person intends to occupy as their home where that amount—
(a) is attributable to the proceeds of the sale of premises formerly occupied by the person as their home;
(b) has been deposited with a housing association as mentioned in paragraph 12; or
(c) is a grant made to the person for the sole purpose of the purchase of a home.

14. An amount received under an insurance policy within the past 6 months in connection with the loss or damage to the premises occupied by the person as their home or to their personal possessions.

15. An amount received within the past 6 months that is to be used for making essential repairs or alterations to premises occupied or intended to be occupied as the person's home where that amount has been acquired by the person (whether by grant or loan or otherwise) on condition that it is used for that purpose.

Other payments

2.540 **16.** A payment made within the past 12 months under Part 8 of the Contributions and Benefits Act (the social fund).

17.—(1) A payment made within the past 12 months by or on behalf of a local authority—
(a) under section 17, 23B, 23C or 24A of the Children Act 1989, section 12 of the Social Work (Scotland) Act 1968 [[2], or section 29 or 30 of the Children (Scotland) Act 1995 or section 37, 38, 109, 110, 114 or 115 of the Social Services and Well-being (Wales) Act 2014]; or
(b) under any other enactment in order to meet a person's welfare needs related to old age or disability, other than living expenses.

(2) In sub-paragraph (1) "living expenses" has the meaning in regulation 66(2).

18.—(1) A payment received within the past 12 months by way of arrears of, or compensation for late payment of—

(a) universal credit;

(b) a benefit abolished by section 33 of the Act; or

(c) a social security benefit which is not included as unearned income under regulation 66(1)(a) or (b).

(2) "Social security benefit" means a benefit under any enactment relating to social security in any part of the United Kingdom [[5]and includes armed forces independence payment under the Armed Forces and Reserve Forces (Compensation Scheme) Order 2011].

[[9]**18ZA.** Any payment within the past 12 months of widowed parent's allowance—

(a) to the survivor of a cohabiting partnership (within the meaning in section 39A(7) of the Contributions and Benefits Act) who is entitled to a widowed parent's allowance for a period before the Bereavement Benefits (Remedial) Order 2023 comes into force, and

(b) in respect of any period of time during the period ending with the day before the survivor makes the claim for a widowed parent's allowance.]

[[8]**18A.** A payment received within the past 12 months by way of local welfare provision including arrears and payments in lieu of local welfare provision.]

19. A payment to a person by virtue of being a holder of the Victoria Cross or George Cross.

[[1]**20.**—[[9](1)] A payment made within the past 12 months of bereavement support payment in respect of the rate set out in regulation 3(2) or (5) of the Bereavement Support Payment Regulations 2017 (rate of bereavement support payment).]

[[9](2) Where bereavement support payment under section 30 of the Pensions Act 2014 (bereavement support payment) has been paid within the past 12 months to the survivor of a cohabiting partnership (within the meaning in section 30(6B) of the Pensions Act 2014) in respect of a death occurring before the day the Bereavement Benefits (Remedial) Order 2023 comes into force, any amount of that payment which is—

(a) in respect of the rate set out in regulation 3(1) of the Bereavement Support Payment Regulations 2017, and

(b) paid as a lump sum for more than one monthly recurrence of the day of the month on which their cohabiting partner died.]

[[3]**21.** Any early years assistance given within the past 12 months in accordance with section 32 of the Social Security (Scotland) Act 2018.]

[[4]**22.** Any funeral expense assistance given within the past 12 months in accordance with section 34 of the Social Security (Scotland) Act 2018.]

[[6]**23.** Any assistance given within the past 52 weeks in accordance with the Carer's Assistance (Young Carer Grants) (Scotland) Regulations 2019.]

[[7]**24.** Any winter heating assistance given within the past 52 weeks in accordance with regulations made under section 30 of the Social Security (Scotland) Act 2018.]

AMENDMENTS

1. Pensions Act 2014 (Consequential, Supplementary and Incidental Amendments) Order 2017 (SI 2017/422) art.43(4) (April 6, 2017).

2. Social Services and Well-being (Wales) Act 2014 and the Regulation and Inspection of Social Care (Wales) Act 2016 (Consequential Amendments) Order 2017 (SI 2017/901) art.15 (November 2, 2017).

3. Social Security (Scotland) Act 2018 (Best Start Grants) (Consequential Modifications and Saving) Order 2018 (SI 2018/1138) art.11 (December 10, 2018).

4. Social Security (Scotland) Act 2018 (Funeral Expense Assistance and Early Years Assistance) (Consequential Modifications and Savings) Order 2019 (SI 2019/1060) art.19(2) (September 16, 2019).

5. Social Security (Capital Disregards) (Amendment) Regulations 2019 (SI 2019/1314) reg.8(2) (October 31, 2019).

6. Social Security (Scotland) Act 2018 (Young Carer Grants, Short-Term Assistance and Winter Heating Assistance) (Consequential Provision and Modifications) Order 2020 (SI 2020/989) art.8 (November 9, 2020).

7. Social Security (Scotland) Act 2018 (Young Carer Grants, Short-Term Assistance and Winter Heating Assistance) (Consequential Provision and Modifications) Order 2020 (SI 2020/989) art.21 (November 9, 2020).

8. Universal Credit (Local Welfare Provision Disregard) (Amendment) Regulations 2022 (SI 2022/448) reg.2(3) (May 4, 2022).

9. Bereavement Benefits (Remedial) Order 2023 (SI 2023/134) art.13 (February 9, 2023).

DEFINITIONS

"close relative"—see reg.2.
"Contributions and Benefits Act"—*ibid.*
"grant"—see regs 2 and 68(7).
"local welfare provision"—see reg.2.
"partner"—*ibid.*
"widowed parent's allowance"—*ibid.*

GENERAL NOTE

2.541 The list of capital that is ignored for the purposes of universal credit is greatly reduced compared with that which applies for the purposes of income support, old style JSA, old style ESA and housing benefit. Many of the provisions in Sch.10 are similar to those that apply for those benefits but not all. Paragraph 11—the disregard of the value of a funeral plan—is new.

The opportunity has been taken to group the disregards in a more coherent and easy to follow structure. The notes below follow that structure and note the equivalences with and differences from the provisions in Sch.10 to the Income Support Regulations (see Vol.V of this series, 2021/22 edition as updated in Cumulative Supplements included in this volume and in mid-year Supplements for detailed discussion). The disregards can apply to notional capital. By virtue of reg.48(2), where any period of six months is specified in Sch.10 it can be extended by the Secretary of State (and on any appeal by a tribunal) if it is reasonable to do so in the circumstances. Any specified period of 12 months is not extendable.

The disregards can apply to capital that a claimant is treated as possessing under reg.48 (notional capital), providing that the terms of the particular paragraph of Sch.10 are satisfied (see discussion in the note to para.6). Although the references in Sch.10 are to a person, not to a claimant, that is merely in accord with 48(2) applying the Sch.10 disregards to the calculation of "a person's capital". Thus when a paragraph in Sch.10 refers to the circumstances of a person it means the person whose capital would otherwise count in the claimant's case, i.e. the claimant or either of joint claimants.

Capital disregards outside Sch.10

Note that, in addition to the categories specified in Sch.10, there are specific disregards of capital in reg.75(4), (5) and (6) (sums derived from compensation for personal injury to claimant), reg.76 (special compensation schemes) and reg.77(3)(a) (assets of company where claimant treated as sole owner or partner). Further, reg.51 of the Universal Credit (Transitional Provisions) Regulations 2014, as inserted by reg.3 of the Universal Credit (Managed Migration Pilot and Miscellaneous Amendments) Regulations 2019 (SI 2019/1152) with effect from July 24, 2019, supplies a transitional capital disregard to claimants who (i) were previously entitled to a tax credit and had capital exceeding £16,000; (ii) are given a migration notice that existing benefits are to terminate; and (iii) claim universal credit within the deadline. The disregard is of any capital exceeding £16,000. The disregard can apply only for 12 assessment periods and ceases (without the possibility of revival) following any assessment period in which the amount of capital the claimant has falls below £16,000. See regs 56 and 57 of the Transitional Provisions Regulations for further provisions on termination of the protection. The £16,000 non-disregarded capital that the claimant by definition possesses will produce an assumed yield as income of £174 per month under reg.72. There is no capital limit for tax credits. Paragraph 7 of Sch.2 to the Transitional Provisions Regulations, inserted by the same Regulations, contains a disregard as capital of any amount paid as a lump sum by way of a "transitional SDP amount" under that Schedule.

See the notes to para.18 below for the additional effect of regs 10A, 10B and 10C (arrears of various benefits disregarded as capital) of the Transitional Provisions Regulations 2014.

With effect from May 29, 2020, reg.26(1)(a) of the Victims' Payments Regulations 2020 (SI 2020/103) (see later in this Part) provides that a victims' payment or a lump sum under those Regulations is to be disregarded as capital or income. Under the Regulations payments are to be made to those injured in a "Troubles-related incident", which is defined in s.10(11) of the Northern Ireland (Executive Formation etc) Act 2019 as "an incident involving an act of violence or force carried out in Ireland, the UK or anywhere in Europe for a reason related to the constitutional status of Northern Ireland or to political or sectarian hostility between people there". In so far as any such payment constitutes income it is not listed in reg.66(1), so is not to be taken into account as unearned income. In so far as it constitutes capital, either initially or on metamorphosing into capital (see the notes to reg.45), it is to be disregarded without any limit as to how long ago the payment was made.

With effect from April 1, 2022, reg.2(1) of the Universal Credit (Energy Rebate Scheme Disregard) Regulations 2022 (SI 2022/257) (see later in this Part) provides that any payment received under the Energy Rebate Scheme 2022 is to be disregarded as capital for 12 months from the date of receipt. That scheme is defined in reg.2(2) of the 2022 Regulations as the scheme to provide financial support in respect of energy bills that was announced in Parliament on February 3, 2022 and any comparable scheme announced by the Welsh or Scottish Ministers. The disregard thus formally applies to all the elements of that scheme, but in practice it can only apply to the £150 rebate to council tax payers in bands A–D or the discretionary payment to vulnerable people who do not pay council tax or whose property is in bands E–H. Other elements of the scheme would not involve payments of capital.

"Cost of living payments" under the Social Security (Additional Payments) Act 2022 and the 2023 Act, both those to recipients of specified means-tested benefits and "disability" payments, are not to be taken into account for any universal credit purposes by virtue of s.8(b) of both Acts.

Finally, note that with effect from May 21, 2020, reg.2(2) of the Universal Credit (Coronavirus) (Self-employed Claimants and Reclaims) (Amendment) Regulations 2020 (SI 2020/522) introduced a disregard as capital for 12 months of any payment made to a self-employed claimant under the Coronavirus Job Retention Scheme or by way of a grant or loan to meet the expenses or losses of the trade, profession or vocation in relation to the outbreak of coronavirus disease. See further discussion in the note to para.7.

However, there was no specific provision for some other coronavirus-related payments. See the notes to reg.66 for the taxable £500 payment, administered by local authorities, made to those in England entitled to a qualifying income-related benefit (including universal credit) who were required by NHS Test and Trace on or after September 28, 2020 (down at least to summer 2021) to self-isolate for 14 (or ten) days, were unable to work from home and would lose income from employment or self-employment and the discretionary payments available to those not entitled to a qualifying benefit. The payments appear to be in the nature of income, in the form of compensation for the loss of earnings that would otherwise have been received. As such they were not to be taken into account as unearned income since they are not listed in reg.66(1). There is, though, the possibility that any amount remaining out of the £500 at the end of the required days of self-isolation, or more probably after the end of the assessment period of receipt, would then be treated as capital under the usual principles (see the notes to para.7 below and to reg.54A for discussion in the context of surplus earnings).

The intention was expressed in the guidance on scheme eligibility that the £500 payments were not to be taken into account as capital for benefit purposes. There was no amendment to the universal credit legislation to secure that result. So far as "legacy benefits" are concerned, the payments, being made by local authorities, appear to have constituted "local welfare provision" within the capital disregard in para.18A of Sch.10 to the Income Support Regulations (see Vol.V of this series, 2021/22 edition as updated in Cumulative Supplements included in this volume and in mid-year Supplements) and the equivalent provisions for other benefits. The phrase is very widely defined in reg.2(1) of those Regulations. There is now, from May 4, 2022, an equivalent disregard in para.18A of the present Schedule, which thus was not in operation at the time the payments were made. The closest provision at the time was para.17 (see the notes below), but that applies only to payments from local authorities under specific legislation that would not cover the Test and Trace payments or under any legislation to meet welfare needs related to old age or disability, but excluding living expenses. The payments are not linked to old age or disability and, even if they were, would fall foul of the living expenses exclusion.

It was announced in the March 2021 budget that an automatic one-off £500 support payment would be made by HMRC to those in receipt of working tax credit (or child tax credit alone if eligible for WTC but income too high for payability), in view of the withdrawal after April 5, 2021 of the temporary uplift to WTC rates during the coronavirus pandemic. The payment was to be made in April 2021 without the need for any claim and under powers in the Coronavirus Act 2020. It was therefore not a payment of WTC and would appear to be in the nature of a capital receipt, rather than income. According to LA Welfare Direct 3/2021, the payment was to be disregarded for housing benefit and universal credit purposes, but there was no amendment of the legislation for the purposes of universal credit (or legacy benefits). The payment does not fall within the disregard for local authority welfare payments in para.17, because it is not made under any of the legislation specified there (see the previous paragraph) or paid by a local authority. No other provision of Sch.10 appears to have applied. Even if the payment were regarded as income, as some kind of supplement to the regular WTC payments, it is not linked to any particular period, so that any unspent sum out of the £500 would appear to become capital under the principles discussed in the notes to reg.45.

The continuing effect of capital disregards

The discussion at a meeting of the Social Security Advisory Committee (SSAC) on December 8, 2021 in relation to the Social Security (Income and Capital Disregards) (Amendment) Regulations 2021 (SI 2021/1405) (see the notes to reg.76) revealed some conceptual problems in the relationship of capital disregards to the calculation of the amount of capital possessed at a particular date. The essence of the problem put to DWP officials was what would happen if a claimant received a compensation payment within the disregard introduced by those regulations, acquired further non-disregarded capital and then spent a substantial amount of capital: how would it be known what pot of capital the expenditure came out of (SSAC minutes December 8, 2021, para.2.2(f))? The answer given in the letter dated January 12, 2022 from the Minister for Welfare Delivery, David Rutley, (Annex C to the minutes) was that:

> "the Department does not attempt to distinguish the capital derived from a compensation payment from other capital (with the exception of personal injury compensation that has been placed in trust). Wherever a claimant has received a payment of capital which is disregarded, whether indefinitely or for a prescribed period, their capital threshold is effectively increased by the amount of the original payment for the duration of that period. This is regardless of whether it was simply paid into a bank account with other funds or held or invested elsewhere."

That approach ought for consistency to apply to all capital disregards applying to payments rather than other assets, though probably if funds derived from any sort of compensation payment are held in a segregated account with no payments in from any other source (whether subject to a trust or not) a payment out of that fund would go to reduce the amount disregarded (see the notes to reg.75). No doubt it is right that for social security purposes no-one should have to get into all the difficulties that have arisen in other areas of the law in identifying whether specific funds that have been paid into some mixed account have been depleted by subsequent payments out. However, it is far from clear how that approach should hold, say, if a payment out is made for a purpose for which the compensation was specifically paid. If part of personal injury compensation, not held in trust or in a segregated account, was specifically to cover disability adaptations to a home, would it be right, after expenditure for that purpose, to continue simply to regard the capital threshold as increased by the amount of the original disregard? Paragraph H2054 of the ADM seems consistent with that view in suggesting that, where an account contains a (disregarded) compensation payment and other capital, it should be accepted that money withdrawn is from the other capital, unless there is evidence that it is from the compensation payment.

There appears to have been a misunderstanding in the discussion of this issue by the SSAC and the DWP in the assumption that an amount of compensation held in trust, e.g. qualifying for the indefinite disregard of personal injury compensation under reg.75(4), would be held in a separate account from a claimant's other assets, so that the conceptual problem would be avoided. However, that does not take into account the decision in *Q v SSWP (JSA)* [2020] UKUT 49 (AAC) that funds held in a joint bank or building society account with someone else are subject to a trust. It is argued in the notes to reg.75(4) that, although the wording of the disregard is different from that being considered in *Q*, the words "in trust" are not a term of art that has some special meaning and so should apply whenever the sum derived from personal injury compensation is subject to a trust. The question then would not be whether the compensation has been placed in trust, in the sense of being put into a specifically created trust, but simply whether the sum is held on trust.

The Sch.10 disregards

The categories of disregards under Sch.10 are as follows:

Para.1	Premises occupied as a person's home;
Para.2	Premises occupied as home by close relative with LCW or over pension age;
Para.3	Premises occupied as home by former partner living apart by force of circumstances;
Para.4	Various premises that person intends to occupy as home;
Para.5	Premises ceased to be occupied as home following estrangement;
Para.6	Premises where taking reasonable steps to dispose;
Para.7	Assets used for purposes of trade etc. being carried on;
Para.8	Assets previously used for purposes of trade etc no longer carried on;
Para.9	Life insurance policies;
Para.10	Pension rights;
Para.11	Funeral plan contracts;
Para.12	Housing association deposits;
Para.13	Amounts to be used to purchase new home;
Para.14	Insurance payments for home or personal possessions;
Para.15	Amounts received to be used for essential repairs or alterations;
Para.16	Social fund payments in past 12 months;
Para.17	Welfare payments in past 12 months;
Para.18	Arrears or compensation for late payment of certain benefits in past 12 months;
Para.18ZA	Arrears of widowed parent's allowance;
Para.18A	Local welfare provision;

Para.19 Victoria Cross and George Cross payments;
Para.20 Lump sum bereavement support payments in past 12 months;
Para.21 Scottish early years assistance in past 12 months;
Para.22 Scottish funeral expense assistance in past 12 months;
Para.23 Scottish young carer grants in past 52 weeks;
Para.24 Scottish winter heating assistance in past 52 weeks.

Premises

2.542 *Paragraph 1* (premises occupied as the home) is equivalent to para.1 of the income support Sch.10 except that it is in terms of premises rather than a dwelling. That change seems to open up considerable uncertainties, since the word "premises" is given no further definition and for income support "dwelling occupied as the home" has a detailed definition in reg.2(1) of the Income Support Regulations, which is first limited to (or perhaps extends to) the dwelling (i.e. residential accommodation: SSCBA, s.137(1)) normally occupied by the claimant as their home and expressly brings in any garage, garden and outbuildings plus any premises not so occupied that it is impracticable or unreasonable to sell separately, in particular any croft land in Scotland. "Premises" could in general have a much wider meaning than residential accommodation (see para.13 of *R(IS) 3/96*), extending to buildings originally intended for other purposes and to land without buildings, such as farmland, paddocks or woodland.

The primary test under para.1 is whether premises as a whole are occupied by a person as their home, i.e., it is submitted, whether it has been made the person's home whatever the intended or normal purpose of the building or whatever, and then what is the extent of the premises that can be said to be occupied as the home. There is no express rule to allow in garages, gardens and outbuildings, but they would plainly be included within the meaning of "premises", as opposed to a "dwelling/residential accommodation", when considering what is occupied as the person's home. Nor, more importantly, is there any rule including premises not so occupied that it is impracticable or unreasonable to sell separately (despite the suggestion to the contrary in relation to croft land in Scotland in ADM para.H2039). So the question comes back to what can be regarded as occupied as the home. If, say, a farmhouse and surrounding farmland etc is all in the same ownership and no-one else has any rights over that land, it could be argued that all of it would be regarded as occupied together as part of the home by the person occupying the farmhouse, even if the farm work was done by employees of the occupier. If the farmland was partly occupied by someone else, e.g. by neighbours allowed by license to graze their sheep on fields, it is submitted that the same result would follow if the occupier of the farmhouse retained full access to the fields at all times. It could be different, though, if the surrounding land was leased to others, when it might well be said that it was no longer occupied by the occupier of the farmhouse. But the particular circumstances of individual cases would have to be considered carefully. For instance, who knows what the answer might be for universal credit if the facts of *R(IS) 3/96* were replicated? The claimant and her husband jointly owned a farmhouse and 42 acres of farm and woodland. She had moved permanently to a residential care home and her husband remained living in the farmhouse. The land was farmed by the husband and their son in partnership, with no payments of rent being made. In substituting a decision in *R(IS) 3/96* itself, Commissioner Mesher held that the disregard equivalent to para.3 did not apply, as the 42 acres could practicably and reasonably be sold separately, assuming, without directly addressing the point, that the 42 acres were not occupied by the husband as his home. But that was in the context of a provision applying, as the Commissioner held, to a dwelling/residential accommodation. It might be different, as the adjudication officer submitted there, if the provision applied to premises more generally. But, on the other hand, it might be said that the land being used for business, rather than personal, purposes was not occupied by the husband as his home, even though he was involved in the business.

Paragraph 1 applies simply to premises occupied by a person as their home, not, as in the income support definition of "dwelling", to residential accommodation "normally" occupied. It is not at all clear that any difference in practical outcome was intended, but the possibility is opened up that mere transient occupation might do, rejected in the particular circumstances of a night shelter in a different context in *OR v SSWP & Isle of Anglesey CC (HB)* [2013] UKUT 65 (AAC). But the reasoning in that case was based on whether the claimant's extremely transient occupation of the shelter there could be "as his home", so that the omission of "normally" would not indicate a different outcome. Conversely, could it be argued that, while the "normally" test plainly covers temporary absences from premises that have been occupied as the home, the same does not apply where the test is simple occupation? ADM para.H2038 asserts that premises usually occupied as the home are disregarded if they are not occupied for a time and the intention is to return to live in the premises as the home, but no reasoning is given for that conclusion. It is submitted that that obviously reasonable outcome can be justified by applying the ordinary meaning of "occupied as their home", under which the notion of a home connotes a continuing existence during temporary absences. Whether such a general approach can properly be condensed into a rule making the major factor the intention to return to live in premises as the home, as in para.H2038, is more doubtful. The matter will not be resolved until some appeal reaches the Upper Tribunal.

It appears still to be the case that a person cannot be said to be occupying premises so as to fall within para.1 until they have moved in for the first time (as in *R(SB) 27/84* and *R(SB) 7/86*), though note the disregard in para.4(1)(a) of premises acquired within the past six months (extendable) that the person intends to occupy as the home. Thus, the "moving in" issue will in practice be much less important for capital disregards than, say, in housing benefit or in establishing qualification for a housing costs element for a renter in universal credit. What amounts to sufficient moving in to conclude that occupation as the home has started will be a question of fact in the particular circumstances of each case. In special circumstances like those in *R(H) 9/05*, where the claimant had had her furniture moved into a new flat and given up her previous tenancy, but did not herself physically go to the flat as scheduled on the day the furniture was moved because she was admitted to hospital, it could properly be concluded, as held by the Deputy Commissioner, that she had occupied (and normally occupied) the flat from that day.

Paragraph 1(2) provides, for the purposes of paras 1 to 5 as a whole, that only one set of premises may be treated as a person's home. That must mean at the same time, so that if a claimant moves from one home to another in the middle of an assessment period, the capital value of both is to be disregarded. The mischief aimed at is concurrent occupation. In income support, there is quite a lot of case law on whether physically separate properties can constitute one dwelling (on which see the notes to reg.2(1) of the Income Support Regulations in the 2021/22 edition of Vol.V of this series, as updated in Cumulative Supplements included in Vol.II and in mid-year Supplements). The principle confirmed in *Secretary of State for Work and Pensions v Miah* [2003] EWCA Civ 1111; [2003] 4 All E.R. 702; *R(JSA) 9/03* was that the expanded definition of "dwelling occupied as the home" required looking at the function served by the concept of a dwelling rather than the bricks and mortar, so that the home was not necessarily confined to a single building. It could be asked whether one building was an annex of the other or whether there was single home on a split site. In *Miah*, the claimant and his wife had eight dependant children. He owned the two houses in the same street in which they lived, with two houses in between. If they had all lived in one house there would have been a breach of the statutory overcrowding rules. Although the Court of Appeal appears not to have expressed a conclusion on the evidence or formally about the finding of a second tribunal that the value of both houses was to be disregarded as the claimant normally occupied both as his home, it was apparently content that that result was a proper one on the evidence. The use of the phrase "set of premises" in para.1(2) strongly suggests that a similar principle should be adopted. However, the answer in particular cases will be heavily fact-specific. For further post-*Miah* examples, see *London Borough of Hackney v GA* [2008] UKUT 26 (AAC) and *Birmingham CC v IB* [2009] UKUT 116 (AAC), both housing benefit cases, and *MM v SSWP (IS)* [2012] UKUT 358 (AAC). A case on the other side of the line is *PJ v SSWP (SPC)* [2014] UKUT 152 (AAC), where the claimant went to live with a daughter for three years to avoid council tax liability on the flat he owned and had previously lived in, leaving his other daughter (a student not counting as an occupier for council tax purposes) in the flat. Although the claimant visited the flat at weekends and stayed more overnight for a period when his student daughter was ill, he was held not to be normally occupying it as his home.

Paragraph 2 (premises occupied by a close relative as their home) is the equivalent of para.4(a) of the income support Sch.10, except that it is restricted to close relatives of the claimant instead of any relative or a partner. The alternative test (to that of having attained state pension credit qualifying age) of the relative having limited capability for work may possibly be more restrictive than that of being incapacitated. Regulations 38–44 only apply to determining whether a *claimant* has limited capability for work, or for work and work-related activity. Thus it is arguable either that the words "limited capability for work" merely have their ordinary meaning or that it is not necessary that the relative be in receipt of any benefit or credit based on a determination as to limited capability for work.

Paragraph 3 (premises occupied by a former partner as their home) is the equivalent of para.4(b) of the income support Sch.10, but with slightly different conditions. The application of para.4(b) is excluded where there has been a divorce from the former partner or a dissolution of a civil partnership as well as where the claimant and the former partner are estranged. The application of para.3 is not automatically excluded by divorce or the dissolution of a civil partnership, but is where there is estrangement, which may or may not follow such procedures, especially after some lapse of time. More important is the positive condition, not present in para.4(b) of the income support Sch.10, that the two are living apart by force of circumstances. That will prevent the application of the disregard for many non-estranged former partners. But it will apply to claimants who are in a residential home and so no longer share a household with their former partner for that reason. See also the potential disregard in para.5 where the claimant has ceased within the previous 6 months (or longer where the former partner is a lone parent) to occupy premises following an estrangement from their former partner.

Estrangement is a slippery concept that has generated case law in other benefits from which it is difficult to take clear guidance, not least because it is hard to see just what policy objective is served by preventing the application of the disregard when the claimant is estranged from the former partner. In the absence of any definition in the legislation, estrangement must be given its ordinary meaning in context. Some difference in expression among decisions, none of which purport to give definitions, is therefore to be expected and too much attention should not be given to such differences that may simply stem from the circumstances of the particular case in which the question was addressed (*CIS/4096/2005* and *AC v SSWP (IS)* [2015] UKUT 49 (AAC)). The discussion below attempts to concentrate on principles on which there is general agreement without citing all the decisions mentioned in past editions.

First, it is well established that estrangement is not the same as separation (*CIS/4843/2002*, *R(IS) 5/07*) and that separation does not necessarily imply estrangement (*R(IS) 5/05*). Nor does divorce or dissolution of a civil partnership necessarily imply estrangement, but no doubt normally the initial circumstances would indicate estrangement as discussed below and there would have to be some real intention to resume living together to found a different conclusion. By definition, to be a former partner the person must at least no longer be a member of the same household as the claimant. It must be remembered that, as pointed out in *R(IS) 5/05*, a person may temporarily be living away from a claimant and yet still be a member of the household. That is so on the general meaning of the term and as the basis of the special rule in reg.3(6), which purports to limit that effect of a temporary absence to six months (the form of reg.3(6) appears to be somewhat circular, because it refers to temporary absence from the claimant's household when a temporary absence would mean that the household was still shared, so "household" may have to mean little more than accommodation). Examples might be where a spouse or partner is in a care or nursing home or hospital or caring for a sick relative or friend in another place for a time that is realistically hoped to be temporary. In such circumstances, the two remain a couple as defined in s.39 of the WRA 2012 and partners, so that the two must claim universal credit as joint claimants. But the value of the premises where the person is staying (if the other partner happened to have an interest in them) could not be disregarded under para.1 (because only one set of premises occupied as the home is covered) or para.2 (because a partner is not a close relative) or para.3 (because the person is not a *former* partner). If the separation has been permanent or open-ended from the outset (so as not to be merely temporary) or becomes non-temporary after a change of circumstances (including the time that it has continued), the person will be a former partner.

If there is separation such as to make the person a former partner, "estrangement" must entail something further in order to give some force to the condition of not being estranged. *R(IS) 5/05* agrees with *R(SB) 2/87* that estrangement has a "connotation of emotional disharmony". That has been accepted in subsequent decisions, but the important matter is the context in which such disharmony is to be assessed. There can be friendly relations between the claimant and former partner although they are estranged for the purposes of the disregard (*R(IS) 5/05*, para.12, *CPC/683/2007*, *CH/377/2007* and *Bristol CC v SJP (HB)* [2019] UKUT 360 (AAC), paras 34–37, where there is a helpful summary of the earlier decisions). The way that Commissioner Rowland put it in *R(IS) 5/05* was that the question was whether the parties had ceased to consider themselves a couple, as has been accepted and applied in later cases. That needs some unpacking because "couple" has a particular meaning within the legislation that by definition cannot be met where the person is a former partner. So the word must be used in a more general everyday sense.

In para.13 of *CPC/683/2007*, Commissioner Jacobs said this:

> "It seems to me that the proper analysis of the relationship between the claimant and his wife is this. They remain married and have no plans to divorce. He would like to resume living with her, but she is opposed to the idea. The reality is that they will never resume living as husband and wife; the claimant accepts that. However, they are not hostile to each other on a personal level and he feels a continuing responsibility towards her. This leads him to help her when she cannot manage on account of her ill-health. In other words, there is no emotional disharmony between the claimant and his wife as adults, but there is emotional disharmony between them as partners. That is a key distinction, because the language used in the legislation is attempting to identify those cases in which the relationship between the parties is such that it is appropriate for their finances to be treated separately for the purposes of benefit entitlement. Once the facts of the case are set out, they seem to me to allow of only one interpretation, which is that the couple are estranged."

The distinction between disharmony as partners and disharmony as adults is a useful one. It is no doubt going too far to say, as the same judge did in *CH/117/2005*, that two people are not estranged if they retain all the indicia of partners apart from physical presence in the same household, at least if that were to be taken out of context to represent a test that separation equals estrangement unless that condition is met. That would not be compatible with a proper consideration of the circumstances of particular cases and an application of the ordinary meaning of estrangement. But it perhaps illustrates one end of the continuum, where although the person is a former partner, because the separation is non-temporary, they and the claimant would be members of the same household if it were not for the circumstances enforcing the separation. At the other end of the continuum are cases where a relationship has broken down such that there is no current prospect of a resumption of living together. Then, no matter how amicable and co-operative the parties might be about, say children, finances and other practical matters, there is estrangement. There is an emotional disharmony between them as partners.

In *CIS/4096/2005*, Commissioner Jupp, in a different context, indicated that estrangement does not require mutuality of feeling. Disharmony can arise from one person's attitude to another even though the other party may not wish the situation to be as it is. The form of para.3 does not ask whether one party is estranged from the other, as for other benefits, but whether the person and the former partner are not estranged. So the question is whether a state of estrangements exists between them. If the realistic position is that the attitude of one party prevents any resumption of a relationship as partners, the fact that the other party did not wish the situation to be as it was or hoped that the estrangement might not be permanent (*CH/377/2007*) does not on its own point against a conclusion that the other party is estranged from the first.

If estrangement is approached in the way suggested above there will be little work for the additional condition of living apart by force of circumstances to do. For the parties not to be estranged something very like that will have to be the case. Note that some people may be in residential care and yet estranged. And someone may be in residential care on a temporary basis, such that the parties remain a couple and the person is not a *former* partner.

Paragraph 4(1)(a) (premises acquired within past 6 months and intends to occupy as the home) is the equivalent of para.2 of the income support Sch.10, with a very slightly wider application. Paragraph 2 requires any extension to the period of 26 weeks from acquisition to be reasonable in the circumstances to enable the claimant to obtain possession and commence occupation. Under para.4(1)(a), provided as always that there is an intention to occupy the premises as the home, the extension to the period of six months under reg.48(2) can be made whenever it is reasonable in the circumstances.

Paragraph 4(1)(b) (commenced steps to obtain possession of premises within the past 6 months) is the equivalent of para.27 of the income support Sch.10. The provisions in sub-para.(2) about when a person is to be deemed to have commenced steps to obtain possession make the conditions the same as under para.27, except that any extension to the period of 6 months under reg.48(2) can be made whenever it is reasonable in the circumstances instead of being linked to enabling obtaining possession and commencing occupation.

Paragraph 4(1)(c) (essential repairs or alterations, commenced within the past 6 months, to render premises fit for occupation) is the equivalent of para.28 of the income support Sch.10, but with a narrower scope. The income support disregard starts from the date on which steps were first taken to effect the repairs, which can cover getting a grant or loan for the cost of the works, applying for permissions or consulting an architect or contractors. In para.4(1)(c) the person must be carrying out the essential repairs or alterations. It is not clear where in the preparatory process that might start. Nor is it entirely clear that alterations essential for occupation by the particular person (e.g. adaptations for someone who is disabled) are covered. The decision in *SH v London Borough of Southwark (HB)* [2023] UKUT 198 (AAC) suggests that the test is not whether the alterations must be required to make the premises fit for occupation by anyone. There, in the context of whether housing benefit could be paid for two properties under reg.7(4) of the Housing Benefit Regulations, Judge Hemingway held that the evaluation of whether repairs were essential should take account of the claimant's individual circumstances, including impairment or vulnerability in consequence of ill-health, as also decided in *CH/393/2002*. Under the supplementary benefit single payments scheme, "essential" was said to mean something like "necessary" in the sense in which luxuries are differentiated from the necessaries of life, importing a test of substantial need

(*R(SB) 10/81*), but no doubt the ordinary word in para.4(1)(c) should be applied in the circumstances of each case rather than some attempted further explanation of it. However, note that if the claimant has already taken up occupation as the home para.1 will apply and that if the premises were acquired within the previous six months (extendable) there is the more general disregard in para.4(1)(a). Regulation 48(2) allows the six months from commencement to be extended as reasonable.

Paragraph 5 (claimant ceased to occupy premises as home following estrangement from former partner) is the equivalent of para.25 of the income support Sch.10, except that it does not automatically apply on divorce or the dissolution of a civil partnership, only on estrangement. See the notes to para.3 for discussion of estrangement. The 6 months under sub-para.(b) can be extended where reasonable in the circumstances under reg.48(2).

The disregard applies in any circumstances for the first six months (extendable where reasonable: reg.48(2)) after the claimant ceases to occupy the previous home (sub-para.(a). Otherwise the premises must be occupied by the former partner as their home and the former partner must be a lone parent (sub-para.(b)). "Lone parent" is not defined in the Regulations or in the WRA 2012 (by contrast it is defined in the Income Support Regulations). It is therefore arguable that the phrase is to be given its ordinary everyday meaning, without any technical tests to do with responsibility or membership of the household or even the age of the children or young persons in question, accepting that it must be the case that the former partner does not have a current partner as defined in reg.2. However, it is also arguable that in the context of the Regulations as a whole the phrase must be taken to refer to someone who is responsible for a child or young person under reg.4. That makes the initial test whether the child normally lives with the person concerned, but where the child normally lives with two or more people, then only one can be taken as responsible and that is the person who has the main responsibility (reg.4(4)). The people concerned can make a joint declaration as to who has main responsibility, subject to decision by the Secretary of State in default of agreement or if the nomination does not reflect the actual arrangements. The issue could be problematic where the claimant and the former partner have children who move between their now separate households on a more or less equal basis. It appears that who has the child benefit is not only not determinative, but may be irrelevant to an assessment which is focused on responsibility in substance (see *MC v SSWP (UC)* [2018] UKUT 44 (AAC) in the notes to reg.4).

Paragraph 6 (commenced taking reasonable steps to dispose of premises within past 6 months) is the equivalent of para.26 of the income support Sch.10. The 6 months can be extended where reasonable in the circumstances under reg.48(2). In both provisions the disregard applies to any premises, not just premises occupied as the home. Thus it should cover land without any building on it (*R(IS) 4/97*).

Steps to dispose of premises can include many preparatory steps before actually putting them on the market. Things that have been accepted include obtaining a solicitor's quotation for sale charges and obtaining an estate agent's valuation (*JT v Leicester CC (CTB)* [2012] UKUT 445 (AAC)), making a genuine approach to another tenant in common to agree a sale (*JH v SSWP* [2009] UKUT 1 (AAC)), bringing ancillary relief proceedings within a divorce suit (*R(IS) 5/05*) or even the bringing of divorce proceedings (*CIS/195/2007*). That last decision suggests that if, once steps have first been taken, there is some temporary suspension of activity (e.g. because of family pressures, threats of violence or efforts at reconciliation), that does not necessarily mean that steps are no longer being taken, but it would all depend on the circumstances. What are "reasonable" steps is a question of fact with a margin of judgment involved, but according to *R(IS) 4/97* the test is an objective one. So if a property is put up for sale at a totally unrealistic price, the disregard would not apply. If the asking price was later lowered to something realistic, it could start to apply and it would be that date at which reasonable steps commenced and at which the primary six months started to run.

In some cases, where reasonable steps stop being taken (as opposed to there being a mere temporary suspension or diminution of activity) and are later resumed it will be right to regard the commencement of reasonable steps as taking place at the beginning, not at the date of the resumption. But that is not necessarily always the case (see *SP v SSWP* [2009] UKUT 255 (AAC)). If premises are genuinely taken off the market and later, in different circumstances, are put on the market again, it is arguable that the disregard can start to be applied afresh, with a new six months starting to run. A gap in the receipt of benefit would not automatically have that effect, but could be one of the relevant circumstances to be taken into account.

It was decided in *CIS/30/1993* that the income support disregard could not apply to premises that the claimant had already disposed of, but was treated as still possessing the value of under the notional capital rule. That was because the income support disregard only applied if the claimant was taking reasonable steps to dispose of the premises, which was impossible as only the new owner could take such steps. That reasoning would apply equally to para.6 as the person who has to be taking the reasonable steps must be the person whose capital would be relevant to the universal credit claim were it not for the effect of reg.48(2) in applying the Sch.10 disregards.

Business assets

2.543 *Paragraph 7* (assets of trade etc. being carried on) is the equivalent of the first part of para.6(1) of the income support Sch.10. Income support para.6 uses the terms of assets of a business owned in whole or in part by the claimant for the purposes of which he is engaged as a self-employed earner. In view of the meaning of self-employed earner, the use here of the terms "used wholly or mainly for the purposes of a trade, profession or vocation" comes to the same thing. Paragraph 7 applies while the claimant is carrying on that trade, profession or vocation. See the notes to reg.64 for when a person is carrying on a trade etc, from which it is clear that a person may be trading in that sense ("in work") while not currently engaged in activities ("at work"). In this respect, it is arguable that the scope of para.7 is broader than that of the income support para.6(1). For those purposes, it has been held that to be "engaged in" a business a claimant must be performing some business activities in some practical sense as an earner (see the discussion of *Chief Adjudication Officer v Knight*, reported as part of *R(IS) 14/98*, in the notes to para.6(1) of the income support Sch.10 in Vol.V of this series). That appears to make the test whether the self-employed person is "at work". But the concept of "carrying on" a trade etc. in para.7 is significantly different. See the notes to para.8 below for the apparent resulting mismatch between the two provisions.

It is no longer necessary to discuss the problems arising from the disregard introduced with effect from May 21, 2020, and still in effect, by reg.2(2) of the Universal Credit (Coronavirus) (Self-employed Claimants and Reclaims) (Amendment) Regulations 2020 (SI 2020/522), because no coronavirus-related payments of the kind covered have been made for some years. See pp.600-601 of the 2023/24 edition of this volume for the relevant payments and problems.

The income support disregard applies to the assets of a business partly or wholly owned by a claimant. Here, para.7 applies to assets wholly or mainly "used" for the purposes of the trade etc. The income support disregard therefore appears to apply to any asset used to any extent beyond the de minimis in the business. For instance, the value of a vehicle used for 10% of the time for self-employment and for 90% of the time for personal purposes would seem to be disregarded under that rule. It is accordingly arguable that the universal credit position would be different, so that the value of the vehicle would not be disregarded under para.7 unless the business use amounted to more than 50%. But, if that test is met, the whole value of the asset is disregarded. There is no scope for any apportionment. By contrast, it seems that the use of the word "used" involves no more restrictive condition than under the income support disregard. There, business assets are distinguished from personal assets by asking whether they are "part of the fund employed and risked in the business" (*R(SB) 4/85*). The question whether assets are used for the purposes of a trade etc is substantially the same.

In answering those questions, the income tax and accounting position are factors to be taken into account, but are not conclusive (*CFC/10/1989*). The Commissioner in *R(SB) 4/85* noted that, while people in a business partnership owe a duty to the other partner(s) to keep business assets severed from and not mixed with their own assets, the same does not apply to sole traders. They can mix their own and business assets together and can freely transfer items from business to personal assets and vice versa. Although so far as money is concerned it is much more straightforward if a self-employed person maintains a business account separate from any personal accounts and keeps receipts and expenditure to the appropriate account, many of those in small-scale self-employment will not maintain any separate bank or building society account. The account may even be a joint account with a person not involved in the business. That in itself is not fatal to the identification of some sums in the mixed account as employed and risked in the business. It becomes a matter of whether there is sufficient evidence (and no doubt it falls to the claimant to come forward with the evidence if there is no separate business account) to be able to identify such an asset. Thus, for instance, if claimants can show that they have a sum of money in a mixed account that is set aside to meet income tax due for payment in the future on their self-employed earnings, that would seem to fall within the scope of this disregard. By contrast, in *CIS/2467/2003* money put by an author into a Maxi ISA, designed for personal savings by medium or long term investment, was found not to have been employed in the business, but to be in the personal sphere as the proceeds of the business. The Commissioner stated that claimants who wished to benefit from the para.6 disregard in relation to money that was not in a separate business account would have to show a clear demarcation between the assets of the business and personal assets. However, it is submitted that that should be taken more as an explanation of why, on the circumstances of the particular case, the claimant had failed to show that he could benefit from the disregard than as a rule of thumb to be applied in place of the principle laid down in *R(SB) 4/85*. Everything depends on the assessment of the evidence in individual cases.

In the particular context of universal credit, the above principles may help to resolve a conundrum stemming from the method of calculating earnings, at least for the self-employed if not for employees. The rule for the self-employed in reg.57 is that income receipts are taken into account in the assessment period in which they are received. The principle that an amount cannot be income and capital at the same time (see *R(IS) 3/93* and *R(IS) 9/08*) would then probably entail that the receipt and funds derived from it could not be capital during that assessment period. But any proceeds left over in future assessment periods would be capital, it appears regardless of whether surplus earnings would be attributed to those periods under reg.54A as result of the amount of the particular receipt. But the proceeds would still be assets used for the purposes of the trade etc, so would be disregarded as capital under para.7. There is no such escape route for employees. But see the notes to reg.54A (at 2.196) for the argument that the amount of any retained earnings to be taken into account as surplus earnings in any assessment period does not count as capital because the application of reg.54A represents a liability that has to be deducted before the metamorphosis from earnings to capital takes place. That argument can work for the self-employed and employees.

R(FC) 2/92 holds that the ownership by an individual of a tenanted house is not in itself a business, although there may come a point, depending on the circumstances, at which the amount of administration and/or activity involved even in the letting out of a single property could amount to self-employment. See also *RM v Sefton Council (HB)* [2016] UKUT 357 (AAC), reported as [2017] AACR 5, where there was an exceptionally comprehensive survey of the existing authorities. It concluded that, apart from the mere carrying out of the duties of a landlord of one dwelling being insufficient, there are no hard and fast rules, merely factors that point one way or the other. But note carefully that for universal credit the test for the disregard is in terms of trade, profession or vocation and that trade is a narrower concept than business (see the discussion, particularly in the context of rented property, in the notes to regs 52 and 77(1) (See 2.299)).

Paragraph 8 (assets of trade etc. that ceased to carry on within the past 6 months) is the equivalent of the second part of para.6(1) and para.6(2) of the income support Sch.10. The disregard is arguably narrower in scope than the income support disregard because it applies only when the claimant has ceased to carry on the trade etc, which may, for the reasons given in the notes to para.7, entail a more definite cessation of trading as a whole, rather than a ceasing to be engaged in activities. Sub-para. (a), where the carrying on of trade ceased for any reason, is limited to circumstances where the claimant is taking reasonable steps to dispose of the assets. Presumably, that allows the value of only some assets, to which that applies, to be disregarded, leaving the value of the rest to count against the capital limits. Under sub-para.(b) the claimant must have ceased to be engaged in carrying on the trade etc because of incapacity (not further defined) and have a reasonable expectation of re-engaging on recovery. That is odd language, because if there has merely been a cessation of engagement in practical activities in the business, with the reasonable expectation of re-engagement once the incapacity is over, the conclusion in most cases would be that the claimant had not ceased to carry on the trade etc., so that the para.7 disregard would still apply. There would only be an easy fit with para.7 if that provision did not apply once a claimant had ceased to be engaged in activities. But on any basis a claimant should not be deprived of a disregard in the circumstances covered by para.8(b). Note that, by contrast with the income support position, incapacity has to be the reason for the cessation of engagement, not merely a reason for a continuation of a cessation started for another reason or a reason for not beginning to play a part in a business for the first time. The period of 6 months since ceasing to be engaged can be extended where reasonable in the circumstances under reg.48(2).

Note that where reg.77 applies (person in a position analogous to that of a sole trader or partner in relation to a company carrying on a trade treated as sole owner or partner and as possessing capital equal to the value of the company's capital, or a share), the value of that deemed capital is disregarded by reg.77(3)(a) while the person is engaged in activities in the course of that trade.

Rights in pensions schemes etc.

2.544 Note first that many provisions in the income support Sch.10 disregarding the capital value of the right to receive various forms of income are not replicated in the present Schedule (e.g. paras 11 (annuities, but see reg.46(3)), 12 (trust funds derived from personal injury compensation, but see reg.75(4)), 13 (life interests and liferents), 16 (capital payable by instalments, but see reg.46(4)), 24 (rent)).

Paragraph 9 (life insurance policies) is the equivalent of para.15 of the income support Sch.10. The latter refers to the surrender value. Paragraph 9 does not, but in the light of reg.49(1), the disregard must apply to whichever of the market value or surrender value has been applied to the policy.

Paragraph 10 (occupational or personal pension schemes) is the equivalent of para.23 of the income support Sch.10. The right to receive a pension from the schemes mentioned is not capable of being bought or sold and so would have no capital value anyway. There is no equivalent in the present Schedule to para.23A of the income support Sch.10 disregarding the value of any funds held under a personal pension scheme. It is no doubt considered that such funds do not form part of the capital of the member of the scheme, whose interests are only in the rights under the scheme rather than in the fund itself.

In the Institute for Government and the Social Security Advisory Committee's 2021 joint report *Jobs and benefits: The Covid-19 challenge* it was recommended that the value of Lifetime ISAs should be disregarded as capital because they are used by individuals, particularly the self-employed who have no access to occupational schemes, as a form of pension provision (pp.23 and 31). That recommendation was rejected in the Government's response of March 22, 2022, in particular on the ground that investments where the government had made a contribution to encourage saving should be taken into account.

Paragraph 11 (funeral plan contracts) has no equivalent in the income support Sch.10.

Amounts earmarked for special purposes

Paragraph 12 (housing association deposits as a condition of occupying the home) is the equivalent of para.9(a) of the income support Sch.10. The latter defines housing association. **2.545**

Paragraph 13(a) (amounts received within the past 6 months attributable to proceeds of sale of previous home to be used for the purchase of premises to be occupied as the home) is the equivalent of para.3 of the income support Sch.10. Under the latter, the sum must be directly attributable to the proceeds of sale, rather than merely attributable. The emphasis of the 6-month condition is different. Under income support para.3 the intention must be to occupy new premises within 26 weeks of the sale of the previous home. Under para.13(a) there is simply a limit (extendable under reg.48(2)) of 6 months from the receipt of the proceeds of sale and no condition that the intention be to occupy the new home within any particular period. See *R(IS) 7/01* on the effect of the test of "is to be used". It was held there that there must not only be an intention to use the proceeds to buy a new home (which can include buying land to build a house on), but also "reasonable certainty" that it will be so used. A mere hope that the proceeds will be used at some future date for another home is not sufficient.

In *EAM v SSWP (UC)* [2020] UKUT 247 (AAC), Judge Poynter declined to follow *R(IS) 7/01* and the other decisions referred to there as being inconsistent with the principle conclusively confirmed in *In re B (Children)* [2008] UKHL 35, [2009] A.C. 11 that there is only one civil standard of proof and that is proof that the fact in issue more probably occurred than not. His view was that to apply a test in terms of any kind of certainty was to place a higher burden on the claimant than the balance of probabilities. Although he agreed with the proposition in *R(IS) 7/01* that a mere genuine intention to use the sum to purchase a new home is not enough, he continued in para.33 that the phrase "is to be used for the purchase of premises" is about "what in all the circumstances of the case (including the claimant's intentions) is likely to happen in practice". Then he said in para.34 that to the extent that the *R(IS) 7/01* test requires a claimant to prove any fact to any standard other than the balance of probabilities he declined to follow that decision.

There are at least two problems in applying *EAM*. One is that it was not necessary to the decision for the judge to reach a definite conclusion on the correctness of *R(IS) 7/01*. On the facts as found by the First-tier Tribunal, the remaining amount attributable to the proceeds of sale of the claimant's home (£37,000) was not enough to buy a new home for her and her partner, so that they would need a mortgage, which on the balance of probabilities they would be unable to secure because of the level of their indebtedness. Accordingly, although the tribunal had been inconsistent on the nature of the test and had seemed to apply a test of practical certainty in concluding that the sum was not to be disregarded, its decision was not set aside because the same result would have followed if Judge Poynter's suggested test had been used. That undermines the basis for not following a reported decision that might otherwise have existed if a First-tier Tribunal or the Secretary of State considered Judge Poynter's reasoning, especially as supported by House of Lords' authority, to be persuasive.

The second problem is that the judge's reasoning appears dubious. There is a slight uncertainty about whether the disagreement with *R(IS) 7/01* extended only to the burden of proving facts necessary to the application of the legislative test or whether it extended also to the burden of showing that that test is met in all the circumstances as established by findings of fact. On balance, the latter seems to be intended. But then the result in accordance with para.33 is that the test to be applied is whether it is more likely than not that the sum will be used for the purchase of premises. Such a test appears, as a matter of the ordinary use of language, to be significantly different from and less restrictive than the legislative test in terms of "is to be used". Arguably, Judge Poynter's approach conflates the nature of the burden of proving that the legislative test is met with the true meaning of that test.

Unless and until *EAM* is taken to the Court of Appeal or is given the status of a reported decision or there is some further decision clarifying the issue (which may well take some years), tribunals may wish to hedge their bets by applying both approaches in the alternative, but only if properly satisfied that the outcome would be the same whichever was applied. If not so satisfied, a choice will have to be made as to whether the reasoning in *EAM* is sufficiently persuasive to be preferred to the approach approved in *R(IS) 7/01*.

A claimant who has a sum attributable to the proceeds of sale of home A and is currently living in home B may claim the advantage of the disregard provided that there is the requisite intention and reasonable certainty of use in relation to home C (*CIS/4269/2003*). However, the change in the condition for universal credit as compared to income support, of having received the sum within the previous six months (extendable) rather than intending to occupy the new home within 26 weeks (extendable) makes such a scenario more difficult to get within the terms of the disregard. The disregard cannot apply if the claimant has already bought a new home prior to the sale of the former home and at the time of the purchase it was not intended that the former home would be sold (*WT v DSD (IS)* [2011] NI Com 203).

Paragraph 13(b) (amounts received within the past 6 months to be used for the purchase of premises to be occupied as the home that have been deposited with a housing association) is the equivalent of para.9(b) of the income support Sch.10. See the notes to para.13(a) for "is to be used". The six months can be extended where reasonable in the circumstances under reg.48(2).

Paragraph 13(c) (grant received in the past 6 months for sole purpose of purchase of a home) appears to be the equivalent of para.37(a) of the income support Sch.10, but without any limitation as to the source of the grant. The definition of "grant" in reg.68(7) (see reg.2) does not seem applicable in the context of para.13(c). See the notes to para.13(a) for "is to be used". The six months can be extended where reasonable in the circumstances under reg.48(2).

Paragraph 14 (amount received within the past 6 months under an insurance policy in connection with loss of or damage to the home or personal possessions) is the equivalent of para.8(a) of the income support Sch.10, but without the condition that the sum be intended for repair and replacement. The 6 months can be extended where reasonable in the circumstances under reg.48(2).

Paragraph 15 (amount received within the past 6 months to be used for essential repairs or alterations to premises occupied or to be occupied as the home, where condition that it be used for that purpose) is the equivalent of para.8(b) of the income support Sch.10. See the notes to para.13(a) on the effect of the test of "is to be used". The 6 months can be extended where reasonable in the circumstances under reg.48(2).

Other payments

2.546 *Paragraph 16* (social fund payments made within the past 12 months) is the equivalent of para.18 of the income support Sch.10. The 12 months is not extendable.

Paragraph 17 (local authority welfare payments made within the past 12 months) appears to be the equivalent of paras 17(1) and (2) and 67 of the income support Sch.10 with some extension, but not so as to replicate the scope of para.18A of that Schedule on "local welfare provision". Under sub-para.(a) only payments by a local authority under the specified legislation, to do with the welfare of children, are disregarded. Under sub-para.(b) there is no restriction to any particular legislative provision as the source of the power to make the payment, but it must be to meet a person's welfare needs related to old age or disability, subject to the exception of payments for living expenses. That is a good deal narrower than the category of "local welfare provision" now, from May 4, 2022, covered by para.18A. See the notes near the beginning of this commentary for the possible consequences for the one-off support payment to be made to working tax credit recipients in April 2021. It must always be asked whether payments constitute income rather than capital. But even if a payment, such as possibly the WTC payment, is income, any unspent sum out of that income will metamorphise into capital under the principles discussed in the notes to reg.45 (and see *R(IS) 3/93* and *R(IS) 9/08*). See the notes to reg.66 for the question of how payments of unearned income should be attributed to assessment periods. The 12 months is not extendable.

Paragraph 18 (arrears or compensation for late payment received within the past 12 months of universal credit and certain social security benefits) is the equivalent of para.7 of the income support Sch.10, although the specification of the other benefits covered is through a different method. The 12 months is not extendable. There is no provision, as there is for income support and other legacy benefits, for a longer disregard for large payments of arrears or compensation where the late payment was the result of official error or an error of law (but see regs 10A, 10B and 10C of the Transitional Provisions Regulations, mentioned below). The benefits abolished by s.33 of the WRA 2012 are income-based JSA, income-related ESA, income support, housing benefit, council tax benefit (already abolished), child tax credit and working tax credit. Benefits falling outside reg.66(1)(a) and (b) and therefore covered by the disregard will include child benefit, attendance allowance, any care or mobility component of disability living allowance, any daily living component or mobility component of personal independence payment and the monthly payments of the new bereavement support payment, as well as Scottish child payments and adult and child disability payments. The category would appear to extend to arrears of discretionary housing payment (DHP), payable under s.69 of the Child Support, Pensions and Social Security Act 2000 and thus within the meaning of "social security benefit" in para.18(2). Thus payments of arrears (or compensation for late payment) of the benefits listed in reg.66(1)(a) or (b), including retirement pension income and new style ESA and JSA, do not attract the capital disregard.

In principle, payments of benefits that would have had the character of income if paid on their due date retain that character when paid in arrears as a lump sum (*R(SB) 4/89* and *CH/1561/2005*, and see *Minter v Kingston upon Hull CC* and *Potter v Secretary of State for Work and Pensions* [2011] EWCA Civ 1155, reported as [2012] AACR 21 on lump sum payments of compensation in settlement of equal pay claims, discussed in the notes to reg.66). In *R(SB) 4/89*, the Commissioner, relying on the principle in *McCorquodale v Chief Adjudication Officer*, reported as *R(SB) 1/88*, held that the income should be taken into account in the periods for which it would have been taken into account if paid on the due dates. In view of the absence of a clear rule in regs.66 and 73 on the assessment period in which payments of unearned income are to be taken into account (see the notes to reg.66), it is arguable that the same principle would apply to universal credit. But there is also a principle that if any amount of income is left over after the end of the period to which it is properly to be attributed that amount metamorphoses into capital (*R(SB) 2/83* and *R(IS) 3/93*). Looking at the date on which the payment of arrears or compensation is made, by definition all the periods to which the income would have been attributed if paid on the due dates would have passed, so that the lump sum would constitute capital from that point on. The disregard would therefore bite at that point, if applicable. If, however, the lump sum should be taken into account as unearned income for a forward period starting with the assessment period in which it is paid, it would not constitute capital in the assessment periods in which it was so attributed, except to the extent that there were amounts left over from that attributed to each succeeding assessment period.

See reg.10A of the Universal Credit (Transitional Provisions) Regulations 2014 (Pt IIB of this volume), inserted with effect from September 11, 2018. This allows a longer period of disregard as capital in cases where a payment of arrears of benefit, or of compensation for arrears due to the non-payment of benefit, amounts to £5,000 or more and the period of entitlement to which the payment relates began before legacy benefits are totally abolished (introductory part of reg.10A(1) and para.(1)(d)). All cases of arrears or compensation for non-payment of benefit are covered. Apparently any benefit can be involved, as there is no special definition of that word. Thus benefits not included in the scope of para.18 are included, as well as the disregard being able to extend beyond 12 months (see below). There is no restriction to cases of official error or error of law. There are then two alternatives. The first (para.(1)(a)(i)) is that the payment is received during a current award of universal credit, in which case the disregard applies for 12 months from the date of receipt if the payment would have been disregarded if the claimant had been entitled to a legacy benefit or SPC. The second (para.(1)(ii)) is that the payment was received during an award of a legacy benefit or SPC and no more than a month elapsed between the ending of that award and the start of entitlement to universal credit. In that case the disregard applies for the same period if the payment was disregarded under the rules of the earlier award.

Regulation 10B of the Transitional Provisions Regulations 2014, inserted with effect from October 31, 2019, applies a disregard as capital for 12 months from the date of receipt to payments of arrears (or compensation for arrears) of maternity allowance (excluded from para.18 because listed in reg.66(1)(b)) of less than £5,000, if the conditions in reg.10A(1)(a)-(d) are met.

Regulation 10C of the Transitional Provisions Regulations 2014, inserted with effect from July 15, 2020, applies a disregard as capital for 12 months from the date of receipt of certain compensatory payments for delay or failure to carry out an assessment for old style contributory ESA, with additional conditions and a potential extension for payments of £5,000 or more.

Note that all these payments would, in accordance with the principles explained above, retain their character as income. Whether that has an effect on universal credit entitlement depends first on how far the period to which the payments falls before the start of the period of any universal credit award. To the extent that it does fall before, there can be no effect. To the extent that it does not there can be a revision under reg.12 of the Decisions and Appeals Regulations 2013. But that depends on whether the benefit concerned is listed in reg.66(1)(b). If not, the payment cannot be taken into account as unearned income.

Paragraph 18ZA (arrears of widowed parent's allowance) and the February 2023 amendment to para.20 on bereavement support payment deal with the consequences of payments of arrears made under the Bereavement Benefits (Remedial) Order 2023.

The legislation on widowed parent's allowance (WPA), abolished on April 5, 2017, and bereavement support payment (BSP) in operation for deaths after April 5, 2017, was declared incompatible with the ECHR by discriminating against children whose parents were cohabiting but not married to each other or in a civil partnership (see *Re McLaughlin's Application for Judicial Review* [2018] UKSC 48, [2018] 1 W.L.R. 4250 and *R (Jackson and others) v Secretary of State for Work and Pensions* [2020] EWHC 183, [2020] 1 W.L.R. 1441 in Vol.I of this series). The Remedial Order allows retrospective claims to be made for those benefits from August 30, 2018 onwards and accordingly for arrears of benefit to be paid if the conditions of entitlement are met. The new para.18ZA, and the amended para.20 on BSP, deal with the consequences of such payments on universal credit entitlement, although with somewhat differing outcomes, stemming from WPA being included as unearned income in reg.66(1)(b)(vi), to be taken into account in full in calculating entitlement, and from BSP not being so included.

The Explanatory Memorandum misleadingly asserts in para.7.15 that the Remedial Order provides for payments of arrears under the Order to be treated as capital and disregarded for the purposes of income-related benefits, in line with assurances that had been given by the government to the Joint Committee on Human Rights and in its response to public consultation on a draft of the Order (see

Draft Bereavement Benefits (Remedial Order 2022: Second Report (HC 834, HL Paper 108) (December 6, 2022), para.61). However, it is absolutely plain that the amendments made by the Order do nothing to deem any payment of arrears to be capital. The new provisions like para.18ZA merely provide for a disregard of the payment for 52 weeks in so far as it is properly to be regarded as capital. It has been firmly established at least since the decision in *R(SB) 4/89* that cumulative arrears of social security benefits that would have been income if paid on time retain their nature as income though paid as a lump sum (see the notes to para.18). Then, as argued in the notes to reg.66 (under the heading *Attribution of unearned income to assessment periods*, 2.270), the monthly amounts of the arrears would be taken into account in the past assessment periods to which they related. That would trigger the Secretary of State's power to revise the decision(s) awarding universal credit in reg.12 of the Decisions and Appeals) Regulations 2013 (Vol.III of this series) for any periods to which the arrears were attributable as income and a resulting overpayment would be recoverable certainly under s.71ZB of the SSAA 1992 (and see in particular subs. (5)), but also possibly under s.74(2) and (4).

That that is the legal position (apart from the s.74(2) point) was effectively conceded by Viscount Younger, the Minister for Work and Pensions in the House of Lords, in a letter of February 2, 2023 to Baroness Sherlock (deposited in the Library of the House of Lords), in which he said this:

> "It is right that usual rules apply in these cases, to ensure that we don't treat cohabitee claimants differently to those claimants who were in a legal union with the deceased. WPA is taken into account as income when assessing entitlement to other means-tested benefits. Where a claimant was in receipt of a legacy income-related benefit during the period of entitlement for WPA, we will offset any overpayment of the relevant benefit from the retrospective lump sum of WPA and pay a net WPA award. Where a claimant was in receipt of Universal Credit during the period of WPA entitlement, the claimant may incur an overpayment of Universal Credit as a consequence of receiving a retrospective WPA award. We will make this clear to claimants, so that they are able to make an informed choice about making a claim."

The Explanatory Memorandum appears not so far to have been corrected, despite the error having been made plain to those responsible, and DMG Memo 2/23 makes no mention of this issue.

Lord Younger's letter states that for universal credit claimants arrears of WPA will be paid in full, with a universal credit overpayment to follow, with no process of abatement (what he calls an offset) of the amount of the arrears payable, as for legacy benefits, but does not explain why. It may be that the administrative and computer systems are not currently capable of carrying out that operation, but there also appears to be a suggestion that there is not a legal power to abate/offset. It might have been thought that, despite the amendment to s.74(2) of the SSAA 1992 in February 2013 allowing abatement where more universal credit has been paid than would have been if a prescribed payment had been made on time, that provision cannot apply because no payments have been prescribed for that purpose in the Social Security (Overpayments and Recovery) Regulations 2013. However, WPA is a prescribed payment under reg.8(1)(i) of the Social Security (Payments, Overpayments and Recovery) Regulations 2008, which thus allows the abatement of such payments. There then seems no reason why, given the specific amendment to the general effect of s.74(2), the abatement process should not be used where it is excess universal credit that had been paid.

A further obstacle has been thought to lie in the exceptionally obscure provisions of reg.16 of the Overpayments and Recovery Regulations 2013 (Vol.III of this series) on offsetting, and in particular para.(4). However, close analysis suggests that reg.16 simply cannot apply where the entitlement to the benefit that then counts as unearned income for the past arises from a new claim, as here. It only applies where an original decision has been revised, superseded or set aside on appeal (para.(1)).

If those arguments are wrong and s.74(2) abatement is not available, recoverability of the overpaid universal credit would undoubtably arise under s.71ZB of the SSAA 1992. It might then be asked why the overpayment of universal credit cannot be deducted from the WPA arrears under s.71ZC and reg.10 of the Overpayment and Recovery Regulations 2013 on recovery by deduction from benefits, which specifies any benefits under Pts 2 to 5 of the SSCBA 1992 that are payable as open to such recovery. But there would then be a problem of timing. There could not be a revision of the decisions awarding universal credit and identifying an overpayment until after there had been a decision on the retrospective WPA claim that specified what amounts the claimant was entitled to and for what periods. Regulation 16 of the Decisions and Appeals Regulations 1999 would not appear to allow suspension of payment of the WPA merely because that might give rise to an overpayment of a different benefit. Thus, if the abatement process under s.74(2) of the SSAA 1992 is not properly available, as it is for legacy benefits, it may be that there is no way of adopting an equivalent process and that the consequences of illicitly delaying payment of the WPA arrears until after the universal credit authorities have made the overpayment recovery decision are too messy to contemplate.

It is therefore to be hoped that the warning to claimants mentioned by Lord Younger will be sufficiently explicit to deter them from spending any of the money that would be needed to cover the universal credit overpayment. The payment of arrears will immediately, because the assessment periods to which it is to be attributed as income will all be in the past, metamorphose into capital on accepted principles (see *R(IS) 3/93* and *R(IS) 9/08* and the notes to reg.18). The new para.18ZA will of course operate to disregard that amount, including that for any periods when there was universal credit entitlement, as capital for 12 months from receipt.

Note that the outcome for BSP (see the amendment to para.20) is different because BSP is not included in the list of benefits in reg.66(1) that count as unearned income for universal credit purposes.

Paragraph 18A (local welfare provision) was introduced with effect from May 4, 2022 to provide a capital disregard for "local welfare provision", as newly defined in reg.2. The definition is in the same terms as for the corresponding disregard that has existed for some time for other means-tested benefits. It covers occasional financial or other assistance given by or on behalf of a local authority or the Scottish or Welsh Ministers to help to meet an immediate short-term need arising out of an exceptional event or circumstances that has to be met to avoid a risk to an individual's well-being or to enable individuals to establish or maintain a settled home. According to the Explanatory Memorandum to the amending regulations (SI 2022/448) that is to bring the universal credit provision into line with that for other means-tested benefits, there never having been any policy intention that such payments should be taken into account as capital, the problem having become particularly apparent in the light of the introduction of the £350 per month "thank you" payments under the Homes for Ukraine scheme and the extension of the Household Support Fund (the successor of the Covid Winter Grant Scheme and the Local Grant Scheme).

Paragraph 19 (Victoria Cross and George Cross) is the equivalent of para.46 of the income support Sch.10.

Paragraph 20 (bereavement support payments) now covers two different elements of these payments. In so far as payments have the nature of income they do not count as unearned income because they are not in the list in reg.66(1). In the first month of entitlement to bereavement support payment (BSP) there is entitlement to a one-off addition to the usual rate, under reg.3(2) or (5) of the Bereavement Support Payment Regulations 2017 (in Vol.I of this series). If that is to be regarded as capital, its amount is disregarded under sub-para.(1) and that disregard will continue to operate for 12 months from receipt if the amount is not spent or disposed of in that first month (see the introductory part of the note to Sch.10 at 2.541).

Any payment of arrears of the ordinary monthly payments would be disregarded as capital under reg.18.

Sub-paragraph (2) was added with effect from February 9, 2023 to deal specifically with the consequences of receipt of a payment of arrears of BSP on a retrospective claim under the Bereavement Benefits (Remedial) Order 2023. See the note to para.18ZA for the general background to such payments. Although a payment of arrears of ordinary monthly payments would in its nature be income attributable to the past assessment periods to which it was attributed, it would on receipt and retention immediately metamorphose into capital, which is then disregarded for 12 months under sub-para.(2). Arguably, the amendment was unnecessary because arrears of BSP are already disregarded as capital for the same period under para.18(1)(c).

Paragraph 21 disregards as capital any Scottish early years assistance, but only where given within the 12 months before the date in question. The restriction of this disregard to receipts within the previous 12 months does not apply to other means-tested benefits (see, for instance, para.75 of Sch.10 to the Income Support Regulations). Early years assistance is not listed in reg.66 of the Universal Credit Regulations 2013, so cannot count as unearned income, although since it takes the form of lump sum payments it probably could not have constituted income in any event.

Paragraph 22 disregards as capital any Scottish funeral expense assistance, but only where given within the 12 months before the date in question. The benefit is implemented by the Funeral Expense Assistance (Scotland) Regulations 2019 (SSI 2019/292) (see Pt XIII of Vol.IV of this series). Funeral expense assistance is not listed in reg.66, so cannot count as unearned income, although since it takes the form of lump sum payments would probably not have constituted income in any event.

Paragraph 23 (Scottish young carer grants) disregards as capital, with effect from November 9, 2020, the annual grants under the specified regulations (SSI 2019/324: see Pt XIII of Vol.IV of this series) received in the previous 52 weeks. The grants of (from April 2024) £383.75, limited to one a year, are payable in Scotland to carers aged 16 to 18 who care for at least 16 hours a week over a 13-week period for a person who normally receives a disability benefit. The 52-week limitation is absent from the equivalent provisions for "legacy benefits". Since the 2019 Regulations came into operation on October 21, 2019, there appears to have been a gap during which the grants were not disregarded as capital for the purposes of universal credit or legacy benefits. Young carer grants are not listed as unearned income in reg.66(1), but appear plainly to be in the nature of capital.

Paragraph 24 (Scottish winter heating assistance) disregards as capital, with effect from November 9, 2020, grants under the Winter Heating Assistance for Children and Young People (Scotland) Regulations 2020 (SSI 2020/352, also in operation from November 9, 2020: see Pt XIII of Vol.IV of this series) received in the previous 52 weeks. There was initially an automatic annual grant in November 2020 to a family of £200 (£251.50 for 2024) for each child entitled to the highest rate of the care component of DLA in the week of September 21–27, 2020. A single annual payment of £58.75 is now available to claimants with awards of qualifying benefits. The 52-week limitation is absent from the equivalent provisions for "legacy benefits". Winter heating assistance is not listed as unearned income in reg.66(1), but appears plainly to be in the nature of capital.

Omissions

A number of categories disregarded for the purposes of income support and old style ESA and JSA are thus not included in the universal credit Sch.10 or regs 75–77. Some cover very specific circumstances, but all are apparently deserving. They include payments of expenses of attending various schemes relating to job-seeking, the value of the right to receive the outstanding amount of capital payable by instalments, payments under a council tax reduction scheme and educational maintenance allowances. **2.547**

Regulation 112

SCHEDULE 11

APPLICATION OF ESA OR JSA SANCTIONS TO UNIVERSAL CREDIT

Moving an ESA sanction to UC

2.548 1. (1) This paragraph applies where—

(a) a person is, or has ceased to be, entitled to an employment and support allowance;

(b) there is a reduction relating to the award of the employment and support allowance under section 11J of the Welfare Reform Act 2007; and

(c) the person becomes entitled to universal credit.

(2) Any reduction relating to the award of the employment and support allowance is to be applied to the award of universal credit.

(3) The period for which the reduction is to have effect is the number of days which apply to the person under regulations 52 and 53 of the ESA Regulations minus—

(a) any days which have already resulted in a reduction to the amount of the employment and support allowance; and

(b) if the award of the employment and support allowance has terminated, any days falling after the date of that termination and before the date on which the award of universal credits starts, and that period is to be added to the total outstanding reduction period.

(4) The amount of the reduction in the award of universal credit for any assessment period in which the reduction is applied is the amount calculated in accordance with regulation 110.

Moving a JSA sanction to UC

2.549 2. (1) This paragraph applies where—

(a) a person is, or has ceased to be, entitled to a jobseeker's allowance;

(b) there is a reduction relating to the person's award of a jobseeker's allowance under section 6J or 6K of the Jobseekers Act 1995; and

(c) the person becomes entitled to universal credit.

(2) Any reduction relating to the award of the jobseeker's allowance is to be applied to the award of universal credit.

(3) The period for which the reduction is to have effect is the number of days which apply to the person under regulations 19 to 21 of the Jobseeker's Allowance Regulations 2013 minus—

(a) any days which have already resulted in a reduction to the amount of the jobseeker's allowance; and

(b) if the award of the jobseeker's allowance has terminated, any days falling after the date of that termination and before the date on which the award of universal credits starts, and that period is to be added to the total outstanding reduction period.

(4) The amount of the reduction in the award of universal credit for any assessment period in which the reduction is applied is the amount calculated in accordance with regulation 110.

Effect of ESA or JSA sanction on escalation of UC sanction

2.550 3. Where—

(a) a reduction in relation to an award of an employment and support allowance or an award of a jobseeker's allowance is applied to an award of universal credit by virtue of paragraph 1 or 2;

(b) there is a subsequent sanctionable failure under section 26 or 27 of the Act; and

(c) the failure giving rise to the reduction in relation to the award of an employment and support allowance or the award of a jobseeker's allowance ("the previous failure") and the reduction period determined for that failure correspond with a failure specified under section 26 or 27 of the Act to which the same reduction period would apply under Chapter 2 of Part 8 of these Regulations,

for the purposes of determining the reduction period for that subsequent failure, the previous failure is to be treated as if it were the corresponding failure under section 26 or 27 of the Act.

GENERAL NOTE

Paragraphs. 1 and 2

2.551 Paragraphs 1 and 2 constitute an important element of the relationship between new style ESA and JSA and universal credit. They provide that where a claimant is entitled to new style ESA or JSA and is subject to a sanction under s.11J of the WRA 2007 or s.6J or 6K of the WRA 2012 and then becomes entitled to universal credit, and also where the claimant ceases to be entitled to new style ESA or JSA, the ESA or JSA reduction is to be applied to the universal credit award. That works in practice if entitlement to ESA or JSA has ceased, but if that entitlement continues, it is the case that the unreduced (see reg.42 of the ESA Regulations 2013 and reg.5 of the JSA Regulations 2013 disapplying the sanctions regime for those benefits in the circumstances of dual entitlement) amount of ESA or JSA counts as income in the calculation of the amount of any universal credit award and so cuts into the amount available for reduction under the universal credit sanction. That sanction cannot as such reduce the amount of new style ESA or JSA payable. It is in the nature of a reduction in the amount of an award of benefit that the reduction cannot exceed the amount of that particular award. That has the anomalous results discussed in the notes to reg.5 of the JSA Regulations 2013 in Vol.I of this series.

The WRA 2012 contains a regulation-making power that could have been used to avoid these anomalous results. This is in para.2 of Sch.5, which applies when a claimant is entitled to both universal credit and a "relevant benefit", i.e. new style ESA or JSA. Paragraph 2(2) allows regulations in particular to provide in such circumstances for no amount to be payable by way of the relevant benefit. A Departmental memorandum to the House of Lords Select Committee on Delegated Powers and Regulatory Reform (see para.1.273) indicated that among the intended uses of the powers in para.2 was to specify in cases of dual entitlement whether the claimant would be paid only universal credit or only the relevant benefit or both. It was also intended to set out, if sanctions were applicable, which benefit was to be reduced first and to provide, if appropriate, that the application of a sanction to one benefit did not increase the amount of another. However, no regulations have been made to carry out those intentions. The only use of para.2 appears to have been in making reg.42 of the ESA Regulations 2013 and reg.5 of the JSA Regulations 2013, under the power in para.2(3), para.2(2) not being mentioned in the list of statutory powers invoked in the preamble to the Regulations. If regulations had provided that when there was dual entitlement no amount of new style ESA or JSA was to be payable, then there would have been no income from the benefit concerned to be taken into account in the calculation of the amount of universal credit payable and any reduction of benefit under a sanction would bite on the whole amount of the universal credit in the ordinary way. The non-application of the work-related and connected requirements for new style JSA and the sanctions regime under new style ESA and JSA would then have been part of a coherent structure. But that is not the actual state of the legislation.

It might be asked whether the provisions for reduction periods under the universal credit provisions to be applied to a new style ESA or JSA award and vice versa supply a way out of the anomalies. The answer is no. Regulation 61 of the ESA Regulations 2013 and reg.30 of the JSA Regulations 2013 only apply where a claimant ceases to be entitled to universal credit and is or becomes entitled to new style ESA or JSA. In those circumstances any universal credit sanction reduction period is applied to the ESA or JSA award. Regulations 61 and 30 do not apply during any period of dual entitlement. By contrast, when the opposite direction is considered, reg.43 of the ESA Regulations 2013 and reg.6 of the JSA Regulations 2013 apply only where the claimant is entitled to new style ESA or JSA subject to a sanction reduction period, becomes entitled to universal credit and *remains* entitled to new style ESA or JSA. But the result is that the reduction ceases to be applicable to the ESA or JSA award. That appears merely to reinforce the position under reg.42 of the ESA Regulations 2013 and reg.5 of the JSA Regulations 2013. The unreduced amount of ESA or JSA counts as income in the calculation of the amount of the universal credit award and only the "topping up" element of universal credit can be subject to reduction.

Paragraph 3

2.552 Under para.3, where a new style ESA or JSA sanction has been applied to universal credit under para.1 or 2, it can count as a "previous sanctionable failure" for the purposes of calculating the length of the reduction period for a subsequent universal credit sanction under s.26 or 27 of the WRA 2012 (see regs 102–104). Where there have been previous universal credit (and these equivalent) sanctionable failures within the previous 365 days including the date of the current sanctionable failure (but not within the previous 14 days), that affects the length of the reduction period. Note that it is not every previous new style ESA or JSA sanction that has that effect under para.3. It is only such a sanction that has been applied to universal credit. The position is thus not the same as under regs 19–21 of the JSA Regulations 2013 where there is express reference to previous universal credit sanctions as well as new style JSA sanctions (and new style ESA sanctions in the case of reg.21) as capable of being previous sanctionable failures. Regulation 19 of the ESA Regulations 2013 refers to previous new style JSA sanctionable failures and universal credit sanctionable failures at the appropriate level as well as to previous new style ESA low-level sanctionable failures. It also appears that an old style ESA or JSA sanctionable failure occurring within the 365 days cannot count as a previous sanctionable failure.

[1 Regulation 24A(4)

SCHEDULE 12

Availability of the Child Element where Maximum Exceeded – Exceptions

Introduction

2.553 1. This Schedule provides for cases where, for the purposes of regulation 24A, an exception applies in relation to a child or qualifying young person for whom a claimant is responsible ("A").

Multiple births

2.554 2. An exception applies where—

(a) the claimant is a parent (other than an adoptive parent) of A;

(b) A was one of two or more children born as a result of the same pregnancy;

(c) the claimant is responsible for at least two of the children or qualifying young persons born as a result of that pregnancy; and

(d) A is not the first in the order of those children or qualifying young persons as determined under regulation 24B.

Adoptions

2.555 3. An exception applies where A has been placed for adoption with, or adopted by, the claimant in accordance with the Adoption and Children Act 2002 or the Adoption and Children (Scotland) Act 2007, but not where—

(a) the claimant (or, if the claimant is a member of a couple, the other member)—

(i) was a step-parent of A immediately prior to the adoption; or

(ii) has been a parent of A (other than by adoption) at any time;

(b) the adoption order made in respect of A was made as a Convention adoption order (as defined, in England and Wales, in section 144 of the Adoption and Children Act 2002 and in Scotland, in section 119(1) of the Adoption and Children Scotland Act 2007); or

(c) prior to that adoption, A had been adopted by the claimant (or, if the claimant is a member of a couple, the other member) under the law of any country or territory outside the British Islands.

Non-parental caring arrangements

2.556 4.—(1) An exception applies where the claimant—

(a) is a friend or family carer in relation to A; or

(b) is responsible for a child who is a parent of A.

(2) In this paragraph, "friend or family carer" means a person who is responsible for A, but is not (or, if that person is a member of a couple, neither member is) A's parent or step-parent and—

(a) is named in a child arrangements order under section 8 of the Children Act 1989, that is in force with respect to A, as a person with whom A is to live;
(b) is a special guardian of A appointed under section 14A of that Act;
(c) is entitled to a guardian's allowance under section 77 of the Contributions and Benefits Act in respect of A;
(d) in whose favour a kinship care order, as defined in section 72(1) of the Children and Young People (Scotland) Act 2014, subsists in relation to A;
(e) is a guardian of A appointed under section 5 of the Children Act 1989 or section 7 of the Children (Scotland) Act 1995;
(f) in whom one or more of the parental responsibilities or parental rights respectively described in section 1 and 2 of the Children (Scotland) Act 1995 are vested by a permanence order made in respect of A under section 80 of the Adoption and Children (Scotland) Act 2007;
(g) fell within any of paragraphs (a) to (f) immediately prior to A's 16th birthday and has since continued to be responsible for A; or
(h) has undertaken the care of A in circumstances in which it is likely that A would otherwise be looked after by a local authority.

Non-consensual conception

5.—(1) An exception applies where— 2.557

(a) the claimant ("C") is A's parent; and
(b) the Secretary of State determines that—
  (i) A is likely to have been conceived as a result of sexual intercourse to which C did not agree by choice, or did not have the freedom and capacity to agree by choice; and
  (ii) C is not living at the same address as the other party to that intercourse ("B").

(2) The circumstances in which C is to be treated as not having the freedom or capacity to agree by choice to the sexual intercourse are to include (but are not limited to) circumstances in which, at or around the time A was conceived—

(a) B was personally connected to C;
(b) B was repeatedly or continuously engaging in behaviour towards C that was controlling or coercive; and
(c) that behaviour had a serious effect on C.

(3) The Secretary of State may make the determination in sub-paragraph (1)(b)(i) only if—

(a) C provides evidence from an approved person which demonstrates that—
  (i) C had contact with that approved person or another approved person; and
  (ii) C's circumstances are consistent with those of a person to whom sub-paragraphs (1)(a) and (1)(b)(i) apply; or
(b) there has been—
  (i) a conviction for—
    (aa) an offence of rape under section 1 of the Sexual Offences Act 2003 or section 1 of the Sexual Offences (Scotland) Act 2009;
    (bb) an offence of controlling or coercive behaviour in an intimate or family relationship under section 76 of the Serious Crime Act 2015; or
    (cc) an offence under the law of a country outside Great Britain that the Secretary of State considers to be analogous to the offence mentioned in sub-paragraph (aa) or (bb) above; or
  (ii) an award under the Criminal Injuries Compensation Scheme in respect of a relevant criminal injury sustained by C,

where it appears likely to the Secretary of State that the offence was committed, or the criminal injury was caused, by B and resulted in the conception of A or diminished C's freedom or capacity to agree by choice to the sexual intercourse which resulted in that conception.

(4) The Secretary of State may make the determination in sub-paragraph (1)(b)(ii) where the only available evidence is confirmation by C that that sub-paragraph applies.

(5) For the purposes of sub-paragraph (2)(a), B was personally connected to C if, at or around the time A was conceived—

(a) they were in an intimate personal relationship with each other; or
(b) they were living together and—
  (i) were members of the same family; or
  (ii) had previously been in an intimate personal relationship with each other.

(6) For the purposes of sub-paragraph (2)(c), B's behaviour had a serious effect on C if—

(a) it caused C to fear, on at least two occasions, that violence would be used against C; or

(b) it caused C serious alarm or distress which had a substantial adverse effect on C's day-to-day activities.

(7) In sub-paragraph (3)—

"approved person" means a person of a description specified on a list approved by the Secretary of State for the purposes of sub-paragraph (3)(a) and acting in their capacity as such;

"Criminal Injuries Compensation Scheme" means the Criminal Injuries Compensation Scheme under the Criminal Injuries Compensation Act 1995; and

"relevant criminal injury" means—

(a) a sexual offence (including a pregnancy sustained as a direct result of being the victim of a sexual offence);

(b) physical abuse of an adult, including domestic abuse; or

(c) mental injury,

as described in the tariff of injuries in the Criminal Injuries Compensation Scheme.

(8) For the purposes of sub-paragraph (5)(b)(i), B and C were members of the same family if, at or around the time A was conceived—

(a) they were, or had been, married to each other;

(b) they were, or had been, civil partners of each other;

(c) they were relatives (within the meaning given by section 63(1) of the Family Law Act 1996);

(d) they had agreed to marry each other, whether or not the agreement had been terminated;

(e) they had entered into a civil partnership agreement (within the meaning given by section 73 of the Civil Partnership Act 2004), whether or not the agreement had been terminated;

(f) they were both parents of the same child; or

(g) they had, or had had, parental responsibility (within the meaning given in regulation 4A(2)) for the same child.

Continuation of existing exception in a subsequent award

2.558 6. An exception applies where—

(a) the claimant ("C") is A's step-parent;

(b) none of the exceptions under paragraphs 2 to 5 above apply;

(c) C has previously been entitled to an award of universal credit as a member of a couple jointly with a parent of A, in which an exception under paragraph 2, 3 or 5 above applied in relation to A;

(d) since that award terminated, each award of universal credit to which C has been entitled has been made—

(i) as a consequence of a previous award having ended when C ceased to be a member of a couple or became a member of a couple; or

(ii) in any other circumstances in which the assessment periods for that award begin on the same day of each month as the assessment periods for a previous award under regulation 21 (assessment periods); and

(e) where, in the award mentioned in sub-paragraph (c), an exception under paragraph 2 above applied in relation to A—

(i) C is responsible for one or more other children or qualifying young persons born as a result of the same pregnancy as A; and

(ii) A is not the first in the order of those children or qualifying young persons as determined under regulation 24B (order of children and qualifying young persons).

AMENDMENT

1. Social Security (Restrictions on Amounts for Children and Qualifying Young Persons) Amendment Regulations 2017 (SI 2017/376) reg.2(1) and (4) (April 6, 2017).

GENERAL NOTE

2.559 See the commentary to regs 24-24B.

The Rent Officers (Universal Credit Functions) Order 2013

(SI 2013/382) (AS AMENDED)

The Secretary of State for Work and Pensions makes the following Order in exercise of the powers conferred by section 122 of the Housing Act 1996.

[*In force April 29, 2013*]

ARRANGEMENT OF REGULATIONS

SCHEDULES

Citation and commencement

1.—This Order may be cited as the Rent Officers (Universal Credit Functions) Order 2013 and comes into force on 29th April 2013. 2.560

Interpretation

2.—In this Order— 2.561

"Welfare Reform Act" means the Welfare Reform Act 2012;

"the Universal Credit Regulations" means the Universal Credit Regulations 2013;

"accommodation" means any residential accommodation whether or not consisting of the whole or part of a building and whether or not comprising separate and self-contained premises;

[2 "assessment period" has the same meaning as in section 40 of the Welfare Reform Act.]

[1 . . .]

"assured tenancy"—

(a) in England [3 . . .], has the same meaning as in Part 1 of the Housing Act 1988, except that it includes—

(i) a tenancy which would be an assured tenancy but for paragraph 2, 8 or 10 of Schedule 1 (tenancies which cannot be assured tenancies) to that Act; and

(ii) a licence which would be an assured tenancy (within the extended meaning given in this definition) were it a tenancy; and

(b) in Scotland, has the same meaning as in Part 2 of the Housing (Scotland) Act 1988, except that it includes—
   (i) a tenancy which would be an assured tenancy but for paragraph 7 or 9 of Schedule 4 (tenancies which cannot be assured tenancies) to that Act; and
   (ii) any other form of occupancy which would be an assured tenancy (within the extended meaning given in this definition) were it a tenancy;

"broad rental market area" has the meaning given in article 3;

"housing payment" means a relevant payment within the meaning of paragraph 3 of Schedule 4 (housing costs element for renters) to the Universal Credit Regulations;

[3 "introductory standard contract" has the meaning given by the Renting Homes (Wales) Act 2016 (see section 16 of that Act);]

"local authority" means—

(a) in relation to England, the council of a district or London borough, the Common Council of the City of London or the Council of the Isles of Scilly;
(b) in relation to Wales, the council of a county or county borough; and
(c) in relation to Scotland, a council constituted under section 2 (constitution of councils) of the Local Government etc. (Scotland) Act 1994;

[3 "private landlord" has the meaning given by the Renting Homes (Wales) Act 2016 (see section 10 of that Act);]

[3 "private registered provider of social housing" has the meaning given by section 80(3) of the Housing and Regeneration Act 2008;]

"provider of social housing" has the meaning given in paragraph 2 of Schedule 4 to the Universal Credit Regulations;

[3 "registered social landlord" means a person registered in the register maintained under section 1 of the Housing Act 1996(61);]

"relevant time" means the time the request for the determination is made or, if earlier, the date the tenancy ends;

[3 "secure contract" has the meaning given by the Renting Homes (Wales) Act 2016 (see section 8 of that Act);]

"service charge payments" has the meaning given in paragraph 7 of Schedule 1 (meaning of payments in respect of accommodation) to the Universal Credit Regulations;

[3 "standard contract" has the meaning given by the Renting Homes (Wales) Act 2016 (see section 8 of that Act), but does not include—

(a) an introductory standard contract,
(b) a prohibited conduct standard contract within the meaning given by the Renting Homes (Wales) Act 2016 (see section 116 of that Act), or
(c) a supported standard contract within the meaning given by the Renting Homes (Wales) Act 2016 (see section 143 of that Act);]

"tenancy" includes—

(a) in England and Wales, a licence to occupy premises; and
(b) in Scotland, any other right of occupancy,

and references to rent, a tenant, a landlord or any other expression appropriate to a tenancy are to be construed accordingly;

"tenant" includes, where the tenant is a member of a couple within the meaning of section 39 of the Welfare Reform Act, the other member of the couple;

"working day" means any day other than—

(a) a Saturday or a Sunday;

(b) Christmas Day or Good Friday; or

(c) a day which is a bank holiday under the Banking and Financial Dealings Act 1971 in any part of Great Britain.

AMENDMENTS

1. Rent Officers (Housing Benefit and Universal Credit Functions) (Amendment) Order 2013 (SI 2013/1544) art.4(2) (September 1, 2013).

2. Rent Officers (Housing Benefit and Universal Credit Functions) (Local Housing Allowance Amendments) Order 2014 (SI 2014/3126) art.4(2) (January 8, 2015).

3. Renting Homes (Wales) Act 2016 (Consequential Amendments to Secondary Legislation) Regulations 2022 (SI 2022/907) Sch.1 para.28.

Broad rental market area determinations

3.—(1) Broad rental market area determinations taking effect on 29th April 2013 are determined in accordance with paragraph (7) and all other broad rental market area determinations are determined in accordance with paragraphs (2) to (6). 2.562

(2) A rent officer must, at such times as the rent officer considers appropriate and if the Secretary of State agrees—

(a) determine one or more broad rental market areas; and

(b) in respect of that broad rental market area, or those broad rental market areas, give to the Secretary of State a notice which identifies the local authority areas and the postcodes contained within the broad rental market area (or each of them).

[2 (2A) The power in paragraph (2) is not limited by paragraph 2(2) of Schedule 1.]

(3) A broad rental market area is an area within which a person could reasonably be expected to live having regard to facilities and services for the purposes of health, education, recreation, personal banking and shopping, taking account of the distance of travel, by public and private transport, to and from those facilities and services.

(4) A broad rental market area must contain—

(a) residential premises of a variety of types, including such premises held on a variety of tenures; and

(b) sufficient privately rented residential premises to ensure that, in the rent officer's opinion, the local housing allowance for the categories of accommodation in the area for which the rent officer is required to determine a local housing allowance is representative of the rents that a landlord might reasonably be expected to obtain in that area.

(5) Every part of Great Britain must fall within a broad rental market area and a broad rental market area must not overlap with another broad rental market area.

(6) Any broad rental market area determination made in accordance with paragraph (2) is to take effect—

(a) on the day the determination is made for the purpose of enabling a rent officer to determine a local housing allowance for that area; and

[4 (b) for all other purposes on the next relevant Monday following the day on which the determination is made.]

(7) For broad rental market area determinations that take effect on 29th April 2013, a rent officer must use the broad rental market area determinations determined in accordance with article 4B of, and Schedule 3B to, the Rent Officers (Housing Benefit Functions) Order 1997 or the Rent Officers (Housing Benefit Functions) (Scotland) Order 1997 that apply on 29th April 2013.

[[3] (8) "Relevant Monday" has the same meaning as in article 4(4).]

AMENDMENTS

1. Rent Officers (Housing Benefit and Universal Credit Functions) (Local Housing Allowance Amendments) Order 2013 (SI 2013/2978) art.4(2) (January 13, 2014).

2. Rent Officers (Housing Benefit and Universal Credit Functions) (Local Housing Allowance Amendments) Order 2016 (SI 2016/1179) art.4(1) and (2) (January 23, 2017).

3. Rent Officers (Housing Benefit and Universal Credit Functions) (Amendment) Order 2017 (SI 2017/1323) art.4(1) and (2) (January 26, 2018).

4. Rent Officers (Housing Benefit and Universal Credit Functions) (Amendment and Modification) Order 2021 (SI 2021/1380) (January 31, 2022).

Local housing allowance determinations

2.563 **4.**—(1) [[5] . . .]

[[5] (1)] [[1] In 2014 and in each subsequent year, on the date specified in paragraph [[5] (2)],] a rent officer must—

(a) for each broad rental market area determine, in accordance with Schedule 1, a local housing allowance for each of the categories of accommodation set out in paragraph 1 of Schedule 1; and
(b) notify the Secretary of State of the local housing allowance determination made in accordance with sub-paragraph (a) for each broad rental market area.

[[1] [[3] [[5] (2)] The date specified for the purposes of paragraph [[5] (1)] is the last working day of January [[6] and also the 31st March 2020].]]

[[4] [[5] (3) Any local housing allowance determination made in accordance with paragraph (1) is to take effect—

(a) in the case of a person with an existing UC entitlement—
    (i) on the relevant Monday where that is the first day of an assessment period for the person in question; or
    (ii) where the relevant Monday is not the first day of an assessment period for that person, on the first day of the next assessment period following that; or
(b) in any other case, on the relevant Monday.]]

[[6] (3A) The determinations made in accordance with paragraph (1) on the 31st March 2020 shall take effect (under paragraph (3)) in place of the determinations made in accordance with paragraph (1) on the 31st January 2020.]

[[5] (4) For the purposes of this article—

"a person with an existing UC entitlement" means a person who is entitled to universal credit on the relevant Monday;

"relevant Monday" means the first Monday in the first tax year that commences following the day on which the determination is made;

"tax year" means a period beginning with 6th April in one year and ending with 5th April in the next.]

AMENDMENTS

1. Rent Officers (Housing Benefit and Universal Credit Functions) (Amendment) Order 2013 (SI 2013/1544), art.4(3) (September 1, 2013).

2. Rent Officers (Housing Benefit and Universal Credit Functions) (Local Housing Allowance Amendments) Order 2013 (SI 2013/2978), art.4(2) (January 13, 2014).

3. Rent Officers (Housing Benefit and Universal Credit Functions) (Local Housing Allowance Amendments) Order 2014 (SI 2014/3126) art.4(3) (January 8, 2015).

4. Rent Officers (Housing Benefit and Universal Credit Functions) (Local Housing Allowance Amendments) Order 2014 (SI 2014/3126) art.4(4) (January 8, 2015).

5. Rent Officers (Housing Benefit and Universal Credit Functions) (Local Housing Allowance Amendments) Order 2015 (SI 2015/1753) art.4(2) (November 2, 2015).

6. Social Security (Coronavirus) (Further Measures) Regulations 2020 (SI 2020/371) reg.4(3)(a) (March 30, 2020).

DEFINITIONS

"accommodation"—see art.2.
"assessment period"—*ibid.*
"broad rental market area"—see arts 2 and 3.

Housing payment determination

5.—Where a rent officer receives a request from the Secretary of State for a determination in respect of housing payments for accommodation let by a provider of social housing, the rent officer must— 2.564

(a) determine in accordance with Schedule 2 whether each of the housing payments specified by the Secretary of State in that request is reasonable for that accommodation; and

(b) where the rent officer determines that a housing payment is not reasonable, determine in accordance with Schedule 2 the amount that is reasonable for the accommodation and notify the Secretary of State of that amount.

DEFINITIONS

"accommodation"—see art.2.
"assessment period"--*ibid.*
"housing payment"—see art.2 and Universal Credit Regs, Sch.4, para.3.

Redeterminations

6.—(1) Where a rent officer has made a determination under article 3, 4 or 5 ("the determination") and paragraph (2) applies, a rent officer must make a further determination ("a redetermination") and notify the Secretary of State of the redetermination. 2.565

(2) This paragraph applies where—

(a) the determination was made under article 3 or 4 and the rent officer considers that there is an error in relation to that determination; or

(b) the determination was made under article 5 and—

(i) the Secretary of State requests that the rent officer makes a redetermination;

(ii) the Secretary of State informs the rent officer that the information supplied when requesting the determination was incorrect or incomplete; or

(iii) the rent officer considers that there is an error in relation to the determination.

(3) Where a rent officer makes a redetermination the rent officer must do so in accordance with the provisions of this Order that applied to the determination and use the same information that was used for the determination except that, where the information used was incorrect or incomplete, the rent officer must use the correct or complete information.

(4) Where a rent officer makes a redetermination by virtue of paragraph (2)(b)(i), the rent officer must have regard to the advice of at least one other rent officer in relation to that redetermination.

Information

2.566 **7.**—Where a rent officer considers that the information supplied by the Secretary of State or a landlord under regulation 40 (information to be provided to rent officers) of the Universal Credit, Personal Independence Payment, Jobseeker's Allowance and Employment and Support Allowance (Claims and Payments) Regulations 2013 is incomplete or incorrect, the rent officer must—

(a) notify the Secretary of State or the landlord of that fact; and

(b) request that the Secretary of State or the landlord supplies the further information or to confirm whether, in their opinion, the information already supplied is correct and, if they agree that it is not, to supply the correct information.

Means of giving notice

2.567 **8.**—Any notice given by a rent officer under this Order may be given in writing or by electronic means unless the Secretary of State requests that notice is given in writing only.

Article 4

SCHEDULE 1

LOCAL HOUSING ALLOWANCE DETERMINATIONS

Categories of accommodation

2.568 **1.** The categories of accommodation for which a rent officer is required to determine a local housing allowance in accordance with article 4 are—

(a) accommodation where the tenant has the exclusive use of only one bedroom and where the tenancy provides for the tenant to share the use of one or more of—

(i) a kitchen;

(ii) a bathroom;

(iii) a toilet; or

(iv) a room suitable for living in;

(b) accommodation where the tenant has the exclusive use of only one bedroom and exclusive use of a kitchen, a bathroom, a toilet and a room suitable for living in;

(c) accommodation where the tenant has the use of only two bedrooms;

(d) accommodation where the tenant has the use of only three bedrooms;

(e) accommodation where the tenant has the use of only four bedrooms.

[1 Local housing allowance for category of accommodation in paragraph 1

2.—(1) Subject to [11 paragraphs] 5 (anomalous local housing allowances) [11 and 7 (minimum local housing allowance)] the rent officer must determine a local housing allowance for each category of accommodation in paragraph 1 as follows. 2.569

[8 [9 (2) The local housing allowance for any category of accommodation is the lower of—

(a) the rent at the 30th percentile determined in accordance with paragraph 3; and

(b) for a category of accommodation listed in column 1 of the following table, the amount listed in column 2 of that table (maximum local housing allowance)—

1. Category of accommodation as specified in paragraph 1	**2. Maximum local housing allowance for that category of accommodation**
paragraph 1(a) (one bedroom, shared accommodation)	[£ 1,439.97]
Paragraph 1(b) (one bedroom, exclusive use)	[£ 1,439.97]
Paragraph 1(c) (two bedrooms)	[£ 1,793.98]
Paragraph 1(d) (three bedrooms)	[£ 2,160.02]
Paragraph 1(e) (four bedrooms)	[£ 3,060.00]]]

(2A) [8 . . .]

(2B) [8 . . .]

(3) [8 . . .]

(3A) [8 . . .]

(4) Where the local housing allowance would otherwise not be a whole number of pence, it must be rounded to the nearest whole penny by disregarding any amount less than half a penny and treating any amount of half a penny or more as a whole penny.]

Rent at the 30th percentile

3.—(1) The rent officer must determine the rent at the 30th percentile in accordance with the following sub-paragraphs. 2.570

(2) The rent officer must compile a list of rents.

[10 (3) The rent officer must compile a list of rents in ascending order of the rents which, in the rent officer's opinion, are payable—

(a) for each category of dwelling specified in paragraph 1—

(i) in England, let under an assured tenancy, or

(ii) in Wales—

(aa) before the day on which section 239 of the Renting Homes (Wales) Act 2016 comes into force, let under an assured tenancy, or

(bb) on or after that day, let under a relevant occupation contract; and

(b) in the 12 month period ending on the 30th day of the September preceding the date of the determination.]

(4) The list must include any rents which are of the same amount.

(5) The criteria for including an assured tenancy [10 or a relevant occupation contract, as the case may be,] on the list of rents in relation to each category of accommodation specified in paragraph 1 are that—

(a) the accommodation let under the assured tenancy [10 or relevant occupation contract] is in the broad rental market area for which the local housing allowance for that category of accommodation is being determined;

(b) the accommodation is in a reasonable state of repair; and

(c) the assured tenancy [10 or relevant occupation contract] permits the tenant to use exclusively or share the use of, as the case may be, the same number and type of rooms as the category of accommodation in relation to which the list of rents is being compiled.

[1 (6) Sub-paragraph (7) applies where the rent officer is not satisfied that the list of rents in respect of any category of accommodation would contain sufficient rents, payable in the 12 month period ending on the 30th day of the September preceding the date of the determination for accommodation in the broad rental market area, to enable a local housing allowance to be determined which is representative of the rents that a landlord might reasonably be expected to obtain in that area.]

(7) In a case where this sub-paragraph applies, the rent officer may add to the list rents for accommodation in the same category in other areas in which a comparable market exists.

(8) Where rent is payable other than monthly the rent officer must use the figure which would be payable if the rent were to be payable monthly by calculating the rent for a year and dividing the total by 12.

(9) When compiling the list of rents for each category of accommodation, the rent officer must—

(a) assume that no-one had sought or is seeking the tenancy who would have been entitled to housing benefit under Part 7 of the Social Security Contributions and Benefits Act 1992(12) or universal credit under Part 1 of the Welfare Reform Act; and

(b) exclude the amount of any rent which, in the rent officer's opinion, is fairly attributable to the provision of services performed or facilities (including the use of furniture) provided for, or rights made available to, the tenant and which would not be classed as service charge payments.

(10) The rent at the 30th percentile in the list of rents ("R") is determined as follows—

(a) where the number of rents on the list is a multiple of 10, the formula is—

$$R = \frac{\text{the amount of the rent at P + the amount of the rent at P1}}{2}$$

where—

(i) P is the position on the list found by multiplying the number of rents on the list by 3 and dividing by 10; and

(ii) P1 is the following position on the list;

(b) where the number of rents on the list is not a multiple of 10, the formula is—

$$R = \text{the amount of the rent at P2}$$

where P2 is the position on the list found by multiplying the number of rents on the list by 3 and dividing by 10 and rounding the result upwards to the nearest whole number.

[[10] (11) In this paragraph, "relevant occupation contract" means—

(a) a secure contract in relation to which the landlord is a registered social landlord, a private registered provider of social housing, or a private landlord,

(b) a standard contract, or

(c) an introductory standard contract in relation to which the landlord is a registered social landlord or a private registered provider of social housing.]

[[1] Maximum local housing allowance

2.571 **4.** [[2] [[4] . . .]]]

Anomalous local housing allowances

2.572 **5.** [[12] Subject to paragraph 7, where—

(a) the rent officer has determined the local housing allowance for each of the categories of accommodation in paragraph 1 in accordance with the preceding paragraphs of this Schedule; and

(b) the local housing allowance for a category of accommodation in paragraph 1(b) to (e) is lower than the local housing allowance for any of the categories of accommodation which precede it,

that local housing allowance is to be the same as the highest local housing allowance which precedes it.

[[5] **5A.** [[8] ...] [[7] [[8]...]]]

6. [[1] [[3] [[4] . . .]]] [[13] *Minimum local housing allowance*

7. Where—

(a) the rent officer has determined the local housing allowance for each of the categories of accommodation in paragraph 1 in accordance with paragraphs 2 and 3 and, where relevant, paragraph 5 (anomalous local housing allowances); and

(b) the local housing allowance as so determined for a category of accommodation is lower than the local housing allowance determined for that category of accommodation on 31st March 2020, that local housing allowance is to be the same as the local housing allowance determined for that category of accommodation on 31st March 2020.]

AMENDMENTS

1. Rent Officers (Housing Benefit and Universal Credit Functions) (Local Housing Allowance Amendments) Order 2013 (SI 2013/2978) art.4(3) (January 13, 2014).

2. Rent Officers (Housing Benefit and Universal Credit Functions) (Local Housing Allowance Amendments) Order 2014 (SI 2014/3126) art.4(5) (January 8, 2015).

3. Rent Officers (Housing Benefit and Universal Credit Functions) (Local Housing Allowance Amendments) Order 2014 (SI 2014/3126) art.4(6) and Sch.3 (January 8, 2015).

4. Rent Officers (Housing Benefit and Universal Credit Functions) (Local Housing Allowance Amendments) Order 2015 (SI 2015/1753) art.4(3) (November 2, 2015).

5. Rent Officers (Housing Benefit and Universal Credit Functions) (Local Housing Allowance Amendments) Order 2016 (SI 2016/1179) art.4(1) and (3) (January 23, 2017).

6. Rent Officers (Housing Benefit and Universal Credit Functions) (Amendment) Order 2017 (SI 2017/1323) art.4 (January 26, 2018).

7. Rent Officers (Housing Benefit and Universal Credit Functions) (Amendment) Order 2018 (SI 2018/1332) art.4 (January 25, 2019).

8. Rent Officers (Housing Benefit and Universal Credit Functions) (Amendment) Order 2020 (SI 2020/27) art.4(1) and (3) (January 30, 2020).

9. Social Security (Coronavirus) (Further Measures) Regulations 2020 (SI 2020/371) reg.4(3)(b) (March 30, 2020).

10. Renting Homes (Wales) Act 2016 (Consequential Amendments to Secondary Legislation) Regulations 2022 (SI 2022/907) Sch.1 para.28.

11. Rent Officers (Housing Benefit and Universal Credit Functions) (Amendment) Order 2024 art.4(2) (January 31, 2024).

12. Rent Officers (Housing Benefit and Universal Credit Functions) (Amendment) Order 2024 art.4(3) (January 31, 2024).

13. Rent Officers (Housing Benefit and Universal Credit Functions) (Amendment) Order 2024 art.4(4) (January 31, 2024).

MODIFICATION

Article 4 of the Rent Officers (Housing Benefit and Universal Credit Functions) (Modification) Order 2023 (SI 2023/6) provided that, for the purposes of determining the local housing allowances in 2023, Sch.1 is to be read as if the following were substituted for para.2(2): **2.573**

> "(2) For all broad rental market areas the local housing allowance for any category of accommodation is the allowance determined for that category of accommodation on 31st March 2020."

For 2022, the same effect (i.e. freezing rates at the 31 March 2020 level) was created by the Rent Officers (Housing Benefit and Universal Credit Functions) (Amendment and Modification) Order 2021 (SI 2021/1380) Art.7. For 2021, the same effect was created by the Rent Officers (Housing Benefit and Universal Credit Functions) (Modification) Order 2020 (SI 2020/1519) Art.4. For the history of paragraph 2 before 31 March 2020, see earlier volumes of this text.

Regulation 18 of the Renting Homes (Wales) Act 2016 (Saving and Transitional Provisions) Regulations 2022 (SI 2022/1172) makes transitional provision for the purpose of determining a local housing allowance under Sch.1. For so long as it is necessary to refer to rents payable before December 1, 2022 (the day on which s.239

of the Renting Homes (Wales) Act 2016 comes into force, abolishing assured tenancies in Wales), the value of rent which, in the rent officer's opinion, would have been payable for a category of dwelling, specified in para.1 of Sch.1 to the 2013 Order, in Wales let under an assured tenancy, is to be deemed to be the rent that would have been payable in relation to the relevant category of dwelling let under a relevant secure or standard contract. "Relevant secure or standard contract" means a secure or standard contract in relation to which the landlord does not meet the landlord condition in s.80(3) of the Housing Act 1985.

Article 5

SCHEDULE 2

HOUSING PAYMENT DETERMINATION

2.574 **1.** The rent officer must determine whether, in the rent officer's opinion, each of the housing payments payable for the tenancy of the accommodation at the relevant time is reasonable.

2. If the rent officer determines under paragraph 1 that a housing payment is not reasonable, the rent officer must also determine the amount of the housing payment which is reasonable.

3. When making a determination under this Schedule, the rent officer must—

(a) have regard to the level of similar payments under tenancies for accommodation which—
  (i) is let by the same type of landlord;
  (ii) is in the same local authority area [[1] (but see paragraph 4)];
  (iii) has the same number of bedrooms; and
  (iv) is in the same reasonable state of repair,

as the accommodation in respect of which the determination is being made;

(b) exclude—
  (i) the cost of any care, support or supervision provided to the tenant by the landlord or by someone on the landlord's behalf;
  (ii) any payments for services performed or facilities (including the use of furniture) provided for, or rights made available to, the tenant which are not service charge payments; and

(c) where the accommodation is let at an Affordable Rent, assume that the rent is reasonable.

4. Where the rent officer is not satisfied that the local authority area contains sufficient accommodation to allow a determination of the housing payments which a landlord might reasonably have been expected to charge, the rent officer may have regard to the level of housing payments in one adjoining local authority area [[1] or one local authority area adjoining an adjoining local authority area or, if the rent officer considers it necessary, more than one such area].

5. For the purposes of this Schedule—

(a) a housing payment is reasonable where it is not higher than the payment which the landlord might reasonably have been expected to obtain for the tenancy at the relevant time;

(b) accommodation is let by the same type of landlord where—
  (i) in a case where the landlord of the accommodation in respect of which the determination is being made is a local authority, the landlord of the other accommodation is also a local authority; and
  (ii) in a case where the landlord of the accommodation in respect of which the determination is being made is a provider of social housing other than a local authority, the landlord of the other accommodation is also a provider of social housing other than a local authority;

(c) accommodation is let at an Affordable Rent where—
  (i) the rent is regulated under a standard by the Regulator of Social Housing under section 194 of the Housing and Regeneration Act 2008(13) ("the 2008 Act") which requires the initial rent to be set at no more than 80% of the local market rent (including service charges); or

(ii) the accommodation is let by a local authority and, under arrangements between the local authority and the Homes and Communities Agency (as established by section 1 of the 2008 Act), the Greater London Authority or the Secretary of State, the rent payable is set on the same basis as would be the case if the rent were regulated under a standard set by the Regulator of Social Housing under section 194 of the 2008 Act which requires the initial rent to be set at no more than 80% of the local market rent (including service charges).

AMENDMENT

1. Rent Officers (Housing Benefit and Universal Credit Functions) (Local Housing Allowance Amendments) Order 2016 (SI 2016/1179) art.4(1) and (4) (January 23, 2017).

DEFINITIONS

"accommodation"—see art.2.
"housing payment"—see art.2 and Universal Credit Regs, Sch.4, para.3.
"local authority"—see art.2.
"provider of social housing"—see art.2 and Universal Credit Regs, Sch.4, para.4.
"relevant time"—see art.2.
"service charge payments"—see art.2 and Universal Credit Regs, Sch.1 para.7.
"tenancy"—see art.2.
"tenant"—*ibid.*

The Universal Credit (Work-Related Requirements) In Work Pilot Scheme and Amendment Regulations 2015

(SI 2015/89)

Made on January 29, 2015 by the Secretary of State under sections 18(5), 22(2), 41(1)(a), (2)(b) and (4) and 42(2) and (3) of the Welfare Reform Act 2012, Part 3 being made with a view to ascertaining the extent to which the provision made by that Part is likely to promote people already in paid work remaining in work, or obtaining or being able to obtain, more work or better paid work, a draft having been laid before, and approved by resolution of, each House of Parliament in accordance with section 43(4) and (6)(b) of the Act, and the Social Security Advisory Committee having agreed in accordance with section 173(1) of the Social Security Administration Act 1992 that proposals in respect of these Regulations should not be referred to it.

[In force February 19, 2015] **2.575**

REGULATIONS REPRODUCED

PART 1

INTRODUCTORY

PART 2

AMENDMENT OF THE UNIVERSAL CREDIT REGULATIONS

PART 3

THE IN WORK PILOT SCHEME

GENERAL NOTE

2.576 See the annotation to reg.99(6) and (6A), the provisions affected by the amendment in reg.3 of the present Regulations, for the context in which the pilot schemes will operate.

PART 1

INTRODUCTORY

Citation and commencement

2.577 **1.** These Regulations may be cited as the Universal Credit (Work-Related Requirements) In Work Pilot Scheme and Amendment Regulations 2015, and come into force at the end of the period of 21 days beginning with the day on which they are made.

Interpretation

2. In these Regulations— 2.578
"the Act" means the Welfare Reform Act 2012;
[1"monthly earnings" has the meaning in regulation 90(6) of the Universal Credit Regulations;]
"qualifying claimant" has the meaning in regulation 7;
"the Universal Credit Regulations" means the Universal Credit Regulations 2013; and
[1 . . .].

AMENDMENT

1. Universal Credit and Miscellaneous Amendments Regulations 2015 (SI 2015/1754) reg.3(2) (November 4, 2015).

PART 2

AMENDMENT OF THE UNIVERSAL CREDIT REGULATIONS

New provision for suspension of mandatory work search and work availability requirements on account of earnings

3. – *The amendments effected by this regulation have been taken into account in the text of the Universal Credit Regulations 2013 elsewhere in this volume.* 2.579

PART 3

THE IN WORK PILOT SCHEME

Provision made for piloting purposes

4.—(1) The following provision is made in accordance with section 41 of the Act to test the extent to which the imposition of work-related requirements on persons already in paid work is likely to promote their remaining in work, or obtaining or being able to obtain, more work or better-paid work. 2.580

(2) Regulation 99 of the Universal Credit Regulations (which provides for the suspension of work search requirements and work availability requirements where the claimant's [1 monthly] earnings from employment or, if the claimant is a member of a couple, their combined [1 monthly] earnings from employment, reach a specified amount) is to apply as if paragraph (6) were omitted.

(3) The provision made by paragraph (2) is to apply only in relation to qualifying claimants who have been selected by the Secretary of State in accordance with regulation 5 and notified of that selection in accordance with regulation 6.

(4) The provision made by paragraph (2) ceases to apply to a person who has been selected in accordance with regulation 5 where—

(a) that person ceases to be a qualifying claimant (but see paragraph (5)); or

(b) the Secretary of State has determined that that provision should cease to apply because—

(i) the person has moved to live in a different geographical area; or

(ii) the Secretary of State has determined that the testing of particular work-related requirements that have been imposed on that person has concluded.

(5) Where a person has been selected in accordance with regulation 5 and, by reason only of an increase or decrease in their [1 monthly] earnings (or, if they are a member of a couple, the [1 monthly] earnings of the other member) the person is no longer a qualifying claimant, paragraph (2) applies again if the person becomes a qualifying claimant again unless, in the intervening period—

(a) paragraph (2) has ceased to apply for another reason; or

(b) the person has ceased to be entitled to universal credit for a continuous period of 6 months or more.

AMENDMENT

1. Universal Credit and Miscellaneous Amendments Regulations 2015 (SI 2015/1754) reg.3(3) (November 4, 2015).

DEFINITIONS

"the Act"—see reg.2.
"claimant"—see WRA 2012 s.40.
"monthly earnings"—see reg.2 and the Universal Credit Regulations 2013 reg.90(6).
"qualifying claimant"—see regs 2 and 7.
"the Universal Credit Regulations"—see reg.2
"work"—see WRA 2012 s.40.
"work availability requirement"—see WRA 2012 ss.40 and 18(2).
"work search requirement"—see WRA 2012 ss.40 and 17(1).
"work-related requirement"—see WRA 2012 ss.40 and 13(2).

Selection of participants

2.581 **5.**—(1) A selection for the purpose of regulation 4 is to be made by the Secretary of State on a random sampling basis from persons who, at the time of the selection, are qualifying claimants.

(2) The Secretary of State may make a selection in accordance with paragraph (1) on more than one occasion and, on each occasion, the Secretary of State may limit that selection to qualifying claimants living in a particular geographical area determined by the Secretary of State or to persons who have become qualifying claimants within a period determined by the Secretary of State.

DEFINITION

"qualifying claimant"—see regs 2 and 7.

Notification of participants

2.582 **6.**—(1) The Secretary of State must notify a claimant in writing when—

(a) the claimant is selected in accordance with regulation 5; and
(b) the provision made by regulation 4(3) ceases to apply to the claimant by virtue of regulation 4(4), unless it is because the claimant is no longer a qualifying claimant by reason only of a change in earnings.

(2) Where, for the purposes of this regulation, the Secretary of State sends a notice by post to the claimant's last known address, it is to be treated as having been given or sent on the day on which it was posted.

(3) Schedule 2 to the Universal Credit, Personal Independence Payments, Jobseeker's Allowance and Employment and Support Allowance (Claims and Payments) Regulations 2013 applies to the delivery of an electronic communication sent by the Secretary of State for the purposes of this regulation in the same manner as it applies to the delivery of electronic communications for the purposes of those Regulations.

DEFINITIONS

"claimant"—see WRA 2012 s.40.
"qualifying claimant"—see regs 2 and 7.

Meaning of "qualifying claimant"

7.—(1) A qualifying claimant is a person who— **2.583**

(a) falls within section 22 of the Act (claimants subject to all work-related requirements);
(b) has [1 monthly] earnings of such an amount (or, if the person is a member of a couple, the couple has combined [1 monthly] earnings of such an amount) that, apart from regulation 4(2), regulation 99(6) of the Universal Credit Regulations would apply;
(c) is not a person on whom the Secretary of State must not impose work-related requirements by virtue of regulation 98 of the Universal Credit Regulations (victims of domestic violence); and
(d) is not a person to whom any of the following paragraphs of regulation 99 of the Universal Credit Regulations (circumstances in which requirements must not be imposed) applies—
    (i) paragraph (3) (which provides for suspension of work search and work availability requirements for various reasons, including imprisonment and treatment for alcohol or drug dependency), except sub-paragraph (a) (claimant attending court as a witness etc.) and sub-paragraph (g) (claimant engaged in a public duty); or
    (ii) paragraph (5)(c) (claimant unfit for work for longer than 14 days).

AMENDMENT

1. Universal Credit and Miscellaneous Amendments Regulations 2015 (SI 2015/1754) reg.3(3) (November 4, 2015).

DEFINITIONS

"the Act"—see reg.2.
"couple"—see WRA ss.40 and 39.

"monthly earnings"—see reg.2 and the Universal Credit Regulations 2013 reg.90(6).
"the Universal Credit Regulations"—see reg.2
"work availability requirement"—see WRA 2012 ss.40 and 18(2).
"work search requirement"—see WRA 2012 ss.40 and 17(1).

Expiry of the pilot scheme

2.584 **8.** This Part ceases to have effect at the end of the period of three years starting with the day on which these Regulations come into force, unless it continues in effect by order of the Secretary of State under section 41(5)(a) of the Act.

GENERAL NOTE

2.585 Part 3 of the Regulations (i.e. regs 4–8) would have expired in February 2018, but has been continued in effect ever since by the Secretary of State making annual orders as envisaged by reg.8. The most recent of those is the Universal Credit (Work-Related Requirements) In Work Pilot Scheme (Extension) Order 2023 (SI 2024/159), which keeps Pt 3 in effect throughout the 12 months beginning on February 19, 2024.

The Universal Credit (Surpluses and Self-employed Losses) (Digital Service) Amendment Regulations 2015

(SI 2015/345)

Made on February 23, 2015 by the Secretary of State in exercise of the powers conferred by s.42(2) and (3) of, and para.4(1), (3)(a) and (4) of Sch. 1 to, the Welfare Reform Act 2012, having been referred to the Social Security Advisory Committee in accordance with s.172(1) of the Social Security Administration Act 1992.

[In force April 11, 2018]

Citation and commencement

2.586 **1.** These Regulations may be cited as the Universal Credit (Surpluses and Self-employed Losses) (Digital Service) Amendment Regulations 2015 and come into force on [[1]11th April 2018].

AMENDMENT

1. Universal Credit (Miscellaneous Amendments, Saving and Transitional Provision) Regulations 2018 (SI 2018/65) reg.7(2) (February 14, 2018).

Carry forward of surplus earnings

2.587 **2.** *[Amendments incorporated into SI 2013/376]*

Self-employed earnings – treatment of losses

3. *[Amendments incorporated into SI 2013/376]* **2.588**

[[1]Saving

4. [(1)–(3) *Omitted*].

(4) In regulation 54A of the Universal Credit Regulations 2013 (as inserted [[2] ...]), "the old award" does not include an award the last day of which fell before [[2]11th April 2018] and, in regulation 57A (as inserted by regulation 3(4)), "unused loss" does not include the loss from an assessment period that [[2]began] before that date.] **2.589**

AMENDMENTS

1. Universal Credit and Miscellaneous Amendments Regulations 2015 (SI 2015/1754) reg.21 (November 3, 2015).

2. Universal Credit (Miscellaneous Amendments, Saving and Transitional Provision) Regulations 2018 (SI 2018/65) reg.7(5) (February 14, 2018).

GENERAL NOTE

At one point during the introduction of UC, the benefit existed in two different forms depending on which computer system was operating in the area for the Jobcentre to which the claim was made: see further the General Note to the Welfare Reform Act 2012 (above). The amendments made by these Regulations applied in Digital (or "Full") Service areas. Regulation 4(1)–(3) preserved the unamended law for Live Service areas. As Live Service areas no longer exist, reg.4(1)–(3) has not been reproduced in this volume. Readers are referred instead to pp.575–576 of Vol.II of the 2021/22 edition. **2.590**

[[1]Transitional provision – temporary de minimis period

5.—(1) For the purposes of applying regulation 54A (surplus earnings) of the Universal Credit Regulations 2013 in relation to a claim for universal credit made in respect of a period that begins before the end of the temporary de minimis period, the meaning of "relevant threshold" in paragraph (6) of that regulation is modified by substituting "£2,500" for "£300". **2.591**

(2) For the purposes of paragraph (1), the "temporary de minimis period" is the period beginning with the coming into force of regulation 54A and ending on 31st March 2019, but may be extended by the Secretary of State if the Secretary of State considers it necessary to do so to safeguard the efficient administration of universal credit.]

AMENDMENT

1. Universal Credit (Miscellaneous Amendments, Saving and Transitional Provision) Regulations 2018 (SI 2018/65) reg.7(6) (February 14, 2018).

General Note

2.592 See the notes to reg.54A of the Universal Credit Regulations 2013 for the effect of this important modification to the initial operation of the surplus earnings rules. Ever since the surplus earnings rules were brought into force, the Secretary of State has exercised her power annually to determine that the "temporary de minimis period" should be extended. The most recent Determination was dated February 22, 2024 and extends that position to April 2025 (see the DWP's Guidance on regulations under the WRA 2012 on *gov.uk*).

The Loans for Mortgage Interest Regulations 2017

(SI 2017/725)

Made on July 5, 2017 by the Secretary of State, in exercise of the powers conferred by sections 4(5), 35(1), 36(2) and (4) of the Jobseekers Act 1995, sections 2(3)(b) and sections 17(1) and 19(1) of the State Pension Credit Act 2002, sections 123(1)(a), 135(1), 137(1) and (2)(d) and 175(1), (3) and (4) of the Social Security Contributions and Benefits Act 1992, sections 4(2)(a), 24(1) and 25(2), (3) and (5)(a) of the Welfare Reform Act 2007, sections 11(3) and (4) and 42(1), (2) and (3)(a) of, and paragraph 1(1) of Schedule 6 to, the Welfare Reform Act 2012 and sections 18, 19 and 21 of the Welfare Reform and Work Act 2016.

This instrument contains only regulations made under, by virtue of, or consequential upon, sections 18, 19 and 21 of the Welfare Reform and Work Act 2016 and is made before the end of the period of 6 months beginning with the coming into force of those sections. Therefore, in accordance with section 173(5) of the Social Security Administration Act 1992, these Regulations are not required to be referred to the Social Security Advisory Committee.
[In force, see reg.1(2)]

Arrangement of Regulations

GENERAL NOTE

In the past, owner-occupiers who are entitled to IS, IBJSA, IRESA, SPC and universal credit could receive benefit to cover some of their housing costs. Such housing costs were paid as part of the applicable amount (IS, IBJSA and IRESA): see reg.17(1)(e) of, and Sch.3 to, the IS Regulations; reg.83(f) of, and Sch.2 to, the JSA Regulations 1996; reg. 67(1)(c) of, and Sch.6 to, the ESA Regulations 2008; or of the guarantee credit (SPC): see reg.6(6)(c) of, and Sch.2 to, the SPC Regulations; or as the housing costs element of universal credit: see s.11 of the WRA 2012 and regs 25 and 26 of, and Schs 1-3 and 5 to, the UC Regs 2013. 2.594

However, from April 6, 2018, these Regulations, which are made under ss.18, 19 and 21 WRWA 2016, provide for housing costs in respect of mortgage interest and interest on home improvement loans, to be replaced by repayable, interest-bearing, loans secured on the claimants' homes by way of a legal charge.

Owner-occupiers may still be eligible for some support under the legislation referenced in the first paragraph of this section; the principal (and in the case of UC, only) category of eligible housing cost is service charge payments.

The bulk of the Regulations have been in force since July 27, 2017. It was therefore possible for the Secretary of State to make an offer of a loan for mortgage interest before April 6, 2018. However, no amount was payable before that date: see reg.8(1)(a). The new rules commenced for practical purposes on April 6, 2018, when regs 18-21 and Sch.5, which repeal the Schedules referred to in the first paragraph of this Note as they relate to mortgage interest payments and interest on home improvement loans, came into force.

Also, on July 27, 2017, ss 20(2)-(7) and (10) of WRWA 2016 were brought into force by reg.2 of the Welfare Reform and Work Act 2016 (Commencement No. 5) Regulations 2017 (SI 2017/802). Among other things, these amend s.8 SSA 1998 to empower the Secretary of State to make decisions about loans under s.18 WRWA

2016. The consequence is that an appeal lies to the First-tier Tribunal against such a decision under s.12 SSA 1998 and thence to the Upper Tribunal under s.11 TCEA 2007.

The remaining parts of s.20 WRWA 2016, which amend the substantive statute law relating to entitlement to housing costs as part of a means-tested benefit were brought into force on April 6, 2018.

It must be stressed that the changes brought about by these Regulations relate exclusively to owner-occupiers. Renters will continue to be entitled to either the housing costs element of universal credit under section 11 of the WRA 2012 and regs 25 and 26 of, and Schs 1-4 to, the UC Regs 2013, or to the Housing Benefit Regulations, or the Housing Benefit (Persons who have attained the qualifying age for state pension credit) Regulations 2006.

Citation and commencement

2.595 1.—(1) These Regulations may be cited as the Loans for Mortgage Interest Regulations 2017.

(2) These Regulations come into force—

(a) for the purposes of regulations 18 to 21, on 6th April 2018;

(b) for all other purposes, on 27th July 2017.

Interpretation

2.596 **2.**—(1) In these Regulations—

"the Act" means the Welfare Reform and Work Act 2016;

[[1] "alternative finance arrangements" has the meaning given in paragraph 5(4) of Schedule 1 to these Regulations;]

"alternative finance payments" has the meaning given in paragraph 5(3) of Schedule 1 to these Regulations;

"applicable amount" means—

(a) in the case of employment and support allowance, the claimant's weekly applicable amount under regulations 67 to 70 of the ESA Regulations;

(b) in the case of income support, the claimant's weekly applicable amount under regulations 17 to 21AA of the IS Regulations;

(c) in the case of jobseeker's allowance, the claimant's weekly applicable amount under regulations 83 to 86C of the JSA Regulations;

(d) in the case of an SPC claimant, the claimant's weekly appropriate minimum guarantee under section 2 of the State Pension Credit Act 2002;

(e) in the case of a UC claimant, the maximum amount of a claimant's award of universal credit under regulation 23(1) of the UC Regulations;

"assessment period" has the meaning given in regulation 21 of the UC Regulations;

"benefit unit" means a single claimant and his or her partner (if any) or joint claimants;

"benefit week" has the meaning given—

(a) in the case of employment and support allowance, in regulation 2 of the ESA Regulations;

(b) the case of income support, in paragraph 4 of Schedule 7 to the Claims and Payment Regulations;

(c) in the case of jobseeker's allowance, in regulation 1 of the JSA Regulations;
(d) in the case of state pension credit, in regulation 1 of the SPC Regulations;

"charge by way of legal mortgage" has the meaning given in section 132(1) of the Land Registration Act 2002;

"child" means a person under the age of 16;

"claimant" means a single claimant or each of joint claimants;

"Claims and Payment Regulations" means the Social Security (Claims and Payments) Regulations 1987;

"close relative" means a parent, parent-in-law, son, son-in-law, daughter, daughter-in-law, step-parent, step-son, step-daughter, brother, sister, or, if any of the preceding persons is one member of a couple, the other member of that couple;

[2 "conveyancer" means—
(a) in England and Wales, a conveyancer within the meaning of rule 217A of the Land Registration Rules 2003;
(b) in Scotland, a solicitor or advocate within the meaning of section 65 of the Solicitors (Scotland) Act 1980, or a conveyancing practitioner as defined in section 23 of the Law Reform (Miscellaneous Provisions) (Scotland) Act 1990;]

"couple" means—
(a) two people who are married to, or civil partners of, each other and are members of the same household;
(b) two people who are not married to, or civil partners of, each other but are living together as a married couple or civil partners;

"disabled person" has the meaning given—
(a) in the case of employment and support allowance, in paragraph 1(3) of Schedule 6 to the ESA Regulations,
(b) in the case of income support, in paragraph 1(3) of Schedule 3 to the IS Regulations;
(c) in the case of jobseeker's allowance, in paragraph 1(3) of Schedule 2 to the JSA Regulations;
(d) in the case of state pension credit, in paragraph 1(2)(a) of Schedule 2 to the SPC Regulations;
(e) in the case of universal credit, in paragraph 14(3) of Schedule 3 to these Regulations;

"dwelling"—
(a) in England and Wales, means a dwelling within the meaning of Part 1 of the Local Government Finance Act 1992;
(b) in Scotland, means a dwelling within the meaning of Part 2 of that Act;

"earned income" has the meaning given in Chapter 2 of Part 6 of the UC Regulations;

"ESA Regulations" means the Employment and Support Allowance Regulations 2008;

"existing claimant" means a claimant who is entitled to a qualifying benefit, including an amount for owner-occupier payments, on 5th April 2018;

"financial year" has the meaning given in section 25(2) of the Budget Responsibility and National Audit Act 2011;

"income" means any income which is, or which is treated as, an individual's, including payments which are treated as earnings, and which is not disregarded, under—

(a) in the case of employment and support allowance, Part 10 of the ESA Regulations;

(b) in the case of income support, Part 5 of the IS Regulations;

(c) in the case of jobseeker's allowance, Part 8 of the JSA Regulations;

(d) in the case of state pension credit, Part 3 of the SPC Regulations;

"IS Regulations" means the Income Support (General) Regulations 1987;

[[1] "joint claimants"—

(a) in the case of jobseeker's allowance means—

(i) members of a joint-claim couple who have jointly made a claim for, and are entitled to, income-based jobseeker's allowance; or

(ii) members of a joint-claim couple who have made a claim for, but are not entitled to, such a benefit by reason only that they have income—

(aa) equal to or exceeding the applicable amount, but

(bb) less than the sum of that applicable amount and the amount of a loan payment applicable to the joint-claim couple;

(b) in the case of universal credit means members of a couple who have jointly made a claim for, and are entitled to, universal credit;]

"joint-claim couple" has the meaning in section 1(4) of the Jobseekers Act 1995;

"JSA Regulations" means the Jobseeker's Allowance Regulations 1996;

"legacy benefit" means income-related employment and support allowance, income support or income-based jobseeker's allowance;

"legacy benefit claimant" means a claimant who is entitled to [[1], or is treated as entitled to,] a legacy benefit;

"legal estate" means any of the legal estates set out in section 1(1) of the Law of Property Act 1925;

"legal owner" means the owner, whether alone or with others, of a legal estate or, in Scotland, a heritable or registered interest, in the relevant accommodation;

"loan agreement" means an agreement entered into by a single claimant and his or her partner (if any), or each joint claimant, and the Secretary of State, which sets out the terms and conditions upon which the loan payments are made to the claimant;

"loan payments" means one or more payments, calculated under regulation 10, in respect of a claimant's liability to make owner-occupier payments in respect of the relevant accommodation;

"loan payments offer date" means the day on which the Secretary of State sends the loan agreement to a claimant;

"Modified Rules" means the Social Security (Housing Costs Special Arrangements) (Amendment and Modification) Regulations 2008;

"new claimant partner" has the meaning given in regulation 7 of the Transitional Provisions Regulations;

"non-dependant" has the meaning given—

(a) in the case of employment and support allowance, in regulation 71 of the ESA Regulations;

(b) in the case of income support, in regulation 3 of the IS Regulations;

(c) in the case of jobseeker's allowance, in regulation 2 of the JSA Regulations;
(d) in the case of state pension credit, in paragraph 1(4) of Schedule 2 to the SPC Regulations;

"owner-occupier payments" has the meaning given in regulation 3(2)(a);

"partner" means—
(a) where a claimant is a member of a couple, the other member of that couple;
(b) where a claimant is married polygamously to two or more members of the claimant's household, all such members;

"person who lacks capacity"—
(a) in England and Wales, has the meaning given in section 2 of the Mental Capacity Act 2005;
(b) in Scotland, means a person who is incapable under section 1(6) of the Adults with Incapacity (Scotland) Act 2000;

"polygamous marriage" means a marriage during which a party to it is married to more than one person and which took place under the laws of a country which permits polygamy;

"qualifying benefit" means income-related employment and support allowance, income support, income-based jobseeker's allowance, state pension credit or universal credit;

"qualifying lender" has the meaning given in section 19(7) of the Act;

"qualifying loan" means—
(a) in the case of a legacy benefit or state pension credit, a loan which qualifies under paragraph 2(2) or (4) of Schedule 1 to these Regulations;
(b) in the case of universal credit, a loan which qualifies under paragraph 5(2) of Schedule 1 to these Regulations;

"qualifying period" means a period of—
(a) [3 three] consecutive assessment periods in which a claimant has been entitled to universal credit;
(b) 39 consecutive weeks in which a claimant—
   (i) has been entitled to a legacy benefit; or
   (ii) is treated as having been entitled to such a benefit under—
      (aa) paragraph 14 of Schedule 3 to the IS Regulations;
      (bb) paragraph 13 of Schedule 2 to the JSA Regulations; or
      (cc) paragraph 15 of Schedule 6 to the ESA Regulations;

"qualifying young person" has the meaning given—
(a) in the case of a legacy benefit, in section 142 of the Social Security Contributions and Benefits Act 1992;
(b) in the case of state pension credit, in regulation 4A of the SPC Regulations;
(c) in the case of universal credit, in regulation 5 of the UC Regulations;

"relevant accommodation" means the accommodation which the claimant occupies, or is treated as occupying, as the claimant's home under Schedule 3;

"relevant date", apart from in regulation 21, means the first day with respect to which a claimant's liability to make owner-occupier payments is met by a loan payment;

[1 "single claimant" means—
(a) an individual who has made a claim for, and is entitled to, a qualifying benefit;

(b) an individual who has made a claim for, but is not entitled to, a legacy benefit or state pension credit by reason only that the individual has, or, if the individual is a member of a couple, they have, income—
(i) equal to or exceeding the applicable amount, but
(ii) less than the sum of that applicable amount and the amount of a loan payment applicable to the individual;]

"single person" means an individual who is not a member of a couple;

"SPC claimant" means a claimant who is entitled to [1, or is treated as entitled to,] state pension credit;

"SPC Regulations" means the State Pension Credit Regulations 2002;

"standard security" has the meaning in Part 2 of the Conveyancing and Feudal Reform (Scotland) Act 1970;

"transitional end day" has the meaning given in regulations 19(1) [1, 19A(1) and (5)] and 20(2);

"Transitional Provisions Regulations" means the Universal Credit (Transitional Provisions) Regulations 2014;

"UC claimant" means a claimant who is entitled to universal credit;

"UC Regulations" means the Universal Credit Regulations 2013; and

"unearned income" has the meaning given in Chapter 3 of Part 6 of the UC Regulations.

(2) For the purposes of these Regulations, a reference to—

(a) entitlement to a qualifying benefit is to be read as a reference to entitlement as determined under the ESA Regulations, IS Regulations, JSA Regulations, SPC Regulations and UC Regulations;

[1(aa) a person being treated as entitled to a qualifying benefit is to be read as a reference to a person who satisfies sub-paragraph (a)(ii) of the definition of "joint claimants" or sub-paragraph (b) of the definition of "single claimant", except in the definition of "qualifying period", regulation 21(5)(b) and paragraph 3 of Schedule 1;]

(b) the claimant's family or to being a member of the claimant's family means a reference to the claimant's partner and any child or qualifying young person who is the responsibility of the claimant or the claimant's partner, where that child or qualifying young person is a member of the claimant's household;

(c) a person being responsible for a child or qualifying young person is to be read as a reference to a person being treated as responsible for a child or qualifying young person in the circumstances specified in—
(i) in the case of employment and support allowance, regulation 156(10) of the ESA Regulations;
(ii) in the case of income support, regulation 15 of the IS Regulations;
(iii) in the case of jobseeker's allowance, regulation 77 of the JSA Regulations;
(iv) in the case of state pension credit and universal credit, regulation 4 of the UC Regulations;

(d) a person being a member of a household is to be read as a reference to a person being treated as a member of the household in the circumstances specified in—
(i) in the case of employment and support allowance, in regulation 156 of the ESA Regulations;
(ii) in the case of income support, in regulation 16 of the IS Regulations;

(iii) in the case of jobseeker's allowance, in regulation 78 of the JSA Regulations;
(iv) in the case of state pension credit and universal credit, in regulation 5 of the SPC Regulations;

(e) a person being engaged in remunerative work is to be read as a reference to a person being treated as engaged in remunerative work—
(i) in the case of employment and support allowance, in regulations 41 to 43 of the ESA Regulations;
(ii) in the case of income support, in regulations 5 and 6 of the IS Regulations;
(iii) in the case of jobseeker's allowance, in regulations 51 to 53 of the JSA Regulations;
(iv) in the case of state pension credit, in paragraph 2 of Schedule 2 to the SPC Regulations.

AMENDMENTS

1. Loans for Mortgage Interest and Social Fund Maternity Grant (Amendment) Regulations 2018 (SI 2018/307), reg.2(1) and (2) (April 6, 2018).
2. Loans for Mortgage Interest (Amendment) Regulations 2021 (SI 2021/131) reg.2(1) and (2) (March 15, 2021).
3. Loans for Mortgage Interest (Amendment) Regulations 2023 (SI 2023/226) reg.2(2) (April 3, 2023).

GENERAL NOTE

Most of the definitions listed above are self-explanatory. Where they are not, they are discussed in the commentary to the regulations in which the defined terms are used. 2.597

The offer of loan payments

3.—(1) The Secretary of State may make an offer of loan payments to a claimant in respect of any owner-occupier payments the claimant is, or is to be treated as, being liable to make in respect of the accommodation which the claimant is, or is to be treated as, occupying as the claimant's home [1 ...] 2.598

(2) For the purposes of paragraph (1)—
(a) owner-occupier payments are—
(i) in the case of a legacy benefit claimant or SPC claimant, payments within the meaning of Part 1 of Schedule 1;
(ii) in the case of a UC claimant, payments within the meaning of Part 2 of Schedule 1;
(b) the circumstances in which a claimant is, or is to be treated as, being liable to make owner-occupier payments are—
(i) in the case of a legacy benefit claimant or SPC claimant, the circumstances specified in Part 1 of Schedule 2;
(ii) in the case of a UC claimant, the circumstances specified in Part 2 of Schedule 2;
(c) the circumstances in which a claimant is, or is to be treated as, occupying accommodation as the claimant's home are—
(i) in the case of a legacy benefit claimant or SPC claimant, the circumstances specified in Part 2 of Schedule 3;

(ii) in the case of a UC claimant, the circumstances specified in Part 3 of Schedule 3.

(3) Where the liability for owner-occupier payments is shared with a person not in the benefit unit, the claimant shall be, or shall be treated as, liable to make owner-occupier payments by reference to the appropriate proportion of the payments for which the claimant is responsible.

[1 ...]

AMENDMENT

1. Loans for Mortgage Interest (Amendment) Regulations 2023 (SI 2023/226) reg.2(3) (April 3, 2023).

DEFINITIONS

"benefit unit"—reg.2(1).
"claimant"—*ibid.*
"couple"—*ibid.*
"earned income"—*ibid.*
"legacy benefit claimant"—*ibid.*
"loan payments"—*ibid.*
"owner-occupier payments"—regs 2(1) and 3(2)(a).
"single person"—reg.2(1).
"SPC claimant"—*ibid.*
"UC claimant"—*ibid.*

GENERAL NOTE

2.599 *Paragraphs (1) and (2)*: Paragraph (1) empowers the Secretary of State to make "an offer of loan payments" in the following circumstances:

- first, the person to whom the offer is made must be a "claimant", defined in reg.2(1) as meaning "a single claimant or each of joint claimants";

- second, the offer can only be made in respect of "any owner-occupier payments".

  For "legacy benefit claimants" (i.e., those who are entitled to, or treated as entitled to, IRESA, IS or IBJSA: see reg.2(1)) and "SPC claimants" these are as defined in Sch.1, Pt 1. For "UC claimants", the definition is in Sch.1, Pt 2: see para.(2)(1)(a).

- third, the claimant must be liable, or treated as liable, to make those payments.

  The circumstances in which legacy benefit claimants and SPC claimants are, or are treated as, liable to make owner-occupier payments are set out in Sch.2, Pt 1. For UC claimants, those circumstances are set out in Sch.2, Pt 2: see para.(2)(1)(b). Where liability is shared, see also para.(2).

- fourth, the owner-occupier payments that the claimant is, or is treated as, liable to make must be in respect of accommodation which they are, or is treated as, occupying as his or her home.

  The circumstances in which legacy benefit claimants and SPC claimants are, or are treated as, occupying accommodation as their home, are set out in Sch.3, Pt 1. For UC claimants, those circumstances are set out in Sch.3, Pt 2: see para.(2)(1)(c).

The Secretary of State's offer will take the form of a draft loan agreement (as defined in reg.2(1)). The requirements for the offer to be accepted are set out in regs 4 and 5.

Paragraph (3) applies where the claimant is jointly liable for owner-occupier payments with someone who is not in the "benefit unit", which is defined by reg.2(1) as meaning "a single claimant and his or her partner (if any) or joint claimants". In those circumstances, the claimant is only treated as liable for—and is therefore only eligible for a loan in respect of—"the appropriate proportion of the payments for which s/he is responsible". "Appropriate proportion" is not defined and its meaning in individual cases may give rise to disputes.

Acceptance of loan payments offer

4. The offer of loan payments is accepted where the Secretary of State has received the loan agreement signed by, in the case of a single claimant, the claimant and his or her partner (if any), or, in the case of joint claimants, each member of the couple, and the documents referred to in regulation 5(2). **2.600**

DEFINITIONS

"claimant"—reg.2(1).
"couple"—*ibid.*
"joint claimants"—*ibid.*
"loan agreement"—*ibid.*
"loan payments"—*ibid.*
"partner"—*ibid.*
"single claimant"—*ibid.*

GENERAL NOTE

Claimants do not have to accept the Secretary of State's offer. But if they do not do so, they will receive no help at all with owner-occupier payments because the legislation allowing such payments to be met by IS, IBJSA, SPC, IRESA or UC has been repealed. **2.601**

To accept the Secretary of State's offer, the claimant—or both joint claimants—must sign the loan agreement and return it to the DWP with the documents set out in reg.5(2). The offer is not accepted until the Department has received the signed agreement ant those documents.

Conditions to meet before the loan payments can be made

5.—(1) The Secretary of State may make the loan payments if— **2.602**

(a) the loan payments offer is accepted in accordance with regulation 4; and

(b) the conditions in paragraph (2) are met.

(2) The conditions are—

(a) in England and Wales—

(i) where all of the legal owners are within the benefit unit, each legal owner has executed a charge by way of legal mortgage in favour of the Secretary of State in respect of the relevant accommodation;

(ii) where one or more legal owners are not within the benefit unit, each legal owner within the benefit unit (if any) has executed an equitable charge in respect of their beneficial interest in the relevant accommodation;

(b) in Scotland, each legal owner within the benefit unit has executed a standard security in respect of his or her interest in the relevant accommodation;

(c) the Secretary of State has obtained the written consent referred to in paragraph (3); and

(d) the information condition in regulation 6 is met within the period of 6 months ending with the day on which the loan payments offer is accepted.

(3) The consent required by paragraph (2)(c) is consent given in writing to the creation of the charge or, in Scotland, the standard security by any person in the benefit unit in occupation of the relevant accommodation, who is not a legal owner.

DEFINITIONS

"benefit unit"—reg.2(1).
"charge by way of legal mortgage"—*ibid.*
"legal owner"—*ibid.*
"loan payments"—*ibid.*
"relevant accommodation"—*ibid.*
"standard security"—*ibid.*

2.603 GENERAL NOTE

Paragraph (1): The drafting of paragraph (1) seems over-cautious. It states that the Secretary of State may make loan payments if the offer is accepted in accordance with reg.4 and the conditions in paragraph (2) are met. However, under reg.4, the offer is only accepted when the Secretary of State receives "the documents referred to in regulation 5(2)", so—at most—all that all that reg.5(1)(b) achieves is to prevent loan payments from being made where the information condition in reg.6 has not been satisfied during the preceding six months: see para.(2)(d).

Paragraphs (2) and (3) require three things. First, all the legal owners of the "relevant accommodation" (*i.e.*, the accommodation which the claimant occupies, or is treated as occupying, as his or her home under Sch.3: see reg.2(1)) must give the Secretary of State security for the repayment of the loan payments (paras (2)(a) and (b)). In other words, they have to create a second mortgage in favour of the Secretary of State. Second, everyone occupying the relevant accommodation who is not a legal owner must consent to the giving of that security (paras (2)(c) and (3)). Third, the information condition in reg.6 must have been satisfied within the period of six months ending on the day on which the loan offer is accepted (para.(2)(d)).

The type of security that must be given depends upon whether the relevant accommodation is in England and Wales or in Scotland and, in the former case, on whether the legal ownership of the relevant accommodation is held entirely by people in the benefit unit or shared with someone outside that unit.

If the relevant accommodation is in England or Wales and the legal ownership is held entirely by those within the benefit unit each legal owner must execute a charge by way of legal mortgage (defined by reg.2(1) as having the same meaning as in s.132(1) of the Land Registration Act 2002) over it. Where the legal ownership of the relevant accommodation is jointly held with someone who is not in the benefit unit, each legal owner must execute an equitable charge over his or her beneficial interest in the property. For the difference between legal and beneficial ownership, see the commentary to reg.46 of the Income Support Regulations in Vol.V and, e.g., *SSWP v LB Tower Hamlets and CT (IS & HB)* [2018] UKUT 25 (AAC) at paras 21-29.

If the relevant accommodation is in Scotland, then each legal owner within the benefit unit must execute a standard security in respect of her/his interest in the relevant accommodation. "Standard security" is defined by reg.2(1) as having "the meaning in Part 2 of the Conveyancing and Feudal Reform (Scotland) Act 1970".

Information condition

6.—(1) The information condition is that the Secretary of State has provided relevant information about the loan payments to a single claimant and his or her partner (if any) or each joint claimant. 2.604

(2) For the purposes of this regulation, "relevant information" is information about the loan payments which must include—

(a) a summary of the terms and conditions included within the loan agreement;

(b) where the circumstances in regulation 5(2)(a)(i) or (b) apply, an explanation that the Secretary of State will seek to obtain a charge or, in Scotland, a standard security in respect of the relevant accommodation;

(c) an explanation of the consent referred to in regulation 5(3); and

(d) information as to where a single claimant and his or her partner (if any) or each joint claimant can obtain further information and independent legal and financial advice regarding loan payments.

DEFINITIONS

"claimant"—reg.2(1).
"loan agreement"—*ibid.*
"loan payments"—*ibid.*
"partner"—*ibid.*
"relevant accommodation"—*ibid.*
"single claimant"—*ibid.*
"standard security"—*ibid.*

GENERAL NOTE 2.605

Taken together, reg.5(2)(d) and reg.6 require that the Secretary of State must have provided the claimant, and any partner, with the information specified in para.(2) at some point during the period of six months ending with the day on which the offer of loan payments is accepted. The regulations do not specify the consequences that are to follow if the information condition is not satisfied, or is not satisfied during that period.

Time of each loan payment

7. Each loan payment shall be made— 2.606

(a) in the case of a UC claimant, at monthly intervals in arrears; and

[[1](b) in the case of a legacy benefit claimant or SPC claimant, at 4 weekly intervals in arrears.]

AMENDMENT

1. Loans for Mortgage Interest and Social Fund Maternity Grant (Amendment) Regulations 2018 (SI 2018/307), reg.2(1) and (3) (April 6, 2018).

DEFINITIONS

"claimant"—reg.2(1).
"legacy benefit claimant"—*ibid.*

"qualifying benefit"—*ibid.*
"qualifying lender"—*ibid.*
"SPC claimant"—*ibid.*
"UC claimant"—*ibid.*

GENERAL NOTE

2.607 Loan payments are always made in arrears. For UC claimants, they are made at monthly intervals, presumably to coincide with the claimant's assessment period. For those on other benefits, payment is 4-weekly in arrears.

Period covered by loan payments

2.608 **8.—**(1) The period in respect of which the loan payments shall be made shall begin on the later of—

(a) 6th April 2018;

(b) in the case of a UC claimant or legacy benefit claimant [2 , except where sub-paragraph (ba) or (bb) applies], the day after the day on which the qualifying period ends;

[2 (ba) in the case of a couple where one member is an SPC claimant receiving loan payments, the first day of entitlement to universal credit as a couple;

(bb) in the case of a couple where one member was formerly an SPC claimant receiving loan payments, the first day of entitlement to universal credit as a couple, if the first day of that entitlement is within the period of one month beginning with the day on which the entitlement to state pension credit ended;]

[1 (c) in the case of an [2 SPC claimant (who is not in a couple)], the first day of entitlement to state pension credit;]

(d) the transitional end day [1;

(e) a date requested by the claimant.]

[1 (2) If the day referred to in [2 sub-paragraphs (a), (b), (c) and (e) of paragraph (1)] is not the first day of the claimant's benefit week, in the case of a legacy benefit claimant or SPC claimant, or assessment period, in the case of a UC claimant, the day referred to shall be the first day of the first benefit week or first assessment period that begins after that date.]

[2 (3) In this regulation, "couple" means a couple entitled to universal credit as joint claimants under regulation 3(2)(a) of the UC Regulations.]

AMENDMENTS

1. Loans for Mortgage Interest and Social Fund Maternity Grant (Amendment) Regulations 2018 (SI 2018/307) reg.2(1) and (4) (April 6, 2018).

2. Loans for Mortgage Interest (Amendment) Regulations 2023 (SI 2023/226) reg.2(4) (April 3, 2023).

DEFINITIONS

"claimant"—reg.2(1).
"legacy benefit claimant"—*ibid.*
"loan payments"—*ibid.*
"qualifying period"—*ibid.*
"SPC claimant"—*ibid.*
"transitional end day"—*ibid.* and regs 19(1), 19A(1) and (5) and 20(2).
"UC claimant"—reg,2(1).

GENERAL NOTE 2.609

Subject to para.(2), entitlement to loan payments begins on—and any entitlement to housing costs therefore ends the day before—the latest of the five days specified in para.(1). Para.(2) modifies that rule by providing that if the day identified by para.(1) is not the first day of an assessment period (for UC claimants) or of a benefit week (for claimants of IS, IBJSA or IRESA), entitlement to loan payments instead begins on the first day of the next assessment period or benefit week.

"Qualifying period"

The phrase "qualifying period" is defined in reg.2(1). 2.610

For UC claimants, the effect of that definition, taken with sub-para.(1)(b) is that there is no entitlement to a loan payment unless they have first been entitled to universal credit for three consecutive assessment periods.

For claimants of IS, IBJSA, or IRESA the effect is that there is no entitlement to a loan payment unless they have been entitled to one of those benefits—or treated as so entitled by the provisions listed in head (1)(b)(ii) of the definition—for 39 consecutive weeks

Those provisions establish linking rules by which two or more periods of entitlement to one of those benefits are, in some circumstances treated as a single period of entitlement: see further Vol.V.

Where a claimant has moved from one of those benefits to another, see Sch.6, para.20(1)(c) to the ESA Regulations in Vol.V; and reg.32 of the Income Support (General) (Jobseeker's Allowance Consequential Amendments) Regulations 1996, and Sch.2, para.18(1)(c) to the JSA Regulations in Vol.V.

See the commentary to reg.9(7) below for the circumstances in which claimants of IS, IBJSA and IRESA who were previously in receipt of loan payments may receive them again without serving a further qualifying period.

Transitional end day

The transitional end day applies where a claimant was entitled to housing costs before April 6, 2018 and benefits from the transitional provisions in regs 19, 19A and 20: see, further, the General Notes to those regulations. 2.611

Duration of loan payments

9.—(1) Subject to paragraph (2), loan payments shall continue to be made indefinitely at the intervals specified in regulation 7. 2.612

(2) If one of the circumstances in paragraph (3) occurs, the Secretary of State shall terminate the loan payments immediately but subject to paragraph (4).

(3) The circumstances are that—

(a) the claimant ceases to be entitled [1, or treated as entitled to,] to a qualifying benefit;

(b) the claimant ceases to be, or to be treated as, liable to make owner-occupier payments under Schedule 2;

(c) the claimant ceases to be, or to be treated as, occupying the relevant accommodation under Schedule 3;

(d) the loan agreement is terminated in accordance with its terms;

[2 ...]

(4) The Secretary of State shall make the loan payments direct to the claimant for the period specified in paragraph (6) if—

(a) a claimant ceases to be entitled to a legacy benefit by reason that, in the case of a single claimant, the claimant or his or her partner (if any), or, in the case of joint claimants, either member of the couple, is engaged in remunerative work; and

(b) the conditions in paragraph (5) are met.

(5) The conditions are that, in the case of a single claimant, the claimant or his or her partner (if any), or, in the case of joint claimants, either member of the couple—

(a) is engaged in remunerative work which is expected to last for a period of no less than 5 weeks;

(b) is still liable or treated as liable to make owner-occupier payments under Schedule 2;

(c) has, for a continuous period of 26 weeks ending with the day on which he or she commences the work referred to in sub-paragraph (a), been entitled to a legacy benefit; and

(d) was, on the day before the day on which he or she commenced the work referred to in sub-paragraph (a), receiving loan payments under these Regulations.

(6) The period specified is the period of 4 weeks commencing with the day on which the relevant person is first engaged in remunerative work.

[[2] (7) If a legacy benefit claimant ceases to be entitled to, or treated as entitled to, a legacy benefit ("the old entitlement") but becomes entitled, or treated as entitled, again to the benefit ("the new entitlement") within the period of 52 weeks beginning with the day on which the claimant ceased to be entitled, or treated as entitled, to the old entitlement, and the claimant wishes to receive loan payments on the basis of the new entitlement, there is no requirement for the claimant to serve a new qualifying period.

(8) If a UC claimant ceases to be entitled to universal credit ("the old entitlement") but becomes entitled again to universal credit ("the new entitlement") within the period of 6 months beginning with the day on which the claimant ceased to be entitled to the old entitlement, and the claimant wishes to receive loan payments on the basis of the new entitlement, there is no requirement for the claimant to serve a new qualifying period.]

AMENDMENTS

1. Loans for Mortgage Interest and Social Fund Maternity Grant (Amendment) Regulations 2018 (SI 2018/307) reg.2(1) and (5) (April 6, 2018).

2. Loans for Mortgage Interest (Amendment) Regulations 2023 (SI 2023/226) reg.2(5) (April 3, 2023).

DEFINITIONS

"claimant"—reg.2(1).
"couple"—*ibid.*
"entitlement"—reg.2(2)(a).
"joint claimants"—reg.2(1).
"legacy benefit"—*ibid.*
"legacy benefit claimant"—*ibid.*
"loan agreement"—*ibid.*
"loan payments"—*ibid.*
"owner-occupier payments"—regs 2(1) and 3(2)(a).
"partner"—reg.2(1).

"qualifying benefit"—*ibid.*
"qualifying period"—*ibid.*
"relevant accommodation"—*ibid.*
"remunerative work"—reg.2(2)(e).
"single claimant"—reg.2(1).
"UC claimant"—*ibid.*

GENERAL NOTE

Paragraph (1). Once loan payments have started they continue indefinitely at monthly intervals for UC claimants, and four-weekly periods for other claimants, until one of the events in para.(2) occurs. **2.613**

Paragraph (2). Loan payments come to an end if:

- the claimant ceases to be entitled, or treated as entitled, to a qualifying benefit (as defined in reg.2(1). However, where the benefit that has ended is IS, IBJSA or IRESA, and the reason that the benefit has come to an end is that the claimant or her/his partner has begun remunerative work, see paras (4)-(6);
- the claimant ceases to be liable, or to be treated as liable, to make owner occupier payments: see reg.3(2)(a) and (b) and Sch.1;
- the claimant ceases to occupy, or to be treated as occupying, the relevant accommodation: see reg.3(2)(c) and Sch.3;
- the loan agreement comes to an end; or
- for UC claimants, the claimant (or either joint claimant) begins to earn an income.

Paragraphs (4)–(6) create a four-week run-on for some claimants who are no longer eligible for loan payments because they have ceased to be entitled to IS, IBJSA or IRESA. The run-on applies if (1) the reason that entitlement to one of those benefits has ended is that the claimant or her/his partner (if any) have started remunerative work; (2) that work is expected to last for at least five weeks; (3) the claimant s still liable, or treated as liable to make owner-occupier payments; (4) on the day that the claimant or her/his partner commences remunerative work, the claimant has been entitled to one or more of those benefits for a continuous period of 26 weeks, and (5) on the previous day had been receiving loan payments.

Paragraph (7) is puzzling. What it appears to say is that where a claimant ceases to be entitled (or treated as entitled) to IS, IBJSA or IRESA but becomes entitled again within the following 52 weeks, it is not necessary for her/him to wait for a further qualifying period before loan payments can be made.

As the rule is about the circumstances in which the qualifying period does not apply, rather than about the circumstances in which loan payments come to an end, it might be thought to belong more naturally in reg.8 than reg.9.

More importantly, the rule has been drafted so narrowly that it seems likely that it will not be of practical benefit. The reference to the claimant becoming "entitled, or treated as entitled, *again* to the benefit" (emphasis added) suggests that the old entitlement and the new entitlement must be to the same benefit. However, the roll-out of universal credit means it is not in practice possible to make a fresh claim for IS, IBJSA or IRESA. Claimants who might otherwise have benefitted from this rule are likely to be required to claim universal credit, in which case, it will be necessary to serve a qualifying period of three consecutive assessment periods. (Note that while the current para.(7) is a version from 2023, it maintains unchanged the wording at issue here.)

Paragraph (8), while also more naturally belonging in reg.8, is more straightforward in its effect: gaps of no more than six months in UC entitlement do not require a claimant to serve a new qualifying period.

Calculation of each loan payment

2.614 **10.**—Subject to any deduction under regulation 14 [[1] or 14A], each loan payment shall be the aggregate of the amounts resulting from regulations 11 and 12.

AMENDMENT

1. Loans for Mortgage Interest and Social Fund Maternity Grant (Amendment) Regulations 2018 (SI 2018/307), reg.2(1) and (6) (April 6, 2018).

GENERAL NOTE

2.615 Regulation 10 is self-explanatory. The amount of each loan payment is calculated by adding together the amount for interest on qualifying loans (calculated under reg.11) and the amount for alternative finance arrangements (calculated under reg.12) and then subtracting any non-dependant deduction that falls to be made under reg.14 and any insurance payment deduction under reg.14A.

Calculation in respect of qualifying loans

2.616 **11.**—(1) Subject to paragraphs (3) and (4), the amount to be included in each loan payment for owner-occupier payments which are payments of interest on qualifying loans is determined as follows.

Step 1

Determine the amount of capital for the time being owing in connection with each qualifying loan to which the owner-occupier payments relate.

Step 2

If there is more than one qualifying loan, add together the amounts determined in step 1.

Step 3

Determine the identified amount which is the lower of—

(a) the amount resulting from step 1 or 2; and

(b) the capital limit specified in paragraph (2)(a) or (b).

If both amounts in (a) and (b) are the same, that is the identified amount.

Step 4

In respect of a legacy benefit claimant or SPC claimant, apply the following formula to achieve a weekly sum—

$$\frac{A \times SR}{52} - I$$

In respect of a UC claimant, apply the following formula to achieve a monthly sum—

$$\frac{A \times SR}{12} - I$$

In either case—

"A" is the identified amount in step 3,

"SR" is the standard rate that applies at the end of the calculation (see regulation 13), and

"I" is the amount of any income, in the case of a legacy benefit or SPC claimant, or unearned income, in the case of a UC claimant, above the claimant's applicable amount.

The result is the amount to be included in each loan payment for owner-occupier payments which are payments of interest on qualifying loans.

(2) The capital limit is—

(a) £200,000—

(i) in the case of a legacy benefit claimant or SPC claimant where the Modified Rules apply;

(ii) in the case of a UC claimant;

(b) £100,000 in all other cases.

(3) In the application of paragraph (2) to a qualifying loan (or any part of a qualifying loan) which was taken out for the purpose of making necessary adaptations to the accommodation to meet the needs of a disabled person—

(a) the qualifying loan (or the part of the qualifying loan) is to be disregarded for the purposes of steps 2 and 3; and

(b) "A" in step 4 is to be read as the amount resulting from step 1 in respect of the qualifying loan (or the sum of those amounts if there is more than one qualifying loan taken out for the purpose of making such adaptations) plus the amount (if any) resulting from step 3 in relation to any other qualifying loan or loans.

(4) Subject to paragraph (5), any variation in the amount of capital for the time being owing in connection with a qualifying loan is not to be taken into account after the relevant date until such time as the Secretary of State recalculates the amount which shall occur—

(a) on the first anniversary of the relevant date; and

(b) in respect of any variation after the first anniversary, on the next anniversary which follows the date of the variation.

(5) In respect of an existing claimant, the Secretary of State shall recalculate the amount of capital owing in connection with a qualifying loan on the anniversary of the date on which the claimant's qualifying benefit first included an amount for owner-occupier payments.

DEFINITIONS

"applicable amount"—reg.2(1).
"claimant"—*ibid.*
"disabled person"—*ibid.*
"existing claimant"—*ibid.*
"income"—*ibid.*
"legacy benefit claimant"—*ibid.*
"Modified Rules"—*ibid.*
"owner-occupier payments"—regs 2(1) and 3(2)(a).
"qualifying benefit"—*ibid.*

"qualifying loan"—*ibid.*
"relevant date"—*ibid.*
"SPC claimant"—*ibid.*
"UC claimant"—*ibid.*
"unearned income"—*ibid.*

GENERAL NOTE

2.617 Regulation 11 provides for the calculation of loan payments in respect of interest of qualifying loans. The calculation of loan payments in respect of alternative finance payments is governed by reg.12.

Under para.(1), there are four steps to that calculation. However, in order to follow those steps, it is first necessary to identify the capital limit applicable to the claimant, by applying the rules in para.(2) and also the "standard interest rate" (see reg.13, below).

Capital Limit

2.618 The general rule is that the capital limit is £100,000 for those claiming IS, IBJSA, IRESA or SPC and £200,000 for those claiming UC: see para.(2)(a)(ii) and (b). There is one exception, and one modification, to that rule.

The exception is in para.(2)(a)(i). Claimants of IS, IBJSA, IRESA and SPC also have a capital limit of £200,000 where the "Modified Rules" apply. That phrase is defined by reg.2(1) as meaning the Social Security (Housing Costs Special Arrangements) (Amendment and Modification) Regulations 2008 (SI 2008/3195): see further Vol.V.

The modification is in paras (3)-(4) and applies where the whole, or part of, a qualifying loan was taken out in order to make "necessary" adaptations to the accommodation to meet the needs of a disabled person (*i.e.*, as defined in reg.2(1)). To avoid circumlocution, this General Note will refer to that purpose as "the specified purpose" even though reg.11 does not itself use that term.

The legislative intention appears to be that any part of a loan taken out for the specified purpose is excluded when the capital limit applies so that if, for example, a claimant on IBJSA with a capital limit of £100,000 has a loan of £250,000, of which £25,000 was taken out for the specified purpose, the loan payment is calculated on capital of £125,000, £100,000 for the part of the loan that was not taken out for the specified purpose plus the £25,000 that was taken out for that purpose.

However, there must be doubt as to whether the modification is effective. Para.(3) states that it has effect in the application of "*paragraph (2)*" to a qualifying loan taken out for the specified purpose. But the modifications in para.(3) relate to Steps 2, 3 and 4 of the calculation (see below), which do not form part of para.(2) but rather para.(1). Para. (2) is about the amount of the capital limit, which is the same irrespective of the amount of the loan (or loans) and the purposes for which those loans were taken out. Indeed, the whole point of the capital limit is that it is a cap on the actual amount of the claimant's loan or loans. It therefore appears that the reference to "paragraph (2)" in the opening words of para.(3) should instead be to "paragraph (1)".

Moreover, even if it is possible to read para.(3) as referring to para.(1) (perhaps by the application of the rule in *Inco Europe Ltd v First Choice Distribution (a firm)* [2000] UKHL 15), the drafting of the modification is unnecessarily complex, and it is arguable that it has effects that are far more favourable to claimants than was intended: see below.

The calculation

2.619 Where the calculation relates to a loan (or loans), no part of which was taken out for the specified purpose, it is relatively straightforward.

Step 1

The first step is to determine the amount of capital owing on each qualifying loan "to which the owner-occupier payments relate". **2.620**

For claimants of IS, IBJSA, IRESA and SPC, "owner-occupier payments" are defined by reg.3(2)(a) and para.2(1)(a), (2) and (4) of Sch.1 by reference to the purposes for which the loans were taken out. To the extent that a loan was taken out for any purpose not specified in para.2(2) of Sch.1, the capital will not be capital "to which the owner-occupier payments relate" and therefore will not be taken into account in the calculation.

By the same reasoning, for claimants of UC, reg.3(2)(a)(ii) and para.5(1)(a) and (2), the owner-occupier payments will relate to the capital if, but only if, it is secured on the relevant accommodation: the purpose for which the loan was taken out is irrelevant.

Step 2

If there is more than one qualifying loan, then the amounts determined separately in Step 1 are added together. **2.621**

Step 3

The Step 1 or (if there is more than one qualifying loan) Step 2 figure is then compared with the claimant's capital limit (see above) and if it is higher than that limit, then the amount of the loan payment is calculated using the capital limit, not the amount of capital the claimant has actually borrowed. **2.622**

Step 4

Step 4 is the last step in the calculation. The standard interest rate (see reg.13) is applied to the amount of capital identified in Step 3 and the product is then divided by either by 12 (to produce a monthly sum for UC claimants) or 52 (to produce a weekly sum for those on other qualifying benefits). **2.623**

Then, finally, if UC claimants have *unearned* income—or those claiming other qualifying benefits have *any* income—in excess of their "applicable amount", the amount of the excess is deducted.

"Applicable amount" is defined in reg.2(1). For IS, IBJSA and IRESA it is the same as the applicable amount used in the calculation of those benefits. For SPC and universal credit, which do not use the concept of an "applicable amount" in the calculation of the award, the applicable amounts for the purpose of Step 4 are, respectively, the appropriate minimum guarantee (see s.2 SPCA 2002) and the maximum amount (see s.8(1) and (2) WRA 2012 and reg.23(1) of the UC Regulations).

Loans to adapt accommodation for disabled persons

How does that calculation differ, if the loan, or loans, or part of any loan is taken out for the specified purpose? As explained above, this depends upon the modifications made by para.(3) (and assumes that—contrary to what it actually says—para.(3) can be read as applying to para.(1), rather than para.(2)). **2.624**

Step 1

At least at this stage, para.(3) does not modify Step 1. **2.625**

Step 2

2.626 At Step 2, any part of the qualifying loan that was taken out to adapt the accommodation for the needs of a disabled person is disregarded: see para.(3)(a).

At this stage of the calculation the disregard of the capital disadvantages the claimant because it has the effect that capital borrowed to meet the needs of a disabled person does not count towards the total to which the standard rate of interest will be applied in Step 4.

As Step 2 only applies "[i]f there is more than one qualifying loan" and para.(3)(a) does not disregard the capital for the purposes of Step 1, the regulation creates the bizarre situation that—at this stage of the calculation—if a claimant has a single qualifying loan which includes amounts that were borrowed to adapt relevant accommodation to meet the needs of a disabled person, then no part of that capital is disregarded. However, if they have two or more such qualifying loans, all such capital is disregarded whichever loan it is part of.

Step 3

2.627 Where the loan includes capital that was borrowed for the specified purpose, it is difficult to work out what Step 3 requires. Para.(3)(a) says that such capital is to be disregarded for the purposes of that step. But from what amount or amounts is it to be disregarded?

Three amounts are mentioned in the unmodified Step 3, the capital limit, the Step 1 amount and the Step 2 amount.

It is not possible to disregard the amount of the loan taken out for the specified purpose from the capital limit because that figure is a notional amount. And, anyway, deducting the disregarded amount from that limit would reduce it and thereby work against the presumed policy intention that capital borrowed for this purpose should not be affected by the capital limit.

That leaves the Step 1 amount and the Step 2 amount. But capital borrowed to adapt accommodation for a disabled person has already been disregarded from the Step 2 amount. Should a second disregard now be made from that amount? And should such capital now be disregarded from the Step 1 amount as well? Given what is said below about the Step 4 calculation, the answers appear to be "no", and "the question is irrelevant".

Step 4

2.628 Where all or part of the qualifying loan (or loans) was taken out for the specified purpose, para.(3)(a) provides that the capital figure ("A" in the formula):

> "... is to be read as the amount resulting from step 1 in respect of the qualifying loan (or the sum of those amounts if there is more than one qualifying loan taken out for the purpose of making such adaptations) plus the amount (if any) resulting from step three in relation to any other qualifying loan or loans."

Finally, the drafting of the modification for loans taken out to adapt accommodation for the needs of a disabled person begins to make some sense. The aggregate of the full amounts of such loans (i.e., the aggregate of the amounts identified in Step 1) is taken into account. Then, in addition, loans, no part of which were taken out for that purpose are taken into account at the Step 3 figure (i.e., to the extent that, cumulatively, they do not exceed the capital limit). That is why no capital was disregarded at Step 1: for specified purpose loans, Step 4 takes the Step 1 figure into account in full without, in effect, going through the Step 3 process (which is why it is irrelevant whether specified purpose capital is disregarded from the Step 1 figure at the Step 3 stage). It is also why capital borrowed for the specified purpose is disregarded from the Step 2 figure: if it were not, it would be double-counted at Step 4.

Discussion

Even though the drafting becomes clear at the Step 4 stage, it is unnecessarily complex. Moreover, the wording does not achieve the result that appears to have been intended. An example may assist: 2.629

Estelle has been awarded IBJSA and is an owner-occupier. Her capital limit is £100,000. However she has a mortgage of £250,000, of which £25,000 was taken out to adapt her home for the needs of her daughter, Brittney, who is a disabled person.

What was (presumably) intended was that the loan payment should be calculated on £125,000 (i.e., the capital limit of £100,000 plus the £25,000 needed to carry out adaptations for Britney) and that is what would have been achieved if the £25,000 had been taken out as a separate loan.

However, Estelle has only one loan and what, because para.(3)(b) does not distinguish between loans and part loans, it appears to have the effect that the whole of that loan is taken into account at the Step 1 figure, namely £250,000.

Moreover, suppose that (before she claimed JSA) Estelle took out a further loan of £75,000 for purposes that are eligible under para.2(4) of Sch.1 but did not include the specified purpose. Para.(3)(b) now appears to have the effect that the second loan is taken into account at the Step 3 figure, which is £75,000 because it is less than Estelle's capital limit. If so, Estelle's loan payments should be calculated on a loan of £325,000.

Revaluation of capital

Even though Step 1 of the calculation says that what is to be determined is the amount of capital *for the time being owing* in connection with each qualifying loan, the Step 1 figure is not in fact revalued every month (for UC claimants) or every week (for other claimants). Instead, except where the claimant is an "existing claimant", the amount is re-calculated annually on the anniversary of the relevant date and on each subsequent such anniversary: see para.(4). For existing claimants, the recalculation is performed on the anniversary of the date on which owner-occupier payments were included in the claimant's qualifying benefit. 2.630

Calculation in respect of alternative finance payments

12.—(1) The amount to be included in each loan payment for owner-occupier payments which are alternative finance payments is determined as follows. 2.631

Step 1

Determine the purchase price of the accommodation to which the alternative finance payments relate.

Step 2

Determine the identified amount which is the lower of—

(a) the amount resulting from step 1; and

(b) the capital limit specified in paragraph (2)(a) or (b).

If both amounts are the same, that is the identified amount.

Step 3

In respect of an SPC claimant, apply the following formula to achieve a weekly sum—

$$\frac{A \times SR}{52} - I$$

In respect of a UC claimant, apply the following formula to achieve a monthly sum—

$$\frac{A \times SR}{12} - I$$

In either case—

"A" is the identified amount in step 2,

"SR" is the standard rate that applies at the date of the calculation (see regulation 13), and

"I" is the amount of any income, in the case of an SPC claimant, or unearned income, in the case of a UC claimant, above the claimant's applicable amount.

The result is the amount to be included in each loan payment for owner-occupier payments which are alternative finance payments.

(2) The capital limit is—

(a) £200,000 in the case of an SPC claimant where the Modified Rules apply or a UC claimant;

(b) £100,000 in all other cases.

(3) For the purposes of paragraph (1), "purchase price" means the price paid by a party to the alternative finance arrangements other than the claimant in order to acquire the interest in the accommodation to which those arrangements relate less—

(a) the amount of any initial payment made by the claimant in connection with the acquisition of that interest; and

(b) the amount of any subsequent payments made by the claimant or any partner to another party to the alternative finance arrangements before—

(i) the relevant date; or

(ii) in the case of an existing claimant, the date on which the claimant's qualifying benefit first included an amount for owner-occupier payments,

which reduce the amount owed by the claimant under the alternative finance arrangements.

(4) Subject to paragraph (5), any variation in the amount for the time being owing in connection with alternative finance arrangements is not to be taken into account after the relevant date until such time as the Secretary of State recalculates the amount which shall occur—

(a) on the first anniversary of the relevant date; and

(b) in respect of any variation after the first anniversary, on the next anniversary which follows the date of the variation.

(5) In respect of an existing claimant, the Secretary of State shall recalculate the amount for the time being owing [[1] in connection with alternative finance arrangements] on the anniversary of the date on which the claimant's qualifying benefit first included an amount for owner-occupier payments.

AMENDMENT

1. Loans for Mortgage Interest and Social Fund Maternity Grant (Amendment) Regulations 2018 (SI 2018/307), reg.2(1) and (7) (April 6, 2018).

DEFINITIONS

"alternative finance payments"—reg.2(1).
"applicable amount"—*ibid.*
"claimant"—*ibid.*
"existing claimant"—*ibid.*
"income"—*ibid.*
"Modified Rules"—*ibid.*
"owner-occupier payments"—regs 2(1) and 3(2)(a).
"partner"—reg.2(1).
"qualifying benefit"—*ibid.*
"qualifying loan"—*ibid.*
"relevant date"—*ibid.*
"SPC claimant"—*ibid.*
"UC claimant"—*ibid.*
"unearned income"—*ibid.*

GENERAL NOTE

For the definition of "alternative finance payments" see Sch.1, para.5(3). **2.632**

The calculation of loan payments made in respect of alternative finance payments is the same as that prescribed by reg.11 in respect of qualifying loans, except that:

- there is no modification where the alternative finance arrangements have been made in order to adapt the dwelling to meet the needs of a disabled person; and (more fundamentally)
- the Step 1 amount (*i.e.*, the capital element of the calculation) is the purchase price of the property (as set out in para.(3)), rather than the amount owing on a qualifying loan.

Standard rate to be applied under regulations 11 and 12

13.—(1) The standard rate is the average mortgage rate published by the Bank of England which has effect on the 5th April 2018. **2.633**

(2) The standard rate is to be varied each time that paragraph (3) applies.

(3) This paragraph applies when, on any reference day, the Bank of England publishes an average mortgage rate which differs by 0.5 percentage points or more from the standard rate that applies on that reference day (whether it applies by virtue of paragraph (1) or by virtue of a previous application of this paragraph).

(4) The average mortgage rate published on that reference day then becomes the new standard rate in accordance with paragraph (5).

(5) Any variation in the standard rate by virtue of paragraphs (2) to (4) shall come into effect at the end of the period of 6 weeks beginning with the day referred to in paragraph (3).

(6) At least 7 days before a variation of the standard rate comes into effect under paragraph (5), the Secretary of State must arrange for notice to be published on a publicly accessible website of—

(a) the new standard rate; and

(b) the day on which the new standard rate comes into effect under paragraph (5).

(7) For the purposes of this Regulation—

"average mortgage rate" means the effective interest rate (non-seasonally adjusted) of United Kingdom resident banks and building societies for loans to households secured on dwellings, published by the Bank of England in respect of the most recent period specified for that rate at the time of publication; and

"reference day" means any day falling on or after 6th April 2018.

DEFINITIONS

"dwelling"—reg.2(1).

GENERAL NOTE

2.634 The interest rate applied in Step 4 of the calculations under regs 11 and 12 is not the contractual rate due under the qualifying loan (or the rate inherent in the alternative finance arrangements) but, rather, the standard rate as determined in accordance with para.(1) and as subsequently varied under paras (2)-(6).

The standard rate, which varies from time to time, is published at the following web address: *https://www.gov.uk/support-for-mortgage-interest/what-youll-get*.

Non-dependant deductions

2.635 **14.—**(1) In the case of a legacy benefit claimant or SPC claimant, a deduction from each loan payment shall be made in respect of any non-dependant in accordance with paragraph (2).

(2) The amount to be deducted is calculated as follows.

Step 1

Identify the amount which is the sum of the loan payment calculated under regulation 10 and the amount of housing costs (if any) paid to a claimant under—

(a) paragraph 17 of Schedule 3 to the IS Regulations;
(b) paragraph 16 of Schedule 2 to the JSA Regulations;
(c) paragraph 18 of Schedule 6 to the ESA Regulations; or
(d) paragraph 13 of Schedule 2 to the SPC Regulations.

Step 2

Identify the total amount of the non-dependant deductions applicable to the claimant under—

(a) paragraph 18 of Schedule 3 to the IS Regulations;
(b) paragraph 17 of Schedule 2 to the JSA Regulations;
(c) paragraph 19 of Schedule 6 to the ESA Regulations; or
(d) paragraph 14 of Schedule 2 to the SPC Regulations.

Step 3

Identify the proportion of the non-dependant deductions applicable to the loan payment and housing costs (if any) in Step 1 by applying the formula—

$$A \times (B \div C)$$

where—
"A" is the total amount of the non-dependant deductions identified in Step 2,
"B" is the amount of the loan payment calculated under regulation 10, and
"C" is the amount identified in Step 1.

The result is the amount of the non-dependant deduction to be made from each loan payment in the case of a legacy benefit claimant or SPC claimant.

DEFINITIONS

"claimant"—reg.2(1).
"ESA Regulations"—*ibid.*
"IS Regulations"—*ibid.*
"JSA Regulations"—*ibid.*
"legacy benefit claimant"—*ibid.*
"non-dependant"—*ibid.*
"SPC claimant"—*ibid.*
"SPC Regulations"—*ibid.*

GENERAL NOTE

For claimants of IB, IBJSA, IRESA and SPC, some housing costs are still available as part their benefit: see the commentary to Sch.3 to the Income Support Regulations in Vol.V. Reg.14 is designed to ensure that such claimants do not have a non-dependant deduction made twice, once as part of their benefits and once under these regulations. This is achieved by adjusting the non-dependant deduction made when calculating the amount of a loan payment in accordance with the formula set out in Step 3. 2.636

Non-dependant deductions are not applied to loan payments where the claimant is on universal credit.

[1 Insurance payment deduction

14A.—(1) In the case of a legacy benefit claimant or UC claimant, where the claimant or the claimant's partner is in receipt of a payment under a policy of insurance taken out to insure against the risk of being unable to maintain owner-occupier payments within the meaning of Schedule 1, a deduction from the loan payment calculated under regulation 10 shall be made equal to the amount received in respect of owner-occupier payments. 2.637

(2) Where the amount referred to in paragraph (1) is equal to or more than the loan payment, the amount of the loan payment shall be zero.]

AMENDMENT

1. Loans for Mortgage Interest and Social Fund Maternity Grant (Amendment) Regulations 2018 (SI 2018/307), reg.2(1) and (8) (April 6, 2018).

DEFINITIONS

"claimant"—reg.2(1).
"legacy benefit claimant"—*ibid.*
"loan payment"—*ibid.*
"owner-occupier payments"—*ibid.* and reg.3(2)(a) and Sch.1
"partner"—reg.2(1).
"UC claimant"—*ibid.*

General Note

2.638 This regulation is self-explanatory. No insurance payment deduction is made where the claimant's qualifying benefit is SPC.

Interest

2.639 **15.**—(1) The Secretary of State shall charge interest on the sum of the loan payments until the earlier of—

(a) the day on which the loan payments and accrued interest are repaid in full;

(b) the event referred to in regulation 16(1)(c) [1;

(c) where the conditions in paragraph (1A) are met, the day on which the Secretary of State sends a completion statement to the claimant.]

[1 (1A) The conditions are—

(a) the claimant requests a completion statement from the Secretary of State in order to repay all of the outstanding amount in accordance with regulation 16(8) and (9); and

(b) the outstanding amount is paid within 30 days beginning with the day on which the completion statement is sent by the Secretary of State to the claimant.

(1B) Where regulation 16(3) applies, the Secretary of State shall continue to charge interest on the outstanding amount until the day referred to in regulation 15(1).]

(2) Interest at the relevant rate shall accrue daily, with effect from the first day a loan payment is made to a qualifying lender or the claimant under regulation 17, and shall be added to the outstanding amount at the end of each month (or part month).

(3) The relevant rate is the interest rate for the relevant period.

(4) For the purposes of this regulation and [2 regulations 16 and 16A], the outstanding amount is the sum of the loan payments and interest which has been charged under paragraph (1).

[1 (4A) For the purposes of this regulation, a "completion statement" means a written statement setting out the outstanding amount owed by the claimant to the Secretary of State.]

(5) The interest rate referred to in paragraph (3) is the weighted average interest rate on conventional gilts specified in the most recent report published before the start of the relevant period by the Office for Budget Responsibility under section 4(3) of the Budget Responsibility and National Audit Act 2011.

(6) The relevant period is the period starting on—

(a) 1st January and ending on 30th June in any year; or

(b) 1st July and ending on 31st December in any year.

Amendments

1. Loans for Mortgage Interest and Social Fund Maternity Grant (Amendment) Regulations 2018 (SI 2018/307), reg.2(1) and (9) (April 6, 2018).

2. Loans for Mortgage Interest (Amendment) Regulations 2021 (SI 2021/131) reg.2(1) and (3) (March 15, 2021).

Definitions

"claimant"—reg.2(1).
"loan payments"—*ibid.*
"qualifying lender"—*ibid.*

General Note

In contrast with reg.13, this regulation is not about the rate of interest that is applied to calculate the amount of loan payments. Rather, it is the rate that the Secretary of State charges on the loan that she has made to the claimant (*i.e.*, by making the loan payments) and which must be repaid in accordance with reg.16. 2.640

The derivation of the rate is complex. Section 4(3) of the Budget Responsibility and National Audit Act 2011 requires the Office for Budget Responsibility ("OBR") to prepare fiscal and economic forecasts "on at least two occasions for each financial year". This is usually done to coincide with the Budget and the Autumn Statement and the forecast, under the title, *Economic and Fiscal Outlook*, is published on the OBR's website (http://obr.uk/publications/). The relevant figure is in a table in that document. It can be located by downloading the document for the relevant period in PDF format and then searching for "weighted average interest rate on conventional gilts" which is the criterion specified in para.(5). That rate is reviewed, twice yearly, with effect from January 1 and July 1: see para.(6). The current rate is published at the following web address: *https://www.gov.uk/support-for-mortgage-interest/repaying-your-loan.*

Repayment

16.—(1) [2 Subject to regulation 16A, the outstanding amount] shall become immediately due and payable, together with any further interest which accrues on that amount under regulation 15, where one of the following events occurs— 2.641

(a) the relevant accommodation is sold;

(b) legal or beneficial title in, or in Scotland, heritable or registered title to, the relevant accommodation is transferred, assigned or otherwise disposed of, unless paragraph (3) applies;

[1 (c) in the case of—

(i) a claimant who is the sole legal owner of the relevant accommodation or the legal owner of the accommodation with someone other than a partner, the claimant's death;

(ii) a claimant with a partner who is the sole legal owner of the relevant accommodation or the legal owner of the accommodation with someone other than the claimant, the partner's death; or

(iii) a claimant and partner who are both legal owners (whether or not with anyone else) of the relevant accommodation, the death of the last member of the couple.]

(2) Subject to paragraphs (4) to (7), repayment shall occur—

(a) in the event described in paragraph (1)(a) or (b), from the proceeds of sale, transfer, assignment or disposition;

(b) in the event described in paragraph (1)(c), from the relevant person's estate.

(3) This paragraph applies where legal or beneficial title is transferred to—

(a) the claimant's partner, following the death of the claimant, where the partner is in occupation of the relevant accommodation; or

[1(aa) the claimant, following the death of the claimant's partner, where the claimant is in occupation of the relevant accommodation; or]

(b) the claimant, from a former spouse or civil partner, under a court order or an agreement for maintenance where the claimant is in occupation of the relevant accommodation.

(4) Where, in England and Wales—

(a) the Secretary of State has a charge by way of legal mortgage over the relevant accommodation; and

(b) there is insufficient equity available in the relevant accommodation to discharge the outstanding amount,

repayment shall be limited to the amount of available equity in the relevant accommodation after any prior ranking charges by way of legal mortgage have been repaid, and, in the event described in paragraph (1)(c), this shall be taken to be the amount of equity at the date of death of the relevant person.

(5) Where, in England and Wales—

(a) the Secretary of State has an equitable charge over one legal owner's equitable interest in the relevant accommodation, repayment shall be limited to the amount of that legal owner's equitable interest in the relevant accommodation and, in the event described in paragraph (1)(c), this shall be taken to be the value of that equitable interest at the date of death of the relevant person;

(b) the Secretary of State has an equitable charge over more than one legal owner's equitable interest in the relevant accommodation, repayment shall be limited to the sum of the equitable interests in the relevant accommodation of all legal owners within the benefit unit and, in the event described in paragraph (1)(c), this shall be taken to be the value of those equitable interests at the date of death of the relevant person.

(6) Where, in Scotland—

(a) the Secretary of State has a standard security over the whole or part of the relevant accommodation; and

(b) there is insufficient equity available in the whole or part of the relevant accommodation over which the standard security is held,

repayment shall be limited to the amount of available equity in the whole or part of the relevant accommodation over which the standard security is held after any prior ranking standard securities have been repaid, and, in the event described in paragraph (1)(c), this shall be taken to be the amount of equity at the date of death of the relevant person.

(7) In the event that the relevant accommodation is sold or legal or beneficial title in, or in Scotland, heritable or registered title to, the relevant accommodation is transferred, assigned or otherwise disposed of for less than market value, the disposal shall be treated as if it occurred at market value for the purposes of repayment.

(8) Subject to paragraph (9), a claimant shall be permitted to repay some or all of the outstanding amount before an event in paragraph (1) occurs if the amount of each repayment is equal to or more than £100.

(9) Where the outstanding amount is less than £100, a claimant shall be permitted to repay that sum in full in one repayment.

AMENDMENTS

1. Loans for Mortgage Interest and Social Fund Maternity Grant (Amendment) Regulations 2018 (SI 2018/307), reg.2(1) and (10) (April 6, 2018).

2. Loans for Mortgage Interest (Amendment) Regulations 2021 (SI 2021/131) reg.2(1) and (4) (March 15, 2021).

DEFINITIONS

"benefit unit"—reg.2(1).
"charge by way of legal mortgage"—*ibid.*
"claimant"—*ibid.*
"legal owner"—*ibid.*
"partner"—*ibid.*
"relevant accommodation"—*ibid.*
"standard security"—*ibid.*

GENERAL NOTE

The loan from the Secretary of State is repayable 2.642

- when the relevant accommodation is sold: see para.(1)(a);
- when the title to the relevant accommodation changes hands (para.1(b)) unless para.(3) applies;
- when the claimant dies unless
  - — the claimant's partner is either the sole legal owner of the relevant accommodation (or the joint legal owner with someone other than the claimant), in which case the loan is repayable when the partner dies; or
  - — the claimant and partner are both legal owners of the relevant accommodation, in which case the loan is repayable on the death of the surviving member of the couple.

In *R (Vincent and others) v Secretary of State for Work and Pensions* [2020] EWHC 1976 (Admin), the High Court (Andrews J) rejected submissions that para.16(1)(a) unlawfully discriminated against the claimants under art.14 ECHR taken together with A1P1 and/or art.8, as severely disabled people with a partner in receipt of Carer's Allowance and/or as dependent children of such persons. A challenge under the Public Sector Equality Duty was also dismissed.

Under para.(3) the loan is not repayable where the title is transferred (otherwise than by way of sale, in which case para.(1)(a) would apply) to the claimant or her/his partner on the death of the other member of the couple, where the person to whom title is transferred is in occupation of the relevant accommodation: see para.(3)(a) and (aa); or where the title is transferred to the claimant from a former spouse or civil partner either by court order or under a maintenance agreement and the claimant is occupying the relevant accommodation: see para.(3)(b).

The lack of any provision that deals with the reverse of the situation described in para.(3)(b) creates an apparent lacuna. What happens if the claimant deserts their spouse or civil partner and the accommodation is then transferred from the claimant to the civil partner? The answer seems to be that the loan, which is secured on the accommodation that has now been transferred to the former partner, becomes repayable under para.(1)(b). The practical answer may be that under para.(2)(a) repayment is to be made "from the proceeds of sale, transfer, assignment or disposition" and, depending upon the terms of the court order or maintenance agreement, there will often be no such proceeds.

Paragraphs (4)-(6) limit the amount repayable to the Secretary of State to the amount of the equity in the relevant accommodation after repayment of prior mortgages and charges.

Paragraph (7) prevents that rule from being abused by selling the relevant accommodation for less than its market value. In those circumstances the sale is treated as if it had been at market value for the purpose of repayment.

Paragraphs (8) and (9) allow the claimant to make voluntary repayments. Each repayment must be at least £100 unless the amount owing is less than £100 in which case the claimant may repay that amount in full in a single repayment.

[1 Transferring the loan between properties

16A.—(1) Subject to paragraph (6), where the conditions in paragraphs (2) and (3) are met, regulation 16 (repayment) applies in relation to the new property referred to in paragraph (2) instead of in relation to the relevant accommodation ("Property 1").

(2) The first condition is that the claimant or the claimant's partner informs the Secretary of State that it is proposed to sell Property 1, and requests that the outstanding amount be transferred from Property 1 to a new property ("Property 2").

(3) The second condition is that prior to the completion of the sale of Property 1—

(a) the conveyancer dealing with the sale of the property has provided a written undertaking to the Secretary of State to do the following—

(i) to discharge the charge (in England and Wales), if any, or standard security (in Scotland), if any, in favour of the Secretary of State; and

(ii) to transfer the outstanding amount to the conveyancer for the claimant or the claimant's partner, if not also acting on their behalf; and

(b) the conveyancer for the claimant or the claimant's partner has provided a written undertaking to the Secretary of State to do the following—

(i) to register a new charge (in England and Wales) or standard security (in Scotland) in favour of the Secretary of State for the outstanding amount in respect of Property 2; and

(ii) if completion of the sale and completion of the purchase do not happen simultaneously to hold the outstanding amount to the order of the Secretary of State until completion of the purchase of Property 2.

(4) Where the Secretary of State meets the reasonable costs incurred by the conveyancer for the claimant or the claimant's partner for the purpose of transferring the loan from Property 1 to Property 2—

(a) these costs may be added to the outstanding amount of the loan; and

(b) any costs added to the outstanding amount are to be considered as a loan payment for the purpose of accruing interest under regulation 15.

(5) For the purposes of sub-paragraphs (a)(ii) and (b)(ii) of paragraph (3)—

(a) in England and Wales, where the available equity in Property 1 as referred to in regulation 16(4), or, as the case may be, the amount of the equitable interest or interests, as referred to in regulation 16(5), is or are less than the outstanding amount, the reference in those sub-paragraphs to the outstanding amount is a reference to the available equity or to the amount of the equitable interest or interests, as the case may be; and

(b) in Scotland, where the available equity in the whole or part of Property 1 over which the standard security is held, as referred to in regulation 16(6), is less than the outstanding amount, the reference in those sub-paragraphs to the outstanding amount is a reference to the available equity.

(6) If completion in respect of Property 2 does not take place within twelve weeks beginning with the date that completion of the sale of Property 1 occurs or by such later date as the Secretary of State may agree then paragraph (1) does not apply and the outstanding amount under regulation 16, together with any future interest which accrues on that amount under regulation 15, shall be immediately due and payable.

(7) For the purposes of this regulation references to a claimant includes a former claimant.

(8) Where, under paragraph (1), the provisions of regulation 16 apply in relation to Property 2, this regulation applies as if any reference to the relevant accommodation were a reference to Property 2 (with no limit to the number of times this regulation may be treated as applying in relation to a new property).]

AMENDMENT

1. Loans for Mortgage Interest (Amendment) Regulations 2021 (SI 2021/131) reg.2(1) and (5) (March 15, 2021).

DEFINITIONS

"claimant"—see reg.2(1).
"partner"—*ibid.*
"relevant accommodation"—*ibid.*
"standard security"—*ibid.*

GENERAL NOTE

Before March 15, 2021 the loan from the Secretary of State was immediately repayable in the circumstances set out in reg.16 with the effect that when the property subject to the Secretary of State's charge was sold, then, whatever the circumstances—even if, for example, the sale was part of a move to accommodation more suited to the needs of a disabled person—the proceeds of sale that might otherwise have been put towards the price of the new property were reduced by the amount that had to be repaid to the Secretary of State. **2.643**

From March 15, 2021, however, the introduction of reg.16A (and the linked amendment to reg.16) mean that, as long as the conditions in paras (2) and (3) are satisfied, the full equity (or the available equity (see para.(5)) in the existing property can be used towards the purchase of the new property. In those circumstances, the Secretary of State's charge over the existing property will be discharged and an equivalent charge registered against the new property on completion.

Those conditions are (a) that the claimant (or the claimant's partner) informs the Secretary of State that it is proposed to sell the existing property, and requests that the outstanding amount secured on that property be transferred to the new property (para.(2)); and (b) (in the normal case of a linked sale and purchase) that before completion of the sale of the existing property, the conveyancer dealing with that sale provides the Secretary of State with a written undertaking to discharge the charge on that property and to register a new charge against the new property (para.(3)). Para.(3) also makes provision for what happens if different conveyancers are acting on the sale and the purchase, or if the sale and purchase are not completed simultaneously. In the latter case the loan becomes immediately repayable if the sale and purchase are separated by more than 12 weeks (para.(6)).

Para.(4) provides for the reasonable legal costs of transferring the charge—but not *all* the legal costs of the sale and purchase—to be paid by the Secretary of State, and added to the amount of the loan, if the loan recipient so requests. Interest will be payable on any such costs on the same basis as on the original loan.

Para.(8) provides that there is no limit on the number of times that the security for the loan from the Secretary of State can be transferred to a new property.

Direct payments to qualifying lenders

2.644 **17.**—(1) Where the circumstances specified in paragraph (2) are met, the loan payments must be made by the Secretary of State direct to a claimant's lender.

(2) The circumstances referred to in paragraph (1) are that—

(a) money was lent to the claimant in respect of which owner-occupier payments in respect of the relevant accommodation are payable to a qualifying lender; and

(b) those owner-occupier payments are taken into account in calculating the amount of each loan payment under regulation 10.

(3) Where the circumstances in paragraph (2) are not met, the loan payments must be made to the claimant.

(4) Schedule 4 has effect in relation to payments made under paragraph (1).

DEFINITIONS

"claimant"—reg.2(1).
"loan payments"—*ibid.*
"owner-occupier payments"—regs 2(1) and 3(2)(a).
"qualifying lender"—*ibid.*
"relevant accommodation"—*ibid.*

GENERAL NOTE

2.645 In most cases, loan payments will be made to the lender rather than to the claimant. In fact, given the breadth of the circumstances specified in para.(2), loan payments will probably only ever be made to the claimant where the lender is not a "qualifying lender" as defined in reg.2(1) and s.19(7)-(9) WRWA 2016. Any financial institution or public authority is likely to come within that definition. All that remains seems to be private loans from one individual to another.

[1 Consequential amendments

2.646 **18.**—(1) Subject to paragraph (2) and regulations 19, 19A and 20, the amendments in Schedule 5 have effect.

(2) The amendments made by Part 2 of Schedule 5 to the Social Security and Child Support (Decisions and Appeals) Regulations 1999 do not apply in relation to any decision or determination about an amount for owner-occupier payments under the substantive regulations as those regulations applied without the amendments made by Part 1 of Schedule 5.

(3) In this regulation, the "substantive regulations" means the ESA Regulations, IS Regulations, JSA Regulations, SPC Regulations and UC Regulations.]

AMENDMENT

1. Loans for Mortgage Interest and Social Fund Maternity Grant (Amendment) Regulations 2018 (SI 2018/307), reg.2(1) and (11) (April 6, 2018).

GENERAL NOTE

The consequential amendments made by Sch.5 have been taken in at the appropriate points in the text of the amended regulations. Those amendments are, however, subject to the transitional provisions made by regs 19, 19A and 20 below. 2.647

[1 Transitional provision: loan offer made before 6th April 2018

19.—(1) Subject to regulation 20, in relation to an existing claimant in a case where the loan payments offer date occurs before 6th April 2018, the amendments made by Schedule 5 shall be treated as though they did not have effect until the earlier of the following days (where that day occurs after 6th April 2018) ("the transitional end day")— 2.648

(a) the day referred to in paragraph (2);

(b) the day after the day on which entitlement to a qualifying benefit ends.

(2) The day referred to is the later of—

(a) in the case of—

(i) a legacy benefit claimant or SPC claimant, where 6th April 2018 is not the first day of the claimant's benefit week, the first day of the first benefit week that begins after 6th April 2018; or

(ii) a UC claimant, where 6th April 2018 is not the first day of the claimant's assessment period, the first day of the first assessment period that begins after 6th April 2018;

(b) the relevant day in paragraph (3).

(3) The relevant day is the day after the day that is the earlier of—

(a) the day on which the Secretary of State receives notification from the claimant that the claimant does not wish to accept the offer of loan payments;

(b) the last day of the period of 4 weeks, beginning with the day after the day on which the Secretary of State has received both the loan agreement and the documents referred to in regulation 5(2), duly executed, where both the loan agreement and the documents are received within the period of 6 weeks beginning with the loan payments offer date; or

(c) the last day of the period of 6 weeks, beginning with the loan payments offer date, where the Secretary of State has not received both the loan agreement and the documents referred to in regulation 5(2), duly executed, within that period.

(4) Where in the case of—

(a) a legacy benefit claimant or SPC claimant, the relevant day referred to in paragraph (3) is not the first day of the claimant's benefit week, then the relevant day shall be the first day of the first benefit week that begins after the relevant day; or

(b) a UC claimant, the relevant day referred to in paragraph (3) is not the first day of the claimant's assessment period, then the relevant day shall be the first day of the first assessment period that begins after the relevant day.]

AMENDMENT

1. Loans for Mortgage Interest and Social Fund Maternity Grant (Amendment) Regulations 2018 (SI 2018/307), reg.2(1) and (12) (April 6, 2018).

DEFINITIONS

"assessment period"—reg.2(1) and reg.21 UC Regs 2013.
"benefit week"—reg.2(1).
"claimant"—*ibid.*
"entitlement"—reg.2(2)(a).
"existing claimant"—reg.2(1).
"legacy benefit claimant"—*ibid.*
"loan agreement"—*ibid.*
"loan payments"—*ibid.*
"loan payments offer date"—*ibid.*
"qualifying benefit"—*ibid.*
"SPC claimant"—*ibid.*
"transitional end day"—*ibid.* and para.(1).
"UC claimant"—reg.2(1).

GENERAL NOTE

2.649 Regs 19, 19A, 20 and 21 all establish transitional rules for "existing claimants" (*i.e.*, those entitled to a qualifying benefit including an amount for owner-occupier payments on April 5, 2018: see reg.2(1)). "Qualifying benefits" are IRESA, IS, IBJSA, SPC and universal credit. Reg.19 applies where the "loan payments offer date" (*i.e.*, the day on which the Secretary of State sent the loan agreement to the claimant under reg.3: see reg.2(1) (again)) was before April 6, 2018. In those circumstances:

- the consequential amendments made by Sch.5 do not come into effect until the "transitional end date": see also reg.8(1)(d); and
- section 11(1), (8), (9) and (11) of the Welfare Reform and Work Act 2016 (consequential amendments) are treated as though they are not in force in relation to the existing claimant: see reg.2(2) of SI 2018/438.

In the circumstances to which reg.19 applies, that date must be after April 6, 2018, and is either, the later of the days specified in para.(2), or (if earlier) the day after the day on which the claimant's entitlement to the qualifying benefit ends.

Ignoring, for the moment, the provisions about the "relevant day", the effect is that where April 6, 2018 is not the first day of the claimant's benefit week, or universal credit assessment period, the claimant continues to receive housing costs as part of his or her qualifying benefit until the first day of the benefit week or assessment period that begins after that date. This will mean that some universal credit claimants will get housing costs as part of their benefit for up to a month more than others purely because of the day of the month on which they first claimed universal credit.

For those claimants whose benefit weeks or assessment periods begin on April 6, 2018—and who are not affected by the rules in paras (3) and (4) about the relevant day—no transitional provision is required, and none has been made.

Paragraphs (3) and (4) deal with the position where the offer of loan payments was made before April 6, 2018 but is not accepted or rejected until after that date. In those circumstances, entitlement to payment of housing costs as part of a qualifying benefit ends and entitlement to a loan potentially begins on the "relevant day". Subject to the adjustment in para.(4), the rules are as follows:

- if the claimant does not execute and return the loan agreement and the other necessary documents so that the Secretary of State receives them by the last day of the period of six weeks beginning with the loan offer date, then the relevant day is the day after the last day of that six-week period;
- if the claimant does execute and return the loan agreement and the other necessary documents so that the Secretary of State receives them by the last day of that six-week period, the relevant day is the day after the last day of the period of four weeks beginning with the day on which the Secretary of State received those documents; and
- if the claimant notifies the Secretary of State that they do not wish to accept the offer of loan payments, the relevant day is the day after the Secretary of State receives that notification.

However, the need for the relevant day to be the first day of a benefit week or a universal credit assessment period means that the days identified by para.(3) are then adjusted by para.(4). If the relevant day is not the first day of a benefit week or assessment period, the first day of the following benefit week or assessment period becomes the new relevant day.

Reg.19 is subject to the rules about those who lack, or may lack, capacity in reg.20.

[1 Transitional provision: loan offer made on or after 6th April 2018

19A.—(1) Subject to regulation 20 and paragraph (4), in relation to an existing claimant in a case where the loan payments offer date does not occur before 6th April 2018, the amendments made by Schedule 5 shall be treated as though they did not have effect until the earlier of the following days (where that day occurs after 6th April 2018) ("the transitional end day")— 2.650

(a) the relevant day in paragraph (2);

(b) the day after the day on which entitlement to a qualifying benefit ends;

(c) the day after the day on which the Secretary of State receives notification from the claimant that the claimant does not wish to receive loan payments.

(2) The relevant day is—

(a) 7th May 2018; or

(b) where the loan payments offer date occurs before 7th May 2018, the relevant day in regulation 19(3)(b) and (c) and (4).

(3) Where in the case of—

(a) a legacy benefit claimant or SPC claimant, the day referred to in paragraph (1)(c), or the relevant day as referred to in paragraph (2)(a), is not the first day of the claimant's benefit week, then that day or that relevant day is the first day of the first benefit week that begins after that day or that relevant day; or

(b) a UC claimant, the day referred to in paragraph (1)(c), or the relevant day as referred to in paragraph (2)(a), is not the first day of the claimant's assessment period, then that day or that relevant day is not the first day of the first assessment period that begins after that day or that relevant day.

(4) Paragraphs (1) to (3) do not apply in relation to an existing claimant where, as at the end of 5th April 2018—

(a) the Secretary of State, or a person authorised to exercise functions of the Secretary of State, has, before 19th March 2018 made a request to the claimant, whether orally or in writing, to provide information that is needed in order for the Secretary of State or that person to—
   (i) take steps to ascertain whether the claimant wishes to receive an offer of loan payments or not; or
   (ii) be able to send to the claimant the loan agreement and documents referred to in regulation 5(2); and

(b) the claimant has not provided that information to the Secretary of State or that person.

(5) Subject to regulation 20, in the case of an existing claimant referred to in paragraph (4), where 6th April 2018 is not the first day of the claimant's benefit week, in the case of a legacy benefit or SPC claimant, or assessment period, in the case of a UC claimant, the amendments made by Schedule 5 shall be treated as though they did not have effect until the first day of the first benefit week or first assessment period that begins after that date ("the transitional end day").

AMENDMENT

1. Loans for Mortgage Interest and Social Fund Maternity Grant (Amendment) Regulations 2018 (SI 2018/307), reg.2(1) and (12) (April 6, 2018).

DEFINITIONS

"assessment period"—reg.2(1) and reg.21 UC Regs 2013.
"benefit week"—reg.2(1).
"claimant"—*ibid.*
"existing claimant"—*ibid.*
"legacy benefit claimant"—*ibid.*
"loan agreement"—*ibid.*
"loan payments"—*ibid.*
"loan payments offer date"—*ibid.*
"qualifying benefit"—*ibid.*
"SPC claimant"—*ibid.*
"transitional end day"—*ibid.* and paras (1) and (5).
"UC claimant"—reg.2(1).

GENERAL NOTE

2.651 For transitional provision generally, see the General Note to reg.19. Reg.19A governs the position where the "loan payments offer date" was *after* April 6, 2018.

Paragraph (1): In those circumstances, the transitional end day is the earliest of the day after the day on which entitlement to a qualifying benefit ends; the day after the day on which the Secretary of State is notified that the claimant does not wish to receive loan payments; and the relevant day as identified in para.(2). Where the transitional end day is determined in accordance with the first two of those alternatives, and is not the first day of the claimant's benefit week (for claimants of IS. IBJSA, IRESA and SPC) or assessment period (for claimants of universal credit), then the date is adjusted to the first day of the claimant's following benefit week or assessment period.

Paragraph (2): Where the loan payments offer date is on or after April 6, 2018 but before May 7, 2018, the relevant day is determined in accordance with reg.19(3)(b) and (c) and (4): see the commentary to those provisions in the General Note to reg.19.

The effect of para.(2)(a) is that where the loan payments offer date is made on or after May 7, 2018, no transitional provision applies. So, entitlement to housing costs will end on May 7, 2018 (or the last day of the benefit week or assessment period that includes May 7, 2018: see para.(3)) and eligibility for loan payments will begin on the date specified in reg.8.

Paragraphs (4) and (5): In some circumstances, the reason why the loan payments offer date is on or after April 6, 2018 is that the Secretary of State—or an authorised person on his behalf: see reg.22—has asked the claimant for information that is needed to establish that they are eligible for loan payments or to complete the loan agreement or other documents and the claimant has not replied. Where that request was made before March 19, 2018, paras (1)-(3) do not apply. The lack of the transitional protection established by those rules means entitlement to housing costs will end on April 6, 2018, subject to the usual adjustments to ensure that the changes come into force on the first day of a benefit period or assessment period: see para.(5).

Reg.19A is subject to the rules about those who lack, or may lack, capacity in reg.20.

[1 Transitional provision: persons who lack capacity or may lack capacity identified before 6th April 2018

20.—(1) Paragraph (2) applies in relation to an existing claimant where, before 6th April 2018— 2.652

(a) the Secretary of State believes that the claimant is a person who lacks capacity to make some or all decisions about accepting an offer of loan payments; or

(b) on the basis of information received by the Secretary of State, the Secretary of State suspects that the claimant is a person who may lack such capacity,

(a "relevant claimant").

(2) In relation to a relevant claimant, the amendments made by Schedule 5 shall be treated as though they were not in force until the day that is the earlier of ("the transitional end day")—

(a) the relevant day in paragraph (3) or (8);

(b) the day after the day on which entitlement to a qualifying benefit ends.

(3) Subject to paragraph (8), the relevant day is the later of—

(a) 5th November 2018;

(b) where, in a case where paragraph (1)(b) applies, the Secretary of State believes before 5th November 2018 that the claimant is a person who lacks capacity as referred to in paragraph (1)(a), the day after the last day of the period of 6 weeks beginning with the day on which the Secretary of State forms that belief;

(c) where an application for a decision referred to in paragraph (7) is made before the later of 5th November 2018 and the relevant day under sub-paragraph (b), the day after the day specified in paragraph (4).

(4) The specified day is—

(a) the last day of the period of 6 weeks beginning with the day on which a person referred to in paragraph (7) ("relevant person") makes a decision referred to in paragraph (7); or

(b) the last day of the period of 6 weeks beginning with the day on which a relevant person receives notification that the application for such a decision is withdrawn.

(5) Where more than one application for a decision as referred to in paragraph (7) is made to a relevant person within the period referred to in paragraph (3)(c), then the periods in paragraph (4) do not start to run until the relevant person has made a decision with respect to the last of the applications to be dealt with, or the relevant person receives notification that all of the applications are withdrawn.

(6) Where an application for a decision as referred to in paragraph (7) is made to more than one relevant person within the period referred to in paragraph (3)(c), then, where the specified day under paragraph (4) would be different as between the applications made to the different relevant persons, the specified day is the later of the two days.

(7) The decisions referred to are—

(a) in England and Wales—

(i) a decision by the Court of Protection whether or not to appoint a deputy under section 16(2) of the Mental Capacity Act 2005 with power to act on the claimant's behalf in respect of accepting an offer of loan payments;

(ii) a decision by the Court of Protection whether or not, by making an order under section 16(2) of the Mental Capacity Act 2005, to decide on behalf of the claimant to accept an offer of loan payments; or

(iii) a decision by the Public Guardian whether or not to register a lasting power of attorney under the Mental Capacity Act 2005 where the power includes power to act on the claimant's behalf with respect to accepting an offer of loan payments; or

(b) in Scotland—

(i) a decision by the sheriff whether or not to make an order under section 58 of the Adults with Incapacity (Scotland) Act 2000 to appoint a guardian with power to act on the claimant's behalf with respect to accepting an offer of loan payments;

(ii) a decision by the sheriff whether or not, by making an intervention order under section 53 of the Adults with Incapacity (Scotland) Act 2000, to decide on behalf of the claimant to accept an offer of loan payments; or

(ii) a decision by the sheriff or the Court of Session whether or not to make an order under the Judicial Factors Act 1849 to appoint a judicial factor with power to act on the claimant's behalf with respect to accepting an offer of loan payments.

(8) Where, in a case where paragraph (1)(b) applies, the Secretary of State believes before 5th November 2018 that the claimant is not a person who lacks capacity as referred to in paragraph (1)(a), the relevant day is the day after the earlier of—

(a) the day specified in paragraph (9);

(b) the day on which the Secretary of State receives notification from the claimant that the claimant does not wish to receive loan payments.

(9) The specified day is—

(a) the last day of the period of 6 weeks beginning with the day on which the Secretary of State forms the belief in paragraph (8); or

(b) where the loan payments offer date occurs during the period in sub-paragraph (a), the day referred to in regulation 19(3)(b) and (c) and (4).

(10) Where in the case of—

(a) a legacy benefit claimant or SPC claimant, the relevant day referred to in paragraph (3) or (8) is not the first day of the claimant's benefit week, then the relevant day shall be the first day of the first benefit week that begins after the relevant day; or

(b) a UC claimant, the relevant day in paragraph (3) or (8) is not the first day of the claimant's assessment period, then the relevant day shall be the first day of the first assessment period that begins after the relevant day.]

AMENDMENT

1. Loans for Mortgage Interest and Social Fund Maternity Grant (Amendment) Regulations 2018 (SI 2018/307), reg.2(1) and (12) (April 6, 2018). The fact that sub-para.7(b) has two heads lettered "(ii)" is a requirement of the amending instrument and is not an editorial error.

DEFINITIONS

"assessment period"—reg.2(1) and reg.21 UC Regs 2013.
"benefit week"—reg.2(1).
"claimant"—*ibid.*
"entitlement"—reg.2(2)(a).
"existing claimant"—reg.2(1).
"legacy benefit claimant"—*ibid.*
"loan agreement"—*ibid.*
"loan payments"—*ibid.*
"loan payments offer date"—*ibid.*
"person who lacks capacity"—*ibid.*
"qualifying benefit"—*ibid.*
"SPC claimant"—*ibid.*
"transitional end day"—*ibid.* and para.(2).
"UC claimant"—*ibid.*

GENERAL NOTE

Regs 19 and 19A are subject to reg.20, which applies where the Secretary of State believes the claimant lacks capacity to make some or all decisions about accepting an offer of loan payments or, on the basis of information he has received, suspects that to be the case. **2.653**

"Person who lacks capacity" is defined by reg.2(1) by reference to (in England and Wales) s.2 of the Mental Health Act 2005 or (in Scotland) as meaning a person who is incapable under s.1(2) of the Adults with Incapacity (Scotland) Act 2000. Under the former provision "a person lacks capacity in relation to a matter if at the material time he is unable to make a decision for himself in relation to the matter because of an impairment of, or a disturbance in the functioning of, the mind or brain". Under the latter, an "adult" is a person who aged 16 or more and "incapable" means incapable of acting, making decisions, communicating decisions, understanding decisions, or retaining the memory of decisions, by reason of mental disorder or of inability to communicate because of physical disability but not where the lack or deficiency in a faculty of communication can be made good by human or mechanical aid.

The capacity of the claimant is a matter of greater concern to the Secretary of State where what the claimant is being offered is a loan rather than a benefit payment. If the claimant lacks capacity to enter into the loan agreement or to execute the Secretary of State's charge or security over the property, the Secretary of State would be at risk that the agreement, and the charge or security, might be invalid.

The transitional provisions are complex but, in summary, have the effect that the new law does not come into force until any question about the claimant's capacity has been resolved.

Transition from legacy benefit to universal credit

2.654 **21.**—(1) Paragraph (3) applies where—

(a) an award of universal credit is made to a claimant who—

(i) was entitled to [1, or was treated as entitled to,] a legacy benefit (a "relevant award") at any time during the period of one month ending with the day on which the claim for universal credit was made or treated as made (or would have been so entitled were it not for termination of that award by virtue of an order made under section 150(3) of the Welfare Reform Act 2012 or the effect of the Transitional Provisions Regulations); or

(ii) was at any time during the period of one month ending with the day on which the claim for universal credit was made or treated as made, the partner of a person ("P") who was at that time entitled to [1, or was treated as entitled to,] a relevant award, where the award of universal credit is not a joint award to the claimant and P;

(b) on the relevant date—

(i) the relevant award included an amount in respect of housing costs under—

(aa) paragraphs 14 to 16 of Schedule 2 to the JSA Regulations;

(bb) paragraphs 16 to 18 of Schedule 6 to the ESA Regulations; or

(cc) paragraphs 15 to 17 of Schedule 3 to the IS Regulations; or

(ii) the claimant was entitled to loan payments under these Regulations; and

(c) the amendments made by Schedule 5 apply in relation to the award of universal credit.

(2) In this regulation, the "relevant date" means—

(a) where paragraph (1)(a)(i) applies and the claimant was not entitled to [1, or was treated as entitled to,] the relevant award on the date on which the claim for universal credit was made or treated as made, the date on which the relevant award terminated;

(b) where paragraph (1)(a)(i) applies, the claimant is not a new claimant partner and he or she was entitled to [1, or was treated as entitled to,] the relevant award on the date on which the claim for universal credit was made, that date;

(c) where paragraph (1)(a)(i) applies, the claimant is a new claimant partner and he or she was entitled to [1, or was treated as entitled to,] the relevant award on the date on which the claim for universal credit was treated as made, that date;

(d) where paragraph (1)(a)(ii) applies, the date on which the claimant ceased to be the partner of P or, if earlier, the date on which the relevant award terminated.

(3) Where this paragraph applies, regulation 8(1)(b) does not apply.

(4) Paragraph (5) applies where paragraph (1)(a) applies and the amendments made by Schedule 5 apply in relation to the award of universal credit, but—

(a) the relevant award did not include an amount in respect of housing costs because the claimant's entitlement (or, as the case may be, P's entitlement) was nil by virtue of—

(i) paragraph 7(1)(b) of Schedule 2 to the JSA Regulations;

(ii) paragraph 9(1)(b) of Schedule 6 to the ESA Regulations; or

(iii) paragraph 8(1)(b) of Schedule 3 to the IS Regulations; or

(b) the amendments made by Schedule 5 applied in relation to the relevant award but the claimant was not entitled to loan payments by virtue of regulation 8(1)(b).

(5) Where this paragraph applies—

(a) the definition of "qualifying period" in regulation 2(1) does not apply; and

(b) "qualifying period" means the period of 273 days starting with the first day on which the claimant (or, as the case may be, P) was entitled to the relevant award, taking into account any period which was treated as a period of continuing entitlement under—

(i) paragraph 13 of Schedule 2 to the JSA Regulations;

(ii) paragraph 15 of Schedule 6 to the ESA Regulations; or

(iii) paragraph 14 of Schedule 3 to the IS Regulations,

provided that, throughout that part of the qualifying period after the award of universal credit is made, receipt of universal credit is continuous and the claimant otherwise qualifies for loan payments under these Regulations.

(6) Paragraph (7) applies where—

(a) a claimant has an award of universal credit which becomes subject to the amendments made by Schedule 5; and

(b) regulation 29 of the Transitional Provisions Regulations applied in relation to the award.

(7) Where this paragraph applies—

(a) where paragraph (3) of regulation 29 of the Transitional Provisions Regulations applied in relation to the award, regulation 8(1)(b) does not apply; and

(b) where paragraph (5) of regulation 29 of the Transitional Provisions Regulations applied in relation to the award, paragraph (5) of this regulation applies in relation to the award.

AMENDMENT

1. Loans for Mortgage Interest and Social Fund Maternity Grant (Amendment) Regulations 2018 (SI 2018/307), reg.2(1) and (13) (April 6, 2018).

DEFINITIONS

"claimant"—reg.2(1).
"entitlement"—reg.2(2)(a).
"ESA Regulations"—reg.2(1).
"IS Regulations"—*ibid.*
"JSA Regulations"—*ibid.*
"legacy benefit"—*ibid.*
"loan payments"—*ibid.*
"new claimant partner"—*ibid.*
"partner"—*ibid.*
"qualifying period"—reg.2(1) as modified by para.(5).
"relevant date"—para.(2).
"Transitional Provisions Regulations"—reg.2(1).

GENERAL NOTE

2.655 This regulation makes transitional provision where a claimant transfers to universal credit from IS, IBJSA or IRESA.

Delegation

2.656 **22.** A function of the Secretary of State under these Regulations may be exercised by a person authorised for that purpose by the Secretary of State.

GENERAL NOTE

2.657 This regulation is made under s.19(5) of the WRWA 2016 which provides that the regulations "may provide for the Secretary of State to make arrangements with another person for the exercise of functions under the regulations".

Regulation 3(2)(a)

SCHEDULE 1

MEANING OF OWNER-OCCUPIER PAYMENTS

PART 1

LEGACY BENEFIT CLAIMANTS AND SPC CLAIMANTS

Application of Part 1

2.658 1. This Part applies to legacy benefit claimants and SPC claimants.

Payments of interest on qualifying loans and alternative finance payments

2.659 2.—(1) "Owner-occupier payments" means—

(a) payments of interest on a loan which qualifies under sub-paragraph (2) or (4); and

(b) in respect of an SPC claimant only, alternative finance payments within the meaning of paragraph 5(3).

(2) A loan qualifies under this sub-paragraph where the loan was taken out to defray monies applied for any of the following purposes—

(a) acquiring an interest in the relevant accommodation; or

(b) paying off another loan which would have qualified under paragraph (a) had it not been paid off.

(3) For the purposes of sub-paragraph (2), references to a loan also include a reference to money borrowed under a hire purchase agreement, as defined in section 189 of the Consumer Credit Act 1974, for any purpose specified in paragraph (a) or (b) of sub-paragraph (2).

(4) A loan qualifies under this sub-paragraph if it was taken out, with or without security, for the purpose of—

(a) carrying out repairs and improvements to the relevant accommodation;

(b) paying any service charge imposed to meet the cost of repairs and improvements to the relevant accommodation;

(c) paying off another loan that would have qualified under paragraphs (a) and (b) had it not been paid off,

as long as the loan is used for that purpose within 6 months beginning with the date of receipt or as soon as reasonably practicable.

(5) In sub-paragraph (4), "repairs and improvements" means any of the following measures undertaken with a view to maintaining the fitness of the relevant accommodation, or any part of the building containing the relevant accommodation, for human habitation—

(a) provision of a fixed bath, shower, wash basin, sink or lavatory, and necessary associated plumbing, including the provision of hot water not connected to a central heating system;

(b) repairs to existing heating systems;

(c) damp proof measures;
(d) provision of ventilation and natural lighting;
(e) provision of drainage facilities;
(f) provision of facilities for preparing and cooking food;
(g) provision of insulation;
(h) provision of electric lighting and sockets;
(i) provision of storage facilities for fuel or refuse;
(j) repairs of unsafe structural defects;
(k) adapting the accommodation for the special needs of a disabled person; or
(l) provision of separate sleeping accommodation for persons of different sexes aged 10 or over but under the age of 20 who live with the claimant and for whom the claimant or the claimant's partner is responsible.

(6) Where a loan is applied only in part for the purposes specified in sub-paragraph (2) or (4), only that portion of the loan which is applied for that purpose shall qualify.

Loans incurred during relevant period

3.—(1) Subject to sub-paragraph (5), loans which, apart from this paragraph, qualify under paragraph 2(2) or (4) shall not so qualify where the loan was incurred during the relevant period. **2.660**

(2) The "relevant period" for the purposes of this paragraph is any period during which the person to whom the loan was made—

(a) is entitled to, or is treated as entitled to, a legacy benefit or state pension credit; or
(b) is living as a member of a family one of whom is entitled to, or is treated as entitled to, a legacy benefit or state pension credit,

together with any period falling between two such periods of entitlement separated by not more than 26 weeks.

(3) For the purposes of sub-paragraph (2), a person shall be treated as entitled to either a legacy benefit or state pension credit during any period when the person, the person's partner, or, where that person is a member of a joint-claim couple, the other member of that couple was not so entitled because—

(a) that person, the person's partner or, where that person is a member of a joint-claim couple, the other member of that couple, was participating in an employment programme specified in regulation 75(1)(a) of the JSA Regulations; and
(b) in consequence of such participation that person, the person's partner, or, where that person is a member of a joint-claim couple, the other member of that couple, was a person engaged in remunerative work and had income equal to or in excess of the applicable amount.

(4) Where a loan which qualifies under paragraph 2(2) was incurred during the relevant period—

(a) for paying off an earlier loan, and that earlier loan qualified under paragraph 2(2) and was incurred during the relevant period; or
(b) to finance the purchase of a property where an earlier loan, which qualified under paragraph 2(2) or (4) and was incurred during the relevant period in respect of another property, is paid off (in whole or in part) with monies received from the sale of that property,

then the amount of the loan to which sub-paragraph (1) applies is the amount (if any) by which the new loan exceeds the earlier loan.

(5) Loans taken out during the relevant period shall qualify as loans under paragraph 2(2) or (4), where a claimant satisfies any of the conditions specified in sub-paragraphs (6), (8) and (9), but—

(a) where the claimant satisfies the condition in sub-paragraph (6), [1 the amount of each loan payment calculated under regulation 10] shall be subject to the additional limitation imposed by sub-paragraph (7); and
(b) where the claimant satisfies the conditions in more than one of these sub-paragraphs, only one sub-paragraph shall apply in the claimant's case, which shall be the one most favourable to the claimant.

(6) The first condition is that—

(a) during the relevant period, the claimant or a member of the claimant's family acquires an interest ("the relevant interest") in the relevant accommodation; and
(b) in the week preceding the week in which the relevant interest was acquired, the claimant or a member of the claimant's family was entitled to housing benefit.

(7) Where the condition in sub-paragraph (6) is satisfied, the amount of the loans which qualify shall initially not exceed the aggregate of—

(a) the housing benefit entitlement referred to in sub-paragraph (6)(b); and
(b) any amount included in the applicable amount of the claimant or a member of the claimant's family [1 relating to housing costs] in that week,
and shall be increased subsequently only to the extent that it is necessary to take account of any increase in the standard rate under regulation 13 arising after the date of acquisition.

(8) The second condition is that the loan was taken out, or an existing loan increased, to acquire alternative accommodation more suited to the needs of a disabled person than the relevant accommodation which was occupied before the acquisition by the claimant.

(9) The third condition is that—
(a) the loan commitment increased in consequence of the disposal of the relevant accommodation and the acquisition of alternative accommodation; and
(b) the change of accommodation was made solely by reason of the need to provide separate sleeping accommodation for persons of different sexes aged 10 or over but under the age of 20 who live with the claimant and for whom the claimant or the claimant's partner is responsible.

PART 2

UC CLAIMANTS

Application of Part 2

2.661 4. This Part applies to UC claimants.

Payments of interest on loans and alternative finance payments

2.662 5.—(1) "Owner-occupier payments" means—
(a) payments of interest on a loan which qualifies under sub-paragraph (2);
(b) alternative finance payments within the meaning of sub-paragraph (3).

(2) A loan qualifies under this sub-paragraph if it is secured on the relevant accommodation.

(3) "Alternative finance payments" means payments that are made under alternative finance arrangements which were entered into to enable a person to acquire an interest in the relevant accommodation.

(4) "Alternative finance arrangements" has the meaning given in Part 10A of the Income Tax Act 2007.

AMENDMENT

1. Loans for Mortgage Interest and Social Fund Maternity Grant (Amendment) Regulations 2018 (SI 2018/307), reg.2(1) and (14) (April 6, 2018).

DEFINITIONS

"alternative finance payments"—reg.2(1) and para. 5(3).
"alternative finance arrangements"—para.5(4).
"applicable amount"—reg.2(1).
"couple"—*ibid.*
"disabled person"—*ibid.*
"entitlement"—reg.2(2)(a).
"family"—reg.2(2)(b).
"income"—reg.2(1).
"joint-claim couple"—*ibid.*
"JSA Regulations"—*ibid.*
"legacy benefit"—*ibid.*
"legacy benefit claimant"—*ibid.*
"owner-occupier payments"—regs 2(1) and 3(2)(a) and paras 2(1) and 5(1).
"partner"—reg.2(1).
"qualifying loan"—*ibid.*
"relevant accommodation"—*ibid.*

"relevant period"—para.3(2).
"repairs and improvements"—para.2(5).
"remunerative work"—reg.2(2)(e).
"SPC claimant"—reg.2(1).
"UC claimant"—*ibid.*

General Note

The phrase, "owner-occupier payments" is defined by reg.2(1) as having "the meaning given in regulation 3(2)(a)" which, in turn, gives effect to this Schedule. 2.663

The rules differ according to whether the claimant is on a "legacy benefit" or SPC, on the one hand, or on universal credit, on the other.

Paragraph 2: For the former group of claimants, owner-occupier payments are interest payments on:

- a loan to acquire an interest in the accommodation occupied, or treated as occupied as the claimant's home (see the definition of "relevant accommodation" in reg.2(1)) (or a loan to refinance such a loan): see para.2(2); or
- a loan to carry out repairs and improvements to the claimant's home, or to pay a service charge to meet the costs of such repairs or improvements (or a loan to refinance such a loan): see para.2(4).

For what counts as a repair or an improvement (para.2(5)), see the commentary to para.16 of Sch.3 to the IS Regulations in Vol.V.

Where a loan is only partly used to acquire an interest in the claimant's home or to carry out repairs and improvements, only that part qualifies for the purpose of para.2(1)(a) with the effect that a loan payment is only available to meet the interest on that part of the loan: see para.2(6).

For SPC claimants only, a payment in respect of "alternative finance arrangements" (see below) is also an owner occupier payment.

Paragraph 3 provides that, subject to the exceptions in sub-para.(5) loans that would otherwise qualify, do not qualify if they are taken out during the "relevant period" as defined in sub-para.(2). If a claimant refinances during the relevant period, then the amount that does not qualify is the amount by which the new loan exceeds the earlier loan: see sub-para.(4).

Paragraph 5: For UC claimants, the loan qualifies if it is secured on the relevant accommodation, irrespective of the purpose for which it was taken out: see sub-para.(1)(a). In addition, a payment in respect of "alternative finance arrangements" is also an owner occupier payment: see sub-para.(1)(b).

Alternative finance payments are defined by sub-para.(3) as payments that are made under "alternative finance arrangements" which were entered into to enable a person to acquire an interest in the relevant accommodation. Under sub-para.(4), "alternative finance arrangements" are defined by reference to Part 10A of the Income Tax Act 2007 and therefore "means ...(a) purchase and resale arrangements, (b) diminishing shared ownership arrangements, (c) deposit arrangements, (d) profit share agency arrangements, and (e) investment bond arrangements" (see section 564A(2) of that Act). All those types of arrangement are further defined by ss 564C–564G, and represent different types of what are known colloquially as an Islamic mortgage in which help from a financial institution to buy real property is structured in ways that do not involve the charging or payment of interest.

Regulation 3(2)(b)

SCHEDULE 2

Circumstances in which a claimant is, or is to be treated as, liable to make owner-occupier payments

PART 1

Legacy benefit claimants and SPC claimants

Application of Part 1

2.664 1. This Part applies to legacy benefit claimants and SPC claimants.

Liable or treated as liable to make payments

2.665 2.—(1) A claimant is liable to make owner-occupier payments where—

(a) in the case of a single claimant, the claimant or the claimant's partner (if any), or, in the case of joint claimants, either member of the couple, has a liability to make the payments;

(2) A claimant is to be treated as liable to make owner-occupier payments where—

(a) all of the following conditions are met—

(i) the person who is liable to make the payments is not doing so;

(ii) the claimant has to make the payments in order to continue occupation of the relevant accommodation; and

(iii) it is reasonable in all the circumstances to treat the claimant as liable to make the payments; or

(b) all of the following conditions are met—

(i) the claimant in practice shares the responsibility for the owner-occupier payments with other members of the household, none of whom are close relatives of, in the case of a single claimant, the claimant or the claimant's partner (if any), or, in the case of joint claimants, either member of the couple;

(ii) one or more of those members is liable to meet those payments; and

(iii) it is reasonable in all the circumstances to treat that member as sharing responsibility.

(3) Where any one or more, but not all, members of the claimant's family are affected by a trade dispute, the owner-occupier payments shall be treated as wholly the responsibility of those members of the family not so affected.

(4) For the purposes of sub-paragraph (2), "trade dispute" has the meaning given in section 244 of the Trade Union and Labour Relations (Consolidation) Act 1992.

Treated as not liable to make payments

2.666 3. A claimant is to be treated as not liable to make owner-occupier payments where the liability to make the payments is owed to a person who is a member of the claimant's household.

PART 2

UC claimants

Application of Part 2

2.667 4. This Part applies to UC claimants.

Liable or treated as liable to make payments

2.668 5.—(1) A claimant is liable to make owner-occupier payments where—

(a) in the case of a single claimant, the claimant or the claimant's partner (if any), or, in the case of joint claimants, either member of the couple, has a liability to make the payments;

(2) A claimant is to be treated as liable to make owner-occupier payments where—

(a) the person who is liable to make the payments is a child or qualifying young person for whom the claimant is responsible;

(b) all of the following conditions are met—

(i) the person who is liable to make the payments is not doing so;

(ii) the claimant has to make the payments in order to continue occupation of the relevant accommodation;

(iii) the claimant's circumstances are such that it would be unreasonable to expect them to make other arrangements; and
(iv) it is otherwise reasonable in all the circumstances to treat the claimant as liable to make the payments; or
(c) the claimant—
(i) has a liability to make the payments which is waived by the person ("P") to whom the liability is owed; and
(ii) the waiver of that liability is by way of reasonable compensation for reasonable repair or re-decoration works carried out by the claimant to the relevant accommodation which P would otherwise have carried out or been required to carry out.

(3) [1 Sub-paragraph (1)] does not apply to a person in a polygamous marriage who is a single claimant by virtue of regulation 3(4) of the UC Regulations.

Treated as not liable to make payments

6. A claimant is to be treated as not liable to make owner-occupier payments— **2.669**
(a) where the liability to make the payments is owed to a person who is a member of the claimant's household;
(b) in respect of any amount which represents an increase in the sum that would otherwise be payable and is the result of—
(i) outstanding arrears of any payment or charge in respect of the relevant accommodation;
(ii) outstanding arrears of any payment or charge in respect of other accommodation previously occupied by the claimant; or
(iii) any other unpaid liability to make a payment or charge; or
(c) where the Secretary of State is satisfied that the liability to make the owner-occupier payments was contrived in order to secure the offer of loan payments or increase the amount of each loan payment.

AMENDMENT

1. Loans for Mortgage Interest and Social Fund Maternity Grant (Amendment) Regulations 2018 (SI 2018/307), reg.2(1) and (15) (April 6, 2018).

DEFINITIONS

"child"—reg.2(1).
"couple"—*ibid.*
"family"—reg.2(2)(b).
"joint claimants"—reg.2(1).
"legacy benefit claimant"—*ibid.*
"loan payments"—*ibid.*
"owner-occupier payments"—regs 2(1) and 3(2)(a).
"member of a household"—reg.2(2)(b).
"partner"—reg.2(1).
"polygamous marriage"—*ibid.*
"qualifying young person"—*ibid.*
"relevant accommodation"—*ibid.*
"single claimant"—*ibid.*
"SPC claimant"—*ibid.*
"trade dispute"—para.2(4).
"UC claimant"—*ibid.*
"UC Regulations"—*ibid.*

GENERAL NOTE

See the commentary to Sch.2 to the UC Regulations, which is to similar effect, except that the grounds on which a claimant is treated as not liable to make owner-occupier payments are more restricted under this Schedule. **2.670**

The fact that sub-para.2(1) has a single head (a) with no head (b) or (c) etc. is not an editorial error.

Regulation 3(2)(c)

SCHEDULE 3

Circumstances in which a claimant is, or is to be, treated as occupying accommodation

PART 1

General

Interpretation

2.671 1.—(1) In this Schedule—

"Abbeyfield Home" means an establishment run by the Abbeyfield Society including all bodies corporate or incorporate which are affiliated to that Society;

"care home"—

(a) in England and Wales, has the meaning given in section 3 of the Care Standards Act 2000;

(b) in Scotland, means a care home service within the meaning of paragraph 2 of Schedule 12 to the Public Services Reform (Scotland) Act 2010,

and in either case includes an independent hospital;

"croft" means a croft within the meaning of section 3(1) of the Crofters (Scotland) Act 1993;

"full-time student" has the meaning given—

(a) in the case of income support, in regulation 61(1) of the IS Regulations;

(b) in the case of jobseeker's allowance, in regulation 1(3) of the JSA Regulations;

(c) in the case of employment and support allowance, in regulation 131 of the ESA Regulations;

(d) in the case of state pension credit, in regulation 1(2) of the SPC Regulations;

"independent hospital"—

(a) in England, means a hospital as defined in section 275 of the National Health Service Act 2006 that is not a health service hospital as defined by that section;

(b) in Wales, has the meaning given in section 2 of the Care Standards Act 2000;

(c) in Scotland means an independent healthcare service as defined in section 10F(1)(a) and (b) of the National Health Service (Scotland) Act 1978;

"medically approved" means certified by a medical practitioner;

"patient" means a person who is undergoing medical or other treatment as an inpatient in a hospital or similar institution;

"period of study" has the meaning given—

(a) in the case of income support and state pension credit, in regulation 2(1) of the IS Regulations;

(b) in the case of jobseeker's allowance, in regulation 1(3) of the JSA Regulations;

(c) in the case of employment and support allowance, in regulation 2 of the ESA Regulations;

"residential accommodation" means accommodation which is a care home, Abbeyfield Home or independent hospital;

"training course" means a course of training or instruction provided wholly or partly by or on behalf of or in pursuance of arrangements made with, or approved by or on behalf of, Skills Development Scotland, Scottish Enterprise, Highlands and Islands Enterprise, a government department or the Secretary of State.

(2) In this Schedule, a reference to a claimant being liable to make owner-occupier payments is to be read as a reference to a person being treated as liable to make owner-occupier payments under Schedule 2.

PART 2

Legacy benefit claimants and SPC claimants

Application of Part 2

2.672 2. This Part applies to legacy benefit claimants and SPC claimants.

Occupying accommodation: general rule

2.673 3.—(1) Subject to the following paragraphs of this Part, the accommodation which the claimant occupies as the claimant's home or, if the claimant is a member of a family, the claimant and the claimant's family occupy as their home, is the accommodation which is normally occupied as the home.

(2) In determining whether accommodation is the accommodation normally occupied as the home for the purposes of sub-paragraph (1), regard shall be had to any other dwelling occupied by the claimant or, if the claimant is a member of a family, by the claimant and the claimant's family, whether or not that other dwelling is in Great Britain.

Full-time study

4.—(1) Subject to sub-paragraph (2), where a claimant is a full-time student or on a training course and is liable to make owner-occupier payments in respect of either (but not both)— 2.674

(a) the accommodation which the claimant occupies for the purpose of attending the course of study or training course; or

(b) the accommodation which the claimant occupies when not attending the course of study or training course,

the claimant shall be treated as occupying as the claimant's home the accommodation in respect of which the claimant is liable to make the owner-occupier payments.

(2) A claimant who is a full-time student shall not be treated as occupying accommodation as the claimant's home for any week of absence from it outside the period of study, other than an absence occasioned by the need to enter hospital for treatment.

Living in other accommodation during essential repairs

5. Where the claimant— 2.675

(a) has been required to move into temporary accommodation by reason of essential repairs being carried out to the accommodation which the claimant occupies as the claimant's home ("the home accommodation"); and

(b) is liable to make owner-occupier payments in respect of either (but not both) the home accommodation or the temporary accommodation,

the claimant shall be treated as occupying as the claimant's home the accommodation in respect of which the claimant is liable to make those payments.

Living in other accommodation due to fear of violence, where a claimant's partner is a full-time student or where moving into new accommodation

6. Where a claimant is liable to make owner-occupier payments in respect of two dwellings, the claimant shall be treated as occupying both dwellings as the claimant's home— 2.676

(a) where—

(i) the claimant has left and remains absent from the accommodation which the claimant occupies as the claimant's home ("the home accommodation") through fear of violence in the home or of violence by a close relative or former partner; and

(ii) it is reasonable that owner-occupier payments should be met in respect of both the claimant's home accommodation and the claimant's present accommodation which the claimant occupies as the home;

(b) in the case of a couple or a member of a polygamous marriage, where—

(i) one partner is a full-time student or is on a training course and it is unavoidable that the members of the couple or polygamous marriage should occupy two separate dwellings; and

(ii) it is reasonable that owner-occupier payments should be met in respect of both dwellings; or

(c) where—

(i) the claimant has moved into new accommodation occupied as the claimant's home, except where paragraph 5 applies, for a period not exceeding four benefit weeks from the first day of the benefit week in which the move occurs; and

(ii) the claimant's liability to make owner-occupier payments in respect of both the new accommodation and the accommodation from which the move was made is unavoidable.

Moving in delayed for certain reasons

7.—(1) Where— 2.677

(a) a claimant was delayed in moving into accommodation ("the new accommodation") and was liable to make owner-occupier payments in respect of that accommodation before moving in; and

(b) the delay was reasonable and one of the conditions in sub-paragraphs (2) to (4) applies,

the claimant shall be treated as occupying the new accommodation as the claimant's home for the period of delay, not exceeding four weeks immediately prior to the date on which the claimant moved into the new accommodation.

(2) The first condition is that the delay occurred in order to adapt the accommodation to meet the needs of the claimant or a member of the claimant's family who is a disabled person.

(3) The second condition is that—

(a) the move was delayed pending local welfare provision to meet a need arising out of the move or in connection with setting up the claimant's home in the new accommodation; and

(b) in the case of a legacy benefit claimant only—

(i) a member of the claimant's family is aged 5 or under;

(ii) the claimant's applicable amount includes a pensioner premium or disability premium under Schedule 2 to the IS Regulations, Schedule 1 to the JSA Regulations or Schedule 4 to the ESA Regulations; or

(iii) a child tax credit is paid for a member of the claimant's family who is disabled or severely disabled for the purposes of section 9(6) of the Tax Credits Act 2002;

(4) The third condition is that the claimant became liable to make owner-occupier payments in respect of the accommodation while the claimant was a patient or was in a residential home.

Temporary absence to try new accommodation of up to 13 weeks

2.678 8.—(1) This sub-paragraph applies to a claimant who enters residential accommodation—

(a) for the purpose of ascertaining whether the accommodation suits the claimant's needs; and

(b) with the intention of returning to the accommodation which the claimant occupies as the claimant's home ("the home accommodation") in the event that the residential accommodation proves not to suit the claimant's needs,

and while in the residential accommodation, the home accommodation is not let or sub-let to another person.

(2) A claimant to whom sub-paragraph (1) applies shall be treated as occupying the home accommodation during the period of absence, not exceeding 13 weeks in which the claimant is resident in the residential accommodation, but only where the total absence from the home accommodation does not exceed 52 consecutive weeks.

Temporary absence of up to 13 weeks

2.679 9. A claimant, except where paragraph 10 applies, shall be treated as occupying accommodation as the claimant's home throughout any period of absence not exceeding 13 weeks, where—

(a) the claimant intends to return to occupy the accommodation as the claimant's home;

(b) the part of the accommodation occupied by the claimant has not been let or sub-let to another person; and

(c)the period of absence is unlikely to exceed 13 weeks.

Absences for certain reasons up to 52 weeks

2.680 10.—(1) Where sub-paragraph (2) applies, a claimant is to be treated as occupying accommodation as the claimant's home ("the home accommodation") during any period of absence from it not exceeding 52 weeks beginning with the first day of that absence.

(2) This paragraph applies where a claimant's absence from the home accommodation is temporary and—

(a) the claimant intends to return to occupy the home accommodation;

(b) the home accommodation has not been let or sub-let;

(c) the claimant is—

(i) detained in custody on remand pending trial or, as a condition of bail, required to reside—

(aa) in a dwelling, other than the home accommodation; or

(bb) in premises approved under section 13 of the Offender Management Act 2007;

(ii) detained pending sentence upon conviction;

(iii) resident in a hospital or similar institution as a patient;

(iv) undergoing or, the claimant's partner or child, or in the case of an SPC claimant, a person who has not attained the age of 20, is undergoing medical treatment, or medically approved convalescence, in accommodation other than residential accommodation;

(v) undertaking a training course;

(vi) undertaking medically approved care of another person;

(vii) undertaking the care of a child or, in the case of an SPC claimant, a person under the age of 20 whose parent or guardian is temporarily absent from the dwelling occupied by that parent or guardian for the purpose of receiving medically approved care or medical treatment;

(viii) a person who is receiving medically approved care provided in accommodation other than a residential home;

(ix) a full-time student to whom paragraph 4(1) or 6(b) does not apply;

(x) a person, other than a person to whom paragraph 8(1) applies, who is receiving care provided in residential accommodation; or

(xi) a person to whom paragraph 6(a) does not apply and who has left the home accommodation through fear of violence in that accommodation, or by a person who was formerly his or her partner or is a close relative; and

(d) the period of the claimant's absence is unlikely to exceed 52 weeks or, in exceptional circumstances, is unlikely substantially to exceed that period.

PART 3

UC CLAIMANTS

Application of Part 3

11. This Part applies to UC claimants. **2.681**

Occupying accommodation: general rule

12.—(1) Subject to the following paragraphs of this Part, the accommodation which the claimant occupies as the claimant's home is the accommodation which the claimant normally occupies the home. **2.682**

(2) Where the claimant occupies more than one dwelling, in determining whether accommodation is the accommodation normally occupied as the home for the purposes of sub-paragraph (1), regard is to be had to all the circumstances including (among other things) any persons with whom the claimant occupies each dwelling.

(3) Where accommodation which a claimant occupies as the claimant's home is situated on or pertains to a croft, croft land used for the purposes of the accommodation is to be treated as included in the accommodation.

Living in other accommodation due to essential repairs

13.—(1) Where a claimant— **2.683**

(a) is required to move into accommodation ("the other accommodation") on account of essential repairs being carried out to the accommodation the claimant occupies as the claimant's home ("the home accommodation");

(b) intends to return to the home accommodation; and

(c) is liable to make owner-occupier payments in respect of either the other accommodation or the home accommodation (but not both),

the claimant is to be treated as occupying as the claimant's home the accommodation in respect of which the owner-occupier payments are made.

Moving homes: adaptations to new home for disabled person

14.—(1) Sub-paragraph (2) applies where— **2.684**

(a) a claimant has moved into accommodation ("the new accommodation") and, immediately before the move, was liable to make owner-occupier payments in respect of the new accommodation; and

(b) there was a delay in moving in to adapt the new accommodation in order to meet the needs of a disabled person.

(2) The claimant is to be treated as occupying both the new accommodation and the accommodation from which the move was made ("the old accommodation") if—

(a) immediately before the move, the claimant was receiving loan payments or, in the case of an existing claimant, a qualifying benefit which includes an amount for owner-occupier payments, in respect of the old accommodation; and

(b) the delay in moving into the new accommodation was reasonable.

(3) A person is disabled under this Part if the person is—

(a) a claimant or any child or qualifying young person for whom the claimant is responsible; and

(b) in receipt of—

(i) the care component of disability living allowance at the middle or highest rate;

(ii) attendance allowance; or

(iii) the daily living component of personal independence payment.

(4) No claimant may be treated as occupying both the old accommodation and the new accommodation under this paragraph for more than one month.

Living in other accommodation due to fear of violence

2.685 15.—[2 Sub-paragraphs (2) and (3) apply] where—

(a) a claimant is occupying accommodation ("the other accommodation") other than the accommodation which the claimant occupies as the claimant's home ("the home accommodation");

(b) it is unreasonable to expect the claimant to return to the home accommodation on account of the claimant's reasonable fear of violence in the home, or by a former partner, against the claimant or any child or qualifying young person for whom the claimant is responsible; and

(c) the claimant intends to return to the home accommodation.

(2) The claimant is to be treated as occupying both the home accommodation and the other accommodation as the claimant's home if—

(a) the claimant is liable to make payments in respect of both the other accommodation and the home accommodation; and

(b) it is reasonable to make loan payments in respect of both the home accommodation and the other accommodation.

(3) Where the claimant is liable to make [2 owner-occupier] payments in respect of one accommodation only, the claimant is to be treated as occupying that accommodation as the claimant's home but only if it is reasonable to make loan payments in respect of that accommodation.

(4) No claimant may be treated as occupying both the home accommodation and the other accommodation under this paragraph for more than 12 months.

Moving in delayed by adaptations to accommodation to meet needs of disabled person

2.686 16.—(1) The claimant is to be treated as having occupied accommodation before the claimant moved into it where—

(a) the claimant has since moved in and, immediately before the move, the claimant is liable to make payments in respect of that accommodation;

(b) there was a delay in moving in that was necessary to enable the accommodation to be adapted to meet the needs of a disabled person; and

(c) it was reasonable to delay moving in.

(2) No claimant may be treated as occupying accommodation under this paragraph for more than one month.

Moving into accommodation following a stay in hospital or care home

2.687 17.—(1) The claimant is to be treated as having occupied accommodation before he or she moved into it where—

(a) the claimant has since moved in and, immediately before the move, the claimant was liable to make payments in respect of that accommodation; and

(b) the liability to make the payments arose while the claimant was a patient or accommodated in a care home (or, in the case of joint claimants, where both individuals were patients or were accommodated in a care home).

(2) No claimant may be treated as occupying the accommodation under this paragraph for more than one month.

Temporary absence exceeding 6 months

2.688 18.—(1) Subject to sub-paragraph (2), a claimant is to be treated as no longer occupying accommodation from which the claimant is temporarily absent where the absence exceeds, or is expected to exceed, 6 months.

(2) Where a claimant who falls within [1 paragraph 15] is temporarily absent from the relevant accommodation, the claimant is to be treated as no longer occupying that accommodation where the absence exceeds, or is expected to exceed, 12 months.

AMENDMENTS

1. Loans for Mortgage Interest and Social Fund Maternity Grant (Amendment) Regulations 2018 (SI 2018/307), reg.2(1) and (16) (April 6, 2018).

2. Loans for Mortgage Interest (Amendment) Regulations 2021 (SI 2021/131) reg.2(1) and (6) (March 15, 2021).

DEFINITIONS

"applicable amount"—reg.2(1).
"benefit week"—*ibid.*
"care home"—para.1(1).
"child"—reg.2(1).
"close relative"—*ibid.*
"couple"—*ibid.*
"croft"—para.1(1).
"disabled person"—reg.2(1).
"dwelling"—*ibid.*
"ESA Regulations"—*ibid.*
"existing claimant"—*ibid.*
"family"—reg.2(2)(b).
"full-time student"—para.1(1).
"IS Regulations"—reg.2(1).
"joint claimants"—*ibid.*
"JSA Regulations"—*ibid.*
"legacy benefit claimant"—*ibid.*
"loan payments"—*ibid.*
"medically approved"—para.1(1).
"owner-occupier payments"—regs 2(1) and 3(2)(a).
"partner"—reg.2(1).
"patient"—para.1(1).
"period of study"—*ibid.*
"polygamous marriage"—reg.2(1).
"qualifying benefit"—*ibid.*
"qualifying young person"—*ibid.*
"relevant accommodation"—*ibid.*
"residential accommodation"—para.1(1).
"SPC claimant"—reg.2(1).
"SPC Regulations"—*ibid.*
"training course"—para.1(1).
"UC claimant"—reg.2(1).

GENERAL NOTE

See the commentary to Sch.3 to the UC Regulations (above), which is to similar effect. **2.689**

Regulation 17

SCHEDULE 4

Direct payments to qualifying lenders

Direct payments

1. Each loan payment made to a qualifying lender directly under regulation 17(1) shall be the amount calculated under paragraph 2 [1 ...] of this Schedule. **2.690**

[1 Determining the amount to be paid to a qualifying lender: one or more qualifying loans

2.—(1) Where one qualifying loan or alternative finance arrangement has been provided to a claimant by a qualifying lender, the amount that is to be paid direct to that lender is the amount of each loan payment. **2.691**

(2) Where more than one qualifying loan or alternative finance arrangement has been provided to a claimant by a qualifying lender, the amount that is to be paid direct to that lender is the amount of each loan payment in respect of each of those loans or alternative finance arrangements added together.]

Determining the amount to be paid to a qualifying lender: more than one qualifying loan

2.692 3. [1 ...]

Qualifying lenders to apply direct payments to discharge of claimant's liability

2.693 4. Where a direct payment is made under regulation 17(1) to a qualifying lender, the lender must apply the amount of the payment determined under either paragraph 2 or 3 of this Schedule towards discharging the claimant's liability to make owner-occupier payments in respect of which the direct payment was made.

Application by qualifying lenders of any amount which exceeds liability

2.694 5.—(1) Where—

(a) a direct payment is made to a qualifying lender under regulation 17(1); and
(b) the amount paid exceeds the claimant's liability to make owner-occupier payments to the qualifying lender,

the qualifying lender must apply the amount of excess in accordance with sub-paragraph (2).

(2) Subject to sub-paragraph (3), the qualifying lender must apply the amount of excess as follows—

(a) first, towards discharging the amount of any liability of the claimant for arrears of owner-occupier payments in respect of the qualifying loan or alternative finance arrangement in question;
(b) if any amount of the excess is then remaining, towards discharging any liability of the claimant to repay—
 (i) the principal sum in respect of the qualifying loan or alternative finance arrangement; or
 (ii) any other sum payable by the claimant to that lender in respect of that qualifying loan or alternative finance arrangement.

(3) Where owner-occupier payments on two or more qualifying loans or alternative finance arrangements are payable to the same qualifying lender, the lender must apply the amount of the excess as follows—

[1 (a) first, towards discharging the amount of any liability of the claimant for arrears of owner-occupier payments in respect of the qualifying loan or alternative finance arrangement in respect of which the excess amount was paid;
(b) if any amount of the excess is then remaining, towards discharging any liability of the claimant to repay—
 (i) in respect of the loan or alternative finance arrangement referred to in paragraph (a), the principal sum or any other sum payable by the claimant to that lender; or
 (ii) in respect of any other loan or alternative finance arrangement, any sum payable by the claimant to that lender where the liability to pay that sum is not already discharged.]

Fees payable by qualifying lenders

2.695 6.—[2 ...]

Election not to be regarded as a qualifying lender

2.696 7.—(1) A body or person who would otherwise be within the definition of "qualifying lender" in the Act—

(a) may elect not to be regarded as such for the purposes of these Regulations by giving notice to the Secretary of State in writing; and
(b) may revoke any such notice by giving a further notice in writing.

(2) In respect of any financial year, a notice under sub-paragraph (1) which is given not later than 1st February before the start of the financial year, takes effect on 1st April following the giving of the notice.

(3) Where a body or person becomes a qualifying lender in the course of a financial year—

(a) any notice of an election by the body or person under sub-paragraph (1)(a) must be given within 6 weeks ("the initial period") beginning with the date on which the body or person becomes a qualifying lender; and
(b) no direct payments may be made under regulation 17(1) to the body or person before the expiry of the initial period.

(4) Sub-paragraph (3)(b) does not apply in any case where—

(a) the person or body gives the Secretary of State notice in writing that that provision should not apply; and

(b) the notice is given before the start of the initial period or before that period expires.

(5) In relation to a notice under sub-paragraph (1)—

(a) where the notice is given by an electronic communication, it must be given in accordance with Schedule 2 of the Universal Credit, Personal Independence Payment, Jobseeker's Allowance and Employment and Support Allowance (Claims and Payments) Regulations 2013;

(b) where the notice is sent by post, it is to be treated as having been given on the day the notice was received.

Provision of information

8.—(1) A qualifying lender must, in respect of the claimant, provide the Secretary of State with information as to— **2.697**

(a) the owner-occupier payments payable by the claimant to the lender;

(b) the amount of the qualifying loan or alternative finance arrangement in respect of which owner-occupier payments are payable;

(c) the purpose for which the qualifying loan or alternative finance arrangement was made;

(d) the amount outstanding on the qualifying loan or alternative finance arrangement;

(e) the amount of arrears of owner-occupier payments due in respect of the qualifying loan or alternative finance payment;

(f) any change in the owner-occupier payments payable by the claimant to the lender; and

(g) the redemption of the qualifying loan or alternative finance arrangement, in the circumstances specified in paragraphs (2), (3) and (6).

(2) The information referred to in paragraph (1)(a) to (e) must be provided at the request of the Secretary of State where the claimant has made a claim for a qualifying benefit, provided that the Secretary of State may only make one request under this paragraph.

(3) The information referred to in paragraph (1)(d) and (f) must be provided where the Secretary of State makes a request for that information on or after the first day in respect of which loan payments are paid, or to be paid, to the qualifying lender on behalf of the claimant ("the first day"), provided that the Secretary of State may only make a request under this paragraph once in each period of 12 months referred to in paragraph (4).

(4) The period of 12 months is the period of 12 months beginning with the first day and each subsequent period of 12 months commencing on the anniversary of that day.

(5) A request may be made under paragraph (3) for the information referred to in paragraph (1)(d) even though that information has been requested in the same 12 month period (as referred to in paragraph (4)) under paragraph (2).

(6) The information referred to in sub-paragraph (1)(g) must be provided to the Secretary of State as soon as reasonably practicable once the qualifying lender has received notice that the qualifying loan or alternative finance arrangement is to be redeemed.

Recovery of sum wrongly paid

9.—(1) In the following circumstances, a qualifying lender must at the request of the Secretary of State repay any amount paid to the lender under regulation 17(1) which ought not to have been paid. **2.698**

(2) The circumstances are that, in respect of a claimant—

(a) the loan payments are terminated under regulation 9(2);

(b) the qualifying loan or alternative finance arrangement in respect of which owner-occupier payments are made has been redeemed; or

(c) both of the conditions in sub-paragraphs (3) and (4) are met.

(3) The first condition is that the amount of each loan payment determined under regulation 10 is reduced as a result of—

(a) the standard rate determined under regulation 13 having been reduced; or

(b) the amount outstanding on the qualifying loan or alternative finance arrangement having been reduced.

(4) The second condition is that no corresponding reduction was made to the amount calculated in respect of the qualifying lender under paragraph 2 or 3 of this Schedule.

(5) A qualifying lender is not required to make a repayment in the circumstances described in sub-paragraph (2)(a) unless the Secretary of State's request is made before the end of the period of two months starting with the date on which the loan payments are terminated.

AMENDMENTS

1. Loans for Mortgage Interest and Social Fund Maternity Grant (Amendment) Regulations 2018 (SI 2018/307), reg.2(1) and (17) (April 6, 2018).
2. Loans for Mortgage Interest (Transaction Fee) (Amendment) Regulations 2020 (SI 2020/666), reg.2 (August 2, 2020).

DEFINITIONS

"the Act"—reg.2(1)
"alternative finance payments"—reg.2(1).
"financial year"—*ibid.*
"loan payments"—*ibid.*
"owner-occupier payments"—regs 2(1) and 3(2)(a).
"qualifying benefit"—reg.2(1).
"qualifying lender"—*ibid.*
"qualifying loan"—*ibid.*

Regulation 18

SCHEDULE 5

CONSEQUENTIAL AMENDMENTS

2.699 *[Omitted]*

2.700 GENERAL NOTE

The consequential amendments made by Sch.5 have been incorporated at the appropriate places in the text of the amended regulations.

The Universal Credit (Managed Migration Pilot and Miscellaneous Amendments) Regulations 2019

(SI 2019/1152)

Made by the Secretary of State for Work and Pensions under the powers conferred by sections 4(2) and 42(1), (2) and (3) of, and paragraph 4(1), (3)(a) and (4) of Schedule 1 to, and paragraph 1(1), 3(1)(a), 4(1), (2)(a), (c) and (d) and (3) and 6(a) of Schedule 6 to, the Welfare Reform Act 2012.

In accordance with section 173(1)(b) of the Social Security Administration Act 1992 the Social Security Advisory Committee has agreed that the proposals in respect of regulations 2 and 7, and certain proposals in respect of regulation 3(8), should not be referred to it. In accordance with section 172(1) of that Act, the Secretary of State has referred all other proposals in respect of these Regulations to the Social Security Advisory Committee.

In accordance with section 176(1) of the 1992 Act, in so far as these Regulations relate to housing benefit, the Secretary of State has consulted with organisations appearing to her to be representative of the authorities concerned in respect of the proposals for these Regulations.

ARRANGEMENT OF REGULATIONS

Citation and commencement

1.—(1) These Regulations may be cited as the Universal Credit (Managed Migration Pilot and Miscellaneous Amendments) Regulations 2019. 2.701

(2) Regulations 2 and 3 and this regulation come into force on 24th July 2019.

(3) Regulations 4 and 5 come into force on 22nd July 2020.

(4) Regulation 6 comes into force on 23rd September 2020.

(5) Regulation 7 comes into force on 27th January 2021.

Managed migration pilot: limit on number of cases migrated

2. [1 ...] 2.702

AMENDMENT

1. Universal Credit (Transitional Provisions) Amendment Regulations 2022 (SI 2022/752) reg.10 (July 25, 2022).

Amendment of the Universal Credit (Transitional Provisions) Regulations 2014: managed migration (including provision for persons previously entitled to a severe disability premium)

3.—(1) The Universal Credit (Transitional Provisions) Regulations 2014 are amended as follows. 2.703

(2)–(8) *(Amendments incorporated into the text of the Transitional Provisions Regulations in Part IIB of this volume)*

Two week run-on of income support, income-based jobseeker's allowance and income-related employment and support allowance: amendment of the Universal Credit (Transitional Provisions) Regulations 2014

4.—(1) The Universal Credit (Transitional Provisions) Regulations 2014 are amended as follows. 2.704

(2)–(7) *(Amendments incorporated into the Transitional Provisions Regulations in Part IIB of this volume)*

2.705 Two week run-on of income-based jobseeker's allowance and income-related employment and support allowance: day appointed for abolition

5.—(1) Subject to paragraph (2) where, in relation to any relevant claim for universal credit, an article ("the specified article") of any Order made under the powers in section 150(3) of the Welfare Reform Act 2012 provides for the coming into force of the amending provisions, the provision in that article for the day appointed is to be read as though the day appointed was the last day of the period of two weeks beginning with the day [1 after the day] mentioned in that provision.

(2) For the purposes of paragraphs (6) and (7) of article 4 of the No.9 Order (conversion to employment and support allowance of awards of incapacity benefit and severe disablement allowance), including as they apply for the purposes of any other Order made under section 150(3) of the Welfare Reform Act 2012, the day appointed by the specified article for the coming into force of the amending provisions shall be treated as though it was the day that applies apart from this regulation.

(3) In this regulation—

"amending provisions" has the meaning given by article 2(1) of the No.9 Order;

"the No.9 Order" means the Welfare Reform Act 2012 (Commencement No.9 and Transitional and Transitory Provision and Commencement No.8 and Savings and Transitional Provisions (Amendment) Order 2013;

"relevant claim for universal credit" means a claim for universal credit made on or after 22nd July 2020 including a claim where, under the article in question, the amending provisions come into force despite incorrect information having been given by the claimant, but excluding any claim that is treated as made by a couple in the circumstances referred to in regulation 9(8) (claims for universal credit by members of a couple) of the Universal Credit, Personal Independence Payment, Jobseeker's Allowance and Employment and Support Allowance (Claims and Payments) Regulations 2013.

AMENDMENT

1. Universal Credit (Managed Migration Pilot and Miscellaneous Amendments) (Amendment) Regulations 2020 (SI 2020/826) reg.2(2) (August 4, 2020).

12 month exemption from the minimum income floor for new claimants

2.706 **6.**—(1) *(Amendment incorporated into the text of the UC Regulations)*

(2) *(Amendment incorporated into the text of the Transitional Provisions Regulations in Part IIB)*

Abolition of restriction on claims by persons entitled to a severe disability premium

2.707 **7.** *(Amendment incorporated into the text of the Transitional Provisions Regulations)*

The Jobseeker's Allowance and Universal Credit (Higher-Level Sanctions) (Amendment) Regulations 2019

(SI 2019/1357)

Made by the Secretary of State for Work and Pensions under the powers conferred by sections 6J(5)(b) and (6), 19(4)(b) and (5), 35(1) and 36(4)(a) of the Jobseekers Act 1995 and sections 26(6)(b) and (7) and 42(1) and (3)(a) of the Welfare Reform Act 2012, the Social Security Advisory Committee having agreed that the proposals in respect of these Regulations should not be referred to it.

ARRANGEMENT OF REGULATIONS

Citation and commencement

1. These Regulations may be cited as the Jobseeker's Allowance and Universal Credit (Higher-Level Sanctions) (Amendment) Regulations 2019 and come into force on 27th November 2019. **2.708**

Amendment of the Jobseeker's Allowance Regulations 1996

2. (*Amendment incorporated into the text of the JSA Regulations 1996 in Part III of Vol. V of this series*) **2.709**

Amendment of the Universal Credit Regulations 2013

3. (*Amendment incorporated into the text of the Universal Credit Regulations 2013*) **2.710**

Amendment of the Jobseeker's Allowance Regulations 2013

4. (*Amendment incorporated into the text of the JSA Regulations 2013 in Part VII of Vol.I of this series*) **2.711**

Transitional provision

5.—(1) Where, on the date that these Regulations come into force, the amount of an award of jobseeker's allowance is subject to a reduction under section 19 of the Jobseekers Act 1995 for a period of 156 weeks, the reduction is to be terminated where, since the date that the reduction took effect, the award has been reduced for a period of at least 26 weeks. **2.712**

(2) Where, on the date that these Regulations come into force, the amount of an award of jobseeker's allowance is subject to a reduction under section 6J of the Jobseekers Act 1995 for a period of 1095 days, the reduction is to be terminated where, since the date that the reduction took effect, the award has been reduced for a period of at least 182 days.

(3) Where, on the date that these Regulations come into force, the amount of an award of universal credit is subject to a reduction under section 26 of the Welfare Reform Act 2012, or which is treated as a reduction under section 26 of that Act by virtue of regulation 32(3) of the Universal Credit (Transitional Provisions) Regulations 2014(**c**), for a period of 1095 days, the reduction is to be terminated where, since the date that the reduction took effect, the award has been reduced for a period of at least 182 days.

The Victims' Payments Regulations 2020

(SI 2020/103)

[In force: February 24, 2020 and May 29, 2020]

The Secretary of State, Northern Ireland Office, makes these Regulations in exercise of the powers conferred by sections 10 and 11 of the Northern Ireland (Executive Formation etc) Act 2019.

The Secretary of State has had regard to advice given by the Commission for Victims and Survivors for Northern Ireland in accordance with section 10(10) of that Act.

PART 1

PRELIMINARY

Citation and commencement and extent

2.713 **1.**—(1) These Regulations may be cited as the Victims' Payments Regulations 2020.

(2) The following provisions come into force on the 24th February 2020—

(a) regulation 1;
(b) regulation 3;
(c) Schedule 1;
(d) paragraph 4(1) of Schedule 2, and regulation 15(8) so far as it relates to that paragraph;
(e) paragraphs 1, 4 and 5 of Schedule 3, and regulation 53 so far as it relates to that paragraph.

(3) The remaining provisions of these Regulations come into force on 29th May 2020.

(4) Except as provided by paragraphs (5) to (7), these Regulations extend to Northern Ireland only.

(5) Regulations 1, 2, 26, 28, 29 and 31 extend to England and Wales, Scotland and Northern Ireland.

(6) The amendments made by paragraph 2 of Schedule 3 extend to England and Wales only.

(7) Any other amendment made by these Regulations has the same extent as the provision it amends.

Disregard of payments and lump sums for certain purposes

26.—(1) A payment of victims' payments or a lump sum is to be disregarded— 2.714

(a) from the calculation of a person's income or capital when determining entitlement to a relevant social security benefit;

(b) for the purposes of an assessment of a person's ability to pay under regulations made under Article 36(6) or 99(5) (cost of providing residential accommodation) of the Health and Personal Social Services (Northern Ireland) Order 1972;

(c) for the purposes of determining whether a person should repay (either fully or in part) an award of criminal injuries compensation where the application for that award was determined before these Regulations come into force.

(2) In paragraph (1)—

"criminal injuries compensation" means compensation under a scheme established under the Criminal Injuries Compensation Act 1995 or the Criminal Injuries Compensation (Northern Ireland) Order 2002;

"relevant social security benefit" means any of the following—

(a) employment and support allowance under—
   (i) Part 1 of the Welfare Reform Act 2007 as it has effect apart from the amendments made by Schedule 3, and Part 1 of Schedule 14, to the Welfare Reform Act 2012 (to remove references to an income-related allowance);
   (ii) Part 1 of the Welfare Reform Act (Northern Ireland) 2007 as it has effect apart from the amendments made by Schedule 3, and Part 5 of Schedule 12, to the Welfare Reform Order (Northern Ireland) 2015 (to remove references to an income related allowance);

(b) housing benefit under—
   (i) Part 7 of the Social Security Contributions and Benefits Act 1992, or
   (ii) Part 7 of the Social Security Contributions and Benefits (Northern Ireland) Act 1992;

(c) income support under—
   (i) Part 7 of the Social Security Contributions and Benefits Act 1992, or
   (ii) Part 7 of the Social Security Contributions and Benefits (Northern Ireland) Act 1992;

(d) jobseeker's allowance under—
   (i) the Jobseekers Act 1995 as it has effect apart from the amendments made by Part 1 of Schedule 14 to the Welfare Reform Act 2012 (to remove references to an income-based allowance);
   (ii) the Jobseekers (Northern Ireland) Order 1995 as it has effect apart from the amendments made by Part 1 of Schedule 12 to the Welfare Reform Order (Northern Ireland) 2015 (to remove references to an income-based allowance);

(e) state pension credit under—
   (i) section 1 of the State Pension Credit Act 2002, or
   (ii) section 1 of the State Pension Credit Act (Northern Ireland) 2002;

(f) universal credit under—
   (i) Part 1 of the Welfare Reform Act 2012, or
   (ii) Part 2 of the Welfare Reform (Northern Ireland) Order 2015.

GENERAL NOTE

2.715 The relevant provisions for universal credit purposes are reg.26(1)(a) and (2)(f). Under the Regulations payments are to be made to those injured in a "Troubles-related incident", which is defined in s.10(11) of the Northern Ireland (Executive Formation etc) Act 2019 as "an incident involving an act of violence or force carried out in Ireland, the United Kingdom or anywhere in Europe for a reason related to the constitutional status of Northern Ireland or to political or sectarian hostility between people there". In so far as any such payment constitutes income it is not listed in reg.66(1) of the Universal Credit Regulations, so would not be taken into account as unearned income for universal credit purposes even without the disregard in reg.26(1)(a). In so far as it constitutes capital, either initially or on metamorphosing into capital (see the notes to reg.54A of the Universal Credit Regulations), it is to be disregarded without any limit as to how long ago the payment was made.

The Employment and Support Allowance and Universal Credit (Coronavirus Disease) Regulations 2020

(SI 2020/289)

GENERAL NOTE

2.716 These Regulations came into force on March 30, 2020, and were subject to several extensions, but finally ceased to have effect from March 24, 2022, by virtue of reg.2 of the Employment and Support Allowance and Universal Credit (Coronavirus Disease) (Amendment) Regulations 2021 (SI 2021/1158). When in force they ensured that ESA claimants who met the eligibility conditions and were infected with Covid-19 (or self-isolating in line with government guidance, or looking after a child (or qualifying young person) who fell into either of these categories) could be treated as having limited capability for work without the requirement to provide any medical evidence or undergo a work capability assessment. They also removed the need for claimants to serve waiting days, enabling ESA to be paid from day one of any claim. For the text of the now repealed Regulations, see the 2021/22 edition of this work at paras 2.706–2.713 of Vol.II.

The Social Security (Coronavirus) (Further Measures) Regulations 2020

(SI 2020/371)

GENERAL NOTE

2.717 These regulations came into force on March 30, 2020 and were subject to several extensions, but finally ceased to have any effect in relation to universal credit on July 31, 2022. The main effect in relation to the imposition of work-related requirements expired on July 31, 2021, but the Universal Credit (Coronavirus) (Restoration of the Minimum Income Floor) Regulations 2021 (SI 2021/807) extended the effect of some parts of reg.2 for the longer period to allow a process of reintroduction of the minimum income floor rules. See the 2022/23 and earlier editions of this volume for the text of the regulations.

The Universal Credit (Coronavirus) (Self-employed Claimants and Reclaims) (Amendment) Regulations 2020

(SI 2020/522)

Made by the Secretary of State for Work and Pensions in exercise of powers conferred by sections 1(1) and 189(1), (4) and (6) of the Social Security Administration Act 1992 and section 42(1) to (3) of, and paragraph 4(1) and (6) of Schedule 1 to, the Welfare Reform Act 2012, it appearing inexpedient by reason of urgency to refer the proposals in respect of these Regulations to the Social Security Advisory Committee.

Citation and commencement

1. These Regulations may be cited as the Universal Credit (Coronavirus) (Self-employed Claimants and Reclaims) (Amendment) Regulations 2020 and come into force on 21st May 2020. **2.718**

Treatment of payments to self-employed universal credit claimants

2.—(1) For the purposes of regulation 57 (self-employed earnings) of the Universal Credit Regulations 2013— **2.719**

(a) a payment under the Self-employment Income Support Scheme is to be treated as a receipt at step 1 of the calculation of self-employed earnings in the assessment period in which the claimant receives that payment; and

(b) no deduction may be made at step 1 of that calculation in respect of expenses comprising the salary or wages paid to an employee in so far as those expenses are covered by a payment under the Coronavirus Job Retention Scheme.

(2) For the purposes of section 5 (financial conditions) and section 8 (calculation of awards) of the Welfare Reform Act 2012, any payment made to a claimant carrying on a trade, profession or vocation—

(a) in relation to a furloughed employee under the Coronavirus Job Retention Scheme; or

(b) by way of a grant or loan to meet the expenses or losses of the trade, profession or vocation in relation to the outbreak of coronavirus disease, is to be disregarded in the calculation of the claimant's capital for a period of 12 months from the date on which it is received.

(3) In this regulation—

"the Coronavirus Job Retention Scheme" means the scheme (as it has effect from time to time) that is the subject of the direction given by the Treasury on 15th April 2020 under section 76 of the Coronavirus Act 2020;

"the Self-employment Income Support Scheme" means the scheme (as it has effect from time to time) that is the subject of the direction given by the Treasury on 30th April 2020 under that section of that Act;

"coronavirus disease" has the meaning given in section 1 of the Coronavirus Act 2020.

General Note

2.720 The highly problematic effect of this provision, and of the new reg.32A of the Claims and Payments Regulations 2013 inserted by reg.3 (reclaims), is discussed in the notes to reg.57 of and para.7 of Sch.10 to the Universal Credit Regulations in the 2023/24 edition of this volume and in earlier editions.

Amendment of the UC etc. Claims and Payments Regulations

2.721 **3.** After regulation 32 (advance claim for and award of universal credit) of the Universal Credit, Personal Independence Payment, Jobseeker's Allowance and Employment and Support Allowance (Claims and Payments) Regulations 2013 insert—

"Reclaims of universal credit after nil award due to earnings

32A.—(1) This regulation applies where—

(a) a claim is made for universal credit, but no award is made because the condition in section 5(1)(b) or 5(2)(b) of the 2012 Act (condition that the claimant's income, or joint claimants' combined income is such that the amount payable would not be less than the prescribed minimum) is not met; or

(b) entitlement to an award of universal credit ceases because that condition is not met.

(2) The Secretary of State may, subject to any conditions the Secretary of State considers appropriate, treat the claimant (or joint claimants) as making a claim on the first day of each subsequent month, up to a maximum of 5, that would have been an assessment period if an award had been made or, as the case may be, if the award had continued".

The Universal Credit (Coronavirus) (Restoration of the Minimum Income Floor) Regulations 2021

(SI 2021/807)

General Note

2.722 These regulations came into force on July 31, 2021 and continued the effect of certain parts of reg.2 of the Social Security (Coronavirus) (Further Measures) Regulations 2020 (SI 2020/371), subject to various qualifications down to July 31, 2022. That was to allow a process of reintroduction of the minimum income floor rules. See the 2022/23 and earlier editions of this volume for the text of the regulations.

The Universal Credit and Jobseeker's Allowance (Work Search and Work Availability Requirements—limitations) (Amendment) Regulations 2022

(SI 2022/108)

Made by the Secretary of State at 10.35 a.m. on February 7, 2022 under sections 6D(4), 6E(3), 35 and 36(2) and (4) of the Jobseekers Act 1995 and sections 17(4), 18(3) and 42(1) to (3) of the Welfare Reform Act 2012 and laid before Parliament at 4.00 pm on February 7, 2002, it appearing to the Secretary of State that by reason of the urgency of the matter it was inexpedient to refer the proposals in respect of these Regulations to the Social Security Advisory Committee.

Citation, commencement and extent

1.—(1) These Regulations may be cited as the Universal Credit and Jobseeker's Allowance (Work Search and Work Availability Requirements—limitations) (Amendment) Regulations 2022 and come into force on 8th February 2022. **2.723**

(2) Any amendment made by these Regulations has the same extent as the provision amended.

Amendment of the Universal Credit Regulations 2013

2. [*Amendment incorporated into the text of reg.97(5) of the Universal Credit Regulations 2013*] **2.724**

Amendment of the Jobseeker's Allowance Regulations 2013

3. [*Amendment incorporated into the text of reg.14(3)(b) of the JSA Regulations 2013 in Vol.I of this series*] **2.725**

Transitional provision

4. Where, on the date that these Regulations come into force, a work search requirement or work availability requirement is limited under regulation 97(4) of the Universal Credit Regulations 2013 or regulation 14(3) of the Jobseeker's Allowance Regulations 2013, the limitation is to end on— **2.726**

(a) the day before the day on which the limitation no longer applies; or

(b) if earlier, 7th March 2022.

General Note

See the notes to reg.97(5) of the UC Regulations 2013 for the doubtful validity of the amendments made by regs 2 and 3 and their very limited practical effect. **2.727**

The Universal Credit (Energy Rebate Scheme Disregard) Regulations 2022

(SI 2022/257)

Made by the Secretary of State under section 42(2) and (3) of, and paragraph 4(1) and (3) of Schedule 1 to, the Welfare Reform Act 2012, the Social Security Advisory Committee having agreed under section 173(1)(b) of the Social Security Administration Act 1992 that the proposals in respect of these Regulations should not be referred to it.

Citation, commencement and extent

2.728 **1.**—(1) These Regulations may be cited as the Universal Credit (Energy Rebate Scheme Disregard) Regulations 2022 and come into force on 1st April 2022.

(2) These Regulations extend to England and Wales and Scotland.

Capital disregard for Energy Rebate Scheme payments

2.729 **2.**—(1) Any payment a person receives under the Energy Rebate Scheme 2022 is to be disregarded for 12 months beginning with the date on which it is received in the calculation of the person's capital for the purpose of Part 1 of the Welfare Reform Act 2012 (Universal Credit).

(2) In this regulation—

"the Energy Rebate Scheme 2022" means the scheme to provide financial support in respect of energy bills which was announced in Parliament by the Chancellor of the Exchequer on 3rd February 2022 and any comparable scheme announced by Welsh Ministers or Scottish Ministers.

GENERAL NOTE

2.730 See the introductory note to Sch.10 to the Universal Credit Regulations 2013 for the effect of these Regulations.

PART IIB

TRANSITIONAL AND SAVINGS PROVISIONS

The Universal Credit (Transitional Provisions) Regulations 2014

2014/1230 (AS AMENDED)

The Secretary of State for Work and Pensions makes the following Regulations in exercise of the powers conferred by section 42(2) and (3) of and paragraphs 1(1) and (2)(b), 3(1)(a) to (c), 4(1)(a), 5(1), (2)(c) and (d) and (3)(a) and 6 of Schedule 6 to the Welfare Reform Act 2012.

In accordance with section 172(1) of the Social Security Administration Act 1992 ("the 1992 Act"), the Secretary of State has referred proposals in respect of these Regulations to the Social Security Advisory Committee.

In accordance with section 176(1) of the 1992 Act and, in so far as these Regulations relate to housing benefit, the Secretary of State has consulted with organisations appearing to him to be representative of the authorities concerned in respect of proposals for these Regulations.

[In force: June 16, 2014]

ARRANGEMENT OF REGULATIONS

PART 1

PART 2

CHAPTER 1

CHAPTER 2

CHAPTER 3

PART 3

ARRANGEMENTS REGARDING CHANGES TO THE CHILD ELEMENT FROM APRIL 2017

PART 4

MANAGED MIGRATION TO UNIVERSAL CREDIT

The Migration Process

Transitional Protection

Ending of Transitional Protection

Miscellaneous

GENERAL NOTE

2.732 The original Universal Credit (Transitional Provisions) Regulations 2013 (SI 2013/386) ("the 2013 Regulations") came into force on April 29, 2013 and provided for the introduction of universal credit to limited categories of claimant. A series of Commencement Orders has subsequently brought into force provisions relating to universal credit for claimants in specified postcodes, accompanied (in those areas) by repeals of the legislation relating to jobseeker's allowance and employment and support allowance for those claimants. The present Regulations ("the 2014 Transitional Regulations") made provision for the second phase of the introduction of universal credit, and represented a change from the structured plans for the roll out of universal credit set out in the 2013 Regulations. These Regulations accordingly provide for some of the more complex transitional situations that will arise when dealing with families and those on a wider range of existing benefits. The House of Lords' Secondary Legislation Scrutiny Committee expressed the following opinion on the draft 2014 Transitional Regulations (First Report, Session 2014/15, footnote omitted):

> "20. In line with an announcement made on 5 December 2013, the Department for Work and Pensions now expects the "majority" of existing benefit claimants to be transferred to Universal Credit by the end of 2017, that is, around 6.5 million people. DWP officials state that "decisions on the later stages of Universal Credit (UC) roll out will be informed by the development of the enhanced IT but some Employment Support Allowance claimants may be moved on to UC more slowly because they have already experienced the move from the old Incapacity Benefit and they would not immediately benefit from the improved work incentives of Universal Credit". The Committee was surprised to see this instrument accompanied by the original cost/benefit analysis from 2012, despite the well-publicised changes to the programme. DWP officials state that "the Impact Assessment published in December 2012 provides information based on the situation once Universal Credit (UC) is fully rolled out. Therefore, as there has not been any significant change since the Impact Assessment was published, we have not published an updated impact assessment for this instrument". However, the House may wish to note that the end date for completion of the transition to Universal Credit has been made more flexible and can be "managed" if problems arise in a particular area. Such changes will be made by Commencement Orders, which are not subject to parliamentary scrutiny. These Regulations also now include provision to allow the Secretary of State discretion temporarily to stop taking Universal Credit claims in certain geographic areas or for certain groups of claimants, so that any issues can be resolved. Where this provision is exercised, anyone prevented from claiming Universal Credit will be able to claim existing benefits or credits."

Note that most of these Regulations are also included in Vol.4 of this series, with extra commentary that focuses on the interaction between claims for tax credits and universal credit.

PART 1

Citation and commencement

1. (1) These Regulations may be cited as the Universal Credit (Transitional Provisions) Regulations 2014. 2.733

(2) These Regulations come into force on 16th June 2014.

Interpretation

2. (1) In these Regulations— 2.734

"the 2002 Act" means the Tax Credits Act 2002;

[6"the 2006 (SPC) Regulations" means the Housing Benefit (Persons who have attained the qualifying age for state pension credit) Regulations 2006;]

"the 2007 Act" means the Welfare Reform Act 2007;

"the Act" means the Welfare Reform Act 2012;

"assessment period" has the same meaning as in the Universal Credit Regulations;

[5"childcare costs element" has the meaning in the Universal Credit Regulations;]

"the Claims and Payments Regulations" means the Universal Credit, Personal Independence Payment, Jobseeker's Allowance and Employment and Support Allowance (Claims and Payments) Regulations 2013;

"contributory employment and support allowance" means a contributory allowance under Part 1 of the 2007 Act as that Part has effect apart from the amendments made by Schedule 3, and Part 1 of Schedule 14, to the Act that remove references to an income-related allowance;

[1 . . .]

[5 "deadline day" has the meaning in regulation 44;]

[6 "the Decisions and Appeals Regulations" means the Universal Credit, Personal Independence Payment, Jobseeker's Allowance and Employment and Support Allowance (Decisions and Appeals) Regulations 2013;]

[5 "earned income" has the meaning in Chapter 2 of Part 6 of the Universal Credit Regulations;]

"existing benefit" means income-based jobseeker's allowance, income-related employment and support allowance, income support, housing benefit and child tax credit and working tax credit under the 2002 Act, but see also [5paragraph (3) and] regulation 25(2);

[5 "final deadline" has the meaning in regulation 46;]

"First-tier Tribunal" has the same meaning as in the Social Security Act 1998;

[5 "HMRC" means Her Majesty's Revenue and Customs;]

"housing benefit" means housing benefit under section 130 of the Social Security Contributions and Benefits Act 1992;

"income-based jobseeker's allowance" has the same meaning as in the Jobseekers Act 1995;

"income-related employment and support allowance" means an income-related allowance under Part 1 of the 2007 Act;

"income support" means income support under section 124 of the Social Security Contributions and Benefits Act 1992;

[5 "indicative UC amount" has the meaning in regulation 54;]

"joint-claim jobseeker's allowance" means old style JSA, entitlement to which arises by virtue of section 1(2B) of the Jobseekers Act 1995;

[5 "migration day" has the meaning in regulation 49;]

[5 "migration notice" has the meaning in regulation 44;]

"new claimant partner" has the meaning given in regulation 7;

"new style ESA" means an allowance under Part 1 of the 2007 Act as amended by the amendments made by Schedule 3, and Part 1 of Schedule 14, to the Act that remove references to an income-related allowance;

"new style JSA" means an allowance under the Jobseekers Act 1995 as amended by the amendments made by Part 1 of Schedule 14 to the Act that remove references to an income-based allowance;

[5 "notified person" has the meaning in regulation 44;]

"old style ESA" means an employment and support allowance under Part 1 of the 2007 Act as that Part has effect apart from the amendments made by Schedule 3, and Part 1 of Schedule 14, to the Act that remove references to an income-related allowance;

"old style JSA" means a jobseeker's allowance under the Jobseekers Act 1995 as that Act has effect apart from the amendments made by Part 1 of Schedule 14 to the Act that remove references to an income-based allowance;

"partner" in relation to a person ("A") means a person who forms part of a couple with A;

[6 "qualifying age for state pension credit" has the meaning given by section 1(6) of the State Pension Credit Act 2002;]

[5 "qualifying claim" has the meaning in regulation 48;]

[2 "qualifying young person" has the same meaning as in the Universal Credit Regulations, but see also regulation 28;]

[4 "severe disability premium" means the premium in relation to an employment and support allowance under paragraph 6 of Schedule 4 to the Employment and Support Allowance Regulations 2008 or, as the case may be, the corresponding premium in relation to income support, old style JSA or housing benefit;]

[1 "specified accommodation" means accommodation to which one or more of sub-paragraphs (2) to (5) of paragraph 3A of Schedule 1 to the Universal Credit Regulations applies;]

[6 "state pension credit" means state pension credit under the State Pension Credit Act 2002;]

[3 "temporary accommodation" means accommodation which falls within Case 1 or Case 2 under paragraph 3B of Schedule 1 to the Universal Credit Regulations;]

"tax credit" (including "child tax credit" and "working tax credit"), "tax credits" and "tax year" have the same meanings as in the 2002 Act;

"the Universal Credit Regulations" means the Universal Credit Regulations 2013;

[5 "total legacy amount" has the meaning in regulation 53;]

[5 "transitional capital disregard" has the meaning in regulation 51;]

[5 "transitional element" has the meaning in regulation 52;]

"Upper Tribunal" has the same meaning as in the Social Security Act 1998.

(2) For the purposes of these Regulations—

(a) the date on which a claim for universal credit is made is to be determined in accordance with the Claims and Payments Regulations;

(b) where a couple is treated, in accordance with regulation 9(8) of the Claims and Payments Regulations, as having made a claim for universal credit, references to the date on which the claim is treated as made are to the date of formation of the couple;

(c) where a regulation refers to entitlement to an existing benefit on the date on which a claim for universal credit is made or treated as made, such entitlement is to be taken into account notwithstanding the effect of regulations 5, 7 and 8 or termination of an award of the benefit before that date by virtue of an order made under section 150(3) of the Act.

[5(3) In these Regulations—

(a) references to an award of income-based jobseeker's allowance are to an award of old style JSA where the claimant is, or joint claimants are, entitled to the income-based allowance; and

(b) references to an award of income-related employment and support allowance are to an award of old style ESA where the claimant is entitled to the income-related allowance.

(4) In regulation 46 (termination of existing benefits if no claim before the deadline) [7 ...] "terminate" in relation to an award of income-based jobseeker's allowance or income-related employment and support allowance means treating that award as if the following provisions had come into force (including where a saving provision has ceased to apply) in relation to that award—

(a) section 33(1)(a) and (b) and (2) of the Act (abolition of benefits);

(b) paragraphs 22 to 26 of Schedule 3 to the Act (abolition of benefits: consequential amendments) and section 33(3) of the Act in so far as it relates to those paragraphs; and

(c) the repeals in Part 1 of Schedule 14 to the Act (abolition of benefits superseded by universal credit) that come into force if a claim is made for universal credit.]

AMENDMENTS

1. Universal Credit (Transitional Provisions) (Amendment) Regulations 2014 (SI 2014/1626) reg.3 (November 3, 2014).

2. Social Security (Restrictions on Amounts for Children and Qualifying Young Persons) Amendment Regulations 2017 (2017/376) reg.3(2) (April 6, 2017).

3. Universal Credit (Miscellaneous Amendments, Saving and Transitional Provision) Regulations 2018 (SI 2018/65) reg.6(3) (April 11, 2018).

4. Universal Credit (Transitional Provisions) (SDP Gateway) Amendment Regulations 2019 (SI 2019/10) reg.2(2) (January 16, 2019).

5. Universal Credit (Managed Migration Pilot and Miscellaneous Amendments) Regulations 2019 (SI 2019/1152) reg.3(2) (July 24, 2019).

6. Universal Credit (Persons who have attained state pension credit qualifying age) (Amendment) Regulations 2020 (SI 2020/655) reg.6(2) (November 25, 2020).

7. Universal Credit (Transitional Provisions) Amendment Regulations 2022 (SI 2022/752) reg.11 and Sch. para.1(2) (July 25, 2022).

DEFINITIONS

"the Act"—see reg.2(1).

GENERAL NOTE

Paragraph (1)

2.735 *"new claimant partner"*: where a single universal credit claimant becomes a member of a couple, and their award terminates, and the other member of the couple was not previously entitled to universal credit as a single person, but an award of universal credit is then made to the couple as joint claimants, then the other member of the couple is known as a "new claimant partner" (see also reg.7).

"new style ESA": in effect, this means (new variant) contribution-based ESA, shorn of its previous income-based element, and as defined in what were originally the Pathfinder areas as from April 29, 2013.

"new style JSA": similarly, this means (new variant) contribution-based JSA, again shorn of its income-related element, and as defined in those Pathfinder areas as from April 29, 2013.

Paragraph (2)(a)

2.736 The normal rule is that the date of a universal credit claim is the date the claim is received, whether electronically or by telephone or, if later, the first day for which the claim is made: see Claims and Payments Regulations 2013, reg.10.

Revocation and saving of the Universal Credit (Transitional Provisions) Regulations 2013

2.737 **3.** (1) The Universal Credit (Transitional Provisions) Regulations 2013 ("the 2013 Regulations") are revoked, subject to the savings in paragraphs (2) to (4).

(2) Chapters 2 and 3 of Part 2 (Pathfinder Group and treatment of invalid claims) of the 2013 Regulations continue to have effect in relation to a claim for universal credit—

(a) which was made before the date on which these Regulations come into force ("the commencement date"); and

(b) in respect of which no payment has been made to the claimant before the commencement date.

(3) Regulation 19 of the 2013 Regulations (advance payments of universal credit) continues to have effect in relation to an advance payment which was made in accordance with that regulation before the commencement date and regulation 17 of these Regulations does not apply to such a payment.

(4) Any other provision of the 2013 Regulations continues to have effect in so far as is necessary to give full effect to paragraphs (2) and (3).

DEFINITIONS

"the 2013 Regulations"–para.(1).
"the commencement date"–para.(2)(a).

General Note

This regulation provides for revocation of the Universal Credit (Transitional Provisions) Regulations 2013 (para.(1)), subject to certain savings (paras.(2)-(4)). These savings concern claimants who claimed universal credit before the date on which the 2014 Transitional Regulations came into force (June 16, 2014) and relate in particular to the treatment of invalid claims and recovery of advance payments of universal credit made under the 2013 Transitional Regulations. The intention is to ensure that the validity of a claim is judged in accordance with the provisions which were in force at the time the claim was made, and that advance payments made under the 2013 Transitional Regulations remain recoverable. 2.738

Part 2

Chapter 1

Secretary of State discretion to determine that claims for universal credit may not be made

4. [[1]...] 2.739

Amendment

1. Universal Credit (Transitional Provisions) Amendment Regulations 2022 (SI 2022/752) reg.2 (July 25, 2022).

[[1]Restriction on claims for universal credit by persons entitled to a severe disability premium

4A.—[[3][[2]...]] 2.740

Amendments

1. Universal Credit (Transitional Provisions) (SDP Gateway) Amendment Regulations 2019 (SI 2019/10) reg.2(3) (January 16, 2019).
2. Universal Credit (Managed Migration Pilot and Miscellaneous Amendments) Regulations 2019 (SI 2019/1152) reg.3(3) (July 24, 2019).
3. Universal Credit (Managed Migration Pilot and Miscellaneous Amendments) Regulations 2019 (SI 2019/1152) reg.7 (January 27, 2021).

General Note

There was a complex background to this provision originally inserted into the Regulations in January 2019. By way of context, universal credit, unlike the legacy means-tested benefits, does not include an equivalent component to severe disability premium (SDP). The Coalition Government maintained that universal credit would simplify means-tested support for disabled people, but disability organisations pointed out that the abolition of SDP could result in vulnerable claimants losing out financially. In response, the Government announced that transitional protection would be available to ensure that people moving onto universal credit did not lose out in cash terms at the point of transfer (i.e. if their universal credit entitlement was lower than their existing legacy benefits). However, it became apparent that transitional protection would only be available to claimants who were subject to "managed migration", i.e. having been required to transfer by the DWP. For claimants moving by "natural migration"—e.g. a change in their circumstances—there would be no such protection. 2.741

This differential treatment was challenged by way of judicial review in the High Court in R *(On the application of TP and AR) v Secretary of State for Work and Pensions* [2018] EWHC 1474 (Admin), in which two claimants previously in receipt of IR-ESA had to claim universal credit following a move to a full service area. In the absence of any equivalent to SDP they suffered a sudden and significant drop in their incomes. The judicial review claim was put on three grounds: (1) the absence of any additional payment in universal credit for those who previously qualified for SDP amounted to unlawful discrimination contrary to art.14 read with art.1 of the First Protocol to the ECHR; (2) the Universal Credit (Transitional Provisions) Regulations 2014 involved unlawful discrimination (on the same basis) because of the absence of any element of transitional protection; and (3) the Secretary of State had breached the Equality Act 2010 by failing to have due regard to the impact of removing the premiums for disabled people when making the Universal Credit Regulations 2013 and the Transitional Provisions Regulations.

In June 2018 Lewis J. dismissed the challenges on the first and third grounds of judicial review, but allowed the application on the second ground, holding that the Transitional Provisions Regulations did not strike a fair balance between the interests of the individual and the community respectively in bringing about a phased transition to universal credit. The impact on the individuals was apparent—their cash payments were now significantly lower than the amounts they had previously received. The Judge found there appeared to have been no consideration given to the justification for requiring the individual to assume the entirety of the difference between their previous benefits and universal credit; this was all the more striking given Government statements over the years that such persons could need assistance and there was a need to define precisely the circumstances in which persons would not receive assistance. In this case, the operation of the implementation arrangements was "manifestly without reasonable foundation" and failed to strike a fair balance (at [88]). The differential treatment was based on status and had not been objectively justified. Accordingly, Lewis J. held that the universal credit implementing arrangements gave rise to unlawful discrimination contrary to art.14 read with art.1 of the First Protocol to the ECHR. The High Court granted a declaration that there was unlawful discrimination, leaving the Secretary of State to determine how to rectify the unlawful discrimination (at [114]). Thus, Lewis J concluded as follows:

> "[113] The 2013 Regulations establishing universal credit do not involve discrimination contrary to Article 14 ECHR in so far as they do not include any element which corresponds to the additional disability premiums payable under the previous regime. Any differential treatment between different groups is objectively justifiable.
>
> [114] The implementing arrangements do at present give rise to unlawful discrimination contrary to Article 14 ECHR read with Article 1 of the First Protocol to the ECHR. There is differential treatment between the group of persons who were in receipt of additional disability premiums (the SDP and EDP) and who transferred to universal credit on moving to a different local housing authority area and so receive less money by way of income related support than they previously received and the group of persons in receipt of SDP and EDP and who move house within the same local housing authority area but are not required to transfer to universal credit and continue to receive the basic allowance and SDP and EDP and suffer no loss of income. That differential treatment is based on status. That differential treatment has not been objectively justified at present. A declaration will be granted that there is unlawful discrimination. The defendant will then be able to determine how to rectify the unlawful discrimination."

In *R (on the application of AR & SXC) v SSWP* [2020] EWCA Civ 37, the Court of Appeal dismissed the Secretary of State's appeal against the judgment of Lewis J. The Department advanced four grounds of appeal. The first was that the judge had been wrong to conclude that there was any appearance of discriminatory treatment against TP and AR. The Court of Appeal rejected this ground for appeal on the basis that "there can be no realistic dispute that there is a difference of treatment between TP and AR on the one hand and, on the other hand, people in an analogous situation, who do not have to apply for universal credit" (at [87]). The second ground of appeal was that the High Court had erred in holding that the difference of treatment in these cases was on the ground of an 'other status' for the purpose of art.14, namely a severely disabled person who moves to a different local authority area. The Court (Rose LJ dissenting) held that residence in a given local authority area could constitute a relevant status. The third ground of appeal was that Lewis J had been wrong to hold that the difference in treatment lacked an objective justification. This ground for appeal failed as, on the evidence that the DWP placed before Lewis J, there appeared to have been no consideration of the difference in treatment between the comparator groups. The final ground for appeal was that the High Court's declaration should have been limited to one that there had been a failure to 'consider' transitional payments, rather than that TP and AR had suffered unlawful discrimination by reason of the difference in payments. This ground was rejected as being based on a misunderstanding of Lewis J's reasoning. Moreover, the Court found that the DWP had failed in its duty of candour and co-operation by omitting to disclose to Lewis J that it had already made a policy decision both to stop moving more severely disabled people onto universal credit and to provide transitional payments for those who had already been transferred.

Following the High Court's decision in *R (on the application of TP and AR) v SSWP*, the DWP agreed to compensate the claimants in the case for the money they had lost as a result of moving onto universal credit, and to make ongoing payments of around £170 a month to reflect future loss which would be paid until changes to the regulations came into force.

The Government's immediate response, more broadly, was to issue a written statement explaining that "in order to support the transition for those individuals who live alone with substantial care needs and receive the Severe Disability Premium", the rules implementing universal credit would be changed. The Government announced that current claimants with an award including SDP who had a change of circumstances (normally meaning they would be subject to natural migration to universal credit) would not in fact move to the new benefit until they qualified for transitional protection—i.e. not until they were subject to "managed migration", i.e. as and when required to migrate by the DWP (written statement HCWS745, June 7, 2018, by the then Secretary of State, Esther McVey MP). The Secretary of State further stated that claimants who had already moved to universal credit and so lost their SDP would receive on-going compensation payments and an additional lump-sum payment to cover the period since they moved.

As a consequence there has been, in effect, a twin-track approach to further developments, namely first the relatively straightforward proposal to stop SDP claimants from transferring from legacy benefits to universal credit and, secondly, the more complex arrangements for providing transitional protection to those who have already transferred or will so transfer in due course.

As to the first track, the Universal Credit (Transitional Provisions) (SDP Gateway) Amendment Regulations 2019 (SI 2019/10), which came into force on January 16, inserted new reg.4A so as to prevent claimants of legacy benefits (IS, IR-ESA, IB-JSA or HB) with SDP from making a claim for universal credit. The exclusion also applies where an award of a legacy benefit has ended within the last month, so long as the claimant continued to satisfy the conditions for entitlement to the SDP. This exclusion is known as the "SDP gateway", although the "SDP roadblock" might be a more accurate description. DWP guidance to staff is available in Memo ADM 01/19 UC *Claimants entitled to Severe Disability Premium* (January 2019). As the Explanatory Memorandum to SI 2019/10 explains, "The regulations provide that these claimants will no longer naturally migrate to UC, but will remain on their existing benefits or be able to claim another existing benefit instead until such time as they are moved to Universal Credit as part of the Department's managed migration process." However, it should be noted that the SDP gateway has been prospectively repealed with effect from January 27, 2021 (see SI 2019/1152, reg.7), in response to the further High Court judgment in *R (on the application of TP, AR and SXC) v Secretary of State for Work and Pensions* [2019] EWHC 1116 (Admin). Swift J held there that the differential treatment between claimants with SDP who have already moved to universal credit and those who are prevented from doing so because of the SDP gateway was not justified (see further below).

As to the second track, it is fair to say that the DWP has had several attempts (to be precise, three goes as at the time of writing) at trying to develop a satisfactory solution for compensating those with financial losses.

First, transitional payment arrangements for claimants who had already moved to universal credit (and so had lost their SDP) were included in the draft Universal Credit (Managed Migration) Regulations laid before Parliament on November 5, 2018. An initial draft had been submitted to the SSAC, which undertook a public consultation on them over summer 2018. In the event, the DWP withdrew the draft regulations following wider concerns about its proposed approach to managed migration.

Secondly, the Department then included provisions on SDP transitional payments in the draft Universal Credit (Managed Migration Pilot and Miscellaneous Amendments) Regulations, laid before Parliament in January 2019. The regulations were subject to the affirmative procedure but no debate or vote took place in either House. In a case brought by the two claimants who had successfully challenged the DWP in the High Court in June 2018 (TP and AR), and a third claimant (SXC), the High Court (Swift J) ruled on May 3, 2019 that the Government's proposed scheme for SDP transitional payments was unlawful (*R (on the application of TP, AR and SXC) v Secretary of State for Work and Pensions* [2019] EWHC 1116 (Admin)). Under the proposed scheme set out in the second set of draft regulations, SDP recipients moving to universal credit on managed migration would receive top-ups of up to £180 a month, while those claimants who had already been subject to natural migration and lost their SDP would have received payments of £80 per months. Swift J. agreed that this difference in treatment could not be justified:

> "[59] ...What needs to be justified extends to the difference in treatment between the SDP migrant group and the Regulation 4A group. The need for some form of explanation for the difference in treatment is all the more striking given the circumstances which, at the beginning of 2018, prompted the Secretary of State to consider the position of severely disabled benefits claimants. This was the point raised by the members of the House of Commons Select Committee on Work and Pensions on the effect that migration to Universal Credit was having on those who had previously been in receipt of SDP, and it was the point considered in the subsequent Departmental presentation (see above, at paragraphs 30 to 33).
>
> [60] No sufficient explanation for the difference in treatment has been provided. The Secretary of State's "bright line"/administrative efficiency submission explains the treatment of the SDP natural migrant group on its own terms, but does not explain why that group is treated differently to the Regulation 4A group. Both groups comprise severely disabled persons; all of whom meet the criteria for payment of SDP (or would continue to meet those criteria but for natural migration). The simple fact of natural migration is not a satisfactory ground of distinction because the trigger conditions for natural migration are not indicative of any material change in the needs of the Claimants (or the other members of the SDP natural migration group), as severely disabled persons. The same point is sufficient to dispose of the further suggestion in Miss Young's witness statement that the Secretary of State considered the SDP natural migrants as being in materially the same position as new welfare benefits claimants (i.e. severely disabled persons presenting themselves to the welfare benefits system for the first time, after the implementation of Universal Credit). There is no logical foundation for that view; if there were a logical foundation for it, it would negate the rationale for regulation 4A of the Transitional Provisions Regulations."

The High Court left it to the Government to decide what should happen next with regard to the regulations. The Court of Appeal subsequently dismissed the Secretary of State's appeal against Swift J's judgment (see *R (on the application of AR & SXC) v SSWP* [2020] EWCA Civ 37). A separate claim by SXC for compensation under the Human Rights Act 1988 was later dismissed by Swift J. (*SXC v Secretary of State for Work and Pensions* [2019] EWHC 2774 (Admin)). This takes us to the third attempt to deal with SDP transitional protection.

Thirdly, the final Universal Credit (Managed Migration Pilot and Miscellaneous Amendments) Regulations (SI 2019/1152) —which unlike the previous versions were subject to the negative procedure—were laid before Parliament on July 22, 2019 and (for present purposes) came into force two days later. They provide, among other things, for transitional payments for claimants who were in receipt of SDP who have already moved to universal credit, comprising ongoing monthly payments and an additional lump-sum covering the period since they moved.

Finally, the SDP gateway was repealed with effect from January 27, 2021 (see reg.7 of the Universal Credit (Managed Migration Pilot and Miscellaneous Amendments) Regulations 2019 (SI 2019/1152)). This was in response to the High Court's decision in *R. (on the application of TP, AR and SXC) v Secretary of State for Work and Pensions* [2019] EWHC 1116 (Admin). The consequence is that affected claimants will move to universal credit if a change of circumstances prompts them to make a claim for universal credit, in which event they may be eligible to be considered for transitional payments (see reg.63 and Sch.2, as substituted by reg.2 of the Universal Credit (Transitional Provisions) (Claimants previously entitled to a severe disability premium) Amendment Regulations 2021 (SI 2021/4)).

See further the judgment of Holgate J in *R. (on the application of TP and AR) v Secretary of State for Work and Pensions* [2022] EWHC 123 (Admin) (*TP and AR No.3*). This judgment includes a helpful analysis of *TP No.1* ([114]–[126]), *TP No.2* ([127]–[137] and the Court of Appeal's judgment in both appeals ([138]–[146]). *TP and AR No.3* is discussed in the commentary to reg.63 below. Note that the Court of Appeal refused (in forthright terms) the Secretary of State's application for permission to appeal against the decision of Holgate J. (CA-2022-000398; January 12, 2023).

CHAPTER 2

Exclusion of entitlement to certain benefits

5.—(1) Except as provided in paragraph (2), a claimant is not entitled to— 2.742

(a) income support;

(b) housing benefit;

(c) a tax credit; or

(d) state pension credit [2 ...],

in respect of any period when the claimant is entitled to universal credit.

(2) Entitlement to universal credit does not preclude the claimant from entitlement—

[1(a) to housing benefit in respect of specified accommodation or temporary accommodation;

(ab) to housing benefit or income support where regulation 8(2A) [3 or 46(1)] applies; [2...]

(b) during the first assessment period for universal credit, where the claimant is a new claimant partner, to—

(i) income support, where an award to which the new claimant partner is entitled terminates, in accordance with regulation 7(4), after the first date of entitlement to universal credit;

(ii) housing benefit, where regulation 7(5)(b) [2 or (c)] applies and an award of housing benefit to which the new claimant partner is entitled terminates after the first date of entitlement to universal credit; [2 ...]

(iii) a tax credit, where an award to which the new claimant partner is entitled terminates, in accordance with the 2002 Act, after the first date of entitlement to universal credit [2; or

(iv) state pension credit, where an award to which the new claimant partner is entitled terminates after the first date of entitlement to universal credit; or

(c) during the last assessment period for universal credit, where the claimant reaches the qualifying age for state pension credit and paragraph 26 of Schedule 1 to the Decisions and Appeals Regulations applies, to housing benefit or state pension credit from the date the claimant reaches that age.]

AMENDMENTS

1. Universal Credit (Managed Migration Pilot and Miscellaneous Amendments) Regulations 2019 (SI 2019/1152) reg.4(2) (July 22, 2020).
2. Universal Credit (Persons who have attained state pension credit qualifying age) (Amendment) Regulations 2020 (SI 2020/655) reg.6(3) (November 25, 2020).
3. Universal Credit (Transitional Provisions) Amendment Regulations 2022 (SI 2022/752) reg.11 and Sch. para.1(3) (July 25, 2022).

DEFINITIONS

"the 2002 Act"—see reg.2(1).
"assessment period"—*ibid.*
"housing benefit"—*ibid.*
"income support"—*ibid.*
"new claimant partner"—*ibid.*
"specified accommodation"—*ibid.*
"tax credit"—*ibid.*

GENERAL NOTE

2.743 This regulation broadly performs the same function as reg.15(1)-(2A) of the 2013 Transitional Regulations. The basic rule is that entitlement to universal credit and entitlement to any of the benefits or tax credits in para.(1) are mutually exclusive. Provision is made to similar effect in relation to "old style JSA" and "old style ESA" by virtue of the various Commencement Orders made under s.150(3) of the Act, which bring into force repeals of the legislation relating to those benefits. References to "old style JSA" and "old style ESA" are to the versions of jobseeker's allowance and employment and support allowance which include an income-based, or income-related, allowance (see reg.2 above).

[1 Entitlement to universal credit and housing benefit: universal credit work allowance

2.744 **5A.** Where a claimant has an award of universal credit and, in any assessment period, is also entitled to housing benefit for temporary accommodation and the award of universal credit does not include an amount for housing costs, regulation 22(2) of the Universal Credit

Regulations (amount of the work allowance) is to apply in relation to that assessment period as if the award did include an amount for housing costs.]

AMENDMENT

1. Universal Credit (Miscellaneous Amendments, Saving and Transitional Provision) Regulations 2018 (SI 2018/65) reg.6(4) (April 11, 2018).

DEFINITIONS

"assessment period"—see reg.2(1).
"housing benefit"—*ibid.*
"temporary accommodation"—*ibid.*
"Universal Credit Regulations"—*ibid.*

GENERAL NOTE

The new reg.5A provides that where in a universal credit assessment period a person is entitled to universal credit (without the housing costs element) and is also entitled to housing benefit for temporary accommodation, then that person is to be treated for the purposes of work allowances in universal credit as though they were entitled to universal credit with the housing costs element. **2.745**

Exclusion of claims for certain existing benefits

6. [1...]

AMENDMENT

1. Universal Credit (Transitional Provisions) Amendment Regulations 2022 (SI 2022/752) reg.3 (July 25, 2022). **2.746**

[1Restriction on claims for housing benefit, income support or a tax credit

6A.—(1) Except as provided by paragraphs (2) to (7) a person may not make a claim for housing benefit, income support, or a tax credit. **2.747**

(2) Paragraph (1) does not apply to a claim for housing benefit in respect of specified accommodation or temporary accommodation.

(3) Paragraph (1) does not apply to a claim for housing benefit that is made during the last assessment period of an award of universal credit, where the claimant reaches the qualifying age for state pension credit and paragraph 26 of Schedule 1 to the Decisions and Appeals Regulations applies, in respect of entitlement arising from the date the claimant reaches that age.

(4) Paragraph (1) does not apply to a claim for housing benefit by a single person who has reached the qualifying age for state pension credit, or a member of a State Pension Credit Act couple where both members have reached that age or a member of a polygamous marriage where all members have reached that age.

(5) Paragraph (1) does not apply to a claim for housing benefit where—

(a) the claim is made by a member of a State Pension Credit Act couple who has reached the qualifying age for state pension credit and the other member has not reached that age; and

(b) one of the savings in the sub-paragraphs of article 4(1) of the Welfare Reform Act 2012 (Commencement No.31 and Savings and Transitional Provisions and Commencement No.21 and 23 and Transitional and Transitory Provisions (Amendment)) Order 2019 applies and the saving has not ceased to have effect under article 4(2) of that Order.

(6) Paragraph (1) does not apply to a claim for a tax credit where a person makes or persons make a claim for child tax credit or working tax credit and on the date on which he or she (or they) makes or make the claim he or she (or they) has or have an award of working tax credit or child tax credit respectively.

(7) Paragraph (1) does not apply to a claim for a tax credit where a person has or had, or persons have or had, an award of child tax credit or working tax credit in respect of a tax year and that person or those persons makes or make (or is or are treated as making) a claim for that tax credit for the next tax year.

(8) For the purposes of this regulation—

(a) "polygamous marriage" has the same meaning as in regulation 3(5) of the Universal Credit Regulations;

(b) "State Pension Credit Act couple" means a couple as defined in section 17(1) of the State Pension Credit Act 2002,

and a reference to the date on which a claim for a tax credit is made is a reference to the date on which such claim is made or treated as made as provided for in the Tax Credits (Claims and Notifications) Regulations 2002.]

AMENDMENT

1. Universal Credit (Transitional Provisions) Amendment Regulations 2022 (SI 2022/752) reg.4 (July 25, 2022).

Termination of awards of certain existing benefits: new claimant partners

2.748 7.—(1) This regulation applies where—

(a) a person ("A") who was previously entitled to universal credit [2 . . .] ceases to be so entitled on becoming a member of a couple;

(b) the other member of the couple ("the new claimant partner") was not entitled to universal credit [2 . . .] immediately before formation of the couple; [5 and]

(c) the couple is treated, in accordance with regulation 9(8) of the Claims and Payments Regulations, as having made a claim for universal credit. [5 ...]

(2) Subject to paragraphs (4) and (5), where this regulation applies, all awards of income support or housing benefit to which the new claimant partner would (were it not for the effect of these Regulations) have been entitled during the relevant period are to terminate, by virtue of this regulation—

(a) on the day before the first date on which the joint claimants are entitled to universal credit in connection with the claim; or

(b) if the joint claimants are not entitled to universal credit, on the day before the first date on which they would have been so entitled, if all of the basic and financial conditions applicable to them had been met; or

(c) if the new claimant partner became entitled to an award after the date on which it would otherwise terminate under sub-paragraph (a) or (b), at the beginning of the first day of entitlement to that award.

(3) For the purposes of this regulation, "the relevant period" is the period starting with the first day of the assessment period (in relation to A's award of universal credit) during which A and the new claimant partner formed a couple and ending with the date of formation of the couple.

(4) Where the new claimant partner was entitled during the relevant period to income support, he or she was at that time a member of a couple and the award included an amount in respect of the new claimant partner and their partner at that time ("P"), the award of income support terminates, by virtue of this regulation, on the date on which the new claimant partner and P ceased to be a couple for the purposes of the Income Support (General) Regulations 1987, unless it terminates on that date in accordance with other legislative provision, or terminated on an earlier date.

(5) An award of housing benefit to which the new claimant partner is entitled does not terminate by virtue of this regulation where—

(a) the award is in respect of [1 specified accommodation] [3 or temporary accommodation]; [4...]

(b) the new claimant partner leaves the accommodation in respect of which housing benefit was paid, in order to live with A [4; or

(c) the new claimant partner has reached the qualifying age for state pension credit and the award is made in accordance with the 2006 (SPC) Regulations.]

(6) Where an award terminates by virtue of this regulation, any legislative provision under which the award terminates on a later date does not apply.

(7) Where the new claimant partner was, immediately before forming a couple with A, treated by regulation 11 as being entitled to a tax credit, the new claimant partner is to be treated, for the purposes of the 2002 Act, as having made a claim for the tax credit in question for the current tax year.

AMENDMENTS

1. Universal Credit (Transitional Provisions) (Amendment) Regulations 2014 (SI 2014/1626) reg.3 (November 3, 2014).

2. Universal Credit (Digital Service) Amendment Regulations 2014 (SI 2014/2887) reg.3(3) (November 26, 2014).

3. Universal Credit (Miscellaneous Amendments, Saving and Transitional Provision) Regulations 2018 (SI 2018/65) reg.6(6)(b) (April 11, 2018).

4. Universal Credit (Persons who have attained state pension credit qualifying age) (Amendment) Regulations 2020 (SI 2020/655) reg.6(5) (November 25, 2020).

5. Universal Credit (Transitional Provisions) Amendment Regulations 2022 (SI 2022/752) reg.5(2) (July 25, 2022).

DEFINITIONS

"the 2002 Act"—see reg.2(1).
"A"—para.7(1)(a).
"the Act"—see reg.2(1).
"assessment period"—*ibid.*
"the Claims and Payments Regulations"—*ibid.*
"housing benefit"—*ibid.*
"income support"—*ibid.*

"new claimant partner"—*ibid.*
"partner"—*ibid.*
"the relevant period"—para.(3).
"specified accommodation"—see reg.2(1).
"tax year"—*ibid.*

GENERAL NOTE

2.749 In broad terms this provision performs the same function as reg.16 of the 2013 Transitional Regulations, with various modifications. As a general rule, all existing benefit or tax credit awards will terminate when an award of universal credit is made to a newly formed couple, one of whom was previously entitled to universal credit and the other to an existing benefit (or tax credit). The mechanics of this process are different for existing benefit and tax credits awards respectively.

Thus where the conditions in para.(1) are met, the new claimant partner's award of income support or housing benefit will terminate as provided for in para.(2). Para.(4) deals with the timing of the termination of an earlier award of income support where the new claimant partner was receiving that benefit together with their own previous partner ("P"). Para.(5) provides for special cases where an award of housing benefit does not end, despite the general rule.

The process is rather more complicated with tax credits – where the new partner is treated as having an ongoing tax credit award by virtue of reg.11, then they are treated as having made a new claim for the current year, whether or not they actually have made such a claim (para.(7)), and any award made under such a deemed claim likewise terminates on the day before the start of the joint award of universal credit.

Paragraph (1)

2.750 The amendments to para.(1)(a) and (b) (the omission of the words "as a single parent") are each subject to the saving provision as set out in reg.5 of the Universal Credit (Digital Service) Amendment Regulations 2014 (SI 2014/2887).

Paragraph (7)

2.751 See further reg.11.

Termination of awards of certain existing benefits: other claimants

2.752 **8.**—(1) This regulation applies where—

(a) a claim for universal credit (other than a claim which is treated, in accordance with regulation 9(8) of the Claims and Payments Regulations, as having been made) is made[4, whether or not subsequently withdrawn].

(b) [4...]

(2) [2Where] this regulation applies, all awards of [3 [2 . . .]] or a tax credit to which the claimant (or, in the case of joint claimants, either of them) is entitled on the date on which the claim is made are to terminate, by virtue of this regulation—

(a) on the day before the first date on which the claimant is entitled to universal credit in connection with the claim; or

(b) if the claimant is not entitled to universal credit, on the day before the first date on which he or she would have been so entitled, if all of the basic and financial conditions applicable to the claimant had been met.

[2 (2A) Subject to paragraph (3), where this regulation applies, an award of [3 income support or] housing benefit to which the claimant is entitled on the day mentioned in paragraph (2)(a) or (b) terminates on the last day of the period of two weeks beginning with the day after that day (whether or not the person is also entitled to an award of [3 . . .] a tax credit).]

[4(2B) This regulation does not apply in the case of a single claimant who has reached the qualifying age for state pension credit or in the case of joint claimants who have both reached the qualifying age for state pension credit.]

(3) An award of housing benefit to which a claimant is entitled in respect of [1 specified accommodation] [2 or temporary accommodation] does not terminate by virtue of this regulation.

(4) Where this regulation applies and the claimant (or, in the case of joint claimants, either of them) is treated by regulation 11 as being entitled to a tax credit—

(a) the claimant (or, as the case may be, the relevant claimant) is to be treated, for the purposes of the 2002 Act and this regulation, as having made a claim for the tax credit in question for the current tax year; and

(b) if the claimant (or the relevant claimant) is entitled on the date on which the claim for universal credit was made to an award of a tax credit which is made in respect of a claim which is treated as having been made by virtue of sub-paragraph (a), that award is to terminate, by virtue of this regulation—

  (i) on the day before the first date on which the claimant is entitled to universal credit; or

  (ii) if the claimant is not entitled to universal credit, on the day before the first date on which he or she would have been so entitled, if all of the basic and financial conditions applicable to the claimant had been met.

(5) Where an award terminates by virtue of this regulation, any legislative provision under which the award terminates on a later date does not apply.

AMENDMENTS

1. Universal Credit (Transitional Provisions) (Amendment) Regulations 2014 (SI 2014/1626) reg.3 (November 3, 2014).

2. Universal Credit (Miscellaneous Amendments, Saving and Transitional Provision) Regulations 2018 (SI 2018/65) reg.6(7) (April 11, 2018).

3. Universal Credit (Managed Migration Pilot and Miscellaneous Amendments) Regulations 2019 (SI 2019/1152) reg.4(3) (July 22, 2020).

4. Universal Credit (Transitional Provisions) Amendment Regulations 2022 (SI 2022/752) reg.5(3) (July 25, 2022).

DEFINITIONS

"the 2002 Act"—see reg.2(1).
"the Act"—*ibid.*
"the Claims and Payments Regulations"—*ibid.*
"housing benefit"—*ibid.*
"income support"—*ibid.*
"specified accommodation"—*ibid.*
"tax credit"—*ibid.*
"tax year"—*ibid.*

GENERAL NOTE

2.753 As a general rule, all existing benefit or tax credit awards will terminate when an award of universal credit is made to a claimant. This regulation essentially performs the same function as reg.7 but for claimants who do not have a new claimant partner.

In *AD (A child, by her litigation friend TD) & PR v SSWP* [2019] EWHC 462 (Admin) the High Court had held that the failure to provide transitional protection for claimants who transferred to universal credit following an incorrect legacy benefit decision was not unlawful.

However, the High Court's decision was reversed by the Court of Appeal in *R (TD & Ors) v SSWP* [2020] EWCA Civ 618.

TD was a single parent entitled to IS, CTC (with a disabled child element) and carer's allowance. Her total entitlement (excluding HB) was £1,005.45 per month. She also received DLA, on behalf of her daughter, of £333.23 per month. In March 2017, the DWP stopped her IS award and her Job Centre advised her to claim universal credit, which was awarded in April 2017. TD's universal credit award was £872.90 a month, which was £136.99 a month less than she had been entitled under the legacy benefits. TD was unable to return to legacy benefits due to the application of regs 8 and 13. In August 2018, the DWP increased her daughter's DLA, meaning she was entitled to the highest rate of the disabled child element of CTC (up to April 2017) and, thereafter, the highest rate of the disabled child element of universal credit. As a result, the household's combined entitlement was now at the same level under universal credit as it would have been had TD continued to receive her legacy benefits. However, TD continued to seek a declaration and damages for the distress caused to them resulting from the drop in income at the time of transfer. She argued that the declaration sought would also benefit others in the same position who remained on a lower entitlement under universal credit.

PR was in receipt of ESA with the SDP and support component, and was also entitled to PIP when, in March 2017, the DWP stopped her ESA. She challenged that decision and claimed universal credit in April 2017. PR's legacy benefits entitled her to receive £814.67 per month, while her universal credit award was £636.58 per month, £178.09 less. The ESA decision was reversed in August 2017 but, as with TD, the 2014 Regulations precluded her from receiving or claiming any legacy benefits after her claim for universal credit.

TD (and her daughter) and PR were given permission for the judicial review challenge on three grounds: (1) that the treatment amounted to unlawful discrimination contrary to art.14 read with art.1 of the First Protocol to the ECHR (and in the case of TD and her daughter, it was said that their art.8 rights were also engaged); (2) that the decision of the Secretary of State to prevent those in the position of these claimants from returning to the legacy system, without providing for transitional protection, was irrational; and (3) that the SSWP had failed to comply with her Public Sector Equality Duty (PSED). In the High Court, May J. dismissed all three grounds.

However, the Court of Appeal accepted the Appellants' argument that, in their cases, the absence of transitional protection constituted discrimination contrary to art.14 of the ECHR. For art.14 purposes, the comparator group was, according to the Court of Appeal, "people who were entitled to legacy benefits and in whose cases no error was made by the Respondent". The High Court's analysis was flawed because, in considering whether the difference of treatment to which the Appellants had been subjected was justified, the judge failed to decide that matter for herself. Instead, the judge rejected the Appellants' case because she was persuaded that justification had been adequately considered by the Secretary of State. The Court of Appeal went on to decide that the difference of treatment was not justified and its effect was manifestly disproportionate for the Appellants, so that their rights under art.14 had been breached. The key consideration was identified in para.83 of the Court's judgment:

> "83...these Appellants were treated as they were despite their successful reviews, for reasons to do with administrative cost and complexity, which have nothing

to do with the merits of their cases; and that the only reason in reality why they moved from legacy benefits to UC was as a result of errors of law by the state itself."

The Court of Appeal gave a declaration that the Appellants' art.14 rights had been breached but added "it will be a matter for the Secretary of State to decide how to respond to a declaration". Whether or not the response will be to introduce transitional protection for all claimants, rather than limiting it to those undergoing "managed migration", remains to be seen. The Court's decision was not based on a finding that the absence of transitional protection was, in general, discrimination contrary to art.14. However, nor did the Court rule that its absence was, in general, justified. As explained above, the Court decided the case by reference to the, hopefully, infrequent circumstance of a misadvised claimant. Whether, in the absence of such circumstances, the UK Government's policy of granting transitional protection to universal credit "managed migrants", but not "natural migrants", falls foul of art.14 remains to be determined.

[1 Transitional housing payment

8A. Where an award of housing benefit terminates under regulation 8 [2 [3or 46]]— 2.754

(a) the claimant is to be treated for the purposes of the Housing Benefit Regulations 2006 as entitled to universal credit during the period of two weeks mentioned in regulation 8(2A) [2 [3or 46(1)]], even if no decision has been made on the claim; [2...]

(b) if a claim for universal credit is made because the claimant moves to new accommodation occupied as the claimant's home, then, notwithstanding anything in the Housing Benefit Regulations 2006, housing benefit is to be paid directly to the claimant during the period of two weeks mentioned in regulation 8(2A) [2 [3or 46(1)]] [2; and

(c) if a claim for universal credit is made by a notified person then, notwithstanding anything in the Housing Benefit Regulations 2006, the weekly amount of housing benefit to which the person is entitled for that period of two weeks is the same as the weekly amount they were entitled to on the first day of that period.]

AMENDMENTS

1. Universal Credit (Miscellaneous Amendments, Saving and Transitional Provision) Regulations 2018 (SI 2018/65) reg.6(8) (April 11, 2018).
2. Universal Credit (Managed Migration Pilot and Miscellaneous Amendments) Regulations 2019 (SI 2019/1152) reg.3(5) (July 24, 2019).
3. Universal Credit (Transitional Provisions) Amendment Regulations 2022 (SI 2022/752) reg.11 and Sch. para.1(4) (July 25, 2022).

DEFINITION

"housing benefit"—see reg.2(1).

GENERAL NOTE

The amendments to reg.8 effective from April 11, 2018 provide for a transitional housing payment for claimants who migrate to universal credit when they are in receipt of housing benefit. In addition, the new reg.8(2A) allows a housing benefit award to continue for a period of two weeks beyond the day on which the person becomes entitled to universal credit. The new reg.8A in turn provides that, pending 2.755

the decision on the claim, the claimant is treated as entitled to universal credit for the purposes of the housing benefit award, and where the claimant makes a claim for universal credit because they have moved home, housing benefit will be paid directly to the claimant for the period of two weeks beginning with the day on which they become entitled to universal credit. The references to regs 46 and 47 provide for the amount of housing benefit to be frozen during the two-week run-on period in a case where the claimant is moved to universal credit.

[[1]Effect on universal credit award of two week run-on of income support, income-based jobseeker's allowance and income-related employment and support allowance

2.756 **8B.** In a case where an award of income support, income-based jobseeker's allowance or income-related employment and support allowance is to continue for two weeks after the commencement of an award of universal credit by virtue of regulation 8(2A) [[2]or 46(1)] or by virtue of regulation 5 (two week run-on of income-based jobseeker's allowance and income-related employment and support allowance: day appointed for abolition) of the Universal Credit (Managed Migration Pilot and Miscellaneous Amendments) Regulations 2019—

(a) regulation 79 of the Universal Credit Regulations applies as if the benefit in question was not included in the list of welfare benefits in section 96(10) of the Act (benefit cap); and

(b) in a case where the claimant has become entitled to an award of new style JSA or new style ESA on the termination of an award of income-based jobseeker's allowance or income-related employment and support allowance, the claimant is to be treated, for the purposes of regulation 73 of the Universal Credit Regulations (unearned income calculated monthly), as if they had been entitled to that award of new style JSA or new style ESA from the first day of the award of universal credit.]

AMENDMENTS

1. Universal Credit (Managed Migration Pilot and Miscellaneous Amendments) Regulations 2019 (SI 2019/1152) reg.4(4) (July 22, 2020).

2. Universal Credit (Transitional Provisions) Amendment Regulations 2022 (SI 2022/752) reg.11 and Sch. para.1(5) (July 25, 2022).

GENERAL NOTE

2.757 This regulation provides for an award of income support, income-based jobseeker's allowance or income-related employment and support allowance to continue for two weeks beyond the date on which it would otherwise have terminated as result of a claim for universal credit (or, in a managed migration case, a failure to make a claim by the deadline day). This reflects a recommendation by the SSAC, which was concerned that claimants who were reliant on (legacy) benefits paid fortnightly should not bear the risk from the Government's policy that universal credit is paid monthly. In the absence of such a run-on, claimants would otherwise be offered the choice between financial hardship (while waiting for the first universal credit payment) or getting into debt with the Department (by requesting an advance payment).

Treatment of ongoing entitlement to certain benefits: benefit cap

2.758 **9.** (1) This regulation applies where a claimant who is a new claimant partner, or who has (in accordance with regulation 26 of [[2] the Claims and Payments Regulations]) been awarded universal credit in respect of a period preceding the date on which the claim for universal credit was made or treated as made—

(a) is entitled, in respect of the whole or part of the first assessment period for universal credit, to a welfare benefit (other than universal credit) mentioned in [[1]section 96(10) of the Act (benefit cap)]; and

(b) is entitled to housing benefit at any time during the first assessment period for universal credit, or would be so entitled were it not for the effect of these Regulations.

(2) Where this regulation applies, regulation 79 of the Universal Credit Regulations applies, in relation to the claimant, as if the benefit in question was not included in the list of welfare benefits in [[1] section 96(10) of the Act].

AMENDMENTS

1. Benefit Cap (Housing Benefit and Universal Credit) (Amendment) Regulations 2016 (SI 2016/909) reg.5(a) (November 7, 2016).

2. Social Security and Universal Credit (Miscellaneous Amendments) Regulations 2023 (SI 2023/543) reg.6(2) (June 29, 2023).

DEFINITIONS

"assessment period"—see reg.2(1).
"housing benefit"—*ibid.*
"new claimant partner"—*ibid.*
"the Universal Credit Regulations"—*ibid.*

GENERAL NOTE

This regulation provides for entitlement to some benefits (i.e. those listed in reg.79(4) of the Universal Credit Regulations 2013) to be disregarded for the purposes of the benefit cap during the claimant's first assessment period for universal credit. This applies where a claimant is entitled to universal credit from a date before the date on which they made a claim, or were treated as making a claim, and they were also previously entitled to housing benefit (which may already have been subject to the benefit cap). 7.759

Treatment of overpayments

10. (1) This regulation applies where— 2.760

(a) an award of universal credit is made to a claimant who was previously entitled to an existing benefit other than a tax credit or a joint-claim jobseeker's allowance; and

(b) a payment of the existing benefit is made which includes payment ("the overpayment") in respect of a period—

(i) during which the claimant is not entitled to that benefit (including non-entitlement which arises from termination of an award by virtue of an order made under section 150(3) of the Act or regulation 7, 8, or 14); and

(ii) which falls within an assessment period for universal credit.

(2) Where this regulation applies, for the purposes of calculating the amount of an award of universal credit in respect of an assessment period—

(a) regulation 66 of the Universal Credit Regulations (what is included in unearned income?) applies as if the overpayment which was made in respect of that assessment period were added to the descriptions of unearned income in paragraph (1)(b) of that regulation; and

(b) regulation 73 of the Universal Credit Regulations (unearned income calculated monthly) does not apply to the overpayment.

(3) In so far as any overpayment is taken into account in calculating the amount of an award of universal credit in accordance with this regulation, that payment may not be recovered as an overpayment under—

(a) the Social Security (Payments on account, Overpayments and Recovery) Regulations 1988;

(b) the Housing Benefit Regulations 2006; or

(c) [1 the 2006 (SPC) Regulations].

AMENDMENT

1. Universal Credit (Persons who have attained state pension credit qualifying age) (Amendment) Regulations 2020 (SI 2020/655) reg.6(6) (November 25, 2020).

DEFINITIONS

"the Act"—see reg.2(1).
"assessment period"—*ibid.*
"existing benefit"—*ibid.*
"joint-claim jobseeker's allowance"—*ibid.*
"overpayment"—para.(1)(b).
"tax credit"—see reg.2(1).
"the Universal Credit Regulations"—*ibid.*

GENERAL NOTE

2.761 This regulation provides that overpayments of existing benefits (other than joint-claim jobseeker's allowance or tax credits) that may arise on transition to universal credit are to be off-set against entitlement to universal credit (para.(1)). Thus, overpayments of existing benefits which may arise on transition to universal credit can be offset as unearned income against the claimant's entitlement to universal credit (para.(2)) and may not then be recovered under other legislation (para.(3)). This is because it will be recovered as unearned income from the universal credit award rather than as an excess payment under existing overpayments legislation.

[1 Arrears of benefit disregarded as capital

2.762 **10A.**—(1) This regulation applies in relation to the calculation of an award of universal credit (the "current award") where the claimant has received a payment of arrears of benefit [2or armed forces independence payment], or a payment made to compensate for arrears due to the non-payment of benefit [2or armed forces independence payment], of £5,000 or more, and the following conditions are met—

(a) the payment—

(i) is received during the current award; or

(ii) was received during an award of an existing benefit or state pension credit (the "earlier award") and the claimant became entitled to the current award within one month of the date of termination of the earlier award;

(b) in the case of a payment falling within sub-paragraph (a)(i), it would be disregarded from the calculation of the claimant's capital if the claimant were entitled to an existing benefit or state pension credit;

(c) in the case of a payment falling within sub-paragraph (a)(ii), it was disregarded from the calculation of the claimant's capital for the purposes of the earlier award; and

(d) the period of entitlement to benefit [[2]or armed forces independence payment] to which the payment relates commences before the first date on which, by virtue of section 33 of the Act (abolition of benefits), no claimant is entitled to an existing benefit.

(2) Where this regulation applies, notwithstanding anything in the Universal Credit Regulations, the payment is to be disregarded from the calculation of the claimant's capital for 12 months from the date of receipt of the payment, or until the termination of the current award (if later).]

[[2](3) "Armed forces independence payment" means armed forces independence payment under the Armed Forces and Reserve Forces (Compensation Scheme) Order 2011.]

AMENDMENTS

1. Social Security (Treatment of Arrears of Benefit) Regulations 2018 (SI 2018/932) reg.8 (September 11, 2018).
2. Social Security (Capital Disregards) (Amendment) Regulations 2019 (SI 2019/1314) reg.9(2) (October 31, 2019).

DEFINITIONS

"armed forces independence payment"—see para.(3).
"current award"—see para.(1).
"earlier award"—see para.(1)(a)(ii).
"existing benefit"—see reg.2(1).

GENERAL NOTE

The UC Regs 2013 provide for arrears of a means-tested benefit, or a payment to compensate for arrears, to be disregarded for a period of 12 months from the date the payment is received (see Sch.10 para.18). As originally enacted, there was no provision for such a payment to be disregarded for a longer period if it had been paid out because of official error. This regulation provides for the longer disregard to apply until the termination of the universal credit award where a payment of arrears of £5,000 or more has been received during an earlier award of an income-related benefit and the claimant becomes entitled to universal credit within one month of their earlier award terminating, or where it has been received during the universal credit award. Thus, the effect is that the arrears in question may be disregarded for the life of the benefit award rather than for the usual maximum of 52 weeks. This additional disregard only applies to a payment that relates to a period of entitlement to benefit which begins before migration of existing benefits to universal credit is completed. 2.763

[[1]Arrears of maternity allowance disregarded as capital

10B.—(1) This regulation applies in relation to the calculation of an award of universal credit where— 2.764

(a) the conditions set out in regulation 10A(1)(a) to (d) are met; and

(b) the claimant has received a payment of arrears of maternity allowance, or a payment made to compensate for arrears due to the non-payment of maternity allowance, of under £5,000.

(2) Where this regulation applies, notwithstanding anything in the Universal Credit Regulations, the payment is to be disregarded from the calculation of the claimant's capital for 12 months from the date of receipt of the payment.

(3) "Maternity allowance" means a maternity allowance under section 35 of the Social Security Contributions and Benefits Act 1992 (state maternity allowance for employed or self-employed earner).]

AMENDMENT

1. Social Security (Capital Disregards) (Amendment) Regulations 2019 (SI 2019/1314) reg.9(3) (October 31, 2019).

DEFINITIONS

"maternity allowance" para.(3).
"Universal Credit Regulations" reg.2(1).

[[1]Compensatory payment disregarded as capital

2.765 **10C.**—(1) This regulation applies in relation to the calculation of an award of universal credit where—

(a) the claimant has received a payment made to rectify, or to compensate for, an error made by an officer of the Department for Work and Pensions which was not caused or materially contributed to by any person outside the Department and which prevented or delayed an assessment of the claimant's entitlement to contributory employment and support allowance; and

(b) the payment is received before the first date on which, by virtue of section 33 of the Act (abolition of benefits), no claimant is entitled to an existing benefit.

(2) Where this regulation applies and the amount of the payment is less than £5,000, the payment is to be disregarded from the calculation of the claimant's capital for 12 months from the date of receipt of the payment.

(3) Where—

(a) this regulation applies;

(b) the amount of the payment is £5,000 or more; and

(c) the conditions set out in regulation 10A(1)(a) and (c) are met,

the payment is to be disregarded from the calculation of the claimant's capital for 12 months from the date of receipt of the payment, or until the termination of the current award (if later).]

AMENDMENT

1. Social Security (Income and Capital) (Miscellaneous Amendments) Regulations 2020 (SI 2020/618) reg.9 (July 15, 2020).

GENERAL NOTE

2.766 Universal credit replaces income-related ESA but not contribution-based ESA. Since, however, it is not possible to have entitlement to both universal credit and the original versions of ESA, the Government introduced new-style ESA in 2013 to provide a benefit which is wholly and exclusively based on National Insurance contributions, and so can be paid alongside universal credit. However, extra-statutory payments have had to be made to provide redress to people affected by initial errors in the way claims for new-style ESA were handled. These extra-statutory payments are intended to restore a claimant's award to as near as possible the amount that should have been payable, were it not for the incorrect advice. Where this payment would otherwise affect an individual's award of universal credit, it will be disregarded under this provision. HM Treasury has provided the DWP with the appropriate cover to disregard the extra-statutory payments for the interim period until the new regulation provided a firm statutory backing.

Ongoing awards of tax credits

11. (1) For the purposes of [[2]these Regulations]— 2.767

(a) a person is to be treated as being entitled to working tax credit with effect from the start of the current tax year even though a decision has not been made under section 14 of the 2002 Act in respect of a claim for that tax credit for that tax year, if the person was entitled to working tax credit for the previous tax year and any of the cases specified in paragraph (2) applies; and

(b) a person is to be treated as being entitled to child tax credit with effect from the start of the current tax year even though a decision has not been made under section 14 of the 2002 Act in respect of a claim for that tax credit for that tax year, if the person was entitled to child tax credit for the previous tax year and any of the cases specified in paragraph (2) applies[[2];]

[[2]and references to an award of a tax credit are to be read accordingly].

(2) The cases are—

(a) a final notice has not been given to the person under section 17 of the 2002 Act in respect of the previous tax year;

(b) a final notice has been given, which includes provision by virtue of subsection (2) or (4) of section 17, or a combination of those subsections and subsection (6) and—

(i) the date specified in the notice for the purposes of section 17(2) and (4) or, where different dates are specified, the later of them, has not yet passed and no claim for a tax credit for the current tax year has been made, or treated as made; or

(ii) a claim for a tax credit has been made, or treated as made, on or before the date mentioned in paragraph (i), but no decision has been made in relation to that claim under section 14(1) of the 2002 Act;

(c) a final notice has been given, no claim for a tax credit for the current year has been made, or treated as made, and no decision has been made under section 18(1) of the 2002 Act in respect of entitlement to a tax credit for the previous tax year; [[1]. . .]

[[1](ca) a final notice has been given and the person made a declaration in response to a requirement included in that notice by virtue of section 17(2)(a), (4)(a) or (6)(a), or any combination of those provisions—

(i) by the date specified on the final notice;

(ii) if not in accordance with paragraph (i), within 30 days following the date on the notice to the person that payments of tax credit under section 24(4) of the 2002 Act have ceased due to the person's failure to make the declaration by the date specified in the final notice; or

(iii) if not in accordance with paragraph (i) or (ii), before 31 January in the tax year following the period to which the final notice relates and, in the opinion of Her Majesty's Revenue and Customs, the person had good reason for not making the declaration in accordance with paragraph (i) or (ii); or]

(d) a final notice has been given and—

(i) the person did not make a declaration in response to provision included in that notice by virtue of section 17(2)(a), (4)(a) or (6)(a), or any combination of those provisions, by the date specified in the notice;

(ii) the person was given due notice that payments of tax credit under section 24(4) of the 2002 Act had ceased due to his or her failure to make the declaration; and

(iii) the person's claim for universal credit is made during the period of 30 days starting with the date on the notice referred to in paragraph (ii) or, where the person is a new claimant partner, notification of formation of a couple with a person entitled to universal credit is given to the Secretary of State during that period.

AMENDMENTS

1. Universal Credit (Miscellaneous Amendments, Saving and Transitional Provision) Regulations 2018 (SI 2018/65) reg.6(9) (February 14, 2018).

2. Universal Credit (Managed Migration Pilot and Miscellaneous Amendments) Regulations 2019 (SI 2019/1152) reg.3(6) (July 24, 2019).

DEFINITIONS

"the 2002 Act"—see reg.2(1).
"new claimant partner"—*ibid.*
"tax credit"—*ibid.*
"tax year"—*ibid.*

GENERAL NOTE

2.768 This regulation provides for a claimant to be treated as entitled to an award of a tax credit in certain cases, for the purposes of regs.7 and 8.

Modification of tax credits legislation: overpayments and penalties

2.769 **12.** (1) This regulation applies where—

(a) a claim for universal credit is made, or is treated as having been made; [3and]

(b) the claimant is, or was at any time during the tax year in which the claim is made or treated as made, entitled to a tax credit [3...];

(c) [3...].

(2) Where this regulation applies, the 2002 Act applies in relation to the claimant with the following modifications.

(3) In section 28—

(a) in subsection (1)—

(i) after "tax year" in both places where it occurs, insert "or part tax year";

[2 (ii) in paragraph (b), for the words from "as if it were" to the end substitute "as an overpayment of universal credit"]

(b) [2. . .]
(c) omit subsection (5);
(d) in subsection (6) omit "(apart from subsection (5))".
[1 (4) [2. . .]]
(5) In section 48 after the definition of "overpayment" insert—
""part tax year" means a period of less than a year beginning with 6th April and ending with the date on which the award of a tax credit terminated,".
(6) In Schedule 2, in paragraph 6(1)(a) and (c) and (2)(a), after "for the tax year" insert "or part tax year".

AMENDMENTS

1. Universal Credit (Transitional Provisions) (Amendment) Regulations 2016 (SI 2016/232) reg.2 (April 1, 2016).
2. Tax Credits (Exercise of Functions in relation to Northern Ireland and Notices for Recovery of Tax Credit Overpayments) Order 2017 (2017/781) art.7 (September 25, 2017).
3. Universal Credit (Transitional Provisions) Amendment Regulations 2022 (SI 2022/752) reg.5(4) (July 25, 2022).

DEFINITIONS

"the 2002 Act"—see reg.2(1).
"the Act"—*ibid.*
"tax credit"—*ibid.*
"tax year"—*ibid.*

GENERAL NOTE

This regulation provides that, where a claim for universal credit is made by a claimant who was previously entitled to a tax credit, the Tax Credits Act 2002 is to apply to that claimant with certain modifications. For a full analysis of the impact of these modifications, see *HMRC v AS (TC)* [2023] UKUT 67 (AAC). The effect is that that any overpayments of tax credits may be treated as overpayments of universal credit and appropriate time limits apply in relation to the imposition of penalties. **2.770**

[1 Modification of tax credits legislation: finalisation of tax credits

12A. (1) This regulation applies where— **2.771**
(a) a claim for universal credit is made, or is treated as having been made [3, or a migration notice is issued and the notified person fails to make a claim on or before the deadline day];
(b) the claimant is, or was at any time during the tax year in which the claim is made or treated as made [3 or in which the deadline day falls], entitled to a tax credit [2...]
(c) [2...]
(2) Subject to paragraph (3), where this regulation applies, the amount of the tax credit to which the person is entitled is to be calculated in accordance with the 2002 Act and regulations made under that Act, as modified by the Schedule to these Regulations ("the modified legislation").
(3) Where, in the opinion of the Commissioners for Her Majesty's Revenue and Customs, it is not reasonably practicable to apply the modified legislation in relation to any case or category of cases, the 2002 Act and regulations made under that Act are to apply without modification in that case or category of cases.]

Amendments

1. Universal Credit (Transitional Provisions) (Amendment) Regulations 2014 (SI 2014/1626) reg.4 (October 13, 2014).
2. Universal Credit (Transitional Provisions) Amendment Regulations 2022 (SI 2022/752) reg.5(5) (July 25, 2022).
3. Social Security and Universal Credit (Migration of Tax Credit Claimants and Miscellaneous Amendments) Regulations 2024 (SI 2024/341) reg.8(3) (April 6, 2024).

Definitions

"the 2002 Act"—see reg.2(1).
"the 2002 Act"—*ibid.*
"the modified legislation"—para.(2).
"tax credit"—see reg.2(1).
"tax year"—*ibid.*

General Note

2.772 This amendment is designed to smooth the transition from receipt of tax credits to an award of universal credit. It re-instates provision for in-year finalisation of tax credits for universal credit claimants (there was no equivalent to reg.17 of, and the Schedule to, the 2013 Transitional Regulations in the original version of the 2014 Transitional Regulations). By doing so, this provision allows tax credits awards to be finalised during the relevant tax year when a tax credit claimant makes the transition to universal credit (see paras.(1) and (2) and the Schedule), rather than after the end of the tax year. This is intended to reduce administrative complexity and confusion for the claimant by providing a clean break from tax credits, thus avoiding the claimant having to revert to providing HMRC with information about their circumstances and income after they have been receiving universal credit for some time. It also should thereby, in theory at least, ensure the claimant has a single interaction with HMRC so that HMRC only have to deal with their case once, as both the stopping of a tax credits award and the finalising of the award are dealt with upon transition to universal credit. In practice the modifications to the normal rules involve considerable complexity; for a full analysis see *HMRC v AS (TC)* [2023] UKUT 67 (AAC), which emphasises that the focus of the modified rules is on income *received in* the part-year period rather than income *attributable to* the part-year period.

Although the intention is that in-year finalisation of tax credits awards is the default approach in the majority of cases, provision has been made (see para.(3)) to allow HMRC to continue to finalise tax credits awards after the end of the tax year, if they think that it is not practicable to apply the modified legislation to a particular case or class of case, e.g. where it proved difficult to verify income that is particularly complex, such as those cases including particular combinations of self-employed and other income. Para.(3) might also be invoked as a contingency to guard against unforeseen operational or IT difficulties.

Appeals etc relating to certain existing benefits

2.773 **13.** (1) This regulation applies where, after an award of universal credit has been made to a claimant—

(a) an appeal against a decision relating to the entitlement of the claimant to income support, housing benefit or a tax credit (a "relevant benefit") is finally determined;
(b) a decision relating to the claimant's entitlement to income support is revised under section 9 of the Social Security Act 1998 ("the 1998 Act") or superseded under section 10 of that Act;

(c) a decision relating to the claimant's entitlement to housing benefit is revised or superseded under Schedule 7 to the Child Support, Pensions and Social Security Act 2000; or

(d) a decision relating to the claimant's entitlement to a tax credit is revised under section 19 or 20 of the 2002 Act, or regulations made under section 21 of that Act, or is varied or cancelled under section 21A of that Act.

(2) Where the claimant is a new claimant partner and, as a result of determination of the appeal or, as the case may be, revision or supersession of the decision the claimant would (were it not for the effect of these Regulations) be entitled to income support or housing benefit during the relevant period mentioned in regulation 7(3), awards of those benefits are to terminate in accordance with regulation 7.

(3) Where the claimant is not a new claimant partner and, as a result of determination of the appeal or, as the case may be, revision, supersession, variation or cancellation of the decision, the claimant would (were it not for the effect of these Regulations) be entitled to a relevant benefit on the date on which the claim for universal credit was made, awards of relevant benefits are to terminate in accordance with regulation 8 [[1] [[2] or 46]].

(4) The Secretary of State is to consider whether it is appropriate to revise under section 9 of the 1998 Act the decision in relation to entitlement to universal credit or, if that decision has been superseded under section 10 of that Act, the decision as so superseded (in either case, "the UC decision").

(5) Where it appears to the Secretary of State to be appropriate to revise the UC decision, it is to be revised in such manner as appears to the Secretary of State to be necessary to take account of—

(a) the decision of the First-tier Tribunal, Upper Tribunal or court, or, as the case may be, the decision relating to entitlement to a relevant benefit, as revised, superseded, varied or cancelled; and

(b) any finding of fact by the First-tier Tribunal, Upper Tribunal or court.

AMENDMENTS

1. Universal Credit (Managed Migration Pilot and Miscellaneous Amendments) Regulations 2019 (SI 2019/1152) reg.4(7) (July 22, 2020).

2. Universal Credit (Transitional Provisions) Amendment Regulations 2022 (SI 2022/752) reg.11 and Sch. para.1(6) (July 25, 2022).

DEFINITIONS

"the 1998 Act"—para.(1)(b).
"the 2002 Act"—see reg.2(1).
"First-tier Tribunal"—*ibid.*
"housing benefit"—*ibid.*
"income support"—*ibid.*
"new claimant partner"—*ibid.*
"relevant benefit"—para.(1)(a).
"tax credit"—see reg.2(1).
"the UC decision"—para.(4).
"Upper Tribunal"—see reg.2(1).

GENERAL NOTE

This regulation deals with appeals which are determined, and decisions about existing benefits which are revised or superseded, after the appellant has become entitled to universal credit (see para.(1)). Entitlement to income support, housing 2.774

benefit or a tax credit arising from an appeal, revision or supersession will terminate in accordance with regulation 7 or 8 (paras.(2) and (3)) and a decision made about entitlement to universal credit may be revised to take account of any findings of fact by the relevant appeal body (paras.(4) and (5)). The equivalent provision in the 2013 Transitional Regulations (reg.18) applied only to new claimants partners; this provision applies to all claimants and not just new claimant partners. See further the note to reg.8 above.

Appeals etc relating to universal credit

2.775 **14.** (1) This regulation applies where—

(a) a decision is made that a claimant is not entitled to universal credit ("the UC decision");

(b) the claimant becomes entitled to income support, housing benefit or a tax credit (a "relevant benefit");

(c) an appeal against the UC decision is finally determined, or the decision is revised under section 9 of the Social Security Act 1998;

(d) an award of universal credit is made to the claimant in consequence of entitlement arising from the appeal, or from the decision as revised; and

(e) the claimant would (were it not for the effect of regulation 5 and this regulation) be entitled to both universal credit and a relevant benefit in respect of the same period.

(2) Subject to paragraph (3), where this regulation applies—

(a) all awards of a relevant benefit to which the claimant would (were it not for the effect of these Regulations) be entitled are to terminate, by virtue of this regulation, at the beginning of the first day of entitlement to that award; and

(b) any legislative provision [2 except regulation 8(2A)] under which an award would otherwise terminate on a later date does not apply.

(3) An award of housing benefit to which a claimant is entitled in respect of [1 specified accommodation] [2 or temporary accommodation] does not terminate by virtue of this regulation.

AMENDMENTS

1. Universal Credit (Transitional Provisions) (Amendment) Regulations 2014 (SI 2014/1626) reg.3 (November 3, 2014).

2. Universal Credit (Miscellaneous Amendments, Saving and Transitional Provision) Regulations 2018 (SI 2018/65) reg.6(10) (April 11, 2018).

DEFINITIONS

"housing benefit"—see reg.2(1).
"income support"—*ibid.*
"relevant benefit"—para.(1)(b).
"specified accommodation"—see reg.2(1).
"tax credit"—*ibid.*
"the UC decision"—para.(1)(a).

GENERAL NOTE

2.776 This regulation concerns the situation where a claimant successfully appeals a decision that they are not entitled to universal credit, or such a decision is revised, but only after the claimant has become entitled to income support, housing benefit or a tax credit. In such a case, the award of the existing benefit terminates at the beginning of the first day of entitlement if there would otherwise be an overlap with the award of universal credit.

CHAPTER 3

Modification of Claims and Payments Regulations in relation to universal credit claimants

15. (1) Where a claim for universal credit is made by a person who was previously entitled to an existing benefit, regulation 26 of the Claims and Payments Regulations (time within which a claim for universal credit is to be made) applies in relation to that claim with the modification specified in paragraph (2). 2.777

(2) In paragraph (3) of regulation 26, after sub-paragraph (a) insert—

"(aa) the claimant was previously in receipt of an existing benefit (as defined in the Universal Credit (Transitional Provisions) Regulations 2014) and notification of expiry of entitlement to that benefit was not sent to the claimant before the date that the claimant's entitlement expired;".

DEFINITIONS

"the Claims and Payments Regulations"—see reg.2(1).
"existing benefit"—*ibid.*

GENERAL NOTE

Where a claim for universal credit is made by a claimant who was previously entitled to an existing benefit, this regulation modifies the application of reg.26(3) of the Claims and Payments Regulations 2013 in relation to the claimant. In practice it means that the time for claiming universal credit may be extended by up to one month, if the claimant was not given advance notice of termination of the award of existing benefit. The aim is to ensure that the same rule applies to claimants making the transition to universal credit from existing benefits as will apply in relation to universal credit and other benefits after the transitional period. 2.778

Persons unable to act

16. (1) Paragraph (2) applies where— 2.779

(a) a person ("P2") has been appointed, or treated as appointed, under regulation 33(1) of the Social Security (Claims and Payments) Regulations 1987 ("the 1987 Regulations") (persons unable to act) to exercise rights and to receive and deal with sums payable on behalf of a person who is unable to act ("P1"); or

(b) a person ("P2") has been appointed under regulation 18(3) of the Tax Credits (Claims and Notifications) Regulations 2002 ("the 2002 Regulations") (circumstances where one person may act for another in making a claim – other appointed persons) to act for a person who is unable to act ("P1") in making a claim for a tax credit.

(2) Where this paragraph applies and P1 is, or may be, entitled to universal credit, the Secretary of State may, if P2 agrees, treat the appointment of P2 as if it were made under regulation 57(1) of the Claims and Payments Regulations (persons unable to act) and P2 may carry out the functions set out in regulation 57(4) of those Regulations in relation to P1.

(3) Paragraph (4) applies where a person ("P2") was appointed, or treated as appointed, under regulation 57(1) of the Claims and Payments Regulations to carry out functions in relation to a person who is unable to act ("P1") and who was, or might have been, entitled to universal credit, but who has ceased to be so entitled, or was not in fact so entitled.

(4) Where this paragraph applies—

(a) the Secretary of State may, if P2 agrees, treat the appointment of P2 as if it were made under regulation 33(1) of the 1987 Regulations and P2 may exercise rights and receive and deal with sums payable in respect of existing benefits on behalf of P1; and

(b) the Board (within the meaning of the 2002 Regulations) may, if P2 agrees, treat the appointment of P2 as if it were made under regulation 18(3) of the 2002 Regulations and P2 may act for P1 in making a claim for a tax credit.

DEFINITIONS

"the 1987 Regulations"—para.(1)(a).
"the 2002 Regulations"—para.(1)(b).
"the Claims and Payments Regulations"—see reg.2(1).
"existing benefit"—*ibid.*
"tax credit"—*ibid.*

GENERAL NOTE

2.780 The effect of this regulation (which had no equivalent provision in the 2013 Transitional Regulations) is that a person who has been appointed to act on behalf of a claimant in relation to existing benefits and/or tax credits may be treated as having been appointed to act on their behalf in relation to universal credit and *vice versa*. This may be particularly relevant where claimants have mental health problems or where they suffer from other conditions that make communication with the Department very difficult or impossible. The aim of the provision is to make the process of transition between existing benefits and universal credit easier for claimants who are in this position.

[[1] Waiting days

2.781 **16A.** [[2]. . .]]

AMENDMENTS

1. Universal Credit (Waiting Days) (Amendment) Regulations 2015 (SI 2015/1362) reg.2(2) (August 3, 2015).
2. Universal Credit (Miscellaneous Amendments, Saving and Transitional Provision) Regulations 2018 (SI 2018/65) reg.6(11) (April 11, 2018).

Advance payments of universal credit

2.782 **17.** (1) This regulation applies where—

(a) the Secretary of State is deciding a claim for universal credit, other than a claim which is treated as having been made, in accordance with regulation 9(8) of the Claims and Payments Regulations;

(b) the claimant is, or was previously, entitled to an existing benefit ("the earlier award"); and

(c) if the earlier award terminated before the date on which the claim for universal credit was made, the claim for universal credit was made during the period of one month starting with the date of termination.

(2) Where this regulation applies—

(a) a single claimant may request an advance payment of universal credit;

(b) joint claimants may jointly request such a payment,

at any time during the first assessment period for universal credit.

(3) Where a request has been made in accordance with this regulation, the Secretary of State may make an advance payment to the claimant, or joint claimants, of such amount in respect of universal credit as the Secretary of State considers appropriate.

(4) After an advance payment has been made under this regulation, payments of any award of universal credit to the claimant or, in the case of joint claimants, to either or both of them, may be reduced until the amount of the advance payment is repaid.

DEFINITIONS

"assessment period"—see reg.2(1).
"the Claims and Payments Regulations"—*ibid.*
"the earlier award"—para.(1)(b).
"existing benefit"—see reg.2(1).

GENERAL NOTE

As a general rule universal credit is payable monthly in arrears (Claims and Payments Regulations 2013, reg.47(1)). Where a claim for universal credit is made by a claimant who was entitled to an existing benefit before they became entitled to universal credit, this regulation allows the claimant to apply for an advance payment of universal credit during their first assessment period (paras.(1) and (2)). The amount of any advance payment is at the discretion of the Secretary of State (para. (3)). Repayment is by reduction of subsequent payments (para.(4)). 2.783

This regulation differs from its predecessor in the 2013 Transitional Regulations (reg.19), in that new claimant partners are now no longer able to request such an advance. Instead, if the new couple require support they will have to apply for a universal credit (change of circumstances) advance. The justification for this change is that it is supposed to reduce complexity in the advance payment process.

Deductions from benefits

18. (1) This regulation applies where— 2.784

(a) an award of universal credit is made to a claimant who—
  (i) was entitled to income-based jobseeker's allowance, income-related employment and support allowance or income support (a "relevant award") on the date on which the claim for universal credit was made or treated as made;
  (ii) is a new claimant partner who was, immediately before forming a couple with a person entitled to universal credit, the partner of a person ("P") who was at that time entitled to a relevant award; or
  (iii) is not a new claimant partner and was, immediately before making a claim for universal credit, the partner of a person ("P") who was at that time entitled to a relevant award, where the award of universal credit is not a joint award to the claimant and P; and
(b) on the relevant date, deductions in respect of fuel costs or water charges were being made under regulation 35 of the Social Security (Claims and Payments) Regulations 1987, in accordance with Schedule 9 to those Regulations.

(2) In this regulation, the "relevant date" means—
(a) where paragraph (1)(a)(i) applies and the claimant is not a new claimant partner, the date on which the claim for universal credit was made;

(b) where paragraph (1)(a)(i) applies and the claimant is a new claimant partner, the date on which the claim for universal credit was treated as made;

(c) where paragraph (1)(a)(ii) or (iii) applies, the date on which the claimant ceased to be the partner of P.

(3) Where this regulation applies, deductions in respect of fuel costs or, as the case may be, water charges, may be made from the award of universal credit in accordance with Schedule 6 to the Claims and Payments Regulations, without the need for any consent which would otherwise be required under paragraph 3(3) of that Schedule.

(4) For the purposes of this regulation, a deduction is to be taken into account even if the relevant award subsequently terminated by virtue of an order made under section 150(3) of the Act, regulation 7 or, as the case may be, regulation 8, before the date on which the deduction was first applied.

DEFINITIONS

"the Act"—see reg.2(1).
"the Claims and Payments Regulations"—*ibid.*
"income-based jobseeker's allowance"—*ibid.*
"income-related employment and support allowance"—*ibid.*
"income support"—*ibid.*
"new claimant partner"—*ibid.*
"partner"—*ibid.*
"relevant award"—para.(1)(a)(i).
"relevant date"—para.(2).

GENERAL NOTE

2.785 Where certain deductions were made from an award of an existing benefit (e.g. for fuel costs or water charges), this regulation allows deductions in respect of the same items to be made from an award of universal credit without the need for the consents which might otherwise be required.

Transition from old style ESA

2.786 **19.** (1) This regulation applies where—

(a) an award of universal credit is made to a claimant who was entitled to old style ESA on the date on which the claim for universal credit was made or treated as made ("the relevant date"); and

[1 (b) on or before the relevant date it had been determined that the claimant had limited capability for work or limited capability for work-related activity (within the meaning of Part 1 of the 2007 Act).]

(2) Where, on or before the relevant date, it had been determined that the claimant [1 had limited capability for work (within the meaning of Part 1 of the 2007 Act)]—

(a) [1 . . .]

(b) the claimant is to be treated as having limited capability for work for the purposes of [1 . . .] section 21(1)(a) of [2the Act; and

(c) the claimant is to be treated as if the determination that they have limited capability for work, for the purposes of regulation 14(1)(b) of the Universal Credit Regulations, was made before the date on which the claimant started receiving education (see regulations 12(2) and 13 of the Universal Credit Regulations).]

(3) [1 . . .]

(4) Where, on or before the relevant date, it had been determined that the claimant [1 had limited capability for work-related activity (within the meaning of Part 1 of the 2007 Act) or was treated as having limited capability for work-related activity]—

(a) regulation 27(3) of the Universal Credit Regulations does not apply; [2 . . .]

(b) the claimant is to be treated as having limited capability for work and work-related activity for the purposes of regulation 27(1)(b) of those Regulations and section 19(2)(a) of [2the Act; and

(c) the claimant is to be treated as if the determination that they have limited capability for work and work-related activity, for the purposes of regulation 14(1)(b) of those Regulations, was made before the date on which the claimant started receiving education.]

(5) Unless the assessment phase applied and had not ended at the relevant date, in relation to a claimant who is treated as having limited capability for work and work-related activity under paragraph (4)(4)(b)—

(a) regulation 28 of the Universal Credit Regulations does not apply; and

(b) the LCWRA element is (subject to the provisions of Part 4 of the Universal Credit Regulations) to be included in the award of universal credit with effect from the beginning of the first assessment period.

(6) For the purposes of this regulation, a determination that the claimant [1 had limited capability for work or, as the case may be, limited capability for work-related activity (within the meaning of Part 1 of the 2007 Act)], is to be taken into account even if the award of old style ESA subsequently terminated (in so far as it was an award of income-related employment and support allowance) before the date on which that determination was made, by virtue of an order made under section 150(3) of the Act.

(7) Where a claimant is treated, by virtue of this regulation, as having limited capability for work or, as the case may be, limited capability for work and work-related activity, the Secretary of State may at any time make a fresh determination as to these matters, in accordance with the Universal Credit Regulations.

(8) In this regulation and in regulations 20 to 27—

[1 "assessment phase" has the same meaning as in the 2007 Act;]

"incapacity benefit" and "severe disablement allowance" have the same meanings as in Schedule 4 to that Act;

[1 "LCWRA element" has the same meaning as in the Universal Credit Regulations.]

(9) For the purposes of this regulation and regulation 20, references to cases in which the assessment phase applied are references to cases in which sections 2(2)(a)[1 and 4(4)(a)] of the 2007 Act applied and references to cases in which the assessment phase did not apply are references to cases in which those sections did not apply.

[1 (10) For the purposes of this regulation, references to a determination that the claimant had limited capability for work do not include a determination made under regulation 30 of the Employment and Support Allowance Regulations 2008 (conditions for treating a claimant as having limited capability for work until a determination about limited capability for work has been made).]

AMENDMENT

1. Employment and Support Allowance and Universal Credit (Miscellaneous Amendments and Transitional and Savings Provisions) Regulations 2017 (SI 2017/204) reg.5(2) (April 3, 2017).

2. Universal Credit (Exceptions to the Requirement not to be receiving Education) (Amendment) Regulations 2021 (SI 2021/1224) reg.3 (December 15, 2021).

DEFINITIONS

"the Act"—see reg.2(1).
"assessment period"—*ibid.*
"assessment phase"—para.(8).
"incapacity benefit"—*ibid.*
"income-based jobseeker's allowance"—see reg.2(1).
"LCW element"—para.(8).
"LCWRA element"—*ibid.*
"old style ESA"—see reg.2(1).
"the relevant date"—para.(1)(a).
"severe disablement allowance"—para.(8).
"support component"—*ibid.*
"the Universal Credit Regulations"—see reg.2(1).
"work-related activity component"—para.(8).

GENERAL NOTE

2.787 The purpose of this apparently complex provision is relatively simple. It provides that a claimant may be treated as having limited capability for work, or limited capability for work and work-related activity, for the purposes of an award of universal credit, if they were previously so assessed for the purpose of old style ESA. If the claimant in question was in the process of assessment of their capability for work in connection with an award of employment and support allowance at the time the award terminated, the assessment period for universal credit will be adjusted accordingly, under reg.20.

Transition from old style ESA before the end of the assessment phase

2.788 **20.** (1) This regulation applies where—

(a) an award of universal credit is made to a claimant who was entitled to old style ESA on the date on which the claim for universal credit was made or treated as made ("the relevant date"); and

(b) on the relevant date, the assessment phase in relation to the claimant applied and had lasted for less than 13 weeks.

(2) Where this regulation applies—

(a) regulation 28(2) of the Universal Credit Regulations (period for which the [1 . . .] LCWRA element is not to be included) does not apply; and

(b) for the purposes of regulation 28 of those Regulations, the relevant period is—

(i) the period of 13 weeks starting with the first day of the assessment phase; or

(ii) where regulation 5 of the Employment and Support Allowance Regulations 2008 (the assessment phase – previous claimants) applied to the claimant, the period which ends when the sum of the periods for which the claimant was previously entitled to old style ESA and the period for which the claimant is entitled to universal credit is 13 weeks.

(3) Where, on the relevant date, the assessment phase in relation to the claimant applied and had not ended and had lasted for more than 13 weeks—

(a) regulation 28 of the Universal Credit Regulations does not apply;

(b) [1 . . .]

(c) if it is subsequently determined in accordance with Part 5 of the Universal Credit Regulations that the claimant has limited capability for work and work-related activity the LCWRA element is (subject to the provisions of Part 4 of those Regulations) to be included in the award of universal credit with effect from the beginning of the first assessment period.

(4) For the purposes of this regulation, the fact that an assessment phase applied in relation to a claimant on the relevant date is to be taken into account even if the award of old style ESA subsequently terminated (in so far as it was an award of income-related employment and support allowance) before that date by virtue of an order made under section 150(3) of the Act.

AMENDMENT

1. Employment and Support Allowance and Universal Credit (Miscellaneous Amendments and Transitional and Savings Provisions) Regulations 2017 (SI 2017/204) reg.5(3) (April 3, 2017).

DEFINITIONS

"the Act"—see reg.2(1).
"assessment period"—*ibid.*
"assessment phase"—see reg.19(8).
"income-based jobseeker's allowance"—*ibid.*
"LCW element"—see reg.19(8).
"LCWRA element"—*ibid.*
"old style ESA"—*ibid.*
"the relevant date"—para.(1)(a).
"the Universal Credit Regulations"—see reg.2(1).

GENERAL NOTE

This regulation provides that where a claimant was in the process of assessment of their capability for work in connection with an award of old style ESA at the time that award terminated, the assessment period for universal credit will be adjusted accordingly. **2.789**

[1 Transition from jobseeker's allowance following an extended period of sickness

20A.—(1) This regulation applies where— **2.790**

(a) the claimant's first day of entitlement to universal credit ("the relevant date"), immediately follows the claimant's last day of entitlement to a jobseeker's allowance; and

(b) immediately before the relevant date, the claimant was treated as capable of work or as not having limited capability for work under regulation 55ZA of the Jobseeker's Allowance Regulations 1996 or regulation 46A of the Jobseeker's Allowance Regulations 2013 (extended period of sickness).

(2) Where this regulation applies—

(a) regulation 28(2) of the Universal Credit Regulations (period for which [1 . . .] LCWRA element is not to be included) does not apply; and

(b) for the purposes of regulation 28 of those Regulations, the relevant period is the period starting with the first day of the period for which the claimant was treated as capable of work or as not having limited capability for work as specified in paragraph (1)(b).]

AMENDMENTS

1. Jobseeker's Allowance (Extended Period of Sickness) Amendment Regulations 2015 (SI 2015/339) reg.6 (March 30, 2015).

2. Employment and Support Allowance and Universal Credit (Miscellaneous Amendments and Transitional and Savings Provisions) Regulations 2017 (SI 2017/204) reg.5(4) (April 3, 2017).

DEFINITIONS

"the relevant date"—para.(1)(a).

"LCW element"—see reg.19(8).

"LCWRA element"—*ibid.*

"the Universal Credit Regulations"—see reg.2(1).

GENERAL NOTE

2.791 The Jobseeker's Allowance (Extended Period of Sickness) Amendment Regulations 2015 (SI 2015/339) enabled jobseeker's allowance claimants suffering from a short (or third) period of sickness to choose to remain on that benefit while on what is termed as an "extended period of sickness" (EPS) for a continuous period of up to 13 weeks in a 12 month period. The same regulations also made provision to enable the employment and support allowance assessment phase (before any additional ESA components become payable) and the universal credit relevant period (before any additional universal credit elements become payable) to be reduced by the time a claimant spends on an EPS. This regulation is accordingly designed to ensure that the calculation of the universal credit relevant period includes the EPS where jobseeker's allowance claimants make a claim for universal credit and move immediately into the universal credit relevant period.

Other claimants with limited capability for work: credits only cases

2.792 **21.** (1) This regulation applies where—

(a) an award of universal credit is made to a claimant who was entitled to be credited with earnings equal to the lower earnings limit then in force under regulation 8B(2)(iv), (iva) or (v) of the Social Security (Credits) Regulations 1975 ("the 1975 Regulations") on the date on which the claim for universal credit was made or treated as made (the "relevant date"); and

(b) neither regulation 19 nor regulation 20 applies to that claimant (whether or not, in the case of joint claimants, either of those regulations apply to the other claimant).

(2) Where, on or before the relevant date, it had been determined that the claimant would have limited capability for work (within the meaning of Part 1 of the 2007 Act) if he or she was entitled to old style ESA—

(a) [1 . . .]

(b) the claimant is to be treated as having limited capability for work for the purposes of [1 . . .] section 21(1)(a) of the Act.

(3) [1 . . .]

(4) Where, on or before the relevant date, it had been determined that the claimant would have limited capability for work-related activity (within the meaning of Part 1 of the 2007 Act) if he or she was entitled to old style ESA—

(a) regulation 27(3) of the Universal Credit Regulations does not apply; and

(b) the claimant is to be treated as having limited capability for work and work-related activity for the purposes of [2regulation 27(1)] of those Regulations and section 19(2)(a) of the Act.

(5) Unless the notional assessment phase applied and had lasted for less than 13 weeks at the relevant date, in relation to a claimant who is treated as having limited capability for work and work-related activity under paragraph (4)—

(a) regulation 28 of the Universal Credit Regulations does not apply; and

(b) the LCWRA element is (subject to the provisions of Part 4 of the Universal Credit Regulations) to be included in the award of universal credit with effect from the beginning of the first assessment period.

(6) Where, on the relevant date, the notional assessment phase in relation to the claimant to whom the award was made applied and had lasted for less than 13 weeks—

(a) regulation 28(2) of the Universal Credit Regulations does not apply; and

(b) for the purposes of regulation 28 of those Regulations, the relevant period is the period of 13 weeks starting with the first day of the notional assessment phase.

(7) Where, on the relevant date, the notional assessment phase in relation to the claimant applied and had not ended and had lasted for more than 13 weeks—

(a) regulation 28 of the Universal Credit Regulations does not apply;

(b) [1 . . .]

(c) if it is subsequently determined in accordance with Part 5 of those Regulations that the claimant has limited capability for work and work-related activity, the LCWRA element is (subject to the provisions of Part 4 of those Regulations) to be included in the award of universal credit with effect from the beginning of the first assessment period.

(8) Where a claimant is treated, by virtue of this regulation, as having limited capability for work or, as the case may be, limited capability for work and work-related activity, the Secretary of State may at any time make a fresh determination as to these matters, in accordance with the Universal Credit Regulations.

(9) For the purposes of this regulation—

(a) a determination that the claimant would have limited capability for work or, as the case may be, limited capability for work-related activity, if the claimant was entitled to old style ESA is to be taken into account even if the claimant subsequently ceased to be entitled as mentioned in paragraph (1)(a) before the date on which that determination was made because he or she became entitled to universal credit;

(b) the fact that a notional assessment phase applied in relation to a claimant on the relevant date is to be taken into account even if the claimant subsequently ceased to be entitled as mentioned in paragraph (1)(a) before that date because the claimant became entitled to universal credit.

(c) references to a determination that the claimant would have limited capability for work if the claimant was entitled to old style ESA do not include a determination made under regulation 30 of the Employment and Support Allowance Regulations 2008 (conditions for treating a claimant as having limited capability for work until a determination about limited capability for work has been made);

(d) references to cases in which the notional assessment phase applied are references to cases in which sections 2(2)(a) [1 and 4(4)(a)] of the 2007 Act would have applied to the claimant if he or she had been entitled to old style ESA in addition to the entitlement mentioned in paragraph (1)(a), but do not include cases in which the claimant is entitled as mentioned in paragraph (1)(a) under regulation 8B(2)(iva) of the 1975 Regulations;

(e) subject to sub-paragraph (f), the "notional assessment phase" is the period of 13 weeks starting on the day on which the assessment phase would have started in relation to the claimant, if he or she had been entitled to old style ESA and sections 2(2)(a) [1 and 4(4)(a)] of the 2007 Act had applied;

(f) the notional assessment phase has not ended if, at the end of the 13 week period referred to in sub-paragraph (e), no determination has been made as to whether a claimant would have limited capability for work (within the meaning of Part 1 of the 2007 Act) if the claimant was entitled to old style ESA.

AMENDMENTS

1. Employment and Support Allowance and Universal Credit (Miscellaneous Amendments and Transitional and Savings Provisions) Regulations 2017 (SI 2017/204) reg.5(4) (April 3, 2017).

2. Social Security and Universal Credit (Miscellaneous Amendments) Regulations 2023 (SI 2023/543) reg.6(3) (June 29, 2023).

DEFINITIONS

"the 1975 Regulations"—para.(1)(a).
"the 2007 Act"—see reg.2(1).
"the Act"—*ibid.*
"assessment period"—*ibid.*
"assessment phase"—see reg.19(8).
"LCW element"—*ibid.*
"LCWRA element"—*ibid.*
"old style ESA"—*ibid.*
"the relevant date"—para.(1)(a).
"the Universal Credit Regulations"—see reg.2(1).

GENERAL NOTE

2.793 This regulation makes similar provision to reg.20 but for claimants who were not entitled to old style ESA, but who were entitled to credits of contributions and earnings on the grounds of limited capability for work. In *JW v SSWP (UC)* [2022] UKUT 117 (AAC) the claimant had been entitled to income-related ESA at the support group rate but her claim ended when her partner took up full-time work. Six months later, the claimant applied for universal credit. The decision-maker and tribunal concluded, applying the general rule in reg.28 of the UC Regs 2013, that she had to wait for a further three months from the start of her universal credit claim before the limited capability for work-related activity (LCWRA) element became payable. However, Judge Wikeley observed that none of the exceptions to the general rule in reg.28 dealt with the situation in which a claimant had previously been entitled to a legacy benefit. Such cases required consideration of the UC (Transitional) Regulations 2014 and especially reg.21. Having concluded that the claimant fell within the terms of reg.8B(2)(a)(iv) of the Social Security (Credits) Regulations 1975 (see reg.21(1))—namely that a person can receive NI credits equivalent to the lower earnings limit for the relevant period if the only reason they are not entitled to ESA is that they did not satisfy the contribution conditions—Judge Wikeley held, allowing the claimant's appeal and re-making the decision under appeal, that reg.21(4) and (5) provided the mechanism for the payment of the LCWRA element from the start of the claimant's universal credit claim rather than after a further waiting period of three months.

Transition from income support payable on the grounds of incapacity for work or disability [1 and other incapacity benefits]

22. (1) This regulation applies where an award of universal credit is made to a claimant [1 (other than a claimant to whom regulation 23 or 24 applies)] who was entitled to income support on the grounds of incapacity for work or disability on the date on which the claim for universal credit was made or treated as made [1 or is entitled to incapacity benefit or severe disablement allowance]. **2.794**

(2) Where this regulation applies—

(a) if it is determined in accordance with Part 5 of the Universal Credit Regulations that the claimant has limited capability for work—

 (i) the claimant is to be treated as having had limited capability for work for the purposes of regulation 27(1)(a) of the Universal Credit Regulations (award to include LCW and LCWRA elements) from the beginning of the first assessment period;

 (ii) regulation 28 of those Regulations (period for which the LCW or LCWRA element is not to be included) does not apply; and

 (iii) the LCW element is (subject to the provisions of Part 4 of the Universal Credit Regulations) to be included in the award with effect from the beginning of the first assessment period;

(b) if it is determined in accordance with Part 5 of the Universal Credit Regulations that the claimant has limited capability for work and work-related activity—

 (i) the claimant is to be treated as having had limited capability for work and work-related activity for the purposes of regulation 27(1)(b) of the Universal Credit Regulations from the beginning of the first assessment period;

 (ii) regulation 28 of those Regulations does not apply; and

 (iii) the LCWRA element is (subject to the provisions of Part 4 of the Universal Credit Regulations) to be included in the award of universal credit with effect from the beginning of the first assessment period.

(3) In this regulation—

"income support on the grounds of incapacity for work or disability" means an award of income support which is an "existing award" within the meaning of Schedule 4 to the 2007 Act.

Amendment

1. Universal Credit (Transitional Provisions) (Amendment) Regulations 2014 (SI 2014/1626) reg.5(1) (October 13, 2014).

Definitions

"the 2007 Act"—see reg.2(1).
"assessment period"—*ibid.*
"incapacity benefit"—see reg.19(8).
"income support"—*ibid.*
"income support on the grounds of incapacity for work or disability"—para.(3).
"LCW element"—see reg.19(8).
"LCWRA element"—*ibid.*
"severe disablement allowance"—*ibid.*
"the Universal Credit Regulations"—see reg.2(1).

General Note

2.795 The process of transition from existing incapacity benefits to universal credit is dealt with in regs.22 to 25. Transition from income support awarded on the grounds of incapacity for work or disability is dealt with in reg. 22 and transition from incapacity benefit or severe disablement allowance is dealt with in regs.23 to 25. In both cases, the limited capability for work (LCW) or limited capability for work and work-related activity (LCWRA) elements may be included in an award of universal credit with effect from the start of the first assessment period, if the claimant is subsequently assessed as having limited capability for work or, in the case of a claimant approaching pensionable age, is entitled to certain other benefits. Regulations 26 and 27 make similar provision to regs.22-25 but in respect of claimants who although they were not entitled to an incapacity benefit were entitled to credits of earnings on the grounds of incapacity for work.

The various amendments to regs 22-26 which came into effect on October 13, 2014 were designed to ensure that incapacity benefit or severe disablement allowance claimants can have the LCW or LCWRA elements applied to their universal credit award, from the start of the first assessment period where they joined or made a universal credit claim, as quickly as possible. This is sought to be achieved by ensuring they either:

- remain in the employment and support allowance conversion process and undergo a work capability assessment to determine whether their existing incapacity award qualifies for conversion to new style ESA, inclusive of either the WRA or support component and where it does, allow this decision to be used to apply the LCW or LCWRA element to their universal credit award; or
- enter the universal credit assessment process and undergo a universal credit work capability assessment to ascertain whether the LCW or LCWRA element should be applied to their award.

Before the October 2014 amendments, claimants who have not commenced ESA conversion had the choice of either entering the universal credit assessment process or waiting until they undergo conversion to ascertain whether the LCW or LCWRA element should be applied to their universal credit award. The amendments are intended to ensure that where the claimant has not entered the ESA conversion process they now have to enter the universal credit process, if they want to be assessed and have the LCW or LCWRA element backdated. The significance of this change is that if they do not enter the universal credit assessment process they would have to wait until they are scheduled for ESA conversion to see if their existing incapacity award qualified for conversion to new style ESA, before the LCW or

LCWRA element could be applied to their universal credit award. This is supposed to avoid any delay in these claimants accessing the additional financial support they will be entitled to if it is decided that they have LCW or LCWRA.

The amending regulations also ensure that where incapacity benefit claimants are in receipt of National Insurance credits only, and are not entitled to the appropriate level or component of a prescribed benefit to allow them to qualify for the LCW or LCWRA element in universal credit, that they will be treated in the same way as those incapacity benefit or severe disablement allowance claimants and will not have to serve the universal credit relevant period but can have the LCW or LCWRA element applied to their universal credit award, with retrospective effect, back to the start of the first assessment period, if it is subsequently determined by a universal credit work capability assessment that they have either LCW or LCWRA.

Transition from other incapacity benefits [1: assessment under the 2010 Regulations]

23. (1) This regulation applies where— 2.796

(a) an award of universal credit is made to a claimant who is entitled to incapacity benefit or severe disablement allowance [1 ("the relevant award")]; and

[1(b) on or before the date on which the claim for universal credit is made or treated as made, a notice has been issued to the claimant under regulation 4 of the Employment and Support Allowance (Transitional Provisions, Housing Benefit and Council Tax Benefit) (Existing Awards) (No.2) Regulations 2010 ("the 2010 Regulations") (notice commencing the conversion phase).]

[1 (1A) Where this regulation applies, regulations 27(3) (award to include LCW and LCWRA elements) and 38 (determination of limited capability for work and work-related activity) of the Universal Credit Regulations do not apply and the question whether a claimant has limited capability for work, or for work and work-related activity, is to be determined, for the purposes of the Act and the Universal Credit Regulations, in accordance with this regulation.]

(2) [1 Where it is determined in accordance with the 2010 Regulations that the relevant award qualifies for conversion into an award in accordance with regulation 7 of those Regulations (qualifying for conversion) and that award includes the work-related activity component]—

(a) [1 . . .];

(b) the claimant is to be treated as having had limited capability for work for the purposes of regulation 27(1)(a) of the Universal Credit Regulations from the beginning of the first assessment period;

(c) regulation 28(1) of those Regulations (period for which LCW or LCWRA element is not to be included) does not apply;

(d) the LCW element is (subject to the provisions of Part 4 of the Universal Credit Regulations) to be included in the award of universal credit with effect from the beginning of the first assessment period; and

(e) the claimant is to be treated as having limited capability for work for the purposes of section 21(1)(a) of the Act.

(3) [1 Where it is determined in accordance with the 2010 Regulations that the relevant award qualifies for conversion into an award in accordance with regulation 7 of those Regulations and that award includes the support component]—

(a) [1 . . .];
(b) the claimant is to be treated as having had limited capability for work and work-related activity for the purposes of regulation 27(1)(b) of the Universal Credit Regulations from the beginning of the first assessment period;
(c) regulation 28(1) of those Regulations does not apply;
(d) the LCWRA element is (subject to the provisions of Part 4 of the Universal Credit Regulations) to be included in the award of universal credit with effect from the beginning of the first assessment period; and
(e) the claimant is to be treated as having limited capability for work and work-related activity for the purposes of section 19(2)(a) of the Act.

AMENDMENT

1. Universal Credit (Transitional Provisions) (Amendment) Regulations 2014 (SI 2014/1626) reg.5(2) (October 13, 2014).

DEFINITIONS

"the 2010 Regulations"—para.(1)(b).
"the Act"—see reg.2(1).
"assessment period"—*ibid.*
"incapacity benefit"—see reg.19(8).
"LCW element"—*ibid.*
"LCWRA element"—*ibid.*
"the relevant award"—para.(1)(a).
"severe disablement allowance"—see reg.19(8).
"support component"—*ibid.*
"the Universal Credit Regulations"—see reg.2(1).
"work-related activity component"—see reg.19(8).

GENERAL NOTE

2.797 See General Note to reg.22.

Transition from other incapacity benefits: claimants approaching pensionable age

2.798 **24.** (1) This paragraph applies where—
(a) an award of universal credit is made to a claimant who is entitled to incapacity benefit or severe disablement allowance;
(b) no notice has been issued to the claimant under regulation 4 (notice commencing the conversion phase) of the Employment and Support Allowance (Transitional Provisions, Housing Benefit and Council Tax Benefit) (Existing Awards) (No.2) Regulations 2010 ("the 2010 Regulations");
(c) the claimant will reach pensionable age (within the meaning of the 2010 Regulations) within the period of one year; and
(d) the claimant is also entitled to—
(i) personal independence payment, where neither the daily living component nor the mobility component is payable at the enhanced rate;
(ii) disability living allowance under section 71 of the Social Security Contributions and Benefits Act 1992 ("the 1992

Act"), where the care component is payable at the middle rate within the meaning of section 72(4) of that Act or the mobility component is payable at the lower rate within the meaning of section 73(11) of that Act (or both components are payable at those rates);

(iii) attendance allowance under section 64 of the 1992 Act, where the allowance is payable at the lower rate in accordance with section 65 of that Act;

(iv) an increase in the weekly rate of disablement pension under section 104 of the 1992 Act (increase where constant attendance needed), where the increase is of an amount which is equal to or less than the amount specified in paragraph 2(a) of Part V of Schedule 4 to that Act; or

(v) any payment based on the need for attendance which is paid as an addition to a war disablement pension (which means any retired pay or pension or allowance payable in respect of disablement under an instrument specified in section 639(2) of the Income Tax (Earnings and Pensions) Act 2003), where the amount of that payment is equal to or less than the amount specified in paragraph 2(a) of Part V of Schedule 4 to the 1992 Act.

(2) Where paragraph (1) applies and paragraph (3) does not apply—

(a) regulation 27(3) of the Universal Credit Regulations (award to include LCW and LCWRA elements) does not apply;

(b) the claimant is to be treated as having limited capability for work for the purposes of regulation 27(1)(a) of those Regulations from the beginning of the first assessment period;

(c) regulation 28(1) of the Universal Credit Regulations (period for which LCW or LCWRA element is not to be included) does not apply;

(d) the LCW element is (subject to the provisions of Part 4 of the Universal Credit Regulations) to be included in the award of universal credit with effect from the beginning of the first assessment period; and

(e) the claimant is to be treated as having limited capability for work for the purposes of section 21(1)(a) of the Act.

(3) This paragraph applies where—

(a) an award of universal credit is made to a claimant who is entitled to incapacity benefit or severe disablement allowance;

(b) no notice has been issued to the claimant under regulation 4 of the 2010 Regulations;

(c) the claimant will reach pensionable age (within the meaning of the 2010 Regulations) within the period of one year; and

(d) the claimant is also entitled to—

(i) personal independence payment, where either the daily living component or the mobility component is (or both components are) payable at the enhanced rate;

(ii) disability living allowance under section 71 of the 1992 Act, where the care component is payable at the highest rate within the meaning of section 72(4) of that Act or the mobility component is payable at the higher rate within the meaning of section 73(11) of that Act (or both components are payable at those rates);

(iii) attendance allowance under section 64 of the 1992 Act, where the allowance is payable at the higher rate in accordance with section 65 of that Act;
(iv) armed forces independence payment under the Armed Forces and Reserve Forces (Compensation Scheme) Order 2011;
(v) an increase in the weekly rate of disablement pension under section 104 of the 1992 Act, where the increase is of an amount which is greater than the amount specified in paragraph 2(a) of Part V of Schedule 4 to that Act; or
(vi) any payment based on the need for attendance which is paid as an addition to a war disablement pension (which means any retired pay or pension or allowance payable in respect of disablement under an instrument specified in section 639(2) of the Income Tax (Earnings and Pensions) Act 2003), where the amount of that payment is greater than the amount specified in paragraph 2(a) of Part V of Schedule 4 to the 1992 Act.

(4) Where paragraph (3) applies (whether or not paragraph (1) also applies)—

(a) regulation 27(3) of the Universal Credit Regulations does not apply;
(b) the claimant is to be treated as having limited capability for work and work-related activity for the purposes of regulation 27(1)(b) of those Regulations from the beginning of the first assessment period;
(c) regulation 28(1) of the Universal Credit Regulations does not apply;
(d) the LCWRA element is (subject to the provisions of Part 4 of the Universal Credit Regulations) to be included in the award of universal credit with effect from the beginning of the first assessment period; and
(e) the claimant is to be treated as having limited capability for work and work-related activity for the purposes of section 19(2)(a) of the Act.

Definitions

"the 1992 Act"—para.(1)(d)(ii).
"the 2010 Regulations"—para.(1)(b).
"the Act"—see reg.2(1).
"assessment period"—*ibid.*
"incapacity benefit"—see reg.19(8).
"LCW element"—*ibid.*
"LCWRA element"—*ibid.*
"severe disablement allowance"—*ibid.*
"the Universal Credit Regulations"—see reg.2(1).
"work-related activity component"—see reg.19(8).

General Note

2.799 See General Note to reg.22.

Transition from other incapacity benefits: supplementary

2.800 **25.** (1) Where an award of universal credit is made to a claimant who is entitled to incapacity benefit or severe disablement allowance, regulation 66 of the Universal Credit Regulations (what is included in unearned income?)

applies to the claimant as if incapacity benefit or, as the case may be, severe disablement allowance were added to the descriptions of unearned income in paragraph (1)(b) of that regulation.

(2) For the purposes of regulations [1 22,] 23 and 24 and this regulation only, incapacity benefit and severe disablement allowance are prescribed benefits under paragraph 1(2)(b) of Schedule 6 to the Act.

AMENDMENT

1. Universal Credit (Transitional Provisions) (Amendment) Regulations 2014 (SI 2014/1626) reg.5(3) (October 13, 2014).

DEFINITIONS

"the Act"—see reg.2(1).
"incapacity benefit"—see reg.19(8).
"severe disablement allowance"—*ibid.*
"the Universal Credit Regulations"—see reg.2(1).

GENERAL NOTE

See General Note to reg.22. **2.801**

Other claimants with incapacity for work: credits only cases where claimant is approaching pensionable age

26. (1) This regulation applies where— **2.802**

(a) an award of universal credit is made to a claimant who was entitled to be credited with earnings equal to the lower earnings limit then in force under regulation 8B(2)(a)(i), (ii) or (iii) of the Social Security (Credits) Regulations 1975 on the date on which the claim for universal credit was made or treated as made;
(b) the claimant will reach pensionable age within the meaning of the Employment and Support Allowance (Transitional Provisions, Housing Benefit and Council Tax Benefit) (Existing Awards) (No.2) Regulations 2010 within the period of one year; and
(c) [1 none of regulations 22, 23 or 24 apply] to that claimant (whether or not, in the case of joint claimants, [1 any] of those regulations apply to the other claimant).

(2) Where the claimant is entitled to a payment, allowance or increased rate of pension specified in regulation 24(1)(d) and is not entitled to a payment, allowance or increased rate of pension specified in regulation 24(3)(d)—

(a) regulation 27(3) of the Universal Credit Regulations (award to include LCW and LCWRA elements) does not apply;
(b) the claimant is to be treated as having limited capability for work for the purposes of regulation 27(1)(a) of those Regulations from the beginning of the first assessment period;
(c) regulation 28(1) of the Universal Credit Regulations (period for which the LCW or LCWRA element is not to be included) does not apply;
(d) the LCW element is (subject to the provisions of Part 4 of the Universal Credit Regulations) to be included in the award of universal credit with effect from the beginning of the first assessment period; and

(e) the claimant is to be treated as having limited capability for work for the purposes of section 21(1)(a) of the Act.

(3) Where the claimant is entitled to a payment, allowance or increased rate of pension specified in regulation 24(3)(d) (whether or not the claimant is also entitled to a payment, allowance or increased rate of pension specified in regulation 24(1)(d))—

(a) regulation 27(3) of the Universal Credit Regulations does not apply;
(b) the claimant is to be treated as having limited capability for work and work-related activity for the purposes of regulation 27(1)(b) of those Regulations from the beginning of the first assessment period;
(c) regulation 28(1) of the Universal Credit Regulations does not apply;
(d) the LCWRA element is (subject to the provisions of Part 4 of the Universal Credit Regulations) to be included in the award of universal credit with effect from the beginning of the first assessment period; and
(e) the claimant is to be treated as having limited capability for work and work-related activity for the purposes of section 19(2)(a) of the Act.

[1 (4) Where the claimant is not entitled to a payment, allowance or increased rate of pension specified in either regulation 24(1)(d) or regulation 24(3)(d)—

(a) if it is determined in accordance with Part 5 of the Universal Credit Regulations that the claimant has limited capability for work—
  (i) the claimant is to be treated as having had limited capability for work for the purposes of regulation 27(1)(a) of the Universal Credit Regulations from the beginning of the first assessment period;
  (ii) regulation 28 of the Universal Credit Regulations does not apply; and
  (iii) the LCW element is (subject to the provisions of Part 4 of the Universal Credit Regulations) to be included in the award with effect from the beginning of the first assessment period; and
(b) if it is determined in accordance with Part 5 of the Universal Credit Regulations that the claimant has limited capability for work and work-related activity—
  (i) the claimant is to be treated as having had limited capability for work and work-related activity for the purposes of regulation 27(1)(b) of the Universal Credit Regulations from the beginning of the first assessment period;
  (ii) regulation 28 of the Universal Credit Regulations does not apply; and
  (iii) the LCWRA element is (subject to the provisions of Part 4 of the Universal Credit Regulations) to be included in the award of universal credit with effect from the beginning of the first assessment period.]

AMENDMENT

1. Universal Credit (Transitional Provisions) (Amendment) Regulations 2014 (SI 2014/1626) reg.5(4) (October 13, 2014).

DEFINITIONS

"the Act"—see reg.2(1).

"assessment period"—*ibid.*
"LCW element"—see reg.19(8).
"LCWRA element"—*ibid.*
"the Universal Credit Regulations"—see reg.2(1).
"the work-related activity component"—see reg.19(8).

GENERAL NOTE

Regulations 26 and 27 make similar provision to regs 22-25 but in respect of claimants who although they were not entitled to an incapacity benefit were entitled to credits of earnings under the Social Security (Credits) Regulations 1975 (SI 1975/556) on the grounds of incapacity for work. **2.803**

Other claimants with incapacity for work: credits only cases

27. (1) This regulation applies where— **2.804**

(a) an award of universal credit is made to a claimant who was entitled to be credited with earnings equal to the lower earnings limit then in force under regulation 8B(2)(a)(i), (ii) or (iii) of the Social Security (Credits) Regulations 1975 on the date on which the claim for universal credit was made or treated as made; and
(b) none of regulations 22, 23, 24 or 26 apply to that claimant (whether or not, in the case of joint claimants, any of those regulations apply to the other claimant).

(2) Where this regulation applies—

(a) if it is determined in accordance with Part 5 of the Universal Credit Regulations that the claimant has limited capability for work—
    (i) the claimant is to be treated as having had limited capability for work for the purposes of regulation 27(1)(a) of the Universal Credit Regulations (award to include LCW and LCWRA elements) from the beginning of the first assessment period;
    (ii) regulation 28 of the Universal Credit Regulations (period for which the LCW or LCWRA element is not to be included) does not apply; and
    (iii) the LCW element is (subject to the provisions of Part 4 of the Universal Credit Regulations) to be included in the award with effect from the beginning of the first assessment period;
(b) if it is determined in accordance with Part 5 of the Universal Credit Regulations that the claimant has limited capability for work and work-related activity—
    (i) the claimant is to be treated as having had limited capability for work and work-related activity for the purposes of regulation 27(1)(b) of the Universal Credit Regulations from the beginning of the first assessment period;
    (ii) regulation 28 of the Universal Credit Regulations does not apply; and
    (iii) the LCWRA element is (subject to the provisions of Part 4 of the Universal Credit Regulations) to be included in the award of universal credit with effect from the beginning of the first assessment period.

DEFINITIONS

"assessment period"—see reg.2(1).

"LCW element"—see reg.19(8).
"LCWRA element"—*ibid.*
"the Universal Credit Regulations"—see reg.2(1).

GENERAL NOTE

2.805 See General Notes to regs 22 and 26.

Meaning of "qualifying young person"

2.806 **28.** Where a person who would (apart from the provision made by this regulation) be a "qualifying young person" within the meaning of regulation 5 of the Universal Credit Regulations is entitled to an existing benefit—

(a) that person is not a qualifying young person for the purposes of the Universal Credit Regulations; and
(b) regulation 5(5) of those Regulations applies as if, after "a person who is receiving" there were inserted "an existing benefit (within the meaning of the Universal Credit (Transitional Provisions) Regulations 2014),".

DEFINITIONS

"existing benefit"—see reg.2(1).
"the Universal Credit Regulations"—*ibid.*

GENERAL NOTE

2.807 This regulation ensures that payments may not be made as part of an award of universal credit in respect of a young person who is entitled to existing benefits in their own right. Such persons cannot be claimed for by a parent or carer for the purposes of the Universal Credit Regulations 2013.

Support for housing costs

2.808 **29.** (1) Paragraph (3) applies where—

(a) an award of universal credit is made to a claimant who—
 (i) was entitled to income-based jobseeker's allowance, income-related employment and support allowance or income support (a "relevant award") at any time during the period of one month ending with the day on which the claim for universal credit was made or treated as made (or would have been so entitled were it not for termination of that award by virtue of an order made under section 150(3) of the Act or the effect of these Regulations); or
 (ii) was at any time during the period of one month ending with the day on which the claim for universal credit was made or treated as made, the partner of a person ("P") who was at that time entitled to a relevant award, where the award of universal credit is not a joint award to the claimant and P; and
(b) on the relevant date, the relevant award included an amount in respect of housing costs under—
 (i) [2 paragraph 16 of Schedule 2] to the Jobseeker's Allowance Regulations 1996 ("the 1996 Regulations");
 (ii) [2 paragraph 18 of Schedule 6] to the Employment and Support Allowance Regulations 2008 ("the 2008 Regulations"); or, as the case may be,

(iii) [2 paragraph 17 of Schedule 3] to the Income Support (General) Regulations 1987 ("the 1987 Regulations").

(2) In this regulation, the "relevant date" means—

(a) where paragraph (1)(a)(i) applies and the claimant was not entitled to the relevant award on the date on which the claim for universal credit was made or treated as made, the date on which the relevant award terminated;

(b) where paragraph (1)(a)(i) applies, the claimant is not a new claimant partner and he or she was entitled to the relevant award on the date on which the claim for universal credit was made, that date;

(c) where paragraph (1)(a)(i) applies, the claimant is a new claimant partner and he or she was entitled to the relevant award on the date on which the claim for universal credit was treated as made, that date;

(d) where paragraph (1)(a)(ii) applies, the date on which the claimant ceased to be the partner of P or, if earlier, the date on which the relevant award terminated.

(3) Where this paragraph applies, paragraph 5 of Schedule 5 to the Universal Credit Regulations (no housing costs element under this Schedule for qualifying period) does not apply.

(4) Paragraph (5) applies where paragraph (1)(a) applies, but the relevant award did not include an amount in respect of housing costs because the claimant's entitlement (or, as the case may be, P's entitlement) was nil by virtue of—

(a) paragraph 6(1)(c) or 7(1)(b) of Schedule 2 to the 1996 Regulations;

(b) paragraph 8(1)(c) or 9(1)(b) of Schedule 6 to the 2008 Regulations; or, as the case may be,

(c) paragraph 6(1)(c) or 8(1)(b) of Schedule 3(4) to the 1987 Regulations.

(5) Where this paragraph applies—

(a) paragraph 5(2) of Schedule 5 to the Universal Credit Regulations does not apply; and

(b) the "qualifying period" referred to in paragraph 5 of that Schedule is the period of [1 273] days starting with the first day on which the claimant (or, as the case may be, P) was entitled to the relevant award, taking into account any period which was treated as a period of continuing entitlement under—

(i) paragraph 13 of Schedule 2 to the 1996 Regulations;

(ii) paragraph 15 of Schedule 6 to the 2008 Regulations; or, as the case may be,

(iii) paragraph 14 of Schedule 3 to the 1987 Regulations,

provided that, throughout that part of the qualifying period after the award of universal credit is made, receipt of universal credit is continuous and the claimant otherwise qualifies for the inclusion of an amount calculated under Schedule 5 to the Universal Credit Regulations in their award.

(6) For the purposes of—

(a) paragraph (1)(b) of this regulation, inclusion of an amount in respect of housing costs in a relevant award is to be taken into account even if the relevant award subsequently terminated by virtue of an order made under section 150(3) of the Act, regulation 7 or, as the case may be, regulation 8, before the date on which that amount was included in the award;

(b) paragraph (5)(b) of this regulation, entitlement to a relevant award is to be treated as having continued until the relevant date even if the award subsequently terminated by virtue of an order made under section 150(3) of the Act, regulation 7 or, as the case may be, regulation 8, before that date.

AMENDMENTS

1. Social Security (Housing Costs Amendments) Regulations 2015 (SI 2015/1647) reg.6 (April 1, 2016).

2. Loans for Mortgage Interest Regulations 2017 (2017/725) Sch.5 para.6 (April 6, 2018).

DEFINITIONS

"the 1987 Regulations"—para.(1)(b)(iii).
"the 1996 Regulations"—para.(1)(b)(i).
"the 2008 Regulations"—para.(1)(b)(ii).
"the Act"—see reg.2(1).
"income-based jobseeker's allowance"—*ibid.*
"income-related employment and support allowance"—*ibid.*
"income support"—*ibid.*
"new claimant partner"—*ibid.*
"partner"—*ibid.*
"qualifying period"—para.(5)(b).
"relevant award"—para.(1)(a)(i).
"relevant date"—para.(2).
"the Universal Credit Regulations"—see reg.2(1).

GENERAL NOTE

2.809 This is a hideously opaque regulation. Where a universal credit claimant or their partner was previously entitled to old style JSA, old style ESA or income support, this regulation allows for any support for housing costs which was included in that award (paras.(1) and (2)), or time spent waiting to qualify for such support (paras. (4)–(6)), to be carried over to the award of universal credit (para.(3)), providing the claimant is entitled to the universal credit housing element. The amendment to para.(5)(b) is subject to the saving provision in reg.8 of the Social Security (Housing Costs Amendments) Regulations 2015 (SI 2015/1647).

Sanctions: transition from old style ESA

2.810 **30.** (1) This regulation applies where—

(a) an award of universal credit is made to a claimant who was previously entitled to old style ESA ("the ESA award"); and
(b) on the relevant date, payments in respect of the ESA award were reduced under regulation 63 of the Employment and Support Allowance Regulations 2008 ("the 2008 Regulations").

(2) In this regulation, the "relevant date" means—

(a) where the claimant was not entitled to old style ESA on the date on which the claim for universal credit was made or treated as made, the date on which the ESA award terminated;
(b) where the claimant is not a new claimant partner and was entitled to old style ESA on the date on which the claim for universal credit was made, that date;
(c) where the claimant is a new claimant partner and was entitled to old style ESA on the date on which the claim for universal credit was treated as made, that date.

(3) Where this regulation applies—

(a) the failure which led to reduction of the ESA award ("the ESA failure") is to be treated, for the purposes of the Universal Credit Regulations, as a failure which is sanctionable under section 27 of the Act;

(b) the award of universal credit is to be reduced in relation to the ESA failure, in accordance with the provisions of this regulation and Chapter 2 of Part 8 of the Universal Credit Regulations (sanctions), as modified by this regulation; and

(c) the reduction is to be treated, for the purposes of the Universal Credit Regulations, as a reduction under section 27 of the Act.

(4) The reduction period for the purposes of the Universal Credit Regulations is a period of the number of days which is equivalent to the length of the fixed period applicable to the person under regulation 63(7) of the 2008 Regulations in relation to the ESA failure, minus—

(a) the number of days (if any) in that period in respect of which the amount of old style ESA was reduced; and

(b) if the ESA award terminated before the first date of entitlement to universal credit in connection with the current award, the number of days (if any) in the period after termination of that award, before the start of the universal credit award.

(5) Accordingly, regulation 101 of the Universal Credit Regulations (general principles for calculating reduction periods) applies in relation to the ESA failure as if, in paragraphs (1) and (3), for "in accordance with regulations 102 to 105", there were substituted "in accordance with regulation 30 of the Universal Credit (Transitional Provisions) Regulations 2014".

(6) For the purposes of this regulation, a determination that payments in respect of the ESA award are to be reduced under regulation 63 of the 2008 Regulations is to be taken into account even if the ESA award subsequently terminated (in so far as it was an award of income-related employment and support allowance) on a date before the date on which that determination was made, by virtue of an order made under section 150(3) of the Act.

DEFINITIONS

"the 2008 Regulations"—para.(1)(b).
"the Act"—see reg.2(1).
"the ESA award"—para.(1)(a).
"the ESA failure"—para.(3)(a).
"income-related employment and support allowance"—*ibid.*
"new claimant partner"—*ibid.*
"old style ESA"—*ibid.*
"relevant date"—para.(2).
"the Universal Credit Regulations"—see reg.2(1).

GENERAL NOTE

Regulations 30 to 34 deal with the treatment of any sanctions which have been imposed on awards of old style JSA and old style ESA, prior to a claimant's transition to universal credit. The underlying principle is one of equivalence of treatment. Such pre-existing sanctions will continue to have effect by way of deductions from the award of universal credit and past sanctions will also be taken into account for **2.811** the purposes of determining the level of sanction applicable to any future sanctionable failure. However, where there is a period of entitlement to an existing benefit between two periods of entitlement to universal credit, any sanctions arising prior to that intervening period will not be taken into account.

So, for example, where a new universal credit claimant was previously entitled to ESA, and subject to an ESA sanction for failure to take part in a work-focussed interview or to undertake a work-related activity, the ESA failure is treated as a sanctionable failure for the purposes of universal credit (paras.(1) and (3)). The reduction period is adjusted accordingly (para.(4)).

Escalation of sanctions: transition from old style ESA

2.812 **31.** (1) This regulation applies where an award of universal credit is made to a claimant who was at any time previously entitled to old style ESA.

(2) Where this regulation applies, for the purposes of determining the reduction period under regulation 104 of the Universal Credit Regulations (low-level sanction) in relation to a sanctionable failure by the claimant, other than a failure which is treated as sanctionable by virtue of regulation 30—

(a) a reduction of universal credit in accordance with regulation 30; and

(b) any reduction of old style ESA under the Employment and Support Allowance Regulations 2008 ("the 2008 Regulations") which did not result in a reduction under regulation 30,

is, subject to paragraph (3), to be treated as arising from a sanctionable failure for which the reduction period which applies is the number of days which is equivalent to the length of the fixed period which applied under regulation 63 of the 2008 Regulations.

(3) In determining a reduction period under regulation 104 of the Universal Credit Regulations in accordance with paragraph (2), no account is to be taken of—

(a) a reduction of universal credit in accordance with regulation 30 if, at any time after that reduction, the claimant was entitled to an existing benefit;

(b) a reduction of old style ESA under the 2008 Regulations if, at any time after that reduction, the claimant was entitled to universal credit, new style ESA or new style JSA, and was subsequently entitled to an existing benefit.

DEFINITIONS

"the 2008 Regulations"—para.(2)(b).
"existing benefit"—see reg.2(1).
"new style ESA"—*ibid.*
"new style JSA"—*ibid.*
"old style ESA"—*ibid.*
"the Universal Credit Regulations"—*ibid.*

GENERAL NOTE

2.813 This provision ensures that any previous ESA fixed period reductions are taken into account when deciding the appropriate reduction period for the purposes of a universal credit sanction.

Sanctions: transition from old style JSA

2.814 **32.** (1) This regulation applies where—

(a) an award of universal credit is made to a claimant who was previously entitled to old style JSA ("the JSA award");
(b) on the relevant date, payments in respect of the JSA award were reduced under section 19 (as it applied either before or after substitution by the Act) or section 19A of the Jobseekers Act 1995 ("the 1995 Act"), or under regulation 69B of the Jobseeker's Allowance Regulations 1996 ("the 1996 Regulations"); and
(c) if the JSA award was made to a joint-claim couple within the meaning of the 1995 Act and the reduction related to—
 (i) in the case of a reduction under section 19 as it applied before substitution by the Act, circumstances relating to only one member of the couple; or,
 (ii) in the case of a reduction under section 19 as it applied after substitution by the Act, a sanctionable failure by only one member of the couple,

the award of universal credit was made to that person.

(2) In this regulation, the "relevant date" means—
(a) where the claimant was not entitled to old style JSA on the date on which the claim for universal credit was made or treated as made, the date on which the JSA award terminated;
(b) where the claimant is not a new claimant partner and was entitled to old style JSA on the date on which the claim for universal credit was made, that date;
(c) where the claimant is a new claimant partner and was entitled to old style JSA on the date on which the claim for universal credit was treated as made, that date.

(3) Where this regulation applies—
(a) the circumstances or failure which led to reduction of the JSA award (in either case, "the JSA failure") is to be treated, for the purposes of the Universal Credit Regulations, as—
 (i) a failure which is sanctionable under section 26 of the Act, where the reduction was under section 19 of the 1995 Act; or
 (ii) a failure which is sanctionable under section 27 of the Act, where the reduction was under section 19A of the 1995 Act or regulation 69B of the 1996 Regulations;
(b) the award of universal credit is to be reduced in relation to the JSA failure, in accordance with the provisions of this regulation and Chapter 2 of Part 8 of the Universal Credit Regulations (sanctions), as modified by this regulation; and
(c) the reduction is to be treated, for the purposes of the Universal Credit Regulations, as a reduction under section 26 or, as the case may be, section 27 of the Act.

(4) The reduction period for the purposes of the Universal Credit Regulations is a period of the number of days which is equivalent to the length of the period of reduction which is applicable to the person under regulation 69, 69A or 69B of the 1996 Regulations, minus—
(a) the number of days (if any) in that period in respect of which the amount of old style JSA was reduced; and
(b) if the award of old style JSA terminated before the first date of entitlement to universal credit in connection with the current award, the number of days (if any) in the period after termination of that award, before the start of the universal credit award.

(5) Accordingly, regulation 101 of the Universal Credit Regulations applies in relation to the JSA failure as if, in paragraphs (1) and (3), for "in accordance with regulations 102 to 105", there were substituted "in accordance with regulation 32 of the Universal Credit (Transitional Provisions) Regulations 2014".

(6) Where the JSA award was made to a joint-claim couple within the meaning of the 1995 Act and the JSA failure related to only one member of the couple, the daily reduction rate for the purposes of the Universal Credit Regulations is the amount calculated in accordance with regulation 70(3) of the 1996 Regulations in respect of the JSA award, divided by seven and rounded down to the nearest 10 pence, unless regulation 111(2) or (3) of the Universal Credit Regulations (daily reduction rate) applies.

(7) Where the daily reduction rate is to be determined in accordance with paragraph (6), regulation 111(1) of the Universal Credit Regulations applies in relation to the JSA failure as if, for the words from "an amount equal to" to the end there were substituted the words "an amount determined in accordance with regulation 32 of the Universal Credit (Transitional Provisions) Regulations 2014".

(8) For the purposes of this regulation, a determination that payments in respect of the JSA award are to be reduced under regulation 69, 69A or 69B of the 1996 Regulations is to be taken into account even if the JSA award subsequently terminated (in so far as it was an award of income-based jobseeker's allowance) on a date before the date on which that determination was made, by virtue of an order made under section 150(3) of the Act.

DEFINITIONS

"the 1995 Act"—para.(1)(b).
"the 1996 Regulations"—para.(1)(b).
"the 2002 Act"—see reg.2(1).
"income-based jobseeker's allowance"—*ibid.*
"the JSA award"—para.(1)(a).
"the JSA failure"—para.(3)(a).
"new claimant partner"—see reg.2(1).
"new style ESA"—*ibid.*
"new style JSA"—*ibid.*
"old style JSA"—*ibid.*
"relevant date"—para.(2).
"the Universal Credit Regulations"—see reg.2(1).

GENERAL NOTE

2.815 This has similar effect for JSA as reg.30 does for ESA. It is designed to ensure that current JSA sanctions carry forward into the universal credit scheme.

Escalation of sanctions: transition from old style JSA

2.816 **33.** (1) This regulation applies where an award of universal credit is made to a claimant who was at any time previously entitled to old style JSA.

(2) Where this regulation applies, for the purposes of determining the applicable reduction period under regulation 102 (higher-level sanction), 103 (medium-level sanction) or 104 (low-level sanction) of the Universal Credit Regulations in relation to a sanctionable failure by the person, other than a failure which is treated as sanctionable by virtue of regulation 32—

(a) a reduction of universal credit in accordance with regulation 32; and
(b) any reduction of old style JSA under section 19 or 19A of the Jobseekers Act 1995 ("the 1995 Act"), or under regulation 69B of the 1996 Regulations which did not result in a reduction under regulation 32,

is, subject to paragraph (3), to be treated as arising from a sanctionable failure for which the reduction period is the number of days which is equivalent to the length of the period which applied under regulation 69, 69A or 69B of the 1996 Regulations.

(3) In determining a reduction period under regulation 102, 103 or 104 of the Universal Credit Regulations in accordance with paragraph (2), no account is to be taken of—

(a) a reduction of universal credit in accordance with regulation 32 if, at any time after that reduction, the claimant was entitled to an existing benefit;
(b) a reduction of old style JSA under section 19 or 19A of the 1995 Act, or under regulation 69B of the 1996 Regulations if, at any time after that reduction, the claimant was entitled to universal credit, new style ESA or new style JSA, and was subsequently entitled to an existing benefit.

DEFINITIONS

"the 1995 Act"—para.(2)(b).
"the 1996 Regulations"—see reg.32(1)(b).
"existing benefit"—see reg.2(1).
"new style ESA"—*ibid.*
"new style JSA"—*ibid.*
"old style JSA"—*ibid.*
"the Universal Credit Regulations"—*ibid.*

GENERAL NOTE

This is the JSA equivalent of reg.31, which applies to ESA. 2.817

Sanctions: temporary return to certain existing benefits

34. If an award of universal credit terminates while there is an outstanding reduction period (within the meaning of regulation 107 of the Universal Credit Regulations) and the claimant becomes entitled to old style JSA, old style ESA or income support ("the relevant benefit") during that period— 2.818

(a) regulation 107 of the Universal Credit Regulations (reduction period to continue where award terminates) ceases to apply; and
(b) the reduction period is to terminate on the first date of entitlement to the relevant benefit.

DEFINITIONS

"income support"—see reg.2(1).
"old style ESA"—*ibid.*
"old style JSA"—*ibid.*
"relevant benefit"—see reg.34.
"the Universal Credit Regulations"—see reg.2(1).

GENERAL NOTE

2.819 This provision has the effect that where a claimant comes off universal credit and claims one of the former benefits (e.g. JSA, because he is no longer in a relevant area), then if he subsequently becomes entitled again to universal credit (e.g. by forming a couple with a universal credit claimant) then the universal credit sanction does not bite, even if it had on the face of it not expired. This is because the reduction period is deemed as having terminated on the first day of the award of the existing benefit such as JSA.

Loss of benefit penalties: transition from existing benefits other than tax credits

2.820 **35.** (1) Subject to paragraph (6), this regulation applies in the cases set out in paragraphs (2) to (4).

(2) The first case is where—

(a) an award of universal credit is made to a claimant who is an offender;

(b) the claimant was entitled to old style JSA, old style ESA, income support or housing benefit ("the earlier award") at any time during the period of one month ending with the date on which the claim for universal credit was made or treated as made (or would have been so entitled were it not for termination of that award by virtue of an order made under section 150(3) of the Act or, as the case may be, the effect of these Regulations); and

(c) payments in respect of the earlier award were, on the relevant date, subject to a restriction under section 6B (loss of benefit in case of conviction, penalty or caution for benefit offence), 7 (repeated benefit fraud) or 8 (effect of offence on joint-claim jobseeker's allowance) of the 2001 Act.

(3) The second case is where—

(a) an award of universal credit is made to a claimant who is an offender;

(b) another person who was the offender's family member (but is no longer their family member) was entitled to old style JSA, old style ESA, income support or housing benefit ("the earlier award") at any time during the period of one month ending with the date on which the claim for universal credit was made or treated as made; and

(c) payments in respect of the earlier award were, on the relevant date, subject to a restriction under section 9 (effect of offence on benefits for members of offender's family) of the 2001 Act.

(4) The third case is where—

(a) an award of universal credit is made to a claimant who is an offender's family member;

(b) the offender, or the claimant, was entitled to old style JSA, old style ESA, income support or housing benefit ("the earlier award") at any time during the period of one month ending with the date on which the claim for universal credit was made or treated as made; and

(c) payments in respect of the earlier award were, on the relevant date, subject to a restriction under section 6B, 7, 8 or, as the case may be, 9 of the 2001 Act.

(5) Where this regulation applies—

(a) any subsequent payment of universal credit to the claimant in respect of an assessment period which falls wholly or partly within the remainder of the disqualification period applicable to the offender is to be reduced in accordance with regulation 36; and

(b) regulation 3ZB of the 2001 Regulations does not apply.

(6) This regulation does not apply if the earlier award was a joint-claim jobseeker's allowance and—

(a) payments in respect of the award were, on the relevant date, subject to a restriction under section 8(2) of the 2001 Act; or

(b) the award of universal credit is not made to joint claimants who were, on the relevant date, both entitled to the joint-claim jobseeker's allowance.

(7) In this regulation and in regulation 36—

"the 2001 Act" means the Social Security Fraud Act 2001;

"the 2001 Regulations" means the Social Security (Loss of Benefit) Regulations 2001;

"disqualification period" has the meaning given in the 2001 Act, interpreted in accordance with the 2001 Regulations;

"earlier award" is to be interpreted in accordance with paragraph (2)(b), (3)(b) or, as the case may be, (4)(b) and, for the purposes of regulation 36, where there is more than one earlier award, the term refers to the award to which the claimant became entitled most recently;

"offender" means an offender within the meaning of the 2001 Act;

"offender's family member" has the same meaning as in the 2001 Act;

"the relevant date" means—

(a) in relation to the first case—

(i) where the claimant was not entitled to the earlier award on the date on which the claim for universal credit was made or treated as made, the date on which the earlier award terminated;

(ii) where the claimant is not a new claimant partner and was entitled to the earlier award on the date on which the claim for universal credit was made, that date;

(iii) where the claimant is a new claimant partner and was entitled to the earlier award on the date on which the claim for universal credit was treated as made, that date;

(b) in relation to the second case, the date on which the person entitled to the earlier award ceased to be the offender's family member or, if the award terminated before that date, the date on which the earlier award terminated;

(c) in relation to the third case—

(i) where the claimant was entitled to the earlier award but that entitlement terminated before the date on which the claim for universal credit was made or treated as made, the date on which the earlier award terminated;

(ii) where the claimant is not a new claimant partner and was entitled to the earlier award on the date on which the claim for universal credit was made, that date;

(iii) where the claimant is a new claimant partner and was entitled to the earlier award on the date on which the claim for universal credit was treated as made, that date;

(iv) where the offender's family member was entitled to the earlier award, the date on which that person ceased to be the offender's family member or, if earlier, the date on which the earlier award terminated.

(8) For the purposes of this regulation, the fact that payments in respect of an earlier award were subject to a restriction is to be taken into account, even if the earlier award subsequently terminated before the date on which payments became subject to a restriction by virtue of an order made under section 150(3) of the Act (in so far as it was an award of income-based jobseeker's allowance or income-related employment and support allowance), regulation 7 or, as the case may be, regulation 8.

DEFINITIONS

"the 2001 Act"—para.(7).
"the 2001 Regulations"—*ibid.*
"the 2002 Act"—see reg.2(1).
"assessment period"—*ibid.*
"the disqualification period"—para.(7).
"earlier award"—*ibid.*
"housing benefit"—see reg.2(1).
"income support"—*ibid.*
"income-based jobseeker's allowance"—*ibid.*
"income-related employment and support allowance"—*ibid.*
"joint-claim jobseeker's allowance"—*ibid.*
"new claimant partner"—*ibid.*
"offender"—para.(7)
"offender's family member"—*ibid.*
"old style ESA"—see reg.2(1).
"old style JSA"—*ibid.*
"the relevant date"—para.(7).

GENERAL NOTE

2.821 This provision (taken with reg.36) has the effect that where a claimant moves to universal credit within one month of the end of an award of an existing benefit and is subject to a loss of benefit penalty, the penalty will in most cases continue on the basis of the rate applicable to the existing benefit for the remainder of the disqualification period. The usual rules relating to calculation of penalties within universal credit will not apply.

Loss of benefit penalties: reduction of universal credit

2.822 **36.** (1) Subject to paragraph (6) [1 and to regulation 38], where regulation 35 applies, the amount of a reduction of universal credit in respect of an assessment period is to be calculated by multiplying the daily reduction rate by the number of days in the assessment period, unless paragraph (2) applies.

(2) Where the disqualification period ends during an assessment period, the amount of the reduction for that assessment period is (subject to paragraph (6)) to be calculated by multiplying the daily reduction rate by the number of days in the assessment period which are within the disqualification period.

(3) Subject to paragraphs (4) and (5), the daily reduction rate where regulation 35 applies is an amount which is equal to—

(a) the monetary amount by which payments in respect of the earlier award were reduced in accordance with section 6B or 7 of the 2001 Act or, as the case may be, regulation 3, 3ZA or 17 of the 2001 Regulations in respect of the last complete week before the relevant date (within the meaning of regulation 35);

(b) multiplied by 52;
(c) divided by 365; and
(d) rounded down to the nearest 10 pence.

(4) Where the monetary amount by which payments in respect of the earlier award would have been reduced would, if the claimant had remained entitled to the earlier award, have changed during the disqualification period because of an order made under section 150 of the Social Security Administration Act 1992 (annual up-rating of benefits)—

(a) the daily reduction rate is to be calculated in accordance with paragraph (3), but on the basis of the new amount by which payments would have been reduced; and
(b) any adjustment to the reduction of universal credit is to take effect from the first day of the first assessment period to start after the date of the change.

(5) Where the earlier award was a joint-claim jobseeker's allowance, the daily reduction rate is an amount which is equal to—

(a) the amount of the standard allowance applicable to the joint claimants under regulation 36 of the Universal Credit Regulations (table showing amounts of elements);
(b) multiplied by 12;
(c) divided by 365;
(d) reduced by 60%; and
(e) rounded down to the nearest 10 pence.

(6) The amount of the reduction under this regulation in respect of any assessment period is not to exceed the amount of the standard allowance which is applicable to the claimant in respect of that period.

AMENDMENTS

1. Universal Credit (Transitional Provisions) (Amendment) Regulations 2014 (SI 2014/1626) reg.6(1) (October 13, 2014).

DEFINITIONS

"the 2001 Act"—see reg.35(7).
"the 2001 Regulations"—*ibid.*
"assessment period"—see reg.2(1).
"the disqualification period"—see reg.35(7).
"earlier award"—*ibid.*
"joint-claim jobseeker's allowance"—see reg.2(1).
"the relevant date"—see reg.35(7).
"the Universal Credit Regulations"—see reg.2(1).

GENERAL NOTE

See General Note to reg.35. Note also that as compared with reg.35 of the 2013 Transitional Regulations provision for the transfer of loss of benefit penalties for fraudulent offences to a universal credit award has been amended in relation to the transfer of penalties from joint-claim JSA awards to an award of universal credit (para.(5)). In these cases the amount of the penalty applied to the universal credit award is reduced by 60%, if only one of the joint JSA claimants is subject to a penalty. This reflects the position in JSA where the member of the joint-claim couple who is not the benefit fraud offender can be paid JSA at the single person's rate. **2.823**

[1 Loss of benefit penalties: transition from working tax credit

2.824 **37.** (1) This regulation applies where an award of universal credit is made to a claimant who—

(a) was previously entitled to working tax credit; and
(b) is an offender, within the meaning of the 2002 Act.

(2) Where this regulation applies, the Social Security (Loss of Benefit) Regulations 2001 apply as if in regulation 3ZB of those Regulations—

(a) in paragraph (1) at the beginning there were inserted "Subject to regulation 38 of the Universal Credit (Transitional Provisions) Regulations 2014,";
(b) "disqualification period" includes a disqualification period within the meaning of the 2002 Act;
(c) "offender" includes an offender within the meaning of the 2002 Act; and
(d) "offender's family member" includes a person who is a member of the family (within the meaning of section 137(1) of the Social Security Contributions and Benefits Act 1992 of a person who is an offender within the meaning of the 2002 Act.]

AMENDMENTS

1. Universal Credit (Transitional Provisions) (Amendment) Regulations 2014 (SI 2014/1626) reg.6(2) (October 13, 2014).

DEFINITIONS

"the 2002 Act"—see reg.2(1).
"working tax credit"—*ibid.*

GENERAL NOTE

2.825 This regulation provides that where a working tax credit (WTC) claimant has a fraud penalty applied to their WTC award, the fraud penalty will be applied to the universal credit standard allowance, for the remaining period of that penalty. As a consequence, reg.38 below ensures that where a claimant has been in receipt of WTC and another existing benefit (e.g. housing benefit) and both awards have had a fraud penalty applied to them, the combination of these penalties will not exceed the universal credit standard allowance in any assessment period. This follows the approach taken with existing Department for Work and Pensions benefits where there is more than one fraud penalty applied to an existing benefit award upon the transition to universal credit.

[1 Loss of benefit penalties: maximum total reduction

2.826 **38.** Where regulations 35 and 37 both apply to a claimant, the total amount of a reduction of universal credit in respect of any assessment period under—

(a) regulation 36; and
(b) regulation 3ZB of the Social Security (Loss of Benefit) Regulations 2001,

must not exceed the amount of the standard allowance which is applicable to the claimant in respect of that period.]

AMENDMENT

1. Universal Credit (Transitional Provisions) (Amendment) Regulations 2014 (SI 2014/1626) reg.6(2) (October 13, 2014).

DEFINITIONS

"assessment period"—see reg.2(1).

GENERAL NOTE

See General Note to reg.37. 2.827

[1 PART 3

ARRANGEMENTS REGARDING CHANGES TO THE CHILD ELEMENT FROM APRIL 2017

Restriction on claims for universal credit during the interim period

39.—[2 ...]] 2.828

AMENDMENTS

1. Social Security (Restrictions on Amounts for Children and Qualifying Young Persons) Amendment Regulations 2017 (2017/376) reg.3(3) (April 6, 2017).
2. Universal Credit (Restriction on Amounts for Children and Qualifying Young Persons) (Transitional Provisions) Amendment Regulations 2019 (SI 2019/27) reg.2 (February 1, 2019).

GENERAL NOTE

The repeal of this regulation is a consequence of the Government's decision to remove the retrospective application of the "two child rule" in universal credit. Under WRWA 2016, Government policy was to provide support in the CTC and universal credit regimes for a maximum of two children (with some exceptions). This rule applied to claims for children born on or after April 6, 2017 (the date that the legislation relating to the policy to provide support for a maximum of two children came into force). During an interim period following the introduction of the policy, new claims for families with three or more children were to be directed to tax credits and the child element in universal credit was to be paid for all children born before April 6, 2017. This interim period was due to come to an end on February 1, 2019. From that date, the policy was to apply to all new claims to universal credit regardless of the date of birth of the child. From that date, new claims for families with three or more children are no longer directed to tax credits and instead are made to universal credit. As a result of the Government announcement of January 11, 2019, families with three or more children will continue to receive an additional amount in universal credit for all children born before April 6, 2017.

[1 Availability of the child element where maximum exceeded – transitionally protected children and qualifying young persons

40.—[2 ...]] 2.829

AMENDMENTS

1. Social Security (Restrictions on Amounts for Children and Qualifying Young Persons) Amendment Regulations 2017 (2017/376) reg.3(3) (April 6, 2017).
2. Universal Credit (Restriction on Amounts for Children and Qualifying Young Persons) (Transitional Provisions) Amendment Regulations 2019 (SI 2019/27) reg.2 (February 1, 2019).

GENERAL NOTE

See General Note to reg.39.

[1 Availability of the child element where maximum exceeded – continuation of exception from a previous award of child tax credit, income support or old style JSA

2.830 **41.**—(1) Where—

(a) the claimant ("C") is the step-parent of a child or qualifying young person ("A"); and

(b) within the 6 months immediately preceding the first day on which C became entitled to an award of universal credit, C had an award of child tax credit, income support or old style JSA in which an exception corresponding with an exception under paragraph 2, 3, 5 or 6 of Schedule 12 to the Universal Credit Regulations applied in respect of A,

paragraph 6 of that Schedule is to apply as if sub-paragraph (c) of that paragraph were satisfied, despite the fact that the previous award was not an award of universal credit.

(2) In this regulation, "step-parent" has the same meaning as in the Universal Credit Regulations.]

AMENDMENT

1. Social Security (Restrictions on Amounts for Children and Qualifying Young Persons) Amendment Regulations 2017 (2017/376) reg.3(3) (April 6, 2017).

[1 Evidence for non-consensual conception where claimant previously had an award of child tax credit

2.831 **42.**—(1) This regulation applies for the purposes of paragraph 5 of Schedule 12(7) to the Universal Credit Regulations (exception for non-consensual conception).

(2) The Secretary of State may treat the condition in sub-paragraph (3)(a) of that paragraph 5 as met if the Secretary of State is satisfied that the claimant has previously provided the evidence referred to in that sub-paragraph to the Commissioners for her Majesty's Revenue and Customs for the purposes of the corresponding exception in relation to child tax credit.]

AMENDMENT

1. Social Security (Restrictions on Amounts for Children and Qualifying Young Persons) Amendment Regulations 2017 (2017/376) reg.3(3) (April 6, 2017).

[1 Abolition of higher amount of the child element for first child or qualifying young person – saving where claimant responsible for a child or qualifying young person born before 6th April 2017

2.832 **43.** Section 14(5)(b) of the Welfare Reform and Work Act 2016(8) (which amends the Universal Credit Regulations by omitting the amount of the child element payable for the first child or qualifying young person) does not apply where the claimant is responsible for a child or qualifying young person born before 6th April 2017.]

AMENDMENT

1. Social Security (Restrictions on Amounts for Children and Qualifying Young Persons) Amendment Regulations 2017 (2017/376) reg.3(3) (April 6, 2017).

[1PART 4

MANAGED MIGRATION TO UNIVERSAL CREDIT

The Migration Process

Migration notice

44.—(1) The Secretary of State may, at any time, issue a notice ("a migration notice") to a person who is entitled to an award of an existing benefit— 2.833

(a) informing the person that all awards of any existing benefits to which they are entitled are to terminate and that they will need to make a claim for universal credit; and

(b) specifying a day ("the deadline day") by which a claim for universal credit must be made.

(2) The migration notice may contain such other information as the Secretary of State considers appropriate.

(3) The deadline day must not be within the period of three months beginning with the day on which the migration notice is issued.

(4) If the person who is entitled to an award of an existing benefit is, for the purposes of that award, a member of a couple or a member of a polygamous marriage, the Secretary of State must also issue the migration notice to the other member (or members).

(5) The Secretary of State may cancel a migration notice issued to any person—

(a) if it has been issued in error; [2 or]

(b) [2...]

(c) in any other circumstances where the Secretary State considers it necessary to do so in the interests of the person, or any class of person, or to safeguard the efficient administration of universal credit.

(6) A "notified person" is a person to whom a migration notice has been issued.]

AMENDMENTS

1. Universal Credit (Managed Migration Pilot and Miscellaneous Amendments) Regulations 2019 (SI 2019/1152) reg.3(7) (July 24, 2019).

2. Universal Credit (Transitional Provisions) Amendment Regulations 2022 (SI 2022/752) reg.11 and Sch. para.1(7) (July 25, 2022).

DEFINITIONS

"deadline day"—see para.(1)(b).
"existing benefit"—see reg.2(1).
"migration notice"—see para.(1).
"notified person"—see para.(6).

GENERAL NOTE

2.834 *The background*

Universal credit was first introduced on April 29, 2013. Initially claimants were required to satisfy the so-called "Pathfinder Group" and later the "gateway" conditions, in what were known as "live service" areas. As from November 26, 2014, it became possible to claim universal credit in "full service" or "digital service" areas without satisfying those criteria. Since December 12, 2018, all GB postcode districts and part-districts have been converted to digital service areas, in which universal credit must be claimed instead of one of the existing benefits (subject to certain exceptions where a legacy benefit may be claimed). Claimants of existing benefits who have had a change of circumstances have moved to universal credit by the process known as "natural migration".

2.835 *The first managed migration pilot*

The next phase in the roll-out of universal credit is "managed migration", whereby claimants of existing benefits are invited to make a claim for universal credit under the new Pt 4 of these Regulations. In the first instance this is being introduced on a pilot basis. This regulation provides for the issue of a migration notice, which in effect formally kick-starts the process of managed migration (although, according to official guidance, "before a migration notice is issued, claimants are informed about the migration process to ensure that they are ready to claim UC": see DMG Ch.M7: *Managed migration pilot and transitional protection* para.M7041). The migration notice informs a person that their existing benefits are to terminate and gives a deadline for claiming universal credit. Note that in the first instance at least this process is limited to a pilot, both geographically and numerically.

The first managed migration pilot, which was originally expected to last for up to 18 months, was confined to the Harrogate area and to a maximum of 10,000 awards of universal credit (see reg.2 (Managed migration pilot: limit on number of cases migrated) of the Universal Credit (Managed Migration Pilot and Miscellaneous Amendments) Regulations 2019 (SI 2019/1152), in force with effect from July 24, 2019). However, the Harrogate pilot was temporarily suspended on March 30, 2020, owing to the coronavirus crisis.

2.836 *The managed migration pilot resumed*

On April 25, 2022, the Secretary of State made the following statement to the House of Commons under the headline of "Completing the Move to Universal Credit by 2024" (HCWS780):

> "In 2012, Parliament voted to end legacy benefits and replace them with a single modern benefit system, Universal Credit (UC). The UC system stood up to the challenges of the pandemic and ensured support was provided for a significant number of new claimants with varying needs across the country. As the rest of government and society returns to business as usual, it is appropriate to resume the process to complete the move to UC by 2024.
>
> There are around 2.6 million households receiving legacy benefits and tax credits who need to move across to UC. The natural migration process, where claimants experience a change in circumstances and consequently move to UC, has largely continued throughout the last two years. The voluntary migration process has also been available throughout. We are taking steps to increase people's awareness of the fact that they could be better off financially if they were receiving Universal Credit, including through the publication of our document, *Completing the Move to Universal Credit*, today on GOV.UK. I will place copies in the libraries of both Houses.
>
> In that document, we set out our analysis which estimates that 1.4 million (55%) of those on legacy benefits or tax credits would receive a higher entitlement on UC than on legacy benefits and would benefit from moving voluntarily,

rather than waiting for a managed migration. This is particularly the case for tax credit claimants, with our analysis estimating around two-thirds of them would benefit. That is why we have included information on UC in this year's renewal forms for current tax credit recipients. It is important for current recipients to satisfy themselves that they would be better off on UC using independent benefit calculators before moving voluntarily, as once the claim is made, recipients cannot revert to tax credits or legacy benefits, nor receive any transitional protection payments. More information is included in the document.

For those claimants who do not choose to move and have not migrated naturally, we will manage their migration to UC. Parliament committed to providing transitional financial protection to those who are moved onto UC through the managed migration process. Whilst many households will be better off financially on UC, for those with a lower calculated award in UC than in their legacy benefits, transitional protection will be provided for eligible households. This means they will see no difference in their entitlement at the point they are moved to UC, provided there is no change in their circumstances during the migration process.

Before the pandemic, the department had started testing processes for managed migration in a pilot based in Harrogate. In 2020, the pilot was stopped to handle the significant increase in new claims for UC resulting from the pandemic. During this pilot there was proactive engagement with 80 people, 38 of these were moved to UC. 35 claimants were better off and only three people required transitional protection. The remainder of moves were not completed before the pilot was stopped. This pilot only involved claimants that the department had an existing relationship with. No claimants on Working Tax Credits were approached directly to commence a Move to UC.

The pilot provided valuable insights. First, while claimants will likely look for support from organisations they already know, such as a local authority, we are no longer assuming that all engagement needs to be managed by that organisation. Second, claimants can and will move autonomously, but some may need more support, particularly on digital access. The pandemic reinforced the importance of claimants being able to manage their own claims online and the strength of this system. Third, claimants can successfully choose a date for their claim, factoring in other income and expenditure points during the month. Finally, the pilot allowed the department to understand the processes and tools required to complete a managed move, such as those needed to calculate transitional protection.

As I have said to the House previously, we are not resuming the Harrogate pilot. We have learned from that experience and our wider experience over the last two years. As we complete the Move to UC, I am absolutely committed to making this a responsible and safe transition. Next month, we will be starting a multi-site approach across the country with a small number of claimants, approximately five hundred initially, being brought into the mandatory migration process. We will continue to develop our processes and systems to scale the migration process and complete by 2024.

We are resuming under existing regulations, though I intend to bring forward to Parliament amendments to the UC Transitional Provisions Regulations, following their consideration by the Social Security Advisory Committee.

Universal Credit is a dynamic welfare system fit for the 21st century. As part of our levelling up agenda to support the British public, we will continue to help people into work and progress in work, taking advantage of the recent reduction in the taper rate and boost to work allowances."

See also the DWP's accompanying press release (*https://www.gov.uk/government/news/managed-move-of-claimants-to-universal-credit-set-to-restart*). The new managed migration process commenced on May 9, 2022, but was confined to just two areas – Bolton and Medway. A coalition of charities has sent the Secretary of State an open letter calling for a halt to the managed migration process because of what they say is the risk to claimants' incomes: *https://www.mind.org.uk/news-campaigns/news/leading-charities-unite-to-tell-uk-government-to-halt-managed-migration/*.

Regulation 2 of the Universal Credit (Managed Migration Pilot and Miscellaneous Amendments) Regulations 2019 (SI 2019/1152), limiting the number of cases migrated to a maximum of 10,000 awards, was revoked with effect from July 25, 2022, by reg.10 of the Universal Credit (Transitional Provisions) Amendment Regulations 2022 (SI 2022/752).

On March 28, 2023 Mr G Opperman, Minister of State for Employment, made the following statement on the timetable for universal credit (*Move to Universal Credit Update*, Statement UIN HCWS678):

> "Since its introduction in 2013, Universal Credit has protected the most vulnerable in society, supported households through periods of financial uncertainty, helped people progress in work and move into better paid jobs. A dynamic benefit that reflects people's needs from month to month, Universal Credit successfully supports millions of people, and ensures that individuals are provided with the support they need to increase their earnings and move into better paid quality jobs.
>
> In April 2022, the Government set out its plan to complete the move to Universal Credit, and published Completing the move to Universal Credit, learning from the pilot that was paused in 2020.
>
> In May 2022, we commenced our Discovery phase. Initially, we issued 500 Migration Notices to households in Bolton and Medway. This notification letter sets out the requirement to make a claim to Universal Credit, to continue to receive financial support from the Government. It advises that they have a minimum of three months to make their claim and provides details of the support available.
>
> Following these initial notifications, we expanded the Discovery phase to Truro and Falmouth in July 2022, Harrow in August 2022, Northumberland in September 2022 and more recently all postcodes in Cornwall during February 2023.
>
> In January 2023, we published our learning from the Earliest Testable Service, which set out our initial learnings from the Discovery phase. It also set out the Department's plans for Move to Universal Credit in 2023/24 and 2024/25.
>
> We are now preparing to increase the numbers of Migration Notices issued and will expand into additional areas, bringing in the whole of Great Britain during 2023/24. Social security is a transferred matter in Northern Ireland.
>
> Through 2023/24, our focus will be on notifying households that receive tax credits only, increasing volumes incrementally each month. As we move into 2024/25, all cases with tax credits (including those on both Employment Support Allowance and tax credits), all cases on Income Support and Jobseeker's Allowance (Income Based) and all Housing Benefit cases (including combinations of these benefits) will be required to move to Universal Credit.
>
> At the point of moving over to Universal Credit (for those claimants moving through the managed migration process), legacy benefit claimants will be assessed for transitional protection and paid where appropriate. The aim of this temporary payment is to maintain benefit entitlement at the point of transition so that claimants will have time to adjust to the new benefit system.
>
> In line with the 2022 Autumn statement, the Government is delaying the managed migration of claimants on income-related Employment Support Allowance (except for those receiving Child Tax Credit) to Universal Credit. Employment Support Allowance claimants are still however able to make a claim for Universal Credit if they believe that they will be better off.
>
> This Government remains committed to making this a smooth and safe transition. As we move to the next phase of Move to Universal Credit, we will continue to build on our learning to ensure the service continues to meet the needs of those required to make the move to Universal Credit."

On December 4, 2023, the DWP issued a letter to local authorities setting out its plans for the sequence of issuing migration notices. The main features were as follows:

- The DWP's aim was to finish issuing migration notices to all claimants in receipt of only tax credits by the end of March 2024.
- The migration plans for 2024/25 include notifying most of the remaining applicable households on legacy benefits of the need to move to universal credit during this period, which include:
  - o residual tax credits cases (including those on both Employment Support Allowance and tax credits and Housing Benefit);
  - o all cases on Income Support and Jobseeker's Allowance (Income Based) and those combined with Housing Benefit and Housing Benefit only cases (except those Housing Benefit only customers living in supported or temporary accommodation).
- The DWP planned to undertake the issuing of migration notices to working age benefit claimants sequentially starting with Income Support (April–June 2024), Employment Support Allowance with Child Tax Credits (July – September 2024) and Jobseeker's Allowance (September 2024). If a Housing Benefit claimant is receiving one of these benefits, they will receive a migration notice.
- From April 2024 the DWP will also invite tax credits claimants with Housing Benefit and then Housing Benefit (only) claimants to move to universal credit.

If this timetable is adhered to, the net effect is that all claimants on tax credits should have moved to universal credit by April 2025.

Paragraphs (1)–(6) 2.837

A person who receives a migration notice is a "notified person" (see para.(6)). A notice is only a migration notice if it contains two pieces of information (although other information may be included (para.(2)). First, the notice must inform "the person that all awards of any existing benefits to which they are entitled are to terminate and that they will need to make a claim for universal credit" (para.(1) (a))—thus transfer is not automatic, and a claim must be made. Second, the notice must also specify the day ("the deadline day") by which a claim for universal credit must be made (para.(1)(b)). Deadline day must not fall within three months of the date of issue of the migration notice (para.(3)) and may be extended (see reg.45). Where couples are concerned each member must be issued with a migration notice (para. (4)). Notices can be cancelled in the circumstances set out in para.(5)).

[1Extension of the deadline day

45.—(1) The Secretary of State may determine that the deadline day should be changed to a later day either— 2.838

(a) on the Secretary of State's own initiative; or

(b) if a notified person requests such a change before the deadline day,

where there is a good reason to do so.

(2) The Secretary of State must inform the notified person or persons of the new deadline day.]

AMENDMENT

1. Universal Credit (Managed Migration Pilot and Miscellaneous Amendments) Regulations 2019 (SI 2019/1152) reg.3(7) (July 24, 2019).

DEFINITIONS

"deadline day"—see reg.44(1)(b).
"notified person"—see reg.44(6).

GENERAL NOTE

2.839 This provides in very general terms for the circumstances in which the deadline for making a universal credit claim following issue of a migration notice can be extended. The deadline may be extended by the Secretary of State on her own initiative or on receipt of a request from the notified person. All that is required (in either instance) is "a good reason to do so". There is no statutory definition of "good reason". The non-exhaustive list of examples in the official guidance refers to cases where the claimant has difficulty completing the universal credit claim because they have a physical or mental health condition, have learning difficulties, are in or about to go in to hospital as an in-patient, have significant caring responsibilities, are homeless or face a domestic emergency (*DMG Chapter M7: Managed migration pilot and Transitional protection* para M7081). Providing the criteria are met, there is no limit to the potential number of extensions that can be made (although cancellation under reg.44(5) may be more appropriate) but in any case the notified person must be advised of the new deadline (para.(2)). The official guidance also asserts that there is no right to a mandatory reconsideration or appeal about being issued with a migration notice, the deadline day or a refusal to extend a deadline or cancel the notice. This guidance is presumably based on the premise that such actions are not "made on a claim for, or on an award of, a relevant benefit" within s.12 SSA 1998 and, as they are not included within Sch.3 to that Act, do not carry a right of appeal. It may, however, be possible to challenge such an action indirectly as a "building block" to an "outcome decision" (e.g. no valid migration notice served so decision to terminate existing award is incorrect). Such a challenge to extension notices may raise issues analogous to those in *R(TC) 1/05*. Failing that, in theory at least, judicial review must be available for a potential challenge.

[1Termination of existing benefits if no claim before the deadline

2.840 **46.**—(1) Where a notified person has not made a claim for universal credit on or before the deadline day, all awards of any existing benefits to which the person is entitled terminate—

(a) in the case of housing benefit, [2 income support, income-based jobseeker's allowance or income-related employment and support allowance,] on the last day of the period of two weeks beginning with the deadline day; and

(b) in the case of [2a tax credit], on the day before the deadline day.

(2) An award of housing benefit to which a claimant is entitled in respect of specified accommodation or temporary accommodation does not terminate by virtue of this regulation.

(3) Where paragraph (1) applies and the notified person makes a claim for universal credit—

(a) after the deadline day; and

(b) on or before the final deadline specified in paragraph (4),

then, notwithstanding anything in regulation 26 of the Claims and Payments Regulations (time within which a claim for universal credit is to be made) as modified by regulation 15 of these Regulations, the award is to commence on the deadline day.

(4) The final deadline is the day that would be the last day of the first assessment period in relation to an award commencing on the deadline day.

(5) [3...]]

AMENDMENTS

1. Universal Credit (Managed Migration Pilot and Miscellaneous Amendments) Regulations 2019 (SI 2019/1152) reg.3(7) (July 24, 2019).
2. Universal Credit (Managed Migration Pilot and Miscellaneous Amendments) Regulations 2019 (SI 2019/1152) reg.4(5) July 22, 2020).
3. Universal Credit (Transitional Provisions) Amendment Regulations 2022 (SI 2022/752) reg.11 and Sch. para.1(8) (July 25, 2022).

DEFINITIONS

"assessment period"—see reg.2(1).
"deadline day"—see reg.44(1)(b).
"existing benefit"—see reg.2(1).
"final deadline"—see para.(4).
"housing benefit"—see reg.2(1).
"migration notice"—see reg.44(1).
"notified person"—see reg.44(6).
"specified accommodation"—see reg.2(1).
"temporary accommodation—*ibid.*

GENERAL NOTE

This provides for termination of all awards of any existing benefits where a notified person does not claim universal credit by the deadline day (para.(1)). However, the DWP has indicated that it has no intention to use these powers during the pilot phase – rather action will be taken to encourage the claimant to make a claim for universal credit. 2.841

In the case of an income-based JSA or income-related ESA, "terminate" means treating the award in the same way as if WRA 2012 s.33(1)(a) or (b) (abolition of those benefits) and associated provisions had come into force. This means that any contribution-based or contributory allowance to which a claimant is entitled becomes an award of new style JSA or new style ESA (as defined in reg.2 of the 2014 Regulations). Where the person claims universal credit by the final deadline (which is the last day of the first assessment period of an award commencing on the deadline day) the award is backdated to the deadline day (paras.(3) and (4)). See also reg.47 (para.(5)).

[1Notified persons who claim as a different benefit unit

47.—[2 ...] 2.842

AMENDMENTS

1. Universal Credit (Managed Migration Pilot and Miscellaneous Amendments) Regulations 2019 (SI 2019/1152) reg.3(7) (July 24, 2019).
2. Universal Credit (Transitional Provisions) Amendment Regulations 2022 (SI 2022/752) reg.6(1) (July 25, 2022).

Transitional Protection

[1Meaning of "qualifying claim"

48. A "qualifying claim" is a claim for universal credit by a single claimant who is a notified person or by joint claimants, both of whom are notified persons, where the claim is made on or before the final deadline (see regulation 46(4)).] 2.843

Amendment

1. Universal Credit (Managed Migration Pilot and Miscellaneous Amendments) Regulations 2019 (SI 2019/1152) reg.3(7) (July 24, 2019).

Definitions

"final deadline"—see reg.46(4).
"notified person"—see reg.44(6).

General Note

2.844 The Secretary of State is required (see new regs 48 and 49) to determine whether transitional protection applies where the person makes a "qualifying claim" as defined by this provision. It follows these arrangements for transitional protection apply only to cases subject to *managed* migration, and not to cases affected by *natural* migration (e.g. owing to a change of circumstances). The two types of transitional protection are a "transitional capital disregard" (reg.51) and a "transitional element" (regs 52 to 55). The *transitional capital disregard* enables claimants entitled to tax credits and with capital above £16,000 to be entitled to universal credit for up to 12 months (technically 12 assessment periods). The *transitional element* is an additional amount of universal credit based on the difference between the total amount of existing benefits and the amount of universal credit entitlement. This is added to the award before income is deducted and erodes as other elements increase.

But see also reg.58, enabling the Secretary of State to specify a later commencement date for an award on a qualifying claim.

See further *FL v Secretary of State for Work and Pensions* [2024] UKUT 6 (AAC), discussed in the note to reg.63 below.

[1Meaning of "migration day"

2.845 **49.** "Migration day", in relation to a qualifying claim, means the day before the first day on which the claimant is entitled to universal credit in connection with that claim.]

Amendment

1. Universal Credit (Managed Migration Pilot and Miscellaneous Amendments) Regulations 2019 (SI 2019/1152) reg.3(7) (July 24, 2019).

Definition

qualifying claim"—see reg.48.

General Note

2.846 Migration day, being the day before the start of a universal credit award, is used as the marker to calculate any transitional protection due.

[1Secretary of State to determine whether transitional protection applies

2.847 **50.**—(1) Before making a decision on a qualifying claim the Secretary of State must first determine whether—

(a) a transitional capital disregard is to apply; or
(b) a transitional element is to be included,

(or both) in the calculation of the award.

(2) But the Secretary of State is not to determine whether a transitional element is to be included in a case [2 where—

(a) notified persons who were a couple for the purposes of an award of an existing benefit when the migration notice was issued are single persons or members of a different couple for the purposes of a claim for universal credit; or

(b) notified persons who were single for the purposes of an award of an existing benefit when the migration notice was issued are a couple for the purposes of a claim for universal credit; or

(c) notified persons who were members of a polygamous marriage for the purposes of an award of an existing benefit when the migration notice was issued are a couple or single persons for the purposes of a claim for universal credit]].

AMENDMENTS

1. Universal Credit (Managed Migration Pilot and Miscellaneous Amendments) Regulations 2019 (SI 2019/1152) reg.3(7) (July 24, 2019).
2. Universal Credit (Transitional Provisions) Amendment Regulations 2022 (SI 2022/752) reg.6(2) (July 25, 2022).

DEFINITIONS

"notified person"—see reg.44(6).
"qualifying claim"—see reg.48.
"transitional capital disregard"—see reg.51.
"transitional element"—see reg.52.

GENERAL NOTE

Subject to the special cases in para.(2), the Secretary of State is under a duty to determine whether transitional protection applies on a qualifying claim. This must be done "*before* making a decision on a qualifying claim". The sequencing is important as otherwise the universal credit conditions of entitlement may not be satisfied or the amount of universal credit to which the claimant might be entitled might be less than any income taken into account. In addition, of course, transitional protection applies only to a qualifying claim (see reg.48), i.e. a claim made on or before the final deadline. Claimants who fail to claim under the managed migration rules will not be entitled to transitional protection even if they manage to make a successful claim at a later date. As the Explanatory Memorandum puts it: 2.848

> "7.4 Provided that existing benefit claimants (and their partner, if they have one) make the UC claim by the deadline day specified in the notification, existing benefits will be paid up until the day before they made their UC claim and Transitional Protection will be considered. If they do not make a new UC claim by the deadline day, their existing benefits will end and will be paid up until the day before that day.
> 7.5 If claimants contact the Department after the deadline date but within one month of their existing benefits ending, their UC claim will automatically be backdated to the deadline date and Transitional Protection can be applied to the UC award. If a claimant does not contact the Department until after a month after the deadline date they were given, their claim will not be considered as a managed migration claim which means their claim will be assessed under the UC regulations5 without the consideration or award of Transitional Protection."

[[1]The transitional capital disregard

2.849 **51.**—(1) A transitional capital disregard is to apply where, on the migration day, the claimant—

(a) is entitled to an award of a tax credit; and

(b) has capital exceeding £16,000.

(2) Where a transitional capital disregard applies, any capital exceeding £16,000 is to be disregarded for the purposes of—

(a) determining whether the financial condition in section 5(1)(a) or 5(2)(a) of the Act (capital limit) is met; and

(b) calculating the amount of an award of universal credit (including the indicative UC amount).

(3) Where a transitional capital disregard has been applied in the calculation of an award of universal credit but, in any assessment period, the claimant no longer has (or joint claimants no longer have) capital exceeding £16,000, the transitional capital disregard is not to apply in any subsequent assessment period.

(4) A transitional capital disregard is not to apply for more than 12 assessment periods.]

AMENDMENT

1. Universal Credit (Managed Migration Pilot and Miscellaneous Amendments) Regulations 2019 (SI 2019/1152) reg.3(7) (July 24, 2019).

DEFINITIONS

"assessment period"—see reg.2(1).

"migration day"—see reg.49.

"tax credit"—see reg.2(1).

GENERAL NOTE

2.850 Tax credit entitlement is not subject to any capital limit whereas universal credit claimants must not have capital over £16,000. The transitional capital disregard allows capital over £16,000 in the hands of former tax credit claimants to be disregarded for 12 months where the relevant conditions are satisfied (the 12 months need not be consecutive). The transitional capital disregard ceases to apply in the circumstances set out in para.(3) or those in reg.56.

[[1]The transitional element

2.851 **52.**—(1) A transitional element is to be included in the calculation of an award if the total amount of any awards of existing benefits determined in accordance with regulation 53 ("the total legacy amount") is greater than the amount of an award of universal credit determined in accordance with regulation 54 ("the indicative UC amount").

(2) Where a transitional element is to be included in the calculation of an award, the amount of that element is to be treated, for the purposes of section 8 of the Act (calculation of awards), as if it were an additional amount to be included in the maximum amount under section 8(2) before the deduction of income under section 8(3).]

AMENDMENT

1. Universal Credit (Managed Migration Pilot and Miscellaneous Amendments) Regulations 2019 (SI 2019/1152) reg.3(7) (July 24, 2019).

DEFINITIONS

"existing benefit"—see reg.2(1).
"indicative UC amount"—see reg.54.
"total legacy amount"—see reg.53.

GENERAL NOTE

Transitional protection in the form of a "transitional element" applies (see para. (1)) if the "total legacy amount" (in effect the previous entitlement under existing benefits on the day before change-over—see reg.53) is more than the "indicative UC amount" (see reg.54). This method has been "designed to provide a balanced, like-for-like comparison of entitlement under the two regimes" (Explanatory Memorandum, para.7.15). Where transitional element applies, the difference is included in the universal credit award as a transitional element. It is treated as an additional amount to be included in the maximum amount of universal credit before the deduction of income (para.(2)). Rounding rules apply as under reg.61. The transitional element is no longer included in an award in the circumstances specified in reg.56. If the indicative UC amount is more than the total legacy amount, then obviously no such element is included. 2.852

[1The transitional element – total legacy amount

53.—(1) The total legacy amount is the sum of the representative monthly rates of all awards of any existing benefits to which a claimant is, or joint claimants are, entitled on the migration day. 2.853

Tax credits

(2) To calculate the representative monthly rate of an award of working tax credit or child tax credit—

(a) take the figure for the daily rate of the award on the migration day provided by HMRC and calculated on the basis of the information as to the claimant's circumstances held by HMRC on that day; and
(b) convert to a monthly figure by multiplying by 365 and dividing by 12.

(3) For the purposes of paragraph (2)(a) "the daily rate" is—

(a) in a case where section 13(1) of the 2002 Act applies (relevant income does not exceed the income threshold or the claimant is entitled to a prescribed social security benefit), the maximum rate of each element to which the claimant is entitled on the migration day divided by 365; and
(b) in any other case, the rate that would be produced by applying regulations 6 to 9 of the Tax Credits (Income Thresholds and Determination of Rates) Regulations 2002(**6**) as if the migration day were a relevant period of one day.

IS, JSA (IB) and ESA (IR)

(4) To calculate the representative monthly rate of an award of income support, income-based jobseeker's allowance or income-related employment and support allowance—

(a) take the weekly rate on the migration day calculated in accordance with—

(i) in the case of income support, Part 7 of the Social Security Contributions and Benefits Act 1992 and the Income Support (General) Regulations 1987,

(ii) in the case of income-based jobseeker's allowance, Part 1 of the Jobseekers Act 1995 and the Jobseeker's Allowance Regulations 1996, or

(iii) in the case of income-related employment and support allowance, Part 1 of the 2007 Act, the Employment and Support Allowance Regulations 2008 and the Employment and Support Allowance (Transitional Provisions, Housing Benefit and Council Tax Benefit) (Existing Awards) (No.2) Regulations 2010,

on the basis of the information held by the Secretary of State on that day; and

(b) convert to a monthly figure by multiplying by 52 and dividing by 12.

(5) The amount of an award of income-related employment and support allowance or income-based jobseeker's allowance is to be calculated before any reduction for a sanction.

(6) Where—

(a) a claimant who is entitled to income-based jobseeker's allowance is also entitled to contribution-based jobseeker's allowance; or

(b) a claimant who is entitled to income-related employment and support allowance is also entitled to a contributory allowance,

then, notwithstanding section 4(8) to (11) of the Jobseekers Act 1995 and section 6(3) to (7) of the 2007 Act (excess over the contributory allowance to be treated as attributable to the income-based, or income-related, allowance) the weekly rate in paragraph (4) is to be calculated as the applicable amount less the claimant's income (if any).

Housing benefit

(7) To calculate the representative monthly rate of an award of housing benefit—

(a) take the weekly rate on the migration day calculated in accordance with Part 7 of the Social Security Contributions and Benefits Act 1992 and the Housing Benefit Regulations 2006, on the basis of the information held by the Secretary of State on that day, and convert to a monthly figure by multiplying by 52 and dividing by 12; or

(b) in a case where the claimant has rent free periods, calculate the annual rate by multiplying the weekly rate (as above) by the number of weeks in the year in respect of which the claimant is liable to pay rent, and convert to a monthly figure by dividing by 12.

(8) For the purposes of paragraph (7), if the migration day falls in a rent free period, the weekly rate of housing benefit is to be calculated by reference to the amount of rent for the last complete week that was not a rent free period.

(9) In paragraphs (7) and (8) "rent free period" has the meaning in regulation 81 of the Housing Benefit Regulations 2006.

(10) In a case where regulation 8(3) (continuation of housing benefit in respect of specified accommodation or temporary accommodation) applies, no amount is to be included in the total legacy amount [2 for housing benefit in respect of specified or temporary accommodation].

The benefit cap

(11) Where—

(a) the existing benefits do not include an award of housing benefit, or they include an award of housing benefit that has been reduced to the minimum amount by virtue of Part 8A of the Housing Benefit Regulations 2006 (the benefit cap);

(b) Part 7 of the Universal Credit Regulations (the benefit cap) applies in the calculation of the indicative UC amount; and

(c) the claimant's total entitlement to welfare benefits (as defined in section 96(10) of the Act) on the migration day is greater than the relevant amount,

the total legacy amount is reduced by the excess (minus the amount for childcare costs referred to regulation 54(2)(b) where applicable) over the relevant amount.

(12) For the purposes of paragraph (11)—

(a) the amount of each welfare benefit is the monthly equivalent calculated in the manner set out in regulation 73 (unearned income calculated monthly) of the Universal Credit Regulations; and

(b) the "relevant amount" is the amount referred to in regulation 80A of those Regulations which is applicable to the claimant.]

AMENDMENTS

1. Universal Credit (Managed Migration Pilot and Miscellaneous Amendments) Regulations 2019 (SI 2019/1152) reg.3(7) (July 24, 2019).

2. Social Security and Universal Credit (Miscellaneous Amendments) Regulations 2023 (SI 2023/543) reg.6(4) (June 29, 2023).

DEFINITIONS

"contributory employment and support allowance"—see reg.2(1).
"the daily rate"—see para.(3).
"existing benefit"—see reg.2(1).
"housing benefit"—*ibid.*
"income support"—*ibid.*
"income-based jobseeker's allowance"—*ibid.*
"income-related employment and support allowance"—*ibid.*
"migration day"—see reg.49.
"HMRC"—see reg.2(1).
"relevant amount"—see para.(11).

"rent free period"—see para.(9).
"tax credit"—see reg.2(1).
"total legacy amount"—see para.(1).

GENERAL NOTE

2.854 The total legacy amount is calculated by adding together the monthly rates of all awards of the existing benefits to which the claimant was entitled on migration day, i.e. the day before the universal credit award starts. That principle is established by para.(1). The remainder of the regulation deals with the necessary arithmetic with respect to tax credits (paras.(2) and (3)), income support, income-based JSA and income-related ESA (paras.(4)–(6)) and housing benefit (paras.(7)–(10)), subject to any benefit cap adjustment (paras.(11)–(12)).

[1The transitional element – indicative UC amount

2.855 **54.**—(1) The indicative UC amount is the amount to which a claimant would be entitled if an award of universal credit were calculated in accordance with section 8 of the Act by reference to the claimant's circumstances on the migration day, applying the assumptions in paragraph (2).

(2) The assumptions are—

(a) if the claimant is entitled to an award of child tax credit, the claimant is responsible for any child or qualifying young person in respect of whom the individual element of child tax credit is payable;

(b) if the claimant is entitled to an award of working tax credit that includes the childcare element, the indicative UC amount includes the childcare costs element and, for the purposes of calculating the amount of that element, the amount of the childcare costs is equal to the relevant weekly childcare charges included in the calculation of the daily rate referred to in regulation 53(2), converted to a monthly amount by multiplying by 52 and dividing by 12;

(c) the amount of the claimant's earned income is—

(i) if the claimant is entitled to an award of a tax credit, the annual amount of any employment income or trading income, as defined by regulation 4 or 6 respectively of the Tax Credits (Definition and Calculation of Income) Regulations 2002, by reference to which the representative monthly rate of that tax credit is calculated for the purposes of regulation 53(2) converted to a net monthly amount by—

(aa) dividing by 12, and

(bb) deducting such amount for income tax and national insurance contributions as the Secretary of State considers appropriate,

(ii) if paragraph (i) does not apply and the claimant is entitled to an award of income support, income-based jobseeker's allowance or income-related employment and support allowance, the amount of earnings by reference to which the representative monthly rate of that benefit was calculated for the purposes of regulation 53(4) to (6) (including nil if none were taken into account) converted to a monthly amount by multiplying by 52 and dividing by 12, or

(iii) if paragraphs (i) and (ii) do not apply, but the claimant had an award of housing benefit, the amount of earnings by reference to which the representative monthly rate of that benefit was calculated for the purposes of regulation 53(7) to (10) (including nil if none were taken into account) converted to a monthly amount by multiplying by 52 and dividing by 12.

(3) If the claimant would not meet the financial condition in section 5(1)(b) of the Act (or, in the case of joint claimants, they would not meet the condition in section 5(2)(b) of the Act) the claimant is to be treated, for the purposes of calculating the indicative UC amount, as if they were entitled to an award of universal credit of a nil amount.

(4) If a transitional capital disregard is to apply, the claimant is to be treated as having met the financial condition in section 5(1)(a) or 5(2)(a) of the Act (capital limit).

(5) The indicative UC amount is to be calculated after any reduction under Part 7 of the Universal Credit Regulations (the benefit cap) but before any reduction under section 26 (higher-level sanctions) or 27 (other sanctions) of the Act.

(6) But there is to be no reduction for the benefit cap under that Part where the amount of the claimant's earned income (or, in the case of a couple their combined earned income) on the migration day, calculated in accordance with paragraph (2)(c), is equal to or exceeds the amount specified in paragraph (1)(a) of regulation 82 (exceptions – earnings) of the Universal Credit Regulations.

(7) The calculation of the indicative UC amount is to be based on the information that is used for the purposes of calculating the total legacy amount, supplemented as necessary by such further information or evidence as the Secretary of State requires.]

AMENDMENT

1. Universal Credit (Managed Migration Pilot and Miscellaneous Amendments) Regulations 2019 (SI 2019/1152) reg.3(7) (July 24, 2019).

DEFINITIONS

"childcare costs element"—see reg.2(1).
"earned income"—*ibid.*
"housing benefit"—*ibid.*
"indicative UC amount"—see reg.54.
"migration day"—see reg.49.
"tax credit"—see reg.2(1).
"total legacy amount"—see reg.53.
"transitional capital disregard"—see reg.51.

GENERAL NOTE

The total legacy amount (reg.53) is a relatively straightforward concept to grasp. **2.856**
It is what the claimant was in fact entitled to under the existing benefit regime. The indicative UC amount is a less readily understandable concept. According to para.(1) it represents the hypothetical amount of universal credit to which the claimant would have been entitled to on migration day (i.e. the day before the universal credit award commenced) but subject to the various assumptions in para.(2). In addition, if the claimant would not meet the income financial condition of entitlement, they are treated for these purposes as being entitled to a nil award (para.(3)). Claimants are also treated as satisfying the capital financial condition where the transitional

capital disregard applies (para.(4)). The indicative UC amount is worked out *after* any reduction due to the benefit cap (but see para.(6)) and *before* any reduction for a sanction (para.(5)).

[[1]The transitional element – initial amount and adjustment where other elements increase

2.857 **55.**—(1) The initial amount of the transitional element is—

(a) if the indicative UC amount is greater than nil, the amount by which the total legacy amount exceeds the indicative UC amount; or

(b) if the indicative UC amount is nil, the total legacy amount plus any amount by which the income which fell to be deducted in accordance with section 8(3) of the Act exceeded the maximum amount.

(2) The amount of the transitional element to be included in the calculation of an award is—

(a) for the first assessment period, the initial amount;

(b) for the second assessment period, the initial amount reduced by the sum of any relevant increases in that assessment period;

(c) for the third and each subsequent assessment period, the amount that was included for the previous assessment period reduced by the sum of any relevant increases (as in sub-paragraph (b)).

(3) If the amount of the transitional element is reduced to nil in any assessment period, a transitional element is not to apply in the calculation of the award for any subsequent assessment period.

(4) A "relevant increase" is [[2], subject to paragraph (5)] an increase in any of the amounts that are included in the maximum amount under sections 9 to 12 of the Act (including any of those amounts that is included for the first time), apart from the childcare costs element.]

[[2](5) In cases where the LCW element is replaced by the LCWRA element, the "relevant increase" is to be treated as the difference between the amounts of those elements.

(6) In this regulation, "LCW element" and "LCWRA element" have the same meaning as in regulation 2 of the Universal Credit Regulations.]

AMENDMENTS

1. Universal Credit (Managed Migration Pilot and Miscellaneous Amendments) Regulations 2019 (SI 2019/1152) reg.3(7) (July 24, 2019).

2. Universal Credit (Transitional Provisions) Amendment Regulations 2022 (SI 2022/752) reg.7 (July 25, 2022).

DEFINITIONS

"assessment period"—see reg.2(1).
"childcare costs element"—*ibid.*
"relevant increase"—see para.(4).
"indicative UC amount"—see reg.54.
"total legacy amount"—see reg.53.
"transitional element"—see reg.52.

General Note

The amount of the transitional element to be included in the calculation of a universal credit award is, for the first assessment period (para.(2)(a)), the initial amount as defined by para.(1). The amount for subsequent periods is governed by para.(2)(b) and (c) as appropriate. In these later periods the amount can be reduced by relevant increases, as defined by para.(4). 2.858

Note, however, Judge Church's judgment in *Secretary of State for Work and Pensions v JA (UC)* [2024] UKUT 52 (AAC), upholding the FTT's decision that the Department's application of reg.55 (and Sch.2) on the facts of that case resulted in unlawful discrimination against the claimant (JA) in breach of s.6 of the HRA 1998 and Art.14 of the ECHR. JA, who had previously been in receipt of income-related ESA with the SDP, made a claim for UC as a result of 'natural migration' (following her move to a different local authority area). She was entitled to stand-alone transitional SDP of £285 for each assessment period (i.e. for each month). She then moved from mainstream accommodation into specified accommodation (supported by housing benefit), and the transitional SDP amount was incorporated into her monthly UC award. She then moved a third time from specified accommodation back into mainstream accommodation with the housing costs element (£369.37) now payable as part of her UC award. However, by virtue of reg.55(2), the UC transitional element was reduced to nil in one fell swoop as the amount of the housing costs element exceeded the SDP transitional sum. The FTT, following the *TP1* line of cases (see commentary to reg.63), decided that reg.55(2) should be disapplied as it was unlawfully discriminatory in reducing the SDP transitional element to nil.

Judge Church dismissed the Secretary of State's appeal to the Upper Tribunal, holding that JA had an "other status" under Art.14 ECHR – the only difference between the status of JA and that of the claimants in *TP1* was that JA's move was from specified accommodation to mainstream accommodation, whereas in *TP1* the move was from one local authority area to another. As such, JA's claim to "other status" was stronger as the move was more closely related to her status as a severely disabled person. Judge Church also agreed with the FTT that JA had been treated differently as compared to someone who moves from mainstream accommodation to a cheaper rental property. Furthermore, the Secretary of State had not shown an objective justification for the discriminatory treatment, e.g. as to why those in JA's position should not be afforded the same protection from a cliff-edge income loss as was found to be necessary in *TP1*. The Upper Tribunal confirmed that the appropriate remedy was to disapply reg.55(2):

> "129. ... Disapplying the provisions to the extent that they discriminate unlawfully against the Claimant and those sharing her status does not require a wholesale unpicking of the Universal Credit scheme. Erosion can still occur, and the transitional protections can be eroded to nothing as claimants enjoy increases in their benefit. What cannot occur is the unfair stripping away of all transitional protection in one fell swoop when a claimant's circumstances change such that they need to move between specified accommodation which is funded via Housing Benefit and non-specified accommodation which attracts the Housing Costs Element of Universal Credit."

[1 Ending of transitional protection

Circumstances in which transitional protection ceases

56.—(1) A transitional capital disregard or a transitional element does not apply in any assessment period to which paragraph (2) or (4) applies, or in any subsequent assessment period. 2.859

Cessation of employment or sustained drop in earnings

(2) This paragraph applies to an assessment period if the following condition is met—

(a) in the case of a single claimant—

(i) it is the assessment period after the third consecutive assessment period in which the claimant's earned income is less than the amount specified in regulation 99(6)(a) of the Universal Credit Regulations ("the single administrative threshold"), and

(ii) in the first assessment period of the award, the claimant's earned income was equal to or more than that threshold; or

(b) in the case of joint claimants—

(i) it is the assessment period after the third consecutive assessment period in which their combined earned income is less than the amount specified in regulation 99(6)(b) of the Universal Credit Regulations ("the couple administrative threshold"), and

(ii) in the first assessment period of the award, their combined earned income was equal to or more than that threshold.

[[2](3) For the purposes of paragraph (2)—

(a) references to the amount specified in regulation 99(6)(a) and 99(6)(b) respectively of the Universal Credit Regulations are to the amount that was applicable on the first day of the award; and

(b) a claimant is to be treated as having earned income that is equal to or more than the single administrative threshold and the couple administrative threshold respectively in any assessment period in respect of which regulation 62 (minimum income floor) of the Universal Credit Regulations applies to that claimant or would apply but for regulation 62(5) of those Regulations (minimum income floor not to apply in a start-up period).]

Couple separating or forming

(4) This paragraph applies to an assessment period in which—

(a) joint claimants cease to be a couple or become members of a different couple; or

(b) a single claimant becomes a member of a couple, unless it is a case where the person may, by virtue of regulation 3(3) of the Universal Credit Regulations (claimant with an ineligible partner), claim as a single person.]

AMENDMENTS

1. Universal Credit (Managed Migration Pilot and Miscellaneous Amendments) Regulations 2019 (SI 2019/1152) reg.3(7) (July 24, 2019).

2. Universal Credit (Administrative Earnings Threshold) (Amendment) Regulations 2023 (SI 2023/7) reg.3 (January 30, 2023).

DEFINITIONS

"assessment period"—see reg.2(1).

"earned income"—*ibid.*

"the couple administrative threshold"—see para.(2)(b)(i).

"the single administrative threshold"—see para.(2)(a)(i).
"transitional capital disregard"—see reg.51.
"transitional element"—see reg.52.

General Note

This provides for the circumstances in which transitional protection ceases. These are where there is a reduction in earnings over a three-month period or where an award ends (including where a couple separate or form—but note the exceptions turning on reg.3(3) of the Universal Credit Regulations). Exceptionally, transitional protection can be carried over to a subsequent award in certain circumstances under new reg.57. **2.860**

[1Application of transitional protection to a subsequent award

57.—(1) Where— **2.861**

(a) a transitional capital disregard is applied, or a transitional element is included, in the calculation of an award, and that award terminates; or

(b) the Secretary State determines (in accordance with regulation 50) that a transitional capital disregard is to apply, or a transitional element is to be included in the calculation of an award, but the decision on the qualifying claim is that there is no entitlement to an award,

no transitional capital disregard is to apply and no transitional element is to be included in the calculation of any subsequent award unless paragraph (2) applies.

(2) This paragraph applies if—

(a) the reason for the previous award terminating or, as the case may be, there being no entitlement to an award, was that the claimant (or joint claimants) had earned income on account of which the financial condition in section 5(1)(b) or 5(2)(b) of the Act (income is such that the amount payable is at least 1p) was not met; and

(b) the claimant becomes entitled to an award within the period of three months beginning with—

(i) where paragraph (1)(a) applies, the last day of the month that would have been the final assessment period of the previous award (had it not terminated), or

(ii) where paragraph (1)(b) applies, the day that would have been the last day of the first assessment period had there been entitlement to an award.

(3) Where paragraph (2) applies in a case where a previous award has terminated, the new award is to be treated for the purposes of regulation 51 (transitional capital disregard), 55 (transitional element – initial amount and adjustment where other elements increase) and 56 (circumstances in which transitional protection ceases) as if it were a continuation of that award.]

Amendment

1. Universal Credit (Managed Migration Pilot and Miscellaneous Amendments) Regulations 2019 (SI 2019/1152) reg.3(7) (July 24, 2019).

Definitions

"assessment period"—see reg.2(1).
"earned income"—*ibid.*

"qualifying claim"—see reg.48.
"transitional capital disregard"—see reg.51.
"transitional element"—see reg.52.

GENERAL NOTE

2.862 The basic rule is that where transitional protection on a universal credit claim has been lost (either because an award with transitional protection has ended or because a qualifying claim with such protection has been disallowed) then it is lost forever (para.(1)). However, there are exceptional cases in which transitional protection once lost can be revived, as in the circumstances set out in para.(2).

[1Miscellaneous

Qualifying claim – Secretary of State may set later commencement day

2.863 **58.** Where the Secretary of State decides a qualifying claim, and it is not a case where the award is to commence before the date of claim by virtue of regulation 46(3) [2...] (claim made by the final deadline) or regulation 26 of the Claims and Payments Regulations (time within which a claim for universal credit is to be made) as modified by regulation 15 of these Regulations, the Secretary of State may determine a day on which the award of universal credit is to commence that is after, but no more than one month after, the date of claim.]

AMENDMENTS

1. Universal Credit (Managed Migration Pilot and Miscellaneous Amendments) Regulations 2019 (SI 2019/1152) reg.3(7) (July 24, 2019).
2. Universal Credit (Transitional Provisions) Amendment Regulations 2022 (SI 2022/752) reg.11 and Sch. para.1(9) (July 25, 2022).

DEFINITION

"qualifying claim"—see reg.48.

GENERAL NOTE

2.864 This enables the Secretary State to set a date for commencement of the award of universal credit up to a month after the date of a qualifying claim (provided it is not a case where the claim is to be backdated). According to the Explanatory Memorandum, this provision "has been included to delay the start date of UC claims if the number of claims that need to be assessed would put pressure on operational capacity to the point of threatening service delivery to claimants" (para.7.13).

[1Minimum income floor not to apply for first 12 months

2.865 **59.** [2...]]

AMENDMENTS

1. Universal Credit (Managed Migration Pilot and Miscellaneous Amendments) Regulations 2019 (SI 2019/1152) reg.3(7) (July 24, 2019).
2. Universal Credit (Managed Migration Pilot and Miscellaneous Amendments) Regulations 2019 (SI 2019/1152) reg.6(2) (September 23, 2020).

General Note

As originally enacted, reg.59 provided for all notified persons who would otherwise be subject to the minimum income floor (under which certain self-employed claimants are to have an assumed level of earnings) to have the 12 month "start-up" period without the requirement to have started their business within the past 12 months. However, reg.63 of the Universal Credit Regulations provides for a 12 month start-up period during which the minimum income floor does not apply. That provision was amended so as to extend the start-up period to all claimants for universal credit who are in gainful self-employment and have not previously been subject to the minimum income floor (even if they have not started their business within the past 12 months). As a result, reg.59 was revoked. 2.866

[[1]Protection for full-time students until course completed

60.—[[2](1)] Where a notified person does not meet the basic condition in section 4(1)(d) of the Act (not receiving education) on the day on which all awards of any existing benefit are to terminate as a consequence of a claim for universal credit because the person is undertaking a full-time course (see regulation 12(2) and 13 of the Universal Credit Regulations), that condition is not to apply in relation to the notified person while they are continuing to undertake that course.] 2.867

[[2](2) Paragraph (1) does not apply to any assessment period in respect of which a transitional element or transitional capital disregard would (if the claimant had been entitled to that element or that disregard) have ceased to apply by virtue of regulation 56 (circumstances in which transitional protection ceases) or regulation 57 (application of transitional protection to a subsequent award).]

Amendments

1. Universal Credit (Managed Migration Pilot and Miscellaneous Amendments) Regulations 2019 (SI 2019/1152) reg.3(7) (July 24, 2019).
2. Universal Credit (Transitional Provisions) Amendment Regulations 2022 (SI 2022/752) reg.8 (July 25, 2022).

Definitions

"existing benefit"—reg.2(1).
"notified person"—see reg.44(6).

General Note

This provides for notified persons who are students, and entitled to existing benefits, to be exempt from the exclusion of full-time students from universal credit until they complete their course. 2.868

[[1]Rounding

61. Regulation 6 of the Universal Credit Regulations (rounding) applies for the purposes of calculating any amount under this Part.] 2.869

Amendment

1. Universal Credit (Managed Migration Pilot and Miscellaneous Amendments) Regulations 2019 (SI 2019/1152) reg.3(7) (July 24, 2019).

[1Effect of revision, appeal etc. of an award of an existing benefit

2.870 **62.**—(1) Nothing in regulation 53 (total legacy amount) or 54 (indicative UC amount) requiring a calculation in relation to the transitional element to be made on the basis of information held on the migration day prevents the Secretary of State from revising or superseding a decision in relation to a claim for, or an award of, universal credit where—

(a) in the opinion of the Secretary of State, the information held on that day was inaccurate or incomplete in some material respect because of—
  (i) a misrepresentation by a claimant,
  (ii) a failure to report information that a claimant was required to report where that failure was advantageous to the claimant, or
  (iii) an official error; or
(b) a decision has been made on or after the migration day on—
  (i) an application made before migration day to revise or supersede a decision in relation to an award of an existing benefit (including the report of a change of circumstances), or
  (ii) an appeal in relation to such an application.

(2) In this regulation "official error" means an error that—

(a) was made by an officer of, or an employee of a body acting on behalf of, the Department for Work and Pensions, HMRC or a local authority that administers housing benefit; and
(b) was not caused, or materially contributed to, by any person outside that body or outside the Department, HMRC or local authority,

but excludes any error of law which is shown to have been such by a subsequent decision of the Upper Tribunal or of a court as defined in section 27(7) of the Social Security Act 1998.]

AMENDMENT

1. Universal Credit (Managed Migration Pilot and Miscellaneous Amendments) Regulations 2019 (SI 2019/1152) reg.3(7) (July 24, 2019).

DEFINITIONS

"HMRC"—see reg.2(1).
"migration day"—see reg.49.
"official error"—see para.(2).
"transitional element"—see reg.52.
"Upper Tribunal"—see reg.2(1).

GENERAL NOTE

2.871 This provision ensures that the requirement to apply the information held at the migration day when calculating transitional protection does not prevent the subsequent revision of the universal credit award in cases of misrepresentation or error or in order to give effect to an outstanding revision or appeal.

[1Claimants previously entitled to a severe disability premium

2.872 **63.** [2Schedules 2 and 3 contain] provision in respect of certain claimants who have been entitled to a benefit which included a severe disability premium.]

AMENDMENTS

1. Universal Credit (Managed Migration Pilot and Miscellaneous Amendments) Regulations 2019 (SI 2019/1152) reg.3(7) (July 24, 2019).
2. Universal Credit (Transitional Provisions) (Amendment) Regulations 2023 (SI 2023/1238) reg.2(2) (February 14, 2024).

DEFINITION

"severe disability premium"—see reg.2(1).

GENERAL NOTE

The original Sch.2 made provision for transitional payments to those claimants who had been entitled to a benefit that included a severe disability premium and moved to universal credit before the SDP gateway came into force (or, in some exceptional cases, while the SDP gateway was in force). Where such a case came to the attention of the Secretary of State, a flat rate payment was to be calculated and paid as a lump sum in respect of each month since the move to universal credit. The same amount was then to continue as a separate monthly payment until the Secretary of State was satisfied that it could be included in the calculation of the award (in the same way as if the claimant has moved to universal credit under the managed migration provisions). Now that the SDP gateway has been revoked, claimants who are entitled to a benefit that includes a severe disability premium will no longer be prevented from claiming universal credit and the new Sch.2 will take effect. When claimants are awarded universal credit, they will now be entitled to the flat rate payment as part of the calculation from the outset. See further the General Note to Sch.2 below. **2.873**

The High Court has held that reg.63 and Sch.2, as originally enacted, discriminated against SDP natural migrants by failing to provide transitional relief for the loss of the enhanced disability premium (EDP), although some compensation was provided for the loss of the SDP: *R. (on the application of TP and AR) v Secretary of State for Work and Pensions* [2022] EWHC 123 (Admin) (*TP and AR No.3*). The claimants, TP and AR, had previously succeeded in the judicial reviews in *TP No.1* and *TP No.2*, which were both upheld in the Court of Appeal (see the commentary on reg.4A above). In *TP and AR No.3*, the claimants argued that the SDP transitional payment of £120 a month constituted unlawful discrimination under art.14 of the ECHR. This was because they had not been compensated for the loss of the EDP. As a result, they were still about £60 a month worse off than had they remained on legacy benefits. Thus, the judicial review challenge related solely to the lack of transitional protection in cases of natural migration to universal credit against the cliff-edge effect of suddenly experiencing the loss of the EDP element (para.74). It was accepted that the claim fell within the ambit of A1P1 of the ECHR for the purposes of art.14. Holgate J furthermore found that there was a difference in treatment (paras 148–151), which was on the ground of an "other status" (paras 152–157), and which could not be justified (paras 158–198). The Judge concluded (at para.196):

> "I am not satisfied on the material before the Court that the broad aims of promoting phased transition, curtailing public expenditure or administrative efficiency required the denial of transitional relief against the loss of EDP for SDP natural migrants. Quite apart from that, I reach the firm conclusion that a fair balance has not been struck between the severity of the effects of the measure under challenge upon members of the SDP natural migrants group and the contribution that that measure makes to the achievement of the defendant's aims, *a fortiori* where there is no connection between the triggering event, the move to a home in a different local authority area, and any rational assessment of the disability needs of a severely disabled claimant."

The Court of Appeal subsequently refused (in forthright terms) the Secretary of State's application for permission to appeal against the decision of Holgate J. (CA-2022-000398, January 12, 2023).

The High Court's decision in *TP and AR No.3* was the context for the Upper Tribunal's decision in *FL v Secretary of State for Work and Pensions* [2024] UKUT 6 (AAC). The claimant's circumstances in *FL* were essentially on all fours with those of the claimants in *TP and AR No.3* as a result of her 'natural migration' to a different local authority area. As such, although she was in receipt of the transitional SDP element, she was still financially worse off as compared with her previous position on legacy benefits as her new universal credit award did not compensate her for the loss of the EDP element. She appealed to the FTT, which dismissed her appeal on the basis that her entitlement had been correctly calculated under the relevant universal credit regulations.

Judge Wikeley allowed FL's further appeal to the Upper Tribunal, noting that "the starting point is the principle that the First-tier Tribunal (and indeed the Upper Tribunal) is not, and should not be, in the business of applying unlawful regulations" (para.39). Furthermore, "this basic principle applies – unless the Tribunal is prohibited from acting by statute – regardless of the species of public law error that infects the regulations in question, e.g. whether they are ultra vires or irrational, or because they breach Convention rights or conflict with rights conferred by primary legislation" (para.39). Given the decision in *TP and AR No.3*, the judge found that the FTT was bound to find that the failure to compensate FL for the loss of the EDP element amounted to a breach of her human rights. The question then was the appropriate remedy.

Judge Wikeley rejected the claimant's primary submission on remedy, namely that a substantial part of reg.48 of the UC (Transitional Provisions) Regulations 2014 should be disapplied so as to provide claimants who were subject to natural migration with the same degree of transitional protection as the managed migration group. This submission was rejected for two reasons. First, it was not reg.48 but rather reg.63 that resulted in the breach of the claimant's human rights. Secondly, disapplying reg.48 would collapse the distinction between managed and natural migration, which would involve "social engineering on a massive scale" such as was properly a matter for Parliament (para.54). However, the claimant's secondary submission on remedy was successful, so the case was remitted to the Secretary of State with a direction that FL's entitlement to universal credit be redecided on a lawful (and so ECHR-compliant) basis.

The Universal Credit (Transitional Provisions) (Amendment) Regulations 2023 (SI 2023/1238) subsequently amended regulation 63 and inserted Schedule 3 so as to compensate claimants for the loss of the EDP. However, these amendments only take effect from February 14, 2014, so there may yet be further episodes in this litigation saga. The Department's response to this saga was subject to adverse comment in the Fifth Report of the House of Lords' Secondary Legislation Scrutiny Committee, published on December 7, 2023 (HL Paper 24).

[1Discretionary hardship payments

2.874 **64.** [2...]

AMENDMENTS

1. Universal Credit (Managed Migration Pilot and Miscellaneous Amendments) Regulations 2019 (SI 2019/1152) reg.3(7) (July 24, 2019).

2. Universal Credit (Transitional Provisions) Amendment Regulations 2022 (SI 2022/752) reg.9 (July 25, 2022).

(2014/1230 Sch.1) (as amended)

Regulation 12A

SCHEDULE [2 1]

MODIFICATION OF TAX CREDITS LEGISLATION (FINALISATION OF TAX CREDITS)

Modifications to the Tax Credits Act 2002

1. Paragraphs 2 to 10 prescribe modifications to the application of the 2002 Act where regulation 12A of these Regulations applies. **2.875**

2. In section 7 (income test)—

(a) in subsection (3), before "current year income" in each place where it occurs, insert "notional";

(b) [3...]

(c) after subsection (4), insert—

"(4A) In this section "the notional current year income" means—

(a) in relation to persons by whom a joint claim for a tax credit is made, the aggregate income of the persons for the part tax year to which the claim relates, divided by the number of days in that part tax year, multiplied by the number of days in the tax year in which the part tax year is included and rounded down to the next whole number of pence; and

(b) in relation to a person by whom a single claim for a tax credit is made, the income of the person for that part tax year, divided by the number of days in that part tax year, multiplied by the number of days in the tax year in which the part tax year is included and rounded down to the next whole number of pence.".

3. In section 17 (final notice)—

(a) in subsection (1)—

(i) omit "the whole or"; and

(ii) in sub-paragraph (a), before "tax year" insert "part";

(b) in subsection (3), before "tax year" insert "part";

(c) in subsections (4)(a) and (4)(b), for "current year" in both places where it occurs, substitute "current part year";

(d) in subsection (5)(a) for "current year" in both places where it occurs, substitute "current part year";

(e) omit subsection (8).

4. In section 18 (decisions after final notice)—

(a) in subsection (1), before "tax year" insert "part";

(b) omit subsections (6) to (9);

(c) in subsection (10), for "subsection (1), (5), (6) or (9)" substitute "subsection (1) or (5)";

(d) in subsection (11)—

(i) after "subsection (5)" omit "or (9)";

(ii) omit paragraph (a);

(iii) in paragraph (b) omit "in any other case,";

(iv) before "tax year" in each place where it occurs, insert "part".

5. In section 19 (power to enquire)—

(a) in subsection (1)(a) and (b), before "tax year" insert "part";

(b) in subsection (3), before "tax year" insert "part";

(c) for subsection (5) substitute—

"(5) "The relevant section 18 decision" means the decision under subsection (1) of section 18 in relation to the person or persons and the part tax year.";

(d) for subsection (6) substitute—

"(6) "The relevant section 17 date" means the date specified for the purposes of subsection (4) of section 17 in the notice given to a person or persons under that section in relation to the part tax year.";

(e) in subsection (11), before "tax year" insert "part";

(f) in subsection (12), before "tax year" in each place where it occurs, insert "part".

6. In section 20 (decisions on discovery)—

(a) in subsection (1), before "tax year" insert "part";

(b) in subsection (4)(a), before "tax year" insert "part";
(c) in subsection (5)(b), before "tax year" insert "part";
(d) in subsection (6)—
 (i) before "tax year" insert "part";
 (ii) in paragraph (a), for "section 18(1), (5), (6) or (9)" substitute "section 18(1) or (5)";
(e) in subsection (7), before "tax year" in each place where it occurs, insert "part".

7. In section 21 (decisions subject to official error), for "18(1), (5), (6) or (9)" substitute "18(1) or (5)".

8. In section 23 (notice of decisions)—
(a) in subsection (1), for "18(1), (5), (6) or (9)" substitute "18(1) or (5)";
(b) in subsection (3)—
 (i) after "18(1)" omit "or (6)";
 (ii) for paragraph (b) substitute—

"(b) the notice of the decision under subsection (1) of section 18,".

9. In section 30(1) (underpayments), before "tax year" in each place where it occurs, insert "part".

10. In section 38 (appeals)—
(a) in subsection (1)(b), before "tax year" insert "part";
(b) for subsection (2), substitute—

"(2) "The relevant section 18 decision" means the decision under subsection (1) of section 18 in relation to the person or persons and the tax credit for the part tax year.".

Modifications to the Tax Credits (Definition and Calculation of Income) Regulations 2002

2.876 11. Paragraphs 12 to 23 prescribe modifications to the application of the Tax Credits (Definition and Calculation of Income) Regulations 2002 where regulation 12A of these Regulations applies.

12. In regulation 2(2) (interpretation), after the definition of "the Macfarlane Trusts" insert—

""part tax year" means a period of less than a year beginning with 6th April and ending with the date on which the award of a tax credit terminated;".

13. In regulation 3 (calculation of income of claimant)—
(a) in paragraph (1)—
 (i) before "tax year" insert "part";
 (ii) in Steps 1 and 2, after "of the claimant, or, in the case of a joint claim, of the claimants" insert "received in or relating to the part tax year";
 (iii) in the second and third sentences of Step 4, before "year" insert "part";
(b) in paragraph (6A), for the words from "ending on 31st March" to the end, substitute "ending on the last day of the month in which the claimant's award of a tax credit terminated";
(c) in paragraph (8)(b), before "year" insert "part".

14. In regulation 4 (employment income)—
(a) in paragraph (1)(a), before "tax year" insert "part";
(b) in paragraph (1)(b), (c), (d), (e), (g) and (k), before "year" insert "part";
(c) in paragraph (1)(f), after "ITEPA" insert "which is treated as received in the part tax year and in respect of which the charge arises in the part tax year";
(d) in paragraph (1)(h), after "week" insert "in the part tax year";
(e) in paragraph (1)(i), for "that year" substitute "the tax year" and after "ITEPA" insert "which is treated as received in the part tax year";
(f) in paragraph (1)(j), after "applies" insert "which is received in the part tax year";
(g) in paragraph (1)(l), for "that year" substitute "the tax year" and after "ITEPA" insert "in respect of which the charge arises in the part tax year";
(h) in paragraph (1)(m), after "paid" insert "in the part tax year";
(i) in paragraph (4), in the first sentence and in the title of Table 1, after "employment income" insert "received in the part tax year";
(j) in paragraph (5), after "calculating earnings" insert "received in the part tax year".

15. In regulation 5 (pension income)—
(a) in paragraph (1), after ""pension income" means" insert "any of the following received in or relating to the part tax year";

(b) in paragraph (2), in the first sentence and in the title of Table 2, after "pension income" insert "received in or relating to the part tax year";
(c) in paragraph (3), after "income tax purposes", insert "in relation to the part tax year".

16. In regulation 6 (trading income)—
(a) re-number the existing regulation as paragraph (1);
(b) in paragraph (1) (as so re-numbered)—
(i) in sub-paragraph (a), for "taxable profits for the tax year" substitute "actual or estimated taxable profits attributable to the part tax year";
(ii) in sub-paragraph (b), for "taxable profit for the" substitute "actual or estimated taxable profit attributable to the part tax";
[4(c) after paragraph (1) insert—
"(2) Actual or estimated taxable profits attributable to the part tax year ("the relevant trading income") is to be calculated by reference to the basis period (determined by reference to paragraph 63 or paragraph 65 of Schedule 1 to the Finance Act 2022, whichever applies) ending with 5th April 2024.
(3) The relevant trading income is to be calculated by—
(a) taking the figure for the actual or estimated taxable income earned in the basis period referred to in paragraph (2);
(b) dividing that figure by the number of days in that period to give the daily figure; and
(c) multiplying the daily figure by the number of days in the part tax year on which the trade, profession or vocation was carried on."]
(3) The relevant trading income is to be calculated by—
(a) taking the figure for the actual or estimated taxable income earned in the basis period;
(b) dividing that figure by the number of days in the basis period to give the daily figure; and
(c) multiplying the daily figure by the number of days in the part tax year on which the trade, profession or vocation was carried on.".

17. In regulation 7 (social security income)—
(a) in paragraph (1), after "social security income" insert "received in the part tax year";
(b) in paragraph (3), in the opening words and in the title of Table 3, after "social security income" insert "received in the part tax year".

18. In regulation 8 (student income), after "in relation to a student" insert ", any of the following which is received in the part tax year".

19. In regulation 10 (investment income)—
(a) in paragraph (1), after "gross amount" insert "received in the part tax year";
(b) in paragraph (1)(e), before "year" insert "part tax";
(c) in paragraph (2), in the opening words and in the title of Table 4, after "investment income" insert "received in the part tax year".

20. In regulation 11(1) (property income)—
(a) omit "annual";
(b) after "taxable profits" insert "for the part tax year".

21. In regulation 12(1) (foreign income), before "year" insert "part tax".

22. In regulation 13 (notional income), after "means income" insert "received in the part tax year".

23. In regulation 18 (miscellaneous income), after "means income" insert "received in the part tax year".

Modifications to the Tax Credits (Income Thresholds and Determination of Rates) Regulations 2002

24. Paragraphs 25 to 27 prescribe modifications to the application of the Tax Credits (Income Thresholds and Determination of Rates) Regulations 2002 where regulation 12A of these Regulations applies. **2.877**

25. In regulation 2 (interpretation)—
(a) [3 ...]
(b) in the definition of "the relevant income" insert "as modified by the Universal Credit (Transitional Provisions) Regulations 2014" at the end.

26. In regulation 7(3) (determination of rate of working tax credit)—
(a) in Step 1, in the definition of "MR", after "maximum rate" insert "(determined in the manner prescribed at the date on which the award of the tax credit terminated)";

(b) [3 ...]

27. In regulation 8(3) (determination of rate of child tax credit)—

(a) in Step 1, in the definition of "MR", after "maximum rate" insert "(determined in the manner prescribed at the date on which the award of the tax credit terminated)";

(b) [3 ...]

Modifications to the Tax Credits (Claims and Notifications) Regulations 2002

2.878 28. Paragraphs 29 to 34 prescribe modifications to the application of the Tax Credits (Claims and Notifications) Regulations 2002 where regulation 12A of these Regulations applies.

29. In regulation 4 (interpretation), omit paragraph (b).

30. Omit regulation 11 (circumstances in which claims to be treated as made).

31. Omit regulation 12 (further circumstances in which claims to be treated as made).

32. In regulation 13 (circumstances in which claims made by one member of a couple to be treated as also made by the other)—

(a) in paragraph (1), after "prescribed by paragraph" omit "(2) or";

(b) omit paragraph (2).

33. In regulation 15(1)(c) (persons who die after making a claim)—

(a) omit "the whole or" and "after the end of that tax year but"; and

(b) for "section 18(1), (5), (6) or (9)" substitute "section 18(1) or (5)".

34. In regulation 33 (dates to be specified in notices)—

(a) in paragraph (a), for the words from "not later than 31st July" to "if later", substitute "not less than 30 days after the date on which the notice is given";

(b) omit paragraph (b) and the "and" which precedes it.

Modification to the Tax Credits (Payment by the Commissioners) Regulations 2002

2.879 35. Paragraph 36 prescribes a modification to the application of the Tax Credits (Payment by the Commissioners) Regulations 2002 where regulation 12A of these Regulations applies.

36. Omit regulation 7 (prescribed circumstances for certain purposes).

Modification to the Tax Credits (Residence) Regulations 2003

2.880 37. Paragraph 38 prescribes a modification to the application of the Tax Credits (Residence) Regulations 2003 where regulation 12A of these Regulations applies.

38. In regulation 3(5)(a) (circumstances in which a person is treated as not being in the United Kingdom)(26), omit "under regulation 11 or 12 of the Tax Credits (Claims and Notifications) Regulations 2002 or otherwise".]

AMENDMENTS

1. Universal Credit (Transitional Provisions) (Amendment) Regulations 2014 (SI 2014/1626) reg.4 (October 13, 2014).

2. Universal Credit (Managed Migration Pilot and Miscellaneous Amendments) Regulations 2019 (SI 2019/1152) reg.3(8) (July 24, 2019).

3. Social Security and Universal Credit (Miscellaneous Amendments) Regulations 2023 (SI 2023/543) reg.6(5) (June 29, 2023).

4. Social Security and Universal Credit (Migration of Tax Credit Claimants and Miscellaneous Amendments) Regulations 2024 (SI 2024/341) reg.8(4) (April 6, 2024).

GENERAL NOTE

2.881 See General Note to reg.12A.

Regulation 63

[1[2 SCHEDULE 2

Claimants previously entitled to a severe disability premium

1. This Schedule applies to an award of universal credit where the following conditions are met in respect of the claimant, or each of joint claimants. 2.882

[3 (2) In paragraph 5(b)(i), the reference to a person being a carer for another person is to the person being entitled to, and in receipt of, a carer's allowance [5or carer support payment] or having an award of universal credit which includes the carer element in respect of caring for that other person.]

[4 (3) In paragraph (2) "carer support payment" means carer's assistance given in accordance with the Carer's Assistance (Carer Support Payment) (Scotland) Regulations 2023.]

4. Where this Schedule applies (subject to paragraphs 6 and 7), a transitional SDP element is to be included in the calculation of the award and the amount of that element is to be treated, for the purposes of section 8 of the Act, as if it were an additional amount to be included in the maximum amount under section 8(2) before the deduction of income under section 8(3).

5. The amount of the transitional SDP element in the first assessment period is—

(a) in the case of a single claimant—

(i) [5£140.97], if the LCWRA element is included in the award, or

(ii) [5£334.81], if the LCWRA element is not included in the award;

(b) in the case of joint claimants—

(i) [5£475.79], [3if the higher SDP rate is payable on the first day of the award and no person becomes a carer for either of them in the first assessment period]

(ii) [5£140.97], if paragraph (i) does not apply and the LCWRA element is included in the award in respect of either of them, or

(iii) [5£334.81], if paragraph (i) does not apply and the LCWRA element is not included in the award in respect of either of them.

6. In respect of the second and each subsequent assessment period, regulation 55(2) (adjustment where other elements increase), regulation 56 (circumstances in which transitional protection ceases) and regulation 57 (application of transitional protection to a subsequent award) are to apply in relation to the transitional SDP element as if it were a transitional element in respect of which the amount calculated in accordance with paragraph 5 was the initial amount.

7. The award is not to include a transitional SDP element where the claim was a qualifying claim and the award is to include a transitional element.

8.(1) In this Schedule—

"LCWRA element" has the meaning in the Universal Credit Regulations;

"the higher SDP rate" is the rate specified in sub-paragraph (ii) of paragraph 11(2)(b) of Schedule 4 to the Employment and Support Allowance Regulations 2008 or, as the case may be, the corresponding rate of a severe disability premium in relation to income support or income-based jobseeker's allowance.]]

[3 (2) In paragraph 5(b)(i), the reference to a person being a carer for another person is to the person being entitled to, and in receipt of, a carer's allowance [5 or carer support payment] or having an award of universal credit which includes the carer element in respect of caring for that other person.]

[4 (3) In paragraph (2) "carer support payment" means carer's assistance given in accordance with the Carer's Assistance (Carer Support Payment) (Scotland) Regulations 2023.]

[3 **9.** For the purposes of paragraph 3(b) and 5(b)(i), paragraph 6(6) of Schedule 4 to the Employment and Support Allowance Regulations 2008 or, as the case may be, the corresponding provision in relation to income support or income-based jobseeker's allowance, is to be disregarded.]

AMENDMENTS

1. Universal Credit (Managed Migration Pilot and Miscellaneous Amendments) Regulations 2019 (SI 2019/1152) reg.3(8) (July 24, 2019).

2. Universal Credit (Transitional Provisions) (Claimants previously entitled to a severe disability premium) Amendment Regulations 2021 (SI 2021/4) reg.2 (January 27, 2021).

3. Social Security and Universal Credit (Miscellaneous Amendments) Regulations 2023 (SI 2023/543) reg.6(6) (June 29, 2023).

4. Carer's Assistance (Carer Support Payment) (Scotland) Regulations 2023 (Consequential Amendments) Order 2023 (SI 2023/1218) art.26 (November 19, 2023).

5. Social Security Benefits Up-rating Order 2024 (SI 2024/242) art.33(a) (April 8. 2024).

GENERAL NOTE

2.883 There have been two operative versions of Sch.2 to these Regulations, introduced by reg.63. The first version of the Schedule was in force from July 24, 2019 while the second version was effective from January 27, 2021. In a case where the first day of an award of universal credit falls before the latter date then the original version of Sch.2 continues to apply (see Universal Credit (Transitional Provisions) (Claimants previously entitled to a severe disability premium) Amendment Regulations 2021 (SI 2021/4) reg.3).

The first version of Sch.2 in the 2014 Regulations provided for transitional payments in respect of certain claimants who were entitled to a severe disability premium (SDP) before claiming universal credit as a result of natural migration (e.g. a claim to universal credit prompted by a change in circumstances). Eligibility was governed by Sch.2 para.1 (all references in this paragraph are to the original version of the Schedule); there was no need for individuals to make a claim, as the DWP set up a specialist team to review universal credit claims and identify those claimants who might be eligible for a SDP transitional payment. The payments were based on a flat rate for each assessment period since the move to universal credit (see Sch.2 para.2). The flat rate was converted into a transitional element after a date determined by the Secretary of State; the effect was that a lump-sum payment was made to cover the period since the claimant moved to universal credit followed by an ongoing monthly payment thereafter (see Sch.2 para.3). Note that any such lump-sum payment was disregarded as capital for 12 months or for the duration of the universal credit award, whichever was longer (see Sch.2 para.7). This provision was necessary as some of the backdated payments were substantial (the average (in the sense of median) lump-sum payment is £2,280: see House of Commons Library, *Universal Credit and the Severe Disability Premium*, Briefing Paper 08494 November 5, 2019, p.7).

The second version of Sch.2, now in force, operates in circumstances where the SDP gateway has been revoked and so claimants who are entitled to a benefit that includes a severe disability premium will no longer be prevented from claiming universal credit. The new Sch.2 will accordingly take effect such that when claimants are awarded universal credit they will be entitled to the flat rate payment as part of the calculation from the outset. Paragraphs 1 to 3 set out the conditions for the application of the new Sch.2. The first condition is that the award must not have been made as consequence of claimant forming a couple with an existing universal credit claimant. The second condition is that the claimant must have been entitled, or the partner of a person entitled, to an award of income support, income-based JSA or income-related ESA that included a severe disability premium within the month before the start of the universal credit award. They must also have continued to meet the conditions for eligibility for a severe disability premium up to and including the first day of that award. Paragraphs 4 to 6 provide for the universal credit award to include a transitional SDP element. This is to be the amount specified in para.5 in the first assessment period and, in subsequent assessment periods, is to be treated as in the same way as if it were a transitional element awarded to a claimant who had moved to universal credit by managed migration. This means that after the first assessment period the amount may decrease if other elements increase or may cease if there is a change of circumstances.

Paragraph 7 prevents duplication by excluding a claimant from receiving a transitional SDP element if they are awarded a transitional element as a consequence of being moved to universal credit by managed migration.

Regulation 63

[[1]SCHEDULE 3

Additional Amounts For Claimants Previously Entitled To An Enhanced Disability Premium, A Disability Premium, A Disabled Child Premium Or A Disabled Child Element In Addition To A Severe Disability Premium

1. This Schedule applies to an award of universal credit where—

(a) in the first assessment period beginning on or after 14th February 2024 the award includes a transitional SDP element by virtue of Schedule 2 or a transitional SDP amount by virtue of that Schedule as saved by regulation 3 of the Universal Credit (Transitional Provisions) (Claimants previously entitled to a severe disability premium) Amendment Regulations 2021, or would have done had it not been eroded to nil by virtue of regulation 55 (the transitional element - initial amount and adjustment where other elements increase); and

(b) at least one of the conditions in paragraph 4 is satisfied.

2. This Schedule does not apply where the claim was a qualifying claim and the award is to include a transitional element.

3. Where this Schedule applies, in the assessment period described in paragraph 1—

(a) the transitional SDP element or, as the case may be, the transitional SDP amount, is to be increased by the additional amount specified in paragraph 5; and

(b) if the transitional SDP element or, as the case may be, the transitional SDP amount, has been reduced to nil by virtue of regulation 55, the additional amount is to be treated as if it were the initial amount of a transitional element calculated under regulation 55(1).

4. The conditions referred to in paragraph 1(b) above are that—

(a) within the month immediately preceding the first day of the award the claimant was entitled (or was a member of a couple the other member of which was entitled) to an award of income support, income-based jobseeker's allowance or income-related employment and support allowance that included an enhanced disability premium, and continued to satisfy the conditions for eligibility for the enhanced disability premium up to and including the first day of the award of universal credit;

(b) within the month immediately preceding the first day of the award the claimant was entitled (or was a member of a couple the other member of which was entitled) to an award of income support or income-based jobseeker's allowance that included a disability premium and continued to satisfy the conditions for eligibility for a disability premium up to and including the first day of the award of universal credit; and/or

(c) within the month immediately preceding the first day of the award the claimant was entitled to an award of income support or income-based jobseeker's allowance that included a disabled child premium, or an award of child tax credit that included the disabled child element at the rate for a child or qualifying young person who is disabled but not severely disabled, and continued to satisfy the conditions for eligibility for the disabled child premium or the disabled child element up to and including the first day of the universal credit award and is entitled in the assessment period described in paragraph 1 to the lower rate of the disabled child addition in universal credit.

5. The additional amount is—

(a) in the case of a single claimant—
   (i) [[2]£89.63] for a claimant meeting the condition in paragraph 4(a);
   (ii) [[2]£183.52] for a claimant meeting the condition in paragraph 4(b); and
   (iii) [[2]£188.86] per disabled child or qualifying young person for a claimant meeting the condition in paragraph 4(c);

(b) in the case of joint claimants—
   (i) [[2]£128.04] for claimants meeting the condition in paragraph 4(a);
   (ii) [[2]£262.48] for claimants meeting the condition in paragraph 4(b); and
   (iii) [[2]£188.86] per disabled child or qualifying young person for claimants meeting the condition in paragraph 4(c).

6. The Secretary of State may, having regard to the efficient administration of universal credit, decide the time and manner in which the payments of the additional amount are to be paid to claimants already in receipt of universal credit on the date this Schedule comes into force.

7. In this Schedule—

"disability premium" means the premium in relation to income-based jobseeker's allowance under paragraph 13 of Part III of Schedule 1 to the Jobseeker's Allowance Regulations 1996 or, as the case may be, the corresponding premium in relation to income support;

"disabled child element" has the meaning in section 9(2)(c) of the Tax Credits Act 2002;

"disabled child premium" means the premium in relation to income-based jobseeker's allowance under paragraph 16 of Part III of Schedule 1 to the Jobseeker's Allowance Regulations 1996, or, as the case may be, the corresponding premium in relation to income support;

"enhanced disability premium" means the premium in relation to income-related employment and support allowance under paragraph 7 of Part 2 of Schedule 4 to the Employment and Support Allowance Regulations 2008 or, as the case may be, the corresponding premium in relation to income support or income-based jobseeker's allowance.]

AMENDMENTS

1. Universal Credit (Transitional Provisions) (Amendment) Regulations 2023 (SI 2023/1238) reg.2(3) (February 14, 2024).

2. Social Security Benefits Up-rating Order 2024 (SI 2024/242) art.33(b) (April 8, 2024).

GENERAL NOTE

Schedule 3 represents a belated official response to the High Court's decision in *R. (on the application of TP and AR) v Secretary of State for Work and Pensions* [2022] EWHC 123 (Admin) (*TP and AR No.3*). Its effect is to add an additional amount of universal credit to claimants entitled (or previously entitled) to the transitional SDP amount or transitional SDP element where e.g. their legacy benefit entitlement included the EDP. Note, however, that the Schedule came into force on February 14, 2024 and is not retrospective in its effect (see para.6). According to official guidance, "Qualifying new natural migration claimants after that date will have the benefit of these changes immediately. For claimants already in receipt of UC the time and manner of the payments will be arranged in due course in a time and manner to be decided by the Secretary of State" (*ADM 01/24: UC - Transitional Provisions - The Additional Amount*, para.3). The Department's response to this saga was subject to adverse comment in the Fifth Report of the House of Lords' Secondary Legislation Scrutiny Committee, published on December 7, 2023 (HL Paper 24). See further the commentary to reg.63 above.

The Universal Credit (Digital Service) Amendment Regulations 2014

(2014/2887)

GENERAL NOTE

2.886 At one point during the introduction of UC, the benefit existed in two different forms depending on which computer system was operating in the area for the Jobcentre to which the claim was made: see further the General Note to the Welfare Reform Act 2012 (above). The amendments made by these Regulations applied in Digital (or "Full") Service areas. Regulation 5 preserved the unamended law for Live Service areas. As Live Service areas no longer exist, reg.5 has not been reproduced in this volume. Readers are referred instead to pp.799–800 of Vol.V of the 2020/21 edition.

The Employment and Support Allowance and Universal Credit (Miscellaneous Amendments and Transitional and Savings Provisions) Regulations 2017

(SI 2017/204)

In Force April 3, 2017

Regulations Reproduced

The Secretary of State for Work and Pensions makes the following Regulations in exercise of the powers conferred by sections 12(1), 17(4), 18(3), 19(2)(d), 25(a) and 42(3)(a) of the Welfare Reform Act 2012 and sections 15(4) and (5) and 34(1) of the Welfare Reform and Work Act 2016.

In accordance with section 173(5)(b) of the Social Security Administration Act 1992, this instrument contains only regulations made by virtue of, or consequential upon, sections 15, 16, 17 and 34 of the Welfare Reform and Work Act 2016 and is made before the end of the period of 6 months beginning with the coming into force of those sections.

In accordance with section 176(1) of the Social Security Administration Act 1992 the Secretary of State has consulted with organisations appearing to him to be representative of the authorities concerned.

General Note

Parts 1-3 of, and Sch.1 to, these Regulations, taken together and ss.15-17 of the Welfare Reform and Work Act 2016, abolish the LCW element of universal credit (and the work-related activity component of ESA) with effect from April 3, 2017 and make a number of consequential amendments. However, for universal credit, the abolition is subject to the transitional and savings provisions in Sch.2, Pt 2, to which effect is given by reg.2. Part 1 of the Schedule contains equivalent provisions for ESA and is reproduced in Vol.V. 2.888

Under Pt.2 of Sch.2, claimants who are found to have—or are treated as having—limited capability for work, but not limited capability for work-related activity, continue to be entitled to the LCW component in the following circumstances:

- There was an award of universal credit immediately before April 3, 2017 and that award included the LCW element, or would have done so if that element were not excluded by the three-month waiting period in reg.28(1) of the Universal Credit Regulations (para.9).
- There was an award of universal credit immediately before April 3, 2017 and that award included the LCWRA element, and it is subsequently decided that the claimant only has limited capability for work (para.10). This only applies where the claimant has had both limited capability for work and limited capability for work-related activity throughout the period from April 3, 2017 to the date on which it is determined that they only have limited capability for work.

- There was a claim for universal credit before April 3, 2017 and—also before that date—the claimant provided medical evidence of having limited capability for work. In those circumstances, the claimant will be entitled to the LCW element even if the determination that they have limited capability for work is not made until after April 3, 2017 and even if that determination is made on revision by the Secretary of State or on appeal by the First-tier Tribunal or Upper Tribunal (para.11).
- Article 24 of the Welfare Reform Act 2012 (Commencement No 9 and Transitional and Transitory Provisions and Commencement No 8 and Savings and Transitional Provisions (Amendment)) Order 2013 (see Part IVB below) provides that, where an award of universal credit is made and subsequently a decision is made to revise or supersede and earlier decision about old style ESA (or old style JSA) (or there is a final decision on an appeal against such a decision) the Secretary of State must consider whether to revise (or, in some circumstances, supersede) the universal credit decision. Where the claim for old style ESA was made, or treated as made, before April 3, 2013 and a decision is made to revise the universal credit decision after that date, then, if the revising decision includes a determination that the claimant has limited capability for work, the LCW element is to be included in the universal credit award (para.12).
- The claimant was entitled to employment and support allowance immediately before April 3, 2017 and remains so entitled until the date on which a subsequent claim for universal credit is made or treated as made (para.13).
- The claimant does not fall within the previous paragraph but was entitled to incapacity credits immediately before April 3, 2017 and remains so entitled until the date on which a subsequent claim for universal credit is made or treated as made (para.14).
- The claimant is entitled to income support on the grounds of incapacity for work or disability, or incapacity benefit or severe disablement allowance immediately before April 3, 2017 and regs 22-24, 26 or 27 of the Universal Credit (Transitional Provisions) Regulations 2014 applies to him or her from then until the date on which a subsequent claim for universal credit is made or treated as made (para.15).

The LCW element continues to be payable under Sch,2, Pt.2 for as long as continues to be entitled to universal credit and to have limited capability for work (para.8(1)(b)). Continuity of entitlement is not broken (i) where the award of universal credit but a further award begins immediately because the claimant ceased to be a member of a couple or became a member of a couple (para.8(2)(a)); or (ii) the award ends because the claimant's income (or the joint claimants' combined income) was too high but a further award is made within six months (para.8(2)(b)).

Citation and commencement

2.889 **1.** These Regulations may be cited as the Employment and Support Allowance and Universal Credit (Miscellaneous Amendments and Transitional and Savings Provisions) Regulations 2017 and come into force on 3rd April 2017.

PART 4

Consequential, transitional and savings provisions

Consequential, transitional and savings provisions

7.—(1) [Omitted] 2.890

(2) Schedule 2 contains transitional and savings provisions.

Regulation 7(2)

SCHEDULE 2

Transitional and savings provisions

PART 2

Universal Credit: transitional and savings provisions

Transitional and savings provisions: General

8.—(1) The amendments made by regulations 4 and 5 and paragraphs 13, 16 and 17 of Schedule 1 do not apply— 2.891

(a) where a claimant has an award of universal credit in any of the circumstances in the following paragraphs; and

(b) for so long as the claimant continues to be entitled to universal credit and to have limited capability for work.

(2) For the purposes of sub-paragraph (1)(b), the reference to continuous entitlement to universal credit includes where an award has terminated and a further award is made and—

(a) immediately before the further award commences, the previous award has terminated because the claimant ceased to be a member of a couple or became a member of a couple; or

(b) within the six months beginning with the date that the further award commences, the previous award has terminated because the financial condition in section 5(1)(b) or, if it was a joint claim, section 5(2)(b), of the Welfare Reform Act 2012 was not met.

(3) In this Part—

"employment and support allowance" means an employment and support allowance under Part 1 of the Welfare Reform Act 2007;

"LCW element" and "LCWRA element" have the meanings in regulation 27 of the Universal Credit Regulations 2013 as it has effect apart from the amendments made by regulation 4(4) (which remove references to the LCW element);

"limited capability for work" has the meaning given in section 37(1) of the Welfare Reform Act 2012.

(4) The Universal Credit, Personal Independence Payment, Jobseeker's Allowance and Employment and Support Allowance (Claims and Payments) Regulations 2013 apply for the purpose of deciding the date on which a claim for universal credit is made or is to be treated as made.

Claimants entitled to the LCW element before 3rd April 2017

9. The first circumstance is where immediately before 3rd April 2017 the award included the LCW element, or would have but for regulation 28(1) of the Universal Credit Regulations 2013, as it has effect apart from the amendments made by regulation 4(5)(a) (which removes the reference to the LCW element). 2.892

Claimants entitled to the LCWRA element before 3rd April 2017

10. The second circumstance is where— 2.893

(a) immediately before 3rd April 2017 the award included the LCWRA element;

(b) on or after 3rd April 2017 a determination that the claimant has limited capability for work is made; and

(c) the claimant had limited capability for work and work-related activity throughout the period beginning immediately before 3rd April 2017 and ending with the date on which the determination that the claimant has limited capability for work is made.

Claimants who are providing evidence of having limited capability for work before 3rd April 2017

2.894 **11.** The third circumstance is where—

(a) before 3rd April 2017—

(i) it falls to be determined whether the claimant has limited capability for work; and

(ii) the claimant has provided evidence of having limited capability for work in accordance with the Social Security (Medical Evidence) Regulations 1976; and

(b) on or after 3rd April 2017 a determination that the claimant has limited capability for work is made on the basis of an assessment under Part 5 of the Universal Credit Regulations 2013, on revision under section 9 of the Social Security Act 1998 or on appeal.

Claimants who appeal or seek revision of a decision relating to employment and support allowance

2.895 **12.** The fourth circumstance is where—

(a) the claimant appeals or seeks revision under section 9 of the Social Security Act 1998 of a decision relating to the entitlement of the claimant to an employment and support allowance, where the claim for employment and support allowance was made or treated as made before 3rd April 2017; and

(b) on or after 3rd April 2017, in accordance with article 24 of the Welfare Reform Act 2012 (Commencement No 9 and Transitional and Transitory Provisions and Commencement No 8 and Savings and Transitional Provisions (Amendment)) Order 2013, the Secretary of State considers it appropriate to revise under section 9 of the Social Security Act 1998 an award of universal credit so as to include the LCW element.

Claimants entitled to employment and support allowance before 3rd April 2017

2.896 13. The fifth circumstance is where immediately before 3rd April 2017 the claimant was entitled to employment and support allowance and remains so entitled throughout the period beginning with 3rd April 2017 and ending with the date on which the claim for universal credit is made or treated as made.

Claimants entitled to be credited with earnings under the Social Security (Credits) Regulations 1975 before 3rd April 2017

2.897 14. The sixth circumstance is where—

(a) immediately before 3rd April 2017—

(i) the claimant entitled to the award was entitled to be credited with earnings equal to the lower earnings limit then in force in respect of a week to which regulation 8B(2)(a)(iv), (iva) or (v) of the Social Security (Credits) Regulations 1975 applies; and

(ii) paragraph 13 does not apply to that claimant; and

(b) the claimant is so entitled in respect of each week that falls in the period beginning with 3rd April 2017 and ending with the date on which the claim for universal credit is made or treated as made.

Claimants entitled to income support or other incapacity benefits before 3rd April 2017

2.898 15. The seventh circumstance is where regulation 22, 23, 24, 26 or 27 of the Universal Credit (Transitional Provisions) Regulations 2014 applies to the claimant throughout the period beginning immediately before 3rd April 2017 and ending with the date on which the claim for universal credit is made or treated as made.

The Universal Credit (Housing Costs Element for claimants aged 18 to 21) (Amendment) Regulations 2017

(SI 2017/252)

Made by the Secretary of State under sections 11(5)(a) and 42(2) and (3) of the Welfare Reform Act 2012. **2.899**

[In force April 1, 2017]

General Note

See the commentary to paras 4A-4C of Sch.4 to the Universal Credit Regulations at paras 2.386 – 2.388 of Vol.V of the 2018/19 edition. **2.900**

These Regulations introduced the exclusions from entitlement to the housing costs element of universal credit contained in paras 4A-4C with effect from April 1, 2017. They were reproduced here because regs 3 and 4 contained transitional protection from those exclusion for, respectively, claimants not living in a digital service area and claimants who had been entitled to housing benefit or had an award of universal credit that included the housing costs element: see further paras 3.731-3.732 of Vol.V of the 2018/19 edition.

The Regulations were revoked with effect from December 31, 2018 by SI 2018/1129, which also revoked paras 4A-4C.

PART III

STATE PENSION CREDIT REGULATIONS

The State Pension Credit Regulations 2002

(SI 2002/1792) (AS AMENDED)

Made by the Secretary of State under s.175(3) to (5) of the Social Security Contributions and Benefits Act 1992, ss.7(4A), 9(4A) and 11(1) and (4) of the Social Security Fraud Act 2001 and ss.1(5), 2(3), (4) and (6), 3(4) to (8), 4(3), 5, 6(2), 7(4) and (7), 9(4) and (5), 12(2) and (3), 15, 16(2) and 17(1) and (2) of the State Pension Credit Act 2002

ARRANGEMENT OF REGULATIONS

PART I

General

PART II

Entitlement and amount

PART III

Income

PART I

General

Citation, commencement and interpretation

3.2 **1.**—(1) These Regulations may be cited as the State Pension Credit Regulations 2002 and shall come into force on 6th October 2003.

(2) In these Regulations—

"the Act" means the State Pension Credit Act 2002;

"the 1992 Act" means the Social Security Contributions and Benefits Act 1992;

[[26] "the 2012 Act" means the Welfare Reform Act 2012;]

[[3] "adoption leave" means a period of absence from work on ordinary or additional adoption leave in accordance with section 75A or 75B of the Employment Rights Act 1996;]

[44 "adult disability payment" has the meaning given in regulation 2 of the Disability Assistance for Working Age People (Scotland) Regulations 2022;]

"the appointed day" means the day appointed under section 13(3) of the Act;

[38 "approved blood scheme" means a scheme established or approved by the Secretary of State, or trust established with funds provided by the Secretary of State, for the purpose of providing compensation in respect of a person having been infected from contaminated blood products;]

[7 "the Armed Forces and Reserve Forces Compensation Scheme" means the scheme established under section 1(2) of the Armed Forces (Pensions and Compensation) Act 2004;]

[27 "armed forces independence payment" means armed forces independence payment under the Armed Forces and Reserve Forces (Compensation Scheme) Order 2011;]

"attendance allowance" means—

(a) an attendance allowance under section 64 of the 1992 Act;
(b) an increase of disablement pension under section 104 or 105 of the 1992 Act;
(c) [29. . .]
(d) [29. . .]
(e) a payment by virtue of article 14, 15, 16, 43 or 44 of the Personal Injuries (Civilians) Scheme 1983 or any analogous payment; or

[18 (f) any payment based on a need for attendance which is paid as part of a war disablement pension, or any other such payment granted in respect of disablement which falls within regulation 15(5)(ac);]

"benefit week" means the period of 7 days beginning on the day on which, in the claimant's case, state pension credit is payable;

[8 "board and lodging accommodation" means accommodation provided to a person or, if he is a member of a family, to him or any other member of his family, for a charge which is inclusive of—

(i) the provision of that accommodation, and
(ii) at least some cooked or prepared meals which both are cooked or prepared (by a person other than the person to whom the accommodation is provided or a member of his family) and are consumed in that accommodation or associated premises,

but not accommodation provided by a close relative of his or of his partner, or other than on a commercial basis;]

"care home" [39 in England] has the meaning it has for the purposes of the Care Standards Act 2000 by virtue of section 3 of that Act [2and in [39 Wales and] Scotland means a care home service];

[22 "care home service" [39 in Wales means a care home service within the meaning of Part 1 of the Regulation and Inspection of Social Care (Wales) Act 2016 which is provided wholly or mainly to persons aged 18 or over and in Scotland] has the meaning assigned to it by paragraph 2 of Schedule 12 to the Public Services Reform (Scotland) Act 2010;]

[47 "carer support payment" means carer's assistance given in accordance with the Carer's Assistance (Carer Support Payment) (Scotland) Regulations 2023;]

[23 "the Caxton Foundation" means the charitable trust of that name established on 28th March 2011 out of funds provided by the Secretary of State for the benefit of certain persons suffering from hepatitis C and other persons eligible for payment in accordance with its provisions;]

[43 "child abuse payment" means a payment from a scheme established or approved by the Secretary of State for the purpose of providing compensation in respect of historic institutional child abuse in the United Kingdom;]

"the Claims and Payments Regulations" means the Social Security (Claims and Payments) Regulations 1987;

"close relative" means a parent, parent-in-law, son, son-in-law, daughter, daughter-in-law, step-parent, step-son, step-daughter, brother, sister, [10 or if any of the preceding persons is one member of a couple, the other member of that couple]

[28 "contribution-based jobseeker's allowance" means an allowance under the Jobseekers Act 1995 as amended by the provisions of Part 1 of Schedule 14 to the 2012 Act that remove references to an income-based allowance, and a contribution-based allowance under the Jobseekers Act 1995 as that Act has effect apart from those provisions;]

[28 "contributory employment and support allowance" means an allowance under Part 1 of the Welfare Reform Act as amended by the provisions of Schedule 3, and Part 1 of Schedule 14, to the 2012 Act that remove references to an income-related allowance, and a contributory allowance under Part 1 of the Welfare Reform Act as that Part has effect apart from those provisions;]

[30 "couple" means—

(a) two people who are married to, or civil partners of, each other and are members of the same household; or

(b) two people who are not married to, or civil partners of, each other but are living together [40 as if they were a married couple or civil partners];]

[1 "the Computation of Earnings Regulations" means the Social Security Benefit (Computation of Earnings) Regulations 1996;

"dwelling occupied as the home" means the dwelling together with any garage, garden and outbuildings, normally occupied by the claimant as his home including any premises not so occupied which it is impracticable or unreasonable to sell separately, in particular, in Scotland, any croft land on which the dwelling is situated;]

"Eileen Trust" means the charitable trust of that name established on 29th March 1993 out of funds provided by the Secretary of State for the benefit of persons eligible for payment in accordance with its provisions;

[16 "the Employment and Support Allowance Regulations" means the Employment and Support Allowance Regulations 2008;]

[19 "enactment" includes an enactment comprised in, or in an instrument made under, an Act of the Scottish Parliament [29 or the National Assembly for Wales];]

[6 "equity release scheme" means a loan—

(a) made between a person ("the lender") and the claimant;

(b) by means of which a sum of money is advanced by the lender to the claimant by way of payments at regular intervals; and

(c) which is secured on a dwelling in which the claimant owns an estate or interest and which he occupies as his home;]

[[20] "foreign state retirement pension" means any pension which is paid under the law of a country outside the United Kingdom and is in the nature of social security;]

"the Fund" means moneys made available from time to time by the Secretary of State for the benefit of persons eligible for payment in accordance with the provisions of a scheme established by him on 24th April 1992 or, in Scotland, on 10th April 1992;

"full-time student" has the meaning prescribed in regulation 61(1) of the Income Support Regulations;

[[12] "the Graduated Retirement Benefit Regulations" means the Social Security (Graduated Retirement Benefit) Regulations 2005;]

[[42][[45]"Grenfell Tower payment" means a payment made for the purpose of providing compensation or support in respect of the fire on 14th June 2017 at Grenfell Tower;]]

[[7]"a guaranteed income payment" means a payment made under article 14(1)(b) or article 21(1)(a) of the Armed Forces and Reserve Forces (Compensation Scheme) Order 2005;]

[[17] "the Health Service Act" means "the National Health Service Act 2006];

"the Health Service (Wales) Act" means "the National Health Service (Wales) Act 2006";]

[[45]"the Horizon system" means any version of the computer system used by the Post Office known as Horizon, Horizon Legacy, Horizon Online or HNG-X;]

[[28] "income-based jobseeker's allowance" means an income-based allowance under the Jobseekers Act 1995;]

[[16] "income-related employment and support allowance" means an income-related allowance under Part 1 of the Welfare Reform Act (employment and support allowance);]

"the Income Support Regulations" means the Income Support (General) Regulations 1987;

[[21] "independent hospital"—

(a) in England, means a hospital as defined by section 275 of the National Health Service Act 2006 that is not a health service hospital as defined by that section;

(b) in Wales, has the meaning assigned to it by section 2 of the Care Standards Act 2000; and

[[22] (c) in Scotland, means an independent health care service as defined in section 10F(1)(a) and (b) of the National Health Service (Scotland) Act 1978;]]

[[17] . . .]

[[14] "the Independent Living Fund (2006)" means the Trust of that name established by a deed dated April 10, 2006 and made between the Secretary of State for Work and Pensions of the one part and Margaret Rosemary Cooper, Michael Beresford Boyall and Marie Theresa Martin of the other part;]

[[17] . . .]

"the Jobseeker's Allowance Regulations" means the Jobseeker's Allowance Regulations 1996;

[[25] "local welfare provision" means occasional financial or other assistance given by a local authority, the Scottish Ministers or the Welsh

Ministers, or a person authorised to exercise any function of, or provide a service to, them, to or in respect of individuals for the purpose of—

(a) meeting, or helping to meet, an immediate short term need—
   (i) arising out of an exceptional event, or exceptional circumstances; and
   (ii) that requires to be met in order to avoid a risk to the well-being of an individual; or
(b) enabling individuals to establish or maintain a settled home, where those individuals have been or, without the assistance, might otherwise be—
   (i) in prison, hospital, a residential care establishment or other institution; or
   (ii) homeless or otherwise living an unsettled way of life;]

[[11] "the London Bombings Relief Charitable Fund" means the company limited by guarantee (number 5505072) and registered charity of that name established on 11th July 2005 for the purpose of (amongst other things) relieving sickness, disability or financial need of victims (including families or dependants of victims) of the terrorist attacks carried out in London on 7th July 2005;]

[[37] "the London Emergencies Trust" means the company of that name (number 09928465) incorporated on 23rd December 2015 and the registered charity of that name (number 1172307) established on 28th March 2017;]

"the Macfarlane (Special Payments) Trust" means the trust of that name, established on 29th January 1990 partly out of funds provided by the Secretary of State, for the benefit of certain persons suffering from haemophilia;

"the Macfarlane (Special Payments) (No.2) Trust" means the trust of that name, established on 3rd May 1991 partly out of funds provided by the Secretary of State, for the benefit of certain persons suffering from haemophilia and other beneficiaries;

"the Macfarlane Trust" means the charitable trust, established partly out of funds provided by the Secretary of State to the Haemophilia Society, for the relief of poverty or distress among those suffering from haemophilia;

[[35] "member of the work-related activity group" means a claimant who has or is treated as having limited capability for work under either—

(a) Part 5 of the Employment and Support Allowance Regulations 2008 other than by virtue of regulation 30 of those Regulations; or
(b) Part 4 of the Employment and Support Allowance Regulations 2013 other than by virtue of regulation 26 of those Regulations;]

[[20] "MFET Limited" means the company limited by guarantee (number 7121661) of that name, established for the purpose in particular of making payments in accordance with arrangements made with the Secretary of State to persons who have acquired HIV as a result of treatment by the NHS with blood or blood products;]

[[42] "the National Emergencies Trust" means the registered charity of that name (number 1182809) established on 28th March 2019;]

[[41]"parental bereavement leave" means leave under section 80EA of the Employment Rights Act 1996;]

[[24] "paternity leave" means a period of absence from work on [[34] . . .] paternity leave by virtue of section 80A or 80B of the Employment Rights Act 1996 [[34] . . .];]

[13 "patient", except in Schedule II, means a person (other than a prisoner) who is regarded as receiving free in-patient treatment within the meaning of regulation 2(4) and (5) of the Social Security (Hospital In-Patients) Regulations 2005;]

"pension fund holder" means with respect to [15 an occupational pension scheme,] a personal pension scheme or retirement annuity contract, the trustees, managers or scheme administrators, as the case may be, of the scheme or contract concerned;

[26 "personal independence payment" means personal independence payment under Part 4 of the 2012 Act;]

"policy of life insurance" means any instrument by which the payment of money is assured on death (except death by accident only) or the happening of any contingency dependent on human life, or any instrument evidencing a contract which is subject to payment of premiums for a term dependent on human life;

[45"the Post Office" means Post Office Limited (registered number 02154540);]

[45"Post Office compensation payment" means a payment made by the Post Office or the Secretary of State for the purpose of providing compensation or support which is—

(a) in connection with the failings of the Horizon system; or

(b) otherwise payable following the judgment in *Bates and Others v Post Office Ltd* ((No. 3) "Common Issues");]

"prisoner" means a person who—

(a) is detained in custody pending trial or sentence upon conviction or under a sentence imposed by a court; or

(b) is on temporary release in accordance with the provisions of the Prison Act 1952 or the Prisons (Scotland) Act 1989,

other than a person detained in hospital under the provisions of the Mental Health Act 1983, or in Scotland, under the provisions of the [9 Mental Health (Care and Treatment) (Scotland) Act 2003] or the Criminal Procedure (Scotland) Act 1995;

[19 "public authority" includes any person certain of whose functions are functions of a public nature;]

"qualifying person" means a person in respect of whom [42 a Grenfell Tower payment [43, a child abuse payment [45, a Windrush payment, a Post Office compensation payment or a vaccine damage payment] has been made or] payment has been made from the Fund [4, the Eileen Trust [20, MFET Limited] [11, the Skipton Fund [23, the Caxton Foundation] [36, the Scottish Infected Blood Support Scheme] [37, [38 an approved blood scheme], the London Emergencies Trust, the We Love Manchester Emergency Fund] [42, the National Emergencies Trust] [46, the Victims of Overseas Terrorism Compensation Scheme] or the London Bombings Relief Charitable Fund]];

[36 "Scottish Infected Blood Support Scheme" means the scheme of that name administered by the Common Services Agency (constituted by section 10 of the National Health Service (Scotland) Act 1978);]

[31 . . .]

[32 "shared parental leave" means leave under section 75E or 75G of the Employment Rights Act 1996;]

[5 "the Skipton Fund" means the ex-gratia payment scheme administered by the Skipton Fund Limited, incorporated on 25th March 2004, for the benefit of certain persons suffering from hepatitis C and other persons eligible for payment in accordance with the scheme's provisions;]

[[28] "universal credit" means universal credit under Part 1 of the 2012 Act;]

[[45]"vaccine damage payment" means a payment made under the Vaccine Damage Payments Act 1979;]

[[46]"the Victims of Overseas Terrorism Compensation Scheme" means the scheme of that name established by the Ministry of Justice in 2012 under section 47 of the Crime and Security Act 2010;]

[[2] "voluntary organisation" means a body, other than a public or local authority, the activities of which are carried on otherwise than for profit;]

"water charges" means—

(a) as respects England and Wales, any water and sewerage charges under Chapter 1 of Part V of the Water Industry Act 1991;

(b) as respects Scotland, any water and sewerage charges under Schedule 11 to the Local Government Finance Act 1992;

in so far as such charges are in respect of the dwelling which a person occupies as his home;

[[37] the We Love Manchester Emergency Fund" means the registered charity of that name (number 1173260) established on 30th May 2017;]

[[16] "the Welfare Reform Act" means the Welfare Reform Act 2007;]

[[43] "Windrush payment" means a payment made under the Windrush Compensation Scheme (Expenditure) Act 2020.]

(3) In these Regulations, unless the context otherwise requires, a member of [[11] a couple] is referred to as a partner and both members are referred to as partners.

[[31] (3A) References in these Regulations to a claimant participating as a service user are to—

(a) a person who is being consulted by or on behalf of—

(i) a body which has a statutory duty to provide services in the field of health, social care or social housing; or

(ii) a body which conducts research or undertakes monitoring for the purpose of planning or improving such services,

in their capacity as a user, potential user, carer of a user or person otherwise affected by the provision of those services; or

[[33] (ab) a person who is being consulted by or on behalf of—

(i) the Secretary of State in relation to any of the Secretary of State's functions in the field of social security or child support or under section 2 of the Employment and Training Act 1973; or

(ii) a body which conducts research or undertakes monitoring for the purpose of planning or improving such functions,

in their capacity as a person affected or potentially affected by the exercise of those functions or the carer of such a person;]

(b) the carer of a person consulted under [[33] sub-paragraphs (a) or (ab)].]

(4) In these Regulations, unless the context otherwise requires, a reference—

(a) to a numbered section is to the section of the Act bearing that number;

(b) to a numbered Part is to the Part of these Regulations bearing that number;

(c) to a numbered regulation or Schedule is to the regulation in, or Schedule to, these Regulations bearing that number;
(d) in a regulation or Schedule to a numbered paragraph is to the paragraph in that regulation or Schedule bearing that number;
(e) in a paragraph to a lettered or numbered sub-paragraph is to the sub-paragraph in that paragraph bearing that letter or number.

AMENDMENTS

1. State Pension Credit (Consequential, Transitional and Miscellaneous Provisions) Regulations 2002 (SI 2002/3019) reg.23(a) (October 6, 2003).

2. State Pension Credit (Consequential, Transitional and Miscellaneous Provisions) (No.2) Regulations 2002 (SI 2002/3197) reg.2 and Sch. para.1 (October 6, 2003).

3. State Pension Credit (Transitional and Miscellaneous Provisions) Amendment Regulations 2003 (SI 2003/2274) reg.2(2) (October 6, 2003).

4. Social Security (Miscellaneous Amendments) (No.2) Regulations 2004 (SI 2004/1141) reg.2(a) (May 12, 2004).

5. Social Security (Miscellaneous Amendments) (No.2) Regulations 2004 (SI 2004/1141) reg.2(b)(iv) (May 12, 2004).

6. Social Security (Housing Benefit, Council Tax Benefit, State Pension Credit and Miscellaneous Amendments) Regulations 2004 (SI 2004/2327) reg.7(2) (October 4, 2004).

7. Social Security (Miscellaneous Amendments) Regulations 2005 (SI 2005/574) reg.2(1) (April 4, 2005).

8. Social Security (Miscellaneous Amendments) (No.2) Regulations 2005 (SI 2005/2465) reg.6(2) (October 3, 2005).

9. Mental Health (Care and Treatment) (Scotland) Act 2003 (Modification of Subordinate Legislation) Order 2005 (SSI 2005/445) art.2 and Sch. para.35(1) (October 3, 2005).

10. Civil Partnership (Pensions, Social Security and Child Support) (Consequential, etc. Provisions) Order 2005 (SI 2005/2877) art.2(3) and Sch.3 para.35(2) (December 5, 2005).

11. Income-related Benefits (Amendment) (No.2) Regulations 2005 (SI 2005/3391) reg.7(2) (December 12, 2005).

12. Social Security (Deferral of Retirement Pensions, Shared Additional Pension and Graduated Retirement Benefit) (Miscellaneous Provisions) Regulations 2005 (SI 2005/2677) reg.13(2) (April 6, 2006).

13. Social Security (Hospital In-Patients) Regulations 2005 (SI 2005/3360) reg.8(2) (April 10, 2006).

14. Independent Living Fund (2006) Order 2007 (SI 2007/2538) art.6(2) (October 1, 2007).

15. Social Security (Miscellaneous Amendments) (No.5) Regulations 2007 (SI 2007/2618) reg.10(2) (October 1, 2007).

16. Employment and Support Allowance (Consequential Provisions) (No.2) Regulations 2008 (SI 2008/1554) reg.4(2) (October 27, 2008).

17. Social Security (Miscellaneous Amendments) (No.6) Regulations 2008 (SI 2008/2767) reg.5(2) (November 17, 2008).

18. Social Security (Miscellaneous Amendments) (No.7) Regulations 2008 (SI 2008/3157) reg.4(2) (January 5, 2009).

19. Social Security (Miscellaneous Amendments) (No.4) Regulations 2009 (SI 2009/2655) reg.5(2) (October 26, 2009).

20. Social Security (Miscellaneous Amendments) (No.2) Regulations 2010 (SI 2010/641) reg.6(3)(a) (April 6, 2010).

21. Health and Social Care Act 2008 (Miscellaneous Consequential Amendments) Order 2010 (SI 2010/1881) art.5 (October 1, 2010).

22. Public Services Reform (Scotland) Act 2010 (Consequential Modifications of Enactments) Order 2011 (SI 2011/2581) art.2 and Sch.2 para.35 (October 28, 2011).

23. Social Security (Miscellaneous Amendments) (No.3) Regulations 2011 (2011/2425) reg.15(2) (October 31, 2011).

24. Social Security (Miscellaneous Amendments) Regulations 2012 (2012/757) reg.5(2) (April 1, 2012).

25. Social Security (Miscellaneous Amendments) Regulations 2013 (SI 2013/443) reg.6(2) (April 2, 2013).

26. Personal Independence Payment (Supplementary Provisions and Consequential Amendments) Regulations 2013 (SI 2013/388) reg.8 and Sch. para.27(2) (April 8, 2013).

27. Armed Forces and Reserve Forces Compensation Scheme (Consequential Provisions: Subordinate Legislation) Order 2013 (SI 2013/591) art.7 and Sch. para.23(2) (April 8, 2013).

28. Universal Credit (Consequential, Supplementary, Incidental and Miscellaneous Provisions) Regulations 2013 (SI 2013/630) reg.33(2) (April 29, 2013).

29. Social Security (Miscellaneous Amendments) (No.3) Regulations 2013 (SI 2013/2536) reg.10(2) (October 29, 2013).

30. Marriage (Same Sex Couples) Act 2013 (Consequential Provisions) Order 2014 (SI 2014/107) art.2 and Sch.1 para.32 (March 13, 2014 for England & Wales only); Marriage and Civil Partnership (Scotland) Act 2014 and Civil Partnership Act 2004 (Consequential Provisions and Modifications) Order 2014 (SI 2014/3229) art.29 and Sch.6 para.23 (December 16, 2014 for the United Kingdom).

31. Social Security (Miscellaneous Amendments) Regulations 2014 (SI 2014/591) reg.7(2) (April 28, 2014).

32. Shared Parental Leave and Statutory Shared Parental Pay (Consequential Amendments to Subordinate Legislation) Order 2014 (SI 2014/3255) art.10(2)(b) (December 31, 2014).

33. Social Security (Miscellaneous Amendments) Regulations 2015 (SI 2015/67) reg.2(2) (February 23, 2015).

34. Shared Parental Leave and Statutory Shared Parental Pay (Consequential Amendments to Subordinate Legislation) Order 2014 (SI 2014/3255) art.10(2)(a) (April 5, 2015).

35. Employment and Support Allowance and Universal Credit (Miscellaneous Amendments and Transitional and Savings Provisions) Regulations 2017 (SI 2017/204) reg.7(1) and Sch.1, para.5(2) (April 3, 2017).

36. Social Security (Scottish Infected Blood Support Scheme) Regulations 2017 (SI 2017/329) reg.5(2) (April 3, 2017).

37. Social Security (Emergency Funds) (Amendment) Regulations 2017 (SI 2017/689) reg.4(2) (June 19, 2017).

38. Social Security (Infected Blood and Thalidomide) Regulations 2017 (SI 2017/870) reg.5(2) (October 23, 2017).

39. Social Security and Child Support (Regulation and Inspection of Social Care (Wales) Act 2016) (Consequential Provision) Regulations 2018 (SI 2018/228) reg.8 (April 2, 2018).

40. Civil Partnership (Opposite-sex Couples) Regulations 2019 (SI 2019/1458) reg.41(b) and Sch.3 Part 2 para.61 (December 2, 2019).

41. Parental Bereavement Leave and Pay (Consequential Amendments to Subordinate Legislation) Regulations 2020 (SI 2020/354) reg.10(2) (April 6, 2020).

42. Social Security (Income and Capital) (Miscellaneous Amendments) Regulations 2020 (SI 2020/618) reg.4(2) (July 15, 2020).

43. Social Security (Income and Capital Disregards) (Amendment) Regulations 2021 (SI 2021/1405) reg.4(2) (January 1, 2022).

44. Social Security (Disability Assistance for Working Age People) (Consequential Amendments) Order 2022 (SI 2022/177) art.8(2) (March 21, 2022).

45. Social Security (Income and Capital Disregards) (Amendment) Regulations 2023 (SI 2023/640) reg.4(2) (July 9, 2023).

46. Social Security (Habitual Residence and Past Presence, and Capital Disregards) (Amendment) Regulations 2023 (SI 2023/1144) reg.5(2)(b) (October 27, 2023).

47. Carer's Assistance (Carer Support Payment) (Scotland) Regulations 2023 (Consequential Amendments) Order 2023 (SI 2023/1218) art.14(2) (November 19, 2023).

Modification

The definition of "prisoner" in regulation 1(2) is modified as from April 8, 2020 by reg.2 of the Social Security (Coronavirus) (Prisoners) Regulations 2020 (SI 2020/409). For details of the modification, see the General Note to this regulation.

Definition

"claimant"—see SPCA 2002 s.17(1).

General Note

Paragraph (2)

"Appointed day": This date was October 6, 2003: see State Pension Credit Act 2002 (Commencement No.5) and Appointed Day Order 2003 (SI 2003/1766 (C.75)). 3.3

"Board and lodging accommodation": On the importance of establishing, in this context, the precise status of someone staying with the claimant (e.g. as sub-tenant, lodger or non-dependant), see *KC v Secretary of State for Work and Pensions (SPC)* [2012] UKUT 114 (AAC).

"Care home": Section 3(1) of the Care Standards Act 2000 provides that "an establishment is a care home if it provides accommodation, together with nursing or personal care" for various categories of person (e.g. the ill, the disabled, those with mental disorders and those with alcohol or drug dependency). An establishment is not a care home if it is a hospital, independent clinic or children's home, or if it is excluded by regulations (see Care Standards Act 2000 s.3(3) and Care Homes Regulations 2001 (SI 2001/3965) reg.3)). For the (slightly differently phrased) Scottish definition of "care home", see Regulation of Care (Scotland) Act 2001 s.2. This defines a "care home" as an establishment in which a care home service is provided, i.e. accommodation together with nursing, personal care, or personal support for people by reason of their vulnerability or need. See further *SA v Secretary of State for Work and Pensions (IS)* [2010] UKUT 345 (AAC); [2011] AACR 16.

"Close relative": This definition is in identical terms to that used in reg.2(1) of the Income Support (General) Regulations 1987 (SI 1987/1967), and therefore will presumably be interpreted in the same way. Thus "brother" and "sister" include half-brothers and half-sisters, and persons who are adopted cease to have any legal relationship with their birth family (*R(SB) 22/87*). 3.4

"Couple": This new streamlined definition is consequential upon the Marriage (Same Sex Couples) Act 2013—see further the Note at the start of this Volume. On the proper approach to the assessment of whether two persons are "living together as husband and wife" (now "living together as if they were a married couple or civil partners" in the statutory definition of couple), see *DK v SSWP* [2016] Scots CSIH 84.

"Dwelling occupied as the home": This also follows the income support definition: see para.2.25 above. See also *ED v Secretary of State for Work and Pensions* [2009] UKUT 161 (AAC), confirming that the basic meaning of this expression "does not extend to any land or other premises not occupied by the person in question, whatever the nature of the other premises" (at para.17). See further *PJ v Secretary of State for Work and Pensions* (SPC) [2014] UKUT 152 (AAC), holding that "a person who chooses for financial reasons not to live in his usual home for a period of three years cannot say that during that period he normally occupies the property as his home" (at para.16).

3.5 *"Full-time student"*: For analysis of the complex case law on this term in the context of income support, see the commentary to Pt VIII of the Income Support (General) Regulations 1987 (SI 1987/1967) in Vol.V of this series.

"Patient": This is the same definition as used for the purposes of income support (see reg.21(3) of the Income Support (General) Regulations 1987 (SI 1987/1967) in Vol.V of this series.

3.6 *"Prisoner"*: This is also the same definition as used for the purposes of income support (see reg.21(3) of the Income Support (General) Regulations 1987 (SI 1987/1967). Note also that as from April 8, 2020, the definition of "prisoner" is to be read as if it did not include a person on temporary release in accordance with the provisions of the Prison Act 1952 (see Social Security (Coronavirus) (Prisoners) Regulations 2020 (SI 2020/409) reg.2). The purpose of this change was to make provision for those individuals on temporary release from a prison in England and Wales due to the outbreak of COVID-19 in Great Britain to access means-tested benefits during the period of that release. The regulations must be kept under review by the Secretary of State and "cease to have effect at the end of the period of eight months beginning on 13th March 2020" (SI 2020/409 reg.6). However, with effect from November 12, 2020, reg.2 of the Social Security (Coronavirus) (Prisoners) Amendment Regulations 2020 (SI 2020/1156) amended reg.6 of SI 2020/409 by substituting "14 months" for "eight months". Subsequently the end date for the regulations was revised to 31 August, 2021 (see the Social Security (Coronavirus) (Miscellaneous Amendments) Regulations 2021 (SI 2021/476), reg.4(6), further amending SI 2020/409, reg.6).

PART II

Entitlement and amount

[1 Disapplication of section 1(1A) of the Social Security Administration Act

3.7 **1A.**—Section 1(1A) of the Social Security Administration Act 1992 (requirement to state a national insurance number) shall not apply to a person who—

(a) is a person in respect of whom a claim for state pension credit is made;
(b) is subject to immigration control within the meaning of section 115(9)(a) of the Immigration and Asylum Act 1999;
(c) does not satisfy the conditions of entitlement to state pension credit as specified in section 1(2); and

(d) has not previously been allocated a national insurance number.]

AMENDMENT

1. Social Security (National Insurance Number Information: Exemption) Regulations 2009 (SI 2009/471) reg.8 (April 6, 2009).

GENERAL NOTE

This provision ensures that there is no requirement for a National Insurance number (NINo) to be allocated to an individual who has no leave to enter or remain in the United Kingdom where that person is a partner of a legitimate benefit claimant. See also the earlier Commissioner's decision *CH/3801/2004*. 3.8

[1 Persons not in Great Britain

2.—(1) A person is to be treated as not in Great Britain if, subject to the following provisions of this regulation, he is not habitually resident in the United Kingdom, the Channel Islands, the Isle of Man or the Republic of Ireland. 3.9

(2) No person shall be treated as habitually resident in the United Kingdom, the Channel Islands, the Isle of Man or the Republic of Ireland unless he has a right to reside in (as the case may be) the United Kingdom, the Channel Islands, the Isle of Man or the Republic of Ireland other than a right to reside which falls within paragraph (3) [9 or (3A)].

(3) A right to reside falls within this paragraph if it is one which exists by virtue of, or in accordance with, one or more of the following—

(a) regulation 13 of the [9 Immigration (European Economic Area) Regulations 2016];

(b) regulation 14 of those Regulations, but only in a case where the right exists under that regulation because the person is—

(i) a jobseeker for the purpose of the definition of "qualified person" in regulation 6(1) of those Regulations, or

(ii) a family member (within the meaning of regulation 7 of those Regulations) of such a jobseeker; [11or]

[5[9(bb) regulation 16 of those Regulations, but only in a case where the right exists under that regulation because the person satisfies the criteria in paragraph (5) of that regulation.]]

(c) [11 . . .]

(d) [11 . . .]

(e) [11 . . .]

[9(3A) A right to reside falls within this paragraph if it exists by virtue of a person having been granted limited leave to enter, or remain in, the United Kingdom under the Immigration Act 1971 by virtue of—

(a) Appendix EU to the immigration rules made under section 3(2) of that Act; [12 . . .]

(b) being a person with a Zambrano right to reside as defined in Annex 1 of Appendix EU to the immigration rules made under section 3(2) of that Act [12; or

(c) having arrived in the United Kingdom with an entry clearance that was granted under Appendix EU (Family Permit) to the immigration rules made under section 3(2) of that Act.]

[10(3B) Paragraph (3A)(a) does not apply to a person who—

(a) has a right to reside granted by virtue of being a family member of a relevant person of Northern Ireland; and

(b) would have a right to reside under the Immigration (European Economic Area) Regulations 2016 if the relevant person of Northern Ireland were an EEA national, provided that the right to reside does not fall within paragraph (3).]

(4) A person is not to be treated as not in Great Britain if he is—

[[13](zza) a person granted leave in accordance with the immigration rules made under section 3(2) of the Immigration Act 1971, where such leave is granted by virtue of—

(i) the Afghan Relocations and Assistance Policy; or

(ii) the previous scheme for locally-employed staff in Afghanistan (sometimes referred to as the ex-gratia scheme);

(zzb) a person in Great Britain not coming within sub-paragraph (zza) or [[14](h)] who left Afghanistan in connection with the collapse of the Afghan government that took place on 15th August 2021;]

[[14](zzc) a person in Great Britain who was residing in Ukraine immediately before 1st January 2022, left Ukraine in connection with the Russian invasion which took place on 24th February 2022 and—

(i) has been granted leave in accordance with immigration rules made under section 3(2) of the Immigration Act 1971; [[15] ...]

(ii) has a right of abode in the United Kingdom within the meaning given in section 2 of that Act;] [[15] ...]

[[15](iii) does not require leave to enter or remain in the United Kingdom in accordance with section 3ZA of that Act;]

[[16](zzd) a person who was residing in Sudan before 15th April 2023, left Sudan in connection with the violence which rapidly escalated on 15th April 2023 in Khartoum and across Sudan and—

(i) has been granted leave in accordance with immigration rules made under section 3(2) of the Immigration Act 1971;

(ii) has a right of abode in the United Kingdom within the meaning given in section 2 of that Act; or

(iii) does not require leave to enter or remain in the United Kingdom in accordance with section 3ZA of that Act;]

[[17](zze) a person who was residing in Israel, the West Bank, the Gaza Strip, East Jerusalem, the Golan Heights or Lebanon immediately before 7th October 2023, who left Israel, the West Bank, the Gaza Strip, East Jerusalem, the Golan Heights or Lebanon in connection with the Hamas terrorist attack in Israel on 7th October 2023 or the violence which rapidly escalated in the region following the attack and—

(i) has been granted leave in accordance with immigration rules made under section 3(2) of the Immigration Act 1971;

(ii) has a right of abode in the United Kingdom within the meaning given in section 2 of that Act; or

(iii) does not require leave to enter or remain in the United Kingdom in accordance with section 3ZA of that Act;]

[[8] (za) a qualified person for the purposes of regulation 6 of the [[9] Immigration (European Economic Area) Regulations 2016] as a worker or a self-employed person;

(zb) a family member of a person referred to in sub-paragraph (za) [[10] . . .];

(zc) a person who has a right to reside permanently in the United Kingdom by virtue of regulation 15(1)(c), (d) or (e) of those Regulations;]

[10(zd) a family member of a relevant person of Northern Ireland, with a right to reside which falls within paragraph (3A)(a), provided that the relevant person of Northern Ireland falls within sub-paragraph (za), or would do so but for the fact that they are not an EEA national;]

[11(ze) a frontier worker within the meaning of regulation 3 of the Citizens' Rights (Frontier Workers) (EU Exit) Regulations 2020;

(zf) a family member of a person referred to in sub-paragraph (ze), who has been granted limited leave to enter, or remain in, the United Kingdom by virtue of Appendix EU to the immigration rules made under section 3(2) of the Immigration Act 1971;]

(g) a refugee within the definition in Article 1 of the Convention relating to the Status of Refugees done at Geneva on 28th July 1951, as extended by Article 1(2) of the Protocol relating to the Status of Refugees done at New York on 31st January 1967;

[6 (h) a person who has been granted leave or who is deemed to have been granted leave outside the rules made under section 3(2) of the Immigration Act 1971 [14 . . .];

(hh) a person who has humanitarian protection granted under those rules;] [7 or]

(i) a person who is not a person subject to immigration control within the meaning of section 115(9) of the Immigration and Asylum Act 1999 and who is in the United Kingdom as a result of his deportation, expulsion or other removal by compulsion of law from another country to the United Kingdom;[3 . . .].

(j) [7 . . .]

(k) [7 . . .]

[10(5) In this regulation—

"EEA national" has the meaning given in regulation 2(1) of the Immigration (European Economic Area) Regulations 2016;

"family member" has the meaning given in regulation 7(1)(a), (b) or (c) of the Immigration (European Economic Area) Regulations 2016 except that regulation 7(4) of those Regulations does not apply for the purposes of paragraphs (3B) and (4)(zd);

"relevant person of Northern Ireland" has the meaning given in Annex 1 of Appendix EU to the immigration rules made under section 3(2) of the Immigration Act 1971.]

[11(6) In this regulation references to the Immigration (European Economic Area) Regulations 2016 are to be read with Schedule 4 to the Immigration and Social Security Co-ordination (EU Withdrawal) Act 2020 (Consequential, Saving, Transitional and Transitory Provisions) Regulations 2020.]

AMENDMENTS

1. Social Security (Persons from Abroad) Amendment Regulations 2006 (SI 2006/1026) reg.9 (April 30, 2006).

2. Social Security (Persons from Abroad) Amendment (No.2) Regulations 2006 (SI 2006/2528) reg.4 (October 9, 2006).

3. Social Security (Habitual Residence) (Amendment) Regulations 2009 (SI 1009/362) reg.4 (March 18, 2009).

4. Treaty of Lisbon (Changes in Terminology or Numbering) Order 2012 (SI 2012/1809) art.3 and Sch. Pt 2 (August 1, 2012).

5. Social Security (Habitual Residence) (Amendment) Regulations 2012 (SI 2012/2587) reg.4 (November 8, 2012).

6. Social Security (Croatia) Amendment Regulations 2013 (SI 2013/1474) reg.4(2) (July 1, 2013).

7. Social Security (Miscellaneous Amendments) (No.3) Regulations 2013 (SI 2013/2536) reg.10(3) (October 29, 2013).

8. Social Security (Habitual Residence) (Amendment) Regulations 2014 (SI 2014/902) reg.4 (May 31, 2014).

9. Social Security (Income-related Benefits) (Updating and Amendment) (EU Exit) Regulations 2019 (SI 2019/872) reg.4(2) (May 7, 2019).

10. Social Security (Income-Related Benefits) (Persons of Northern Ireland—Family Members) (Amendment) Regulations 2020 (SI 2020/683) reg.4(2) (August 24, 2020).

11. Immigration and Social Security Co-ordination (EU Withdrawal) Act 2020 (Consequential, Saving, Transitional and Transitory Provisions) (EU Exit) Regulations 2020 (SI 2020/1309) reg.59 (December 31, 2020).

12. Immigration (Citizens' Rights etc.) (EU Exit) Regulations 2020 (SI 2020/1372) reg.13 (December 31, 2020).

13. Social Security (Habitual Residence and Past Presence) (Amendment) Regulations 2021 (SI 2021/1034) reg.2 (September 15, 2021).

14. Social Security (Habitual Residence and Past Presence) (Amendment) Regulations 2022 (SI 2022/344) reg.2 (March 22, 2022).

15. Social Security (Habitual Residence and Past Presence) (Amendment) (No.2) Regulations 2022 (SI 2022/990) reg.2(1) and (2)(c) (October 18, 2022).

16. Social Security (Habitual Residence and Past Presence) (Amendment) Regulations 2023 (SI 2023/532) reg.2 (May 15, 2023).

17. Social Security (Habitual Residence and Past Presence, and Capital Disregards) (Amendment) Regulations 2023 (SI 2023/1144) reg.2(1) and 2(2)(c) (October 27, 2023).

General Note

3.10 It is a fundamental requirement of entitlement to the state pension credit that the claimant "is in Great Britain" (SPCA 2002 s.1(2)(a)). In this context note *EC v Secretary of State for Work and Pensions* [2010] UKUT 93 (AAC); [2010] AACR 39, where it was held that state pension credit is a special non-contributory benefit within art.10a of Regulation 1408/71 and so is payable only to those living in Great Britain. In its original form this provision simply adopted the habitual residence test from the income support scheme as a means of determining whether a person was "in Great Britain" for the purposes of pension credit. This was then supplemented by the addition of the right to reside test as from May 1, 2004. However, as from April 30, 2006, the provision was recast in its current form (and has subsequently also been further amended). The new reg.2 reflects the evolution of the right to reside test and in particular the coming into force of Directive 2004/38. Note also the special dispensation for those temporarily absent from Great Britain (reg.3) and those being treated abroad under NHS provisions (reg.4).

For a full analysis of both the habitual residence and the right to reside rules, see the commentary to reg.21AA of the Income Support (General) Regulations 1987 and the Immigration (European Economic Area) Regulations 2016 in Vol.V in this series. For detailed discussion of the position of persons subject to immigration control, see Part V of this Volume.

The pre-April 30, 2006 version of reg.2 was considered by Commissioner Jacobs in *CPC/3588/2006* and by Commissioner Rowland in *CPC/1072/2006*; the claimant's appeal in the latter case was dismissed by the Court of Appeal in

Patmalniece v Secretary of State for Work & Pensions [2009] EWCA Civ 621 and then by the Supreme Court ([2011] UKSC 11; [2011] AACR 34). The Supreme Court held that s.1 of the Act and reg.2 had to be read as a whole. The test under reg.2(2) was constructed in such a way that it was more likely to be satisfied by a UK national than by a national of another Member State. In terms of EU law, that meant that although it was not directly discriminatory on grounds of nationality, it was indirectly discriminatory and so had to be justified. The purpose of the right to reside test was to safeguard the UK's social security system from exploitation by those who wished to enter in order to live off income-related benefits rather than to work. That was a legitimate reason for the imposition of the test. It was independent of nationality, arising from the principle that only those who were economically or socially integrated with the host Member State should have access to its social assistance system. There was, therefore, sufficient justification for the discrimination arising from reg.2(2). The position of Irish nationals—who met the requirements of reg.2(2) even though they did not have a right to reside in the UK and were not habitually resident there—was protected by art.2 of the Protocol on the Common Travel Area. It was not discriminatory not to extend the same entitlement to the nationals of other Member States.

Commissioner Jacobs has analysed the post-April 30, 2006 version of reg.2 in **3.11** *CPC/2134/2007* and *CPC/3764/2007*. In *CPC/2134/2007* the claimant, a Lithuanian national, arrived in the UK in 2000, and unsuccessfully claimed asylum. She abandoned her asylum appeal when Lithuania joined the EU in May 2004. She claimed state pension credit in January 2006 but her claim was not decided until October 2006, when it was refused on the basis that she had no right to reside. Commissioner Jacobs acknowledged that the claimant had been in the UK for more than five years but ruled that she had no permanent right of residence. Pre-accession periods of residence could not be taken into account (following *GN (EEA Regulations: five years' residence) Hungary* [2007] UKAIT 73). The claimant had not exercised any EU right either before or after accession.

In *CPC/3764/2007* Commissioner Jacobs likewise confirmed that a pre-accession period of residence by a Slovakian national between 1997 and 2004 could not be taken into account (see also *R(IS) 3/08*). The Commissioner also analysed in detail the argument of the claimant's representative based on proportionality, concluding that the circumstances were "not sufficiently exceptional to justify ignoring the terms of the legislation governing the right to reside" (at para.46).

See also *Secretary of State v AA* [2009] UKUT 249 (AAC), where the issue was whether the claimant had a right to reside where he was a dependant of his son, who was in employment and held both British and Spanish nationality and with whom he had gone to live on a rent-free basis. Upper Tribunal Judge Rowland distinguished *McCarthy v Secretary of State for the Home Department* [2008] EWCA Civ 641, ruling that on a literal construction of the Immigration (European Economic Area) Regulations 2006 (SI 2006/1003) "a Spanish national is therefore an EEA national to whom regulation 6 applies, even if he or she also holds British nationality" (at para.16). In *HG v Secretary of State (SPC)* [2011] UKUT 382 (AAC), a decision issued after the judgment of the ECJ in *McCarthy v Secretary of State for the Home Department* (C-434/09). [2011] All E.R. (EC) 729, it was accepted that the claimant, a Polish national, was dependent upon her daughter, Mrs D. Judge Jacobs, taking the same approach as Judge Rowland in *Secretary of State v AA* [2009] UKUT 249 (AAC), held that Mrs D had a right to reside in the UK under the Immigration (EEA) Regulations 2006:

> "9. The claimant is a family member of Mrs D under regulation 7(1)(c) as a dependent direct relative in her ascending line. As such, she has a right to reside under regulation 14(2) if Mrs D has a permanent right to reside. Mrs D has resided for the requisite period of five years to acquire that right under regulation 15(1)(a), provided two conditions are satisfied. One is that she is 'an EEA

national'. She satisfies that condition by virtue of the definitions in regulation 2(1), under which an EEA national is a national of an EEA State other than the United Kingdom. Mrs D, as I have said, is Polish. The other condition is that she has resided in the United Kingdom in accordance with the 2006 Regulations. She would do so if she has resided as a worker. Under regulation 4(1)(a) a worker means 'a worker within the meaning of Article 39 of the Treaty'. The Secretary of State accepts that the evidence shows that Mrs D was a worker within the case law of the European Court of Justice. Article 39 is a Treaty provision and so free of the limitations on the scope of Directive 2004/38. There is, therefore, no impediment to Mrs D relying on that status for the purposes of the 2006 Regulations."

3.12 The decision of the Deputy Commissioner in *CPC/1433/2008* has been reversed by the Court of Appeal in *Pedro v Secretary of State for Work and Pensions* [2009] EWCA Civ 1358; [2010] AACR 18. The claimant was a 62-year-old Portuguese national who had come to the UK to live with her son, who worked here. She had largely been financially dependent upon him and had claimed JSA and later state pension credit. The Court of Appeal stressed that the aim of Directive 2004/38 was to strengthen the right of free movement in the EU. Furthermore, an EU citizen who wished to work in another state might be deterred from doing so if he knew that his elderly, but not then dependent, mother would not be regarded as his dependant for the purposes of art.2(2) were she to join him and later become dependent upon him. Thus no such impediment should be placed in his way (*Metock and Minister voor Vreemdelingenzaken en Integratie v Eind* (C-291/05) [2008] All E.R. (EC) 371). Whether someone had the status of a dependent family member was a question of fact (*Centre Public d'Aide Sociale, Courcelles v Lebon* (C-316/85) [1987] E.C.R. 2811). Article 2(2)(d) did not specify when the dependency had to have arisen, nor did it require that the relative had to be dependent in the country of origin. Accordingly, proof of the claimant's dependence on her son in the UK would suffice under art.2(2)(d), and as the tribunal had already found as a fact that she was dependent on him, she was entitled to state pension credit. On the importance of fact-finding where there is a claim of dependency on a relative, see also *LA v SSWP* [2010] UKUT 109 (AAC).

For a discussion of what may be needed to lose habitual residence, see *KS v SSWP* [2010] UKUT 156 (AAC), holding that a VSO volunteer who went to India for more than two years had not lost his UK habitual residence.

Secretary of State for Work and Pensions v LL (SPC) [2014] UKUT 136 (AAC), concerning a Belgian pensioner supported in the UK by her daughter, who was unemployed at the material time, confirms that the effect of para.(2) and (3)(b)(ii) is that a right to reside is excluded for the family member of a jobseeker. See also *Secretary of State for Work and Pensions v LZ (SPC)* [2014] UKUT 147 (AAC), holding that the lack of a registration certificate prevented the claimant (a 64-year-old Polish woman living with her brother in the UK) as an "extended family member" from being treated as the "family member" of her brother, with the consequence that she too had no right to reside.

3.13 *CPC/3588/2006*, referred to above in the context of the pre-April 2006 version of the legislation, also decided that a residence permit is only evidence and does not of itself create a right to reside. This was confirmed by the ECJ in *Dias v SSWP (C-325/09)* [2012] AACR 36. See also *MD v SSWP (SPC)* [2016] UKUT 319 (AAC), in which a Turkish Cypriot had been wrongly issued with an EEA certificate of permanent residence. Judge Rowland held that the residence certificate "is capable of proving the right of permanent residence in the absence of adequate evidence to the contrary but it does not confer a right of permanent residence and was insufficient to prove such a right in the present case in the face of uncontested evidence that the claimant had not qualified for a right of permanent residence" (at para.15).

For an illustration of a case in which self-employed was found to be "marginal and ancillary" (the claimant was self-publishing his life story) rather than "genuine and effective", see *SSWP v HH (SPC)* [2015] UKUT 583 (AAC).

Paragraph (4)(i)

On the meaning of a "person subject to immigration control" within sub-para.(4)(i), see *OO v Secretary of State for Work and Pensions (SPC)* [2013] UKUT 335 (AAC). A spouse who falls within that definition is not treated as part of the claimant's household for SPC purposes, i.e. when calculating the claimant's applicable amount or income. The tribunal in this case had failed to distinguish between a spouse being "sponsored" for immigration purposes and a person being subject to a sponsorship undertaking (under immigration law, written sponsorship undertakings cannot apply to a spouse). The claimant's statement on his SPC claim form that his wife was sponsored to be in the UK was accurate (he had not stated that he had signed a written undertaking). The DWP, which had wrongly assumed that his wife was a person subject to immigration control (rather than having been given indefinite leave to remain, as in fact was the case), had failed to make proper enquiries as to her true immigration status. The resulting overpayment was, therefore, due to official error and was not recoverable. The entitlement decision was remitted to a new tribunal for detailed findings on the claimant's means which were required to determine his entitlement to SPC. 3.14

[1 Persons temporarily absent from Great Britain

3.—(1) A claimant's entitlement to state pension credit while the claimant is temporarily absent from Great Britain is to continue but for no longer than— 3.15

(a) 4 weeks, provided the absence is not expected to exceed 4 weeks;
(b) 8 weeks, where paragraph (2) applies; or
(c) 26 weeks, where paragraph (3) applies,

provided the claimant continues to satisfy the other conditions of entitlement.

(2) This paragraph applies where the absence is not expected to exceed 8 weeks and is in connection with the death of—

(a) the claimant's partner or a child or qualifying young person normally living with the claimant; or
(b) a close relative of—
 (i) the claimant;
 (ii) the claimant's partner; or
 (iii) a child or qualifying young person normally living with the claimant,

and the Secretary of State considers that it would be unreasonable to expect the claimant to return to Great Britain within 4 weeks.

(3) This paragraph applies where the absence is not expected to exceed 26 weeks and is solely in connection with—

(a) the claimant undergoing—
 (i) treatment for an illness or physical or mental impairment by, or under the supervision of, a qualified practitioner; or
 (ii) medically approved convalescence or care as a result of treatment for an illness or physical or mental impairment, where the claimant had that illness or impairment before leaving Great Britain; or
(b) the claimant accompanying his or her partner or a child or qualifying young person normally living with the claimant for treatment or convalescence or care as mentioned in sub-paragraph (a).

(4) In this regulation and in regulation 5—

"medically approved" means certified by a registered medical practitioner;
"qualified practitioner" means a person qualified to provide medical treatment, physiotherapy or a form of treatment which is similar to, or related to, either of those forms of treatment.]

DEFINITIONS

"close relative"—see reg.1(2).
"medically approved"—see para.(4).
"partner" —see reg.1(2).
"qualified practitioner"—see *ibid.*
"qualifying young person"—see reg.4A.

AMENDMENT

1. Housing Benefit and State Pension Credit (Temporary Absence) (Amendment) Regulations 2016 (SI 2016/624) reg.4(2) (July 28, 2016).

GENERAL NOTE

3.16 The generosity of the statutory provisions governing continuing entitlement to state pension credit for claimants temporarily absent from Great Britain has waxed and waned over the years. Initially, the general rule was that entitlement could only continue for up to four weeks. After October 2008, it became possible for pension credit to continue for up to 13 weeks during a temporary absence from GB, where the absence was unlikely to exceed 52 weeks. However, from 2008 there was no time limit in cases where the absence from GB was in order to receive medical treatment under NHS arrangements. But in November 2015, as part of the Spending Review and Autumn Statement, the Chancellor of the Exchequer announced that "The government will end the payment of Housing Benefit and Pension Credit to claimants who travel outside of Great Britain for longer than 4 weeks consecutively, from April 2016."

In the event these changes did not come into force until July 28, 2016 (see further below on transitional protection). According to official statements, the temporary absence period was reduced (in most cases) from 13 weeks to four weeks so as to achieve fairness in the benefits system, balancing the burden on taxpayers with support for claimants on low incomes. The four-week rule also aligns the new provisions for both housing benefit and state pension credit with universal credit.

The starting point now is the rule in the new reg.(3)(1)(a) that entitlement to state pension credit while the claimant is temporarily absent from Great Britain continues but for no longer than four weeks, "provided the absence is not expected to exceed 4 weeks". This default rule is subject to two exceptions.

3.17 The first exception (reg.3(1)(b) and 3(2)) is in the case of temporary absence from GB in connection with the death of a partner, a child or young person (see the new reg.4A). In such a case the four-week period can be extended by a further four weeks, if it would be unreasonable to expect a return to GB within four weeks. This exception also applies where the temporary absence is in connection with the death of a "close relative" (on which see the definition in reg.1(1)) of the claimant, or of their partner or of a child or young person normally living with the claimant

The second exception (reg.3(1)(c) and 3(3)) is in the event of temporary absence from GB due to the need to receive medical treatment or convalescence. In this type of case pension credit may continue for up to 26 weeks. Where the claimant is accompanying their partner or a child or a young person who lives with them for medical treatment or convalescence outside GB, then pension credit may also continue for up to 26 weeks. The effect of this amendment is simultaneously to broaden the range of circumstances where the medical exemption can apply (broadly equivalent to the position in universal credit) – so e.g. the exception is not confined to NHS arrangements – but to cap the previously indefinite period of continued entitlement at 26 weeks.

The new temporary absence from rules for pension credit claimants also apply to members of the claimant's household as well as the claimant (see amendments to reg.5 below).

Note also the transitional protection that may apply. Regulation 5(3) of the amending regulations provides that "Regulation 4 shall not apply in respect of a person who is temporarily absent from Great Britain on 28th July 2016 until the day that person returns to Great Britain." **3.18**

The amending regulations were the subject of a report by the SSAC, following an abridged consultation period (a report unhelpfully published in July 2016 under the same title as the regulations, namely *Housing Benefit and State Pension Credit (Temporary Absence) (Amendment) Regulations 2016 (S.I. 2016 No. 624)*). The Committee made a number of recommendations in respect of the new temporary absence provisions as they affected housing benefit claimants, some of which were accepted in part (e.g. a modification for housing benefit claimants who are victims of domestic violence). The government rejected a more general proposal that the default position be set at a temporary absence limit of eight weeks, rather than four weeks, which the SSAC had considered "would capture the hardest cases that are likely to be impacted by these proposals". The government also dismissed a proposal that decision makers be given discretion to extend the allowable period in individual cases where good cause was shown. This suggestion was rejected on the basis that it "would provide uncertainty for both customer and decision makers, as well as the potential for additional administrative costs".

[1 Persons temporarily absent from Great Britain on 6th October 2008

3A. [2 . . .]] **3.19**

AMENDMENTS

1. Social Security (Miscellaneous Amendments) (No.4) Regulations 2008 (SI 2008/2424) reg.3(3) (October 6, 2008).

2. Housing Benefit and State Pension Credit (Temporary Absence) (Amendment) Regulations 2016 (SI 2016/624) reg.4(3) (July 28, 2016).

GENERAL NOTE

This regulation, repealed with effect from July 28, 2016, was in effect a spent provision giving transitional protection for those claimants who were already temporarily absent from Great Britain on October 6, 2008. **3.20**

Persons receiving treatment outside Great Britain

4. [1 . . .] **3.21**

AMENDMENT

1. Housing Benefit and State Pension Credit (Temporary Absence) (Amendment) Regulations 2016 (SI 2016/624) reg.4(4) (July 28, 2016).

GENERAL NOTE

This regulation was repealed with effect from July 28, 2016. For the position of persons receiving treatment outside Great Britain, see now the new reg.3(3) above. **3.22**

[1 Meaning of "qualifying young person"

3.23 **4A.**—(1) A person who has reached the age of 16 but not the age of 20 is a qualifying young person for the purposes of these Regulations—

(a) up to, but not including, the 1st September following the person's 16th birthday; and

(b) up to, but not including, the 1st September following the person's 19th birthday, if the person is enrolled on, or accepted for, approved training or a course of education—

(i) which is not a course of advanced education within the meaning of regulation 12(3) of the Universal Credit Regulations 2013;

(ii) which is provided at a school or college or provided elsewhere but approved by the Secretary of State for the purposes of regulation 5 of the Universal Credit Regulations 2013; and

(iii) where the average time spent during term time in receiving tuition, engaging in practical work or supervised study or taking examinations exceeds 12 hours per week.

(2) Where the young person is aged 19, he or she must have started the education or training or been enrolled on or accepted for it before reaching that age.

(3) The education or training referred to in paragraph (1) does not include education or training provided by means of a contract of employment.

(4) "Approved training" means training in pursuance of arrangements made under section 2(1) of the Employment and Training Act 1973 or section 2(3) of the Enterprise and New Towns (Scotland) Act 1990 which is approved by the Secretary of State for the purposes of regulation 5 of the Universal Credit Regulations 2013.

(5) A person who is receiving universal credit, a contributory employment and support allowance, a contribution-based jobseeker's allowance, an income-related employment and support allowance, an income-based jobseeker's allowance or income support is not a qualifying young person.]

AMENDMENT

1. Housing Benefit and State Pension Credit (Temporary Absence) (Amendment) Regulations 2016 (SI 2016/624) reg.4(5) (July 28, 2016).

DEFINITIONS

"approved training"—see para.(4).
"contribution-based jobseeker's allowance"—see reg.1(2).
"contributory employment and support allowance"—see *ibid.*
"income-related employment and support allowance"—see *ibid.*
"income-based jobseeker's allowance"—see *ibid.*
"universal credit"—see *ibid.*

Persons treated as being or not being members of the same household

3.24 **5.**—(1) A person is to be treated as not being a member of the same household as the claimant if—

(a) he is living away from the claimant and—

(i) he does not intend to resume living with the claimant; or
(ii) his absence is likely to exceed 52 weeks except where there are exceptional circumstances (for example the person is in hospital or otherwise has no control over the length of his absence), and the absence is unlikely to be substantially more than 52 weeks;

(b) he or the claimant is permanently in a care home [[4]or an independent hospital];
(c) he or the claimant is, or both are—
(i) detained in a hospital provided under [[2] the provisions of the Mental Health Act 1983, the [[3] Mental Health (Care and Treatment) (Scotland) Act 2003], or the Criminal Procedure (Scotland) Act 1995; or]
(ii) detained in custody pending trial or sentence upon conviction or under a sentence imposed by a court; or
(iii) on temporary release in accordance with the provisions of the Prison Act 1952 or the Prison (Scotland) Act 1989;

(d) the claimant is abroad and does not satisfy [[2] . . .] regulation 3 (persons [[7] temporarily] absent from Great Britain);
(e) [[5] . . .]
[[7] (f) except in circumstances where paragraph (1A) applies, he is absent from Great Britain;]
[[1](g) [[2]. . .]
(h) he is a person subject to immigration control within the meaning of section 115(9) of the Immigration and Asylum Act 1999.]

[[5] [[7] (1A) A person is to be treated as being a member of the same household as the claimant while he is absent from Great Britain but for no longer than—

(a) 4 weeks, provided the absence is not expected to exceed 4 weeks;
(b) 8 weeks, where paragraph (1B) applies; or
(c) 26 weeks, where paragraph (1C) applies.

(1B) This paragraph applies where the absence is not expected to exceed 8 weeks and is in connection with the death of—

(a) a child or qualifying young person normally living with the person; or
(b) a close relative of—
(i) the person;
(ii) the person's partner; or
(iii) a child or qualifying young person normally living with the person,

and the Secretary of State considers that it would be unreasonable to expect the person to return to Great Britain within 4 weeks.

(1C) This paragraph applies where the absence is not expected to exceed 26 weeks and is solely in connection with—

(a) the person undergoing—
(i) treatment for an illness or physical or mental impairment by, or under the supervision of, a qualified practitioner; or
(ii) medically approved convalescence or care as a result of treatment for an illness or physical or mental impairment, where the person had that illness or impairment before leaving Great Britain; or

(b) the person accompanying his partner or a child or qualifying young person normally living with the person for treatment or convalescence or care as mentioned in sub-paragraph (a).]

(2) Subject to [8paragraphs (1) and (5)], partners shall be treated as members of the same household notwithstanding that they are temporarily living apart.

[6. . .]

[8(3) Paragraph (5) applies where a claimant ("C"), who has attained the qualifying age, would otherwise not be entitled to either state pension credit or universal credit, because—

(a) but for that paragraph, C would be a member of the same household as a partner who has not attained the qualifying age and therefore a member of a mixed-age couple excluded from state pension credit by virtue of section 4(1A), and

(b) C is neither entitled to universal credit jointly with that partner, nor entitled to universal credit as a single person, in one of the cases set out in paragraph (4).

(4) The cases are where C is not entitled to universal credit because C has attained the qualifying age and—

(a) any of the following paragraphs of regulation 3 of the Universal Credit Regulations 2013 (couples) applies, and in the case of paragraph (ii) below, one of the following circumstances applies—

(i) paragraph (3) (treatment of certain couples—universal credit may only be claimed as a single person);

(ii) paragraph (4) (treatment of polygamous marriages), so that C is not entitled to universal credit because C may only claim universal credit either as one of two parties to a polygamous marriage to be treated as a couple where the other party has also attained the qualifying age, or as a remaining party to such a marriage to be treated as single;

(iii) paragraph (6) (absence from the household—universal credit may only be claimed as a single person); or

(b) C lost joint entitlement to universal credit as part of a mixed-age couple due to one of the following changes of circumstances taking effect from a date (namely the first day of the universal credit assessment period in which the change occurred) that is earlier than when, but for paragraph (5), the same change would take effect for the purposes of state pension credit, those changes being where—

(i) C and their partner are no longer a couple; or

(ii) C is party to a marriage that is no longer polygamous and C's remaining spouse has attained the qualifying age.

(5) Where this paragraph applies—

(a) C and their partner, who are to be treated as a non-polygamous couple in accordance with sub-paragraph (a)(ii) of paragraph (4), or who are no longer parties to a polygamous marriage in accordance with sub-paragraph (b)(ii), are to be treated as members of the same household as each other but not of that of any party (or parties) with whom they are not part of a couple in accordance with those provisions; or

(b) C, who is to be treated as single in accordance with sub-paragraph (a)(i) to (iii) of paragraph (4), or is single in accordance with sub-paragraph (b)(i), is to be treated as though C is not a member of the same household as any party (or parties) with whom C is not part of a couple in accordance with those provisions,

where paragraph (4)(a) applies, with effect from the date on which the relevant paragraph of regulation 3 of the Universal Credit Regulations 2013 first applies to C, or, where paragraph (4)(b) applies, with effect from the date referred to in paragraph (4)(b) on which C lost entitlement to universal credit.

(6) In this regulation—

(a) in relation to universal credit entitlement, "assessment period" has the meaning prescribed by regulation 21 of the Universal Credit Regulations 2013;

(b) "mixed-age", in respect of a couple or a marriage, means where one member has attained the qualifying age and the other has not;

(c) the definition in sub-paragraph (b) includes a polygamous marriage where at least one party to the marriage has attained the qualifying age and at least one has not; and

(d) "polygamous marriage" means a marriage during which a party to it is married to more than one person and which took place under the laws of a country that permits polygamy.]

AMENDMENTS

1. State Pension Credit (Consequential, Transitional and Miscellaneous Provisions) (No.2) Regulations 2002 (SI 2002/3197) reg.2 and Sch. para.2 (October 6, 2003).

2. State Pension Credit (Transitional and Miscellaneous Provisions) Amendment Regulations 2003 (SI 2003/2274) reg.2(5) (October 6, 2003).

3. Mental Health (Care and Treatment) (Scotland) Act 2003 (Modification of Subordinate Legislation) Order 2005 (SSI 2005/445) art.2 and Sch. para.35(2) (October 3, 2005).

4. Social Security (Care Homes and Independent Hospitals) Regulations 2005 (SI 2005/2687) reg.6 and Sch.5 para.2 (October 24, 2005).

5. Social Security (Miscellaneous Amendments) (No.4) Regulations 2006 (SI 2006/2378) reg.14(2) (October 2, 2006).

6. Social Security (Miscellaneous Amendments) (No.4) Regulations 2008 (SI 2008/2424) reg.3(4) (October 6, 2008).

7. Housing Benefit and State Pension Credit (Temporary Absence) (Amendment) Regulations 2016 (SI 2016/624) reg.4(6) (July 28, 2016).

8. Universal Credit (Persons who have attained state pension credit qualifying age) (Amendment) Regulations 2020 (SI 2020/655) reg.2(2) (November 25, 2020).

MODIFICATION

The definition of "prisoner" in regulation 1(2) is modified as from April 8, 2020 by reg.3 of the Social Security (Coronavirus) (Prisoners) Regulations 2020 (SI 2020/409). For details of the modification, see the General Note to this regulation.

DEFINITIONS

"appropriately qualified"—see para.(3) and reg.3(4).
"care home"—see reg.1(2).
"claimant"—see SPCA 2002 s.17(1).
"close relative"—see reg.1(2).
"medically approved"—see reg.3(4).
"partner"—see reg.1(2).
"qualified practitioner"—see reg.3(4).
"qualifying young person"—see reg.4A.
"young person"—see para.(3) and reg.3(4).

General Note

3.25 This provision is modelled on the parallel rule relating to income support (see Income Support (General) Regulations 1987 (SI 1987/1967) reg.16, in Vol.V of this series), although the drafting is a little more straightforward. The starting point is that partners (i.e. members of a married or unmarried couple) are treated as members of the same household "notwithstanding that they are temporarily living apart" (para.(2)). In other words, membership of the same household does not cease simply because one partner is temporarily living elsewhere. This basic rule is then subject to the exceptions set out in para.(1), which replicate in part those that apply to income support.

Note that para.(1)(c)(iii) is "to be read as if the words 'the Prison Act 1952 or' were omitted" (see Social Security (Coronavirus) (Prisoners) Regulations 2020 (SI 2020/409) reg.3). The purpose of this change was to make provision for those individuals on temporary release from a prison in England and Wales due to the outbreak of COVID-19 in Great Britain to access means-tested benefits during the period of that release. In particular, it enables a person temporarily released from a prison in England and Wales to be included as a member of a claimant's household. The regulations must be kept under review by the Secretary of State and ceased to have effect on August 31, 2021 (see SI 2021/476 reg.4(6) amending SI 2020/409 reg.6).

Amount of the guarantee credit

3.26 **6.**—(1) Except as provided in the following provisions of these Regulations, the standard minimum guarantee is—

(a) [5£332.95] per week in the case of a claimant who has a partner;
(b) [5£218.15] per week in the case of a claimant who has no partner.

(2) Paragraph (3) applies in the case of—

(a) prisoners; and
(b) members of religious orders who are fully maintained by their order.

(3) In a case to which this paragraph applies—

(a) section 2(3) has effect with the substitution for the reference to the standard minimum guarantee in section 2(3)(a) of a reference to a [2nil] amount; and
(b) except in the case of a person who is a remand prisoner, [2 nil] is the prescribed additional amount for the purposes of section 2(3)(b).

(4) Except in a case to which paragraph (3) applies, an amount additional to that prescribed in paragraph (1) shall be applicable under paragraph (5) if the claimant is treated as being a severely disabled person in accordance with paragraph 1 of Part I of Schedule I.

(5) The additional amount applicable is—

(a) except where paragraph (b) applies, [5£81.50] per week if paragraph 1(1)(a), (b) or (c) of Part I of Schedule I is satisfied; or
(b) [5£163.00] per week if paragraph 1(1)(b) of Part I of Schedule I is satisfied otherwise than by virtue of paragraph 1(2)(b) of that Part and no one is entitled to and in receipt of an allowance under section 70 of the 1992 Act [4or carer support payment] [1, or has an award of universal credit which includes the carer element under regulation 29 of the Universal Credit Regulations 2013,] in respect of caring for either partner.

(6) Except in a case to which paragraph (3) applies, an amount additional to that prescribed in paragraph (1) shall be applicable—

(a) if paragraph 4 of Part II of Schedule I is satisfied (amount applicable for carers);

(b) in accordance with Part III of Schedule I (amount applicable for former claimants of income support or income-based jobseeker's allowance); [3 . . .]

(c) except where paragraph (7) applies, in accordance with Schedule II (housing costs) [3; or]

[3 (d) except where paragraph (11) applies, or entitlement ceases by virtue of paragraph (14), in accordance with Schedule IIA (additional amount applicable for claimants responsible for a child or qualifying young person).]

(7) This paragraph applies in the case of a person who has been detained in custody for more than 52 weeks pending trial or sentence following conviction by a court.

(8) The amount applicable if paragraph 4 of Part II of Schedule I is satisfied is [5£45.60] per week, and in the case of partners, this amount is applicable in respect of each partner who satisfies that paragraph.

(9) In the case of a remand prisoner paragraph (6) shall apply as if sub-paragraphs (a) and (b) were omitted.

(10) In this regulation, "remand prisoner" means a person who, for a period not exceeding 52 weeks, has been detained in custody on remand pending trial or, as a condition of bail, required to reside in a hostel approved under section 27(1) of the Probation Service Act 1993 or, as the case may be, detained pending sentence upon conviction.

[3 (11) This paragraph applies in the case of a person who is awarded, or who is treated as having an award of, a tax credit under the Tax Credits Act.

(12) For the purposes of paragraph (11)—

(a) a person is to be treated as having an award of a working tax credit with effect from the start of the current tax year even though a decision has not been made under section 14 of the Tax Credits Act in respect of a claim for that tax credit for that tax year, if the person was awarded a working tax credit for the previous tax year and any of the cases specified in paragraph (13) applies; and

(b) a person is to be treated as having an award of a child tax credit with effect from the start of the current tax year even though a decision has not been made under section 14 of the Tax Credits Act in respect of a claim for that tax credit for that tax year, if the person was awarded a child tax credit for the previous tax year and any of the cases specified in paragraph (13) applies.

(13) The cases specified for the purposes of paragraph (12) are—

(a) a final notice has not been given to the person under section 17 of the Tax Credits Act in respect of the previous tax year;

(b) a final notice has been given which includes provision by virtue of subsection (2) or (4) of section 17, or a combination of those subsections and subsection (6), and—

(i) the date specified in the notice for the purposes of section 17(2) and (4) or, where different dates are specified, the later of them has not passed and no claim for a tax credit for the current tax year has been made or treated as made; or

(ii) a claim for a tax credit has been made or treated as made on or before the date mentioned in paragraph (i), but no decision has been made in relation to that claim under section 14 of that Act; or

(c) a final notice has been given, no claim for a tax credit for the current tax year has been made or treated as made, and no decision has been made under section 18(1) of the Tax Credits Act in respect of an award of a tax credit for the previous tax year.

(14) Entitlement to the additional amount specified in Schedule IIA ceases where a person is awarded a tax credit in the circumstances specified in paragraph (15) or (16).

(15) The circumstances specified in this paragraph are—

(a) the person was awarded a tax credit for the previous tax year which was not terminated by Her Majesty's Revenue and Customs under section 16 of the Tax Credits Act;

(b) a final notice has been given to the person under section 17 of the Tax Credits Act in respect of that tax year; and

(c) either—

(i) the person makes a declaration during the period of 30 days following the cessation of payment of a tax credit made under section 24(4) of the Tax Credits Act; or

(ii) the person makes a declaration after the end of the period of 30 days following the cessation of payment of a tax credit made under section 24(4) of the Tax Credits Act but before 31st January of the tax year following the period to which the notice relates, and, in the opinion of Her Majesty's Revenue and Customs, the person had good reason for not making the declaration by the date specified in paragraph (13)(b).

(16) The circumstances specified in this paragraph are that a decision under section 14(1), 15(1), 16(1), 18(1), (5), (6) or (9), 19(3) or 20(1) or (4) of the Tax Credits Act is revised in favour of the claimant following—

(a) a revision by virtue of section 21 of the Tax Credits Act;

(b) a request for a review under section 21A of the Tax Credits Act;

(c) an appeal under section 38 of the Tax Credits Act; or

(d) a revision, in any other circumstances, of a decision by Her Majesty's Revenue and Customs relating to an award of a tax credit under the Tax Credits Act.

(17) In this regulation—

"a tax credit" includes a child tax credit and a working tax credit;

"the Tax Credits Act" means the Tax Credits Act 2002;

"child tax credit" means a child tax credit under and by virtue of section 8 of the Tax Credits Act;

"working tax credit" means a working tax credit under and by virtue of section 10 of the Tax Credits Act and includes the child care element by virtue of section 12 of that Act.]

AMENDMENTS

1. Universal Credit and Miscellaneous Amendments Regulations 2015 (SI 2015/1754) reg.16(2) (November 4, 2015).

2. Social Security Benefits Up-rating Order 2017 (SI 2017/260) art.25(2) and Sch.13 (April 10, 2017).

3. State Pension Credit (Additional Amount for Child or Qualifying Young Person) (Amendment) Regulations 2018 (SI 2018/676), reg.2(2) and (3) (February 1, 2019).

4. Carer's Assistance (Carer Support Payment) (Scotland) Regulations 2023 (Consequential Amendments) Order 2023 (SI 2023/1218) art.14(3) (November 19, 2023).
5. Social Security Benefits Up-rating Order 2024 (SI 2024/242) art.29(2) (April 8, 2024).

Definitions

"the 1992 Act"—see reg.1(2).
"child tax credit"—see para.(17)
"claimant"—see SPCA 2002 s.17(1).
"partner"—see reg.1(3).
"prisoner"—see reg.1(2).
"remand prisoner"—see para.(10).
"a tax credit"—see para.(17).
"the Tax Credits Act"—see *ibid.*
"working tax credit"—see *ibid.*

General Note

Paragraph (1)

The general conditions of entitlement to state pension credit are set out in s.1 of the SPCA 2002, with the supplementary conditions for the guarantee credit component contained in s.2. The amount of the guarantee credit is the "appropriate minimum guarantee" for claimants with no income and the difference between that figure and the person's income in other cases (s.2(2)). The "appropriate minimum guarantee" is comprised of the "standard minimum guarantee" and such other amounts as may be prescribed. This provision sets out the amount of the "standard minimum guarantee" for individual claimants and couples respectively. The "standard minimum guarantee" therefore performs broadly the same function as the age-related personal allowance taken together with the former pensioner premium in the income support scheme before that was subject to amendments consequential upon the coming into force of the SPCA 2002. This figure is then aggregated together with other prescribed amounts as set out in the remaining paragraphs of this regulation and Sch.1 to these Regulations to produce the "appropriate minimum guarantee" (or applicable amount in income support terms). The calculation used to arrive at the final guarantee credit is then as provided for by s.2(2) of the SPCA 2002, as described above. 3.27

Paragraphs (2) and (3)

As with income support (see the Income Support (General) Regulations 1987 (SI 1987/1967) Sch.7 paras 7 and 8, in Vol.V of this series), prisoners and those fully maintained by their religious orders effectively have no entitlement to the guarantee credit, as their living costs are met from other sources. They also have a nil entitlement to the savings credit (reg.7(3)). 3.28

See further *CSPC/677/2007*, the lead case of several involving claims for state pension credit by nuns who were all members of a Carmelite closed order. Any income received by an individual nun was paid into a monastery account, which held the funds in common. Commissioner May QC held that in these circumstances the nuns were fully maintained by their order; no distinction could be made between those nuns who contributed their own income and those who had no income. Nor could any distinction be made between those orders which were self-maintaining and those which were not. The Commissioner also held that neither art.1 of Prot.1 nor art.8 of the European Convention on Human Rights was engaged.

Furthermore, in *Secretary of State for Work and Pensions v Sister IS and KM* [2009] UKUT 200 (AAC), where the claimants were Benedictine and Carmelite nuns, a three-judge panel of the Upper Tribunal ruled that: (1) the expression "religious order" in reg.6(2)(b) is to be read in the broader sense of that term found in dictionaries; it is not limited to those religious communities subject to a centralised authority or control; (2) the nuns in question were fully maintained from funds held by their orders, and that it did not matter from what source the funds originated (whether by their own work or any entitlement to benefits which contributed to the order's funds); and (3) it was possible to remove any element of religious discrimination (if there was one) in reg.6(2)(b) "by removing the reference to religion. That would leave the provision to apply to 'members of religious orders who are fully maintained by their order'."

The claimant's further appeal to the Court of Appeal was dismissed in *Scott v Secretary of State for Social Security* [2011] EWCA Civ 103; [2011] AACR 23. The Court held that the Upper Tribunal had not misdirected itself as to the proper construction of the phrase "fully maintained"; the proposition that "full maintenance" was only conceptually possible if the recipient of the funds was making no contribution could not be read into the Regulations. There was no doubt that the claimant was being "fully maintained" by her community when she made her claim. Her work was not for her own personal benefit, but exclusively for the trust, in return for which she received the benefit of bed and board under the trust arrangements in place. It followed that her maintenance was provided by the trust, rather than, as the Upper Tribunal had found, directly from her own efforts.

Paragraphs (4) and (5)

3.29 Section 2(7) of the SPCA 2002, which mirrors SSCBA 1992 s.135(5), requires an additional amount to be prescribed (for the purposes of calculating the "appropriate minimum guarantee") for severely disabled people. The qualifying criteria for this additional amount, which essentially performs the same function as the severe disability premium in the income support scheme, are set out in para.1 of Sch.1 to these Regulations. See further *DB (as executor of the estate of OE) v SSWP and Birmingham CC (SPC)* [2018] UKUT 46 (AAC). See *HT v SSWP (AA)* [2020] UKUT 57 (AAC) for an example of a case where receipt of an equivalent Polish disability benefit qualified for these purposes.

Paragraphs (6)–(10)

3.30 Further additional amounts for the purposes of calculating the "appropriate minimum guarantee" are prescribed for carers, former claimants of income support or income-based jobseeker's allowance, in respect of housing costs and for claimants entitled to the standard minimum guarantee who are responsible for a child or qualifying young person but do not have an award of a tax credit.

This last type of additional amount was introduced to compensate for the abolition of child tax credit by the Welfare Reform Act 2012. The amendment ensures that low income pensioners who are responsible for a child or young person continue to receive financial support akin to CTC. The criteria for the award of such an additional amount are set out in the new Sch.IIA. This Schedule applies to a claimant who is responsible for a "child" or "qualifying young person" (para.1); defines the terms "child" and "qualifying young person" (para.2); sets out the circumstances in which a person is, or is not, to be treated as responsible for a child or qualifying young person (paras 3 to 8); specifies the additional amount of benefit applicable to a claimant where he or she is responsible for a child or qualifying young person (the amount is increased if the child or qualifying young person is entitled to DLA or PIP or if they are certified as severely sight impaired or blind) (para.9); and provides for a higher amount to be payable where the eldest child or qualifying young person was born before April 6, 2017 (para.10).

Paragraphs (8)–(10)

3.31 The amount of the carer additional amount is set out in para.(8); the other additional amounts are detailed in Pt III of Sch.1, and Sch.2 to these Regulations respectively. Prisoners and fully maintained members of religious orders are not eligible for such additional amounts. Furthermore, those who have been detained in custody for more than 52 weeks pending trial or sentence following conviction are not eligible for housing costs. Note also that remand prisoners are in any event not eligible for the additional amounts prescribed for carers and for former claimants of income support or income-based jobseeker's allowance (paras (9) and (10)).

Paragraphs (11)–(17)

3.32 The effect of the addition of para.(6)(d) is to provide for the payment of an additional amount to a pension credit claimant who is entitled to the standard minimum guarantee, so long as that claimant is responsible for a child or qualifying young person and does not have an award of a tax credit (see paras (11) and (14)). Paragraph 11 provides for a person "who is awarded, or who is treated as having an award of, a tax credit" to be excluded from entitlement to the additional amount for a child or QYP. The relevant circumstances are as defined by paras (12) and (13). Paragraph (14) provides for a person to cease to be entitled to such an additional amount "where a person is awarded a tax credit in the circumstances specified in paragraph (15) or (16)".

Savings Credit

3.33 **7.**—(1) The percentage prescribed for the purposes of determining—

(a) the maximum savings credit is [2 60 per cent];

(b) "amount A" in section 3(4) is [2 60 per cent];

(c) "amount B" in section 3(4) is [2 40 per cent].

(2) The amount prescribed for the savings credit threshold is [3£189.90] for a claimant who has no partner and [3£301.22] for a claimant who has a partner.

(3) The maximum savings credit shall be taken to be [2 nil] in the case of—

(a) prisoners; and

(b) members of religious orders who are fully maintained by their order.

[1(4) If a calculation made for the purposes of paragraph (1)(b) or (c) results in a fraction of a penny, that fraction shall, if it would be to the claimant's advantage, be treated as a penny; otherwise it shall be disregarded.]

AMENDMENTS

1. State Pension Credit (Consequential, Transitional and Miscellaneous Provisions) Regulations 2002 (SI 2002/3019) reg.23(d) (October 6, 2003).

2. Social Security Benefits Up-rating Order 2017 (SI 2017/260), art.25(3) and (6) and Sch.13 (April 10, 2017).

3. Social Security Benefits Up-rating Order 2024 (SI 2024/242) art.29(3) (April 8, 2024).

DEFINITIONS

"claimant"—see SPCA 2002 s.17(1).
"partner"—see reg.1(3).
"prisoner"—see reg.1(2).

GENERAL NOTE

3.34 See annotations to s.3 of the SPCA 2002 for a full explanation as to the calculation of the savings credit. This regulation prescribes the relevant percentages (para.(1)) for the purposes of that calculation, specifies the savings credit threshold for individuals and couples (para.(2)) and excludes prisoners and fully maintained members of religious orders (para.(3)).

[1 Limitation of savings credit for certain mixed-age couples

3.35 **7A.**—A person who is a member of a mixed-age couple, is not entitled to a savings credit unless one of the members of the couple—

(a) has been awarded a savings credit with effect from a day before 6th April 2016 and was entitled to a savings credit immediately before 6th April 2016, and

(b) remained entitled to a savings credit at all times since the beginning of 6th April 2016.]

AMENDMENT

1. Pension Credit (Amendment) Regulations 2015 (SI 2015/1529) reg.2(2) (April 6, 2016).

DEFINITION

"couple"—see reg.1(2).

GENERAL NOTE

3.36 The first requirement for entitlement to the savings credit element of pension credit, as originally enacted, was that the claimant (or their partner) was at least 65 (State Pension Credit Act 2002, s.3(1)). However, as a result of amendments made by the Pensions Act 2014, there is no longer access to the savings credit element for those claimants reaching state pension age on or after April 6, 2016 unless they are a member of a couple where their partner reached state pension age before that date (known as "a mixed-age couple"). Section 3ZA of the 2002 Act provides the enabling power for entitlement to the savings credit to be so restricted and defines what is meant by a "mixed-age couple". This regulation specifies the conditions which must be met for a mixed-age couple to qualify for savings credit. Although the drafting of the regulation suggests that there are only two pre-conditions, in reality there are three. First, one member must have attained state pension age before April 6, 2016. Secondly, that person must have been entitled to savings credit immediately before April 6, 2016. Thirdly, that individual must have been entitled to savings credit at all times since that date.

Special groups

3.37 **8.**—Schedule III shall have effect in the case of members of polygamous marriages and [1 persons serving a sentence of imprisonment detained in hospital].

AMENDMENT

1. Social Security (Persons Serving a Sentence of Imprisonment Detained in Hospital) Regulations 2010 (SI 2010/442) reg.4(2) (March 25, 2010).

GENERAL NOTE

3.38 Section 12 of the SPCA 2002 enables special provision to be made for members of polygamous marriages. Special provision for other persons is authorised by the general regulation-making powers in SSCBA 1992 s.175 which apply in this context by virtue of SPCA 2002 s.19(1).

Qualifying income for the purposes of savings credit

9.—For the purposes of section 3 (savings credit), all income is to be treated as qualifying income except the following which is not to be treated as qualifying income— 3.39

(a) working tax credit;
(b) incapacity benefit;
(c) a contribution-based jobseeker's allowance [2 . . .]
(d) severe disablement allowance;
(e) maternity allowance;
(f) payments referred to in regulation 15(5)(d) (maintenance payments).
[1 (g) contributory employment and support allowance.]

AMENDMENTS

1. Employment and Support Allowance (Consequential Provisions) (No.2) Regulations 2008 (SI 2008/1554) reg.4(3) (October 27, 2008).
2. Universal Credit (Consequential, Supplementary, Incidental and Miscellaneous Provisions) Regulations 2013 (SI 2013/630) reg.33(3) (April 29, 2013).

GENERAL NOTE

WTC and the other benefits and payments listed here are excluded from the definition of qualifying income for the purpose of calculating the savings credit under SPCA 2002 s.3. 3.40

In *CPC/4177/2005* Commissioner May QC dismissed a challenge to reg.9(d) based on Directive 79/7 (equal treatment). The Commissioner ruled that art.4 of the Directive was engaged for the purposes of the savings credit element of pension credit (but not for the guaranteed credit). The Commissioner then held that there was no discrimination and so no breach of art.4 of the Directive. However, the reasoning in this decision may be revisited in subsequent decisions–e.g. it is less than clear that it is permissible to "sever" pension credit into its constituent elements, given that jobseeker's allowance is treated as one benefit (see *Hockenjos v Secretary of State for Social Security* [2001] EWCA Civ 624; [2001] 2 C.M.L.R. 51). It should also be noted that in *CPC/4177/2005* the claimant did not attend the Commissioner's oral hearing and was unrepresented.

In *CPC/4173/2007* the claimant, aged 76, lived with her husband, aged 61, who received incapacity benefit. Her husband's incapacity benefit did not count as qualifying income for the purposes of savings credit by virtue of reg.9(b). The claimant argued that this was discriminatory as a woman of the same age as her husband would have received retirement pension (which does count as qualifying income). Commissioner Howell QC held that reg.9 does not contravene art.14 of the European Convention, as there was no differential treatment by reason of status. The Commissioner also ruled that there was no breach of Council Directive 79/7/EEC on equal treatment, as the circumstances fell squarely within the exclusion in art.7, which related to the determination of pensionable ages. Moreover, the Sex Discrimination Act 1975 had no application in this context.

Assessed income period

10.—(1) For the purposes of section 6(2)(b) (circumstances in which the Secretary of State is prevented from specifying an assessed income period), the circumstances are— 3.41

(a) in the case of partners, one partner is under the age of 60; or

(b) state pension credit is awarded, or awarded at a higher rate, because an element of the claimant's retirement provision which is due to be paid to the claimant stops temporarily.

[[2] (c) that—

(i) the Secretary of State has sent the claimant the notification required by regulation 32(6)(a) of the Claims and Payments Regulations; and

(ii) the claimant has not provided sufficient information to enable the Secretary of State to determine whether there will be any variation in the claimant's retirement provision throughout the period of 12 months beginning with the day following the day on which the previous assessed income period ends.]

(2) The circumstances prescribed for the purposes of section 7(4) (circumstances in which assessed amounts are deemed not to change) are that—

[[4] (a) except where sub-paragraph (b) applies, the arrangements under which the assessed amount is paid contain no provision for periodic increases in the amount payable; or]

(b) the assessed income comprises income from capital other than income to which paragraph (7) applies.

(3) Paragraphs (4) and (5) do not apply where the assessed amount comprises income from capital.

(4) Where the Secretary of State is informed that the arrangements under which the assessed amount is paid contains provision—

(a) for the payment to be increased periodically;

(b) for the date on which the increase is to be paid; and

(c) for determining the amount of the increase, the assessed amount shall be deemed to increase from the day specified in paragraph (5) by an amount determined by applying those provisions to the amount payable apart from this paragraph.

[[3] (5) The day referred to in this paragraph is—

(a) in a case to which paragraph (5A) applies—

(i) where the first increased payment date is the day on which the benefit week begins, that day;

(ii) where head (i) does not apply, the first day of the next benefit week which begins after that increased payment date;

(b) in a case to which paragraph (5A) does not apply—

(i) where the second increased payment date is the day on which the benefit week begins, that day;

(ii) where head (i) does not apply, the first day of the next benefit week following that increased payment date.

(5A) This paragraph applies where the period which—

(a) begins on the date from which the increase in the assessed amount is to accrue; and

(b) ends on the first increased payment date,

is a period of the same length as the period in respect of which the last payment of the pre-increase assessed amount was made.

(5B) In paragraphs (5) and (5A)—

"increased payment date" means a date on which the increase in the assessed amount referred to in paragraph (4) is paid as part of a periodic payment [[4] . . .]; and "pre-increase assessed amount" means the assessed amount prior to that increase.]

(6) Except where paragraph (4) applies, the assessed amount shall be deemed to increase—

[[3] (a) on the day in April each year on which increases under section 150 (1)(c) of the Administration Act come into force if that is the first day of a benefit week but if it is not from the next following such day; and]

(b) by an amount produced by applying to the assessed amount the same percentage increase as that applied for the purposes of additional pensions under section 150(1)(c) and 151(1) of the Administration Act.

(7) Where the assessed amount comprises income from capital, it shall be deemed to increase or decrease—

(a) on the first day of the next benefit week to commence [[1]on or after] the day on which the income increases or decreases; and

(b) by an amount equal to the change in the claimant's income produced by applying to his income changes made to the yields capital is deemed to produce, or to the capital amounts, specified in regulation 15(6), or to both if both are changed.

(8) [[5] . . .]

AMENDMENTS

1. State Pension Credit (Consequential, Transitional and Miscellaneous Provisions) Regulations 2002 (SI 2002/3019) reg.23(e) (October 6, 2003).

2. State Pension Credit (Transitional and Miscellaneous Provisions) Amendment Regulations 2003 (SI 2003/2274) reg.2(6) (October 6, 2003).

3. State Pension Credit (Miscellaneous Amendments) Regulations 2004 (SI 2004/647) reg.3(2) and (3) (April 5, 2004).

4. State Pension Credit (Amendment) Regulations 2005 (SI 2005/3205) reg.2(2) (December 18, 2005).

5. Social Security (Miscellaneous Amendments) (No.4) Regulations 2006 (SI 2006/2378) reg.14(3) (October 2, 2006).

DEFINITIONS

"the Administration Act"—see SPCA 2002 s.17(1).
"assessed income period"—see *ibid.*
"benefit week"—see reg.1(2).
"claimant"—see SPCA 2002 s.17(1).
"increased payment date"—see para.(5B).
"partner"—see reg.1(3).
"pay day"—see para.(8).
"pre-increase assessed amount"—see para.(5B).
"retirement provision"—see SPCA 2002 ss.7(6) and 17(1).

GENERAL NOTE

The "assessed income period" was central to the original conception of the state pension credit. Recognising that the traditional weekly means test of income support has been an important factor in the relatively low take-up of that benefit amongst pensioners, the Government initially adopted a very different strategy for state pension credit. Section 6(1) of the SPCA 2002 imposed a duty on the Secretary of State to specify an assessed income period when making a decision on a state pension credit claim. In normal circumstances, the assessed income period was fixed at five 3.42

years from the date that decision took effect (SPCA 2002 s.9(1)). The principle then was that changes in the pensioner's income during that period need not be reported and thus any increases in income did not, of themselves, result in disentitlement or run the risk of overpayments accruing. Instead, the claimant's income throughout the five-year period was deemed to be the same as the income at the outset (*ibid.*, and s.7(3)), subject to deemed cost of living increases (*ibid.* and s.7(4)).

See further *CPC/0206/2005*, discussed in the note to State Pension Credit Act 2002 s.7 and *CPC/1928/2005*, discussed in the note to s.9 of that Act.

However, as a result of the Pensions Act 2014, assessed income periods will be phased out as from April 2016. As a result, any change in retirement income will in future need to be reported to the Department when it occurs, triggering a review and change in benefit award where appropriate.

Paragraph (1)

3.43 Section 6(2) of the SPCA 2002 provides that the Secretary of State is prevented from specifying a standard assessed income period under s.6(1) in two categories of case. The first is where an assessed income period is already in force in the claimant's case by virtue of an earlier application of the s.6 rule. The second comprises "such other circumstances as may be prescribed" (SPCA 2002 s.6(2)(b)). This paragraph prescribes two such types of case. The first is where the claimant is a member of a couple and one partner is aged under 60. This inevitably increases the likelihood that they are in (or may re-enter) the labour market and so a five-year "deeming rule" may be inappropriate. The second is where there has been a temporary cessation of the claimant's retirement provision leading to an award (or higher award) of state pension credit.

Presumably the insertion of reg.10(1)(c) should be read as being preceded by the word "or" at the end of reg.10(1)(b).

Paragraph (2)

3.44 As explained in the General Note above, the normal rule is that the amount of income fixed at the date of claim (the "assessed amount") is deemed to be the claimant's income throughout the assessed income period, subject to cost of living increases (SPCA 2002 s.7(3) and (4)). The prescribed cost of living increases in a claimant's assessed income do not operate where there is no clause in the claimant's pension scheme or annuity contract which provides for such periodic increases in the amount payable. The assessed amount is also not periodically uprated where it comprises income from capital (except income covered by para. (7) below).

Paragraphs (3)–(5)

3.45 Many occupational and personal schemes will include provisions for periodic (typically annual) increases in the amount payable, which also specify when such increases are to be paid and how they are to be calculated. Where the Secretary of State is informed that such arrangements exist, then para.(4) enables the claimant's assessed income to be increased accordingly, reflecting such improvements in pension provision. The increase is deemed to apply from the start of the benefit week if the increase under the pension scheme is due to be paid on that day or, failing that, from the start of the next benefit week (para.(5)). For cases not covered by para.(4), see para.(6). These provisions do not apply where the assessed income comprises income from capital (para.(3); see further para (7)).

Paragraph (6)

3.46 In the event that the pension scheme does not include a provision which meets the criteria of para.(4), the default position is that the assessed amount is increased in line with the percentage increase stipulated by the Secretary of State as the amount by which additional pensions are to be increased.

Paragraph (7)

If the assessed amount comprises income from capital, it is deemed to increase (or decrease) in line with the tariff income rule under reg.15(6). 3.47

Retirement provision in assessed income period

11.—[1 (1) Where an element of a person's retirement provision ceases to be payable by one source but— 3.48

(a) responsibility for that element is assumed by another source, income from both those sources shall be treated as income from the same source; or

(b) in consequence of that element ceasing, income of a different description becomes payable from a different source, that income shall be treated as income of the same description from the same source as the element which ceased to be payable.

[1 (2) For the purposes of section 7(6) (meaning of retirement provision) of the Act, a foreign state retirement pension is to be treated as a benefit under the 1992 Act.]

AMENDMENT

1. Social Security (Miscellaneous Amendments) (No.2) Regulations 2010 (SI 2010/641) reg.6(4) (April 13, 2010).

DEFINITION

"retirement provision"—see ss.7(6) and 17(1) of the SPCA 2002.

GENERAL NOTE

The purpose of this provision is to ensure that the assessed income period continues notwithstanding the fact that responsibility for a pensioner's retirement provision changes (e.g. from one pension provider to another). The addition of para. (2) was designed to reverse the effect of *CPC/571/2008*. 3.49

End of assessed income period

12.—An assessed income period shall end [2 . . .] 3.50

(a) [2 at such time as] the claimant no longer satisfies a condition of entitlement to state pension credit;

(b) [2 at such time as] payments of an element of the claimant's retirement provision which is due to be paid to him stops temporarily or the amount paid is less than the amount due and in consequence his award of state pension credit is superseded under section 10 of the Social Security Act 1998;

(c) [2 at such time as] a claimant who has no partner is provided with accommodation in a care home [1 or an independent hospital] other than on a temporary basis [2;

(d) if, apart from this sub-paragraph, it would have ended on a date falling within the period specified in column 1 of the table in Schedule IIIA, on the corresponding date shown against that period in column 2 of that table.]

AMENDMENTS

1. Social Security (Care Homes and Independent Hospitals) Regulations 2005 (SI 2005/2687) reg.6 and Sch.5 para.3 (October 24, 2005).

2. State Pension Credit (Amendment) Regulations 2015 (SI 2015/1529) reg.2(3) (April 6, 2016).

DEFINITIONS

"assessed income period"—see SPCA 2002 ss.6, 9 and 17(1).
"care home"—see reg.1(2).
"claimant"—see SPCA 2002 s.17(1).
"partner"—see reg.1(3).
"retirement provision"—see ss.7(6) and 17(1) of the SPCA 2002.

GENERAL NOTE

3.51 The Assessed Income Period (AIP), a feature of pension credit from its introduction in 2003, removed the requirement for many recipients aged 65 and over to notify the DWP of changes to their retirement provision (i.e. savings and non-state pensions) during a set period. The maximum length of an AIP was five years in the case of recipients under the age of 75 when their AIP was set, but an indefinite period for those aged 75 or over. Changes which would increase the award could still be notified during an AIP and lead to a change in the award; changes that would reduce the award were assessed if they are notified, but the award itself was not changed until the end of the AIP.

Thus the normal rule was that the assessed income period would last for five years (SPCA 2002 s.9(1)). The primary legislation provides for various exceptions to this principle, namely where the claimant becomes (or ceases to be) a member of a couple, reaches the age of 65 or (in the case of a couple) where their partner attains 65 (*ibid.*, and s.9(4)). The regulation originally provided for just three further and restricted circumstances in which that period will end before the expiry of five years—where the claimant no longer satisfies a condition of entitlement (para.12(a)), where there is a fall in income provided by way of retirement provision (para.12(b)), and where a single claimant goes into long-term care (para.12(c)). The underlying thinking is that instead of having to report the multitudinous changes of circumstances required under the income support scheme, state pension credit claimants will only have to report the sorts of significant life changes which have to be reported in any event for state pension purposes (e.g. bereavement, remarriage, moving into a care home).

As a result of the amendments made by the Pensions Act 2014 (see s.28), there is now a fourth and further situation in which assessed income periods will cease. This restriction is far more significant. The effect of the Pensions Act 2014 is to limit the application of the AIP legislation to decisions that took effect *before* April 6, 2016. Consequently, and as from April 6, 2016, no new AIPs have been or will be set. Where this change takes effect, any change in retirement provision must accordingly be reported by the claimant when it occurs, triggering an immediate review and (where appropriate) a change of the pension credit award. The position with AIPs already set before April 6, 2016 is that they will remain valid beyond that date, until such time as they end—whether through natural expiry, being phased out early, or under the existing rules on reporting changes of circumstances.

3.52 The effect of the new reg.12(d) is to bring to an end all pre-April 6, 2016 AIPs within three years (being the necessary time frame to achieve the annual expenditure savings agreed in the Government's 2013 Spending Round; the removal of the AIP is expected to generate savings of approximately £80 million per year by 2020/21). As a result, and as from April 2016, existing AIPs due to end on a date between April 2016 and March 2019 will run their course until they end (in whatever circumstances under the current rules); and existing AIPs that would otherwise be due to end after March 2019 will be brought forward to end on a specified date between July 2016 and March 2019. Consequently, by April 2019, the only AIPs still in existence should be those that were set indefinitely prior to April 6, 2016 (and where the claimants' circumstances have remained unchanged). The details of those AIPs which will be ended early are set out in a table to these Regulations, added as Schedule IIIA. Column 1 of the table in Sch.IIIA sets out the dates when these AIPs were originally due to be terminated, while Column 2 of Sch.IIIA provides the new dates on which they will now end. The Department's intention is that recipients with a fixed-term AIP which is to be ended early will receive a letter giving six months' advance notice of their revised end-date. The table contains several gaps between some of the months; the purpose of this which is to allow the Department's Operations branch to distribute and manage the prescribed volumes, including customer contact and explanation of benefit revision. As the fixed-term AIPs come to an end, the intention is that in future periodic case reviews will be conducted on those cases. These are generally conducted on a three-yearly basis, but the intervals for reviews are not set out in existing legislation and can therefore be applied more flexibly in practice.

The decision to abolish AIPs was taken as part of the 2013 Spending Round. The policy justification was that when AIPs were introduced, it was assumed that pensioners are more likely to have relatively stable income and capital. However, the Government has argued that this assumption has not proved to be correct. In particular, recent analysis suggests that pensioners' financial circumstances change more significantly than was anticipated (see DWP, *Abolition of Assessed Income Periods for Pension Credit; Impact Assessment*, October 2013, especially pp.10–11). As a result, fixing retirement provision for a long period has allowed some recipients to keep their benefit despite obtaining higher amounts of capital or new income streams—whereas if an AIP were not in place in these cases, the award would be either reduced or removed entirely.

Small amounts of state pension credit

13.—Where the amount of state pension credit payable is less than 10 pence per week, the credit shall not be payable unless the claimant is in receipt of another benefit payable with the credit. 3.53

Definition

"claimant"—see SPCA 2002 s.17(1).

General Note

This applies the same de minimis rule as operates in the income support scheme (Social Security (Claims and Payments) Regulations 1987 (SI 1987/1968) reg.26(4)): see Vol.III). 3.54

[1Part-weeks

13A.—(1) The guarantee credit shall be payable for a period of less than a week ("a part-week") at the rate specified in paragraph (3) if— 3.55

(a) the claimant was entitled to [3 universal credit,] income support [2, an income-related employment and support allowance] or an income-based jobseeker's allowance immediately before the first day on which the conditions for entitlement to the credit are satisfied; and

(b) the claimant's entitlement to the credit is likely to continue throughout the first full benefit week which follows the part-week.

(2) For the purpose of determining the amount of the guarantee credit payable in respect of the part-week, no regard shall be had to any income of the claimant and his partner.

(3) The amount of the guarantee credit payable in respect of the part-week shall be determined—

(a) by dividing by 7 the weekly amount of the guarantee credit which, taking into account the requirements of paragraph (2), would be payable in respect of a full week; and then

(b) multiplying the resulting figure by the number of days in the part-week,

any fraction of a penny being rounded up to the nearest penny.]

AMENDMENTS

1. State Pension Credit (Consequential, Transitional and Miscellaneous Provisions) Regulations 2002 (SI 2002/3019) reg.23(f) (October 6, 2003).

2. Employment and Support Allowance (Consequential Provisions) (No.2) Regulations 2008 (SI 2008/1554) reg.4(4) (October 27, 2008).

3. Universal Credit (Consequential, Supplementary, Incidental and Miscellaneous Provisions) Regulations 2013 (SI 2013/630) reg.33(4) (April 29, 2013).

DEFINITIONS

"a part-week"—see para.1.

"benefit week"—see reg.1(2).

"claimant"—see SPCA 2002 s.17(1).

"partner"—see reg.1(3).

GENERAL NOTE

3.56 This regulation provides for a simple means of ensuring continuity of payment for claimants transferring from income support or income-based jobseeker's allowance to state pension credit. Claimants in such circumstances are entitled to a part-week payment of the guarantee credit to take them up to the start of their first week on state pension credit. This part week payment is paid irrespective of the claimant's income (or that of their partner) (para.(2)). Note that there is no provision for part week payments of the savings credit.

[[1]Date on which benefits are treated as paid

3.57 **13B.**—(1) The following benefits shall be treated as paid on the day of the week in respect of which the benefit is payable—

(a) severe disablement allowance;

(b) short-term and long-term incapacity benefit;

(c) maternity allowance;

(d) contribution-based jobseeker's allowance [[4] . . .]

[[3] (e) contributory employment and support allowance.]

(2) All benefits except those mentioned in paragraph (1) shall be treated as paid on the first day of the benefit week in [[2] . . .] which the benefit is payable.]

AMENDMENTS

1. State Pension Credit (Consequential, Transitional and Miscellaneous Provisions) Regulations 2002 (SI 2002/3019) reg.23(f) (October 6, 2003).

2. State Pension Credit (Consequential, Transitional and Miscellaneous Provisions) (No.2) Regulations 2002 (SI 2002/3197) reg.2 and Sch. para.3 (October 6, 2003).

3. Employment and Support Allowance (Consequential Provisions) (No.2) Regulations 2008 (SI 2008/1554) reg.4(5) (October 27, 2008).

4. Universal Credit (Consequential, Supplementary, Incidental and Miscellaneous Provisions) Regulations 2013 (SI 2013/630) reg.33(5) (April 29, 2013).

DEFINITION

"benefit week"—see reg.1(2).

GENERAL NOTE

This provision is a good example of the topsy-turvy principle of statutory drafting. The general rule, as enshrined in para.(2), is that a social security benefit is treated as being paid on the first day of the benefit week in which the benefit is payable. The "benefit week" is the period of seven days beginning on the day in which, in the claimant's case, the state pension credit is payable (reg.1(2)). The exceptions to this general principle are then listed in para.(1). Employment and support allowance, incapacity benefit, severe disablement allowance and jobseeker's allowance are all normally paid fortnightly in arrears from the date of claim (Social Security (Claims and Payments) Regulations 1987 (SI 1987/1968) regs 24(1), 26A(1) and 26C(1)). Maternity allowance is usually payable on Fridays (Social Security (Claims and Payments) Regulations 1987 (SI 1987/1968) reg.24(4)). 3.58

PART III

Income

Calculation of income and capital

14.—The income and capital of— 3.59

(a) the claimant; and
(b) any partner of the claimant,

shall be calculated in accordance with the rules set out in this Part; and any reference in this Part to the claimant shall apply equally to any partner of the claimant.

DEFINITIONS

"claimant"—see SPCA 2002 s.17(1).
"income"—see *ibid.*, and s.15.
"partner"—see reg.1(3).

GENERAL NOTE

On the definition of "income", see SPCA 2002 s.15(1) and regs 15–18 and reg.24 below. On the meaning of "capital", see regs 19–23 below. The normal rules on aggregating the income and capital resources of married and unmarried couples apply to state pension credit as to other means-tested benefits (SPCA 2002 s.5). 3.60

The approach to income is rather different to the income support scheme, under which claimants are required to report every element of their income and capital and any changes as they occur. For state pension credit purposes, the categories of income to be disclosed by claimants are set out in SPCA 2002 ss.15 and 16 and in this Part of the Regulations, taken together with Schs IV, V and VI, which deal with disregards and calculation. There is, therefore, no need to report forms of income which are not listed in these statutory provisions (e.g. charitable payments and compensation for personal injuries).

Income for the purposes of the Act

3.61 **15.**—(1) For the purposes of section 15(1)(e) (income), all social security benefits are prescribed except—

[[31](za) universal credit;]

(a) disability living allowance;

[[16] (aa) personal independence payment;]

[[17] (ab) armed forces independence payment;]

(b) attendance allowance payable under section 64 of the 1992 Act;

(c) an increase of disablement pension under section 104 or 105 of the 1992 Act;

(d) a payment under regulations made in exercise of the power conferred by paragraph 7(2)(b) of Part II of Schedule 8 to the 1992 Act;

(e) an increase of an allowance payable in respect of constant attendance under paragraph 4 of Part I of Schedule 8 to the 1992 Act;

(f) any child special allowance payable under section 56 of the 1992 Act;

(g) any guardian's allowance payable under section 77 of the 1992 Act;

(h) any increase for a dependant, other than the claimant's partner, payable in accordance with Part IV of the 1992 Act;

(i) any social fund payment made under Part VIII of the 1992 Act;

(j) child benefit payable in accordance with Part IX of the 1992 Act;

(k) Christmas bonus payable under Part X of the 1992 Act;

[[1](l) housing benefit;

[[15] . . .]

[[21](n) bereavement support payment under section 30 of the Pensions Act 2014;]

(o) statutory sick pay;

(p) statutory maternity pay;

[[14] (q) ordinary statutory paternity pay payable under Part 12ZA of the 1992 Act;

(qa) [[19] . . .]

[[18] (qb) statutory shared parental pay payable under Part 12ZC of the 1992 Act;]

[[26](qc) statutory parental bereavement pay payable under Part 12ZD of the 1992 Act;]

(r) statutory adoption pay payable under Part 12ZB of the 1992 Act;

[[23] (ra) carer's allowance supplement payable under section 81 of the Social Security (Scotland) Act 2018;]

[[24](rb) early years assistance given in accordance with section 32 of the Social Security (Scotland) Act 2018;]

[[25](rc) funeral expense assistance given in accordance with section 34 of the Social Security (Scotland) Act 2018;]

[[27](rd) any Scottish child payment assistance given in accordance with section 79 of the Social Security (Scotland) Act 2018;]

[[28](re) any assistance given in accordance with the Carer's Assistance (Young Carer Grants) (Scotland) Regulations 2019;]

[[29](rf) short-term assistance given in accordance with regulations made under section 36 of the Social Security (Scotland) Act 2018;]

[30(rg) winter heating assistance given in accordance with regulations made under section 30 of the Social Security (Scotland) Act 2018;]

[32(rh) disability assistance given in accordance with regulations made under section 31 of the Social Security (Scotland) Act 2018;]

(s) any benefit similar to those mentioned in the preceding provisions of this paragraph payable under legislation having effect in Northern Ireland.]

[13 (2) For the purposes of section 15(1)(f) (foreign social security benefits) of the Act, income includes—

(a) all foreign social security benefits which are similar to the social security benefits prescribed under paragraph (1), and

(b) any foreign state retirement pension.]

(3) Where the payment of any social security benefit prescribed under paragraph (1) [22, or retirement pension income to which section 16(1)(za) to (e)(2) applies,] is subject to any deduction (other than an adjustment specified in paragraph (4)) the amount to be taken into account under paragraph (1) [22, or section 16(1)(za) to (e),] shall be the amount before the deduction is made.

(4) The adjustments specified in this paragraph are those made in accordance with—

(a) the Social Security (Overlapping Benefits) Regulations 1979;

[8 (b) regulation 2 of the Social Security (Hospital In-Patients) Regulations 2005;]

(c) section 30DD or section 30E of the 1992 Act (reductions in incapacity benefit in respect of pensions and councillor's allowances);

[9 (d) section 3 of the Welfare Reform Act (deductions from contributory allowance);]

[22 (e) section 14 of the Pensions Act 2014 (pension sharing: reduction in the sharer's section 4 pension);

(f) section 45B or 55B of the Social Security Contributions and Benefits Act 1992 (reduction of additional pension in Category A retirement pension and shared additional pension: pension sharing)];

[33(g) regulation 16(2) of the Carer's Assistance (Carer Support Payment) (Scotland) Regulations 2023.]

(5) For the purposes of section 15(1)(j) (income to include income of prescribed descriptions), income of the following descriptions is prescribed—

[10 (a) a payment made—

(i) under article 30 of the Naval, Military and Air Forces Etc. (Disablement and Death) Service Pensions Order 2006, in any case where article 30(1)(b) applies; or

(ii) under article 12(8) of that Order, in any case where sub-paragraph (b) of that article applies;]

[4(aa) a guaranteed income payment;

(ab) a payment made under article 21(1)(c) of the Armed Forces and Reserve Forces (Compensation Scheme) Order 2005 [10, in any case where article 23(2)(c) applies];]

[10 (ac) any retired pay, pension or allowance granted in respect of disablement or any pension or allowance granted to a widow, widower or surviving civil partner in respect of a death due to service or war injury under an instrument specified in section 639(2) of the Income Tax (Earnings and Pensions) Act 2003, where such payment does not fall within paragraph (a) of the definition of "war disablement pension" in section 17(1) of the State Pension Credit Act 2002 or, in respect of any retired pay or pension granted in respect of disablement, where such payment does not fall within paragraph (b) of that definition;]

[20(b) a pension paid by a government to victims of National Socialist persecution;]

(c) payments under a scheme made under the Pneumoconiosis, etc. (Worker's Compensation) Act 1979;

(d) payments made towards the maintenance of the claimant by his spouse [6, civil partner, former spouse or former civil partner] or towards the maintenance of the claimant's partner by his spouse [6, civil partner, former spouse or former civil partner], including payments made—

(i) under a court order;

(ii) under an agreement for maintenance; or

(iii) voluntarily;

(e) payments due from any person in respect of board and lodging accommodation provided by the claimant [5 . . .];

[11 (f) royalties or other sums paid as a consideration for the use of, or the right to use, any copyright, design, patent or trade mark;] [2. . .]

[11 (g) any payment in respect of any—

(i) book registered under the Public Lending Right Scheme 1982; or

(ii) work made under any international public lending right scheme that is analogous to the Public Lending Right Scheme 1982;]

[2 (h) any income in lieu of that specified in—

(i) paragraphs (a) to (i) of section 15(1) of the Act, or

(ii) in this regulation;

(i) any payment of rent made to a claimant who—

(i) owns the freehold or leasehold interest in any property or is a tenant of any property;

(ii) occupies part of that property; and

(iii) has an agreement with another person allowing that person to occupy that property on payment of rent.]

[3(j) any payment made at regular intervals under an equity release scheme;]

[7 (k) PPF periodic payments.]

[12 (6) For the purposes of section 15(2) (deemed income from capital) and subject to regulation 17(8) (capital to be disregarded), a claimant's capital shall be deemed to yield a weekly income of—

(a) £1 for each £500 in excess of £10,000; and

(b) £1 for any excess which is not a complete £500.]

(7) [13 . . .]

(8) [13 . . .]

AMENDMENTS

1. State Pension Credit (Consequential, Transitional and Miscellaneous Provisions) Regulations 2002 (SI 2002/3019) reg.23(g) (October 6, 2003).

2. State Pension Credit (Transitional and Miscellaneous Provisions) Amendment Regulations 2003 (SI 2003/2274) reg.2(7) (October 6, 2003).

3. Social Security (Housing Benefit, Council Tax Benefit, State Pension Credit and Miscellaneous Amendments) Regulations 2004 (SI 2004/2327) reg.7(3) (October 4, 2004).

4. Social Security (Miscellaneous Amendments) Regulations 2005 (SI 2005/574) reg.2(2) (April 4, 2005).

5. Social Security (Miscellaneous Amendments) (No.2) Regulations 2005 (SI 2005/2465) reg.6(3) (October 3, 2005).

6. Civil Partnership (Pensions, Social Security and Child Support) (Consequential, etc. Provisions) Order 2005 (SI 2005/2877) art.2(3) and Sch.3 para.35(3) (December 5, 2005).

7. Social Security (Miscellaneous Amendments) Regulations 2006 (SI 2006/588) reg.4(2) (April 6, 2006).

8. Social Security (Hospital In-Patients) Regulations 2005 (SI 2005/3360) reg.8(3) (April 10, 2006).

9. Employment and Support Allowance (Consequential Provisions) (No.2) Regulations 2008 (SI 2008/1554) reg.4(6) (October 27, 2008).

10. Social Security (Miscellaneous Amendments) (No.7) Regulations 2008 (SI 2008/3157) reg.4(3) (January 5, 2009).

11. Social Security (Miscellaneous Amendments) Regulations 2009 (SI 2009/583) reg.5(2) (April 6, 2009).

12. Social Security (Deemed Income from Capital) Regulations 2009 (SI 2009/1676) regs 2 and 3 (November 2, 2009).

13. Social Security (Miscellaneous Amendments) (No.2) Regulations 2010 (SI 2010/641) reg.6(5) (April 13, 2010).

14. Social Security (Miscellaneous Amendments) Regulations 2012 (2012/757) reg.5(3) (April 1, 2012).

15. Council Tax Benefit Abolition (Consequential Provision) Regulations 2013 (SI 2013/458) reg.3 and Sch.1 (April 1, 2013).

16. Personal Independence Payment (Supplementary Provisions and Consequential Amendments) Regulations 2013 (SI 2013/388) reg.8 and Sch. para.27(3) (April 8, 2013).

17. Armed Forces and Reserve Forces Compensation Scheme (Consequential Provisions: Subordinate Legislation) Order 2013 (SI 2013/591) art.7 and Sch. para.23(3) (April 8, 2013).

18. Shared Parental Leave and Statutory Shared Parental Pay (Consequential Amendments to Subordinate Legislation) Order 2014 (SI 2014/3255) art.10(3)(b) (December 31, 2014).

19. Shared Parental Leave and Statutory Shared Parental Pay (Consequential Amendments to Subordinate Legislation) Order 2014 (SI 2014/3255) art.10(3)(a) (April 5, 2015).

20. Social Security (Income-Related Benefits) Amendment Regulations 2017 (2017/174) reg.4(2) (March 20, 2017).

21. Pensions Act 2014 (Consequential, Supplementary and Incidental Amendments) Order 2017 (SI 2017/422) art.21(2) (April 6, 2017).

22. Social Security (Miscellaneous Amendments) Regulations 2017 (SI 2017/1015) reg.10(2) and (3) (November 16, 2017).

23. Social Security (Scotland) Act 2018 (Consequential Modifications) Order 2018 (SI 2018/872), art.4 (September 3, 2018).

24. Social Security (Scotland) Act 2018 (Best Start Grants) (Consequential Modifications and Saving) Order 2018 (SI 2018/1138), art.7(2) (December 10, 2018).

25. Social Security (Scotland) Act 2018 (Funeral Expense Assistance and Early Years Assistance) (Consequential Modifications and Savings) Order 2019 (SI 2019/1060) art.11(2) (September 16, 2019).

26. Parental Bereavement Leave and Pay (Consequential Amendments to Subordinate Legislation) Regulations 2020 (SI 2020/354) reg.10(3) (April 6, 2020).

27. Social Security (Scotland) Act 2018 (Information-Sharing and Scottish Child Payment) (Consequential Provision and Modifications) Order 2020 (SI 2020/482) art.5(2) (November 9, 2020).

28. Social Security (Scotland) Act 2018 (Young Carer Grants, Short-Term Assistance and Winter Heating Assistance) (Consequential Provision and Modifications) Order 2020 (SI 2020/989) art.4(2) (November 9, 2020).

29. Social Security (Scotland) Act 2018 (Young Carer Grants, Short-Term Assistance and Winter Heating Assistance) (Consequential Provision and Modifications) Order 2020 (SI 2020/989) art.11(2) (November 9, 2020).

30. Social Security (Scotland) Act 2018 (Young Carer Grants, Short-Term Assistance and Winter Heating Assistance) (Consequential Provision and Modifications) Order 2020 (SI 2020/989) art.17(2) (November 9, 2020).

31. Universal Credit (Persons who have attained state pension credit qualifying age) (Amendment) Regulations 2020 (SI 2020/655) reg.2(3) (November 25, 2020).

32. Social Security (Scotland) Act 2018 (Disability Assistance, Young Carer Grants, Short-term Assistance and Winter Heating Assistance) (Consequential Provision and Modifications) Order 2021 (SI 2021/886) art.13(2) (July 26, 2021).

33. Carer's Assistance (Carer Support Payment) (Scotland) Regulations 2023 (Consequential Amendments) Order 2023 (SI 2023/1218) art.14(4) (November 19, 2023).

DEFINITIONS

"the 1992 Act"—see reg.1(2).
"attendance allowance"—see *ibid.*
"board and lodging accommodation"—see *ibid.*
"capital"—see SPCA 2002 s.17(1).
"care home"—see reg.1(2).
"claimant"—see SPCA 2002 s.17(1).
"income"—see *ibid.*
"partner"—see reg.1(2).

GENERAL NOTE

Paragraph (1)

3.62 The presumption under SPCA 2002 s.15(1)(e) is that social security benefits count as income for the purposes of calculating entitlement to state pension credit. There is, however, an extensive list of exceptions here. Note also that there are disregards that apply to certain forms of income, as specified in reg.17(7) and Sch.IV below.

Paragraph (2)

3.63 This provision was amended in order to reverse the effect of *SSWP v JK* [2009] UKUT 55 (AAC). If income is received in a currency other than Sterling, the value of any payment is determined by taking the Sterling equivalent on the date that payment is made (reg.17(6)).

Paragraph (3)

3.64 The effect of this rule is that payments of prescribed social security benefits are taken into account gross, i.e. before any deductions are applied (e.g. under the Social Security (Claims and Payments) Regulations 1987 (SI 1987/1968) reg.35 and Sch.9). This is subject to the exceptions specified in para.(4).

Paragraph (5)

3.65 Section 15(1)(j) is a catch-all provision that enables the Secretary of State to prescribe other forms of income not caught by any of the other provisions. As regards sub-para.(5)(b), the amended version gives effect to Judge Williams' decision in *MN v Bury Council and SSWP (HB)* [2014] UKUT 187 (AAC), where it was held that compensation pension payments made by the Dutch Government to victims of Nazi persecution should be treated in the same way as payments made under schemes administered by the German and Austrian governments for the purposes of calculating entitlement to housing benefit. The same disregard rules now apply across all means-tested benefits to all those victims of Nazi persecution, irrespective of the person's nationality and regardless of the national government making the payments.

As regards board and lodging accommodation (sub-para.(5)(e)), and on the importance of establishing the precise status of someone staying with the claimant (e.g. as a sub-tenant, lodger or non-dependant), see *KC v Secretary of State for Work and Pensions (SPC)* [2012] UKUT 114 (AAC).

Note that neither s.15 of the Act nor reg.15 seem to include as assessable income for state pension credit purposes regular payments of income from a benevolent institution (e.g. the Royal British Legion) or from a family member: see *AMS v SSWP (PC) (final decision)* [2017] UKUT 381 (AAC) at para.13.

Paragraph (6)

The tariff income rule for state pension credit is markedly more generous to claimants than that which applies in the income support scheme. In particular, the assumed rate of return is halved. The rule for state pension credit is that the claimant is assumed to receive £1 per week for every £500 or part thereof over the threshold of £10,000. Thus a state pension credit claimant with £14,000 in savings will have a deemed income of £8 per week from that capital. A person of working age with £10,000 in capital is excluded from entitlement to income support. Note also that there is no upper capital limit for state pension credit, and that the threshold for the tariff income rule was raised to £10,000 for all claimants, and not just those in residential care and nursing homes, with effect from November 2, 2009. **3.66**

Retirement pension income

16.—There shall be added to the descriptions of income listed in section 16(1) (retirement pension income) the following [1paragraphs]— **3.67**

"(k) any sum payable by way of pension out of money provided under the Civil List Act 1837, the Civil List Act 1937, the Civil List Act 1952, the Civil List Act 1972 or the [1Civil List Act 1975];

[1(l) any payment, other than a payment ordered by a court or made in settlement of a claim, made by or on behalf of a former employer of a person on account of the early retirement of that person on grounds of ill-health or disability;]

[2(m) any payment made at regular intervals under an equity release scheme;]"

[4(n) any payment made under the Financial Assistance Scheme Regulations 2005.]

AMENDMENTS

1. State Pension Credit (Consequential, Transitional and Miscellaneous Provisions) (No.2) Regulations 2002 (SI 2002/3197) reg.2 and Sch. para.3 (October 6, 2003).

2. Social Security (Housing Benefit, Council Tax Benefit, State Pension Credit and Miscellaneous Amendments) Regulations 2004 (SI 2004/2327) reg.7(4) (October 4, 2004).

3. State Pension Credit (Amendment) Regulations 2005 (SI 2005/3205) reg.2(3) (December 18, 2005).

DEFINITION

"income"—see SPCA 2002 ss.15 and 17(1).

GENERAL NOTE

3.68 Readers with republican tendencies will doubtless be reassured to see that pensions paid from the Civil List count as retirement pension income for the purposes of SPCA 2002 s.16(1). More prosaically, payments made by virtue of early retirement on ill-health grounds (other than those ordered by court or agreed under the settlement of a claim) also count.

Calculation of weekly income

3.69 **17.**—(1) Except where paragraph (2) and (4) apply, for the purposes of calculating the weekly income of the claimant, where the period in respect of which a payment is made—

(a) does not exceed a week, the whole of that payment shall be included in the claimant's weekly income;

(b) exceeds a week, the amount to be included in the claimant's weekly income shall be determined—

(i) in a case where that period is a month, by multiplying the amount of the payment by 12 ad dividing the product by 52;

(ii) in a case where that period is three months, by multiplying the amount of the payment by 4 and dividing the product by 52;

(iii) in a case where that period is a year, by dividing the amount of the payment by 52;

(iv) in any other case, by multiplying the amount of the payment by 7 and dividing the product by the number of days in the period in respect of which it is made.

(2) Where—

(a) the claimant's regular pattern of work is such that he does not work the same hours every week; or

(b) the amount of the claimant's income fluctuates and has changed more than once,

the weekly amount of that claimant's income shall be determined—

(i) if, in a case to which sub-paragraph (a) applies, there is a recognised cycle of work, by reference to his average weekly income over the period of the complete cycle (including, where the cycle involves periods in which the claimant does no work, those periods but disregarding any other absences); or

(ii) in any other case, on the basis of—

(aa) the last two payments if those payments are one month or more apart;

(bb) the last four payments if the last two payments are less than one month apart; or

(cc) such other payments as may, in the particular circumstances of the case, enable the claimant's average weekly income to be determined more accurately.

(3) For the purposes of paragraph (2)(b) the last payments are the last payments before the date the claim was made or treated as made or, if there is a subsequent supersession under section 10 of the Social Security Act 1998, the last payments before the date of the supersession.

(4) If a claimant is entitled to receive a payment to which paragraph (5) applies, the amount of that payment shall be treated as if made in respect of a period of a year.

(5) This paragraph applies to—

[3 (a) royalties or other sums received as a consideration for the use of, or the right to use, any copyright, design, patent or trade mark;]

[3 (b) any payment in respect of any—

(i) book registered under the Public Lending Right Scheme 1982; or

(ii) work made under any international public lending right scheme that is analogous to the Public Lending Right Scheme 1982;] [1 and

(c) any payment which is made on an occasional basis.]

(6) Where payments are made in a currency other than Sterling, the value of the payment shall be determined by taking the Sterling equivalent on the date the payment is made.

(7) Income specified in Schedule IV is to be disregarded in the calculation of a claimant's income.

(8) Schedule V shall have effect so that—

(a) the capital specified in Part I shall be disregarded for the purpose of determining a claimant's income; and

(b) the capital specified in Part II shall be disregarded for the purpose of determining a claimant's income under regulation 15(6).

[1(9) The sums specified in Schedule VI shall be disregarded in calculating—

(a) the claimant's earnings; and

[3 (b) any amount to which paragraph (5) applies where the claimant is the first owner of the copyright, design, patent or trademark, or an original contributor to the book or work referred to in paragraph (5)(b).]

(9A) For the purposes of paragraph (9)(b), and for that purpose only, the amounts specified in paragraph (5) shall be treated as though they were earnings.]

(10) [1Subject to regulation [217B(6)] (deduction of tax and contributions for self-employed earners),] in the case of any income taken into account for the purpose of calculating a person's income, there shall be disregarded—

(a) any amount payable by way of tax;

(b) any amount deducted by way of National Insurance Contributions under the 1992 Act or under the Social Security Contributions and Benefits (Northern Ireland) Act 1992;

(c) [2 . . .].

[1(11) In the case of the earnings of self-employed earners, the amounts specified in paragraph (10) shall be taken into account in accordance with paragraph (4) or, as the case may be, paragraph (10) of regulation 13 of the Computation of Earnings Regulations, as having effect in the case of state pension credit.]

AMENDMENTS

1. State Pension Credit (Consequential, Transitional and Miscellaneous Provisions) Regulations 2002 (SI 2002/3019) reg.23(h) (October 6, 2003).

2. State Pension Credit (Consequential, Transitional and Miscellaneous Provisions) (No.2) Regulations 2002 (SI 2002/3197) reg.2 and Sch. para.5 (October 6, 2003).

3. Social Security (Miscellaneous Amendments) Regulations 2009 (SI 2009/583) reg.5(3) (April 6, 2009).

Definitions

"claimant"—see SPCA 2002 s.17(1).
"Computation of Earnings Regulations"—see reg.1(2).
"income"—see SPCA 2002 s.17(1).

General Note

Paragraph (1)

3.70 This follows the precedent of income support by providing for the same simple method of converting payments of income into weekly equivalents (Income Support (General) Regulations 1987 (SI 1987/1967) reg.32(1), in Vol.V of this series). This is subject to the special rules for irregular patterns of work (para.(2)) and for payments of royalties and other occasional payments (paras (4) and (5)).

In *R(PC) 3/08* the Commissioner rejected the Secretary of State's argument that "capital" has a special meaning in the state pension credit scheme. The Commissioner held that the general rule applied, namely that a payment of income (there state retirement pension, paid four-weekly) did not metamorphose into capital until the expiry of a period equal in length to the period in respect of which it was paid. The Commissioner applied the general principle to that effect as stated in *R(IS)3/93*, notwithstanding the absence in the state pension credit scheme of an equivalent provision to reg.29(2) of the Income Support (General) Regulations 1987. The Commissioner held that the state pension credit system "must operate on an assumed notion of a period of attribution" (para.24).

See also *PS v Secretary of State for Work and Pensions (SPC)* [2016] UKUT 21 (AAC), where the claimant had been paid arrears of his army pension in 2008, for a period going back to March 2006. The DWP subsequently sought to recover from the claimant an overpayment of pension credit, including the period from March 2006 to the date of receipt of the arrears. The First-tier Tribunal confirmed this decision. However, Judge Ward allowed the claimant's further appeal, ruling that for pension credit purposes income payable in arrears falls to be attributed *forward* from the date of receipt rather than *backwards* over the period in respect of which it was earned (see paras 14–17). In doing so Judge Ward followed *R(PC) 3/08* at para.24.

Paragraphs (2) and (3)

3.71 This is yet another variant on the various legislative measures devised to deal with the problematic question of accommodating those with irregular working patterns into a means-tested benefit system. The rule is modelled on but also departs from the traditional income support approach (see Income Support (General) Regulations 1987 (SI 1987/1967) reg.32(6)).

Paragraphs (4) and (5)

3.72 Royalties and other occasional payments are treated as paid in respect of a year, in contrast to the income support rule (Income Support (General) Regulations 1987 (SI 1987/1967) reg.30(2)).

Paragraph (6)

3.73 Any banking charges or commission payable when converting payments of income in other currencies into Sterling are disregarded (Sch.IV para.16).

Paragraph (7)

3.74 See the annotations to Sch.IV.

Paragraph (8)

3.75 Schedule V is divided into two Parts. Part I specifies those forms of capital which are to be disregarded for the purpose of calculating the claimant's income. This extensive list is modelled on Sch.10 to the Income Support (General)

Regulations 1987 (SI 1987/1967). Part II contains a more limited list of categories of capital which are to be disregarded solely for the purposes of calculating notional income.

Paragraph (9)

This links to Sch.VI, which carries forward the standard £5, £10 and £20 disregards on earnings that apply in the income support scheme to the state pension credit system. However, there is no hours rule for state pension credit, so it matters not whether a pensioner is working under or over 16 hours a week. **3.76**

Paragraph (10)

This is similar to the income support rule (see Income Support (General) Regulations 1987 (SI 1987/1967) reg.36(3)). The principal difference is that the income support rule applies to earnings, whereas this rule applies to all income. The income support rule permits a deduction from earnings representing 50 per cent of the amount of any occupational or personal pension scheme contributions. The parallel provision for state pension credit purposes is to be found in reg.17A(4A) below. **3.77**

Paragraph (11)

See also reg.17B. **3.78**

[[1]Treatment of final payments of income

17ZA.—(1) Save where regulation 13B applies, this regulation applies where— **3.79**

(a) a claimant has been receiving a regular payment of income;
(b) that payment is coming to an end or has ended; and
(c) the claimant receives a payment of income whether as the last of the regular payments or following the last of them ("the final payment").

(2) For the purposes of regulation 17(1)—

(a) where the amount of the final payment is less than or equal to the amount of the preceding, or the last, regular payment, the whole amount shall be treated as being paid in respect of a period of the same length as that in respect of which that regular payment was made;
(b) where the amount of the final payment is greater than the amount of that regular payment—
    (i) to the extent that it comprises (whether exactly or with an excess remaining) one or more multiples of that amount, each such multiple shall be treated as being paid in respect of a period of the same length as that in respect of which that regular payment was made; and
    (ii) any excess shall be treated as paid in respect of a further period of the same length as that in respect of which that regular payment was made.

(3) A final payment referred to in paragraph (2)(a) shall, where not in fact paid on the date on which a regular payment would have been paid had it continued in payment, be treated as paid on that date.

(4) Each multiple and any excess referred to in paragraph (2)(b) shall be treated as paid on the dates on which a corresponding number of regular payments would have been made had they continued in payment.

(5) For the purposes of this regulation, a "regular payment" means a payment of income made in respect of a period—

(a) referred to in regulation 17(1)(a) or (b) on a regular date; or
(b) which is subject to the provisions of regulation 17(2).]

AMENDMENT

1. State Pension Credit (Miscellaneous Amendments) Regulations 2004 (SI 2004/647) reg.3(4) (April 5, 2004).

DEFINITIONS

"the final payment"—see para.(1)(c).
"regular payment"—see para.(5).

GENERAL NOTE

3.80 This regulation provides for the treatment of final payments of income. The rule applies whenever the claimant has been receiving a regular payment of income (a term which is wider than it first appears; see para.(5) and below), those payments come to an end and a final payment is made (para.(1)). The basic rule is that where the final payment of income is less than or equal to the previtous payment of income, then the whole of the final payment is attributed to the normal period for such payments (para.(2)(a); and see para.(3) for the date on which the final payment may be treated as paid). If, however, the final payment exceeds the usual or "regular payment", then it is treated as applying to a series of sequential periods, depending on the number of multiples involved (para.(2)(b); and see para.(4) for the dates on which such multiple payments may be treated as paid). Paragraph (5) defines "regular payment" by reference to reg.17(1) and (2); the effect of this is that irregular patterns of work may nevertheless give rise to a "regular payment" for the purpose of this provision (see reg.17(2)(b)(ii)).

[[1]Earnings of an employed earner

3.81 **17A.**—(1) For the purposes of state pension credit, the provisions of this regulation which relate to the earnings of employed earners, shall have effect in place of those prescribed for such earners in the Computation of Earnings Regulations.

(2) Subject to paragraphs [[2](3), (4) and 4(A)], "earnings" in the case of employment as an employed earner, means any remuneration or profit derived from that employment and includes—

(a) any bonus or commission;
(b) any payment in lieu of remuneration except any periodic sum paid to a claimant on account of the termination of his employment by reason of redundancy;
(c) any payment in lieu of notice;
(d) any holiday pay;
(e) any payment by way of a retainer;
(f) any payment made by the claimant's employer in respect of expenses not wholly, exclusively and necessarily incurred in the performance of the duties of the employment, including any payment made by the claimant's employer in respect of—
 (i) travelling expenses incurred by the claimant between his home and place of employment;
 (ii) expenses incurred by the claimant under arrangements made for the care of a member of his family owing to the claimant's absence from home;
(g) the amount of any payment by way of a non-cash voucher which has been taken into account in the computation of a person's earnings in accordance with Part V of Schedule 3 to the Social Security (Contributions) Regulations 2001;

(h) statutory sick pay and statutory maternity pay payable by the employer under the 1992 Act;

[4 (i) [7 . . .] statutory paternity pay payable under Part 12ZA of the 1992 Act;

(ia) [7 . . .];]

[6 (ib) statutory shared parental pay payable under Part 12ZC of the 1992 Act;]

[8 (ic) statutory parental bereavement pay payable under Part 12ZD of the 1992 Act;]

(j) statutory adoption pay payable under Part 12ZB of the 1992 Act;

(k) any sums payable under a contract of service—

(i) for incapacity for work due to sickness or injury; or

(ii) by reason of pregnancy or confinement.

(3) "Earnings" shall not include—

(a) subject to paragraph (4), any payment in kind;

(b) any payment in respect of expenses wholly, exclusively and necessarily incurred in the performance of the duties of the employment;

(c) any occupational pension;

(d) any lump sum payment made under the Iron and Steel Re-adaptation Benefits Scheme;

[2(e) any payment of compensation made pursuant to an award by an employment tribunal in respect of unfair dismissal or unlawful discrimination.]

[3 (f) any payment in respect of expenses arising out of the [5 claimant participating as a service user]

(4) Paragraph (3)(a) shall not apply in respect of any non-cash voucher referred to in paragraph (2)(g).

[2(4A) One half of any sum paid by a claimant by way of a contribution towards an occupational pension scheme or a personal pension scheme shall, for the purpose of calculating his earnings in accordance with this regulation, be disregarded.]

(5) In this regulation "employed earner" means a person who is gainfully employed in Great Britain either under a contract of service, or in an office (including elective office) with emoluments chargeable to income tax under Schedule E.]

AMENDMENTS

1. State Pension Credit (Consequential, Transitional and Miscellaneous Provisions) Regulations 2002 (SI 2002/3019) reg.23(i) (October 6, 2003).

2. State Pension Credit (Consequential, Transitional and Miscellaneous Provisions) (No.2) Regulations 2002 (SI 2002/3197) reg.3(1) (October 6, 2003).

3. Social Security (Miscellaneous Amendments) (No.4) Regulations 2009 (SI 2009/2655) reg.5(3) (October 26, 2009).

4. Social Security (Miscellaneous Amendments) Regulations 2012 (SI 2012/757) reg.5(4) (April 1, 2012).

5. Social Security (Miscellaneous Amendments) Regulations 2014 (SI 2014/591) reg.7(3) (April 28, 2014).

6. Shared Parental Leave and Statutory Shared Parental Pay (Consequential Amendments to Subordinate Legislation) Order 2014 (SI 2014/3255) art.10(4)(c) (December 31, 2014).

7. Shared Parental Leave and Statutory Shared Parental Pay (Consequential Amendments to Subordinate Legislation) Order 2014 (SI 2014/3255) art.10(4)(a) and (b) (April 5, 2015).

8. Parental Bereavement Leave and Pay (Consequential Amendments to Subordinate Legislation) Regulations 2020 (SI 2020/354) reg.10(4) (April 6, 2020).

DEFINITIONS

"claimant"—see para.(2)(a).
"Computation of Earnings Regulations"—see reg.1(2).
"employed earner"—see para.(5).
"occupational pension scheme"—see SPCA 2002 s.17(1).
"personal pension scheme"—see *ibid.*

GENERAL NOTE

3.82 This provides a comprehensive definition of "earnings" for employed earners who claim state pension credit which is independent of the rules contained in the Social Security (Computation of Earnings) Regulations 1996 (SI 1996/2745). In contrast, reg.17B below specifically applies the 1996 Regulations to the assessment of the earnings of *self*-employed earners, subject to certain modifications. The rules governing employed earners in this regulation follow closely (but do not entirely mirror) those that apply to the definition of an employed earner's earnings for the purposes of income support (see Income Support (General) Regulations 1987 (SI 1987/1967) reg.35, in Vol.V of this series).

[1Earnings of self-employed earners

3.83 **17B.**—(1) For the purposes of state pension credit, the provisions of the Computation of Earnings Regulations in their application to the earnings of self-employed earners, shall have effect in so far as provided by this regulation.

(2) In their application to state pension credit, regulations 11 to 14 of the Computation of Earnings Regulations shall have effect as if—

[2(za) "board and lodging accommodation" has the same meaning as in [3 regulation 1(2)];]

(a) "claimant" referred to a person claiming state pension credit and any partner of the claimant;

(b) "personal pension scheme" referred to a personal pension scheme—

(i) as defined in section 1 of the Pension Schemes Act 1993; or

(ii) as defined in section 1 of the Pension Schemes (Northern Ireland) Act 1993.

(3) In regulation 11 (calculation of earnings of self-employed earners), paragraph (1) shall have effect, but as if the words "Except where paragraph (2) applies" were omitted.

(4) In regulation 12 (earnings of self-employed earners).

(a) paragraph (1) shall have effect;

(b) [5 the following paragraph shall be added after paragraph (1)]

"(2) Earnings does not include—

(a) where a claimant occupies a dwelling as his home and he provides in that dwelling board and lodging accommodation for which payment is made, those payments;

[5 (b) any payment made by a local authority to a claimant with whom a person is accommodated by virtue of arrangements made under—

[9 (i) section 22C(2) of the Children Act 1989 (ways in which looked after children are to be accommodated and maintained),]

[9 (ia) section 81(2) of the Social Services and Well-being (Wales) Act

2014 (ways in which looked after children are to be accommodated and maintained),]

[[8](ii) section 26 or 26A of the Children (Scotland) Act 1995 (manner of provision of accommodation to child looked after by local authority and duty to provide continuing care), or]

(iii) regulations 33 or 51 of the Looked After Children (Scotland) Regulations 2009 (fostering and kinship care allowances and fostering allowances);]

(c) any payment made "by a voluntary organisation in accordance with section 59(1)(a) of the Children Act 1989 (provision of accommodation by voluntary organisations);

(d) any payment made to the claimant or his partner for a person ('the person concerned') who is not normally a member of the claimant's household but is temporarily in his care, by—

(i) a health authority;

(ii) a local authority;

(iii) a voluntary organisation;

(iv) the person concerned pursuant to section 26(3A) of the National Assistance Act 1948; [[4] . . .]

[[6] (iva) [[11] an integrated care board established under Chapter A3 of Part 2 of the National Health Service Act 2006];

(ivb) [[12]NHS England]; [[7] . . .]]

(v) [[6] . . .]

[[4] (vi) a Local Health Board established under section 16BA of the National Health Service Act 1977 or established by an order made under section 11 of the Health Service (Wales) Act;] [[7][[9] . . .]

(vii) the person concerned where the payment is for the provision of accommodation in respect of the meeting of that person's needs under section 18 or 19 of the Care Act 2014 (duty and power to meet needs for care and support);] [[9] or

(viii) the person concerned where the payment is for the provision of accommodation to meet that person's needs for care and support under section 35 or 36 of the Social Services and Well-being (Wales) Act 2014 (duty and power to meet care and support needs of an adult);]

[[8](da) any payment or part of a payment made by a local authority in accordance with section 26A of the Children (Scotland) Act 1995 (duty to provide continuing care) to a person ("A") which A passes on to the claimant where A—

(i) was formerly in the claimant's care;

(ii) is aged 16 or over; and

(iii) continues to live with the claimant;]

[[10](db) any payment made to a claimant under section 73(1)(b) of the Children and Young People (Scotland) Act 2014 (kinship care assistance);]

(e) any sports award [[2] being an award made by one of the Sports Councils named in section 23(2) of the National Lottery etc. Act 1993 out of sums allocated to it for distribution under that section]

(5) In regulation 13 (calculation of net profit of self-employed earners)—

(a) for paragraphs (1) to (3), the following provision shall have effect—

"(1) For the purposes of regulation 11 (calculation of earnings of self-employed earners), the earnings of a claimant to be taken into account shall be—

(a) in the case of a self-employed earner who is engaged in employment on his own account, the net profit derived from that employment;

(b) in the case of a self-employed earner whose employment is carried on in partnership, his share of the net profit derived from that employment less—

(i) an amount in respect of income tax and of social security contributions payable under the Contributions and Benefits Act calculated in accordance with regulation 14 (deduction of tax and contributions for self-employed earners); and

(ii) one half of any premium paid in the period that is relevant under regulation 11 in respect of a retirement annuity contract or a personal pension scheme";

(b) paragraphs (4) to (12) shall have effect.

(6) Regulation 14 (deduction of tax and contributions for self-employed earners) shall have effect.]

AMENDMENTS

1. State Pension Credit (Consequential, Transitional and Miscellaneous Provisions) Regulations 2002 (SI 2002/3019) reg.23(i) (October 6, 2003).

2. State Pension Credit (Consequential, Transitional and Miscellaneous Provisions) (No.2) Regulations 2002 (SI 2002/3197) reg.3(2) (October 6,2003).

3. Social Security (Miscellaneous Amendments) (No.2) Regulations 2005 (SI 2005/2465) reg.6(4) (October 3, 2005).

4. Social Security (Miscellaneous Amendments) (No.7) Regulations 2008 (SI 2008/3157) reg.4(4) (January 5, 2009).

5. Social Security (Miscellaneous Amendments) (No.5) Regulations 2010 (SI 2010/2429) reg.6 (November 1, 2010).

6. National Treatment Agency (Abolition) and the Health and Social Care Act 2012 (Consequential, Transitional and Saving Provisions) Order 2013 (SI 2013/235) art.11 and Sch.2 para.54(3) (April 1, 2013) (England and Wales only).

7. Care Act 2014 (Consequential Amendments) (Secondary Legislation) Order 2015 (SI 2015/643) reg.19(1) and (2) (April 1, 2015).

8. Children and Young People (Scotland) Act 2014 (Consequential Modifications) Order 2016 (SI 2016/732) art.4(2) (August 5, 2016).

9. Social Services and Well-being (Wales) Act 2014 and the Regulation and Inspection of Social Care (Wales) Act 2016 (Consequential Amendments) Order 2017 (SI 2017/901) regs.9(2) and 24 (November 3, 2017).

10. Social Security and Child Support (Care Payments and Tenant Incentive Scheme) (Amendment) Regulations 2017 (SI 2017/995) reg.4(2) (November 7, 2017).

11. Health and Care Act 2022 (Consequential and Related Amendments and Transitional Provisions) Regulations 2022 (SI 2022/634) reg.99 and Sch. (July 1, 2022).

12. Health and Care Act 2022 (Further Consequential Amendments) (No. 2) Regulations 2023 (SI 2023/1071) reg.107 and Sch. (November 6, 2023).

DEFINITIONS

"board and lodging accommodation"—see para.(2)(za).

"claimant"—see para.(2)(a).

"Computation of Earnings Regulations"—see reg.1(2).
"dwelling occupied as the home"—see *ibid.*
"personal pension scheme"—see para.(2)(b).
"retirement annuity contract"—see SPCA 2002 s.16(3).

GENERAL NOTE

The earnings of self-employed earners for the purposes of state pension credit are calculated in accordance with the Social Security (Computation of Earnings) Regulations 1996 (SI 1996/2745) (on which see Vol.I in this series), subject to the modifications made by this regulation. Thus the special rule relating to royalties does not apply (para.(3)), as special provision is made for such payments for the purposes of state pension credit (see reg.17(4) and (5)). There is also a more extensive list of disregards to be applied when calculating earnings (para.(4)). 3.84

In *CPC/3373/2007* Deputy Commissioner Poynter held that the state pension credit scheme does not permit a claimant to offset a loss from self-employment income against his other sources of income. There is no equivalent within the state pension credit scheme to what used to be s.380 of the Income and Corporation Taxes Act 1988 (now Income Tax Act 2007 s.64). Accordingly, where a claimant makes a loss on self-employed income, the net profit for the purposes of state pension credit is nil, and not a negative figure. But note also that on the particular facts of that case the Deputy Commissioner held that the Secretary of State had not shown a relevant changes of circumstances such as to justify a supersession of the award of benefit to the claimant.

Notional income

18.—[2 (1) A claimant who has attained the qualifying age shall be treated as possessing the amount of any retirement pension income— 3.85

(a) to which section 16(1)[7(za)] to (e) applies,
(b) for which no claim has been made, and
(c) to which the claimant might expect to be entitled if a claim for it were made,

but only from the date on which that income could be expected to be acquired if a claim for it were made.

(1A) Paragraph (1) is subject to paragraphs (1B) [3, (1CA) and 1(CB)].

(1B) Where a claimant—

(a) has deferred entitlement to retirement pension income to which section 16(1)(a) to (c) applies for at least 12 months, and
(b) would have been entitled to make an election under Schedule 5 or 5A to the 1992 Act or under Schedule 1 to the Graduated Retirement Benefit Regulations,

he shall be treated for the purposes of paragraph (1) as possessing the amount of retirement pension income to which he might expect to be entitled if he were to elect to receive a lump sum.

[3 (1C) Paragraphs (1CA) and (1CB) apply for the purposes of paragraph (1) (or, where applicable, paragraph (1) read with paragraph (1B)).

(1CA) Where a benefit or allowance in payment in respect of the claimant would be adjusted under the Social Security (Overlapping Benefits) Regulations 1979 [9or regulation 16(2) of the Carer's Assistance (Carer Support Payment) (Scotland) Regulations 2023] if the retirement pension income had been claimed, he shall be treated as possessing that income minus the benefit or allowance in payment.

(1CB) Where a benefit or allowance in payment in respect of the claimant would require an adjustment to be made under the Social Security

(Overlapping Benefits) Regulations 1979 to the amount of retirement pension income payable had it been claimed, he shall be treated as possessing that retirement pension income minus the adjustment which would be made to it.]

(1D) A claimant who has attained the qualifying age shall be treated as possessing income from an occupational pension scheme which he elected to defer, but only from the date on which it could be expected to be acquired if a claim for it were made.]

(2) Where a person, [5 who has attained the qualifying age], is a person entitled to money purchase benefits under an occupational pension scheme or a personal pension scheme, or is a party to, or a person deriving entitlement to a pension under, a retirement annuity contract, and—

(a) he fails to purchase an annuity with the funds available in that scheme where—
  (i) he defers, in whole or in part, the payment of any income which would have been payable to him by his pension fund holder;
  (ii) he fails to take any necessary action to secure that the whole of any income which would be payable to him by his pension fund holder upon his applying for it, is so paid; or
  (iii) income withdrawal is not available to him under that scheme; or

(b) in the case of a retirement annuity contract, he fails to purchase an annuity with the funds available under that contract,

the amount of any income foregone shall be treated as possessed by him, but only from the date on which it could be expected to be acquired were an application for it to be made.

(3) The amount of any income foregone in a case to which either head (i) or (ii) of paragraph (2)(a) applies shall be the [8 rate of the annuity which may have been purchased with the fund and is to be determined by the Secretary of State, taking account of information provided by the pension fund holder in accordance with regulation 7(5) of the Social Security (Claims and Payments) Regulations 1987].

(4) The amount of any income foregone in a case to which either head (iii) of paragraph (2)(a) or paragraph (2)(b) applies shall be the income that the claimant could have received without purchasing an annuity had the funds held under the relevant scheme or retirement annuity contract been held under a personal pension scheme or occupational pension scheme where income withdrawal was available and shall be determined in the manner specified in paragraph (3).

(5) In paragraph (2), "money purchase benefits" has the meaning it has in the Pensions Scheme Act 1993.

(6) [1 Subject to [4 the following paragraphs],] a person shall be treated as possessing income of which he has deprived himself for the purpose of securing entitlement to state pension credit or increasing the amount of that benefit.

[1 (7) Paragraph (6) shall not apply in respect of the amount of an increase of pension or benefit where a person, having made an election in favour of that increase of pension or benefit under Schedule 5 or 5A to the 1992 Act or under Schedule 1 to the Graduated Retirement Benefit Regulations, changes that election in accordance with regulations made under Schedule 5 or 5A to that Act in favour of a lump sum.

[7 (7ZA) Paragraph (6) shall not apply in respect of the amount of an increase of pension where a person, having made a choice in favour of that increase of pension under section 8(2) of the Pensions Act 2014, alters that choice in favour of a lump sum, in accordance with Regulations made under section 8(7) of that Act.

(7ZB) Paragraph (6) shall not apply in respect of the amount of an increase of pension where a person, having made a choice in favour of that increase of pension in accordance with Regulations made under section 10 of the Pensions Act 2014 which include provision corresponding or similar to section 8(2) of that Act, alters that choice in favour of a lump sum, in accordance with Regulations made under section 10 of that Act which include provision corresponding or similar to Regulations made under section 8(7).]

[4 (7A) Paragraph (6) shall not apply in respect of any amount of income other than earnings, or earnings of an employed earner, arising out of the [6 claimant participating as a service user]

(8) In paragraph (7), "lump sum" means a lump sum under Schedule 5 or 5A to the 1992 Act or under Schedule 1 to the Graduated Retirement Benefit Regulations.]

[7 (8A) In paragraph (7ZA), "lump sum" means a lump sum under section 8 of the Pensions Act 2014.

(8B) In paragraph (7ZB), "lump sum" means a lump sum under Regulations made under section 10 of the Pensions Act 2014.]

[2 (9) For the purposes of paragraph (6), a person is not to be regarded as depriving himself of income where—

(a) his rights to benefits under a registered pension scheme are extinguished and in consequence of this he receives a payment from the scheme, and

(b) that payment is a trivial commutation lump sum within the meaning given by paragraph 7 of Schedule 29 to the Finance Act 2004.

(10) In paragraph (9), "registered pension scheme" has the meaning given in section 150(2) of the Finance Act 2004.]

AMENDMENTS

1. Social Security (Deferral of Retirement Pensions, Shared Additional Pension and Graduated Retirement Benefit) (Miscellaneous Provisions) Regulations 2005 (SI 2005/2677) reg.13(3) (April 6, 2006).

2. Social Security (Miscellaneous Amendments) (No.4) Regulations 2006 (SI 2006/2378) reg.14(4) (October 2, 2006).

3. Social Security (Miscellaneous Amendments) (No.5) Regulations 2007 (SI 2007/2618) reg.10(3) (October 1, 2007).

4. Social Security (Miscellaneous Amendments) (No.4) Regulations 2009 (SI 2009/2655) reg.5(4) (October 26, 2009).

5. Social Security (Miscellaneous Amendments) (No.2) Regulations 2010 (SI 2010/641) reg.6(6) (April 6, 2010).

6. Social Security (Miscellaneous Amendments) Regulations 2014 (SI 2014/591) reg.7(4) (April 28, 2014).

7. Pensions Act 2014 (Consequential, Supplementary and Incidental Amendments) Order 2015 (SI 2015/985) art.24(2) (April 6, 2016).

8. Social Security (Miscellaneous Amendments) Regulations 2017 (SI 2017/1015) reg.10(2)(a) (November 16, 2017).

9. Carer's Assistance (Carer Support Payment) (Scotland) Regulations 2023 (Consequential Amendments) Order 2023 (SI 2023/1218) art.14(5) (November 19, 2023).

DEFINITIONS

"claimant"—see SPCA 2002 s.17(1).
"income"—see *ibid.*
"lump sum"—see paras (8A) and (8B).
"money purchase benefits"—see para.(5).
"occupational pension scheme"—see SPCA 2002 s.17(1).
"pension fund holder"—see reg.1(2).
"personal pension scheme"—see SPCA 2002 s.17(1).
"qualifying age"—see SPCA 2002 s.1(6).
"retirement annuity contract"—see *ibid.*, and s.16(3).
"retirement pension income"—see SPCA 2002 ss.16 and 17(1).

GENERAL NOTE

3.86 This regulation provides for three types of notional income: certain forms of pension income which have not been applied for or have been deferred (para.(1)), income foregone under a money purchase benefits pension scheme or under a retirement annuity contract (paras (2)–(5)), and cases of income deprivation for the purpose of securing entitlement to (or increasing the amount of) state pension credit (para.(6)). Note also that Pt II of Sch.V lists various forms of capital which are to be disregarded in determining a person's notional income.

Paragraph (1)

3.87 The general rule is that pension income which the claimant could expect to receive on application is to be deemed to be notional income. The reference to SPCA 2002 s.16(1)(za)–(e) has the effect of confining this provision to various categories of state retirement pension income under the SSCBA 1992 or its Northern Ireland equivalent. The inclusion of the cross-reference to s.16(1)(za) in subs.(1)(a) means that for the purposes of pension credit a person is to be treated as receiving their new state pension while they are deferring it. Notional income also includes income from an occupational pension scheme which the claimant has chosen to defer. Other forms of income from private pension arrangements may be caught by paras (2)–(5).

Paragraphs (2)–(5)

3.88 These provisions mirror those that apply to income support (Income Support (General) Regulations 1987 (SI 1987/1967) reg.42(2A)–(2C), in Vol.V of this series; see further *BRG v SSWP (SPC)* [2014] UKUT 246 (AAC). The amendment to para.(3), made with effect from November 16, 2017, was designed to reverse the effect of Judge Humphrey's decision in *SSWP v IG (SPC)* [2018] UKUT 228 (AAC), where it was held that notional amounts from a personal pension scheme that had assets valued at less than the initial investment should be treated as payments of capital by instalments (and not income). However, in the event the Upper Tribunal's decision was reversed by the Court of Appeal in *SSWP v Goulding* [2019] EWCA Civ 839.

Paragraph (6)

3.89 This is expressed in the same terms as the notional income and notional capital rules for income support, and so the same principles apply ((Income Support (General) Regulations 1987 (SI 1987/1967) regs 42(1) and 51(1), in Vol.V of this series).

Paragraphs (7ZA) and (7ZB)

3.90 The effect of these provisions is that a person who changes their choice of a weekly increase to a lump sum in respect of the new state pension is not penalised by being treated as still possessing the extra income. See further paras.(8A) and (8B) for definitions.

[1Calculation of capital in the United Kingdom

19.—Capital which a claimant possesses in the United Kingdom shall be calculated at its current market or surrender value less— 3.91

(a) where there would be expenses attributable to sale, 10 per cent; and
(b) the amount of any encumbrance secured on it.]

AMENDMENT

1. Social Security (Miscellaneous Amendments) (No.5) Regulations 2007 (SI 2007/2618) reg.10(4) (October 1, 2007).

DEFINITIONS

"capital"—see SPCA 2002 s.17(1).
"claimant"—see *ibid.*

GENERAL NOTE

This is in the same terms as the parallel provision in the income support scheme (see Income Support (General) Regulations 1987 (SI 1987/1967) reg.49, in Vol.V of this series. See also *GE v Department for Communities (PC)* [2016] NICom 73, where the claimant's capital consisted of a part ownership as tenant in common of a property which was her former matrimonial home. Commissioner Stockman observed that "there is no market for the type of interest in property which the [claimant] possesses. Where there is no market, it follows that the current market value of the respondent's interest is likely to be, as the tribunal has found, nominal" (para.41). 3.92

Calculation of capital outside the United Kingdom

20.—Capital which a claimant possesses in a country outside the United Kingdom shall be calculated— 3.93

(a) in a case where there is no prohibition in that country against the transfer to the United Kingdom of an amount equal to its current market or surrender value in that country, at that value;
(b) in a case where there is such a prohibition, at the price which it would realise if sold in the United Kingdom to a willing buyer,

less, where there would be expenses attributable to sale, 10 per cent, and the amount of any encumbrance secured on it.

DEFINITIONS

"capital"—see SPCA 2002 s.17(1).
"claimant"—see *ibid.*

GENERAL NOTE

This is in the same terms as the parallel provision in the income support scheme (see Income Support (General) Regulations 1987 (SI 1987/1967) reg.50, in Vol.V of this series). 3.94

Notional capital

21.—[2(1) A claimant shall be treated as possessing capital of which he has deprived himself for the purpose of securing entitlement to state pension credit or increasing the amount of that benefit except to the extent that the capital which he is treated as possessing is reduced in accordance with regulation 22 (diminishing notional capital rule).] 3.95

[3 (2) A person who disposes of a capital resource for the purpose of—
(a) reducing or paying a debt owed by the claimant; or
(b) purchasing goods or services if the expenditure was reasonable in the circumstances of the claimant's case,
shall be regarded as not depriving himself of it.]

[1(3) Where a claimant stands in relation to a company in a position analogous to that of a sole owner or partner in the business of that company, he shall be treated as if he were such sole owner or partner and in such a case—
(a) the value of his holding in that company shall, notwithstanding regulation 19 (calculation of capital), be disregarded; and
(b) he shall, subject to paragraph (4), be treated as possessing an amount of capital equal to the value or, as the case may be, his share of the value of the capital of that company and the foregoing provisions of this Chapter shall apply for the purposes of calculating that amount as if it were actual capital which he does possess.

(4) For so long as a claimant undertakes activities in the course of the business of the company, the amount which he is treated as possessing under paragraph (3) shall be disregarded.

(5) Where under this regulation a person is treated as possessing capital, the amount of that capital shall be calculated in accordance with the provisions of this Part as if it were actual capital which he does possess.]

AMENDMENTS

1. State Pension Credit (Consequential, Transitional and Miscellaneous Provisions) Regulations 2002 (SI 2002/3019) reg.23(j) (October 6, 2003).
2. State Pension Credit (Consequential, Transitional and Miscellaneous Provisions) (No.2) Regulations 2002 (SI 2002/3197) reg.2 and Sch. para.6 (October 6, 2003).
3. State Pension Credit (Miscellaneous Amendments) Regulations 2004 (SI 2004/647) reg.3(5) (April 5, 2004).

DEFINITIONS

"capital"—see SPCA 2002 s.17(1).
"claimant"—see *ibid.*

GENERAL NOTE

3.96 Readers who are well acquainted with the income support system will be familiar with the concept of notional capital, that is capital which the claimant is deemed to possess even though he or she does not actually have such resources. This is, therefore, essentially an anti-avoidance provision in the context of means-tested benefits. Section 15(6) of the SPCA 2002 (which mirrors SSCBA 1992 s.163(5)) provides the legislative authority for such a rule in the state pension credit scheme. The notional capital rule enshrined in this regulation contains some parallels with the equivalent rule in the income support scheme (Income Support (General) Regulations 1987 (SI 1987/1967) reg.51, in Vol.V of this series), but is also different. In particular, the state pension credit rule operates only where there is a deprivation of capital with a view to claiming or increasing entitlement to benefit (para.(1)) or where the claimant is a sole trader or a partner in a business which is a limited company (paras (3) and (4)). There is, therefore, no equivalent to the income support rules governing failures to apply for capital which is available, payments to third parties by someone else on the claimant's behalf or retention of capital received on behalf of a third party (Income Support (General) Regulations 1987 (SI 1987/1967) reg.51(2) and (3)).

See also *MC v SSWP* [2010] UKUT 29 (AAC) for guidance on how the presumption of a resulting trust may operate in the context of a transaction between family members.

Paragraph (1)

3.97 The general rule is expressed in similar terms to Income Support (General) Regulations 1987 (SI 1987/1967) reg.51(1). The Secretary of State must accordingly show that: (1) the claimant has deprived him or herself of actual capital, and (2) this was done with the purpose of securing or increasing entitlement to state pension credit. As to (1), the traditional approach has been that "deprive" does not carry a special legal meaning and is a matter of ordinary English (*R(SB) 38/85, R(SB) 40/85*). However, these authorities will have to be applied with some care in the context of state pension credit as, unlike in the income support scheme, para.(2) below gives specific examples of what is not to be regarded as a deprivation. The supplementary benefit and income support case law on the claimant's purpose in making the deprivation will presumably apply equally here given the statutory language is the same in this respect (see commentary at para.2.419 in Vol.V of this series). There is, however, no express exception for capital for personal injuries compensation held in trust or administered by the court (contrast Income Support (General) Regulations 1987 (SI 1987/1967) reg.51(1)(a) and (c)).

Paragraph (2)

3.98 This is an interesting provision which has no direct parallel in the analogous rule that applies under the income support scheme (Income Support (General) Regulations 1987 (SI 1987/1967) reg.51). That said, it appears to be an attempt to illustrate what is not to be regarded as an act of deprivation. Thus, a disposal for the purpose of either reducing or paying a debt owed by the claimant, or in purchasing goods or services "if the expenditure was reasonable in the circumstances of the claimant's case", is not to be seen as a deprivation. Under the income support scheme, such disposals would be seen as a deprivation and the argument would then revolve around the claimant's purpose in making such a disposal. Typically the claimant would argue that the payment was solely for some other purpose, and not with a view to claiming or increasing entitlement to benefit. The position under the state pension credit scheme would appear to be different and perhaps weighted more in favour of the claimant. If the claimant is able to demonstrate that one of the circumstances in para.(2) applies, then there has been no deprivation and the issue as to the claimant's purpose need not be explored. This construction is strengthened by the repeal of the qualifying phrase "Without prejudice to the generality of paragraph (1)" as from April 5, 2004. That amendment also repealed the provision which automatically deemed a disposal by way of a gift to a third party to be a deprivation. However, it remains open to decision-makers and tribunals to find that such a gift was a deprivation made with the intent of securing (or increasing) entitlement to pension credit.

Paragraphs (3) and (4)

3.99 These two paragraphs establish an artificial method for dealing with one person companies and analogous enterprises. In summary, the value of the individual's shareholding itself is disregarded (para.(3)(a)) but the claimant is treated as possessing a proportionate share of the company's capital (para.(3)(b)). However, so long as the individual undertakes activities in the course of the business, the amount produced by para.(3)(b) is disregarded (para.(4)). See further the commentary on the parallel provisions in reg.51(4) and (5) of the Income Support (General) Regulations 1987 (SI 1987/1967).

Paragraph (5)

3.100 As the claimant's capital is to be calculated as though it were actual capital, it follows that notional capital is assumed to yield a weekly income on the basis set out in reg.15(6). It also means that any relevant capital disregards under reg.17(8) and Sch.V must be applied to the notional capital (by analogy with *CIS/231/1991*).

Diminishing notional capital rule

3.101 **22.**—(1) Where a claimant is treated as possessing capital under regulation 21(1) (notional capital), the amount which he is treated as possessing—

(a) in the case of a week that is subsequent to—
  (i) the relevant week in respect of which the conditions set out in paragraph (2) are satisfied, or
  (ii) a week which follows that relevant week and which satisfies those conditions,

shall be reduced by an amount determined under paragraph (2);

(b) in the case of a week in respect of which sub-paragraph (1)(a) does not apply but where—
  (i) that week is a week subsequent to the relevant week, and
  (ii) that relevant week is a week in which the condition in paragraph (3) is satisfied,

shall be reduced by the amount determined under paragraph (3).

(2) This paragraph applies to a benefit week where the claimant satisfies the conditions that—

(a) he is in receipt of state pension credit; and
(b) but for regulation [[1]21(1)], he would have received an additional amount of state pension credit in that benefit week;

and in such a case, the amount of the reduction for the purposes of paragraph (1)(a) shall be equal to that additional amount.

(3) Subject to paragraph (4), for the purposes of paragraph (1)(b) the condition is that the claimant would have been entitled to state pension credit in the relevant week, but for regulation [[1]21(1)], and in such a case the amount of the reduction shall be equal to the aggregate of—

(a) the amount of state pension credit to which the claimant would have been entitled in the relevant week but for regulation [[1]21(1)];
(b) the amount of housing benefit (if any) equal to the difference between his maximum housing benefit and the amount (if any) of housing benefit which he is awarded in respect of the benefit week, within the meaning of regulation 2(1) of the Housing Benefit (General) Regulations 1987 (interpretation), which includes the last day of the relevant week;
(c) the amount of council tax benefit (if any) equal to the difference between his maximum council tax benefit and the amount (if any) of council tax benefit which he is awarded in respect of the benefit week which includes the last day of the relevant week, and for this purpose "benefit week" [[2] means a period of 7 consecutive days beginning on a Monday and ending on a Sunday].

(4) The amount determined under paragraph (3) shall be re-determined under that paragraph if the claimant makes a further claim for state pension credit and the conditions in paragraph (5) are satisfied, and in such a case—

(a) sub-paragraphs (a) to (c) of paragraph (3) shall apply as if for the words "relevant week" there were substituted the words "relevant subsequent week"; and

(b) subject to paragraph (6), the amount as re-determined shall have effect from the first week following the relevant subsequent week in question.

(5) The conditions are that—

(a) a further claim is made 26 or more weeks after—

(i) the date on which the claimant made a claim for state pension credit in respect of which he was first treated as possessing the capital in question under regulation [[1]21(1)]; or

(ii) in a case where there has been at least one re-determination in accordance with paragraph (4), the date on which he last made a claim for state pension credit which resulted in the weekly amount being re-determined; or

(iii) the date on which he last ceased to be in receipt of state pension credit, whichever last occurred; and

(b) the claimant would have been entitled to state pension credit but for regulation [[1]21(1)].

(6) The amount as re-determined pursuant to paragraph (4) shall not have effect if it is less than the amount which applied in that case immediately before the re-determination and in such a case the higher amount shall continue to have effect.

(7) For the purpose of this regulation—

(a) "relevant week" means the benefit week in which the capital in question of which the claimant has deprived himself within the meaning of regulation [[1]21(1)]—

(i) was first taken into account for the purpose of determining his entitlement to state pension credit; or

(ii) was taken into account on a subsequent occasion for the purpose of determining or re-determining his entitlement to state pension credit on that subsequent occasion and that determination or re-determination resulted in his beginning to receive, or ceasing to receive, state pension credit;

and where more than one benefit week is identified by reference to heads (i) and (ii) of this sub-paragraph the later or latest such benefit week;

(b) "relevant subsequent week" means the benefit week which includes the day on which the further claim or, if more than one further claim had been made, the last such claim was made.

AMENDMENTS

1. State Pension Credit (Consequential, Transitional and Miscellaneous Provisions) (No.2) Regulations 2002 (SI 2002/3197) reg.2 and Sch. para.7 (October 6, 2003).

2. Council Tax Benefit Abolition (Consequential Provision) Regulations 2013 (SI 2013/458) reg.4 and Sch.2 para.6 (April 1, 2013).

DEFINITIONS

"benefit week"—see reg.1(2).
"capital"—see SPCA 2002 s.17(1).
"claimant"—see *ibid.*
"relevant week"—see para.(7)(a).

"relevant subsequent week"—see para.7(b).

General Note

3.102 This diminishing notional capital rule is, in all material respects, identical to that which operates under the income support scheme (Income Support (General) Regulations 1987 (SI 1987/1967) reg.51A, in Vol.V of this series). Thus if the amount of notional capital has the effect of removing entitlement to state pension credit altogether, owing to the application of the tariff income rule in reg.15(6) above, that notional capital is to be treated as reducing each week in accordance with para.(1)(b) and (3). In such a case the weekly reduction is by a sum representing the aggregate of the state pension credit which would have been received in the absence of such notional capital plus the proportion of rent and council tax not met by housing benefit and council tax benefit respectively. In other cases, the interaction of the notional capital rule and the tariff income rule will reduce rather than extinguish entitlement to state pension credit. In this type of situation the notional capital is to be treated as reducing each week by the amount by which the state pension credit would be increased in the absence of such notional capital (para.(1)(a) and (2)). Paragraphs (4)–(6) provide for redetermination and recalculation in the event of a fresh claim being made.

Capital jointly held

3.103 **23.**—Where a claimant and one or more persons are beneficially entitled in possession to any capital asset they shall be treated as if each of them were entitled in possession to the whole beneficial interest therein in an equal share and the foregoing provisions of this Part shall apply for the purposes of calculating the amount of capital which the claimant is treated as possessing as if it were actual capital which the claimant does possess.

Definitions

"capital"—see SPCA 2002 s.17(1).
"claimant"—see *ibid.*

General Note

3.104 This provision is essentially in the same terms as the parallel and notoriously problematic provision in the income support scheme (see Income Support (General) Regulations 1987 (SI 1987/1967) reg.52, in Vol.V of this series). For a valuable reminder that in cases where capital is held jointly "the market value of such an interest in circumstances such as these is not by any means the same thing as half the entire value of the freehold with vacant possession", see *AM v SSWP* [2010] UKUT 134 (AAC), para.5, applying *R(IS) 5/07*. However, its impact in the context of state pension credit is likely to be much less as there is no capital rule as such. It will, however, have effect for the purpose of calculating the value of the claimant's capital for the purpose of attributing the deemed tariff income under reg.15(6).

Income paid to third parties

3.105 **24.**—(1) Any payment of income, other than a payment specified in [1 paragraphs (2) or (3)], to a third party in respect of the claimant shall be treated as possessed by the claimant.

(2) Paragraph (1) shall not apply in respect of a payment of income made under an occupational pension scheme or in respect of a pension or other periodical payment made under a personal pension scheme where—

(a) a bankruptcy order has been made in respect of the person in respect of whom the payment has been made or, to Scotland, the estate of that person is subject to sequestration or a judicial factor has been appointed on that person's estate under section 41 of the Solicitors (Scotland) Act 1980;

(b) the payment is made to the trustee in bankruptcy or any other person acting on behalf of the creditors; and

(c) the person referred to in sub-paragraph (a) and his partner does not possess, or is not treated as possessing, any other income apart from that payment.

[1 (3) Paragraph (1) shall not apply in respect of any payment of income arising out of the [2 claimant participating as a service user.]

AMENDMENTS

1. Social Security (Miscellaneous Amendments) (No.3) Regulations 2011 (2011/2425) reg.15(4) (October 31, 2011).

2. Social Security (Miscellaneous Amendments) Regulations 2014 (SI 2014/591) reg.7(5) (April 28, 2014).

DEFINITIONS

"claimant"—see SPCA 2002 s.17(1).
"income"—see SPCA 2002 ss.15 and 17(1).
"occupational pension scheme"—see SPCA 2002 s.17(1).
"partner"—reg.1(3).
"personal pension scheme"—see *ibid.*

GENERAL NOTE

The claimant is deemed to possess income which is paid to a third party by someone in respect of the claimant. This is subject to the exceptions set out in para.(2), which is in identical terms to regs 42(ZA)(d) and 51(3A)(c) of the Income Support (General) Regulations 1987 (SI 1987/1967), in Vol.V of this series, which apply to notional income and notional capital respectively for income support purposes. 3.106

See further *BL v SSWP (SPC)* [2018] UKUT 4 (AAC) (discussed in the commentary on s.15 of the 2002 Act), in which the claimant directed pension payments to his separated wife. Judge Farbey QC rejected a submission that payments to third parties should be discounted from income unless they are deployed for the alimentation of the claimant. In that case, "Standard Life paid the claimant's wife in lieu of the claimant; and the payments were treated as maintenance payments made by him. I do not regard the tribunal as having erred in law by concluding that, in these circumstances, Standard Life made the payments for the claimant's purposes and so 'in respect of' the claimant" (at para.48).

[1Rounding of fractions

24A.—Where any calculation under this Part results in a fraction of a penny that fraction shall, if it would be to the claimant's advantage, be treated as a penny; otherwise it shall be disregarded.] 3.107

AMENDMENT

1. State Pension Credit (Consequential, Transitional and Miscellaneous Provisions) Regulations 2002 (SI 2002/3019) reg.23(k) (October 6, 2003).

GENERAL NOTE

This reflects the normal rule for means-tested benefits (see Income Support (General) Regulations 1987 (SI 1987/1967) reg.27). 3.108

Part IV

Loss of benefit

Loss of benefit

3.109 **25.**—[*Omitted.*]

General Note

3.110 This regulation amends the Social Security (Loss of Benefits) Regulations 2001 (SI 2001/4022); the relevant changes are incorporated in Vol.III in this series.

SCHEDULES

Regulation 6(4)

SCHEDULE I

Part I

Circumstances in which persons are treated as being or not being severely disabled

Severe disablement

3.111 **1.**—(1) For the purposes of regulation 6(4) (additional amounts for persons severely disabled), the claimant is to be treated as being severely disabled if, and only if—

(a) in the case of a claimant who has no partner—

(i) he is in receipt of attendance allowance [7, the care component of disability living allowance at the highest or middle rate prescribed in accordance with section 72(3) of the 1992 Act [12,] the daily living component of personal independence payment at the standard or enhanced rate in accordance with section 78(3) of the 2012 Act [12, the daily living component of adult disability payment at the standard or enhanced rate in accordance with regulation 5 of the Disability Assistance for Working Age People (Scotland) Regulations 2022] [8 or armed forces independence payment]]; and

(ii) no person who has attained the age of 18 is normally residing with the claimant, nor is the claimant normally residing with such a person, other than a person to whom paragraph 2 applies; and

(iii) no person is entitled to and in receipt of an allowance under section 70 of the 1992 Act ([2 carer's allowance]) [13or carer support payment] [10 , or has an award of universal credit which includes the carer element,] in respect of caring for him;

(b) in the case of a claimant who has a partner—

(i) both partners are in receipt of attendance allowance [7, the care component of disability living allowance at the highest or middle rate prescribed in accordance with section 72(3) of the 1992 Act [12,] the daily living component of personal independence payment at the standard or enhanced rate in accordance with section 78(3) of the 2012 Act [12, the daily living component of adult disability payment at the standard or enhanced rate in accordance with regulation 5 of the Disability Assistance for Working Age People (Scotland) Regulations 2022] [8 or armed forces independence payment]]; and

(ii) no person who has attained the age of 18 is normally residing with the partners, nor are the partners normally residing with such a person, other than a person to whom paragraph 2 applies;

and either a person is entitled to, and in receipt of, an allowance under section 70 of the 1992 Act [13or carer support payment] [10, or has an award of universal credit which includes the carer element,] in respect of caring for one only of the partners or, as the case may be, no person is entitled to, and in receipt of, such an allowance [10 under section 70 [13or carer support payment], or has an award of universal credit which includes the carer element,] in respect of caring for either partner;

(c) in the case of a claimant who has a partner and to whom head (b) does not apply—

(i) either the claimant or his partner is in receipt of attendance allowance [[7], the care component of disability living allowance at the highest or middle rate prescribed in accordance with section 72(3) of the 1992 Act [[12],] or the daily living component of personal independence payment at the standard or enhanced rate in accordance with section 78(3) of the 2012 Act [[12], the daily living component of adult disability payment at the standard or enhanced rate in accordance with regulation 5 of the Disability Assistance for Working Age People (Scotland) Regulations 2022] [[8] or armed forces independence payment]]; and

[[9] (ii) the other partner is certified as severely sight impaired or blind by a consultant ophthalmologist; and;]

(iii) no person who has attained the age of 18 is normally residing with the partners, nor are the partners normally residing with such a person, other than a person to whom paragraph 2 applies; and

(iv) no person is entitled to and in receipt of an allowance under section 70 of the 1992 Act [[13]or carer support payment] [[10], or has an award of universal credit which includes the carer element, in] respect of caring for the person to whom head (c) (i) above applies.

(2) A person shall be treated—

(a) for the purposes of sub-paragraph (1) as being in receipt of attendance allowance or, as the case may be, [[7], the care component of disability living allowance at the highest or middle rate prescribed in accordance with section 72(3) of the 1992 Act [[12],] or the daily living component of personal independence payment at the standard or enhanced rate in accordance with section 78(3) of the 2012 Act [[12], the daily living component of adult disability payment at the standard or enhanced rate in accordance with regulation 5 of the Disability Assistance for Working Age People (Scotland) Regulations 2022] [[8] or armed forces independence payment]], for any period—

(i) before an award is made but in respect of which the allowance [[7]or payment] is awarded; or

(ii) not covered by an award but in respect of which a payment is made in lieu of an award;

(b) for the purposes of sub-paragraph (1)(b) as being in receipt of attendance allowance or the care component of disability living allowance at the highest or middle rate prescribed in accordance section [[1]72(3)] of the 1992 Act if he would, but for his being a patient for a period exceeding 28 days, be so in receipt;

[[7] (ba) for the purposes of sub-paragraph (1)(b) as being in receipt of the daily living component of personal independence payment at the standard or enhanced rate in accordance with section 78 of the 2012 Act if he would, but for regulations made under section 86(1) (hospital in-patients) of that Act, be so in receipt;]

[[12] (bb) for the purposes of sub-paragraph (1)(b) as being in receipt of the daily living component of adult disability payment at the standard or enhanced rate in accordance with regulation 5 of the Disability Assistance for Working Age People (Scotland) Regulations 2022, if that person would, but for regulation 28 (effect of admission to hospital on ongoing entitlement to Adult Disability Payment) of those Regulations, be so in receipt;]

(c) for the purposes of sub-paragraph (1), as not being in receipt of an allowance under section 70 of the 1992 Act [[13]or carer support payment] [[10], or as having an award of universal credit which includes the carer element,] for any period before [[5] the date on which the award is first paid].

[[9] (3) For the purposes of sub-paragraph (1)(c)(ii), a person who has ceased to be certified as severely sight impaired or blind on regaining his eyesight shall nevertheless be treated as severely sight impaired or blind, as the case may be, and as satisfying the requirements set out in that sub-paragraph for a period of 28 weeks following the date on which he ceased to be so certified.]

[[10] (4) For the purposes of this paragraph, a person has an award of universal credit which includes the carer element if the person has an award of universal credit which includes an amount which is the carer element under regulation 29 of the Universal Credit Regulations 2013.]

Persons residing with the claimant whose presence is ignored

2.—(1) For the purposes of paragraph 1(1)(a)(ii), (b)(ii) and (c)(iii), this paragraph applies to the persons specified in the following sub-paragraphs. 3.112

(2) A person who—

(a) is in receipt of attendance allowance [[7], the care component of disability living allowance at the highest or middle rate prescribed in accordance with section 72(3) of the 1992 Act [[12],] the daily living component of personal independence payment at the standard or enhanced rate in accordance with section 78(3) of the 2012 Act [12, the daily living component of adult disability payment at the standard or enhanced rate in accordance with regulation 5 of the Disability Assistance for Working Age People (Scotland) Regulations 2022] [8 or armed forces independence payment]];

[9 (b) is certified as severely sight impaired or blind by a consultant ophthalmologist;

(c) is no longer certified as severely sight impaired or blind in accordance with head (b) but was so certified not more than 28 weeks earlier;]

(d) lives with the claimant in order to care for him or his partner and is engaged by a charitable or voluntary organisation which makes a charge to the claimant or his partner for the services provided by that person;

(e) is a partner of a person to whom head (d) above applies; or

(f) is a person who is [3 a qualifying young person [11 within the meaning of regulation 4A] or] child [11 as defined in section 40 of the 2012 Act].

(3) Subject to sub-paragraph (4), a person who joins the claimant's household for the first time in order to care for the claimant or his partner and immediately before he joined the household, the claimant or his partner was treated as being severely disabled.

(4) Sub-paragraph (3) applies only for the first 12 weeks following the date on which the person first joins the claimant's household.

(5) A person who is not a close relative of the claimant or his partner and—

(a) who is liable to make payments on a commercial basis to the claimant or his partner in respect of his occupation of the dwelling;

(b) to whom the claimant or his partner is liable to make payments on a commercial basis in respect of his occupation of that person's dwelling; or

(c) who is a member of the household of a person to whom head (a) or (b) applies.

(6) Subject to paragraph 3(3), a person who jointly occupies the claimant's dwelling and who is either—

(a) co-owner of that dwelling with the claimant or the claimant's [1partner] (whether or not there are other co-owners); or

(b) jointly liable with the claimant or the claimant's partner to make payments to a landlord in respect of his occupation of that dwelling.

(7) Subject to paragraph 3(3), a person who is a partner of a person to whom sub-paragraph (6) applies.

3.—(1) For the purposes of paragraphs 1 and 2, a person resides with another only if they share any accommodation except a bathroom, a lavatory or a communal area, but not if each person is separately liable to make payments in respect of his occupation of the dwelling to the landlord.

(2) In sub-paragraph (1), "communal area" means any area (other than rooms) of common access (including halls and passageways) and rooms of common use in sheltered accommodation.

(3) Paragraph 2(6) and (7) applies to a person who is a close relative of the claimant or his partner only if the claimant or his partner's co-ownership, or joint liability to make payments to a landlord in respect of his occupation, of the dwelling arose either before 11th April 1988, or, if later, on or before the date upon which the claimant or the claimant's partner first occupied the dwelling in question.

Part II

Amount applicable for carers

3.113 **4.**—(1) For the purposes of regulation 6(6)(a), this paragraph is satisfied if any of the requirements specified in sub-paragraphs (2) to (4) are met.

(2) A claimant is, or in the case of partners either partner is, or both partners are, entitled to an allowance under section 70 of the 1992 Act ([2 carer's allowance]) [13or carer support payment].

(3) Where an additional amount has been awarded under regulation 6(6)(a) but—

(a) the person in respect of whose care the allowance [13or payment] has been awarded dies; or

(b) the person in respect of whom the additional amount was awarded ceases to be entitled or ceases to be treated as entitled to the allowance [13or payment],

this paragraph shall be treated as satisfied for a period of eight weeks from the relevant date specified in sub-paragraph (4).

(4) The relevant date for the purposes of [1sub-paragraph (3) is]—

(a) the Sunday following the death of the person in respect of whose care the allowance

[13or payment] has been awarded (or beginning with the date of death if the death occurred on a Sunday);

(b) where sub-paragraph (a) does not apply, the date on which the person who has been entitled to the allowance [13or payment] ceases to be entitled to that allowance [13or payment].

5.—For the purposes of paragraph 4, a person shall be treated as being entitled to and in receipt of an allowance under section 70 of the 1992 Act [13or carer support payment] for any period not covered by an award but in respect of which a payment is made in lieu of an award.

PART III

Amount applicable for former claimants of income support [6, income-based jobseeker's allowance or income-related employment and support allowance]

6.—(1) If on the relevant day the relevant amount exceeds the provisional amount, an additional amount ("the transitional amount") equal to the difference shall be applicable to a claimant to whom sub-paragraph (2) applies. 3.114

(2) This sub-paragraph applies to a claimant who, in respect of the day before the relevant day, was entitled to either income support [6, an income-based jobseeker's allowance or an income-related employment and support allowance.]

(3) The relevant day is the day in respect of which the claimant is first entitled to state pension credit.

(4) The provisional amount means the amount of the appropriate minimum guarantee applicable to the claimant on the relevant day but for this paragraph.

(5) The relevant amount means the amount which, on the day before the relevant day, was the claimant's applicable amount—

(a) for the purposes of determining his entitlement to income support; [6 . . .]

(b) for the purpose of determining his entitlement to an income-based jobseeker's allowance,

less any of the following amounts included in it—

(i) any amount determined in accordance with paragraph 2 of Schedule 2 to the Income Support Regulations or paragraph 2 of Schedule 1 to the Jobseeker's Allowance Regulations;

(ii) any amount by way of a residential allowance applicable in accordance with paragraph 2A of Schedule 2 to the Income Support Regulations or paragraph 3 of Schedule 1 to the Jobseeker's Allowance Regulations;

(iii) any amount by way of family premium applicable in accordance with paragraph 3 of Schedule 2 to the Income Support Regulations or paragraph 4 of Schedule 1 to the Jobseeker's Allowance Regulations;

(iv) any amount by way of disabled child premium applicable in accordance with paragraph 14 of Schedule 2 to the Income Support Regulations or paragraph 16 of Schedule 1 to the Jobseeker's Allowance Regulations; and

(v) any amount in respect of a person other than the claimant or his partner by way of enhanced disability premium applicable in accordance with paragraph 13A of Schedule 2 to the Income Support Regulations [6, paragraph 7 of Schedule 4 to the Employment and Support Allowance Regulations] or paragraph 15A of Schedule 1 to the Jobseeker's Allowance Regulations [6; or

(c) for the purposes of determining his entitlement to income-related employment and support allowance.]

(6) In determining the relevant amount under sub-paragraph (5), the applicable amount shall be increased by an amount equal to the amount (if any) payable to the claimant in accordance with Part II of the Income Support (Transitional) Regulations 1987 (transitional protection) or regulation 87(1) of the Jobseeker's Allowance Regulations (transitional supplement to income-based jobseeker's allowance).

(7) If—

(a) paragraph 1 of Schedule 7 to the Income Support Regulations or paragraph 1 of Schedule 5 to the Jobseeker's Allowance [1 Regulations] applied to the claimant or his partner on the day before the relevant day; but

(b) paragraph 2(2) of Schedule 3 does not apply to the claimant or his partner on the relevant day;

then for the purposes of this paragraph the relevant amount shall be determined on the assumption that the provision referred to in sub-paragraph (7)(a) did not apply in his case.

(8) Subject to sub-paragraph (9), the transitional amount shall—

(a) be reduced by a sum equal to the amount (if any) by which the appropriate minimum guarantee increases after the relevant day;

(b) cease to be included in the claimant's appropriate minimum guarantee from the day on which—

(i) the sum mentioned in head (a) above equals or exceeds the transitional amount; or

(ii) the claimant or the claimant's partner ceases to be entitled to state pension credit.

(9) For the purposes of sub-paragraph (8), there shall be disregarded—

(a) any break in entitlement not exceeding 8 weeks; and

[4 (b) any amount by which the appropriate minimum guarantee of a patient is increased on 10th April 2006 by virtue of the substitution of paragraph 2 of Schedule 3.]

[1 (10) This sub-paragraph applies where the relevant amount included an amount in respect of housing costs relating to a loan—

(a) which is treated as a qualifying loan by virtue of regulation 3 of the Income Support (General) Amendment and Transitional Regulations 1995 or paragraph 18(2) of Schedule 2 to the Jobseeker's Allowance Regulation [6 or paragraph 20(2) of Schedule 6 to the Employment and Support Allowance Regulations]; or

(b) the appropriate amount of which was determined in accordance with paragraph 7(6C) of Schedule 3 to the Income Support Regulations as in force prior to 10th April 1995 and maintained in force by regulation 28(1) of the Income-related Benefits Schemes (Miscellaneous Amendments) Regulations 1995.

(11) Where sub-paragraph (10) applies, the transitional amount shall be calculated or, as the case may be, recalculated, on the relevant anniversary date determined in accordance with paragraph 7(4C) of Schedule II ("the relevant anniversary date") on the basis that the provisional amount on the relevant day included, in respect of housing costs, the amount calculated in accordance with paragraph 7(1) of Schedule II as applying from the relevant anniversary date and not the amount in respect of housing costs determined on the basis of the amount of the loan calculated in accordance with paragraph 7(4A) of that Schedule.

(12) The transitional amount as calculated in accordance with sub-paragraph (11) shall only be applicable from the relevant anniversary date.]

AMENDMENTS

1. State Pension Credit (Consequential, Transitional and Miscellaneous Provisions) (No.2) Regulations 2002 (SI 2002/3197) reg.2 and Sch. para.8 (October 6, 2003).

2. State Pension Credit (Transitional and Miscellaneous Provisions) Amendment Regulations 2003 (SI 2003/2274) reg.2(8) (October 6, 2003).

3. Social Security (Young Persons) Amendment Regulations 2006 (SI 2006/718) reg.6(3) (April 10, 2006).

4. Social Security (Miscellaneous Amendments) Regulations 2006 (SI 2006/588) reg.4(3) (April 10, 2006).

5. Social Security (Miscellaneous Amendments) Regulations 2007 (SI 2007/719) reg.4 (April 2, 2007).

6. Employment and Support Allowance (Consequential Provisions) (No.2) Regulations 2008 (SI 2008/1554) reg.4(7) (October 27, 2008).

7. Personal Independence Payment (Supplementary Provisions and Consequential Amendments) Regulations 2013 (SI 2013/388) reg.8 and Sch. para.27(4)(a) (April 8, 2013).

8. Armed Forces and Reserve Forces Compensation Scheme (Consequential Provisions: Subordinate Legislation) Order 2013 (SI 2013/591) art.7 and Sch. para.23(4) (April 8, 2013).

9. Universal Credit and Miscellaneous Amendments (No.2) Regulations 2014 (SI 2014/2888) reg.3(4)(a) (November 26, 2014).

10. Universal Credit and Miscellaneous Amendments Regulations 2015 (SI 2015/1754) reg.16(3) (November 4, 2015).

11. Housing Benefit and State Pension Credit (Temporary Absence) (Amendment) Regulations 2016 (SI 2016/624) reg.4(7) (July 28, 2016).

12. Social Security (Disability Assistance for Working Age People) (Consequential Amendments) Order 2022 (SI 2022/177) art.8(3) (March 21, 2022).

13. Carer's Assistance (Carer Support Payment) (Scotland) Regulations 2023 (Consequential Amendments) Order 2023 (SI 2023/1218) art.14(6) (November 19, 2023).

GENERAL NOTE

Schedule I sets out the criteria for the award of additional guarantee credit amounts, on the same basis as under the income support scheme, for severely disabled pensioners (Pt I), for carers (Pt II) and for pensioners with entitlement to transitional additions (Pt III). Regulation 6 is the principal provision governing the guarantee credit and lists the actual weekly amounts for the principal additional elements. 3.115

Paragraph 1

According to *CPC/2021/2008* (at paras 56–64), the reference to a person being "in receipt of attendance allowance" is to be read as meaning "in actual receipt of attendance allowance" rather than being "entitled to but not actually in receipt of attendance allowance", notwithstanding the absence of a provision equivalent to para.14B of Sch.2 to the Income Support (General) Regulations 1987 (SI 1987/1967). See further *DB (as executor of the estate of OE) v SSWP and Birmingham CC (SPC)* [2018] UKUT 46 (AAC), in which Judge Mitchell concluded that the legislator "intended to link the additional amount for severe disability to factual receipt of attendance allowance rather than its payability" (at para.53). See *HT v SSWP (AA)* [2020] UKUT 57 (AAC) for an example of a case where receipt of an equivalent Polish disability benefit qualified for these purposes. 3.116

Paragraphs 2 and 3

In *CPC/1446/2008*, Deputy Commissioner Wikeley considered whether a claimant was "residing with" a non-dependent within the meaning of Sch.1 paras 2 and 3. The Deputy Commissioner followed *CSIS/652/2003* in preferring *CSIS/2532/2003* to *CIS/185/1995* on the parallel income support rules. According to the Deputy Commissioner, a kitchen may therefore form part of shared accommodation even if the claimant personally does not visit the kitchen so long as he uses it in some other way (e.g. storage or for a third party to prepare meals). However, in *RK v SSWP* [2008] UKUT 34 (AAC) Judge Rowland was prepared to accept that a person does not necessarily share a kitchen merely because meals are prepared for him or her there. Judge Rowland also agreed with the outcomes of the appeals in *CSIS/185/1995*, *CIS/2532/2003*, *CSIS/652/2003* and *CPC/1446/2008* if not all of the reasoning. Judge Rowland took the view that "residing with" means "living in the same household as". On the facts a claimant who was confined to her bedroom in her son's house shared accommodation with her son and so normally resided with him, and so was not entitled to a severe disability premium. See further, *ST v Secretary of State for Work and Pensions* [2009] UKUT 269 (AAC). 3.117

Regulation 6(6)(c)

SCHEDULE II

HOUSING COSTS

Housing costs

1.—(1) Subject to the following provisions of this Schedule, the housing costs applicable to a claimant in accordance with regulation 6(6)(c) are those costs— 3.118

(a) which the claimant or, if he has a partner, his partner is, in accordance with paragraph 3, liable to meet in respect of the dwelling occupied as the home which he or his partner is treated as occupying; and

(b) which qualify [41 under paragraph 13].

(2) [41 . . .]

(3) For the purposes of sub-paragraph (2)(a), a person shall not cease to be a disabled person on account of his being disqualified for receiving benefit or treated as capable of work by virtue of the operation of section 171E of the 1992 Act (incapacity for work, disqualification, etc.) [19 or disqualified for receiving employment and support allowance or treated as not having limited capability for work in accordance with regulations made under section 18 of the Welfare Reform Act (disqualification)].

(4) In this Schedule, "non-dependant" means any person, except someone to whom sub-paragraph (5), (6) or (7) applies, who normally resides with the claimant.

(5) This sub-paragraph applies to—

(a) a partner of the claimant or any person under the age of [13 20] for whom the claimant or the claimant's partner is responsible;

(b) a person who lives with the claimant in order to care for him or for the claimant's partner and who is engaged for that purpose by a charitable or voluntary organisation which makes a charge to the claimant or the claimant's partner for the care provided by that person;

(c) the partner of a person to whom head (b) above applies.

(6) This sub-paragraph applies to a person, other than a close relative of the claimant or the claimant's partner—

(a) who is liable to make payments on a commercial basis to the claimant or the claimant's partner in respect of his occupation of the claimant's dwelling; [2or]

(b) [2. . .]

(c) who is a member of the household of a person to whom head (a) [2 . . .] above applies.

(7) This sub-paragraph applies to—

(a) a person who jointly occupies the claimant's dwelling and who is either—

(i) co-owner of that dwelling with the claimant or the claimant's partners (whether or not there are other co-owners); or

(ii) jointly liable with the claimant or the claimant's partner to make payments to a landlord in respect of his occupation of that dwelling;

(b) a partner of a person to whom head (a) above applies.

(8) For the purpose of sub-paragraphs (4) to (7) a person resides with another only if they share any accommodation except a bathroom, a lavatory or a communal area but not if each person is separately liable to make payments in respect of his occupation of the dwelling to the landlord.

(9) In sub-paragraph (8), "communal area" means any area (other than rooms) of common access (including halls and passageways) and rooms of common use in sheltered accommodation.

Remunerative work

3.119 **2.**—(1) Subject to the following provisions of this paragraph, a person shall be treated for the purposes of this Schedule as engaged in remunerative work if he is engaged, or, where his hours of work fluctuate, he is engaged on average, for not less than 16 hours a week, in work for which payment is made or which is done in expectation of payment.

(2) Subject to sub-paragraph (3), in determining the number of hours for which a person is engaged in work where his hours of work fluctuate, regard shall be had to the average of hours worked over—

(a) if there is a recognisable cycle of work, the period of one complete cycle (including, where the cycle involves periods in which the person does no work, those periods but disregarding any other absences);

(b) in any other case, the period of 5 weeks immediately prior to the date of claim, or such other length of time as may, in the particular case, enable the person's weekly average hours of work to be determined more accurately.

(3) Where, for the purposes of sub-paragraph (2)(a), a person's recognisable cycle of work at a school, other educational establishment or other place of employment is one year and includes periods of school holidays or similar vacations during which he does not work, those periods and any other periods not forming part of such holidays or vacations during which he is not required to work shall be disregarded in establishing the average hours for which he is engaged in work.

(4) Where no recognisable cycle has been established in respect of a person's work, regard shall be had to the number of hours or, where those hours will fluctuate, the average of the hours, which he is expected to work in a week.

(5) A person shall be treated as engaged in remunerative work during any period for which he is absent from work referred to in sub-paragraph (1) if the absence is either without good cause or by reason of a recognised, customary or other holiday.

(6) A person on income support or an income-based jobseeker's allowance for more than 3 days in any benefit week shall be treated as not being in remunerative work in that week.

(7) A person shall not be treated as engaged in remunerative work on any day on which the person is on maternity leave [4, paternity leave [33, shared parental leave] [42, parental bereavement leave] or adoption leave,] or is absent from work because he is ill.

(8) A person shall not be treated as engaged in remunerative work on any day on which he is engaged in an activity in respect of which—

(a) a sports award has been made, or is to be made, to him; and

(b) no other payment is made or is expected to be made to him [2, and for the purposes of this sub-paragraph, "sports award" means an award made by one of the Sports Councils named in section 23(2) of the National Lottery etc. Act 1993 out of sums allocated to it for distribution under that section.]

(9) In this paragraph "benefit week"—

(a) in relation to income support, has the same meaning as in regulation 2(1) of the Income Support Regulations;

(b) in relation to jobseeker's allowance, has the same meaning as in regulation 1(3) of the Jobseeker's Allowance Regulations.

Circumstances in which a person is liable to meet housing costs

3.—A person is liable to meet housing costs where— 3.120

(a) the liability falls upon him or his partner but not where the liability is to a member of the same household as the person on whom the liability falls;

(b) because the person liable to meet the housing costs is not meeting them, the claimant has to meet those costs in order to continue to live in the dwelling occupied as the home and it is reasonable in all the circumstances to treat the claimant as liable to meet those costs;

(c) he in practice shares the housing costs with other members of the household none of whom are close relatives either of the claimant or his partner, and—

(i) one or more of those members is liable to meet those costs, and

(ii) it is reasonable in the circumstances to treat him as sharing responsibility.

Circumstances in which a person is to be treated as occupying a dwelling as his home

4.—(1) Subject to the following provisions of this paragraph, a person shall be treated as occupying as his home the dwelling normally occupied as his home by himself or, if he has a partner, by himself and his partner, and he shall not be treated as occupying any other dwelling as his home. 3.121

(2) In determining whether a dwelling is the dwelling normally occupied as the claimant's home for the purposes of sub-paragraph (1) regard shall be had to any other dwelling occupied by the claimant or by him and his partner whether or not that other dwelling is in Great Britain.

(3) Subject to sub-paragraph (4), where a claimant who has no partner is a full-time student or is on a training course and is liable to make payments (including payments of mortgage interest or, in Scotland, payments under heritable securities or, in either case, analogous payments) in respect of either (but not both) the dwelling which he occupies for the purpose of attending his course of study or his training course or, as the case may be, the dwelling which he occupies when not attending his course, he shall be treated as occupying as his home the dwelling in respect of which he is liable to make payments.

(4) A full-time student shall not be treated as occupying a dwelling as his home for any week of absence from it, other than an absence occasioned by the need to enter hospital for treatment, outside the period of study, if the main purpose of his occupation during the period of study would be to facilitate attendance on his course.

(5) Where a claimant has been required to move into temporary accommodation by reason of essential repairs being carried out to the dwelling normally occupied as his home and he is liable to make payments (including payments of mortgage interest or, in Scotland, payments under heritable securities or, in either case, analogous payments) in respect of either (but not both) the dwelling normally occupied or the temporary accommodation, he shall be treated as occupying as his home the dwelling in respect of which he is liable to make those payments.

(6) Where a person is liable to make payments in respect of two (but not more than two) dwellings, he shall be treated as occupying both dwellings as his home only—

(a) where he has left and remains absent from the former dwelling occupied as the home through fear of violence in that dwelling or of violence by a close relative or former partner and it is reasonable that housing costs should be met in respect of both his former dwelling and his present dwelling occupied as the home; or

(b) in the case of partners, where one partner is a full-time student or is on a training course and it is unavoidable that he or they should occupy two separate dwellings and reasonable that housing costs should be met in respect of both dwellings; or

(c) in the case where a person has moved into a new dwelling occupied as the home, except where sub-paragraph (5) applies, for a period not exceeding four benefit weeks [[15] from the first day of the benefit week where the move takes place on that day, but if it does not, from the first day of the next following benefit week] if his liability to make payments in respect of two dwellings is unavoidable.

(7) Where—

(a) a person has moved into a dwelling and was liable to make payments in respect of that dwelling before moving in; and

(b) he had claimed state pension credit before moving in and either that claim has not yet been determined or it has been determined but—

(i) an amount has not been included under this Schedule; or

(ii) the claim has been refused and a further claim has been made within four weeks of the date on which the claimant moved into the new dwelling occupied as the home; and

(c) the delay in moving into the dwelling in respect of which there was liability to make payments before moving in was reasonable and—

(i) that delay was necessary in order to adapt the dwelling to meet the disablement needs of the claimant, his partner or a person under the age of [[13] 20] for whom either the claimant or his partner is responsible; or

(ii) the move was delayed pending [[27] local welfare provision or] the outcome of an application under Part VIII of the 1992 Act for a social fund payment to meet a need arising out of the move or in connection with setting up the home in the dwelling; or

(iii) the person became liable to make payments in respect of the dwelling while he was a patient or was in a care home [[11] or an independent hospital],

he shall be treated as occupying the dwelling as his home for any period not exceeding four weeks immediately prior to the date on which he moved into the dwelling and in respect of which he was liable to make payments.

[[11] (8) This sub-paragraph applies to a person who enters a care home or an independent hospital—

(a) for the purpose of ascertaining whether that care home or independent hospital suits his needs, and

(b) with the intention of returning to the dwelling which he normally occupies as his home should, in the event that, the care home or independent hospital prove not to suit his needs,

and while in the care home or independent hospital, the part of the dwelling which he normally occupies as his home is not let, or as the case may be, sub-let to another person.]

(9) A person to whom sub-paragraph (8) applies shall be treated as occupying the dwelling he normally occupies as his home during any period (commencing with the day he enters the [[11] care home or independent hospital]) not exceeding 13 weeks in which the person is resident in the [[11] care home or independent hospital], but only in so far as the total absence from the dwelling does not exceed 52 weeks.

(10) A person, other than a person to whom sub-paragraph (11) applies, shall be treated as occupying a dwelling as his home throughout any period of absence not exceeding 13 weeks, if, and only if—

(a) he intends to return to occupy the dwelling as his home; and

(b) the part of the dwelling normally occupied by him has not been let or, as the case may be, sub-let to another person; and

(c) the period of absence is unlikely to exceed 13 weeks.

(11) This sub-paragraph applies to a person whose absence from the dwelling he normally occupies as his home is temporary and—

(a) he intends to return to occupy the dwelling as his home; and

(b) while the part of the dwelling which is normally occupied by him has not been let or, as the case may be, sub-let; and

(c) he is—

[[8] (i) detained in custody on remand pending trial or, as a condition of bail, required to reside—

(aa) in a dwelling, other than the dwelling he occupies as his home; or

(bb) in premises approved under [[21] section 13 of the Offender Management Act 2007]

or, detained pending sentence upon conviction; or]

(ii) resident in a hospital or similar institution as a patient; or

(iii) undergoing or, as the case may be, his partner or a person who has not attained the age of [13 20] and who is dependent on him or his partner is undergoing, in the United Kingdom or elsewhere, medical treatment, or medically approved convalescence, in accommodation other than in a care home [11 or an independent hospital]; or
(iv) following, in the United Kingdom or elsewhere, a training course; or
(v) undertaking medically approved care of a person residing in the United Kingdom or elsewhere; or
(vi) undertaking the care of a person under the age of [13 20] whose parent or guardian is temporarily absent from the dwelling normally occupied by that parent or guardian for the purpose of receiving medically approved care or medical treatment, or
(vii) a person who is, whether in the United Kingdom or elsewhere, receiving medically approved care provided in accommodation other than a care home [11 or an independent hospital]; or
(viii) a full-time student to whom sub-paragraph (3) or (6)(b) does not apply; or
(ix) a person, other than a person to whom sub-paragraph (8) applies, who is receiving care provided in a care home [11 or an independent hospital]; or
(x) a person to whom sub-paragraph (6)(a) does not apply and who has left the dwelling he occupies as his home through fear of violence in that dwelling, or by a person who was formerly his partner or is a close relative; and

(d) the period of his absence is unlikely to exceed a period of 52 weeks or, in exceptional circumstances, is unlikely substantially to exceed that period.

(12) A person to whom sub-paragraph (11) applies is to be treated as occupying the dwelling he normally occupies as his home during any period of absence not exceeding 52 weeks beginning with the first day of that absence.

(13) In this paragraph—
(a) "medically approved" means certified by a medical practitioner;
(b) "training course" means such a course of training or instruction provided wholly or partly by or on behalf of or in pursuance of arrangements made with, or approved by or on behalf of [22 Skills Development Scotland], Scottish Enterprise, Highlands and Islands Enterprise, a government department or the Secretary of State.

Housing costs not met

5.—(1) No amount may be met under the provisions of this Schedule— 3.122
(a) in respect of housing benefit expenditure; or
(b) where the claimant is in accommodation which is a care home [11 or an independent hospital] except where he is in such accommodation during a temporary absence from the dwelling he occupies as his home and in so far as they relate to temporary absences, the provisions of paragraph 4(8) to (12) apply to him during that absence.

[1(1A) In paragraph (1), "housing benefit expenditure" means expenditure in respect of which housing benefit is payable as specified in regulation 10(1) of the Housing Benefit (General) Regulations 1987 but does not include any such expenditure in respect of which an additional amount is applicable under regulation 6(6)(c) (housing costs).]

(2)–(13) [41 . . .]

Apportionment of housing costs

6.—(1) Where the dwelling occupied as the home is a composite hereditament and— 3.123
(a) before 1st April 1990 for the purposes of section 48(5) of the General Rate Act 1967 (reduction of rates on dwellings), it appeared to a rating authority or it was determined in pursuance of subsection (6) of section 48 of that Act that the hereditament, including the dwelling occupied as the home, was a mixed hereditament and that only a proportion of the rateable value of the hereditament was attributable to use for the purpose of a private dwelling; or
(b) in Scotland, before 1st April 1989 an assessor acting pursuant to section 45(1) of the Water (Scotland) Act 1980 (provision as to valuation roll) has apportioned the net annual value of the premises including the dwelling occupied as the home between the part occupied as a dwelling and the remainder,

the additional amount applicable under this Schedule shall be such proportion of the amounts applicable in respect of the hereditament or premises as a whole as is equal to the proportion of the rateable value of the hereditament attributable to the part of the hereditament used for the purposes of a private tenancy or, in Scotland, the proportion of the net annual value of the premises apportioned to the part occupied as a dwelling house.

(2) Subject to sub-paragraph (1) and the following provisions of this paragraph, where the dwelling occupied as the home is a composite hereditament, the additional amount applicable under this Schedule shall be the relevant fraction of the amount which would otherwise be applicable under this Schedule in respect of the dwelling occupied as the home.

(3) For the purposes of sub-paragraph (2), the relevant fraction shall be obtained in accordance with the formula—

$$\frac{A}{A + B}$$

where—

"A" is the current market value of the claimant's interest in that part of the composite hereditament which is domestic property within the meaning of section 66 of the Act of 1988;

"B" is the current market value of the claimant's interest in that part of the composite hereditament which is not domestic property within that section.

(4) In this paragraph—

"composite hereditament" means—

(a) as respects England and Wales, any hereditament which is shown as a composite hereditament in a local non-domestic rating list;

(b) as respects Scotland, any lands and heritages entered in the valuation roll which are part residential subjects within the meaning of section 26(1) of the Act of 1987;

"local non-domestic rating list" means a list compiled and maintained under section 41(1) of the Act of 1988;

"the Act of 1987" means the Abolition of Domestic Rates, Etc. (Scotland) Act 1987;

"the Act of 1988" means the Local Government Finance Act 1988.

(5) Where responsibility for expenditure which relates to housing costs met under this Schedule is shared, the additional amounts applicable under this Schedule shall be calculated by reference to the appropriate proportion of that expenditure for which the claimant is responsible.

The calculation for loans

3.124 **7.**—[41 . . .]

General provisions applying to housing costs

3.125 **8.**—[41 . . .]

The standard rate

3.126 **9.**—[41 . . .]

Excessive Housing Costs

3.127 **10.**—[41 . . .]

Loans on residential property

3.128 **11.**—[41 . . .]

Loans for repairs and improvements to the dwelling occupied as the home

3.129 **12.**—[41 . . .]

[41 Housing costs]

3.130 **13.**—(1) Subject to the deduction specified in sub-paragraph (2) and the reductions applicable in sub-paragraph (5), there shall be met under this paragraph the amounts, calculated on a weekly basis, in respect of the following housing costs—

(a) payments by way of rent or ground rent relating to a long tenancy [14 . . .];

(b) service charges;

(c) payments by way of rentcharge within the meaning of section 1 of the Rentcharges Act 1977;

(d) payments under a co-ownership scheme;

(e) payments under or relating to a tenancy or licence of a Crown tenant;

(f) where the dwelling occupied as the home is a tent, payments in respect of the tent and the site on which it stands.

(2) Subject to sub-paragraph (3), the deductions to be made from the weekly amounts to be met under this paragraph are—

(a) where the costs are inclusive of any of the items mentioned in paragraph 5(2) of Schedule I to the Housing Benefit (General) Regulations 1987 (payment in respect of fuel charges), the deductions prescribed in that paragraph unless the claimant provides evidence on which the actual or approximate amount of the service charge for fuel may be estimated, in which case the estimated amount;

(b) where the costs are inclusive of ineligible service charges within the meaning of paragraph 1 of Schedule I to the Housing Benefit (General) Regulations 1987 (ineligible service charges) the amounts attributable to those ineligible service charges or where that amount is not separated from or separately identified within the housing costs to be met under this paragraph, such part of the payments made in respect of those housing costs which are fairly attributable to the provision of those ineligible services having regard to the costs of comparable services;

(c) any amount for repairs and improvements, and for this purpose the expression "repairs and improvements" has [[41] the meaning in sub-paragraph (7)].

(3) Where arrangements are made for the housing costs, which are met under this paragraph and which are normally paid for a period of 52 weeks, to be paid instead for a period of 53 weeks, or to be paid irregularly, or so that no such costs are payable or collected in certain periods, or so that the costs for different periods in the year are of different amounts, the weekly amount shall be the amount payable for the year divided by 52.

(4) Where the claimant or the claimant's partner—

(a) pays for reasonable repairs or redecorations to be carried out to the dwelling he occupies; and

(b) that work was not the responsibility of the claimant or his partner; and

(c) in consequence of that work being done, the costs which are normally met under this paragraph are waived, then those costs shall, for a period not exceeding eight weeks, be treated as payable.

(5) Where in England and Wales an amount calculated on a weekly basis in respect of housing costs specified in sub-paragraph (l)(e) (Crown tenants) includes water charges, that amount shall be reduced—

(a) where the amount payable in respect of water charges is known, by that amount;

(b) in any other case, by the amount which would be the likely weekly water charge had the property not been occupied by a Crown tenant.

[[1](6) In this paragraph—

(a) "co-ownership scheme" means a scheme under which a dwelling is let by a housing association and the tenant, or his personal representative, will, under the terms of the tenancy agreement or of the agreement under which he became a member of the association, be entitled, on his ceasing to be a member and subject to any condition stated in either agreement, to a sum calculated by reference directly or indirectly to the value of the dwelling;

(b) "Crown tenant" means a person who occupies a dwelling under a tenancy or licence where the interest of the landlord belongs to Her Majesty in right of the Crown or to a government department or is held in trust for Her Majesty for the purposes of a government department except (in the case of an interest belonging to Her Majesty in right of the Crown) where the interest is under the management of the Crown Estate Commissioners [[34] or a relevant person];

(c) "housing association" has the meaning assigned to it by section 1(1) of the Housing Associations Act 1985;

(d) "long tenancy" means a tenancy granted for a term of years certain exceeding twenty one years, whether or not the tenancy is, or may become, terminable before the end of that term by notice given by or to the tenant or by re-entry, forfeiture (or, in Scotland, irritancy) or otherwise and includes a lease for a term fixed by law under a grant with a covenant or obligation for perpetual renewal unless it is a lease by sub-demise from one which is not a long tenancy[[34]; and

(e) "relevant person", in relation to any property, rights or interests to which section 90B(5) of the Scotland Act 1998 applies, means the person who manages that property or those rights or interests.]]

[[41] (7) For the purposes of sub-paragraph (2)(c), "repairs and improvements" means any of the following measures undertaken with a view to maintaining the fitness of the dwelling for human habitation or, where the dwelling forms part of a building, any part of a building containing that dwelling—

(a) provision of a fixed bath, shower, wash basin, sink or lavatory, and necessary associated plumbing, including the provision of hot water not connected to a central heating system;
(b) repairs to existing heating system;
(c) damp proof measures;
(d) provision of ventilation and natural lighting;
(e) provision of drainage facilities;
(f) provision of facilities for preparing and cooking food;
(g) provision of insulation of the dwelling occupied as the home;
(h) provision of electric lighting and sockets;
(i) provision of storage facilities for fuel or refuse;
(j) repairs of unsafe structural defects;
(k) adapting a dwelling for the special needs of a disabled person; or
(l) provision of separate sleeping accommodation for persons of different sexes aged 10 or over but under the age of 20 who live with the claimant and for whom the claimant or the claimant's partner is responsible.]

Persons residing with the claimant

3.131 **14.**—(1) Subject to the following provisions of this paragraph, the following deductions from the amount to be met under the preceding paragraphs of this Schedule in respect of housing costs shall be made—

(a) in respect of a non-dependant aged 18 or over who is engaged in any remunerative work, [48£124.55];
(b) in respect of a non-dependant aged 18 or over to whom paragraph (a) does not apply, [48£19.30].

(2) In the case of a non-dependant aged 18 or over to whom sub-paragraph [4(1)(a)] applies because he is in remunerative work, where the claimant satisfies the Secretary of State that the non-dependant's gross weekly income is—

(a) less than [48£176.00], the deduction to be made under this paragraph shall be the deduction specified in sub-paragraph [(1)(b)];
(b) not less than [48£176.00] but less than [48£256.00], the deduction to be made under this paragraph shall be [48£44.40];
(c) not less than [48£256.00] but less than [48£334.00], the deduction to be made under this paragraph shall be [48£60.95];
(d) not less than [48£334.00] but less than [48£445.00], the deduction to be made under this paragraph shall be [48£99.65];
(e) not less than [48£445.00] but less than [48£554.00], the deduction to be made under this paragraph shall be [48£113.50].

(3) Only one deduction shall be made under this paragraph in respect of partners and where, but for this sub-paragraph, the amount that would fall to be deducted in respect of one partner is higher than the amount (if any) that would fall to be deducted in respect of the other partner, the higher amount shall be deducted.

(4) In applying the provisions of sub-paragraph (2) in the case of partners, only one deduction shall be made in respect of the partners based on the partners' joint weekly income.

(5) Where a person is a non-dependant in respect of more than one joint occupier of a dwelling (except where the joint occupiers are partners), the deduction in respect of that non-dependant shall be apportioned between the joint occupiers (the amount so apportioned being rounded to the nearest penny) having regard to the number of joint occupiers and the proportion of the housing costs in respect of the dwelling occupied as the home payable by each of them.

(6) No deduction shall be made in respect of any non-dependants occupying the dwelling occupied as the home of the claimant, if the claimant or any partner of his is—

[32 (a) certified as severely sight impaired or blind by a consultant ophthalmologist, or who is within 28 weeks of ceasing to be so certified; or]
(b) receiving in respect of himself either—
   (i) an attendance allowance; or
   (ii) the care component of the disability living allowance27; [29 . . .]
   (iii) the daily living component of personal independence payment];[29 [45 . . .]
   [45(iiia) the daily living component of adult disability payment; or]
   (iv) armed forces independence payment.]

(7) No deduction shall be made in respect of a non-dependant—

(a) if, although he resides with the claimant, it appears to the Secretary of State that the dwelling occupied as his home is normally elsewhere; or

(b) if he is in receipt of a training allowance paid in connection with [21 youth training] under section 2 of the Employment and Training Act 1973 or section 2 of the Enterprise and New Towns (Scotland) Act 1990; or

(c) if he is a full-time student during a period of study or, if he is not in remunerative work, during a recognised summer vacation appropriate to his course; or

[2(cc) if he is a full-time student and the claimant or his partner has attained the age of 65;]

(d) if he is aged under 25 and in receipt of income support or an income-based jobseeker's allowance; or

[14 (dd) in respect of whom a deduction in the calculation of a rent rebate or allowance falls to be made under regulation 55 (non-dependant deductions) of the Housing Benefit (Persons who have attained the qualifying age for state pension credit) Regulations 2006; or]

(e) if he is not residing with the claimant because he has been [12 an in-patient residing in a hospital or similar institution] for a period in excess of [352] weeks, or is a prisoner; and in calculating any period of [352] weeks, any 2 or more distinct periods separated by one or more intervals each not exceeding 28 days shall be treated as a single period [10; or]

[10 (f) if he is in receipt of state pension credit;]

[19 (g) if he is aged less than 25 and is in receipt of [27 income-related] employment and support allowance which does not include an amount under section [20 . . .] 4(4) [35 . . .] of the Welfare Reform Act [35 (component) or is not a member of the work-related activity group]] [30; or

(h) if he is aged less than 25 and is entitled to an award of universal credit which is calculated on the basis that he does not have any earned income;]

(8) In the case of a non-dependant to whom sub-paragraph (1) applies because he is in remunerative work, there shall be disregarded from his gross income—

[45(a) any attendance allowance, disability living allowance, armed forces independence payment, personal independence payment or adult disability payment received by him;]

(b) any payment from the Macfarlane Trust, the Macfarlane (Special Payments) Trust, the Macfarlane (Special Payments) (No.2) Trust ("the Trusts"), the Fund, the Eileen Trust [23, MFET Limited] [25, the Skipton Fund, the Caxton Foundation] [37, the Scottish Infected Blood Support Scheme][39, [40 an approved blood scheme], the London Emergencies Trust, the We Love Manchester Emergency Fund] [43, the National Emergencies Trust] [47, the Victims of Overseas Terrorism Compensation Scheme] or the Independent Living [20 Fund (2006)]; and

[43(ba) any Grenfell Tower payment;]

[44(bb) any child abuse payment;

(bc) any Windrush payment;]

[46(bd) any Post Office compensation payment;]

(c) any payment in kind;

[41 (d) any payment made under or by a trust, established for the purpose of giving relief and assistance to disabled persons whose disabilities were caused by the fact that during their mother's pregnancy she had taken a preparation containing the drug known as Thalidomide, and which is approved by the Secretary of State.]

[30 (9) For the purposes of sub-paragraph (7)(h), "earned income" has the meaning given in regulation 52 of the Universal Credit Regulations 2013.]

Rounding of fractions

15.—Where any calculation made under this Schedule results in a fraction of a penny, that fraction shall be treated as a penny. **3.132**

AMENDMENTS

1. State Pension Credit (Consequential, Transitional and Miscellaneous Provisions) Regulations 2002 (SI 2002/3019) reg.23(1) (October 6, 2003).

2. State Pension Credit (Consequential, Transitional and Miscellaneous Provisions) (No.2) Regulations 2002 (SI 2002/3197) reg.2 and Sch. para.9 (October 6, 2003).

3. Social Security (Hospital In-Patients and Miscellaneous Amendments) Regulations 2002 (SI 2003/1195) reg.8(2) (May 21, 2003).

4. State Pension Credit (Transitional and Miscellaneous Provisions) Amendment Regulations 2003 (SI 2003/2274) reg.2(9)(a) (October 6, 2003).

5. Social Security (Housing Costs Amendments) Regulations 2004 (SI 2004/2825) reg.2(2) (November 28, 2004).

6. Social Security (Housing Costs Amendments) Regulations 2004 (SI 2004/2825) reg.2(3) (November 28, 2004).

7. Social Security (Housing Costs Amendments) Regulations 2004 (SI 2004/2825) reg.2(4) (November 28, 2004).

8. Social Security (Housing Benefit, Council Tax Benefit, State Pension Credit and Miscellaneous Amendments) Regulations 2004 (SI 2004/2327) reg.7(5)(a) (April 4, 2005).

9. Social Security (Housing Benefit, Council Tax Benefit, State Pension Credit and Miscellaneous Amendments) Regulations 2004 (SI 2004/2327) reg.7(5)(b)(i) (April 4, 2005).

10. Social Security (Housing Benefit, Council Tax Benefit, State Pension Credit and Miscellaneous Amendments) Regulations 2004 (SI 2004/2327) reg.7(5)(b)(ii) (April 4, 2005).

11. Social Security (Care Homes and Independent Hospitals) Regulations 2005 (SI 2005/2687) reg.6 and Sch.5 para.5 (October 24, 2005).

12. Social Security (Hospital In-Patients) Regulations 2005 (SI 2005/3360) reg.8(4) (April 10, 2006).

13. Social Security (Young Persons) Amendment Regulations 2006 (SI 2006/718) reg.6(4) (April 10, 2006).

14. Social Security (Miscellaneous Amendments) (No.4) Regulations 2006 (SI 2006/2378) reg.14(5) (October 2, 2006).

15. Social Security (Miscellaneous Amendments) (No.5) Regulations 2006 (SI 2006/3274) reg.4(1) (January 8, 2007).

16. Social Security (Miscellaneous Amendments) (No.5) Regulations 2007 (SI 2007/2618) reg.10(5) (October 1, 2007).

17. Social Security (Housing Costs and Miscellaneous Amendments) Regulations 2007 (SI 2007/3183) reg.5 (December 17, 2007).

18. Social Security (Miscellaneous Amendments) Regulations 2008 (SI 2008/698) reg.5 (April 14, 2008).

19. Employment and Support Allowance (Consequential Provisions) (No.2) Regulations 2008 (SI 2008/1554) reg.4(8) (October 27, 2008).

20. Employment and Support Allowance (Miscellaneous Amendments) Regulations 2008 (SI 2008/2428) reg.41(4) (October 27, 2008).

21. Social Security (Miscellaneous Amendments) (No.6) Regulations 2008 (SI 2008/2767) reg.5(4) (November 17, 2008).

22. Social Security (Miscellaneous Amendments) Regulations 2009 (SI 2009/583) reg.5(4) (April 6, 2009).

23. Social Security (Miscellaneous Amendments) (No.2) Regulations 2010 (SI 2010/641) reg.6(3)(b) (April 6, 2010).

24. Social Security (Housing Costs) (Standard Interest Rate) Amendment Regulations 2010 (SI 2010/1811) reg.2(1)(c) and (2) (October 1, 2010).

25. Social Security (Miscellaneous Amendments) (No.3) Regulations 2011 (2011/2425) reg.15(5) (October 31, 2011).

26. Employment and Support Allowance (Duration of Contributory Allowance) (Consequential Amendments) Regulations 2012 (SI 2012/913) reg.6 (May 1, 2012).

27. Social Security (Miscellaneous Amendments) Regulations 2013 (SI 2013/443) reg.6(3) (April 2, 2013).

28. Personal Independence Payment (Supplementary Provisions and Consequential Amendments) Regulations 2013 (SI 2013/388) reg.8 and Sch. para.27(5) (April 8, 2013).

29. Armed Forces and Reserve Forces Compensation Scheme (Consequential Provisions: Subordinate Legislation) Order 2013 (SI 2013/591) art.7 and Sch. para.23(5) (April 8, 2013).

30. Universal Credit (Consequential, Supplementary, Incidental and Miscellaneous Provisions) Regulations 2013 (SI 2013/630) reg.33(6) (April 29, 2013).
31. Social Security (Miscellaneous Amendments) Regulations 2014 (SI 2014/591) reg.7(6) (April 28, 2014).
32. Universal Credit and Miscellaneous Amendments (No.2) Regulations 2014 (SI 2014/2888) reg.3(4)(b) (November 26, 2014).
33. Shared Parental Leave and Statutory Shared Parental Pay (Consequential Amendments to Subordinate Legislation) Order 2014 (SI 2014/3255) art.10(5) (December 31, 2014).
34. Crown Estate Transfer Scheme 2017 (SI 2017/524) art.8 and Sch.5, para. 94 (April 1, 2017).
35. Employment and Support Allowance and Universal Credit (Miscellaneous Amendments and Transitional and Savings Provisions) Regulations 2017 (SI 2017/204) reg.7(1) and Sch.1, para.5(3) (April 3, 2017).
36. Employment and Support Allowance and Universal Credit (Miscellaneous Amendments and Transitional and Savings Provisions) Regulations 2017 (SI 2017/204) reg.7(1) and Sch.1, para.14 (April 3, 2017).
37. Social Security (Scottish Infected Blood Support Scheme) Regulations 2017 (SI 2017/329) reg.5(3)(a) (April 3, 2017).
38. Social Security Benefits Up-rating Order 2017 (SI 2017/260) art.25(4) and Sch.13 (April 10, 2017).
39. Social Security (Emergency Funds) (Amendment) Regulations 2017 (SI 2017/689) reg.4(3)(a) (June 19, 2017).
40. Social Security (Infected Blood and Thalidomide) Regulations 2017 (SI 2017/870) reg.5(3)(a) and (4) (October 23, 2017).
41. Loans for Mortgage Interest Regulations 2017 (SI 2017/725) reg.18 and Sch.5, para.4 (April 6, 2018).
42. Parental Bereavement Leave and Pay (Consequential Amendments to Subordinate Legislation) Regulations 2020 (SI 2020/354) reg.10(5) (April 6, 2020).
43. Social Security (Income and Capital) (Miscellaneous Amendments) Regulations 2020 (SI 2020/618) reg.4(3) (July 15, 2020).
44. Social Security (Income and Capital Disregards) (Amendment) Regulations 2021 (SI 2021/1405) reg.4(3) (January 1, 2022).
45. Social Security (Disability Assistance for Working Age People) (Consequential Amendments) Order 2022 (SI 2022/177) art.8(4) (March 21, 2022).
46. Social Security (Income and Capital Disregards) (Amendment) Regulations 2023 (SI 2023/640) reg.4(3) (July 9, 2023).
47. Social Security (Habitual Residence and Past Presence, and Capital Disregards) (Amendment) Regulations 2023 (SI 2023/1144) reg.5(3)(a) (October 27, 2023).
48. Social Security Benefits Up-rating Order 2024 (SI 2024/242) art.29(4) (April 8, 2024).

GENERAL NOTE

This Schedule, dealing with housing costs, follows the pattern of the income support scheme (Income Support (General) Regulations 1987 (SI 1987/1967) Sch.3), as now extensively amended (and substituted) by the Loans for Mortgage Interest Regulations 2017 (SI 2017/725). Note that although paras.7–12 were repealed by those Regulations (see Sch.5, para.4(c)), there are transitional rules for existing claimants—see regs 19, 19A and 20 of those Regulations and the commentary in Part IIA of this Volume. 3.133

Paragraph 3

On the application of para.3(b), see *Secretary of State for Work and Pensions v DP* [2009] UKUT 225 (AAC), confirming that "there had to be an immediate threat to the continued occupation of the home, not a theoretical possibility of this happening in the future" (agreeing with *CIS/14/1993*). See further *AH v SSWP* [2010] UKUT 353 (AAC). 3.134

Paragraph 4

3.135 The purpose of para.4 is to make it clear that "in general, for the purpose of entitlement to housing costs, a person is only occupying the dwelling normally occupied by him as his home if he is living there": *PJ v Secretary of State for Work and Pensions* (SPC) [2014] UKUT 0152 (AAC) at para.15. The claimant and his wife had moved out of their flat as they could no longer afford the council tax. One of their daughters lived in the flat for a while, and when she was ill the claimant and/or his wife would stay overnight at the flat to look after her. However, they were staying over to care for the daughter in *her* home, and not because it was the *claimant's* home.

The amendment to para.4(6)(c) made by Social Security (Miscellaneous Amendments) (No.5) Regulations 2006 (SI 2006/3274) reg.4(1) does not apply to any person covered by reg.36(6) of the State Pension Credit (Consequential, Transitional and Miscellaneous Provisions) Regulations 2002 (SI 2002/3019) (i.e. persons entitled to income support immediately before the appointed day). In such cases para.4(6)(c) is to be read as if after "four benefit weeks" there were inserted "from the first day of the benefit week in which the move occurs": Social Security (Miscellaneous Amendments) (No.5) Regulations 2006 (SI 2006/3274) reg.4(2) and (3).

Paragraphs 7–12

3.136 Paragraphs 7–12 were repealed by para.4(c) of Sch.5 to the Loans for Mortgage Interest Regulations 2017 (SI 2017/725) subject to transitional rules for existing claimants—see regs 19, 19A and 20 of those Regulations and the commentary in Part IIA of this Volume.

Paragraph 13(1)(a): ground rent relating to a long tenancy

3.137 On the meaning of "long tenancy" (see para.(6)(d)) under Scots law, see *NR v Secretary of State for Work and Pensions* [2013] UKUT 0647 (AAC), dealing with the requirement that the tenancy be capable of registration (see also *R(H) 3/07*). Judge J.N. Wright QC held that in principle this requirement did not apply in Scotland, because although a lease for 20 years or more requires to be registered to be effectual against singular successors (i.e. successors in title), under Scots law a tenancy might be enforceable only against the granter. This did not assist the tenant on the facts, as there was no written agreement, and Scots law requires a lease for more than one year to be in writing. The decision also confirms that caravan park periodical fees for mobile homes will normally fall under the housing benefit scheme.

Paragraph 13(1)(b): service charges

3.138 The treatment of service charges for the purposes of entitlement to pension credit was considered by the Commissioner in *R(PC) 1/07*. Tribunals cannot assume that where a proportion of service charges are met by the Supporting People programme, the balance necessarily constitute eligible housing costs under para.13. In *R(PC) 1/07* the evidence before the tribunals lacked "any detail of what the scheme manager did other than in relation to general counselling and support, and nowhere was there any indication of what proportion of his time a scheme manager spent on activities said to relate to the provision of adequate accommodation" (at para.18). The Commissioner agreed:

> "with the remark of the Commissioner in paragraph 9 of *CPC/968/2005* that a "broad approach" is called for: for example, a decision-maker or tribunal supplied with the terms of the lease relating to services and service charges, a breakdown of the service charges, details of what service charges (if any) are met by the Supporting People programme, and a statement from the scheme manager as to how his working time is usually divided up should normally be able to make a reasoned estimate of how much of the service charges in dispute are eligible or ineligible. Each case will, however, inevitably turn on its own facts and evidential requirements will vary" (at para.23).

See also *R(PC) 2/08*, which deals with several technical issues concerned with how an award of state pension credit should be adjusted for housing costs after estimated service charges have been finalised.

The case law on the treatment of eligible service charges was considered further in *DL v Secretary of State for Work and Pensions* [2013] AACR 22; [2013] UKUT 29 (AAC). This review of the authorities confirmed that charges for maintenance, repairs, cleaning, and utility charges for communal areas and gardens are eligible (*CIS/1459/1995*); charges for reserve fund contributions for accommodation costs are eligible (*CPC/968/2005* and *CIS/667/2002*); staffing costs fairly attributable to the provision of adequate accommodation based on what the staff actually do in the particular development or similar developments are eligible (*R(PC) 1/07* and *CPC/977/2007*); and other administrative costs, which cannot be neatly categorised, should be apportioned in the same ratio as eligible and non-eligible charges in the rest of the budget (*R(PC) 1/07* and *CPC/968/2005*), rather than in the same ratio as eligible and non-eligible charges in the staff costs budget only (as held in *R(IS) 2/07*).

Paragraph 13(2)(c) and (7): repairs and improvements

In practice the absence of documentation to support claims for loans taken out to pay for repairs and improvements is often a problem when the work in question was undertaken some years ago. As Judge Lane pointed out in *KWA v Secretary of State for Work and Pensions (SPC)* [2011] UKUT 10 (AAC), "the tribunal cannot pluck figures out of the air" (at para.7). Thus: **3.139**

> "There are two principles which come into play where there is a lack of evidence on an issue. The first is that parties to tribunal proceedings have a duty to cooperate with the tribunal. If a party has not done all that he could reasonably do to provide evidence which lies within his purview, a tribunal is entitled to determine an issue dependent upon that evidence against him: *Kerr v Department for Social Development* [2004] UKHL 23, per Lady Hale of Richmond [62, 63]. The second is that if, at the end of the day, an issue cannot be resolved because of the lack of evidence, it will be decided against the party who had the burden of proving it. In this case, the burden is on the claimant" (at para.8).

Judge Lane also observed that "'repairs and improvements' must be carried out with a view to maintaining fitness for human habitation. That is a low standard. It does not reflect the highest standards of living a person may wish to have. Moreover, the work done is only a repair and improvement if it falls within one of the categories (a)–(l). There is no discretion to award housing costs in relation to works which do not fall within the headings set out" (at para.12).

The scope of para.13(7)(l) (or rather its predecessor, para.12(2)(l), now repealed) was considered by Judge Jacobs in *CPC/2038/2008*. A loan taken out to provide separate sleeping accommodation may be taken out before a child reaches the age of 10 and still be covered by this provision; how far in advance will depend on the circumstances of the particular case (broadly following *CIS/14657/1996* and *CIS/5119/2001* and not following *CIS/1678/1999*).

Regulation 6(6)(d)

[1 SCHEDULE IIA

ADDITIONAL AMOUNT APPLICABLE FOR CLAIMANTS RESPONSIBLE FOR A CHILD OR QUALIFYING YOUNG PERSON

General

1. This Schedule applies to a claimant who is responsible for a child or qualifying young person. **3.140**

2.—(1) In this Schedule—

"child" means a person under the age of 16;

"qualifying young person" has the meaning given in regulation 4A.

(2) Whether a claimant is responsible for a child or qualifying young person for the purposes of this Schedule is determined in accordance with paragraphs 3 to 8.

Child or qualifying young person normally living with the claimant

3.141 **3.**—(1) Subject to sub-paragraph (2), a claimant is responsible for a child or qualifying young person who normally lives with the claimant.

(2) A claimant is not responsible for a qualifying young person if the two of them are living as a couple.

(3) Where a child or qualifying young person normally lives with two or more persons who are not a couple, only one of them is to be treated as responsible, and that is the person who has the main responsibility for that child or qualifying young person.

(4) The persons referred to in sub-paragraph (3) may jointly nominate for the purposes of this Schedule which of them has the main responsibility for the child or qualifying young person, but the Secretary of State may determine that question—

(a) if there is no joint nomination; or

(b) if a nomination or change of nomination does not, in the opinion of the Secretary of State, reflect the arrangements between those persons.

Child or qualifying young person looked after by a local authority

3.142 **4.**—(1) Except where sub-paragraph (3) applies, a claimant is to be treated as not being responsible for a child or qualifying young person during any period when the child or qualifying young person is looked after by a local authority.

(2) A child or qualifying young person is treated as looked after by a local authority for the purposes of sub-paragraph (1) if that child or qualifying young person is looked after by a local authority within the meaning of section 22 of the Children Act 1989, section 17(6) of the Children (Scotland) Act 1995 or section 74 of the Social Services and Well-being (Wales) Act 2014.

(3) This sub-paragraph applies to any period—

(a) which is in the nature of a planned short term break, or is one of a series of such breaks, for the purpose of providing respite for the person who normally cares for the child or qualifying young person; or

(b) during which the child or qualifying young person is placed with, or continues to live with, their parent or a person who has parental responsibility for them.

(4) For the purposes of sub-paragraph (3), a person has parental responsibility if they are not a foster parent and—

(a) in England and Wales, they have parental responsibility within the meaning of section 3 of the Children Act 1989, or

(b) in Scotland, they have any or all of the legal responsibilities or rights described in sections 1 or 2 of the Children (Scotland) Act 1995.

Prisoners

3.143 **5.** The claimant is to be treated as not being responsible for a child or qualifying young person during any period when the child or qualifying young person is a prisoner.

Temporary absence in Great Britain

3.144 **6.** A claimant is to be treated as not being responsible for a child or qualifying young person during periods of temporary absence of the child or qualifying young person in Great Britain if the period of absence is likely to exceed 52 weeks, except where there are exceptional circumstances (for example, the child or qualifying young person is in hospital), and the absence is unlikely to be substantially more than 52 weeks.

Temporary absence outside Great Britain

3.145 **7.**—(1) A claimant is to be treated as not being responsible for a child or qualifying young person if the child or qualifying young person is temporarily absent from Great Britain for longer than—

(a) 4 weeks, or where the absence is expected to exceed 4 weeks;

(b) where sub-paragraph (2) applies—

(i) 8 weeks; or

(ii) where the absence is expected to exceed 8 weeks; or

(c) where sub-paragraph (3) applies—

(i) 26 weeks; or

(ii) where the absence is expected to exceed 26 weeks.

(2) This sub-paragraph applies where the absence of the child or qualifying young person is in connection with the death of—

(a) the claimant's partner or a child or qualifying young person normally living with the claimant; or

(b) a close relative of—

(i) the claimant;

(ii) the claimant's partner; or
(iii) a child or qualifying young person normally living with the claimant,

and the Secretary of State considers that it would be unreasonable to expect the child or qualifying young person to return to Great Britain within 4 weeks.

(3) This sub-paragraph applies where the absence of the child or qualifying young person is solely in connection with—

(a) the child or qualifying young person undergoing—
  (i) treatment for an illness or physical or mental impairment by, or under the supervision of, a qualified practitioner; or
  (ii) medically approved convalescence or care as a result of treatment for an illness or physical or mental impairment, where the child or qualifying young person had that illness or impairment before leaving Great Britain; or
(b) the child or qualifying young person accompanying the claimant or the claimant's partner for convalescence or care as mentioned in sub-paragraph (a).

(4) In this paragraph—

"medically approved" means certified by a registered medical practitioner;

"qualified practitioner" means a person qualified to provide medical treatment, physiotherapy or a form of treatment which is similar to, or related to, either of those forms of treatment.

Death of child or qualifying young person

8.—(1) If a child or qualifying young person for whom a claimant is responsible dies, the claimant is to be treated as responsible for that child or qualifying young person until— **3.146**

(a) the end of the period of eight weeks starting with the day on which the child or qualifying young person dies; or
(b) in the case of a qualifying young person, the date on which he or she would have attained the age of 20, if earlier.

(2) The additional amount applicable to the claimant during the period in which they are treated as responsible for a child or qualifying young person under sub-paragraph (1) is to be calculated in accordance with paragraph 9 on the basis of the circumstances which existed on the day before the day on which the child or qualifying young person died.

Amount of additional payment

9.—(1) The additional amount applicable to a claimant to whom this Schedule applies is— **3.147**

(a) subject to paragraph 10, [4£66.29] for each child or qualifying young person; and
(b) a further amount of—
  (i) [4£35.93] where sub-paragraph (2) applies; or
  (ii) [4£112.21] where sub-paragraph (3) applies.

(2) This sub-paragraph applies where the claimant is responsible for a child or qualifying young person who is entitled to a disability living allowance [2, child disability payment (within the meaning given in regulation 2 of the Disability Assistance for Children and Young People (Scotland) Regulations 2021)] [3, adult disability payment] or personal independence payment.

(3) This sub-paragraph applies where the claimant is responsible for a child or qualifying young person who is—

(a) entitled to the care component of disability living allowance at the highest rate [3, the daily living component of adult disability payment at the enhanced rate] or the daily living component of personal independence payment at the enhanced rate; or
[2(aa) entitled to the care component of child disability payment at the highest rate in accordance with regulation 11(5) of the Disability Assistance for Children and Young People (Scotland) Regulations 2021; or]
(b) certified as severely sight impaired or blind by a consultant ophthalmologist.

Amount for the eldest child or qualifying young person born before 6th April 2017

10. In a case where the eldest child or qualifying young person for whom the claimant is responsible was born before 6th April 2017, the amount prescribed in paragraph 9(1)(a) in respect of that child or qualifying young person is [4£76.79]. **3.148**

AMENDMENTS

1. State Pension Credit (Additional Amount for Child or Qualifying Young Person) (Amendment) Regulations 2018 (SI 2018/676), reg.2(4) (February 1, 2019).

2. Social Security (Scotland) Act 2018 (Disability Assistance for Children and Young People) (Consequential Modifications) Order 2021 (SI 2021/786) art.10 (July 26, 2021).

3. Social Security (Disability Assistance for Working Age People) (Consequential Amendments) Order 2022 (SI 2022/177) art.8(5) (March 21, 2022).
4. Social Security Benefits Up-rating Order 2024 (SI 2024/242) art.29(5) and (6) (April 8, 2024).

DEFINITIONS

"child"—see para.2(1).
"close relative"—see reg.1(2).
"couple"—see *ibid.*
"medically approved"—see para.7(4).
"personal independence payment"—see reg.1(2).
"prisoner"—see *ibid.*
"qualified practitioner"—see para.7(4).
"qualifying young person"—see para.2(1).

GENERAL NOTE

3.149 This Schedule sets out the criteria for the award of an additional amount to a state pension credit claimant who qualifies for the guarantee credit and has responsibility for a child or qualifying young person (see reg.6(6)(d)). Claimants who receive tax credits are excluded from entitlement, as this provision is designed to compensate for the abolition of CTC (see reg.6(11)–(17)).

Paragraph 2

3.150 This paragraph applies the standard definitions, so a "child" means someone under the age of 16, while "qualifying young person" (QYP) is a person who has reached the age of 16 but not the age of 20, and has enrolled or been accepted in full-time, non-advanced education or approved training before the age of 19 (see reg.4A).

Paragraph 3

3.151 A person is treated as responsible for a child or QYP who normally lives with them (but not if they are living together with a QYP as a couple). In cases where a child or QYP resides with two or more people who are not a couple, only one person can be treated as responsible for a child or QYP, namely the person who has the "main responsibility". They may nominate which of them has the main responsibility. If they cannot agree, or where it is considered that the nomination does not reflect the arrangements for the child or QYP, the Secretary of State has the discretion to decide who has main responsibility. These rules broadly reflect those that apply to universal credit, albeit with some minor drafting differences: see UC Regs 2013 reg.4(2)–(5).

Paragraph 4

3.152 A person is to be treated as *not* responsible for a child or QYP during any period for which the child or QYP is looked after by a local authority. This is subject to exceptions for planned short term breaks (or one of a series of such breaks) for the purpose of providing the responsible person with a respite period. There is also an exception for periods where the child or QYP is placed with (or continues to live with) their parent or a person who has parental responsibility for them. These rules reflect those that apply to universal credit: see UC Regs 2013 reg.4A.

Paragraph 5

3.153 A person cannot be treated as responsible for a child or QYP for any time that the child or QYP is a prisoner, as defined by reg.1(2).

Paragraphs 6 and 7

A claimant is treated as not responsible for a child or QYP if they are away from the claimant and the absence is likely to exceed a specified period. Paragraph 6 deals with temporary absences of the child or QYP *in* Great Britain while para.7 deals with temporary absences *outside* Great Britain. 3.154

Where a child or QYP is absent from the claimant but remains within Great Britain, the claimant can be treated as responsible for them as long as the absence is not expected to be for more than 52 weeks (para.6). If it was known at the start of the absence that it will exceed 52 weeks, responsibility ceases from the start of the absence, unless there are exceptional circumstances (e.g. that the child or QYP is in hospital and the absence is not expected to be substantially longer than 52 weeks).

If the absence is outside Great Britain, then the length of time for which a claimant is treated as responsible varies according to the circumstances as detailed by para.7.

Paragraph 8

Where a child or QYP dies, there is a run-on period of 8 weeks, to allow the claimant time to adjust to their new circumstances, thus aligning provision with the rules for housing benefit. 3.155

Paragraphs 9 and 10

These paragraphs set out the relevant weekly rates, depending on the circumstances of the child or QYP. 3.156

Regulation 8

SCHEDULE III

Special Groups

Polygamous marriages

1.—(1) The provisions of this paragraph apply in any case to which section 12 (polygamous marriages) applies if the claimant is taken to be "the person in question" for the purposes of that section. 3.157

(2) The following provision shall apply instead of section 3(1)—

"(1) The first condition is that, if the claimant is taken [1 . . .] to be "the person in question" for the purposes of section 12 (polygamous marriages)—
(a) the case is one to which that section applies; and
(b) any one or more of the persons falling within subsection (1)(c) of that section [12 has attained pensionable age before 6 April 2016 and] has attained the age of 65 [12 (before, on or after that date)].".

(3) The following provision shall apply instead of section 4(1)—

"(1) A claimant is not entitled to state pension credit if, taking the claimant to be 'the person in question' for the purposes of section 12 (polygamous marriages)—
(a) the case is one to which that section applies; and
(b) any one or more of the other persons falling within subsection (1)(c) of that section is entitled to state pension credit.".

(4) The following provision shall apply instead of section 5—

"5.—Income and capital of claimant, spouses, etc.

(1) This section applies in any case to which section 12 (polygamous marriages) applies if the claimant is taken to be 'the person in question' for the purposes of that section.

(2) In any such case, the income and capital of each of the other persons falling within subsection (1)(c) of that section shall be treated for the purposes of this Act as income and capital of the claimant, except where regulations provide otherwise.".

(5) In regulation 6 (amount of the guarantee credit), for paragraph (1) there shall be substituted—

"(1) Except as provided in the following provisions of these Regulations, in a case to which section 12 (polygamous marriages) applies if the claimant is taken to be 'the person in question' for the purposes of that section the standard minimum guarantee is the sum of—
(a) [14£332.95] per week in respect of the claimant and any one spouse of the claimant's; and
(b) [14£114.80] per week in respect of for each additional spouse (whether of the claimant or that spouse) who falls within section 12(1)(c).".

(6) The maximum savings credit shall be determined on the assumption that the standard minimum guarantee is the amount prescribed for partners under regulation 6(1)(a).

(7) In regulation 7 (savings credit) for paragraph (2) there shall be substituted—

"(2) In any case to which section 12 (polygamous marriages) [2applies] if the claimant is taken to be 'the person in question' for the purposes of that section, the amount prescribed for the savings credit threshold is [14£301.22]."

[11 (7A) The following provision shall apply instead of regulation 7A (limitation of savings credit for certain mixed-age couples)—

"7A.—(1) This regulation applies if, taking the claimant to be the person in question for the purposes of section 12 (polygamous marriages),—
(a) the case is one to which that section applies; and
(b) at least one of the persons falling within subsection (1)(c) of that section had attained pensionable age before 6 April 2016 and at least one of those persons had not.

(2) Where this regulation applies, the claimant is not entitled to a savings credit unless the claimant—
(a) has been awarded a savings credit with effect from a day before 6 April 2016 and was entitled to a savings credit immediately before that date; and
(b) remained entitled to a savings credit at all times since the beginning of 6 April 2016."]

(8) In regulations [10 3, [6. . .],5, [16(8),] 10,12 and 14 and in paragraph [36(5)(b)(v)] of Schedule 1 and in Schedule 2, any reference to a partner includes also a reference to any additional spouse to whom this paragraph applies.

(9) For the purposes of regulation 6(5)(a) and (b), paragraph 1(1)(b)(i) of Part I of Schedule I is satisfied only if both partners and each additional spouse to whom this paragraph applies are in receipt of attendance allowance [8, the care component of disability living allowance at the highest or middle rate prescribed in accordance with section 72(3) of the 1992 Act [12 ,] the daily living component of personal independence payment at the standard or enhanced rate in accordance with section 78(3) of the 2012 Act [12, the daily living component of adult disability payment at the standard or enhanced rate in accordance with regulation 5 of the Disability Assistance for Working Age People (Scotland) Regulations 2022] [9 or armed forces independence payment]].

(10) For the purposes of regulation 6(5)(a), paragraph 1(1)(c) of Part I of Schedule 1 is only satisfied if—
(a) both partners and each additional spouse to whom this paragraph applies all fall within either paragraph 1(1)(c)(i) or paragraph 1(1)(c)(ii); and
(b) at least one of them falls within paragraph 1(1)(c)(i); and
(c) at least one of them falls within paragraph 1(1)(c)(ii) but not paragraph 1(1)(c)(i); and
(d) either paragraph 1(1)(c)(iv) is satisfied or a person is entitled to and in receipt of an allowance under section 70 of the 1992 Act [13or carer support payment] in respect of caring for one or more, but not all, the persons who fall within paragraph 1(1)(c)(i).

(11) Any reference in this paragraph to an additional spouse to whom this paragraph applies is a reference to any person who is an additional spouse (whether of the claimant's or of a spouse of the claimant's) falling within subsection (1)(c) of section 12 if the claimant is taken to be "the person in question" for the purposes of that section.

Persons serving a sentence of imprisonment detained in hospital

3.158 [4**2.** —[7 (1) Sub-paragraph (2) applies in the case of a claimant ("C") who satisfies either of the following conditions.

(1A) The first condition is that—
(a) C is being detained under section 45A or 47 of the Mental Health Act 1983 (power of higher courts to direct hospital admission; removal to hospital of persons serving sentences of imprisonment etc.); and
(b) in any case where there is in relation to C a release date within the meaning of section 50(3) of that Act, C is being detained on or before the day which the Secretary of State certifies to be that release date.

(1B) The second condition is that C is being detained under—

(a) section 59A of the Criminal Procedure (Scotland) Act 1995 (hospital direction); or

(b) section 136 of the Mental Health (Care and Treatment) (Scotland) Act 2003 (transfer of prisoners for treatment of mental disorder).]

(2) In the case of a claimant to whom paragraph (1) applies—

(a) section 2(3) has effect with the substitution of a reference to a nil amount for the reference to the standard minimum guarantee in paragraph (a) [[5], and [[11] nil] is the prescribed additional amount for the purposes of paragraph (b)] and

(b) the maximum amount of savings credit shall be taken to be [[11] nil]].

AMENDMENTS

1. State Pension Credit (Consequential, Transitional and Miscellaneous Provisions) Regulations 2002 (SI 2002/3019) reg.23(m) (October 6, 2003).

2. State Pension Credit (Consequential, Transitional and Miscellaneous Provisions) (No.2) Regulations 2002 (SI 2002/3197) reg.2 and Sch. para.10 (October 6, 2003).

3. State Pension Credit (Transitional and Miscellaneous Provisions) Amendment Regulations 2003 (SI 2003/2274) reg.2(10) (October 6, 2003).

4. Social Security (Hospital In-Patients) Regulations 2005 (SI 2005/3360) reg.8(5) (April 10, 2006).

5. Social Security (Miscellaneous Amendments) Regulations 2006 (SI 2006/588) reg.4(4) (April 10, 2006).

6. Social Security (Miscellaneous Amendments) (No.4) Regulations 2008 (SI 2008/2424) reg.3(5) (October 6, 2008).

7. Social Security (Persons Serving a Sentence of Imprisonment Detained in Hospital) Regulations 2010 (SI 2010/442) reg.4(2) (March 25, 2010).

8. Personal Independence Payment (Supplementary Provisions and Consequential Amendments) Regulations 2013 (SI 2013/388) reg.8 and Sch. para.27(6) (April 8, 2013).

9. Armed Forces and Reserve Forces Compensation Scheme (Consequential Provisions: Subordinate Legislation) Order 2013 (SI 2013/591) art.7 and Sch. para.23(6) (April 8, 2013).

10. Housing Benefit and State Pension Credit (Temporary Absence) (Amendment) Regulations 2016 (SI 2016/624) reg.4(8) (July 28, 2016).

11. Social Security (Miscellaneous Amendments No. 5) Regulations 2017 (SI 2017/1187) reg.5(3) (December 21, 2017).

12. Social Security (Disability Assistance for Working Age People) (Consequential Amendments) Order 2022 (SI 2022/177) art.8(6) (March 21, 2022).

13. Carer's Assistance (Carer Support Payment) (Scotland) Regulations 2023 (Consequential Amendments) Order 2023 (SI 2023/1218) art.14(7) (November 19, 2023).

14. Social Security Benefits Up-rating Order 2024 (SI 2024/242) art.29(7) (April 8, 2024).

GENERAL NOTE

Paragraph 2

This paragraph was amended with effect from March 25, 2010 in response to the Court of Appeal's decision in *R. (on the application of D & M) v Secretary of State for Work and Pensions* [2010] EWCA Civ 18. The Court of Appeal had held that the previous wording meant that a person subject to an indeterminate sentence of imprisonment who was being detained in hospital for treatment for mental disorder would be eligible for DWP benefits when the tariff part of the sentence had been served. This was regarded as contrary to Government policy. The amended paragraph provides a revised form of words which is intended to ensure that such a person continues to be excluded from benefits when the tariff date has passed. **3.159**

Regulation 12

[1 SCHEDULE IIIA

Date on which certain fixed length assessed income periods end

3.160

Column 1 *Period in which the assessed income period would end apart from regulation 12(d)*	*Column 2* *Date on which assessed income period is to end*
1st April 2019 to 14th April 2019	14th July 2016
15th April 2019 to 30th April 2019	28th July 2016
1st May 2019 to 14th May 2019	14th August 2016
15th May 2019 to 31st May 2019	28th August 2016
1st June 2019 to 14th June 2019	14th October 2016
15th June 2019 to 30th June 2019	28th October 2016
1st July 2019 to 14th July 2019	14th November 2016
15th July 2019 to 31st July 2019	28th November 2016
1st August 2019 to 14th August 2019	14th December 2016
15th August 2019 to 31st August 2019	28th December 2016
1st September 2019 to 14th September 2019	14th February 2017
15th September 2019 to 30th September 2019	28th February 2017
1st October 2019 to 14th October 2019	14th March 2017
15th October 2019 to 31st October 2019	28th March 2017
1st November 2019 to 14th November 2019	14th April 2017
15th November 2019 to 30th November 2019	28th April 2017
1st December 2019 to 14th December 2019	14th June 2017
15th December 2019 to 31st December 2019	28th June 2017
1st January 2020 to 14th January 2020	14th July 2017
15th January 2020 to 31st January 2020	28th July 2017
1st February 2020 to 14th February 2020	14th September 2017
15th February 2020 to 29th February 2020	28th September 2017
1st March 2020 to 14th March 2020	14th October 2017
15th March 2020 to 31st March 2020	28th October 2017
1st April 2020 to 14th April 2020	14th December 2017
15th April 2020 to 30th April 2020	28th December 2017
1st May 2020 to 14th May 2020	14th January 2018
15th May 2020 to 31st May 2020	28th January 2018
1st June 2020 to 14th June 2020	14th March 2018
15th June 2020 to 30th June 2020	28th March 2018
1st July 2020 to 14th July 2020	14th April 2018
15th July 2020 to 31st July 2020	28th April 2018
1st August 2020 to 14th August 2020	14th June 2018
15th August 2020 to 31st August 2020	28th June 2018
1st September 2020 to 14th September 2020	14th July 2018
15th September 2020 to 30th September 2020	28th July 2018
1st October 2020 to 14th October 2020	14th August 2018
15th October 2020 to 31st October 2020	28th August 2018
1st November 2020 to 14th November 2020	14th October 2018
15th November 2020 to 30th November 2020	28th October 2018
1st December 2020 to 14th December 2020	14th November 2018
15th December 2020 to 31st December 2020	28th November 2018
1st January 2021 to 14th January 2021	14th January 2019
15th January 2021 to 31st January 2021	28th January 2019
1st February 2021 to 14th February 2021	14th February 2019
15th February 2021 to 28th February 2021	28th February 2019
1st March 2021 to 14th March 2021	14th March 2019
15th March 2021 to 5th April 2021	28th March 2019]

AMENDMENT

1. State Pension Credit (Amendment) Regulations 2015 (SI 2015/1529) reg.2(4) (April 6, 2016).

GENERAL NOTE

See the notes to reg.12 above and to s.2(6) of the State Pension Credit Act 2002. 3.161

Regulation 17(7)

SCHEDULE IV

AMOUNTS TO BE DISREGARDED IN THE CALCULATION OF INCOME OTHER THAN EARNINGS

1.—In addition to any sum which falls to be disregarded in accordance with paragraphs 3 to 6, £10 of any of the following, namely— 3.162

(a) a war disablement pension (except insofar as such a pension falls to be disregarded under paragraph 2 or 3);

(b) a war widow's or war widower's pension;

[7 (ba) unless paragraph 1(a) or (b) applies, any payment described in regulation 15(5)(ac) (except insofar as such a payment falls to be disregarded under paragraph 2 or 3);]

(c) a pension payable to a person as a [6 widow, widower or surviving civil partner] under [7. . .]any power of Her Majesty other wise than under an enactment to make provision about pensions for or in respect of persons who have been disabled or have died in consequence of service as members of the armed forces of the Crown;

[4 (cc) a guaranteed income payment] [7 and, if the amount of that payment has been abated to less than £10 by a [8 pension or payment falling within article 31(1)(a) or (b) of the Armed Forces and Reserve Forces (Compensation Scheme) Order 2005], so much of [8 that pension or payment] as would not, in aggregate with the amount of [8 any] guaranteed income payment disregarded, exceed £10];

(d) a payment made to compensate for the non-payment of such a pension [4 or payment] as is mentioned in any of the preceding sub-paragraphs;

(e) a pension paid by the government of a country outside Great Britain which is analogous to any of the [4 pensions or payments mentioned in sub-paragraphs (a) to (cc) above];

[9 (f) a pension paid by a government to victims of National Socialist persecution.]

2.—The whole of any amount included in a pension to which paragraph 1 relates in respect of—

(a) the claimant's need for constant attendance;

(b) the claimant's exceptionally severe disablement.

3.—Any mobility supplement under [7 article 20 of the Naval, Military and Air Forces Etc. (Disablement and Death) Service Pensions Order 2006] (including such a supplement by virtue of any other scheme or order) or under article 25A of the Personal Injuries (Civilians) Scheme 1983 or any payment intended to compensate for the non-payment of such a supplement.

[7 **4.**—Any supplementary pension under article 23(2) of the Naval, Military and Air Forces Etc. (Disablement and Death) Service Pensions Order 2006 (pensions to surviving spouses and surviving civil partners) and any analogous payment made by the Secretary of State for Defence to any person who is not a person entitled under that Order.]

5.—In the case of a pension awarded at the supplementary rate under article 27(3) of the Personal Injuries (Civilians) Scheme 1983 (pensions to [6 widows, widowers or surviving civil partners]), the sum specified in paragraph 1(c) of Schedule 4 to that Scheme.

6.—(1) Any payment which is—

(a) made under any of the Dispensing Instruments to a [6 widow, widower or surviving civil partner] of a person—

(i) whose death was attributable to service in a capacity analogous to service as a member of the armed forces of the Crown; and

(ii) whose service in such capacity terminated before 31st March 1973; and

[7 (b) equal to the amount specified in article 23(2) of the Naval, Military and Air Forces Etc. (Disablement and Death) Service Pensions Order 2006.]

(2) In this paragraph "the Dispensing Instruments" means the Order in Council of 19th December 1881, the Royal Warrant of 27th October 1884 and the Order by His Majesty of 14th January 1922 (exceptional grants of pay, non-effective pay and allowances).

7.—£10 of any widowed parent's allowance to which the claimant is entitled under section 39A of the 1992 Act.

[[2]**7A.**—£10 of any widowed mother's allowance to which the claimant is entitled under section 37 of the 1992 Act.]

8.—(1) Where the claimant occupies a dwelling as his home and he provides in that dwelling board and lodging accommodation, an amount, in respect of each person for whom such accommodation is provided for the whole or any part of a week, equal to—

(a) where the aggregate of any payments made in respect of any one week in respect of such accommodation provided to such person does not exceed £20.00, 100 per cent of such payments; or

(b) where the aggregate of any such payments exceeds £20.00, £20.00 and 50 per cent of the excess over £20.00.

(2) [[5]. . .]

9.—If the claimant—

(a) owns the freehold or leasehold interest in any property or is a tenant of any property; and

(b) occupies a part of that property; and

(c) has an agreement with another person allowing that person to occupy another part of that property on payment of rent and—

(i) the amount paid by that person is less than £20 per week, the whole of that amount; or

(ii) the amount paid is £20 or more per week, £20.

10.—Where a claimant receives income under an annuity purchased with a loan, which satisfies the following conditions—

(a) that the loan was made as part of a scheme under which not less than 90% of the proceeds of the loan were applied to the purchase by the person to whom it was made of an annuity ending with his life or with the life of the survivor of two or more persons (in this paragraph referred to as "the annuitants") who include the person to whom the loan was made;

(b) that at the time the loan was made the person to whom it was made or each of the annuitants had attained the age of 65;

(c) that the loan was secured on a dwelling in Great Britain and the person to whom the loan was made or one of the annuitants owns an estate or interest in that dwelling;

(d) that the person to whom the loan was made or one of the annuitants occupies the dwelling on which it was secured as his home at the time the interest is paid; and

(e) that the interest payable on the loan is paid by the person to whom the loan was made or by one of the annuitants,

the amount, calculated on a weekly basis, equal to—

(i) where, or insofar as, section 369 of the Income and Corporation Taxes Act 1988 (mortgage interest payable under deduction of tax) applies to the payments of interest on the loan, the interest which is payable after deduction of a sum equal to income tax on such payments at the applicable percentage of income tax within the meaning of section 369(1A) of that Act;

(ii) in any other case the interest which is payable on the loan without deduction of such a sum.

11.—(1) Any payment, other than a payment to which sub-paragraph (2) applies, made to the claimant by Trustees in exercise of a discretion exercisable by them.

(2) This sub-paragraph applies to payments made to the claimant by Trustees in exercise of a discretion exercisable by them for the purpose of—

(a) obtaining food, ordinary clothing or footwear or household fuel;

(b) the payment of rent, council tax or water charges for which that claimant or his partner is liable;

(c) meeting housing costs of a kind specified in Schedule 2;

(d) [[1]. . .].

(3) In a case to which sub-paragraph (2) applies, £20 or—

(a) if the payment is less than £20, the whole payment; or

(b) if, in the claimant's case, £10 is disregarded in accordance with paragraph 1(a) to (f), [[1] or paragraph 7] [[2] or 7A] £10 or the whole payment if it is less than £10.

(4) For the purposes of this paragraph—

"ordinary clothing and footwear" means clothing or footwear for normal daily use, but does not include school uniforms, or clothing and footwear used solely for sporting activities; and

"rent" means eligible rent for the purposes of the Housing Benefit (General) Regulations

1987 less any deductions in respect of non-dependants which fall to be made under regulation 63 (non-dependant deductions) of those Regulations.

12.—Any increase in [7 pension or allowance under Part 2 or 3 of the Naval, Military and Air Forces Etc. (Disablement and Death) Service Pensions Order 2006] paid in respect of a dependent other than the pensioner's [7 . . .] [6 partner].

13.—Any payment ordered by a court to be made to the claimant or the claimant's partner in consequence of any accident, injury or disease suffered by [2the person] to whom the payments are made.

14.—Periodic payments made to the claimant or the claimant's partner under an agreement entered into in [2 . . .] settlement of a claim made by [2 that person] for an injury suffered by him.

15.—Any income which is payable outside the United Kingdom for such period during which there is a prohibition against the transfer to the United Kingdom of that income.

16.—Any banking charges or commission payable in converting to Sterling payments of income made in a currency other than Sterling.

17.—[7 . . .]

[3**18.** Except in the case of income from capital specified in Part II of Schedule V, any actual income from capital.]

[10**19.** Any amount of carer support payment that is in excess of the amount the claimant would receive if they had an entitlement to carer's allowance under section 70 of the 1992 Act.]

AMENDMENTS

1. State Pension Credit (Consequential, Transitional and Miscellaneous Provisions) Regulations 2002 (SI 2002/3019) reg.23(n) (October 6, 2003).

2. State Pension Credit (Consequential, Transitional and Miscellaneous Provisions) (No.2) Regulations 2002 (SI 2002/3197) reg.2 and Sch. para.11 (October 6, 2003).

3. State Pension Credit (Transitional and Miscellaneous Provisions) Amendment Regulations 2003 (SI 2003/2274) reg.2(11) (October 6, 2003).

4. Social Security (Miscellaneous Amendments) Regulations 2005 (SI 2005/574) reg.2(7) and (8)(d) (April 4, 2005).

5. Social Security (Miscellaneous Amendments) (No.2) Regulations 2005 (SI 2005/2465) reg.6(5) (October 3, 2005).

6. Civil Partnership (Pensions, Social Security and Child Support) (Consequential, etc. Provisions) Order 2005 (SI 2005/2877) art.2(3) and Sch.3 para.35(4) (December 5, 2005).

7. Social Security (Miscellaneous Amendments) (No.7) Regulations 2008 (SI 2008/3157) reg.4(5) (January 5, 2009).

8. Social Security (Miscellaneous Amendments) (No.4) Regulations 2009 (SI 2009/2655) reg.5(5) (October 26, 2009).

9. Social Security (Income-Related Benefits) Amendment Regulations 2017 (2017/174) reg.4(2) (March 20, 2017).

10. Carer's Assistance (Carer Support Payment) (Scotland) Regulations 2023 (Consequential Amendments) Order 2023 (SI 2023/1218) art.14(8) (November 19, 2023).

GENERAL NOTE

This Schedule performs the same function in relation to state pension credit as Sch.9 to the Income Support (General) Regulations 1987 (SI 1987/1967) (see Vol.V of this series) does in the context of income support, although the list of disregards is much less extensive (reflecting the different nature of state pension credit). 3.163

Paragraph 1

See Income Support (General) Regulations 1987 (SI 1987/1967) Sch.9 para.16 (although that also includes widowed mother's allowance and widowed parent's allowance: see para.(7)). 3.164

Paragraph 3

See Income Support (General) Regulations 1987 (SI 1987/1967) Sch.9 para.8. 3.165

Paragraphs 4–6

3.166 See Income Support (General) Regulations 1987 (SI 1987/1967) Sch.9 paras 54–56.

Paragraphs 7–7A

3.167 See Income Support (General) Regulations 1987 (SI 1987/1967) Sch.9 para.16(g) and (h).

Paragraph 8

3.168 See Income Support (General) Regulations 1987 (SI 1987/1967) Sch.9 para.20.

Paragraph 9

3.169 This is a more generous provision than the nearest equivalent under the income support scheme. Income Support (General) Regulations 1987 (SI 1987/1967) Sch.9 para.19 provides that, for the purposes of income support, only the first £4 a week of income from a sub-tenant is disregarded (plus a slightly larger prescribed figure where the rent charged includes an amount for heating). This provision grants a state pension credit claimant in similar circumstances a disregard of up to £20 a week on payments from a sub-tenant or licensee.

Paragraph 10

3.170 See Income Support (General) Regulations 1987 (SI 1987/1967) Sch.9 para.17.

Paragraph 11

3.171 See Income Support (General) Regulations 1987 (SI 1987/1967) Sch.9 para.15 for the closest equivalent under the income support scheme.

Paragraphs 13–14

3.172 These are more generous rules than apply to income support. The rule there is that sums paid by way of personal injuries compensation and held under a trust are disregarded as capital (Income Support (General) Regulations 1987 (SI 1987/1967) Sch.10 para.12), but payments made out of the fund to the claimant count as income or capital in the normal way. The rule for state pension credit is that payments made in compensation for personal injuries under a court order or following a settlement do not count as income. The repeal of the word "final" in the first amendment to para.14 (so that it reads "in settlement of" and not "in final settlement of ") presumably ensures that the benefit of this provision will be gained by pensioners who receive provisional awards of personal injuries damages under the Supreme Court Act 1981 s.32A.

Paragraphs 15–16

3.173 See Income Support (General) Regulations 1987 (SI 1987/1967) Sch.9 paras 23–24.

Regulation 17(8)

SCHEDULE V

INCOME FROM CAPITAL

PART I

Capital disregarded for the purpose of calculating income

3.174 **1.**—Any premises acquired for occupation by the claimant which he intends to occupy as his home within 26 weeks of the date of acquisition or such longer period as is reasonable in the circumstances to enable the claimant to obtain possession and commence occupation of the premises.

[3 **1A.**—The dwelling occupied by the claimant as his home but only one home shall be disregarded under this paragraph.]

2.—Any premises which the claimant intends to occupy as his home, and in respect of which he is taking steps to obtain possession and has sought legal advice, or has commenced legal proceedings, with a view to obtaining possession, for a period of 26 weeks from the date on which he first sought such advice or first commenced such proceedings whichever is the earlier, or such longer period as is reasonable in the circumstances to enable him to obtain possession and commence occupation of those premises.

3.—Any premises which the claimant intends to occupy as his home to which essential repairs or alterations are required in order to render them fit for such occupation, for a period of 26 weeks from the date on which the claimant first takes steps to effect those repairs or alterations, or such longer period as is necessary to enable those repairs or alterations to be carried out.

4.—Any premises occupied in whole or in part—

(a) by a [6 person who is a close relative, grandparent, grandchild, uncle, aunt, nephew or niece of the claimant or of his partner] as his home where that person [18 has attained the qualifying age for state pension credit or is incapacitated];

(b) by the former partner of the claimant as his home; but this provision shall not apply where the former partner is a person from whom the claimant is estranged or divorced [9 or with whom he had formed a civil partnership that has been dissolved].

5.—Any future interest in property of any kind, other than land or premises in respect of which the claimant has granted a subsisting lease or tenancy, including sub-leases or sub-tenancies.

6.—(1) Where a claimant has ceased to occupy what was formerly the dwelling occupied as the home following his estrangement or divorce from [9, or dissolution of his civil partnership with,] his former partner, that dwelling for a period of 26 weeks from the date on which he ceased to occupy that dwelling or, where the dwelling is occupied as the home by the former partner who is a lone parent, for so long as it is so occupied.

(2) In this paragraph—

(a) "dwelling" includes any garage, garden and outbuildings, which were formerly occupied by the claimant as his home and any premises not so occupied which it is impracticable or unreasonable to sell separately, in particular, in Scotland, any croft land on which the dwelling is situated;

(b) "lone parent" means a person who has no partner and who is responsible for, and a member of the same household as, a child; and

(c) "child" means a person [12 who is a qualifying young person [31 within the meaning of regulation 4A] or] a child [31 as defined in section 40 of the 2012 Act].

7.—Any premises where the claimant is taking reasonable steps to dispose of the whole of his interest in those premises, for a period of 26 weeks from the date on which he first took such steps, or such longer period as is reasonable in the circumstances to enable him to dispose of those premises.

8.—All personal possessions.

9.—The assets of any business owned in whole or in part by the claimant and for the purposes of which he is engaged as a self-employed earner or, if he has ceased to be engaged, for such period as may be reasonable in the circumstances to allow for disposal of those assets.

[1**9A.**—The assets of any business owned in whole or in part by the claimant if—

(a) he is not engaged as a self-employed earner in that business by reason of some disease or bodily or mental disablement; but

(b) he intends to become engaged (or, as the case may be, re-engaged) as a self-employed earner in that business as soon as he recovers or is able to become engaged, or re-engaged, in that business,

[3 . . .].]

10.—The surrender value of any policy of life insurance.

11.—The value of any funeral plan contract; and for this purpose, "funeral plan contract" means a contract under which—

(a) the claimant makes one or more payments to another person ("the provider");

(b) the provider undertakes to provide, or secure the provision of, a funeral in the United Kingdom for the claimant on his death; and

(c) the sole purpose of the plan is to provide or secure the provision of a funeral for the claimant on his death.

12.—Where an ex-gratia payment has been made by the Secretary of State on or after 1st February 2001 in consequence of the imprisonment or [2internment] of—

(a) the claimant;

(b) the claimant's partner;

(c) the claimant's deceased spouse [9 or deceased civil partner]; or

(d) the claimant's partner's deceased spouse [9 or deceased civil partner],

by the Japanese during the Second World War, an amount equal to that payment.

13.—(1) Subject to sub-paragraph (2), the amount of any trust payment made to a claimant or a claimant's partner [3 who is]—

(a) [3 . . .] a diagnosed person;

(b) [3a diagnosed person's partner or] was a diagnosed person's partner at the time of the diagnosed person's death;

(c) [3 . . .] a parent of a diagnosed person, a person acting in place of the diagnosed person's parents or a person who was so acting at the date of the diagnosed person's death.

(2) Where [3 a trust payment is made to]—

(a) [3 a person referred to in sub-paragraph (1)(a) or (b), that sub-paragraph] shall apply for the period beginning on the date on which the trust is made and ending on the date on which [3 that person] dies;

(b) [3 a person referred to in sub-paragraph (1)(c), that sub-paragraph] shall apply for the period beginning on the date on which the trust payment is made and ending two years after that date.

(3) Subject to sub-paragraph (4), the amount of any payment by a person to whom a trust payment has been made or of any payment out of the estate of a person to whom a trust payment has been made, which is made to a claimant or a claimant's partner [3 who is]—

(a) [3 . . .] the diagnosed person;

(b) [3 a diagnosed person's partner or] was a diagnosed person's partner at the date of the diagnosed person's death; or

(c) [3 . . .] a parent of a diagnosed person, a person acting in place of the diagnosed person's parents or a person who was so acting at the date of the diagnosed person's death.

(4) Where [3 a payment referred to in sub-paragraph (3) is made to]—

(a) [3 a person referred to in sub-paragraph (3)(a) or (b), that sub-paragraph] shall apply for the period beginning on the date on which the payment is made and ending on the date on which [3 that person] dies;

(b) [3 a person referred to in sub-paragraph (3)(c), that sub-paragraph] shall apply for the period beginning on the date on which the payment is made and ending two years after that date.

(5) In this paragraph, a reference to a person—

(a) being the diagnosed person's partner;

(b) acting in place of the diagnosed person's parents,

at the date of the diagnosed person's death shall include a person who would have been such a person or a person who would have been so acting, but for the diagnosed person [8 residing in a care home or independent hospital].

(6) In this paragraph—

"diagnosed person" means a person who has been diagnosed as suffering from, or who, after his death, has been diagnosed as having suffered from, variant [3 Creutzfeldt]-Jakob disease;

"relevant trust" means a trust established out of funds provided by the Secretary of State in respect of persons who suffered, or who are suffering, from variant [3 Creutzfeldt]-Jakob disease for the benefit of persons eligible for payments in accordance with its provisions;

"trust payment" means a payment under a relevant trust.

14.—[16 (1)] The amount of any payment, other than a war disablement pension or a war widow's or widower's pension, to compensate for the fact that the claimant, the claimant's partner, the claimant's deceased spouse [9 or deceased civil partner] or the claimant's partner's deceased spouse [9 or deceased civil partner]—

(a) was a slave labourer or a forced labourer;

(b) had suffered property loss or had suffered personal injury; or

(c) was a parent of a child who had died, during the Second World War.

[16 (2) In sub-paragraph (1), "war disablement pension" and "war widow's or widower's pension" include any payment described in regulation 15(5)(ac).]

15.—(1) Any payment made under [20 or by] the Macfarlane Trust, the Macfarlane (Special Payments) Trust, the Macfarlane (Special Payments) (No.2) Trust ("the Trusts"), the Fund, the Eileen Trust [19, MFET Limited] [4, the [15 Independent Living Fund (2006)] [10, the Skipton Fund [21, the Caxton Foundation] [33, the Scottish Infected Blood Support Scheme] [35, [36 an approved blood scheme], the London Emergencies Trust, the We Love Manchester Emergency Fund] [42, the National Emergencies Trust [52, the Victims of Overseas Terrorism Compensation Scheme] or the London Bombings Relief Charitable Fund]].

[42 (1A) Any Grenfell Tower payment [48, child abuse payment, Windrush payment [50, Post Office compensation payment or vaccine damage payment] or any payment made by the Child

Migrants Trust (registered charity number 1171479) under the scheme for former British child migrants.]

(2) Any payment by or on behalf of a person who is suffering or who suffered from haemophilia or who is or was a qualifying person, which derives from a payment made under [20 or by] any of the Trusts to which sub-paragraph (1) refers [42, or from a Grenfell Tower payment,] [48, a child abuse payment [50, a Windrush payment, a Post Office compensation payment or a vaccine damage payment] and which is made to or for the benefit of that person's partner or former partner from whom he is not, or where that person has died was not, estranged or divorced [9 or with whom he has formed a civil partnership that has not been dissolved or, where that person has died, had not been dissolved at the time of that person's death].

(3) Any payment by or on behalf of the partner or former partner of a person who is suffering or who suffered from haemophilia or who is or was a qualifying person provided that the partner or former partner and that person are not, or if either of them has died were not, estranged or divorced [9 or, where the partner or former partner and that person have formed a civil partnership, the civil partnership has not been dissolved or, if either of them has died, had not been dissolved at the time of the death], which derives from a payment made under [20 or by] any of the Trusts to which sub-paragraph (1) refers [42, or from a Grenfell Tower payment,] [48, a child abuse payment [50, a Windrush payment, a Post Office compensation payment or a vaccine damage payment] and which is made to or for the benefit of the person who is suffering from haemophilia or who is a qualifying person.

(4) Any payment by a person who is suffering from haemophilia or who is a qualifying person, which derives from a payment under [20 or by] any of the Trusts to which sub-paragraph (1) refers [42, or from a Grenfell Tower payment,] [48, a child abuse payment [50, a Windrush payment, a Post Office compensation payment or a vaccine damage payment] where—

- (a) that person has no partner or former partner from whom he is not estranged or divorced [9 or with whom he has formed a civil partnership that has not been dissolved], nor any child who is or had been a member of that person's household; and
- (b) the payment is made either—
  - (i) to that person's parent or step-parent, or
  - (ii) where that person at the date of the payment is a child or a student who has not completed his full-time education and has no parent or step-parent, to any person standing in the place of his parent,

but only for a period from the date of the payment until the end of two years from that person's death.

(5) Any payment out of the estate of a person who suffered from haemophilia or who was a qualifying person, which derives from a payment under [20 or by] any of the Trusts to which sub-paragraph (1) refers [42, or from a Grenfell Tower payment,] [48, a child abuse payment [50, a Windrush payment, a Post Office compensation payment or a vaccine damage payment] where—

- (a) that person at the date of his death (the relevant date) had no partner or former partner from whom he was not estranged or divorced [9 or with whom he has formed a civil partnership that had not been dissolved], nor any child who was or had been a member of his household; and
- (b) the payment is made either—
  - (i) to that person's parent or step-parent, or
  - (ii) where that person at the relevant date was a child or a student who had not completed his full-time education and had no parent or step-parent, to any person standing in place his parent,

but only for a period of two years from the relevant date.

[51(5A) Any payment out of the estate of a person, which derives from a payment to meet the recommendation of the Infected Blood Inquiry in its interim report published on 29th July 2022 made under or by the Scottish Infected Blood Support Scheme or an approved blood scheme to the estate of the person, where the payment is made to the person's son, daughter, step-son or step-daughter.]

(6) In the case of a person to whom or for whose benefit a payment referred to in this paragraph is made, any capital resource which derives from any payment of income or capital made under or deriving from any of the Trusts [42, or from a Grenfell Tower payment] [48, a child abuse payment [50, a Windrush payment, a Post Office compensation payment or a vaccine damage payment].

(7) For the purposes of sub-paragraphs (2) to (6), any reference to the Trusts shall be construed as including a reference to the Fund [5, the Eileen Trust [19, MFET Limited] [10, the Skipton Fund [21, the Caxton Foundation] [33, the Scottish Infected Blood Support Scheme]

[35, [36 an approved blood scheme] the London Emergencies Trust, the We Love Manchester Emergency Fund] [42, the National Emergencies Trust] [52, the Victims of Overseas Terrorism Compensation Scheme], and the London Bombings Relief Charitable Fund]].

(8) In this paragraph—

"child" means any person [12 who is a qualifying young person [31 within the meaning of regulation 4A] or] a child [31 as defined in section 40 of the 2012 Act];

"course of study" means any course of study, whether or not it is a sandwich course and whether or not a grant is made for undertaking or attending it;

"qualifying course" means a qualifying course as defined for the purposes of Parts II and IV of the Jobseeker's Allowance Regulations;

"sandwich course" has the meaning given in regulation 5(2) of the Education (Student Support) Regulations 2001, regulation 5(2) of the Education (Student Loans) (Scotland) Regulations 2000 or regulation 5(2) of the Education (Student Support) Regulations (Northern Ireland) 2000, as the case may be;

"student" means a person, other than a person in receipt of a training allowance, who is attending or undertaking—

(a) a course of study at an educational establishment; or

(b) a qualifying course;

"training allowance" means an allowance (whether by way of periodical grants or otherwise) payable—

(a) out of public funds by a Government department or by or on behalf of the Secretary of State, [17 Skills Development Scotland,] Scottish Enterprise or Highlands and Islands Enterprise;

(b) to a person for his maintenance or in respect of a member of his family; and

(c) for the period, or part of the period, during which he is following a course of training or instruction provided by, or in pursuance of arrangements made with, that department or approved by that department in relation to him or so provided or approved by or on behalf of the Secretary of State, [17 Skills Development Scotland,] Scottish Enterprise or Highlands and Islands Enterprise,

but it does not include an allowance paid by any Government department to or in respect of a person by reason of the fact that he is following a course of full-time education, other than under arrangements made under section 2 of the Employment and Training Act 1973 or is training as a teacher [2. . .].

[7 **15A.**—[10. . . .]]

16.—[1(1)] An amount equal to the amount of any payment made in consequence of any personal injury to the claimant or, if the claimant has a partner, to the partner.

[1(2) Where the whole or part of the payment is administered—

[13(a) by the High Court or the County Court under rule 21.11(1) of the Civil Procedure Rules 1998, or the Court of Protection, or on behalf of a person where the payment can only be disposed of by order or direction of any such court;]

(b) in accordance with an order made under [13 . . .] rule 36.14 of the Ordinary Cause Rules 1993 or under rule 128 of those Rules; or

(c) in accordance with the terms of a trust established for the benefit of the claimant or his partner,

the whole of the amount so administered.]

17.—Any amount specified in paragraphs 18 to 20 [16 or 20B]—

(a) in a case where there is an assessed income period, until the end of that period or until the expiration of one year from the date of payment, whichever is the later; or

(b) in any other case, for a period of one year beginning with the date of receipt.

18.—Amounts paid under a policy of insurance in connection with the loss of or damage to the property occupied by the claimant as his home and to his personal possessions.

19.—So much of any amounts paid to the claimant or deposited in the claimant's name for the sole purpose of—

(a) purchasing premises which the claimant intends to occupy as his home; or

(b) effecting essential repairs or alterations to the premises occupied or intended to be occupied by the claimant as his home.

20.—(1) Any amount paid—

(a) by way of arrears of benefit;

(b) by way of compensation for the late payment of benefit; or

(c) in lieu of the payment of benefit;

[3 (d) any payment made by a local authority (including in England a county council), or by the [16 Welsh Ministers], to or on behalf of the claimant or his partner relating to a service which is provided to develop or sustain the capacity of the claimant or his partner to live independently in his accommodation] [23; or

(e) by way of local welfare provision including arrears and payments in lieu of local welfare provision; or

(f) in consequence of a reduction of council tax under section 13, 13A or 80 of the Local Government Finance Act 1992 (reduction of liability of [42 council tax;

(g) to rectify, or to compensate for, an error made by an officer of the Department for Work and Pensions which was not caused or materially contributed to by any person outside the Department and which prevented or delayed an assessment of the claimant's entitlement to contributory employment and support allowance.]

(2) In paragraph (1), "benefit" means—

(a) attendance allowance under section 64 of the Contributions and Benefits Act;

(b) disability living allowance;

[24 (ba) personal independence payment;]

[25 (bb) armed forces independence payment;]

(c) income support;

(d) income-based jobseeker's allowance;

(e) housing benefit;

(f) state pension credit;

(g) [3 . . .]

(h) [3 an increase of a disablement pension under section 104 of the Contributions and Benefits Act (increase where constant attendance needed), and any further increase of such a pension under section 105 of that Act (increase for exceptionally severe disablement)];

(i) any amount included on account of the claimant's exceptionally severe disablement [3 or need for constant attendance] in a war disablement pension or [16 any other such amount described in regulation 15(5)(ac)].

[1(j) council tax benefit;

(k) social fund payments;

(l) child benefit;

(m) [3 . . .]

(n) child tax credit under the Tax Credits Act 2002;]

[14 (o) income-related employment and support allowance] [26;

(p) universal credit;]

[34 (q) bereavement support payment under section 30 of the Pensions Act 2014;]

[39 (r) early years assistance given in accordance with section 32 of the Social Security (Scotland) Act 2018;]

[40(s) funeral expense assistance given in accordance with section 34 of the Social Security (Scotland) Act 2018;]

[41(t) maternity allowance under section 35 of the 1992 Act (state maternity allowance for employed or self-employed earner).]

[43(u) any Scottish child payment assistance given in accordance with section 79 of the Social Security (Scotland) Act 2018];

[44(v) any assistance given in accordance with the Carer's Assistance (Young Carer Grants) (Scotland) Regulations 2019.]

[45(w) short-term assistance given in accordance with regulations made under section 36 of the Social Security (Scotland) Act 2018;]

[46(x) winter heating assistance given in accordance with regulations made under section 30 of the Social Security (Scotland) Act 2018.]

[47(y) disability assistance given in accordance with regulations made under section 31 of the Social Security (Scotland) Act 2018.]

[3**20A.**—(1) Subject to sub-paragraph (3), any payment of £5,000 or more to which paragraph 20(1)(a), (b) or (c) applies, which has been made to rectify, or to compensate for, an official error [38 or an error on a point of law] relating to a [42 relevant benefit, or to which paragraph 20(1)(g) applies, and which has been] received by the claimant in full on or after the day on which he became entitled to benefit under these Regulations.

(2) Subject to sub-paragraph (3), the total amount of any payment disregarded under—

(a) paragraph 7(2) of Schedule 10 to the Income Support (General) Regulations 1987;

(b) paragraph 12(2) of Schedule 8 to the Jobseeker's Allowance Regulations 1996;

[16. . .]

[14 or

(e) paragraph 11(2) of Schedule 9 to the Employment and Support Allowance Regulations,]

[16 (f) paragraph 9(2) [42 or 9A] of Schedule 6 to the Housing Benefit Regulations 2006;

(g) paragraph 22 of Schedule 6 to the Housing Benefit (Persons who have attained the qualifying age for state pension credit) Regulations 2006;

(h) paragraph 9(2) of Schedule 5 to the Council Tax Benefit Regulations 2006; [26 . . .]

(i) paragraph 22 of Schedule 4 to the Council Tax Benefit (Persons who have attained the qualifying age for state pension credit) Regulations 2006;] [26 or

(j) [27 paragraph 18] of Schedule 10 to the Universal Credit Regulations 2013;]

[42(k) regulations 10A to 10C of the Universal Credit (Transitional Provisions) Regulations 2014;]

where the award during which the disregard last applied in respect of the relevant sum either terminated immediately before the relevant date or is still in existence at that date.

(3) Any disregard which applies under sub-paragraph (1) or (2) shall have effect until the award comes to an end.

(4) In this paragraph—

"the award", except in sub-paragraph (2), means—

(a) the award of State Pension Credit under these Regulations during which the relevant sum or, where it is received in more than one instalment, the first instalment of that sum is received; or

(b) where that award is followed immediately by one or more further awards which begins immediately after the previous award ends, such further awards until the end of the last award, provided that, for such further awards, the claimant—

(i) is the person who received the relevant sum;

(ii) is the partner of that person; or

(iii) was the partner of that person at the date of his death;

"official error"—

(a) where the error relates to housing benefit [22 . . .] has the meaning given by regulation 1(2) of the Housing Benefit and Council Tax Benefit (Decisions and Appeals) Regulations 2001;
and

(b) where the error relates to any other relevant benefit, has the meaning given by regulation 1(3) of the Social Security and Child Support (Decisions and Appeals) Regulations 1999;

"the relevant date" means the date on which the claimant became entitled to benefit under the Act;

"relevant benefit" means any benefit specified in paragraph 20(2); and

"the relevant sum" means the total payment referred to in sub-paragraph (1) or, as the case may be, the total amount referred to in sub-paragraph (2).]

[49 **20AA.** Any payment of a widowed parent's allowance made pursuant to section 39A of the 1992 Act (widowed parent's allowance)—

(a) to the survivor of a cohabiting partnership (within the meaning in section 39A(7) of the 1992 Act) who is entitled to a widowed parent's allowance for a period before the Bereavement Benefits (Remedial) Order 2023 comes into force, and

(b) in respect of any period of time during the period ending with the day before the survivor makes the claim for a widowed parent's allowance,

but only for a period of 52 weeks from the date of receipt of the payment.]

[16 **20B.**—Any arrears of supplementary pension which is disregarded under paragraph 4 of Schedule 4 (amounts to be disregarded in the calculation of income other than earnings) or of any amount which is disregarded under paragraph 5 or 6 of that Schedule.]

21.—Where a capital asset is held in a currency other than sterling, any banking charge or commission payable in converting that capital into sterling.

22.—The value of the right to receive income from an occupational pension scheme or a personal pension scheme.

23.—The value of a right to receive income from a under a retirement annuity contract.

[11 **23A.**—Where a person elects to be entitled to a lump sum under Schedule 5 or 5A to the 1992 Act or under Schedule 1 to the Graduated Retirement Benefit Regulations, or is treated as having made such an election, and a payment has been made pursuant to that election, an amount equal to—

(a) except where sub-paragraph (b) applies, the amount of any payment or payments made on account of that lump sum;

(b) the amount of that lump sum,

but only for so long as that person does not change that election in favour of an increase of pension or benefit.]

[30 **23AA.** Where a person chooses a lump sum under section 8(2) of the Pensions Act 2014 or in accordance with Regulations made under section 10 of that Act which include provision corresponding or similar to section 8(2) of that Act, or fails to make a choice, and a lump sum payment has been made, an amount equal to—

(a) except where sub-paragraph (b) applies, the amount of any payment or payments made on account of that lump sum;

(b) the amount of that lump sum,

but only for so long as that person does not alter that choice in favour of an increase of pension.]

[[17] **23B.**—Any payment made under Part 8A of the 1992 Act (entitlement to health in pregnancy grant).]

[[21] **23C.**—Any payments made [[28] . . .]—

(a) [[28] by virtue of regulations made under] section 57 (direct payments) of the Health and Social Care Act 2001;

[[28] (b) as a direct payment as defined in section 4(2) of the Social Care (Self-directed Support) (Scotland) Act 2013; [[29] . . .]

(c) [[28] by virtue of regulations made under] sections 12A to 12C (direct payments for health care) of the National Health Service Act 2006] [[29][[37] . . .]

(d) under sections 31 to 33 of the Care Act 2014 [[37] (direct payments); or

(e) by virtue of regulations made under section 50 or 52 of the Social Services and Well-being (Wales) Act 2014 (direct payments).].]

[[32] **23D.**—(1) Any payment made by a local authority in accordance with section 26A of the Children (Scotland) Act 1995.

(2) Subject to sub-paragraph (3), any payment or part of a payment made by a local authority in accordance with section 26A of the Children (Scotland) Act 1995 to a person ("A") which A passes on to the claimant.

(3) Sub-paragraph (2) only applies where A—

(a) was formerly in the claimant's care;

(b) is aged 16 or over; and

(c) continues to live with the claimant.]

[[34] **23E.** [[49] (1)] A payment of bereavement support payment in respect of the rate set out in regulation 3(2) or (5) of the Bereavement Support Payment Regulations 2017 (rate of bereavement support payment), but only for a period of 52 weeks from the date of receipt of the payment.]

[[49] (2) Where bereavement support payment under section 30 of the Pensions Act 2014 is paid to the survivor of a cohabiting partnership (within the meaning in section 30(6B) of the Pensions Act 2014) in respect of a death occurring before the day the Bereavement Benefits (Remedial) Order 2023 comes into force, any amount of that payment which is—

(a) in respect of the rate set out in regulation 3(1) of the Bereavement Support Payment Regulations 2017, and

(b) paid as a lump sum for more than one monthly recurrence of the day of the month on which their cohabiting partner died,

but only for a period of 52 weeks from the date of receipt of the payment.]

[[36] **23F.** Any payment made under or by a trust, established for the purpose of giving relief and assistance to disabled persons whose disabilities were caused by the fact that during their mother's pregnancy she had taken a preparation containing the drug known as Thalidomide, and which is approved by the Secretary of State.]

Part II

[[1]Capital disregarded only for the purposes of determining deemed income] 3.175

24.—The value of the right to receive any income under a life interest or from a life rent.

25.—The value of the right to receive any rent except where the claimant has a reversionary interest in the property in respect of which rent is due.

26.—The value of the right to receive any income under an annuity or the surrender value (if any) of such an annuity.

27.—[[3] . . .]

28.—Where property is held under a trust, other than—

(a) a charitable trust within the meaning of the Charities Act 1993; or

(b) a trust set up with any payment to which paragraph 16 of this Schedule applies, and under the terms of the trust, payments fall to be made, or the trustees have a discretion to make payments, to or for the benefit of the claimant or the claimant's partner, or both, that property.

AMENDMENTS

1. State Pension Credit (Consequential, Transitional and Miscellaneous Provisions) Regulations 2002 (SI 2002/3019) reg.23(o) (October 6, 2003).

2. State Pension Credit (Consequential, Transitional and Miscellaneous Provisions) (No.2) Regulations 2002 (SI 2002/3197) reg.2 and Sch. para.12 (October 6, 2003).

3. State Pension Credit (Transitional and Miscellaneous Provisions) Amendment Regulations 2003 (SI 2003/2274) reg.2(12) (October 6, 2003).

4. Social Security (Miscellaneous Amendments) (No.2) Regulations 2004 (SI 2004/1141) regs 3(3) and 3(4)(d) (May 12, 2004).

5. Social Security (Miscellaneous Amendments) (No.2) Regulations 2004 (SI 2004/1141) regs 3(5) and 3(6)(d) (May 12, 2004).

6. Social Security (Housing Benefit, Council Tax Benefit, State Pension Credit and Miscellaneous Amendments) Regulations 2004 (SI 2004/2327) reg.7(6) (October 4, 2004).

7. Income-related Benefits (Amendment) Regulations 2005 (SI 2005/2183) reg.6 (August 5, 2005).

8. Social Security (Care Homes and Independent Hospitals) Regulations 2005 (SI 2005/2687) reg.6 and Sch.5 para.6 (October 24, 2005).

9. Civil Partnership (Pensions, Social Security and Child Support) (Consequential, etc. Provisions) Order 2005 (SI 2005/2877) art.2(3) and Sch.3 para.35(5) (December 5, 2005).

10. Income-related Benefits (Amendment) (No.2) Regulations 2005 (SI 2005/3391) reg.7(3) (December 12, 2005).

11. Social Security (Deferral of Retirement Pensions, Shared Additional Pension and Graduated Retirement Benefit) (Miscellaneous Provisions) Regulations 2005 (SI 2005/2677) reg.13(4) (April 6, 2006).

12. Social Security (Young Persons) Amendment Regulations 2006 (SI 2006/718) reg.6(5) (April 10, 2006).

13. Social Security (Miscellaneous Amendments) (No.4) Regulations 2006 (SI 2006/2378) reg.14(6) (October 2, 2006).

14. Employment and Support Allowance (Consequential Provisions) (No.2) Regulations 2008 (SI 2008/1554) reg.4(9) (October 27, 2008).

15. Social Security (Miscellaneous Amendments) (No.6) Regulations 2008 (SI 2008/2767) reg.5(5) (November 17, 2008).

16. Social Security (Miscellaneous Amendments) (No.7) Regulations 2008 (SI 2008/3157) reg.4(6) (January 5, 2009).

17. Social Security (Miscellaneous Amendments) Regulations 2009 (SI 2009/583) reg.5(4) and (5) (April 6, 2009).

18. Social Security (Equalisation of State Pension Age) Regulations 2009 (SI 2009/1488) regs 22 and 23 (April 10, 2010).

19. Social Security (Miscellaneous Amendments) (No.2) Regulations 2010 (SI 2010/641) reg.6(3)(c) (April 6, 2010).

20. Social Security (Miscellaneous Amendments) (No.2) Regulations 2010 (SI 2010/641) reg.6(2) (April 6, 2010).

21. Social Security (Miscellaneous Amendments) (No.3) Regulations 2011 (2011/2425) reg.15(6) and (7) (October 31, 2011).

22. Council Tax Benefit Abolition (Consequential Provision) Regulations 2013 (SI 2013/458) reg.3 and Sch.1 (April 1, 2013).

23. Social Security (Miscellaneous Amendments) Regulations 2013 (SI 2013/443) reg.6(4) (April 2, 2013).

24. Personal Independence Payment (Supplementary Provisions and Consequential Amendments) Regulations 2013 (SI 2013/388) reg.8 and Sch. para.27(7) (April 8, 2013).

25. Armed Forces and Reserve Forces Compensation Scheme (Consequential Provisions: Subordinate Legislation) Order 2013 (SI 2013/591) art.7 and Sch. para.23(7) (April 8, 2013).

26. Universal Credit (Consequential, Supplementary, Incidental and Miscellaneous Provisions) Regulations 2013 (SI 2013/630) reg.33(7) (April 29, 2013).

27. Social Security (Miscellaneous Amendments) (No.3) Regulations 2013 (SI 2013/2536) reg.10(4) (October 29, 2013).

28. Social Care (Self-directed Support) (Scotland) Act 2013 (Consequential Modifications and Savings) Order 2014 (SI 2014/513) art.2 and Sch. para.7 (April 1, 2014).

29. Care Act 2014 (Consequential Amendments) (Secondary Legislation) Order 2015 (SI 2015/643) reg.19(1) and (2) (April 1, 2015).

30. Pensions Act 2014 (Consequential, Supplementary and Incidental Amendments) Order 2015 (SI 2015/1985) reg.24(2) (April 6, 2016).

31. Housing Benefit and State Pension Credit (Temporary Absence) (Amendment) Regulations 2016 (SI 2016/624) reg.4(9) (July 28, 2016).

32. Children and Young People (Scotland) Act 2014 (Consequential Modifications) Order 2016 (SI 2016/732) art.4(3) (August 5, 2016).

33. Social Security (Scottish Infected Blood Support Scheme) Regulations 2017 (SI 2017/329) reg.5(3)(b) (April 3, 2017).

34. Pensions Act 2014 (Consequential, Supplementary and Incidental Amendments) Order 2017 (SI 2017/422) art.21(3) (April 6, 2017).

35. Social Security (Emergency Funds) (Amendment) Regulations 2017 (SI 2017/689) reg.4(3)(b) (June 19, 2017).

36. Social Security (Infected Blood and Thalidomide) Regulations 2017 (SI 2017/870) reg.5(3)(b) and 5(5) (October 23, 2017).

37. Social Services and Well-being (Wales) Act 2014 and the Regulation and Inspection of Social Care (Wales) Act 2016 (Consequential Amendments) Order 2017 (SI 2017/901) reg.9(3) (November 3, 2017).

38. Social Security (Treatment of Arrears of Benefit) Regulations 2018 (SI 2018/932), reg.4 (September 11, 2018).

39. Social Security (Scotland) Act 2018 (Best Start Grants) (Consequential Modifications and Saving) Order 2018 (SI 2018/1138), art.7(3) (December 10, 2018).

40. Social Security (Scotland) Act 2018 (Funeral Expense Assistance and Early Years Assistance) (Consequential Modifications and Savings) Order 2019 (SI 2019/1060) art.11(2) (September 16, 2019).

41. Social Security (Capital Disregards) (Amendment) Regulations 2019 (SI 2019/1314) reg.4(2) (October 31, 2019, reg.4(2)).

42. Social Security (Income and Capital) (Miscellaneous Amendments) Regulations 2020 (SI 2020/618) reg.4 (July 15, 2020).

43. Social Security (Scotland) Act 2018 (Information-Sharing and Scottish Child Payment) (Consequential Provision and Modifications) Order 2020 (SI 2020/482) art.5 (November 9, 2020).

44. Social Security (Scotland) Act 2018 (Young Carer Grants, Short-Term Assistance and Winter Heating Assistance) (Consequential Provision and Modifications) Order 2020 (SI 2020/989) art.4(3) (November 9, 2020).

45. Social Security (Scotland) Act 2018 (Young Carer Grants, Short-Term Assistance and Winter Heating Assistance) (Consequential Provision and Modifications) Order 2020 (SI 2020/989) art.11(3) (November 9, 2020).

46. Social Security (Scotland) Act 2018 (Young Carer Grants, Short-Term Assistance and Winter Heating Assistance) (Consequential Provision and Modifications) Order 2020 (SI 2020/989) art.17(3) (November 9, 2020).

47. Social Security (Scotland) Act 2018 (Disability Assistance, Young Carer Grants, Short-term Assistance and Winter Heating Assistance) (Consequential Provision and Modifications) Order 2021 (SI 2021/886) art.13(3) (July 26, 2021).

48. Social Security (Income and Capital Disregards) (Amendment) Regulations 2021 (SI 2021/1405) reg.4(4) (January 1, 2022).

49. Bereavement Benefits (Remedial) Order 2023 (SI 2023/134) art.10 and Sch. para.5 (February 9, 2023).

50. Social Security (Income and Capital Disregards) (Amendment) Regulations 2023 (SI 2023/640) reg.4(4) (July 9, 2023).

51. Social Security (Infected Blood Capital Disregard) (Amendment) Regulations 2023 (SI 2023/894) reg.2 (August 30, 2023).

52. Social Security (Habitual Residence and Past Presence, and Capital Disregards) (Amendment) Regulations 2023 (SI 2023/1144) reg.5(3)(b) (October 27, 2023).

General Note

3.176 This Schedule includes many of the same disregards as are to be found in Sch.10 to the Income Support (General) Regulations 1987 (SI 1987/1967) (see Vol.V of this series). However, the function of the two Schedules is conceptually different. The purpose of Sch.10 in the income support scheme is to provide for disregards to be applied in calculating the claimant's capital with a view to seeing whether the relevant capital threshold is exceeded. The purpose of this Schedule is to specify disregards which apply in the assessment of capital which is then used for calculating the claimant's income under the tariff income rule in reg.15(6), there being no capital rule as such in the state pension credit scheme. That said, the actual drafting of these provisions follows closely the parallel provisions in the income support schemes. But note also that the disregards in this Schedule are subdivided into two categories: those which are disregarded for the purpose of calculating income (Pt I) and those disregarded—which are fewer in number—for the purpose of calculating notional income (Pt II).

Paragraph 1

3.177 See Income Support (General) Regulations 1987 (SI 1987/1967) Sch.10 para.2. The claimant's own home (Sch.2 para.1 of the 1987 Regulations) is disregarded for state pension credit purposes by para.1A below.

Paragraphs 2–3

3.178 See Income Support (General) Regulations 1987 (SI 1987/1967) Sch.10 paras 27–28.

Paragraphs 4–5

3.179 See Income Support (General) Regulations 1987 (SI 1987/1967) Sch.10 paras 4 and 5.

Paragraph (4)(a) provides for the disregard of the value of a second property where that property is occupied by someone who is aged 60 or over or is incapacitated and who is a relative of the pension credit claimant or their partner. Note that the original drafting of para.(4) meant that the disregard applied only if the occupier of the property was a close relative of the pension credit claimant himself (or herself). The amended formulation applies the disregard equally where the occupier is a close relative of the claimant's partner. The original wording reflected a drafting oversight, and the Minister has indicated that extra-statutory payments will be considered to anyone who lost out (*Hansard*, HC Vol. 421, col. 140W, May 10, 2004).

Paragraph 4(b) makes similar provision where the claimant's former partner occupies the property. This disregard is not available if the claimant is divorced or estranged from their ex-partner (or a civil partnership has been dissolved). On the meaning of "estranged", see *CPC/0683/2007*, following *R(IS) 5/05* and *CH/0177/2005*.

Paragraph 6

3.180 This applies the more generous housing benefit disregard (see, e.g. Housing Benefit (General) Regulations 1987 (SI 1987/1971) Sch.5 para.24) in preference to the more limited disregard in the Income Support (General) Regulations 1987 (SI 1987/1967) Sch.10 para.25. Thus the disregard on a former family home is for 26 weeks where the claimant moves out following a relationship breakdown, and beyond that time if the remaining partner is a lone parent (until such time as that status ceases).

Paragraph 7

See Income Support (General) Regulations 1987 (SI 1987/1967) Sch.10 para.26. **3.181**

Paragraph 8

See Income Support (General) Regulations 1987 (SI 1987/1967) Sch.10 para.10 **3.182**
(although the qualification in the income support provision is not repeated here).

Paragraphs 9–9A

See Income Support (General) Regulations 1987 (SI 1987/1967) Sch.10 **3.183**
para.6(1) and (2).

Paragraph 10

See Income Support (General) Regulations 1987 (SI 1987/1967) Sch.10 para.15. **3.184**
See further *AB v SSWP* [2010] UKUT 343 (AAC), where the claimant wrote to the DWP asking for a recalculation of his pension credit and for it to be backdated, as he now realised that on his claim form he had declared details of the surrender value of a life insurance policy which should not have been counted as part of his capital resources. His benefit was recalculated as from the date of the letter. Judge Ovey held that the tribunal had erred in treating the information supplied by the claimant as a notification of a change of circumstances rather than revelation of a mistake in the calculation of the original award, and had further failed to consider whether there had been an official error in the making of that award.

Paragraph 11

This has no direct parallel under the income support scheme. **3.185**

Paragraph 12

See Income Support (General) Regulations 1987 (SI 1987/1967) Sch.10 para.61. **3.186**

Paragraphs 13–14

See Income Support (General) Regulations 1987 (SI 1987/1967) Sch.10 paras 64–65. **3.187**

Paragraph 15

See Income Support (General) Regulations 1987 (SI 1987/1967) Sch.10 para.22. **3.188**

Paragraph 16

Payments in respect of compensation for personal injuries are disregarded for both **3.189**
capital and income purposes (see also Sch.IV paras 13 and 14). Paragraph 16(2) deals with the specific example of funds held in court: see Income Support (General) Regulations 1987 (SI 1987/1967) Sch.10 paras 44 and 45.

Paragraphs 17–19

These paragraphs are designed to fulfil broadly the same functions as the disre- **3.190**
gards Income Support (General) Regulations 1987 (SI 1987/1967) Sch.10 paras 3 and 8. These disregards, however, last for one year rather than the "26 weeks or such longer period as is reasonable in the circumstances" qualification that applies under the income support scheme. See *DG v SSWP (SPC)* [2010] UKUT 241 (AAC), confirming that for the purposes of the disregard in paras 17(b) and 19 time runs from the actual date of receipt of the funds, regardless of whether the claimant is actually in the UK at the time in question.

Paragraph 20

See Income Support (General) Regulations 1987 (SI 1987/1967) Sch.10 para.7. **3.191**

Paragraph 21

See Income Support (General) Regulations 1987 (SI 1987/1967) Sch.10 para.21. **3.192**
See also reg.17(6).

Paragraph 22

3.193 See Income Support (General) Regulations 1987 (SI 1987/1967) Sch.10 para.(23).

Paragraph 23AA

3.194 The effect of this provision is that an amount equal to the pre-tax amount of the lump-sum payment paid where a person changes their choice of payment of the new state pension is to be disregarded for life, so long as that person does not change their choice to a weekly increase.

Paragraphs 24–26

3.195 See Income Support (General) Regulations 1987 (SI 1987/1967) Sch.10 paras 13, 24 and 11 respectively.

Regulation 17(9)

SCHEDULE VI

Sums Disregarded from Claimant's Earnings

3.196 **1.**—(1) In a case where a claimant is a lone parent, £20 of earnings.

(2) In this paragraph—

(a) "lone parent" means a person who has no partner and who is responsible for, and a member of the same household as, a child;

(b) "child" means a person [4 who is a qualifying young person [11 within the meaning of regulation 4A] or] a child [11 as defined in section 40 of the 2012 Act].

2.—In a case of earnings from employment to which sub-paragraph (2) applies, £20.

(2) This paragraph applies to employment—

[9 (a) a part-time fire-fighter employed by a fire and rescue authority under the Fire and Rescue Services Act 2004 or by the Scottish Fire and Rescue Service established under section 1A of the Fire (Scotland) Act 2005;]

(b) as an auxiliary coastguard in respect of coast rescue activities;

(c) in the manning or launching of a lifeboat if the employment is part-time;

[1(d) a member of any territorial or reserve force prescribed in Part I of Schedule 6 to the Social Security (Contributions) Regulations 2001].

[1**2A.**—Where a person is engaged in one or more of the employments specified in paragraph 2 but his earnings derived from those employments are less than £20 in any week and he is also engaged in any other employment, so much of his earnings from that other employment as would not in aggregate with the amount of his earnings disregarded under paragraph 2 exceed £20.]

[2 **2B.**—Where only one member of a couple is in employment specified in paragraph 2(2), so much of the earnings of the other member of the couple as would not, in aggregate with the earnings disregarded under paragraph 2, exceed £20.]

3.—(1) If the claimant or one of the partners is a carer, or both partners are carers, £20 of any earnings received from his or their employment.

(2) In this paragraph the claimant or his partner is a carer if paragraph 4 of Part II of Schedule I (amount applicable for carers) is satisfied in respect of him.

4.—(1) £20 is disregarded if the claimant or, if he has a partner, his partner—

(a) is in receipt of—

(i) long-term incapacity benefit under section 30A of the 1992 Act;

(ii) severe disablement allowance under section 68 of that Act;

(iii) attendance allowance;

(iv) disability living allowance under section 71 to 76 of that Act;

(v) any mobility supplement under [6 article 20 of the Naval, Military and Air Forces Etc. (Disablement and Death) Service Pensions Order 2006](including such a supplement by virtue of any other scheme or order) or under article 25A of the Personal Injuries (Civilians) Scheme 1983; [5 . . .]

[1(vi) the disability element or the severe disability element of working tax credit under Schedule 2 to the Working Tax Credit (Entitlement and Maximum Rate) Regulations 2002; or]

[5 (vii) employment and support allowance; [7 . . .]]

[7 (viii) personal independence payment; [7 . . .]]

[12 (viiia) adult disability payment;]

[8 (ix) armed forces independence payment; or]

[10 (b) is or are certified as severely sight impaired or blind by a consultant ophthalmologist.]

(2) Subject to sub-paragraph (4), £20 is disregarded if the claimant or, if he has a partner, his partner has, within a period of 8 weeks ending on the day in respect of which the claimant first satisfies the conditions for entitlement to state pension credit, had an award of income support [5, income-based jobseeker's allowance or income-related employment and support allowance] and—

(a) £20 was disregarded in respect of earnings taken into account in that award;

(b) the person whose earnings qualified for the disegard in employment after the termination of that award.

(3) Subject to sub-paragraph (4), £20 is disregarded if the claimant or, if he has a partner, his partner, immediately before attaining pensionable age—

(a) had an award of state pension credit; and

(b) a disregard under paragraph 4(1)(a)(i) or (ii) was taken into account in determining that award.

(4) The disregard of £20 specified in sub-paragraphs (2) and (3) applies so long as there is no break, other a break which does not exceed eight weeks—

(a) in a case to which sub-paragraph (2) refers, in a person's entitlement to state pension credit or in employment following the first day in respect of which state pension credit is awarded; or

(b) in a case where sub-paragraph (3) applies, in the person's entitlement to state pension credit since attaining pensionable age.

(5) [1. . .].

[1**4A.**—(1) £20 is the maximum amount which may be disregarded under any of paragraphs 1, 2, 3 or 4 notwithstanding that—

(a) in the case of a claimant with no partner, he satisfies the requirements of more than one of those paragraphs or, in the case of paragraph 4, he satisfies the requirements of more than one of the sub-paragraphs of that paragraph; or

(b) in the case of [3 couples], both partners satisfy one or more of the requirements of paragraphs 2, 3 and 4.

(2) Where, in a case to which sub-paragraph (1)(b) applies, the amount to be disregarded in respect of one of the partners ("the first partner") is less than £20, the amount to be disregarded in respect of the other partner shall be so much of that other partner's earnings as would not, in aggregate with the first partner's earnings, exceed £20.]

5.—Except where the claimant or his partner qualifies for a £20 disregard under the preceding provisions of this Schedule—

(a) £5 shall be disregarded if a claimant who has no partner has earnings;

(b) £10 shall be disregarded if a claimant who has a partner has earnings.

6.—Any earnings [1, other than any amount referred to in regulation 17(9)(b),] derived from any employment which ended before the day in respect of which the claimant first satisfies the conditions for entitlement to state pension credit.

[1**7.**—Any banking charges or commission payable in converting to Sterling payments of earnings made in a currency other than Sterling.]

AMENDMENTS

1. State Pension Credit (Consequential, Transitional and Miscellaneous Provisions) (No.2) Regulations 2002 (SI 2002/3197) reg.2 and Sch. para.13 (October 6, 2003).

2. State Pension Credit (Transitional and Miscellaneous Provisions) Amendment Regulations 2003 (SI 2003/2274) reg.2(13) (October 6, 2003).

3. Civil Partnership (Pensions, Social Security and Child Support) (Consequential, etc. Provisions) Order 2005 (SI 2005/2877) art.2(3) and Sch.3 para.35(6) (December 5, 2005).

4. Social Security (Young Persons) Amendment Regulations 2006 (SI 2006/718) reg.6(6) (April 10, 2006).

5. Employment and Support Allowance (Consequential Provisions) (No.2) Regulations 2008 (SI 2008/1554) reg.4(10) (October 27, 2008).

6. Social Security (Miscellaneous Amendments) (No.7) Regulations 2008 (SI 2008/3157) reg.4(7) (January 5, 2009).
7. Personal Independence Payment (Supplementary Provisions and Consequential Amendments) Regulations 2013 (SI 2013/388) reg.8 and Sch. para.27(8) (April 8, 2013).
8. Armed Forces and Reserve Forces Compensation Scheme (Consequential Provisions: Subordinate Legislation) Order 2013 (SI 2013/591) art.7 and Sch. para.23(8) (April 8, 2013).
9. Social Security (Miscellaneous Amendments) (No.3) Regulations 2013 (SI 2013/2536) reg.10(5) (October 29, 2013).
10. Universal Credit and Miscellaneous Amendments (No.2) Regulations 2014 (SI 2014/2888) reg.3(4)(c) (November 26, 2014).
11. Housing Benefit and State Pension Credit (Temporary Absence) (Amendment) Regulations 2016 (SI 2016/624) reg.4(10) (July 28, 2016).
12. Social Security (Disability Assistance for Working Age People) (Consequential Amendments) Order 2022 (SI 2022/177) art.8(7) (March 21, 2022).

DEFINITIONS

"attendance allowance"—see reg.1(2).
"child"—see para.1(2).
"claimant"—see SPCA 2002 s.17(1).
"lone parent"—see para.1(2).
"partner"—see reg.1(3).
"pensionable age"—see SPCA 2002 s.17(1).

GENERAL NOTE

3.197 This Schedule performs the same function in relation to state pension credit as Sch.8 to the Income Support (General) Regulations 1987 (SI 1987/1967) (see Vol.V of this series) does in the context of income support. Thus the standard disregard on earnings is £5 a week for a single claimant and £10 a week for a couple (para.5). There are then various special cases (e.g. lone parents, carers, disabled claimants and those active pensioners who are still involved in various emergency services in a part-time capacity) where the disregard is £20 a week. Note that the maximum weekly disregard is £20 even where both members of a couple satisfy one of the tests for the maximum disregard (para.(4A)).

There is, however, one significant difference from income support: although the same earnings disregards apply, there is no 16-hours rule in the context of state pension credit. On the other hand, the low level of the earnings disregards is hardly an incentive for pensioners (or their partners) to work extra hours.

The typographical error in para.4(2)(b) ("disegard" for "disregard") appears in the original version of the Regulations and, as at the time of writing, has not been corrected.

PART IV

THE SOCIAL FUND

The Social Fund Cold Weather Payments (General) Regulations 1988

(SI 1988/1724) (AS AMENDED)

Made by the Secretary of State under ss.32(2A) and 84(1) of the Social Security Act 1986 and s.166(1) to (3A) of the Social Security Act 1975

GENERAL NOTE

Section 138(2) of the Contributions and Benefits Act provides that payments may be made out of the social fund "to meet expenses for heating, which appear to the Secretary of State to have been or to be likely to be incurred in cold weather". That power has been used to make these Regulations and also the Social Fund Winter Fuel Payment Regulations 2000 (see below). 4.1

The cold weather payments scheme was introduced in April 1988 and, although there have been subsequent technical changes, has had substantially the same structure since November 1, 1991. That structure is as follows:

- Every postcode in Great Britain is linked to a weather site accredited by the Met Office. Until October 31, 2016, the link was prescribed by Schedules 1 and 2 to these Regulations. However, from November 1, 2016, those Schedules were revoked by SI 2016/876 and the link is instead designated by the Secretary of State under reg.2A. According to the Explanatory Memorandum to that SI, the aim of the change was "to enable the Secretary of State to vary weather station designations relevant to cold weather payments without the need for new legislation every time a variation is needed".
- If a period of cold weather (i.e. seven consecutive days during which the average daily temperature is below 0°C) is forecast for, or recorded by, the weather site that is linked to a postcode district then any claimant whose home is in that district and who satisfies the conditions in reg.1A is entitled to a cold weather payment of (currently) £25.
- There is no need for a claim. However, a cold weather payment cannot be made after September 28 following the winter which included the period of cold weather (26 weeks beginning with March 31) (see reg.2(6)).

The decision to make a payment is made by a decision-maker but there is no notification in cases where a payment is not made. As it is not possible to make a claim, a person who does not receive a payment to which s/he thinks s/he is entitled must request a negative decision before there is something to appeal against.

For a historical review of the Scheme see pp.338–353 of the 3rd edition ofT. Buck, *The Social Fund—Law and Practice* (3rd edn) (London: Sweet & Maxwell, 2009), pp.338–353.

Citation, commencement and interpretation

1.—(1) These regulations may be cited as the Social Fund Cold Weather Payments (General) Regulations 1988 and shall come into force on 7th November 1988. 4.2

(2) In these Regulations, unless the context otherwise requires—

[[11] "the 2012 Act" means the Welfare Reform Act 2012;]

[[9] "the Act" means the Social Security Contributions and Benefits Act 1992;]

[[7] "the Welfare Reform Act" means the Welfare Reform Act 2007;]

"the General Regulations" means the Income Support (General) Regulations 1987;

[4[12"the Met Office" means the Met Office of the [18Department for Science, Innovation and Technology];]]

[9 . . .]

[2"claimant" means a person who is claiming or has claimed income support [6, state pension credit [7, income-based jobseeker's allowance [11, income-related employment and support allowance or universal credit [15 or who is in receipt of owner-occupier loan payments]]]];]

[9"cold weather payment" means a payment to meet expenses for heating made out of the social fund under section 138(2) of the Act and these Regulations;

"family" has the meaning given to it in section 137 of the Act and the General Regulations;]

[2"forecast" means a weather forecast produced by the [12 Met] Office [4. . .] and supplied to the [8 Department for Work and Pensions] on a daily basis [4 between 1st November in any year and 31st March in the following year,] which provides the expected average mean daily temperature for a period of 7 consecutive days;

"forecasted period of cold weather" means a period of 7 consecutive days, during which the average of the mean daily temperature for that period is forecasted to be equal to or below 0 degrees celsius; and for the purposes of this definition where a day forms part of a forecasted period of cold weather it shall not form part of any other such forecasted period;]

"home" means the dwelling, together with any garage, garden and outbuildings normally occupied by the claimant as his home, including any premises not so occupied which it is impracticable or unreasonable to sell separately [17 ...];

[4"income-based jobseeker's allowance" has the same meaning in these Regulations as it has in the Jobseekers Act 1995 by virtue of section 1(4) of that Act;]

[7"income-related employment and support allowance" means an income-related allowance under Part 1 of the Welfare Reform Act (employment and support allowance);]

[9"income support" means income support under Part 7 of the Act;]

[6 . . .]

"mean daily temperature" means, in respect of a day, the average of the maximum temperature and minimum temperature recorded at a [16 site] for that day;

[14 13 "member of the support group" means a person who has or is treated as having limited capability for work-related activity under Part 6 of the Employment and Support Allowance Regulations 2008;]

[14 13 "member of the work-related activity group" means a person who has or is treated as having limited capability for work under Part 5 of the Employment and Support Allowance Regulations 2008 other than by virtue of regulation 30 of the Employment and Support Allowance Regulations 2008;]

[2"overlap period" means any period of a day or days, where a day forms part of a recorded period of cold weather and also forms part of a forecasted period of cold weather;]

[15 "owner-occupier loan payments" means loan payments made under the Loans for Mortgage Interest Regulations 2017;]

[6 . . .]

[9 . . .]

[4"postcode district" means a Post Office postcode district [5except in the case of any postcode district which is identified with an alpha suffix which shall, for the purposes of these Regulations, be treated as if it forms part of a postcode district which is identified without that suffix]];

"recorded period of cold weather" means a period of 7 consecutive days, during which the average of the mean daily temperature recorded for that period was equal to or below 0 degrees celsius; and for the purposes of this definition where a day forms part of a recorded period of cold weather it shall not form part of any other such recorded period;

[6 "state pension credit" has the meaning given by section 1(1) of the State Pension Credit Act 2002]

[4. . .]

[4 [16 "site" means a site accredited by the Met Office in relation to which a period of cold weather may be forecasted or recorded for the purposes of these Regulations;]]

[11 "universal credit" means universal credit under Part 1 of the 2012 Act;]

[9 "winter period" means the period beginning on 1st November in any year and ending on 31st March in the following year.]

[6 . . .]

[1 (2A) [6 . . .]]

(3) In these Regulations, unless the context otherwise requires, a reference to a numbered regulation is to the regulation in these Regulations bearing that number and a reference in a regulation to a numbered paragraph or sub-paragraph is to the paragraph or sub-paragraph in that regulation bearing that number.

AMENDMENTS

1. Social Fund (Miscellaneous Amendments) Regulations 1990 (SI 1990/580) reg.3 (April 9, 1990).

2. Social Fund Cold Weather Payments (General) Amendment No.2 Regulations 1991 (SI 1991/2238) reg.2 (November 1, 1991).

3. Social Fund Cold Weather Payments (General) Amendment (No.2) Regulations 1992 (SI 1992/2448) reg.2 (November 1, 1992).

4. Social Fund Cold Weather Payments (General) Amendment Regulations 1996 (SI 1996/2544) reg.2 (November 4, 1996).

5. Social Fund Cold Weather Payments (General) Amendment Regulations 1997 (SI 1997/2311) reg.2 (November 1, 1997).

6. Social Fund Cold Weather Payments (General) Amendment Regulations 2005 (SI 2005/2724) reg.3 (November 1, 2005).

7. Employment and Support Allowance (Consequential Provisions) (No.2) Regulations 2008 (SI 2008/1554) reg.6(1) and (2) (October 27, 2008).

8. Social Fund Cold Weather Payments (General) Amendment Regulations 2008 (SI 2008/2569) reg.2(1) and (2) (November 1, 2008).

9. Social Fund Cold Weather Payments (General) Amendment Regulations 2010 (SI 2010/2442) reg.2(1) and (2) (November 1, 2010).

10. Transfer of Functions (Her Majesty's Land Registry, the Meteorological Office and Ordnance Survey) Order 2011 (SI 2011/2436) art.6 and Sch.2 para.6 (November 9, 2011).

11. Social Fund Cold Weather Payments (General) Regulations 1988 (SI 2013/248) reg.2(1) and (2) (November 1, 2013).

12. Social Fund Cold Weather Payments (General) (Amendment) Regulations 2016 (SI 2016/876) reg.2(1) and (2) (November 1, 2016).

13. Employment and Support Allowance and Universal Credit (Miscellaneous Amendments and Transitional and Savings Provisions) Regulations 2017 (SI 2017/204) reg.7(1) and Sch.1, Pt.1, para.2(1) and (3) (April 3, 2017).

14. Employment and Support Allowance (Miscellaneous Amendments and Transitional and Savings Provision) Regulations 2017 (SI 2017/581) reg.2 (June 23, 2017, subject to the transitional and savings provision in reg.10).

15. Loans for Mortgage Interest Regulations 2017 (SI 2017/725) reg.18 and Sch.5 para.10(1) and (2) (April 6, 2018).

16. Social Fund and Social Security (Claims and Payments) (Amendment) Regulations 2020 (SI 2020/600) reg.3(1) and (2) (July 9, 2020).

17. Social Security (Scotland) Act 2018 (Winter Heating Assistance) (Consequential Modifications) Order 2022 (SI 2022/1018) art.2 (November 1, 2022).

18. Secretaries of State for Energy Security and Net Zero, for Science, Innovation and Technology, for Business and Trade, and for Culture, Media and Sport and the Transfer of Functions (National Security and Investment Act 2021 etc) Order 2023 (SI 2023/424) Sch. para.25 (May 3, 2023).

General Note

4.3 Most of the definitions in reg.1 are self-explanatory. The following merit additional comment.

"Home": The definition is the same as the definition of "dwelling occupied as the home" in reg.2(1) of the Income Support General Regulations. See the notes to that regulation in Vol.V of this series.

"Forecasted period of cold weather": The definition covers any period of seven consecutive days (i.e. not necessarily a calendar week) during which the average of the mean daily temperature (as defined) for that period is forecasted to be equal to or less than 0°C. If a day falls into a forecasted period of cold weather it cannot count in any other forecasted period, but it can be part of a "recorded period of cold weather" (see the definition of that phrase and of "overlap period"). The possibility of relying on a forecast without having to wait until a period of cold weather has actually been recorded allows the cold weather payment to be made nearer to the time when the need to incur additional heating expenses arises.

4.4 "*Overlap period*": On the assumption that weather forecasts are occasionally correct, a day that falls within a "forecasted period of cold weather" will sometimes also fall within a "recorded period of cold weather". Such a day (or days) form an "overlap period". For the treatment of overlap periods, see reg.2(3)–(5).

"Recorded period of cold weather": The definition covers any period of seven consecutive days (i.e. not necessarily a calendar week) during which the average of the mean daily temperature (as defined) recorded for that period was equal to or less than 0°C. If a day falls into a recorded period of cold weather it cannot count in any other recorded period, but it can be part of a "forecasted period of cold weather" (see the definition of that phrase and of "overlap period"). The possibility of relying upon recorded temperatures means that a cold weather payment can be made in respect of a period of cold weather that was not forecast.

[1 10 Prescribed description of persons

4.5 **1A.**—(1) A cold weather payment may be made in the circumstances prescribed by regulation 2 to a person who satisfies the following conditions.

(2) The first condition is that, in respect of at least one day during the recorded or the forecasted period of cold weather specified in regulation 2(1)(a), the person has been awarded—

(a) state pension credit;

(b) income support;
(c) an income-based jobseeker's allowance; [13 . . .]
(d) an income-related employment and support allowance [13; [19 ...]
(e) universal credit] [19; or
(f) owner-occupier loan payments and is treated as entitled to a benefit specified in sub-paragraphs [20 (b)] to (d).]
[20 (g) owner-occupier loan payments and is treated as entitled to state pension credit.]

(3) The second condition (which applies only if the person ("P") falls within paragraph (2)(b), [13 (c), [19 (d), (e) or (f)]] is that, in respect of the day to which paragraph (2) relates—

(a) P's family includes a member aged less than 5;
(b) where P has been awarded income support, P's applicable amount includes one or more of the premiums specified in paragraphs 9 to 14 of Part 3 of Schedule 2 to the General Regulations;
(c) where P has been awarded a jobseeker's allowance, P's applicable amount includes one or more of the premiums specified in paragraphs 10 to 16 of Part 3 of Schedule 1 to the Jobseeker's Allowance Regulations 1996;
[17 (d) P's child tax credit includes a disability element within the meaning of section 9(3) of the Tax Credits Act 2002;] [13 . . .]
(e) where P has been awarded an employment and support allowance, [15 and]—
 (i) [15 P's applicable amount includes] one or more of the premiums specified in paragraphs 5 to 7 of Schedule 4 to the Employment and Support Allowance Regulations 2008, or
 (ii) P is a member of the work-related activity group or is a member of the support group; [19 ...]]
[13 (f) where P has been awarded universal credit—
 (i) the award includes an amount under section 10(2) of the 2012 Act (child or qualifying young person who is disabled); or
 [16 (ii) P has limited capability for work or limited capability for work and work-related activity as construed in accordance with regulations 39 and 40 of the Universal Credit Regulations 2013]] [19; or
(g) where P has been awarded owner-occupier loan payments, P's applicable amount, if P were entitled to a benefit specified in paragraph (2) (b) to (d), would include one or more of the premiums specified in—
 (aa) where P is treated as entitled to income support, paragraphs 9 to 14 of Part 3 of Schedule 2 to the General Regulations;
 (bb) where P is treated as entitled to jobseeker's allowance, paragraphs 10 to 16 of Part 3 of Schedule 1 to the Jobseeker's Allowance Regulations 1996;
 (cc) where P is treated as entitled to employment and support allowance, paragraphs 5 to 7 of Schedule 4 to the Employment and Support Allowance Regulations 2008.]

[19(3A) In [20 paragraphs (2) and (3)], a person being treated as entitled to a benefit has the meaning given to it in regulation 2(2)(aa) of the Loans for Mortgage Interest Regulations 2017.]

(4) The third condition (which does not apply to a person who comes [11 within] paragraph (3)(a) or (d)) is that the person does not reside in—

(a) a care home;
(b) an independent hospital;

(c) an establishment run by the Abbeyfield Society or by a body corporate or incorporate which is affiliated to that Society; or

(d) accommodation provided under section 3(1) of, and Part 2 of the Schedule to, the Polish Resettlement Act 1s947 (provision by the Secretary of State of accommodation in camps).

[13 (4A) In relation to a person who has been awarded universal credit, the third condition applies as if paragraph (4)(d) were omitted.]

(5) In paragraph (4) —

(a) "care home" in England [18 ...] has the meaning assigned to it by section 3 of the Care Standards Act 2000, [18 in Wales means a care home service within the meaning of Part 1 of the Regulation and Inspection of Social Care (Wales) Act 2016 which is provided wholly or mainly to persons aged 18 or over] and in Scotland means a care home service as defined by [12 paragraph 2 of schedule 12 to the Public Services Reform (Scotland) Act 2010];

(b) "independent hospital"—

(i) in England, means a hospital as defined by section 275 of the National Health Service Act 2006 that is not a health service hospital as defined by that section;

(ii) in Wales, has the meaning assigned to it by section 2 of the Care Standards Act 2000; and

(iii) in Scotland, means an independent healthcare service as defined in [12 section 10F(1)(a) and (b) of the National Health Service (Scotland) Act 1978].]

[13 (6) The fourth condition, which applies only where the person has been awarded universal credit and their award of universal credit does not include an amount under section 10(2) of the 2012 Act (child or qualifying young person who is disabled) is that—

(a) in a case where a cold weather payment is payable in relation to a recorded period of cold weather as mentioned in regulation 2(1)(a)(i), the person was not in employment or gainful self-employment on any day during that period; or

(b) in a case where a cold weather payment is payable in relation to a forecasted period of weather as mentioned in regulation 2(1)(a)(ii), the person is not in employment or gainful self-employment on the day when the [14 Met] Office supplies the Department for Work and Pensions with the forecast.

(7) For the purpose of paragraph (6)—

(a) "employment" means employment under a contract of service, or in an office, including an elective office;

(b) a person is in gainful self-employment where—

(i) they are carrying on a trade, profession or vocation as their main employment;

(ii) their earnings from that trade, profession or vocation are treated as self-employed earnings for the purpose of regulations made under section 8(3) of the 2012 Act; and

(iii) the trade, profession or vocation is organised, developed, regular and carried on in expectation of profit.]

[21 (8) The fifth condition is that the person's home is in England or Wales.]

AMENDMENTS

1. Social Fund Cold Weather Payments (General) Amendment No.3 Regulations 1991 (SI 1991/2448) reg.2 (November 1, 1991).
2. Social Fund Cold Weather Payments (General) Amendment Regulations 1993 (SI 1993/2450) reg.2 (November 1, 1993).
3. Social Fund Cold Weather Payments (General) Amendment Regulations 1996 (SI 1996/2544) reg.3 (November 4, 1996).
4. State Pension Credit (Consequential, Transitional and Miscellaneous Provisions) Regulations 2002 (SI 2002/3019) reg.31 (October 6, 2003).
5. Social Security (Removal of Residential Allowance and Miscellaneous Amendments) Regulations 2003 (SI 2003/1121) reg.3 (October 6, 2003).
6. Social Fund Cold Weather Payments (General) Amendment Regulations 2004 (SI 2004/2600) reg.2 (November 1, 2004).
7. Social Security (Care Homes and Independent Hospitals) Regulations 2005 (SI 2005/2687) reg.9 (October 24, 2005).
8. Social Fund Cold Weather Payments (General) Amendment Regulations 2008 (SI 2008/2569) reg.2(1) and (3) (October 27, 2008).
9. Health and Social Care Act 2008 (Miscellaneous Consequential Amendments) Order 2010 (SI 2010/1881) regs 2 and 6 (October 1, 2010).
10. Social Fund Cold Weather Payments (General) Amendment Regulations 2010 (SI 2010/2442) reg.2(1) and (3) (November 1, 2010).
11. Social Fund Cold Weather Payments (General) Amendment Regulations (No.2) 2010 (SI 2010/2591) reg.3(1) November 1, 2010.
12. Public Services Reform (Scotland) Act 2010 (Consequential Modifications of Enactments) Order 2011(SI 2011/2581) art.2 and Sch.2 para.15 (October 28, 2011).
13. Social Fund Cold Weather Payments (General) Regulations 1988 (SI 2013/248) reg.2(1) and (3)–(6) (November 1, 2013).
14. Social Fund Cold Weather Payments (General) (Amendment) Regulations 2016 (SI 2016/876) reg.2(1) and (3) (November 1, 2016).
15. Employment and Support Allowance and Universal Credit (Miscellaneous Amendments and Transitional and Savings Provisions) Regulations 2017 (SI 2017/204) reg.7(1) and Sch.1, Pt.1, para.2(1) and (3) (April 3, 2017).
16. Employment and Support Allowance and Universal Credit (Miscellaneous Amendments and Transitional and Savings Provisions) Regulations 2017 (SI 2017/204) reg.7(1) and Sch.1, Pt.2, para.11 (April 3, 2017).
17. Social Fund (Amendment) Regulations 2017 (SI 2017/271) reg.2 (April 6, 2017).
18. Social Security and Child Support (Regulation and Inspection of Social Care (Wales) Act 2016) (Consequential Provision) Regulations 2018 (SI 2018/228) reg.3 (April 2, 2018).
19. Loans for Mortgage Interest Regulations 2017 (SI 2017/725) reg.18 and Sch.5 para.10(1) and (3) (April 6, 2018).
20. Loans for Mortgage Interest (Amendment) Regulations 2021 (SI 2021/131) reg.3 (March 15, 2021).
21. Social Security (Scotland) Act 2018 (Winter Heating Assistance) (Consequential Modifications) Order 2022 (SI 2022/1018) art.2 (November 1, 2022).

DEFINITIONS

"the Act"—see reg.1(2).
"the General Regulations"—*ibid.*
"claimant"—*ibid.*
"family"—*ibid.*
"forecasted period of cold weather"—*ibid.*
"income-based jobseeker's allowance"—*ibid.*
"income support"—*ibid.*
"recorded period of cold weather"—*ibid.*

General Note

4.6 Regulation 1A sets out the five conditions which a claimant must satisfy in order to receive a cold weather payment. The second, third and fourth conditions do not apply to all claimants. However, where they apply, the conditions are cumulative so failure to satisfy any of them means that no cold weather payment can be made.

The first condition is that the claimant must either actually have been awarded (i.e. an underlying entitlement will not suffice) SPC, IS, income-based JSA, income-related ESA or universal credit, or owner-occupier loan payments—defined in reg.1(2) as meaning loan payments made under the Loans for Mortgage Interest Regulations 2017: see above—and in that latter case be treated as entitled to IS, IBJSA, SPC or IRESA under reg.2(2)(a) and (aa) of those Regulations, for at least one day in the relevant (forecasted or recorded) period of cold weather.

The second condition is that, unless the claimant has been awarded SPC (or has been awarded owner-occupier loan payments and is treated as entitled to SPC), then—for that day—either:

- his or her family must include a child under five;
- the claimant has an award of child tax credit which includes an individual element for a disabled, or severely disabled, child or qualifying young person;
- (if the claimant has been awarded IS or income-based JSA) his or her applicable amount must include one of the pensioner or disability premiums;
- (if the claimant has been awarded income-related ESA) he or she is in the work-related activity group or the support group, or his or her applicable amount must include either one of the pensioner or disability premiums; or
- (if the claimant has been awarded universal credit) the award includes either the disabled child addition (i.e. the additional amount of the child element payable for a child or qualifying young person who is disabled); or the claimant has limited capability for work or limited capability for work-related activity. Those who qualify on the basis that their award includes the LCW element or the LCWRA element must also satisfy the fourth condition.
- (if the claimant has been awarded owner-occupier loan payments) but is treated as entitled to either IS, IBJSA or IRESA (see above), his or her applicable amount for that benefit would include one of the premiums specified in the third to fifth bullet points above.

4.7 The third condition applies to claimants who do not have a child under five in their family and who do not have an award of child tax credit which includes one of the individual elements specified above. It is that the claimant does not reside in a care home or independent hospital (as defined in each case in para.(5)) or (for claimants who are not in receipt of universal credit: see para.(4A)) in an Abbeyfield Home or accommodation provided under the specified provisions of the Polish Resettlement Act 1947.

The fourth condition applies to claimants who have an award of universal credit that does not include the disabled child addition (i.e. those who have limited capability for work or work-related activity (see above)). It is that the claimant is not in gainful employment or self-employment (as defined in para.(7)) during the period of cold weather in respect of which the cold weather payment is payable.

The fifth condition is that the person's home is in England or Wales.

Since no claim for a cold weather payment is possible, the decision maker will identify qualifying claimants from Departmental records and make a payment automatically.

[1 **Prescribed circumstances**

4.8 **2.**—(1) The prescribed circumstances in which [9 a cold weather payment may be made] are—

[7 (a) subject to paragraphs (1A), (1B) and (3) to (6)—

(i) there is a recorded period of cold weather at a primary [8 site], or
(ii) there is a forecasted period of cold weather at a primary [8 site], and]

(b) the home of the claimant is, or by virtue of paragraph (2)[7 . . .] is treated as, situated in a postcode district in respect of which the [8 site] mentioned in sub-paragraph (a)(i) or, as the case may be, (a)(ii) is the designated [8 site].]

(c) [2. . .]

[5 [7 (1A) For the purposes of paragraph (1)(a)(i), where a primary [8 site] is unable to provide temperature information in respect of a particular day, the mean daily temperature on that day—

(a) at the secondary [8 site], or
(b) where there is no secondary [8 site] designated, or where the secondary [8 site] is unable to provide temperature information in respect of that day, at the alternative [8 site],

is to be used to determine whether or not there is a recorded period of cold weather at the primary [8 site].]

[7 (1B) For the purposes of paragraph (1)(a)(ii), where the Met Office is unable to produce a forecast in respect of a particular period at a primary [8 site], the forecast in respect of that period produced—

(a) at the secondary [8 site], or
(b) where there is no secondary [8 site] designated, or where the secondary [8 site] is unable to produce a forecast in respect of that period, at the alternative [8 site],

is to be used to determine whether or not there is a forecasted period of cold weather at the primary [8 site].]]

[7 (2) For the purposes of this regulation, where the home of the claimant is not situated within a postcode district for which a primary [8 site] is designated, it is to be treated as situated within a postcode district—

(a) which, in the opinion of the Met Office, is the most geographically and climatologically representative of that postcode district, and
(b) for which a primary [8 site] is designated.]

(3) Subject to paragraphs (4) and (5) where a recorded period of cold weather is joined by an overlap period to a forecasted period of cold weather a payment under paragraph (1) may only be made in respect of the forecasted period of cold weather.

(4) Where—

(a) there is a continuous period of forecasted periods of cold weather, each of which is linked by an overlap period; and
(b) the total number of recorded periods of cold weather during that continuous period is greater than the total number of forecasted periods of cold weather,

a payment in respect of the last recorded period of cold weather may also be made under paragraph (1).

[6 (5) Where—

(a) a claimant satisfies the conditions in regulation 1A and paragraph (1) in respect of a recorded period of cold weather, and
(b) a payment in respect of the recorded period of cold weather does not fall to be made by virtue of paragraph (4), and
(c) the claimant does not satisfy the conditions in regulation 1A in respect of the forecasted period of cold weather which is linked to the recorded period of cold weather by an overlap period,

a cold weather payment may be made in respect of that recorded period of cold weather.

(6) A cold weather payment may not be made after the end of the period of 26 weeks beginning with the last day of the winter period in which the period of cold weather concerned falls.]

[7 (7) For the purposes of this regulation—

"alternative [8 site]" means a [8 site]—

(a) which, in the opinion of the Met Office, is the most geographically and climatologically representative for the postcode district in which the home of the claimant is situated, and

(b) is able to provide temperature information—

(i) for the purposes of paragraph (1A), for the relevant day, or

(ii) for the purposes of paragraph (1B), for the production of a forecast for the relevant period;

"primary [8 site]" means a [8 site] designated for a postcode district in accordance with regulation 2A(1);

"secondary [8 site]" means a [8 site] designated for a postcode district in accordance with regulation 2A(2).]

AMENDMENTS

1. Social Fund Cold Weather Payments (General) Amendments No.2 Regulations 1991 (SI 1991/2238) reg.3 (November 1, 1991).

2. Social Fund Cold Weather Payments (General) Amendment No.3 Regulations 1991 (SI 1991/2448) reg.3 (November 1, 1991).

3. Social Fund Cold Weather Payments (General) Amendment (No.2) Regulations 1992 (SI 1992/2448) reg.3 (November 1, 1992).

4. Social Fund Cold Weather Payments (General) Amendment Regulations 1996 (SI 1996/2544) reg.4 (November 4, 1996).

5. Social Fund Cold Weather Payments (General) Amendment Regulations 1997 (SI 1997/2311) reg.3 (November 1, 1997).

6. Social Fund Cold Weather Payments (General) Amendment Regulations 2010 (SI 2010/2442) reg.2(1) and (4) (November 1, 2010).

7. Social Fund Cold Weather Payments (General) (Amendment) Regulations 2016 (SI 2016/876) reg.2(1) and (4) (November 1, 2016).

8. Social Fund and Social Security (Claims and Payments) (Amendment) Regulations 2020 (SI 2020/600) reg.3(1) and (3) (July 9, 2020).

DEFINITIONS

"the Act"—see reg.1(2).
"the General Regulations"—*ibid.*
"claimant"—*ibid.*
"family"—*ibid.*
"forecasted period of cold weather"—*ibid.*
"home"—*ibid.*
"income support"—*ibid.*
"overlap period"—*ibid.*
"postcode district"—*ibid.*
"recorded period of cold weather"—*ibid.*
"[8 site]"—*ibid.*

GENERAL NOTE

4.9 Regulation 2 prescribes the circumstances in which a cold weather payment is to be made. The principal rule is established by para.1(a) and (b): a period of cold weather (i.e. seven consecutive days) must be either recorded or forecast at the weather site relevant to the claimant's home. The two conditions are alternatives so that the cold weather payment is payable even if a forecasted period of cold weather does not materialise or if there is a recorded period of cold weather that was not forecast.

Under para.(1), the relevant weather site will normally be the one designated for the relevant postcode district pursuant to reg.2A(1). However, if that weather site is unable to provide temperature information, the relevant site is the secondary site designated pursuant to reg.2A(2): see para.(2)(a). If the secondary site is also unable to provide temperature information, or if no secondary site has been designated, the relevant weather site will be the alternative site as defined in para.(7): see para.(2)(b).

Paragraphs (3)–(5) are designed to prevent double payment. An individual day can only count as part of one recorded period of cold weather or one forecasted period of cold weather (see the definitions in reg.1(2)), although it can be part of both a recorded and a forecasted period. Where there is a recorded period of cold weather which coincides wholly or partly with the forecasted period, there is then an overlap period, again defined in reg.1(2). The general rule in those circumstances is that the cold weather payment is only payable for the forecasted period (para.(3)) because the policy is to make the payment before the extra heating is required if possible. That rule is subject to two exceptions:

- where there is a continuous series of overlapping forecasted periods and recorded periods which includes more recorded periods than forecasted periods, a cold weather payment can also be made for the final recorded period (para.(4)); and
- where para.(4) does not apply and the claimant does not satisfy the conditions in reg.1A for any day of the forecasted period, but does satisfy those conditions for at least one day of the recorded period, then a payment can be made for the recorded period (para.(5)).

[1 Designation of primary and secondary [2 sites]

2A.—(1) The Secretary of State must designate a primary [2 site] for each postcode district. 4.10

(2) The Secretary of State may designate a secondary [2 site] for each postcode district.]

Amendment

1. Social Fund Cold Weather Payments (General) (Amendment) Regulations 2016 (SI 2016/876) reg.2(1) and (5) (November 1, 2016).
2. Social Fund and Social Security (Claims and Payments) (Amendment) Regulations 2020 (SI 2020/600) reg.3(1), (4) and (5) (July 9, 2020).

General Note

There were originally 55 primary weather stations. At the time of going to press, there are 101 designated primary sites. The increase is intended to improve the sensitivity of the scheme. 4.11

[1 Publication of designations

2B.—(1) The Secretary of State must publish details of a designation under regulation 2A. 4.12

(2) Publication under paragraph (1) may be in such manner as the Secretary of State considers appropriate.]

Amendment

1. Social Fund Cold Weather Payments (General) (Amendment) Regulations 2016 (SI 2016/876) reg.2(1) and (5) (November 1, 2016).

General Note

4.13 The Secretary of State must publish details of the designation "in such manner as [she] considers appropriate". The current list (which dates from February 2017) can be found in Chapter L4: *Universal Credit – Social Fund – Cold Weather Payments* of *Advice for Decision Making*. There is a cold weather payment postcode checker at *https://coldweatherpayments.dwp.gov.uk/*.

[1 Review and variation of designations

4.14 **2C.**—(1) The Secretary of State must, in accordance with paragraph (2), review a designation under regulation 2A to determine if it remains appropriate.

(2) Each designation must be reviewed every 12 months, in the period beginning with 1st November and ending with 31st October.

(3) If, on review, or at any other time, the Secretary of State is of the opinion that a designation is no longer appropriate, the Secretary of State must—

(a) vary the designation in such manner as the Secretary of State considers expedient, and

(b) publish details of the varied designation.

(4) Publication under paragraph (3)(b) may be in such manner as the Secretary of State considers appropriate.

(5) When determining whether to vary a designation, the Secretary of State must have regard to any recommendation made by the Met Office.

(6) For the purposes of this regulation, whether a designation is appropriate includes, in particular, whether the [2 site] designated—

(a) is geographically and climatologically representative for the relevant postcode district, and

(b) provides accurate temperature information.]

Amendment

1. Social Fund Cold Weather Payments (General) (Amendment) Regulations 2016 (SI 2016/876) reg.2(1) and (5) (November 1, 2016).

2. Social Fund and Social Security (Claims and Payments) (Amendment) Regulations 2020 (SI 2020/600) reg.3(1) and (6) (July 9, 2020).

General Note

4.15 Designations under reg.2A must be reviewed annually taking into account the matters in para.(6) and any recommendation made by the Met Office (para.(5)). If, as a result of the review, the Secretary of State decides to vary the designation, he must publish details of the variation, again "in such manner as [he] considers appropriate" (paras (3)(b) and (4)).

Prescribed amount

4.16 **3.**—[1 . . .] The amount of the payment in respect of each period of cold weather shall be [2 3£25].

Amendments

1. Social Fund Cold Weather Payments (General) Amendment No.2 Regulations 1991 (SI 1991/2238) reg.4 (November 1, 1991).

2. Social Fund Cold Weather Payments (General) Amendment Regulations 1995 (SI 1995/2620) reg.2 (November 1, 1995).

3. Social Fund Cold Weather Payments (General) Amendment Regulations (No. 2) 2010 (SI 2010/2591) reg.2(1) November 1, 2010.

GENERAL NOTE

Payment is at the fixed rate of £25 for each week which counts under regs 1A and 2. 4.17

The weekly rate was originally set at £5 in 1988. It was then increased to £6 in February 1991, to £7 in November 1994 and to £8.50 in November 1995. For the periods from November 1, 2008 to March 31, 2009, and from November 1, 2009 to March 31, 2010, reg.3 was modified by, respectively, reg.3 of the Social Fund Cold Weather Payments (General) Amendment Regulations 2008 (SI 2008/2569) and reg.3 of the Social Fund Cold Weather Payments (General) Amendment Regulations 2009 (SI 2009/2649). In each case, the effect of the modification was that the weekly amount of £8.50 increased to £25 for any period of cold weather which began during either of the above periods. That increase was made permanent with effect from November 1, 2010.

Effect and calculation of capital

4.—[1 . . .] 4.18

AMENDMENT

1. Social Fund Cold Weather Payments (General) Amendment No.2 Regulations 1991 (SI 1991/2238) reg.5 (November 1, 1991).

GENERAL NOTE

There is no capital limit for cold weather payments. 4.19

SCHEDULES

Regulation 2(1), (1A) and (2)

[18 SCHEDULE 1

IDENTIFICATION OF STATIONS AND POSTCODE DISTRICTS

[19 . . .]] 4.20

AMENDMENTS

1. Social Security Cold Weather Payments (General) Amendment Regulations 2000 (SI 2000/2690) reg.2 (November 1, 2000).
2. The Social Fund Cold Weather Payments (General) Amendment Regulations 2002 (SI 2002/2524) reg.2 (November 1, 2002).
3. Social Fund Cold Weather Payments (General) Amendment Regulations 2003 (SI 2003/2605) reg.2 and Sch.1 (November 1, 2003).
4. Social Fund Cold Weather Payments (General) Amendment (No.2) Regulations 2003 (SI 2003/3203) reg.2 (November 28, 2003).
5. Social Fund Cold Weather Payments (General) Amendment Regulations 2004 (SI 2004/2600) reg.3 (November 1, 2004).
6. Social Fund Cold Weather Payments (General) Amendment Regulations 2005 (SI 2005/2724) reg.4 and Sch.1 (November 1, 2005).
7. Social Fund Cold Weather Payments (General) Amendment Regulations 2006 (SI 2006/2655) reg.3 and Sch.1 (November 1, 2006).
8. Social Fund Cold Weather Payments (General) Amendment Regulations 2007 (SI 2007/2912) reg.3 and Sch.1 (November 1, 2007).

9. Social Fund Cold Weather Payments (General) Amendment Regulations 2008 (SI 2008/2569) reg.2(1) and (4) (November 1, 2008).

10. Social Fund Cold Weather Payments (General) Amendment Regulations 2009 (SI 2009/2649) reg.2(1) and (2) and Sch.1 (November 1, 2009).

11. Social Fund Cold Weather Payments (General) Amendment Regulations 2010 (SI 2010/2442) reg.2(1) and (5) (November 1, 2010).

12. Social Fund Cold Weather Payments (General) Amendment Regulations 2011 (SI 2011/2423) reg.2(1) and Sch.2 (November 1, 2011).

13. Social Fund Cold Weather Payments (General) Amendment Regulations 2012 (SI 2012/2280) reg.2(1) (November 1, 2012).

14. Social Fund Cold Weather Payments (General) Amendment (No.2) Regulations 2012 (SI 2012/2379) reg.2 (November 1, 2012).

15. Social Fund Cold Weather Payments (General) Amendment (No.2) Regulations 2013 (SI 2538/2013) reg.2(1) and Sch.1 (November 1, 2013).

16. Social Fund Cold Weather Payments (General) Amendment Regulations 2014 (SI 2014/2687) reg.2(1) and Sch.1 (November 1, 2014).

17. Social Fund Cold Weather Payments (General) Amendment Regulations 2015 (SI 2015/183) reg.2 (March 23, 2015).

18. Social Fund Cold Weather Payments (General) Amendment (No.2) Regulations 2015 (SI 2015/1662) reg.2(1) and Sch.1 (November 1, 2015).

19. Social Fund Cold Weather Payments (General) (Amendment) Regulations 2016 (SI 2016/876) reg.2(1) and (6) (November 1, 2016).

Regulation 2(1A)(a) and 2(1B)(a)

[13 SCHEDULE 2

SPECIFIED ALTERNATIVE STATIONS

4.21 [14 . . .]]

AMENDMENTS

1. Social Fund Cold Weather Payments (General) Amendment Regulations 1999 (SI 1999/2781) reg.3 and Sch.2 (November 1, 1999).

2. Social Fund Cold Weather Payments (General) Amendment Regulations 2003 (SI 2003/2605) reg.3 and Sch.2 (November 1, 2003).

3. Social Fund Cold Weather Payments (General) Amendment Regulations 2005 (SI 2005/2724) reg.5 and Sch.2 (November 1, 2005).

4. Social Fund Cold Weather Payments (General) Amendment Regulations 2006 (SI 2006/2655) reg.4 and Sch.2 (November 1, 2006).

5. Social Fund Cold Weather Payments (General) Amendment Regulations 2007 (SI 2007/2912) reg.4 and Sch.2 (November 1, 2007).

6. Social Fund Cold Weather Payments (General) Amendment Regulations 2008 (SI 2008/2569) reg.2(1) and (6) (November 1, 2008).

7. Social Fund Cold Weather Payments (General) Amendment Regulations 2009 (SI 2009/2649) reg.2(1) and (3) and Sch.2 (November 1, 2009).

8. Social Fund Cold Weather Payments (General) Amendment Regulations 2010 (SI 2010/2442) reg.2(1) and (6) (November 1, 2010).

9. Social Fund Cold Weather Payments (General) Amendment Regulations 2011 (SI 2011/2423) reg.2(2) and Sch.2 (November 1, 2011).

10. Social Fund Cold Weather Payments (General) Amendment Regulations 2012 (SI 2012/2280) reg.2(2) (November 1, 2012).

11. Social Fund Cold Weather Payments (General) Amendment (No.2) Regulations 2013 (SI 2538/2013) reg.2(2) and Sch.2 (November 1, 2013).

12. Social Fund Cold Weather Payments (General) Amendment Regulations 2014 (SI 2014/2687) reg.2(2) and Sch.2 (November 1, 2014).
13. Social Fund Cold Weather Payments (General) Amendment (No.2) Regulations 2015 (SI 2015/1662) reg.2(2) and Sch.2 (November 1, 2015).
14. Social Fund Cold Weather Payments (General) (Amendment) Regulations 2016 (SI 2016/876) reg.2(1) and (6) (November 1, 2016).

The Social Fund Winter Fuel Payment Regulations 2000

(SI 2000/729)

Made by the Secretary of State under ss.138(2) and (4) and 175(1), (3) and (4) of the Social Security Contributions and Benefits Act 1992 and ss.5(1)(a) and (i), and 189(1) and (4) of the Social Security Administration Act 1992 and s.16(1) and s.79(1) and (4) of, and para.3 of Sch.5 to, the Social Security Act 1998 [In force April 3, 2000]

General Note

In November 1997, the Government announced that all pensioner households would receive a one-off payment in the winter of 1998 (and another in 1999) towards their fuel bills. These payments would be in addition to any cold weather payments which might be awarded under the Social Fund Cold Weather Payments (General) Regulations 1998 (above). As is the case under those regulations, no separate claim needs to be made for a winter fuel payment. Entitlement simply depends on the person being ordinarily resident in Great Britain and over the qualifying age on at least one day in the "qualifying week" (see reg.1(2)). 4.22

The qualifying age was originally pensionable age (i.e. 60 for a woman and 65 for a man). However, in *R. v Secretary of State for Social Security, Ex p. Taylor* (C–382/98)(ECJ, December 16, 1999), the ECJ held that the different qualifying ages for men and women constituted unlawful discrimination on the ground of sex contrary to Directive 79/7/EEC. The qualifying age was therefore equalised at 60 for both women and men from the winter of 2000–2001 and remained at that level until April 6, 2010 when the gradual process of increasing pensionable age for women began. The qualifying age is now the same as for state pension credit, i.e. pensionable age in the case of a woman, and in the case of a man, the age which is pensionable age for a woman born on the same day.

Citation, commencement and interpretation

1.—(1) These Regulations may be cited as the Social Fund Winter Fuel Payment Regulations 2000 and shall come into force on 3rd April 2000. 4.23

(2) In these Regulations—

[5 "care home" in England [15 ...] has the meaning assigned to it by section 3 of the Care Standards Act 2000, [15 in Wales, means a care home service within the meaning of Part 1 of the Regulation and Inspection of Social Care (Wales) Act 2016 which is provided wholly or mainly to persons aged 18 or over] and in Scotland means a care home service as defined by [11 paragraph 2 of schedule 12 to the Public Services Reform (Scotland) Act 2010];]

[6 [12 13 "couple" means—

(a) two people who are married to, or civil partners of, each other and are members of the same household; or

(b) two people who are not married to, or civil partners of, each other but are living together [16 as if they were a married couple or civil partners];]]

"free in-patient treatment" shall be construed in accordance with regulation [7 2(4) and (5) of the Social Security (Hospital In-Patients) Regulations 2005];

[8 "income-related employment and support allowance" means an income-related allowance under Part 1 of the Welfare Reform Act (employment and support allowance);]

[14 . . .]

[5 10 "independent hospital"—

(a) in England, means a hospital as defined by section 275 of the National Health Service Act 2006 that is not a health service hospital as defined by that section;

(b) in Wales, has the meaning assigned to it by section 2 of the Care Standards Act 2000; and

(c) in Scotland, means an independent healthcare service as defined in [11 section 10F(1)(a) and (b) of the National Health Service (Scotland) Act 1978];]

[9 "qualifying age for state pension credit" means—

(a) in the case of a woman, pensionable age; or

(b) in the case of a man, the age which is pensionable age in the case of a woman born on the same day as the man;]

"qualifying week" means in respect of any year the week beginning on the third Monday in the September of that year;

[5 . . .]

"partner" means a member of—

(a) [6 a couple]; or

(b) a polygamous marriage;

[5 . . .] and

[4 "state pension credit" has the meaning assigned to it by section 1 of the State Pension Credit Act 2002;]

[1 . . .]

[2 (3) [5 . . .] in these Regulations a person—

(a) is in residential care if, disregarding any period of temporary absence, he resides in—

[5 (i) a care home;

(ii) an independent hospital; or]

(iii) accommodation provided under section 3(1) of the Polish Resettlement Act 1947 (provision by the Secretary of State of accommodation in camps),

throughout the qualifying week and the period of 12 weeks immediately before the qualifying week;

(b) lives with another person if—

(i) disregarding any period of temporary absence, they share accommodation as their mutual home; and

(ii) they are not in residential care.

[5 . . .]

(4) In these Regulations, unless the context otherwise requires, a reference—

(a) to a numbered regulation is to the regulation in these Regulations bearing that number; and

(b) in a regulation to a numbered paragraph is to the paragraph in that regulation bearing that number.

AMENDMENTS

1. Social Fund Winter Fuel Payment (Amendment) Regulations 2000 (SI 2000/2864) reg.2(a)(1) (November 13, 2000).
2. Social Fund Winter Fuel Payment (Amendment) Regulations 2001 (SI 2001/3375) reg.2(2) (November 2, 2001).
3. Social Security (Removal of Residential Allowance and Miscellaneous Amendments) Regulations 2003 (SI 2003/1121) reg.5 (October 6, 2003).
4. Social Fund Winter Fuel Payment (Amendment) Regulations 2004 (SI 2004/2154) reg.2(a) (September 20, 2004).
5. Social Security (Care Homes and Independent Hospitals) Regulations 2005 (SI 2005/2687) reg.8 (October 24, 2005).
6. Civil Partnership (Pensions, Social Security and Child Support) (Consequential, etc. Provisions) Order 2005 (SI 2005/2877) art.2(3) and Sch.3 para.32 (December 5, 2005).
7. Social Security (Hospital In-Patients) Regulations 2005 (SI 2005/3360) reg.7 (April 10, 2006).
8. Employment and Support Allowance (Consequential Provisions) (No.2) Regulations 2008 (SI 2008/1554) reg.7(1) and (2) (October 27, 2008).
9. Social Security (Equalisation of State Pension Age) Regulations 2009 (SI 2009/1488) reg.19 (April 6, 2010).
10. Health and Social Care Act 2008 (Miscellaneous Consequential Amendments) Order 2010 (SI 2010/1881) regs 2 and 5 (October 1, 2010).
11. Public Services Reform (Scotland) Act 2010 (Consequential Modifications of Enactments) Order 2011(SI 2011/2581) art.2 and Sch.2 para.29 (October 28, 2011).
12. Marriage (Same Sex Couples) Act 2013 (Consequential Provisions) Order 2014 (SI 2014/107) reg.2 and Sch.1 para.28 (March 13, 2014). The amendment extends to England and Wales only (see SI 2014/107 art.1(4)).
13. Marriage and Civil Partnership (Scotland) Act 2014 and Civil Partnership Act 2004 (Consequential Provisions and Modifications) Order 2014 (SI 2014/3229) art.29 and Sch.6 para.19 (December 16, 2014). The amendment relates only to Scotland (see SI 2014/3229, art.3(4)) but is in the same terms as the amendments made in relation to England and Wales by SI 2014/107 (see point 12 above).
14. Social Security (Miscellaneous Amendments) Regulations 2015 (SI 2015/67) reg.4(1)(a) (February 23, 2015).
15. Social Security and Child Support (Regulation and Inspection of Social Care (Wales) Act 2016) (Consequential Provision) Regulations 2018 (SI 2018/228) reg.6 (April 2, 2018).
16. Civil Partnership (Opposite-sex Couples) Regulations 2019 (SI 2019/1458) reg.41 and Sch.3 Pt.2 para.58 (December 2, 2019).

GENERAL NOTE

"qualifying age for state pension credit": As a result of the progressive increase in the retirement age for women, pensionable age for men and women is now the same for anyone born after December 5, 1953.

Social fund winter fuel payments

[1 **2.**—(1) Subject to paragraphs (2) [6 to (4)] and regulation 3 of these Regulations, and regulation 36(2) of the Social Security (Claims and Payments) Regulations 1987, the Secretary of State shall pay to a person who— 4.24

[6 (a) in respect of any day falling within the qualifying week is—

(i) ordinarily resident in Great Britain; or
(ii) habitually resident in [8 any of the countries listed in the Schedule to these Regulations]; and]

[5 (b) in or before the qualifying week has attained the qualifying age for state pension credit,]

a winter fuel payment of—

(i) £500 unless he is in residential care or head (ii)(aa) applies; or
(ii) £250 if [3 state pension credit] [4 , an income-based jobseeker's allowance or an income-related employment and support allowance] has not been, nor falls to be, paid to him in respect of the qualifying week and he is—
(aa) in that week living with a person to whom a payment under these Regulations has been, or falls to be, made in respect of the winter following the qualifying week; or
(bb) in residential care.

(2) Where such a person has attained the age of 80 in or before the qualifying week—

(a) in paragraph (1)(i), for the sum of £500 there shall be substituted the sum of £600; and

[2(b) in paragraph (1)(ii), for the sum of £250 there shall be substituted the sum of £500, except that—
(i) where he is in that week living with a person to whom a payment under these Regulations has been, or falls to be, made in respect of the winter following that week who has also attained the age of 80 in or before that week, or
(ii) where he is in residential care,

there shall be substituted the sum of £300.]

(3) Where such a person has not attained the age of 80 in or before the qualifying week but he is a partner of and living with a person who has done so, in paragraph (1)(i) for the sum of £500 there shall be substituted the sum of £600.]

[6 (4) A person does not qualify for a winter fuel payment by virtue of falling within paragraph [7 (1)(a)(ii)] above unless—

(a) they are a person to whom Council Regulation (EC) No 1408/71 [9, as amended from time to time,] on the application of social security schemes to employed persons, to self-employed persons and to members of their families moving within the Community, or Regulation (EC) No 883/2004 [9, as amended from time to time,] of the European Parliament and of the Council on the coordination of social security systems, applies; and
(b) they are able to demonstrate a genuine and sufficient link to the United Kingdom social security system.]

AMENDMENTS

1. Social Fund Winter Fuel Payment (Amendment) Regulations 2003 (SI 2003/1737) reg.2 (September 1, 2003).

2. Social Fund Winter Fuel Payment (Amendment) (No.2) Regulations 2003, (SI 2003/2192) reg.2 (September 3, 2003).

3. Social Fund Winter Fuel Payment (Amendment) Regulations 2004 (SI 2004/2154) reg.2(b) (September 20, 2004).

4. Employment and Support Allowance (Consequential Provisions) (No.2) Regulations 2008 (SI 2008/1554) reg.7(1) and (3) (October 27, 2008).

5. Social Security (Equalisation of State Pension Age) Regulations 2009 (SI 2009/1488) reg.20 (April 6, 2010).
6. Social Fund Winter Fuel Payment (Amendment) Regulations 2013 (SI 2013/1509) reg.2(1) and (2) (September 16, 2013).
7. Social Security (Miscellaneous Amendments) Regulations 2015 (SI 2015/67) reg.4(1)(b) (February 23, 2015).
8. Social Fund Winter Fuel Payment (Amendment) Regulations 2014 (SI 2014/3270) reg.2(1) and (2) (September 21, 2015).
9. Social Security (Updating of EU References) (Amendment) Regulations 2018 (SI 2018/1084) reg.4 and Sch. para.9 (November 15, 2018).

DEFINITIONS

"qualifying week"—see reg.1(2).
"residential care"—see reg.1(3).

GENERAL NOTE

Regulation 2 sets out the conditions of entitlement to a winter fuel payment. A person qualifies if: **4.25**

(a) He or she is either ordinarily resident in Great Britain, or in one of the countries listed in the Schedule to the Regulations, in the qualifying week (i.e. the week commencing on the third Monday in September (see reg.1(2)).

Claimants who qualify on the basis of habitual residence in a scheduled country must also fall within the personal scope of Regulation (EC) No. 1408/71 or of Regulation (EC) 883/2004 and have a "genuine and sufficient link to the United Kingdom social security system": see para.(4) and Vol.III of the 2020/21 edition (as updated in Vol.III).

Until the winter of 2015/16, winter fuel payments were payable to people who were habitually resident in any EEA state (or Switzerland) rather than only to those who were habitually in a scheduled country. The effect of the amendment made by SI 2014/3270 with effect from September 21, 2015 is that those who are habitually resident in Cyprus, France, Greece, Malta, Portugal and Spain no longer qualify. According to the explanatory memorandum to SI 2014/3270 the average winter temperature (November to March) in the warmest part of the United Kingdom is 5.6°C. The policy is to exclude from entitlement those who are habitually resident in EEA states where the average winter temperature is warmer. The memorandum goes on to state:

> "7.7 DWP is aware there will be people who live in cold regions of "warm" countries who will not be eligible for a Winter Fuel Payment. However, we would have to implement the scheme on a regional basis throughout the EEA in order to make a Winter Fuel Payment for even some of these people. DWP considered this very carefully but concluded that it would introduce disproportionate complexity and administrative costs. Therefore, the scheme has to be administered on a countrywide basis using the average winter temperature for each EEA country to determine where Winter Fuel Payments will be payable."

For the winter of 2019/20 the qualifying week ran from Monday, September 16 to Sunday, September 22, 2019; for the winter of 2020/21, it ran from Monday, September 21 to Sunday, September 27, 2020; and for the winter of 2021/22, it will run from Monday, September 20 to Sunday, September 26, 2021.

(b) He attains the qualifying age for state pension credit before the end of the qualifying week. To have been eligible for the winter 2021/22, the claimant must have been born on or before October 5, 1954. To be eligible for the winter 2021/22 s/he must have been born on or before September 26, 1955.

People who meet these conditions may nevertheless be excluded from entitlement if reg.3 applies to them.

The drafting of reg.2 is quite unnecessarily opaque and must be read with reg.3 to be fully understood. Careful analysis discloses that, subject to what is said below about modification, it prescribes four rates of payment—£300, £200, £150 and £100—which apply as follows.

4.26 Claimants who live alone, or are the only person in their household who qualify for the winter fuel payment, receive either £200 (reg.2(1)(b)(i)) or £300 if they have reached the age of 80 by the end of the qualifying week (reg.2(2)(a)). Those rates do not apply to claimants in residential care.

For claimants who live with another person, who also qualifies for a winter fuel payment (described in this note as a "qualifying person"), the position is more complicated:

- If the qualifying person is the claimant's *partner* and has been awarded SPC, income-based JSA or income-related ESA, then the claimant is excluded from entitlement (reg.3(1)(a)(i)). The effect, at least in the normal case where the couple do not live with a third (or fourth, etc.) person who is also a qualifying person, is that, as the claimant has been excluded, the partner becomes the only person in the household who qualifies for the payment and therefore receives the £200 rate under reg.2(1)(b)(i), or, if the partner or the claimant is over 80, the £300 rate under reg.2(2)(a) or reg.2(3) respectively.

- The converse also applies. Where it is the *claimant* who has been awarded SPC, income-based JSA or income-related ESA, and he/she lives with a partner who would otherwise be a qualifying person, then his or her partner is excluded from entitlement by reg.3(1)(a)(i) and it is therefore the claimant who is entitled to receive the £200 rate under reg.2(1)(b)(i).

- Subject to that, claimants who have *not* been awarded SPC, income-based JSA or income-related ESA, receive £100 (reg.2(1)(b)(ii)(aa). That appears to be the case even if the qualifying people have been awarded SPC, income-based JSA or income-related ESA, as long as they are not the claimant's partner. That rate is increased to £200 for a claimant aged 80 or over (reg.2(2)(b)), unless the qualifying person is also aged 80 or over, in which case it is increased to £150 reg.2(2)(b)(i).

- The rate payable where the claimant has been awarded SPC, income-based JSA or income-related ESA and lives with qualifying person, who is not his or her partner, and who has also been awarded SPC, income-based JSA or income-related ESA is unclear.

  The point turns on the meaning of the words "or head (ii)(aa) applies" in reg.2(1)(b)(i). Does head (aa) apply whenever a claimant lives with a qualifying person, or does it only apply when the additional requirement that the claimant has not been awarded SPC, income-based JSA or income-related ESA is satisfied? The former interpretation is the more natural: the additional requirement is contained in the main body of subpara.(ii) but not in head (aa) itself, so if it was intended to refer to it why not refer to the whole subparagraph rather than just head (aa)? But on that view, neither the claimant, nor the qualifying person receives a payment: reg.2(1)(b)(i) does not apply (because head (ii)(aa) does) and no other rate has been prescribed that expressly covers the situation in the first sentence of this bullet point.

> It cannot have been intended to leave two people, both of whom are reliant on income-related benefits, without a winter fuel payment that is paid to many people who are much better off financially. Therefore one is driven to the latter interpretation. On that view, head (ii)(aa) does not apply in the circumstances under discussion (because the claimant has an award of SPC, income-based JSA or income-related ESA for the qualifying week) and so the claimants (and the qualifying people) are entitled to £200 under reg.2(1)(b)(i) (if they are aged 79 or less) or £300 (if they are aged 80 or over).

The test for whether one person lives with another for these purposes, is established in reg.1(3)(b). It provides a person lives with another person if, disregarding any period of temporary absence, they share accommodation as their mutual home and are not in residential care (as defined below).

Claimants who are in residential care are only entitled if they have *not* been awarded SPC, income-based JSA or income-related ESA for the qualifying week, in which case they get £100 (reg.2(1)(b)(ii)(bb)) or, if they are 80 or over, £150 (reg.2(2)(b)(ii)). Claimants in residential care who do have an award of SPC, income-based JSA or income-related ESA for the qualifying week are excluded from entitlement. With effect from February 23, 2015, the new reg.3(1)(a)(iv)—which appears to have been introduced to address criticisms of the drafting made in previous editions—confirms that this is the case. People count as being in residential care if they have resided in a care home an independent hospital or a Polish Resettlement Home for a continuous period of at least 13 weeks ending with the last day of the qualifying week: see reg.1(3)(a). Temporary absences are disregarded when calculating the 13-week period. 4.27

The position is further complicated by the fact that the above rates of payment were temporarily modified by:

- reg.2 of the Social Fund Winter Fuel Payment (Temporary Increase) Regulations 2008 (SI 2008/1778) during "the 2008–09 winter" (defined as "the winter which follows the qualifying week beginning on 15th September 2008");
- reg.2 of the Social Fund Winter Fuel Payment (Temporary Increase) Regulations 2009 (SI 2009/1489) during "the 2009–2010 winter" (defined as "the winter which follows the qualifying week beginning on 21st September 2009"); and
- reg.2 of the Social Fund Winter Fuel Payment (Temporary Increase) Regulations 2010 (SI 2010/1161) during "the 2010-2011 winter" (defined as the winter which follows the qualifying week beginning on September 20, 2010).

On each occasion, the modifications took the form of a temporary increase in so that the £100 rate in regs 2(1)(b)(ii) became £125; the £100 figure in reg.2(2)(b) became £125; the £200 rate in regs 2(1)(b)(i), (2)(a) and (3), became £250; the £200 rate in reg.2(2)(b) became £275; the £150 rate in reg.2(2)(b) became £200; and the £300 rate in regs 2(2)(a) and 2(3) became £400.

In respect of the winter of 2022/23, yet another temporary modification was made, but at different rates. For the winter that follows the qualifying week beginning on September 19, 2022, reg.2 of the Social Fund Winter Fuel Payment (Temporary Increase) Regulations 2022 (SI 2022/813) modified the 2000 Regulations as follows:

- the £100 rate in regs 2(1)(b)(ii) and 2(2)(b) became £250;
- the £200 rate in regs 2(1)(b)(i), (2)(a) and (3) became £500;
- the £200 rate in reg.2(2)(b) became £350;
- the £150 rate in reg.2(2)(b) became £300; and
- the £300 rate in regs 2(2)(a) and 2(3) became £600.

Those 2022/23 rates will be maintained for the winter of 2023/24: Social Fund Winter Fuel Payment (Temporary Increase) Regulations 2023 (SI 2023/549), coming into force on September 18, 2023.

Note that it is possible to be "ordinarily resident" in more than one country: see *CIS/1691/2014*.

Persons not entitled to a social fund winter fuel payment

4.28 **3.**—(1) Regulation 2 shall not apply in respect of a person who—

(a) is [5 throughout the qualifying week]—

[4 (i) a partner of, and living with, a person who attained the qualifying age for state pension credit in or before the qualifying week and to whom state pension credit, an income-based jobseeker's allowance or an income-related employment and support allowance has been, or falls to be, paid in respect of the qualifying week;]

(ii) receiving free in-patient treatment and has been receiving free in-patient treatment for more than 52 weeks; or

(iii) detained in custody under a sentence imposed by a court; or

[7 (iv) in residential care and is a person to whom state pension credit, an income-based jobseeker's allowance or an income-related employment and support allowance has been, or falls to be, paid in respect of the qualifying week; or]

(b) subject to paragraph (2), has not made a claim for a winter fuel payment [5 on or before the 31st March] following the qualifying week in respect of the winter following that week.

(2) Paragraph (1)(b) shall not apply where—

(a) a payment has been made by virtue of regulation 4(1) [5 on or before the 31st March] following the qualifying week in respect of the winter following that week; or

(b) regulation 4(2) applies.

[6 (3) No person is entitled to a winter fuel payment for the winter of 1997 to 1998, 1998 to 1999 or 1999 to 2000 unless they have made a claim for such a payment on or before 31st March 2014.]

AMENDMENTS

1. Social Fund Winter Fuel Payment (Amendment) Regulations 2000 (SI 2000/2864) reg.2(a)(ii) (November 13, 2000).

2. Social Fund Winter Fuel Payment (Amendment) Regulations 2004 (SI 2004/2154) reg.2(c) (September 20, 2004).

3. Employment and Support Allowance (Consequential Provisions) (No.2) Regulations 2008 (SI 2008/1554) reg.7(1) and (4) (October 27, 2008).

4. Social Security (Equalisation of State Pension Age) Regulations 2009 (SI 2009/1488) reg.21 (April 6, 2010).

5. Social Security (Miscellaneous Amendments) Regulations 2012 (SI 2012/757) reg.18 (April 1, 2012).

6. Social Fund Winter Fuel Payment (Amendment) Regulations 2013 (SI 2013/1509) reg.2(1) and (3) (September 16, 2013).

7. Social Security (Miscellaneous Amendments) Regulations 2015 (SI 2015/67) reg.4(1)(c) (February 23, 2015).

DEFINITIONS

"free in-patient treatment"—see reg.1(2).

"qualifying week"—*ibid.*

GENERAL NOTE

Regulation 3 excludes certain people from entitlement to a winter fuel payment even if they fall within reg.2(a) and (b). There are five categories: 4.29

(a) partners of people who were entitled to state pension credit, income-based jobseeker's allowance or income-related employment and support allowance throughout the qualifying week (reg.3(1)(a)(i)). This is to prevent double payment;

(b) people who, throughout the qualifying week, have been receiving free in-patient treatment (see the notes to reg.21(3) of the Income Support Regulations) for more than 52 weeks (reg.3(1)(a)(ii));

(c) people serving a custodial sentence throughout the qualifying week (reg.3(1)(a)(iii)). Note that the reference to "a sentence imposed by a court" excludes those in prison on remand;

(d) people in residential care who were entitled to state pension credit, income-based jobseeker's allowance or income-related employment and support allowance during the qualifying week; and

(e) anyone who does not automatically receive a winter fuel payment under reg.4 and who fails to claim it by March 31 in the following year. There is an exception for refugees to whom reg.4(2) applies. In *CIS 2337/2004*, Commissioner Jacobs held that the time limit in reg.3(1)(b) does not infringe claimants' rights under art.1 of the First Protocol to the European Convention on Human Rights even when a payment has been made without a claim in respect of previous years. The time limit did not deprive claimants of any rights but merely defined the scope of those rights. In *Walker-Fox v Secretary of State for Work and Pensions* [2005] EWCA Civ 1441 (*R(IS) 3/06*), the Court of Appeal held (overruling the decision of the Deputy Commissioner in *CIS/488/2004*) that the March 31 time limit applied for the winters of 2000/01 and 2001/02 in cases in which the claimant had to rely on Regulation 1408/71, even though the UK Government did not accept that there was an entitlement in such cases until July 2002 (i.e. after those time limits had expired). In this context, see also *CIS/3555/2004*. The final time limit for claiming a winter fuel payment for the winters of 1997/1998, 1998/1999 and 1999/2000 is March 31, 2014 (see para.(3)).

A claim for a winter fuel payment may be made using one of the forms at *http://www.gov.uk*. Typing the words "winter fuel payment claim" into the search box on the home page gives a link to the forms (one for those living in Great Britain and the other for those living in another EEA country or Switzerland). Proof of age will usually be required. Claiming in other ways may be acceptable, as long as it is done in writing, but—unless to do so would risk missing the absolute time limit for claiming—it is better to use the appropriate form, if possible.

Making a winter fuel payment without a claim

4.—(1) Subject to paragraph (2), the Secretary of State may [3 on or before the 31st March] of the year following the year in which the qualifying week falls make a winter fuel payment under regulation 2 in respect of the preceding winter to a person who (disregarding regulation 3(b)) appears from official records held by the Secretary of State to be entitled to a payment under that regulation. 4.30

(2) Where a person becomes entitled to income support [1 [2 , state pension credit or an income-related employment and support allowance]] in respect

of the qualifying week by virtue of a decision made after that week that section 115 of the Immigration and Asylum Act 1999 (exclusions) ceases to apply to him the Secretary of State shall make a winter fuel payment to that person under regulation 2 in respect of the winter following the qualifying week.

(3) Subject to paragraph (4), for the purposes of paragraphs (1) and (2) official records held by the Secretary of State as to a person's circumstances shall be sufficient evidence thereof for the purpose of deciding his entitlement to a winter fuel payment and its amount.

(4) Paragraph (3) shall not apply so as to exclude the revision of a decision under section 9 of the Social Security Act 1998 (revision of decisions) or the supersession of a decision under section 10 of that Act (decisions superseding earlier decisions) or the consideration of fresh evidence in connection with the revision or supersession of a decision.

AMENDMENTS

1. Social Fund Winter Fuel Payment (Amendment) Regulations 2004 (SI 2004/2154) reg.2(d) (September 20, 2004).

2. Employment and Support Allowance (Consequential Provisions) (No.2) Regulations 2008 (SI 2008/1554) reg.7(1) and (5) (October 27, 2008).

3. Social Security (Miscellaneous Amendments) Regulations 2012 (SI 2012/757) reg.18 (April 1, 2012).

DEFINITION

"qualifying week"—see reg.1(2).

GENERAL NOTE

4.31 Regulation 4 empowers (but does not oblige) the Secretary of State to make winter fuel payments on the basis of Benefits Agency records and without an express claim being made. At the outset, the information in those records is deemed to be sufficient evidence of entitlement or non-entitlement (see reg.4(3)) but reg.4(4) permits the initial decision to be revised or superseded in the normal way if further information comes to light. Those who consider themselves to be entitled to a winter fuel payment but do not receive one automatically may make a claim for it, provided they do so by March 31 in the year following the qualifying week (see reg.3(1)(b)). In cases where the Secretary of State does not make an automatic payment, there is no right of appeal against that omission. This is because omitting to make a payment does not give rise to a "decision" against which there is a right of appeal (see *CIS/751/2005* and *CIS/840/2005*, the latter decision doubting the decision of the Deputy Commissioner in *CIS/4088/2004*). In *CIS/840/2005*, the Commissioner explained the point as follows:

> "9. . . . I do not consider that, where the Secretary of State does not decide to make a payment under regulation 4(1), he is obliged to issue a decision not to make a payment. Indeed, it seems to me that he is not entitled, before 31 March of the relevant year, to issue a decision not to make a payment to a person who may be entitled to one, because that person may still make a claim within the time allowed by regulation 3(1)(b) and might establish his entitlement on the claim. He can make a decision under regulation 4 to make a payment but otherwise it seems to me that he must leave matters open and await a possible claim."

And, of course, after March 31 the Secretary of State's power to make the payment ends in any event by virtue of reg.3(1)(b).

For the effect of reg.4(2) before June 14, 2007, see p.1246 of Vol.II of the 2007 edition. The paragraph now appears to be otiose following the revocation of reg.21ZB of the Income Support Regulations. However, it has not itself been revoked.

In *CIS 2497/2002* an argument was raised that the operation of reg.4 discriminated indirectly against men on the grounds of their sex contrary to Directive 79/7. The evidence was that those selected by the Secretary of State to receive a winter fuel payment without a claim had been identified from official records of those receiving social security benefits (including retirement pension) in the qualifying week. As the pensionable age for women is lower than that for men, it was argued that there would be significantly more women than men in that category. However, Commissioner Mesher rejected that argument on the basis that, even if the operation of the rules allowing the Secretary of State to make payments without a claim was discriminatory, the claimant had not been disadvantaged by reg.4 but by "the overall and identical time-limit [i.e. March 31, after the winter in question] set for claims and for the making of payments without a claim".

In *JE v Secretary of State for Work and Pensions (SF)* [2022] UKUT 12 (AAC), the appellant relied on discrimination arguments which were in substance quite similar to those rejected in *CIS 2497/2002*, but made them in the context of the Human Rights Act 1998 instead of EU law. Upper Tribunal Judge Wikeley dismissed the appeal.

Revocations

5.—The Social Fund Winter Fuel Payment Regulations 1998, the Social Fund Winter Fuel Payment Amendment Regulations 1998 and the Social Fund Winter Fuel Payment Amendment Regulations 1999 are hereby revoked. **4.32**

[1 Regulation 2

SCHEDULE

4.33

Countries
Republic of Austria
Kingdom of Belgium
Republic of Bulgaria
Republic of Croatia
Czech Republic
Kingdom of Denmark
Republic of Estonia
Republic of Finland
Federal Republic of Germany
Republic of Hungary
Republic of Iceland
Republic of Ireland
Republic of Italy
Republic of Latvia
Principality of Liechtenstein
Republic of Lithuania
Grand Duchy of Luxembourg
Kingdom of the Netherlands
Kingdom of Norway
Republic of Poland
Republic of Romania
Slovak Republic
Republic of Slovenia
Kingdom of Sweden
Swiss Confederation.]

AMENDMENT

1. Social Fund Winter Fuel Payment (Amendment) Regulations 2014 (SI 2014/3270) reg.2(1) and (3) (September 21, 2015).

The Social Fund Maternity and Funeral Expenses (General) Regulations 2005

(SI 2005/3061) (AS AMENDED)

Made by the Secretary of State under sections 138(1)(a) and (4) and 175(1), (3) and (4) of the Social Security Contributions and Benefits Act 1992, after agreement by the Social Security Advisory Committee that proposals in respect of these Regulations should not be referred to it

[In force December 5, 2005]

ARRANGEMENT OF REGULATIONS

PART I

GENERAL

PART II

PAYMENTS FOR MATERNITY EXPENSES

PART III

PAYMENTS FOR FUNERAL EXPENSES

GENERAL NOTE

4.35 With effect from December 5, 2005, these Regulations replaced the Social Fund Maternity and Funeral Expenses (General) Regulations 1987 in their entirety. However, with a few exceptions, the effect was intended to consolidate those regulations and to produce a (greatly needed) simplification in the structure and wording of the rules for funeral payments.

The main changes were:

- a new definition of "couple" in reg.3(1) to reflect the coming into force of the Civil Partnership Act 2004. The definition has since been amended to reflect the coming into force of the Marriage (Same Sex Couples) Act 2013;

- a cosmetic change to the definition of "family" in reg.3(1). The definition now refers to "polygamous marriage" rather than a "polygamous relationship";
- the exclusion from the "immediate family member test" in reg.8(1) of students aged less than 19 who are in non-advanced education. Previously only those in advanced education were excluded (see reg.8(4)(a) of the former regulations);
- a large increase in the categories of people that are excluded from the "closer contact" test in reg.8(6)–(8) so that those categories are now the same as the categories of people who are exempt from the "immediate family member test" (cf. reg.8(8)(b) with reg.7(7) of the former regulations); and
- the metrification of references to distance.

Part I

General

Citation and commencement

1.—(1) These Regulations may be cited as the Social Fund Maternity and Funeral Expenses (General) Regulations 2005 and shall come into force on 5th December 2005. **4.36**

Revocation

2.—The Regulations specified in the Schedule are revoked to the extent specified there. **4.37**

General Note

The Schedule has not been reproduced. Its effects are noted at paras 3.197 and 3.200–3.204 of the Supplement to the 2005 edition. **4.38**

Interpretation

3.—(1) In these Regulations— **4.39**

"the Act" means the Social Security Contributions and Benefits Act 1992;

[[3] "the 1995 Act" means the Jobseekers Act 1995;

"the 2007 Act" means the Welfare Reform Act 2007;

"the 2012 Act" means the Welfare Reform Act 2012;]

[[1] "the Employment and Support Allowance Regulations" means the Employment and Support Allowance Regulations 2008;]

"the Income Support Regulations" means the Income Support (General) Regulations 1987;

"the Jobseeker's Allowance Regulations" means the Jobseeker's Allowance Regulations 1996;

"absent parent" means a parent of a child who has died where—

(a) that parent was not living in the same household with the child at the date of that child's death; and

(b) that child had his home, at the date of death, with a person who was responsible for that child for the purposes of Part IX of the Act;

[[2] "adoption agency" has the meaning given in section 2 of the Adoption and Children Act 2002;

"adoption order" means an order made under section 46 of the Adoption and Children Act 2002;]

"child" means a person under the age of 16 or a young person within the meaning of regulation 14 of the Income Support Regulations or, as the case may be, of regulation 76 of the Jobseeker's Allowance Regulations;

[5 "child arrangements order" means a child arrangements order as defined in section 8(1) of the Children Act 1989 which consists of, or includes, arrangements relating to either or both of the following—

(i) with whom the child is to live, and

(ii) when the child is to live with any person;]

"child tax credit" means a child tax credit under section 8 of the Tax Credits Act 2002;

"claimant" means a person claiming a social fund payment in respect of maternity or funeral expenses;

"close relative" means a parent, parent-in-law, son, son-in-law, daughter, daughter-in-law, step-parent, step-son, step-son-in-law, step-daughter, step-daughter-in-law, brother, brother-in-law, sister or sister-in-law;

"confinement" means labour resulting in the [2 birth] of a living child, or labour after 24 weeks of pregnancy resulting in the [2 birth] of a child whether alive or dead;

[4 6 "couple" means—

(a) two people who are married to, or civil partners of, each other and are members of the same household; or

(b) two people who are not married to, or civil partners of, each other but are living together [11 as if they were a married couple or civil partners];]

"family" means—

(a) a couple and any children who are members of the same household and for whom at least one of the couple is responsible;

(b) a person who is not a member of a couple and any children who are members of the same household and for whom that person is responsible;

(c) persons who are members of a polygamous marriage who are members of the same household and any children who are also members of the same household and for whom a member of the polygamous marriage is responsible [3 except where the claimant is in receipt of universal credit,];

[7 . . .]

[8 . . .]

"funeral payment" has the meaning given in regulation 7(1);

[2 "guardian" means a person appointed as a guardian or special guardian under section 5 or 14A of the Children Act 1989;]

"health professional" means—

(a) a registered medical practitioner, or

(b) a registered nurse or registered midwife;

"immediate family member" means a parent, son or daughter;

"income-based jobseeker's allowance" has the same meaning as it has in the Jobseekers Act 1995 by virtue of section 1(4) of that Act;

[1 "income-related employment and support allowance" means an income-related allowance under Part 1 of the Welfare Reform Act (employment and support allowance);]

"occupational pension scheme" has the same meaning as in the Pension Schemes Act 1993;

[9 "owner-occupier loan payments" means loan payments made under the Loans for Mortgage Interest Regulations 2017;]

[2 "parental order" means an order made under section 30 of the Human Fertilisation and Embryology Act 1990 or section 54 [10 or section 54A] of the Human Fertilisation and Embryology Act 2008;]

"partner" means where a person—

(a) is a member of a couple, the other member of that couple;

(b) is married polygamously to two or more members of his household, any such member [3 except that paragraph (b) does not apply where the claimant is in receipt of universal credit,];

[2 "placed for adoption" has the meaning given in section 18 of the Adoption and Children Act 2002;]

"person affected by a trade dispute" means a person—

(a) to whom section 126 of the Act applies; or

(b) to whom that section would apply if a claim for income support were made by or in respect of him;

"prescribed time for claiming" means the appropriate period during which a Sure Start Maternity Grant or, as the case may be, a funeral payment, may be claimed pursuant to regulation 19 of, and Schedule 4 to, the Social Security (Claims and Payments) Regulations 1987;

[2 "qualifying order" has the meaning given in regulation 3A;

"residence order" means a residence order as defined in section 8, and made under section 10, of the Children Act 1989;]

[5 . . .]

"still-born child", in relation to England and Wales, has the same meaning as in section 12 of the Births and Deaths Registration Act 1926 and, in relation to Scotland, has the same meaning as in section 56(1) of the Registration of Births, Deaths and Marriages (Scotland) Act 1965;

"Sure Start Maternity Grant" is to be construed in accordance with regulation 5;

[3 "universal credit" means universal credit under Part 1 of the 2012 Act;]

"working tax credit" means a working tax credit under section 10 of the Tax Credits Act 2002.

[2 (1A) References in these Regulations to—

(a) section 5, 8, 10 or 14A of the Children Act 1989,

(b) section 2, 18, 46 or 66 of the Adoption and Children Act 2002,

are to be construed as including a reference to a provision (if any) in legislation which has equivalent effect in Scotland, Northern Ireland, the Channel Islands or the Isle of Man.]

(2) For the purposes of Part III of these Regulations, persons shall be treated as members of the same household where—

(a) they are married to each other, or in a civil partnership with each other, and are living in the same care establishment, or

(b) they were partners immediately before at least one of them moved permanently into such an establishment,

and at least one of them is resident in a care establishment as at the date of death of the person in respect of whom a funeral payment is claimed.

(3) In paragraph (2), "care establishment" means—

(a) a care home,

(b) an Abbeyfield Home, or

(c) an independent hospital,

as defined in regulation 2(1) of the Income Support Regulations [1 or regulation 2(1) of the Employment and Support Allowance Regulations].

(4) For the purposes of these Regulations—

(a) persons are to be treated as not being members of the same household in the circumstances set out in regulation 16(2) and (3)(a), (b) and (d) of the Income Support Regulations [1 , in regulation 156 of the Employment and Support Allowance Regulations] or, as the case may be, in regulation 78(2) and (3)(a) to (c) of the Jobseeker's Allowance Regulations;

(b) [3 except where the claimant is in receipt of universal credit,] a person shall be treated as a member of a polygamous marriage where, during the subsistence of that marriage, a party to it is married to more than one person and the ceremony of marriage took place under the law of a country which permits polygamy.

[9 (5) For the purposes of these Regulations, a person being treated as entitled to a benefit has the meaning given to it in regulation 2(2)(aa) of the Loans for Mortgage Interest Regulations 2017.]

AMENDMENTS

1. Employment and Support Allowance (Consequential Provisions) (No.2) Regulations 2008 (SI 2008/1554) reg.8(1) and (2) (October 27, 2008).

2. Social Fund Maternity Grant Amendment Regulations 2010 (SI 2010/2760) reg.2 (December 13, 2010).

3. Social Fund (Maternity and Funeral Expenses) Amendment Regulations 2013 (SI 2013/247) reg.2 (April 1, 2013) (Note that the extraneous comma at the end of the definition of "partner" is required by SI 2013/247 and is not an editorial error).

4. Marriage (Same Sex Couples) Act 2013 (Consequential Provisions) Order 2014 (SI 2014/107) reg.2 and Sch.1 para.37 (March 13, 2014). The amendment extends to England and Wales only (see SI 2014/107, art.1(4)).

5. Child Arrangements Order (Consequential Amendments to Subordinate Legislation) Order 2014 (SI 2014/852) art.12(1) and (2) (April 22, 2014).

6. Marriage and Civil Partnership (Scotland) Act 2014 and Civil Partnership Act 2004 (Consequential Provisions and Modifications) Order 2014 (SI 2014/3229) art.29 and Sch.6 para.26 (December 16, 2014). The amendment relates only to Scotland (see SI 2014/3229 art.3(4)) but is in the same terms as the amendments made in relation to England and Wales by SI 2014/107 (see point 4 above).

7. Social Fund (Amendment) Regulations 2017 (SI 2017/271) reg.3 (April 6, 2017).

8. Social Fund Funeral Expenses Amendment Regulations 2018 (SI 2018/61) regs 3 and 4 (April 2, 2018).

9. Loans for Mortgage Interest Regulations 2017 (SI 2017/725) reg.18 and Sch.5 para.9(1) and (2) (April 6, 2018).

10. Human Fertilisation and Embryology Act 2008 (Remedial) Order 2018 (SI 2019/1413) art.3(2) and Sch.2 para.2 (January 3, 2019).

11. Civil Partnership (Opposite-sex Couples) Regulations 2019 (SI 2019/1458) reg.41 and Sch.3 Pt.2 para.81 (December 2, 2019).

GENERAL NOTE

Paragraph (1)

4.40 Regulation 3 defines the terms commonly used in these Regulations. Where relevant, these will be noted at the appropriate places in the commentary below. The following should, however, be noted:

"Close relative": The definition is narrower than the equivalent definitions in reg.2(1) of the Income Support Regulations and reg.1(3) of the Jobseeker's

Allowance Regulations because, although it includes a "step-son-in-law" and a "step-daughter-in-law", it does not specify that the partner of a close relative is also a close relative. So, for example, the unmarried partner or civil partner of the claimant's son (or a person with whom the claimant's son lives as if they were civil partners) is a "close relative" for the purposes of IS and JSA but not of maternity grants or funeral payments. For the position of "half-blood" and adoptive relationships, see the commentary to reg.2(1) of the Income Support Regulations.

"Confinement": Note that a payment can be made for a stillbirth only if it occurs after the 24th week of the pregnancy.

"Couple": The definition is the same as for IS and JSA—see the note to the definition in reg.2(1) of the Income Support Regulations in Vol.V of this series. In some circumstances where the members of a couple are living apart, they are deemed not to be members of the same household—see the note to para.(4)(a) below. For the position where at least one member of the couple lives in a "care establishment" see paras (2) and (3).

"Family": See the commentary on the definition of "family" in s.137(1) of the Contributions and Benefits Act in Vol.V of this series. The definition in para.(1) is differently worded from that definition (which applies for IS purposes) and the equivalent definition in s.35(1) of the Jobseekers Act. But, subject to the commentary to para.(4)(a) below, the consequences of the definition are the probably the same for all claimants other than those in polygamous marriages and their children (who are included in the definition for the purposes of maternity grants and funeral payments but not of IS or JSA). (For the circumstances in which a person is to be treated as a member of a polygamous marriage, see para.(4)(b).)

For the circumstances in which a person is "responsible" for a child see reg.4A below.

"Still-born child": The definition referred to is "a child which has issued forth from its mother after the 24th week of pregnancy and which did not at any time after being completely expelled from its mother draw breath or show any other signs of life."

Paragraphs (2) and (3)

For "*care home*", "*Abbeyfield Home*" and "*independent hospital*", see reg.2(1) of the Income Support Regulations and the commentary to that regulation in Vol.V of this series. 4.41

Paragraph 4(a)

See the commentary to reg.16 of the Income Support Regulations in Vol.V of this series. The general rule in that regulation (and reg.78 of the Jobseeker's Allowance Regulations and reg.156 of the ESA Regulations) is that family members are treated as continuing to be members of the same household even though one or more of them is temporarily living away from the others. That general rule is subject to the exceptions listed in paras (2) and (3) of reg.16. Previous editions of this work have expressed the view that the operation of para.(4)(a) is problematical because, whilst it incorporates the exceptions into the rules for maternity grants and funeral payments (other than the exceptions relating to residential care, which are dealt with in paras (2) and (3)) and goes further than reg.16 by deeming people within those exceptions *not* to be members of the same household, it does not incorporate the general rule. If that were correct, it would follow that, in cases that do not fall within the exceptions, the general law applies to the question of whether membership of a household endures through a temporary absence (see *England v Secretary of State for Social Services* [1982] 3 F.L.R. 222; *Taylor v Supplementary Benefit Officer (R(FIS) 5/85)*; *Santos v Santos* [1972] 2 All E.R. 246). However, in *SSWP v LD (IS)* [2010] UKUT 77 (AAC), the Upper Tribunal held that the general rule in reg.16(1) (or, 4.42

by implication, in regs 78 and 156) does apply to maternity grants and funeral payments. Judge Levenson stated:

> "16. Regulation 3(4)(a) of the 2005 regulations refers to not being treated as a member of the same household in the circumstances set out in regulation 16(2) of the 1987 regulations. Those circumstances refer to paragraph 16(1) of the 1987 regulations not applying if paragraph 16(2) applies. The logic of this is that 16(1) is also incorporated into the story by the wording of regulation 3(4)(a). There is no doubt that before the deceased moved away from the claimant, they were partners living in the same household. The First-tier Tribunal was clearly satisfied, as am I, that the deceased was only temporarily living away from the claimant. Regulation 16(1) of the 1987 regulations requires that they continue to be treated as members of the same household. That being the case, they continued to be a couple for the purposes of regulation 7(8)(a) of the 2005 regulations."

In any event, the couple in that case continued to be members of the same household whilst living in different places.

Paragraph (4)(b)

4.43 This applies the usual social security rule regarding polygamous marriages (i.e. that the marriage is polygamous at any time during which it is actually, rather than potentially, polygamous) to maternity grants and funeral payments.

[1 Provision against double payment: Sure Start Maternity Grants

4.44 **3A.**—(1) In this regulation—

(a) "C" is the child in respect of whom a Sure Start Maternity Grant has been claimed;

(b) "first grant" is a first Sure Start Maternity Grant [3 or a Best Start Grant] in respect of C;

[3 (c) "subsequent grant" is, in respect of C—

(i) a second or subsequent Sure Start Maternity Grant; or

(ii) if a Best Start Grant has been given, a first Sure Start Maternity Grant;

(d) "Best Start Grant" is a grant given to a qualifying individual under Regulations made under section 32 of the Social Security (Scotland) Act 2018 in connection with having, or expecting to have, a new baby in the family.]

(2) Subject to paragraph (3), a [3 subsequent] grant may not be awarded if a first grant has been awarded.

(3) A [3 subsequent] grant may be awarded to a person ("P") if the following conditions are satisfied.

(4) The first condition is that P—

(a) alone, or together with another person, has been granted a qualifying order; or

(b) falls within regulation 5(3)(b), (d), (e) or (f).

(5) The second condition is that P—

(a) has not already received a first grant; or

(b) was not, at the time a first grant was claimed, a member of the family of a person to whom a first grant has been paid.

(6) A qualifying order is one of the following types of order—

(a) an adoption order;

(b) a parental order;

(c) a [2 child arrangements] order.]

AMENDMENTS

1. Social Fund Maternity Grant Amendment Regulations 2010 (SI 2010/2760) reg.2 (December 13, 2010).

2. Child Arrangements Order (Consequential Amendments to Subordinate Legislation) Order 2014 (SI 2014/852) art.12(1) and (3) (April 22, 2014).

3. Social Security (Scotland) Act 2018 (Best Start Grants) (Consequential Modifications and Saving) Order 2018 (SI 2019/1138) art.3(1) and (2) (December 10, 2018).

GENERAL NOTE

Paragraph (2) sets out the general rule is that only one maternity grant or Best Start Grant (collectively in this Note, a "grant") may be paid for any individual child. That rule is subject to the exceptions set out in paras (3)–(5). 4.45

Those exceptions allow a second grant to be paid in circumstances where the claimant did not receive the first grant (and was not a family member of the person who received the first grant when that grant was claimed)—see para.(5)—and either:

- the claimant has been granted a "qualifying order" (defined by para.(6) as an adoption order, a parental order or a child arrangements order);
- the claimant is responsible for a child aged under 12 months in the circumstances set out in reg.5(3)(b) below;
- the claimant (or claimant's partner) has been appointed the guardian of a child under 12 months and is responsible for that child (i.e. where reg.5(3)(d) applies);
- the claimant (or claimant's partner) is responsible for a child aged under 12 months who has been "placed for adoption" by an "adoption agency" (i.e. where reg.5(3)(e) applies and see the commentary to that provision for the definition of the terms in quotation marks); or
- (in certain circumstances) the claimant (or claimant's partner) has adopted a child aged under 12 months under the laws of a country outside the UK (i.e. where reg.5(3)(f) applies).

The various types of "qualifying order" are defined further by reg.3(1). An "adoption order" is an order made under s.46 of the Adoption and Children Act 2002. A "parental order" is an order made under either s.30 of the Human Fertilisation and Embryology Act 1990 or s.54 of the Human Fertilisation and Embryology Act 2008 (which replaced s.30 with effect from April 6, 2010). Such an order provides for a child who has been born following a surrogate pregnancy to be treated in law as the child of the couple in whose favour it is granted. A "child arrangements order" is "a child arrangements order as defined in section 8(1) of the Children Act 1989 which consists of, or includes, arrangements relating to either or both of the following (i) with whom the child is to live, and (ii) when the child is to live with any person".

Note that, even if none of the above exceptions applies, only a lawful payment bars another payment—see *CG/30/1990*. So, where the first payment was made to the partner of the maternity grant claimant (who was the income support claimant) and not to her, this did not prevent her receiving a payment.

[1 Provision against double payment: funeral payments

4.—(1) Subject to paragraph (2), no funeral payment shall be made under these Regulations if such a payment [3 , or an award of funeral expense assistance given in accordance with regulations made under section 34 of the Social Security (Scotland) Act 2018,] has already been made in respect of any funeral expenses arising from the death of the same person. 4.46

(2) A further funeral payment may be made in respect of any funeral expenses arising from the death of a person in respect of which such a payment has already been made where—

(a) the decision pursuant to which the funeral payment was awarded has been revised; and

(b) the further amount of the award as revised, together with the amount of the funeral payment already paid in respect of the death of that person, does not exceed the amount of any funeral payment which may be awarded pursuant to regulation 9.]

[2 (3) No funeral payment may be made under these Regulations for an item or service for which payment has been received under The Social Fund (Children's Funeral Fund for England) Regulations 2019, unless the amount paid under those Regulations is less that the total amount charged for the item or service, in which case a payment may be made for an amount not exceeding the remainder of the amount charged.]

AMENDMENTS

1. Social Fund Maternity Grant Amendment Regulations 2010 (SI 2010/2760) reg.2 (December 13, 2010).

2. Social Fund (Children's Funeral Fund for England) Regulations 2019 (SI 2019/1064) reg.6 (July 23, 2019).

3. Social Security (Scotland) Act 2018 (Funeral Expense Assistance and Early Years Assistance) (Consequential Modifications and Savings) Order 2019 (SI 2019/1060) art.3(1) and (2) (September 16, 2019, subject to the saving in art.4).

GENERAL NOTE

4.47 As amended, the effect of reg.4 is that only one of the following payments may be made in respect of any individual death:

- a funeral payment;
- a Children's Funeral Fund payment under SI 2019/1064 (see below); or
- Scottish funeral expense assistance under SSI 2019/292 (see Pt XIII of Vol.IV of this series).

There are two exceptions. The first is where the decision to award the funeral payment is revised so as to increase the amount of the claimant's entitlement after the original (smaller) payment has been made. In such a case, a further payment may be made (subject to the overall maximum prescribed by reg.9). The second is where the amount paid from the Children's Funeral Fund was less that the total charge for the item or service. In such a case, the balance can be met by a funeral payment: see para.(3).

PART II

PAYMENTS FOR MATERNITY EXPENSES [1 IN ENGLAND AND WALES]

AMENDMENT

1. Social Security (Scotland) Act 2018 (Best Start Grants) (Consequential Modifications and Saving) Order 2018 (SI 2019/1138) art.3(1) and (3) (December 10, 2018).

[1 Persons to be treated as responsible for children

4.48 **4A.**—(1) For the purposes of this Part, subject to paragraph (4), a person ("P") is to be treated as responsible for a child if paragraph (2) or (3) applies.

(2) This paragraph applies if—

(a) P is receiving child benefit in respect of the child, unless P is a child in respect of whom another person is receiving child benefit; or

(b) no one is receiving child benefit in respect of the child but the child usually lives with P.

(3) This paragraph applies where P is receiving child benefit in respect of a child who is in receipt of child benefit in respect of another child in which case P is to be treated as responsible for both children.

(4) P is not to be treated as responsible for a child if the child is—

(a) being looked after by a local authority within the meaning of section 22 of the Children Act 1989, or section 93 of the Children (Scotland) Act 1995, [2 or section 74 of the Social Services and Well-being (Wales) Act 2014,] unless the child usually lives with P; or

(b) detained in custody pending trial or sentence upon conviction or under a sentence imposed by a court.]

AMENDMENTS

1. Social Fund Maternity Grant Amendment Regulations 2011 (SI 2011/100) reg.2 (January 24, 2011).

2. Social Services and Well-being (Wales) Act 2014 and the Regulation and Inspection of Social Care (Wales) Act 2016 (Consequential Amendments) Order 2017 (SI 2017/901) art.10 (November 3, 2017).

GENERAL NOTE

It is only possible for claimants to qualify for a maternity grant under regs.5(3) (b)–(e) below if they (or, sometimes, their partners) are "responsible for" the child in respect of whom the grant is to be made. From January 24, 2011 reg.4A defines the circumstances in which a person is to be treated as responsible for a child for the purposes of these Regulations. 4.49

The general rule is that the person receiving child benefit for the child is responsible. But that does not apply where a person is receiving child benefit for a child who is herself the parent of, and receiving child benefit for, another child. In those circumstances, the first person mentioned is responsible for both children. If no-one receives child benefit for the child, then the person with whom the child usually lives is responsible.

Under para.(4), no-one is responsible for—and therefore reg.5(3)(b)–(e) do not apply with respect to—children who are looked after by a local authority or are detained in custody. The only exception is where a child who is looked after by a local authority nevertheless usually lives with another person. In those circumstances, the person with whom the child usually lives is responsible.

[2 Entitlement

5.—(1) Subject to [3 regulations 5A and 6], a payment of £500 to meet maternity expenses (referred to in these Regulations as a "Sure Start Maternity Grant") shall be made in respect of a child or still-born child where the following conditions are satisfied. 4.50

(2) The first condition is that the claimant or the claimant's partner has, in respect of the date of the claim for a Sure Start Maternity Grant, been awarded—

(a) income support;

(b) state pension credit;

(c) an income-based jobseeker's allowance;

(d) working tax credit where the disability element or the severe disability element of working tax credit as specified in regulation 20(1)(b) and (f) of the Working Tax Credit (Entitlement and Maximum Rate) Regulations 2002(11) is included in the award;

(e) child tax credit [5 which includes an individual element or a disability element referred to in section 9(3) of the Tax Credits Act 2002]; [4 . . .]

(f) an income-related employment and support allowance [4; [6 ...]

(g) universal credit] [6; or

(h) owner-occupier loan payments and is treated as entitled to a benefit specified in sub-paragraphs (a) to (c) and (f).]

(3) The second condition is that—

(a) the claimant or, if the claimant is a member of a family, one of the family is pregnant or has given birth to a child or a still-born child;

[3 (b) the child's parents are not partners at the date of the claim and the claimant—

(i) is the parent (but not the mother) of the child (who must not exceed the age of twelve months at the date of the claim), or is responsible for that parent, and

(ii) is responsible for the child;]

(c) the claimant or the claimant's partner—

(i) has been granted a qualifying order in respect of a child who does not exceed the age of twelve months at the date of the claim, and

(ii) is responsible for the child;

(d) the claimant or the claimant's partner—

(i) has been appointed the guardian of a child who does not exceed the age of twelve months at the date of the claim, and

(ii) is responsible for the child;

(e) a child who does not exceed the age of twelve months at the date of the claim has been placed for adoption with the claimant or the claimant's partner by an adoption agency and the claimant or the claimant's partner is responsible for the child; or

(f) the claimant or the claimant's partner has adopted a child who does not exceed the age of twelve months at the date of the claim and that adoption falls within section 66(1)(c) to (e) of the Adoption and Children Act 2002 (meaning of adoption).

(4) [8 ...]

(5) The [8 third] condition is that the claim is made within the prescribed time for claiming a Sure Start Maternity Grant.]

[7 (6) The [8 fourth] condition is that the claimant lives in England or Wales.]

AMENDMENTS

1. Employment and Support Allowance (Consequential Provisions) (No.2) Regulations 2008 (SI 2008/1554) reg.8(1) and (3) (October 27, 2008).

2. Social Fund Maternity Grant Amendment Regulations 2010 (SI 2010/2760) reg.2 (December 13, 2010).

3. Social Fund Maternity Grant Amendment Regulations 2011 (SI 2011/100) reg.2 (January 24, 2011).

4. Social Fund (Maternity and Funeral Expenses) Amendment Regulations 2013 (SI 2013/247) reg.2(4) (April 1, 2013).

5. Social Fund (Amendment) Regulations 2017 (SI 2017/271) reg.3 (April 6, 2017).

6. Loans for Mortgage Interest Regulations 2017 (SI 2017/725) reg.18 and Sch.5 para.9(1) and (3) (April 6, 2018).

7. Social Security (Scotland) Act 2018 (Best Start Grants) (Consequential Modifications and Saving) Order 2018 (SI 2018/1138) art.3(1) and (4) (December 10, 2018).

8. Social Fund Maternity and Funeral Expenses (General) and Social Security (Claims and Payments) (Amendment) Regulations 2023 (SI 2023/545) reg.3 (June 8, 2023).

General Note

Regulation 5 sets out the four conditions of entitlement for a one-off lump sum payment of £500 per child (see para.(1)) called a "Sure Start Maternity Grant". Those conditions are: 4.51

- the claimant (or the claimant's partner) must be in receipt of a qualifying benefit (para.(2));
- the claimant, (or, in some cases, the claimant's partner or a member of the claimant's family) must be either pregnant or, have given birth to a child, or have become responsible for a child aged less than 12 months in certain specified circumstances (para.(3));
- except in the case of a still-birth, the claimant (or the claimant's partner) must have received advice from a health professional (para.(4)); and
- the claim for the maternity grant must have been made within the time limit (para.(5)); and
- (from December 10, 2018) the claimant must live in England and Wales (para.(6)).

All five conditions must be satisfied to qualify for the grant. In addition there are restrictions on entitlement where the claimant (or the claimant's partner) is a person affected by a trade dispute (see reg.6) and, from January 24, 2011 (but subject to the transitional protection in reg.3 of SI 2011/100: see below) where another member of the claimant's family is under 16.

Qualifying benefits—para. (2)

These are listed in sub-paras (a)–(h) of para.(2) and are largely self-explanatory. 4.52

For tax credits generally, see Vol.IV. In *GC v SSWP (SF)* [2010] UKUT 100 (AAC), it was accepted by the Secretary of State that the reference in reg.7 to "having an award" of CTC or WTC was to the award under s.14 TCA 2002, rather than the subsequent determination of entitlement under s.18 of that Act. Presumably the same is true of the requirement in para.(1) that the claimant should have "been awarded" tax credits.

WTC comprises seven separate elements, namely the basic, disabled, 30-hour, second adult, lone parent, childcare, and severe disability elements (see TCA s.11 2002 and reg.3 of the Working Tax Credit (Entitlement and Maximum Rate) Regulations 2002 ("the WTC Regulations")). WTC is a qualifying benefit for a maternity grant if either the disability element (under reg.9 of the WTC Regulations) or the severe disability element (under reg.17) is included in the calculation of the claimant's "maximum annual rate of working tax credit" under reg.20 of the WTC Regulations.

The rule for CTC looks equally straightforward but is problematic. Until April 5, 2017, para.(2)(e) provided that CTC was a qualifying benefit for a maternity grant if it was "payable at a rate higher than the family element". The effect of that rule was that CTC was only a qualifying benefit to the extent that the taper did not completely extinguish the individual element(s) paid in respect of each child or qualifying young 4.53

person for whom the claimant (or one of joint claimants) was responsible (see the commentary under the hearing, *"Family element"* in para.5.32 of Vol.II of the 2016/17 edition). However, from April 6, 2017, SI 2017/271 amended para.(2)(e) to provide that CTC was a qualifying benefit if it "includes an individual element or a disability element referred to in section 9(3) of the Tax Credits Act 2002". On first impression therefore, it appears that the rule for CTC is being brought into line with that for WTC so that it is a qualifying benefit if certain elements are included in the calculation of the award and the rate at which the award is payable is no longer relevant. However, the problem arises when it is realised that the "individual element" (i.e. as defined by TCA 2002 s.9(3)) is included in *every* award of CTC. A claimant is (or joint claimants are) entitled to an individual element "in respect of each child or qualifying young person for whom the person is, or either of them is or are, responsible": see s.9(2)(b). It is inevitable that anyone who is awarded CTC will be responsible for at least one child or qualifying young person because otherwise the basic condition of entitlement to that tax credit in TCA 2002 s.8(1) will not be satisfied. On that basis, everyone who has been awarded CTC is in receipt of a qualifying benefit for a maternity grant.

The Explanatory Memorandum for SI 2017/271 says:

> "This instrument amends the Social Fund Maternity and Funeral Expenses (General) Regulations 2005 in consequence of the changes to the family element of Child Tax Credit that will take effect from 6 April 2017. Entitlement to a Sure Start Maternity Grant and Funeral Expenses Payment from 6 April 2017 will be linked to the award of an individual element or disability element of Child Tax Credit, as from this date not all claimants awarded Child Tax Credit will be awarded the family element. The intention of this change is to ensure that all claimants who would have qualified for a Sure Start Maternity Grant or Funeral Expenses Payment prior to 6 April 2017 will continue to do so."

so it seems unlikely that the intention was to extend entitlement. However, what matters is the meaning of what the legislator has said, rather than what they meant to say. It is even difficult to argue that an award of CTC no longer includes the individual element where that element has been extinguished by the taper because that is not consistent with the use of the word "includes" in para.(2)(d).

The qualifying benefit must have been awarded to the claimant or to her partner. Whether or not a claimant has a partner is a matter of law, and her own views on the point are relevant factors to be taken into account but are not conclusive of that issue—see *CIS/2031/2003* in which the Commissioner advised tribunals that:

> ". . . the question of whether a claimant has a partner is intrinsic to the very question of entitlement to a grant and in an appeal against a refusal of a grant which depends on the question of entitlement to a qualifying benefit, a tribunal should always enquire whether the person applying for the grant has a partner".

4.54 In that appeal, the claimant was entitled to a maternity grant because her (undisclosed) partner had been entitled to IS at the relevant date, albeit not in respect of her.

To meet the condition in para.(2), it is necessary for a qualifying benefit to have been awarded "in respect of the date of claim". It is not necessary that the qualifying benefit should actually have been paid by that date. Further, although para.(1)(a) appears to require that a qualifying benefit "has . . . been awarded", an award of made *after* the date of the claim for the maternity grant but which covers the date of claim will suffice (see *SSWP v FS (IS)* [2010] UKUT 18 (AAC) at para.27 and *GC v SSWP* [2010] UKUT 100 (AAC)). For what happens when a decision refusing a grant has been made and a qualifying benefit is subsequently awarded, see under "*Time limit for claims*" (below).

Pregnancy, birth and becoming responsible for a child under 12 months—para.(3)

4.55 When reg.5 was completely recast with effect from December 13, 2010, the main change was to extend the list of circumstances (now set out in para.(3)) in which a maternity grant can be made. That list now takes into account the decision of the Court of Appeal in *Francis v Secretary of State for Work and Pensions* [2005] EWCA Civ 1303, *R(IS) 6/06* (and see further p.1332 of Vol.II of the 2010/11 edition), which held that the refusal (under the former reg.5(1)(b)) of a maternity grant to a parent who had obtained a residence order (in circumstances in which a grant would have been made if she had obtained an adoption order) discriminated against her contrary to arts 8 and 14 of the ECHR. It also creates new entitlements to a maternity grant in the circumstances set out in sub-paras (b), (d), (e) and (f).

For the definitions of "family", parent" and "still-born child" see reg.3 and the commentary to that regulation. For "qualifying order" see regs 3(1) and 3A(6) and the commentary to the latter. For "responsible for the child" see reg.4A.

Sub-paragraphs (a)–(f) are alternative rather than cumulative so it is sufficient to satisfy any one of them. The issues to which they give rise will normally be simple ones of fact.

Sub-paragraph (a)—The phrase "is pregnant" in sub-para.(a) means that an advance payment can be made where a child is to be born to the claimant or a member of her/his family. In other cases, entitlement can only arise after the event. 4.56

Sub-paragraph (b)—was amended with effect from January 24, 2011 by SI 2011/100. Its original wording (which was in effect from December 13, 2010 to January 23, 2011) was as follows:

> "(b) the claimant is the parent (but not the mother) of a child not exceeding the age of twelve months at the date of the claim and is responsible for the child and the child's parents are not partners at the date of the claim;".

The effect of that wording was to confer entitlement on a father of a child under 12 months who is responsible for that child and who is not the partner of the child's mother. The amended wording continues to cover those circumstances but also confers entitlement where:

- the child is less than 12 months old;
- the mother or father of the child is a child her/himself; and
- the claimant is responsible for the mother or father and is also responsible for the child.

The drafting would have been clearer if the amendment had dealt with those two, very different, cases by using different sub-paragraphs.

Sub-paragraph (d)—"Guardian" is defined by reg.3(1) as "a person appointed as a guardian or special guardian under section 5 or 14A of the Children Act 1989". 4.57

Sub-paragraph (e)—"Adoption agency" is defined by reg.3(1) as having the meaning set out in s.2 of the Adoption and Children Act 2002. That Act provides that a local authority or a "registered adoption society" "may be referred to as an adoption agency". "Registered adoption society" is itself defined (subject to a proviso) as a "voluntary organisation which is an adoption society registered under Pt 2 of the Care Standards Act 2000 (c. 14). . .". Regulation 3(1) also defines "placed for adoption" by reference to s.18 of the 2002 Act which empowers an adoption agency to place a child for adoption with prospective adopters and, following such a placement, to leave the child with them as prospective adopters.

Sub-paragraph (f)—Section 66(1)(c)–(e) of the Adoption and Children Act 2002 covers:

- an adoption under the law of a country or territory outside the British Islands, in which the Hague Convention (i.e. the Convention on Protection of Children and Co-operation in respect of Intercountry Adoption, concluded at the Hague on 29th May 1993) is in force that has been certified in pursuance of Article 23(1) of that Convention (see also s.144 of the 2002 Act);
- an "overseas adoption" as defined by s.87 of the 2002 Act; and

- an adoption recognised by the law of England and Wales and effected under the law of any other country.

Double payments—Where sub-paras (b), (d), (e) or (f) apply, it will sometimes be possible for the claimant to be awarded a maternity grant even if such a grant has previously been paid to another person: see reg.3A.

Health and welfare advice—para. (4)

4.58 Under para.(4), either the claimant or her partner (if she has one) must have received advice on the health and welfare of the child from a "health professional" (as defined in reg.3) before a maternity grant can be paid. For obvious reasons, this requirement does not apply if the child is still-born (see sub-para.(a)). Where the claim is made before the birth of the child, advice must also have been given about the health of the mother.

Time limit for claims—para. (5)

4.59 Under para.(5), it is a condition of entitlement to a maternity grant that it should have been claimed within the time limit for doing so. That time limit is prescribed by reg.19(1) of, and Sch.4 para.8 to, the Claims and Payments Regulations as amended with effect from October 18, 2018, by reg.2 of the Social Security (Claims and Payments) (Social Fund Maternity Grant) (Amendment) Regulations 2018 (SI 2018/989) (see Vol.III). Before that date, each of the six-month time limits set out below were three-month time limits.

The time limit depends upon which sub-paragraph of reg.5(3) is the basis for the claim. Where the claim is based on pregnancy or the birth of a child (reg.5(3)(a)), the time limit is the period beginning 11 weeks before the first day of the expected week of confinement and ending six months after the actual date of confinement. A claim based on the grant of a qualifying order (reg.5(3)(c)) must be made within six months after the date the order is made. A claim based on appointment as a guardian (reg.5(3)(d)), or placement for adoption (reg.5(3)(e)) must be made within six months after the date on which the appointment took effect or the placement was made. A claim based on a foreign adoption (reg.5(3)(f)) must be made within six months after the date on which the adoption either took effect or was recognised under UK law.

The time limit for claims based on reg.5(3)(b) is six months from the date the claimant became responsible for the child.

4.60 The time limit in Sch.4 para.8 cannot be extended. However if a claim for a maternity grant is refused because (at the date of that claim) a qualifying benefit not yet been awarded then, as long as the qualifying benefit is claimed within 10 working days of the original claim for the maternity grant, a further claim made within three months of a subsequent award of the qualifying benefit is treated as made on the date of the original claim, or the date the qualifying benefit was awarded, whichever is later (Claims and Payments Regulations, regs 6(16)–(18) and (22)). There is no provision in the legislation to extend the 10 working days limit: see *MW v SSWP (IS)* [2017] UKUT 291 (AAC) at para.41.

When deciding whether the claim for the qualifying benefit was made within 10 working days time limit, it is the date on which the claim form was received by the relevant office that counts. A claim for council tax benefit (or housing benefit) that is backdated and therefore "treated as made" within the 10-day period will not suffice—see *CIS/3416/2004* (a case about funeral payments, for which the rules are identical).

Another way of dealing with the problem caused by a subsequent award of a qualifying benefit is by seeking a revision of the earlier decision to refuse the original claim. Under reg.3(3) of the Decisions and Appeals Regulations (see Vol.III). the Secretary of State has power to revise that decision where the application for a revision is made within one month of the notification of the original refusal, or within the six months' time limit, whichever is later. So far those time limits are less generous to claimants than the rules in reg.6(16)–(18) of the Claims and Payments Regulations. The potential advantage of this route is that the time limit may be extended under reg.4 of the Decisions and Appeals Regulations up to 13 months from the date of notification of the original decision. If the qualifying benefit was not awarded until after the expiry of the primary time limit, that might amount to "special circumstances . . . as a result of [which] it was not practicable for the application to be made within the time limit"—see reg.4(4)(c) of those Regulations. Note, however, that there is no right of appeal against a refusal by the Secretary of State to extend time under reg.4 (see *R(TC) 1/05*).

As this way around the time limit problem involves seeking a revision of the original decision, rather than a supersession, it cannot be used where the claimant is subsequently awarded but with effect from a date after the claim for the maternity grant: see *MW v SSWP (IS)* [2017] UKUT 291 (AAC) at paras 44–45.

Living in England and Wales—para.(6)

Until December 9, 2018 maternity grants were payable to anyone living in Great Britain who met the conditions of entitlement. However, as part of the devolution of social security to the Scottish Parliament, those living in Scotland became eligible to a pregnancy and baby grant paid under s.32 of, and Sch.6 to, the Social Security (Scotland) Act 2018 and the Early Years Assistance (Best Start Grants) (Scotland) Regulations 2018 (SSI 2018/370) (see Pt XIII of Vol.IV of this series). As a consequence, maternity grants are now only payable to those living in England and Wales. 4.61

There will presumably be cases in which a claimant could be said to be living in both England and Wales and Scotland. However, the provision against double payment in reg.3A (as amended), and in Sch.2 to SSI 2018/370, will prevent such a claimant receiving both a maternity grant and a pregnancy and baby grant in respect of the same child.

[[1] [2] Entitlement where another member of the claimant's family is under the age of 16

5A.—(1) In this regulation— 4.62

(a) "C" means the child or still-born child in respect of whom a Sure Start Maternity Grant is claimed; and

(b) "existing member of the family" has the meaning given in paragraph (2) or, as the case may be, (3).

(2) Where a parent of C ("P") is under the age of 20 and a member of the claimant's family, "existing member of the family" means any member of the claimant's family who is also a child of P, apart from C or any other child born as a result of the same pregnancy as C.

(3) In any other case, "existing member of the family" means any member of the claimant's family apart from—

(a) C;

(b) any other child born as a result of the same pregnancy as C;

(c) any child whose parent is under the age of 20 and a member of the claimant's family [[3];

(d) any child—

(i) who was not, at the time of the child's birth, a child of the claimant (or, where the claimant has a partner at the date of claim, the claimant's partner); and

(ii) whose age, at the time that the claimant (or, where the claimant has a partner at the date of claim, the claimant's partner) first became responsible for that child, exceeded 12 months.]

(4) Subject to the following provisions of this regulation, a Sure Start Maternity Grant shall not be awarded if, at the date of claim, any existing member of the family is under the age of 16.

(5) Where C is one of two or more children—

(a) born or still-born as a result of the same pregnancy, or
(b) (if the claim is made before the confinement in a case where regulation 5(3)(a) applies) who are expected to be born as a result of the same pregnancy,
(c) the number of Sure Start Maternity Grants to be awarded is to be determined in accordance with paragraphs (6) and (7).

(6) Where at the date of claim no existing member of the family is under the age of 16 a Sure Start Maternity Grant is to be awarded in respect of each of the children mentioned in paragraph (5).

(7) Where at the date of claim any existing member of the family is under the age of 16 then—
(a) where each of those existing members of the family under the age of 16 was born as a result of separate pregnancies, a Sure Start Maternity Grant is to be awarded for all but one of the children mentioned in paragraph (5); and
(b) where two or more of those existing members of the family under the age of 16 were born as a result of a single pregnancy, the number of Sure Start Maternity Grants to be awarded in respect of the children mentioned in paragraph (5) is the number of children mentioned in paragraph (5) minus the maximum number of existing members of the family born as a result of a single pregnancy.]

[[4] (8) A Sure Start Maternity Grant shall be awarded if—
(a) at the date of claim, any existing member of the family is under the age of 16;
(b) the claimant is a person to whom paragraph (9) or (10) applies;
(c) no Sure Start Maternity Grant has been awarded to the claimant—
  (i) where the claimant is a person to whom paragraph (9) applies, on or after 15th August 2021;
  (ii) where the claimant is a person to whom paragraph (10) applies, on or after 24th February 2022; and
(d) the other conditions for entitlement to the grant are satisfied.

(9) This paragraph applies where the claimant is—
(a) a person who is granted leave in accordance with the immigration rules made under section 3(2) of the Immigration Act 1971 ("the 1971 Act") by virtue of—
  (i) Appendix Afghan Relocations and Assistance Policy of those rules; or
  (ii) the previous scheme for locally-employed staff in Afghanistan (sometimes referred to as the ex-gratia scheme); or
(b) a person in Great Britain not coming within sub-paragraph (a) who left Afghanistan in connection with the collapse of the Afghan government that took place on 15th August 2021.

(10) This paragraph applies where the claimant is a person who was residing in Ukraine immediately before 1st January 2022, who left Ukraine in connection with the Russian invasion which took place on 24th February 2022 and who —
(a) has a right of abode in the United Kingdom within the meaning given in section 2 of the 1971 Act;
(b) has been granted leave in accordance with immigration rules made under section 3(2) of the 1971 Act;
(c) has been granted, or is deemed to have been granted, leave outside those rules; or

(d) does not require leave to enter or remain in the United Kingdom in accordance with section 3ZA of the 1971 Act.]

AMENDMENTS

1. Social Fund Maternity Grant Amendment Regulations 2011 (SI 2011/100) reg.2 (January 24, 2011).
2. Social Fund Maternity Grant Amendment Regulations 2012 (SI 2012/1814) reg.2 (August 13, 2012).
3. Loans for Mortgage Interest and Social Fund Maternity Grant (Amendment) Regulations 2018 (SI 2018/307) reg.3 (April 6, 2018).
4. Social Fund Maternity and Funeral Expenses (General) and Social Security (Claims and Payments) (Amendment) Regulations 2023 (SI 2023/545) reg.3 (June 8, 2023).

GENERAL NOTE

From January 24, 2011, a maternity grant cannot generally be awarded if any "existing member of the family" is under the age of 16. That general rule is now stated in para.(4). **4.63**

For the definition of "family" see the commentary to reg.3(1). "Existing member of the family" is defined by paras (2) and (3). The phrase normally means any member of the family apart from the child for whom the maternity grant is claimed ("C"), any other child born as a result of the same pregnancy as C and any child whose parent is under the age of 20 and a member of the claimant's family (para.(3)).

However, where C's parent ("P") is under 20 and the claim is made by another member of the family (i.e. normally, a grandparent), "existing member of the family" means any child of P, apart from C or any other child born as a result of the same pregnancy as C, who is also a member of the claimant's family (para.(2)). That definition has the effect that the a maternity grant can be awarded for C even if there are other members of the family (excluding children born as a result of the same pregnancy as C) who are under 16, as long as P is not the parent of those other family members.

Paragraph (6), taken together with para.(5), provides that where more than one child is born (or still born or expected to be born) as a result of the same pregnancy and there is no other family member under the age of 16, a maternity grant is payable for each child. Presumably this provision has been included out of an abundance of caution because the consequence appears to follow in any event. In those circumstances, the definition of "existing member of the family " in para.(3) would remove the other child born as a result of the same pregnancy from the scope of the restriction in para.(4) even if para.(6) did not exist. **4.64**

Paragraph (7), taken together with para.(5), introduces a further exception the first time from August 13, 2012. Where more than one child is born (or still born or expected to be born) as a result of the same pregnancy, then a maternity grant is to be awarded in respect of the additional child or children born even if other existing members of the family are under 16. As the explanatory memorandum to SI 2012/1814 states:

> "For example, if a claimant has an existing child but then has twins, one further [maternity grant] will be paid on the basis that the claimant already has existing baby items from the first child but needs additional baby items in respect of the second twin. If they have one existing child and then have triplets, two more grants will be paid and so on."

Paragraph (7)(b) modifies that principle where there have been previous multiple births in the family (or, more technically, where two or more of the existing members of the family under the age of 16 were born as a result of a single pregnancy).

Regulation 3 of SI 2012/1814 (see below) contains transitional provisions which mean that claimants cannot take advantage of the more generous terms of the new reg.5A where: **4.65**

- the claim is based on reg.5(3)(a), was made before the birth and before August 13, 2012 and the expected date of confinement is before October 29, 2012;
- the claim is based on reg.5(3)(a), was made after the birth and the birth took place before October 29, 2012;
- the claim is based on reg.5(3)(c) and the qualifying order was made before October 29, 2012;
- the claim is based on reg.5(3)(d) and the appointment as guardian took effect before October 29, 2012;
- the claim is based on reg.5(3)(e) and the child is placed for adoption with the claimant or the claimant's partner before October 29, 2012; and
- the claim is based on reg.5(3)(f) and the adoption took effect before October 29, 2012.

For claims affected by the transitional provisions, the former version of reg.5A continues to apply: see pp.1393–1394 of Vol.II of the 2012/13 edition.

In *LS v SSWP (SF)* [2014] UKUT 298 (AAC), it was submitted that reg.5A is ultra vires on the ground that the Secretary of State had not complied with the public sector equality duty in s.71 of the Race Relations Act 1976 as amended when making it. The Upper Tribunal (Judge Levenson) rejected that submission.

In *SK and LL v SSWP* [2020] UKUT 145 (AAC), the Upper Tribunal (Judge Church) held that reg.5A discriminated unlawfully against:

- refugees with "pre-flight children" (i.e. those with an existing child but who were unlikely to have been able to bring that child's baby things to the UK when fleeing persecution) contrary to art.14 read with art.8 and A1P1 of the Convention; and
- those having their first biological child while already responsible for a child who came into their care after reaching 12 months old contrary to art.14 read with A1P1 of the Convention.

Judge Church disapplied reg.5A in the cases before him and, there being no dispute as to the other conditions of entitlement, awarded the claimants a Sure Start Maternity Grant.

Persons affected by a trade dispute

4.66 **6.**—(1) Where the claimant or the claimant's partner is a person affected by a trade dispute, a Sure Start Maternity Grant shall be made only if—

(a) in the case where the claimant or the claimant's partner is in receipt of income support or income-based jobseeker's allowance, the trade dispute has, at the date of the claim for that payment, continued for not less than six weeks; or

(b) in the case where the claimant or the claimant's partner is in receipt of—

(i) working tax credit where the disability element or the severe disability element of working tax credit as specified in regulation 20(1)(b) and (f) of the Working Tax Credit (Entitlement and Maximum Rate) Regulations 2002 is included in the award, or

(ii) child tax credit [1 which includes an individual element or a disability element referred to in section 9(3) of the Tax Credits Act 2002]

(2) In paragraph (1)(b), the relevant claim means the claim in respect of which a tax credit of the type referred to in head (i) or (ii) of that subparagraph was awarded.

AMENDMENT

1. Social Fund (Amendment) Regulations 2017 (SI 2017/271) reg.3 (April 6, 2017).

GENERAL NOTE

Regulation 3 defines "person affected by a trade dispute" by reference to s.126 of the Social Security Contributions and Benefits Act 1992, which refers on to s.14 of the old style Jobseekers Act 1995 (see the notes to those provisions in Vol.V of this series). **4.67**

If the claimant (or her/his partner) is affected by a trade dispute then there is no entitlement to a maternity grant unless, either, that dispute is of at least six weeks' duration or the family is entitled to one of the tax credits specified in sub-para.(b) by virtue of a claim made before the trade dispute started. See the General Note to reg.5 for an argument that every award of CTC "includes" an individual element.

It may sometimes be difficult to tell when a trade dispute started, since the dispute is to be distinguished from the stoppage of work due to it.

PART III

PAYMENTS FOR FUNERAL EXPENSES [1 IN ENGLAND AND WALES]

AMENDMENT

1. Social Security (Scotland) Act 2018 (Funeral Expense Assistance and Early Years Assistance) (Consequential Modifications and Savings) Order 2019 (SI 2019/1060) art.3(1) and (3) (September 16, 2019, subject to the saving in art.4).

Funeral payments: entitlement

7.—(1) In these Regulations— **4.68**

(a) "funeral payment" means a social fund payment to meet funeral expenses of a deceased person;

(b) "responsible person" means the person who accepts responsibility for the funeral expenses.

(2) Subject to regulation 8, a funeral payment shall be made where each of the conditions referred to in paragraphs (3) to [6 (9A)] is satisfied.

(3) The first condition is that, in respect of the date of the claim for a funeral payment, the responsible person or his partner is a person to whom paragraph (4) applies.

(4) This paragraph applies to a person—

(a) who has an award of—

(i) income support,

(ii) state pension credit,

(iii) income-based jobseeker's allowance,

(iv) working tax credit where the disability element or the severe disability element of working tax credit as specified in regulation 20(1)(b) and (f) of the Working Tax Credit (Entitlement and Maximum Rate) Regulations 2002 is included in the award,

(v) child tax credit [4 which includes an individual element or a disability element referred to in section 9(3) of the Tax Credits Act 2002],

(vi) housing benefit, or

(vii) [3 . . .] [2 . . .

(viii) income-related employment and support allowance; [5 ...]]

[3 (ix) universal credit] [5; or

(x) owner-occupier loan payments and is treated as entitled to a benefit specified in sub-paragraphs (i) to (iii) and (viii).]

(b) [3 . . .]

(5) The second condition is that the deceased was ordinarily resident in the United Kingdom at the date of his death.

(6) The third condition is that the claim is made within the prescribed time for claiming a funeral payment.

(7) The fourth condition is that the claimant is the responsible person or the partner of the responsible person.

(8) The fifth condition is that—

(a) the responsible person was the partner of the deceased at the date of death; or

(b) in a case where the deceased was a child and—

(i) there is no absent parent, or

(ii) there is an absent parent who, or whose partner, is a person to whom paragraph (4) applied as at the date of death,

the responsible person was the person, or the partner of the person, responsible for that child for the purposes of Part IX of the Act as at the date of death; or

(c) in a case where the deceased was a still-born child, the responsible person was a parent, or the partner of a parent, of that still-born child as at the date when the child was still-born; or

(d) in a case where the deceased had no partner and neither sub-paragraph (b) nor (c) applies, the responsible person was an immediate family member of the deceased and it is reasonable for the responsible person to accept responsibility for those expenses; or

(e) in a case where the deceased had no partner and none of sub-paragraphs (b), (c) and (d) applies, the responsible person was either—

(i) a close relative of the deceased, or

(ii) a close friend of the deceased,

and it is reasonable for the responsible person to accept responsibility for the funeral expenses.

(9) The sixth condition is that the funeral takes place—

(a) in a case where paragraph (10) applies, in a member State of the European Union, Iceland, Liechtenstein [1, [8 Norway, Switzerland or the United Kingdom]];

(b) in any other case, in the United Kingdom.

[6 (9A) The seventh condition is that the claimant lives in England and Wales.]

[1 [7 (10) This paragraph applies where the responsible person or the responsible person's partner is—

(a) a qualified person within the meaning of regulation 6(1)(b) (worker) or (c) (self-employed person) of the Immigration (European Economic Area) Regulations 2016 (the EEA Regulations);

(b) a person who retains the status referred to in sub-paragraph (a) pursuant to regulation 6(2) or (4) of the EEA Regulations;

(c) a person who is a family member of a person referred to in sub-paragraph (a) or (b) within the meaning of regulation 7(1) of the EEA Regulations; or

(d) a person who has a right to reside permanently in the United Kingdom by virtue of regulation 15(1)(c), (d) or (e) of the EEA Regulations;

(e) a person granted indefinite leave to enter, or remain in, the United Kingdom under the Immigration Act 1971 by virtue of Appendix EU to the immigration rules made under section 3(2) of that Act.]]

[[7] (11) References in this regulation to the Immigration (European Economic Area) Regulations 2016 are to be read with Schedule 4 to the Immigration and Social Security Co-ordination (EU Withdrawal) Act 2020 (Consequential, Saving, Transitional and Transitory Provisions) Regulations 2020.]

AMENDMENTS

1. Social Security (Persons from Abroad) Amendment Regulations 2006 (SI 1026/2006) reg.8(2) (April 30, 2006).
2. Employment and Support Allowance (Consequential Provisions) (No.2) Regulations 2008 (SI 2008/1554) reg.8(1) and (4) (October 27, 2008).
3. Social Fund (Maternity and Funeral Expenses) Amendment Regulations 2013 (SI 2013/247) reg.2(5) (April 1, 2013).
4. Social Fund (Amendment) Regulations 2017 (SI 2017/271) reg.3 (April 6, 2017).
5. Loans for Mortgage Interest Regulations 2017 (SI 2017/725) reg.18 and Sch.5 para.9(1) and (4) (April 6, 2018).
6. Social Security (Scotland) Act 2018 (Funeral Expense Assistance and Early Years Assistance) (Consequential Modifications and Savings) Order 2019 (SI 2019/1060) art.3(1) and (4) (September 16, 2019, subject to the saving in art.4).
7. Immigration and Social Security Co-ordination (EU Withdrawal) Act 2020 (Consequential, Saving, Transitional and Transitory Provisions) (EU Exit) Regulations 2020 (SI 2020/1309) reg.62 (December 31, 2020 at 11.00 pm).
8. Social Fund Funeral Expenses Payment (Amendment) Regulations 2021 (SI 2021/65) reg.2 (February 15, 2021).

GENERAL NOTE

For the legislative history of funeral payments see pp.1229–1230 of Vol.II of the 2005 edition. **4.69**

This regulation, together with reg.8, governs the right to funeral payments. Regulation 7 sets out the conditions of entitlement and reg.8 makes supplementary provision and contains two exclusory rules which disqualify some claimants who would otherwise have been entitled.

Regulation 7 specifies seven conditions of entitlement, all of which must be satisfied (para.(2)):

- the claimant (or her/his partner) must have an award of a qualifying benefit or be a person in respect of whom council tax benefit in the form of second adult rebate could be awarded (paras (3) and (4));
- the deceased must have been ordinarily resident in the UK (para.(5));
- a claim must have been made within the time limit (para.(6));
- the claimant (or her/his partner) must be a "responsible person" (para.(7));
- the responsible person must be sufficiently closely connected to the deceased (para.(8));
- the funeral must take place in the UK or (in certain circumstances) in an EEA state (paras (9)–(11)); and
- the claimant must live in England or Wales (para.(9A)).

Each of these conditions requires consideration in more detail.

Qualifying benefit

4.70 Under paras (3) and (4), the benefits that qualify a claimant for a funeral payment include all those that are qualifying benefits for a sure start maternity grant (see the commentary to reg.5) with the addition of housing benefit.

For the family element of child tax credit, see the note to the relevant definition in reg.3.

Before April 1, 2013, the first condition was also satisfied if the claimant (or her/his partner) was a person in respect of whom a second adult rebate could be awarded: see the former sub-para.(4)(b). Secondly adult rebate was an alternative form of council tax benefit, which was abolished with effect from that date. For further details of the position before April 1, 2013, see p.1397 of Vol.II of the 2012/13 edition.

4.71 The award of the qualifying benefit must be in respect of the date of claim for the funeral payment. See the notes to reg.5(1) and *GC v SSWP* (SF) [2010] UKUT 100 (AAC). Also note *CIS/2059/1995*. In that case the claimant's claim for a funeral payment had been rejected on the ground that he was not entitled to income support. However, the consequence of the Commissioner allowing his appeal against the decision refusing income support was that the basis for the rejection of his claim for a funeral payment had gone. Thus the tribunal's decision on that appeal, although sound when it was given, had become erroneous and it too had to be set aside.

A person "has an award" of income-based JSA (and therefore satisfies the condition in para.(4)(a)(iii)) while serving the waiting days (i.e. under Jobseekers Act 1995 Sch.1 para.4 and reg.46 of the JSA Regulations 1996) before entitlement to that benefit begins: *SSWP v SJ (IS)* [2015] UKUT 127 (AAC).

The requirement that claimants should be in receipt of a qualifying benefit has been held not to infringe their Convention rights under the Human Rights Act 1998, see *CIS/3280/2001*, *CIS/1722/2002* and *Faith Stewart v SSWP* [2011] EWCA Civ 907, [2012] AACR 9, upholding *SSWP v FS (SF)* [2010] UKUT 18 (AAC). It has also been held that failure of the scheme to provide for the personal representative of an insolvent estate to be eligible for a payment was neither irrational nor an infringement of the Convention: see *RM v SSWP (IS)* [2010] UKUT 220 (AAC).

Ordinary residence in the UK

4.72 The deceased must be ordinarily resident in the UK at the date of his death. Ordinary residence "connotes residence in a place with some degree of continuity and apart from accidental and temporary absences" (see *R(P) 1/78* at para.7). As the requirement is one of ordinary residence, not presence, a claim can be made in respect of a UK resident who dies, for example, while on holiday abroad for the cost of the funeral in the UK (although the cost of transporting the body back to the UK would not be covered, except possibly under reg.9(2)(g)).

The time limit

4.73 Under Claims and Payments Regulations, reg.19(1) and Sch.4 para.9, the time for claiming a funeral payment begins on the date of the death and ends six months after the date of the funeral. Otherwise the rules in this area are the same as for maternity grants—see the note to reg.5.

The six-month time limit begins to run on the day after the funeral and ends on the day six months later that corresponds to the day of the month on which the funeral took place: see *SSWP v SC (SF)* [2013] UKUT 607 (AAC) in which the funeral took place on July 26, 2011 and the time limit, which was then three months, ended on October 26, 2011 so that a claim made on October 27, 2011 was out of time.

Responsible person

4.74 The claimant (or her/his partner) must be a "responsible person", which is defined by para.(1)(b) as "the person who accepts responsibility for the funeral expenses".

In *CSB/488/1982*, it was held that the fact that someone else makes the arrangements does not mean that the claimant has not taken responsibility for the costs. The test is not who is responsible for arranging the funeral. The question is whether the claimant (or partner) has entered into a contractual relationship with the funeral director. Often the fact that the claimant's name appears on the funeral director's account will be sufficient evidence of that. But if someone else's name appears that does not necessarily mean that the claimant has not accepted responsibility because that person may, on a correct legal analysis, have been acting as the claimant's (or partner's) agent. In *CIS/12344/1996* the claimant's son made the funeral arrangements; his mother was unable to do so because of her age and the sudden death of her husband. The bill was in his name and he paid it before the claim for a social fund funeral payment was made. It is held that the son had been acting as agent for his mother and the fact that the account was addressed to him did not detract from this. The claimant had accepted responsibility for the funeral costs. In *R(IS) 6/98* the Commissioner retracts his statement in *CIS/12344/1996* that it was necessary for the undertakers to know of the agency. The concept of the "undisclosed principal" in the law of agency allowed an agency to exist even where this was not disclosed to the third party, provided that the agent had in fact had authority beforehand. But if there was no agency at the time the funeral debt was incurred, it was not open to a person to intervene later and claim to be legally responsible for the debt (although depending on the circumstances a novation may achieve that result, see below). In *VC v SSWP (IS)* [2010] UKUT 189 (AAC), the Upper Tribunal stressed the importance of making sufficient findings of fact as to the nature of any agreement between the claimant and any other putative responsible person.

Agency must be distinguished from a novation, or transfer, of the contract as occurred in *R(IS) 9/93*. The Commissioner follows *CSB/423/1989* in holding that if another person has initially made a contract with the undertakers the claimant may assume liability for the funeral costs by a novation of the contract under which the claimant assumes the other person's liability and the undertakers release the other person from his liability. The novation requires the consent of all three parties, but no consideration or further payment is necessary. Providing that the claimant comes within one of the heads of what is now sub-para.(e) and has assumed responsibility for the costs before the decision is made (or possibly before the claim is made) the condition is satisfied. Often, arrangements will be made without thinking about the legal niceties, and a commonsense view should be taken.

Legal issues can also arise if the closest relative lacks the legal capacity to accept a contractual liability to the undertakers. In *C1/01-02(SF)* the Commissioner had to decide whether a 16-year-old boy could legally "accept responsibility" for the expenses of his mother's funeral under the Northern Ireland equivalent of reg.7. She held that, in the particular circumstances of that case (where the claimant was the deceased's eldest child, 16-years old, had become the tenant of the family home and there was no other parent whose whereabouts were known) those expenses were a "necessary" for him so that he was obliged to pay a reasonable price for them under s.3 of the Sale of Goods Act 1979 even though he did not have capacity to make a binding contract to pay them.

Connection with the deceased

Paragraph 8 identifies the person who may claim a funeral expenses payment on the basis of how closely he or she was related to, or connected with, the deceased. There are two different hierarchies depending on whether the deceased was an adult or a child. 4.75

If the deceased was an adult then, under sub-para.(a), the claimant must be his or her partner. If the deceased had no partner at the date of death then, under sub-para.(d), the claim may be made by an "immediate family member" (i.e. a parent, son or daughter—see reg.3(1)) if it is reasonable for him or her to take responsibility for the funeral expenses. If the deceased dies without a partner or an immediate family member (or if there was an immediate family member but it is not reasonable for him or her to take responsibility for the funeral expenses), then, under subpara. (e), the claim may be made by a "close relative" (i.e. a parent, parent-in-law, son, son-in-law, daughter, daughter-in-law, step-parent, step-son, step-son-in-law, step-daughter, step-daughter-in-law, brother, brother-in-law, sister or sister-in-law—again see reg.3(1)) or a close friend. Again, a close relative or close friend, must show that it was reasonable for him or her to take responsibility for the funeral expenses. In the very rare case where the deceased's partner also dies before the deceased's funeral without making a claim for a funeral payment, then the deceased is treated as not having had a partner at the date of his or her death—see reg.8(4).

If the deceased was a child then the first question to ask is whether s/he was still-born. If so, then the claimant must be one of the child's parents or a person who was the partner of one of the child's parents at the date of the death (sub-para.(c)). If not, then the claimant must be the person responsible for the child at the date of death (or his or her partner), unless there is an absent parent (defined in reg.3(1)) who (or whose partner) was not receiving a qualifying benefit at the date of death (sub-para.(b)). If no-one qualifies under sub-paras (b) or (c) then, as for adults, the claimant must be an "immediate family member", or failing this, a "close relative" or a close friend. A person is responsible for a child if s/he is counted as such for the purposes of child benefit.

4.76 If there is more than one "immediate family member" then, unless the claimant is the deceased's partner, see also reg.8(1) and (2).

In any case where the claimant is a close relative (other than an immediate family member) or a close friend of the deceased, s/he must also establish that it was reasonable for him or her to accept responsibility for the funeral expenses. Regulation 8(5) states that this "shall be determined by the nature and extent of his contact with the deceased". *R(IS) 3/98* holds that in deciding this question, regard should be had to the person's relationship with the deceased as a whole and not just during the period immediately preceding the date of death. The claimant had claimed a funeral payment in respect of his late father whom he had not seen for 24 years. He was the only close relative. The Commissioner decided that the lack of contact over the previous 24 years did not automatically erase the contact they had had in the preceding 30 years. It was not unreasonable for a son to wish to pay his last respects to his father whatever the reasons for their estrangement. See also *CIS/13120/1996* (claimant divorced from the deceased only two weeks before his death after 40 years of marriage), a decision on the law as in force up to June 5, 1995 (although the actual result would be different on the current law). The fact that it is reasonable for one person to assume responsibility for the cost of a funeral does not mean that it is not reasonable for someone else to do so (*CIS/13120/196*).

If there is more than one close relative then see reg.8(6)–(8).

It will be apparent from the above that an ex-partner (or someone who is no longer treated as a partner), or a relative who is not a close relative, will have to qualify under the category of close friend. According to the Decision Makers Guide, in considering whether a person was a close friend of the deceased, the depth of the relationship will be more important than its duration. In *CIS/788/2003* the deceased was a boy who had died at the age of three months. The child's mother was herself a minor and the funeral directors refused to enter into a contract with her for that reason. The child's grandmother therefore undertook responsibility for the expenses and claimed a funeral payment. Commissioner Turnbull held that the grandmother could be treated as a "close friend" of the deceased. The Secretary of State had argued that as child benefit had been paid to the child's mother, she would have satisfied what is now reg.7(8)(b)(ii) if she had accepted responsibility for the funeral expenses and therefore that the words equivalent to "none of sub-paragraphs (b), (c) and (d) applies" in sub-para.(e) were not satisfied. The Commissioner rejected that argument. The provision about the receipt of child benefit "did not apply" because there was no real possibility of the mother taking responsibility for the funeral expenses. Neither the existence of a family relationship between the grandmother and the child nor the child's very young age prevented her from being treated as his "close friend" for the purposes of the regulation.

Place of funeral

4.77 Paragraph (9) provides that the "funeral" must take place in the UK unless para.(10) (as qualified by para.(11)) applies. The effect is that funeral payments can still be made where the responsible person (or partner) has settled status under the EU Scheme or falls within one of the provisions of the 2016 Regulations that are listed in para.(10)(a)–(d), as those provisions are preserved and modified by Sch.4 to SI 2020/1309: see further Vol.V.

Until April 2, 2018, "funeral" was defined by reg.3(1) as "a burial or cremation". However, that definition was revoked by reg.4 of SI 2018/61, leaving the word undefined. The result must be that, for the purposes of the Regulations, "funeral" is to be treated as an ordinary word of the English language, rather than as a term of art (and reg.9(3)(ba) does contemplate that a funeral payment may be made in respect of one cost of "the disposal of the body of the deceased, whether by burial, cremation *or otherwise*" (emphasis added)). The most important funeral costs that are eligible for a funeral payment, however, remain those incurred as a result of burial or cremation (see reg.9(3)(a) and (b)), but not both (see reg.9(5)).

In *JEC v Secretary of State for Work and Pensions (SF)* [2021] UKUT 243 (AAC), Upper Tribunal Judge Caldwell QC decides that in relation to the reg.7(9) requirement for a funeral to take place in the UK (or, in certain circumstances, an EU/EFTA state), "for the purposes of the 2005 Regulations a 'funeral' is one event that involves disposal of the deceased's body" [para.37].

JEC does not address situations where there is no body, and the Secretary of State has subsequently issued guidance [ADM Memo 17/21, para.6]: "In the case where there is no body or remains of the deceased, a payment may be made for a single commemorative event."

In those cases in which a funeral that takes place in an EEA country remains eligible for a funeral payment, financial help with the funeral expenses is available that would not be available where the funeral takes place in other countries. This has led to a number of attempts to argue that the rule (and its predecessor which required the funeral to take place in the UK) were unlawfully discriminatory. Apart from the challenge in *O'Flynn v Adjudication Officer* (C–237/94) (R(IS) 4/98) in which the former absolute requirement that the funeral must take place in the UK was held to be contrary to EU law (as to which see pp.1231–1232 in Vol.II of the 2005 edition), these were all unsuccessful:

- In *R. v Secretary of State for Social Security, Ex p. Nessa, The Times*, November 15, 1994, the High Court rejected an argument that the predecessor rule was unlawful under the Race Relations Act 1976. Section 75 of that Act stated that it applied to acts done by ministers, as it applied to acts done by a private person. But Auld J held that acts of a governmental nature, such as the making of regulations, were not subject to the control of the 1976 Act as they were not acts of a kind that could be done by a private person.

- In *CIS/3150/1999* a challenge to the validity of the rule on the basis that it was ultra vires and irrational was rejected.

- In *CIS 4769/2001* the Commissioner rejected a challenge under the Human Rights Act: the rule was not directly discriminatory and the Commissioner was not persuaded either that there was any indirect discrimination against the claimant, a Muslim of Pakistani origin, or that, if there was such discrimination, it had not been established that it was not objectively justified.

- In *Esfandiari v SSWP* [2006] EWCA Civ 282 (*R(IS) 11/06*), the Court of Appeal also held the rule did not discriminate unlawfully against recent migrants. Giving the judgment of the Court, Carnwath LJ stated:

  "8. . . . I find it impossible to see this as a case of 'discrimination' in any relevant sense. The state made provision for a suitable burial in the UK for all those of inadequate means, regardless of personal characteristics or status. There was no obligation on the state to do so, and certainly no obligation to do more. It was open to each appellant to take advantage of this provision, but each chose not to do so for understandable, but entirely personal, reasons.

9. The only way in which this can be represented as 'discriminatory' is by characterising them as members of a 'group', that of recent migrants to this country; and then finding 'indirect' discrimination, in that as a group (so it is assumed) they are more likely than other comparable groups to have retained family links with their countries of origin, and therefore more likely to want their loved ones to be buried there. Such reasoning seems to me, with respect, wholly artificial. Without demeaning the strength and sincerity of the wishes of these appellants as individuals, it is not obvious that recent migrants, as a group, are particularly likely to prefer a burial in their country of origin, rather than in the country they have made their home. In any event there may be many other categories of people resident in this country, who, given the choice, might elect for a burial abroad for themselves or their loved ones, whether for religious, family, social or purely sentimental reasons. They may have spouses from another country, who have retained their native family links; they may have spent large parts of their lives in another country; they may have children who have moved to another country. Such wishes are understandable and to be respected; but it is not the job of the state to satisfy them. Nor does the sharing of such desires render those who have them a 'group' requiring special protection under Article 14."

- Alternatively, if the rule was regarded as discriminatory then that discrimination was objectively justified.

In *CIS/1335/2004*, the claimant's husband died while they were on holiday in Spain. Because she could not afford to have his body flown back to the UK, he was cremated in Spain. His ashes were then interred in England. The Commissioner confirmed the Secretary of State's decision to refuse a funeral payment. The "funeral" was the Spanish cremation and not the subsequent burial of ashes in the UK. Therefore, the actual cost of the burial did not qualify under reg.9(3)(a) and the other UK costs could only qualify as other funeral expenses under reg.9(3)(g) as incidental to, or consequential upon, the cremation in Spain if the claimant was in principle entitled to a funeral payment in respect of that cremation. That was not the case because the claimant was neither a migrant worker nor a family member of such a worker within the provisions set out in para.(10). The result was that the rule treated UK citizens less favourably than citizens of other Member States exercising rights in the UK under EU law. However, that discrimination was not unlawful under EU law or under ECHR art.14, taken together with art.1 of the First Protocol. From April 30, 2006 para.(10) applies to nationals of Switzerland as well as to nationals of Iceland, Liechtenstein and Norway—and to members of their families as defined by art.2 of the Rights of Residence Directive—as if those nationals were EU nationals (see reg.10(g) of SI 1026/2006).

Country where the claimant lives

4.78 From September 16, 2019, para.(9A) requires that a claimant must live in England or Wales to be entitled to a funeral payment. Claimants who live in Scotland must claim funeral expense assistance from the Scottish Ministers: see the Funeral Expense Assistance (Scotland) Regulations 2019 (SSI 2019/292) in Part XIII of Vol.IV of this series, particularly reg.9.

Funeral payments: supplementary

8.—(1) Subject to paragraph (2), the claimant shall not be entitled to a funeral payment where the responsible person is an immediate family member, a close relative or a close friend of the deceased and— 4.79

(a) there are one or more immediate family members of the deceased;
(b) one or more of those immediate family members or their partners are not persons to whom regulation 7(4) applied as at the date of death; and
(c) any of the immediate family members referred to in sub-paragraph (b) was not estranged from the deceased at the date of his death.

(2) Paragraph (1) shall not apply to disentitle the claimant from a funeral payment where the immediate family member who meets the description specified in sub-paragraph (c) of that paragraph is at the date of death—

(a) a person who has not attained the age of 18;
(b) [1 a qualifying young person within the meaning of section 142 of the Act (child and qualifying young person);]

[2 (bb) a qualifying young person under section 10(5) (prescription of qualifying young person) of the Welfare Reform Act 2012;]

(c) a person who has attained the age of 18 but not the age of 19 and who is attending a full-time course of advanced education, as defined in regulation 61 of the Income Support Regulations, or, as the case may be, a person aged 19 or over but under pensionable age who is attending a full-time course of study, as defined in that regulation, at an educational establishment;
(d) a person in receipt of asylum support under section 95 of the Immigration and Asylum Act 1999;
(e) a member of, and fully maintained by, a religious order;
(f) being detained in a prison, remand centre or youth custody institution and either that immediate family member or his partner is a person to whom regulation 7(4) applied immediately before that immediate family member was so detained;
[3(ff) a person resident in a care establishment within the meaning of regulation 3(3), whose accommodation and care costs are met in whole or in part by a local authority within the meaning of the Local Government Act 1972 or the Local Government etc (Scotland) Act 1994;]
(g) a person who is regarded as receiving free in-patient treatment within the meaning of the Social Security (Hospital In-Patients) Regulations 1975, or the Social Security (Hospital In-Patients) Regulations (Northern Ireland) 1975, and either that immediate family member or his partner is a person to whom regulation 7(4) applied immediately before that immediate family member was first regarded as receiving such treatment; or
(h) a person ordinarily resident outside the United Kingdom.

(3) Paragraphs (4) to (8) apply for the purposes of regulation 7(8)(d) and (e).

(4) The deceased shall be treated as having had no partner where the deceased had a partner at the date of death and—

(a) no claim for funeral expenses is made by the partner in respect of the death of the deceased; and
(b) that partner dies before the date upon which the deceased's funeral takes place.

(5) Whether it is reasonable for the responsible person to accept responsibility for meeting the expenses of a funeral shall be determined by the nature and extent of his contact with the deceased.

(6) Paragraph (7) applies (subject to paragraph (8)) in a case where the deceased had one or more close relatives.

(7) If, on comparing the nature and extent of any close relative's contact with the deceased and the nature and extent of the responsible person's contact with the deceased, any such close relative was—

(a) in closer contact with the deceased than the responsible person,

(b) in equally close contact with the deceased and neither that close relative nor his partner, if he has one, is a person to whom regulation 7(4) applies,

the claimant shall not be entitled to a funeral payment.

(8) However paragraph (7) shall not apply where the close relative who was in—

(a) closer contact with the deceased than the responsible person, or (as the case may be)

(b) equally close contact with the deceased,

is at the date of death of a description specified in any of sub-paragraphs (a) to (h) of paragraph (2).

(9) In a case where the responsible person is the partner of the person who was a close relative, immediate family member or (as the case may be) close friend of the deceased, references in the preceding provisions of this regulation, and in regulation 7(8)(d) and (e), to the responsible person are to be construed as references to the responsible person's partner.

AMENDMENTS

1. Social Security (Miscellaneous Amendments) Regulations 2006 (SI 2006/588) reg.6 (April 10, 2006).

2. Social Fund (Maternity and Funeral Expenses) Amendment Regulations 2013 (SI 2013/247) reg.2(6) (April 1, 2013).

3. Social Fund Funeral Expenses Amendment Regulations 2018 (SI 2018/61) regs 3 and 5 (April 2, 2018).

GENERAL NOTE

4.80 Apart from making supplementary provision that has already been noted in the commentary to reg.7, reg.8 contains two important exclusory rules.

The first, in para.(1), disentitles a claimant who was not the deceased's partner if there are any immediate family members of the deceased (other than those excluded under para.(2)) who, or whose partners, have not been awarded a qualifying benefit, unless they were estranged from the deceased.

The second, in paras (6)–(8), disentitles a claimant who was not the deceased's partner if any close relative (other than one excluded under para.(2)) either had closer contact with the deceased or had equal contact and was not (or his or her partner was not) in receipt of qualifying benefit. This is a separate test from that in para.(1) so that estrangement from the deceased is not directly relevant in a claim where there are no immediate family members (*CIS/3534/2007* and *MS v SSWP* [2009] UKUT (AAC) 201).

4.81 To avoid confusion between the two rules, it is necessary to pay close regard to the distinction between "immediate family members" and "close relatives". In everyday language a brother or sister, for example, might be regarded as an immediate family member. As defined in reg.3(1), however, the *only* "immediate family members" are parents, sons and daughters. As people in those categories are also "close relatives", *both* exclusory rules apply to them.

Other relatives, however, (i.e. brothers, sisters, sons-in-law, daughters-in-law, parents-in-law, brothers-in-law, sisters-in-law, step-parents, step-children and step-children-in-law) are "close relatives only" and not "immediate family members". For the reasons given below, the first exclusory rule does not usually apply to them. Except where they have claimed in circumstances where there is an immediate family member (i.e. where the immediate family member has not claimed because it is not reasonable for him or her to take responsibility got the funeral expenses), they will be subject to the second exclusory rule only.

Immediate family members not in receipt of a qualifying benefit

The first exclusory rule will normally only apply to claims by an "immediate family member". This is because, where there is an "immediate family member", a claim by a "close relative" or "close friend" is only possible in circumstances where it is not reasonable for the immediate family member to take responsibility for the funeral expenses (see reg.7(8)(e) and, e.g. *CIS/788/2003*). 4.82

The meaning of the provision corresponding to para.(1) in the 1987 Regulations was considered in *CIS/2288/1998*. Read as a whole, the paragraph means that the claimant is not entitled to a funeral payment if there is at least one (other) immediate family member who not estranged from the deceased and neither that family member nor his or her partner was in receipt of a qualifying benefit.

A further point arose in *CIS/1218/1998*. The claimant had applied for a funeral payment in respect of his late mother. His sister was not in receipt of a qualifying benefit. The tribunal decided that what is now para.(1)(b) referred to *both* the claimant and his sister and since he was in receipt of a qualifying benefit the disentitlement imposed by the paragraph did not apply. The AO appealed, contending that if the tribunal's interpretation was correct, no claim would ever be caught by the provision since it was a requirement under what is now reg.7(3) and (4) that the responsible person be in receipt of a qualifying benefit. In addition, there would be no need to exempt those immediate family members now listed in para.(2) from the operation of the provision. The Commissioner agreed; in his view the immediate family members referred to in sub-paras (a) and (b) did not include the responsible person.

"Estrangement" has "connotations of emotional disharmony" (*R(SB) 2/87*) and may exist even though financial support is being provided. In *C1/01–02(SF)*, the Commissioner stated that "[m]ere disagreement is not sufficient to constitute estrangement, there must be something akin to treating as a stranger for a sufficient period of time". On the facts of that case estrangement had taken place between the claimant's grandparents and his mother (who had a drink problem) "in that there was a deliberate decision to sever relationships due to the strong disapproval and anger which the grandparents felt about the deceased's drinking and the strong desire which they felt that this lifestyle should change and had to change before any relationships could be resumed." In *CIS/4498/2001* the claimant's deceased mother had suffered from senile dementia as a result of which she could not communicate with anyone or recognise family members and his sister—the other "immediate family member"—had lived in Australia for 10 years but had returned to Britain on at least three occasions because of her mother's ill-health. Quoting his earlier decision in *CIS/5321/1998*, Commissioner Henty stated: 4.83

> "The appropriate OED definition of 'estranged', accepted in *CIS/5119/97* is, 'to alienate in feeling or affection'. I might put a gloss on that such as 'not to be on speaking terms'. The evidence before the tribunal points, I think, not at so much as an alienation of feeling or affection—the emphasis being on 'alienation', a concept which involves some form of positive consideration—but a drifting apart which to my mind connotes something short of alienation. Of course a long period of 'drifting apart' may lead to the inference that there had been an alienation, but such is not, in my view, the case here'. Those considerations are equally applicable here. Had such a break down in relation occurred before the on set of the mother's incapacity, then estrangement there would have been. But the inca-

pacity by itself is not estrangement, and neither is the fact that the sister had been in Australia for some 10 years."

In *CIS 1228/2004*, Commissioner Fellner held "that registering a death is [not] enough *in itself* to show that the person who does so *cannot* have been estranged from the deceased" (original emphasis).

In *CIS/4096/2005*, Commissioner Jupp reviewed the authorities on estrangement (in the context of reg.13(1)(d) of the Income Support Regulations) and concluded that there was no requirement of mutuality in feeling for estrangement to exist, as had been suggested by the Commissioner in *CIS/4498/2001*. Disharmony can arise from one person's attitude to another even though the other party may not wish the situation to be as it is. The position has to be judged from the point of view of (in the context of funeral payments) the surviving immediate family member who is being considered and not from the point of view of the deceased.

4.84 The concept of "estrangement" is also relevant to the capital disregard in para. (4) of Sch.10 to the Income Support Regulations, Sch.8 to the JSA Regulations and Sch.5 to the State Pension Credit Regulations. However, caution needs to be exercised when applying the case law on that provision to funeral payments. In *CPC/683/2007*, the Commissioner noted that "the language used in [that] legislation is attempting to identify those cases in which the relationship between the parties is such that it is appropriate for their finances to be treated separately for the purposes of benefit entitlement". That is not the same as the context in which estrangement needs to be considered on a claim for a funeral payment.

What happens if—as may well be the case even in relatively close families—the claimant simply does not know whether or not any of the other immediate family members or close relatives is in receipt of a qualifying benefit: where does the burden of proof lie? This was one of the issues considered by the House of Lords in *Kerr v Department for Social Development* [2004] UKHL 23 (*R 1/04 (SF)*). In that case, which concerned the Northern Ireland equivalent of the current reg.8, the claimant was the eldest of three brothers and a sister who, although living in the Belfast area, had not been in touch with each other for over 20 years. One of the brothers died and the claimant was traced by the police and agreed to accept financial responsibility for the funeral. He claimed a funeral payment which was refused without any enquiry by the Department into whether the surviving brother and sister had been awarded a qualifying benefit, an question which, of course, the Department was better placed to answer than the claimant. The issue was therefore whether Mr Kerr had to prove a negative—that neither his sister or brother were in receipt of a qualifying benefit—or whether the Department had to show that they were. Giving the judgment of the House, Baroness Hale said, in a passage which has profound implications for social security administration generally:

> "61. Ever since the decision of the Divisional Court in *R. v Medical Appeal Tribunal (North Midland Region), Ex p Hubble* [1958] 2 QB 228, it has been accepted that the process of benefits adjudication is inquisitorial rather than adversarial. Diplock J. as he then was said this of an industrial injury benefit claim at p.240:
>
>> 'A claim by an insured person to benefit under the Act is not truly analogous to a lis inter partes. A claim to benefit is a claim to receive money out of the insurance funds . . . Any such claim requires investigation to determine whether any, and if so, what amount of benefit is payable out of the fund. In such an investigation, the minister or the insurance officer is not a party adverse to the claimant. If analogy be sought in the other branches of the law, it is to be found in an inquest rather than in an action.'
>
> 62. What emerges from all this is a co-operative process of investigation in which both the claimant and the department play their part. The department is the one which knows what questions it needs to ask and what information it needs to have in order to determine whether the conditions of entitlement have been met. The claimant is the one who generally speaking can and must supply that information.

But where the information is available to the department rather than the claimant, then the department must take the necessary steps to enable it to be traced.

63. If that sensible approach is taken, it will rarely be necessary to resort to concepts taken from adversarial litigation such as the burden of proof. The first question will be whether each partner in the process has played their part. If there is still ignorance about a relevant matter then generally speaking it should be determined against the one who has not done all they reasonably could to discover it. As Mr Commissioner Henty put it in decision *CIS/5321/1998*, 'a claimant must to the best of his or her ability give such information to the AO as he reasonably can, in default of which a contrary inference can always be drawn.' The same should apply to information which the department can reasonably be expected to discover for itself."

In this case, the claim was allowed because the Department had failed to ask Mr Kerr the necessary questions and could not "use its own failure to ask questions which would have led it to the right answer to defeat the claim" (at para.65). Baroness Hale also addressed the position which would have existed if both the claimant and the Department had done everything which was legally required of them but it had still not proved possible to ascertain the true position? In that case:

"66. This will not always be sufficient to decide who should bear the consequences of the collective ignorance of a matter which is material to the claim. It may be that everything which could have been done has been done but there are still things unknown. The conditions of entitlement must be met before the claim can be paid. . . It may therefore become relevant to ask whether a particular matter relates to the conditions of entitlement or to an exception to those conditions. In this case, the department argues that all the elements, including those in regulation 6(6) [equivalent to reg.8(7) of the current GB regulations], are conditions of entitlement, so that the claimant must bear the consequences of ignorance. The claimant argues that the conditions of entitlement are laid down in regulation 6(1), supplemented where relevant by paragraphs (2) and (5) [regs 7 and 8((4) and (5) of the current GB Regulations]. Paragraphs (3) and (4), which go together, and paragraph (6) [reg.8(1),(2) and (7) of the current GB regulations] are exceptions.

67. The structure and wording of the regulation support the claimant's case. Conditions (a), (b), (c) and (d) in regulation 6(1) are clearly established. The claimant qualifies as a 'close relative' under condition (e)(iv)(aa) but this also requires that it be reasonable for him to accept responsibility. Under regulation 6(5) the question 'whether it is reasonable for a person to accept responsibility for meeting the expenses of the funeral shall be determined by the nature and extent of that person's contact with the deceased'. The tribunal decided that it was reasonable for the claimant, as the eldest son who had grown up with his brother, to accept that responsibility, despite the fact that they had not been in contact with one another for many years. That conclusion is not challenged in this appeal, in my view rightly. For the reasons given earlier, there is a strong public interest in encouraging families to take responsibility for the speedy and seemly burial of their deceased relatives.

68. Regulation 6(3) provides that the person who has made himself responsible 'shall not be entitled' if there is a more appropriate immediate family member. That this is a disentitling provision is made clear by regulation 6(4), which states that 'Paragraph (3) shall not apply to *disentitle* the responsible person' (my emphasis) in the circumstances there set out. In the same way, paragraph 6(6) provides that if there is a close relative who is either in closer contact or in equally close contact and not receiving benefits or having capital, the responsible person 'shall not be entitled' to the payment. These paragraphs are therefore worded in terms of exceptions rather than qualifying conditions. If anything, this interpretation is supported by the legislative history given earlier, as the existence of a more suitable relative was added as an exception or qualification to the basic rule.

69. This, therefore, is a case in which the department should bear the burden of the collective ignorance and pay the claim."

Paragraph (2) sets out the circumstances in which the claimant may remain entitled to a funeral payment even if s/he has an immediate family member who is not in receipt of a qualifying benefit. These are largely self-explanatory and include where the immediate family member is under 18, a qualifying young person for child benefit purposes, in certain types of full-time education, in receipt of asylum support, ordinarily resident outside the UK or—in some circumstances—in hospital or in prison.

Closer contact

4.85 Under paras (6)–(8), if the responsible person is an immediate family member, another close relative or a close friend (see para.(3)), and the deceased had one or more close relatives (para.(6)), the nature and extent of their contact with the deceased will be compared (para.(7)).

This is a separate test from deciding whether it is reasonable for the person to have accepted responsibility for the funeral costs (see para.(5)), as confirmed in *R(IS) 3/98*. If any close relative had closer contact, the claimant will not be entitled to a funeral payment (para.(7)(a)). If the contact was equally close, a payment will also be refused if the close relative (or their partner) is not getting a qualifying benefit (see para.(7)(b)). But this rule does not apply if at the date of death the close relative concerned came within any of the categories listed in para.(2) (see above).

Close contact will be a question of fact in each case. It should be noted that the test involves having regard to the nature as well as the extent of the contact. Thus this will bring in issues of quality as well as quantity. *CIS/8485/1995* states that, when considering the question of contact with the deceased, tribunals should adopt a broad brush, commonsense approach. The amount of time spent with the deceased is only one factor, and the nature of the contact should be judged not just by visits, letters, etc. but also by the quality of the contact. So if the claimant's half-brother's unpredictable nature had affected his relationship with his late mother, that should have been taken into account in assessing the nature of his contact with her. The guidance given to decision-makers by the Decision Makers Guide is that they "should consider the overall nature and extent of the contact with the deceased given the circumstances of the individual. For example, domestic or work responsibilities may prevent a close relative from keeping in regular contact with the deceased but the nature of the contact may be equally as close as a close friend who visited every day." The guidance suggests that factors to be considered include the nature of the relationship, frequency of contact, type of contact, domestic or caring assistance given to the deceased, social outings and holidays, domestic or work responsibilities and estrangements or arguments with the deceased (paras 39181–39182).

4.86 As the Deputy Commissioner pointed out in *CIS/3534/2007*, whether or not the close relative was estranged from the deceased is not legally relevant to the test in para.(7). However, the existence of estrangement may be relevant as a matter of fact. It is suggested that a close relative who was not estranged from the deceased will normally have been in closer contact with the deceased than a close relative who was so estranged.

The question of how para.(7)(b) applies in the situation where none of the close relatives was in contact with the deceased at all—i.e. whether the phrase "in equally close contact" includes circumstances in which there was an equal lack of contact—was considered, obiter, by three members of the House of Lords in the *Kerr* case (above). Lord Scott was of the view that it did not. To read "equally close contact" as meaning "equal contact" was to rewrite the statutory language and to ignore the significance of the words "close" and "in"—one cannot be "in" a "close" lack of contact. Where there was no contact at all, then none of the sub-paras of what is now para.(7) was applicable. Further, the question was not whether any of the close relatives "had had close contact with the deceased in the past" but "whether they were 'in equally close contact' with him at the time of his death" (paras 26–35). By contrast Lord Hope held (at para.9) that the test in what is now para.(7)(b) was not necessarily limited to the state of affairs which existed at the time of the deceased's death:

> "Regulation [8(7)] assumes that where there is 'contact' the question of 'closeness' is put in issue, however slight or remote in time that may be. I do not find anything in the regulation to indicate that the contact must have been current at, or immediately before, the date of the deceased's death. The period of time during which a comparison of the nature and extent of the contact is to be undertaken is not specified. The conclusion which I would draw from this is that there is no restriction as to the time of this contact. In my opinion the first question which the adjudicator must ask himself is whether the relevant person had any 'contact' with the deceased at all at any time. If he did, the question of the relative 'closeness' of that contact in comparison with the contact of the responsible person can and must be asked and answered."

Baroness Hale (at para.70), whilst agreeing with Lord Scott that it was "harder to see how 'was . . . in equally close contact' can cover contact which ended 20 years earlier", preferred not to express any view on the issue. It is disappointing that when the regulations were re-drafted in 2005, the opportunity was not taken to clarify the point one way or another.

Amount of funeral payment

9.—(1) A funeral payment shall be an amount sufficient to meet any relevant expenditure less any amount which falls to be deducted under regulation 10. 4.87

(2) In paragraph (1), "relevant expenditure" means any costs to which paragraph (3) applies which fall to be met or have been met by the responsible person (or a person acting on behalf of the responsible person), inclusive of any available discount on those costs allowed by the funeral director or by any other person who arranges the funeral.

(3) This paragraph applies to the following costs—

(a) where the deceased is buried—

[1 (i) the necessary costs of obtaining a new burial plot for the deceased and a right of burial in that plot, whether or not that right is exclusive]

(ii) the fees levied in respect of a burial by the authority or person responsible for the provision and maintenance of cemeteries for the area where the burial takes place, [3 and] the fees levied by a private grave-digger, in so far as it is necessary to incur those fees;

(b) where the deceased is cremated—

(i) the fees levied in respect of a cremation by the authority or person responsible for the provision and maintenance of crematoria for the area where the cremation takes place in so far as it is necessary to incur those fees;

(ii) [1 ...]

(iii) [1 ...]

(iv) the fee payable for the removal of any device as defined for the purposes of the Active Implantable Medical Devices Regulations 1992 save that, where that removal is carried out by a person who is not a registered medical practitioner, no more than £20 shall be met in respect of that fee;

[1(ba) the cost of obtaining any medical reference, report or other documentation required in connection with the disposal of the body of the deceased, whether by burial, cremation or otherwise;]

(c) the cost of obtaining any documentation, production of which is necessary in order to release any assets of the deceased which may be deducted from a funeral payment pursuant to regulation 10;

(d) where the deceased died at home or away from home and it is necessary to transport the deceased within the United Kingdom in excess of 80 kilometres (approximately 50 miles) to the funeral director's premises or to the place of rest, the reasonable cost of transport in excess of 80 kilometres;

(e) where transport is provided by a vehicle for the coffin and bearers and by one additional vehicle, from the funeral director's premises or the place of rest to the funeral and—

(i) the distance travelled, in the case of a funeral which consists of a burial where no costs have been incurred under sub-paragraph (a)(i) above, exceeds 80 kilometres; or

(ii) the distance travelled, in the case of any other funeral, necessarily exceeds 80 kilometres,

the reasonable cost of the transport provided, other than the cost in respect of the first 80 kilometres of the distance travelled;

(f) the necessary cost of one return journey for the responsible person, either for the purpose of making arrangements for, or for attendance at, the funeral; and

(g) any other funeral expenses which shall not exceed [2 £1,000] in any case.

(4) Paragraphs (2) and (3) have effect subject to the following provisions.

(5) Paragraph (3)(a) does not apply to costs in connection with burial of the deceased's ashes (where he was cremated).

(6) All references to 80 kilometres shall be construed as applying to—

(a) in a case to which paragraph (3)(d) applies, the combined distance from the funeral director's premises or the deceased's place of rest to the place of death and of the return journey;

(b) in a case to which paragraph (3)(e) applies, the combined distance from the funeral director's premises or the deceased's place of rest to the funeral and of the return journey.

(7) The cost of items and services referred to in paragraph (3)(a), (b), (d) and (e) shall not include any element in the cost of those items and services which relates to a requirement of the deceased's religious faith.

(8) Paragraph (3)(e)(i) includes costs only to the extent that, together with the costs referred to under paragraph (3)(a)(ii), they do not exceed the costs which would have been incurred under—

(a) paragraph (3)(a)(i) and (ii), and

(b) where appropriate, paragraph (3)(e)(ii),

if it had been necessary to purchase for the deceased a new burial plot [1 with a right of burial in that plot, whether or not that right is exclusive].

(9) Paragraph (3)(f) includes costs only to the extent that they do not exceed the costs which would have been incurred in respect of a return journey from the home of the responsible person to the location where the necessary costs of a burial or, as the case may be, cremation referred to in paragraph (3)(a) or (b) would have been incurred.

(10) Where items and services have been provided on the death of the deceased under a pre-paid funeral plan or under any analogous arrangement—

(a) no funeral payment shall be made in respect of items or services referred to in paragraph (3) which have been provided under such a plan or arrangement; and

(b) paragraph (3)(g) shall have effect in relation to that particular claim as if for the sum [2 £1,000], there were substituted the sum "£120".

AMENDMENTS

1. Social Fund Funeral Expenses Amendment Regulations 2018 (SI 2018/61) regs 3 and 6 (April 2, 2018).

2. Social Fund Funeral Expenses Payment (Coronavirus) (Amendment) Regulations 2020 (SI 2020/405) reg.2 (in relation to deaths occurring on or after April 8, 2020: see reg.3).

3. Social Fund and Social Security (Claims and Payments) (Amendment) Regulations 2020 (SI 2020/600) reg.2 (July 9, 2020).

GENERAL NOTE

Regulation 9 defines "relevant expenditure", i.e. the expenses that are eligible to be met by a funeral payment. Under para.(1) the amount of the funeral payment is the total relevant expenditure less any deduction that falls to be made under reg.10. 4.88

A payment can be made for the expenses that are listed in para.(3)(a)–(f) (except for those that have been met by a pre-paid funeral plan or similar arrangement (para.(10)(a)), together with up to £700 for other funeral expenses, or £120 if some of the funeral costs have been met under a pre-paid funeral plan or similar arrangement, (paras (3)(g) and (10)(b)). For funeral plans, see also reg.10(e) and the commentary on that provision.

It will be noted that some of sub-paras (a)–(f) in para.(3) contain an express limitation to "reasonable" costs and some do not (in others the word "necessary" is used). On a previous form of this provision *R(IS) 14/92* considered that the word "reasonable" should be read into the listed categories even where it was not expressed. But in *CIS/6818/1995* the Commissioner concluded that what was said about reasonableness in *R(IS) 14/92* was not an essential part of the decision. He expressed the view (which was also not necessary to his decision) that each sub-paragraph in what is now reg.8(3) contained its own complete test and that there was no room for any further conditions to be implied. In view of the quite specific nature of the items or services covered by para.(3)(a)–(f) it is suggested that the approach of *CIS/6818/1995* is to be preferred.

Any element in the burial or transport costs that relates to a requirement of the deceased's religious faith will not be met (para.(7))—see *CSIS/42/1996*, which held that a vigil is a requirement of the Roman Catholic faith.

Burial and cremation—paras 3(a) and (b)

Paragraph (3)(a)(i) allows "the necessary costs of purchasing a new burial plot for the deceased". The meaning of the word "necessary" in a predecessor of this paragraph was considered in *R(IS) 18/98*. The Commissioner decided that it implied that any expense over that which was properly required was to be excluded. However, its effect was not to require the purchase of the cheapest possible plot without regard to any other consideration. Account should be taken of the proximity to the deceased's residence while he was alive and of the deceased's religion, so that, for example a person of the Greek Orthodox faith was entitled to be buried in an area set aside for people of that faith. 4.89

A funeral payment may be awarded for the cost of either a cremation or a burial but not both. Costs in connection with the burial of cremated ashes are not eligible (para.(5)).

See also in this context *CIS/1335/2004* discussed in the commentary to reg.7(10) (above).

Transport costs—paras (3)(d)–(f)

4.90 Paragraphs (3)(d) and (e) allow certain transport costs for distances (i.e. the combined distance of the outward and return journey (para.(3)), in excess of 80km (about 50 miles) to be met. For the calculation of the 80km, see para.(6).

R(IS) 11/91 decided that the deceased's "home" in para.(3)(d) was the accommodation where he normally lived prior to his death, as opposed to his "home town".

Where the costs of transport and burial in an existing plot (i.e. usually away from where the deceased lived) exceed the purchase and burial costs of a new plot, plus any necessary transport costs (i.e. the costs of burying locally), para.(3)(e)(i) provides that such costs will be met up to the level of the local burial costs (para. (8))

Paragraph (3)(f) covers the necessary costs of one return journey for the responsible person for arranging the funeral or attending it. The journey is not restricted to a journey within the UK but see para.(9) which limits the costs that will be met to those of a return journey from the responsible person's home to the place where the "necessary" funeral costs would have been incurred (although the drafting is not entirely clear, it is understood that the intention is to restrict payment of travel costs to those that would have been incurred if the funeral had taken place in the UK). *CIS 16957/1996* decides that although sub-para.(f) refers to a "return journey" it did also apply where the claimant only undertook a single journey (her husband had died away from home and she had travelled home to attend the funeral). Others who are relatives of the deceased may be eligible for a community care grant for the cost of travel to and from a funeral in the UK (see Social Fund direction 4(b)(ii)). The applicant must be a member of a family containing a claimant in receipt of income support or income-based JSA.

Other expenses

4.91 The expenses to be covered by para.(3)(g) are not specified but will include items such as a funeral director's fees (including the cost of a coffin which cannot be met under either para.(3)(a) or (b)—see *CIS/2651/2003* and *CIS 2607/2003*), church fees or flowers. But there is no definition of funeral expenses and so any expense that is a funeral expense should be allowed. Thus, in *CIS/1345/2004*, Commissioner Williams held that "suitable funeral attire" might amount to a funeral expense within sub-para. (g). The test was not, as had been suggested by the Secretary of State, whether the expense was "wholly exclusively and necessarily required for the funeral". There was no basis in law for restricting the scope of the paragraph beyond the words actually used in the sub-para. The only tests for applying sub-para.(g) were:

"(i) Were the expenses in fact funeral expenses that took into account any relevant discounts?

(ii) If so, were the expenses met by the claimant or partner (or will they be)?

(iii) If so, were they of a nature covered by any of the provisions in regulation [9(3)(a) to (f)]?

(iv) If not, do they exceed the set sum?

If they do not, they are allowable."

It should be noted, however, that in *CIS/1924/2004*, Commissioner Fellner held that, although flowers were capable of amounting to a funeral expense within the sub-para., obituary notices and the cost of a memorial stone and flower container were not. There is a clear tension between these two decisions: if the *CIS/1345/2004* test had been applied to the items disallowed in *CIS/1924/2004*, it seems probable that some, at least, would have been allowed.

Under para.(3)(g) there is no limit on the funeral expenses that are to be met, other than the £1,000 ceiling. There is therefore nothing to prevent para.(3)(g) being used to pay for the cost of items or services in para.(3)(a)–(f) that have not been fully met or—as para.3(g) is not mentioned in para.(7)—to cover the cost of a religious requirement.

Payment of funeral expenses

A funeral payment will be made even if the costs have already been met by the claimant, his partner, or a person acting on their behalf. If the funeral costs have not been paid any funeral payment is to be made direct to the creditor—see reg.35(2) of the Claims and Payments Regulations. 4.92

Deductions from an award of a funeral payment

10.—(1) There shall be deducted from the amount of any award of funeral payment which would otherwise be payable— 4.93

(a) [4 subject to paragraph (1A)] the amount of any assets of the deceased which are available to the responsible person (on application or otherwise) or any other member of his family without probate or letters of administration, or (in Scotland) confirmation, having been granted;

(b) the amount of any lump sum due to the responsible person or any other member of his family on the death of the deceased by virtue of any insurance policy, occupational pension scheme or burial club, or any analogous arrangement;

[8 (c) . . .]

(d) the amount of any funeral grant, made out of public funds, in respect of the death of a person who was entitled to a war disablement pension;

(e) in relation to a pre-paid funeral plan or any analogous arrangement—

(i) where the plan or arrangement had not been paid for in full prior to the death of the deceased, the amount of any sum payable under that plan or arrangement in order to meet the deceased's funeral expenses;

(ii) where the plan or arrangement had been paid for in full prior to the death of the deceased, the amount of any allowance paid under that plan or arrangement in respect of funeral expenses.

[4 (1A) For the purposes of regulation 10(1)(a), arrears of the following benefits payable to the deceased as at the date of death are excluded from the assets of the deceased—

(a) attendance allowance under Part 3 of the Act;

(b) bereavement allowance under Part 2 of the Act;

(c) carer's allowance under Part 3 of the Act;

[9 (ca) carer support payment under the Carer's Assistance (Carer Support Payment) (Scotland) Regulations 2023;]

(d) child benefit under Part 9 of the Act;

(e) child tax credit under section 8 of the Tax Credits Act 2002(8);

(f) council tax benefit under Part 7 of the Act;

(g) disability living allowance under Part 3 of the Act;

(h) employment and support allowance under—

(i) Part 1 of the 2007 Act as amended by Schedule 3, and Part 1 of Schedule 14, to the 2012 Act (to remove references to an income-related allowance); or

(ii) Part 1 of the 2007 Act as it has effect apart from the amendments made by Schedule 3, and Part 1 of Schedule 14, to the 2012 Act;

(i) exceptionally severe disablement allowance under Part 5 of the Act;
(j) guardian's allowance under Part 3 of the Act;
(k) housing benefit under Part 7 of the Act;
(l) incapacity benefit under Part 2 of the Act;
(m) income support under Part 7 of the Act;
(n) industrial death benefit under Part 5 of the Act;
(o) industrial injuries disablement benefit under Part 5 of the Act;
(p) jobseeker's allowance under—

(i) the 1995 Act as amended by Part 1 of Schedule 14 to the 2012 Act (to remove references to an income-based allowance); or
(ii) the 1995 Act as it has effect apart from the amendments made by Part 1 of Schedule 14 to the 2012 Act;

(q) maternity allowance under Part 2 of the Act;
(r) personal independence payment under Part 4 of the 2012 Act;
(s) reduced earnings allowance under Part 5 of the Act;
(t) severe disablement allowance under Part 3 of the Act;
(u) state pension credit under section 1 of the State Pension Credit Act 2002;
(v) state retirement pension under Parts 2 or 3 of the Act;
[[6] (va) a state pension under Part 1 of the Pensions Act 2014;]
(w) universal credit under Part 1 of the 2012 Act;
(x) war disablement pension under an instrument specified in section 639(2) of the Income Tax (Earnings and Pensions) Act 2003(10) in respect of the death or disablement of any person;
(y) war widow's pension under an instrument specified in section 639(2) of the Income Tax (Earnings and Pensions) Act 2003 in respect of the death or disablement of any person;
(z) war widower's pension under an instrument specified in section 639(2) of the Income Tax (Earnings and Pensions) Act 2003 in respect of the death or disablement of any person;
(aa) widowed mother's allowance under Part 2 of the Act;
(bb) widowed parent's allowance under Part 2 of the Act;
(cc) widow's pension under Part 2 of the Act;
(dd) winter fuel payment under Part 8 of the Act;
(ee) working tax credit under section 10 of the Tax Credits Act 2002] [[5];
(ff) armed forces independence payment under the Armed Forces and Reserve Forces (Compensation Scheme) Order 2011.]

[[8] (2) . . .]
[[8] (3) . . .]

AMENDMENTS

1. Income-related Benefits (Amendment) (No.2) Regulations 2005 reg.8 (December 12, 2005).

2. Social Security (Miscellaneous Amendments) (No.2) Regulations 2010 (SI 2010/641) reg.7 (April 6, 2010).

3. Social Security (Miscellaneous Amendments) (No.3) Regulations 2011 (SI 2011/2425) reg.18 (October 31, 2011).

4. Social Fund (Maternity and Funeral Expenses) Amendment Regulations 2013 (SI 2013/247) reg.2 (April 1, 2013).

5. Armed Forces and Reserve Forces Compensation Scheme (Consequential Provisions: Subordinate Legislation) Order 2013 (SI 2013/591) art.7 and Sch. para.32 (April 8, 2013).
6. Pensions Act 2014 (Consequential, Supplementary and Incidental Amendments) Order 2015 (SI 2015/1985) art.27 (April 6, 2016).
7. Social Security (Emergency Funds) (Amendment) Regulations 2017 (SI 2017/689) reg.5 (June 19, 2017).
8. Social Fund Funeral Expenses Amendment Regulations 2018 (SI 2018/61) regs 3 and 7 (April 2, 2018).
9. Carer's Assistance (Carer Support Payment) (Scotland) Regulations 2023 (Consequential Amendments) Order 2023 (SI 2023/1218) art.16 (November 19, 2023).

General Note

The amounts listed in reg.10 are deducted from the amount calculated under reg.9. Those amounts do not include the value of the deceased's estate but, by virtue of s.78(4) of the Administration Act any funeral payment from the social fund may be recovered from the estate (i.e. not just those assets available to the responsible person without a grant of probate or letters of administration: see para.(1)(a)) as if it were a funeral expense—see further the commentary to s.78 in Vol.III. 4.94

Paragraph (1) specifies the amounts that are to be deducted.

Sub-paragraph (a): Under the Administration of Estates (Small Payments) Act 1965 certain sums can be distributed from the estate to beneficiaries without a grant of probate or letters of administration. The current limit is £5,000. In addition many statutes regulating Post Office and building society accounts, savings certificates, etc. (but not, after privatisation, Trustee Savings Bank accounts) allow payment to be made after the owner's death. There is a similar power for most social security benefits. One problem is that these provisions are generally merely permissive, so that payment cannot be demanded as of right. In *R(IS) 14/91* the Commissioner indicates that in straightforward cases it may be concluded that such an amount is available on application. However, the circumstances (e.g. some dispute between next of kin of equal status) may point to the opposite conclusion. *R(IS) 14/91* also decides that evidence of availability of assets from the date of death up to the date of the decision on the claim is relevant. Thus where the claim was made on the date of death, a sum of £1300 in the deceased's building society account was available, although the claimant did not obtain the money until a week later. Nor was that conclusion defeated by the fact that before the decision the claimant had distributed or spent most of the money. 4.95

In *PA v SSWP (SF)* [2010] UKUT 42 (AAC), the deceased left no partner or surviving close relatives. The funeral was arranged by his carer, who claimed a funeral payment as a close friend. That claim was refused, ultimately because he did not provide evidence of the deceased's estate, the Secretary of State drawing the inference that the amount available to the claimant was sufficient to extinguish any entitlement. Allowing the appeal, Judge Mesher pointed out that reg.10(1)(a) "does not contain a rule that the value of the deceased's estate or of any assets within the estate is always to be set against the amount of a funeral payment that would otherwise be awarded". It only applies where those assets are "available" and available "to the claimant or some member of this family". There was some evidence that the claimant had approached the deceased's bank to try to obtain the balance standing to the credit of his account. According to that evidence, Judge Mesher remarked (at para.11):

> "The bank said that if there was money in the account a cheque would be sent to the funeral directors. There was not in fact an indication that money would have been paid over to the claimant, a person apparently not entitled to any share of Mr O's estate and not an executor under a will or an administrator on intestacy. Nor was there a clear indication that such a person would be provided with a copy of the closing bank statement."

As there was no other evidence to suggest that the deceased had (or had in the past had) significant capital, and as the burden of proof on the issue was on the Secretary of State (para.14), Judge Mesher awarded the claimant a funeral payment on the basis that reg.10(1)(a) did not apply.

4.96 Funeral expenses are a first charge on the estate (*R(SB) 18/84*). If there are liquid assets in the estate, these may be immediately available for funeral expenses regardless of other debts. In *R(IS) 12/93* arrears of attendance allowance for the deceased were paid to the claimant as next of kin. The Commissioner holds that the arrears were available. Since they exceeded the cost of the funeral, no award was made.

However, from April 1, 2013, arrears of the benefits listed in para.(1A) (including attendance allowance) do not form part of the deceased's assets for these purposes and therefore no deduction can be made in respect of them under para.(1)(a).

In *TG v SSWP (SF)* [2015] UKUT 571 (AAC), the claimant made an internet transfer of £2,500 from his late mother's bank account to his own shortly before his mother died on a Sunday afternoon. However, as Sunday was not a business day, the deceased's bank statements did not show the money leaving her account until the following day. Whether or not the claimant was entitled to a funeral payment depended upon whether the sum of £2,500 was an asset of the deceased at the time of her death.

4.97 Judge Rowley accepted the Secretary of State's submission in support of the appeal that "... where a transfer is ordered prior to death, notwithstanding that the transaction does not clear until after the death, the funds which are the subject of the transfer are, generally speaking, no longer 'assets of the deceased' available to the responsible person". That proposition was subject to any contrary provision in the contractual arrangements between the deceased and her bank. However, there was no such provision in *TG*. Rather, the evidence from the bank was that when one of its customers transferred funds using internet banking the funds would be applied to the payee's account within minutes even if the transfer were made on a non-business day, and even though, in those circumstances, the payment would only show on the customer's statement as being paid on the next following business day.

The claimant said that his mother had owed him the money and that he had made the transfer on her instructions. However, the First-tier Tribunal did not accept that the transfer represented a genuine reimbursement of money owed to the claimant. Rather, it viewed the transaction as a means of reducing the mother's estate prior to her death. Judge Rowley held that the motivation behind the transfer was irrelevant. The question to be determined was whether there were assets of the deceased that were available to the responsible person. If the transfer was validly made, then the transferred assets did not fall within reg.10(1)(a).

4.98 *Sub-paragraph (b):* For this sub-paragraph to apply, the amount must be due to the claimant or a member of his family (defined in reg.3(1)). Due must mean legally due. Sometimes such a member will have a clear legal entitlement under an insurance policy or a pension scheme. Sometimes trustees may have a discretion as to who should be paid a lump sum. In these circumstances no amount can be legally due until the trustees have exercised that discretion.

In *PA v SSWP* [2010] UKUT 157 (AAC), the deceased's daughter had taken out insurance policies on her mother's life. In England and Wales children do not have an insurable interest in the lives of their parents and it was therefore arguable that the proceeds of those policies were not "due" within the meaning of subpara.(b). However, Judge Levenson held that the insurance company had accepted the premiums and a court (or the regulatory institutions of the insurance industry) would have enforced payment. Even if what the daughter had entered into could not technically be an "insurance policy" it was an "analogous arrangement" within the subparagraph.

Where a policy has become fully-paid up, and could have been, but was not, encashed before the deceased's death the test is whether the proceeds of the policy were due and paid on a triggering event other than the death: see *PA* (above) and *SSWP v GB (IS)* [2020] UKUT 316 (AAC).

Sub-paragraph (c): Until April 1, 2018, any contribution towards funeral expenses which had been actually been received by the claimant or a family member from a charity or a relative of the claimant or the deceased was deducted from any funeral payment. See pp.1566-1567 of Vol.II of the 2017/18 edition for commentary on the former provision. The rule was revoked by SI 2018/61 with effect from April 2, 2018. The fact that no charitable payments are now deducted from a funeral payment means that it is no longer necessary to have specific disregards for payments from the charities formerly listed in para.(2) and defined in para.(3). Those paragraphs were therefore also revoked. **4.99**

Sub-paragraph (d): This paragraph is straightforward. **4.100**

Sub-paragraph (e): Any amount payable under a pre-paid funeral plan or similar arrangement will be deducted. In order to avoid a double deduction, it is necessary to interpret this deduction as applying when a funeral plan pays a cash benefit to the responsible person or other relative of the deceased and reg.9(10) as applying where payment under the plan has been made direct to the funeral director. This interpretation is supported by the use of the words "[w]here items and services have been provided . . . under a pre-paid funeral plan . . ." in reg.9(10). **4.101**

Paragraph (1A): Arrears of these benefits that had not been paid to the deceased at the date of her/his death do not count as "assets of the deceased" for the purposes of the rule in para.(1)(a). **4.102**

The Social Fund Maternity Grant Amendment Regulations 2012

(SI 2012/1814)

Made by the Secretary of State for Work and Pensions under ss.138(1)(a) and (4) and 175(1), (3) and (4) of the Social Security Contributions and Benefits Act 1992, the Social Security Advisory Committee having agreed that proposals in respect of these regulations should not be referred to it.

GENERAL NOTE

See the commentary to reg.5A of the Social Fund Maternity and Funeral Expenses (General) Regulations 2005 (above). **4.103**

Citation, commencement and interpretation

1.—(1) These Regulations may be cited as the Social Fund Maternity Grant Amendment Regulations 2012. **4.104**

(2) They come into force on 13th August 2012.

(3) In these Regulations, "the principal Regulations" means the Social Fund Maternity and Funeral Expenses (General) Regulations 2005 and expressions defined in those Regulations have the same meaning in these Regulations.

Amendment of the principal Regulations

2.—*[For the amendments made by reg.2, see reg.5A of the Social Fund Maternity and Funeral Expenses (General) Regulations 2005]* **4.105**

Transitional provisions

4.106 **3.**—(1) The substitution made by regulation 2 does not apply in a case where any of paragraphs (2) to (7) apply.

(2) This paragraph applies in a case where—

(a) the claimant falls within regulation 5(3)(a) of the principal Regulations;

(b) the claim is made before C's birth;

(c) the claim is made before 13th August 2012; and

(d) the expected date of confinement is before 29th October 2012.

(3) This paragraph applies in a case where—

(a) the claimant falls within regulation 5(3)(a) or (b) of the principal Regulations;

(b) the claim is made after C's birth; and

(c) C is born before 29th October 2012.

(4) This paragraph applies in a case where—

(a) the claimant falls within regulation 5(3)(c) of the principal Regulations; and

(b) the qualifying order is made before 29th October 2012.

(5) This paragraph applies in a case where—

(a) the claimant falls within regulation 5(3)(d) of the principal Regulations; and

(b) the appointment as guardian takes effect before 29th October 2012.

(6) This paragraph applies in a case where—

(a) the claimant falls within regulation 5(3)(e) of the principal Regulations; and

(b) C is placed for adoption with the claimant or the claimant's partner before 29th October 2012.

(7) This paragraph applies in a case where—

(a) the claimant falls within regulation 5(3)(f) of the principal Regulations; and

(b) the adoption referred to in that provision takes effect before 29th October 2012.

(8) In this regulation, "C" means the child or still-born child in respect of whom a Sure Start Maternity Grant is claimed.

The Social Security (Scotland) Act 2018 (Best Start Grants) (Consequential Modifications and Saving) Order 2018

(SI 2018/1138)

Made by the Secretary of State under sections 104 and 113(4) and (5) of the Scotland Act 1998(1).

[In force December 10, 2018]

PART 1

INTRODUCTORY

Citation, commencement and extent

1.—(1) This Order may be cited as the Social Security (Scotland) Act 2018 (Best Start Grants) (Consequential Modifications and Saving) Order 2018. **4.107**

(2) This Order comes into force immediately after the coming into force of the first Regulations made under section 32 of the Social Security (Scotland) Act 2018.

(3) Each amendment made by this Order has the same extent as the provision to which it relates.

GENERAL NOTE

The first Regulations made under s.32 of the Social Security (Scotland) Act 2018 were the Early Years Assistance (Best Start Grants) (Scotland) Regulations 2018 (SSI 2018/370)—see Pt XIII of Vol.IV of this series—which came into force on December 10, 2018. **4.108**

PART 2

AMENDMENTS AND SAVING IN RELATION TO SURE START MATERNITY GRANTS

Interpretation

2. In this Part, "the 2005 Regulations" means the Social Fund Maternity and Funeral Expenses (General) Regulations 2005(3). **4.109**

Amendment of the 2005 Regulations

3. *[Omitted]* **4.110**

Saving in relation to the amendment of the 2005 Regulations

4.—(1) The amendments made to the 2005 Regulations in article 3 are of no effect in relation to a claim for Sure Start Maternity Grant made before the date on which the first Regulations made under section 32 of the Social Security (Scotland) Act 2018 come into force. **4.111**

(2) In paragraph (1), "Sure Start Maternity Grant" has the meaning given in the 2005 Regulations.

The Social Security (Scotland) Act 2018 (Funeral Expense Assistance and Early Years Assistance) (Consequential Modifications and Savings) Order 2019

(SI 2019/1060)

Made by the Secretary of State under sections 104 and 113(2), (4) and (5) of the Scotland Act 1998.

[In force September 16, 2019]

Articles Reproduced

Part 1

Introductory

Part 2

Amendments and Savings in Relation to Funeral Payments

PART 1

Introductory

Citation, commencement and extent

4.113 **1.**—(1) This Order may be cited as the Social Security (Scotland) Act 2018 (Funeral Expense Assistance and Early Years Assistance) (Consequential Modifications and Savings) Order 2019.

(2) This Order comes into force as follows:

(a) [*Omitted as relating to Northern Ireland*]

(b) all other provisions, immediately after the coming into force of the first Regulations made under section 34 of the Social Security (Scotland) Act 2018.

(3) Each amendment made by this Order has the same extent as the provision being amended.

General Note

The first Regulations made under s.34 of the Social Security (Scotland) Act 2018 were the Funeral Expense Assistance (Scotland) Regulations 2019 (SSI 2019/292) which came into force on September 16, 2019 (see Pt XIII of Vol.IV of this series). 4.114

PART 2

Amendments and savings in relation to funeral payments

Interpretation

2. In this Part: 4.115

(a) the "2005 Regulations" means the Social Fund Maternity and Funeral Expenses (General) Regulations 2005;
(b) [*Omitted as relating to Northern Ireland*]

Amendment of the 2005 Regulations

3. [*Omitted: see the amended text of reg.4 and reg.7 of the 2005 Regulations (above)*] 4.116

Saving in relation to the amendments of the 2005 Regulations

4.—(1) The amendments made to the 2005 Regulations in article 3 are of no effect in relation to a claim for a funeral payment made before the date on which the first Regulations made under section 34 of the Social Security (Scotland) Act 2018 come into force. 4.117

(2) In paragraph (1), "funeral payment" has the meaning given in regulation 7(1)(a) of the 2005 Regulations.

The Social Fund (Children's Funeral Fund for England) Regulations 2019

(SI 2019/1064)

[In force July 23, 2019]

Made by the Secretary of State under sections 138(1)(a) and (4) and 175(1), (3), (4) and (5) of the Social Security Contributions and Benefits Act 1992, and sections 1(1) and (1C), and 5(1)(a), (i) and (j), and (1A), and 189(1), (4), (5), (5A) and (5B) of the Social Security Administration Act 1992, the Social Security Advisory Committee having agreed under section 173(1)(b) of the Social Security Administration Act 1992, that the proposals in respect of these Regulations should not be referred to it.

Arrangement Of Regulations

General Note

4.119 These Regulations establish a "Children's Funeral Fund payment" (a "CFF payment"), which is a new type of funeral payment from the social fund. It is payable if the person who has died was under the age of 18 at the date of his or her death (reg.3(1)(a)(i), or a stillborn child as defined (reg.3(1)(a)(ii)), and the funeral takes place in England on or after 23 July 2019 (reg.3(1)(b)). The payment is to be the amount of any fees charged by a burial or cremation authority or of any associated expenses (reg.3(4)). "Fees charged by a burial or cremation authority" are defined in reg.4 and "associated expenses" in reg.5. Both regulations contain an anti-abuse provision that restricts the amount payable to "what the Secretary of State considers to be reasonable in the circumstances" (regs 4(2) and 5(2)) Further, no payment can be made in respect of "any element which relates exclusively to a requirement of the religious faith of the deceased or the family of the deceased" (regs 4(3) and 5(3)).

CFF payments have two notable new features. First, there is no means-testing. A payment can be made if the requirements of regs 3-6 are met irrespective of the income and assets of the person who has died and of his or her parents. Second, a claim for fees charged by a burial or cremation authority may *only* be made by the burial or cremation authority that charges those fees. Claims for "associated expenses" may be made by a burial authority, a cremation authority, a funeral director, or "the person responsible for the purchase of a listed item". Given the nature of associated expenses, the person responsible for the purchase is likely to be the funeral director unless the funeral is arranged privately. The time limit for making a claim is the same as for a funeral payment under the Social Fund Maternity and Funeral Expenses (General) Regulations 2005 (see reg.2(1) of the Claims and Payments Regulations 1979 as amended by reg.7).

Regulation 6 contains provisions against double payment. Under para.(1), there is an absolute bar on more than one CFF payment being made for the same listed item. Para.(2), together with the amended reg.4 of the 2005 Regulations and reg.8(5) of the Funeral Expense Assistance (Scotland) Regulations 2019 (SSI 2019/292, Part XIII of Vol.IV of this series), govern how the main funeral expenses scheme for England and Wales and the funeral expense assistance scheme in Scotland interrelate.

Note, finally, that in Wales a contribution of £500 towards the funeral costs of a child can be claimed when registering the child's death: see further *https://gov.wales/child-funeral-and-other-related-costs-information-html.*

Citation, commencement and extent

4.120 **1.**—(1) These Regulations may be cited as the Social Fund (Children's Funeral Fund for England) Regulations 2019 and come into force on 23rd July 2019.

(2) Subject to paragraph (3), these Regulations extend to England and Wales only.

(3) Regulations 7 and 8 extend to England and Wales, and Scotland.

Interpretation

2. In these Regulations— 4.121

"associated expenses" means the expenses referred to in regulation 5;

"burial authority" means a person responsible for the management of a burial ground;

"claimant" means—

(a) with respect to claims in relation to fees charged by a burial or cremation authority, the burial authority or cremation authority in question;

(b) with respect to claims in relation to associated expenses, a burial authority, a cremation authority, a funeral director, or the person responsible for the purchase of a listed item;

"cremation authority" means a person responsible for the management of a crematorium;

"fees charged by a burial or cremation authority" means the fees referred to in regulation 4;

"funeral" means erecting a memorial in a case where there is no body, or the burial or cremation of a body (whether or not the burial or cremation is accompanied by the erection of a memorial);

"listed item" means an item or service referred to in regulation 4(1) or regulation 5(1);

"qualifying age" means an age less than 18 years old.

Entitlement

3.—(1) A claimant is entitled to a Children's Funeral Fund payment in relation to a funeral, where— 4.122

(a) the deceased was—

(i) of qualifying age at the time of death; or

(ii) a stillborn child as defined in section 41 of the Births and Deaths Registration Act 1953, born after the 24th week of pregnancy;

(b) the funeral takes place in England on or after 23rd July 2019; and

(c) were it not for these Regulations, those fees or expenses would be chargeable to a person involved in the organisation of the funeral.

(2) Section 1(1A) of the Social Security Administration Act 1992 (the requirement to provide evidence of a national insurance number in order to make a claim) is disapplied in relation to a claim for a Children's Funeral Fund payment.

(3) Subject to regulation 6, a claimant may be awarded more than one Children's Funeral Fund payment in relation to a funeral.

(4) In this regulation, a "Children's Funeral Fund payment" means a payment out of the social fund in the amount of any fees charged by a burial or cremation authority or of any associated expenses.

DEFINITIONS

"claimant"—see reg.2.
"cremation authority"—*ibid.*
"fees charged by a burial or cremation authority"—see regs 2 and 4.
"funeral"—see reg.2.
"qualifying age"—*ibid.*

Fees charged by a burial or cremation authority

4.123 **4.**—(1) Fees charged by a burial or cremation authority are—

(a) where the deceased is buried—

(i) the fees for obtaining a burial plot and a right of burial for the deceased in that plot, whether or not that right is exclusive;

(ii) the fees levied in respect of a burial by the burial authority or the person responsible for the provision and maintenance of cemeteries for the area where the burial takes place;

(b) where the deceased is cremated—

(i) the fees levied in respect of the cremation by the cremation authority or person responsible for the provision and maintenance of crematoria for the area where the cremation takes place;

(ii) fees levied for a private post mortem examination where this is necessary for the cremation to be authorised;

(c) the fees levied for the scattering of ashes;

(d) the fees levied for the burial of ashes;

(e) the fees levied for the storage of ashes in a columbarium or similar receptacle until the point where the deceased, if alive, would have ceased to be of qualifying age;

(f) the fees levied in respect of obtaining permission to erect a memorial;

(g) where it is a condition of the right of burial, the maintenance fees of the place of burial until the point where the deceased, if alive, would have ceased to be of qualifying age;

(h) fees levied for renewal of the right of exclusive use of the burial plot until the point where the deceased, if alive, would have ceased to be of qualifying age;

(i) any other fees the Secretary of State considers to be appropriate.

(2) Fees charged by a burial or cremation authority are limited to what the Secretary of State considers to be reasonable in the circumstances.

(3) Fees charged in accordance with paragraph (1) must not include any element which relates exclusively to a requirement of the religious faith of the deceased or the family of the deceased.

DEFINITIONS

"burial authority"—see reg.2.
"cremation authority"—*ibid.*
"qualifying age"—*ibid.*

Associated expenses

4.124 **5.**—(1) Associated expenses are—

(a) where the deceased is buried, the fees levied by a private grave-digger, inclusive of the fees levied for the removal and replacement of headstones and kerbing;

(b) where the deceased is cremated—

(i) the fees payable for the removal of any active implantable medical device as defined in regulation 2 of the Medical Devices Regulations 2002 save that, where that removal is carried out by a person who is not a registered medical practitioner no more than £20 may be met in respect of that removal;

(ii) the fees levied for the completion of cremation certification;

(c) the price of a coffin, shroud, or casket in which the deceased is buried or cremated;

(d) the price of an appropriate receptacle for storage of cremated remains where the receptacle in which the cremated remains are returned is unsuitable for this purpose.

(2) Associated expenses are limited to what the Secretary of State considers to be reasonable in the circumstances.

(3) Associated expenses charged in accordance with paragraph (1) must not include any element which relates exclusively to a requirement of the religious faith of the deceased or the family of the deceased.

Provisions against double payment

6.—(1) No payment may be made for a listed item under these Regulations where a payment has already been made under these Regulations for that listed item in relation to the same funeral. **4.125**

(2) No payment may be made for a listed item under these Regulations if—

(a) a payment for the listed item has been made in respect of funeral expenses arising from the death of the same person under the Social Fund Maternity and Funeral Expenses (General) Regulations 2005; or

(b) a payment for the listed item has been made in respect of funeral expenses arising from the death of the same person under Regulations made under section 34 of the Social Security (Scotland) Act 2018,

unless the amount paid under those Regulations is less than the total amount charged for the listed item, in which case a payment may be made for an amount not exceeding the remainder of the amount charged for the listed item.

Amendment of the Social Fund Maternity and Funeral Expenses (General) Regulations 2005

7. [*Omitted: see reg.4 (Provision against double payment: funeral expenses) of the 2005 Regulations, above.*] **4.126**

Amendment of the Social Security (Claims and Payments) Regulations 1987

8. [*Omitted: see reg.2(1) (Interpretation) of the 1987 Regulations in Vol.III.*] **4.127**

PART V

PERSONS SUBJECT TO IMMIGRATION CONTROL

The Social Security (Immigration and Asylum) Consequential Amendments Regulations 2000

(SI 2000/636) (AS AMENDED)

Made by the Secretary of State under ss.115(3), (4) and (7), 1235) and (6), 166(3) and 167 of the Immigration and Asylum Act 1999, ss.64(1), 68(4), 70(4), 71(6), 123(1)(a), (d) and (e), 135(1), 136(3) and (4), 137(1) and (2) (i) and 175(1), (3) and (4) of the Social Security Contributions and Benefits Act 1992, ss.5(1)(a) and (b), 189(1) and (4) and 191 of the Social Security Administration Act 1992, ss.12(1) and (2), 35(1) and 36(2) and (4) of the Jobseekers Act 1995

[In force April 3, 2000]

GENERAL NOTE

The United Kingdom's withdrawal from the European Union

The United Kingdom left the European Union on January 31, 2020 at 11.00 pm and the transitional "Implementation Period" during which EU law continued to apply ended on December 31, 2020 at 11.00 pm. These Regulations are reproduced below as they are worded with effect from January 1, 2021. For the law that applied during the Implementation Period, see pp.913–926 of Vol.V of the 2020/21 edition.

Persons subject to immigration control 5.1

These regulations are made under s.115 of the Immigration and Asylum Act 1999 (see Part I above), which excludes "persons subject to immigration control" from entitlement to specified non-contributory benefits (including universal credit). Regulation 2 and the Schedule provide for exceptions to that exclusion. The combined effect of those provisions is as follows.

"Person subject to immigration control" is defined by s.115(9). Note first of all that a British citizen can never be a person subject to immigration control for social security purposes—*R(PC)2/07*. Until December 31, 2020 at 11.00 pm, neither could EEA nationals, but that is no longer the case. Except for those EEA nationals with transitional protection under SI 2020/1209 (see further Vol.V), the rules for EEA nationals are the same as for nationals of any other country outside the Common Travel Area.

Nationals of such countries are subject to immigration control if they are within one of the following four categories:

(a) A person who requires leave to enter or remain in the UK but does not have it

This category (s.115(9)(a)) covers illegal entrants, overstayers, people who are 5.2
subject to a deportation order, those allowed temporary admission to the UK and, subject to *R(SB) 11/88* (below), anyone whose immigration status has yet to be determined (other than those EEA nationals with transitional protection under SI 2020/1209 (see further Vol.V)). It does not apply to EEA nationals who have settled or pre-settled status because both groups have leave to remain which does not fall within s.115(9)(b)–(d) (albeit for a limited period in the case of those with pre-settled status).

The practice of the Home Office is to grant temporary admission to asylum seekers (except those who are detained) pending investigation of their claims (see *CIS/3108/97*). Section 115 therefore has the effect of excluding all asylum seekers from benefit. Asylum seekers who are destitute will instead receive support from a Home Office agency, the National Asylum Support Service, under ss.95–100 of the Immigration and Asylum Act.

For social security purposes, whether or not a person requires leave to enter or remain in the UK is a matter for the decision-maker (or, on appeal, for the First-tier Tribunal or Upper Tribunal) to determine and any decision by the Home Office is not binding (*R(SB) 11/88* but see *R(SB) 2/85* and *R(SB) 25/85* as to the terms on which leave is granted).

By s.3ZA(1) of the Immigration Act 1971, an Irish national does not require leave to enter or remain in the UK unless directions have been given under section 3ZA(2) (which permits exclusion where the Home Secretary decides it is "conducive to the public good") or s/he is an "excluded person" for the purposes of section 8B. Nationals of the Isle of Man and the Channel Islands have freedom of travel within the UK and do not require leave to enter (Immigration Act 1971 s.1(3)).

For the position where leave to enter or remain-or British citizenship-is obtained by fraud, see the decisions of the Upper Tribunal in *R v HMRC and Kirklees Metropolitan BC (CH & CTC)* [2020] UKUT 379 (Judge Hemingway) and *ED v SSWP* [2020] UKUT 352 (AAC) (Judge Perez).

(b) A person who has leave to enter or remain but subject to a condition that he does not have recourse to public funds

5.3 Limited leave to enter or remain subject to there being no recourse to public funds is given under s.33(1) of the Immigration Act 1971. From April 6, 2016, "public funds" are defined by rule 6 of the Immigration Rules as attendance allowance, severe disablement allowance, carer's allowance, disability living allowance, income support, (the former) council tax benefit and housing benefit, a social fund payment, child benefit, income-based JSA, income-related ESA, state pension credit, child tax credit, working tax credit, universal credit, personal independence payment, council tax reduction, certain publicly funded housing, and payments from local welfare funds under s.1 of the Localism Act 2011, the Welfare Funds (Scotland) Act 2015, or regulations made under art.135 of the Welfare Reform (Northern Ireland) Order 2015. Note however the clarifications of that definition in rules 6A–6C, as follows:

> "6A. For the purpose of these Rules, a person (P) is not to be regarded as having (or potentially having) recourse to public funds merely because P is (or will be) reliant in whole or in part on public funds provided to P's sponsor unless, as a result of P's presence in the United Kingdom, the sponsor is (or would be) entitled to increased or additional public funds (save where such entitlement to increased or additional public funds is by virtue of P and the sponsor's joint entitlement to benefits under the regulations referred to in paragraph 6B).
>
> 6B. Subject to paragraph 6C, a person (P) shall not be regarded as having recourse to public funds if P is entitled to benefits specified under section 115 of the Immigration and Asylum Act 1999 by virtue of regulations made under subsections (3) and (4) of that section or section 42 of the Tax Credits Act 2002. For an example of this principle, see *OD v SSWP (JSA)* [2015] UKUT 0438 (AAC).
>
> 6C. A person (P) making an application from outside the United Kingdom will be regarded as having recourse to public funds where P relies upon the future entitlement to any public funds that would be payable to P or to P's sponsor as a result of P's presence in the United Kingdom, (including those benefits to which P or the sponsor would be entitled as a result of P's presence in the United Kingdom under the regulations referred to in to paragraph 6B)."

The circumstances in which a "no recourse to public funds" condition will be imposed are set out in Appendix FM to the Immigration Rules. In *R. (on the application of W (A Child)) v Secretary of State for the Home Department* [2020] EWHC 1299 (Admin), the Divisional Court (Bean LJ and Chamberlain J) summarised the provisions of that Appendix as follows:

> "16. As a result [*i.e.*, of the events set out earlier in the judgment], the criteria for deciding whether to impose or lift the NRPF condition were included in the

Immigration Rules. That was done by way of amendment to Appendix FM to the Immigration Rules. Appendix FM provides a number of bases on which a person may be granted LTR with a view to eventual settlement by virtue of a connection with a family member who is a British citizen, settled in the UK or a refugee or person entitled to humanitarian protection. There are separate provisions governing applications for entry clearance or LTR as a partner (D-ECP and D-LTRP), a child (D-ECC and DLTRC) and a parent (D-ECPT and D-LTRPT) of such a person. The rules for those applying as partners and parents stipulate that entry clearance or LTR, if granted, will be subject to a condition of NRPF "unless the decision-maker considers, with reference to paragraph GEN 1.11A, that the applicant should not be subject to such a condition". The rules for those applying as children provide that the child will be subject to the same condition as the parent.

17. Paragraph GEN 1.11A provides as follows:

> "Where entry clearance or leave to remain as a partner, child or parent is granted under paragraph D-ECP.1.2., D-LTRP.1.2., D-ECC.1.1., DLTRC.1.1., D-ECPT.1.2. or D-LTRPT.1.2., it will normally be granted subject to a condition of no recourse to public funds, unless the applicant has provided the decision-maker with:
> (a) satisfactory evidence that the applicant is destitute as defined in section 95 of the Immigration and Asylum Act 1999; or
> (b) satisfactory evidence that there are particularly compelling reasons relating to the welfare of a child of a parent in receipt of a very low income."

In *Re W*, the Divisional Court held (at [73]) that:

> "The NRPF regime ... [does] not adequately recognise, reflect or give effect to the Secretary of State's obligation not to impose, or to lift, the condition of NRPF in cases where the applicant is not yet, but will imminently suffer inhuman or degrading treatment [*i.e.*, by becoming destitute] without recourse to public funds. In its current form the NRPF regime is apt to mislead caseworkers in this critical respect and gives rise to a real risk of unlawful decisions in a significant number of cases. To that extent it is unlawful."

It is suggested, however, that it is not open to a tribunal to decide on an appeal against a decision refusing a social security benefit on the basis that the claimant is a person subject to immigration control, that a no recourse to public funds condition that has in fact been imposed, should not have been: see *R(SB) 2/85* and *R(SB) 25/85* below. Such an argument must be pursued by an appeal against the immigration decision or by judicial review. However, different considerations potentially apply following the decision of a Divisional Court of the Queen's Bench Division in *ST and VW v Secretary of State for the Home Department* [2021] EWHC 1085 (Admin) which declared that the No Recourse to Public Funds Scheme as a whole does not comply with s.55 of the Borders, Citizenship and Immigration Act 2009.

For this category (s.115(9)(b)) and the following two (s.115(9)(c) and (d)) to apply, it is necessary that the person should actually require leave to enter or remain in the UK. So, for example, if the Home Office mistakenly grants conditional leave to a person who is in fact a British citizen and does not require leave at all, the mistake does not cause that person to become subject to immigration control for social security purposes (see *R(SB) 11/88*). However, where leave is required, the decision of the Home Office as to the terms on which leave is granted is conclusive (see *R(SB) 2/85* and *R(SB) 25/85*). A proper statement of the terms of leave should be obtained from the Home Office (*CSSB/137/82*).

Until October 28, 2013 there was one exception to the exclusion from benefit in s.115(9)(b). However, that exception was abolished with effect from October

29, 2013, by reg.9(1) and (3) of the Social Security (Miscellaneous Amendments) (No.3) Regulations 2013 (SI 2013/2536). For details of the law as it stood before that date, see pp.375, 800–801 and 809–810 of Vol.II of the 2013/14 edition.

(c) A person who has leave to enter or remain which was given as a result of a maintenance undertaking

5.4 "Maintenance undertaking" is defined by s.115(10) as "a written undertaking given by another person in pursuance of the immigration rules to be responsible for [the claimant's] maintenance and accommodation". Under r.35 of the Immigration Rules such undertakings may be demanded from "a sponsor of a person seeking leave to enter or variation of leave to enter or remain in the United Kingdom" but are normally only required from the sponsors of elderly or other dependent relatives.

Rule 6 defines "sponsor" as meaning:

> "the person in relation to whom an applicant is seeking leave to enter or remain as their spouse, fiancé, civil partner, proposed civil partner, unmarried partner, same-sex partner or dependent relative, as the case may be, under paragraphs 277 to 295O or 317 to 319 or the person in relation to whom an applicant is seeking entry clearance or leave as their partner or dependent relative under Appendix FM."

A promise of support given by someone who is not a "sponsor" as so defined cannot amount to a "maintenance undertaking" for the purposes of s.115(10) or para.3 of the Schedule: see *Leeds City Council v EO (HB)* [2019] UKUT 96 (AAC).

The purpose of the undertaking is to reinforce a condition that the person seeking leave to enter or remain should not have recourse to public funds by

- demonstrating that the sponsor has sufficient resources to maintain and accommodate the relative without the latter claiming public funds; and
- making the sponsor legally "liable to maintain" the relative. This has the effect that, if the Secretary of State does for any reason have to pay income support to the relative (and, in most cases, the mere existence of an undertaking will mean that the relative has no such entitlement), the sponsor may, in certain circumstances, be subject to a criminal penalty and the Secretary of State may recoup the benefit paid by making a complaint in a magistrates' court (see, respectively ss.105 and 106 of the SSAA 1992 in Vol.III).

The requirement in the definition that the undertaking has been given "in pursuance of the immigration rules" cannot mean "in pursuance of a requirement in the immigration rules" because the decision whether to ask for an undertaking is a discretionary one. Rather, it means "under" or "further to" the immigration rules, see *CIS/1697/2004*, paras 41 and 42. In that case, the Deputy Commissioner held that it was sufficient that the sponsor was making a promise in furtherance of the claimant's application for indefinite leave to remain.

It is not necessary that the undertaking should be given on one of the official Home Office forms (either Form RON 112 or the Form SET(F) that replaced it)—see *R. (Begum) v Social Security Commissioner* [2003] EWHC 3380 (QB), QBD (Sir Christopher Bellamy), November 6, 2003 confirming *CIS/2474/1999*, *CIS/2816/2002* and, on this point, *CIS/47/2002*. Those forms "are expressly in the language of undertaking and emphasise the significance of such undertakings" (see Rix LJ at [36] of *Ahmed v Secretary of State for Work & Pensions* [2005] EWCA Civ 535, CA (May, Rix and Jacob LJJ), April 19, 2005 (reported as *R(IS) 8/05*). But if an official form is not used, consideration may need to be given to whether the document signed by the sponsor amounts to an "undertaking" at all. In *Ahmed* the Court of Appeal held (upholding the Commissioner in *CIS/426/2003* and disagreeing, on this point, with the Commissioner in *CIS/47/2002* in which the disputed document was in similar terms) that the issue is one of substance rather than form and that the legal test is whether or not the document contains a promise or agreement about what the sponsor will do in the future rather than a statement about his or her present abilities and intentions:

> "**47.** . . . It seems to me that an undertaking has to be something in the nature of a promise or agreement and the language that 'I am able and willing to maintain and accommodate' is language which has reference, essentially, to current ability and intention and does not amount to a promise for the future. The essence of an undertaking is a promise as to the future, as typically found in the language 'I will.'
>
> **48.** I accept that the use of any particular language is not a condition precedent. The absence of an express reference to 'I undertake', such as is found in the Home Office's forms, or to 'I promise' or 'I agree', will not necessarily be critical if it is still clear that the substance of what is said is a promise for the future." (per Rix LJ)

So, the declaration in the *Ahmed* case that the sponsor was "able and willing to maintain and accommodate the applicant without recourse to public funds and in suitable accommodation" was not an undertaking because it only related to present facts and intentions. For a further example (in which the opposite conclusion was reached on the facts) see *CIS/1697/2004.* That decision also holds that neither a Commissioner, nor (by necessary implication) a tribunal, has any power to grant rectification of a defective maintenance undertaking . **5.5**

In *CIS 3508/2001* it was held that leave to enter or remain was given "as a result of" a maintenance undertaking if the existence of that undertaking was a factor in the decision to grant leave. It does not have to be the only, or even a major, factor. It is sufficient that it was of some relevance. It seems that that will almost always be the case if the immigration decision-maker acts within the Immigration Rules. In *Shah v Secretary of State for Work and Pensions* [2002] EWCA Civ 285 (reported as *R(IS) 2/02)*, the Court of Appeal held that a maintenance undertaking should be regarded as a continuing obligation and therefore applied even if the claimant had left the UK (thereby causing his or her indefinite leave to remain to lapse) and had been made a fresh grant of indefinite leave to remain as a returning resident on his or her return. *Shah* was decided under the pre-April 2000 law, but it is suggested that the same principles also apply to s.115(9)(c).

Under the principles set out by the House of Lords in *Kerr v Department for Social Development* [2004] UKHL 23; *R1/04 (SF)*, it is for the Secretary of State to show that the maintenance undertaking was a factor in the decision to grant leave: see *R(PC) 1/09.* In that case, where the decision to grant leave was made outside the Immigration Rules, the causal connection could not be inferred and had not been established: see also *SSWP v SS (SPC)* [2010] UKUT 485 (AAC) and *SJ v SSWP* [2015] UKUT 505 (AAC).

People who are granted leave to enter or remain as a result of a maintenance undertaking are not entitled to income support or income-based JSA until they have been resident in the UK for a period of at least five years from the date of entry or the date on which the undertaking was given, whichever is later. The only exceptions are where the sponsored immigrant becomes a British citizen during the five-year period (see *R(PC) 2/07*) and where the person (or all the people if there was more than one) who gave the maintenance undertaking has died before the end of the five-year period. See para.3 of Pt I of the Schedule. The five years' residence need not be continuous: it can be made up of shorter periods (see paras 74–75 of the Commissioner's decision in *R(IS) 2/02*). In *CPC/1035/2005* the Commissioner considered the position of a Pakistani national who had been given leave to enter the UK under a maintenance undertaking. Since entering the UK in October 1996, she had returned to Pakistan for periods of 17 months, nearly 14 months and 21 months in order to look after her parents. In July 2004, over 7½ years after she first entered, she claimed—and, in August 2004, was refused—SPC. The Commissioner upheld that refusal. Although it was not necessary for the claimant to be physically present in the UK in order to be resident here, "whether a person is or is not resident in a particular place during a period of physical absence depends on a calculus consisting of the duration and circumstances of the absence". Some absences affect residence simply on account of their length. Each period of absence had to be considered individually but none of the periods listed above, not even the shortest, was compatible with the claimant remaining resident in the UK. It followed that as the claimant had not been resident in the UK for nearly 58 months (4 years and 10 months) of the period between October 1996 and August 2004, she had not been resident for a total of five years since the date of her entry and was therefore still excluded from benefit.

Sponsored immigrants are not excluded from social fund payments (see para.4 of Pt II of the Schedule) but in practice are unlikely to be eligible for anything other than a winter fuel payment. This is because, as persons subject to immigration control, they are excluded from the qualifying benefits for maternity and funeral expenses payments, budgeting loans and cold weather payments. Sponsored immigrants are also not excluded from entitlement to attendance allowance, severe disablement allowance, (the former) health in pregnancy grants, carer's allowance, disability living allowance, personal independence payment or child benefit.

(d) A person who has leave to enter or remain only because he is appealing against certain immigration decisions

5.6 Section 115(9)(d) provides that a person who "has leave to enter or remain in the United Kingdom only as a result of paragraph 17 of Schedule 4 [*i.e.*, Sch.4 to the Immigration and Asylum Act 1999 itself]" is a person subject to immigration control. Para.17 of Sch.4 was repealed by Sch.9, para.1 to the Nationality, Immigration and Asylum Act 2002 with effect from 1 April 2003. However, *EE v City of Cardiff (HB)* [2018] UKUT 418 (AAC) the Upper Tribunal held that s.17(2) of the Interpretation Act 1978 has the effect that the reference to para.17 of Schedule 4 in s.115(9)(d) must be read as a reference to that provision as re-enacted in section 3C(1) and (2)(b) and (c) of the Immigration Act 1971.

Under s.82 of the 2002 Act (the successor to s.61 of the 1999 Act referred to in to para.17 of Sch.4 to that Act), a person with limited leave to enter or remain in the UK has a right of appeal against a decision to vary, or to refuse to vary, his leave. Section 3C of the Immigration Act 1971 provides that while such an appeal is pending, the leave to which the appeal relates and any conditions subject to which it was granted continue to have effect. *EE* holds that of s.115(9)(d) is therefore now that those whose leave has automatically been extended by s.3C are persons subject to immigration control. (See the General Note to s.115 of the Immigration and Asylum Act 1999, earlier in this volume, for a brief analysis of why *EE* may not be correctly decided.)

The former section 3D of the Immigration Act 1971 (which was in force from 31 August 2006 to 30 November 2016) is also potentially relevant. It applied where a person's leave to enter or remain in the United Kingdom is "varied with the result that he has no leave to enter or remain in the United Kingdom, or ... is revoked" and had the effect that the former leave to enter or remain was extended during any period when the person was appealing against it. The reference in s.115(9)(d) to paragraph 17 of Schedule 4 is not to be treated as a reference to section 3D—see *EE* (above) at paras 37-40—so anyone within s.3D was not a person who "requires leave to enter or remain in the United Kingdom but does not have it" within s.115(9)(a): see *GO v HMRC (CHB)* [2018] UKUT 328 (AAC).

The ECSMA Agreement and the European Social Charter

5.7 Nationals of those countries that have ratified the European Convention on Social and Medical Assistance ("the ECSMA Agreement") or the European Social Charter (both of which are treaties concluded under the auspices of the Council of Europe (ETS Nos 14 and 35 respectively) are not excluded from income support, income-based jobseeker's allowance, income-related ESA, housing benefit, social fund payments or (before April 1, 2013) council tax benefit: see *OD v SSWP (JSA)*

[2015] UKUT 438 (AAC). Until the amendment of reg.2(1A) by SI 2020/1505 with effect from January 1, 2021 there was no exclusion from universal credit either.

This affects EEA Nationals and nationals of Turkey (ECSMA Agreement and Social Charter), Switzerland (Social Charter) and the Republic of Northern Macedonia (Social Charter). Turkey ratified the Social Charter on November 24, 1999 and the ECSMA Agreement on December 2, 1996. Switzerland ratified the Social Charter on May 6, 1976 and Northern Macedonia ratified it on March 31, 2005. Records of which States have ratified a Council of Europe treaty are maintained by the Council's Treaty Office and are available from its website at *http://www.conventions.coe.int/*.

Note, finally, that there are two European Social Charters. For the purposes of these regulations it is the original Charter (which was opened for signature in Turin on October 18, 1961) that is relevant, not the Revised Social Charter (ETS 163) (which was opened for signature in Strasbourg on May 3, 1996).

The meaning of "lawfully present" was considered by the House of Lords in *Szoma v Secretary of State for Work and Pensions* [2005] UKHL 64 (reported as *R(IS) 2/06*). That appeal was a challenge to the decision of the Court of Appeal in *Kaya v Haringey LBC* [2001] EWCA Civ 677, in which it had been held, following the decision of the House of Lords in *In re Muisi* (reported *sub nom. R. v Home Secretary Ex p. Bugdaycay* [1987] A.C. 514), that a person granted temporary admission to the UK could not be "lawfully present" because he or she was deemed by s.11 of the Immigration Act 1971 not to be present in the UK at all. In *Szoma*, their Lordships overruled *Kaya* and held that lawful presence did not require

> ". . . more by way of positive legal authorisation for someone's presence in the UK than that they are at large here pursuant to the express written authority of an immigration officer provided for by statute."

Note that an ECSMA national who is not excluded from benefit by virtue of para.4 of Pt I of the Schedule, may nevertheless be excluded by virtue of the habitual residence and right to reside tests—see *Yesiloz v Camden LBC and SSWP* [2009] EWCA Civ 415 *(R(H) 7/09)*.

Spouses and family members of EEA nationals

Until December 31, 2020 at 11.00 pm, a person who was not an EEA national 5.8
but who was a family member of such a national was not excluded from social fund payments (and certain non-contributory, non-means-tested benefits covered by Vol.I: see para.1 of Pt II of the Schedule). In *CDLA/708/2007*, the Deputy Commissioner held that para.1 only applied where the EEA national is "exercising his or her rights or freedoms under the EEA Agreement (whether or not he or she also has equivalent rights under EC law) and where the family member is a person who has rights under the EEA Agreement as a family member. However, in *JFP v DSD (DLA)* [2012] NI Com 267, the Chief Commissioner of Northern Ireland declined to follow *CDLA/708/2007*. In his view, there was no reason not to give para.1 of Pt II of the Schedule its natural meaning so that s.115 did not exclude any family member of any EEA national from entitlement to attendance allowance, disability living allowance, carer's allowance, child benefit, a social fund payment or any of the other benefits set out in the heading to that Part of the Schedule. In *MS v SSWP (DLA)* [2016] UKUT 42 (AAC) a judge of the Upper Tribunal in Great Britain considered the reasoning in both decisions and preferred that in *CDLA/708/2007*. The judge's views on this point were *obiter* because he had already decided that the claimant did not satisfy the conditions of entitlement to DLA. However, in *SSWP v AS (CA)* [2021] UKUT 24 (AAC), the Upper Tribunal (Judge Ward) also followed the decision of the Deputy Commissioner (albeit for additional reasons) in an appeal that turned on the point. The decision in *SSWP v AS* creates a conflict of precedent between Great Britain and Northern Ireland. The strict position has always been that the FTT in Great Britain was bound to follow

CDLA/708/2007 and appeal tribunals in Northern Ireland were bound by the decision of the Chief Commissioner. However, most tribunals in Great Britain would in practice have regarded themselves as free to follow *JFP v DSD* because, although it was given in another jurisdiction, it was of considerable persuasive authority, had considered *CDLA/708/2007* in detail, and disapproved it. That line of argument is no longer open following *MS v SSWP* and *SSWP v AS*.

However, that conflict of precedent is unlikely to have much practical effect: para.1 of Pt II of the Schedule was revoked with effect from December 31, 2020 at 11.00 pm, by reg.57 of the Immigration and Social Security Co-ordination (EU Withdrawal) Act 2020 (Consequential, Saving, Transitional and Transitory Provisions) (EU Exit) Regulations 2020 (SI 2020/1309), so the issue will no longer arise in the future.

As regards entitlement to social fund payments, see the note on sponsored immigrants (above) as to the practical restrictions on eligibility.

Reciprocal agreements

5.9 Under art.217 (ex-238 TEC) of the Treaty on the Functioning of the European Union, the EU "may conclude with one or more States or international organisations agreements establishing an association involving reciprocal rights and obligations, common action and special procedure".

Before the end of the Implementation Period, paras 2 and 3 of Pt II of the Schedule applied to "association agreements" under art.217 that provided for equal treatment in the field of social security of workers who are nationals of the signatory State and their families. In those circumstances, nationals of the non-EU State who were lawfully working in the UK and members of their families who were living with them were not excluded by s.115 from entitlement to social fund payments, attendance allowance, SDA, the former health in pregnancy grants, carer's allowance, DLA and child benefit. For further details, see p.920 of Vol.V of the 2020/21 edition.

From January 1, 2021 (and see below for the position for the final hour of December 31, 2020), A person who is lawfully working in Great Britain and is a national of a State with which the UK has concluded an agreement which replaces in whole or in part a former association agreement under art.217 is not excluded from entitlement to the above benefits.

The habitual residence test and the right to reside

5.10 Note that, even if claimants are not excluded from benefit as a person subject to immigration control, entitlement to universal credit, IS, IBJSA, IRESA, HB and SPC is also dependent upon their being (or treated as being) habitually resident (including, where appropriate, satisfying the right to reside test: see Vol.V).

Citation, commencement and interpretation

5.11 **1.**—(1) These Regulations may be cited as the Social Security (Immigration and Asylum) Consequential Amendments Regulations 2000.

(2) These Regulations shall come into force on 3rd April 2000.

(3) In these Regulations—

"the Act" means the Immigration and Asylum Act 1999;

"the Attendance Allowance Regulations" means the Social Security (Attendance Allowance) Regulations 1991;

"the Claims and Payments Regulations" means the Social Security (Claims and Payments) Regulations 1987;

"the Contributions and Benefits Act" means the Social Security Contributions and Benefits Act 1992;

[[1] . . .];

"the Disability Living Allowance Regulations" means the Social Security (Disability Living Allowance) Regulations 1991;

[2 "the Employment and Support Allowance Regulations" means the Employment and Support Allowance Regulations 2008;]

[1 . . .];

"the Income Support Regulations" means the Income Support (General) Regulations 1987;

"the Invalid Care Allowance Regulations" means the Social Security (Invalid Care Allowance) Regulations 1976;

"the Jobseeker's Allowance Regulations" means the Jobseeker's Allowance Regulations 1996;

[3 "personal independence payment" means personal independence payment under Part 4 of the Welfare Reform Act 2012;]

"the Persons from Abroad Regulations" means the Social Security (Persons from Abroad) Miscellaneous Amendments Regulations 1996;

"the Severe Disablement Allowance Regulations" means the Social Security (Severe Disablement Allowance) Regulations 1984.

[2 "income-related employment and support allowance" means an income-related allowance under Part 1 of the Welfare Reform Act 2007 (employment and support allowance) [4 ;

"universal credit" means universal credit under Part 1 of the Welfare Reform Act 2012].]

(4) In these Regulations, unless the context otherwise requires, a reference—

(a) to a numbered regulation or Schedule is to the regulation in, or the Schedule to, these Regulations bearing that number;

(b) in a regulation or Schedule to a numbered paragraph is to the paragraph in that regulation or Schedule bearing that number.

AMENDMENTS

1. Housing Benefit and Council Tax Benefit (Consequential Provisions) Regulations 2006 (SI 2006/217) reg.3 and Sch.1 (March 6, 2006).

2. Employment and Support Allowance (Consequential Provisions) (No.2) Regulations 2008 (SI 2008/1554) reg.69(1) and (2) (October 27, 2008).

3. Personal Independence Payment (Supplementary Provisions and Consequential Amendments) Regulations 2013 (SI 2013/388) reg.8 and Sch. para.23(1) and (2) (April 8, 2013).

4. Universal Credit (Consequential, Supplementary, Incidental and Miscellaneous Provisions) Regulations 2013 (SI 2013/630) reg.31(1) and (2) (April 29, 2013).

GENERAL NOTE

With effect from April 7, 2003 the definition of "the Claims and Payments Regulations" was revoked in so far as it related to child benefit and guardian's allowance (reg.43 of and Pt I of Sch.3 to the Child Benefit and Guardian's Allowance (Administration) Regulations 2003). The definition remains in force for the purposes of other benefits. 5.12

Persons not excluded from specified benefits under section 115 of the Immigration and Asylum Act 1999

2.—(1) For the purposes of entitlement to income-based jobseeker's allowance, income support, a social fund payment, [11 or] [3 income-related 5.13

employment and support allowance] [11 ...] as the case may be, a person falling within a category or description of persons specified in Part I of the Schedule is a person to whom section 115 of the Act does not apply.

[8 (1A) For the purposes of entitlement to [11 housing benefit under the Contributions and Benefits Act, state pension credit under the State Pension Credit Act 2002, or] universal credit [11 , as the case may be,] a person falling within a category or description of persons specified in [10 paragraphs 2 and 3] of Part I of the Schedule is a person to whom section 115 of the Act does not apply.]

(2) For the purposes of entitlement to attendance allowance, severe disablement allowance, [1 carer's allowance], disability living allowance, a social fund payment [4 , health in pregnancy grant] or child benefit under the Contributions and Benefits Act [7 or personal independence payment], as the case may be, a person falling within a category or description of persons specified in Part II of the Schedule is a person to whom section 115 of the Act does not apply.

(3) For the purposes of entitlement to child benefit, attendance allowance or disability living allowance under the Contributions and Benefits Act [7 or personal independence payment], as the case may be, a person in respect of whom there is an Order in Council made under section 179 of the Social Security Administration Act 1992 giving effect to a reciprocal agreement in respect of one of those benefits, as the case may be, is a person to whom section 115 of the Act does not apply.

[10 (3A) For the purposes of entitlement to child benefit under the Contributions and Benefits Act, a person—

(a) who is lawfully working in Great Britain; and
(b) who is a national of a State with which the United Kingdom has concluded an agreement which replaces, in whole or in part, an agreement under Article 217 of the Treaty on the Functioning of the European Union which makes provision for the receipt of family allowances for members of their family who are legally resident in the United Kingdom,

is a person to whom section 115 of the Act does not apply.]

(4) For the purposes of entitlement to—

(a) income support, a social fund payment, housing benefit [6 . . .] under the Contributions and Benefits Act, [3 or income-related employment and support allowance,] as the case may be, a person who is entitled to or is receiving benefit by virtue of paragraph (1) or (2) of regulation 12 of the Persons from Abroad Regulations is a person to whom section 115 of the Act does not apply;
(b) attendance allowance, disability living allowance, [1carer's allowance, severe disablement allowance, a social fund payment or child benefit under the Contributions and Benefits Act, as the case may be, a person who is entitled to or is receiving benefit byvirtue of paragraph (10) of regulation 12 is a person to whom section 115 of the Act does not apply.

[2(c) state pension credit under the State Pension Credit Act 2002, a person to whom sub-paragraph (a) would have applied but for the fact that they have attained the qualifying age for the purposes of state pension credit, is a person to whom section 115 of the Act does not apply.]

[5 (5) For the purposes of entitlement to [8 universal credit,] income support, [8 an income-based jobseeker's allowance under the Jobseekers

Act 1995], an [8 income-related] employment and support allowance or a social fund payment under the Contributions and Benefits Act, as the case may be, a person who is an asylum seeker within the meaning of paragraph (4) of regulation 12 who has not ceased to be an asylum seeker by virtue of paragraph (5) of that regulation is a person to whom section 115 of the Act does not apply.]

(6) For the purposes of entitlement to housing benefit [6 . . .] or a social fund payment under the Contributions and Benefits Act, as the case may be, a person to whom regulation 12(6) applies is a person to whom section 115 of the Act does not apply.

[2 (7) For the purposes of entitlement to state pension credit under the State Pension Credit Act 2002, a person to whom paragraph (5) would have applied but for the fact that they have attained the qualifying age for the purposes of state pension credit, is a person to whom section 115 of the Act does not apply.

(8) [9 . . .]]

AMENDMENTS

1. Social Security Amendment (Carer's Allowance) Regulations 2002 (SI 2002/2497) reg.3 and Sch.2 (April 1, 2003).

2. State Pension Credit (Transitional and Miscellaneous Provisions) Amendment Regulations 2003 (SI 2003/2274) reg.6 (October 6, 2003).

3. Employment and Support Allowance (Consequential Provisions) (No.2) Regulations 2008 (SI 2008/1554) reg.69(1) and (3) (October 27, 2008).

4. Health in Pregnancy Grant (Entitlement and Amount) Regulations 2008 (SI 2008/3108) reg.8(2) (January 1, 2009).

5. Social Security (Miscellaneous Amendments) (No.5) Regulations 2009 (SI 2009/3228) reg.3(5) (January 25, 2010).

6. Council Tax Benefit Abolition (Consequential Provision) Regulations 2013 (SI 2013/458) reg.3 and Sch.1 (April 1, 2013).

7. Personal Independence Payment (Supplementary Provisions and Consequential Amendments) Regulations 2013 (SI 2013/388) reg.8 and Sch. para.23(1) and (3) (April 8, 2013).

8. Universal Credit (Consequential, Supplementary, Incidental and Miscellaneous Provisions) Regulations 2013 (SI 2013/630) reg.31(1) and (3) (April 29, 2013).

9. Social Security (Miscellaneous Amendments) (No.3) Regulations 2013 (SI 2013/2536) reg.9(2) (October 29, 2013).

10. Social Security and Tax Credits (Miscellaneous and Coronavirus Amendments) Regulations 2021 (SI 2021/495) reg.4 (May 13, 2021).

11. Social Security and Council Tax Reduction Schemes (Amendment) Regulations 2022 (SI 2022/449) reg.2 (May 3, 2022).

Transitional arrangements and savings

12.— *Omitted* 5.14

GENERAL NOTE

Reg.12 makes transitional provision for those who claimed asylum before April 3, 2000 (when the Immigration and Asylum Act 1999 came into force) and whose claims have not subsequently been decided or abandoned. The regulation remains in force but has not been reproduced because, more than 21 years after April 3, 5.15

2000, it is doubtful whether it now applies to anyone and, even if it does, it has not given rise to a significant number of appeals for many years.

For the text of the regulation, and commentary, see pp.923–925 of Vol.V of the 2020/21 edition.

Regulation 2

SCHEDULE

Persons not Excluded from Certain Benefits under Section 115 of the Immigration and Asylum Act 1999

Part I

5.16 *Persons not excluded under section 115 of the Immigration and Asylum Act from entitlement to [5 universal credit,] income-based jobseeker's allowance, income support, [3 income-related employment and support allowance,] a social fund payment, housing benefit or council tax benefit.*

1. [9 ...]

[8 **2.** A person who is lawfully working in Great Britain and is a national of a State with which—

(a) [10 ...]

(b) the United Kingdom has concluded an agreement which replaces in whole or in part [10 an agreement under Article 217 of the Treaty on the Functioning of the European Union] which has ceased to apply to, and in, the United Kingdom, providing, in the field of social security, for the equal treatment of workers who are nationals of the signatory State and their families.]

3. A person who—

(a) has been given leave to enter or remain in, the United Kingdom by the Secretary of State upon an undertaking by another person or persons pursuant to the immigration rules within the meaning of the Immigration Act 1971, to be responsible for his maintenance and accommodation; and

(b) has been resident in the United Kingdom for a period of at least five years beginning on the date of entry or the date on which the undertaking was given in respect of him, whichever date is the later.

4. A person who is a national of a state which has ratified the European Convention on Social and Medical Assistance (done in Paris on 11th December 1953) or a state which has ratified the Council of Europe Social Charter (signed in Turin on 18th October 1961) and who is lawfully present in the United Kingdom.

Part II

5.17 *Persons not excluded under section 115 of the Immigration and Asylum Act from entitlement to attendance allowance, severe disablement allowance, [1carer's allowance], disability living allowance, [4 personal independence payment,] a social fund payment [2 , Health in Pregnancy Grant] or child benefit.*

1. [9 ...]

[8 **2.** A person who is lawfully working in Great Britain and is a national of a State with which—

(a) [10 ...]

(b) the United Kingdom has concluded an agreement which replaces in whole or in part [10 an agreement under Article 217 of the Treaty on the Functioning of the European Union] which has ceased to apply to, and in, the United Kingdom, providing, in the field of social security, for the equal treatment of workers who are nationals of the signatory State and their families.]

3. A person who is a member of a family of, and living with, a person specified in paragraph 2.

4. A person who has been given leave to enter, or remain in, the United Kingdom by the Secretary of State upon an undertaking by another person or persons pursuant to the immigration rules within the meaning of the Immigration Act 1971, to be responsible for his maintenance and accommodation.

AMENDMENTS

1. Social Security Amendment (Carer's Allowance) Regulations 2002 (SI 2002/2497) reg.3 and Sch.2 (April 1, 2003).
2. Health in Pregnancy Grant (Entitlement and Amount) Regulations 2008 (SI 2008/3108) reg.8(3) (January 1, 2009).
3. Employment and Support Allowance (Consequential Provisions) (No.2) Regulations 2008 (SI 2008/1554) reg.69(1) and (5) (October 27, 2008).
4. Personal Independence Payment (Supplementary Provisions and Consequential Amendments) Regulations 2013 (SI 2013/388) reg.8 and Sch. para.23(1) and (4) (April 8, 2013).
5. Universal Credit (Consequential, Supplementary, Incidental and Miscellaneous Provisions) Regulations 2013 (SI 2013/630) reg.31(1) and (4) (April 29, 2013).
6. Social Security (Croatia) Amendment Regulations 2013 (SI 2013/1474) reg.8 (July 1, 2013).
7. Social Security (Miscellaneous Amendments) (No.3) Regulations 2013 (SI 2013/2536) reg.9(3) (October 29,2013).
8. Social Security, Child Benefit and Child Tax Credit (Amendment) (EU Exit) Regulations 2019 (SI 2019/1431) reg.2 (December 31, 2020 at 11.00 pm).
9. Immigration and Social Security Co-ordination (EU Withdrawal) Act 2020 (Consequential, Saving, Transitional and Transitory Provisions) (EU Exit) Regulations 2020 (SI 2020/1309) reg.57 (December 31, 2020 at 11.00 pm).
10. Social Security, Child Benefit and Child Tax Credit (Amendment) (EU Exit) Regulations 2020 (SI 2020/1505) reg.2(1) and (3) (January 1, 2021).

GENERAL NOTE

See under the heading, *Reciprocal agreements*, above. **5.18**

For the period of one hour between December 31, 2020 at 11.00 pm (when SI 2020/1309 came into effect) and January 1, 2021 (when it was further amended by SI 2020/1505), para.2 read as follows:

"2. A person who is lawfully working in Great Britain and is a national of a State with which—

(a) the European Union has concluded an agreement under Article 217 of the Treaty on the Functioning of the European Union (an "EU Agreement") providing, in the field of social security, for the equal treatment of workers who are nationals of the signatory State and their families; or

(b) the United Kingdom has concluded an agreement which replaces in whole or in part an EU Agreement in sub-paragraph (a) which has ceased to apply to, and in, the United Kingdom, providing, in the field of social security, for the equal treatment of workers who are nationals of the signatory State and their families."

SOCIAL SECURITY VOLUME V SUPPLEMENT 2024/2025

General Editor
Nick Wikeley, M.A. (Cantab)

Commentary by

John Mesher, B.A., B.C.L. (Oxon), LL.M. (Yale)
Retired Judge of the Upper Tribunal
Emeritus Professor of Law, University of Sheffield

Tom Royston, M.A. (Cantab)
Barrister

Nick Wikeley, M.A. (Cantab)
Judge of the Upper Tribunal,
Emeritus Professor of Law, University of Southampton

Consultant Editor
Child Poverty Action Group

Sweet & Maxwell

PREFACE

This is the 2024/25 Cumulative Supplement to Volume V in this series, *Income Support and the Legacy Benefits 2021/22*. For more detail on the background to this initiative, we refer readers to the separate Note on Restructuring the *Social Security Legislation* series as set out at p.xiii of the 2023/24 edition of Volume II (and the other volumes of that edition). The Note explains the process of restructuring the series to reflect the fact that universal credit has now become the default working-age means-tested benefit for new claims in the social security system. This has resulted in some re-ordering of material across the volumes to provide readers with a clear and coherent explanation (at least so far as we can) of the various social security benefits.

A specific part of that restructuring process was that no new edition of Volume V has been published since 2021/22. That was because there were then estimated to be only (sic) about 1.5 million households still in receipt of income support and old style ESA and JSA, a number that will continue to fall with the combined effect of "natural migration" and "managed migration" to universal credit, so giving rise to a diminishing number of appeals that are likely to involve any of the legacy benefits. Instead, this Cumulative Supplement incorporates the up-dating for Volume V contained in the 2021/22 Supplement, the Supplements contained in Volume II 2022/23 and 2023/24 and in mid-year Supplements, as well as subsequent amendments up to April 8, 2024. The internal structure of the Cumulative Supplement for Volume V, *Income Support and the Legacy Benefits 2021/22*, follows the same model as the main volume. It is anticipated that the same approach will be followed in succeeding years, although this will be kept under close review if the plans for a more rapid migration process for all income support and old style ESA and JSA claimants are maintained. Readers are therefore advised not to dispose of their copies of the 2021/22 Volume V, which will in the future almost certainly only be updated by way of such Supplements.

As to the content of this Supplement, there have, of course, been the usual routine amendments to primary legislation and to regulations since the 2023/24 mid-year Supplement, including the April 2024 up-rating of benefits, and a number of new decisions, including on general issues such as the calculation of capital.

We renew our thanks for the flexibility and forbearance of the publishers and for a great deal of help from a number of sources. Those include, in particular, the Child Poverty Action Group as advisory editor to this series. We remain grateful for this assistance in our task of providing an authoritative reflection on the current state of the law. Users of the series, and its predecessor works, have over the years contributed to their effectiveness by providing valuable comments on our commentary, as well as pointing out where the text of some provision has been omitted in error, or become garbled, or not been brought fully up to date. In providing such feedback, users of the work have helped to shape the content and ensure the accuracy of our material, and for that we continue to be grateful. That is all the more important given the major restructuring that has taken place. We therefore hope that users of the work will continue to provide such helpful input and feedback. Please write to the General Editor of the series, Emeritus Professor Nick Wikeley, c/o School of Law, University of Southampton, Highfield, Southampton SO17 1BJ, email: njw@soton.ac.uk, and he will pass on any comments received to the appropriate commentator.

Our gratitude also goes to the President of the Social Entitlement Chamber of the First-tier Tribunal and her colleagues there for continuing the now long tradition of help and encouragement in our endeavours.

We would also like to draw attention to what we have said in the main Preface to Volume II about Mark Rowland's tremendous contribution over some 30 years to the development and success of the *Social Security Legislation* series.

August 2024

John Mesher
Tom Royston
Nick Wikeley

CONTENTS

PAGES OF MAIN VOLUMES AFFECTED BY MATERIAL IN THIS SUPPLEMENT

Main volume page affected	Relevant paragraph in supplement
VOLUME V	
p.15	5.001
p.18	5.002
pp.19–20	5.003
p.33	5.004
p.72	5.005
p.81	5.006
p.124	5.007
p.133	5.008
p.226	5.009
p.229	5.010
p.275	5.011
p.314	5.012
pp.329–331	5.013
p.355	5.014
p.385	5.015
pp.393–396	5.016
p.412	5.017
p.421	5.018
pp.431–433	5.019
p.438	5.020
p.439	5.021
pp.440–441	5.022
p.443	5.023
p.446	5.024
p.449	5.025
p.451	5.026
p.457	5.027
p.467	5.028
p.482	5.029
pp.520–523	5.030
p.526	5.031
p.527	5.032
p.539	5.033
p.542	5.034
p.550	5.035
pp.571–572	5.036
p.605	5.037
p.606	5.038
p.631	5.039

Main volume page affected	Relevant paragraph in supplement
p.642	5.040
p.644	5.041
p.646	5.042
p.648	5.043
p.651	5.044
p.665	5.045
p.676	5.046
p.676	5.047
p.677	5.048
p.680	5.049
p.680	5.050
p.681	5.051
p.682	5.052
pp.684–685	5.053
p.685	5.054
p.689	5.055
p.695	5.056
p.697	5.057
p.707	5.058
p.709	5.059
p.711	5.060
p.714	5.061
p.717	5.062
p.721	5.063
p.722	5.064
p.722	5.065
p.722	5.066
p.722	5.067
p.773	5.068
p.785	5.069
p.787	5.070
p.787	5.071
pp.851–852	5.072
pp.872–873	5.073
p.896	5.074
pp.902–903	5.075
pp.910–912	5.076
p.923	5.077
p.970	5.078
pp.974–977	5.079
p.1014	5.080
p.1021	5.081
p.1023	5.082
p.1027	5.083
pp.1029–1030	5.084
p.1054	5.085
p.1055	5.086
pp.1059–1060	5.087
pp.1071–1072	5.088
p.1080	5.089

Main volume page affected	Relevant paragraph in supplement
p.1081	5.090
p.1086	5.091
p.1087–1088	5.092
p.1091	5.093
p.1120	5.094
pp.1120–1122	5.095
p.1138	5.096
p.1144	5.097
p.1146	5.098
p.1147	5.099
p.1149	5.100
p.1151	5.101
p.1153	5.102
p.1156	5.103
p.1165	5.104
p.1166	5.105
pp.1167–1168	5.106
p.1168	5.107
p.1172	5.108
p.1177	5.109
p.1184	5.110
p.1187	5.111
p.1188	5.112
p.1205	5.113
pp.1209, 1214, 1218, 1219 and 1221	5.114–5.117
p.1230	5.118
pp.1238–1239	5.119
p.1250	5.120
p.1260	5.121
p.1302	5.122
pp.1334–1135	5.123
p.1336	5.124
p.1340	5.125
pp.1341–1342	5.126
p.1373	5.127
p.1377	5.128
p.1378	5.129
p.1382	5.130
pp.1406–1407	5.131
p.1409	5.132
p.1411	5.133
p.1413	5.134
pp.1431–1432	5.135
p.1437	5.136
p.1438	5.137
pp.1494–1496	5.138
pp.1507–1514	5.139
pp.1525–1532	5.140
p.1540	5.141
p.1542	5.142

Main volume page affected	Relevant paragraph in supplement
p.1544	5.143
p.1546	5.144
p.1549	5.145
p.1554	5.146
p.1556	5.147
p.1556	5.148
pp.1558–1559	5.149
p.1559	5.150
p.1563	5.151
pp.1565–1566	5.152
p.1579	5.153
p.1579	5.154
p.1613	5.155
p.1613	5.156
p.1615	5.157
pp.1663–1664	5.158
pp.1670–1672	5.159
pp.1670–1672	5.160
p.1674	5.161
p.1681	5.162
pp.1681–1683	5.163
p.1732	5.164
p.1734	5.165
p.1734	5.166
p.1735	5.167
pp.1735–1736	5.168
p.1738	5.169
p.1742	5.170
p.1745	5.170
p.1793	5.171
p.1798	5.172
pp.1826–1829	5.173
pp.1889–1891	5.174
p.1890	5.175
pp.1891–1892	5.176
pp.1892–1893	5.177
p.1893	5.178

TABLE OF CASES

TABLE OF COMMISSIONERS' DECISIONS

TABLE OF EUROPEAN LEGISLATION

TABLE OF STATUTES

TABLE OF STATUTORY INSTRUMENTS

PART I

SOCIAL SECURITY STATUTES

p.15, *amendment to the Social Security Contributions and Benefits Act 1992 s.126(7) (Trade disputes)*

With effect from April 8, 2024, art.22 of the Social Security Benefits Up-rating Order 2024 (SI 2024/242) substituted "£50.00" for "£47.00" (as had been in effect from April 10, 2023) in subs.(7). **5.001**

p.18, *annotation to the Social Security Contributions and Benefits Act 1992 s.126(5)(b) (Trade disputes—relevant sum)*

Note that the amount of the "relevant sum" for the purposes of s.126(5) (b) is specified in subs.(7), not (6). With effect from April 8, 2024 the sum was increased to £50 (see the entry for p.15). **5.002**

pp.19–20, *annotation to the Social Security Contributions and Benefits Act 1992 s.134(1) (Exclusions from benefit)*

In the Institute for Government and the Social Security Advisory Committee's 2021 joint report *Jobs and benefits: The Covid-19 challenge* it was noted that if the capital limit had risen in line with prices since 2006 it would be close to £23,500 (or £25,000: different figures are given) and recommended that the limit should be increased to £25,000 and subsequently automatically indexed to maintain its real value (pp.22 and 31). That recommendation was summarily rejected in the Government's response of March 22, 2022. **5.003**

p.33, *annotation to the old style Jobseekers Act 1995 GENERAL NOTE*

The two remaining prohibitions on claiming universal credit have now been removed. The former exception for "frontier workers" was removed with effect from March 30, 2022 by the Welfare Reform Act 2012 (Commencement No.34 and Commencement No.9, 21, 23, 31 and 32 and Transitional Provisions (Amendment)) Order 2022 (SI 2022/302) and the discretion given to the Secretary of State under reg.4 of the Transitional Provisions Regulations 2014 (SI 2014/1230) to determine (for the safeguarding of efficient administration or ensuring the efficient testing of administrative systems) that no claims for universal credit were to be accepted in an area or category of case was removed with effect from July 25, 2022 by reg.2 of the Universal Credit (Transitional Provisions) Amendment Regulations 2022 (SI 2022/752). There is thus now no exception, however remote, to the proposition that any new claim for JSA can only be for new style JSA. **5.004**

p.72, *annotation to the Jobseekers Act 1995 s.13(1) (Income and capital: income-based jobseeker's allowance)*

In the Institute for Government and the Social Security Advisory Committee's 2021 joint report *Jobs and benefits: The Covid-19 challenge* it was noted that if the capital limit had risen in line with prices since 2006 it would be close to £23,500 (or £25,000: different figures are given) and recommended that the limit should be increased to £25,000 and subsequently automatically indexed to maintain its real value (pp.22 and 31). That recommendation was summarily rejected in the Government's response of March 22, 2022. **5.005**

p.81, *annotation to the old style Jobseekers Act 1995 s.15(2) (Effect on other claimants—trade disputes)*

5.006 With effect from April 8, 2024 the "prescribed sum" for the purposes of s.15(2)(d) was increased to £50 (see the entry for p.1086).

p.124, *correction to the old style Jobseekers Act 1995 s.20E (Contracting out)*

5.007 The text in s.20E(1)–(3) should be replaced with the following:

"(1) The following functions of the Secretary of State may be exercised by, or by employees of, such person (if any) as the Secretary of State may authorise for the purpose, namely—

(a) [2...]
(b) [2...]
(c) [2...]
(d) [3...]
(e) [3...]
(f) [3...]

(2) The following functions of officers of the Secretary of State may be exercised by, or by employees of, such person (if any) as the Secretary of State may authorise for the purpose, namely—

(a) specifying places and times, and being contacted, under section 8;
(b) entering into or varying any jobseeker's agreement under section 9 or 10 and referring any proposed agreement or variation to the Secretary of State under section 9 or 10;
(c) giving notifications under section 16[2...];
(d) [2...].

(3) Regulations may provide for any of the following functions of the Secretary of State to be exercisable by, or by employees of, such person (if any) as the Secretary of State may authorise for the purpose—

(a) any function under regulations under section 8,[2...] 17A[2...][3...], except the making of an excluded decision (see subsection (4));
(b) the function under section 9(1) of the 1998 Act (revision of decisions) so far as relating to decisions (other than excluded decisions) that relate to any matter arising under any such regulations;
(c) the function under section 10(1) of the 1998 Act (superseding of decisions) so far as relating to decisions (other than excluded decisions) of the Secretary of State that relate to any matter arising under any such regulations;
(d) any function under Chapter 2 of Part 1 of the 1998 Act (social security decisions), except section 25(2) and (3) (decisions involving issues arising on appeal in other cases), which relates to the exercise of any of the functions within paragraphs (a) to (c)."

p.133, *annotation to the old style Jobseekers Act 1995 s.35 (Interpretation—definition of "employment officer")*

5.008 Note in relation to the schemes whose providers have been designated as employment officers that the Work Programme has ceased to operate and that reg.8(3) of the SAPOE Regulations has been revoked with effect from March 22, 2022 (see the entry for p.1187).

PART II

INCOME SUPPORT REGULATIONS

p.226, *amendments to list of regulations for the Income Support (General) Regulations 1987 (SI 1987/1967)* 5.009

Insert the following entries between the entries for regs 66B and 67:

"66C. Treatment of fee loans
66D. Treatment of loans for specific purposes"

p.229, *amendments to the Income Support (General) Regulations 1987 (SI 1987/1967) reg.2 (Interpretation)*

With effect from July 26, 2021, Sch.1 para.2 of the Social Security (Scotland) Act 2018 (Disability Assistance for Children and Young People) (Consequential Modifications) Order 2021 (SI 2021/786) inserts the following definitions: 5.010

"child disability payment" has the meaning given in regulation 2 of the DACYP Regulations;
"DACYP Regulations" means the Disability Assistance for Children and Young People (Scotland) Regulations 2021;

With effect from January 1, 2022, reg.2(2) of the Social Security (Income and Capital Disregards) (Amendment) Regulations 2021 (SI 2021/1405) inserts the following definitions:

"child abuse payment" means a payment from a scheme established or approved by the Secretary of State for the purpose of providing compensation in respect of historic institutional child abuse in the United Kingdom;"
"Windrush payment" means a payment made under the Windrush Compensation Scheme (Expenditure) Act 2020;"

With effect from January 1, 2022, reg.2(2) of the Social Security (Income and Capital Disregards) (Amendment) Regulations 2021 (SI 2021/1405) inserts ", a child abuse payment or a Windrush payment" into the definition of "qualifying person", after "Grenfell Tower payment".

With effect from March 21, 2022, art.2(2) of the Social Security (Disability Assistance for Working Age People) (Consequential Amendments) Order 2022 (SI 2022/177) inserts the following definition:

"adult disability payment" has the meaning given in regulation 2 of the Disability Assistance for Working Age People (Scotland) Regulations 2022;

With effect from July 9, 2023, reg.2 of the Social Security (Income and Capital Disregards) (Amendment) Regulations 2023 (SI 2023/640) amends reg.2 as follows:

- for the definition of "Grenfell Tower payment" substitute—""Grenfell Tower payment" means a payment made for the purpose of providing compensation or support in respect of the fire on 14th June 2017 at Grenfell Tower;";
- insert the following definitions:
  - "the Horizon system" means any version of the computer system used by the Post Office known as Horizon, Horizon Legacy, Horizon Online or HNG-X;

- "the Post Office" means Post Office Limited (registered number 02154540);
- "Post Office compensation payment" means a payment made by the Post Office or the Secretary of State for the purpose of providing compensation or support which is—
  (a) in connection with the failings of the Horizon system; or
  (b) otherwise payable following the judgment in Bates and Others v Post Office Ltd ((No. 3) "Common Issues") (10);
- "vaccine damage payment" means a payment made under the Vaccine Damage Payments Act 1979(11);";

- in the definition of "qualifying person", for "or a Windrush payment" substitute ", a Windrush payment, a Post Office compensation payment or a vaccine damage payment".

With effect from October 27, 2023, reg.3 of the Social Security (Habitual Residence and Past Presence, and Capital Disregards) (Amendment) Regulations 2023 (SI 2023/1144) amends reg.2 as follows:

- in the definition of "qualifying person", after "the National Emergencies Trust" insert ", the Victims of Overseas Terrorism Compensation Scheme";
- insert the following definition:

  "the Victims of Overseas Terrorism Compensation Scheme" means the scheme of that name established by the Ministry of Justice in 2012 under section 47 of the Crime and Security Act 2010;

With effect from November 19, 2023, art.5 of the Carer's Assistance (Carer Support Payment) (Scotland) Regulations 2023 (Consequential Amendments) Order 2023 (SI 2023/1218) amends reg.2 as follows:

after the definition of "care home" insert—

""carer support payment" means carer's assistance given in accordance with the Carer's Assistance (Carer Support Payment) (Scotland) Regulations 2023;".

p.275, *amendments to the Income Support (General) Regulations 1987 (SI 1987/1967) reg.4 (Temporary absence from Great Britain)*

5.011 With effect from July 26, 2021, Sch.1 para.3 of the Social Security (Scotland) Act 2018 (Disability Assistance for Children and Young People) (Consequential Modifications) Order 2021 (SI 2021/786) makes the following amendment:

In reg.4(2)(c)(v)(aa) after "allowance", insert ", the care component of child disability payment at the highest rate in accordance with the DACYP Regulations (see regulation 11(5) of those Regulations)".

With effect from March 21, 2022, art.2(3) of the Social Security (Disability Assistance for Working Age People) (Consequential Amendments) Order 2022 (SI 2022/177) makes the following amendment:

In reg.4(2)(c)(v)(aa) (temporary absence from Great Britain):

(a) for "or" after "armed forces independence payment" substitute ",";

(b) after "personal independence payment" insert "or the enhanced rate of the daily living component of adult disability payment".

p.314, *annotation to the Income Support (General) Regulations 1987 (SI 1987/1967) reg.17 (Applicable amounts)*

The Social Security (Coronavirus) (Further Measures) Regulations 2020 (SI 2020/371), followed by the Universal Credit (Extension of Coronavirus Measures) Regulations 2021 (SI 2021/313), had the effect that for the 18 months to October 2021, the standard allowances of UC were uplifted by £20 per week. Similar measures were employed for working tax credit: the Coronavirus Act 2020 s.77, followed by the Coronavirus Act 2020 Functions of Her Majesty's Revenue and Customs (Covid-19 support scheme: working households receiving tax credits) Direction (7 April 2021). 5.012

Recipients of IS, ESA and JSA did not receive an uplift. In *R(T) v Secretary of State for Work and Pensions*, the legality of this differential treatment was challenged (unsuccessfully) as being unlawfully discriminatory contrary to the ECHR.

In [2022] EWHC 351 (Admin) (18 February 2022) the High Court: (i) rejected the claim that there was unlawful discrimination against people with the status of being a legacy benefit claimant, on the basis that being a legacy benefit claimant was not a status within the scope of ECHR art.14 (paras 22–24); and (ii) rejected the claim that there was unlawful discrimination against disabled people, on the basis that the discrimination was justified (paras 30–38). Permission to appeal to the Court of Appeal was refused on point (i) but given on point (ii). In [2023] EWCA Civ 24 (17 January 2023), the Court of Appeal confirmed that the disability discrimination was justified. The Secretary of State's focus was on prioritising people likely to be facing a recent reduction in income, and on adopting an approach she considered technically practicable (paras 53–54). In that context, the High Court did not err by deciding that the limitation of uplift to UC and WTC was a proportionate means of achieving a legitimate aim.

pp.329–331, *amendment to the Income Support (General) Regulations 1987 (SI 1987/1967) reg.21AA (Special cases: supplemental—persons from abroad)*

The text in the main volume at para.2.167 should be replaced with the following: 5.013

"[1 Special cases: supplemental—persons from abroad

21AA.—(1) "Person from abroad" means, subject to the following provisions of this regulation, a claimant who is not habitually resident in the United Kingdom, the Channel Islands, the Isle of Man or the Republic of Ireland.

(2) No claimant shall be treated as habitually resident in the United Kingdom, the Channel Islands, the Isle of Man or the Republic of Ireland unless he has a right to reside in (as the case may be) the United Kingdom, the Channel Islands, the Isle of Man or the Republic of Ireland other than a right to reside which falls within paragraph (3) [12 or (3A)].

(3) A right to reside falls within this paragraph if it is one which exists by virtue of, or in accordance with, one or more of the following—

(a) regulation 13 of the [12 Immigration (European Economic Area) Regulations 2016];

(b) regulation 14 of those Regulations, but only in a case where the right exists under that regulation because the claimant is—

(i) a jobseeker for the purpose of the definition of "qualified person" in regulation 6(1) of those Regulations, or

(ii) a family member (within the meaning of regulation 7 of those Regulations) of such a jobseeker; [14 or]

[7 [12(bb) regulation 16 of those Regulations, but only in a case where the right exists under that regulation because the claimant satisfies the criteria in paragraph (5) of that regulation;]]

[14 (c)–(e) . . .]

[12 (3A) A right to reside falls within this paragraph if it exists by virtue of a claimant having been granted limited leave to enter, or remain in, the United Kingdom under the Immigration Act 1971 by virtue of—

(a) Appendix EU to the immigration rules made under section 3(2) of that Act; [15 . . .]

(b) being a person with a Zambrano right to reside as defined in Annex 1 of Appendix EU to the immigration rules made under section 3(2) of that Act.] [15; or

(c) having arrived in the United Kingdom with an entry clearance that was granted under Appendix EU (Family Permit) to the immigration rules made under section 3(2) of that Act.]

[13 (3B) Paragraph (3A)(a) does not apply to a person who—

(a) has a right to reside granted by virtue of being a family member of a relevant person of Northern Ireland; and

(b) would have a right to reside under the [12 Immigration (European Economic Area) Regulations 2016] if the relevant person of Northern Ireland were an EEA national, provided that the right to reside does not fall within paragraph (3).]

(4) A claimant is not a person from abroad if he is—

[17(zza) a person granted leave in accordance with the immigration rules made under section 3(2) of the Immigration Act 1971, where such leave is granted by virtue of—

(i) the Afghan Relocations and Assistance Policy; or

(ii) the previous scheme for locally-employed staff in Afghanistan (sometimes referred to as the ex-gratia scheme);

(zzb) a person in Great Britain not coming within sub-paragraph (zza) or [18 (h)] who left Afghanistan in connection with the collapse of the Afghan government that took place on 15th August 2021;]

[18(zzc) a person in Great Britain who was residing in Ukraine immediately before 1st January 2022, left Ukraine in connection with the Russian invasion which took place on 24th February 2022 and—

(i) has been granted leave in accordance with immigration rules made under section 3(2) of the Immigration Act 1971; [19 . . .]

(ii) has a right of abode in the United Kingdom within the meaning given in section 2 of that Act;] [19 or

(iii) does not require leave to enter or remain in the United Kingdom in accordance with section 3ZA of that Act;]

[20(zzd) a person who was residing in Sudan before 15th April 2023, left Sudan in connection with the violence which rapidly escalated on 15th April 2023 in Khartoum and across Sudan and—

(i) has been granted leave in accordance with immigration rules made under section 3(2) of the Immigration Act 1971;

(ii) has a right of abode in the United Kingdom within the meaning given in section 2 of that Act; or

(iii) does not require leave to enter or remain in the United Kingdom in accordance with section 3ZA of that Act;]

[21(zze) a person who was residing in Israel, the West Bank, the Gaza Strip, East Jerusalem, the Golan Heights or Lebanon immediately before 7th October 2023, who left Israel, the West Bank, the Gaza Strip, East Jerusalem, the Golan Heights or Lebanon in connection with the Hamas terrorist attack in Israel on 7th October 2023 or the violence which rapidly escalated in the region following the attack and—

(i) has been granted leave in accordance with immigration rules made under section 3(2) of the Immigration Act 1971;

(ii) has a right of abode in the United Kingdom within the meaning given in section 2 of that Act; or

(iii) does not require leave to enter or remain in the United Kingdom in accordance with section 3ZA of that Act;]

[10(za) a qualified person for the purposes of [16 regulation 6 of the Immigration (European Economic Area) Regulations 2016] as a worker or a self-employed person;

(zb) a family member of a person referred to in sub-paragraph (za) [13 . . .];

(zc) a person who has a right to reside permanently in the United Kingdom by virtue of regulation 15(1)(c), (d) or (e) of those Regulations;]

[13(zd) a family member of a relevant person of Northern Ireland, with a right to reside which falls within paragraph (3A)(a), provided that the relevant person of Northern Ireland falls within sub-paragraph (za), or would do so but for the fact that they are not an EEA national;]

[14(ze) a frontier worker within the meaning of regulation 3 of the Citizens' Rights (Frontier Workers) (EU Exit) Regulations 2020;

(zf) a family member, of a person referred to in sub-paragraph (ze), who has been granted limited leave to enter, or remain in, the United Kingdom by virtue of Appendix EU to the immigration rules made under section 3(2) of the Immigration Act 1971;]

(g) a refugee within the definition in Article 1 of the Convention relating to the Status of Refugees done at Geneva on 28th July 1951, as extended by Article 1(2) of the Protocol relating to the Status of Refugees done at New York on 31st January 1967;

[3[9(h) a person who has been granted leave or who is deemed to have been granted leave outside the rules made under section 3(2) of the Immigration Act 1971 [18 . . .];

(hh) a person who has humanitarian protection granted under those rules;] [9 or]

(i) a person who is not a person subject to immigration control within the meaning of section 115(9) of the Immigration and Asylum Act and who is in the United Kingdom as a result of his deportation, expulsion or other removal by compulsion of law from another country to the United Kingdom; [5 . . .] [9 . . .]

[13 (5) In this regulation—

"EEA national" has the meaning given in regulation 2(1) of the Immigration (European Economic Area) Regulations 2016;

"family member" has the meaning given in regulation 7(1)(a), (b) or (c) of the Immigration (European Economic Area) Regulations 2016 except that regulation 7(4) of those Regulations does not apply for the purposes of paragraphs (3B) and (4)(zd);

"relevant person of Northern Ireland" has the meaning given in Annex 1 of Appendix EU to the immigration rules made under section 3(2) of the Immigration Act 1971.]

[[14] (6) In this regulation references to the Immigration (European Economic Area) Regulations 2016 are to be read with Schedule 4 to the Immigration and Social Security Co-ordination (EU Withdrawal) Act 2020 (Consequential, Saving, Transitional and Transitory Provisions) Regulations 2020.]"

AMENDMENTS

1. Social Security (Persons from Abroad) Amendment Regulations 2006 (SI 1026/2006) reg.6(3) (April 30, 2006).

2. Social Security (Lebanon) Amendment Regulations 2006 (SI 2006/1981) reg.2 (July 25, 2006). The amendment ceased to have effect from January 31, 2007.

3. Social Security (Persons from Abroad) Amendment (No. 2) Regulations 2006 (SI 2006/2528) reg.2 (October 9, 2006).

4. Social Security (Bulgaria and Romania) Amendment Regulations 2006 (SI 2006/3341) reg.2 (January 1, 2007).

5. Social Security (Habitual Residence) (Amendment) Regulations 2009 (SI 2009/362) reg.2 (March 18, 2009).

6. Social Security (Miscellaneous Amendments) (No. 3) Regulations 2011 (SI 2011/2425) reg.7(1) and (3) (October 31, 2011).

7. Social Security (Habitual Residence) (Amendment) Regulations 2012 (SI 2012/2587) reg.2 (November 8, 2012).

8. Social Security (Croatia) Amendment Regulations 2013 (SI 2013/1474) reg.2 (July 1, 2013).

9. Social Security (Miscellaneous Amendments) (No. 3) Regulations 2013 (SI 2013/2536) reg.4(1) and (5) (October 29, 2013).

10. Social Security (Habitual Residence) (Amendment) Regulations 2014 (SI 2014/902) reg.2(1) (May 31, 2014).

11. Social Security (Updating of EU References) (Amendment) Regulations 2018 (SI 2018/1084) reg.4 and Sch. para.6 (November 15, 2018).

12. Social Security (Income-related Benefits) (Updating and Amendment) (EU Exit) Regulations 2019 (SI 2019/872) reg.2 (May 7, 2019).

13. Social Security (Income-Related Benefits) (Persons of Northern Ireland—Family Members) (Amendment) Regulations 2020 (SI 2020/683) reg.2 (August 24, 2020).

14. Immigration and Social Security Co-ordination (EU Withdrawal) Act 2020 (Consequential, Saving, Transitional and Transitory Provisions) (EU Exit) Regulations 2020 (SI 2020/1309) reg.53 (December 31, 2020 at 11.00pm).

15. Immigration (Citizens' Rights etc.) (EU Exit) Regulations 2020 (SI 2020/1372) reg.8 (December 31, 2020 at 11.00 pm).

16. Social Security (Income-related Benefits) (Updating and Amendment) (EU Exit) Regulations (SI 2019/872) reg.2 (May 7, 2019).

17. Social Security (Habitual Residence and Past Presence) (Amendment) Regulations 2021 (SI 2021/1034) reg.2 (September 15, 2021).

18. Social Security (Habitual Residence and Past Presence) (Amendment) Regulations 2022 (SI 2022/344) reg.2 (March 22, 2022).

19. Social Security (Habitual Residence and Past Presence) (Amendment) (No. 2) Regulations 2022 (SI 2022/990) reg.2 (October 18, 2022).

20. Social Security (Habitual Residence and Past Presence) (Amendment) Regulations 2023 (SI 2023/532), reg.2 (May 15, 2023).

21. Social Security (Habitual Residence and Past Presence, and Capital Disregards) (Amendment) Regulations 2023, reg.2 (SI 2023/1144) (October 27, 2023).

p.355, *annotation to the Income Support (General) Regulations 1987 (SI 1987/1967) reg.23 (Calculation of the income and capital of members of claimant's family and of a polygamous marriage)*

In line 4 of p.355, for "on the exclusion of", substitute "so as to exclude" and in line 5 for "s.11", substitute "ss.11 and 12". 5.014

p.385, *annotation to the Income Support (General) Regulations 1987 (SI 1987/1967) reg.35(1)(d) (Earnings of employed earners—holiday pay)*

Replace the second paragraph of 2.265 (starting "Holiday pay") with the following: 5.015

Holiday pay outside this sub-paragraph is to be treated as capital (reg.48(3)), with no disregard. It then appears that it cannot be taken into account as actual income, whether it would in the absence of reg.48(3) be regarded as earnings under the general meaning in reg.35(1) or as income other than earnings. In either case there is also a disregard (Sch.8, paras 1–2, and Sch.9, para.32).

pp.393–396, *annotation to the Income Support (General) Regulations 1987 (SI 1987/1967) reg.37 (Earnings of self-employed earners)*

SSWP v MA (ESA) [2024] UKUT 131 (AAC) decides that the fact that the claimant's income was derived from the criminal enterprise of buying and selling stolen bikes on an industrial scale did not prevent it counting as earnings from self-employment. If for some reason that did not work, it would count as income other than earnings. Although the main point in the case was whether the claimant's activity constituted "work", so as to cause him to be treated as not entitled to ESA under reg.40 of the ESA Regulations 2008 (which it did), it was possible that there were some weeks in which he did not work in which the self-employed earnings would be relevant. 5.016

The two Business Interruption Loan Schemes and the Bounce Back Loan Scheme ceased to operate on March 31, 2021, to be replaced by the Recovery Loan Scheme.

p.412, *annotation to the Income Support (General) Regulations 1987 (SI 1987/1967) reg.40(1) (Calculation of income other than earnings)*

Add to the non-exhaustive list of benefits disregarded as income under Sch.9, various Scottish benefits (paras 81–85 of Sch.9). 5.017

p.421, *amendment to the Income Support (General) Regulations 1987 (SI 1987/1967) reg.42(4ZB) (Notional income—exceptions)*

With effect from January 1, 2022, reg.2(3) of the Social Security (Income and Capital Disregards) (Amendment) Regulations 2021 (SI 2021/1405) amended para.(4ZB) by substituting the following for "a payment of income which is a Grenfell Tower payment": 5.018

"any of the following payments of income—
(a) a Grenfell Tower payment;
(b) a child abuse payment;
(c) a Windrush payment."

All of those payments are defined in reg.2(1). See the entry for p.684 for discussion of the nature of child abuse and Windrush payments.

With effect from July 9, 2023, reg.2(3) of the Social Security (Income and Capital Disregards) (Amendment) Regulations 2023 (SI 2023/640) amended reg.42(4ZA) by inserting the following after sub-para.(c):

"(d) a Post Office compensation payment."

Such payments are newly defined in reg.2(1), where there is now also an expanded definition of Grenfell Tower payments. See the entry for pp.684–685 for the background.

pp.431–433, *annotation to the Income Support (General) Regulations 1987 (SI 1987/1967) reg.42(4) and (4ZA) (Notional income—third parties)*

5.019 Note the extended exception to the operation of para.(4) (see the entry for p.421).

p.438, *annotation to the Income Support (General) Regulations 1987 (SI 1987/967) reg.45 (Capital limit)*

5.020 In the Institute for Government and the Social Security Advisory Committee's 2021 joint report *Jobs and benefits: The Covid-19 challenge* it was noted that if the capital limit of £16,000 had risen in line with prices since 2006 it would be close to £23,500 (or £25,000: different figures are given) and recommended that the limit should be increased to £25,000 and subsequently automatically indexed to maintain its real value (pp.22 and 31). That recommendation was summarily rejected in the Government's response of March 22, 2022.

p.439, *annotation to the Income Support (General) Regulations 1987 (SI 1987/1967) reg.46 (Calculation of capital)*

5.021 At some point, the valuation of digital assets, such as non-fungible tokens, cryptocurrency etc., may have to be addressed, including how they fit into the notions of capital and of personal possessions. There is extensive discussion of the existing legal framework in the Law Commission's *Digital Assets: Consultation Paper* (Law Com. No.256, July 28, 2022). Now see *Digital Assets: Final report* (Law Com. No.412, June 27, 2023). The DWP universal credit guidance on the treatment of capital deposited in the House of Commons library (as collected in the Resources section of the Rightsnet website) suggests that cryptoassets, including cryptocurrency, be treated as investments, with a 10% deduction from valuation for expenses of sale. If cryptocurrency were to be treated like any other money, para.21 of Sch.10 on commission or banking charges for conversion into sterling would need consideration.

pp.440–441, *annotation to the Income Support (General) Regulations 1987 (SI 1987/1967) reg.46 (Calculation of capital)*

The text in the paragraph starting "See also" on p.440 to the paragraph ending "had ceased." on p.441 should be deleted. 5.022

Insert the following text on p.441 between the paragraph starting "However" and the heading "*Beneficial ownership*":

Interests under a will or intestacy when someone has died

The DMG (paras 29169-29175) contains guidance adopting in para.29174 the general principle that a beneficiary under a will or intestacy has no legal or equitable interest in any specific property while the estate remains unadministered. The personal representative in those circumstances has full ownership of the assets of the estate. That principle was applied by the Tribunal of Commissioners in *R(SB) 5/85*, relying on the foundational Privy Council decision in *Commissioner of Stamp Duties (Queensland) v Livingston* [1965] A.C. 694.

However, there are two important qualifications. The first is that, even where the *Livingston* principle applies, the beneficiary has a right to have the deceased's estate properly administered. That is a chose in action that has a market value. It can be transferred and can be borrowed against. Depending on the particular circumstances, the market value can be considerable and not far off the value that would be put on the asset(s) in question if owned outright. That point was made clearly by Commissioner Howell in para.28 of his decision in *R(IS) 1/01* and nothing to the contrary was said in the Court of Appeal in *Wilkinson v Chief Adjudication Officer*, reported as part of *R(IS) 1/01*, in upholding the Commissioner's decision. Nor is *R(SB) 5/85* to the contrary: the Commissioners there expressly noted that the claimant had a chose in action (para.7). It is submitted that that is the basis on which the later decision of Commissioner Howell in *CIS/1189/2003* is to be supported. The claimant there was the sole residuary beneficiary under her mother's will and the estate, whose main asset was a property that the claimant did not live in, remained unadministered for several years, so that the property had not actually vested in the claimant. In para.11, the Commissioner said that the claimant was beneficially entitled to the property from the date of her mother's death subject only to the formalities needed to perfect her title, so that for all practical purposes she had an entitlement equivalent to full beneficial ownership. That proposition can easily be misinterpreted, but in para.12, the Commissioner noted that as the claimant was the sole *residuary* beneficiary, it was para.28 of *R(IS) 1/01* that was applicable. So the valuation was of the claimant's chose in action, but in the circumstances the difference in value from that of full beneficial ownership was negligible.

The second qualification is that the position may be different where there has been a specific gift of some asset, as was the case in *R(IS) 1/01*, where the will of the claimant's mother gave the claimant and her brother equal shares in some income bonds and other money in a bank account and in a property. The matter was put very strongly by Commissioner Howell in para.27 of his decision, where he said that the *Livingston* principle had:

> "never had any application to property specifically devised or bequeathed by a will. Such property becomes in equity the property of the legatee as

> soon as the testator dies, subject only to the right of the personal representative to resort to it for payment of debts if the remainder of the estate is insufficient for this purpose [citations omitted]."

No specific comment on that proposition was made in the judgments of the Court of Appeal in *Wilkinson*, but Mummery LJ did note generally that the evidence did not suggest that there was any question of the executors needing to have recourse to the property for payment of debts or that there was any other legal obstacle to the immediate completion of the administration of the estate and to an assent by the executors vesting the property in the names of the claimant and her brother as joint owners. That strongly suggests that what was being considered was a valuation of the claimant's chose in action, rather than of some equitable interest. It is submitted that that is the proper approach. The valuation would therefore be sensitive to the possibilities mentioned by Mummery LJ in the particular case, as well as to the value of the underlying asset. That approach would hold also for personal property or money, although there it should be noted that the process of the personal representative giving an assent, i.e. an indication that a certain asset is not required for administration purposes and may pass under the will or (possibly) an intestacy into the ownership of the beneficiary, does not need to be in writing and may be implied from conduct.

p.443, *annotation to the Income Support (General) Regulations 1987 (SI 1987/967) reg.46 (Calculation of capital—claimant holding as trustee)*

5.023 In line 10 of the paragraph starting "One particular", insert the following between "return it" and the full stop:

> "(a result most recently confirmed by the decision of the Privy Council in the *Prickly Bay* case)"

p.446, *annotation to the Income Support (General) Regulations 1987 (SI 1987/967) reg.46 (Calculation of capital—claimant holding as trustee)*

5.024 Note, in relation to the discussion of cases in which the *Quistclose* principle has or has not been applied, that the Privy Council in *Prickly Bay Waterside Ltd v British American Insurance Co Ltd* [2022] UKPC 8; [2022] 1 W.L.R. 2087, while accepting the value of summaries of principles, in particular of those established by the judgment of Lord Millett in *Twinsectra Ltd v Yardley* [2002] 2 A.C. 164, warned against not going back to the "core analysis" in that judgment. It was emphasised again that it is not enough that money is provided for a particular purpose. The question is whether the parties intended that the money should be at the free disposition of the recipient. An intention that it should not be need not be mutual, in the sense of being shared or reciprocated, but could be imposed by one party and acquiesced in by the other. A *Quistclose* trust is a default trust, so can be excluded or moulded by the terms of the parties' express agreements. In the particular case, involving complex commercial transactions in which a sum was loaned to a bank that contracted to guarantee payment of the purchase price of a property on future completion, it was significant to the outcome that a *Quistclose* trust had not been established that there had been no requirement that the sum be segregated by the bank from its other funds. It is submitted that in other contexts, such as family or other relatively informal arrangements more likely to be encountered in the social security context, a lack of segregation, say into a separate account, would not carry nearly such weight.

p.449, *annotation to the Income Support (General) Regulations 1987 (SI 1987/1967) reg.46 (Calculation of capital—claimant holding as trustee)*

5.025 Note, in relation to the decision in *Marr v Collie*, that the Court of Appeal (*Williams v Williams* [2024] EWCA Civ 42; [2024] 4 W.L.R. 10) has applied what it described as the "long-standing principle of equity that property acquired in joint names for business purposes would be presumed to be held beneficially as tenants in common rather than as joint tenants with the accidents of survivorship". There was nothing in *Stack v Dowden* or *Jones v Kermott* relied on in the domestic context to suggest that that principle had been undermined or affected in any way.

p.451, *annotation to the Income Support (General) Regulations 1987 (SI 1987/1967) reg.46 (Calculation of capital—claimant holding as trustee)*

5.026 Note the decision of the Supreme Court, by a majority of three to two, in *Guest v Guest* [2022] UKSC 27; [2022] 3 W.L.R. 911 on proprietary estoppel and the nature of the remedies available in equity. Lord Briggs, giving the majority judgment, conducted an exhaustive survey of the English and Australian case law, as well as academic debate, and rejected the theory that the aim of the remedy was to compensate the person given a promise or assurance about the acquisition of property for the detriment suffered in reliance on the promise or assurance, rather than primarily to hold the person who had given the promise or assurance to the promise or assurance, which would usually prevent the unconscionability inherent in the repudiation of the promise or assurance that had been detrimentally relied on (paras 71 and 61). However, the remedy was a flexible one dependent on the circumstances. Lord Briggs summarised the principles as follows:

> "74. I consider that, in principle, the court's normal approach should be as follows. The first stage (which is not in issue in this case) is to determine whether the promisor's repudiation of his promise is, in the light of the promisee's detrimental reliance upon it, unconscionable at all. It usually will be, but there may be circumstances (such as the promisor falling on hard times and needing to sell the property to pay his creditors, or to pay for expensive medical treatment or social care for himself or his wife) when it may not be. Or the promisor may have announced or carried out only a partial repudiation of the promise, which may or may not have been unconscionable, depending on the circumstances.
>
> 75. The second (remedy) stage will normally start with the assumption (not presumption) that the simplest way to remedy the unconscionability constituted by the repudiation is to hold the promisor to the promise. The promisee cannot (and probably would not) complain,

for example, that his detrimental reliance had cost him more than the value of the promise, were it to be fully performed. But the court may have to listen to many other reasons from the promisor (or his executors) why something less than full performance will negate the unconscionability and therefore satisfy the equity. They may be based on one or more of the real-life problems already outlined. The court may be invited by the promisor to consider one or more proxies for performance of the promise, such as the transfer of less property than promised or the provision of a monetary equivalent in place of it, or a combination of the two.

76. If the promisor asserts and proves, the burden being on him for this purpose, that specific enforcement of the full promise, or monetary equivalent, would be out of all proportion to the cost of the detriment to the promisee, then the court may be constrained to limit the extent of the remedy. This does not mean that the court will be seeking precisely to compensate for the detriment as its primary task, but simply to put right a disproportionality which is so large as to stand in the way of a full specific enforcement doing justice between the parties. It will be a very rare case where the detriment is equivalent in value to the expectation, and there is nothing in principle unjust in a full enforcement of the promise being worth more than the cost of the detriment, any more than there is in giving specific performance of a contract for the sale of land merely because it is worth more than the price paid for it. An example of a remedy out of all proportion to the detriment would be the full enforcement of a promise by an elderly lady to leave her carer a particular piece of jewellery if she stayed on at very low wages, which turned out on valuation by her executors to be a Faberge worth millions. Another would be a promise to leave a generous inheritance if the promisee cared for the promisor for the rest of her life, but where she unexpectedly died two months later."

Winter v Winter [2024] EWCA Civ 699, in another farm case, has explored the requirement of detriment in some detail, in particular holding that when deciding whether a claimant has suffered detriment as a result of reliance on an assurance, the court must weigh any non-financial disadvantage against any financial benefit even where the disadvantage is not susceptible to quantification, and even though it is a difficult exercise.

Thus, in circumstances where proprietary estoppel might be in play (as would probably now be the case on similar facts to *R(SB) 23/85* and *R(SB) 7/87*), great care would be needed in establishing the primary facts and, outside the clearest cases, in a deeper investigation of the principles of law governing the nature of any remedy available. And would a repudiation of a promise when the promisor would otherwise be forced to rely on a means-tested benefit be unconscionable? However, even if it were to be concluded that the claimant did not hold the property in question on trust for someone else, the possibility of a claim in equity, e.g. for some monetary compensation, may well affect the valuation of the property.

p.457, *amendment to the Income Support (General) Regulations 1987 (SI 1987/1967) reg.48(10) (Income treated as capital—exceptions)*

With effect from January 1, 2022, reg.2(4) of the Social Security (Income and Capital Disregards) (Amendment) Regulations 2021 (SI 2021/1405) amended para.(10) by inserting the following after sub-para.(ab): 5.027

> "(ac) which is a child abuse payment;
> (ad) which is a Windrush payment; or"

Both of those payments are defined in reg.2(1). See the entry for p.684 for discussion of their nature. The "or" following sub-para.(ab), omitted in error in the main volume, has also been removed.

With effect from July 9, 2023, reg.2(4) of the Social Security (Income and Capital Disregards) (Amendment) Regulations 2023 (SI 2023/640) amended reg.48(10) by omitting "or" at the end of sub-para.(ad) and inserting the following:

> "(ae) which is a Post Office compensation payment."

Such payments are newly defined in reg.2(1), where there is now also an expanded definition of Grenfell Tower payments (see sub-para.(ab)). See the entry for pp.684–685 for the background.

With effect from October 27, 2023, reg.3(3)(a) of the Social Security (Habitual Residence and Past Presence, and Capital Disregards) (Amendment) Regulations 2023 (SI 2023/1144) amended reg.48(10)(c) by inserting ", the Victims of Overseas Terrorism Compensation Scheme" after "the National Emergencies Trust". That scheme is newly defined in reg.2(1). See the entry for pp.684–685 for the background.

p.467, *amendment to the Income Support (General) Regulations 1987 (SI 1987/1967) reg.51(3B) (Notional capital—exceptions)*

With effect from January 1, 2022, reg.2(5) of the Social Security (Income and Capital Disregards) (Amendment) Regulations 2021 (SI 2021/1405) amended para.(3B) by substituting the following for "a payment of capital which is a Grenfell Tower payment": 5.028

> "any of the following payments of capital—
> (a) a Grenfell Tower payment;
> (b) a child abuse payment;
> (c) a Windrush payment."

All of those payments are defined in reg.2(1). See the entry for p.684 for discussion of the nature of child abuse and Windrush payments.

With effect from July 9, 2023, reg.2(5) of the Social Security (Income and Capital Disregards) (Amendment) Regulations 2023 (SI 2023/640) amended reg.51(3B) by inserting the following after sub-para.(c):

> "(d) a Post Office compensation payment;
> (f) a vaccine damage payment."

Such payments are newly defined in reg.2(1), where there is now also an expanded definition of Grenfell Tower payments (see sub-para.(a)). See the entry for pp.684–685 for the background.

With effect from October 27, 2023, reg.3(3)(b) of the Social Security (Habitual Residence and Past Presence, and Capital Disregards) (Amendment) Regulations 2023 (SI 2023/1144) amended reg.51(3A)(a) by inserting ", the Victims of Overseas Terrorism Compensation Scheme" after "the National Emergencies Trust". That scheme is newly defined in reg.2(1). See the entry for pp.684–685 for the background.

p.482, *annotation to the Income Support (General) Regulations 1987 (SI 1987/1967) reg.51(1) (Notional capital—deprivation)*

5.029 See the entry for pp.1029–30 for the acceptance of the position under reg.113(1) of the JSA Regulations 1996 in *DB v DfC (JSA)* [2021] NICom 43. There, it was found that the claimant had deprived herself of capital while in receipt of income-related ESA. It was inherently improbable that when doing so, more than a year before she claimed JSA, she had possible entitlement to JSA or income support in mind. The tribunal had failed to make necessary findings of fact in concluding that her purpose had been the securing of entitlement to JSA. The principle would apply even more so to reg.51(1), where the test of purpose is still restricted to income support (but contrast the position reg.115(1) of the ESA Regulations 2008).

The decision also illustrates that on a new claim neither the decision-maker nor a tribunal on appeal is bound by the findings of fact on capital that have underpinned a decision of non-entitlement on capital grounds. The basis of the ESA decision, that the claimant as at that date still had actual capital of more than £40,000, did not have to be adopted on the JSA claim.

pp.520–523, *annotations to the Income Support (General) Regulations 1987 (SI 1987/1967) reg.61 (Interpretation—students—meaning of "Full-time course")*

5.030 The principles derived from the case law, taking into account Court of Appeal decisions not all of which are discussed in the main volume, have recently very helpfully been summarised by Judge Rowley in para.19 of *BK v SSWP (UC)* [2022] UKUT 73 (AAC) (some references added by annotator):

"a. Whether or not a person is undertaking a full-time course is a question of fact for the tribunal having regard to the circumstances in each particular case (*R/SB 40/83* at [13]; *R(SB) 41/83* at [12]). Parameters have been set, as appear below:

b. The words 'full-time' relate to the course and not to the student. Specifically, they do not permit the matter to be determined by reference to the amount of time which the student happens to dedicate to their studies (*R/SB 40/83* at [14], [15]; *R(SB) 2/91* at [7]; *R(SB) 41/83* at [11]).

c. Evidence from the educational establishment as to whether or not the course is full-time is not necessarily conclusive, but it ought to be accepted as such unless it is inconclusive on its face, or is challenged by relevant evidence which at least raises the possibility that it ought to be rejected (*R/SB 40/83* at [18]), and any evidence adduced in

Judge Poynter formulated the correct test to be applied, without the *CH/4429/2006* limitation and in line with the established approach in other areas of social security law, as follows:

> "139. I therefore conclude that "reasonable steps" means steps that are reasonable in all the circumstances including all the personal characteristics of the individual who was eligible to have applied for the student loan. That includes strong conscientious religious or other objections to the payment of interest.
> 140. I would, however, add that all the circumstances includes the interests of the wider public as represented by the Secretary of State and that assessing reasonableness will need to give those interests weight (see paragraphs 190–191 below). Without being prescriptive, I suggest that an omission to acquire a loan that is based on purely financial considerations is unlikely to outweigh those interests."

He rejected the Secretary of State's submission that that approach would involve direct discrimination against claimants who did not share his particular religious views. That was because (para.142):

> "[t]he line drawn by my interpretation is not between Muslims and non-Muslims nor even between people who have conscientious objections to taking out a student loan and those who don't. Rather it is between, on the one hand, any student whose personal circumstances as a whole are such that—for whatever reason—he cannot take reasonable steps to acquire a student loan and, on the other, all students who are not so circumstanced. Those two groups are not in analogous situations. The latter could reasonably acquire the loan that [the regulation] takes into account as their income. The former cannot."

The judge also rejected the submission that his interpretation would make the housing benefit scheme unworkable and invite numerous, possibly opportunistic, claims, pointing out the limited scope for students to qualify for housing benefit (as for other means-tested benefits, including income support), the fact that to benefit from the rule the claimant would have to turn down the advantages of actually receiving the loan on offer and the difficulties that claimants might have in showing a genuine conscientious religious or other objection to the payment of interest. The latter point might easily be tested by seeing if the particular claimant had any interest-bearing bank or building society accounts, a credit card or a non-Sharia mortgage. Finally, there was the limiting factor of the need to take into account when judging reasonableness the interests of the wider public, in the form of the government policy that the costs of education are usually to be funded from the education budget rather than the social security benefit.

However, in substituting his own decision in IB Judge Poynter had no doubt that the claimant's personal circumstances, in particular his sincere and strongly held religious conviction that it would be a major sin to pay interest, outweighed any loss to public funds or dent in the government's general policy.

The result is that at the moment there are two conflicting decisions of equal authority. A First-tier Tribunal may therefore choose to follow the decision whose reasoning it finds more convincing. In doing so it can give weight to the fact that IB contains a detailed review of the reasoning in *CH/4429/2006*.

p.542, *amendment to the Income Support (General) Regulations 1987 (SI 1987/1967) reg.66D (Treatment of special support loans)*

5.034 With effect from April 1, 2024, reg.3 of the Social Security and Universal Credit (Migration of Tax Credit Claimants and Miscellaneous Amendments) Regulations 2024 (SI 2024/341) amended reg.66D by substituting the following for the existing text and heading:

> **"Treatment of loans for specific purposes**
>
> **66D.** A loan under the Education (Student Support) Regulations 2011 or regulations made under section 73 of the Education (Scotland) Act 1980 that is intended to meet the cost of books, equipment, travel or childcare is to be disregarded as income."

The new form of reg.66D is intended to ensure that special support loans under a scheme to be introduced for full-time students by the Scottish government from the beginning of academic year 2024/25 are to be disregarded as income in same way as special support loans in England and Wales. Although the new form no longer refers to the definition of "special support loan" in reg.68 of the Education (Student Support) Regulations 2011, the restriction to loans intended (i.e., by necessary implication, intended by the awarding authority) to meet the cost of books, equipment, travel or childcare excludes loans under those regulations for other purposes. See reg.62 for the disregard of grants, as opposed to loans, for similar and other purposes.

p.550, *amendments to the Income Support (General) Regulations 1987 (SI 1987/1967) Sch.1B (Prescribed categories of persons)*

5.035 With effect from July 26, 2021, Sch.1 para.4 of the Social Security (Scotland) Act 2018 (Disability Assistance for Children and Young People) (Consequential Modifications) Order 2021 (SI 2021/786) makes the following amendments:

- In para.4(a) of Sch.1B (persons caring for another person):
  - in para.(i), after "Contributions and Benefits Act" insert ", the care component of child disability payment at the highest or middle rate in accordance with the DACYP Regulations (see regulation 11(5) of those Regulations),";
  - in para.(iii), after "disability living allowance", insert ", child disability payment";
  - after para.(iiia), insert "(iiib) the person being cared for ("P") has claimed entitlement to the care component of child disability payment in accordance with regulation 24 (when an application is to be treated as made and beginning of entitlement to assistance) of the DACYP Regulations, an award at the highest or middle rate has been made in respect of P's claim, and where the period for which the award is payable has begun, P is in receipt of that payment;".

With effect from March 21, 2022, art.2(4)–(5) of the Social Security (Disability Assistance for Working Age People) (Consequential Amendments) Order 2022 (SI 2022/177) makes the following amendments:

- In para.4(a) (persons caring for another person) of Sch.1B (prescribed categories of person):
    - in sub-para.(i):
        - for "or" after "(see regulation 11(5) of those Regulations)," substitute ",";
        - after "2012 Act" insert "or the daily living component of adult disability payment at the standard or enhanced rate in accordance with regulation 5 of the Disability Assistance for Working Age People (Scotland) Regulations 2022";
    - in sub-para.(iii):
        - for "or" after "armed forces independence payment" substitute ",";
        - after "personal independence payment" insert "or adult disability payment";
    - after sub-para.(iv) insert "(v)the person being cared for has claimed entitlement to the daily living component of adult disability payment in accordance with regulation 35 (when an application is to be treated as made and beginning of entitlement to assistance) of the Disability Assistance for Working Age People (Scotland) Regulations 2022, an award at the standard or enhanced rate has been made in respect of that claim and, where the period for which the award is payable has begun, that person is in receipt of the payment;".
- In para.7A (certain persons in receipt of the daily living component of personal independence payment) of Sch.1B:
    - in the heading, after "personal independence payment" insert "or adult disability payment";
    - after "at the enhanced rate" insert "or the daily living component of adult disability payment at the enhanced rate".

With effect from November 19, 2023, art.5 of the Carer's Assistance (Carer Support Payment) (Scotland) Regulations 2023 (Consequential Amendments) Order 2023 (SI 2023/1218) makes the following amendments to paragraph 4(b) of Schedule 1B:

- after "carer's allowance" insert "or carer support payment";
- for "that allowance" substitute "a carer's allowance".

pp.571–572, *amendments to the Income Support (General) Regulations 1987 (SI 1987/1967) Sch.2 (Applicable amounts)*

The text in the main volume at paras 2.606–2.626 should be replaced with the following: **5.036**

Regulations 17 [3 (1)] and 18

"SCHEDULE 2

APPLICABLE AMOUNTS

[35 PART I

PERSONAL ALLOWANCES

2.606 **1.**—The weekly amounts specified in column (2) below in respect of each person or couple specified in column (1) shall be the weekly amounts specified for the purposes of regulations 17(1) and 18(1) (applicable amounts and polygamous marriages).

Column (1) *Person or Couple*	*Column (2)* *Amount*
(1) Single claimant aged— (a) except where head (b) or (c) of this sub-paragraph applies, less than 18; [28(b) less than 18 who falls within any of the circumstances specified in paragraph 1A;] (c) less than 18 who satisfies the condition in [65 paragraph 11(1)(a)] (d) not less than 18 but less than 25; (e) not less than 25.	(1) (a) [86 £71.70]; (b) [86 £71.70]; (c) [86 £71.70]; (d) [86 £71.70]; (e) [86 £90.50].
(2) Lone parent aged— (a) except where head (b) or (c) of this sub-paragraph applies, less than 18; [28(b) less than 18 who falls within any of the circumstances specified in paragraph 1A;] (c) less than 18 who satisfies the condition in [65 paragraph 11(1)(a)] (d) not less than 18.	(2) (a) [86 £71.70]; (b) [86 £71.70]; (c) [86 £67.20]; (d) [86 £90.50].
[28(3) Couple— (a) where both members are aged less than 18 and— (i) at least one of them is treated as responsible fora child; or (ii) had they not been members of a couple, each would have qualified for income support under regulation 4ZA [71 or income-related employment and support allowance]; or (iii) the claimant's partner satisfies the requirement of section 3(1)(f)(iii) of the Jobseekers Act 1995 (prescribed circumstances for persons aged 16 but less than 18); or (iv) there is in force in respect of the claimant's partner a direction under section 16 of the Jobseekers Act 1995 (persons under 18: severe hardship); (b) where both members are aged less than 18 and head (a) does not apply but one member of the couple falls within any of the circumstances specified in paragraph 1A;	(3) (a) [86 £108.30]; (b) [86 £71.70];
Column (1) *Person or Couple*	*Column (2)* *Amount*

(c) where both members are aged less than 18 and heads (a) and (b) do not apply;	(c) [86 £71.70];
(d) where both members are aged not less than 18;	(d) [86 £142.25];
(e) where one member is aged not less than 18 and the other member is a person under 18 who—(2) (i) qualifies for income support under regulation 4ZA [71 or income-related employment and support allowance], or who would so qualify if he were not a member of a couple; or (ii) satisfies the requirements of section 3(1)(f)(iii) of the Jobseekers Act 1995 (prescribed circumstances for persons aged 16 but less than 18); or (iii) is the subject of a direction under section 16 of the Jobseekers Act 1995 (persons under 18: severe hardship);	(e) [86 £142.25];
(f) where the claimant is aged not less than 18 but less (f) than 25 and his partner is a person under 18 who— (i) would not qualify for income support under regulation 4ZA [71 or income-related employment and support allowance] if he were not a member of a couple; and (ii) does not satisfy the requirements of section 3(1)(f)(iii) of the Jobseekers Act 1995 (prescribed circumstances for persons aged 16 but less than 18); and (iii) is not the subject of a direction under section 16 of the Jobseekers Act 1995 (persons under 18: severe hardship);	(f) [86 £71.70];
(g) where the claimant is aged not less than 25 and his (g) partner is a person under 18 who— (i) would not qualify for income support under regulation 4ZA [71 or income-related employment and support allowance] if he were not a member of a couple; and (ii) does not satisfy the requirements of section 3(1)(f)(iii) of the Jobseekers Act 1995 (prescribed circumstances for persons aged 16 but less than 18); and (iii) is not the subject of a direction under section 16 of the Jobseekers Act 1995 (persons under 18: severe hardship).]]	(g) [86 £90.50].

[28 **1A.**—(1) The circumstances referred to in paragraph 1 are that— **2.607**

(a) the person has no parents nor any person acting in the place of his parents;

(b) the person—

(i) is not living with his parents nor any person acting in the place of his parents; and

(ii) in England and Wales, was being looked after by a local authority pursuant to a relevant enactment who placed him with some person other than a close relative of his; or in Scotland, was in the care of a local authority under a relevant enactment and whilst in that care was not living with his parents or any close relative, or was in custody in any institution to which the Prison Act 1952 or the Prisons (Scotland) Act 1989 applied immediately before he attained the age of 16;

(c) the person is in accommodation which is other than his parental home, and which is other than the home of a person acting in the place of his parents, who entered that accommodation—

(i) as part of a programme of rehabilitation or resettlement, that programme being under the supervision of the probation service or a local authority; or

(ii) in order to avoid physical or sexual abuse; or

(iii) because of a mental or physical handicap or illness and needs such accommodation because of his handicap or illness;

(d) the person is living away from his parents and any person who is acting in the place of his parents in a case where his parents are or, as the case may be, that person is, unable financially to support him and his parents are, or that person is—

(i) chronically sick or mentally or physically disabled; or

(ii) detained in custody pending trial or sentence upon conviction or under sentence imposed by a court; of

(iii) prohibited from entering or re-entering Great Britain; or

(e) the person of necessity has to live away from his parents and any person acting in the place of his parents because—

(i) he is estranged from his parents and that person; or

(ii) he is in physical or moral danger; or

(iii) there is a serious risk to his physical or mental health.

(2) In this paragraph—

(a) "chronically sick or mentally or physically disabled" has the same meaning it has in regulation 13(3)(b) (circumstances in which persons in relevant education are to be entitled to income support);

(b) in England and Wales, any reference to a person acting in place of a person's parents includes a reference to—

(i) where the person is being looked after by a local authority or voluntary organisation who place him with a family, a relative of his, or some other suitable person, the person with whom the person is placed, whether or not any payment is made to him in connection with the placement; or

(ii) in any other case, any person with parental responsibility for the child, and for this purpose "parental responsibility" has the meaning it has in the Children Act 1989 by virtue of section 3 of that Act;

(c) in Scotland, any reference to a person acting in place of a person's parents includes a reference to a local authority or voluntary organisation where the person is in their care under a relevant enactment, or to a person with whom the person is boarded out by a local authority or voluntary organisation whether or not any payment is made by them.]

2.608 [[35] **2.**—[[59] . . .]]

2.609 [[17] **2A.**—[[55] . . .]]

Part II

Regulations 17[**3** (1)](c) [[3] and 18(1)](d)

Family Premium

2.610 **3.**—[[59] . . .]

Part III

Regulations 17[**3** (1)](d) [**3** and 18(1)](e)

Premiums

2.611 **4.**—Except as provided in paragraph 5, the weekly premiums specified in Part IV of this Schedule shall, for the purposes of regulations 17[[3](1)](d)[[3] and 18(1)](e), be applicable to a claimant who satisfies the condition specified in [[42] paragraphs 8A] [[10] to 14ZA] in respect of that premium.

5.—Subject to paragraph 6, where a claimant satisfies the conditions in respect of more than one premium in this Part of this Schedule, only one premium shall be applicable to him and, if they are different amounts, the higher or highest amount shall apply.

[58 **6.**—(1) Subject to sub-paragraph (2), the following premiums, namely—

(a) a severe disability to which paragraph 13 applies;

(b) an enhanced disability premium to which paragraph 13A applies;

(c) [59 . . .]; and

(d) a carer premium to which paragraph 14ZA applies,

may be applicable in addition to any other premium that may apply under this Schedule.

(2) An enhanced disability premium in respect of a person shall not be applicable in addition to—

(a) a pensioner premium under paragraph 9 or 9A; or

(b) a higher pension premium under paragraph 10.]

7.—[10(1) Subject to sub-paragraph (2)] for the purposes of this Part of this Schedule, once a premium is applicable to a claimant under this Part, a person shall be treated as being in receipt of any benefit—

(a) in the case of a benefit to which the Social Security (Overlapping Benefits) Regulations 1979 applies, for any period during which, apart from the provisions of those Regulations, he would be in receipt of that benefit; [85 . . .]

(b) for any period spent by a claimant in undertaking a course of training or instruction provided or approved by the [12 Secretary of State [68 . . .]] under section 2 of the Employment and Training Act 1973 [11, or by [69 Skills Development Scotland,] Scottish Enterprise or Highlands and Islands Enterprise under section 2 of the Enterprise and New Towns (Scotland) Act 1990,] [7 or for any period during which he is in receipt of a training allowance]. [85 ; and

(c) in the case of carer support payment, for any period during which, apart from regulation 16 of the Carer's Assistance (Carer Support Payment) (Scotland) Regulations 2023, he would be in receipt of that benefit.]

[10(2) For the purposes of the carer premium under paragraph 14ZA, a person shall be treated as being in receipt of [49 carer's allowance] by virtue of sub-paragraph (1)(a) [87 or carer support payment by virtue of sub-paragraph (1)(c)] only if and for so long as the person in respect of whose care the allowance [85 or payment] has been claimed remains in receipt of attendance allowance [15 , [75 . . .] the care component of disability living allowance at the highest or middle rate prescribed in accordance with section 37ZB(3) of the Social Security Act [SSCBA, s.72(3)]] [82 , the care component of child disability payment at the highest or middle rate prescribed in accordance with the regulation 11(5) of the DACYP Regulations] [75 or the daily living component of personal independence payment at the standard or enhanced rate in accordance with section 78(3) of the 2012 Act] [83 , the daily living component of adult disability payment at the standard or enhanced rate in accordance with regulation 5 of the Disability Assistance for Working Age People (Scotland) Regulations 2022] [76 or armed forces independence payment].]

Lone Parent Premium

8.—[29 . . .]. 2.612

[42 Bereavement Premium

8A.—[67 . . .]] 2.613

[Pensioner premium for persons under 75

[54 **9.**—The condition is that the claimant has a partner aged [70 not less than the qualifying age for state pension credit] but less than 75.] 2.614

Pensioner premium for persons 75 and over

[54 **9A.**—The condition is that the claimant has a partner aged not less than 75 but less than 80.]] 2.615

Higher Pensioner Premium

10.—[54 (1) [65 Subject to sub-paragraph (6), the] condition is that— 2.616

(a) the claimant's partner is aged not less than 80; or

(b) the claimant's partner is aged less than 80 but [70 not less than the qualifying age for state pension credit] and either—

(i) the additional condition specified in [58 paragraph 12(1)(a), (c) or (d)] is satisfied; or

(ii) the claimant was entitled to, or was treated as being in receipt of, income support and—

(aa) the disability premium was or, as the case may be, would have been, applicable to him in respect of a benefit week within eight weeks of [70 the day his partner attained the qualifying age for state pension credit]; and

(bb) he has, subject to sub-paragraph (3), remained continuously entitled to income support since his partner attained [70 the qualifying age for state pension credit].]

(2) [. . .]

(3) For the purposes of this paragraph and paragraph 12—

(a) once the higher pensioner premium is applicable to a claimant, if he then ceases, for a period of eight weeks or less, to be entitled to [41or treated as entitled to] income support, he shall, on becoming re-entitled to income support, thereafter be treated as having been continuously entitled thereto;

(b) in so far as [54 sub-paragraph (1)(b)(ii) is] concerned, if a claimant ceases to be entitled to [41or treated as entitled to] income support for a period not exceeding eight weeks which includes [70 the day his partner attained the qualifying age for state pension credit], he shall, on becoming re-entitled to income support, thereafter be treated as having been continuously entitled thereto.

[33 (4) In the case of a claimant who is a welfare to work beneficiary, references in sub-paragraphs (1)(b)(ii) [65 . . .] and (3)(b) to a period of 8 weeks shall be treated as references to a period of [64 104 weeks].]

[41 (5) For the purposes of this paragraph, a claimant shall be treated as having been entitled to and in receipt of income support throughout any period which comprises only days on which he was participating in an employment zone programme and was not entitled to income support because, as a consequence of his participation in that programme, he was engaged in remunerative work or had income in excess of his applicable amount as prescribed in Part IV.]

[65 (6) The condition is not satisfied if the claimant's partner to whom sub-paragraph (1) refers is a long-term patient.]

Disability Premium

2.617 **11.**—[65 (1) Subject to sub-paragraph (2), the] condition is that—

(a) where the claimant is a single claimant or a lone parent, [54 . . .] the additional condition specified in paragraph 12 is satisfied; or

(b) where the claimant has a partner, either—

[54 (i) the claimant satisfies the additional condition specified in paragraph [58 12(1)(a), (b), (c) or (d)]; or]

(ii) his partner [70 has not attained the qualifying age for state pension credit] and the additional condition specified in [58 paragraph 12(1)(a), (c) or (d)] is satisfied by his partner.

[65 (2) The condition is not satisfied if—

(a) the claimant is a single claimant or a lone parent and (in either case) is a long-term patient;

(b) the claimant is a member of a couple or polygamous marriage and each member of the couple or polygamous marriage is a long-term patient; or

(c) the claimant is a member of a couple or a polygamous marriage and a member of that couple or polygamous marriage is—

(i) a long-term patient; and

(ii) the only member of the couple or polygamous marriage to whom sub-paragraph (1)(b) refers.]

Additional condition for the Higher Pensioner and Disability Premiums

2.618 **12.**—(1) Subject to sub-paragraph (2) and paragraph 7 the additional condition referred to in paragraphs 10 and 11 is that either—

(a) the claimant or, as the case may be, his partner—

(i) is in receipt of one or more of the following benefits: attendance allowance, [15 disability living allowance, [76 armed forces independence payment,] [75 personal independence payment,] [83 adult disability payment,] [50 the disability element or the severe disability element of working tax credit as specified in regulation 20(1)(b) and (f) of the Working Tax Credit (Entitlement and Maximum Rate) Regulations 2002]], mobility supplement, [25 long-term incapacity benefit] under [22 Part II of the Contributions and Benefits Act or severe disablement allowance under Part III of that Act] [1but, in the case of

[25 long-term incapacity benefit] or severe disablement allowance only where it is paid in respect of him]; or

(ii) is provided by the Secretary of State with an invalid carriage or other vehicle under section 5(2) of the National Health Service Act 1977 (other services) or, in Scotland, under section 46 of the National Health Service (Scotland) Act 1978 (provision of vehicles) or receives payments by way of grant from the Secretary of State under paragraph 2 of Schedule 2 to that 1977 Act (additional provisions as to vehicles) or, in Scotland, under that section 46; or

[77 (iii) is certified as severely sight impaired or blind by a consultant ophthalmologist; or]

[26 (b) the claimant—

(i) is entitled to statutory sick pay or [27 is, or is treated as, incapable of work,] in accordance with the provisions of Part XIIA of the Contributions and Benefits Act and the regulations made thereunder (incapacity for work), and

(ii) has been so entitled or so incapable [27, or has been treated as so incapable,] for a continuous period of not less than—

(aa) 196 days in the case of a claimant who is terminally ill within the meaning of section 30B(4) of the Contributions and Benefits Act; or

(bb) [63 subject to [65 paragraph 2A] of Schedule 7] 364 days in any other case; and for these purposes any two or more periods of entitlement or incapacity separated by a break of not more than 56 days shall be treated as one continuous period; or]

[54 (c) the claimant's partner was in receipt of long-term incapacity benefit under Part II of the Contributions and Benefits Act when entitlement to that benefit ceased on account of the payment of a retirement pension under that Act [81 or a state pension under Part 1 of the Pensions Act 2014] and—

(i) the claimant has since remained continuously entitled to income support;

(ii) the higher pensioner premium or disability premium has been applicable to the claimant; and

(iii) the partner is still alive;

(d) except where paragraph [63 2A [65 . . .]] of Schedule 7 (patients) applies, the claimant or, as the case may be, his partner was in receipt of attendance allowance [75, disability living allowance [83, personal independence payment or adult disability payment]]—

(i) but payment of that benefit has been suspended under the [60 Social Security (Attendance Allowance) Regulations 1991 [75, the Social Security (Disability Living Allowance) Regulations 1991 or regulations made under section 86(1) (hospital in-patients) of the 2012 Act]] or otherwise abated as a consequence of the claimant or his partner becoming a patient within the meaning of regulation 21(3); and

(ii) a higher pensioner premium or disability premium has been applicable to the claimant.]

[34(1A) In the case of a claimant who is a welfare to work beneficiary, the reference in sub-paragraph (1)(b) to a period of 56 days shall be treated as a reference to a period of [64 104 weeks].]

[77 (2) For the purposes of sub-paragraph (1)(a)(iii), a person who has ceased to be certified as severely sight impaired or blind on regaining his eyesight shall nevertheless be treated as severely sight impaired or blind, as the case may be, and as satisfying the additional condition set out in that sub-paragraph for a period of 28 weeks following the date on which he ceased to be so certified.]

(3) [26 . . .]

(4) For the purpose of [58 sub-paragraph (1)(c) and (d)], once the higher pensioner premium is applicable to the claimant by virtue of his satisfying the condition specified in that provision, if he then ceases, for a period of eight weeks or less, to be entitled to income support, he shall on again becoming so entitled to income support, immediately thereafter be treated as satisfying the condition in [58 sub-paragraph (1)(c) and (d)].

[4(5) For the purposes of sub-paragraph (1)(b), once the disability premium is applicable to a claimant by virtue of his satisfying the additional condition specified in that provision, he shall continue to be treated as satisfying that condition for any period spent by him in undertaking a course of training provided under section 2 of the Employment and Training Act 1973 [7 or for any period during which he is in receipt of a training allowance].]

[25(6) For the purposes of [58 sub-paragraph (1)(a)(i) and (c)], a reference to a person in receipt of long-term incapacity benefit includes a person in receipt of short-term incapacity benefit at a rate equal to the long-term rate by virtue of section 30B(4)(a) of the Contributions and Benefits Act (short-term incapacity benefit for a person who is terminally ill), or who would be or would have been in receipt of short-term incapacity benefit at such a rate but for the fact that the rate of short-term incapacity benefit already payable to him is or was equal to or greater than the long-term rate.]

[40 [61 . . .]]

Severe Disability Premium

2.619 **13.**—(1) The condition is that the claimant is a severely disabled person.

(2) For the purposes of sub-paragraph (1), a claimant shall be treated as being a severely disabled person if, and only if—

(a) in the case of a single claimant[19, a lone parent or a claimant who is treated as having no partner in consequence of sub-paragraph (2A)]—

(i) he is in receipt of attendance allowance [15 [75 . . .] the care component of disability living allowance at the highest or middle rate prescribed in accordance with section 37ZB(3) of the Social Security Act [SSCBA, s.72(3)]] [75 or the daily living component of personal independence payment at the standard or enhanced rate in accordance with section 78(3) of the 2012 Act] [83 , the daily living component of adult disability payment at the standard or enhanced rate in accordance with regulation 5 of the Disability Assistance for Working Age People (Scotland) Regulations 2022] [76 or armed forces independence payment], and

(ii) subject to sub-paragraph (3), he has no non-dependants aged 18 or over [23 normally residing with him or with whom he is normally residing,] and

(iii) [41 no person is entitled to, and in receipt of, [49 a carer's allowance] under section 70 of the Contributions and Benefits Act [85 or has an award of universal credit which includes the carer element] in respect of caring for him;]

(b) [42 in the case of a claimant who] has a partner—

(i) he is in receipt of attendance allowance [15, [75 . . .] the care component of disability living allowance at the highest or middle rate prescribed in accordance with section 37ZB(3) of the Social Security Act [SSCBA, s.72(3)]] [75 or the daily living component of personal independence payment at the standard or enhanced rate in accordance with section 78(3) of the 2012 Act] [83 , the daily living component of adult disability payment at the standard or enhanced rate in accordance with regulation 5 of the Disability Assistance for Working Age People (Scotland) Regulations 2022] [76 or armed forces independence payment]; and

(ii) his partner is also in receipt of such an allowance or, if he is a member of a polygamous marriage, all the partners of that marriage are in receipt thereof; and

(iii) subject to sub-paragraph (3), he has no non-dependants aged 18 or over [23 normally residing with him or with whom he is normally residing,]

and either [41 a person is entitled to, and in receipt of, [49 a carer's allowance] [85 or carer support payment] [80 or has an award of universal credit which includes the carer element] in respect of caring for only one of the couple or, in the case of a polygamous marriage, for one or more but not all the partners of the marriage or, as the case may be, no person is entitled to, and in receipt of, such an allowance] [85 or payment] [80 or has such an award of universal credit] in respect of caring for either member of the couple or any partner of the polygamous marriage.

[19 (2A) Where a claimant has a partner who does not satisfy the condition in sub-paragraph (2)(b)(ii), and that partner is [77 severely sight impaired or blind or treated as severely sight impaired or blind] within the meaning of paragraph 12(1)(a)(iii) and (2), that partner shall be treated for the purposes of sub-paragraph (2) as if he were not a partner of the claimant.]

(3) For the purposes of sub-paragraph (2)(a)(ii) and (2)(b)(iii) no account shall be taken of—

(a) a person receiving attendance allowance [15, [75 . . .] the care component of disability living allowance at the highest or middle rate prescribed in accordance with section 37ZB(3) of the Social Security Act [SSCBA, s.72(3)]] [75 or the daily living component of personal independence payment at the standard or enhanced rate in accordance with section 78(3) of the 2012 Act] [83 , the daily living component of adult disability payment at the standard or enhanced rate in accordance with regulation 5 of the Disability Assistance for Working Age People (Scotland) Regulations 2022] [76 or armed forces independence payment]; or

(b) [21 . . .]

(c) subject to sub-paragraph (4), a person who joins the claimant's household for the first time in order to care for the claimant or his partner and immediately before so joining the claimant or his partner was treated as a severely disabled person; [19 or (d) a person who is [77 severely sight impaired or blind or treated as severely sight impaired or blind] within the meaning of paragraph 12(1)(a)(iii) and (2).]

[1(3A) For the purposes of sub-paragraph (2)(b) a person shall be treated [41 . . .]

(a) [41 as being in receipt of] attendance allowance [15, or the care component of disability living allowance at the highest or middle rate prescribed in accordance with section 37ZB(3) of the Social Security Act [SSCBA, s.72(3)]] if he would, but for his being a patient for a period exceeding 28 days, be so in receipt;

(b) [41 as being entitled to and in receipt of [49 a carer's allowance] [85 or carer support payment] [80 or having an award of universal credit which includes the carer element] if he would, but for the person for whom he was caring being a patient in hospital for a period exceeding 28 days, be so entitled and in receipt [80 of carer's allowance [85 or carer support payment] or have such an award of universal credit].]]

[75 (c) as being in receipt of the daily living component of personal independence payment at the standard or enhanced rate in accordance with section 78(3) of the 2012 Act if he would, but for a suspension of benefit in accordance with regulations under section 86(1) (hospital in-patients) of the 2012 Act, be so in receipt [83 ;

(d) as being in receipt of the daily living component of adult disability payment at the standard or enhanced rate in accordance with regulation 5 of the [84 Disability Assistance for Working Age People (Scotland) Regulations 2022], if they would, but for regulation 28 (effect of admission to hospital on ongoing entitlement to Adult Disability Payment) of those Regulations, be so in receipt.]]

[22(3ZA) For the purposes of sub-paragraph (2)(a)(iii) and (2)(b), no account shall be taken of an award of [49 a carer's allowance] [85 carer support payment] [80 or universal credit which includes the carer element] to the extent that payment of such an award is back-dated for a period before [66 the date on which the award is first paid].]

(4) Sub-paragraph (3)(c) shall apply only for the first 12 weeks following the date on which the person to whom that provision applies first joins the claimant's household.

[45 (5) In sub-paragraph (2)(a)(iii) and (b), references to a person being in receipt of [49 a carer's allowance] [80 or as having an award of universal credit which includes the carer element] shall include references to a person who would have been in receipt of that allowance [80 or had such an award] but for the application of a restriction under section [72 6B or] 7 of the Social Security Fraud Act 2001 (loss of benefit provisions).]

[80 (6) For the purposes of this paragraph, a person has an award of universal credit which includes the carer element if the person has an award of universal credit which includes an amount which is the carer element under regulation 29 of the Universal Credit Regulations 2013.]

[43 Enhanced disability premium

13A.—[76 (1) Subject to sub-paragraph (2), the condition is that— **2.620**

(a) the claimant; or

(b) the claimant's partner, if any, who has not attained the qualifying age for state pension credit, is a person to whom sub-paragraph (1ZA) applies.

(1ZA) This sub-paragraph applies to the person mentioned in sub-paragraph (1) where—

(a) armed forces independence payment is payable to that person;

(b) the care component of disability living allowance is, or would, but for a suspension of benefit in accordance with regulations under section 113(2) of the Contributions and Benefits Act or but for an abatement as a consequence of hospitalization, be payable to that person at the highest rate prescribed under section 72(3) of that Act; [82 . . .

(ba) the care component of child disability payment is payable to that person at the highest rate in accordance with the DACYP Regulations (see regulation 11(5) of those Regulations); [83 . . .]]

(c) the daily living component of personal independence payment is, or would, but for regulations made under section 86(1) (hospital in-patients) of the 2012 Act, be payable to that person at the enhanced rate in accordance with section 78(2) of that Act [83]; or

(d) the daily living component of adult disability payment is, or would, but for regulation 28 (effect of admission to hospital on ongoing entitlement to Adult Disability Payment) of the [84 Disability Assistance for Working Age People (Scotland) Regulations 2022], be payable to that person at the enhanced rate in accordance with regulation 5 of those Regulations.]]

[73 (1A) Where the condition in sub-paragraph (1) ceases to be satisfied because of the death of a child or young person, the condition is that the claimant [74 or partner] is entitled to child benefit in respect of that person under section 145A of the Contributions and Benefits Act (entitlement after death of child or qualifying young person).]

[65 (2) The condition is not satisfied if the person to whom sub-paragraph (1) refers is—

(a) [50 . . .]

(b) a single claimant or a lone parent and (in either case) is a long-term patient;

(c) a member of a couple or polygamous marriage and each member of the couple or polygamous marriage is a long-term patient; or

(d) a member of a couple or polygamous marriage who—

(i) is a long-term patient; and

(ii) is the only member of the couple or polygamous marriage to whom sub-paragraph (1) refers.]

Disabled Child Premium

2.621 **14.**—[59 . . . 65]

[10 Carer premium

2.622 **14ZA.**—(1) [13 Subject to sub-paragraphs (3) and (4),] the condition is that the claimant or his partner is, or both of them are, [41 entitled to [49 a carer's allowance] under section 70 of the Contributions and Benefits Act] [85 or carer support payment].

(2) [57 . . .]

[41 [48 (3) Where a carer premium is awarded but—

(a) the person in respect of whose care the [49 carer's allowance] [85 or carer support payment] has been awarded dies; or

(b) in any other case the person in respect of whom a carer premium has been awarded ceases to be entitled [57 . . .] to [49 a carer's allowance] [85 or carer support payment],

the condition for the award of the premium shall be treated as satisfied for a period of eight weeks from the relevant date specified in sub-paragraph (3A) below.

(3A) The relevant date for the purposes of sub-paragraph (3) above shall be—

(a) [57 where sub-paragraph (3)(a) applies,] the Sunday following the death of the person in respect of whose care [49 a carer's allowance] [85 or carer support payment] has been awarded or the date of death if the death occurred on a Sunday;

(b) [57 . . .]

(c) in any other case, the date on which the person who has been entitled to [46 a carer's allowance] [85 or carer support payment] ceases to be entitled to that allowance [85 or payment].]

(4) Where a person who has been entitled to [49 a carer's allowance] [85 or carer support payment] ceases to be entitled to that allowance [85 or payment] and makes a claim for income support, the condition for the award of the carer premium shall be treated as satisfied for a period of eight weeks from the date on which—

[48 (a) the person in respect of whose care the [49 carer's allowance] [85 or carer support payment] has been awarded dies;

(b) [57 . . .]

[57 (c) in any other case, the person who has been entitled to a carer's allowance [85 or carer support payment] ceased to be entitled to that allowance [85 or payment].]]]]

[3 Persons in receipt of concessionary payments

2.623 **14A.**—For the purpose of determining whether a premium is applicable to a person [12 under paragraphs 12 to 14ZA], any concessionary payment made to compensate that person for the non-payment of any benefit mentioned in those paragraphs shall be treated as if it were a payment of that benefit.]

[8 Person in receipt of benefit

2.624 **14B.**—For the purposes of this Part of this Schedule, a person shall be regarded as being in receipt of any benefit if, and only if, it is paid in respect of him and shall be so regarded only for any period in respect of which that benefit is paid.]

[37 Part IV

Weekly Amounts of Premiums Specified in Part III

2.625

Column (1) *Premium*	*Column (2)* *Amount*
15.—(1) [29 . . .] [42(1A) [67 . . .]] [54(2) Pensioner premium for persons to whom paragraph 9 applies. (2A) Pensioner premium for persons to whom paragraph 9A applies. (3) Higher pensioner premium for persons to whom paragraph 10 applies.]	(1) [29 . . .]. [42 (1A) [67 . . .]] (2) [87 £190.70] (2A) [87 £190.70] (3) [87 £190.70]
(4) Disability Premium— (a) where the claimant satisfies the condition in [65 paragraph 11(1)(a)]; (b) where the claimant satisfies the condition in [65 paragraph 11(1)(b)].	(4) (a) [87 £42.50]. (b) [87 £60.60].
(5) Severe Disability Premium— (a) where the claimant satisfies the condition in paragraph 13(2)(a); (b) where the claimant satisfies the condition in paragraph 13(2)(b). (i) if there is someone in receipt of [49 a carer's allowance] or if he or any partner satisfies that condition only by virtue of paragraph 13(3A); (ii) if no-one is in receipt of such an allowance.	(5) (a) [87 £81.50]; (b) (i) [87 £81.50]; (ii) [87 £163.00];
(6) [59 . . .]	(6) [59 . . .]
(7) Carer Premium—	(7) [87 £45.60] in respect of each person who satisfied the condition specified in paragraph 14ZA.]
[43 (8) Enhanced disability premium where the conditions in paragraph 13A are satisfied—	(8) (a) [59 . . .] (b) [87 £20.85] in respect of each person who is neither— (i) a child or young person; nor (ii) a member of a couple or a polygamous marriage, in respect of whom the conditions specified in paragraph 13A are satisfied: (c) [86 £27.90] where the claimant is a member of a couple or a polygamous marriage and the conditions specified in paragraph 13A are satisfied in respect of a member of that couple or polygamous marriage.]

PART V

ROUNDING OF FRACTIONS

2.626 **16.** Where income support is awarded for a period which is not a complete benefit week and the applicable amount in respect of that period results in an amount which includes a fraction of a penny that fraction shall be treated as a penny."

AMENDMENTS

1. Income Support (General) Amendment Regulations 1988 (SI 1988/663) reg.29 (April 11, 1988).
2. Income Support (General) Amendment No. 3 Regulations 1988 (SI 1988/1228) reg.9 (September 12, 1988).
3. Income Support (General) Amendment No. 4 Regulations 1988 (SI 1988/1445) reg.19 (September 12, 1988).
4. Income Support (General) Amendment No. 5 Regulations 1988 (SI 1988/2022) reg.17(*b*) (December 12, 1988).
5. Income Support (General) Amendment No. 5 Regulations 1988 (SI 1988/2022) reg.17(*a*) (April 10, 1989).
6. Income Support (General) Amendment Regulations 1989 (SI 1989/534) reg.5 (October 9, 1989).
7. Income Support (General) Amendment No. 3 Regulations 1989 (SI 1989/1678) reg.6 (October 9, 1989).
8. Income Support (General) Amendment Regulations 1990 (SI 1990/547) reg.17 (April 9, 1990).
9. Income Support (General) Amendment No. 2 Regulations 1990 (SI 1990/1168) reg.2 (July 2, 1990).
10. Income Support (General) Amendment No. 3 Regulations 1990 (SI 1990/1776) reg.8 (October 1, 1990).
11. Enterprise (Scotland) Consequential Amendments Order 1991 (SI 1991/3870) art.9 (April, 1991).
12. Income Support (General) Amendment Regulations 1991 (SI 1991/236) reg.2 (April 8, 1991).
13. Income Support (General) Amendment No. 4 Regulations 1991 (SI 1991/236) reg.15 (August 5, 1991).
14. Income Support (General) Amendment No. 4 Regulations 1991 (SI 1991/1559) reg.15 (October 7, 1991).
15. Disability Living Allowance and Disability Working Allowance (Consequential Provisions) Regulations 1991 (SI 1991/2742) reg.11(4) (April 6, 1992).
16. Income Support (General) Amendment Regulations 1992 (SI 1992/468) reg.6 (April 6, 1992).
17. Social Security Benefits (Amendments Consequential Upon the Introduction of community Care) Regulations 1992 (SI 1992/3147) reg.2 (April 1, 1993).
18. Social Security Benefits (Miscellaneous Amendments) Regulations 1993 (SI 1993/518) reg.5 (April 1, 1993).
19. Income-related Benefits Schemes (Miscellaneous Amendments) (No. 2) Regulations 1993 (SI 1993/1150) reg.3 (May 25, 1993).

[20.]

21. Income-related Benefits Schemes (Miscellaneous Amendments) (No. 4) Regulations 1993 (SI 1993/2119) reg.18 (October 4, 1993).
22. Income-related Benefits Schemes (Miscellaneous Amendments) (No. 5) Regulations 1994 (SI 1994/2139) reg.30 (October 3, 1994).
23. Income-related Benefits Schemes (Miscellaneous Amendments) (No. 6) Regulations 1994 (SI 1994/3061) reg.2(3) (December 2, 1994).
24. Income-related Benefits Schemes (Miscellaneous Amendments) Regulations 1995 (SI 1995/516) reg.24 (April 10, 1995).

25. Disability Working Allowance and Income Support (General) Amendment Regulations 1995 (SI 1995/482) reg.16 (April 13, 1995).

26. Disability Working Allowance and Income Support (General) Amendment Regulations 1995 (SI 1995/482) reg.17 (April 13, 1995).

27. Income-related Benefits Schemes and Social Security (Claims and Payments) (Miscellaneous Amendments) Regulations 1995 (SI 1995/2303) reg.6(8) (October 2, 1995).

28. Income Support (General) (Jobseeker's Allowance Consequential Amendments) Regulations 1996 (SI 1996/206) reg.23 and Sch.2 (October 7, 1996).

29. Child Benefit, Child Support and Social Security (Miscellaneous Amendments) Regulations 1996 (SI 1996/1803) reg.39 (April 7, 1997).

30. Income-related Benefits and Jobseeker's Allowance (Personal Allowances for Children and Young Persons) (Amendment) Regulations 1996 (SI 1996/2545) reg.2 (April 7, 1997).

31. Income-related Benefits and Jobseeker's Allowance (Amendment) (No. 2) Regulations 1997 (SI 1997/2197) regs 7(5) and (6)(a) (October 6, 1997).

32. Social Security Amendment (Lone Parents) Regulations 1998 (SI 1998/766) reg.12 (April 6, 1998).

33. Social Security (Welfare to Work) Regulations 1998 (SI 1998/2231) reg.13(3)(a) (October 5, 1998).

34. Social Security (Welfare to Work) Regulations 1998 (SI 1998/2231) reg.13(3)(b) (October 5, 1998).

35. Social Security Benefits Up-rating Order 1999 (SI 1999/264) art.18(3) and Sch.4 (April 12, 1999).

36. Social Security Benefits Up-rating Order 1999 (SI 1999/264) art.18(4)(b) (April 12, 1999).

37. Social Security Benefits Up-rating Order 1999 (SI 1999/264) art.18(5) and Sch.5 (April 12, 1999).

38. Social Security Amendment (Personal Allowances for Children and Young Persons) Regulations 1999 (SI 1999/2555) reg.2(1)(b) and (2)(April 10, 2000).

39. Social Security and Child Support (Tax Credits) Consequential Amendments Regulations 1999 (SI 1999/2566) reg.2(2) and Sch.2 Pt II (October 5, 1999).

40. Social Security (Miscellaneous Amendments) (No. 2) Regulations 1999 (SI 1999/2556) reg.2(8) (October 4, 1999).

41. Social Security (Miscellaneous Amendments) Regulations 2000 (SI 2000/681) reg.4 (April 3, 2000).

42. Social Security Amendment (Bereavement Benefits) Regulations 2000 (SI 2000/2239) reg.2(3) (April 9, 2001).

43. Social Security Amendment (Enhanced Disability Premium) Regulations 2000 (SI 2629) reg.2(c) (April 9, 2001).

44. Social Security Amendment (Residential Care and Nursing Homes) Regulations 2001 (SI 2001/3767) reg.2 and Sch. Pt I para.14 (April 8, 2002).

45. Social Security (Loss of Benefit) (Consequential Amendments) Regulations 2002 (SI 2002/490) reg.2 (April 1, 2002).

46. Social Security Amendment (Residential Care and Nursing Homes) Regulations 2001 (SI 2001/3767) reg.2 and Sch. Pt I para.14 (as amended by Social Security Amendment (Residential Care and Nursing Homes) Regulations 2002 (SI 2002/398) reg.4(2)) (April 8, 2002).

47. Social Security Amendment (Personal Allowances for Children and Young Persons) Regulations 2002 (SI 2002/2019) reg.2 (October 14, 2002).

48. Social Security Amendment (Carer Premium) Regulations 2002 (SI 2002/2020) reg.2 (October 28, 2002).

49. Social Security Amendment (Carer's allowance) Regulations 2002 (SI 2002/2497) reg.3 and Sch.2 (April 1, 2003).

50. Social Security (Working Tax Credit and Child Tax Credit) (Consequential Amendments) Regulations 2003 (SI 2003/455) regs 1(5) and 2 and Sch.1 para.20(b) (April 7, 2003).

51. Social Security Benefits Up-Rating Order 2003 (SI 2003/526) art.17(3) and Sch.2 (April 7, 2003).

52. Social Security Benefits Up-Rating Order 2003 (SI 2003/526) art.17(5) and Sch.3 (April 7, 2003).

53. Social Security Benefits Up-Rating Order 2003 (SI 2003/526) art.17(4) (April 7, 2003).

54. State Pension Credit (Consequential, Transitional and Miscellaneous Provisions) Regulations 2002 (SI 2002/3019) reg.29(5) (October 6, 2003).

55. Social Security (Removal of Residential Allowance and Miscellaneous Amendments) Regulations 2003 (SI 2003/1121) reg.2 and Sch.1 para.6 (October 6, 2003).

56. Social Security (Hospital In-Patients and Miscellaneous Amendments) Regulations 2003 (SI 2003/1195) reg.3 (May 21, 2003).

57. Social Security (Miscellaneous Amendments) (No. 2) Regulations 2003 (SI 2003/2279) reg.2(3) (October 1, 2003).

58. Income Support (General) Amendment Regulations 2003 (SI 2003/2379) reg.2 (October 6, 2003).

59. Social Security (Working Tax Credit and Child Tax Credit) (Consequential Amendments) Regulations 2003 (SI 2003/455) reg.2 and Sch.1 para.20 (April 6, 2004, except in "transitional cases" and see further the note to reg.17 of the Income Support Regulations).

60. Social Security (Miscellaneous Amendments) (No. 2) Regulations 2004 (SI 2004/1141) reg.6 (May 12, 2004).

61. Social Security (Back to Work Bonus and Lone Parent Run-on) (Amendment and Revocation) Regulations 2003 (SI 2003/1589) reg.2(d) (October 25, 2004).

62. Civil Partnership (Pensions, Social Security and Child Support) (Consequential, etc. Provisions) Order 2005 (SI 2005/2877) art.2(3) and Sch.3 para.13(3) (December 5, 2005).

63. Social Security (Hospital In-Patients) Regulations 2005 (SI 2005/3360) reg.4 (April 10, 2006).

64. Social Security (Miscellaneous Amendments) (No. 4) Regulations 2006 (SI 2006/2378) reg.5(7) (October 2, 2006).

65. Social Security (Miscellaneous Amendments) Regulations 2007 (SI 2007/719) reg.2(7) (April 9, 2007). As it relates to paras 13A(2)(a) and 14, the amendment only affects "transitional cases". See further the note to reg.17 of the Income Support Regulations and the commentary below.

66. Social Security (Miscellaneous Amendments) Regulations 2007 (SI 2007/719) reg.2(7)(e) (April 2, 2007).

67. Social Security (Miscellaneous Amendments) (No. 5) Regulations 2007 (SI 2007/2618) reg.2 and Sch. (October 1, 2007).

68. Social Security (Miscellaneous Amendments) Regulations 2008 (SI 2008/698) reg.2(12) (April 14, 2008).

69. Social Security (Miscellaneous Amendments) Regulations 2009 (SI 2009/583) reg.2(1) and (3) (April 6, 2009).

70. Social Security (Equalisation of State Pension Age) Regulations 2009 (SI 2009/1488) reg.3 (April 6, 2010).

71. Social Security (Miscellaneous Amendments) (No. 2) Regulations 2010 (SI 2010/641) reg.2(1) and (9) (April 13, 2010).

72. Social Security (Loss of Benefit) Amendment Regulations 2010 (SI 2010/1160) reg.10(1) and (3) (April 1, 2010).

73. Social Security (Miscellaneous Amendments) Regulations 2011 (SI 2011/674) reg.3(5) (April 11, 2011).

74. Social Security (Miscellaneous Amendments) (No. 3) Regulations 2011 (SI 2011/2425) reg.7(1) and (7) (October 31, 2011).

75. Personal Independence Payment (Supplementary Provisions and Consequential Amendments) Regulations 2013 (SI 2013/388) reg.8 and Sch. para.11(1) and (5) (April 8, 2013).

76. Armed Forces and Reserve Forces Compensation Scheme (Consequential Provisions: Subordinate Legislation) Order 2013 (SI 2013/591) art.7 and Sch. para.4(1) and (5) (April 8, 2013).
77. Universal Credit and Miscellaneous Amendments (No. 2) Regulations 2014 (SI 2014/2888) reg.3(2)(a) (November 26, 2014).
78. Welfare Benefits Up-rating Order 2015 (SI 2015/30) art.6 and Sch.1 (April 6, 2015).
79. Social Security Benefits Up-rating Order 2015 (SI 2015/457) art.14(5) and Sch.3 (April 6, 2015).
80. Universal Credit and Miscellaneous Amendments Regulations 2015 (SI 2015/1754) reg.14 (October 28, 2015).
81. Pensions Act 2014 (Consequential, Supplementary and Incidental Amendments) Order 2015 (SI 2015/1985) art.8(1) and (3) (April 6, 2016).
82. Social Security (Scotland) Act 2018 (Disability Assistance for Children and Young People) (Consequential Modifications) Order 2021 (SI 2021/786) Sch.1 para.5 (July 26, 2021).
83. Social Security (Disability Assistance for Working Age People) (Consequential Amendments) Order 2022 (SI 2022/177) art.2(6) (March 21, 2022).
84. Social Security (Disability Assistance for Working Age People) (Consequential Amendments) (No. 2) Order 2022 (SI 2022/530) art.2(2) (June 6, 2022).
85. Carers Assistance (Carer Support Payment) (Scotland) Regulations 2023 (Consequential Amendments) Order 2023 (SI 2023/1218) art.5 (November 19, 2023).
86. Social Security Benefits Up-rating Order 2024 (SI 2024/242) art.20(3) and Sch.2 (April 8, 2024).
87. Social Security Benefits Up-rating Order 2024 (SI 2024/242) art.20(5) and Sch.3 (April 8, 2024).

DEFINITIONS

"adult disability payment"—see reg.2(1).
"attendance allowance"—*ibid.*
"benefit week"—*ibid.*
"child"—see SSCBA s.137(1).
"child disability payment"—see reg.2(1).
"claimant"—*ibid.*
"close relative"—*ibid.*
"couple"—*ibid.*
"the DACYP Regulations"—*ibid.*
"disability living allowance"—*ibid.*
"family"—see SSCBA s.137(1).
"invalid carriage or other vehicle"—see reg.2(1).
"lone parent"—*ibid.*
"mobility supplement"—*ibid.*
"non-dependent"—see reg.3.
"partner"—see reg.2(1).
"personal independence payment"—*ibid.*
"polygamous marriage"—*ibid.*
"preserved right"—see reg.2(1) and reg.19.
"single claimant"—see reg.2(1).
"Social Security Act"—*ibid.*
"welfare to work beneficiary"—*ibid.*
"young person"—*ibid.*, reg.14.

For the General Note to Sch.2, see Vol.V paras 2.627–2.650.

p.605, *amendments to the Income Support (General) Regulations 1987 (SI 1987/1967) Sch.3 para.18 (Housing costs—non-dependant deductions)*

5.037 With effect from April 8, 2024, art.20(6) of the Social Security Benefits Up-rating Order 2024 (SI 2024/242) makes the following amendments:

- in sub-paragraph (1)(a) for "£116.75" substitute "£124.55";
- in sub-paragraph (1)(b) for "£18.10" substitute "£19.30";
- in sub-paragraph (2)(a) for "£162.00" substitute "£176.00";
- in sub-paragraph (2)(b)—
  (i) for "£41.60" substitute "£44.40";
  (ii) for "£162.00" substitute "£176.00"; and
  (iii) for "£236.00" substitute "£256.00";
- in sub-paragraph (2)(c)—
  (i) for "£57.10" substitute "£60.95";
  (ii) for "£236.00" substitute "£256.00"; and
  (iii) for "£308.00" substitute "£334.00";
- in sub-paragraph (2)(d)—
  (i) for "£93.40" substitute "£99.65";
  (ii) for "£308.00" substitute "£334.00"; and
  (iii) for "£410.00" substitute "£445.00"; and
- in sub-paragraph (2)(e)—
  (i) for "£106.35" substitute "£113.50";
  (ii) for "£410.00" substitute "£445.00"; and
  (iii) for "£511.00" substitute "£554.00".

p.606, *ERRATUM Income Support (General) Regulations 1987 (SI 1987/1967) Sch.3 para.18 (Housing costs—non-dependant deductions)*

An amendment was made to para.18 by the Social Security (Income and Capital) (Miscellaneous Amendments) Regulations 2020 (SI 2002/618) reg.2(1)(1) (July 15, 2020), adding the words "any Grenfell Tower payment, or". That amendment is incorrectly shown as being to the start of para.18(8)(a). It in fact adds those words at the start of para.18(8)(b).

p.606, *amendments to the Income Support (General) Regulations 1987 (SI 1987/1967) Sch.3 para.18 (Housing costs—non-dependant deductions)*

5.038 With effect from July 26, 2021, para.6 of Sch.1 to the Social Security (Scotland) Act 2018 (Disability Assistance for Children and Young People) (Consequential Modifications) Order 2021 (SI 2021/786) inserts into sub-paragraph (6)(b), after paragraph (ii), "(iia) the care component of child disability payment;" and inserts into sub-paragraph (8)(a), after "disability living allowance", ", child disability payment".

With effect from January 1, 2022, reg.2(6) of the Social Security (Income and Capital Disregards) (Amendment) Regulations 2021 (SI 2021/1405) inserts into para.18(8)(b), after "Grenfell Tower payment", ", child abuse payment or Windrush payment".

With effect from March 21, 2022, art.2(7) of the Social Security (Disability Assistance for Working Age People) (Consequential Amendments) Order 2022 (SI 2022/177) makes the following amendments:

in para.18(6)(b)(iii) omit "or" at the end;
after para.18(6)(b)(iii) insert "(iiia) the daily living component of adult disability payment; or"; and
in para.18(8)(a), for "or personal independence payment" substitute ", personal independence payment, adult disability payment".

With effect from July 9, 2023, reg.2 of the Social Security (Income and Capital Disregards) (Amendment) Regulations 2023 (SI 2023/640) amends para.18 as follows:

- in paragraph 18(8)(b) (non-dependant deductions), for "or Windrush payment" insert ", Windrush payment or Post Office compensation payment".

p.631, *amendment to the Income Support (General) Regulations 1987 (SI 1987/1967) Sch.8, para.6A (Sums to be disregarded in the calculation of earnings)*

With effect from November 19, 2023, art.5(5) of the Carer's Assistance (Carer Support Payment) (Scotland) Regulations 2023 (Consequential Amendments) Order 2023 (SI 2023/1218) amended para.6A(1) by inserting "or carer support payment" after "carer's allowance" in the first place where that occurs. Carer support payment is newly defined in reg.2(1) by reference to the Scottish legislation (see the entry for p.229). 5.039

p.642, *amendments to the Income Support (General) Regulations 1987 (SI 1987/1967) Sch.9 paras 6 and 9 (Sums to be disregarded in the calculation of income other than earnings—mobility component and AA, care component and daily living component)*

With effect from March 21, 2022, art.2(8)(a) of the Social Security (Disability Assistance for Working Age People) (Consequential Amendments) Order 2022 (SI 2022/177) amended para.6 to read as follows (square brackets indicate only the present amendment, those indicating previous amendments having been omitted): 5.040

"**6.**—The mobility component of disability living allowance[,] the mobility component of personal independence payment [or the mobility component of adult disability payment]."

With effect from March 21, 2022, art.2(8)(b) of the same Order amended para.9 to read as follows (square brackets indicate only the present amendment, those indicating previous amendments having been omitted):

"**9.**—Any attendance allowance, the care component of disability living allowance[,] the daily living component of personal independence payment [or the daily living component of adult disability payment]."

"Adult disability payment" is defined in reg.2(1) by reference to reg.2 of the Disability Assistance for Working Age People (Scotland) Regulations 2022 (SSI 2022/54) (see Vol.IV of this series).

p.644, *amendment to the Income Support (General) Regulations 1987 (SI 1987/1967) Sch.9 para.21(2) (Sums to be disregarded in the calculation of income other than earnings—income in kind)*

5.041 With effect from January 1, 2022, reg.2(7)(a) of the Social Security (Income and Capital Disregards) (Amendment) Regulations 2021 (SI 2021/1405) amended sub-para.(2) by inserting ", a child abuse payment or a Windrush payment" after "Grenfell Tower payment". All of those payments are defined in reg.2(1). See the entry for pp.684–685 for discussion of the nature of child abuse and Windrush payments.

p.646, *amendment to the Income Support (General) Regulations 1987 (SI 1987/1967) Sch.9 para.27(da) (Sums to be disregarded in the calculation of income other than earnings—payments for persons temporarily in care of claimant)*

5.042 With effect from July 1, 2022, reg.99 of and Sch. to the Health and Care Act 2022 (Consequential and Related Amendments and Transitional Provisions) Regulations 2022 (SI 2022/634) amended para.27(da) by substituting the following for the text after "(da)":

"an integrated care board established under Chapter A3 of Part 2 of the National Health Service Act 2006;"

With effect from November 6, 2023, reg.2 of the Health and Care Act 2022 (Further Consequential Amendments) (No.2) Regulations 2023 (SI 2023/1071) amended para.27(db) by substituting "NHS England" for "the National Health Service Commissioning Board".

p.648, *amendment to the Income Support (General) Regulations 1987 (SI 1987/1967) Sch.9 para.39(1A) (Sums to be disregarded in the calculation of income other than earnings)*

5.043 With effect from January 1, 2022, reg.2(7)(b) of the Social Security (Income and Capital Disregards) (Amendment) Regulations 2021 (SI 2021/1405) amended para.39 by substituting the following for sub-para.(1A):

"(1A) Any—
(a) Grenfell Tower payment;
(b) child abuse payment;
(c) Windrush payment."

In addition, reg.2(7)(c) amended sub-paras (2) to (6) by inserting ", a child abuse payment or a Windrush payment" after "Grenfell Tower payment" in each place where those words occur. All of those payments are defined in reg.2(1).

See the entry for pp.684–685 (Sch.10 (Capital to be disregarded) para.22) for some technical problems arising from the date of effect of these amendments. Because all the payments so far made from the approved historic institutional child abuse schemes and from the Windrush Compensation Scheme have been in the nature of capital, the question of disregarding income has not yet arisen.

With effect from July 9, 2023, reg.2(7) of the Social Security (Income and Capital Disregards) (Amendment) Regulations 2023 (SI 2023/640) amended para.39(1A) by adding the following after head (c):

"(d) a Post Office compensation payment."

Such payments are newly defined in reg.2(1), where there is now also an expanded definition of Grenfell Tower payments (see head (a)). With effect from the same date, the words substituted in sub-paras (2) to (6) have been further amended by substituting ", a Windrush payment, a Post Office compensation payment or a vaccine damage payment" for "or a Windrush payment". "Vaccine damage payment" is also newly defined in reg.2(1). See the entry for pp.684-685 for the background.

p.651, *amendments to the Income Support (General) Regulations 1987 (SI 1987/1967) Sch.9 (Sums to be disregarded in the calculation of income other than earnings)*

With effect from July 26, 2021, art.11(2) of the Social Security (Scotland) Act 2018 (Disability Assistance, Young Carer Grants, Short-term Assistance and Winter Heating Assistance) (Consequential Provision and Modifications) Order 2021 (SI 2021/886) inserted the following after para.85: 5.044

> "**86**. Any disability assistance given in accordance with regulations made section 31 of the Social Security (Scotland) Act 2018."

The first regulations made under s.31 of the 2018 Act were the Disability Assistance for Children and Young People (Scotland) Regulations 2021 (SSI 2021/174), also in effect from July 26, 2021, providing for the benefit known as a child disability payment. The regulations also authorise the payment of short-term assistance, to be disregarded under para.85. The Disability Assistance for Working Age People (Scotland) Regulations 2022 (SSI 2022/54), in effect from March 21, 2022, providing for the benefit known as adult disability payment, were also made under s.31, but the two potential elements (mobility component and daily living component) have been specifically covered by para.6 and para.9 from that date (see the entry for p.642). Short-term assistance under reg.62 of the 2022 Regulations is disregarded under para.85.

With effect from November 19, 2023, art.5(6) of the Carer's Assistance (Carer Support Payment) (Scotland) Regulations 2023 (Consequential Amendments) Order 2023 (SI 2023/1218) inserted the following after para.86:

> "**87**. Any amount of carer support payment that is in excess of the amount the claimant would receive if they had an entitlement to carer's allowance under section 70 of the Contributions and Benefits Act."

Carer support payment (CSP) is newly defined in reg.2(1) by reference to the Scottish legislation (see the entry for p.229). Note that CSP in general counts as income and that the disregard is limited to any excess of the amount of the CSP over what the claimant would have been entitled to in carer's allowance under British legislation. That is in accordance with the Fiscal Framework Agreement governing the provision of devolved benefits in Scotland (see para.6.9 of the Explanatory Memorandum to SI 2023/1218). Initially, CSP is to be paid at the same rate as carer's allowance.

p.665, *annotations to the Income Support (General) Regulations 1987 (SI 1987/1967) Sch.9 paras 6 and 9 (Sums to be disregarded in the calculation of income other than earnings—mobility component and AA, care component and daily living component)*

5.045 Note the amendments to paras 6 and 9 on p.642 to take account of the introduction of Scottish adult disability payment (see Vol.IV of this series).

p.676, *annotation to the Income Support (General) Regulations 1987 (SI 1987/1967) Sch.9, para.31A (Sums to be disregarded in the calculation of income other than earnings—local welfare provision)*

5.046 No doubt, payments from the Household Support Fund, initially in operation from October 2021 to March 2022, and later extended in tranches to September 2024, constituted "local welfare provision", as with the schemes mentioned in the main volume. See para.18A of Sch.10 for the capital disregard.

p.676, *annotation to the Income Support (General) Regulations 1987 (SI 1987/1967) Sch.9 para.34 (Sums to be disregarded in the calculation of income other than earnings—payments by trade unions during trade disputes)*

5.047 The relevant sum was increased to £50 with effect from April 8, 2024 (see the entries for pp.15 and 18).

p.677, *annotation to the Income Support (General) Regulations 1987 (SI 1987/1967) Sch.9 para.39 (Sums to be disregarded in the calculation of income other than earnings—payments from certain funds), and for the extensions from July 2023 to Post Office compensation payments and vaccine damage payments*

5.048 See the entries for pp.648 and 684 for the extension in a new sub-para. (1A) of the funds covered to child abuse compensation payments from certain schemes and to payments under the Windrush Compensation Scheme.

p.680, *annotation to the Income Support (General) Regulations 1987 (SI 1987/1967) Sch.9 para.84 (Sums to be disregarded in the calculation of income other than earnings—Scottish child payment)*

5.049 As at April 2024 the weekly amount of the Scottish child payment is £26.70.

p.680, *annotation to the Income Support (General) Regulations 1987 (SI 1987/1967) Sch.9 para.85 (Sums to be disregarded in the calculation of income other than earnings—Scottish short-term assistance)*

5.050 Provision for short-term assistance under s.36 of the Social Security (Scotland) Act 2018, thus falling within para.85, has been made by reg.42 of and Sch. to the Disability Assistance for Children and Young People (Scotland) Regulations 2021 (SSI 2021/174), with effect from July 26, 2021, and by reg.62 of and Sch. to the Disability Assistance for Working Age People (Scotland) Regulations 2022 (SSI 2022/54), with effect from March 21, 2022.

p.681, *amendment to the Income Support (General) Regulations 1987 (SI 1987/1967) Sch.10, para.7(1)(a) (Capital to be disregarded)*

With effect from July 26, 2021, art.11(3) of the Social Security (Scotland) Act 2018 (Disability Assistance, Young Carer Grants, Shortterm Assistance and Winter Heating Assistance) (Consequential Provision and Modifications) Order 2021 (SI 2021/886) substituted "84, 85 or 86" for "84 or 85". See the entry for p.651 for the new para.86 of Sch.9. 5.051

p.682, *amendment to the Income Support (General) Regulations 1987 (SI 1987/1967) Sch.10 para.7A (Capital to be disregarded—widowed parent's allowance)*

With effect from February 9, 2023, para.1(a) of the Schedule to the Bereavement Benefits (Remedial) Order 2023 (SI 2023/134) inserted the following after para.7 of Sch.10: 5.052

"**7A.** Any payment of a widowed parent's allowance made pursuant to section 39A of the Contributions and Benefits Act (widowed parent's allowance)—

(a) to the survivor of a cohabiting partnership (within the meaning in section 39A(7) of the Contributions and Benefits Act) who is entitled to a widowed parent's allowance for a period before the Bereavement Benefits (Remedial) Order 2023 comes into force, and

(b) in respect of any period of time during the period ending with the day before the survivor makes the claim for a widowed parent's allowance,

but only for a period of 52 weeks from the date of receipt of the payment."

The legislation on widowed parent's allowance (WPA), abolished on April 5, 2017, and bereavement support payment (BSP) in operation for deaths after April 5, 2017, was declared incompatible with the ECHR by discriminating against children whose parents were cohabiting but not married to each other or in a civil partnership (see *Re McLaughlin's Application for Judicial Review* [2018] UKSC 48; [2018] 1 W.L.R. 4250 and *R(Jackson) v Secretary of State for Work and Pensions* [2020] EWHC 183 (Admin); [2020] 1 W.L.R. 1441 in Vol.I of this series). The Remedial Order allows retrospective claims to be made for those benefits from August 30, 2018 onwards and accordingly for arrears of benefit to be paid if the conditions of entitlement are met. The new para.7A, and the amended para.72 on BSP, deal with the consequences of such payments on income support entitlement, although with somewhat differing outcomes.

The Explanatory Memorandum misleadingly asserts in para.7.15 that the Remedial Order provides for payments of arrears under the Order to be treated as capital and disregarded for the purposes of income-related benefits, in line with assurances that had been given by the government to the Joint Committee on Human Rights and in its response to public consultation on a draft of the Order (see *Draft Bereavement Benefits (Remedial Order 2022: Second Report* (HC 834, HL Paper 108) (December 6, 2022), para.61). However, it is absolutely plain that the amendments made by the Order do nothing to deem any payment of arrears to be capital. The new provisions like para.7A merely provide for a disregard of the payment for 52 weeks in so far as it is properly to be regarded as capital. It has been firmly established at least since the decision in *R(SB) 4/89* (see para.2.245 of the 2021/22 main volume) that cumulative arrears of social security benefits that would have been income if paid on time retain their nature as income though paid as a lump sum. Then, as a result of regs 29 and 31 the periodical payments are to be treated for income support purposes as paid on the date on which they were due to be paid (i.e. in the past) for the payment period starting with that date. Thus, if a claimant receiving a sum of arrears of WPA had been in receipt of income support (or another "legacy" income-related benefit) for some part of the period to which the WPA is properly to be attributed as income (subject to the £10 per week disregard under Sch.9 para.16(h)) that would trigger the Secretary of State's power to revise the decision(s) awarding income support (Social Security and Child Support (Decisions and Appeals) Regulations 1999 (SI 1999/991) reg.3(7) and SSA 1998 s.9(3) in Vol.III of this series) and, if exercised, the creation of an overpayment that would be recoverable under the SSAA s.74, either by abatement of the amount payable by way of arrears of WPA or, if that was not exercised by recovery from the claimant.

That that is the legal position was effectively conceded by Viscount Younger, the Minister for Work and Pensions in the House of Lords, in a letter of February 2, 2023 to Baroness Sherlock (deposited in the Library of the House of Lords), in which he said this:

> "It is right that usual rules apply in these cases, to ensure that we don't treat cohabitee claimants differently to those claimants who were in a legal union with the deceased. WPA is taken into account as income when assessing entitlement to other means-tested benefits. Where a claimant was in receipt of a legacy income-related benefit during the period of entitlement for WPA, we will offset any overpayment of the relevant benefit from the retrospective lump sum of WPA and pay a net WPA award. Where a claimant was in receipt of Universal Credit during the period of WPA entitlement, the claimant may incur an overpayment of Universal Credit as a consequence of receiving a retrospective WPA award. We will make this clear to claimants, so that they are able to make an informed choice about making a claim."

The Explanatory Memorandum appears not so far to have been corrected and DMG Memo 2/23 makes no mention of this issue.

There remains something for the new para.7A to bite on. Because of the £10 weekly disregard, even if the abatement process is applied over the entire period to which the arrears of WPA are attributed, there will be some amount of arrears payable, which according to accepted principle would metamorphose from income into capital at the end of the period to which it is properly attributable as income (see *R(IS) 3/93* and paras 2.208 and 2.209 of the 2020/21 main volume). Such capital is to be disregarded for 52 weeks, as would capital deriving from weeks in the past in which no income-related benefit was in payment. If the abatement process had been available but did not take place, it is arguable that the arrears of income would only metamorphose into capital after deduction of the liability to recovery of the overpayment (*R(SB) 2/83* and *R(SB) 35/83*).

Note that the outcome for BSP (see the amendment to para.72) is different because BSP is disregarded entirely as income for income support purposes (Sch.9 para.80).

pp.684–685, *amendment to the Income Support (General) Regulations 1987 (SI 1987/1967) Sch.10 para.22 (Capital to be disregarded)*

With effect from January 1, 2022, reg.2(8)(a) of the Social Security (Income and Capital Disregards) (Amendment) Regulations 2021 (SI 2021/1405) amended sub-para.(1A) by inserting ", child abuse payment, Windrush payment" after "Grenfell Tower payment" and amended sub-paras (2) to (6) by inserting ", a child abuse payment or a Windrush payment" after "Grenfell Tower payment" in each place where those words occur. All of those payments are defined in reg.2(1). 5.053

There are some technical problems with the addition only with effect from January 1, 2022 of the disregards of payments from approved schemes providing compensation in respect of historic institutional child abuse in the UK (para.(1)(a)(vii)) and from the Windrush Compensation Scheme. All the schemes so far in existence provide payments in the nature of capital.

The Explanatory Memorandum to the amending regulations reveals that four child abuse compensation schemes had been approved by the Secretary of State as at January 1, 2022: under the Historical Institutional Abuse (Northern Ireland) Act 2019; under the Redress for Survivors (Historical Child Abuse in Care) (Scotland) Act 2021; the London Borough of Lambeth Redress Scheme and the London Borough of Islington's proposed support payment scheme. All provide one-off capital payments. The Memorandum also reveals that payments under the Northern Ireland and Lambeth schemes could have been made prior to January 1, 2022. The application of the disregards provided under SI 2021/1405 to such pre-January 2022 payments has been authorised by a ministerial direction from the Secretary of State, acting under "common law powers" (see the letters of December 3, 2021 between the Permanent Secretary and the Secretary of State, published on the internet). The Windrush Compensation Scheme has also been making payments for some time. The correspondence above states that extra-statutory arrangements agreed with HM Treasury provided for the disregard in practice of such payments in means-tested benefits from the outset. It might be thought that the delay in putting that outcome on a proper statutory basis is symptomatic of the way in which the victims of that scandal have been treated.

Those arrangements raise questions as to what a tribunal on appeal should do if it has evidence of receipt prior to January 1, 2022 of a payment that would have been disregarded under the amendments if it had been received on or after that date. The legislation that a tribunal is bound to apply would not allow a disregard of such a payment unless it fell within an existing "personal injury" disregard in para.12 or 12A (possible for some historic institutional child abuse payments, though not for payments to next of kin or those who had merely been in "harm's way" or for Windrush Compensation Scheme payments). However, if an express submission from the DWP recorded the practical result of the application of the disregard either on the basis of a ministerial direction or an extra-statutory arrangement, it would appear that the issue of the treatment of the payment would not arise on the appeal (see SSA 1998 s.12(8)(a)) and it is submitted that it would then be irrational for the tribunal to exercise its discretion to consider the issue nonetheless. If evidence of a payment that had not been taken into account as capital emerged in the course of an appeal, but there was no express DWP submission to explain that outcome, it is submitted that a tribunal with knowledge of the matters mentioned above could still legitimately conclude that the issue did not arise on the appeal and decline to exercise its discretion under s.12(8)(a). Memo DMG 15/21 on the effect of the amendment to Sch.10 says nothing about these questions, although it does name the currently approved historic institutional child abuse schemes and give the date of approval (December 10, 2021).

With effect from July 9, 2023, reg.2(8) of the Social Security (Income and Capital Disregards) (Amendment) Regulations 2023 (SI 2023/640) amended para.22(1A) by adding the following after "Windrush payment":

> ", Post Office compensation payment or vaccine damage payment"

Such payments are newly defined in reg.2(1), where there is now also an expanded definition of Grenfell Tower payments. With effect from the same date, the words substituted in sub-paras (2) to (6) have been further amended by substituting ", a Windrush payment, a Post Office compensation payment or a vaccine damage payment" for "or a Windrush payment".

The definition of "Post Office compensation payment" in reg.2(1) applies to any payments for compensation or support from the Post Office or the Secretary of State in connection with the failings of the Horizon computer accounting system (also defined in reg.2(1)) or the decision in the named test case on the Post Office's liability to the now famous group of 555 postmasters within the Group Litigation Order (GLO). The neutral citation number of the decision, as set out in a footnote to the amending regulation, is [2019] EWHC 606 (QB). Following on that and a consequent decision (the Horizon Issues judgment) a settlement was agreed, but the claimants actually received only a small proportion of the overall figure, the remainder being taken up by funding costs. Paragraph 7.3 of the Explanatory Memorandum describes the compensation schemes in being as at July 2023:

> "Government has announced funding to enable the Post Office to deliver compensation schemes and arrangements for various cohorts of postmasters, including the Historical Shortfall Scheme, compensation arrangements for postmasters whose convictions were overturned and a compensation scheme for postmasters who did not receive remuneration during a suspension period, to address issues expressly identified by the parties during the court proceedings or flowing from the Common Issues and Horizon Issues judgments. In March 2022, the Government agreed to provide funding to ensure that the claimants received compensation on a similar basis to other postmasters. A Department for Business and Trade scheme to deliver that outcome opened for applications in March 2023."

No doubt any compensation paid following the proposals announced in February 2024 for the automatic quashing of a much wider range of convictions than hitherto will fall within the condition of being "in connection with the failings of the Horizon system".

With effect from August 30, 2023, reg.2(1)(a) of the Social Security (Infected Blood Capital Disregard) (Amendment) Regulations 2023

(SI 2023/894) amended para.22 by inserting the following after sub-para.(5):

> "(5A) Any payment out of the estate of a person, which derives from a payment to meet the recommendation of the Infected Blood Inquiry in its interim report published on 29th July 2022 made under or by the Scottish Infected Blood Support Scheme or an approved blood scheme to the estate of the person, where the payment is made to the person's son, daughter, step-son or step-daughter."

Sir Brian Langstaff's interim report recommended that an interim payment of £100,000 should be made to all those infected from contaminated blood and blood products and all bereaved partners already registered on one of the four UK infected blood support schemes and those who registered before the inception of any future scheme. The Government committed that where the infected person or their bereaved partner died after registering for such a scheme but before the interim payment could be made, it would be paid to their estate. The amendment is intended to secure that a payment derived from an interim infected blood compensation payment from the estate will be disregarded as capital for income support purposes if it is made to a deceased person's son, daughter, step-son or step-daughter.

With effect from October 27, 2023, reg.3(3)(c) of the Social Security (Habitual Residence and Past Presence, and Capital Disregards) (Amendment) Regulations 2023 (SI 2023/1144) amended para.22(1) and (7) by inserting ", the Victims of Overseas Terrorism Compensation Scheme" after "the National Emergencies Trust" in both places. That scheme is newly defined in reg.2(1). It was set up under s.47 of the Crime and Security Act 2010 and is administered by the Criminal Injuries Compensation Authority. It enables compensation to be paid to persons injured and to partners or close family members of persons killed, where the injury or death is directly attributable to a designated incident. Payments for personal injury would be disregarded as capital under paras 12 and 12A (indefinitely only if held on trust, otherwise for 52 weeks), but will now if necessary be disregarded indefinitely under para.22, along with payments to family members (not previously covered). The amending regulations were made under urgency procedures following the UK's designation of some aspects of the violence in Israel from October 7, 2023 as incidents of terrorism, but many other incidents have been designated (as listed on the scheme's website). The official view, as set out in the note to para.16 of ADM Memo 17/23 is that capital retained from payments received before October 27, 2023 will be covered by the terms of the new provision as from that date:

> "While the classification of the Hamas attack on Israel on 7.10.23 has raised the need to disregard payments under the Victims of Overseas Terrorism Compensation scheme as capital, the regulations will cover any and all payments made under the scheme. There is no intention to differentiate between compensation payments made to victims of different terrorism attacks which are recognised under the compensation scheme."

The same view was expressed in a statement made to the Social Security Advisory Committee (see footnote 2 to para.1.6 of the minutes of the meeting of December 16, 2023).

p.685, *amendment to the Income Support (General) Regulations 1987 (SI 1987/1967) Sch.10 para.29 (Capital to be disregarded—payments in kind)*

5.054 With effect from January 1, 2022, reg.2(8)(b) of the Social Security (Income and Capital Disregards) (Amendment) Regulations 2021 (SI 2021/1405) amended para.29 by inserting ", child abuse payment or Windrush payment" after "Grenfell Tower payment". All of those payments are defined in reg.2(1). See also the entry for pp.684–685.

p.689, *amendment to the Income Support (General) Regulations 1987 (SI 1987/1967) Sch.10 para.72 (Capital to be disregarded—bereavement support payment)*

5.055 With effect from February 9, 2023, para.1(b) of the Schedule to the Bereavement Benefits (Remedial) Order 2023 (SI 2023/134) amended para.72 by making the existing text sub-para.(1) and inserting the following:

"(2) Where bereavement support payment under section 30 of the Pensions Act 2014 is paid to the survivor of a cohabiting partnership (within the meaning in section 30(6B) of the Pensions Act 2014) in respect of a death occurring before the day the Bereavement Benefits (Remedial) Order 2023 comes into force, any amount of that payment which is—

(a) in respect of the rate set out in regulation 3(1) of the Bereavement Support Payment Regulations 2017, and

(b) paid as a lump sum for more than one monthly recurrence of the day of the month on which their cohabiting partner died,

but only for a period of 52 weeks from the date of receipt of the payment."

See the entry for p.682 for the general background. The operation of this amendment is much more straightforward than that of the new para.7A on widowed parent's allowance. Although a payment of arrears of bereavement support payment (BSP) is in its nature a payment of income and attributable to the past period in respect of which it is due, the payment could not affect any entitlement to income support in that past period because it would be disregarded entirely as income (Sch.9 para.80). The amount of the arrears would thus immediately metamorphose into capital, which would then be disregarded under para.72(2) subject to the 52 week limit.

p.695, *annotation to the Income Support (General) Regulations 1987 (SI 1987/1967) Sch.10 (Capital to be disregarded)*

5.056 In the list of categories of disregards of capital, insert the following between the entry for para.7 and the entry for para.8:

"*Para.7A* Arrears of widowed parent's allowance;"

p.697, *annotation to the Income Support (General) Regulations 1987 (SI 1987/1967) Sch.10 (Capital to be disregarded)*

With effect from June 28, 2022 "Cost of living payments" under the Social Security (Additional Payments) Act 2022 (see Part I of Vol.II of this series), both those to recipients of specified means-tested benefits and "disability" payments, are not to be taken into account for any income support purposes by virtue of s.8(b) of the Act. The same effect was achieved with effect from March 23, 2023 in relation to payments under the Social Security (Additional Payments) Act 2023 (s.8(b) of that Act). See Pt I of Vol.II for the text of both Acts. 5.057

p.707, *annotation to the Income Support (General) Regulations 1987 (SI 1987/1967) Sch.10 (Capital to be disregarded–arrears of certain benefits)*

With effect from October 18, 2021, the Social Security Benefits (Claims and Payments) (Amendment) Regulations 2021 (SI 2021/1065) have permitted the payment of arrears of many benefits to be made in instalments, where necessary to protect the interests of the beneficiary and the latter agrees. Once such payments become capital (see the main volume), presumably the 52-week limit on the para.7(1) disregard runs separately from the date of receipt of each instalment. The application of the conditions in para.7(2) for a longer disregard might be more problematic. 5.058

p.709, *annotation to the Income Support (General) Regulations 1987 (SI 1987/1967) Sch.10 para.7A (Capital to be disregarded—arrears of widowed parent's allowance)*

Insert the following before the note to para.8:

"Paragraph 7A 5.059

This new disregard as capital of arrears of widowed parent's allowance was introduced with effect from February 9, 2023. See the entry for p.682 for the text and discussion of its effect."

p.711, *annotation to the Income Support (General) Regulations 1987 (SI 1987/1967) Sch.10 para.12 (Capital to be disregarded—trusts derived from payments made in consequence of personal injury)*

Note that *R(IS) 15/96*, mentioned in para.2.819, holds that payments made under the Criminal Injuries Compensation Scheme are in consequence of personal injury. 5.060

p.714, *annotation to the Income Support (General) Regulations 1987 (SI 1987/1967) Sch.10 para.18A (Capital to be disregarded—local welfare provision)*

There has been no specific provision made under Sch.10 (or the equivalent old style ESA or JSA provisions) to disregard 2022 Energy Rebate Scheme payments as capital, as has been done for universal credit in the Universal Credit (Energy Rebate Scheme Disregard) Regulations 2022 (SI 2022/257) (see Pt II of Vol.II). That is because the payments to be administered by local authorities (the £150 council tax rebate for properties in bands A–D and under the discretionary scheme for the vulnerable) are considered already to be covered by para.18A. 5.061

p.717, *annotation to the Income Support (General) Regulations 1987 (SI 1987/1967) Sch.10, para.28 (Capital to be disregarded—premises intended to be occupied: essential repairs or alterations needed)*

5.062 In the second paragraph of this annotation in the main volume, the reference to the Housing Benefit Regulations should be to para.28 of Sch.6, not para.27 of Sch.5. Further, the works must be required to make the property fit for occupation by the claimant, not fit for human habitation as suggested in the first paragraph. There might sometimes be no difference in the practical effect, but sometimes there will be. In *SH v London Borough of Southwark (HB)* [2023] UKUT 198 (AAC), Judge Hemingway held in para.23, in the context of reg.7(4) of the Housing Benefit Regulations, that the evaluation of whether repairs were essential had to take account of the claimant's individual characteristics, including impairment or vulnerability in consequence of ill-health, as had also been decided by Commissioner Williams in *CH/393/2002*. "Essential" probably means something like "necessary" in the sense in which luxuries are differentiated from the necessaries of life, importing a test of substantial need *(R(SB) 10/81* on the supplementary benefit single payments scheme), but the ordinary word in para.28 should be applied rather than some attempted further explanation.

p.721, *annotation to the Income Support (General) Regulations 1987 (SI 1987/1967) Sch.10 para.72 (Capital to be disregarded—bereavement support payments)*

5.063 See the entry for p.689 for the text of the amendment with effect from February 9, 2023 extending this disregard to arrears of payments made under the Bereavement Benefits (Remedial) Order 2023 (SI 2023/134) and discussion of its effect.

p.722, *annotation to the Income Support (General) Regulations 1987 (SI 1987/1967) Sch.10 para.77 (Capital to be disregarded—Scottish young carer grants)*

5.064 The amount of the annual young carer grant increased to £383.75 with effect from April 1, 2024.

p.722, *annotation to the Income Support (General) Regulations 1987 (SI 1987/1967) Sch.10 para.78 (Capital to be disregarded—Scottish winter heating assistance)*

5.065 The amount of the annual child winter heating payment increased to £251.50 with effect from April 1, 2024.

Further regulations (the Winter Heating Assistance (Low Income) (Scotland) Regulations 2023 (SSI 2023/16)) introduce, from January 25, 2023, one-off annual payments of (from April 1, 2024) £58.75 for certain recipients of income-related benefits (see Vol.IV of this series).

p.722, *annotation to the Income Support (Liable Relatives) Regulations 1990 (SI 1990/1777) reg.2 (Prescribed amounts for the purposes of section 24A of the Act)*

With effect from November 19, 2023, art.7 of the Carer's Assistance (Carer Support Payment) (Scotland) Regulations 2023 (Consequential Amendments) Order 2023 (SI 2023/1218) amended reg.2(1)(e) by inserting "or carer support payment under the Carer's Assistance (Carer Support Payment) (Scotland) Regulations 2023," after "carer's allowance". 5.066

p.742, *amendment to the Fines (Deductions from Income Support) Regulations 1992 (SI 1992/2182) reg.4 (Deductions from offender's income support, universal credit, state pension credit or jobseeker's allowance)*

With effect from October 29, 2021, reg.2 of the Fines (Deductions from Income Support) (Miscellaneous Amendments) Regulations 2021 (SI 2021/1077) substitutes a new reg.4(1B): 5.067

> "(1B) The amount that may be deducted under paragraph (1A) is 5 per cent. of the appropriate universal credit standard allowance for the offender for the assessment period in question, as specified under regulation 36 of the UC Regulations."

This amendment follows the decision of Kerr J in *R. (Blundell) v SSWP* [2021] EWHC 608 (Admin); [2021] P.T.S.R. 1342, where the Secretary of State's policy on deductions was found to be unlawfully fettering her discretion about the amount to deduct under reg.4(1B). The new regulation removes that discretion, by limiting deductions to the smallest amount which could previously have been deducted.

p.773, *amendment to the Child Support Maintenance Calculation Regulations 2012 (SI 2012/2677) reg.44 (Flat rate)*

With effect from November 19, 2023, arts.1(2) and 22 of the Carer's Assistance (Carer Support Payment) (Scotland) Regulations 2023 (Consequential Amendments) Order 2023 (SI 2023/1218) deleted the "and" at the end of reg.44(1)(h), inserted "and" at the end of reg.44(1)(i) and inserted a new reg.44(1)(j) as follows: 5.068

> (j) carer support payment under the Carer's Assistance (Carer Support Payment) (Scotland) Regulations 2023.

PART III

OLD STYLE JOBSEEKER'S ALLOWANCE REGULATIONS

p.785, *amendments to list of regulations for the Jobseeker's Allowance Regulations 1996 (SI 1996/207)*

5.069 Insert the following entry between the entries for regs 136B and 137:

"136C. Treatment of loans for specific purposes"

p.787, *annotation to the Jobseeker's Allowance Regulations 1996 (SI 1996/207)*

5.070 Insert the following text at the end of the GENERAL NOTE as a new paragraph:

Note that after July 25, 2022, there are no longer any circumstances in which it is possible to make a new claim for old style JSA: see the entry for p.33.

p.787, *amendments to the Jobseeker's Allowance Regulations 1996 (SI 1996/207), reg.1 (Citation, commencement, interpretation and application)*

5.071 With effect from July 26, 2021, Sch.3 para.2 of the Social Security (Scotland) Act 2018 (Disability Assistance for Children and Young People) (Consequential Modifications) Order 2021 (SI 2021/786) inserts the following definitions:

- "child disability payment" has the meaning given in regulation 2 of the DACYP Regulations;
- "DACYP Regulations" means the Disability Assistance for Children and Young People (Scotland) Regulations 2021;

With effect from January 1, 2022, reg.3(2) of the Social Security (Income and Capital Disregards) (Amendment) Regulations 2021 (SI 2021/1405) inserts the following definitions:

- "child abuse payment" means a payment from a scheme established or approved by the Secretary of State for the purpose of providing compensation in respect of historic institutional child abuse in the United Kingdom;"
- "Windrush payment" means a payment made under the Windrush Compensation Scheme (Expenditure) Act 2020;"

With effect from January 1, 2022, reg.3(2) of the Social Security (Income and Capital Disregards) (Amendment) Regulations 2021 (SI 2021/1405) inserts ", a child abuse payment or a Windrush payment" into the definition of "qualifying person", after "Grenfell Tower payment".

With effect from March 21, 2022, art.5 of the Social Security (Disability Assistance for Working Age People) (Consequential Amendments) Order 2022 (SI 2022/177) inserts the following definition:

"adult disability payment" has the meaning given in regulation 2 of the Disability Assistance for Working Age People (Scotland) Regulations 2022;

With effect from July 9, 2023, reg.3 of the Social Security (Income and Capital Disregards) (Amendment) Regulations 2023 (SI 2023/640) amends reg.1 as follows:

- for the definition of "Grenfell Tower payment" substitute—"“Grenfell Tower payment” means a payment made for the purpose of providing compensation or support in respect of the fire on 14th June 2017 at Grenfell Tower;";
- insert the following definitions:
  - “the Horizon system” means any version of the computer system used by the Post Office known as Horizon, Horizon Legacy, Horizon Online or HNG-X;
  - “the Post Office” means Post Office Limited (registered number 02154540);
  - “Post Office compensation payment” means a payment made by the Post Office or the Secretary of State for the purpose of providing compensation or support which is—
    - (a) in connection with the failings of the Horizon system; or
    - (b) otherwise payable following the judgment in Bates and Others v Post Office Ltd ((No. 3) “Common Issues”)(10);
  - “vaccine damage payment” means a payment made under the Vaccine Damage Payments Act 1979(11);";
- in the definition of “qualifying person”, for “or a Windrush payment” substitute “, a Windrush payment, a Post Office compensation payment or a vaccine damage payment”.

With effect from October 27, 2023, reg.4 of the Social Security (Habitual Residence and Past Presence, and Capital Disregards) (Amendment) Regulations 2023 (SI 2023/1144) amends reg.1 as follows:

- in the definition of “qualifying person”, after “the National Emergencies Trust” insert “, the Victims of Overseas Terrorism Compensation Scheme”;
- insert the following definition:

  “the Victims of Overseas Terrorism Compensation Scheme” means the scheme of that name established by the Ministry of Justice in 2012 under section 47 of the Crime and Security Act 2010(20);

With effect from November 19, 2023, art.8 of the Carer's Assistance (Carer Support Payment) (Scotland) Regulations 2023 (Consequential Amendments) Order 2023 (SI 2023/1218) amends reg.1 as follows:

after the definition of “care home” insert—

"“carer support payment” means carer's assistance given in accordance with the Carer's Assistance (Carer Support Payment) (Scotland) Regulations 2023;".

pp.851–852, *Annotation to the Jobseeker's Allowance Regulations 1996 (SI 1996/207) reg.16 (Further circumstances in which a person is to be treated as available: permitted period)*

Note that there has been no amendment to reg.16, equivalent to that made for universal credit and new style JSA purposes by SI 2022/108 (see the notes to reg.97(4) and (5) of the Universal Credit Regulations 2013 in Pt II of Vol.II of this series and to reg.14(3) of the JSA Regulations 2013 in Vol.I of this series), to reduce the maximum length of a “permitted period” from 13 weeks to four. **5.072**

pp.872–873, *Annotation to the Jobseeker's Allowance Regulations 1996 (SI 1996/207) reg.20 (Further circumstances in which a person is to be treated as actively seeking employment: permitted period)*

5.073 Note that there has been no amendment to reg.20, equivalent to that made for universal credit and new style JSA purposes by SI 2022/108 (see the notes to reg.97(4) and (5) of the Universal Credit Regulations 2013 in Pt II of Vol.II of this series and to reg.14(3) of the JSA Regulations 2013 in Vol.I of this series), to reduce the maximum length of a "permitted period" from 13 weeks to four.

p.896, *amendments to the Jobseeker's Allowance Regulations 1996 (SI 1996/207) reg.46(1) (Waiting days)*

5.074 With effect from November 19, 2023, art.8(3) of the Carer's Assistance (Carer Support Payment) (Scotland) Regulations 2023 (Consequential Amendments) Order 2023 (SI 2023/1218) amended reg.46(1)(a) and (d) by substituting ", carer's allowance or carer support payment" for "carer's llowance" in both places. Carer support payment is newly defined in reg.1(3) by reference to the Scottish legislation (see the entry for p.787).

pp.902–903, *amendments to the Jobseeker's Allowance Regulations 1996 (SI 1996/207) reg.48(2) and (3) (Linking periods)*

5.075 With effect from November 19, 2023, art.8(4) of the Carer's Assistance (Carer Support Payment) (Scotland) Regulations 2023 (Consequential Amendments) Order 2023 (SI 2023/1218) amended reg.48(2)(a) and (3) by inserting "or carer support payment" after "Benefits Act" in para.(2)(a) and after "carer's allowance" in para.(3). Carer support payment is newly defined in reg.1(3) by reference to the Scottish legislation (see the entry for p.787).

pp.910–912, *amendments to the Jobseeker's Allowance Regulations 1996 (SI 1996/207) reg.51 (Remunerative work)*

5.076 The text in the main volume at para.3.166 should be replaced with the following:

"Remunerative work

51.—(1) For the purposes of the Act "remunerative work" means—

(a) in the case of [5 a claimant], work in which he is engaged or, where his hours of work fluctuate, is engaged on average, for not less than 16 hours per week; and

(b) in the case of any partner of the claimant, work in which he is engaged or, where his hours of work fluctuate, is engaged on average, for not less than 24 hours per week; [1 and

(c) in the case of a non-dependant, or of a child or young person to whom paragraph 18 of Schedule 6 refers, work in which he is engaged or, where his hours of work fluctuate, is engaged on average, for not less than 16 hours per week,] and for those purposes, [3 "work" is work] for which payment is made or which is done in expectation of payment.

(2) For the purposes of paragraph (1), the number of hours in which [5 a claimant] or his partner is engaged in work shall be determined—

(a) where no recognisable cycle has been established in respect of a person's work, by reference to the number of hours or, where those hours are likely to fluctuate, the average of the hours, which he is expected to work in a week;

(b) where the number of hours for which he is engaged fluctuate, by reference to the average of hours worked over—

(i) if there is a recognisable cycle of work, and sub-paragraph (c) does not apply, the period of one complete cycle (including, where the cycle involves periods in which the person does not work, those periods but disregarding any other absences);

(ii) in any other case, the period of five weeks immediately before the date of claim or the date of [4 supersession], or such other length of time as may, in the particular case, enable the person's average hours of work to be determined more accurately;

(c) [7 . . .]

(3) In determining in accordance with this regulation the number of hours for which a person is engaged in remunerative work—

(a) that number shall include any time allowed to that person by his employer for a meal or for refreshments, but only where the person is, or expects to be, paid earnings in respect of that time;

(b) no account shall be taken of any hours in which the person is engaged in an employment or scheme to which any one of paragraphs (a) to (h) of regulation 53 (person treated as not engaged in remunerative work) applies;

(c) no account shall be taken of any hours in which the person is engaged otherwise than in an employment as an earner in caring for—

(i) a person who is in receipt of attendance allowance [1 . . .] [9 , the care component of disability living allowance at the highest or middle rate [11 the care component of child disability payment at the highest or middle rate in accordance with regulation 11(5) of the DACYP Regulations] [10 , armed forces independence payment] [12 . . .] the daily living component of personal independence payment at the standard or enhanced rate] [12 , or the daily living component of adult disability payment at the standard or enhanced rate]; or

(ii) a person who has claimed an attendance allowance [1 . . .] [9, disability living allowance [11 child disability payment] [10 , armed forces independence payment] [12 . . .] personal independence payment] [12 or adult disability payment], but only for the period beginning with the date of claim and ending on the date the claim is determined or, if earlier, on the expiration of the period of 26 weeks from the date of claim; or

(iii) another person [2 and] is in receipt of [6 carer's allowance] under Section 70 of the [1 Benefits Act [13 or carer support payment]; or

(iv) a person who has claimed either attendance allowance or disability living allowance and has an award of attendance allowance or the care component of disability living allowance at one of the two higher rates prescribed under section 72(4) of the Benefits Act for a period commencing after the date on which that claim was made] [9 ; or

[11 (iva) a person who has claimed child disability payment and has an award of the care component of child disability payment at the highest or middle rate in accordance with regulation 11(5) of the DACYP Regulations for a period commencing after the date on which the claim was made;] or

(v) a person who has claimed personal independence payment and has an award of the daily living component at the standard or enhanced rate under section 78 of the 2012 Act for a period commencing after the date on which that claim was made] [10 ; or

[12 (va) a person who has claimed adult disability payment and has an award of the daily living component at the standard or enhanced rate under regulation 5 of the Disability Assistance for Working Age People (Scotland) Regulations 2022 for a period commencing after the date on which that claim was made;] or

(vi) a person who has claimed and has an award of armed forces independence payment for a period commencing after the date on which that claim was made.]

[8 . . .]"

AMENDMENTS

1. Jobseeker's Allowance (Amendment) Regulations 1996 (SI 1996/15160) reg.9 (October 7, 1996).

2. Jobseeker's Allowance (Amendment) Regulations 1996 (SI 1996/1516) reg.20 and Sch. (October 7, 1996).

3. Social Security (Miscellaneous Amendments) Regulations 1997 (SI 1997/454) reg.2(5) (April 7, 1997).

4. Social Security Act 1998 (Commencement No. 11, and Savings and Consequential and Transitional Provisions) Order 1999 (SI 1999/2860 (C.75)) art.3(1) and (12) and Sch.12 para.5 (October 18, 1999)

5. Jobseeker's Allowance (Joint Claims) Regulations 2000 (SI 2000/1978) reg.2(5) and Sch.2 para.14 (March 19, 2001).

6. Social Security (Miscellaneous Amendments) Regulations 2003 (SI 2003/511) reg.3(4) and (5) (April 1, 2003).

7. Social Security (Miscellaneous Amendments) Regulations 2009 (SI 2009/583) reg.4(1) and (4) (April 6, 2009).

8. Social Security (Miscellaneous Amendments) (No. 3) Regulations 2011 (SI 2011/2425) reg.10(1) and (3) (October 31, 2011).

9. Personal Independence Payment (Supplementary Provisions and Consequential Amendments) Regulations 2013 (SI 2013/388) reg.8 and Sch. para.16(1) and (3) (April 8, 2013).

10. Armed Forces and Reserve Forces Compensation Scheme (Consequential Provisions: Subordinate Legislation) Order 2013 (SI 2013/591) art.7 and Sch. para.10(1) and (3) (April 8, 2013).

11. Social Security (Scotland) Act 2018 (Disability Assistance for Children and Young People) (Consequential Modifications) Order 2021 (SI 2021/786) Sch.3 para.3 (July 26, 2021).

12. Social Security (Disability Assistance for Working Age People) (Consequential Amendments) Order 2022 (SI 2022/177) art.5(3) (March 21, 2022).

13. Carer's Assistance (Carer Support Payment) (Scotland) Regulations 2023 (Consequential Amendments) Order 2023 (SI 2023/1218) art.8 (November 19, 2023).

DEFINITIONS

"the Act"—see reg.1(3).
"adult disability payment"—*ibid.*
"attendance allowance"—*ibid.*
"the Benefits Act"—see Jobseekers Act s.35(1).
"child"—*ibid.*
"child disability payment"—see reg.1(3).
"claimant"—see Jobseekers Act s.35(1).
"date of claim"—see reg.1(3).
"DACYP Regulations"—*ibid.*
"disability living allowance"—*ibid.*
"earnings"—*ibid.*
"employment"—see reg.3.
"partner"—see reg.1(3).
"payment"—*ibid.*
"personal independence payment"—*ibid.*
"week"—*ibid.*
"young person"—*ibid.*, reg.76.
For the General Note to reg.51, see Vol.V paras 3.167–3.169.

p.923, *amendment to the Jobseeker's Allowance Regulations 1996 (SI 1996/207) reg.55ZA(2)(a) (Extended period of sickness)*

With effect from July 1, 2022, reg.4(1) of the Social Security (Medical Evidence) and Statutory Sick Pay (Medical Evidence) (Amendment) (No. 2) Regulations 2022 (SI 2022/630) omitted the words "a doctor's" between "form of" and "statement". 5.077

p.970, *annotation to the Jobseeker's Allowance Regulations 1996 (SI 1996/207) reg.83 (Applicable amounts)*

On the lawfulness of not uplifting the amounts paid in IS, JSA and ESA by £20 per week (as was done with UC for 18 months during the coronavirus pandemic), see the annotation to the Income Support (General) Regulations 1987 (SI 1987/1967) reg.17 (Applicable amounts), above. 5.078

pp.974–977, *amendments to the Jobseeker's Allowance Regulations 1996 (SI 1996/207) reg.85A (Special cases: supplemental—persons from abroad)*

The text in the main volume at para.3.278 should be replaced with the following: 5.079

"**85A.**—(1) "Person from abroad" means, subject to the following provisions of this regulation, a claimant who is not habitually resident in the United Kingdom, the Channel Islands, the Isle of Man or the Republic of Ireland.

[[10] (2) No claimant shall be treated as habitually resident in the United Kingdom, the Channel Islands, the Isle of Man or the Republic of Ireland unless—

(a) [12 subject to the exceptions in paragraph (2A),] the claimant has been living in any of those places for the past three months; and

(b) the claimant has a right to reside in any of those places, other than a right to reside which falls within paragraph (3) [13 or (3A)].]

[12 (2A) The exceptions are where the claimant has at any time during the period referred to in paragraph (2)(a)—

(a) paid either Class 1 or Class 2 contributions by virtue of regulation 114, 118, 146 or 147 of the Social Security (Contributions) Regulations 2001 or by virtue of an Order in Council having effect under section 179 of the Social Security Administration Act 1992; or

(b) been a Crown servant posted to perform overseas the duties of a Crown servant; or

(c) been a member of Her Majesty's forces posted to perform overseas the duties of a member of Her Majesty's forces.]

(3) A right to reside falls within this paragraph if it is one which exists by virtue of, or in accordance with, one or more of the following—

(a) regulation 13 of the [13 Immigration (European Economic Area) Regulations 2016]; [15 or]

[7[13(aa) regulation 16 of those Regulations, but only in a case where the right exists under that regulation because the claimant satisfies the criteria in paragraph (5) of that regulation;]]

(b) [15 . . .]

(c) [15 . . .]

[13 (3A) A right to reside falls within this paragraph if it exists by virtue of a claimant having been granted limited leave to enter, or remain in, the United Kingdom under the Immigration Act 1971 by virtue of—

(a) Appendix EU to the immigration rules made under section 3(2) of that Act; [16 . . .]

(b) being a person with a Zambrano right to reside as defined in Annex 1 of Appendix EU to the immigration rules made under section 3(2) of that Act.] [16; or

(c) having arrived in the United Kingdom with an entry clearance that was granted under Appendix EU (Family Permit) to the immigration rules made under section 3(2) of that Act.]

[14 (3B) Paragraph (3A)(a) does not apply to a person who—

(a) has a right to reside granted by virtue of being a family member of a relevant person of Northern Ireland; and

(b) would have a right to reside under the Immigration (European Economic Area) Regulations 2016 if the relevant person of Northern Ireland were an EEA national, provided that the right to reside does not fall within paragraph (3A).]

(4) A claimant is not a person from abroad if he is—

[16(zza) a person granted leave in accordance with the immigration rules made under section 3(2) of the Immigration Act 1971, where such leave is granted by virtue of—

(i) the Afghan Relocations and Assistance Policy; or

(ii) the previous scheme for locally-employed staff in Afghanistan (sometimes referred to as the ex-gratia scheme);

(zzb) a person in Great Britain not coming within sub-paragraph (zza) or [17 (h)] who left Afghanistan in connection with the collapse of the Afghan government that took place on 15th August 2021;]

[[17](zzc) a person in Great Britain who was residing in Ukraine immediately before 1st January 2022, left Ukraine in connection with the Russian invasion which took place on 24th February 2022 and—

(i) has been granted leave in accordance with immigration rules made under section 3(2) of the Immigration Act 1971; [[18] . . .]

(ii) has a right of abode in the United Kingdom within the meaning given in section 2 of that Act;] [[18] or

(iii) does not require leave to enter or remain in the United Kingdom in accordance with section 3ZA of that Act;]

[[19](zzd) a person who was residing in Sudan before 15th April 2023, left Sudan in connection with the violence which rapidly escalated on 15th April 2023 in Khartoum and across Sudan and—

(i) has been granted leave in accordance with immigration rules made under section 3(2) of the Immigration Act 1971(10);

(ii) has a right of abode in the United Kingdom within the meaning given in section 2 of that Act(11); or

(iii) does not require leave to enter or remain in the United Kingdom in accordance with section 3ZA of that Act;]

[[20](zze) a person who was residing in Israel, the West Bank, the Gaza Strip, East Jerusalem, the Golan Heights or Lebanon immediately before 7th October 2023, who left Israel, the West Bank, the Gaza Strip, East Jerusalem, the Golan Heights or Lebanon in connection with the Hamas terrorist attack in Israel on 7th October 2023 or the violence which rapidly escalated in the region following the attack and—

(i) has been granted leave in accordance with immigration rules made under section 3(2) of the Immigration Act 1971;

(ii) has a right of abode in the United Kingdom within the meaning given in section 2 of that Act; or

(iii) does not require leave to enter or remain in the United Kingdom in accordance with section 3ZA of that Act;]

[[11](za) a qualified person for the purposes of regulation 6 of the [[13] Immigration (European Economic Area) Regulations 2016] as a worker or a self-employed person;

(zb) a family member of a person referred to in sub-paragraph (za) [[14] . . .];

(zc) a person who has a right to reside permanently in the United Kingdom by virtue of regulation 15(1)(c), (d) or I of those Regulations;]

[[14](zd) a family member of a relevant person of Northern Ireland, with a right to reside which falls within paragraph (3A)(a), provided that the relevant person of Northern Ireland falls within sub-paragraph (za), or would do so but for the fact that they are not an EEA national;]

[[15](ze) a frontier worker within the meaning of regulation 3 of the Citizens' Rights (Frontier Workers) (EU Exit) Regulations 2020;

(zf) a family member, of a person referred to in sub-paragraph (ze), who has been granted limited leave to enter, or remain in, the United Kingdom by virtue of Appendix EU to the immigration rules made under section 3(2) of the Immigration Act 1971;]

(g) a refugee within the definition in Article 1 of the Convention relating to the Status of Refugees done at Geneva on 28th July 1951, as extended by Article 1(2) of the Protocol relating to the Status of Refugees done at New York on 31st January 1967;

[3[9(h) a person who has been granted leave or who is deemed to have been granted leave outside the rules made under section 3(2) of the Immigration Act 1971 [17 . . .]]

(hh) a person who has humanitarian protection granted under those rules;] [9 or]

(i) a person who is not a person subject to immigration control within the meaning of section 115(9) of the Immigration and Asylum Act and who is in the United Kingdom as a result of his deportation, expulsion or other removal by compulsion of law from another country to the United Kingdom; [5 . . .]

[9 . . .]

[14 (5) In this regulation—

"EEA national" has the meaning given in regulation 2(1) of the Immigration (European Economic Area) Regulations 2016;

"family member" has the meaning given in regulation 7(1)(a), (b) or (c) of the Immigration (European Economic Area) Regulations 2016 except that regulation 7(4) of those Regulations does not apply for the purposes of paragraphs (3B) and (4)(zd);

"relevant person of Northern Ireland" has the meaning given in Annex 1 of Appendix EU to the immigration rules made under section 3(2) of the Immigration Act 1971.]

[15 (6) In this regulation references to the Immigration (European Economic Area) Regulations 2016 are to be read with Schedule 4 to the Immigration and Social Security Co-ordination (EU Withdrawal) Act 2020 (Consequential, Saving, Transitional and Transitory Provisions) Regulations 2020.]"

AMENDMENTS

1. Social Security (Persons from Abroad) Amendment Regulations 2006 (SI 1026/2006) reg.7(3) (April 30, 2006).

2. Social Security (Lebanon) Amendment Regulations 2006 (SI 2006/1981) reg.3 (July 25, 2006). The amendment ceased to have effect from January 31, 2007.

3. Social Security (Persons from Abroad) Amendment (No. 2) Regulations 2006 (SI 2006/2528) reg.3 (October 9, 2006).

4. Social Security (Bulgaria and Romania) Amendment Regulations 2006 (SI 2006/3341) reg.3 (January 1, 2007).

5. Social Security (Habitual Residence) (Amendment) Regulations 2009 (SI 2009/362) reg.3 (March 18, 2009).

6. Social Security (Miscellaneous Amendments) (No. 3) Regulations 2011 (SI 2011/2425) reg.10(1) and (7) (October 31, 2011).

7. Social Security (Habitual Residence) (Amendment) Regulations 2012 (SI 2012/2587) reg.3 (November 8, 2012).

8. Social Security (Croatia) Amendment Regulations 2013 (SI 2013/1474) reg.3 (July 1, 2013).

9. Social Security (Miscellaneous Amendments) (No. 3) Regulations 2013 (SI 2013/2536) reg.6(1) and (8) (October 29,2013).

10. Jobseeker's Allowance (Habitual Residence) Amendment Regulations 2013 (SI 3196/2013) reg.2 (January 1, 2014).

11. Social Security (Habitual Residence) (Amendment) Regulations 2014 (SI 2014/902) reg.3 (May 31, 2014).

12. Jobseeker's Allowance (Habitual Residence) Amendment Regulations 2014 (SI 2014/2735) reg.3 (November 9, 2014).

13. Social Security (Income-related Benefits) (Updating and Amendment) (EU Exit) Regulations 2019 (SI 2019/872) reg.3 (May 7, 2019).

14. Social Security (Income-Related Benefits) (Persons of Northern Ireland—Family Members) (Amendment) Regulations 2020 (SI 2020/683) reg.3 (August 24, 2020).

15. Immigration and Social Security Co-ordination (EU Withdrawal) Act 2020 (Consequential, Saving, Transitional and Transitory Provisions) (EU Exit) Regulations 2020 (SI 2020/1309) reg.55 (December 31, 2020 at 11.00 pm).

16. Social Security (Habitual Residence and Past Presence) (Amendment) Regulations 2021 (SI 2021/1034), reg.2 (September 15, 2021).

17. Social Security (Habitual Residence and Past Presence) (Amendment) Regulations 2022 (SI 2022/344) reg.2 (March 22, 2022).

18. Social Security (Habitual Residence and Past Presence) (Amendment) (No. 2) Regulations 2022 (SI 2022/990) reg.2 (October 18, 2022).

19. Social Security (Habitual Residence and Past Presence) (Amendment) Regulations 2023 (SI 2023/532), reg.2 (May 15, 2023).

20. Social Security (Habitual Residence and Past Presence, and Capital Disregards) (Amendment) Regulations 2023, reg.2 (SI 2023/1144) (October 27, 2023).

p.1014, *amendment to the Jobseeker's Allowance Regulations 1996 (SI 1996/207) reg.105(10A) (Notional income—exceptions)*

With effect from January 1, 2022, reg.3(3) of the Social Security (Income and Capital Disregards) (Amendment) Regulations 2021 (SI 2021/1405) amended para.(10A) by inserting the following after sub-para.(ab): 5.080

"(ac) a child abuse payment;
(ad) a Windrush payment;"

Those payments are defined in reg.1(3). See the entry for pp.684–685 for discussion of the nature of those payments.

With effect from July 9, 2023, reg.3(3) of the Social Security (Income and Capital Disregards) (Amendment) Regulations 2023 (SI 2023/640) amended reg.105(10A) by inserting the following after sub-para.(ad):

"(ae) a Post Office compensation payment;"

Such payments are newly defined in reg.1(3), where there is now also an expanded definition of Grenfell Tower payments (see sub-para.(ab)). See the entry for pp.684-685 for the background.

p.1021, *annotation to the Jobseeker's Allowance Regulations 1996 (SI 1996/207) reg.107 (Capital limit)*

In the Institute for Government and the Social Security Advisory Committee's 2021 joint report *Jobs and benefits: The Covid-19 challenge* it was noted that if the capital limit of £16,000 had risen in line with prices since 2006 it would be close to £23,500 (or £25,000: different figures are given) and recommended that the limit should be increased to £25,000 and subsequently automatically indexed to maintain its real value (pp.22 and 31). That recommendation was summarily rejected in the Government's response of March 22, 2022. 5.081

p.1023, *amendment to the Jobseeker's Allowance Regulations 1996 (SI 1996/207) reg.110(10) (Income treated as capital—exceptions)*

5.082 With effect from January 1, 2022, reg.3(4) of the Social Security (Income and Capital Disregards) (Amendment) Regulations 2021 (SI 2021/1405) amended para.(10) by inserting the following after sub-para.(ab):

"(ac) which is a child abuse payment;
(ad) which is a Windrush payment; or"

Those payments are defined in reg.1(3). See the entry for pp.684–685 for discussion of the nature of those payments. The "or" following sub-para. (ab), omitted in error in the main volume, has also been removed.

With effect from July 9, 2023, reg.3(4) of the Social Security (Income and Capital Disregards) (Amendment) Regulations 2023 (SI 2023/640) amended reg.110(10) by omitting "or" at the end of sub-para.(ad) and inserting the following:

"(ae) which is a Post Office compensation payment;"

Such payments are newly defined in reg.1(3), where there is now also an expanded definition of Grenfell Tower payments (see sub-para.(ab)). See the entry for pp.684–685 for the background.

With effect from October 27, 2023, reg.4(3)(a) of the Social Security (Habitual Residence and Past Presence, and Capital Disregards) (Amendment) Regulations 2023 (SI 2023/1144) amended reg.110(10)(c) by inserting ", the Victims of Overseas Terrorism Compensation Scheme" after "the National Emergencies Trust". That scheme is newly defined in reg.1(3). See the entry for pp.684–685 on income support for the background.

p.1027, *amendment to the Jobseeker's Allowance Regulations 1996 (SI 1996/207) reg.113(3B) (Notional capital—exceptions)*

5.083 With effect from January 1, 2022, reg.3(5) of the Social Security (Income and Capital Disregards) (Amendment) Regulations 2021 (SI 2021/1405) amended para.(3B) by substituting the following for "a payment of capital which is a Grenfell Tower payment":

"any of the following payments of capital—

(a) a Grenfell Tower payment;
(b) a child abuse payment;
(c) a Windrush payment."

All of those payments are defined in reg.1(3). See the entry of pp.684–685 for discussion of the nature of child abuse and Windrush payments.

With effect from July 9, 2023, reg.3(5) of the Social Security (Income and Capital Disregards) (Amendment) Regulations 2023 (SI 2023/640) amended reg.113(3B) by inserting the following after sub-para.(c):

"(d) a Post Office compensation payment;
(e) a vaccine damage payment."

Such payments are newly defined in reg.1(3), where there is now also an expanded definition of Grenfell Tower payments (see sub-para.(a)). See the entry for entry for pp.684–685 for the background.

With effect from October 27, 2023, reg.4(3)(b) of the Social Security (Habitual Residence and Past Presence, and Capital Disregards) (Amendment) Regulations 2023 (SI 2023/1144) amended reg.113(3A)(a) by inserting ", the Victims of Overseas Terrorism Compensation Scheme" after "the National Emergencies Trust". That scheme is newly defined in reg.1(3). See the entry for pp.684–685 on income support for the background.

pp.1029–1030, *annotation to the Jobseeker's Allowance Regulations 1996 (SI 1996/207) reg.113(1) (Notional capital—deprivation)*

DB v DfC (JSA) [2021] NICom 43 takes the same approach as set out in the main volume to the scope of the Northern Ireland equivalent (in identical terms) of reg.113(1). The claimant had been entitled to old style ESA. On November 25, 2016 the decision was given that she was not entitled from August 2015, apparently on the basis that, although she asserted that she had disposed of some £40,000 of capital that she said did not belong to her, it was her capital and she had not shown that she had disposed of it. She claimed old style JSA on September 14, 2017. On October 16, 2017 it was decided that she was not entitled, on the basis that her actual capital exceeded £16,000, despite her further assertions of having depleted bank accounts. A revision of that decision and submissions made on appeal were hopelessly confused as between actual and notional capital, but the decision of October 16, 2017 was never formally changed. The appeal tribunal found that the claimant had deprived herself of more than £40,000 in 2016 for the principal purpose of bringing her capital below the limits to obtain benefits including JSA, so that she was treated as having notional income over £16,000 after the application of the diminishing notional capital rule (reg.114). The Chief Commissioner held, as had been submitted by the DfC, that because reg.113(1) could only bite when the claimant's purpose was securing entitlement to or increasing the amount of old style JSA or income support, the appeal tribunal had failed to make the necessary findings of fact or show that it had applied the legally correct approach. It was inherently improbable that when depriving herself of capital while in receipt of ESA, more than a year before she claimed JSA, the claimant had possible entitlement to JSA in mind. 5.084

The decision also illustrates that on a new claim neither the decision-maker nor a tribunal on appeal is bound by the findings of fact on capital that have underpinned a decision of non-entitlement on capital grounds. The basis of the ESA decision, that the claimant as at that date still had actual capital of more than £40,000, did not have to be adopted on the JSA claim.

p.1054, *annotation to the Jobseeker's Allowance Regulations 1996 (SI 1996/207) reg.136(4) and (5) (Treatment of student loans and postgraduate loans)*

See the entry for p.539 on income support for details of the decision in *IB v Gravesham BC and SSWP (HB)* [2023] UKUT 193 (AAC); [2024] P.T.S.R. 130 on when a claimant cannot acquire a loan by taking reasonable steps to do so. 5.085

p.1055, *amendment to the Jobseeker's Allowance Regulations 1996 (SI 1996/2077) reg.136C (Treatment of special support loans)*

5.086 With effect from April 1, 2024, reg.2 of the Social Security and Universal Credit (Migration of Tax Credit Claimants and Miscellaneous Amendments) Regulations 2024 (SI 2024/341) amended reg.136C by substituting the following for the existing text and heading:

> **"Treatment of loans for specific purposes**
> **136C.** A loan under the Education (Student Support) Regulations 2011 or regulations made under section 73 of the Education (Scotland) Act 1980 that is intended to meet the cost of books, equipment, travel or childcare is to be disregarded as income."

The new form of reg.136C is intended to ensure that special support loans under a scheme to be introduced for full-time students by the Scottish government from the beginning of academic year 2024/25 are to be disregarded as income in same way as special support loans in England and Wales. Although the new form no longer refers to the definition of "special support loan" in reg.68 of the Education (Student Support) Regulations 2011, the restriction to loans intended (i.e., by necessary implication, intended by the awarding authority) to meet the cost of books, equipment, travel or childcare excludes loans under those regulations for other purposes. See reg.131 for the disregard of grants, as opposed to loans, for similar and other purposes.

pp.1059–1060, *amendments to the Jobseeker's Allowance Regulations 1996 (SI 1996/207) reg.140 (Hardship payments)*

5.087 With effect from July 26, 2021, Sch.3 para.4 of the Social Security (Scotland) Act 2018 (Disability Assistance for Children and Young People) (Consequential Modifications) Order 2021 (SI 2021/786) makes the following amendments to reg.140(1)(h):

- in para.(i), after "Benefits Act", insert ", the care component of child disability payment at the highest or middle rate in accordance with regulation 11(5) of the DACYP Regulations";
- in para.(ii), after "disability living allowance", insert ", child disability payment";
- after para.(iii), insert "(iiia) has claimed child disability payment and has an award of the care component of child disability payment at the highest or middle rate in accordance with regulation 11(5) of the DACYP Regulations for a period commencing after the date on which the claim was made; or".

With effect from March 21, 2022, art.5 of the Social Security (Disability Assistance for Working Age People) (Consequential Amendments) Order 2022 (SI 2022/177) makes the following amendments to reg.140(1)(h):

- in para.(i):
    - after "DACYP Regulations" for "or" substitute ",";
    - after "the 2012 Act" insert ", the daily living component of adult disability payment at the standard or enhanced rate in

accordance with regulation 5 of the Disability Assistance for Working Age People (Scotland) Regulations 2022";

- in para.(ii):
  - after "armed forces independence payment" for "or" substitute ",";
  - after "personal independence payment" insert "or adult disability payment";
- after para.(iv) insert "(iva) has claimed adult disability payment and has an award of the daily living component of adult disability payment at the standard or enhanced rate in accordance with regulation 5 of the Disability Assistance for Working Age People (Scotland) Regulations 2022 for a period commencing after the date on which that claim was made; or".

pp.1071–1072, *amendments to the Jobseeker's Allowance Regulations 1996 (SI 1996/207) reg.146A (Meaning of "couple in hardship")*

With effect from July 26, 2021, Sch.3 para.5 of the Social Security (Scotland) Act 2018 (Disability Assistance for Children and Young People) (Consequential Modifications) Order 2021 (SI 2021/786) makes the following amendments to reg.146A(1)(e): 5.088

- in para.(i), after "Benefits Act", insert ", the care component of child disability payment at the highest or middle rate in accordance with regulation 11(5) of the DACYP Regulations";
- in para.(ii), after "disability living allowance", insert ", child disability payment";
- after para.(iii), insert "(iiia) has claimed child disability payment and has an award of the care component of child disability payment at the highest or middle rate in accordance with regulation 11(5) of the DACYP Regulations for a period commencing after the date on which the claim was made; or".

With effect from March 21, 2022, art.5(5) of the Social Security (Disability Assistance for Working Age People) (Consequential Amendments) Order 2022 (SI 2022/177) makes the following amendments to reg.146A(1)(e):

- in para.(i):
  - after "armed forces independence payment", for "or" substitute ",";
  - after "the 2012 Act" insert ", or the daily living component of adult disability payment at the standard or enhanced rate in accordance with regulation 5 of the Disability Assistance for Working Age People (Scotland) Regulations 2022";
- in para.(ii):
  - after "armed forces independence payment", for "or" substitute ",";
  - after "personal independence payment" insert "or adult disability payment";
- after para.(iv) insert "(iva) has claimed adult disability payment and has an award of the daily living component at the standard or enhanced rate in accordance with regulation 5 of the Disability Assistance for Working Age People (Scotland) Regulations 2022

for a period commencing after the date on which that claim was made; or".

p.1080, *amendment to the Jobseeker's Allowance Regulations 1996 SI 1996/207), reg.150 (amount of a jobseeker's allowance payable)*

5.089 With effect from November 19, 2023, art.8 of the Carer's Assistance (Carer Support Payment) (Scotland) Regulations 2023 (Consequential Amendments) Order 2023 (SI 2023/1218) makes the following amendment to reg.150(2):

after "carer's allowance," insert "carer support payment,".

p.1081, *amendment to the Jobseeker's Allowance Regulations 1996 SI 1996/207), reg.153 (modification in the calculation of income),*

5.090 With effect from November 19, 2023, art.8 of the Carer's Assistance (Carer Support Payment) (Scotland) Regulations 2023 (Consequential Amendments) Order 2023 (SI 2023/1218) makes the following amendment to reg.153(c):

after "carer's allowance," insert "carer support payment,".

p.1086, *amendment to the Jobseeker's Allowance Regulations 1996 (SI 1996/207) reg.172 (Trade disputes: prescribed sum)*

5.091 With effect from April 8, 2024, art.27 of the Social Security Benefits Up-rating Order 2024 (SI 2024/242) substituted "£50.00" for "£47.00" (as had been in effect from April 10, 2023) in reg.172.

pp.1087–1088, *amendments to the Jobseeker's Allowance Regulations 1996 (SI 1996/207) Sch.A1 (Categories of members of a joint-claim couple who are not required to satisfy the conditions in section 1(2B)(b))*

5.092 With effect from July 26, 2021, Sch.3 para.6 of the Social Security (Scotland) Act 2018 (Disability Assistance for Children and Young People) (Consequential Modifications) Order 2021 (SI 2021/786) makes the following amendments to para.3(a) (member caring for another person):

- in para.(i), after "Benefits Act", insert ", the care component of child disability payment at the highest or middle rate in accordance with regulation 11(5) of the DACYP Regulations";
- in para.(iv), after "disability living allowance", insert ", child disability payment";
- after para.(v), insert "(va) the person being cared for ("P") has claimed entitlement to the care component of child disability payment in accordance with regulation 24 (when an application is to be treated as made and beginning of entitlement to assistance) of the DACYP Regulations, an award at the highest or middle rate has been made in respect of P's claim, and where the period for which the award is payable has begun, P is in receipt of that payment;"

With effect from March 21, 2022, art.5(6) of the Social Security (Disability Assistance for Working Age People) (Consequential Amendments) Order 2022 (SI 2022/177) makes the following amendments to para.3(a) (member caring for another person):

- in para.3(a)(i) (member caring for another person):
  - after "armed forces independence payment" for "or" substitute ",";
  - after "the 2012 Act" insert "or the daily living component of adult disability payment at the standard or enhanced rate in accordance with regulation 5 of the Disability Assistance for Working Age People (Scotland) Regulations 2022";
- in para.3(a)(iv):
  - after "armed forces independence payment" for "or" substitute ",";
  - after "personal independence payment" insert "or adult disability payment";
- in para.3(a)(vi) omit "or" at the end; and
- after para.3(a)(vi) insert "(via) the person being cared for has claimed entitlement to the daily living component of adult disability payment in accordance with regulation 35 (when an application is to be treated as made and beginning of entitlement to assistance) of the Disability Assistance for Working Age People (Scotland) Regulations 2022, an award of the standard or enhanced rate of the daily living component has been made in respect of that claim and, where the period for which the award is payable has begun, that person is in receipt of that payment; or"

With effect from November 19, 2023, art.8 of the Carer's Assistance (Carer Support Payment) (Scotland) Regulations 2023 (Consequential Amendments) Order 2023 (SI 2023/1218) makes the following amendment to para.3(b):

after "carer's allowance," insert "or carer support payment".

p.1091, *amendments to the Jobseeker's Allowance Regulations 1996 (SI 1996/207) Sch.1 (Applicable amounts)*

Substitute the following for paras 3.479–3.508 5.093

Regulations 83 and 84(1)

"SCHEDULE 1

APPLICABLE AMOUNTS

[9 PART I

PERSONAL ALLOWANCES

3.479 **1.**—The weekly amounts specified in column (2) below in respect of each person or couple specified in column (1) shall be the weekly amounts specified for the purposes of regulations 83 [28 84(1), 86A and 86B] (applicable amounts and polygamous marriages).

Column (1) *Person or Couple*	*Column (2)* *Amount*
(1) Single claimant aged—	1.
(a) except where head (b) or (c) of this sub-paragraph applies, less than 18;	(a) [56 £71.70];
(b) less than 18 who falls within paragraph (2) of regulation 57 and who— (i) is a person to whom regulation 59, 60 or 61 applies [1 . . .]; or (ii) is the subject of a direction under section 16;	(b) [56 £71.70];
(c) less than 18 who satisfies the condition in [33 paragraph 13(1)(a)] of Part 3;	(c) [56 £71.70];
(d) not less than 18 but less than 25;	(d) [56 £71.70];
(e) not less than 25.	(e) [56 £90.50];
(2) Lone parent aged—	2.
(a) except where head (b) or (c) of this sub-paragraph applies, less than 18;	(a) [56 £71.70];
(b) less than 18 who falls within paragraph (2) of regulation 57 and who— (i) is a person to whom regulation 59, 60 or 61 applies [1 . . .]; or (ii) is the subject of a direction under section 16;	(b) [56 £71.70];
(c) less than 18 who satisfies the condition in [33 paragraph 13(1)(a)] [2 of Part 3];	(c) [56 £71.70];
(d) not less than 18.	(d) [56 £90.50].
(3) Couple—	3.
(a) where both members are aged less than 18 and— (i) at least one of them is treated as responsible for a child; or (ii) had they not been members of a couple, each would have been a person to whom regulation 59, 60 or 61 (circumstances in which a person aged 16 or 17 is eligible for a jobseeker's allowance) applied or (iii) had they not been members of a couple, the claimant would have been a person to whom regulation 59, 60 or 61 (circumstances in which a person aged 16 or 17 is eligible for a	(a) [56 £108.30];
Column (1) *Person or Couple*	*Column (2)* *Amount*

Column (1) *Person or Couple*	*Column (2)* *Amount*
jobseeker's allowance) applied and his partner satisfies the requirements for entitlement to income support [36 or an income-related employment and support allowance] other than the requirement to make a claim for it; or	
[1(iv) they are married [31 or civil partners]and one member a of the couple is person to whom regulation 59, 60 or 61 applies and the other member is registered in accordance with regulation 62; or	
(iva) they are married [31 or civil partners] and each member of the couple is a person to whom regulation 59, 60 or 61 applies; or]	
(v) there is a direction under section 16 (jobseeker's allowance in cases of severe hardship) in respect of each member; or	
(vi) there is a direction under section 16 in respect of one of them and the other is a person to whom regulation 59, 60 or 61 applies [1 . . .], or	
(vii) there is a direction under section 16 in respect of one of them and the other satisfies requirements for entitlement to income support [36 or an income-related employment and support allowance] other than the requirement to make a claim for it;	
(b) where both members are aged less than 18 and sub-paragraph (3)(a) does not apply but one member of the couple falls within paragraph (2) of regulation 57 and either— (i) is a person to whom regulation 59, 60 or 61 applies [1 . . .]; or (ii) is the subject of a direction under section 16 of the Act;	(b) [56 £71.70];
(c) where both members are aged less than 18 and neither head (a) nor (b) of sub-paragraph (3) applies but one member of the couple— (i) is a person to whom regulation 59, 60 or 61 applies [1 . . .]; or (ii) is the subject of a direction under section 16;	(c) [56 £71.70];
(d) where both members are aged less than 18 and none of heads (a), (b) or (c) of sub-paragraph (3) apply but one member of the couple is a person who satisfies the requirements of [33 paragraph 13(1)(a)];	(d) [56 £71.70];
[35 (e) where— (i) both members are aged not less than 18; or (ii) one member is aged not less than 18 and the other member is a person who is— (aa) under 18, and (bb) treated as responsible for a child;]	(e) [56 £142.75];
(f) where [35 paragraph (e) does not apply and] one member is aged not less than 18 and the other member is a person under 18 who— (i) is a person to whom regulation 59, 60 or 61 applies [1 . . .]; or (ii) is the subject of a direction under section 16; [38 or	(f) [56 £142.75];

(iii) satisfies requirements for entitlement to income support or who would do so if he were not a member of a couple, other than the requirement to make a claim for it; or (iv) satisfies requirements for entitlement to an income-related employment and support allowance other than the requirement to make a claim for it;] (g) where one member is aged not less than 18 but less than 25 and the other member is a person under 18— (i) to whom none of the regulations 59 to 61 applies; or (ii) who is not the subject of a direction under section 16; and (iii) does not satisfy requirements for entitlement to income support [36 or an income-related employment and support allowance] disregarding the requirement to make a claim for it; (h) where one member is aged not less than 25 and the other member is a person under 18— (i) to whom none of the regulations 59 to 61 applies; or (ii) is not the subject of a direction under section 16; and (iii) does not satisfy requirements for entitlement to income support [36 or an income-related employment and support allowance] disregarding the requirement to make a claim for it.	(g) [56 £71.70]; (h) [56 £90.50].
2.—[30 . . .]	
3.—[29 . . .]	

Part II

Family Premium

3.480 **4.**—[30 . . .]

Part III

Premiums

3.481 **5.**—Except as provided in paragraph 6, the weekly premiums specified in Part IV of this Schedule shall for the purposes of regulations 83(e) and 84(1)(f), be applicable to a claimant who satisfies the condition specified in [4 15 paragraphs 9A] to 17 in respect of that premium.

6.—Subject to paragraph 7, where a claimant satisfies the conditions in respect of more than one premium in this Part of this Schedule, only one premium shall be applicable to him and, if they are different amounts, the higher or highest amount shall apply.

[16 **7.**—(1) Subject to sub-paragraph (2), the following premiums, namely—

(a) a severe disability premium to which paragraph 15 applies;

(b) an enhanced disability premium to which paragraph 15A applies;

(c) [30 . . .]; and

(d) a carer premium in which paragraph 17 applies,

may be applicable in addition to any other premium which may apply under this Part of this Schedule.

(2) An enhanced disability premium in respect of a person shall not be applicable in addition to—

(a) a pensioner premium under paragraph 10 or 11; or
(b) a higher pensioner premium under paragraph 12.]

8.—(1) Subject to sub-paragraph (2) for the purposes of this Part of this Schedule, once a premium is applicable to a claimant under this Part, a person shall be treated as being in receipt of any benefit—

(a) in the case of a benefit to which the Social Security (Overlapping Benefits) Regulations 1979 applies, for any period during which, apart from the provisions of those Regulations, he would be in receipt of that benefit; [55 ...]
[3(b) for any period spent by a claimant in undertaking a course of training or instruction provided or approved by the Secretary of State [35 . . .] under section 2 of the Employment and Training Act 1973, or by [37 Skills Development Scotland,] Scottish Enterprise or Highlands and Islands Enterprise under section 2 of the Enterprise and New Towns (Scotland) Act 1990 or for any period during which he is in receipt of a training allowance [55 ... ; and
(c) in the case of carer support payment, for any period during which, apart from regulation 16 of the Carer's Assistance (Carer Support Payment) (Scotland) Regulations 2023, he would be in receipt of that benefit.]]

(2) For the purposes of the carer premium under paragraph 17, a person shall be treated as being in receipt of [24 carer's allowance] by virtue of sub-paragraph (1)(a) [55 or carer support payment by virtue of sub-paragraph (1)(c)] only if and for so long as the person in respect of whose care the allowance [48 or payment] has been claimed remains in receipt of attendance allowance, [46 the care component of disability living allowance at the highest or middle rate prescribed in accordance with section 72(3) of the Benefits Act [52 , the care component of child disability payment at the highest or middle rate prescribed in accordance with regulation 11(5) of the DACYP Regulations] [47 , armed forces independence payment] [53 ,] the daily living component of personal independence payment at the standard or enhanced rate prescribed in accordance with section 78(3) of the 2012 Act] [53 , or the daily living component of adult disability payment at the standard or enhanced rate prescribed in accordance with regulation 5 of the Disability Assistance for Working Age People (Scotland) Regulations 2022].

Lone Parent Premium

9.—[4 . . .] 3.482

[15 Bereavement Premium

9A.—[34 . . .]] 3.483

Pensioner premium for persons [40 over the qualifying age for state pension credit]

10.—The condition is that the claimant— 3.484

(a) is a single claimant or lone parent who has attained [40 the qualifying age for state pension credit]; or
(b) has attained [40 the qualifying age for state pension credit] and has a partner; or
(c) has a partner and the partner has attained [40 the qualifying age for state pension credit] but not the age of 75.

Pensioner premium where claimant's partner has attained the age of 75

11.—The condition is that the claimant has a partner who has attained the age of 75 but not the age of 80. 3.485

Higher Pensioner Premium

12.—(1) [33 Subject to sub-paragraph (5), the] condition is that— 3.486

(a) the claimant is a single claimant or lone parent who has attained [40 the qualifying age for state pension credit] and either—
    (i) satisfies one of the additional conditions specified in paragraph 14(1)(a), (c), [51 (ca), (cb),] (e), (f) [51, (fa)] or (h); or
    (ii) was entitled to either income support or income-based jobseeker's allowance [12, or was treated as being entitled to either of those benefits and the disability premium was or, as the case may be, would have been,] applicable to him in respect of a benefit week within 8 weeks of [40 the date he attained the qualifying age for state pension credit] and he has, subject to sub-paragraph (2), remained continuously entitled to one of those benefits since attaining that age; or
(b) the claimant has a partner and—
    (i) the partner has attained the age of 80; or

(ii) the partner has attained [40 the qualifying age for state pension credit] but not the age of 80, and the additional conditions specified in paragraph 14 are satisfied in respect of him; or

(c) the claimant—

(i) has attained [40 the qualifying age for state pension credit];

[3(ii) satisfies the requirements of either sub-head (i) or (ii) of paragraph 12(1)(a); and]

(iii) has a partner.

(2) For the purposes of this paragraph and paragraph 14—

(a) once the higher pensioner premium is applicable to a claimant, if he then ceases, for a period of eight weeks or less, to be entitled to either income support or income-based jobseeker's allowance [12 or ceases to be treated as entitled to either of those benefits], he shall, on becoming re-entitled to either of those benefits, thereafter be treated as having been continuously entitled thereto;

(b) in so far as sub-paragraphs (1)(a)(ii) and (1)(c)(ii) are concerned, if a claimant ceases to be entitled to either income support or an income-based jobseeker's allowance [12 or ceases to be treated as entitled to either of those benefits] for a period not exceeding eight weeks which includes [40 the date he attained the qualifying age for state pension credit], he shall, on becoming re-entitled to either of those benefits, thereafter be treated as having been continuously entitled thereto.

[8(3) In this paragraph where a claimant's partner is a welfare to work beneficiary, sub-paragraphs (1)(a)(ii) and (2)(b) shall apply to him as if for the words "8 weeks" there were substituted the words "[32 104 weeks]".]

[12 (4) For the purposes of this paragraph, a claimant shall be treated as having been entitled to income support or to an income-based jobseeker's allowance throughout any period which comprises only days on which he was participating in an employment zone programme and was not entitled to—

(a) income support because, as a consequence of his participation in that programme, he was engaged in remunerative work or had income in excess of the claimant's applicable amount as prescribed in Part IV of the Income Support Regulations; or

(b) a jobseeker's allowance because, as a consequence of his participation in that programme, he was engaged in remunerative work or failed to satisfy the condition specified in section 2(1)(c) or in section 3(1)(a).]

[33 (5) The condition is not satisfied if—

(a) the claimant is a single claimant or a lone parent and (in either case) is a long-term patient;

(b) the claimant is a member of a couple or polygamous marriage and each member of the couple or polygamous marriage is a long-term patient; or

(c) the claimant is a member of a couple or a polygamous marriage and a member of that couple or polygamous marriage is—

(i) a long-term patient; and

(ii) the only member of the couple or polygamous marriage to whom sub-paragraph (1)(b) or (c) refers.]

Disability Premium

3.487 **13.** [33 —(1) Subject to sub-paragraph (2), the] condition is that the claimant—

(a) is a single claimant or lone parent who has not attained [40 the qualifying age for state pension credit] and satisfies any one of the additional conditions specified in paragraph 14(1)(a), (c), [51 (ca), (cb),] (e), (f) [51, (fa)] or (h); or

(b) has not attained [40 the qualifying age for state pension credit], has a partner and the claimant satisfies any one of the additional conditions specified in paragraph 14(1)(a), (c), [51 (ca), (cb),] (e), (f) [51, (fa)] or (h); or

(c) has a partner and the partner has not attained [40 the qualifying age for state pension credit] and also satisfies any one of the additional conditions specified in paragraph 14.

[33 (2) The condition is not satisfied if—

(a) the claimant is a single claimant or a lone parent and (in either case) is a long-term patient;

(b) the claimant is a member of a couple or polygamous marriage and each member of the couple or polygamous marriage is a long-term patient; or

(c) the claimant is a member of a couple or polygamous marriage and a member of that couple or polygamous marriage—

(i) is a long-term patient; and
(ii) is the only member of the couple or polygamous marriage to whom the condition in sub-paragraph (1)(b) or (c) refers.]

Additional conditions for Higher Pensioner and Disability Premium

14.—(1) The additional conditions specified in this paragraph are that— **3.488**

(a) the claimant or, as the case may be, his partner, is in receipt [25 the disability element or the severe disability element of working tax credit as specified in regulation 20(1)(b) and (f) of the Working Tax Credit (Entitlement and Maximum Rate) Regulations 2002] or mobility supplement;
(b) the claimant's partner is in receipt of severe disablement allowance;
(c) the claimant or, as the case may be, his partner, is in receipt of attendance allowance or disability living allowance or is a person whose disability living allowance is payable, in whole or in part, to another in accordance with regulation 44 of the Claims and Payments Regulations (payment of disability living allowance on behalf of third party);
[46 (ca) the claimant or, as the case may be, his partner, is in receipt of personal independence payment or is a person whose personal independence payment is payable, in whole or in part, to another in accordance with regulation 58(2) of the Universal Credit etc. Claims and Payments Regulations (payment to another person on the claimant's behalf);]
[53 (caa) the claimant or, as the case may be, the claimant's partner, is in receipt of adult disability payment or is a person whose adult disability payment is payable, in whole or in part, to another in accordance with regulation 33 of the Disability Assistance for Working Age People (Scotland) Regulations 2022 (making payments);]
[47 (cb) the claimant or, as the case may be, the claimant's partner, is in receipt of armed forces independence payment or is a person whose armed forces independence payment is payable, in whole or in part, to another in accordance with article 24D of the Armed Forces and Reserve Forces (Compensation Scheme) Order 2011;]
(d) the claimant's partner is in receipt of long-term incapacity benefit or is a person to whom section 30B(4) of the Benefits Act (long term rate of incapacity benefit payable to those who are terminally ill) applies;
(e) the claimant or, as the case may be, his partner, has an invalid carriage or other vehicle provided to him by the Secretary of State under section 5(2)(a) of and Schedule 2 to the National Health Service Act 1977 or under section 46 of the National Health Service (Scotland) Act 1978 or provided by the Department of Health and Social Services for Northern Ireland under article 30(1) of the Health and Personal Social Services (Northern Ireland) Order 1972, or receives payments by way of grant from the Secretary of State under paragraph 2 of Schedule 2 to the Act of 1977 (additional provisions as to vehicles) or, in Scotland, under section 46 of the Act of 1978;
(f) the claimant or, as the case may be, his partner, is a person who is entitled to the mobility component of disability living allowance but to whom the component is not payable in accordance with regulation 42 of the Claims and Payments Regulations (cases where disability living allowance not payable);
[46 (fa) the claimant or, as the case may be, his partner, is a person who is entitled to the mobility component of personal independence payment but to whom the component is not payable in accordance with regulation 61 of the Universal Credit etc. Claims and Payments Regulations (cases where mobility component of personal independence payment not payable);]
[53 (fb) the claimant or, as the case may be, the claimant's partner, is a person who is entitled to the mobility component of adult disability payment but to whom the component is not payable in accordance with regulation 34(6) of the Disability Assistance for Working Age People (Scotland) Regulations 2022 (amount and form of adult disability payment);]
(g) the claimant's partner was either—
(i) in receipt of long term incapacity benefit under section 30A(5) of the Benefits Act immediately before attaining pensionable age and he is still alive;
(ii) entitled to attendance allowance or disability living allowance but payment of that benefit was suspended in accordance with regulations under section 113(2) of the Benefits Act or otherwise abated as a consequence of [2 the partner] becoming a patient within the meaning of regulation 85(4) (special cases), [53 ; . . .]
(iii) entitled to personal independence payment but no amount is payable in accordance with regulations made under section 86(1) (hospital in-patients) of the 2012 Act] [53 ; or

(iv) entitled to adult disability payment but no amount is payable in accordance with regulation 28 (effect of admission to hospital on ongoing entitlement to Adult Disability Payment) of the Disability Assistance for Working Age People (Scotland) Regulations 2022;]

and [53 in any of the cases described in sub-paragraphs (i) to (iv),]the higher pensioner premium or disability premium had been applicable to the claimant or his partner;

[48 (h) the claimant or, as the case may be, his partner, is certified as severely sight impaired or blind by a consultant ophthalmologist.]

[48 (2) For the purposes of sub-paragraph (1)(h), a person who has ceased to be certified as severely sight impaired or blind on regaining his eyesight shall nevertheless be treated as severely sight impaired or blind, as the case may be, and as satisfying the additional condition set out in that sub-paragraph for a period of 28 weeks following the date on which he ceased to be so certified.]

Severe Disability Premium

3.489 **15.**—(1) In the case of a single claimant, a lone parent or a claimant who is treated as having no partner in consequence of sub-paragraph (3), the condition is that—

(a) he is in receipt of attendance allowance [46 , the care component of disability living allowance at the highest or middle rate prescribed in accordance with section 72(3) of the Benefits Act [47 , armed forces independence payment] [53 ,] the daily living component of personal independence payment at the standard or enhanced rate in accordance with section 78(3) of the 2012 Act] [53 , or the daily living component of adult disability payment at the standard or enhanced rate in accordance with regulation 5 of the Disability Assistance for Working Age People (Scotland) Regulations 2022]; and

(b) subject to sub-paragraph (4), there are no non-dependants aged 18 or over normally residing with him or with whom he is normally residing; and

[11(c) no person is entitled to, and in receipt of, [24 a carer's allowance] under section 70 of the Benefits Act [55 or carer support payment] [50 or has an award of universal credit which includes the carer element] in respect of caring for him;]

(2) Where the claimant has a partner, the condition is that—

(a) the claimant is in receipt of attendance allowance [46 , the care component of disability living allowance at the highest or middle rate prescribed in accordance with section 72(3) of the Benefits Act [47 , armed forces independence payment] [53 ,] the daily living component of personal independence payment at the standard or enhanced rate in accordance with section 78(3) of the 2012 Act] [53 , or the daily living component of adult disability payment at the standard or enhanced rate in accordance with regulation 5 of the Disability Assistance for Working Age People (Scotland) Regulations 2022]; and

(b) the partner is also in receipt of a qualifying benefit, or if he is a member of a polygamous marriage, all the partners of that marriage are in receipt of a qualifying benefit; and

(c) subject to sub-paragraph (4), there is no non-dependant aged 18 or over normally residing with him or with whom he is normally residing; and

(d) either—

(i) [11 no person is entitled to, and in receipt of, [24 a carer's allowance] under section 70 of the Benefits Act [55 or has an award of universal credit which includes the carer element] in respect of] caring for either member of the couple or all the members of the polygamous marriage; or

(ii) a person is engaged in caring for one member (but not both members) of the couple, or one or more but not all members of the polygamous marriage, and in consequence is [11 entitled to] [24 a carer's allowance] under section 70 of the Benefits Act [55 or carer support payment] [50 or has an award of universal credit which includes the carer element].

(3) Where the claimant has a partner who does not satisfy the condition in sub-paragraph (2)(b), and that partner is [48 severely sight impaired or blind or treated as severely sight impaired or blind] within the meaning of paragraph 14(1)(h) and (2), that partner shall be treated for the purposes of sub-paragraph (2) as if he were not a partner of the claimant.

(4) The following persons shall not be regarded as a non-dependant for the purposes of sub-paragraphs (1)(b) and (2)(c)—

(a) a person in receipt of attendance allowance [46 , the care component of disability living allowance at the highest or middle rate prescribed in accordance with section 72(3) of the Benefits Act [47 , armed forces independence payment] [53 ,] the daily living component of personal independence payment at the standard or enhanced rate in accordance with section 78(3) of the 2012 Act] [53 , or the daily living component of adult disability payment at the standard or enhanced rate in accordance with regulation 5 of the Disability Assistance for Working Age People (Scotland) Regulations 2022];

(b) subject to sub-paragraph (6), a person who joins the claimant's household for the first time in order to care for the claimant or his partner and immediately before so joining the claimant or his partner satisfied the condition in sub-paragraph (1) or, as the case may be, (2);

(c) a person who is [48 severely sight impaired or blind or treated as severely sight impaired or blind] within the meaning of paragraph 14(1)(h) and (2).

(5) For the purposes of sub-paragraph (2), a person shall be treated [11 . . .] (a) [11 as being in receipt of] attendance allowance, or the care component of disability living allowance at the highest or middle rate prescribed in accordance with section 72(3) of the Benefits Act if he would, but for his being a patient for a period exceeding 28 days, be so in receipt;

[46 (aa) as being in receipt of the daily living component of personal independence payment at the standard or enhanced rate in accordance with section 78 of the 2012 Act if he would, but for regulations made under section 86(1) (hospital in-patients) of the 2012 Act, be so in receipt;]

[53 (ab) as being in receipt of the daily living component of adult disability payment at the standard or enhanced rate in accordance with regulation 5 of the Disability Assistance for Working Age People (Scotland) Regulations 2022 if they would, but for regulation 28 (effect of admission to hospital on ongoing entitlement to Adult Disability Payment) of those Regulations be so in receipt;]

[11(b) as being entitled to and in receipt of [24 a carer's allowance] [55 or carer support payment] [50 or having an award of universal credit which includes the carer element] if he would, but for the person for whom he was caring being a patient in hospital for a period exceeding 28 days, be so entitled and in receipt [50 of carer's allowance or have such an award of universal credit].]

(6) Sub-paragraph (4)(b) shall apply only for the first 12 weeks following the date on which the person to whom that provision applies first joins the claimant's household.

(7) For the purposes of sub-paragraph (1)(c) and (2)(d), no account shall be taken of an award of [24 carer's allowance] [55 carer support payment] [50 or universal credit which includes the carer element] to the extent that payment of such an award is backdated for a period before [34 the date on which the award is first paid].

(8) A person shall be treated as satisfying this condition if he would have satisfied the condition specified for a severe disability premium in income support in paragraph 13 of Schedule 2 to the Income Support Regulations by virtue only of regulations 4 to 6 of the Income Support (General) Amendment (No. 6) Regulations 1991 (savings provisions in relation to severe disability premium) and for the purposes of determining whether in the particular case regulation 4 of those Regulations had ceased to apply in accordance with regulation 5(2)(a) of those Regulations, a person who is entitled to an income-based jobseeker's allowance shall be treated as entitled to income support.

[20 (9) In sub-paragraphs (1)(c) and (2)(d), references to a person being in receipt of [24 a carer's allowance] [50 or as having an award of universal credit which includes the carer element] shall include references to a person who would have been in receipt of that allowance [50 or had such an award] but for the application of a restriction under section [39 6B or] 7 of the Social Security Fraud Act 2001 (loss of benefit provisions).]

[50 (10) For the purposes of this paragraph, a person has an award of universal credit which includes the carer element if the person has an award of universal credit which includes an amount which is the carer element under regulation 29 of the Universal Credit Regulations 2013.]

[16 Enhanced disability premium

15A.—[46 (1) Subject to sub-paragraph (2), the condition is that— **3.490**

(a) the claimant; or

(b) the claimant's partner (if any), is a person who has not attained the qualifying age for state pension credit and is a person to whom sub-paragraph (1ZA) applies.

(1ZA) This sub-paragraph applies to the person mentioned in sub-paragraph (1) where—

(a) the care component of disability living allowance is, or would, but for a suspension of benefit in accordance with regulations under section 113(2) of the Benefits Act or but for an abatement as a consequence of hospitalisation, be payable to that person at the highest rate prescribed under section 72(3) of the Benefits Act; or

[52 (aa) the care component of child disability payment is payable to that person at the highest rate in accordance with regulation 11(5) of the DACYP Regulations; or]

(b) the daily living component of personal independence payment is, or would, but for a suspension of benefits in accordance with regulations under section 86(1) (hospital in-patients) of the 2012 Act, be payable to that person at the enhanced rate in accordance with section 78(2) of the 2012 Act] [47 ; or

[53 (ba) the daily living component of adult disability payment is, or would, but regulation 28 (effect of admission to hospital on ongoing entitlement to Adult Disability Payment) of the Disability Assistance for Working Age People (Scotland) Regulations 2022, be payable to that person at the enhanced rate in accordance with regulation 5 of those Regulations]

(c) armed forces independence payment is payable to that person.]

[42 (1A) Where the condition in sub-paragraph (1) ceases to be satisfied because of the death of a child or young person, the condition is that the claimant is entitled to child benefit in respect of that person under section 145A of the Benefits Act (entitlement after death of child or qualifying young person).]

[33 (2) The condition is not satisfied where the person to whom sub-paragraph (1) refers is—

(a) a child or young person—

(i) whose capital if calculated in accordance with Part 8 of these Regulations in like manner as for the claimant, except as provided in regulation 106(1), would exceed £3,000; or

(ii) who is a long-term patient;

(b) a single claimant or a lone parent and (in either case) is a long-term patient;

(c) a member of a couple or polygamous marriage and each member of the couple or polygamous marriage is a long-term patient; or

(d) a member of a couple or polygamous marriage who is—

(i) a long-term patient; and

(ii) the only member of the couple or polygamous marriage to whom sub-paragraph (1) refers.]]

Disabled Child Premium

3.491 **16.**—[30 . . . 33]

Carer Premium

3.492 **17.**—(1) Subject to sub-paragraphs (3) and (4), the condition is that the claimant or his partner is, or both of them are, [11 entitled to] [24 a carer's allowance] under section 70 of the Benefits Act [55 or carer support payment].

(2) [28 . . .]

[23 (3) Where a carer premium is awarded but—

(a) the person in respect of whose care the [24 carer's allowance] [55 or carer support payment] has been awarded dies; or

(b) in any other case the person in respect of whom a carer premium has been awarded ceases to be entitled [28 . . .] to [24 a carer's allowance] [55 or carer support payment], the condition for the award of the premium shall be treated as satisfied for a period of eight weeks from the relevant date specified in sub-paragraph (3A) below.

(3A) The relevant date for the purposes of sub-paragraph (3) above shall be—

(a) [28 where sub-paragraph (3)(a) applies,] the Sunday following the death of the person in respect of whose care [24 a carer's allowance] [55 or carer support payment] has been awarded or the date of death if the death occurred on a Sunday;

(b) [28 . . .]

(c) in any other case, the date of which the person who has been entitled to [24 a carer's allowance] [55 or carer support payment] ceases to be entitled to that allowance [55 or payment].]

(4) Where a person who has been entitled to [24 a carer's allowance] [55 or carer support payment] ceases to be entitled to that allowance [55 or payment] and makes a claim for a jobseeker's allowance, the condition for the award of the carer premium shall be treated as satisfied for a period of eight weeks from the date on which—

[23(a) the person in respect of whose care the [24 carer's allowance] [55 or carer support payment] has been awarded dies;

(b) [28 . . .]

[28 (c) in any other case, the person who has been entitled to a carer's allowance [55 or carer support payment] ceased to be entitled to that allowance [55 or payment].]]

Persons in receipt of concessionary payments

18.—For the purpose of determining whether a premium is applicable to a person under paragraphs 14 to 17, any concessionary payment made to compensate that person for the non-payment of any benefit mentioned in those paragraphs shall be treated as if it were a payment of that benefit. 3.493

Person in receipt of benefit

19.—For the purposes of this Part of this Schedule, a person shall be regarded as being in receipt of any benefit if, and only if, it is paid in respect of him and shall be so regarded only for any period in respect of which that benefit is paid. 3.494

PART IV

WEEKLY AMOUNTS OF PREMIUMS SPECIFIED IN PART III

Premium	*Amount*
20.—(1) [4 . . .]	(1) [4 . . .]
(1A) [34 . . .];	(1A) [34 . . .];
(2) Pensioner premium for persons [40 who have attained the qualifying age for state pension credit]— (a) where the claimant satisfies the condition in paragraph 10(a); (b) where the claimant satisfies the condition in paragraph 10(b). (c) where the claimant satisfies the condition in paragraph 10(c).	(2) (a) [57 £127.65]; (b) [57 £190.70]; (c) [57 £190.70];
(3) Pensioner premium for claimants whose partner has attained the age of 75 where the claimant satisfies the condition in paragraph 11;	(3) [57 £190.70];
(4) Higher Pensioner Premium— (a) where the claimant satisfies the condition in paragraph 12(1)(a); (b) where the claimant satisfies the condition in paragraph 12(1)(b) or (c).	(4) (a) [57 £127.65]; (b) [57 £190.70];
(5) Disability Premium— (a) where the claimant satisfies the condition in [33 paragraph 13(1)(a)]; (b) where the claimant satisfies the condition in [33 paragraph 13(1)(b) or (c)].	(5) (a) [57 £42.50]; (b) [57 £60.60].
(6) Severe Disability Premium— (a) where the claimant satisfies the condition in paragraph 15(1); (b) where the claimant satisfies the condition in paragraph 15(2)— (i) if there is someone in receipt of [24 a carer's allowance] or [2 if any partner of the claimant] satisfies that condition by virtue of paragraph 15(5); (ii) if no-one is in receipt of such an allowance.	(6) (a) [57 £81.50]; (b) (i) [57 £81.50] (ii) [57 £163.00]
(7) [30 . . .]	(7) [30 . . .]
(8) Carer Premium.	(8) [57 £45.60] in respect of each person who satisfied the condition specified in paragraph 17.

Premium	*Amount*
[16 (9) Enhanced disability premium where the conditions in paragraph 15A are satisfied.]	[16 (9) (a) [30 . . .] (b) [57 £20.85] in respect of each person who is neither— (i) a child or young person; nor (ii) a member of a couple or a polygamous marriage, respect of whom the in conditions specified in paragraph 15A are satisfied;
	(c) [57 £29.75] where the claimant is a member of a couple or a polygamous marriage and the conditions specified in paragraph 15A are satisfied in respect of a member of that couple or polygamous marriage.]

[14 PART IVA

PREMIUMS FOR JOINT-CLAIM COUPLES

3.497 **20A.**—Except as provided in paragraph 20B, the weekly premium specified in Part IVB of this Schedule shall, for the purposes of regulations 86A(c) and 86B(d), be applicable to a joint-claim couple where either or both members of a joint-claim couple satisfy the condition specified in paragraphs 20E to 20J in respect of that premium.

20B.—Subject to paragraph 20C, where a member of a joint-claim couple satisfies the conditions in respect of more than one premium in this Part of this Schedule, only one premium shall be applicable to the joint-claim couple in respect of that member and, if they are different amounts, the higher or highest amount shall apply.

[16 **20C.**—(1) Subject to sub-paragraph (2), the following premiums, namely—

(a) a severe disability premium to which paragraph 20I applies;
(b) an enhanced disability premium to which paragraph 20IA applies; and
(c) a carer premium to which paragraph 20J applies,

may be applicable in addition to any other premium which may apply under this Part of this Schedule.

(2) An enhanced disability premium in respect of a person shall not be applicable in addition to—

(a) a pensioner premium under paragraph 20E; or
(b) a higher pensioner premium under paragraph 20F.]

20D.—(1) Subject to sub-paragraph (2) for the purposes of this Part of this Schedule, once a premium is applicable to a joint-claim couple under this Part, a person shall be treated as being in receipt of any benefit—

(a) in the case of a benefit to which the Social Security (Overlapping Benefits) Regulations 1979 applies, for any period during which, apart from the provisions of those Regulations, he would be in receipt of that benefit; [55 ...]
(b) for any period spent by a person in undertaking a course of training or instruction provided or approved by the Secretary of State under section 2 of the Employment and Training Act 1973, or by [37 Skills Development Scotland,] Scottish Enterprise or Highlands and Islands Enterprise under section 2 of the Enterprise and New Towns (Scotland) Act 1990, or for any period during which he is in receipt of a training allowance [55 ; and
(c) in the case of carer support payment, for any period during which, apart from regulation 16 of the Carer's Assistance (Carer Support Payment) (Scotland) Regulations 2023, he would be in receipt of that benefit.]

(2) For the purposes of the carer premium under paragraph 20J, a person shall be treated as being in receipt of [24 carer's allowance] by virtue of sub-paragraph (1)(a) [55 or carer support payment by virtue of sub-paragraph (1)(c)] only if and for so long as the person in respect of

whose care the allowance [55 or payment] has been claimed remains in receipt of attendance allowance, [46 the care component of disability living allowance at the highest or middle rate prescribed in accordance with section 72(3) of the Benefits Act [52 or the care component of child disability payment at the highest or middle rate in accordance with regulation 11(5) of the DACYP Regulations]or the daily living component of personal independence payment at the standard or enhanced rate in accordance with section 78(3) of the 2012 Act [53, the daily living component of adult disability payment at the standard or enhanced rate in accordance with regulation 5 of the [54 Disability Assistance for Working Age People (Scotland) Regulations 2022] [47 or armed forces independence payment]].

Pensioner premium where one member of a joint-claim couple has attained [40 the qualifying age for state pension credit]

20E.—The condition is that one member of a joint-claim couple has attained [40 the qualifying age for state pension credit]but not the age of 75. 3.498

Higher Pensioner Premium

20F.—(1) [33 Subject to sub-paragraph (5), the] condition is that one member of a joint claim couple— 3.499

(a) has attained [40 the qualifying age for state pension credit] but not the age of 80, and either the additional conditions specified in paragraph 20H are satisfied in respect of him; or

(b) has attained [40 the qualifying age for state pension credit] and—

(i) was entitled to or was treated as entitled to either income support or an income-based jobseeker's allowance and the disability premium was or, as the case may be, would have been applicable to him in respect of a benefit week within 8 weeks of [40 the date he attained the qualifying age for state pension credit] and he has, subject to sub-paragraph (2), remained continuously entitled to one of those benefits since attaining that age; or

(ii) was a member of a joint-claim couple who had been entitled to, or who had been treated as entitled to, a joint-claim jobseeker's allowance and the disability premium was or, as the case may be, would have been applicable to that couple in respect of a benefit week within 8 weeks of [40 the date either member of that couple attained the qualifying age for state pension credit] and the couple have, subject to that sub-paragraph (2), remained continuously entitled to a joint claim jobseeker's allowance since that member attained that age.

(2) For the purpose of this paragraph and paragraph 20H—

(a) once the higher pensioner premium is applicable to a joint-claim couple, if that member then ceases, for a period of 8 weeks or less, to be entitled or treated as entitled to either income support or income-based jobseeker's allowance or that couple cease to be entitled to or treated as entitled to a joint-claim jobseeker's allowance, he shall or, as the case may be, that couple shall, on becoming re-entitled to any of those benefits, thereafter be treated as having been continuously entitled thereto;

(b) in so far as sub-paragraph (1)(b)(i) or (ii) is concerned, if a member of a joint-claim couple ceases to be entitled or treated as entitled to either income support or an income-based jobseeker's allowance or that couple cease to be entitled to or treated as entitled to a joint-claim jobseeker's allowance for a period not exceeding 8 weeks which includes [40 the date either member of that couple attained the qualifying age for state pension credit], he shall or, as the case may be, the couple shall, on becoming re-entitled to either of those benefits, thereafter be treated as having been continuously entitled thereto.

(3) In this paragraph, where a member of a joint-claim couple is a welfare to work beneficiary, sub-paragraphs (1)(b)(i) and (2)(b) shall apply to him as if for the words "8 weeks" there were substituted the words "[32104 weeks]".

(4) For the purposes of this paragraph, a member of a joint-claim couple shall be treated as having been entitled to income support or to an income-based jobseeker's allowance or the couple of which he is a member shall be treated as having been entitled to a joint-claim jobseeker's allowance throughout any period which comprises only days on which a member was participating in an employment zone scheme and was not entitled to—

(a) income support because, as a consequence of his participation in that scheme, he was engaged in remunerative work or had income in excess of the claimant's applicable amount as prescribed in Part IV of the Income Support Regulations; or

(b) a jobseeker's allowance because, as a consequence of his participation in that scheme, he was engaged in remunerative work or failed to satisfy the condition specified in section 2(1)(c) or the couple of which he was a member failed to satisfy the condition in section 3A(1)(a).

[33 (5) The condition is not satisfied if the member of the joint-claim couple to whom sub-paragraph (1) refers is a long-term patient.]

[33 Disability Premium

3.500 **20G.**—(1) Subject to sub-paragraph (2), the condition is that a member of a joint-claim couple has not attained [40 the qualifying age for state pension credit] and satisfies any one of the additional conditions specified in paragraph 20H.

(2) The condition is not satisfied if—

(a) paragraph (1) only refers to one member of a joint-claim couple and that member is a long-term patient; or

(b) paragraph (1) refers to both members of a joint-claim couple and both members of the couple are long-term patients.]

Additional conditions for Higher Pensioner and Disability Premium

3.501 **20H.**—(1) The additional conditions specified in this paragraph are that a member of a joint-claim couple—

(a) is in receipt of [26 the disability element or the severe disability element of working tax credit as specified in regulation 20(1)(b) and (f) of the Working Tax Credit (Entitlement and Maximum Rate) Regulations 2002] or mobility supplement;

(b) is in receipt of severe disablement allowance;

(c) is in receipt of attendance allowance or disability living allowance or is a person whose disability living allowance is payable, in whole or in part, to another in accordance with regulation 44 of the Claims and Payments Regulations (payment of disability living allowance on behalf of third party);

[46 (ca) is in receipt of personal independence payment or is a person whose personal independence payment is payable, in whole or in part, to another in accordance with regulation 58(2) of the Universal Credit etc. Claims and Payments Regulations (payment to another person on the claimant's behalf);]

[53 (caa) is in receipt of adult disability payment or is a person whose adult disability payment is payable, in whole or in part, to another in accordance with regulation 33 of the Disability Assistance for Working Age People (Scotland) Regulations 2022 (making payments);]

[47 (cb) is in receipt of armed forces independence payment or is a person whose armed forces independence payment is payable, in whole or in part, to another in accordance with article 24D of the Armed Forces and Reserve Forces (Compensation Scheme) Order 2011;]

(d) is in receipt of long-term incapacity benefit or is a person to whom section 30B(4) of the Benefits Act (long-term rate of incapacity benefit payable to those who are terminally ill) applies;

(e) has been entitled to statutory sick pay, has been incapable of work or has been treated as incapable of work for a continuous period of not less than—

(i) 196 days in the case of a member of a joint-claim couple who is terminally ill within the meaning of section 30B(4) of the Benefits Act; or

(ii) 364 days in any other case,

and for these purposes, any two or more periods of entitlement or incapacity separated by a break of not more than 56 days shall be treated as one continuous period;

[36 (ee) has had limited capability for work or has been treated as having limited capability for work for a continuous period of not less than—

(i) 196 days in the case of a member of a joint-claim couple who is terminally ill within the meaning of regulation 2(1) of the Employment and Support Allowance Regulations; or

(ii) 364 days in any other case,

and for these purposes any two or more periods of limited capability for work separated by a break of not more than 12 weeks is to be treated as one continuous period;]

(f) has an invalid carriage or other vehicle provided to him by the Secretary of State under section 5(2)(a) of, and Schedule 2 to, the National Health Service Act 1977 or under section 46 of the National Health Service (Scotland) Act 1978 or provided by the Department of Health and Social Services for Northern Ireland under article 30(1) of the Health and Personal Social Services (Northern Ireland) Order 1972, or receives payments by way of grant from the Secretary of State under paragraph 2 of Schedule 2 to the Act of 1977 (additional provisions as to vehicles) or, in Scotland, under section 46 of the Act of 1978;

(g) is a person who is entitled to the mobility component of disability living allowance but to whom the component is not payable in accordance with regulation 42 of the Claims and Payments Regulations (cases where disability living allowance not payable);

[46 (ga) is a person who is entitled to the mobility component of personal independence payment but to whom the component is not payable in accordance with regulation 61 of the Universal Credit etc. Claims and Payments Regulations (cases where mobility component of personal independence payment not payable);]

[53 (gb) is a person who is entitled to the mobility component of adult disability payment but to whom the component is not payable in accordance with regulation 34(6) of the Disability Assistance for Working Age People (Scotland) Regulations 2022 (amount and form of adult disability payment);]

(h) was either—

(i) in receipt of long-term incapacity benefit under section 30A(5) of the Benefits Act immediately before attaining pensionable age and he is still alive; or

(ii) entitled to attendance allowance or disability living allowance but payment of that benefit was suspended in accordance with regulations under section 113(2) of the Benefits Act or otherwise abated as a consequence of either member of the joint-claim couple becoming a patient within the meaning of regulation 85(4) (special cases), [46 [53 . . .]

(iii) entitled to personal independence payment but no amount is payable in accordance with regulations under section 86(1) (hospital in-patients) of the 2012 Act,] [53 or

(iv) entitled to adult disability payment but no amount is payable in accordance with regulation 28 (effect of admission to hospital on ongoing entitlement to Adult [54 Disability Payment) of the Disability Assistance for Working Age People (Scotland) Regulations 2022,]

and [53 in any of the cases described in paragraphs (i) to (iv)], the higher pensioner premium or disability premium had been applicable to the joint-claim couple; or

[48 (l) is certified as severely sight impaired or blind by a consultant ophthalmologist.]

(2) [41 . . . [32 . . .]]

[48 (3) For the purposes of sub-paragraph (1)(i), a person who has ceased to be certified as severely sight impaired or blind on regaining his eyesight shall nevertheless be treated as severely sight impaired or blind, as the case may be, and as satisfying the additional condition set out in that sub-paragraph for a period of 28 weeks following the date on which he ceased to be so certified.]

Severe Disability Premium

20I.—(1) The condition is that— 3.502

(a) a member of a joint-claim couple is in receipt of attendance allowance [46 , the care component of disability living allowance at the highest or middle rate prescribed in accordance with section 72(3) of the Benefits Act [47 , armed forces independence payment] [53 ,] the daily living component of personal independence payment at the standard or enhanced rate in accordance with section 78(3) of the 2012 Act] [53 , or the daily living component of adult disability payment at the standard or enhanced rate in accordance with regulation 5 of the Disability Assistance for Working Age People (Scotland) Regulations 2022]; and

(b) the other member is also in receipt of such an allowance, or if he is a member of a polygamous marriage, all the partners of that marriage are in receipt of a qualifying benefit; and

(c) subject to sub-paragraph (3), there is no non-dependant aged 18 or over normally residing with the joint-claim couple or with whom they are normally residing; and

(d) either—

(i) no person is entitled to, and in receipt of, [24 a carer's allowance] [55 or carer support payment] under section 70 of the Benefits Act [50 or has an award of universal credit which includes the carer element] in respect of caring for either member or the couple or all the members of the polygamous marriage; or

(ii) a person is engaged in caring for one member (but not both members) of the couple, or one or more but not all members of the polygamous marriage, and in consequence is entitled to [24 a carer's allowance] under section 70 of the Benefits Act [55 or carer support payment] [50 or has an award of universal credit which includes the carer element].

(2) Where the other member does not satisfy the condition in sub-paragraph (1)(b), and that member is [48 severely sight impaired or blind or treated as severely sight impaired or blind] within the meaning of paragraph 20H(1)(i) and (2), that member shall be treated for the purposes of sub-paragraph (1) as if he were not a member of the couple.

(3) The following persons shall not be regarded as non-dependant for the purposes of sub-paragraph (1)(c)—

(a) a person in receipt of attendance allowance [46 , the care component of disability living allowance at the highest or middle rate prescribed in accordance with section 72(3) of the Benefits Act [47 , armed forces independence payment] [53 ,] the daily living component of personal independence payment at the standard or enhanced rate in accordance with section 78(3) of the 2012 Act] [53 , or the daily living component of adult disability payment at the standard or enhanced rate in accordance with regulation 5 of the Disability Assistance for Working Age People (Scotland) Regulations 2022];

(b) subject to sub-paragraph (5), a person who joins the joint-claim couple's household for the first time in order to care for a member of a joint claim couple and immediately before so joining, that member satisfied the condition in sub-paragraph (1);

(c) a person who is [48 severely sight impaired or blind or treated as severely sight impaired or blind] within the meaning of paragraph 20H(1)(i) and (2).

(4) For the purposes of sub-paragraph (1), a member of a joint-claim couple shall be treated—

(a) as being in receipt of attendance allowance, or the care component of disability living allowance at the highest or middle rate prescribed in accordance with section 72(3) of the Benefits Act if he would, but for his being a patient for a period exceeding 28 days, be so in receipt;

(b) as being entitled to and in receipt of [24 a carer's allowance] [55 or carer support payment] [50 or having an award of universal credit which includes the carer element] if he would, but for the person for whom he was caring being a patient in hospital for a period exceeding 28 days, be so entitled and in receipt [50 of carer's allowance [55 or carer support payment] or have such an award of universal credit].

[46 (c) as being in receipt of the daily living component of personal independence payment at the standard or enhanced rate in accordance with section 78 of the 2012 Act if he would, but for regulations made under section 86(1) (hospital in-patients) of the 2012 Act, be so in receipt.]

[53 (d) as being in receipt of the daily living component of adult disability payment at the standard or enhanced rate in accordance with regulation 5 of the [54 Disability Assistance for Working Age People (Scotland) Regulations 2022], if he would, but for regulation 28 (effect of admission to hospital on ongoing entitlement to Adult Disability Payment) of those Regulations, be so in receipt]

(5) Sub-paragraph (3)(b) shall apply only for the first 12 weeks following the date on which the person to whom that provision applies first joins the joint-claim couple's household.

(6) For the purposes of sub-paragraph (1)(d), no account shall be taken of an award of [24 carer's allowance] [55 or carer support payment] [50 or universal credit which includes the carer element] to the extent that payment of such an award is back-dated for a period before [34 the date on which the award is first paid].

[20 (7) In sub-paragraph (1)(d), the reference to a person being in receipt of [24 a carer's allowance] [55 or carer support payment] [50 or as having an award of universal credit which includes the carer element] shall include a reference to a person who would have been in receipt of that allowance [58 or payment] [50 or had such an award] but for the application of a restriction under section [39 6B or] 7 of the Social Security Fraud Act 2001 (loss of benefit provisions).]

[50 (8) For the purposes of this paragraph, a person has an award of universal credit which includes the carer element if the person has an award of universal credit which includes an amount which is the carer element under regulation 29 of the Universal Credit Regulations 2013.]

[16 Enhanced disability premium

3.503 **20IA.**—[46 (1) Subject to sub-paragraph (2), the condition is that in respect of a member of a joint-claim couple who has not attained the qualifying age for state pension credit—

(a) the care component of disability living allowance is, or would, but for a suspension of benefit in accordance with regulations under section 113(2) of the Benefits Act or but for an abatement as a consequence of hospitalisation, be payable at the highest rate prescribed under section 72(3) of the Benefits Act; or

(b) the daily living component of personal independence payment is, or would, but for regulations made under section 86(1) (hospital in-patients) of the 2012 Act, be payable at the enhanced rate in accordance with section 78(2) of the 2012 Act [[53], the daily living component of adult disability payment is, or would, but for regulation 28 (effect of admission to hospital on ongoing entitlement to Adult Disability Payment) of the [[54] Disability Assistance for Working Age People (Scotland) Regulations 2022], be payable at the enhanced rate under those Regulations,] [[47] or armed forces independence payment is payable].]

[[33] (2) The condition is not satisfied if—

(a) paragraph (1) only refers to one member of a joint-claim couple and that member is a long-term patient; or

(b) paragraph (1) refers to both members of a joint-claim couple and both members of the couple are long-term patients.]]

Carer Premium

20J.—(1) Subject to sub-paragraphs (3) and (4), the condition is that either or both members of a joint-claim couple are entitled to [[28] . . .] [[24] a carer's allowance] under section 70 of the Benefits Act [[55] or carer support payment]. **3.504**

(2) [[28] . . .]

[[23] (3) Where a carer premium is awarded but—

(a) the person in respect of whose care the [[24] carer's allowance] [[55] or carer support payment] has been awarded dies: or

(b) in any other case the member of the joint-claim couple in respect of whom a carer premium has been awarded ceases to be entitled [[28] . . .] to [[24] a carer's allowance] [[55] or carer support payment],

the condition for the award of the premium shall be treated as satisfied for a period of eight weeks from the relevant date specified in sub-paragraph (3A) below.

(3A) The relevant date for the purposes of sub-paragraph (3) above shall be—

(a) [[28] where sub-paragraph (3)(a) applies,] the Sunday following the death of the person in respect of whose care [[24] a carer's allowance] [[55] or carer support payment] has been awarded or beginning with the date of death if the death occurred on a Sunday;

(b) [[28] . . .]

(c) in any other case, the date on which that member ceased to be entitled to [[24] a carer's allowance] [[55] or carer support payment].]

(4) Where a member of a joint-claim couple who has been entitled to [[24] a carer's allowance] [[58] or carer support payment] ceases to be entitled to that allowance [[55] or payment] and makes a claim for a jobseeker's allowance jointly with the other member of that couple, the condition for the award of the carer premium shall be treated as satisfied for a period of eight weeks from the date on which—

[[23](a) the person in respect of whose care the [[24] a carer's allowance] [[55] or carer support payment] has been awarded dies;

(b) [[28] . . .]

(c) [[28] in any other case, the person who has been entitled to a carer's allowance [[55] or carer support payment] ceased to be entitled to that allowance [[55] or payment].]]

Member of a joint-claim couple in receipt of concessionary payments

20K.—For the purpose of determining whether a premium is applicable to a joint-claim couple under paragraphs 20H to 20J, any concessionary payment made to compensate a person for the non-payment of any benefit mentioned in those paragraphs shall be treated as if it were a payment of that benefit. **3.505**

Person in receipt of benefit

20L.—For the purposes of this Part of this Schedule, a member of a joint-claim couple shall be regarded as being in receipt of any benefit if, and only if, it is paid in respect of him and shall be so regarded only for any period in respect of which that benefit is paid. **3.506**

PART IVB

Premium	*Amount*
20M.—	
(1) Pensioner premium where one member of a joint-claim couple [40 has attained the qualifying age for state pension credit] and the condition in paragraph 20E is satisfied.	(1) [58 £190.70].
(2) Higher Pensioner Premium where one member of a joint-claim couple satisfies the condition in paragraph 20F.	(2) [58 £190.70].
(3) Disability Premium where one member of a joint-claim couple satisfies the condition in paragraph [33 20G(1)].	(3) [58 £60.60].
(4) Severe Disability Premium where one member of a joint-claim couple satisfies the condition in paragraph 20I(1)— (i) if there is someone in receipt of [24 a carer's allowance] or if either member satisfies that condition only by virtue of paragraph [16 20I(4)]; (ii) if no-one is in receipt of such an allowance.	(4) (i) [58 £81.50]; (ii) [58 £163.00].
Premium	*Amount*
(5) Carer Premium.	(5) [58 £45.60] in respect of each person who satisfied the condition specified in paragraph 20J.]
[16 (6) Enhanced disability premium where the conditions specified in paragraph 20IA are satisfied.	(6) [58 £29.75] where the conditions in paragraph 20IA are satisfied in respect of a member of a joint-claim couple.]

PART V

ROUNDING OF FRACTIONS

3.508 **21.**—Where an income-based jobseeker's allowance is awarded for a period which is not a complete benefit week and the applicable amount in respect of that period results in an amount which includes a fraction of one penny that fraction shall be treated as one penny."

AMENDMENTS

1. Jobseeker's Allowance (Amendment) Regulations 1996 (SI 1996/1516) reg.18 (October 7, 1996).

2. Jobseeker's Allowance (Amendment) Regulations 1996 (SI 1996/1516) reg.20 and Sch. (October 7, 1996).

3. Social Security and Child Support (Jobseeker's Allowance) (Miscellaneous Amendments) Regulations 1996 (SI 1996/2538) reg.2(11) (October 28, 1996).

4. Child Benefit, Child Support and Social Security (Miscellaneous Amendments) Regulations 1996 (SI 1996/1803) reg.44 (April 7, 1997).

5. Income-related Benefits and Jobseeker's Allowance (Personal Allowances for Children and Young Persons) (Amendment) Regulations 1996 (SI 1996/2545) reg.2 (April 7, 1997).

6. Income-related Benefits and Jobseeker's Allowance (Amendment) (No. 2) Regulations 1997 (SI 1997/2197) reg.7(5) and (6)(b) (October 6, 1997).

7. Social Security Amendment (Lone Parents) Regulations 1998 (SI 1998/766) reg.14 (April 6, 1998).

8. Social Security (Welfare to Work) Regulations 1998 (SI 1998/2231) reg.14(3) (October 5, 1998).

9. Social Security Amendment (Personal Allowances for Children and Young Persons) Regulations 1999 (SI 1999/2555) reg.2(1)(b) and (2) (April 10, 2000).

10. Social Security and Child Support (Tax Credits) Consequential Amendments Regulations 1999 (SI 1999/2566) reg.2(2) and Sch.2 Pt III (October 5, 1999).

11. Social Security (Miscellaneous Amendments) Regulations 2000 (SI 2000/681) reg.4(3) (April 3, 2000).

12. Social Security Amendment (Employment Zones) Regulations 2000 (SI 2000/724) reg.4 (April 3, 2000).

13. Social Security Amendment (Personal Allowances for Children) Regulations 2000 (SI 2000/1993) reg.2 (October 23, 2000).

14. Jobseeker's Allowance (Joint Claims) Regulations 2000 (SI 2000/1978) reg.2(5) and Sch.2 para.53 (March 19, 2001).

15. Social Security Amendment (Bereavement Benefits) Regulations 2000 (SI 2000/2239) reg.3(2) (April 9, 2001).

16. Social Security Amendment (Enhanced Disability Premium) Regulations 2000 (SI 2629) reg.5(c) (April 9, 2001).

17. Social Security Amendment (Joint Claims) Regulations 2001 (SI 2001/518) reg.2(7) (March 19, 2001).

18. Social Security Amendment (Bereavement Benefits) Regulations 2000 (SI 2000/2239) reg.3(2)(c) (April 9, 2001).

19. Social Security Amendment (Residential Care and Nursing Homes) Regulations 2001 (SI 2001/3767) reg.2 and Sch. Pt II para.18 (April 8, 2002).

20. Social Security (Loss of Benefit) (Consequential Amendments) Regulations 2002 (SI 2002/490) reg.2 (April 1, 2002).

21. Social Security Amendment (Residential Care and Nursing Homes) Regulations 2001 (SI 2001/3767) reg.2 and Sch. Pt II para.18 (as amended by Social Security Amendment (Residential Care and Nursing Homes) Regulations 2002 (SI 2002/398) reg.4(3)) (April 8, 2002).

22. Social Security Amendment (Personal Allowances for Children and Young Persons) Regulations 2002 (SI 2002/2019) reg.2 (October 14, 2002).

23. Social Security Amendment (Carer Premium) Regulations 2002 (SI 2002/2020) reg.3 (October 28, 2002).

24. Social Security (Miscellaneous Amendments) Regulations 2003 (SI 2003/511) reg.3(4) and (5) (April 1, 2003).

25. Social Security (Working Tax Credit and Child Tax Credit) (Consequential Amendments) Regulations 2003 (SI 2003/455) regs 1(9), 3 and Sch.2 para.20(b) (April 7, 2003).

26. Social Security (Working Tax Credit and Child Tax Credit) (Consequential Amendments) Regulations 2003 (SI 2003/455) regs 1(9), 3 and Sch.2 para.20(e) (April 7, 2003).

27. Social Security (Hospital In-Patients and Miscellaneous Amendments) Regulations 2003 (SI 2003/1195) reg.6 (May 21, 2003).

28. Social Security (Miscellaneous Amendments) (No. 2) Regulations 2003 (SI 2003/2279) reg.3(3) (October 1, 2003).

29. Social Security (Removal of Residential Allowance and Miscellaneous Amendments) Regulations 2003 (SI 2003/1121) reg.4 and Sch.2 para.9 (October 6, 2003).

30. Social Security (Working Tax Credit and Child Tax Credit) (Consequential Amendments) Regulations 2003 (SI 2003/455) reg.3 and Sch.2 para.20 (April 6, 2004, except in "transitional cases" and see further the note to regs 83 and to 17 of the Income Support Regulations).

31. Civil Partnership (Pensions, Social Security and Child Support) (Consequential, etc. Provisions) Order 2005 (SI 2005/2877) art.2(3) and Sch.3 para.26(11) (December 5, 2005).

32. Social Security (Miscellaneous Amendments) (No. 4) Regulations 2006 (SI 2006/2378) reg.13(10) (October 1, 2006).

33. Social Security (Miscellaneous Amendments) Regulations 2007 (SI 2007/719) reg.3(8) (April 9, 2007). As it relates to paras 15(2)(a) and 16, the amendment only affects "transitional cases". See further the note to reg.17 of the Income Support Regulations and the commentary below.

34. Social Security (Miscellaneous Amendments) (No. 5) Regulations 2007 (SI 2007/2618) reg.2 and Sch. (October 1, 2007).

35. Social Security (Miscellaneous Amendments) Regulations 2008 (SI 2008/698) reg.4(14) (April 14, 2008).

36. Employment and Support Allowance (Consequential Provisions) (No. 2) Regulations 2008 (SI 2008/1554) reg.3(1) and (24) (October 27, 2008).

37. Social Security (Miscellaneous Amendments) Regulations 2009 (SI 2009/583) reg.4(1) and (3) (April 6, 2009).

38. Social Security (Students and Miscellaneous Amendments) Regulations 2009 (SI 2009/1575) reg.3 (August 1, 2009).

39. Social Security (Loss of Benefit) Amendment Regulations 2010 (SI 2010/1160) reg.11(1) and (3) (April 1, 2010).

40. Social Security (Equalisation of State Pension Age) Regulations 2009 (SI 2009/1488) reg.13 (April 6, 2010).

41. Employment and Support Allowance (Transitional Provisions, Housing Benefit and Council Tax Benefit) (Existing Awards) (No. 2) Regulations 2010 (SI 2010/1907) reg.26(1) and Sch.4 para.1A(3) (as amended by the Employment and Support Allowance (Transitional Provisions, Housing Benefit and Council Tax Benefit) (Existing Awards) (No. 2) (Amendment) Regulations 2010 (SI 2010/2430) reg.15) (November 1, 2010).

42. Social Security (Miscellaneous Amendments) Regulations 2011 (SI 2011/674) reg.7(7) (April 11, 2011).

43. Social Security Benefits Up-rating Order 2012 (SI 2012/780) art.25(3) and Sch.13 (April 9, 2012).

44. Social Security Benefits Up-rating Order 2012 (SI 2012/780) art.25(5) and Sch.14 (April 9, 2012).

45. Social Security Benefits Up-rating Order 2012 (SI 2012/780) art.25(6) and Sch.15 (April 9, 2012).

46. Personal Independence Payment (Supplementary Provisions and Consequential Amendments) Regulations 2013 (SI 2013/388) reg.8 and Sch. para.16(1) and (7) (April 8, 2013).

47. Armed Forces and Reserve Forces Compensation Scheme (Consequential Provisions: Subordinate Legislation) Order 2013 (SI 2013/591) art.7 and Sch. para.10(1) and (7) (April 8, 2013).

48. Universal Credit and Miscellaneous Amendments (No. 2) Regulations 2014 (SI 2014/2888) reg.3(3) (November 26, 2014).

49. Welfare Benefits Up-rating Order 2015 (SI 2015/30) art.9 and Sch.3 (April 6, 2015).

50. Universal Credit and Miscellaneous Amendments Regulations 2015 (SI 2015/1754) reg.15 (October 28, 2015).

51. Universal Credit and Jobseeker's Allowance (Miscellaneous Amendments) Regulations 2018 (SI 2018/1129) reg.2 (November 28, 2018).

52. Social Security (Scotland) Act 2018 (Disability Assistance for Children and Young People) (Consequential Modifications) Order 2021 (SI 2021/786) Sch.3 paras 7–8 (July 26, 2021).

53. Social Security (Disability Assistance for Working Age People) (Consequential Amendments) Order 2022 (SI 2022/177) art.7 (March 21, 2022).

54. Social Security (Disability Assistance for Working Age People) (Consequential Amendments) (No. 2) Order 2022 (SI 2022/530) art.3(2) (June 6, 2022).

55. Carers Assistance (Carer Support Payment) (Scotland) Regulations 2023 (Consequential Amendments) Order 2023 (SI 2023/1218) art.8 (November 19, 2023).

56. Social Security Benefits Up-rating Order 2024 (SI 2024/242) art.26(3) and Sch.8 (April 8, 2024).

57. Social Security Benefits Up-rating Order 2024 (SI 2024/242) art.26(5) and Sch.9 (April 8, 2024).

58. Social Security Benefits Up-rating Order 2024 (SI 2024/242) art.26(6) and Sch.10 (April 8, 2024).

DEFINITIONS

"adult disability payment"—see reg.1(3).
"attendance allowance"—*ibid.*
"the Benefits Act"—see Jobseekers Act s.35(1).
"child"—*ibid.*
"child disability payment"—*ibid.*
"claimant"—*ibid.*
"couple"—see reg.1(3).
"DACYP Regulations"—*ibid.*
"disability living allowance"—*ibid.*
"family"—see Jobseekers Act s.35(1).
"invalid carriage or other vehicle"—see reg.1(3).
"lone parent"—*ibid.*
"mobility supplement"—*ibid.*
"non-dependent"—see reg.2.
"partner"—see reg.1(3).
"personal independence payment"—*ibid.*
"polygamous marriage"—*ibid.*
"preserved right"—*ibid.*
"single claimant"—*ibid.*
"welfare to work beneficiary"—*ibid.*
"young person"—see reg.76.

For the General Note to Sch.1, see Vol.V paras 3.509–3.518.

p.1120, *amendments to the Jobseeker's Allowance Regulations 1996 (SI 1996/207) Sch.2 para.17 (Non-dependant deductions)*

With effect from April 8, 2024, art.26(7) of the Social Security Benefits Up-rating Order 2024 (SI 2024/242) makes the following amendments: 5.094

- in sub-paragraph (1)(a) for "£116.75" substitute "£124.55";
- in sub-paragraph (1)(b) for "£18.10" substitute "£19.30";
- in sub-paragraph (2)(a) for "£162.00" substitute "£176.00";
- in sub-paragraph (2)(b)—
  - (i) for "£41.60" substitute "£44.40";
  - (ii) for "£162.00" substitute "£176.00"; and
  - (iii) for "£236.00" substitute "£256.00";
- in sub-paragraph (2)(c)—
  - (i) for "£57.10" substitute "£60.95";
  - (ii) for "£236.00" substitute "£256.00"; and
  - (iii) for "£308.00" substitute "£334.00";
- in sub-paragraph (2)(d)—
  - (i) for "£93.40" substitute "£99.65";
  - (ii) for "£308.00" substitute "£334.00"; and
  - (iii) for "£410.00" substitute "£445.00"; and

- in sub-paragraph (2)(e)—
  (i) for "£106.35" substitute "£113.50";
  (ii) for "£410.00" substitute "£445.00"; and
  (iii) for "£511.00" substitute "£554.00".

pp.1120–1122, *amendments to the Jobseeker's Allowance Regulations 1996 (SI 1996/207) Sch.2 para.17 (Housing costs—non-dependant deductions)*

5.095 With effect from July 26, 2021, Sch.3 para.9 of the Social Security (Scotland) Act 2018 (Disability Assistance for Children and Young People) (Consequential Modifications) Order 2021 (SI 2021/786) makes the following amendments to Sch.2 para.17:

- in sub-para.(6)(b), at the end of para.(ii), insert "or (iia) the care component of child disability payment;"
- in sub-para.(8)(a), after "disability living allowance", insert ", child disability payment".

With effect from January 1, 2022, reg.3(6) of the Social Security (Income and Capital Disregards) (Amendment) Regulations 2021 (SI 2021/1405) inserts into para.17(8)(b), after "Grenfell Tower payment", ", child abuse payment or Windrush payment".

With effect from March 21, 2022, art.5(8) of the Social Security (Disability Assistance for Working Age People) (Consequential Amendments) Order 2022 (SI 2022/177) makes the following amendments to Sch.2 para.17:

- after para.17(6)(b)(iii) (non-dependant deductions), insert "(iiia) the daily living component of adult disability payment;";
- in para.17(8)(a):
  - after "armed forces independence payment" for "or" substitute ",";
  - after "personal independence payment" insert "or adult disability payment".

With effect from July 9, 2023, reg.3 of the Social Security (Income and Capital Disregards) (Amendment) Regulations 2023 (SI 2023/640) amends para.17 as follows:

- in paragraph 17(8)(b) (non-dependant deductions), for "or Windrush payment" insert ", Windrush payment or Post Office compensation payment".

p.1138, *amendment to the Jobseeker's Allowance Regulations 1996 (SI 1996/207) Sch.6 para.7(1) (Sums to be disregarded in the calculation of earnings)*

5.096 With effect from November 19, 2023, art.8(10) of the Carer's Assistance (Carer Support Payment) (Scotland) Regulations 2023 (Consequential Amendments) Order 2023 (SI 2023/1218) amended para.7(1) by inserting "or carer support payment" after "carer's allowance" in the first place where that occurs. Carer support payment is newly defined in reg.1(3) by reference to the Scottish legislation (see the entry for p.787).

p.1144, *amendment to the Jobseeker's Allowance Regulations 1996 (SI 1996/207) Sch.6A para.2(1) (Sums to be disregarded in the calculation of earnings of members of joint-claim couples)*

With effect from November 19, 2023, art.8(11) of the Carer's Assistance (Carer Support Payment) (Scotland) Regulations 2023 (Consequential Amendments) Order 2023 (SI 2023/1218) amended para.2(1) by inserting "or carer support payment" after "carer's allowance" in the first place where that occurs. Carer support payment is newly defined in reg.1(3) by reference to the Scottish legislation (see the entry for p.787). **5.097**

p.1146, *amendment to the Jobseeker's Allowance Regulations 1996 (SI 1996/207) Sch.7 para.7 (Sums to be disregarded in the calculation of income other than earnings—mobility component)*

With effect from March 21, 2022, art.5(9)(a) of the Social Security (Disability Assistance for Working Age People) (Consequential Amendments) Order 2022 (SI 2022/177) amended para.7 to read as follows (square brackets indicate only the present amendment, those indicating previous amendments having been omitted): **5.098**

"**7.**—The mobility component of disability living allowance[,] the mobility component of personal independence payment [or the mobility component of adult disability payment]."

"Adult disability payment" is defined in reg.1(3) by reference to reg.2 of the Disability Assistance for Working Age People (Scotland) Regulations 2022 (SSI 2022/54) (see Vol.IV of this series).

p.1147, *amendment to the Jobseeker's Allowance Regulations 1996 (SI 1996/207) Sch.7 para.10 (Sums to be disregarded in the calculation of income other than earnings—attendance allowance, care component of DLA or daily living component)*

With effect from March 21, 2022, art.5(9)(b) of the Social Security (Disability Assistance for Working Age People) (Consequential Amendments) Order 2022 (SI 2022/177) amended para.10 to read as follows (square brackets indicate only the present amendment, those indicating previous amendments having been omitted): **5.099**

"**10.**—Any attendance allowance, the care component of disability living allowance[,] the daily living component of personal independence payment [or the daily living component of adult disability payment]."

"Adult disability payment" is defined in reg.1(3) by reference to reg.2 of the Disability Assistance for Working Age People (Scotland) Regulations 2022 (SSI 2022/54) (see Vol.IV of this series).

p.1149, *amendment to the Jobseeker's Allowance Regulations 1996 (SI 1996/207) Sch.7 para.22(2) (Sums to be disregarded in the calculation of income other than earnings—income in kind)*

With effect from January 1, 2022, reg.3(7)(a) of the Social Security (Income and Capital Disregards) (Amendment) Regulations 2021 (SI 2021/1405) amended sub-para.(2) by inserting ", a child abuse payment **5.100** or a Windrush payment" after "Grenfell Tower payment". All of those payments are defined in reg.1(3). See the entry for pp.684–685 for discussion of the nature of child abuse and Windrush payments.

p.1151, *amendment to the Jobseeker's Allowance Regulations 1996 (SI 1996/207) Sch.7 para.28(da) (Sums to be disregarded in the calculation of income other than earnings—payments for persons temporarily in care of claimant)*

5.101 With effect from July 1, 2022, reg.10 of the Health and Care Act 2022 (Consequential and Related Amendments and Transitional Provisions) Regulations 2022 (SI 2022/634) amended para.28 by substituting the following for sub-para.(da):

"(da) an integrated care board established under Chapter A3 of Part 2 of the National Health Service Act 2006;"

Note that sub-para.(dzb) seems to be out of the proper order in the 2021/22 main volume.

With effect from November 6, 2023, reg.4 of the Health and Care Act 2022 (Further Consequential Amendments) (No.2) Regulations 2023 (SI 2023/1071) amended para.28(db) by substituting "NHS England" for "the National Health Service Commissioning Board".

p.1153, *amendments to the Jobseeker's Allowance Regulations 1996 (SI 1996/207) Sch.7 para.41 (Sums to be disregarded in the calculation of income other than earnings)*

5.102 With effect from January 1, 2022, reg.3(7)(b) of the Social Security (Income and Capital Disregards) (Amendment) Regulations 2021 (SI 2021/1405) amended para.41 by substituting the following for sub-para.(1A):

"(1A) Any—
(a) Grenfell Tower payment;
(b) child abuse payment;
(c) Windrush payment."

In addition, reg.3(7)(c) amended sub-paras (2) to (6) by inserting ", a child abuse payment or a Windrush payment" after "Grenfell Tower payment" in each place where those words occur. All of those payments are defined in reg.1(3).

See the entry for pp.684–685 (Income Support Regulations, Sch.10 (capital to be disregarded) para.22) for some technical problems arising from the date of effect of these amendments. Because all the payments so far made from the approved historic institutional child abuse compensation schemes and from the Windrush Compensation Scheme have been in the nature of capital, the question of disregarding income has not yet arisen.

With effect from July 9, 2023, reg.3(7) of the Social Security (Income and Capital Disregards) (Amendment) Regulations 2023 (SI 2023/640) amended para.41(1A) by adding the following after head (c):

"(d) Post Office compensation payment."

Such payments are newly defined in reg.1(3), where there is now also an expanded definition of Grenfell Tower payments (see head (a)). With effect from the same date, the words substituted in sub-paras (2) to (6) have been further amended by substituting ", a Windrush payment, a Post Office compensation payment or a vaccine damage payment" for "or a Windrush payment". "Vaccine damage payment" is also newly defined in reg.1(3). See the entry for pp.684–685 for the background.

p.1156, *amendments to the Jobseeker's Allowance Regulations 1996 (SI 1996/207) Sch.7 (Sums to be disregarded in the calculation of income other than earnings)*

With effect from July 26, 2021, art.12(2) of the Social Security (Scotland) Act 2018 (Disability Assistance, Young Carer Grants, Shortterm Assistance and Winter Heating Assistance) (Consequential Provision and Modifications) Order 2021 (SI 2021/886) inserted the following after para.81: 5.103

> "**82**. Any disability assistance given in accordance with regulations made section 31 of the Social Security (Scotland) Act 2018."

The first regulations made under s.31 of the 2018 Act were the Disability Assistance for Children and Young People (Scotland) Regulations 2021 (SSI 2021/174), also in effect from July 26, 2021, providing for the benefit known as a child disability payment. The regulations also authorise the payment of short-term assistance, to be disregarded under para.81. The Disability Assistance for Working Age People (Scotland) Regulations 2022 (SSI 2022/54), in effect from March 21, 2022, providing for the benefit known as adult disability payment, were also made under s.31, but the two potential elements (mobility component and daily living component) have been specifically covered by para.7 and para.10 from that date (see the entries for pp.1146 and 1147). Short-term assistance under reg.62 of the 2022 Regulations is disregarded under para.81.

With effect from November 19, 2023, art.8(12) of the Carer's Assistance (Carer Support Payment) (Scotland) Regulations 2023 (Consequential Amendments) Order 2023 (SI 2023/1218) inserted the following after para.82:

> "**83**. Any amount of carer support payment that is in excess of the amount the claimant would receive if they had an entitlement to carer's allowance under section 70 of the Benefits Act."

Carer support payment (CSP) is newly defined in reg.1(3) by reference to the Scottish legislation (see the entry for p.787). Note that CSP in general counts as income and that the disregard is limited to any excess of the amount of the CSP over what the claimant would have been entitled to in carer's allowance under British legislation. That is in accordance with the Fiscal Framework Agreement governing the provision of devolved benefits in Scotland (see para.6.9 of the Explanatory Memorandum to SI 2023/1218). Initially, CSP is to be paid at the same rate as carer's allowance.

p.1165, *amendment to the Jobseeker's Allowance Regulations 1996 (SI 1996/207) Sch.8 para.12(1)(a) (Capital to be disregarded)*

5.104 With effect from July 26, 2021, art.12(3) of the Social Security (Scotland) Act 2018 (Disability Assistance, Young Carer Grants, Shortterm Assistance and Winter Heating Assistance) (Consequential Provision and Modifications) Order 2021 (SI 2021/886) substituted "80, 81 or 82" for "80 or 81". See the entry for p.1156 for the new para.82 of Sch.7.

p.1166, *amendment to the Jobseeker's Allowance Regulations 1996 (SI 1996/207) Sch.8 para.12A (Capital to be disregarded—widowed parent's allowance)*

5.105 With effect from February 9, 2023, para.3(a) of the Schedule to the Bereavement Benefits (Remedial) Order 2023 (SI 2023/134) inserted the following after para.12:

> **"12A.** Any payment of a widowed parent's allowance made pursuant to section 39A of the Contributions and Benefits Act (widowed parent's allowance)—
> (a) to the survivor of a cohabiting partnership (within the meaning in section 39A(7) of the Contributions and Benefits Act) who is entitled to a widowed parent's allowance for a period before the Bereavement Benefits (Remedial) Order 2023 comes into force, and
> (b) in respect of any period of time during the period ending with the day before the survivor makes the claim for a widowed parent's allowance,
>
> but only for a period of 52 weeks from the date of receipt of the payment."

The legislation on widowed parent's allowance (WPA), abolished on April 5, 2017, and bereavement support payment (BSP) in operation for deaths after April 5, 2017, was declared incompatible with the ECHR by discriminating against children whose parents were cohabiting but not married to each other or in a civil partnership (see *Re McLaughlin's Application for Judicial Review* [2018] UKSC 48; [2018] 1 W.L.R. 4250 and *R(Jackson) v Secretary of State for Work and Pensions* [2020] EWHC 183 (Admin); [2020] 1 W.L.R. 1441 in Vol.I of this series). The Remedial Order allows retrospective claims to be made for those benefits from August 30, 2018 onwards and accordingly for arrears of benefit to be paid if the conditions of entitlement are met. The new para.12A, and the amended para.65 on BSP, deal with the consequences of such payments on old style JSA entitlement, by providing for them to be disregarded as capital for 52 weeks from receipt. See the entry for p.682 on income support for the effect of the payment of arrears of WPA being in its nature a payment of income to be taken into account (subject to a £10 per week disregard under para.17(i) of Sch.7 to the JSA Regulations 1996) against entitlement in past periods (allowing revision and the creation of an overpayment) and the misleading state of para.7.15 of the Explanatory Memorandum to the Order.

pp.1167–1168, *amendments to the Jobseeker's Allowance Regulations 1996 (SI 1996/207) Sch.8 para.27 (Capital to be disregarded)*

With effect from January 1, 2022, reg.3(8)(a) of the Social Security (Income and Capital Disregards) (Amendment) Regulations 2021 (SI 2021/1405) amended sub-para.(1A) by inserting ", child abuse payment, Windrush payment" after "Grenfell Tower payment" and amended sub-paras (2) to (6) by inserting ", a child abuse payment or a Windrush payment" after "Grenfell Tower payment" in each place where those words occur. All of those payments are defined in reg.1(3). 5.106

See the entry for pp.684–685 (Income Support Regulations Sch.10 (Capital to be disregarded) para.22) for some technical problems with the addition only with effect from January 1, 2022 of the disregards of payments from approved schemes providing compensation in respect of historic institutional child abuse in the UK and from the Windrush Compensation Scheme. All the schemes so far in existence provide payments in the nature of capital. That entry also contains information about the nature of the schemes involved, including the child abuse compensation schemes so far approved.

With effect from July 9, 2023, reg.3(8) of the Social Security (Income and Capital Disregards) (Amendment) Regulations 2023 (SI 2023/640) amended para.27(1A) by adding the following after "Windrush payment":

> ", Post Office compensation payment or vaccine damage payment."

Such payments are newly defined in reg.1(3), where there is now also an expanded definition of Grenfell Tower payments. With effect from the same date, the words substituted in sub-paras (2) to (6) have been further amended by substituting ", a Windrush payment, a Post Office compensation payment or a vaccine damage payment" for "or a Windrush payment". See the entry for pp.684–685 on income support in this Supplement.

With effect from August 30, 2023, reg.2(1)(b) of the Social Security (Infected Blood Capital Disregard) (Amendment) Regulations 2023 (SI 2023/894) amended para.27 by inserting the following after sub-para.(5):

> "(5A) Any payment out of the estate of a person, which derives from a payment to meet the recommendation of the Infected Blood Inquiry in its interim report published on 29th July 2022 made under or by the Scottish Infected Blood Support Scheme or an approved blood scheme to the estate of the person, where the payment is made to the person's son, daughter, step-son or step-daughter."

See the entry for pp.684–685 on income support for the background.

With effect from October 27, 2023, reg.4(3)(c) of the Social Security (Habitual Residence and Past Presence, and Capital Disregards) (Amendment) Regulations 2023 (SI 2023/1144) amended para.27(1) by inserting ", the Victims of Overseas Terrorism Compensation Scheme" after "the National Emergencies Trust". That scheme is newly defined in reg.1(3).

See the entry for pp.684–685 on income support for the background.

p.1168, *amendment to the Jobseeker's Allowance Regulations 1996 (SI 1996/207) Sch.8 para.31 (Capital to be disregarded—payments in kind)*

With effect from January 1, 2022, reg.3(8)(b) of the Social Security (Income and Capital Disregards) (Amendment) Regulations 2021 (SI 2021/1405) amended para.31 by inserting ", a child abuse payment or a Windrush payment" after "Grenfell Tower payment". All of those payments are defined in reg.1(3). See also the entry for pp.684–685. 5.107

p.1172, *amendment to the Jobseeker's Allowance Regulations 1996 (SI 1996/207) Sch.8 para.65 (Capital to be disregarded—bereavement support payment)*

5.108 With effect from February 9, 2023, para.3(b) of the Schedule to the Bereavement Benefits (Remedial) Order 2023 (SI 2023/134) amended para.65 by making the existing text sub-para.(1) and inserting the following:

> "(2) Where bereavement support payment under section 30 of the Pensions Act 2014 is paid to the survivor of a cohabiting partnership (within the meaning in section 30(6B) of the Pensions Act 2014) in respect of a death occurring before the day the Bereavement Benefits (Remedial) Order 2023 comes into force, any amount of that payment which is—
>
> (a) in respect of the rate set out in regulation 3(1) of the Bereavement Support Payment Regulations 2017, and
>
> (b) paid as a lump sum for more than one monthly recurrence of the day of the month on which their cohabiting partner died,
>
> but only for a period of 52 weeks from the date of receipt of the payment."

See the entry for p.682 on income support for the general background. The operation of this amendment is much more straightforward than that of the new para.12A on widowed parent's allowance. Although a payment of arrears of bereavement support payment (BSP) is in its nature a payment of income and attributable to the past period in respect of which it is due, the payment could not affect any entitlement to old style JSA in that past period because it would be disregarded entirely as income (Sch.7 para.76). The amount of the arrears would thus immediately metamorphose into capital, which would then be disregarded under para.65(2) subject to the 52 week limit.

p.1177, *annotation to the Jobseeker's Allowance Regulations 1996 (SI 1996/207) Sch.8 (Capital to be disregarded)*

5.109 With effect from June 28, 2022 "Cost of living payments" under the Social Security (Additional Payments) Act 2022, both those to recipients of specified means-tested benefits and "disability" payments are not to be taken into account for any old style JSA purposes by virtue of s.8(b) of the Act. The same effect was achieved with effect from March 23, 2023 in relation to payments under the Social Security (Additional Payments) Act 2023 (s.8(b) of that Act). See Pt I of Vol.II for the text of both Acts.

p.1184, *annotation to the Jobseeker's Allowance (Schemes for Assisting Persons to Obtain Employment) Regulations 2013 (SI 2013/276)*

5.110 Note the doubts expressed in the note to reg.3 in the 2021/22 main volume about the validity of the prescription of the Work and Health Programme in reg.3(8C) and in the entry below for p.1187 about the validity of the prescription of the Restart Scheme in reg.3(8D).

p.1187, *amendment to the Jobseeker's Allowance (Schemes for Assisting Persons to Obtain Employment) Regulations 2013 (SI 2013/276) reg.3 (Schemes for assisting persons to obtain employment)*

With effect from March 14, 2022, reg.2(3) of the Jobseeker's Allowance (Schemes for Assisting Persons to Obtain Employment) (Amendment) Regulations 2022 (SI 2022/154) amended reg.3 by omitting para.(8) and by inserting the following after para.(8C): **5.111**

> "(8D) The Restart Scheme is a scheme which provides support for a period of up to 12 months for claimants who have been unemployed for 9 months or more and reside in England and Wales."

The Explanatory Memorandum to SI 2022/154 (note that a revised Memorandum, not labelled as such in its heading but with an additional "001" in the version online, was issued on April 13, 2022) explains that the Work Programme no longer exists. There is therefore no controversy about the removal of para.(8), which described that scheme.

However, the introduction of the new para.(8D) is of very doubtful validity. That is because s.17A(1) of the old style Jobseekers Act 1995 only allows claimants to be required to participate in schemes designed to assist them to obtain employment that are of a "prescribed description". The Supreme Court in *R. (Reilly and Wilson) v SSWP* [2013] UKSC 68; [2014] 1 A.C. 453 held that the Jobseeker's Allowance (Employment, Skills and Enterprise Scheme) Regulations 2011 (SI 2011/917) reg.2 did not satisfy that test because it did not add anything to the description of the schemes in the Act itself, which was necessary for the requirement for a prescribed description to have any point. Regulation 2 had provided that the Employment, Skills and Enterprise Scheme (ESES) meant a scheme of that name within s.17A and provided pursuant to arrangements by the Secretary of State that was designed to assist claimants to obtain employment or self-employment and which might include for any individual work-related activity, including work experience or job search. The Supreme Court must therefore have regarded the reference to the possible inclusion of work-related activity as too vague to constitute any kind of description of what the scheme involved. The Court agreed that it was not necessary in the case of the ESES to explore how much detail needed to be included in the regulations to comply with s.17A(1), as no description at all was given.

The amendment contained in SI 2022/154 may therefore not be on all fours with the ESES Regulations reg.2, because the new para.(8D) could be said to contain *some* description of the Restart Scheme, in identifying the categories of claimants who could be directed to the Restart Scheme, the maximum length of the scheme and that it would provide support (although arguably that word, in conjunction with the other specified elements, is also so vague as not to constitute any meaningful description at all). If it is accepted that there is *some* description, the question then, as in *R. (Smith) v SSWP* [2015] EWCA Civ 229 on the Jobseeker's Allowance (Mandatory Work Activity Scheme) Regulations 2011 (SI 2021/688), would be whether there is sufficient description for the purposes of s.17A(1). In *Smith*, Underhill LJ suggested at para.25 that the natural reading of "prescribed description" connoted "no more than an indication of the character of the scheme provided for, such as a scheme in which the claimant was required to undergo training or education or to work with a mentor, or—as here—to do work or work-related activity". So the CA held that the mention of work or work-related activity, with the specification of maximum weekly hours and length of participation, was enough for the MWAS Regulations to be valid. Although the present amendment specifies which claimants fall into the scope of the Restart Scheme and the maximum length, it says nothing worthwhile about the nature of the scheme. All it says is that it "provides support", nothing about what kind of support or who it will be provided by. Equally, if not more, important, it says nothing about what a claimant is to be expected to do by way of participation. What does it mean to have "support" thrust on a claimant? The argument that the new para.(8D) provides an insufficient description seems very strong. It might be thought that the Explanatory Memorandum betrays the faulty approach in paras 7.8 and 7.9, where it is said that the current legislation "lists" the employment schemes claimants can be required to participate in and that the amendment adds the Restart Scheme to the list. To be valid, and to carry the requirement to participate backed by sanctions, a regulation must not merely "list" a scheme, but must describe it.

The Explanatory Memorandum records that the Restart Scheme was already in existence through 12 providers in England and Wales, initially for universal credit claimants who had spent 12 to 18 months uninterrupted time in the Intensive Work Search Regime (i.e. subject to all work-related requirements), but now with the time reduced to nine months. Because of improved labour market conditions the opportunity arose to widen the eligibility criteria to provide intensive employment support for old style JSA claimants that had previously only been available to limited groups. The Scheme is still only available in England and Wales. The emphasis is said to be on positive engagement with the claimant to encourage participation, with the requirement to participate being "used as a backstop where reasonable attempts at engagement fail without good reason" (para.6.7). However, it is stated that claimants who fail to comply with the requirement to participate in compulsory activities may be issued with a low-level sanction (para.6.6). It is far from clear that "compulsory activities" are adequately described by the term "support" in para.(8D).

The policy paper *How the Restart Scheme will work* (January 18, 2022, updated April 26, 2022, available on the gov.uk website) states:

> "Through regular contact with all participants, providers will develop a strong understanding of individuals' employment history, skills, aspirations and support needs to develop the right package of support to help each participant succeed.
>
> For some this might be bespoke training to take advantage of opportunities in a growth sector or to succeed in a major recruitment exercise, for others it might be support to get the right certificate to take up a job in a different industry such as construction or transport or to update skills such as IT."

That document thus gets to a description of the scheme, but as there is no reference to it in para.(8D) there can be no reliance on its description merely by use of the label "Restart Scheme".

Providers will be given letters of empowerment under reg.17 authorising them to exercise the functions of the Secretary of State to issue notices requiring participation (reg.5) or that that requirement has ceased (reg.6(3)(a)) (Explanatory Memorandum, para.6.3). It is understood that providers and employees will not be designated as "employment officers" under s.35 of the old style Jobseekers Act 1995, so that they will have no power to issue jobseeker's directions under s.19A(2)(c).

p.1188, *annotation to the Jobseeker's Allowance (Schemes for Assisting Persons to Obtain Employment) Regulations 2013 (SI 2013/276) reg.3 (Schemes for assisting persons to obtain employment)*

Note, in addition to the points made in the entry for p.1187, that in the last paragraph of the existing note the reference to s.19(2)(c) should be to s.19A(2)(c). **5.112**

PART IV

OLD STYLE EMPLOYMENT AND SUPPORT ALLOWANCE REGULATIONS

p.1205 *amendments to list of regulations for the Employment and Support Allowance Regulations 2008 (SI 2008/794)*

Substitute the following for the text of the entry for reg.139A: 5.113

"139A. Treatment of loans for specific purposes"

p.1209, 1214, 1218, 1219 and 1221 *amendments to the Employment and Support Allowance Regulations 2008 (SI 2008/794) reg.2 (Interpretation)*

With effect from July 26, 2021, Sch.9 para.2 of the Social Security (Scotland) Act 2018 (Disability Assistance for Children and Young People) (Consequential Modifications) Order 2021 (SI 2021/786) adds the following definitions: 5.114

"child disability payment" has the meaning given in regulation 2 of the DACYP Regulations;

"the DACYP Regulations" means the Disability Assistance for Children and Young People (Scotland) Regulations 2021;

With effect from January 1, 2022, reg.7(2) of the Social Security (Income and Capital Disregards) (Amendment) Regulations 2021 (SI 2021/1405) inserts the following definitions:

"child abuse payment" means a payment from a scheme established or approved by the Secretary of State for the purpose of providing compensation in respect of historic institutional child abuse in the United Kingdom;"

"Windrush payment" means a payment made under the Windrush Compensation Scheme (Expenditure) Act 2020;"

With effect from January 1, 2022, reg.7(2) of the Social Security (Income and Capital Disregards) (Amendment) Regulations 2021 (SI 2021/1405) inserts ", a child abuse payment or a Windrush payment" into the definition of "qualifying person", after "Grenfell Tower payment".

With effect from March 21, 2022, art.11 of the Social Security (Disability Assistance for Working Age People) (Consequential Amendments) Order 2022 (SI 2022/177) adds the following definition:

"adult disability payment" has the meaning given in regulation 2 of the Disability Assistance for Working Age People (Scotland) Regulations 2022;

With effect from April 4, 2022, reg.2(1) of the Universal Credit and Employment and Support Allowance (Terminal Illness) (Amendment) Regulations 2022 (SI 2022/260) amends the definition of "terminally ill" by substituting for "6 months", "12 months".

With effect from July 9, 2023, reg.7(2)(a) of the Social Security (Income and Capital Disregards) (Amendment) Regulations 2023 (SI 2023/640) substituted for the definition of "Grenfell Tower payment" the following new definition: 5.115

""Grenfell Tower payment" means a payment made for the purpose of providing compensation or support in respect of the fire on 14th June 2017 at Grenfell Tower;".

5.116 With effect from July 9, 2023, reg.7(2)(b) of the Social Security (Income and Capital Disregards) (Amendment) Regulations 2023 (SI 2023/640) inserted at the appropriate places the following new definitions:

- ""the Horizon system" means any version of the computer system used by the Post Office known as Horizon, Horizon Legacy, Horizon Online or HNG-X;";"
- ""the Post Office" means Post Office Limited (registered number 02154540);";"
- ""Post Office compensation payment" means a payment made by the Post Office or the Secretary of State for the purpose of providing compensation or support which is—
  (a) in connection with the failings of the Horizon system; or
  (b) otherwise payable following the judgment in *Bates and Others v Post Office Ltd* ((No. 3) "Common Issues");";"
- ""vaccine damage payment" means a payment made under the Vaccine Damage Payments Act 1979;".

With effect from October 27, 2023, reg.8(2) of the Social Security (Habitual Residence and Past Presence, and Capital Disregards) (Amendment) Regulations 2023 (SI 2023/1144) inserts the following definitions:

- in the definition of "qualifying person" after "the National Emergencies Trust" insert ", the Victims of Overseas Terrorism Compensation Scheme";
- after the definition of "vaccine damage payment" insert— "'the Victims of Overseas Terrorism Compensation Scheme' means the scheme of that name established by the Ministry of Justice in 2012 under section 47 of the Crime and Security Act 2010;";

With effect from November 19, 2023, art.19(2) of the Carer's Assistance (Carer Support Payment) (Scotland) Regulations 2023 (Consequential Amendments) Order 2023 (SI 2023/1218) inserts the following definition after the definition of "carer's allowance":

> "'carer support payment' means carer's assistance given in accordance with the Carer's Assistance (Carer Support Payment) (Scotland) Regulations 2023;".

5.117 With effect from July 9, 2023, reg.7(2)(c) of the Social Security (Income and Capital Disregards) (Amendment) Regulations 2023 (SI 2023/640) substituted ", a Windrush payment, a Post Office compensation payment or a vaccine damage payment" for "or a Windrush payment" in the definition of "qualifying person".

p.1230, *revocation of the Employment and Support Allowance Regulations 2008 (SI 2008/794) reg.6 (The assessment phase—a claimants appealing against a decision)*

5.118 Strictly speaking, reg.6 was *revoked* by reg.9(5) of the Social Security (Miscellaneous Amendments) (No. 3) Regulations 2010/840 (rather than *omitted* by the annotator).

pp.1238–1239, *amendment of the Employment and Support Allowance Regulations 2008 (SI 2008/794) reg.18 (Circumstances in which the condition that the claimant is not receiving education does not apply)*

Regulation 18 now reads, as amended, as follows: 5.119

"Paragraph 6(1)(g) of Schedule 1 to the Act does not apply where the claimant is entitled to a disability living allowance [3, child disability payment] [2, armed forces independence payment] [4,] [1 personal independence payment] [4 or adult disability payment]."

In addition, the following notes should be added to the list of

AMENDMENTS:

3. Social Security (Scotland) Act 2018 (Disability Assistance for Children and Young People) (Consequential Modifications) Order 2021 (SI 2021/786) Sch.9 para.3 (July 26, 2021).

4. Social Security (Disability Assistance for Working Age People) (Consequential Amendments) Order 2022 (SI 2022/177) art.11(3) (March 21, 2022).

p.1250, *amendment to the Employment and Support Allowance Regulations 2008 (SI 2008/794) reg.21 (Information required for determining capability for work)*

With effect from July 1, 2022, reg.4(2) of the Social Security (Medical Evidence) and Statutory Sick Pay (Medical Evidence) (Amendment) (No. 2) Regulations 2022 (SI 2022/630) omitted the words "a doctor's" between "form of" and "statement". 5.120

p.1260, *annotation to the Employment and Support Allowance Regulations 2008 (SI 2008/794) reg.24 (Matters to be taken into account in determining good cause in relation to regs 22 or 23)*

See, however, the successful application for a new inquest in *Dove v HM Assistant Coroner for Teesside and Hartlepool, Rahman and SSWP* [2023] EWCA Civ 289. Mrs Dove's daughter, Jodey, had died of an overdose shortly after her ESA award had been stopped. Jodey, who had been in receipt of ESA for several years, had a history of mental health problems, suicidal ideation and overdoses, as well as physical ill-health. In 2016, on a periodic review, she asked the DWP for a home visit. The DWP neglected to deal with that request and required her to attend an HCP assessment, which she failed to do. The DWP decided that Jodey had shown neither good cause for the failure to attend nor that she had limited capability for work. Jodey's ESA was duly stopped on February 7, 2017, and she died a fortnight later. Mrs Dove believed that the withdrawal of benefit had created extra stress and contributed to her daughter's death. The coroner ruled that questioning the DWP's decisions was beyond her remit under the Coroners and Justice Act 2009. 5.121

Mrs Dove applied to the High Court under the Coroners Act 1988 s.13, seeking two remedies: (a) to quash the coroner's suicide verdict; and (b) to order a new inquest covering the circumstances surrounding her daughter's death. Mrs Dove submitted that (1) the coroner's inquiry was insufficient in scope and should have covered the DWP's failings; (2) those failings meant that the state was in breach of ECHR art.2, so requiring a wider inquiry; (3) fresh evidence (in the form of an expert psychiatrist's report, obtained after the inquest, which concluded it was likely that Jodey's mental state would have been substantially affected by the decision to stop her benefits and an ICE report on a complaint about the DWP's handling of Jodey's claim) showed that a new inquest was necessary. At first instance the Divisional Court ([2021] EWHC 2511 (Admin); Warbey LJ, Farbey J and HH Judge Teague QC) dismissed the application on all three grounds.

However, the Court of Appeal allowed Mrs Dove's appeal and directed a fresh inquest ([2023] EWCA Civ 289: Lewis LJ, William Davis LJ and Whipple LJ). The Court ruled that the psychiatrist's report (but not the ICE report) was fresh evidence making it desirable in the interests of justice to hold a fresh inquest (*R v HM Coroner for North Humberside and Scunthorpe Ex p. Jamieson* [1995] Q.B. 1). Thus, "it is in the interests of justice that Mrs Dove and her family should have the opportunity to invite a coroner, at a fresh inquest, to make a finding of fact that the Department's actions contributed to Jodey's deteriorating mental health and, if that finding is made, to invite the coroner to include reference to that finding in the conclusion on how Jodey came by her death" (per Whipple LJ at [72]). One of the reasons for the Court reaching this conclusion was that "there is a public interest in a coroner considering the wider issue of causation raised on this appeal. If Jodey's death was connected with the abrupt cessation of benefits by the Department, the public has a legitimate interest in knowing that. After all, the Department deals with very many people who are vulnerable and dependent on benefits to survive, and the consequences of terminating benefit payments to such people should be examined in public, where it can be followed and reported on by others who might be interested in it."

p.1302, *annotation to the Employment and Support Allowance Regulations 2008 (SI 2008/794) reg.35 (Certain claimants to be treated as having limited capability for work-related activity)*

5.122 For further examples of the need for sufficient fact-finding and adequate reasons in appeals where reg.35 is in issue, see *MH v SSWP (ESA)* [2021] UKUT 90 (AAC) and *CT v SSWP (ESA)* [2021] UKUT 131 (AAC). On the importance of tribunals in universal credit appeals (that turn on the equivalent provision to reg.35 in Sch.9 para.4) ensuring they have been provided with an accurate list of work-related activities, see *KS v SSWP (UC)* [2021] UKUT 132 (AAC). Secretary of State appeal responses on such appeals may not have included accurate lists of work-related activities until after July 2020.

pp.1334–1335, *amendment of the Employment and Support Allowance Regulations 2008 (SI 2008/794) reg.64D (The amount of a hardship payment)*

5.123 The text in the main volume at para.4.174 should be replaced with the following:

"[1 The amount of a hardship payment

64D.—[2 (1) A hardship payment is either—

(a) 80% of the prescribed amount for a single claimant as set out in paragraph (1)(a) of Part 1 of Schedule 4 where—

(i) the claimant has an award of employment and support allowance which does not include entitlement to a work-related activity component under section 4(2)(b) of the Welfare Reform Act 2007 as in force immediately before 3rd April 2017; and

(ii) the claimant or any other member of their family is either pregnant or seriously ill; or

(b) 60% of the prescribed amount for a single claimant as set out in paragraph (1)(a) of Part 1 of Schedule 4 in any other case.]

(2) A payment calculated in accordance with paragraph (1) shall, if it is not a multiple of 5p, be rounded to the nearest such multiple or, if it is a multiple of 2.5p but not of 5p, to the next lower multiple of 5p.]"

AMENDMENTS

1. Employment and Support Allowance (Sanctions) (Amendment) Regulations 2012 (SI 2012/2756) reg.6 (December 3, 2012).

2. Employment and Support Allowance (Exempt Work Hardship Amounts) (Amendment) Regulations 2017 (SI 2017/205) reg.5 (April 3, 2017).

p.1336, *annotation to the Employment and Support Allowance Regulations 2008 (SI 2008/794) reg.67 (Prescribed amounts)*

On the lawfulness of not uplifting the amounts paid in IS, JSA and ESA by £20 per week (as was done with UC for 18 months during the coronavirus pandemic), see the annotation to the Income Support (General) Regulations 1987 (SI 1987/1967) reg.17 (Applicable amounts), above. 5.124

p.1340, *annotation to the Employment and Support Allowance Regulations 2008 (SI 2008/794) reg.69 (Special cases)*

Concerning the definition of 'prisoner', in *JC v Secretary of State for Work and Pensions* [2024] UKUT 13 (AAC) (08 January 8, 2024), §30 Upper Tribunal Judge Jones holds that reg.69(2) 'should be interpreted as providing a restricted definition of a prisoner as being one detained or sentenced for a criminal offence or detained or sentenced to imprisonment by a criminal court rather than including a finding of guilt and sentence by a civil court in respect of a civil contempt of court'. The reasoning for this is to achieve parity with past judicial interpretation of primary legislation depriving prisoners of benefit—see currently s.113(1)(b) SSCBA 1992. That provision states that benefits under Parts II to V of the Act shall not be received by or payable in respect of any person for any period during which the person 'is undergoing imprisonment or detention in legal custody'. In *R(S) 8/79*, §8 the Commissioner found imprisonment in this sense 'means only imprisonment imposed by a court exercising criminal jurisdiction'. 5.125

pp.1341–1342, *amendment to the Employment and Support Allowance Regulations 2008 (SI 2008/794) reg.70 (Special cases: supplemental—persons from abroad)*

The text in the main volume at para.4.187 should be replaced with the following: 5.126

"Special cases: supplemental—persons from abroad

70.—(1) "Person from abroad" means, subject to the following provisions of this regulation, a claimant who is not habitually resident in the

United Kingdom, the Channel Islands, the Isle of Man or the Republic of Ireland.

(2) A claimant must not be treated as habitually resident in the United Kingdom, the Channel Islands, the Isle of Man or the Republic of Ireland unless the claimant has a right to reside in (as the case may be) the United Kingdom, the Channel Islands, the Isle of Man or the Republic of Ireland other than a right to reside which falls within paragraph (3) [8 or (3A)].

(3) A right to reside falls within this paragraph if it is one which exists by virtue of, or in accordance with, one or more of the following—

(a) regulation 13 of the [8 Immigration (European Economic Area) Regulations 2016];

(b) regulation 14 of those Regulations, but only in a case where the right exists under that regulation because the claimant is—

(i) a jobseeker for the purpose of the definition of "qualified person" in regulation 6(1) of those Regulations; or

(ii) a family member (within the meaning of regulation 7 of those Regulations) of such a jobseeker; [10 or]

[4[8(bb) regulation 16 of those Regulations, but only in a case where the right exists under that regulation because the claimant satisfies the criteria in paragraph (5) of that regulation;]]

(c) [10 . . .]

(d) [10 . . .]

(e) [10 . . .]

[8 (3A) A right to reside falls within this paragraph if it exists by virtue of a claimant having been granted limited leave to enter, or remain in, the United Kingdom under the Immigration Act 1971 by virtue of—

(a) Appendix EU to the immigration rules made under section 3(2) of that Act; [11 . . .];

(b) being a person with a Zambrano right to reside as defined in Annex 1 of Appendix EU to the immigration rules made under section 3(2) of that Act.] [11; or

(c) having arrived in the United Kingdom with an entry clearance that was granted under Appendix EU (Family Permit) to the immigration rules made under section 3(2) of that Act.]

[9 (3B) Paragraph (3A)(a) does not apply to a person who—

(a) has a right to reside granted by virtue of being a family member of a relevant person of Northern Ireland; and

(b) would have a right to reside under the Immigration (European Economic Area) Regulations 2016 if the relevant person of Northern Ireland were an EEA national, provided that the right to reside does not fall within paragraph (3).]

(4) A claimant is not a person from abroad if the claimant is—

[12(zza) a person granted leave in accordance with the immigration rules made under section 3(2) of the Immigration Act 1971, where such leave is granted by virtue of—

(i) the Afghan Relocations and Assistance Policy; or

(ii) the previous scheme for locally-employed staff in Afghanistan (sometimes referred to as the ex-gratia scheme);

(zzb) a person in Great Britain not coming within sub-paragraph (zza) or [13 (h)] who left Afghanistan in connection with the collapse of the Afghan government that took place on 15th August 2021;]

[13(zzc) a person in Great Britain who was residing in Ukraine immediately before 1st January 2022, left Ukraine in connection with the Russian invasion which took place on 24th February 2022 and—
(i) has been granted leave in accordance with immigration rules made under section 3(2) of the Immigration Act 1971; [14 . . .]
(ii) has a right of abode in the United Kingdom within the meaning given in section 2 of that Act;] [14 or
(iii) does not require leave to enter or remain in the United Kingdom in accordance with section 3ZA of that Act;]

[15(zzd) a person who was residing in Sudan before 15th April 2023, left Sudan in connection with the violence which rapidly escalated on 15th April 2023 in Khartoum and across Sudan and—
(i) has been granted leave in accordance with immigration rules made under section 3(2) of the Immigration Act 1971;
(ii) has a right of abode in the United Kingdom within the meaning given in section 2 of that Act; or
(iii) does not require leave to enter or remain in the United Kingdom in accordance with section 3ZA of that Act;]

[16(zze) a person who was residing in Israel, the West Bank, the Gaza Strip, East Jerusalem, the Golan Heights or Lebanon immediately before 7th October 2023, who left Israel, the West Bank, the Gaza Strip, East Jerusalem, the Golan Heights or Lebanon in connection with the Hamas terrorist attack in Israel on 7th October 2023 or the violence which rapidly escalated in the region following the attack and—
(i) has been granted leave in accordance with immigration rules made under section 3(2) of the Immigration Act 1971;
(ii) has a right of abode in the United Kingdom within the meaning given in section 2 of that Act; or
(iii) does not require leave to enter or remain in the United Kingdom in accordance with section 3ZA of that Act;]

[7(za) a qualified person for the purposes of regulation 6 of the [8 Immigration (European Economic Area) Regulations 2016] as a worker or a self-employed person;

(zb) a family member of a person referred to in sub-paragraph (za) [9 . . .];

(zc) a person who has a right to reside permanently in the United Kingdom by virtue of regulation 15(1)(c), (d) or (e) of those Regulations;]

[9(zd) a family member of a relevant person of Northern Ireland, with a right to reside which falls within paragraph (3A)(a), provided that the relevant person of Northern Ireland falls within sub-paragraph (za), or would do so but for the fact that they are not an EEA national;]

[10(ze) a frontier worker within the meaning of regulation 3 of the Citizens' Rights (Frontier Workers) (EU Exit) Regulations 2020;

(zf) a family member of a person referred to in sub-paragraph (ze), who has been granted limited leave to enter, or remain in, the United Kingdom by virtue of Appendix EU to the immigration rules made under section 3(2) of the Immigration Act 1971;]

(g) a refugee within the definition in Article 1 of the Convention relating to the Status of Refugees done at Geneva on 28th July 1951, as extended by Article 1(2) of the Protocol relating to the Status of Refugees done at New York on 31st January 1967;

[6(h) a person who has been granted leave or who is deemed to have been granted leave outside the rules made under section 3(2) of the Immigration Act 1971 [13 . . .]

(i) a person who has humanitarian protection granted under those rules; [6 or]

(j) a person who is not a person subject to immigration control within the meaning of section 115(9) of the Immigration and Asylum Act and who is in the United Kingdom as a result of deportation, expulsion or other removal by compulsion of law from another country to the United Kingdom; [1 . . .]

(k) [6 . . .]

(l) [1 [6 . . .]]]

[9 (5) In this regulation—

"EEA national" has the meaning given in regulation 2(1) of the Immigration (European Economic Area) Regulations 2016;

"family member" has the meaning given in regulation 7(1)(a), (b) or (c) of the Immigration (European Economic Area) Regulations 2016 except that regulation 7(4) of those Regulations does not apply for the purposes of paragraphs (3B) and (4)(zd);

"relevant person of Northern Ireland" has the meaning given in Annex 1 of Appendix EU to the immigration rules made under section 3(2) of the Immigration Act 1971.]

[10 (6) References in this regulation to the Immigration (European Economic Area) Regulations 2016 are to be read with Schedule 4 to the Immigration and Social Security Co-ordination (EU Withdrawal) Act 2020(Consequential, Saving, Transitional and Transitory Provisions) Regulations 2020.]"

Amendments

1. Social Security (Habitual Residence) (Amendment) Regulations 2009 (SI 2009/362) reg.9 (March 18, 2009).

2. Social Security (Miscellaneous Amendments) (No. 3) Regulations 2011 (SI 2011/2425) reg.23(1) and (7) (October 31, 2011).

3. Treaty of Lisbon (Changes in Terminology or Numbering) Order 2012 (SI 2012/1809) art.3(1) and Sch.1 Pt.2 (August 1, 2012).

4. Social Security (Habitual Residence) (Amendment) Regulations 2012 (SI 2012/2587) reg.2 (November 8, 2012).

5. Social Security (Croatia) Amendment Regulations 2013 (SI 2013/1474) reg.7 (July 1, 2013).

6. Social Security (Miscellaneous Amendments) (No. 3) Regulations 2013 (SI 2013/2536) reg.13(1) and (24) (October 29, 2013).

7. Social Security (Habitual Residence) (Amendment) Regulations 2014 (SI 2014/902) reg.7 (May 31, 2014).

8. Social Security (Income-related Benefits) (Updating and Amendment) (EU Exit) Regulations 2019 (SI 2019/872) reg.7 (May 7, 2019).

9. Social Security (Income-Related Benefits) (Persons of Northern Ireland –Family Members) (Amendment) Regulations 2020 (SI 2020/638) reg.7 (August 24, 2020).

10. Immigration and Social Security Co-ordination (EU Withdrawal) Act 2020 (Consequential, Saving, Transitional and Transitory Provisions) (EU Exit) Regulations 2020 (SI 2020/1309) reg 73 (December 31, 2020 at 11.00 pm).

11. Immigration (Citizens' Rights etc.) (EU Exit) Regulations 2020 (SI 2020/1372) reg.23 (December 31, 2020 at 11.00 pm).

12. Social Security (Habitual Residence and Past Presence) (Amendment) Regulations 2021 (SI 2021/1034) reg.2 (September 15, 2021).

13. Social Security (Habitual Residence and Past Presence) (Amendment) Regulations 2022 (SI 2022/344) reg.2 (March 22, 2022).

14. Social Security (Habitual Residence and Past Presence) (Amendment) (No. 2) Regulations 2022 (SI 2022/990) reg.2 (October 18, 2022).

15. Social Security (Habitual Residence and Past Presence) (Amendment) Regulations 2023 (SI 2023/532) reg.2(1) and 2(2)(f) (May 15, 2023).

16. Social Security (Habitual Residence and Past Presence, and Capital Disregards) (Amendment) Regulations 2023, reg.2 (SI 2023/1144) (October 27, 2023).

Modification

Regulation 70 is modified by Sch.1 para.10A of the Employment and Support Allowance (Transitional Provisions, Housing Benefit and Council Tax Benefit) (Existing Awards) (No. 2) Regulations 2010 (SI 2010/1907) as amended for the purposes specified in reg.6(1) of those Regulations. For the details of the modification, pp.1410–1452 of Vol.I of the 2020/21 edition.

Definition

"Immigration and Asylum Act"—reg.2(1).

p.1373, *amendment to the Employment and Support Allowance Regulations 2008 (SI 2008/794) reg.107(10A) (Notional income—exceptions)*

With effect from January 1, 2022, reg.7(3) of the Social Security (Income and Capital Disregards) (Amendment) Regulations 2021 (SI 2021/1405) amended para.(10A) by substituting the following for "a payment of income which is a Grenfell Tower payment": 5.127

"any of the following payments of income—
(a) a Grenfell Tower payment;
(b) a child abuse payment;
(c) a Windrush payment."

All of those payments are defined in reg.2(1). See the entry for p.684 for discussion of the nature of child abuse and Windrush payments.

With effect from July 9, 2023, reg.7(3) of the Social Security (Income and Capital Disregards) (Amendment) Regulations 2023 (SI 2023/640) amended reg.107(5A) by inserting the following after sub-para.(c):

"(d) a Post Office compensation payment."

Such payments are newly defined in reg.2(1), where there is now also an expanded definition of Grenfell Tower payments (see sub-para.(a). See the entry for pp.684–685 on income support in this Supplement.

p.1377, *annotation to the Employment and Support Allowance Regulations 2008 (SI 2008/794) reg.110 (Capital limit)*

In the Institute for Government and the Social Security Advisory Committee's 2021 joint report *Jobs and benefits: The Covid-19 challenge* it was noted that if the capital limit of £16,000 had risen in line with prices since 2006 it would be close to £23,500 (or £25,000: different figures are given) and recommended that the limit should be increased to £25,000 and subsequently automatically indexed to maintain its real value (pp.22 and 31). That recommendation was summarily rejected in the Government's response of March 22, 2022. 5.128

p.1378, *amendment to the Employment and Support Allowance Regulations 2008 (SI 2008/794) reg.112(8) (Income treated as capital—exceptions)*

5.129 With effect from January 1, 2022, reg.7(4) of the Social Security (Income and Capital Disregards) (Amendment) Regulations 2021 (SI 2021/1405) amended para.(8) by substituting the following for sub-para.(b):

"any—
(a) Grenfell Tower payment;
(b) child abuse payment;
(c) Windrush payment."

All of those payments are defined in reg.2(1). See the entry for p.684 for discussion of the nature of child abuse and Windrush payments.

With effect from July 9, 2023, reg.7(4) of the Social Security (Income and Capital Disregards) (Amendment) Regulations 2023 (SI 2023/640) amended reg.112(8)(b) by inserting the following after head (iii):

"(iv) Post Office compensation payment."

Such payments are newly defined in reg.2(1), where there is now also an expanded definition of Grenfell Tower payments (see head (a)). See the entry for pp.684–685 on income support for the background.

With effect from October 27, 2023, reg.8(3)(a) of the Social Security (Habitual Residence and Past Presence, and Capital Disregards) (Amendment) Regulations 2023 (SI 2023/1144) amended reg.112(8)(a) by inserting ", the Victims of Overseas Terrorism Compensation Scheme" after "the National Emergencies Trust". That scheme is newly defined in reg.2(1). See the entry for pp.684–685 on income support for the background.

p.1382, *amendment to the Employment and Support Allowance Regulations 2008 (SI 2008/794) reg.115(5A) (Notional capital—exceptions)*

5.130 With effect from January 1, 2022, reg.7(5) of the Social Security (Income and Capital Disregards) (Amendment) Regulations 2021 (SI 2021/1405) amended para.(5A) by substituting the following for "a payment of capital which is a Grenfell Tower payment":

"any of the following payments of capital—
(a) a Grenfell Tower payment;
(b) a child abuse payment;
(c) a Windrush payment."

All of those payments are defined in reg.2(1). See the entry for p.684 for discussion of the nature of child abuse and Windrush payments.

With effect from July 9, 2023, reg.7(5) of the Social Security (Income and Capital Disregards) (Amendment) Regulations 2023 (SI 2023/640) amended reg.115(5A) by inserting the following after sub-para.(c):

"(d) a Post Office compensation payment;
(e) a vaccine damage payment."

Such payments are newly defined in reg.2(1), where there is now also an expanded definition of Grenfell Tower payments (see sub-para.(a)). See the entry for pp.684–685 on income support in this Supplement.

With effect from October 27, 2023, reg.8(3)(b) of the Social Security (Habitual Residence and Past Presence, and Capital Disregards) (Amendment) Regulations 2023 (SI 2023/1144) amended reg.115(5)(a) by inserting ", the Victims of Overseas Terrorism Compensation Scheme" after "the National Emergencies Trust". That scheme is newly defined in reg.2(1). See the entry for pp.684–685 on income support for the background.

pp.1406–1407, *annotation to the Employment and Support Allowance Regulations 2008 (SI 2008/794) reg.137(4) and (5) (Treatment of student loans and postgraduate loans)*

See the entry for p.539 on income support for details of the decision in *IB v Gravesham BC and SSWP (HB)* [2023] UKUT 193 (AAC); [2024] P.T.S.R. 130 on when a claimant cannot acquire a loan by taking reasonable steps to do so. 5.131

p.1409, *amendment to the Employment and Support Allowance Regulations 2008 (SI 2008/794) reg.139A (Treatment of special support loans)*

With effect from April 1, 2024, reg.5 of the Social Security and Universal Credit (Migration of Tax Credit Claimants and Miscellaneous Amendments) Regulations 2024 (SI 2024/341) amended reg.139A by substituting the following for the existing text and heading: 5.132

> **"Treatment of loans for specific purposes**
> **139A.** A loan under the Education (Student Support) Regulations 2011 or regulations made under section 73 of the Education (Scotland) Act 1980 that is intended to meet the cost of books, equipment, travel or childcare is to be disregarded as income."

The new form of reg.139A is intended to ensure that special support loans under a scheme to be introduced for full-time students by the Scottish government from the beginning of academic year 2024/25 are to be disregarded as income in same way as special support loans in England and Wales. Although the new form no longer refers to the definition of "special support loan" in reg.68 of the Education (Student Support) Regulations 2011, the restriction to loans intended (i.e., by necessary implication, intended by the awarding authority) to meet the cost of books, equipment, travel or childcare excludes loans under those regulations for other purposes. See reg.132 for the disregard of grants, as opposed to loans, for similar and other purposes.

pp.1411, *amendment to the Employment and Support Allowance Regulations 2008 (SI 2008/794) reg.144 (Waiting days)*

With effect from November 19, 2023, art.19(4) of the Carer's Assistance (Carer Support Payment) (Scotland) Regulations 2023 (Consequential Amendments) Order 2023 (SI 2023/1218) amended reg.144(2)(a) by inserting ", carer support payment" after "carer's allowance". 5.133

p.1413, *annotation to the Employment and Support Allowance Regulations 2008 (SI 2008/794) reg.145 (Linking rules)*

For more detailed analysis see the commentary on SSCBA 1992 s.30C(1) (c) in Vol.I of the 2011/12 edition of this work (at paras 1.67–1.77). 5.134

pp.1431–1432, *amendments to the Employment and Support Allowance Regulations 2008 (SI 2008/794) reg.158 (Meaning of "person in hardship")*

5.135 With effect from July 26, 2021, Sch.9 para.4 of the Social Security (Scotland) Act 2018 (Disability Assistance for Children and Young People) (Consequential Modifications) Order 2021 (SI 2021/786) makes the following amendments to reg.158:

- In para.(3):
  - in sub-para.(c), after "disability living allowance", insert ", child disability payment";
  - in sub-para.(d)(ii), after "disability living allowance", insert ", child disability payment".
- For para.(7), substitute:
  "(7) In this regulation, "care component" means—

(a) the care component of disability living allowance at the highest or middle rate prescribed under section 72(3) of the Contributions and Benefits Act; or

(b) the care component of child disability payment at the highest or middle rate provided for in regulation 11(5) of the DACYP Regulations.".

With effect from March 21, 2022, art.11(4) of the Social Security (Disability Assistance for Working Age People) (Consequential Amendments) Order 2022 (SI 2022/177) makes the following amendments to reg.158(3):

- in sub-para.(b):
  - after "armed forces independence payment" for "or" substitute ",";
  - after "daily living component" insert "or the daily living component of adult disability payment";
- in sub-para.(c):
  - after "armed forces independence payment" for "or" substitute ",";
  - after "personal independence payment", insert "or adult disability payment";
- in sub-para.(d):
  - in para.(i):
    - after "armed forces independence payment" for "or" substitute ",";
    - after "daily living component" insert "or the daily living component of adult disability payment";
  - in para.(ii):
    - after "armed forces independence payment" for "or" substitute ",";
    - after "personal independence payment", insert "or adult disability payment".

p.1437, *amendment to the Employment and Support Allowance Regulations 2008 (SI 2008/794) reg.165 (entitlement for less than a week—amount of anemployment and support allowance payable)*

5.136 With effect from November 19, 2023, art.19 of the Carer's Assistance (Carer Support Payment) (Scotland) Regulations 2023 (Consequential Amendments) Order 2023 (SI 2023/1218) amends reg.165(3) as follows:

after "carer's allowance" insert ", carer support payment".

p.1438, *amendment to the Employment and Support Allowance Regulations 2008 (SI 2008/794) reg.167 (modification in the calculation of income)*

With effect from November 19, 2023, art.19 of the Carer's Assistance (Carer Support Payment) (Scotland) Regulations 2023 (Consequential Amendments) Order 2023 (SI 2023/1218) amends reg.167(d) as follows: 5.137

after "carer's allowance" insert ", carer support payment".

pp.1494–1496, *annotation to the Employment and Support Allowance Regulations 2008 (SI 2008/794) Sch.2 Activity 17 (Appropriateness of behaviour with other people, due to cognitive impairment or mental disorder)*

Consideration of Activity 17 may require the disclosure of Unacceptable Customer Behaviour (UCB) forms as provided in confidence by the DWP to HMCTS: *MH v SSWP (ESA)* [2021] UKUT 90 (AAC). 5.138

pp.1507–1514, *amendments to the Employment and Support Allowance Regulations 2008 (SI 2008/794) Sch.4 (Amounts)*

Substitute the following for paras 4.420–4.429 5.139

Regulations 67(1)(a) and (2) and 68(1)(a) and (b)

"SCHEDULE 4

AMOUNTS

PART 1

PRESCRIBED AMOUNTS

1. The weekly amounts specified in column (2) in respect of each person or couple specified in column (1) are the weekly amounts specified for the purposes of regulations 67(1) and 68 (prescribed amounts and polygamous marriages). 4.420

(1) *Person or Couple*	*(2)* *Amount*
(1) *Single claimant—* (a) who satisfies the conditions set out in section 2(2) [12 . . .] or 4(4) [12 . . .] of the Act [13 or who is a member of the work-related activity group]; (b) aged not less than 25 (c) aged less than 25.	(1) (a) [16 £90.50]; (b) [16 £90.50]; (c) [16 £71.70];
(2) Lone parent [6 or a person who has no partner and who is responsible for and a member of the same household as a young person]— (a) who satisfies the conditions set out in section 4(4) [12 ...] of the Act[13 or who is a member of the work-related activity group and satisfies the conditions set out in Part 2 of Schedule 1 to the Act]; (b) aged not less than 18; (c) aged less than 18.	(2) (a) [16 £90.50]; (b) [16 £90.50]; (c) [16 £71.70];

(1) *Person or Couple*	*(2)* *Amount*
(3) Couple—	(3)
(a) where both members are aged not less than 18;	(a) [16 £192.25];
(b) where one member is aged not less than 18 and the other member is a person under 18 who— (i) [3 if that other member had not been a member] of a couple, would satisfy the requirements for entitlement to income support other than the requirement to make a claim for it; or (ii) [3 if that other member had not been a member] of a couple, would satisfy the requirements for entitlement to an income-related allowance; or (iii) satisfies the requirements of section 3(1)(f)(iii) of the Jobseekers Act (prescribed circumstances for persons aged 16 but less than 18); or (iv) is the subject of a direction under section 16 of that Act (persons under 18: severe hardship);	(b) [16 £192.25];
(c) where the claimant satisfies the conditions set out in section 4(4) [12 . . .] of the Act [13 or the claimant is a member of the work-related activity group and satisfies the conditions set out in Part 2 of Schedule 1 to the Act] and both members are aged less than 18 and— (i) at least one of them is treated as responsible for a child; or (ii) had they not been members of a couple, each would have qualified for an income-related allowance; or (iii) had they not been members of a couple the claimant's partner would satisfy the requirements for entitlement to income support other than the requirement to make a claim for it; or (iv) the claimant's partner satisfies the requirements of section 3(1)(f)(iii) of the Jobseekers Act (prescribed circumstances for persons aged 16 but less than 18); or (v) there is in force in respect of the claimant's partner a direction under section 16 of that Act (persons under 18: severe hardship);	(c) [16 £192.25];
(d) where both members are aged less than 18 and— (i) at least one of them is treated as responsible for a child; or (ii) had they not been members of a couple, each would have qualified for an income-related allowance; or (iii) had they not been members of a couple the claimant's partner satisfies the requirements for entitlement to income support other than a requirement to make a claim for it; or (iv) the claimant's partner satisfies the requirements of section 3(1)(f)(iii) of the Jobseekers Act (prescribed circumstances for persons aged 16 but less than 18); or	(d) [15 £101.50];

(1) *Person or Couple*	*(2)* *Amount*
(v) there is in force in respect of the claimant's partner a direction under section 16 of that Act (persons under 18: severe hardship);	
(e) where the claimant is aged not less than 25 and the claimant's partner is a person under 18 who— (i) would not qualify for an income-related allowance if the person were not a member of a couple; (ii) would not qualify for income support if the person were not a member of a couple; (iii) does not satisfy the requirements of section 3(1)(f)(iii) of the Jobseekers Act (prescribed circumstances for persons aged 16 but less than 18); and (iv) is not the subject of a direction under section 16 of that Act (persons under 18: severe hardship);	(e) [16 £90.50];
(f) where the claimant satisfies the conditions set out in section 4(4) [12 . . .] of the Act [13 or the claimant is a member of the work-related activity group and satisfies the conditions set out in Part 2 of Schedule 1 to the Act] and the claimant's partner is a person under 18 who— (i) would not qualify for an income-related allowance if the person were not a member of a couple; (ii) would not qualify for income support if the person [1 were] not a member of a couple; (iii) does not satisfy the requirements of section 3(1)(f)(iii) of the Jobseekers Act (prescribed circumstances for persons aged 16 but less than 18); and (iv) is not the subject of a direction under section 16 of that Act (persons under 18: severe hardship);	(f) [16 £90.50];
(g) where the claimant satisfies the conditions set out in section 4(4) [12 . . .] of the Act [13 or the claimant is a member of the work-related activity group and satisfies the conditions set out in Part 2 of Schedule 1 to the Act] and both members are aged less than 18 and paragraph (c) does not apply;	(g) [16 £90.50];
(h) where the claimant is aged not less than 18 but less than 25 and the claimant's partner is a person under 18 who— (i) would not qualify for an income-related allowance if the person were not a member of a couple; (ii) would not qualify for income support if the person were not a member of a couple; (iii) does not satisfy the requirements of section 3(1)(f)(iii) of the Jobseekers Act (prescribed circumstances for persons aged 16 but less than 18); and (iv) is not the subject of a direction under section 16 of that Act (persons under 18: severe hardship);	(h) [16 £71.70];
(i) where both members are aged less than 18 and paragraph (d) does not apply.	(i) [16 £71.70].

Regulations 67(1)(b) and 68(1)(c)

PART 2

PREMIUMS

4.421 **2.** Except as provided in paragraph 4, the weekly premiums specified in Part 3 of this Schedule are, for the purposes of regulation 67(1)(b) and 68(1)(c), to be applicable to a claimant who satisfies the condition specified in paragraphs 5 to 8 in respect of that premium.

3. An enhanced disability premium in respect of a person is not applicable in addition to a pensioner premium.

4.—(1) For the purposes of this Part of this Schedule, once a premium is applicable to a claimant under this Part, a person is to be treated as being in receipt of any benefit—

(a) in the case of a benefit to which the Social Security (Overlapping Benefits) Regulations 1979 applies, for any period during which, apart from the provisions of those Regulations, the person would be in receipt of that benefit; and

(b) for any period spent by a person in undertaking a course of training or instruction provided or approved by the Secretary of State under section 2 of the Employment and Training Act 1973, or by [3 Skills Development Scotland] or Highlands and Islands Enterprise under section 2 of the Enterprise and New Towns (Scotland) Act 1990, or for any period during which the person is in receipt of a training allowance]. [15 ; and

(c) in the case of carer support payment, for any period during which, apart from regulation 16 of the Carer's Assistance (Carer Support Payment) (Scotland) Regulations 2023, he would be in receipt of that benefit.]

[7 (2) For the purposes of the carer premium under paragraph 8, a person is to be treated as being in receipt of a carer's allowance by virtue of sub-paragraph (1)(a) [15 or carer support payment by virtue of sub-paragraph (1)(c)] only if and for so long as the person in respect of whose care the allowance [15 or payment] has been claimed

(a) attendance allowance;

(b) the care component of disability living allowance at the highest or middle rate prescribed in accordance with section 72(3) of the Contributions and Benefits Act; [8 . . .]

(c) the daily living component of personal independence payment at the standard or enhanced rate in accordance with section 78(3) of the 2012 Act [8 [14 . . .

(ca) the daily living component of adult disability payment at the standard or enhanced rate in accordance with regulation 5 of the Disability Assistance for Working Age People (Scotland) Regulations 2022; or]

(d) armed forces independence payment.]]

Pensioner premium

4.422 **5.** The condition is that the claimant or the claimant's partner has attained the qualifying age for state pension credit.

Severe disability premium

4.423 **6.**—(1) The condition is that the claimant is a severely disabled person.

(2) For the purposes of sub-paragraph (1), a claimant is to be treated as being a severely disabled person if, and only if—

(a) in the case of a single claimant, a lone parent [6 , a person who has no partner and who is responsible for and a member of the same household as a young person] or a claimant who is treated as having no partner in consequence of sub-paragraph (3)—

(i) the claimant is in receipt of the care component [7 , the daily living component] [14 , the daily living component of adult disability payment] [8 , armed forces independence payment] [5 or attendance allowance];

(ii) subject to sub-paragraph (4), the claimant has no non-dependants aged 18 or over normally residing with the claimant or with whom the claimant is normally residing; and

(iii) no person is entitled to, and in receipt of, [11 a carer's allowance [15 or carer support payment] or has an award of universal credit which includes the carer element] in respect of caring for the claimant;

(b) in the case of a claimant who has a partner—

(i) the claimant is in receipt of the care component [7 , the daily living component] [14 , the daily living component of adult disability payment] [8 , armed forces independence payment] [5 or attendance allowance];

(ii) the claimant's partner is also in receipt of the care component [7 , the daily living component] [14 , the daily living component of adult disability payment] [8 , armed forces independence payment] or attendance allowance or, if the claimant is a member of a polygamous marriage, all the partners of that marriage are in receipt of the care component [7 , the daily living component] [14 , the daily living component of adult disability payment] [8 , armed forces independence payment] or attendance allowance; and

(iii) subject to sub-paragraph (4), the claimant has no non-dependants aged 18 or over normally residing with the claimant or with whom the claimant is normally residing,

and, either a person is entitled to, and in receipt of, a carer's allowance [15 or carer support payment] [11 or has an award of universal credit which includes the carer element] in respect of caring for only one of the couple or, in the case of a polygamous marriage, for one or more but not all the partners of the marriage or, as the case may be, no person is entitled to, and in receipt of, such an allowance [15 or payment] [11 or has such an award of universal credit] in respect of caring for either member of the couple or any partner of the polygamous marriage.

(3) Where a claimant has a partner who does not satisfy the condition in sub-paragraph (2)(b)(ii) and that partner is blind or severely sight impaired or is treated as blind or severely sight impaired that partner is to be treated for the purposes of sub-paragraph (2) as if the partner were not a partner of the claimant.

(4) For the purposes of sub-paragraph (2)(a)(ii) and (b)(iii) no account is to be taken of—

(a) a person receiving attendance allowance, [7 the daily living component] [14 , the daily living component of adult disability payment] [8 , armed forces independence payment] or the care component;

(b) subject to sub-paragraph (7), a person who joins the claimant's household for the first time in order to care for the claimant or the claimant's partner and immediately before so joining the claimant or the claimant's partner was treated as a severely disabled person; or

(c) a person who is blind or severely sight impaired or is treated as blind or severely sight impaired.

(5) For the purposes of sub-paragraph (2)(b) a person is to be treated—

(a) as being in receipt of attendance allowance or the care component if the person would, but for the person being a patient for a period exceeding 28 days, be so in receipt;

(b) as being entitled to, and in receipt of, a carer's allowance [15 or carer support payment] [11 or having an award of universal credit which includes the carer element] if the person would, but for the person for whom the person was caring being a patient in hospital for a period exceeding 28 days, be so entitled and in receipt [11 of carer's allowance or have such an award of universal credit] .

[7(c) as being in entitled to, and in receipt of, the daily living component if the person would, but for regulations under section 86(1) (hospital in-patients) of the 2012 Act, be so entitled and in receipt.]

[14 (d) as being in entitled to, and in receipt of, the daily living component of adult disability payment if the person would, but for regulation 28 (effect of admission to hospital on ongoing entitlement to Adult Disability Payment) of the Disability Assistance for Working Age People (Scotland) Regulations 2022, be so in receipt.]

(6) For the purposes of sub-paragraph (2)(a)(iii) and (b), no account is to be taken of an award of carer's allowance [15 or carer support payment] [11 or universal credit which includes the carer element] to the extent that payment of such an award is backdated for a period before the date on which the award is first paid.

(7) Sub-paragraph (4)(b) is to apply only for the first 12 weeks following the date on which the person to whom that provision applies first joins the claimant's household.

(8) In sub-paragraph (2)(a)(iii) and (b), references to a person being in receipt of a carer's allowance [11 or as having an award of universal credit which includes the carer element] are to include references to a person who would have been in receipt of that allowance [11 or had such an award] but for the application of a restriction under section [4 6B or] 7 of the Social Security Fraud Act 2001 (loss of benefit provisions).

(9) [11 (a)] In this paragraph—

[9 "blind or severely sight impaired" means certified as blind or severely sight impaired by a consultant ophthalmologist and a person who has ceased to be certified as blind or severely sight impaired where that person's eyesight has been regained is, nevertheless, to be treated as blind or severely sight impaired for a period of 28 weeks following the date on which the person ceased to be so certified;]

"the care component" means the care component of disability living allowance at the highest or middle rate prescribed in accordance with section 72(3) of the Contributions and Benefits Act.

[11 (b) A person has an award of universal credit which includes the carer element if the person has an award of universal credit which includes an amount which is the carer element under regulation 29 of the Universal Credit Regulations 2013.]

Enhanced disability premium

4.424 7.—(1) Subject to sub-paragraph (2), the condition is that—

(a) the claimant's applicable amount includes the support component; [7 . . .]
(b) the care component of disability living allowance is, or would, but for a suspension of benefit in accordance with regulations under section 113(2) of the Contributions and Benefits Act or, but for an abatement as a consequence of hospitalisation, be payable at the highest rate prescribed under section 72(3) of that Act in respect of—
   (i) the claimant; or
   (ii) the claimant's partner (if any) who is aged less than the qualifying age for state pension credit [7 ; [8 . . .]
(c) the daily living component is, or would, but for regulations made under section 86(1) (hospital in-patients) of the 2012 Act, be payable at the enhanced rate under section 78(2) of that Act in respect of—
   (i) the claimant; or
   (ii) the claimant's partner (if any) who is aged less than the qualifying age for state pension credit"]; [14 . . .
(ca) the daily living component of adult disability payment is, or would, but for regulation 28 (effect of admission to hospital on ongoing entitlement to Adult Disability Payment) of the Disability Assistance for Working Age People (Scotland) Regulations 2022, be payable at the enhanced rate under section 78(2) of those Regulations in respect of—
   (i) the claimant; or
   (ii) the claimant's partner (if any) who is aged less than the qualifying age for state pension credit; or]
(d) armed forces independence payment is payable in respect of—
   (i) the claimant; or
   (ii) the claimant's partner (if any) who is aged less than the qualifying age for state pension credit.]

(2) An enhanced disability premium is not applicable in respect of—

(a) a claimant who—
   (i) is not a member of a couple or a polygamous marriage; and
   (ii) is a patient within the meaning of regulation 69(2) and has been for a period of more than 52 weeks; or
(b) a member of a couple or a polygamous marriage where each member is a patient within the meaning of regulation 69(2) and has been for a period of more than 52 weeks.

Carer premium

4.425 8.—(1) Subject to sub-paragraphs (2) and (4), the condition is that the claimant or the claimant's partner is, or both of them are, entitled to a carer's allowance under section 70 of the Contributions and Benefits Act [15 or carer support payment].

(2) Where a carer premium is awarded but—

(a) the person in respect of whose care the carer's allowance [15 or carer support payment] has been awarded dies; or
(b) in any other case the person in respect of whom a carer premium has been awarded ceases to be entitled to a carer's allowance [15 or carer support payment], the condition for the award of the premium is to be treated as satisfied for a period of 8 weeks from the relevant date specified in sub-paragraph (3).

(3) The relevant date for the purposes of sub-paragraph (2) is—

(a) where sub-paragraph (2)(a) applies, the Sunday following the death of the person in respect of whose care a carer's allowance [15 or carer support payment] has been awarded or the date of death if the death occurred on a Sunday; or

(b) in any other case, the date on which the person who has been entitled to a carer's allowance [15 or carer support payment] ceases to be entitled to that allowance [15 or payment].

(4) Where a person who has been entitled to a carer's allowance [15 or carer support payment] ceases to be entitled to that allowance [15 or payment] and makes a claim for an income-related allowance, the condition for the award of the carer premium is to be treated as satisfied for a period of 8 weeks from the date on which—

(a) the person in respect of whose care the carer's allowance [15 or carer support payment] has been awarded dies; or

(b) in any other case, the person who has been entitled to a carer's allowance [15 or carer support payment] ceased to be entitled to that allowance [15 or payment].

Persons in receipt of concessionary payments

9. For the purpose of determining whether a premium is applicable to a person under paragraphs 6, 7 and 8, any concessionary payment made to compensate that person for the non-payment of any benefit mentioned in those paragraphs is to be treated as if it were a payment of that benefit. **4.426**

Persons in receipt of benefit

10. For the purposes of this Part of this Schedule, a person is to be regarded as being in receipt of any benefit if, and only if, it is paid in respect of the person and is to be so regarded only for any period in respect of which that benefit is paid. **4.427**

PART 3

WEEKLY AMOUNT OF PREMIUMS SPECIFIED IN PART 2

11.— **4.428**

Premium	*Amount*
(1) Pension premium for a person to whom paragraph 5 applies who—	(1)
(a) is a single claimant and—	(a)
(i) [12 . . .];	(i) [12 . . .];
(ii) is entitled to the support component; or	(ii) [17 £79.95];
[12(iii) is not entitled to the support component;]	(iii) [17 £127.65];
(b) is a member of a couple and—	(b)
(i) [12 . . .]	(i) [12];
(ii) is entitled to the support component; or	(ii) [17 £143.00];
[12 (iii) is not entitled to the support component;]	(iii) [17 £190.70];
(2) Severe disability premium—	(2)
(a) where the claimant satisfies the condition in paragraph 6(2)(a);	(a) [17 £181.50];
(b) where the claimant satisfies the condition in paragraph 6(2)(b)—	(b)
(i) if there is someone in receipt of a carer's allowance or if the person or any partner satisfies that condition only by virtue of paragraph 6(5);	(i) [17 £81.50];
(ii) if no-one is in receipt of such an allowance.	(ii) [17 £163.00].

(3) Carer premium.	(3) [17 £45.60]; in respect of each person who satisfies the condition specified in [1 paragraph 8(1)].
(4) Enhanced disability premium where the conditions in paragraph 7 are satisfied.	(4)(a) [17 £20.85]; in respect of each person who is neither— (i) a child or young person; nor (ii) a member of a couple or a polygamous marriage, in respect of whom the conditions specified in paragraph 7 are satisfied; (b) [17 £29.75]; where the claimant is a member of a couple or a polygamous marriage and the conditions specified in [1 paragraph 7] are satisfied in respect of a member of that couple or polygamous marriage.

Regulation 67(3)

PART 4

[12 THE COMPONENT]

4.429 **12.** [12 . . .].

13. The amount of the support component is [17 £44.70]."

AMENDMENTS

1. Employment and Support Allowance (Miscellaneous Amendments) Regulations 2008 (SI 2008/2428) reg.14 (October 27, 2008).
2. Social Security (Miscellaneous Amendments) Regulations 2009 (SI 2009/583) reg.10(2) (April 6, 2009).
3. Social Security (Miscellaneous Amendments) (No. 4) Regulations 2009 (SI 2009/2655) reg.11(1) and (16) (October 26, 2009).
4. Social Security (Loss of Benefit) Amendment Regulations 2010 (SI 2010/1160) reg.12(1) and (3) (April 1, 2010).
5. Social Security (Miscellaneous Amendments) (No. 3) Regulations 2011 (SI 2011/2425) reg.23(14) (October 30, 2011).
6. Social Security (Work-focused Interviews for Lone Parents and Partners) (Amendment) Regulations 2011 (SI 2011/2428) reg.5(5) (October 30, 2011).
7. Personal Independence Payment (Supplementary Provisions and Consequential Amendments) Regulations 2013 (SI 2013/388) reg.8 and Sch. para.40(1) and (5) (April 8, 2013).
8. Armed Forces and Reserve Forces Compensation Scheme (Consequential Provisions: Subordinate Legislation) Order 2013 (SI 2013/591) art.7 and Sch. para.37(1) and (5) (April 8, 2013).
9. Universal Credit and Miscellaneous Amendments (No. 2) Regulations 2014 (SI 2014/2888) reg.3(7)(a) (November 26, 2014).

10. Welfare Benefits Up-rating Order 2015 (SI 2015/30) art.11(1) and Sch.4 (April 6, 2015).
11. Universal Credit and Miscellaneous Amendments Regulations 2015 (SI 2015/1754) reg.19 (November 4, 2015).
12. Employment and Support Allowance and Universal Credit (Miscellaneous Amendments and Transitional and Savings Provisions) Regulations 2017 (SI 2017/204) reg.2(1) and (4) (April 3, 2017).
13. Employment and Support Allowance (Miscellaneous Amendments and Transitional and Savings Provision) Regulations 2017 (SI 2017/581) reg.7(1) and (4) (June 23, 2017, subject to the transitional and savings provision in reg.10).
14. Social Security (Disability Assistance for Working Age People) (Consequential Amendments) Order 2022 (SI 2022/177) art.11(5) (March 21 2022).
15. Carers Assistance (Carer Support Payment) (Scotland) Regulations 2023 (Consequential Amendments) Order 2023 (SI 2023/1218) art.19 (November 19, 2023).
16. Social Security Benefits Up-rating Order 2024 (SI 2024/242) art.30(2) and Sch.11 (April 8, 2024).
17. Social Security Benefits Up-rating Order 2024 (SI 2024/242) art.30(4) and Sch.12 (April 8, 2024).
18. Social Security Benefits Up-rating Order 2024 (SI 2024/242) art.30(7) (April 8, 2024).

For the General Note to Sch.4, see Vol.V para.4.430.

pp.1525–1532, *amendments to the Employment and Support Allowance Regulations 2008 (SI 2008/794) Sch.6 (Housing costs)*

With effect from July 26, 2021, Sch.9 para.5 of the Social Security (Scotland) Act 2018 (Disability Assistance for Children and Young People) (Consequential Modifications) Order 2021 (SI 2021/786) makes the following amendments to Sch.6: 5.140

- In para.15(11)(b) (linking rule), after "disability living allowance", insert ", child disability payment".
- In para.19(6)(b) (non-dependent deductions), after sub-para.(ii), insert "(iia) the care component of child disability payment;".

With effect from January 1, 2022, reg.7(6) of the Social Security (Income and Capital Disregards) (Amendment) Regulations 2021 (SI 2021/1405) inserts into para.19(8)(b), after "Grenfell Tower payment", ", child abuse payment or Windrush payment".

With effect from March 21, 2022, art.11(5) of the Social Security (Disability Assistance for Working Age People) (Consequential Amendments) Order 2022 (SI 2022/177) makes the following amendments to Sch.6:

- in para.15(11)(b) (linking rule):
  - after "armed forces independence payment" for "or" substitute ",";
  - after "personal independence payment", insert "or adult disability payment";
- in para.19(8)(a) (non-dependent deductions):
  - after "armed forces independence payment" for "or" substitute ",";
  - after "personal independence payment", insert "or adult disability payment";

- at the end of para.19(6)(b)(iii) omit "or";
- after para.19(6)(b)(iii) insert "(iiia) the daily living component of adult disability payment; or".

With effect from April 8, 2024, art.30(7) of the Social Security Benefits Up-rating Order 2024 (SI 2024/242) makes the following amendments:

- in sub-paragraph (1)(a) for "£116.75" substitute "£124.55";
- in sub-paragraph (1)(b) for "£18.10" substitute "£19.30";
- in sub-paragraph (2)(a) for "£162.00" substitute "£176.00";
- in sub-paragraph (2)(b)—
  (i) for "£41.60" substitute "£44.40";
  (ii) for "£162.00" substitute "£176.00"; and
  (iii) for "£236.00" substitute "£256.00";
- in sub-paragraph (2)(c)—
  (i) for "£57.10" substitute "£60.95";
  (ii) for "£236.00" substitute "£256.00"; and
  (iii) for "£308.00" substitute "£334.00";
- in sub-paragraph (2)(d)—
  (i) for "£93.40" substitute "£99.65";
  (ii) for "£308.00" substitute "£334.00"; and
  (iii) for "£410.00" substitute "£445.00"; and
- in sub-paragraph (2)(e)—
  (i) for "£106.35" substitute "£113.50";
  (ii) for "£410.00" substitute "£445.00"; and
  (iii) for "£511.00" substitute "£554.00".

With effect from July 9, 2023, reg.7 of the Social Security (Income and Capital Disregards) (Amendment) Regulations 2023 (SI 2023/640) amends para.19 as follows:

- in paragraph 19(8)(b) (non-dependant deductions), for "orWindrush payment" insert ", Windrush payment or Post Office compensation payment".

p.1540, *amendments to the Employment and Support Allowance Regulations 2008 (SI 2008/794) Sch.8 paras 8 and 11 (Sums to be disregarded in the calculation of income other than earnings—mobility component and AA, care component and daily living component)*

5.141 With effect from March 21, 2022, art.11(7)(a) of the Social Security (Disability Assistance for Working Age People) (Consequential Amendments) Order 2022 (SI 2022/177) amended para.8 to read as follows (square brackets indicate only the present amendment, those indicating previous amendments having been omitted):

"**8.**—The mobility component of disability living allowance[, the mobility component of adult disability payment] or the mobility component of personal independence payment.]."

With effect from March 21, 2022, art.11(7)(b) of the same Order amended para.11 to read as follows (square brackets indicate only the present amendment, those indicating previous amendments having been omitted):

"**11.**—Any attendance allowance, the care component of disability living allowance[,] the daily living component [or the daily living component of adult disability payment]."

"Adult disability payment" is defined in reg.2(1) by reference to reg.2 of the Disability Assistance for Working Age People (Scotland) Regulations 2022 (SSI 2022/54) (see Vol.IV of this series).

p.1542, *amendment to the Employment and Support Allowance Regulations 2008 (SI 2008/794) Sch.8 para.22(2) (Sums to be disregarded in the calculation of income other than earnings—income in kind)*

With effect from January 1, 2022, reg.7(7)(a) of the Social Security (Income and Capital Disregards) (Amendment) Regulations 2021 (SI 2021/1405) amended sub-para.(2) by inserting ", a child abuse payment or a Windrush payment" after "Grenfell Tower payment". All of those payments are defined in reg.2(1). See the entry for pp.684–685 for discussion of the nature of child abuse and Windrush payments. 5.142

p.1544, *amendment to the Employment and Support Allowance Regulations 2008 (SI 2008/794) Sch.8 para.29(da) (Sums to be disregarded in the calculation of income other than earnings—payments for persons temporarily in care of claimant)*

With effect from July 1, 2022, reg.99 of and Sch. to the Health and Care Act 2022 (Consequential and Related Amendments and Transitional Provisions) Regulations 2022 (SI 2022/634) amended para.29(da) by substituting the following for the text after "(da)": 5.143

"an integrated care board established under Chapter A3 of Part 2 of the National Health Service Act 2006;"

With effect from November 6, 2023, reg.28 of the Health and Care Act 2022 (Further Consequential Amendments) (No.2) Regulations 2023 (SI 2023/1071) amended para.29(db) by substituting "NHS England" for "the National Health Service Commissioning Board".

p.1546, *amendments to the Employment and Support Allowance Regulations 2008 (SI 2008/794) Sch.8 para.41 (Sums to be disregarded in the calculation of income other than earnings)*

With effect from January 1, 2022, reg.7(7)(b) of the Social Security (Income and Capital Disregards) (Amendment) Regulations 2021 (SI 2021/1405) amended para.41 by substituting the following for sub-para.(1A): 5.144

"(1A) Any—
(a) Grenfell Tower payment;
(b) child abuse payment;
(c) Windrush payment."

In addition, reg.7(7)(c) amended sub-paras (2) to (6) by inserting ", a child abuse payment or a Windrush payment" after "Grenfell Tower payment" in each place where those words occur. All of those payments are defined in reg.2(1).

See the entry for pp.684–685 (Income Support Regulations Sch.10 (capital to be disregarded) para.22) for some technical problems arising from the date of effect of these amendments. Because all the payments so far made from the approved historic institutional child abuse compensation schemes and from the Windrush Compensation Scheme have been in the nature of capital, the question of disregarding income has not yet arisen.

With effect from July 9, 2023, reg.3(7) of the Social Security (Income and Capital Disregards) (Amendment) Regulations 2023 (SI 2023/640) amended para.41(1A) by adding the following after head (c):

"(d) Post Office compensation payment."

Such payments are newly defined in reg.2(1), where there is now also an expanded definition of Grenfell Tower payments (see head (a)). With effect from the same date, the words substituted in sub-paras (2) to (6) have been further amended by substituting ", a Windrush payment, a Post Office compensation payment or a vaccine damage payment" for "or a Windrush payment". "Vaccine damage payment" is also newly defined in reg.2(1). See the entry for pp.684–685 on income support in this Supplement.

p.1549, *amendments to the Employment and Support Allowance Regulations 2008 (SI 2008/794) Sch.8 (Sums to be disregarded in the calculation of income other than earnings)*

5.145 With effect from July 26, 2021, art.16(2) of the Social Security (Scotland) Act 2018 (Disability Assistance, Young Carer Grants, Short-term Assistance and Winter Heating Assistance) (Consequential Provision and Modifications) Order 2021 (SI 2021/886) inserted the following after para.73:

"**74.** Any disability assistance given in accordance with regulations made section 31 of the Social Security (Scotland) Act 2018."

The first regulations made under s.31 of the 2018 Act were the Disability Assistance for Children and Young People (Scotland) Regulations 2021 (SSI 2021/174), also in effect from July 26, 2021, providing for the benefit known as a child disability payment. The regulations also authorise the payment of short-term assistance, to be disregarded under para.73. The Disability Assistance for Working Age People (Scotland) Regulations 2022 (SSI 2022/54), in effect from March 21, 2022, providing for the benefit known as adult disability payment, were also made under s.31, but the two potential elements (mobility component and daily living component) have been specifically covered by para.8 and para.11 from that date (see the entry for p.1540). Short-term assistance under reg.62 of the 2022 Regulations is disregarded under para.73.

With effect from November 19, 2023, art.19(8) of the Carer's Assistance (Carer Support Payment) (Scotland) Regulations 2023 (Consequential Amendments) Order 2023 (SI 2023/1218) inserted the following after para.74:

"**75.** Any amount of carer support payment that is in excess of the amount the claimant would receive if they had an entitlement to carer's allowance under section 70 of the Contributions and Benefits Act."

Carer support payment (CSP) is newly defined in reg.2(1) by reference to the Scottish legislation (see the entry for p.1211). Note that CSP in general counts as income and that the disregard is limited to any excess of the amount of the CSP over what the claimant would have been entitled to in carer's allowance under British legislation. That is in accordance with the Fiscal Framework Agreement governing the provision of devolved benefits in Scotland (see para.6.9 of the Explanatory Memorandum to SI 2023/1218). Initially, CSP is to be paid at the same rate as carer's allowance.

p.1554, *annotation to the Employment and Support Allowance Regulations 2008 (SI 2008/794) Sch.9 para.73 (Sums to be disregarded in the calculation of income other than earnings—Scottish short-term assistance)*

Provision for short-term assistance under s.36 of the Social Security (Scotland) Act 2018, thus falling within para.73, has been made by reg.42 of and Sch. to the Disability Assistance for Children and Young People (Scotland) Regulations 2021 (SSI 2021/174), with effect from July 26, 2021, and by reg.62 of and Sch. to the Disability Assistance for Working Age People (Scotland) Regulations 2022 (SSI 2022/54), with effect from March 21, 2022. 5.146

p.1556, *amendment to the Employment and Support Allowance Regulations 2008 (SI 2008/794) Sch.9 para.11(1)(a) (Capital to be disregarded)*

With effect from July 26, 2021, art.16(3) of the Social Security (Scotland) Act 2018 (Disability Assistance, Young Carer Grants, Short-term Assistance and Winter Heating Assistance) (Consequential Provision and Modifications) Order 2021 (SI 2021/886) substituted "72, 73 or 74" for "72 or 73". See the entry for p.1549 for the new para.74 of Sch.8. 5.147

p.1556, *amendment to the Employment and Support Allowance Regulations 2008 (SI 2008/794) Sch.9 para.11A (Capital to be disregarded—widowed parent's allowance)*

With effect from February 9, 2023, para.11(a) of the Schedule to the Bereavement Benefits (Remedial) Order 2023 (SI 2023/134) inserted the following after para.11: 5.148

"**11A.** Any payment of a widowed parent's allowance made pursuant to section 39A of the Contributions and Benefits Act (widowed parent's allowance)—

(a) to the survivor of a cohabiting partnership (within the meaning in section 39A(7) of the Contributions and Benefits Act) who is entitled to a widowed parent's allowance for a period before the Bereavement Benefits (Remedial) Order 2023 comes into force, and

(b) in respect of any period of time during the period ending with the day before the survivor makes the claim for a widowed parent's allowance,

but only for a period of 52 weeks from the date of receipt of the payment."

The legislation on widowed parent's allowance (WPA), abolished on April 5, 2017, and bereavement support payment (BSP) in operation for deaths after April 5, 2017, was declared incompatible with the ECHR by discriminating against children whose parents were cohabiting but not married to each other or in a civil partnership (see *Re McLaughlin's Application for Judicial Review* [2018] UKSC 48; [2018] 1 W.L.R. 4250 and *R. (Jackson) v Secretary of State for Work and Pensions* [2020] EWHC 183 (Admin); [2020] 1 W.L.R. 1441 in Vol.I of this series). The Remedial Order allows retrospective claims to be made for those benefits from August 30, 2018 onwards and accordingly for arrears of benefit to be paid if the conditions of entitlement are met. The new para.11A, and the amended para.60 on BSP, deal with the consequences of such payments on old style ESA entitlement, by providing for them to be disregarded as capital for 52 weeks from receipt. See the entry for p.682 on income support for the effect of the payment of arrears of WPA being in its nature a payment of income to be taken into account (subject to a £10 per week disregard under para.17(i) of Sch.8 to the ESA Regulations 2008) against entitlement in past periods (allowing revision and the creation of an overpayment) and the misleading state of para.7.15 of the Explanatory Memorandum to the Order.

pp.1558–1559, *amendments to the Employment and Support Allowance Regulations 2008 (SI 2008/794) Sch.9 para.27 (Capital to be disregarded)*

5.149 With effect from January 1, 2022, reg.7(8)(a) of the Social Security (Income and Capital Disregards) (Amendment) Regulations 2021 (SI 2021/1405) amended sub-para.(1A) by inserting ", child abuse payment, Windrush payment" after "Grenfell Tower payment" and amended sub-paras (2) to (6) by inserting ", a child abuse payment or a Windrush payment" after "Grenfell Tower payment" in each place where those words occur. All of those payments are defined in reg.2(1).

See the entry for pp.684–685 (Income Support Regulations Sch.10 (Capital to be disregarded) para.22) for some technical problems with the addition only with effect from January 1, 2022 of the disregards of payments from approved schemes providing compensation in respect of historic institutional child abuse in the UK and from the Windrush Compensation Scheme. All the schemes so far in existence provide payments in the nature of capital. That entry also contains information about the nature of the schemes involved, including the child abuse compensation schemes so far approved.

With effect from July 9, 2023, reg.3(8) of the Social Security (Income and Capital Disregards) (Amendment) Regulations 2023 (SI 2023/640) amended para.27(1A) by adding the following after "Windrush payment":

", Post Office compensation payment or vaccine damage payment."

Such payments are newly defined in reg.2(1), where there is now also an expanded definition of Grenfell Tower payments. With effect from the same date, the words substituted in sub-paras (2) to (6) have been further amended by substituting ", a Windrush payment, a Post Office compensation payment or a vaccine damage payment" for "or a Windrush payment". See the entry for pp.684–685 on income support in this Supplement.

With effect from August 30, 2023, reg.2(1)(f) of the Social Security (Infected Blood Capital Disregard) (Amendment) Regulations 2023 (SI 2023/894) amended para.27 by inserting the following after sub-para.(5):

"(5A) Any payment out of the estate of a person, which derives from a payment to meet the recommendation of the Infected Blood Inquiry in its interim report published on 29th July 2022 made under or by the Scottish Infected Blood Support Scheme or an approved blood scheme to the estate of the person, where the payment is made to the person's son, daughter, step-son or step-daughter."

See the entry for pp.684–685 on income support for the background.

With effect from October 27, 2023, reg.8(3)(c) of the Social Security (Habitual Residence and Past Presence, and Capital Disregards) (Amendment) Regulations 2023 (SI 2023/1144) amended para.27(1) and (7) by inserting ", the Victims of Overseas Terrorism Compensation Scheme" after "the National Emergencies Trust" in both places. That scheme is newly defined in reg.2(1). See the entry for pp.684–685 on income support for the background.

p.1559, *amendment to the Employment and Support Allowance Regulations 2008 (SI 2008/794) Sch.9 para.31 (Capital to be disregarded—payments in kind)*

With effect from January 1, 2022, reg.7(8)(b) of the Social Security (Income and Capital Disregards) (Amendment) Regulations 2021 (SI 2021/1405) amended para.31 by inserting ", a child abuse payment or a Windrush payment" after "Grenfell Tower payment". All of those payments are defined in reg.2(1). See also the entry for pp.684–685. 5.150

p.1563, *amendment to the Employment and Support Allowance Regulations 2008 (SI 2008/794) Sch.9 para.60 (Capital to be disregarded—bereavement support payment)*

With effect from February 9, 2023, para.11(b) of the Schedule to the Bereavement Benefits (Remedial) Order 2023 (SI 2023/134) amended para.60 by making the existing text sub-para.(1) and inserting the following: 5.151

"(2) Where bereavement support payment under section 30 of the Pensions Act 2014 is paid to the survivor of a cohabiting partnership (within the meaning in section 30(6B) of the Pensions Act 2014) in respect of a death occurring before the day the Bereavement Benefits (Remedial) Order 2023 comes into force, any amount of that payment which is—

(a) in respect of the rate set out in regulation 3(1) of the Bereavement Support Payment Regulations 2017, and

(b) paid as a lump sum for more than one monthly recurrence of the day of the month on which their cohabiting partner died,

but only for a period of 52 weeks from the date of receipt of the payment."

See the entry for p.682 on income support for the general background. The operation of this amendment is much more straightforward than that of the new para.111A on widowed parent's allowance. Although a payment of arrears of bereavement support payment (BSP) is in its nature a payment of income and attributable to the past period in respect of which it is due, the payment could not affect any entitlement to old style ESA in that past period because it would be disregarded entirely as income (Sch.8, para.68). The amount of the arrears would thus immediately metamorphose into capital, which would then be disregarded under para.60(2) subject to the 52 week limit.

pp.1565–1566, *annotation to the Employment and Support Allowance Regulations 2008 (SI 2008/794) Sch.9 (Capital to be disregarded)*

5.152 With effect from June 28, 2022 "Cost of living payments" under the Social Security (Additional Payments) Act 2022, both those to recipients of specified means-tested benefits and "disability" payments are not to be taken into account for any old style ESA purposes by virtue of s.8(b) of the Act. The same effect was achieved with effect from March 23, 2023 in relation to payments under the Social Security (Additional Payments) Act 2023 (s.8(b) of that Act). See Pt I of Vol.II for the text of both Acts.

p.1579, *amendment to the Employment and Support Allowance (Work-Related Activity) Regulations 2011 (SI 2011/1349) reg.2 (Interpretation)*

5.153 With effect from November 19, 2023, arts1(2) and 21(2) of the Carer's Assistance (Carer Support Payment) (Scotland) Regulations 2023 (Consequential Amendments) Order 2023 (SI 2023/1218) amended para. (1) by inserting ", "carer support payment"" after "carer's allowance".

p.1579, *amendment to the Employment and Support Allowance (Work-Related Activity) Regulations 2011 (SI 2011/1349) reg.3 (Requirement to undertake work-related activity)*

5.154 With effect from November 19, 2023, arts1(2) and 21(3) of the Carer's Assistance (Carer Support Payment) (Scotland) Regulations 2023 (Consequential Amendments) Order 2023 (SI 2023/1218) amended para. (2) by deleting the word "and" at the end of para,(2)(c) and inserting the new sub-paragraph "(ca) is not entitled to carer support payment; and".

PART V

UNIVERSAL CREDIT COMMENCEMENT ORDERS

p.1613, *amendment of the Welfare Reform Act 2012 (Commencement No.9 and Transitional and Transitory Provisions and Commencement No.8 and Savings and Transitional Provisions (Amendment)) Order 2013 (SI 2013/983) art.5A (Transitional provision where Secretary of State determines that claims for universal credit may not be made: effect on claims for employment and support allowance and jobseeker's allowance)*

With effect from March 30, 2022, art.5 and Sch.1 para.1(2) of the Welfare Reform Act 2012 (Commencement No. 34 and Commencement No. 9, 21, 23, 31 and 32 and Transitional and Transitory Provisions (Amendment)) Order 2022 (SI 2022/302) omitted the phrase "or article 4(11) of the Welfare Reform Act 2012 (Commencement No. 32 and Savings and Transitional Provisions) Order 2019 (no claims for universal credit by frontier workers)" in art.5A(1). But note also the next entry. **5.155**

p.1613, *revocation of the Welfare Reform Act 2012 (Commencement No.9 and Transitional and Transitory Provisions and Commencement No.8 and Savings and Transitional Provisions (Amendment)) Order 2013 (SI 2013/983) art.5A (Transitional provision where Secretary of State determines that claims for universal credit may not be made: effect on claims for employment and support allowance and jobseeker's allowance)*

With effect from July 25, 2022, reg.11 of, and Sch. para.2(2) to, the Universal Credit (Transitional Provisions) Amendment Regulations 2022 (SI 2022/752) revoked art.5A. **5.156**

p.1615, *amendments to the Welfare Reform Act 2012 (Commencement No. 9 and Transitional and Transitory Provisions and Commencement No. 8 and Savings and Transitional Provisions (Amendment)) Order 2013 (SI 2013/983) art.6 (Transitional provision: where the abolition of income-related employment and support allowance and income-based jobseeker's allowance is treated as not applying)*

With effect from March 30, 2022, art.5 and Sch.1 para.1(3) of the Welfare Reform Act 2012 (Commencement No. 34 and Commencement No. 9, 21, 23, 31 and 32 and Transitional and Transitory Provisions (Amendment)) Order 2022 (SI 2022/302) omitted the phrase "or article 4(11) of the Welfare Reform Act 2012 (Commencement No. 32 and Savings and Transitional Provisions) Order 2019 (no claims for universal credit by frontier workers)" in art.6(1)(e)(ii). **5.157**

With effect from July 25, 2022, reg.11 of, and Sch. para.2(3) to, the Universal Credit (Transitional Provisions) Amendment Regulations 2022 (SI 2022/752) omitted para.(1)(e)(ii) in art.6 and the "or" preceding it.

pp.1663–1664, *annotation to the Welfare Reform Act 2012 (Commencement No.20 and Transitional and Transitory Provisions and Commencement No.9 and Transitional and Transitory Provisions (Amendment)) Order 2014 (SI 2014/3094)*

Article 6 of SI 2014/3094 (Transitory provision: claims for housing benefit, income support or a tax credit) was revoked with effect from July **5.158**

25, 2022, by reg.11 of, and Sch. para.5 to, the Universal Credit (Transitional Provisions) Amendment Regulations 2022 (SI 2022/752).

pp.1670–1672, *amendment of the Welfare Reform Act 2012 (Commencement No.21 and Transitional and Transitory Provisions) Order 2015 (SI 2015/33) art.6 (Transitional provision: claims for housing benefit, income support or a tax credit)*

5.159 With effect from March 30, 2022, art.5 and Sch.1 para.2 of the Welfare Reform Act 2012 (Commencement No. 34 and Commencement No. 9, 21, 23, 31 and 32 and Transitional and Transitory Provisions (Amendment)) Order 2022 (SI 2022/302) omitted the phrase "or by virtue of article 4(11) of the Welfare Reform Act 2012 (Commencement No. 32 and Savings and Transitional Provisions) Order 2019" in art.6(11). But note also the next entry.

pp.1670–1672, *revocation of the Welfare Reform Act 2012 (Commencement No.21 and Transitional and Transitory Provisions) Order 2015 (SI 2015/33) art.6 (Transitional provision: claims for housing benefit, income support or a tax credit)*

5.160 With effect from July 25, 2022, reg.11 of, and Sch. para.3 to, the Universal Credit (Transitional Provisions) Amendment Regulations 2022 (SI 2022/752) revoked art.6.

p.1674, *annotation to the Welfare Reform Act 2012 (Commencement No.23 and Transitional and Transitory Provisions) Order 2015 (SI 2015/634) (General Note)*

5.161 Delete the letter "a" after "These" in line 3 of the General Note at para.5.116.

p.1681, *amendment of the Welfare Reform Act 2012 (Commencement No.23 and Transitional and Transitory Provisions) Order 2015 (SI 2015/634) art.7 (Transitional provision: claims for housing benefit, income support or a tax credit)*

5.162 With effect from March 30, 2022, art.5 and Sch.1 para.3 of the Welfare Reform Act 2012 (Commencement No. 34 and Commencement No. 9, 21, 23, 31 and 32 and Transitional and Transitory Provisions (Amendment)) Order 2022 (SI 2022/302) omitted the phrase "or by virtue of article 4(11) of the Welfare Reform Act 2012 (Commencement No. 32 and Savings and Transitional Provisions) Order 2019" in art.7(2). But note also the next entry.

pp.1681–1683, *revocation of the Welfare Reform Act 2012 (Commencement No.23 and Transitional and Transitory Provisions) Order 2015 (SI 2015/634) art.7 (Transitional provision: claims for housing benefit, income support or a tax credit)*

5.163 With effect from July 25, 2022, reg.11 of, and Sch. para.6 to, the Universal Credit (Transitional Provisions) Amendment Regulations 2022 (SI 2022/752) revoked art.7.

p.1732, *amendment to the Welfare Reform Act 2012 (Commencement No. 31 and Savings and Transitional Provisions and Commencement No. 21 and 23 and Transitional and Transitory Provisions (Amendment)) Order 2019 (SI 2019/37) art.2 (Interpretation)*

With effect from July 25, 2022, reg.11 of, and Sch. para.4(2) to, the Universal Credit (Transitional Provisions) Amendment Regulations 2022 (SI 2022/752) omitted "and article 8(2)(b)" in art.2(3). 5.164

p.1734, *amendment to the Welfare Reform Act 2012 (Commencement No. 31 and Savings and Transitional Provisions and Commencement No. 21 and 23 and Transitional and Transitory Provisions (Amendment)) Order 2019 (SI 2019/37) art.6 (Transitional provision: termination of awards of housing benefit)*

With effect from July 25, 2022, reg.11 of, and Sch. para.4(3) to, the Universal Credit (Transitional Provisions) Amendment Regulations 2022 (SI 2022/752) substituted "in regulation 2 of the Universal Credit (Transitional Provisions) Regulations 2014" for "respectively in sub-paragraphs (h) and (l) of article 7(11) of the No.23 Order" in art.6(4). 5.165

p.1734, *amendment to the Welfare Reform Act 2012 (Commencement No. 31 and Savings and Transitional Provisions and Commencement No. 21 and 23 and Transitional and Transitory Provisions (Amendment)) Order 2019 (SI 2019/37) art.7 (Transitional provision: application to housing benefit of the rules in universal credit for treatment of couples and polygamous marriages)*

With effect from July 25, 2022, reg.11 of, and Sch. para.4(4) to, the Universal Credit (Transitional Provisions) Amendment Regulations 2022 (SI 2022/752) substituted "regulation 6A of the Universal Credit (Transitional Provisions) Regulations 2014" for "article 6 of the No. 21 Order or article 7 of the No. 23 Order" in art.7(1)(a)(i). 5.166

p.1735, *amendment of the Welfare Reform Act 2012 (Commencement No. 31 and Savings and Transitional Provisions and Commencement No. 21 and 23 and Transitional and Transitory Provisions (Amendment)) Order 2019 (SI 2019/37) art.8 (Transitional provision: where restrictions on claims for universal credit are in place)*

With effect from March 30, 2022, art.5 and Sch.1 para.4 of the Welfare Reform Act 2012 (Commencement No. 34 and Commencement No. 9, 21, 23, 31 and 32 and Transitional and Transitory Provisions (Amendment)) Order 2022 (SI 2022/302) inserted "or" at the end of art.8(1)(a) and omitted both art.8(1)(c) and the "or" preceding it. But note also the next entry. 5.167

pp.1735–1736, *revocation of the Welfare Reform Act 2012 (Commencement No. 31 and Savings and Transitional Provisions and Commencement No. 21 and 23 and Transitional and Transitory Provisions (Amendment)) Order 2019 (SI 2019/37) art.8 (Transitional provision: where restrictions on claims for universal credit are in place)*

With effect from July 25, 2022, reg.11 of, and Sch. para.4(5) to, the Universal Credit (Transitional Provisions) Amendment Regulations 2022 (SI 2022/752) revoked art.8. 5.168

p.1738, *amendment of the Welfare Reform Act 2012 (Commencement No. 32 and Savings and Transitional Provisions) Order 2019 (SI 2019/167) art.1 (Citation and interpretation)*

5.169 With effect from March 30, 2022, art.4(3) of the Welfare Reform Act 2012 (Commencement No. 34 and Commencement No. 9, 21, 23, 31 and 32 and Transitional and Transitory Provisions (Amendment)) Order 2022 (SI 2022/302) omitted art.1(3).

p.1742, *amendment of the Welfare Reform Act 2012 (Commencement No. 32 and Savings and Transitional Provisions) Order 2019 (SI 2019/167) art.4 (Appointed day—coming into force of universal credit provisions and abolition of income-related employment and support allowance and income-based jobseeker's allowance: persons resident outside Great Britain)*

5.170 With effect from March 30, 2022, art.4(4) of the Welfare Reform Act 2012 (Commencement No. 34 and Commencement No. 9, 21, 23, 31 and 32 and Transitional and Transitory Provisions (Amendment)) Order 2022 (SI 2022/302) omitted art.4(11).

p.1745, *insertion of new Commencement Order at para.5.188 onwards.*

The Welfare Reform Act 2012 (Commencement No. 34 and Commencement No. 9, 21, 23, 31 and 32 and Transitional and Transitory Provisions (Amendment)) Order 2022

SI 2022/302 (C.12)

The Secretary of State makes the following Order in exercise of the powers conferred by section 150(3) and (4)(a), (b)(i) and (c) of the Welfare Reform Act 2012:

Arrangement Of Articles

Citation

5.188 **1.** This Order may be cited as the Welfare Reform Act 2012 (Commencement No. 34 and Commencement No. 9, 21, 23, 31 and 32 and Transitional and Transitory Provisions (Amendment)) Order 2022.

Interpretation

2. In this Order— 5.189

"the No. 9 Order" means the Welfare Reform Act 2012 (Commencement No. 9 and Transitional and Transitory Provisions and Commencement No. 8 and Savings and Transitional Provisions (Amendment)) Order 2013;
"the No. 32 Order" means the Welfare Reform Act 2012 (Commencement No. 32 and Savings and Transitional Provisions) Order 2019.

Full commencement of universal credit

3. 30th March 2022 ("the appointed day") is the appointed day for the coming into force of the provisions of the Welfare Reform Act 2012 listed in Schedule 2 (universal credit provisions coming into force in relation to certain claims and awards) to the No. 9 Order, in so far as they are not already in force. 5.190

Removal of restriction preventing frontier workers from claiming universal credit

4.—(1) The amendments of the No. 32 Order set out in paragraphs (3) and (4) have effect from the appointed day. 5.191
(2) The No. 32 Order is amended as follows.
(3) In article 1 (citation and interpretation), omit paragraph (3).
(4) In article 4 (appointed day—coming into force of universal credit provisions and abolition of income-related employment and support allowance and income-based jobseeker's allowance: persons resident outside Great Britain), omit paragraph (11).

Consequential amendments

5. The consequential amendments set out in the Schedule have effect from the appointed day. 5.192

Article 5

SCHEDULE

Consequential Amendments

1.—(1) The No. 9 Order is amended as follows. 5.193
(2) In article 5A (transitional provision where Secretary of State determines that claims for universal credit may not be made: effect on claims for employment and support allowance and jobseeker's allowance), in paragraph (1) omit "or article 4(11) of the Welfare Reform Act 2012 (Commencement No. 32 and Savings and Transitional Provisions) Order 2019 (no claims for universal credit by frontier workers)".
(3) In article 6 (transitional provision: where the abolition of income-related employment and support allowance and income-based jobseeker's allowance is treated as not applying), in paragraph (1)(e)(ii) omit "or article 4(11) of the Welfare Reform Act 2012 (Commencement No. 32 and Savings and Transitional Provisions) Order 2019 (no claims for universal credit by frontier workers)".

2.—(1) The Welfare Reform Act 2012 (Commencement No. 21 and Transitional and Transitory Provisions) Order 2015 is amended as follows.

(2) In article 6 (transitional provision: claims for housing benefit, income support or a tax credit), in paragraph (11) omit "or by virtue of article 4(11) of the Welfare Reform Act 2012 (Commencement No. 32 and Savings and Transitional Provisions) Order 2019".

3.—(1) The Welfare Reform Act 2012 (Commencement No. 23 and Transitional and Transitory Provisions) Order 2015 is amended as follows.

(2) In article 7 (transitional provision: claims for housing benefit, income support or a tax credit), in paragraph (2) omit "or by virtue of article 4(11) of the Welfare Reform Act 2012 (Commencement No. 32 and Savings and Transitional Provisions) Order 2019".

4.—(1) The Welfare Reform Act 2012 (Commencement No. 31 and Savings and Transitional Provisions and Commencement No. 21 and 23 and Transitional and Transitory Provisions (Amendment)) Order 2019 is amended as follows.

(2) In article 8 (transitional provision: where restrictions on claims for universal credit are in place)—

(a) at the end of paragraph (1)(a) insert "or"; and

(b) omit subparagraph (1)(c) and the "or" preceding it.

PART VI

TRANSITIONAL, SAVINGS AND MODIFICATIONS PROVISIONS

PART VII

IMMIGRATION STATUS AND THE RIGHT TO RESIDE

p.1793, *annotation to the Immigration (European Economic Area) Regulations 2016 (SI 2016/1052) (General Note—EEA nationals and their family members with pre-settled status)*

In *R. (Fratila) v SSWP* [2021] UKSC 53; [2022] P.T.S.R. 448 the Supreme Court allowed the appeal by the Secretary of State against a decision of the Court of Appeal which had found the domestic right to reside test unlawfully discriminatory contrary to art.18 of the TFEU for treating EU nationals with pre-settled status differently to UK nationals. The judgment of the Court of Appeal had become unsustainable following the decision of the CJEU, in *CG v Department for Communities* (C-709/20) [2021] 1 W.L.R. 5919, that such a provision is not contrary to art.18 of the TFEU, or Directive 2004/38. 5.171

However, what the Supreme Court elected not to address (since it was a new point, which would have required new evidence) was the implications for the domestic Regulations of what had also been said in *CG* about the Charter of Fundamental Rights of the European Union (the Charter). The Court of Justice had stated:

> "[93] . . . [Where] a Union citizen resides legally, on the basis of national law, in the territory of a Member State other than that of which he or she is a national, the national authorities empowered to grant social assistance are required to check that a refusal to grant such benefits based on that legislation does not expose that citizen, and the children for which he or she is responsible, to an actual and current risk of violation of their fundamental rights, as enshrined in Articles 1, 7 and 24 of the Charter. Where that citizen does not have any resources to provide for his or her own needs and those of his or her children and is isolated, those authorities must ensure that, in the event of a refusal to grant social assistance, that citizen may nevertheless live with his or her children in dignified conditions. In the context of that examination, those authorities may take into account all means of assistance provided for by national law, from which the citizen concerned and her children are actually entitled to benefit."

Important questions arising from *CG* are:

- whether the Charter has any ongoing application, since the end of the transition period in December 2020, for EU nationals resident in the UK on the basis of pre-settled status; and
- what if any substantive or procedural requirements are imposed on the Secretary of State by the obligation to 'check' that Charter rights will not be breached.

In *SSWP v AT (UC)* [2022] UKUT 330 (AAC) (December 12, 2022), a three-judge panel addressed those questions. It dismissed the Secretary of State's appeal against a decision that a destitute parent who was also a victim of domestic violence was entitled to UC. Though her only right of residence was on the basis of her pre-settled status, the refusal of UC would breach her Charter rights. The panel decided that by virtue of the Withdrawal Agreement, the Charter does indeed continue to apply following the end of the transition period where a person is residing in the UK with pre-settled status. It also decided that *CG* does indeed impose a requirement on the Secretary of State (and by extension the FTT) to check in individual cases that there is no breach of Charter rights. It gives guidance on how that check should be conducted. The Secretary of State made a second appeal to the Court of Appeal; the Court of Appeal unanimously dismissed it: [2023] EWCA Civ 1307 (November 8, 2023). On February 7, 2024, the Supreme Court refused the Secretary of State permission to appeal any further.

Several further questions about the operation of the domestic regulations still await definitive judicial determination.

First, is the domestic right to reside test unlawful in its application to people with PSS (or at least subject to disapplication in individual cases) on the basis that:

- there is a right to equal treatment under Art.23 Withdrawal Agreement for all those with pre-settled status, given the way that the UK implemented Art.18 WA? The argument runs that grants of pre-settled status constitute 'residence on the basis of this agreement' within the meaning of Art.23, which triggers an equal treatment right and distinguishes the position from pre-WA cases given that claimants such as Fratila and CG were not residing 'on the basis of' Directive 2004/38/EC, and as such had no equal treatment right. In a homelessness eligibility context, this argument has been accepted at county court level in one case, *Hynek v Islington* K40CL206 (HHJ Saunders, 24 May 2024), and rejected (obiter) in another, *C v Oldham* [2024] EWCC 1 (22 May 2024). It has been rejected by the High Court in *Fertre v Vale of White Horse District Council* [2024] EWHC 1754 (KB) (8 July 2024). No application for permission to appeal was made in either County Court case; a PTA application is pending with the Court of Appeal in *Fertre*.
- it discriminates unlawfully against EEA nationals in comparison with third country nationals, contrary to Art.14 ECHR and s.3 HRA 1998?
- it is ultra vires s.4(5) WRA 2012?

Those arguments were raised in *AT* at the Upper Tribunal stage, but never required determination, because of AT's success on her 'dignity' point.

Second, what kind of residence is necessary to be within the scope of Art.10 WA? Neither the decided *AT* 'dignity' basis for disapplying the domestic right to reside test in individual cases, nor the potential 'equal treatment' argument for setting the domestic right to reside test aside altogether, could apply where a person is outside the scope of the Citizens Rights part of the WA. Relatedly, is a grant of EUSS leave conclusive evidence that a person is in the scope of the WA, or does there exist a category of persons granted PSS or SS who have domestic law rights only? Art.10(1)(a) applies to 'Union citizens who exercised their right to reside in the United Kingdom in accordance with Union law before the end of the transition period and continue to reside there thereafter'. It might be suggested that the requirement to 'continue to reside there thereafter' requires residence in accordance with EU law (ie exercising a positive EU law right of residence) at least until, and perhaps even beyond, the end of the transition period. See *Secretary of State for the Home Department v Abdullah* [2024] UKUT 66 (IAC), e.g. [68]. However, the contrary – and, it is suggested, better – argument is that once there has been a pre-transition period of residence, continuous factual residence thereafter is sufficient. The 'continuous residence in accordance with EU law' position would be textually strained, and hard to reconcile with analysis of analogous wording in *Secretary of State for Work and Pensions v Gubeladze* [2019] UKSC 31, [2019] AC 885, [76]-[92]. It would also generate great uncertainty: it would mean that there was indeed a class of persons with PSS or SS who have domestic law rights only, but nobody would know who they were until a dispute arose about their rights, potentially years or even decades later.

Third, can people with leave under the EUSS who are neither EU citizens nor their family members (i.e. EFTA state members) rely on the *AT* principle of protection against a breach of the right to dignity?

p.1798, *annotation to the Immigration (European Economic Area) Regulations 2016 (SI 2016/1052) (General Note—Overview)*

In *FN v SSWP (UC)* [2022] UKUT 77 (AAC), Judge Ward records an example of the evidential problems which can arise for claimants seeking to demonstrate a right of residence under these Regulations: 5.172

> "[4] . . . On the (erroneous) basis that it was necessary to demonstrate that the husband was a 'qualified person', the claimant, by her social worker, had informed the DWP that she and her daughter had fled the family home due to domestic violence and that the claimant had obtained a non-molestation order against her husband. His name, date of birth, national insurance number and details of his then current and previous employers were provided to the DWP, who were asked to contact them, as although the social worker had had some contact with the husband, he had been uncooperative in providing the information necessary.
>
> [5] On mandatory reconsideration, the DWP upheld the original decision saying that the Data Protection Act prevented them from providing the information relating to the husband that had been requested.
>
> [6] On appeal, the DWP indicated they could provide information if in response to a tribunal or court order. The claimant's representatives emailed the FtT on 6 February 2020 explaining this and asking for an order to be made. The email did not on its face identify that the claimant and her husband were estranged due to domestic violence and that may have contributed to why the District Tribunal Judge (DTJ) refused the application, saying, put shortly, that the husband should get them and send them to the DWP and that the FtT would only become involved if the parties had exhausted their own efforts. This prompted a follow-up email on 16 March 2020 explaining the background of domestic abuse and providing a copy of the non-molestation order. The DTJ remained adamant, indicating that the order did not prevent the claimant from contacting her husband through solicitors and until there was evidence that an attempt had been made to do so and had been unsuccessful the decision remained unaltered. Subsequently, on 26 May 2020 a registrar did make an order for the evidence to be supplied by DWP but it was not, despite the representative sending a follow-up email. The case was then listed as a paper hearing, without further notification to the claimant or her representative, and decided [adversely to the claimant]."

As the facts of *FN* indicate, problems are particularly likely where a right of residence may derive from a family member from whom the claimant is estranged. A Tribunal's failure to exercise the FTT's inquisitorial duty to seek evidence of a right of residence, including by establishing details about a relative's identity and possible rights of residence, may constitute an error of law. See, e.g. *AS v SSWP (UC)* [2018] UKUT 260 (AAC); *ZB v SSWP* CIS/468/2017 unreported April 25, 2019 ([21]: "an award of benefit is not a prize rewarding only the most adept"), and *PM v SSWP (IS)* [2014] UKUT 474 (AAC). It is clear from those decisions that the Tribunal can direct the Secretary of State to provide information she holds about an estranged family member. Further, while the Secretary of State appears to consider that due to her data protection obligations she can provide information about such a third party only if ordered to do so by a court or tribunal, there is room for doubt about whether that view is in fact correct, as noted in *ZB* at [19].

pp.1826–1829, *annotation to the Immigration (European Economic Area) Regulations 2016 (SI 2016/1052) reg.4 ("Worker", "self-employed person", "self-sufficient person" and "student")*

Self-sufficient persons

5.173 In *VI v Commissioners for HMRC* (C–247/20 O) (September 30, 2021) at [56]–[64], AG Hogan's opinion described a "fundamental question" in that case as "probably" being whether free access to the NHS satisfies the requirement to have CSI, and lamented that the UK Government had not made any submissions about that issue. However, the AG did not express an opinion on the answer, and advised the Court not to do so either.

Surprisingly, the court's judgment ([2022] EUECJ C-247/20 [2022] 1 W.L.R. 2902) did give an answer, and the answer was that free access to the NHS does satisfy the CSI requirement:

> "[68] In the present case, it is apparent from the documents before the Court that VI and her son were affiliated during the period in question, namely from 1 May 2006 to 20 August 2006, to the United Kingdom's public sickness insurance system offered free of charge by the National Health Service.
>
> [69] In that regard, it must be recalled that, although the host Member State may, subject to compliance with the principle of proportionality, make affiliation to its public sickness insurance system of an economically inactive Union citizen, residing in its territory on the basis of Article 7(1)(b) of Directive 2004/38, subject to conditions intended to ensure that that citizen does not become an unreasonable burden on the public finances of that Member State, such as the conclusion or maintaining, by that citizen, of comprehensive private sickness insurance enabling the reimbursement to that Member State of the health expenses it has incurred for that citizen's benefit, or the payment, by that citizen, of a contribution to that Member State's public sickness insurance system (judgment of 15 July 2021, *A (Public health care)* (C–535/19) EU:C:2021:595 at [59]), the fact remains that, once a Union citizen is affiliated to such a public sickness insurance system in the host Member State, he or she has comprehensive sickness insurance within the meaning of Article 7(1)(b).

> [70] Furthermore, in a situation, such as that in the main proceedings, in which the economically inactive Union citizen at issue is a child, one of whose parents, a third-country national, has worked and was subject to tax in the host State during the period at issue, it would be disproportionate to deny that child and the parent who is his or her primary carer a right of residence, under Article 7(1)(b) of Directive 2004/38, on the sole ground that, during that period, they were affiliated free of charge to the public sickness insurance system of that State. It cannot be considered that that affiliation free of charge constitutes, in such circumstances, an unreasonable burden on the public finances of that State."

That decision is obviously inconsistent with a long line of domestic authority, cited in the main volume commentary: for example *Ahmad v Secretary of State for the Home Department* [2014] EWCA Civ 988; *FK (Kenya) v Secretary of State for the Home Department* [2010] EWCA Civ 1302; *W (China) and X (China) v Secretary of State for the Home Department* [2006] EWCA Civ 1494 and *VP v SSWP (JSA)* [2014] UKUT 32 (AAC) and *SSWP v GS (PC) (European Union law: free movement)* [2016] UKUT 394 (AAC); [2017] AACR 7.

VI falls within the scope of art.89 of the Withdrawal Agreement (as a CJEU reference made before the end of the Transition Period). As such, it so far appears to be uncontentious that *VI* is directly binding, in relation to periods before December 31, 2020, and that the old domestic authorities should no longer be followed. See *WH v Powys County Council and SSWP* [2022] UKUT 203 (AAC), para.3.

In *SSWP v WV (UC)* [2023] UKUT 112 (AAC) the Upper Tribunal shows one way in which *VI* may have practical application for a person reliant on benefit income. A Belgian national was a carer for his disabled wife who received income-related ESA. The amount of social assistance decreased due to the claimant's presence in the household: the loss of some premiums, and the inclusion of carer's allowance (which is social security not social assistance), more than offset the increase to couple rates. UTJ Ward decided the claimant had a right to reside at that time as a self-sufficient person. Until *VI*, the claimant's argument would have foundered on the comprehensive sickness insurance requirement, but *VI* meant that the claimant met it. When the couple then claimed universal credit, the relatively modest additional cost which awarding that benefit to the couple rather than just awarding it to his UK national spouse as a single person (and only for the 23 months until the claimant qualified for settled status), along with the cost of similar such claims which would also now fall to be allowed, was not an "unreasonable burden" on the UK social assistance system. Consequently, the claimant did not lose his right to reside as a self-sufficient person, and was therefore entitled to a joint award of universal credit.

pp.1889–1891, *modification to the Immigration (European Economic Area) Regulations 2016 reg.16 (SI 2016/1052) (Derivative right to reside)*

As explained in the main text, the 2016 Regulations continue to apply as saved and modified by the Immigration and Social Security Co-ordination (EU Withdrawal) Act 2020 (Consequential, Saving, Transitional and Transitory Provisions) (EU Exit) Regulations 2020 (SI 2020/1309). 5.174

With effect from February 2, 2023, by amending the 2020 Regulations, reg.5 of the Immigration (Restrictions on Employment etc.) (Amendment) (EU Exit) Regulations 2023 (SI 2023/12) makes additional modifications to the saved reg.16 of the 2016 Regulations:

- in paragraph (3)(b), after "a worker" insert "or a self-employed person";
- in paragraph (7), after sub-paragraph (c), insert— "(d) "selfemployed person" does not include a person treated as a selfemployed person under regulation 6(4);"

p.1890, *erratum—Immigration (European Economic Area) Regulations 2016 (SI 2016/1052), reg.16 (Derivative right to reside)*

5.175 There is an error in the first of the two parallel versions of reg.16(12) (i.e. the version stated as now applying to those with pre-settled status). The words "unless that decision" should be deleted from that version.

pp.1891–1892, *annotation to the Immigration (European Economic Area) Regulations 2016 (SI 2016/1052) reg.16 (Derivative right to reside)*

Primary carers of self-sufficient children

5.176 The main volume General Note discusses a pending reference to the CJEU in *Bajratari v Secretary of State for the Home Department* [2017] NICA 74. The Court's judgment (C-93/18) was delivered on October 2, 2019 ([2020] 1 W.L.R. 2327). It agreed with AG Szpunar and held (at [53]), that a Union citizen minor can meet the requirement to have sufficient resources not to become an unreasonable burden on the social assistance system of the host Member State during his period of residence, "despite his resources being derived from income obtained from the unlawful employment of his parent, a third-country national without a residence card and work permit".

pp.1892–1893, *annotation to the Immigration (European Economic Area) Regulations 2016 (SI 2016/1052) reg.16 (Derivative right to reside)*

Primary carer of children of migrant workers in education

5.177 The main volume General Note asserts: "Where primary carers are also jobseekers (in the EU sense of that term), they cannot be denied social assistance on the basis of the derogation in art.24(2) of the Citizenship Directive". There is now domestic authority for that proposition: *Sandwell MBC v KK and SSWP (HB)* [2022] UKUT 123 (AAC).

p.1893, *annotation to the Immigration (European Economic Area) Regulations 2016 reg.16 (SI 2016/1052) (Derivative right to reside)*

Primary carers of previously self-sufficient children with a right of permanent residence

5.178 Regulation 16(2) and reg.16(5) address the position of carers of *Chen* children and of *Zambrano* children respectively (*Zhu and Chen v Home Secretary* (C-200/02); *Zambrano v Office national de l'emploi (ONEm)* (C-34/09)). It might be thought that both groups are in essentially the same position, insofar as the carer's right of residence does not generate a right to reside triggering social security entitlement. However, the difference is that the *Chen* child may eventually acquire a right of permanent residence under Directive 2004/38 art.16. The situation of primary carers of *previously* self-sufficient children who *now* have a right of permanent residence is not recognised in domestic law. But in *FE v HMRC (CHB*) [2022] UKUT 4 (AAC) the Upper Tribunal decides that it is necessary to treat that category differently, and recognise their right of access to social assistance.

INDEX

LEGAL TAXONOMY

FROM SWEET & MAXWELL

This index has been prepared using Sweet and Maxwell's Legal Taxonomy. Main index entries conform to keywords provided by the Legal Taxonomy except where references to specific documents or non-standard terms (denoted by quotation marks) have been included. These keywords provide a means of identifying similar concepts in other Sweet & Maxwell publications and online services to which keywords from the Legal Taxonomy have been applied. Readers may find some minor differences between terms used in the text and those which appear in the index. Suggestions to *sweetandmaxwell.taxonomy@thomson.com*.

(All references are to paragraph number)

ISBN 978-0-331-24094-8
PIBN 11039450

Volume complete

SCHRIFTEN

DER

PHYSIKALISCH-ÖKONOMISC GESELLSCHAFT

ZU

KÖNIGSBERG i. Pr.

SECHSUNDZWANZIGSTER JAHRGANG.

1885.

KÖNIGSBERG.

IN COMMISSION BEI KOCH & REIMER.

1886.

Von der physikalisch-ökonomischen Gesellschaft herausgegeben (in Commission in der Buchhandlung von Koch & Reimer, Königsberg) sind erschienen:

I. Beiträge zur Naturkunde Preussens:

1) **Mayr**, Dr. G., Die Ameisen des baltisch. Bernsteins. (5 Taf.) gr. 4°. 1868. 6 Mk.

2) **Heer**, Prof. Dr., Miocene baltische Flora. (30 Taf.) gr. 4°. 1869. 30 Mk.

3) **Steinhardt**, E. Th. G., Die bis jetzt in preuss. Geschieben gefundenen Trilobiten. (6 Taf.) gr. 4°. 1874. 6 Mk.

4) **Lentz**, Prof. Dr., Katalog der Preussischen Käfer. Neu bearbeitet. gr. 4°. 1879. 2 Mk. 50 Pf.

5) **Klebs**, Richard, Dr., Der Bernsteinschmuck der Steinzeit. (12 Taf.) gr. 4°. 1882. 10 Mk.

II. Schriften der physikalisch-ökonomischen Gesellschaft: Jahrgang I—VII (1860—66), IX bis XXVI. (1868—85) à 6 Mk. Jahrgang VIII. (1867) Pr. 15 Mk.

Davon sind als Separatabdrücke erschienen:

Albrecht, Dr. P., Gedächtnissrede auf Prof. Dr. G. Zaddach. 50 Pf.

Berendt, Prof. Dr. G., Marine Diluvialfauna in Westpreussen. (1 Taf.) 1866. 50 Pf.

— — Nachtrag zur marinen Diluvialfauna in Westpreussen. (1 Taf.) 1867. 50 Pf.

— — Marine Diluvialfauna in Ostpreussen und 2. Nachtrag zur Diluvialfauna Westpreussens. (1 Taf.) 1874. 50 Pf.

— — Vorbemerkungen zur geologischen Karte der Provinz Preussen. (1 Tafel.) 1866. 60 Pf.

— — Die Bernsteinablagerungen und ihre Gewinnung. (1 Taf.) 1866. 1 Mk.

— — Erläuterungen zur geologischen Karte Westsamlands. 1. Theil: Verbreitung und Lagerung der Tertiärformationen. (1 Taf.) 1866. 50 Pf.

— — Beitrag zur Lagerung und Verbreitung des Tertiärgebirges im Bereiche der Provinz Preussen. (1 Tafel.) 1867. 75 Pf.

— — Geologie des kurischen Haffs und seiner Umgebung. (6 Taf.) 1868. 6 Mk.

— — Pommerellische Gesichtsurnen. (6 Taf.) 1872. 3 Mk.

— — Altpreuss. Küchenabfälle am frischen Haff. (13 Holzschn.) 1875. 40 Pf.

— — Notizen a. d. russischem Grenzgebiete nördlich der Memel. 1876. 25 Pf.

Berendt u. Troost, Ueber ein Bernsteinvorkommen bei Cap Sable in Maryland. 1870. 30 Pf.

Blümner, Prof. Dr., Ueber Schliemanns Ausgrabungen in Troja. 1876. 60 Pf.

Caspary, Prof. Dr. R., Bericht über den botanischen Verein der Provinz Preussen für 1875 1,30 Mk.; für 1876 2 Mk.; für 1877, 1878, 1879, 1880, 1881, 1882, 1883, 1884 à 1,50 Mk.

Cleve, Prof. P. T. u. **Jentzsch**, Dr. A., Ueber einige diluviale und alluviale Diatomeenschichten Norddeutschlands. 1882. 2 Mk.

Dewitz, Dr. H., Alterthumsfunde in Westpreussen. (4 Holzschn.) 1874. 30 Pf.

— — Ueber ostpreussische Silur-Cephalopoden. (1 Taf.) 1879. 1 Mk.

Dorn, Prof. Dr. E., Die Station zur Messung von Erdtemperaturen zu Königsberg (1 Taf.) 1872. 1,50 Mk.

— — Beobachtungen vorgenannter Station in den Jahren 1873, 1874, 1875, 1876, 1877, 1878 à Jahrgang 60 Pf.

Elditt, H., Caryoborus (Bruchus) gonagra Fbr. und seine Entwickelung in der Cassia. 1860. 75 Pf.

Franz, Dr. J., Festrede aus Veranlassung von Bessel's hundertjährigem Geburtstag. 1884. 1 Mk.

Grenzenberg, Die Makrolepidopteren d. Provinz Preussen. 1869. 1,30 Mk.

— — 1. Nachtrag dazu. 1876. 30 Pf.

SCHRIFTEN

DER

PHYSIKALISCH-ÖKONOMISCHEN GESELLSCHAFT

ZU

KÖNIGSBERG i. Pr.

SECHSUNDZWANZIGSTER JAHRGANG.

1885.

KÖNIGSBERG.

IN COMMISSION BEI KOCH & REIMER.

1886.

Inhalt des XXVI. Jahrganges.

[illegible]

Sitzungsberichte.

Verzeichniss der Mitglieder

der

physikalisch-ökonomischen Gesellschaft

am 1. Juli 1885*).

Protector der Gesellschaft.

Herr Ober-Präsident der Provinz Ostpreussen Dr. v. Schlieckmann. 6. 4. 82.

Vorstand.

1. Sanitätsrath Dr. med. Schiefferdecker, Präsident. 15. 12. 48.
2. Medicinalrath Professor Dr. Moeller, Director. 8. 1. 47.
3. Stadtrath Lottermoser, Secretair. 17. 6. 64.
4. Commerzienrath Weller, Cassen-Curator. 29. 6. 60.
5. Hofapotheker Hagen, Rendant. 30. 6. 51.
6. Dr. Otto Tischler, Bibliothekar und auswärtiger Secretair. 1. 12. 65.

Ehrenmitglieder.

1. Herr v. Dechen, Wirkl. Geh. Rath, Oberberghauptmann, Dr., Excellenz, Bonn. 5. 3. 80.
2. „ Friederici, Director a. D. 6. 4. 32.
3. „ v. Helmersen, General, Excellenz, St. Petersburg, Wassili-Ostrow 7. Linie No. 2. 5. 4. 78.
4. „ W. Hensche, Dr., Medicinalrath, Stadtältester. 24. 10. 23.
5. „ v. Horn, Dr., Wirklicher Geh. Rath, Ober-Präsident a. D., Excellenz, Berlin W, Landgrafenstrasse 11. 4. 6. 69.
6. „ Emile Levasseur, Membre de l'Institut in Paris. 7. 6. 78.
7. „ Neumann, Dr., Professor, Geh. Regierungsrath. 16. 2. 27.
8. „ v. Rénard, Dr., Geheimrath in Moskau. 19. 12. 62.
9. „ v. Scherzer, Dr., Ministerialrath, K. K. Generalconsul in Genua. 4. 6. 80.
10. „ Torell, Dr., Professor in Stockholm. 3. 12. 80.
11. „ Virchow, Dr., Professor, Geheimrath in Berlin. 3. 12. 80.

*) Die beigesetzten Zahlen bezeichnen Tag und Jahr der Aufnahme.

Ordentliche Mitglieder.

1. Herr Albrecht, Dr., Dir. d. Prov.-Gewerbeschule a. D. 16. 6. 43.
2. „ Andersch, A., Comm.-R. 21. 12. 49.
3. „ Andersch, Consul, Medenau. 5. 6. 44.
4. „ Aschenheim, Dr., Prassnicken. 4. 6. 68.
5. „ Baenitz, C., Dr., Lehrer. 1. 12. 65.
6. „ v. Batocki-Bledau. 4. 12. 68.
7. „ Baumgart, Dr., Professor. 6. 12. 73.
8. „ Baumgarten, Dr., Prof. 1. 12. 76.
9. „ Becker, Apothenbesitzer. 3. 12. 80.
10. „ Becker, M., Commerz.-Rath. 7. 12. 82.
11. „ Becker, J., Kaufmann. 7. 12. 82.
12. „ Beer, Rechtsanwalt. 1. 6. 82.
13. „ v. Behr, Oberlehrer, Prof. 12. 6. 46.
14. „ Benecke, Dr. med., Prof. 7. 6. 67.
15. „ Berent, Dr., 7. 12. 77.
16. „ Bernecker, Bankdirector. 4. 6. 80.
17. „ Bertholdt, Dr. med., Prof. 4. 12. 68.
18. „ Besch, Oberlehrer. 6. 6. 73.
19. „ Bessel-Lorck, Königl. Landes-Bauinspektor. 6. 12. 83.
20. „ Bezzenberger, Dr., Prof. 6. 12. 83.
21. „ Bielitz, Major. 4. 12. 74.
22. „ Bienko, Partikulier. 2. 6. 60.
23. „ Bieske, Reg.-Bauführer. 6. 12. 83.
24. „ Blochmann, Dr. 4. 6. 80.
25. „ Böhm, Oberamtmann. 1. 7. 59.
26. „ Bohn, Dr. med., Professor. 21. 12. 60.
27. „ Bon, Buchhändl. u. Rittergutsbesitzer. 1. 6. 66.
28. „ Born, Apothekenbesitzer. 7. 12. 82.
29. „ Braun, Candidat. 3. 12. 80.
30. „ Bujack, Dr., Oberlehrer. 13. 12. 61.
31. „ Burchard, Geheimrath. 2. 6. 76.
32. „ Burow, Dr., Professor. 27. 6. 62.
33. „ Caspary, J., Dr., Professor. 3. 12. 80.
34. „ Caspary, R., Dr., Professor. 1. 7. 59.
35. „ Cholevius, L., Dr., Oberlehrer. 5.6.68.
36. „ Chun, Dr., Professor. 6. 12. 83.
37. „ Cohn, J., Commerzienrath. 3. 12. 69.
38. „ Conditt, B., Kaufmann. 19. 12. 62.
39. „ Conrad, Rittergutsbesitzer in Görken p. Trömpau. 7. 6. 78.
40. „ Coranda, Dr. 4. 12. 84.
41. „ Crüger, Posthalter u. Kaufm. 1.12.81.
42. „ Cynthius, Kreisphysikus, Sanitätsrath, Dr. 5. 6. 74.
43. „ Czwalina, Dr., Gymnasial-Lehrer. 3. 12. 69.
44. „ Davidsohn, M., Kaufmann. 7. 12. 82.
45. „ Devens, Polizei-Präsident. 1. 12. 76.
46. „ Döbbelin, Zahnarzt. 7. 6. 72.
47. Herr Dohrn, Dr., Prof., Geh. Medicinalrath. 6. 12. 83.
48. „ Douglas, Rentier. 28. 6. 61.
49. „ Ehlert, Otto, Kaufmann. 17. 6. 64.
50. „ Eichert, Apothekenbesitzer. 6. 6. 73.
51. „ Ellendt, Dr., Oberlehrer, Professor. 6. 12. 67.
52. „ Erdmann, Dr. med. 1. 6. 82.
53. „ Falkenheim, Dr. med. 4. 6. 77.
54. „ Falkson, Dr. med. 1. 7. 59.
55. „ Falkson, R., Dr., Privatdocent. 7. 12. 82.
56. „ Fischer, Ober-Landesgerichts-Rath. 21. 12. 60.
57. „ Fleischer, Rittmeister. 5. 6. 84.
58. „ Franz, Dr. 7. 12. 77.
59. „ Friedländer, Dr., Prof., Geheimrath. 23. 12. 59.
60. „ Fröhlich, Dr. 7. 6. 72.
61. „ Fuhrmann, Oberlehrer. 13. 12. 61.
62. „ Gädeke, H., Geh. Commerzienrath. 16. 12. 36.
63. „ Gädeke, Rittergutsbesitzer, Powayen. 6. 6. 79.
64. „ Gamm, Fabrikant. 2. 6. 76.
65. „ Gebauhr jun., Kaufm. 7. 12. 77.
66. „ Glede, Hauptm., Amtsrath. 29. 6. 49.
67. „ v. d. Goltz, Freiherr, Dr., Professor. 26. 6. 63.
68. „ Graf, Stadtrath. 1. 12. 81.
69. „ v. Gramatzki, Landesdir. 5. 6. 84.
70. „ v. Gramatzki, Rentier. 21. 12. 60.
71. „ Grünhagen, Dr., Professor. 1. 12. 81.
72. „ Grun, Baurath. 7. 6. 78.
73. „ Grunewald, Fabrikant chirurgischer Instrumente. 3. 12. 80.
74. „ Grunewald, Zimmermstr. 7. 12. 77.
75. „ Gutzeit, Buchhändler. 5. 12. 79.
76. „ Guthzeit, Dr. med. 5. 6. 74.
77. „ Haarbrücker, F., Kaufm. 6. 12. 72.
78. „ Häbler, Gen.-Landsch.-R. 6. 12. 64.
79. „ Hagen, Stadtrath. 6. 6. 79.
80. „ Hagen, Hofapotheker. 30. 6. 51.
81. „ Hagen, Justizrath. 6. 12. 83.
82. „ Hay, Dr. med., Privatdocent. 1. 6. 59.
83. „ Hay, A., Partikulier 1. 12. 81.
84. „ Heilmann, Rentier. 5. 6. 65.
85. „ Hennig, Dr. 6. 12. 78.
86. „ Herbig, Apothekenbesitzer. 4. 6. 80.
87. „ Hermann, Dr., Professor. 4. 12. 84.
88. „ Hertz, Dr. med. 7. 12. 82.
89. „ Heydeck, Professor. 6. 12. 73.
90. „ Heumann, Fabrikdirector. 6. 6. 79.

91. Herr Hieber, Dr. med. 10. 6. 70.
92. " Hirsch, Dr. med., Sanit.-R. 2. 7. 52.
93. " Hirschfeld, Dr., Professor. 6. 12. 78.
94. " Hirschfeld, Dr. 6. 6. 79.
95. " Hoffmann, Bürgermeister. 6. 12. 72.
96. " Holldack, Kaufmann. 11. 6. 85.
97. " Jacobson, Julius, Geh. Medicinalrath, Dr. med., Prof. 1. 7. 59.
98. " Jaffé, Dr., Professor. 6. 12. 73.
99. " Jentzsch, Dr., Privatdocent. 4. 6. 75.
100. " Jereslaw, Lion, Kaufm. 1. 12. 76.
101. " Ihlo, Dr. 3. 12. 75.
102. " Ipsen, Stadtrath. 6. 6. 79.
103. " Kade, Prem.-Lieutenant. 4. 12. 84.
104. " Kahle, Apothekenbesitzer. 3. 12. 75.
105. " Karow, akadem. Maler. 6. 12. 83.
106. " Kemke, Kaufmann. 21. 12. 60.
107. " Klebs, Dr., Geologe an der K. geolog. Landesanstalt in Berlin. 4. 6. 77.
108. " Kleiber, Prof., Director. 6. 12. 72.
109. " Klien, Dr. 4. 6. 77.
110. " Kluge, Generalagent. 7. 12. 77.
111. " Knobbe, Dr., Oberlehrer. 15. 12. 43.
112. " Koch, Buchhändler. 3. 12. 75.
113. " Kowalewski, Apotheker. 6. 12. 67.
114. " Krah, Landes-Baurath. 2. 6. 76.
115. " Krahmer, Justizrath. 21. 12. 60.
116. " Kratz, Director der Ostpr. Südbahn. 4. 6. 77.
117. " Krause, Amtsgerichtsrath. 3. 12. 69.
118. " Kreiss, Generalsecretair, Hauptm. 4. 6. 75.
119. " Krohne, Kaufmann. 5. 12. 79.
120. " Krüger, Director der Ostpr. Südbahn. 11. 6. 85.
121. " Künow, Conservator. 4. 12. 74.
122. " Kunze, Apothekenbesitzer. 7. 12. 77.
123. " Landsberg, Dr. 6. 12. 83.
124. " Langendorff, Dr., Prof. 4. 12. 84.
125. " Laser, Dr. med. 21. 12. 60.
126. " Lehmann, Dr. med. 24. 12. 59.
127. " v. Leibitz, Hauptmann. 5. 6. 84.
128. " Lentz, Dr., Professor. 1. 7. 59.
129. " Leo, Stadtrath. 7. 12. 77.
130. " Liedtke, Prediger. 5. 6. 74.
131. " Lindemann, Dr., Prof. 6. 12. 83.
132. " Lobach, Partikulier. 19. 12. 62.
133. " Lohmeyer, Dr., Prof. 3. 12. 69.
134. " Lossen, Dr., Professor. 17. 6. 78.
135. " Lottermoser, Stadtrath. 17. 6. 64.
136. " Luchhau, Dr. 4. 6. 80.
137. " Ludwich, Dr., Professor. 6. 6. 79.
138. " Luther, Dr., Professor. 25. 6. 47.
139. " Magnus, Dr. med., Sanitäts-Rath. 4. 7. 51.
140. " Magnus, E., Dr. med. 5. 6. 68.
141. " Magnus, L., Kaufmann. 3. 12. 80.
142. Herr Marek, Dr., Professor. 6. 12. 78.
143. " Maschke, Dr. med. 10. 6. 70.
144. " Meier, Ivan, Kaufmann. 3. 12. 69.
145. " Merguet, Oberlehrer. 5. 6. 74.
146. " Meschede, Dr., Director. 6. 12. 73.
147. " Meyer, O., Kaufmann. 11. 6. 85.
148. " Meyer, Dr. 3. 12. 80.
149. " Michels, Chefredacteur. 1. 6. 82.
150. " Michelson, Dr. 6. 12. 83.
151. " Milentz, Apothekenbes. 23. 12. 59.
152. " Mischpeter, Dr., Realschullehrer. 7. 6. 72.
153. " Möller, Dr., Professor, Medicinalrath. 8. 1. 47.
154. " v. Morstein, Oberlehrer, Dr., 4. 12. 74.
155. " Motherby, Rittergutsbes. in Arnsberg p. Creuzburg. 6. 6. 79.
156. " Müller, Rector. 7. 6. 67.
157. " Müller, Secretair der Kunstakademie. 1. 12. 76.
158. " Münster, Dr. med., Prof. 4. 6. 80.
159. " Müttrich, Dr. med. 21. 12. 60.
160. " Musack, Fabrikbesitzer. 4. 12. 74.
161. " Nath, Dr., Reg.- und Medicinalrath. 11. 6. 85.
162. " Naumann, Apotheker. 24. 6. 57.
163. " Naunyn, Dr., Professor. 4. 12. 74.
164. " Neumann, Dr., Prof., Medicinalrath. 23. 12. 59.
165. " Nötling, Dr. 3. 12. 80.
166. " Olck, Oberlehrer. 7. 6. 72.
167. " v. Olfers, Dr., Rittergutsbesitzer in Metgethen. 7. 6. 72.
168. " Oltersdorf, Kaufmann. 4. 6. 80.
169. " Packheiser, Apothekenbes. 7. 6. 72.
170. " Pape, Dr., Professor. 6. 12. 78.
171. " Passarge, Oberlandesgerichts-Rath. 13. 12. 61.
172. " Patze, Apotheker und Stadtrath. 29. 6. 38.
173. " Peise, Corpsapotheker. 7. 6. 78.
174. " Peter, Kaufmann. 7. 12. 77.
175. " Peters, Oberlehrer. 4. 6. 77.
176. " Petruschky, Dr., Professor, Ober-Stabsarzt. 1. 12. 65.
177. " Pincus, Medicinalrath, Dr., Professor. 4. 12. 68.
178. " Prin jun., Kaufmann. 6. 12. 78.
179. " Rauscher, Oberlandesgerichts-Rath. 7. 12. 82.
180. " Richter, Dr., Prof., Departements-Thierarzt. 13. 12. 61.
181. " Ritthausen, Dr., Prof. 23. 12. 59.
182. " Rosenfeld, H., Kaufm. 7. 6. 78.
183. " Rupp, Dr. med. 6. 12. 72.
184. " Saalschütz, Dr., Professor. 6. 6. 73.
185. " Samter, Dr. med. 29. 6. 60.

186. Herr Samuel, Dr. med., Prof. 23. 12. 57.
187. „ Samuelson, Dr. 7. 6. 83.
188. „ Sanio, Realschullehrer. 1. 6. 82.
189. „ Sauter, Dr., Director a. D. der höheren Töchterschule. 16. 12. 53.
190. „ Schauinsland, Dr. 6. 12. 83.
191. „ Schellong, Dr. 4. 12. 84.
192. „ Schepke, Kaufmann. 7. 12. 77.
193. „ Schiefferdecker, Realschul-Direct. a. D. 17. 12. 41.
194. „ Schiefferdecker, Dr., Sanitätsrath. 15. 12. 48.
195. „ Schimmelpfennig, Kaufm. 6. 6. 79.
196. „ Schlesinger, Dr. med. 19. 12. 62.
197. „ Schmidt, Dr., Director d. städtischen Realschule. 23. 12. 59.
198. „ Schmidt, E., Rentier. 1. 6. 82.
199. „ Schneider, Dr. med., Prof. 4. 6. 69.
200. „ Schönborn, Geheimer Medicinalrath. Dr., Professor. 4. 12. 74.
201. „ Schreiber, Dr., Professor. 3. 12. 80.
202. „ Schröder, Dr. 3. 12. 80.
203. „ Schröter, Dr. med. 23. 12. 59.
204. „ Schröter, Commerzienrath. 7. 12. 77.
205. „ Schüssler, Apothekenbes. 1. 12. 81.
206. „ Schuhmacher, Dr. med. 4. 12. 68.
207. „ Schwanbeck, Dr. med. 6. 12. 72.
208. „ Schwenkner, Apotheker. 1. 12. 81.
209. „ Selke, Oberbürgermeister. 3. 12. 75.
210. „ Seydel, Dr. 6. 6. 79.
211. „ Seydler, Apotheker. 4. 12. 74.
212. „ Simon, Geheimer Commerzienrath. 7. 12. 77.
213. „ Simon, Dr. jur., Kaufm. 7. 12. 77.
214. „ Simony, Civilingenieur. 1. 6. 66.
215. „ Simsky, C., chirurg. Instrumentenmacher. 1. 6. 66.
216. „ Sommer, Dr., Prof. 23. 12. 59.
217. Herr Sommerfeld, Dr. med. 7. 12. 52.
218. „ Sotteck, Dr. med., Sanitätsrath. 17. 12. 52.
219. „ Spirgatis, Dr., Professor. 17. 12. 56.
220. „ Spriegel, Kaufmann. 7. 12. 77.
221. „ v. Steinberg-Skirbs, Dr., Generalarzt z. D. 2. 6. 76.
222. „ Stellter, O., Justizrath. 21. 12. 60.
223. „ Stetter, Dr. med., Privatdocent. 7. 12. 82.
224. „ Symanski, Landgerichtsrath. 9. 6. 71.
225. „ Theodor, Stadtrath a. D. 7. 12. 77.
226. „ Tieffenbach, Gymnasial-Lehrer. 6. 12. 73.
227. „ Tischler, Dr. 1. 12. 65.
228. „ Tischler, Gutsbesitzer, Losgehnen. 5. 6. 74.
229. „ Unterberger, Dr. 7. 6. 83.
230. „ Vogelgesang, Dr. 5. 6. 74.
231. „ Walter, Dr., Professor. 3. 12. 75.
232. „ Warkentin, Stadtrath. 6. 12. 73.
233. „ Wedthoff, Ober-Reg.-Rath. 9. 6. 71.
234. „ Weger, Dr., Sanitätsrath. 14. 6. 39.
235. „ Weller, Commerzienrath. 29. 6. 60.
236. „ Weller, L., Kaufmann. 4. 6. 80.
237. „ Wendland, Director der Ostpr. Südbahn. 6. 12. 72.
238. „ Wiedemann, Landesrath. 4. 6. 80.
239. „ Wiehler, F., Kaufmann. 7. 12. 77.
240. „ Wilutzky, Ad., Hof-Lithograph. 10. 6. 70.
241. „ Winbeck, Feuerwerks-Hauptmann. 4. 6. 80.
242. „ Wyszomierski, Dr., Russ. Consul. 5. 6. 68.
243. „ Zacharias, Dr. med., Sanitätsrath. 2. 7. 52.
244. „ Zimmermann, Apotheker. 4. 6. 80.

Auswärtige Mitglieder.

1. Herr Albrecht, Dr., Professor in Brüssel. 1. 6. 77.
2. Alterthums-Gesellschaft in Elbing.
3. Herr Anger, Dr., Director, Graudenz. 4. 12. 74.
4. „ Arppe, Ad. Ed., Prof. der Chemie in Helsingfors. 19. 12. 62.
5. „ v. Baehr, Rittergutsbes., Gr. Ramsau p. Wartenburg. 6. 6. 79.
6. „ Baxendell, Jos., Secretair der naturforsch. Gesellschaft zu Manchester. 19. 12. 62.
7. Herr Benefeldt, Rittergutsbes., Quoossen p. Gallingen. 5. 6. 84.
8. „ Berendt, Dr., Professor, Berlin NW, Dorotheenstr. No. 61. 1. 6. 66.
9. „ Behrens, Alb., Rittergutsbesitzer auf Seemen bei Gilgenburg. 19. 12. 62.
10. „ Berent, Rittergutsbesitzer auf Arnau. 1. 12. 65.
11. „ Beyrich, Dr., Prof., Geh. Bergrath in Berlin, Franz. Str. 29. 6. 12. 67.
12. „ Blell, Rentier, Lichterfelde b. Berlin. 5. 12. 79.

13. Herr Böhm, Rittergutsbesitzer, Glaubitten per Korschen. 7. 6. 72.
14. " v. Bönigk, Freiherr, Major a. D., Postdirector in Demmin in Pommern. 1. 12. 76.
15. " Börnstein, Dr., Prof. in Berlin NW, Platz am neuen Thor 1 A. 6. 12. 72.
16. " v. Bohlschwing, Rittergutsbesitzer, Schönbruch, Kreis Friedland, Ostpr. 6. 12. 78.
17. " Bresgott, Kreisbaumstr., Mohrungen. 5. 12. 79.
18. " Brischke, G., Hauptlehrer a. D., Langfuhr bei Danzig. 29. 6. 60.
19. " v. Bronsart, Rittergutsbesitzer auf Schettnienen per Braunsberg. 21. 12. 60.
20. " Bruhn, Oscar, Kaufmann, Insterburg. 5. 12. 79.
21. " Brusina Spiridion, Vorsteher der zoolog. Sammlungen am naturhistor. Museum in Agram. 4. 12. 74.
22. " Buchinger, Dr., Prof. in Strassburg. 6. 12. 67.
23. " Buhse, Fr., Dr., Director des naturforsch. Vereins zu Riga. 9. 6. 71.
24. " de Caligny, Anatole, Marquis, Château de Sailly pr. Fontenay St. Père. 7. 2. 66.
25. " v. Cesati, Vincenz, Baron in Neapel. 19. 12. 62.
26. " Claassen, Rittergutsbes., Warnikam p. Ludwigsort. 3. 12. 80.
27. Conradi'sche Stiftung in Jenkau. 18. 12. 63.
28. Copernikus-Verein in Thorn. 7. 12. 66.
29. Herr Copes, F. S., Dr., New-Orleans. 6. 12. 72.
30. " Crüger, Dr. philos. in Tilsit. 3. 12. 69.
31. " Czudnowitz, Dr., Insterburg. 1.12.81.
32. " Daemers de Cachard, L., Professor in Brüssel. 7. 6. 78.
33. " Danehl, Rector in Zinten. 7. 6. 78.
34. " Dittrich, Lehr. in Wormditt. 6.12.78.
35. " zu Dohna-Schlodien, Graf, Obermarschall, Burggraf, Excell., p.Lauk. 21. 12. 61.
36. " Dorn, Dr., Professor in Darmstadt, Bessunger Wilhelmsstrasse No. 10. 7. 6. 72.
37. " Dohrn, C. A., Dr., Präsident des entomologischen Vereins in Stettin. 29. 6. 60.
38. " Donath, Rittergutsbes., Ruttkowitz per Soldau. 7. 12. 77.
39. " Dorien, Dr. med., Sanitätsrath, Lyck. 19. 12. 62.
40. Herr Dorr, Dr., Oberlehrer, Elbing. 6.12.78.
41. " Dromtra, Ottom., Kaufmann in Allenstein. 13. 12. 61.
42. " Drope, Pächter in Grünlinde p. Grünhayn. 7. 12. 77.
43. " Duchartre, P., Professor der Botanik und Mitglied der Akademie zu Paris. 19. 12. 62.
44. " Eckert, Landschaftsrath, Czerwonken per Lyck. 7. 6. 78.
45. " Erchenbrecher, Dr., Salzbergwerk Neu-Stassfurt p. Stassfurt. 5. 12. 79.
46. " Erikson, Director des Königl. Gartens in Haga bei Stockholm. 4. 12. 67.
47. " Fleck, Justizrath, Conitz. 4. 12. 74.
48. " Flügel, Felix, Dr., Leipzig. 18. 12. 63.
49. " Frankenstein, Rittergutsbes., Wiese p. Reichenbach, Kreis Pr. Holland. 6. 12. 78.
50. " Frisch, A., Oberamtmann auf Stanaitschen. 16. 12. 64.
51. " Fröhlich, Lehrer in Thorn. 3. 12. 75.
52. " Fröhlich, Rendant in Culm. 7. 12. 77.
53. " Geinitz, Dr., Prof., Geh. Hofrath, Dresden. 1. 12. 76.
54. " Genthe, Herm., Dr., Director, Hamburg. 10. 6. 70.
55. " Gerstaeker, Dr., Prof., Greifswald. 19. 12. 62.
56. " Giesebrecht, Dr., Prof., München. 1. 6. 59.
57. " v. Glasow, Lieutenant, Lokehnen per Wolittnick. 3. 12. 80.
58. " Goltz, Dr., Prof., Strassburg. 4. 12. 68.
59. " Gandoger in Arnas (Rône) per Villa franche France. 7. 12. 82.
60. " v. Gossler, Minister der Geistlichen, Unterrichts- u. Medizinal-Angelegenheiten, Excellenz, Berlin. 4. 6. 69.
61. " Gottheil, E., i. New-Orleans. 6.12.72.
62. " Greiff, Wirkl. Geh. Rath, Excellenz, Berlin, Genthinerstr. 13. 1. 12. 71.
63. " Grentzenberg, Kaufmann, Danzig. 21. 12. 60.
64. " Grenda, Landgerichtsrath in Lyck. 2. 6. 76.
65. " Grewingk, Dr., Professor in Dorpat. 16. 12. 64.
66. " Güllich, Forstkassenrendant, Braunsberg. 7. 12. 77.
67. " Gürich, Regierungsrath in Breslau. 6. 12. 72.
68. " Hagedorn, Dr., Mohrungen. 11.6.85.
69. " Hagen, Dr., Professor, Cambridge, Amerika. 15. 12. 43.
70. " Hagen, A., Stadtrath in Berlin. 2. 7. 52.

130. Herr Nagel, R., Dr., Professor, Oberlehrer in Elbing. 18. 12. 63.
131. Naturwissenschaftlicher Verein in Bromberg. 7. 6. 67.
132. Herr Neumann, Amtsgerichtsrath in Mohrungen. 5. 12. 79.
133. „ Oelrich, Rittergutsbesitzer, Bialutten p. Illowo, Kr. Neidenburg. 19. 12. 62.
134. „ Oudemans, A. J. A., Professor in Amsterdam. 17. 6. 64.
135. „ Pavenstädt, Rittergutsbesitzer in Weitzdorf p. Rastenburg. 1. 12. 76.
136. „ Pehlke, Kaufm., Bartenstein. 4. 6. 80.
137. „ Peter, Dr., Conservator in München, Türkenstrasse 51 III. 7. 6. 83.
138. „ Podlech, Gutsbesitzer in Mollehnen. 5. 6. 74.
139. „ Pöpke, Bohrunternehmer, Anklam. 5. 6. 84.
140. „ Praetorius, Dr., Professor, Oberlehrer in Conitz. 4. 12. 74.
141. „ Prang, Apotheker, Bartenstein. 5. 12. 79.
142. „ Preuschoff, Propst in Tolkemit. 18. 12. 63.
143. „ v. Prinz, Baron, Rittergutsbesitzer auf Plinken p. Germau. 1. 12. 76.
144. „ v. Pulszki, F., Ritter, Director des Königl. Ungar. National-Museums in Budapest. 1. 12. 76.
145. „ v. Puttkamer, Minister des Innern, Berlin, Excellenz. 1. 12. 71.
146. „ Puttlich, Rittergutsbesitzer, Sandlack p. Bartenstein. 5. 6. 84.
147. „ Radde, Dr., Direct. des Kaukasischen Museums in Tiflis. 5. 6. 74.
148. „ Rast, Gutsbesitzer, Schippenbeil. 9. 6. 71.
149. „ v. Recklinghausen, Professor in Strassburg. 17. 6. 64.
150. „ Reissner, E., Dr., Prof. in Dorpat. 9. 12. 62.
151. „ v. Rode, Gutsbesitzer, Babbeln bei Gr. Karpowen. 4. 6. 80.
152. „ v. Rode, Landschaftsrath, Rauschken per Usdau. 2. 6. 76.
153. „ Romer, Dr., Prof., Grosswardein. 4. 12. 72.
154. „ Rosenbohm, Apotheker, Graudenz. 5. 12. 79.
155. „ Rumler, Oberlehrer, Gumbinnen. 4. 6. 77.
156. „ Rygh, Dr., Professor in Christiana. 7. 12. 77.
157. „ v. Sadowski, Dr. in Krakau. 1. 12. 76.
158. „ Salomon, Pfarrer in Enzuhnen per Trakehnen. 13. 12. 61.
159. Herr v. Sanden, Rittergutsbesitzer, Raudonatschen p. Kraupischken. 3. 12. 80.
160. „ v. Saucken, Rittergutsbesitzer auf Tarputschen p. Insterburg. 16. 12. 64.
161. „ Scharlok, J., Apotheker in Graudenz. 7. 6. 67.
162. „ Schenk, Dr., Professor, Geh. Hofrath in Leipzig. 27. 6. 62.
163. „ Schiefferdecker, Dr. med., Prosector in Göttingen. 6. 12. 72.
164. „ Schlicht, Kreisschulinspector in Rössel. 16. 2. 78.
165. „ Schliemann, H., Dr. in Athen. 4. 6. 77.
166. „ Schreiber, Dr., Lehrer a. d. Königl. technischen Lehranstalten in Chemnitz. 1. 12. 76.
167. „ Schuhmann, Landgerichtsrath in Braunsberg. 6. 12. 73.
168. „ Seidlitz, Dr., Charlottenthal p. Ludwigsort. 4. 6. 77.
169. „ de Selys-Longchamp, E., Baron, Akademiker in Lüttich. 2. 6. 60.
170. „ Semper, O., in Altona. 1. 12. 76.
171. „ Senoner, Adolph, in Wien. 27. 6. 62.
172. „ Seydler, Fr., Rector in Braunsberg. 29. 6. 60.
173. „ Siegfried, Rittergutsbes. auf Skandlack per Barten. 28. 6. 61.
174. „ Siegfried, Rittergutsbes. auf Carben bei Heiligenbeil. 6. 12. 72.
175. „ Siegfried, Rittergutsbes. auf Pluttwinnen p. Laptau. 6. 12. 78.
176. „ Simson, E., Dr., Präsident d. Reichsgerichts, Wirkl. Geh. Rath, Excell., Leipzig. 4. 7. 51.
177. „ Skrzezka, Dr., Prof., Geh. Medicinalrath in Berlin. 28. 6. 61.
178. „ Sohnke, Dr., Prof., Jena. 16. 12. 64.
179. „ Sonntag, Ad., Dr. med., Kreisphysikus, Sanitätsrath in Allenstein. 13. 12. 61.
180. „ Steinhardt, Dr., Oberlehrer i. Elbing. 6. 12. 72.
181. „ Steppuhn, Rittergutsbes., Liekeim per Bartenstein. 7. 12. 77.
182. „ Stöckel, Generalsecretair, Stobingen per Insterburg. 3. 12. 75.
183. „ Strüvy, Rittergutsbesitzer, Worlack per Landsberg, Ostpr. 1. 12. 76.
184. „ v. Tettau, Freiherr, Rittergutsbes. auf Tolks p. Bartenstein. 21. 12. 60.
185. „ Thiel, Dr., Sanitätsrath, Kreisphysik. in Bartenstein. 6. 12. 72.
186. „ Todaro, A., Dr., Professor, Senator, Director des botanischen Gartens in Palermo. 1. 12. 76.

187. Herr Treichel, Rittergutsbesitzer, Hoch-Paleschken p. Alt-Kischau. 2. 6. 76.
188. „ Tulasne, L. R., Akademiker in Paris. 9. 12. 62.
189. „ Vigouroux, Schulinspect. in Wartenburg. 4. 12. 74.
190. „ Vogt, C., Professor, Genf. 1. 12. 71.
191. „ Voigdt, Dr., Pfarrer a. D., Rittergutsbesitzer auf Dombrowken. 11. 6. 41.
192. „ Wahlberg, P. E., best. Secretair der Akademie der Wissenschaften zu Stockholm. 19. 12. 62.
193. „ Wahlstedt, L. J., Dr. in Lund. 17. 6. 64.
194. „ Waldeyer, Dr., Professor in Berlin. 19. 12. 62.
195. „ Wangerin, A., Dr., Prof. in Halle a. d. S., Burgstr. 27. 6. 12. 73.
196. Herr Wartmann, Dr., Prof. in St. Gallen. 17. 6. 64.
197. „ Waterhouse, G. R., Esq. Dir. d. Brit. Mus. in London. 18. 12. 63.
198. „ Weiss, Apotheker in Caymen per Wulfshöfen. 6. 12. 72.
199. „ Werdermann, Rittergutsbesitzer auf Corjeiten p. Germau. 7. 6. 78.
200. „ Wiebe, Geh. Regierungs-Baurath in Berlin. 19. 12. 62.
201. „ Worsaae, Kammerherr u. Museumsdirector in Copenhagen. 7. 12. 77.
202. „ v. Zander, Dr., Landrath in Heinrichswalde. 7. 6. 78.
203. „ Ziehe, Dr., prakt. Arzt in Gerdauen. 6. 12. 78.
204. „ Zinger, Lehrer, Pr. Holland. 5. 6. 84.

Bericht

über die 23. Versammlung des preussischen botanischen Vereins zu Memel am 7. October 1884.

Vom Vorstande.

In Memel fand diese Versammlung dem 1883 in Marienburg gefassten Beschlusse gemäss unter gefälliger Geschäftsführung des Herrn Apotheker E. Berger statt. Die schon am 6. Oktober mit dem Insterburg-Memel'er Eisenbahnzuge um $3^1/_2$ Uhr Nachmittags in Memel eingetroffenen Theilnehmer unternahmen sofort unter Führung des Herrn Berger und Herrn Gymnasiallehrer Kühnemann eine Exkursion nach dem Sandkruge auf der kurischen Nehrung, die bis zur Meeresküste von der Haffseite überschritten wurde. Es wurden als bemerkenswerth Silene parviflora Pers. und Gypsophila paniculata, hier höchst verbreitet, gefunden. Der Abend vereinigte die Angekommenen und viele Memeler zu geselliger Unterhaltung im Gasthause von Karl Fischer.

Daselbst eröffnete der Vorsitzende, Professor Rob. Caspary, den 7. Oktober Morgens $8^1/_2$ Uhr die Sitzung des Vereins. Mit warmem Dank theilt er mit, dass auch für das Jahr 1. April 1884/85 von dem hohen Landtage der Provinz Ostpreussen die gewöhnliche Unterstützung von 900 Mk. geneigtest dem Verein bewilligt sei und dass durch ein Geschenk von 630 Mk. eines Mitgliedes es möglich geworden, eine grössere Thätigkeit als je zuvor zu entwickeln, indem 3 Sendboten Sommer über ausgesendet seien: Dr. Lange zur ergänzenden Erforschung der Kreise Danzig, Neustadt, Kartaus und Berent, Stud. Alfred Lemcke der Kreise Danzig und Neustadt, Stud. Emil Knoblauch zur Untersuchung des Kreises Memel. Die Zahl der Vereinsmitglieder habe die frühere Höhe im letzten Jahre wenig überschritten.*) Mit Bedauern wird mitgetheilt, dass der zweite Vorsitzende, Professor Dr. Prätorius, durch Krankheit in seiner Familie, Conrektor Seydler, erster Schriftführer, wie auch Scharlok-Graudenz durch ihre eigene leidende Gesundheit an der Theilnahme an

*) Eine Beilage bringt ein Verzeichniss der Mitglieder, die im Juni 1885 an Zahl 416 betrug.

der Versammlung verhindert seien. Wie gewöhnlich werden dann zuerst die Sendungen der Abwesenden der Versammlung vorgelegt. Dr. Bethke verliest folgende

Mittheilung des Herrn Conrektor Fr. Seydler.

Ich sammelte 1. im Kreise Braunsberg den 17. Mai auf einem Abhange im sog. Hohlen Grunde zw. Lisettenhof und der Wecklitzmühle bei Braunsberg **Vicia lathyroides** zahlreich; Saxifraga granulata mit Uredo Saxifragarum und Capsella Bursa pastoris mit Uredo candida auf allen Theilen; 22. Mai auf sumpfigem Torfboden, zw. der Kl. Amtsmühle und Regitten **Carex caespitosa**, Stellaria uliginosa; 30. Mai an einem Graben auf der bei Braunsberg zw. der Mehlsack'er Chaussee und der Sekundärbahn belegenen Wiese verschiedene Formen von **Carex acuta**, darunter solche mit 6 bis 8 kurzen gedrängt untereinander stehenden weiblichen Aehren, die sämmtlich von langen Deckblättern unterstützt sind (vielleicht Carex personata Fr.?); 3. Juni an der Wecklitzmühle bei Braunsberg Heleocharis uniglumis, unter der grossen Linde bei Huntenberg **Potentilla collina**, auf trockenen Anhöhen bei Huntenberg Botrychium Lunaria; 4. Juni auf dem Eisenbahndamme zw. Einsiedel und dem Braunsberg'er Bahnhofe Medicago lupulina var. stipularis Wallr., Senecio vulgaris + vernalis; 13. Juni am rechten Passargeufer auf der Aue bei Braunsberg Hieracium praealtum var. **Bauhini** mit fast glattem bräunlichem Stengel, schwach gewimperten lanzettförmigen Blättern und blühenden Ausläufern; 15. Juni auf der Wiese zw. der Sekundärbahn und der Mehlsack'er Chaussee Polygonum Bistorta mit 2 Aehren, auf hartem Lehmacker zw. der Kl. Amtsmühle und Regitten **Ranunculus arvensis**; 21. Juni bei Julienhöhe zw. Huntenberg und Kälberhaus **Achyrophorus maculatus** mit 3 und mehreren Köpfen; 24. Juni auf dem Eisenbahndamme zw. dem Empfangsgebäude und dem Güterschuppen die hier von mir bis jetzt noch nicht gesehene ***Matricaria discoides*** und die doppeltästigen sterilen Stengel von Equisetum arvense; 27. Juni zw. Grafenmorgen und dem Braunsberg'er Bahnhofe Valeriana sambucifolia, Senecio erraticus, Bromus racemosus; 29. Juni auf sumpfiger Wiese an der Haltestelle Tiedmannsdorf Aira caespitosa L., **var altissima** Lmk. und **Carex caespitosa**; im Bruche zw. genannter Haltestelle und Kl. Tromp **Scheuchzeria palustris**, Juncus filiformis, **Carex limosa**; in der Waldschlucht am linken Ufer der Passarge zw. Kl. Tromp und Pettelkau die eben im Aufblühen begriffene ***Astrantia maior*** in reichlicher Anzahl. Es ist dies der dritte von mir im Kreise Braunsberg entdeckte Standort dieser schönsten der bei uns wildwachsenden Umbelliferen. Nicht minder gross war meine Freude, als ich an der Mündung der Schlucht am hohen Passargeufer die von mir schon lange gesuchte ***Onobrychis viciifolia*** zahlreich und in schönster Blüthe fand. Schon Stadtrath Patze hatte diese Pflanze am 15. Juni 1872 an derselben Stelle beobachtet und mir damals darüber Folgendes brieflich mitgetheilt: „Ich habe am hohen Passargeufer an pflanzenreicher Stelle die Onobrychis viciifolia Scop. in reichlicher Menge gefunden und bin überzeugt, dass diese Pflanze durch Kultur nicht hierher gekommen sein kann, weil die bebauten Ländereien vom Standorte durch waldige Höhen getrennt sind und ziemlich fern liegen und auch nicht durch die Passarge der Same angeschwemmt sein kann, da der höchste Wasserstand derselben, wohl nie den Standort erreicht." Diese Ansicht theile auch ich und um so mehr, da der langjährige Verwalter von Gr. Tromp: Herr Hartung, von dem Anbau dieser Pflanze nie etwas gehört hat. Ich glaube daher mit Sicherheit annehmen zu können, dass diese schöne Papilionacee hier wildwachsend vorkommt. An derselben Stelle unter Onobrychis fand ich auch in Menge die von mir in den Kreisen Braunsberg und Heiligenbeil bisher noch nicht beobachtete *Sanguisorba minor*. Ich sammelte ferner auf den bewaldeten Höhen Viola mirabilis, Actaea spicata, Asarum europaeum, Campanula persicifolia mit ästigem Stengel und sehr grossen Blüthen, Hieracium boreale; in der Schlucht am Bache sehr grosse Exemplare von Cystopteris fragilis, auf offener Stelle die weissblühende Polygala vulgaris, im Garten zu Gr. Tromp auf Grasplätzen Crepis nicaeensis; 21. Juli am kleinen See bei Schillgehnen bei Braunsberg Myosotis caespitosa, Peplis Portula, **Scirpus compressus** Pers., Juncus supinus; in Schillgehnen selbst an den Zäunen Inula Helenium und Dipsacus silvester; 22. Juli zw. Frauenburg und Narz Melampyrum arvense, Asparagus officinalis, Spergula arvensis var. laricina Wulf., Pimpinella magna, Sedum boloniense, auf sumpfiger Stelle am Narzbach **Epipactis palustris**, Salix cuspidata, Orchis incarnata, Juncus supinus und squarrosus, auf der Höhe daselbst **Achyrophorus maculatus**, Polygonatum anceps.; 25. Juli in Braunsberg hinter den Scheunen am Regitten'er Mühlenfliess **Festuca distans**, am Chausseegraben Festuca arundinacea; 9. August auf dem Bruche zw. Kälberhaus und Huntenberg Veronica longifolia mit zusammengesetzten Aehren, Utricularia vulgaris, Hypericum tetrapterum, **Betula humilis**, Salix rosmarinifolia, Juncus alpinus; 13. August bei Schillgehnen Bromus arvensis, Glyceria plicata, zw. Kloppschen und Schillgehnen Armeria vulgaris, auf trockenem, sandigem Acker am Walde bei Schalmey Arnoseris pusilla, Teesdalea nudicaulis, Aphanes arvensis, Centunculus minimus; 25. August zw. der Sekundärbahn und der Lindenau'er Chaussee bei Braunsberg **Festuca arundinacea, Polygonum Bistorta** mit 2—5 langgestielten Nebenähren, Anthemis tinctoria (früher hier nicht vorgekommen), Succisa pratensis mit ungewöhnlich langen Hüllblättern, Equisetum palustre var. polystachium, **Lolium perenne** und **Festuca elatior;** 30. August auf der Wiese zw. Grafenmorgen und dem Bahnhofe Thalictrum angustifolium, auf dem Eisenbahndamme die Blätter von Tussilaga Farfara dicht mit Uredo Tussilaginis befallen. — 2. Im Kreise Heiligenbeil: 6. Juni im Rossen'er Walde bei Einsiedel an zwei Stellen **Linnaea borealis** in voller Blüthe, Myosotis versicolor an Ackerändern zw. dem Walde und Rossen; 12. Juni im Schutzbezirk Damerau der Oberförsterei Födersdorf in der sog. Kupferrinne unter Carpinus Betulus *Veronica montana*. Es ist dies der zweite von mir in Ostpreussen entdeckte Standort dieser seltenen Pflanze. Daselbst sammelte ich noch **Carex pilosa** und elongata, ferner Pirola minor, Asarum europaeum L., Sanicula europaea, auf offenem Waldboden Vicia cassubica L., Hieracium floribundum Wimm und Grab., Anthoxanthum odoratum L. var. villosum Loisl; 14. Juni auf Haideboden zw. Einsiedel und Rossen Nardus stricta, im Rossen'er Walde Viola canina var. lucorum Rchb.; 24. Juli im Walde zw. Rossen und Gerlachsdorf Monotropa Hypopitys, Circaea alpina, am Rande der Runenwiese Chaerophyllum bulbosum; 26. Juli im Rehteichbruche bei Rosen **Lycopodium Sclago** in Menge, Pirola rotundifolia, minor und secunda, Juncus alpinus, **Polystichum cristatum**; 27. Juli in dem Flüsschen Jäcknitz zw. Jäcknitz und Woyditten Potamageton crispa und alpina, Lysimachia thyrsiflora, an der Brücke bei

Jäcknitz **Erythraea pulchella**; 20. August bei Gerlachsdorf das bisher von mir noch nicht gefundene *Verbascum nigro + Lychnites*, ferner Rumex Hydrolapatum mit Uredo Rumicum, Populus pyramidalis mit Uredo populina Pers. — 3. Im Kreise Mohrungen: 11. Juli am Ewingsee bei Saalfeld Ranunculus Lingua, Cicuta virosa in grosser Menge, im Ewingsee und in den Zu- und Abflüssen Elodea canadensis, auf dem Michelsberge Veronica spicata, **Helianthemum vulgare**, Tragopogon pratensis, Verbascum thapsiforme, Coronilla varia; 12. Juli im Kunzendorf'er zur Forst Alt-Christburg gehörigen Forstrevier Circaea alpina, Geranium palustre mit gekerbten Blumenblättern, Maianthemum bifolium mit Aecidium Convallariae, Fagus silvatica, Rubus saxatilis, Lathyrus silvester, Asperula odorata, Stachys silvatica, Polypodium Dryopteris, Equisetum pratense, Pirola minor und secunda, im Klostocksee Utricularia vulgaris, Juncus alpinus, am Wege zw. dem Kunzendorf'er Forstrevier und Ebenau Genista tinctoria; 13. Juli am Wege zw. Tabern und Prohnen auf unbebautem Boden Anthyllis Vulneraria in Menge, in einer Schlucht bei Prohnen Daphne Mezereum, Ervum silvaticum, Astragalus glycyphyllos, Lathyrus silvester, Carlina vulgaris, Betonica officinalis; 14. Juli in der Waldschlucht bei Protheinen zw. Calmen und Vorwerk Polygonatum anceps, **Circaea lutetiana**, Asarum europaeum, Mercurialis perennis, Paris quadrifolia, Viola mirabilis, Lonicera Xylosteum, Hepatica triloba; auf dem Schlossberge (Grewose) zw. der Altstadt und Königsee, der durch eine tiefe Schlucht, durch welche die Sorge fliesst, durchnitten wird und vielleicht noch von keinem Botaniker gründlich untersucht ist, das in Ostpreussen seltene *Pleurospermum austriacum*, die daselbst nur an wenigen Stellen vorkommende **Glyceria plicata**, ferner Campanula latifolia, Circaea lutetiana und alpina, Viola mirabilis, Mespilus monogyna und Oxyacantha, Viburnum Opulus, Cornus sanguinea, Daphne Mezereum, Brachypodium silvaticum, Hypericum montanum, Actaea spicata, Equisetum pratense und hiemale L., Cystopteris fragilis; am Wege zw. Cöllmen und Grewose Ononis arvensis, am Wege zw. Glanden und Grewose Melilotus officinalis Desf., zw. Terpen und Segertswalde Anthemis tinctoria. Schliesslich noch die Mittheilung, dass der praktische Arzt Herr Hagedorn in Mohrungen so freundlich war, mir ein Photographie von Juniperus communis L. var. pyramidalis zu übersenden, welcher in natura 8 m hoch ist, die Höhe des Stammes bis zur Verästelung 16 cm, der Umfang des Stammes daselbst 135 cm und die einzelnen Aeste in der Höhe von 150 cm über dem Boden im Umfang von 28—47 cm. Dieser merkwürdige, riesige Wachholder befindet sich im Kreise Mohrungen am Wege zw. Güldenboden und Gelbitten. Ein über 3 m hohes, sehr schön gewachsenes Exemplar des Pyramiden-Wachholders fand ich diesen Sommer im Garten des Gutsbesitzers Herrn Matern-Anticken im Braunsberg'er Kreise.

Hauptlehrer Kremp-Memel übermittelt der Versammlung einen Gruss von Kantor Grabowski-Marienburg, verhindert persönlich zu erscheinen.

Der Vorsitzende vertheilt dann eine sehr reiche Sammlung von getrockneten, vorzüglich aufgelegten Pflanzen der Umgebung von Graudenz, von Scharlok eingeschickt. Es waren:

Allium fallax Schrader aus dem Rondsen'er Wäldchen. — **Alyssum calycinum L.** racemis racemosis. Südliche Festungsplantage. — **Anthericum ramosum L.**, aus dem Rondsen'er Wäldchen. — **Aquilegia vulgaris L.** fr. atrata Koch von St. Beatenberg

i. d. Schweiz. — **Aristolochia Clematitis L.**, von dem ehemals Salomon'schen Acker. — **Artemisia scoparia W. K.**, der Grundblattrosetten wegen selbst gezogen. — **Asperula tinctoria L.**, aus dem Rondsen'er Wäldchen. — **Aspidium Lonchitis Sw.**, von der St. Beatenberg'er Alp, Schweiz. — **Asplenium Ruta muraria L.**, aus den Wallmauern des Hornwerkes. — **Avena pratensis L.** Südliche Festungsplantage. — **Bromus asper L.**, aus der Schlucht von Eliesenthal, Kreis Kulm. — **Bromus sterilis L.** Adl. Dombrowken und **Brom. tectorum L.** Festungsplantage. Je ein Exemplar von jedem in 1 Umschlage, des Vergleiches wegen. — **Campanula Rapunculus L.**, aus der Schweiz stammend. — **Carduus acanthoides L. flore albo.** Paparczyn, Kreis Kulm. — **Collomia grandiflora Douglas**, aus dem Nahethale bei Idar. — **Eryngium planum L.** Festungsplantage. — **Euphorbia Esula Scopoli**, aus dem Rondsen'er Wäldchen. — **Euphorbia exigua L.**, aus dem Nahethale bei Sobernheim stammend. — **Euphorbia Lathyris L.** — **Euphorbia stricta L.**, aus dem Nahethale bei Sobernheim stammend. — **Galanthus nivalis L. normalis.** Eliesenthaler Schlucht, Kreis Kulm und **Gal. nival. L. f. Scharlokii Caspary**, aus einem Garten in Sobernheim, je beide in 1 Umschlage des Vergleiches wegen. — **Impatiens Nolitangere L. flor. cleistogamis** und dieselbe **flor. cleistogamis nebst Uebergängen**; die aus dem Ellerbruch bei Mischke stammende normale Pflanze hat sich in etwa 5 Jahren so in meinem viel trockenern Garten verändert. Nach mündlicher Mittheilung des H. Rosenbaum ist dieser Uebergang zur Cleistogamie auch im Walde von Fronau, Kreis Kulm zu finden — **Lathyrus tuberosus L.** Aecker dicht an der Südgrenze der Festungsplantage. — **Libanotis montana All. f. sibirica Koch.** Südliche Festungsplantage. — **Linaria Elatine L.**, aus dem Nahethale bei Sobernheim. — **Lithospermum officinale L.** Bei Sartowitz, Kreis Schwetz. — **Lolium perenne L. f. composita Thuillier.** Adl. Dombrowken, Kreis Graudenz. — **Matricaria inodora L. flor. ligulatis.** Adl. Dombrowken, Kreis Graudenz. — **Orobanche Galii Duby.** Südliche Festungsplantage. — **Osmunda regalis L.** Vom grossen Moor bei Bremen. — **Oxalis stricta L.** Sehr lästiges Gartenunkraut. — **Physalis Alkekengi L.** Von Stein am Stad bei Regenburg. — **Pleurospermum austriacum Hoffm.** Wald, südlich von Oliva, Kreis Danzig. — **Polygala comosa L.** Adl. Dombrowken, Kreis Graudenz. — **Polygonum aviculare L. f. monspeliense Thieb.**, eingeschickt von Frl. Julie Reichel, gesammelt in Heiligenbrunn bei Langefuhr, Kreis Danzig. — **Potentilla mixta Nolte.** Grenze von Liniec und Paparczyn, Kreis Kulm. — **Potentilla norvegica L.** Torfmoor. Radmannsdorf, Kreis Kulm. — **Potentilla procumbens Sibthp.** Grenze von Liniec und Paparczyn, Kreis Kulm. — **Potentilla recta L.** Südliche Festungsplantage. — **Pulmonaria angustifolia + obscurum.** Wäldchen von Liniec, Kreis Kulm. — **Rosa alpina L.** Von St. Beatenberg i. d. Schweiz. — **Salix myrtilloides L.** Sphagnetum bei Gottersfeld, Kreis Kulm. — **Salvia pratensis L. flore albo.** Südliche Festungsplantage. — **Sedum reflexum L. f. rupestris.** Nördlich von Paparczyn, Kreis Kulm. — **Setaria verticillata P. B.** Gartenunkraut. — **Tragopogon maior L.** Bei Sartowitz, Kreis Schwetz. — **Urtica pilulifera L.** und **Ur. pil. f. Dodartii**, beide aus Thüringen. — **Viola mirabilis L.** Wäldchen von Stremoczyn. — **Xanthium strumarium L. f. arenaria Lasch.** Adl. Dombrowken, Kreis Graudenz.

Die Apotheker Ludwig-Christburg und Rosenbohm-Graudenz senden der Versammlung Grüsse; auch Lehrer Frölich-Thorn, der 1884 bei Thorn folgende wichtigere Pflanzen gefunden hat:

Cerastium triviale Lk. b. nemoralis Uechtr. Schlucht bei Kisin. — **Veronica verna L. fr. longistyla** L. G. Fröl. Blätter unten kermesin, Blüthen etwas grösser als bei der fr. brevistyla G. Fröl., der Griffel etwa ½ so lang als die Kapsel, überragt diese weit, während bei fr. brevistyla der Griffel etwa ⅓ so lang als die Kapsel, diese nicht oder kaum überragt.*) Cosson und Sturm bilden die fr. brevistyla, Reichenbach die fr. longistyla ab. Ascherson und Garcke beschreiben die fr. brevistyla. Der Winkel der Ausrandung zw. den Kapsellappen ist bei beiden Formen stumpf-, recht- und spitzwinklig; bei der fr. longistyla von Thorn meist spitzwinklig. Beide Pflanzen wachsen bei Thorn an geschiedenen Standorten und sind samengetreu, wie Herr Frölich durch Aussaat in Töpfen und Kasten fand. Weitere Beobachtungen auch anderwegen wünschenswerth. — **Linaria cymbalaria** Festungsmauer von Thorn in der Nähe des Garnisongerichtsgebäudes — **Bunias orientalis**, Aecker südlich von Neu-Weisshof — **Bromus asper.** b. serotinus Schlucht bei Kisin — **Carex flacca** und **distans**, Schlucht zw. Plutowo und Kielp. — **Ervum hirsutum** L. **var. fissum** G. Frölich. Die bei der gewöhnlichen Form halb-pfeilförmigen Nebenblätter sind in 3—4 ungleich lange und breite, fast borstige Zipfel mehr oder weniger tief gespalten; auf Aeckern bei Neu-Weisshof. — **Koeleria cristata** Pers. c. pyramidata Lmck. Schonung östlich von Otloschin. — Bei Kisin hat Herr Frölich, wie früher Rosenbohm und Preuss, vergebens nach Betula nana gesucht.

Apotheker Jansen-Pr. Eylau schickt der Versammlung ein Verzeichniss der bisher von ihm um Pr. Eylau gefundenen Moose, das vervollständigt, später veröffentlicht werden wird.

Auf Antrag des Vorsitzenden wird den Herren Prätorius, Seydler und Scharlok telegraphisch das Bedauern der Versammlung ausgedrückt, dass sie ihr nicht beiwohnen konnten.

Von John-Reichenbach, ehedem auf Plicken, jetzt in Oberstraass bei Zürich, sind aus der Umgebung von Zürich folgende getrocknete Pflanzen, die vertheilt werden, eingetroffen:

Stachys silvatica, Galium cruciatum, Gymnadenia conopea, Listera ovata, Orchis maculata, Lysimachia nemorum, Cynanchum Vincetoxicum, Salvia pratensis, Cephalanthera pallens, Cypripedium Calceolus, Euphorbia Cyparissias, Pinguicula vulgaris, Ophrys Arachnites, Ophrys muscifera, Bellidiastrum Michelii, Neottia Nidus avis, Lilium Martagon, Sedum album, Ononis repens, Succisa pratensis, Colchicum autumnale, Leontopodium alpinum, Nigritella angustifolia, Aster alpinus, Rhododendron hirsutum, Eupatorium cannabinum, Tamus communis, Gentiana asclepiadea, Equisetum Telmateia, Epipactis palustris, Gymnadenia odoratissima, Polygala Chamaebuxus, Spiraea Aruncus, Tofieldia calyculata, Orobanche minor, Helianthemum vulgare.

Von Pfarrer Preuschoff, ehedem in Tannsee, jetzt in Tolkemit, sind folgende Pflanzen zur Vertheilung eingesandt:

Gagea arvensis, Tannsee, 22. 4. 84. — **Holosteum umbellatum** von ebendaher Mai. — **Androsace septentrionalis**, Halbstadt auf d. Sande, 25. 5. 84. — **Sherardia arvensis**, Grasplatz im Pfarrgarten zu Tannsee. — **Vicia lathyroides**, Halbstadt auf dem Sande,

*) Beide Formen sind durch Preussen, wie das Herbarium des königl. botan. Gartens nachweist, verbreitet, wenn auch bisher nicht unterschieden. Casp.

25. 5. 84. — **Nonnea pulla**, aus Graudenz in meinen Garten verpflanzt, 9. 6. 84. — **Aristolochia Clematitis**, um Marienburg nicht selten, 19. 6. 84. — **Potamogeton pectinata**, Teich im Pfarrgarten zu Ladekopp, 29. 8. 84. — **Artemisia scoparia**, Nogatdamm bei Halbstadt, August 84. — **Phleum pratense** mit Stützblatt unter der Aehre bei Tannsee. — **Plantago arenaria**, Rehhof, Kr. Stuhm, auf Sandäckern, 16. 7. 84. — **Falcaria Rivini**, Marienwerder an der Chaussee, 18. 7. 84. — **Polystichum spinulosum** von Buchwalde bei Pr. Holland, 3. 6. 84. — **Fontinalis antipyretica** von Halbstadt, Kreis Marienburg, im Bruch, August 84. — **Riccia natans**, Lupenhorst, Kr. Elbing, in einem Graben, 16. 10. 83.

Herr Apotheker Weiss-Caymen sendet der Versammlung seinen Gruss und folgende Pflanzen: **Geum strictum + urbanum** in 2 Formen, die schon im Bericht über die Marienburg'er Versammlung erwähnt sind; die Griffeltheile der älteren verhalten sich, wie $1:2-2^1/_2$, die der neuen, wie $1:2^1/_2-3$ — **Geum rivale + strictum** von 2 Stauden. — **Valeriana sambucifolia** — **Medicago sativa.** In einem Gerstenfelde bei Caymen. Juli 1884. Für Caymen neu — **Albersia Blitum**, auf einem bekrauteten Feldwege nach dem südlich vom Schlosse liegenden Gemüsegarten. Septbr. 1884. Neu für Caymen. — **Rosa mollis** Smith ad venustam transiens. Nach Christ's Bestimmung. Zw. Wangen und Waldhaus Bendisen. — **Polygonum minus + Persicaria.** Aug. 1884. In den Furchen eines Kartoffelfeldes. — **Pulmonaria officinalis** L. fr. obscura. Unter der normalen Form. 1884. Selten!

Pharmazeut Paul Schmitt-Tilsit sendet zur Vertheilung folgende 1884 gesammelte Pflanzen:

Von den Putschinen bei Tilsit: **Juncus balticus**, I. **filiformis**, I. **bufonius**, I. **fuscoater**, **Scabiosa columbaria** a. **ochroleuca**, **Trifolium agrarium**, **Erythraea Centaurium**, **Tragopogon heterospermus** und **Silene tartarica**; aus dem Barsduhnen'er Walde bei Heydekrug: **Linnaea borealis** und von den Kalkfelsen bei Zweischlinge bei Bielefeld in Westfalen: **Asplenium Trichomanes** und **Polypodium vulgare.**

Stadtrath Patze-Königsberg sendet folgende Pflanzen, welche von ihm im August dieses Jahres bei Gallehnen im Kreise Pr. Eylau gesammelt wurden:

Mentha silvestris, Trifolium pratense floribus albis, Galinsoga parviflora und Vicia villosa floribus albis.

Seminarist Max Grütter sendet aus Kreis Thorn 1884 gesammelt: **Asplenium Trichomanes** 14. 4., Niedermühle; **Botrychium Matricariae** Spr. 10. 4., daselbst; **Thesium ebracteatum** 1. 6., Smolnik; **Sarothamnus scoparius** 1. 6., daselbst; **Veronica austriaca** 2. 6., Wald bei Fort IV; **Pirola uniflora** 2. 6., Barbarken; **Potentilla norvegica** 2. 6., Fort IV; **Medicago minima** 4. 6., Abhang bei Grünhof; *Lythrum Hyssopifolia* vom Seminaristen Sich bei Gremboczyn, September 1883 gefunden. Neu für Preussen. Aus Kreis Stuhm auch 1884 gesammelt: **Anemone nemorosa** b. purpurea 11. 5., Wengern; **Viola mirabilis** 11. 5., daselbst; **Andromeda poliifolia** 22. 5., Konradswalde; **Luzula sudetica** b. **pallescens** 22. 5., Damerau'er See; **Cerastium brachypetalum** 25. 5., Wengern, bis 0,5 m lang; **Avena caryophyllea** 15. 6., zw. Willenberg und Wengern; **Peplis Portula** 7. 7., zw. Wengern und Braunswalde; **Pleurospermum austriacum** 7. 7., Wengern; **Salix nigricans** 13. 7., Konradswalde; **Alchemilla arvensis** 13. 7., Konradswalde; **Centunculus minimus** 6. 9., Wengern; **Gentiana cruciata** 2 Standorte bei Wengern; **Salix livida**, **Eriophorum gracile** bei Konradswalde. Von Kreis Marienburg: **Chenopodium**

murale 21. 7., Seminargarten in Marienburg; **Vicia lathyroides** 15. 6., Bahndamm bei Kaldowe. Auch einige seltenere Pflanzen aus dem Posenschen sendet Grütter.

Herr Lehrer Peil-Sackrau, Kreis Graudenz, schickt zur Vertheilung:

Vicia silvatica (zw. Barchnau und Pelplin), **Linaria cymbalaria** (Graudenz'er Festungsmauer), **Polycnemum arvense** (Felder bei Gr. Wolz, Kr. Graudenz), **Dianthus arenarius** (Bingsberge, Kr. Graudenz), **Ceterach officinarum** (Graudenz'er Festungsmauer), **Chaiturus Marrubiastrum** (Sackrau), **Alchemilla arvensis, Selinum Carvifolia, Silene chlorantha** (Bingsberge), **Linaria minor** (Sackrau), **Pedicularis palustris, Epipactis latifolia** (Bingsberge), **Sisymbrium Sinapistrum** (Bingsberge), **Anemone silvestris** (zw. Sackrau und Wolz), **Paris quadrifolia** (Jammi'er Forst), **Polygonatum officinale, Sedum palustre, Asperula tinctoria** (Bingsberge), **Stellaria glauca, Eriophorum gracile** (Bruch auf den Bingsbergen), **Festuca heterophylla** (Jammi'er Forst), **Arabis Gerardi, Geranium molle, Pulmonaria angustif. + officinalis** (Burg-Belchau'er Wald). **Petasites officinalis, Lathraea squamaria, Galeopsis Ladanum** b. **latifolium, Chaerophyllum aromaticum** und **Melampyrum arvense** (von Seminarist K. Peil bei Danzig gesammelt).

Ferner sendet Herr Peil einige auffallende Formen: **Monotropa Hypopitys**, a) hirsuta, bei der die untern Blüthenäste 5—6 cm lang gestielt und beblättert sind; **Companula Trachelium**, sehr gross, wahrscheinlich niederliegend, denn die Blüthenstiele einseitswendig, bis 30 cm lang, mehrblüthig; **Trifolium pratense** fl. albo; dasselbe mit vergrünten Blüthen; **Gagea pratensis** mit einer Wurzelknolle am überirdischen, oben blühenden Stengel.

Herr L. Frank-Gumbinnen berichtet, dass er in seinem Hausgarten ein vor 23 Jahren gepflanztes Exemplar von Ginkgo biloba habe, das von Reitenbach-Plicken bezogen und aus einem Kern erwachsen war, jetzt von 4,20 m Höhe bei einem Stammumfang von 0,65 m. Auch sendet Herr Frank blühenden Epheu aus seinem Garten, der an einem Baume gezogen wird und vor 21 Jahren gepflanzt ist.

Dr. **Julius Lange** erstattet dann

Bericht über seine botanische Erforschung der Kreise Danzig, Neustadt, Kartaus und Berent.

Durch Herrn Professor Caspary war mir der Auftrag zu Theil geworden, im Sommer des Jahres 1884 gewisse Theile der Kreise Danzig, Neustadt, Kartaus und Berent in botanischer Beziehung zu untersuchen. Meine Forschung begann am 4. Mai und zwar von Zuckau aus, Kr. Kartaus. — 4. Mai. Zw. Zuckau und Babenthal im Stangenwalde'r Forst: Hierochloa australis, Daphne Mezereum, Lathraea squamaria. Krissau, Alt Glintsch. An einem Bache zw. Neu-Glintsch und Zuckau: Gagea minima, Corydalis fabacea. — 5. Mai. Rechtes Radauneufer zw. Zuckau und Babenthal: Aconitum variegatum, Holosteum umbellatum. Linkes Radauneufer südlich von Borkau: Gagea pratensis. Patocka, Wald nördlich von Bortsch: Mercurialis perennis. Fliessenkrug, Kelpin. — 6. Mai. Zw. Kelpin und Burchardswo: Aiuga pyramidalis, Rubus Bellardi. Kartaus, Seeresen, Borrowo. Im Walde nordöstlich vom Borrowo-See: Pulsatilla vernalis, Hierochloa australis. Zw. Borkau und Zuckau: Gagea pratensis. — 7. Mai. Zw. Zuckau und Saranowken: Gagea pratensis. Smolsin. Am nordwestl. Ufer des Glemboki-See: Arabis arenosa. Am Zittno-See: Equisetum hiemale. Borrowokrug. Wald östlich von Pechbude: Viola mirabilis. Linkes Radauneufer zw. Drahthammerbrücke und Borkau: Lamium maculatum, Mercurialis perennis, Corydalis fabacea, C. cava, Aconitum variegatum, Viola mirabilis, Vicia lathyroides. — 8. Mai. Linkes Radauneufer zw. Zuckau und Ellernitz: Arabis arenosa. An der Chaussee bei Ellernitz: Petasites officinalis. Linkes Radauneufer zw. Ellernitz und der Lappinen'er Pappfabrik: Holosteum umbellatum, Gagea minima, G. pratensis, Aconitum variegatum, Lathraea squamaria, Viola mirabilis, Corydalis fabacea. Lappinener See, Helenenhof. Im Dorfe Rheinfeld an der Strasse 2 Ahornbäume mit Viscum album. — 9. Mai. An der Stolpe zw. Zuckau und Mehlken: Equisetum pratense, Corydalis fabacea. Seefeld. Zw. Kobissau u. U. F. Seeresen: Carex montana (1 Exemplar). Borkau. — Den 10. Mai. Mahlkau. Im Wäldchen nördlich von Exau: Corydalis fabacea. Exau-See. Tockar, Czeczau, Gr. Mischau. — 12. Mai. Wald nordöstlich von Zuckau: Viola mirabilis, Lathraea squamaria, Lamium maculatum. Pempau, Ramkau, Czapeln, Ellernitz. Uebersiedelung nach Hoppendorf, etwa 2 Meilen südwestlich von Zuckau.

13. Mai. Von Hoppendorf nach Kamehlen: Aiuga pyramidalis. Zw. Kamehlen und Jäcknitz: Lycopodium clavatum. Pollenczyn. Am Pollenczyn'er See: Lycopodium Selago. Tiefenthal, Neuendorf, Maidahnen, Bortsch. — 14. Mai. Zw. Hoppendorf und Semlin: Ledum palustre, Corydalis fabacea. Zw. Semlin und Kelpin: Pulsatilla pratensis. Kartaus, Hoppendorf. — 15. Mai. Zw. Semlin und Gorrenczyn: Pulsatilla pratensis, Vicia lathyroides. Zw. Gorrenczyn und Ostritz: Myosotis versicolor. Remboczewo, Smentau, Löszno, Semlin. — 16. Mai. Fitschkau. Zw. Fliessenkrug und Babenthal: Pulsatilla pratensis, P. vernalis, Pulmonaria angustifolia, Asarum europaeum. Bortsch. — 17. Mai. Zw. Kamehlen und Neuendorf: Viola silvatica + canina. Zw. Neuendorf und Michaelshütte: Carex pilulifera. Zw. Michaelshütte und Ndr. Klanau: Viola mirabilis, Polypodium vulgare. Buchenwäldchen nördlich von Ndr. Klanau: Viola Riviniana + canina, Potentilla cinerea. Ndr. Hütte, Krönken. — 19. Mai. An der Chaussee von Hoppendorf nach Eggertshütte: Viola silvatica + arenaria. Schlawkau. Am Westufer des Schlawkau-Sees: Corydalis fabacea, Asperula odorata. Zw. Schlawkau und Konty: Potentilla opaca. Zw. Konty und Schöneberg: Viola Riviniana + canina. Thurmberg, Fischershütte. — 20. Mai. U. F. Rehhof. Wilhelmsdorf. An einem Bache östlich von Wilhelmsdorf: Asarum europaeum. Rechtes Radauneufer zw. Wilhelmsdorf und Fliessenkrug: Aconitum variegatum, Viola mirabilis, Corydalis fabacea, Paris quadrifolia, Trollius europaeus. Linkes Radauneufer zw. Fliessenkrug u. d. Drahthammerbrücke: Pulsatilla pratensis, Myosotis sparsiflora, Alliaria officinalis, Geranium silvaticum, Polygonatum multiflorum, Convallaria maialis. Babenthal, Bortsch. Uebersiedelung nach Osterwick in der Danziger Niederung.

22. Mai. Im sogenannten Bruch, nordwestlich von Osterwick: Carex riparia. Elodea canadensis, Berula angustifolia, Myosurus minimus. — 23. Mai. Zw. Osterwick und Schönwarling: Senecio paluster, Holosteum umbellatum, Euphorbia Esula. Zw. Schönwarling und Hohenstein: Saxifraga granulata. Von Hohenstein nach Kolling: Holosteum umbellatum. Güttland. In Kriefkohl an Zäunen: Asperugo procumbens. — 24. Mai. Zw. Osterwick und Wossitz: Holosteum umbellatum. Zw. Wossitz und Gemlitz: Cynoglossum officinale, Fragaria elatior. Auf dem Weichsel-Aussendeich zw. Gemlitz und der Stüblau'er Wachtbude: Petasites tomentosa, Salix amygdalina

var. concolor und discolor, Holosteum umbellatum. Stüblau. — 26. Mai. Zw. Osterwick und dem Grossen Sandberg: Senecio paluster, Saxifraga tridactylites. Schönwarling. Zw. Rosenberg und Grebin: Saxifraga tridactylites, Holosteum umbellatum. Herrngrebin. — 27. Mai. Zw. Wossitz und Stüblau: Conium maculatum, Salix cinerea + aurita, Carex Schreberi. Auf dem Stüblau'er Aussendeich: Equisetum hiemale, Viburnum Opulus. — 28. Mai. Zw. Osterwick und Herrn-Grebin: Camelina microcarpa. Zw. Herrn-Grebin und Schönau: Valerianella olitoria. Herzberg. An der Chaussee von Gr. Zünder nach Trutenau: Hieracium praealtum a. genuinum 1 verum. Auf einer Wiese zw. Trutenau und Wossitz: Lepidium campestre. — 30. Mai. Rechtes Motlau-Ufer zw. Osterwick und Kriefkohl: Ranunculus arvensis. Zw. Kriefkohl und Güttland: Adonis aestivalis. Zw. Güttland und dem Aussendeich: Salix cinerea + viminalis. Aussendeich zw. Güttland und Stüblau: Carex Schreberi, Viburnum Opulus. Aussendeich zw. Güttland und Dirschau: Holosteum umbellatum, — 31. Mai. Linkes Motlau-Ufer zw. Osterwick und Herrn-Grebin: Conium maculatum. Im Mühlengarten von Herrn-Grebin: Geranium phaeum, Alliaria officinalis Zw. Herrn-Grebin und Sperlingsdorf: Sinapis arvensis var. orientalis. Zw. Sperlingsdorf und Landau: Geranium molle. Graben zw. Landau und Müggenhall: Chara foetida, Valerianella olitoria. Zw. Müggenhall und Rostau: Saxifraga tridactylites. Grebin. — Den 2. Juni. Im Dorfe Trutenau: Hieracium praealtum. Trutenau. Herzberg. — 3. Juni. Zw. Gr. u. Kl. Zünder: Matricaria Chamomilla, Myosurus minimus, Orchis latifolia. Zw. Kl. Zünder und Gottswalde: Geranium pusillum. Zw. Gottswalde und Herzberg: Salix repens var. rosmarinifolia, Viola canina, Luzula sudetica a. pallescens. — 4. Juni. Zw. Gr. Zünder und Gemlitz: Salix nigricans. Zw. Gemlitz und Stüblau: Carex Schreberi. Auf dem Aussendeich zw. Stüblau und der Gemlitz'er Wachtbude: Salix cinerea + viminalis, Barbarea stricta. In einem Teiche westlich von der Geml. Wachtbude: Potamogeton lucens. Aussendeich zw. d. Geml. und d. Langfeld'er Wachtbude: Euphorbia lucida. Zw. d. Langf. Wachtbude und Langfelde: Crataegus Oxyacantha. Zw. Langfelde und Gr. Zünder: Acer Negundo angepflanzt. — 6. Juni. An der Chaussee von Gr. Zünder nach Letzkau: Sium latifolium, Vicia tetrasperma. Zw. Letzkau und der Letzkau'er Wachtbude: Scirpus radicans. Zw. d. Letzk. und Käsemark'er Wachtbude: Barbarea stricta, Salvia pratensis, Erysimum hieraciifolium, Eryngium planum. Käsemark. — 7. Juni. Zw. Kl. Zünder u. d. Lauenkrug: Carex vulpina. An der Heringslake zw. d. Lauenkrug u. d. Heringskrug: Thalictrum flavum. Auf d. Weichsel-Aussendeich zw. d. Heringskrug und d. Käsemark. Wachtbude: Barbarea stricta, Eryngium planum, Orchis latifolia, Erysimum hieraciifolium, Crataegus monogyna. Zw. Käsemark und Letzkau: Thalictrum flavum. — 9. Juni. An der Chaussee von Trutenau nach Schönau: Acer campestre, Hieracium praealtum, Lysimachia thyrsiflora, Stellaria nemorum, Diplotaxis tenuifolia, Barbarea stricta, Aquilegia vulgaris. Schönau, Wotzlaff, Gottswalde, Herzberg. Uebersiedelung nach Quaschin, Kreis Neustadt.

13. Juni. An der Chaussee von Quaschin nach Kölln: Equisetum hiemale, Viola Riviniana + canina. An einem Bache westlich von Quaschin: Arnoseris pusilla, Geranium silvaticum. Oestlich von Bojahn: Spartium scoparium, Ornithopus perpusillus, Scorzonera humilis. Zw. Bojahn und Kölln: Ranunculus polyanthemos, Aiuga genevensis. Köllner See. — 14. Juni. Torfbruch südlich von Quaschin:

Nardus stricta, Andromeda poliifolia. An einem Bache südwestl. von Quaschin: Scorzonera humilis. Im Wäldchen südlich von Quaschin: Spergula Morisonii, Luzula multiflora. Espenkrug. Am Espenkr. See: Juncus filiformis, Ranunculus reptans, Hydrocotyle vulgaris, Ornithopus perpusillus, Turritis glabra; in dem See Isoëtes lacustris, Litorella lacustris. — 16. Juni. Im Walde südlich von Gr. Katz: Helianthemum vulgare, Pirola secunda, P. uniflora, Scorzonera humilis, Lycopodium Selago, Asperula odorata, Stellaria uliginosa. Von Gr. Katz nach Quaschin: Mespilus monogyna, Ornithopus perpusillus. — 17. Juni. Zw. Quaschin und Gr. Tuchom: Veronica Anagallis, Helianthemum vulgare, Spergula Morisonii. Am Tuchom'er See: Valeriana sambucifolia, Spartium scoparium, Phegopteris Dryopteris, Hieracium Auricula, Actaea spicata, Paris quadrifolia, Polygonatum multiflorum. — 18. Juni. Am Wittstock'er See (südöstlich von Espenkrug): Myosotis versicolor, Viburnum Opulus, Hieracium Auricula, Stellaria uliginosa. Barnewitz. An einem Bache zw. Ramkau und Julienthal: Vicia angustifolia a. segetalis Aschers. — 19. Juni. Im Walde südlich von Gr. Katz: Milium effusum, Aconitum variegatum, Lysimachia nemorum, Carex remota, C. silvatica, Ranunculus polyanthemos, Galium boreale, Orobus niger, Platanthera bifolia. — 20. Juni. Uebersiedelung nach Schönwalde.

21. Juni. Am Gossentinbach zw. Schönwalde und Gr. Dennemörse: Stachys palustris, Ornithopus perpusillus, Alectorolophus minor, Myosotis versicolor. Im Walde südöstlich von Gr. Dennemörse: Pirola uniflora, Lysimachia nemorum. Gr. Ottalsin-See: Myosotis versicolor, Juncus filiformis, Isoëtes lacustris, Litorella lacustris, Salix aurita + nigricans, Nitella flexilis, Hieracium Auricula, Empetrum nigrum, Salix pentandra. Kl. Ottalsin-See. In Jellentschhütte an der Dorfstrasse: Archangelica officinalis. — 23. Juni. Zw. Schönwalde und Gr. Dennemörse: Galeopsis Ladanum, Matricaria Chamomilla, Spartium scoparium. Am Gossentinbach südöstlich von Gr. Dennemörse: Linum catharticum, Scorzonera humilis, Myosotis hispida, Ranunculus polyanthemos, Blechnum Spicant, Pirola uniflora. Am Mühlenteich in Jellentschhütte: Carex leporina, Nitella flexilis, Ranunculus reptans, Peplis Portula. — 24. Juni. Auf einem Torfbruch am Südende des Steinkrug'er Sees: Scirpus caespitosus, Andromeda poliifolia, Vaccinium Oxycoccos, V. uliginosum, Ledum palustre. Steinkruger See: Isoëtes lacustris, Empetrum nigrum. Am See von Köllnerhütte: Andromeda poliifolia, Epilobium montanum. — 25. Juni. Zw. Schönwalde und Grabowitz: Arnoseris pusilla, Armeria vulgaris. Von Grabowitz nach d. U. F. Wigodda: Pulsatilla vernalis, Scorzonera humilis, Achyrophorus maculatus, Lycopodium annotinum. Am südlichsten der 3 Seen von Wigodda: Juncus filiformis, Hydrocotyle vulgaris, Salix repens. Zw. Pretoschin und Grabowitz: Pirola uniflora, Milium effusum. — 26. Juni. Zw. Schönwalde und dem Schwarzen See (südlich von Pretoschin): Saxifraga granulata. Am Schwarzen See: Peplis portula, Juncus supinus, Viola palustris + epipsila. Am Gossentinbach südlich von Pretoschin: Equisetum hiemale, Lysimachia nemorum, Carex remota. In Pretoschin an der Dorfstrasse: Cynoglossum officinale, Euphorbia Peplus. Zw. Pretoschin u. d. U. F. Wigodda: Pirola secunda, Asperula odorata, Lysimachia nemorum. An den beiden Seen nordwestlich von d. U. F. Wigodda: Hydrocotyle vulgaris, Stellaria glauca, Lysimachia thyrsiflora, Ledum palustre. Zw. Wigodda und Schönwalde: Ornithopus perpusillus, Vicia angustifolia, Carex remota, Pirola chlorantha, Orobus

niger, Ranunculus polyanthemos. — 27. Juni. Zw. Schönwalde u. Okuniewo: Spergula Morisonii. Am Okuniewo-See: Veronica scutellata L. var. parmularia, Juncus filiformis, Campanula patula. Zw. Okuniewo und Bieschkowitz: Achyrophorus maculatus, Pirola uniflora, Pulsatilla vernalis. Bieschkowitz-See: Isoëtes lacustris, Juncus supinus, Lycopodium inundatum, ***Montia lamprosperma***, Veronica scutellata zusammen mit var. parmularia, Carex limosa, C. filiformis, Scheuchzeria palustris. Zw. Bieschkowitz und Schönwalde: Ornithopus perpusillus. — 28. Juni. Zw. Schönwalde und Steinkrug: Quercus sessiliflora. Nordufer des Steinkrug'er Sees: Veronica scutellata und var. parmularia. Zw. Steinkrug und Bieschkowo: Campanula persicifolia, Polypodium Dryopteris. An den Seen von Bieschkowo: Veronica scutellata und var. parmularia, Alectorolophus minor. Marchowia-See: Potamogeton alpina, P. praelonga, P. obtusifolia, Butomus umbellatus, Myriophyllum alterniflorum, Veronica scut. var. parm., Juncus supinus var. fluitans, Ranunculus reptans, Valeriana dioica, Sanicula europaea. Zw. Kölln und Steinkrug: Botrychium Lunaria, Myosotis hispida. — 30. Juni. Zw. Gr. und Kl. Dennemörse: Turritis glabra, Hypericum quadrangulum. Zw. Kl. Dennemörse und Lebno: Arctostaphylos Uva ursi, Pulsatilla vernalis, Spergula Morisonii, Conium maculatum. Zw. Lebno und Smasin: Luzula albida, Utricularia vulgaris, Empetrum nigrum. An der Gossentin nördlich von Smasin: Vicia silvatica, Geranium palustre, Aconitum variegatum, Asarum europaeum, Viola mirabilis, Polygonatum multiflorum, Rubus saxatillis, Mercurialis perennis.

1. Juli. Uebersiedlung nach Seefeld (Kreis Kartaus). — 2. Juli. Zw. Seefeld und Exau: Clinopodium vulgare, Trifolium hybridum. Am See von Exau: Potamogeton perfoliata, Veronica scutellata var. parmularia, Alectorolophus minor, Rubus saxatilis. — 3. Juli. Zw. Seefeld und Czeczau: Thalictrum aquilegifolium, Sparganium ramosum, Pirola minor und chlorantha, Carex remota. Zw. Czeczau u. d. Huss-See: Campanula persicifolia. Huss-See: Potamogeton mucronata, Blechnum Spicant, Drosera longifolia, Lycopodium Selago, Pirola chlorantha, P. minor, P. secunda, Ranunculus Lingua. Zw. Warznau und Tockar: Chenopodium Bonus Henricus. Zw. Tockar u. Exau: Peucedanum Oreoselinum. — 5. Juli. Gelonken-See (südl. v. Wittstock-See): Ranunculus reptans, Salix repens, Isoëtes lacustris, Drosera longifolia. Wittstock-See: Ranunculus reptans, Drosera longifolia, Oxycoccos, Isoëtes lacustris, Lobelia Dortmanna, Scirpus acicularis, Avena praecox. Zw. dem Wittstock-See und Klossau: Galeopsis Ladanum. Zalense. — 7. Juli. Zw. Seefeld und Zalense: Coronilla varia, Ononis repens, Hypericum quadrangulum. Zw. Zalense und Willamowo: Hieracium laevigatum. Zw. Pomiczyn und Pomiczynscahütte: Pirola minor. Pomiczynscahütte, Schwarzhütte. — 8. Juli. Von Seefeld nach Kobissau: Ervum hirsutum, Vicia villosa. Zw. Kobissau und Smolsin: Salvia pratensis, Dianthus Carthusianorum. Tuchlinko-See (südwestlich vom Smolsin): Ranunculus reptans, Veronica scutellata var. parmularia, ***Potamogeton marina*** (neu für Westpreussen). Glemboki-See: Ranunculus reptans, Veronica scutellata var. parmularia, Chara fragilis, Hydrocotyle vulgaris, Rubus saxatilis, Salix repens b. fusca Wimm., S. pentandra, Actaea spicata, **Laserpitium latifolium**, Hypericum montanum. Carlikauer See: Campanula persicifolia var. eriocarpa, Hydrocotyle vulgaris, Salix nigricans. — 9. Juli. Im Walde nordwestlich von Borrowokrug: Pirola rotundifolia, Neottia Nidus avis, Platanthera bifolia, Monotropa Hypopitys. Zittno-See: Selinum Carvifolia, Lysimachia thyrsiflora, ***Isoëtes***

lacustris, Paris quadrifolia. Zw. Zittno und Smolsin: Dianthus deltoides, Milium effusum, Peucedanum Oreoselinum. — 10. Juli. An dem Bache zw. Exau und Klossau: Aconitum variegatum, Hypericum quadrangulum, Pirola rotundifolia, Pimpinella magna, Digitalis grandiflora, Trollius europaeus, ***Bupleurum longifolium.*** Zw. Klossau und Tockar: Hieracium umbellatum.

11. Juli: Uebersiedelung von Seefeld nach Borkau. — 12. Juli. Linkes Radauneufer zw. Borkau und der Drahthammerbrücke: Hypericum tetrapterum, Camelina microcarpa, Epipactis latifolia, **Chaerophyllum hirsutum,** Trifolium alpestre, Digitalis ambigua, Hypericum montanum, Polygonatum multiflorum und officinale, Campanula persicifolia var. hispida, Pimpinella magna, **Laserpitium latifolium,** Cornus sanguineus, Lilium Martagon, Orobus niger, Crepis biennis, Geranium sanguineum Bromus asper, **Bupleurum longifolium,** Aconitum variegatum, Paris quadrifolia, Actaea spicata, Listera ovata, Hieracium cymosum. Auf einem Abhange südlich von der Drahthammerbrücke: Tragopogon pratensis, Asperula odorata. Im Walde südlich von Borrowo: Pirola minor, P. uniflora, Paris quadrifolia, Aconitum variegatum, Polygonatum officinale, Platanthera bifolia, Pirola rotundifolia. — 14. Juli. Rechtes Radauneufer zw. Ruthken und Babenthal: **Chaerophyllum hirsutum, Bupleurum longifolium,** Hypericum quadrangulum und montanum, Lilium Martagon, Neottia Nidus avis, Triticum caninum, **Pleurospermum austriacum,** Epipactis latifolia. An einem Bache im Walde südlich von Babenthal: **Chaerophyllum hirsutum,** Sanicula europaea, Thalictrum angustifolium. An der Chaussee von Babenthal nach Zuckau: Anthericus ramosus, Aquilegia vulgaris, Lathyrus silvester, Crepis virens. — 15. Juli. Zw. Borkau und Seeresen: Veronica spicata, Helianthemum vulgare. Seeresen-See: Myosotis caespitosa. Am Wodsno-See: Drosera longifolia, Anthericus ramosus, Geranium sanguineum, Ribes rubrum. Mehsau. Zw. Pechbude und dem Borrowo-See: Senecio silvaticus, Monotropa Hypopitys. Am Borrowo-See: Ranunculus reptans, Scheuchzeria palustris, Drosera longifolia, Litorella lacustris. Im Walde nordöstlich vom Borrowo-See: Selinum Carvifolia, Lilium Martagon, Geranium sanguineum. — 16. Juli. Von Borkau nach der Zuckau'er Papiermühle: Geranium palustre, Berula angustifolia. An der Stolpe zw. der Zuckau'er Papiermühle und Mehlken: **Polemonium coeruleum,** Lathyrus silvester, Thalictrum angustifolium, Eriophorum latifolium. Abhang südöstlich von Mehlken: **Centaurea austriaca,** Chaerophyllum aromaticum. Sumpf zw. Smolsin und Borkau: Carex filiformis. — 19. Juli: Linkes Radauneufer zw. Borkau und Zuckau: Triticum caninum, Geranium pratense, Stachys silvatica, Listera ovata, **Chaerophyllum hirsutum,** Allium oleraceum, Fragaria collina, Phleum Boehmeri, Trollius europaeus, **Libanotis montana.** Rechtes Radauneufer zw. Zuckau und Ottomin: Salix nigricans. Zw. Ottomin und Ruthken: Crepis virens. — 21. Juli. In einem Sumpf südöstlich. von Ruthken: Peplis Portula. Zw. Neu- und Alt-Glinsch: Papaver dubium. Im Stangenwalde'r Forst zw. Alt-Glintsch und Babenthal: Pirola rotundifolia, Selinum Carvifolia, Monotropa Hypopitys. Im Walde zw. Babenthal und der Radaune: **Chaerophyllum hirsutum,** Bromus asper, **Bupleurum longifolium,** Actaea spicata, **Pleurospermum austriacum,** Pirola chlorantha, Orobus niger.

23. Juli: Uebersiedelung nach Hoppendorf. 24. Juli. Zw. Hoppendorf und Semlin: Campanula Trachelium, Saponaria officinalis. Von Semlin nach Kelpin: Crepis biennis, Anthemis tinctoria. An den Seen zw. Kelpin und Mehsau: Myosotis

caespitosa, Empetrum nigrum, Scheuchzeria palustris, Rhynchospora alba, Drosera longifolia, **Litorella lacustris.** Rechtes Radauneufer zw. Fliessenkrug und Wilhelmshof: Armeria vulgaris, Asarum europaeum, **Polygonatum verticillatum**, Crepis biennis, Rubus suberectus. Sümpfe bei Neuhof. — 26. Juli. Zw. Semlin und Kartaus: Scabiosa columbaria, Sticta pulmonaria, Lathyrus silvester. Am Stillen See (südlich vom Krugsee): Carex filiformis, Rubus saxatilis, Glyceria nemoralis. Am Krugsee: Myosotis caespitosa. Zw. Kartaus und Burchardswo: Rubus Bellardi. Am Firkus-See: Peplis Portula. Im Walde westlich vom Firkus-See: **Laserpitium prutenicum,** Pimpinella magna. — 28. Juli. Zw. Semlin und Gorrenczyn: Stellaria glauca, Ononis repens. An der Radaune zw. Gorrenczyn und Ostritz: Sagina nodosa. Am Trzebno-See: Aiuga genevensis, Clinopodium vulgare, Lolium remotum. Am Ostritz-See zw. Ostritz und Ndr. Brodnitz: Stachys annua, Linaria minor, Thalictrum minus, **Arabis hirsuta.** Am Gr. Brodno-See zw. Ndr. Brodnitz und Remboszewo: Pimpinella magna, Ranunculus Lingua, Listera ovata. Zw. Remboszewo u. Dombrowo: Monotropa Hypopitys. — 29. Juli. Eggertshütte. Schlawkau. Am See von Schlawkau: Viola mirabilis, Stachys silvatica, Ranunculus Lingua. Zw. Konty und Ostritz: Coronilla varia. Zw. Ostritz und Colano: Asperula odorata, Scabiosa columbaria, Lathyrus silvester. — 30. Juli. An einem Bache östlich von Hoppendorf, der bei Fliessenkrug in die Radaune mündet: Selinum Carvifolia, Salix pentandra, Pimpinella magna, Viola mirabilis, Aconitum variegatum, **Laserpitium prutenicum.** — 31. Juli. Zw Eggertshütte und Fischerhütte: Avena praecox. Zw. Fischerhütte und Fustpeterhütte: Carlina vulgaris. Kapellenhütte. Am See von Kapellenhütte: Carex filiformis. Starkhütte, Kamehlen. Zw. Kamehlen und Hoppendorf: Juncus squarrosus. — 2. August. Zw. Kamehlen und Tiefenthal: Agrostis alba b. gigantea. Am Pollenczin'er See: Scirpus acicularis, Polygonum mite, Hieracium boreale b. chlorocephalum, Agrimonia odorata, Carlina vulgaris, Lycopodium complanatum. Von Tiefenthal nach Ndr. Klanau. Am See von Ndr. Klanau: Ranunculus Lingua. Zw. Ndr. Klanau und Michaelshütte: Actaea spicata. — 3. August. Hoppendorf, Fitschkau. Im Wäldchen nördlich von Fitschkau: **Chaerophyllum hirsutum,** Orobus niger, Triticum caninum, Viola mirabilis, **Libanotis montana,** Centaurea austriaca, Alliaria officinalis. Zw. Fliessenkrug und Babenthal: Scabiosa columbaria. Auf dem rechten Radauneufer zw. Fliessenkrug und Babenthal: Botrychium Matricariae (1 Exempl.), Lathyrus silvester, Bromus asper, **Chaerophyllum hirsutum,** Campanula latifolia. — 4. August. Zw. Bortsch und Ober-Sommerkau: Selinum Carvifolia, Galium verum, Centaurea austriaca. Am Sommerkau'er See: Circaea lutetiana, Glyceria nemoralis, Rumex sanguineus, Orobus niger, Sanicula europaea, Carex silvatica, **Chaerophyllum hirsutum,** Ranunculus Lingua, Lycopodium Selago. Am Glamke-See: Polygonatum multiflorum, Viola mirabilis.

6. August: Uebersiedelung nach Stendsitz. 7. August. Zw. Stendsitz und dem Radaune-See: Aiuga genevensis. Am Kopinsko-See: Hydrocotyle vulgaris, Drosera longifolia, Potamogeton graminea b. heterophylla, Sparganium minimum, Utricularia vulgaris. Im Dorfe Borruczyn: Verbena officinalis, Conium maculatum. See von Borruczyn. Am Radaunesee südlich von Lonczyn: Rumex maximus, R. aquaticus, Aiuga genevensis, Mercurialis perennis, Sanicula europaea, Scabiosa columbaria, Ranunculus Lingua. Auf der Halbinsel nördlich von Lonczyn: **Libanotis montana,** Thalictrum minus, **Aconitum variegatum,** Pimpinella magna, Veronica Teucrium.

Lonczyn, Stendsitz. — 8. August. Zw. Stendsitz und Gollubien: Hypochoeris glabra. Kniewo-See: Myriophyllum alterniflorum, Scirpus setaceus, Carlina vulgaris. Schönberg. Sycorczyn. Am Dlugi-See (östlich von Skorzewo): Myriophyllum alterniflorum, Scirpus acicularis. Skorzewo, Stendsitz. — 9. August. Zw. Stendsitz und Seedorf: Setaria viridis. Zw. Seedorf und Alt-Czapel: Geranium silvaticum, Pirola media. Am Brück-See: Drosera longifolia, Scabiosa columbaria. Am Südufer des Ostritz-Sees: Ainga genevensis, Actaea spicata, Viola mirabilis, Circaea lutetiana, Pirola rotundifolia und **media, Cephalanthera rubra, Cypripedium Calceolus,** Sanicula europaea, Epipactis latifolia, Aconitum variegatum, Listera ovata, Agrimonia odorata. — 11. August. Zw. Stendsitz und Pierszewo: Thalictrum aquilegifolium, **Pirola media,** Sticta pulmonaria. Lonken-See: **Myriophyllum alterniflorum,** Geranium columbinum. Am Kosel-See: Ranunculus reptans, Hydrocotyle vulgaris. Zw. dem Koselsee und Alt-Czapel: Rubus suberectus. In Alt-Czapel: Verbena officinalis. Stein-See: **Myriophyllum alterniflorum,** Carlina vulgaris. Schulzen-See: **Myriophyllum alterniflorum.** Zw. Gr. Pierszewo und Gollubien: Malva Alcea, Rubus Bellardi. — 12. August. Am Nordufer des Ostritzsees: Thalictrum minus, Euphorbia Cyparissias, Stachys annua, St. silvatica, Hedera Helix. Von Ndr.-Brodnitz nach Ober-Brodnitz: Selinum carvifolia. Lindenhof. — 13. August. Am Radaune-See zw. Lindenhof und Schnurken: Pimpinella magna, Onobrychis viciifolia, Viola mirabilis, Convallaria maialis, Paris quadrifolia, Dianthus barbatus, Arabis Gerardi, Agrimonia odorata. Zw. Schnurken und Max: Ononis repens. An der Chaussee von Max nach Borruczyn: Onobrychis viciifolia. Am Radaune-See zw. Borruczyn und Zuromin: Linaria minor, Salix pentandra, Actaea spicata. — 14. August. In einem Torfbruch südlich von Stendsitz: Gentiana Amarella. Bobernitz. Am Bobernitz-See: Drosera longifolia, Hydrocotyle vulgaris. Owsnitz. Am Gr. Dlugi-See: Pulsatilla vernalis, Hydrocotyle vulgaris, Polygonatum officinale, **Cynanchum Vincetoxicum,** Geranium sanguineum, Orobus niger, **Laserpitium latifolium,** Lilium Martagon, Actaea spicata. Kl. Dlugi-See, Gostomie, Stendsitz. — 16. August. Von Gostomie nach Gostomken: Astragalus arenarius. Gostomkener See: Juncus alpinus, Eriophorum latifolium, Hydrocotyle vulgaris, Potamogeton mucronata, Gypsophila muralis, Aiuga genevensis. Am Borrowo-See (Kr. Berent): Hydrocotyle vulgaris, **Laserpitium latifolium,** Lycopodium annotinum, Arctostaphylos Uva ursi, **Pirola media,** P. umbellata. Glinken, Gostomie. Gostomie'r Mühlenteich, Reinwasserbach. — 18. August. Klukowahütte. Mischischewitz. In der Sucha-Schlucht: Potentilla procumbens, Drosera longifolia, Hydrocotyle vulgaris. Auf einem Abhange im Dorfe Sulleczyn: **Libanotis montana.** Am Gustinsch-See: Hydrocotyle vulgaris, **Aplenium Trichomanes, Polygonatum verticillatum.** Am Gostkowo-See: Scabiosa columbaria. Wensiorry. — 19. August. Zw. Stendsitz und Riebenhof: Carduus acanthoides. Zw. Riebenhof und Niesolowitz: Lolium remotum, Hydrocotyle vulgaris. Am Ostrowitt'er See: Alchemilla arvensis. Am Dlugi-See (bei Niesolowitz): Juncus capitatus. Wensiorry, Krähwinkel.

21. August. Uebersiedelung nach Alt-Kischau (Kreis Berent). — 22. August. Im Dorfe Alt-Kischau: Nepeta Cataria, Galeopsis pubescens. Rechtes Ferseufer zw. Alt-Kischau und Schwarznau: Ranunculus Lingua, Berula angustifolia, Poa serotina Von Schwarznau nach Blumfelde: Marrubium vulgare. Rechtes Ferseufer zw. Boschpohl und Ober-Mahlkau: Potamogeton fluitans, Thalictrum angustifolium, Pimpinella

magna. Auf einer sumpfigen Wiese nördlich vom Cziesien-See: Saxifraga Hirculus, Dianthus superbus, Epipactis palustris, Eriophorum latifolium. Cziesien-See. Vielle-See: **Euonymus verrucosa**, Mercurialis perennis. An der Chaussee von Gora nach Alt-Kischau: Ameria vulgaris. — 23. August. Am See südlich vom Wege zw. Alt-Kischau und Fersenau: Lycopodium inundatum, Hydrocotyle vulgaris. Am Krangen-See: Senecio paluster, Dianthus superbus. Fersenau. Kosellen-See. Am Czerwonnek-See: Drosera longifolia. Czengardlo, Konarschin. — 25. August. Kl. Okonin. An dem See südlich von Kl. Okonin: Pirola umbellata, Galium boreale, Polygonatum officinale, Pulsatilla vernalis. Grünthal. Dunaiken-See: Potamogeton praelonga. Nordöstlich von Kasub im Walde: Dianthus arenarius, Lycopodium annotinum. Dlugi-See bei Lippe. An einem Bache von Trenkkrug nach der Lippe'r Mühle: Holcus mollis. Strugga. — 26. August. Im Forste Okonin zw. Ob.-F. Okonin und Unt. F. Kl. Bartel: Polygonatum officinale, Geranium sanguineum, **Peucedanum Cervaria**, Lilium Martagon. An den Seen nordöstlich von d. Unt.-F. Kl. Bartel: Hydrocotyle vulgaris, Juncus supinus, Rhynchospora alba, Lycopodium Selago, Pirola umbellata, P. minor, P. secunda, Arctostaphylos Uva ursi, Calamagrostis neglecta. Zw. Kl. und Gr. Bartel: Thalictrum minus. Zw. Gr. Bartel und Alt-Kischau: Geranium sanguineum, Arctostaphylos Uva ursi, Pirola umbellata. — 27. August. Zw. Prziawitzno und d. Unt.-F. Gribno: Pulsatilla vernalis, Prunella grandiflora, Anthericus ramosus. Grosser Sumpf nordöstlich von d. Unt.-F. Gribno: Hypericum tetrapterum. Am Moos-See: Juncus alpinus. Am See südwestlich von d. Unt.-F. Gribno: Salix pentandra, Scabiosa columbaria. An den Seen bei d. Unt.-F. Gribno: Hypericum tetrapterum, Hydrocotyle vulgaris. Zw. Unt.-F. Gribno und Unt.-F. Holzort: Arctostaphylos Uva ursi, Dianthus arenarius. Zw. Unt.-F. Holzort und Wigonin: Lilium Martagon, Prunella grandiflora. — 28. August. Am Dlugi-See (nördlich von Przia-witzno): Erythraea Centaurium. An den Seen südlich von Bzengardlo: Juncus alpinus, Verbascum phlomoides, Hydrocotyle vulgaris. Am Sand-See: Myosotis caespitosa, Stachys annua, Lolium remotum. Zw. Konadschin und Alt-Kischau: Panicum filiforme.

29. August. Uebersiedelung nach Pogutken. — 30. August. Pogutken, Koschmin. Zw. Koschmin und Gora: Armeria vulgaris, Conium maculatum. Ostufer des Vielle-Sees: Brachypodium pinnatum, Vicia cassubica, Cuscuta Epithymum. Am Wiechol-See: Geranium dissectum, Polygonatum officinale, ***Euonymus verrucosus***, Vicia cassubica, Agrimonia odorata. Im Frauen-See: Potamogeton graminea b. heterophylla, **Myriophyllum alterniflorum.** An der Chaussee südlich von Gora: Centaurea maculosa. Zw. d. Frauen-See und Babidol: Armeria vulgaris, Hydrocotyle vulgaris, Aiuga reptans. Neuhof. — 1. Septbr. Zw. Pogutken und Kleschkau: Scabiosa columbaria, Armeria vulgaris. An d. grossen Torfsumpf südlich von Jarischau: Juncus supinus, Peplis Portula. An den Seen zw. Kleschkau und Lindenberg: Ranunculus reptaus, **Myriophyllum alterniflorum,** Drosera longifolia. Im Langen-See: **Myriophyllum alterniflorum,** ***Isoëtes lacustris,*** Ranunculus reptans. Zw. Gr. Semlin und Jeseritz: Vicia cassubica. Unt. F. Killa. — 2. September. Zw. Pogutken und Gladau: Pirola minor, Asperula odorata. Decka'scher See: **Myriophyllum alterniflorum,** Drosera longifolia. Lonken-See: Drosera longifolia, **Myriophyllum alterniflorum.** Am Gebrowo-See: Ranunculus Lingua. Gladau, Gilnitz. Zw. Gilnitz und Pogutken: Galium

boreale, Rubus Bellardi. — 3. September. Auf dem rechten Ferseufer zw. Pogutken und Reinwasser: **Potamogeton fluitans,** Picris hieracioides, Agrimonia odorata. Schwarzhof. Bukowitz. Im Sobowitz'er Forst zw. Schwarzhof und Unt.-F. Thiloshain: Hypericum quadrangulum.

Von Professor Dr. Prätorius trifft ein Päckchen mit Pflanzen von Konitz zur Vertheilung ein. Es waren:

Gentiana cruciata L. Insel im Müskendorf'er See 24. 7. 84. Neu für Konitz. — **Gentiana Pneumonanthe** L. Sandkrug 7. 9. 84. — **Lepidium ruderale** L. Bahnhof. 13. 9. 84. Neu für Konitz. — **Carlina acaulis** L. 7. 9. 84. — **Pedicularis Sceptrum Carolinum** L. Abrau 2. 8. 84. — **Pedicularis silvatica** L. Sandkrug 7. 9. 84. — **Swertia perennis** L. Abrau 2. 8. 84. — **Tofieldia calyculata** Whlnb. Abrau 22. 7. und 17. 8. 84. — **Gymnadenia conopea** R. Br. Abrau 10. 7. 84. — **Agrimonia odorata** Mill. Insel im Müskendorf'er See 24. 7. 84. — **Potentilla procumbens** Sibth. Sandkrug 7. 9. 84. — **Stachys annua** L. Walkmühl 13. 7. 84. — **Origanum vulgare** L. Insel im Müskendorf'er See 24. 7. 84. — **Epipactis palustris** Crntz. Abrau 10. 7. 84. — **Saxifraga Hirculus** L. Abrau 22. 7. 84 und Walkmühl 24. 7. 84. — **Alchemilla arvensis** Scop. Weg nach Kl. Konitz am Waldrande 22. 6. 84. — **Geranium molle** L. Zandersdorf 14. 6. 84. — **Veronica opaca** Fr. Mai und Juni. — **Veronica polita** Fr. Mai und Juni. — **Pirola chlorantha** Sw. 22. 6. 84. — **Anemone patens** L. Bergelau 27. 4. 84. — **Anemone vernalis** L. Bergelau 27. 4. 84. — **Betula humilis.** Abrau 2. 8. 84. — **Carex Pseudo-Cyperus** L. Abrau 17. 8. 84. — **Molinia coerula.** Abrau 17. 8. 84. — **Astragalus Cicer** L. Abrau 22. 7. 84. — **Centaurea austriaca** Willd. Abrau 2. 8. 84. **Serratula tinctoria** L. Abrau 2. 8. 84. — **Erythraea Centaurium** Pers. Abrau 22. 7. 84., roth und weissblühend. — **Caltha palustris** L. Mit Umwandlung von Stengelblättern in Blumenblätter. 29. 4. 84. — **Narcissus poëticus** L. mit Doppelblüthen.

Professor Prätorius fügt folgende von Conrad Rosentreter, einem Schüler von ihm, bei Dirschau gesammelte Pflanzen bei:

Veronica longifolia L. 15. 8. 84. — **Reseda luteola** L. 25. 8. 84. — **Hordeum murinum** L. 25. 8. 84. — **Lactuca scariola** L. 25. 8. 84. — **Eryngium planum** L. 15. 8. 84. — **Xanthium italicum Mor.** 25. 8. 84. — **Stachys lanata.** 25. 8. 84., wild am Weichseldamm eine Meile oberhalb Dirschau.

Die Herren Apotheker Siemering und Oberlehrer Berent in Tilsit beglückwünschen die Versammlung durch Telegramm.

Herr Stud. Alfred Lemcke erstattet dann

Bericht über die botanische Erforschung der Kreise Danzig und Neustadt.

Ich hatte von Herrn Professor Caspary den Auftrag erhalten, eine ergänzende Untersuchung der Flora der Kreise Danzig und Neustadt, deren Erforschung Herr Professor Caspary seit vielen Jahren, Herr Dr. Bethke 1882 und Herr Dr. Abromeit im Vorjahre betrieben hatten, zu unternehmen. Ich begab mich deshalb am 3. Mai 1884 nach Praust und begann von hier aus meine Excursionen am 4. Mai.

Zunächst untersuchte ich den südwestlichen Theil des Kreises Danzig, wo ich in dem Saskoczin'er Walde: *Carex pilosa* (erster Standort westlich der Weichsel) vorfand. Dann suchte ich den zwischen den beiden Weichselmündungen gelegenen

Landstrich ab und ging allmälig längs dem Strande nach Norden bis Grossendorf vor. Von Putzig aus fuhr ich nach Hela hinüber und untersuchte die Halbinsel von Hela bis Grossendorf.

Dann ging ich in den südlichen Theil des Kreises Neustadt, untersuchte zunächst die Waldungen südlich vom Rhedathal und endlich die Umgegend von Smasin.

Leider musste ich einer Krankheit wegen meine Excursionen schon am 22. August einstellen.

In den Forsten des Kreises Danzig fand ich häufiger: Corydalis cava, C. intermedia, Mercurialis perennis, Polypodium vulgare, Lonicera Hylosteum, Viola mirabilis. **Scirpus rufus** beobachtete ich nur an zwei Stellen, südwestlich von Brösen und zwischen der Möwenschanze bei Weichselmünde und dem Binnensee.

Verbreitet im Kreise Neustadt sind folgende Pflanzen: Spartium scoparium, Empetrum nigrum, Ornithopus perpusillus, Hierochloa australis, Lycopodium annotinum, Avena praecox, Pinguicula vulgaris, in der Nähe der Küste Orchis maculata, Phegopteris polypodioides, Polypodium vulgare, Lysimachia nemorum, Carex glauca, Juncus squarrosus, Astragalus arenarius, Actaea spicata, Hypericum humifusum, Neottia Nidus avis, Monotropa Hypopitys, Ononis repens, Euphorbia Esula, Aiuga pyramidalis. Seltener fand ich: Listera ovata, Goodyera repens, Pirola uniflora, P. umbellata, P. chlorantha, Blechnum Spicant, Lycopodium Selago, Carex silvatica, Hypericum montanum, Digitalis ambigua, Cardamine hirsuta b. silvatica, Aconitum variegatum, Melica uniflora, Erica Tetralix, Avena caryophyllea, Cystopteris fragilis, Scirpus caespitosus, Myosotis versicolor, Aquilegia vulgaris, Thalictrum aquilegifolium, Armeria vulgaris, Plantago maritima, Hierochloa borealis, Juncus filiformis.

Selten beobachtete ich in den von mir untersuchten Gegenden: Pulsatilla vernalis, Listera cordata, Botrychium matricariifolium, B. simplex, Ophioglossum vulgatum, Festuca silvatica, Bromus asper, Juncus obtusifloras, Trifolium fragiferum, Thalictrun flavum, Polystichum montanum, Myosotis sparsiflora, Circaea lutetiana, Veronica montana, Lathyrus paluster, Elymus europaeus, Scirpus uniglumis, Carex dioica und C. pulicaris.

Im Bachthal der Bohlschau fand ich in grosser Menge: ***Struthiopteris germanica*** (2. Standort westlich der Weichsel).

Für die Unterstützung, die ich von Herrn Oberpräsidenten von Ernsthausen und von den Herren Rittergutsbesitzern Pieper-Smasin und Tümmler-Dembogorsz erhalten habe, statte ich hiermit meinen herzlichen Dank ab.

Die wichtigsten Ergebnisse der einzelnen Ausflüge sind folgende:

4. 5. 84. Längs Radauneufer zw. Praust und Gute Herberge: Gagea pratensis Z^3, G. minima $V^2 Z^3$. Im Wäldchen bei den Drei Schweinsköpfen: Viola odorata, **Corydalis intermedia** (1 Ex.). Auf dem Kirchhof von Bankau: Viscum album auf Tilia ulmifolia. Zw. Bankau und Prangschin: Viscum album auf Tilia ulmif. und Populus Tremula, Gagea minima. — 6. 5. 84. Zw. Praust und Schwintsch: Gagea pratensis, **Veronica polita** $V^1 Z^{23}$. In der Salau'er Forst: Viola Riviniana + silvatica, Monotropa Hypopitys. Zw. Saalau und Artschau: Gagea pratensis; im Dorfe Gischkau: Petasites officinalis. — 7. 6. 84. Zw. Prangschin und Bankau: Veronica agrestis, Asarum europaeum, Adoxa moschatellina, Gagea pratensis, **Corydalis**

intermedia $V^3 Z^3$, Equisetum hiemale. — 8. 5. 84. Im Bankau'er Walde: Carex montana, Polystichum cristatum. Am Ottomin'er See: Hierochloa australis Z^3, Neottia Nidus avis, Asperula odorata, Daphne Mezereum. Zw. Borgfeld und St. Albrecht: Petasites officinalis. — 9. 5. 84. Im nördlichen Theil des Saskoczin'er Waldes: **Corydalis intermedia** (Frucht) und **cava** (flor. alb. u. 4 Ex. c. flor. rubr.), Viola mirabilis, Paris quadrifolia, Asperula odorata. Im südlichen Theil des Saskoczin'er Waldes: Neottia Nidus avis, **Carex pilosa** $V^2 Z^{2-3}$, Mercurialis perennis, Polygonatum multiflorum. — 10. 5. 84. Regen. — 11. 5. 84. Zw. Praust und Schwintsch: Barbaraea vulgaris, Valerianella olitoria. In den Schluchten der Kladau bei Gr. Kleschkau: Viola mirabilis, **Corydalis cava** (c. flor. alb. et rubr.) $V^3 Z^4$, Lathraea squamaria $V^4 Z^4$ Daphne Mezereum, Corydalis intermedia $V^2 Z^2$. — 12. 5. 84. Im östlichen Theil des Sobbowitz'er Waldes: Carex montana. Ufer der Kladau zw. dem Sobbowitz'er Wald und Kladau: Mercurialis perennis, **Ranunculus cassubicus** $V^2 Z^3$, Thalictrum aquilegifolium (Knospen), Viola mirabilis $V^3 Z^4$, Viola Riviniana + silvatica, Alliaria officinalis $V^1 Z^3$, **Aconitum variegatum** (Kraut) $V^2 Z^4$. Ueber Kladau, Suckczyn, Russoczyn nach Praust. — 13. 5. 84. Im Uhlkau'er Walde: Pirola uniflora, Viola Riviniana + silvatica. Ueber Lagschau, Klempin nach Senslau. Im Dorfe Senslau: Viscum album auf Populus tremula. — 14. 5. 84. Regen. — 15. 5. 84. Uebersiedelung nach Neufahrwasser.

16. 5. 84. Auf der Westerplatte: Fedia olitoria ($V^3 Z^2$), Carex Schreberi, Vicia lathyroides $V^4 Z^3$. Haide östlich von Weichselmünde: Spergula Morisonii $V^3 Z^5$, Carex ericetorum. Heubude, durch den westlichen Theil der Münd'schen Forst. Zwischen den Dünen an der Badeanstalt von Weichselmünde: Hierochloa borealis $V^2 Z^3$. — 18. 5. 84. Ballastplätze auf dem linken Ufer der Weichsel bei Neufahrwasser: Potentilla cinerea, Vicia lathyroides $V^3 Z^4$. — Zw. Neufahrwasser und Brösen, im Wäldchen bei Brösen: Hierochloa borealis Z^3, Pirola uniflora $V^2 Z^3$. Am Strande **Scirpus rufus** $V^1 Z^2$. Auf feuchtem Boden zw. den Dünen zw. Brösen und Glettkau: Empetrum nigrum. Zw. Glettkau und Zoppot: Ornithopus perpusillus $V^2 Z^2$, Vicia lathyroides, Viola canina + silvatica. Oliva'er Forst, zw. Zoppot und Josephau: Hierochloa australis, Viola Riviniana + silvatica. — 19. 5. 84. Zw. Brösen und Oliva: Vicia lathyroides, Carex Schreberi. Auf dem Karlsberg bei Oliva: Carex montana. Oliva'er Forst zw. Oliva und Schmierau: Pulsatilla vernalis, Hierochloa australis, Vicia lathyroides. Zw. Schmierau und Grenzlau: Anemone nemorosa (c. fl. rubr.), Hierochla australis. Zw. Grenzlau und Zoppot: Aquilegia vulgaris, Pulmonaria officinalis, Actaea spicata, Thalictrum aquilegifolium. — 21. 5. 84. Auf der Westerplatte: Geranium molle. Westlich von der Möwenschanze bei Weichselmünde, am Binnensee: **Scirpus rufus** $V^1 Z^4$. Südlich von der Möwenschanze: Euphorbia Esula. Haide zw. Weichselmünde und der Münd'schen Forst: Vicia lathyroides, Carex Schreberi. Am Weichselufer zw. der Mündung und Sandkathen (Schleuse): Hierochloa borealis. Am Weichselufer zw. Sandkathen und Heubude: Valerianella olitoria, Carex riparia. —

22. 5. 84. Uebersiedelung nach Oliva. — 23. 5. 84. Oliva'er Forst zw. Kenneberg und Strauchmühle: Hierochloa australis, Lathraea squamaria $V^2 Z^2$, Polygonatum anceps. Zw. Strauchmühle und Wittstock: Lycopodium Selago. Ueber U.-F. Schäferei nach Oliva. — 24. 5. 84. Am Glettkau-Fliess zw. Oliva und Glettkau:

Eupatorium cannabinum, Juncus balticus. Zw. Glettkau und Saspe: Pinguicula vulgaris (V[1] Z[4]), Myosotis versicolor, Avena praecox. Zw. Saspe und Saspe'r See: Ranunculus Lingua, Vicia lathyroides, **Polygala amara** V[1] Z[2]. Am Saspe'r See: Hierochloa borealis. Zw. Saspe'r See und Neufahrwasser: Carex Schreberi. — 25. 5. 84. Zw. Neufahrwasser und Legan: Alyssum calycinum, Hierochloa borealis. Gräben südlich vom Saspe'r See: ***Potamogeton densa*** V[2] Z[4]. — 26. 5. 84. Feiertag. — 27. 5. 84. Wiesen zw. Glettkau und Zoppot: Pinguicula vulgaris Z[4]. Auf den Strandtriften: Juncus balticus, Vicia lathyroides. In Zoppot: Alliaria officinalis.

28. 5. 84. Uebersiedelung nach Neufahrwasser. — 29. 5. 84. Hagel und Regen. Nachmittag auf der Westerplatte: Asperugo procumbens, **Bunias orientalis.** — 30. 5. 84. Westerplatte: Reseda lutea. Am Binnen-See: Scirpus rufus. An der Möwenschanze: Triglochin maritima. In der Münd'schen Forst: Pirola uniflora. Gr. Haid-See. Zw. Heubude und Weichselmünde: Carex riparia, Hierochloa borealis. — 31. 5. 84. Wiesen nordöstlich von Weichselmünde: Empetrum nigrum. In der Münd'schen Forst: Quercus sessiliflora, Spergula Morisonii, Asperugo procumbens. Seestrand nördlich der Münd'schen Forst bis zum Weichseldurchbruch von 1840: Orchis incarnata, Thalictrum aquilegifolium, Equisetum hiemale. Südrand der Münd'schen Forst zw. dem Durchbruch der Weichsel bei Neufähr und Heubude: Carex Schreberi, Sempervivum soboliferum V[2] Z[4], Polygonatum anceps, Polystichum cristatum, Spergula Morisonii.

4. 6. 84. Uebersiedelung nach Oliva. — 5. 6. 84. Zw. Oliva und Pelonken: Geranium molle. Oliva'er Forst zw. dem vierten Hof von Pelonken und der Ziegelbrennerei: Monotropa Hypopitys, Hierochloa australis, Polygonatum anceps, Actaea spicata, Neottia Nidus avis. Zw. Pelonken und Jeschkenthal: Viscum album auf Populus tremula und Tilia ulmifolia. Im Jeschkenthal'er Wäldchen: Polygonatum anceps, V[2] Z[2]. — 6. 6. 84. Zw. Glettkau und Zoppot: Potentilla opaca, Botrychium Lunaria V[2] Z[3], **B. matricariifolium** V[1] Z[2], Pinguicula vulgaris V[2] Z[3]. — 7. 6. 84. Zw. Bahnhof Oliva und Kenneberg: Asperugo procumbens, Carex pallescens. Zw. Kenneberg und Grenzlau: Pirola uniflora. Zw. Grenzlau und Taubenwasser: Potentilla opaca. Zw. Taubenwasser und Zoppot: Actaea spicata. — 8. 6. 84. Zw. Oliva und Schmierau: Geranium molle, Ornithopus perpusillus. Zw. Schmierau und Taubenwasser, Oliva'er Forst: Neottia Nidus avis, Polygonatum anceps, Hierochloa australis, Viola canina + silvatica. Taubenwasser. Zw. Josephau (Josefshof) und Bernadowa: Rubus saxatilis, Equisetum hiemale, Myosotis hispida. — 9. 6. 84. Bernadowa, Koliebken. In Strandschluchten zw. Koliebken und Zoppot: Asperugo procumbens, Fragaria elatior V[1] Z[3-4], Actaea spicata, Polygonatum multiflorum; auf den Strandtriften zw. Koliebken und Zoppot: Valerianella olitoria, Euphorbia Esula, Triglochin maritima. — 10. 6. 84. Zw. Oliva und Schwabenthal: Hordeum murinum, Orchis incarnata, Valerianella olitoria; nordwestlich von Ernsthof: Viscum album auf Tilia ulmifolia; zw. Schwabenthal und Freudenthal: Lathraea squamaria V[3] Z[3], Orchis latifolia; zw. Freudenthal und Gluckau: Orchis incarnata, Potentilla opaca; Kokoschken und Hoch-Kelpin. In den Schluchten am Striess-Bache zw. Kl. Kelpin und Matemblewo: Viola mirabilis (Frucht) V[3] Z[2], **Aconitum variegatum** (Laub), Hierochloa australis, Neottia Nidus avis, Sanicula europaea. Ueber Brentau und Silberhammer nach Oliva. — 11. 6. 84. Regen. —

12. 6. 84. Zw. Oliva und Ernstthal: Asperugo procumbens, Valerianella olitoria; zw. Ernstthal und Lobeckshof: Polygonatum anceps und P. multiflorum, Aquilegia vulgaris $V^2 Z^4$; zw. Jeschkenthal und Matemblewo: Scorzonera humilis. — 14. 6. 84. Saspe. Zw. Weishof-Saspe und Glettkau: Hippuris vulgaris $V^1 Z^3$; Strandtriften zw. Glettkau und Zoppot: Botrychium Lunaria, Vicia lathyroides, Juncus balticus, Orchis latifolia, **Botrychium matricariifolium** (1 Expl.). — 15. 6. 84. Zw. Oliva und Glettkau unter Gebüsch: **Myosotis sparsiflora** $V^1 Z^2$; zw. Glettkau und Zoppot auf den Strandtriften: Avena praecox $V^2 Z^4$, Myosotis versicolor $V^1 Z^2$, **Botrychium simplex** (10 Ex.), Ornithopus perpusillus $V^3 Z^2$, Pinguicula vulgaris $V^3 Z^3$, Botrychium Lunaria $V^4 Z^2$, **Botrychium matricariifolium** $V^1 Z^1$; zw. Zoppot und Thalmühle: Orchis incarnata, **Myosotis hispida**; im Wäldchen bei Thalmühle: Crepis paludosa, Listera ovata $V^2 Z^3$, Orchis maculata $V^2 Z^3$, Thalictrum aquilegifolium. — 16. 6. 84. Umzug nach Kielau. — 17. 6. 84. Zw. Bahnhof Kielau und Pogorsz: Orchis incarnata; zw. Pogorsz und Rahmel: Ornithopus perpusillus $V^2 Z^2$, Carex stellulata, Avena praecox, Pinguicula vulgaris $V^1 Z^2$. Von Rahmel über Sagorsz nach Kielau. — 18. 6. 84. Zw. Kielau und Gdingen durch die Kielau'er Forst, in einer Waldschlucht: Pinguicula vulgaris $V^3 Z^3$, Geranium sanguineum, Polygonatum anceps. Dann Regen. — 19. 6. 84. Zw. Kielau und Gdingen, längs der Chaussee: Chenopodium Bonus Henricus; zw. Gdingen und Adlers Horst: Myosotis versicolor, Carex flacca, Viola mirabilis $V^2 Z^3$ (Laub), Trifolium alpestre, **Hieracium echioides** $V^2 Z^{3-4}$, Actaea spicata; von Adlers-Horst über Hoch-Redlau, Gdingen nach Kielau. — 20. 6. 84. sammelte ich zwischen Zoppot und Glettkau ausser den oben erwähnten Pflanzen noch Botrychium simplex und B. matricariifolium.

21. 6. 84. Uebersiedelung nach Ziessau. — 22. 6. 84. Im Kielau-Bruch zw. dem Kielau-Bach an der Kielau-Pogorsz'er Chaussee und Oxhöft: Orchis incarnata und O. latifolia, **Scirpus uniglumis** $V^3 Z^3$, Eriophorum latifolium $V^3 Z^2$. Von Oxhöft über Oblusz, Pogorsz nach Ziessau. — 23. 6. 84. Zw. Rheda und Schmelz, in der Gnevau'er Forst: Listera ovata, Orchis maculata $V^2 Z^2$, Eriophorum latifolium $V^1 Z^2$, Ervum cassubicum, Sanicula europaea, Carex silvatica, Orobus niger $V^1 Z^3$, Neottia Nidus avis, Rubus Bellardi, Lysimachia nemorum $V^1 Z^3$, **Ophioglossum vulgatum** (Laub) $V^2 Z^{2-3}$, **Carex glauca**, Polygonatum anceps, Pirola uniflora $V^3 Z^2$. Schmelz. In Sagorcz: Chenopodium Bonus Henricus; zw. Sagorcz und Ziessau: Trifolium alpestre. — 25. 6. 84. Zw. Ziessau und U.-F. Starapila, in der Kielau'er Forst: Lysimachia nemorum, Lycopodium Selago und annotinum, Carex silvatica, C. remota, Ervum cassubicum, **Polygala amara** $V^1 Z^3$, **Cardamine hirsuta b. silvatica** $V^2 Z^3$, Pirola uniflora und chlorantha; zw. U.-F. Starapila und U.-F. Piekelken: Geranium sanguineum; in den Schluchten am Sagorcz-Bach zw. den beiden Unterförstereien: **Cardamine hirsuta b. silvatica** $V^1 Z^1$, Listera ovata; zw. U.-F. Piekelken und Lensitz, Kilau'er Forst: **Rubus Bellardi**, Pulsatilla vernalis (2 Expl., Frucht); zw. Lensitz u. Ziessau: Pirola uniflora $V^1 Z^5$. — 26. 6. 84. Zw. Ziessau und Völtzendorf: Pirola umbellata, Scorzonera humilis; zw. Völtzendorf und U.-F. Krückenwald längs Katz-Bach: Thalictrum aquilegifolium, Lysimachia nemorum, Platanthera bifolia; zw. U.-F. Krückwald u. Kl. Katz längs dem Katz-Bach: Lysimachia nemorum, Orchis incarnata, Eriophorum latifolium; zw. Kl. Katz und Völtzendorf: Ervum cassubicum, Pirola uniflora, P. chlorantha, Avena caryophillea. — 27. 6. 84. Zw. Ziessau und Dembogorsz: Ononis repens, Blyssmus

compressus; im Kielau-Bruch: Eriophorum latifolium; Kielauer' Forst, Revier Eichberg: Epipactis latifolia (Laub), Pirola chlorantha und umbellata, Monotropa Hypopitys a. hirsuta, Ervum cassubicum, Carex remota; Dembogorsz Eichberg. Im Kielau-Bruch zw. Eichberg und Ziessau: Carex dioica V^2 Z^4, Orchis incarnata, **Carex pulicaris** V^3 Z^{3-4}, Pinguicula vulgaris (Frucht) Z^3.

28. 6. 84. Uebersiedelung nach Dembogorsz. — 29. 6. 84. Pogorsz. Zw. Oxhöft und Neu-Oblusz: Avena praecox, Ononis repens. — 30. 6. 84. Regen. — 1. 7. 84. Auf Strandhügel südöstlich von Oxhöft: Marrubium vulgare. Nachmittag Regen. 2. 7. 84. Zw. Dembogorsz und Amalienfelde: **Erica Tetralix** V^1 Z^3, Myosotis versicolor; in der Babidole oder Hexenschlucht, am Strande zw. Amalienfelde u. Neu-Oblusz: **Blechnum Spicant** Z^3, Pirola umbellata, Calamagrostis silvatica. Auf Strandhügeln zw. dem Hexengrund und Ostrow-Grund: Actaea spicata, Viola mirabilis (Laub), Listera ovata. Nachmittag im Kielau-Bruch, zw. Casimir und Vorwerk zu Dembogorsz: Orchis latifolia, **Carex pulicaris** V^1 Z^3, C. dioica, Avena caryophyllea und praecox. — 3. 7. 84. Zw. Dembogorsz und Amalienfelde: Avena caryophyllea; zw. Amalienfelde und Mechlinken, auf bewaldeten Strandhügeln: Viola mirabilis, Avena caryophyllea, Ribes alpinum, Listera ovata, Trifolium alpestre; zw. Mechlinken und Rewa: Hippuris vulgaris, Triglochin maritima. Im Brück'schen Moor zw. Rewa und Casimir: Juncus balticus, Butomus umbellatus, Hippuris vulgaris, Orchis incarnata, Pinguicula vulgaris; Gräben: Hydrocotyle vulgaris, Eriophorum latifolium, Listera ovata V^1 Z^3, Carex dioica V^3 Z^4, **Carex pulicaris** V^2 Z^3; über Casimir, Rahmel nach Dembogorsz: Pinguicula vulgaris, Avena praecox und caryophyllea. — 4. und 5. 8. 84 Regen. — 6. 8. 84. Zw. Pierwoschin und Brück: Hypericum montanum; in Brück: Saponaria officinalis; zw. Brück und dem Strömming-Fliess: Hippuris vulgaris, Scirpus compressus, Triglochin maritima; zw. Strömming-Fliess und Eichberg: **Carex pulicaris** V^2 Z^4, C. dioica. — 7. 7. 84. Zw. Pogorsz und Kilau: Avena praecox. Kielau'er Forst, Revier Eichberg: Orchis maculata, Carex filiformis.

9. 7. 84. Uebersiedelung nach Putzig. — 10. 7. 84. Ueberfahrt nach Hela mit Dampfer Putzig. — 11. 7. 84. Wald nördlich von Hela: Empetrum nigrum V^3 Z^3, **Erica Tetralix** V^2 Z^3, **Listera cordata** V^1 Z^4, Avena praecox; im Dorfe Hela: Hordeum murinum. — 12. 7. 84. Zw. Hela und dem Hela'er Leuchtthurm: Elymus arenarius, Hieracium umbellatum fr. linariifolium, Empetrum nigrum V^4 Z^5, Juncus balticus, Erica Tetralix V^3 Z^3, Avena praecox. Zw. Hela'er und Heisternest'er Leuchtthurm, auf den Dünen am äussern Seestrande: **Pisum maritimum** V^3 Z^2, Linaria odora V^3 Z^{1-2}, **Erica Tetralix** V^3 Z^3, Juncus squarrosus, Eriophorum latifolium, Orchis maculata, **Listera cordata**; zw. den Dünen des Nordufers: **Lycopodium inundatum**; im Walde: Andromeda poliifolia, Monotropa Hypopitys; zw. Heisternest'er Leuchtthurm und Hela: Erica Tetralix, Empetrum nigrum, **Goodyera repens**, Glaux maritima. — 13. 7. 84. Zw. Hela und Heisternest'er Leuchtthurm: Senecio viscosus, Avena praecox, Erica Tetralix, Carex filiformis, Hydrocotyle vulgaris, Goodyera repens, Linaria odora; zw. Heisternest'er Leuchtthurm und Danzig'er Heisternest: Glaux maritima, Avena praecox, **Erica Tetralix**, Hydrocotyle vulgaris; zw. Danzig'er und Putzig'er Heisternest: Triglochin maritima. — 15. 7. 84. Zw. Putzig'er Heisternest und Kussfeld: Cakile maritima, Hippuris vulgaris, Armeria vulgaris, Triglochin maritima, **Erythraea linariifolia** V^2 Z^3, **Plantago maritima** V^3 Z^3, Lathyrus paluster V^1 Z^2, Scirpus Taber-

naemontani, Hydrocotyle vulgaris, Pirola uniflora, P. umbellata und P. chlorantha, **Listera cordata** V^2 Z^2, L. ovata V^3 Z^4, Agrostis canina, Glaux maritima, Salix pentandra; zw. Kussfeld und Ceynowa: Pisum maritimum, Linaria odora, Ammophila baltica V^3 Z^3, **Spergularia salina** V^2 Z^{3-4}, Glaux maritima, Juncus balticus, Plantago maritima. — 16. 7. 84. Ruhetag. — 17. 7. 84. Zw. Putzig und Döhling's Ziegelei: Phleum pratense b. nodosum, Calamagrostis arundinacea, C. lanceolata, Geranium molle, Aquilegia vulgaris; zw. Döhling's Ziegelei und Blondzikau: Avena praecox, Butomus umbellatus; zw. Blondzikau und Celbau: Sperganium simplex, Geranium pratense. — 18. 7. 84. Zw. Blondzikau und Sellistrau: **Erica Tetralix** V^2 Z^2, **Scirpus caespitosus** V^1 Z^3, S. compressus; am Gisdepka-Bach zw. Schmollin und Oslamin: Lysimachia nemorum V^1 Z^3, Scrophularia alata, **Lappa nemorosa** V^1 Z^1; zw. Oslamin und Rutzau: Silene nutans, Equisetum hiemale, Thalictrum flavum V^1 Z^3, **Rubus Bellardi** V^2 Z^2, Hippophae rhamnoides, Avena praecox; zw. Rutzau und Putzig: Hypericum montanum. — 19. 7. 84. Zw. Putzig und Celbau: Alopecurus geniculatus; an den kleinen Tümpeln westlich vom Putzig-Polchau'er Wege: Triodia decumbens, Avena praecox, **Scirpus uniglumis** V^3 Z^4, **Erica Tetralix** V^2 Z^2, Phleum pratense b. bulbosum; zw. Kl. Schlatau und Rekau: Ornithopus perpusillus; zw. Rheda und Rekau, in der Darslub'er Forst, Revier Rekau: Pulmonaria obscura, **Melica uniflora** V^3 Z^2, Orobus niger, Monotropa Hypopitys b. hirsuta, Mercurialis perennis, Sanicula europaea, Neottia Nidus avis, **Brachypodium silvaticum**, Epipactis latifolia (Laub), Trifolium alpestre, **Rubus Bellardi**, Hypericum montanum, Actaea spicata; zw. Rekau und Polchau: Avena caryophyllea; zw. Polchau und Schmollin: Alchemilla arvensis, Phleum pratense b. bulbosus; in Schmollin: Verbena officinalis; zw. Schmollin und Putzig: Alchemilla arvensis, Hypericum humifusum. — 20. 7. 84. Regen. — 21. 7. 84. Vormittags zw. Putzig und Zrada: Sparganium simplex, Ranunculus Lingua, Epipactis palustris V^3 Z^2, Dianthus superbus V^2 Z^4. — Nachmittags Uebersiedelung nach Rheda. — 22. 7. 84. Anhaltender Regen. — 23. 7. 84. Zw. Rheda und Neustadt: Chenopodium Bonus Henricus; auf dem Garnierberg bei Neustadt: Actaea spicata, **Brachypodium silvaticum**, Carex silvatica, C. remota, Lysimachia nemorum, **Veronica montana** V^2 Z^{3-4}, **Rubus Bellardi**, Circaea lutetiana V^3 Z^3, **Melica uniflora** V^3 Z^2, Calamagrostis arundinacea, Ervum cassubicum. Auf den Cedronwiesen zw. der Schlossmühle und der Ziegelei: Polemonium coeruleum V^3 Z^2; Neustädt'er Forst, zw. Ziegelei und Neustadt, östlich vom Cedronthal: Orobus niger, Daphne Mezereum, **Festuca silvatica** V^3 Z^3, Neottia Nidus avis, Carex remota, C. silvatica, **Rubus Bellardi** V^1 Z^1, Pirola umbellata, Monotropa Hypopitys a. hirsuta; zw. Cedronmühle und U.-F. Ottiliensruh: Circaea alpina, Lysimachia nemorum, **Blechnum Spicant** V^2 Z^2. — 24. 7. 84. In einer Schlucht der Gnewau'er Forst, gegenüber dem Bahnhof von Rheda: **Lappa nemorosa 1** Expl.; in der Gnewau'er Forst zw. Rheda und Mehlken: Ervum cassubicum, Monotropa Hypopitys, **Goodyera repens** V^1 Z^4, **Melica uniflora** V^2 Z^4, **Rubus Bellardi**, **Veronica scutellata var. parmularia**, Crepis virens; längs östl. Cedron-Quellfluss zw. Mehlken und Neustädt'er Ziegelei: Hydrocotyle vulgaris, Listera ovata, Lysimachia nemorum, Thalictrum aquilegifolium, Orchis maculata, Mercurialis perennis, Hypericum montanum, Rubus Bellardi. Dann Regen, der auch am 25. 7. 84 anhielt. — 26. 7. 84. Zw. Rheda und Neustadt: Alchemilla arvensis, Hypericum montanum; in der Gnewau-Neustädt'er Forst: Rubus Bellardi, Achillea

Ptarmica, Ervum cassubicum, Avena caryophyllea, Monotropa Hypopitys, Orchis maculata, Viola mirabilis, Mercurialis perennis, Pirola chlorantha, Lysimachia nemorum, Listera ovata, **Cardamine hirsuta** b. **silvatica** V^2 Z^3, Circaea alpina V^3 Z^4, Lathyrus silvester, **Brachypodium silvaticum**, Lycopodium Selago, **Blechnum Spicant** V^3 Z^{1-2}. Wald südl. von Neustadt: Aspidium cristatum, **Rubus Bellardi**, **Blechnum Spicant** V^3 Z^4, Cystopteris fragilis; auf den Cedronwiesen zw. Neustadt und der Ziegelei: Orchis maculata, **Rubus Sprengelii** V^1 Z^2, Melandrium rubrum; auf dem Kellerberg bei Neustadt: **Blechnum Spicant** V^4 Z^3, **Aspidium montanum** V^1 Z^3; Schmechau, Pelzau. — 27. 7. 84. Zw. Rheda und Sbichau: Clinopodium vulgare, **Rubus Bellardi**, Monotropa Hypopitys, Pirola secunda; zw. Sbichau und Neuhof: Achillea Ptarmica; zw. Neuhof und Bieschkowitz: Andromeda poliifolia; zw. Bieschkowitz und Borrowo: Anthericum ramosum V^3 Z^2; am Borrowo-See: Juncus filiformis, **Rubus Bellardi**, **Blechnum Spicant** V^2 Z^1, Hydrocotyle vulgaris; zw. Borrowo und Wispau: Anthericum ramosum; zw. Gnewau und Rheda: Rubus Bellardi V^3 Z^2, Pirola uniflora V^1 Z^1. — 30. 7. 84. Zw. Rheda und Pelzau, am Nordrande der Gnewau'er Forst: Pirola secunda, **Goodyera repens**, Festuca gigantea, **Cardamine hirsuta** b. **silvatica**, **Bromus asper**, **Brachypodium silvaticum** V^2 Z^3, Rubus Bellardi, Circaea lutetiana, Mercurialis perennis, in einer Schlucht südöstlich von Pelzau: **Cardamine hirsuta** b. **silvatica** V^1 Z^2, Lysimachia nemorum, Orchis maculata; Avena praecox. — 31. 7. 84. Zw. Putzig und Schwarzau: **Scirpus uniglumis** V^2 Z^3, Triglochin maritima, Thalictrum flavum (Laub.), **Spergularia salina** V^2 Z^2, **Erythraea linariifolia** V^3 Z^2; in Gräben an der Mündung der Plutnitz: **Nasturtium officinale** V^2 Z^2; Strandwiesen zw. der Plutnitz-Mündung und Schwarzau: Alopecurus geniculatus, Trifolium fragiferum V^3 Z^4; zw. Schwarzau und Grossendorf auf Strandwiesen: Ligustrum vulgare, **Plantago maritima** V^4 Z^3, **Spergularia salina** V^1 Z^4, Avena praecox, Radiola linoides V^4 Z^5, Hippuris vulgaris, **Erythraea linariifolia** V^3 Z^3, Geranium palustre; in Strandgräben südöstlich von Grossendorf: **Potamogeton trichoides**, Myriophyllum verticillatum, Utricularia vulgaris, **Juncus obtusiflorus** V^1 Z^3. Vom 1. 8. 84 bis 9. 8. 84 musste ich einer heftigen Erkältung wegen meine Excursionen einstellen.

Am 10. 8. 84 siedelte ich nach Smasin über. 11. 8. 84. Am Gossentin-Bach zw. Smasin und Abbau Melwin: **Aconitum variegatum** V^2 Z^3, Geranium palustre, Festuca gigantea V^3 Z^2, Viola mirabilis (Laub), Polygonatum anceps, Mercurialis perennis V^3 Z^3, Euonymus europaea, **Digitalis ambigua** V^3 Z^4, **Bromus asper** V^1 Z^3, Thalictrum aquilegifolium V^3 Z^{2-4}, Lycopodium Selago V^3 Z^{2-3}, Aiuga pyramidalis, **Cardamine hirsuta** b. **silvatica** V^1 Z^3, Lysimachia nemorum V^3 Z^3, Achillea Ptarmica; am Gossentinbach zw. Abbau Mellwin und Mühle Barlomin: Scirpus silvaticus, Circaea alpina V^3 Z^3, Lysimachia nemorum V^3 Z^4, ***Strutiopteris germanica*** V^3 Z^5, **Brachypodium silvaticum** V^2 Z^3, Avena caryophyllea V^4 Z^{2-3}; zw. Barlomin'er Mühle und Barlomin: Achillea Ptarmica; zw. Barlomin und Wischetzin im Barlomin'er Walde: Carex remota, Molinia coerulea b. arundinacea, Monotropa Hypopitys; zw. Wischetzin und Smasin, am Hohlwege im Smasin'er Walde: **Digitalis ambigua** V^2 Z^3. — 12. 8. 84. Regen. — 13. 8. 84. Bruch im Südosten von Smasin: Empetrum nigrum, Salix pentandra, Carex glauca, **Scirpus caespitosus** V^3 Z^4; Bruch östlich vom vorigen: **Scirpus caespitosus** V^1 Z^2, Empetrum nigrum, Geranium palustre; im Wäldchen nordwestlich von Smasin: Digitalis ambigua V^1 Z^3, Carex silvatica V^3 Z^2; **Aconitum variegatum** V^1 Z^1, **Bromus asper**, Festuca gigantea, Asarum europaeum; am

Nordwestufer des Wischetzin'er Sees am Wege zw. Smasin und Wischetzin: *Erica Tetralix* $V^1 Z^2$. — 14. 8. 84. Zw. Smasin und Grünberg: Achillea Ptarmica; zw. Grünberg und Pretoschin: **Rubus Bellardi**; über Glashütte nach Neuhof; im Walde von Dennemörse: **Scirpus caespitosus.** — 15. 8. 84. Am Gossentin-Bach zw. Smasin und Zemblau'er Mühle: Geranium palustre, Pulmonaria officinalis $V^2 Z^3$, **Centaurea austriaca** $V^2 Z^2$, *Polygonatum verticillatum* $V^1 Z^3$, Mercurialis perennis $V^2 Z^4$, Calamagrostis lanceolata $V^3 Z^3$, Scrophularia alata; in Torfgräben: Myriophyllum spicatum, Molinia coerulea b. arundinacea; Salix pentandra; zw. Zemblau'er Mühle und Lewinko: Achillea Ptarmica; im und am Lewinko-See: **Myriophyllum alterniflorum** (einen Gürtel um den See bildend), **Elatine Hydropiper** $V^2 Z^2$; im und am Miloschewo-See: **Myriophyllum alterniflorum, Chara aspera** $V^1 Z^5$ (in 1⅓—2' tiefem Wasser), Butomus umbellatus; am bewaldeten Ostufer des Miloschewo-See: Ribes alpinum, Rubus Bellardi; über Lewinko, Pobloz, Idasruh nach Smasin. — 17. 8. 84. Zw. Smasin und Zemblau: Geranium palustre, Mentha silvestris $V^1 Z^3$; zw. Zemblau und Bendargau: **Lycopodium inundatum.** — 18. 8. 84. Zw. Smasin und Grüneberg: Hypericum humifusum; Grüneberg, Pretoschin, Soppieschin, Biala; kl. Moorwiese südwestlich von Biala: Juncus filiformis; am Teufels-See im Walde zw. Biala u. U.-F. Pentkowitz: **Veronica scutellata var. parmularia,** Avena praecox, Hydrocotyle vulgaris; *Polystichum montanum* $V^1 Z^3$, Monotropa Hypopitys; in den Schluchten am westl. Quellfliess des Cedronbaches: Mercurialis perennis. Circaea alpina, Lysimachia nemorum, Lycopodium Selago, **Blechnum Spicant** $V^1 Z^3$, **Cardamine hirsuta** b. **silvatica** $V^1 Z^2$; zw. der Neustadt'er Ziegelei und der Cedron-Mühle in den bewaldeten Schluchten des rechten Cedron-Ufers: **Blechnum Spicant** $V^3 Z^2$, Circaea lutetiana, **Festuca silvatica** $V^1 Z^3$, **Bromus asper,** Mercurialis perennis, **Rubus Bellardi, Elymus europaeus** $V^1 Z^3$, **Melica uniflora** $V^2 Z^2$; auf den Cedron-Wiesen: **Polemonium coeruleum**; zw. der Cedron-Mühle und dem Kellerberg: **Blechnum Spicant, Aspidium montanum** $V^2 Z^2$; über Soppieschin, Pretoschin, Grüneberg nach Smasin. — 19. 8. Ruhetag. — 20. 8. Zw. Smasin und Lebno: Salix pentandra, Hypericum tetrapterum, Orchis maculata, Eriophorum latifolium, Platanthera bifolia. — 21. 8. Zw. Lebno und Schönwalderhütte: Ornithopus perpusillus, Alchemilla arvensis, **Aster longifolius** (verwildert), Vaccinium uliginosum; an einem Torfsee: Empetrum nigrum; an einem Waldsumpf: Peplis Portula, Veronica scutellata var. parmularia; in Torfbrüchen zw. Schönwalderhütte und Steinkrug'er See: **Scirpus caespitosus** $V^3 Z^4$, Achillea Ptarmica, Rhynchospora alba $V^2 Z^3$; im u. am Steinkrug'er See: Isoëtes lacustris fr. falcata, Avena praecox. — 22. 8. 84. Zw. Smasin und Carolinenhof: Empetrum nigrum, Hypericum humifusum, Achillea Ptarmica; im Walde westlich von Smasin: Paris quadrifolius, **Festuca silvatica** $V^2 Z^3$, Thalictrum aquilegifolium, **Digitalis ambigua**, Neottia Nidus avis; am kl. Waldsee im Smasin'er Wald: Carex filiformis $V^3 Z^2$; zw. Carolinenhof und Strepsch: Hypericum humifusum, **Carlina vulgaris,** Molinia coerulea b. arundinacea, Ervum cassubicum, Orchis maculata, Achillea Ptarmica, Bidens cernuus b. minimus; im und am See von Strepsch: **Elatine Hydropiper** $V^1 Z^3$, Peplis Portula, **Myriophyllum alterniflorum**; Pobloz; in einem Torfsee am Wege zw. Strepsch und Pobloz: Vaccinium uliginosum; am Zemblau'er Mühlenteich: Potamogeton crispa, **Polemonium coeruleum** (Laub.).

Es wird um 12 Uhr eine Frühstückspause von ½ Stunde gemacht.

1883 waren in Marienburg die Herren Prof. Lentz und Apotheker Eichert zu Prüfern der Kasse erwählt. Da Herr Eichert verreist war und Herr Professor Spirgatis, den der Vorsitzende für Herrn Eichert einzutreten aufforderte, sich verhindert sah, übernahm Herr Gartenmeister Einicke mit Herrn Prof. Lentz die Prüfung der Kasse. Ihr Bericht wird verlesen. Die Einnahme betrug 1884 3257,65 Mk., die Ausgabe 3184,49 Mk., mithin Bestand 73,16 Mk. 1000 Mk. wurden kapitalisirt und es sind 11725 Mk. Kapital vorhanden. Auf diesen Bericht hin wird die Kassenführung von der Versammlung für richtig erklärt. Zu Prüfern der Kasse für 1885 werden die Herren Prof. Dr. Spirgatis und Apotheker Mielentz erwählt. Pr. Stargardt wird als Versammlungsort für 1885 ausersehen, wo Herr Apotheker Siewert die Geschäftsführung übernehmen will. Der Vorstand wird durch Acclamation von Neuem erwählt und beschlossen, die muthmasslich für 1885 zur Verfügung stehenden 1200 Mk. zur Ergänzung der Untersuchungen der Kreise Memel, Kartaus, Berent und Danzig zu verwenden.

Dr. Heidenreich-Tilsit bringt: Struthiopteris germanica von Friedrichsgnade an der Equitte. Dann Juncus balticus und Tragopogon heterospermus von den Dünen westlich von der Stadt Tilsit, auf denen Dr. Heidenreich jetzt auch Salix daphnoides Vill., neu für Tilsit, aufgefunden hat. Ferner: Trifolium spadiceum von den Puszinen, Coenolophium Fischeri vom Memelufer bei Tilsit, Laserpitium prutenicum aus Polen vom waldigen Memelufer bei Kowno, Alnus pubescens Tausch, Ranunculus auricomus b. fallax Wimmer, Bidens radiatus, Centaurea maculosa, Achillea cartilaginea, Chaeturus Marrubiastrum, Gladiolus imbricatus, Ononis hircina aus der Nähe von Tilsit.

Es laufen dankende Telegramme von Professor Prätorius und Conrektor Seydler ein.

Stud. Emil Knoblauch erstattet dann seinen

Bericht über die botanische Erforschung des Kreises Memel.

Die Untersuchung des Kreises Memel von Seiten des preussisch-botanischen Vereins wurde 1884 von Herrn Professor Caspary mir übertragen. Sie dauerte vom 7. Mai bis 12. September, während welcher Zeit ich den Kreis zweimal bereiste. Der Kreis Memel ist waldarm; die meist privaten Wälder des nördlichen Theils sind (mit Ausnahme der angepflanzten Memel'er „Plantagen") Laubwälder; die des südlichen Theils werden von der königl. Klooschen'er Forst gebildet. Die Hauptbäume des nördlichen Theils sind Betula verrucosa und pubescens, daneben findet man Sorbus aucuparia, Populus tremula, Quercus pedunculata, Alnus glutinosa und incana, Fraxinus excelsior, Tilia ulmifolia, Prunus Padus, Juniperus communis, Rhamnus Frangula; in der Lappenischke und in Wäldern bei Baugskorallen treten auch Pinus silvestris und Picea excelsa als Hauptwaldbäume auf; die der Klooschen'er Forst sind Pinus silvestris, Picea excelsa, Betula pubescens und verrucosa, ferner Populus tremula, Quercus pedunculata, Rhamnus Frangula, Sorbus aucuparia, Fraxinus excelsior, Alnus glutinosa. Eine interessante Ausbeute lieferten die Flussthäler der Dange, Schmeltelle, Minge, Wewirczo; von Bachthälern ist besonders das der Ekitte zu erwähnen. — Von meinen Funden sind neu für Ostpreussen ***Carex pulicaris,*** V^3 Z^2

im Kreise, und *Myrica Gale* (westlich und nordwestlich von Prökuls); von *Potamogeton salicifolia Wolfg.* fand ich den 2. Standort für Ostpreussen und Deutschland.

Bemerkenswerth ist die Verbreitung folgender Pflanzen im Kreise: der seit Kannenberg im Kreise nicht gefundenen *Sesleria coerulea* (40 Standorte; südlich von der Minge noch nicht beobachtet), ferner der *Pinguicula vulgaris* (75 Standorte, namentlich im Löbarten'er, Dt. Crottingen'er und Baugskorallen'er Gebiet) *Primula farinosa* (85) *).

Von seltneren Pflanzen fand ich: Lycopodium inundatum (2: Prökuls, Zenkuhnen), L. Selago, Polygonatum verticillatum (6: Bebruhne, Ekitte, Miszeiken, Löbarten, Minge), Eriophorum latifolium (11), Equisetum arvense b. boreale Ruprecht (30), E. hiemale (17), Linnaea borealis (12), Ranunculus fluitans (Minge, Aglohne), Carex pulicaris (10), C. fulva Good. (14), C. flacca, Ophioglossum vulgatum (3), Trifolium spadiceum (8), Microstylis monophylla (2), Gentiana Pneumonanthe (3); nur im nördlichen Theile der Kreises beobachtete ich: Alyssum montanum (1), Arabis Gerardi (2), Festuca arundinacea (3), Coralliorrhiza innata (1), Triticum iunceum (1), T. acutum (1), Lappa nemorosa (1), Brachypodium silvaticum (2), Centaurea austriaca (1), Pedicularis Sceptrum Carolinum (1); im südlichen Theile: Myrica Gale (9), Gladiolus imbricatus (3), Stellaria Frieseana, Listera cordata (2), Liparis Loeselii (1), Drosera anglica (2), Carex limosa (1), Cyperus fuscus (1).

Am 3. 7. 84 fand Herr Gutsbesitzer Scheu-Löbarten im Gehölz von Dautzkurr-Narmund **Epipactis palustris,** und **Microstylis monophylla** (zum 1. Male im Kreise.)

Anderweitig häufige Pflanzen sind im Kreise Memel selten, wovon ich hervorhebe: Asperula odorata (1), Circaea alpina (4), Carex Pseudo-Cyperus (1), Malachium aquaticum (Minge, Wewircze, Olisse.)

Nur in und bei der Stadt Memel sah ich: Chenopodium Vulvaria, Onopordon Acanthium, Epipactis rubiginosa (1), Ononis repens, Aster Tripolium (Nordermole), Centaurea paniculata, Hippophaë rhamnoides, Silene tartarica (Sandkrug, daselbst auch S. parviflora Pers.); fast ausschliesslich bei Memel: Echium vulgare, nur bei der Stadt Memel und in Schwarzort: Lepidium ruderale. Memel'er Ballastpflanzen sind: Diplotaxis tenuifolia, D. muralis, Sisymbrium Sinapistrum, Carduus nutans, Reseda lutea, R. Luteola; jedenfalls eingeschleppt sind Gypsophila paniculata (am Sandkruge, in der Plantage am Leuchtthurm, bis zur holl. Mütze, selbst noch bei Immersatt) und Elaeagnus argentea Pursh.

Häufigere Pflanzen sind: Carex caepitosa (verbreitet im Crottingen'er Gebiet**): 10), Elscholzia Patrini (10), Archangelica officinalis (14: Dange, Minge, Schmeltelle, Kanal, Wewircze), Cichorium Intybus (16, davon 10 im Memel'er Gebiet), Berteroa incana (17, 13 bei Memel, 4 bei Prökuls), Lappa minor (19), Campanula patula (23, im Aszpurwen'er Gebiet), Asarum europaeum (25, 17 im Baugskorallen'er, 6 im Crottingen'er Gebiet), Scirpus silvaticus (26), Carex flava a. vulg. (28) und b. Oederi (49), Melica nutans (28), Radiola linoides (28), Achyrophorus maculatus (33, namentlich im südl. Theil), Ledum palustre (33, bes. im Aszpurwen'er, Prökuls'er und Miszeiken'er Gebiet), Arctostaphylus Uva ursi (34 im südl. Theil), Juncus

*) Eingeklammerte Zahlen hinter Pflanzennamen geben die ungefähre Zahl der beobachteten Standorte an.

**) Diese Gebiete sind die Gebiete der Excursionen von den einzelnen Wohnorten aus.

squarrosus (39, bes. im Aszpurwen'er, Prökuls'er, Miszeiken'er, Löbarten'er Gebiet), Ranunculus polyanthemus (39, bes. im Aszpurwen'er, Löbarten'er, Prökuls'er Gebiet), Lycopodium annotinum (42, namentl. im südl. Theil), Dianthus deltoides (43), Drosera rotundifolia (46), Potentilla cinerea (48, namentl. im nördl. Theil im Gebiete der Dange und Schmeltelle, Ekitte, Minge, aber auch in dem der Wewircze), Juncus alpinus (51), Paris quadrifolia (51, namentl. im Crottingen'er und Baugskorallen'er Gebiet), Solanum Dulcamara (54), Artemisia Absinthium (58), Empetrum nigrum (62, bes. im südl. Theil), Gnaphalium silvaticum (63), Alectorolophus minor (67), Anchusa officinalis (70), Rubus saxatilis (73), Nardus stricta (75), **Pinguicula vulgaris** (75), Myosotis caespitosa (76), **Salix livida** (83, bes. im Baugskorallen'er, Löbarten'er und Miszeiken'er Gebiet), **Primula farinosa** (85).

Allen Herren, die mich bei meiner Untersuchung freundlichst unterstützt haben, sage ich auch an dieser Stelle meinen verbindlichsten Dank, insbesondere Herrn Landrath Cranz, Herrn Oberförster Schoeppfer-Klooschen, Herrn Apotheker Berger-Memel, den Herren Rittergutsbesitzern Frenzel auf Baugskorallen, Corallischken und Grünheide, Ruppel-Gr. Tauerlauken, C. Ogilvin-Aszpurven, Scheu-Löbarten, Schulz-Szernen, v. Schulze-Zenkuhnen, v. Schulze-Miszeiken, Sperber-Prökuls, Herrn Pfarrer Jussas-Dt. Crottingen und Herrn Hauptlehrer Kremp-Memel.

Hiernach gebe ich die hauptsächlichen Ergebnisse der einzelnen nach der Generalstabskarte angestellten Excursionen. — 7. 5. 84. Hinreise nach Memel, wo ich bis zum 14. 5. blieb. — 8. 5. 84. Gr. Tauerlauken, Purmallebach. — 9. 5. 84. Regen. — 10. 5. 84. In Seebad Försterei: Arabis arenosa, **Vicia lathyroides** V^1 Z^5; zw. Försterei und holländ. Mütze: **Chimophila umbellata** V^1 Z^3, **Polypodium vulgare**. Mellneraggen (kaufm. Plantage), Leuchtthurm, Bommelsvitte. — 11. 5. 84. Bachthal südl. von Kl. Tauerlauken: **Vicia lathyroides**. Ringel: Elodea canadensis V^5 Z^5. Oestlich von Gr. Tauerlauken: Viola odorata. Grünthal: Petasites tomentosus, Barbaraea arcuata. — 12. 5. 84. Carlsberg, Gr. Szarde, Schmelz. — 13. 5. 84. Bach zw. Zenkuhnen und Thaleiken-Jakob: Elodea canadensis; zw. Buddelkehmen und Carlsberg: Equisetum arvense b. boreale.

15. 5. 84. Umzug nach Dt. Crottingen, unterwegs an der Chaussee gefunden: Sesleria coerulea südlich von Gr. Tauerlauken V^1 Z^2; ferner zw. Gr. Tauerlauken und Paul-Narmund kurz vor Kilometerstein 7,8 V^1 Z^2 und zw. 10,0 und 10,5 V^2 Z^{2-3}; zw. Paul-Narmund und Dt. Crottingen V^{1-2} Z^2, z. B. vor 12,4, 12,9 und 13,7. — 15. 5. 84. Zw. Dt. Crottingen und Dange: **Sesleria coerulea** V^1 Z^3, **Polygala amara**; zw. Stanszen und Dt. Crottingen: Sesleria coerulea V^1 Z^1 vor 14,2. — 16. 5. 84. Linkes Dangeufer zw. Dt. Crottingen und Dautzin-Niklau: Sesleria coerulea, **Corydalis intermedia** (V^1 Z^5 gegenüber Dt. Crottingen). Zw. Dt. Crottingen und Gut Crottingen: Sesleria coerulea V^2 Z^{2-3}; zw. Gut Crottingen und Bajohr-Görge: Sesleria coerulea V^3 Z^{1-3}, Elodea canadensis. — 17. 5. 84. Dange zw. Dt. Crottingen und Dautzin-Niklau: Elodea canadensis V^4 Z^5; zw. Ekitten und Matzständen: Senecio vernalis, S. paluster, Stratiotes aloides. — 18. 5. 84. Dangewiesen zw. Stanszen und Claus-Puszen: **Sesleria coerulea** V^3 Z^5; Thal südlich von Claus-Puszen. — 19. 5. 84. Gehölz westlich von Dt. Crottingen: **Mercurialis perennis, Viola mirabilis** Z^5. Zw. Patra und Ulszeiken-Jahn: Sesleria coerulea V^2 Z^{2-3}; zw. Ulszeiken und Brusdeilinen und zw. Brusdeilinen und Szeichen: Sesleria coerulea Z^4. Chaussee

von Brusdeilinen und Szurlig: Sesleria coerulea V^4 Z^5, **Polygala amara** V^3 Z^1; zw. Szurlig und Immersatt: Sesleria coerulea V^3 Z^2; in Immersatt: **Carex Schreberi**. Zw. Nimmersatt und Strand: ***Alyssum montanum*** Z^5. Zw. Karkelbek und Perkam und zw. Perkam und Darguszen: **Sesleria coerulea**; zw. Darguszen und Labatag-Michel: Sesleria coerulea V^1 Z^2, Polygala amara V^3 Z^{1-3} (blau und weiss). — 20. 5. 84. Gehölz zw. Patra und Szodeiken-Jakob: Viola canina + silvatica, V. mirabilis, Sesleria coerulea, **Polygala amara**. Zw. Patra und Ilgauden-Mauserim, in Gehölz westl. am Wege: Hepatica triloba; am Wege: Sesleria coerulea V^{2-3} Z^3. — 21. 5. 84. Zw. Szudebarsden und Bahne: Sesleria coerulea V Z^3; Wald zw. Wallehnen und Talutten: **Carex flacca** V Z^3; zw. Wallehnen und Girngallen-Gedmin: **Carex flacca**; in Lappenischke: **Sesleria coerulea** V^3 Z^4; Lappenischke zw. Girngallen und Adl. Lappenischken: Lathyrus montanus; zw. Adl. Lappenischken und Gr. Kurschen: **Polygala amara**. — 22. 5. 84. Zw. Einnahren und Paul-Narmund: Sesleria coerulea V^3 Z^3 und V^1 Z^{3-4} zw. 10,8 und 12,4. Zw. Paul-Narmund und Collaten, Chaussee: **Polygala amara**. Wald nordöstlich von Collaten, Podszeit-Niklau, Sperrkersten. — 23. 5. 84. Labatag-Michel. — 24. 5. 84. Zw. Gaussen und Raiszen-Jetkandt: Sesleria coerulea V^2 Z^3; Gehölz nordwestlich von Raiszen: Sesleria coerulea, auch zw. Raiszen und Ilgauden-Mauserim; zw. Ilgauden und Kiacken: **Polygala amara**, im Walde: **Sesleria coerulea** Z^5, **Viola epipsila**. Zw. Kiaken und Ramutten-Jahn: Sesleria coerulea, Polygala amara V^3 Z^1; zw. Ramutten und Uszneiten und zw. Brusdeilinen und Perkam: Sesleria coerulea, Polygala amara. — 25. 5. 84. Zw. Zarthen und Kl. Kurschen, und zw. Gr. Kurschen und Dautzin-Thoms: Sesleria coerulea, Polygala amara (blau und weiss); zw. Dautzin-Thoms und Zarthen: Sesleria coerulea.

26. 5. 84. Umzug nach Baugskorallen. Zw. Baugskorallen und dem Walde: **Polygala amara**. Mikaitischken'er Wald, südl. Theil: Viola canina + silvatica. — 27. 5. 84. In der Baugst östlich von Corallischken: Elodea canadensis. Wald nordwestlich von Corallischken: **Polygala amara**; zw. Szabern-Wittko und Carlshof: Viola canina + silvatica; an der Ekitte: Lonicera Xylosteum, Mercurialis perennis, **Polygala amara**; letztere auch am Landweg von Corrallischken zur Chaussee. In Baugskorallen: **Symphytum officinale**. — 28. 5. 84. Baugskorallen'er Wald: **Ranunculus cassubicus, Sesleria coerulea** Z^{2-4}, **Polygala amara**; zw. Birkenwalde und Plicken: **Sesleria coerulea** V^4 Z^{2-5}, Polygala amara: zw. Plicken und Truszen: Polygala amara, Sesleria coerulea; zw. Truszen und Woiduszen: Sesleria coerulea; zw. Meddicken und Graumen: Sesleria coerulea, **Polygala amara**. Chaussee zw. Birkenwalde und Baugskorallen: **Sesleria coerulea**. — 29. 5. 84. Wald von Packmohren südlich der Ekitte: Viola canina + silvatica, Polygala amara; linkes Ekitteufer zw. Johannishof und Packmohren: Trollius europaeus, Lathyrus vernus, Acer platanoides, Viola canina + silvatica, **Struthiopteris germanica**. — 30. 5. 84. Wald östlich von Kl. Jagschen: Mercurialis perennis. Zw. Smilginen und Duatzkucken: **Ranunculus cassubicus**. — 31. 5. 84. Kallnischken, Truszellen, Ilgauden-Paul, Corallischken. — 1. 6. 84. In Bachmann: Viola odorata, Symphytum officinale, Petasites officinalis (angepflanzt, im Kreise nicht wild gefunden). — 2. 6. 84. Ekitte zw. Szabern-Wittko und Carlshof: **Polygonatum verticillatum**. Corallischken. — 3. 6. 84. Zw. Bajohr-Mitzko und Dargwill-Szodeiken: Viola mirabilis; Matzkiken, Dargwill-Szodeiken, Todden-Jakob, Dawillen. Zw. Laugallen und Todden: Polygala

amara, **Sesleria coerulea** V^{2-3} Z^{2} (südlichster Standort). — 4. 6. 84. Mikaitischken'er Wald, südl. Theil: Lathyrus vernus; Wiese zw. nördl. und südl. Theil: **Polygala amara.** — 5. 6. 84. Zw. Szabern-Wittko und Johannishof, rechtes Ekitte-Ufer: **Arabis Gerardi**; Wald links der Ekitte zw. Packmohren und Plicken: Hepatica triloba, Viola mirabilis, **Orchis mascula β. speciosa Host, Eriophorum latifolium. Carex dioica, C. filiformis.** — 6. 6. 84. Regen. — 7. 6. 84. Chaussee zw. Baugskorallen und Grünheide, und zw. Grünheide und Dinwethen: Polygala amara. Zw. Kaitienen und Matz-Masuhren: Lathyrus montanus. Ilgauden, Raddeilen. Ekitte gegenüber Friedrichsgnade: Mercurialis perennis; Wald von Packmohren nördl. der Ekitte: Orchis mascula β. speciosa. Rechtes Ekitte-Ufer zw. Johannishof und Szabern-Wittko: **Geranium silvaticum**; dasselbe zw. Carlshof und Friedrichsgnade: **Struthiopteris germanica**, Viola canina + silvatica.

8. 6. 84. Umzug nach Miszeiken. — 9. 6. 84. Miszeiken'er Park: **Asperula odorata** V^{1} Z^{2-3} (einziger Standort im Kreise), **Milium effusum, Ranunculus cassubicus,** Viola canina + silvatica; Schmeltelle: ***Polygonatum verticillatum*** V^{1} Z^{2}, Mercurialis perennis, Viola mirabilis, Hepatica triloba, Cornus sanguinea. Miszeiken'er Wald: Andromeda poliifolia. — 10. 6. 84. Zw. Miszeiken und Hennig-Haus: Orchis latifolia, Barbaraea arcuata. Wald zw. Löbarten und Ilgejahnen: **Listera ovata.** Zw. Löbarten und Dautzkurr-Narmund: Orchis mascula β. speciosa. In Kerren-Görge: Barbaraea stricta. Zw. Schweppeln und Eglien-Görge auf früherer Waldstelle: Trollius europaeus. — 11. 6. 84. Miszeiken'er Wald: Astragalus glycyphyllus (von Herrn v. Schulze mir gezeigter Standort). Südl. von Januszen: Salix livida + aurita; zw. Januszen und Kl. Daupern: Salix livida + aurita, Platanthera bifolia, Equisetum arvense b. boreale; zw. Slapsil und Bajohr-Mitzko: **Equisetum hiemale**, Vaccinium Oxycoccos, Salix repens c. vulg. Wimm.; zw. Schlapszil u. Gr. Daupern: Carex dioica. Schmeltelle gegenüber Gr. Daupern: **Thalictrum aquilegifolium.** — 12. 6. 84. Kischken-Görge, Kischken'er Wald: Carex Goodenoughii fr. iuncella Fr., ***Linnaea borealis*** V^{1} Z^{4}. —. 13. 6. 84. Daupern'er Moor: **Rubus Chamaemorus**, Carex dioica, ***Scirpus caespitosus.*** — 14. 6. 84. Schmeltelle. Rechtes Ufer zw. Miszeiken und Sziluppen: Equisetum palustre b. polystachyum, Barbaraea stricta, Salix rubra, Poa compressa, **Ranunculus divaricatus** in der Schmeltelle. Rechtes Ufer zw. Sziluppen und Zenkuhnen: Barbaraea stricta, Equisetum arvense b. boreale. Heide östlich von Zenkuhnen: **Eriophorum latifolium.** Gehölz nördlich von Zenkuhnen: Ulmus montana, Lathyrus vernus, L. montanus; zw. Zenkuhnen und Sziluppen, Weg östlich der Schmeltelle: Orchis mascula b. speciosa. Linkes Schmeltelle-Ufer zw. Januszen-Görge, Gr. und Kl. Daupern. Nordrand des Miszeiken'er Waldes: **Carex flacca.** — 15. 6. 84. Miszeiken'er Park: **Actaea spicata** V^{1} Z^{3-4}, Ulmus montana (ein Baum).

16. 6. 84. Umzug nach Löbarten. — Folgenden Minge-Theilen: 1) zw. Sudmanten-Haus und Dawillen, 2) zw. Szernen und Gedminnen, 3) zw. Gedminnen und Baiten, 4) zw. Szernen und Gröszuppen und 5) zw. Gröszuppen und Rooken ist gemeinsam: **Petasites tomentosus**; den ersten 4: **Ranunculus fluitans** (in der Minge) und Equisetum arvense b. boreale; den ersten 3: **E. hiemale**; Theil 1, 3 und 4: Thalictrum aquilegifolium; Theil 1, 2, 4 und 5: Barbaraea stricta, Saponaria officinalis; Theil 2, 4 und 5: Ranunculus polyanthemus, Solanum Dulcamara. — 1) Dem Walde zw. Löbarten und Ilgejahnen, 2) Gehölz zw. Baben und Galten und 3) von Dautz-

kurr-Narmund, 4) Szernen'er Gutswald ist **Viola epipsila** gemeinsam (in 1 und 4 auch V. epipsila + palustris); in 1, 2, 3: **Eriophorum latifolium**, Equisetum arvense b. boreale; in 2, 4: Aspidium cristatum, Ranunculus polyanthemus; in 1 und 3: Orchis mascula β. speciosa; in 2 und 3: **Carex pulicaris** zus. mit **C. fulva Good.** — 16. 6. 84. Wald zw. Löbarten und Ilgejahnen: Stratiotes aloides, **Carex paradoxa,** C. dioica, Platanthera bifolia. — 17. 6. 84. Zw. Hennig-Haus und Skranden-Niklau: Orchis mascula β) speciosa. Schmeltelle zw. Zenkuhnen und Buddelkehmen. — 18. 6. 84. Szernen'er Gutswald: Listera ovata. Szernen'er Wald nördl. d. Chaussee: **Equisetum hiemale** $V^1 Z^2$. Minge zw. Szernen und Gröszuppen: Eriophorum latifolium; Szernen'er Wald südl. d. Chaussee: **Linnaea borealis.** — 19. 6. 84. Rechtes Mingeufer zw. Sudmanten-Haus und Darwillen: Lychnis Viscaria, **Cynanchum Vincetoxicum,** Aspidium cristatum, **Trifolium spadiceum,** Spiraea Filipendula, **Struthiopteris germanica, Cystopteris fragilis,** Astragalus glycyphyllus. Zw. Stanz-Tramm und Baiten: Spiraea Filipendula, Thalictrum flavum; zw. Baiten und Griegszen: Spiraea Filipendula; zw. Griegszen und Kiaunoden: **Geranium silvaticum,** Lychnis Viscaria, **Trifolium spadiceum, Ribes alpinum, Carex fulva,** Thalictrum flavum, Petasites tomentosus (an der Minge). — 20. 6. 84. Zw. Sudmanten-Haus und der Minge: Senecio vernalis; Minge zw. Sudmanten und Kalwen: Barbaraea stricta, **Struthiopteris germanica** Z^4, Cynanchum Vincetoxicum, **Cystopteris fragilis,** Thalictrum aquilegifolium. — 21. 6. 84. Minge zw. Szernen und Gedminnen: Veronica Teucrium. Zw. Szernen und Gedminnen: Aspidium cristatum Phegopteris polypodiodes, **Viola epipsila,** Calla palustris. In der Minge zw. Gedminnen und Baiten: ***Potamogeton salicifolia Wolfg.;*** an d. Minge: Veronica Teucrium, Cynanchum Vincetoxicum, **Fragaria viridis,** Ulmus effusa. — 22. 6. 84. Ilgejahnen'er Wald: Trifolium spadiceum. Zw. Thalciken-Jakob und Kiaunoden-Görge: Aspidium cristatum, Equisetum hiemale, Silene nutans. — 23. 6. 84. Szernen'er Wald südl. d. Chaussee: Lathyrus montanus, Astragalus arenarius, **Chimophila umbellata,** Carex arenaria. Zw. Kl. und Gr. Jodicken: Carex arenaria; zw. Gr. Jodicken und der Chaussee: Senecio paluster, Carex teretiuscula. Chaussee zw. Kissinnen und Szernen: Anthemis tinctoria. — 24. 6. 84. Zw. Löbarten und Dautzkurr-Narmund: **Trifolium spadiceum, Botrychium Lunaria.** Gehölz von Dautzkurr: ***Carex pulicaris*** (neu für Ostpreussen), **Epipactis latifolia,** ***Polygonatum verticillatum.*** Kiefernwald zw. Dautzkurr und Jodeischen-Jahn: Platanthera bifolia. — 25. 6. 84. Gehölz südl. von Birbindschen (Nausseden-Jakob): **Viola epipsila.** Gehölz von Deutzkurr-Narmund: **Listera ovata,** Mercurialis perennis, **Carex flacca.** — Umzug nach Prökuls.

26. 6. 84. Woweriszken, Buttken'er Wald: **Chimophila umbellata, Pirola chlorantha.** Minge zw. Woweriszken und Protniszken: **Veronica Teucrium, Allium oleraceum** $V^1 Z^3$, Geranium pratense. **Ranunculus fluitans** in d. Aglohne. Zw. Gut Stragna und Mingekrug: Barbaraea stricta; zw. Mingekrug und Prökuls: Geranium pratense. — 27. 6. 84. ***Myrica Gale*** (neu für Ostpreussen) auf der Haide westl. vom Bahnhof Prökuls. — 28. 6. 84. Linkes Mingeufer zw. Klooschen und Swentwokarren: Stratiotes aloides (Tümpel). Kr. Heidekrug. In Gut Kukoreiten: Viola epipsila. Kieferngehölz westl. v. Bahnhof Kukoreiten: Aspidium cristatum, Iszlitz-Bruch: Calla palustris, **Sparganium minimum Fr.** — 29. 6. 84. Uszwaad- und Bruceschwa-Wiesen gemeinsam: **Triglochin maritimum, Hippuris vulgaris, Calamagrostis neglecta,** Potamogeton graminea b. heterophylla. Wäldchen der Oberförsterei Klooschen

(Jag. 51): Ranunculus fluitans (in d. Minge). In der Kliszub: **Scirpus Tabernaemontani**, an der Kliszub: Triglochin maritimum, Hippuris vulgaris. Nordöstl. v. Drawöhnen: Calamagrostis neglecta, Triglochin maritimum; Brucschwa-Wiesen: Scirpus Tabernaemontani. — 30. 6. 84. Tyrusmoor (Jag. 113), Szwenzeln'er Moor. Südwestl. v. Bahnhof Prökuls: **Euphorbia Cyparissias** V^1 Z^3; westl. desselben: Platanthera bifolia, ***Myrica Gale*** V^{1-3} Z^{2-4} (zw. Aeckern). Heide östl. v. Tyrusmoor: ***Myrica Gale***, Carex dioica; Tyrusmoor (Jag. 113): ***Myrica Gale*** V^3 Z^5, Potamogeton graminea b. heterophylla Fr. Szwenzeln'er Moor: **Rubus Chamaemorus**, Aspidium cristatum, ***Scirpus caespitosus***. — 1. 7. 84. Westl. des Bahnhofs Prökuls, **Sarothamnus scoparius** V^2 Z^3, Phegopteris Dryopteris. Zw. Prökuls und Darzeppeln; ***Myrica Gale***. In Darzeppeln: ***Myrica Gale***, Aspidium cristatum. Zw. Darzeppeln und Waschken: Carex arenaria, Scabiosa ochroleuca. In Kindschen-Bartel: Senecio paluster. Luseze. Jag. 87: Dianthus arenarius, westlich von Jag. 91 und 90 der Luseze: Scirpus Tabernaemontani, Triglochin maritimum. Wilhelmskanal zw. Jag. 88 und Schäferei: Carex arenaria, Dianthus arenarius; zw. Schäferei (Kanal) und Waschken: Triglochin maritimum; zw. Nibbern und Kooden: Lychnis Viscaria. — 2. 7. 84. Jag. 67: Platanthera bifolia. Am Kanal westl. von Jag. 60: Barbaraea stricta; von Jag. 67: **Lathyrus paluster**. Jag. 68: Thalictrum flavum. Jag. 70: Pirola uniflora; Jag. 71: Aspidium cristatum, **Circaea alpina**. — 3. 7. 84. In Szudnaggen: **Symphytum officinale**. Am Kanal östl. von Jag. 68: Senecio vernalis. Jag. 63: Barbaraea stricta, Thalictrum flavum (am Kanal), ***Gladiolus imbricatus*** (Südrand d. Jagens). Wiese südl. v. Jag. 65: Triglochin maritimum, Thalictrum flavum, ***Gladiolus imbricatus***; im Jag. 64: Thalictrum flavum. Ostsüdöstl. v. Darzeppeln: **Lycopodium inundatum** V^1 Z^{2-3}. Zw. Kooden und Prökuls: Spiraea Filipendula. — 4. 7. 84. Schutzbezirk Schwarzort: **Stellaria Frieseana**, Aspidium spinulosum b. dilatatum Hoffm., Koeleria cristata, **Linnaea borealis, Tragopogon floccosus**, Pirola uniflora. Ostseestrand von Schwarzort: Astragalus arenarius, Carex arenaria.

5. 7. 84. Umzug nach Aszpurwen. — 6. 7. 84. Wiesen östl. der Jagen 44: **Carex dioica, Eriophorum latifolium.** Jag. 39: Lathyrus vernus. Jag. 43: Phegopteris polypodioides. — 7. 7. 84. Jag. 46: **Circaea alpina** V^1 Z^4. Jag. 49: **Scirpus caespitosus.** Zw. Pöszeiten und Paaszkenkrug: **Trifolium spadiceum,** Triticum repens a. genuinum 2. aristatum Aschsn.; zw. Paaszkenkrug und Posingen, Landweg: Astragalus glycyphyllus; zw. Paaszkenkrug u. Szidellen: **Aiuga genevensis.** Zw. Paaszken und Kojellen, Gehölz nordwestl. von Paaszken: Thalictrum aquilegefolium, Ulmus montana With. Dorf Aszpurwen: **Triglochin maritimum.** — 8. 7. 84. Jag. 36: Lathyrus montanus, **Geranium sanguineum.** Südsüdwestl. von Gut Aszpurwen: **Echium vulgare** (im Innern des Kreises sehr selten), **Geranium molle.** Rechtes Aisseufer zw. Aszpurwen und Degeln: **Silene nutans.** Linkes Ufer zw. Degeln und Braszken: **Aiuga genevensis.** — 9. 7. 84. Jag. 20, 23—25. — 10. 7. 84. Rechtes Aisseufer zw. Aszpurwen und Dwielen: **Equisetum hiemale.** Jag. 50: **Salix livida + aurita.** Zw. Piktagen und Gellszinnen: **Trifolium spadiceum** (auch zw. Paaszken und Bielischken), **Carex pulicaris, C. dioica;** nordwestl. d. Gehölzes zw. Gelszinnen und Grabszten: **Equisetum hiemale.** Zw. Grabszten und Kojellen: Triticum repens b. caesium aristatum. Zw. Forsthaus und Dorf Aszpurwen: Platanthera bifolia. — 11. 7. 84. Gut Aszpurwen: Leonurus Cardiaca. Jag. 24: Carex arenaria; Jag. 21: **Listera cordata** V^1 Z^1

(2 Ex.). — 12. 7. 84. Westl. v. Degeln: Koeleria cristata. Jag. 27: **Listera cordata** V^2 Z^{2-3}. Wewirsze zw. Stoneiten und Stankaiten: Geranium palustre, Campanula persicifolia, Mercurialis perennis. — 13. 7. 84. Wewircze zw. Szeppoten und Begeden: Cornus sanguinea, **Aiuga genevensis, Senecio paludosus.** Jag. 15: **Microstylis monophylla** V^3 Z^1, Carex paniculata, **Eupatorium cannabinum**, Thalictrum aquilegifolium; Jag. 17: **Chimophila umbellata**; Jag. 18: Campanula persicifolia b. **eriocarpa DC., Geranium sanguineum,** Lychnis Viscaria; Wiese nordwestl. desselben: **Eriophorum latifolium,** Thalictrum aquilegifolium, Carex dioica, **Viola epipsila,** Aspidium cristatum, **Epipactis palustris, Liparis Loeselii** (1 Ex.), **Drosera anglica, Carex limosa.** In Begeden: Leonurus Cardiaca. — 14. 7. 84. Jag. 13: Veronica spicata, **Chimophila umbellata.** Jag. 4: **Aiuga genevensis.** In Grünheide bei Saugen: Koeleria cristata. Jag. 18: Lathyrus silvester; Jag. 19: **Carex Pseudo-Cyperus** (einziger Standort), Festuca rubra b. dumetorum L. (als Art) (= b. villosa Koch), Calla palustris, **Pirola chlorantha.** Zw. Norkaten und Kebbeln: Carex arenaria, Koeleria cristata. Linkes Wewirczeufer zw. Stankaiten und Aisseknen: Rumex aquaticus. — 15. 7. 84. Wiese östl. von Jag. 42: **Silene nutans.**

16. 7. 84. Umzug nach Memel. Bürgerfeld'er Memels: Potamogeton graminea b. heterophylla. Dange östlich von Königswäldchen: **Allium oleraceum.** Am Swiane-Teich: Calla palustris. — 17. 7. 84. In Begleitung des Herrn Hauptlehrer Schiemann nach der Plantage. Alter Ballastplatz in Memel: Echium vulgare, **Reseda lutea,** Onopordon Acanthium. Bommelsvitte'scher Kirchhof: **Sisymbrium Sinapistrum,** Vitte'scher Kirchhof: Echium vulgare. Zw. Bommelsvitte und Leuchtthurm, nördlicher Weg: **Hippophaë rhamnoides, Ononis repens** V^2 Z^5, Astragalus glycyphyllus; nördlicher Weg: **Elaeagnus argentea Pursch, Thalictrum minus, Centaurea paniculata.** Glacis des Plantagenfort: Centaurea paniculata, Diplotaxis tenuifolia, **Reseda Luteola.** Plantage zw. Leuchtthurm und Melneraggen'er Kirchhof: **Botrychium Matricariae** V^1 Z^3. Memel, Veitstrasse: **Chenopodium Vulvaria**; zw. Steinthor und Kallnischken: dasselbe, **Scirpus Tabernaemontani** an der Dange, Sisymbrium Sinapistrum. — 18. 7. 84. Schmelz (Chaussee): Onopordon Acanthium, Saponaria officinalis (dies auch am sog. Oberweg); Götzhöfen'er Kirchhof: **Thalictrum minus** V^1 Z^{2-3}. In Rumpischken: Symphytum officinale; zw. Rumpischken und Chaussee: **Malva silvestris.** Kurische Nehrung, Haff zw. nördl. Badeweg und dem obern Sandkruge: Rosa rubiginosa, **Elaeagnus argentea, Festuca arundinacea** (Südermole), **Malva silvestris.** Südlich vom obern Sandkruge: Elaeagnus argentea, **Silene Otites** und S. parviflora Pers., **S. tartarica.** Neuer Ballastplatz in Memel; **Matricaria discoides, Diplotaxis muralis.** — 19. 7. 84. Schwarzort, zw. Dorf und Bernsteincolonie: **Petasites tomentosus**; Grikiun: Aspidium cristatum, **Circaea alpina, Stellaria uliginosa**; Blocksberg: **Lycopodium Selago.** Ostseestrand: **Corispermum intermedium.** Weg südlich von Dorf Schwarzort, Haffseite: **Scirpus Tabernaemontani, Senecio silvaticus, Rumex maritimus.** Dorf: **Symphytum officinale.** — 20. 7. 84. Begleitet von Herrn Gymnasiallehrer Kühnemann. Oestlich von den Schiessständen an der städtischen Plantage: Typha latifolia, **Botrychium Matricariae, Ophioglossum vulgatum** V^3 Z^{1-3}. Park des Gasthauses Gr. Tauerlauken (westlich der Chaussee): Cuscuta europaea.

21. 7. 84. Umzug nach Gr. Tauerlauken. — Linkes Dange-Ufer in Kl. Tauerlauken: **Nasturtium barbaraeoides Tausch**, Limnanthemum nymphaeoides (Dange),

Festuca gigantea, Petasites tomentosus (auch an der Dange zw. Kl. Tauerlauken und Daugallen). Bachthal südlich von Kl. Tauerlauken: **Eupatorium cannabinum.** — 22. 7. 84. Begleitet von Herrn Kühnemann. Nordöstl. Theil der städt. Plantage: Platanthera bifolia, Pirola uniflora, Aspidium cristatum, **Allium oleraceum, Ophioglossum vulgatum** (südlich von Schiessstand I), **Botrychium Matricariae** (östlicher Rand der Plantage). Städtische Plantage: **Lolium italicum A. Br.** (verbreitet); im südlichen Theil: **Equisetum hiemale** V^1 Z^5, **Epipactis rubiginosa** V^1 Z^3 (westlich vom Plantagenfort), **Medicago media Pers.**; Nordermole: **Carduus nutans** V^1 Z^2, Diplotaxis muralis, D. tenuifolia, **Atriplex litorale, Rumex paluster, Aster Tripolium, Triglochin maritimum, Festuca arundinacea, F. distans.** Westnordwestlich vom Leuchtthurm (Badeweg): Ononis repens. Kaufmännische Plantage: **Corallorrhiza innata** südöstlich von Försterei in jungem Erlengehölz V^2 Z^3. Zw. Försterei und holländ. Mütze: Koeleria cristata, **Sarothamnus scoparius,** Ulmus montana With., Pinus Pumilio (angepflanzt), **Monotropa Hypopitys var. glabra** unter Kiefern. Palwen zw. holländ. Mütze und Gedwill-Paul: **Botrychium Matricariae** V^2 Z^1. Zw. Gedwill und Gr. Tauerlauken: Calla palustris. — 23. 7. 84. Dange zw. Gr. Tauerlauken und Purmallen: **Epilobium roseum,** Rumex aquaticus, **Allium oleraceum, Fragaria viridis,** Barbaraea stricta, Geranium palustre. Purmallebach östlich der Chaussee: Acer platanoides, Epilobium roseum. Südermole: Diplotaxis tenuifolia, **Triglochin maritimum,** Anthemis tinctoria, Corispermum intermedium, **Carduus nutans** V^1 Z^4 (auf Ballast). Dünen zw. Nehrungsfort und obern Sandkrug: **Silene parviflora Pers.** und **S. tartarica.** — 24. 7. 84. Dange bei Megallen und Gündullen. Zw. Elkitten und Matzständen: Geranium palustre, Trollius europaeus, **Allium oleraceum.** Zw. Gwilden und Oberhof: Spiraea Filipendula, Veronica spicata. Ringelbach: **Rumex aquaticus,** Geranium palustre, **Epilobium hirsutum.** — 25. 7. 84. Städtische Plantage, nördlicher Theil: Pirola uniflora. Palwen südlich von Försterei: **Botrychium Matricariae** V^1 Z^1, Salix repens a. vulg. In Försterei: **Sarothamnus scoparius,** Koeleria cristata. Am Collaten'er See: Calla palustris, **Typha latifolia,** Ranunculus polyanthemus. Zw. Podszeit-Niklau und Collaten: Geraniun palustre. — 26. 7. 84. Gr. Tauerlauken'er Bach, östl. und westl. d. Chaussee: **Campanula latifolia;** östlich der Chaussee: Stellaria Holostea. Bach westlich derselben, auf d. Palwe: Koeleria cristata, **Corispermum intermedium.** — 27. 7. 84. Derselbe Bach westl. der Chaussee, nördl. Arm: **Allium oleraceum,** Campanula latifolia. In Gr. Trauerlauken: **Populus nigra** (1 Baum), daran **Nepeta Cataria.** — 28. 7. 84. Ostseestrand zw. Leuchtthurm und dem nördl. Mellneraggen: **Salsola Kali** V^{2-3} Z^2, **Ammophila baltica;** Strand westl. des letztern: Corispermum intermedium, Salix rubra, Ammophila baltica. Südl. von Försterei: **Ononis repens** V^3 Z^5. Strand zw. Försterei und holländ. Mütze: Ammophila baltica, Corispermum intermedium; holländ. Mütze, Abhänge: **Silene nutans;** in der Plantage: **Pirola chlorantha.** Zw. Gr. Trauerlauken und Purmallen, westl. der Chaussee: Calla palustris. — 29. 7. 84. Ruhetag.

30. 7. 84. Regen und Umzug nach Wallehnen. — 31. 7. 84. Lappenischke zw. Wallehnen und Girngallen-Gedmin: **Carex flacca, C. fulva, Scirpus compressus, Viola epipsila.** Lappenischke nördl. d. Weges Wallehnen-Woiduszen: **Sesleria coerulea.** In Girngallen: **Lemna gibba.** Zw. Girngallen und Adl. Lappenischken (Lappenischke): **Viola epipsila.** Zw. Adl. Lappenischken und Gr. Kurschen: Geranium palustre. Westrand der Lappenischke südlich v. Gr. Kurschen: Trollius europaeus, **Trifolium**

spadiceum. Zw. Wittauken und Gr. Kurschen: Trollius europaeus, **Carex fulva.** Zw. Gr. Kurschen und Corallen, und zw. C. und Dorf Szudebarsden: **Trifolium spadiceum.** — 1. 8. 84. Linkes Bebruhneufer in Wallehnen: **Allium oleraceum, Struthiopteris germanica,** *Polygonatum verticillatum.* — 2. 8. 84. Zw. Dt. Crottingen und Patra-Jahn: **Sesleria coerulea,** in d. Gehölz südl. d. Weges: **Ranunculus cassubicus,** Geranium palustre; in Patra: Anthemis tinctoria. Zw. Labatag-Michel und Darguszen: **Carex flacca.** Ostseestrand westl. v. Karkelbek: Ammophila baltica (beides auch zw. Karkelbek und Immersatt), Corispermum intermedium, Ustilago Hypodites Fr. auf Ammophila arenaria, **Potamogeton mucronata** und Ranunculus divaricatus, in d. Ostsee, **Triticum iunceum, T. acutum.** Wäldchen westl. v. Immersatt: **Gypsophila paniculata,** Koeleria cristata (auch zw. Immersatt und Uszeneiten); in Zeipen: **Echium vulgare.**

3. 8. 84. Umzug nach Baugskorallen. — 3. 8. 84. Baugskorallen'er Wald: **Eriophorum latifolium,** Mercurialis perennis, Ulmus montana With. — 4.8.84. Mikaitischken'er Wald, südl. Theil: Aspidium cristatum, Thalictrum flavum. In Plicken: Saponaria officinalis, Leonurus Cardiaca. Zw. Packmohren und Peleiken-Claus: **Carex flacca, Serratula tinctoria.** Ekitte, zw. Raddeilen und Urbicken: Geranium palustre, **Campanula rapunculoides, Silene nutans.** — 5. 8. 84. In Szabern-Wittko: **Fragaria viridis.** Rechtes Ekitteufer zw. Szabern und Johannishof: **Polygonatum verticillatum** V^1 Z^3. In Johannishof: Aspidium cristatum. Ekitte zw. Szabern und Carlshof: **Polygonatum verticillatum** V^{2-3} Z^{3-4}, **Lappa nemorosa, Actaea spicata** V^3 Z^{1-2}. — 6. 8. 84. Rechtes Ufer der Ekitte zw. Carlshof und Friedrichsgnade: **Astragalus glycyphyllus;** Wald nordwestl. v. Corallischken: Thalictrum flavum, **Lathyrus niger.** — 7. 8. 84. Packmohren-Wald, südl. d. Ekitte: **Centaurea austriaca,** nördl. d. Ekitte: **Trifolium spadiceum.** Zw. Packmohren und Raddeilen: **Carex flacca, C. fulva, C. pulicaris, Trifolium spadiceum,** Trollius europaeus. Rechtes Ekitteufer zw. Raddeilen und Friedrichsgnade: Viola mirabilis. Wald südl. v. Friedrichsgnade, nördl. d. Ekitte: **Carex fulva.** — 8. 8. 84. Rechtes Ekitteufer zw. Urbicken und Ekitten: Spiraea Filipendula, **Campanula latifolia, Struthiopteris germanica,** Trollius europaeus, **Epilobium roseum.** Ekitten'er Schlossberg: **Fragaria viridis, Scabiosa ochroleuca.** Zw. Ekitten und Dautzin-Niklau: **Fragaria viridis.** Linkes Dangeufer zw. Dautzin und Dt. Crottingen: Spiraea Filipendula, Geranium palustre, **Fragaria viridis.** Westöstl. Weg nach Peleiken: **Fragaria viridis.**

9. 8. 84. Umzug nach Miszeiken. Miszeiken'er Wald, nordwestl. Theil: **Viola epipsila.** Schmeltelle: **Struthiopteris germanica, Triticum caninum,** Cuscuta europaea. — 10. 8. 84. Zw. neuem Ballastplatz und Lootsenthurm Memels: **Plantago arenaria, Rumex maritimus, Catabrosa aquatica;** zw. Lootsenthurm und Bommelsvitte: **Glyceria plicata;** Nordermole: Rumex aquaticus. — 11. 8. 84. Miszeiken'er Wald: Aspidium cristatum, **Rubus suberectus Anders.** — 12. 8. 84. Schmelltelle. Rechtes Ufer zw. Miszeiken und Sziluppen, und zw. Sziluppen und Zenkuhnen: **Triticum caninum.** Gehölz nördl. v. Zenkuhnen: **Milium effusum.** Schmeltelle zw. Zenkuhnen und Buddelkehmen: **Campanula latifolia,** Schmeltelle: Sparganium ramosum. — 13. 8. 84. Zw. Buddrücken und Althof-Memel: Spiraea Filipendula. Dangeabhänge östl. v. Königswäldchen: **Serratula tinctoria, Ranunculus polyanthemus,** Geranium palustre, **Fragaria viridis.** Dange zw. Königswäldchen und Kl. Tauerlauken: **Trollius europaeus, Achillea**

Ptarmica V[2] Z[3] gegenüber Kl. Tauerlauken. — 14. 8. 84. Zw. Gr. und Kl. Daupern, Landweg südl. d. Chaussee: **Salix livida + aurita, Pedicularis Sceptrum Carolinum** V[1] Z[2], **Carex fulva, C. dioica**; zw. Schlapszil u. Bajohr-Mitzko: **Carex fulva, C. pulicaris, Salix triandra + viminalis** (b. hippophaifolia Wimm.); zw. Schlapszil u. Gr. Daupern, Gehölz: **Carex fulva, C. pulicaris, C. flacca**. — 15. 8. 84. Zw. Birbindschen und Grambowischken: **Gentiana Amarella** V[2] Z[3]; Gehölz südl. d. ersteren; Calla palustris. Kischken'er Wald: Platanthera bifolia. Wald zw. Löbarten und Ilgejahnen: Aspidium spinulosum b., **dilatatum**; Heide zw. Skranden und Zenkuhnen: **Lycopodium inundatum** V[1] Z[3] (2. Standort).

17. 8. 84. Umzug nach Löbarten. — 18. 8. 84. Minge zw. Sudmanten und Dawillen: Geranium palustre, **Senecio paludosus, Triticum caninum.** Zw. Griegszen und Kiaunoden: Viola mirabilis; zw. Szernen und Kalwen: Geranium palustre. — 19. 8. 84. Szernen'er Wald südlich der Chaussee: **Viola arenaria, Pirola chlorantha.** Szernen'er Gutswald: Cuscuta europaea, Epilobium roseum. Zw. Kiaunoden-Görge und Spengen: Spiraea Filipendula. In Kindszen: **Epilobium roseum**; zw. Kischken-Bartel (Kairin) und der Luseze: **Dianthus arenarius.** Luseze, Jag. 87: Koeleria cristata. Zw. Försterei Starrischken und der Schmelz'er Kanalbrücke: Carex arenaria, **Elymus arenarius**, Senecio viscosus, **Dianthus arenarius.** Oestliches Kanalufer zw. der Schmelz'er Brücke und der Luseze: Senecio viscosus, **Echium vulgare.** Torfbruch zw. Grutzeiken und Labatag-Michel-Purwin: **Ranunculus Lingua.** — 21. 8. 84. Buttken'er Wald: Aspidium cristatum, **Lycopodium Selago**, Aspidium spinulosum b. **dilatatum.** Zw. Rooken und Gröszuppen: **Ranunculus Lingua** in der Kissuppe; zw. Gröszuppen und Szernen'er Wald: **Juncus capitatus.** Minge westlich desselben: **Triticum caninum**, Stellaria uliginosa, Cuscuta europaea. — 22. 8. 84. Zw. Thaleiken-Jakob und Kiaunoden-Görge: Potamogeton graminea b. heterophylla. Gehölz von Dautzkurr: **Eupatorium cannabinum, Rubus suberectus**, Aspidium cristatum. — 23. 8. 84. Minge zw. Szernen und Gedminnen: **Allium oleraceum**, Triticum caninum, **Malachium aquaticum** V[1] Z[2]. Zw. Szernen und Gedminnen: **Eupatorium cannabinum, Carex pulicaris.** Minge zw. Gedminnen und Baiten: **Thalictrum flavum.** Zw. Kalwen und Löbarten: **Scirpus compressus.** — 24. 8. 84. Nordrand des Löbarten'er Waldes: **Achillea Ptarmica** (von Herrn Gutsbesitzer Scheu gefunden).

25. 8. 84. Umzug nach Aszpurwen. — In Jagen 12, 38—40, 43, 46, 47: **Rubus suberectus Anders.**; in Jagen 15, 42, 47: Phegopteris Dryopteris; in Jagen 32, 33, 37, 42, 45, 47: Andromeda poliifolia; in 35, 38, 40, 45, 47: Ledum palustre; in 32, 34, 35, 49, 50: **Rhynchospora alba**; in 19, ?5: Vaccinium Oxycoccos; in 34, 40, 46: Equisetum arv. b. boreale; in 47, 40/41: Platanthera bifolia; in 5, 12, 30, 32/33: Veronica spicata; in 14, 15, 19: **Rumex aquaticus.** — 25. 8. 84, Jagen 40/41: **Viola epipsila.** — 26. 8. 84. Jagen 26: **Monotropa Hypopitys** β. **hirsuta.** In Blimatzen: **Chenopodium Botrys** (Gartenunkraut). Jagen 31: **Lycopodium Selago** V[1] Z[2]. Rechtes Aisse-Ufer zw. Degeln und Aszpurwen: **Malachium aquaticum.** — 27. 8. 84. Jagen 34: Aspidium cristatum. Wewircze zw. Szeppoten und Begeden: Rumex aquaticus, **Malachium aquaticum.** — 28. 8. 84. Wewircze zw. Stoneiten und Stomkaiten: **Senecio paludosus, Cyperus fuscus** V[3] Z[1]. Jagen 19: **Lycopodium Selago** V[1] Z[4], **Stellaria uliginosa, Epipactis latifolia.** — 29. 8. 84. Jagen 15: **Ranunculus cassubicus**, Campanula persicifolia **var. eriocarpa DC.** Jagen 11: Spiraea Filipendula; 4: Koeleria cristata: in Grün-

heide bei Saugen: Veronica spicata; Jagen 1/6: **Viola arenaria**; Jagen 1: **Botrychium Matricariae** V¹ Z²—⁴, **Ophioglossum vulgatum** V¹ Z². — 30. 8. 84. Jagen 50 (Posingen'er Moor): **Rubus Chamaemorus.** Rechtes Aisse-Ufer zw. Aszpurwen und Degeln: **Cuscuta europaea.** — 31. 8. 84. In Gut Stragna: **Symphytum officinale.** — 1. 9. 84. Zw. Pöszeiten und Dorf Aszpurwen (Chaussee): **Aiuga genevensis**; zw. Paaszken und Kojellen: **Triticum caninum** (Aglohne). Zw. Szilleningken (Ortstafel) und Szaukeln (Kreuzweg): **Gentiana Amarella** V¹ Z²—³.

3. 9. 84. Umzug nach Prökuls. — 4. 9. 84. Szwenzeln'er Moor: **Rhynchospora alba,** Calla palustris, **Scheuchzeria palustris, Drosera anglica.** — 5. 9. 84. Weg v. Prökuls nach dem Wäldchen südlich von Darzeppeln (nordöstlich von Tyrusmoor): **Myrica Gale.** Südlich von diesem Wäldchen: **Rhynchospora alba**; in demselben: **Gentiana Pneumonanthe, Carex fulva, Myrica Gale**; Tyrusmoor, Jagen 113: Aspidium cristatum, **Utricularia minor** (Gräben), **Rumex maritimus** (Gräben am Vorwerk von Pempen); Jagen 114: **Myrica Gale, Rubus fissus Lindl.**; am Kanal: Senecio viscosus. — 6. 9. 84. Rechtes Minge-Ufer zw. Mingekrug und Prökuls. — 7. 9. 84. Park des Gutes Prökuls: Festuca gigantea. — 8. 9. 84. Luseze, Jagen 62, 64, 67, 69: **Rubus suberectus**; 64: **Serratula tinctoria. Gladiolus imbricatus** auf dem Jodeglinen'er Moor (Wiesen), mir von Herrn Förster Sorge-Schäferei angegebener Standort. Wilhelmskanal zw. Luseze und Meyenhof: **Elymus arenarius,** Thalictrum flavum, **Salsola Kali,** Senecio viscosus. — 9. 9. 84. Rechtes Minge-Ufer zw. Prökuls und Woweriszken: **Veronica Teucrium,** Geranium palustre. — 10. 9. 84. Nach Memel. — 11. 9. 84. Weg von Gr. Tauerlauken nach den Palwen, westlich der Chaussee: **Botrychium Matricariae**; in den kleinen Gehölzen nördlich der städt. Plantage Memels: **Gentiana Pneumonanthe, Ophioglossum vulgatum,** Platanthera bifolia; zw. Försterei und holländ. Mütze in einem Thale westlich des Weges: **Gentiana Pneumonanthe.** — 12. 9. 84. Rückreise nach Königsberg.

Alle 3 Sendboten des botanischen Vereins: Dr. Lange, Stud. Lemcke und Stud. Knoblauch vertheilen zahlreiche von ihnen gesammelten Pflanzen an die Anwesenden.

Vom Conservator des kön. bayr. Harbariums in München, Herrn Dr. Alb. Peter ist eine reiche Sendung von Pflanzen der bayrischen Alpen eingegangen, die mit grossem Dank von den Anwesenden in Empfang genommen werden.

Herr Apotheker Kühn-Trakehnen berichtet Folgendes:

18. 5. 84. Lamium dissectum bei Trakehnen und Taukenischken. Im Taukenischken'er Walde: Ribes alpinum, Daphne Mezereum, Euonymus europaea und verrucosa, Thalictrum aquilegifolium. — 2. 6. 84. Packledimmen'er Moor: Orchis Morio, Salix depressa und rosmarinifolia, Rubus Chamaemorus, Drosera rotundifolia, Empetrum nigrum. — 3. 6. 84. Zw. Trakehnen und Bajohrgallen a. d. Rodupp: Alnus incana, Viburnum Opulus. — 19. 7. 84. Moor zw. Danzkehmen und Pabalen: Luzula sudetica, Juncus alpinus, Carex Pseudo-Cyperus, Thalictrum simplex, Rumex aquaticus, Salix depressa, Carex teretiuscula. — 27. 7. 84. Zw. Mehlkehmen und Lenkmischken a. d. Pissa: Heracleum sibiricum var. longifolium Koch., Potamogeton mucronata, Rumex aquaticus, Carex paniculata. Bei Nassawen auf dem Catharinenberge: Euonymus verrucosa, Campanula cervicaria, bononiensis, persicifolia var. eriocarpa, Vicia cassubica. In der Schlucht bei Jägersthal: Euonymus verrucosa, Laser-

pitium latifolium, Campanula bononiensis und persicifolia var. eriocarpa, Digitalis ambigua. Im Walde von Jägersthal: Astragalus arenarius var. glabrescens. — 28. 8. 84. Packledimmen'er Moor: Carex Pseudo-Cyperus, Salix pentandra, Utricularia vulgaris. Viele dieser Pflanzen vertheilt Herr Apotheker Kühn.

Herr Stud. Carl Braun giebt an die Anwesenden folgende Pflanzen aus:

Salix alba + fragilis, Pulvergang zw. Cosse und Neue Bleiche bei Königsberg (13. 9. 84). — Sweertia perennis L., Bruch zw. Jungferndorf und Fuchshöfen (3. 9. 84). — Trollius europaeus L., Wiese zw. Jungferndorf und Fuchshöfen (14. 6. 84). — Polystichum Thelypteris Roth., Bruch zw. Jungferndorf und Fuchshöfen (8. 8. 84). — Ranunculus Lingua, ebendaher (8. 8. 84). — Catabrosa aquatica Pal. de Beauv., ebendaher (14. 6. 84). — Betula humilis Schrank, ebendaher (3. 9. 84). — Bidens cernuus L. b. radiatus, ebendaher (25. 8. 83). — Eupatorium cannabinum L., in einem Graben der Jungferndorf'er Wiesen (8. 8. 84). — Hierochloa borealis, R. et S., Chaussee zw. Kraussen und Steinbeck (1. 7. 83). — Erythraea Centaurium Pers., Süssenthal'er Seegebiet, Kr. Allenstein (24, 8. 81).

Dr. Bethke vertheilt:

Rumex crispus + paluster (Weichsel-Ufer bei Wachbude Letzkau im Danzig'er Werder); aus den russischen Ostseeprovinzen: Salix livida, Gentiana Amarella, Pedicularis Sceptrum Carolinum, Trifolium spadiceum, Circaea intermedia, Phegopteris Robertianum, Cardamine Impatiens, Platanthera viridis, Gladiolus imbricatus, Gymnadenia conopea, Ophioglossum vulgatum und Lunaria rediviva. Von demselben werden dann noch zur Ansicht vorgelegt: Cirsium heterophyllum aus Kurland, Viola arenaria + mirabilis und V. riviniana + silvatica mit zahlreichen Wurzelsprossen.

Dr. Abromeit giebt an die Anwesenden folgende Pflanzen aus:

Brachypodium silvaticum: Rominten'er Heide bei Theerbude. — Asperula Aparine MB.: Rominteufer bei Theerbude. — Carex pilosa Scop.: Rominten'er Haide von der „Königshöhe". — Ophioglossum vulgatum: am Fichtenwald bei Gumbinnen. Lolium italicum: Rasenplätze am linken Pissaufer in Gumbinnen. — Crepis biennis: zwischen Blumberg und Gumbinnen. — Epilobium tetragonum b. adnatum Griseb.: am Wege zwischen Cranz und Grenz. — Stellaria frieseana Ser.: Friedrichstein'er Wald südlich von Löwenhagen. — ***Potamogeton densa L.:*** Graben am rechten Pregelufer zwischen Cosse und Dammkrug bei Königsberg. Neu für Ostpreussen. — Geranium columbinum: Aus dem botan. Garten. — G. dissectum: von Königsgarten; hierselbst auf vielen Rasenplätzen. — Potentilla digitato — flabellata A. Br.: aus d. botan. Garten. Wurde vom Bahnhof Löwenhagen, wo sie 1882 Herr Prof. Caspary entdeckte, nach dem botan. Garten gebracht. — Juncus Gerardi Loisl.: aus dem botan. Garten. Eingesandt 1881 von der Nordmoole bei Pillau von Herrn Apotheker Koschorrek. — Stachys silvestris + palustris = St. ambigua: aus dem botan. Garten. Eingesandt 1877 aus Appelwerder, Kreis Dt. Crone, von Herrn Ruhmer. — Bupleurum longifolium: aus dem botan. Garten. Eingesandt 1882 von Herrn Dr. Bethke aus dem Radaunethal von Unter-Kahlbude, Kreis Danzig. — Dianthus Armeria (glatte Form): aus dem botan. Garten. Eingesandt 1881 von Herrn Lehrer Kalmus, der ihn zwischen Güldenboden und Rapendorf entdeckte. — Dracocephalum Ruyschiana: aus dem botan. Garten. Eingesandt 1881 von Dr. Abromeit aus den Maynabergen bei Zimnawodda, Kreis Neidenburg. — Adenophora liliifolia Ledeb.: aus dem botan.

Garten. Eingesandt 1881 von Dr. Abromeit von den Ochsenbergen (Forst Napiwodda), Kr. Neidenburg. — Campanula persicifolia var. hispida Del.: aus dem botan. Garten. Eingesandt 1881 von Dr. Abromeit vom Abhang am Commosin'er Seeabfluss zw. Commosin und Terten, Kr. Neidenburg.

Herr Apotheker H. Eichholz in Rhein, Kreis Lötzen schickt: 1) 2 schöne Exempl. Carlina acaulis von Rhein, 2) zerzupfte Arnica-Blüthen von Friedrichshof, Kreis Ortelsburg, wo die Leute zu medizinischem Gebrauch die Blüthen sammeln. Septbr. 1884.

Der Vorsitzende legt dann einige seltene Pflanzen vor, die Herr Schulamtskandidat Kurpiun 1884 im Kreis Lötzen gefunden hat: **Festuca borealis** 19. 9. in $^1/_2$ m Tiefe. Woysack-See. — **Alisma arcuatum** Michal. fr. graminifolia Casp. 13. 8. Westseite des Löwentin-Sees. — **Betula humilis**, Nordufer des Szimon-Sees auf einer Wiese, 23. 8.

Herr Stud. Anton Collin sendet folgende Pflanzen aus Kreis Insterburg, 1884 gesammelt, ein: **Thalictrum simplex.** Am Angerappufer beim grossen Exercierplatz. 24. 7. 84. — An der Angerapp zw. Insterburg u. Luxenberg. 28. 7. 84. — Zw. Pieragienen und Tammowischken. 14. 9. 84. Bei und unterhalb Karalene am Pissaufer. 17. 9. 84. Die drei letzteren Standorte sind neu. — **Hypericum montanum.** 28. 7. 84. Auf den hohen Angerapp-Ufern zw. Pieragienen und Tammowischken (neu für Kreis Insterburg). — **Vicia pisiformis.** 28. 7. 84. Zw. Pieragienen und Tammowischken. — **Vicia dumetorum.** 28. 7. 84. Zw. Pieragienen und Tammowischken. — **Vicia cassubica.** 14. 9. 84. Abhänge bei Siegmanten. — **Anthericum ramosum.** 19. 9. 84. Abhang bei Siegmanten. — **Filago arvensis.** 14. 9. Acker bei Tammowischken. — **Aster Novi Belgii L. fr. squarrosa Nees.** 17. 9. 84. Unter Weiden am Pissa-Ufer zw. Trackinnen und Karalene.

Herr Apotheker Kascheike hat 12. 7. 1884 im Stadtwalde von Drengfurth, wo er in früheren Jahren Orobanche pallidiflora W. et. Gr. auf Cirsium oleraceum entdeckt hatte, diese Orobanche auf Cirsium palustre gefunden und an den Vorsitzenden gesendet.

Herr Apotheker Borck-Stolpemünde hat von dem Ballastplatz dieser Stadt **Fumaria micrantha,** Herr Rittergutsbesitzer von Bronsart-Schettnienen: **Puccinia Malvacearum** auf Malva silvestris in Schettnienen, daselbst 1884 zum ersten Mal aufgefunden, Herr Lehrer Flick-Goldapp: **Botrychium Matricariae** Spr. von einem Sandfelde zw. dem Militärschiessstande und dem neugepflanzten Kiefernwäldchen, wo die Pflanze in einigen hundert Exemplaren wuchs, an Prof. Caspary eingeschickt.

Der Vorsitzende berichtet dann über seine eigenen Excursionen. Vom 29. Mai bis 8. Juni hat er die Südwestecke des Kreises Neustadt von Buckowin, Kreis Lauenburg, aus untersucht. Im Park von Buckowin sind auf dem Nordostabhange **Poa sudetica** und **Luzula albida** reichlich vorhanden; erstere auch nebst **Melampyrum silvaticum** und **Polygonatum verticillatum** am Grenzbach zw. Okkalitz und Labuhn. **Erica Tetralix** ist in dem Südwestzipfel des Kreises Neustadt nur nördlich vom Wooksee und an einigen Stellen zw. Wilhelmsdorf und Kantschin, wie auch im Lauenburg'er Kreise nördlich von Bukowin in einigen Torfsümpfen und zwischen Jezow und Dzinzelitz vorhanden, findet sich aber, wie sonst angegeben worden ist, in den jetzt völlig geschundenen Torfsümpfen um Wahlendorf nicht. **Scirpus caespitosus** in einem Torfbruch westlich von Kantschin.

Untersuchung der Gewässer des Kreises Danzig und Neustadt.

Vom 17. Juli bis 9. September 1884 hat der Vorsitzende zum grössten Theil die Gewässer des Kreises Danzig und alle des Kreises Neustadt untersucht, mit Ausnahme einiger, die er schon 1877 befahren hatte. **Nuphar pumilum** Smith. ist von ihm in 7 Seen gefunden. In einem kleinen Torfsee westlich von Leesen, Kreis Danzig und im Kreise Neustadt in 6 Seen: im Schwarzsee bei Lessnau, daselbst schon in früherer Zeit von ihm entdeckt, im Langen-See, südöstlich von Lessnau, hier schon von Abromeit gefunden, im Torfsee Poglews $2^1/_2$ km südwestlich von Gr. Domachau, im Torfsee, Jagen 68 Forst von Darslub, im Hungersee bei Mühle Warschkau, im Torfsee bei einem Abbau südlich von Mühle Warschkau.

Der Bastard Nuphar **luteum** + **pumilum** wurde in 6 Seen gefunden; im Kreise Neustadt: im See Poglews, eben erwähnt, im Schwarzsee von Lessnau (hat hier 37,7 pCt. schlechten Blüthenstaub), im Langen-See bei Abbau Lessnau, im See, Karpionki (daselbst schon 1877 vom Vorsitzenden entdeckt); im Kreise Kartaus: See südlich von Kl. Tuchom; im Kreise Danzig: Torfsee westlich von Leesen.

Nuphar luteum fr. **rupropetalum** Casp. wurde im Sasp'er-See, wo es schon Klinsmann entdeckte, im Mühlenteich von Oliva, der an der Chaussee nach Cöln liegt und im Mühlenteich von Conradshammer, im nördlichen Teich, aufgefunden.

Nymphaea candida ooarpa erythrocarpa semiaperta fand sich nur in einem See: dem von Nenkau, **Nymphaea alba** sphaerocarpa in sehr vielen.

11 Arten von Characeen wurden gefunden. **Nitella gracilis** im Langen-See, südwestlich von Lessnau, im Kl. See von Jagen 68 der Darslub'er Forst bei Lessnau, im „Verwachsenen See" bei Bieschkowo; **Nitella opaca** im Kl. See von Jagen 68 des Darslub'er Forstes; **Nitella flexilis**, Loch im Sphagnetum des östlichen Wittstock'er Sees; **Nitella mucronata** in einem Tümpel an der Ostseite des Sees von Ottomin; in 14 Seen ausserdem wurden sterile unbestimmbare Nitellen, Abthlg.: Monarthrodactylae, angetroffen; **Nitella nidifica** reichlich im Putzig'er Wiek fast überall, 1 Expl. im Loch der Westerplatte. **Chara ceratophylla** im See von Zarnowitz und im See von Ottomin; Chara fragilis in 10 Seen; Chara foetida in 6 Seen; Chara aspera im Putzig'er Wiek und im See von Zarnowitz; **Chara baltica** im Putzig'er Wiek; **Chara crinita**, bloss weiblich, wie stets, im Putzig'er Wiek.

Isoëtes lacustris ist in 16 Seen des Kreises Neustadt von mir festgestellt. v. Klinggraeff II hatte eine Form aus dem Gr. Ottalsin'er See mit fast glatten Makrosporen var. **leiospora** benannt, sie aber nur bei einer einzigen Blattform, der **patula** Gay, nachgewiesen. Die **leiospora** v. Kl. kommt aber unter allen den Blättern nach verschiedenen Gestalten von Isoët. lac. in den Neustädt'er Seen als: fr. stricta Gay, elatior Gay, longifolia Mott. et. Vend., die bis $27^1/_2$ cm lang wird, und falcata Tausch vor. v. Klinggraeff hat den Beweis nicht geliefert, dass die Makrosporen der leiospora reif und ausgebildet seien. Die Vermuthung lag nahe, dass sie unreif seien. Prof. Caspary hat jedoch dadurch, dass es ihm gelang, an frisch im März 1885 geholtem Material, Keimung der glatten Makrosporen und Erzeugung junger Pflanzen zu beobachten, den Beweis gefunden, dass jene Makrosporen wirklich reif seien und mithin eine Form leiospora anzuerkennen ist.

Isoëtes echinospora Dur. hat Prof. Caspary in einem neuen See, dem Grabowke-See bei Wigodda mit Isoët. lac. daselbst zusammen, entdeckt, so dass nun drei Seen mit Isoët. echinosp. im Kreise Neustadt bekannt sind.

Es mag folgender kurzer Bericht über die See-Untersuchungen hier seine Stelle finden, wobei die zahlreich gesammelten Wassermoose vorläufig unberücksichtigt bleiben. Die Seen sind alle befahren, wenn sie nicht zu seicht oder zu sumpfig in der Umgebung waren. Den 17. 7. 84. Sasper-See: **Potamogeton trichoides**, Elodea canad. — 18. 7. Loch der Westerplatte: Zanichellia palustris, 1 Expl. Nitella nidif. und sehr wenige Pflanzen von Chara baltica. Chara connivens, die Bänitz als Handelswaare 1872 dort zahlreich sammelte, wie Ch. aspera, sind daselbst verschwunden. **Juncus Gerardi** am Ufer zahlreich; am mittleren jetzt trockenen Loch der Westerplatte **Carex distans**. — 19. 7. Die 3 Haideseen bei Heubude. Im Kl. Haide-See an der Försterei: Utricularia minor. — 21. 7. Die Heubude'r (faule) Laake, die todte Weichsel, die 5 Kolke bei östlich Neufähr. Im grossen südlichen Kolk, der allein auf der Generalstabskarte steht, Elodea can. Hauptpflanze; **Scirpus rufus** auf dem Nordufer und **Carex distans**. — 22. 7. Die Schutenlaake, die todte Weichsel bei Gansekrug. Salvinia natans nicht vorhanden, einst da von Bail gefunden. — 23. 7. Die 14 Teiche, welche das Gletkau'er Mühlenfliess speisst; die im königl. Garten von Oliva fortgelassen. Chara foetida longibractata im obersten Teich (Fournirmühlenteich), wie in mehreren andern. **Festuca silvatica** am Ostufer des obersten Teichs. Elodea can. und Potamogeton rufescens in sehr vielen; **Oryza clandestina** am Teich des Rippenhammers und am Dahlmann'schen Teich zu Conradshammer gehörig; an letzterem auch Senecio barbaraeifolius.

24. 7. Uebersiedelung von Neufahrwasser nach Quaschin. — 25. 7. Espenkrug'er See: **Isoët. lac.** fr. stricta, patula und falcata Tausch*) meist leiospora, selten vulgaris. Oestlicher Wittstock-See: **Potamogeton crispa + praelonga** Casp. Z^3 V^3, **Isoët. lac.** stricta, sehr wenig. Ranunculus aquatilis Z^2 V^3. — 26. 7. See von Kl. Tuchom. — 27. 7. Torfloch südlich vom vorigen See nach Kl. Mischau zu: Nuphar luteum + pumilum. — 28. 7. See von Kl. Mischau; See von Leesen; Torf-See 1½ km westlich von Leesen: Utricularia minor, Eriophorum gracile, siehe auch oben. — 29. 7. Szaben-See bei Hoch-Kelpin, Nenkau'er See (siehe oben), See von Ottomin (siehe oben). — 30. 7. Nord-Ufer des Espenkrug'er See's. — 31. 7. Dorf-See von Köln, östlicher und westlicher Machowie-See: Myriophyllum alternifl. Die von anderer Seite gemachte Angabe, dass im östlichen Machowie-See Nuphar intermedium Ledeb., welches der Bastard zw. Nuphar luteum und pumilum ist, vorkomme, beruht auf unrichtiger Bestimmung einer kleinen Form von Nuphar luteum. — 1. 8. Bozanken-See, Czartowo-See, See Swinak: Myriophyllum alternifl. — 2. 8. Espenkrug'er See, Nord-Ufer noch einmal nach Wassermoosen abgesucht. — 3. 8. Strauchmühlenteich und die 4 dabei befindlichen kleinen Fischteiche. Im Quellthal davon: Glyceria nemoralis. Pulvermühlenteich. — 4. 8. Zw. Espenkrug und Legan: Polygonum tataricum.

Uebersiedelung nach Köln. Pfarrwald von Köln: Lysimachia nemorum. — 5. 8. See von Hawowanno: Myriophyllum alternifl., Geranium molle am Ufer;

*) Dieser Name ist vor 1847 gegeben, also der älteste für die Form mit zurückgekrümmten Blättern.

Przerosla-See (= Verwachsener See); Langer Okuniewo-See; Dorf-See von Okuniewo. — 6. 8. Steinkrug'er See: **Isoët. lac.** fr. patula, subfalcalta, stricta, substricta; Makrosporen warzig, also fr. vulgaris; nur einige Exemplare verschiedener Blattgestalten waren fast glatt und wahrscheinlich noch unreif. Leckno-See: Litorella lacustris, aber keine Isoët. lac., die in diesem See von anderer Seite angegeben ist. — 7. 8. Ost- und Nord-Ufer des Sees von Leckno abgesucht. Der westliche Wittstock-See: **Isoët. lac.** fr. stricta, patula, falcata; die Makrosporen alle fast glatt, also leiospora. Der Bresenken-See. — 8. 8. Gr. Ottalsin'er See: Myriophyllum alternifl., **Isoët. lac.** fr. falcata, patula, stricta, substricta; Alles leiospora; der Kl. Ottalsin'er See. — 9. 8. See Sawiart bei Bieschkowitz: Scirpus setaceus, Juncus capitatus, Potentilla procumbens, Lobelia dortm.; See von Bieschkowitz: Litorella lacustris, Lobel. dortm., **Isoët. lac.** fr. patula und stricta, theils leiospora, theils vulgaris. Torf-See von Bieschkowitz. — 11. 8. Gelonken-See: Lobelia, Litorella, **Isoët. lac.** fr. stricta, patula und subpatula, longifolia, letztere mit bis 27½ cm langen Blättern; alle Formen: leiospora; Abfluss des westlichen Wittstock-Sees in den Mühlenteich von Jellenschhütte; in letzterem **Isoët. lac.** fr. stricta, subfalcata, auch tenuifolia u. patula. Makrosporen mit schwachen Höckern und leiospora. Moos-See im Dennemörse'r Walde. — 12. 8. Warznauer See (Fluss-See): Blechnum boreale, Juncus supinus fluitans in einem Torfloch; 2 Torftümpel zw. Warznau'er Hütte und Kowalewo; Torftümpel Nordostost von Kowalewo. — 13. 8. Die Torftümpel zw. Bojahn und Gloddau; Torftümpel südlich von Gloddau. — 14. 8. Uebersiedelung von Köln nach Bieschkowitz.

15. 8. See Grabowke: Lobelia dortm., **Isoët lac.** vulgaris fr. patula, substricta u. patentistima; ***Isoëtes echinospora*** Dur.; See Czarno-Dombrowo (Schwarzsee), südliches Seechen in Pretoschin: Lycopodium inundatum; Seechen nördlich von Pretoschin am Wege nach Ustarbau; See von Ustarbau, stark erniedrigt: Ranunculus reptans, Lobel. dortm., **Isoët. lac.** vulg. stricta, alle 3 meist auf dem trockenen Ufer. Die Tümpel nördlich von Ustarbau im freien Felde. — 16. 8. See von Wigodda: **Isoët. lac. vulg.** fr. stricta und patula; See Kripko nordwestl. von Wigodda. — 18. 8. Borowo-See: **Isoët. lac.** vulg. fr. patula und stricta, Lobel. dortm.; See von Wispau; See in Jagen 51 des gräflichen neustädt. Forstes: Eriophorum gracile. — 19. 8. Uebersiedelung nach Putzig. — 20. 8. Putziger Wiek dicht bei Putzig, siehe in Betreff der Charen und Nitella oben; Zostera marina, **Ruppia rostellata,** Zanichellia palustris; Plutnitz: **Nasturtium officinale,** grosse Polster im Fluss bildend. — 21. 8. Vier Torftümpel Nordwest von Brunhausen (Miruschin): Erica Tetralix, Scirpus caespitosus. Nacht in Karwenbruch. — 22. 8. Der östliche und westliche Ostrau-See die Tümpel südwestlich von Ostrau. Erica Tetralix zw. der Brücke von Tupadel und Ostrau reichlich. — 23. 8. Untersuchung des Putzig'er Wiek zw. Putzig und Ceynowo auf dem Boot des Herrn Dr. med. Borchert: Potamogeton pectinata (Trewo poln.) in 10—12' tiefem bräkischem Wasser. Tümpel NO von Grossendorf: **Ranunculus confusus** Godron. Neu für Preussen. Von Grossendorf auf dem Putzig'er Wiek nach Putzig mit eigenem Boot zurück; überall die genannten Characeen und **Ruppia rostellata.** — 24. 8. Die Plutnitz oberhalb der nördlichsten Brücke. — 25. 8. Putziger Wiek zw. Oslanin und Rowa mit Herrn Dr. Borchert-Putzig. Dieselben Characeen wie bei Putzig, Ruppia rost. und Zanich. pal. — 26. 8. Uebersiedelung nach Mechau. Schwarzsee bei Lessnau (siehe oben unter Nuphar), ***Drosera inter-***

media. — 27. 8. Noch einmal derselbe Schwarzsee; See im Garten des Guts Lessnau; Torfsee westlich von Lessnau; Langer See südwestl. von Lessnau (siehe oben unter Nuphar und Nitella); Kl. See bei Jagen 68 des Darslub'er Forstes (siehe oben unter Nuphar und Nitella); Stubbenteich. — 28. 8. Der Gute-See (See von Gallitza): Litor. lac., **Isoët. lac.** vulg. fr. stricta und patula; Teich der Warschkau'er Mühle; der Tiefe See bei Warschkau'er Mühle: Juncus obtusiflorus, hier schon von Abromeit entdeckt; Hunger-See südwestl. von Warschkau-Mühle (siehe oben wegen Nuphar); See Poglews, 2½ km westlich von Gr. Dommatau (siehe oben unter Nuphar). — 29. 8. Nochmals See Poglews. Uebersiedelung nach Zarnowitz. — 30. 8. See von Zarnowitz (siehe oben unter Chara): Chara foetida und fragilis.

31. 8. Zw. Zarnowitz und Gelsin an mehreren Tümpeln: Erica Tetralix und an feuchten torfigen Stellen: Lycopodium inundatum. — 1. 9. Uebersiedelung nach Lusin. Tümpel bei Abbau Warschkau (siehe oben bei Nuphar). — 2. 9. Einige Tümpel nördlich von Lusin; Torftümpel östlich vom Gut Platenrode. — 3. 9. See von Wischetzin; der Tiefe See von Wischetzin. Nacht in Barlomin. — 4. 9. Uebersiedelung nach Okkalitz; Okkalitz'er (Wussow'er) See. Pirola media im Hohlwege, der unweit davon nach Ost liegt. — 5. 9. See von Wahlendorf; See Karpionki; Orkan verhinderte eine genaue Untersuchung: **Isoët. lac.** vulg. fr. stricta, patula und subpatula; Wook-See: **Isoët. echinospora** Dur. bis 4' tief; der Weisse See (Moszisch) östlich vom Wege zw. Wahlendorf und Werder: Litor. lac., Lobelia, Scirp. caesp. Ostufer; Isoëtes nicht zu finden. — 6. 9. See Dombrowo westlich vom Wege zw. Wahlendorf und Werder: Scirpus caespit. am Westufer, Myriophyll. alternifl., **Isoëtes lac.** Z V, Lobelia, Litorella. Tümpel von Schrödersfelde, Kreis Cartaus. — 8. 9. Kl. Torfsee östlich von Wilhelmsdorf. Erica Tetralix auf einem feuchten Stück Heideland zw. Wilhelmsdorf und Linde, Torfsee von Poblotz: Lycopodium inundatum. — 9. 9. Torfsee südwestlich von Wahlendorf und die sämmtlichen Torftümpel zw. Wahlendorf und Vorwerk Wahlendorf südwestlich und südöstlich von Wahlendorf. Nirgend Erica Tetralix, ausser im Norden vom Wooksee. See Karpionki. Weisser See, Westufer: Polystichum Oreopteris.

Schliesslich spricht der Vorsitzende denjenigen Herren seinen warmen Dank aus, die ihn mit Rath und That, besonders durch Gastfreundschaft in seinen Unternehmungen unterstützten, den Herren Dr. med. Borchert-Putzig, Rittergutsbesitzern Dix-Köln, Heering-Okkalitz, v. Zelewski-Barlomin, Herrn Gutspächter v. Santen-Bieschkowitz und Herrn Administrator Polehn-Quaschin.

Um 4 Uhr Schluss der Sitzung. Bald darauf Festessen, dem auch Herr Oberbürgermeister König beiwohnt.

Den 8. Oktober Vormittags wird die Nordermole und Plantage unter Führung der Apotheker Herren Berger, Groening und des Herrn Gymnasiallehrer Kühemann von den Vereinsmitgliedern besucht.

Die Marklücken der Coniferen.

Von

Carl Fritsch.

Hierzu Tafel I. und II.

Wohl ist es eine bekannte Erscheinung bei krautigen Pflanzen, dass durch Lostrennung, Zerreissung oder Zerstörung ausgebildeter Zellen Marklücken entstehen. Dass aber durch die nicht erfolgte Streckung der Markzellen bei holzigen Gewächsen auf schizogenem Wege auch Lücken entstehen können, dafür bieten die Coniferen ein gutes Beispiel.

Die Marklücke derselben entdeckte vor nun 11 Jahren Herr Professor Caspary bei Picea excelsa, P. alba; Abies balsamea, A. pectinata, A. sibirica; Larix europaea. Ihm verdankt vorliegende Arbeit ihre Entstehung. Derselbe sagt in der betreffenden Anmerkung*): „Bei . . . . (obigen) und gewiss bei anderen Coniferen zeigt sich die merkwürdige Erscheinung, die unbekannt zu sein scheint, dass normal das Mark in seiner ganzen Breite durch eine quere Lücke an den Stellen unterbrochen ist, wo sich ein neuer Jahresschoss als Fortsetzung des vorhandenen Schosses oder ein Seitenspross anschliesst." Da mir von Herrn Professor Caspary das reiche Coniferenmaterial des königl. botanischen Gartens bereitwilligst zur Untersuchung überlassen wurde, so kann ich das Vorkommen der Lücke noch bei folgenden Coniferen angeben: Picea alkokiana, P. Engelmanni, P. Menziesii, P. nigra mariana, P. obovata, P. polita, P. sitchensis, P. Tschugatzkoi; Abies cephalonica, A. Fraseri, A. magnifica glauca, A. Maximowiczii, A. nobilis, A. nordmanniana, A. panachaica, A. Pindrow, A. Veitchii; Larix dahurica, L. leptolepis; Cedrus Deodara.

„Die Lücke findet sich nicht bei Tsuga canadensis; Pinus Pumilio, P. Strobus, P. Cembra, P. Laricio; Taxus baccata", sagt Professor Caspary a. a. O. Diesen kann ich noch anfügen: Pinus silvestris; Juniperus communis, J. virginiana; Cryptomeria japonica; Taxodium sempervirens; Araucaria excelsa; Podocarpus macrophylla; Prumnopytis elegans; Gingko biloba; Cephalotaxus drupacea; Torreya nucifera. Es scheint somit das Vorkommen der Marklücke auf die Arten der Gattungen Picea, Abies, Larix und Cedrus beschränkt zu sein; allen anderen aber zu fehlen.

Die vier, in der Familie der Coniferen vereinigten Gruppen der Cupressineen, Abietineen, Podocarpeen und Taxineen bieten im Bau ihres Markes zwei Reihen, die, wenn auch durch einzelne Uebergänge verbunden, dennoch scharf von einander getrennt sind, dar. So scharf ist der Unterschied im Bau des Markes, dass er leicht mit unbewaffnetem Auge wahrgenommen werden kann. Auf der einen Seite, der die

---

*) Caspary: Die Krummfichte. Schriften der physikal. ökonom. Gesellschaft. Königsberg 1874. Anmerkung Seite 114.

Cupressineen, Podocarpeen und Taxineen angehören, zeigt das Mark nichts Auffallendes; im Mark der Abietineen dagegen sieht man eine regelmässige, an die Enden der Jahrestriebe gebundene Abwechselung zwischen weissen und braunen Markschichten. Das Genauere will ich bei den einzelnen untersuchten Arten, deren Reihe ich nach Carrière folgen lasse, angeben:

1. Grp. Cupressineen.

Es wurde Juniperus communis L., J. virginiana L., Cryptomeria japonica Don, Taxodium sempervirens Hook. und zwar die beiden ersten durch mehrere auf einander folgende, die beiden letzten nur im letzten und vorletzten Jahrestriebe untersucht. Besonders wurde auf das Mark in der Höhe der Seitenknospen geachtet. Immer fand sich dasselbe aus parenchymatischen, wenig verdickten und gleich grossen Zellen, die in der Jugend, Taxodium am 17. VII. 84, Cryptomeria am 21. VII. 84, Stärke führen, im Alter, Juniperus, vertrocknet und gebräunt waren, gebildet. In ganz gleichmässigem Zuge durchlief das Mark die untersuchten Aeste und zeigte an keiner Stelle eine besondere Färbung. Es bot überhaupt bei der mikroskopischen Untersuchung nicht den geringsten Unterschied vom Mark der meisten Angiospermen dar.

2. Grp. Podocarpeen.

Dasselbe Verhalten zeigte das Mark von Podocarpus macrophylla Don und Prumnopytis elegans Phil., von denen die letzten und vorletzten Triebe an Seitenästen untersucht wurden.

3. Grp. Taxineen.

Das Mark von Taxus baccata L., Cephalotaxus drupacea Sieb. et Zucc. und Gingko biloba L. besteht aus ähnlichen Zellen wie das der meisten Angiospermen und stimmt im Bau vollkommen mit dem der vorhergehenden Coniferen überein. Dagegen zeigt Torreya nucifera Sieb. et Zucc. eine Abweichung. Zur Untersuchung diente ein frischer dreijähriger Seitentrieb, der im zweiten und dritten Jahre Knospen gebildet hatte. Während das Mark des Triebes nichts vom allgemeinen Typus Abweichendes zeigte, war etwas über dem Abgange des Knospenmarkes ersteres von einer vier Zellen breiten Scheidewand durchsetzt, welche ihre convexe Seite nach oben kehrte. Der Längendurchmesser dieser Zellen steht senkrecht auf dem Längendurchmesser der regelmässigen Markzellen; die Zellwände sind stärker als gewöhnlich verdickt. Durch Jod liess sich am 12. Juli 1884 sowohl in der Scheidewand, wie im übrigen Marke, Stärke nachweisen. Erwähnen will ich, das Torreya sich durch die am Aste bleibenden Knospenschuppen von den übrigen Taxineen unterscheidet und an die folgende Gruppe erinnert.

4. Grp. Abietineen.

Hier zeigt das Mark in seinem Bau die grössten Verschiedenheiten. Während auf der einen Seite Tsuga ein Mark, welches durch das Auftreten querliegender Binden von verdickten Zellen an Torreya erinnert, besitzt, finden sich bei Abies und Picea dieselben verdickten Zellen, unterhalb derselben aber auch eine Lücke, welche das ganze Mark quer durchbricht. Bei Larix ist in einigen Zweigen die Lücke nachweisbar, in anderen nur die Scheidewand, und bei Pinus fehlt beides, obwohl das Mark an der Abgangsstelle der Seitenäste eine auffallende Bräunung hat. Araucaria endlich zeigt ein regelmässig gebautes, den Cupressineen ähnliches Mark.

1. Tsuga canadensis Carr.

Das Mark des Jahrestriebes besitzt in seiner mittleren Länge längsgestreckte parenchymatische, wenig verdickte Zellen, die nur halb so breit wie lang sind. Gegen das Ende des Triebes dagegen bleibt der Längendurchmesser der Zellen an Grösse zurück, ja er wird gleich dem Querdurchmesser, und kubische Zellen bilden das Endmark. In der Höhe der Knospenschuppen finden sich im Mark sogar Zellen, deren Querdurchmesser grösser als der Längendurchmesser, deren Zellwand stärker als die vorhergehender und folgender Markzellen verdickt ist. Dadurch fallen sie als eine das Mark querdurchsetzende Scheidewand auf, die sich in die Knospenschuppen fortzusetzen scheint. Diese stehen nämlich auf einem wulstartigen Ringe, der im Präparate nach Art eines Stieles die Knospenschuppen trägt. Die mittleren Zellen dieses Ringes, über dessen Natur ich noch nichts aussagen kann, haben dieselbe Beschaffenheit wie die der Scheidewand im Mark des tragenden Astes, und bisweilen glaube ich durch das Holz hindurch einen Zusammenhang beider wahrgenommen zu haben.

2. Abies balsamea Mill.

Wie die vorhergehende zeigt diese nordamerikanische Tanne in der Höhe der Seitenäste eine das Mark quer durchsetzende Scheidewand, Fig. 1, s, die aus fünf bis acht Zellreihen bestehend, bald gerade, meist aber etwas gewölbt erscheint. Die Wölbung ist bald der Spitze, bald dem Grunde zugekehrt, öfters in der Mitte eingesenkt. An ihre obere Zellreihe setzt sich, wie es — Figur 1, m — zeigt, das Mark, während die untere öfters an einen Hohlraum grenzt.

In der ruhenden Knospe — Fig. 2 — ist diese Scheidewand, s, ebenfalls deutlich; sie trennt das Knospenmark, m, vom Mark, a, des vorhergehenden Jahrestriebes. Die Markzellen dieses sind in der Nähe der Scheidewand rundlich eiförmig und theilweise ohne Inhalt und mit gebräunten Zellwänden, theilweise auch mit Protoplasma und Stärke gefüllt und mit farblosen Wänden. Diese letzteren Zellen, — ich will sie lebensfähig, die ersteren im Gegensatz dazu abgestorben nennen, ohne mir deshalb ein Urtheil über ihre physiologische Thätigkeit zu erlauben, — grenzen mit ihren Wänden eng an einander und schliessen kleine tetraedrische Zwischenzellräume ein; die ersteren dagegen sind mehr oder weniger zusammengefallen, so dass eine Berührung der Zellwände nur an wenigen Punkten stattfindet. In Folge dessen sind grosse Zwischenzellräume vorhanden, die vielleicht durch den Schnitt noch vergrössert werden. Je näher der Scheidewand, desto mehr fehlen die lebensfähigen Zellen, desto zahlreicher sind die abgestorbenen. Die letzten Reihen bestehen nur aus diesen. Häufig haben sie jeden Zusammenhang mit den Scheidewandzellen verloren, zuweilen aber grenzen sie hie und da vereinzelt an diese. So findet sich hier ein grosser Zwischenzellraum, die Marklücke, l.

In der fortwachsenden Spitze, an der sich eine einzelne Spitzenzelle nicht findet, besteht das Mark im Längsschnitt aus vier- bis sechseckigen, mit Protoplasma und Stärke angefüllten Zellen, deren Wände wenig verdickt sind, — Fig. 3. — Die Länge und Breite der Zellen ist sehr verschieden.

Im älteren Jahrestrieb sind die Markzellen bedeutend in die Länge gestreckt, zwei- bis viermal so lang wie breit — Fig. 4, m. — Diese stehen, wie es in Fig. 4 zu sehen, senkrecht auf den Scheidewandzellen, s. Doch nicht der ganze Trieb besitzt gleiche Zellen. Verfolgt man die Markzellen von einer Scheidewand zur Spitze des Triebes, so erkennt man, dass diese langen Zellen mehr und mehr durch kurze ersetzt werden, dass der Zusammenhang zwischen den einzelnen Zellen lockerer wird. Bald treten einzelne kubische Zellen auf. Ja in der Nähe der jüngeren Scheidewand besitzen die Zellen nicht einmal mehr Zellwände, die sich unter deutlichen Winkeln schneiden, sondern sie haben eine runde oder eiförmige Gestalt angenommen; ihr Zusammenhang ist der grossen Zwischenzellräume wegen äusserst lose, ihr Inhalt mehr oder weniger gebräunt. Sie zeigen grosse Neigung selbst am befeuchteten Messer zu kleben und fortgerissen zu werden. In jüngeren Aesten liegen sie öfters der Scheidewand fest an — Fig. 1 l, — in älteren sind sie zusammengefallen, vertrocknet. Dadurch wird eine Lücke gebildet.

Aehnlich ist das Mark in dem vorhergehenden Jahrestriebe gebildet. Ich verweise, um Wiederholungen zu vermeiden, auf Fig. 1, die den horizontalen (s. w. u.) Längsschnitt des 1879er und 1880er Markes und der Scheidewand darstellt und zwar eines Präparates, das eine Lücke nicht zeigt. Ich besitze ausserdem solche mit Lücke. Es sind die ältesten Schosse, die ich untersuchen konnte. Da der typische Bau keine Abweichungen zeigt, so folgere ich, dass diese eben dargelegten Verhältnisse sich auch in älteren Aesten wiederfinden werden. Die Lücke findet sich demnach nicht in jedem Ende eines Jahresschosses oder in jedem Grund eines Seitensprosses. Vielmehr richtet sich ihr Vorkommen nach dem Alter des Triebes; je älter der untersuchte Trieb, desto sicherer darf man auf das Vorhandensein einer Lücke rechnen, weil in diesen die abgestorbenen Zellen immer zahlreicher und mehr vertrocknet sind. Sie zeigt sich namentlich in trocknen Aesten gross und deutlich. In älteren lebenden ist sie, je nachdem der Schnitt geführt wird, bald mehr, bald weniger deutlich. Schnitte, von der Spitze zum Grunde geführt, geben eine grössere, in umgekehrter Richtung geführte, eine kleinere Lücke, weil die Zellen durch das Messer bald zusammengeschoben, bald von einander getrennt werden. Immer aber verkleinerte sich die Lücke noch, wenn ein Tropfen Wasser hinzugegeben wurde, da dann die Zellwände ihre alte Spannung und Form erhielten. Die Lücke entsteht niemals durch Theilung oder Zerreissung besonders dazu ausgebildeter Zellen, sondern ist ein vergrösserter Zwischenzellraum. Ihre Grösse ist auch nichts primäres, von vorne herein Angelegtes, sondern etwas sekundäres, von dem Alter und der Feuchtigkeit des Astes Abhängiges. Ein Grund für ihr Entstehen ist das Zusammenfallen der obersten Markzellen eines Jahresschosses, welchem die tiefer liegenden, gewöhnlichen Markzellen und die höher liegenden Scheidewandzellen ihrer stärker verdickten Wände wegen nicht folgen können.

Doch ist nicht zu verkennen, dass die Grösse auch von dem Wachsthum des Astes abhängig ist. Wenn sich die Holzzellen in die Länge strecken, so wird damit die Scheidewand weiter von den obersten Markzellen entfernt, die Lücke vergrössert. Unterbleibt die stärkere Streckung, so bleibt auch die Lücke klein, oder fehlt gänzlich.

Die Lücke ist ferner durch alle Jahrgänge hindurch von gleicher Beschaffenheit. Ueberall, wo sie angetroffen wurde, war sie von Luft erfüllt; niemals wurde in ihr Harz oder Flüssigkeit gefunden.

Um über die Veränderungen der Scheidewandzellen Klarheit zu bekommen, wurde in der Endknospe, sowie in den beiden vorhergehenden Jahresabschnitten der Hohlraum und die gemeinsame Wand der Scheidewandzellen gemessen. Dieserhalb wurden auch die Präparate in doppelter Weise angefertigt; es wurden einmal Medianschnitte und zweitens Schnitte durch die Axe zweiten Grades und den Grund des Jahrestriebes geführt. Die Schnitte letzter Art treffen also die Axe ersten Grades unter einem mehr oder weniger grossen Winkel, der von der Neigung der Axe zweiten Grades abhängt; da aber diese Shnitte letzter Art sich der Wagrechten annähern, so nenne ich sie horizontale Längsschnitte. Sie wurden zugleich so angelegt, dass sie durch die Axe der Knospen dritten Grades gingen.

Im Allgemeinen liegt der längste Durchmesser der Zellen senkrecht zur Wachsthumsrichtung des Astes; obwohl auch Zellen, deren Länge und Breite gleich, ja deren grösste Ausdehnung der Axe des Triebes parallel ist, getroffen werden, wie es Fig. 5 zeigt. Diese giebt die unteren Scheidewandzellen der ruhenden Endknospe wieder. Primäre Zellwand ist überall deutlich; die starken sekundären Verdickungen werden von Porenkanälen durchzogen. Das Verhältniss des Längen- zum Höhendurchmesser und zur Dicke der Wand zwischen zwei Zellräumen stellt sich an den Medianschnitten im Mittel aus je fünf Messungen:

1. in der Endknospe 1881: L : H : D = 22,5 : 10 : 5,5
2. in der Endknospe 1880: L : H : D = 24,5 : 10 : 6
3. in der Endknospe 1879: L : H : D = 29 : 11 : 6,5

Die absoluten Werte für die Länge des Zellraumes waren für 1881 = 0,0261 mm, für 1880 = 0,0284 mm und für 1879 = 0,0336 mm; für die Höhe des Zellraumes ergab sich 1881 = 0,0116 mm, für 1880 = 0,0116 mm, für 1879 = 0,0127 mm; die gemeinsame Wand zweier benachbarter Zellen war 1881 = 0,0064 mm, 1880 = 0,0069 mm, 1879 = 0,0079 mm stark. Somit hat in diesen drei Jahren eine Vergrösserung des Zellraumes nach Länge und Höhe, sowie eine Verdickung der Zellwände stattgefunden.

Auch die horizontalen Längsschnitte ergeben ähnliche Resultate. Das Verhältniss des Längendurchmessers zum Höhendurchmesser und zur Dicke der gemeinsamen Wand ist für

1881: L : H : D = 20,5 : 10,5 : 6.
1880: L : H : D = 22 : 13 : 7,5
1879: L : H : D = 21 : 16 : 6,5

Die berechneten Messungen stellen den Längendurchmesser für 1881 = 0,0238 mm, für 1880 = 0,0255 mm und für 1879 = 0,0244 mm; die Höhe ist für 1881 = 0,0121 mm, für 1880 = 0,015 mm und für 1879 = 0,0185 mm; die gemeinsame Wand ist 1881 = 0,0069 mm, 1880 = 0,0087 mm, 1879 = 0,0075 mm dick. Zeigt auch die Längenausdehnung in 1879, sowie die Dicke der Zellwand gegen 1880 bei diesen zweiten Messungen eine Abnahme, die ihre Erklärung in der verschiedenen Stärke der untersuchten Aeste findet, so ist doch gegen 1881 eine, nur durch selbstständiges Wachsthum erklärliche Vergrösserung bemerkbar. Woraus der Schluss, dass die Scheidewandzellen ihr Leben länger als die übrigen Markzellen bewahrt haben, gerechtfertigt erscheint. Ist auch dieses Wachsthum nicht so lebhaft und von grossen Gestalts-

veränderungen begleitet gewesen, so hat doch eine Verdickung der Zellwände, sowie eine Vergrösserung der Scheidewandzellen nach allen drei Dimensionen stattgefunden.

Vergleicht man die Zahlen für die Längendurchmesser der Scheidewandzellen in den Medianschnitten und in den horizontalen Längsschnitten mit einander, so findet man, dass die Länge in den ersteren grösser ist. Sie übertrifft die letzeren 1881 um 0,0023 mm, 1880 um 0,0029 mm und 1879 um 0,004 mm. Es entspricht dieses, mit dem Alter zunehmende Plus einem stärkeren Wachsthum der Scheidewandzellen in der Richtung der Mediane, also parallel der Richtung der Schwerkraft; es stimmt vollständig mit der Wachsthumsart des Astes überein.

In der Theilung begriffene Zellen wurden in keiner Scheidewand, wohl aber ab und zu dünnere, der Längsaxe des Astes mehr oder weniger parallele Scheidewände angetroffen. Eine Zellvermehrung kann, wenn sie überhaupt stattgefunden, nur in einseitiger Richtung eingetreten sein. Die Scheidewand war nämlich im Mittel aus fünf Messungen, nur für 1879 sind vier Zählungen gemacht, in der Wachsthumsrichtung des Astes 1881 fünf, 1880 sieben und 1879 fünf Zellen hoch. Hieraus dürfte wohl kaum eine Zellvermehrung in der Wachsthumsrichtung des Astes, die die Scheidewand durch neue Zellreihen verstärken würde, abzuleiten sein. Gegen diese Annahme sprechen ferner die geringen Unterschiede in der Höhe der gemessenen Zellräume, während doch durch eine Theilung in dieser Richtung gerade die Höhe bedeutend verkürzt erscheinen müsste. Senkrecht zur Höhe bestand die Scheidewand der Länge nach 1881 aus zehn, 1880 aus neunzehn und 1879 aus fünfzehn neben einanderliegenden Zellen. Wenn also eine Vermehrung der Scheidewandzellen stattgefunden, so hat sie wahrscheinlich nur, dem Dickenwachsthum des Astes folgend, zu der Verbreiterung der Scheidewand beigetragen und die Zellwände sind mehr oder weniger zur Astaxe parallel angelegt.

Daraus folgt dann, dass die allgemeine Gestalt der Scheidewandzellen durch das Wachsthum nicht wesentlich verändert ist. Die Zellen haben die Form unregelmässiger Prismen mit drei oder vier, mehr oder weniger gewölbten Seiten, so dass sie bisweilen an die Eiform erinnern. Die Gestalt der Zellen an getrennten zu beobachten, war trotz der sorgfältigsten Mazeration mit Wasser, Säuren, Alkalien oder chlorsaurem Kali und Salpetersäure nicht möglich, weil sich eine einzelne Zelle nicht herauspräpariren liess. Die Zellen erscheinen ferner in der Richtung der Astaxe zusammengedrückt und besitzen stark verdickte Wände mit einfachen Poren, die, soweit beobachtet, also bis ins dritte Jahr, geschlossen sind. Ob sie in späteren Jahren offen sind, kann ich nicht sagen.

Auch in der Zapfenaxe — Fig. 6 — findet sich in der Höhe der untersten Schuppen eine ähnliche, zehn bis zwölf Zellen starke Scheidewand, s, doch ist unterhalb derselben keine Lücke, sondern ein eigenthümliches Zellgewebe, l, und an dieses schliessen sich die rundlichen Markzellen, a, welche, dem Stiele angehörend, ohne Lückenbildung zum Astmarke übergehen. Dieses zwischen der Scheidewand, s, und dem Mark des Zapfenstieles, a, liegende Zellgewebe, dessen Glieder in mehr oder weniger radialen Reihen angeordnet, dünnwandig, ohne Zwischenzellräume an einander liegen, widersteht der Schwefelsäure ungemein lange; durch Jod und Schwefelsäure wird es nach Quellen in Kalilauge blau. Diese in ihren Reaktionen korkähnliche Zellschicht sitzt auf dem Mark des Zapfenstieles wie ein Zündhütchen auf dem

Piston, so dass das Ende des letzteren vollständig, auch zum Theil seitlich von der Scheidewand abgeschlossen ist. Dieses korkähnliche Zellgewebe findet sich in jedem Zapfen; niemals an seiner Stelle eine Lücke. Das Mark der Zapfenspindel besteht aus Parenchym mit stark verdickten, porösen Wänden, m; es zeigt keine Zwischenzellräume.

3. Abies nobilis Lindl.

Am Grunde des dreijährigen Triebes fand sich eine eilf bis zwölf Zellen dicke Scheidewand, deren untere sechs Schichten heller gefärbt sind und Stärke führen. Die Scheidewand ist nach oben convex, nach unten concav. Das sich anschliessende junge Mark erscheint dem blossen Auge hellbraun, führt aber Stärke; das alte Mark ist dunkelbraun. Einige runde Zellen dieses sitzen an der Scheidewand fest; doch ist die Hauptmasse derselben so zusammengeschrumpft, dass über und seitlich vom alten Markkörper eine deutliche Lücke vorhanden ist.

Jod zeigt in einigen Zellen Stärke; daneben liegen leere Zellen. Jod und conzentrirte Schwefelsäure so zu dem in Wasser befindlichen Präparat zugesetzt, dass das jüngste Holz und die Markzellen blau, die älteren Holzzellen gelbgrün wurden, ertheilte einigen älteren runden Markzellen auch eine blaue Farbe, zwischen ihnen lagen aber unveränderte braune. Die sechs untersten Zellreihen der Scheidewand waren gequollen, aber ungefärbt, die oberen braunen unverändert. Erst längere Einwirkung von Jod und Schwefelsäure machte alles blau, zuerst die innere Wandverdickung der hellen Scheidewandschicht. Es sind sonach die Wände der Scheidewandzellen aus einer anderen Modification des Zellstoffes gebildet, die den Reagentien länger widersteht, als die jungen Mark- und Holzzellen.

Am Grunde des diesjährigen Triebes lag eine sechszellige, nach oben convexe, nach unten concave Scheidewand, unter derselben die Lücke. Auch hier waren die drei oberen Zellreihen heller als die unteren gefärbt. Im alten Mark liegen zwischen braunen und stärkefreien Zellen helle mit Stärke. Es scheint hier eine Vermehrung der Scheidewandzellen auch in der Höhe, in der Richtung der Astaxe vorzukommen.

Die im Wachsthum begriffene Endknospe zeigte am 17. VII. 1884 noch keine Anlage der Scheidewand und Lücke. Doch grenzten rundliche Markzellen an solche mit mehr oder weniger zu einander senkrechten Wänden, die der Spitze zulagen.

4. Abies magnifica glauca Hort.

In einem vertrockneten Zweige war eine fünfzellige Scheidewand mit darunter liegender Lücke vorhanden.

5. Abies Fraseri Lindl.

Am Grunde des diesjährigen Triebes geht fürs blosse Auge ein feiner brauner Strich, der nach der Spitze zu concav ist, durch das Mark. Es sind dies die oberen rundlichen, abgestorbenen Zellen des vorjährigen Markes. Ueber diesen, durch eine Lücke getrennt, liegt die aus sechs Zellreihen in senkrechter Richtung bestehende Scheidewand. Der Zellraum der Scheidewandzellen ist im Durchschnitt elliptisch, der grösste Durchmesser liegt senkrecht zur Wachsthumsrichtung des Astes. Der Inhalt war am 21. VII. 1884 Protoplasma mit grossem Zellkern, Stärke fehlte. Diese fand sich aber in einem anderen am 28. VI. 1885 untersuchten Aste. Die Zellwand war stets hell und sehr dick, auch von einfachen, im Durchschnitt elliptisch geschlossenen Poren durchsetzt, die namentlich leicht nach Zusatz von Alkohol, welcher die jüngste Verdickung von der vorhergehenden im Präparate deutlich unterscheidbar machte, kenntlich.

Innerhalb der Knospe sind zwei Arten von Markzellen erkennbar; die unteren so lang wie breit und etwas abgerundet, die oberen, fünf Reihen, quergestreckt und verdickt. Dann folgt das gewöhnliche Mark der Knospen. Alle Zellen enthalten reichliches Protoplasma. Die fünf Reihen quergestreckter Zellen werden die Scheidewand.

6. Abies nordmanniana Spach.

Auch diese südkaukasische Tanne zeigt ebenso wie die nordamerikanischen eine Scheidewand und Lücke. Am Grunde eines vorjährigen Astes bestand die Scheidewand aus vier helleren und vier bis fünf dunkleren Zellreihen, von denen die ersteren unteren Stärke führten. Das ältere, dem blossen Auge braun erscheinende Mark war teilweise aus Stärke haltigen, lebenden, theilweise aus abgestorbenen Zellen gebildet. Zwischen den gewöhnlichen Markzellen und der Scheidewand war eine spaltenartige, schmale Lücke. Das jüngere Mark führte am 21. VII. 84 keine Stärke.

Die Scheidewand des diesjährigen Triebes hatte drei helle und vier dunkele Zellschichten und war durch einen schmalen Spalt vom darunter liegenden Mark getrennt. Nirgends konnte Stärke nachgewiesen werden.

Das Mark der Endknospe zeigte über dem Ansatz der untersten Schuppen eine Verengerung, in der die nach oben concave Scheidewand liegt. Die Zellen derselben sind, wie gewöhnlich, quergestreckt; ihre Wände stärker verdickt. In keiner der sieben Zellreihen konnte Stärke nachgewiesen werden, wohl aber reichliches Protoplasma. Das darunter liegende ältere Mark war in den oberen Reihen gebräunt, wenn auch noch keine Lücke gebildet war. Das Knospenmark bestand aus fast kubischen Zellen.

7. Abies pectinata DC.

In der Endknospe ist eine fünf bis sechs Zellen dicke und zwölf bis dreizehn Zellen lange Scheidewand vorhanden. Das darunter liegende, alte Mark, welches durch eine spaltenartige Lücke von derselben getrennt ist, besteht aus rundlichen, lockeren Zellen und zeigt eine kleine Verbreiterung gegen die Knospe hin. Die ältere, ebenso dicke aber fünfzehn bis sechszehn Zellen breite Scheidewand war gegen das vorhergehende rundzellige und gebräunte Mark convex, gegen das jüngere concav. Poren waren in den stark verdickten Wänden nur selten erkennbar, immer aber sehr reichliches Protoplasma. Eine Lücke war ausgebildet.

8. Abies cephalonica Lk.

Eine zehn bis elf Zellen dicke und achtzehn bis neunzehn Zellen lange Scheidewand trennt das Knospenmark von dem des letzten Triebes. Unter ihr ist eine kleine spaltenförmige Lücke erkennbar. Auch in dem zwei Jahre älteren Mark ist eine achtzehn bis neunzehn Zellen lange und sieben bis acht Zellen dicke Scheidewand, die nur in äusserst losem Zusammenhange mit dem älteren Mark steht, erkennbar.

9. Abies panachaica Heldreich.

Zwischen dem etwas blasig aufgetriebenen alten Mark, dessen runde Zellen zwar unter sich, doch wenig mit den angrenzenden Zellen in Zusammenhang stehen und daher meist eine Lücke erkennen lassen, und dem Knospenmark liegt eine sieben bis acht Zellen dicke Scheidewand. Einen besonderen Anblick boten am 28. II. 1882. die mit Stärke reichlich gefüllten Scheidewandzellen zwischen dem 1879/80er Triebe. Während die älteren äusseren Theile der Zellwand gut erhalten und keine Schichten in ihm getrennt waren, waren die später gebildeten Schichten nur lose und ringförmig den älteren angelegt; und daher erschien bei schwächerer Vergrösserung die Scheidewand aus runden porösen Zellen zu bestehen.

10. **Abies Pindrow Spach.**

Am Grunde des vorjährigen Triebes war eine acht Zellen breite Scheidewand vorhanden, deren fünf obere Reihen braun gefärbt waren. Die darunter befindliche Lücke wurde von hellwandigen, mit Stärke gefüllten Markzellen gebildet; über der Scheidewand war am 17. VII. 1884 noch keine Stärke im Mark. Die äusserlich abgerundete Knospe zeigt ein stumpfendendes grünes Mark ohne Scheidewand und Lücke.

11. **Abies sibirica Ledeb.**

In der Endknospe, sowie in den Seitenknospen eines kräftigen Astes ist eine sieben Zellen dicke Scheidewand, deren Breite von einundzwanzig Zellen in der Endknospe, von zehn bis elf in den Seitenknospen gebildet wird. Die Poren der stark verdickten Scheidewandzellen sind nicht durchbrochen. Eine Lücke ist in einem Aste deutlich; in einem anderen nicht ausgebildet. Das ältere Mark besteht aus meist braunen elliptischen Zellen.

12. **Abies Pinsapo Boiss.**

Am Grunde des zweijährigen Triebes findet sich eine in senkrechter Richtung sieben Zellreihen starke Scheidewand; unter ihr eine Lücke. Das darüberliegende Mark erschien dem Auge braun; das darunter liegende weiss. Letzteres besteht aus kugligen Zellen, die ebenso wie die Scheidewandzellen Stärke führen. Das darüber liegende, einjährige Mark besteht aus langgestreckten Zellen mit stärker verdickten Wänden; im Inhalte aber konnte Stärke nicht nachgewiesen werden.

Die Wände der Scheidewand nahmen bei Jod dieselbe braungelbe Farbe wie die Holzzellen an; ein Zusatz von Schwefelsäure färbte sie unter Aufquellen blau. Hierbei zeigte sich die Wandverdickung aus zwei Schichten bestehend, da die innere Verdickung sofort, die äussere bedeutend später blau wurde. Zwischenzellstoff war nicht vorhanden. Kalilauge bewirkte ein gleichmässiges Aufquellen. Das junge Ende hatte am 17. VII. 84 eine schwach gewölbte Oberfläche. Sein Mark war im unteren Ende aus lang parenchymatischen, im oberen schon aus kugelförmigen Zellen gebildet; alle Zellen mit feinkörnigem Protoplasma gefüllt. Die Scheidewand war nicht angelegt.

13. **Abies Veitchii Carr.**

Diese japanesische Tanne hat am Grunde des zweijährigen Triebes eine fünf- bis sechszellige Scheidewand, die nach unten concav ist. Nach oben schliessen sich wie bei den Anderen längere Zellen des jüngeren, nach unten rundliche des älteren Markes so an, dass keine Lücke vorhanden ist. Dagegen führen alle Stärke. Am Grunde des diesjährigen Triebes ist aber unter der nach oben convexen und fünf bis sechs Reihen starken Scheidewand eine deutliche Lücke, zumal die runden alten Markzellen braun und zusammengefallen erscheinen und keine Stärke führen.

14. Abies Maximowiczii K. L. B. 1883 *)

Am Grunde des vorjährigen Triebes war eine fünf bis sechs Zellreihen starke Scheidewand, deren obere drei Reihen braun, vorhanden. Die unteren hellen Schichten führten Stärke, die dem jüngeren Marke am 21. VII. 1884 fehlte. Am Grunde des diesjährigen Triebes fand sich eine ebenso starke Scheidewand mit drei hellen, Stärke führenden Schichten. Die älteren Markzellen waren zum Theil braun und leer, zum Theil hell und mit Stärke gefüllt. Das junge Mark zeigte keine Stärke, die sich aber schon in den Markstrahlen vorfand. Eine Lücke wurde unter keiner Scheidewand angetroffen.

15. Picea excelsa Lk.

Figur 7 stellt einen am 19. April 1885 angefertigten Längsschnitt durch die Endknospe eines neunjährigen Stammes dar. Zwischen den entfernten Knospenschuppen liegt der junge kugelförmige Trieb, an dessen Rande die Nadeln als Kerbung hervortreten. Je näher der Spitze desto kleiner sind die Nadeln; der Scheitel ist ohne dieselben. Eine einzelne Scheitelzelle war nicht vorhanden. Der Innenraum des Triebes wird von gleichmässigen kubischen Zellen, m, mit reichem Inhalt gebildet. Unter diesen setzt eine zehn bis elf Reihen dicke Wand, s, quer durch das Mark. Ihre grösste Dicke liegt in der Mitte des Astes; nach den Seiten wird sie dünner, da die Zellenzahl abnimmt. Die Länge der Scheidewand von links nach rechts hängt von der Stärke des Triebes ab. Bei vier Gipfelknospen von Aesten fand ich sie zu 1,653 — 1,392 — 1,682 — 1,682 mm; im Mittel ist sie = 1,602 mm lang. Die entsprechende Dicke am Rande war = 0,145 — 0,1856 — 0,116 — 0,261 mm; im Mittel = 0,1769 mm; die Dicke in der Mitte betrug = 0,29 — 0,2958 — 0,29 — 0,348 mm, durchschnittlich = 0,306 mm. Diese Scheidewand wird am Rande meist von sechs, in der Mitte von zehn Reihen stark verdickter Zellen gebildet, welche ohne Zwischenräume an einander schliessen. Sie enthalten viel Protoplasma und einen grossen Zellkern; Stärke und Kernkörperchen konnte ich nicht erkennen. Die Verdickung ist von zahlreichen Poren durchsetzt, wie es Fig. 8 veranschaulicht; Fig. 9 giebt einige Zellen im Verbande. Die Poren erweitern sich zu kleinen Höfen; die Scheidewand zwischen denselben ist deutlich sichtbar. Ich erhielt folgende Maasse, die ich im Mittel aus je fünf Messungen angebe: Länge des Porenganges = 0,0045 mm; Breite des Zellraumes = 0,0108 mm; Länge desselben = 0,0332 mm; Wandstärke zwischen zwei Zellen = 0,0098 mm. Der Durchmesser des Zellkernes im kürzeren Zellendurchmesser gemessen war = 0,0087 mm, im längeren Zellendurchmesser = 0,0096 mm. Da der Anblick der Zellen und des Kernes ganz gleich ist, ob man den Medianschnitt oder senkrecht dazu einen horizontalen Schnitt führt, so folgt für den Zellkern eine etwas abgeplattete Kugelgestalt und für die Zellen selbst eine Form, die dem Rotationsellipsoid nahe kommt; das beweisst auch der Querschnitt durch die Scheidewand. Die mittlere Länge der Zellen, von Scheidewand zu Scheidewand, ist = 0,0422 mm; die Breite = 0,0198 mm.

Der untere Rand der Markscheidewand ist nicht eben, sondern zeigt Ausbuchtungen, welche es klar erscheinen lassen, dass von ihr die darunter liegenden

---

*) „Fragliche Tanne aus der kgl. Landesbaumschule; nur in einem Jahre angezeigt. Ist nicht Picea Maximowiczii; hält alle Unbill des Klimas ohne Schaden aus." (Prof. Caspary.)

Markzellen gewaltsam abgerissen sind. Diese Wand bildet den oberen Rand der Lücke; der untere wird von kugligen bis eiförmigen, porösen Markzellen gebildet, die häufig durch Zwischenzellräume getrennt sind. Inhalt ist nicht vorhanden; die Zellwand — Fig. 10 — hin und wieder gebräunt. Der Gesammtanblick macht den Eindruck eines vertrocknenden Zellgewebes, das nur lose am Holzrohr hängt und leicht herausfällt. Durch Wasserzusatz kann es in seine frühere Spannung gebracht und die Lücke geschlossen werden. Auf diese verkürzten Zellen folgt dann das aus langgestreckten, inhaltleeren Parenchymzellen bestehende Mark des vorjährigen Triebes. An dieses, m in Fig. 11, schliesst sich dann unmittelbar die Scheidewand, s, mit ihren queren, jetzt inhaltleeren Zellen an, deren Lumen in der Breite = 0,0267 mm, in der Länge = 0,0336 mm ist. Die gemeinsame Wand zwischen zwei Zellen ist = 0,0104 mm stark.

Darunter liegt die Lücke, l. Es folgen die abgestorbenen, rundlichen Markzellen, Fig. 12, mit gebräunten Zellwänden, in denen die Poren nur noch äusserst selten erkennbar. Alkohol und Terpentinöl entfernte die Farbe nicht; Kalilauge lässt die Zellwand aufquellen. Diese Zellen werden seltener; es traten zwischen sie einige mit ungefärbten Zellwänden und deutlichen Poren, Fig. 13. Letztere Zellen sind weiter abwärts in der Mehrzahl und dann folgt die gewöhnliche Zellform des Markes, die dann wieder an die Querzellen der Scheidewand, Fig. 14, grenzen.

Markzellen sowohl wie die Scheidewandzellen sind ohne Inhalt, mit ungefärbten Zellwänden und einfachen, geschlossenen Poren.

So wiederholt sich der Bau des Markes durch jedes Jahr bis zum verfolgten neunten, in welchem die Zellräume = 0,015 mm breit und 0,0232 mm lang sind. Die Verdickung zwischen zwei Zellen war = 0,0104 mm stark. Nur die abgestorbenen und gebräunten Zellen des älteren Markes fallen beim Schneiden leichter als früher heraus, wodurch dann die Lücke vergrössert erscheint. Auch in den Aesten findet man denselben regelmässigen Bau des Markes wie im Stamme.

Immer ist das Mark in der Nähe des Endes eines Jahrestriebes, nämlich da, wo äusserlich die Knospenschuppen der Rinde eingewachsen sind, von einer mehr oder weniger dicken Scheidewand, die ungefähr die Gestalt einer planconvexen Linse hat, durchsetzt. Die Zellen derselben sind eiförmig bis elliptisch; besitzen stark verdickte Wände, die von Porenkanälen häufig durchbrochen sind. Der Zellinhalt ist Protoplasma und ein grosser kugliger Zellkern. Eine Vergrösserung des Zellraumes findet mit dem Alter statt, da die Maasse der Zellen älterer Scheidewände grösser als die der Endknospe sind. Dagegen zeigt das neunte Jahr, dass die Scheidewandzellen kürzer geworden sind, dass sie sich in der Richtung des Radius des Stammes verkleinert haben; was mit dem Verhalten des Markes bei Holzpflanzen übereinstimmen würde. Unterhalb der Scheidewand findet sich eine, der Grösse nach sehr verschiedene Lücke, die niemals mit Harz oder Terpentinöl gefüllt angetroffen wurde. Sie ist ein Zwischenzellraum, der durch die Streckung des Holzrohres, welcher die rundlichen älteren Markzellen nicht folgten, entstanden ist. Die Grösse der Lücke schwankt je nach dem Wassergehalt des untersuchten Theiles der Pflanze; sie ist in trockenen Pflanzentheilen grösser als in feuchten. Ja sogar in der Endknospe des Stammes wird sie während des Winters grösser als während des Frühlings gesehen.

In abgefallenen Zapfen konnte ich weder Scheidewand noch Lücke finden.

16. Picea Menziesii Carr.

Am Grunde des vorjährigen Triebes ist eine sechs bis sieben Zellenreihen starke Scheidewand vorhanden, deren bedeutend verdickte Zellwände zwei Schichten, die bei Jodzusatz noch deutlicher wurden, zeigen. Unter der Scheidewand wird eine Lücke durch die zusammengetrockneten, rundlichen Zellen des älteren Markes gebildet, doch führen diese ebenso wie die Scheidewandzellen Stärke. Am Grunde des diesjährigen Triebes ist eine fünf- bis sechszellige Scheidewand, die nicht wie die vorhergehende biconvex, sondern nach der Spitze zu concav, nach unten convex ist; darunter ist eine deutliche Lücke.

Die Endknospe des untersuchten Astes war am 16. VII. 1884 oben glatt und schon in Ruhe. Sie zeigte dreierlei Gestalten der Markzellen. Unten und inmitten der Knospe waren die Zellen regelmässig polyëdrisch, der Querdurchmesser gleich dem Längendurchmesser. Näher der Spitze waren acht bis neun Reihen entschieden quergestreckter Zellen, die ebenso wie die vorhergehenden Chlorophyll führen, vorhanden. Ueber diesen befinden sich vier bis fünf Reihen quadratischer, Blattgrün freier Zellen, die die Oberhaut bilden.

17. Picea sitchensis Carr.

Am 17. VII. 1884 war am Grunde des diesjährigen Triebes eine fünf- bis sechszellige Scheidewand, an deren unterem Rande einige alte Markzellen festsassen. Zwischen diesen und dem alten Mark war eine deutliche Lücke. Stärke war nirgend vorhanden. Die fortwachsende Endknospe hatte eine Scheidewand noch nicht angelegt.

18. Picea alba Lk.

Der Medianschnitt der Gipfelknospe eines Astes zeigte unter der aus acht bis neun Zellreihen bestehenden Scheidewand jedesmal eine Lücke, die durch das Fehlen der rundlichen Markzellen hervorgerufen wurde. Die Zellen der Scheidewand haben den schon bei P. Menziesii und P. excelsa beschriebenen Bau; es sind stark verdickte, poröse und eng an einander liegende polyëdrische Zellen mit reichlichem Inhalt. Die einjährige Scheidewand besteht ebenfalls aus neun Zellreihen; doch ist sie gegen das ältere Mark convex. Dieses besteht aus rundlichen, lockeren Zellen, welche durch den Schnitt leicht fortgeführt werden. Das übrige Mark besteht aus langem Parenchym. Diese sowie die drei ersten Zellreihen der Scheidewand haben einen dichten protoplasmatischen Inhalt.

19. Picea mariana nigra.

Untersucht wurde die Endknospe und einige Seitenknospen eines Astes. In allen war eine Scheidewand, aus sechs bis sieben Reihen stark verdickter Zellen bestehend, vorhanden. Die Zellen derselben enthielten am 23. III. 1882 wohl reichlich Protoplasma, doch keine Stärke. Diese fand sich aber in den grosskernigen Zellen des jungen Markes und hin und wieder in den rundlichen, lockeren Zellen des vorhergehenden Markes. Am Ende desselben war eine Lücke vorhanden.

Die Scheidewand und eine kleine Lücke fand sich auch am Anfang des vorhergehenden Triebes. Erstere bestand aus sieben Zellreihen und ist nach oben zu gewölbt, die oberen drei Zellreihen unterscheiden sich von den unteren durch eine dunklere Farbe. Während ein helles, durchsichtiges Protoplasma die Markzellen füllt, ist in den Scheidewandzellen ein dunkles. Stärke war in keinem nachweisbar.

20. Picea obovata Ledeb.

Zur Untersuchung wurden Medianschnitte durch den diesjährigen und vorjährigen Trieb eines Astes am 1. II. 1882 geführt. Die Endknospe zeigte eine aus sechs bis sieben Zellreihen bestehende Scheidewand. Darunter, im älteren Mark, war bei jedem Schnitt wahrscheinlich durch Ankleben der rundlichen, locker zusammenhängenden Zellen am Messer eine auffallend grosse Lücke. Darüber lag Parenchym mit reichlichem Inhalt. Die vorjährige Scheidewand begrenzte auf der untern Seite ein Mark, das aus längeren, parenchymatischen, auf umfangreichen Schnitten im Zickzack angeordneten Zellen bestand. Das unter der Scheidewand und dieser meist anliegende ältere Mark bestand aus leeren unregelmässig runden Zellen mit auffallend dünnen Scheidewänden, erst in einiger Entfernung nahm die Zellwand die gewöhnliche Dicke an.

21. Picea Tschugatzkoi Hort.*)

Während in einem abgestorbenen Aste die Lücke sehr deutlich, war am Grunde eines diesjährigen, frischen Zweiges nur eine siebenzellige Scheidewand und keine Lücke ausgebildet. Das ältere Mark bestand in seinem jüngsten Theile aus runden lockeren Zellen. In der Endknospe war am 27. VII. 1884 weder Scheidewand noch Lücke.

22. Picea Morinda Lk.

In der durchschnittenen Endknospe eines Astes erkennt das unbewaffnete Auge nach der Spitze zu ein dunkelgrünes, nach dem Grunde zu ein hellgrünes Mark. Ersteres besteht aus weiten, in der Wachsthumsrichtung gestreckten Zellen; letzteres aus sechs Reihen quergestreckter Zellen mit verdickten Wänden; doch enthielten diese am 17. VII. 1884 weder Chlorophyll noch Stärke. Es sind die Scheidewandzellen. Auf diese folgt ein grossmaschiges Mark, dessen vier- bis sechseckige Zellen wagrecht von links nach rechts die grösste Axe haben und kein Chlorophyll und keine Stärke führen. Zwischen Scheidewand und altem Mark war keine Lücke.

Am Grunde des 1883er Triebes liegt eine fünf Zellen dicke Scheidewand und unter derselben braune und helle, rundliche Markzellen. Eine Lücke war nicht ausgebildet; Stärke nicht nachweisbar.

Der Trieb des Jahres 1882 hatte am Grunde eine in der Axe siebenzellige nach unten convexe Scheidewand, in deren Zellen Stärke angetroffen wurde. Obwohl keine Lücke ausgebildet war, so bestand das ältere Mark aus runden, der grossen Zwischenzellräume wegen lockeren Zellen, deren Wände zum Theil hell, zum Theil braun gefärbt waren, nur die hellwandigen enthielten Stärke. Diese war in dem über der Scheidewand liegenden jüngeren Mark noch nicht nachweisbar.

In todten Aesten war unter jeder Scheidewand eine grosse Lücke.

Es zeigt diese im westlichen Himalaya in 2000 bis 3000 Meter Höhe wachsende Fichte sehr deutlich die Veränderung der am Ende des Triebes befindlichen Markzellen. Diese sind in der Endknospe polyëdrisch, runden sich im ersten Jahre ab und bilden im zweiten grosse Zwischenzellräume. Dass dieselben nicht zu einer

*) „P. Tschugatzkoi Hort ist wahrscheinlich Picea obovata Ledeb" (Prof. Caspary.)

Marklücke zusammenfliessen, zu deren Ausbildung alle Verhältnisse gegeben sind, könnte man vielleicht dem veränderten Klima, das eine beträchtliche Streckung der Holzzellen nicht gestattet, diese ebenso wie die ganze Pflanze am richtigen Wachsthum hindern wird, zuschreiben. Ob aber nicht auch bei uns in älteren Aesten eine Lückenbildung eintritt, kann ich nicht sagen, da ich solche nicht erhalten konnte.

23. Picea polita Carr.

Untersucht wurde ein Seitenzweig vom Stammgrunde am 17. VII. 1882. Am Grunde des vorjährigen Triebes war eine deutliche Lücke und darüber eine zehn Zellen starke Scheidewand, die nach oben eben, nach unten convex erschien, erkennbar. Die unteren drei Zellreihen besassen helle Wände und führten Stärke; die übrigen waren braunwandig und stärkefrei. Die darüber liegenden Markzellen waren mit Stärke gefüllt. Das obere Ende des alten Markes war braun, abgestorben und ohne Stärke; diese fand sich erst in einiger Entfernung. Auch zwischen dem dies- und vorjährigen Triebe befand sich Lücke und Scheidewand. Letztere war sieben- bis achtreihig; ihre vier unteren Reihen bestanden aus hellwandigen Zellen. Stärke war in ihr ebensowenig wie in den darunter liegenden runden Markzellen vorhanden; sie fand sich erst in den langgestreckten Markzellen.

Die im Wachsthum begriffene Endknospe zeigte noch keine Differenzirung der Markzellen.

24. Picea alkokiana Carr.

Am 15. III. 1882 war in der Knospe eines Astes die Scheidewand im Mark deutlich erkennbar. Unterschied sie sich von den älteren Markzellen auch nur durch die stärker verdickten Wände und den festeren Zusammenhang ihrer Zellen, so war sie doch gegen die wenig verdickten Zellen des Knospenmarkes scharf abgegrenzt. In dünneren Schnitten war eine Lücke zwischen einigen an der Scheidewand fest sitzen gebliebenen Markzellen und den übrigen vorhanden; in dickeren fehlte sie. Offenbar war also die Lücke nur durch das Messer, an dem die dünnwandigen, locker zusammenhängenden Zellen kleben blieben, und nicht in der Endknospe durch das Wachsthum entstanden.

Die vorjährige und auch die vorhergehende dreijährige Scheidewand zeigte eine Differenzirung ihres Gewebes. Während in der Knospe die Scheidewand aus fünf gleichartigen Zellreihen bestand, zeigte der Ast am Anfange der Jahrestriebe über vier bis fünf Reihen gleichfalls hellwandiger Zellen drei bis vier mit weniger verdickten Wänden, an welche dann die langgestreckten Markzellen des jüngeren Triebes sich anlegten. Die Markzellen am Ende des älteren Triebes waren eiförmig, hellwandig, mit braunem, harzigem Inhalte und durch grosse Zwischenzellräume von einander getrennt. Obwohl die Präparate stets Lücken zeigten, so möchte ich doch annehmen, dass diese durch Fortreissen der sehr harzreichen Markzellen entstanden sind, da einige derselben, wenn auch nur vereinzelt an der Scheidewand sassen. Es lag die Lücke, abweichend von allen anderen, nicht zwischen Scheidewand und altem Mark, sondern innerhalb dieses. Vielleicht passen auf diese, an das wärmere japanesische Klima gewöhnte Fichte dieselben Erwägungen wie bei P. Morinda. Es sind auch hier alle Verhältnisse zur Lückenbildung gegeben; dass dieselbe nicht eingetreten, mag an der geringen Streckung des Holzkörpers in den untersuchten Aesten liegen.

25. **Picea Engelmanni Carr.**

Am Grunde des diesjährigen Triebes ist eine sieben bis acht Zellen starke Scheidewand mit drei hellen unteren Reihen vorhanden. Darunter liegt die Lücke.

Das Mark der Endknospe besteht aus ziemlich regelmässigen vier- und sechseckigen, Chlorophyll haltigen Zellen, über welchen drei bis vier Zellreihen ohne Chlorophyll liegen. Die Endknospe war am 16. VII. 84 abgeplattet und nicht mehr im Fortwachsen begriffen; eine Scheidewand aber nicht erkennbar.

Am Grunde des vorjährigen Triebes befindet sich eine oben ebene, unten convexe Scheidewand, die von neun bis zehn Zellreihen gebildet wird, von denen wiederum die unteren drei hellere, stärker verdickte Wände besitzen. An diese setzen sich ohne ausgebildete Lücke die runden Zellen des älteren Markes, die meist noch lebensfähig sind, da sie Stärke enthalten. Stärke findet sich auch in den Scheidewandzellen und den langen Zellen des darüber liegenden Markes.

26. **Larix europaea DC.**

Auch bei der Lärche sind, wie bei Tanne und Fichte, die einzelnen Jahrestriebe der Aeste an den manschettenartigen Knospenschuppen äusserlich erkennbar. Ihnen entsprechen im Marke aber zwei Scheidewände. Beide finden sich in allen Aesten an den Grenzen verschiedenartiger Triebe.

Das Mark wird im älteren Theile aus gestrecktem Parenchym, dessen Wände mässig verdickt und stark porös sind und unter rechten Winkeln auf einander treffen, gebildet; hin und wieder finden sich in ihm kubische Zellen. Letztere werden, je näher dem Jahresende, desto zahlreicher; ihr längster Durchmesser liegt senkrecht zur Wachsthumsrichtung. Sie allein mit ihrem braunen Inhalt bilden schliesslich das Mark, doch setzen sich ohne Lücke stärker verdickte, poröse Zellen von unregelmässiger Gestalt an. Zwischen diesen und den jüngeren Markzellen geht in Form eines grossen Bogens, von der Markscheide beginnend, eine vier bis fünf Zellreihen starke Wand hindurch, deren Zellen ebenso stark wie die vorhergehenden verdickt und porös sind, die aber durch ihre Gestalt leicht auffallen. Sie sind in der Wachsthumsrichtung des Astes zusammengedrückt; dagegen ist ihr Querdurchmesser bedeutend vergrössert. Ihre oberste Reihe stösst an das junge Mark.

Die Endknospe der Zweige geht meist, wahrscheinlich durch das Aneinanderschlagen der Aeste während eines Windes verloren, denn häufig fehlt sie. Bedeutend umfangreicher als der Zweig sitzt sie wie eine kleine, von Schuppen umgebene Kugel an demselben. Von den ähnlichen Nadelzweigen unterscheidet sie sich dadurch, dass ihre äussersten Schuppen meist grün sind. Medianschnitte zeigten, dass das Mark aus runden Zellen, die wegen ihres lockeren Zusammenhanges und grossen Harzreichthumes leicht durch das Messer entfernt werden, besteht. Hierauf folgt in der Höhe der untersten Knospenschuppen eine vierzellige, nach unten gewölbte Scheidewand; zwischen ihr und dem älteren Mark ist meist eine Lücke. Ueber der Scheidewand beginnt ein aus kubischen Zellen bestehendes Mark, das nach der Knospe zu sich erweitert und in der Erweiterung aus sehr dünnwandigen Zellen besteht. Dieses ist wiederum von dem grünen Knospenmark, welches die Gestalt eines spitzen Kegels hat, durch eine vierreihige Scheidewand stärker verdickter, blattgrünfreier Zellen geschieden.

Sonach zeigt Larix europaea sowohl in der Endknospe wie in älteren Trieben, am Jahresende abweichend von den früheren Coniferen zwei Scheidewände, unter deren erster eine Lücke in trockenen Aesten stets, in frischen, saftigen seltener angetroffen wird. Die Markzellen zwischen den beiden Scheidewänden werden während des Wachsthums verdickt; hier habe ich niemals eine Lücke gesehen.

In diesem Bau gleicht die Endknospe vollständig den Nadelzweigen, von denen Fig. 15 einen fünfjährigen darstellt. In diesen ist Holz, H, und Mark, M, deutlich getrennt, ersteres besitzt auch Markstrahlen. Das Mark besteht aus ebensoviel gesonderten Körpern, m, wie der Zweig Jahre zählt. Jeder Markkörper ist durch eine mehr oder weniger grosse Lücke, b, vom vorhergehenden getrennt. Die meisten Zellen sind kuglig, zuweilen mit braunem Inhalt. Nach unten schliessen sie an eine zwei- bis vierzellige Wand, s, quergestreckter Zellen, die mit den Markscheidezellen fest verbunden, wahrscheinlich durch sie und den Holzkörper nach Art der Markstrahlen hindurchgehen. Die Spitze wird von einem kurzen Kegel, a, grüner Zellen gebildet, der von Schuppen umgeben ist und auf einer vier- bis fünfzelligen Scheidewand ruht. Zellkern und Protoplasma war in ihren Zellen deutlich; Poren und Stärke am 4. IV. 82 nicht erkennbar.

Die Seitenäste eines Hauptastes beginnen mit rundlichen, porösen und etwas verdickten Markzellen, die ohne Zwischenräume an einander schliessen. Darüber liegen kubische Markzellen, die allmählich in gestreckte übergehen. Auf diesen nur wenig Zellen hohen Markkörper folgen vier bis fünf Reihen kubischer, stark verdickter Zellen, welche nach Art der Scheidewand, nach oben concav, nach unten convex, das Mark durchsetzen. Unterhalb dieser Wand habe ich häufig, doch nicht immer, eine Lücke gesehen.

Auch das Mark in der Axe der männlichen Blüthe ist vom vorhergehenden der darunter liegenden Axe durch eine Scheidewand getrennt. Letzteres scheint eine ähnliche Gliederung wie das der Nadelzweige zu besitzen und besteht wie dort aus runden Zellen. Das Mark der Zapfenaxe besteht aus lang gestreckten, inhaltreichen Zellen, die ihres baldigen Hinwelkens wegen bedeutendere Veränderungen nicht erleiden.

Die weibliche Blüthe hat im Stiel grüngefärbtes, in der Spindel farbloses Mark. Eine Scheidewand in der Höhe der untersten Knospenschuppen fehlt; wohl aber ist eine Reihe querliegender, wenig verdickter Zellen am äussersten Grunde des Stieles, fast noch im Holzkörper des tragenden Astes, vorhanden.

Durch das Auftreten zweier Scheidewände im Knospenmarke, die ein Stück desselben aus dem innigen Zusammenhangemit den anderen Markzellen reissen und sie zu eigener Entwickelung zwingen, weicht Larix von den anderen Abietineen ab. Da eine Lückenbildung nur zwischen der unteren Scheidewand und dem älteren Mark auftritt, so kann man den ganzen Zellcomplex, der am Grunde des jüngeren Markes liegt und sich von diesem durch die stärker verdickten und anders geformten Zellen unterscheidet, als Scheidewand auffassen. Es käme dann Larix eine dreischichtige Scheidewand zu.

27. Larix dahurica Turcz.

Aeste und Nadelzweige zeigen denselben, soeben beschriebenen Bau.

28. Larix leptolepis Gord.

Ausser in den Aesten und Nadelzweigen, die mit den vorhergehenden übereinstimmen, findet sich eine Scheidewand als trennende Schicht auch zwischen dem Mark des die weibliche Blüte tragenden Theiles der Axe und dem darunter liegenden Theil derselben Axe.

29. Cedrus Deodara Loud.

Sie bietet ihres Harzreichthumes und des dünnen Markes wegen der Untersuchung einige Schwierigkeit dar, die bei den Nadeln tragenden Zweigen noch grösser ist. In den Aesten endet jeder Jahrestrieb mit braunen, rundlichen, lockeren Zellen, die durch Zusammenfallen die Lücke bilden; zum Theil auch durch das Messer, an dem sie leicht kleben bleiben, entfernt werden. Ueber diesen beginnt das junge Mark ohne eine Scheidewand quergestreckter Zellen mit in der Axe verlängertem Parenchym.

Auch in den Nadelzweigen war eine Querwand verdickter Zellen nicht vorhanden, aber eine ziemlich unvermittelte Abwechselung runder und langer Markzellen. Beide enthielten am 16. VII. 84 Chlorophyll und Stärke. Die runden Zellen wurden aus der Mitte des Markes wohl durch den Schnitt entfernt, denn sie sassen an der Markscheide zum Theil noch fest und grenzten dort an die langen Markzellen.

Cedrus Deodara zeigt demnach die Möglichkeit einer Lückenbildung ohne die einer Scheidewand.

30. Pinus silvestris L.

Die äusserlich von mehreren häutigen Schuppen bedeckte Endknospe war am 12. IX. 84 im Inneren vollständig grün. Das Mark besteht aus fast kubischem Parenchym mit reichlichem Protoplasma und Zellkern. Poren waren nicht sichtbar. Von den mehr rundlichen und Stärke führenden Holzzellen waren sie leicht zu unterscheiden. Durch das weitere Wachsthum werden die unteren Markzellen eines Triebes bedeutend in die Länge gestreckt, während die des oberen Endes sich gleichmässiger nach allen drei Dimensionen ausdehnen.

In einem siebenjährigen Triebe zeigte das Mark folgenden, sich jedes Jahr wiederholenden Bau. Jeglicher Zellinhalt ist im Mark verschwunden. Die Zellwand besitzt eiförmig längliche, unregelmässig vertheilte, undurchbrochene Poren. Die Gestalt der Zellen ist aber sehr verschieden. Zwischen langgestrecktem Parenchym. liegen verschieden zahlreich kurze Zellen mit gebräunten Zellwänden. Diese letzteren nehmen je näher dem Triebende desto mehr an Zahl zu, so dass in der Höhe des nächstjährigen Astquirles nur diese braunwandigen, hier aber rundlichen Zellen vorhanden sind. Ueber den Astansatz hinaus nimmt die Zahl dieser Zellen wieder ab und es treten Zellen der vorher beschriebenen Art wieder auf. Scheidewand und Lücke habe ich hier so wenig wie in jüngeren Aststücken gefunden. Trotzdem ist man im Stande, mit unbewaffnetem Auge an der Farbe des Markes die Jahresgrenze eines Triebes anzugeben, da das ältere Mark gebräunt, das jüngere weiss erscheint

31. Pinus Strobus L.

Die Endknospe eines Astes zeigt ein aus regelmässigem, scharfwinkligem Parenchym gebildetes Mark, dessen Zellen auf dem Medianschnitt breiter als lang und mit Protoplasma gefüllt sind. Nach dem Grunde der Knospe zu setzen sich quadratische Zellen mit abgerundeten Wänden an. Eine Lücke oder Scheidewand ist nicht vorhanden.

In älteren Zweigen sind die kubischen Zellen braun gefärbt und nicht bedeutend vergrössert, während die jüngeren sich in die Länge gestreckt und zuweilen einen Zickzackverlauf haben; gleichsam als wenn sie nicht in gerader Richtung, sondern nur durch seitliches Ausbiegen den nöthigen Raum für ihre Streckung finden konnten. Lücke oder Scheidewand wurde bei keinem der untersuchten Aeste angetroffen.

Auch die übrigen Arten: Pinus Cembra L., P. mitis Mich., P. Pumilio Haenke, P. densiflora Sieb. et Zucc., P. Laricio Poir. zeigten nirgends Lücke oder Scheidewand; stets aber hatte beim Jahreswechsel eine Gestaltsveränderung der Markzellen stattgefunden, die schon dem unbewaffneten Auge durch die braune und weisse Färbung auffiel. Es fanden sich am Ende eines jeden Jahrestriebes nach unten kubische Zellen mit braunen Wänden, nach oben lang gestrecktes Parenchym mit hellen Zellwänden.

37. Araucaria excelsa R. Br.

Schon äusserlich unterscheidet sich die untersuchte Vertreterin der von Carrière den Abietineen angefügten Unterordnung von den ächten Abietineen durch das gänzliche Fehlen der Knospenschuppen. Am Grunde eines 1 dcm langen Zweiges, dessen Alter sich daher nicht angeben lässt, ist weder Lücke noch Scheidewand vorhanden. Das Mark besteht aus Stärke führendem Parenchym, dessen Zellen doppelt so lang wie breit sind. Auch an den Abgangsstellen der Seitenäste zeigt das Mark des Hauptastes dieselben Verhältnisse; nirgend eine Lücke, Scheidewand oder eine Gestaltsveränderung der Zellen. Ebenso besitzt die Gipfelknospe nur ein gleichmässiges, an die Junipereen erinnerndes Mark.

Nach meinen Untersuchungen bietet das Mark der Araucaria excelsa, der Cupressineen, Podocarpeen und Taxineen, mit Ausnahme von Torreya nucifera, nicht den geringsten Unterschied vom Mark der meisten Angiospermen dar. Es besteht überall aus Parenchym, dessen Zellen gleich gross, wenig verdickt und ohne Zwischenzellräume an einander gelagert sind. Torreya nucifera zeigt ein ähnlich gebautes Mark, das aber in der Höhe der Axen zweiten Grades von einer Scheidewand querliegender Zellen durchsetzt ist. Diese Conifere vermittelt dadurch den Uebergang zum Mark der Abietineen, bei welchen allen — mit Ausnahme der Araucaria excelsa, deren Mark im Baue mit dem der Cupressineen übereinstimmt, — am Ende des Jahrestriebes eine durch die Farbe der Wände der Markzellen hervorgebrachte Grenze zwischen altem und jungem Marke deutlich ist. Mit der Farbe ändert sich gleichzeitig die Form und Gestalt der Markzellen. In seinem mittleren Verlaufe besteht bei ihnen allen das Mark eines Jahrestriebes aus lang gestrecktem Parenchym; am Ende des Triebes dagegen aus kubischen oder eiförmigen Zellen, welche durch mehr oder weniger häufige Zwischenzellräume einen lockeren Verband haben. Ueber diesen alten Markzellen findet sich eine Lücke im Marke bei den Arten der Gattungen Abies, Picea, Larix und Cedrus Deodara. Die Lücke fehlt im Marke von Tsuga canadensis und den Arten der Gattung Pinus. Oberhalb der Lücke, oder, wenn diese nicht ausgebildet, in der Höhe der Knospenschuppen findet sich im Marke eine Scheidewand quergestreckter Zellen bei Tsuga canadensis, den Arten von Abies, Picea und Larix. Die Scheidewand fehlt im Marke von Cedrus Deodara und den

Pinus-Arten. Ueberhaupt wird das Vorkommen der Markscheidewand durch die äusserlich an der Rinde bleibenden Knospenschuppen angezeigt; alle Coniferen mit bleibenden Knospenschuppen besitzen eine das Mark quer durchsetzende Scheidewand; den Coniferen mit hinfälligen Knospenschuppen fehlt sie.

Demnach würde man, wenn der Versuch einer Eintheilung der Coniferen nach den anatomischen Merkmalen des Markes gewagt werden sollte, folgende Gruppen unterscheiden müssen:

I. Coniferen ohne Lücke und ohne Scheidewand:
   1. Im Marke sind die Enden der Jahrestriebe nicht zu erkennen: Junipereen, Podocarpeen, Taxineen s. p., Araucaria excelsa.
   2. Die Enden der Jahrestriebe sind im Marke erkennbar: Pinus silvestris, P. Cembra, P. Strobus, P. mitis, P. Pumilio, P. densiflora, P. Laricio.

II. Coniferen ohne Lücke aber mit Scheidewand:
   1. Die Markzellen am Ende eines Jahrestriebes sind von den vorhergehenden und folgenden nicht verschieden: Torreya nucifera.
   2. Am Ende des Jahrestriebes ist eine andere Form von Markzellen vorhanden: Tsuga canadensis.

III. Coniferen mit Lücke, ohne Scheidewand: Cedrus Deodara.

IV. Coniferen mit Lücke und mit Scheidewand: Arten der Gattungen: Abies, Picea und Larix.

Die Scheidewand dieser drei letzten Gattungen ist keine von der geographischen Verbreitung der Arten oder äusseren Einflüssen abhängige Eigenthümlichkeit. Sie findet sich ebensowohl bei europäischen, wie asiatischen und nordamerikanischen Tannen, Fichten und Lärchen. Ebenso sicher ist sie in abgestorbenen, wie absterbenden und lebenden Aesten und Stämmen vorhanden. Sie ist eine Eigenthümlichkeit der gesund fortwachsenden Pflanze und findet sich immer, wie schon erwähnt, in der Höhe der bleibenden Knospenschuppen im Marke. Sie entsteht am Ende eines jeden Sommers. Auf ihre Anlage hat die Temperatur einigen Einfluss. Die Scheidewand wird nicht gleichzeitig bei allen Arten angelegt; sondern es legen die aus südlicheren, wärmeren Gegenden bei uns gezogenen Exemplare diese früher, die aus kälteren später an. Die aus dem nordwestlichen Amerika stammende Abies nobilis hatte am 17. VII. 1884 noch keine Scheidewand, während die in Pennsilvanien und Carolina einheimische Abies Fraseri dieselbe am 21. VII. 1884 besass; Picea Tschugatzkoi aus Sibirien und vom Altai hatte am 27. VII. 1884 noch keine Scheidewand, aber in Picea Morinda aus dem westlichen Himalaya war sie am 17. VII. 1884 schon fertig; Picea excelsa hatte am 27. VII. 1884 noch keine Scheidewand.

Der jüngste, bei Abies Fraseri und Picea Menziesii beobachtete Zustand waren mehrere, so im Marke angelegte Zellen, dass ihr grösster Durchmesser senkrecht zur Wachsthumsrichtung des Astes sich befand. Sie führten im Protoplasma Chlorophyll (Picea Menziesii). Die Zellen scheinen sich nicht in der Wachsthumsrichtung des Astes zu vermehren, sondern in radialer, dem Dickenwachsthum des Astes und Stammes folgender Richtung (Abies balsamea). Die neunjährige Scheidewand von Picea excelsa zeigt in dieser Richtung eine Verkürzung der Zellendurchmesser. Ihre Vergrösserung besteht in einer gleichmässigen Streckung nach allen

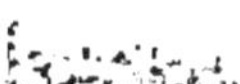

drei Dimensionen des Raumes (Abies balsamea, Picea excelsa); in Aesten ist die Streckung in senkrechter Richtung die bedeutendste (Abies balsamea). Die ausgebildeten Zellen sind bald unregelmässige Prismen mit gewölbten Seiten, bald eiförmig gestaltet. Sie sind länger als die umgebenden Markzellen lebensfähig und enthalten reichlich Protoplasma und einen kugligen Zellkern; ja sie führen zu gewissen Zeiten auch Stärke. Ihre bedeutende Wandverdickung, die von zahlreichen, geschlossenen Poren durchbrochen wird, zeigt zwei Schichten; die äussere ist gewöhnlicher Zellstoff, die innere eine den Reagentien länger widerstehende Modifikation desselben (Abies nobilis, A. Fraseri). Eine Verharzung der Zellwände wurde nicht wahrgenommen, wenn auch einige Reihen der Scheidewandzellen später braune Wände erhalten (Picea polita, P. Engelmanni, P. alkokiana). Scheidewände anderer Arten haben soweit sie durch eine Reihe von Jahren verfolgt werden konnten, Zellwände von gleicher Farbe. Abgesehen von der Färbung, zeigt nur die Gattung Larix eine dreischichtige aus verschiedenen Zellformen gebildete Scheidewand; Abies und Picea nicht.

Mit der Scheidewand in innigem Zusammenhange steht die Marklücke der Coniferen in sofern als diese mit Sicherheit nur in den Arten von Abies, Picea und Larix zu finden ist. Eine Lücke ohne Scheidewand hat Cedrus Deodara; andererseits findet sich die Scheidewand, aber keine Lücke bei Torreya nucifera und Tsuga canadensis, bei welch letzterer eine Lücke noch am ersten, der veränderten Endzellen des alten Markes wegen, erwartet werden könnte.

Von diesen drei Ausnahmen abgesehen, findet sich die Marklücke in allen vegetativen Axen von Abies-, Picea- und Larix-Arten da im Marke, wo „ein neuer Jahresschoss als Fortsetzung des vorhandenen Schosses oder ein Seitenspross sich anschliesst.“ Sie liegt unterhalb der Scheidewand und über dem Ende des älteren Markes und trennt beide in ihrer ganzen Breite.

Die Marklücke ist nie durch Zerreissung oder Auflösung von Zellen entstanden, wohl aber durch Loslösen ganzer Zellen des Markendes eines Jahrestriebes von den Scheidewandzellen. Ihre Entstehung hängt von zwei im eigenen Bau und Leben des Holz- und Markkörpers gegebenen Verhältnissen ab. Der erste Grund ist die Veränderung der Endzellen des Markes eines Jahrestriebes.

Diese Zellen sind polyëdrisch angelegt und berühren sich mit ihren Zellwänden (P. Morinda); später runden sie sich mehr und mehr zur Ei- oder Kugelform ab, wodurch grössere Zwischenzellräume auftreten. Dadurch wird ein lebhafterer Saftaustausch der Zellen unter sich und mit den umgebenden Zellgeweben erschwert; diese Markzellen sind zu ihrer weiteren Ausbildung auf die eigenen Vorräthe angewiesen und vertrocknen nach Verbrauch derselben. Ihre wenig verdickten Wände fallen mehr und mehr zusammen. Die Zwischenzellräume werden namentlich zwischen den Scheidewandzellen und den obersten Markzellen grösser und bilden in ihrer Gesammtheit die Lücke. Aeussere Einflüsse, wie etwa Frost oder Hitze, können zu dieser Ausbildung nicht Veranlassung gewesen sein, da die Zellen schon im Hochsommer nicht nur bei den aus dem Süden stammenden, sondern selbst bei unseren einheimischen Coniferen verkümmert sind. Der Grund dafür muss im eigenen, inneren Leben des Baumes gesucht werden.

Der zweite Grund für die Entstehung der Marklücke liegt im Wachsthum des Holzkörpers, dessen Zellen sich bedeutend nach ihrer Anlage in die Länge strecken. Hierdurch wird die an der Markscheide befestigte Scheidewand von den darunter liegenden, sich nicht streckenden Markzellen des Jahresendes entfernt.

Die Lücke ist das Resultat der gemeinschaftlichen Wirkung beider Lebensvorgänge. Die Grösse derselben steht aber in innigem Zusammenhange mit jeder von beiden. So lange die Endzellen des älteren Markes sich lebenskräftig ausdehnen oder eine Streckung der Holzzellen der Jugend oder der veränderten Wachsthumsweise des Klimas wegen nicht stattgefunden, so lange ist eine Lücke nicht vorhanden (Picea Morinda, P. alkokiana). Das kann zeitlich bei den einzelnen Arten, ja selbst in den verschiedenen Theilen des Exemplares sehr verschieden sein. Ich besitze z. B. Längsschnitte durch die Endknospe von Picea excelsa mit sehr verschieden grossen Lücken. Die im Winter angefertigten Präparate zeigen eine grosse deutliche Lücke; die im Frühjahre angefertigten dagegen haben theils nur spaltenförmige, theils deutliche Lücken. Immerhin wird in älteren und daher trockneren Aesten und Stämmen mit grösserer Sicherheit eine Lücke angetroffen, als in Endknospen und jungen Trieben, weil in ersteren die Holzzellen sich gestreckt, das Markende des Jahresschosses vertrocknet ist; in letzteren dagegen die Markendzellen häufiger noch lebenskräftig, ihre Zellwände durch Feuchtigkeit gespannt und die Holzzellen wenig in die Länge gestreckt sind. Sonach ist die Grösse der Lücke auch von dem Alter und der Feuchtigkeit des Stammes und der Aeste abhängig. Vergessen darf schliesslich nicht werden, dass die Grösse der Marklücke auch durch die Schnittführung geändert werden kann, wie ich es bei Abies balsamea und Picea alkokiana erwähnt habe.

Die Marklücke unterliegt demnach mancherlei Einflüssen, die auf ihre Grösse und ihr Entstehen wirken, und die Frage nach dem zeitlich zuerst eintretenden, also ursächlichen Einfluss ist nicht leicht zu beantworten, zumal die direkte Beobachtung keinerlei Anhalt bietet. Die natürlichste Ursache scheint mir die Längsstreckung der Holzzellen zu sein, denn durch sie findet alles Uebrige die einfachste Erklärung. Dadurch erklärt sich leicht der lose Zusammenhang der Markzellen am Ende des Jahresschosses, ihr schnelles Absterben und Vertrocknen gleicht Zellen, die aus dem Zusammenhange gerissen sind. Deshalb erscheint es auch nicht befremdlich, wenn hin und wieder einige Markzellen an der Scheidewand sitzend angetroffen werden.

Ihrer Natur nach gehört die Marklücke zu den Luft führenden Zwischenzellräumen, niemals habe ich sie von Terpentin oder Harz, wie es Sachs in seinem Lehrbuche der Botanik IV. pag. 517 für den Stamm der Coniferen angiebt, erfüllt gesehen.

Bericht

über die

in den Sitzungen

der

physikalisch-ökonomischen Gesellschaft

zu Königsberg in Pr.

gehaltenen Vorträge im Jahre 1885.

Sitzung am 8. Januar 1885.

Der Vorsitzende begrüsst die Versammlung und bezeichnet das verflossene Jahr als ein für die Gesellschaft glückliches. Die Geologen sind mit den Aufnahmen in der Provinz weiter fortgeschritten, die Sammlungen und Bibliothek sind bedeutend vermehrt, letztere wird theilsweisse translocirt werden müssen, da die jetzigen Räume nicht mehr ausreichen, derselbe spricht die Hoffnung aus, dass auch das neue Jahr sich glücklich gestalten werde.

Zur Statistik der Gesellschaft übergehend bemerkt er, dass dieselbe jetzt zählt: 1 Protector, 13 Ehren-, 251 ordentliche und 217 auswärtige Mitglieder, gegen 1 Protector, 17 Ehren-, 262 ordentliche und 217 auswärtige Mitglieder beim Beginn des vorigen Jahres. Durch den Tod sind ihr entrissen: 1 Ehrenmitglied, Geheimer Archivrath Dr. Lisch in Schwerin, 2 ordentliche Mitglieder, Commerzienrath Wiehler und Geheimer Medicinalrath Professor Dr. v. Wittich, 9 auswärtige Mitglieder 1) Hotelbesitzer Braune-Insterburg, 2) Rittergutsbesitzer Bernhardi-Loelken, 3) Prof. Dr. Brücke in Wien, 4) Forstrath Prof. Dr. Hartig in Braunschweig, 5) Regierungs-Medicinalrath Dr. Hoogeweg in Münster, 6) Pastor Kowall in Pussen (Kurland), 7) Rittergutsbesitzer Siegfried in Kirschnehnen, 8) Prof. Stannius in Rostock, 9) Geheimer Commerzienrath Warschauer in Berlin. Die Gesellschaft wird Allen ein ehrendes Andenken bewahren.

Der Vorsitzende verliest darauf ein Schreiben des Zweigcomités der zoologischen Station in Neapel, in welchem um einmalige Beiträge gebeten wird. Er bemerkt, dass bereits zweimal über die Station in unseren Sitzungen berichtet ist, dass derselben grosse Ausgaben bevorstehen, indem ein Dampfer reparirt und ein neuer angeschafft werden soll, und dass das Institut dauernd im Wachsen begriffen ist; die Subventionen der Regierung reichen nicht aus. Eine Liste zur Zeichnung von Beiträgen wurde ausgelegt. Die Sammlung ergab 90 Mk., welche an das Comité abgeführt sind.

Herr Professor Dr. Merkel hielt einen Vortrag über das Alter.

Herr Dr. Tischler legt den ihm von der Frau Kammerherr Sehested auf Broholm zum Geschenk gemachten zweiten Theil des Sehested'schen Werkes: „Archaeologiske Undersögelser 1878—81 af N. F. B. Sehested“ vor, welches nach dem Tode des Verfassers von der Familie herausgegeben ist. Dies Werk ist ebenso wie der erste Theil

(Fortidsminder og Oldsager fra Egnen om Broholm 1878) auf das Glänzendste ausgestattet und mit der allergrössten Gründlichkeit und Genauigkeit abgefasst, so dass beide Theile als bisher unerreichte, geradezu klassische Muster der Erforschung und Bearbeitung eines abgeschlossenen kleineren Gebietes dastehen. Der zweite Theil bringt die Ausgrabungsberichte von weiteren Hügeln der Broncezeit — wobei die früher sogenannten Diademe sich als Halskragen erwiesen, die Fortsetzung des Flachgräberfeldes von Møllegaardsmark etc. und die Ausgrabung einiger Hügel aus Addit Skov in Jütland etc., im Ganzen die Fortsetzung der exacten Ausgrabungsberichte des ersten Theiles. Die von Madsen und Magnus Petersen ausgeführten Kupferstiche sind geradezu als Kunstwerke zu betrachten. Der Vortragende hatte selbst das Glück, mehrere Tage die Gastfreundschaft der Familie Sehested zu geniessen, welche nach seinem Tode in würdiger Pietät das von dem Verstorbenen begonnene Werk fortführt. Er konnte die in einem eigens dazu errichteten Hause untergebrachten reichen Funde genau studiren und auch die Resultate der Versuche verfolgen, die Sehested unternommen hatte, um die Technik und Arbeitsweise der Steinzeit zu ergründen.

Ueber diese Versuche berichtet der vorliegende Band eingehend. Dieselben sind in äusserst gründlicher Weise ausgeführt und haben zu recht überraschenden Resultaten geführt. Es werden Steinäxte geschliffen, durch Holzblätter mit Sand gesägt, ferner dieselben durch massive oder hohle Stäbe gebohrt mittelst eines Bogens oder Drillbohrers (mit Holz, Knochen oder Horn). Aehnliche Versuche hatte der Vortragende auch früher gemacht*) — was in obigem Werke erwähnt ist — und an diesem Orte vorgezeigt. (Die Stücke befinden sich im Provinzial-Museum.) Die Sehested'schen Arbeiten sind viel umfassender und bestehen in einer sehr ausgedehnten Versuchsreihe.

Nun handelte es sich aber noch darum, zu zeigen, dass man mit den Steingeräthen auch wirklich arbeiten könne, und dies gelang in überraschendster Weise, wobei sich auch die früher immer ausgesprochene Ansicht, dass solche Arbeiten, ebenso wie die Herstellung der Geräthe, einen ungeheueren Zeitaufwand erfordern, als Fabel erwies. Sehested erbaute ein vollständiges Blockhaus aus Kiefern nur mit Hilfe von Feuerstein-Aexten, Meisseln und Schabern. Die Bäume wurden gefällt — ein Probestück eines in 11 Minuten mit einer Feuersteinaxt abgehauenen Stammes hat Sehested unserem Provinzial-Museum zum Geschenk gemacht — entästet, entrindet, zugespitzt, in einander gefugt, das Dach aufgesetzt und eine Thüre in ein besonderes Gerüst gehängt. So entstand in ziemlich kurzer Zeit ein zierliches Häuschen. Zu den Arbeiten im Walde wurde folgende Zeit gebraucht: Zum Fällen von 63 Bäumen von 0,30 m Dicke 2½ Arbeitstage (ein Tag à 10 Stunden), 60 von 0,09 m in 5 Stunden (½ Tag), Herausschleppen 2 Arbeitstage, Entästeln 4½, Entrinden 5 Tage, in Summa auf 1 Mann berechnet 14½ Arbeitstage. Die Aexte blieben dabei vollständig scharf und unbeschädigt, nur von einer lösten sich beim Abhauen der Aeste (es wurden über 6000 abgehauen) einige lange Splitter. Um das Haus fertig zu stellen, wurden dann noch 66½ Arbeitstage verbraucht, incl. Schleifen der Steingeräthe, also in Summa 81.

*) Schriften der physikalisch-ökonomischen Gesellschaft 1880. Sitzungsberichte p. 16—18.

Jetzt steht das kleine Gebäude unter schattigen Bäumen am Wasser, die Werkzeuge, mit denen es hergestellt in sich bergend, das Zauberhaus, an dem die Landleute Abends nur mit abergläubischer Scheu vorbeieilen.

Der Vortragende zeigt ferner im Anschluss an die in der Sitzung vom 1. April 1881 gemachten Mittheilungen, eine Anzahl Jütischer Töpfe und die Werkzeuge, die zu ihrer Fertigstellung gebraucht wurden, wie sie im ersten Bande des Sehested'schen Werkes beschrieben sind, alles ein Geschenk der Familie Sehested an das Provinzial-Museum. Die Töpfe zeigen, wie damals erörtert, dass auch ohne Drehscheibe Gefässe von vollendet gerundeter Form hergestellt werden können, und dann ist auch ihre schwarzglänzende Oberfläche bemerkenswerth, die besonders in den mit einem Stein aufpolirten einfachen Ornamenten einen durchaus metallischen, vollständig graphitähnlichen Glanz zeigt, und dabei ist Graphit absolut nicht zur Anwendung gekommen, sondern der Glanz und die Schwärze nur durch Brennen der Töpfe in einem glimmenden, rauchenden, reducirenden Feuer erzeugt.

Nun ist solche schwarze Topfwaare in einem grossen Theile des östlichen Europas, besonders wie es scheint, bei slavischen Nationen verbreitet, geht aber allmählich immer mehr ein, so dass wir es hier ebenso wie in Jütland mit einer interessanten, dem Untergange verfallenden Industrie zu thun haben, obwohl diese Gefässe beim Kochen sogar manche Vorzüge vor den glasirten haben.

Im südlichen Westpreussen wurden früher die sogenannten Kassubischen Töpfe in grosser Masse producirt, während jetzt die Industrie eingegangen ist. Unser eifriges Mtiglied, Herr Apotheker Scharlock in Graudenz, hat noch einige solche Töpfe erstehen können und 3 Stück gütigst dem Provinzial-Museum zum Geschenk gemacht. Ebenso gab er 2 Thongefässe, die er zum Versuche den in Steinkisten gefundenen nachgebildet hatte, und aus Thon gebrannt ein Modell der unten (in seinem Bericht) beschriebenen Blockscheibe. Zugleich hat Herr Scharlock die Notizen über die Fabrikation dieser Gefässe gesammelt und dabei den Töpfermeister Maschlitzki zu Rathe gezogen. Es sind dadurch eine Reihe von Thatsachen bezüglich auf eine dem Untergange verfallende, zum Theil primitive Technik zusammengekommen, welche werth sind, der Vergessenheit entrissen und hier fixirt zu werden. Der von Herrn Scharlock freundlichst eingesandte Bericht wird daher weiter unten unverkürzt mitgetheilt und der Vortragende wird dankbar sein, wenn auch anderweitig ähnliche Studien gemacht und ihm übermittelt würden.

Der Vortragende fand bei seiner vorjährigen Reise durch Galizien und Ungarn besonders in den Gewerbe-Museen von Krakau und Lemberg eine Menge solcher schwarzen unglasirten Gefässe haupsächlich aus Ostgalizien, auch aus der Ukraine. In Galizien ragten die Töpfereien von Wertelka durch ihre anmuthigen Formen hervor, welche entschieden an klassische erinnern, so dass es fast den Anschein hat, als ob hier seit der römischen Occupation Daciens eine gewisse stilistische Tradition sich latent bis auf die Neuzeit forterhalten hat, wie wir es ja in manchen Gebirgsländern finden (so z. B. die Tauschirkunst in Spanien).

Nähere Notizen über diese südöstlichen schwarzen Töpfe sollen noch gesammelt und gelegentlich mitgetheilt werden.

Diese Gefässe, sowohl die Kassubischen als die Galizischen, sind abweichend von den Jütischen auf der Drehscheibe gefertigt. In der Decoration ähnen sie ihnen aber darin, dass sie durch flach eingedrückte glänzende Streifen oder Kreisschnörkel verziert sind, die mit einem stumpfen Instrumente, Feuerstein oder dergleichen, vor dem Brande aufpolirt sind. Sie haben ein besonderes Interesse für uns, da die merkwürdigen 3 gedrehten, entschieden importirten Henkeltöpfe von Warnikam (aus spät römischer Zeit) in ähnlicher Methode decorirt sind; sie zeigen nämlich ganz flach mit stumpfen Instrumenten in den noch nicht gebrannten, aber schon ziemlich erhärteten Thon eingedrückte Streifensysteme. Wenn man nun bedenkt, dass gerade in Galizien zu derselben Zeit (c. 4. Jahrhundert v. Chr. eine Anzahl ähnlicher Gefässe entdeckt sind (die bei anderer Gelegenheit publicirt werden sollen), so weisen jene Ostpreussischen auf eine südöstliche Quelle hin. Sie sind nicht rein römisch, doch jedenfalls unter römischen Einfluss entstanden und ihre Form und zum Theil die Technik hat sich einigermaassen in den schwarzen Thongefässen besonders von Wertelka erhalten.

In solcher Weise wirft die moderne Haus- und Landtöpferei noch manches Licht auf die prähistorische Gefässfabrikation. Da die Jütischen Töpfe eine so vollkommene aus freier Hand hergestellte Rundung zeigen, so ist es nicht nöthig, für die prähistorischen Töpfe, besonders für die in der Form oft sehr vollendeten aus Westpreussischen Steinkisten, eine andere Technik, z. B. die Blockscheibe anzunehmen, eine Annahme, die Herr Scharlock, der gerade auf die Blockscheibe hingewiesen hat, auch für zulässig erklärt.

Ueber das ehemals in Preussen übliche Drehen des Töpfergeschirrs auf der Blockscheibe uud das Schwarzbrennen desselben, zweier untergegangener, nnd in Berücksichtigung der vorgeschichtlichen preussischen Begräbnissurnen bemerkenswerther Herstellungsweisen von Thongeräthen. Von Scharlok.

Als ich vor etwa 20 Jahren anfing, die vorgeschichtlichen Alterthümer unserer Gegend zu sammeln, von denen ich Kunde erhielt, wurden die meisten mir nicht zum Zwecke der künftigen Begründung eines öffentlichen Museums, wie Graudenz jetzt ein solches in seinem Stadtmuseum besitzt, als einstweiliges Eigenthum übergeben, sondern höchstens zur naturgetreuen Nachbildung geliehen, gewöhnlich unter der ganz ausdrücklichen Bedingung der Eigenthümer, die Gegenstände ihnen unversehrt und möglichst bald wieder zurückzugewähren.

Wenn ich auch voraussah, dass, wie es wirklich geschehen ist, manche werthvollen Stücke bei ihren Eigenthümern unnachweisbar verloren gegangen sind, so gelang es mir doch, 30 und einige facta similia in mehrstückigen Auflagen anzufertigen.

Von diesen Auflagen, soweit sie eben gefördert waren, erhielten je eine, unter der Bedingung Kenntniss fördernder oder lückenfüllender Gegengaben:

der jetzt verstorbene Professor E. Desor zu Neuchatel,
das Lindenschmidtsche Museum zu Mainz,
das Museum germanischer Alterthümer zu Nürnberg,
die naturforschende Gesellschaft in Danzig,
die Alterthumsgesellschaft Prussia zu Königsberg in Preussen,
die physikalisch-ökonomische Gesellschaft zu Königsberg in Preussen,

das Alterthümer-Museum zu Weissenfels,
das kulturhistorische Museum zu Buxtehude,
und endlich, nebst allen auch den in meinem Besitz befindlichen Originalen, das Stadtmuseum zu Graudenz.

Von Herrn von Ossowski zu Krakau, welcher den grössten Theil der in meinem Besitz befindlichen Urnen gezeichnet und gemessen hat, empfing ich als Gegengabe einige Photographien bemerkenswerther Alterthümer.

Aus Weissenfels erhielt ich das Lichtbild einer auf einem Urnenscherben vor dem Brennen eingeritzten sehr merkwürdigen Zeichnung, vom Herrn Professor Desor aber erhielt ich eine nicht unbeträchtliche Anzahl lauter lückenfüllender und zugleich sehr lehrreicher Original-Gegengaben aus den Pfahlbauten des Neuchateller Sees: — unter diesen letzteren auch das Scherbenstück eines sehr dicken Gefässes aus gebranntem Thon mit eingeknetetem grobem Kies, welches Gefäss augenscheinlich aus freier Hand geformt worden ist, denn es zeigt an seiner Innenseite die Eindrücke schlanker Finger, welche glättend in senkrechter und an der Aussenseite solcher, die in wagerechter Richtung gestrichen haben.

In jener Zeit (vor etwa 20 Jahren) war man sehr geneigt anzunehmen, dass die in Westpreussen gefundenen Begräbniss-Gefässe aus gebranntem Thon, deren Wände und wagrecht laufende Verzierungen verbogen und nicht geradelaufend sind, aus freier Hand geformt worden wären.

Auch wurden vereinzelte Stimmen laut, welche behaupteten, die schwarze und graue Farbe der vorgeschichtlichen Thongefässe stamme von Graphit her, und solche mit glänzend schwarzer Oberfläche seien glasirt.

Schon in früher Jugend, noch als Knabe in meiner Vaterstadt, bin ich sehr viel in der Werkstatt des Töpfermeisters Napp daselbst gewesen, habe mit grosser Lust von Allem, was darin vorging Kenntniss und Theil daran genommen, habe auch auf der Scheibe gedreht, in Thon modellirt und mit vor dem Brennofen gesessen. Ich habe diese Theilnahme für die Thonbildnerei nicht bloss nicht verloren, sondern deren in dem Maasse mehr gewonnen, als ich als Jüngling und Mann vielfach die Gelegenheit fand und wahrnahm, mich in Ziegeleien, Steingut-, Porcellan- und Thonwaarenfabriken umzusehen, und mit meinen steigenden chemischen und physikalischen Kenntnissen immer tiefere Einsicht, auch in die Nebenzweige dieses Kunsthandwerks zu gewinnen.

Jene Annahmen über das Herstellen dünnwandiger Urnen mit wagerechten Verzierungslinien aus freier Hand wollte mir nicht in den Sinn, so lange sie nicht durch Beweise erhärtet war.

Die Verwendung von Graphit, wie sie zur Herstellung der feuerfesten Graphittigel stattfindet, hier in der norddeutschen Ebene, in der kein Graphit vorkommt, zur Erzeugung der schwarzen Bestattungsurnen, schien mir ein entschiedener Irrthum zu sein, besonders, nachdem ich in den ersten Jahrzehnten meiner Ansiedelung hier in Graudenz, vom Jahre 1837 an, zu jedem Jahrmarkte grosse Mengen von matt-schwarz-grauen, dem rohen Eisenguss sehr ähnlichen, auch mit glänzenden Strichen verzierten Töpferwaaren, wagenweise ankommen, auspacken und verkaufen sah. Kochtöpfe mit einem Henkel, Schmoortriegel (Töpfe) mit 2 Henkeln, Triegel oder Tiegel (Pfannen) mit einer walzig-wagerecht abstehenden Handhabe mit und ohne Füsse, und Testen (Schalen, Schüsseln, auch als Deckel zu gebrauchen) innen glatte, oder auch durch rhomboidisch sich kreuzende Einritzungen rauh gemachte, sog. Tobakstesten, um sich selbst seinen Schnühwke (Schnupftabak) zu reiben, selbst solche, mit 2 Henkeln und einem durchlöcherten Boden versehene, als Durchschlag zu brauchende sowie wirkliche Deckel mit einem Knopfe zum Anfassen, waren die Hauptgeschirre. Die Art war unter dem Namen „Kaschubsche Töpf" ganz allgemein bekannt, die Geschirre zeigten sehr gefällige Gestalten, eine flotte Mache, und waren aus einem, trotz der reichlichen Beimengung von nur mässig feinem Sande, offenbar sehr bildsamem Thone hergestellt. Das Geschirr war sehr billig; das zum Kochen bestimmte wurde aber nicht blos deshalb in fast allen Küchen verwendet, sondern, weil von ihm behauptet wurde, dass es aufs Feuer gesetzt, nicht so leicht zerspringe als das aus reinerem und feinerem Thon gebrannte rohe oder glasirte. Manches Geschirr hielt für manche Flüssigkeiten nicht ganz dicht, sondern sickerte durch nach Art der Alkárazzas und diesem Uebelstande suchten die Köchinnen dadurch abzuhelfen, dass sie das neue Geschirr mit Fett einliessen.

In dem Maasse als die Porcellan-, Gusseisen und die verschiedenen Arten der Eisenblechgefässe im Preise sanken und eine immer allgemeinere Verwendung fanden, wurden auch immer weniger „Kaschubsche Töpfe" gebraucht und zu Markt gebracht, bis vor etwa 35—30 Jahren diese Jahrmarktswaare gänzlich ausblieb.

Als diejenigen Stimmen der Alterthumsforscher laut wurden, die da meinten, dass die hier gefundenen schwarzgrauen Urnen ihre Farbe einer Beimengung von Graphit verdankten, suchte ich vergebens hier am Orte noch einige solcher altmodischen Kaschub'schen Töpfe aufzutreiben, oder auch nur zu erfahren, wo dieselben früher angefertigt worden waren oder etwa noch gemacht würden; und nur den langen und unermüdlich fortgesetzten Bemühungen des Fräulein Adelheid Brüss in Tuchel, jetzt Frau Buchhändler Weber in Königsberg verdankte ich die letzten Geschirre dieser Art, welcher der Töpfermeister Maslonkowski zu Kamionken bei Neuenburg in Westpreussen noch gemacht hatte, sowie ein Stückchen ungebrannten, drehfertigen Thones. Diesen letzten Rest von Fabrikaten eines, wie es scheint, eben untergegangenen Gewerbebetriebes theilte ich zwischen der naturforschenden Gesellschaft in Danzig, der physikalisch-ökonomischen Gesellschaft in Königsberg und dem städtischen Museum in Graudenz.

Meine Bitte, mir einige von dem hiesigen Töpfermeister Maschlitzki alten Urnen nach nachgebildete Gefässe mit schwarz zu brennen, konnte der Töpfermeister Maslonkowski zu Kamionken bei Neuenburg nicht mehr erfüllen, da ihn Krankheit gezwungen hatte, die Topfdreherei aufzugeben, und ich seinen Vorschlag als für mich zu kostspielig und umständlich von der Hand weisen musste, der dahin ging, hier in Graudenz das zur Füllung eines Ofens erforderliche Geschirr anfertigen und in Kamionken brennen zu lassen.

Noch lange, ehe die Mittheilung des Herrn Dr. Tischler in Königsberg in den Schriften der physikalisch-ökonomischen Gesellschaft 1881, Sitzungsbericht p. 13/14 (nach Sehested: Fortidsminder og oldsager fra Egnen on Broholm p. 345—351) über die noch gegenwärtig auf Jütland gebräuchliche Herstellung von dünnwandigen fast gar nicht oder nur nur kaum verbogenen, auch mit Strichverzierungen geschmückten und schwarz gebrannten Töpfergeschirren aus freier Hand, bekannt gemacht wurde, zeigte ich dem bereits genannten Töpfermeister Maschlitzki von hier meine zum grössten Theil aus Steinkistengräbern hiesiger Gegend stammenden Bestattungsurnen nebst Deckeln und Schalen mit der Bitte, mir seine Ansicht darüber mitzutheilen, wie dieselben wohl gemacht worden wären, indem ich ihm zugleich auch sagte, dass sich Ansichten dafür geltend machten, dass dieselben aus freier Hand hergestellt, durch Graphit schwarz gefärbt, oder auch wohl glasirt sein könnten.

Nach Herrn Maschlitzkis Ansicht befindet sich unter den jetzt im Graudenzer Museum befindlichen Urnen keine mit einer Glasur überzogene; die glänzenden Urnen, Deckel, Schalen oder deren Scherben verdanken ihren Glanz nur einer Politur des getrockneten Geschirrs vor dem Brande, die erhalten wird, wenn man das Gefäss mit einem harten und glatten Gegenstande einem Flaschenboden, einem polirten Feuersteine oder dergleichen glatt reibt, wodurch es einen Spekglanz erhält. Damit dieser Glanz recht lebhaft werde, muss die zu polirende Stelle keine groben Körner enthalten, weshalb sie mit Schlicker (den beim feinen Abdrehen gewonnenen Schlamm) oder auch mit sehr fein geschlemmtem Thon überzogen wird. Bei der grossen Urne aus Ksiondsken, und bei der kleinen Deckelurne aus dem Klinzkauer Steinkistengrabe ist der Gegensatz des polirten Halses und des durch eingedrückten Granitgrus grobkörnig glimmerglitzernd gemachten Bauches mit feinem Kunstgefühl zu wohlthuender Wirkung gebracht worden. Bei einigen anderen Urnen ist der Versuch, diese schmückenden Gegensätze hervorzubringen, weniger gelungen, bei den meisten garnicht versucht. Die schwarzgraue Farbe ist in der Weise erzeugt, wie bei den Kaschubschen Töpfen, wovon weiter die Rede sein wird.

Einige wenige Geschirre, vorzugsweise aber der zerbrochene schalenartige Deckel mit Falz aus den weissen Bergen bei Paparzyn, Kreis Kulm, verdankt seinen schönen Glanz zwar auch dem Poliren, aber die tiefschwarze Oberfläche auf der röthlichgrauen Scherbenmasse verdankt er dem Ueberfange mit einem Schlickerbeisatz, der den Töpfern nicht mehr bekannt, aber keine Glasur ist.

Der schweizerische, dicke ganz offenbar aus freier Hand gemachte und die Streichspuren der Finger zeigende Scherben ist von ganz anderer Masse und ganz anders gearbeitet, als die alten westpreussischen Urnen und deren Scherben. Dass auch diese aus freier Hand gemacht sein sollen, ist zu bezweifeln, dahingegen wäre eine andere Erklärung vielleicht zutreffender.

Bevor nämlich die Töpfer auf der jetzt ganz allgemein und nur allein noch gebräuchlichen Töpferscheibe drehten, drehten sie auf der Blockscheibe oder dem Blocke, welcher auch auf alten Zunftpetschaften noch abgebildet ist.

Die Töpferscheibe besteht aus einer senkrechten starken eisernen an den betreffenden sich reibenden Stellen sauber abgedrehten Spindelstange, die mit ihrem stumpf zugespitzten unteren Ende in einer im Boden befestigten Pfanne aus Stirnholz und kurz unter ihrem oberen Ende in einer festen, zu öffnenden und zu schliessenden Gabelstange, mit der Innenseite einer Speckschwarte umhüllt, läuft und gut in Oel gehalten wird.

Auf dem oberen Ende trägt sie die kleinere Kopfscheibe oder den Scheibenkopf, auf welchem der Thon zu Geschirren gestaltet wird, und kurz über dem unteren Ende eine grössere, dickere und recht schwere Scheibe, das Scheiben- oder Fussblatt, das der Töpfer mit seinen nackten Fusssohlen in drehende Bewegung setzt, und das zugleich als Schwungrad dient. Steht die Spindel genau senkrecht in festen Leitungen, wird sie hinreichend in gutem Oele gehalten, und sind Kopfscheibe und Fussblatt eben und vollkommen fest in einem Winkel von genau 90 Gr. an der Spindel angebracht, so bildet das Ganze mit dem dazu gehörigen Sitze für den Dreher eine zwar sehr einfache, aber recht leicht zu handhabende und zuverlässig arbeitende Maschine, auf der er, wenn er sonst nur fest im Kreuz und in den Oberarmen, und feinfühlig und geschickt in den Unterarmen, Händen und Fingern ist, die saubersten Dreharbeiten herstellen kann.

Ein Anderes war es aber mit dem Block oder der Blockscheibe. Diese bestand aus dem walzenrunden fest in den Boden gesetzten, trockenen, geglätteten und nicht mehr biegsamen Stämmchen eines jungen Hartholz-Baumes.

Auf diese feststehende oben stumpf zugespitzte Spindel wurde ein drehbares Gestell gehängt. Dieses bestand aus einem an seiner oberen Seite ebenen Klotze aus hartem Holze, dem Scheibenkopfe. In die untere Seite dieses Klotzes oder Blockes wurde eine Vertiefung als Pfanne hineingearbeitet, bestimmt, den Spindelkopf aufzunehmen und sich auf ihm zu drehen. Es waren ferner noch mehrere, gewöhnlich sechs nicht durchgehende Löcher in diese Unterseite des Blockes gebohrt oder auch wohl nur mit einem glühenden Eisen hineingebrannt, in welche Löcher eben so viele gerade, glatte: trockene, steife junge Hartholz-Stämmchen oder auch vom Drechsler gedrehte Sprossen eingesetzt und fest verkeilt wurden, die gleichlaufend mit ihren anderen Enden in eine grössere klotzartige Scheibe, den Fussblock oder auch Fussblatt, eingesetzt und gleichfalls fest verkeilt wurden. In der Mitte dieses Fussblockes befand sich ein Loch, das möglichst genau, jedoch ohne sich zu klemmen um den Spindelstamm herumgriff.

Stülpte man nun das ganze Gestell, bestehend aus dem durch Sprossen mit dem Scheibenkopfe verbundenen Fussblocke über den Spindelstamm, so dass der Scheibenkopf mit seiner Pfanne auf die Spindelstammspitze zu stehen kam, so hatte man gleichfalls eine mit den Füssen in Bewegung zu setzende Maschine, auf deren oberer Fläche man Thongefässe drehen konnte, und dies war die Blockscheibe.

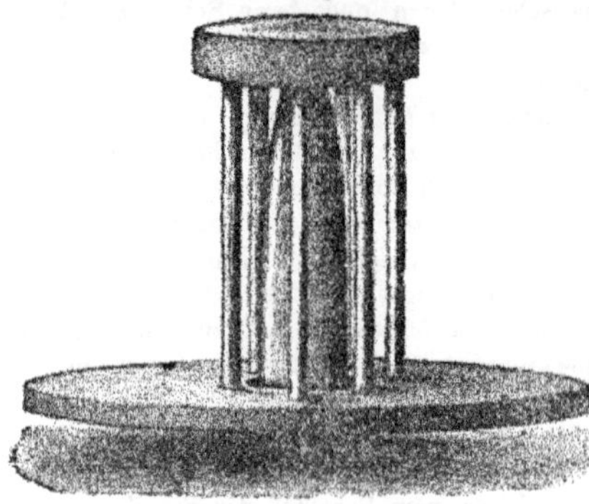

Blockscheibe nach einem von Maschlitzki in Thon angefertigtem Modell.

Während aber eine gut gebaute Töpferscheibe sich ganz gleichmässig wagerecht mit ihrer fest verbundenen senkrechten Eisenspindel um ihre Achse dreht, kann auch der bestgebaute Block diese Drehung nicht ohne gewisse schlackernde und wippende Abweichungen sowohl aus der senkrechten, als auch aus der wagerechten Richtung machen. Zur Milderung dieses Uebelstandes wurde die Stammspindel da, wo sich der Fussblock um sie drehte mit in Theer getränkten Leinenlappen umwickelt, und ebenso, wie die Spindelspitze nebst Kopfpfanne ordentlich mit Theer geschmiert erhalten. Damit das Fussblatt die gehörige Schwere bekam und auch als Schwungrad von einem Fusstoss eine Weile in Bewegung blieb, wurden ihm möglichst viel grosse Eisennägel eingeschlagen und Eisenreifen umgelegt. Die das Blatt mit dem Kopf verbindenden Sprossen waren aber besonders bei einem leichten, schlecht schwingenden Block, bei welchem fortwährend getreten werden musste, eine Plage für den Dreher, weil er sich die Fussknöchel daran wund stiess und rieb, die deshalb für diese Arbeit mit Lappen bebunden wurden.

Es ist wohl erklärlich, dass selbst ein geschickter Dreher nicht gleich mit jedem Blocke gute Arbeit liefern konnte, sondern sich erst mit seinem wackeligen Werkzeuge eingearbeitet haben musste. Es wird aber auch erklärlich erscheinen, dass selbst der geschicklichste Dreher auf seinem ihm ganz vertrauten Blocke niemals so gute und genaue Arbeit liefern konnte als auf einer guten Scheibe, denn alle, auf einem Klotz gedrehten Geschirre werden immer Seitenwände haben, die sich bei genauer Prüfung etwas schief erweisen und wagerechte Linien in den Rändern, Bauch- und Halsansätzen oder Verzierungen zeigen, die in kürzeren oder längeren Wellen von den gleichmässig wagerechten Linien abweichen. Genau diese Eigenschaften haben die in den Steinkistengräbern und die in der blossen Erde gefundenen Urnen und anderen Gefässe des Graudenzer Stadtmuseums, womit aber nicht behauptet werden soll, dass diese wirklich so gemacht sind, sondern nur, dass sie, wenn sie auf dem Blocke gedreht worden wären, so aussehen müssten, als es der Fall ist."

Herr Maschlitzki theilte mir ferner noch Folgendes mit:

Im Königreiche Polen, südlich von Gollub, betrieben vor etwa 50 Jahren noch viele kleinere Landleute neben ihrer Ackerwirthschaft die Töpferei als häusliches Gewerbe. Wo dies der Fall war, befand sich in der Wohnstube neben dem Fenster der Block mit der Sitzbank des Drehers, und gut drehbarer Thon war stets vorräthig. Je nachdem nun die Landwirthschaft Zeit liess, oder ein Jahrmarkt in der Nähe war, jüdische Feiertage oder sonst eine gute Gelegenheit bevorstand, die Geschirre zu verkaufen. wurden solche gedreht, getrocknet, gebrannt und nicht blos für den eigenen Gebrauch, sondern eben auch zum Verkauf.

Viele Kinder solcher Landleute gingen, natürlich erst nur zum Zeitvertreib, an den Drehblock des Vaters, wenn derselbe gerade leer stand und erreichten bald eine ganz anerkennenswerthe Geschicklichkeit, und eben aus diesen Kindern gingen dann, vorzugsweise die Dreher hervor, welche wunderbar saubere Arbeiten trotz ihres doch so mangelhaften Werkzeuges, des wackeligen Blockes, fertig stellten.

Je mehr Sand dem Thone beigemengt war, desto besser trocknete er, aber die Waare war mürber; je reiner der Thon war, desto leichter bekam er Risse beim Trocknen, aber desto härter und fester war auch das Geschirr.

Dieses wurde theils roh gebrannt, theils nach einer älteren Art, die auch jetzt noch in Tolkemit gebräuchlich sein soll, glasirt, nämlich geknispelt.

Während beim wirklichen Glasiren Quarzsand und Bleioxyd oder wie der Töpfer es nennt, Versatzsand mit Bleiasche oder auch Bleiglätte nur für sich oder mit färbenden Metallaschen versetzt, unter Wasser auf einer Präparirmühle zum feinsten Schlamm zerrieben, schmanddünn mit Wasser angerührt, sehr gleichmässig und dünn über das trockene Stück gegossen und dann gebrannt wird, wobei sich Bleiglas (kieselsaures Bleioxyd) bildet und das Stück mit einer dünnen aufgeschmolzenen Glasurschicht bedeckt, wird beim Knispeln nur feiner Versatz, d. i. Quarzsand mit Bleiasche oder Bleiglätte in einer Test' gemengt, auf das zuvor mit einem dünnen aus Roggenmehl und Wasser gekochten noch nassen Kleister (Schlicht) bestrichene Gefäss gesiebt, getrocknet und dann gebrannt.

Die Juden kauften nur unglasirtes Geschirr unmittelbar aus dem Ofen, weil das geknispelte nach ihrer Glaubensmeinung durch den Anstrich mit Mehlkleister für den „Ostrigen Gebrauch" verunreinigt worden war.

Wenn die erforderliche Menge von Geschirr fertig war, wurde der Brennofen hergerichtet.

Derselbe war ein Feld-Kesselofen und auf folgende Art hergestellt*): Es wurde ein länglich rundes Loch mit senkrechten Wänden in den Boden gegraben, von ungefähr 5 Fuss grösstem Durchmesser und 2—3 Fuss Tiefe und zu jedem Schmalende dieses Loches ein schräg hinabführender Zugang, der am Ofen so viel tiefer war, dass der vor dem Schörloche (Feuerloche) stehende Brenner bequem den Ofeninhalt übersehen und das Brennen (Schören) besorgen konnte.

Die Sohle des Ofens wurde mit Ziegelbrocken in Lehm glatt ausgelegt und die Seitenwände wurden ebenso mit Ziegeln und Lehm glatt aus- und so hoch aufgemauert, dass sie etwa 2 Fuss in die Erde kamen und wohl noch etwas mehr über die Erde herausreichten.

An jedem Schmalende wurde ein kleines Gewölbeloch zum Einlegen des Holzes und Feuers, das Feuerloch, Schür- oder Schörloch ausgespart. Ungefähr 6—9 Zoll vor jedem der beiden Feuerlöcher an der Innenseite des Ofens wurde eine senkrechte dünne feste Wand aus Ziegeln in Lehm aufgemauert, und dicht über dem Feuerloche mit der Ofenwand durch Ziegeln verbunden, Ständer genannt. An diese beiden Ständer sich anschliessend wurde, gleichlaufend mit der Umfassungsmauer, noch eine kleine dünne und niedrige Mauer aus Ziegelsteinen und Ziegelbrocken aufgesetzt, welche Zwischenräume von etwa 3 Zoll zwischen sich liessen. Auf die Kante dieser Aufmauerung wurden mit dem einen Ende Ziegeln gelegt, die mit dem anderen Ende auf einem kleinen Vorsprunge in der Umfassungsmauer ruhten, und auch etwa 3 Zoll von einander entfernt waren, so dass an jeder Seite, von Schörloch zu Schörloch in der unteren Ofenecke ein Kanal mit durchbrochenen Wänden, der Schörgang (Schürgang) herumlief.

Nachdem dieser ganz hergestellt war, wurde der mittlere Theil des Ofens, reichlich so hoch als der Schörgang mit Ziegelbrocken und Geschirrscherben locker aufgefüllt, wobei die sich von selbst zwischen ihnen bildenden Zwischenräume belassen wurde. Diese Aufschüttung, deren Oberfläche möglichst eben gelegt wurde, hiess der Hals. Auf diesem Halse wurden nun die zu brennenden und getrockneten Geschirre möglichst dicht aufgestellt (aufgeflien, aufgefleiet), indem man zu unterst und zunächst dem Schörgange das stehende Geschirr, Töpfe, Kannen u. dgl. aufrecht und möglichst dicht aneinander gepackt, hineinsetzte und in der Mitte bis über 1 Fuss hoch über den Ofenrand hinaus aufbaute. Das Flachzeug, Schüsseln, Testen, Deckel u. dgl., wurde dagegen vom Rande aus, schräg nach der Mitte zu angelegt, so dass es ganz oben

*) Das von Maschlitzki in Thon angefertigte Modell eines solchen Feldofens hat Herr Scharlock noch nachträglich der Gesellschaft zum Geschenk gemacht.

kuppelartig das übrige Zeug bedeckte, und dass die Spitze dieses Kuppelgewölbes wohl als ein 3 Fuss hoher Aufbau über den Ofenrand hervorragte. Bei nicht glasirtem Geschirr wurden die grösseren Stücke auch noch voll kleiner gepackt. Der so beschickte Ofen wurde nun mit Scherbeln (Scherben zerbrochener Geschirre von früheren Bränden herrührend, 3—5 Zoll hoch bedeckt, bescherbelt) und das Brennen konnte beginnen.

Schon bei dem Einsetzen wurden in den Feuerlöchern kleine Feuerchen angezündet, die zwar den Töpfer durch ihren Rauch etwas belästigten, ihm aber durch dessen Entweichen zeigten, ob die Beschickung gut oder schlecht gemacht war, und nebenbei auch das den Ofen füllende Geschirr schon anwärmten. Nun aber wurden die in den Feuerlöchern entzündeten Holzscheite in den Schörgängen weiter geschoben und neue Scheite eingelegt, wo denn die Flammen und die Hitze nicht blos durch die in den Schörgängen befindlichen Zwischenräume, sondern auch durch die im Halse befindlichen Lücken hindurch schlugen und das ganze Geschirr gleichmässig umspülten. Das Feuern begann sehr allmählich mit Kleinfeuer und steigerte sich vorsichtig bis zum Starkfeuer, wobei der Brenner, indem er das Aeussere des Ofens fleissig beobachtete, hiernach das Vertheilen der Feuerbrände in den Schörlöchern leitete. Wenn nun das Geschirr gar, der Brand fertig war, was man daran erkannte, dass die Asche des verbrannten Holzes als trockener weisslicher Staub auf der Oberfläche des Ofens erschien, und in der Dunkelheit der Ofen wie eine Gluth aussah, dann wurden beim Herunterbrennen der letzten Kühlfeuer die Feuerlöcher schnell vermauert, und der Ofen wurde zum Abkühlen sich selbst überlassen. War dies nun, je nach Umständen in 6—9 Stunden geschehen, dann wurde er erst abgescherbelt und dann ausgepackt, wo bei gelungenem Brande das Geschirr fest und klingend war, bei dem Rohzeuge die Farbe, entsprechend den Eigenschaften des Thones roth bis weisslich-gelbgrau und bei der glasirten Waare die Glasur gut und gleichmässig geflossen erschien.

Nun gab es aber noch eine andere Art des Brennens, bei dem die Oefen mit ihren Schörgängen ebenso beschaffen waren und das Einsetzen des Geschirres, sowie das Brennen bis zum Garwerden ganz in der beschriebenen Weise betrieben wurde. War dieser Punkt aber eingetreten und der Ofen in voller Gluth, dann wurden schnell die Schörgänge mit recht fettem Kiehn gefüllt, die Feuerlöcher so schnell wie irgend möglich vermauert und der ganze Ofen, besonders aber die aufgebaute Kuppel mit Rasen und mit Erde dicht und fest zugedeckt."

Nach dem Verkühlen sah das ausgepackte Geschirr nun aber dunkel-schwarzgrau aus, genau so, wie die „Kaschubschen Töpfe".

Die Töpfer, welche ihr Geschirr so brannten, hiessen „Schwarzbrenner.

Die ganz grauschwarzen Begräbniss-Urnen und Scherben stammen von ganz wohlgelungenen, die heller grauen und graufleckigen von theilweise misslungenen Schwarzbränden her.

Der bereits erwähnte in dem Paparzyner Steinkistengrabe in den weissen Bergen 1879 gefundene und im Graudenzer Stadtmuseum unter No. 327 vorhandene Deckelscherben mit der tiefschwarzen Farbe auf der bräunlich-grauen Innenmasse ist nicht glasirt, wohl aber gut polirt und mit einem Schlicker überzogen, der mit einer, uns Töpfern jetzt nicht mehr bekannten Masse versetzt ist, welche bei dem letzten Beschicken des Ofens mit Kiehn diese schöne tiefschwarze Färbung angenommen hat.

So weit Herr Maschlitzki.

Wenn nun auch nicht mehr festgestellt werden kann, ob unsere Urnen nach Art der Jütischen Töpfe aus freier Hand aus einem auf festem Brette gedrehten Thonklumpen oder auf Blockscheiben gedreht, mit Torf gar und schwarzgebrannt, oder nach Art der Kaschubschen Töpf mit Holz ge- und mit Kiehn schwarzgebrannt worden sind, so ist es doch von Wichtigkeit, durch einen Fachmann einen noch auf eigener Anschauung beruhenden Bericht über eine ältere bereits fast vergessene Art des Topfdrehens und des Schwarzbrennens zu haben, der für die Herstellung der schwarzgrauen Begräbniss-Urnen, Töpfe und Schalen auch nicht schlechthin ausgeschlossen ist, wenn die Gestaltung aus der auf fester Unterlage gedrehten Thonmasse auch sicher sehr lange Zeit zuvor geübt worden ist, ehe man zum Geschirrdrehen auf dem Blocke kam.

Als ich zuerst im Jahre 1837 von den Kaschubschen Töpfen hörte, meinte ich, sie seien nur schwarz berusst; als ich aber die ersten neuen für meine Wirthschaft gekauften schwarzgrauen Töpfe zu Gesicht bekam, die gar nicht abfärbten und auch im Innern des Scherbens ebenso beschaffen waren, wusste ich mir diese Sache nicht zu erklären. Nachdem es mit der allgemeineren Einführung der Gasbeleuchtung aber mehrfach beobachtet wurde, dass das Leuchtgas, welches eigentlich nur aus dem starkleuchtenden Doppelt-Kohlenwasserstoff bestehen sollte, beim zu starken Erhitzen der Gasretorten in den kaum leuchtenden Einfach-Kohlenwasserstoff verwandelt wird, indem es einen Theil seines Kohlenstoffes an den heissen Retortenwänden in Gestalt einer grauschwarzen, fast diamantharten Masse (der Retortenkohle) absetzt, von der bei den ersten sogenannten elektrischen Sonnen feine Stifte als Elektricitätsleiter und Pole benutzt wurden, da war es mir gar nicht mehr zweifelhaft, dass hier in dem hellroth glühenden Topfgeschirr ein der Retortenkohle entsprechender Kohlenstoff aus den an ätherischem Oel und Leuchtgas so reichen Destillations- und Verkohlungserzeugnissen des Kiehns abgesetzt würde, der die nicht abschmutzende Gusseisenfarbe des Kaschubschen Geschirres erzeuge.

Die Sache wurde mir sehr anschaulich, als Marsh die gleichlaufende Entdeckung machte, dass Arsenwasserstoff durch eine glühende Glasröhre geleitet, seinen Arsen in Gestalt eines spiegelnden grauen Ringes absetzt, worauf die jetzt allgemein gebräuchliche Marsh'sche Methode gegründet wurde, um Arsenik bei chemischen Untersuchungen zu ermitteln, auszuscheiden und demnächst durch andere Prüfungsmittel zweifellos festzustellen.

Die Ursache der tief schwarzen polirten Schicht auf den grauen Urnendeckelscherben von Paparzin, den ich hier beifüge, habe ich durch chemische Untersuchung nicht mehr ermitteln können. Es ist mir auch nicht mehr gelungen, eine solche Schicht durch Versuche herzustellen, weil diejenigen Urnen mit körnig rauhen, glimmerschillernden Bäuchen und glatten polirten Hälsen, die Herr Maschlitzki einigen alten Ursprungsurnen auf mein Gesuch nachgebildet hatte, von dem Schwarzbrenner Maslonkowski in Kamionken nicht mehr mitgebrannt werden konnten, und bei dem Versuche als rothe Töpferwaare aus dem gewöhnlichen Töpferofen kamen, welchen Versuch Herr Maschlitzki mit wenig Vertrauen und nur auf mein ganz besonderes Bitten ausführte, nämlich die mit Fett getränkten, fest in Sägespäne verpackten und mit einer dicken Sandschicht überschütteten Urnen, jede in einem besonderen zugedeckten Topfe mitzubrennen.

Diese in der Gestalt, dem rauhen Bauch und dem glatten Halse ge-, in der Farbe beim Brennen aber misslungenen Nachbildungen habe ich der physikalisch-ökonomischen Gesellschaft übergeben.

Zur Herstellung eines tiefschwarz werdenden Ueberzuges beim Schwarzbrennen habe ich bei einigen der Maschlitzkischen Urnen dem Ueberfangsschlick ziemlich viel von dem gelb-bräunlichen, schlammfeinen aus Eisen-Oxydul-Oxyd-Hydrat bestehenden Eisenocker beimengen lassen, der sich an den Osträndern des alten Weichselüberschwemmungsgebietes da bildet, und oft ganze Wiesengräben ausfüllt, wo von Mergelschichten herrührende kalkhaltige mit solchen Quellen sich mischen, die schwefelsaures, von zersetztem Schwefelkies herrührendes Eisen-Oxydul-Oxyd enthalten. Solcher Eisenocker verliert beim Brennen in offenem Feuer sein Hydratwasser, verwandelt sich zum grossen Theil in Oxyd, und wird dann, wenn dies in der Glühhitze mit hinreichendem Kohlenwasserstoff in Berührung kommt und bleibt zu schwarzem Oxydul reducirt, worauf auch die Herstellung des Ferrum oxydulatum nigrum mehrerer alter Pharmacopoeen beruhte.

Mein Versuch musste fehlschlagen, weil nicht die Kohlenwasserstoff-Atmosphäre hergestellt werden und erhalten bleiben konnte, die in der Glühhitze des Schwarzbrennofens herrscht und bis zum Verkühlen darin bleibt.

Obwohl die mit einem polirten Feuersteinkeil, wie die mit einem glatten Flaschenboden geriebene Oberfläche eines feinen Schlicküberfanges beim Reiben einen auch nach dem Brennen bleibenden Speckglanz annimmt, so meine ich doch, dass der Glanz mancher Urnen und Urnenscherben ein stärkerer sei, als der, der allein auf diese Schwarzbrennerart erzeugt wird und glaube, ein solcher sei zu erreichen, wenn dem reinen oder dem ockerhaltigen Thonschlick eine bindende Masse beigemischt würde, die eine feste, glänzende schwer verbrennliche Kohle giebt. Solche Kohlen werden von stickstoffhaltigen Körpern gebildet. Als hierzu geeignet halte ich ihres Käsegehaltes wegen etwas eingedampfte Magermilch, der man, damit ihr Käsestoff nicht gerinne, ein wenig Sodaauflösung oder Blut, dem man, damit sein Faserstoff nicht gerinne, etwas Essig zusetzen müsste. Die stickstoffhaltige Kohle beider ist glänzend, dicht und schwer verbrennlich und dürfte die Verfolgung dieser Idee wahrscheinlich zu einem erwünschten Ziele führen.

Ich selbst bin leider schon längst durch andere Arbeiten, die meine Zeit vollständig in Anspruch nehmen, verhindert, meine Versuche in dieser Richtung fortzusetzen.

Sitzung am 5. Februar 1885.

Herr Dr. Paucritius, welcher vom 23. April bis 26. Mai 1884 die Passarge bereist hatte, hielt einen Vortrag über dieselbe. Die Passarge entspringt zwischen Grieslienen und Hohenstein in einer grossen moorigen Wiese, circa 160 m über dem Meeresspiegel. Sie zieht sich hier aus mehreren kleinen Sprinden zusammen und besitzt beim Passiren der Hohensteiner Chaussee bereits eine Breite von 0,90 m, während die Tiefe 0,1—0,5 m beträgt. Der Grund ist moorig, versandet jedoch sehr bald und lässt hier und da Mergel durchblicken.

Der ganze Lauf des Flusses beträgt 120 km und ist in nordnordwestlicher Richtung. Die Passarge durchfliesst in ihrem oberen Lauf 5 Seen: den Hohensteiner Stadt-, den Wemitter-, den Sarong-, den Langguter- und Eissing-See. Ferner wird der Fluss in seinem Laufe von 11 Mühlen gesperrt. Die Breite des Flusses beträgt im Maximum etwas über 30 m und steht im umgekehrten Verhältnisse zur Tiefe, indem mit zunehmender Tiefe immer eine Verengerung des Flussbettes stattfindet. Die Tiefe schwankt von 0,2 bis circa 6 m, an einer, in der Nähe der Braunsberger Kreuzkirche gelegenen Stelle. Sie mündet mit 1—2 m Tiefe.

Die sich an Breite und Tiefe anschliessende Strömung des Flusses ist stark und schwankt zwischen 1 und 2,5 m in der Sekunde, jedoch lässt sich eine feste Zahl für den oberen Lauf des Flusses kaum aufstellen, da hier die Strömung durch die vielen Mühlen zu stark beeinflusst wird.

Die Ufer des Flusses sind grösstentheils bergig und machen breiten Wiesenthälern nur an wenigen Orten Platz, z. B. von Sporthenen bis Spanden, während ein schmales Wiesenufer häufiger den Fluss umsäumt. Die hohen Ufer sind viel bewaldet, die Wiesenufer fast immer von Erlen, seltener von Weiden eingefasst.

Der Flussgrund ist grössentheils Sand, im oberen Lauf oft grober Kies und an Orten mit dicht herantretenden hohen Ufern steinig. Schlickig dagegen ist der Grund selten, höchstens ein schmaler Saum am Ufer.

Eine genaue Beschreibung der Flora war dem Vortragenden nicht möglich, da zur Zeit der Bereisung wenig davon vorhanden war, ihn interessirte vorzüglich das massenhafte, für die Fischerei wichtige Vorkommen von Pflanzen. Der ganze Oberlauf des Flusses bis zum Sarong-See verwächst fast vollständig durch Krautbänke von Myriophyllum, hinter dem Sarong-See tritt Potamogeton, Nuphar luteum, Nymphea alba, Sagittaria sagittifolia und Elodea canadensis häufig auf. Der untere Lauf des Flusses ist möglichst frei.

Die Beschaffenheit der 5 durchflossenen Seen ist in Kurzem folgendes: Der Hohensteiner Stadtsee ist ein gleichförmig sich vertiefendes Becken von ca. 25 Morgen Grösse und 5 m Tiefe. Das Ostufer ist bewaldet und das ganze Ufer von einer Kiesbank umgeben, letzteres haben alle 5 Seen gemein. Der Wemitter-See, circa 180 Morgen gross, und der Sarong-See von 600 Morgen zeigen gleiche Verhältnisse, indem beide ohne flache Buchten zu haben, von der sie umgebenden Kiesbank steil abfallen. Das Becken beider Seen ist gleichförmig muldenartig und hat als grösste Tiefe bei ersterem 14 m, bei letzterem 16 m. Die Ufer des Wermitter-Sees sind wenig erhaben und kahl, während der Sarong-See hohes Nord- und Südufer hat. Seine schmalen Ost- und Westufer (Ein- und Ausfluss der Passarge) sind Wiesenufer. Das Nordufer des Sarong-Sees ist bewaldet und von Rohr umsäumt. Der Grund beider Seen ist Moder. Die beiden letzten Seen, der Langguter- und der Eissing, zeigen wieder gleiche Verhältnisse. Beide zeichnen sich durch vorzüglich klares Wasser, festen Grund und grosse Tiefe aus. Der Langguter-See hat als grösste Tiefe 26 m, die Gleichförmigkeit seines Beckens wird nur durch 2 Erhebungen, welche als Inseln hervortreten, gestört, er ist mit Bäumen umpflanzt, wenn nicht

Wald seine wenig hohen Ufer bedeckt, die noch mit Rohrkämpen bewachsen sind. Der Eissing-See ist bis 47 m tief, doch ist sein Becken durch fortwährende Unebenheiten gestört, die die Fischerei sehr mühsam machen, ausserdem tritt die Elodea so mächtig auf, dass Schleppnetze nicht zu brauchen sind. Die Ufer sind grösstentheils erhaben, wenig bewaldet und mit Rohr eingefasst.

Die den Fluss bevölkernde Fische sind folgende: 1) Flussbarsch (Perca fluviatilis) im ganzen Flusslaufe, wo es die Tiefe gestattet, besonders reichlich im Sarong- und Wemitter-See, 2) Kaulbarsch (Acerina cernua) in den Seen häufiger als im Fluss, 3) Kaulkopf (Cottus gobio), zwischen Kalkstein und Schwenkitten häufig, 4) Stichling (Gasterosteus aculeatus) im ganzen Fluss und den Seen häufig, hat in den letzten Jahren an Zahl sehr abgenommen, 5) Quappe (Lota vulgaris) wird immer seltener, 6) Karpfen (Cyprinus carpio) wird unterhalb Braunsberg nicht zu selten gefangen, oberhalb gar nicht, 7) Karausche (Carassius vulgaris) und 8) Schleihe (Tinca vulgaris) in den Seen, 9) Barbe (Barbus fluviatilis) nicht zu häufig, 10) Gründling (Gobio fluviatilis) häufiger im oberen, als im unteren Lauf, 11) Bitterling (Rhodeus amarus) im Fluss selten, in den Seen etwas häufiger, 12) Bressem (Abramis brama) nur im unteren Lauf nicht häufig, der Eissing-See in grösserer Menge, jedoch in letzter Zeit sehr zurückgegangen, 13) Zärthe (Abramis vimba) nur als Haffeinwanderer zu betrachten, 14) Gieben (Blicca björkna) an der Mündung häufig, oberhalb und in den Seen seltener, 15) Uckelei (Alburnus lucidus) im Sarong- und Wemitter-See in ungeheurer Menge, auch im oberen Flusslauf ziemlich häufig, 16) Rapfen (Aspius rapax) sehr selten, 17) Rothauge (Scardinius erythrophthalmus) in der ganzen Passarge, besonders im Eissing-See, 18) Plötze (Leuciscus rutilus) im Flusse häufig, sehr zahlreich im Sarong- und Wemitter-See, 19) Döbel (Squalius cephalus) häufig, 20) Häsling (Squalius leuciscus) ziemlich zahlreich, 21) Nase (Chondrostoma nasus) um Schwenkitten in kolossaler Menge, 22) Schlammpitzker (Cobitis fossilis), 23) Schmerle (Cobitis barbatula), 24) Steinbeisser (Cobitis taenia) nicht zu selten, 25) Stint (Osmerus eperlanus) als Haffeinwanderer, 26) Lachs (Trutta salar), 1827 sollen die letzten gefangen sein, 27) Bachforelle (Trutta fario) nicht zu selten, 28) Hecht (Esox lucius) im mittleren Lauf ziemlich häufig, besonders im Eissing, 29) Aal (Anguilla vulgaris) fast vollständig verschwunden, 30 Flussneunauge (Petromyzon fluviatilis) unterhalb Braunsberg in grosser Menge, 31) Bachneunauge (Petromyzon Planeri) im oberen Lauf sehr häufig. Von grosser Wichtigkeit ist auch der Krebs (Astacus fluviatilis), der die Passarge und die Seen in grosser Menge bevölkert.

Der grösste Feind der Fische ist der Mensch, der durch sinnlose Raubfischerei den Bestand des Flusses äusserst reducirt. Als zweiter Räuber ist die Fischotter zu nennen, welche namentlich den mittleren und unteren Lauf unsicher macht. Von den Vögeln, welche den Fischen nachstellen, nannte Redner: den grauen Reiher, die Sumpf- oder Wiesenweihe und den Eisvogel. Fischadler sind selten, Kormorane nie beobachtet. Unter den Fischen selbst befinden sich auch Räuber, wie Hecht und Barsch, als Laichräuber wurden Kaulkopf, Stichling und Aal bezeichnet.

Der Fluss ist grösstenteils von den Adjacenten und Mühlenbesitzern gegen geringen Pachtzins verpachtet, der Ertrag wäre höher, wenn für geeignete Laichplätze gesorgt wäre. Wie willkommen solche den Fischen sind, zeigt die in folgender Weise betriebene Raubfischerei: es werden in der Nähe der Ufer Pfähle eingeschlagen und dazwischen Kieferäste gelegt, da diese Stellen mit grosser Vorliebe von Barsch und Plötze aufgesucht werden, so stellt man Reusen darunter auf, in welchen sich die Fische fangen. Im Eissing-See wird ein sehr ergiebiger Krebsfang betrieben.

Redner wirft die Frage auf, ob eine rationelle Bewirthschaftung der Passarge und ihrer Seen im Stande ist, höhere Erträge zu liefern, und bejaht dieselbe. Die kostbaren Fische müssen vermehrt und die Raubfischerei möglichst beschränkt werden. Für die Vermehrung des Lachses und Aales ist gesorgt, auch hat die Königl. Regierung den Bau von 3 Lachsleitern angeordnet und die Mühlenbesitzer haben die Anlage von Aalleitern zugesagt, um die Lachsforelle zu vermehren, müssen Schonreviere angelegt werden. Die Raubfischerei liesse sich durch Bildung von Genossenschaften längst des Flusses beseitigen.

Herr Dr. Jentzsch sprach über die Aufgaben, der Heimathskunde Ostpreussens, er wünschte die Herausgabe eines Atlasses zu billigem Preise, welcher alles enthalten sollte, was auf die Heimathskunde Bezug hat, neue Angabe von Eisenbahnen, Chausseen, Flüssen, Seen, Waldverhältnissen, Verbreitung der verschiedenen Confessionen etc. Er war der Ansicht, dass derselbe eine weite Verbreitung finden würde.

Sitzung am 5. März 1885.

Herr Dr. Jentzsch legte 119 Messtischblätter in photographischen Copien der Generalstabsaufnahme vor, die noch nicht veröffentlicht sind und die er der Güte des Generalstabes verdankt. Es waren Aufnahmen aus Ost- und Westpreussen; von allen Messtischblättern, welche später photographisch vervielfältigt werden, sind der Gesellschaft zum Selbstkostenpreise Exemplare zugesichert. Der Vorsitzende sprach dem Generalstabe und Herrn Dr. Jentzsch den Dank der Gesellschaft aus.

Herr Professor Dr. E. Berthold hielt einen Vortrag über die objectiv wahrnehmbaren Veränderungen der belichteten Netzhaut. Nach einer kurzen Beschreibung des gröberen anatomischen Baues des Auges schildert der Vortragende die feine histiologische Structur der Netzhaut und versucht dieselbe durch in sehr vergrössertem Maassstabe hergestellten Abbildungen (die Retina von Max Schultze) zur Anschauung zu bringen. Von den verschiedenen Schichten, aus denen die Netzhaut gebildet wird, stellen die Stäbchen und Zapfen, wie das seit der Entdeckung der Radialfasern der Netzhaut durch H. Müller (1851) feststeht, die letzten Endigungen des nervus opticus dar, sie sind als die eigentlichen percipirenden Elemente der Netzhaut aufzufassen. Es lässt sich leicht beweisen, dass die Schichten der Netzhaut, welche vor den Stäbchen und Zapfen liegen, und der Sehnerv selbst vom Lichte nicht erregt werden.

Der Eintrittsstelle des Sehnerven entspricht nämlich eine dunkle Stelle im Gesichtsfelde, der sogenannte blinde Fleck (von Mariotte in der Mitte des 17. Jahrhunderts entdeckt). Fixirt man bei geschlossenem linken Auge ein kleines auf ein Blatt Papier gezeichnetes Kreuz mit dem rechten Auge, so kann man durch entsprechende Annäherung dieses Blattes an das beobachtende Auge einen kleinen Kreis, der rechts vom Kreuz gezeichnet ist, zum Verschwinden bringen. Nähert man nun das Blatt dem Auge noch mehr, so tritt der Kreis wieder im Gesichtsfelde auf. Es giebt also eine ganz bestimmte Entfernung dies Blattes vom Auge, in welcher der Kreis aus dem Gesichtsfelde verschwindet. Untersucht man genauer, auf welche Stelle des Augengrundes hierbei der Kreis fallen würde, so findet man, dass es die Eintrittsstelle des Sehnerven ist. Der beste Beweis für die Richtigkeit der Anschauung, dass es die Stäbchen- und Zapfenschicht ist, durch welche das Bild im Auge zur Wahrnehmung gelange, ist die von H. Müller gegebene Erklärung des Purkinjèschen Aderversuches. Durch seitliche Beleuchtung der Sclera des menschlichen Auges lassen sich die Schatten der baumförmig verzweigten Netzhautgefässe zur Beobachtung bringen. Da sich die Blutgefässe bis an die Zwischenkörnerschicht der Netzhaut erstrecken, so bleiben zur Perception ihres Schattenbildes nur die äusseren Körner mit den Stäbchen und Zapfen zur Auswahl übrig. Dass letztere mit den äusseren Körnern in continuo stehen, wies H. Müller nach, somit mussten die Stäbchen oder Zapfen, oder beide zusammen die Nervenenden sein (siehe Max Schultzes Anatomie und Physiologie der Retina p. 3). Waren auch hiermit die Endapparate des Sehnerven, in denen seine Erregung stattfinden müsse, gefunden, so wusste man doch über den eigentlichen Vorgang dieser Erregung, über die Art, wie die Aetherschwingungen in den Stäbchen und Zapfen zur Wirkung kommen, noch nichts Genaueres. Nach der Daguerreschen Entdeckung der Wirkung des Lichtes auf Jodsilber stellte Moser, der frühere Professor der Physik an unserer Universität, zuerst die geistreiche Hypothese auf, dass die Netzhauterregung auf einem photochemischen Processe beruhe, eine Hypothese, welche 1876 eine glänzende Bestätigung fand. Vor der ausführlichen Schilderung dieser photochemischen Processe sind jedoch die photoelectrischen Eigenschaften der Netzhaut zu erwähnen. E. du Bois-Reymond hatte schon 1849 nachgewiesen, dass bei einer Verbindung des künstlichen Querschnittes oder des natürlichen Längsschnittes des Sehnerven mit einem beliebigen Punkte der Aussenfläche des Augapfels, vorzugsweise der Hornhaut, ein electrischer Strom vorhanden sei. Dabei zeigte es sich, dass der Querschnitt des Nerven sich constant negativ verhielt gegen jeden beliebigen Punkt der Aussenfläche des Augapfels. Sechszehn Jahre später nahm Holmgren die Untersuchungen wieder auf. Er konnte im wesentlichen die von du Bois-Reymond aufgestellte Thatsache bestätigen. Er ging aber noch einen bedeutungsvollen Schritt weiter, indem er die naheliegende Vermuthung, dass eine Schwankung der Retinaströme eintreten werde, wenn die Netzhaut des Auges der Wirkung des Lichtes ausgesetzt werde, durch den Versuch zur Gewissheit erhob. Die Stromesschwankung spiegelt gleichsam den Erregungsvorgang im Auge ab und stellt das bis dahin nicht aufgewiesene Zwischenglied zwischen den Lichtbildern auf der Retina und der Lichtempfindung im Gehirn dar. Kehren wir jetzt zu den photochemischen Eigenschaften der Netzhaut zurück, so muss zuerst die Mittheilung von Fr. Boll (weiland Professor in Rom) vom 12. November 1876 an die Berliner

Akademie erwähnt werden, dass die Stäbchenschicht der Retina aller Geschöpfe im lebenden Zustande nicht farblos sei, wie man bisher meinte, sondern purpurroth. Im Leben, sagt Boll, würde die Eigenfarbe der Netzhaut beständig durch das ins Auge fallende Licht verzehrt, in der Dunkelheit wiederhergestellt, und im Tode halte sie sich nur einige Augenblicke. Diese purpurrothe Farbe der Netzhaut, der sogenannte Sehpurpur, hat die Eigenschaft auch im Tode nur durch das Licht gebleicht zu werden, er ist ganz unabhängig vom physiologisch frischen Zustande der Netzhaut. Schützt man einzelne Stellen einer auf Glas ausgebreiteten Netzhaut, die mit einem dünnen Deckglase bedeckt wird, durch millimeterbreite Staniolstreifen, welche man auf das Deckglas aufklebt, vor den Strahlen des Lichtes, so zeigen sich nach Abnahme des Deckglases, an den von Staniolstreifen geschützten Stellen schöne Bänder unveränderten Purpurs, also ein positives Photogramm (Kühne). Ist die Netzhaut gebleicht, so kehrt der Sehpurpur weder im Dunkeln, noch in anders farbenem Licht zurück. So lange aber die Retina im Auge auf der Chorioidea nur hinter capillaren Schichten des Glaskörpers Luft und Licht ausgesetzt blieb, erhielt sich stets der Sehpupur. Man kann sich leicht davon überzeugen, dass es nur die Chorioidea mit dem Retinaepithel ist, welche den Purpur vor dem Bleichen im Lichte schützt. Ja, die gebleichte Netzhaut gewinnt sogar ihren Sehpurpur wieder, wenn sie recht glatt auf das entblösste Pigment der Retina zurückgelegt wird. Die Netzhaut verhält sich also nicht nur wie eine photographische Platte, sondern wie eine photographische Werkstatt, worin der Arbeiter durch Auftragen neuen lichtempfindlichen Materials die Platte immer wieder vorbereitet und zugleich das alte Bild verwischt (Kühne). Es gelang Kühne, den Sehpurpur durch Galle zu lösen und rein darzustellen. Da der Sehpurpur nur in den Stäbchen und nie in den Zapfen der Netzhaut des Menschen und vieler Thiere vorkommt, da ferner die Macula lutea, die Stelle unseres schärfsten Sehens, die wir zum Fixiren gebrauchen, nur Zapfen allein enthält, so ist damit bewiesen, dass der Sehpurpur zum Sehen nicht unbedingt erforderlich ist. Nach kurzer Erwähnung Drapers, dass die Erregung der belichteten Netzhaut durch Erwärmung derselben zu erklären sei, dass also unter dem Finfluss des Lichtes photothermische Vorgänge in der Netzhaut stattfinden können, geht der Vortragende zu den erst kürzlich von Th. W. Engelmann entdeckten photomechanischen Veränderungen der Netzhaut über. Engelmann fand, dass die Zapfeninnenglieder sich unter Einwirkung des Lichtes verkürzen, im Dunkeln verlängern. Es scheint aber nur der an Protoplasma erinnernde Theil des Zapfeninnengliedes von der Limitans externa bis an das Aussenglied beweglich zu sein. Er bleibt daher immer in Continuität mit dem zugehörigen Zellkörper der äusseren Körnerschicht. Seine Verkürzung ist von Verdickung, seine Streckung von Verdünnung begleitet, deren Betrag die Annahme von Volumsänderungen auszuschliessen scheint. Er verhält sich also in dieser Beziehung wie contractiles Protoplasma oder Muskelfasern. Genau so wie die Zapfeninnenglieder bewegen sich auch unter gleichen Beleuchtungsbedingungen die Pigmentzellen der Netzhaut. Man könnte daraus schliessen, dass beide Bewegungen in causaler Beziehung zu einander ständen derart, dass die eine Erscheinung nicht ohne die andere eintreten könne. Es giebt jedoch Bedingungen, unter denen die Zapfen sich maximal verkürzen, ohne dass das Pigment sich aus der Dunkelstellung entfernt und umgekehrt. Die photomechanischen Reactionen der Pigmentzellen oder Zapfen treten bei Belichtung nur eines Auges stets in beiden Augen gleichzeitig auch bei geköpften Fröschen auf, wenn das Gehirn erhalten blieb. Nach Zerstörung des Gehirns mit Messer oder Nadel blieben die Lichtwirkungen stets auf das direct beleuchtete Auge beschränkt. Man ist daher gezwungen, eine durch Nervenbahnen vermittelte Association der Zapfen- und Pigmentzellen beider Augen, also ein sympathisches Zusammenwirken beider Netzhäute anzunehmen. Trotz unserer jetzigen Kenntniss von elektrischen, chemischen, thermischen und mechanischen Veränderungen der belichteten Netzhaut, die bei der Sehnervenerregung sicherlich eine wichtige Rolle zu spielen haben, bleibt uns der eigentliche Vorgang der Erregung, wie also die vorhingenannten Veränderungen in der Netzhaut eine Lichtempfindung zur Folge haben, einstweilen, ja vielleicht für immer, ein ungelöstes Räthsel.

Herr Professor Dr. Chun sprach über die antropomorphen Affen. An der Hand einer neuerdings für das zoologische Museum erworbenen Collection von Gorilla- und Orangschädeln suchte er einerseits die Differenzen zwischen jugendlichen und erwachsenen Thieren, sowie andererseits zwischen den menschlichen Schädeln und denen der antropomorphen Affen klar zu legen. Insbesondere betonte er die Wichtigkeit der Schädelnähte für das Verständniss des physiognomischen Habitus der erwachsenen Thiere und wies namentlich darauf hin, dass bei den antropomorphen Affen im Gegensatz zum Menschen auffällig lange die Nähte an der Basis des Hirnschädels persistiren. Da relativ frühe die Stirnnaht, Pfeilnaht und Lambdanaht schwindet, während noch länger die Nähte des Gesichtsschädels getrennt bleiben, so erklärt sich die starke Prognathie des Gesichtsschädels bei dem erwachsenen Thiere. Ja, nach dem Alter zeigen die Orangschädel auffallende Differenzen — ein Umstand, der irrthümlich zur Aufstellung mehrerer in Borneo vorkommenden Orangarten Veranlassung gab. Der Vortragende entschied sich indessen für das Vorkommen zweier Arten von Orangs, deren eine kleinere im unzugänglichen Innern von Borneo heimisch ist, und stützte sich bei dessen Auffassung auf einen vorgezeigten Schädel, der von allen bisher beschriebenen auffällig abweicht, insofern er keine Andeutung der mächtigen Muskelkämme aufweist, obwohl er einem ganz alten Thiere angehört. Den Schluss des Vortrags bildeten unter Demonstrationen eines neuerdings für das zoologische Museum erworbenen weiblichen Gorillas und des wohlerhaltenen Kopfes eines Nasenaffen Bemerkungen über die historische Entwickelung unserer Kenntnisse und über die Lebensweise des antropomorphen Affen.

Herr Dr. Tischler legt das Werk: „Fundstatistik der vorrömischen Metallzeit im Rheingebiete" von Freiherr v. Tröltsch vor. Es ist dies Werk mit Freude zu begrüssen, als der erste Versuch, das in zahlreichen Sammlungen Süddeutschlands zerstreute Material übersichtlich zu gruppiren. Die nächste Hauptaufgabe der vergleichenden Archäologie besteht darin, die Funde und Formen nach ihrer Zeitstellung und ihrem localen Vorkommen zu ordnen. Die erste Aufgabe kann nur durch eingehende kritische Untersuchung und Vergleichung der Funde gelöst werden, und ist vom Verfasser die Gruppirung nach Broncezeit, Hallstädter- und La Tène-Periode, unternommen. Die alte Eintheilung der Vorgeschichte in Stein-, Bronze- und Eisenzeit kann, obwohl lange Zeit heftig bekämpft, auch für das hier in Betracht kommende Gebiet vollständig aufrecht erhalten werden, nur passt sie nicht mehr in dieser Allgemeinheit. Die vorrömische Eisenzeit gliedert sich in die Hallstädter- und La Tène-Periode. Aber auch in der Bronzezeit kann man deutlich verschiedene Phasen unterscheiden: Eine ältere, durchaus reine Bronzezeit, die in zahlreichen Hügeln von Böhmen an durch Süddeutschland bis nach Frankreich hinein vollständig gleichmässig auftritt, und eine jüngere, wie sie in den meisten Bronzestationen der Schweizer Pfahlbauten vertreten ist. Diese letztere läuft nun zeitlich entschieden eine Weile der Hallstädter Eisenperiode parallel; es finden sich einige Stücke (getriebene Bronzegefässe, Bronzerasirmesser, Ringe, Formen der Bronzeschwerter) sowohl unter den Funden der einen wie der anderen Kategorie — es sind zwei Culturströmungen, die eine Zeit lang, zum Theil local getrennt, nebeneinander hergehen. Wenn man die Formen also in einzelne Kategorien einordnen will, machen gerade diese eine gewisse Schwierigkeit, sie müssten eigentlich noch eine gesonderte Klasse bilden. Ebenso ist der Uebergang der Hallstädter zur La Tène-Periode — Culturen, die auf der Höhe ihrer Entwickelung durchaus von einander verschieden sind — eine noch näher aufzuklärende Phase. Manche Formen, wie z. B. die hohlen aufgeschlitzten Armringe sind beiden gemeinsam. Wenn man daher bei einzelnen Stücken nicht ganz sicher ist, ob ihre Stellung eine ganz richtige ist, so berührt indessen dies den Hauptinhalt des Werkes durchaus nicht und schmälert seinen Werth nicht im Mindesten.

Hier hat der Verfasser die wichtigsten typischen Formen in deutlicher Zeichnung dargestellt und dann für jede Form die Vorkommnisse in Süddeutschland und der Schweiz mitgetheilt mit Berücksichtigung der Funde in den Nachbargebieten, Frankreich, Italien, Oesterreich, Gegenden, welche aber nicht in gleicher Vollständigkeit behandelt werden konnten. Es stützt sich die Zusammenstellung hauptsächlich auf die eigenen Studien des Verfassers in den zahlreichen Museen des Gebietes. Diese Arbeit ist von grosser Bedeutung. Man kann die Verbreitung aller einzelnen Formen studiren, man erkennt die Existenz gewisser auf kleinere Gebiete beschränkten Localformen, man ersieht die Sammlungen, in denen sich die betreffenden Stücke befinden. Alles dies sind wichtige und unentbehrliche Hilfsmittel für den, welcher tiefer in die Lösung der urgeschichtlichen Fragen eindringen wll, und werden jedem — wie der Vortragende in einzelnen Fällen selbst empfunden hat — von grösstem Nutzen sein. Denn das Werk will eben in die Fragen selbst noch nicht eindringen, es ist eine Vorstudie, die erst, indem sie richtig angewandt wird, ihren vollen Nutzen gewährt.

Es ist natürlich, dass bei dem grossen Eifer, mit dem man in Süddeutschland jetzt an den meisten Orten die prähistorische Forschung verfolgt, jährlich eine Fülle neuer Entdeckungen hinzukommt, dass somit die Aufzählung unvollständig wird. Das konnte aber nicht anders erwartet werden, und es musste die Arbeit einmal begonnen werden. Solche Ergänzungen können von zweierlei Art sein, entweder Funde von schon bekannten Formen, die dann also wesentlich nichts neues bringen, oder Formen, die in einem bestimmten Gebiete geradezu neu sind. Letzteres ist seltener der Fall, stösst doch aber gelegentlich jedem auf, der nach einer Reihe von Jahren die Sammlungen wieder durchsieht. Besonders tritt dies jetzt ein, weil, angeregt durch die Wirksamkeit der deutschen anthropologischen Gesellschaft, eine Reihe von Localforschern entstanden ist, welche kleinere, früher unberücksichtigte Gebiete ihren Forschungen unterzieht. Dadurch werden grosse Lücken in den Fundorten beseitigt, und so dürften gerade die Karten des Werkes, welche die Verbreitung der nach den chronologischen Hauptabschnitten geordneten Fundgruppen darstellen, späterhin mehr ausgefüllt werden, und besonders diese Karten werden an Bedeutung wesentlich gewinnen, wenn die östlichen und westlichen Nachbargebiete — Oesterreich und Frankreich erst klarer dargestellt sein werden.

Von den Karten hat wohl die grösste Bedeutung die der Verbreitung der vorrömischen Münzen. Es ist wahrscheinlich, dass diese merkwürdigen Stücke schon früher die Aufmerksamkeit erregt haben, als viele andere Alterthümer, und dass diese Karte bereits ein ziemlich grosses Bild gewähren wird.

Besonders hervorzuheben ist das äusserst geringe Eindringen der Münzen nach Norddeutschland, während die La Tène-Cultur sonst hier glänzend vertreten ist.

Diese Unvollkommenheiten liegen in der Natur der Sache begründet, da eben ja solche statistische Zusammenstellungen ewig unvollständig bleiben müssen.

Was aber bisher vorhanden war, hat der Verfasser in äusserst vollständiger Weise mit grösster Mühe zusammengebracht und sich dadurch ein grosses Verdienst um die Wissenschaft erworben. Es gilt nun das Werk zu vervollständigen und weiter auszudehnen.

Herr Dr. Tischler legt ferner die Copie eines zu Rondsen bei Graudenz gefundenen Bronzeeimers vor. Das Original befindet sich mit den Rondsener Funden im Alterthums-Museum zu Graudenz. Die Copie ist von Herrn Florkowski, Conservator dieses Museums, in Gyps und Steinpappe ausgeführt und in den Farben des Originals bemalt. Sie ist vorzüglich gelungen und der Preis von 15 Mk., für den sie Herr Florkowski an Museen ablässt, ein durchaus mässiger. Dieser Eimer gehört zu einer interessanten Klasse von Bronzegefässen, auf die besonders Undset aufmerksam gemacht hat*). Diese vasenförmigen Eimer, deren Henkel nach unten in 2 Fortsätze gespalten auslaufen, sind vollständig oder meist nur sehr fragmentarisch in einer Anzahl von Exemplaren gefunden zu Neuhof bei Ueckermünde (Pommern), 2 bei Lüneburg, zu Borgfeld (vielleicht) und Böhlsen (Hannover) zu Meisdorf bei Ballensted (Pr. Sachsen). Zu Münsterwalde bei Marienwerder (Westpreussen) ist ein ähnlich geformter Bronzeeimer nur mit verschiedenen Henkeln gefunden (Berliner Museum), in dem ein zusammengebogenes Spät-La Tène-Schwert lag.

Der Inhalt des als Aschen-Urne dienenden Rondsener**) Eimers war ein zusammengebogenes zweischneidiges Spät-La Tène-Schwert mit Bronceschcide, ein ein-

---

*) Undset: Das erste Auftreten des Eisens in Nord-Europa. Hamburg 1882. p. 528 Bronceeimer wie Taf. XXIV Fig. 1: p. 237, 283, 288.

**) Eine kurze Beschreibung dieses interessanten Gräberfeldes siehe Zeitschrift für Ethnologie. Berlin 1886 Heft 1.

schneidiges Schwert, eine eiserne Spät-La Tène-Fibel, Schildhenkel und ein räthselhaftes Bronzegeräth.

Das Schwert ist denen von Alesia nahe verwandt und mit einem des Spät-La Tène-Gräberfeldes von Nauheim fast identisch. Wir haben hier also einen Fund vor uns, der annähernd der Mitte des 1. Jahrhunderts v. Chr. angehört. Das Gräberfeld von Rondsen gehört zum Theil dieser Periode, zum Theil der frühen Kaiserzeit (ca. 1. Jahrh. n. Chr.) an und ist daher seine Erforschung für die Erkenntniss dieser Uebergangsperiode um Christi Geburt in Westpreussen, die bisher in Ostpreussen fast gar nicht vertreten ist, von ganz besonderer Wichtigkeit. Interessant ist das Factum, welches sich hier wie an zahlreichen anderen Funden Norddeutschlands (Schlesien, Pommern, Pr. Sachsen, Hannover) herausstellt, dass am Ende des 1. Jahrh. v. Chr. die Stämme, welche diese Gegenden bewohnten, die also nur Germanen sein können, dieselben Waffen führten als die Gallier, die Bewohner des jetzigen Frankreichs.

Sitzung am 2. April 1885.

Herr Professor Dr. Marek bespricht in seinem Vortrage über Moorcultur die Ursachen, welche zur Torfbildung Veranlassung geben, die Pflanzen, welche die Moore zusammensetzen, die verschiedenen Arten der Moore, deren geographische Verbreitung, stoffliche Zusammensetzung und Vertheilung in den verschiedenen Provinzen Preussens. Die alten Provinzen Preussens enthalten 260,4 Quadratmeilen Moor, Ostpreussen 36,4 Quadratmeilen. Im Ganzen dürfte die Ausdehnung der Moore in Preussen incl. der neuen Provinzen auf 2 Millionen Hectar geschätzt werden. Die Asche frischer Torfpflanzen ist reich an Alkalien. Durch den Vertorfungsprocess treten Veränderungen ein, die sich sowohl auf die äussere Beschaffenheit des Moores, wie in der stofflichen Zusammensetzung der Moorasche kundgiebt. Die Alkalien werden ausgelaugt und der Gehalt an Kalk, Phosphorsäure, Eisen und Thonerde nimmt relativ zu. Nach Art der Entstehung sind zwei Hauptgruppen von Mooren zu unterscheiden. Grünlands- und Hochmoore. Erstere sind kalkreicher und erfordern eine andere Cultur wie Hochmoore. Redner bespricht hierauf die verschiedentlichen Nutzungen der Moore und deren Culturen. Bei den letzteren werden die Ueberdüngungen mit Erde und Compost, die künstlichen Düngungen, das Brennen der Moore, die Entwässerungen, die Rigolculturen, die Rimpausche Dammcultur und die in Holland vornehmlich zur Ausführung gebrachte Fehncultur besonders besprochen und dabei vielfach auf die neuen auf Moorkultur bezugnehmenden wissenschaftlichen Untersuchungen eingehend Rücksicht genommen.

Herr Professor Dr. R. Caspary spricht über zwei Sporenpflanzen, die im Norden und auf den europäischen Gebirgen stellenweise mit Ausschluss der Schweizer Alpen auf dem Boden von Seen vorkommen und kleinen nicht blühenden Binsen ähnlich sehen: Isoëtes lacustris L. und echinospora Durieu. Sie finden sich auch in Preussen. Isoët. lac. in 35 Seen (Kreis Neustadt, Carthaus, Berent, Allenstein). Isoët. echinospora in 3 (Kreis Neustadt). Isoët. lac. wird lebend aus Seen des Kreises

Neustadt vorgezeigt und ihre verschiedenen Formen, die kleinere bis etwa 12 cm hoch mit aufrechten Blättern (fr. stricta), die mit geraden bis zu 15 cm hohen, gespreizten Blättern (fr. patens), die mit zurückgekrümmten gespreizten Blättern, die schon vor 1847 von Tausch in Böhmen gefunden und von ihm als fr. falcata bezeichnet ist, an die sich fr. circinata J. Gay mit zum Theil uhrfederig aufgerollten Blättern anschliesst, besprochen. Ferner eine Form mit sehr langen Blättern: longifolia bis 27 cm lang, bei uns vorkommend. Die Blätter legen sich, wenn die Pflanze aus dem Wasser gezogen wird, in 1—3 Büscheln pinselförmig zusammen, was an lebenden Pflanzen dargethan wird. Diese Form wächst auf moorigem Boden in der Tiefe der Seen von 5—9 Fuss und tiefer und bildet die Hauptbestände der Pflanze, die oft wiesenartig sind. Davon ist als Extrem eine fr. maxima von A. Blytt in Norwegen aufgestellt, die bis 1½ Fuss hoch wird. v. Klinggraeff II. hat eine Spielart mit glatten Sporen (fr. leiospora) unterschieden, die er besonders im Ottalsiner See, Kreis Neustadt, gefunden hat; er behauptet, dass bei dieser glattsporigen Pflanze die Blätter um 45 Gr. abstehen; dieses ist nicht allgemein richtig. Glatte Sporen kommen bei allen Formen vor. v. Klinggraeff II. hätte die Verpflichtung gehabt, zu beweisen, dass die glatten Sporen keine unreifen seien. Die Frage nach der Reife der Sporen hat sich v. Klinggraeff gar nicht gestellt. Um sie zu beantworten, hat Professor Caspary sich aus 3 Seen des Kreises Neustadt, dessen sämmtliche Seen er 1884 in 8 Wochen untersuchte, Ende März frische Isoëtes lacustris kommen lassen. Die Sporen der äusseren Blätter waren jedenfalls als reife zu betrachten, auch sie zeigten sich glatt; obenein haben sie gekeimt. Die fr. leiospora ist also anzuerkennen. Isoëtes echinospora hat Professor Caspary in einem neuen See des Kreises Neustadt entdeckt: im Grabowke, zwischen Bieschkowitz und Försterei Wigodda.

Sitzung am 7. Mai 1885.

Der Vorsitzende widmete nachstehenden Nachruf dem Geheimen Rath Professor Dr. **Carl Theodor Ernst von Siebold.**

Seitdem wir zum letzten Mal versammelt waren, hat die Gesellschaft eines ihrer ältesten und berühmtesten Mitglieder durch den Tod verloren, einen Mann, welcher zwar kein geborener Preusse war, aber durch eine Reihe von Jahren mehr für die Naturgeschichte von Ost- und Westpreussen geleistet hat, als irgend ein anderer. Carl Theodor Ernst v. Siebold ist am 7. April d. J. in München nach längerem Siechthum 81 Jahre alt gestorben.

Der Verstorbene gehörte der berühmten Gelehrten-Familie dieses Namens an, welche seit der Mitte des vorigen Jahrhunderts eine ununterbrochene Reihe von bedeutenden Aerzten und Naturforschern hervorgebracht hat. Alle diese Herren waren in Würzburg ansässig, nur einer starb in Berlin, alle waren Mediciner und zum grössten Theil berühmte Geburtshelfer, alle waren Professoren und selbst zwei Frauen in der Familie studirten Geburtshilfe und erlangten die academische Doctorwürde.

Unser Carl v. Siebold war ein Grosssohn des ersten berühmten Gelehrten jener Familie, des Carl Kaspar v. Siebold, welcher zu Niedeck im Herzogthum Jülich

1736 geboren, später nach Würzburg übersiedelte und dort der Stammvater der Gelehrtenfamilie wurde. Carl v. Siebold erblickte in Würzburg am 16. Februar 1804 das Licht der Welt, empfing dort seine Schul- und Universitätsbildung, ging aber später nach Berlin und absolvirte dort seine Examina als Arzt, so dass er unmittelbar danach in unsere Provinz als Kreisphysicus nach Heilsberg kam. Hier fing er an sich neben seiner Amtsthätigkeit mit zoologischen Arbeiten zu beschäftigen und sich namentlich dem Studium der Fauna des Landes zuzuwenden.

Diese Bestrebungen erregten in dem jungen arbeitslustigen Mann bald den Wunsch, in einer grösseren, namentlich in einer Universitätsstadt zu leben, wo literarische Hilfsmittel und der Verkehr mit anderen Gelehrten jede wissenschaftliche Thätigkeit fördern mussten. In Königsberg hatte damals Carl Ernst v. Bär seine grossen Arbeiten über die Entwickelung des Eies der Säugethiere beendigt und genoss einen bedeutenden Ruf, es lag daher nahe, dass unser Carl v. Siebold hierher zu kommen strebte, was ihm auch im Jahre 1834 gelang, indem er das hiesige Stadtphysicat bekam. Leider aber machte sich die Sache nicht so, wie v. Siebold erwartet hatte, Herr v. Bär verliess bald darauf Königsberg, um einem Ruf an die Academie in Petersburg Folge zu leisten, und als sich Siebold habilitiren wollte, um v. Bärs Vorlesungen fortzusetzen, konnte er die Erlaubniss dazu nicht erlangen, weil er katholisch, die Albertina aber damals streng lutherisch war. Obgleich v. Siebold für seine Thätigkeit hier einige Gesinnungsgenossen fand und damals auch Mitglied unserer Gesellschaft wurde, welche die Erforschung der Naturgeschichte der Provinz auf ihr Programm geschrieben hatte, so war ihm doch seine ganze Stellung verleidet und er verliess Königsberg schon nach einem Jahre, um in Danzig als Director der Entbindungs- und Hebammenlehranstalt einzutreten, zu welchem Amte er 1839 auch das Stadtphysicat übernahm. So war denn unser v. Siebold wie alle Mitglieder der Familie Geburtshelfer geworden.

Aber die Beschäftigung mit zoologischen und vergleichend anatomischen Arbeiten war ihm doch zu sehr ans Herz gewachsen, als dass er sich gänzlich von ihr hätte lossagen können. So gab er die Danziger Stellung schon 1840 wieder auf, um als Professor für sein Specialfach nach Erlangen zu gehen.

In die Jahre von 1834—1854, also bis lange nach dem Fortgange von Danzig fallen die Arbeiten v. Siebolds über die Naturgeschichte preussischer Thiere. Als er Danzig verliess, nahm er in einer kurzen Ansprache an die Provinz, welche im 25. Bande der „Preussischen Provinzialblätter" abgedruckt ist, Abschied von derselben und erklärte, dass er auch in späteren Jahren für seine hier begonnenen Arbeiten weiter thätig sein werde. Diese Zusage hat er in vollem Maasse erfüllt, denn wie bereits angeführt wurde, gehen seine Arbeiten bis in das Jahr 1854. Eine der ersten Arbeiten im Jahre 1836 betraf das mehrfach beobachtete Vorkommen des Oleanderschwärmers in der Provinz Westpreussen, im Jahre 1837 berichtigte er einen Irrthum über das angebliche Vorkommen von Schildkröten in der Ostsee. Es war nämlich eine lebende Carettschildkröte in der Nähe von Danzig aus der See gefischt worden, die im Mittelländischen Meere lebt. v. Siebold wies nach, dass dieses Thier nur durch Zufall auf einem Schiff aus südlichen Gegenden in die Ostsee gekommen und dort über Bord gefallen sein könne. Im Jahre 1838 veröffentlichte v. Siebold einen grösseren Aufsatz über die Kolumbatzer Fliege in Preussen, und diesmal trat unser

Forscher nicht blos als Zoologe, sondern auch als Physicus auf. Es hatte sich nämlich jene Fliege, eine Species der Gattung Simulia, die auch sonst bei uns beobachtet war, in grossen Schwärmen gezeigt und Kühe auf der Weide überfallen und getödtet. v. Siebold interessirte sich sofort lebhaft für die Sache; sammelte die betreffenden Beobachtungen aus der Gegend von Danzig und gab an, wie man das Vieh vor solchen Angriffen schützen und hinterher curiren könne.

In den Jahren 1837—1842 hat v. Siebold wiederholt kritische und ergänzende Aufsätze über die damals neu erschienenen Werke: 1) Lorecks Fauna prusica, 2) Bujacks Naturgeschichte der höheren Thiere veröffentlicet und hat noch zuletzt 1842 eine grössere Arbeit als „Neue Beiträge zur Wirbelthierfauna Preussens" folgen lassen.

Für die höheren in der Provinz Preussen vorkommenden Thiere war, wie wir gesehen haben, mancherlei geschehen. Von den Mollusken aber wusste man wenig und von den Gliederthieren waren auch nur die Käfer in früherer Zeit von Kugelan und Illiger theilweise bearbeitet worden. Hier griff nun v. Siebold mit Eifer an, sammelte, was er von niederen Thieren bekommen konnte, suchte die noch niemals bearbeiteten Ordnungen möglichst sicher zu bestimmen und veröffentlichte als erste Grundlage der Kenntniss unserer Fauna in den Jahren 1838 bis 1851 nacheinander 13 Verzeichnisse preussischer Mollusken und Insecten. Jeder der sich in jener Zeit mit entomologischen Sammlungen und Studien beschäftigt hat, wird sich noch dankbar jener Publikationen v. Siebolds erinnern, von welchen viele auch bis jetzt ihren vollen Werth behalten haben und der Fortsetzung harren.

Im Jahre 1840 folgte v. Siebold einem Rufe nach Erlangen, ging 1845 nach Freiburg im Breisgau, wohin er als Professor der Physiologie, vergleichenden Anatomie und Zoologie berufen worden, dann 1850 nach Breslau als Professor der Physiologie; zuletzt aber 1853 nach München als Professor der Physiologie und vergleichenden Anatomie, später auch der Zoologie.

Während dieser Zeit der Wanderungen veröffentlichte v. Siebold eine Reihe von wissenschaftlichen Arbeiten, welche sich meistens auf die Fortpflanzung und Metamorphose der Gliederthiere bezogen, 1848 auch ein Lehrbuch der vergleichenden Anatomie der wirbellosen Thiere. 1849 begründete er mit Kölliker zusammen die „Zeitschrift für wissenschaftliche Zoologie", ein Werk, das stets an der Spitze der zoologischen Literatur gestanden hat.

In München, woselbst v. Siebold über 30 Jahre thätig gewesen ist, traten die bedeutendsten Arbeiten an die Oeffentlichkeit, unter anderem im Jahre 1854 das Werk über Band- und Blasenwürmer, 1856 die Schrift über „die wahre Parthenogenesis bei Schmetterlingen und Bienen", ein Thema, welches von ihm selbst und anderen fortgesetzt bearbeitet wurde und vielfach ganz neue und interessante Vorgänge aus dem Leben der Insecten bekannt werden liess. 1863 erschien ein Buch, an welchem Siebold sehr lange gearbeitet hatte, nämlich „die Süsswasserfische von Mitteleuropa". Hier handelte es sich nämlich darum, die ganz eigenthümlichen Lebenserscheinungen der in grossen Tiefen der schweizerischen und bayerischen Alpenseen lebenden Fische zu ergründen. Als der Verfasser bei Gelegenheit der Naturforscherversammlung nach Königsberg gekommen war, machte er von hier aus eine Excursion nach den masurischen Seen; um auch diese auf ihre Fische zu untersuchen und fand auch hier manches Interessante. Zwischen diesen grossen Arbeiten hat v. Siebold fortwährend kleine Aufsätze über verschiedene Gegenstände aus dem Gebiete der Physiologie, Biologie, Zoologie u. s. w. meist in Zeitschriften veröffentlicht, so dass die Gesammtzahl der einzelnen von ihm publicirten Arbeiten eine sehr grosse ist, auf welche hier natürlich nicht näher eingegangen werden kann.

Schon aus den kurzen Mittheilungen über das Leben unseres Gelehrten geht hervor, dass derselbe ein Mann von grosser Arbeitskraft war, der Bedeutendes geschaffen hat. Vor allem aber müssen wir hervorheben, dass unser eigenes Vaterland, die Provinz Preussen, diesem Manne sehr viel verdankt, und dass es unsere Pflicht ist, sein Andenken stets hoch zu halten.

Der Vorsitzende ersuchte als äusseres Zeichen der Achtung und Verehrung, die der Verstorbene stets genossen, die Anwesenden, sich von ihren Plätzen zu erheben, was bereitwilligst geschah.

Herr Dr. Tischler spricht unter Vorzeigung von Abbildungen über die Darstellungen von Waffen und Costümen auf alten Bronzen der Hallstadt-Italischen Periode. Während zu Beginn der Eisenzeit in Italien nördlich und südlich des Apennins eine annähernd gleiche Cultur herrschte, trat später eine scharfe Trennung und eine verschiedenartige Entwickelung ein. Im Süden bildet sich die eigentlich etruskische Cultur aus, während nördlich die grosse Nekropole von Bologna in continuirlich fortschreitender Folge ein ganz anderes Bild gewährt, bis ca. im 5. Jahrhundert vor Christi die Etrusker ihre Eroberungen nördlich über den Apennin ausdehnten, worauf dann eine Ausgleichung stattfand, wie sie auf dem Begräbnissplatze der Certosa zu Bologna zu Tage tritt. Es stimmt dies Verhältniss wenig zu der Annahme einer Einwanderung der Etrusker von Norden, während der Einzug einer vielleicht nicht sehr grossen Schaar von der Seeseite, die mit der unterworfenen einheimischen Bevölkerung verschmolz, sich viel besser mit den archäologischen Verhältnissen verträgt. Nördlich vom Apennin kann man eine Reihe verschiedener Gebiete unterscheiden, die sich östlich über die Alpen hinaus und dann um die ganze Kette herum durch Oesterreich, Süddeutschland bis nach Frankreich (Franche Comté, Burgund) hinein erstrecken, die alle in ihrer Cultur und Hinterlassenschaft einen gemeinsamen Zug aufweisen. Besonders stehen die aneinander grenzenden Gebiete immer in naher Verwandtschaft, wenngleich sie in der Gesammtheit ihres Inventars sich gegeneinander abgrenzen. Je weiter man aber nach Westen kommt, desto grössere Unterschiede gegen den östlichen Ausgangspunkt treten zu Tage. Wenn nun die Geräthe und Schmucksachen, die wir in den zahlreichen Gräbern dieser sogenannten Italo-Hallstädter Periode finden, zum Theil einander sehr ähnen, so dass sie anfänglich jedenfalls aus einer gemeinsamen Quelle stammen, so treten andererseits in jenen getrennten Gebieten eine Menge Localformen auf, welche auf eine hochentwickelte einheimische Industrie und Technik daselbst schliessen lassen. Zu den früher schon systematisch untersuchten Gebieten, dem von Bologna und von Hallstadt, sind neuerdings andere dazwischenliegende getreten, so das Euganeische Gebiet, in welchem die Nekropole von Este durch Prosdocimi gründlich erforscht ist, und das Krainer Gebiet, wo die Nekropole von Watsch, die Hügel von St. Margareten u. a. m. in das Wiener Hofmuseum, das Provinzialmuseum von Laibach und die Sammlung des Fürsten Ernst zu Windischgrätz in Wien ganz ausserordentliche archäologische Schätze geliefert haben. Ein näheres Eingehen in diese interessanten Entdeckungen ist hier nicht angänglich. Es soll nur ein besonders wichtiger Punkt herausgegriffen werden. In Norditalien wie in Krain und benachbarten Gegenden Südtirols sind eine Anzahl von Bronzeeimern (meist die konisch verjüngenden situlae) gefunden mit figürlichen Darstellungen aus dem häuslichen und kriegerischen Leben. Die besterhaltenen sind eine Situla zu Bologna, eine zu Este (woselbst noch mehrere andere), eine zu Watsch in Krain. Am letzteren Orte ist noch ein prächtiges Gürtelblech mit einer Kampfscene gefunden (im Besitze von Fürst Windischgrätz). Die zahlreichen übrigen Gefässe sind nur in Fragmenten vorhanden. Die Gefässe sind in mehrere Zonen getheilt, deren unterste meist einen Zug phantastischer Thiere, Einhörner, Sphinxe, geflügelte Löwen etc. enthält. In den andern finden sich kriegerische Aufzüge und die verschiedenartigsten Scenen des öffentlichen und Privatlebens dargestellt. So zeigt die Situla von Bologna das Opfer mit allen Vorbereitungen, ein Mahl, Preiskämpfer — eine oft sich wiederholende Darstellung —, den Hirten, den Holzhauer etc. Zu Este wird u. a. ein Pferdekauf dargestellt. Der Eimer von Watsch bringt einen pomphaften Leichenzug mit dem Leichenschmaus und den obligaten Preiskämpfern. Alle diese Gefässe zeigen in ihren zwar recht unkünstlerisch aber doch realistisch treu gehaltenen Darstellungen eine durchaus übereinstimmende Tracht. Die Männer haben meist flache, gemusterte Tellermützen, die Priester mehrfach breitkrämpige Hüte, die vollständig den jetzigen Jesuitenhüten ähnen. Wir sehen hier anliegende Kleider mit Aermeln und enganliegende ärmellose Umhängemäntel, gewürfelt oder in senkrecht herablaufende gemusterte Streifen getheilt. Die Frauen haben ein enganliegendes Unterkleid mit Aermeln, darüber ein Oberkleid mit einer den Kopf umhüllenden Kapuze. Hosen sind nicht bemerkbar. Interessanter ist aber noch die Bewaffnung, welche besonders auf der Situla von Bologna und dem Gürtelbleche von Watsch erscheint. Auf der obersten Zone jenes Eimers tritt ein langer Zug von Kriegern auf in vier verschiedenen Waffengattungen, drei Trupps Fussoldaten und ein Trupp Reiterei. Die Reiter und ein Trupp Fussoldaten haben Celte von der Form mit breiter dünner Klinge mit Flügeln, wie sie aus Eisen und Bronze sich in den Gräbern Krains und Norditaliens findet. Die übrigen tragen Lanzen, eine längere mit Lanzenfuss oder eine kürzere. Die Schilde der Lanzenträger sind von drei Formen: oval, mehr viereckig und rund. Wahrscheinlich enthielten sie keine Metalltheile, es hat sich davon auch nichts in den Gräbern erhalten. Die Kleidung besteht in einer kurzärmeligen, verzierten Jacke. Am interessantesten sind aber die Helme, deren jeder Trupp einen anderen trägt. Die Reiter haben einen mit rundem Kopf und breiter Krämpe, wie ein ganz entsprechender zu Hallstadt gefunden ist. Die Infanteristen mit leichtem Speer tragen einen Helm mit grossem, hinten lang herabhängenden Helmkamme, wie ihn alle drei Krieger auf dem Gürtelbleche zu Watsch besitzen. Entsprechende Helme sind zu Watsch gefunden, die vorne und hinten ein Häkchen tragen, eines in Gestalt eines Pferdekopfes, zum Befestigen des Kammes und oben zur seitlichen Begrenzung derselben entweder zwei Bronzekämme oder zwei Figuren, die das Abgleiten desselben verhindern. Ein ähnlicher ist auf einem Fragmente von Matrei dargestellt. Die mit Celten bewaffneten Infanteristen tragen einen kegelförmigen Helm; vielleicht stellt ein zu Oppeano gefundenes kegelförmiges, mit Thierfiguren bedecktes Bronzegefäss einen solchen Helm vor. Höchst auffallend sind die Helme der schweren Infanterie, oben in eine Spitze auslaufend und unten herum mit Buckeln besetzt. Man würde sich von ihnen kein rechtes Bild machen können, wenn nicht glücklicherweise zu Watsch mehrere solche Helme entdeckt wären, die, obwohl in Einzelheiten etwas abweichend, doch unzweifelhaft in diesen merkwürdigen Abbildungen dargestellt sind. Dieselbe bestanden aus einem mit Leder überzogenen Geflecht gespaltener Haselruthen und waren aussen rundherum mit sechs gewölbten Bronzescheiben besetzt und oben von einer siebenten in eine hohe Eisenspitze auslaufenden gekrönt. Die Zwischenräume waren dicht mit kleinen Bronzeknöpfchen oder Nägelchen mit runden Köpfen ausgefüllt. Aehnliche Helme scheinen auch auf einem Fragmente von St. Marein in Krain dargestellt zu sein. So finden sich die dargestellten Trutz- und Schutzwaffen also auch sämmtlich in den Gräbern wieder, woselbst das Schwert fehlt, das auch keiner dieser Krieger trägt — während es in Hallstadt und Süddeutschland so häufig ist. — Welchem Volke aber diese Eimer zuzuschreiben sind, ist noch schwer zu entscheiden. Es scheint fast, als ob die Euganeer und Krainer einander näher stehen, und auffallend ist es jedenfalls, dass man die merkwürdigsten Helme gerade nur in Krain gefunden hat. Sollte also hier das Centrum der Fabrikation gelegen haben, so könnte der Bologneser Eimer als ein versprengtes Stück angesehen werden.*) Doch muss dies noch als durchaus offene Frage betrachtet werden, das Alter der Objecte lässt sich annähernd in das 6. Jahrhundert v. Chr. setzen. Waffen und Costüme von wesentlich verschiedenem Charakter zeigt die gravirte Bronceshceide eines prachtvollen, zu Hallstadt gefundenen Schwertes, welches einer jüngeren Zeit, dem Beginne der La Tène-Periode angehört und in seiner Form mit den Schwertern von den grossen Begräbnissplätzen der Champagne übereinstimmt. Die Schilde zeigen längliche Buckel, wie sie sich in diesen Gräbern mehrfach gefunden haben, während die Helme nicht den in gallischen Gräbern gefundenen trichterförmigen entsprechen und wahrscheinlich nicht aus Metall, sondern aus Leder bestehen — die Helme des gemeinen Volkes. Aeusserst roh erscheinen gegen diese immerhin noch ziemlich primitiven Darstellungen die Abbildungen auf den Felszeichnungen Schwedens, wo man aber auf einer solchen zu Nedre Hede und Oester Röd noch immer den Bronceschild mit getriebenen Buckeln, wie er ja im Norden mehrfach gefunden ist, und die Schwertscheide mit dem für die Hallstädter Schwerter charakteristischen Endbeschlage erkennen kann.

Herr Dr. Richard Klebs sprach über neue geologische Beobachtungen über die Verbreitung der Braunkohlen in Ostpreussen. Das Bestreben Braunkohlen zu

*) Die Beschreibung einer 2. Situla von Bologna (Brizio: Sulla nuova situla di Bronzo figurata trovata in Bologna. Deputazione di storia patria di Romagna 1884 kam dem Vortragenden erst nach Druck dieses Auszuges zu Gesicht. Dieselbe enthält Wagenwettfahrten, Kriegeraufzüge etc. Brizio setzt sie zeitlich noch später, ins 4. Jahrhundert, was doch fraglich.).

finden, welche abbauwürdig seien, ist in unserer Provinz seit langer Zeit sehr rege gewesen. An verschiedenen Orten sind in früheren Jahren Unternehmungen in grösserem und kleinerem Maassstabe vorgenommen worden, welche aber bis jetzt stets ungünstige Resultate gegeben haben. Nicht allein sind diese vielfachen Bohrungen etc. dadurch ohne Nutzen gewesen, dass sie keine produktive Kohle gaben, sondern mehr dadurch, dass die dabei erlangten Resultate nicht in der Weise Geologen von Fach zugänglich gemacht sind, dass sie wissenschaftlich verwerthet werden konnten. Denn gerade die Braunkohlenformation in Ostpreussen bietet aus Gründen, die der Vortragende näher erläuterte, selbst dem Fachmann grosse Schwierigkeiten in der Parallelisirung der Schichten aus verschiedenen Gegenden. Bis jetzt ist unsere genaue Kenntniss über die Braunkohlen in ihrer Lagerung nur auf zwei, vielleicht drei Gebiete beschränkt; auf das des samländischen Strandes, welches Professor Dr. Zaddach klassisch bearbeitet, und auf das von Heilsberg, welches der Vortragende in den Jahren 1881 bis 1884 studirt hat. Die Heiligenbeiler Kohlen sind vom Vortragenden im Jahre 1878 allerdings gleichfalls untersucht worden, indes nicht in der speciellen Weise wie die vom Samland und von Heilsberg, weil Zeit und Umstände das Eingehen auf alle Details unmöglich machten. Der Vortragende ging dann auf die Gliederung unseres Tertiärs ein, zu welchem die Braunkohlenformation gehört, und auf die Horizonte in welchen die Kohlen selbst lagern. Aus der oberen Etage der Braunkohlenformation ist als mächtigstes Flötz das von Warnicken bekannt, welches 2 m, aus der mittleren Etage das von Gr. Hubnicken, welches 1,7 m stark ist. Aehnlich sind die Mächtigkeitsverhältnisse bei Birkenau und Warnikam in der Gegend von Heiligenbeil. Bei Heilsberg erreichen an einzelnen Stellen die Kohlen 3 m Mächtigkeit und lagern in einem geologischen Horizont, welcher die Zaddachsche obere und mittlere Abtheilung der Braunkohlenformation in sich begreift. Gerade bei Heilsberg konnte die Schichtenfolge des ostpreussischen Tertiärs sehr eingehend studirt werden, da der Vortragende auf Kosten des Staates Schürfarbeiten im grösseren Maassstabe vornehmen konnte und zwei Bohrlöcher, welche der durch Brunnenanlagen in unserer Provinz rühmlichst bekannte Herr Pöpke aus Anclam der guten Sache wegen vornehmen liess, Profile bis zu 60 m Mächtigkeit lieferten. Sehr unterstützt wurden die Heilsberger Untersuchungen durch den Gräfeschen Bohrapparat, den der Vortragende zu schnellen Bohrungen bis zu 10 m sehr empfahl und dessen Construction und einfache Handhabung er erläuterte. Ausser den Kohlen aber bietet das Heilsberger Tertiär noch das Interessante, dass nach Ansicht des Vortragenden die im Simserthale zu Tage tretenden Thone zu den tiefsten Ablagerungen in dem ostpreussischen Tertiär gehören und Schichten entsprechen, wie wir solche von Geidau in 87—194, in Markehnen von 92—110, in Königsberg durchschnittlich in 55—65 m Tiefe kennen. Danach würde in geringer Tiefe unter dem Spiegel der Simser die Kreideformation bei Heilsberg anstehen und ein Uebergreifen der eigentlichen Braunkohlen- über die glaukonitische (Bernstein-) Formation stattfinden. In Zusammenhang hiermit dürften dann auch die fraglichen Kreideaufschlüsse von Jäcknitz bei Zinten und von Wackern bei Pr. Eylau zu bringen sein. Der Vortragende ging dann auf die Verbreitung der eigentlichen Kohle bei Heilsberg und auf die Schichtenstörungen in derselben näher ein und erläuterte an einer Reihe von Photographien und Fundstücken den Einfluss der einzelnen Diluvialschichten auf die dortige Braunkohlenformation und wies auf die wissenschaftlich äusserst interessante Thatsache hin, dass sich in der ältesten Diluvialzeit bei Heilsberg stellenweise eine Süsswasserfauna entwickelt habe.

Hierauf hielt Herr Dr. Franz, Observator der Sternwarte, einen Vortrag über: Messungen des Magnetismus von eisernen Tiefbrunnenröhren und Eisenbahnschienen in Königsberg. Am 25. April theilte mir Herr Dr. Jentzsch mit, dass er soeben erfahren habe, dass sich an dem noch nicht ganz vollendeten Tiefbrunnen in der Trainkaserne auf dem Oberhaberberge hierselbst magnetische Erscheinungen zeigten, und bat mich die Sache zu untersuchen. Sofort begab ich mich dorthin und sah, dass allerdings Eisentheile, welche dem oberen Ende der über 200 m langen eisernen Brunnenröhre etwa bis auf 3 cm genähert wurden, angezogen und festgehalten wurden; die Brunnenröhre ist also stark magnetisch. Ueber die Ursache des Magnetismus kann kein Zweifel bestehen; dieselbe ist im Erdmagnetismus zu suchen. Denn ebenso wie jedes Eisenstäbchen, welches einem Magnetpole genähert und durch Influenz oder Vertheilung des Magnetismus zu einem Magneten gemacht wird, so wird auch jeder Stab durch den Erdmagnetismus magnetisch und zwar um so mehr, je mehr er die Richtung einer im Schwerpunkt aufgehängten Magnetnadel, einer Inklinationsnadel hat, und nur dann wird er nicht magnetisirt, wenn er senkrecht zur Richtung der Inklinationsnadel steht. Der Magnetismus tritt aber auch um so stärker auf, je länger die Eisenstücke sind, je mehr Masse sie haben und je länger sie in der für die Entstehung des Magnetismus günstigen Stellung bleiben. Da wir es hier nun mit Eisenröhren von 200 m Länge zu thun haben, die bereits seit 2½ Jahren in derselben senkrechten Stellung sind, so bestehen hier Verhältnisse von aussergewöhnlicher Grösse welche zu genauerer Untersuchung und zu einer Messung einladen. Daher versuchte ich am 27. April mit einer Magnetnadel 1. an dem Tiefbrunnen der Trainkaserne auf dem Oberhaberberg und ebenso 2. an dem fast vollendeten, über 250 m tiefen Brunnen der Kürassierkaserne auf dem Schlossplatz, 3. am Südende der Schienen der Pferdebahn in der Kronenstrasse und 4. am Nordende der Schienen der Ostpreussischen Südbahn auf den Südbahnhof Messungen des Magnetismus zu machen, da bei allen diesen Punkten aus demselben Grunde starker Magnetismus vermuthet werden musste. Es wurde erstens die Ablenkung und zweitens die Schwingungsdauer der Magnetnadel beobachtet. Um die Ablenkung zu finden, wurde die Magnetnadel in gleichen, gemessenen Entfernungen (1 m, 0,5 m und so weiter) östlich und westlich vom Polende so gehalten, dass in beiden Fällen der Nullpunkt ihres Zifferblatts nach demselben Azimut oder derselben Himmelsgegend hinzeigte, und dann die Stellung der Magnetnadel auf dem Zifferblatt abgelesen. Das Mittel beider Ablesungen giebt den magnetischen Meridian, die halbe Differenz der Ablesungen die Ablenkung an, welche die Magnetnadel durch den Pol (das Ende der Brunnenröhre oder der Schienen) erfährt. Nach dem Satze vom Parallellogramm der Kräfte ist die Horizontalkomponente der anziehenden Kraft des Magnetpols dem Sinus des Ablenkungswinkels, die Horizontalkomponente des Erdmagnetismus dem Cosinus dieses Winkels proportional. Ihr Verhältniss ist also gleich der trigonometrischen Tangente des Ablenkungswinkels. — Um die Schwingungsdauer zu finden, wurde die Anzahl der Schwingungen der Magnetnadel in 10 Sekunden nach der Taschenuhr gezählt und die Schwingungsdauer der Magnetnadel auf der Sternwarte, wo sie nur unter dem Einfluss des Erdmagnetismus stand, mit dem Chronograph durch gleichzeitiges Einregistriren mit den Sekundenschlägen einer Pendeluhr bestimmt. Ebenso wie bei Pendelschwingungen gilt hier die Relation:

$$T = \sqrt{\frac{c}{g}}$$

wenn T die Schwingungsdauer, c eine Konstante, die vom Trägheitsmoment und der magnetischen Stärke der Magnetnadel abhängig ist, und g die Horizontalkomponente der auf die Nadel wirkenden Anziehungskräfte ist. Es ist aber $g^2 = h^2 + m^2$, wenn h die Horizontalkomponente des Erdmagnetismus, m die Horizontalkomponente des Magnetismus des Pols in der gemessenen Entfernung ist. Die Messungen, sowohl der Ablenkungen wie auch der Schwingungsdauer, die in verschiedenen horizontalen Entfernungen von den Polen, d. h. von den Enden der Brunnenröhren und der Eisenbahnschienen gemacht wurden, zeigten, dass die anziehende Kraft nicht dem Quadrate der Entfernung, sondern nahezu der einfachen Entfernung proportional ist. So überraschend diese Erscheinung Anfangs erschien, so wird sie doch durch die Theorie bestätigt. Denn bei diesen Magneten von so aussergewöhnlicher Länge ist der entfernte Pol zunächst ohne Einfluss auf die Magnetnadel. Bei dem nahen Pole, also bei Brunnenröhren bei dem oberen Pole ist aber der Magnetismus nicht in einem Punkte concentrirt, sondern über eine längere Strecke von mindestens mehreren Metern nahezu gleichmässig vertheilt. Wir haben es also mit der Anziehung nicht eines Punktes, sondern einer auf einer Seite unbegrenzten graden Linie auf die Magnetnadel zu thun. Die Anziehung einer unendlich langen Linie auf einen Punkt ist aber, wie man durch eine einfache Integration erkennt, umgekehrt proportional der einfachen Entfernung, und ebenso gilt dies für die Horizontalkomponente der Anziehung einer einseitig unbegrenzten Linie, da diese die Hälfte der Anziehung der beiderseitig unbegrenzten Linie ist. Hiermit sind die Messungen in verschiedenen Entfernungen berechnet und auf 1 m Abstand reducirt. Störende Eisenwasser beeinträchtigten die Messungen, die mit dem primitiven Apparat natürlich nur rohe sein konnten, und daher beschränke ich mich darauf, die Resultate in abgerundeten Zahlen anzugeben. Vergleicht man die Horizontalkomponente der Anziehung, in 1 m Entfernung vom Pole, mit der Horizontalkomponente des Erdmagnetismus, so findet man bei dem Südende der Schienen der Pferdeeisenbahn Anziehung $= \frac{1}{4}$ des Erdmagnetismus, bei dem Nordende der Schienen der Südbahn denselben Werth, bei dem Tiefbrunnen der Kürassierkaserne Anziehung $= \frac{3}{4}$ des Erdmagnetismus, bei der Trainkaserne dagegen Anziehung fünfzehnmal so gross wie der Erdmagnetismus! Am 5. Mai mass ich den Magnetismus auf der Kürassierkaserne noch einmal, nachdem zur Hinablassung des kupfernen Filters neue Eisenmassen in die Brunnenröhre hineingeführt waren, und fand ihn wesentlich verstärkt. Die Anziehung ergab sich in 1 m Entfernung fünfmal so gross wie der Erdmagnetismus. Allerdings spricht der Umstand, dass die Magnetnadel hier eine starke Inklination von 68 Grad hat, dafür, dass senkrechte Eisenmassen unter gleichen Umständen stärker magnetisch werden als wagrechte, aber der auffallend starke Magnetismus des Tiefbrunnens der Trainkaserne erscheint als eine nicht genügend aufgeklärte Erscheinung. Schliesslich sei noch erwähnt, dass natürlich überall der Magnetismus in dem von der Theorie geforderten Sinne auftrat. Nennt man den Pol der Magnetnadel, welcher nahezu nach Norden zeigt, den Nordpol, so hatten die Tiefbrunnen oben einen Südpol ebenso das Südende der Pferdebahn, dagegen war das Nordende der Eisenbahn ein Nordpol.

Herr Rittmeister **Fleischer** machte darauf aufmerksam, dass bei den Bohrungen in der Trainkaserne Dynamitexplosionen angewandt seien und die Erschütterungen vielleicht zur Verstärkung des Magnetismus beigetragen hätten. Auch sei der Brunnen im Winter zugedeckt und unbeobachtet gewesen und daher vielleicht das allmähliche Entstehen des Magnetismus an demselben nicht früher bemerkt worden.

Sitzung am 11. Juni 1885.

Herr Professor L. **Hermann** hielt einen Vortrag über neuere Untersuchungen betreffend die thierische und menschliche Bewegung, besonders mit Hilfe der Momentan-Photographie.

Der Vortragende entwickelte die Principien der Gangtheorie der Gebrüder Weber, und die von ihnen angewandten Untersuchungsmethoden. Ferner erörterte er die besonders von Marey erfundenen graphischen Verfahren zur Registrirung sämmtlicher Acte und Grössen im menschlichen und thierischen Gange und im Fluge der Vögel. Sodann ging er auf die von Muybridge in San-Francisco zuerst eingeführte Methode der Momentan-Photographie, und auf deren Umgestaltung durch Marey näher ein, und zeigte Kopien so gewonnener Bilderreihen vor. Zum Schluss machte der Vortragende Bemerkungen über das Schwimmen, und über die mechanische Bedeutung der Schwimmblase der Fische.

Herr Dr. **Klien** sprach: „Ueber einige pflanzenphysiologische Versuche." Auf dem Gebiete der Erforschung der Pflanzenernährung bedient man sich vorzugsweise zweier Culturmethoden: der Wasser- und Sandcultur. Diese beiden Methoden unterscheiden sich dadurch von einander, dass bei ersterer nur destillirtes Wasser verwendet wird, in welchem die zur Anwendung kommenden Nährstoffe theils gelöst, theils suspendirt sind, während bei der Sandcultur ausgewaschener Sand als Medium zur Verwendung gelangt, der mit bestimmten Nährstoffen durchtränkt wird. Die Wassercultur hat aber gegenüber der andern den Vorzug, dass sie mit reinen Materialien arbeiten kann und auch die Pflanzen bis zur Wurzelspitze herunter sichtbar sind. Zur Ernährung und zum Aufbau des Pflanzenkörpers sind bestimmte Elementarstoffe absolut unentbehrlich, doch werden auch entbehrliche Elemente in geringeren, einige aber auch nicht selten in grösseren Mengen (Silicium, Mangam) von den Pflanzen aufgenommen.

Ausser Wasser sind es: Kali, Kalk, Magnesia, Eisenoxyd, Kohlensäure, Salpetersäure, Schwefelsäure, Phosphorsäure und Chlor, welche zur Ernährung chlorophyllgrüner Pflanzen durchaus nothwendig sind, und darum diese Stoffe — ausser Kohlensäure — in einer Normalnährstofflösung nicht fehlen dürfen. In geeigneter Weise kann man diese Nährstoffe etwa in folgenden Verbindungen und Mengenverhältnissen den Pflanzen in Lösung zuführen: 0,207 g Chlorkalium, 0,456 g salpetersauren Kalk, 0,171 g schwefelsaures Magnesia, 0,133 g phosphorsaures Eisenoxyd und 0,033 g phosphorsaures Kali. Die Kohlensäure, welche der Lösung nicht zugefügt wird, erhält die Pflanze in hinreichender Menge aus der atmosphärischen Luft. Der Referent hat in solcher Nährstofflösung, welche 1 g des genannten Salzgemisches in einem Liter Wasser gelöst enthielt, viele Pflanzen bis zur vollkommensten Entwickelung gebracht. Es wurden z. B. Zuckerrüben mit 15 pCt. Zucker, Kartoffelknollen mit 19 pCt. Stärke, die verschiedensten Getreidearten mit sehr schön ausgebildeten Körnern und auch Holzgewächse mehrere Jahre lang unter solchen Culturbedingungen erzogen. Fehlt natürlich nur einer der unentbehrlichen Nährstoffelemente, so wird das Wachsthum der Pflanze vollständig unterdrückt und es kann daher durch eine einseitige Zufuhr eines im Boden fehlenden Nährstoffelementes die Unfruchtbarkeit desselben eventuell plötzlich beseitigt werden. Ist somit die Wasserculturmethode recht dazu geeignet, für jeden in die Pflanze aufgenommenen Baustoff die Bedeutung nachforschen zu können, welche ihm in den im Organismus sich abspielenden Vorgängen zufällt, so benutzt man diese Methode auch mit Vortheil zur Nachforschung über die Wirkung verschiedener krankheitserregender Stoffe (Gifte) auf das Wachsthum der Pflanzen. In der hiesigen Versuchsstation wurden in der letzten Zeit mehrere derartige Arbeiten ausgeführt, welche auch praktische Bedeutung hatten. So wurde z. B. dem Referenten ein rhodanhaltiges Ammoniak-Superphosphat zur Prüfung eingeschickt, welches bei der Abscheidung des Ammoniaks aus dem Leuchtgase auf trocknem Wege gewonnen worden war und was eventuell im grossen Maassstabe fabricirt werden sollte, wenn dessen Gehalt an Rhodanammonium (Schwefelcyanammonium) den Kulturpflanzen nicht schädlich sein sollte. Der Düngungsversuch auf dem Felde hatte ergeben, dass nach erfolgter Düngung die Pflänzchen von Gerste und Hafer in den ersten Wochen auffallend zurückblieben, ein krankes Aussehen bekamen, die Blattspitzen braungelb wurden und vertrockneten. Nach einigen Wochen erholten sich zwar die Pflänzchen der mit dem rhodanhaltigen Dünger bestreuten Parzellen wieder und suchten den auf den anderen Flächen wachsenden Pflanzen nachzueilen. Immerhin konnte die verloren gegangene Vegetationszeit nicht wieder eingeholt werden, was eine geringere Ernteausbeute zur Folge hatte. Nebenbei wurden auch Wasserculturversuche in rhodanhaltiger Nährstofflösung angestellt und auch Gerste und Hafer als Versuchspflanzen gewählt. Wo einem Liter Nährstofflösung 0,09 g reines Rhodanammonium zugefügt worden war, begannen die Keimpflänzchen bald an zu kränkeln und gingen nach und nach zu Grunde, während eine gleiche Anzahl Pflänzchen nach dem Hinzufügen von reinem schwefelsaurem Ammoniak, welches derselben Menge Stickstoff im Rhodanammonium entsprach, sich kräftig weiterentwickelten. Bei älteren Pflanzen mit 6—8 Blättchen schienen obige Mengen Rhodan keinen schädlichen Einfluss auszuüben, doch erkrankten sie bald bei Vermehrung des Rhodans um das Doppelte und selbst bei fast ausgewachsenen Pflanzen führte eine Zufuhr von 0,1 g pro Liter nach einiger Zeit den Tod herbei, während schwefelsaures Ammoniak in ziemlich grossen Mengen immer mit günstigem Erfolge der Nährstofflösung beigegeben werden konnte. Namentlich in den Blattspitzen der in rhodanhaltiger Lösung erzogenen Pflanzen konnte die Gegenwart von Rhodan mittelst Eisenchloridlösung mit grösster Schärfe nachgewiesen werden und nehmen somit die Pflanzen Rhodan in unveränderter Form auf. Nach den Untersuchungsresultaten scheint es, als wenn die Zersetzung des Rhodans unter dem Einfluss des Lichtes im oberirdischen Theile der Pflanze vor sich ginge und die Zersetzungsprodukte erst störend wirkten. — Vom Referenten wurden zwei gleichalterige Haferpflanzen vorgezeigt, von denen die eine zu einem Liter Nährstofflösung 0,1 g reines Rhodanammonium vor 14 Tagen zugefügt bekommen hatte, während in die Lösung der anderen Pflanze anstatt Rhodanammonium die entsprechende Menge schwefelsaures Ammoniak gegeben worden war. Bei der Rhodanpflanze hatte das Wachsthum aufgehört, die Blätter waren weiss-gelb geworden und die sonstige Krankheit zeigte grosse Aehnlichkeit mit derjenigen, welche man bei Einwirkung von schwefliger Säure auf das Pflanzenwachsthum beobachten kann. Die in rhodanfreier Lösung gewachsene Pflanze war vollkommen gesund und stand im üppigsten Wachsthum.

Es folgte die **General-Versammlung**, der nur die Wahl neuer Mitglieder oblag. Es wurden gewählt

zu ordentlichen Mitgliedern:

Herr Kaufmann Holldack,
" Eisenbahndirector Krüger,
" Kaufmann O. Meyer,
" Regierungs-Medicinalrath Dr. Nath;

zum auswärtigen Mitgliede:

Herr Dr. Hagedorn in Mohrungen.

Lottermoser.

Sitzung am 1. Oktober 1885.

Herr Dr. Klien hielt einen Vortrag über den Einfluss der Qualität des Bodens auf die Beschaffenheit der Pflanzen.

Er theilte zunächst mit, dass die von ihm in der letzten Sitzung vorgezeigte ³/₄ Meter hohe Haferpflanze, welche vom Samen aus in Nährstofflösung — also unter Ausschluss von Wurzelboden gewachsen sei — eine Höhe von 1,8 Meter erreicht und eine sehr grosse Samenmenge produzirt hätte.

Die Mineralstoffe, welche zur Ernährung und vollständigen Ausbildung der Pflanzen nöthig sind, sind nicht gleichartig bei sämmtlichen Pflanzen vertheilt, sondern die Menge und Zusammensetzung der mineralischen Nährstoffe (Asche) ändert sich bei den verschiedenen Pflanzenfamilien und ist auch in den einzelnen Pflanzentheilen zu verschiedenen Jahreszeiten eine andere. Zu ihrer Ernährung nehmen die Pflanzen aber auch meist viel grössere Mengen von Nährstoffen auf, als sie zur Ausbildung nöthig haben, wenn sie in einem sehr fruchtbaren Erdreiche wachsen. Der Aschengehalt der Pflanzen ist so gewissermassen mit ein Zeichen für die Ueppigkeit und Nährkraft eines Bodens. Die Fruchtbarkeit wird aber nicht allein durch den Gehalt an Gesammtnahrung im Boden bedingt, sondern sie hängt vor Allem von demjenigen Nährstoffe ab, welcher in geringster Menge darin vertreten ist; der im Minimum vorhandene Nährstoff muss darum vom Landwirth und Gärtner gesucht und künstlich ersetzt werden. Die Beschaffenheit der Pflanzen und ihrer Früchte wird wesentlich von der Nährstoffmischung im Boden beeinflusst, wofür der Redner zahlreiche Beispiele anführte. Sandig-lehmiger und nährstoffreicher Boden mit durchlassendem Untergrund, der sich leicht erwärmt und in lebhaftem Verkehr mit der Atmosphäre steht, giebt bei ausreichender Pflege und guter Bearbeitung mit das nahrhafteste und gesundeste Futter, während nährstoffarme, kalte und undurchlässige Böden sehr geringwerthige Futterpflanzen produziren. Stickstoffreichthum des Bodens begünstigt die Entwickelung der Blattorgane und liefert im Allgemeinen eiweissreiche Pflanzen mit einem relativ verminderten Gehalt an stickstofffreien Extractstoffen (Kohlenhydrate), während umgekehrt die Phosphorsäure in Begleitung von Kali, Magnesia etc. die Fruchtbildung und das Ausreifen der Pflanzenindividuen fördert. Der assimilirbare Stickstoff reagirt aber viel stärker auf den Pflanzenorganismus, als die genannten Mineralstoffe, so dass er bei einigem Vorwalten die die Fruchtbildung beeinträchtigt und das Ausreifen verhindert, oder im Uebermaass die Pflanzen zum Vergeilen bringt. Ueberreich an Stickstoff ist z. B. die Jauche. Darum hat man bei der Spüljaucherieselung, welche jetzt auch für Königsberg Interesse gewinnt, mit mancherlei Schwierigkeiten zu kämpfen. Hierzu kommt noch, dass in der Spüljauche der Gehalt an Kochsalz so bedeutend ist, dass es viele Pflanzen giebt, denen leicht zu grosse Mengen davon geboten werden. Die Beeinträchtigung wächst mit der geilen Entwickelung, weil bei andauernd trockener Hitze im Sommer die Salzkonzentration grösser wird und dann selbst weniger empfindliche Pflanzen geschädigt werden. Könnte die Spüljauche nur von 20 Menschen auf ein Hektar Land ausgebreitet werden, so würde man unter diesen Bedingungen allerdings bauen können, was Landwirthschaft und Gärtnerei überhaupt hervorzubringen vermögen. Hierauf muss aber eine Rieselwirthschaft, die nicht ad libitum rieseln kann, ein für allemal verzichten, zumal die gewöhnliche Schwemmkanalisation gerade zu den Zeiten die meiste Spüljauche liefert, wo sie am wenigsten für den Pflanzenbau zu gebrauchen ist. Die Auswahl der Pflanzen für Rieselland ist darum sehr wichtig. Zunächst eignen sich für solches Land am besten die Gemüsepflanzen, worauf die Grünfutterpflanzen und einige Gräser folgen. Das Rieselheu ist in Folge des hohen Salzgehaltes sehr hygroskopisch und lässt sich darum schwer aufbewahren und trocken erhalten. Bohnen, Erbsen, Wicken etc. werden leicht von Pilzkrankheiten befallen, die Hackfrüchte gern von Insekten und Würmern heimgesucht und verläuft der Reifeprozess bei den Getreidearten höchst ungleichmässig. Längere Zeit stark gerieselte Ländereien liefern schliesslich Pflanzen, die so reich an Stickstoff und Kali sind, dass sie als konzentrirte Jauche aufgefasst und zum Düngen anderer Ländereien benutzt werden könnten. Was der Landwirth unter Raubbau versteht, ist für die Rieselwirthschaft das rationelle Ziel hinsichtlich des Stickstoffs. Es muss nur dafür gesorgt werden, dass die im Minimum vorhandenen Nährstoffe (Phosphorsäure) ebenfalls den Rieselfeldern gegeben werden. Für Grossstädte ist die Spüljauchenrieselung ein noch immer nicht gelöstes Problem. Vor Allem hat man hier neben passender Oberflächengestaltung der Rieselfelder für die erforderliche Drainage und für wirksame Entwässerung zu sorgen. Dann müssten die Rieselanlagen so beschaffen sein, dass die Spüljauchenpächter ad libitum rieseln können, also dass sie zu jeder Zeit die ihnen überflüssig erscheinende Jauche zurückweisen dürfen; das erforderliche Quantum Flüssigkeit müssten sie jedoch bestimmt erhalten, wenn das Deficit auch nur durch Fluss- oder Grundwasser gedeckt würde. Endlich hätte der Rieselpächter noch dafür zu sorgen, dass das Nährstoffverhältniss im Rieselboden ein möglichst günstiges ist, so dass eine Zufuhr von geeigneten Hilfsdüngemitteln (Phosphate) anzuwenden wäre.

Unter diesen schwierigen Umständen würde dann auch die Spüljauchenrieselung äusserst lohnend werden, indem die meisten unserer Kulturpflanzen sich auf solchen Rieselboden von recht guter Beschaffenheit gewinnen lassen würden.

Herr Professor Dr. Langendorff bespricht die Abbe'schen Ansichten über das Zustandekommen des mikroskopischen Bildes und über die Grenzen des mikroskopischen Unterscheidungsvermögens und erörtert einige praktische Verbesserungen, die an neueren Mikroskopen getroffen sind.

Sitzung am 5. November 1885.

Herr Dr. Jentzsch legte Messtischblätter des Generalstabes vor, welche der Gesellschaft für die Herstellungskosten überlassen sind. Bereits früher sind solche schon der Gesellschaft vorgezeigt. Die erste Gruppe enthielt 160 Blätter und wurde für den Selbstkostenpreis uns abgegeben, die zweite Gruppe von 39 Blättern ist zum Geschenk gemacht, die dritte, jetzt vorliegende Gruppe von 27 Blättern wie schon erwähnt uns für die Herstellungskosten überlassen. Die Aufnahme von Ost- und Westpreussen ist fast fertig, doch sind erst wenige Blätter veröffentlicht. Die Blätter sind dadurch so werthvoll, dass man die Höhe jeden Ortes vom Meeresspiegel leicht ablesen kann, da sie Höhencurven enthalten.

Der Vorsitzende sprach dem Generalstabe den Dank der Gesellschaft aus.

Herr Oberlehrer Czwalina sprach über „Neuere Forschungen über Entstehung und Verbreitung der Gewitter". Nach Sohnke liegt an Gewittertagen die Grenzschicht in der Luft, über welcher Frost herscht, viel tiefer als sonst; das wird bewiesen durch Luftschichtfahrten und die Vergleichung der Temperatur an verschieden hohen Beobachtungsorten, die bei Gewittern eine viel schnellere Temperaturabnahme als sonst zeigen. Letzteres, von Sohnke für Freiburg im Breisgau und einen Ort des Schwarzwaldes nachgewiesen, zeigt sich nach Beobachtungen von Assmann ebenso deutlich in Thüringen, wo die Spitze des Inselberges mit verschiedenen Städten in Bezug auf die Temperaturerniedrigung verglichen wurde. Ueberhaupt aber senkt sich die Grenzfläche des Frostes nach Mittag beträchtlich. Aufsteigende Luftströme nun, durch die Erwärmung des Bodens veranlasst, und also auch Nachmittags am häufigsten auftretend, müssen um so höher sich erheben, je mehr Feuchtigkeit sie enthalten und in je kältere Luft sie kommen. Durch die Ausdehnung in grösserer Höhe wird ihr Wasserdampf zu kleinen Wassertröpfchen, dabei wird Wärme frei und diese giebt neuen Auftrieb. Kommen nun diese warmen, mit Wassertröpfchen beladenen Luftströme in kalte, Eiskrystallchen führende Schichten, so entsteht Gewitter. Man beobachtet auch immer über den aufsteigenden Cumuluswolken eine Cirrhusschicht, wenn ein Gewitter beginnt, und der Anfang desselbrn fällt bei weitem am häufigsten in die frühen Nachmittagsstunden, wo die aufsteigenden Luftströme am leichtesten in die nöthige Höhe gelangen. — Die Elektricität des Gewitters entsteht nun dadurch, dass die Wassertröpfchen und Eistheilchen sich aneinander reiben. Das ist leicht experimentell nachzuweisen, wenn man komprimirte feuchte Luft ausströmen lässt; die bei der Ausdehnung durch die Abkühlung entstehenden Wassertröpfchen machen alle Metalle durch ihre Reibung negativ, Eis positiv elektrisch; letzteres umsomehr, je kälter es ist, aber nicht mehr, wenn es mit einer Schmelzschicht von Wasser bedeckt ist, so dass also Wasser an Wasser reibend keine Elektricität hervorruft. Es sind aber bei diesen Versuchen besondere Vorsichtsmassregeln nothwendig: die Ausströmungsöffnung darf nicht zu klein sein und der Hahn muss sehr schnell geöffnet werden; sonst reiben sich die Wassertröpfchen bereits an der Ausströmungsröhre selbst und übertragen auf das entgegenstehende Metall ihre eigene positive Elektricität. Die Nichtbeachtung dieses Umstandes macht die Versuche von Koppe über Entstehung von Elektricität durch Reibung warmer und kalter Luftströme ungiltig, der auch das Gewitter nur auf letzteren Vorgang zurückführen wollte. Die mächtigen Entladungen des Blitzes werden dadurch erklärt, dass die kleinen Wassertröpfchen zu gröseren Regentropfen zusammenfliessen, die im Vergleich zu jenen eine viel kleinere Oberfläche haben, auf der also die Spannung der Elektricität sehr steigen muss. Von der Verbreitung der Gewitter handeln besonders v. Bezold für Bayern und Assmann für Mitteldeutschland. Ersterer hat die Akten der Feuerversicherung, die in Bayern staatlich ist, in Bezug auf zündende Blitze verglichen, und zieht nur solche in Betracht. Da zeigt sich nun zuerst, dass seit 50 Jahren die Häufigkeit der zündenden Blitze beträchtlich, fast auf das Dreifache, zugenommen hat; diese Zunahme ist aber nicht kontinuirlich, sondern wechselt mit Jahren geringerer Blitzhäufigkeit ab, und der Gang dieser Erscheinung zeigt eine merkwürdig genaue Uebereinstimmung mit der Periode der Sonnenflecken, so dass die Jahre, in welche das Maximum der letzteren fällt, die geringste Anzahl von zündenden Blitzen aufweisen. Die Städte zeigen dem flachen Lande gegenüber eine viel geringere, noch nicht halb so grosse Blitzgefahr. In Bayern ziehen die schadenbringenden Gewitter regelmässig auf zwei grossen Strassen vom Bodensee nach Osten und vom nördlichen Schwarzwalde nach Nordosten; der westliche Böhmerwald ist wenig von ihnen betroffen. In Mitteldeutschland entstehen Gewitter sehr oft lokal und breiten sich nicht weit aus, so dass, während jeder einzelne Beobachtungsort im Jahre nur wenig über 20 Gewitter hat, im ganzen Gebiet deren jährlich 150 gezählt werden. Sie bewirken dort eine gleichmässigere Vertheilung des Regens; in den gewitterfreien Monaten ist die Ostseite der Gebirge viel trockener als die Westseite; Hagelschläge aber treffen ganz vorzugsweise die Niederungen östlich von Gebirgszügen. Zum Schluss legt der Vortragende eine merkwürdige Photographie eines Blitzes vor, auf welcher sich drei parallele Züge nebeneinander zeigen und die wohl nur so zu erklären ist, dass der Blitz oscillirend mehrmals hintereinander dieselbe Bahn zurückgelegt hat. Er erwähnt dabei, dass er diese seltene Erscheinung am 2. Juli dieses Jahres selbst sehr schön zwischen Tapiau und Arnau vom Dampfer aus beobachtete. Wohl 50 bis 60 Blitze fuhren dieselbe Bahn 2- bis 3mal, mehrere 4- bis 5mal, ja einer sogar 8mal unmittelbar hintereinander vom Himmel zur Erde. Er forderte auf, auf ähnliche Vorkommnisse zu achten.

Herr Dr. Jentzsch sprach über den Nachweis einer Interglacialzeit für Norddeutschland.

Sitzung am 3. Dezember 1885.

Herr Professor Chun sprach über das Verhältniss zwischen Fläche und Masse im thierischen Körper. Er suchte nachzuweisen, dass der komplizirte Bau der höheren Thiere in erster Linie durch ihre Grösse bedingt wird insofern durch Bildung neuer Flächen das bei der Vergrösserung entstehende Missverhältniss zwischen Volumen und Oberfläche ausgeglichen wird. An der Hand der Rechnung wurde das Verhältniss zwischen Fläche und Masse eines Infusors als annähernd gleich demjenigen einer Schlange gefunden und schliesslich wurde betont, dass die Energie der Leistung gleich grosser Thiere bedeutender ist bei den mit günstiger entwickelter Fläche als bei den mit relativ ungünstiger ausgestatteten. Schliesslich wurde der Versuch gemacht, die Erscheinungen der Zelltheilung und Faltung der Keimblätter aus dem angedeuteten Gesichtspunkt zu erklären.

Herr Dr. Franz macht Mittheilungen über den teleskopischen, periodischen Tuttleschen Kometen, welcher in diesem Jahre nach den Rechnungen des Königsberger Astronomen Joh. Rahts wieder aufgefunden ist. Der Komet wurde am 9. Januar 1790 von Méchain in Paris entdeckt und von ihm selbst vom 9. Januar bis 1. Februar und von Messier vom 11. bis 22. Januar beobachtet. Méchains Beobachtungen sind aber nirgends veröffentlicht worden. Im Jahre 1858 wurde am 4. Januar von Tuttle in Cambridge bei Boston (Mass.) und unabhängig davon am 11. Januar von Bruhns in Berlin ein Komet entdeckt, dessen Elemente grosse Aehnlichkeit mit denen des Méchainschen Kometen von 1790 zeigten. Die Identität beider Kometen, die von Tuttle in Amerika und von Pape in Europa vermuthet war, wurde zur Gewissheit erhoben, als aus den Beobachtungen von 1858 folgte, dass der Lauf des Kometen einer parabolischen Bahn nicht angeschlossen werden konnte, sondern eine Ellipse mit einer Umlaufszeit von nahe 14 Jahren erforderte. In der Zwischenzeit war der Komet viermal und zwar in den Jahren 1803, 1817, 1830 und 1844 unbemerkt zum Perihel zurückgekehrt. Im Jahre 1830 hätte er wohl beobachtet werden können; allein da er nur in den Morgenstunden vor Sonnenaufgang sichtbar war, blieb er unentdeckt. In den übrigen 3 Jahren und ebenso bei der diesjährigen Erscheinung war er kaum sichtbar, weil die Richtung von der Erde nach dem Kometen nahe an der Sonne vorbeiging und der Komet weit von der Erde entfernt blieb. Nun unternahmen gleichzeitig Clausen in Dorpat und Friedrich Tischler in Königsberg die schwierige Aufgabe, durch Berechnung der Störungen, welche der Komet zwischen 1790 und 1858 von den Planeten erlitten hatte, die beiden Erscheinungen von 1790 und 1858 mit einander zu verbinden. Am genauesten wurden die Störungen von Tischler berechnet und so Fundamente geschaffen, mit Hilfe derer eine Vorausberechnung für die nächste Erscheinung des Kometen möglich war. Tischler, der leider im französischen Kriege 1870 fiel, hat auch kurze Zeit vor seinem Tode noch die Bahnelemente für 1871 berechnet, und nachdem dieselben in seinen hinterlassenen Papieren von Luther aufgefunden waren, gelang es nach einer von Hind in Greenwich daraus berechneten Aufsuchungstabelle den beiden Beobachtern Borelly in Marseille und Winneke in Karlsruhe, den Kometen am 12. beziehungsweise 15. Oktober 1871 wieder aufzufinden. Er wurde auf der nördlichen Halbkugel bis zum 15. Dezember und in Kapstadt bis zum 30. Januar 1872 beobachtet. Diese neuen Beobachtungen suchte nun Rahts, dem der Vortragende die vorstehenden Mittheilungen im wesentlichen verdankte, mit denen von 1858 möglichst gut in Verbindung zu bringen, und mit Hilfe der dadurch sich ergebenden Bahnelemente berechnete er sorgfältig die Störungen von Mars, Jupiter und Saturn nach der Hansen-Tietjenschen Methode, während er die Störungen von Merkur, Venus, Erde und Uranus nach der Besselschen Methode dadurch berücksichtigte, dass er den Kometen auf den gemeinsamen Schwerpunkt derselben und der Sonne bezog. Aus den sich so ergebenden Bahnelementen leitete Rahts eine Ephemeride ab, nach der der Komet am 8. August 1885 von Perrotin in Nizza aufgefunden und bis zum 22. August zwölfmal dort beobachtet wurde. Der Komet war nur in jeder Nacht 10 bis 15 Minuten lang schwach sichtbar, denn kaum war er nach seinem Aufgange sichtbar geworden, so verschwand er auch bald in der anbrechenden Morgendämmerung. So ist es nur der genauen Vorausberechnung (der Komet wich von dem vorausberechneten Orte nur 12 Sekunden in Rektascension und 5 Bogenminuten in Deklination ab) zu verdanken, dass es gelang, den Kometen in der diesjährigen, so ungünstigen Erscheinung wenigstens auf einer Sternwarte wieder aufzufinden.

Herr Dr. Franz machte dann einige kurze Mittheilungen über den Andromedanebel. Von diesem hellen, selbst mit blossem Auge sichtbaren Nebelfleck und seinen beiden Nachbarnebeln legte er eine schöne Zeichnung vor, die nach Beobachtungen am grossen Refraktor zu Cambridge bei Boston (Mass.) von Trourelot gemacht ist. Nahe bei der dichtesten Stelle des Nebels leuchtete plötzlich am 16. August 1885 ein neuer Stern 6. bis 7. Grösse auf, auf den Dr. Hartwig in Dorpat zuerst aufmerksam machte und der bald immer schwächer wurde, so dass er im Anfang Dezember 12. Grösse und kaum noch sichtbar war. Sein Ort wurde mit dem hiesigen Heliometer, so oft es anging, gemessen.

Auf Anregung des Herrn Professor Caspary wurde noch über den prachtvollen Sternschnuppenfall vom 27. November 1885 berichtet, der durch den Durchgang der Erde durch einen Theil, vermuthlich den ersten Kopf des Bielaschen Kometen verursacht wurde und eine Wiederholung des Phänomens vom 27. November 1872 war. Trotz vielfach trüben Himmels zählte Dr. Franz 300 Sternschnuppen in 14 und nachher ebenso viele in 9 Minuten und fand als Radiant derselben: Rektascension 24° 27′, Deklination 44° 17′ für 7 Uhr Abends. Hieraus und aus der Umlaufszeit des Bielaschen Kometen leitete er folgende Elemente ab:

Periheldurchgang	1885 Dezember 27,9
mittlere tägliche Bewegung . .	536″ 06′
Neigung	13° 12′
Knoten	245° 42′
Perihel	111° 0′
Excentricitätswinkel	49° 6′

welche gut mit den Elementen des Bielaschen Kometen übereinstimmen und aus denen eine Ephemeride zur Aufsuchung der Kometen auf der südlichen Halbkugel abgeleitet wurde.

Herr Dr. Jentzsch knüpfte an den Vortrag Bemerkungen über Meteoriten an, die theils aus nickelhaltigem Eisen theils aus anderen Gesteinen mit schön krystallisirten Mineralien wie Olivin bestehen.

Derselbe legte Quarz mit eingesprengtem Golde aus Venezuela vor, ein Geschenk des Herrn Simski, dann Photographien von Sprudellöchern und schliesslich einen Atlas von Gesteinphotographien, ein Geschenk des Verfassers Dr. Lehmann. Es ist schwierig Gesteine abzubilden oder zu photographiren. Dr. Lehmann hatte dieselben angeschliffen und dann photographiren lassen, durch dieses Verfahren war die Struktur deutlich zu erkennen. Dr. Jentzsch sprach über die Bildung krystallisirter Schiefer und kam zu dem Schluss, dass es mechanische Ursachen sind, die zur Bildung derselben Anlass gegeben haben.

Es wurde zur **General-Versammlung** übergegangen und die Wahl neuer Mitglieder zunächst vorgenommen.

Zu ordentlichen Mitgliedern wurden gewählt:

1. Herr Privatdocent Dr. Brandt,
2. „ Direktor Busch (leider bereits verstorben),
3. „ Hauptmann Donisch,
4. „ Dr. Gisevius,
5. „ Professor Dr. Hahn,
6. „ Dr. Rahts, Assistent an der Sternwarte,
7. „ Professor Dr. Stieda,
8. „ Oberlehrer Dr. Wittrin.

Zu auswärtigen Mitgliedern:

1. Herr Geologe Dr. Ebert in Neustadt W.-P.,
2. „ Dr. Kade in Berlin.

Schliesslich erfolgte die Wahl des Vorstandes durch die vorgeschriebene Zettelwahl. Der bisherige Vorstand wurde einstimmig wiedergewählt, so dass derselbe für das nächste Jahr zusammengesetzt ist wie folgt:

Präsident: Sanitätsrath Dr. Schiefferdecker,
Direktor: Medizinalrath Professor Dr. Möller,
Sekretair: Stadtrath Lottermoser,
Kassenkurator: Kommerzienrath Weller,
Rendant: Hofapotheker Hagen,
Bibliothekar und auswärtiger Sekretair: Dr. Tischler.

Lottermoser.

Bericht für 1885

über die

Bibliothek der physikalisch-ökonomischen Gesellschaft

von

Dr. Otto Tischler.

Die Bibliothek befindet sich im Provinzial-Museum der Gesellschaft, Lange Reihe 7, 2 Treppen hoch. Bücher werden an die Mitglieder gegen vorschriftmässige Empfangszettel Vormittags bis 12 und Nachmittags von 2 Uhr an ausgegeben. Dieselben müssen spätestens nach 3 Monaten zurückgeliefert werden.

Verzeichniss

derjenigen Gesellschaften, mit welchen die physikalisch-ökonomische Gesellschaft in Tauschverkehr steht, sowie der im Laufe des Jahres 1885 eingegangenen Werke.

(Von den mit † bezeichneten Gesellschaften kam uns 1885 keine Sendung zu.)

Die Zahl der mit uns in Tauschverkehr stehenden Gesellschaften hat 1885 um folgende 9 zugenommen:

Frankfurt a. M. Verein für Geschichte und Alterthumskunde.
Lübben. Niederlausitzer Gesellschaft für Anthropologie und Urgeschichte.
Meiningen. Hennebergischer alterthumsforschender Verein.
Worms. Alterthumsverein.
Toulouse. Société archéologique du Midi de la France.
Florenz. Sezione fiorentina della Società Africana d'Italia.
Budapest. Archäologische Abtheilung des königl. Ungarischen National-Museums.
Trentschin. Naturwissenschaftlicher Verein des Trentschiner Comitats.
Lissabon. Section des travaux géologiques de Portugal.

Nachstehendes Verzeichniss bitten wir zugleich als Empfangsbescheinigung ansehen zu wollen statt jeder besonderen Anzeige. Besonders danken wir noch den Gesellschaften, welche auf Reclamation durch Nachsendung älterer Jahrgänge dazu beigetragen haben, Lücken in unserer Bibliothek auszufüllen. In gleicher Weise sind wir stets bereit solchen Reclamationen nachzukommen, soweit es der Vorrath der früheren Bände gestattet, den wir immer zu ergänzen streben, so dass es von Zeit zu Zeit möglich wird, auch augenblicklich ganz vergriffene Hefte nachzusenden.

Diejenigen Herren Mitglieder der Gesellschaft, welche derselben ältere Jahrgänge der Schriften zukommen lassen wollen, werden uns daher im Interesse des Schriftentausches zu grossem Danke verpflichten.

Wir werden fortan allen Gesellschaften, mit denen wir in Correspondenz stehen, unsere Schriften franco durch die Post zusenden und bitten soviel als möglich den gleichen Weg einschlagen zu wollen, da sich dies viel billiger herausstellt als der Buchhändlerweg. Etwaige Beischlüsse bitten wir ergebenst an die resp. Adresse gütigst befördern zu wollen.

Belgien.

1. Brüssel. Académie Royale des sciences des lettres et des arts. 1) Bulletin, 3. Serie 6 (Année 52). 3. Serie 7, 8 (53). 2) Mémoires couronnés et Mémoires des savants Etrangers in 4° 45, 46. 3) Mém. cour. et autres Mém. in 8° 36. 4) Mémoires de l'Académie in 4° 45. 5) Annuaire 50, 51 (1884, 85).
2. Brüssel. Académie Royale de Médecine. Bulletin, 3. Serie 19 (1885).
3. Brüssel. Société Entomologique Belge. Annales 28, 29 (1884, 85).
4. Brüssel. Société malacologique de Belgique. 1) Annales 15 (1880) 18 (1883). 2) Procès-verbaux (auch in den Annalen enthalten) 14 (1885) p. 1—79.
5. Brüssel. Société Royale de botanique de Belgique. Bulletin 24 (1885).
† 6. Brüssel. Commissions Royales d'art et d'archéologie.
7. Brüssel. Société Belge de Microscopie. 1) Annales 9. 2) Bulletin (auch in den Annalen enthalten) 11 1 — 12 1.
8. Brüssel. Société Belge de Géographie. Bulletin 9 (1885).
† 9. Brüssel. Observatoire Royal.
10. Brüssel. Société d'Anthropologie. Bulletin 3 (1884, 85).
11. Lüttich. Société Royale des sciences. Mémoires, 2. Serie 12.
12. Lüttich. Société géologique de Belgique. 1) Annales 10, 11. Tables générales Tome 1—10. 2) Catalogue des ouvrages de géologie, de minéralogie et de paléontologie et des cartes géologiques qui se trouvent dans les principales bibliothèques de Belgique, par Dewalque. Liège. 1884.

† 13. Lüttich. Institut archéologique.

† 14. Namur. Société archéologique.

Dänemark.

15. Kopenhagen. Kongelig Dansk Videnskabernes Selskab (Société Royale des sciences). 1) Oversigt over Forhandlinger. Bulletin 1884 2. 3. 1885 1. 2. 2) Skrifter, naturvidenskabelig og matematisk Afdeling (Mémoires, Classe des sciences) 6 Raekke I 11, II 7, III 1, 3.

† 16. Kopenhagen. Naturhistorisk Forening.

17. Kopenhagen. Kongelig Dansk Nordisk Oldskrift Selskab (Société royale des antiquaires du Nord). 1) Aarböger for Nordisk Oldkyndighed og Historie 1884 4. Tillaeg. 1885 1–3.

18. Kopenhagen. Botanisk Forening, Botanisk Tidskrift 14 4.

Deutsches Reich.

† 19. Altenburg. Naturforschende Gesellschaft des Osterlandes.

† 20. Augsburg. Naturhistorischer Verein.

† 21. Bamberg. Naturforschende Gesellschaft.

† 22. Bamberg. Historischer Verein für Oberfranken.

23. Berlin. K. Preussische Akademie der Wissenschaften. 1) Sitzungsberichte 1884 40 bis Schluss. 1885 1–39. 2) Abhandlungen. Physikalische 1884 (2 Hefte).

24. Berlin. Botanischer Verein für die Provinz Brandenburg. Verhandlungen Jahrgang 26 (1884).

25. Berlin. Deutsche geologische Gesellschaft. Zeitschrift 36 4 (1884). 37 1, 2, 3. (1885).

26. Berlin. Verein zur Beförderung des Gartenbaues in den Preussischen Staaten. Gartenzeitung, Jahrgang IV 1885.

† 27. Berlin. Physikalische Gesellschaft.

28. Berlin. Kgl. Landes-Oekonomie-Collegium. Landwirthschaftliche Jahrbücher 14 (1885).

29. Berlin. Gesellschaft naturwissenschaftlicher Freunde. Sitzungsberichte 1884.

30. Berlin. Gesellschaft für Anthropologie, Ethnologie und Urgeschichte. Verhandlungen 1884 Octb. bis Decbr., 1885 Jan. bis Mai.

31. Berlin. Geologische Landesanstalt und Bergakademie. 1) Geologische Specialkarte von Preussen und den Thüringischen Staaten (1/25000), je 1 Blatt, mit 1 Heft Erläuterungen. Gradabtheilung 45 13–15, 19–21, 25–27. 55 24, 30. 56 19, 23–25, 29, 30. 57 19–21, 25–27. 2) Abhandlungen zur geologischen Specialkarte IV 4, V 2 mit Atlas, V 3, 4, VI 1 mit Atlas, VI 2, VII 1.

32. Berlin. Kaiserlich Statistisches Amt. 1) Monatshefte 1885. 2) Statistik des Deutschen Reichs. Neue Folge. 5 (Landw. Betriebstatistik n. d. allg. Berufszählung 5/6 1882). 6 (Gewerbestatistik n. d. Berufszählung 5/6 1882. 13 (Kriminalst. 1883). 14 (Ausw. Waarenverkehr 1884). 15 (Ausw. Waaren-

verkehr 1884 2). 16 2 (D. Wasserstrassen 1884). 17 1 (St. der Seeschifffahrt 1884.) 3) Statistisches Jahrbuch für das Deutsche Reich 6 (1885).

33. Berlin. K. Preussisches Statistisches Bureau. Zeitschrift 25 (1885) 1—3.

34. Bonn. Naturhistorischer Verein der Preussischen Rheinlande und Westfalens. 1) Verhandlungen 41 2 (1884), 42 1. 2) Autoren und Sachregister zu den Bänden 1—40.

† 35. Bonn. Verein von Alterthumsfreunden im Rheinlande.

36. Braunsberg. Historischer Verein für Ermland. Zeitschrift für die Geschichte und Alterthumskunde des Ermlandes VIII 1 (1884).

† 37. Braunschweig. Verein für Naturwissenschaft.

38. Bremen. Naturwissenschaftlicher Verein. Abhandlungen 9 2.

39. Bremen. Geographische Gesellschaft. Deutsche geograph. Blätter. VIII (1885).

40. Breslau. Schlesische Gesellschaft für vaterländische Cultur. Jahresbericht 62.

41. Breslau. Verein für das Museum Schlesischer Alterthümer. Schlesiens Vorzeit in Wort und Bild. Bericht 58, 59 (Bd. IV 14, 15).

42. Breslau. Verein für Schlesische Insectenkunde. Zeitschrift für Entomologie 10.

43. Breslau. K. Oberbergamt. Production der Bergwerke, Salinen und Hütten im Preussischen Staate i. J. 1884.

† 44. Chemnitz. Naturwissenschaftliche Gesellschaft.

45. Chemnitz. Kgl. Sächsisches meteorologisches Institut. Jahrbuch II (1884).

† 46. Coburg. Anthropologischer Verein.

† 47. Colmar. Société d'histoire naturelle.

48. Danzig. Naturforschende Gesellschaft. 1) Schriften. Neue Folge VI 2. 2) Bericht über die Verwaltung der Sammlungen des Westpr. Provinzial-Museums 1885.

49. Darmstadt. Verein für die Erdkunde und mittelrheinisch geologischer Verein. Notizblatt. Neue Folge 5.

50. Darmstadt. Historischer Verein für das Grossherzogthum Hessen. 1) Archiv für Hessische Geschichte und Alterthumskunde 15 3. 2) Quartalsblätter 1884. 1885 1, 2. 3) Die Einhard Basilika zu Steinbach.

† 51. Dessau. Naturhistorischer Verein.

52. Donaueschingen. Verein für Geschichte und Naturgeschichte der Baar und angrenzenden Landestheile. Schriften 5 (1885).

53. Dresden. Verein für Erdkunde. Jahresbericht 21.

54. Dresden. Naturwissenschaftliche Gesellschaft Isis. Festschrift zur Feier des 50 jährigen Bestehens 14/5 1885.

† 55. Dresden. Gesellschaft für Natur- und Heilkunde. Jahresbericht 1884/85.

† 56. Dürkheim a. d. H. Pollichia, naturwissenschaftlicher Verein der Rheinpfalz.

57. Eberswalde. Forstakademie. 1) Beobachtung der forstlich meteorologischen Stationen. Jahrgang 10 (1884) 7—12. 11 (85) 1—6. 2) Jahresbericht 10 (1884).

† 58. Elberfeld. Naturwissenschaftliche Gesellschaft.

59. Emden. Naturforschende Gesellschaft. Jahresbericht 1883/84.

60. Emden. Gesellschaft für bildende Kunst und vaterländische Alterthümer. Jahrbuch VI 2.

61. Erfurt. Akademie gemeinnützíger Wissenschaften. Jahrbuch. Neue Folge. Heft 12, 13.
† 62. Erlangen. Physikalisch-medicinische Societät.
† 63. Frankfurt a. M. Senkenbergische naturforschende Gesellchaft.
64. Frankfurt a. M. Physikalischer Verein. Jahresbericht 1883/84.
65. Frankfurt a. M. Verein für Geographie und Statistik.
66. Frankfurt a. M. Verein für Geschichte und Alterthumskunde. 1) Mittheilungen IV, V 1—3, VI 1, 2. VII. 2) Verzeichniss der Abhandlungen und Notizen zur Geschichte Frankfurts. 3) Donner v. Richter und Riese: Heddernheimer Ausgrabungen. Frankfurt 1885.
67. Freiburg im Breisgau. Naturforschende Gesellschaft. Verhandlungen 8 3.
† 68. Fulda. Verein für Naturkunde.
† 69. Gera. Verein von Freunden der Naturwissenschaften.
70. Giessen. Oberhessische Gesellschaft für Natur- und Heilkunde. Hoffmann: Resultate der wichtigsten pflanzen-phänologischen Beobachtungen in Europa. Giessen 1885.
† 71. Görlitz. Naturforschende Gesellschaft.
72. Görlitz. Oberlausitzische Gesellschaft der Wissenschaften. Neues Lausitzisches Magazin 61 1.
73. Göttingen. K. Gesellschaft der Wissenschaften. Nachrichten 1884.
74. Greifswald. Naturwissenschaftlicher Verein für Vorpommern und Rügen. Mittheilungen 16.
75. Greifswald. Geographische Gesellschaft. Jahresbericht 2 (1883—84).
76. Güstrow. Verein der Freunde der Naturgeschichte in Meklenburg. Archiv 38 (1884).
77. Halle. Kaiserlich Leopoldino - Carolinische Deutsche Akademie der Naturforscher. Leopoldina 21 (1885).
78. Halle. Naturforschende Gesellschaft. 1) Abhandlungen 16 3. 2) Berichte über die Sitzungen 1884.
79. Halle. Naturwissenschaftlicher Verein für Sachsen und Thüringen. Zeitschrift für Naturwissenschaften. 4. Folge 3 6. 4 1—4.
† 80. Halle. Verein für Erdkunde.
† 81. Hamburg. Naturwissenschaftlicher Verein von Hamburg-Altona.
82. Hamburg. Verein für naturwissenschaftliche Unterhaltung. Verhandlungen 1882—82.
83. Hamburg. Geographische Gesellschaft. Mittheilungen 1885.
† 84. Hanau. Wetterauische Gesellschaft für die gesammte Naturkunde.
85. Hannover. Naturhistorische Gesellschaft. Jahresbericht 33 (1882—83.)
86. Hannover. Historischer Verein für Niedersachsen. 1) Nachricht 27. 2) Africa auf der Ebstorfer Weltkarte von Sommerbrodt.
87. Hannover. Geographische Gesellschaft. Jahresbericht 6 (1884/85).
† 88. Hannover. Gesellschaft für Microscopie.
† 89. Heidelberg. Naturhistorisch-medicinischer Verein.
90. Jena. Gesellschaft für Medicin und Naturwissenschaft. Jenaische Zeitschrift für Naturwissenschaft 19 1—3. Suppl. 1, 2 (Sitzungsberichte).

91. Insterburg. Alterthumsgesellschaft. 1) v. Schack: Der Kriegszug des Ordens nach der Insel Gothland und die Vernichtung der Vitalienbrüder im Jahre 1398 (Vorlesung a 6/3 1885). 2) Hoening: Der Generalbescheid des Insterburgischen Amts i. J. 1638 (Vortrag 30/1 1885). 3) Polenz: Chronik der in Ostpreussen gelegenen Seiner Hoheit dem Herzoge von Anhalt gehörigen Norkittenschen Güter (abgeschlossen 1881). 4) Jahresbericht 1884/85. 5) Verzeichniss der Sammlungen 1885. 6) Ehmcke: Die ausgestorbenen und aussterbenden Thiere Ostpreussens.

92. Insterburg. Landwirthschaftlicher Centralverein für Littauen und Masuren. 1) Georgine, landwirthschaftliche Zeitschrift. Jahrgang 53 (1885). 2) Jahresbericht 1884.

† 93. Karlsruhe. Naturwissenschaftlicher Verein.

94. Karlsruhe. Grossherzogliches Alterthums-Museum. 1) Die Grossherzogliche Alterthumssammlung in Karlsruhe. Antike Bronzen. Darstellungen in unveränderlichem Lichtdrucke. Herausgegeben von Wagner. Neue Folge II, III. 2) Wagner: Hügelgräber und Urnenfriedhöfe in Baden und Karlsruhe 1885.

† 95. Kassel. Verein für Naturkunde.

† 96. Kassel. Verein für Hessische Geschichte und Landeskunde.

† 97. Kiel. Universität.

98. Kiel. Naturwissenschaftlicher Verein für Schleswig-Holstein. Schriften 6 1.

99. Kiel. Ministerial-Commission zur Erforschung der Deutschen Meere. Ergebnisse der Beobachtungsstationen an den Deutschen Küsten. 1884.

† 100. Kiel. Schleswig-Holsteinisches Museum für vaterländische Alterthümer.

† 101. Klausthal. Naturwissenschaftlicher Verein Maja.

102. Königsberg. Alt-Preussische Monatsschrift, herausgegeben von Reicke und Wichert. 22 (1885).

103. Königsberg. Ostpreussischer Landwirthschaftlicher Central-Verein. Königsberger Land- und forstwirthschaftliche Zeitung 21 (1884).

† 104. Landshut. Botanischer Verein.

105. Leipzig. Sächsische Gesellschaft der Wissenschaften. 1) Abhandlungen der mathematisch-physikalischen Klasse 13 2–4. 2) Berichte über die Verhandlungen der math.-phys. Klasse 1884, 1885.

106. Leipzig. Verein für Erdkunde. 1) Mittheilungen 1884. 2) Geistbeck (Dr. Alois): Die Seen der Deutschen Alpen, mit Atlas 1883.

107. Leipzig. Naturforschende Gesellschaft. Sitzungsberichte. Jahrgang 11 (1884).

108. Leipzig. Museum für Völkerkunde. Bericht 12 (1884).

109. Leipzig. Geologische Landesuntersuchung des Königreichs Sachsen. Specialkarte des Königreichs Sachsen 1/25000, je 1 Blatt mit 1 Blatt Erläuterungen. Blatt 13, 30, 41, 57, 124, 135, 144, 151, 152, 154—156.

110. Lübben. Nieder-Lausitzer Gesellschaft für Anthropologie und Urgeschichte. Mittheilungen Heft 1.

111. Lübeck. Naturhistorisches Museum. Jahresbericht 1884.

† 112. Lüneburg. Naturwissenschaftlicher Verein für das Fürstenthum Lüneburg.

113. Magdeburg. Naturwissenschaftlicher Verein. Jahresber. 13—15 (1882—84).
114. Mannheim. Verein für Naturkunde. Jahresbericht 1883/84.
† 115. Marburg. Gesellschaft zur Beförderung der gesammten Naturwissenschaften.
116. Marienwerder. Historischer Verein für den Regierungsbezirk Marienwerder. Zeitschrift Heft 13—15.
117. Meiningen. Hennebergischer alterthumsforschender Verein. 1) Beiträge zur Geschichte deutschen Alterthums 4 (1841), 5 (1845). Neue Beiträge 1 (1858), 3 (1867), 4 (1883). 2) Einladungsschrift zur 15. Jahresfestfeier 14/11 1847. 3) Einladungsschrift zur Feier des 50jährigen Bestehens 1882.
118. Metz. Académie. Mémoires, 2 Periode 62 (3. Serie 10) 1880/81.
119. Metz. Société d'histoire naturelle. Bulletin. 2. Ser. 16.
120. Metz. Verein für Erdkunde. Jahresbericht 6 (1883—84).
121. München. K. Bairische Akademie der Wissenschaften. 1) Sitzungsberichte der mathematisch-physikalischen Klasse 1885 1—3. 2) Abhandlungen der mathematisch-physikalischen Klasse 15 2.
122. München. Geographische Gesellschaft. Jahresbericht 9 (1884).
123. München. Historischer Verein von Oberbayern. 1) Oberbayrisches Archiv für vaterländische Geschichte 42. 2) Jahresbericht 46, 47 (1883—84).
124. Münster. Westphälischer Provinzialverein für Wissenschaft und Kunst. Jahresbericht 13 (1884).
† 125. Neisse. Philomathie.
126. Nürnberg. Naturhistorische Gesellschaft. Jahresbericht 1884.
127. Nürnberg. Germanisches Museum. 1) Anzeiger I 1 (1884). 2) Mittheilungen I 1 (1884). 3) Katalog der im Germ. Mus. befindlichen Glasgemälde aus älterer Zeit 1884. 4) v. Borch: Beiträge zur Rechtsgeschichte des Mittelalters mit besonderer Rücksicht auf die Ritter und Dienstmannen fürstlicher und gräflicher Herkunft.
128. Offenbach. Verein für Naturkunde. Bericht 24, 25.
† 129. Oldenburg. Oldenburger Landesverein für Alterthumskunde.
130. Osnabrück. Naturwissenschaftlicher Verein. Jahresbericht 6 (1883—84).
† 131. Passau. Naturhistorischer Verein.
132. Posen. Gesellschaft der Freunde der Wissenschaften.
133. Regensburg. Zoologisch-mineralogische Gesellschaft. Correspondenzblatt 38.
134. Regensburg. K. Bairische botanische Gesellschaft. Flora, allgemeine botanische Zeitung. Neue Reihe 42 (ganze 67) 1884.
† 135. Reichenbach im Vogtlande. Vogtländischer Verein für allgemeine und specielle Naturkunde.
136. Schmalkalden. Verein für Hennebergische Geschichte und Landeskunde. Zeitschrift. Supplementheft 3 (Geisthirt: Historia Schmalcaldica III).
137. Schwerin. Verein für Mecklenburgische Geschichte und Alterthumskunde. Jahrbücher und Jahresberichte 50 (1885).
138. Sondershausen. Botanischer Verein für Thüringen. Irmischia, Correspondenzblatt des Vereins 4 12, 5 (1885) 1—9.
139. Stettin. Entomologischer Verein. Entomologische Zeitung. Jahrgang 45.

140. Stettin. Gesellschaft für Pommersche Geschichte und Alterthumskunde. Baltische Studien 35.
141. Strassburg. Commission für die geologische Landesuntersuchung von Elsass-Lothringen. Abhandlungen zur geologischen Specialkarte. Band II 3 mit Atlas, III 1, IV 1, 2.
142. Stuttgart. Verein für vaterländische Naturkunde in Würtemberg. Jahreshefte 41.
143. Stuttgart. Königlich Statistisches Landes-Amt. Würtembergische Vierteljahrshefte für Landesgeschichte. Jahrgang 7 (1883).
† 144. Thorn. Towarzystwa Naukowego.
145. Tilsit. Litauische Literarische Gesellschaft. Mittheilungen Heft 10.
† 146. Trier. Gesellschaft für nützliche Forschungen.
147. Wiesbaden. Nassauischer Verein für Naturkunde. Jahrbücher 37.
148. Wiesbaden. Verein für Nassauische Alterthumskunde und Geschichtsforschung. Annalen 18.
149. Worms. Alterthumsverein. 1) Die Römische Abtheilung des Paulus-Museums zu Worms von A. Weckerling. 2) Geschichte des Archivs der weiland freien Stadt und freien Reichsstadt Worms (Boos: Bericht über Neuordnung des Archivs 1882). 3) Becker: Beiträge der Frei- und Reichsstadt Worms und und der daselbst seit 1527 errichteten höheren Schulen. 1880. 4) Soldau: Der Reichstag zu Worms 1521 (1883).
† 150. Würzburg. Physikalisch-medicinische Gesellschaft.
151. Zwickau. Verein für Naturkunde. Jahresbericht 1884.

Frankreich.

152. Albeville. Société d'Emulation. Bulletin 1881—84.
† 153. Amiens. Société Linnéenne du Nord de la France.
154. Apt. Société litéraire scientifique et artistique.
155. Auxerre. Société des sciences historiques et naturelles de l'Yonne. Bulletin 38 2.
156. Besançon. Société d'Emulation du Doubs. Mémoires 5. Serie 8 (1883).
† 157. Bordeaux. Académie nationale des sciences belles lettres et arts.
158. Bordeaux. Société Linnéenne. Actes 37 (4 Serie 7).
159. Bordeaux. Société des sciences physiques et naturelles. Mémoires 3. Serie 1.
160. Bordeaux. Société de géographie commerciale. Bulletin 2. Serie 8 (1885).
† 161. Caën. Société Linnéenne de Normandie.
† 162. Caën. Académie des sciences arts et belles lettres.
† 163. Caën. Association Normande.
† 164. Chambéry. Académie de Savoie.
165. Cherbourg. Société nationale des sciences naturelles et mathématiques. 1) Mémoires 24 (3. Ser. 4). 2) Catalogue de la Bibliothèque 3.
† 166. Dijon. Académie des sciences arts et belles lettres.

† 167. **Dijon.** Société d'agriculture et d'industrie agricole du département de la Côte d'or.
† 168. **La Rochelle.** Société des sciences naturelles de la Charente inférieure.
† 169. **Lille.** Société des sciences, de l'agriculture et des arts.
170. **Lyon.** Académie des sciences des helles lettres et des arts. Mémoires, Classe des sciences 27.
171. **Lyon.** Société Linnéenne. Annales, Nouvelle Série 30 1 1883.
172. **Lyon.** Société d'agriculture, d'histoire naturelle et des arts utiles. 5. Serie 6 (1883).
† 173. **Lyon.** Muséum d'histoire naturelle.
† 174. **Lyon.** Association des amis des sciences naturelles.
† 175. **Lyon.** Société d'anthropologie.
176. **Montpellier.** Académie des sciences et des lettres. Mémoires de la section de Médécine 8 3.
† 177. **Nancy.** Académie de Stanislas.
† 178. **Paris.** Académie des sciences.
179. **Paris.** Société centrale d'horticulture. Journal. 3. Serie 7 (1885).
† 180. **Paris.** Société de botanique de France.
181. **Paris.** Société de géographie. 1) Bulletin 1885. 2) Comte rendu des séances de la commission centrale 1885.
† 182. **Paris.** Société zoologique d'acclimation.
183. **Paris.** Société philomatique. Bulletin. 7. Serie 9 1–3. (1884–85).
184. **Paris.** Société d'Anthropologie. Bulletin. 3. Serie 7 4, 5, 8 1–3.
† 185. **Paris.** Ministère de l'Instruction publique.
186. **Paris.** Ecole polytechnique. Journal, Cahier 54.
187. **Rochefort.** Société d'agriculture des helles lettres et des arts.
† 188. **Semur.** Société des sciences historiques et naturelles.
† 189. **Toulouse.** Académie des sciences, inscriptions et helles lettres. Mémoires 8. Serie 6.
190. **Toulouse.** Société archéologique du midi de la France. Séances 1/4—22/7 1884.
191. **Alger.** Société algérienne de climatologie des sciences physiques et naturelles. Bulletin 21 (1884).

Grossbritannien und Colonieen.

192. **Cambridge.** Philosophical society. Proceedings V 1–4.
† 193. **Dublin.** Royal Irish Academy.
† 194. **Dublin.** Royal geological society of Ireland.
195. **Dublin.** Royal Dublin Society. Scientific transactions. 2. Ser. Vol. III 4–6.
196. **Edinburgh.** Botanical society. Transactions and Proceedings 15 2, 16 1 (1885).
197. **Edinburgh.** Geological society. Transactions IV 3, V 1.
198. **Glasgow.** Natural history society. Proceedings V 3, I 1.

† 199. Liverpool. Literary and philosophical Society.
200. London. Royal Society. 1) Proceedings 37, 38 235–39. 2) Philosophical transactions 175 1, 2. 3) List of Members 1/12 1884.
201. London. Linnean Society. 1) Journal of Zoology 17 103, 18, 19 106. 2) Journal of Botany 21 134–137. 3) List of Members 1884–85.
202. London. Henry Woodward. Geological Magazine. 2. Ser. Decade III. Vol. II (1885).
† 203. London. Nature.
204. London. Anthropological Institute of Great Britain and Ireland. Journal 14 4, 15 1, 2.
205. London. Chamber of Commerce. Journal IV 36–46.
† 206. Manchester. Philosophical society.
207. Calcutta. Asiatic Society of Bengal. 1) Journal 53 Part. I Special Number 1884. Part. II 3. 54. Part. I 1, 2. Part. II 1, 2. 2) Proceedings 1884 11. 1885 1–8. 3) Centenary Review of the Asiatic Society from 1784–1883.
208. Calcutta. Geological survey of India. 1) Memoirs in 8° 21. 2) Records 18 1–3. 3) Memoirs in 8° (Palaeontologia Indica) Ser. IV, Vol. I 4, 5. III 5. (Indian posttertiary Vertebrata). Ser. X, Vol. III 6. (Indian tertiary and posttertiary Vertebrata). Ser. XIII, Vol. IV 3, 4, 5. (Salt Range Fossils). Ser. XIV I 3 fasc. V (Tertiary and upper cretaceous fossiles of Western Sund).
† 209. Montreal. Royal Society of Canada.
† 210. Montreal. Geological and natural history survey of Canada.
† 211. Ottawa. Field naturalists club.
212. Shanghai. China branch of the Royal Asiatic society. Journal. New ser. 18 (1883). 19 (1884). 20 1–3. (85).
213. Sydney. Royal Society of N. S. Wales. 1) Journal and Proceedings 17 (1883). 18 (84). 2) Ferdinand v. Müller: Index perfectus ad Caroli Linnaei species plantarum nempe earum primam editionem. Melbourne 1880.
214. Toronto. Canadian Institute. Proceedings II 3. III 1, 2.
215. Wellington. New Zealand Institute. 1) Transactions and Proceedings 17 (1884). 2) Annual report on the Colonial Museum and laboratory 10 (1883/84).

Holland und Colonieen.

216. Amsterdam. Koninglijke Akademie van Wetenschapen. 1) Verslagen en Mededeelingen. Afdeeling Naturkunde 19, 20. 2) Jaarboek 1883.
217. Amsterdam. Koninglijke Zoologisk Genootschap „Natura artis magistra". Bijdragen tot de Dierkunde. Afl. 2.
218. s'Gravenhag. Nederlandsch Entomologische Vereeniging. Tijdschrift voor Entomologie 27 3, 4. 28 1, 2.
219. Groningen. Genootschap ter Bevoordering der naturkundigen Wetenschapen. Verslag 83, 84.
220. Haarlem. Hollandsche Maatschappij ter Bevordering van Nijverheid. Tijdschrift 4 Reeks. Deel 9 (1885).

221. **Haarlem.** Hollandsche Maatschappij ter Bevordering der naturkundigen Wetenschapen (Société Hollandaise des sciences). Archives néerlandaises des sciences exactes et naturelles 19 3–5. 20 1–3.
222. **Haarlem.** Musée Teyler. Archives 2. Ser. II 2.
† 223. **Leyden.** Herbier Royal.
224. **Leyden.** Nederlandsche Dierkundige Vereenigung. Tijdschrift IV 2–4.
† 225. **Luxembourg.** Institut Royal Grandducal.
† 226. **Luxembourg.** Section historique de l'Institut Royal Grand-ducal.
227. **Luxembourg.** Société de botanique. Mémoires 9—10 (1883—84).
228. **Nijmwegen.** Nederlandsche botanische Vereenigung. Nederlandsch Kruidkundig Archief 2. Ser. IV 3.
† 229. **Utrecht.** Physiologisch Laboratorium der Utrechtsche Hoogeschool.
† 230. **Utrecht.** Kon. Nederlandsch Meteorologisch Instituut.
231. **Batavia.** Kon. Naturkundige Vereeniging in Nederlandsch Indie. 1) Naturkundig Tijdschrift voor Nederl. Indie. 44 (8. Ser. 5). 2) Catalogus der Bibliothek.
† 232. **Batavia.** Bataviaasch Genootschap der Kunsten en Wetenschapen.
233. **Batavia.** Magnetisch en meterologisch Observatorium. 1) Regenwaarnemingen in Nederlandsch Indie. 6 (1884). 2) Observations made at the magnetical Observatory at Batavia VI 2 part 1, 2.

Italien.

234. **Bologna.** Accademia delle scienze. Memorie 3. Ser. 5.
235. **Catania.** Accademia Gioenia di scienze naturali. Atti 3. Ser. 18.
236. **Florenz.** Accademia economica agraria dei Georgofli. Atti 4. Ser. 8 (63 im Ganzen).
237. **Florenz.** T. Caruel: Nuovo giornale botanico italiano 17 (1885).
238. **Florenz.** Società Italiana di antropologia etnologia e psicologia comparata. 14 3, 4. 15 1, 2.
239. **Florenz.** Sezione fiorentina della Società Africana d'Italia. Bulletino I 1, 2.
† 240. **Genua.** Giacomo Doria. Museo civico.
241. **Mailand.** Reale Istituto Lombardo. Rendiconti 2. Ser. 18 (1885).
† 242. **Mailand.** Società Italiana di scienze naturali.
243. **Modena.** Società dei naturalisti. 1) Memorie 3. Ser. 2, 3. 2) Rendiconti delle adunanze 3. Ser. 1, 2 (1883, 84).
† 244. **Neapel.** Accademia delle scienze fisiche e matematiche.
245. **Neapel.** Deutsche zoologische Station. Mittheilungen 6.
246. **Neapel.** Società africana d'Italia. Bulletino 4 1–5. (1885).
247. **Padua.** Società Veneto-Trentina. Atti IX 3.
† 248. **Palermo.** Reale Accademia di scienze lettere e belle arti.
249. **Pisa.** Società Toscana di scienze naturali. 1) Memorie IV 3. 2) Processi verbali IV p. 144–266. VI 6.

250. Reggio nell' Emilia. Bulletino di paletnologia Italiana, 10 11, 12. 11 1–10. (1885).

251. Rom. R. Accademia dei Lincei. 1) Transunti 3. Ser. VIII 1–16. 2) Rendiconti I 1–27. 3) Osservazioni meteorologiche fatte al R. Osservatorio del Campidoglio. Lugliol-Dicenbre 1884.

552. Rom. Società geografica italiana. Bulletino 2. Ser. X (1885).

253. Rom. Comitato geologico d'Italia. Bolletino 16 1–10. (1885).

† 254. Sassari. Circolo di scienze mediche e naturali.

255. Turin. R. Accademia delle scienze. 1) Atti 21. 2) Bolletino dell' Osservatoria della regia Università 19 (1884). 3) L'Ottica di Claudio Tolomeo da Eugenio scrittore del Secolo XII ridotta in Latino sovra la traduzione araba di un testo inperfetto, pubbicata da Gilberto Gori (Torino 1885.)

† 256. Venedig. Istituto Veneto di scienze lettere ed arti.

† 257. Verona. Accademia d'agricoltura, commercio ed arti.

Japan.

258. Yokuhama. Deutsche Gesellschaft für Natur- und Völkerkunde Ost-Asiens. Mittheilungen IV 33.

† 259. Tokio. Seismological Society of Japan.

Mexico.

† 260. Mexico. Sociedad de geografia y estadistica de la republica mexicana.

† 261. Mexico. Museo nacional.

Nord-Amerika (Union).

† 262. Albany. N. Y. Albany Institute.

263. Boston. American Academy of Arts and sciences. Proceedings 20 (New Series 12).

264. Boston. Society of natural history. 1) Proceedings 22 23. 2) Memoirs III 8–10.

† 265. Cambridge. Peabody Museum of american archaeology.

266. Cambridge. Museum of comparative Zoology at Harvard College. 1) Bulletin XI 7–11. XII 1, 2. 2) Memoirs X 4. XIV No. 1 Part. 1. XVI. 3) Annal report 25 (1884–85).

† 267. Chicago. Academy of science.

† 268. Cincinnati. Ohio Mechanic's Institute.

† 269. Columbus. Landbaubehörde.

† 270. Davenport (Jowa). Academy of natural sciences.

† 271. Indianopolis. State of Indiana.

272. Jowa-City. Professor Gustavus Hinrichs. 1) Weather Service. 1. Report Sept.-Dec. 1881, 1882. 2. Biennial report of the Central Station 3. 3) Bulletin Jan.-May 1883. 4. Season in Jowa. Calender for 1884.

† 273. Little Rock. State of Arkansas.

† 274. Madison. Wisconsin Academy of arts and lettres.

† 275. Milwaukee. Naturhistorischer Verein von Wiskonsin.

† 276. New-Haven. Conecticut Academy of arts and sciences.

277. New-York. Academy of Sciences. Annals III 3–6.

278. Philadelphia. Academy of natural sciences. Proceedings 1884 3. 1885 1. 2.

279. Philadelphia. American philosophical Society for promoting useful knowledge. 1) Proceedings 22 117–119. 2) Register of papers published in the transactions and proceedings of the A. Ph. S. 1881.

280. Salem. American association for the advancement of science. Proceedings of the meeting 32.

281. Salem. Essex Institute. Bulletin 16 (1884).

† 282. Salem. Peabody Academy of science.

283. San Francisco. California Academy of sciences. Bulletin 1884 2, 3.

† 284. St. Louis. Academy of science.

285. Washington. Smithsonian Institution. 1) Smithsonian report 1883. 2) Contributions to knowledge 24, 25.

286. Washington. Departement of agriculture. Report 1884.

† 287. Washington. War Department.

† 288. Washington. Treasury Department.

289. Washington. U. S. Geological Survey. Monographs 7—8.

Oesterreich-Ungarn.

† 290. Aussig. Naturwissenschaftlicher Verein.

291. Bistritz. Gewerbeschule. Jahresbericht 11.

292. Bregenz. Vorarlberger Museumsverein. Jahresbericht 23 (1883—84).

293. Brünn. K. K. Mährisch-Schlesische Gesellschaft zur Beförderung des Ackerbaues, der Natur- und Landeskunde. Mittheilungen 64 (1884).

294. Brünn. Naturforschender Verein. Verhandlungen 22.

295. Budapest. K. Ungarische Akademie der Wissenschaften. 1) Ungarische Revue 1885 1–10. 2) Mathematisch-naturwissenschaftliche Berichte aus Ungarn II. 3) Almanach 1885. 4) Nemzetgazdasági és Statistikai Évkönyv (Statistisches Jahrbuch II 1884). 5) Matematikai és természettudomanyi Értesitö (Naturwissenschaftlicher und mathematischer Anzeiger) III 1–5. (1884). 6) Matematikai Értekezések (Mathematische Abhandlungen XI 1–9. 7) Természettudomanyi Értekezések (Naturwissenschaftliche Abhandlungen XIV 2–8.

296. Budapest. K. Ungarisches National-Museum. Természetrajzi Füzetek (Naturhistorische Hefte, Ungarisch mit Deutscher Revue) IX 1, 2.

297. Budapest. K. Ungarisches National-Museum. Archäologische Abtheilung.

Archaeologiai Értesitö (Archäologischer Anzeiger) 3, 4 (1870). 6 (72). 7 (73). 9 (75). 13 († 6,9). 14 († 2). Neue Folge I 2 (82). II (83). III 1, 2. (84). IV 1, 2 (84). V 1–3 (85).

298. Budapest. Ungarische geologische Anstalt. Mittheilungen aus dem Jahrbuche VII 2–4.

299. Budapest. Maghyaroni Földtani Tàrsulat (Ungarische geologische Gesellschaft) Földtani Közlöny (Geologische Mittheilungen) 15 (1885).

† 300. Budapest. Magyar természettudományi Társulat (Ungarischer naturwissenschaftliche Gesellschaft). Die Vergangenheit und Gegenwart der K. Ungarischen naturwissenschaftlichen Gesellschaft. Budapest 1885.

† 301. Gratz. Naturwissenschaftlicher Verein für Steiermark.

302. Hermannstadt. Siebenbürgischer Verein für Naturwissenschaften. Verhandlungen und Mittheilungen 34, 35.

303. Hermannstadt. Verein für Siebenbürgische Landeskunde. Archiv 19 3. 20 1, 2.

304. Innsbruck. Ferdinandeum. Neue Folge 29.

305. Innsbruck. Naturwissenschaftlich medicinischer Verein. Bericht 14 (1883/84).

306. Késmark. Ungarischer Karpathenverein. Jahrbuch 12 (1885).

307. Klagenfurt. Naturhistorisches Landes-Museum für Kärnthen. 1) Jahresbericht 17. 2) Bericht über die Wirksamkeit 1884. 3) Seeland: Diagramme der magnetischen und meteorologischen Beobachtungen 1884.

† 308. Klausenburg. Siebenbürgischer Museumsverein.

309. Klausenburg. Magyar növénytani Lapok (Ungarische botanische Blätter, herausgegeben von August Kanitz) VIII.

310. Krakau. K. Akademie der Wissenschaften. 1) Rozprawy i sprawozdania z Posiedzén (Sitzungsberichte 12). 2) Pamietnik IX. 3) Zbiór Wiadomósci do Antropologii Krajowéj (Sammlung von anthropologischen Berichten). Dodatok do Tomo IX: Sprawa Wykopalisk Mnikowskich. 4) Franke: Jan Bozek (J. Broscius) Akademik Krakowski 1585—1652.

311. Linz. Museum Francisco-Carolinum. Bericht 43.

† 312. Linz. Verein für Naturkunde in Oesterreich ob der Enns.

† 313. Prag. K. Böhmische Gesellschaft der Wissenschaften.

314. Prag. Naturhistorischer Verein Lotos. Lotos, Jahrbuch für Naturwissenschaft. Neue Folge 6 (ganze 34).

315. Prag. Museum des Königreichs Böhmen. Památky archaeologické XII 9–12

316. Pressburg. Verein für Natur- und Heilkunde. Mittheilungen 16.

317. Reichenberg i Böhmen. Verein der Naturfreunde.

† 318. Salzburg. Gesellschaft für Landeskunde. 1) Geschichte der Stadt Salzburg von Zillner 1885. 1) Mittheilungen 25 (1885).

319. Trentschin. Trencsen megyei természettudományi egylet (Naturwissenschaftlicher Verein des Trentschiner Comitats). Évkönyv (Jahrbuch) 7 (1885).

† 320. Triest. Società Adriatica di scienze naturali.

† 321. Triest. Museo civico di storia naturale.

† 322. Wien. K. K. Akademie der Wissenschaften.

323. Wien. Geologische Reichsansalt. 1) Jahrbuch 34 4. 35 1–3. 2) Verhand-

lungen 1884 13 bis Schluss. 1885 1. 3) Abhandlungen XI 1. 4) Die Meteoriten-Sammlung des K. K. Mineralogischen Hofkabinets von Dr. A. Brezina (Sep. aus d. Jahrbuch 1885, Heft I).

324. Wien. K. K. Geographische Gesellschaft. Mittheilungen 27 (Neue Folge 17) 1884.

325. Wien. K. K. Zoologisch botanische Gesellschaft. Verhandlungen 34 (1884). 35 1. Personen- und Ortsregister 3. Reihe 1871—80.

326. Wien. Anthropologische Gesellschaft. Mittheilungen 14 (Neue Folge 4) 4. 15 1.

327. Wien. Verein zur Verbreitung naturwissenschaftlicher Kenntnisse. Mittheilungen 24 (1883/84).

328. Wien. Oesterreichische Centralanstalt für Meteorologie und Erdmagnetismus. Jahrbücher. Neue Folge 20 (1883).

329. Wien. Verein für Landeskunde von Niederösterreich. 1) Topographie von Niederösterreich II 14, 15. 2) Blätter. Neue Folge 13 (1884).

Portugal.

† 330. Lissabon. Academia real das Sciencias.

331. Lissabon. Secção das trabalhos geologiques de Portugal (Section des travaux géologiques Communicacões I (1885).

Russland.

332. Dorpat. Naturforschende Gesellchaft. 1) Schriften I. 2) Sitzungsberichte VII 1. 3) Archiv für die Naturkunde Liv-, Est- und Kurlands. 2. Ser. X 1.

333. Dorpat. Gelehrte estnische Gesellschaft. Verhandlungen 12 (1884).

334. Helsingfors. Finska Vetenskaps Societet (Societas scientiarium fennica). 1) Bidrag till kännedom af Finlands Natur och Folk 39—42. 2) Öfversigt af Förhandlingar 26 (1883—84). 3) Acta XIV.

† 335. Helsingfors. Finlands geologiska undersökning.

336. Helsingfors. Societas pro fauna et flora fennica. Meddelanden 11.

† 337. Helsingfors. Finska fornminnesförening (Suomen Muinaismuisto).

338. Mitau. Kurländische Gesellschaft für Litteratur und Kunst. Sitzungsberichte 1883.

339. Moskau. Société impériale des naturalistes. Bulletin 1884 2.

340. Moskau. Musées public et Roumiantzow. Numismatisches Kabinet. Catalog der Münzen I (1884).

341. Odessa. Société des naturalistes de la nouvelle Russie. Sapiski IX, X 1.

342. Petersburg. Kaiserliche Akademie der Wissenschaften. 1) Mémoires 32 1—18. 33 1. 2) Bulletin 30 1, 2.

343. Petersburg. Observatoire physique central. Annalen 1883.

344. Petersburg. Societas entomologica Rossica. Horae 18 (1884).

345. Petersburg. K. Russische Geographische Gesellschaft. 1) Iswestija (Bulletin) 21 (1885). 2) Otschet 1884.

346. Petersburg. K. Botanischer Garten. Acta horti petropolitanis (Trudy) VIII 3. IX 1.
347. Petersburg. Comité géologique. 1) Memoires II 1 (Allgemeine geologische Karte von Russland. Blatt 71). 2) Iswestija (Bulletin) 4 (1885) 1–3.
348. Riga. Naturforschender Verein. Correspondenzblatt 27, 28.

Schweden und Norwegen.

† 349. Bergen. Museum.
† 350. Drontheim. K. Norsk. Videnskabernes Selskab.
† 351. Gothenburg. Vetenskaps och Vitterhets Samhället.
† 352. Kristiania. K. Norsk Universitet.
† 353. Kristiania. Videnskabernes Selskab.
354. Kristiania. Forening til Norske fortids mindesmerkers Bevaring. 1) Aarsberetning 1883. 2) Kunst och Handverk fra Norges Fortid (Nicolaysen). Heft IV.
355. Kristiania. Den Norske Nordhavs Expedition 1876—78 (herausgegeben von der Norwegischen Regierung). XII. Zoologie (Spongidae von G. Armauer Hansen.) XIII. Zoologie (Pennatulidae von Danielsen und Koren.) XIII. Zoologie (Crustaceae I. a. b. von Sars.)
† 356. Kristiania. Geologische Landesuntersuchung von Norwegen.
357. Lund. Universität. 1) Acta Universitalis Lundensis 20 (Mathematik und Naturwissenschaft.) 2) Accessionskatalog der Bibliothek. 1883. 1884.
358. Stockholm. K. Vetenskaps Akademie Oefversigt af Förhandlingar 41 6–10, 42 1–5.
359. Stockholm. K. Vitterhets historie och Antiquitets Akademie. 1) Antiquarisk Tidskrift VII. 4. 2) Månadsblad 1884.
360. Stockholm. Entomologiska Förening. Entomologisk Tidskrift 5 3–4.
† 361. Stockholm. Bohusläns Hushållnings-Selskap.
362. Stockholm. Geologiska Förening. Förhandlingar. VII. 8–13.
363. Stockholm. Sveriges geologiska Undersökning. (Institut Royal géologique.) 1) Ser. Aa. Geologische Karte 1:80000 mit je 1 Heft. Beschreibung 87. 93. 95. 96. 2) Ser. Ab. Karte im Massstab 1:200000 Blatt 8. 3) Ser. C. Mémoires diverses 69. 70. 72. 73. (4°). 67. 68. 71. 74—77. (8°).
364. Tromsö. Museum. 1) Aarshefter 8. 2) Aarsberetning 1884.
365. Upsala. Société Royale des sciences (Regia Societas scientiarum). 1) Nova Acta XII. 2. 2) Bulletin mensuel de l'Observatoire météorologique de l'Université d'Upsal 16 (1884).

Schweiz.

366. Basel. Naturforschende Gesellschaft. Verhandlungen VII. 3.
367. Bern. Naturforschende Gesellschaft. Mittheilung 1884 2. 3. 1885.
368. Bern. Allgemeine Schweizerische Gesellschaft für die gesammten Natur-

wissenschaften. Verhandlungen der 67. Jahresversammlung zu Luzern. Compte rendu des travaux présentés à la 67. Session à Lucerne. 16—18. September 1884.

369. Bern. Geologische Commission der schweizerischen naturforschenden Gesellschaft. 1) Geologische Karte der Schweiz 1:100 000 Blatt 14. 2) Matériaux pour la Carte géologique de la Suisse. Livr. 18 (Descr. géol. de Vaud, Fribourg et Bern avec un tableau des terrains et 13 planches).

370. Bern. Universität. 83 akademische Schriften.

371. Chur. Naturforschende Gesellschaft Graubündtens. Jahresbericht 27. 28.

† 372. Frauenfeld. Thurgauische naturforschende Gesellschaft.

373. Genf. Société de physique et d'histoire naturelle.

374. Genf. Société de géographie. Le Globe 24 1. 2. (1885.)

375. Lausanne. Société Vaudoise des sciences naturelles. Bulletin XX. 91. XXI. 92.

† 376. Neuchâtel. Société des sciences naturelles.

377. Schaffhausen. Schweizer Entomologische Gesellschaft. Mittheilungen VII. 2–4.

378. St. Gallen. Naturwissenschaftliche Gesellschaft. Bericht 1882/83.

379. Zürich. Naturforschende Gesellschaft. Vierteljahrsschrift 26—29.

380. Zürich. Antiquarische Gesellschaft. 1) Anzeiger für Schweizerische Alterthumskunde 1885. 2) Mittheilungen. XXI. 6.

Süd-Amerika.

† 381. Buenos-Aires. Museo publico.

382. Buenos-Aires. Sociedad Cientifica Argentina Annales XIX.

383. Cordoba. Academia nacional de Cienceas de la Republica Argentina. 1) Boletin VI. 2–4. 2) Actas V. 2.

† 384. Rio de Janeiro. Instituto historico geografico e etnografico de Brasil.

385. Rio de Janeiro. Museo nacional. Conférence faite au Musée au présence de sa M. M. impériale 11. 11. 1884 par le Dr. Ladislas Netto.

Angekauft 1885.

Globus. Illustrirte Zeitschrift für Länder- und Völkerkunde 47, 48 (1885).

Petermann. Geographische Mittheilungen 1885. Ergänzungsheft 74—80.

Annalen der Physik und Chemie. Neue Folge 24—26 (1885). Beiblätter 9 (1885).

Archiv für Anthropologie XVI.

Zeitschrift für Ethnologie 17 (1885).

Th. v. Bayer. Reiseeindrücke und Skizzen aus Russland. Stuttgart. J. G. Cotta 1885.

Bock. Im Reiche des weissen Elephanten. 14 Tage im Lande und am Hofe des Königs von Siam. Deutsch von Schröter. Leipzig. F. Hirt & Sohn. 1885.

Forbes. Wanderungen eines Naturforschers im Malayischen Archipel 1878—1883. A. d. Engl. von R. Teuscher. Bd. I. Jena. Costenoble 1886.

Jaworsky. Reise der Russichen Gesandschaft in Afghanistan und Buchara in den Jahren 1878—79. (A. d. Russischen von Petri). Bd. II. Jena. Costenoble 1885.

Kolberg. Nach Equador. Freiburg. Herder. 1885.

Lansdell. Russisch Central-Asien nebst Kuldscha, Buchara, China, Merw. Deutsch von H. v. Wobeser. I. II. Leipzig. Hirt & Sohn. 1885.

Nordenskiöld. Studien und Forschungen, veranlasst durch meine Reisen im hohen Norden. Populär-wissenschaftliches Supplement der Umseglung Asiens und Europa's auf der Vega. Leipzig. F. A. Brockhaus. 1885.

Prschewalsk. Reisen in Tibet und im oberen Laufe des gelben Flusses. (A. d. Russischen von Stein-Nordheim). Jena. H. Costenoble. 1885.

Radloff. Aus Sibirien. Lose Blätter aus dem Tagebuche eines reisenden Lisguisten. 2. Bände. Leipzig. F. O. Weigel. 1884.

Retzius. Finnland. Schilderungen aus seiner Natur, seiner alten Cultur. Deutsch von Appel. Berlin. G. Reimer. 1885.

Sellin. Das Kaiserreich Brasilien. (Das Wissen der Gegenwart 36, 37. Der Welttheil Amerika 2, 3). Leipzig. G. Freitag. 1885.

Schliemann. Tiryns. Der Prähistorische Palast der Könige von Tiryns. Leipzig. F. A. Brockhaus. 1886.

Stanley. Der Congo. 2 Bände. Deutsche Ausgabe. Leipzig. F. A. Brockhaus. 1885.

Thomson. Durch Massai-Land. Forschungsreise in Ost-Africa zu den Schneebergen und wilden Stämmen zwischen dem Kilimandscharo und Victoria Njansa (Deutsch von Freeden). Leipzig. F. A. Brockhaus. 1885.

Werner. Das Kaiserreich Ostindien und die angrenzenden Gebirgsländer n. d. Reisen der Gebrüder Schlaginweit und anderer neuerer Forscher dargestellt. Jena. Costenoble 1884.

Zöller. Die deutschen Besitzungen an der westafrikanischen Küste: Das Togo-Land und die Sklavenküste. Stuttgart. W. Spemann. 1885.

Expedition zur Erforschung der Ostsee. Berlin 1873.

Kolmodin. Sverges Siluriska Ostracoder. Upsala 1869.

v. Könen. Paleocene Fauna von Kopenhagen. Göttingen 1885.

Lindström. Authezoa perforata of Gotland. Stockholm 1870.

Messtischblätter von Ost- und Westpreussen: 149 Blatt photographische Copien. (Gegen Erstattung der Herstellungskosten 146 Blatt von d. Königl. Landesaufnahme, 3 Blatt von d. Königl. Geolog. Landesanstalt.)

Nötling. Fauna d. baltischen Cenoman-Geschiebe. Berlin 1885.

Palaeontographica, herausgegeben von Zittel. Bd. 32. Stuttgart 1885/86.

Römer. Lethaea erratica. Berlin 1885.

Schmidt. Russisch-Deutsches Wörterbuch. Leipzig 1884.

Zittel. Handbuch der Paläontologie. Bd. I. Lief. 8. München 1885.

Geschenke 1885.

Ninni. Rapporte a. s. e. il ministro di agricoltura, industria e commercio sui progressi della dita grege par estendere la pescicoltura ad introdure la cocleo coltura nel fondo situato nei comuni censuari di Lugugnana e Caorle. Roma. 1885.

Jentzsch. Beiträge zum Ausbau d. Glacialhypothese. Berlin 1885. (Verf.).

Kleinert. Der Gypsstock von Wapno. Bromberg. 1878. (Verf.)

J. Lehmann. 10 Blatt Photographien von Strudellöchern des Chemnitzthales. (Verf.)

Messtischblätter von Ost- und Westpreussen: 39 Blatt photographischer, Copien (von d. Königl. Landesaufnahme [Generalstab]).

Produktion der Bergwerke, Salinen und Hütten im preussischen Staate im Jahre 1884. Berlin 1885. (Von Herrn Oberpräsident von Schlieckmann).

Reuter. Die Beyrichien der obersilurischen Diluvialgeschiebe Ostpreussens. Königsberg 1885. (Verf.).

Seeck. Beitrag zur Kenntniss der granitischen Diluvialgeschiebe in Ost- und Westpreussen. Königsberg 1885. (Verf.)

Trautschold. Traces de l'étage tongrien près de Kamyschloff. Jekaterinburg 1882.

Wada. Die Kaiserl. Geologische Reichsanstalt von Japan. Berlin 1885. (Diese beiden von Dr. Jentzsch.)

Wahnschaffe. Gletschererscheinungen b. Velpke u. Daundorf. Berlin 1880.

do. Entstehung d. oberen Diluvialsandes. Berlin 1881.

do. Vorkommen geschiebefreien Thones in den obersten Schichten des unteren Diluviums b. Berlin. Berlin 1882.

do. Glaciale Druckerscheinungen im norddeutschen Diluvium. Berlin 1882.

Druck von R. Leupold in Königsberg in Pr.

Erklärung der Abbildungen.

Fig. 1. *Abies balsamea.* Horizontaler Längsschnitt durch das zweitjüngste (1879) Stammende. 28. XII. 1881. $\frac{24}{1}$.
M. das Mark, *H.* das Holz, *R.* die Rinde, *S.* Knospenschuppe. *a.* = rundliche, meist gebräunte Markzellen am Ende des 1879er Markes, *l.* = oberste, häufig fehlende Zellreihen, an deren Stelle die Lücke, *s.* = Scheidewand, *m.* = Markzellen des 1880er Triebes.

„ 2. *A. balsamea.* Medianschnitt der ruhenden Knospe eines Astes am 24. XII. 1881. $\frac{22}{1}$.
a. = älteres Mark, *l.* = Lücke, *s.* = Scheidewand, *m.* = Knospenmark, *r.* = ringförmiger Träger der Knospenschuppen = *k.*, *h.* = Harzbehälter in demselben.

„ 3. *A. balsamea.* Medianschnitt der fortwachsenden Spitze eines Astes am 16. VII. 1881. $\frac{140}{1}$. Markzellen.

„ 4. *A. balsamea.* Medianschnitt am Grunde des diesjährigen und Ende des vorjährigen Triebes eines Astes. 16. VII. 1881. $\frac{140}{1}$.
s. = oberste Zellen der Scheidewand, *m.* = Markzellen.

„ 5. *A. balsamea.* Medianschnitt der 1881er Endknospe eines Astes. 24. XII. 1881. $\frac{900}{1}$. Zellen vom unteren Rande der Scheidewand.

„ 6. *A. balsamea.* Längsschnitt der Zapfenaxe. $\frac{24}{1}$.
a. = Mark des Zapfenstieles, *l.* = korkähnliches Gewebe, *s.* = Scheidewand, *m.* = Mark der Zapfenspindel.

„ 7. *Picea excelsa.* Längsschnitt durch die ruhende Endknospe des Stammes. 19. IV. 1885. $\frac{12}{1}$.
a. = altes Mark, *l.* = Lücke, *s.* = Scheidewand, *m.* = Knospenmark.

Fig. 8. *P. excelsa.* Einzelne Zelle der jüngsten Scheidewand. 10. I. 1882. $\frac{300}{1}$.

„ 9. *P. excelsa.* Mehrere Zellen der jüngsten Scheidewand im Verbande. 10. I. 1882. $\frac{600}{1}$.

z. = Zellenraum, *k.* = Zellkern, *p.* = Pore, *w.* = Zellwand.

„ 10. *P. excelsa.* Längsschnitt der Endknospe. 10. I. 1882. $\frac{140}{1}$. Markzellen im Verbande vom Ende des vorjährigen Triebes.

„ 11. *P. excelsa.* Medianschnitt des 1880er Triebes eines Stammes. 14. II. 1882. $\frac{24}{1}$.

a. = altes Mark, *l.* = Lücke, *s.* = Scheidewand, *m.* = junges Mark.

„ 12 *P. excelsa.* Medianschnitt des 1880er Triebes. 14. II. 1882. $\frac{140}{1}$. Veränderte Markzellen am Ende des Schosses.

„ 13. *P. excelsa.* Medianschnitt wie v. $\frac{140}{1}$. Unveränderte, poröse Markzellen in der Nähe des Triebendes.

„ 14. *P. excelsa.* Medianschnitt wie v. $\frac{140}{1}$. *m.* = jüngere Markzellen (1880) vom Beginn des Triebes, *s.* = oberste Scheidewandzellen.

„ 15. *Larix europaea.* Längsschnitt eines fünfjährigen Nadelzweiges. *M.* = Mark, *H.* = Holz, *a.* = Spitze des Zweiges, *m.* = einzelner Markkörper, *s.* = dessen Scheidewand, *l.* Lücke.

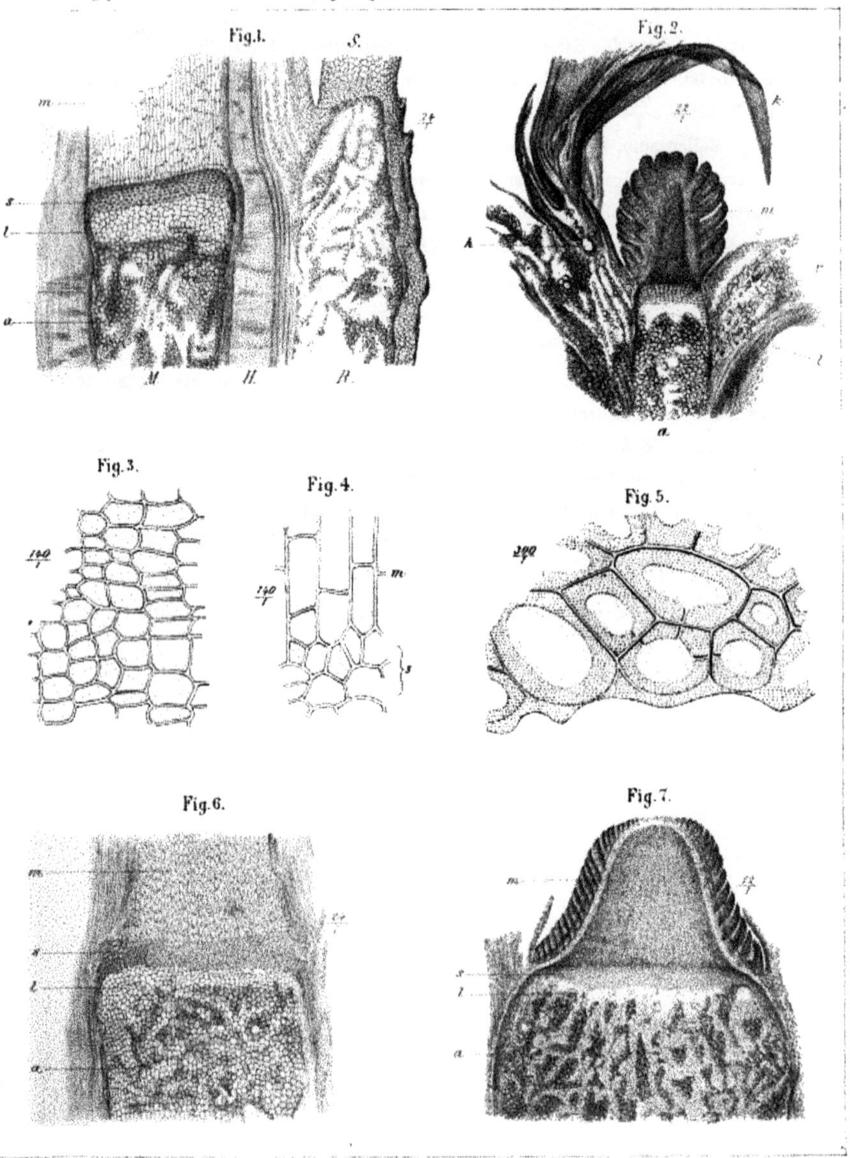

C. Fritsch u. Dr. Treibel gez.

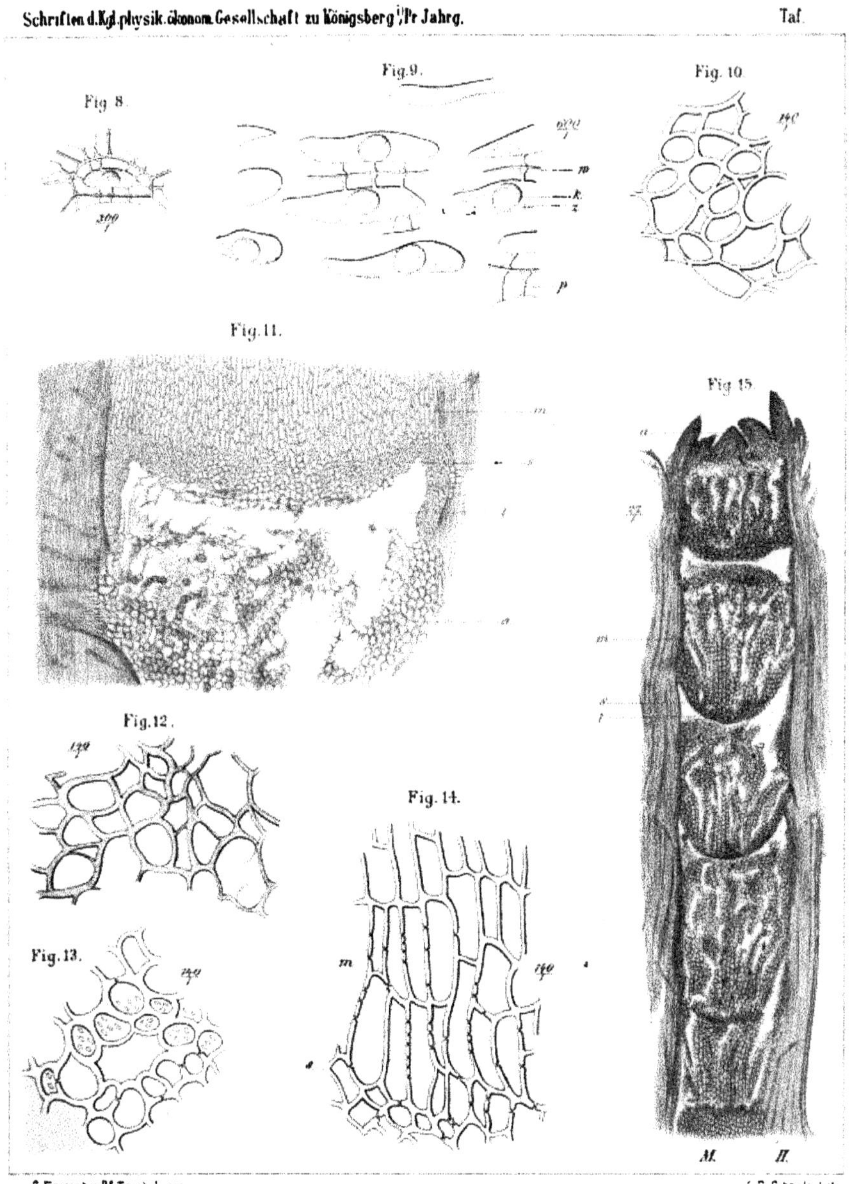

C. Fritsch u. Dr. Tesebel gez.

C. F. Schmidt lith.

SCHRIFTEN

DER

PHYSIKALISCH-ÖKONOMISCHEN GESELLSCHAFT

ZU

KÖNIGSBERG i. Pr.

SIEBENUNDZWANZIGSTER JAHRGANG.

1886.

KÖNIGSBERG.
IN COMMISSION BEI KOCH & REIMER.
1887.

Inhalt des XXVII. Jahrganges.

Abhandlungen.

Sitzungsberichte.

Verzeichniss der Mitglieder

der

physikalisch-ökonomischen Gesellschaft

am 1. Juli 1886*).

Protector der Gesellschaft.

Herr Ober-Präsident der Provinz Ostpreussen Dr. v. Schlieckmann. 6. 4. 82.

Vorstand.

1. Sanitätsrath Dr. med. Schiefferdecker, Präsident. 15. 12. 48.
2. Medicinalrath Professor Dr. Moeller, Director. 8. 1. 47.
3. Stadtrath Lottermoser, Secretair. 17. 6. 64.
4. Commerzienrath Weller, Cassen-Curator. 29. 6. 60.
5. Hofapotheker Hagen, Rendant. 30. 6. 51.
6. Dr. Otto Tischler, Bibliothekar und auswärtiger Secretair. 1. 12. 65.

Ehrenmitglieder.

1. Herr v. Dechen, Wirkl. Geh. Rath, Oberberghauptmann, Dr., Excellenz, Bonn. 5. 3. 80.
2. " W. Hensche, Dr., Medicinalrath, Stadtältester. 24. 10. 23.
3. " v. Horn, Dr., Wirklicher Geh. Rath, Ober-Präsident a. D., Excellenz, Berlin W, Landgrafenstrasse 11. 4. 6. 69.
4. " Emile Lavasseur, Membre de l'Institut in Paris. 7. 6. 78.
5. " Neumann, Dr., Professor, Geh. Regierungsrath. 16. 2. 27.
6. " v. Rénard, Dr., Geheimrath in Moskau. 19. 12. 62.
7. " v. Scherzer, Dr., Ministerialrath, K. K. Generalconsul in Genua. 4. 6. 80.
8. " Torell, Dr., Professor, Geheimrath in Berlin. 3. 12. 80.
9. " Virchow, Dr., Professor, Geheimrath in Berlin. 3. 12. 80.

---

*) Die beigesetzten Zahlen bezeichnen Tag und Jahr der Aufnahme.

Ordentliche Mitglieder.

1. Herr Albrecht, Dr., Dir. d. Prov.-Gewerbeschule a. D. 16. 6. 43.
2. " Andersch, A., Comm.-R. 21. 12. 49.
3. " Aschenheim, Dr., Prassnicken. 4. 6. 68.
4. " Baenitz, C., Dr., Lehrer. 1. 12. 65.
5. " v. Batocki-Bledau. 4. 12. 68.
6. " Baumgart, Dr. Professor. 6. 12. 73.
7. " Baumgarten, Dr., Prof. 1. 12. 76.
8. " Becker, Apothekenbesitzer. 3. 12. 80.
9. " Becker, M., Commerz.-Rath. 7. 12. 82.
10. " Becker, J., Kaufmann. 7. 12. 82.
11. " Beer, Rechtsanwalt. 1. 6. 82.
12. " v. Behr, Oberlehrer, Prof. 12. 6. 46.
13. " Berent, Dr. 7. 12. 77.
14. " Bernecker, Bankdirector. 4. 6. 80.
15. " Bertholdt, Dr. med., Prof. 4. 12. 68.
16. " Besch, Oberlehrer. 6. 6. 73.
17. " Bessel-Lorck, Königl. Landes-Bauinspector. 6. 12. 83.
18. " Bezzenberger, Dr. Prof. 6. 12. 83.
19. " Bielitz, Major. 4. 12. 74.
20. " Bienko, Partikulier. 2. 6. 60.
21. " Bieske, Reg.-Bauführer. 6. 12. 83.
22. " Blochmann, Dr. 4. 6. 80.
23. " Böhm, Oberamtmann. 1. 7. 59.
24. " Bohn, Dr. med., Professor. 21. 12. 60.
25. " Bon, Rittergutsbesitzer. 1. 6. 66.
26. " Born, Apothekenbesitzer. 7. 12. 82.
27. " Brandt, Dr., Privatdocent. 3. 12. 85.
28. " Braun, Candidat. 3. 12. 80.
29. " Bujack, Dr., Oberlehrer. 13. 12. 61.
30. " Caspary, J., Dr., Professor. 3. 12. 80.
31. " Caspary, R., Dr., Professor. 1. 7. 59.
32. " Cholevius, L., Dr., Oberlehrer. 5. 6. 68.
33. " Chun, Dr., Professor. 6. 12. 83.
34. " Cohn, J., Commerzienrath. 3. 12. 69.
35. " Conditt, B., Kaufmann. 19. 12. 62.
36. " Conrad, Rittergutsbesitzer in Görken p. Trömpau. 7. 6. 78.
37. " Coranda, Dr. 4. 12. 84.
38. " Crüger, Posthalter u. Kaufm. 1. 12. 81.
39. " Cynthius, Kreisphysikus, Sanitätsrath, Dr. 5. 6. 74.
40. " Czwalina, Dr., Gymnasial-Lehrer. 3. 12. 69.
41. " Döbbelin, Zahnarzt. 7. 6. 72.
42. " Dohrn, Dr., Prof., Geh. Medicinalrath. 6. 12. 83.
43. " Donisch, Hauptmann. 3. 12. 85.
44. " Douglas, Rentier. 28. 6. 61.
45. " Eichert, Apothekenbesitzer. 6. 6. 73.
46. " Ellendt, Dr., Oberl., Prof. 6. 12. 67.
47. Herr Erdmann, Dr. med. 1. 6. 82.
48. " Falkenheim, Dr. med. 4. 6. 77.
49. " Falkson, Dr. med. 1. 7. 59.
50. " Falkson, R., Dr., Privatdocent. 7. 12. 82.
51. " Fischer, Ober-Landesgerichts-Rath. 21. 12. 60.
52. " Fleicher, Rittmeister. 5. 6. 84.
53. " Fleischmann, Dr., Prof. 27. 5. 86.
54. " Franz, Dr. 7. 12. 77.
55. " Friedländer, Dr., Prof., Geheimrath. 23. 12. 59.
56. " Fröhlich, Dr. 7. 6. 72.
57. " Fuhrmann, Oberlehrer. 13. 12. 61.
58. " Gädeke, H., Geh. Commerzienrath. 16. 12. 36.
59. " Gädeke, Rittergutsbesitzer, Powayen. 6. 6. 79.
60. " Gamm, Fabrikant. 2. 6. 76.
61. " Gebauhr jun., Kaufm. 7. 12. 77.
62. " Gisevius, Dr. 3. 12. 85.
63. " Graf, Stadtrath. 1. 12. 81.
64. " v. Gramatzki, Landesdir. 5. 6. 84.
65. " Grünhagen, Dr., Professor. 1. 12. 81.
66. " Grunewald, Fabrikant chirurgischer Instrumente. 3. 12. 80.
67. " Grunewald, Zimmermstr. 7. 12. 77.
68. " Gutzeit, Buchhändler. 5. 12. 79.
69. " Guthzeit, Dr. med. 5. 6. 74.
70. " Haarbrücker, F., Kaufm. 6. 12. 72.
71. " Häbler, Gen.-Landsch.-R. 6. 12. 64.
72. " Hagen, Stadtrath. 6. 6. 79.
73. " Hagen, Hofapotheker. 30. 6. 51.
74. " Hagen, Justizrath. 6. 12. 83.
75. " Hahn, Dr., Professor. 3. 12. 85.
76. " Hay, Dr. med., Privatdocent. 1. 6. 59.
77. " Hay, A., Partikulier. 1. 12. 81.
78. " Heilmann, Rentier. 5. 6. 65.
79. " Hennig, Dr. 6. 12. 78.
80. " Herbig, Apothekenbesitzer. 4. 6. 80.
81. " Hermann, Dr., Professor. 4. 12. 84.
82. " Hertz, Dr. med. 7. 12. 82.
83. " Heydeck, Professor. 6. 12. 73.
84. " Heumann, Fabrikdirector. 6. 6. 79.
85. " Hieber, Dr. med. 10. 6. 70.
86. " Hirsch, Dr. med., Sanit.-R. 2. 7. 52.
87. " Hirschfeld, Dr., Professor. 6. 12. 78.
88. " Hirschfeld, Dr. 6. 6. 79.
89. " Hoffmann, Bürgermeister. 6. 12. 72.
90. " Holldack, Kaufmann. 11. 6. 85.
91. " Hueser, Ingenieur. 27. 5. 86.
92. " Jacobson, Julius, Geh. Medicinalrath, Dr. med., Prof. 1. 7. 59.

93. Herr Jaffé, Dr., Professor. 6. 12. 73.
94. " Jentzsch, Dr., Privatdocent. 4. 6. 75.
95. " Jereslaw, Lion, Kaufm. 1. 12. 76.
96. " Ihlo, Dr. 3. 12. 75.
97. " Ipsen, Stadtrath. 6. 6. 79.
98. " Kade, Prem.-Lieutenant. 4. 12. 84.
99. " Kahle, Apothekenbesitzer. 3. 12. 75.
100. " Karow, akadem. Maler. 6. 12. 83.
101. " Klebs, Dr., Geologe an der K. geolog. Landesanstalt in Berlin. 4. 6. 77.
102. " Kleiber, Prof., Director. 6. 12. 72.
103. " Klien, Dr. 4. 6. 77.
104. " Kluge, Generalagent. 7. 12. 77.
105. " Knobbe, Dr., Oberlehrer. 15. 12. 43.
106. " Koch, Buchhändler. 3. 12. 75.
107. " Kowalewski, Apotheker. 6. 12. 67.
108. " Krah, Landes-Baurath. 2. 6. 76.
109. " Krahmer, Justizrath. 21. 12. 60.
110. " Krause, Amtsgerichtsrath. 3. 12. 69.
111. " Kreiss, Generalsecretair, Hauptm. 4. 6. 75.
112. " Krohne, Kaufmann. 5. 12. 79.
113. " Krüger, Director der Ostpr. Südbahn. 11. 6. 85.
114. " Künow, Conservator. 4. 12. 74.
115. " Kunze, Apothekenbesitzer. 7. 12. 77.
116. " Langendorff, Dr., Prof. 4. 12. 84.
117. " Laser, Dr. med. 21. 12. 60.
118. " Lehmann, Dr. med. 24. 12. 59.
119. " v. Leibitz, Hauptmann. 5. 6. 84.
120. " Lentz, Dr., Professor. 1. 7. 59.
121. " Leo, Stadtrath. 7. 12. 77.
122. " Liedtke, Prediger. 5. 6. 74.
123. " Lindemann, Dr., Prof. 6. 12. 83.
124. " Lohmeyer, Dr., Prof. 3. 12. 69.
125. " Lossen, Dr., Professor. 17. 6. 78.
126. " Lottermoser, Stadtrath. 17. 6. 64.
127. " Lucbbau, Dr. 4. 6. 80.
128. " Ludwich, Dr., Professor. 6. 6. 79.
129. " Luther, Dr., Professor. 25. 6. 47.
130. " Magnus, Dr. med., Sanitäts-Rath. 4. 7. 51.
131. " Magnus, E., Dr. med. 5. 6. 68.
132. " Magnus, L., Kaufmann. 3. 12. 80.
133. " Marek, Dr., Professor. 6. 12. 78.
134. " Maschke, Dr. med. 10. 6. 70.
135. " Meier, Ivan, Kaufmann. 3. 12. 69.
136. " Merguet, Oberlehrer. 5. 6. 74.
137. " Meschede, Dr., Director. 6. 12. 73.
138. " Meyer, O., Kaufmann. 11. 6. 85.
139. " Michels, Chefredacteur. 1. 6. 82.
140. " Michelson, Dr. 6. 12. 83.
141. " Milentz, Apothekenbes. 23. 12. 59.
142. " Mischpeter, Dr., Realschullehrer. 7. 6. 72.
143. " Möller, Dr., Professor, Medicinal-Rath. 8. 1. 47.
144. Herr v. Morstein, Oberlehrer, Dr. 4. 12. 74.
145. " Motherby, Rittergutsbes. in Arnsberg p. Creuzburg. 6. 6. 79.
146. " Müller, Rector. 7. 6. 67.
147. " Müller, Secretair der Kunstakademie. 1. 12. 76.
148. " Münster, Dr. med., Prof. 4. 6. 80.
149. " Musack, Fabrikbesitzer. 4. 12. 74.
150. " Nath, Dr., Reg.- und Medicinalrath. 11. 6. 85.
151. " Naumann, Apotheker. 24. 6. 57.
152. " Naunyn, Dr., Professor. 4. 12. 74.
153. " Neumann, Dr., Prof., Medicinalrath. 23. 12. 59.
154. " Neumann, Prem.-Lieut. 27. 5. 86.
155. " Olck, Oberlehrer. 7. 6. 72.
156. " v. Olfers, Dr., Rittergutsbesitzer in Metgethen. 7. 6. 72.
157. " Oltersdorf, Kaufmann. 4. 6. 80.
158. " Packheiser, Apothekenbes. 7. 6. 72.
159. " Pape, Dr., Professor. 6. 12. 78.
160. " Passarge, Oberlandesgerichts-Rath. 13. 12. 61.
161. " Patze, Apotheker und Stadtrath. 29. 6. 38.
162. " Peise, Corpsapotheker. 7. 6. 78.
163. " Peter, Kaufmann. 7. 12. 77.
164. " Peters, Oberlehrer. 4. 6. 77.
165. " Pincus, Medicinalrath, Dr., Professor. 4. 12. 68.
166. " Prin jun., Kaufmann. 6. 12. 78.
167. " Rahts, Dr. 3. 12. 85.
168. " Rauscher, Oberlandesgerichts-Rath. 7. 12. 82.
169. " Richter, Dr., Prof., Departements-Thierarzt. 13. 12. 61.
170. " Ritthausen, Dr., Prof. 23. 12. 59.
171. " Rosenfeld, H., Kaufm. 7. 6. 78.
172. " Rupp, Dr. med. 6. 12. 72.
173. " Saalschütz, Dr., Professor. 6. 6. 73.
174. " Samter, Dr. med. 29. 6. 60.
175. " Samuel, Dr. med., Prof. 23. 12. 57.
176. " Sanio, Realschullehrer. 1. 6. 82.
177. " Sauter, Dr., Director a. D. der höheren Töchterschule. 16. 12. 53.
178. " Schellong, Dr. 4. 12. 84.
179. " Schepke, Kaufmann. 7. 12. 77.
180. " Schiefferdecker, Realschul-Direct. a. D. 17. 12. 41.
181. " Schiefferdecker, Dr., Sanitätsrath. 15. 12. 48.
182. " Schimmelpfennig, Kaufm. 6. 6. 79.
183. " Schlesinger, Dr. med. 19. 12. 62.
184. " Schmidt. E., Rentier. 1. 6. 82.
185. " Schneider, Dr. med., Prof. 4. 6. 69.
186. " Schönborn, Geheimer Medicinalrath. Dr., Professor. 4. 12. 74.

187. Herr Schreiber, Dr., Professor. 3. 12. 80.
188. „ Schröder, Dr. 3. 12. 80.
189. „ Schröter, Dr. med. 23. 12. 59.
190. „ Schröter, Commerzienrath. 7.12.77.
191. „ Schüssler, Apothekenbes. 1. 12. 81.
192. „ Schuhmacher, Dr. med. 4. 12. 68.
193. „ Schwanbeck, Dr. med. 6. 12. 72.
194. „ Schwenkner, Apotheker. 1. 12. 81.
195. „ Selke, Oberbürgermeister. 3. 12. 75.
196. „ Seydel, Dr. 6. 6. 79.
197. „ Seydler, Apotheker. 4. 12. 74.
198. „ Simon, Geheimer Commerzienrath. 7. 12. 77.
199. „ Simon, Dr. jur., Kaufm. 7. 12. 77.
200. „ Simony, Civilingenieur. 1. 6. 66.
201. „ Simsky, C., chirurg. Instrumentenmacher. 1. 6. 66.
202. „ Sommer, Dr., Prof. 23. 12. 59.
203. „ Sommerfeld, Dr. med. 7. 12. 52.
204. „ Sotteck, Dr. med., Sanitätsrath. 17. 12. 52.
205. „ Spirgatis, Dr., Professor. 17. 12. 56.
206. „ v. Steinberg-Skirbs, Dr., General-Arzt z. D., 2. 6. 76.
207. „ Stellter, O., Justizrath. 21. 12. 60.
208. „ Stetter, Dr. med., Privatdocent. 7. 12. 82.
209. „ Stieda, Dr., Professor. 3. 12. 85.
210. „ Symanski, Landgerichtsrath. 9.6.71.
211. Herr Theodor, Stadtrath a. D. 7. 12. 77.
212. „ Tieffenbach, Gymnasial-Lehrer. 6. 12. 73.
213. „ Tischler, Dr., 1. 12. 65.
214. „ Tischler, Gutsbesitzer, Losgehnen. 5. 6. 74.
215. „ Unterberger, Dr. 7. 6. 83.
216. „ Vanhöffen, Oberlehrer. 27. 5. 86.
217. „ Vogelgesang, Dr. 5. 6. 74.
218. „ Volkmann, Dr., Professor. 27.5.86.
219. „ Walter, Dr., Professor. 3. 12. 75.
220. „ Warkentin, Stadtrath. 6. 12. 73.
221. „ Wedthoff, Ober-Reg.-Rath. 9.6.71.
222. „ Weger, Dr., Sanitätsrath. 14. 6. 39.
223. „ Weller, Commerzienrath. 29. 6. 60.
224. „ Weller, L., Kaufmann. 4. 6. 80.
225. „ Wendland, Director der Ostpr. Südbahn. 6. 12. 72.
226. „ Wiehler, F., Kaufmann. 7. 12. 77.
227. „ Wilutzky, Ad., Hof-Lithograph. 10. 6. 70.
228. „ Winbeck, Feuerwerks-Hauptmann. 4. 6. 80.
229. „ Wittrin, Dr., Oberlehrer. 3. 12. 85.
230. „ Wyszomierski, Dr., Russ. Consul. 5. 6. 68.
231. „ Zacharias, Dr. med., Sanitätsrath. 2. 7. 52.
232. „ Zimmermann, Apotheker. 4. 6. 80

Auswärtige Mitglieder.

1. Herr Albrecht, Dr., Professor in Brüssel. 1. 6. 77,
2. Alterthums-Gesellschaft in Elbing.
3. Herr Anger, Dr., Director, Graudenz. 4. 12. 74.
4. „ Arppe, Ad. Ed., Prof. der Chemie in Helsingfors. 19. 12. 62.
5. „ v. Baehr, Rittergutsbes., Gr. Ramsau p. Wartenburg. 6. 6. 7:.
6. „ Baxendell, Jos., Secretair der naturforsch. Gesellschaft zu Manchester. 19. 12. 62.
7. „ Benefeldt, Rittergutsbes., Quoossen p. Gallingen. 5. 6. 84.
8. „ Berendt, Dr., Professor, Berlin NW, Dorotheenstr. No. 61. 1. 6. 66.
9. „ Behrens, Alb., Rittergutsbesitzer auf Seemen bei Gilgenburg. 19. 12. 62.
10. „ Berent, Rittergutsbesitzer auf Arnau. 1. 12. 65.
11. „ Beyrich, Dr., Prof., Geh. Bergrath in Berlin, Franz. Str. 29. 6. 12. 67.
12. Herr Blell, Rentier, Lichterfelde b. Berlin. 5. 12. 79.
13. „ Böhm, Rittergutsbesitzer, Glaubitten per Korschen. 7. 6. 72.
14. „ v. Bönigk, Freiherr, Major a. D., Postdirector in Demmin in Pommern. 1. 12. 76.
15. „ Börnstein, Dr., Prof. in Berlin NW, Platz am neuen Thor 1A. 6. 12. 72.
16. „ v. Bohlschwing, Rittergutsbesitzer, Schönbruch, Kreis Friedland, Ostpr. 6. 12. 78.
17. „ Bresgott, Kreisbaumst., Mohrungen. 5. 12. 79.
18. „ v. Bronsart, Rittergutsbesitzer auf Schettnienen per Braunsberg. 21. 12. 60.
19. „ Bruhn, Oscar, Kaufmann, Insterburg. 5. 12. 79.
20. „ Brusina Spiridion, Vorsteher der zoolog. Sammlungen am naturhistor. Museum in Agram. 4. 12. 74.

21. Herr Buchinger, Dr., Prof. in Strassburg. 6. 12. 67.
22. " Buhse, Fr., Dr., Director des naturforsch. Vereins zu Riga. 9. 6. 71.
23. " de Caligny, Anatole, Marquis, Château de Sailly pr. Fontenay St. Père. 7. 2. 66.
24. " Canestrini, Dr., Professor in Padua. 17. 6. 64.
25. " v. Cesati, Vincenz, Baron in Neapel. 19. 12. 62.
26. " Claassen, Rittergutsbes., Warnikam p. Ludwigsort. 3. 12. 80.
27. Conradi'sche Stiftung in Jenkau. 18. 12. 63.
28. Copernikus-Verein in Thorn. 7. 12. 66.
29. Herr Copes, F. S., Dr., New-Orleans. 6. 12. 72.
30. " Czudnowitz, Dr., Insterburg. 1.12.81.
31. " Daemers de Cachard, L., Professor in Brüssel. 7. 6. 78.
32. " Danehl, Rector in Zinten. 7. 6. 78.
33. " Dittrich, Lehr. in Wormditt. 6.12.78.
34. " zu Dohna-Schlodien, Graf, Obermarschall, Burggraf, Excell., p. Lauk. 21. 12. 61.
35. " Dorn, Dr., Professor in Halle a. d. S., Burgstrasse 21. 7. 6. 72.
36. " Dohrn, C. A., Dr., Präsident des entomologischen Vereins in Stettin. 29. 6. 60.
37. " Dorien, Dr. med., Sanitätsrath, Lyck. 19. 12. 62.
38. " Dorr, Dr., Oberlehrer, Elbing. 6.12.78.
39. " Dromtra, Ottom., Kaufmann in Allenstein. 13. 12. 61.
40. " Drope, Pächter in Grünlinde p. Grünhayn. 7. 12. 77.
41. " Duchartre, P., Professor der Botanik und Mitglied der Akademie zu Paris. 19. 12. 62.
42. " Ebers, Dr., Neustadt, Westpr. 3.12.85.
43. " Eckert, Landschaftsrath, Czerwonken per Lyck. 7. 6. 78.
44. " Erchenbrecher, Dr., Salzbergwerk Neu-Stassfurt p. Stassfurt. 5. 12. 79.
45. " Erikson, Director des Königl. Gartens in Haga bei Stockholm. 4. 12. 67.
46. " Flügel, Felix, Dr., Leipzig. 18.12.63.
47. " Frisch, A., Oberamtmann auf Stanaitschen. 16. 12. 64.
48. " Fröhlich, Lehrer in Thorn. 3.12.75.
49. " Fröhlich, Rendant in Culm. 7.12.77.
50. " Geinitz, Dr., Prof., Geh. Hofrath, Dresden. 1. 12. 76.
51. " Gerstaeker, Dr., Prof., Greifswald. 19. 12. 62.
52. Herr Giesebrecht, Dr., Prof., München. 1. 6. 59.
53. " v. Glasow, Lieutenant, Lokehnen per Wolittnick. 3. 12. 80.
54. " Gandoger in Aras (Rhône). 7.12.82.
55. " v. Gossler, Minister der Geistlichen, Unterrichts- und Medizinal-Angelegenheiten, Excellenz, Berlin. 4. 6. 69.
56. " Gottheil, E., i. New-Orleans. 6.12.72.
57. " Greiff, Wirkl. Geh. Rath, Excellenz, Berlin, Genthinerstr. 13. 1. 12. 71.
58. " Grentzenberg, Kaufmann, Danzig. 21. 12. 60.
59. " Grenda, Landgerichtsrath in Lyck. 2. 6. 76.
60. " Grewingk, Dr., Professor in Dorpat. 16. 12. 64.
61. " Güllich, Forstkassenrendant, Braunsberg. 7. 12. 77.
62. " Gürich, Regierungsrath in Breslau. 6. 12. 72.
63. " Haber, Lehrer, Lüneburg. 27. 5. 86.
64. " Hagedorn, Dr., Mohrungen. 11.6.85.
65. " Hagen, Dr., Professor, Cambridge, Amerika. 15. 12. 43.
66. " Hagen, A., Stadtrath in Berlin. 2. 7. 52.
67. " Hagen, Gutsbesitzer auf Gilgenau per Passenheim. 4. 6. 69.
68. " Hartung, G., Dr. in Heidelberg, per Adr. A. J. Ernst in Heidelberg. 2. 7. 58.
69. " Hasemann, Kreisschulinspector, Marienwerder. 7. 12. 82.
70. " Hasenbalg, Director in Sprottau. 3. 12. 75.
71. " Hecht, Dr., Kreisphysikus in Neidenburg. 19. 12. 62.
72. " Helmholtz, Dr., Prof., Geh. Rath in Berlin. 21. 12. 49.
73. " Helwich, Apotheker, Bischofstein. 3. 12. 80.
74. " Hensche, Rittergutsbesitzer auf Pogrimmen p. Kleschowen. 7. 6. 67.
75. " v. Heyden, Major z. D., Dr. in Bockenheim, Schlossstrasse. 1. 6. 66.
76. " Heubach, Rittergutsbesitzer in Kapkeim per Lindenau. 6. 6. 79.
77. " Hilbert, Dr., Sensburg. 27. 6. 81.
78. " Hinrichs, G., Professor in Jowa-city. 1. 12. 65.
79. Historischer Verein in Marienwerder.
80. Herr Hooker, Dr., Jos. Dalton, R. N., F. R., S., F. L. S. etc. Royal Gardens, Kew. 19. 12. 62.
81. " Horn, Amtm., Oslanin b. Putzig. 7.6.72.

82. Herr Horn, Rechtsanwalt, Insterburg. 7. 12. 77.
83. „ Hoyer, Gutsbesitzer in Swaroschin per Dirschau. 3. 12. 75.
84. „ Hundertmark, Pfarrer, Insterburg. 3. 12. 80.
85. „ Issel, Arthur, Dr., Professor, Genua. 4. 12. 74.
86. „ Jensen, Dr., Director in Dalldorf bei Berlin. 1. 6. 82.
87. „ Kade, Dr., Berlin. 3. 12. 85.
88. „ Kaesewurm, C., Darkehmen. 4.12.74.
89. „ Kascheike, Apotheker in Drengfurth. 21. 12. 60.
90. „ Kersand, Dr., Geh. Ober-Medicinalrath in Berlin, Tempelhofer Ufer 31. 4. 12. 68.
91. „ King, V. O., Dr. in New-Orleans. 6. 12. 72.
92. „ Kirchhoff, Dr., Prof., Geheimrath in Berlin. 15. 12. 48.
93. „ Knoblauch, Dr., Prof., Geheimrath in Halle a. S. 23. 12. 59.
94. „ Koch, Rittergutsbes. auf Powarben per Trömpau. 28. 6. 61.
95. „ Körnicke, Dr., Prof. in Poppelsdorf. 21. 12. 60.
96. „ Krauseneck, Rittergutsbesitzer auf Schanwitz p. Gutenfeld. 7. 12. 77.
97. „ Krauseneck, Buchdruckereibesitzer in Gumbinnen. 4. 6. 77.
98. „ Krieger, Dr., Oberlehrer, Tilsit. 3. 12. 69.
99. „ Kröhnert, Lehrer, Sportehnen per Liebstadt. 5. 12. 79.
100. „ Krosta, Dr., Stadtschulrath in Stettin. 4. 6. 69.
101. „ Krosta, Pfarrer, Rydzewen p. Milken. 1. 2. 76.
102. „ Kühn, Reg.-Rath in Breslau. 3.12.75.
103. „ Kuhn, Landrath in Fischhausen. 1. 12. 65.
104. „ Lange, Dr., Professor in Kopenhagen. 12. 6. 64.
105. „ Lefèvre, T., in Brüssel. 1. 12. 76.
106. „ Le Jolis, Dr. in Cherbourg. 27. 6. 62.
107. „ Leistner, Dr. i. Eydtkuhnen. 1.6.82.
108. „ Lepkowski, Dr., Prof. in Krakau. 1. 12. 76.
109. „ Lindenschmit, L., Dr., Director des römisch-germanisch. Museums in Mainz. 3. 12. 75.
110. „ Lipschitz, Dr., Professor in Bonn. 21. 12. 55.
111. Litterarischer Verein Mohrungen. 27. 5. 86.
112. Herr Lovén, Prof. in Stockholm. 6. 12. 67.
113. Herr Mack, Rittergutsbes., Althof-Ragnit. 4. 6. 77.
114. „ Maske, Rentier, Göttingen. 26. 6. 63.
115. „ Meibauer, Rechtsanwalt in Conitz. 4. 12. 74.
116. „ Meyer, A., Pächter, Schwesternhof b. Caymen p. Wulfshöfen. 4.12.74.
117. „ Meyer, Dr., Kreisphysikus in Heilsberg. 1. 6. 82.
118. „ Minden, Partikulier in Dresden, Altstadt, Winkelmannstr. 24, part. 17. 12. 52.
119. „ Möhl, H., Dr., Schriftführer des naturhistorischen Vereins in Cassel. 5. 6. 68.
120. „ Mörner, Dr., Sanitätsrath, Kreisphysikus in Pr. Stargardt. 17.6.64.
121. „ Momber, Professor, Oberlehrer in Danzig. 10. 6. 70.
122. „ Mühl, Amtsgerichtsrath a. D. und Stadtrath in Breslau, Gr. Feldstr. 10. 8. 12. 72.
123. „ Mühl, Forstmeister in Wiesbaden. 6. 2. 72.
124. „ Müttrich, Dr., Prof. in Neustadt-Eberswalde. 1. 7. 59.
125. „ Nagel, R., Dr., Professor, Oberlehrer in Elbing. 18. 12. 63.
126. Naturwissenschaftlicher Verein in Bromberg. 7. 6. 67.
127. Herr Neumann, Amtsgerichtsrath in Mohrungen. 5. 12. 79.
128. „ Oelrich, Rittergutsbesitzer, Bialutten p. Illowo, Kr. Neidenburg. 19.12.62.
129. „ Oudemans, A. J. A., Professor in Amsterdam. 17. 6. 64.
130. „ Pavenstädt, Rittergutsbesitzer in Weitzdorf p. Rastenburg. 1. 12. 76.
131. „ Pehlke, Kaufm., Bartenstein. 4.6.80.
132. „ Peter, Dr., Conservator in München, Türkenstrasse 51 III. 7. 6. 83.
133. „ Podlech, Gutsb. in Mollehnen. 5.6.74.
134. „ Pöpke, Bohrunternehmer, Anklam. 5. 6. 84.
135. „ Praetorius, Dr., Professor, Oberlehrer in Conitz. 4. 12. 74.
136. „ Prang, Apotheker, Bartenstein. 5. 12. 79.
137. „ Preuschoff, Propst in Tolkemit. 18. 12. 63.
138. „ v. Pulszki, F., Ritter, Director des Königl. Ungar. National-Museums in Budapest. 1. 12. 76.
139. „ v. Puttkamer, Minister des Innern, Berlin, Excellenz. 1. 12. 71.
140. „ Puttlich, Rittergutsbesitzer, Sandlack p. Bartenstein. 5. 6. 84.

141. Herr Radde, Dr., Direct. des Kaukasischen Museums in Tiflis. 5. 6. 74.
142. „ Rast, Gutsbesitzer, Schippenbeil. 9. 6. 71.
143. „ v. Recklinghausen, Professor in Strassburg. 17. 6. 64.
144. „ Reissner, E., Dr., Prof. in Dorpat. 9. 12. 62.
145. „ v. Rode, Gutsbesitzer, Babbeln bei Gr. Karpowen. 4. 6. 80.
146. „ v. Rode, Landschaftsrath, Rauschken per Usdau. 2. 6. 76.
147. „ Romer, Dr., Prof., Grosswardein. 4. 12. 72.
148. „ Rosenbohm, Apotheker, Graudenz. 5. 12. 79.
149. „ Rumler, Oberlehrer, Gumbinnen. 4. 6. 77.
150. „ Rygh, Dr., Professor in Christiana. 7. 12. 77.
151. „ v. Sadowski, Dr. in Krakau. 1. 12. 76.
152. „ v. Sanden, Rittergutsbesitzer, Raudonatschen p. Kraupischken. 3. 12. 80.
153. „ Scharlok, J., Apotheker in Graudenz. 7. 6. 67.
154. „ Schenk, Dr., Professor, Geh. Hofrath in Leipzig. 27. 6. 62.
155. „ Schiefferdecker, Dr. med., Prosector in Göttingen. 6. 12. 72.
156. „ Schlicht, Kreisschulinspector in Rössel. 16. 2. 78.
157. „ Schliemann, H., Dr. in Athen. 4. 6. 77.
158. „ Schreiber, Dr., Lehrer a. d. Königl. technischen Lehranstalten in Chemnitz. 1. 12. 76.
159. „ Schuhmann, Landgerichtsrath in Braunsberg. 6. 12. 73.
160. „ Seidlitz, Dr., Charlottenthal p. Ludwigsort. 4. 6. 77.
161. „ de Selys-Longchamp, E., Baron, Akademiker in Lüttich. 2. 6. 60.
162. „ Semper, O., in Altona. 1. 12. 76.
163. „ Senoner, Adolph, in Wien. 27. 6. 62.
164. „ Seydler, Fr., Rector in Braunsberg. 29. 6. 60.
165. „ Siegfried, Rittergutsbes. auf Skandlack per Barten. 28. 6. 61.
166. „ Siegfried, Rittergutsbes. auf Carben bei Heiligenbeil. 6. 12. 72.
167. „ Siegfried, Rittergutsbes. auf Pluttwinnen p. Laptau. 6. 12. 78.
168. Herr Simson, E., Dr., Präsident d. Reichsgerichts, Wirkl. Geh. Rath, Excell., Leipzig. 4. 7. 51.
169. „ Sohnke, Dr., Prof., Jena. 16. 12. 64.
170. „ Sonntag, Ad., Dr. med., Kreisphysikus, Sanitätsrath in Allenstein. 13. 12. 61.
171. „ Steinbardt, Dr., Oberlehrer i. Elbing. 6. 12. 72.
172. „ Steppuhn, Rittergutsbes., Liekeim per Bartenstein. 7. 12. 77.
173. „ Stöckel, Generalsecretair, Stobingen per Insterburg. 3. 12. 75.
174. „ Strüvy, Rittergutsbesitzer, Worlack per Landsberg, Ostpr. 1. 12. 76.
175. „ v. Tettau, Freiherr, Rittergutsbes. auf Tolks p. Bartenstein. 21. 12. 60.
176. „ Thiel, Dr., Sanitätsrath, Kreisphysik. in Bartenstein. 6. 12. 72.
177. „ Todaro, A., Dr., Professor, Senator, Director des botanischen Gartens in Palermo. 1. 12. 76.
178. „ Treichel, Rittergutsbesitzer, Hoch-Paleschken p. Alt-Kischau. 2. 6. 76.
179. „ Tulasne, L. R., Akademiker in Paris. 9. 12. 62.
180. „ Vigouroux, Schulinspect. in Wartenburg. 4. 12. 74.
181. „ Vogt, C., Professor, Genf. 1. 12. 71.
182. „ Voigdt, Dr., Pfarrer a. D., Rittergutsbesitzer auf Dombrowken. 11. 6. 41.
183. „ Wahlberg, P. E., best. Secretair der Akademie der Wissenschaften zu Stockholm. 19. 12. 62.
184. „ Wahlstedt, L. J., Dr. in Lund. 17. 6. 64.
185. „ Waldeyer, Dr., Professor in Berlin. 19. 12. 62.
186. „ Wangerin, A., Dr., Prof. in Halle a. d. S., Burgstr. 27. 6. 12. 73.
187. „ Wartmann, Dr., Prof. in St. Gallen. 17. 6. 64.
188. „ Waterhouse, G. R., Esq. Dir. d. Brit. Mus. in London. 18. 12. 63.
189. „ Weiss, Apotheker in Caymen per Wulfshöfen. 6. 12. 72.
190. „ Werdermann, Rittergutsbesitzer auf Corjeiten p. Germau. 7. 6. 78.
191. „ Wiebe, Geh. Regierungs-Baurath in Berlin. 19. 12. 62.
192. „ v. Zander, Dr., Landrath in Heinrichswalde. 7. 6. 78.
193. „ Ziehe, Dr., prakt. Arzt in Gerdauen. 6. 12. 78.
194. „ Zinger, Lehrer, Pr. Holland. 5. 6. 84.

Einige neue Pflanzenreste aus dem samländischen Bernstein.

Von

Robert Caspary.

Nebst Tafel I.

Ausser 8 Pflänzchen der Lebermoose, in 5 Bernsteinstücken enthalten, sind alle andern im Folgenden von mir beschriebenen Pflanzenreste königsberger Sammlungen entnommen, denen der Herren Dr. med. Sommerfeldt, Apotheker Kowalewski, Professor Schumann, jetzt dem altstädt. Gymnasium gehörig, der Firma Stantien & Becker, der meinigen und ganz besonders der des Herrn Konservator Künow.

Lebermoose.

Goeppert (Goeppert u. Berent der Bernstein, u. die in ihm befindl. Pflanz. d. Vorwelt 1845 S. 113 — angeführt unter I) beschrieb 3 Arten Lebermoose, gab auch dazu unbrauchbare Abbildungen. Goeppert (Ueber die Bernsteinflora. Monatsber. Berlin. Akad. 1853, angeführt als II) behauptete, dass die 3 von ihm früher beschriebenen Arten noch jetzt lebenden angehörten und führte 8 andere ausserdem auf, die er alle mit jetzt lebenden identificirt, wozu in keinem einzigen Falle ein hinlänglicher Grund vorlag. Mit Recht erklärt sich Gottsche (Botan. Centralblatt Bd. XXV 1886 95 u. 121) gegen dies Verfahren, verwirft die Bezeichnungen Goepperts u. giebt den 28 Pflänzchen, die er in 28 Bernsteinstücken fand, neue Namen, aber — fügt keine Beschreibungen oder Abbildungen hinzu, so dass seine Arbeit unbenutzbar ist. Ich habe in 35 Bernsteinstücken 39 Lebermoosreste gesehen, die ich in folgenden 17 Arten, eine davon mit einer Spielart, beschrieben habe.

1. Jungermannia sphaerocarpoides Casp. Blätter ganzrandig, einlappig, umgekehrt-eiförmig, rundlich, unterer Rand an der Axe aufgekrümmt, so dass der aufgerichtete Theil $^1/_4$—$^1/_3$ des oberen Blatttheils beträgt; das Blatt also auf der untern Seite am Hinterrande sackartig; Blätter 2-zeilig, wagrecht und sich deckend oder weitläuftiger und unter grossen spitzen Winkeln schief zur zickzackigen Axe gerichtet. (Bild 1 u. 2). 2 Bruchstücke.

Ich sah das Original der Goeppert'schen Jungermannia sphaerocarpa des Bernstein's (Goeppert II.), welches er für identisch mit Jung. sphaerocarpa Hook. hält, die jetzt in England, Frankreich und in Deutschland, in letzterem jedoch höchst selten, lebt. Ich untersuchte von der jetzt lebenden Pflanze Nro. 495 von Rabenhorst's Hep. europ. aus Dresdens Nähe, kann aber den Beweis der Identität mit der fossilen

Pflanze nicht für erbracht halten um so weniger als von der fossilen nur kurze Stückchen ohne Fructifikation gefunden sind; die fossile Pflanze ist der jetzt lebenden nur ähnlich. Bei der fossilen Pflanze ist der aufgeschlagene Hinterrand des Blattes breiter und länger, als bei der der Jetztwelt angehörigen.

2. Jungermannia dimorpha Casp. Das fadenförmige Stämmchen im untern Theil mit 2-zeiligen, kleinen, kurz-eiförmigen oder kurz länglich eiförmigen, auf ihrer Spitze 2-zahnigen, selten dreizahnigen weitläuftig stehenden Blättern besetzt, die weniger breit als der Stamm sind. Sie gehen gegen die Endknospe zu in umgekehrt eiförmige, breitere dicht liegende, sich dachziegelig deckende, ganzrandige Blätter über. Beiblätter (Amphigastria) nicht da. (Bild 3 u. 4). 1 Stämmchen.

3. Phragmicoma magnistipulata Casp. Blätter zweizeilig, wagerecht und sich dachziegelig deckend, oder von der Axe unter grossen spitzen Winkeln abstehend, umgekehrt-eiförmig, schief, ganzrandig, einlappig, am Hinterrande unterseits sackförmig dadurch, dass der Saum desselben sich nach der Stammspitze aufschlägt. Die Breite des aufgeschlagenen Theils $1/5 - 1/4$ der des wagerechten obern Blatttheils. Der umgeschlagene Theil verläuft allmälig am Seitenrande des Blatts in diesen und ist am Hinterrande mehr oder weniger geschwungen. Beiblätter gross, ihre Breite $1/4 - 1/3$ der ganzen Laubbreite, umgekehrt-eiförmig, ganzrandig, das untere das obere deckend. (Bild 5). 1 Bruchstück.

4. Phragmicoma contorta Casp. (Jungermannites contortus Goepp. et Berendt. I 114 Taf. VI Fig. 40 u. 41. Lejeunia serpyllifolia Goepp. II (nicht Libert). Blätter schief-eiförmig, ganzrandig, breit abgerundet, einlappig, 2-zeilig, dachziegelig sich deckend, oder auch von der Axe schief abstehend; der Hinterrand geschwungen, sein Saum etwas aufgerichtet, (so dass ein kleiner Sack entsteht) und erst am Seitenrande in den Rand des oberen Blatttheils übergehend; Beiblätter querrechteckig, Ecken gerundet, Oberrand breit und sanft ausgerandet; das untere deckt das obere. (Bild 6). 1 Stämmchen.

Dies Moos hat die obigen Synonyme Goepperts, wie mich Goepperts Original des berlin. mineral. Museums belehrte. Es ist von Lejeunia serpyllifolia Libert (vergleiche die Abbildung bei Hook. Brit. Jung. t. 42) sehr verschieden, welche Beiblätter hat, die rundlich sind und spitzwinklig und tief 2-spaltig.

5. Phragmicoma suborbiculata Casp. (Radula complanata Goepp. nicht Dumort. nach Goepp. II gemäss dem Original Goepperts in Berendt's Sammlung). Blätter schief-umgekehrt-eiförmig, einlappig, Hinterrand sackbildend aufgeschlagen, gewölbt, der aufgeschlagene Theil allmälig am Seitenrande des oberen Blatttheils in diesen verlaufend; Blätter zweizeilig, dachziegelig sich deckend, wagrecht, Beiblätter rundlich, querelliptisch, nierenförmig, das untere das obere deckend, so breit als der vierte Theil der Laubbreite. (Bild 7). 1 Stämmchen, nämlich Goepperts Original.

Kann Radula complanata Dum. nicht sein, da diese sehr grosse Hinterlappen hat und keine Beiblätter.

Var. **sinuata** Casp. Hinterrand des Blatts meist geschwungen; der sackartig aufgeschlagene Theil etwa $1/4$ der Breite des oberen Blatttheils, nicht $1/6 - 1/7$, wie bei der Hauptform; der aufgeschlagene Theil des Hinterrandes nimmt etwas mehr als die Hälfte seiner Länge, nicht wie bei der Hauptform fast dessen ganze Länge ein. (Bild 8). 1 Stämmchen. Einige zwischen der Hauptform und Spielart in den

Eigenschaften vermittelnde Blätter machten die Trennung beider Reste als die verschiedenen Arten nicht zulässig.

6. **Lejeunia latiloba Casp.** Blatt 2-lappig, Vorderlappen etwa doppelt so lang, als der Hinterlappen, schief umgekehrt-eiförmig, ganzrandig, vor dem Übergang in den Hinterlappen am Hinterrande stark geschwungen, konkav; Hinterlappen rechteckig oder eiförmig-rechteckig, etwa $^1/_3$ so breit als der Vorderlappen, obere Aussenspitze breit gerundet, nicht über die Bucht zwischen Vorder- und Hinterlappen vorgezogen; Blätter 2-zeilig, wagrecht, dachziegelig; Beiblätter fast kreisrund, etwas elliptisch, mit schmalem und spitzwinkligem Ausschnitt oben, der $^3/_8$—$^1/_2$ der Länge des Beiblatts beträgt, Lappen spitzwinklig und spitz. Die Breite der Beiblätter beträgt fast $^1/_6$ der Breite des ganzen Laubes. (Bild 9). 2 Stämmchen in 2 verschiedenen Bernsteinstücken.

Ist der Lejeunia serpyllif. Lib. ähnlich.

7. **Lejeunia Schumanni Casp.** Vorderlappen nierenförmig-kreisrund, ganzrandig, da wo er an den Hinterlappen stösst bogig nach aussen begränzt, ohne alle Schwingung. Blätter 2-zeilig, wagrecht, dachziegelig. Hinterlappen eiförmig-dreieckig, ganzrandig, aufgeschlagen, etwa halb so breit und halb so lang, als der Vorderlappen; die nach aussen gewandte Spitze gerundet. Beiblätter gross, kreisrund-nierenförmig, etwa $^1/_3$ so breit als das Laub, bis zur Hälfte der Höhe gespalten, die 2 Lappen spitz oder zugespitzt, Seitenrand jederseits 1—2-buchtig, zum Theil mit einem Zahn, selten ganzrandig. (Bild 10). 2 Stämmchen in 2 Bernsteinstücken.

Dem verstorbenen Professor Dr. Julius Schumann, Oberlehrer am altstädtischen Gymnasium zu Ehren benannt.

8. **Lejeunia pinnata Casp.** Blätter 2-zeilig, ohne sich zu decken, 2-lappig. Vorderlappen kurz-länglich, fast doppelt so lang als breit, ganzrandig, fast lineal, Spitze breit gerundet. Hinterlappen fast dreieckig, nicht ganz halb so lang als der Vorderlappen, an der Axe lang angeheftet, nach ihrer Spitze hinauflaufend, einen Sack mit dem Vorderlappen bildend, am oberen Rande gerundet, und hier nach aussen mit einem spitzen Zahn, auch zum Theil noch mit kleineren der Axe näher liegenden. Beiblätter weitläuftig, fast elliptisch, kurz länglich, tief spitzwinklig bis zur halben Länge gespalten mit 2 spitzen, spitzenwinkligen Lappen oben. (Bild 26. Die beiden obern Blätter a u. b, sonst fast zerstört, zeigen die Hinterlappen unversehrt). 1 Fetzen, dessen linke Seite zerstört war.

9. **Madotheca linguifera Casp.** Blatt zweilappig; Vorderlappen breit umgekehrt-eiförmig, wagrecht, flach oder schwach am Seitenrande zurückgekrümmt; Blätter 2-zeilig, dachziegelig. Hinterlappen gross, $^2/_3$—$^3/_4$ so lang als der Vorderlappen, und wohl mehr als halb so breit, länglich-eiförmig, stets mit den Seitenrändern etwas nach aussen gerollt, n a c h h i n t e n g e r i c h t e t. Beiblatt lanzettlich, zungenförmig, fast 4 mal so lang als breit, allmälig zugespitzt, spitz oder spitzlich, selten doppelt breiter und gespalten. (Bild 11). 1 Stämmchen, das an den meisten Stellen auf der untern Seite sehr schlecht erhalten ist und an der besten auch durch Zersetzung gelitten hat.

Ist von Madotheca platyphylla Dum. und laevigata Dum. der Jetztzeit sehr verschieden durch die verhältnissmässig bedeutendere Grösse der Hinterlappen, deren Richtung schiefabwärts, während sie bei den genannten lebenden Pflanzen, schief-aufrecht ist und das schmale, lanzettliche, spitze Beiblatt, das bei den beiden lebenden Arten sehr breit und stumpf ist.

10. Lophocolea polyodus Casp. Blätter einlappig, eiförmig, oben 2zahnig, Zähne spitz, Ausschnitt auch spitz und spitzwinklig, in den jüngern Blättern die Zähne zurückgekrümmt. Blätter auf den Zweigspitzen dachziegelig, später entfernter stehend und sich nicht, oder wenig deckend, wagrecht. Beiblätter nierenförmig, 5—7zahnig oder spaltig, Zähne 1—3mal so lang als breit, öfters mit 1—2 Seitenzähnen. (Bild 12 und 13). 1 Stämmchen.

Verwandt der Loph. heterophylla N. v. E. (vgl. Hook. Brit. Jung. tab. 31), jedoch ist bei ihr die Ausrandung der Blätter gerundet und die Beiblätter sind nur 2—3spaltig; verwandt auch mit Loph. Hookeriana N. v. E. (als Jungerm. bidentata in Hook. Brit. Jung. t. 30), jedoch ist die Ausrandung der Blätter auch bei ihr nicht so scharf und spitzwinklig und meist gerundet, die Beiblätter 2—3spaltig, die Lappen lang lanzettlich und mit ähnlichen Lappen zum Theil seitlich versehen.

11. Radula oblongifolia Casp. Vorderlappen ein drittel bis fast doppelt so lang als breit, schief-eiförmig oder die längeren fast lineallänglich, breit gerundet, Hinterlappen schief-rautenförmig, $^{2}/_{5}$ bis fast $^{2}/_{3}$ so lang als der Vorderlappen und $^{1}/_{2}$—$^{2}/_{3}$ so breit als dieser, äussere obere Spitze abgerundet, stumpf, Blätter wagrecht, sich mehr oder weniger dachziegelig deckend. Beiblätter nicht vorhanden (Bild 25). Viele und astreiche Stammstückchen in einem Stück Bernstein.

Der Radula complanata ähnlich, jedoch sind die Vorderlappen der fossilen Pflanze beträchtlich länger.

12. Frullania primigenia Casp. Durchmesser des Laubes in wagrechter Richtung 0,198—0,318 mm; Vorderlappen umgekehrt eiförmig, theils sich deckend und dachziegelig, theils unter spitzen Winkeln von der Axe abstehend. Die aufgerollten Hinterlappen umgekehrt eiförmig, unten gestutzt, ihre Br. und Lge. = [1]) 0,085 und 0,1136
[2]) 0,0494 und 0,125

Beiblätter nicht zu finden. Einige junge Kapselanlagen da; die entwickeltste F (Bild 14 von der Seite und 15 von oben) hat noch einige umgekehrt eiförmige, stumpfe, spitzliche grössere Hüllblätter und endlich 3 sehr grosse, ganz glatte (nicht wie bei Frull. dilatata warzige), die der eiförmigen innersten Hülle, von der nur die Spitze vorsteht, dicht anliegen. — Ein verästeltes Stämmchen, leider an vielen Stellen durch fremdartige Stoffe und Zerstörung undeutlich.

13. Frullania truncata Casp. Vorderlappen wagrecht, kurz-länglich-eiförmig, breit abgerundet auf der Spitze, Hinterlappen aufgerollt umgekehrt-eiförmig, unten gestutzt, 0,06—0,10 mm etwa breit an dickster Stelle und $^{5}/_{4}$ bis annähernd doppelt so lang, Beiblätter spatelförmig, oben mit tiefem und spitzwinkligem Einschnitt, Lappen auf der Spitze gestutzt, ungefähr so breit oben als der Grund des Beiblatts, die gestutzte Fläche zum Theil gezähnelt. (Bild 16 und 21). 19 Stämmchen in 19 Bernsteinstücken. Die Beiblätter fehlen in den meisten Pflänzchen und die Zugehörigkeit zu dieser Art ist daher nur nach der Grösse und sonstigen übereinstimmenden Verhältnissen bei solchen Resten ermittelt. Einzelne Stämmchen mit gipfelständiger Kapselanlage, die jedoch über eine abgeplattete Kugel von 0,47 mm Durchmesser und 0,369 mm Höhe nie hinausgekommen war. Die Blätter dachziegelig sich deckend oder ziemlich weitläuftig und vereinzelt bei einigen Exemplaren.

14. Frullania varians Casp. Vorderlappen rundlich, umgekehrt-eiförmig, ganzrandig, Hinterlappen aufgerollt, umgekehrt-eiförmig, unten gestutzt, 0,9—0,10 mm im dicksten Theil breit, entweder gewölbt oder die Aussenseite auf die Innenseite eingesunken und somit der Hinterlappen aussen napfförmig; Beiblätter spatelförmig, oben gezähnelt, oder auch wohl 2lappig, durch einen mittleren Einschnitt (Bild 17 und 18.). Ein verästeltes Stämmchen. Der Oberlappen wagrecht oder später abstehend.

15. Frullania tenella Casp. Vorderlappen schief kurz länglich, umgekehrt-eiförmig, Hinterlappen aufgerollt, umgekehrt-eiförmig, unten gestutzt, 0,08—0,09 mm im breitsten Theil breit und $^{1}/_{3}$—$1^{1}/_{2}$mal so lang. Beiblatt fast elliptisch oder kurz eiförmig, oben tief spitzwinklig gespalten, Lappen spitz, Seiten gewölbt oder selten mit einem Zahn auf der Seite (Bild 21). 2 Stammstückchen, zum Theil sehr schlecht erhalten, in 2 Bernsteinstücken. Etwas grösser als vorige Art, Beiblätter, wie die von Lejeunia latiloba Bild 9 und L. pinnata Bild 26.

16. Frullania acutata Casp. Vorderlappen eiförmig, ganzrandig, kurz zugespitzt, Spitze spitzlich. Hinterlappen aufgerollt, umgekehrt-eiförmig, unten gestutzt. Beiblätter länger wie breit, fast elliptisch, oben mit tiefem spitzwinkligem Einschnitt, Lappen spitz und spitzwinklig, Seiten gewölbt, ganzrandig oder mit einem Zahn. (Bild 23). Ein Stämmchen und eine abgerissne Zweigspitze (Bild 24), welche Hüllblätter einer Fructifikation oben zeigte.

17. Frullania magniloba Casp. (Jungermannites Neesianus Goepp. et Ber. I. S. 113 Taf. VI. Fig. 34—37. Jungermannia crenulata Goepp., nicht Sm., vrgl. Göppert II). Vorderlappen umgekehrt-eiförmig, ganzrandig, an der Zweigspitze wagrecht, dachziegelig, weiter ab abstehend, Br. : Lge. = 0,24 mm: 0,27 mm (Mittel aus 4 Messungen). Hinterlappen gross, aufgerollt, walzig-eiförmig, unten gestutzt, oben gerundet. Br. : Lge. = 0,138 mm : 0,223 mm.

Beiblätter nicht vorhanden (Bild 19 und 20). 1 Stämmchen, Original Goeppert's von seiner Hand bezeichnet mit: „Jungermannia crenulata. Breslau. Den 2. Febr. 1868"; kann jedoch Jungermannia crenulata, die Hinterlappen nicht hat (vgl. Hook. Brit. Jung. t. 73), nicht sein, sondern ist eine ächte Frullania. Goeppert identificirt Jungermannia crenulata Sm. (Goeppert II., S. 9. Sonderabdruck) mit seinem Jungermannites Neesianus (Goeppert und Berent I Taf. VI. Fig. 34—37). Das Original Goepperts seiner Abbildung a. O. habe ich nicht gesehen; es ist aber ohne Zweifel mit seinem andern Original von 1868 nicht identisch und Goeppert hat 2 verschiedene Pflanzen als Jungerm. crenulata bezeichnet.

Ist der Frullania dilatata N. v. E. der Jetztwelt nicht ganz unähnlich, aber abgesehen davon, dass die fossile Pflanze nicht in allen Theilen vorliegt, also Identität durchaus nicht ausgesprochen werden könnte, hat Frull. dil. rundliche nicht umgekehrt-eiförmige, mit längerem Grunde dem Stamm aufsitzende, kürzere Vorderlappen und verhältnissmässig auch kürzere und breitere Hinterlappen.

Unter den Lebermoosen, die ich im Bernstein sah, ist keines, das aus dem Rahmen der Gattungen, die das mittlere Europa heute hat, hinausfällt, aber auch keines, das mit einer jetzt lebenden Art für identisch gehalten werden kann.

Koniferen.

18. Pinus cembrifolia Casp. 5 Nadeln in einem Kleinzweige, unten durch Schuppenblätter, von denen nur der Grund geblieben ist, zusammengehalten. Leider die Länge der Nadeln nicht bestimmbar, in einem der 2 Stücke, die mir zu Gebot standen, $52^1/_2$ mm lang, aber die Spitzen fehlten. Auf der Rückseite der einzelnen Nadeln, welche 0,819 mm breit sind, keine Spaltöffnungen, auf den Seitenflächen 3—4 Reihen elliptischer Spaltöffnungen. Die Aussenkanten der Nadeln haben oben einige weitläuftige Zähne, die Innenkante hat solche Zähne in ihrem ganzen Verlauf. — Die Nadeln von Pinus Strobus sind dünner, die von Pinus Cembra denen der fossilen Pflanze an Dicke gleich; daher der Name. 2 Bernsteinstücke mit je einem Exemplar; jedoch nur die Scheide an einem unten erhalten.

19. Cupressinanthus Casp. Dieser Gattungsname soll nur bezeichnen, dass männliche Blüthen von Cupressineen gemeint sind, die vorläufig einer bestimmten Gattung nicht zugewiesen werden können.

C. polysaccus Casp. Männliche Blüthe 15 mm lang, zwischen den Spitzen der Staubblätter 5—6 mm dick. Ordnung der Staubblätter vielleicht 8/21. Unten einige der Axe anliegende dicke schuppenartige Hochblätter mit Spaltöffnungen unten auf den Seiten des Rückens, und Franzensaum am Rande. Die Staubblätter lang-länglich, bis 3 mm lang, 1,1—1,2 mm breit, fast unter 60° abstehend, nachenförmig, Spitze gerundet, wie der Rand eingekrümmt; Staubsäcke zu 8—9 um den Grund der Staubblätter auf den Blattkissen, scheinbar auf der Axe, unter dem Blatt etwa 6, über ihm 2—3, jedoch keiner in der Mediane. Staubsäcke eiförmig, kurz länglich 0,35—0,44 mm hoch; reissen unregelmässig auf.

20. Cupressinanthus magnus Casp. Männliche Blüthe 12 mm lang, $4^1/_2$ zwischen den Spitzen der Stammblätter im Durchmesser. Alle Blätter in der Blüthe in 3zähligen Quirlen, unten 2 Quirle dicker, schuppenartiger der Axe angedrückter Hochblätter; die Staubblätter dreieckig-eiförmig, nachenförmig, stehen fast wagrecht ab, sind kurz gestielt; Rand zart sägezahnig; Staubsäcke kuglig, 8—9 um den Grund jedes Staubblatts, auf der obern Seite bloss 3—4, keiner in der Mediane oben über dem Blatt, sie sitzen scheinbar der Axe, d. h. dem Blattkissen auf. Durchmesser der Säcke, die unregelmässig aufreissen, 0,26—0,33 mm. Eine Blüthe.

21. Widdringtonites oblongifolius Goepp. fr. longifolia Casp. Blätter lineal-lanzettlich, $2^1/_2$—$3^1/_2$ mm, ja über 4 mm lang, und 0,4—0,416 mm breit, oder gegen die Mitte zu sehr schwach verbreitert und von da an wieder an Breite abnehmend, spitz, breit sitzend, am Stamm hinablaufend, Blattkissen durch 2 Furchen, je eine rechts und links begrenzt, innere Seite des Blattes mit schwach vortretender Mittelrippe und auch etwas erhabenem Rande gesäumt, zwischen Rand und Mittelrippe durchweg ein Spaltöffnungsstreif. Rücken schwach gewölbt, ohne sichtbare Mittelrippe, am Grunde rechts und links beginnt ein Spaltöffnungsstreif, der sich über die Blattkissen (scheinbar auf der Axe) weit hinunterzieht. — Einige vielblättrige Äste. — Blätter nach $^3/_8$ geordnet unter spitzen Winkeln ziemlich gerade abstehend.

22. Widdringtonites lanceolatus Casp. Blätter auch, wie es scheint, nach $^3/_8$ geordnet, lineal-lanzettlich, breit sitzend, am Stamm hinablaufend, Blattkissen durch je eine Furche rechts und links begrenzt, Blätter spitz, $3^1/_2$—4 mm lang und etwa

0,6 mm breit, Mittelrippe mit 2 Längserhabenseiten unten stark vorspringend; zwischen diesen und zwei andern Längserhabenheiten in der Nähe des Randes längs der ganzen Unterseite des Blattes rechts und links je ein Spaltöffnungsstreif vorhanden, der sich auch über das Blattkissen (scheinbar über die Axe) hinzieht. Oben 3 Längserhabenseiten, eine mittlere und 2 seitliche, auch zwischen diesen rechts und links je ein Spaltöffnungsstreif über die ganze Blattlänge verlaufend. — 1 Ästchen.

23. **Sequoia Sternbergii Heer.** Blätter nach $^{2}/_{5}$ wahrscheinlich gestellt, $3^{1}/_{2}$—4 mm lang und 1 mm breit. — 1 Aststück.

24. **Sequoia Coutsiae Heer.** Form mit schuppenartigen, eingekrümmten Blättern. — 2 Aststückchen.

Acerinea.

25. **Acer Scharlokii Casp.** 2 Blüthen dicht neben und übereinander. Blüthe fast 5 mm hoch, Stiel nicht da. Kelchblätter 4 (?), lineal, stumpf, 4—5 mal so lang als breit, gewimpert. Blumenblätter lineal, etwa 3 mal so lang als die Kelchblätter, unter grossen spitzen Winkeln abstehend, gewimpert; es scheinen 6 (?) jeder Blüthe zuzukommen, denn es sind 12 (?) da, wahrscheinlich fehlen einige. Staubblätter 13 da; wahrscheinlich fehlen einige, $^{1}/_{4}$ an Länge etwa die Blumenblätter überragend; Antheren kurz elliptisch, oben und unten ausgerandet, unbehaart, 4-fächrig, mit Längsriss aufspringend. 1 Exemplar. — Herrn Apotheker Julius Scharlok in Graudenz zu Ehren benannt, dem eifrigen und geschickten Erforscher der Flora des Kreises Graudenz.

Oxalidacea.

26. **Oxalidites brachysepalus Casp.** Eine junge Frucht $6^{1}/_{4}$ mm lang, mit fünf, $^{1}/_{2}$ mm langen freien fadenförmigen Griffelresten oben; Frucht fünffurchig und 5-kantig, länglich, doppelt so lang als breit ohne die Griffel und ohne den Blüthenstiel, fast ellipsoidisch, oben gestutzt, in der Mitte am breitesten; 5 unterständige nierenförmige am Rande etwas ausgefressen krause Kelchblätter. 1 Stück.

Campanulacea?

27. **Carpolithus specularioides Casp.** Ein anscheinend drehrunder Fruchtknoten von $2^{1}/_{2}$ mm Länge, dessen Grund leider fehlt, trägt 5 spatelig-lineale Kelchblätter. Alle übrigen Blüthentheile fehlen. Der ganze Rest ist 8 mm hoch; er sieht einer jungen Frucht, deren Korolle mit den Staubblättern und dem Griffel abgeworfen sind, von Specularia Speculum DC. höchst ähnlich, ohne dass mit Sicherheit in ihm eine Campanulacee nachgewiesen ist.

Cupulifera.

28. **Quercus Klebsii Casp.** Perigon kreiselförmig (trichterig-glockig), $2^{1}/_{2}$—3 mm lang, oben etwa $1^{3}/_{4}$ mm breit, unbehaart, fünfzahnig, Zähne dreieckig, ungefähr so hoch als breit, spitzlich, Staubblätter etwa 9—10, wenig das Perigon überragend; Antheren elliptisch, oben und unten etwas ausgerandet, oder die Spitze (auf demselben Blüthestande) schwach und stumpflich mukronat. Brakteen lineal-lanzettlich, ungefähr so lang als das Perigon; Blüthenaxe dicht mit Sternhaaren besetzt. — 1 Blüthestand. Benannt nach dem Staatsgeologen Herrn Dr. Richard Klebs.

Pilze.

29. Stilbum succini Casp. Etwa $^1/_2$ mm hoch, Stiel in der Mitte 0,1 mm dick, Kopf stark gewölbt, mit stumpfer Kante am Grunde, 0,216 mm im Durchmesser, Sporen schon verstreut, jedoch noch viele auf dem Kopf und auch dem Stiel haftend, elliptisch, 0,0066—0,0079 lang, braunroth. — 1 Ex. auf einer Unterlage, die wahrscheinlich Vogelkoth ist. Ausgezeichnet erhalten, dem Stilbum vulgare sehr ähnlich.

26. Gonatobotrys primigenia Casp. Aufrehte Fäden 0,074 — 0,199 mm hoch und 0,0042—0,0071 mm dick. Im untern Theil die Fäden schmutzig tiefbraun, und hier selten mit gerader Seitenwand, oft etwas wellig, meist fast rosenkranzartig, indem Einschürungen mit Anschwellungen dicht bei einander wechseln. Oben sitzen auf den letzten 2—3 Anschwellungen ringsum viele fast gestielte elliptische durchscheinende schmutzig braune Sporen, etwa 0,0019 mm lang und fast halb so breit. Die letzte Anschwellung ist meist eiförmig, zugespitzt, fast farblos und trägt auf der Spitze einen Sporenhaufen. — Auf einem nicht sicher deutbaren Blütherest. Ist dem Gonatobotrys fusca Saccardo Fung. ital. 48 ähnlich, aber die angeschwollenen Glieder stehen bei dem fossilen Pilz ganz dicht.

31. Ramularia oblongispora Casp. Kurze aufrechte Fäden 0,045—0,051 mm hoch und 0,0028—0,0042 mm dick sind fast farblos, gegliedert. Die Glieder 2—3 mal so lang als breit, fast walzig oder tonnenartig, Fäden oben 1—4 ästig, die Glieder der Äste fallen als elliptische Keimkörner ab. — Auf dem Griffel eines Blüthenrestes. Die Gattung Ramularia fasse ich in der Weise, wie Saccardo l. c. 995 u. ff.

32. Torula heteromorpha Casp. Fäden, die aus kurz elliptischen oder fast länglichen, schmutzig-braunen Gliedern bestehen, die 0,0057—0,0071 mm im Durchmesser haben und nur so lang oder wenig länger sind; oft haben die Fäden auch Äste; 3—30 solcher Glieder, die dicht auf einander folgen, endigen beiderseits mit langem dünnem vegetativem Faden, der nur 0,0011—0,0014 mm dick ist und selten Gliederung erkennen lässt. — Frei ohne Unterlage in einem Stück Bernstein.

33. Torula globulifera Casp. Verästelte Fäden bestehen aus kuglichen oder fast kuglichen tief schmutzig-braunen Zellen, die 0,0026—0,0066 mm im Durchmesser haben. Selten zwischen ihnen vegetative auch verästelte sehr dünne walzige Fäden von 0,0013 mm Durchmesser. — Mehrere Haufen oder Bruchstücke dieses Pilzes frei in einem Stück Bernstein; auch auf einer nicht erkennbaren Unterlage.

34. Acremonium succineum Casp. Über Blätter und Axe von Widdringtonites oblongifolius Goepp. fr. longifolia ziehen sich oberflächlich tief-braune 0,0042 mm dicke verästelte walzige Fäden hin, die hie und da senkrecht ebenso dicke und 0,085—0,096 mm hohe Fäden aufsteigen lassen, die mit einem umgekehrt eiförmigem, fast kuglichem Kopf von etwa 0,0227 mm Länge und 0,017 mm Breite endigen.

Beobachtungen

der

Station zur Messung der Temperatur der Erde

in verschiedenen Tiefen

im botanischen Garten zu Königsberg in Pr.

Januar 1879 bis December 1880.

Herausgegeben von Dr. E. **Mischpeter.**

Da Herr Professor Dr. E. Dorn, jetzt in Halle, durch andere Arbeiten an der Herausgabe der Beobachtungen verhindert ist, so habe ich dieselbe übernommen. Die restierenden Jahrgänge will ich so schnell wie es irgend möglich ist bearbeiten, und es erfolgen hier zunächst die beiden Jahrgänge 1879 und 1880 der Beobachtungen in derselben Anordnung wie die früheren.

Am 22./23. Februar 1879 wurde die Station von einem sehr bedauerlichen Unfall betroffen. Am 23. Februar erhielt ich von Herrn Gartenmeister Einicke, der die Ablesungen an den Thermometern macht, die Nachricht, dass er das Quecksilber bei E_{24} nicht zu sehen vermöge. Eiligst begab ich mich nach dem botanischen Garten und überzeugte mich, dass das Thermometer äusserlich durchaus unverletzt, jedoch das Quecksilber bei demselben vor der Skala vollständig verschwunden war. Das deutete natürlich auf einen Bruch an irgend einer Stelle unterhalb des Erdbodens. Bis heute ist die Sache unaufgeklärt, und die Beobachtungen konnten vom 22. Februar 1879 an E_{24} nicht mehr gemacht werden.

Am 18. Januar 1879 stellte ich eine Bestimmung der Nullpunkte bei den Thermometern I^1 und IV an, fand dieselben jedoch gegen meine Bestimmung am 20. April 1877 unverändert.

Der Quecksilberfaden bei Thermometer VII riss in der Zeit vom 1. bis 7. December 1879 wiederholt. Erst am 9. December konnte ich eine ernstliche Reparatur vornehmen, die auch von dauerndem Erfolg war. Für die Berechnung des Monatsmittels sind die entsprechenden Angaben von IV benutzt.

Januar 1879.

Luftthermometer.

III. In Glas			IV. In Kupfer			1' frei			VII.		
7	2	8	7	2	8	7	2	8	7	2	8
	5,96	3,33	4,68	6,03	3,32	4,90	5,90	3,48	5,08	6,62	3,62
	0,63	0,35	0,15	0,43	− 0,05	0,96	0,32	0,45	0,47	0,27	1,04
0,86	0,27	0,87	− 0,76	0,53	0,58	− 0,60	0,19	0,45	− 0,11	0,47	0,85
1,75	0,39	− 1,75	− 1,40	0,15	− 1,78	− 1,71	0,02	− 1,45	− 0,88	− 0,22	− 1,58
	− 0,22	− 5,10	− 2,22	− 0,29	− 4,75	− 2,14	− 1,18	− 4,60	− 2,09	− 1,72	− 4,40
	0,83	− 5,47	− 2,36	− 0,09	− 5,60	− 2,14	− 0,75	− 5,25	− 2,21	− 0,88	− 5,57
	− 3,77	−15,53	− 8,52	− 5,23	−15,01	− 7,79	− 5,08	−14,20	− 8,32	− 4,98	−15,56
	− 1,67	− 6,35	− 5,70	− 2,98	− 6,18	− 5,46	− 3,09	− 6,12	− 5,89	− 3,25	− 6,49
	− 7,52	− 9,09	− 8,81	− 8,28	− 8,95	− 8,62	− 8,19	− 8,79	− 8,90	− 8,58	− 9,06
	− 7,00	− 7,88	− 1,93	− 7,47	− 7,71	−11,62	− 7,44	− 7,75	−11,86	− 7,56	− 7,88
	− 3,85	− 4,66	− 5,80	− 3,93	− 4,75	− 5,59	− 4,09	− 4,60	− 5,98	− 4,43	− 4,81
	− 3,79	− 4,58	− 5,23	− 3,97	− 4,70	− 5,12	− 3,96	− 4,30	− 5,27	− 4,28	− 4,70
	− 3,45	− 4,94	− 5,33	− 3,70	− 4,75	− 5,16	− 3,70	− 4,60	− 5,49	− 4,05	− 4,69
	− 2,16	− 3,60	− 4,27	− 2,36	− 3,52	− 4,17	− 2,44	− 3,43	− 4,43	− 2,90	− 3,51
4,16	− 3,37	− 6,68	− 4,61	− 3,56	− 6,66	− 4,21	− 3,57	− 6,55	− 4,43	− 3,55	− 6,80
	− 3,59	− 5,39	− 6,66	− 4,17	− 5,89	− 6,37	− 4,43	− 4,60	− 6,60	− 5,04	− 5,97
	− 4,34	− 5,06	− 4,75	− 4,27	− 5,09	− 4,30	− 4,30	− 4,73	− 4,81	− 4,78	− 5,19
	− 3,49	− 6,27	− 5,04	− 3,80	− 6,08	− 4,64	− 3,88	− 5,59	− 4,97	− 3,98	− 6,04
	− 3,08	− 6,07	− 5,99	− 3,37	− 5,60	− 5,41	− 3,47	− 5,16	− 5,73	− 4,13	− 5,49
	− 3,04	− 6,87	− 5,60	− 3,33	− 6,85	− 5,16	− 3,34	− 6,46	− 5,35	− 4,05	− 7,18
	− 7,48	− 9,38	− 7,51	− 8,03	− 9,05	− 7,82	− 7,75	− 8,62	− 7,60	− 8,70	− 9,24
	− 3,45	− 9,90	−12,27	− 6,37	− 9,58	−11,62	− 6,85	− 9,30	−12,39	− 6,80	− 9,85
13,12	− 6,44	− 4,58	−12,79	− 6,66	− 4,46	−12,48	− 6,55	− 4,30	−13,01	− 6,80	− 4,51
	− 0,70	− 1,35	− 3,80	− 1,30	− 1,40	− 3,78	− 1,27	− 1,27	− 3,74	− 1,04	− 1,34
	1,68	− 2,56	− 1,26	0,91	− 2,36	− 0,96	0,80	− 2,41	− 0,76	0,62	− 2,21
	− 3,45	− 4,66	− 7,99	− 4,27	− 4,70	− 7,11	− 4,56	− 4,64	− 7,34	− 5,27	− 4,78
	− 2,32	− 3,85	− 4,37	− 2,74	− 3,80	− 2,87	− 3,04	− 3,78	− 4,21	− 3,55	− 3,82
	0,83	− 1,75	− 1,88	0,15	− 1,74	− 1,71	0,06	− 1,62	− 1,68	− 0,22	− 1,68
	− 5,59	− 8,13	− 4,27	− 6,08	− 8,04	− 4,21	− 6,03	− 7,75	− 4,51	− 6,42	− 8,21
7,94	− 1,83	−15,85	−17,71	− 9,87	−15,78	−17,52	− 9,91	− 4,93	−17,85	− 9,85	−15,79
9,06	− 6,19	−15,58	−18,67	−11,45	−15,80	−17,97	−11,20	− 4,63	−19,67	−11,29	−15,29
5,97	− 2,61	− 5,75	− 5,89	− 3,17	− 5,67	− 5,57	− 3,64	− 5,39	− 5,85	− 3,90	− 5,68

Februar 1879.

III. In Glas			IV. In Kupfer			1' frei			VII.		
7	2	8	7	2	8	7	2	8	7	2	8
19,56	− 6,68	−14,92	−19,68	−10,88	− 4,20	−18,69	− 6,87	−15,05	−18,61	−10,90	−14,91
16,86	− 5,79	− 6,08	−13,37	− 5,80	− 6,08	−13,21	− 5,99	− 6,07	−13,89	− 6,42	− 6,12
18,92	− 0,70	−10,35	−13,95	− 6,18	− 9,91	−13,13	− 6,46	−10,67	−13,28	− 5,53	−10,28
7,88	− 0,22	−10,20	− 7,71	− 4,85	− 9,89	− 7,69	− 5,16	−10,14	− 7,98	− 5,23	− 9,70
11,91	− 5,06	− 9,05	−13,37	− 5,09	− 8,62	−12,33	− 5,53	− 9,42	−12,13	− 5,96	− 9,09
3,45	0,27	− 1,40	− 3,22	− 0,14	− 1,71	− 3,00	− 0,41	− 1,43	− 3,36	− 0,30	− 1,41
1,08	1,80	1,59	1,01	1,74	1,19	0,89	1,41	1,80	1,31	1,92	2,00
2,48	2,20	2,36	2,61	1,97	2,09	2,27	2,14	2,32	2,39	2,50	2,77
2,60	3,01	3,04	2,96	2,89	3,05	2,76	2,65	3,01	2,85	3,08	3,36
4,08	3,89	1,78	3,76	3,47	1,75	3,68	3,05	1,80	4,23	3,08	2,00
3,81	4,62	3,56	3,85	4,39	3,38	3,68	4,00	4,01	4,08	4,12	4,31
1,31	5,31	1,73	1,69	4,53	1,79	1,61	4,25	1,84	2,08	4,01	1,81
0,16	0,59	− 0,33	− 0,19	− 0,05	− 0,56	0,02	0,02	− 0,77	− 0,22	0,00	− 0,76
1,23	− 0,16	− 2,26	− 1,21	− 0,05	− 2,14	− 1,18	− 0,63	− 2,24	− 1,15	− 0,68	− 1,91
5,35	9,16	− 2,74	− 5,13	− 2,26	− 2,57	− 6,67	0,02	− 3,04	− 4,28	− 1,42	− 2,21
2,66	− 1,83	− 2,26	− 2,36	− 2,22	− 1,80	− 1,67	− 2,14	− 2,56	− 2,41	− 2,37	− 2,13
6,86	− 2,56	− 4,65	− 6,05	− 3,32	− 4,60	− 6,30	− 3,21	− 4,92	− 4,89	− 3,66	− 4,81
6,26	0,95	− 2,26	− 6,17	− 0,24	− 2,05	− 3,87	− 0,32	− 2,24	− 4,13	− 1,07	− 2,13
1,95	1,68	− 0,14	− 1,83	0,10	− 0,41	− 1,62	0,49	− 0,42	− 1,83	− 0,08	− 0,30
1,63	1,68	− 2,26	− 1,60	0,91	− 2,05	− 1,23	0,58	− 2,24	− 1,37	0,16	− 2,18
7,88	6,77	− 1,21	− 7,61	0,05	− 2,14	− 7,62	− 0,41	− 2,24	− 7,94	0,89	− 2,13
0,67	2,20	− 3,22	0,06	1,39	− 3,74	0,58	0,93	− 3,01	− 0,14	0,71	− 2,63
2,66	9,52	− 2,02	− 2,60	2,70	− 1,62	− 2,31	1,96	− 2,08	− 2,53	2,00	− 2,18
	2,93	0,91	0,53	2,46	0,89	0,80	2,27	1,15	0,85	2,39	1,35
	2,68	− 0,05	− 0,29	1,97	0,02	0,02	1,71	− 0,14	0,16	1,62	0,19
	0,95	0,53	− 0,19	0,03	0,45	− 0,11	0,45	0,59	− 0,49	0,85	0,85
	1,67	0,19	0,00	0,91	0,02	0,02	0,38	0,27	0,00	1,04	0,47
4,14	2,68	− 0,11	− 3,56	1,68	− 0,28	− 3,36	1,28	− 0,30	− 3,44	1,23	− 0,50
3,54	1,49	− 2,14	− 3,36	− 0,33	− 2,11	− 3,16	− 0,31	− 2,22	− 3,07	− 0,42	− 2,00

Januar 1879.

Erdthermometer

		1' tief			2' tief			4' tief			8' tief	16' tief	24' tief
		7	2	8	7	2	8	7	2	8	7	7	7
2,76	1,46	0,96	1,15	1,12	1,74	1,82	1,76	4,04	4,03	4,02	7,11	9,30	9,12
0,39	0,22	1,09	1,09	1,11	1,87	1,88	1,88	3,99	3,99	3,97	7,04	9,29	9,12
0,22	0,29	1,10	1,15	1,21	1,76	1,91	1,94	3,95	3,94	3,93	6,80	9,24	9,13
0,19	0,11	1,19	1,20	1,18	1,95	1,93	1,95	3,92	3,91	3,89	6,87	9,23	9,12
0,23	— 0,35	1,22	1,21	1,17	1,93	1,94	1,87	3,88	3,87	3,86	6,87	9,21	9,11
0,19	— 0,21	1,15	1,18	1,16	1,94	1,94	1,93	3,86	3,86	3,85	6,81	9,16	9,09
— 0,49	— 2,01	1,10	1,09	1,06	1,93	1,92	1,93	3,85	3,83	3,81	6,78	9,15	9,08
— 0,44	— 1,26	1,01	1,00	0,98	1,91	1,85	1,91	3,80	3,79	3,79	6,71	9,09	9,08
— 2,26	— 2,00	0,92	0,82	0,78	1,84	1,80	1,75	3,77	3,74	3,73	6,65	9,06	9,08
— 3,07	— 2,99	0,63	0,56	0,51	1,70	1,63	1,50	3,71	3,70	3,69	6,58	9,04	9,07
— 1,48	— 1,43	0,46	0,44	0,45	1,52	1,48	1,47	3,67	3,66	3,68	6,58	9,01	9,06
— 1,30	— 1,41	0,42	0,40	0,40	1,42	1,39	1,37	3,65	3,60	3,60	6,48	9,00	9,06
— 1,30	— 1,46	0,40	0,34	0,34	1,34	1,32	1,29	3,60	3,50	3,49	6,46	8,98	9,06
— 1,97	— 1,08	0,32	0,31	0,31	1,28	1,26	1,25	3,47	3,43	3,42	6,38	8,93	9,05
— 1,24	— 1,93	0,31	0,32	0,30	1,22	1,22	1,20	3,39	3,39	3,39	6,34	8,91	9,04
— 1,65	— 1,73	0,24	0,19	0,27	1,16	1,15	1,13	3,33	3,31	3,31	6,27	8,87	9,04
— 1,60	— 1,69	0,06	0,17	0,17	1,09	1,09	1,08	3,27	3,26	3,22	6,23	8,86	9,03
— 1,60	— 2,11	0,12	0,10	0,04	1,03	1,04	1,01	3,22	3,20	3,19	6,18	8,82	9,03
— 1,73	— 1,94	0,06	0,02	0,04	0,91	0,96	0,92	3,15	3,14	3,14	6,13	8,81	9,02
— 1,49	— 2,14	0,01	0,01	0,00	0,91	0,90	0,88	3,12	3,03	3,05	6,09	8,77	9,01
— 2,97	— 3,30	— 0,11	— 0,14	— 0,20	0,85	0,85	0,82	3,04	3,01	3,01	6,01	8,72	8,99
— 3,38	— 4,03	— 0,34	— 0,41	— 0,49	0,81	0,77	0,74	2,98	2,98	2,94	5,97	8,69	8,99
— 3,92	— 3,00	— 0,70	— 0,82	— 0,76	0,70	0,68	0,60	2,91	2,89	2,88	5,96	8,67	8,98
— 1,38	— 1,16	— 5,58	— 0,49	— 0,31	0,58	0,56	0,58	2,86	2,83	2,83	5,86	8,66	8,97
— 0,50	— 0,95	— 0,26	— 0,22	— 0,18	0,57	0,55	0,57	2,79	2,76	2,76	5,85	8,66	9,03
— 1,98	— 2,13	— 0,15	— 0,24	— 0,32	0,58	0,56	0,54	2,75	2,72	2,72	5,78	8,62	8,99
— 1,70	— 1,83	— 0,40	— 0,44	— 0,41	0,52	0,52	0,48	2,69	2,67	2,67	5,74	8,57	8,97
— 1,78	— 0,84	— 0,31	— 0,31	— 0,28	0,41	0,49	0,49	2,65	2,63	2,61	5,69	8,55	8,96
— 1,97	— 2,63	— 0,20	— 0,24	— 0,29	0,42	0,48	0,49	2,60	2,58	2,58	5,62	8,51	8,95
— 4,39	— 6,09	— 0,70	— 0,96	— 1,14	0,47	0,44	0,37	2,58	2,57	2,56	5,60	8,49	8,95
— 5,78	— 6,42	— 1,63	— 1,87	— 1,17	0,29	0,25	0,21	2,53	2,53	2,51	5,55	8,47	8,94
— 1,54	— 1,82	0,08	0,21	0,23	1,18	1,18	1,16					8,88	9,04

Februar 1879.

		1' tief			2' tief			4' tief			8' tief	16' tief	24' tief
		7	2	8	7	2	8	7	2	8	7	7	7
— 5,98	— 6,53	— 1,55	2,49	2,46	0,13	0,08	0,05	2,49	2,46	2,45	5,49	8,45	8,92
— 5,19	— 4,53	— 2,79	2,30	2,51	0,15	0,15	0,22	2,40	2,36	2,34	5,45	8,41	8,92
— 4,08	— 5,08	— 2,42	2,42	2,24	0,20	0,22	0,24	2,33	2,30	2,28	5,42	8,38	8,91
— 3,81	— 4,75	— 2,32	2,21	2,12	0,27	0,28	0,30	2,23	2,22	2,19	5,34	8,34	8,89
— 4,26	— 4,66	— 2,39	2,49	2,26	0,34	0,40	0,40	2,16	2,10	2,04	5,31	8,31	8,89
— 2,10	— 2,05	— 2,22	1,96	1,69	0,41	0,43	0,40	2,06	2,03	2,01	5,28	8,28	8,89
— 0,65	— 0,12	— 1,90	1,11	0,86	0,32	0,26	0,23	2,01	1,95	1,95	5,21	8,25	8,89
0,38	— 0,51	— 0,55	0,40	0,25	0,11	0,14	0,05	1,95	1,91	1,86	5,16	8,25	8,87
0,76	— 0,92	— 0,11	0,09	0,05	0,02	0,02	0,04	1,87	1,88	1,88	5,13	8,21	8,88
1,14	0,78	0,01	0,34	0,06	0,09	0,08	0,10	1,87	1,86	1,87	5,07	8,18	8,86
1,76	1,25	0,08	0,10	0,11	0,11	0,11	0,12	1,87	1,86	1,85	5,05	8,16	8,85
2,46	1,06	0,14	0,14	0,14	0,18	0,14	0,17	1,83	1,82	1,83	5,01	8,14	8,86
0,22	0,20	0,19	0,16	0,16	0,19	0,17	0,17	1,83	1,83	1,82	4,96	8,11	8,84
0,23	0,08	0,17	0,16	0,17	0,19	0,19	0,18	1,82	1,83	1,83	4,89	8,06	8,80
0,42	0,22	0,18	0,23	0,18	0,21	0,24	0,20	1,82	1,84	1,83	4,85	8,03	8,77
— 0,27	— 0,05	0,22	0,22	0,21	0,22	0,20	0,20	1,83	1,82	1,82	4,84	8,01	8,78
— 0,75	— 1,08	0,22	0,19	0,19	0,22	0,21	0,21	1,80	1,82	1,82	4,80	7,99	8,76
— 0,13	— 0,27	0,18	0,19	0,20	0,21	0,20	0,21	1,81	1,83	1,84	4,74	7,93	8,74
0,04	0,09	0,19	0,19	0,21	0,21	0,23	0,24	1,84	1,83	1,84	4,73	7,93	8,73
0,07	— 0,18	0,22	0,21	0,22	0,24	0,25	0,26	1,84	1,83	1,82	4,68	7,88	8,72
0,19	— 0,35	0,18	0,19	0,18	0,29	0,30	0,28	1,77	1,82	1,83	4,64	7,85	8,72
0,09	0,10	0,17	0,19	0,20	0,29	0,29	0,33	1,84	1,84	1,86	4,63	7,82	8,70
0,43	0,26	0,24	0,19	0,18	0,34	0,35	0,35	1,87	1,87	1,87	4,62	7,82	
0,22	0,26	0,06	0,20	0,19	0,36	0,36	0,37	1,88	1,87	1,88	4,59	7,78	
0,87	0,22	0,19	0,22	0,23	0,38	0,37	0,39	1,88	1,88	1,88	4,56	7,76	
0,23	0,25	0,23	0,22	0,22	0,41	0,41	0,42	1,88	1,88	1,89	4,54	7,73	
0,85	0,22	0,23	0,24	0,23	0,44	0,46	0,47	1,89	1,89	1,90	4,50	7,68	
	0,26	0,24	0,22	0,23	0,48	0,46	0,50	1,90	1,91	1,93	4,48	7,67	
					0,12	0,11	0,13	1,95	1,94	1,94	4,93	8,00	

März 1879.

Luftthermometer											
III. In Glas			IV. In Kupfer			1' frei					
7	2	8	7	2	8	7	2	8	7	2	8
	10,73	— 3,85	— 2,65	3,32	— 3,98	— 2,40	1,71	— 3,09	— 2,79	2,00	— 3,44
	8,67	— 5,31	— 3,08	2,46	— 5,33	— 2,57	1,66	— 4,60	— 3,25	2,58	— 5,35
	1,88	— 0,14	— 0,66	1,49	— 0,19	— 0,71	1,11	0,02	— 0,96	0,85	— 0,29
	2,08	— 0,27	— 0,91	1,73	0,34	— 0,54	1,41	0,23	— 1,37	1,06	0,39
	5,35	— 1,02	— 0,43	3,56	— 0,91	— 0,24	3,05	— 0,67	— 0,38	2,27	— 0,68
	6,24	1,92	1,10	4,63	1,97	1,10	3,95	1,84	1,15	3,97	2,00
	7,62	— 0,02	0,82	4,58	0,05	0,76	3,48	0.15	0,77	3,54	0,08
	3,81	1,64	— 1,26	3,08	1,73	— 0,20	2,52	1,75	0,08	2,31	1,70
	5,55	1,47	0,05	4,29	1,49	0,54	3,48	1,75	0,77	3,43	1,96
	4,26	2,20	1,39	3,80	2,22	1,53	3,57	2.18	1,58	3,49	2,50
	2,97	— 0,62	1,97	2,26	— 0,43	1,96	2,09	— 0,71	2,00	2,00	— 0,68
2,64	1,99	— 1,71	— 2,94	— 0,26	— 1,50	— 2,97	— 0,84	— 2,57	— 2,71	— 1,07	— 1,45
1,51	0,91	— 3,45	— 1,94	— 0,66	— 3,22	— 1,71	— 0,84	— 3,00	— 1,83	— 1,37	— 3,28
1,83	5,55	— 3,45	— 2,36	1,01	— 3,32	— 2,53	— 0,45	— 3,25	— 2,49	— 0,99	— 2,88
5,71	4,22	— 4,58	— 5,84	0,77	— 4,85	— 5,59	— 0,84	— 4,73	— 6,04	— 0,96	— 4,51
8,69	4,42	— 4,66	— 8,09	0,26	— 4,75	— 7,53	— 0,41	— 4,39	— 7,98	0,08	— 4,96
10,87	6,01	— 6,60	—10,49	1,11	— 6,47	— 9,48	— 0,02	— 5,37	—10,23	0,39	— 5,89
8,69	1,80	0,19	— 7,99	0,77	0,10	— 7,32	0,89	0,11	— 7,86	0,20	0,20
1,02	3,89	— 1,02	— 1,40	2,56	— 0,91	— 1,36	2,18	— 0,71	— 1,91	1,62	— 0,68
2,72	6,85	— 2,24	— 2,46	4,10	— 1,88	— 2,14	2,31	— 2,01	— 2,64	2,16	— 1,88
	5,96	— 5,87	— 7,61	0,53	— 5,81	— 7,32	— 1,62	— 5,03	— 7,37	— 1,45	— 4,89
	6,24	— 3,93	— 8,09	1,49	— 3,80	— 7,32	0,36	— 3,43	— 7,94	1,23	— 3,86
	5,35	— 5,51	— 7,04	— 0,29	— 5,41	— 6,89	— 1,27	— 5,03	— 7,07	— 1,64	— 5,65
	6,24	— 4,26	— 8,57	1,49	— 4.13	— 8,06	0,02	— 3,78	— 8,32	0,16	— 3,98
	4,22	— 3,65	— 6,08	1,01	— 3,32	— 5,56	0,02	— 3,00	— 6,00	— 0,52	— 2,98
	0,99	— 4,66	— 4,75	— 0,69	— 4,65	— 4,43	— 0,50	— 4,21	— 5,19	— 1,72	— 4,18
	8,75	— 3,45	— 4,27	3,61	— 3,22	— 4,21	0,98	— 2,87	— 4,66	0,31	— 2,98
	8,19	— 3,04	— 6,66	4,39	— 2,84	— 6,37	1,32	— 2,83	— 6,50	1,00	— 2,75
	14,77	— 2,04	— 5.23	8,25	— 1,88	— 4,76	4,47	— 1,27	— 5,35	3,27	— 1,45
	3,89	1,47	— 2,84	2,94	1,49	— 2,44	2,52	1,41	— 2,98	1,73	1,62
	6,57	1,99	1.11	5,16	1,01	1,02	4,47	1,15	0,85	4,23	1,56
— 3,44	+ 5,32	— 2,10	— 3,16	+ 2,35	— 1,98	— 2,89	+ 1,31		— 3,41	1,10	— 1,78

April 1879.

7	2	8	7	2	8	7	2	8	7	2	8
2,20	13,59	4,22	1,87	10,04	4,00	1,66	8,57	3,91	1,62	8,70	4,31
3,78	21,27	8,27	3,82	17,42	7,77	3,14	15,17	7,67	3,16	15,53	8,47
4,82	21,27	9,77	4,39	17,80	9,35	4,84	16,04	9,53	4,31	16,60	10,09
4,91	18,34	5,08	4,39	14,60	4,73	4,25	19,09	5,04	4,54	13,00	5,47
2,60	15,87	4,62	2,86	11,87	4,39	2,18	9.97	4,63	2,08	9,78	5,00
2,44	8,43	5,55	2,46	8,06	5,35	2,48	7,80	5,34	2,39	7,86	5,85
0,06	12,08	3,01	0,19	8,78	2,94	0,02	7,24	3,05	0,45	7,51	3,35
2,89	7,46	5,84	2,65	6,46	5,84	2,70	6,87	5,73	2,54	5,97	5,85
2,76	15,58	2.48	2,17	11,14	2,46	2,18	9,89	2,96	2,04	9,51	2,77
0,43	6,65	0,71	0,15	5,85	0,82	0,15	4,81	0,89	0,22	3,93	0,93
1,51	11,59	2,72	1,01	8,49	2,94	0,98	7,26	3,39	0,85	6,93	2,96
1,84	5,35	4,22	1,78	4,53	4,15	1,71	4,43	4,01	1,42	4,19	4,31
2,60	6,12	3,81	2,46	5,11	3,90	2,89	4,95	3,91	2,27	4,70	4,01
1,23	8,75	2,60	0,91	6,76	2,56	1,10	6,67	2,71	1,08	5.47	2,77
3,49	15,17	0,35	3,18	11,14	1,97	2,74	9,62	1,28	2,23	8,93	1,27
2,60	6,77	9,24	2,26	5,98	9,11	2,27	5,77	9,10	2,00	6,16	9,70
5,08	18,95	8,19	4,49	17,85	8,85	4,34	17,17	8,66	4,16	17,59	8,82
10,87	6,82	7,84	9,79	5,95	7,28	9,44	5,21	7,37	9,70	4,70	7,39
3,41	8,97	3,01	3,92	3,42	3,08	3,39	3,69	2,61	3,27	3,46	3,54
4,14	9,68	2,20	3,42	7,48	2,12	2,96	6,93	2,52	2,77	6,24	2,77
3,61	21,27	8,67	3,42	18,14	8,39	3,48	16,43	8,75	3,35	16,22	9,12
7,58	19,11	12,85	6,90	16,45	13,21	6,84	15,87	12,87	6,62	15,87	13,06
10,82	17,20	6,24	10,66	15,10	6,82	10,83	11,87	7,28	10,17	14,42	6,74
5,08	15,91	2,68	4,68	11,62	2,94	4,81	10,13	3.48	4,08	8,85	2,77
3,38	8,19	4,06	3,52	7,53	4,00	3,61	6,93	4.34	3,54	6,62	4,04
4,10	4,70	3,01	3,95	4,49	3,04	4,00	4,60	3,18	3,66	4,20	3,03
4,34	5,48	4,84	4,23	5,21	4,89	4,31	5,21	4,34	3,97	5.08	4,70
5,08	7,21	3,57	4,87	6,90	3,61	4,43	6.84	3.91	4,58	6,74	3,85
4,62	11,06	4,70	4,49	9,35	4,68	4,55	8,66	4.81	4,31	7,86	4,81
5,23	9,89	7,66	5,16	9,02	7.42	5,21	8,32	7.71	5,24	8.66	7.70

März 1879.

Erdthermometer												
" tief		1' tief			2' tief			4' tief			8' tief	16' tief
2	8	7	2	8	7	2	8	7	2	8	7	7
0,48	0,29	0,24	0,23	0,24	0,50	0,50	0,50	1,91	1,92	1,93	4,47	7,66
0,51	0,26	0,24	0,25	0,25	0,52	0,53	0,53	1,92	1,94	1,94	4,47	7,62
0,20	0,28	0,24	0,24	0,24	0,54	0,54	0,53	1,92	1,95	1,94	4,45	7,60
0,25	0,31	0,24	0,23	0,26	0,53	0,57	0,57	1,95	1,95	1,94	4,41	7,45
0,72	0,21	0,26	0,26	0,25	0,57	0,56	0,58	1,95	1,94	1,95	4,41	7,45
1,20	0,65	0,26	0,27	0,27	0,59	0,59	0,60	1,95	1,95	1,98	4,40	7,51
1,55	0,23	0,24	0,26	0,26	0,61	0,61	0,62	1,94	1,96	1,96	4,37	7,47
1,20	0,89	0,25	0,27	0,28	0,64	0,62	0,63	1,96	1,97	1,97	4,36	7,47
1,95	0,73	0,26	0,28	0,29	0,64	0,65	0,65	1,96	1,98	1,99	4,35	7,44
2,01	1,13	0,29	0,28	0,29	0,68	0,67	0,68	1,99	1,99	1,99	4,34	7,41
1,60	0,37	0,32	0,29	0,29	0,71	0,68	0,69	1,99	1,98	2,00	4,33	7,41
0,22	0,08	0,28	0,29	0,30	0,71	0,69	0,73	1,97	1,98	1,99	4,30	7,45
0,18	− 0,29	0,31	0,32	0,37	0,74	0,74	0,74	1,99	1,99	1,98	4,30	7,46
0,40	0,14	0,31	0,32	0,32	0,75	0,77	0,77	1,97	1,99	1,99	4,27	7,40
0,27	− 0,05	0,33	0,34	0,34	0,78	0,78	0,78	1,98	2,01	2,03	4,24	7,32
0,26	0,21	0,34	0,35	0,36	0,84	0,83	0,86	2,02	2,01	2,03	4,25	7,27
0,36	− 0,15	0,35	0,36	0,37	0,81	0,84	0,85	2,00	2,02	2,03	4,25	7,26
0,08	0,08	0,35	0,38	0,38	0,84	0,86	0,87	2,01	2,02	2,03	4,20	7,22
0,48	0,24	0,38	0,38	0,40	0,87	0,87	0,88	2,01	2,03	2,03	4,20	7,19
0,25	0,26	0,40	0,42	0,43	0,89	0,90	0,89	2,02	2,04	2,05	4,18	7,18
0,33	− 0,92	0,40	0,41	0,41	0,91	0,92	0,91	2,05	2,07	2,02	4,18	7,15
0,41	0,28	0,37	0,41	0,42	0,91	0,93	0,94	2,05	2,05	2,05	4,17	7,11
0,29	− 1,77	0,37	0,37	0,44	0,93	0,92	0,96	2,04	2,05	2,03	4,15	7,11
0,35	− 0,41	0,29	0,31	0,31	0,89	0,88	0,89	2,05	2,05	2,04	4,13	7,07
0,23	− 0,39	0,25	0,28	0,32	0,85	0,86	0,87	2,03	2,04	2,02	4,12	7,04
− 0,09	− 1,29	0,26	0,28	0,30	0,84	0,84	0,84	2,03	2,02	2,02	4,11	7,03
0,31	− 0,32	0,22	0,26	0,28	0,83	0,83	0,83	2,01	2,02	2,01	4,11	7,01
0,81	− 0,12	0,21	0,23	0,25	0,82	0,81	0,79	2,00	2,01	2,01	4,09	7,00
2,19	0,26	0,17	0,20	0,26	0,78	0,78	0,79	1,99	1,99	1,98	4,07	6,97
0,17	0,38	0,28	0,27	0,30	0,79	0,76	0,78	1,97	1,97	1,98	4,08	6,94
1,19	0,42	0,30	0,30	0,30	0,77	0,79	0,79	1,95	1,96	1,98	4,05	6,93
0,67	0,06	0,31	0,30	0,31	0,74	0,74	0,75	1,99	1,99	2,00	4,25	7,28

April 1879.

" tief 2	" tief 8	1' 7	1' 2	1' 8	2' 7	2' 2	2' 8	4' 7	4' 2	4' 8	8' 7	16' 7
4,47	8,42	0,30	0,33	0,33	0,79	0,81	0,83	1.94	1,94	1,95	4,04	6,91
[illegible]	7,86	0,36	0,56	0,56	0,81	0,86	0,90	1,94	1,94	1,95	4,02	6,90
[illegible]	6,95	0,56	1,11	1,63	1,02	1,67	1,36	1,94	1,94	1,94	4,03	6,90
[illegible]	7,96	1,57	2,45	2,93	1,59	1,77	2,00	1,94	1,96	1,99	4,01	6,86
[illegible]	4,56	2,14	2,66	3,32	2,07	2,18	2,33	1,99	2,02	2,06	3,97	6,84
[illegible]	4,55	2,67	2,82	3,07	2,47	2,48	2,51	2,09	2,12	2,16	3,97	6,81
[illegible]	3,85	2,52	2,61	2,94	2,56	2,54	2,54	2,21	2.23	2,27	3,98	6,82
[illegible]	4,54	2.62	2,78	3,12	2,55	2,56	2,66	2,31	2,34	2,38	3,96	6,79
[illegible]	4 42	2,97	3,46	3,97	2,74	2,82	2,98	2,42	2.44	2.50	3,97	6,77
[illegible]	2,44	3,25	3,13	3,27	3,09	3,06	3,04	2,56	2,60	2,64	3,99	6,77
[illegible]	4,20	2,59	3,27	3,85	2,94	2,96	3,04	2,72	2,77	2,80	4,01	6,73
[illegible]	8,81	3,47	5,44	3,55	3,26	3,26	3,28	2,85	2,88	2,90	4,01	6,71
[illegible]	8,73	3,24	3,39	3 53	3,26	3,26	3,29	2,97	3,00	3,03	4,02	6,69
[illegible]	8,50	3.22	3,32	3,55	3,28	3,67	3,30	3,06	3,09	3,14	4,06	6,68
[illegible]	4,96	3,21	4,29	4,99	3,31	3,44	3,71	3,14	3,19	3,20	4,08	6,66
[illegible]	6,98	3,97	3,83	4,23	3,82	3.74	3,77	3,23	3,27	3,35	4.12	6,66
[illegible]	6,87	4,42	6,24	4,82	3,92	4,56	4.08	3,45	3,45	3,41	4,15	6,64
[illegible]	8,01	5,27	4,58	6,77	4,33	3,99	4,87	3,45	3,38	3,54	4,17	6,63
[illegible]	8,58	5,84	3,08	4,91	5,08	4,99	4,81	3,63	3,70	3,76	4,20	6,61
[illegible]	8,68	4,23	4,27	4,38	4,54	4,40	4,37	3,83	3,88	3,91	4,22	6,60
[illegible]	8,56	3,98	4,99	6,05	4,18	4,29	4,58	3,92	3,94	3,98	4,27	6,58
[illegible]	[illegible]	5,64	6,50	7,50	4,89	5,04	5,45	3,98	4,03	4,05	4,31	6,58
[illegible]	[illegible]	7,48	6,50	8,22	5,83	6,01	6,26	4,09	4,16	4,22	4,35	6,56
[illegible]	[illegible]	7,22	7,92	7,20	6,33	6,30	6,26	4,33	4,40	4,46	4,38	6,54
[illegible]	[illegible]	6,84	6,14	6,26	6,15	6,01	5,94	4,60	4,63	4,69	4,46	6,53
[illegible]	[illegible]	5,96	5,83	5,76	5,85	5,75	5,69	4,75	4,77	4,81	4,49	6,51
[illegible]	[illegible]	5,48	4,48	5,62	5,55	5,48	5,51	4,82	4,82	4,83	4,55	6,50
[illegible]	[illegible]	5,34	5,60	5,75	5,42	5,41	5,42	4,86	4,86	4,86	4,60	6,48
[illegible]	[illegible]	5,50	5,62	5,80	5,43	5,41	5,44	4,86	4,87	4,88	4,66	6,47
[illegible]	[illegible]	5,71	5,84	6,11	5,48	5,49	5.56	4,89	4,89	4,91	4.71	6,46
[illegible]	[illegible]	3.56	3.88	4.47	3.75	3.81	3.86	3.22	3.32	3.35	4.19	6.67

März 1879.

	Luftthermometer											
	III. In Glas			IV. In Kupfer			I' frei			VII.		
	7	2	8	7	2	8	7	2	8	7	2	8
1	— 2,92	10,78	— 3,85	— 2,65	3,32	— 3,98	— 2,40	1,71	— 3,09	— 2,79	2,00	— 3,44
2	— 3,37	8,67	— 5,31	— 3,08	2,46	— 5,33	— 2,57	1,66	— 4,60	— 3,25	2,58	— 5,85
3	— 1,23	1,88	— 0,14	— 0,66	1,49	— 0,19	— 0,71	1,11	0,02	— 0,96	0,85	— 0,22
4	— 1,02	2,08	— 0,27	— 0,91	1,73	0,34	— 0,54	1,41	0,23	— 1,37	1,06	0,39
5	— 0,58	5,35	— 1,02	— 0,43	3,56	— 0,91	— 0,24	3,05	— 0,67	— 0,38	2,27	— 0,68
6	1,11	6,24	1,92	1,10	4,63	1,97	1,10	3,95	1,84	1,15	3,97	2,00
7	0,95	7,62	— 0,02	0,82	4,58	0,05	0,76	3,48	0,15	0,77	3,54	0,08
8	— 0,30	3,81	1,64	— 1,26	3,08	1,73	— 0,20	2,52	1,75	0,08	2,31	1,70
9	0,51	5,55	1,47	0,05	4,29	1,49	0,54	3,48	1,75	0,77	3,48	1,95
10	1,59	4,26	2,20	1,39	3,80	2,22	1,53	3,57	2,18	1,58	3,43	2,50
11	2,00	2,97	— 0,62	1,97	2,26	— 0,43	1,96	2,09	— 0,71	2,00	2,00	— 0,68
12	— 2,64	1,39	— 1,71	— 2,94	— 0,26	— 1,50	— 2,87	— 0,84	— 2,57	— 2,71	— 1,07	— 1,45
13	— 1,51	0,91	— 3,45	— 1,94	— 0,66	— 3,22	— 1,71	— 0,84	— 3,00	— 1,83	— 1,37	— 3,28
14	— 1,83	5,55	— 3,45	— 2,36	1,01	— 3,32	— 2,53	— 0,45	— 3,25	— 2,49	— 0,99	— 2,98
15	— 5,71	4,23	— 4,58	— 5,84	0,77	— 4,85	— 5,59	— 0,84	— 4,73	— 6,04	— 0,96	— 4,51
16	— 8,69	4,42	— 4,66	— 8,09	0,26	— 4,75	— 7,53	— 0,41	— 4,30	— 7,08	0,08	— 4,36
17	—10,87	6,04	— 6,60	—10,49	1,11	— 6,47	— 9,48	— 0,02	— 5,37	—10,23	0,39	— 5,89
18	— 8,69	1,80	0,19	— 7,09	0,77	0,10	— 7,32	0,89	0,11	— 7,86	0,20	0,29
19	— 1,02	3,89	— 1,02	— 1,40	2,56	— 0,91	— 1,36	2,18	— 0,71	— 1,91	1,62	— 0,68
20	— 2,72	6,85	— 2,21	— 2,46	4,10	— 1,88	— 2,14	2,31	— 2,01	— 2,64	2,16	— 1,83
21	— 7,48	5,96	— 5,87	— 7,61	0,53	— 5,81	— 7,32	— 1,62	— 5,03	— 7,37	— 1,45	— 4,89
22	— 8,57	6,24	— 3,93	— 8,09	1,49	— 3,80	— 7,32	0,86	— 3,43	— 7,94	1,23	— 3,96
23	— 7,16	5,35	— 5,51	— 7,04	— 0,29	— 5,41	— 6,89	— 1,27	— 5,03	— 7,07	— 1,64	— 5,65
24	— 8,77	6,24	— 4,26	— 8,57	1,49	— 4,13	— 8,06	0,02	— 3,78	— 8,32	0,16	— 3,66
25	— 6,27	4,22	— 3,65	— 6,08	1,01	— 3,32	— 5,56	0,02	— 3,00	— 6,00	— 0,52	— 2,98
26	— 4,74	0,39	— 4,66	— 4,75	— 0,69	— 4,65	— 4,43	— 0,50	— 4,21	— 5,19	— 1,72	— 4,18
27	— 3,93	3,75	— 3,45	— 4,27	3,61	— 3,22	— 4,21	0,98	— 2,87	— 4,66	0,31	— 2,98
28	— 6,56	8,19	— 3,04	— 6,66	4,39	— 2,84	— 6,37	1,33	— 2,83	— 6,50	1,00	— 2,75
29	— 4,98	14,77	— 2,01	— 5,23	8,25	— 1,88	— 4,76	4,47	— 1,27	— 5,35	3,27	— 1,45
30	— 2,64	3,89	1,47	— 2,84	2,94	1,49	— 2,41	2,52	1,41	— 2,98	1,73	1,62
31	1,39	6,57	1,39	1,11	5,16	1,01	1,02	4,47	1,15	0,85	4,23	1,56
	— 3,44	+ 5,92	— 2,10	— 3,16	+ 2,35	— 1,98	— 2,89	+ 1,81	— 1,80	— 3,41	1,10	— 1,78

April 1879.

	7	2	8	7	2	8	7	2	8	7	2	8
1	2,20	13,59	4,23	1,87	10,04	4,00	1,66	8,57	3,91	1,63	8,70	4,31
2	3,73	21,27	8,27	3,32	17,42	7,77	3,14	15,17	7,67	3,16	15,53	8,47
3	4,82	21,27	9,77	4,39	17,80	9,35	4,34	16,04	9,53	4,31	16,60	10,09
4	4,91	18,34	5,03	4,39	14,60	4,73	4,25	13,09	5,04	4,54	13,00	5,47
5	2,60	15,37	4,62	2,36	11,87	4,39	2,18	9,97	4,63	2,08	9,78	5,00
6	2,44	8,43	5,55	2,46	8,06	5,35	2,48	7,80	5,34	2,39	7,86	5,85
7	— 0,06	12,08	3,01	— 0,19	8,73	2,94	0,02	7,24	3,05	— 0,45	7,51	3,35
8	2,89	7,46	5,84	2,65	6,46	5,84	2,70	6,87	5,73	2,54	5,97	5,85
9	2,76	15,58	2,48	2,17	11,14	2,46	2,18	9,89	2,96	2,04	9,51	2,77
10	0,43	6,65	0,71	0,15	5,35	0,32	0,15	4,81	0,89	— 0,22	3,93	0,98
11	1,51	11,59	2,72	1,01	8,49	2,94	0,98	7,26	3,39	0,85	6,98	2,96
12	1,84	5,35	4,22	1,78	4,53	4,15	1,71	4,43	4,04	1,42	4,19	4,31
13	2,60	6,12	3,81	2,46	5,11	3,90	2,39	4,95	3,91	2,27	4,70	4,01
14	1,23	8,75	2,60	0,91	6,76	2,56	1,10	6,67	2,74	1,08	5,47	2,77
15	3,49	15,17	0,35	3,18	11,14	1,97	2,74	9,62	1,28	2,23	8,93	1,27
16	2,60	6,77	9,21	2,26	5,98	9,11	2,27	5,77	9,10	2,00	6,16	9,70
17	5,03	18,95	8,19	4,49	17,83	8,35	4,84	17,17	8,66	4,16	17,59	8,82
18	10,37	6,32	7,34	9,79	5,35	7,28	9,44	5,21	7,37	9,70	4,70	7,39
19	3,41	3,97	3,01	3,32	3,42	3,08	3,39	3,69	2,61	3,27	3,46	3,54
20	4,14	9,68	2,20	3,42	7,43	2,12	2,96	6,93	2,52	2,77	6,24	2,77
21	3,61	21,27	8,67	3,42	18,14	8,39	3,48	16,48	8,75	3,35	16,22	9,12
22	7,58	19,11	12,85	6,90	16,45	13,21	6,84	15,87	12,87	6,62	15,37	13,08
23	10,82	17,20	6,24	10,68	15,10	6,32	10,83	14,87	7,28	10,17	14,42	6,74
24	5,03	15,91	2,08	4,68	11,62	2,94	4,81	10,18	3,48	4,08	8,85	2,77
25	3,83	8,13	4,06	3,52	7,53	4,00	3,61	6,93	4,34	3,54	6,62	4,04
26	4,10	4,70	3,01	3,95	4,49	3,04	4,00	4,60	3,18	3,66	4,20	3,08
27	4,34	5,43	4,34	4,29	5,21	4,39	4,34	5,21	4,34	3,97	5,08	4,70
28	5,03	7,21	3,57	4,87	6,90	3,61	4,43	6,81	3,91	4,58	6,74	3,85
29	4,62	11,06	4,70	4,49	9,35	4,68	4,55	8,60	4,81	4,81	7,88	4,81
30	5,23	9,89	7,66	5,16	9,03	7,42	5,21	8,32	7,71	5,24	8,66	7,70
	3,89	11,76	5,03	3,60	9,71	4,70	3,55	8,95	5,17	3,44	8,66	4,65

März 879.

Erdthermometer													
1" tief			1' tief			2' tief			4' tief			8' tief	16' ti
7	2	8	7	2	8	7	2	8	7	2	8	7	7
	0,43	0,29	0,24	0,23	0,24	0,50	0,50	0,50	1,91	1,92	1,93	4,47	7,66
0,22	0,51	0,26	0,24	0,25	0,25	0,52	0,53	0,53	1,92	1,94	1,94	4,47	7,62
0,06	0,20	0,23	0,24	0,24	0,24	0,54	0,54	0,53	1,92	1,95	1,94	4,45	7,60
0,24	0,26	0,31	0,24	0,23	0,26	0,53	0,57	0,57	1,95	1,95	1,94	4,41	7,45
0,25	0,72	0,21	0,26	0,26	0,25	0,57	0,56	0,58	1,95	1,94	1,95	4,41	7,45
0,24	1,20	0,65	0,26	0,27	0,27	0,59	0,59	0,60	1,95	1,95	1,98	4,40	7,51
0,29	1,56	0,23	0,24	0,26	0,26	0,61	0,61	0,62	1,94	1,96	1,96	4,37	7,47
0,19	1,20	0,89	0,25	0,27	0,28	0,64	0,62	0,63	1,96	1,97	1,97	4,36	7,47
0,29	1,95	0,73	0,26	0,28	0,29	0,64	0,65	0,65	1,96	1,98	1,99	4,35	7,44
0,84	2,01	1,13	0,29	0,28	0,29	0,68	0,67	0,68	1,99	1,99	1,99	4,34	7,41
1,06	1,60	0,87	0,32	0,29	0,29	0,71	0,68	0,69	1,99	1,98	2,00	4,33	7,41
− 0,19	0,22	0,03	0,28	0,29	0,30	0,71	0,69	0,73	1,97	1,98	1,99	4,30	7,45
− 0,10	0,18	− 0,29	0,31	0,32	0,37	0,74	0,74	0,74	1,99	1,99	1,98	4,30	7,46
− 0,27	0,40	0,14	0,31	0,32	0,32	0,75	0,77	0,77	1,97	1,99	1,99	4,27	7,40
− 0,74	0,27	− 0,05	0,33	0,34	0,34	0,78	0,78	0,78	1,98	2,01	2,03	4,24	7,32
− 1,18	0,26	0,21	0,34	0,35	0,36	0,84	0,83	0,86	2,02	2,01	2,03	4,25	7,27
− 2,29	0,36	− 0,15	0,35	0,36	0,37	0,81	0,84	0,85	2,00	2,02	2,03	4,25	7,26
− 2,59	0,03	0,08	0,35	0,38	0,38	0,84	0,86	0,87	2,01	2,02	2,03	4,20	7,22
− 0,18	0,48	0,24	0,38	0,38	0,40	0,87	0,87	0,88	2,01	2,03	2,03	4,20	7,19
− 0,21	0,25	0,26	0,40	0,42	0,43	0,89	0,90	0,89	2,02	2,04	2,05	4,18	7,18
− 2,48	0,33	− 0,92	0,40	0,41	0,41	0,91	0,92	0,91	2,05	2,07	2,02	4,18	7,15
− 2,82	0,41	0,28	0,37	0,41	0,42	0,91	0,93	0,94	2,05	2,06	2,05	4,17	7,11
− 3,26	0,29	− 1,77	0,37	0,37	0,44	0,93	0,92	0,96	2,04	2,05	2,03	4,15	7,11
− 3,84	0,35	− 0,41	0,29	0,31	0,31	0,89	0,88	0,89	2,05	2,05	2,04	4,13	7,07
− 2,85	0,28	− 0,39	0,25	0,28	0,32	0,85	0,86	0,87	2,03	2,04	2,02	4,12	7,04
− 1,99	0,09	− 1,29	0,26	0,28	0,30	0,84	0,84	0,84	2,03	2,02	2,02	4,11	7,03
− 2,18	0,81	− 0,32	0,22	0,26	0,28	0,83	0,83	0,83	2,01	2,02	2,01	4,11	7,01
− 3,29	0,81	− 0,12	0,21	0,23	0,25	0,82	0,81	0,79	2,00	2,01	2,01	4,09	7,00
− 2,76	2,19	0,26	0,17	0,20	0,26	0,78	0,78	0,79	1,99	1,99	1,98	4,07	6,97
− 1,02	0,17	0,38	0,28	0,27	0,30	0,79	0,76	0,78	1,97	1,97	1,98	4,08	6,94
0,83	1,12	0,42	0,30	0,30	0,30	0,77	0,79	0,79	1,95	1,96	1,98	4,05	6,93
− 0,99	0,67	0,06	0,31	0,30	0,31	0,74	0,74	0,75	1,99	1,99	2,00	4,25	7,28
0,46	4,47	3,42	0,30	0,33	0,38	0,79	0,81	0,83	1,94	1,94	1,95	4,04	6,91
1,19	10,66	7,86	0,36	0,56	0,56	0,81	0,86	0,90	1,94	1,94	1,95	4,02	6,90
2,23	11,84	6,25	0,56	1,11	1,63	1,02	1,67	1,36	1,94	1,94	1,94	4,03	6,90
2,38	10,99	7,36	1,57	2,45	2,93	1,59	1,77	2,00	1,94	1,96	1,99	4,01	6,86
1,74	9,07	4,56	2,14	2,66	3,32	2,07	2,13	2,33	1,99	2,02	2,06	3,97	6,84
2,24	5,44	4,55	2,67	2,82	3,07	2,47	2,48	2,51	2,09	2,12	2,16	3,97	6,81
1,11	6,37	3,35	2,52	2,61	2,94	2,56	2,54	2,54	2,21	2,23	2,27	3,98	6,82
2,48	4,85	4,54	2,62	2,78	3,12	2,55	2,56	2,66	2,31	2,34	2,38	3,96	6,79
2,31	9,02	4,42	2,97	3,46	3,97	2,74	2,82	2,98	2,42	2,44	2,50	3,97	6,77
1,63	4,19	2,44	3,25	3,13	3,27	3,09	3,06	3,04	2,56	2,60	2,64	3,99	6,77
1,02	7,54	4,20	2,59	3,27	3,85	2,94	2,96	3,04	2,72	2,77	2,80	4,01	6,73
2,40	4,08	3,81	3,47	5,44	3,55	3,26	3,26	3,28	2,85	2,88	2,90	4,01	6,71
2,48	4,37	3,73	3,24	3,39	3,53	3,26	3,26	3,29	2,97	3,00	3,08	4,02	6,69
1,97	6,54	3,50	3,22	3,32	3,55	3,28	3,67	3,30	3,06	3,09	3,14	4,06	6,68
2,33	11,37	4,24	3,21	4,29	4,99	3,31	3,44	3,71	3,14	3,19	3,20	4,08	6,66
2,48	4,78	6,38	3,97	3,83	4,23	3,82	3,74	3,77	3,28	3,27	3,35	4,12	6,66
4,65	12,96	6,67	4,42	6,24	4,82	3,92	4,56	4,08	3,45	3,45	3,41	4,15	6,64
7,30	5,74	8,01	5,27	4,58	6,77	4,35	3,99	4,87	3,45	3,88	3,54	4,17	6,63
4,46	4,40	3,53	5,84	3,08	4,91	5,09	4,99	4,81	3,63	3,70	3,76	4,20	6,61
3,22	5,74	3,08	4,23	4,27	4,38	4,54	4,40	4,37	3,83	3,88	3,91	4,22	6,60
8,10	12,60	8,56	3,93	4,99	6,05	4,18	4,29	4,58	3,92	3,94	3,98	4,27	6,58
5,69	13,92	11,18	5,64	6,50	7,50	4,89	5,04	5,45	3,98	4,08	4,06	4,31	6,58
5,78	13,20	8,66	7,43	6,50	8,22	5,83	6,01	6,26	4,09	4,16	4,22	4,35	6,56
6,15	10,07	5,82	7,22	7,92	7,20	6,33	6,30	6,26	4,33	4,40	4,46	4,38	6,54
4,69	6,68	5,93	6,34	6,14	6,26	6,15	6,01	5,94	4,60	4,63	4,69	4,46	6,53
5,05	5,62	4,59	5,96	5,83	5,76	5,85	5,75	5,69	4,75	4,77	4,81	4,49	6,51
4,74	5,66	5,27	5,43	4,48	5,62	5,55	5,48	5,51	4,82	4,83	4,88	4,55	6,50
4,98	6,78	5,89	5,84	5,60	5,75	5,42	5,41	5,42	4,86	4,86	4,86	4,60	6,48
4,92	7,48	5,85	5,50	5,62	5,80	5,43	5,41	5,44	4,86	4,87	4,88	4,66	6,47
5,52	7,42	7,20	5,71	5,84	6,11	5,48	5,49	5,56	4,89	4,89	4,91	4,71	6,46

Mai 1879.

Luftthermometer

III. In Glas			IV. In Kupfer			I' frei					
7	2	8	7	2	8	7	2	8	7	2	8
	4,30	8,49	4,68	4,63	3,61	4,73	4,64	8,91	4,39	4,81	3,54
	8,92	3,89	3,90	8,25	8,30	3,91	7,37	4,21	3,39	6,93	8,93
	21,76	2,89	5,45	15,97	2,84	5,17	13,57	8,74	4,78	11,04	3,16
	23,63	4,80	4,87	18,04	4,29	4,60	15,26	4,90	4,35	13,24	4,62
	26,07	8,59	6,73	21,57	8,35	6,10	16,63	8,66	5,47	14,58	8,93
	25,46	11,92	10,28	20,70	11,62	10,61	18,11	11,83	9,40	16,87	12,01
	9,40	0,99	7,48	8,68	2,70	7,46	18,01	3,48	6,70	7,20	2,00
3,65	9,40	3,41	4,05	8,25	3,42	8,13	7,37	8,91	2,73	7,01	3,77
4,06	10,70	7,46	4,00	10,28	7,18	3,91	9,53	7,87	3,93	9,32	7,39
9,32	10,29	6,65	8,87	9,59	6,56	8,94	9,48	6,93	8,66	8,85	6,81
5,31	6,49	4,62	5,35	6,69	4,63	5,42	6,07	4,77	5,08	5,70	4,70
4,62	5,79	4,42	4,68	5,59	4,39	4,77	5,55	4,55	4,39	5,08	4,39
6,12	22,53	5,03	5,98	18,00	4,87	5,60	15,95	5,64	5,85	13,04	5,16
11,02	21,27	5,84	11,73	18,72	5,74	11,70	16,57	6,20	9,32	14,98	5,59
9,04	23,90	7,05	9,76	19,35	6,90	9,36	17,34	7,41	7,51	15,07	7,01
8,67	23,71	6,65	14,38	19,69	6,61	8,01	17,17	7,37	8,16	14,30	6,78
9,89	21,88	5,43	14,66	16,79	5,60	8,44	15,17	6,50	8,85	12,39	5,85
6,44	16,51	13,22	6,13	14,52	13,22	6,07	14,44	13,22	5,85	13,84	13,08
12,73	19,23	15,17	12,49	18,24	14,66	12,57	17,84	14,74	12,77	17,86	15,07
12,73	25,83	9,89	12,89	23,22	9,69	11,83	20,56	10,10	10,85	18,97	9,78
10,70	29,25	11,71	10,47	24,77	11,62	10,40	23,11	12,14	10,09	19,88	11,70
14,48	31,94	12,42	13,00	28,06	12,85	14,27	25,52	12,91	13,16	22,78	12,47
14,48	31,04	14,11	13,45	27,58	13,89	13,57	25,69	14,31	13,08	23,93	14,98
15,25	32,19	14,77	13,55	27,68	14,52	14,65	26,38	14,74	14,30	23,77	14,54
14,97	25,13	17,20	14,00	25,61	16,70	14,31	23,37	16,91	14,84	23,20	16,98
16,59	26,56	20,17	16,45	23,70	19,54	16,04	22,98	19,71	15,68	22,93	20,18
18,62	32,06	22,49	18,03	30,62	21,87	18,33	28,58	21,90	18,66	28,51	22,78
18,88	29,49	21,68	18,64	28,20	21,42	18,93	27,33	21,42	18,89	27,39	21,41
19,31	30,72	22,57	18,92	27,63	22,25	18,63	27,07	22,07	18,81	26,16	22,70
13,95	30,72	15,01	13,94	25,74	14,71	13,87	23,80	15,35	13,77	25,39	14,69
15,90	23,38	16,80	15,68	22,59	16,45	15,52	21,98	16,91	16,90	22,78	16,49
		10,32	10,04	18,64	10,20	10,01	17,58	10,57	9,64	16,02	10,98

Juni 1879.

III. In Glas			IV. In Kupfer			I' frei					
7	2	8	7	2	8	7	2	8	7	2	8
15,17	13,86	19,84	15,15	28,16	13,06	15,00	24,36	18,89	15,45	23,62	19,65
17,00	23,23	15,78	16,45	24,67	15,49	16,17	23,02	16,04	16,22	21,56	15,64
	25,34	19,64	14,42	23,70	19,85	13,96	22,07	19,49	14,69	22,78	19,65
	17,20	11,67	16,55	16,45	11,72	16,30	16,13	12,48	16,68	15,37	11,70
	18,10	9,48	9,81	12,54	9,69	9,88	12,27	10,00	9,05	10,51	9,40
10,70	21,76	10,21	10,56	16,94	9,79	10,40	16,48	10,40	10,09	14,77	10,09
9,40	24,52	12,81	9,16	21,09	12,59	9,10	20,35	13,00	9,20	18,51	12,39
	27,86	13,55	11,14	25,64	13,17	11,18	23,11	14,00	10,47	21,22	13,16
	24,12	14,44	13,70	21,04	14,33	13,70	19,92	14,74	13,58	19,57	14,22
	32,15	14,11	11,62	25,98	13,98	11,88	25,22	14,52	11,16	22,62	14,14
	30,64	17,12	13,26	26,51	16,60	13,03	23,80	17,00	13,08	23,17	16,98
	29,12	16,80	14,04	25,64	16,45	13,83	24,19	16,91	14,69	22,09	16,60
15,17	33,61	13,95	14,52	28,59	14,04	14,40	26,15	14,91	15,45	24,04	13,54
	31,67	15,17	14,23	26,27	14,76	14,40	25,52	15,61	14,42	23,17	14,69
	17,00	13,39	13,80	16,16	13,07	13,70	15,52	13,87	13,24	15,15	13,48
	29,82	17,61	12,40	26,61	17,42	12,57	24,75	17,73	12,89	24,08	17,74
	31,70	22,57	18,97	28,68	21,98	18,50	27,68	22,11	19,27	27,70	22,51
9,76	21,27	15,78	19,85	20,42	15,59	19,19	19,92	16,04	19,65	19,65	16,18
7,61	28,03	18,83	17,37	27,58	18,07	16,91	24,68	18,97	16,71	25,00	19,27
	32,27	17,94	15,97	30,29	17,66	15,83	25,52	18,24	15,84	25,12	18,18
	30,64	21,68	17,61	29,13	21,28	17,00	25,52	21,55	17,74	26,54	21,56
	29,49	20,78	18,14	29,37	20,66	17,98	26,77	20,78	17,36	25,39	20,79
	24,86	16,11	15,63	23,41	16,07	15,70	21,21	16,74	15,45	19,76	15,92
	27,81	16,80	16,35	20,61	16,45	15,61	22,16	16,91	15,84	22,51	16,68
	19,97	15,66	16,94	19,56	15,49	16,48	18,29	16,04	16,60	18,62	15,84
14,15	16,31	13,43	14,04	15,97	13,36	14,31	15,61	13,65	13,92	15,45	13,85
15,58	15,58	14,61	14,76	15,49	14,52	14,74	14,44	14,65	14,69	13,92	14,42
16,47	26,15	15,99	16,31	24,53	15,73	15,17	22,07	16,26	15,45	19,73	15,84
17,20	20,73	15,33	16,94	20,32	15,10	16,48	22,01	15,61	16,79	18,98	15,48
14,89	18,14	14,44	14,66	17,90	14,33	14,70	17,08	14,63	14,77	17,25	14,58

Mai 1879.

Erdthermometer

1" tief			1' tief			2' tief			4' tief			8' tief	16' tief
7	2	8	7	2	8	7	2	8	7	2	8	7	7
5,19	5,39	4,93	5,85	5,72	5,66	5,60	5,57	5,55	4,92	4,94	4,94	4.77	6,46
4,64	6,62	5,46	5,34	5,44	5,73	5,44	5,40	5,42	4,98	4,98	4,99	4.77	6,46
5,08	14,29	7,06	5,50	6,67	7,54	5.48	5,61	5,93	4,98	4,99	4,99	4,84	6,45
4,98	14,52	7,57	6,37	7,01	7,80	6,09	6,12	6,37	5,02	5,04	5,07	4,88	6,44
5,57	15,90	9,97	6,70	7,66	8,71	6,40	6,44	6,76	5,08	5,16	5,18	4,91	6,43
7,88	16,68	11,76	7,84	8,77	9,65	7,01	7,10	7,39	5,22	5,26	5,32	4,95	6,43
8,04	9,61	6,89	8,72	8,67	8,50	7,59	7,62	7,62	5,37	5,46	5,55	4,99	6,43
8,10	7,64	5,85	7,21	7,01	7,10	7,31	7,09	6,99	5,57	5,64	5,67	5,03	6,41
8,28	8,95	7,98	6,37	6,67	7,06	6,74	6,64	6,66	5,69	5,70	5,71	5,07	6,41
7,44	9,08	7,35	6,90	7,22	7,29	6,66	6,69	6,78	5,71	5,72	5,71	5,13	6,42
6,49	6,83	6,06	7,12	6,93	6,86	6,79	6,72	6,71	5,73	5,74	5,78	5,21	6,42
5.51	6,31	5,66	6,48	6,45	6,42	6,57	6,43	6,44	5,72	5,77	5,78	5,23	6,42
5,77	12,73	7,66	6,21	6,82	7,54	6,85	6,88	6,55	5,77	5,79	5,78	5,27	6,40
6,23	15,80	9,34	6,97	8,21	9,01	6,69	6,82	7,15	5,75	5,79	5,81	5,30	6,40
7,47	16,97	10.54	8,03	9,25	9,92	7,36	7,51	7,76	5,80	5,85	5,90	5,35	6,41
7,64	16,89	10,35	8,06	9,48	10,22	7,93	7,99	8,23	5,90	5,98	6,05	5,39	6,40
8,86	16,36	10,01	9,08	9,74	10,39	8,82	8,40	8,53	6,06	6,21	6,22	5,43	6.40
7,80	11,97	11,58	9,35	9,12	9,50	8,66	8,50	8,51	6,29	6,35	6,40	5,50	6,41
11,06	15,09	13.39	9,52	10,15	10,61	8,56	8,66	8,83	6,47	6,50	6,57	5,53	6.42
10,46	17,62	12,34	10,11	10,72	11,82	9,01	9,11	9,82	6,60	6,67	6,71	5,56	6,41
10,14	20,02	13,97	10,48	11,35	12,32	9,43	9,53	9,85	6,81	6,85	6,92	5,63	6.41
11,77	21,43	14,66	11,43	12,24	13,13	10,07	10,19	10,48	7,00	7,09	7,14	5,69	6,41
12,14	21,26	15,16	12,05	12,90	13,53	10,65	10,75	10,99	7,25	7,31	7.43	5,75	6,42
13,30	22,36	16,26	12.73	13,10	14,06	11,15	11,21	11,47	7,53	7,64	7,72	5,82	6,42
13,21	20,48	17,05	13,27	14,01	14,47	11,69	11,73	11,89	7,83	7,94	8,02	5,92	6,41
14,86	20,60	18,28	13,79	14,41	14,96	12,03	12,12	12,31	8,13	8 50	8,33	6,02	6,46
15,95	28,75	20,12	14.47	15,30	16,08	12,51	12,64	12,94	8,40	8 50	8 61	6,07	6,44
17,05	28,80	20,95	15,59	16,28	17,00	13,25	13,36	13,66	8,73	8 80	8,83	6,17	6,45
17,86	22,76	19,46	16,39	16,73	17,15	13,97	14,03	14,24	9,08	9'13	9,29	6,29	6,45
15,48	21,64	17,20	16,29	16,32	16,59	14,82	14,26	14,81	9.46	9'56	9,66	6,41	6,46
14.64	18,76	16,75	15,55	15,59	15.59	14,21	14.04	14.03	9,82	9'88	9,94	6,52	6.46
9.68	15,58	11,64	9.09	10,18	10,70	8,83	8,86	9,02	6,54	6,61	6,65	5,46	6,43

Juni 1879.

1" tief			1' tief			2' tief			4' tief			8' tief	16' tief
7	2	8	7	2	8	7	2	8	7	2	8	7	7
14,26	21,10	18,21	14,71	15,16	15,89	13,57	13,66	13,86	10,06	10,08	10,15	6,69	6,50
15,65	18,89	16,72	13,42	15,34	15,61	14,04	13,94	14.00	10 22	10,21	10,32	6,82	6,51
14,14	19,20	17,89	14,87	15,17	15,67	13,95	13,86	13,97	10,34	10.36	10,42	6,93	6,50
15,74	16,21	14,32	13,28	15,17	15,09	14,04	13,97	13,96	10 49	10,51	10,55	7,06	6,51
11,89	13,46	12,21	13,93	13,73	13,69	13,08	13,46	13,34	10,60	10,61	10,64	7,21	6,51
11,52	14,12	12,29	13,00	12,94	13,11	13,04	12,82	12,75	10,65	10,65	10,66	7,33	6,53
10,19	16,98	14,13	12,89	12,71	13,22	12,57	12,42	12,45	10,61	10,61	10,58	7,45	6,53
11,81	19,10	15,18	12,92	13,48	14,15	12,54	12,50	12,68	10,57	10,54	10,52	7,57	6,57
13,29	16,24	14,81	13,59	13,66	13,94	12,85	12,80	12,86	10,51	10,51	10,52	7,66	6,59
12,20	19,74	15,69	13,19	13,06	14,48	12,79	12,77	12,93	10,52	10,52	10,54	7,76	6,61
13,16	19,00	16,61	13,87	14,16	14,77	13,09	13,04	13,19	10,54	10,54	10,56	7,84	6,61
13,84	20.42	17,05	14,27	14,78	15,36	13,34	13,36	13,53	10,63	10,63	10,65	7,93	6,64
14,31	21,58	16,64	14,80	15,25	15,89	13,74	13,73	13,89	10,70	10,74	10,77	7,98	6,67
14,93	21,87	17,33	15,37	15,63	16,23	14,10	14,12	14,26	10,84	10,86	10,95	8,05	6,68
14,81	15,24	14.75	15,56	15,15	15,02	14,37	14,26	14,17	11,01	11,04	11,09	8,15	6,73
12,76	20,72	17,39	14,15	14,70	14,44	13,93	13,81	13,93	11,14	11,17	11,20	8,19	6,74
16,23	22,81	20,40	15,26	15,93	16,73	14,16	14,21	14,46	11,22	11,24	11,27	8,29	6,76
17,76	19,24	16,75	16.57	16,52	16,42	14,85	14,88	14,93	11,39	11,35	11,43	8,36	6,80
15 81	21,94	18,42	15,75	16,12	16,57	14.82	14,89	14,90	11,50	11,55	11,59	8,41	6,82
16,19	23,24	19,07	16,28	16,64	17,25	15,00	15,01	15,22	11,66	11,63	11,75	8,53	6,84
16,60	22,20	20,81	16,72	16,93	14,43	15,40	15,37	15.51	11,82	11,84	11,94	8,60	6,87
16,81	24,19	20,30	17,19	17,54	18,03	15,63	15,67	15,83	12,00	12,01	12,06	8,73	6,92
17,91	20,01	17,62	17,54	17,35	17.86	16,02	15,97	15,96	12,15	12,20	12,27	8.79	6 94
15,88	20,87	17,98	16,65	16,80	17,10	15,84	15,70	15,72	12,35	12,36	12,40	8,87	6,96
[illegible]	17,28	16,51	16,47	16,32	15,55	15,72	15,58	15,53	12,49	12,50	12,54	8,96	6,93
	15,83	14,75	15,85	15,70	15,54	15,37	15,24	15,14	12,56	12,57	12,58	9,05	7,02
	15,02	14,94	15,02	14,95	14,95	14,90	14,75	14,69	12 60	12,59	12,53	9,15	7,03
	20,98	17.07	14.56	15,16	15,91	14,50	14,41	14.88	12,57	12,53	12,55	9,25	7,06
	18,91	16,46	15,00	15,80	16,03	14,83	14,80	14,88	12,54	12,50	12,52	9,36	7.13
	16,27	15,07	15,30	15,26	15,18	14,86	14,74	14,69	12,52	12,53	12,53	9,48	7.13

Juli 1879.

	Luftthermometer											
	III. In Glas			IV. In Kupfer			1' frei			VII.		
	7	2	8	7	2	8	7	2	8	7	2	8
1	15,46	26,81	14,20	15,63	26,12	13,94	14,44	21,85	14,57	14,61	19,46	14,80
2	14,85	28,27	22,08	14,57	26,61	21,33	14,35	24,49	21,30	14,69	25,00	21,98
3	12,89	15,58	15,78	12,97	15,49	15,49	13,44	15,21	15,17	12,77	14,96	15,26
4	13,47	20,53	14,20	13,12	19,83	14,04	13,35	19,40	14,65	13,54	19,80	14,08
5	13,26	15,58	13,95	12,83	14,66	13,60	12,57	14,81	13,74	13,27	14,88	13,65
6	13,75	15,99	13,95	13,55	15,59	13,26	13,00	15,35	13,83	13,54	14,34	13,92
7	13,37	24,72	14,52	15,05	23,08	14,52	14,44	20,44	14,95	14,22	17,36	14,80
8	15,37	26,07	15,99	15,15	25,78	15,87	14,31	21,64	16,22	14,46	20,03	15,84
9	15,58	22,69	18,34	15,49	21,77	17,52	14,95	19,92	17,64	14,77	19,65	17,82
10	14,77	23,30	14,20	14,62	22,50	14,04	14,52	21,08	14,74	14,88	20,03	14,15
11	13,47	25,83	13,63	13,75	22,74	13,07	13,30	20,35	13,87	12,77	18,13	13,92
12	13,22	18,67	13,55	12,93	17,56	13,07	12,91	14,83	13,44	12,85	14,58	13,85
13	13,67	30,80	15,99	13,45	28,30	15,78	12,64	22,59	16,13	13,24	20,87	15,92
14	13,95	29,37	19,84	13,55	27,09	19,49	13,65	24,19	19,40	13,92	23,39	19,84
15	15,66	16,80	16,47	15,59	16,55	15,97	15,82	16,48	16,17	15,57	15,68	16,60
16	14,65	28,19	17,69	14,52	27,09	17,42	14,31	24,06	18,11	14,69	23,09	17,70
17	15,83	34,96	17,32	15,83	31,35	16,94	15,61	27,33	17,77	15,68	24,42	17,28
18	17,28	29,00	16,80	17,42	30,62	16,45	16,48	26,55	17,38	17,21	24,31	16,60
19	16,11	33,49	16,51	15,97	29,85	16,35	16,04	26,81	17,12	15,45	24,31	16,22
20	15,09	17,81	16,39	15,97	18,14	16,11	16,13	17,68	16,91	15,64	16,98	16,52
21	22,08	33,37	13,95	21,77	30,86	14,04	21,55	28,71	14,22	21,94	27,08	14,30
22	17,69	17,61	16,68	17,52	17,42	16,55	17,47	17,86	16,95	17,26	17,36	16,60
23	16,64	18,26	15,99	16,55	17,90	15,49	16,82	17,00	16,13	16,45	16,45	16,14
24	15,54	31,45	14,97	15,87	28,59	14,90	15,17	22,54	15,17	15,64	21,30	15,07
25	12,44	15,25	14,15	12,40	14,90	14,04	12,66	14,74	14,22	12,02	14,49	14,88
26	13,55	15,17	13,55	13,41	14,52	13,12	13,44	14,22	13,44	13,35	14,34	13,62
27	14,15	25,67	14,56	13,89	23,51	14,18	13,53	20,13	14,95	14,46	19,19	14,69
28	15,58	24,16	13,99	15,25	22,74	13,60	14,74	18,97	14,31	14,77	17,66	13,92
29	15,99	27,09	16,07	15,59	25,54	15,97	14,83	20,87	16,04	14,93	19,61	15,84
30	14,86	31,94	16,16	14,33	28,64	15,97	14,40	24,06	16,74	14,15	22,62	16,07
31	15,25	30,64	16,72	15,25	27,58	16,21	15,00	22,97	16,91	14,69	22,05	16,60
	15,03	21,36	15,77	14,90	23,00	15,43	14,70	20,67	15,88	14,84	19,46	15,69
	August 1879.											
1	16,39	33,90	16,88	16,84	29,51	16,55	15,95	27,15	17,43	15,72	23,39	16,98
2	15,99	35,28	16,92	15,68	30,72	16,45	15,95	28,45	17,34	16,07	24,92	16,98
3	15,83	34,02	17,77	15,68	29,76	17,52	15,95	26,29	18,11	15,30	25,85	17,51
4	14,89	35,52	23,90	14,90	32,32	22,74	14,87	28,54	22,71	13,92	27,60	23,47
5	19,72	38,77	20,37	19,45	35,46	20,12	19,23	31,55	20,78	19,84	29,24	20,11
6	15,09	26,97	29,53	15,00	25,74	20,32	15,65	24,57	20,56	15,07	23,17	20,52
7	18,42	29,25	13,95	18,14	28,06	14,04	18,20	26,68	14,83	18,32	26,27	13,92
8	14,97	28,52	15,25	15,00	25,74	15,00	14,74	21,77	16,04	14,88	20,03	15,37
9	14,21	19,35	15,70	14,14	19,01	15,59	14,22	18,76	16,04	14,11	18,59	15,99
10	13,55	24,64	13,75	13,65	24,09	14,42	13,79	18,03	14,09	13,54	17,03	14,15
11	14,56	15,50	14,11	14,42	15,84	14,66	14,52	15,00	14,48	14,69	14,88	14,42
12	16,39	21,85	15,05	16,11	22,84	16,45	15,70	19,58	15,26	15,76	18,59	15,07
13	15,37	23,30	16,51	15,25	21,43	16,16	15,43	20,35	17,00	15,37	19,54	16,60
14	16,47	30,02	16,55	15,97	25,16	16,45	15,95	23,15	17,34	16,49	23,28	16,90
15	16,15	24,20	15,01	16,07	20,42	16,62	15,82	20,35	15,61	15,45	20,03	15,07
16	11,82	24,85	11,92	11,62	21,87	11,62	11,96	21,30	11,96	12,39	21,48	12,89
17	11,85	22,49	13,95	11,14	20,42	13,75	11,48	20,01	14,74	11,74	20,52	14,22
18	12,00	22,49	14,36	11,62	20,42	14,33	12,05	13,88	15,26	12,12	20,26	14,77
19	14,36	19,52	16,64	14,33	19,11	16,07	14,31	17,68	16,65	14,03	18,18	16,80
20	16,43	22,00	15,37	16,35	20,80	15,15	16,22	20,35	15,82	15,84	20,45	15,45
21	13,55	23,30	16,96	13,55	22,25	16,94	13,70	21,21	17,34	14,90	20,45	17,28
22	14,56	27,37	22,08	14,52	25,45	21,52	14,74	24,75	21,55	14,69	23,85	22,13
23	18,62	28,60	17,61	18,38	27,38	17,42	18,11	26,51	18,20	18,13	27,08	17,48
24	14,36	21,76	16,08	14,52	21,18	16,21	14,48	20,35	16,04	14,22	20,87	17,86
25	15,50	28,30	14,28	15,25	21,38	14,04	15,26	21,17	15,17	15,45	19,50	14,69
26	15,17	21,76	15,17	14,76	20,80	14,90	14,74	20,44	15,95	15,07	20,71	15,80
27	15,17	19,58	12,40	15,00	18,38	12,25	15,17	17,86	13,14	14,99	17,78	12,77
28	13,55	15,17	15,99	13,41	15,00	15,63	13,44	14,83	15,87	13,46	15,18	16,30
29	18,67	21,68	16,39	18,28	20,39	16,21	18,20	19,58	16,39	18,81	19,35	16,60
30	15,58	20,05	15,37	15,34	19,85	15,00	15,17	18,20	15,52	15,18	18,13	15,57
31	13,02	20,05	14,97	13,07	19,25	14,90	13,22	18,03	15,17	13,35	18,61	15,26
	15,22	25,10	16,23	15,08	22,93	15,77	15,42	21,71	16,54	14,82	21,20	16,84

Juli 1879.

Erdthermometer

1" tief			1' tief			2' tief			4' tief			8' tief	16' tief
7	2	8	7	2	8	7	2	8	7	2	8	7	7
14,26	20,08	15,87	14,71	15,08	15,47	14,52	14,58	14,51	12,51	12,51	12,51	9,49	7,16
13,99	21,71	19,48	14,98	15,48	16,18	14,57	14,54	14,70	12,52	12,52	12,51	9,57	7,20
15,11	15,50	15,84	16,07	15,71	15,65	14,94	14,93	14,91	12,52	12,52	12,56	9,61	7,22
13,48	17,26	15,34	14,87	15,05	15,20	14,68	14,54	14,55	12,58	12,59	12,58	9,67	7,27
13,51	14,88	14,64	14,79	14,71	14,88	14,55	14,38	14,37	12,58	12,58	12,58	9,73	7,27
13,41	14,93	14,33	14,41	14,40	14,43	14,30	14,18	14,12	12,58	12,56	12,57	9,81	7,34
14,02	18,90	15,60	14,15	14,61	15,09	14,01	13,97	14,10	12,52	12,50	12,50	9,83	7,36
14,02	18,78	16,01	14,77	14,78	15,00	14,30	14,18	14,23	12,49	12,47	12,47	9,87	7,41
14,36	19,26	17,04	14,70	15,10	15,60	14,26	14,27	14,40	12,46	12,46	12,53	9,93	7,42
14,75	19,24	16,06	15,31	16,34	15,95	14,56	14,60	14,67	12,47	12,48	12,51	9,99	7,46
13,62	18,21	14,86	15,20	15,10	15,21	14,70	14,59	14,58	12,50	12,51	12,52	9,99	7,49
13,91	14,98	14,17	14,71	14,48	14,46	14,49	14,34	14,27	12,58	12,56	12,58	10,05	7,53
13,09	19,67	16,42	14,07	14,60	15,28	14,07	14,01	14,17	12,56	12,56	12,57	10,07	7,58
13,79	19,33	17,95	14,92	15,16	15,70	14,42	14,40	14,52	12,56	12,56	12,57	10,12	7,61
15,75	16,04	16,15	15,02	15,49	15,52	14,73	14,73	14,74	12,57	12,57	12,60	10,15	7,64
14,45	20,36	17,62	15,93	15,53	15,98	14,63	14,61	14,74	12,62	12,63	12,65	10,20	7,66
14,96	22,20	18,15	15,53	15,90	16,59	14,80	14,84	15,06	12,67	12,68	12,70	10,23	7,70
16,08	22,78	18,25	16,20	16,62	17,25	15,29	15,31	15,52	12,74	12,76	12,78	10,25	7,74
16,19	22,40	18,20	16,73	16,88	17,50	15,76	15,72	15,93	12,84	12,90	12,93	10,31	7,79
16,54	17,38	17,06	16,98	16,86	16,77	16,01	15,92	15,90	12,99	13,02	13,05	10,36	7,80
19,95	22,38	14,81	17,18	16,50	16,01	15,75	15,60	15,68	13,17	13,14	13,12	10,41	7,85
17,42	17,65	17,28	17,14	17,01	16,95	16,01	16,07	16,00	13,18	13,20	13,22	10,42	7,86
16,63	16,51	16,44	16,55	16,33	16,32	15,90	15,77	15,77	13,28	13,32	13,34	10,48	7,89
14,87	20,25	16,88	15,70	15,91	16,36	15,52	15,40	15,47	13,35	13,36	13,39	10,51	7,92
13,96	14,73	14,70	15,70	15,34	15,24	15,46	15,31	15,19	13,37	13,38	13,40	10,58	7,96
14,03	14,27	14,08	14,92	14,71	14,65	14,96	14,77	14,68	13,37	13,35	13,35	10,64	8,01
14,28	18,14	15,69	16,55	14,71	15,24	14,51	14,41	14,51	13,31	13,27	13,30	10,68	8,02
14,61	17,07	15,17	14,93	14,90	15,16	14,63	14,55	14,61	13,23	13,19	13,19	10,73	8,06
14,03	17,50	16,01	14,57	14,80	15,24	14,55	14,47	14,56	13,17	13,15	13,13	10,76	8,08
14,65	20,14	17,12	15,03	15,48	16,01	14,67	14,68	14,85	13,12	13,12	13,12	10,79	8,11
15,21	19,80	17,58	15,72	16,01	16,44	15,06	15,05	15,21	13,11	13,11	13,12	10,85	8,15
14,61	18,46	16,27	15,41	15,47	15,72	14,86	14,79	14,85	12,81	12,82	12,83	10,20	7,66

August 1879.

1" tief			1' tief			2' tief			4' tief			8' tief	16' tief
7	2	8	7	2	8	7	2	8	7	2	8	7	7
15,88	21,80	18,14	16,10	16,44	17,01	15,38	15,40	15,57	13,18	13,18	13,19	10,83	8,16
15,98	23,30	18,84	16,51	16,96	17,63	15,74	15,78	16,00	13,22	13,25	13,28	10,87	8,19
16,31	22,04	18,76	17,07	17,14	17,50	16,17	16,21	16,22	13,33	13,40	13,41	10,88	8,24
15,09	19,84	21,28	17,05	17,61	18,35	16,29	16,34	16,54	13,56	13,52	13,53	10,91	8,27
18,46	25,96	21,26	18,11	18,71	19,26	16,85	16,97	17,16	13,59	13,64	13,66	10,95	8,29
17,25	21,80	20,19	18,61	18,54	18,78	17,18	17,32	17,38	13,65	13,80	13,88	10,98	8,31
18,18	23,48	17,26	18,29	18,62	18,76	17,36	17,32	17,40	14,05	14,00	14,08	11,05	8,34
15,85	19,88	17,43	17,60	17,57	17,83	17,15	16,95	16,95	14,11	14,15	14,19	11,09	8,38
15,34	19,89	16,81	17,04	16,94	17,11	16,81	16,59	16,58	14,20	14,20	14,20	11,16	8,41
15,08	17,05	15,45	16,57	16,30	16,29	16,39	16,17	16,09	14,24	14,22	14,24	11,20	8,46
14,98	15,11	15,07	15,84	15,61	15,60	15,92	15,67	15,61	14,21	14,18	14,17	11,28	8,48
15,22	16,86	15,83	15,38	15,47	15,72	15,42	15,33	15,35	14,14	14,12	13,82	11,31	8,48
15,06	18,85	17,20	15,41	15,80	16,20	15,30	15,30	15,41	14,06	13,96	14,01	11,37	8,52
15,34	20,86	17,93	15,78	16,30	16,92	15,48	15,52	15,71	13,98	14,00	13,96	11,41	8,54
16,01	19,60	16,94	16,46	16,67	16,89	15,84	15,86	15,91	13,94	13,97	13,96	11,45	8,57
13,49	19,75	13,49	15,85	16,21	15,84	15,81	15,72	15,81	13,98	14,00	13,97	11,48	8,58
13,16	18,72	16,12	15,70	15,95	16,31	15,74	15,60	15,64	13,98	13,99	14,00	11,50	8,61
13,70	19,25	16,44	15,70	16,06	16,50	15,61	15,54	15,64	13,98	13,98	13,98	11,53	8,64
14,66	16,18	16,15	15,86	15,70	15,77	15,64	15,50	15,48	13,94	13,94	13,98	11,55	8,67
15,35	18,93	16,90	15,54	16,07	16,48	15,36	15,40	15,54	13,93	13,95	13,95	11,58	8,69
14,15	19,40	17,47	15,66	15,96	16,44	15,49	15,44	15,56	13,91	13,90	13,95	11,62	8,74
15,33	21,62	19,87	16,09	16,67	17,23	15,67	15,61	15,89	13,93	13,93	13,94	11,66	8,78
17,20	22,68	19,02	16,97	17,58	18,00	16,14	16,25	16,41	13,93	13,94	13,97	11,64	8,79
15,69	18,55	17,27	17,23	17,20	17,20	16,50	16,41	16,42	14,02	14,05	14,07	11,66	8,80
15,93	19,87	16,74	16,72	16,94	17,16	16,24	16,22	16,28	14,12	14,14	14,15	11,68	8,81
15,18	19,60	17,08	16,37	16,71	17,03	16,16	16,08	16,15	14,18	14,20	14,22	11,71	8,87
15,59	17,90	15,37	16,44	16,51	16,54	16,10	16,02	16,00	14,22	14,22	14,22	11,74	8,88
14,29	14,67	15,66	15,80	15,45	15,44	15,81	15,61	15,50	14,22	14,22	14,22	11,76	8,92
16,90	18,05	16,88	15,65	16,03	16,28	15,39	15,44	15,55	14,20	14,18	14,20	11,80	8,95
15,32	16,72	16,08	15,91	15,81	15,93	15,58	15,45	15,48	14,16	14,13	14,16	11,84	8,98
13,95	18,23	16,17	15,39	15,73	16,06	15,39	15,28	15,39	14,13	14,11	14,10	11,88	9,03
15,47	19,56	17,26	16,41	16,59	16,90	16,00	15,96	15,97	13,98	13,95	13,96	11,37	8,59

September 1879.

Luftthermometer

	III. In Glas			IV. In Kupfer			1' frei			VII.		
	7	2	8	7	2	8	7	2	8	7	2	8
1	14,77	19,07	12,32	14,52	18,04	12,21	14,88	17,25	12,83	11,69	16,79	12,69
2	13,14	16,72	12,44	12,73	15,97	12,25	13,00	15,26	12,83	13,54	14,49	12,69
3	11,59	15,17	15,25	11,62	15,00	15,25	11,70	14,95	15,17	14,51	15,15	15,45
4	13,34	23,30	14,56	13,17	21,38	14,33	13,35	20,05	15,17	13,54	21,18	14,88
5	12,57	18,83	9,40	12,59	18,00	9,02	10,92	17,12	10,61	12,77	16,22	10,01
6	7,74	18,62	13,26	8,01	17,42	13,07	8,32	17,34	13,44	7,70	17,36	13,54
7	8,27	22,90	15,26	8,59	21,28	15,00	8,88	20,87	15,17	8,93	21,52	15,45
8	12,36	29,25	21,68	12,40	27,48	20,80	12,57	26,29	20,87	12,39	27,70	21,56
9	17,40	28,92	21,27	17,03	27,38	20,90	17,34	26,59	21,21	17,44	27,50	21,56
10	17,81	23,10	15,15	17,90	21,38	15,10	17,90	20,05	15,39	17,74	20,03	15,30
11	12,12	22,69	13,75	12,25	21,18	13,55	12,57	19,92	14,22	12,20	17,93	14,03
12	11,92	26,07	14,97	11,87	23,60	14,81	12,57	20,87	15,20	12,01	20,66	15,26
13	10,49	21,60	14,48	10,56	20,32	14,52	10,83	19,66	14,74	10,70	19,57	14,69
14	14,61	25,87	18,62	14,66	23,99	18,04	14,83	23,29	13,69	14,49	24,31	18,89
15	15,70	18,02	10,74	15,68	17,80	10,56	15,82	17,51	11,57	15,64	16,68	11,24
16	10,27	21,52	13,55	10,42	20,08	13,45	10,74	19,19	14,40	10,55	18,43	13,84
17	12,44	20,13	12,98	12,45	19,35	12,73	12,78	18,97	13,35	12,31	18,81	13,35
18	9,32	23,96	15,66	9,21	22,50	15,49	9,66	21,73	15,95	9,43	22,09	15,99
19	13,22	25,34	18,91	13,17	24,19	18,38	18,44	23,71	18,97	13,16	24,54	19,27
20	15,99	24,72	15,99	15,97	23,51	15,59	16,39	21,12	16,26	15,88	21,26	16,22
21	13,79	19,23	15,87	13,94	18,63	15,25	14,74	17,90	15,95	14,11	18,13	15,84
22	13,39	25,05	16,11	13,21	23,51	15,78	13,78	22,76	16,13	13,05	23,39	16,22
23	12,28	22,41	15,01	12,35	20,90	14,76	12,70	20,26	15,70	12,20	20,68	15,26
24	11,96	18,38	16,07	12,01	17,23	15,87	12,23	16,91	15,91	12,01	17,32	15,99
25	12,73	22,06	14,48	12,64	20,80	14,28	12,66	19,82	14,74	13,16	20,11	14,69
26	11,59	19,97	11,10	11,38	18,77	10,95	11,57	18,37	11,70	11,24	18,78	11,62
27	6,00	20,05	11,92	5,96	18,14	11,72	6,59	17,77	12,57	6,24	18,32	12,39
28	10,40	16,92	11,92	9,98	16,35	11,96	10,70	15,87	12,27	10,23	15,45	12,01
29	10,49	16,35	11,51	10,56	15,68	11,33	11,09	14,83	12,01	10,58	15,07	11,24
30	10,78	15,17	10,70	10,76	14,90	10,42	11,09	14,74	11,13	10,77	14,05	10,98
	12,27	21,21	13,55	12,26	20,15	14,24	12,82	19,95	15,14	12,31	19,26	14,73

October 1879.

	III. In Glas			IV. In Kupfer			1' frei			VII.		
	7	2	8	7	2	8	7	2	8	7	2	8
1	7,86	17,12	10,29	7,77	16,45	10,08	8,36	15,70	10,79	7,86	15,81	10,97
2	7,05	16,68	11,02	7,14	15,97	10,66	7,63	15,26	11,36	7,05	15,34	11,24
3	10,82	14,36	9,20	10,76	14,14	8,87	11,09	13,87	9,53	10,93	13,92	9,48
4	6,08	15,78	10,21	6,08	14,62	10,56	6,50	14,31	10,61	6,24	14,30	10,47
5	9,20	12,98	8,75	9,07	11,76	8,08	9,31	11,40	9,01	9,24	12,39	9,32
6	8,19	15,99	10,29	7,48	14,81	10,18	7,80	14,70	10,92	8,55	14,30	10,47
7	10,83	14,77	9,16	10,28	13,65	9,21	10,49	13,48	9,79	10,55	13,24	9,40
8	7,86	12,98	7,25	7,77	12,11	7,18	8,23	12,27	8,23	8,08	12,16	7,82
9	3,06	12,85	7,05	3,18	12,11	6,99	3,91	12,14	7,89	3,54	11,61	7,47
10	10,62	12,77	9,16	10,52	12,11	9,11	10,74	11,40	9,44	10,55	11,24	9,32
11	6,65	13,34	6,16	6,70	11,28	5,94	6,97	10,92	6,84	7,01	10,66	7,01
12	8,79	12,73	8,67	8,73	12,59	8,39	8,92	12,14	8,66	8,93	12,39	9,12
13	3,89	12,12	10,62	4,00	11,91	10,42	4,51	11,40	10,49	4,43	11,32	10,62
14	11,55	9,36	4,34	9,50	8,01	4,15	9,10	7,93	4,86	8,93	8,39	4,78
15	3,09	8,67	1,39	2,84	7,18	1,49	3,39	6,93	2,23	3,35	7,31	1,31
16	1,84	7,86	2,44	2,07	6,66	2,46	2,61	6,50	3,05	2,00	6,54	2,77
17	1,98	14,23	1,59	2,07	7,77	1,59	1,27	6,50	2,27	1,73	7,51	2,39
18	0,99	2,93	2,98	1,11	2,94	3,04	1,69	3,14	3,39	1,15	2,47	3,24
19	0,43	6,89	4,70	0,72	6,75	4,63	1,10	6,54	5,03	0,98	6,54	5,00
20	6,81	11,50	8,67	7,04	11,24	8,85	7,02	11,27	8,57	7,12	11,70	8,82
21	6,81	8,75	4,62	7,04	8,49	4,58	6,80	8,14	4,86	6,93	8,08	4,85
22	5,03	8,27	5,43	4,87	7,91	5,85	5,34	7,89	5,73	5,08	7,70	5,85
23	3,01	7,05	7,25	2,99	6,90	7,28	3,59	7,03	7,37	3,24	7,01	7,39
24	6,97	13,67	8,43	6,90	12,40	8,25	6,97	10,96	8,44	7,01	10,47	8,55
25	8,07	11,10	6,04	8,73	10,76	5,85	8,75	10,40	6,41	8,95	10,81	6,64
26	5,92	9,24	8,85	5,94	9,21	8,25	6,07	9,10	8,36	5,85	9,32	8,55
27	8,55	10,98	8,43	8,54	10,76	8,85	8,57	10,66	8,75	8,55	10,70	8,85
28	7,33	9,56	6,08	7,42	9,81	5,94	7,58	9,10	6,16	7,70	8,81	6,03
29	5,43	7,66	6,65	5,49	7,72	6,80	5,73	7,63	7,02	5,58	7,58	7,01
30	6,65	8,67	6,24	6,80	8,39	6,42	6,93	8,34	6,93	6,74	8,16	6,55
31	1,72	11,50	1,55	1,78	8,39	1,49	2,27	6,53	2,18	2,39	7,47	[illegible]
	6,10	11,36	6,87	5,91	10,46	6,75	6,36	10,13	7,26	6,33	10,17	[illegible]

September 1879.

Erdthermometer													
1" tief			1' tief			2' tief			4' tief			8' tief	16' tief
7	2	8	7	2	8	7	2	8	7	2	8	7	7
15,07	16,89	14,49	15,74	15,75	15,70	15,43	15,37	15,33	14,07	14,08	14,07	11,90	9,01
13,60	15,43	14,24	15,03	15,02	15,07	15,16	14,94	14,99	14,04	14,04	14,02	11,86	9,03
12,73	14,32	14,65	14,50	14,42	14,52	14,78	14,64	14,62	13,98	13,95	13,98	11,89	9,06
13,77	17,85	15,48	14,43	14,84	15,12	14,55	14,58	14,59	13,90	13,89	13,85	11,94	9,11
11,57	16,50	13,37	14,56	15,30	14,85	14,56	14,49	14,50	13,80	13,76	13,77	11,89	9,11
10,38	15,81	14,15	13,76	13,98	16,56	14,32	14,16	14,17	13,73	13,73	13,72	11,92	9,12
10,67	18,43	15,68	13,94	14,14	14,71	14,11	14,04	14,13	13,64	13,62	13,58	11,95	9,17
13,08	21,36	19,09	14,34	15,03	15,88	14,23	14,34	14,61	13,53	13,52	13,52	11,93	9,19
16,87	22,74	20,40	16,10	16,70	17,38	15,01	15,25	15,51	13,52	13,51	13,53	11,97	9,23
17,63	19,25	16,55	17,17	16,98	16,81	15,86	15,88	15,87	13,59	13,62	13,69	11,96	9,25
13,96	18,81	15,70	15,92	15,96	16,09	15,67	15,54	15,49	13,73	13,77	13,80	11,87	9,28
13,96	18,89	15,94	15,58	15,63	15,78	15,38	15,28	15,29	13,79	13,81	13,84	11,94	9,28
12,98	17,90	15,68	15,21	15,38	15,69	15,20	15,09	15,14	13,82	13,83	13,84	11,95	9,32
14,83	20,70	18,43	15,40	16,00	16,53	15,11	15,21	15,34	13,81	13,83	13,81	11,92	9,34
15,98	17,03	14,80	16,27	16,20	15,95	15,54	15,53	15,48	13,81	13,81	13,81	11,92	9,35
11,90	18,22	15,28	14,80	15,17	15,42	15,13	15,03	14,99	13,83	13,87	13,85	11,93	9,35
13,43	17,39	14,87	14,97	15,28	15,47	14,96	14,92	14,96	13,82	13,83	13,81	11,94	9,39
11,89	19,41	16,54	14,72	15,17	15,65	14,85	14,83	14,91	13,79	13,80	13,77	11,95	9,39
14,26	20,49	18,48	15,32	15,87	16,40	14,99	15,07	15,23	13,75	13,77	13,75	11,96	9,43
16,45	18,55	16,75	16,22	16,23	16,28	15,42	15,45	15,47	13,74	13,83	13,79	11,97	9,44
15,22	16,70	16,08	15,92	15,82	15,80	15,46	15,44	15,36	13,83	13,83	13,85	12,00	9,47
14,56	20,20	16,96	15,47	15,96	16,34	15,23	15,29	15,39	13,85	13,99	13,88	11,98	9,49
13,87	18,77	16,54	15,67	15,90	16,18	15,39	15,37	15,42	13,96	13,90	13,88	11,99	9,50
13,82	15,81	15,84	15,69	15,43	15,46	15,40	15,29	15,22	13,87	13,90	13,90	11,99	9,51
13,65	17,03	15,28	15,02	15,07	15,24	15,03	14,97	14,94	13,90	13,91	13,89	12,01	9,53
12,91	16,24	13,66	14,80	14,86	14,88	14,85	14,79	14,75	13,86	13,88	13,85	12,01	9,54
9,60	16,84	13,56	13,93	14,19	14,39	14,50	14,38	14,32	13,80	13,82	13,79	12,03	9,56
12,02	14,67	13,29	14,00	13,97	14,04	14,26	14,18	14,11	13,73	13,72	13,69	12,03	9,58
12,22	13,72	12,74	13,74	13,67	13,66	14,02	13,94	13,87	13,64	13,60	13,57	12,06	9,59
11,99	13,85	12,84	13,39	13,50	13,61	13,74	13,69	13,67	13,54	13,55	13,47	12,06	9,60
13,45	17,09	14,22	15,38	15,25	15,50	14,93	14,93	14,92	13,78	13,77	13,76	11,95	9,32

October 1879.

1" tief 7	1" tief 2	1" tief 8	1' tief 7	1' tief 2	1' tief 8	2' tief 7	2' tief 2	2' tief 8	4' tief 7	4' tief 2	4' tief 8	8' tief 7	16' tief 7
10,33	14,17	12,09	13,00	13,09	13,16	13,54	13,45	13,39	13,41	13,39	13,35	12,05	9,61
9,81	13,83	12,40	12,65	12,80	12,92	13,27	13,18	13,17	13,29	13,28	13,25	12,04	9,62
11,55	13,01	11,53	12,77	12,76	12,77	13,10	13,06	13,04	13,18	13,15	13,11	12,04	9,65
8,77	13,13	11,17	12,11	12,22	12,32	12,84	12,75	12,68	13,07	13,04	12,99	12,00	9,67
10,31	11,55	10,38	12,07	12,02	11,96	12,63	12,50	12,45	12,96	12,89	12,83	12,00	9,70
9,24	14,26	11,88	11,56	12,07	12,35	12,30	12,29	12,36	12,80	12,76	12,72	11,97	9,71
11,03	13,93	11,19	12,18	12,50	12,48	12,38	12,44	12,44	12,66	12,64	12,61	11,95	9,71
10,12	13,11	10,57	12,03	12,33	12,34	12,39	12,40	12,38	12,57	12,55	12,52	11,92	9,72
7,94	11,77	9,73	11,42	11,48	11,57	12,22	12,05	12,00	12,49	12,47	12,43	11,89	9,74
10,67	11,35	10,36	11,32	11,41	11,40	11,87	12,83	11,80	12,35	12,37	12,33	11,85	9,77
8,62	11,41	9,23	11,01	11,27	11,27	11,68	11,65	11,62	12,26	12,25	12,22	11,81	9,77
9,26	10,99	9,68	10,69	10,74	10,87	11,49	11,36	11,32	12,17	12,12	12,08	11,76	9,77
7,13	10,51	10,20	10,34	10,40	10,53	11,19	11,09	11,04	12,03	12,01	11,95	11,74	9,80
10,91	9,19	7,71	10,75	10,57	10,12	11,07	11,03	10,97	11,85	11,90	11,84	11,69	9,82
5,92	8,22	5,67	9,52	9,47	9,24	10,72	10,56	10,56	11,75	11,74	11,68	11,65	9,82
4,89	7,90	5,65	8,54	8,65	8,61	10,05	9,90	9,76	11,62	11,55	11,50	11,59	9,82
2,76	7,65	5,03	7,79	7,90	7,03	9,46	9,35	9,19	11,38	11,37	11,28	11,55	9,83
3,91	4,59	4,82	7,48	7,26	7,21	9,00	8,84	8,71	11,14	11,07	11,01	11,49	9,85
3,51	6,29	5,87	6,92	7,01	7,20	8,50	8,41	8,39	10,88	10,80	10,73	11,43	9,86
6,57	9,39	8,80	7,31	7,81	8,15	8,38	8,45	8,55	10,64	10,57	10,50	11,38	9,87
7,26	8,11	6,47	8,31	8,39	8,36	8,74	8,80	8,83	10,40	10,36	10,32	11,31	9,91
6,80	7,89	7,02	7,98	8,06	8,13	8,73	8,71	8,69	10,28	10,25	10,22	11,19	9,87
5,15	7,26	7,45	7,78	7,84	7,97	8,63	8,59	8,59	10,17	10,15	10,12	11,15	9,88
7,35	9,93	8,56	8,06	8,35	8,51	8,59	7,65	8,71	10,07	9,95	10,03	11,07	9,90
8,75	9,61	7,90	8,66	8,84	8,86	8,83	8,93	8,92	9,98	9,95	9,94	11,01	9,90
6,93	8,40	8,38	8,37	8,35	8,46	8,91	8,84	8,87	9,93	9,91	9,90	10,91	9,90
6,48	9,86	8,01	8,62	8,87	9,01	8,89	8,96	9,03	9,87	9,88	9,88	10,84	9,93
8,83	10,62	7,72	8,96	8,92	8,89	9,11	9,10	9,09	9,86	9,85	9,84	10,78	9,92
6,81	7,83	7,70	8,55	8,48	8,50	9,04	8,96	8,94	9,84	9,83	9,82	10,75	9,92
7,49	8,47	7,85	8,42	8,49	8,57	8,88	8,87	8,85	9,81	9,80	9,80	10,63	9,91
5,14	8,19	5,14	8,19	8,27	8,10	8,81	8,78	8,76	9,74	9,74	9,73	10,58	9,92
7,75	10,01	8,62	9,78	9,88	9,93	10,49	10,51	10,50	11,43	11,41	11,40	11,48	9,81

November 1879.

Luftthermometer

0,19
5,92

1,19
1,80
1,23

15,81

12,96

10,10
2,96

1,96
1,07
2,16
0,27
2,24
0,51
2,12

November 1879.

Erdthermometer

1" tief			1' tief			2' tief			4' tief			8' tief	16' tief
7	2	8	7	2	8	7	2	8	7	2	8	7	7
3,87	4,85	5,23	7,25	6,93	6,87	8,44	8,25	8,08	9,68	9,68	9,65	10,51	9,90
6,18	6,37	5,93	7,08	7,12	7,17	7,93	7,91	7,89	9,59	9,54	9,50	10,47	9,91
5,21	5,64	4,37	6,37	7,00	6,87	7,86	7,85	7,75	9,45	9,42	9,37	10,44	9,93
3,56	5,83	3,61	5,97	6,53	6,47	7,57	7,48	7,44	9,30	9,26	9,23	10,37	9,90
2,95	6,66	5,84	6,49	6,19	6,52	7,27	7,18	7,21	9,18	9,13	9,09	10,34	9,91
4,80	5,23	4,45	5,96	6,45	6,36	7,24	7,20	7,15	9,00	8,94	8,91	10,27	9,91
3,16	6,38	5,88	5,96	6,19	6,35	7,02	6,98	6,96	8,86	8,81	8,88	10,21	9,90
4,41	5,89	5,79	6,19	6,15	6,31	6,94	6,80	6,92	8,71	8,69	8,65	10,14	9,89
4,87	6,41	6,47	6,03	6,17	6,34	6,86	6,85	6,85	8,60	8,57	8,55	10,08	9,88
6,16	6,09	5,85	6,55	6,57	6,58	6,96	6,98	7,02	8,43	8,48	8,47	10,01	9,88
5,67	6,78	4,62	6,56	6,59	6,57	7,02	7,03	7,01	8,44	8,35	8,56	9,96	9,89
2,87	3,75	3,77	5,90	5,66	5,59	6,86	6,72	6,62	8,36	8,33	8,32	9,86	9,86
2,97	3,66	3,72	5,37	5,27	5,28	6,45	6,36	6,31	8,28	8,25	8,22	9,81	9,85
3,71	4,17	3,89	5,21	5,20	5,26	6,20	6,13	6,10	8,15	8,10	8,08	9,74	9,85
2,68	2,51	2,21	5,07	4,84	4,74	6,05	5,95	5,87	8,00	7,96	7,94	9,69	9,84
1,68	2,18	1,57	4,32	4,19	4,07	5,63	5,52	5,39	7,86	7,82	7,78	9,63	9,83
0,24	1,80	0,45	3,68	3,59	3,45	5,18	5,03	4,90	7,70	7,66	7,59	9,55	9,81
− 0,10	0,15	0,17	2,96	2,86	2,73	4,64	4,53	4,39	7,49	7,45	7,38	9,47	9,79
− 0,46	0,15	− 0,26	2,58	2,51	2,39	4,22	4,12	4,01	7,25	7,19	7,12	9,39	9,79
0,06	0,18	0,64	2,33	2,35	2,39	3,96	3,82	3,79	7,01	6,94	6,87	9,32	9,78
1,38	1,93	2,00	2,59	2,72	2,88	3,77	3,80	3,81	6,77	6,70	6,69	9,23	9,77
1,92	2,51	2,31	3,03	3,13	3,23	3,89	3,94	4,00	6,57	6,52	6,50	9,16	9,75
2,04	2,99	3,09	3,27	3,14	3,48	4,06	4,08	4,12	6,44	6,40	6,39	9,07	9,74
2,84	3,18	0,10	3,66	3,70	3,13	4,25	4,24	4,25	6,39	6,33	6,30	8,96	9,72
2,33	− 0,27	− 1,43	3,76	2,76	2,43	4,31	4,10	3,90	6,32	6,27	6,24	8,91	9,72
− 3,04	− 1,15	− 2,46	1,94	1,82	1,62	3,63	3,51	3,12	6,21	6,19	6,13	8,77	9,70
− 3,13	− 1,70	− 0,98	1,31	1,23	1,18	3,07	2,97	2,87	6,05	6,00	5,96	8,69	9,67
− 1,09	− 0,27	− 0,54	1,14	1,12	1,15	2,72	2,65	2,62	5,86	5,80	5,74	8,61	9,66
− 0,45	0,04	− 0,38	1,13	1,14	1,16	2,54	2,51	2,50	5,64	5,60	5,54	8,51	9,65
− 1,48	− 1,61	− 2,55	1,12	1,07	1,03	2,45	2,42	2,39	5,47	5,42	5,39	8,41	9,62
2,18	3,01	2,44	4,36	4,34	4,32	5,50	5,43	5,37	7,70	7,66	7,66	9,58	9,81

December 1879.

1" tief			1' tief			2' tief			4' tief			8' tief	16' tief
7	2	8	7	2	8	7	2	8	7	2	8	7	7
− 3,97	− 3,28	− 4,29	0,83	0,75	0,60	2,31	2,25	2,16	5,29	5,26	5,22	8,35	9,61
− 5,41	− 4,63	− 5,55	0,41	0,27	0,10	1,95	1,91	1,82	5,15	5,10	5,06	8,33	9,60
− 5,38	− 4,32	− 3,54	− 0,14	− 0,24	− 0,18	1,60	1,52	1,45	4,98	4,93	4,89	8,18	9,59
− 4,01	− 4,15	− 6,64	− 0,24	− 0,28	− 0,42	1,37	1,29	1,21	4,79	4,72	4,69	8,10	9,58
− 6,29	− 5,61	− 6,08	− 0,84	− 0,95	− 1,07	1,17	1,02	0,96	4,57	4,54	4,48	8,00	9,55
− 5,84	− 4,90	− 5,02	− 1,14	− 1,27	− 1,23	0,80	0,73	0,68	4,38	4,33	4,28	7,88	9,51
− 7,20	− 6,87	− 7,96	− 1,54	− 1,75	− 1,98	0,57	0,49	0,41	4,18	4,16	4,09	7,79	9,50
− 9,87	− 8,38	− 9,14	− 2,61	− 2,08	− 2,96	0,26	0,16	0,06	4,00	3,94	3,89	7,70	9,48
− 7,47	− 6,02	− 5,24	− 3,19	− 2,98	− 2,74	− 0,05	− 0,09	− 0,13	3,78	3,75	3,69	7,58	9,44
− 6,20	− 5,06	− 4,76	− 2,48	− 2,52	− 2,35	− 0,16	− 0,19	− 0,20	3,59	3,54	3,48	7,49	9,43
− 4,30	− 3,00	− 2,84	− 2,16	− 1,95	− 1,73	− 0,22	− 0,20	− 0,21	3,39	3,45	3,29	7,35	9,40
− 2,14	− 1,84	− 1,99	− 1,42	− 1,27	− 1,18	− 0,12	− 0,10	− 0,05	3,22	3,19	3,16	7,25	9,36
− 3,36	− 2,98	− 2,59	− 1,12	− 1,21	− 1,24	− 0,01	0,00	− 0,02	3,11	3,05	3,04	7,15	9,34
− 2,16	− 1,77	− 1,48	− 1,14	− 1,06	− 0,97	− 0,01	0,02	0,02	2,99	2,96	2,93	7,02	9,32
− 0,97	− 0,84	− 0,66	− 0,79	− 0,68	− 0,62	0,04	0,06	0,08	2,91	2,87	2,86	6,96	9,29
− 0,60	− 0,34	− 0,14	− 0,49	− 0,43	− 0,35	0,09	0,13	0,13	2,84	2,82	2,80	6,81	9,25
0,10	0,19	0,10	− 0,25	− 0,19	− 0,14	0,17	0,18	0,19	2,79	2,79	2,77	6,73	9,24
0,11	0,11	0,12	− 0,08	− 0,06	− 0,04	0,20	0,21	0,21	2,74	2,73	2,72	6,60	9,18
− 0,45	0,07	− 0,52	− 0,02	− 0,01	0,01	0,25	0,25	0,25	2,70	2,69	2,68	6,53	9,18
0,02	0,48	0,23	0,00	0,02	0,02	0,29	0,31	0,32	2,67	2,66	2,64	6,45	9,15
0,22	0,24	0,22	0,04	0,07	0,07	0,33	0,34	0,36	2,64	2,64	2,64	6,35	9,11
− 0,19	0,22	− 0,81	0,08	0,09	0,09	0,40	0,42	0,36	2,64	2,62	2,62	6,27	9,06
− 0,05	0,21	0,23	0,09	0,10	0,11	0,43	0,46	0,46	2,61	2,61	2,61	6,26	9,04
0,35	0,25	0,24	0,14	0,12	0,14	0,50	0,50	0,51	2,61	2,60	2,60	2,16	9,02
− 0,10	0,18	0,40	0,16	0,14	0,16	0,53	0,54	0,56	2,60	2,60	2,60	6,08	8,97
0,22	0,34	0,24	0,15	0,16	0,17	0,58	0,57	0,59	2,60	2,59	2,59	6,03	8,96
− 0,02	0,18	− 1,48	0,18	0,18	0,18	0,61	0,64	0,66	2,59	2,60	2,59	5,96	8,90
− 3,81	− 2,87	− 3,55	0,04	− 0,06	− 0,21	0,65	0,65	0,64	2,59	2,59	2,59	5,89	8,87
− 2,14	− 0,58	0,01	− 0,44	− 0,34	− 0,18	0,61	0,60	0,58	2,59	2,58	2,58	5,86	8,84
0,20	0,28	0,32	− 0,23	0,08	0,06	0,58	0,62	0,61	2,57	2,58	2,58	5,80	8,81
0,28	0,29	0,24	0,11	0,13	0,15	0,64	0,64	0,64	2,59	2,60	2,58	5,75	8,77
− [illegible]	− 1,85	− 2,18	− 0,54	− 0,58	− 0,54	0,53	0,51	0,50	3,31	3,29	3,26	6,79	9,24

Januar 1880.

Luftthermometer

III. In Glas			IV. In Kupfer			Frei				VII.	
7	2	8	7	2	8	7	2	8	7	2	8
1,10	0,59	– 0,30	– 0,81	0,48	– 0,43	– 0,71	0,36	– 0,41	– 0,88	0,39	– 0,30
1,83	0,83	2,28	– 1,88	0,72	2,12	– 1,88	0,76	1,92	– 1,88	0,96	2,43
	2,12	2,00	0,43	2,22	2,07	0,54	1,88	2,27	0,85	2,19	2,47
	2,85	1,88	1,07	2,46	1,57	1,66	2,27	1,66	2,91	2,39	2,19
	2,60	1,23	2,70	2,16	1,20	2,52	2,18	1,15	2,89	2,47	1,23
	2,04	2,52	0,91	2,07	2,36	0,89	1,96	2,18	0,96	2,00	2,47
	3,61	0,59	2,46	3,13	0,19	2,52	2,74	0,28	2,02	3,08	0,85
	2,12	3,49	0,34	2,13	3,32	0,54	1,88	3,05	0,77	2,08	3,02
	10,29	– 2,33	0,24	2,36	– 2,36	0,28	1,75	– 1,71	0,77	2,23	– 1,83
	2,16	– 2,96	– 5,41	– 2,26	– 2,84	– 4,56	– 2,14	2,36	– 5,04	– 2,60	– 2,00
4,18	1,43	– 0,23	– 3,90	– 1,50	– 0,14	– 3,61	– 1,27	0,02	– 4,05	– 1,83	– 0,47
0,75	0,51	0,59	0,67	0,34	0,53	1,23	0,36	0,45	0,70	0,20	0,47
	1,80	0,67	0,87	1,59	0,58	1,10	1,32	0,49	1,04	1,15	0,02
	1,31	– 2,40	0,15	0,83	– 2,36	0,28	0,63	– 2,28	0,99	0,62	– 1,83
	0,94	– 4,66	– 4,75	– 1,78	– 4,65	– 4,39	– 1,80	– 4,30	– 3,90	– 1,07	– 4,05
	3,21	– 5,71	– 5,04	– 3,42	– 5,70	– 4,64	– 2,91	– 5,16	– 4,74	– 3,74	– 5,65
	3,04	– 9,66	– 8,33	– 4,51	– 9,29	– 7,84	– 5,59	– 8,71	– 8,47	– 6,61	– 9,86
	8,80	– 9,28	–13,85	– 8,95	– 9,29	–12,70	– 8,49	– 8,62	–13,51	– 9,47	– 9,55
14,12	8,93	–10,88	–14,34	– 9,31	–10,55	–13,43	– 8,92	– 9,91	–14,80	–10,48	–10,42
	4,74	– 6,00	–11,21	– 5,13	– 6,56	–10,86	– 5,25	– 6,46	–11,97	– 5,57	– 6,72
	1,83	–11,91	– 3,70	– 2,07	–11,83	– 3,34	– 2,23	–11,03	– 3,66	– 2,60	–11,90
	5,87	– 5,55	–13,37	– 6,18	– 5,56	–12,57	– 6,33	– 5,28	–13,55	– 7,37	– 5,42
	0,22	– 9,94	– 6,66	– 0,53	–10,15	– 6,29	– 0,84	– 9,18	– 6,61	– 1,53	– 9,85
	0,99	– 3,29	– 5,51	0,15	– 3,47	– 5,37	0,58	– 3,61	– 5,65	0,06	– 2,79
	5,92	– 2,75	– 3,18	2,11	– 2,84	– 3,43	1,22	– 2,40	– 2,79	0,66	– 2,60
	9,00	–10,71	– 7,47	0,05	–10,49	– 6,56	– 1,37	– 9,78	– 7,26	– 1,53	–10,23
12,20	3,01	– 7,96	–12,03	– 4,75	– 7,80	–11,20	– 5,26	– 7,49	–11,52	– 3,44	– 7,56
11,35	9,48	–10,63	–11,35	0,53	–10,49	–10,56	– 1,61	– 9,48	–11,07	– 2,21	–10,04
	10,29	– 6,27	– 4,88	2,46	– 6,28	– 4,21	0,06	– 5,73	– 4,05	0,47	– 6,04
	7,13	–10,05	–11,16	– 0,43	–10,01	–10,25	– 2,57	– 8,96	–10,61	– 3,21	– 9,39
12,56	9,48	– 7,28	–12,41	1,01	– 7,24	–11,53	– 1,27	– 6,63	–11,60	– 1,07	– 6,51
4,86	+ 1,45	– 4,06	– 4,84	– 0,77	– 4,06	– 4,46	– 1,27	– 3,74	– 4,64	– 1,38	– 3,80

Februar 1880.

7	2	8	7	2	8	7	2	8	7	2	8
9,09	10,49	– 3,45	– 8,91	2,94	– 3,80	– 8,28	1,45	– 3,30	– 8,47	2,39	– 2,90
9,42	6,89	– 8,84	– 9,53	– 0,77	– 8,67	– 8,29	– 1,84	– 7,84	– 8,86	– 2,49	– 8,62
8,21	7,86	0,59	– 7,85	1,97	0,53	– 7,56	0,80	0,45	– 8,13	0,08	0,59
0,99	1,80	1,07	0,91	1,54	1,11	1,23	1,32	0,89	0,95	1,54	1,23
0,06	1,07	– 0,90	0,05	0,67	– 0,91	0,02	0,63	– 0,63	– 0,30	0,17	– 0,68
4,74	– 1,19	0,75	– 4,75	– 1,80	0,63	– 4,17	– 1,18	0,54	– 4,43	– 1,15	0,85
1,10	0,79	0,31	– 1,21	0,43	0,34	– 1,14	0,23	0,45	– 1,37	0,08	0,39
2,72	11,02	– 2,12	– 2,70	8,11	– 2,12	– 2,48	2,39	– 1,27	– 2,52	2,39	– 1,79
4,34	11,10	– 0,77	– 4,08	5,84	– 0,77	– 3,66	2,83	– 0,50	– 3,74	2,39	– 0,84
4,94	8,55	– 3,85	– 4,18	4,39	– 3,80	– 3,52	0,89	– 3,00	– 4,21	0,08	– 3,62
6,68	– 1,02	– 1,23	– 6,47	– 1,16	– 1,16	– 5,76	– 0,84	– 0,84	– 6,04	– 1,83	– 1,15
0,90	1,48	– 0,62	– 0,71	1,20	– 0,76	– 0,75	0,80	– 0,67	– 0,99	0,39	– 0,60
4,66	0,59	– 1,02	– 4,37	0,05	– 0,91	– 4,26	– 0,41	– 0,93	– 4,51	– [illegible]	– 0,99
1,43	0,19	– 1,75	– 1,50	– 0,53	– 1,78	– 1,31	– 0,58	– 1,40	– 1,45	– 1,02	– 1,75
2,56	3,97	– 4,58	– 2,55	0,34	– 5,13	– 2,44	– 0,84	– 3,96	– 2,60	– 1,75	– 4,78
5,71	– 2,64	– 5,75	– 5,83	– 3,70	– 5,60	– 5,16	– 4,17	– 5,41	– 5,73	– 5,08	– 5,73
5,95	– 5,19	–11,83	– 5,80	– 6,08	–11,64	– 5,77	– 6,87	–11,36	– 6,19	– 7,48	–11,90
16,41	– 9,98	–14,64	–16,06	–11,93	–14,68	–15,65	–12,18	–14,20	–16,16	–13,28	–14,95
15,41	–10,69	– 9,90	–15,20	– 9,77	– 9,15	–14,72	–10,08	– 9,05	–15,48	–10,50	– 9,28
3,93	2,68	2,60	– 3,66	2,32	2,46	– 3,70	2,09	2,31	– 3,74	2,39	2,77
2,60	2,68	1,89	2,70	2,56	1,80	2,91	2,74	1,15	2,85	2,77	1,31
1,11	1,15	– 0,22	1,11	0,77	– 0,71	0,89	0,54	– 0,41	0,93	0,47	– 0,83
3,77	– 3,04	– 3,69	– 3,56	– 3,32	– 4,17	– 3,43	– 3,00	– 3,52	– 3,62	– 3,90	– 4,13
6,96	11,67	– 3,85	– 6,86	7,77	– 4,13	– 6,25	1,53	– 3,52	– 6,61	– 0,60	– 2,98
6,68	2,85	– 1,02	– 6,66	0,53	– 1,30	– 6,25	0,45	– 0,92	– 6,34	– 0,76	– 1,07
1,23	0,59	1,47	– 1,11	0,34	1,32	– 1,09	0,40	1,32	– 0,93	0,58	1,54
0,11	0,19	– 0,22	0,15	– 0,14	– 0,43	0,15	– 0,11	– 0,41	0,17	– 0,49	– 0,19
4,34	2,60	0,71	– 4,37	1,59	0,67	– 3,87	1,32	0,71	– 1,51	1,23	1,23
1,47	1,80	3,49	1,30	1,78	3,29	1,11	1,58	3,26	1,35	2,00	3,73
		– 2,32	– 4,18	0,22	– 2,47	– 3,92	– 0,69	– 2,11	– 4,16	– 1,12	– 0,23

Januar 1880.

Erdthermometer													
1" tief			1' tief			2' tief			4' tief			8' tief	16' tief
7	2	8	7	2	8	7	2	8	7	2	8	7	7
0,05	0,09	0,14	0,14	0,15	0,15	0,65	0,65	0,67	2,56	2,58	2,56	5,71	8,74
− 0,27	0,18	0,19	0,16	0,15	0,16	0,68	0,69	0,68	2,55	2,53	2,54	5,67	8,71
0,22	0,44	0,40	0,19	0,20	0,20	0,70	0,72	0,71	2,55	2,55	2,54	5,62	8,67
0,44	0,54	0,39	0,24	0,21	0,22	0,76	0,75	0,74	2,55	2,53	2,54	5,58	8,64
0,71	0,57	0,42	0,24	0,24	0,56	0,78	0,75	0,79	2,54	2,53	2,54	5,57	8,61
0,30	0,69	0,75	0,25	0,26	0,28	0,75	0,83	0,81	2,54	2,54	2,52	5,52	8,58
0,89	1,05	0,22	0,28	0,29	0,26	0,84	0,85	0,84	2,54	2,54	2,53	5,47	8,54
0,22	0,72	1,14	0,29	0,31	0,29	0,87	0,88	0,88	2,54	2,54	2,53	5,45	8,52
0,22	1,06	0,23	0,30	0,34	0,31	0,89	0,92	0,90	2,54	2,54	2,56	5,41	8,48
− 0,25	− 0,06	− 0,12	0,26	0,33	0,33	0,94	0,93	0,95	2,56	2,54	2,54	5,36	8,43
− 0,59	− 0,28	− 0,02	0,33	0,35	0,38	0,96	0,96	0,94	2,49	2,54	2,56	5,34	8,40
0,18	0,22	0,22	0,39	0,41	0,40	0,99	1,02	0,99	2,55	2,56	2,56	5,29	8,38
0,26	0,25	0,23	0,44	0,45	0,45	1,03	1,03	1,03	2,55	2,56	2,57	5,25	8,34
0,26	0,30	0,26	0,48	0,48	0,50	1,05	1,06	1,07	2,56	2,56	2,56	5,24	8,31
− 0,81	0,20	− 0,58	0,51	0,54	0,51	1,09	1,10	1,09	2,55	2,57	2,57	5,22	8,28
− 0,75	− 0,25	− 0,74	0,51	0,55	0,54	1,09	1,10	1,09	2,55	2,58	2,57	5,18	8,24
− 1,18	− 0,80	− 1,57	0,53	0,53	0,52	1,12	1,11	1,11	2,56	2,58	2,57	5,14	8,22
− 2,20	− 1,78	− 2,06	0,48	0,42	0,42	1,12	1,08	1,07	2,58	2,58	2,57	5,13	8,20
− 2,55	− 2,22	− 2,43	0,38	0,33	0,29	1,08	1,02	1,01	2,57	2,57	2,55	5,11	8,17
− 3,26	− 1,88	− 1,96	0,20	0,19	0,20	0,97	0,96	0,96	2,55	2,55	2,57	5,06	8,14
− 1,07	− 0,73	− 1,81	0,19	0,22	0,20	0,92	0,89	0,89	2,54	2,54	2,54	5,06	8,09
− 2,81	− 2,18	− 1,87	0,11	0,08	0,06	0,87	0,85	0,82	2,51	2,50	2,50	5,02	8,07
− 1,96	− 1,07	− 1,94	0,02	0,04	0,05	0,79	0,78	0,78	2,41	2,46	2,46	5,00	8,04
− 1,71	− 0,87	− 1,13	0,00	0,01	0,10	0,75	0,74	0,72	2,44	2,42	2,43	4,98	8,00
− 1,21	− 0,18	− 0,51	0,04	0,05	0,08	0,71	0,70	0,71	2,40	2,39	2,38	4,97	7,98
− 1,74	− 0,84	− 2,22	0,06	0,04	0,00	0,71	0,71	0,68	2,37	2,34	2,35	4,92	7,94
− 3,36	− 1,73	− 2,50	− 0,14	− 0,17	− 0,20	0,68	0,66	0,62	2,33	2,32	2,32	4,90	7,92
− 3,65	− 1,24	− 2,85	− 0,37	− 0,41	− 0,38	0,59	0,57	0,56	2,29	2,29	2,30	4,87	7,89
− 2,93	− 0,73	− 1,79	− 0,61	− 0,54	− 0,38	0,56	0,49	0,47	2,28	2,24	2,26	4,84	7,86
− 3,51	− 1,52	− 3,09	− 0,59	− 0,65	− 0,64	0,46	0,43	0,42	2,22	2,22	2,23	4,82	7,84
− 4,29	− 1,49	− 2,83	− 0,91	− 0,93	− 0,82	0,38	0,31	0,29	2,19	2,18	2,18	4,78	7,81
− 1,16	− 0,44	− 0,89	0,14	0,14	0,16	0,83	0,82	0,82	2,48	2,48	2,48	5,21	8,26

Februar 1880.

1" tief 7	1" tief 2	1" tief 8	1' tief 7	1' tief 2	1' tief 8	2' tief 7	2' tief 2	2' tief 8	4' tief 7	4' tief 2	4' tief 8	8' tief 7	16' tief 7
− 3,66	− 0,55	− 0,99	− 1,03	− 0,97	− 0,63	0,26	0,24	0,28	2,13	2,14	2,16	4,77	7,78
− 3,15	− 1,04	− 2,76	− 0,73	− 0,85	− 0,71	0,27	0,23	0,22	2,08	2,07	2,07	4,73	7,74
− 3,71	− 0,89	− 0,67	− 1,12	− 1,00	− 0,41	0,21	0,16	0,12	2,04	2,04	2,00	4,66	7,72
− 0,14	0,06	0,10	− 1,22	− 0,32	− 0,24	0,19	0,18	0,20	2,00	2,00	1,99	4,66	7,70
0,19	0,13	0,15	− 0,89	− 0,08	− 0,03	0,26	0,25	0,26	1,96	1,95	1,95	4,65	7,69
− 0,90	− 0,46	− 0,14	− 0,79	− 0,03	− 0,01	0,28	0,27	0,28	1,95	1,94	1,94	4,60	7,65
− 0,28	− 0,19	− 0,08	− 0,83	− 0,01	− 0,01	0,29	0,30	0,31	1,93	1,92	1,93	4,56	7,63
− 0,58	0,25	0,21	0,03	0,02	0,04	0,33	0,31	0,32	1,90	1,90	1,91	4,54	7,60
− 1,44	0,28	0,13	0,01	− 0,03	0,00	0,35	0,35	0,34	1,91	1,91	1,91	4,51	7,58
− 0,93	0,13	− 0,38	0,03	0,03	− 0,04	0,35	0,36	0,37	1,91	1,88	1,91	4,48	7,54
− 2,18	− 0,29	− 0,64	− 0,07	− 0,12	− 0,12	0,35	0,38	0,37	1,91	1,89	1,89	4,46	7,52
− 0,47	− 0,15	− 0,12	− 0,06	− 0,07	− 0,02	0,38	0,37	0,38	1,89	1,88	1,89	4,43	7,50
− 1,56	− 0,66	− 0,64	− 0,05	− 0,16	− 0,14	0,42	0,38	0,38	1,90	1,89	1,89	4,41	7,46
− 0,72	− 0,55	− 0,63	− 0,12	− 0,10	− 0,09	0,37	0,38	0,39	1,88	1,89	1,89	4,36	7,45
− 0,79	− 0,41	− 1,20	− 0,07	− 0,08	− 0,09	0,41	0,39	0,39	1,89	1,87	1,88	4,37	7,42
− 1,91	− 1,77	− 2,22	− 0,19	− 0,30	− 0,36	0,41	0,39	0,37	1,87	1,87	1,86	4,34	7,39
− 2,41	− 2,63	− 4,00	− 0,49	− 0,59	− 0,71	0,36	0,33	0,31	1,86	1,85	1,87	4,31	7,37
− 6,67	− 6,17	− 7,00	− 1,36	− 1,79	− 2,09	0,22	0,17	0,08	1,86	1,85	1,84	4,29	7,35
− 7,85	− 6,58	− 6,38	− 2,70	− 2,90	− 2,85	− 0,01	− 0,13	− 0,20	1,82	1,81	1,81	4,26	7,32
− 4,48	− 1,37	− 0,38	− 2,75	− 2,20	− 1,55	− 0,31	− 0,34	− 0,29	1,79	1,76	1,76	4,23	7,29
0,04	0,18	− 0,17	− 0,83	− 0,63	− 0,47	− 0,25	− 0,10	− 0,07	1,76	1,70	1,71	4,27	7,29
0,21	0,21	− 0,27	− 0,30	− 0,24	0,05	0,02	0,04	0,08	1,66	1,65	1,65	4,22	7,27
− 0,60	− 1,10	− 0,72	− 0,14	− 0,17	− 0,25	0,09	0,09	0,11	1,63	1,63	1,64	4,19	7,24
− 2,89	− 0,09	− 1,09	− 0,47	− 0,65	− 0,49	0,12	0,10	0,08	1,64	1,60	1,62	4,18	7,23
− 3,34	− 0,06	− 0,58	− 0,73	− 0,76	− 0,57	0,07	0,05	0,04	1,60	1,60	1,59	4,13	7,18
− 0,67	− 0,27	− 0,01	− 0,43	− 0,39	− 0,30	0,07	0,06	0,11	1,60	1,59	1,61	4,13	7,17
− 0,04	0,16	0,14	− 0,21	− 1,17	− 0,14	0,11	0,13	0,13	1,57	1,58	1,59	4,07	7,15
− 0,94	0,02	0,04	− 0,11	− 0,14	− 0,10	0,15	0,13	− 0,26	1,59	1,59	1,58	4,02	7,11
0,20	0,20	0,23	− 0,05	− 0,03	− 0,02	0,17	0,17	0,13	1,56	1,58	1,56	3,98	7,10
− 1,44	− 0,82	− 1,04	− 0,61	− 0,51	− 0,43	0,20	0,20	0,21	1,83	1,82	1,82	4,27	7,43

Luftthermometer											
III. In Glas			IV. In Kupfer			I' frei			VII.		
7	2	8	7	2	8	7	2	8	7	2	8
	4,87	3,93	2,46	4,39	4,00	1,93	3,78	3,31	2,39	4,62	4,16
	4,70	2,52	2,21	4,19	2,46	2,18	3,65	2,52	2,77	4,39	2,93
	6,57	6,24	4,10	6,23	6,08	3,82	5,21	5,47	4,31	6,16	6,62
	6,16	0,91	1,49	4,49	0,72	1,75	4,51	0,89	1,85	4,12	0,85
	3,41	0,99	1,87	3,04	1,01	1,66	2,70	1,02	1,92	2,69	1,08
	3,41	− 2,28	− 0,62	2,22	− 2,36	− 0,67	1,23	− 1,71	− 0,68	0,08	− 1,72
	4,95	2,72	2,11	4,77	2,56	1,84	4,68	2,52	2,31	4,78	2,89
2,40	4,22	− 2,64	− 2,26	1,11	− 2,50	− 2,05	0,67	− 2,14	− 2,05	− 0,22	− 2,29
1,43	5,43	0,99	− 1,50	2,60	0,91	− 1,36	1,88	0,80	− 1,75	0,70	1,28
1,10	17,81	3,00	− 1,16	12,73	2,99	− 0,93	9,23	3,05	− 0,68	7,31	3,16
	9,24	− 2,24	0,05	3,90	− 2,26	0,15	2,31	− 1,57	0,35	0,55	− 1,83
	6,65	− 6,68	− 4,99	1,11	− 6,27	− 4,82	− 2,14	− 5,33	− 5,04	− 4,92	− 6,96
	9,48	− 4,66	− 8,57	4,00	− 4,61	− 7,57	2,61	− 3,78	− 8,13	− 0,60	− 4,28
	2,68	− 1,27	− 5,94	1,59	− 1,21	− 4,95	1,15	− 0,94	− 5,43	0,08	− 1,07
	3,51	− 1,63	− 3,90	3,90	− 1,59	− 3,70	2,96	− 1,18	− 3,74	1,35	− 1,45
	6,53	0,07	− 1,40	4,97	0,05	− 1,27	3,31	0,26	− 1,26	3,04	0,08
	2,60	− 4,74	− 0,29	0,05	− 4,75	− 0,50	− 0,73	− 4,30	− 0,60	− 1,91	− 4,65
	1,39	− 6,52	− 8,47	− 1,78	− 6,18	− 7,98	− 2,23	− 5,33	− 8,32	− 4,74	− 6,08
3,57	1,80	− 0,38	− 3,47	1,30	− 0,53	− 3,00	1,11	− 0,32	− 3,51	0,98	− 0,90
1,43	2,85	− 1,51	− 1,40	1,35	− 1,74	− 1,36	0,58	− 1,41	− 1,56	0,08	− 1,64
1,43	1,07	− 1,02	− 1,40	0,53	− 1,11	− 1,14	0,98	− 0,93	− 1,45	0,55	− 1,34
9,50	8,67	− 5,02	− 9,34	3,42	− 4,75	− 8,92	1,75	− 4,09	− 9,47	− 0,96	− 4,51
4,14	14,77	− 0,34	− 4,13	7,57	− 0,43	− 3,57	5,77	0,02	− 4,70	2,54	0,90
0,11	2,60	− 0,30	0,05	1,27	− 0,43	0,06	1,66	− 0,07	− 0,22	1,23	0,08
1,71	13,06	− 1,71	− 1,74	8,73	− 1,74	− 1,27	7,37	− 1,13	− 1,72	6,54	− 1,07
2,16	12,32	− 1,58	− 2,07	8,25	− 1,88	− 1,80	7,19	− 1,05	− 2,02	5,31	− 0,84
1,11	6,65	− 0,50	− 1,16	5,85	− 0,71	− 0,84	5,21	− 0,41	− 0,88	4,70	− 0,98
3,60	13,47	− 2,24	− 3,66	9,35	− 2,36	− 3,21	7,89	− 1,91	− 3,74	5,20	− 1,90
	1,80	0,59	− 0,53	1,49	0,53	− 0,41	1,75	0,71	− 0,68	1,31	0,39
	3,09	1,39	− 0,14	2,60	1,49	0,02	2,39	1,53	− 0,30	1,81	1,62
0,46	15,66	2,12	− 0,66	12,49	1,87	− 0,63	10,23	2,18	− 0,99	1,77	2,19
	6,90	− 0,70	− 1,79	4,80	− 0,69	− 2,00	3,18	− 0,43	− 1,71	1,90	− 0,46
	3,33	1,80	0,19	2,56	1,63	0,45	2,57	1,75	0,20	1,77	1,86
	6,34	1,80	0,43	5,25	1,87	0,58	4,77	2,39	0,27	4,04	2,27
0,83	3,01	0,19	0,05	3,26	0,05	0,45	1,75	0,06	0,51	1,66	0,08
0,06	1,55	0,47	0,05	1,20	0,53	0,20	1,32	0,54	0,30	1,12	0,47
1,80	19,76	9,48	1,74	16,94	8,99	1,75	13,96	1,29*)	1,62	12,96	9,82
5,43	19,23	8,79	5,12	16,07	8,73	4,69	15,30	8,57	5,08	13,35	8,97
5,35	6,16	4,62	5,02	5,84	4,53	5,21	5,47	4,77	4,85	5,47	4,70
2,36	5,19	3,17	2,22	4,49	3,28	2,52	4,55	3,39	2,08	4,04	3,20
3,13	17,28	1,88	2,94	12,85	1,74	2,83	11,61	2,27	2,47	10,09	1,66
2,04	7,86	4,87	1,74	6,90	4,77	2,09	6,93	4,95	1,70	6,04	4,97
4,38	12,20	6,24	4,04	11,14	6,22	4,12	10,44	6,41	3,85	9,59	6,85
4,46	22,08	3,53	4,29	17,08	3,52	4,47	15,95	3,91	3,93	13,46	3,77
5,39	21,27	8,06	5,45	17,42	7,67	4,84	16,04	8,10	3,31	13,92	8,98
6,44	22,28	12,32	6,51	18,38	12,11	6,41	17,43	12,23	5,93	16,98	12,47
9,73	22,74	9,89	9,40	19,54	9,79	9,53	19,40	10,74	9,62	17,06	10,47
7,94	18,02	3,63	7,77	14,52	3,52	7,93	14,40	4,25	7,47	12,81	3,70
5,84	26,48	13,39	5,94	22,40	12,69	6,07	21,30	13,09	5,20	19,50	13,62
11,51	30,23	15,42	11,14	24,67	15,00	10,83	23,89	15,17	10,97	21,94	15,76
13,95	32,87	8,87	14,52	27,92	10,56	13,18	27,24	9,53	13,16	24,81	8,63
6,36	23,96	9,43	6,32	19,21	9,07	6,93	17,77	9,79	5,83	15,58	9,32
10,62	28,15	11,92	10,42	24,92	11,62	10,31	23,84	11,96	10,32	22,70	12,01
9,08	23,71	12,73	10,18	20,56	12,45	9,93	19,49	13,00	8,27	18,21	13,16
11,92	15,58	10,70	12,01	14,52	10,32	11,31	14,74	11,09	10,32	14,69	11,24
8,59	9,08	9,08	9,45	8,54	8,83	8,66	9,19	9,10	7,78	9,05	9,01
7,86	11,92	6,57	7,77	11,43	6,51	7,80	10,87	6,73	8,16	11,12	7,16
7,98	21,68	4,22	7,77	16,59	4,00	7,58	15,53	5,24	7,31	11,24	5,08
7,13	14,77	2,20	6,99	11,38	2,02	6,67	10,40	3,14	6,24	7,86	2,77
5,88	10,37	2,20	5,84	9,40	2,36	5,61	9,10	2,61	5,39	8,28	2,81
3,41	18,83	1,39	4,10	12,40	1,39	3,39	11,40	2,09	2,69	6,58	1,79
3,33	19,64	5,03	2,94	15,00	4,97	2,83	13,48	5,60	2,39	10,09	5,63

März 1880.

Erdthermometer													
1" tief			1' tief			2' tief			4' tief			8' tief	16' tief
7	2	8	7	2	8	7	2	8	7	2	8	7	7
0,59	0,61	0,66	0,02	0,04	0,04	0,19	0,17	0,19	1,54	1,57	1,57	3,97	7,09
0,54	1,00	0,63	0,08	0,08	0,11	0,20	0,20	0,19	1,56	1,57	1,58	4,00	7,07
1,13	1,68	1,77	0,12	0,12	0,12	0,22	0,20	0,22	1,57	1,56	1,56	4,02	7,05
0,61	2,32	1,57	0,14	0,17	0,16	0,23	0,23	0,25	1,57	1,57	1,58	4,03	7,03
0,72	1,34	0,67	0,18	0,18	0,19	0,25	0,24	0,25	1,57	1,57	1,59	4,00	6,99
0,24	0,83	0,26	0,20	0,22	0,21	0,27	0,26	0,28	1,57	1,58	1,58	3,97	6,96
0,25	1,42	1,21	0,22	0,20	0,21	0,29	0,29	0,30	1,58	1,56	1,58	4,01	6,95
0,26	1,07	0,27	0,22	0,22	0,24	0,31	0,32	0,33	1,58	1,59	1,59	3,93	6,92
0,07	0,22	0,32	0,23	0,23	0,22	0,32	0,36	0,36	1,60	1,58	1,59	3,89	6,89
0,19	4,58	1,61	0,23	0,27	0,25	0,36	0,37	0,37	1,59	1,58	1,59	3,89	6,89
0,22	2,92	0,26	0,23	0,26	0,16	0,38	0,41	0,40	1,59	1,63	1,61	3,87	6,86
— 0,40	0,27	— 0,55	0,25	0,25	0,18	0,42	0,43	0,43	1,61	1,62	1,63	3,82	6,84
— 1,40	0,77	— 0,12	0,25	0,25	0,24	0,43	0,44	0,45	1,62	1,63	1,62	3,81	6,80
— 1,23	0,41	0,24	0,25	0,27	0,25	0,46	0,47	0,45	1,62	1,63	1,63	3,78	6,79
— 0,95	1,46	0,22	0,24	0,26	0,26	0,46	0,48	0,47	1,63	1,65	1,63	3,78	6,77
— 0,18	0,77	0,22	0,25	0,26	0,25	0,48	0,48	0,50	1,65	1,64	1,65	3,79	6,76
— 0,28	0,39	— 0,19	0,27	0,26	0,26	0,51	0,50	0,53	1,64	1,65	1,65	3,79	6,72
— 1,71	0,24	— 1,09	0,25	0,26	0,25	0,53	0,54	0,53	1,65	1,66	1,66	3,74	6,70
— 0,95	0,03	0,11	0,24	0,24	0,25	0,54	0,54	0,56	1,65	1,66	1,67	3,80	6,69
— 0,46	0,20	0,08	0,25	0,24	0,26	0,56	0,56	0,57	1,66	1,66	1,67	3,72	6,66
— 0,42	0,18	0,19	0,26	0,25	0,25	0,57	0,58	0,57	1,68	1,68	1,68	3,72	6,65
— 2,80	0,71	— 0,33	0,24	0,23	0,25	0,58	0,60	0,59	1,68	1,69	1,69	3,68	6,62
— 1,40	2,01	0,23	0,24	0,25	0,25	0,58	0,59	0,62	1,68	1,69	1,70	3,68	6,59
— 0,22	0,25	0,20	0,26	0,27	0,27	0,61	0,62	0,63	1,70	1,70	1,70	3,69	6,57
— 0,06	3,63	0,25	0,27	0,28	0,29	0,64	0,65	0,65	1,70	1,72	1,72	3,68	6,57
— 0,02	3,87	— 0,10	0,30	0,30	0,27	0,68	0,68	0,70	1,70	1,72	1,71	3,67	6,55
0,07	2,29	0,06	0,29	0,32	0,34	0,73	0,73	0,76	1,70	1,72	1,71	3,64	6,53
— 0,28	5,08	2,20	0,36	0,46	0,47	0,80	0,82	0,83	1,72	1,72	1,64	3,64	6,52
0,06	1,29	0,71	0,43	0,60	0,54	0,85	0,87	0,85	1,73	1,73	1,74	3,62	6,49
0,19	1,35	0,98	0,53	0,56	0,60	0,91	0,90	0,92	1,74	1,74	1,76	3,63	6,51
0,11	6,68	2,13	0,52	0,88	1,05	0,91	0,97	1,05	1,76	1,76	1,76	3,62	6,46
— 0,21	1,59	0,47	0,25	0,28	0,28	0,50	0,50	0,51	1,63	1,65	1,65	3,80	6,80

April 1880.

1" tief 7	2	8	1' tief 7	2	8	2' tief 7	2	8	4' tief 7	2	8	8' tief 7	16' tief 7
0,43	1,72	1,43	0,87	0,86	0,90	1,15	1,12	1,14	1,78	1,78	1,79	3,61	6,44
0,68	2,75	1,78	0,87	1,01	1,13	1,16	1,16	1,22	1,80	1,80	1,82	3,61	6,43
0,61	1,23	0,77	0,97	0,93	0,99	1,25	1,22	1,25	1,82	1,83	1,84	3,59	6,41
0,33	1,05	0,85	0,90	0,90	0,94	1,25	1,24	1,23	1,86	1,87	1,87	3,59	6,39
0,11	8,32	6,66	0,95	1,54	2,39	1,25	1,36	1,58	1,87	1,89	1,98	3,58	6,36
3,35	10,32	7,67	2,63	3,53	4,35	1,94	2,23	2,59	1,90	1,92	1,93	3,59	6,34
5,21	5,37	4,92	4,27	4,10	4,07	3,04	3,16	3,23	1,98	2,03	2,10	3,59	6,37
3,29	4,00	3,61	3,74	3,54	3,53	3,27	3,24	3,22	2,04	2,28	2,34	3,59	6,33
2,26	9,07	4,48	3,32	3,81	4,31	3,19	3,25	3,41	2,44	2,51	2,46	3,60	6,29
2,90	5,40	4,66	3,81	3,84	4,06	3,53	3,47	3,55	2,63	2,69	2,74	3,61	6,28
3,90	7,88	6,44	3,92	4,42	4,87	3,63	3,68	3,84	2,81	2,85	2,90	3,64	6,27
4,80	13,15	6,31	4,52	5,26	5,90	4,02	4,10	4,36	2,97	3,04	3,06	3,68	6,27
4,02	13,15	8,22	5,17	5,73	6,41	4,56	4,69	4,81	3,13	3,20	3,27	3,74	6,23
5,24	13,72	10,43	5,77	6,42	7,24	5,02	5,09	5,35	3,34	3,42	3,47	3,74	6,22
8,42	15,73	11,00	7,09	7,81	8,46	5,70	5,90	6,20	3,58	3,64	3,72	3,79	6,22
8,23	14,12	7,88	8,02	8,43	8,66	6,53	6,63	6,81	3,86	3,96	4,04	3,83	6,20
5,63	13,60	12,01	8,13	8,02	8,89	6,77	6,74	6,94	4,20	4,29	4,36	3,88	6,18
9,50	17,81	13,84	8,63	9,28	10,67	7,31	7,35	7,67	4,48	4,26	4,62	3,95	6,17
11,11	19,83	12,94	9,78	10,53	11,15	8,03	8,21	8,50	4,75	4,86	4,93	4,01	6,15
8,68	14,00	11,05	10,04	9,83	10,00	8,68	8,59	8,59	5,11	5,24	5,32	4,08	6,15
9,41	17,92	13,05	9,38	10,11	10,79	8,53	8,54	8,75	5,47	5,55	5,69	4,18	6,13
9,42	15,92	12,90	10,13	10,26	10,86	8,95	8,93	9,05	5,70	5,81	5,87	4,26	6,11
10,53	18,74	12,08	10,53	10,55	10,87	9,17	9,17	9,27	5,98	6,05	6,12	4,37	6,11
8,93	10,61	10,14	10,22	10,04	8,06	9,28	9,15	9,14	6,21	6,30	6,35	4,47	6,11
8,74	10,09	8,45	9,45	9,30	9,22	8,96	8,81	8,75	6,44	6,48	6,51	4,60	6,08
7,44	11,36	8,10	8,57	8,65	8,96	8,50	8,34	8,34	6,57	6,61	6,62	4,70	6,08
6,68	10,00	6,75	8,29	8,29	8,43	8,22	8,08	8,06	6,63	6,64	6,65	4,81	6,08
6,74	7,66	5,18	7,58	7,40	7,32	7,91	7,86	7,58	6,64	6,63	6,62	4,91	6,07
8,78	9,43	5,37	6,45	6,59	7,09	7,20	6,29	6,99	6,58	6,60	6,55	5,02	6,06
4,27	9,13	6,60	6,53	6,65	6,96	6,96	6,84	6,84	6,49	6,47	6,41	5,12	6,05
5,48	10,29	7,52	6,01	6,25	6,56	5,49	5,49	5,51	4,04	4,08	4,13	4,02	6,22

Mai 1880.

	Luftthermometer											
	III. In Glas			IV. In Kupfer			I' frei			VII.		
	7	2	8	7	2	8	7	2	8	7	2	8
1	8,09	14,77	8,67	6,66	13,55	8,25	6,20	12,78	8,66	5,66	12,01	9,05
2	10,70	18,42	12,32	10,66	17,13	11,87	10,14	17,34	12,01	10,47	15,95	12,39
3	9,08	28,19	12,23	9,64	22,74	11,67	9,66	21,77	12,14	8,66	18,24	12,39
4	9,89	18,02	12,81	10,31	16,60	12,69	10,27	16,04	13,00	9,28	15,18	12,96
5	13,55	19,31	13,63	13,07	18,00	13,55	12,57	17,74	13,87	12,39	16,71	13,84
6	15,17	17,86	11,84	14,81	16,50	11,62	14,05	15,61	11,89	13,62	16,11	11,89
7	7,86	15,21	5,43	7,57	9,89	4,92	7,80	9,19	5,64	7,66	8,63	5,51
8	7,25	11,51	7,46	6,70	10,95	7,23	6,67	10,53	7,71	6,85	10,01	7,35
9	7,66	8,55	5,43	7,28	7,91	5,40	7,37	8,14	5,90	6,62	7,55	5,98
10	6,12	8,19	9,81	6,08	7,96	9,64	6,07	8,01	9,53	6,24	7,86	9,82
11	8,27	11,18	7,86	8,01	10,66	7,38	8,23	10,27	8,01	7,97	9,78	7,78
12	8,75	14,36	7,46	8,39	12,49	7,38	8,13	12,23	7,93	7,55	10,05	7,39
13	13,95	25,59	15,05	13,41	22,50	14,57	12,96	21,21	14,91	13,43	20,41	14,84
14	16,07	15,89	14,48	15,39	15,10	14,04	14,70	15,17	14,40	14,69	15,84	14,34
15	14,11	28,19	11,14	13,55	24,96	10,66	13,35	22,59	11,27	12,96	19,50	10,85
16	11,63	26,72	6,57	16,56	23,70	6,42	10,06	21,21	7,37	11,16	16,87	6,08
17	5,55	19,27	1,59	5,06	15,15	1,77	5,21	13,00	2,52	4,12	7,66	1,78
18	4,54	17,77	1,72	4,00	14,04	1,44	4,12	12,57	2,61	3,16	7,39	2,12
19	4,26	17,61	1,51	4,00	15,00	1,05	3,57	13,00	1,66	3,27	8,16	1,00
20	3,21	11,30	5,03	2,94	10,23	4,39	2,74	9,79	5,34	3,12	8,47	5,39
21	8,43	14,97	11,10	7,91	13,65	10,66	7,28	13,00	10,49	7,20	12,16	10,89
22	9,08	15,58	8,67	8,73	13,80	8,25	8,49	13,00	8,75	8,74	11,47	8,74
23	10,54	11,92	8,27	9,98	10,85	7,87	9,66	10,83	8,23	9,93	10,47	8,16
24	10,21	13,55	10,37	9,81	12,88	10,18	8,84	12,48	10,53	9,70	12,77	10,77
25	10,29	23,71	10,70	10,18	18,87	10,18	9,10	17,77	10,49	9,97	14,61	10,62
26	12,57	26,89	11,10	12,21	22,79	10,47	11,27	22,59	11,24	12,01	17,32	10,97
27	13,06	34,79	22,28	12,30	31,56	21,62	11,96	28,54	21,21	12,39	27,58	21,84
28	20,57	35,64	22,41	19,83	32,13	21,77	19,27	30,60	21,64	20,41	29,73	20,79
29	10,29	17,69	10,41	10,08	16,16	10,28	10,74	15,26	10,92	10,47	13,92	10,13
30	11,51	13,95	10,71	11,14	12,64	10,56	11,18	12,78	11,01	10,85	12,01	10,62
31	10,62	14,96	13,14	10,32	13,55	13,07	10,74	13,44	13,00	10,47	13,00	13,16
	9,93	18,42	10,04	9,87	16,25	9,71	9,43	15,43	10,13	9,37	13,79	9,98

Juni 1880.

	7	2	8	7	2	8	7	2	8	7	2	8
1	13,79	24,64	16,80	13,07	21,57	16,45	12,66	20,44	16,30	12,85	19,65	16,83
2	15,42	32,79	15,78	14,62	28,20	15,49	14,27	26,81	16,13	15,07	22,89	15,45
3	14,77	34,79	19,45	14,14	30,19	18,92	13,78	28,97	18,97	14,88	24,66	19,50
4	15,87	15,17	12,08	14,66	15,10	11,77	14,74	13,83	12,57	15,36	15,37	12,77
5	14,93	24,32	10,41	14,42	21,77	10,28	13,96	19,49	10,87	14,38	17,74	10,09
6	6,65	14,77	10,09	6,61	13,07	9,79	6,93	12,57	10,01	7,01	11,62	10,09
7	9,89	13,14	10,41	9,69	12,45	10,03	10,31	12,14	10,23	10,12	11,70	10,47
8	11,51	21,35	10,29	11,14	16,84	9,98	11,40	16,48	10,57	11,54	13,54	10,22
9	12,73	24,60	11,51	12,21	21,28	11,14	12,05	19,92	11,61	12,01	18,13	11,24
10	12,40	27,37	20,70	12,11	25,16	20,17	11,70	24,23	20,05	12,39	23,24	20,41
11	17,73	30,64	13,55	17,28	25,64	13,26	16,91	25,95	14,22	16,52	20,79	13,24
12	16,76	34,71	22,90	16,02	29,51	22,25	16,44	30,26	22,93	14,96	25,39	22,47
13	21,19	34,96	18,02	20,32	30,34	17,56	20,31	30,60	18,20	20,49	26,58	18,59
14	20,45	23,63	22,49	19,35	21,28	21,77	19,53	20,91	21,30	18,81	21,29	21,64
15	18,06	28,72	18,83	17,23	24,43	18,04	16,91	23,80	18,20	17,06	22,05	18,51
16	15,99	31,04	18,42	15,54	25,40	17,80	15,17	26,21	18,03	15,64	21,67	17,93
17	16,88	30,56	17,32	15,97	26,61	16,94	16,00	27,46	17,68	16,03	23,56	17,06
18	16,80	31,45	16,55	16,03	27,24	16,07	16,13	26,38	16,40	15,84	23,85	16,83
19	17,86	30,64	13,95	16,99	25,78	14,04	17,00	26,38	14,74	16,98	20,95	13,82
20	11,51	21,27	11,10	11,43	17,90	10,95	11,61	19,06	12,05	11,81	14,90	10,85
21	13,63	22,83	12,73	13,21	19,54	12,59	12,78	20,44	13,44	13,31	16,98	12,89
22	13,34	31,45	14,36	12,97	26,32	14,04	13,00	27,59	15,17	13,24	21,45	14,08
23	13,91	32,59	21,39	13,45	28,25	21,04	13,48	28,11	21,21	13,39	25,85	21,10
24	17,49	26,56	18,02	16,73	24,57	17,56	16,65	22,93	18,63	16,30	22,82	17,70
25	18,22	20,45	17,65	17,42	19,93	17,47	17,68	20,18	18,11	16,98	20,08	17,70
26	15,99	22,20	14,61	15,34	19,83	14,33	15,61	19,66	14,83	15,18	18,40	14,65
27	15,99	20,94	12,73	15,25	17,90	12,25	15,34	18,63	12,96	14,84	15,92	12,43
28	13,55	29,61	15,99	13,02	24,33	15,49	12,57	24,57	16,25	13,16	20,19	18,22
29	13,89	22,04	15,58	13,21	19,35	15,10	13,87	19,06	15,61	13,70	18,36	15,57
30	16,23	29,00	16,80	16,07	23,80	16,59	16,39	22,93	17,04	16,14	21,56	16,90
	14,43	26,26	15,68	14,52	22,45	15,31	14,51	22,53	15,83	14,19	20,00	15,54

Mai 880.

	9,49	8,56	6,52	6,83	7,41	6,79	6,76	6,84	6,36	6,35	6,38	5,20	6,06
	13,35	11,18	7,27	8,00	8,84	7,01	6,14	7,38	6,26	6,27	6,26	5,28	6,06
	13,20	11,85	8,49	8,92	9,80	7,71	7,80	8,06	6,26	6,31	6,32	5,34	6,06
	12,72	11,93	9,42	9,50	9,95	8,37	8,42	8,56	6,35	6,50	6,47	5,38	6,06
	13,83	12,53	9,89	10,02	10,33	8,76	8,83	8,94	6,54	6,60	6,65	5,44	6,08
	13,23	12,35	10,28	10,47	10,66	9,11	9,19	9,31	6,74	6,80	6,87	5,48	6,08
	10,13	8,61	10,36	10,09	9,89	9,39	9,33	9,28	6,96	7,02	7,07	5,53	6,08
	9,57	9,03	9,02	10,49	9,18	9,01	8,81	8,84	7,16	7,16	7,23	5,59	6,09
	8,47	7,58	8,87	8.74	8,65	8,71	8,63	8,54	7,25	7,29	7,25	5,64	6,09
	7,77	8,57	8,26	8,09	8,17	8,37	8,24	8,18	7,29	7,28	7,32	5,72	6,11
	9,26	8,71	8,28	8,40	8,57	8,12	8,12	8,17	7,27	7,25	7,25	5,78	6,13
,20	10,52	9,10	8,43	8,60	8,90	8,20	8,18	8,27	7,23	7,22	7,24	5,87	6,13
,31	14,84	13,56	8,87	9,53	10,33	8,87	8,43	8,73	7,22	7,23	7,26	5,93	6,13
,32	13,38	13,40	10,58	10,82	11,08	9,21	9,38	9,53	7,28	7,30	7,37	5,99	6,14
,96	16,17	13,15	11,01	11,30	11,85	9,77	9,82	10,06	7,45	7,51	7,55	6,04	6,17
,10	15,54	10,71	11,08	11,20	11,49	10,23	10,15	10,21	7,67	7,73	7,77	6,10	6,18
,48	10,32	7,02	10,34	9,88	9,83	10,15	9,90	9,74	7,89	7,92	7,99	6,14	6,18
,38	9,08	6,52	8,68	8,49	8,75	9,38	9,08	8,96	8,02	8,03	8,03	6,20	6,19
,92	8,70	5,61	7,95	7,88	8,01	8,72	8,49	8,37	8,01	7,96	7,98	6,27	6,19
,06	7,99	7,03	7,26	7,31	7,75	8,18	8,00	7,98	7,91	7,87	7,84	6,34	6,20
,54	9,87	9,40	7,60	7,95	8,35	7,98	7,98	8,03	7,76	7,75	7,69	6,41	6,23
,50	10,57	9,51	8,45	8,64	8,98	8,24	8,30	8,40	7,66	7,63	7,64	6,45	6,25
,74	9,75	9,13	8,86	8,87	9,02	8,57	8,51	8,59	7,63	7,64	7,64	6,52	6,25
,36	10,59	10,29	8,71	8,87	9,24	8,58	8,56	8,67	7,66	7,67	7,69	6,56	6,26
,06	13,19	10,99	9,28	9,53	10,07	8,78	8,82	9,01	7,70	7,72	7,74	6,59	6,29
,08	14,81	12,05	9,89	10,26	10,95	9,22	9,28	9,51	7,77	7,77	7,83	6,62	6,30
,43	18,09	17,33	10,53	11,18	12,81	9,80	9,86	10,22	7,88	7,91	7,97	6,67	6,30
,53	21,00	19,41	12,72	13,36	14,33	10,88	11,15	11,56	8,05	8,11	8,19	6,69	6,33
,11	13,60	12,47	13,89	13,34	13,06	12,09	12,08	12,01	8,34	8,44	8,53	6,72	6,34
,33	12,09	11,55	12,23	12,00	11,91	11,74	11,58	11,46	8,72	8,80	8,86	6,78	6,37
,01	12,13	12,36	11,56	11,50	11,57	11,27	11,17	11,11	8,97	9,01	9,04	6,84	6,38
,07	12,02	10,69	9,50	9,68	9,98	9,06	8,99	9,11	7,46	7,49	7,51	6,07	6,18

Juni 1880.

,18	16,59	15,02	11,63	11,86	12,55	11,10	11,10	11,28	9,08	9,11	9,12	6,98	6,41
,07	18,03	16,02	12,51	12,90	13,75	11,53	11,60	11,90	9,17	9,17	9,23	7,00	6,41
,48	19,40	17,57	13,55	13,82	14,66	11,29	12,35	12,02	9,29	9,32	9,41	7,09	6,43
,69	14,33	13,96	14,53	14,23	14,04	13,03	13,03	12,99	9,50	9,56	9,64	7,15	6,45
,53	15,40	13,46	13,48	13,46	13,74	12,83	12,70	12,73	9,76	9,80	9,87	7,24	6,46
,56	13,44	11,53	12,78	12,37	12,51	12,60	12,35	12,23	9,95	9,99	10,04	7,31	6,48
,83	12,33	10,99	11,97	11,94	11,82	12,00	11,84	11,74	10,06	10,08	10,09	7,41	6,51
,11	13,85	11,70	12,20	11,72	12,00	11,81	11,59	11,70	10,09	10,06	10,08	7,45	6,52
,14	15,42	12,56	11,59	11,83	12,31	11,54	11,45	11,53	10,07	10,05	10,05	7,60	6,55
,73	18,05	16,83	11,73	12,22	13,28	11,50	11,51	11,76	10,04	10,03	10,04	7,68	6,56
,11	21,12	16,25	13,42	14,10	15,09	12,20	12,39	12,81	10,04	10,04	10,07	7,76	6,59
,18	23,27	20,94	14,60	15,25	16,55	13,22	13,33	13,78	10,14	10,20	10,26	8,82	6,61
,25	24,86	19,79	16,56	17,12	17,98	14,44	14,62	15,04	10,37	10,47	10,59	7,89	6,62
,47	20,57	20,82	17,45	17,45	17,94	15,43	15,44	15,61	10,73	10,84	10,97	7,94	6,65
,85	21,23	18,36	17,56	17,50	17,77	15,77	15,74	15,83	11,13	11,24	11,36	8,00	6,66
,78	21,29	18,19	16,45	16,46	17,17	15,67	15,40	15,47	11,52	11,61	11,70	8,11	6,68
,27	22,33	18,63	16,37	16,65	17,48	15,50	15,38	15,53	11,81	11,84	11,90	8,21	6,73
,80	23,25	18,60	16,73	17,11	17,85	15,72	15,63	15,84	11,98	12,00	12,06	8,31	6,73
,94	22,64	17,38	16,94	17,11	17,80	15,99	15,86	16,04	12,15	12,18	12,28	8,44	6,76
,62	18,41	15,04	16,63	16,33	16,66	16,05	15,82	15,75	12,33	12,42	12,41	8,54	6,79
,24	18,91	15,76	15,58	15,74	16,88	15,56	15,33	15,37	12,48	12,51	12,53	8,66	6,82
,24	21,84	17,09	15,46	15,83	16,82	15,31	15,17	15,32	12,55	12,55	12,56	8,79	6,82
,17	23,20	20,31	16,07	16,54	17,57	15,51	15,45	15,69	12,58	12,59	12,63	8,91	6,86
,28	23,07	19,67	17,40	17,63	18,37	16,10	16,14	16,39	12,65	12,67	12,75	9,03	6,90
,26	20,59	19,14	17,70	17,84	18,36	16,58	16,55	16,69	12,80	12,85	12,92	9,12	6,90
,79	20,52	17,44	17,71	17,80	18,05	16,76	16,67	16,94	13,00	13,06	13,10	9,23	6,95
,74	18,93	15,75	17,06	17,12	17,20	16,62	16,44	16,41	13,20	13,24	13,26	9,34	6,98
,59	21,40	17,77	16,04	16,36	17,26	16,81	15,94	16,04	13,31	13,33	13,38	9,44	7,01
,09	17,70	16,73	16,73	16,49	16,70	16,81	16,07	16,03	13,38	13,35	13,41	9,55	7,02
,01	20,33	17,68	16,82	16,51	17,08	15,94	15,84	15,94	13,41	13,41	13,43	9,65	7,08

Juli 1880.

Luftthermometer

19,14
18,54

19,75
15,83

16,88

August

12,65	19,68	13,14	11,91	17,18	12,59	11,92	14,40	12,96	11,81	16,18	13,50
14,07	15,25	14,03	13,50	14,04	14,14	12,66	14,18	14,05	13,16	18,92	14,30
16,72	28,84	16,89	16,21	22,25	15,54	15,61	23,71	16,48	15,34	20,22	16,03
15,54	16,80	17,36	15,25	16,07	17,08	15,61	16,44	17,04	15,64	15,99	17,06
	20,05	18,42	16,31	19,73	18,09	16,48	19,40	18,29	16,22	19,54	18,55
16,51	22,41	17,61	16,11	20,46	17,04	16,17	20,01	17,21	16,23	19,84	17,44
	27,57	19,31	15,87	24,33	18,58	16,17	21,85	19,06	16,30	21,61	19,35
	33,57	18,99	16,55	31,45	18,63	16,65	27,33	18,87	16,49	26,16	19,50
	26,15	18,10	16,85	24,96	17,90	16,39	22,59	18,20	16,23	22,02	18,33
	24,36	18,02	16,70	22,25	17,90	16,91	21,55	18,63	16,90	20,33	18,51
	29,00	19,89	20,17	26,17	19,64	19,03	25,95	20,26	19,65	24,46	20,08
	31,41	23,10	19,73	28,25	22,39	19,49	27,60	22,89	19,76	25,77	23,09
	33,97	23,71	20,32	35,81	23,22	19,83	30,56	23,93	20,41	28,00	23,74
21,76	36,53	18,83	20,94	33,14	18,43	21,21	31,64	18,72	21,67	28,08	19,27
	31,45	21,19	19,83	27,58	20,80	19,92	26,64	21,51	19,57	24,19	21,10
18,91	32,27	19,19	18,77	26,22	18,97	19,10	24,92	19,62	18,59	23,39	19,27
18,67	27,73	17,69	18,19	23,82	17,42	18,63	23,15	18,20	18,21	21,86	18,18
19,23	32,67	15,68	18,52	26,41	15,89	18,16	25,30	16,04	17,86	21,41	15,84
15,50	33,90	14,56	15,00	26,66	14,13	14,73	25,03	15,61	13,15	21,94	14,99
19,95	31,86	17,53	13,65	25,16	16,94	14,09	23,80	17,47	14,73	23,01	17,55
13,95	33,90	16,39	13,55	26,90	16,40	14,22	25,18	17,00	13,84	23,85	16,94
14,40	28,19	16,88	13,55	24,19	16,74	14,13	24,57	17,68	13,62	23,89	17,36
15,68	27,37	17,23	15,20	23,99	17,08	15,21	24,57	18,16	15,57	22,82	17,78
16,89	27,62	16,11	15,97	24,24	15,97	16,48	24,79	17,21	16,49	23,36	16,90
	28,11	15,29	14,52	24,19	15,10	14,48	24,14	16,23	14,38	22,86	15,92
	26,97	13,14	11,52	20,12	13,12	12,27	19,92	13,87	11,62	19,08	13,54
9,97	26,97	12,82	9,74	20,46	12,60	9,75	20,28	13,13	9,74	18,97	12,77
10,82	19,56	15,09	10,66	18,00	15,00	11,48	18,20	15,52	11,16	17,96	15,30
12,57	27,62	15,17	12,49	22,15	14,81	12,70	21,64	15,87	12,85	19,99	15,49
11,51	31,86	14,86	11,24	25,74	14,14	11,83	26,16	15,48	11,35	22,51	15,07
12,73	29,00	16,88	12,49	25,40	16,74	13,35	25,86	17,47	12,09	23,58	[illegible]

Juli 1880.

Erdthermometer													
1" tief			1' tief			2' tief			4' tief			8' tief	16' tief
7	2	8	7	2	8	7	2	8	7	2	8	7	7
16,35	23,81	18,82	16,65	17,28	18,15	16,03	16,04	16,33	13,42	13,41	13,47	9,76	7,10
17,59	21,42	19,39	17,66	17,69	18,20	16,60	16,56	16,70	13,48	13,49	13,55	9,85	7,13
17,54	23,03	20,42	17,84	18,04	18,69	16,82	16,78	16,97	13,60	13,62	13,67	9,93	7,16
18,04	20,59	20,66	18,14	18,10	18,53	17,14	17,06	17,12	13,74	13,79	13,82	10,02	7,20
17,28	19,21	17,78	18,25	18,03	18,06	17,22	17,14	17,12	13,88	13,93	13,97	10,11	7,28
14,86	16,06	14,99	17,04	16,64	16,43	16,88	16,62	16,41	14,04	14,06	14,07	10,19	7,27
13,96	21,19	18,96	15,69	16,19	17,11	16,03	15,83	16,00	14,11	14,07	14,07	10,27	7,30
16,14	22,40	20,30	16,91	17,30	18,08	16,27	16,28	16,48	14,05	14,02	14,07	10,36	7,35
17,28	25,12	22,60	17,77	18,32	19,48	16,79	16,84	17,13	14,02	14,04	14,05	10,44	7,37
18,45	25,55	22,24	18,98	19,40	20,20	17,60	17,61	17,87	14,11	14,14	14,19	10,52	7,41
19,39	18,95	18,33	19,78	19,29	19,09	18,23	18,17	18,10	14,26	14,34	14,40	10,59	7,46
16,05	23,98	20,42	17,93	18,19	19,09	17,75	17,51	17,62	14,52	14,56	14,59	10,65	7,50
17,27	23,81	19,69	18,58	18,80	19,50	17,81	17,73	17,89	14,66	14,67	14,70	10,73	7,52
18,66	24,57	20,53	18,81	19,27	19,89	18,02	17,96	18,15	14,74	14,75	14,80	10,81	7,58
17,71	25,00	20,85	19,19	19,47	20,19	18,33	18,23	18,41	14,85	14,89	14,92	10,90	7,61
17,28	24,54	21,39	19,26	19,40	20,31	18,54	18,39	18,57	14,98	15,00	15,04	10,99	7,64
17,95	26,06	23,08	19,65	19,92	20,89	18,77	18,69	18,91	15,12	15,14	15,18	11,06	7,68
20,34	22,35	19,84	20,43	20,46	20,52	19,24	19,24	19,25	15,25	15,30	15,34	11,15	7,72
18,51	23,29	19,71	19,44	19,64	19,95	19,04	18,85	18,87	15,42	15,47	15,51	11,24	7,77
17,76	21,07	18,29	19,20	19,04	19,27	18,83	18,64	18,59	15,56	15,60	15,56	11,34	7,82
15,75	16,52	16,25	18,41	17,85	17,73	18,46	18,18	17,95	15,61	15,62	15,63	11,44	7,86
15,13	19,98	16,77	17,03	17,08	17,55	17,53	17,34	17,26	15,62	15,60	15,59	11,51	7,88
13,73	20,01	17,93	16,64	16,79	17,52	17,12	16,89	16,94	15,51	15,47	15,45	11,61	7,95
15,17	18,57	16,21	17,01	16,98	17,26	17,04	16,90	16,93	15,39	15,38	15,34	11,70	7,99
15,64	18,05	16,90	16,62	16,74	17,06	16,80	16,67	16,69	15,30	15,25	15,25	11,75	8,03
15,86	19,46	17,76	16,53	16,78	17,33	16,63	16,52	16,64	15,19	15,15	15,14	11,83	8,05
15,46	15,96	15,18	16,84	16,46	16,32	16,70	16,58	16,46	15,10	15,09	15,09	11,87	8,11
15,06	20,53	17,80	15,92	17,11	17,19	16,22	16,11	16,27	15,06	15,04	15,02	11,92	8,12
15,85	18,20	17,33	16,86	16,87	17,19	16,49	16,46	16,52	14,97	14,97	14,95	11,96	8,17
14,98	16,82	17,09	16,54	16,45	16,68	16,48	16,37	16,33	14,93	14,94	14,92	11,98	8,24
15,16	16,90	16,21	16,25	16,46	16,66	16,26	16,17	16,22	14,92	14,92	14,91	12,01	8,27
16,65	21,14	18,83	17,77	17,94	18,39	17,34	17,25	17,31	14,69	14,70	14,72	10,99	7,68

August 1880.

7	2	8	7	2	8	7	2	8	7	2	8	7	7
13,70		14,66	15,96	15,53	15,59	16,13	15,91	15,80	14,86	14,86	14,84	12,03	8,30
13,26		14,63	15,02	14,88	15,03	15,56	15,37	15,31	14,81	14,77	14,77	12,05	8,33
14,77		17,42	14,94	15,43	16,23	15,18	15,16	15,35	14,68	14,65	14,60	12,07	8,36
15,70		17,04	16,08	15,93	16,08	15,63	15,60	15,61	14,54	14,53	14,53	12,09	8,42
16,30		18,12	16,12	16,26	16,66	15,69	15,69	15,81	14,50	14,49	14,51	12,11	8,45
16,50		17,92	16,70	16,82	17,10	15,98	16,04	16,14	14,49	14,49	14,52	12,12	8,49
16,29		18,65	16,70	16,81	17,39	16,21	16,16	16,31	14,55	14,56	14,58	12,12	8,53
16,26		19,00	16,99	17,22	17,80	16,44	16,39	16,56	14,62	14,62	14,66	12,13	8,57
16,99		18,96	17,46	17,57	18,07	16,72	16,70	16,83	14,66	14,68	14,73	12,13	8,62
17,40		18,79	17,70	17,57	17,85	16,98	16,91	16,93	14,76	14,80	14,84	12,19	8,64
18,39		20,68	17,73	18,23	18,88	16,98	17,04	17,24	14,87	14,88	14,94	12,14	8,67
18,87		21,96	18,63	18,86	19,53	17,48	17,52	17,68	14,97	14,99	15,08	12,17	8,71
19,70		22,99	19,31	19,53	20,22	17,95	18,00	18,18	15,11	15,16	15,20	12,20	8,75
20,40		21,44	20,00	20,30	20,82	18,52	18,56	18,75	15,27	15,36	15,39	12,23	8,78
19,81		21,75	19,94	19,88	20,90	18,87	18,74	18,80	15,52	15,56	15,61	12,30	8,83
19,47		20,52	19,77	19,71	19,94	18,83	18,73	18,75	15,71	15,78	15,80	12,33	8,86
19,13		20,02	19,57	19,53	19,89	18,71	18,64	18,67	15,88	15,92	15,93	12,38	8,89
17,86		18,54	18,99	19,02	19,36	18,59	18,43	18,45	15,99	16,02	16,03	12,45	8,92
16,02		18,11	18,25	18,29	18,81	18,29	18,08	18,08	16,06	16,09	16,08	12,52	8,95
15,17		18,66	17,85	17,88	18,30	17,98	17,77	17,75	16,06	16,08	16,06	12,58	8,99
15,33	21,02	17,97	17,65	17,76	18,30	17,70	17,57	17,63	16,03	16,03	15,99	12,67	9,12
15,08	23,15	19,16	17,34	18,08	18,75	17,52	17,48	17,66	15,96	15,94	15,94	12,73	9,15
[illegible]	23,86	19,64	17,69	18,45	19,15	17,67	17,62	17,86	15,91	15,89	15,89	12,79	9,10
[illegible]	24,54	19,55	18,28	19,00	19,61	17,92	17,94	18,16	15,89	15,89	15,89	12,84	9,12
[illegible]	23,56	19,00	18,24	18,68	19,35	18,09	18,01	18,18	15,90	15,92	15,91	12,88	9,14
[illegible]	21,15	16,58	17,82	17,90	18,27	18,01	17,80	17,76	15,98	15,97	15,94	12,91	9,17
[illegible]	21,32	16,25	16,64	17,13	17,71	17,48	17,26	17,27	15,94	15,96	15,92	12,94	9,21
[illegible]	17,59	16,08	15,64	16,42	16,66	17,07	16,84	16,77	15,87	15,84	15,81	12,98	9,24
[illegible]	21,68	17,78	16,15	16,81	17,55	16,57	16,56	16,70	15,75	15,73	15,69	13,00	9,28
[illegible]	23,99	[illegible]	16,53	17,24	18,02	16,73	16,72	16,95	15,62	15,63	15,58	13,04	9,31
[illegible]	23,59	[illegible]	16,96	17,66	18,45	16,96	16,95	17,19	15,56	15,54	15,55	13,06	9,34

September 1880.

Luftthermometer

	III. In Glas			IV. In Kupfer			1' frei			VII.		
	7	2	8	7	2	8	7	2	8	7	2	8
1	12,04	30,96	19,56	11,82	26,75	19,16	12,14	25,48	19,49	12,01	25,50	19,73
2	15,17	26,97	15,99	14,62	24,57	15,97	14,83	23,84	16,87	14,69	23,77	16,64
3	17,73	24,08	16,72	17,04	21,28	16,50	17,34	20,91	17,08	16,79	20,64	16,98
4	17,12	23,30	15,00	16,89	21,09	15,00	17,21	21,38	15,70	16,98	20,03	15,76
5	12,93	31,24	20,17	12,69	28,06	19,83	13,13	25,84	20,26	12,77	25,50	20,41
6	17,90	28,68	17,45	17,42	25,78	17,08	17,77	25,35	17,86	17,36	25,81	17,86
7	17,61	23,83	17,12	17,32	21,87	16,89	17,43	21,47	17,17	17,36	20,91	17,06
8	14,56	22,20	14,28	14,28	18,97	14,14	14,44	17,94	14,57	14,88	18,82	14,77
9	12,57	24,20	11,02	12,25	20,27	10,76	12,61	19,62	11,31	12,58	19,57	11,02
10	10,98	20,94	10,78	10,47	17,76	10,28	10,66	18,20	11,28	10,17	16,30	11,24
11	11,02	19,11	9,56	10,71	16,31	9,59	11,05	16,44	9,97	10,55	16,45	9,98
12	6,89	19,39	11,59	6,46	16,94	11,28	6,84	16,61	11,70	7,01	16,98	12,01
13	7,70	22,28	11,51	7,62	18,87	11,24	7,80	18,11	11,27	7,89	18,24	12,12
14	7,05	21,68	13,43	7,09	18,87	13,45	7,37	18,24	13,44	7,47	18,43	13,77
15	11,43	21,88	11,71	10,90	19,73	11,62	11,53	19,23	12,57	11,04	17,97	12,54
16	9,56	22,69	16,15	9,21	20,42	15,87	9,89	20,56	16,30	9,62	19,35	16,22
17	13,47	20,94	13,75	13,21	18,14	13,65	13,61	18,20	13,87	13,46	17,82	13,92
18	11,10	21,84	14,36	10,76	20,80	14,17	11,09	19,92	14,65	11,32	19,65	14,69
19	12,65	19,48	14,03	12,11	18,14	13,55	12,57	16,91	14,44	12,58	16,71	14,30
20	13,34	19,80	12,73	12,88	18,77	12,30	13,13	18,46	12,57	12,96	18,59	12,69
21	11,30	12,16	10,62	11,14	11,72	10,42	11,36	11,27	10,92	11,47	11,62	10,93
22	13,39	16,11	13,55	13,17	15,25	13,31	13,00	15,26	13,61	13,39	14,99	13,54
23	11,59	13,39	10,95	11,14	12,59	10,90	11,18	12,66	10,92	11,01	12,54	11,16
24	10,86	13,55	11,51	10,80	12,69	11,14	11,14	12,35	11,44	11,04	12,39	11,54
25	9,16	15,99	11,51	8,87	14,76	11,81	9,10	14,44	12,05	9,09	14,15	12,20
26	12,24	13,95	12,57	11,91	13,21	12,85	12,01	14,00	12,70	12,12	13,24	12,85
27	10,82	19,89	10,86	10,85	17,32	10,90	11,05	17,04	11,01	11,04	16,14	11,36
28	9,32	22,28	10,86	9,21	19,59	10,96	9,62	19,75	11,48	15,15	18,86	11,47
29	12,24	18,54	8,59	12,35	16,84	8,54	12,57	16,65	9,31	12,39	15,26	9,48
30	12,24	14,03	11,35	12,30	13,45	11,24	12,57	13,26	11,27	12,69	13,54	11,43
	12.17	21,84	13,31	11,91	18,69	13,12	12,30	18,64	13,56	12,29	17,94	13,67

October 1880.

	III. In Glas			IV. In Kupfer			1' frei			VII.		
	7	2	8	7	2	8	7	2	8	7	2	8
1	6,36	15,78	10,45	6,08	13,45	10,28	6,24	13,00	10,66	6,47	12,85	10,58
2	11,71	13,06	12,52	11,76	12,59	12,40	11,61	12,66	12,57	12,30	12,69	12,86
3	10,49	8,67	5,51	10,42	7,28	5,35	10,49	7,63	5,77	10,98	7,78	6,08
4	5,27	5,23	6,04	5,11	4,68	6,13	5,55	5,38	6,24	5,47	6,24	6,78
5	6,81	13,55	8,27	6,56	11,87	8,15	6,59	11,70	8,49	6,81	11,43	8,55
6	7,86	18,83	13,75	7,82	17,08	13,55	8,01	16,78	13,78	7,89	16,52	13,84
7	13,75	15,25	12,32	13,75	14,71	12,11	13,96	14,52	12,23	14,30	14,49	12,31
8	5,92	12,73	6,28	5,98	10,28	6,42	6,11	10,40	5,98	6,24	9,62	6,62
9	3,37	10,21	5,03	3,32	7,77	5,11	3,48	7,80	5,30	3,66	7,39	5,35
10	2,28	8,59	5,03	2,41	7,28	5,06	2,70	6,98	5,21	2,39	6,16	5,20
11	3,41	10,94	3,89	3,42	8,97	4,19	3,57	9,01	4,34	3,46	8,55	4,54
12	— 0,22	12,57	3,81	— 0,29	10,08	3,56	0,15	9,84	4,12	0,27	9,82	4,27
13	2,32	5,84	6,69	2,36	5,84	6,32	2,83	5,94	6,50	2,89	5,58	6,55
14	7,78	9,60	3,81	7,62	7,77	3,76	7,37	7,80	3,82	7,74	7,66	3,98
15	1,23	8,35	7,86	1,15	7,28	7,87	1,36	7,02	7,93	1,62	6,85	8,16
16	8,92	11,10	6,24	8,92	10,56	6,32	9,10	10,06	6,50	9,40	10,43	6,66
17	7,25	12,12	8,27	7,23	11,14	8,15	8,19	10,83	8,23	7,31	10,77	8,47
18	8,06	10,70	8,67	7,87	10,13	8,59	8,19	9,97	8,66	8,05	10,01	8,63
19	7,13	9,81	3,41	7,14	8,73	2,94	7,19	8,36	2,61	7,09	8,39	3,54
20	— 1,02	9,08	2,72	— 1,01	7,09	2,89	— 0,84	6,63	2,87	— 0,41	5,78	2,81
21	3,41	3,73	2,60	3,52	3,90	2,46	3,61	3,48	3,05	3,93	3,93	3,16
22	0,55	7,65	— 0,62	0,34	4,39	— 0,53	0,67	3,18	— 0,41	0,85	3,27	— 0,15
23	— 1,83	6,24	— 1,83	— 1,83	3,90	— 1,78	— 1,58	3,57	— 1,23	— 1,71	2,96	— 1,58
24	— 3,60	7,38	— 1,19	— 3,61	4,87	— 1,26	— 3,34	3,95	— 0,84	— 3,82	2,89	— 0,96
25	0,35	8,79	0,71	0,29	5,55	0,53	0,46	4,77	1,32	0,58	4,70	1,19
26	0,19	2,60	4,54	0,10	2,46	4,19	0,15	2,52	4,34	0,20	2,81	4,54
27	3,49	4,78	0,19	3,42	3,42	0,05	3,57	4,21	0,54	3,54	3,58	0,51
28	— 0,10	0,99	— 0,22	0,00	0,77	— 0,14	0,15	0,80	— 0,20	0,08	0,70	— 0,30
29	0,19	1,80	6,24	0,05	1,59	5,89	0,39	1,75	6,03	0,47	1,08	6,24
30	0,23	2,64	— 0,22	0,15	1,87	— 0,05	0,45	1,84	— 0,28	0,30	2,00	— 0,22
31	1,27	6,73	3,01	0,87	5,06	2,99	1,32	4,30	3,09	1,35	4,31	3,16
	2,96	8,86	4,96	3,30	7,49	4,89	3,91	7,31	5,07	4,17	7,16	5,19

September 1880.

Erdthermometer

1" tief 7	1" tief 2	1" tief 8	1' tief 7	1' tief 2	1' tief 8	2' tief 7	2' tief 2	2' tief 8	4' tief 7	4' tief 2	4' tief 8	8' tief 7	16
14,32	24,69	19,81	17,30	17,84	18,66	17,22	17,15	17,37	15,53	15,54	15,54	13,09	
15,51	24,13	18,99	17,57	18,13	18,80	17,38	17,34	17,54	15,54	15,54	15,56	13,09	
17,57	23,10	18,32	18,09	18,29	18,53	17,58	17,56	17,63	15,56	15,58	15,60	13,12	
17,36	20,20	17,75	17,93	18,12	18,28	17,55	17,52	17,56	15,62	15,63	15,63	13,13	
14,48	24,46	20,32	17,10	17,77	18,74	17,34	17,31	17,47	15,65	15,66	15,65	13,13	
17,74	23,97	19,59	18,22	18,74	19,16	17,61	17,99	17,85	15,67	15,67	15,69	13,16	
17,74	20,98	18,45	18,38	18,57	18,75	17,91	17,81	17,86	15,71	15,73	15,73	13,17	
16,00	18,05	15,37	17,80	17,76	17,44	17,69	17,53	17,43	15,76	15,77	15,79	13,18	
13,75	19,56	14,69	16,37	16,62	16,81	17,04	16,84	16,79	15,78	15,80	15,77	13,20	
12,05	17,76	13,60	15,46	15,62	15,83	16,43	16,19	16,13	15,73	15,70	15,67	13,21	
12,01	15,77	12,06	14,80	14,93	14,93	15,82	15,61	15,47	15,59	15,56	15,48	13,23	
8,66	16,78	13,18	13,41	13,86	14,42	15,06	14,83	14,84	15,40	15,35	15,29	13,25	
8,49	18,07	13,62	13,36	13,90	14,59	14,63	14,58	14,60	15,17	15,10	15,08	13,25	
9,64	18,13	14,47	13,50	14,03	14,76	14,51	14,40	14,53	14,94	14,86	14,80	13,25	
12,09	18,70	11,37	14,02	14,69	15,21	14,54	14,55	14,71	14,71	14,67	14,64	13,25	
11,26	18,44	16,23	14,16	14,66	15,40	14,68	14,62	14,80	14,56	14,54	14,54	13,23	
13,77	16,58	14,46	14,98	15,02	15,12	14,95	14,90	14,91	14,48	14,45	14,45	13,22	
11,92	18,86	15,65	14,26	15,01	15,50	14,73	14,70	14,86	14,43	14,40	14,41	13,18	
13,61	15,75	14,69	14,96	14,88	15,05	14,95	14,88	14,90	14,38	14,35	14,37	13,15	
13,15	16,65	13,53	14,59	14,70	14,72	14,79	14,72	14,70	14,34	14,34	14,32	13,11	
12,87	13,23	12,44	14,27	14,08	13,96	14,59	14,48	14,38	14,31	14,28	14,27	13,07	
12,71	14,78	14,65	13,61	13,87	14,09	14,18	14,13	14,14	14,25	14,22	14,19	13,06	
12,71	13,21	12,48	13,94	13,67	13,67	14,17	14,05	14,01	14,14	14,12	14,11	13,02	
12,04	13,68	12,67	13,33	13,64	13,54	13,87	13,81	13,78	14,05	14,03	14,00	12,98	
12,62	13,52	12,81	13,01	13,00	13,24	13,70	13,55	13,52	13,97	13,93	13,90	12,98	
12,29	13,66	12,97	13,12	13,30	13,39	13,50	13,49	13,50	13,84	13,82	13,79	12,93	
11,78	16,23	12,75	13,08	13,36	13,65	13,46	13,46	13,44	13,73	13,72	13,69	12,91	
10,75	18,61	13,31	12,98	13,64	14,08	13,47	13,46	13,59	13,65	13,64	13,61	12,87	
12,30	14,60	11,87	13,31	13,43	13,49	13,61	13,54	13,58	13,57	13,57	13,57	12,82	
11,93	13,14	12,53	12,87	12,92	13,06	13,45	13,29	13,26	13,55	13,52	13,50	12,82	
13,14	17,18	14,88	14,99	14,41	15,56	15,43	15,41	15,32	14,75	14,77	14,75	13,10	

October 1880.

1" tief 7	1" tief 2	1" tief 8	1' tief 7	1' tief 2	1' tief 8	2' tief 7	2' tief 2	2' tief 8	4' tief 7	4' tief 2	4' tief 8	8' tief 7	16
9,09	13,54	11,17	12,30	12,45	12,60	13,11	12,98	12,95	13,46	13,44	13,42	12,78	
11,58	11,78	11,89	12,35	12,34	12,36	12,90	12,82	12,77	13,35	13,34	13,29	12,74	
11,38	10,28	7,94	12,20	10,97	12,57	12,70	12,60	12,49	13,23	13,20	13,16	12,70	
6,56	7,41	7,27	11,43	10,10	9,92	12,06	11,72	12,50	13,12	13,06	13,01	12,66	
7,58	11,28	9,53	9,83	10,18	10,58	11,19	11,11	11,15	12,92	12,83	12,81	12,60	
8,20	13,86	12,88	10,15	10,68	11,33	11,15	11,14	11,26	12,65	12,60	12,54	12,58	
13,05	13,97	12,69	11,81	12,25	12,42	11,61	11,82	11,97	12,47	12,42	12,39	12,53	
8,46	10,98	8,24	11,63	11,31	11,11	12,02	11,87	11,73	12,37	12,34	12,33	12,48	
5,43	7,49	6,64	9,88	9,50	9,36	11,37	11,06	10,83	12,34	12,32	12,28	12,41	
4,90	6,98	6,23	8,67	8,54	8,58	10,43	11,17	10,04	12,23	12,15	12,11	12,36	
4,94	9,10	6,10	8,22	8,50	8,65	9,80	9,69	9,67	12,01	11,91	11,85	12,30	
3,39	9,92	6,34	7,79	8,17	8,44	9,47	9,34	9,35	11,73	11,66	11,59	12,24	
4,32	6,01	6,60	7,67	7,57	7,71	9,21	9,04	8,96	11,46	11,39	11,53	12,19	
7,51	9,44	5,76	8,08	8,57	8,45	8,96	9,04	9,11	11,21	11,14	11,07	12,11	
8,88	7,51	7,51	7,61	9,69	7,98	8,97	8,85	8,83	10,98	10,93	10,87	12,05	
8,90	9,95	8,12	8,49	8,90	9,02	8,96	9,07	9,20	10,80	10,75	10,71	11,95	
7,57	10,02	8,65	8,72	8,99	9,21	9,26	9,28	9,40	10,64	10,64	10,60	11,86	
8,25	9,42	8,56	9,08	9,16	9,24	9,43	9,44	9,49	10,59	10,58	10,58	11,77	
7,73	8,40	5,03	8,95	8,94	8,49	9,46	9,42	9,36	10,54	10,54	10,55	11,68	
2,98	6,74	4,45	7,10	7,09	7,28	8,89	8,61	8,50	10,51	10,49	10,47	11,01	
8,84	4,45	3,71	6,49	6,52	6,49	8,20	8,02	7,92	10,41	10,34	10,29	11,52	
1,81	4,19	1,59	5,67	5,37	5,28	7,60	7,83	7,12	10,18	10,12	10,05	11,48	
[illegible]	4,59	1,07	4,48	4,73	4,98	6,72	6,54	6,50	9,95	9,86	9,78	11,39	
[illegible]	3,89	0,95	4,37	4,23	4,87	6,32	6,12	6,04	9,64	9,55	9,46	11,31	
[illegible]	4,76	1,81	3,98	4,37	4,58	5,87	5,80	5,84	9,33	9,24	9,15	11,23	
[illegible]	2,02	3,60	3,94	3,81	4,00	5,70	5,56	5,49	9,02	8,93	8,84	11,15	
[illegible]	5,07	2,73	4,45	4,70	4,85	5,56	5,62	5,69	8,75	8,67	8,61	11,04	
[illegible]	[illegible]	0,83	4,17	3,98	3,72	5,61	5,48	5,67	8,52	8,45	8,42	10,93	
[illegible]	[illegible]	4,53	3,41	3,36	3,86	5,13	5,01	4,98	8,34	8,27	8,20	10,82	
[illegible]	[illegible]	0,93	4,39	4,01	3,72	5,17	5,19	5,09	8,12	8,05	8,01	10,69	
[illegible]	[illegible]	3,00	3,21	3,39	3,78	4,86	4,75	4,79	7,95	7,88	7,84	10,58	

Novem[illegible]r 1880.

			Luftthermometer								
	In Glas		IV. In Kupfer			I' frei					
	2	8	7	2	8	7	2	8	7	2	8
	5,43	0,59	0,58	3,80	0,53	0,80	3,48	0,80	0,70	3,93	0,70
	1,89	− 1,02	− 0,48	1,39	− 1,26	− 0,88	1,41	− 0,84	− 0,68	1,35	− 0,84
	4,62	− 3,04	− 2,89	2,94	− 3,18	− 2,53	2,18	− 2,66	− 2,00	1,96	− 2,87
4,66	3,89	− 1,02	− 4,65	1,89	− 1,01	− 4,47	0,58	− 0,71	− 4,51	0,31	− 0,84
1,80	4,66	0,79	1,87	4,05	0,72	1,88	4,04	1,28	1,96	3,81	1,00
3,41	7,46	3,93	3,33	6,65	3,90	3,26	6,76	4,04	3,16	6,93	4,28
5,11	7,98	6,40	5,16	7,18	6,32	5,21	6,97	6,46	5,16	7,05	6,89
	5,80	5,31	5,55	5,50	5,16	5,94	5,25	5,30	5,58	5,70	5,47
	6,65	− 2,24	0,29	2,67	− 2,41	0,36	1,02	− 1,88	0,66	1,23	− 1,41
2,24	2,12	− 1,77	− 2,36	0,77	− 1,59	− 2,14	0,71	− 1,31	− 2,13	0,47	− 1,87
5,06	3,57	− 1,31	− 4,75	1,49	− 1,30	− 4,43	0,89	− 1,01	− 4,32	0,66	− 1,29
	3,57	0,59	− 1,01	2,41	0,63	− 1,01	2,18	0,89	− 0,72	1,92	1,04
	6,21	6,49	3,32	5,84	6,62	3,48	5,68	6,33	3,62	5,97	6,54
7,46	8,35	10,29	7,48	8,15	9,98	7,89	8,62	9,66	8,16	8,63	10,88
9,08	6,85	8,89	8,73	6,27	3,80	8,88	6,37	3,91	9,32	6,62	4,08
	6,24	1,80	1,11	4,00	1,44	1,32	3,82	2,35	1,31	3,50	1,92
	11,10	6,65	8,78	9,69	6,43	8,75	9,57	6,50	9,01	9,74	6,70
	6,20	5,43	6,03	5,91	5,54	6,16	6,07	5,64	6,35	6,01	5,77
	4,38	6,24	0,19	4,05	5,94	0,36	4,17	6,11	0,60	4,12	6,28
5,15	2,20	0,11	5,12	1,63	0,00	5,12	1,62	0,02	5,20	1,62	0,04
1,51	7,46	− 2,00	− 1,61	5,35	− 2,17	− 1,50	3,95	− 1,50	− 1,15	3,85	− 1,45
	1,76	0,19	− 3,08	1,25	0,05	− 2,66	1,02	0,36	− 2,60	1,23	− 0,47
	1,80	− 0,02	0,96	1,59	− 0,19	1,10	1,71	0,02	1,23	1,70	0,08
1,15	6,82	− 0,50	1,01	4,82	− 0,48	1,23	3,22	− 0,32	1,23	2,77	− 0,19
1,07	7,05	4,30	1,01	5,25	4,34	1,15	4,47	4,21	1,15	4,23	4,81
	6,89	4,62	5,25	6,61	4,49	5,30	6,33	4,77	5,47	6,47	4,70
	7,05	5,84	5,74	7,01	5,79	5,73	7,02	5,64	5,78	7,39	5,81
5,15	5,47	4,62	4,97	5,11	4,58	5,12	5,25	4,77	5,27	5,31	4,70
	5,03	4,74	4,34	4,87	3,80	4,34	4,90	4,86	4,43	5,00	4,91
4,62	5,93	5,84	4,63	5,84	5,64	4,68	5,81	5,64	4,93	5,78	5,85
2,14	5,45	2,52	2,15	4,43	2,37	2,29	4,17	2,64	2,72	4,17	2,67

December 1880.

5,96	4,99	3,93	5,74	4,87	3,90	5,90	4,81	4,08	6,04	5,08	4,04
3,21	4,34	1,43	3,18	4,44	1,44	3,18	4,34	1,32	3,16	4,74	1,99
− 1,67	0,99	− 6,40	− 1,59	− 0,48	− 6,18	− 2,01	− 2,01	− 6,83	− 1,75	− 2,56	− 5,81
− 5,68	− 1,71	− 9,50	− 5,56	− 0,66	− 9,58	− 5,50	− 4,73	− 9,48	− 5,27	− 5,27	− 9,18
− 2,79	1,39	− 0,70	− 2,74	0,10	− 0,43	− 2,48	1,29	− 1,10	− 2,49	1,50	− 0,56
− 7,56	− 0,50	− 0,71	− 7,42	− 5,70	−10,68	− 7,11	− 6,89	−10,43	− 7,18	− 8,09	−10,42
− 7,40	3,53	− 2,40	− 7,32	2,07	− 2,17	− 6,93	2,79	− 2,14	− 7,18	3,50	− 2,21
1,64	2,92	4,70	1,25	2,07	4,41	1,53	2,09	4,47	1,63	2,23	4,78
4,82	6,08	2,16	5,06	5,40	1,92	4,68	4,51	1,84	5,24	5,47	2,00
− 1,27	10,62	− 0,22	− 0,91	7,28	− 0,09	− 1,18	3,05	− 0,28	− 0,72	2,89	− 0,30
0,83	10,29	1,03	0,77	5,50	1,01	0,89	3,52	0,69	1,15	3,35	1,13
0,31	4,62	1,64	0,53	3,90	1,59	0,63	3,74	1,32	0,77	3,03	1,02
1,07	4,72	− 1,02	0,82	2,22	− 0,91	0,71	1,28	− 1,27	0,77	1,46	− 0,96
− 2,56	5,84	− 4,56	− 2,55	2,89	− 4,89	− 2,40	− 0,41	− 4,47	− 2,41	− 0,30	− 4,06
− 8,05	3,37	− 6,02	− 8,19	− 0,06	− 6,37	− 7,84	− 1,58	− 6,46	− 7,86	− 1,79	− 6,19
− 6,07	− 3,14	− 7,32	− 5,94	− 3,75	− 7,14	− 5,68	− 3,43	− 6,89	− 5,96	− 4,13	− 7,14
− 5,47	− 0,62	− 7,08	− 5,51	− 1,01	− 7,42	− 5,03	− 2,14	− 7,19	− 5,09	− 2,21	− 7,08
−12,01	− 9,09	− 8,25	−11,93	− 9,43	− 7,71	− 1,41	− 9,05	− 7,44	−11,45	− [illegible]	− 7,94
− 0,46	2,08	1,80	− 0,76	1,59	1,49	− 1,27	1,83	1,82	− 0,22	1,62	1,70
2,60	1,88	0,31	2,17	1,49	0,29	2,09	1,32	0,36	2,62	1,46	0,47
1,07	4,22	3,61	1,01	3,95	3,47	1,15	3,83	3,44	1,08	4,31	3,85
0,48	3,58	− 1,63	0,05	1,78	− 1,88	0,19	0,11	− 1,71	0,53	0,39	− 1,45
− 1,48	− 0,42	− 1,31	− 1,64	− 0,66	− 1,21	− 1,92	− 0,71	− 1,09	− 1,84	[illegible] 0,09	− 1,07
1,39	0,99	0,67	1,78	0,96	0,53	1,49	0,75	0,54	1,51	0,93	0,81
3,41	3,37	2,00	2,75	2,94	1,59	3,44	2,87	1,83	3,62	3,24	1,85
− 0,82	1,80	1,51	− 0,77	1,49	1,25	− 0,67	1,15	1,15	− 0,68	1,50	1,54
0,35	6,85	− 0,86	0,29	3,13	− 1,01	0,53	1,10	− 0,71	[illegible]	1,08	− 0,60
− 3,25	3,67	− 3,65	− 3,42	5,06	− 3,42	− 3,17	2,83	− 3,17	− 3,06	1,00	− 3,32
− 0,86	0,91	2,20	− 0,91	0,77	1,97	− 0,73	0,08	2,01	[illegible] 0,84	1,23	2,31
3,21	4,66	3,61	3,04	4,84	3,42	2,87	4,00	3,48	3,16	4,16	3,54
0,91	4,78	1,51	1,20	4,19	1,49	1,10	3,87	1,71	1,01	3,93	1,62

November 1880.

		Erdthermometer										
			1' tief			2' tief						
2	8	7	2	8	7	2	8					
	1,93	3,63	3,55	3,39	4,81	4,76						10,35
	0,77	3,19	3,33	3,35	4,62	4,56	4,54			7,51		10,33
	0,66	2,89	3,08	3,22	4,40	4,32	4,35					10,33
	0,24	2,63	2,59	2,53	4,24	4,13	4			7,16		10,32
	1,89	2,43	2,77	3,00						6,99		10,31
	4,24	3,25	3,59	4,01								10,30
	5,49	4,45	4,74	4,95				6,75	6,76	6,72		10,29
	5,86	5,12	5,25	5,32						6,72		10,27
	0,64	4,96	4,50	4,06						6,79		10,26
	0,54	3,27	3,04	2,80				6,80				10,24
	0,33	2,53	2,51	2,47						6,78		10,21
	1,20	2,30	2,40	2,58								10,19
4,54	5,21	2,97	3,39	3,88								10,17
8,03	8,74	4,87	5,62	6,12								10,16
7,88	4,26	6,69	6,91	6,43						6,31		10,14
4,42	2,71	5,13	4,81	4,73						6,38		10,11
8,14	6,19	5,03	5,70	5,97								10,09
6,13	5,87	5,86	5,83	5,95								10,05
4,18	4,80	5,40	5,05	5,06								9,99
3,20	1,89	5,31	5,17	4,66	5,61	5,61	5,51	6,67		6,68		10,00
4,47	0,84	3,70	3,73	3,79	5,13	4,91				6,61		9,98
0,61	0,58	3,07	2,85	2,74	4,56	4,35				6,57		9,95
1,93	1,16	2,61	2,73	2,85	3,97	3,91				6,35		9,93
3,11	1,03	2,54	2,78	2,84	3,79	3,78				6,17		9,90
3,98	3,42	2,52	2,73	3,16	3,69	3,67				6,01		9,87
5,41	4,00	3,59	4,06	4,31	3,91	4,10	4,26			5,88		9,84
5,95	5,64	4,26	4,57	4,87	4,43	4,53	4,63			5,84		9,82
5,19	4,69	4,97	4,99	4,98	4,80	4,91	4,89			5,86		9,80
4,91	4,89	4,87	4,58	4,90	5,05	5,05	5,06			5,94		9,75
5,00	5,50	5,00	5,11	5,27	5,12	5,16	5,23			6,00		9,72
3,95	3,15	3,97	4,08	4,14	4,66	4,69	4,71	6,59	6,57	6,56	9,07	10,09

December 1880.

5,27	4,75	5,42	5,85	5,84	5,31	5,36	5,40	6,02	6,08	6,04	8,08	9,69
4,32	2,85	4,91	4,83	4,77	5,34	5,25	5,21	6,07	6,08	6,10	7,97	9,67
0,88	0,23	3,74	3,40	3,03	4,82	4,68	4,47	6,12	6,11	6,11	7,95	9,63
0,24	− 0,63	2,67	2,56	2,38	4,14	3,98	3,85	6,08	6,03	6,01	7,91	9,60
0,09	0,23	2,10	2,03	2,00	3,59	3,48	3,38	5,92	5,89	5,84	7,88	9,58
− 0,77	− 2,61	1,82	1,74	1,59	2,24	3,15	3,06	5,75	5,68	5,64	7,84	9,56
− 0,29	0,03	1,40	1,36	1,41	2,91	2,81	2,77	5,54	5,48	5,45	7,82	9,53
0,28	0,68	1,41	1,43	1,46	2,70	2,67	2,62	5,36	5,29	5,25	7,77	9,51
2,75	1,89	1,46	1,55	1,73	2,56	2,53	2,56	5,17	5,17	5,13	7,72	9,47
2,18	0,39	1,65	1,71	1,67	2,57	2,54	2,54	5,05	4,98	4,97	7,69	9,45
3,08	0,88	1,64	1,76	1,89	2,50	2,49	2,54	4,93	4,88	4,85	7,62	9,43
2,54	1,66	1,68	1,80	2,04	2,52	2,51	2,57	4,81	4,78	4,77	7,55	9,40
1,31	0,33	1,88	1,82	1,77	2,53	2,56	2,52	4,70	4,68	4,66	7,47	9,37
0,22	− 0,05	1,57	1,57	1,49	2,44	2,42	2,38	4,62	4,58	4,60	7,40	9,34
0,21	− 0,75	1,36	1,39	1,32	2,35	2,31	2,28	4,54	4,51	4,50	7,32	9,31
− 0,60	− 1,23	1,19	1,20	1,16	2,22	2,18	2,17	4,47	4,43	4,43	7,24	9,28
− 0,29	− 1,62	1,09	1,09	1,08	2,13	2,08	2,07	4,40	4,36	4,34	7,16	9,25
− 2,67	− 2,72	0,85	0,88	0,79	2,05	1,99	1,93	4,33	4,30	4,27	7,10	9,22
0,04	0,22	0,90	0,80	0,84	1,90	1,86	1,85	4,24	4,22	4,22	7,01	9,20
0,39	0,22	0,86	0,80	0,89	1,83	1,81	1,79	4,17	4,15	4,18	6,94	9,17
1,20	1,26	0,94	0,97	0,93	1,81	1,80	1,80	4,10	4,08	4,06	6,88	9,15
0,54	0,26	0,95	0,98	0,99	1,76	1,75	1,75	4,04	3,99	3,95	6,85	9,13
0,15	0,10	0,97	0,99	1,00	1,74	1,74	1,76	3,94	3,92	3,89	6,77	9,10
0,39	0,39	1,04	1,04	1,05	1,75	1,75	1,75	3,88	3,87	3,87	6,71	9,07
2,45	1,64	1,14	1,25	1,40	1,77	1,80	1,83	3,84	3,82	3,80	6,65	9,05
0,73	0,73	1,32	1,30	1,31	1,90	1,91	1,90	3,78	3,78	3,77	6,58	9,01
1,99	0,24	1,23	1,29	1,26	1,83	1,89	1,88	3,75	3,75	3,75	6,49	8,97
1,32	− 0,85	1,18	1,27	1,13	1,87	1,88	1,88	3,74	3,71	3,73	6,45	8,94
0,26	0,55	1,10	1,15	1,17	1,84	1,88	1,82	3,69	3,71	3,69	6,38	8,91
3,28	2,94	1,24	1,42	1,82	1,83	1,86	1,94	3,68	3,67	3,66	6,33	8,90
3,28	1,97	1,21	2,03	2,16	2,14	2,19	2,25	3,65	3,64	3,64	6,26	8,86

Monatsmittel 1879.

	Luftthermometer											
	III. In Glas			IV. In Kupfer			1' frei			VII.		
	7	2	8	7	2	8	7	2	8	7	2	8
Januar . .	— 5,97	— 2,61	— 5,75	— 5,89	— 3,17	— 5,67	— 5,57	— 3,64	— 5,39	— 5,85	— 3,90	— 5,63
Februar . .	— 3,54	1,49	— 2,14	— 3,36	— 0,33	— 2,11	— 3,16	— 0,31	— 2,22	— 3,07	— 0,42	— 2,00
März . . .	— 3,44	5,32	— 2,10	— 3,16	+ 2,35	— 1,98	— 2,89	1,31	— 1,80	— 3,44	1,10	— 1,78
April . . .	3,89	11,76	5,03	3,60	9,71	4,70	3,55	8,95	5,17	3,44	8,66	4,65
Mai . . .	10,35	21,26	10,32	10,04	18,64	10,20	10,01	17,58	10,57	9,64	16,02	10,38
Juni . . .	15,17	24,06	15,83	14,78	23,17	15,62	14,60	21,53	15,59	14,78	20,59	15,78
Juli . . .	15,03	24,36	15,77	14,90	23,00	15,43	14,70	20,67	15,88	14,84	19,46	15,69
August . .	15,22	25,10	16,23	15,08	22,93	15,77	15,42	21,71	16,54	14,82	21,20	16,34
September .	12,27	21,21	13,55	12,26	20,15	14,24	12,82	19,35	15,14	12,34	19,29	14,73
October . .	6,10	11,36	6,87	5,91	10,46	6,75	6,36	10,13	7,26	6,38	10,17	7,23
November .	— 0,07	3,43	0,38	0,08	2,32	0,35	0,13	2,14	0,81	0,31	2,07	1,13
December .	— 6,38	— 1,88	— 5,74	— 5,95	— 3,99	— 5,78	— 6,00	— 3,93	— 5,34	— 5,98	— 3,96	— 5,73
Jahresmittel	5,31	12,14	5,69	4,86	10,44	5,63	4,99	9,62	6,02	4,85	9,19	5,89

Monatsmittel 1880.

	III. In Glas 7	III. 2	III. 8	IV. In Kupfer 7	IV. 2	IV. 8	1' frei 7	1' frei 2	1' frei 8	VII. 7	VII. 2	VII. 8
Januar . .	— 4,86	+ 1,45	— 4,06	— 4,84	— 0,77	— 4,06	— 4,46	— 1,27	— 3,74	— 4,64	— 1,38	— 3,80
Februar . .	— 4,32	2,04	— 2,32	— 4,18	0,22	— 2,47	— 3,92	— 0,69	— 2,14	— 4,16	— 1,12	— 2,25
März . . .	— 1,81	6,30	— 0,70	— 1,79	4,80	— 0,69	— 2,00	3,18	— 0,43	— 1,71	1,90	— 0,46
April . . .	5,79	16,51	6,46	5,74	13,73	6,36	5,61	13,00	6,46	5,22	11,53	6,70
Mai . . .	9,93	18,42	10,04	9,87	16,25	9,71	9,43	15,43	10,13	9,37	13,79	9,96
Juni . . .	14,43	26,26	15,68	14,52	22,45	15,31	14,51	22,53	15,88	14,19	20,00	15,54
Juli . . .	17,09	28,27	17,98	16,49	24,88	17,52	16,36	23,74	17,95	16,50	22,00	17,95
August . .	15,96	27,90	17,35	15,51	24,09	16,84	15,65	23,14	17,49	15,59	21,79	17,41
September .	12,17	21,84	13,31	11,91	18,69	13,12	12,20	18,64	13,56	12,29	17,94	13,67
October . .	8,96	8,86	4,96	3,90	7,49	4,89	3,91	7,31	5,07	4,17	7,16	5,19
November .	2,14	5,49	2,52	2,15	4,43	2,37	2,29	4,17	2,64	2,72	4,17	2,67
December .	— 1,16	2,56	— 1,16	— 1,21	1,63	— 1,33	— 1,13	0,80	— 1,30	— 0,79	0,78	— 1,15
Jahresmittel	5,78	13,83	6,67	5,67	11,49	6,46	5,70	10,83	6,79	5,73	9,72	6,79

Monatsmittel 1879.

Erdthermometer														
1" tief			1' tief			2' tief			4' tief			8' tief	16' tief
7	2	8	7	2	8	7	2	8	7	2	8	7	7
— 1,86	— 1,54	— 1,82	0,08	0,21	0,23	1,18	1,18	1,16	3,32	3,30	3,29	6,31	8,88
— 1,24	— 0,62	— 0,82	— 0,42	— 0,42	— 0,35	0,12	0.11	0,13	1,95	1,94	1,94	4,93	8,00
— 0,99	0,67	0,06	0,31	0,30	0,31	0,74	0,74	0,75	1,99	1,99	2,00	4,25	7,28
3,36	7,76	5,55	5,56	3,88	4,47	3,75	3,81	3,86	3,22	3,32	3,35	4,19	6,67
9,63	15,58	11,64	9,69	10,28	10,70	8,83	8,86	9,02	6,54	6,61	6,65	5,46	6,43
14,56	19,07	16,57	15,11	15,26	15,44	14,25	14,17	14,27	11,29	11,30	11,34	8,15	6,76
14,81	18,46	16,27	15,41	15,47	15,72	14,86	14,79	14,85	12,81	12,82	12,83	10,20	7,66
15,47	19,56	17,26	16,41	16,59	16,90	16,00	15,96	15,97	13,98	13,95	13,96	11,37	8,59
13,45	17,09	14,22	15,38	15,25	15,50	14,93	14,93	14,92	13,78	13,77	13,76	11,95	9,32
7,75	10,01	8,62	9,78	9,88	9,93	10,49	10,51	10,50	11,43	11,41	11,40	11,48	9,81
2,18	3,01	2,44	4,36	4,34	4,32	5,50	5,43	5,37	7,70	7,66	7,66	9,58	9,81
— 2.61	— 1,85	— 2,18	— 0,54	— 0,53	— 0,54	0,53	0.51	0,50	3,31	3,29	3,26	6.79	9,24
6,21	8,93	7,32	7,59	7,54	7,82	7,59	7,61	7,61	7,61	7,61	7,62	7,89	8,20

Monatsmittel 1880.

1" tief 7	2	8	1' tief 7	2	8	2' tief 7	2	8	4' tief 7	2	8	8' tief 7	16' tief 7
— 1,16	— 0,44	— 0,89	0,14	0,14	0,16	0,83	0,82	0,82	2,48	2,48	2,48	5,21	8,26
— 1,44	— 0,82	— 1,04	— 0,61	— 0,51	— 0,43	0,20	0,20	0,21	1,83	1,82	1,82	4,27	7,43
— 0,21	1,59	0,47	0,25	0,28	0,28	0,50	0,50	0,51	1,63	1,65	1,65	3,80	6,80
5,48	10,29	7,52	6,01	6,25	6,56	5,49	5,49	5,51	4.04	4,08	4,13	4,02	6,22
9,07	12,02	10,69	9,50	9,68	9,98	9,06	8,99	9,11	7,46	7,49	7,51	6,07	6,18
14,47	19,41	16,69	15,16	15,31	15,89	14,38	14,29	14,43	11,29	11,32	11,34	8,22	6,98
16,65	21,14	18,83	17,77	17,94	18,39	17,34	17,25	17,31	14,69	14,70	14,72	10,99	7,68
16,17	21,09	18,66	17,50	17,76	18,24	17,10	17,16	17,26	15,36	15,37	15,38	12,46	8,84
13,14	17,18	14,88	14,99	14,41	15,56	15,45	15,41	15,32	14,75	14,77	14,75	13,10	9,79
5,25	7,49	6,04	7,76	7,82	7,89	8,96	8,89	8,86	10,92	10,87	10,83	11,86	10,32
2,91	3,95	3,15	3,97	4,08	4,14	4.66	4,69	4,71	6,59	6,57	6,56	9,07	10,09
0,33	1.10	0,44	1,61	1,70	1,71	2.55	2,52	2,53	4.66	4,63	4.62	7.22	9.28
6,72	9,49	7,95	7,81	7,82	8,20	8,04	8,02	8,05	7,98	7,98	7,99	8,02	8,15

Bericht

über die 24. Versammlung des preussischen botanischen Vereins zu Pr. Stargard am 6. October 1885.

Vom Vorstande.

Mit einer Tafel.

Dem in Memel 1884 gefassten Beschlusse gemäss wurde die Versammlung des preussischen botanischen Vereins 1885 zu Pr. Stargard am 6. October abgehalten. Die Herren Apotheker H. Sievert, Gymnasiallehrer Schöttler und Apotheker C. Steinbrück hatten gefälligst die Geschäftsführung in Pr. Stargard übernommen und in sehr gelungener Weise durchgeführt.

Die schon am 5. October angelangten Mitglieder des Vereins machten am Nachmittage dieses Tages nach dem Schützenhause und von da längs der Ferse im königlichen Belauf Kochankenberg eine Exkursion unter Führung der Herren Gymnasiallehrer Schöttler, Dr. Riechert und Apotheker Steinbrück. Trotz vorgerückter Jahreszeit wurden noch gefunden: Tunica prolifera, **Potentilla rupestris** (in Blüthe), Armeria vulgaris, Seseli annuum, Digitalis ambigua, **Ervum pisiforme**, Viola mirabilis, Euonymus europaeus wenig, und **Euonymus verrucosus** sehr zahlreich, aber bloss kleine Sträucher. Professor Caspary, der die Gegend vor 13 Jahren untersucht hatte, konnte sicher angeben, dass damals nur sehr wenige Exemplare von letzter Pflanze vorhanden waren; sie hatten sich seitdem bedeutend vermehrt. Im Schiesshause wurde die Aufmerksamkeit auf einen stark verzweigten Ast einer Ulme gelenkt, der aus dem Gerichtsgarten stammte und zahlreiche Knollen aufwies, die mit Beiknospen bedeckt waren. Die Ursache dieser Missbildung konnte natürlich nicht ermittelt werden. Der Wirth des Schiesshauses schenkte eine Photographie dieser auffallenden Bildung dem Vorsitzenden des Vereins.

Nach eingetretener Dunkelheit und kurzer Rast im Schützenhause kehrten die Theilnehmer an der Exkursion nach Pr. Stargard zurück und verbrachten den Abend im Saale des R. Wolff'schen Gasthauses in geselliger Unterhaltung, an der zahlreiche Bürger der gastlichen Stadt sich lebhaft betheiligten. Herr Bürgermeister Mörner hiess die bereits erschienenen Mitglieder des Vereins im Namen der Stadt willkommen, worauf ihm der Vorsitzende des Vereins Professor Caspary mit warmen Worten dankte. Der Direktor des königlichen Gymnasiums Herr Dr. Heinze hielt an die Versammelten eine Ansprache, in welcher er die Zwecke des Vereins darlegte, sie zur Unterstützung lebhaft empfahl und dadurch bewirkte, dass sofort von den Anwesenden eine nicht unerhebliche Zahl als Mitglieder in den Verein eintrat.

Am folgenden Tage, den 6. October, früh $8^{1}/_{2}$ Uhr eröffnete Professor Caspary die Sitzung im Saale des Gasthauses von R. Wolff. Er giebt an, dass die Mitgliederzahl im letzten Jahre sich nur wenig vermehrt habe, bedauert den Tod des Pfarrer Carolus-Plauthen, theilt mit, dass die in Memel gefassten Beschlüsse über die Vereinsthätigkeit so viel als möglich ausgeführt seien, der Kreis Memel sei zum zweiten Mal von stud. rer. nat. Knoblauch untersucht, die Kreise Neustadt und Berent ergänzungsweise von stud. rer. nat. Lemcke, die Umgegend von Neuenburg und der Kreis Schwetz von Lehrer Grütter-Lnianno, eine grosse Zahl Seen etwa 189 der Kreise Berent und Kartaus habe er selbst (der Vorsitzende) seine früheren Untersuchungen derselben ergänzend näher erforscht. Professor Caspary stattet Grüsse von vielen Vereinsmitgliedern ab, die verhindert waren, zum Theil durch die ungleiche Lage der Herbstferien in Ost- und Westpreussen, an der Versammlung theilzunehmen, nämlich von den Herren John Reitenbach-Oberstrass bei Zürich, Oberlehrer Kuck-Insterburg, Apotheker Weiss dem älteren Caymen, Apotheker Kühn-Insterburg, Ross-Berlin, Apotheker Rosenbohm-Graudenz, Apotheker Kunze dem jüngeren Königsberg, Lehrer Frölich-Thorn, Dr. Preuss-Thorn, Apotheker Ludwig-Christburg, v. Hohmeier-Stolp, Dr. med. Hilbert-Sensburg, stud. rer. nat. Otto Strübing. Durch Krankheit verhindert waren Scharlok-Graudenz und der erste Schriftführer des Vereins, Conrektor Seydler. Dann legt der Vorsitzende die von den Abwesenden eingegangenen Mittheilungen und Geschenke zur Vertheilung vor.

Apotheker Kühn schickt aus dem Kreise Darkehmen: Carex Schreberi, Cirsium acaule, Bidens radiatus (1 Exempl.) u. cernuus, Geranium columinumb u. G. dissectum, Gypsophila muralis, Polygonum minus, Veronica opaca, Calamintha Acinos, Carex vulpina, Salix depressa, Carex vulgaris, C. digitata, C. muricata, Galeopsis pubescens, Campanula bononiensis u. rapunculoides, Glyceria plicata, Isopyrum thalictroides, Adoxa moschatellina, Acer Pseudoplatanus, Cirsium rivulare.

Stud. rer. nat. O. Strübing sendet folgende von ihm 1884 gesammelten Schweizerpflanzen: *) Pinguicula vulgaris L., Katzensee C. Z. — P. alpina L., Trichterhauser Mühle C. Z. — Veronica saxatilis Scop., Gotthardhospiz-Hospenthal C. U. — Schoenus nigricans L., Trichterhauser Mühle C. Z. — Eriophorum Scheuchzeri Hopp., Gotthardhospiz-Hospenthal C. U. — Phleum alpinum L., Airolo-Val Tremula C. T. — Poa alpina L., Airolo-Val Tremula C. T. — Poa alpina v. vivipara, Adermatt C. U. — Galium rubrum L., Airolo C. T. — G. montanum Vill., Airolo-Val Tremula C. T. — Alchemilla alpina L., Rigi C. Schwyz. — Globularia cordifolia L., Speer C. Gl. — Plantago alpina L., Speer C. Gl. — P. montana Lam., Speer C. Gl. — Viola biflora L., Val Tremula C. T. — V. tricolor v. alpestris, Gotthardhospiz-Hospenthal C. U. — Drosera intermedia Hayn., Pfäffikoner See C. Z. — Bupleurum stellatum L., Gotthardpass C. U. — Azalea procumbens L., Gotthardhospiz C. U. — Nonnea lutea, Sonnenberg C. Z. — Primula farinosa L., Kloster Einsiedeln C. Schwyz. — Primula viscosa All., Gotthardhospiz C. U. — Soldanella pusilla Baumg., Pilatus C. Luzern. —

*) C. bedeutet Canton, Z. Zürich, T. Tessin, Gl. Glarus, U. Uri, G. Graubündten.

S. alpina L., Rigi Staffel C. Schwyz. — Androsace Chamaejasme Host, Speer C. Gl. — Gentiana campestris L., Ponte-Samaden C. G. — G. nivalis L., Albulapasshöhe C. G. — G. verna L., Pilatus C. Luzern. — G. acaulis L., Rigi C. Schwyz. — Campanula pusilla Haenke, Raggatz-Pfeffers C. St. Gallen. — Phyteuma haemisphaericum L., Engadin C. G. — Ph. pauciflorum L., Speer C. Gl. — Ph. betonicifolium Vill., Sentis C. Appenzell. — Ph. Halleri All., Airolo C. T. — Rumex nivalis Heg., Gotthardhospiz-Hospenthal C. U. — Polygonum alpinum L., Speer C. Gl. — Epilobium Fleischeri Hochst., Morteratschgletscher C. T. — Dianthus silvestris Wulf, Furkapass C. Unterwalden. — Gypsophila repens L., Abalapass C. T. — Silene rupestris L., Airolo C. T. — S. acaulis L., Speer, Gotthard, Glarnisch. — Alsine laricifolia Crantz, Morteratschgletscher. — Cherleria sedoides L., Morteratschgletscher. — Sempevivrum montanum L., Engadin C. G. — S. tectorum L., Pontresina C. G. — Saxifraga aspera L., Rhonegletscher C. Unterwalden. — S. aizoides L., Schynpass C. G. — S. stellaris L., Andermatt-Göschenen C. U. — S. rotundifolia L., Teufelsbrücke C. U. — S. exarata Vill., Glärnisch C. Gl. — Reseda lutea L., Waldshut (Baden). — Euphorbia verrucosa Lam., Altstätten C. Z. — Dryas octopetala L., Speer C. Gl. — Sieversia montana Sprgl., Pilatus C. Luzern. — Rosa pomifera Herrm., Airolo C. G. — Ranunculus aconitifolius L., Rigi C. Schwyz. — R. alpestris L., Rigi C. Schwyz. — Pedicularis rostrata L., Gotthardhospiz-Hospenthal C. U. — P. tuberosa L., Gotthardhospiz-Hospenthal C. U. — P. foliosa L., Speer C. Gl. — Erynus alpinus L., Speer C. Gl. — Linaria alpina Mill., Albulapasshöhe C. G. — Teucrium montanum L., Julierpass C. G. — T. Chamaedrys L., Schynpass C. G. — Calamintha alpina Lam., Airolo C. T. — Hutschinsia alpina R. Br. Gotthardhospiz C. U. — Polygala Chamaebuxus L., Ütli C. Z. — P. corsica Bor., Airolo C. T. — Coronilla montana Scop, Pontresina, Bad St. Moritz C. G. — Trifolium alpinum L., Engadin C. G. — Bellidiastrum Michelii Cass., Uto Staffel C. Z. — Leontopodium alpinum Cass., Piz Languard C. G. — Aster alpinus L., Bergün-Weissenstein C. G. — Achillea atrata L., Morteratschgletscher C. G. — Crepis alpestris Tausch, Hospenthal C. U. — Homogyne alpina Cass., Rigi C. Schwyz. — Hieraciam Jacquini Vill., Hohentwiel (Baden). — Leucanthemum alpinum Lam., Furkapass C. Unterwalden. — Orchis fusca Jacq., Sihlthal C. Z. — Gymnedenia conopea R. Br., Albiskette C. Z. — Nigritella angustifolia Rich., Bergün-Weissenstein C. G. — Carex ornithopoda Willd., Sihlwald C. Z. — C. firma Host., Gotthardhospiz C. U. — C. Davalliana Sm., Ütli C. Z. — Arum maculatum L., Sihlwald C. Z. — Botrychium Lunaria Sm., Hospenthal-Andermatt C. U.

Sehr interessant ist, dass Herr Strübing im Lunau'er Walde, Kreis Kulm, auf dem seinem Vater gehörigen Theil, zwischen Zalesie und Waldhof, Vorwerk von Paparczyn, in einem Bruch ein Sträuchlein Salix myrtilloides L. entdeckt hat; 5. Standort im Kreise Kulm.

Apotheker Weiss-Caymen der ältere sendet: Rosa mollis Sm. f. ad venustam vergens, determ. Christ. An Gräben zwischen Wangen und Waldhaus Bendisen. Juni-August 1885. — Geum strictum + urbanum, f. ad urbanum vergens et f. ad strictum vergens. Caymen: an Grabenufern zwischen Gebüsch. — Geum rivale + strictum. Caymen 1885. — Lappa maior + tomentosa. Caymen. August 1885. leg. Walter Weiss. — Silene noctiflora L. Felder bei Caymen. — Euphorbia Chamaesyce L. Aus dem Garten des Herrn Weiss in Caymen; aus Samen getrockneter Pflanzen, welche im botanischen Garten zu Breslau verwildert waren, gezogen. — Cuscuta europaea L. b) Viciae Koch et Schönh. Wickenfeld bei Sielkeim.

Apotheker Weiss sendet auch auf Ersuchen des Vorsitzenden über die von ihm bei Caymen aufgefundenen 2 Formen von Geum strictum + urbanum folgende Beschreibung: *„Sehr veränderlich.* **Pollen:** Kaum nennenswerth gut; **Blüthen:** Hiervon oft die Hälfte gleich nach dem Verblühen absterbend; Fruchtköpfchen kaum halb so gross als die der Eltern. **Früchtchen:** Meist sehr verkümmert (1—2 mm lang), ein geringer Prozentsatz 4—6 mm lang mit längerem Griffel, dem Fruchtkopf ein gehörntes Aussehen gebend. — **Wurzel** stärker, tiefer wurzelnd als die von strictum. Geruch von **mir** nie bemerkt. — **Stengel:** Etwas gebogen aufsteigend und dunkelbraun in abnehmender Färbung bis zum zweiten Laubblatt, dann grün und gerade aufsteigend; von Nebenblatt- und Blattstielleisten kantig, stark mit theils abstehenden, theils abwärtsgebogenen borstlichen Haaren — unter den Nebenblättern stärker — besetzt; geringer die Nebenaxen und oft fast kahl die stielrunden Fruchtstiele. Kleine warzenartige Erhöhungen wie bei strictum sehr selten. — **Wurzelblätter.** Endlappen: Dreitheilig oder -lappig, mehr oder weniger ausgebuchtet mit in Grösse und Form sehr wechselnden Fiederblättchen. Bebaarung am stärksten an den sehr hervortretenden Blattnerven und den Seiten der Blattlappen (Wimperhaare), weniger am Stengel, aber stets stärker als bei urbanum. — **Laubblätter:** Bis zur obersten Verzweigung des Stengels dreilappig, die untere lang gestielt mit 2—6 Fiederblättchen, die obern meistens ohne dieselben und kurz gestielt, zuletzt lanzettlich ungetheilt. — **Nebenblätter:** In der Grösse und Form sehr verschieden, meistens grösser als bei strictum, mit sehr hervortretenden Nerven; Zahnung und Behaarung wie bei den Wurzelblättern. — **Blüthen- und Fruchtstengel: Aufsteigend oder etwas geneigt.** — **Blumenblätter: Wagerecht abstehend,** grösser als bei urbanum, in der Form etwas — oft in einer Blüthe — verschieden. — **Kelchlappen:** Nach dem Erblühen meistens **bis an den Stengel und bleibend** zurückgeschlagen. Durch Zusammenwachsen von Kelchlappen und Kelchanhängsel wird solches bisweilen verhindert, ähnlich wie bei strictum. — **Fruchtköpfchen:** Halbkugelförmig; die Früchtchen bald locker wie bei urbanum, bald dicht anliegend und seitrückwärts gebogen wie bei strictum. — **Griffel:** Im Anfange sehr verschieden gefärbt, später die jeder Pflanze eigenthümliche Farbe annehmend, welche dem Fruchtkopf entweder eine **rothbraune** oder **fahl röthlich** oder **gelblich grüne Farbe** ertheilt. Auch wechseln die Längenverhältnisse der einzelnen Theile je nach der Farbe desselben."

„Durch dieses fühle ich mich veranlasst, zwei Formen, welche ich in Folgendem zu präcisiren mir erlaube, anzunehmen:

Alte Form. An Bekannte bereits unter dem vorl. N. f. ad strictum vergens verabfolgt.	**Neue Form,** ad urbanum vergens.

Griffel (bei Lupenvergrösserung).

1. **Gelbgrünlich** ähnlich wie bei strictum.	1. Rothbraun.
2. Die obere Hälfte des untern Theils **öfter** röthlich gefleckt.	2. Die obere Hälfte des untern Theils mit gelbgrünlichen Flecken.

Alte Form.	Neue Form.

Längenverhältnisse der einzelnen Theile.

3. Unterer Griffeltheil 2—2½ mal so lang als der etwas behaarte obere.	3. 2½—3 mal so lang als der etc. obere.

Haare der Früchtchen

4. Bedecken den untern Griffeltheil bis zu ⅔.	4. Bis zur Hälfte.

Fruchtkopfbau

5. Vorwaltend an **strictum** erinnernd.	5. Oft fast zum Verwechseln an urbanum erinnernd.

Blüthezeit: Juni, Juli bis August. (Erste Blüthe etwa den 10. Juni). Höhe 60—100 auch 120 cm."

Dr. med. Hilbert von Tossens in Oldenburg nach Sensberg übergesiedelt sandte der Versammlung folgende Pflanzen. Von Tossens, Oldenburg 1884 gesammelt: Salicornia herbacea, Obione portulacoides, Schoberia maritima, Aster Tripolium, Artemisia maritima. — Aus dem Kreise Sensburg 1885 gesammelt: Drosera rotundifolia, Parnassia palustris, Andromeda poliifolia, Equisetum palustre, Utricularia vulgaris, Equisetum hiemale, und was besonders Interesse erregte: Salix myrtilloides von 2 Standorten, aus dem sogenannten „Kessel" bei Sensburg (25. August 1885) und von „der Insel", langgestreckte Halbinsel im Czos-See bei Sensburg. Dass Salix myrtilloides bei Sensburg wuchs, hatte der Vorsitzende schon 1875 erkannt, indem er fand, dass ein von Apotheker Aschmann bei Sensburg gesammelter Weidenzweig, der ohne Zeit- und nähere Ortsangabe im Herbarium des königlichen botanischen Gartens lag und von Professor E. Meyer unrichtig als Salix livida bestimmt war, Salix myrtilloides ist.

Pharmazeut Schmitt-Graudenz sendet zur Ansicht: „**Anemone ranunculoides flor. tribus.** Wald zwischen Orle und Mühle Slupp, Kreis Graudenz. Mai 1885. — **Anemone silvestris.** Blätter aus dem Rondsen'er Wäldchen. Juli 1885. — **Puccinia Adoxae.** Wald zwischen Orle und Mühle Slupp. — **Aecidium Ranunculacearum** auf Anemone nemorosa. Wald bei Orle. April 1885. — **Puccinia Euphorbiacearum** auf Euphorbia Esula. Bei Klodtken sehr häufig. Mai 1885. — **Paris quadrif.** mit 5 und 6 Blättern. Park von Mischke. Mai 1885. — **Thesium ebracteatum L.** Von einem neuen Standort im Kreise Graudenz dem Rondsen'er Wäldchen. Mai 1885. — *Zur Vertheilung:* **Androsace septentrionalis L.** Von einem neuen Standorte im Kreise Graudenz: Grandfeld und Dorfkirchhof bei Rondsen. Mai 1885. — **Armeria vulgaris Willd. Graudenz.** Festungsabhänge. **Schwetz.** Marsau, Lubin. Juni 1885. — **Astragalus arenarius L.** Rondsener Wäldchen. Juli 1885. — **Campanula sibirica L.** Festungswälle, Wallgräben. Juli 1885. — **Carex digitata L.** Weichselabhänge bei Stremoczyn. Mai 1885. — **Colutea arborescens L.** Verwildert in den Festungsplantagen. Juli 1885. — **Epipactis rubiginosa.** Rondsener Wäldchen. Juli 1885. — **Eryngium planum L.** Im Weichselgebiete häufig. Juli 1885. — **Falcaria Rivini Host.** Im Weichselgebiete häufig. Juli 1885. — **Helian-**

themum vulgare L. Rondsener Wäldchen und Festungsgebiet. Juli 1885. — **Hyssopus officinalis L.** Verwildert in ehemaligen Gärten der Festung. Juli 1885. — **Nonnea pulla DC.** Zuchthauskirchhof und Festungsabhänge. Juli 1885. — **Mercurialis perennis L.** Ossaabhänge bei Mühle Slupp und bei Stremoczyn. Mai 1885. — **Ononis hircina Jacq.** Kuntersteiner Wiesen, Kreis Graudenz, Weichselland bei Michelau, Kreis Schwetz, 1885, sowie Memelufer bei Tilsit 1884. — **Ornithopus perpusillus Brot.** Auf einigen Gräbern des Zuchthauskirchhofes. Juli 1885. — **Paris quadrifolius L.** Park von Mischke. Mai 1885. — **Prunella grandiflora Jacq.** Festungsabhänge. Juli 1885. — **Pulmonaria angustifolia L.** Im Rondsen'er Wäldchen. Mai 1885. — **Salvia pratensis L.** Festungsabhänge, Dorf Marsau, Kreis Schwetz. Juli 1885. — **Salix myrtilloides L.** Von den durch Scharlok und Rosenbohm entdeckten Standorten, zwei Sphagneten bei Gottersfeld, Kreis Kulm. Juli 1885. — **Saxifraga granulata L.** Sandige Hügel bei Mühle Slupp, Weichselufer zwischen Stremoczyn und Rondsen. Mai 1885. — **Saxifraga tridactylites L.** Acker am Rudnick-See. Mai 1885."

Herr Lehrer Georg Froelich-Thorn sendet folgende Mittheilungen über seine Exkursionen im Kreise Pr. Stargard und Marienwerder: „28. 5. 85. Pelplin, Oberförsterei Pelplin, Adl. Lipinken, Marienwill, Neuhof. O.-F. Pelplin. Lathyrus montanus. — Adl. Lipinken: Saxifraga tridactylites, Arabis Gerardii, Carex canescens, Alchemilla vulg. — **Barbaraea vulgaris.** — Pelpliner Forst zw. Adl. Lipinken und Marienwill: Lathyrus montanus. **Aquilegia vulgaris.** Rubus saxatilis, R. Idaeus, **Evonymus verrucosa,** Asperula odorata, Hepatica triloba, Hierochloa australis, Salvia pratensis b) rostrata, Ranunculus polyanthemus, Convallaria maialis, Lonicera Xylosteum. — Acker bei Neuhof: Equisetum silvaticum.

Pelplin. Chenopodium Bonus Henricus, Geum intermedium Willd., Fragaria moschata, Falcaria Rivini, Ranunculus arvensis, Allium Scorodoprasum.

29. 5. Pelplin-Rauden-Alt Liebenau-Sprauden (Kr. Marienwerder), Wola: Barbaraea vulgaris. — Rauden: Falcaria Rivini, Ranunculus arvensis. — Raudenmühle: Petasites officinalis. — Auf einem Hügel zw. Raudenmühle und Alt Liebenau: *Orchis mascula.* — In der Niederung zw. Alt Liebenau und Sprauden: *Adonis aestivalis* unter Weizen Z⁴. — An der Chaussee zw. Alt Liebenau und Sprauden: Aiuga genevensis.

30. 5. Zw. Raikau und dem Forst: Fragaria viridis, Salvia pratensis b) rostrata, Aiuga genevensis. — Im Wäldchen südlich von Raikau: Sambucus racemosa (anscheinend wild). — Acker zw. Raikau und Pelplin: Camelina microcarpa, Equisetum silvaticum.

29. Juli 1885. Im Wäldchen bei Rosenthal bei Pelplin: Sambucus racemosa, Calamagrostis neglecta. — Pelplin: Camelina microcarpa, Anthemis Cotula, Panicum humifusum, Sisymbrium officinale b) leiocarpum. — An der Chaussee b. Polko: Trifolium elegans. — Oberförsterei Pelplin: Chenopodium polyspermum a) cymosum. — Acker bei Adl. Lipinken: Polygonum Convolvulus b) pterocarpum. — Im Unterholz nordwestlich von Adl. Lipinken: Verbascum Thapsus, Hypericum montanum, Ervum cassubicum, Lilium Martagon, **Cimicifuga foetida,** Vicia tenuifolia, **Peucedanum Cervaria, Scabiosa columbaria.** — In der Wengermuz bei Roppoch: Potamogeton alpina.

30. 7. 85. Dorf Rauden: Anthemis Cotula, **Atriplex roseum, Atriplex hastatum.** — Am Wege von Rauden nach der Niederung: Conium maculatum, **Trifolium fragi-**

ferum, Dipsacus silvester, Verbena officinalis, Melilotus officinalis. — Abhänge östlich von Rauden: Picris hieracioides, Melampyrum arvense, Stachys recta, Scabiosa ochroleuca. — Niederung längs der Abhänge zwischen Alt Liebenau und Rauden: Allium oleraceum, Sonchus arvensis b) laevipes. — Unter Getreide in der Nähe der Schlucht zw. Sprauden und Adl. Liebenau: Astragalus Cicer, Lathyrus tuberosus. In der Schlucht: Vicia tenuifolia (Frucht), Veronica Teucrium, Astragalus Cicer, Allium oleraceum. — Dorf Adl. Liebenau: Chenopodium Bonus Henricus, Coronopus Ruellii."

Ausserdem sendet Herr Froelich zur Vertheilung aus der Gegend von Thorn: Ervum hirsutum fr. fissa Fröl., Luzula sudetica, Omphalodes scorpioides, Phleum Boehmeri fr. vivipara, Ostericum pal., Sisymbrium Sinap., Euphorbia dulc., Scabiosa suaveolens.

Scharlok-Graudenz sendet zur Vertheilung Impatiens Nolim tangere fl. cleistogam. in seinem Garten gewachsen und *Ranunculus Steveni* Andrzejowski von einer Wiese bei Klodtken, von Scharlok daselbst 1884 entdeckt.

Von Ranunculus Steveni Andr. schickt Scharlok ausserdem eine beträchtliche Menge von Umrisszeichnungen in natürlicher Grösse, die von seiner Enkelin Frl. Anna Keibel angefertigt waren, zur Ansicht der Versammelten. Die Zeichnungen waren von folgender eingehender Beschreibung aller einzelnen Theile der Pflanze und Angabe der Literatur begleitet.

Ranunculus Steveni Andrz. bei Graudenz.

(Mit Abbildung.)

Literatur: Besser, Enum. 1822, p. 22. — Reichenbach in Flora 1822, p. 292. Wimmer et Grabowski, Fl. Sil. 1829, p. 132 (als Ran. acris β. serotinus). — Reichenbach, Fl. excurs. 1833, p. 724. — Reichenbach, Icones fl. germ. VIII 1838, p. 11. — Ledebour, Fl. ross. I (1842), p. 41 (als Ran. acris var.) — v. Klinggraeff, Fl. v. Preussen, 1848, p. 8. — Koch, Syn. Ed. III Pars I 1857, p. 15 (als Form von R. acris.) — Neilreich, Diagnosen 1867, p. 5. — Knapp, Pflanz. Galiziens u. d. Bukowina 1872, 288. — Fiek-Uechtritz, Flora 1881, p. 12.

Beschreibung des Ranunc. Stev.,

gefunden auf einer Wiese bei Mühle Klodtken, in Gemeinschaft von Ranunculus acer L. und R. repens L. Mai und Juni 1885.

Grundaxe dick fleischig, etwas spröde, wagrecht, bis schrägaufsteigend-kriechend, mit langen und ziemlich dicken Wurzelfasern; meist nur mit einer Endknospe, weit seltener sich theilend und mit 2 Endknospen.

Länge eines Jahrestriebes, gemessen bei 6 Pflanzen vom vorjährigen bis zum diesjährigen Stengel 34, 38, 41, 42, 42, 43 mm. — Gesammtlänge von dem, in seine Gefässbündel sich auflösenden Ende bis zum Stengel der blühenden Pflanze, gemessen bei 4 Pflanzen, 55, 74, 76, 90 mm.

Ihr Gipfel ist im Frühlinge, besonders aber im Herbste mit den stark behaarten Scheiden der frischen Grundblätter umgeben. Sowie diese verwesen, hinterlassen sie zuerst den in seine Gefässbündel sich auflösenden Blattgrund, und, wenn auch dieser verwest ist, an den Stellen der Blattnarben kurze, steife, anliegende Haare.

Bei jungen Sommertrieben, die frisch grünlich-weiss aussehen, aber beim Trocknen dunkel werden, rücken die schwarzen Scheidengründe mit ihren Gefässbündeln auseinander, wodurch die Axe das Ansehen eines Equisetum erhält.

So oft es mir gelang, auch das älteste Ende der Grundaxe mit aus der Erde zu bekommen, fand ich dies aus einer mit Humus gefüllten Röhre bestehend, die aus einer dicken brüchigen, in ihre Gefässbündel sich auflösenden Haut gebildet war.

Diese Verwesung scheint mit dem 3. Altersjahre der Axe einzutreten, und ihrem Gipfeltriebe zu folgen.

Stengel stielrund, einfach oder von der Mitte ab verzweigt, mit feinen, anliegenden Haaren in der Jugend dicht besetzt; sowie die Stengel in die Länge treiben, rücken die Haare auseinander, sitzen dann oft recht weitläuftig, und fallen endlich ab, so dass der untere Theil alter Stengel gewöhnlich kahl ist. Bis 0,8 m hoch.

Bei Pflanzen von gleicher Höhe ist der Stengel dicker als bei R. acer L., hat dünnere Seitenwandungen und eine weichere Behaarung wie dieser, ist immer nur grün und niemals bläulich bereift.

Grundblätter langgestielt. Spreiten bei kreisförmigem Umriss und herzförmigem Grunde 3 theilig, 5 lappig, mit meist 3 zipfeligen, keilförmigen, eingeschnitten gezähnten Lappen.

Die Stiele umfassen mit etwas bauchigen Scheiden die Grundaxe, verschmälern sich über der Scheide, sind in ihrer Mitte ganz flach, und im Grunde und unter den Spreiten tiefer rinnig. Die Scheiden sind innen glatt. aussen mit mässig weichen und langen Haaren sehr dicht besetzt, dieselben liegen am Grunde der Scheide an, werden höher hinauf abstehend bis zu einem Winkel von 90°, legen sich dann wieder an und sind kurz über der Scheide wieder angepresst; sie sind grüngelblich bis fuchsig, und werden späterhin dunkelbraun. — Die Stiele sind kurz über den Scheiden am dichtesten, jung und kurz dichter, ausgewachsen ziemlich spärlich, mit anliegenden weichen Haaren bedeckt, von denen aber viele bis zum Vermodern der Stiele bleiben.

Stengelblätter. Die unteren den Grundblättern ähnlich, und manchmal ziemlich lang gestielt, die höheren handförmig, kurzgestielt, die oberen fast sitzend, eingeschnitten mit 3—5 zähnigen, linienlanzettlichen etwas keilförmigen Zipfeln, die alleroberston sitzend, sehr schmal, aus etwas breiterem Grunde zugespitzt.

Sämmtliche Blattspreiten sind mit seidenweichen Haaren besetzt; an den Oberseiten sind diese kürzer, und stehen weniger dicht; an den Unterseiten sind sie länger, stehen bei der Blattentfaltung sehr dicht, und sind dann seidenglänzend, rücken aber bei dem Auswachsen der Spreite auseinander.

Bei vielen Grund- und auch noch bei manchen unteren Stengelblättern findet sich an der untern Seite des Spreitengrundes ein schmaler Gürtel schwärzlicher Haare, der sich bis auf den Gipfel des Blattstiels erstreckt, aber diese Farbe beim Trocknen verliert.

Blüthenstand ein lockeres Dichasium mit langen Blüthenstielen.

Blüthenstiele stielrund, nicht gefurcht, fast seidenartig behaart, besonders dicht unter den Blüthen oder gar unter den Knospen.

Kelche ausgebreitet.

Kelchblätter eiförmig, etwas ausgehöhlt, mit häutigem Rande, der meist gelb ist, auf dem Rücken langseidenhaarig, an der Spitze des stumpfen Knickes mit einer dunkleren, schwärzlichröthlichen Linie.

Blumenkronblätter mit einer Honigschuppe versehen; — mit kurzem Nagel; Seiten schwach abgerundet; Spitze abgerundet, ganzrandig, aber auch ausgerandet und eingekerbt; — goldgelb.

Staubblätter und Blüthenstaub. In einer Blüthe wurden gezählt: 57 Staubgefässe, deren Fäden 0,75 bis 3,00 mm lang und deren Beutel 1,20 bis 1,75 mm lang waren; 697 gute, strotzende Blüthenstaubkörner = 49,221 % gute, 54 zweifelhafte, 665 schlechte (zusammen 719 schlechte) Blüthenstaubkörner = 50,779 % schlechte. In einer anderen Blüthe von einer anderen Pflanze: 62 Staubgefässe mit Fäden 2,00 bis 3,00 mm lang und Beuteln 1,25 bis 1,45 mm lang; 917

gute strotzende Blüthenstaubkörner = 63,285 % gute, 383 sehr zweifelhafte, 149 ganz schlechte, (zusammen 532 schlechte) = 36,715 % schlechte.

Fruchtköpfchen kuglig, nicht verlängert.

Früchtchen unregelmässig-verkehrt eirund-kugelförmig, etwas gewölbt, nach dem kaum abgesetzten Rande zu etwas abgeflacht; — ganz reif dunkelbraun mit kaum hellerem Rande; — kahl; — und mit dem Griffel gekrönt.

Der Griffel steigt aus breitem, flachem Grunde bis etwa zu $^1/_5$ der ganzen Frucht auf, und biegt sich mit seiner stumpflichen Spitze kurz schnabelförmig nach der vorgestreckten Bauchseite des Früchtchens um; er trägt auf dem Scheitel, ein wenig an der Rückenseite herablaufend, die an den hervorragenden, erhärteten Papillen erkennbare Narbe, die viel heller als das Früchtchen, an der Spitze fast weiss ist.

Mit dem Griffel gemessene Früchte ergaben (in mm) das Verhältniss Länge: Breite = 2,60 mm : 1,90 mm; 2,70 : 1,60; 3,00 : 2,00; 3,10 : 2,00; 3,50 : 1,90; 3,60 mm : 2,40 mm.

Fruchtboden unbehaart.

Eine mit Blattschuppenresten besetzte Grundaxe bildete Jacob Sturm in seiner Flora von Deutschland XIII. 7. 1802 bei Ranunculus Traunsteineri Hoppe ab.

Die Grundaxe treibt mitunter von einem Stengel aus nach zwei entgegengesetzten Richtungen je einen Stammspross.

Bei 2 Pflanzen mit sehr langen, schmalen Lappen, auch einigen spreizenden Zipfeln und Zähnen glaubte ich auf den Bastard R. acer + Steveni schliessen zu dürfen. Bei einer dieser Pflanzen ist diese Meinung als irrig erwiesen, weil die Pflanze 87,73 % gute Blüthenstaubkörner hatte, doch bin ich zweifelhaft, ob ich sie dem R. acer oder dem R. Steveni zuzählen soll.

Die vorstehende Beschreibung ist gegeben um eine weitere Nachforschung nach Ranunculus Steveni im Vereinsgebiet zu veranlassen. Fernere Beobachtungen, besonders Kreuzung mit Ranunc. acer werden über seine Artrecht zu entscheiden haben.

Im Anschluss an diese Mittheilungen über Ran. Steveni waren zur Vergleichung ebenso ausführliche über Ranunc. acer und R. lanuginosus beigelegt, auch getrocknete Exemplare von Ran. montanus W. und R. Gouani W. Hoffentlich veröffentlicht Herr Scharlok selbst einmal das Wesentliche dieser Untersuchungen. Der knappe Raum verbietet die Darlegung derselben an dieser Stelle.

Ein Telegramm von Herrn Max Hoyer, Lehrer an der Landwirthschaftsschule zu Schweidnitz in Schlesien beglückwünscht die Versammlung.

Von Dr. Paul Preuss-Thorn sind an Herrn Gymnasiallehrer Schoettler Pflanzen zur Vertheilung eingesandt, theilweise aus Berlins Umgegend und dem westlich. Deutschland (Gentiana germanica, Centaurea solstitialis, Polygala amara, Astragulus danicus, Bupleurum rotundif., Orchis laxifl., O. Rivini, Avena praecox, Sanguisorba minor, Osmunda regalis, Linaria spuria, Aiuga Chamaepitys, Illecebrum verticillatum, Drosera intermedia, Epilobium tetragonum), theils aus der Weichselgegend (Chaeturus Marrubiastrum, Thesium intermedium, Liparis Loeselii, Alsine viscosa, Allium ursinum, Astragalus Cicer, Orchis ustulata, Gentiana amarella, Oxytropis pilosa, Juncus capitatus, Fumaria Vaillantii, Lycopodium inundatum, Linaria Elatine, Allium acutangulum, Trifolium Lupinaster, Lavatera thuringica, Androsace septentrionalis, Inula hirta). Es war leider unmöglich von letzteren, die allein für den Verein ein näheres Interesse haben, während der Versammlung ein genaueres Verzeichniss zu nehmen.

Es folgt dann der

Bericht über die botanischen Exkursionen in den Kreisen Neustadt, Kartaus und Berent

von stud. rer. nat. Alf. Lemcke.

Um ergänzende Untersuchungen der Kreise Neustadt, Kartaus und Berent im Auftrage des botan. Vereins für den Spätsommer zu unternehmen, begab ich mich zunächst nach Occalitz, wo ich am 4. August anlangte und bei Herrn Rittergutsbesitzer Hering sehr freundliche Aufnahme fand. Ich untersuchte von Occalitz aus den Südwestzipfel des Kreises Neustadt östlich bis zur Leba und südlich bis zum Gr. Klenczan-See. 5. 8. 95. Zwischen Occalitz und dem Occalitz-Labuhn'er Grenzbach: Hydrocotyle vulgaris (in einem Tümpel am Wege); am Occalitz-Labuhn'er Grenzbach) zwischen dem Occalitz-Labuhn'er Weg und Wussow): Avena flavescens, **Polygonatum verticillatum** V[2] Z[2], **Festuca silvatica** V[2] Z[4], Carex remota, C. silvatica, Orchis maculata, **Aquilegia vulgaris** (Frucht), Glyceria nemoralis, Thalictrum aquilegif., ***Carex pulicaris*** V[1] Z[2], ***Juncus obtusiflorus*** V[1] Z[3], Monotropa Hypopitys, Circaea alpina und **Circaea lutetiana** V[1] Z[4], Triticum caninum, Achillea Ptarmica; am Südufer desselben Baches im Kreise Lauenburg (Pommern) von der Grenze des Neustädt'er Kreises bis Wussow: Clinopodium vulgare, Anthericum ramosum, Hypericum montanum, Pimpinella magna; zwischen Wussow und dem Wussow-See im Kreise Lauenburg: Monotropa Hypopitys b) hirsuta, Lilium Martagon (Laub), auf einer Waldwiese: Hydrocotyle vulgaris, in der Wussow'er Forst Lycopodium Selago V[1] Z[2], **Goodyera repens** V[2] Z[2], Stachys annua V[2] Z[2]; am Wussow-See im Kreise Lauenburg: Rhynchospora alba V[1] Z[3], im Kreise Neustadt: Viola epipsila, **Veronica scutellata var. parmularia.** 6. 8. 85. Wiesen zwischen Occalitz und Werder: Scirpus uniglumis, Geranium palustre, Juncus filiformis, Thalictrum aquilegifolium, **Centaurea austriaca** V[3] Z[3]; in Werder: Chenopodium polyspermum; Haide zwischen Werder und Kanterschin: **Erica Tetralix** V[1] Z[5], Eriophorum latifolium, Viola epipsila, zwischen Kanterschin und Dzinzelitz: **Erica Tetralix** V[1] Z[2], Juncus squarrosus; zwischen Dzinzelitz und Poppow, im Kreise Lauenburg: Anthyllis Vulneraria, Ornithopus perpusillus, Trifolium alpestre. 7. 8. 85. Im Dorfteich von Occalitz: Potamogeton pusilla; am Wege zwischen Occalitz und Werder: Chenopodium Bonus Henricus; am ersten kleinen See nördlich vom Wege zwischen Werder-Wilhelmsdorf und Abbau Wilhelmsdorf: Drosera longifolia V[1] Z[3], am zweiten kleinen Tümpel nördlich bei Abbau-Wilhelmsdorf: Viola epipsila, Peplis Portula; zwischen Abbau Wilhelmsdorf und Linde: Hypericum humifusum, in einem Wäldchen nördlich vom Wege: Anthyllis Vulneraria; zwischen Linde und Grünlinde: **Pulsatilla vernalis** (Blätter), **Juncus supinus fr. fluitans** (in einem Tümpel). In Wahlendorf: Chenopodium Bonus Henricus; Westufer des Sees von Wahlendorf: **Scirpus setaceus** V[3] Z[5], **Veronica scutellata var parmularia** V[2] Z[4], Peplis Portula; Südufer des Dombrowo-See: **Myriophyllum alterniflorum** (am ganzen Seerande in 2 Fuss Wassertiefe), **Scirpus setaceus** V[2] Z[2], Litorella lacustris, **Veronica scutellata var. parmularia, Isoëtes lacustris** (ausgeworfen); am Westufer des See's auf sumpfiger Wiese: Drosera longifolia; im Walde am Nordufer des Dombrowo-See: Monotropa Hypopitys fr. hirsuta. Regen. 8. 8. 85. Moszick-See, östlich vom Wege zwischen Werder und Wahlendorf: **Myriophyllum**

alterniflorum V^4 Z^3, Litorella lacustris (in 1 Fuss Wassertiefe rings um den See), **Scirpus setaceus** V^3 Z^{1-3}, **Veronica scutellata var. parmularia** V^1 Z^2, **Lobelia dortmanna** (Laub; ausgeworfen); hohes Südufer des Moszick-See: **Pirola media** V^2 Z^2, **Aspidium montanum** V^2 Z^3; am Wege zwischen dem Moszick-See und Wahlendorf: Radiola linoides V^1 Z^2, Ornithopus perpusillus; Ostufer des Wahlendorf'er Sees: **Scirpus setaceus**, Peplis Portula, **Elatine Hydropiper** V^3 Z^{2-3}, Potentilla norvegica (an der Dorfstrasse); Bruch am Nordufer des Wook-See: **Erica Tetralix** V^1 Z^3, **Rhynchospora alba** V^4 Z^5; im NO. des Wook-Sees: **Lobelia dortmanna** (in 1—4 Fuss Wassertiefe, in grosser Menge). Lycopodium inundatum V^1 Z^5 (am Südufer des Sees); **Sparganium simplex fr. fluitans** (am Westufer des Sees). — Anhaltender Regen. — 9. 8. 85. Occalitzer Wald: Pirola uniflora V^2 Z^{2-3}, Polygonatum anceps. Anhaltender Regen. 10. 8. 85. Haide an der Werder-Buckowin'er Grenze, an einem Sumpfe: **Erica Tetralix** V^1 Z^3, **Scirpus caespitosus** V^2 Z^4, Eriophorum latifolium; **Lycopodium complanatum b) Chamaecyparyssus** V^3 Z^4; am kleinen See südwestlich von Wahlendorf: Rhynchospora alba Z^3, Scheuchzeria palustris V^2 Z^2, Juncus supinus, Sparganium minimum: an einem Tümpel südlich davon: Sparganium minimum; im und am Karpionki-See: Litorella lacustris, **Isoëtes lacustris**, Sparganium minimum, **Juncus supinus fr. fluitans**, Stellaria uliginosa, **Lobelia dortmanna** (Laub), **Elatine Hydropiper.** 11. 8. 85. Am Occalitz-Labuhn'er Grenzbach: **Bromus asper**, Carex silvatica, **Brachypodium silvaticum**, Rumex sanguineus fr. genuina, ausser den am 5. 8. 85. erwähnten Pflanzen; im Labuhn'er Walde, Kreis Lauenburg: Molinia coerulea fr. silvatica; am Bache zwischen Labuhn und Wussow, Kreis Lauenburg in Pommern: Actaea spicata, Triticum caninum, Bromus asper, Brachypodium silvaticum, Crepis virens, Pulsatilla vernalis (Laub); zwischen Wussow und Occalitz am Bache, der bei Wussow mit dem südlichern Occalitz-Labuhn'er Grenzbach zusammenfliesst, im Kreise Lauenburg: Brachypodium silvaticum; im Kreise Neustadt: **Potamogeton alpina** V^2 Z^4, **Blechnum Spicant** V^1 Z^3, **Rubus Bellardi** Z^2, **Polygonatum verticillatum** V^1 Z^2, Cardamine amara. 12. 8. 85. Torfbruch südlich vom Wege zwischen Wilhelmsdorf und Kanterschin: **Scirpus caespitosus**, Salix aurita + repens; an einem Tümpel südlich vom Wege: Ranunculus divaricatus, Juncus supinus, **Scirpus setaceus**, Bidens minimus, Radiola linoides, **Veronica scutellata var. parmularia**; zwischen Kanterschin und Klutschau, auf einem Lehmacker: Chenopodium Bonus Henricus; Leba-Thal zwischen Klutschau und Abbau Strepsch: Helianthemum Chamaecystus, Scrophularia aquatica; im Flusse: Sagittaria sagittifolia; in Strepsch: Chenopodium Bonus Henricus; zwischen Miloschewo und Linde: Helianthemum vulgare, **Scirpus caespitosus.**

13. 8. 85. Ueberfahrt nach Mirchau, Kreis Kartaus. Zwischen Mirchau und Bontsch: Agrimonia odorata, **Brachypodium silvaticum.** Regen und Gewitter. 14. 8. 85. Zwischen Mirchau und Neue Mühle: **Atriplex hortense**, Triticum caninum, Rumex sanguineus; zwischen Neue Mühle und Libagosch-See: Phegopteris polypodioides; Mirchau'er Forst, Jagen 74: Glyceria nemoralis, Calamagrostis lanceolata, **Blechnum Spicant**; Nordostufer des Libagosch-See: Pirola uniflora, Lycopodium annotinum, Circaea alpina; Nordufer des Sees östlich vom Gr. Klenczan-See: Sanicula europaea, Hydrocotyle vulgaris, Hypericum montanum, **Rubus Bellardi**, Ranunculus Lingua; Nordufer des Gr. Klenczan-See: Sparganium minimum, **Rubus Bellardi**, **Scirpus setaceus** V^1 Z^2, Radiola linoides, **Pulsatilla vernalis** (Laub), Potamogeton compressa;

zwischen Kaminitzamühl und U. F. Mirchau, in der Mirchau'er Forst: **Pirola media** V^1 Z^2. 15. 8. 85. Anhaltender Regen ebenso 16. 8. 85 Nachmittag Exkursion nach den kleinen Waldseen südlich vom Mirchau-Kaminitza'er Wege. Ich fand an beiden Seen: Scheuchzeria palustris, Carex limosa, Rhynchospora alba, **Scirpus caespitosus.** Am See in Jagen 69: **Scirpus caespitosus.** 17. 8. 85. Zwischen Mirchau und Strissabudda an einer Steinmauer: **Asplenium Trichomanes** V^1 Z^4; zwischen Strissabudda und Staniszewo: Origanum vulgare; in Staniszewo: Chenopodium Bonus Henricus; am Damnitza-Bach zwischen Staniszewo und Glusino: Vicia villosa. Regen. 18. 8. 85. Zwischen Mirchau und U. F. Mirchau: **Rubus Bellardi, Blechnum Spicant** (in Jag. 66); zwischen U. F. Mirchau und Libagosch-See: Lathyrus silvester fr. ensifolius, **Blechnum Spicant**; Südwestufer des Libagosch-See: **Rubus Bellardi, Blechnum Spicant,** Circaea alpina; Südufer des Kl. Klenczan-See: Stellaria glauca; Südufer des Gr. Klenczan-See: Hydrocotyle vulgaris, Circaea alpina, **Festuca silvatica** V^2 Z^4, Lycopodium Selago, Radiola linoides, Lycopodium inundatum, Stellaria glauca, **Rubus Bellardi**; |im und am Biala-See: **Chara aspera, Rubus Bellardi.** 19. 8. 85. Mirchauer Forst zwischen Mirchau und Libagosch-See: **Blechnum Spicant**; Waldsee westlich vom Wege im Jagen 94: Carex filiformis, C. limosa, Scheuchzeria palustris; in der Mirchau'er Forst Jagen 102: **Laserpitium prutenicum**; zwischen Kobillass und Grünlinde: Stachys annua, **Stachys arvensis** V^2 Z^4; zwischen Grünlinde und Linde: **Pulsatilla vernalis** (Laub); in Linde: Pulicaria vulgaris; zwischen Linde und Abbau Strepsch: **Pimpinella magna** γ.) **laciniata Wallr.**; von Strepsch über Miloschewo nach Nowahutta; am Wege zwischen den beiden letzten Dörfern: Lathyrus silvester fr. ensifolius; zwischen Nowahutta und Mirchau: Stellaria glauca. 20. 8. 85. Zwischen Mirchau und Neue Mühle: Pimpinella nigra; Leba-Ufer zwischen Nowahutta und Miloschewo: Geranium pratense, **Potamogeton alpina,** Vicia villosa, Rumex sanguineus; zwischen Miloschewo und Lewinno, Wald südlich vom Wege: **Lycopodium complanatum** V^1 Z^5; über Bendargau längs Damnitza-Bach bis Glusino und über Staniszewo nach Strissabudda; zwischen Strissabudda und Mirchau: Agrimonia odorata.

22. 8. 85. Ueberfahrt nach Gr. Czapielken, im Südosten des Kreises Kartaus. 23. 8. 85. Nach Eisenhammer Luisenhof; Bembernitz-Fliess zw. Luisenhof u. Ober-Kahlbude: Actaea spicata V^2 Z^3, Viola mirabilis V^3 Z^{2-3}, Asarum europaeum V^2 Z^2, **Aconitum variegatum** V^3 Z^2, Pulmonaria obscura, **Digitalis ambigua** V^3 Z^{1-2}, Mercurialis perennis V^2 Z^3, **Bromus asper** V^2 Z^2, **Struthiopteris germanica** V^3 Z^3, Lathyrus niger V^1 Z^2, **Festuca silvatica** V^2 Z^2; zwischen Ober-Kahlbude und Oel-Mühle längs linkem Radaune-Ufer, Kreis Danzig: Thalictrum minus V^4 Z^2, Mentha silvestris a) nemorosa V^2 Z^2, Asarum europaeum V^1 Z^3, Thalictrum aquilegifolium V^1 Z^3, Hypericum montanum, Polygonum dumetorum, Oenothera biennis, Alliaria officinalis V^1 Z^2, **Struthiopteris germanica** V^1 Z^3, **Digitalis ambigua** V^1 Z^3, Origanum vulgare, **Bromus asper** V^2 Z^2, **Tunica prolifera** V^2 Z^3, Anthericum ramosum V^1 Z^3; zwischen Oel-Mühle und Nieder-Prangenau: Pimpinella nigra; zwischen Nieder-Prangenau und Ziegelei Babenthal: Carlina vulgaris, Pimpinella nigra, Agrimonia odorata; zwischen Ziegelei Babenthal und Gr. Czapielken in der Stangenwald'er Forst: Polygonatum anceps, **Digitalis ambigua** V^1 Z^1. 24. 8. 85. Zwischen Gr. Czapielken und Buschkau: Achillea Ptarmica, in der Stangenwald'er Forst: **Brachypodium silvaticum,** Geranium sanguineum, Carex remota, Pirola uniflora V^2 Z^2, **Rubus Bellardi,** Cuscuta Epithymum

auf Tragopogon prat. und Plantago lanceol.; in der bewaldeten Schlucht südlich von Ober-Buschkau: Actaea spicata V^3 Z^2, Thalictrum aquilegifolium V^1 Z^2, **Brachypodium silvaticum** V^3 Z^2, **Aconitum variegatum** V^1 Z^3, **Bromus asper** V^2 Z^3, **Festuca silvatica** V^1 Z^3, **Ranunculus cassubicus** (Grundblätter) V^1 Z^2, Lathyrus niger; linkes Ufer der Kladau zw. Buschkau und Meisterswalde: **Aconitum variegatum** V^2 Z^3, Thalictrum aquilegifolium, Triticum caninum V^1 Z^3; Nordufer des Mariensee: **Elatine Hydropiper** V^3 Z^4, **Myriophyllum alterniflorum, Callitriche autumnalis,** Limosella aquatica, Potamogeton graminea fr.) heterophylla, Potamogeton pusilla. — 25. 8. 85. Zw. Gr. Czapielken und Helenenhof: Pimpinella nigra, Festuca rubra fr. arenaria, Achillea Ptarmica; Lappin'er See, Südostufer: Stellaria glauca, Litorella lacustris V^3 Z^4, Limosella aquatica; zw. dem Nordende des Lappin'er See und Kl. Czapielken: Avena flavescens. — 26. 8. 85. Zw. Gr. Czapielken und Marschau, längs Bembernitz-Fliess: **Aconitum variegatum** V^4 Z^{1-2}, Thalictrum augustifolium V^2 Z^2, **Bromus asper** V^2 Z^3, Neottia Nidus avis V^1 Z^1 (Fr.), **Digitalis ambigua** V^3 Z^2, Thalictrum aquilegifolium V^2 Z^3, **Festuca silvatica** V^1 Z^3, Polygonatum anceps, Paris quadrifolius, **Brachypodium silvaticum** V^1 Z^2, Carex silvatica V^1 Z^3, Mercurialis perennis V^1 Z^3; zw. Marschau und Sommerkau'er See, am Waldrande nördlich vom Wege: Actaea spicata V^2 Z^2, **Digitalis ambigua** V^2 Z^{1-2}, **Centaurea austriaca** (1 Ex.); zw. Sommerkau'er See und Krug Babenthal: **Centaurea austriaca** V^1 Z^4, **Digitalis ambigua** V^2 Z^3, **Aquilegia vulgaris** (Frucht) V^1 Z^2. In der Schlucht südlich vom Krug Babenthal zw. der Chaussee und der Radaune: Saponaria officinalis, **Salix pruinosa**, Helianthemum Chamaecystus, Viola mirabilis, Lonicera Hylosteum, **Bromus asper**, Thalictrum aquilegifolium, **Lilium Martagon** (Fr.), Asarum europaeum, **Digitalis ambigua, Aconitum variegatum, Brachypodium silvaticum**, Mercurialis perennis, **Bupleurum longifolium** V^3 Z^2; am rechten Radaune-Ufer zw. Krug Babenthal und Ruthken dieselben Pflanzen mit Ausnahme der drei zuerst aufgezählten, ausserdem: Triticum caninum, Actaea spicata, Lathyrus niger, Scabiosa columbaria, Hypericum montanum, Carlina vulgaris, Polygonatum anceps, **Epipactis latifolia** V^2 Z^2; von Ruthken nach Rheinfeld, Ostufer des Rheinfeld'er See: **Veronica scutellata var. parmularia.** — 27. 8. 85. Lappiner See, Nordwestufer: Litorella lacustris, Hypericum montanum, Pimpinella nigra; zw. Lappin und Lichtenfeld: Salix aurita + repens; Lichtenfeld'er See: Limosella aquatica, Peplis Portula; Grabenrand zw. Lichtenfeld'er und Rheinfeld'er See: **Centaurea austriaca** V^1 Z^3; in Rheinfeld: Chenopodium Bonus Henricus; zw. Rheinfeld und Krissau: **Gentiana campestris,** Helianthemum vulgare, Scabiosa columbaria V^1 Z^2, Eriophorum latifolium. — 28. 8. 85. Forst zw. Gr. Czapielken und Stangenwalde: **Rubus Bellardi**; Schlucht in der Stangenwald'er Forst östlich von der Chaussee: Paris quadrifolius, Lycopodium Selago; an der Chaussee zw. Stangenwalde und Mariensee: Pimpinella nigra; Insel im Marien-See.

29. 8. 85. Ueberfahrt nach Kleschkau, Kreis Berent. 30. 8. 85—2. 9. 85 krank. 3. 9. 85. Zw. Kleschkau und dem Langen See: Alchemilla arvensis; am und im Langen See: **Elatine Hydropiper,** Limosella aquatica; an den nordöstlich davon gelegenen Seen: Hypericum humifusum, **Myriophyllum alterniflorum,** Limosella aquatica, **Elatine Hydropiper, Ranunculus reptans**; zw. Lindenberg und Krangen: Mentha silvestris; zwischen Krangen und Grabowitz, Kreis Pr. Stargard an einem kleinen Waldsee: Scheuchzeria palustris, **Juncus supinus fr. fluitans,** Utricularia vulgaris und **intermedia** (in einem torfigen Graben), Carex limosa; Ferseufer zw. Grabowitz und Reinwasser,

Kreis Berent: Sagittaria sagittifolia, Polygonum dumetorum, Scabiosa columbaria; zw. Reinwasser und Waldowken: Carlina vulgaris; zw. Woldowken und Kleschkau: Melilotus officinalis, Anthyllis Vulneraria, Vicia villosa. — 4. 9. 85. Rückkehr nach Königsberg.

Von Oberlehrer Witt-Löbau langt eine Sendung Pflanzen zur Vertheilung aus Kreis Löbau an: Linnaea borealis Gron., Alt-Eiche. — Saxifraga Hirculus L., Kellerode. — Equisetum hiemale L., Rinnek. — Carlina vulgaris L., Rinnek und Kosten. — Centaurea maculosa Lmk., Rinnek. — Thesium ebracteatum Hayne, Rosenthal. — Arabis arenosa Scop., Rosenthal. — Hypericum montanum L., Kosten. — Hypericum humifusum L., Zajonskowo. — Marrubium vulgare L., Mortung. — Arnoseris minima Sk., Zajonskowo. — Cimicifuga foetida L., Kosten. — Hieracium praealtum Vill., Kosten. — Phegopteris Dryopteris Fée., Kosten. — Aspidium spinulosum Sw., Kosten. — Aspidium Thelypteris Sw., Kosten. — Cystopteris fragilis, Forstrevier Kosten.

Conrector Seydler-Braunsberg sendet folgenden Bericht über seine botanischen Excursionen von 1885 ein:

„Bei dem schönen Herbstwetter im vorigen Jahre blühten noch eine Menge Pflanzen zum zweiten Male, so dass ich noch am 1. November auf einem kurzen Ausfluge in die nächste Umgebung von Braunsberg nicht weniger als 65 in schönster Blüthe sammeln konnte, darunter Anagallis phoenicea, Berteroa incana, Centaurea Cyanus, Campanula rapunculoides, Gypsophila muralis, Knautia arvensis, Matricaria Chamomilla, Ranunculus acer, Rubus Idaeus, Tragopogon orientalis, Tithymalus Esula, Peplus und helioscopius. Den 21. November hatte ich Gelegenheit, im Garten des Herrn Rittergutsbesitzers v. Brandt-Rossen einen blühenden an einer Pyramidenpappel sich gegen 20 Fuss emporklammernden **Epheu** zu beobachten. Am 9. März 1885 starben in der Kl. Amtsmühle zu Braunsberg zwei Kinder im Alter von 3 und 4 Jahren in Folge des Genusses der Wurzelstöcke des Wasserschierlings (Cicuta virosa). An demselben Tage übersandte mir Herr Gutsbesitzer Grube-Koggenhöfen bei Elbing aus seinem Garten **blühende Epheuzweige** von einem Stamme, der 30 Jahre alt ist und $2^1/_2$ Fuss über dem Erdboden einen Durchmesser von 3 Zoll hat. Am 18. März erhielt ich durch Herrn Gutspächter Kähler-Ottenhagen aus dem Gutsgarten in Gr. Barthen bei Löwenhagen **Hedera Helix mit reifen Früchten.**

Ich sammelte im Kreise Braunsberg den 2. Mai bei Rodelshöfen Ribes nigrum und rubrum, Prunus Padus, Oxalis Acetosella; den 13. Mai am linken Passargeufer Lamium amplexicaule und maculatum, Veronica hederifolia, Salix purpurea u. a.; den 23. Mai auf dem rechten Passargeufer in der Aue bei Braunsberg **Potentilla collina** und Tithymalus Esula mit Aecidium Euphorbiae; den 3. Juni in Pfahlbude an der Mündung der Passarge Alliaria officinalis, Barbaraea stricta, Petasites tomentosus, Orchis incarnata; den 6. Juni im Walde zwischen Hagendorf, Lichtnau und Packhausen Calla palustris, Cardamine amara, **Valeriana simplicifolia, Pirola uniflora,** ***Listera cordata, Veronica montana*** (der dritte von mir in Ostpreussen aufgefundene Standort), Thysselinum palustre, Drosera rotundifolia, **Ranunculus cassubicus,** Stellaria glauca und uliginosa, **Carex Schreberi**; am Wege zwischen Lichtwalde und Packhausen Orchis Morio, am Ackerrande am Torfbruch bei Lichtwalde **Myosotis versicolor**; den 9. Juni auf der Wiese zwischen der Sekundärbahn und der Lindenau'er

Chaussee Hesperis matronalis, verwildert, Bromus racemosus; den 12. Juni auf der Aue bei Braunsberg Tithymalus Esula in den verschiedensten Formen mit einfachem Stengel ohne Doldenstrahlen, mit blühenden und nicht blühenden Aesten, mit schmalen und breiteren Blättern; den 17. Juni in der Umgebung des Braunsberg'er Bahnhofs **Matricaria discoides**, zwischen Grafenmorgen und der Ostbahn Crepis biennis, Thalictrum angustifolium und die seltene Form von Leucanthemum vulgare Lmk. **ohne Strahl**; den 26. Juni am Haffufer bei Frauenburg Archangelica officinalis in Menge, **Scirpus Tabernaemontani** und maritimus, Juncus alpinus; an der Baudebrücke Achillea Millefolium var. **lanata**, Anthericum ramosum, Vicia cassubica, **Spiraea Filipendula**, Platanthera bifolia Rchb. mit mehreren Stengelblättern; den 24. Juni auf dem sumpfigen Moor zwischen der Kl. Amtsmühle und Regitten ***Crepis succisifolia***, auf der Aue am rechten Passargeufer bei Braunsberg zum ersten Male ***Bunias orientalis***; den 2. Juli im Garten des Herrn Baurath Bertram hierselbst **Lathyrus sativus**, verwildert; den 4. Juli zwischen dem Bahnhofe und Güterschuppen ***Plantago arenaria***, eine wandernde Pflanze, bisher von mir bei Braunsberg nicht gesehen, ebenso ***Potentilla digitato-flabellatata*** Al. Br. et Bouch.; den 5. Juni unter den Eichen bei Rodelshöfen Dianthus Armeria, ***Dianthus Armeria + deltoides***, Hypericum quadrangulum, Equisetum arvense var. nemorosum in 2—3 Spitzen auslaufend; zwischen der Badestelle in der Passarge und Rodelshöfen ***Allium Scorodoprasum***; den 7. Juli am Waldrande zwischen Fehlau und Zagern Leucanthemum vulgare mit auffallend starker Behaarung, im Grunde bei Zagern Coronaria flos cuculi mit gefüllten Blumen, bei Fehlau Galium verum und ochroleucum; den 9. Juli auf dem rechten Passargeufer Myosotis caespitosa, Juncus compressus und auf einem Acker Calendula officinalis, wahrscheinlich mit Gartendünger hierher gebracht; den 12. Juli im Walschthale bei Mehlsack ***Equisetum maximum***; den 14. Juli im Braunsberg'er Stadtwald Rubus Bellardi, zwischen dem Stadtwalde und Marienfelde **Hypericum humifusum**, Ranunculus polyanthemus, Juncus squarrosus und filiformis; den 28. Juli im kalthöfener Walde bei der Kl. Amtsmühle Serratula tinctoria, **Digitalis ambigua**, an der Landstrasse zwischen der Kl. Amtsmühle und Birkmannshöfchen Galium ochroleucum Wlf. unter den Eltern; den 31. Juli am rechten Passargeufer zwischen der Ziegelei und dem Chausseehause Salix amygdalina var. discolor zum zweiten Male in diesem Jahre blühend; den 1. August zwischen der Mühle und der Eisenbahnbrücke bei Bömenhöfen **Mentha silvestris**; **Laserpitium prutenicum** und ausser der Hauptform noch ein monströses Exemplar mit durchwachsener Dolde. Herr Rittergutsbesitzer Höpfner-Bömenhöfen machte mich auf ein mit schwedischem Klee (Trifolium hybridum) bestandenes durch ein Insekt verheertes Feld aufmerksam. Sämmtliche Blätter waren durch den kleinen Rüsselkäfer Apion Trifolii vollständig skelettirt. Ich sammelte ferner noch im Kreise Braunsberg den 20. August an der Sandgrube am Oberthor bei Braunsberg **Geranium dissectum**, Veronica opaca Fr., an der alten Stadtmauer am Oberthor **Chenopodium murale**; den 22. August auf der sumpfigen Moorwiese zwischen Regitten und der Kl. Amtsmühle **Dianthus superbus** in Menge; den 24. August am linken Passargeufer zwischen Braunsberg und der Kreuzkirche Artemisia Absinthium, im Graben an der Sekundärbahn Festuca arundinacea, Equisetum palustre var. polystachyum in verschiedenen Formen; den 1. September an den Scheunen in der Ritterstrasse **Festuca distans**, auf dem evangelischen Kirchhofe Stenactis annua, verwildert; den 2. September im Braunsberg'er Stadtwalde **Vinca minor** (ob wirklich wild, ist noch festzustellen), Laserpitium prutenicum, ausser der Hauptform auch die mit kahlem Stengel, auf den Aeckern zwischen dem Walde und Marienfelde Veronica serpyllifolia var. **tenella**, Radiola linoides, Aphanes arvensis; den 19. September auf Aeckern bei Braunsberg **Lamium hybridum** zahlreich.

Im Kreise Heiligenbeil sammelte ich den 11. Juni im königl. Forstrevier Damerau zwischen Braunsberg und Heiligenbeil Ranunculus polyanthemus, Thalictrum aquilegifolium, ***Veronica montana***, **Vinca minor**, ***Carex pilosa*** und pilulifera, **Festuca silvatica**, Neottia Nidus avis, Phegopteris Dryopteris und polypodioides, Cystopteris fragilis Bernh.; den 19. Juni im Rossen'er Walde Rhamnus Frangula mit Aecidium Rhamni, **Polypodium vulgare**, Galium boreale, auf dem Mühlenberge Sempervivum soboliferum mit **Uredo Sempervivi**; den 18. Juli bei Otten auf einem mit Cuscuta Trifolii Bab. befallenen Kleefelde **Crepis nicaeensis**, im naheliegenden Gebüscche Hieracium boreale, am Bache **Aconitum variegatum**, Pimpinella magna, Asperula odorata, Triticum caninum und vulgare mit begrannter Aehre. Hier hatte ich auch Gelegenheit, ein Rübenfeld zu beobachten, welches durch die Larven der Rübenblattwespen (Athalia spinarum) gänzlich zerstört war; sämmtliche Blätter waren skelettirt. Ich sammelte ferner im Kreise Heiligenbeil den 19. Juli im Walde bei Pellen **Pyrola chlorantha**, Rubus saxatilis, bei Jäcknitz am Wege der nach Zinten führt **Erythraea pulchella**, welche jetzt nach der Drainage nur noch in geringer Zahl vorkommt. — Den 26. Juli machte ich auf dem Dampfer Braunsberg eine Ausflucht nach Gr. Bruch auf der frischen Nehrung, Kreis Fischhausen. Die Exkursion war nicht sehr ergiebig. In dem königl. Forstrevier, welches die Breite der Nehrung einnimmt, sammelte ich **Pirola chlorantha**, minor, **uniflora** und secunda, Epipactis atrorubens, Erigeron acer var. **droebachensis**, Astragalus arenarius, roth und weiss blühend, Hieracium umbellatum var. **coronopifolium**, Honckenya peploides, Potentilla reptans, Anthyllis Vulneraria var. **maritima**, Sedum boloniense, Artemisia Absinthium, Arabis arenosa, Equisetum hiemale und ausserdem noch zu bestimmende Rubi und Lichenes.

Bei einem Besuche in Ottenhagen, Kreis Königsberg, sammelte ich den 5. August auf Haideboden an der Chaussee zwischen Ottenhagen und Lindenau Alectorolophus maior var. **angustifolius**, Scabiosa ochroleuca, am Waldrande bei Gr. Barthen Dianthus arenarius, Veronica spicata mit einer und mehreren endständigen Trauben, Potentilla cinerea, nur Blattexemplare mit Aecidium Potentillae, Senecio erraticus, Hieracium umbellatum var. **linariifolium**.

Zur Ansicht und Bestimmung wurden mir eingesandt: 1) Von Herrn Gymnasiallehrer Krieger den 27. Mai bei Liebemühl gesammelte Pflanzen als: Paris quadrifolius, Actaea spicata, **Viola mirabilis**, ***Ajuga pyramidalis***, Cerastium arvense, Lonizera Xylosteum, Scorzonera humilis, Pirola uniflora, Asperula odorata; von demselben aus der Gegend zw. Pillau und Neuhäuser Scabiosa ochroleuca, Artemisia campestris var. sericea, Anthyllis Vulneraria, Eryngium maritimum, Astragalus arenarius, Epipactis atrorubens und von der Chaussee zwischen Alt-Pillau und Neuhäuser **Tithymalus Cyparissias**; 2) von Herrn Dr. med. Hagedorn aus der königl. Forst Taberbrück, Belauf Pörschken bei Sonnenborn, Kreis Mohrungen, ***Lilium Martagon***; 3) von Herrn Bauinspector Friedrich aus der Umgegend von Braunsberg Clavaria flava; 4) von Herrn Lehrer Desmarowitz den 4. September im Walde bei Kreuzdorf bei Frauenburg gesammelt:

Calla palustris mit zwei Blüthenscheiden; 5) von Herrn Landrath Oberg zwei seltene Pilze, **Peziza onotica** aus dem Stadtwalde und **Peziza cochleata** aus seinem Garten; 6) von meinem Zöglinge, dem Tertianer Schrade, einen flachen Zapfen von Pinus silvestris aus dem Rossen'er Walde bei Braunsberg."

Schliesslich wurde eine grosse Anzahl seltener Pflanzen, die Conrector Seydler eingeschickt hatte, an die Anwesenden vertheilt.

Herr stud. rer. nat. Knoblauch erstattet dann

Bericht über die botanische Untersuchung des Kreises Memel im Jahre 1885.

Die von Herrn Professor Caspary mir übertragene zweite Untersuchung des Kreises Memel wurde von mir in der Zeit vom 7. Mai bis 15. September 1885 ausgeführt. Ich bereiste den Kreis zweimal und untersuchte ihn ergänzend mit Rücksicht auf meine vorjährigen Exkursionen.

Von meinen Funden seien besonders hervorgehoben: Poa sudetica (22. 6. 85), Campanula Cervicaria (10. 9. 85), Lunaria rediviva (7. 7. 85), Gymnadenia conopea, Inula salicina, Epilobium tetragonum (18. 7. 85), Goodyera repens (27. 7. 85), Utricularia intermedia, Thalictrum simplex (5. 8. 85), Helianthemum Chamaecistus (19. 8. 85), Trifolium fragiferum, von Ballastpflanzen: Salvia verticillata (1. Südermole Memels, 2. Chaussee nördlich von Purmallen, Lepidium latifolium (19. 8. 85) und Bunias orientalis (1. städtischer Kirchhof Memels, 2. Nordermole, 3. Immersatt). — Herr Gutsbesitzer Scheu-Löbarten fand Juni 85 Avena flavescens auf Mingewiesen südlich Pilatischken (Schmidt-Matz) rechts der Minge zwischen Sudmanten-Hans und Dawillen.

Für die Unterstützung meiner Untersuchungen namentlich von Seiten des Herrn Landrath Cranz, des Herrn Oberförster Schoeppfer-Klooschen, der Herren Gutsbesitzer Scheu-Löbarten, v. Schulze-Miszeiken, v. Dressler-Friedrichsgnade, des Herrn Pfarrer Jussas-Dt. Crottingen und des Herrn Dr. Labes-Pröculs sage ich besten Dank.

Folgendes sind die Hauptergebnisse meiner Exkursionen.

Vom 7. bis 11. 5. 85 in Miszeiken. — 7. 5. 85. Zw. Miszeiken und Kerren-Görge: Elodea canadensis. Dautzkurr-Narmund. — 8. 5. 85. Miszeikener Park: Carex digitata, Lathyrus vernus; zw. Kl. Daupern und der Chaussee: Equisetum hiemale V^1 Z^4. Zw. Todden-Jacob und Dautzkurr-Krieger: Equisetum hiemale, **Viola arenaria**; zw. D.-K. und Dawillen: Viola arenaria. Zw. Galten und Jodeischen: Saponaria officinalis. — 9. 5. 85. Schmeltelle. Rechtes Ufer zw. Miszeiken und Sziluppen: Equisetum boreale. Gehölz nördlich von Zenkuhnen: **Lathraea squamaria** V^1 Z^3, **Corydalis intermedia**, Gagea minima. Kaufmännische Plantage östlich von Mellneraggen: Lycopodium Selago V^1 Z^2, Veronica hederifolia (auch zw. Leuchtthurm und Bommelsvitte). — 11. 5. 85. Rechtes Schmeltelleufer zw. Zenkuhnen und Buddelkehmen: Gagea minima, Corydalis intermedia.

12. 5. 85. Umzug nach Löbarten. — Rechtes Mingeufer zw. Sudmanten-Hans und Dawillen: Viola arenaria, V. mirabilis, Lathyrus vernus, Asarum europaeum, Veronica Teucrium. Gehölz zw. Griegszen und Kiaunoden: Corydalis intermedia, Mercurialis perennis, Stellaria Holostea, Hepatica triloba, Ranunculus cassubicus. Minge zw. Baiten und Gedminnen: Gagea minima, Lathyrus vernus, Thalictrum

aquilegifolium, Viola arenaria; Minge zw. G. und Szernen: Th. aquilegifolium, Lonicera Xylosteum, Lycopodium Selago; westlich des Szernen'er Gutswaldes: **Carex stricta Good**, Chara fragilis. — 13. 5. 85. Zw. Löbarten und Ilgejahnen: Senecio vernalis; zw. Mauszellen und Chaussee: Carex caespitosa. — 15. 5. 85. Minge zw. Szernen und Gröszuppen: **Carex stricta**; Minge zw. G. und Rooken: Thalictrum aquilegifolium; Minge zw. der Kissuppe und Buttken: **Veronica Teucrium.** Zw. Rooken und Jodicken: **Polygala amara.** Chaussee zw. Kissinnen und Szernen: Viola arenaria. — 18. 5. 85. Zw. Hennig-Hans und Jodeischen: Polygala amara. Zw. Dawillen und Todden-Jacob: Viola arenaria + canina, Equisetum hiemale; zw. Nausseden und Laugallen: Polygala amara. Wald östlich von Kl. Jagschen: Lathyrus vernus, L. montanus, Ranunculus cassubicus. — 19. 5. 85. Zw. Girngallen und Adl. Lappenischken: Carex flacca; in d. Lappenischke zw. G. und Wallehnen: **Carex pulicaris.** — 20. 5. 85. Szernener Gutswald: Viola arenaria, **Phegopteris polypodioides**, Ph. Dryopteris, Carex caespitosa, Equisetum boreale. Zw. Szernen und Jurgen: **Botrychium Lunaria.** — 21. 5. 85. In Szernen: Symphytum officinale. — 22. 5. 85. Luseze, Jag. 67: Phegopteris Dryopteris; Jag. 66: Viola epipsila, Carex caespitosa; Jag. 61: Thalictrum flavum; Gestell zw. Jag. 62 und 61: Viola epipsila + palustris; Jag. 62: **Carex paradoxa**; westlicher Theil von Jag. 67: Carex digitata. In Oberförsterei Klooschen 700 Rothbuchen gepflanzt, gut gedeihend, 2 Ex. etwa 15 m hoch. — 23. 5. 85. Schmeltelle zw. Buddelkehmen und Gr. Szarde: Ranunculus bulbosus, Equisetum boreale. Zw. Löbarten und Dautzkurr: Polygala amara. — 25. 5. 85. Zw. Hennig-Hans und Jodeischen: **Sesleria coerulea.** Gehölz von Dautzkurr: Carex caespitosa. Zw. Löbarten und Sudmanten-Hans: Ranunculus bulbosus; Minge zw. S. und Szernen: Lonicera Xylosteum. Zw. Löbarten und Hennig-Hans: Barbaraea arcuata.

26. 5. 85. Umzug nach Blimatzen. — Chaussee nördlich von Forsthaus Aszpurwen: **Sesleria coerulea** V^1 Z^2. Wewirsze zw. Stoneiten und Stankaiten: **Struthiopteris germanica**, Phegopteris Dryopteris, Asarum europaeum, Viola mirabilis, Aspidium cristatum, Lathyrus vernus, Astragalus glycyphyllus, **Aiuga genevensis**, Lychnis Viscaria, Spiraea Filipendula. Aisse gegenüber Aissehnen: Thalictrum aquilegifolium. — 27. 5. 85. Jag. 21, 22, 27, 31, 34, 35: Andromeda poliifolia. Jag. 26: Equisetum boreale; Jag. 32, 34: Phegopteris Dryopteris. — 28. 5. 85. Zw. Degeln und Blimatzen: **Aiuga genevensis.** Jag. 40: Carex digitata, Lathyrus vernus. Jag. 38: L. montanus. Jag. 41, 34: Phegopteris Dryopteris. Jag. 43: **Phegopteris polypodioides.** Jag. 39: Lathyrus vernus. — 29. 5. 85. Jag. 50: Polygala amara. Zw. Paaszkenkrug und Paaszken: Sesleria coerulea. Weg nordwestlich von Paaszkenkrug: Viola arenaria, **Sesleria coerulea.** Zw. Paaszken und Kojellen: **Orchis mascula β. speciosa,** Equisetum boreale; zw. Gellszinnen und Piktazen: Polygala amara. — 31. 5. 85. Wewirsze zw. Szeppoten und Begeden: **Struthiopteris germanica, Geranium silvaticum.** Jag. 15: Listera ovata. Wiese nordwestlich von Jag. 18: Mercurialis perennis, **Polygonatum verticillatum, Daphne Mezereum,** Viola mirabilis, Orchis incarnata, Arabis arenosa. Jag. 19: Carex paradoxa.

1. 6. 85. Umzug nach Pröculs. — Gehölz westlich des Bahnhofs Pröculs: Pirola uniflora, Equisetum boreale, Carex arenaria, **Myrica Gale, Botrychium Lunaria,** Orchis mascula β. speciosa. Tyrusmoor, Jag. 114: Typha latifolia, Aspidium cristatum, Calla palustris; am Kanal: Botrychium Lunaria und Alyssum calycinum. —

2. 6. 85. In den Wäldchen nordöstlich vom Tyrusmoor: **Scirpus pauciflorus.** Zw. Dorf Stragna und Grezen: Orchis incarnata. — 3. 6. 85. Linkes Mingeufer zw. Gut Pröculs und Protniszken: **Allium Scorodoprasum** V[1] Z[2]. Buttken'er Wald: Viola epipsila, Cornus sanguinea. — 4. 6. 85. — 5. 6. 85. Szwenzelner Moor: Senecio paluster, Carex paniculata. — 6. 6. 85. Kr. Heidekrug. Zw. Gr. Szlaszen und Russ: Carex filiformis. Zw. Brionischken und Colonie Bredszull: **Cenolophium Fischeri Koch.** Bredzuller Moor: Rubus Chamaemorus. Ibenhorster Forst, Jag. 102: Carex riparia. Jag. 111: Milium effusum, Ulmus effusa. Jag. 123: Stellaria frieseana. Jag. 133: Lathyrus paluster. — 7. 6. 85. Jag. 39: Carex paradoxa. Jag. 128: Stellaria uliginosa. — 8. 6. 85. Werder Helena: **Hierochloa borealis.** 9. 6. 85. Kr. Memel: Luseze, Jag. 73: **Stellaria frieseana,** Viola epipsila, Mercurialis perennis, **Circaea alpina, Polypodium vulgare.** — 10. 6. 85. Jag. 69: Carex digitata. Jag. 68: Polygala amara; östlich desselben (Kanal): **Lathyrus paluster,** Symphytum officinale, Thalictrum flavum. Jag. 77: Stellaria frieseana, Circaea alpina, Polypodium vulgare. Jag. 86: **Listera cordata** V[1] Z[2], **Chimophila umbellata, Linnaea borealis** (auch in 85). In Jag. 62 u. 67: Hepatica triloba; in Jag. 67: Asarum europaeum. — 11. 6. 85. O. F. Klooschen (Wäldchen): Equisetum boreale, **Ranunculus fluitans** (in der Minge).

12. 6. 85. Umzug nach Memel. — Zw. Kl. Tauerlauken und der Ringel: Barbaraea arcuata, **Fragaria viridis.** Dange zw. Kl. Tauerlauken und Daugallen: Equisetum boreale. Bachthal südlich von Kl. T.: Lychnis Viscaria, Fragaria viridis, Crataegus monogyna. — 13. 6. 85. Bürgerfelder Memels: Symphytum officinale. Dange zw. Luisenhof und Kl. Tauerlauken: **Ranunculus Lingua,** Carex paradoxa, Salix rubra, Spiraea Filipendula, Echium vulgare, Lychnis Viscaria. Dange zw. Gr. Tauerlauken und Purmallen: **Struthiopteris germanica** V[1] Z[2], **Botrychium Lunaria** V[1] Z[2-3]. Purmallebach östlich der Chaussee: Phegopteris Dryopteris, **Ph. polypodioides.** Palwen nördlich der städtischen Plantage: **Scirpus pauciflorus.** — 15. 6. 85. Zw. Bommelsvitte und Leuchtthurm, nördlicher Weg: **Euphorbia Esula,** Silene nutans, **Geranium molle** (Gehölz). Plantage Memels: Equisetum boreale; am Swiane-Teich: Carex teretiuscula, **Corallorrhiza innata.** — 16. 6. 85. Städtischer Kirchhof und Nordermole: **Bunias orientalis.** Zw. Bommelsvitte und Leuchtthurm: **Valerianella olitoria.** — 17. 6. 85. Glacis des Plantagenfort: Echium vulgare, Tragopogon floccosus, **Alyssum calycinum.** Kur. Nehrung, südlich des Sandkruges: **Polygala comosa** (Plantage).

18. 6. 85. Umzug nach Dt. Crottingen. — Dange östlich von Dt. Crottingen: Carex flacca, **Potentilla reptans** (Abhänge). — 19. 6. 85. Linkes Dangeufer zw. Dt. Crottingen und Dautzin-Niclau: **Polygonatum verticillatum, Stellaria uliginosa,** Geum urbanum + rivale, Ranunculus cassubicus, Viola mirabilis, **Actaea spicata,** Orchis mascula β. speciosa, Carex dioica, **Eriophorum latifolium,** Serratula tinctoria. — 20. 6. 85. Bahne oberh. Gut Szudebarsden: Orchis mascula β. speciosa, **Vicia silvatica.** Bebruhne zw. Schule Wallehnen und der Dange: **Potentilla reptans, Arabis Gerardi** V[1] Z[3], Ulmus montana With, **Geranium silvaticum.** Bach südlich von Talutten: **Polygonatum verticillatum** Z[2]. — 22. 6. 85. Zw. der Dange und Zarthen, zw. Wallehnen und Woiduszen, zw. Corallen und Dorf Szudebarsden: **Scirpus pauciflorus.** In der Lappenischke zw. Wallehnen und Girngallen: **Daphne Mezereum,** Ranunculus cassubicus, Cornus sanguinea, **Eriophorum latifolium;** ebenda zw. G. und Adl. Lappenischken: ***Poa sudetica,*** Ulmus effusa. — 23. 6. 85. Dange zw. Gündullen und Megallen: Scirpus pauciflorus,

Botrychium Lunaria, Silene nutans. — 24. 6. 85. Nordermole Memels: Gypsophila paniculata, Centaurea paniculata. Südermole: **Hippophaë rhamnoides.** Kur. Nehrung, Hirschwiese: Lathyrus paluster. In der Ostsee zw. Sandkrug und Schwarzort: **Zostera marina.** — 25. 6. 85. Schwarzorter Strand: **Chimophila umbellata** und Salix livida (Wäldchen). Grikiun: **Carex Pseudo-Cyperus,** C. digitata, Polypodium vulgare. — 26. 6. 85. Zw. Gasthaus Collaten und Paul-Narmund: Geranium pratense. — 27. 6. 85. Gehölz zw. Dt. Crottingen und Patra: Scirpus pauciflorus, Carex fulva, C. dioica. Wald zw. Ilgauden und Kiacken: Serratula tinctoria, Orchis mascula β. speciosa, **Polygonatum verticillatum,** Carex fulva, C. paradoxa. Zw. Gibbischen und der Chaussee: Scirpus pauciflorus, **Listera ovata,** Carex fulva. Zw. Szurlig und Immersatt: **Polygala comosa, Calamagrostis neglecta;** in J.: **Bunias orientalis.** — 29. 6. 85. Gehölz nördlich von Stanz-Schlaudern: Carex fulva, Orchis mascula β. speciosa, **Geranium silvaticum,** Scirpus pauciflorus. — 30. 6. 85. Gehölz zw. Patra und der Nimmersatt'er Chaussee: **Trifolium spadiceum, Carex pulicaris.** Zw. Gut Collaten und Podszeit-Niclau: **Nasturtium barbaraeoides Tausch.** Kiefernwald nördlich vom Collaten'er See: Polypodium vulgare, **Fragaria moschata.** — 1. 7. 85. Zw. Brusdeilinen und Szeipen, Gehölz: Carex fulva, **C. pulicaris.** Zw. Szeipen und Grabben: Trifolium spadiceum, Typha latifolia. — 2. 7. 85. Rechtes Ekitteufer zw. Szabern und Johannishof: Struthiopteris germanica, Actaea spicata, Vicia silvatica, Triticum caninum. Zw. Carallischken und Grünheide: Carex flacca. — 3. 7. 85. Baugskorallener Wald: Carex fulva, C. pulicaris, Rubus suberectus, Trifolium spadiceum, Equisetum hiemale, **Pedicularis Sceptrum Carolinum, Gymnadenia conopea.** Mikaitischkener Wald: die beiden Letzteren und Listera ovata, Hieracium caesium.

5. 7. 85. Umzug nach Plicken. — 6. 7. 85. Packmohrener Wald, südlich der Ekitte: Listera ovata, Scirpus pauciflorus, **Pedicularis Sceptrum Carolinum, Inula salicina,** Ranunculus cassubicus, Orchis incarnata; **Arabis Gerardi** und **Hieracium cymosum** an der Ekitte. Ekitte bis Friedrichsgnade. — 7. 7. 85. Rechtes Ekitteufer zw. Friedrichsgnade und Raddeilen: Cystopteris fragilis, **Polygonatum verticillatum,** Actaea spicata; linkes Ufer: ***Lunaria rediviva*** V[2] Z[3—4], Stellaria Holostea, **Asperula odorata** V[1] Z[2—3]. Gehölz nordwestlich Corallischken: **Pimpinella magna.**

9. 7. 85. Umzug nach Miszeiken. — Zw. Baugskorallen und Dinwethen: Carex flacca. — 10. 7. 85. Zw. Miszeiken und Hennig-Hans: Scirpus pauciflorus. — 11. 7. 85. Miszeikener Wald: Campanula persicifolia var. eriocarpa; Miszeikener Park: Festuca gigantea. Schmeltelle zw. Park und Podszeit-Stankus: Ranunculus divaricatus, Sparganium ramosum. — 13. 7. 85. Dauperner Moor: Aspidium cristatum, **Scheuchzeria palustris,** Rhynchospora alba. Zw. Gr. und Kl. Daupern, Weg südlich der Chaussee: Scirpus pauciflorus, **Carex pulicaris, Gladiolus imbricatus.** Zw. Slapzil und Bajohr-Mitzko: **Gymnadenia conopea** V[1] Z[2—3].

14. 7. 85. Umzug nach Löbarten. — Minge zw. Sudmanten und Dawillen: Fragaria viridis, **Allium Scorodoprasum, Scirpus acicularis, Actaea spicata,** Hieracium caesium, Campanula persicifolia var. eriocarpa, Mercurialis perennis, Lonicera Xylosteum, Cuscuta europaea. — 15. 7. 85. Wald zw. Löbarten und Ilgejahnen: Carex fulva, C. pulicaris, Scirpus pauciflorus. Gehölz von Dautzkurr-Narmund: Epilobium parviflorum. — 16. 7. 85. Minge zw. Szernen und Gedminnen: Fragaria viridis, **Epipactis latifolia** V[1] Z[2], Circaea alpina, **Potamogeton lucens** (in der Minge), Struthio-

pteris germanica (Bach), Thalictrum flavum. Minge zw. Gedminnen und Baiten: Equisetum hiemale, Senecio paludosus. Zw. B. und Griegszen: Scirpus pauciflorus, Carex pulicaris, Eriophorum latifolium. — 17. 7. 85. Schmeltelle zw. Sziluppen und Zenkuhnen: Sparganium ramosum. Gehölz nördlich von Zenkuhnen: Festuca gigantea, Epilobium roseum, Eupatorium cannabinum. Schmeltelle zw. Zenkuhnen und Buddelkehmen: Cornus sanguinea, Viola mirabilis, Triticum caninum, Vicia silvatica. Zw. Gut Dumpen und der Szernen'er Chaussee: Sparganium minimum, Scirpus pauciflorus. — 18. 7. 85. Szernen'er Gutswald: Circaea alpina, **Epilobium tetragonum, Glyceria plicata Fr., Microstylis monophyllos.** Schutzbezirk Szernen, Jag. 141: **Carlina vulgaris.** Zw. Grabszten und Margen: Carex pulicaris, C. dioica; zw. Margen und Sznauksten: Scirpus pauciflorus, Geranium sanguineum. — 19. 7. 85. Szernener Wald, südlich der Chaussee: Verbascum Thapsus, Carlina vulgaris (Jag. 130), Monotropa Hypopitys fr. glabra (Jag. 139), **Potamogeton pusilla** und Chara fragilis, Senecio silvaticus. Linkes Mingeufer westlich des Szernen'er Waldes: Epilobium roseum, **Scirpus compressus,** Chara fragilis. — 20. 7. 85. In Löbarten: Anagallis arvensis. Zw. Dötzken und Jodeischen-Jahn: **Carex Pseudo-Cyperus;** zw. J.-J. und Nausseden-Jacob: Monotropa Hypopitys β. hirsuta. — 21. 7. 85. Zw. Memel und Gr. Tauerlauken: Triticum caninum. In Gr. Szarde: Nepeta Cataria. Schmeltelle in Sudmanten: Potamogeton crispa. Zw. Casparischken und Labatag: Scirpus pauciflorus. — 22. 7. 85. Gehölz südlich von Nausseden-Jacob: Rubus suberectus; zw. Baben und Grambowischken: **Carex pulicaris,** C. fulva, C. dioica, **Gymnadenia conopea, Inula salicina,** Sparganium minimum, Agrostis canina. — 23. 7. 85· Minge zw. Sudmanten und Szernen: Scirpus compressus.

24. 7. 85. Umzug nach Pröculs. — 25. 7. 85. Rechtes Mingeufer zw. Pröculs und Woweriszken: **Nasturtium barbaraeoides Tsch.,** Rubus suberectus, Cuscuta europaea. Linkes Ufer zw. Mingekrug und Gut Pröculs: Geranium silvaticum; ebenda zw. Gut Pröculs und Protniszken: **Libanotis montana,** Nasturtium barbaraeoides. Südlich des Buttken'er Waldes: **Lycopodium inundatum.** Wald, südwestlicher Theil: **Microstylis monophyllos;** östlich des Waldes: **Ranunculus Lingua.** — 26. 7. 85. Tyrusmoor, Jag. 114: Carex Pseudo-Cyperus, Utricularia vulgaris. Luseze, Jag. 71: Rubus plicatus f. umbrosa, Jag. 78: Monotropa Hypopitys. — 27. 7. 85. Jag. 64: Triticum caninum, **Gladiolus imbricatus;** Jag. 63: **Carex riparia;** Jag. 79: Senecio silvaticus; Jag. 86: **Goodyera repens.** — 28. 7. 85. Zw. Bratziszken und der Minge, Bach: Ranunculus Lingua. Zw. Wilkieten und Zillkoten: Lycopodium inundatum V^1 Z^3. — 29. 7. 85. Tyrusmoor, Jag. 113: **Utricularia intermedia,** U. vulgaris. Drawöhne zw. Meyenhof und Stryck: **Alisma arcuatum fr. graminifolium Casp.,** Scirpus maritimus, **Potamogeton lucens.** Szwenzelner Moor: Agrostis canina, Ultricularia vulgaris. — 31. 7. 85. Weiden und Heiden zw. Wilkomeden und Kebbeln: Carex pulicaris, Scirpus pauciflorus, Agrostis canina. Wäldchen der O. F. Klooschen: Libanotis montana, Epipactis latifolia. — 1. 8. 85. Carlsberg, Schmelz. Luseze, Jag. 89: **Linnaea borealis.**

2. 8. 85. Umzug nach Aszpurwen. — 3. 8. 85. Jag. 30: Chimophila umbellata. Jag. 35: Monotropa Hypopitys b. hirsuta. — 4. 8. 85. Jag. 36—38, 40, 42, 44. — 5. 8. 85. Wewirsze zw. Szeppoten und Begeden: Silene nutans, **Thalictrum simplex,** Wiese nördlich von Jag. 18: **Gymnadenia conopea;** Abhang nördlich von Jag. 18: Vicia silvatica, Botrychium Lunaria, Geranium sanguineum. — 6. 8. 85. · Jag. 39 u. 41. — 7. 8. 85. Zw. Szaukeln und Dorf Asz-

purwen: Lolium temulentum. — 8. 8. 85. Wäldchen zw. Paaszkenkrug und Szidellen: Equisetum hiemale. Grabszten, Jurgen. — 10. 8. 85. Jag. 50: Utricularia minor. Zw. Degeln und Szaukeln: **Lycopodium inundatum** V[1] Z[3], Gentiana Amarella. Zw. Sz. und Szilleningken: Scirpus compressus; zw. Aglohnen und Paaszken: **Chara foetida** fr. longibracteata.

11. 8. 85. Umzug nach Heidekrug. — Augstumal'er Torfbruch westlich von Trackseden: Rubus Chamaemorus, Utricularia vulgaris. Linkes Sziesze-Ufer zw. Heidekrug und Werden: Silene tatarica. — 12. 8. 85. Wald zw. Szibben und Grabuppen: Viola arenaria. Rechtes Sziesze-Ufer zw. G. und Werden: Trifolium alpestre, Rubus plicatus.

13. 8. 85. Umzug nach Skirwieth (Kr. Heidekrug). — In Russ an der Pokallna: **Achillea cartilaginea, Cucubalus baccifer.** In Skirwieth: Malachium aquaticum. — 14. 8. 85. Ibenhorst'er Forst, Jag. 39: Orchis latifolia, Carex Pseudo-Cyperus. — 17. 8. 85. In Colonie Bismarck: Elssholzia Patrini.

18. 8. 85. Umzug nach Gr. Tauerlauken. — 19. 8. 85. Nordermole Memels: Campanula rapunculoides. Zw. Bommelsvitte und Leuchtthurm, südlicher Weg: **Helianthemum Chamaecistus**; nördlicher Weg: Allium oleraceum, ***Lepidium latifolium L.*** a. glabrum. Bommelsvitte'scher Kirchhof: **Falcaria Rivini**, Medicago media. — 20. 8. 85. Städt. Plantage, Ostrand südlich des Swiane-Teichs: **Gentiana Pneumonanthe.** Zw. Memel und Gr. Tauerlauken: Gentiana Amarella. — 21. 8. 85. Städt. Plantage, südlicher Theil: Malachium aquaticum. Kaufmännische Plantage, an einem Graben nördlich des Mellneraggen'er Kirchhofs: **Corallorrhiza innata.** Zw. Seebad Försterei und holländ. Mütze: Campanula persicifolia b) eriocarpa; Ostseestrand: Elodea canadensis und **Potamogeton zosterifolia** von der See ausgeworfen. — 22. 8. 85. Dange zw. Luisenhof und Kl. Tauerlauken: **Utricularia intermedia.** — 23. 8. 85. Kur. Nehrung, Haffseite zw. Sandkrug und Hirschwiese: **Trifolium fragiferum**, Festuca arundinacea, Atriplex litorale. Hirschwiese: Rumex maritimus, Scirpus acicularis, Senecio paluster. — 25. 8. 85. Dangewiesen zw. Kl. Tauerlauken und Königswäldchen: Epipactis palustris, **Centaurea austriaca**, Agrostis canina, **Carex limosa.** In Bommelsvitte, Plantagenstrasse: Chenopodium Vulvaria. Gr. Tauerlaukener Bach: **Chaerophyllum aromaticum.** — 26. 8. 85. Dange zw. Gr. Tauerlauken und Purmallen: Cuscuta europaea, Rubus suberectus, **Holcus mollis.** Purmallebach östlich der Chaussee: Nasturtium barbaraeoides. Gündullener Bach: Epilobium parviflorum, Triticum caninum, Mentha sativa.

27. 8. 85. Umzug nach Dt. Crottingen. — In Dt. Crottingen: **Typha angustifolia.** Zw. Adl. Gut Crottingen und Szlaaszen: Fumaria officinalis, Typha latifolia, **Mentha aquatica**, Ranunculus Lingua. — 28. 8. 85. Bahne zw. Gut Szudebarsden und Wittinnen: Astragalus glycyphyllos, Mentha aquatica, Triticum caninum, Allium oleraceum, **Potentilla reptans.** Lappenischke zw. Girngallen und Adl. Lappenischken: **Brachypodium silvaticum, Milium effusum, Circaea lutetiana.** — 29. 8. 85. Zw. Gaussen und Szodeiken-Jacob: Gentiana Amarella, **Nasturtium barbaraeoides**; zw. Altszeiken-Jahn und Patra: Gentiana Amarella. — 31. 8. 85. Zw. Blinden und Karkelbek: Agrostis canina, Gentiana Amarella. Zw. Nimmersatt und Strand: Silene tatarica; in N.: Cuscuta Epithymum. — 1. 9. 85. Zw. Immersatt und Szurlig: ***Alyssum montanum***; zw. Szeipen und Grabben: Nasturtium barbaraeoides. — 2. 9. 85. In Gr.

Tauerlauken: Cystopteris fragilis. — 3. 9. 85. Südermole Memels: Aster Tripolium, Trifolium fragiferum, Scirpus maritimus, Ononis repens, **Salvia verticillata**, Papaver dubium. Dünen südlich des Sandkruges: Malachium aquaticum. Dünen zw. Sandkrug und Schwarzort: Ammophila baltica, Salix daphnoides + repens. — 5. 9. 85. Schwarzorter Wald, Theil nördlich der Försterei: Rubus suberectus, Linnaea borealis, Hieracium caesium, Aspidium spinulosum b) dilatatum. — 6. 9. 85. Schwarzorter Strand, südlich des Rettungsschuppen: Salix daphnoides + repens; zw. Station 22 und 23: **Lathyrus maritimus, Eryngium maritimum.** Haffseite südlich von Dorf Schwarzort: **Peplis Portula.** — 7. 9. 85. Zw. Stanszen und Dt. Crottingen: Cuscuta Epithymum. — 8. 9. 85. Linkes Ekitteufer zw. Friedrichsgnade und Raddeilen: Campanula latifolia, **Brachypodium silvaticum.** Ekitte gegenüber Johannishof: Brachypodium silvaticum. — 9. 9. 85. Zw. Gr. Kurschen und Gaaszen: Gentiana Amarella. — 10. 9. 85. Bebruhne zw. Schule Wallehnen und der Dange: Brachypodium silvaticum. Lappenischke zw. Girngallen und Adl. Lappenischken: **Campanula Cervicaria**, in den beiden südlichen Jagen: **Polygonatum verticillatum.** — 11. 9. 85. Zw. Plicken und Schattern: Gentiana Amarella. — 12. 9. 85. Nach Memel. — 14. 9. 85. Wald zw. Löbarten und Ilgejahnen: **Lycopodium inundatum.** — 15. 9. 85. Rückreise nach Königsberg.

Herr Lehrer Max Grütter in Lnianno erstattet dann

Bericht über seine Exkursionen in der Umgegend von Neuenburg und Lnianno.

20. Juli. **Neuenburg, Hübschmann'sche Schlucht bei Neuthal, Schluchten bei Unterberg und Weide, Sprindt, Belauf Doberau bis zur Ostbahn. Auf einer Mauer an der evangelischen Kirche:** Linaria Cymbalaria Z^2; **an der Fähre:** Potentilla supina; **in der Hübschmann'schen Schlucht:** Libanotis montana Z^3, Cimicifuga foetida, Dianthus deltoides, Chaerophyllum aromaticum; **in der Unterberg'er Schlucht:** Vicia tenuifolia Z^{4-5}, Melampyrum arvense Z^3, Circaea lutetiana Z^3, Daphne Mezereum, Phegopteris Dryopteris Z^2, Epilobium montanum, Ophioglossum vulgatum Z^2; **auf Aeckern zw. Unterberg und Weide:** Alchemilla arvensis, Salsola Kali; **in Weide:** Conium maculatum, Physalis Alkekengi Z^{4-5}; **Schlucht zw. Weide und Sprindt:** Dianthus Armeria Z^2, Hedera Helix, Carex remota; **auf Aeckern daselbst:** Alsine viscosa, Juncus capitatus Z^1; **an einem Tümpel:** Centunculus minimus; **im Belauf Doberau:** Scabiosa Columbaria, Peucedanum Cervaria Z^1, Carex montana Z^3, Lycopodium annotinum; **zwei kleine Tümpel an der Bahn; am nördlichen:** Scheuchzeria palustris, Eriophorum gracile, Salix myrtilloides Z^3; **am südlichen:** Rhynchospora alba, Drosera anglica. — 21. Juli. **Neuenburg, Stadtwald, See in demselben, Bruch nördlich vom See, zurück durch den Stadtwald, Brüche vor demselben. — Zw. Neuenburg und dem Stadtwalde unweit des alten Kirchhofes:** Ophioglossum vulgatum Z^{2-3}, Botrychium Matricariae Z^2, Teesdalea nudicaulis; **im Stadtwalde:** Ervum cassubicum Z^3, Pirola chlorantha, Carex montana (2 Standorte), Carex pilulifera; **am See im Stadtwalde:** Scheuchzeria palustris, Carex limosa, Carex filiformis, Malaxis paludosa Z^3, Salix myrtilloides (mit etwas behaarten Blättern) Z^1; **im Bruch nördlich vom See:** Scheuchzeria palustris, Malaxis paludosa Z^{3-4}, Rhynchospora alba Z^4; **im Stadtwalde:** Lilium Martagon, Carex montana, Thesium ebracteatum, Laserpitium prutenicum, Aquilegia vulgaris, Hypericum montanum; **auf Brüchen vor**

dem Stadtwalde: Juncus supinus b) fluitans, Dianthus deltoides Carex limosa; Ammophila arenaria **auf Sand zw. dem Stadtwalde und Sprindt.** — 22. Juli. **Neuenburg, Ziegelei an der Weichsel, Hundeschlucht, Kozielec, Wessel, Fiedlitz, Münsterwalde, Münsterwald'er Forst, Brüche bei Hartigswalde, Osterwitt, Pienonskowo, Eichstädt, Bochlin, Neuenburg. Bei Neuenburg:** Anthemis Cotula; **Abhänge an der Weichsel zw. der Ziegelei und der Hundeschlucht:** Brachypodium pinnatum, Libanotis montana, Dianthus prolifer, Inula salicina Z^2; **Acker unweit der Hundeschlucht:** Alchemilla arvensis, Euphorbia exigua Z^{3-4}; **in der Hundeschlucht:** Gentiana cruciata Z^{3-5}, Cimicifuga foetida Z^2, Picris hieracioides, Daphne Mezereum, Brachypodium pinnatum, Brachypodium silvaticum Z^{2-3}, Ervum silvaticum, Inula salicina, Digitalis ambigua; **Kozielec'er Wald:** Gentiana cruciata Z^{1-2}, Dianthus deltoides, Epilobium montanum; **im Walde zw. Kozielec und Wessel:** Laserpitium prutenicum, Serratula tinctoria, Peucedanum Cervaria Z^3, Trifolium rubens Z^{2-3}, Microstylis monophyllos Z^3, Prunella grandiflora Z^2, Epipactis rubiginosa; **zw. Wessel und Fiedlitz:** Spiraea Filipendula, Allium fallax, Peucedanum Cervaria, Lathyrus niger, Microstylis monophyllos Z^{1-2}, Pirus torminalis Z^1, Digitalis ambigua; **zw. Fiedlitz und Münsterwalde:** Aquilegia vulgaris; **in der Kämpe:** Rosa rubiginosa, Silene tatarica, Petasites tomentosus, Cucubalus baccifer; **am Weichselabhang südl. von Münsterwalde:** Gentiana cruciata Z^2, Dianthus prolifer; **in Münsterwalde:** Amarantus retroflexus; **in der Münsterwald'er Forst:** Digitalis ambigua, Cimicifuga foetida Z^1, Spiraea Filipendula; **auf Brüchen bei U. F. Hartigswalde:** Carex dioica, Alchemilla vulgaris, Carex paradoxa, Scirpus compressus; **in einem Gehölz zw. Osterwitt und Pienonskowo:** Carlina vulgaris, Leontodon hispidus nebst Leontodon hastilis. — 23. Juli. **Neuenburg, Belauf Doberau, Bruch südlich vom Stadtwaldsee; grosser Bruch bei Doberau; zwei Brüche an der Ostbahn östl. vom Czarne-See; zw. dem Czarne- und Lonk'er See; am Lonk'er See; Belauf Mittelwald, Bruch südlich vom Czarne-See; Bruch südlich vom Lonk'er-See; Kl. Plochotschin; Kl. Warlubien über Sprindt nach Neuenburg. Bruch im Belauf Doberau, rechts vom Wege nach Doberau:** Peplis Portula, Veronica scutellata, Juncus supinus; **im Belauf Doberau:** Lathyrus niger, Peucedanum Cervaria, Anthyllis Vulneraria Z^1, Carex montana; **Bruch südl. vom See im Stadtwalde:** Polystichum cristatum; **Bruch nordwestl. von Doberau:** Carex filiformis, Carex limosa; Rhynchospora alba, Scheuchzeria palustris; Drosera rotundifolia Z^{2-3}, Drosera intermedia V^3 Z^5, Drosera anglica Z^1; Malaxis paludosa Z^1, Salix myrtilloides Z^1, Betula pubescens mit Frucht, Drosera obovata; **zwei Brüche an der Bahn, auf dem südlichen:** Carex limosa, Malaxis paludosa, Carex dioica, Drosera anglica; Scheuchzeria palustris; **in einem Gehölz zwischen dem Czarne- und Lonk'er-See:** Carlina vulgaris; **in einem Erlenbruch am Wege nach Espenhöhe:** Circaea alpina; **am Lonk'er See:** Stellaria glauca, Polygala comosa, Salix nigricans Z^1, Liparis Loeselii Z^1; **im Belauf Mittelwald:** Carex pilulifera, Carex montana; Peucedanum Cervaria; **auf dem Bruch südlich vom Czarne-See:** Radiola linoides, Drosera anglica Z^2; **im Bruch südlich vom Lonk'er See:** Scheuchzeria palustris; Rhynchospora alba; Drosera anglica; Carex limosa, Drosera obovata; Malaxis paludosa, Liparis Loeselii, Carex filiformis; **zw. dem Lonk'er See und Kl. Plochotschin:** Carex pilulifera, Hypochoeris glabra, Ammophila arenaria, Alchemilla arvensis, Teesdalea nudicaulis. — 24. Juli. **Vormittag und Nachmittag bis 4 Uhr Regen. Dann Exkursion nach der Schlucht bei Neuthal.** Rosa tomentosa, Dianthus Armeria Z^2, Seseli annuum, Fragaria collina, Picris hieracioides, Brachypodium pinnatum, Rosa rubiginosa, Melampyrum arvense Z^3,

Carlina vulgaris, Crepis paludosa, Daphne Mezereum, Lonicera Xylosteum, Mercurialis perennis. — 25. Juli. **Neuenburg, Milewo, Milewo'er Wald, Bruch zw. Czarne-See und Sabudownia, Belauf Mittelwald, Rad-See, Schrewin, Südufer des Radsees. Neuenburg an der Hardenberg'er Chaussee:** Verbena officinalis, Cuscuta Epithymum auf Achillea Millefolium und Artemisia campestris; **in Milewo:** Datura Stramonium, Stachys annua Z^{1-2}, Amarantus retroflexus, Conium maculatum; **im Milewo'er Walde:** Carex pilulifera, Pirola chlorantha, Teesdalea nudicaulis; **auf dem Bruch im Milewo'er Walde:** Polystichum cristatum, Carex limosa, Rhynchospora alba, Scheuchzeria palustris; **auf dem Bruch zw. Czarne-See und Sabudownia:** Scheuchzeria palustris, Eriophorum gracile, Senecio paluster; **Belauf Mittelwald:** Gypsophila fastigiata; **bei Espenhöhe:** Galeopsis versicolor; **am Nord-Ufer des Rad-Sees:** Cyperus fuscus; Naias maior (von den Wellen angespülte Zweige am Ufer); **im Walde nördlich von Schrewin:** Prunus Padus, Cytisus, capitatus; **am Südufer des Radsees:** Salix nigricans, Carex distans, Epipactis palustris, Senecio paludosus. **Ein anhaltender, heftiger Regen nöthigt mich zur Rückkehr; auf derselben noch gefunden: im Belauf Mittelwald:** Lathyrus silvester, Digitalis ambigua; **auf dem Lehmwege im Walde:** Chenopodium polyspermum Z^1, Setaria glauca, Hypochoeris glabra. — 27. Juli. **Neuenburg, Konschitz, Unterberg, Weide, Kl. und Gr. Kommorsk, Gr. Sibsau, Ober-Grupp'er Forst, Flötenau, Ellsenau, Nieder-Gruppe, Gr. Lubin, Sanskau, Montau, Treul, Konschitz. Bei Konschitz:** Chenopodium glaucum, Amarantus Blitum, Lactuca Scariola; **bei Unterberg:** Epilobium roseum, Setaria glauca; **bei Weide;** Salsola Kali; **Kl. Kommorsk:** Echinospermum Lappula; **in Gr. Kommorsk:** Chenopodium glaucum, Chenopodium rubrum, Potentilla supina; **zw. Gr. Kommorsk und Gr. Sibsau:** Scabiosa ochroleuca, Erythraea pulchella Z^{1-2}, Scirpus compressus; **in Gr. Sibsau:** Verbena officinalis, Datura Stramonium; **in der Nähe des Drei Mohren-Kruges:** Koeleria glauca; **in der Nähe der Montaubrücke zw. Nieder-Gruppe und Gr. Lubin:** Rumex Hydrolapathum, **in der Montau:** Elodea canadensis, **bei Gr. Lubin in der Kämpe:** Cucubalus baccifer, Reseda Luteola; **bei Vorwerk Sanskau am Weichseldamm:** Sisymbrium Sinapistrum Z^{2-3}, Senecio saracenicus; **in der Kämpe:** Lathyrus paluster, Thalictrum flavum; Achillea cartilaginea; **auf einem Kartoffelacker bei Vorwerk Sanskau:** Chenopodium polyspermum; **am Damm zw. Gr. und Kl. Sanskau:** Stenactis annua, Verbascum Blattaria Z^1; **zw. Kl. Sanskau und Montau:** Reseda Luteola, Silene tatarica; **in Montau unweit des Damm-Kruges:** Conium maculatum; **bei Treul:** Dipsacus silvester; Achillea cartilaginea; **zw. Treul und Konschitz:** Scirpus maritimus. — 28. Juli. **Neuenburg, Nordufer des Doberau'er Sees, Belauf Doberau, Bel. Mittelwald, Bruch am Udschitz-See im Fronza'er Walde, Blissawen, Gr. Wolfsbruch, Südspitze des Montassek-Sees, U. F. Hammer, Heidemühl, Gr. Plochotschin'er Wald, Neuenburg. Am NO. Ufer des Doberau'er Sees:** Botrychium Matricariae Z^{2-3}, Ophioglossum vulgatum Z^4; **am Nordufer desselben:** Drosera anglica Z^2, Cyperus flavescens Z^{2-3}, Centunculus minimus Z^2, Juncus capitatus Z^2; **Belauf Doberau, zw. Jagen 6 und 10:** Lycopodium complanatum; **Belauf Mittelwald:** Gypsophila fastigiata; **auf dem Bruch am Udschitz-See:** Carex dioica; **an einem Graben bei Blissawen:** Cyperus flavescens; Potentilla supina; **auf dem Sphagnetum am Südende des Montussek-Sees:** Carex limosa, Drosera anglica; **im Gr. Plochotschin'er Walde zw. Heidemühl und der Försterei:** Silene tatarica Z^2, Erigeron acer b) droebachiensis, Oxytropis pilosa (auf zwei Stellen Z^1 und Z^2), **östl. von der Försterei:** Digitalis ambigua, Lycopodium complanatum. — 29. Juli. **Anhaltender Regen.** — 30. Juli. **Neuenburg, Sprindt, Südufer** des **Doberau'er Sees, Bel. Doberau, Sawadda, Sawadda-See, Kl. Warlubien, Kl. Plochotschin, Gr. Plochotschin'er Wald, Montau bis Bunkau'er Mühle, Bunkau'er Wald, Warlubien, Sprindt, Neuenburg. Auf feuchtem Sande am Rande der Bülowsheid'er Forst bei Sprindt:** Centunculus minimus, Peplis Portula, Avena caryophyllea, Radiola linoides; **im Belauf Doberau zw. Sprindt und dem See:** Peucedanum Cervaria Z²; **am Südufer des Doberau'er Sees:** Radiola linoides, Avena caryophyllea, Salix aurita + repens, Botrychium Matricariae Z³⁻⁴, Eriophorum gracile, Drosera anglica, Scheuchzeria palustris, Carex limosa; **im Belauf Doberau:** Thalictrum minus, Goodyera repens Z¹⁻², Erigeron acer b) droebachiensis, Gypsophila fastigiata; **östlich von Sawadda in einer jungen Schonung:** Sempervivum soboliferum; **am Sawadda-See:** Senecio viscosus, Salsola Kali, Scirpus compressus; **im Sawadda-See:** Potamogeton pectinata; **an einem Graben bei Kl. Plochotschin:** Carex vesicaria Z³; **auf einem Ackerrande zw. Kl. Plochotschin und dem Walde:** Valerianella dentata, Trifolium fragiferum Z², Setaria glauca; **am Rande des Plochotschin'er Waldes:** Alchemilla arvensis V⁵ Z⁵; **auf einem Torfstich im Pl. Walde:** Carduus nutans V² Z²; **in der Nähe der Montau:** Phegopteris Dryopteris, Hedera Helix; **in der Hagen'er Forst an einem Bache, der zur Montau fliesst:** Agrimonia odorata, Cimicifuga foetida Z³; **an der Montau:** Daphne Mezereum, Phegopteris Dryopteris, Ribes alpinum; **im Bunkau'er Walde am Wege nach Warlubien:** Botrychium rutaceum Z¹⁻², Silene tatarica Z³, Juncus squarrosus; **zw. Warlubien und Sprindt:** Anthyllis Vulneraria. — 31. Juli. **Neuenburg, Konschitz, Montau, Weichseldamm bis Treul, Damm zw. Treul und der Montau, Montau abwärts bis zur Brücke. Zw. Konschitz und der Montau-Brücke:** Cuscuta lupuliformis auf Salix amygdalina und viminalis, Achillea cartilaginea, Polygonum dumetorum, Galeopsis versicolor; **an der Montau bis zum Weichseldamm:** Limosella aquatica, Potentilla supina, Cuscuta lupuliformis, Leersia oryzoides, Chenopodium polyspermum, Acorus Calamus; **in der Montau:** Elodea canadensis; **in der Kämpe:** Euphorbia lucida Z⁵, Thalictrum flavum, Potentilla supina, Petasites officinalis, Senecio saracenicus; **am Weichseldamm:** Reseda Luteola, Erisymum hieraciifolium, Conium maculatum, Campanula sibirica Z¹, Euphorbia lucida; **am Montaudamm:** Silene tatarica, Dipsacus silvester; **auf einem Acker an der Montau unweit der letzten Schleuse:** Lolium temulentum, Silene noctiflora, Linaria minor. — 1. August. **Neuenburg, Kozielec'er Wald, Wessel, Fiedlitz, Münsterwalde, Münsterwald'er Forst bei Wessel. An den bewaldeten Abhängen am Wege von Neuenburg nach Münsterwalde, westl. von Kozielec:** Phleum Boehmeri, Sedum boloniense, Fragaria collina; **im Kozielec'er Walde bis zur Försterei:** Impatiens Noli tangere; **im Walde zw. der Försterei und Gr. Wessel:** Thalictrum minus, Thalictrum aquilegifolium, Digitalis ambigua, Spiraea Filipendula, Serratula tinctoria, Carlina vulgaris, Laserpitium prutenicum, Lathyrus pisiformis Z²⁻³, Prunella grandiflora, Dracocephalum Ruyschiana Z⁴, Trifolium rubens Z¹, Microstylis monophyllos Z³, Epipactis rubiginosa, Daphne Mezereum, Cimicifuga foetida (Blätter), Lathyrus niger, Peucedanum Cervaria; **in Kl. Wessel:** Geranium molle; **zw. Kl. Wessel und Fiedlitz:** Pirola uniflora, Sanicula europaea, Aconitum variegatum (Blätter), Gypsophila fastigiata, Pulmonaria angustifolia, Dianthus deltoides; **zw. Fiedlitz und Münsterwalde:** Aquilegia vulgaris (Blätter), Ervum cassubicum, Lathyrus silvester, Platanthera bifolia; **auf einem Acker am Rande der Münsterwald'er Forst:** Oxalis stricta; **in der Münsterwald'er Forst** zw. **Münsterwalde und Gr. Wessel:** Lycopodium complanatum, Galium verum b) ochroleucum, Daphne Mezereum, Phegopteris Dryopteris, Sanicula europaea, Epipactis rubiginosa, Trollius europaeus, Polygonatum multiflorum. — 3. August. **Abreise nach Lnianno. Nachmittag Exkursion nach dem See zu beiden Seiten der Bahn. Zw. Lnianno und dem See:** Salsola Kali, Lolium remotum, Radiola linoides, Avena praecox, Veronica scutellata b) parmularia, Hypericum humifusum, Juncus squarrosus, Lycopodium inundatum, Gnaphalium luteo-album, Centunculus minimus; **am und auf dem Sphagnetum nördlich von der Bahn:** Peplis Portula, Veronica scutellata b) permularia, Juncus supinus, Scheuchzeria palustris, Rhynchospora alba, Drosera anglica, Drosera intermedia V^3 Z^5, Utricularia minor, Carex limosa, Eriophorum gracile, Lycopodium inundatum, Drosera obovata, Carex filiformis; **am Bahndamm zw. beiden Sphagneten:** Hieracium Auricula, Alchemilla arvensis, Potentilla norvegica, Veronica scutellata b) parmularia, Erigeron acer b) droebachiensis; **auf dem Sphagnetum südlich von der Bahn:** Rhynchospora alba, Scheuchzeria palustris, Drosera intermedia, Drosera anglica, Eriophorum gracile, Andromeda poliifolia, Carex limosa, Lycopodium inundatum, Carex filiformis, Ledum palustre, Utricularia minor und intermedia Z^1; **am Sphagnetum südlich von der Bahn:** Radiola linoides, Juncus squarrosus, Drosera anglica, Lycopodium inundatum, Hydrocotyle vulgaris, Avena praeco5, Drosera intermedia, Juncus Tenageia, Gnaphalium luteo-album, Hypericum humifusum, Peplis Portula; **in Lnianno:** Sisymbrium officinale b) leiocarpum, Oxalis stricta. — 4. August. **Lnianno, See südöstl. von Lnianno, Johannisberg'er Holz, Bialle-Wiese, zurück durch das Johannisberg'er Holz nach Lnianno. Am See südöstl. von Lnianno:** Peplis Portula, Juncus squarrosus, Lycopodium inundatum, Hypericum humifusum, Veronica scutellata b) parmularia, Scirpus setaceus, Centunculus minimus, Gnaphalium luteo-album, Potentilla norvegica; **im Johannisberg'er Holz:** Carlina acaulis, Larix decidua, Luzula sudetica b) pallescens, Botrychium Lunaria, Botrychium rutaceum (je zwei Standorte), Achyrophorus maculatus, Lathyrus silvester, Carlina vulgaris, Pulmonaria angustifolia, Leontodon hastilis nebst L. hispidus, Carlina acaulis b) caulescens, Orchis maculata, Erigeron acer b) droebachiensis; **auf der Bialle-Wiese:** Equisetum silvaticum, Salix aurita + repens, Salix depressa, Epipactis palustris, Crepis succisifolia, Saxifraga Hirculus, Carex paradoxa; in einem Birkenbruch: Betula humilis; **auf dem Rückwege im Johannisberg'er Holz:** Dianthus arenarius, Carex pilulifera, Euphorbia Cyparissias, Carlina acaulis. — 5. August. **Lnianno, Stenzlau, Wiesen am Mukrz-Fliess, Belauf Rehhof, Bieszewo- und Czarnowo-See, Cisbusch, Wiese zw. Cisbusch und dem Ebensee, Hutta, Eichwald, Lnianno. Auf Aeckern zw. Lnianno und Stenzlau:** Setaria glauca, Arnoseris pusilla; **auf einer Wiese:** Hieracium Auricula; **auf Wiesen am Mukrz-Fliess:** Vaccinium uliginosum, Juncus squarrosus, Equisetum silvaticum, Rumex Hydrolapathum, Alectorolophus minor, Hypericum humifusum; **in einem Gebüsch am Mukrz-Fliess:** Serratula tinctoria, Hieracium boreale; **auf einem Bruch im Belauf Rehhof:** Radiola linoides, Hydrocotyle vulgaris, Veronica sentellata b) parmularia, Potentilla norvegica Z^1, Peplis Portula; **im Belauf Rehhof:** Carlina acaulis, Lycopodium complanatum; **am Bieszewo-See:** Drosera anglice, Andromeda poliifolia, Carex limosa, Utricularia minor, Hydrocotyle vulgaris; **am Czarnowo-See:** Inula salicina Z^5 (auf einer Wiese), Drosera anglica, Carex limosa, Ledum palustre; **auf einem Leinacker östl. v. Mukrz:** Lolium remotum;

auf einem anderen bei Eibenhorst: Camelina dentata; **im Cisbusch:** Stellaria nemorum, Crepis paludosa, Milium effusum, Taxus baccata, Phegopteris Dryopteris, Circaea alpina, Euonymus verrucosus, Asperula odorata; **auf Wiesen zw. Cisbusch und dem Ebensee:** Epipactis palustris, Polygala comosa, Saxifraga Hirculus, Alectorolophus minor, Betula humilis, Carex vesicaria, Succisa pratensis; **auf einem Acker unweit des Hutta'er Kirchhofes:** Alchemilla arvensis, Alsine viscosa, Setaria glauca; **am Kirchhof von Hutta:** Sempervivum soboliferum, Sarothamnus scoparius; **bei Eichwald:** Chondrilla iuncea; Hypericum humifusum. — 6. August. **Lnianno, Bahndamm bis Mukrz-Fliess, Wiesen am Mukrz-Fliess; im Belauf Rehhof an der Bahn, Czarnowo-See, Mukrz, Mukrz-See, Cisbusch, Wiesen südl. vom Cisbusch; Hutta, Andreasthal, Lnianno. Am Bahndamm:** Dianthus arenarius, Hypochoeris glabra, Potentilla collina, Radiola linoides, Arnoseris pusilla, Avena caryophyllea, Hypericum humifusum, Juncus squarrosus, Gypsophila fastigiata, Ervum hirsutum, Carlina acaulis; **auf den Wiesen am Mukrz-Fliess:** Sanguisorba officinalis, Veronica scutellata b) parmularia, Potentilla digitato-flabellata, Salix aurita + repens, Epipactis palustris; **im Belauf Rehhof in der Nähe des Mukrz-Fliess:** Orchis maculata, Hypericum quadrangulum, Alectorolophus minor, Epipactis palustris, Dracocephalum thymiflorum, Hypericum humifusum, Potentilla procumbens; **auf Wiesen zw. Mukrz-Fliess und Czarnowo-See:** Carex dioica, Serratula tinctoria; **am Czarnowo-See:** Scheuchzeria palustris; **im Bel. Lindenbusch zw. Czarnowo-See und Mukrz:** Hedera Helix, Lycopodium Selago, Quercus sessiliflora; **in Mukrz:** Malva neglecta; **am Mukrz-See:** Cyperus fuscus, Chenopodium rubrum; **auf Aeckern am Westufer des Mukrz-See:** Camelina dentata, Lolium remotum, Centunculus minimus, Juncus capitatus, Radiola linoides, Myosurus, minimus, Alsine viscosa, Alectorolophus minor; **auf Wiesen westl. vom Cisbusch:** Betula humilis; **im Cisbusch:** Hedera Helix, Melica uniflora Z[4], Brachypodium silvaticum; **auf Brüchen südlich vom Cisbusch:** Listera ovata, Salix livida, Gymnadenia, conopea (2 Standorte), Pedicularis Sceptrum Carolinum, Potentilla collina. — 7. August. **Kleiner See südl. von Lnianno, See südl. vom Bahnhof, Andreasthal, Gehölz westl. von Wentfin. Darauf Regen. Am Seechen südl. von Lnianno:** Potentilla norvegica, Lycopodium inundatum Z[3], Drosera anglica, Drosera intermedia, Scirpus setaceus Z[3], Juncus Tenageia Z[2-3], Veronica scutellata b) parmularia, Centunculus minimus, Rhynchospora alba Z[2]; **am See südl. vom Bahnhof:** Hydrocotyle vulgaris, Potentilla norvegica, Gnaphalium luteo-album, Juncus Tenageia, Juncus capitatus, Veronica scutellata b) parmularia; **auf dem Sphagnetum des Sees:** Lycopodium inundatum, Drosera obovata Z[2], Rhynchospora alba, Ledum palustre; **auf Aeckern zw. dem See und Andreasthal:** Centunculus minimus, Hypericum humifusum, Arnoseris, pusilla, Hieracium Auricula, Hypochoeris glabra, Juncus capitatus, Medicago lupulina a) genuina, Polycnemum arvense unter Ornithopus sativus, Alsine viscosa; **auf Aeckern zw. Andreasthal und Wentfin:** Alsine viscosa, Juncus capitatus, Setaria glauca, Alchemilla arvensis; **auf einem kleinen Bruch:** Scheuchzeria palustris; Rhynchospora alba; **an demselben:** Hydrocotyle vulgaris; **am Wege vom Bruch nach dem Gehölz:** Avena caryophyllea; **auf den Brüchen am Gehölz:** Lycopodium inundatum, Vaccinium uliginosum, Carex vesicaria; **im Gehölz:** Lathyrus silvester, Salix Caprea, Carlina acaulis; Drosera anglica **auf einem kleinen Bruch zw. dem Gehölz und Wentfin.** — 8. August. **Lnianno, Sternbach, Rischkefliess bis Rischke, Marienfelde, See-**

nördl. von Lnianno. In Lnianno: Malva rotundifolia und Malva neglecta; **auf Aeckern zw. Lnianno und Sternbach:** Potentilla collina, Centunculus minimus, Scirpus setaceus Z^1, Juncus capitatus Z^{2-3}; **bei Sternbach:** Viscum album auf Populus monilifera, Sinapis alba (verwildert), Sinapis arvensis (einziger Standort), Amarantus retroflexus; **im Gutsgarten:** Dianthus deltoides, Amarantus Blitum, Oxalis stricta; **an einem Tümpel zw. Sternbach und Rischke:** Carex vesicaria, Hypericum humifusum; **am Rischke-Fliess:** Epilobium roseum, Carex flava, Selinum Carvifolia, Leersia oryzoides, Hypericum montanum, Rumex maximus, Rumex Hydrolapathum, Lactuca muralis, Rumex aquaticus; **am Abhange am Fliess:** Elymus arenarius auf zwei Stellen Z^{1-2} und Z^4; **an einem Graben zw. Rischke und Marienfelde:** Carlina vulgaris 0,60—0,80 m hoch, (vielköpfig, 1 Exemplar mit 12 Köpfen), Hieracium Auricula, Hieracium laevigatum, Potentilla norvegica Z^{1-3}, Potentilla procumbens; **am Marienfeld'er See:** Carex vesicaria, Potentilla mixta, Potentilla collina; **in Marienfelde:** Chenopodium polyspermum, Sisymbrium officinale (verum! im Gebiete sehr selten); **zw. Marienfelde und Lnianno:** Onopordon Acanthium, Avena caryophyllea, Erythraea pulchella, Carlina acaulis, Thesium ebracteatum, Scorzonera humilis, Alectorolophus minor, Juncus squarrosus, Centunculus minimus, Alsine viscosa; **am See nördl. von Lnianno:** Hieracium Auricula, Limosella aquatica, Cyperus fuscus, Scirpus lacustris, Scirpus Tabernaemontani, Potentilla supina, Galium Mollugo b) ochroleucum. Auf meinen Frühjahrsexkursionen fand ich **bei Laskowitz in einem kleinen Birkengehölz:** Ulex europaeus, Sambucus racemosa; **am Schwarzwasser zw. U. F. Grüneck und Ottersteig:** Crepis praemorsa, Polystichum spinulosum b) dilatatum, Triticum caninum; **im Cisbusch:** Lathraea Squamaria, Taxus baccata, Euonymus verrucosus, Phegopteris Dryopteris; **im Forstrevier Lindenbusch, Bel. Grünhof:** Sanicula europaea, Silene infracta; im Sommer **im Bel. Rehhof:** Pirola media; **in der Charlottenthal'er Forst bei Bremin:** Gymnadenia conopea. — Sehr interessant waren die Exkursionen, die ich im Spätsommer unternahm. Auf diesen fand ich am 12. August. **Am Rischke-Fliess:** Rubus nemorosus; **im Fliess:** Potamogeton pectinata; **in der Sternbach'er Forst:** Carex montana, Geranium molle. — 19. August. **Gatzki:** Chenopodium urbicum, Alsine viscosa. — 20. August. **Am Bahndamm bei Falkenhorst:** Rudbeckia hirta; **am Fliess zw. Falkenhorst u. Dritschmin:** Mimulus luteus, Trifolium fragiferum; **auf Aeckern bei Dritschmin:** Polycnemum arvense, Avena strigosa; **in Dritschmin:** Stachys annua, Verbena officinalis, Pulicaria vulgaris, Chenopodium urbicum, Elscholzia Patrini; **auf dem Torfstich westl. von Falkenhorst:** Hieracium pratense + Pilosella. — 23. August. **Bei Marienthal:** Lycopodium inundatum; **auf einer Wiese bei Stenzlau:** Polygonum Bistorta (aus der Aehre kommen viele ziemlich langgestielte, kleinere Aehren). — 26. August. **Am Ebensee:** Cirsium acaule, Rubus nemorosus; **im Ebensee:** Potamogeton curvifolia, Potamogeton pectinata, P. perfoliata. **Blondźminer See:** Lycopodium inundatum, Rubus nemorosus, Carlina vulgaris; **auf den Sumpfwiesen westlich vom Ebensee:** Gentiana Cruciata (leider waren die Wiesen kurz vorher gemäht); **auf Aeckern am Ebensee:** Centunculus minimus. — 29. August. **Am See südl. von Lnianno an der Bahn:** Cyperus flavescens (auf zwei Stellen); **am See auf der Nordseite der Bahn:** Cyperus fuscus. — 30. August. **Am Bach zw. Neuhaus und Rischke'r Wiese:** Lycopodium Selago, Epilobium tetragonum; **auf der Rischke'r Wiese:** Saxifraga Hirculus, Leersia oryzoides, Hieracium pratense;

Abhänge am Pruski-Fliess zw. Rischke'r Wiese und Wiersch: Phegopteris polypodioides, Cystopteris fragilis, Viola mirabilis, Actaea spicata, Cimicifuga foetida, Polypodium vulgare, Epilobium roseum; **am Hammer-Fliess zw. Hammer und Lischin:** Lycopodium inundatum, Rubus nemorosus; **auf Aeckern bei Lischin:** Linaria arvensis. — 31. August. **Auf dem grossen Bruch zw. Lnianno und Schiroslaw:** Salix myrtilloides, Sal. myrt. + repens, Utricularia minor, Utricularia intermedia, Scheuchzeria palustris, Rhynchospora alba, Carex limosa, Potamogeton graminea nebst f. heterophylla (beide blühend); **am Südrande des Bruches:** Potentilla procumbens; **auf einem Acker nördl. vom Bruch:** Senecio viscosus; **in Schiroslaw:** Marrubium vulgare, Pulicaria vulgaris, Stachys arvensis, Nepeta Cataria; **in Falkenhorst:** Marrubium vulgare. — 2. September. **Bei Eichdorf:** Botrychium Matricariae. — 3. September. **In Wentfin:** Chenopodium urbicum, Pulicaria vulgaris; **auf einem Bruch zw. Lnianno und Wentfin:** Scheuchzeria palustris, Carex limosa, Trifolium fragiferum. — 5. September. **Mehrere kleine Brüche am Wege nach Schiroslaw:** Salix myrtilloides, Lycopodium inundatum, Scheuchzeria palustris, Gnaphalium luteo-album, Potentilla norvegica, Cyperus fuscus, Carex filiformis, Juncus Tenageia, Rhynchospora alba; **auf einer Sumpfwiese nordöstl. von Marienfelde:** Saxifraga Hirculus, Epipactis palustris; **an einem Tümpel unweit Schiroslaw:** Potentilla procumbens, Gnaphalium luteo-album. — 9. September. **Brüche zw. Dritschmin und Falkenhorst, südl. von der Bahn:** Potentilla norvegica, Potentilla procumbens, Juncus Tenageia, Juncus supinus, Gnaphal. luteo-album. — 10. September. **Am See südöstl. von Lnianno:** Cyperus flavescens; **auf Wiesen zw. Abbau Lnianno und Wentfin:** Hieracium Auricula, Cirsium acaule nebst f. caulescens, Erythraea pulchella, Trifolium fragiferum; **auf Aeckern bei Abbau Wentfin:** Linaria minor, Silene noctiflora. — 11. September. **An einem feuchten Platze am Wege v. Lnianno nach Wentfin:** Veronica scutellata b) parmularia; **zwei Tümpel bei Abbau Wentfin:** Hydrocotyle vulgaris, Juncus capitatus, Centunculus minimus, an beiden: Cyperus flavescens; **am Nordrande des Berges zw. Siemkau und Jesiorken:** Cirsium acaule nebst b) caulescens, Gentiana Amarella; **Wiese bei Hintersee:** Gentiana Amarella, Cirsium acaule (1 Exemplar caulescens); **auf Aeckern zw. Hintersee und Andreasthal:** Centunculus minimus; **auf Heiden:** Lycopodium inundatum, Hydrocotyle vulgaris, Botrychium Matricariae.

Nachträglich die Mittheilung, dass ich am 7. Juli 1885 bei Bahnhof Lnianno ***Lepidium micranthum*** Ledeb. var. apetalum, offenbar durch den Eisenbahnverkehr aus Russland eingeschleppt, fand.

Es wird eine ³/₄ stündige Pause fürs Frühstück um 12¹/₂ Uhr gemacht.

Nach Wiedereröffnung der Sitzung theilt der Vorsitzende den Bericht über die Kasse mit, welche die Herren Professor Dr. Lentz und Apotheker Mielentz geprüft haben.

Königsberg, den 3. October 1885.

„In der dreiundzwanzigsten Versammlung des preussischen botanischen Vereins zu Memel am 7. October 1884 wurden zu Prüfern der Kasse des botanischen Vereins erwählt Apothekenbesitzer Mielentz und Prof. Spirgatis. In Vertretung des letzteren hatte Prof. Dr. Lentz die Güte das Amt zu übernehmen. Gedachte Herren fanden sich am 3. October 1885 bei dem Schatzmeister Herrn Apothekenbesitzer Schuessler ein und fanden bei der Revision folgendes Resultat vor:

Nach Einsicht des Kassenbuches betrug

die Einnahme	2 919 Mk.	26 Pf.
die Ausgabe	2 429 „	85 „
Bestand	489 Mk.	41 Pf.

Dieser Bestand von 489 Mk. 41 Pf. wurde richtig vorgefunden.

Die laut Kassenabschluss vom 30. September 1884 nachgewiesenen 4 proc. Ostpreuss. Pfandbriefe im Betrage von . . . . 11 725 Mk.
und die im Laufe des Jahres 1885 angekauften 4 proc. Pfandbriefe No. 10 836 über 1000 Mk. . . . . 1 000 „

12 725 Mk.

zwölftausend siebenhundert fünfundzwanzig Mark waren ebenfalls vorhanden; ebenso auch die zugehörigen Coupons.

Lentz. Mielentz."

Auf diesen Bericht hin wird die Kasse von der Versammlung für richtig geführt erklärt. Zu Prüfern der Kasse werden fürs nächste Jahr die Herren Apotheker Packheiser und Eichert erwählt.

Für Abhaltung der nächsten Versammlung sind Einladungen von Sensburg und Insterburg eingegangen; der letzteren Stadt wird der bequemeren Lage wegen der Vorzug gegeben.

Es wird dann beschlossen die muthmasslich für 1886 dem Verein zur Verfügung stehenden 1 200 Mk. zu verwenden 1) zur Untersuchung des Kreises Strassburg, 2) des Kreises Ortelsburg, 3) zur Erforschung mangelhaft bekannter Stellen der Kreise Kartaus und Berent.

Der bisherige Vorstand wird durch Acclamation wieder gewählt.

Herr Professor Dr. Prätorius legt dann folgende für den Kreis Konitz neue oder seltene Pflanzen vor und vertheilt sie an die Anwesenden:

Lobelia Dortmanna L. Kl. Barsch-See. 30. 8. 85. Neu für Konitz. — **Gagea arvensis** Schult. Auf dem Acker des Besitzers Sengers hinter dem Pulverhause unweit des Schind-Angers in grosser Menge. 28. 4. 85. — **Malva borealis** Wallman, (M. rotundifolia L.). Im Dorfe Schlagenthin in Menge 12. 8. 85. Sonst ist hier statt derselben als Strassenunkraut nur Malva neglecta Wallr. — **Mentha silvestris** L. Neuer Standort an den Quellen hinter dem Schützenhause. 25. 8. 85. — **Mentha silvestris** L. v. nemorosa Willd. Walkmühl 26. 7. 85. Ebenfalls neuer Standort. — **Botrychium rutaefolium** A. Br. Exercierplatz 19. 6. 85. Am 7. Juli 1885 ist dieser bisher brachgelegene Platz umgepflügt worden. — **Botrychium matricoriaefolium** A. Br. wie vorige. — **Botrychium Lunaria** Sw. In ungeheurer Menge an der Schanze des Exercierplatzes. 19. 6. 85. — **Alectorolophus minor.** W. und Grab. Auf dem Exercierplatze neben der Chaussee. Neuer Standort. 19. 6. 85. — **Pedicularis silvatica** L. Kl. Barsch-See. 30. 8. 85. — **Erythraea Centaurium** Pers. Gr. Barsch-See. 30. 8. 85. — **Erythraea Centaurium** aus Abrau weissblühend, an derselben Stelle Jahr für Jahr. 25. 7. 85. — **Carlina acaulis** L. Königl. Wald bei Ragnitz. 30. 8. 85. Neuer Standort. — **Sweertia perennis** L. Abrau. 12. 8. 85. — **Tofieldia calyculata** Whlnb. Abrau. 25. 7. 85 und 12. 8. 85. — **Epilobium palustre** L. Abrau. 12. 8. 85. **Lysimachia vulgaris** L. sehr weichhaarig. Chausseeböschung im Walde bei Buschmühl. 30. 8. 85. — **Linnaea borealis** L. Der alte Standort hinter Kathrinchenkrug an der Chaussee. Blühend. 5. 7. 85. — **Lycopodium complanatum** L. Gr. Barsch-See. 30. 8. 85. — **Pulsatilla patens** Mill. 19. 4. 85. Stadtwald bei Buschmühl. — **P. vernalis** Mill. Wie vorige. — **Asclepias Vincetoxicum** L. Zweite Insel im Müskendorf'er See. 20. 6. 85. — **Veronica longifolia** L. Zweite Insel im Müskendorf'er See. 20. 6. 85. — **Veronica latifolia** L. Erste Insel im Müskendorf'er See. 20. 6. 85. — **Cornus alba** L. Zweite Insel im Müskendorf'er See. 20. 6. 85. — **Salix pentandra** L. Zweite Insel im Müskendorf'er See. 20. 6. 85. — **Salix daphnoides** Vill. Wie vorige. — **Arabis hirsuta** Scp. Zweite Insel im Müskendorf'er See. 20. 6. 85. — **Hieracium praemorsum** L. Erste Insel im Müskendorf'er See. 20. 6. 85. — **Dianthus superbus** L. Abrau und Walkmühl. 25 7. 85. — **Dianthus deltoides** L. Abrau-Schlagenthin. 25. 7. 85. — **Centaurea austriaca** Willd. Abrau. 25. 7. 85. — **Gymnadenia conopea** R. Br. Abrau. 25. 7. 85. — **Epipactis palustris** Cratz. Abrau. 25. 7. 85. — **Saxifraga Hirculus** L. Abrau. 25. 7. 85. — **Astragalus Cicer** L. Abrau. 25. 7. 85. — **Hypericum quadrangulum** L. Abrau. 25. 7. 85. — **Betonica officinalis** L. mit zwei Blüthenähren. Abrau. 25. 7. 85. — **Cardamine amara** L. violett in Menge in einem Graben unweit des Schützenhauses. 22. 5. 85. — **Iris germanica** L. viertheilig. 19. 6. 84. In meinem Garten. — **Cineraria hybrida** W. Topfpflanze. Blüthe durchwachsen. 31. 3. 85. — **Pirus malus** L. aus meiner Baumschule mit fiedertheiligen Blättern, maulbeerähnlich. Sommer 1885.

Professor Prätorius legt von Herrn Gymnasiallehrer Zielinski-Konitz blühende Lobelia Dortmanna L. aus dem Kl. Barsch-See, Kr. Schlochau, 21. 7. 85, vor.

Herr Kantor Grabowski-Marienburg vertheilte Achillea cartilaginea und Amarantus retroflexus und zeigt ein bei Marienburg gefundenes Exemplar von Verbascum Blattaria vor.

Herr Lehrer Peil-Sackrau vertheilt folgende im Kreise Graudenz gesammelte Pflanzen: I. Aus der **Jammi'er Forst:** Asperula odorata. Bltr. v. unten nach oben zu 5, 6, 8 bis 10 in Wirteln. Myriophyllum verticillatum. Stellaria uliginosa. Carex montana. C. digitata. C. canescens. Polypodium vulgare. Spergula Morisonii. Viola palustris. Neottia Nidus avis. Lycopodium annotinum. L. clavatum. Phegopteris Dryopteris. Impatiens Noli tangere mit cleistogamen Blüthen. Circaea alpina. Milium effusum. Festuca heterophylla Haenke. Euphrasia officinalis c.) nemorosa. Mit blauen Blüthen. — II. Zwischen **Orle und Mühle Slupp:** Myosotis silvatica. Viola silvestris. — III. An der **Ossa bei Mühle Slupp:** Mercurialis perennis. Saxifraga granulata. Corydalis cava. Adoxa Moschatellina. Mit Puccinia Adoxae DC. auf den Blättern. — IV. Bei **Klodtken:** Euphorbia Cyparissias. Corydalis intermedia. — V. In und bei **Festung Graudenz:** Linaria Cymbalaria. Asplenium Ruta muraria. Ceterach officinarum. Picris hieracioides. Salvia verticillata. — VI. Bei **Parsken,** in der Weichselkämpe: Hierochloa odorata. — VII. Im **Burg Belchau'er** Walde: Paris quadrifolius. Mit 3 bis 6 Blättern. Primula officinalis. Mit 2, 3, 15, 16, 18, 19 bis 25 Blüthen. Lathyrus vernus Bernh. Mit 1 bis 2 Blüthen. Erigeron acer. Ueber 70 cm lang. — VIII. Im Dorfe **Sackrau.** Auf Aeckern und an Wegen. Veronica persica. Chaiturus Marrubiastrum. Barbaraea stricta, mit Blüthen und Früchten. Verbena officinalis. Ebenso. Chenopodium urbicum. — IX. Auf den **Bingsbergen,** zwischen **Sackrau** und **Wolz.** Mycrostylis mophyllos. Gymnadenia conopea. Oxytropis pilosa. Orobanche Galii. Darunter auch sehr reichblüthige Pflanzen, mit mehr als 20 Blüthen. **Orobanche coerulescens.** Campanula sibirica. Verbascum nigrum. Lithospermum officinale. Chimophila umbellata. Erysimum hieraciifol. Trifolium rubens. Pirola minor.

Probst Preuschoff-Tolkemit vertheilt und bespricht folgende Pflanzen aus der Umgebung von Tolkemit, Kreises Elbing: „**Pleurospermum austriacum**, in Schluchten und auf buschigen Hügeln bei Tolkemit. — Centaurea austriaca, Lehmberg bei Tolkemit, zahlreich. — **Rubus pyramidalis**, Kaltenbach (villicaulis. Köhler), buschreiche Schlucht bei Neuendorf. — Rubus saxatilis. — Aconitum variegatum, an einem Bach. — Stachys annua, Pfefferberge bei Tolkemit. — **Saxifraga tridactylites**, Kleeacker am Wege nach der alten Burg. — **Galium aristatum**, häufig in Gebüschen. — Vicia cassubica, auf buschigen Hügeln zahlreich. — Kakile maritima und Diplotaxis muralis, am Haff. — Corydalis solida, in Gärten häufig. — Corydalis cava, an einem Bache. — Holosteum umbellatum, auf Aeckern. — Circaea lutetiana, Kadinen im Walde, massenhaft. — Bromus racemosus, Haffwiesen bei Steinort. — Brachypodium silvaticum, unter Gebüschen zahlreich. — Luzula albida, bei Kadinen, Panklau in Wäldern, reichlich. — **Struthiopteris germanica**, längs des Mühlenbachs, häufig. — Equisetum pratense, Tolkemit, sehr verbreitet. — Aus andern Kreisen: Bromus sterilis, Buchwalde Kr. Pr. Holland, an der Kanal-Böschung. — Fontinalis antipyretica, die Form aus stehendem und die aus fluthendem Wasser, erstere Halbstadt, Kr. Marienburg, letztere Waldbach bei Buchwalde. — Amblystegium riparium, Torftümpel bei Rehhof, Kr. Stuhm. — **Bromus asper**, Waldrand bei Revier Rachelshof, Kr. Stuhm. 16. 7. 84. — Derselbe zeigte noch zwei Missbildungen vor: Glyceria spectabilis, an deren Rispe fast alle Aehrchen zu Blattschösslingen ausgewachsen sind; und einen fasciirten Blüthenstengel von Hesperis matronalis."

Hierauf vertheilte Dr. Abromeit seine im Kreise Neustadt 1883 gesammelten Pflanzen, die auf der Fahrt zwischen Königsberg und Marienburg Behufs Besuch der Versammlung des preuss. botan. Vereins verloren, von Dr. Lange später in den Händen eines Eisenbahnbeamten in Danzig durch Zufall entdeckt, durch Apotheker Dr. von der Lippe-Danzig dem Eisenbahnbeamten abgekauft und dem Vorsitzenden des Vereins zur Verfügung gestellt waren. Nähere Angaben über diese Pflanzen sind im Bericht über die Marienburg'er Versammlung von 1883 enthalten. Von neuen Standorten aus der Umgebung von Gumbinnen werden von Dr. Abromeit vertheilt: **Equisetum variegatum** Schleich (neu für Ostpreussen), Agrimonia pilosa, Asperula Aparine, Stachys arvensis.

Dr. Abromeit vertheilt ferner im Namen des abwesenden Dr. Bethke Rumex ucranicus und Salix daphnoides + repens.

Cand. Richard Schultz: **Broesk'er Feldmark:** Oxalis stricta, Myosotis hispida, Agrimonia odorata, Melampyrum arvense, Euphorbia Esula, Utricularia vulgaris, Helichrysum arenarium, Gagea arvensis, Cynoglossum officinale (selten), Anthyllis Vulneraria (eingeschleppt), Spiraea salicifolia, Ranunculus arvensis, Centaurea Scabiosa, Veronica longifolia (1 Exemplar), Eryngium planum, Coronilla varia, Achillea cartilaginea, Thalictrum flavum, Sparganium simplex. Salvinia natans (in der Vorfluth zw. Neunhuben und Ladekopp.) — **Am Weichseldamm bei Schoeneberg, Kr. Marienburg:** Saponaria officinalis (gefüllt), Eryngium planum. — Wald bei **Faule-Lake bei Pasewark,**

Kr. Danzig: Aspidium spinulosum, Polypodium Dryopteris, Hydrocotyle vulgaris, Goodyera repens, Polypodium vulgare, Anthyllis Vulneraria (Seestrand), Cakile maritima, Linaria odora.

Professor Caspary berichtet dann über seine eigenen Exkursionen. Den 21. Mai 1885 untersuchte der Vorsitzende den Karpionki und Wooksee bei Wahlendorf von Bukowin aus um die Frühjahrszustände von Isoëtes lac. u. echinospora kennen zu lernen. Vom 23. Mai bis 30. Mai erforschte er die Gegend westlich, nord- und südwestlich von Barlomin, Kreis Neustadt, wo er der Gastfreundschaft des Herrn von Zelewski-Barlomin sich erfreute. Abgesehen von Pflanzen dieser Gegend, die schon von Abromeit, Lange und Lemcke daselbst gefunden waren, sind zu erwähnen: Viscum album auf einer Salix alba im Garten von Barlomin, **Polyporus hispidus** auf einer Rothbuche im Park von Barlomin, Myosotis hispida Thal der Leba oberhalb Paraschin, Corydalis intermedia im Thal der Gossentin, nördlich von Smasin und der Leba zwischen Niederlowitz und Paraschin, auch im Park von Barlomin; **Botrychium ramosum Aschers.** Wegseite nördlich von Leba, und in Menge auf einem Hügel im Wiesenthal Südost von Wischetzin; **Melampyrum silvaticum** Thal der Gossentin, Feldmark Barlomin, unter Gebüsch von Carpinus Betulus; Lycopodium Selago, Wald von Schloss Platen; Struthiopteris germanica; beginnt im südlichsten Punkt des Gebiets von Barlomin im Thal der Gossentin und geht bis Barlomin'er Mühle; stellenweise in grösster Fülle. Der Vorsitzende erstattet dann

Bericht über die Untersuchung vieler Seen der Kreise Berent, Konitz und Kartaus 1885 ausgeführt.

Den 19. Juli fuhr ich über Pr. Stargard, wo ich mit Herrn Sievert und Steinbrück die Vorbereitung der heutigen Versammlung besprach nach Hochstüblau, wo ich bei Herrn Apotheker Settmacher Aufnahme fand. Auf dem Bahnhof in Pr. Stargardt: **Salvia verticillata**, die eine immer grössere Verbreitung mittelst der Eisenbahnen in unsern Gegenden erlangt. — 20. Juli. Tümpel an der Chaussee Hochstüblau-Struga bei Stein 29 und 27,5. Frauensee zu Gora gehörig: **Myriophyllum alternifl.**, Schnapsee (Horczalka) zwischen dem See Wichol und Frauensee: Scirpus Tabern.; Wichol: Scirp. Tabern. — 20. Juli. See Vielle bei Gora: Glyceria nemoralis und plicata, Westufer; Czisien-See, Teich von Dobrik, See Czerwonnak. — 22. Juli. Thesium ebracteatum Chaussee Berent-Hochstüblau zwischen Stein 30,2 und 30,3. See Prczedgorsz (Gastsee) bei Gora: **Callitriche autumnalis, Myriophyllum alterniflor.**, *Alisma natans* Z^4 V^1, östlichster Fundort dieser Pflanze, soweit bisher bekannt; Fersensee, südwest. von der Kirche in Pogutken: Myriophyll. vertic.; See Stafke und Staruch. — 23. 7. Westlichster Tümpel bei Kl. Pallubin; Tümpel dicht am Wege zw. Neuhof und Gora. Die 3 Torfseen im Belauf Weissbruch: Melonken-See, Runder See, Langer See. See von Decka: **Litorella lacustris, Isoëtes lacustris** vulgaris und leiospora elatior subpatula und patula. Nacht in Decka bei Herrn Engler. — 24. 7. 85. See Lonke: **Myrioph. altern.**; Strehsau'er See: **Nuphar pumilum, Nuphar** luteum + pumilum, **Potamogeton crispa + praelonga** wenig, vor Jahren darin häufiger; See Gebrowo bei Gladau. — 25. 7. Der Lange See bei Kleschkau: **Nitella opaca, Myriophyll. alternifl., Potamogeton crispa + praelonga**; vergebens nach der im See 1884 von Dr. Lange entdeckten Isoët. lac. gesucht, fortgesetzt durch sehr heftigen Wind gestört; **Ranunculus reptans** am Ufer und bis 1½ Fuss Wassertiefe. Rokitke-See: **Myriophyll. altern.**; See Modscharlo: **Myriophyll. altern.**, Chara fragilis. — 27. 7. Gladau'er See; See von Alt-Fietz, von Schadrau, Schadrau'er Torfsee, östlich vom Dorf. Nacht in Decka. — 28. 7. Schwarzer See in Gr. Boschpot; See von Neu-Englers-Hütte; See von Wulfen: **Myriophyll. altern.** — 29. 7. Noch einmal den Langen See bei Kleschkau nach Isoët. lac. untersucht, in Begleitung des Gastwirth Döring in Kleschkau, der früher 2 Jahre Gehilfe im kön. botan. Garten zu Königsberg gewesen war und mir im Frühjahr Auswürflinge von Isoët. aus dem See geschickt hatte. Wieder heftiger Wind. Vergebens nach dem Standort der Isoët. im See gesucht, aber einige ausgeworfene Blätter von Isoët. gefunden, welche die Pflanze als var. leiospora ergaben. See von Lindenberg: **Myriophyll. altern.** Torfbruchloch nordwestlich von Kleschkau. — 30. 7. See Piaceczenko, See Dlugi bei Lippe; in letzterem **Chara cerotophylla** und **Naias maior.** See Katschmarski, See Czarni östlich von Kassub: **Chara cerotophylla.** Der Duze-See westlich vom vorigen: Chara cerat.; kleiner Torfsee westlich vom vorigen; See südwestl. von Dunaiken; östlicher See in Grünthal, sogenannter Kl. Grünthal'er See: Chara fragilis. — 31. 7. Torfsee westlich von Kobilla; der See „Schlunk" bei Orle; Torfsee westlich von Orle. Nacht in Czarnikau bei Herrn Hauptmann Höpner. — 1. August 85. See von Garczunko: **Myriophyll. alternifl.**, Elatine Hydropiper, **Callitriche autumnalis,** *Ranunculus confervoides* Fr. schon 1873 von mir gefunden, in der Schälung hauptsächlich am Südufer, blüht noch. Ganz wie die Pflanze Lapplands, die ich 1868 daselbst fand; Chara fragilis. Bukowo-See (Bukowice der Generalstabskarte) **Isoëtes lacustris** vulgaris minor, elatior, patula und subpatula, schon 1878 daselbst von mir entdeckt, **Myriophyll. alternifl.** Kl. Bukowko, östlich vom vorigen. — 3. Aug. Der westl. See bei Grünthal (Gr. Grünthal'er See). See von Kl. Okonin: Chara fragilis. Torfsee südlich von Quarschnau. See von Wigonin: Chara fragilis, **Ch. contraria, Ch. aspera.** — 4. Aug. Uebersiedelung nach **Fersenau** (Bartischowlas). — 5. 8. Der Krangensee: Chara fragilis, Scirpus Tabernaem., Dianthus superbus, Malaxis Loeselii auf dem Torfufer ohne Sphagnum. Kosellen-See. Kl. Czerwonnek. Czerwonnek bei Ruda: Chara fragilis. — 6. 8. See Przywloszno vom Czerwonnek westlich: am Westende Saxifraga Hirculus und Hieracium vulgatum im Gebüsch eines Sphagnetums, Scirpus Tabern. See von Lossiner Thal: Chara fragilis. Kottelsee bei Olpuch: **Chara contraria,** Ch. fragilis. Seechen westl. vom Kottelsee: Chara fragilis Z. — 7. 8. 2 Tümpel bei Fosshütte, Torfbruch zwischen Neubukowitz und Olpuch, See Chonzi (Chondschi), Chossen der Generalstabskarte: **Chara contraria,** Ch. fragilis. 3 Torftümpel südlich vom vorigen. Der Dranczt-See (Sandsee der Karte, welcher Namen an Ort und Stelle unbekannt ist) bei Barlogi: **Chara contraria,** Ch. fragilis, Ch. Ceratophylla, *Nitella batrachosperma* A. Br., neu für Preussen, nur 2 Ex. im dicken Schlamm des Bodens trotz allem Suchen zu finden. Das Suchen freilich durch Regen und Gewitter behindert. — 8. 8. Babbie-See südlich von Konarschin: Chara fragilis, **Potamogeton rutila** Z^2 V^2. 2 Torfseen südlich vom vorigen. Tümpel östlich vom Babbie-See. Gr. Pruczonka, dicht am Dranczt: Chara fragilis. Dieselbe Chara im Kl. Pruczonka. Dlugi zw. Konarschin und Fersenau: Chara fragilis. — 10. 8. Pfaffensee bei Fersenau: Chara fragilis. Der Czarlinek; Viola epipsila im Sphagnetum. See von Prziawitzno. Seechen Sdrojek, nördlich von Wigonin: **Utricularia intermedia,** Chara fragilis. **Potamogeton rutila.** Teich von

Gr. Bartel. See Niribno, östl. von Gr. Bartel: Chara fragilis, Utricularia minor. See Karaschnik — 11. 8. Sei bei Oberförsterei Okonin: Chara ceratophylla und fragilis.

12. Aug. Uebersiedelung nach der kön. Försterei Gribno zu Herrn Forstaufseher Bacher. Gribno-See: Chara fragilis, **Chara contraria** und Ch. foetida fr. longibracteata. Wirfusssee: **Chara contraria.** — 13. 8. See südlich von der kön. Försterei Holzort: Chara fragilis, **Potamogeton rutila.** See südwestl. vom vorigen: **Chara intermedia,** Ch. fragilis. See östlich von Försterei Holzort: Chara fragilis. See Westnordnord von Försterei Holzort: Chara fragil., Utricularia vulg. See südwestl. vom vorigen: **Chara intermedia,** Ch. frag., Potentilla procumbens Sibth. am Ufer. 4 Tümpel bei letzterem See. See Westnordnord vom vorigen: **Chara foetida** fr. longibracteata macroteles, Ch. fragilis, **Oryza clandestina.** — 14. 8. See südlich vom Wege zwischen Gribno und Gr. Bartel: **Chara foetida** fr. longibracteata, Ch. fragilis. 4 kleine Seen fast südlich vom vorigen; 3 davon mit Chara frag. Der Weisssee südwestlich von den vorigen. Kleiner See im Walde nördlich vom Wege zw. Gr. Bartel und Gribno: Chara fragilis. — 15. 8. Der Moossee Westnordnord von Gribno: **Utricularia intermedia** in grösster Menge Z^3 V^3, Utr. vulgaris Z^1 V^1, Utr. minor Z^2 V^2, Chara fragilis longibracteata. Tümpel nordöstlich und ein anderer nordwestlich vom vorigen. 7 grössere oder kleinere Torftümpel südöstlich vom Dranczt-See; in ihnen zum Theil Chara frag. — 17. 8. Der Ferdinandsbruch südwestlich von Gribno: Chara fragilis, **Potamogeton rutila.** See Smolske, östlich von Bonk: Chara frag., **Potamog. rutila, Centunculus minimus,** Radiola Milleg. 4 Tümpel östlich von Bonk; im südöstlichsten: **Chara foetida** longibracteata, Potamogeton pusilla tenuissima. Teich der Mühle Bonk.

18. Aug. Uebersiedelung nach Borsk. Auf Aeckern östlich von Borsk viel Potycnemum arvense. See von Klitzkau. — 19. Aug. Ostseite des Wdzidze-Sees vom Ausfluss des Schwarzwassers bei Borsk bis Zabroddi am Golluhn von 5 Uhr früh an um möglichst wenig Wind und Wellen auf dem riesigen See zu haben untersucht: **Chara ceratophylla,** Ch. fragilis, **Ch. contraria** in der nördlichsten Bucht nördlich von Lippa; **Elodea canad.** im Wdzidze und Golluhn, **Potamogeton lucens + praelonga.** Torfloch zw. Zabrodden und Lippa, anderes nördlich von Ribaken; der See Kukuhko nordöstl. von Ribaken. Polycnemum arvense zw. Ribaken und Borsk. — 20. 8. Südufer des Wdzidze von der Schleuse am Ausfluss des Schwarzwassers bis nach Wildau (Prczitania): **Chara iubata** (wenig und schlecht), **Ch. stelligera** (desgleichen), Ch. ceratophylla, Ch. fragilis; die 3 südlichen Inseln des Wdzidze. See Pomarczyn in Weitsee. See Grzybor, westlich von Czyste: **Chara intermedia, Ch. contraria,** Ch. ceratophylla, Ch. fragilis auch fr. Hedwigii. See von Czyste: **Chara aspera,** Ch. contraria, Ch. ceratophylla. — 21. 8. See Krzywe nördlich von Czyste. See Lonzek östlich vom vorigen. See Goninko, nördlich von Wildau: Chara fragilis. Auf den Wiesen nördlich davon **Saxifraga Hirculus.** See Joninko nördlich vom vorigen.

22. Aug. Uebersiedelung nach Dzimmianen am See von Dzimmianen: Lycopodium inundatum. — 23. 8. 2 Torflöcher zw. Dzimmianen und Trzebuhn. Dorfsee von Trzebuhn. See von Zajonskowo: Chara fragilis, Rhynchospora alba, Hydrocotyle vulg. 2 Torftümpel südwestl. vom vorigen See. See Ababino östlich von dem von Zajonskowo: Chara ceratophylla und fragilis. See Trzebionko, östlich vom vorigen: Chara fragilis fr. longibracteata. Der westliche Radolino: Chara ceratophylla und frag.; östlicher Radolino: Chara fragilis. — 25. 8. See von Slonnen: Chara

frag. Torfsee von Mechowo: **Elodea canad.** Z[4] V[4] seit wenig Jahren in dem See. Unbekannt, wie sie dahin gekommen ist.

26. Aug. Uebersiedelung von Dzimmianen nach Gr. Podless zu Frau Schnee auf Gr. Podless. — 27. 8. See Ploczicz bei Rottenberg: **Chara intermedia,** Ch. ceratophylla und Ch. fragilis, **Cladium Mariscus,** nicht mehr so zahlreich als vor 12 Jahren. Tümpel südwestlich vom Ploczicz. Der Czabienko Westnordnord von Gr. Podless. See Czartofke Südsüdost von Gr. Klinsch.

28. Aug. Uebersiedelung nach Putz zu Herrn Rittergutsbesitzer Pieper auf Putz. — 29. 8. 2 Tümpel bei Putzhütte. See Policzewko: **Lobelia dort., Litorella lac.** See von Dobrogosch: **Myriophyll. altern.,** Limosella aquatica. Leider ist von Isoëtes lac. und Lobelia dort., welche beiden Pflanzen ich 1863 und 1864 in ausserordentlicher Fülle in dem See fand, gar nichts mehr vorhanden; diese Pflanzen sind durch wiederholte Erniedrigung des Wasserspiegels vernichtet und jetzt ist dieser vor Jahren so höchstinteressante See, ein ausserordentlich pflanzenarmer Sandsee. Von Litorella, früher auch sehr zahlreich in ihm, fand ich noch nicht ½ Dutzend Exemplare auf dem trocknen Ufer. Der grosse Schweinebudensee: **Litorella lac., Lobelia dortm., Myriophyll. altern., Isoëtes lacustr.** vulgaris elatior, longifolia, patula, subfalcata, 14 bis 24½ cm lang. Der kleine Schweinebudensee. Der Galgensee: **Myrioph. altern.** — 31. 8. See von Wentfie. See Bebrowo. Der Amtssee bei Berent. See Wrzedzunko zw. Kreis Berent und Kartaus: Chara frag. See Dlugi bei Skorczewo: **Myriophyll. altern.** — 1. Septbr. 2 Tümpel bei Heringshütte. Tümpel in Recknitz. See von Bendomin: **Myrioph. altern., Isoëtes lac.** vulg. elatior und longifolia, patula und subpatula. Nitella sp. steril bedeckt fast den ganzen Seeboden. Agrimonia odorata am Westufer. Torfsee südlich vom vorigen: Nuphar luteum, **Nuphar pumilum** und **Nuphar luteum + pumilum.** Torfsee südwestlich vom vorigen: **Nuphar luteum + pumilum.** Teich der Kulla-Mühle: **Oryza clandestina.** Teich der Mühle Bendomin abgeflossen. — 2. 9. See von Putz. Torfsee südlich von Jeziorken. Torftümpel südlich vom vorigen. Torftümpel westlich vom vorigen: Rhynchospora alba, Drosera longifolia, Scheuchzeria pal. Dorfsee in Neu-Barkoschin: **Myrioph. altern.** In Lubahn Libanotis montana. Sandsee bei Neukrug: **Myrioph. altern., Callitriche autumnalis;** Pontentilla norvegica und Gnaphalium luteo-album am Ufer. Torfsee bei Grauhof.

3. Septbr. Uebersiedelung nach Hoppendorf, Kreis Kartaus. — 4. 9. See von Schlafkau. Tümpel südlich von Eggertshütte: Peplis Portula. Zw. Eggertshütte und Starkhütte: **Gentiana campestris.** Torfsee von Kapellenhütte. See von Pollenczyn: **Myrioph. altern., Elatine Hydropiper.**

5. Septbr. Uebersiedelung nach Kelpin. Gr. Kelpin'er See: Litorella lac. Kl. Kelpin'er See: Litor. lac. Siecym-See, Rosensee. — 6. 9. **Pleurospermum austr., Aconitum variegat., Mercurialis perenn.,** Thalictrum aquilegif. in einer Schlucht des rechten Radauneufers östlich von Kelpin. — 7. 9. Torfsee Stuczino, nördlich von Kelpin: Gentiana camp., Utricularia minor. See Okunowo: **Litorella lac., Elatine Hydropiper.** See von Mehsau: **Callitriche autumnalis, Litorella lac., Nitella gracilis.** See von Seeresen: **Callitriche autumnalis,** Chara frag. Torfsee südlich vom Borowo-Kruge: **Elatine Hydropiper.** Karlikau'er See (Borowo-See): **Lobelia dortm., Isoëtes lacustris,** meist leiospora, seltner vulgaris, minor, depauperata, elatior, patula, subpatula. — 8. 9. Zittno-See: Chara frag., **Lobelia dortm., Isoëtes lac.** vulgaris und leiospora minor,

elatior, subpatula, patula und patentissima, **Callitriche autumnal.** See Glemboki: Chara fragilis, **Potamogeton crispa + praelonga, Litorella lac.**

9. Septbr. Uebersiedelung nach Exau zu Herrn Keier. — 10. 9. See von Exau. In diesem mit Potamogeton natans, P. perfoliata, P. obtusifolia, P. praelonga, P. crispa, P. zosterifolia, Ceratophyllum demersum und Chara fragilis, die Moor mit Kalk lieben und im moorigen Theil des Sees lebten: **Lobelia dortm., Litorella lac., Elatine Hydropiper, Isoëtes lacustris** vulgaris patula elatior auf festem, steinigem, sandigem Boden auf der Südostseite. 6 Torftümpel und Seen bei Seefeld. In dem westlich vom Wege zw. Seefeld und Kable: Chara frag., Elatine Hydropiper. Nördlich von Seefeld: **Gentiana campestris.** — 11. 9. Dorfsee von Smolsin. See Tuchlinek, südöstlich von Smolsin: **Litorella lac., Elatine Hydropiper, Isoëtes lac.**, vulgaris patula und subpatula, zugleich mit Potamogeton pus. und graminea, Utricularia vulgaris und andere Sumpfwasserpflanzen. Im Verbindungsgraben zw. diesem See und dem Glemboki, in dem 1884 Dr. Lange Potamog. marina entdeckte, war aufgeräumt und nichts davon zu finden.

12. 9. Uebersiedelung von Exau nach Stangenwalde. — 14. 9. See von Lappin. Hier wieder **Elatine Hydropiper, Litorella lac., Isoëtes lac.** vulgaris patula und elatior, falcata mit Sumpfwasserpflanzen wie Potamogeton natans, P. pus., P. crispa + praelonga, P. crispa, P. obtusifolia, P. lucens, Chara fragilis, **Callitriche autumnalis, Elodea canadensis**, welche letztere ich öfters zusammen mit Isoëtes mit der Gabel in die Höhe brachte. Seen von Rheinfeld und Lichtenfelde. — 15. 9. Niedersommerkau'er See bei Neuhof: Chara fragilis, Spur. Glamke-See: **Chara ceratophylla**, Ch. fragilis. Der Kl. See bei Glasberg. — 16. 9. Von Stangenwalde nach Praust und zurück nach Königsberg. Mein Pferd verkaufte ich an einen Juden aus Schiedlitz bei Danzig in Stangenwalde auf 3 M. Handgeld. Es wurde verabredet, dass der Jude in Praust, nachdem ich Boot, Wagen u. s. w. auf die Eisenbahn daselbst gebracht hätte, das Pferd in Empfang nehmen und den Rest des Kaufgeldes zahlen sollte. Der Jude war jedoch zur verabredeten Zeit nicht in Praust. Ich liess das Pferd in einem vorherbestimmten Gasthof zurück, von wo der Jude es sich den nächsten Tag geholt hat. Er zahlte aber nicht, verweigerte auch Zahlung auf einen Postauftrag und als ich die Sache einem Rechtsanwalt in Danzig übergeben wollte, erfuhr ich von diesem, dass der Jude zahlungsunfähig sei und nicht einmal die Staatssteuern von ihm einzutreiben seien. So hat der Jude das Pferd für 3 M. gehabt.

Es ist also Myriophyll. altern. von mir 1885 in 19 Seen gefunden, darunter in vielen neuen, Isoët. lac. in 10, darunter in 6 neuen, Callitriche autum. in 7, Litorella lac. in 8, Lobelia dort. in 5, Elatine Hydropiper in 8, Potamogeton rutila in 5, Potam. lucens + praelonga in 1, P. crispa + praelonga in 3, **Ranunculus confervoides** in 1, Ran. reptans in 2, Nuphar pumilum in 2, Nuphar luteum + pumilum in 2, Chara ceratophylla in 9, Ch. contraria in 8, Ch. foetida in 4, Ch. intermedia in 3, Ch. aspera in 2, Ch. fragilis in mehr als 30, Nitella gracilis, Nitella opaca, **Nitella batrachosperma**, Chara iubata, Ch. stelligera, ferner Alisma natans, Naias maior, Oryza clandestina in je einem See von mir gefunden.

Dr. Abraham vertheilt aus der Flora von Elbing: Salvinia natans, Petasites albus und Circaea alpina.

Es sei noch bemerkt, dass Herr Semprich, Vorsteher der Präparandenanstalt in Pr. Stargardt, ein Exemplar von Potentilla recta, bei Pr. Stargardt in den Anlagen zwischen Stadt und Schiesshaus gefunden, mehreren auf der Versammlung Anwesenden vorzeigte.

Der Seminarist Erich Sich hat 1884 und 1885 in einem Graben seines Heimathsdorfes Gremboczyn Kr. Thorn Lythrum Hyssopifolia L. gefunden und dem Vorsitzenden wiederholentlich mitgetheilt.

Schluss der Sitzung um $4^1/_2$ Uhr.

Es folgte nun das Festessen, bei dem es sehr heiter zuging. Auf Vorschlag von Kantor Grabowski werden Telegramme an Scharlok und Konrector Seydler gesandt, die Bedauern über deren Abwesenheit ausdrücken.

Gedächtnissrede

auf

J. J. A. Worsaae

gehalten in der Sitzung der physikalisch-ökonomischen Gesellschaft am 4. März 1886

von

Dr. Otto Tischler.

Am 15. August 1885 ereilte ein plötzlicher Tod den Director der Königlichen Museen zu Kopenhagen, den Kammerherrn Worsaae, noch im Vollbesitze seiner körperlichen und geistigen Frische. Der Tod Worsaae's, welcher Mitglied der physikalisch-ökonomischen Gesellschaft war, ist für die Wissenschaft ein unermesslicher Verlust, dessen Grösse um so klarer hervortritt, wenn ich es versuche, an dieser Stelle die Bedeutung des Mannes für die Entwicklung der Alterthumskunde darzulegen.

Worsaae war nicht der Begründer dieser neuen Disciplin, er hat sie aber erst zum Range einer Wissenschaft erhoben, und um daher seine Thätigkeit voll zu verstehen, müssen wir uns zuerst der vor ihm liegenden Periode zuwenden, sehen was er vorfand, und was er daraus geschaffen hat.

Im 17. Jahrhundert entstanden die fürstlichen Kunst- und Raritätenkammern, in denen ohne viel Verständniss alles Mögliche durcheinander gesammelt wurde, Bilder, Gegenstände des Kunstgewerbes, besonders Kuriositäten und Raritäten, hin und wieder auch Alterthümer und Naturalien. Diese ungeordneten Sammlungen haben aber doch ihre hohe Bedeutung, denn aus ihnen sind allmählich durch Abspaltung die naturhistorischen und Kunst-Museen entstanden, jetzt die Zierden der Hauptstädte Europa's. Die älteste und vorzüglichste war die 1616 gegründete Gottorpische Kunstkammer, welche 1751 nach Kopenhagen gelangte. Aus der Mitte desselben Jahrhunderts datirt die Begründung der Berliner, in der heidnische Alterthümer nur spärlich Aufnahme fanden. Erst seit 1798 wurde hier durch Ankauf verschiedener Privatsammlungen viel in dieser Richtung geleistet, bis die nordischen Alterthümer 1830 als eigene Sammlung abgezweigt wurden. Wenn im 18. Jahrhundert auch mancherlei, natürlich recht unwissenschaftliche Nachgrabungen stattgefunden hatten und mancherlei Gegenstände in die Kunstkammern gelangten, so war doch nur in Mecklenburg-Schwerin etwas Bedeutenderes geleistet worden. Die früheren Funde wurden dann durch den Grossherzog Friedrich Franz 1804 in Ludwigslust vereint, und man muss zugeben, dass in Förderung der Alterthumskunde Mecklenburg zunächst in Europa und nachher noch lange Zeit in Deutschland den ersten Rang einnahm. Die Sammlung wurde durch systematische Nachgrabungen und eingelieferte Funde unter den Directoren v. Oertzen und Schroeter reichlich vermehrt, bis 1836 Lisch die Leitung übernahm und für sie eine neue Aera eröffnete.

Der skandinavische Norden war abgesehen von einzelnen in der Kopenhagener Kunstkammer aufbewahrten Funden nicht in gleicher Weise vorgeschritten wie Mecklenburg. Erst im 19. Jahrhundert begann sich hier ein lebhafteres Interesse für die Vorzeit und die vaterländischen Alterthümer zu regen. 1806 begründete Nyerup das Museum nordischer Alterthümer im Anschluss an die Bibliothek im runden Thurm zu Kopenhagen, welches am 1. Februar 1807 eingeweiht wurde. Zugleich erfolgte die Einsetzung der Königlichen Commission für Aufbewahrung der Alterthümer, die bis 1847 bestand. Die Kriegsereignisse riefen eine Stockung hervor, und erst 1816 als Thomsen eintrat, der bis 1865 Director des Museums blieb, nahm die Sammlung den ungeheuren Aufschwung, der sie zur grossartigsten Europa's gemacht hat. Neben dem Museum entstand 1825 die Nordische Alterthums-Gesellschaft, hauptsächlich durch Rafn gegründet, welcher bis zu seinem Tode 1864 ihr beständiger Secretär blieb. Diese Gesellschaft beschäftigte sich zunächst ausschliesslich mit der Herausgabe der nordischen und isländischen Sagen. Erst später trat sie dem Museum näher und stellte der Commission ihre Publikationen zur Verfügung, so dass sich seit Mitte der dreissiger Jahre ein immer erfreulicheres Zusammenwirken entwickelte. Die Mitte der dreissiger Jahre ist überhaupt für die Entwickelung der Nordischen Alterthumskunde eine Epoche von einschneidender Bedeutung.

Es hatten in den verschiedensten Gegenden Deutschland's verdiente Männer eine Menge einzelner Ausgrabungen unternommen und die Resultate derselben publicirt, so u. a. Büsching, Dorow, Kruse, Danneil, besonders Wilhelmi in Sinsheim, dessen Berichte zu dem Besten gehören, was in älterer Zeit geliefert worden ist, u. a. m. Es galt aber nun das doch bereits recht stark angewachsene Material zu ordnen und in ein System zu bringen.

Da tritt als ein Merkstein in der Geschichte der Alterthumskunde der „Leitfaden zur nordischen Alterthumskunde" herausgegeben von der Königlichen Gesellschaft für Nordische Alterthumskunde hervor, der 1836 in dänischer, 1837 in deutscher Sprache herauskam, und dessen zweite Abtheilung „Kurzgefasste Uebersicht über Denkmäler und Alterthümer aus der Vorzeit des Nordens" Thomsen verfasst hatte. Thomsen stellt hier die Eintheilung der Urzeit in das Stein-, Bronce- und Eisenzeitalter auf, das berühmte Drei-Perioden-System. Er behauptet, dass Bronce vor dem Eisen in Gebrauch gewesen und dass die im Norden gefundenen Geräthe zum grossen Theil im Lande selbst angefertigt seien. Fast zu gleicher Zeit wurde diese Theorie noch von anderen Forschern, wenn auch nicht in ganz so präciser Form ausgesprochen. Lisch in Schwerin, welcher dort auf Schroeter folgte gab das von jenem begonnene Werk Friderico-Francisceum heraus, die Abbildungen der grossherzoglichen Alterthümer zu Ludwigslust. Den Text verfasste Lisch selbstständig; er erschien 1837, war aber schon 1836 gedruckt. Lisch kam hier auch auf die Dreitheilung, die er aber nicht so scharf als Thomsen präcisirte. Hingegen gebührt ihm das grosse Verdienst, dass er die verschiedenen Klassen der Gräber genau beschrieb, ordnete und darauf drang, dass die beieinander gefundenen Gegenstände auch in der Sammlung zusammengehalten würden, ein Prinzip, das er fortan in seiner Sammlung durchführte. Ferner hatte als Dritter Danneil in Salzwedel auch eine solche Gliederung erkannt, indem er 1836 in einem Generalbericht über Ausgrabungen in der Umgegend von Salzwedel in Förstemann's Neuen Mittheilungen 1836 Gräber unterscheidet, die Kupfer oder Kupfer-Composition und solche, die Eisen enthalten. Diese Eintheilung ist aber immer nicht so präsise auseinandergesetzt als im Dänischen Leitfaden.

Thomsen hat die Eintheilung also zuerst ausgesprochen; die dänische Ausgabe des Leitfadens hat das älteste Datum. Bereits 1830 hatte er das Princip dieser Eintheilung dem Reichs-Antiquar Hildebrand aus Stockholm auseinander gesetzt und in den nächsten Jahren die Kopenhagener Alterthümer danach geordnet. Doch sind diese 3 Forscher unbedingt unabhängig von einander fast gleichzeitig auf die Idee gekommen, die Entdeckung lag so zu sagen in der Luft. Uebrigens ist auch nicht Thomsen der erste, sondern 1813 hatte schon Vedel-Simonsen die Eintheilung der Kulturgeschichte in Stein-, Kupfer- und Eisen-Alter vorgeschlagen. Doch hatte dies weiter keinen Einfluss auf den Gang der Wissenschaft und blieb ziemlich unbeachtet. Erst 1836 trat die neue folgenschwere Entdeckung in's Leben.

Nach diesem Prinzip hatte Thomsen nun die Kopenhagener Alterthümer geordnet und sie in grosse Suiten nach ihrem Material eingereiht. Es war dadurch ein festerer Boden gewonnen, man konnte das gewaltige Material besser überblicken. Hiermit war aber auch ein gewisses Ziel erreicht und man wäre nach der bisher angewandten Methode nicht viel weiter gekommen. Das Ordnen der Fundobjecte nach Formenreihen führte dazu, die einzelnen Funde auseinander zu reissen, was ein weiteres Studium ausserordentlich erschwerte. Zudem waren gerade in Dänemark diese Stücke weniger durch gründliche systematische Ausgrabungen gewonnen, sondern verdankten mehr dem Zufalle oder den Nachforschungen von Dilettanten ihren Ursprung, die nicht sehr zuverlässige Berichte darüber anfertigten. Man hatte mit den noch vorhandenen Denkmälern und den in der Erde ruhenden Alterthümern wenig Fühlung, welche unbemerkt in wahrhaft erschreckender Weise verschwanden. Ebenso war die wissenschaftliche Verwerthung der Fundobjecte meist eine verkehrte. Zu sehr knüpfte man noch an historische Ueberlieferungen und schriftliche Nachrichten, unbekümmert darum, ob sie bis an die Objecte aus jener fernen Urzeit heranreichten. Auch in Deutschland wucherten solche Phantasien und auf luftige Deductionen gegründete Combinationen üppig empor. Es fehlten auch die Mittel, die Alterthümer der verschiedenen Länder zu vergleichen. Abbildungen gab es noch sehr wenig, die Gelehrten klebten noch zu sehr an der Scholle — nur Reisen nach dem classischen Italien waren üblich. Kurz, bei den ausserordentlichen Verdiensten, die sich Thomsen erworben hatte, war doch ein neuer Impuls nöthig, eine neue Methode der Forschung, eine neue jugendliche Kraft.

Und da trat gerade im geeigneten Momente Worsaae ein.

Jens Jacob Asmussen Worsaae war am 14. März 1821 zu Veile in Jütland geboren, woselbst sein Vater Amtsverwalter war. Er besuchte das Gymnasium zu Horsens, bezog 1838 die Universität zu Kopenhagen und wurde bald darauf Thomsens Assistent.

Nachdem er einige Ausgrabungen im Inlande geleitet und beschrieben hatte, besuchte er in den Jahren 1842—45 zu verschiedenen Malen, mit Staatsunterstützungen versehen, Schweden, Norwegen und Deutschland, 1846—47 die britischen Inseln, 1851—52 England und Frankreich. Er konnte dadurch seinen Gesichtskreis bedeutend erweitern, die Alterthümer aller dieser Länder studiren und mit einander vergleichen.

Die Hauptfrüchte dieser Reisen und der Studien im Lande sind neben zahlreichen kleineren, folgende Publicationen: „Dänemarks Vorzeit durch Alterthümer und Grabhügel beleuchtet (dänisch 1843, deutsch 1844); Die nationale Alterthumskunde in Deutschland, Reisebemerkungen (dänisch und deutsch 1846); Blekingsche Denkmäler aus dem heidnischen Alterthum in ihrem Verhältniss zu den übrigen scandinavischen und europäischen Alterthumsdenkmälern (dänisch und deutsch 1846/47); Die Dänen und Nordmänner in England, Schottland und Irland (dänisch und deutsch 1852)." Es würde hier zu weit führen, die von dem unermüdlichen Fleisse Worsaaes zeugenden zahlreichen kleineren Publicationen aufzuführen, es können nur die wichtigeren, bahnbrechenden hervorgehoben werden. In obigen Werken, besonders in den Blekingschen-Denkmälern, legte nun Worsaae die Grundzüge der neuen Methode, nach der die Archäologie arbeiten musste, dar. Er zeigte, dass es vor allem darauf ankäme den Charakter der Denkmäler, die Fund- und Lagerungsverhältnisse genau zu studiren; die Gegenstände müssen dann ihrer Form nach mit einander verglichen werden und die Objecte einer Gruppe und eines Landes mit denen der übrigen. Durch diese Vergleichungen gelingt es zunächst das Aeltere vom Jüngeren zu unterscheiden und ferner die gleichzeitig existirenden lokal getrennten Gebiete zu fixiren — ein ideales Ziel, welches allerdings noch lange nicht erreicht ist. Wenn man dann die Verschiebung dieser einzelnen Gebiete im Laufe der Zeiten verfolgt, so kann man die Völkerbewegungen in einer Periode ermitteln, in die noch kein Strahl geschriebener Ueberlieferung dringt und durch die Aehnlichkeit einzelner Objecte im Norden mit denen südlicher Regionen erkennt man die Handels- und Culturbewegungen, die von den Centren alter Civilisation sich weit hin in die dunklen Barbarenländer erstreckten. Die Sitten und Gebräuche dieser Barbaren treten uns selbst vor Augen und sie erscheinen uns lange nicht mehr so barbarisch als die befangene Meinung des Volkes und der Gelehrten früher annahm.

Alles dies sind die Grundsätze der sogenannten „Vergleichenden Archäologie."

Sie sind jetzt das Gemeingut aller Forscher und kommen uns nun so selbstverständlich vor, dass man sich kaum denken kann, sie wären einst nicht befolgt worden. Und doch ist es ausser Lisch, der einige derselben schon hervorhob, besonders das Studium der Grab- und Lagerungsverhältnisse, der aber trotz seines rastlosen Arbeitens wegen des kleinen Gebiets, das er allein übersehen konnte, nicht weitere Blicke gewinnen konnte, erst Worsaae gewesen, der sie klar und deutlich aussprach und in seinen Arbeiten auch sofort befolgte. Man kann ihn daher mit vollem Rechte den „Schöpfer der vergleichenden Archäologie" nennen.

Wie erwähnt zog er selbst bereits daraus die Consequenzen und versuchte besonders in den Blekingschen Denkmälern aus den Denkmalen selbst die Besiedelung des Nordens in den verschiedenen Perioden und deren Zusammenhang mit den südlicher gelegenen Regionen zu entwickeln. Auf eine eingehendere Detailbehandlung der Formen wird hier verzichtet und mehr die Resultate der Studien, die Worsaae in dieser Beziehung unternommen hat, mitgetheilt.

Während man die Zeit bis 1847 als seine Studienjahre bezeichnen kann, beginnt nun die Hauptperiode seiner wissenschaftlichen Thätigkeit, die während eines Zeitraums von fast 20 Jahren gleichmässig fortschreitend dahinfloss. Ausserdem trat er aber im Sinne seiner Methode der Erforschung der Alterthümer praktisch näher, als er 1847 zum Inspecteur der Dänischen Alterthümer gemacht wurde und in die Commission zur Erhaltung derselben eintrat, deren Obliegenheiten er nach ihrer Auflösung seit 1849 allein erfüllte. In Begleitung eines Zeichners konnte er das Land bereisen, das Vorhandene aufnehmen, soweit angänglich systematische Grabungen veranstalten, für die Erhaltung der Denkmäler sorgen. Nicht nur den prähistorischen Alterthümern wandte er seine Aufmerksamkeit zu, sondern auch den aller späteren Zeiten und hier wurde durch Restauration der Kirchen und ähnlicher Bauten viel geleistet. 1861 wurde er Conservator der Alterthümer und Denkmäler Dänemark's. Erst 1873 wurden seitens des Staats grössere Mittel bewilligt zur Inventarisirung und zum Ankauf solcher Denkmäler und Gräber, die nicht in Staatsländereien liegen, so dass seitdem 900 Denkmäler jeder Art für die Zukunft gesichert sind und nach und nach planmässig erforscht werden können. Die Instruktionen, die er im Beginne seiner Thätigkeit und später veröffentlichte, trugen wesentlich dazu bei, beim Volk den Sinn und das Verständniss für diese Denkmäler zu wecken. Das Arbeiten auf freiem Felde schult erst den Archäologen und Niemand wird das rechte Verständniss für die Alterthümer haben, der diese Schule nicht durchgemacht hat.

Nun galt es aber die sich immer riesiger anhäufenden Resultate weiter zu verarbeiten. Thomsen hatte durch seine Eintheilung den ersten glücklichen Schritt auf diesem Wege gethan, Nilson in Schweden hatte ein anschauliches Bild der Cultur der Steinzeit durch Vergleich mit den Völkern, welche noch jetzt auf einer ähnlichen Stufe der Civilisation stehen, gegeben. Das waren aber erst Anfänge. Bei der zeitlichen Abgrenzung der Perioden war Thomson noch in schwere Irrthümer verfallen: man kann ihn darob nicht tadeln, denn es fehlten noch manche Zwischenglieder und sind ja ähnliche Irrthümer noch bis in sehr neue Zeit ausgesprochen worden. Worsaae erkannte nun, dass die Eintheilung in drei Hauptperioden nicht genüge, und dass alle diese einen sehr langen Zeitraum einnehmenden Abschnitte sich noch weiter gliederten, doch schritt diese Erkenntniss auch erst nach und nach vor, so dass manche Anschauungen der früheren Arbeiten in späteren berichtigt werden mussten.

Bereits Mitte der vierziger Jahre schloss er aus der Beschaffenheit der Steingeräthe auf einen älteren und jüngeren Abschnitt der Steinzeit. Doch erst seit 1850 konnte er sichere Anhaltspunkte gewinnen, seit er mit Olsen den ersten jener gewaltigen Küchenabfallswälle zu Meilgaard in Jütland untersuchte und hier eine viel primitivere Cultur mit roh zugeschlagenen Feuersteingeräthen als in den grossen Grabkammern mit ihren feingeschliffenen Werkzeugen entdeckte, Funde an die sich ähnliche auf den kleinen dänischen Inseln reihten. Ebenso fand er eine wesentliche Verschiedenheit der Broncealterthümer heraus in der Form, wie in den Grabgebräuchen. Er unterschied die ältere Bronzezeit mit Leichenbestattung und die jüngere mit Leichenbrand, in welcher ganz besonders häufig reiche Broncevorräthe in den Mooren, die in der Vorzeit Seen vorstellten, deponirt waren. Die Formen beider Abschnitte zeigen eine durchgehende Verschiedenheit. Diese Ansichten, welche im Laufe der fünfziger Jahre sich bald klärten, entwickelte er eingehend 1859 in den Verhandlungen der Dänischen Gesellschaft der Wissenschaften und später noch mehrfach in wenig modificirter Form. Noch früher gelangte er zu der Einsicht, dass das Eisenalter, welches anfangs nur in seinen jüngsten Phasen bekannt war, und das man daher erst 500 n. Chr. hatte beginnen lassen, viel weiter zurückreiche, bis in die römische Kaiserzeit, bis in den Beginn unserer Aera. Schon 1843 in Dänemarks Vorzeit hatte er die Anwesenheit römischer Alterthümer in Dänemark constatirt, eine Entdeckung, die durch spätere Entdeckungen wesentlich bestätigt wurde und in seiner Abhandlung Jernalderens Beygedelse i Danmark (der Anfang des Eisenalters in Dänemark, Annaler for Nordisk Oldkyndighed 1847) näher auseinandergesetzt und in mehreren folgenden Abhandlungen 1850—53 weiter entwickelt wurde. So kam er dazu, ein älteres Eisenalter, das ungefähr den Zeitraum von 0—450 n. Chr. einnimmt auszuscheiden. Eine besondere Stütze erhielt diese Ansicht durch die Entdeckung des grossen Thorsberg (Brarup) Moorfundes in Schleswig, den Worsaae von 1857 an behandelte. Am vollständigsten setzte dann Worsaae sein System in dem Werke „Om Slesvigs eller Sønderjyllands Oldtidsminder" (Schleswig'sche Denkmäler, Kopenhagen 1865) auseinander, so dass er also von 1859—1865 dasselbe zum Abschluss brachte. Worsaae zweigte von der jüngeren Eisenzeit noch eine mittlere ab, welche den Zeitraum von 450 bis 700 ausfüllt und deren Formenreihe sich von denen der angrenzenden Perioden wesentlich unterscheidet.

Zugleich führte er in diesem Werke nochmals das gründlich aus, was er in den Bleknigschen Denkmälern versucht hatte, was er aber jetzt in Folge der inzwischen gewonnenen Kenntniss in weit vollständigerer, richtiger und sicherer Weise vollbringen konnte. Er suchte in allen diesen einzelnen Unterperioden die Völkerverschiebungen im scandinavischen Norden in Verbindung mit denen des benachbarten Europa's zu entwickeln, ein Versuch, den er in wenig mehr veränderter Form noch in einer Reihe späterer Publicationen wiederholte:

> „Die Colonisation Russlands und des scandinavischen Nordens (Dänisch und Französisch 1872, 73). Die Vorgeschichte des Nordens nach gleichzeitigen Denkmälern (Dänisch und Deutsch 1878, 1881). Das Stein- und Bronce-Alter in der alten und neuen Welt (Dänisch und Französisch 1879, 80)."

Es traten im Ganzen keine wesentlich neuen Gesichtspunkte mehr hervor, wenngleich im Einzelnen manche neue Resultate den stets wachsenden Erfahrungen Worsaae's zu verdanken sind. Es ist auch weniger neues Detail — mit Ausnahme des dritten citirten Werkes — was uns hier entgegentritt, sondern der Abschluss von Worsaae's archäologischer Anschauung. Ein wesentlich neuer Punkt wird in den neuesten Werken gerade erst angedeutet. Es zeigt sich nämlich, dass auch in Dänemark das Eisenalter noch mehrere Jahhunderte v. Chr. zurückreicht. Es sind aus der La Tène Zeit eine ganze Reihe von Funden gemacht, die zuerst Undset in seinem epochemachenden Werke „Das erste Auftreten des Eisens in Nord-Europa 1881" zusammengefasst und die sich seitdem noch bedeutend gemehrt haben. Diese Periode welche mehrere Jahrhunderte v. Chr. umfasst, und deren Erkenntniss erst die letzte Lücke in unserer Kenntniss der Urgeschichte Nord- und Mittel-Europa's geschlossen hät, ist in dem Kopenhagener Museum aber schon seit längerer Zeit als besondere vorrömische Gruppe abgesondert.

Die Hauptformen der Alterthümer in den verschiedenen Perioden sowohl der heidnischen Zeit als des Mittelalters und der Renaissance bildete Worsaae in dem Buche „Nordiske Oldsager i det Kgl. Museum i Kjöbenhavn (Nordische Alterthümer im Königl. Museum zu Kopenhagen. Erste Auflage 1854, Zweite Auflage 1859) ab. Dies Werk ist der Vorläufer der ähnlichen Werke, welche später in den anderen scandinavischen Reichen erschienen und ist daher besonders oft citirt worden, wenn es galt gewisse Formen genau zu bezeichnen.

Es fehlte nicht an Angriffen auf Worsaae's System. Die Zweitheilung des Steinalters bekämpfte sein Landsmann Steenstrup eifrig, ist aber unterlegen. Auch gegen die Gliederung der Broncezeit in eine ältere und jüngere Periode ist gerade in Dänemark Opposition gemacht, während sie Montelius in Schweden acceptirt, ja noch viel weiter durchgeführt hat. Ferner wird die Gliederung des Eisenalters von Hildebrand in Schweden etwas anders aufgefasst, welcher die ältere und mittlere Eisenzeit enger zusammenzieht. Doch sind diese Differenzen nicht von besonders einschneidender Bedeutung und kann ihre sachgemässe Verhandlung nur dazu dienen der Wahrheit näher zu kommen. Die täglich wachsende Erfahrung bringt ja auch immer neue und vervollkommnete Anschauungen.

Hingegen bedrohte das eben fertiggestellte Gebände plötzlich ein Sturm, der es fast umzustürzen schien.

1864 begannen deutscherseits die Angriffe auf das Dreiperiodensystem, welche manchmal an Heftigkeit fast den Character politischer und religiöser Streitigkeiten annahmen, und die das rein sachliche öfters aus den Augen setzten. In unberechtigter nationaler Aufwallung wurde das System als dänische Beeinflussung und Ueberhebung angegriffen, eine Auffassung, welcher Lisch, der ganz unabhängige Mitschöpfer des Systems, energisch entgegentrat. Von nationaler Ueberhebung ist, wenn man die ruhig und objectiv gehaltenen Schriften Worsaaes und der anderen scandinavischen Forscher studirt, wohl keine Spur zu finden; auch ist es ja ein grosser Theil des ausserhalb Scandinaviens gelegenen Norddeutschlands, das an dieser bestrittenen Cultur der Bronzezeit participirt, und die Scandinavier räumen selbst ein, dass ihnen diese Cultur von Süden her zugegangen sei. Der Kampf hatte aber das Gute, dass es jetzt galt die Grundlagen der Archäologie immer mehr durch inductives, vergleichendes Studium zu sichern, denn die einfach a priori ausgesprochene Ansicht: „es ist dies oder jenes nicht möglich" hat sich oft genug als irrig bewiesen. Und man muss zugestehen, dass gerade die scandinavischen Gelehrten die Lösung der Fragen wesentlich gefördert haben, da in den drei Ländern zunächst eine feste Organisation der archäologischen Wissenschaft existirt, und besonders da gerade die Gelehrten der jüngeren Generation durch reichliche Staatsstipendien in den Stand gesetzt waren, die europäischen Sammlungen zu wiederholten Malen im weitesten Maasse zu studiren. Die eingehenden Forschungen, welchen sich die Entdeckungen in Süddeutschland, Oesterreich, der Schweiz, Italien anschlossen, haben dem Drei-Periodensystem zu einem von dem grössten Theile der Archäologen anerkannten Siege verholfen. Ueberall in Europa und auch über die Grenzen der Erdtheile hinaus tritt die Bronce früher als das Eisen auf, geht aber bei Waffen und Geräthen nachher noch längere Zeit mit dem Eisen parallel. Ebenso hat die genaueste Kenntniss der Broncen aus den Mittelmeerländern gelehrt, dass der bei weitem grösste Theil der nordischen Bronzen nicht importirt, sondern wirklich im Lande selbst angefertigt worden ist. Es tritt die Gliederung in den einzelnen Regionen Europa's wohl etwas verschieden auf, man muss die Eintheilung danach modificiren, auch erweitern und dann die correspondirenden Abschnitte von den verschiedenen lokalen Gebieten in Parallele bringen, aber für den scandinavischen Norden hat die Wornaae'sche Gliederung, wenn man noch die La Tène Periode einschaltet, ihre volle Giltigkeit behalten, abgesehen von einigen Abänderungen untergeordneter Natur. Worsaae ward es noch vergönnt diesen Sieg seiner Ideen und den überwiegenden Umschwung der Meinungen bei der wissenschaftlichen Welt zu erleben. Die Zeiten, in welchen auf Congressen ein Redner, der den verpönten Ausdruck „Bronzezeit" gebrauchte, sich wegen dieses „Scandinavismus" zu entschuldigen für nöthig hielt, sind glücklicherweise vorüber.

Die Jahre nach 1865 brachten ausser einigen kleineren auf die Spätzeit bezüglichen Abhandlungen, über das Begräbnis von Mammen, über die Cultur der Vikinger, jene oben bereits erwähnten Abhandlungen, welche im Wesentlichen die in den Schleswig'schen Alterthümern auseinandergesetzten Anschauungen wiederholten, zum Theil noch etwas weiter ausführten. Nur ein neuer Gedanke beherrschte Worsaae in diesem letzten Abschnitte seines Lebens immer mehr und drängte seine Untersuchungen in eine neue Richtung, die sich jedoch von der streng inductiven Richtung der vergleichenden Archäologie etwas entfernte.

Im Jahre 1866 suchte er die so häufig vorkommenden massenhaften in Mooren, d. h. einstigen Seen, oder unter grossen Steinen aufgefundenen Depots von Bronzesachen durch religiöse Bräuche zu erklären. Er dehnte diese Annahme auch auf Eisengeräthe und Waffen aus und führte dies 1867 besonders in Bezug auf die gewaltigen Moorfunde der älteren Eisenzeit weiter aus. Er war der Ansicht, dass letztere Opfer an die Götter seien: nach einer gewonnenen Schlacht hätte man wahrscheinlich die Kriegsbeute in heilige Seen versenkt, nachdem die Waffen zum Theil unbrauchbar gemacht waren; eine Ansicht, die er durch Belege aus den historisch mitgetheilten Gebräuchen verschiedener älterer Völker, der Gallier, der Cimbern wahrscheinlich zu machen suchte. Die Annahme dehnte er dann auf die meisten kleineren Depot's der Bronzezeit und auch auf viele bis in ein hohes Alter hineinreichenden der Steinzeit aus, Depot's welche natürlich auch in Friedenszeiten den Göttern als Opfer dargebracht seien. Dass gerade die grossen Moorfunde eine solche Bedeutung haben ist sehr wohl möglich, vielleicht ist es aber doch gewagt, auch die kleineren Depot's zum grössten Theile auf diese Weise erklären zu wollen, die immerhin, wenn ihnen überhaupt eine symbolische Bedeutung zukommt, auch mit bestimmten Grabgebräuchen in Verbindung stehen können.

Diese Richtung nach der religiösen Seite der Forschung verfolgte er dann nach mehreren anderen Seiten. In der Abhandlung über die Darstellungen der Goldbracteaten (dänisch und französisch 1870) brachte er dieselben mit der altnordischen Götter- und Heldensage in Verbindung. Besonders aber verfolgte er diese Ideen in seiner letzten grösseren Schrift „The Industrial arts of Danmark 1882", in welcher er die Entwicklung des grössten Theils der Ornamente aller Perioden der Vorzeit als durch religiöse und symbolische Vorstellungen bedingt darstellte. Es ist ja Thatsache, dass die religiösen Vorstellungen besonders bei den auf einer primitiveren Culturstufe stehenden Völkern auf Gebräuche und Ornamente einen ungemein grossen Einfluss geübt haben, und das Vieles Jahrtausende hindurch, selbst beim Wechsel der Religionen sich bis auf die Gegenwart fortgepflanzt hat. Da aber bei diesen Schlüssen die strenge Induction mehr den Conjecturen weichen muss, ist es ja immerhin möglich gar manche Erscheinung noch anders zu deuten.

Im Jahre 1865 beginnt der letzte wichtige Abschnitt seiner Thätigkeit, er tritt jetzt als Organisator auf. 1864 war Rafn, 1865 Thomsen gestorben. Beide Männer hatten ein Leben reich an Arbeit, reich an wissenschaftlichen Erfolgen hinter sich. Damit ihre grossartigen Schöpfungen erfolgreich weiter gedeihen konnten war aber eine Auffrischung, eine Reform nöthig. Die Alterthumsgesellschaft nahm eine neue Organisation an, die sich den Anforderungen der Zeit mehr anpasste und besonders auch die archäologische Richtung besser vertreten konnte. Worsaae wurde Vice-Präsident — Präsident war der König Christian IX., 1866 wurde Worsaae Director des Museums, und in beiden Richtungen, besonders in letzterer konnte er nun seine Thätigkeit voll entfalten. Der Zeitpunkt war auch ein besonders günstiger, wieder eine Epoche von hervorragender Wichtigkeit in der Geschichte der Archäologie.

Gerade am Anfange der 60er Jahre verbreitete sich das Interesse für die vorhistorische Archäologie in allen Kreisen der wissenschaftlichen überhaupt der gebildeten Welt, nachdem diese Disciplin vorher von einer doch nur kleinen Zahl Fachgelehrter gepflegt worden war. Zahlreiche Jünger strömten der neuen Wissenschaft zu auch in den Ländern, wo sie vorher nicht mit demselben Eifer, wie im Norden gepflegt worden war, und so hat sie in den letzten 25 Jahren einen Aufschwung genommen, wie wenig andere Disciplinen. Besonders zog die inductive Methode der vergleichenden Archäologie, welche mit der naturwissenschaftlichen eine grosse Verwandtschaft besitzt, an und erst auf diesem Wege konnte man hoffen zu sicheren Resultaten zu kommen.

Diesen Studien galt es nun das enorme Material des Kopenhagener Alterthums-Museums in vollster Weise zugänglich zu machen, und hier konnte Worsaae jetzt voll seine segensreiche Thätigkeit entfalten, den Principien, die er schon lange vertreten hatte, Geltung verschaffen. Die Sammlung, welche aus dem Runden Thurm nach Christianborg Schloss und 1854 nach Prindsenspalais übergesiedelt war, ordnete er nun soweit es noch anging nach ganz neuen Principien. Die Eintheilung in die drei Hauptperioden wurde beibehalten, aber dieselbe nach seinem System noch weiter fortgeführt: ferner wurden in den einzelnen Abschnitten die geographisch getrennten Bezirke auseinander gezogen und endlich die zusammen in Gräbern oder anderweitig bei einander gefundenen Objecte beisammen aufgestellt. So kann man jetzt die zeitlichen Veränderungen in den verschiedenen Theilen des Landes deutlich verfolgen. Worsaae wurde bei der Aus- und Weiterführung dieses Werkes durch eine Reihe tüchtiger Gehilfen erfolgreich unterstützt und sein belebender und anregender Einfluss hat es verstanden immer neue Kräfte heranzuziehen, so dass wir auch nach seinem so sehr zu beklagenden Tode über die gedeihliche Fortführung seines Werkes vollständig beruhigt sein können.

Bis jetzt wurde nur die prähistorische Seite der Dänischen Forschung in's Auge gefasst. Die Ziele aber waren viel weiter gesteckt. Es sollte das ganze nationale Leben und die Entwicklung der Cultur auch bis in die neueren Zeiten hinein dargestellt werden. Dies war in Dänemark umsomehr angezeigt, als in Scandinavien aus der heidnischen bis in die neueste Zeit eine fortlaufende Entwicklung vorliegt, welche durch keine fremde Invasion wie in Norddeutschland unterbrochen ist. Wie weit diese Continuität allerdings in das höchste Alterthum zurückreicht ist noch fraglich.

Im Nordischen Museum waren die Funde und Ueberreste auch aus dem Mittelalter und der neueren Zeit bis 1660 aufgestellt, bis zum Beginne des Souveränen Königthum's. Eine zeitliche Fortsetzung ist die historische Sammlung der Dänischen Könige im Rosenborg Schloss, so recht Worsaae's eigene Schöpfung. Bereits 1858 war er Inspecteur derselben geworden und konnte hier voll das chronologische Princip zur Geltung bringen. Die ziemlich ungeordnete Sammlung wurde von ihm ganz umgestaltet. Die Räume wurden streng chronologisch gegliedert; er suchte aus den verschiedenen Königlichen Schlössern die Einrichtungen, Mobiliar, die Schmucksachen, kurz den ganzen Besitz der einzelnen Könige oder hervorragender Personen zusammen und bildete so in jedem einzelnen Raume eine abgeschlossene Sammlung, welche ausschliesslich den Charakter dieser Periode repräsentirte, wobei die Porträts von Zeitgenossen den Eindruck noch erhöhten. Nothwendige Restaurationen dienten dazu, das Ganze noch einheitlicher zu gestalten. So entstand in Rosenborg ein Schmuckkästchen, wie man es nirgends wieder antrifft, in welchem der Spaziergang durch die Zimmerreihe ein höchst belehrendes Bild über die fort- oder auch zurückschreitende Kunst und Cultur in ihren Höhepunkten vor Augen führt.

Worsaae wollte diese Entwicklung noch weiter fortführen von 1848 bis auf die Neuzeit und zur Ergänzung auch in einem neuen Volks-Museum die Culturentwickelung in den breiten Schichten des Volkes darstellen. Doch war es ihm nicht mehr vergönnt, diesen grossartigen Plan durchzuführen.

Mit dem Nordischen Museum im Prindsenspalais übernahm Worsaae 1866 auch noch ein zweites grossartiges, das Ethnographische, welches durch seine sehr reiche Sammlung von Eskimogeräthen besonders geeignet war die primitive Cultur der alten Europäischen Steinzeit zu illustriren. Diese nach einem bestimmten Plane von Thomsen geordnete Sammlung — die Gruppen waren nach Klimaten auseinander gezogen — ordnete Worsaae nach seinem chronologisch-geographischen Princip neu. Die prähistorischen Alterthümer der ausserdänischen Völker wurden zu einer eigenen comparativen Abtheilung zusammengestellt, und die Sammlungen der modernen Völker nach Racen und Volksstämmen ethnographisch wissenschaftlich geordnet.

Die Art und Weise Museen zu ordnen, sowohl was die Auswahl des Stoffes als die Anordnung desselben betrifft ist eine äusserst wichtige, zumal gegenwärtig in allen Fächern ein so massenhaftes Material zusammengebracht wird, dass eine zweckmässige Verwaltung, welche sowohl für das Studium des wissenschaftlichen Forschers wie für die Anschauung und Belehrung der grossen Menge genügen soll, auf ernste Schwierigkeiten stösst. Hierüber entwickelte Worsaae ein Jahr vor seinem Tode in einer kleinen Schrift (Ueber die Ordnung archäologisch-historischer Museen innerhalb und ausserhalb des Nordens, Dänisch und Französisch 1884) äusserst beherzigenswerthe Grundsätze, welche, da sie aus der Feder eines so erfahrenen Museums-Direktors kommen, ganz besondere Beachtung verdienen.

Bei dieser vielseitigen schöpferischen Thätigkeit war es natürlich, dass Worsaae unter seinen Fachgenossen eine hervorragende Stellung einnahm und mit denselben in engster Verbindung stand. Nachdem 1867 bei Gelegenheit der Pariser WeltAusstellung der erste internationale Congress für prähistorische Archäologie stattgefunden hatte, wiederholten sich dieselben in periodischen Zwischenräumen. Es wurde dadurch den Gelehrten die beste Gelegenheit gegeben die Alterthümer der verschiedenen Länder Europas kennen zu lernen und zu studiren und durch persönliche Berührung mit den Fachgenossen die grosse Arbeit an dem gemeinsamen internationalen Werke zu fördern. Worsaae nahm an den meisten Congressen Theil und spielte daselbst eine hervorragende Rolle. Dem Congress 1869 zu Kopenhagen präsidirte er. Der Reise zu einem russischen Congresse 1869 nach Moskau und den hier gemachten Studien verdankt die schon erwähnte Schrift über die Besiedelung Russlands und des scandinavischen Nordens ihren Ursprung, in welcher er u. a. die Annahme bekämpft als sei Scandinavien von Russland aus besiedelt worden.

In Bezug auf die äusseren Lebensverhältnisse ist noch nachzuholen, dass Worsaae 1854 Professor für Alterthumskunde wurde, 1874 Cultusminister unter Fonnesbeck wurde, ein Amt, das er nach einem Jahre niederlegte und welches der ganzen Richtung seiner Thätigkeit wenig entsprach. Am 15. August 1885 beschloss dann ein jäher Tod das Leben dieses in voller Rüstigkeit dastehenden Mannes, dessen nie ruhenden Geist noch immer neue grossartige Pläne erfüllten.

Es gebührt sich schliesslich neben dem Manne der Wissenschaft und Arbeit auch noch des Menschen zu gedenken.

Worsaae's mildes, liebenswürdiges Wesen hat nicht wenig zu seinen grossen Erfolgen beigetragen. Ein Freund der dänischen Könige, von grossem Ansehen und Einfluss in den höheren Gesellschaftskreisen, war er ebenso populär im Volke. So war er im Stande das Verständniss für seine Bestrebungen in den weitesten Kreisen zu erwecken und die Sache zu einer nationalen zu machen, d. h. nicht im Sinne einseitiger nationaler Ueberhebung, sondern nationaler Betheiligung. Sanft in seinem Urtheile liess er auch abweichende Ansichten gelten und trat ihnen nicht schroff entgegen, wenn sie von dem Geiste und dem Bestreben wissenschaftlicher Forschung durchdrungen waren. Als väterlicher Freund stand er den jungen Gelehrten zur Seite, die unter seiner Aegide sich heranbildeten und, wenn die Ansichten auch in manchen Punkten von den seinigen abweichen, ist es doch sein Geist, der diese neue Generation leitet und auf die richtigen Bahnen gelenkt hat.

Wir Ausländer haben auch in vollstem Masse Gelegenheit gehabt diese Seite seines Wesens kennen zu lernen und nach jeder Richtung hin dankbar auszunutzen. Dem fremden Forscher wurden die Schätze des Kopenhagener Museums in liberalster, unbeschränkter Weise zur Verfügung gestellt, bereitwillig jede Unterstützung und Auskunft ertheilt; dem fremden Besucher, bei welchem Worsaae Interesse für sein Museum erblickte, erklärte er seine Alterthümer und zwar meist in dessen jedesmaliger Landessprache.

So ist in Worsaae ein Mann dahin gegangen, gleich bedeutend als Forscher, als Organisator, als Mensch.

Verzeichniss
einer Sammlung Ost- und Westpreussischer Geschiebe

eingesandt von **Dr. Alfred Jentzsch** in Königsberg, geordnet und theilweise bestimmt von

Hjalmar Lundbohm in Stockholm.*)

28 Proben von **Gneiss.** Grau oder roth; im Allgemeinen grob, deutlich geschichtet; darunter mehrere Varietäten von **Granatgneiss.**

Ein Handstück eines mittelkörnigen grauen, glimmerreichen Gneisses mit banfkorngrossen Granaten stammt aus einem 28,6 Kubikmeter haltenden Block von Königsberg; ein anderes Handstück von grobem glimmerreichem Gneiss aus einem sehr grossen Block, welcher bei Sykorczyn, Kreis Berent in Westpreussen, 200 Meter über der Ostsee lag.

Die vorliegenden Stücke sind gesammelt bei Königsberg, Rauschen im Samland, Labiau, Mohrungen, Insterburg, Goldap, Lötzen, Pr. Holland, Heilsberg und Lyck in Ostpreussen, sowie von Pr. Stargardt und Thorn in Westpreussen.

Keines der Handstücke ist so charakteristisch, dass seine Heimath mit Sicherheit bestimmt werden kann. Vermuthungsweise kann man für den Granatgneiss Södermanland, für den grauen Gneiss Reslagen als Heimath ansehen; aber ähnliche Gesteine treten an vielen andern Orten in Schweden auf.

19 Proben von **Hornblendegneiss, Hornblendeschiefer, Dioritschiefer etc.** Dieselben sind im Allgemeinen feinkörnig; mehrere enthalten Granaten; doch gleichen sie nicht dem granatführenden Dioritschiefer Schonens und Hallands. Fundorte: Königsberg, Rauschen, Pillau, Memel, Insterburg, Dar-

Auch für diese Gesteine kann der Ursprung nicht bestimmt werden.

*) Die Sammlung befindet sich im Bureau der geologischen Landesuntersuchung Schwedens. Zu jedem der untersuchten Stücke werden Duplikate, welche von demselben Block geschlagen sind, mit gleicher Nummer im Provinzial-Museum zu Königsberg aufbewahrt. Die Sammlung repräsentirt sämmtliche im November 1880 im Provinzial-Museum vorhanden gewesenen Varietäten krystallinischer Geschiebe Ostpreussens. Das Manuskript ist durch A. Jentzsch aus dem Schwedischen übersetzt.

kehmen, Heilsberg, Heiligenbeil, Schippenbeil, Mohrungen in Ostpreussen, sowie Pr. Stargardt und Graudenz in Westpreussen.

22 Proben von **Diorit.** Theils feinkörnig und feldspatharm, theils mittelkörnig, theils mit porphyrartig in einer feinkörnigen, gewöhnlich helleren Grundmasse eingesprengten Hornblende-Krystallen. Fundorte: Königsberg, Rauschen, Heiligenbeil, Labiau, Goldap, Heilsberg in Ostpreussen und Danzig in Westpreussen.

Mehrere der porphyrartigen Diorite gleichen denen, welche auf den Blättern Hvetlanda und Nydala in Småland vorkommen. Aber ähnliche Varietäten treten auch anderwärts in Schweden auf.

75 Proben von **Hälleflintgneiss, Glimmerschiefer** und **Hälleflinta** von Königsberg, Wormditt, Kruglanken, Mehlauken, Darkehmen, Wehlau, Heiligenbeil, Pr. Holland, Arys, Passenheim, Rauschen, Schippenbeil, Landsberg, Heilsberg, Insterburg, Kurische Nehrung, Mohrungen, Zinten in Ostpreussen, und von Rosenberg, Pr. Stargardt, Thorn, Dirschau, Elbing, Carthaus in Westpreussen, sowie aus der Provinz Posen.

Sowohl unter den Hälleflinten als unter den Hälleflintgneissen finden sich einige, welche den Småländischen gleichen; aber dass sie wirklich dorther stammen, ist doch keineswegs sicher. Die meisten Proben sind unbestimmbar.

Die charakteristischsten Proben sind:

No. 8013 von Königsberg }
„ 5501 „ „ } weisser gestreckter, ziemlich grober Glimmerschiefer.
„ 7503 „ Kruglanken }

Dieselben haben auffallende Aehnlichkeit mit den hellen Glimmerschiefern des nordöstlichen Schonens. Bekanntlich wird dieses Gestein gerade nach Königsberg behufs Verwendung als Schleifstein exportirt, und es liegt daher die Annahme nahe, dass diese Gesteine auf solche Weise dahin gelangt sind.

In den Norrländischen Schiefern finden sich nach Svenonius sehr untergeordnete Lagen, welche mit einem der Handstücke eine gewisse Aehnlichkeit besitzen.

No. 2734, 2195 und 5399 von Königsberg. Dunkler, fast schwarzer, sehr feinkörniger, in dem einen Stück fast dichter Glimmerschiefer, mit grossen kantigen oder abgerundeten Krystallen von Andalusit.

Solche Schiefer finden sich in Vestmanland und Nerike und wahrscheinlich nördlich vom Westende des Hjelmar-Sees, sowie lose Blöcke in Nyköpings Län und in einem Rullstensås bei der Station Rosersberg. Doch scheinen diese sämmtlich gröber als die vorliegenden Geschiebe zu sein. Andalusitführende Glimmerschiefer treten auch als untergeordnete Einlagerungen des Hälleflinthgneisses in Ångermanland sowie in den nordischen „gelben Schiefern“ auf.

59 Proben von **Granit**, worunter folgende bemerkenswerth:

No. 8889 von Königsberg. Grauer, mittelkörniger Granit mit hellgrauem Quarz schwarzem Glimmer, einem vielleicht als Cordierit zu bezeichnenden Mineral; weissem, stark verwittertem Plagioklas und ziemlich grossen Zwillingskrystallen von Orthoklas.

Das Gestein ist sehr ähnlich dem Granit von Striegau in Schlesien. Ein schwedischer Granit gleichen Aussehens ist (wahrscheinlich) nicht bekannt.

No. 8891 von Königsberg. Rothgrauer porphyrartiger Granit; feinkrystallinische Grundmasse mit kleinen runden Quarzkörnern, etwas grösseren gelben Plagioklas-Krystallen und einzelnen Orthoklas-Krystallen; ausserdem Hornblende.

Vielleicht von Småland.

No. 2022 von Königsberg. Hellgrauroth, mittelkörnig.

Vexiö-Granit von Småland?

No. 8943 von Königsberg. Grober weisser Augengranit mit schwarzem Glimmer.

Dasselbe Gestein findet sich als lose Blöcke in den Schären bei Stockholm.

No. 5489 von Königsberg. Die bis 11 Centimeter grossen braunrothen Orthoklas-Krystalle liegen in einer feinkörnigen Grundmasse desselben Feldspaths mit zuckerkörnigem, bisweilen grünem Quarz.

Gleicht einigermassen dem Granit aus der Gegend von Eknö zwischen Vestervik und Oskarshamn in Småland. Auch dieser hat weissen und grünlichen zuckerkörnigen Quarz mit manchmal gleich grossen Feldspath-Krystallen, ist aber gewöhnlich bedeutend reicher an Glimmer.

No. 8918 von Königsberg. Rother, grobkörniger Granit mit dunkelrothem Orthoklas und hellgrauem Quarz; Pegmatitähnlich; Glimmer fehlt beinahe ganz.

Von Småland?

No. 7119 von Königsberg. Rother grobkörniger Granit.	Gleicht dem Granit vom Festlande bei Virbo in Småland.
No. 8916 von Königsberg. Rother mittelkörniger Granit mit zuckerkörnigem Quarz.	Sehr ähnlich gewissen Småländischen Graniten, z. B. dem von Helgerum, südlich von Vestervik.
No. 5776 und 5790 von Rauschen im Samland. Graurother Augengranit. Fein- bis mittelkörnige Grundmasse, runde und kantige dunkle Quarzkörner; zolllange Krystalle von hellem Orthoklas und ziemlich grosse Krystalle feingestreifter, mit kleinen Quarzkörnchen erfüllter Plagioklase.	Das Gestein ist ausserordentlich charakteristisch; aber seine Heimath ist nicht mit Sicherheit anzugeben.
No. 8911 von Königsberg. Rother, fein- bis mittelkörniger glimmerarmer Granit mit fast schwarzem Quarz.	Nicht sicher bestimmbar. Aehnelt den Åländischen Ganggraniten.
No. 8917 von Königsberg. Blassrother feinkörniger Granit mit grossen Krystallen von Feldspath, dunkelm Quarz, etwas Hornblende, mit Andeutung von Rapakiwi-Struktur.	Wahrscheinlich von Åland.
No. 9376 von Königsberg. Grobkörniger hellrother Granit mit deutlicher Rapakiwi-Struktur.	Åland.
No. 8906 von Königsberg. Grob- bis mittelkörniger hellrother Granit mit Hornblende und mit hellem und dunklem Quarz.	Åland.
No. 8907 von Königsberg und No. 7248 von Lyck. Rother feinkörniger Granit mit vereinzelten grösseren Feldspath-Krystallen; in Drusenhöhlungen sitzen Krystalle von Feldspath, Quarz und Flussspath.	Åland oder Vesternorrland.
No. 8915 von Königsberg. Mittelkörniger rother Gneiss mit viel Feldspath und mit einem gelben Verwitterungsprodukt.	Wahrscheinlich von Norrland.
No. 8895 von Königsberg. Gleicht dem vorigen, ist aber bedeutend stärker verwittert.	Vielleicht von Norrland.

No. 8909 von Königsberg. Grobkörniger rother Granit mit dunkeln Quarz und ausserordentlich viel Hornblende.

Aehnelt einigermassen einem der Åländischen Granite.

No. 7848 von Mohrungen in Ostpreussen. Rother, mittelkörniger, prophyrartiger Granit.

Gleicht dem porphyrartigen Granit von Dalarne.

No. 7396 von Heiligenbeil, Ostpreussen. Rapakiwi mit 1—2 Zoll langen Feldspathkrystallen, die mit einem schmalen Ring hellgrauen Feldspathes umgeben sind.

Finland.

Die übrigen Granite sind fein- bis grobkörnig, roth oder grau, mit oder ohne Augenstruktur. Einige derselben gleichen gewissen Småländischen Graniten, sind aber doch nicht mit Sicherheit bestimmbar. Die meisten Proben stammen von Königsberg und Rauschen; die übrigen von den nämlichen Fundorten, wie die Gneisse.

34 Proben von **Pegmatit**, von denselben Fundpunkten.

Das Heimathsgebiet kann nicht bestimmt werden.

53 Proben von **Porphyr**, meist von den gleichen Lokalitäten. Die bemerkenswerthesten sind:

No. 8900 von Königsberg. Rother Quarzporphyr; in der dichten dunkelrothen Grundmasse liegen grosse runde Quarzkörner und hellrothe Feldspathkrystalle.

Åland.

No. 5782 von Rauschen. In einer feinkörnigen stark verwitterten graugelben Grundmasse liegen grosse verwitterte Feldspathkrystalle mit runden oder eckigen grauen Quarzkörnern.

Gleicht im Habitus einigermassen dem porphyrartigen Granit von Åland.

No. 7203 von Elbing in Westpreussen. Quarzporphyr mit kleinen Einschlüssen eines schwarzen Gesteins. Kleines schlechtes Handstück.

Vielleicht von Åland?

No. 2025 und 5646 von Lyck, No. 5762 und 5786 von Rauschen, No. 7300 von Wormditt und No. 8887 von Königsberg. Rother Quarz-Porphyr. Grundmasse dicht mit kleinen runden oder eckigen dunkeln Quarzen und sehr kleinen spärlichen hellrothen Feldspath-Krystallen.

No. 8805, 8884, 8894, 8897, 8913 und 8914 von Königsberg und No. 7829 von Pr. Stargardt in Westpreussen. Porphyr mit brauner Grundmasse, sehr zahlreichen kleinen gelbrothen Feldspath-Krystallen und sehr kleinen dunkeln Quarzkörnern.

Gleichen im allgemeinen Habitus dem Elfdalener-Porphyr, sind aber nicht besonders typisch. „Rother“ und „schwarzer Orrlok“ haben ungefähr gleiches Aussehen, aber es fehlt ihnen der Quarz.

No. 2065 von der Kurischen Nehrung, Ostpreussen. Rothe Grundmasse mit gelben und rothen Feldspath-Krystallen.

Dala-Porphyr „Kåtilla“.

No. 7832 von Pr. Stargardt, Westpreussen. Dunkle Grundmasse mit kleinen rothen Feldspath-Krystallen.

Gleicht einigermassen dem Dalaporphyr „Mjågen“.

No. 5768 von Rauschen im Samland. Braune Grundmasse mit hellen Feldspath-Krystallen und spärlichen Quarzen.

Gleicht im allgemeinen Habitus dem Dalaporphyr, ist aber nicht besonders typisch.

No. 5640 und 5708 von Thorn in Westpreussen. Rothe Grundmasse, hellgrüner Feldspath.

Vielleicht von Dalarne.

No. 2243 von Heilsberg in Ostpreussen. Rothe Grundmasse, hellrothe Feldspath-Krystalle.

Vielleicht von Dalarne.

No. 7854 von Heilsberg. Dunkel graubraune Grundmasse, hellere grünliche Feldspath-Krystalle.

Vielleicht von Dalarne.

No. 5720 von Thorn. Braunrothe flasrige Grundmasse; kleine rothe Feldspath-Krystalle.

Dalarnes „Loka-Risberg“.

No. 2411 von Königsberg. Braungraue dichte Grundmasse, bohnenförmige kleine Feldspath-Krystalle und blaue Quarze.

Småländischer Gangporphyr.

Unter den übrigen Porphyren finden sich viele mit felsitischer Grundmasse, welche nicht bestimmbar sind; ausserdem granitartige Porphyre, Diorit- und Diabas-Porphyr, theils von in Schweden unbekanntem Typus, theils solchen Gesteinen gleichend, welche als lose Blöcke im westlichen Norrland und anstehend an vielen anderen Stellen in Schweden auftreten. Einige der Handstücke gleichen gewissen Porphyren in der durch Feddersen aus Jütland mitgebrachten Geschiebesammlung.

1 Probe (No. 1501) eines grünen Gesteins aus dem Samland.	Gleicht dem „Phonolith" von Dalarne.

20 Proben von **Diabas**, von welchen 6 Stücke dem sogenannten Åsby-Typus angehören, nämlich:

No. 5390 von Darkehmen, Ostpreussen. Kleines schlechtes Handstück mit röthlichem Feldspath. No. 7194 von Elbing, Westpreussen. Grobkörniger typischer Åsby-Diabas. No. 5796 von Rauschen, Ostpreussen. Mittelkörnig. No. 7468 von Mohrungen in Ostpreussen. Kleines verwittertes Stück, mittelkörnig, mit etwas röthlichem Feldspath. No. 6979 von Heiligenbeil, Ostpreussen. Feinkörnig, typisch. Nach Angabe des Etiketts ist das Gestein durch Verwitterung oberflächlich schalenförmig abgesondert. No. 7317 von Landsberg in Ostpreussen. Spaltenausfüllung von Augit, Chlorit etc. in feinkörnigem Diabas, wie bei den Spaltenausfüllungen, welche man oft in dem Diabas von Vesternorrland antrifft.	Von welchen der bekannten Fundorte des Åsby-Diabas (Dalarne, Jemtland, Vesternorrland, Helsingland, Gestrikland etc.) diese Geschiebe stammen, dürfte wahrscheinlich selbst bei mikroskopischer Untersuchung nicht zu entscheiden sein.

Die übrigen Diabas-Proben bestehen zumeist aus schwarzem feinkörnigem bis dichtem Trapp: viele sind von eigenthümlicher Art, aber bis auf Weiteres unbestimmbar. Ausserdem finden sich einige Proben von groben, Gabbro ähnlichen Gesteinen.

26 Proben von **Mandelstein** und ähnlichen Felsarten. Darunter sind hervorzuheben:

No. 4170 von Kruglanken, Ostpreussen. Verwittert; Grundmasse anscheinend braun; Mandeln von rothem feinkörnigem Feldspath und grünem Chlorit.

Wahrscheinlich von Gefle.

Unter den Mandelsteinen haben mehrere grosse Aehnlichkeit mit solchen, die als Geschiebe auf Gotland vorkommen, deren Heimath gleichfalls unbekannt ist.

33 Proben von **Sandstein** und **Conglomerat**. Unter den Sandsteinen gleichen 3 Stücke dem rothen Sandstein von Dalarne und Norrland, nämlich No. 8791 von Königsberg, No. 5834 von Mehlauken, No. 5820 von Rauschen, sämmtlich ostpreussische Fundorte.

Viele der Sandsteine und Conglomerate gleichen dem Sandstein vom Kalmarsund, sowie gewissen Varietäten aus der Sparagmit-Formation und Visingsö-Formation von Småland.

Ferner gleichen No. 2179 aus Ostpreussen, No. 7840 von Wormditt und No. 9378 von Memel sehr dem Phosphorit-Conglomerat von Gislöf in Schonen; aber die Kugeln scheinen nicht wie bei dem letzteren aus Phosphorit zu bestehen.

Unter den übrigen Sandsteinen und Conglomeraten gleichen viele cambrischen, silurischen und noch jüngeren Gesteinen Schwedens, doch ist es unmöglich, ihre Heimath zu bestimmen.

Ausser den vorstehend aufgezählten Proben, finden sich noch 14 Stücke sedimentären und körnigen Kalksteines, verschiedene schieferartige Gesteine etc., deren Ursprung nicht bestimmt werden kann.

Wie aus dem Obigen hervorgeht, bestehen die allermeisten Geschiebe aus Felsarten, welche in weiten Gebieten Schwedens gemein sind, und deren Herkunft folglich nicht mit grösserer Sicherheit bestimmt werden kann. Nur diejenigen Granite und Porphyre, welche, wie oben angegeben, von Åland, Finland, Dalarne und Vesternorrland (die beiden letztgenannten Landschaften liegen im mittelsten Schweden) herstammen, nur diese sind hinreichend charakteristisch, um als Leitgeschiebe dienen zu können. Alle übrigen indessen, vielleicht mit ein Paar Ausnahmen, können von der östlichen Küste Schwedens herstammen.

Ueber Tertiaerpflanzen von Grünberg in Schl. aus dem Provinzial-Museum zu Königsberg in Pr.

Von

Hermann Engelhardt,

Oberlehrer in Dresden.*)

Ueber die mir zur Bestimmung freundlichst übersendeten Tertiaerpflanzen aus dem plastischen Thone von Grünberg habe ich Folgendes zu berichten:

Obgleich mir eine immerhin ansehnliche Zahl von grösseren und kleineren Thonstücken vorlag, so vermochte ich doch nur wenige Arten nachzuweisen, weil die Blattreste zweier tertiaerer Bäume auf ihnen fast allen Raum in Anspruch nehmen, nämlich die von Ficus tiliaefolia Al. Br. sp. und Alnus Kefersteinii Göpp. sp. Erstere sind in allen Grössen, welche verschiedene Alter repräsentiren, vertreten, ganz wie es die Funde von Sagan zeigten, die mir früher von anderer Seite zur Bestimmung übergeben worden waren. (Vgl. Sitzgsb. d. naturw. Gesellsch. Isis in Dresden. 1877. S. 18—20.) Hier wie dort liegen sie nicht vereinzelt neben-, sondern oft vielfach über- und durcheinander, zuweilen förmliche Schichten bildend. Da sie auch an von Göppert untersuchten Arten (Vgl. Palaeontogr. II.) in reichlicher Zahl auftreten (von ihm Ficus aequalifolia und F. grandifolia genannt), so muss nothwendiger Weise geschlossen werden, dass diese Art zur Tertiaerzeit im Gebiete des heutigen Niederschlesiens die verbreitetste und in Menge von Exemplaren auftretende Art gewesen ist. Die Blätter der anderen Art bieten eine wahre Musterkarte von Formen dar, zeigen sich aber leider nur selten am Rande gut erhalten, während die Nervation fast nichts zu wünschen übrig lässt.

Die übrigen Pflanzenreste treten nur vereinzelt auf. Von Phragmites oeningensis Al. Br. (auch von Sagan nachgewiesen) sind Blattfetzen, einmal mit dem Pilze

---

*) Vergl. Sitzungsber. phys.-oek. Gesellsch. 186 p. 20. Die betr. Blattabdrücke sind vom Königl. Oberbergamt Breslau der Gesellschaft geschenkt und „sämmtlich von Grünberg in einer Thonlage im unmittelbaren Hangenden des 2 Lachter mächtigen Braunkohlenlagers."

Ueber die Lagerung der dortigen Schichten vergl. Giebelhausen, Zeitschr. f. Berg-, Hütten- und Salinenwesen. Bd. XIX. und Berendt, das Tertiaer im Bereiche der Mark Brandenburg, Sitzungsbericht d. K. preuss. Akad. d. W. zu Berlin vom 30. Jui 1885.

Sphaeria Trogii Heer besetzt, und Rhizomstücke vorhanden. Interessant sind die langen Bänder von Potamogeton amblyphyllus Beck, a ch ein Kätzchen von Juglans, das die Staubgefässe noch erkennen liess und, weil Juglans bilinica Ung bei Sagan nachgewiesen werden konnte, vielleicht zu dieser Art gehört; sonst waren nur noch Juncus retractus Heer, ein Fragment von der Einzelfrucht des Acer otopterix Göpp. (von Göppert irrthümlicher Weise zu Acer giganteum gezogen) und Rindenstücke mit einer Rhizomorpha-Art zu beobachten, wenn ich von einem Käferflügel, der jedenfalls einem Rüssler zuzusprechen ist, völlig absehe.

Die Hauptvertreter dieser Florula sind vom Tongrien bis zur Oeninger Stufe vielfach nachgewiesen worden, Juncus retractus Heer kennt man aus dem Aquitanien und Helvetien, Potamogeton amblyphyllus Beck nur aus dem Oligocän Sachsens. (Vgl. Beck, Das Oligocän von Mittweida. Zeitschr. d. Deutschen geol. Gesellsch. 1882. S. 756. Tfl. 31. Fig. 7.)

Einen Schluss auf das geologische Alter der Schichten, die diese Reste einer untergegangenen Pflanzenwelt in sich bergen, zu machen, ist nur erlaubt, wenn wir anderwärts in Niederschlesien gefundene Reste mit zu Hilfe nehmen. Da zeigt sich dann sofort, dass diese mit Schossnitz nicht zu vereinen sind. Amenoseuron Noeggerathiae Göpp. und Pterocarpus giganteum Göpp. sp. können nur tropische Formen sein; Apocynophyllum helveticum Heer, Daphnogene Ungeri Heer, Anona cacaoides Zenk. sp., Potamogeton amblyphyllus Beck sind in Deutschland nur im Oligocän gefunden worden, Osmunda Heeri Gaud. in der Schweiz nur im Aquitanien.

Wenn nun bei der geringen Zahl von Arten, die man aus dem niederschlesischen Tertiaer bisher kennen gelernt hat, eine immerhin grosse Anzahl auf das Oligocän hinweisen, so wird es sehr wahrscheinlich, dass man es mit einer oligocänen Flora zu thun hat, freilich, wenn man die übrigen Reste mit berücksichtigt, mit einer, die wahrscheinlich das Ende dieser Zeit bezeichnen dürfte.

Ueber Fern- und Druckwirkungen.

Vortrag,

gehalten in der physikalisch-ökonomischen Gesellschaft zu Königsberg in Pr. am 4. November 1886

von

Paul Volkmann.

Der vorliegende Gegenstand ist zwar abstrakt, aber nicht ohne Interesse. Veranlassung zur Wahl desselben gab mir die Wahrnehmung, dass die Frage nach den in der Natur wirkenden Kräften — ob Druck- ob Fern-Kräfte — in den letzten Decennien physikalischer Forschung in ein neues Stadium getreten zu sein scheint. Eine völlige Erledigung haben die einschlagenden Fragen bisher nicht gefunden, ja ein Theil der Physiker steht noch mit Abneigung derartigen Untersuchungen gegenüber.

Die folgende Darstellung will über den vorliegenden Stoff berichten. Insofern der ganze Gegenstand der mathematischen Physik angehört, auf der einen Seite also eine mathematische Behandlung fordert, auf der andern aber gerade hier eine solche vermieden werden soll, wird man nicht mehr erwarten dürfen, als die Gesichtspunkte angedeutet zu finden, nach denen die Forschung in dieser Richtung sich bisher entwickelt hat und vielleicht noch entwickeln wird.

Das umfangreiche Gebiet der physikalischen Erscheinungen ist bisher zu einem Theil auf Druckwirkungen, zu einem anderen auf Fernwirkungen zurückgeführt. Es lässt sich nicht leugnen, dass die Druckwirkungen unserem Anschauungsvermögen näher stehen. Die Undurchdringlichkeit sei es der Materie, sei es der kleinsten Theile derselben, vermöge der an derselben Stelle des Raumes nicht gleichzeitig zwei ponderable Massen sich befinden können, zwingt uns z. B. die Möglichkeit von Stössen auf, und diese geben die Mittel zur grobsinnlichsten Anschauung einer Druckwirkung.

Die Annahme von Fernwirkungen steht hingegen unserem Anschauungsvermögen unvermittelt gegenüber. Wenn wirklich zwei Himmelskörper durch den leeren Raum hindurch in die Ferne auf einander einwirken, so scheint es von vornherein ausgeschlossen, dass unser Causalitätsbedürfniss in irgend einer Auffassung dieses Vorgangs jemals seine Befriedigung wird finden können. Wir können ja die Gesetze aufstellen, nach denen die Bewegung der Himmelskörper vor sich geht, aber dem wahren Grunde der Erscheinung sind wir darum keinen Schritt näher gekommen. Wir lernen uns bescheiden, wie das schon früher, in neuerer Zeit zumal von Kirchhoff betont ist, die in der Natur vorkommenden Erscheinungen zu beschreiben — Vollständigkeit und Einfachheit dabei als oberstes Ziel einer wissenschaftlichen Darstellung im Auge behaltend.

Historische Thatsache ist nun, dass wir der Einführung von unvermittelt fernwirkenden Kräften in die theoretischen Speculationen seit Newton eine Epoche der Physik verdanken, welche bis in die neueste Zeit hineinreicht. Es wird daher naturgemäss sein, mit den Fernwirkungen zunächst der ponderabeln Materie zu beginnen.

In der Natur haben wir es mit ausgedehnten Massen zu thun. Die Kräfte solch ausgedehnter räumlich getrennter Massen auf einander werden sofern die Kräfte durch die Entfernung bedingt sind, von der Anordnung der Masse im Raum, bei homogener Dichtigkeit also von der geometrischen Gestalt der Massen abhängen. Es wird alles darauf ankommen, das Gesetz für die Wirkung zweier Massenelemente, Massenpunkte auf einander, das Elementargesetz für die Wirkung ponderabler Massen abzuleiten, vorausgesetzt, dass es gestattet ist von der Wirkung der Theile durch einfache Summation zu der Wirkung des Ganzen überzugehen.

Es bedurfte eines Genies das Problem in dieser Weise zu fassen — und damit nicht genug — sich auch analytisch die Mittel zu schaffen vom unendlich Kleinen zum Endlichen, von den Elementarwirkungen zu den Totalwirkungen überzugehen. Newton war es, der das Elementargesetz der Wirkung der ponderabeln Materie nach dem umgekehrten Verhältniss des Quadrats der Entfernung und nach der Proportionalität der als Quantität der Trägheit definirten ponderabeln Massen aufstellte, der durch Erfindung der Infinitesimalrechnung d. h. der Differential- und Integral-Rechnung die Mittel schuf, aus der Wirkung der Massenelemente aufeinander die Wirkung endlich ausgedehnter Massen durch Integration berechnen zu können.

Es ist sicherlich die Ableitung des Gravitationsgesetzes aus den Keplerschen Gesetzen der grösste und weittragendste Schritt, welcher im Gebiet der physikalischen Forschung je gemacht ist. War einmal das Gravitationsgesetz für die Wirkung ponderabler Materie richtig erkannt, dann lag es nahe in demselben einen Leitstern für die physikalische Forschung nach den Gesetzen anderer Fernwirkungen zu erblicken, so der Wirkung electrostatischer und magnetischer Massen.

Newton war seiner Zeit soweit vorausgeeilt, dass es erst eines Jahrhunderts bedurfte, bis Coulomb für die Wirkung dieser eben erwähnten imponderabeln Massen das nach ihm benannte Gesetz aufstellte und erkannte, ein Gesetz, welches eigentlich mit dem Newtonschen vollkommen identisch ist, es erheischte nur die imponderable Masse eine Definition, in der man auf die mechanische Krafteinheit zurückzugehen hatte. Dabei wurden in Folge der hier auftretenden anziehenden und abstossenden Kräfte positive und negative Massen unterschieden, eine Bezeichnungsweise, die in Folge ihrer Bequemlichkeit bis auf den heutigen Tag beibehalten ist, aber nicht in der Natur der Sache ihren Grund hat. Ferner boten die magnetischen Fluida die Schwierigkeit, dass dieselben in den kleinsten Theilen der ponderabeln Materie stets vereint in gleichen Quantitäten vorkamen, nicht aber einzeln auf einen Körper übertragen werden konnten.

Ganz neue und bis dahin ungeahnte Gebiete sollten der Physik durch die Entdeckung des Galvanismus am Ende des vorigen Jahrhunderts erschlossen werden.

1820 führte ein Zufall auf die Entdeckung der Einwirkung galvanischer Ströme auf eine Magnetnadel. Die Einwirkung auch galvanischer Ströme unter einander war dadurch sehr wahrscheinlich gemacht und wurde von Ampère aufgefunden.

Die Fruchtbarkeit der Newtonschen Principien war damals vollkommen erfasst, es durfte nicht lange dauern, bis auch für die zwischen galvanischen Strömen und Magneten bestehenden sogenannten electromagnetischen Kräfte und für die zwischen galvanischen Strömen unter einander bestehenden sogenannten electrodynamischen Kräfte das Gesetz der Elementarwirkung aufgestellt war. Die umgekehrte Proportionalität mit dem Quadrat der Entfernung lag der Analogie mit den Elementargesetzen von Newton und Coulomb nahe und erwies sich auch hier als richtig. Es traten aber weiter hier neue Gesichtspunkte hinzu: Die Bedingungen für das Newtonsche und Coulombsche Gesetz waren punktförmige Massen in einer bestimmten Entfernung von einander. Durch zwei Punkte ist nur eine feste Richtung die der Verbindungslinie gegeben, wie konnte also nach dem Satz vom zureichenden Grunde die Kraft anders, als in der Richtung der Verbindungslinie wirken. Die Elemente, durch welche die electromagnetischen und electrodynamischen Wirkungen bedingt sind, verhalten sich anders; die Stromrichtung fordert hier ein Stromelement als Linienelement zu fassen.

Bei einer elektromagnetischen Elementarwirkung ist daher abgesehen von der Grösse und Richtung der Verbindungslinie auch der Winkel der Richtung des Stromelements mit der Verbindungslinie, ferner die Ebene, in der Stromelement und Verbindungslinie liegen und damit auch die Senkrechte auf dieser Ebene gegeben.

Die Beobachtung entschied — seltsam genug aber darum von um so grösserer Wichtigkeit — dass die elektromagnetische Wirkung in dieser Senkrechten stattfände. — Die drehende Bewegung unserer Dynamomaschinen beruht darauf — die Richtung der Wirkung innerhalb dieser Senkrechten gab eine Regel von Ampère an, die Abhängigkeit der Wirkung endlich von der Neigung der Stromelemente gegen die Verbindungslinie wurde von Biot und Savart, bezw. Laplace festgesetzt.

Bei einer elektrodynamischen Elementarwirkung ist abgesehen von der Grösse und Richtung der Verbindungslinie auch der Winkel, den jedes der Stromelemente mit der Verbindungslinie sowie der Winkel der Stromelemente gegeneinander, ferner zwei Ebenen, in denen je eines der Stromelemente und die Verbindungslinie liegt und damit auch die beiden Senkrechten auf diesen Ebenen gegeben.

Es war Ampère, der, nachdem er überhaupt die electrodynamische Fernwirkung entdeckt, zuerst auch ein Elementargesetz für dieselbe aufstellte. Danach fand die Wirkung wieder in der Richtung der Verbindungslinie statt, ausserdem wurde die Abhängigkeit von den verschiedenen Winkeln, welche oben aufgeführt sind, gegeben.

Bei der Aufstellung dieser Elementargesetze für die electromagnetischen und electrodynamischen Wirkungen ist aber noch ein weiterer Gesichtspunkt zu erwägen. In allen Beobachtungen, auf welche sich diese Elementargesetze gründeten, war mit geschlossenen Strömen beobachtet worden. Es ist fraglich, ob man ein Stromelement als solches isolirt vom übrigen Strom betrachten darf und ob diese Elementargesetze die einzig möglichen sind.

Die Trennung eines Stromelementes vom übrigen Strom, der in sich geschlossen ist, war jedenfalls nur eine analytische Operation ohne jede physikalische Bedeutung, und so durften in der That diese Elementargesetze nicht als die einzig möglichen betrachtet werden. In der That ist z. B. von Grassmann ein electrodynamisches Elementargesetz aufgestellt, nach dem die Wirkung nicht in die Richtung der Verbindungslinie fällt, welches aber auf geschlossene Ströme angewandt zu denselben Resultaten führt.

So kam es denn im weiteren Verlauf vielmehr darauf an Ausdrücke für die electromagnetischen und electrodynamischen Wirkungen aufzustellen, welche in der einfachsten Weise gleich auf geschlossene Ströme sich bezogen. Dieses leisteten die sogenannten electromagnetischen und electrodynamischen Potentialausdrücke, Ausdrücke von der weittragendsten Bedeutung für die Wissenschaft, auf welche nicht näher eingegangen werden kann, nur darf hier nicht unerwähnt bleiben, dass wir dieselben unserem berühmten Ehrenmitgliede F. E. Neumann verdanken.

Nach Aufstellung dieser einzig durch die Erfahrung geforderten Ausdrücke für die Wirkung geschlossener Ströme konnte dann rückwärts wieder der Versuch gemacht werden möglichst einfache Elementargesetze zu finden. Helmholtz unternahm solche Untersuchungen, gleichzeitig bemüht electrische Bewegungen zu realisiren, welche ungeschlossenen Strömen — Stromelementen gleichkommen. Das von ihm aufgestellte Potentialgesetz liefert nicht nur Kräfte in der Richtung der Verbindungslinie, sondern auch Drehungsmomente der Elemente auf einander.

Wir haben hier noch einer anderen Auffassung der electrodynamischen Fernwirkungen zu gedenken. Durch das Bestreben eine Theorie des Galvanismus auf die Electrostatik zu begründen — wie es in der Mitte dieses Jahrhunderts sich geltend machte — wurde gleichzeitig bedingt, die Kräfte zwischen Stromelementen auf Punktkräfte zurückzuführen. Dann aber mussten ganz neue Momente in das Elementargesetz treten. Hatte man den electrischen Strom zu fassen als Bewegung electrostatischer Massen in gewissen Richtungen, so konnten als neu die Geschwindigkeiten, ja die Beschleunigungen dieser Massen in das Elementargesetz eingeführt werden. Die Aufstellung solcher Gesetze konnte wieder mit gewisser Willkür erfolgen, so lange man dabei nur auf Beobachtungen geschlossener Ströme zurückging. So stellten W. Weber, Riemann, Clausius Grundgesetze auf, in denen sei es die Entfernungsgeschwindigkeit d. i. die Geschwindigkeit, mit der sich die Entfernung ändert, sei es die relative, sei es endlich die absolute Geschwindigkeit der Theilchen eine Rolle spielt. Auf der einen Seite führten diese Gesetze zu mechanisch schweren Bedenken, theilweise wurde das Princip der Gleichheit von actio und reactio aufgegeben, theilweise die Möglichkeit eröffnet ins Unbegrenzte Arbeit zu schaffen. Auf der andern Seite aber hatte die Aufstellung dieser Gesetze das Gute zu neuen experimentellen Untersuchungen anzuregen, so ergab sich z. B. das Beobachtungsresultat, dass mechanisch fortgeführte Electricität, wir sagen electrische Convection wirklich electrodynamisch wirksam ist.

Die weiter an diese Gesetze knüpfende Discussion hat dann immer mehr auf die Nothwendigkeit hingewiesen, nicht blos von einer Fernwirkung durch den leeren Raum zu sprechen, sondern auch das Zwischenmedium als solches in den Kreis der Betrachtung zu ziehen.

Ich muss es mir hier versagen auf diese ebenso interessanten wie geistvollen Speculationen einzugehen, durch welche sich an die erwähnten Grundgesetze anknüpfende Erörterungen auszeichneten. Es konnte mir hier nur darauf ankommen vorzuführen, einer wie mannigfachen Entwickelung der Begriff der Fernwirkung fähig ist. Ebenso würde es mich zu weit von meinem Gegenstande abbringen, wollte ich hier auch die sogenannten Inductionserscheinungen in den Kreis meiner Betrachtung ziehen. Vom Newtonschen Standpunkt hat man in denselben eben auch nur eine aus der Ferne wirkende electromotorische Kraft zu sehen.

Ich will mich jetzt vielmehr zu Erscheinungen wenden, welche geeignet sind den Uebergang von Fernwirkungen zu Druckwirkungen zu finden:

Das Gesetz von der umgekehrten Proportionalität mit dem Quadrat der Entfernung kommt auch noch in anderen Gebieten der Physik vor. Wir wissen, dass die Intensität der Lichtstrahlung ebenso wie der Wärmestrahlung durch den leeren Raum im umgekehrten Quadrat der Entfernung abnimmt, eine Thatsache, die mit der geometrischen Anschauung in unmittelbaren Zusammenhang gebracht werden kann, ein Vorgang, der zu den Fernwirkungen im Sinne des Newtonschen Gesetzes eine vollkommene Analogie bildet. Nun aber hat man von jeher Anstoss daran genommen, wie sinnlich so wahrnehmbare Erscheinungen, wie die Licht- und Wärmestrahlung, durch einen leeren Raum sich fortpflanzen könne; man glaubte daher hier schon lange der Annahme eines Zwischenmediums zu bedürfen, um sich die Fortpflanzbarkeit der Strahlung vorstellen zu können. Dieses Bedürfniss trat ebenso in der Emanationstheorie, nach der, sei es Licht, sei es Wärme, von dem strahlenden Körper durch kleine Particel mit sehr grosser gradliniger Geschwindigkeit in die Ferne vermittelt wird, wie in der Undulationstheorie auf, nach der sich das vermittelnde Medium selbst im Schwingungszustand befindet.

So wurde der Begriff des Äthers in die Wissenschaft eingeführt. Allenthalben vorhanden und doch unseren Sinnen nirgends zugänglich, ergaben sich grosse Elasticität, geringe Dichte und dabei Incompressibilität als die Haupteigenschaften desselben, eine Verbindung von Eigenschaften, welche den Äther ebenso scharf von den gasförmigen, wie von den flüssigen und festen Zuständen der sinnlich wahrnehmbaren Materie unterschied.

Wenn wir uns nun fragen, wie es komme, dass bei so gleichen Gesetzen, wie sie die Änderung der Gravitation und die Intensität der Strahlung mit der Entfernung befolgen, der Vorgang der Strahlung die Einführung eines Zwischenmediums gefordert hat, und die Wirkung z. B. der Gravitation bisher ohne eine solche behandelt ist, so kann ich den Grund nur darin sehen, dass unser Körper zur Aufnahme der einen Einwirkung Organe hat, zur directen Aufnahme der anderen ihm aber solche fehlen. Die Physik hat uns längst gelehrt, unsere sinnlichen Wahrnehmungen ihrem objectiven Werth nach zu schätzen. Ebenso wie wir nur quantitativ unterschiedene Reize, als da sind Licht- und Wärme-Strahlen, durch verschiedene Organe aufnehmen und auf diese Weise als ganz verschiedene Qualitäten deuten, so können uns für die directe sinnliche Aufnahme irgend welcher anderer Kräfte Organe fehlen, dahin gehören die bisher betrachteten Fernwirkungen.

Nehmen wir nun aber auch für das Zustandekommen dieser Fernwirkungen ein Zwischenmedium als nothwendig an, dann geben wir eben die Möglichkeit einer directen Fernwirkung auf, dann haben wir es, wie bei der Licht- und Wärme-Strahlung in der That eben mit Druckwirkungen zu thun, welche räumlich und zeitlich auf einander folgend die scheinbare Fernwirkung zu Stande bringen.

Die Frage, ob die Gravitation und die anderen fernwirkenden Kräfte als Druckkräfte im eben erwähnten Sinn gefasst werden müssen, scheint der Beobachtung nicht unzugänglich. Wenn die Fernkräfte in analoger Weise Zeit brauchen zu ihrer Wirkung, wie man von der Fortpflanzungsgeschwindigkeit des Lichts spricht, dann erscheint mir die Annahme eines Zwischenmediums auch in der Theorie der Gravitation mit Nothwendigkeit geboten. Die Schwere auf der Erdoberfläche ist ganz geringen Änderungen durch die verschiedene Stellung des Mondes und der Sonne gegen den Horizont unterworfen. Würden wir nun z. B. beobachten, dass die Schwere ein Minimum wird in demselben Moment, in welchem wir den Durchgang der Sonne durch den Meridian beobachten, so müssten wir sagen: Die Wirkung der Gravitation pflanzt sich mit derselben Geschwindigkeit, wie das Licht fort. Es sind solche Instrumente angegeben und construirt worden, welche diese geringen Aenderungen der Schwere angeben sollen, am bekanntesten ist das Horizontalpendel von Zöllner, aber die bisherigen Beobachtungen scheiterten daran, dass das Instrument nicht hinreichend erschütterungsfrei aufgestellt werden konnte.

Wenn wir nun versuchen wollen die Fernwirkungen auf Druckwirkungen zurückzuführen, so haben wir zunächst die verschiedenen Druckwirkungen zu erwähnen, welche die theoretische Physik behandelt. Ich sagte schon am Anfang, dass die grobsinnlichste Anschauung zu einer Druckwirkung der einfache Stoss bietet. Aber mit diesem Stossbegriff kommen wir nicht weit, viel fruchtbarer ist der Druckbegriff, wie ihn die Elasticitätstheorie und die Hydrodynamik unter Berücksichtigung der Reibung bietet.

Wir sagen ein beliebiges Medium befindet sich im natürlichen Zustand, wenn keine Druckwirkungen im Innern derselden stattfinden. Ändern wir jetzt auf irgend eine Weise die Lage der Theilchen des Mediums gegeneinander, finden in irgend einer Weise jetzt Dilatationen und Compressionen statt, dann werden im Innern desselben elastische Druck- resp. Zugkräfte rege, welche die Tendenz haben den natürlichen Zustand wieder herzustellen. Es folgt so als die eine allgemeine Theorie der Druckwirkungen die Elasticitätstheorie; und in der That ist die Undulationstheorie der Licht- und Wärme-Strahlung so vom Standpunkt der Elasticitätstheorie aus begründet und entwickelt worden.

In der Elasticitätstheorie haben wir es mit unendlich kleinen Verschiebungen materieller Theile gegen einander zu thun, bei denen jeder Theil doch im Grossen und Ganzen an seiner Stelle bleibt. In der Hydrodynamik treten endliche Verschiebungen materieller Theile auf, bei denen die gesammte in Betrachtung kommende Masse im Grossen in Bewegung ist. Unter Berücksichtigung der Reibung entspringt hier der Druck aus der Geschwindigkeitsdifferenz benachbarter Theile.

In einem ganz andern Gebiete wurde zuerst gezeigt, wie hier das Problem in Angriff zu nehmen und analytisch zu behandeln sei. Fourier war es hierin ganz gleich dem grossen Newton, welcher in der Theorie der Wärmeleitung das Problem formulirte und analytisch löste.

War Newton bei den Fernwirkungen auf Elementarkräfte zurückgegangen,

d. h. auf die Wirkung zweier punktförmiger Massen, so liess sich bei dem — einer hydrodynamischen durch Reibung hervorgerufenen Druckwirkung analogen — Vorgang der Wärmeleitung das Problem nicht in gleicher Weise in Angriff nehmen, hier musste für die Wirkung innerhalb — wenn auch noch immer kleiner Räume — so zu sagen ein Pauschquantum genommen werden, ein Ansatz für das Resultat eines ziemlich complicirten Processes, dessen Zerlegung in Elementarwirkungen auf Schwierigkeiten stösst.

Dieser Ansatz in Fouriers Theorie der Wärmeleitung war der, dass die senkrecht durch ein Flächenelement im Innern eines der Wärmeleitung ausgesetzten Körpers strömende Wärmemenge proportional der Grösse des Flächenelements, der Temperaturänderung längs des Normalenelements zu dieser Fläche im Verhältniss zur Länge dieses Normalenelements sei.

Dieser Ansatz von Fourier bildet vollkommen das Analogon zum Gravitationsgesetz von Newton. Hatte Newton in der Erfindung der Infinitesimalrechnung auch die analytischen Mittel zur Verwerthung seines Gesetzes gegeben, so lieferte Fourier durch die nach ihm benannten Reihen vollständig die Mittel die aus der Natur seines Ansatzes sich ergebenden partiellen Differentialgleichungen zu lösen — eine That, die für die weitere Entwickelung der Physik ebenso wie der Mathematik von weittragender Bedeutung wurde. Rechnen wir von Newton eine Epoche der Physik, so beginnt mit Fourier eine zweite.

In der Theorie der Flüssigkeitsreibung tritt an Stelle der Temperaturänderung die Geschwindigkeitsänderung und es ist danach die normal zu einem Flächenelement in Folge der Reibung entstehende Druckwirkung proportional der Componente der Geschwindigkeitsänderung längs des Normalenelementes im Verhältniss zur Länge desselben. Die mathematische Formulirung ist also ganz dieselbe, nur die physikalische Deutung ist eine verschiedene.

Wenn wir nun daran gehen wollen die Fernwirkung durch die Druckwirkung zu ersetzen, werden wir in den allgemeinen Formeln der Elasticitätstheorie und der Hydrodynamik consequent alle fernwirkenden Kräfte ganz auszuschliessen haben.

Sir William Thomson hat 1842 gezeigt, wie vollkommen identisch die Electrostatik mit der Theorie der stationären Wärmeleitung begründet werden könne; wir wollen uns ausdrücken, wie die fernwirkenden Kräfte der Gravitation und der Electrostatik durch die durch Reibung entstehenden Druckkräfte der Hydrodynamik ersetzt werden können. Es wird genügen einige in der Electrostatik und Wärmeleitung analogen Begriffe anzudeuten, zugleich wird die künstliche Unterscheidung zwischen positiver und negativer Electricität dadurch in ein neues jedenfalls naturgemässes Licht gestellt. Ein positiv electrischer Körper entspricht danach einer Wärmequelle, ein negativ electrischer Körper einem Wärmeabzug, einer Kältequelle. Die positiv electrische Oberfläche eines Leiters einer Oberfläche, durch welche Wärme in den Körper strömt, die negativ electrische Oberfläche eines Leiters einer Oberfläche, durch welche Wärme aus dem Körper strömt.

Es würde nun der Versuch nahe liegen, auch die electromagnetischen und electrodynamischen Kräfte so in Beziehung zur Theorie der Wärmeleitung beziehungsweise der Hydrodynamik zu bringen. Solche Versuche sind nicht gemacht, dagegen liegt der Versuch vor, alle fernwirkenden Kräfte auf Elasticitätsdruck- und zugkräfte zurückzuführen.

Wir haben hier eines Mannes zu gedenken, dessen Originalität zu allen Zeiten ebenso bewundert werden wird wie seine Meisterschaft, eines Mannes, der in der Art seiner Forschung von seinen Zeitgenossen völlig unverstanden, die Welt mit einer Reihe Entdeckungen bereicherte, welche in ihrer Fruchtbarkeit noch in ferne Zeiten reichen werden — nicht allein für die Wissenschaft: Faraday. Es entspricht vollkommen dem Bildungs- und Entwickelungsgange dieses wunderbaren Geistes, wenn er unbekümmert um die thatsächlich vorhandenen Errungenschaften und Begriffe der Wissenschaft so zu sagen von vorne anfing. Eben darum, weil Faraday nicht mit gebräuchlichen Begriffen und Bezeichnungen operirte, konnte es nicht ausbleiben, dass seine Mitwelt eigentlich nur seine Entdeckungen hinnahm und nicht danach fragte, wie er sie gefunden.

Es ist das Verdienst Maxwells uns Faraday näher geführt, seine Sprache so zu sagen in die uns geläufige von Newton ererbte übertragen, seine Ableitungen mathematisch formulirt zu haben. Es hat sich durch Maxwells Forschung die in der Geschichte der Physik jedenfalls beispiellose Thatsache herausgestellt, dass Faraday, ohne selbst Matthematiker zu sein, sich einer so präcisen Ausdrucksweise bedient, dass sie Schritt für Schritt einer mathematischen Formulirung vollkommen gleichwerthig ist; dabei operirt Faraday mit Begriffen, die in ihrer Wichtigkeit bis dahin nur eine mathematische Behandlung des Gegenstandes erkannt hatte — ich denke an die Rolle, welche bei ihm der Begriff des Potentials spielt.

Faraday's Sprache entspringt einer unmittelbaren Anschauung. Wo Newton fernwirkende Kräfte zwischen zwei Massen setzte, da sah Faraday schon durch Anwesenheit einer wirkenden Masse in dem unermesslichen Raum ein Kraftfeld, durch Kraftlinien erfüllt und diese gaben ihm eine vollkommen übersichtliche Anschauung über die Kraftvertheilung im Raume, d. h. über die Kraftwirkung auf andere Körper innerhalb des Kraftfeldes. Die Beobachtung hat diese Kraftlinien in ihrem Verlauf festzustellen und die Angabe derselben bei Existenz eines Massenelements, allgemeiner eines Wirkungselements ersetzt bei Faraday vollkommen die früher erwähnten Elementargesetze der fernwirkenden Kräfte.

Für gravitirende, electrostatische, magnetische Punktmassen verlaufen die Kraftlinien geradlinig von den Punktmassen aus nach dem Unendlichen. Die electromagnetischen Kraftlinien eines geradlinigen Stromes sind concentrische Kreise, deren Centrum in der Axe des Stromes liegt und deren Ebene senkrecht zu derselben steht. Im Falle eines magnetischen Kraftfeldes lassen sich die Kraftlinien in einfacher Weise zur Darstellung bringen. Man streue Eisenfeilspäne auf die Ebene eines gespannten Bogens Papier und halte einen Magneten dicht darunter; die Späne ordnen sich dann in Curven, welche mit Kraftlinien des Magneten nahe zusammenfallen.

Maxwell unternahm es in seinem berühmten Buch über Electricität und Magnetismus uns die Faraday'sche Theorie in mathematischer Form darzustellen. Hier wird die Fernwirkung durch elastische Druckwirkung vollkommen ersetzt. Das Zwischenmedium befindet sich danach in einem Zwangszustande. Es würde mich zuweit führen, hier die Art dieses Zwangszustandes für ein electrostatisches, magnetisches oder electromagnetisches Feld zu beschreiben. Es mag erwähnt werden, wie einfach sich von diesem Standpunkt Maxwell der Schlüssel zu einer electromagnetischen Lichttheorie ergab.

Ich will aber hervorheben, dass Maxwell in der Beschreibung dieses Zwangszustandes noch nicht den letzten Schritt zur Erkenntniss der Rolle sieht, welche das Zwischenmedium zur Erklärung der Fernwirkungen aus Druckwirkungen zu spielen hat. Es wird darauf ankommen festzustellen, wie der Zwangszustand innerhalb des Zwischenmediums zu Stande kommt und wie er erhalten bleibt. Es ist möglich, dass die Theorie der Molecularkräfte hier berufen ist einzugreifen; schon hat sich dieselbe unter Einführung der Annahme, dass die Molecularkräfte nur für unendlich kleine Entfernungen wirken, für alle endlichen Entfernungen aber verschwinden, in der sogenannten Capillaritätstheorie als sehr fruchtbar bewiesen.

Mit diesem Fernblick auf eine vielleicht noch zu durchlaufende Bahn will ich schliessen. Wenn es wahr ist, dass die Wissenschaft nach einheitlichen Principien und nach einer einheitlichen Darstellung ringen soll, so haben wir jetzt einen Standpunkt gewonnen, von dem dieses möglich erscheint.

Wie verschieden treten doch die mannigfachen Kräfte der Natur, sei es direct unseren Sinnen, sei es indirect durch ihre Wirkung auf äussere Erscheinungen uns entgegen. Hier erscheinen auf räthselhafte Weise Einwirkungen zwischen Himmelskörpern auf einander oder zwischen Magnet und Eisen nach Gesetzen, die lange gesucht werden mussten, dort wird momentan fast mit dem Auftreten einer Lichtquelle ein Lichtstrahl in unermessliche Entfernungen entsandt, hier erfolgt ein langsam stetiger Wärmeausgleich innerhalb eines Körpers, dort schlägt uns von einer fernen Wärmequelle im kalten Raume strahlende Wärme entgegen.

Wie mannigfach die Art der Erscheinungen, wie gross die Täuschung der Sinne, wie erhebend das Bewusstsein die Fülle der Räthsel, wenn auch nicht lösen, so doch nach einheitlichen Grundsätzen ordnen zu können!

Senecio vernalis W. et K. schon um 1717 in Ostpreussen gefunden.

Von

Rob. Caspary.

v. Klinggräff I. (2. Nachtrag zur Flora der Provinz Preussen 1866, 105) sagt: „Wahrscheinlich ist Senecio vernalis erst zu Anfang dieses Jahrhunderts von Osten und Süden her in das Gebiet (d. h. in die ungetrennte Provinz Preussen) eingewandert, seit 1826 von mir bei Marienwerder und schon einige Jahre früher von Lottermoser bei Rastenburg, von List bei Tilsit beobachtet."

Es liegt aber der Beweis vor, dass die Vermuthung, dass Senecio vernalis erst zu Anfang dieses Jahrhunderts nach Preussen eingewandert ist, unrichtig ist und dass die Pflanze bereits um 1717 in dieser Provinz und zwar in der Mitte von Ostpreussen bei Angerburg vom dortigen Probst Helwing gefunden ist.

Georg Andreas Helwing wurde 1691 Adjunkt seines Vaters, der Geistlicher in Angerburg war, 1725 Probst in Angerburg und starb 1748. Bei ihm hielt sich vom Frühjahr 1717 an längere Zeit der Student der Medicin Mathias Ernst Boretius, später Prof. ordinar. tertius der medicin. Facultät in Königsberg, der Botanik zu lesen hatte, starb 1738, auf, um bei Helwing, dem Verfasser der Flora quasi modo genita und der Florae campana und ausgezeichnetem Pflanzenkenner, botanische Kenntnisse sich zu erwerben. Boretius verfertigte 1717 unter Helwings Aufsicht Herbarien, die an verschiedene hervorragende Leute ausgegeben wurden. In den „Wochentlichen Königsbergischen Frag- und Anzeigungs-Nachrichten" vom Jahre 1737, No. 27, einer Zeitschrift, die über alle Dinge des praktischen Lebens, Handelssachen, Häuserbeleihungen, angekommene Schiffe, Wittinnen, polnische Juden u. s. w. Nachrichten gab, aber auch Abhandlungen der beträchtlichsten Gelehrten der Königsberg'er Universität, z. B. auch von Immanuel Kant, brachte, — in dieser Zeitschrift sagt Boretius in einer Abhandlung: „Von Nana oder Ananas und deren Frucht": ‚Nach diesen (d. h. den preussischen Botanikern Wigand, Wolff, Mentzel, Loesel, Gottsched) hat der in dieser Kunst (d. h. Botanik) hocherfahrene und unermüdete Herr M. Georg Andreas Helwing, jetziger wohlverordneter Probst in Angerburg, in den preussischen Wäldern, Gesträuchen und Feldern noch fast einst so viel aufgesuchet, so wie solches die unter seiner Aufsicht vor 20 Jahren verfertigte Herbaria viva, davon eines die Ehre hat in Sr. Königl. Majestät von Pohlen Königl. Bibliotheque in Dresden aufgehoben zu sein, stattsam an den Tag legen." Diese Abhandlung wurde 1737 veröffentlicht; die Herbarien sind mithin 1717 von Boretius angefertigt. Das, was der damalige König von Polen und Sachsen erhielt, ist leider in Dresden 1848 bei der Revolution verbrannt, oder, wie es auch heisst, nach Petersburg gekommen. Eines wurde an den Stadtsecretär von Danzig: Jacob Theodor Klein gegeben. Drei sind in Königsberg, eins auf der königl. Bibliothek, eins in der städtischen und eins in der des königl. botanischen Gartens. Letzteres hat Carl August Hagen, Verfasser der Chloris bor. und Preussens Pflanzen besessen und ist vor Kurzem von dem Enkel Hagens, dem jetzigen Hofapotheker Hagen, dem königl. botan. Garten geschenkt worden. Es besteht in 5 dicken Bänden aus Schreibpapier in Schweinsleder gebunden in Fol., in denen die Pflanzen aufgeklebt, mit den langen Namen, die sie zu Helwings Zeit führten, versehen und meist auch von C. G. Hagens Hand mit den Linné'schen Namen bezeichnet sind. Auf Blatt 66 des IV. Bandes befindet sich ein 27 cm hohes bewurzeltes Exemplar von Senecio vernalis aufgeklebt, das 2 Hauptblüthenstengel gehabt hat, von denen einer sehr gut erhalten, der andere seines Blüthenstandes beraubt ist. Die Rosette von 10 Grundblättern ist gut erhalten. Beigeschrieben ist von Helwing oder Boretius: „Jacobaea Senecionis folio incano perennis Raji hist. 285." Nach Linné (Richt. Cod. Linn. No. 6282*) ist „Jacobaea Senecionis folio incano perennis Ray" Senecio silvaticus und darauf fussend hat C. G. Hagen eigenhändig zu dem Helwing'schen Exemplar den unrichtigen Namen hinangeschrieben: „Senecio silvaticus."

Da in dem Helwing'schen Herbar einige Gartenpflanzen sich befinden, liegt der Gedanke nicht gerade fern, dass auch dies Exemplar von Senecio vernalis einem Garten entnommen sei. Aber wie kann man sich vorstellen, dass zu jener Zeit Senec. vernalis in irgend einem Garten gebaut sei? Eine Zierpflanze ist er nicht und der Gedanke, dass er in einem botan. Garten als werthvoll für die Wissenschaft schon damals gezogen wurde, hat nicht das mindeste für sich. In dem Verzeichniss der im kurfürstl. Garten zu Königsberg gezogenen Pflanzen von Titius 1654 steht keine Pflanze, die darauf gedeutet werden könnte.

Jedoch beweist ein Umstand, dass jenes Exemplar des Senecio vernalis aus Angerburgs Umgegend entnommen ist. Im Suppl. der Flora quasi modo genita, welches Juni 1726 erschien, führt Helwing: „Jacobaea Senecionis folio incano perennis" auf und giebt als Fundorte bei Angerburg an: „Auf den Kehlischen und Ogonschen Aeckern in arenosis." Ich besitze das Exemplar des Suppl., welches einst Eigenthum des preuss. Floristen J. C. Wulff war und später C. G. Hagen gehörte. Auch hier hat Hagen an den Rand geschrieben: „Senecio silvaticus". Kehlen ist ein Dorf im Kreise Angerburg 1/2 Meile südlich von Angerburg am Schwenzait-See; „Ogonsche Aecker" sind ohne Zweifel die von Ogonken, einem Dorf 1 Meile südöstlich von Angerburg an demselben See. Die Standorte der Jacobaea Senecionis folio incano perennis des Probst Helwing stimmen vortrefflich mit Sen. vern.: „in arenosis" und „auf Aeckern" und die Blüthezeit „Majo" auch. Die Angabe: auf Aeckern, passt nicht gut auf Senecio silvaticus, der meist in Nadelwäldern, selten auf Feldern vor-

*) Das Citat von Ray hist. p. 258 ist in Bezug auf die Seitenzahl unrichtig; soll heissen 285.

kommt und die Blüthezeit „Majo" auch nicht, da Senecio silvatic. von Ende Juli bis Herbst blüht.

Es liegt hier also klar der Fall vor, dass der ausgezeichnetste Pflanzenkenner einer Gegend, dies war C. G. Hagen für Preussen seiner Zeit, Senecio vernal. verkannt und falsch bestimmt hat, obgleich die Pflanze schon ein Jahrhundert früher in Preussen existirte. Kann dies nicht auch anderwegen geschehen sein? Und kann man sicher schliessen, wenn in einer Gegend bisher Senec. vernal. nicht beobachtet ist, aber ein Botaniker, der scharfsichtiger als seine Vorgänger ist, die Pflanze nun in ihr findet und richtig erkennt, dass die Pflanze nach jenem Ort eben eingewandert sei?

Dazu kommt, dass Sen. vern. ein sehr neckisches Auftreten hat, weil die Zahl, in der er erscheint, in den einzelnen Jahren sehr schwankt. Als ich 1859 nach Königsberg kam, fand ich vor dem Ausfallsthor, durch welches ich fast täglich gehe, um einen Spaziergang auf der Festungsfläche zu machen, einige wenige Exemplare der Pflanze; in den folgenden Jahren nahmen sie zu; in einigen Jahren waren manche Stellen der Wälle ganz gelb davon; dann verschwand die Pflanze wieder bis auf einzelne Exemplare. Wäre nun Jemand hinzugekommen, der die frühere Erfahrung nicht hatte, er hätte auf den Gedanken kommen können: jetzt wandert die Pflanze hier an diesem Orte ein. Dieselbe Erfahrung ist anderwegen gemacht, so in Schlesien und in Westpreussen. Dr. Bethke theilt mir mit, dass bei Pr. Friedland die Felder, besonders Kleefelder, so mit Senec. vern. zeitweise besetzt gewesen seien, als ob die Pflanze gesät worden war; dann ist sie wieder bis auf wenige Exemplare verschwunden. Dieselbe Beobachtung machte ich zwischen Hohenstein und Praust bei Danzig. 1878 hatte die königl. Regierung in Westpreussen befohlen, die Pflanze auszurotten und ich bekam von mehreren Orten der Kreise Rosenberg, Mohrungen, Marienwerder Exemplare mit der Anfrage zugeschickt, ob dies die zu vertilgende „Wucherblume" sei? Ohne Zweifel würde sie auch in jenen Kreisen von selbst nachgelassen haben bedrohlich aufzutreten.

In Preussen ist mit richtiger Erkenntniss der Art Senecio vernalis 1822 von Lottermoser in Rastenburg, bei dieser Stadt gefunden, also in demselben Jahre, in dem er in Schlesien zuerst entdeckt ist. Aus dem Nachlass des Prof. Eysenhardt sind 12 Briefe Lottermosers an ihn gerettet; jetzt im Besitz des königl. botan. Gartens. In einem vom 12. Juni 1822 zeigt Lottermoser Prof. Eysenhardt von Rastenburg aus an, dass er Senecio vernalis daselbst gefunden habe und fügt hinzu: „Die beiden beikommenden Exemplare sind noch nicht die beiden äussersten Extreme der Varietäten auf trockenem und fettem Boden." Eysenhardt trug Senecio vernal. in Folge dessen in die handschriftliche Liste der merkwürdigeren bei Rastenburg wild wachsenden Pflanzen ein und veröffentlichte ihn (vergl. Eysenhardt. De accurata plantarum comparatione adnexis observationibus in florem prussicam. Diss. inaug. 12. Mai 1823 p. 14) als neu für Preussen mit einem i. v. dahinter. Wenn v. Klinggräff a. O. angiebt, dass auch List in Tilsit vor 1826 Senecio vernal. dort gefunden habe, so liegt mir kein Belag vor, der dafür oder dagegen spricht und ich muss jene Angabe dahingestellt sein lassen. Ein Exemplar des Sen. vern. ist im hiesigen königl. Herbar von List bei Tilsit gesammelt vorhanden, aber leider, wie andere von Kannenberg bei Stuhm, von Albers bei Gumbinnen vor langer Zeit gesammelte ohne Zeitangabe. Die handschriftlichen Aufzeichnungen von List, eingetragen von ihm in ein mit

Schreibpapier durchschossenes Exemplar der Chloris bor., welche mir vorliegen, geben auch kein Datum für Senecio vern. bei Tilsit an. In Polen wird Sen. vern. zuerst 1824 von Schubert (catalogue des plantes du jardin bot. de Varsovie p. 227) mit dem Zusatz: „um Warschau", angegeben und Waga (Fl. polska II 1848 p. 414) sagt: „Wächst fast überall."

Aelter als der Name Senecio vern., der in den Icones plant. rar. Hung. von Waldstein und Kitaibel 1802 zuerst auftritt, sind einige Namen, die von Gilibert in Grodno gegeben und wahrscheinlich damit synonym sind und weil sie älter als die Bezeichnung von Waldstein und Kitaibel sind, Interesse wegen des Fundorts haben. Gilibert hat 1781 nach Ledeb. (Fl. ross. II) in seiner Fl. litbuan. inchoata III p. 201 und 202 der Pflanze die Namen Jacobaea sinuata und J. incana, ferner nach Georgi (Beschreibung des russ. Reichs III. 4. S. 1242) 1800 die Bezeichnung Senecio nebrodensis beigelegt. Leider fehlt mir gerade Theil III der Fl. lithuan. inchoa. von Gilibert, aber Jacobaea sinuata und incana führt er mit Beschreibungen wieder in Exercitia phytolog. von 1792, S. 165 und 166 auf. Es frägt sich, sind die Gilibert'schen Namen wirklich synonym mit Senec. vernal.? Da Gilibert zu seiner Jacobaea sinuata die Abbildung 401 von Barrelier Icon. pl. per Galliam, Hispaniam et Ital. observat. anführt, die Linné (Richt. Cod. Linn. 6283) zu Senecio nebrodensis zieht und Gilib. zur Jacobaea incana das Bild Barrelier's 262 mit dem Beisatz angiebt: bene exprimit illam (sc. Jacobaeam incanam) tabula Barrelieri 262, welche die alpine Senecio incana L. darstellt, so könnte man wegen dieser offenbar auf Sen. vern. nicht passenden Bestimmungen zweifelhaft werden, ob Gilibert wirklich Senecio vernalis bei Grodno gefunden habe, und nur unter jenen falschen Benennungen veröffentlicht. Seine Diagnosen der Grodno'er Pflanzen sind jedoch der Art, dass sie auf keine andern Pflanzen, die daselbst wachsen, bezogen werden können; auch passt die Blüthezeit Mai und Juni. Er scheint daher richtig anzunehmen, dass Gilibert schon um 1781 Senecio vern. gekannt hat, wenn er ihn auch in zwei Arten spaltete. Immer ist Gilibert's Fund noch 67 Jahre später als Helwings, der die früheste Kunde von Sen. vern. liefert.

Ascherson (Verhandl. des botan. Vereins der Provinz Brandenburg, 3. und 4. Heft, 1861 und 62, 152) hat dargelegt, warum Giliberts Name Jacobaea incana nicht gelten kann, obgleich er früher als Senec. vern. gegeben ist.

War Senec. vern. schon 1717 bei Angerburg in der Mitte Ostpreussens als Bürger der dortigen Flora vorhanden, so liegt der Schluss nahe, dass er auch sonst zu der Zeit im übrigen Preussen bereits eingebürgert war, wie weit nach West und ob er damals schon das ganze Gebiet, in dem er sich heute findet, inne hatte, bis zur Elbe und einige Meilen westlich von ihr, lässt sich freilich nicht angeben. Die Unbekanntschaft der frühern Botaniker mit der Pflanze, ihr zeitweises sehr ungleiches Auftreten, haben zur Meinung, dass sie, die längst eingebürgert war, nach West von Süd und Ost wandere, selbst innerhalb Preussens, noch gegen die Mitte dieses Jahrhunderts Anlass gegeben. v. Klinggräff I (A. O.), der sie zuerst 1826 bei Marienwerder beobachtete, sagt: „Damals bei Marienwerder noch sparsam, 10 Jahre später schon gemein. Noch später weiter nördlich, z. B. in den Gegenden von Saalfeld, Elbing, Danzig vorgedrungen, hat er sich gegenwärtig über die ganze Provinz verbreitet." Diese angebliche Wanderung ist durch nichts bewiesen, hat im Gegentheil ohne Zweifel nicht stattgefunden.

Wer sich über die vermeintlichen oder wirklichen Wanderungen in Schlesien, der Mark und Sachsen unterrichten will, vergl. Wimmer (Fl. v. Schlesien, 1857. 268), der Ostwinde zu Verbreitern der Pflanze in Schlesien macht, was anderwegen nachgeschrieben ist, obgleich diese Vermuthung durch nichts bewiesen ist und die Sache ganz anders liegen kann, Ascherson (Verhandl. d. bot. Vereins der Provinz Brandenburg A. O.) und Maass (A. O. 27. Jahrg. 1885 IX ff.).

Es wäre sehr wünschenswerth, dass in den ältesten brandenburgischen, schlesischen, sächsischen und pommerschen Herbarien nachgesucht würde, ob sich darin nicht auch Senecio vernalis aus einer Zeit, die vor der der vermeintlichen Einwanderung in diese Provinzen liegt, finden liesse.

Königsberg, 4. November 1886.

Keine Trüffeln bei Ostrometzko.

Von

Rob. Caspary.

Ein in seinen Angaben und Erinnerungen höchst zuverlässiger Freund, der in Königsberg geboren und daselbst fast immer gelebt hatte, theilte mir vor langer Zeit mit, dass ehedem in der Gewürzhandlung von Rudolph Häbler in Königsberg sogenannte „Thorn'er Trüffeln" zu haben gewesen seien. Der Inhaber dieses Geschäfts, der es zu der Zeit, als mir diese Mittheilung gemacht wurde, besass und an den ich mich desshalb wandte, wusste nichts davon. Da nach meiner Kenntniss in Preussen Trüffeln nur auf der Nonnenkämpe bei Kulm — seit mehr als fünfzig Jahren schon — gefunden sind, interessirte mich jene Angabe meines Freundes über „Thorn'er Trüffeln" sehr und ich schrieb daher an Herrn Busch auf Archidiakonka, Kreis Thorn, Vorsitzenden des landwirthschaftlichen Vereins des Kreises Thorn und bat ihn, die Sache in der nächsten Sitzung dieses Vereins zur Sprache zu bringen. Herr Busch antwortete unter dem 2. November 1874: „Ew. Hochwohlgeboren theile ich ergebenst mit, dass Ich ihr geschätztes Schreiben vom 10. v. M. dem Verein vorgelegt und angefragt habe, ob noch ein anderer Fundort für Trüffeln bekannt sei, als die Nonnenkämpe bei Kulm. Diese Frage wurde verneint; keinem der Mitglieder ist bekannt, dass sonst noch irgend wie hier Trüffeln in der Gegend gefunden werden." Damit nicht zufrieden, wandte ich mich mit derselben Frage an den Lehrer am Gymnasium zu Thorn, Adolph Hein. Ed. Müller. Dieser antwortete am 10. November 1874: „In den 34 Jahren meines Hierseins, von denen ich eine ziemliche Reihe hindurch theils allein, theils mit dem verstorbenen v. Nowitzki, dem wohl kaum ein Winkelchen im Thorn'er Kreise unbekannt geblieben ist, zu botanischen Exkursionen verwandte, habe ich niemals irgend etwas vom Vorhandensein von Trüffeln gehört. Auch die Kaufleute, die ich gefragt habe, darunter einen 70jährigen, der mit dem alten Häbler in geschäftlicher Verbindung stand, wissen nichts davon, dass jemals ein Trüffelhandel über Thorn existirt habe. Es wird daher wohl jedenfalls eine Verwechselung mit Kulm sein."

Ich war nach diesem negativen Ergebniss nicht wenig verwundert, aus der Feder von Ascherson (Verhandl. des botan. Vereins der Provinz Brandenburg 1881 S. 133) in einer Abhandlung über „Speisetrüffeln im nordöstlichen Deutschland" zu lesen: „Bei Ostrometzko, gerade in der Biegung des Weichselstromes nach Norden, ungefähr gegenüber der Mündnng der Brahe, hat Herr Rittergutsbesitzer v. Alvensleben, wie er Herrn Director Hüttig mittheilte, Trüffeln in lohnender Menge gefunden.“ Ostrometzko liegt im Kreise Kulm; ich habe in diesem Kreise, ferner in dem angrenzenden Graudenz und Thorn viele Bekannte, der preuss. botan. Verein hat dort viele Mitglieder, und von einer so interessanten Entdeckung, wie die von „Trüffeln in lohnender Menge,“ d. h. also für den Handel lohnend doch wohl, sollte mir Niemand etwas berichtet haben, wenn sie wirklich gemacht war? Ich fragte daher bei Herrn Erbtruchsess A. v. Alvensleben auf Ostrometzko, der im Kreise Kulm viele Güter besitzt und dessen Majorat: Erxleben in Sachsen liegt, wegen des Trüffelfundes an und erhielt unter dem 7. Mai 1881 die Antwort, „dass die Angabe jedenfalls ein Irrthum sei.“ Ich beauftragte Herrn Apotheker Eugen Rosenbohm, der 1881 die Kreise Graudenz, Kulm, Thorn botanisch als Reisender des preussischen botanischen Vereins besuchte, sich überall nach etwa gefundenen Trüffeln zu erkundigen. Wieder bloss negatives Ergebniss. Jedoch fand sich, dass bei einzelnen Gutsbesitzern im Gutsgarten gefundenes Sleroderma vulgare mit in Graudenz gekauften Trüffeln vermengt, zu Trüffelwurst verbraucht wurde. Dies bewies eine Probe solcher im Haushalt angewandter Trüffeln, die Frau Gutsbesitzer Vogel auf Nielub Herrn Rosenbohm gab, obgleich ich ausser Stande war, da die Stückchen wirklicher Trüffel von zu jungen Exemplaren kamen und keine ausgebildeten Sporen hatten, die Art der Trüffel zu bestimmen.

Ich theilte Herrn Professor Ascherson mit, dass die Angaben Hüttigs auf Irrthum beruhen müssen und ersuchte um Berichtigung. In Folge dessen beanstandete Ascherson (a. o. 24. Jahrg. 1883 S. 23) in einer Sitzung des botan. Vereins der Provinz Brandenburg vom 31. März 1882 die Angabe über Speisetrüffeln bei Ostrometzko „als nicht hinlänglich beglaubigt“, jedoch giebt Bail (botan. Centralblatt 1881, Bd. V, S. 293) in einem Bericht über jenen erwähnten Vortrag Aschersons an, dass er auch schon von dem Vorkommen von Trüffeln bei Ostrometzko gehört habe und ebenso ein Mitglied des brandenb. botan. Vereins O. v. Semen, dass ihm schon vor 15 Jahren davon in Bromberg mitgetheilt sei. Hüttig, Gärtner, der von Herrn v. Alvensleben nach Ostrometzko berufen war, damit er seinem Gärtner daselbst den Obstbaumschnitt lehre, räumte die Möglichkeit ein, dass nicht Herr v. Alvensleben ihm jene Mittheilung über den Trüffelfund bei Ostrometzko gemacht habe, hielt indess aufrecht, dass er die Mittheilung in Ostrometzko selbst erhalten habe.

Hat nun einer derer, die die Nachricht von Trüffeln bei Ostrometzko verbreiteten oder bestätigten, Hüttig, Bail, v. Semen, Trüffeln von da gesehen? Niemand!

Hat einer der Genannten Forschungen an Ort und Stelle angestellt, um den Grund jenes Gerüchts zu ermitteln? Niemand!

1883 untersuchte ich die Seen der Kreise Graudenz, Kulm und Thorn und kam auch nach Ostrometzko; ich verhandelte die Trüffelangelegenheit nun mündlich mit Herrn v. Alvensleben und dessen Beamten: Herrn Oberförster Gusovius und Administrator Rehse. Ich hörte von allen Seiten, dass Trüffeln in Ostrometzko nicht gefunden seien und ich erfuhr nun auch die Umstände, die zu der falschen Nachricht möglicher Weise Veranlassung gegeben haben konnten. Herr v. Alvensleben theilte mir mit, dass auf seinem Gute Gierkowo, Kreis Thorn, beim Drainiren in der Erde haselnussgrosse, grauschwarze Knollen gefunden seien, die ihm als „Trüffeln" gebracht seien, aber dies seien sie entschieden nicht; jedoch wisse er nicht, was sie seien. Ich bat um solche Knollen und erhielt sie frisch schon den folgenden Tag, 1. Septbr. 1883, in grosser Menge. Die Knollen waren die von Equisetum palustre L., denn die Stengeläste, die nur noch an wenigen hafteten, waren 6kantig. Dann theilte mir Herr Oberförster Gusovius mit, dass vor sehr langer Zeit, als noch der Vorbesitzer von Ostrometzko, Herr v. Schönborn, Schwiegervater des Herrn v. Alvensleben, auf Ostrometzko lebte, starb 1874, einmal von einem der Güter desselben: Fronau, Kreis Kulm, welches 7 Meilen in der Luftlinie von Ostrometzko nach Nordost liegt, eine Kiste mit angeblichen „Trüffeln" geschickt sei, die der damalige Gärtner in Ostrometzko: Rossbigall, als solche beanstandet und er (der Oberförster) sofort als „Boviste" bezeichnet habe. Ich fragte, ob mir diese Pilze nicht gezeigt werden könnten. Nein! sagte der Oberförster, ich kann Ihnen jetzt keine besorgen. Jedoch begleitete mich der Oberförster mehrere Tage als Führer nach den Seen und Altwassern der Weichsel bei Ostrometzko und als ich auf einem dieser Ausflüge in einem sandigen Wege im Belauf Striesau zu Ostrometzko gehörig, einige Exemplare von Scleroderma vulgare fand, sagte der Oberförster, dass er mit Bestimmtheit in diesen Pilzen die „Trüffeln" von Fronau wieder erkenne.

Mit dem Nachweise, dass keine Trüffeln bei Ostrometzko gefunden sind, dass dies Gerücht aber auf Verkennung von Schachtelhalmknollen und Scleroderma beruhe, ist es hoffentlich ein für alle Mal beseitigt. Wer es aufrecht erhalten will, muss consequenter Weise behaupten, dass in ganz Ost- und Westpreussen, auch Pommern Trüffeln vorhanden seien, denn in diesen Provinzen wird Scleroderma vulg. nicht bloss oft gefunden, sondern auf zahlreichen Gütern „Trüffel" genannt, aufgesucht und als Trüffel verspeist, was in Ostrometzko nicht einmal geschehen ist. Von solcher Verkennung und Benutzung des Scleroderma vulgare einige Beispiele. Oben ist schon bemerkt, dass in Nielub bei Briesen, Kreis Thorn, Scleroderma als Trüffel benutzt ist. Bail führt ebenfalls (Centralblatt 1881 VI. 136) zwei Fälle für Güter an, auf denen Sclerod. vulg. als „Trüffel" genossen ist.

Herr Rittergutsbesitzer Schielke auf Tautschkon, Kreis Neidenburg, theilte mir, als ich dort war, 1862, mit, dass er in seinem Garten „Trüffeln" habe, die zu wirthschaftlichen Zwecken benutzt würden. Als ich mich einige Jahre später an ihn der „Trüffeln" wegen wandte, war Herr Schielke schon todt, aber sein Schwiegersohn, Herr Rittmeister Kaul auf Kattlewo bei Löbau, Kreis Löbau, schrieb mir unter dem 7. October 1874, dass in diesem Jahr in Tauschken keine „Trüffeln" gewachsen seien, er sie aber in seinem Garten auch habe. Zugleich schickte er einige. Es waren diese Pilze Scleroderma vulg. In Tautschken und Kattlewo sind sie auch gegessen. Herr Rittmeister Kaul schreibt: „Vor einigen Jahren wurde eine Probe der hiesigen Trüffel nach Hamburg an eine Delicatessenhandlung geschickt. Dieselbe erklärte die Trüffel für gut und machte auch ein Gebot auf dieselbe, welches jedoch nicht acceptirt wurde, da die Absicht, ein Handelsgeschäft zu machen, nicht vorlag." Zugleich theilte mir Herr Rittmeister Kaul mit, dass auch auf dem Gute Gr. Koschlau, Kreis Neidenburg, Trüffeln gefunden würden und Frau Elise Möller, deren Mann ehedem Gr. Koschlau besass, veranlasste, dass mir „Trüffeln" von dort geschickt wurden, die Scleroderma vulg. waren; auch schreibt Frau Möller: „Sie sind der Gesundheit nicht nachtheilig; wir haben sie gegessen; ihr Aussehen ist ganz das der ächten Trüffel, sie haben aber, wenn sie gekocht sind, nicht den würzigen Geruch und Geschmack wie diese und sind mithin nicht als Delicatesse zu bezeichnen." Den 2. Septbr. 1875 wies mir Herr v. Zitzewitz auf Bornzin bei Stolp in Pommern im Garten dieses Guts „Trüffeln" nach, die Scleroderma vulg. waren; ebenso im Park im Sande in Gr. Krien, demselben Herrn gehörig.

Den 28. Juli 1879 sagten mir Herr Major v. Restorf auf Klotainen, Kreis Heilsberg, und Frau Gemahlin, dass bei ihnen im Garten „Trüffeln" wachsen. Sie wurden mir mit der Frage, ob es ächte seien, vorgelegt; es war Scleroderma vulg. Ich erfuhr, dass diese „Trüffel" zu Trüffelleberwurst verwendet würde und dass Herr Major v. Restorf nebst Frau und auch ihre Verwandten diese „Trüffelwurst" ohne jeden Schaden gegessen hätten. Die mit Scleroderma bereitete Trüffelwurst hätte schwarze Punkte, der Geschmack sei durch den Pilz gar nicht verändert; die Behauptung: solche Trüffelwurst schmecke besser, als gewöhnliche, beruhe auf Einbildung; ihre „Trüffel" schmecke nach nichts.

In Preussen speisen also viele Menschen, gewiss hunderte, alljährlich Scleroderma vulg. ohne Nachtheil. Göppert aber (50. Jahresbericht der schles. Ges. für vaterl. Cultur 1873, 114. Otto, Hamburger Garten- u. Blumenzeitung 1877, 64 u. 65) stellt Scleroderma vulg. als Gift von „grosser Intensivität" dar, führt jedoch als Belag dafür nur einen Fall an. Ist denn in diesem Fall zweifellos festgestellt, dass die giftige Wirkung einer verspeisten „Sauce" dem Scleroderma zuzuschreiben war? Konnte darin nicht etwas anderes Giftiges sein? Der Fall scheint gar nicht dazu angethan die giftige Wirkung von Scleroderma zu beweisen und steht obenein den höchst zahlreichen Fällen des nicht nachtheiligen Genusses von Scleroderma in „Trüffelwurst" vereinzelt gegenüber. Auch in dem Falle von angeblicher Vergiftung durch Scleroderma vulg., den Bail anführt (Centralblatt A. O.), ist es durchaus nicht erwiesen, dass die giftige Wirkung von Scleroderma ausging. Vergiftungserscheinungen kommen zu öfters bei ganzen Familien nach gemeinsamem Genuss von Speisen auch sonst vor, ohne dass Pilze dabei mitwirkten und ohne dass die Ursache sich genau feststellen liesse. Finden sich solche Vergiftungsvorgänge da vor, wo auch Pilze genossen sind, so wird vielleicht mit Unrecht diesen die nachtheilige Wirkung zugeschoben. W. G. Smith (Garden. chron. 1885 p. 48) theilt mit, dass in Epping Forest Scleroderma vulg. gesammelt würde, damit Puten gefüllt und diese schon gebraten in London als mit „Trüffeln" gefüllte verkauft und gegessen würden. Er äussert seine Entrüstung über diesen Betrug, weiss aber von Schädlichkeit der Wirkung nichts zu berichten. Es sind also zuverlässige, wissenschaftliche Untersuchungen, nicht Behauptungen oder Vermuthungen über die Frage: ist Scleroderma vulg. giftig oder nicht, nöthig.

Königsberg, den 9. November 1886.

Ostpreussische Grabhügel.

I.

Von

Dr. Otto Tischler.

(Hierzu Tafel III—VI.)

Einleitung.

Die Provinz Ostpreussen besitzt noch gegenwärtig eine ziemlich grosse Anzahl von Grabhügeln, welche weit in das 1. Jahrtausend v. Chr. zurückreichen. Dieselben fallen aber immer mehr der steigenden Cultur, dem intensiveren Landbau und besonders dem stetig fortschreitenden Ausbau des Chausseenetzes zum Opfer, wobei leider oft diese ehrwürdigen Denkmäler einer uralten Vorzeit in einer der Wissenschaft durchaus keinen Nutzen bringenden Weise zerstört werden. Der jetzige Bestand ist daher nur noch ein schwacher Rest des einst vorhandenen, und es gilt denselben soviel als möglich in einer den strengsten Anforderungen der Alterthumsforschung entsprechenden Weise zu untersuchen.

Dieser Aufgabe haben sich die beiden hiesigen Gesellschaften, die **Physikalisch-ökonomische** und die Alterthumsgesellschaft **Prussia** unterzogen und so im Laufe der letzten beiden Decennien ein beträchtliches äusserst wichtiges systematisches Material zusammengebracht. Schon früher hatten Gelehrte eine grosse Zahl dieser Hügel geöffnet, vielfach aber auch Dilettanten dieselben ziemlich planlos zerstört, so dass bei der relativen Armuth an Metallsachen viele dieser letzteren Grabungen für die Wissenschaft von geringer Wichtigkeit waren. Aber doch haben sie manche Bronze und manche Urne zu Tage gefördert, deren Bedeutung durch die systematischen Grabungen jetzt in klares Licht gestellt wird, so dass immerhin ein Theil dieser planlos oder zufällig gewonnenen Objecte doch noch von Nutzen ist.

Die seitens der Physikalisch-ökonomischen Gesellschaft unternommenen systematischen Ausgrabungen sollen in einer Reihe fortlaufender Abhandlungen veröffentlicht werden. Zunächst wird eine Beschreibung des Baues der einzelnen Hügel, der Fund- und Grabverhältnisse und der einzelnen Fundobjecte gegeben werden. Da die Hügel, welche den Gegenstand dieser vorliegenden 1. Abhandlung bilden, nur einen Theil des Inventars enthielten, welches diese ganze Gräbergruppe geliefert hat, so sollen die allgemeinen Betrachtungen und Schlussfolgerungen auf die nächsten Abhandlungen verschoben werden, welche dies Inventar wesentlich vervollständigen, und aus demselben Grunde sollen die Vergleiche diesmal auf das Nöthigste beschränkt bleiben. Eine Uebersicht über die älteren, publicirten Ausgrabungen wird sich dann später auch besser an die genaueren Beschreibungen der Hügelgräber anschliessen.

Methode der Ausgrabung.

Im Folgenden will ich die Methode auseinandersetzen, die ich in mehr als 10jähriger Praxis ausgebildet und nach und nach entwickelt habe, welche für Ostpreussen, wo man nur mit mässigen Hügeln bis ca. 20 m Durchmesser zu thun hat, für alle Fälle genügen dürfte und die sich im Laufe dieser Zeit immer mehr und mehr bewährt hat. Meine ersten Ausgrabungen wurden noch nicht mit all den Hilfsmitteln, die ich später anwandte, ausgeführt, so dass hier wohl noch hin und wieder kleine Missstände eintraten, die bei den späteren nicht mehr vorkamen. Bei den manchmal viel grösseren Hügeln in anderen Gegenden Europas werden sich in Bezug auf die Bewältigung der ungleich grösseren Erd- und Steinmassen bedeutendere Schwierigkeiten ergeben, welche andere, umfassendere Massregeln erfordern. Ebenso wird die veränderte Bauart solcher Hügel oft eine ganz andere Angriffsmethode bedingen, auf die hier, wo zunächst die einheimischen Verhältnisse berücksichtigt werden sollen, nicht näher eingegangen werden kann, zumal sich bei uns auch keine Gelegenheit zu solchen Studien bot.

Meine Methode schliesst sich, besonders in Bezug auf die Messung und Aufzeichnung, wesentlich an die von Cohausen*) beschriebene an, einige Modificationen wird man beim Vergleich leicht erkennen.

Dem Praktiker, welcher selbst gräbt, wird manches in der folgenden Auseinandersetzung pedantisch oder zu detaillirt erscheinen, da viele Operationen so einfach sind, dass jeder von selbst darauf kommen, oder vieles nach seiner Bequemlichkeit modificiren würde. Manche der erprobten kleinen Handgriffe dürften aber doch dazu beitragen die Arbeit schneller und sicherer zu gestalten und werden daher fast übermässig ausführlich dargestellt. Ausserdem gewährt die Kenntniss der Ausgrabungsmethode einen Schluss auf die Sicherheit der gewonnenen Resultate.

Vor allen kommt es darauf an, während des Verlaufes der Grabung den Bau des Hügels, alle Steinconstructionen, die Lage jedes einzelnen Objectes möglichst schnell und bequem zu messen und aufzuzeichnen, für welchen Zweck ich die Cohausensche Methode als die allerbeste erprobt habe.

Vom höchsten Punkte des Hügels werden gleich weit entfernt nach Nord und nach Süd am Fusse 2 Pfähle eingeschlagen. Eine ängstliche Genauigkeit ist nicht erforderlich, da man die Richtung nachher mit der Boussole fest bestimmen kann. Man lässt dann durch zwei Arbeiter eine genügend lange Schnur an die

---

*) Annalen des Vereins für Nassauische Alterthumskunde und Geschichtsforschung. Wiesbaden. Bd. XII (1873) p. 245. 246.

Pfähle halten, nimmt die Mitte und geht soweit hinaus bis die Schnur straff gespannt ist. An dieser Stelle lässt man einen Pfahl einschlagen, erst auf einer Seite (O), dann auf der andern (W). Bei richtig abgemessener Schnur erhält man zwei Pfähle am Fusse des Hügels, deren Verbindungslinie auf derjenigen der beiden ersten senkrecht steht. Es ist nothwendig diese ziemlich starken Pfähle recht fest einzuschlagen und nöthigenfalls mit Steinen zu umpacken — was immer erforderlich wird, sobald man unten noch auf Steine stösst — damit sie sich im Laufe der Arbeit nicht im mindesten verrücken können.

Es kommt nun darauf an diese Pfähle durch zwei sich berührende horizontale Schnüre, welche also auf einander senkrecht stehen, zu verbinden. Ich wende dazu eine kleine Röhrenlibelle mit Diopter an, die mit einer Nuss über einer Hülse beweglich ist, welche auf den Zapfen eines ganz leichten Stativs gestellt wird. Auf diesen Zapfen schraube ich auch gelegentlich eine kleine Broussole. (Am bequemsten ist dazu ein geologischer Compass mit Dioptern, unter dem man einen kleinen Untersatz mit Nuss anschraubt. Die gemessene Richtung kann man leicht aufzeichnen, indem man den Compas auf das nach Nord orientirte Papier setzt, die Nadel in der gemessenen Richtung einspielen lässt, ein Lineal an den Fuss des Compass legt und die Richtung zieht). Die käuflichen einfachen Diopterlibellen der obigen Art haben keine feinere Einstellung, was das Arbeiten bedeutend verzögert. Man kann sich ein solches Instrument aber leicht umändern lassen, indem man das Unterstück abnimmt und zwischen dies und die Bodenplatte eine Zwischenplatte einlegt, die an einem Ende schwach federnd festsitzt, am andern durch eine Schraube von der obern ein wenig entfernt werden kann, wie die Objecttische bei manchen billigen Mikroskopen. Wenn man dann die grobe Einstellung mit der Hand vornimmt, geht die Arbeit sehr schnell von Statten.

Man stellt dies Stativ in die Verlängerung des einen Durchmessers ausserhalb des Hügels, z. B. nach S., visirt dann nach dem S.-Pfahle und nach den beiden rechts und links, O. und W. An diesen visirten, in einem Niveau befindlichen Punkten werden Nägel lose eingeschlagen. Dasselbe macht man an der gegenüberliegenden (N.) Seite und erhält auf den Pfählen ONW. wieder drei in einem anderen Niveau liegenden Punkte. Auf OW. hat man also zwei Niveaus übereinander. Durch Probiren findet man nun leicht zwei Punkte, welche gleich hoch über jedem entsprechenden Punktpaare liegen, deren Verbindungslinie den Gipfel des Hügels berührt. Den Niveaupunkt an dem dritten Pfahle muss man um die Entfernung von der einen entsprechenden Niveaulinie erhöhen, an dem vierten um die andere. Die beiden somit erhöhten horizontalen Schnüre werden sich dann in ihren Mittelpunkten berühren; die Methode ist völlig genau genug. Es ist aber nicht nöthig, dass sie grade den Gipfel des Hügels berühren, wenn sich z. B. seitwärts noch kleine Erhöhungen befinden. Die Schnüre werden an je einem Nagel festgebunden, über den anderen durch einen angebundenen Stein gespannt, so dass sie stets, so oft sie bei der Arbeit hinderlich sind, aufgerollt werden können.

So lässt sich die Lage jedes Punktes bequem nach drei Coordinaten bestimmen. Man stellt über demselben einen Stock senkrecht auf und misst dessen Entfernung von beiden Schnüren mit dem Bandmasse. Dann wird eine Schnur an einem Nagel festgebunden und von einem Arbeiter über die Schnur des anderen

Paares so lange, ohne diese zu drücken, hingeführt, bis sie genau über dem zu messenden Punkte liegt, wo man mit einem Massstabe die Tiefe misst. In Ostpreussen genügt ein solcher von 2 m Länge. Die Bezeichnung eines Punktes wird also folgendermassen notirt, beispielsweise: 3,5 O. 4,7 N. z = 1,4, d. h. 3,5 östlich von der NS.-Linie, 4,7 nördlich von der OW.-Linie, 1,4 unter dem Niveau der Schnüre. Bei dem Aufmessen habe ich dies Niveau mit dem Gipfel des Hügels nicht immer übereinstimmend genommen, beim Ausarbeiten des Protokolls kann man immer von der Höhe des Gipfels als Null-Ebene ausgehen.

Diese Masse trägt man gleich auf carrirtes, am besten in Millimeter getheiltes Papier ein, welches auf einem kleinen Brettchen mit Heftstiften befestigt ist und bei Regenwetter mit übergestecktem Wachstuch geschützt wird. Wenn man bei Steinconstructionen einige Steine auf diese Weise einträgt, kann man die übrigen leicht und sicher aus freier Hand einzeichnen.

Cohausen a. a. O. schlägt eine auf dem Felde zu fertigende Setzwage vor. An einer Ruthe befestigt man eine Schnur, in deren Mitte ein Stein eingeknüpft wird, während von der Mitte der Ruthe eine ebenfalls einen Stein tragende Schnur herunterhängt. Diese Ruthe soll dann mittelst Umschlingung in die Mitte der horizontal zu spannenden Schnur gesteckt werden, welche dann an einem Ende so lange verschoben wird, bis beide Steinchen übereinander hängen. Die herabhängende Mitte soll dann horizontal sein, ebenso wie die gespannte Schnur. Dies Instrument fand ich aber viel zu ungenau, auch als ich mir ein präciseres aus Messing hatte fertigen lassen. Zumal bei Wind war ein sicheres Einspielen so schwer zu erzielen, dass sich nur sehr unzuverlässige Resultate ergaben. Auch wurden die Schnüre so bedeutend herabgezogen, dass man sie erheblich oberhalb des Gipfels führen, also recht hoch an den Pfählen befestigen musste. Wenn man sich an die Ausgrabung von Hügeln macht, ist es doch nöthig mancherlei mitzunehmen, so dass die obige kleine Libelle nebst Stativ das Gepäck nicht wesentlich vermehrt. In der Nähe der See kann man oft nach dem Meereshorizont die Schnüre spannen.

Für den Fall, dass es durchaus nicht gelingt, vier starke, genügend lange Pfähle aufzutreiben, was in sehr armen, dünnbevölkerten Gegenden eintreten könnte, wird man eine andere weniger bequeme Methode anwenden. Man zeichnet dann auf einem Messtische einfachster Construction. Die gut angefertigte Tischplatte wird mittelst eingeschraubter Hülse auf einen mittelst einer Nuss allseitig beweglichen Zapfen gesetzt, der auf einem **soliden** Stative befestigt ist. Mittelst aufgesetzter Libelle wird die Platte horizontal gestellt und mittelst eines Diopterlineals nach einem festen Punkte orientirt, während das Stativ immer über ein und demselben ausserhalb des Hügels befindlichen Punkte steht. Man visirt dann mit dem Diopterlineal von dem festen Mittelpunkte des Tisches nach dem zu bestimmenden Object, nimmt die Entfernung mit dem Bandmaasse und trägt sie in richtiger Reduction längs der Kante des Lineals auf (also Darstellung mittelst Polarcoordinaten). Die Messung der Höhen resp. Tiefen wird man durch Nivellement mittelst jener Diopterlibelle von einem bestimmten festen Punkte aus vornehmen, eine viel umständlichere Operation. Da der Messtisch immer feststeht, thut man gut, auf einem kleinen Zeichenbrettchen diese Punkte zu copiren und hierauf im Hügel selbst die Zeichnung der Steinconstructionen zu vollenden.

Man kann auch ausserhalb des Hügels ein Quadrat von vier Schnüren spannen, die dann durch vier niedrige Pfähle befestigt werden und von diesen aus messen, doch kommen dieselben bald mit der ausgeworfenen Erde in Conflict und das Nivellement ist ebenso mühsam.

Es ist die Cohausensche Methode immer die bei Weitem bequemste und empfehlenswertheste. Wenn man lange Pfähle nicht an Ort und Stelle erhält, wird man gut thun, sie anderweitig zu kaufen und heranzuschaffen.

Der weitere Verlauf der Grabung wird genau protokollirt. Um fernere Details, wie den Bau der Steinkisten etc. genauer einzeichnen zu können, habe ich mir das Notizbuch aus einem gröber carrirten Papier binden lassen.

Wenn die horizontalen Schnüre gezogen sind, wird zunächst das Profil des Hügels nach zwei Querschnitten aufgenommen. Man steckt das eine Ende des Bandmaasses am Kreuzungspunkte der Schnüre fest und misst nach allen vier Richtungen von Meter zu Meter die Tiefe der Oberfläche unter der Schnur mit dem Maassstabe. Diese Profile kann man auf dem carrirten Papiere parrallel ihren Richtungen ausserhalb der Stelle, welche der Grundriss des Hügels einnehmen wird, eintragen.

Während dieser Operationen können alle irgend disponiblen Arbeiter schon rüstig ans Werk gehen, wenn nur die unter den Schnüren befindlichen Streifen geschont werden.

Oft muss noch die Abholzung des Hügels vorangehen, wobei Bäume und Sträucher aber zunächst nur über der Wurzel abgehauen oder abgesägt werden dürfen.

Am besten ist es, wenn man den Hügel schichtenweise abtragen kann, so dass alle Steinconstructionen klar zu Tage treten und bis zum Schlusse sichtbar bleiben. Das ist aber nur bei kleinen Hügeln bis zu ca. 10 m Durchmesser möglich, wo die Erde noch bequem von der Mitte aus bis über den Rand geworfen werden kann. Bei grösseren Hügeln müsste sie noch einmal bewegt werden, eine entschiedene Arbeitsverschwendung, falls nicht der bei der Planirung selbst interessirte Besitzer die Erde sofort wegfährt, ein stets sehr willkommener Fall. Bei grösseren Hügeln muss die Abtragung daher in zwei Abtheilungen vorgenommen werden, was bei unseren Hügeln von bis zu 20 m Durchmesser genügt und gut durchzuführen geht.

Man trägt dann zuerst den äusseren Mantel in eine Breite von ca. 5 m ab und lässt die Erde möglichst weit nach aussen werfen. Ein Theil der Arbeiter schält die Rasendecke ab, während andere den äussersten Steinkranz des Hügels verfolgen und blosslegen. Unsere Hügel sind meist aus Schichten von Steinen und Erde aufgebaut. Es muss zuerst immer die über den Steinen liegende Erdschicht abgegraben werden, weil schon in den höheren Schichten oft kleinere Objecte vorkommen, dann erst darf die nächstfolgende Steinschicht ausgebrochen werden. So fährt man fort bis zum Boden des Hügels.

Um die Schichtung des Hügels zu erkennen, lässt man unter einem oder unter zwei Schnüren vom Rande an einen mässig breiten Graben bis auf die Sohle des Hügels soweit wie möglich nach der Mitte zu legen (die bei schneller oder pfuscherhafter Durchwühlung eines Hügels ausschliesslich, aber etwas breiter angelegten Kreuzgräben). Die eine Wand muss genau unter der Schnur liegen, so dass man die Stein- und Erdschichten messen und in das Profil des Hügels einzeichnen kann. Sobald regelmässige Steinlager oder andere Constructionen zu Tage treten, werden sie in den Grundplan eingezeichnet, wobei es genügt, nur einige Steine genau zu messen. Wenn sie eingezeichnet sind, kann man sie entfernen und später den ganz steinfreien Raum wieder mit Erde vollwerfen.

Unsere ostpreussischen Hügel enthalten in der Regel sehr viel Steine — ich habe einem Hügel bis über 100 Cubikmeter entnommen. Es müssen daher ein bis zwei Paar Arbeiter fortwährend die Steine wegtragen und auf Haufen werfen, falls sie nicht vom Besitzer fortgefahren werden können.

Wenn der Mantel abgetragen ist, kann man es mit dem Kerne ebenso machen und die Erde in den nun freigewordenen äusseren Ring — immer möglichst weit — werfen. Diese Zweitheilung genügt bei uns.

Cohausen empfiehlt schmälere Ringgräben und zieht es vor, die stehende Wand anzugreifen, anstatt schichtweise abzutragen. Ich halte das für nicht so praktisch da die hier zu Tage tretenden Metallobjecte viel leichter beschädigt werden können, zumal die Arbeiter äusserst schwer von der Angewohnheit abzubringen sind, hervorragende Gegenstände aus der Wand herauszuziehen, wobei diese, falls ihre Constitution nicht unerschütterlich ist, meist zerbrochen werden. Bei vorsichtigem, schichtenweisem Abtragen von oben, was selbst die ungeübtesten Arbeiter schnell begreifen, wird viel weniger zerstört und lassen sich grössere Objecte, die doch meist horizontal liegen, leichter frei machen.

Die frei zwischen Steinen stehenden Urnen sind meist zerdrückt, und müssen ihre Scherben sorgfältig gesammelt werden, sowie die dazwischen liegenden Objecte. In der Regel sind sie aber in grösseren oder kleineren Steinkisten eingeschlossen, welche frei gelegt, sorgfältig ausgemessen und aufgezeichnet werden müssen, am besten in etwas grösserem Maasstabe.

Man wird diese Kisten in der Regel an den grösseren platten Decksteinen erkennen, denen daher besondere Aufmerksamkeit zuzuwenden ist.

Wenn die Kiste frei steht und abgezeichnet ist, kann man die Steine entfernen und die darin stehenden Urnen, wie andere Objecte nach der später mitzutheilenden Methode heben.

Im Norden der Provinz sind die Kisten und anderen Urnen, wie sich weiter unten zeigen wird, durch den ganzen Hügel vertheilt, und man muss daher die Abtragung des ganzen Hügels vornehmen, um sicher zu sein, dass man ihn vollständig ausgebeutet hat, wenn auch manchmal die mittlere Hauptkiste sich als ausgeraubt erweist. Weiter südlich, wo eine grosse Kiste auf der Südseite des Hügels auftritt, und wo man den Verlauf dieser grossen Steine leicht erkennt, ist es zweckmässig, mit einem Theile der Arbeiter diese grosse Kiste möglichst bald frei zu machen, während die anderen auf die gewöhnliche Weise arbeiten, um den Verlauf der Steinsetzungen zu erforschen. Stellt es sich dann heraus, dass die Kiste schon ausgeraubt ist, wobei die grossen Träger und Decksteine oft noch an Ort und Stelle um- oder durcheinander geworfen liegen, so kann man die Arbeit bald aufgeben, während man dies im Samlande nicht thun darf, da hier oft noch eine gute Nachlese zu halten ist.

Die Urnen in den Kisten sind in der Regel besser erhalten als die frei zwischen Steinen stehenden und halten, selbst wenn zersprungen, doch meist in der Form zusammen. Die alte Regel, sie erst ordentlich an der Luft trocknen zu lassen, ehe man sie hebt, ist zwar ganz zweckmässig, aber bei dringender Zeit — da man solche Sachen über Nacht nicht draussen lassen darf — oder bei Regenwetter oft nicht ausführbar, aber auch nicht erforderlich. Ich habe bei anderer *) Gelegenheit meine Methode zur Hebung und Conservirung der Urnen eingehend auseinandergesetzt, die sich nun seit einer Reihe von Jahren bestens bewährt hat, und die hier kurz wiederholt werden soll.

Um die Urnen in dem Zustande, wie sie sich in der Erde befinden, selbst wenn sie schon ziemlich zersprungen sind, zu heben und zu transportiren, kann man 2 Methoden anwenden, eine entsprechende Beschnürung oder einen Gypsverband, welche zweite auch für Alterthumsgegenstände jeder Art höchst zweckmässig ist.

Die Beschnürung eignet sich mehr für besser erhaltene Urnen mit wenig bewegtem Profil und kommt für unsere Hügelgräber weniger in Betracht. Bei Mangel an Gyps wird man aber dazu schreiten müssen.

Um den Hals der Urne legt man möglichst hoch einen vorher fest (mit Kreuzknoten) geknüpften Bindfadenreif, vorausgesetzt, dass sie sich nach unten erweitert. Unten, so tief als möglich legt man einen zweiten Reif, indem man den Bindfaden durch seine Endschlinge fest zieht. Das freie Ende führt man dann in die Höhe, zieht es mittelst einer Packnadel mit krummer Spitze unter dem oberen Reif durch, geht dann schräge herab unter dem unteren Reif hindurch und steigt dann weiter immer im Zickzack herauf und herab, so dass die ganze Urne trommelartig beschnürt wird. Wenn man den Faden von Zeit zu Zeit festzieht, werden die beiden Reifen allmählich auch recht fest an die Urne gezogen, der obere nach unten, der untere nach oben und selbst eine schon ziemlich zersprungene Urne hält noch gut zusammen, vorausgesetzt dass man bei der Arbeit vorsichtig ist. An defecten oder sehr zersprungenen Stellen kann man Papier unterlegen, das später durch die Beschnürung festgedrückt wird. (In der citirten ersten Abhandlung empfahl ich die ganze Beschnürung mit einem einzigen Bindfaden, indem der heraufsteigende Bindfaden erst um den Hals geschlungen wurde und dann herabstieg. Das ist weniger zweckmässig, da der Faden, wenn er schliesslich zu dicht an der Verschlingungsstelle des oberen Ringes durchgezogen wird, leicht das ganze lockern und zum Herabfallen bringen kann. Auch ist bei der neuen Methode nur eine Person nöthig, während früher beim ersten Anfange immer noch eine zweite halten musste.) Die so beschnürte und gehobene Urne kann man der Sicherheit wegen nochmals in Zeug, oder in Ermanglung selbst in Papier schnüren nach derselben Methode. Bei sehr grossen Urnen wende ich eigens dazu mitgenommene Säcke, in welche sie hineingesteckt werden, an, bei kleineren kann man Zeugstücke nehmen. Diese Methode kann auch bei Regenwetter angewendet werden und ertragen die Urnen nun den Transport ganz ruhig.

Von weit grösserer Bedeutung ist aber die Methode des Gypsverbandes.

Man legt die Urne soweit nach unten frei, als es bei ihrem Erhaltungszustande räthlich erscheint und entfernt auch den Deckel, wenn er nicht ganz fest ist und lose sitzt, nicht. Man legt dann um den Hals einen schmalen Zeugstreifen, der aber auch durch Papier ersetzt werden kann, und zieht ihn durch umgelegten Heftzwirn, dessen Ende nicht abgeschnitten wird, mässig fest. In einer emaillirten eisernen

*) O. Tischler: Das Ausgraben von Urnen und deren weitere Behandlung. Correspondenzblatt der Deutschen anthropologischen Gesellschaft 1883 12. 1884 8.

Schale (diese ist der Haltbarkeit wegen ein für allemal vorzuziehen) rührt man gebrannten Gyps in Wasser an, taucht bereitgehaltene viereckige Papierstreifen mit einer Kante in diesen Brei und klebt sie auf den Zeugstreifen nach oben und nach unten, so dass sie sowohl die Mündung der Urne verschliessen als den freien Theil des Bauches einhüllen. Mit dem Zwirn überzieht man das ganze nach allen möglichen Richtungen. Dann taucht man eine zweite Lage Papierstücke mit einer Seite ganz im Gypsbrei, streicht sie dicht auf die erste an und zieht den Bindfaden immer fest darüber. Wenn man das Ganze noch mit Gypsbrei überstreicht, erhält man einen dicht anliegenden Verband aus Papier, Gyps und Bindfaden, den man nun auf dieselbe Weise durch Auflegen von dickerem Papier so lange verstärkt, als man es für erforderlich hält. Exponirtere Stellen wie der Rand, eckige Vorsprünge müssen natürlich einen etwas dickern Mantel erhalten. Sehr hervorragende Glieder, wie Henkel etc. umkleidet man vorher mit Sand. Wenn dieser oberste Verband angelegt ist, macht man die Urne wieder weiter so tief frei, als ihre Konsistenz erlaubt, klebt auf dem untersten Gypsrand neue Papierstreifen und legt ganz ebenso den zweiten Papier-Gyps-Bindfadenmantel um, was in der Regel genügen wird. Steht die Urne auf Sand oder Erde, so verlängert man ihn ein wenig unter ihrem Boden. Dann wird sie mit dem Spaten unterhalb des Bodens gehoben, mit geschicktem Schwung umgekehrt und mit dem Kopf in weiche Erde gesetzt — auf untergelegtes Papier der Reinlichkeit wegen. Man kratzt unten die überschüssige Erde ab, schliesst die freie Oeffnung durch Papierstreifen, die man auf den Mantel klebt und verstärkt den Verband soweit erforderlich. Ein Etikett muss man immer über die Mündung der Urne legen, da es hier vollständig gesichert ist. Um sich unter den eingegypsten Urnen leichter zu orientiren, kann man ein zweites mittelst Bindfaden an dem etwas emporgehobenen Zwirne anbinden und diese Stelle noch gut übergypsen. Denn eine sorgfältige, womöglich mehrfache Etikettirung ist ein Haupterforderniss. Schlimmer ist es, wenn die Urne, wie häufig vorkommt, auf einer Steinfliese steht. Ist diese klein, so thut man vielfach gut sie mit einzugypsen, nachdem man den Zwischenraum möglichst mit Sand ausgefüllt hat. Denn oft stehen die Urnen auf diesen Fliesen so fest, dass der Boden beim Abheben leicht ausbricht, und auf den Boden kommt es bei den Urnen der Hügelgräber sehr an. Man muss diese Trennung mit Messer und Nadel langsam zu vollziehen suchen, und bricht doch noch etwas aus, so werden die sorgfältig gesammelten Scherben später eingeklebt, falls sie nicht ganz zerfallen. Stehen 2 Urnen so dicht aneinandergepresst, dass sie sich eng berühren, manchmal sogar etwas eingedrückt haben, so muss man die Papierstreifen, Fäden und Gypsverband um diese Contactstelle führen, indem man beide Urnen gleichzeitig in Verband legt. Sollten die Urnen doch an dieser Stelle ausbröckeln, so sind sie wenigstens im Uebrigen erhalten und können hier leicht ergänzt werden, ein besonderer Vorzug der Methode. Auf dieselbe Weise kann man eine Menge dicht gedrängter Urnen einer ganzen Steinkiste gleichzeitig in Verband legen.

Gyps ist auch sehr zweckmässig bei difficilen Objecten aus Bronce oder anderem Material zu verwenden, und es ist daher durchaus geboten zu jeder Ausgrabung von vorneherein eine grössere Quantität Gyps mitzunehmen. Da es bei längerer Arbeit schwer fällt in der Nähe guten Gyps zu erhalten, lasse ich denselben aus Königsberg (d. h. dem nächsten Centralpunkte) kommen in Postpacketen zu

10 Pfd., in doppeltem Sack aus starkem Papier und noch in Zeug eingenäht. So kann er, ohne zu stäuben, versandt werden, der Postbote bringt ihn sicher bis in die abgelegensten Gegenden, die Hüllen werden bei weiterem Arbeiten verbraucht und die Transportkosten betragen höchstens 5 Pf. pro Pfund.

Kleinere Objecte legt man annähernd frei, d. h. schneidet einen Erdklotz um sie los, bedeckt sie wieder mit Erde, macht einen kleinen Erdwall herum und übergiesst das ganze mit dickem Gypsbrei. Bei grösseren Stücken muss man Holzstäbchen, Aeste, zerspaltene Cigarrendeckel hinein oder herüberlegen, um dem Gyps mehr Festigkeit zu verleihen. Bei noch grösseren lege ich, um Gyps zu sparen, einen Rahmen aus Cigarrenbrettchen um und auf den Klotz und lege dann den Verband in alter Weise aus Gyps, Papier und Zwirn an. Wo solche grössere Objecte in Masse zu erwarten sind, nehme ich eine Anzahl etwas dickerer Brettchen mit, die auf dem Felde zu viereckigen Rahmen zusammengenagelt und übergestülpt werden. Die Deckbretter werden dann aber am besten nicht aufgenagelt, sondern aufgeschroben, um Erschütterungen zu vermeiden. Das Umkehren ist bei kleinen Stücken leicht, man muss den Erdklotz nur immer ziemlich tief durchschneiden. Bei grösseren muss man eine Reihe kleiner Brettchen in der Richtung der geringsten Breite durchschieben, nöthigenfalls mit 2 längs gelegten Stäben und mit einander über dem Gypsklumpen verschlingen. Bei sehr grossen, flachen Stücken, wo ein übergestülpter Rahmen empfehlenswerth, muss man den Erdklumpen unmittelbar an der Unterseite dieses Rahmens mit einem langen schmalen zugeschärftem Brette oder besser mit einem zu diesem Zwecke eigens bestimmten dicken Eisenlineale gewissermassen durchsägen. Unmittelbar dahinter schiebt man immer schmale Brettchen nach. Nach vollendeter Durchsägung kann man sie genügend festschlingen, den Kasten umkehren und auf der Unterseite einen geeigneten Verschluss anbringen. Bei den einfachen Gypsklumpen legt man auf den glatten Sand, in den man allenfalls einige Vertiefungen schneiden kann, eine Lage geölten, oder zwei gewöhnlichen weichen Papiers — um das Oeffnen zu erleichtern — und giesst dann eine Gypsschicht über die nach oben gekehrte Unterseite, worauf man beide Hälften fest zusammenbindet. Jedermann wird beim arbeiten leicht herausfinden, wie am bequemsten vorzugehen ist, dabei aber die ungemeine Bequemlichkeit des Gypses sowohl beim Ausgraben als beim Verpacken der Fundstücke kennen lernen.

Wenn die Gegenstände zu Hause angekommen sind, kann man den Verband der Urnen leicht lösen, da der Gyps neben Papier und Zwirn ja eigentlich nur eine untergeordnete Rolle spielt. Man schneidet mit einer spitzen Scheere hinein und kann die Lagen leicht abblättern. Man lässt die Urne dann gut trocknen und kann sehr mürbe oder mit leicht abbröckelnder Glättschicht versehene Stücke während der successiven Entfernung des Verbandes tränken. Bei poröser Oberfläche zieht Wasserglaslösung gut ein und giebt eine grosse Festigkeit. Bei glatter, dichter Oberfläche bleibt aber ein weisslicher Anflug von Kieselsäure zurück, der sich nicht gut entfernen lässt. Hier kann die ganz ausgetrocknete Urne mit einer Lösung von gebleichtem Schellack in Spiritus, dem sehr wenig Ricinusöl zugesetzt ist, getränkt werden. Den zurückbleibenden Glanz nimmt man der gefestigten Urne durch vorsichtiges Abwaschen mit Spiritus, was nur bei bunten Urnen sein Bedenken haben kann. Das Reinigen solcher mürben Stücke ist daher sehr vorsichtig vorzunehmen und auch vor dem im allgemeinen, besonders bei Lehmboden, erforderlichen Waschen mit Wasser ist zunächst zu prüfen, ob dadurch nicht Reste von Farbe oder andere Verzierungen der Oberfläche zerstört werden können.

Ueber das Zusammensetzen der Urnen aus ihren Scherben ist a. a. O. ausführlich gesprochen.

Die in Gyps eingeschlossenen Bronzen oder Objecte anderer Natur kann man nun auch noch, ehe sie aus dem Gypskästchen gehoben werden, wesentlich festigen und dadurch Objecte retten, welche bei der blossen Berührung ganz oder theilweise zerfallen wären.

Man hebt die eine Seite des Gypsmantels ab und reinigt das Stück soweit es seine Consistenz erlaubt. Feste Stücke wird man natürlich abwaschen, bei sehr mürben und mehligen geht das nicht an, man wird daher den Rest der Erde vorläufig nicht entfernen können, sondern man tränkt das vollständig ausgetrocknete Stück gründlich mit einer Lösung von gebleichtem Schellack in Spiritus, der ein paar Tropfen Ricinusöl zugesetzt werden können, um die Masse nach dem Trocknen weniger spröde werden zu lassen. Man muss dies fortsetzen, so lange noch irgend Lack in die Bronze einzieht, wobei natürlich ziemlich viel durch den Sand aufgesogen wird. Wenn alles fest ist, kann man die anhaftende Erde und den Sand wieder vorsichtig aufweichen, indem man aus einem Tropfgläschen (einer ausgezogenen Glasröhre mit übergestülptem, kurzem, geschlossenem Gummischlauche) tropfenweise Alkohol zusetzt. Dabei muss die Bronze noch fest bleiben oder sehr wenig aufgeweicht werden. Die Erde entfernt man dann mit Stichel, Nadel, Pinsel. Wenn diese Seite ganz frei präparirt ist, bedeckt man sie mit Sand, giesst wieder Gyps herüber und deckt die andere Seite ab. Sollte die Schellacklösung nicht genügend durchgedrungen sein, so muss man sie nochmals tränken, im Uebrigen behandelt man sie wie die erste.

Bei grösseren Objecten, wie Bronzegefässen, die in unseren Hügeln bisher noch nicht vorgekommen sind, würde man den Gypsmantel stückweise entfernen, die Bronze tränken und präpariren, und dann zu einer benachbarten Stelle übergehen, nachdem man über die erste einen massiven Gypsüberzug gegossen hat. Es erhält dann nach und nach das Gefäss einen aus einzelnen Stücken bestehenden soliden Gypsmantel, der so zusammengesetzt ist, als ob man einen Abguss des Gefässes machen wollte, und der sich, wenn die Arbeit beendet, d. h. wenn die Innenseite gereinigt ist, leicht auseinandernehmen lässt. Um das Anhaften des Gypses zu verhindern, bedeckt man die freien Stellen mit dünner Sandschicht. Papier ist weniger zu empfehlen, weil dasselbe an den Rändern oder falls man von der Rückseite nochmals tränkt, leicht anhaften könnte und dann später mühsamer zu entfernen ist als einzelne Sandkörner. An vollständig zerbröckelnden Stellen wird man an der Innenseite eine festere Unterlage ankleben: wenn solche ganz zerbröckelten oder zerfallenen Stellen also auch nicht immer erhalten werden können, so kann man nach dieser Methode doch noch äusserst difficile Objecte retten.

Die Anwendung auf Objecte jeder anderen Art, Knochen, Eisensachen, Glas-Perlen oder Gefässe etc. etc. ergiebt sich ganz von selbst und wird jedermann in praxi den Umständen gemäss verfahren können, so dass die Berücksichtigung anderer noch eintretender Fälle nun überflüssig sein dürfte.

Die Grabhügel bei Birkenhof.

Auf dem Gut Birkenhof, Kreis Fischhausen, ca. 2500 m nördlich Heiligen Creutz in der Nordwest-Ecke des Samlandes befanden sich eine grosse Menge von Grabhügeln rund um das Gehöft herum, von denen eine Anzahl schon beinahe spurlos verschwunden ist, und von denen ich nur durch die Mittheilungen des Besitzers, Herrn Gutsbesitzer Grötzner Kenntniss erhielt. Mit denen, welche jetzt noch existiren oder kenntlich sind, mögen es mindestens 14 gewesen sein, von denen 4 schon vollständig abgetragen waren. Die anderen zerfallen in 3 Gruppen: a) ca. 1400 Schritt S.-O. vom Gehöft 4 Hügel, 3 davon dichter beisammen, in maximo 200 Schritt entfernt, der 4te ca. 400 Schritt weiter nach N. Die 3 beisammen liegenden Hügel hat Herr Dewitz (Dr. Dewitz zur Zeit Custos im zoologischen Museum zu Berlin) 1873 geöffnet. b) 1600 Schritt östlich vom Gehöft, ca. 1200 Schritt von Gruppe a entfernt 3 Hügel, die zum Theil in neuerer Zeit von Herrn Grötzner abgetragen sind. c) 700 Schritt NNW vom Gehöft eine Gruppe von 3 einander fast berührenden Hügeln, von denen ich einen 1877 ausgrub.

Die Hügel liegen hier, wie vielfach, in kleinen Gruppen beisammen und bevorzugen besonders die Kuppen von Höhenzügen, so dass sie manchmal schon von ferne auffallen und der Landschaft ein characteristisches Gepräge verleihen; so soll auch die ca. 700 Schritt WNW vom Gehöft liegende höchste Kuppe (auf der Generalstabskarte mit der Höhenzahl 190′ bezeichnet) einen solchen Grabhügel, oder wie sie hier zu Lande genannt werden „Kapurne“ getragen haben. Bei der Beschreibung der Hügel beginne ich mit dem von mir abgegrabenen, weil hierüber die genauesten Messungen und Aufzeichnungen vorliegen, welche einige dunkele Punkte in den anderen Berichten zum Theil aufklären. Noch detaillirtere Berichte befinden sich bei den Acten der Museums, aus denen hier nur das Wesentliche mitgetheilt wird.

Hügel I.

(In der Nordgruppe, ausgegraben von O. Tischler vom 27. Nov. — 3 Dec. 1877 mit 10 Mann in Summa 60 [allerdings kurze] Arbeitstage.)

Der Hügel wurde schichtweise abgetragen, die mittlere Erde noch einmal nach aussen geworfen; dies war natürlich eine Arbeitsverschwendung. Ich konnte aber so die in diesem Hügel (dem ersten, den ich ausgrub) besonders klaren Steinconstructionen vollständig frei legen. Es waren zum Messen die horizontalen Kreuzschnüre gezogen (wie stets bei meinen Grabungen), aber noch keine Gräben längs denselben angelegt.

Der Durchmesser des Hügels war ca. 15 m, derselbe lässt sich immer schwer ganz genau feststellen, weil die Kante meist verpflügt ist und der Beginn der glockenförmigen Erhöhung nicht mehr scharf hervortritt. Die Höhe muss ca. 1,50 gewesen sein, doch steigt der natürliche Boden nach Westen etwas in die Höhe, liegt hier also flacher unter dem Gipfel.

Den Aufbau des Hügels erläutert beistehende Skizze (Fig. I), wo nur die regelmässigen Steinconstructionen, die Steinkisten und einzelne Urnen dargestellt, die Steine des Pflasters und der Deckschichten aber fortgelassen sind.

Aussen umgaben den Hügel zwei Kränze regelmässig, dicht aneinandergelegter grosser Steine von 47—50 cm Durchmesser, der äussere von 7,5 mittleren Radius also 15 m Durchmesser (die Mitten der Steine gerechnet), der innere von 5,95 bis 6,15 Radius also ca. 12 m Durchmesser. Der innere ist nicht ganz genau kreisförmig, doch sind die Abweichungen nicht sehr bedeutend. Beim äusseren waren durch's Ackern schon manche Steine entfernt, er wird aber geschlossen gewesen sein und ist darnach ergänzt gezeichnet, während beim inneren kein Stein fehlte. Nur auf der Südseite zeigten beide Kräntze eine correspondirende Lücke von 1,7 Breite, die besonders beim inneren nicht mehr zufällig erscheint, zumal hier auch das Bodenpflaster im Halbkreis zurückweicht. Zwischen beiden Kränzen war der über 1 m breite Zwischenraum ganz steinfrei. Von dem inneren an erstreckte sich auf dem Niveau des natürlichen Bodens bis zu der mittleren ovalen Mauer ein Pflaster kleiner Steine von 20—25 cm Durchmesser.

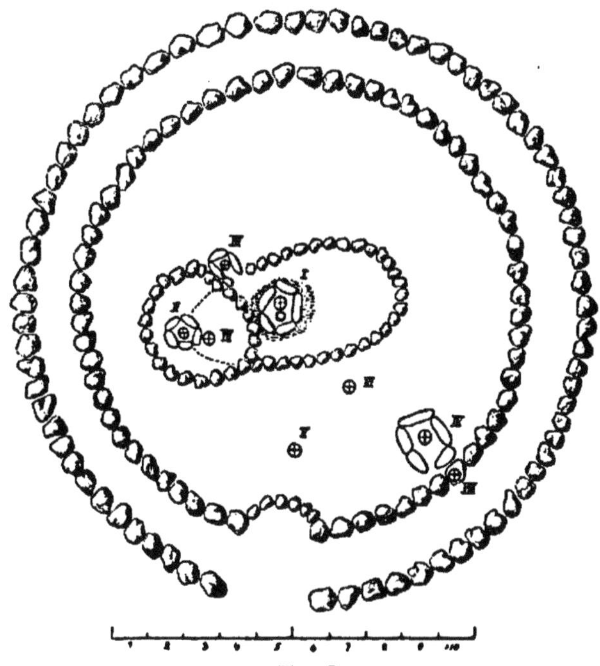

Figur I.

In der Mitte des Hügels zog sich von Westen nach Osten ein aus 3 Schichten übereinandergelegter Steine erbaute ovale Mauer hin, die ursprünglich wohl ca. 6,50 m Länge, 3,30 Breite hatte (wenn man die ungestörte Hälfte ergänzt denkt, wie durch die Punkte des Planes angedeutet), mit ihrer Mitte ziemlich genau im Mittelpunkte des Hügels. Dieselbe war an den Seiten Ost, Süd, West noch in derselben Höhe — im Westen 0,58 m unter dem Gipfel, also vom Boden aus ca. 1 m hoch erhalten, im Norden war sie niedriger, vielleicht bei Nachbegräbnissen etwas zerstört (oder beim Abgraben Anfangs nicht so beachtet); im allgemeinen trat sie aber vollständig ausgesprochen hervor und war unten durch seitliche Steine genügend verstärkt.

Bis an diese Mauer erstreckte sich das Bodenpflaster, darüber ein Erdmantel bis zur obersten Schicht der Mauer, und dann zog sich eine dreifache Schicht von Kopfsteinen über den ganzen Hügel, welche noch von einer die Steine manchmal nicht ganz verhüllenden Erdschicht bedeckt war.

Die ovale Mauer war also wohl der ursprüngliche Mittelbau und beherbergte in ihrer Mitte die erste, bedeutendste, centrale Kiste (I). Sie ist aber jedenfalls bei einem späteren Begräbnisse in ihrem westlichen Theile gestört worden. Man muss annehmen, dass sie hier abgebrochen wurde, worauf man im Niveau des Bodens einen etwas unregelmässigen Kreis grosser Steine von 3,20 Durchmesser legte, aber darauf im Westen und Süden (hier jedenfalls) die Mauer wieder aufbaute, jedoch nicht ganz genau, so dass sie an der Berührungsstelle mit dem Reste der früheren Mauer einen einspringenden Winkel bildet (wie der Grundplan deutlich zeigt). Im Osten geht der Kranz grosser Steine unten durch das Oval, eine Brücke zwischen beiden Wänden bildend. Das jetzt etwas unregelmässige, veränderte Oval hat 1,40 m Länge. In seiner Mitte befand sich die

Centrale Steinkiste I. Dieselbe stand ca. 1,50 m unter dem Gipfel auf dem natürlichen Erdboden. Alle diese kleineren Kisten haben einen ähnlichen Bau. Sie werden von einer Zahl vertikaler Träger gebildet, einfacher Granitgeschiebe, deren Innenseite man möglichst platt gewählt hat, die aber doch ziemlich unregelmässig und daher zum Bau regelmässiger viereckiger Kisten wenig geeignet sind. Sandsteinplatten, die sich dazu viel besser eignen, trifft man weit seltener, daher bilden reguläre vierseitige Kisten fast die Ausnahme, man findet zwei auch mehr Träger an einer Seite, wodurch die Form oft recht unregelmässig, fünfeckig oder von verwandter Form wird; manchmal sind auch mehrere Steine übereinandergelegt, um eine Wand zu bilden. Die Fugen sind besonders bei grösseren Trägern noch durch kleine Steine verzwickt, und unten dienen mehrfache Reihen vorgelegter Steine zur Sicherung der Träger. Ueber den Trägern liegen einer oder mehrere verbindende möglichst glatte Decksteine, die aber, wenn aus Granit, manchmal doch noch ziemlich dick sind. Es finden aber auch Abweichungen statt, wie gerade bei vorliegender Kiste, man trifft mehrere Steinschichten, auch Steinhaufen drüber. Der Boden ist in der Regel mit kleinen glatten Fliesen, am liebsten aus Sandstein bedeckt. Die Maasse variiren sehr, von 2 m Länge (was selten) bis herab zu 0,70; 1,60 Breite bis 0,60, die Höhe 0,70 und darunter, im Allgemeinen sind die Samländischen Kisten ziemlich klein, gehen sogar bis zu sehr unbedeutenden Dimensionen herab, wie die folgende Beschreibung zeigen wird.

Die Kiste I war von 5 Trägern von in maximo 68 cm Höhe, 40—80 Breite, 15—20 Dicke gebildet, die gewissermassen im Fünfeck standen und aussen gut von schützenden horizontalen Steinschichten umstellt waren. Sie war nicht durch Decksteine geschlossen, sondern von 3 Schichten flacher Steine gewissermassen gewölbeartig überdeckt, so dass sich eine Art Kuppe über ihr erhob. Von einem wirklichen Gewölbe oder einer sich tragenden Ueberkragung war natürlich nicht die Rede, wenn auch die unterste Schicht nur ringförmig den Trägern auflag. Man hatte die Steine erst auf die mit Erde angefüllte Kiste gelegt, suchte ihren Druck aber möglichst zu mindern, woher man z. B. in die oberste Schicht einen Mahlstein legte der sich wölbend in die zweite herunterreichte.

Diese grossen ausgehöhlten Mahlsteine finden sich vielfach in den Hügeln, besonders zur Bedeckung von Kisten verwandt, also ein sicheres Zeichen, dass sie schon damals zum Mahlen oder Quetschen des Getreides verwandt wurden, mithin dass das Volk dieser Grabhügel Getreide baute.

Die Kiste hatte aussen die Dimensionen ca. 100 × 100 cm, innen 90 × 70. In ihr standen 2 Thongefässe, nördlich eine grosse Aschen-Urne mit schalenförmigem Deckel (Tfl. III (I) Fig. 1 und 1a. Inventar des Provinzial-Museums No. 1243, 1244) mit gebrannten Knochen angefüllt, ohne jede Beigabe.

Die Knochen in allen Urnen der Hügelgräber liegen dicht beisammen, oft in verhältnissmässig kleinen Raum gestopft, so dass manchmal nur noch wenig Erde in der Urne Platz hatte. Sie sind sorgfältig nach dem Brande ausgelesen, von Erde befreit und ziemlich grobstückig. Dies ist ein wesentlicher Unterschied gegen die gewaltigen Urnen der Samländischen Gräberfelder, wo die Knochen nur einen kleinen Theil der Urne einnehmen, manchmal in der Erde zerstreut sind und im Allgemeinen in kleineren Stücken auftreten.

Die Urne hatte 2 kleine Henkel, welche aber schon in alter Zeit abgebrochen sein müssen, dies zeigt auch die alte, verwitterte Bruchfläche. Eine nähere Beschreibung dieser und der folgenden Thongefässe und Beigaben wird erst am Schlusse im Zusammenhang gegeben werden.

Südlich davon stand ein grosser Henkelkrug mit einer flachen auf der Unterseite durch Nägeleindrücke verzierten Thonschale bedeckt (Tfl. III (I) Fig. 2 und 2a. Inventar. 1245, 1246. Der Deckel ist verkehrt, mit der characteristischen Unterseite nach oben gezeichnet). Der Krug hatte einen Doppelhenkel, der untere ist aber auch schon in alter Zeit abgebrochen. Er war nur mit Erde angefüllt, ist mithin ein Beigefäss. Von den Schutzsteinschichten der Kiste zog sich bis in die Ost-Ecke des Ovals ein Zickzackstreif von Steinen, und im Süd-Ost lag an der Mauer ein Steinhaufen, sonst war der innere ovale Raum nur mit Erde erfüllt. Unter den äusseren Steinschichten zog sich eine Aschenschicht hin, sie noch etwas überragend, die auch auf der Westseite der Kiste hervortrat. In ihr fanden sich einige Scherben- und Knochenstückchen, und ein Fragment eines kleinen Bronzeringchens. Vielleicht war dies die ursprüngliche Brandstelle, wo der Scheiterhaufen für das erste Grab des Hügels errichtet war, nach dessen Beseitigung man dann die Steinkiste erbaute.

Kiste II. Der westliche Theil des Ovals war im Allgemeinen mit Erde erfüllt. Im Niveau des Bodens lief der erwähnte Steinkranz herum, in dessen Mitte excentrisch die kleine Kiste II mit dem oberen Rande 1,46 tief, also in den natürlichen Boden eingetieft stand. Sie war aus 5 etwas unregelmässigen Trägern gebildet mit einem inneren Raume von 80 × 65 cm. Darüber lag kein Deckstein, es befand sich aber etwas seitlich ein die Kiste theilweise überdeckender ca. 1 m hoher

Steinhaufen, der ungefähr bis in die Höhe der Mauerkrone reichte. In der Kiste stand eine Aschen-Urne ohne Deckel (Tfl. III (I) Fig. 3. Inventar 1247) voll Knochen, zwischen denen sich nur das Violinstegförmige Bernsteinstück Tfl. VI (IV) Fig. 2 fand. Neben der Urne dicht an sie angeschmiegt lag die Bronze-Nadel mit gebogenem Halse Tfl. VI (IV) Fig. 1.

Ungefähr 5 cm unter dem Rande der Urne zog sich in einem grossen Theil des Kreises eine mit Kohlenstückchen durchsetzte Aschenschicht hin, die in der Südost-Ecke unter dem Steinhaufen besonders deutlich war. Hier scheint also auch eine Brandstelle gewesen zu sein — wahrscheinlicher wird aber der Scheiterhaufen des ersten centralen Begräbnisses soweit gereicht haben, denn man dürfte kaum so nahe dem ersten Grabe ein neues Feuer angezündet haben. In der Brandschicht fanden sich wenig Knochenreste und ein Paar Scherben eines kleinen Gefässes.

Kiste III. In der einspringenden Ecke, wo die Ost- und West-Abtheilung des Ovals zusammenstossen, fand sich aussen an die Mauer angelehnt eine kleine Kiste, mit je einem Träger an zwei Seiten, zwei an der dritten, die vierte Seite schloss die Mauer. Ob ein Deckstein vorhanden, ist nicht constatirt, da die Kiste erst an den Trägern erkannt wurde. In ihr stand auf einer Steinplatte eine Aschen-Urne mit einer flachen Steinplatte zugedeckt (Tfl. III (I) Fig. 4. Inventar 1250), am Boden 1,15 tief, also höher wie der Boden der Centralkiste, ohne Inhalt als Knochen.

Kiste IV. Im Süd-Osten ganz dicht am inneren Kranze, also weit ausserhalb der Mauer stand eine ziemlich geräumige Kiste in der Richtung NW—SO mit je einem Träger auf drei, zwei auf der vierten Seite, die nicht ganz dicht schlossen, von 55—86 cm Breite, 52—91 Höhe, 8—17 Dicke. Der Boden lag 1,25 tief im Niveau des Pflasters, oben erreichten die Steine den Hügel. Decksteine fehlten, sie können aber wohl fortgenommen sein, da sie jedenfalls zu Tage traten. In der Kiste stand eine Aschen-Urne mit Deckel (Tfl. III (I) Fig. 5, 5a. Inventar 1252, 1251), zwischen den Knochen Nichts.

Ausserdem fanden sich noch an verschiedenen Stellen des Hügels Urnen und Scherben zwischen den Steinen ohne schützende Kiste, die daher ausserordentlich zerdrückt waren und grösstentheils nicht mehr zu restauriren gingen.

Kiste V. An der Südseite des Hügels, dicht an der Lücke, S 3,56 W 0,57 z 1,07; (die Mitte des Hügels ist S 0,9 W 0,3 m) ohne erkennbare Kiste, daher von den Steinen vollständig auseinandergedrückt, fanden sich die Reste einer Aschen-Urne (Inventar 1257), welche noch zu restauriren ging. Dieselbe ähnt in der Form der Urne 1252 aus Urne IV, hat nur einen schlankeren Hals.

Kiste VI. S 2,33 O 1,05 z 1,08. Einige Scherben einer Aschen-Urne zwischen den Steinen. Es gelang nicht sie irgendwie zusammenzusetzen.

Kiste VII. S 0,94 W 3 z 0,93. Beinahe über Kiste II in einer höheren Schicht zwischen Steinen (ohne Kiste) eine ganz zerdrückte Aschen-Urne (nicht zusammengesetzt).

Kiste VIII. Am inneren Kranze südöstlich von Kiste IV fanden sich Scherben einer verzierten Aschen-Urne (Inventar 1258) und Reste des Deckels. Diese

Scherben sind entschieden zerstreut und bei einer, glücklicherweise äusserst unbedeutenden Beschädigung des Hügels aus einer benachbarten Stelle hierher geworfen. Sie ähnen den Urnen IV und V.

Ausserdem fanden sich Scherben vereinzelt an verschiedenen Stellen des Hügels verstreut. Diese Reste waren aber so unbedeutend, dass sie nicht von zerstörten Aschen-Urnen herrühren konnten, sondern beim Zuwerfen des Hügels wohl mit der Erde hineingelangten.

Aus der Vertheilung der Kisten und isolirten Urnen ergiebt sich, dass der Grabhügel nicht gleich in der jetzigen Form, sondern erst nach und nach aufgeschüttet wurde, da es kaum anzunehmen ist, dass man die grossen Steinmassen immer bei einem frischen Begräbnisse weggenommen und wieder aufgelegt habe. Ganz genau kann man den Bau wohl nicht verfolgen, er dürfte sich aber ungefähr folgendermassen gestaltet haben. Zuerst verbrannte man wahrscheinlich den Leichnam in der Mitte des Ovals auf einem von Osten nach Westen gerichteten Scheiterhaufen, sammelte die Knochen sorgfältig und baute in der Mitte des ausgebrannten Scheiterhaufens die centrale Kiste. Die Mauer muss auch schon jetzt erbaut sein, weil man sie theilweise einriss, um die zweite, etwas jüngere Kiste einzugraben, und dann wieder aufbaute. Die Mauer wurde dann mit Erde ausgefüllt, wie weit man nun den äusseren Hügel aufschüttete und ob die beiden äusseren Kränze jetzt schon gelegt wurden, lässt sich nicht mit Sicherheit entscheiden. Die Kiste III baute man später aussen an die Mauer, deren Inneres jetzt nicht mehr gerührt wurde. Endlich muss die jüngste Kiste IV angelegt sein, als der Hügel schon seine jetzige Form und Grösse hatte. Es folgt daraus wohl, dass der Hügel anfangs nicht so hoch gewesen, da man bei den späteren Gräbern sich nicht der Mühe unterzog bis auf den Boden in der Mitte herabzusteigen. Die isolirten Urnen grub man dann nach Entfernung einiger Steine in geringerer Tiefe des fertigen Hügels ein. Die Kiste IV, Urne V und die Scherben VIII werden also jünger sein als die mittleren Urnen, haben auch einen von jener abweichenden, unter sich aber übereinstimmenden Character.

Dewitz hat 1873 die drei südöstlichen Hügel eröffnet, allerdings nicht vollständig abgetragen, wie ich später bemerken konnte. Die nachfolgenden Beschreibungen stützen sich auf den von Herrn Dr. Dewitz zum Zweck dieser Publication zur Disposition gestellten Bericht, der hier etwas modificirt wiedergegeben wird. Die erhaltenen Thongefässe befinden sich im Provinzialmuseum, hingegen sind die wenigen Beigaben leider nicht erhalten.

Hügel II.

Ein Hügel von ca. 16 m Durchmesser, 1,70 Höhe, der schon etwas angegriffen gewesen war. Am Rande fand Dewitz grosse Steinmassen, die sich kreisförmig um den Hügel herumzogen und einen Steinkranz von einigen Fuss Breite in der Erde bildeten. Dies war jedenfalls kein eigentlicher Kranz, sondern Reste der Deckschichten. Die mittlere Steinmauer, die sonst immer auftritt, hatte Dewitz nicht bemerkt, entweder, wie er anführt, weil schon viele Steine herausgenommen waren, oder weil er erst bei den späteren Hügeln auf diese Mauer aufmerksam geworden. Ungefähr in der Mitte des Hügels stand mit der Längsaxe von Süden nach Norden eine ziemlich grosse Steinkiste ca. 2,20 m lang, 1,60 breit, im Inneren 1,25 × 0,94 und 0,63 tief, nicht ordentlich rechtwinkelig, denn die Träger waren dicke unregelmässige Steine von 0,30—0,45 Dicke, so dass im Innern von annähernd glatten Wänden nicht die Rede war. Nur am Südende stand auf beiden Längsseiten ein 0,94 langer, 0,62 hoher, 0,15 dicker ziemlich platter Stein. Mehrere platte nur einige Zoll dicke Decksteine (nach Dewitz Zeichnung 4), auf denen kopfgrosse Steine lagen, schlossen die Kiste. Den Boden deckten platte Fliesen von 0,30—0,60 Breite und Länge, 5—8 cm Dicke.

In der Kiste standen unregelmässig 10 Thongefässe. 5 Aschen-Urnen mit Knochen, 5 leere Beigefässe. Von den Aschen-Urnen waren 4 mit Deckeln versehen, umgestülpten flachen Schalen, auf der fünften lag als schützende Decke ein kleines Thongefäss (nicht vorhanden). Eine der beiden grössten dieser Urnen enthielt zwischen den Knochen einen fingerdicken Eisenring von 5 cm Durchmesser (leider nicht vorhanden, die Beschreibung unklar) die andere (Tfl. III (I) Fig. 8. Inventar 629) ein durch Rost unkenntlich gemachtes Eisenstück und ein 4 cm langes, 2,5 breites, 1,6 dickes Bernsteinstückchen (alles nicht vorhanden). Eine dritte Urne der Kiste ist die kleine Aschen-Urne Tfl. IV (II) Fig. 1 mit dem dazu gehörigen Deckel (unten Fig. 2 im Text). Die anderen Urnen zerfielen vollständig beim Herausnehmen.

Von den Beigefässen war das grösste (21 cm hoch) mit einer platten Schale zugedeckt und hatte einen Doppelhenkel wie Tfl. III (I) Fig. 2 (nicht erhalten). Die anderen waren unbedeckt und näherten sich in der Form theils diesem, theils den Aschen-Urnen (d. h. wohl theils mit, theils ohne Henkel. Eins davon ist der kleine Krug Tfl. VI (II) Fig. 3. Inventar 621. Auf den Fliesen stand noch eine deckelartige Schale (Dewitz meint vielleicht ein heruntergefallener Deckel). Auf dem Boden der Kiste zog sich durch Kohle schwarz gefärbter Sand hin.

An der Südwest-Seite des Hügels zwischen den Steinen fanden sich noch Scherben von 3—4 vollständig zerdrückten Urnen (nicht mitgebracht). Dazwischen gebrannte Knochen, ein Fragment eines kleinen Bronzeringes von ca. 1 cm Durchmesser, und ein rohes Bernsteinstück von der Grösse einer Kartoffel.

Hügel III.

Der Hügel, 200 Schritt nordöstlich von II auf einer anderen Höhe, mass 15 m im Durchmesser, 1,70 Höhe; zahlreiche Steine ragten aus der Erddecke heraus. Am Rande fand Dewitz einen breiten Gürtel aus Steinen von 30—60 cm Durchmesser in einer Schicht, selten in zwei übereinander. Der äussere Kranz und die Deckschicht sind hier wohl nicht auseinandergehalten. Da dieser Theil des Hügels nicht bis auf den Grund abgetragen wurde (wie ich später sah), so ist das wahrscheinlich existirende Bodenpflaster auch nicht constatirt worden, ebenso wie beim vorigen Hügel. Innerhalb dieses Gürtels trat eine 5,6 m Durchmesser haltende kreisförmige Mauer auf, 30—60 cm unter dem Rasen, 60 cm hoch und ungefähr ebenso dick. An der Südseite verband sie sich mit dem äussern Gürtel, d. h. die Deckschicht reichte wohl hier heran. Innerhalb der Mauer befanden sich 2 Kisten.

Kiste I. Im Centrum aus vielen theils platten, theils runden Steinen erbaut, von denen keiner bis zum oberen Rande reichte, daher das Innere nicht sehr regelmässig, mehr rundlich. Der Durchmesser des Hohlraumes ca. 1,1 m, die Höhe 0,78. Decksteine waren (nach der Zeichnung) 2, der Boden mit vielen kleinen Steinen ausgelegt. Auf diesem standen 6 Thongefässe. Die drei grössten sind Aschen-Urnen mit Knochen (2 erhalten: Tfl. IV (II) Fig. 4 Inventar 625, und Inventar 632, nicht abgebildet). 2 waren mit Deckeln versehen (es existiren im Museum verschiedene Deckelfragmente, von denen sich aber nicht constatiren lässt, welcher Urne sie zuzutheilen sind), die dritte (Inventar 632) mit einem aufrechtstehenden Henkelkruge, also einem Beigefässe zugedeckt (nicht vorhanden). Von den anderen beiden Beigefässen mit Henkeln ist ein grosser weiter Krug Tfl. III (I) Fig. 9 (Inventar 624) erhalten; ein kleines Henkeltöpfchen von 8 cm Höhe ist nicht mitgebracht.

Kiste II an der Nordseite unmittelbar an der Mauer von runden Steinen umsetzt, innen von Osten nach Westen 94 cm lang, 47 breit, 62 hoch. An der Südseite war ein grosser ziemlich platter Träger, die anderen nicht so gross, Ost und West je einer, mehrere flache Decksteine, der Boden mit Fliesen belegt. Darin standen drei Thongefässe, eine grosse ca. 30 cm hohe Aschen-Urne mit einer Schale zugedeckt, aber so zerdrückt, dass nicht einmal die Form zu erkennen war; zwischen den Knochen ein bearbeitetes Bernsteinstück (nicht vorhanden). Daneben zwei Beigefässe, Henkeltöpfe, Tfl. III (I) Fig. 6 Inventar 630, und III (I) Fig. 7 Inventar 631, beide ohne Deckel. Ob ausserhalb der Mauer noch Aschen-Urnen sich befinden, ist nicht untersucht worden.

Hügel IV

ca. 100 Schritt südwestlich II, von ähnlichen Dimensionen wie III. Am Rande war ein Ring der Deckschicht zu constatiren, im Innern eine kreisförmige Mauer von 6,3 m Durchmesser, 2—3 Steine von 15—47 cm neben und aufeinandergelegt, so dass der Kranz 47—63 cm hoch und breit wurde. Im Innern waren zwei Kisten, eine centrale und eine an der Südseite, beide in Bau und Grösse denen in Hügel III analog, nur dass die äussere Kiste hier an der Süd- dort an der Nord-Seite lag. Es fehlten den Kisten aber die Decksteine und sie erwiesen sich als bereits ausgeraubt, so dass nur äusserst wenig kleine Scherbenstückchen noch vorgefunden werden konnten. Die von Dewitz untersuchten Hügel zeigten also mit I das Analoge, dass durch eine innere Mauer, die hier kreisförmig, dort oval, eine mittlere Abtheilung begrenzt war, welche mehrere Steinkisten enthielt, die zum Theil etwas grösser und urnenreicher waren als bei I. Die äusseren regelmässigen Kränze, welche hier auch vorhanden gewesen sein mögen, sind nicht verfolgt worden.

Hügel V.

Von Herrn Gutsbesitzer Grötzner ist noch ein Hügel abgetragen worden, über den keine näheren Berichte vorliegen. Das interessanteste Fundstück ist der aus ihm stammende Bronzecelt Tfl. VI (IV) Fig. 4 Inventar 2037—39. Dass derselbe wirklich aus einem solchen Hügel stammt und zum Grabe gehört, wurde durch einen ganz identischen Celt, den ich 1884 in einem analogen Hügel zu Ihlnicken (unweit Birkenhof) im centralen Grabe fand, bestätigt.

Beschreibung der Fundgegenstände.

Thongefässe.

Die Thongefässe zerfallen in zwei deutlich unterschiedene Klassen, Aschen-Urnen und Beigefässe. Erstere dienten zum Aufbewahren der gebrannten und zerschlagenen Knochen, letztere waren Gebrauchsgefässe des gewöhnlichen Lebens, welche den Todten ins Grab mitgegeben wurden, zum Theil vielleicht mit Speise und Trank gefüllt, wovon sich hier allerdings keine Spur vorfand.

Eine Beschreibung von Thongefässen giebt nur ein annähernd so anschauliches Bild als gute Abbildungen, wohl aber kann eine Zusammenstellung der Maasse bei vergleichenden Betrachtungen von Nutzen sein, wenn es sich darum handelt gewisse Kategorien zu characterisiren und gegen einander abzugrenzen.

Ich habe bereits in einer früheren Abhandlung*) eine Reihe von Maassen vorgeschlagen und möchte die Methode noch nach einer Richtung hin erweitern. Zur Characterisirung des Profils einer Urne kommt es darauf an, dasselbe durch die rechtwinkligen Coordinaten einer Anzahl Punkte zu bestimmen. Wenn man diese auf Papier aufträgt und durch gerade Linien verbindet, oder durch nach Gutdünken gezogene gekrümmte, so erhält man ein annäherndes Bild des Profils. Die hervorragendsten Dimensionen der Urne sind ihre Höhe und ihre grösste Weite, die zur Abkürzung nur mit Weite bezeichnet werden soll. Ausserdem sind die Bodenfläche und der obere Rand fest bestimmt, deren Durchmesser also auch Cardinaldimensionen. Der untere Theil des Bauches geht fast immer in sanfter Biegung vom Boden nach der Weite, hier wäre also im allgemeinen keine Zwischendimension nöthig; viel mannigfaltiger ist aber der Verlauf oberhalb der Weite. Die Urne kann convex bis zum Rande verlaufen, oder wie es wohl meist der Fall, nach convexer Krümmung in die entgegengesetzte übergehen; oft schnürt sie sich ein, um dann zum Rande hin sich wieder auszuweiten, oder es setzt sich gegen den gewölbten Bauch der obere Theil mehr gradlinig ab, mehr oder minder stark getrennt. Den oberen Theil wird man den Hals nennen, seine Abgrenzung ist aber eine sehr unbestimmte; wo eine Einschnürung existirt, ist sie ganz scharf, auch dann, wenn dieser Hals deutlich gegen den Bauch abgesetzt erscheint; bei allmählichem Verlaufe der Krümmung, wie in den vorliegenden Urnen ist eine solche Zone aber schwer genau zu fixiren. Wenn wir den Boden als Null-Punkt mit 0 bezeichnen, die Zone der (grössten) Weite mit w, den Rand mit r und die (oft unbestimmte) Stelle des beginnenden Halses mit h, so hätte man an diesen Stellen Durchmesser und Höhe zu messen: Do Durchmesser des Bodens, (Höhe = 0); Dw grösste Weite, Hw Höhe dieser Zone; Dr Durchmesser der Mündung, Hr Gesammthöhe der Urne. Diese Dimensionen sind also sicher. Dh, Hh sind nicht so fest, das ist aber auch nicht nöthig, da sie immer einen wichtigen Punkt des Profils geben werden. Ist dasselbe sehr gegliedert, so wird man noch mehr Zonen haben müssen, und wenn die Urne einen besonders abgesetzten Fuss hat, wird man auch hier unten den Durchmesser und die Höhe dieser Einschnürung nehmen. Kurz, es würde erforderlich sein, soviel Punkte

*) O. Tischler, Ostpreussische Gräberfelder. Schriften der physikalisch-ökonomischen Gesellschaft XIX. 1878, p. 169.

zu messen, dass das durch ihre gradlinige Verbindung entstandene Profil eine annähernde Vorstellung der Urne gewährt. Um Verwechselungen zu verhindern, sei bemerkt, dass H als Höhe immer gross geschrieben werden soll, die Höhe des Halsanfangs h klein (es schien mir immer dieser Buchstabe am zweckmässigsten). Bei den folgenden Messungen ist die unbestimmte Zone h nicht berücksichtigt worden; ich überlasse es anderen Forschern zu versuchen, ob sich bei complicirteren Profilen durch Zuhilfenahme dieser oder von noch mehr Zonen übersichtliche Resultate erzielen lassen; allzuweit wird man diese Messungen wohl nicht ausdehnen, da sie der Anschauung doch nie so zu Hilfe kommen, wie eine Zeichnung. Man kann diesen trockenen Zahlen aber doch eine gewisse Anschaulichkeit abgewinnen, und hiermit möchte ich den Versuch machen, die Methode der Craniologie in die Urnenkunde einzuführen.

Die absoluten Zahlen prägen sich unserer Vorstellung nicht ein, es kommt nur auf ihre Verhältnisse an, wenn man die Form der Urne einigermassen erfassen will. Es können diese Verhältnisse als Indices der Urne eingeführt werden. Die Höhe durch die Weite $\frac{Hr}{Dw}$ sei der Höhenindex (H), er zeigt an ob die Urne hoch oder platt ist; die Querdimensionen werden dann durch die Weite, die Höhendimensionen durch die Höhe dividirt: $\frac{Dr}{Dw}$ = (r) heisse der Randindex, er sagt, ob die Urne eng oder weithalsig ist; $\frac{Do}{Dw}$ = (b — Boden) der Bodenindex, ob der Boden klein oder gross; $\frac{Hw}{Hr}$ (Hw) der Weitenhöhenindex, ob die Weite hoch oder tief sitzt. Letzterer hängt oft mit einem langen Halse zusammen, aber nicht immer. Zur Unterscheidung sollen die Indexzeichen immer eingeklammert verwandt werden. Auf Indices für den Hals habe ich vorläufig verzichtet, um diese Methode möglichst einfach zu gestalten.

Die Messungen lassen sich nicht so genau als die craniometrischen anstellen, weil trotz des guten äusseren Anscheins diese freihändigen Urnen weder in Bezug auf Rundung noch auf gleichmässige Höhe der Zonen fehlerfrei sind, auf Differenzen von einigen Millimetern kommt es aber auch nicht an bei den Indices. Dr und Do lassen sich sehr bequem messen, ebenfalls Dw mit einem zweischenkligen- oder mit einem Stangentasterzirkel. Hw ist oft nicht so scharf zu fixiren, auch an den einzelnen Seiten verschieden, man muss einen Mittelwerth nehmen. Für Hr legt man ein Lineal auf den Rand und misst seine Entfernung von der Tischfläche auf beiden Seiten, da oft der Boden schief (eigentlich die Urne) oder nicht ganz eben ist. Man könnte auch bequemere Apparate hierzu construiren, doch genügen schon einfache Hilfsmittel. Bei den einzelnen Maassen wird man daher meist einige Millimeter Spielraum annehmen können. Die Indices berechnet man als Decimalbrüche und multiplicirt sie mit 100. Die zweite Stelle, (welche in der Tabelle unten angegeben) wird aber immer um einige Einheiten unsicher sein.

Nach dieser Methode sind hier die Dimensionen und Indices der vorhandenen Aschen-Urnen gemessen und angegeben. In der letzten Columne erfolgt die Wanddicke der Urne dicht unterhalb des Randes. Die Bezeichnungen bedeuten:

I I = Hügel I, Kiste oder Urne I. Die Tafeln sind nach der Nummerirung der Separatabhandlung gerechnet, also I für III (I).

	Do	Dw	Dr	Hw	Hr	(H)	(r)	(b)	(Hw)	Dicke
	cm									mm
I I (1243) Tfl. I 1	9,5	30,5	21,5	12,5	26,5	87	70	31	47	7
I II (1247) Tfl. I 3	8,5	24	16	8	20,5	85	66	36	40	5
I III (1250) Tfl. I 4	8	29	19	11	26	90	65	28	42	5
I IV (1252) Tfl. I 5	0	24,5	13	10	20	82	53	0	50	6—7
I V (1257) nicht abgebildet	0	22	12	11	21,5	100	54	0	50	4, tiefer 5
II a (629) Tfl. I 8	11—11,5	29,5	18,5	11	24,5	83	63	ca. 38	45	7
II b (626) Tfl. II 1	8,5	17	12,5	6,5	15,5	91	74	50	42	6
III Ia (632) nicht abgebildet	8	22	18	10	21	96	82	36	48	8
III Ib (625) Tfl. II 4	7	21	12,5	10	20	95	60	33	50	7

Aus dieser Tabelle ersieht man schon, dass die Aschen-Urnen in zwei verschiedene Kategorien zerfallen.

a) Die Urnen des ersten Typus I I, II, III, II a, b, an die sich die etwas abweichende III Ia anschliesst, haben einen auf der Unterseite recht platt gedrückten Bauch, dessen Weite ziemlich tief liegt, unter der Mitte — Weitenhöhenindex unter 50 bis 40 herab, nur bei der abweichenden III Ia fast 50. Die Wölbung geht unten in ziemlich stumpfem Winkel in den kleinen Boden über [(b) = 30—35 d. i. ca. $^1/_3$] nur bei der kleinen Urne III Ib grösser, 50 = $^1/_2$. Der Boden ist aber immer vorhanden und deutlich ausgesprochen. Die Kante ist oft sehr stumpf, manchmal aber mit einem kleinen Wulst umgeben. Hin und wieder ist der Boden sogar schwach gewölbt, so dass die Stabilität der Urnen keine erhebliche ist und erst durch die Umfüllung mit Erde gesichert wird. (Bei den Abbildungen, welche sämmtlich in $^1/_4$ natürlicher Grösse mit der camera lucida gezeichnet sind, war es nicht immer möglich dies genau wiederzugeben, weil sonst zu unschöne Projectionen der Urnen herausgekommen wären, es ist zum Theil aber doch zu erkennen.) Der Bauch geht nach oben mit sanfter Schweifung und ohne besondere Begrenzung in den concav gebogenen Hals über, nur bei III Ia findet sich ein kleiner Absatz beim Uebergange zu dem besonders weiten Halse. Die Oeffnung ist recht weit (weithalsig), der Randindex (r) 65—74 also ca. $^2/_3$, nur bei III Ia sehr gross 82.

Die Urnen sind sämmtlich aus reinem, mit gröberem Sande oder zerstossenen Granitstückchen gemengten Thone angefertigt, welche Beimengung aber lange nicht das grobe Korn hat wie in den grossen Urnen der jüngeren samländischen Gräberfelder, und sind dann mit einer feineren Thonschicht überzogen. Sie sind alle aus freier Hand gefertigt und trotzdem meist von vorzüglicher Rundung und oft recht sauberer Ausführung; dass eine solche ohne Drehscheibe und sonstige Hilfsmittel zu erzielen geht, lehrt die Herstellung der Tatertöpfe in Jütland, welche von Sehested ausführlich beschrieben ist.*) Dann sind sie gut geglättet, einige vollständig wie I II, II b, meist aber nur am oberen Theile, während der untere, unterhalb der Weite, absichtlich rauh gemacht ist, um die Urnen besser halten zu können. Der Brand

*) Sehested: Fortidsminder og Oldsager fra Egnen om Broholm, p. 245—251. Bericht darüber: Schriften der physikalisch-ökonomischen Gesellschaft 22 (1881) Sitzungsberichte p. 14

hat in nicht russendem Feuer stattgefunden, wodurch sie eine hell gelbbraune Farbe erhielten, die kleineren Gefässe oft völlig fleckenlos. Die Urnen erscheinen somit in Form und Herstellung durchaus nicht roh, sind auch, zumal die kleineren, nicht sehr dickwandig, oben an der Mündung 5—7 mm — nur die plumpern IIIIa dicker — also bei weitem feiner und eleganter als die bereits erwähnten weit jüngeren Aschen-Urnen der samländischen Gräberfelder, ein warnendes Beispiel, dass man aus der Masse und Beschaffenheit der Scherben allein nicht auf ihren Zeitunterschied schliessen darf.

Diese Urnen sind manchmal durch ein angesetztes Henkelpaar und noch durch eingedrückte Ornamente verziert.

Die einander gegenüberstehenden, horizontal durchbohrten, oft recht kleinen Henkel konnten nur zum Durchziehen einer Trageschnur benutzt werden, dürften aber wohl mehr ornamental sein, da sie kaum im Stande waren, die gefüllte Urne zu tragen, die man ja auch am rauhen Boden hielt; so sind sie auch manchmal schon in alter Zeit abgebrochen wie bei II (Tfl. I1). Sie fanden sich bei II (Tfl. I1), IIII (Tfl. I4), IIa (Tfl. I8), IIb (Tfl. II1) und IIIIa, nur bei III (Tfl. I3) nicht. Sie sitzen meist unmittelbar über der Weite. Die meisten Urnen dieser Gattung waren unverziert, nur bei IIa (Tfl. I8) findet sich eine Zone von Fingereindrücken um die Weite und eine Zone schräger Kerben, die wohl mit einem zugespitzten Hölzchen in dem weichen Thon gezogen sind, unmittelbar unter den etwas höher stehenden Henkeln.

b) Von abweichendem Typus sind die Urnen IIV (Tfl. I5), IV und jedenfalls auch die Urne IVIII, von der nur ein paar Scherben übrig geblieben. Die Weite liegt in der Mitte der Urne (Hw 1 = 50 d. i. 1/2) und die Mündung ist erheblich kleiner (engerer Hals (r) = c 50 d. i. 1/2). Der Boden ist abgerundet (b) = 0!), es existirt also kein eigentlicher Boden, es sind dies Urnen ohne Stehfläche. Man hat vielfach angenommen, dass Urnen ohne Stehfläche älter seien, als solche mit Boden, was diese Funde aber durchaus nicht bestätigen, denn beide Urnen stammen aus den äusseren Lagen des Hügels und sind unbedingt jünger als die Urnen mit Stehfläche des inneren Ovals. Uebrigens findet sich die Stehfläche sowohl bei den Thongefässen der älteren Bronzezeit, deren Gräber jetzt auch in Ostpreussen nachgewiesen sind, wie besonders zur neolithischen Zeit. Diese Urnen waren also noch viel unstabiler als die vorigen und konnten nur in Erde fest stehen. Die untere Hälfte ist ziemlich dickwandig, was ihr relativ bedeutendes Gewicht verräth bei dünner oberer Wand (4 bis 7 mm). Da der obere Theil des Bauches sich mehr zusammenzieht, tritt ein etwas mehr begrenzter Hals auf.

Beide Urnen sind ohne Henkel, aber verziert. Am unteren Ende des Halses gehen einige scharf eingerissene, horizontale Linien um den Hals, bei IIV (Tfl. I5) 2, an der einen Seite noch eine 3te, bei IV—5. Von diesen steigen Gruppen von 5—6 parallelen Linien schräge herab bis fast zur Weite, die in ihrer Richtung abwechseln. Dies häufig vorkommende Ornament soll „alterirend schräge Strichgruppen“ heissen. Sie sind unten nicht begrenzt, nur bei den wenigen Scherben von Urne IVIII (1258), wo sich dieselben Gruppen finden, gehen unterhalb derselben parallele Zickzacklinien mit scharfen Ecken in unsicherer Führung um das Gefäss herum. Die Urnen sind gut geglättet, überhaupt von sorgfältiger Fabrikation.

Diese eingerissenen Linien haben einen ganz eigenen Character, der besonders von dem der später zu beschreibenden Beigefässe völlig abweicht. Sie sind scharf eingerissen, und während die flachere Seite der Furche einigermaassen glatt bleibt, zeigen sich auf der steileren eine Menge Aussprünge, auch an Stellen, wo noch der Sand liegt, die also beim Reinigen gar nicht gestört sind. Die Führung ist eine unsichere, es kommen geradezu Seitensprünge in den Linien vor. Ich halte es daher für sicher, dass diese Linien mit einem scharfen Instrument, (Messer oder Stichel) in die gebrannten Urnen eingeritzt sind. Im weichen Thon mit einem stumpfen Instrument gezogene Linien zeigen ein sanftes, wenig vertieftes Profil und eine gute sichere Führung, wenn auch Unregelmässigkeiten vorkommen. Bei Linien, die mit scharfer Spitze in weichem Thon gezogen werden (wie bei anderen Urnen aus Hügelgräbern) haben dieselben oft emporgequollenen Ränder, welche ja allerdings auch beseitigt werden können, zeigen aber immer eine sichere Führung und glatten Verlauf. Versuche, die ich mit scharfen Spitzen an glatten Urnenscherben vornahm, lieferten ein Resultat, welches ganz jenen 3 Urnen entsprach. Wenn man das Instrument schräge hielt, blieb die eine Seite glatt, an der anderen traten die Absprünge auf, und so oft man auf ein gröberes Korn der Grundmasse traf, sprang der Stichel seitwärts, ganz in derselben Weise, wie bei den echten alten Furchen. Versuche in festgetrockneten, alten Thonplatten, die allerdings keine gröberen Körnchen enthielten, ergaben auch eine glatte Linienführung, indem der Thon sich mehlig herausschabte, aber nicht bröckelte. Demnach dürfte obige Annahme bewiesen sein. Eine Urne von etwas abweichender Form ist IIIIb (Tfl. II4) mit mittlerer Halsweite (r) = 60), hoher Weite (Hw) = 50) und kleinen Boden (b) = 33). Die obere Hälfte ist glatt, die untere sehr rauh. Die Weite umgiebt ein hervorragender schräge gekerbter Wulst, unterhalb dessen 2 kleine Henkel sitzen.

Die meisten dieser Urnen trugen Deckel, flache Schalen, die über den Rand herüberragen, (Uebergreifende Deckel oder **Schalendeckel**), so die Urnen II, IV, VIII (Fragmente), IIa, b und die meisten Aschen-Urnen, die Dewitz fand, von welch' letzteren noch vier Stück (zum Theil kleine Fragmente, 622, 623, 645, 646) vorhanden sind. Urne IIII war mit einem flachen Stein zugedeckt, nur III ganz ohne Deckel, dies also eine Ausnahme von den Urnen in Kisten. Diese Deckel sind flach gewölbte Schalen mit einem kleinen Boden, hin und wieder auch vollständig flach gewölbt ohne Boden (Deckel 627 zu IIb und das Fragment 622). Der Rand ist manchmal schwach ausgeschweift, schneidet aber unten ziemlich gerade ab. Die Masse der vorhandenen sind (wobei Dr = Dw):

	Dr	Do	Hr	(H)	(b)	Dicke	Bemerkungen.
	cm					mm	
II (1244) Tfl. I1a	30	10	7	23	33	am Rande 8	
IIV (1251) Tfl. I5a	23	7,5	5,5	24	33	4	
IIa (629) Tfl. I8a	26	10,5	7,8	30	40	8	
IIb (627) Fig. 2 im Text	15,5	0	ca. 4	25	0	6	Mit Loch.
623 (Dewitz) Fig. II2	ca. 25	9,5	7	ca. 30	ca. 38	8, Mitte 14	Fragment, ergänzt gezeichnet.
622 (Dewitz)		0			0	10—11	Fragment mit Loch.
645 (Dewitz)						8, Mitte 10	Fragment.
646 (Dewitz)						8, Mitte 10	Fragment mit Boden, mit Loch.

Eine Eigenthümlichkeit einiger Deckel, die auch in anderen Hügeln häufig wiederkehrt, ist ein mitten im Deckel befindliches Loch (bei II b, Fig. 2 anbei) bei 623 und 646 von 2,0--2,5 cm Durchmesser, welches in den noch ungebrannten Deckel, oft nicht sehr geschickt eingebohrt wurde. Die Löcher zeigen deutlich, dass diese Scherben ausschliesslich zu Deckeln der Aschen-Urnen bestimmt waren, da sie dadurch zu jedem anderen Gebrauche untauglich gemacht wurden. Es muss das wohl mit religiösen Anschauungen und damit zusammenhängenden Grabgebräuchen in Verbindung stehen.

Fig. 2.

Die Deckel sind in Folge ihres Gebrauches auch nur auf der Aussenseite verziert, durch um den Rand herumgehende Zonen von Eindrücken. Deckel von Urne II a (Tfl. I 8a) durch drei Reihen von Fingereindrücken, der isolirte Deckel 623 (Tfl. II 2) durch zwei Reihen hurzer Kerben. Wie die Abdrücke der Finger lehren, waren es kleine Finger mit kurzen Nägeln, es werden also Frauen oder Mädchen diese Verzierung vorgenommen haben, wenn nicht die ganze Topffabrikation, wie noch jetzt in Jütland. Die übrigen Deckel sind glatt. I I (Tfl. I 1a) hat am Rande einen kleinen Henkel, der nur rein ornamental sein kann.

Die **Beigefässe** sind in den Birkenhöfer Hügeln (sonst nicht immer), sämmtlich grössere oder kleinere Krüge mit ziemlich breiten, nicht dicken Henkeln, die von dem Rande bis dicht über die Weite herabgehen und auch zum Halten dienten. Bei 2 Gefässen fand sich ein Doppelhenkel, d. h. 2 übereinander stehende, ähnlich geformte Henkel, welche zusammen die Länge des gewöhnlichen einfachen einnehmen; der Krug H I I (Tfl. I2), wo der untere Henkel schon in alter Zeit abgebrochen war (die untere Ansatzstelle ist in der Zeichnung nicht genügend markirt) und ein von Dewitz beschriebener (in seinem Bericht skizzirter) aus Hügel II, der nicht erhalten ist. Die Dimensionen und Verhältnisse ergeben sich aus folgender Tabelle:

Beigefässe.	Do	Dw	Dr	Hw	Hr	(H)	(r)	(b)	(Hw)	Dicke am Rande	Henkelbreite
	cm									mm	cm
I I (1245) Tfl. I 2	8,5	24,5	13,7	8	21	86	56	33	38	4	ca. 4
II (621) Tfl. II 3	5	11	9	3,5	8,5	77	81	45	41	4	2,6
III I (624) Tfl. I 9	12	22	18	7	13	60	82	54	54	ca. 6	3
III IIα (630) Tfl. I 6	6,5	12	8	4	11	90	67	54	36	5	2,5
III IIβ (631 Tfl. I 7	8	20	12	7	20	100	60	40	35	5	3,5

Man ersieht aus den Indices, wie aus den Zeichnungen, dass diese Krüge in den Proportionen erheblich variiren. Einige sind sehr flach und weit wie II (Tfl. II 3), und III I (Tfl. I 9) wo der Höhenindex 77, bei ersterem sogar 60. Der Randindex ist bei beiden c. 80, andere höher und schlanker mit langem Halse und entsprechendem Henkel; so kann man IIIIIβ (Tfl. I7) als wirklich elegant in den Formen bezeichnen.

Die Oberfläche ist stets gut geglättet und einige Male decorirt. Bei dem kleinen Kruge IIIIIα (Tfl. I6) findet sich unterhalb des Halses eine Zone kurzer senkrechter Kerben. Beim Krug II (Tfl. I2) ziehen sich unterhalb des Halses und an der Weite 2 Ringe eingedrückter Punkte herum, die unterhalb des Henkels einen Zwischenraum frei lassen und sich schräge beiderseits des Henkels nach aussen herabsteigend vereinen. Die Zonen sind verbunden durch alternirend schräge Strichgruppen. Die Gruppen von 4—5 Linien sind recht stumpf und flach gezogen, nicht ganz correct, wahrscheinlich in dem schon etwas betrockneten, jedenfalls ungebrannten Gefässe mit einem stumpfspitzigen Stab aus Holz oder Knochen, woher sie sich vollständig von den hart eingerissenen Linien bei IIV (Tfl. I5) unterscheiden. Beim Kruge III IIβ (Tfl. I7) gehen am unteren Ende des Halses, beim Henkelansatz zwei, etwas höher eine vertiefte, ebenso flach und sanft gezogene Linie herum. Von den unteren steigen wieder alternirend schräge Strichgruppen herab; die obere Zone erfüllen zum grössten Theile schraffirte Dreiecke, d. h. herabhängende Dreiecke, bei denen parallel zu einer Seite mehrere Striche im Innern gezogen sind (alle stumpf). Für diese Urne will ich probeweise die Hals-Indices angehen. Wenn man den Hals am oberen Reif beginnen lässt, ist Hh 13, Dh 14 also (Hh) 65, (Dh) 70, rechnet man ihn vom unteren Reifen, beim Henkelansatz, Hh 10, Dh 18, (Hh) 50, (Dh) 90. Die Beigefässe waren in der Regel unbedeckt, nur in zwei Fällen mit Deckeln versehen. Einmal erwähnt Dewitz in Hügel II einen Krug mit Doppelhenkel von einer Schale bedeckt. Der zweite Krug mit Doppelhenkel (II Tfl. I2) trug einen ganz eigenthümlich geformten Deckel, eine platte Scheibe von 21 cm Durchmesser, 13—15 mm dick aus mässig feinem, aber nicht geglätteten Thon. Der dicke Rand und eine Seite sind über und über durch unregelmässig aufgesetzte Fingereindrücke verziert. Merkwürdigerweise lag die verzierte Seite nach unten, und ist nur der Deutlichkeit wegen nach oben gezeichnet.

Bronze-Geräthe.

Die Ausbeute an Bronzegeräthen war eine geringe, wie überhaupt anderweitige Beigaben in den Hügeln immer nur spärlich vorkommen. Ausser dem ganz unbedeutendem Fragmente eines kleinen Bronzeringchens aus der Brandschicht von Hügel I, sind es nur eine Bronzenadel aus Hügel I und ein Bronzecelt aus Hügel V. Die Bronzenadel Tfl. IV, Fig. 1 (Inv. 1249). Die Nadel hat ca. 1/4 ihrer Länge vom Kopf entfernt eine Biegung von ca. 113° mit abgerundeter Ecke. Diese Nadeln sollen „Nadeln mit umgebogenem Halse" genannt werden.

Sie ist in Summa 20 cm lang, der umgebogene Theil 5,5 cm lang, 4 mm dick. Er endet in einen kegelförmigen Kopf und ist mit 4 kleinen Ringen garnirt, die nicht umgelegt, sondern umgegossen sind. Sie ist jedenfalls nach einem Wachsmodell à moule perdu gegossen, was besonders die kleinen, etwas plump geformten Ringe beweisen, welche an einer Stelle eine Art Naht zeigen, die aber nicht klafft, sondern verschmolzen ist. Auch sind sie etwas unterschnitten, würden also aus keiner Form herausgeben. Diese Eigenthümlichkeit lässt sich aber leicht erklären, wenn man annimmt, dass sie ursprünglich aus Wachs geformt waren.

Der Bronzecelt aus Hügel V Tfl. IV Fig. 5 (2037—39), eines der allerschönsten Stücke, welches die Ostpreussischen Hügelgräber geliefert haben, ist von Herrn Gutsbesitzer Grötzner-Birkenhof beim Abtragen eines Hügels gefunden und würde, da von den begleitenden Thongefässen Nichts erhalten ist, in seiner Zeitstellung weniger gesichert erscheinen, wenn ich nicht glücklicherweise 1884 einen Celt ganz desselben Charakters, von grösster Ansehnlichkeit, in einem Grabhügel zu Ihlnicken, Kreis Fischhausen, eine gute halbe Meile von Birkenhof entfernt gefunden hätte, wo die begleitenden Thongefässe zeigten, dass man es mit der Periode der Birkenhöfer Hügel, wie sie in den centralen Kisten vertreten ist, zu thun hatte.

Der Celt ist ein Hohlcelt (von Olshausen, Verl. d. Berliner Anthr. Ges. 1885 p. 364 ff. Tüllencelt genannt) d. h. innen hohl mit einem Loch (Tülle) zur Aufnahme des Holzstieles, von dem noch Reste vorhanden sind. Er ist deutlich gegliedert, indem oben ein kurzer cylindrischer Theil mit ein wenig gewölbten Seitenwänden oberhalb nach der Mündung durch zwei gekerbte vortretende, nach unten durch einen Reifen begrenzt wird. Wir können diesen Theil den Kopf nennen. Dann zieht er sich ein wenig zusammen, bleibt fast gleich breit und verbreitet sich hierauf in concaver Biegung bis zu der gegen den Henkel schräge emporsteigenden, fast gar nicht gekrümmten Schneide (deren Ecken etwas beschädigt sind). Den mittleren Theil, wo Durchmesser und Rundung fast gleich bleibt, möchte ich den Hals, den unteren Theil wo letzterer sich nach beiden Seiten verbreitet, nach der Schneide, aber dachförmig zuschärft, das Blatt nennen. Diese Terminologie könnte in manchen Fällen die Beschreibung erleichtern; oft dürfte die Grenze zwischen den einzelnen Gliedern allerdings eine ganz unsichere, allmählig verlaufende sein, besonders zwischen Hals und Blatt, wie gerade im vorliegenden Falle. Der Durchmesser des Randreifs ist p (d. h. parallel zur Schneide) 22,5 mm, s (senkrecht) 24; der grösste Durchmesser des Kopfes p 24, s 26; der Tülle unterhalb des Kopfes p 20, s 23, innerer Durchmesser der Tülle oben p 19, s 21. Die Länge vom Rande bis zur Schneidenmitte 110, Breite der Schneide ca. 45; innere Länge der Tülle 81, also Länge des vollen Theils des Blatts ca. 30. Die Tülle ist also oben ein wenig oval, senkrecht zur Schneide breiter, zieht sich dann aber in dieser Richtung mehr zusammen, und endet unten keilförmig mit gekrümmter Schneide parallel der äussern. Innen hat sie nicht die erhöhten Rippen, welche sich oft in der Tülle der Celte finden (Olshausen, Verb. d. Berliner Anthrop. Ges. 1885 p. 449 ff.), nur eine etwas rauhe Oberfläche. Die Tülle hat keine Kanten und der Hals verläuft bis ca. 50 mm vom Rande gerundet, worauf sich in allmählichem Uebergange das Blatt parallel der Schneide verbreitert, senkrecht darauf zuschärft, und von der Schmalseite in die Breitseite mit nicht sehr scharfen Kanten übergeht. Diese Kanten vereinigen sich nicht auf den Breitseiten des Blattes, wo sie manchmal eine Art gewölbter Kante gegen den Hals bilden. Ebenso wenig begleiten erhöhte Ränder oder Furchen diese Kanten. Von der Mitte des Kopfes nach dem Halse steigt ein Henkel herab 23 mm lang, in der Mitte schmäler als an den Enden, 3,5 mm resp. 11,5. Er hat ausserhalb eine gerundete Mittelkante, innen eine schärfere. Wir wollen die Seite dieses Henkels als hintere bezeichnen, da sie, wie sich später zeigen wird, dem Schafte, also der Hand näher sass.

Man könnte nach obiger Terminologie die Beschreibung kurz so fassen:

„Gehenkelter Hohlcelt mit gewölbtem durch gekerbte Reife begrenztem Kopfe, kurzem rundem Halse, der allmählich in das lange Blatt mit rückwärts ansteigender gerader Schneide verläuft. Henkel von der Mitte des Kopfes zum Halse absteigend." (Wenn nichts bemerkt wird, soll der Henkel immer der Schneide parallel stehen, ist er senkrecht, so heisst dies „Henkel in Querstellung").

Die Oberfläche der Celts zeigt jetzt das schöne Dunkelgrün der edelsten Patina und ist an den Stellen, wo der Rost keine Gruben gefressen hat, von vorzüglicher Glätte und Glanz. Von Gussnäthen ist keine Spur vorhanden (mit Ausnahme einer Stelle), während alle anderen gewöhnlichen Celte unserer Sammlung auf jeder Querseite eine entlang gehende, nicht fortgenommene Nath zeigen. Es wäre nicht möglich gewesen, eine Nath so spurlos zu beseitigen, was besonders bei den Reifen am Kopfe hätte hervortreten müssen. Der Celt kann nach dem Gusse an der Oberfläche nicht überarbeitet, sondern muss in seinem tadellosen Glanze aus der Form hervorgegangen sein. Dass dies bei der damaligen sehr hohen Stufe des Bronzegusses möglich war, zeigen einzelne Stücke mit zum Theil gegossenen Verzierungen, welche in ausgezeichneter Schärfe dastehen, auf keine andere Weise hergestellt sein können, und zugleich beweisen, dass nach dem Gusse kein Sandkorn mehr die glatte Gusshaut berührt hat. (So z. B. der Celt Madsen, Afb. af Danske Oldsager. Bronzealderen 20, Fig. 5 von Fynen., Kopenhagen 18000, und vor allem ein Schwert aus der früheren Milanischen Sammlung im Besitze der Antiquitätenhändler Egger zu Budapest, wo ein Theil der Ornamente gegossen, wie u. a. die concentrischen Kreise, andere Ornamente nachher geschlagen sind, beides Meisterwerke alten Bronzegusses.) Es findet sich aber eine rauhe Stelle am Celt mit höckriger Oberfläche ohne Glanz und Patina, unterhalb des Henkels von seinen inneren Enden ausgehend, sich etwas ausweitend bis zum unteren Kopfreifen, so dass sie ein Sechseck bildet, 23 mm lang, 17 mm breit. In der Mitte, genau unter dem Henkel, läuft hier eine niedrige Gussnath entlang, ebenso eine unbedeutende, auf der Unterseite des, besonders an den Enden etwas rauhen Henkels, welche in der Mitte fast verschwindet. Bei dem ganz analogen Iblnicker Celt (der in einer der nächsten Abhandlungen beschrieben werden soll) findet sich dieselbe durch Glanz und Patina abstechende 6eckige Stelle, jedoch ein wenig sauberer als hier. Man kann sich demnach den Guss nur auf folgende Weise vorstellen: Das ganze Stück ist wieder in verlorener Form, à moule perdu, nach Wachsmodell gegossen — kurz gesagt mittelst Wachsguss. Ueber einem Thonkern für die Höhlung, den man über Feuer schwach gebrannt hatte, formte man den Celt aus Wachs mit seinen Reifen am Kopf. Dann wurde über diesem Wachsmodell sehr fein geschlemmter Thon in breiigem Zustande mit dem Pinsel oder ähnlich aufgetragen, aussen gröbere Schichten, die mit dem Kern so vereinigt wurden, dass für Eingussöffnung und Windlöcher Platz blieb, hierauf durch schwaches Brennen das Wachs ausgeschmolzen und dann die Bronce eingegossen. Der äussere nun härter gebrannte Thonmantel musste nachher zerschlagen werden. Das schmelzende Wachs tränkte den Thon, wodurch die Bronce eine ungemein glatte Oberfläche erhielt, die man vielleicht noch polirte, aber nicht mehr schliff. Dass man hierdurch im Alterthume Resultate erzielte, die unser Staunen erregen, zeigen einige der oben erwähnten, ungemein scharfen gegossenen Ornamente, die unbedingt nicht mehr nachgearbeitet sind. Wenn der Thonmantel auch ungetrennt die Höhlung des Henkels durchdrungen hätte, so lag die Gefahr nahe, beim Zerschlagen des Mantels den Henkel vermöge des in ihm sitzenden Thonzapfens mit abzusprengen. Daher setzte man hier einen Thonkern ein, der aber aus 2 Stücken bestehen musste, damit man ihn auseinander und herausnehmen konnte. Man hat also jedenfalls, ehe man den Henkel aus Wachs bildete, einen seiner inneren Form entsprechenden Thonklumpen auf das Wachs gesetzt und nach dem Henkel geformt, mit einer oberen flachen Rinne für denselben. Dann wurde derselbe zerschnitten und über Feuer getrocknet, damit er mit dem später aufgetragenen feinen Thon nicht zusammenklebte. Ueber den nochmals aufgesetzten beiden Hälften des Kerns wurde nun der Wachshenkel geformt, der an den Seiten noch ein wenig in diesen Kern hinein ragte, in der Mitte ziemlich frei lag. Der untere Kopfwulst war rund herumgeformt vor Ansatz des Henkels, wie man an seinen Rudimenten an dieser Stelle noch erkennt, ist aber durch den aufgesetzten Kern etwas auseinander gedrückt. Diese schwach gebrannten Kerne konnten durch das Wachs nicht mehr geglättet werden, daher die rauhere Oberfläche und die Nath an der Berührungsstelle beider Kernstücke, welche man beide nicht mehr glättete, was man doch jedenfalls gethan hätte, wenn der andere Theil der Oberfläche noch einer Glättung oder einem Schliff unterzogen wäre. Von grossem Interesse ist ferner die Verzierung des Celts.

Die beiden Reifen oberhalb und der unterhalb des Kopfes sind durch eingeschlagene Striche gekerbt. Diese Kerben gehen schräge, wechseln aber von Zeit zu Zeit ihre Richtung (es tritt dies auf Tfl. IV Fig. 4 schon hervor wird aber durch nebenstehende Figur noch deutlicher aufgerollt dargestellt). Auf den oberen beiden Reifen geht die Verzierung rund herum, beim unteren ist der rauhe Theil der Oberfläche nicht decorirt, zumal hier der Reif etwas zerdrückt wurde. Es findet ein mehrmaliger Wechsel der Richtung statt, wie aus nebenstehender Figur zu ersehen; es treten also hier auch alternirend schräge Strichgruppen auf, dem Ornamente der Urnen analog. Dies Ornament ist für die Schlussperiode der Nordischen Bronzezeit oder den Ausgang der Hallstädter Periode charakteristisch. Der erste Ausgangspunkt desselben stammt von kantigen Drähten her, welche, an einzelnen Stellen festgeklammert, nach derselben Seite gewunden wurden, so dass in Wirklichkeit ein Wechsel der Torsion erfolgte. Solche Ringe treten als kleine Spiralringe aus doppeltem Golddraht schon früh auf, in einer älteren Periode der Bronzezeit.*) Die Windungen werden dann aber auch durch einfache schräge Kerben imitirt, und grössere Bronzedrahtringe (Armringe)

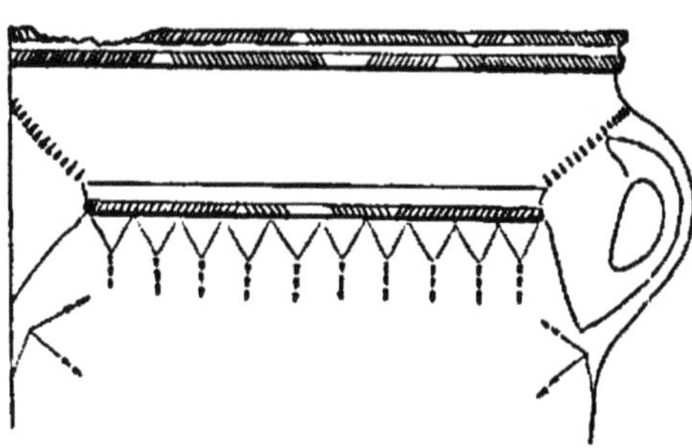

Figur 8.

*) Olshausen: Ueber Spiralringe (Verhandl. d. Berliner Anthropologischen Gesellschaft am 17. Juli 1886) p. 450, 467.

aus Bronze mit imitirter doppelter Torsion finden sich gerade am Ende der Hallstädter Periode (der Zeit unserer Celts), so z. B. ein Armring aus einer Gesichts-Urne zu Sullenczyn, Westpreussen. Die wechselnde Torsion, die echte wie die imitirte, spielt überhaupt zu dieser Zeit bei Halsringen eine grosse Rolle, (wie bei den Ringen Lindenschmits, Alterth. d. h. V. Bd. I Heft XI Tfl. 3. Montelius Antiquités Suédoises Fig. 227, 229) es war daher natürlich, dass man den Celt so decorirte, als ob Drahtringe mit wechselnder Torsion beiderseits um den Kopf gewickelt wären, um ihn zu begrenzen. Oberhalb des unteren Reifen befindet sich noch eine scharf gegen den Kopf abgesetze Furche, welche bereits durch den Guss hergestellt ist.

Unterhalb des Kopfes am oberen Ende des Halses geht eine Reihe von Dreiecken mit abwärts gerichteter Spitze herum, unter der drei ganz kleine spitze Dreiecke je eine herabsteigende Linie bilden. Ein Bogen solcher kleinen spitzen Dreieckchen zieht sich am Kopf vom unteren Reifen an ausserhalb um die rauhe Stelle über den Henkel herüber mit den Spitzen nach aussen. Vom unteren Ende des Henkels laufen sechs Strahlen aus, von jeder Seite 3 divergirende, so dass die beiden mittleren sich unterhalb des Henkels zu einem Dreieck vereinen; in ihrer Verlängerung sind dann wieder 2 kleine scharfe Dreiecke mit den Spitzen nach aussen eingeschlagen. Am oberen Theile des Henkels laufen neben der Mitte 2 Punktreihen entlang, welche durch ganz schwache Furchen, die sich über dem Henkel wölben, verbunden sind. Diese Verzierungen erhalten aber ein ganz besonderes Interesse, wenn man die Art und Weise studirt, auf welche sie hergestellt sind.

Der Celt kam also aus dem Guss unverziert mit den Reifen und der Furche zwischen den oberen beiden, sowie zwischen der unteren und dem Kopfe. Die Verzierungen sind sämmtlich eingeschlagen und ihre Natur lässt sich neben Betrachtung bei schwacher Vergrösserung (ich bin bis zu 25 facher mit zusammengesetztem Mikroskope gegangen), besonders gut durch Abdruck derselben in Thon erkennen. Ich verwende zu diesem Zwecke Plastilin, einen mit Fett durchkneteten Thon, welcher immer dieselbe Consistenz behält und stets zur Hand ist, auch reinlicher arbeitet, wie der erst mit Wasser angefeuchtete gewöhnliche Bildhauerthon. Man drückt ihn ohne weiteres auf das Ornament, das man nötigenfalls ein wenig benetzt. Dies Material ist auch sehr bequem für Studien auf Reisen. Man kann die Abdrücke dann in Pappschächtelchen durch 2 in verschiedenen Richtungen durchgesteckte Stecknadeln fixiren und bequem transportiren oder in Cartoncouverts per Post versenden, ein Hilfsmittel, wovon ich (s. weiter unten) jetzt behufs vergleichender Studien über die Ornamente dieses Celts Gebrauch gemacht habe. Die langen Linien der grossen Dreiecke sind mittelst eines Hiebes eingeschlagen; lange, schmale Linien, die sich nach den Enden etwas verjüngen. Die kleinen punktartigen Dreieckchen sind gewissermassen eingeschlagene Tetraëder. Die beiden längeren Flächen schneiden sich auf dem Boden in ziemlich stumpfer Kante, die dritte kleine ist auf dieser Kante senkrecht und fällt daher nach der Vertiefung ein. Die sämmtlichen Kanten bleiben bei der vollen Reihe recht scharf und ebenso die drei Winkel des Dreiecks an der Oberfläche, deren unterster recht spitz ist. Sie sind also mit einer meisselförmigen Punze mit ziemlich stumpf dachförmiger Schneide und darauf senkrechten Seitenwänden eingeschlagen. Diese Punze konnte nur von Stahl sein. Bei anderer

Gelegenheit habe ich eingehend über die zu Kopenhagen gemachten Versuche und meine Fortsetzung derselben, sowie weitere Studien*) gesprochen, welche deutlich zeigten, dass die specifisch nordischen Bronzen nicht nur mit Bronzepunzen bearbeitet werden konnten, sondern auch sind. Mit den Bronzeplatten und Bronzen, die ich mir 1877 in Kopenhagen anfertigen liess, habe ich jetzt bei Untersuchung dieses Celts selbst neue Versuche angestellt, zum Vergleich gegendie Wirkung der Stahlpunzen. Die Versuche zeigten nun, dass die Verzierungen der Birkenhöfer Celts mit Stahlpunzen geschlagen sind. Wenn man die Punze schräge aufsetzt und ihr einen Hammerschlag giebt, so erfolgt ein dreieckiger Eindruck wie die vorliegenden, der auf einem Ende sehr spitz zuläuft, auf dem anderen in kurzer Seite abbricht. Nur bei Stahl liess sich die volle Gleichmässigkeit und Schärfe einer ganzen Reihe erzielen; bei Bronzepunzen liess sich das erste Dreieck ziemlich ebenso scharf herstellen, während die Schneide sich hier bald abstumpfte, so dass die breite Seite des Dreiecks sich abrundete. Ebenso waren die langen Linien nur mittelst einer breiteren Stahlpunze mit ein wenig convex gekrümmter Schneide zu erzielen, die in der Mitte tiefer und breiter eindrang, nach den Seiten hin fein auslaufende Furchen bildete. Wenn der Celt auch leicht gekrümmt war, lagen diese Linien manchmal fast eben; man hätte mit Bronze, da eine convexe Schneide sich bald gerade schlägt, also nicht diese scharf auslaufenden Furchen erzielen können. Die Eindrücke am Henkel waren mit einer Doppelpunze, d. h. einer solchen mit 2 Spitzen geschlagen, die dazwischen liegende concave Vertiefung der Schneide markirte sich durch die schwachen über den Henkel gehenden Furchen, was besonders gut beim Abdruck mit Plastilin hervortrat. Die Kerben über die Kopfreifen waren aber auch mittelst einer Punze mit concaver Schneide geschlagen, die demnach auch mit Spitzen endete, welche sich einige Male in der Furche oberhalb des untersten Reifens und oben am Halse als kleine eingeschlagene Punkte am Ende der Kerben abgedrückt hatten. Diese Punkte waren hier nicht beabsichtigt; es hatte die scharfe convexe Schneide der Punze Furchen von etwas convexem Verlauf über den Reif geschlagen — was erst beim Abdruck des Plastilins deutlich hervortrat. Dabei blieben die Furchen immer gleichmässig; das wäre bei Bronzepunzen unmöglich, die concave Schneide wäre nach wenig Hieben breit und gerade geschlagen. Also ist hier mit Stahlwerkzeugen operirt worden. Das ist aber weiter nicht wunderbar, da in den Gräbern dieser Zeit schon Eisen auftritt — so in den Dewitz'schen Berichten, ferner verschiedene eiserne Schwanenhals-Nadeln in Gräbern dieses Typus. Die Funde sind ziemlich jung und fallen an das Ende einer Broncezeit, wo hier im Osten Eisen schon im höherem Maasse zur Anwendung kam (so besonders um diese Zeit in der Provinz Posen), während Bronze zu Werkzeugen und Waffen wohl noch das entschiedene Uebergewicht behauptete.

Bei der Untersuchung zahlreicher scandinavischer Bronzen hatte ich gefunden, dass die dem nordischen Gebiet ausschliesslich angehörigen Stücke nur mit Bronze-

---

*) Archiv für Anthropologie X: Sophus Müller, Zur Bronzealterfrage p. 39. Mittheilungen der Anthropol. Gesellschaft zu Wien XII, Verb. d. anthropol. Congress zu Salzburg: Tischler über die Decoration der alten Bronzegeräthe p. 50 ff.

werkzeugen decorirt, und dass die Einwendungen, welche Hostmann*) dagegen erhoben hat, durchaus unbegründet sind. Er nahm besonders an, dass Reihen von Häkchen, S förmigen Figuren, Doppelpunktreihen nur mit eigens dazu geschliffenen Punzen geschlagen seien, die natürlich nur aus Stahl bestehen können, weil es unmöglich ist Bronzepunzen nach 2 und 3 Hieben jedesmal in der richtigen Weise zuzuschleifen. Ich fand aber, dass alle diese Figuren durch mehrfache Schläge eines schmalen gradschneidigen Meissels hervorgebracht sind, und gelang es mir jetzt bei meinen neuen Versuchen, so ungeübt wie ich bin, ähnliche hervorzubringen. Bei den Originalen kann man deutlich wahrnehmen, wie dieser kleine Meissel nach einigen Figuren stumpf wird und wieder geschliffen werden musste. Das kann also nur Bronze sein, denn weiches Eisen wäre der härteren Bronze gegenüber immer im Nachtheil. Bei No. 8 p. 47 l. c. erwähnt Horstmann ein Hängegefäss der Neu-Strelitzer Sammlung. Ich konnte dasselbe an einer Photographie, die ich der Güte des Herrn Obermedicinalrath Dr. Götz verdankte, genau studieren, hatte es auch in Händen gehabt, sandte aber, da die Verzierungen wirklich verdächtig aussahen, an Herrn Dr. von Buchwald, Conservator der Grossherzoglichen Sammlung zu Neu-Strelitz Plastilin, worin er gütigst ein paar Abdrücke machte von einer scheinbar mit Doppelpunzen eingeschlagenen Zone auf dem Hängegefässe und einem gekerbten erhabenen Reifen auf einem tutulusförmigen Deckel, Verzierungen, die mit den Birkenhöfer scheinbar Aehnlichkeit hatten. Jetzt trat aber der Unterschied deutlich hervor. Die Kerben zeigten im Abdruck, dass sie mit einer völlig geradschneidigen Punze eingeschlagen waren, wie dies mit Bronze vorzüglich geht. Ebenso trugen die Doppelpunktreihen einen anderen Character. Es waren Reihen von einander zugekehrten kleinen Dreiecken, die sich manchmal auch etwas rundeten — aber nie so abgesetzt rund wie die Birkenhöfer. Diese waren durch eine Furche oder Einschnürung verbunden und durchaus nicht immer gleich gross oder ganz gleich lang. Ich konnte Eindrücke vollständig wie die vorliegenden erzielen, indem ich eine schmale meisselförmige Punze erst etwas schräge mit der einen Ecke, dann mit der anderen einschlug, wodurch das eingeschnürte Doppeldreieck entstand, wobei es möglich war, eine Menge solcher Doppelpunkte, die sich immermehr abrundeten, einzuschlagen, bis es nöthig war, die Punze wieder zu schleifen. Ebenso liessen sich (freilich von mir etwas ungeschickt) die Sartigen Figuren durch 4—5 Schläge herstellen. Hostmann meint, dass eine vierfache Reihe von kleinen rautenartigen Eindrücken zwischen diesen Doppelpunktzonen nicht mit Bronzepunzen hatte hergestellt sein können, weil dieselben ganz gleichmässig wären und weil die Punze nach jedem Hiebe (über 2080 Mal) hatte geschliffen werden müssen. Versuche lehrten das Gegentheil, abgesehen davon, dass die Rauten nicht so gleichmässig sind. Punzen mit ebener Endfläche von 3- oder 4eckigem Querschnitte, nach dem hin sie sich sehr stumpf zuspitzen, können sehr viele Eindrücke hervorbringen ohne sich wesentlich abzunutzen. Aus alledem geht unzweifelhaft hervor, dass diese Hängekessel und Tutuli mit Bronzepunzen decorirt sind.

Ich musste auf diese vergleichenden Studien und Versuche, wohl etwas zu ausführlich, eingehen, weil die Birkenhöfer Ergebnisse vielleicht die Beweiskraft der

*) Archiv für Anthropologie X: Zur Technik der alten Bronzeindustrie, speciell p. 44 ff.

früheren Untersuchungen hätten erschüttern können, die aber gerade vollständig bestätigt wurden. Es wäre ja schliesslich nicht wunderbar gewesen, wenn bei diesen Bronzekesseln, die in die jüngste Zeit der west-nordischen Bronzezeit fallen, wo weiter östlich (besonders in Posen) das Eisen schon in Gebrauch war, Stahlinstrumente auch bereits nach Mecklenburg gelangt wären. Aber doch ist hier die Anwendung der Bronzepunzen zweifellos constatirt. Die Untersuchung ist nicht immer so leicht wie bei den schönen Strelitzer Gefässen und bei den wunderbar erhaltenen Celten von Birkenhof und Ihlnicken; man wird daher nicht in allen Fällen die Schlüsse mit solcher Sicherheit ziehen können. Bei meinen Versuchen fand ich, wie merkwürdig leicht es für mich ungeübten war, längere scharfe Linien mit Bronzepunzen zu schlagen, welche vollständig den alten entsprachen, weit mehr als die mit Sthahlpunzen geschlagenen. Es ist daher unbegreifflich, wie die Sachverständigen Herr Dr. Karmarsch und Herr F. Behmer in Hannover ein entgegengesetztes technisches Gutachten*) abgeben konnten, welches später noch manchmal kritiklos angeführt worden ist.

In dem Henkel des Celts hing ein 4eckiger Bronzedraht mit 2 Endhaken, 3—3,5 mm lang, 2,5—3,5 dick; mit dem kleineren hing er im Henkel, der grössere, der kurz vor dem Ende eine kleine Furche trägt, war wohl um den Holzstiel gebogen, so den Celt festhaltend. Diese Befestigung mittelst eines Bronzehakens dürfte wohl eine seltene Ausnahme sein und glaube ich, war das auch nicht die ursprüngliche Bestimmung des Stückes. Der kleinere Haken zeigt eine geringe (in der Zeichnung nicht sichtbare) Biegung der Spitze. Ich glaube dies Stück ist ein in der Schleife zerbrochener Gürtelhaken, ähnlich wie der später zu beschreibende Schleifenhaken Tfl. IV 8 von Grosskuhren, dem er völlig ähnt — besonders spricht dafür die seittliche Biegung des kürzeren Hakenendes. Er muss aber schon in alter Zeit zerbrochen sein, was einige Stellen alter unverletzter Patina am Ende dieses Hakens beweisen, und wurde dann an dem Seitenarme etwas ungeschickt gebogen, um den Celt an dem ins Grab mitgegebenen Stiel zu befestigen. Also seine ursprüngliche Bestimmung war dies jedenfalls nicht.

Der Haken sass auf der inneren, dem Schaft zugewandten Seite, durch welche Lage die unsaubere Stelle unter dem Henkel verdeckt war, auch ist dies die naturgemässe Befestigung. Vom Holzschaft haben sich noch einige Reste erhalten, soweit er in der Tülle steckte, wo ihn die Durchtränkung mit Kupfersalz conservirte; ausserhalb derselben ist er nicht abgeschnitten oder abgebrochen, sondern abgefault, so dass er hier jetzt in einer mürben zerfaserten Oberfläche endet. Ob man den ganzen Stiel mitgab, lässt sich schwer entscheiden, da es nicht mehr zu constatiren geht, ob er innerhalb oder ausserhalb der Aschen-Urnen lag. Bei den Eisenlanzen und Celten einer späteren Zeit, in deren Höhlung sich noch Holzreste finden, ist es klar, dass man den Schaft abbrechen musste, um sie der Urne anvertrauen zu können. Hier wird der knieförmig gebogene Stiel immer noch so lang gewesen sein, dass man ihn an dem längeren Ende mit dem zerbrochenen Gürtelhaken festklammern konnte. Der Stiel (Tfl. IV Fig. 4—a, b) ist ein natürlicher etwas gebogener Ast, dessen erhaltener Rest ungefähr von der Mitte an zugeschärft

*) Archiv für Anthropologie X p. 62.

ist und in einer 3—4 mm breiten gerade abgestumpften Schneide endet. Dieselbe ist durch kurze Schnitte hergestellt. Mit was für einer Art Messer, ist fraglich (ob Bronze oder Eisen) da wir aus dieser Zeit kein Messer besitzen, nur ein Bronzemesser aus einer weit älteren Periode. Das Material des Stieles ist nach der Untersuchung von Herrn Professor Caspary Rothbuchenholz. Rothbuche kommt im Samlande jetzt nicht mehr als natürlicher Waldbaum vor, sondern findet sich nur in nachweisbar einst angesäten Beständen im Pilzenwalde bei Neuhäuser und zu Rogehnen. Wohl aber existiren jetzt prachtvolle Wälder an der andern Seite des frischen Haffs von der Passarge nach Westen zu, so dass man aus diesem Stiele weder Schlüsse auf eine einstige grössere Verbreitung der Rothbuche, noch auf eine weit entlegene Ursprungsstelle des Celts ziehen kann.

Dieser Celt hat eine Form, die bisher nur in Ostpreussen vorgekommen ist. Gehenkelte Hohlcelte mit gewölbtem Kopf, der sich deutlich vom Halse abtrennt, sind in Ostpreussen in grosser Menge gefunden, so ein schön verzierter Prunkcelt in einem Depotfunde zu Gross-Söllen bei Bartenstein, (in der Sammlung des Herrn Blell-Lichterfelde), und eine Menge einfacher, roherer Celte mit schlecht beseitigten Gussnäthen in den verschiedenen Sammlungen, welche also die gewöhnlichen Gebrauchsgeräthe repräsentiren, während jene drei schön verzierten Celte jedenfalls Prunkwaffen waren. Bei allen findet sich ein deutlicher Absatz des mehr oder minder breiten gewölbten Kopfes gegen den anfangs geradlinig verlaufenden Hals. Analoge Celte habe ich bisher nirgends gefunden, weder publicirt noch bei meinen Studien in den Sammlungen der verschiedensten Gegenden Europas, besonders nicht in den uns zunächst liegenden Gebieten der jüngeren reichen Bronzecultur, im Scandinavisch-norddeutschen und in Ungarn.*) Es finden sich manchmal 1 oder 2 wulstartige Reifen um die Oeffnung, zwischen oder unter denen der Henkel beginnt; ferner ist durch 2 Reifengruppen mitunter der Kopf abgegliedert, aber er verläuft dann geradwandig ungewölbt (Montelius Antiquités Suédoises 149 aus dem Täckhammarfluss in Södermanland; WorsaaeNordiske Oldsager 194 aus Dänemark). Scheinbar verwandt ist ein Celt von Bognes in Seeland (Montelius: Om Tidslestämming inom Bornsålderen**) Tfl. II 20), welcher am oberen Ende des Halses Dreiecke trägt, von deren Spitzen Linien herabsteigen, und oberhalb wie unterhalb des Kopfes je 2 gekerbte nicht heraustretende Reifen. Der Kopf ist aber cylindrisch, ungewölbt und durch sich kreuzende Linien schraffirt. Ausserdem gehört der Celt einem Grabe aus viel früherer Zeit an (welche ich, die Perioden 2 und 3 von Montelins zusammenziehend als Periode von Peccatel bezeichnen möchte — die Begründung an anderem Orte), die Aehnlichkeit aber ist doch nur eine scheinbare. Das einzige Stück mit gewölbtem Kopfe ist ein henkelloser Celt, von immerhin wesentlich verschiedener Form, von Långbro (Södermanland-Schweden. Montelius Antiquités Suédoises 144) aus der jüngsten Bronzezeit. Somit stehen diese Ostpreussischen Henkelcelte mit gewölbtem Kopfe noch vollständig isolirt da; wir können sie als einheimische Produkte auffassen, welche

*) Wenn sich irgendwo Celte von verwandten Typen vorfinden sollten, würde ich für eine Mittheilung nebst kleiner Skizze sehr dankbar sein. Dieselben werden dann bei späterer Besprechung der Ihlnicker Celts zur Verwendung kommen.

**) K. Vitterhets historie och Antiquitets Akademiens Handlingar. Stockholm XIII (1885).

einer späten Periode, nämlich der beginnenden Eisenzeit angehören. Dass solche Stücke sich selten in Gräbern finden, beruht wohl auf dem Brauche, dass man den Todten zur Zeit der Birkenhöfer Hügel nur sehr wenige und einfache Schmucksachen mitgab; die Depot und Einzelfunde beweisen aber, dass viel mehr Broncegeräthe zu jener Zeit im Lande waren, vor allem Celte dieses ostpreussischen Typus, ähnliche Verhältnisse wie sie zur jüngeren Bronzezeit weiter westlich vorkamen.

Eisengeräthe.

Dewitz erwähnt 2 sehr verrostete Eisengeräthe in 2 Urnen des Hügels II, einen fingerdicken Ring von 5 cm Durchmesser, und ein ganz verrostetes Eisenstück in Urne 629 (Tfl. I Fig. 8). Sie sind leider nicht mehr vorhanden; es kann nur ihre Anwesenheit in Aschen-Urnen dieser Zeit constatirt werden.

Bernsteinschmuck.

Von ganz besonderer Bedeutung sind die Formen des Bernsteinschmucks in diesen Hügeln. Man findet oft rohen Bernstein, manchmal in ganz bedeutenden Quantitäten, bearbeitete Stücke seltener. Dewitz erwähnt einige der Art, aus Hügel II in derselben Aschen-Urne 629 ein 4 cm langes, 2,5 breites, 1,6 dickes Bernsteinstück (das nicht als roh angegeben wird) und ein bearbeitetes Bernsteinstück aus Hügel III Kiste II. Sie sind beide nicht vorhanden.

Der Hügel I hat in Urne II ein höchst merkwürdiges Stück geliefert (Inventar 1248 Tfl. VI (IV) Fig. 2). Ein flaches Stück von in maximo 8 mm Dicke, grösster Länge 41, grösster Breite 23, das auf einer Seite ziemlich flach, auf der anderen schwach gewölbt ist. Die obere Kante ist etwas gebogen und läuft in 2 stumpfe Hörnchen aus, unter denen sich 2 tiefe Einschnitte befinden, von wo die convexen Seiten nach unten wieder in 2 Hörnchen auslaufen, welche durch die concave Unterkante verbunden sind. Für diese eigenthümliche Form dürfte sich die Bezeichnung „violinstegförmige Bernsteinstücke" empfohlen, welche ein mehr oder minder deutliches Bild der verschiedenen Varianten dieses Typus giebt und die ich schon im Kataloge der Berliner prähistorischen Ausstellung 1880 p. 414 angewendet habe. Die Einschnitte sind, wie man deutlich sieht, mit einem scharf schneidenden Instrumente gemacht, nicht mit Feuerstein, auf dieselbe Weise sind die Ränder geschnitten. Die Seiten zeigen 3 Facetten, der obere und untere Rand sind mehr abgerundet. Das Loch ist cylindrisch, an der platten Seite ein wenig enger, von ca. 2 mm Durchmesser. Es ist glatt, scheint aber nicht absolut gerade. Das Stück ist mit einer zersprungenen Rinde bedeckt und schimmert gegen das Licht gehalten prachtvoll rubinroth; also der echte viel besprochene „ambre rouge." Nichts destoweniger ist dies, wie bereits an anderem Orte erwähnt,*) nur eine rothe Verwitterungsrinde, die eigentliche Farbe des Stückes, die an einigen abgebröckelten Partieen etwas zu Tage tritt, ist ein recht helles Klar, was bei dem roth erscheinenden Bernstein immer der Fall ist. So fand ich z. B., dass die dünnen rubinroth durchscheinenden Bernsteinfourniere in den Fürstengräbern von Ludwigsburg und Hundersingen in Württemberg (Museum Stuttgart), welche beiläufig mit dem Birkenhöfer Stück

*) Klebs: Der Bernsteinschmuck der Steinzeit. Königsberg 1882 p. 8.

ziemlich gleichaltrig sind, innen aus einem vollkommen klaren, ganz hellgelben Bernstein bestehen, wie kleine Splitterchen unzweifelhaft beweisen.

Dies merkwürdige Bernsteinstück steht nicht vereinzelt da. Das Provinzial-Museum besitzt ein zweites Stück, Inventar 1260, als Geschenk von Herrn Kowalewski. Dasselbe ist angekauft und wird ungefähr aus der Gegend von Gross Hubnicken, nicht weit von Birkenhof, jedenfalls ursprünglich aus einem Grabhügel stammen. Es (Tfl. IV 4) hat ein mehr dreieckiges Aussehen, indem die Oberkante aus 2 sich in einem stumpfen abgerundeten Winkel verbindenden Seiten besteht. Die Hörnchen sind sehr stumpf. Der Einschnitt liegt daher auf beiden Seiten recht tief und die unteren Hörnchen gleich darunter, verbunden durch die leicht eingebogene Unterseite. Die Breite vom Scheitel bis in die Mitte der Unterseite ist 32 mm, die grösste Länge 45, die Dicke an der Oeffnung 10 mm, unten 8. Beide Seiten sind ziemlich flach, die oberen Ränder bestehen aus 2 Facetten, die sich in einem stumpfen Winkel treffen, die einspringenden Winkel zwischen den Hörnchen und die Unterkante sind abgerundet, man bemerkt hier langgezogene Ritzen. Die Bohrung ist ziemlich glatt und cylindrisch. Man kann diese Cylinder von beiden Seiten verfolgen, sie treffen sich in der Mitte und bilden einen kleinen Grath. Das Loch hat ca. 4 mm Durchmesser. Auf den beiden Facetten der oberen Ränder findet sich je eine Reihe kreisförmiger Gruben, ebenso auf beiden platten Seiten je eine Reihe längs der oberen Kanten, längs der unteren und von dem Loch 3 Reihen ausstrahlend nach den unteren Ecken und der Mitte, endlich noch je 1 über den einspringenden Winkeln der Seiten. Diese Gruben haben ein ziemlich flachgewölbtes Profil; sie sie sind Kugelcaletten, was man sehr gut durch einen Abdruck in Plastilin erkennt, zeigen zum Theil ganz scharfe feine concentrische Reifen auf ihrem Boden, und haben alle dieselbe Krümmung, auch annähernd dieselbe Grösse. In der Provinz sind noch 2 ähnliche Stücke gefunden worden, eines in einem Grabhügel der Warnicker Forst (auch nahe Birkenhof) im Provinzial-Museum No. 1904, dass in der nächsten Abhandlung abgebildet werden soll, und eins im Prussia-Museum aus einem Grabhügel von Rantau, ebenfalls im Samlande.

Alle diese Stücke haben einen höchst eigenthümlichen Character. Sie erinnern ihrer Form nach entfernt, auch durch das Grubenornament und besonders durch die eingeritzten Striche des Warnicker Stückes an den Bernsteinschmuck der Steinzeit. Diese Aehnlichkeit fällt noch mehr auf bei den weiter unten zu beschreibenden Hängestücken von Warschken (Tfl. IV Fig. 9 und Fig. 5 im Text) und Mollehnen (Fig. 6 im Text), die an die unregelmässigen Hängestücke, letzteres an die axtförmigen entschieden erinnern (cf. die Abbildungen bei Klebs, Bernsteinschmuck der Steinzeit. Königsberg 1882). Es tritt also die Frage auf, ob die Zeitbestimmung, die ich in dieser Arbeit gegeben (welche ich mit Herrn Dr. Klebs zusammen verfasst habe) unrichtig war, ob diese Schmuckstücke bis tief in die Hügelgräberzeit im Gebrauch gewesen seien, oder ob endlich diese Stücke zur Steinzeit gearbeitet, in die Erde gerathen und von dem Erbauer der Hügel wieder aufgefunden und verwendet seien. Ein solcher Brauch ist in jüngeren Perioden öfters wirklich nachweisbar.

So fand ich im Gräberfeld zu Greibau in einem Grabe des 3. oder 4. Jahrhunderts n. Chr. ein Bernsteinhängestück, welches mit Sicherheit der Steinzeit entstammte, das sich aber durch seine Verwitterungsrinde und seine Form vollständig von den zahlreichen Bernsteinstücken dieser Spätzeit unterschied. Für die Hügelgräber, wo Stücke von obigem Character nun schon in grösserer Anzahl gefunden sind, dürfte eine solche Annahme wohl nicht zulässig sein, denn die genaue Untersuchung der Stücke zeigt, dass sie von denen der Steinzeit in der Technik vollständig verschieden sind. Bereits der glatte Schnitt der Breitseiten und besonders der schmalen Seitenflächen, die scharfen Kanten bei dem Mollehner Stück, und die sichere Führung des schneidenden Messers zeigen, dass sie durch Metallmesser hergestellt sind. Die schmalen eingeritzten Linien am Rande des Warnicker Stückes sind frei und sicher gezogen, nicht so breit und vielfach ausgefasert, wie die Linien zur Steinzeit. Vollends ist aber die Bohrung durchaus verschieden, bei diesen Stücken unter sich aber übereinstimmend, und hier kommen aufklärend noch eine Reihe von Stücken zu Hilfe, welche im Sommer 1886 zu Rantau in Hügeln ausgegraben sind, die einer noch früheren Periode, der älteren Bronzezeit angehören (der Periode von Peccatel).

Das Gemeinschaftliche aller dieser Bohrungen besteht darin, dass sie glatt, im Innern ziemlich gleich weit verlaufen, aber bei längeren Stücken nicht immer ganz gerade hindurchgehen. Sie unterschieden sich wesentlich von den Bohrungen zur Steinzeit, von denen die Tafeln genannten Werkes eine genügende Vorstellung geben. Man findet bei diesen meist die sich stark kegelförmig nach innen von beiden Seiten verjüngenden Löcher mit sehr starker Reifelung. Die schwierigsten Objecte sind die langen Röhrenperlen Tfl. I, wo man diese starke Reifelung im Innern und eine Röhre von beiderseits nach der Mitte unregelmässig abnehmendem Lumen bemerkt. Die Bernsteinstücke von Rantau gehören einer Periode an, welche mit den Gräbern der älteren Bronzezeit in Mecklenburg, denen von Peccatel, Friedrichsruhe und vielen anderen ungefähr übereinstimmt und zugleich mit einer älteren Abtheilung der Hallstädter Periode oder der Necropolen Oberitaliens, eine Ansicht, die bei der Beschreibung dieser Gräber näher begründet werden soll. In allen diesen Gräbern finden sich Bernsteinstücke mit besonders langen feinen Bohrungen, so u. a. in den Grabhügeln bei Friedrichsruhe in Mecklenburg,*) auf dem Gräberfelde zu Kazmierz (Posen, Sammlung des Herrn Fehlan), zu Hallstadt selbst**) und zu Rantau. Hier zeigen dünne Platten parallel der Platte feine Bohrungen von bis 26 mm Länge, feiner als sie meist in den Bernsteinperlen der Gräberfelder n. Chr. vorkommen. Die Rantauer Bohrungen sind in sich gleichweit, die Röhren aber nicht immer gerade. Ich dachte daher anfangs, ob dieselben nicht mit heissem Draht durchgebrannt sein könnten, eine jetzt noch oft übliche Methode, und stellte Versuche in dieser Richtung an. Wenn man den Draht in der Gasflamme rothglühend macht, geht es leicht und schnell und mit gekrümmtem Draht kann man gekrümmte Löcher herstellen. Dann entstehen aber fast immer Sprünge im Bernstein, so dass er leicht auseinanderfällt. Um diese zu vermeiden, darf man den Draht nur sehr mässig erhitzen, wie es die Alten, denen keine solche Flammen zur Disposition standen, gewiss gethan hätten — dann geht

*) Jahrb. d. Vereins f. Mecklenburgische Geschichte und Alterthumskunde 47 Tfl. VI Fig. 2.
**) Sacken: Das Grabfeld von Hallstadt Tfl. 17.

die Arbeit aber recht langsam vorwärts. Die Röhre überzieht sich ferner innen mit einer glänzenden Schmelzrinde, welche ich fortzuschleifen versuchte, indem ich denselben Draht in Sand eintauchte und in der Röhre herumdrehte. Nun waren einige der kleineren Rantauer Perlen in der Mitte durchgebrochen und gestatteten eine genauere Beobachtung der Röhre, in welcher sich feine parallele Reifen zeigten, wie ich sie beim Ausscheuern mit Sand nicht annähernd hervorbringen konnte. Es musste daher die scheinbar so bequeme Erklärung des Durchbrennens aufgegeben werden. Die modernen Perlen werden mittelst eines vierkantigen, vorne spitzen Stichels durchgebohrt, und geben so ein ganz gerades Loch, ähnlich verfuhr man wohl auch bei den Perlen der 1. Jahrhunderte n. Chr. Ich versuchte eine Bohrung mit Messingdraht, der vorne zu einer etwas breiteren Schneide ausgeklopft und angeschliffen war. Derselbe wurde in den schraubenförmigen Stiel eines Bohrers gesteckt und durch eine auf- und abzuschiebende Hülse schnell umgedreht — ein mit dem Bogen gedrehter Bohrer, den man in den alten Zeiten gewiss kannte, hätte dieselben Dienste geleistet. Die Bohrung ging ausgezeichnet und schnell vor sich, und als das Stück nachher durchschnitten wurde, zeigten sich innen dieselben feinen Reifen als an dem Rantauer Stück. Weil die Schneide etwas breiter war als der Draht, behielt die Drehungsaxe nicht stets dieselbe Lage und so ging das Loch etwas gekrümmt aber mit demselben Lumen hindurch, ganz wie bei den alten Stücken. Es liessen sich die feinen langen Löcher also mit dem noch härteren Bronzedraht gewiss sehr gut herstellen. Zur Zeit der Birkenhöfer Hügel war Eisen allerdings schon bekannt und daher die Bohrung dieser Löcher gar nicht schwer, es war aber Eisen nicht erforderlich. Man bohrte die Löcher von einer Seite wohl meist ganz durch und bohrte von der andern Seite nur nach, um das Loch auszuputzen, daher der kleine Absatz an der Stelle, wo die Bohrungen sich treffen — die sich daher nie verfehlten, wie manchmal zur Steinzeit. Die Gruben auf dem Hubnicker Stück Tfl. IV Fig. 3 lassen sich auch leicht und sehr schnell mit einem glühenden Nadelkopf einbrennen, aber durch Ausscheuern mit Sand konnte ich ebenfalls nicht die feinen concentrischen Reifen hervorbringen, welche den Boden der Grube bedecken; selbst bei feinem Sand waren sie gröber und unregelmässig und können demnach auch nur mit Metall ausgedreht sein, durch einem Bohrer mit schwach gekrümmter Schneide, gleichgiltig ob er aus Bronze oder aus Eisen war. Ich habe nochmals alle unsere von Schwarzort oder aus Steinzeitgräbern stammenden Bernsteinstücke hiermit verglichen, immer waren die Gruben mehr kegelförmig, mit starken oft abgesetzten Reifen und einer sehr deutlichen kleinen Grube in der Tiefe, wie man sie mittelst eines Feuersteinsplitters vollkommen nachahmen konnte, also durchaus verschieden. Bei dem Mollehner Stück (unten Fig. 6) sind die Gruben tiefer, mit einem spitzeren Instrument hergestellt aber ebensowenig im Steinzeitcharakter.

Wir haben also wirklich characteristische Bernsteinformen in der älteren Bronzezeit Ostpreussens, als auch besonders in der jüngeren oder der beginnenden Eisenzeit, d. h. in den uns beschäftigenden Hügeln. (Es sind hier schon Anschauungen vorweg zur Anwendung gebracht, deren eingehende Begründung erst in einer späteren Abhandlung erfolgen kann.) Auffallend und noch nicht recht erklärlich ist nun die Verwandschaft dieser letzteren Stücke mit denen der Steinzeit. Der Zeitunterschied dieser beiden Perioden, den ich bei andrer Gelegenheit zu begründen gesucht habe,*) wird durch die Entdeckung von Gräbern einer älteren Bronzezeit in den Rantauer Hügeln noch gesteigert und andrerseits zeigt die grundverschiedene Keramik der Steinzeit (besonders der kurischen Nehrung), welche mit der in den Kupferstationen der Schweiz (z. B. Vinelz) geradezu **identisch** ist, dass wir vollberechtigt sind, diese Periode so hoch heraufzurücken, und dass von einem Nebeneinanderbestehen dieser alten Cultur und dem jüngeren Bronze- resp. beginnenden Eisenalter in so wenig entfernten Gebieten nicht die Rede sein kann. Es bleibt die Klärung dieser Frage also noch künftigen Entdeckungen vorbehalten.

Grabhügel bei Finken.

Auf dem Territorium des Gutes Finken, Kreis Fischhausen, nach Dorf Schalben zu, ca. 3000 m von Birkenhof, ist von Herrn Heilmann ein Hügelgrab geöffnet und der erhaltene Inhalt dem Provinzial-Museum gütigst übermittelt worden. Es ist der Deckel einer Aschen-Urne und einige Bronzegegenstände gerettet worden.

Der Urnendeckel (No. 1307) hat die Dimensionen Do 12 Dr 29 Hr 8,5: (b) 42 H (30), bewegt sich also in den gewöhnlichen Dimensionen, mit etwas grossem Boden. Der Rand ist etwas ausgebogen und trägt einen kleinen Henkel von 4 cm Länge, 2 Breite. Der Deckel ist besonders auf der Aussenseite vorzüglich geglättet in graubrauner Farbe.

Aus dem Grabe sind erhalten eine Pincette, ein Stück eines Armringes und ein Spiralring.

Die Pincette (Inventar 1298 Tfl. IV 5) ist 82 mm lang, an der Schneide ca. 42 mm breit (die Ecken sind ausgesprungen). Die Seitenkanten gehen concav nach aussen von der längliche Oese, an deren unterem Ende die Blätter dicht zusammenliegen; die Blechdicke beträgt an der Oese 1,5 mm, unmittelbar darüber 1 mm, und nimmt nach unten bis 0 8 mm ab, die Schneiden selbst sind etwas dicker, 1 mm. Die Pincette ist auf jedem Blatt durch 2 parallel den Seitenkanten gezogene Furchen verziert und durch von hinten eingeschlagene Buckelreihen entlang der Schneide, entlang den Seitenkanten hinauf bis 46 unterhalb und entlang der Mittellinie bis 23 mm unterhalb des oberen Endes. Die Buckel sind auf dem umgebogenen Blech von hinten eingeschlagen, die Linien aber erst nach der Biegung mit Stahlwerkzeugen gezogen, denn sie sind äusserst scharf, continuirlich laufend und zeigen eine parallele Streifung, ferner setzen sie unterhalb der Oese ab und beginnen hier wieder ganz schmal. Die eine Linie war etwas verfehlt, zuerst ganz schwach nahe dem Rande gezogen und dann nochmals etwas weiter, wobei sie die Buckel anschnitt und wellenförmig drüber hinweglief was deutlich zeigte, dass diese Linien nicht geschlagen waren. Pincetten von ähnlicher Form sind in Ostpreussen noch mehrfach gefunden: eine zu Stapornen, Kreis Fischausen (Prussia-Museum), aus einem Hügel mit von hinten eingeschlagenen Buckeln und mit seitlich röhrenartig verlängerter Oese; eine zweite ebenfalls mit kleiner Röhre mit eingeschlagenen Dreiecken von unbekanntem Fundort; eine unten ähnlich breite, aber mit schmälerem Stiele, in gleicher Weise mit Buckeln verziert von Kickelhof bei Elbing (Museum

*) Bernsteinschmuck der Steinzeit p. 62 ff. Schriften der physikalisch-ökonomischen Gesellschaft XXIII (1882) p. 32 ff.

Elbing). Ganz entsprechende Pincetten finden sich ausserhalb Ostpreussens nicht, die der westpreussischen Gesichts-Urnen sind wesentlich verschieden mit langen schmalen Stielen, die sich erst unten zu dreieckigen Blättern entwickeln, (welche Form übrigens in Ostpreussen doch auch noch vorkommt, so in einem Hügelgrabe dieser Periode zu Trulack, Kreis Fischhausen, (Prussia-Museum), oder wie Undset XIV 9. In Pommern treten schon ähnliche verbreiterte mit Buckeln auf. Im Gebiete der nordischen Bronze-Cultur — Mecklenburg, Scandinavien finden sich in der jüngsten Bronzezeit verwandte Formen wie die Birkenhöfer mit einzelnen getriebenen Buckeln (Friderico-Franciscеum Tfl. 19, Madsen: Bronsalderen Tfl. 28, Montelius Ant. suéd. 200) nur abweichend im Uebrigen verziert, durch eingeschlagene Wellenlinien und ähnliche Ornamente des Styls dieser Region. Eine gewisse Analogie ist also doch vorhanden bei allen Verschiedenheiten und demnach zu erwarten, das auch durch Westpreussen und Hinterpommern noch eine Verbindung entdeckt wird. Südwärts scheint eine solche ganz ausgeschlossen.

Der Armring (1299 Tfl. IV 6) von gedrücktem Querschnitt mit etwas schärferen Rändern, innen etwas flacher als aussen, (1,8 mm dick, 3 breit, nach dem Endknopfe zu 2,5 mm und 3), verdickt sich nach dem Ende etwas und wird hier durch 3 flache Einschnürungen in 2 kleine und einen grösseren Endknopf gegliedert. Letzterer hat eine Endfläche von 3,6 mm Höhe, 5 Breite, mit gewölbter Ober-, flacher Unterkante und 2 schrägen nach aussen emporsteigenden Seitenkanten. Diese Form mit den etwas grösseren, aber immer noch recht kleinen Endknöpfen erinnert ein wenig an Armringe, welche in Süddeutschland und Frankreich gegen Ende der Hallstädter beim Uebergange zur La Tène-Periode auftreten.

Der Spiralring (1306 Tfl. IV 7) ist in eine Reihe einzelner Stücke zerbrochen, so dass man weder seine volle Länge beurtheilen kann, noch wie er endete. Er hat 42 mm äusseren Durchmesser und einen nicht ganz runden Querschnitt von 1,65—1,8 mm Durchmesser. Die parallel laufenden Längslinien des ein wenig facettirten Drahtes zeigen, dass derselbe wohl gezogen war, da es durch Hämmern schwer möglich gewesen wäre dieselben so gleichmässig herzustellen, doch soll diese Frage hier noch offen gelassen werden.

Hügelgrab bei Gross-Kuhren.

Aus einem Hügelgrabe bei Grosskuhren unweit Finken, über das alle ferneren Angaben fehlen, sind durch Vermittlung des Herrn Apotheker Kowalewski von Herrn Inspector Hassenstein eine Aschen-Urne und ein Bronzehaken dem Provinzial-Museum übermittelt worden.

Die Aschen-Urne (Inventar 1253) ist die grösste aller im Museum aufbewahrten: Do 13 Dw 42 Dr 29 Hw 19—20 Hr 35,7, obere Randdicke 10 mm, also (H) 85 (r) 70 (b) 31 (Hw) ca. 55, demnach ziemlich weit- und kurzhalsig (mit hoher Weite) sonst ähnlich Tfl. I 1 von Birkenhof. Nur der Boden ist durch einen kleinen senkrechten Absatz noch schärfer characterisirt. Der obere Theil ist geglättet, der untere von der Weite an aber ganz besonders rauh, so dass man die groben Fingerspuren vom horizontalen Verstreichen bemerkt. Im Ganzen ist die Urne etwas schief und unsymetrisch, was bei ihrer Grösse vollständig erklärlich.

Der Gürtelhaken (1254 Tfl. IV 8 besteht aus zwei 50 mm langen Schenkeln (Stangen), die sich zu einem 11 mm langen schleifenartigen Haken umbiegen. Auf der anderen Seite biegen sie sich in gerundeten Ecken zu 2 senkrecht abstehenden Seitenarmen um, deren Enden 51 mm von einander entfernt sind. Der Haken besteht aus einer viereckigen Bronzestange von 3,6 mm Breite, 3,0 mm Dicke (von vorne nach hinten), ist an den Kanten durch schräge Kerben etwas gewellt, die auch in der Zeichnung hervortreten und sich kaum erkennbar über die ebenen Flächen herüberziehen. Man sieht deutlich, dass dies ursprünglich ein tordirter Draht war, der nachher viereckig gehämmert wurde, wodurch die alte Torsion nicht vollständig verschwand, sondern besonders an den Kanten noch etwas hervortrat.

Man nennt diese Haken Gürtelhaken, weil sie jedenfalls zum Schliessen eines Leder- oder Zeuggürtels dienten, welcher um die abstehenden Enden herumgelegt und wohl zusammengenäht war. Der Haken spielt v. Chr. eine grosse Rolle und wird erst nach dieser Epoche durch die Schnalle ersetzt. Die oft bedeutenden und unbequemen Dimensionen solcher Haken würden den Zweck nicht verhindern, wenn man an die riesigen Gürtel mancher jetzigen Stämme, wie der Tyroler denkt — es ist dabei aber nicht unmöglich dass sie auch noch andere Riemen als den Leibgurt schlossen, doch nennt man sie frei von jeder Hypothese wohl am bequemsten Gürtelhaken. Die obige Form ist durch die Schleife, in der die beiden Stangen sich zum Haken umbiegen, ganz besonders characterisirt, wir können sie Schleifenhaken nennen.

Diese höchst eigenthümliche Form ist über ein sehr grosses Gebiet verbreitet. In Ostpreussen also zunächst der verbogene zerbrochene Haken von Birkenhof (p. 144) Tfl. IV Fig. 4, den man später in den Henkel des Celts hing. Ferner aus einem Hügelgrabe bei Loppöhnen, Kreis Fischhausen*) (im Museum der Prussia). Hier biegen sich die Seitenarme bis in die Mitte der Stangen in die Höhe und rollen sich dann zu 2 Flachspiralen auf. Diese Spiralen kann man nicht als etwas Wesentliches, Characteristisches betrachten, da sie bei vielen Schleifenhaken fehlen, sie sind nur ein zu dieser (aber auch zu anderen) Zeiten beliebtes Ornament. In der Provinz Posen kommt ein Haken fast identisch mit dem Gross-Kuhrenschen vor, (die Arme enden nur in kleine Knöpfchen) — zu Kazmierz;**) ein zweiter sehr viel zierlicherer, dessen untere Enden sich in kleine, nicht abstehende Spiralen aufrollen und dessen beide Drähte von Ringen umgeben sind, zu Nadziejewo.***) Ein scheinbar ähnlicher Haken, der aber viel weniger regelmässig aus rundem Draht gebogen ist, stammt aus einem Grabhügelfunde der ältesten Bronzezeit zu Weizen in Baden†) und steht den übrigen unter sich ziemlich übereinstimmenden Haken ferner. Hingegen ist ein in der Form mit den ostpreussischen identischer mit geraden Seitenarmen in einem Pfahlbau des Lac de Bourget in Savoyen, Station Le Saut gefunden; ein zweiter kleiner, dessen Enden sich einmal umrollen zu einfachen Oesen, ebenda Station Grésine.††) In der grossen Necropole von Bologna auf dem Besitzthum des

*) Undset: Das erste Auftreten des Eisens in Nord-Europa. Tfl. XVI 4.

**) Undset l. c. XII 8. Album der prähistorischen Ausstellung zu Berlin 1880 Sect. IV Tfl. 4.

***) Undset Tfl. XII 9.

†) Album der Berliner prähistorischen Ausstellung 1880 Sect. VII Tfl. 13.

††) Perrin: Etude préhistorique sur la Savoie. Paris-Chambéry 1870 Tfl. XII 19. XIX 18.

Herrn Arnoaldi Veli sind 3 verwandte Gürtelhaken gefunden,*) einer genau wie der von Gross-Kuhren, bei den beiden andern befindet sich zwischen den Längsstangen und dem Querarme ein reich gegliedertes Mittelstück. Dann greifen die Haken aber in einen Ring, der an einer ähnlichen Querstange sitzt. Es ist hier also die Oese erhalten, welche am anderen Ende des Gürtels sass, und die in unsern Gräbern zu fehlen scheint. Weiter östlich ist zu Domahida in Ungarn**) ein Haken aus Kupfer gefunden in einem grossen Kupfer- und Bronze-Depotfund. Die Längsstangen sind hier ganz verschwunden. Die beiden Drähthe rollen sich gleich, wie sie vom Haken zurückkommen, zu je einer grossen Spirale auf. In demselben Funde kommen mehrere sogenannte Brillenspiralen vor, d. h. 2 Spiralen, welche durch eine Oese miteinander verbunden sind. Pulszky fasst dieselben als die Oesen auf, die Gegenstücke, in welche der Haken hineingriff, ähnlich (auch in der Form) den Haken und Oesen bei den jetzigen Damenkleidern (in Oesterreich-Ungarn „Manderl" und „Weiberl" genannt). Aehnliche Schleifenhaken mit Spiralen und ganz kurzen Stangen in sehr kleinem Maassstabe, und dazu gehörige Oesen, weit geöffnete Bogen, die nicht in Spiralen sondern in kleine Haken auslaufen, und ein zierlicher Haken mit Endspiralen und langen Stangen sind in einem Grabhügel des Hagenauer Waldes im Elsass gefunden (in der schönen Sammlung des Herrn Bürgermeisters Nessel in Hagenau). Sie sind gewissermassen eine Miniaturausgabe des Domahidahaken (und werden deshalb erst hier erwähnt). Endlich sind auf dem Gräberfeld zu Koban am Kaukasus***) 2 Haken gefunden mit geraden Längsstangen, welche sich am untern Ende in Spiralen aufwickeln — also in der Form dem von Loppöhnen am nächsten stehen. Einer riesig gross 12,5 cm lang, 11,6 breit; der zweite 5 lang, 5,8 breit.

Die Verbreitung der Schleifenhaken über ein so grosses Gebiet steht wohl mit einem inneren Zusammenhange derselben in Verbindung, der aber hier noch nicht verfolgt werden kann. Die Zeit der einzelnen Haken fällt (was später genauer begründet wird) in die Hallstädter Periode, die Zeit der italienischen Necropolen; doch werden die obigen Funde nicht gleichaltrig sein. Für die jüngsten möchte ich die ostpreussisch-posenschen ansehen, für die ältesten die kaukasischen.

Die Grabhügel bei Warschken.

Auf dem Territorium des Gutes Warschken, Kreis Fischhausen, ca. 3000 m nord-westlich von Germau befanden sich eine grosse Menge von Grabhügeln, von denen der Besitzer, Herr Gutsbesitzer Kemm bereits eine Menge planirt hat. Dieselben lagen zum Theil im Felde an der Grenze zwischen Warschken und Lesnieken unweit vom Landwege von Sorgenau nach Fischhausen, woselbst Herr Dr. Klebs einen Hügel abgegraben hat, über den mit den damit in Verbindung stehenden Lesnieker Hügeln zusammen in der nächsten Abhandlung berichtet werden soll. Eine andere Gruppe befindet sich in dem nördlich von Warschken sich nach dem von Palmnicken nach Germau gehenden Wege erstreckenden Wäldchen. Hier war noch ein ganz, und dicht daneben ein fast intacter Hügel, dicht südlich von diesem Wege und etwas

*) Gozzadini: Scavi fatti dal S. Arnoaldi Veli presso Bologna Tfl. X 10. 12. 13.
**) Pulszky: Die Kupferzeit in Ungarn. p. 31 Fig. 5.
***) Virchow: Das Gräberfeld von Koban. p. 47. 48. Tfl. VI 8. XI 10.

tiefer im Walde, 2 schon ausgebeutete Hügel vorhanden. Die beiden ersten babe ich ausgegraben. Sie gewährten dadurch ein ganz besonderes Interesse, dass in ihnen Begräbnisse aus verschiedenen Zeiten auftraten, welche durch die zwar spärlichen, zum Theil recht unansehnlichen und schlecht erhaltenen, aber dafür um so wichtigeren Metallbeigaben ganz scharf characterisirt wurden, so dass hier zum ersten Male die Gräber der La Tène Periode in ihrer Stellung zu den älteren klar erkannt werden konnten.

Hügel I.

(Vom 18. October bis 24. October 1882 ausgegraben von O. Tischler, in Summa 34 Arbeitstage.)

Der Durchmesser des Hügels ist 15 m, die Höhe ca. 1,50, der natürliche Boden liegt aber im Westen ca. 0,70 tiefer als im Osten, daher der Querschnitt nicht ganz symmetrisch, und die Höhe schwerer genau zu fixiren. Den Plan des Hügels veranschaulicht der anbei folgende Grundriss, in welchem die Hauptsteinconstructionen und Urnen gezeichnet, die Steine des Deck- und Bodenpflasters aber der Uebersicht wegen fortgelassen sind, und das nebenstehende Profil im Süd-Nord-durchschnitt — die Zeichnung ist nach Norden orientirt. Im Hügel waren eine Reihe von concentrischen Kränzen aus Steinen von 30—40 cm Durchmesser regelmässig gelegt und deutlich zu verfolgen. 1. Der äusserste Kranz von 13,40 NS 13,20 OW Durchmesser, also fast kreisförmig, dessen Steine mit ihrer Oberfläche in folgender Tiefe (horizontal unter dem Gipfel) lagen: N 1,30 O 0,93 S 1,30 W 1,63 mit der Unterseite auf dem natürlichen Boden. 2. Ein zweiter Kranz von 10,60 m Durchmesser, etwas höher, mit der Unterseite tief N 1,23 O 0,87 W 1,23 (mit der Oberseite ca. 0,25 höher), also mit der Unterseite 7—13 cm über der Oberseite des ersten Kranzes, im Ganzen

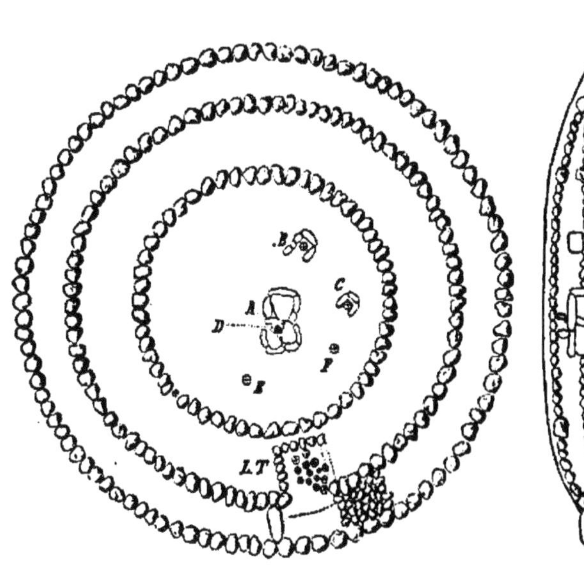

Figur 4.

ca. 40 cm höher. Man hatte hier also wohl schon einen kleinen Erdhügel aufgeschüttet, denn so hoch steigt der natürliche Boden nicht auf diese kurze Strecke, auch lag der Boden der centralen Kiste ziemlich im Niveau des äusseren Kranzes. Der Raum zwischen beiden Kränzen war steinfrei, nur neben der Stelle LT des Grundrisses war er durch ein viereckiges Pflaster kleiner Steine von ca. 1,60 m Breite überbrückt. Circa 1,50 m westlich davon verband beide Kränze ein sehr grosser hervorragender Stein von 1,15 m Länge, 0,35 m Dicke, der senkrecht tief in den Boden gekeilt war. Von Kranz 2 zog sich in sanfter Wölbung ein Grundpflaster kleiner Steine über den Boden des Hügels, in der Mitte ca. 85 tief, also jedenfalls über einem aufgeschütteten Erdhügel, zumal die centrale Kiste noch 60 cm tiefer herabsteigt. Ferner stieg vom zweiten Kranze eine obere (Deck-) Steinschicht empor, sich über den ganzen Hügel erstreckend, welche ihrerseits von 10—20 cm Erde bedeckt war, meist einfach, oft fanden sich doch aber mehrere Steine übereinander, man hat den Erdhügel wohl dicht mit Steinen belegt und dann nochmals beschüttet. Zwischen beiden Steinschichten lag ein Erdkern. 3. Weiter nach innen waren an Stelle der centralen Mauer der Birkenhöfer Hügel als innere Abgrenzung 2 übereinanderliegende Steinkränze von etwas verschiedenem Durchmesser zu erkennen, die sich aus den Boden- und Decksteinen deutlich hervorhoben, der untere von 7,40, der obere von 6,60 Durchmesser, ca. 40 cm höher als der untere. Der obere an der Oberseite tief N 0,45 O 0,40 S 0,45 W 0,57. Bis zu diesem oberen Kranze stieg die Steindecke sehr stark, von hier nach der Mitte nur noch schwach, ca. 0,20, so dass der Hügel eine steilere Böschung und eine sehr flache Kuppe von 6,5 m Durchmesser hatte, was im Felde noch viel mehr hervortrat als bei dem kleinen Massstabe des Profilplanes. Innerhalb dieser Mauer (oder dieses Doppelkranzes) fanden sich 3 Steinkisten und 4 einzelstehende mit Steinen umstellte Aschen-Urnen.

Kiste A. Von der Mitte des Hügels nach Süden verlaufend, also ein wenig excentrisch. Sie bestand aus 2 aneinander gebauten Kisten a und b. Die nördliche a war jedenfalls die ursprüngliche, da sie regelmässiger und centraler ist; b ist später angebaut, daher ist der Süd-Träger von a zugleich ein Nord-Träger von b. Die bis 1,30—1,40 herabsteigenden Träger (bis auf die natürliche Bodenoberfläche) sind innen ziemlich flache, aussen unregelmässige Granitfindlinge von 50—60 cm Höhe, die nach oben manchmal spitz zulaufen, auch nicht immer in demselben Niveau enden, die aber mit kleinen Steinen in den klaffenden Fugen gut verzwickt und auch nach Füllung der Kiste oben belegt sind, so dass die Decksteine doch ein genügendes Widerlager fanden. Kiste a hatte an 3 Seiten einen, an der vierten 2 Träger, von denen einer ein ausgehöhlter Mahlstein, ebenso wie der oberseits flache Deckstein. Kiste b hatte ausser dem Grenzträger noch 4 eigene und 2 Decksteine, deren Oberfläche 60 cm tief lag. Kiste a hatte einen inneren Raum von ca. 45×40 cm, b von ca. 70×60 (alle diese Maasse sind wegen der unregelmässigen Gestalt der Kisten und Träger nur annähernd).

Kiste Aa enthielt eine grosse Aschen-Urne (Inventar 4370 Tfl. II 8), bedeckt mit einem merkwürdigerweise verkehrt, d. h. mit der hohlen Seite nach oben liegenden Deckel (welcher umgekehrt gezeichnet ist um die convexe Seite sichtbar zu machen). Sie stand auf einer Steinfliese und da alle Urnen dieses Hügels ziemlich weich und zersprungen waren, bröckelte der Boden beim Heben stark ab; sein Maass konnte daher nur annähernd genommen werden. Die Urne hatte aber eine Stehfläche und ist im Uebrigen richtig zusammengesetzt worden. Da ich erst im Verlaufe dieser Hügelgrabung die ersten unvollkommenen Versuche mit Gyps machte, gelang es nur einen Theil der sehr mürben und zerbröckelten, zum Theil fest auf Fliesen stehenden Urnen zu retten und zusammenzusetzen, während sich dies bei vielen andern, zumal den frei zwischen Steinen stehenden nicht mehr als möglich erwies. Zwischen den Knochen in der Urne fand sich das bearbeitete Bernsteinstück Tfl. IV 9 Inventar 4395.

In Kiste b standen 2 Aschen-Urnen und ein Beigefäss auf Fliesen. Auf Urne 1 (Tfl. II 10 No. 4371) lag ein durchlochter Deckel wieder verkehrt, mit der hohlen Seite nach oben, auf Urne 2 ein schalenförmiger Deckel mit Henkel (Tfl. III Fig. 1 No. 4372) in gewöhnlicher Weise. Die Urne 2 selbst und das Beigefäss sind nicht erhalten. Neben Urne 1 lag die Brozenadel Tfl. IV Fig. 10 No. 4936, eine „Schwanenhalsnadel" (siehe unten).

Kiste B. 1,5 m nördlich von A stand auf dem Bodenpflaster eine kleine Kiste von Nordost nach Südwest orientirt (sie wurde, wie dies bei solchen kleinen Kisten leicht vorkommen kann, erst erkannt, nachdem schon einige Steine entfernt waren, konnte also nicht mehr vollständig gezeichnet werden). An 2 Seiten hatte sie je 1, an einer 3 Träger, ihr innerer Raum betrug 45×40, die Höhe ca. 30, die Unterkanten lagen 80 cm tief. Darin stand eine Aschen-Urne (No. 4374 Tfl. III Fig. 2) ohne Deckel und ein Beigefäss (No. 4375 Tfl. II a), zwischen ihnen eine Bronzenadel mit umgebogenem Halse (No. 4397 Tfl. IV 11) an die Aschen-Urne geschmiegt.

Kiste C. 1,5 m östlich von A, auf dem Bodenpflaster. 0,83 tief, eine kleine Kiste von 4 Trägern 30—40 cm hoch und breit, wovon einer eine 5 cm dicke Sandsteinplatte, was hier nicht häufig vorkommt (der Deckstein war unbemerkt entfernt). Darin stand auf einer Fliese eine — nicht erhaltene — Aschen-Urne. Ausserdem finden sich an noch 3 Stellen innerhalb der Mauer Aschen-Urnen ohne Kisten, die zum Theil so zerdrückt waren, dass sie nicht mehr restaurirt werden konnten.

Urne D. Am Westrande der Kiste A zwischen beiden Abtheilungen gerade auf der Decke 63 cm tief (nicht erhalten).

Urne E. Circa 1 m fast südlich von A auf dem Bodenpflaster 85 cm tief (d. h. mit dem Boden). In ihr lagen 5 rohe, unbearbeitete Stücke Bernstein.

Urne F (4379). 1 m östlich der Südost-Ecke von A, auf dem Bodenpflaster, 83 cm tief, eine Aschen-Urne mit Deckel, von der nur der untere Theil erhalten ist, der Deckel aber vollständig ergänzt werden konnte.

Urne G. Am oberen Kranze der Mauer zwischen Steinen der Deckschicht, südöstlich von der Mitte, 85 cm tief, eine Aschen-Urne (nicht erhalten).

Der Bau des Hügels ist also so aufzufassen, dass man zuerst die Kiste Aa auf dem natürlichen Boden erbaute, nachher daran Ab. Darnach schüttete man einen flachen Erdhügel auf und bedeckte ihn mit dem unteren Pflaster, das sich bis gegen 60 cm an der Kiste über dem Boden erhob. Ob dann schon alle 3 Kränze gleichzeitig gelegt wurden, lässt sich nur schwer entscheiden. Die Kisten auf dem Grundpflaster sind jedenfalls jünger und noch jünger müssen die isolirten Urnen sein, besonders G zwischen den Steinen der Mauer, welche für die übrigen doch eine einschliessende Bedeutung hatte.

Stelle L. T. Am Südende des Hügels, östlich von der südnördlichen Linie fand sich eine merkwürdige Stelle, ein Nachbegräbniss ganz verschiedener Natur, welches hier den ursprünglichen Bau des Hügels ersichtlich gestört hatte. Das Grundpflaster erstreckte sich ungestört noch ca. 30 cm bis ausserhalb des dritten Kranzes (Mauer), senkte sich dann plötzlich um ca. eines Steines Höhe und zog sich im Osten 1,40 tief, im Westen ca. 1,25, als Pflaster kleiner Steine ca. 2 m lang nach aussen, 1,40 breit mit leichter Abweichung nach Osten. Es war nach Norden durch den Abfall des Grundpflasters begrenzt, nach Westen anfangs durch einen ähnlichen Abfall, der nachher in eine Reihe grösserer Steine auslief, welche in dem erwähnten sehr grossen von 120 cm Länge, 40 Dicke, 70—80 Höhe endete. Letzterer machte anfangs den Eindruck eines irgendwoher herabgewälzten Denksteines, war aber völlig festgekeilt, schien ganz ungerührt und steht zu der ganzen Anlage doch wohl in Beziehung. Oestlich war ein ähnlicher Abfall (dem aber nicht solche Beachtung geschenkt wurde, da man beim Abräumen von dieser Seite erst auf die Stelle stiess). Nach Süden erstreckte sich das Pflaster ein wenig über die Zone des zweiten Kranzes, der auf dieser Stelle fehlte. Zwischen Kranz I und II fand sich dann im Osten dieser Stelle die erwähnte Steinbrücke, die mit der Anlage wohl in Verbindung steht. Vielleicht sind es die dem Hügel entnommenen, wieder regelmässig gelegten Steine, so dass zwischen ihnen und dem grossen Steine ein Zugang zu diesem Pflaster entstände. — Doch das sind nur Vermuthungen. Innerhalb des Ringes des zweiten Kranzes und dem Nordrande des Pflasters standen auf einem Raume von 1 × 0,90 m auf der Ostseite des Pflasters eine Menge Urnen dicht aneinander, unten noch meist von kleinen Steinen umstellt und gestützt. Durch diese und die Last der darüber liegenden waren sie dermassen zerdrückt, umgeworfen, auseinandergerissen und ineinandergeschoben, dass sie sich nur sehr fragmentarisch heben liessen. Eine solche Sachlage ist die schlimmste und könnte man dabei auch mit Gypsverband wenig anfangen, höchstens einige grössere Fragmente retten; es bleibt nichts übrig, als die Scherben einzeln mühsam bloss zu legen und zwischen den Steinen herauszuziehen, wobei, wenn sie feucht und mürbe sind (wie im vorliegenden Falle), natürlich viel zerbröckelt. Genau liess sich die Zahl der Urnen nicht feststellen, es waren ca. 14 Scherbenstellen, die aber zum Theil continuirlich in einander übergingen. Es gelang davon 5 grössere und 2 kleinere Urnen (Beigefässe) zusammen zu setzen (und zu ergänzen), die in ihrer restaurirten Gestalt in durchaus richtigen Verhältnissen (Tfl. III 4—10) gezeichnet sind. Da diese Urnen, sowie die dazwischen gefundenen Metallgegenstände eine vollständig gesonderte Stellung den übrigen Gräbern des Hügels gegenüber einnehmen, sollen sie im Zusammenhange erst nach Besprechung der anderen Funde beider Hügel behandelt werden. Wahrscheinlich nicht damit in Zusammenhang steht ein östlich von dieser Stelle auf dem Pflaster gefundenes Bernsteinstück (4405, Fig. 5 im Text) und ein kleines Bronzestück, die wohl älteren Gräbern des Hügels zuzurechnen sind.

Hügel II.

(Am 25. und 26. October 1882 mit 8 Arbeitern von O. Tischler ausgegraben.)

Der Hügel lag unmittelbar südlich an I anstossend, am Abhange der Höhe, deren Kuppe dieser bedeckte, war daher schief angelegt, so dass die Erddecke nach

Norden fast horizontal verlief, nach Süden steil abfiel. Ihn umgab ein Kranz grosser Steine von 9 m Durchmesser in sehr wechselndem Niveau, tief im Norden 0,30, Osten 0,80, Süden 1,35, Westen 0,90, so dass man für die mittlere Höhe des Hügels ungefähr 1 m annehmen kann. Ein continuirlicher äusserer Kranz konnte nicht constatirt werden, nur einige isolirte Steine, die vielleicht einem Kranz von 11,20 Durchmesser angehört haben, von denen jedenfalls schon viele fortgenommen waren. Der Hügel war mit einer Steindecke überwölbt, die stellenweise doppelt, besonders in der Mitte. Ein Bodenpflaster existirte nicht. Im Uebrigen war er aus sandigen Lehm aufgeschüttet. Innerhalb des Kranzes fanden sich 2 Steinkisten.

Kiste A. Wenig nördlich vom Centrum (ihre Mitte Norden 0,90, Westen 0,20) die centrale Kiste A, im Osten und Süden von je 1 Träger, Norden und Westen von je 2 platten Trägern gebildet — nur 2 davon ausgehöhlte Mahlsteine, alle 50—60 cm hoch. Auf ihren inneren Kanten ruhte der Deckstein 60×40 cm, ca. 20 cm dick, auf den oberen Flächen der Träger noch kleinere platte Steine; so dass die ganze Decke ziemlich flach war. Die Fugen waren wieder alle gut verzwickt und Steine als Streben herumgesetzt. Die Decke der Kiste lag 0,45 tief, der Boden 1,05, der innere Erdwürfel hatte 60×40 cm Fläche, 40 Höhe. In der Kiste standen 2 Aschen-Urnen mit Deckel, unmittelbar aneinanderstossend, No. 1 Tfl. II Fig. 7 Inventar 4409, No. 2 Tfl. II Fig. 5 Inventar 4410, zwischen ihnen die Bronzenadel, Tfl. IV Fig. 11 Inventar 4414, die defect erhalten ist. Bodenfliesen waren nicht vorhanden. Im Nordwesten, dicht an der Kiste, erstreckte sich eine schwarze Brandschicht von 1 m Länge, 0,60 Breite, 5 cm Dicke, aus Aschen und Kohlen bestehend, in halber Höhe der Kiste. Vielleicht war dies die ursprüngliche Brandstelle, in welche die Kiste noch etwas eingetieft ist.

Kiste B. Im südlichen Theile des Hügels lag eine zweite ziemlich grosse Kiste B (die Nordwest-Ecke O 0,20 S 1,60), die aber schon erbrochen und theilweise gestört war, doch wohl nur beim Bäume roden. Es fehlten die Decksteine und ein Theil der Träger. Nördlich stand 1 Träger, im Westen 2; östlich 1, der zweite fehlte. Die Träger waren 60—70 cm breit, 70—80 hoch, 25—35 dick. Ihre obere Fläche lag 45 tief, die untere 1,15—1,20 (der Boden fällt ja hier stark). Der Inhalt war auch ziemlich geplündert. Es fand sich aber noch eine intacte Aschen-Urne (No. 4411 Tfl. II Fig. 6), über welcher ein Bruchstück einer sehr dicken Urne (4412) mit der hohlen Seite nach oben lag, scheinbar wie eine Art Deckel. Es ist dies aber jedenfalls nur ein Fragment einer anderen zertrümmerten Urne dieser Kiste (II B 2), welches man beim Wühlen in derselben hier heraufgelegt hatte, glücklicherweise jene Urne verschonend. Daneben fand sich der untere Theil einer anderen Aschen-Urne (B 3 4413), deren oberer Theil früher zerstört war, und in einer anderen Ecke einige Knochen und Scherben. Die Kiste hat einst jedenfalls noch mehr Urnen enthalten.

Thongefässe.

Die Dimensionen der Thongefässe beider Hügel (mit Ausnahme der auf dem Pflaster L. T. gefundenen) ergeben sich aus folgender Tabelle:

	Do	Dw	Dr	Hw	Hr	(H)	(r)	(b)	(Hw)	Rand-Dicke	Bemerkungen.
										mm	
Aschen-Urne I Aa (4370) Tfl. II8	?	32,8	24,9	15	ca. 27	82	76	?	55	7—8	Rand ausgebröckelt, Boden do.
„ I Ab1 (4371) Tfl. II10	ca. 14	30,2	22	12—13	26,5 über	88 über	73	46?	46—49 unter	7—8	2 Henkel.
„ I B (4374) Tfl. III2	8,8	21,5	15?	10	20	93	70	41	50	7	am Rand fehlte viel, 2 Henkel.
„ II A1 (4409) Tfl. II7	0	27,6	15	7	22,7	82	54	0	31	7	
„ II A2 (4410) Tfl. II5	0	23,5	13,7	ca. 7	19,3	82	59	0	36	7	
„ II B1 (4411) Tfl. II6	0	22	16,5	14	19,3	88	75	0	73	7	
Deckel zu I Aa Tfl. II8a	8,5		30		14	46		28		8	
„ „ I Ab1 Tfl. II10a	7		27,8		9,4	34		25		8	mit Loch.
„ „ I Ab2 (4372) Tfl. III1	7		20		7	35		35			mit Henkel.
Beigefäss I B (4375) Tfl. II9	5,5	13	10	5—6	13	100	77	42	40—46	4	

Hiernach zerfallen die erhaltenen Aschen-Urnen (wie es die Abbildungen noch deutlicher zeigen) in zwei verschiedene Kategorien, mit Stehfläche (I A, I Ab 1, I B) und ohne Stehfläche mit gerundetem Boden (II A 1, 2. II B).

1. Die Urnen mit Stehfläche ähnen den Birkenhöfer in Form und Dimensionen. Die Höhe ist annähernd dieselbe (H) = 82—93 (Bi 85—96) der sonst geschweifte Hals im Allgemeinen etwas weiter, (h) = 70—77 (Bi 63—70), die Weite liegt bei I Aa etwas höher, sonst auch immer unter der Mitte. Der Boden ist eine kleine Fläche, aber doch vorhanden, er liess sich nicht genau messen, da er bei Aa, b ausgebröckelt, aber doch in seinem Absatz zu erkennen war, die Zeichnung ist nach der übrigen Form der Urne richtig. Der Theil oberhalb der Weite (wir sagen einfach obere Theil) ist geglättet, der untere absichtlich rauh gemacht. Bei I B (Tfl. III 2) begann die Rauhung schon oberhalb der Weite und verschwand wieder unten dicht oberhalb des Bodens. Aa hatte keine Henkel, die anderen beiden ein Paar kleine oberhalb der Weite in gewöhnlicher Weise. Ausserdem sind noch die unteren Partieen von 2 anderen Urnen erhalten, mit einigen Stücken des Halses, welche sich nicht mehr vollständig wieder herstellen liessen, aber doch die grosse Aehnlichkeit mit den oben beschriebenen zeigten: Urne I F (4379) hat einen ebenen Boden von 8,5 Durchmesser und ist auch an der Unterseite geglättet. Urne II B 3 (4413) hat einen etwas rundlichen, aber deutlich abgesetzten Boden von 8,5 Durchmesser und zeigt auch, soweit erhalten, die Form dieser Klasse.

2. Einen ganz anderen Typus haben die drei anderen Urnen. II A 1, 2 haben einen ziemlich platten, sehr wenig gewölbten Boden, sind aber durchaus ohne Stehfläche oder irgend einen Absatz gegen den Bauch hin, II B (Tfl. II 6) hat einen unten eiförmig gerundeten Bauch. Die ersten beiden haben einen engen Hals wie die entsprechenden Birkenhöfer, (r) = 54—59 (Bi 53—54), nur II B einen sehr weiten (74). Die Weite liegt bei den ersten tief, bei B ungewöhnlich hoch. A 1 besitzt einen langen ziemlich characterisirten Hals, der bei A 2 fehlt. A 1, 2 sind vollständig sauber geglättet, B ist bis oben hin sehr rauh, nur am obersten Halse ein wenig geglättet und von röthlich-braunem Thone. Das Stück Scherbe (No. 4412), das über B lag, stammte allem Anschein nach

ebenfalls von einer sehr dickwandigen Urne ohne Stehfläche her und seine Dicke steigerte sich von 11—20 mm — in Birkenhof war der Boden dieser Thongefässe ebenfalls sehr dick.

Beide Klassen von Urnen sind besonders noch durch ihre Deckel verschieden.

Die Urnen der ersten Kategorie hatten übergreifende oder Schalen-Deckel, von denen 3 erhalten sind, I Aa (Tfl. II 8a), I Ab 1 (Tfl. II 10a) und Ab 2 (Tfl. III 1, die Urne nicht erhalten). Sie haben ähnliche Proportionen wie die Birkenhöfer, nur der erste ist etwas höher. Der zu I Ab 2 gehörige ist unterhalb des Randes (wegen der Terminologie bei der Beschreibung umgekehrt gedacht) etwas eingezogen und bildet dann eine Kante, von der ab er sich in gewöhnlicher Weise wölbt, zwischen welcher und dem unteren Rande ein kleiner Henkel sitzt. Alle 3 haben flache Böden [(b) = 25—35], nur I Ab 1 darin ein Loch von ca. 2 cm Durchmesser. I Aa (Tfl. II 8) ist durch 4 nicht besonders genaue Reihen von Fingereindrücken verziert. Auffallend war es, dass bei Aa und Ab 1 die Deckel umgekehrt mit der hohlen Seite nach oben lagen, ein durchaus ungewöhnlicher Fall

Vollständig verschieden sind die Deckel bei den Urnen ohne Stehfläche II A 1 (II Fig. 7a) II A 2 (II Fig 5a) denen sich I F (Tfl. III 3) anschliesst, welcher allerdings einer nur zum Theil erhaltenen Urne mit Stehfläche zugehört hat. Diese sind oben gewölbt oder flach und gehen auf der Unterseite in einen etwas zurücktretenden cylindrischen Theil über, welcher in das Innere der Urne hineinpasst und sie stöpselartig verschliesst. Diese Deckel sollen daher Stöpseldeckel heissen, der obere Theil der Kopf, der untere der Cylinder.*) Der Kopf hat einen über den Cylinder mehr oder weniger hervorragenden Rand, hinter dem er bei A 1, 2 einsinkt, um sich dann flach schalenartig zu wölben, während er bei B seiner ganzen Ausdehnung nach eben verläuft. Seine untere Wand ist der oberen entsprechend, geht daher bei gewölbten Deckeln auch gewölbt in den Cylinder über, bei plattem Kopf in scharfem Winkel. Der untere Rand des Cylinders ist wie dieser selbst meist nicht besonders sauber und gleichmässig gearbeitet. Die Dimensionen dieser 3 Deckel sind: II A 1 (II Fig. 7a): Durchmesser des Kopfes 17,7, des Cylinderrandes 13, Höhe des Cylinders von der Unterseite an 2,2—3, Loch 2 mm. Bei II A 2 (II Fig. 5) dieselben Zahlen 14, 11,5—11,8, 3,5—4. Bei I F (III Fig. 5) Durchmesser des Kopfes 16, des Cylinders 14, Cylinderhöhe von unten 2,7 von der Oberseite an. Alle 3 Deckel haben ein Loch in der Mitte.

Die Stöpseldeckel kommen hier und bei den Urnen des Provinzial-Museums aus ostpreussischen Hügeln, überwiegend bei Urnen ohne Stehfläche vor, nur die Urne I F hat eine deutliche Stehfläche und den Formcharacter dieser Urnen, bildet immerhin eine Ausnahme, ist aber schon ein Aussenbegräbniss, also jedenfalls jünger wie die centralen Urnen mit Schalendeckeln. Ferner ist Hügel II gewiss

---

*) Ich glaube die Bezeichnung Stöpseldeckel bezeichnet das Characteristische dieser Form in allen ihren Varianten (so z. B. Tfl. III 3) mehr als die bisherige Benennung „Mützendeckel“. Virchow, der hauptsächlich auf diese interessante Form aufmerksam gemacht hat, spricht bereits von „der stöpselartigen Verlängerung“. Verhandl. d. Berliner Gesellschaft für Anthropologie 1874 p. 113.

jünger als I, dem er erst angebaut wurde als dieser keine Urnen mehr aufnahm, seine Urnen sind also auch jünger. Diese haben aber überwiegend keine Stehfläche jedoch Stöpseldeckel, nur bei II B 3 findet sich noch eine Stehfläche. Sehr weit werden die Hügel zeitlich nicht auseinanderliegen, wie die Metallbeigaben lehren, aber für diese Hügel und noch für andere steht es fest dass die Urnen ohne Stehfläche und die Stöpseldeckel erst später auftreten als die mit Stehfläche und Schalendeckel, welche dann immerhin noch nicht ausser Gebrauch kamen.

Von Beigefässen ist nur eines erhalten (No. 4375) in Kiste B (Tfl. II 9), dasselbe ähnt in seiner Form den Aschen-Urnen, ist nur etwas höher. Oberhalb der Weite gehen 2 horizontale Linien herum, zwischen denen Gruppen von je 3 alternirend schrägen Linien herabsteigen, nicht sehr exact im weichen Thon gezogen, da sie die anderen Linien theilweise durchschneiden. Henkelkrüge wie in Birkenhof fanden sich hier nicht.

Die Bronzebeigaben der älteren Gräber.

In Kiste I B lag eine Bronzenadel mit umgebogenem Halse (Tfl. IV 11), der Birkenhöfer nahe verwandt. Sie ist gestreckt über 20 cm lang (die äusserste Spitze fehlt), der gebogene Hals 6,5; am Kopf 4,5 mm, unten 3 dick. Unter dem kegelförmigen Kopfe hat sie 4 durch Einschnürungen getrennte Reifen.

Die Nadeln Tfl. IV Fig. 10 und 11 aus Kiste I Ab und II A haben einen anderen Character. Der Draht biegt sich unter dem Kopfe in Form einer vollen Welle. Wenn der Draht eine Biegung in Form einer halben Welle erleidet, so dass er nach dieser einmaligen Einbiegung in die vorige Richtung zurücktritt (wie bei den La Tène-Nadeln in einem grossen Theile Norddeutschland's, cf. Undset l. c. Tfl. XXVI 16—19 u. a. m.) möge dies heissen: Nadeln mit einfacher Einbiegung. Bei der vorliegenden in Form einer vollen Welle gekrümmten Nadel macht der Draht 2 Einbiegungen; diese Form kann man mit einem der archäologi-Terminologie nicht fremden Ausdruck als Schwanenhalsnadel bezeichnen. Der Kopf der Nadel IV Fig. 10 ist kegelförmig, den Hals schmückt noch ein kleiner Reif, bei IV 12 war er auch kegelförmig, zerfiel aber. Die kegelförmigen Köpfe sind bei den ostpreussischen Nadeln sehr häufig, es kommen aber auch andere Formen vor wie Halbkugeln, rundliche und oft auch recht reich profilirte Endknöpfe, welche bei der Beschreibung anderer Grabhügel in der nächsten Abhandlung besprochen und abgebildet werden sollen.

Diese Schwanenhalsnadeln haben ihre Hauptverbreitung im nordöstlichen Deutschland. Zahlreich kommen sie in den ostpreussischen Hügelgräbern des Samlands vor, in den westpreussischen Steinkistengräbern mit Gesichts-Urnen und gehen dann durch Pommern bis nach Mecklenburg hinein. In Dänemark sind sie schon seltener, in Schweden und in Norwegen ist je 1 gefunden. Ausserordentlich häufig sind sie in den Flachgräberfeldern Posens und Schlesiens und ziehen sich in die Mark und Lausitz hinein. Die westlichsten Stücke in Mitteldeutschland dürften eine Nadel von Aderstedt bei Bernburg (Museum Bernburg, Album der Berliner Ausstellung 1880 Section IV 7) und eine Rollennadel mit Schwanenhals von Passmarke bei Schlieben (ibid Section VI Tfl. 1, Provinzial-Museum Halle) sein; sonstige habe ich in den Museen zu Halle und Jena nicht gefunden. Vollständig fehlen sie dann in Böhmen, wo es mir weder in den Sammlungen noch durch Nachfrage gelang eine zu entdecken. Sie fehlen dann, wie es scheint auch fernerhin in Oesterreich und in ganz Ungarn. Zu Hallstadt findet sich nur 1 Nadel mit ähnlicher doppelter Biegung, die in einen Spiralkopf übergeht. Hingegen treten sie wieder in Baiern und Würtemberg auf und finden sich noch in der Franche Comté in den Grabhügeln des Plateau von Alaise, sind aus diesen Gegenden aber nicht in solchen Massen vorhanden wie in den Sammlungen Ost-Deutschlands, wo doch wohl ihre Hauptheimath ist.*) Merkwürdig, dass sie gerade an so diagonal entgegengesetzten Gebieten vorkommen, zwischen denen ich den vermittelnden Uebergang vorläufig noch nicht nachweisen kann; der einzige Verbindungsweg scheint durch Thüringen nach Baiern zu gehen.

Was nun die Zeitstellung**) dieser Nadeln betrifft, so soll dieselbe erst in einer späteren Abhandlung an der Hand eines vollständigen Gesammtmaterials genauer begründet werden. Wir können daher hier nur die Resultate annähernd vorweg nehmen. Die Dauer der Nadelform wird immer keine ganz kurze sein, was wir auch aus den vorliegenden Hügelgräbern entnehmen. Die Veränderung der Thongefässformen in den Warschker Hügeln lässt doch auf eine etwas längere Dauer derselben schliessen, während die Nadelform dieselbe bleibt; ferner ist es wohl wahrscheinlich, dass die Eisennadeln die jüngsten sein werden. Am weitesten zeitlich zurück kann man die Nadeln in den Posenschen Flachgräberfeldern verfolgen, wo bereits Objecte aus einer älteren Zeit der Hallstädter Periode auftreten (Schwerter, Eisencelte, Bronzerasirmesser etc.), während sie bei den westpreussischen Gesichts-Urnen an das Ende dieser Periode, in dem Uebergang zur La Tène-Periode fallen. Ueberall im Norden gehören sie der jüngsten Bronzezeit an, welche ungefähr mit dem Schlusse der Hallstädter Periode gleichaltrig sein muss, und auch die Grabhügel der Franche Comté fallen in ganz dieselbe Zeit. Wir kommen demnach überall ungefähr auf das 5. Jahrhundert v. Chr., vielleicht den Anfang des 4.

Die Nadeln mit umgebogenem Halse und kegelförmigem Kopfe wie Tfl. IV 1, 11 haben nicht einen gleich grossen Verbreitungsbezirk, sondern scheinen in dieser Form völlig auf Ostpreussen beschränkt zu sein. Bereits in Westpreussen sind keine mehr gefunden, ebensowenig in dem weiteren Bezirk der Schwanenhalsnadeln. In der Mark sind zu derselben Periode einige Nadeln mit rundlichem Kopfe

*) Chantre. Premier age du fer Pl. 34 8, 38 8, 9. Ueber die Funde in Südwestdeutschland: Tröltsch, Fundstatistik der vorrömischen Metallzeit No. 76a. Speciell in Mecklenburg: Beltz, Das Ende der Bronzezeit in Mecklenburg (Mecklenb. Jahrbücher 51). Ueber die Funde in Ostdeutschland und Scandinavien finden sich die nöthigen Nachweise bei Undset, die Nadeln treten in Posen und Schlesien noch viel massenhafter auf als es nach der hier gegebenen Darstellung scheinen könnte.

**) Betreffs der Gliederung der urgeschichtlichen Entwicklung v. Chr., die an dieser Stelle noch nicht näher begründet werden soll, verweise ich vorläufig besonders auf das bahnbrechende Werk von Undset. „Das erste Auftreten des Eisens in Nordeuropa," zumal auf die Einleitung, und auf eine von mir in der Westdeutschen Zeitschrift V (1886) p. 169—199 gegebene Besprechung der Werke von Wagner, und Faudel und Bleicher über Gräber Baden's und des Elsass, wo ich die Gliederung für Südwestdeutschland näher zu begründen gesucht habe.

gefunden, welche sich im oberen Theile etwas biegen, aber nicht mit so scharfem Knick (Rauschendorf im Märkischen Museum, Müschen im Museum für Völkerkunde). Im Hauptgebiet der Nordischen Bronzecultur, Mecklenburg und Skandinavien finden sich eine Menge Nadeln, deren Hals sich nicht weit vom Kopfe scharf umbiegt; diese tragen dann als Kopf eine durch eine Reihe erhöhter concentrischer Kreise gerippte Scheibe (wie Montelius Ant. suéd. 217) oder einen rundlichen Kopf der äquatorial mit 4 im Kreuz stehenden Knöpfchen und einem an der Spitze besetzt ist (ibid. Fig. 215), auch sogar einen Menschenkopf (Madsen: Bronsealderen I Tfl. 26 9). Vielfach sind die Schafte dieser Nadeln mit alternirend schrägen Strichgruppen verziert, dem characteristischen Ornament der Zeit. Es giebt allerdings eine ziemlich weit verbreitete Form von Nadeln mit umgebogenem Halse, die an der Stelle der Biegung eine Oese haben, wie Undset X Fig. 11, welche sich von Schlesien durch Posen und die Mark bis nach Pommern erstrecken. In Ostpreussen sind sie (identisch mit der abgebildeten von Polkwitz-Schlesien) jetzt in Grabhügeln der älteren Bronzezeit (Peccatel-Periode) zu Rantau, Kreis Fischhausen, und Slaszen, Kreis Memel, in grösserer Menge gefunden als wohl in ganz Schlesien. Sie sind demnach viel älter und können mit den abgebildeten IV 1, 11 in gar keine Beziehung gebracht werden. Wenn wir also in dem nördlichen Gebiete in derselben Periode auch entfernte Analogien für die Art der Biegung finden, stehen die ostpreussischen Nadeln doch isolirt da und sind als lokale Modificationen des weit verbreiteten Typus der Schwanenhalsnadeln aufzufassen.

Was nun die Bedeutung dieser Nadeln betrifft, so ist sie schwer genau festzustellen, weil die Gräber dieser Periode sämmtlich Brandgräber sind. Wahrscheinlich sind es nicht Haar- sondern Gewandnadeln, wofür besonders die riesige Entwicklung mancher scandinavischen Formen spricht. Die Umbiegung würde dann dazu dienen, dass die Falte der beiden übereinandergelegten Gewänder sich fester anschmiegt, und dass die Nadel sich weniger leicht auszieht, was besonders durch die doppelte Biegung erzielt wird. Daher spielen die Nadeln auch gerade in den zur Zeit fibellosen Ländern des östlichen Deutschlands eine solche Rolle; Ost- und Westpreussen haben gar keine, Posen einige Fibeln von ungarischer Form und 2 altitalische, welche wohl noch älter als diese Nadeln sind, geliefert. Demnach wären es also wahrscheinlich Gewandnadeln.

Bernsteinschmuck.

Roher Bernstein fand sich hier, wie häufig in diesen Hügeln, in der Aschen-Urne E des Hügels I 5 Stücke.

In Hügel I Urne Aa lag das bearbeitete Stück Tfl. I Fig. 9 (4395). Dasselbe ist nicht ganz regelmässig viereckig ca. 38 mm lang, 20 breit, in der Mitte ca. 8 mm dick, ziemlich roh gearbeitet, ein natürliches Stück, dem nur noch ein wenig nachgeholfen ist. Er hat jetzt eine röthliche, aussen matt bräunliche Verwitterungsrinde und ist innen jedenfalls hell klar. Das Loch von ca. 4 mm ist von 2 Seiten eingebohrt, aber gut cylindrisch mit einem kleinen Absatz am Zusammenstoss beider Cylinder. Oben ist es von der durchgezogenen Schnur etwas ausgescheuert, wie in der Zeichnung ersichtlich.

Figur 5.

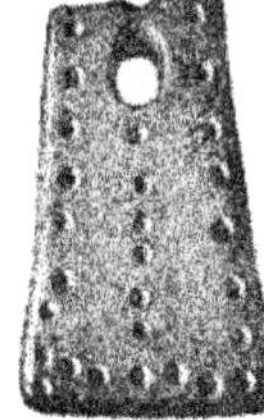

Figur 6.

Ein zweites Stück (anbei Fig. 5) No. 4405 lag östlich von der Stelle L. T.; es lässt sich daher nicht ganz genau feststellen, ob es dazu gehört oder in die ältere Zeit fällt. Es ist kumstfarben mit dicker Rinde, ziemlich roh und sowohl in alter Zeit als jetzt beschädigt, so dass sich die Form nicht mehr genau constatiren lässt. Vielleicht war es auch einst länglich viereckig nach der Ausscheuerung zu schliessen, welche die Trageschnur über dem ovalen Loch hervorgebracht hat, was zugleich zeigt, dass dies wirklich ein Schmuckstück. Das ovale Loch von 8×5 mm Durchmesser war vielleicht ein ursprüngliches Astloch im Bernstein. Jetzt hat das Stück die mittleren Dimensionen 31 × 26, grösste Dicke 9 mm.

Anbei erfolgt zum Vergleich noch ein Hängestück Fig. 6 (No. 3448) aus einer Urne eines eben solchen Hügelgrabes von **Mollehnen**, Kreis Fischhausen (welches erst in späterer Abhandlung besprochen werden soll). Es ist trapezoidisch oben ,16 unten 29 mm breit, 37 lang, oben in der Mitte 6,5 am Rande 6; unten in der Mitte 5,5, am Rande 4,5 dick, sehr scharf geschnitten mit fast rechtwinkligen Kanten und beinahe ebenen Flächen, nur nach der Mitte ein wenig gewölbt. Das Loch ist genau cylindrisch, zeigt aber auch die Abnutzung. An der Oberkante findet sich der (in der Zeichnung sichtbare) Rest einer früheren Bohrung, in der das Stück einst durchgebrochen war. Es ist verziert mit Reihen von Gruben längs der Seiten- und unteren Kante und einer mittleren Reihe von der Oeffnung nach unten, also einigermassen ähnlich dem violinstegförmigen Stück von Hubnicken Tfl. IV 3. Die Löcher sind scharf eingedreht mit einem Bohrer mit schärferer Spitze, zeigen aber nur ganz feine Reifelung, so dass sie sich wie das ganze Stück der Technik noch durchaus von den in der Form analogen Stücken der Steinzeit unterscheiden.

Die Urnengruppe L. T. in Hügel I.

Von den ganz ungemein zerdrückten Urnen der Gruppe zwischen Kranz 2 und 3 des Hügels I gelang es leider nur eine kleine Zahl aus den einzelnen aufgelesenen Scherben zusammenzusetzen und zu ergänzen. Daher konnten die Maasse auch nicht immer mit genügender Genauigkeit genommen werden, doch entsprechen die in folgender Tabelle mitgetheilten Dimensionen ziemlich nahe der Wirklichkeit und sind die Formen auf Tfl. III durchaus richtig wiedergegeben.

Gruppe L. T.	Do	Dw	Dr	Hw	Hr	(H)	(r)	(b)	(Hw)	Dicke	
Aschen-Urne 1 (4381) Tfl. III6	10	17,5	14	9	14	80	80	58	64	6	
„ 2 (4382) Tfl. III8	10	26,5	14,5	11,7	19,3	73	55	38	60	6	Doppel-henkel.
„ 4 (4384) Tfl. III7	7	16	13	7,7	12,5	78	81	44	61	6	
„ 5 (4385) Tfl. III5	13	26	ca. 16	ca. 12	ca. 22	85	61	50	55	7	
„ 6 (4386) Tfl. III4	12,3	24,5	16	12	21,8	89	65	50	55	7	
Beigefäss 3 (4383) Tfl. III9	4,3	8,9	7,2	3,5	8	90	81	50	44	5	
„ 7 (4387) Tfl. III10	3,8	6,3	5,5	ca. 3	6,4	100	88	60	47	5	mit Henkel.

Bei den 5 Aschen-Urnen liegt die Weite über der Mitte [(Hw) 55—64) bei einigen sogar recht hoch. Der Rand ist verhältnissmässig enger als bei den früheren Urnen mit Stehfläche [(r) 55—65], nur bei den Urnen mit hoher Weite, also kurzem Obertheil (Urne 1, 4) ist er weiter [(r) ca. 80]. Die Umbiegung um die Weite geht in schärferer Kante, manchmal aber in sanfter Wölbung vor sich, ist aber immer eine entschiedene, und es geht dann die Wand schräge, nur sehr sanft geschweift nach oben, manchmal am Rande sich ein wenig ausweitend, manchal aber gerade abgeschnitten. Der Untertheil ist viel steiler als bei jenen Urnen, fast gerade oder wenig gebogen und bildet daher einen weniger stumpfen Winkel mit dem immer scharf abgesetzten, grösseren Boden [(b) 44—58]. Man kann diese Form daher annähernd mit 2 aufeinandergesetzten, abgestumpften Kegeln, die an der Basis in schärferer oder gerundeter Kante in einander übergehen, vergleichen, ein abgestumpfter Doppelkegel. Die Urnen sind aus einem dunkel graubraun gebrannten mit Steinchen durchsetztem Thon, meist aber aus einem Hellroth gebrannten, gebildet und dann mit einer jetzt graugelbbraunen gut polirten feineren Glätteschicht bedeckt, die meisten vollständig geglättet, nur bei No. 6 (Tfl. III4) am Untertheil von der Weite an gerauht ist.

Von Verzierungen sind zu erwähnen bei Urne 1 (Tfl. III6) 2 nebeneinanderstehende kleine Knöpfchen (horizontale Doppelknöpfe) an 4 Stellen der Weitenkante. Besonders schön verziert ist die Urne No. 2 (Tfl. III8). Sie hat zunächst einen Doppelhenkel entlang des oberen Kegels, der sich aber (wie der Vergleich mit dem defecten von Birkenhof (Tfl. I2) zeigt) wesentlich von den früheren unterscheidet. Er ist schmaler (2,2—2,3 breit) und dicker, mit kleineren Löchern, im ganzen mehr gradlinig, am oberen und unteren Ende, wie in der Mitte durch stark abgebogene Stege mit der Wand verbunden; auf dem Rücken hat er eine breite vertiefte Furche. Oberhalb der Weite geht eine hübsche Verzierung herum. Von einer tief und breit in den weichen Thon gezogenen Furche steigen Gruppen von 2 kurzen Strichen herab, mit denen etwas tiefer ziemlich an der Weite gleiche Gruppen abwechseln. Dieselben sind durch 1 oder 2 schräge Linien verbunden, entweder die einander zugewandten inneren Enden durch je 1 Linie, manchmal noch die oberen Enden der höheren Zone mit dem mittleren oberen der tieferen durch eine zweite.

Die kleinen Gefässe 3 (Tfl. III9) und 7 (Tfl. III10) sind jedenfalls nur Beigefässe. No. 3 trägt an der Weite 2 von oben nach unten zusammengedrückte, ziemlich spitze Hörnchen; um die Weite geht eine Reihe runder Grübchen herum, die an den Hörnchen bis zur Spitze emporsteigt, während auf jeder Seite der Hörnchen je 2 Gruben senkrecht hinabgehen. Ueber denselben zieht sich ein Kranz von mit der Spitze nach oben gerichteten Dreiecken herum, in deren jedem sich 2 gekreuzte, den Seiten parallele Linien befinden. No. 7 (Tfl. III 10) ist ein kleines Henkeltöpfchen mit sehr weiter Oeffnung, bei dem man aber den Verlauf des Henkels mit rundlichem Querschnitt nicht mehr genau bestimmen kann.

Beigaben.*)

Zwischen diesen Scherben, den zerdrückten Urnen entstammend, lagen einige unbedeutende Metallsachen, durch das Feuer entstellt, zum Theil beschmolzen oder mit Schlacken bedeckt, zerbrochen, kurz keine Cabinetsstücke. Und doch waren diese unansehnlichen, defecten Fibeln wichtiger als die prachtvollen, reichverzierten silbernen Fibeln, wie sie unsere Gräberfelder in so verschwenderischer Fülle liefern.

An einer Stelle lagen zusammen 2 Fibeln, 1 kleine Bronzeflachspirale und ein kleines Stück Bronzering.

Die Bronze-Fibel No. 4400, Tfl. IV 13 hat den Fuss verloren und ist am Bügel mit einem Gemisch von beschmolzener Bronze und Knochenresten überdeckt, aber doch lässt sich durch den Vergleich mit den bekannten Formen ihr Character vollständig enträthseln und danach sind die fehlenden Theile auf der Tafel punktirt mit voller Sicherheit angedeutet. Der Bügel geht am oberen Ende des Halses in die Spirale über (eingliedrig). Diese windet sich um eine Eisenaxe, macht 7 Windungen nach links, geht dann als obere Sehne über die Rolle nach rechts und kehrt in 8 Windungen zurück um in die Nadel überzugehen. Die Spirale ist ca. 33 mm lang, 6, 5 im Durchmesser. Nach unten macht der Hals ein scharfes Knie nach dem Fuss zu, der aber abgebrochen und nicht mehr vorhanden war. Der Fuss bog sich unten um und ging als Schlussstück in die Höhe, dieses fehlt aber auch, erst an dem erwähnten Knie kann man das oberste Ende wieder erkennen. Schliesslich war es ungefähr in der Mitte des Halses durch eine Hülse mit ihm verbunden, doch ist diese Stelle ganz mit beschmolzenen Bronzeklumpen bedeckt, lässt sich demnach im Detail nur undeutlich verfolgen, kann aber nach der ganzen Form der Fibel nicht anders gewesen sein. Ein annäherndes Bild dieser Verbindung giebt die gleichaltrige, wenn auch im Einzelnen etwas verschiedene Fibel Taf. IV, Fig. 16 von St. Lorenz.

Die zweite eiserne Fibel (4401) ist noch defecter, so dass auf eine Zeichnung verzichtet wurde. Die vorhandenen Stücke characterisiren sie aber vollständig: Die Eisenspirale mit oberer Sehne von ca. 11 mm Durchmesser von 4 Windungen, ein Theil des Bügelhalses mit dem verbundenen Schlussstück und der hintere Theil des Fusses mit der nach vorne weit geöffneten Nadelhalter-Rinne, also auch im Character von Tfl. IV, 16, nur länger: Eine La Tène-Fibel mit verbundenem Schlussstück.

---

*) In Bezug auf die Terminologie und weitere Gliederung der La Tène-Periode ist ausser den p. 162 citirten Werken zu vergleichen: Tischler: 1. Ueber Gliederung der La Tène-Periode, Correspondenzblatt der Deutschen Gesellschaft für Anthropologie. 1885, p. 157 ff. 2. Archäologische Studien aus Frankreich, Schriften der physikalisch-ökonomischen Gesellschaft. XXV. (1884) p. 18 ff. 3. Ein kurzer Bericht: Schrift. d. physikal.-ökonomischen Gesellschaft. XXIII. Sitzungsber. p. 18—23.

Das Bronzestück Tfl. IV, Fig. 14 (4402) ist eine kleine Flach-Spirale von 7,2 mm Durchmesser aus-vierkantigem Draht, im Feuer beschmolzen und unvollständig; die beiden in der Abbildung ersichtlichen Zäpfchen sind nur geschmolzene Bronzetröpfchen. Was sie bedeuten ist unklar. Endlich war an dieser Stelle noch ein kleines Stückchen eines dünnen Bronzedrahtes vorhanden.

An einer anderen Stelle fand sich ein Stückchen Bronzedraht von 2 mm Durchmesser auf dem eine kobalt-blaue transparente Glas-Perle zwischen 2 opakweissen sass. Alle Perlen waren beschmolzen und müssen nicht unter 9 mm Durchmesser gehabt haben. Dies kann ein Ohrring gewesen sein, wie man ihn ja auch in den Ohren der noch älteren Gesichtsurnen findet. Diese Perlen haben zwar weder in Form noch in Färbung etwas besonders characteristisches, wichtig ist aber, dass hier weisses opakes Glas, weisses Email, auftritt, welches sonst in den Gräbern der nordischen Bronzezeit und der Hallstädter Periode als Grundmasse der Perlen nicht gefunden ist. In Ostpreussen kommen gerade bei sicheren La Tène-Funden, wie in den zunächst zu beschreibenden Grabhügeln von St. Lorenz, weisse Email-Perlen neben blauen vor; diese weissen Perlen tragen öfters kleine blaue Ringe mit blauem Mittelpunkt (weisse Augen-Perlen) und sind mehrfach in Aschen-Urnen von La Tène-Character (besonders Doppelkegeln mit Doppelhenkel) gefunden, aber in der Regel beschmolzen, so in einer Urne aus einem Grabe bei Rudau, Kreis Fischhausen (Provinzial-Museum No. 4565—4567) und in ganz analogen Urnen aus Grabhügeln des Kalkberges bei Rantau, Kreis Fischhausen (Prussia-Museum). Eine schöne Bronze-Nadel mit gradem Fuss und grossem halbkreisförmigen, mit solchen weissen Augenperlen garnirtem Bügel ist ein Einzelfund von Wiskiauten, Kr. Fischhausen (Prussia-Museum). Aehnliche Perlen scheinen anderweitig gerade nicht häufig zu sein. Eine ganz identische weisse Perle mit den blau geringelten Augen ist zusammen mit einer blauen, auf einem kleinen Bronzeringe zu Bussy le Château in der Champagne auf einem Begräbnissplatze der La Tène-Periode gefunden (Museum St. Germain 13191); eine andere sehr grosse mit mehreren Reihen solcher blauen Ringe zu Tschmy im Kaukasus (Museum Wien). Da sie entschieden importirt sind, so ist zu hoffen, dass sie sich noch mehrfach finden werden. In Römischer Zeit tritt weiss als Grund ebenfalls auf und in der Völkerwanderungsperiode besonders auf Bornholm massenhaft, aber in ganz anderen Formen und Mustern. Weissgrundige Perlen aus Hügelgräbern scheinen demnach in Ostpreussen und weiterhin für die mittlere La Tène-Periode characteristisch zu sein.

An einer anderen Stelle lag ein kleines Bronzegehänge No. 4404 Tfl. IV 15. An einem dünnen Bronzeringchen hängt ein etwas dickerer, der durch's Feuer zu einer kleinen Platte umgeschmolzen ist.

No. 4399, wieder an einer anderen Stelle, ist ein Stückchen eines Armbandes (wahrscheinlich) von viereckigem Querschnitt 6,5—7 mm breit, 3,5 dick, das auf der Aussenseite 3 Rippen trägt, aber sonst wenig characteristisches bietet. Bereits erwähnt ist, dass sich etwas östlich von dieser Stelle das Bernsteinstück No. 4405 (Fig. 5 p. 164) und ein kleines Stück dicken Bronzedrahts fand, von denen es zweifelhaft ist, ob sie noch hierher zu rechnen sind.

Die Ausbeute ist also an und für sich winzig, aber sie characterisirt die ganze Gruppe L. T. vollständig. Die Fibeln beweisen, dass alle diese Urnen zur mittleren La Tène-Periode gehören. Man hat also zu dieser späteren Zeit an einer äusseren Stelle eines älteren Hügels ein Nachbegräbniss gehalten, ein Loch in die Steindecke des Hügels gegraben, die Urnen dicht aneinander auf das untere Pflaster gesetzt, mit Steinen umstellt und mit Steinen wieder überdeckt.

Hügelgräber bei St. Lorenz.

Bei St. Lorenz, Kreis Fischhausen, ist von Herrn Professor Berendt 1872 und von Herrn Professor v. Wittich je ein Grabhügel geöffnet worden.

Hügel I.

Derselbe ist 1872 von Herrn Professor Berendt und Herrn Gutsbesitzer Fröhlich geöffnet. Nach dem Bericht, welchen mir Herr Professor Berendt für diese Publication zur Dispositon gestellt hat, ist die nachfolgende Beschreibung angeordnet.

Der Hügel hatte einen Durchmesser von 9 m, eine Höhe von 1,25—1,50, war übrigens schon früher stark in Angriff genommen gewesen von der Nordwestseite aus. Nach Abräumung des Rasens und der Erde fand sich am Rande ein Steinkreis und dann durch einen schmalen, grabenartigen Zwischenraum getrennt ein zweiter etwas breiterer, in höherer Lage mehrfach durch die früheren Nachgrabungen unterbrochen. Diese Kreise bestanden nach der von Herrn Professor Berendt angefertigten Skizze und Beschreibung nicht aus 1 Kranz, sondern aus mehreren Reihen nebeneinander liegender Steine, der äussere im Südwest fast nur aus einer einfachen Reihe, er verbreiterte sich aber von Südwest durch Nord und Ost bis zu der dreifachen Breite. Der innere war ungleich breiter, aber wie gesagt, vielfach unterbrochen. Im Südwest fand sich zwischen beiden Kränzen eine Steinbrücke, ein viereckiges Pflaster kleiner Steine, unter dem sich aber absolut keine Reste von Urnen zeigten. Es ist diese Brücke also derselben Bildung im Hügel I von Warschken analog. Im Süden, immer noch $^1/_4$ Quadrat entfernt fand sich hier wieder am innern Kranz eine dichtgedrängte Gruppe von La Tène-Urnen, und bei einem Hügel von Rantau, welcher ebenfalls diese La Tène-Gruppe am Rande barg, zeigte sich zwischen den äusseren Kränzen ebenfalls eine solcheSteinbrücke, so dass sie wirklich zu diesem Nachbegräbnisse der La Tène-Zeit in Beziehung zu stehen scheint, obwohl ihre Bedeutung dann vollständig dunkel bleibt. Innerhalb des zweiten Kranzes fand sich ein regelmässig gewölbter Steinkern in Form einer Kugelcalotte, mit einer Einsenkung in der Mitte von der früheren Zerstörung herrührend; nur oben lagen einige grosse Steine (ob von der zerstörten Centralkiste herrührend?) sonst nur kopfgrosse. Der Kern ergab nichts mehr, er war geplündert. In der Zone des inneren Kranzes fanden sich aber noch mehrere Grabstellen; im Osten eine Steinkiste mit flachen Trägern, deren Deckstein schon fehlte, in ihr 2 Aschen-Urnen auf Steinfliesen, die aber nicht erhalten wurden. Im Südosten war eine zweite ganz zerstörte Grabkammer, in der nur noch einige Scherben lagen.

Im Süden ungefähr dicht innerhalb der Kranzstelle trat nun eine Anlage auf, ganz analog der La Tène-Gruppe im Hügel I zu Warschken, ca. 1 m tief unter der Hügeloberfläche standen eine Menge Urnen dicht aneinander, vielleicht gegen 12. von denen aber nur die beiden 1. No. 437 (Tfl. III 11), 2. No. 435 (Tfl. III 12) ein

Fragment mit 3fachem Henkel No. 444 (Tfl. III_{13}) und ein Fragment einer flachen Schale 3. No. 440 erhalten sind. Nach Norden und Westen begrenzten 2 grosse, innen flache, etwas verschobene Steine diese Gruppe, es scheint das aber doch keine wirkliche Kiste gewesen zu sein, da die Stelle ziemlich unberührt war; die Steine mögen auch dem grossen Steine an der Stelle L. T. in Warschken analog gewesen sein. Es hat in diesem Hügel also ebenfalls eine Bestattung zu 2 verschiedenen Zeiten stattgefunden wie in Hügel I Warschken; eine ältere in Steinkisten, aus denen aber nichts mehr gerettet ist und eine jüngere zur La Tène-Zeit, eine dicht aneinander gepackte Menge von Urnen am Rande. Zwischen diesen Urnen lagen einige Beigaben aus Eisen und Bronze, durch Feuer sehr beschädigt, theilweise ganz unkenntlich gemacht, deren Reste aber doch genügen, um wieder die Periode dieser Urnen zu bestimmen, wobei dieselben Resultate herauskommen als zu Warschken. Sie sollen nachher mit den folgenden zusammen beschrieben werden, weil sie denen des nächsten Hügels ganz analog sind.

Hügel II.

Ueber diesen, von dem jetzt verstorbenen Herrn Professor v. Wittich ausgegrabenen Hügel fehlen alle näheren Notizen. Die Funde, welche derselbe dem Provinzial-Museum übergeben hat, zeigen aber, dass ganz ähnliche Verhältnisse wie im vorigen Hügel vorgelegen haben, vor allem Begräbnisse zu 2 verschiedenen Perioden. Aus den älteren Gräbern der Kistenzeit ist nur ein Deckel No. 398 Tfl. III_{15} erhalten, dann aber mehrere characteristische Scherben einer La Tène-Gruppe und zwischen diesen eine Anzahl beschmolzener Objecte aus Eisen, Bronze, Glas der La Tène-Periode angehörig. Eine Urne No. 408 Tfl. III_{14} fand ich, als ich die Leitung des Museums übernahm, noch mit ihrem vollen Inhalt an Knochen und Eisengeräthen (Tfl. IV, Fig. 27—28) vor und habe sie selbst entleert. Die Fundstücke sprechen demnach für sich selbst und gewähren eine willkommene Ergänzung zu den anderweitig gewonnenen Resultaten.

Thongefässe.

Die Dimensionen der erhaltenen Thongefässe beider Hügel sind folgende:

	Do	Dw	Dr	Uw	Hr	(H)	(r)	(b)	(Hw)	Rand Dicke	
Aschen-Urne I_1 (437) Tfl. III_{11}	13	24,8	ca. 16	16	25,4	102	65	52	63	6	
• I_2 (435) Tfl. III_{12}	13	29,4	ca. 23	8,5	15,8	54	78	44	54	7	
Schale I_3 (440) nicht abgeb.	ca. 15		ca. 20		ca. 5,3	ca. 26		ca. 75		9—12	Fragment, Masse sehr ungenau.
Aschen-Urne II (408) Tfl. III_{14}	ca. 14	26,6	15,5	10	20,6	78	58	53	49	7	
Aelterer Deckel II (398) Tfl. III_{15}	6	15	13,5	5,8	7,8						

Unter diesen nimmt Tfl. III 15 eine besondere Stelle ein. Wahrscheinlich ist dies ein Stöpseldeckel einer älteren Urne des Hügels II, da hier jedenfalls ältere Gräber existirt haben werden. Dieser Deckel ist ziemlich hoch und hat einen besonders abgesetzten, etwas vorspringenden Boden und einen wenig über den Cylinder hervortretenden Rand. Dass es ein Deckel ist, keine Schale (die dann umgekehrt hätte gezeichnet werden müssen) wird auch durch das seitlich in der Wölbung befindliche Loch bestätigt. Dies unregelmässige Loch von 13—18 mm Durchmesser ist alt und nicht etwa beim Ausgraben in dem erweichten Thon gestossen. Denn es fand sich noch die Erde des Hügels in seinen Wänden und ausserdem zeigen diese die graubraune Farbe der glatteren Oberfläche, während die gröbere Innenschicht roth gebrannt ist. Höchst eigenthümlich ist diese seitliche Stellung des Loches, welches das Gefäss zu jedem anderen Gebrauche untauglich macht.

Die übrigen Gefässe schliessen sich trotz einiger Abweichungen in ihrem Hauptcharacter den früher behandelten Urnen der La Tène-Periode an: sie haben den Typus des abgestumpften Doppelkegels. Die Urnen Tfl. III 11, 12 aus Hügel I sind die eine sehr hoch, die andere sehr flach, daher müssen ihre Indices abweichen, die Böschung ist ziemlich dieselbe wie bei III 4—8. Urne III 12 ist fast gradlinig in beiden Theilen, schneidet oben gerade ab und ist vollkommen geglättet, graubraun, III 11 im Untertheil sehr hoch und rauh, oben glätter und weitet sich am Rande ein wenig aus, um die Weite laufen Kerben. III 13 ist ein 3facher dicker Henkel (Hügel I No. 4, Inventar 444) mit dicken Stegen, der oben in den Rand eines Gefässes übergeht, welches III 8 vollständig analog gewesen sein muss. Dreifache Henkel kommen seltener vor, während von Doppelkegel-Urnen der La Tène-Periode mit Doppelkenkeln in beiden Königsberger Museen jetzt eine grosse Menge existirt (z. B. Rantau, Rudau — Provinzial-Museum, Kalkberg bei Rantau — Prussia) Urne Tfl. III 14 (488) aus Hügel II hat sehr ähnliche Forman und Indices wie Tfl. III 5 von Warschken, nur die Weite liegt ein wenig tiefer. Oberhalb derselben zieht sich eine decorirte Zone herum, die unten durch eine gezogene Linie, oben durch einen kleinen Absatz begrenzt wird. In derselben steigen Gruppen von 4 Strichen herunter, zwischen denen schräge Gruppen von 3—4 Strichen immer von den beiden Enden von 2 Paaren ungefähr nach der Mitte der mittleren gehen. Von den übrigen Gefässen aus Hügel II sind nur einzelne Bruchstücke erhalten. Von einer Urne (396) Stücke der ornamentirten Zone oberhalb der Weite, 2 horizontale Linien durch schräge Linien so verbunden, dass 2 Reihen mit den Spitzen sich berührender Dreiecke gebildet werden, zwischen denen Rhomben liegen. Diese Dreiecke sind durch Striche parallel einer Seite schraffirt und zwar die beiden Reihen in verschiedenen Richtungen. No. 387 ist ein Obertheil, ein abgestumpfter Kegel mit grader Wand Dw 17, Dr 11, Hh—Hw = 10, also (r) 65, demnach völlig den La Tène-Urnen entsprechend.

Metallbeigaben.

Die Metallbeigaben sind zumeist im Feuer gewesen, daher die aus Eisen noch ziemlich erhalten, die aus Glas oder aus Bronze aber stark beschmolzen, so dass von ihnen meist nur undeutliche Reste übrig geblieben sind, welche vielfach nicht gestatten, die einstige Form zu erkennen, ganz anders, als die schön erhaltenen Beigaben der Steinkistengräber aus einer älteren Zeit. Wenn demnach ein Theil der folgenden Gegenstände schwer zu deuten ist, so wird ihre Abbildung, soweit sie noch erkennbar sind, doch gegeben, da diese Fragmente vielleicht später durch besser erhaltene Stücke erklärt werden können.

Von grösster Bedeutung ist es, dass in jedem Hügel 1 Eisenfibel gefunden ist. Fibel Tfl. IV 16 (450) in Hügel I (abgebildet schon im Katalog der Berliner prähistorischen Ausstellung, p. 415 Fig. 8. und hiernach Undset Tfl. XVI, Fig. 5). Der Bügel geht in die Spirale über, macht links 2 Windungen, geht mit oberer Sehne auf die andere Seite und nach 2 Windungen in die Nadel über. Die Spiralrolle hat ca. 14 mm Länge, 8 mm Durchmesser. Der sanft gebogene Bügel geht in scharfem Knick zum Fuss über, neben welchem sich der Nadelhalter als weit geöffnete Rinne längs aus empor biegt. Das zurückgebogene Schlussstück steigt herauf und ist mit dem Halse durch eine kleine ringförmige Hülse, das Verbindungsstück, welche beide umschliesst, verbunden.

Die Fibel (383) in Hügel II ist leider so zerbrochen, dass sie sich nicht gut zeichnen liess. Die erhaltenen Reste charakterisiren sie aber doch vollkommen als La Tène-Fibel ähnlicher Form. Der Eisenbügel von 3—3,5 mm Durchmesser geht in eine Spiralrolle von 18 mm Durchmesser über. Erhalten ist ferner die Verbindungsstelle zwischen Hals und Schlussstück (Tfl. IV 20, tritt in der Zeichnung nicht deutlich genug vor), wo beide Theile durch eine kugliche hinten offene Eisenhülse zusammen gehalten werden.

Die Bronzen sind zum Theil recht schwer zu deuten, Tfl. IV Fig. 17 (No. 441) und IV 18 (No. 442) beide aus Hügel I haben denselben Typus; von ersterem Stück ist mehr erhalten, man sieht hier ein plattes annähernd dreieckiges Bronzestück, welches an der äusseren Schmalseite durch 2 Perlreihen verziert ist, auf welche 3 schmälere Querrippen folgen; hinter diesen ziehen sich 4 Längsrippen bis an das schmale Ende der Platte, worauf diese mit kurzer Biegung in einen ca. 4 mm dicken Hals übergeht. Hier ist das Stück (alt) abgebrochen. Die eine Platte ist durch Feuer gekrümmt, die andere auf der Rückseite mit angeschmolzenen Glasmassen bedeckt. Nach dem Halse zu schliessen, möchte ich diese Stücke für Nadelköpfe halten und habe nach dieser Conjectur das eine Stück hypothetisch mit einfacher Einbiegung ergänzt. Entfernte Analogien bieten Nadeln mit schaufelförmigem Kopf der La Tène-Periode: Undset XXVIII 8 von Oersdorf, Schleswig-Holstein XIV 4 von Seefeld, Westpreussen, beide aus Eisen.

In Grabhügel II fanden sich einige Stücke Eisendraht: Tfl. IV 21 (No. 380) ein Stück eines ein wenig gebogenen kantigen Drahtes von 2,5 mm Durchmesser, dessen flach geklopftes Ende sich in 1½ Windungen einrollt, Tfl. IV 22 (381) ein Stück eines ähnlichen Eisendrahts mit etwas unregelmässiger Rolle. Zugleich fanden sich Stücke Eisendraht (Tfl. IV 23 No. 377, 378), auf die weisse Email-Perlen von 3,5—4 mm Durchmesser aufgestreift sind. Jetzt lässt sich nicht mehr beurtheilen, wie diese Stücke zusammenhingen und einst aussahen. Vielleicht sind es Stücke von Nadeln, zumal im Prussia-Museum sich die erwähnte, der La Tène-Zeit angehörige Nadel von Wiskiauten befindet, deren Hals mit weissen Augen-Perlen besetzt ist. Dies weisse opake Glas ist in beiden Hügeln durch eine Menge beschmolzener Reste vertreten. In II fanden sich noch einige beschmolzene Perlen (No. 373 374) die einst rundlich, von ca. 8—9 mm Durchmesser, waren. Besonders I hat eine Menge von Glas-Schlacken geliefert, die zum Theil an Bronzen angeschmolzen sind, auch um dünne vierkantige Drähte von 2,2×2,5 mm Durchmesser herumgehen. Es waren jedenfalls Ohrringe wie das Ringfragment von Warschken mit blauen und weissen Perlen. Ein kleiner ziemlich erhaltener Ohrring ist Tfl. IV24 (375) aus Hügel II von 1,6—2 mm Drahtdicke und 20 mm mittlerem Durchmesser und einem umgebogenen Ende, welcher aber durchaus keine Verwandschaft mit den slavischen Schläfenringen (Hakenringen) hat. An den sonst ziemlich intacten Ring ist eine weisse Email-Perle angeschmolzen, die wohl nur beim Ringe gelegen, nicht auf ihm gesessen hat. Das weisse opake Glas wiederholt sich in characteristischer Weise also bei allen diesen La Tène-Funden.

Von grösseren Stücken sind ferner gefunden: Stücke eines dickeren Ringes (Tfl. IV26 No. 372) in Hügel II, wovon 4 Stücke erhalten: das grosse gebogene links gezeichnete besteht aus 2 schon in alter Zeit auseinander gebrochenen, ferner das Stück rechts und ein kurzes stark beschmolzenes, zusammen 233 mm lang; da jedenfalls noch mehreres fehlt, ist dies zum Armring zu viel, muss also ein Halsring gewesen sein. Die Verzierung des Ringes ist theilweise noch erkennbar, zum Theil aber durch den Brand verdorben. In der Mitte ist der Ring dicker bis ca. 6 mm, nimmt dann nach den Enden bis 4 mm ab. Dieser dickste Theil ist auf einer Seite gerippt, auf der anderen glatt, letztere muss die Innenseite gewesen sein, jetzt ist der Ring verbogen. An dem einen Ende (dem unten gezeichneten) kommen dann 2 Gruppen von pfeilförmigen Furchen (Sparrenornament) und wieder Rippen, ein Ornament, dass sich auf dem isolirten Stück fortsetzt (Rippen, doppelte Sparrengruppe), während am anderen Ende 2 Gruppen von alternirend schrägen Furchen auftreten, alles nur auf einer Hälfte. Ein vollkommenes Bild könnte man also von diesem Ringe erst erhalten, wenn sich einst ein analoger besser erhaltener fände.

Der Ring Tfl. IV25 (No. 376) aus Hügel II ist besser erhalten und unbeschmolzen, ein ovaler Ring von 48 × 30 mm Durchmesser und einem Querschnitt von 2,3 × 1,6 mm, aussen gewölbt, innen platt, ziemlich scharfkantig, an den Enden grade abgeschnitten. Da er ziemlich klein, so ist er vielleicht ein Kinderarmring gewesen.

In Hügel I fanden sich noch folgende schwer entzifferbare Bronzereste. Tfl. IV19 (445) ein gebogenes Stück Bronze, am oberen Ende (neuerdings) abgebrochen, am schmalen Ende 8 mm, tiefer 10,5 breit, 1,5 dick. Es ist geschweift und wird parallel den Contouren von 2 Furchen beiderseits durchzogen und einer mittleren, so dass es scheint, als ob 3 aneinander liegende Drähte eine Schleife bilden, wodurch in der Mitte eine Oeffnung von 3,3 mm Breite entsteht. Es sind dies aber nicht 3 nachträglich durch das Feuer zusammengeschmolzene Drähte, sondern wirklich eine gefurchte Platte, wie man besonders an dem frische Bruche deutlich erkennt. Dieses Fragment hat Aehnlichkeit mit Ringen, welche Olshausen eingehend behandelt hat (Verh. d. Berliner Anthrop. Ges. 17. Juli 1886 p. 433 ff., speciell 478, 479); es treten hier an einem Ende 3 einander umschliessende Drahtschleifen auf (l. c. p. 479, dadurch hervorgebracht, dass ein einfacher Draht an einem Ende durch 5 Umbiegungen sich in eine flache Spirale legt (I P^5 nach Olshausens Bezeichnung, oder ein doppelter Draht durch 2 Umbiegungen (II P^2); es könnten solche Ringe in Bronzeguss imitirt sein, wie eine Imitation eines Ringes aus Doppeldraht mit einer Endschleife bei einem Armringe von Grossendorf bei Putzig-Westpreussen (Sammlung Blell-Gross Lichterfelde) auftritt in einem Depotfunde der jüngeren Bronzezeit. Die Ringe, welche nun hier imitirt sein würden, kommen allerdings in sehr alten Gräbern vor (l. c. 478 z. B.

Mönitz in Mähren), welche der ältesten Bronzezeit zuzurechnen sind, so dass ein Zusammenhang doch ausgeschlossen erscheint.

Ob dies Stück ein voller Fingerring war, ist jetzt nicht mehr zu ersehen.

No. 443 (nicht abgebildet, da theilweise sehr undeutlich) besteht aus 2 aneinanderstossenden gewölbten Scheibchen, jede von 9,5 Durchmesser, welche kleine Spiralen imitiren, indem sich eine Furche spiralig bis nach der Mitte zieht, das Ganze ist aber 1 Stück; also dieselbe Technik wie im vorigen Falle.

No. 439 ist ein aus 2 zusammengegossenen kleinen Ringchen von 8 mm Durchmesser bestehendes Stück, ziemlich defect und beschmolzen. Letztere beiden Stücke werden wohl zu irgend einem Hängeschmuck gedient haben.

Die Urne Tfl. III 14 (408) aus Hügel II, welche erst im Museum nachträglich von mir entleert wurde, enthielt einige höchst bemerkenswerthe Eisengeräthe zwischen den Knochen, keine Spur von Bronze. Tfl. IV Fig. 27 (No. 392) ist eine dünne Eisenplatte, die an einigen Stellen zerbröckelte; die fehlenden Stellen sind nach den vorhandenen Spuren jedenfalls richtig ergänzt gezeichnet, nur bleibt in den Dimensionen eine kleine Unsicherheit. Die Platte ist ein wenig oval von 110×100 mm Durchmesser, durch eine Reihe von hinten eingeschlagener Falten und Buckel verziert. Eine Reihe Buckel läuft entlang des Randes, 2 Reihen in der Richtung von 2 aufeinander senkrechten Durchmessern. Längs des längeren Durchmessers läuft beiderseits eine doppelte Falte quer durch; beim kürzern hören dieselben an den ersten Falten auf, bildet aber mit je 2 anderen Doppelfalten 4 Quadrate in den Ecken, deren jedes einen Buckel enthält. Die Dicke der Platte kann wegen des Rostes nicht gut genau gemessen werden, sie beträgt am Rande ca. 1 mm. Aus ihrer Rückseite treten kleine Nieten heraus von ca. 5 mm Länge, die aber auf der Vorderseite keine grossen Köpfe tragen und hier des Rostes wegen nicht zu erkennen sind. Es sind jetzt nur 2 vorhanden, müssen aber wohl mehr existirt haben, wahrscheinlich 4. Die beiden erhaltenen stehen unsymmetrisch, die eine in der Verlängerung des dritten Horizontalfaltenpaares (von oben) rechts, die andere unterhalb des linken Vertikalpaares. Eine ähnlich flache dünne Eisenplatte ist mir nur noch aus dem Provinzial-Museum zu Trier bekannt, wo zwischen den Römischen Gräbern der Vorstadt Paulin auf dem früheren Beckerschen Grundstück isolirt 2 Gräber aus der weit älteren Früh-La Tène-Zeit entdeckt wurden: das eine mit Lanze, Bronzering und Früh-La Tène-Schwert, das andere mit einer analogen Lanze und einer runden ebenen Eisenscheibe von ca. 130 mm Durchmesser, 1,3 mm Dicke und gekerbtem Rande, an welchem 6 Nägel von 18 mm Länge gesessen hatten (das Stück ist nur theilweise erhalten). Demnach scheinen diese Scheiben männliche Schmuckstücke zu sein. Als Schildbesatz wären sie doch zu dünn, vor allem unbrauchbar, da sie vollständig eben, und gerade die ostpreussische Scheibe dürfte man auch nicht als Schildzierrath auffassen, da in diesen Gräbern gar keine Waffen vorkommen. Es kann dann wohl nur eine Zierscheibe sein, die vielleicht auf dem Gürtel befestigt gewesen war.

Tfl. IV 28 (No. 390) ist ein halbkreisförmiges Eisenmesser mit halbrundem Rücken und Schneide, in der Mitte ca. 19 mm, am Ende $17^1/_2$, am Rücken ca. 1,5 mm dick, was aber schwer zu messen ging. Das eine Ende ist abgerundet, das andere abgebrochen, vielleicht auch einst rund.

Die Eisenmesser dieser Form sind als Nachbildungen der älteren Bronzemesser zu betrachten, wie solche in den Pfahlbauten der Schweiz, den Hügelgräbern des mittleren Frankreichs, aus der Hallstädter Periode und auch im Norden zur jüngeren Bronzezeit in verschiedenen Modificationen vorkommen. Diese krummschneidigen, meist fast symmetrischen Messer ohne Stiel sollen halbkreisförmige genannt werden (da man mit dem zweckmässigeren Ausdrucke „mondförmige" meist die südlichen gestielten Bronzemesser bezeichnet). Dieselben finden sich im Norden weit verstreut und eine lange Zeit hindurch vom Ende der Hallstädter Periode bis in die frührömische Zeit hinein. Die Messer dieses letzten Abschnittes, die in Ostpreussen (Dolkeim), Pommern (Porzanzig), Meklenburg Bornholm (mehrfach), Jütland (Thy, Gjetrupgaard), Gotland (Sojvide*) gefunden sind, haben eine Schneide, die wirklich in einem Halbkreise, manchmal (Sojvide) sogar noch mehr gebogen ist, eine concentrische oft ziemlich kleine Innenseite und sind an den Enden radial abgeschnitten — sie gehen nicht mehr in die mittlere Kaiserzeit hinein. Die älteren Messer sind flacher und schmäler, so dass sie meist nicht einen Halbkreis ausfüllen, an den Enden abgerundet oder stumpf zugespitzt, mitunter unsymmetrisch, stehen daher alle dem abgebildeten Muster ziemlich nahe. Zu den ältesten dürfte ein Messer aus einer Bronzeciste zu Pansdorf bei Lübeck gehören**), ferner ein schmales Messer von Passmarke bei Schlieben, Pr. Sachsen***) mit grade abgeschnittenen Enden, zusammen mit einer Schwanenhals-Rollennadel gefunden. Auf Sylt†) im Kroockhook ein zweispitziges Messer in einer später beigesetzten Aschen-Urne; ein fast identisches, nur auf einer Seite mehr abgerundetes, auf der anderen Seite spitzeres Messer zu Dombrowo††) (Kr. Karthaus-Westpreussen) in einem Grabe mit Gesichts-Urnen. Ein mehr in die Länge gestrecktes, an einem Ende spitzes, am anderen stumpfes Eisenmesser ist zu Trzcebcz†††), Kr. Kulm (Westpreussen) unter dem Mittelstein eines Steinkreises gefunden, welcher mit einem benachbarten weit grösseren neolithischen Steinkreise unbedingt nichts zu thun hatte. In der Provinz Sachsen zu Schollene ein Messer mit einer La Tène-Nadel zusammen. In der Mark ein Messer zu Hohen-Wutzow mit La Tène-Fibeln, eines zu Rauschendorf (Märkisches Museum, von hier sehr verschiedenaltrige Sachen), beide Messer an einem Ende stumpfspitzig, am anderen abgebrochen, so dass sie unsymmetrisch sein können. Auch in Baiern zu Stublang (Oberfranken***†) ist ein ähnliches gefunden in Hügeln der jüngeren Hallstädter Periode. Die noch älteren Eisenmesser in Posen (Kazmierz), der Lausitz (Chöne) unterscheiden sich bereits durch eine viel geringere Krümmung bei derselben Schmalheit und ziemlich radiale Begrenzung, so dass sie einen noch kleineren Bogen bei bedeutenderer absoluter Grösse bilden. Verwandte Messer mit längeren oder kürzeren Stielen, die in dem Gebiete vorkommen, sollen jetzt ausser Betracht gelassen werden. Die Messer waren also

*) Schriften der Danziger naturforschenden Gesellschaft. Neue Folge III 2 p. 12 Fig. 26. Friderico-Francisceum Tfl. XVII 12. Aarböger for Nordisk Oldkyndighed 1870 Tfl. V 6. Aarböger 1875 Tfl. II 6. Montelius Ant. Suéd. 266.

**) Undset l. c. p. 300 Fig. 21.

***) Berliner Album Sect. VI Tfl. 1.

†) Handelmann: Die amtlichen Ausgrabungen auf Sylt Tfl. II 3.

††) Ossowski: Monumenta Poloniae praehistorica Tfl. XXI 8.

†††) Ossowski ibid XXXII 11. Zeitschrift des historischen Vereins für Marienwerder II p. 82 Tfl. XII 5.

***†) Hermann: Die heidnischen Grabhügel Oberfranken. Bericht des Bamberger historischen Vereins V Tfl. IX 118.

eine ziemlich lange Zeit in Gebrauch. Was ihre Bedeutung anbetrifft, so sind es wahrscheinlich Rasirmesser, wie sie ja auch meist bezeichnet werden. In den Gräberfeldern n. Chr., welche besonders in Ostpreussen ein überaus vollständiges Inventar liefern, kommen in den reicheren Männergräbern neben dem grossen Messer immer kleine convexe Messer vor, gestielte, in der frühen Kaiserzeit (ca. erstes und Anfang des zweiten Jahrhunderts) auch halbkreisförmige und zwar zusammen mit allerlei Toilettengeräth, Pincette, Ohrlöffel, während sie, zumal die halbkreisförmigen in Frauengräbern sich nicht finden, also entschieden eine männliche Beigabe sind. Solche kleine gekrümmte Messer schneiden auch, wie Versuche mit Scalpels zeigten, ganz gut, zumal wenn es gilt kleinere Stellen zu rasiren. Es liegt daher kein Grund vor, diese Benutzung der halbkreisförmigen Messer zu bezweifeln.

Das dritte Stück Tfl. IV29 (391) ist ein dünnes dreieckiges Eisenblech von unter 1 mm Dicke. Die Ecken sind theilweise abgebrochen, so dass seine Form und Bedeutung nicht genau bestimmbar ist. Längs der 3 Kanten zieht sich eine Reihe sehr feiner Buckel hin. Es kann dies ein Klapperblech sein, wie solche aus Bronze öfters an Ketten in den Ohren der westpreussischen Gesichts-Urnen hängen.

Wenn die Beigaben dieser Urne also zum Theil auch ihre Analogien in einer etwas früheren Periode, dem Beginne der La Tène-Zeit fänden, so weist doch das Auftreten der halbkreisförmigen Messer noch zur Kaiserzeit auf eine Continuität der Form während der ganzen Periode hin, und der Stil der Aschen-Urne reiht sie vollständig den übrigen La Tène-Urnen an.

Schluss.

Die bisher beschriebenen Hügel haben also gezeigt, dass in vielen derselben Brandgräber aus zwei völlig getrennten Perioden vorkommen.

Die älteren, in Steinkisten oder einzeln stehenden Urnen, gehören dem Ende der Hallstädter Periode an, parallel der jüngsten nordischen Bronzezeit, wo hier im Osten Eisen schon mehr in Gebrauch kam, während man zu Waffen und Geräthen wohl noch überwiegend Bronze benutzte. Nur unter dieser Einschränkung könnte man sie als Gräber einer jüngeren Bronzezeit, die mit der beginnenden Eisenzeit zusammenfällt, bezeichnen. Vor sie treten die erst jüngst in ihrer vollen Bedeutung erkannten Skelett-Gräber einer älteren Bronzezeit, der Periode von Peccatel, während eine Menge einzeln gefundener Randcelte auf eine noch ältere Zeit die von Pile-Leubingen (Montelins Periode I) hinweisen.

Die Beigaben in oder neben den Urnen sind unverbrannt, aber geringfügig. Besonders characteristisch treten die Schwanenhalsnadeln auf und die mit umgebogenem Halse. Die später zu beschreibenden Hügel werden dies Inventar noch wesentlich vervollständigen: von Nadeln kommen noch hinzu die hier zufällig nicht gefundenen Rollennadeln, am oberen Ende platt geklopft und in eine Rundung eingerollt; ferner verschiedene Armbänder, worunter die Stöpselarmbänder am wichtigsten, hohle, innen längsgeschlitzte Reifen, deren eines Ende sich stöpselartig in das andere schiebt, eine gerade in Süddeutschland am Ende der Hallstädter Periode häufige Form. Grössere und feinere Bronzen kommen in den Gräbern selten vor, doch zeigen die beiden Prunkcelte mit gewölbtem Kopfe, dass die zahlreich in Einzel- und Depôtfunden auftretenden unverzierten Celte mit gewölbtem Kopfe derselben Zeit angehören, Gebrauchsgeräthe und zugleich als ausschliesslich ostpreussische Formen Produkte einer einheimischen Fabrikation waren. Auf eine solche lassen auch noch andere lokale Formen schliessen, ein dicker grosser Ring mit imitirter Torsion (einmal mit der für diese Zeit characteristischen imitirten „wechselnden Torsion“ in einem Depôtfunde zu Willkühnen, Kr. Königsberg), dessen ösenartig umgebogene Enden in lange schnabelartige Fortsätze auslaufen, „Bügelring mit Vogelkopfenden“. Diese Form, welche nur einmal sicher in einem Grabe dieser Periode gefunden ist (Fritzer Forst bei Königsberg. Bericht der Gesellschaft Prussia 1885—86), kommt in Ost-Preussen ausserordentlich häufig in Einzel- und Depôtfunden vor und geht nur etwas westlich über Danzig hinaus (Tempelburg, Kr. Danzig, Brünhausen, Kr. Neustadt. Verhandlungen der Berliner anthr. Gesellschaft 1883, p. 219 Fig. A), ist aber weder weiter westlich noch südlich gefunden. Demnach hatte Ostpreussen beim Uebergang der Bronze- zur Eisenzeit eine einheimische Bronze-Industrie. Wenn diese auch nicht so reich entwickelt war, als in dem westlicheren Hauptgebiet der nordischen Bronzecultur (Pommern, Mecklenburg bis Skandinavien), so findet sich doch in beiden Gebieten der gemeinsame Zug, dass die Brandgräber ärmlicher ausgestattet wurden, während die meisten Bronzen sich in freier Erde, westlich besonders noch in Mooren finden. Diese beiden Gebiete erscheinen demnach für diese Periode einander näher gerückt, wie jetzt nun auch in der älteren Bronzezeit.

Die jüngeren Gräber gehören der mittleren La Tène-Periode an. Lange standen die Funde aus den St. Lorenzer Hügeln isolirt da, woher auch Undset, welcher zuerst die ostpreussischen Gräber aus vorrömischer Zeit in ihrem Zusammenhang mit den europäischen Gesammtverhältnissen erfasst hat (l. c. 150 ff.), die wahre Bedeutung dieser Funde damals noch nicht erkennen konnte. Erst die Ausgrabungen zu Warschken brachten hierin volle Klarheit, so dass sowohl die Beisetzungsverhältnisse als auch die Formen der La Tène-Urnen deutlich hervortraten. Jetzt nach Feststellung des Urnentypus zeigt es sich, dass die La Tène-Gräber in Ostpreussen viel zahlreicher sind, als man Anfangs vermuthen konnte. Während in Westpreussen im Zusammenhange mit ganz Norddeutschland die La Tène-Periode in grossen Flachgräberfeldern auftritt, welche continuirlich in die frühe Kaiserzeit hineingehen, deren östlichste bekannte Punkte Willenberg bei Marienburg und Rondsen bei Graudenz sind, beide noch östlich der Weichsel und Nogat, finden sich in Ostpreussen, speciell im Samlande die La Tène-Gräber bis jetzt als Nachbegräbnisse dicht aneinander gepackter Urnen am Rande älterer Hügel. Die Beigaben sind leider fast immer durch Feuer stark beschädigt. Ausser den vier beschriebenen Fibeln ist nur noch eine fünfte Bronzefibel der Mittel- La Tène-Zeit einzeln zu Kirpehnen (Prussia-Museum) gefunden worden. Somit ist eine grosse Lücke in der Urgeschichte Ostpreussens ausgefüllt worden.

In den nächsten Abhandlungen soll für beide Zeitabschnitte eine Menge von neuem Material gebracht werden, welches die bisher gewonnenen Resultate wesentlich vervollständigt und sicherer begründet,

Inhalts-Uebersicht.

Erklärung der Tafeln.

Die abgebildeten Gegenstände befinden sich sämmtlich im Provinzial-Museum der physikalisch-ökonomischen Gesellschaft, und ist ihnen hier die betreffende Inventarnummer beigefügt. Die Urnen Tafel III—V (I—III) sind in $^1/_4$, die Beigaben VI (IV) in $^2/_3$ der natürlichen Grösse gezeichnet.

Tafel III (I).

Hügelgräber zu Birkenhof.

Fig. 1. Aschen-Urne aus Hügel I I (1243) mit Deckel (1244). 2. Beigefäss I I (1245) mit Deckel (1246). 3. Aschen-Urne I II (1247). 4. Aschen-Urne I III (1250). 5. Aschen-Urne I V (1252) mit Deckel (1251). 6. Beigefäss III II a (630). 7. Beigefäss III II β (631). 8. Aschen-Urne II (629). 9. Beigefäss III I (624).

Tafel IV (II).

Hügelgräber von Birkenhof Fig. 1—4.

1. Aschen-Urne II b (626). 2. Deckel (623). 3. Beigefäss II (621). 4. Aschen-Urne (III b (625).

Hügelgräber von Warschken Fig. 5—10.

5. Aschen-Urne II A 2 mit Stöpseldeckel (4410). 6. Aschen-Urne II B (4411). 7. Aschen-Urne II A 1 mit Stöpseldeckel (4409). 8. Aschen-Urne I A a mit Schalendeckel (4370). 9. Beigefäss I B (4375). 10. Aschen-Urne I A b 1 (4371).

Tafel V (III).

Aeltere Urnen von Warschken Fig. 1—8.

1. Schalendeckel IAb_2 (4372). 2. Aschen-Urne IB (4374). 3. Stöpseldeckel IF (4379).

Urnen der La Tène-Gruppe aus Hügel I, Warschken.

4. Aschen-Urne 6 (4386). 5. Aschen-Urne 5 (4385). 6. Aschen-Urne 1 (4381). 7. Aschen-Urne 4 (4384). 8. Aschen-Urne 2 mit Doppelhenkel (4382). 9. Beigefäss 3 (4383). 10. Beigefäss 10 (4387).

Aus den Hügelgräbern von St. Lorenz Fig. 11—15 (11—14 La Tène-Periode).

11. Aschen-Urne I_1 (437). 12. Aschen-Urne I_2 (435). 13. Dreifacher Henkel einer Aschen-Urne I_4 (444). 14. Aschen-Urne II (408). 15. Stöpseldeckel einer älteren Urne aus Hügel II (398).

Tafel VI (IV).

Birkenhof Fig. 1—2, 4: 1. Nadel mit umgebogenem Hals I_{II} (1248). 2. Violinstegförmiges Bernsteinstück I_{II} (1248).

Gegend von Gr. Hubnіken: 3. Violinstegförmiges Bernsteinstück (1260).

4. **Birkenhof** Hügel V: Bronzecelt mit einem zerbrochenen Gürtelhaken zur Befestigung des Stiels. 4a—b. Rest des Holzstiels aus Rothbuchenholz (2037—39).

Flaken Fig. 5—7: 5. Bronzepincette (1298). 6. Armring (1299). 7. Spiralring (1306).

Gross-Kuhren Fig. 9: Gürtelhaken (1254).

Warschken, ältere Gräber, Fig. 9—12: 9. Bernsteinhängestück I Aa (4395). 10. Schwanenhalsnadel I Ab (4396). 11. Nadel mit umgebognem Hals I B (4397). 12. Schwanenhalsnadel II A (4414).

Warschken I aus der La Tène-Gruppe: 13. Bronze-La Tène-Fibel mit verbundenem Schlussstück (4400). 14. Kleine Spirale (beschmolzen) (4402). 15. Zwei ineinander hängende Ringe (4404).

St. Lorenz-La Tène-Periode Fig. 16—29: 16. Eisen-La Tène-Fibel I (450). 17. Bronze-Nadelkopf (?) I (441). 18. Desgl. (442). 19. Stück eines Bronze-Schleifenringes I (445). 20. Hals mit dem verbundenen Schlussstück einer Eisen-La Tène-Fibel II (383). 21. 22. Eisendrahtstücke, am Ende eingerollt II (380. 381). 23. Eisendrahtstücke mit weissen Email-Perlen II (377. 378). 24. Ohrring mit weisser Email-Perle II (375). 25. Kleiner Armring II (376). 26. Fragmente eines Halsringes II (372).

Fig. 27—29 aus **II. Urne** 488 Tfl. V $(III)_{14}$: 27. Eiserne Zierplatte (392). 29. Eisernes Zierblech (391). 30. Halbkreisförmiges Eisenmesser (390).

Abbildungen im Text:

Trüffeln und trüffelähnliche Pilze in Preussen.

Von

R. Caspary.

Hierzu Tafel VII und VIII.

Im Anschluss an den vorhergehenden Aufsatz scheint es mir zweckmässig, die Trüffeln, die in Preussen bisher gefunden und von mir untersucht sind, und die ihnen ähnlichen, mit ihnen möglicherweise zu verwechselnden ganz oder halb unterirdischen Pilze genauer zu beschreiben, wozu ich mich um so mehr veranlasst fühle, als ich in den letzten Jahren Neues auf diesem Gebiet nicht erlangt habe, aber sicher mancher hierher gehörige Pilz noch im Lande vorhanden ist und vielleicht einige Leser dieser Zeilen bewogen werden, gelegentlich ihnen vorkommende unterirdische Pilze mir einzuschicken. Es sollen erwähnt werden von den Trüffeln (Tuberacei Tul.): Tuber mesentericum, T. Borchii, Chaeromyces maeandriformis, Hydnotria Tulasnei, und von den trüffelähnlichen Pilzen aus der Abtheilung der Hymenogastrei: Gautieria graveolens, Rhizopogon rubescens, Melanogaster variegatus, Scleroderma vulgare, von den Hirschbrunstpilzen (Elaphomyceae): Elaphomyces granulatus, variegatus und anthracinus, endlich Pisolithus crassipes.

Tuberacei Tul.

Knollenförmige Pilze mit mäandrischen Gängen im Innern, welche mit Schläuchen, die meist 1—8 Sporen bilden, ausgekleidet sind.

Gattung Tuber (Trüffel).

Corda Icon. fung. 1854 VI 75. **Kugelige oder annähernd kugelige, unterirdische Pilze, mit mehr oder weniger derber, geschlossener Hülle umgeben, Inneres weich, bräunlich oder gelblich, mit gehirnartig gewundenen, dunkler bräunlichen oder schwärzlichen Gängen durchzogen, deren Wänden die kurzen, elliptischen Schläuche aufsitzen, die 1—6 elliptische Sporen enthalten, deren äussere Haut maschig-bienenwabig ist.**

Die Unterscheidung der Gattung Tuber mit maschig-bienenwabiger Aussenhaut der Sporen von Oogaster Corda Icon. VI. 70 mit warzigen oder stacheligen Sporen erscheint ganz begründet.

Tuber mesentericum.

Vittadini Monographia Tuberacearum 1831. 40. Tab. III, fig. XIX — **Tulasne** Fungi hypogaei. Parisiis 1851. 139. Tab. V. fig. V. Tab. VII. fig. IV, tab. XVII fig. I. — **Zobel** in Corda Icon. VI 82 als Tuber culinare Zobel b. aestivum Zobel.

Die derbe äussere Kruste ist schwarzgrau, in unregelmässige, vier- bis sechseckige, fast pyramidale, bis 1 mm hohe, am Grunde im Durchmesser 3—10 mm messende Erhabenheiten zerklüftet, deren Kanten scharf, meist kammartig vorspringen und die selten eine Spitze, meist statt ihrer eine unregelmässige Vertiefung tragen; die Seitenflächen der Pyramiden oft mit Längsrissen versehen. Inneres bräunlich-weisslich, mit sehr zahlreichen, unregelmässig hin- und hergewundenen braunen, sporenführenden Linien. In dem weisslichen Zwischengewebe oft eine dunkle, graue Linie, parallel mit den braunen Windungen und zwischen ihnen. Sporensäcke kurz, elliptisch, gestielt, mit 1—6, meist 3—4 Sporen. Sporen elliptisch, im Umfange mit 12—17 Strahlen.

Tuber mesent. kommt in Preussen, diess immer als das alte Königreich, Ost- und Westpreussen genommen, nur auf der „Nonnenkämpe“ nach unserem bisherigen Wissen vor, einer länglichen Insel etwas oberhalb Kulm am rechten Weichselufer. Von der Nonnenkämpe ist die Trüffel seit mehr als 50 Jahren bekannt. Diese Insel, etwa 1500 Morgen gross, mit einem Waldbestande von etwa 1000 Morgen*), bildet einen eigenen Belauf: die Nonnenkämpe, unter einem Waldwärter stehend, zur Oberförsterei Lindenbusch gehörig. Ihr Boden ist der braun-graue Schlick der Weichsel, stellenweise Sand. Als Waldbäume werden besonders Rüstern, ausserdem auch Eichen, Eschen und Hainbuchen gezogen; Schwarz- und Weisspappeln kommen vereinzelt ausser den Beständen vor. Die Eichen sind nur mittelgross, riesig aber sind viele Stämme von Populus alba, — ich maass einen, der 3′ über dem Boden, 15′ 3″ 9‴ im Umfang und eine Höhe von 80′ hatte, — und Populus nigra L. (nicht P. monilifera Ait., die so oft mit ihr verwechselt wird) — ich maass einen, der 16′ 7″ 9‴ Umfang 3′ vom Boden und 120—130′ Höhe hatte. Die Trüffel wächst einige Zoll unter der Bodenoberfläche. Unter welcher Baumart, kann ich nicht sagen; es heisst: Eichen, kommt nicht in grosser Menge vor und wird durch Schweine gesucht. Als ich die Nonnenkämpe den 19. und 20. Aug. 1883 besuchte, war leider der frühere Waldwärter Egidy fort und der neue hatte noch keine Trüffeln gefunden und wusste sie auch nicht zu suchen. Ueberhaupt sind in den letzten Jahren dort keine Trüffeln mehr gefunden. Bail (D)**) hatte die Nonnenkämpe am 7. und 8. October 1879 besucht und eine Trüffelsuche mit Schweinen mitgemacht. Es wäre zu wünschen, dass der Bericht an einer allgemein zugänglicheren Stelle, als in der Danzig'er Zeitung gegeben worden wäre. Ich bekam die Trüffel der Nonnenkämpe im Herbst 1873 durch

*) Ich verdanke diese Angabe dem jetzigen Förster, Herrn Bethkenhagen.

) Ich werde Bail's Nachrichten über von mir in gegenwärtiger Abhandlung erwähnte Pilze in folgender Weise aufführen: **Bail (A) = **Bail** Schrift. naturf. Ges. v. Danzig. 3. Bd. 2. Hft. 1873, 6 und 7. — **Bail (B)** = **Bail** a. O. 4. Bd. 3. Hft. 1878. 9 ff. — **Bail (C)** = **Bail** Schrift. d. physik. ökon. Ges. z. Königsberg. 19. Jahrg. 1878. 73. — **Bail (D)** = **Bail** Danziger Zeitung 12. Novbr. 1879 No. 11869. — **Bail (E)** = **Bail** Schrift. naturf. Ges. i. Danzig. 4. Bd. 4. Hft. 1880. 63 ff. — **Bail (F)** = **Bail.** Botan. Centralblatt von Uhlworm. V. Bd. 1881. 291 ff. — **Bail (G)** = **Bail** Üb. Tub. aestiv. und mesent., wie über falsche Trüffeln. A. O. Bd. VI. 155.

Apotheker Julius Scharlok in Graudenz, den 8. November 1875 durch den Lehrer am Cadettencorps in Kulm, Herrn Dr. Schubart und den 31. October 1876 durch Herrn Rittergutsbesitzer Max Reichel auf Paparczyn, Kreis Kulm. Etwa 43 Stück der Nonnenkämpe'r Trüffel habe ich erhalten. Ich habe am 3. November 1876 in der Sitzung der physik.-ökon. Gesellschaft darüber berichtet (Schriften der physik.-ökon. Gesellschaft in Königsberg 1876, Jahrg. 17, Sitzungsberichte 32). Dass die Nonnenkämpe'r Trüffel Tuber mesentericum Vit. ist, ist nicht zweifelhaft, ob aber Tuber mesent. nicht mit Tub. aestivum Vit. (a. O. 38) identisch ist, ist eine Frage, für die ich die Entscheidung nicht übernehmen mag. Beide sind sich so ähnlich, dass **Tulasne** (a. O. 138) als Unterschied nur die dunkeln Linien, welche Tub. mesent. in dem hellen, unfruchtbaren Gewebe in der Mitte zwischen den dunkeln Sporenreihen hat, aufführt. Diese dunkeln Linien sind aber auch nicht stets da. **Zobel** (in Corda Icon. fung. 1854. 81 ff.) führt zwar noch andere geringe Unterschiede auf, zieht aber Tub. aestiv., Tub. mesent. und fünf andere, etwas abweichende Formen von Tuber, die zum Theil höchst schwach charakterisirt sind, als Spielarten einer Art, die er **Tuber culinare** nennt, zusammen. **Ball** (G 136) stimmt Zobel so weit zu, dass er auch Tub. aestivum und mesent. als zwei Arten nicht unterscheidet. Ich kann die in Betracht kommenden, bisher unterschiedenen Formen des Tub. culinare Zobel nicht beurtheilen, da ich nicht im Stande bin, sie mir zu verschaffen. Ein Nachfolger wird aber vielleicht Schwierigkeiten haben, die Trüffel der Nonnenkämpe zu erlangen, wenn er sie braucht, und es scheint mir daher angemessen, einen Beitrag zur Entscheidung über den Werth des Tub. culinare Zobel dadurch zu geben, dass ich die Trüffel der Nonnenkämpe genauer beschreibe. Die folgenden Angaben sind von mir seiner Zeit am lebenden Pilz gemacht.

Die fast kugeligen, eiförmigen oder nierenförmigen, oder wie aus mehreren fast kugeligen Pilzen zusammengesetzten Trüffeln (Bild 1, 2, 3), die eine Grube, die als Ansatzpunkt hätte betrachtet werden können, wie sie von Vittadini und Tulasne angegeben wird, mit Sicherheit nie zeigten, maassen nach den drei senkrecht auf einander stehenden Richtungen des Raums:

	Breite	Höhe	Länge
1.	44 mm	44 mm	69 mm
2.	50 „	40 „	55 „
3.	44 „	38 „	56 „
4.	42 „	39 „	55 „
5.	30 „	28 „	42 „
6.	36 „	25 „	37 „

Diese Maasse übertreffen die, welche **Tulasne** für den Pilz angiebt, bedeutend, denn ihr Durchmesser ist nach ihm nur 20—35 mm. Ich unterliess leider, die einzelnen zu wiegen. **Ball** (D) giebt an, dass er 38 Trüffeln in einem Pfunde gehabt habe und dass der Waldwärter **Egidy** einmal eine Trüffel von 18 Loth Schwere gefunden habe. Die frischen Pilze hatten einen sehr durchdringenden, eigenthümlichen, unbeschreiblichen Geruch, der zugleich etwas Säuerliches und Weingeistiges hatte. **Ball** (D) bezeichnet den Geruch einer Knolle als Senfgeruch, eine im Innern schon braune hatte gar keinen, sonst sei er bei den anderen sehr stark unangenehm, aber schwer zu vergleichen gewesen. **Vittadini** spricht von

„Odor — moschatus". Moschusartig ist er entschieden nicht. Der Geschmack des frischen Pilzes soll nach **Vittadini** „amariusculus" sein; dies war auch nicht der Fall; ich fand den Geschmack ähnlich dem frischer Wallnuss, fast ölig.

Die feuchte Oberfläche des frischen Pilzes ist tief grau-schwarz, die des getrockneten heller grau-schwarz. **Vittadini** nennt ihn „nigerrimum", was nicht zutrifft.

Die Oberfläche ist mit ungleich grossen, meist 5- oder seltener 4- oder 6-eckigen pyramidalen, ungleichen und unregelmässigen Erhabenheiten, die bis 1 mm hoch sind, bedeckt: Bild 4 und 5, welche photographischeAufnahmen in etwa viermaliger Vergrösserung darstellen. Die pyramidalen Erhabenheiten haben meist scharfe Seitenkanten, die bei den trockenen oft noch viel stärker, fast flügelartig vorspringen. Die Spitzen der Pyramiden sind selten da, meist findet sich statt der Spitze eine unregelmässige Vertiefung. Die Seitenflächen der Pyramiden zeigen oft noch unregelmässige, scharfkantige Risse, die von der Spitze nach dem Grunde verlaufen; grosse Pyramiden von 7 mm und mehr im Durchmeseer des Grundes haben mehr solcher Risse, 7 und mehr, als kleinere Pyramiden von 3—4 mm Durchmesser des Grundes; solche kleinere haben nur 3—4 solcher Risse.

Das Innere zeigt auf dem Querschnitt: Bild 6, welche Zeichnung nach einer Photographie in natürlicher Grösse gegeben ist, unter einer etwa 1 mm dicken, schwarzen Rinde in weisser oder bräunlich-weisser Füllung sehr dichte, unregelmässig hin- und hergekrümmte, streckenweise sich parallel laufende, oft stumpf endende, anastomosirende, grau-braune Linien von $^1/_{10}$—$^4/_5$ mm, ja 2 mm Dicke.

Bei schwacher Vergrösserung unter dem Mikroskop: Bild 7, sieht man eine äusserste braunschwarze oder tiefbraune 0,0749—0,083 mm dicke Schicht, zersetzt in den äussersten Theilen, welche Zell-Zwischenräume nicht hat, tief-braun in den Zellwänden gefärbt, ohne Inhalt ist und allmälich in der Farbe heller werdend, in farbloses, lockeres Gewebe übergeht, das sich zwischen die grau-braunen, gehirnartigen Windungen der Sporengänge fortsetzt. Es hat eben so wenig Inhalt, wie die schwarz-braune Kruste in ihren Zellen, hat aber Zell-Zwischenräume. Die Zellen desselben sind 0,0016—0,0049 mm dick und etwa 2—4 mal so lang, aber so wirr durcheinandergeschlungen, dass selbst 219malige Vergrösserung im Querschnitt einzelne Zellen nicht erkennen lässt: Bild 8. Von diesem farblosen, scheinbar inhaltsleeren Gewebe gehen die Sporensäcke aus, denen es dicht anliegt. Es waren zahlreiche, anscheinend jüngere Zustände der Sporensäcke vorhanden; da aber die Mehrzahl der sonstigen Sporensäcke schon ausgefärbte Sporen hatte, schien es mir zweifelhaft, dass die anscheinend jungen Sporensäcke sich in normalem Zustande befanden. Eher waren es verkümmerte. Die in ihnen vorhandenen farblosen, elliptischen, scheinbar jungen Sporen enthielten zahlreiche Oeltropfen, ohne schon die netzförmige Aussenschicht der Haut entwickelt zu haben. Bei schwacher Vergrösserung: Bild 7, zeigt sich in dem weisslichen Zwischengewebe an vielen Stellen eine dunkle, graue oder bräunlich-graue Linie, parallel mit der Grenze der benachbarten grau-braunen mäandrischen Sporengänge. Tulasne legt auf sie als Unterschied zwischen T. aestivum, dem sie fehle, und Tub. mesent., das sie zeige, Gewicht. Auf getrockneten Querschnitten der Trüffel der Nonnenkämpe ist nichts von diesen dunkeln Zwischenlinien zu sehen.

Die Sporensäcke sind farblos, eiförmig oder umgekehrt eiförmig, fast elliptisch, etwas gestielt: Bild 9, 10, 11, 12, mit 1—6 Sporen. Bei dem Pilz, den ich Herbst 1873 erhielt, fand ich nur 1—4 Sporen in je einem Sack, 1 und 2 am häufigsten, 3 selten, 4 nur einmal. In den Trüffeln, die ich am 8. November 1875 bekam, waren 1—6 Sporen selten, 2 auch nicht häufig, 3—5 am häufigsten in je einem Sacke. In den Sporensäcken war ausser den Sporen noch etwas Plasma vorhanden, das durch Jod stark gebräunt wurde. Die Sporen sind elliptisch, die Innenschicht ihrer Haut lichtbraun, die äussere, viel dickere, netzförmig-wabenartige Schicht ist farblos und nur da, wo drei Wände von drei Maschen zusammenstossen, in der Kante lichtbraun. Es hat daher jede Spore lichtbraune Strahlen um sich, und zwar 12—17, kleinere Sporen weniger als grosse. Die Maschen der Aussenschicht sind 5—7seitig. Die Sporen sind einzellig, gefüllt mit farblosem Oel.

Die Sporen sind sehr ungleich an Grösse. Sie sind meist desto kleiner, je grösser an Zahl sie in einem Sporangium entwickelt sind; die grössten sind die, welche einzeln in einem Sporangium gebildet wurden.

Eine Trüffel hatte:

	Sporensack Breite : Länge	Spore: Breite : Länge
1) Sporensack (einschliesslich Stiel) mit einer Spore	0,0633 mm : 0,0949 mm	0,0416 mm : 0,0449 mm
2) Sporensack mit 2 Sporen	0,0699 mm : 0,0949 mm	0,0383 mm : 0,0416 mm
3)	0,0733 mm : 0,0949 mm	0,0399 mm : 0,0433 mm
4) Sporensack mit 4 Sporen	0,0716 mm : 0,0833 mm	0,0299 mm : 0,0349 mm
5) Sporensack mit 5 Sporen	0,0666 mm : 0,1083 mm	0,0299 mm : 0,0349 mm
6) Sporensack mit 6 Sporen	0,0633 mm : 0,0849 mm	0,0266 mm : 0,0333 mm

Eine andere Trüffel hatte:

		Sporen:
7) Sporensack mit 3 Sporen	0,0633 mm : 0,0899 mm	0,0316 mm : 0,0349 mm
8) Sporensack mit 4 Sporen	0,0666 mm : 0,1166 mm	0,0333 mm : 0,0349 mm
9) Sporensack mit 5 Sporen	0,0699 mm : 0,100 mm	0,0249 mm : 0,0366 mm

Eine 3. Trüffel hatte:

10) Sporensack mit 2 Sporen:
0,0783 mm : 0,0649 mm — 0,0366 mm : 0,0499 mm
(Dieser Sack quer breiter als lang.)

Einige einsporige Sporangien einer 4. Trüffel hatten:

Breite : Länge = 1) 0,0666 mm : 0,0833 mm
2) 0,0633 „ : 0,0749 „
3) 0,0683 „ : 0,0783 „

Einige zweisporige dieser 4. Trüffel maassen:

Breite : Länge = 4) 0,0683 mm : 0,0783 mm
5) 0,0616 „ : 0,0766 „
6) 0,0666 „ : 0,0799 „

Einige dreisporige Sporangien derselben 4. Trüffel maassen:

Breite : Länge = 7) 0,0683 mm : 0,0882 mm
8) 0,0549 „ : 0,0882 „
9) 0,0716 „ : 0,0783 „

Ein viersporiges Sporangium derselben Trüffel maass:

Breite : Länge = 10) 0,0633 mm : 0,0749 mm

Eine Spore dieses letztern viersporigen Sporangiums maass:

Breite : Länge = 0,0333 mm : 0,0349 mm

Eine Spore aus einem einsporigen Sporangium dieser 4. Trüffel hatte:

Breite : Länge = 0,0483 mm : 0,0566 mm

2 Sporen aus einem zweisporigen Sporangium dieser 4. Trüffel maassen:

Breite : Länge = 1) 0,0399 mm : 0,0516 mm
2) 0,0366 „ : 0,0483 „

2 Sporen aus dreisporigem Sporangium hatten:

Breite : Länge = 0,0333 mm : 0,0433 mm
0,0466 „ : 0,0583 „

Steht die Grösse der Sporen in umgekehrtem Verhältniss zu der in einem Sporangium entwickelten Zahl derselben, so scheint die Grösse der Sporensäcke in keinem festen Verhältniss zur Zahl der Sporen, die sie entwickeln, zu stehen.

Im Mittel haben jene 16 Sporen, die gemessen wurden: Breite : Länge = 0,0306 mm : 0,0426 mm. Tulasne giebt Br. : Lge. an = 0,0256 mm : 0,032—0,0384 mm.

Die Sporen der Nonnenkämpe'r Trüffel sind also nicht unbeträchtlich grösser als die des Tub. mesentericum, das Tulasne untersuchte.

Die Unterschiede der Nonnenkämpe'r Trüffel mit Tub. mesentericum Tulasne sind daher folgende:

Tub. mesent. nach Tulasne.	Tub. mesent. der Nonnenkämpe.
1) „Sporangiis 4—6 sporis.“	1) Sporangien mit 1—6 Sporen, meist 3—5.
2) Die Sporen sind kleiner: Breite : Länge = 0,0256 mm : 0,032—0,0384 mm	2) Sporen grösser: Breite : Länge = 0,0306 mm : 0,0426 mm
3) Die Trüffeln kleiner: 20—35 mm im Durchmesser.	3) Die Trüffeln grösser: 25—69 mm und mehr im Durchmesser.

Nach Tulasne's Abbildung, Tab. V. v. sind die braunen Sporengänge zum Theil (Bild v; 6.) viel breiter (1—3 mm breit) und geringer an Zahl, als die der Trüffel der Nonnenkämpe.

Ob diese Unterschiede eine Spielart begründen können oder nicht, müssen weitere Beobachtungen des Tub. mesent. an andern Orten lehren.

Fuckel (Symb. myc. 247) giebt die Grösse der Sporen (Breite : Länge = 24 : 36 mm) bei Tub. mesent. auch kleiner an, als die Trüffel der Nonnenkämpe sie hat.

Die einzigen lebenden Exemplare einer nicht preuss. Trüffel, die ich zu Tub. mesent. rechnete und untersuchen konnte, erhielt ich am 29. October 1876 von Herrn Hermann von Gutschmid von Jena. Sie waren bei Jena von einem Händler mit Hunden gesucht. Der Händler erbot sich, Herrn von Gutschmid auf Trüffeljagd mitzunehmen. Es waren diese 10 Trüffeln, die ich empfing, der Trüffel der Nonnenkämpe sonst gleich, die Farbe nur etwas heller, mehr bräunlich-schwarz-grau und die pyramidalen Höcker etwas breiter. Unter 24 Sporangien hatten 6 fünf Sporen, 6 vier Sporen, 3 drei Sporen, 3 zwei Sporen, 6 eine Spore. Die Sporensäcke mit Stiel hatten:

Breite : Länge = 1) 0,0599 mm : 0,0899 mm
2) 0,0766 „ : 0,0982 „ , 3sporiger Sack
3) 0,0649 „ : 0,0932 „ , 4sporiger Sack

Die Sporen hatten Breite : Länge = 1) 0,0299 mm : 0,0349 mm
2) 0,0299 „ : 0,0366 „
3) 0,0283 „ : 0,0383 „
4) 0,0299 „ : 0,0349 „
5) 0,0349 „ : 0,0466 „
6) 0,0316 „ : 0,0449 „

Im Mittel hatten diese 6 Sporen also
Breite : Länge = 0,0307 mm : 0,0393 mm
sie standen also an Grösse den Sporen der Nonnenkämpe näher, als die Tulasne's.

Tuber Borchii.

Vitt. l. c. 44, Tab. I. Fig. III. — **Tulasne** Fung. hypog. 145., Tab. V. Fig. I. Tab. XXI. XIII. — **Tuber elegans Corda** Icon. VI. 79. Tab. XIX. Fig. 139. (non Tub. Borchii Corda). — **Tuber album Bulliard** Champ. 80., Tab. 404, Fig. A et B (nach Tulasne). — **Tuber album Lespiault** Ann. sc. nat. 3. ser. Tom. II., 317, Tab. VI.

Aussen lichtbraun, unregelmässig rundlich, eiförmig oder kuglig mit wenigen seichten Furchen, 13—32 mm im Durchmesser, schwach behaart, innen licht-graubraun, durchzogen mit zahlreichen, wenig gekrümmten oder geraden anastomosirenden weisslichen Linien, die am Rande in die Rindenschicht auslaufen. Sporensäcke eiförmig-elliptisch mit 1—4 Sporen. Sporen elliptisch oder kuglig mit netzförmiger wabenartiger farbloser Aussenhaut; auf der dem Beschauer zugekehrten Seite 17 bis über 100 Maschen.

Ich erhielt diesen Pilz, der bisher nirgend in Deutschland gefunden zu sein scheint, zuerst 4. November 1876 von Professor Dr. Prätorius in Konitz. Professor Prätorius hatte die Güte für den botanischen Garten in Königsberg den 2. November 1876 einige Exemplare von Carlina acaulis im Kiefernwalde von Krojanten auszugraben und fand bei dieser Gelegenheit in 6—7 Zoll Tiefe 3 Exemplare dieser Trüffel, wovon ich sofort das kleinste und grösste erhielt (Bild 13 und 15 von aussen und Bild 14 und 16 durchschnitten dargestellt). Auch die andern Darstellungen Bild 17—22 sind nach diesen 2 Exemplaren gegeben. Stimmten diese 2 Trüffeln auch nicht in jeder Beziehung mit der von Tuber Borchii von Vittadini, Tulasne, Corda und Lespiault gegebenen Beschreibung, so stimmte doch keine andere bisher beschriebene Trüffel besser als Tuber Borchii Vitt., für die ich den Pilz daher bestimmte. Die Abweichungen, wovon später, liessen sich durch die Jugendlichkeit der Exemplare erklären. Ich untersuchte sie sofort und bat Professor Prätorius um mehr und gereiftere Pilze. Den 26. November suchte Professor Prätorius von Neuem nach Tuber Borchii an der Stelle, wo er es früher gefunden hatte, aber der Boden war mehr als Fusstief gefroren und es wurde vergebens gesucht. Die Gegend ist hügelig und sandig mit niedern Kiefern, dem Rest eines Waldausläufers, etwas Heidekraut und andern Heidepflanzen bedeckt. Ich erhielt dann unter dem 4. November 1877 wieder Tuber Borchii von Professor Prätorius und am 7. December 1878 fand Professor Prätorius den Pilz von Neuem an der früheren Stelle, ich erhielt davon sechs Exemplare. Prätorius schreibt dabei: „Eins der 6 Exemplare ist weiss, die anderen sind röthlich und waren auch schon so in der Erde gefärbt." — „Dieser Pilz ist also, wie jetzt durch 3 auf einander folgende Jahre festgestellt worden, an der bezeichneten Stelle konstant. Selten ist er aber jedenfalls. Man muss ein gutes Stück umgraben, bevor man ihn findet. Auch diesmal fand ich ihn nur in 2 vereinzelten Exemplaren und alle übrigen wie in einem Nest in einer Tiefe von 5—6 Zoll." Ich berichtete über Tuber Borchii Vitt. nach dem Funde des Professor Prätorius in der Sitzung am 1. December 1876 der physik.-ökonomischen Gesellschaft (Schriften physikalisch-ökonomisch. Gesellsch. Königsberg. Sitzungsberichte 1876 34) unter Vorzeigung der mir übersandten Exemplare und der Zeichnungen (Bild 13—22).

Tuber Borchii Vitt. von Krojanten hat einen grössten Durchmesser von 14 bis 23 mm bei den einzelnen Pilzen. Sie sind aussen licht-braun (Bild 13 und 15), heller, fast gelblich-weiss in einigen unregelmässigen Furchen.

Im Innern (Bild 14 und 16) sind die Pilze licht grau-braun, das grössere etwas tiefer in der Farbe, durchzogen mit gekrümmten, oder geraden, meist kurzen, anastomosirenden weissen Linien, die am Rande in die Rindenschicht auslaufen.

Das Mikroskop ergab folgendes Nähere. Die Rindenschicht besteht aus isodiametrischem Parenchym (Bild 17 a—c), dessen äusserste Lagen licht-braun sind, die inneren zahlreicheren sind farblos und ohne Zellzwischenräume. Es folgt dann im Innern ein dichtes Gewebe, welches bald der Länge, bald der Quere nach verlief und sich dicht an die höchst zahlreichen, farblosen, kuglig-eiförmigen, ungestielten, Sporensäcke anlegte. Dieses die Sporensäcke enthaltende an Masse überwiegende Gewebe war, obgleich unter dem Mikroskop farblos, fürs blosse Auge das braune. Die braunen Sporen bewirkten diese Färbung. Die weissen Streifen und Gänge bestehen aus demselben Parenchym, welches jedoch lockerer an diesen Stellen ist, keine Sporensäcke zwischen sich hat, wohl aber Luft (Bild 17, b, b, b). Die Zellen des Parenchyms zwischen den Sporensäcken sind 0,0033 bis 0,0049 mm dick und hie und da mit Querwänden versehen.

Die Sporensäcke waren in den Pilzen, die ich bekam, stets von höchst ungleicher Reife. Einige, die jüngsten, waren mit einer, das Licht stark brechenden, fast gleichartigen Flüssigkeit erfüllt, fast ohne körniges Plasma. Andere, ältere, hatten viel körniges Plasma. Einige hatten ganz junge, kuglige Sporen (Bild 18), mit gleichmässiger nicht körniger Flüssigkeit erfüllt, recht dicker, grünlicher, völlig glatter Haut, ohne Spur von Maschen. Solch eine Spore hatte 0,0249 mm im Durchmesser. Vorgeschrittenere (Bild 19), zeigten ausser etwas körnigem Plasma grosse Oeltropfen und über der dicken, grünlich-bläulichen Haut eine farblose, helle Schicht, welche bereits den Anfang der Maschen als zarte Strahlen im Umfange, aber nicht von oben erkennen liess. Durchmesser der Spore Bild 19 0,0266 mm. Bild 18 und 19 stellen diese jungen Sporen in Glycerin gesehen dar. Weitere Entwicklung zeigt die Sporen zwar farblos, aber schon mit deutlich maschiger Aussenschicht und noch vielem Plasma und Oel im Innern. Endlich bei erwachsenen Sporen ist die innere Haut lichtbraun, mit farbloser dicker das Maschenwerk bildender Schicht umgeben (Bild 22). Im Innern birgt die reife Spore farblose Oeltröpfchen. Die helle Aussenschicht ist in den Kanten, wo drei Maschen zusammenstossen lichtbraun; die Spore ist also mit lichtbraunen Strahlen umgeben. Die Zahl der Maschen, welche die reifen Sporen auf der dem Beschauer zugekehrten Seite zeigen, wechselt sehr, von 10 bis über 100; ich zählte 10, 17, 18, 25, 32, 42, 61, 64, und über 100.

Jod färbte die Häute aller Sporen schwach bräunlich, den Inhalt der Sporensäcke, auch derer, die schon reife Sporen hatten, tief braun. Die unreifen Sporen werden im Inhalt gebräunt, die reifen kaum tiefer in der Farbe. Jod und Schwefelsäure färbte nichts blau.

Auch für **Tuber Borchii** ergab sich, wie für Tuber mesentericum, dass die Sporen in einem Sacke desto grösser sind, je weniger ihrer darin entstehen.

Dafür folgende Messungen als Beweis.

	Sporensack. Durchmesser.	**Spore**		Durchmesser der Maschen.
		Durchmesser mit der helleren netzförmigen Hautschicht.	Durchmesser ohne die hellere Hautschicht.	
1	Breite : Länge = 0,0716 mm : 0,0916 mm Einsporig.	Breite : Länge = 0,0499 mm : 0,0566 mm	Breite : Länge = 0,0416 mm : 0,0483 mm	0,0066 mm
2	Sack mit einer kugligen Spore.	= 0,0516 mm : 0,0516 mm	= 0,0433 mm : 0,0433 mm	
3	= 0,0833 mm : 0,0966 mm Einsporig.	= 0,0549 mm : 0,0649 mm	= 0,0416 mm : 0,0516 mm	
4	= 0,0849 mm : 0,0866 mm Einsporig.	= 0,0516 mm : 0,0633 mm	= 0,0406 mm : 0,0516 mm	
5	Sack mit 2 kugligen braunen Sporen.	1. Spore = 0,0383 mm : 0,0383 mm 2. Spore = 0,0466 mm : 0,0466 mm	= 0,0299 mm : 0,0299 mm = 0,0383 mm : 0,0383 mm	
6	Sack mit 2 kugligen Sporen = 0,0716 mm : 0,0779 mm	1. Spore = 0,0366 mm : 0,0366 mm 2. Spore = 0,0533 mm : 0,0533 mm		
7	Sack mit 2 kugligen Sporen = 0,0749 mm : 0,0916 mm	1. Spore = 0,038 mm : 0,038 mm 2. Spore = 0,0499 mm : 0,0499 mm		
8	Sack mit 3 Sporen = 0,0866 mm : 0,1093 mm	Längster Durchmesser der Sporen: 1. Spore 0,0483 mm 2. " 0,0416 " 3. " 0,0399 "		
9	Sack mit 4 Sporen.	Längster Durchmesser der Sporen: 1. Spore 0,0383 mm mit 2. " 0,0383 " " 3. " 0,0366 " " 4. " 0,0249 " "	 40 Strahlen ringsum. 40 " u. 17 Maschen. 42 " u. 18 " 30 " u. 10 "	0,0049 mm

Tulasne giebt von den Sporensäcken an: Br.: Lge. = 0,065, : 0,06—0,08; die des Pilzes von Konitz mit reifen Sporen haben in Extrem Br.: Lge. = 0,0716 —

0,0866 : 0,0779—0,103. Die Sporensäcke des Konitz'er Pilzes sind also meist etwas grösser, als die des französischen Tuber Borchii, welche Tulasne maass. Von den Sporen giebt Tulasne die Grösse an: Br.: Lge. = 0,025 — 0,035 : 0,035 — 0,040 mm. Die Sporen des Konitz'er Pilzes sind meist beträchtlich grösser.

Der Konitz'er Pilz hatte auf der Aussenseite nur wenige Haare und zwar einfache. Tulasne giebt von diesen Haaren an, dass sie auch am Grunde, obgleich selten, ästig seien; ästige sah ich nicht.

Der Konitz'er Pilz weicht noch in folgenden Punkten von den Beschreibungen Vittadini's, Tulasne's und Lespiault's ab:

1) „Odor fortis, terrosus, subaromaticus." Vitt. „L'odeur de cette Truffe est extrêmement forte et désagréable, surtout à l'époque de sa maturité; on peut la comparer à celle du gaz d'éclairage." Lespiault. So auch Tulasne. Der Konitz'er Pilz roch anfangs sehr schwach nach dem Durchschneiden, wonach lässt sich nicht angeben; am 3. Tage schon roch er gar nicht mehr. Uebrigens sagt Vittadini vom jungen Pilz: „caro initio inodora".

2) „Crescit solitarie ac vix subterraneum." Vitt. Der Konitz'er Pilz wurde in Sandboden 5—7 Zoll unter der Erde gefunden und auch in Nestern.

3) „Caro — demum rufo-fusca, nigrescens." Vitt. „Chair d'abord blanche, prenant ensuite une teinte d'un bistre violacé et marbrée de veines blanchâtres" Lespin. „Parenchyma sporigerum initio albidum, postea senescendo griseum, fuligineo-violaceum aut rufo-fuscum evadit et quidem veluti nigrescit; venis aeriferis primum albis tandemque subfuscis." Tul. Die Sporengänge sah ich nicht anders als graubraun beim Konitz'er Pilz und das Zwischengewebe weiss oder weisslich; bräunliches Violett oder gar Schwärzung sah ich im Innern nicht bei dem frischen Pilz.

4) „Asci brevissime caudati." Tul. Corda (Icon. VI. Tafel XIX. 139 Bild 2) bildet einen solch gestielten Sporensack ab. Ich sah von einer Cauda an ihnen nichts; der Sack: Bild 20, hat nur eine höchst kurze Zuspitzung am Grunde. Auch Lespin. bildet die Sporensäcke fast ganz kuglich ohne Anhang ab.

„Novembri mense maturescere incipit, Aprili evanescit," sagt Vittadini. Dies für den Pilz in Italien. Es kann also ohne Zweifel für den Konitz'er Pilz, der ja so viel weniger Wärme, als die italienischen Artgenossen bis November, in welchem Monat ihn Professor Prätorius ausgrub, erhielt, Gewicht darauf gelegt werden, dass er sich erst im Anfange der Reifezeit befand, also noch nicht ganz ausgefärbt im Innern war und auch noch nicht den Geruch des reifen Pilzes erlangt hatte. Dadurch fallen die unter 1) und 3) aufgeführten Unterschiede fort.

Den Ausschlag für die Bestimmung des Konitz'er Pilzes als Tuber Borchii gab mir die höchst zahlreiche Felderung der Spore, wie sie keine andere Trüffelart hat. Die Abbildungen von **Lesplault** zeigen die Sporen allerdings nur mit wenigen Feldern — ich fand aber sogar solche, die noch weniger, blos 10 auf einer Seite hatten —, jedoch **Corda's** Tub. elegans, das er von **Lesplault** erhalten hatte und das französischen Ursprungs war, hat schon viel mehr Felder auf einer Seite der Sporen, obgleich bei den schematisirten Zeichnungen **Corda's** grosse Genauigkeit nicht erwartet werden darf. **Tulasne** (l. c. Tafel XXL XIII. bildet 2 Sporen mit so viel Feldern ab, dass diese Darstellungen durchaus die Sporen des Konitz'er Pilzes auch wiedergeben. Dass **Tulasne** mit Unrecht **Corda's** Tuber Borchii l. c. Tab. XIX., Fig. 137, für synonym mit Tuber Borchii Vitt. anführt, hat **Zobel** (bei Corda a. O.) längst gezeigt.

Bail (D) giebt an, dass ihm der Waldwärter der Nonnenkämpe noch zwei andere Trüffelarten ausser dem Tuber mesentericum geschickt habe, darunter Tuber rufum Pico. Die 4. Trüffelart nennt Bail mit Namen nicht. Ich habe nichts davon gesehen.

Chaeromyces. Vitt. L. c. 50.

Knollenförmige, rundliche Pilze mit glatter, derber, weisslicher oder gelblicher Hülle; Inneres weisslich mit unregelmässig gewundenen, bräunlichen Linien, in welchen die Sporensäcke liegen. Sporensäcke, ei-keulenförmig, (umgekehrt flaschenförmig), mit 4—8, meist 6 Sporen. Sporen kuglig mit zahlreichen stumpflichen oder spitzlichen, oder gestutzten, fast walzigen Warzen besetzt

Chaeromyces albus. Casp.

Chaeromyces maeandriformis Vitt. l. c. 1831. 51. Tab. II. Fig. I. und Tab. IV. Fig. X. **Berkeley et Broome.** On Brit. hypogaeus fung. Ann. and mag. nat. hist. XIII. 80. **Tulasne** l. c. 170. — **Rhizopogon albus Corda** in **Sturm** Pilze Deutschlands 1841 19. und 20. Hft. t. 14, bloss die Abbildung, da die Beschreibung durch Vermengung mit Tuber magnatum Vitt. verwirrt ist. Ebenso **Corda** Icon. fung. V. 67 Tab. V. Fig. 44. **Rhizopogon magnatum** Corda (non Vitt.) Icon. fung. V. 67. Tab. V. Fig. 45. — **Tuber album Sowerby** Eng. fungi a. 1797 Tab. 310. Die übrigen Synonyme siehe bei Tul. a. O. Eine Diagnose der Art erscheint überflüssig, weil sie die einzige der Gattung zu sein scheint. Nach **Vittadini's** eigener Angabe (vergl. Tulasne p. 171) ist die 2. von ihm aufgestellte Art: Chaer. gangliformis wohl nur eine Form von Chaer. maeandr.

Tulasne hat glücklicher Weise durch Einsicht in Originale diesen Pilz von der Verwirrung, die er mit Tuber magnat. Vitt. erfahren hatte, klargestellt, auch ermittelt, dass Tuber album Sowerby und der engl. Botaniker Chaeromyces maeandrif. Vitt. ist. Es muss also der Name des Pilzes Chaeromyces albus heissen.

Der Pilz ist so selten, dass Tulasne ihn lebend nicht sah. Er hat ihn trocken aus **England** und zwar das Original **Sowerby's**, **Italien**, Originale **Vittadini's** und **Corda's** aus **Böhmen** gesehen. In England ist nach **Broome u. Berkeley** a. O. der Pilz seit Sowerby, der keinen Fundort nennt, nicht gefunden, obgleich in Wiltshire und Sommersetshire danach viel gesucht ist. Aber **Cooke** (Handbook brit. Fung. 742) berichtet, dass der Pilz bei Highgate 1860 wieder beobachtet sei.

Es giebt **Goeppert** (Jahrbuch des schlesischen Forstvereins für 1871. Breslau 1872. 404 und nachmals Hedwigia X. 1871. 168) das Vorkommen des Chaeromyces maeandriformis Vittadini in Oberschlesien an und nähere Fundorte dafür im 50. Jahresbericht der schles. Ges. für vaterländische Cultur 1873 p. 118. Er erklärt diese Trüffel nach Krombholz und Corda für essbar, sie würde sogar der echten Trüffel wegen ihres feinen Geschmacks zu kulinarischen Zwecken vorgezogen und Goeppert empfiehlt sie daher als Handelswaare sehr. In der That wird auch Chaeromyces albus als Trüffel in Böhmen verkauft, wie eine Probe bewies, die ich durch Herrn Sucker-Arklitten

1878 aus Karlsbad erhielt. Aber Krombholz und Corda haben Chaeromyces maeandriformis leider mit dem geschätzten Tuber magnatum Vitt. verwirrend vermengt. Der blosse Name Chaeromyces d. h. „Schweinepilz" zeigt schon, dass Vittadini ihn nur gut fand für Schweine, nicht für Menschen. Und Vittadini sagt ausdrücklich vom Chaeromyces maeandrifor. „Nullum habet usum et rarissime in foro exstat una cum veris tuberibus". — „Interdum tamen pro Tubere magnatum venditur, cuius caro formam et colorem Chaeromycis maeandriformis quodammodo refert." — „Immaturi apud nonnullos esculenti. Maturos tamen ob intensissimum et nauseosum, quem spirant, odorem, comedi posse haud credam." Es ist daher mehr als wahrscheinlich, dass Goeppert das geschätzte Tuber magnatum mit Chaeromyces maeandriform. Vitt. verwechselt hat, obgleich Tulasne a. O. schon hinlänglich die Verwirrung beider bei den Vorgängern, auf die Goeppert sich beruft, Krombholz und Corda nachgewiesen hatte.

Die Nachricht des Director Hüttig, der irrthümlich das Vorkommen von Trüffeln bei Ostrometzko angab, dass in Schweden Chaeromyces maeandriformis „die weisse Trüffel" gefunden sei, (Verhandlungen des botanischen Vereins der Provinz Brandenburg XXIV. Jahrg. 1883, Sitzungsbericht 57) bedarf näherer Prüfung, da die Angabe, dass diese „weisse deutsche Trüffel" in Deutschland sehr gesucht sei, auch eine Verwechslung mit Tuber magnatum vermuthen lässt. Weder von der schlesischen noch der schwedischen „weissen Trüffel" werden die Sporen beschrieben, deren Beschreibung doch allein dem Leser Bürgschaft für eine wissenschaftlich richtige Bestimmung sein kann.

Um so interessanter ist es, dass Chaeromyces albus sicher bei Bischofstein in Ostpreussen vorhanden ist.

Herr Caplan Braun, früher in Bischofstein, jetzt in Gutstadt, hat den Pilz von 1872 bis 1878 jedes Jahr bei Bischofstein an vier verschiedenen Orten gefunden. Ueber die Fundorte macht mir Herr Kaplan Braun folgende nähere Angaben. Alle vier befinden sich am Waldrande an Abhängen, welche die Nachmittagssonne bescheint. Die Pilze sind immer zwischen dem 25. Juli und 15. August gefunden. Sie verriethen ihr Dasein auch bevor sie gesehen wurden durch den starken Geruch nach Bibergeil (castoreum) und konnten, wenn man dem Geruch nachging, gefunden werden. 1. Den 3. August 1872 wurden zwei bis drei Pilze ostsüdsüdlich von Bischofstein, etwa zwei Kilometer von der Stadt im Bischofstein'er Walde, = Lackmedie, Lackmedienwald, korrumpirt vom Volk, in „Lackmühlwald", welchen Namen auch die Generalstabskarte hat, am Abhange des Berges von Herrn Kaplan Braun gefunden, auf welchem der Damerau'er Kirchensteig in den beginnenden Wald, nach dem Trautenau'er Waldhause zu geht, beinahe im Mittelpunkt dieser Abhangsfläche und zwar halb aus der Erde hervorstehend, unter älteren Tannen (d. h. Picea excelsa Link). Hier ist der Pilz fast alljährlich wieder gefunden mit Cantharellus cibarius, Boletus edulis, B. subtomentosus, B. scaber, B. luteus L., B. piperatus, Ammanita muscaria; im Spätherbst daselbst Hydnum repandum und imbricat. Boden sandig mit wenig Lehmbeimengung, mit Gras und wenig Moos bedeckt und mit Vaccinium Myrt., V. vitis idaea, Calluna vulg., Solidago virgaur. und Platanthera bifolia. 2. Der zweite Standort ist vom genannten etwa einen halben Kilometer nach Ost entfernt und liegt von Bischofstein aus gerechnet links neben dem Hauptwege nach dem Dorfe Dameran gleich vor dem Trautenau'er Waldhause im Trautenau'er Walde. Es ist der Anfang des Waldweges, der von dem genannten Waldhause vom Damerau'er Hauptwege links ab in den Wald geht. Dort fand der Lehrer Beckmann von Bischofstein 1873 ein sehr grosses Exemplar, das einen filzigen Wurzelgrund hatte. Die eine Hälfte desselben erhielt Herr Apotheker Hellwich-Bischofstein, die andere hat Herr Kaplan Braun mit Gänseleber zu einer Pastete verarbeiten lassen. Diese ass er mit dem damaligen Bürgermeister von Bischofstein Tausch. Letzterem schmeckte das Gericht ausgezeichnet, dem Herrn Kaplan aber nicht, und er überliess dem Herrn Bürgermeister die Trüffelschnitte. An dieser Stelle ist später kein Exemplar mehr gefunden. Wahrscheinlich war der Pilz von den Schweinen des Waldwärters frühzeitig verzehrt. Boden hier mehr lehmig als sandig. 3. Der dritte Standort liegt von Bischofstein beinahe drei Kilometer nordöstlich im Lackmedienwalde (Bischofstein'er Walde). Von der Chaussee, welche in östlicher Richtung nach Rössel führt, geht man links nach der städtischen Försterei und von dieser in nördlicher Richtung etwa einen halben Kilometer weit bis zu einer grossen feuchten Wiese, über diese weg bis an den Waldrand, wo der Boden ansteigt; dort am Anfange des Waldrandes fand Herr Kaplan Braun mit zwei Bischofstein'er Lehrern neben ein paar Erlenbäumen beinahe noch auf der Wiese drei Chaeromyces von der Grösse einer mässigen Kartoffel. 4. Der 4. Fundort ist westlich von Bischofstein etwa zwei bis drei Kilometer weit neben dem Wege, welcher durch den zum Gute Senkitten gehörigen Wald nach dem Dorfe Schulen geht. Wo der Weg in diesen Wald tritt, steht von Bischofstein aus links noch vor dem Walde ein etwas verfallenes gemauertes Kapellchen, dahinter ist eine kleine nach dem Walde (Westen) zu geneigte Anhöhe, die mit Kiefern besetzt ist und da ist der Fundort. Der Wald wird von den Bischofsteinern meist Schulen'er Wald genannt. Hier fand Herr Kaplan Braun den 13. August 1877 ein schönes Exemplar. Späterhin ist Herr Kaplan Braun nicht mehr an diese Stelle gelangt. Boden hier Sand mit wenig Lehm und denselben Pflanzen, die der erste Fundort hat, die übrigens auch an dem 2. und 3. Fundorte nicht fehlen.

Ich habe Chaeromyces maean. wiederholt 1875 und 76 von Herrn Kaplan Braun erhalten.

Von dem Exemplar des Lehrer Beckmann bekam ich durch Herrn Apotheker Eugen Hellwich September 1875 eine grössere Zahl getrockneter Scheiben. Die Pilze waren mittelgrossen oder selbst grossen Kartoffeln nicht unähnlich, fast kuglige, länglich-rundliche oder rundlich-eiförmige, unregelmässig wulstige und flach gefurchte Knollen; trocken, wie ich sie nur sah, da ich sie stets erst nach Rückkehr von mehrwöchentlicher Abwesenheit erhielt, weisslich-bräunlich, stellenweisse braun und bräunlich-weisslich, Inneres weiss-gelblich mit braunen dichten maeandrischen Linien. Herr Kaplan Braun schrieb mir in Bezug auf ein Exemplar, das ich von ihm am 18. August 1876 erhielt, dass es bei der Herausnahme aus der Erde eine fast ganz weisse nur wenig gelbliche Farbe hatte. „Diese ist aber in fast 24 Stunden bedeutend gelblicher, ja an einzelnen Stellen sogar gelb-rothbräunlich geworden. Ich trug den Pilz in der Hand nach Hause, aber sobald er an der Luft sich befand, krochen aus seiner Oberfläche allenthalben eine Menge kleiner Maden heraus." Leider waren alle Pilze, die ich erhielt, madig und sind deshalb später stark zerstört. Da die übersandten Pilze mir stets erst trocken in die Hand kamen, und dann sehr wurmstichig waren, mit mehreren stärkeren Vertiefungen, kann ich nichts darüber aussagen, ob sie eine Ansatzstelle (Bewurzelungsstelle) haben oder nicht. Das grösste Exemplar, das des Lehrer Beckmann, hatte Herr Apotheker Hellwig frisch gewogen; es wog 265 g. Am 25. September 1876 mass ich zwei der Pilze, die Herr Kaplan Braun schon den 8. September gefunden hatte, die also auch schon trocken waren. Eines mass nach drei auf einander senkrechten Richtungen 45 mm, 64 mm und 73 mm, das andere 46 mm, 49 mm, 53 mm. Beide waren faulig und voll brauner stachlicher Larven. Schnitte zeigten die Sporensäcke nicht mehr deutlich; sie liessen sich nicht mehr herausarbeiten und ihre Haut nicht mehr erkennen. Die Sporen waren jedoch meist reif. Ihre Maasse folgen unter 2. Der erste Pilz, den ich erhielt, hatte nur unreife Sporen. Die Säcke waren ei-keulenförmig, farblos und enthielten nicht blos 8, sondern häufig 4, 5, 6, meist 6 noch glatte kugliche Sporen. Erst einige der grössesten hatten flache Warzen schon auf der Haut. Die unreifen Sporen maassen erst zwischen 0,0183 bis 0,0233mm im Durchmesser. Reife Sporen hatten die Schnitte des Pilzes des Lehrer Beckmann. Die Sporen sind lichtbräunlich bei durchfallendem Licht, die äussere Schicht mit derben walzigen oder pyramidalen, gestutzten, bisweilen selbst oben verdickten, oder gekrümmten Stacheln besetzt, die zwei bis dreimal so lang als breit sind. 21 Stacheln und mehr im Umkreise. Der Durchmesser der Sporen war:

1. Pilz des Lehrers Beckmann:

	0,0183 mm
	0,0266 „
	0,0283 „
	0,0333 „
die meisten	0,0283 „

2. Der Pilz, den Kaplan Braun am 8. September 1886 fand, hatte den Durchmesser der Sporen:

ohne Warzen:	mit Warzen:
1) 0,0233 mm	1) 0,0283 mm
2) 0,0216 „	2) 0,0283 „
3) 0,0249 „	3) 0,0324 „
4) 0,0233 „	4) 0,0337 „

3. Ein Pilz, der am 17. August 1876 gefunden war, hatte im Durchmesser der Sporen:

ohne Warzen:	mit Warzen:
1) 0,0233 mm	1) 0,0291 mm
2) 0,0241 „	2) 0,0274 „
3) 0,0266 „	3) 0,0316

Tulasne a. O. 170 giebt die Sporen wieder kleiner an, nämlich 0,019 bis 0,022 im Durchmesser. Jedenfalls waren die, welche ich maass, weniger eingetrocknet, als die, welche Tulasne hatte.

Hydnotria Berkl. and Broome.

Berkl. and Broom. Ann. und Mag. nat. hist. XVIII p. 78. **Tulasne** l. c. 127. **Zobel** in Corda Icon. fung. VI 61 — **Hydnobolites sp. Berkl. et Broome.** Ann. und Mag. nat. hist. XIII 357.

Fast kuglig, braunroth, mit unregelmässigen, ins Innere führenden Furchen; Hüllschicht wenig entwickelt, Inneres braunroth, mit weitläufigen, unregelmässigen, et-

was maeandrischen Höhlungen. Sporensäcke lang, keulig, um die Höhlungen ein- bis zweireihig liegend, achtsporig. Sporen fast zweireihig, röthlich-braun mit unregelmässigen, grossen, flachen Erhabenheiten besetzt.

Hydnotria Tulasnei Berkl. et Br. l. c. Tulasne l. c.; Zobel l. c.

Am 17. August 1869 erhielt ich ein Exemplar dieses Pilzes, damals noch nicht in Preussen gefunden, durch Herrn Apotheker **Otto Kascheike** in Drengfurth geschickt, welches nebst einigen anderen Exemplaren von dem gräflich Lehndorff'schen Hegemeister Herrn Walther, wohnhaft in Forsthaus Mittenort bei Steinort, Ostpr., im Belauf Mauerwald (Kreis Angerburg), etwa 1500 Schritt vom Mauersee, in lehmigsandigem Boden gefunden war. Ein Exemplar war von Hirschen ausgekratzt; der Hegemeister suchte weiter nach und fand noch einige. Es ist am Fundort Weissbuchen- und Eichenbestand. Da damals in Königsberg Tulasne's Werk: Fung. hyp. noch nicht vorhanden war, schickte ich den Pilz an Prof. De. Bary, der ihn bestimmte.

Das mir gesandte Exemplar war nicht vollständig reif. Ein Sporensack, den ich herausarbeitete, maass 0,0466 mm in Breite und 0,183 mm in Länge. Sporensäcke lang keulig ohne unten so dünn und verschmälert zu sein, wie Tulasne und Corda sie zeichnen. Sie waren ganz allmälig nach unten zugespitzt. Die meisten Säcke hatten noch glatte, farblose oder lichtbraune, kuglige Sporen; einige Sporen, die reif zu sein schienen, da sie röthlich-braun nnd mit Erhabenheiten besetzt waren, hatten im Durchmesser 1) 0,0333 mm; 2) 0,0349 mm; 3) 0,0366 mm. Tulasne giebt ihren Durchmesser auf etwa 0,035 mm an, was mit meinen Messungen stimmt.

Hydnotria Tulasnei Berk. et Br. scheint die einzige Art der Gattung zu sein. Zwar hat **Zobel** bei Corda a. O. noch eine andere: Hydnotria carnea Zobel (Corda), bei der die Sporen einreihig in den Säcken liegen sollen, die Sporen auf den Abbildungen viel grössere Wülste haben und die Sporensäcke nur einreihig um die Höhlungen liegen, während bei Hydn. Tulasnei die Sporen fast zweireihig sein, die Sporen weniger hohe Erhabenheiten haben und die Säcke zweireihig um die Höhlungen sich entwickeln sollen. Aber Tulasne a. O. 128, der originale Bruchstücke der Hydnotria carnea Zobel (Rhizopogon carneus Corda) untersuchte, sagt: „fungus iste habitu et interna structura Hydnotriam Tulasnei plane refert". Auf gewisse Widersprüche in der Beschreibung und Abbildung Tulasne's und der Angaben über Hydnotria Tulasnei von Berk. et Broom, Tulasne und Corda hat Zobel a. O. aufmerksam gemacht.

Bail (B 10) giebt an, **Hydnotria Tulasnei** mit „mehrreihigen Sporen" — **Tulasne** und **Corda** bilden sie nur mit zweireihigen oder fast zweireihigen Sporen ab und **Zobel** l. c. nennt sie „in ascis inordinate nidulantes" — bei Jäschkenthal, Pelonken und Kahlbude gefunden zu haben. Dagegen habe er in Schlesien eine Hydnotria mit einreihigen Sporen schon früher gesammelt und veröffentlicht, die er für **Hydnotria carnea** Zobel (Corda) hielt. Ich empfing Ende November 1877 von **Bail** ein Stück einer Hydn. Tulasnei, von ihm bei Pelonken gefunden; die Sporen lagen zweireihig in den Säcken, die ich aus dem sehr abgetrockneten Pilzstück nicht gut herausarbeiten konnte. Sporen braunroth, undurchscheinend, mit einer grösseren oder minderen Zahl von flachen Warzen auf der Aussenschicht. Da die Warzen ungleich hoch waren, hatte dieselbe Spore in verschiedenen Richtungen oft ungleichen Durchmesser. Sie maassen: 1) 0,0333 mm; 2) 0,0349 mm; 3) 0,0366 bis 0,0416 mm.

Bild 31 stellt eine Spore von aussen dar.

Elaphomyces Fr.

Hüllschicht dick, hart, geschlossen, Inneres grosskammerig, indem dünne, unfruchtbare, lichtere Gewebsstreifen grössere Anhäufungen von sporentragenden Fadenmassen netzartig umschliessen. Sporensäcke auf den Fadenenden endständig, 1—8sporig. Sporen kuglig, höckerig, endlich nach Abwelkung des unfruchtbaren Gewebes ein Pulver im Innern der Hüllschicht bildend.

Als Autor der Gattung Elaphomyces wird von **Fries** Syst. III 57 **Nees** genannt, jedoch ohne Citat. **Vittadini** (Monogr. Tuber 62) macht es ebenso. **Tulasne** (Fung. hyp. 100) citirt ein Werk von **Nees** „Syn. gen. plant. mycet. p. LXVIII", das ich nirgend finden kann, und „Pl. offic. p. I.", das ich auch nicht zu deuten vermag. **Rabenhorst** Deutschlands cryptog. Pilze I. 291 giebt auch für die Gattung **Nees** als Autor ohne Citat, aber für „Elaphomyces granulatus" heisst es: „Nees in litt". Und wahrscheinlich ist der Name Elaphomyces zuerst brieflich an Fries ausgesprochen. Wichtig für die Sporenbildung ist **Tulasne** Ann. sc. nat. 2. Ser. t. XVI. p. 1 ss. Es wird bei der Hülle meist ein „cortex", die äusserste Schicht derselben, und die „Peridie", die innere Schicht der Hülle, unterschieden; da aber cortex und Peridie nur Theile einer und derselben Gewebsmasse sind, unterscheide ich sie nur als Schichten derselben; bei El. variegatus kommt obenein noch eine zwischen der äusseren und inneren Schicht liegende dritte hinzu.

Elaphomyces granulatus Fries (Syn. III. 58).

Tulasne Fung. hyp. 109. **Hülle 1 bis 1¼ mm dick, aussen heller oder dunkler gelb-braun oder grau-braun, zartwarzig, Warzen ¼ bis ⅓ mm am Grunde im Durchmesser, abgerundet oder seltener spitzlich, weniger hoch als breit; Querschnitt der Hülle mit äusserer dünner gelbbrauner Schicht und dicker innerer weisser, oder diese weisse Schicht nach Innen gleichfarbig, blass kermesin-grau. Sporen kuglig, zartwarzig, kermesin-schwarz, Durchmesser im Mittel 0,0272 mm, in den Extremen 0,0235 bis 0,0309 mm.**

Tulasne giebt an, dass die Sporen zu 1—8 in einem Schlauch entstehen. Die Grösse derselben von 10 preussischen verschiedenen Fundorten gemessen, wobei nur die mittleren und grössten, aber nicht die kleinsten, wohl keimunfähigen, berücksichtigt sind, war:

1) 0,0183—0,0249 mm
2) 0,028 —0,034 „
3) 0,024 —0,034 „
4) 0,0239—0,0307 „
5) 0,0186—0,0293 „
6) 0,0239—0,0323 „
7) 0,0199—0,0307 „

8)	0,0239—0,0307	‚
9)	0,0266—0,0323	‚
10)	0,0279—0,0310	‚
Mittel	0,0235—0,0309 mm.	

Tulasne giebt 0,0235—0,03 mm als Durchmesser der Sporen an, was mit den vorstehenden Messungen stimmt.

Elaph. granulatus liegt mir von folgenden Fundorten vor: 1) **Kreis Memel.** Czernener Gutswald. Scheu-Löbarten 1867. Durch Cand. E. Knoblauch. — 2) **Kreis Tilsit.** Schilleningkener Wald. 1877. Apotheker G. Fromm. — Dingkener Forst. 1877. Apotheker Oskar Siemering. — 3) **Kreis Gumbinnen.** Serpenten 1874, durch J. Reitenbach-Plicken. — Buyliener Forst 1872, durch J. Reitenbach-Plicken. — 4) **Kreis Wehlau.** Allenburger Stadtwald 1880, durch Apotheker E. Rosenbohm. — 5) **Kreis Insterburg.** Nähe von Norkitten 1877, durch Apotheker Hempel-Norkitten. — 6) **Kreis Rastenburg.** Wald von Fürstenau 1877, durch Apotheker O. Kascheike-Drengfurth. — 7) **Kreis Friedland** Ostpr. Pohibels bei Schippenbeil 1879, durch Direktor Dr. Sauter. — 8) **Kreis Heiligenbeil.** Stadtwald von Zinten. Apotheker G. Fromm. — Belauf Brandenburg'er Heide bei Ludwigsort 1880. Königl. Förster Holländer. Durch Prof. Dr. Lentz. — Auch daselbst von mir gefunden. — 9) **Kreis Pr. Eylau.** Wald von adl. Tollkeim 1877, durch Superintendenten Lehmann - Schmoditten. — 10) **Kreis Rössel.** Wald von Teistimmen 1876, durch Apotheker E. Hellwich-Bischofsstein. — Bei Bischofsstein 1877. Kaplan Braun-Bischofsstein. — Bischofsstein, durch Apotheker E. Hellwich - Bischofsstein. — 11) **Kreis Fischhausen.** Kaporn'sche Haide bei Moditten 1863 und Elenskrug 1877. Gefunden unter der an diesen Orten für den königl. botanischen Garten angekauften Haideerde. — 12) **Kreis Johannisburg.** Königl. Forstbelauf Weissuhnen bei Rudczany 1882. Königl. Förster Nicolai. — 13) **Kreis Osterode.** Taberbrücker Forst, Jagen 202. 1882. Stud. P. Preuss. — 14) **Kreis Kartaus.** Königl. Forstbelauf Glinow 1877. Königl. Förster Henicke. — 15) **Kreis Flatow.** Königl. Forstbelauf Kl. Lutau. Forstsekretär Herrmann - Kl. Lutau 1878, durch Apotheker E. Rosenbohm.

Bail (E. 64) giebt El. granulatus von Groddeck, Kreis Schwetz, an.

An den meisten aufgezählten Orten fand sich Elaph. granul. unter Kiefern, wenige Zoll unter der Erdoberfläche unter Moos. Ob Elaphomyces auf Kiefernwurzeln schmarotzt oder in symbiotischem Verhältniss mit ihnen lebt, ist durch die Untersuchung von **Reess** (Botan. Zeitung 1880. 729 ff. 1885. 748. Berichte deutsch. botan. Ges. III. 293 und Bd. III. S. IXIII) noch nicht klar gestellt. Es sind mir aber auch Angaben gemacht, dass Elaph. granul. unter Tannenstubben, d. h. denen von Picea excelsa, gefunden sei, so im Walde von Fürstenau bei Drengfurth und im Allenburg'er Stadtwalde, wo El. granul. unter „Picea exc. und Pinus silv. beim Roden“ gesammelt wurde und ich selbst habe zwei Exemplare El. gran. unter Picea excelsa in der Brandenburg'er Haide bei Ludwigsort gefunden. Aber Kiefern waren am letzten Ort ganz in der Nähe und ihre Wurzeln konnten leicht bis dicht an den Rothtannenstamm hinangehen. So wahrscheinlich auch im Walde von Fürstenau. Sicher ist also Elaph. gran. auf Picea excelsa nicht nachgewiesen.

Elaphomyces variegatus Vitt. Monog. Tub. 1831. 68.

Tulasne Fung. hyp. 108. — **Elaphomyces muricatus** Fries 1829. Sys. III 59. — **Elaph. vulg.** γ. variegatus **Corda** in **Sturm** Pilze Deutschlands. 1841. 19. und 20. Heft, Tafel 9. Ist der Name von Fries: El. muricat. wirklich dem El. varieg. Vitt. zukommend, so hat der erstere Name, weil er der frühere ist, zu gelten.

Hülle $^{5}/_{4}$ bis 3 mm dick, dicker als bei E. granul., aussen heller oder dunkler gelbbraun, derbwarzig, Warzen kegelig oder fast pyramidal, undeutlich 4- bis 6-kantig, unten $^{1}/_{3}$ bis $^{1}/_{2}$ mm im Durchmesser, spitz oder stumpf, oft so hoch als breit; Querschnitt der Hülle mit äusserer brauner, dünner Schicht, mittlerer dünner, gelblicher oder weisser, oder licht bräunlich-weisser; dann die 1 bis $1^{1}/_{2}$ mm dicke innerste, bläulich-graue, oder sehr licht kermesingraue, die entweder gleichfarbig und gleichartig ist, oder aus groben, kantigen Körnern zusammengesetzt, ohne Farbenunterschied, oder zwischen groben, sshwärzlich-grauen Körnern hell-röthlich-graue Gewebsmasse zeigt. Sporen schwarz-violett, kuglig, sehr zartwarzig, Durchmesser im Mittel 0,0211 mm, in den Extremen 0,0196 mm bis 0,0226 mm.

Der kuglige Pilz hat eine sehr harte Schaale, welche die des El. granulatus an Dicke sehr übertrifft. Ich sah den Pilz nur von 13—22 mm im Durchmesser. Ich habe mehrere Exemplare, bei denen die Warzen von zwei Grössen sind, grosse, dicke und kleine, schmale. Die letzteren stehen zwischen den ersteren und umgeben sie einreihig als Einfassung. In anderen Exemplaren findet dieser Unterschied nicht oder wenig statt.

Die Sporen, die ich für gut entwickelt halten konnte, maassen in den Extremen, wie folgt, in vier Pilzen von vier verschiedenen Fundorten:

1)	0,0216—0,0249 mm
2)	0,0186—0,0213 „
3)	0,0186—0,0219 „
4)	0,0199—0,0226 „
im Mittel	0,0196—0,0226 mm.

Tulasne l. c. giebt 0,02—0,022 mm als Durchmesser der Sporen an, welches mit meinen Befunden stimmt.

Ich habe den Pilz von folgenden preussischen Fundorten vor mir: 1) **Kreis Gumbinnen.** Serpenten 1872, durch John Reitenbach-Plicken. 1. Ex. — 2) **Kreis Johannisburg.** Königl. Forstbelauf Weissuhnen bei Rudczany. Königl. Förster Nicolai. 1882. 2 Exx. — 3) **Kreis Schlochau.** Peterkau. Durch Prof. Dr. Prätorius. 3 Exx. 1878. — 4) **Kreis Flatow.** Königl. Vandsburg'er Forstbelauf Kl. Lutau. Forstsekretär Herrmann. Durch Apotheker E. Rosenbohm. 1878.

Bail (E 64) giebt Elaphom. variegatus bei Jäschkenthal, Ottomin, Pelonken, in Danzigs Nähe an.

Die Abbildung **Corda's** bei Sturm zeigt in der Hülle hellere, körnige Stücke, geschieden durch dunklere Gewebstheile, gerade umgekehrt, wie ich es bei einigen Exemplaren vor mir habe.

Tulasne sagt, dass Elaph. variegatus ebenso allgemein verbreitet sei, als El. granulatus. Diess ist sicher in Preussen nicht der Fall. Unter einer grösseren Zahl von El. granulatus von einem Fundorte fanden sich immer nur ein oder wenige Exemplare von El. varieg. und nur an wenigen Orten.

Elaphomices anthracinus.

Vitt. Mon. Tub. 66. Tab. III. Fig. VIII. Tulasne Fung. hyp. 106.

Pilz fast kuglig, aussen glanzlos, tief braunschwarz, wie verkohlt, glatt, in Vertiefungen warzig, Warzen 1/3 — 1/2 mm im Durchmesser, flach, stumpf. Hülle 1 1/2 mm dick, äussere Schicht 1/2 mm stark, ganz schwarz, glänzend auf dem Schnitt, innere 1 mm dick, weiss. Sporen kuglig, schwarz, derbwarzig, 0,0297 bis 0,0311 mm im Durchmesser.

Der Pilz befand sich unter einer Sendung von Elaph. granulatus, die ich von königl. Förster **Henecke** aus dem königl. Forstbelauf Glinow, Kreis Kartaus, 1877 erhielt, in einem ganzen Exemplar und zwei zerbrochenen. Die Pilze maassen 17—20 mm im Durchmesser und waren unter Kiefern, die mit Rothbuchen gemischt standen, gefunden.

Hymenogastrei Tul.

Knollig gestaltete Pilze mit nicht von selbst sich öffnender Hülle, mit Höhlungen im Innern, die mit länglichen Zellen (Basidien) ausgekleidet sind, auf denen sich oben zu 2 bis 8 Sporen abschnüren und endlich abfallen.

Gautieria Vittadini.

Vitt. l. c. 25 — **Corda** l. c. fung. v. 28. VI. 33. Anleitg. p. LXXXIII et 114. — **Klotzsch** Fl. regni boruss. t. 464. — **Tulasne** l. c. 62.

Ohne Hüllschicht, der Körper des Pilzes mit rundlichen, länglichen oder linealen, unregelmässig sich krümmenden, nach aussen sich öffnenden Höhlungen durchzogen, die mit länglichen Basidien und Cysten (letzteres nach Bail, E 63) **ausgekleidet sind. Sporen je 2 umgekehrt eiförmig-elliptisch oder fast doppelt-spindelförmig, längsfurchig.**

Gautieria graveolens Vitt. l. c.

Rundlich länglich, mit einfachem Wurzelstrang, ausser den kleinen sporenführenden keine leeren Höhlungen, Sporen elliptisch, gegen den Grund zugespitzt, kurz gestielt, daher fast umgekehrt-eiförmig, mit 7—9 schwach hervorragenden Längsrippen und Furchen, Geruch nach Asa foetida (Knoblauch).

Bail (C) legte auf der Versammlung des preuss. botan. Vereins zu Neustadt eine bei Jäschkenthal bei Danzig, April 1877 von ihm gefundene Gautieria als morchelliformis Vitt. vor. Ich konnte der Versammlung nicht beiwohnen, erbat mir aber eine Probe des Pilzes und erhielt den 5. November desselben Jahres die Hälfte eines Pilzes, den **Bail** den 28. Oktober an der früheren Stelle gesammelt hatte. Der Pilz roch stark nach Asa foetida und es ergab sich bei näherer Untersuchung, dass es **Gautieria graveolens** Vitt. war, wovon sich auf meine Mittheilung und Beweislegung hin **Bail** (C 73, B 9, E 63) überzeugte. Ueber die Gestalt des Pilzes konnte ich nicht urtheilen, da das Stück ohne Schutz im Brief mir zugeschickt war und stark durch die Post zusammengedrückt, in meine Hand kam; auch hatte es nichts von Wurzelgeflecht, welches Vitt. bei G. graveolens als einfachen Strang, bei G. morchelliformis als sehr verzweigt und ausgebreitet beschreibt und abbildet. Die anderen Unterschiede beider Pilze stelle ich der besseren Uebersicht wegen einander gegenüber:

Gant. morchellif.	Gant. graveolens.
1. „Cellulae internae et externae maiusculae". Vitt. Sie sind von Vitt. l. c. Tab. III, VI als Höhlen abgebildet, die bis 3 mm breit und bis 6 mm lang sind.	1. Cellulae internae et externae minutae, poriformes" Vitt. Sie werden kaum halb so gross, als die von G. morchellif. von Vitt. l. c. Tab. IV. XIII. abgebildet.
2. „Odor specificus intensissimus Dictamni albi quodammodo analogus". Vitt.	2. „Odor fortissimus, vix tolerandus quasi cepae emarcidae". Vitt.
3. Sporen: Breite : Länge = 0,0095—0,0125 mm : 0,019— 0,023 mm. Tulasne l. c.	3. Sporen: Breite : Länge = 0,008—0,009 mm : 0,016 mm. Tulasne l. c.
4. Die Wände zwischen je zwei Sporenkammern zeigen noch zahlreiche, lufthaltige, nicht Sporen tragende Hohlräume und sind mehr als doppelt so dick als die von G. graveolens. Corda Icon. VI. p. 34, Tab. VII, Fig. 62.	4. Die Wände zwischen je 2 Sporenkammern sind fast ohne leere Höhlungen und dünn. Corda l. c. Tab. VII. 63.
5) „Sporae ellipsoideae, utrinque subacutae pallide luteo-fuscae". Corda l. c. und Abbildung l. c.	5. Sporae obovato-ellipsoideae, vertice obtusae, luteolae" Corda l. c. und Abbildung.

Der Danzig'er Pilz stimmte gut mit G. graveolens Vitt., Tulasne und Corda, aber nicht mit G. morchelliformis. Die Sporen des Danzig'er Pilzes (Bild 24—28 von der Seite, 29 und 30 vom Scheitel gesehen) hatten folgende Maasse.

1) Br. : Lge. : = 0,0099 : 0,0166 mm
0,0107 : 0,0157 „
0,0099 : 0,0174 „
0,0091 : 0,0157 „
0,0099 : 0,0199 „
0,0083 : 0,0149 „
0,0091 : 0,0149 „
0,0116 : 0,0183 „
0,0083 : 0,0149 „
0,0083 : 0,0166 „
0,0099 : 0,0216 „
0,0091 : 0,0149 „

Mittel: 0,0090 : 0,0167 mm.

Das Mittel stimmt also gut mit Tulasne's Grössenangabe der Sporen von G. graveol.

Die Farbe des Danzig'er Pilzes ist wohl nicht ganz sicher angebbar, da er acht Tage alt in meine Hände kam. Er war aussen umbrafarbig-grau. Hüllschicht nicht wahrnehmbar. Innen ist er umbra-lackbraun; eine dicke weisse Ader, die sich baumartig verzweigt, zog sich über mehr als $^3/_4$ der Länge des kurz-länglichen Stückes, das ich hatte, welches 24 mm breit und 35 mm lang war; Dicke wegen der Quetschung nicht bestimmbar. Ausser dieser weissen baumartigen Ader ist der Pilz für's blosse Auge umbra-lackbraun. Die Lupe jedoch zeigt schon, dass diese Farbe nur der Auskleidung der Sporenkammern zukommt und dass das Gewebe zwischen denselben tiefgrau, etwas durchscheinend und fast knorpelartig erscheint. Bei durchfallendem Licht unter dem Mikroskop zeigt sich die Sporenmasse umbrafarbig, die einzelnen Sporen aber umbra-lackfarbig. Die Sporenkammern sind klein, bis 2 mm lang und etwa $^1/_3$ mm breit; unter dem Mikroskop gemessen waren zwei Höhlungen in Breite : Länge =

1) 0,039 — 0,266 : 1,473 mm,
2) 0,146 : 0,28 mm.

Die Zwischenwände zwischen je zwei Sporenkammern bestehen aus dicht und eng in einander gewebten farblosen Fäden ohne alle Höhlungen; auch in der weissen Ader sind keine Höhlungen. Die Sporen sind umgekehrt-eiförmig, elliptisch, mit stielartiger Spitze unten, stumpf abgerundet oben; sie haben 7 bis 8 deutliche Längsrippen, die sich gut erkennen lassen (Bild 29 und 30), wenn man die Sporen auf den Scheitel stellt. Diese Wandverdickungen sind sehr ungleich breit, oft ist ein solches Längsband getheilt oder gegabelt. Die Verdickungen sind dunkler, als die dünneren Zwischenräume. In den Sporen sind zahlreiche, farblose Oeltropfen. Die Farbe der Sporen liegt in ihrer Wand.

Aus dieser Darlegung ergiebt sich, dass der von Klotzsch (in Dietrich Fl. reg. bor. No. 464) als Gautieria morchelliformis abgebildete und beschriebene Pilz nicht dies, sondern Gaut. graveolens ist; dass ferner Tulasne (l. c. 62) den Pilz von Klotzsch mit Unrecht zu Gaut. maeandrifor. stellt. Klotzsch's Exemplar war von Wallroth bei Nordhausen gefunden. Da Bail (in Nees von Essenbeck und Henry System der Pilze V. Abtheilung 9 Taf. 27) die Abbildung der dargestellten vermeintlichen Gaut. morchellif. von Klotzsch entnommen hat, ist auch von Bail Gaut. graveolens dargestellt.

Rhizopogon Tulasne.

Tulasne, Fungi hyp. 85. Daselbst die weiteren Synonyme.

Hüllschicht des knolligen Pilzes geschlossen, mit wurzelartigen verzweigten Fäden, die vom untern Theil ausgehen, umhüllt. Gewebe des Innern gleichmässig mit zahlreichen kleinen, rundlichen, kugligen, eiförmigen Höhlungen, welche mit den sporenbildenden Zellen (Basidien) ausgekleidet sind. Sporen länglich, glatt, durchscheinend zu 2 bis 8 auf einer Tragzelle (Basidie).

Rhizopogon rubescens.

Tulasne Giornale bot. ital. II. 58. **Tulasne** Fung. hypog. 89.

Jung in der Erde weiss, an der Luft die Hüllschicht erröthend. Wurzelgeflecht gering, Hüllschicht dünn, frisch $^5/_{10}$ bis $^4/_{10}$ mm, trocken $^1/_{10}$ bis $^1/_4$ mm dick. Sporen zu fünf bis acht auf einer Tragzelle, sehr kurz gestielt, länglich, zwei bis dreimal so lang als breit, sehr blass grünlich, in Menge licht olivengrün; Breite : Länge im Mittel = 0,0027 : 0,0073 mm.

Ich erhielt den Pilz zuerst Herbst 1873 von Professor Dr. Prätorius in Konitz, dann 25. September 1874 von Neuem und zwar 39 Stück, den 29. September desselben Jahres folgte eine weitere Sendung. 1876 erhielt ich ein Exemplar schon den 2. Juni, mehrere den 23. September desselben Jahres, eins den 7. Oktober 1879. Sandige Schiessstände bei Konitz. — 18. Oktober 1876 empfing ich ein Exemplar des Pilzes aus dem ehemaligen Lunau'er Walde, jetzt zu Paparczyn gehörig, Kreis Kulm, von Apotheker Scharlok. Herbst 1881 bekam ich von Apotheker Eugen Rosenbohm aus dem Walde von Fronau, Kreis Kulm, mehrere Exemplare von Rhiz. rubescens. — Den 6. September 1883 fand ich im sandigen Kiefernwalde bei Regencia-Mühle, Kreis Thorn, mehrere Pilze der Art. — Den 21. Juli 1878 sammelte ich einige Exx. in der Forst Thurbruch zwischen Rederitz und Machlin, Kreis Dt. Krone, auf grandigem Wege im Kiefernwalde und in demselben Kreise und Jahre östlich von Klein Nakel auf sandigem Wege im Kiefernwalde den 12. August auch einige Pilze der Art. Ferner den 30. August desselben Jahres in demselben Kreise auf sandigem Wege im Kiefernwalde zwischen Drogenmühle und dem Gr. Plötzensee einige Exx. — und den 27. August 1878 im Sande im Stadtwalde von Tütz, südlich vom See Pinnow, einige andere. — Den 20. Oktober 1878 erhielt ich einige Exx. aus einer Kiefernschonung auf Gut Neu-Tuchel, bei Tuchel, Kreis Tuchel, von Herrn Max Hoyer, damals Student der Landwirthschaft in Königsberg. — Professor Prätorius empfing den Pilz von einem Schüler schon Mitte Mai 1875 aus der Schlochau'er Gegend. Bail (B. 11. E. 64) giebt Rhizop. rub. an bei Pelonken, am Karlsberge, Zoppot bei Danzig und bei Groddeck, Kreis Schwetz.

In Ostpreussen fand ich Rhizop. rub. im Kreise Allenstein 1879 auf sandiger Wegseite südwestlich von Kl. Gimmern (18. August) und 19. August auf sandigem Wege zwischen Rentienen und Schillings; ferner 23. August 1880 in sandiger Kiefernschonung am Südostzipfel des Gr. Plauzig'er Sees. Den 10. September 1877 schickte mir Oberlehrer W. Krüger aus sandiger Kiefernhaide des Stadtwaldes von Tilsit einige Knollen des Rhiz. rub.

Die Pilze wurden immer im Sande in der Nähe von Kiefern gefunden und hoben meist die Spitze etwas über das Erdreich empor.

Die jungen Pilze waren unter der Erde ganz weiss mit braunem Wurzelgeflecht umgeben. Aus der Erde herausgenommen, wurden sie in der Hüllschicht blass-rosig: Bild 32. Der Querschnitt: Bild 33, zeigt das Innere ganz weiss, aber die durchschnittene Hüllschicht auch im Innern rosig. Allmälig mit der Heranbildung der höchst blass, einzeln kaum grünlich bei durchfallendem Licht erscheinenden Sporen (Bild 45), die aber in einiger Menge doch schon grünlich erscheinen, färbt sich das Innere des Pilzes blass schmutzig-grünlich (Bild 35), während die Hüllschicht sich noch auf dem Schnitt röthet. Bald hört aber die Röthung der Hüllschicht auch auf dem Querschnitt auf. Aussen ist mit der Heranbildung der Sporen die Hüllschicht auch unter der Erde licht gelblich-bräunlich geworden, während das Wurzelgeflecht grösser und dunkelbraun geworden ist (Bild 46). Die Röthung der Hüllschicht tritt bisweilen bei recht weit vorgeschrittener Reife noch ein. So war die Aussenseite bei den Pilzen, die ich zwischen Rentienen und Schillings fand, schon lichtbraun, dennoch war sie oft noch stark geröthet. Endlich durch die immer mehr heranwachsende Menge der Sporen färbt sich das Innere auf dem Querschnitt dunkelolivengrün (Bild 36). Zuletzt wird auch die Aussenseite schmutzig-braun-grün, im Innern verflüssigt sich das ganze Gewebe in schmutzig-schwärzlich-grüne Jauche, wie Tulasne angiebt, indem das Gewebe zwischen den Sporenkammern selbst schmutziggrünlich wird und so gefärbt verwest. Der ganze Pilz ist dann sehr weich und platzt bei geringer Berührung.

Ich sah die Pilze von 15 mm bis 62 mm im Durchmesser. Einer aus der Nähe von Rentienen hatte in den drei Hauptrichtungen 31, 48 und 62 mm Durchmesser, also schwankte die Grösse von der einer Haselnuss bis zu der einer mässig grossen Kartoffel. Die Knollen waren fast kuglig oder abgeplattet rundlich und durch flache meridiane Einschnürungen wulstig oder eiförmig-länglich (Bild 46), oder langlänglich mit einer Einschnürung. Das ästige tiefbraune Wurzelgeflecht war mehr oder minder kräftig entwickelt und umgab meist vom Anheftungspunkte am Grunde aus den ganzen Pilz bis über den Scheitel (Bild 46).

Hüllschicht aussen glatt, frisch $^{3}/_{10}$ bis $^{4}/_{10}$ mm dick, die in Bild 37 mass 0,366 mm. Der gestrocknete Pilz hat eine viel dünnere Hüllschicht. Ich fand sie beim getrockneten $^{1}/_{10}$—$^{1}/_{4}$ mm dick, ganz dunkelbraun oder nur den äusseren Theil braun, den inneren weisslich. Ich sah keinen Fall, dasss die Hüllschicht irgend wo fehlte, wie Tulasne angiebt: „peridio interdum hinc inde subevanido vel varie rimoso". Auch kann die Hüllschicht nur im Verhältniss zu der dickeren, die Rh. luteolus haben soll, sehr dünn („tenuissimum" Tul.) genannt werden. In der Hüllschicht verlaufen die sehr zarten, dicht liegenden Fäden, aus denen sie besteht, parallel zur Aussenseite. Die äusseren Schichten verwittern, werden braun und dadurch färbt sich auch die Peridie lichtbraun, dann braun, endlich schmutzigschwarz-braun.

Die Sporenkammern des Innern sind (Bild 37) kurz oder lang-länglich, gerade oder gekrümmt, anfangs weiss, wie das lockere Zwischengewebe, später durch die grünlichen Sporen olivenfarbig. Die Sporenkammern sind auf's Dichteste mit den Tragzellen der Sporen ausgefüttert: Bild 38. die Tragzellen (Basidien) der Sporen sind lang-lineal, oben keulig verdickt (Bild 39—44) und tragen auf dieser verdickten Spitze 5—8 elliptische Sporen, selten eine oder die andere auf der Seite (Bild 41). Diese Sporen sind kurz gestielt, nicht sitzend. Tulasne schreibt ihnen ein sterigma brevissimum vix conspicuum zu. Die Stielchen waren jedoch auf's Deutlichste sichtbar und hafteten an den Sporen, wenn sie abgefallen waren (Bild 45).

Tulasne zieht Hymenangium virens Klotzsch (Dietrich Fl. regni bor. 382) zu Rhyzopogon rubescens. Es stimmen die Abbildungen a—d des ganzen Pilzes einigermaassen; die der Abbildung des durchschnittenen Pilzes kann aber nur nach getrocknetem Exemplar gemacht sein und die Abbildung, welche die Basidien, die alle 4 langgestielte Sporen tragen, darstellt, ist ganz unzutreffend. Ich sah vier Sporen und solch lange Stiele nie. Zwischen den Basidien bildet Klotzsch einige kegelförmige „Antheren" ab. Ich habe mich ganz vergebens bemüht, solche zu finden. Tulasne giebt 2—8 Sporen für eine Tragzelle an, ich sah nur 5—8 auf einer; geringere Zahlen nie.

Die Sporen enthalten zarte, plasmatische Körnchen, öfter zwei grössere Tröpfchen und sind drehrund.

Jod bräunt die reifen Sporen etwas, das Gewebe fast gar nicht. Jod und verdünnte Schwefelsäure färben Gewebe und Sporen braun, die Sporen dunkel.

Die Sporen maassen in Br. : Lge. =

I. von Konitz:	1) 0,0033 : 0,0083	mm
	2) 0,0033 : 0,0066	„
	3) 0,0033 : 0,0099	„
	4) 0,0024 : 0,0074	„
	5) 0,0024 : 0,0074	„
II. Lunau'er Wald:	6) 0,0033 : 0,0085	„
	7) 0,0033 : 0,0074	„
III. Tilsit'er Stadtwald:	8) 0,0028 : 0,0072	„
	9) 0,0028 : 0,0079	„
	10) 0,0028 : 0,0050	„
IV. Neu-Tuchel:	11) 0,0021 : 0,0079	„
	12) 0,0021 : 0,0072	„
	13) 0,0021 : 0,0050	„
Mittel:	0,0027 : 0,0073	mm.

Nach Tulasne Fung. hyp. 90 ist die Br. : Lge. = 0,003 : 0,007 bis 0,009 mm; diese Angabe passt zu den obigen Messungen.

Tulasne Fung. hyg. 90 giebt an, dass der Pilz sehr schwach, fast gar nicht riecht. Aus der Erde genommen, riecht der Pilz nach meinen Beobachtungen kaum. Die erste Sendung, welche ich von Konitz erhielt, roch nach 3—4 Tagen nicht sehr stark, aber widerlich. Zwei Freunde erklärten, die Pilze röchen wie menschliche Leichen, die erst wenige Tage alt sind. Die zweite Sendung von Konitz entwickelte in zwei sehr faulen, innen ganz breiigen Pilzen einen entschiedenen Knoblauchgeruch, und in einem recht faulen einen sehr deutlichen Geruch nach Blausäure.

Tulasne Fung. hyp. 90 giebt an, dass der getrocknete Pilz hart sei, aussen rauh und innen die höchst zahlreichen, ziemlich leeren Sporenkammern behalte. Für diese Angabe wird vorausgesetzt, dass der Pilz noch nicht reif ist, weil in der Reife das Gewebe zwischen den Sporenkammern zerfliesst („Septa in pultem solvuntur" l. c. 90. — „Carne tandem toto fatiscente" l. c. 89). Ich finde jedoch, dass der getrocknete Pilz sich je nach seiner Reife verschieden zeigt. Unreife, die erst wenige Sporen entwickelt haben oder keine, sind trocken innen lichtbraun und zeigen ebenso gefärbte, sehr kleine Höhlungen durchweg selbst fürs blosse Auge. Fast reife zeigten getrocknet im Innern eine sehr grosse, unregelmässige, fast den ganzen Pilz durchziehende Höhlung, die durch's Eintrocknen entstand und gegen den Rand zu die kleinen Sporenkammern ganz gefüllt mit schwarz-grünen, dicken Sporenmassen, oder auch (in demselben Pilz) leere an anderen Stellen; die Scheidewände zwischen den gefüllten Kammern lichtbraun und sehr dünn.

Die Unterschiede zwischen Rhizopogon luteolus Tul. und Rh. rubesens Tul. erscheinen sehr gering und lassen sich noch nicht recht beurtheilen, da Rh. luteol. jedenfalls zu wenig bekannt ist. Möglicher Weise sind beide nur Formen eines Pilzes, nicht zwei Arten.

Rhiz. lut. soll nach **Tulasne** schmutzig-gelblich-weiss, später olivenfarbig sein; Rh. rub. anfangs weiss unter der Erde, in der Luft erröthend, endlich braungelblich und olivenfarbig. Das vom Farbenunterschiede in der Jugend hergenommene Merkmal lässt uns aber bei älteren Pilzen ganz im Stich. Die Hüllschicht bei Rh. luteol. soll dick, fast ledrig, die von Rh. rub. sehr dünn sein und hier und da sogar fehlen. Letzteres sah ich nicht. Was ist aber dünn, was dick, wenn nicht

Maasse angegeben werden? Rh. luteol. soll von stark entwickelten, wurzelartigen Fäden umgeben sein, Rh. rub. nur von sehr sparsamen. Ich fand das Wurzelgeflecht, das Rh. rub. umgiebt, recht beträchtlich bisweilen. Wie unterscheidet man aber ein reichliches und ein sparsames ohne sichere Maassangaben? Die Sporenkammern von Rh. lut. sollen zuletzt fast ganz mit Sporen gefüllt sein, die des Rh. rub. „semper vacuae (lacunae scil.) nec unquam sporis ex integro repletae". **Tul.** Wie unterscheidet man lacunae subfarctae und solche, die weniger gefüllt sind, ohne bestimmte Maasse? Die Scheidewände zwischen den Sporenkammern sollen bei Rh. lut. immer weiss bleiben und mit dieser Farbe verfliessen, die von Rh. rub. schliesslich olivengrün werden und so gefärbt verfliessen. Ich habe in dieser Beziehung keine Beobachtungen machen können, finde aber bei getrockneten, fast reifen Pilzen von Rhiz. rub. die Scheidewände bräunlich oder weisslich bräunlich zwischen den schwarz-olivenfarbigen ganz mit Sporen gefüllten Kammern. Die Sporen von Rh. lut. sollen ohne Stiel auf den Basidien sitzen, wie sie Tul. auch abbildet, aber waren sie reif? Sie sollen sehr klein („minutissimae") von Rh. lut. sein, die von Rh. rub. grösser, aber **Tulasne** giebt ein Maass für die von Rh. lut. nicht an. Endlich soll Rh. lut. zuletzt stark und fast nach Koth (oder „quasi stercorius") riechen, **Tul.** l. c. 87, dagegen Rh. rub. sehr schwach oder gar nicht riechen. Dass Rh. rub. jedoch zuletzt recht stark und verschiedenartig riecht, habe ich dargelegt. Kurz die Unterschiede beider Pilze bedürfen weiterer Untersuchung.

Bail (C 73, B 11, E 64) giebt Rh. lut. bei Heubude und Bordel bei Danzig an. „Die Exemplare wurden im Innern schmierig und rochen dann ganz wie Menschenkoth, und zwar sehr energisch" (D 64). Ich kenne den Pilz überhaupt nicht, auch nicht von Danzig. Meine Bitte um ihn wurde mir abgeschlagen.

Melanogaster.

Corda in J. Sturm Dlds. Flora III. 11. 1. (1831); Icon. fung. V. 23; VI. 31 und 45, tab. IX. **Tulasne** Fung. hyp. 92, daselbst die Synonyme.

Hüllschicht des rundlichen knollenförmigen Pilzes glatt, wergartig, von wenig Wurzelgeflecht umgeben, das Innere mit zahlreichen rundlichen oder länglichen Sporenkammern, die von dem Gewebe, das die Tragzellen der Sporen entwickelt, ganz erfüllt werden. Tragzellen mit 4, oder 3 bis 5 glatten gestielten Sporen.

Melanogaster variegatus.

Tul. Ann. sc. nat. 2. Ser. XIX. 1843 p. 377. Tab. 17 fig. 22. **Octaviana variegata Vittadini** l. c. 16. Tab. III fig. 4.

Unregelmässig rundlich, anfangs aussen ockerfarbig, fast goldgelb, endlich braun. Füllung der Sporenkammern schwärzlich, Zwischenwände weiss-gelb. Sporen umgekehrt eiförmig, fast walzig oder elliptisch, braunschwarz, Spitze gerundet, Grund gestutzt, mit glashellem Reste des Stiels, Br. : Lge. (ohne Stiel) = 0,0045 : 0,0082 mm.

Der Pilz ist von Herrn Gutsbesitzer Plehn auf Lubochin, Kreis Schwetz Juli 1876 auf seinem Gute Lubochin in lehmigem Sande 2—3 Zoll unter der Erdoberfläche unter Laubholz: Carpinus Betulus, Betula verrucosa, Populus Tremula nach Mittheilung des Finders entdeckt.

Ich bekam zwei Stücke von zwei verschiedenen Pilzen den 1. November 1876 durch Prof. **Bail** (B 11., E 63). Aus diesen Stücken kann ich über die Gestalt des Pilzes nichts Genaues angeben. Der Pilz war nach ihnen ungefähr wallnussgross. Da die Pilze mehr als ein Vierteljahr alt und trocken waren, konnte ich nur die Sporen (Bild 4) untersuchen. Sie sassen nie mehr den Tragzellen auf, hatten aber einen glashellen Rest am gestutzten Grunde. Sie hatten ohne Stiel:

Br. : Lge. = 1) 0,0049 : 0,0083 mm
2) 0,0041 : 0,0087 „
3) 0,0041 : 0,0074 „
4) 0,0049 : 0,0087 „

Mittel 0,0045 : 0,0082 mm.

Tulasne a. O. giebt die Br. : Lge. an = 0,004 : 0,0064 mm. Er beschreibt sie als atro-brunneae (sc. sporae), semipellucidae. Ich fand sie undurchsichtig. **Bail** (E 63) giebt ihre Br. : Lge. nur an = 0,003 : 0,006 mm und **Bail** (D) berichtet, dass er den Pilz auf der Nonnenkämpe gefunden habe. **Melanogaster ambiguus Tul.** giebt **Bail** (E 62) an, 1877 und 1878 im Jäschkenthal'er Walde bei Danzig gefunden zu haben und beschreibt den Pilz genauer. Ich habe ihn nicht gesehen.

Sclerodermei.

Fries (ex parte) Pl. homonom. 134.

Knollenförmige Pilze, ungestielt oder mit derbem Stiel, Hülle dick, Inneres vielkammerig, Kammern rundlich-eckig, ganz gefüllt mit dem Sporen bildenden Gewebe, geschieden durch Streifen von unfruchtbarem. Sporen, kuglig, warzig, gebildet auf den kuglig angeschwollenen Endzellen (Basidien) des fruchtbaren Gewebes zu 2 bis 4.

Scleroderma.

Pers. Syn. Fung. p. XIV 150. **Nees** Syst. 132. **Fries** Syst. myc. III 44. **Corda** Jcon. V 24.

Abgeplattet-kuglige Pilze, ungestielt oder sehr kurz gestielt, Grund in Wurzeläste zertheilt, Hülle mehr oder weniger dick, derb, lederig, glatt oder gefeldert rissig, Sporenkammern ohne ihnen eigene besondere Hülle, Sporen gestachelt und warzig verdickt. Die Hülle wird endlich unregelmässig oben zersetzt.

Scleroderma vulgare Fr. Syst. myc. III 46.

Abgeplattet-kuglig, umgestielt oder fast ungestielt, Hülle ledrig, schmutzig weisslich, oft rissig gefeldert, dadurch fast warzig, die Felder bräunlich, Inneres, wenn die Sporen im ersten Zustande der Reife sind, blauschwarz, weiss gefeldert, später, nach Zersetzung des Zwischengewebes grau-grünlich-braun. Sporen kuglig, anfangs bei durchfallendem Licht blauschwarz, wenn reif, schmutzig braun

bei durchfallendem Licht, stachelig, Stacheln spitzlich oder gestutzt, 16 bis 25, ja 30 im Umkreise, fast doppelt so hoch als breit, Oberfläche etwas netzförmig. Durchmesser der Sporen im Mittel 0,0146 mm, in den Extremen 0,0108 bis 0,0199 mm.

Ueber die Sporenbildung vergl. **Tulasne** Ann. sc. nat. 1842. II. Ser. Tom. XVII 5.

Die Sporen maassen in reifem Zustande:

1) 0,0149—0,0199	mm	(Ponarien)
2) 0,0149—0,0183	„	(Gr. Koschlau)
3) 0,0112—0,0146	„	(Piditten)
4) 0,0115—0,0146	„	(Lansker Ofen)
5) 0,0115—0,0151	„	(Pilzenkrug)
6) 0,0108—0,0144	„	(Gelguhnen)
7) 0,0149—0,0166	„	(Konitz)
8) 0,0116—0,0149	„	(Lorenz)
9) 0,0132—0,0166	„	(Zw. Liniets u. Paparczin)
10) 0,0182—0,0199	„	(Bornzin, Pommern)
= 0,0146	mm.	

Die Sporen der getrockneten, reifen Pilze, die eine pulvrig-flockige Masse von grau-grün-brauner Farbe im Innern haben und bei denen das Zwischengewebe zwischen den Kammern und den Sporen in unkenntliche Fetzen übergegangen ist, zeigen nach allen Richtungen Stacheln, 16—25, selten mehr, im Umkreise. Diese Stacheln sind spitz oder gestutzt, die Sporen sind bei durchfallendem Licht schmutzig dunkelbraun. Netzförmige Verdickung ist meist nur stellenweise auf ihrer Haut zu erkennen. Ganz anders ist die Farbe der Sporen im ersten Reifezustande, nämlich blauschwarz bei durchfallendem und auffallendem Licht. Dabei zeigt sich in diesem ersten Reifezustande, wenn das Zwischengewebe zwischen den Kammern und den Sporen noch da ist, eine helle Haut rings um die Spore: Bild 48, welche oft zwischen den Stacheln gewölbt ist, und die dunkle Haut ist überall netzförmig. Behandlung mit koncentrirter Schwefelsäure entfernt die helle Haut: Bild 49 und 50. Von Bild 50 ist durch's Messer, mit dem eine dünne Platte aus der noch fest zusammenhängenden Sporenmasse geschnitten wurde, ein Stück der Sporenhaut fortgenommen. Weder über die Farbenänderung der Sporen noch über das Verschwinden der Haut zwischen den Stacheln konnte ich zweifeln, da ich die Sporen farbig bei der Untersuchung in drei Fällen gezeichnet hatte und die schmutzig braun gewordenen an demselben Pilz, der getrocknet wurde, später mit der Zeichnung vergleichen konnte. Ebenso war die Haut in einem Falle sicher bei dem getrockneten Pilz später verschwunden. Ich finde, dass **Tulasne** (Ann. sc. nat. II. Ser. 17. Tome 1842, p. 8. Tab. 1. Fig. 8) die Haut zwischen den Stacheln beobachtet hat. Er deutet sie jedoch anders, denn er hat nicht gefunden, dass die Haut zwischen den Stacheln nur im Jugendzustande der Spore eigen ist und später verschwindet, sondern er spricht die Muthmaassung aus, dass sie eine Eigenthümlichkeit der Sporen von Scleroderma verrucosum Fr. sei, während die Sporen, welche einfache Stacheln haben, dem Scler. vulgare und Bovista Fr. angehörten. „Cependant“, fügt er hinzu, „ces trois espèces étant, à ce quil nous semble, fort difficile à distinguer, nous n'osons pas nous flatter d'être parvenus sans erreur à ces déterminations“. In Widerspruch mit dieser Auffassung zieht er jedoch in der Erklärung von Taf. 1 (a. O. p. 17) die stachligen Sporen und die mit Haut zwischen den Stacheln zu Scceleroderma vulg. Am besten von diesen 3 Arten von Sclerod. von Fries (Sclerod. vulgare, Sc. Bovista und verrucosum) unterscheiden sich Scler. vulgare und verruc., weil Scl. verruc. einen Stiel hat (Bull. Champ. t. 24 besonders bei Sowerby 311). Aber zu Sc. verr. können die Pilze, die ich mit der Haut zwischen den jugendlichen Sporen versehen fand, nicht gehören, weil sie garnicht oder kaum gestielt waren, auch ihre Peridie viel zu hart ist, besonders bei den getrockneten. „Peridio tenui fragili" sagt Fries (Syst. myc. III 49) von Scler. verr. Ich möchte, soweit ich die Frage beurtheilen kann: sind jene Fries'schen 3 Arten anzuerkennen oder nicht, mit: Nein! antworten, denn Scler. vulgare, welche Art mir nur annehmbar erscheint, schwankt in Betreff des Daseins oder der Abwesenheit eines Stiels., der Glätte, Felderung, Warzigkeit oder Höckrigkeit der Hülle, ferner deren Dicke so stark und die Fries'schen Unterschiede jener vermeintlichen 3 Arten sind so unbedeutend und so wenig scharf, dass sie zur Unterscheidung von 3 Arten nicht anwendbar erscheinen.

Sclerod. vulgare ist in Preussen an folgenden Orten beobachtet; ich habe den Pilz von allen gesehen, von den meisten vor mir. 1) **Kreis Fischhausen.** Zw. Pilzen-Krug und Gut Neuhäuser 1880. — Garten von Neuhäuser (Douglas'sches Grundstück) am Fusse alter Acer platanoides. 1874. W. Hensche — Weide bei Widitten in der Kaporn'schen Haide 1874. — 2) **Kreis Heiligenbeil.** Belauf Brandenburg'er Haide bei Ludwigsort 1880. — 3) **Kreis Wehlau.** Neuhof bei Tapiau. Ränder der Gartenwege. Gutsbesitzer Gallandi 1885 mit Anfrage: ob es Trüffeln wären. — 4) **Kreis Heilsberg.** Wald von Scharnick und Lingenau 1877. G. Klebs. — Klotainen. Ränder der Gartenwege 1879. Frau Major von Restorf. — 5) **Kreis Rössel.** Bei Bischofsstein. Kaplan Braun 1877. — 6) **Kreis Lyck.** Czerwonken bei Lyck. E. Rosenbohm 1875. 7) **Kreis Allenstein.** Belauf Lansker Ofen, Jagen 82. Bruch auf Torferde. 1880. — Nordwest von Gelguhnen. Wegseite 1880. — 8) **Kreis Mohrungen.** Ponarien bei Liebstadt. 1874. Graf A. v. d. Gröben. — 9) **Kreis Neidenburg.** Gr. Koschlau 1874. Frau Elise Möller. — 10) **Kreis Ortelsburg.** Zwischen Schwentainen und Grünwalde 1886. Dr. Abromeit. — Zwischen Kollozeygrond und Waldpusch 1886. Dr. Abromeit. — Zwischen Friedrichsfelde und Forstbelauf Kopittko 1886. Dr. Abromeit. — 11) **Kreis Osterode.** Mühlen, Gutsgarten. Administrator F. Wernitz 1884. Mit Anfrage: ob der Pilz eine Trüffel sei. — 12) **Kreis Löbau.** Katlewo bei Löbau 1874. Rittmeister Kaul. — 13) **Kreis Graudenz.** Haus Lopatken, im Garten 1879. Scharlok. — Kiefernwald bei Gruppe 1877. Scharlok. — Oberförsterei Jammi, Belauf Dossotschin 1882. — 14) **Kreis Kulm.** Grenzgraben zwischen Linietz und Paparczin 1877. Scharlok. — Garten von Weidenhof 1882. — 15) **Kreis Marienburg.** Bei Marienburg. Probst Preuschoff-Tolkemit. — 16) **Kreis Danzig.** Pelonken 1877. Scharlok. — 17) **Kreis Berent.** Lorenz, Gutsgarten 1875. — Zwischen Konarschin und Gribno im Kiefernwalde 1885. Sand. — Zwischen Wigonin und Gr. Bartel. Sand. Kiefernwald. — 19) **Kreis Kartaus.** Belauf Stanischau, Oberförsterei Mirchau. Gestell zwischen Jagen 9 und 17. 1877. — 20) **Kreis Konitz.** Garten in Gr. Paglau 1877. Prof. Prätorius. — In der Nähe des Schützenhauses von Konitz 1877. Prof. Prätorius und mehrmals schon 1875 von Prof. Prätorius erhalten; öfters etwas gestielt. — 21) **Kreis Flatow.** Kujaner Haide 1878. E. Rosenbohm. Im Sande des

Weges zwischen Radawnitz und Franziskowo 1881. — 22) **Kreis Dt.-Krone.** Im Sande zwischen Stabitz und Freudenfier 1878.

Der Durchmesser des Kopfs des Sclerod. vul. ist 30—80 mm. Es wächst im Sande, der etwas Lehm enthält, an Wegrändern, an Gartenwegen, auf kurzgrasigen Weiden, auch auf Torf.

Der Pilz lässt sich also durchaus nicht in allen Kreisen Preussens bisher nachweisen, obgleich zu vermuthen ist, dass er fast in allen vorkommt.

Pisolithus.

Albert. et Schwein. Conspect. Fung. 1805. 82. **Polysaccum Desportes** et **DC.** Rapp. voy. I. 8. 1807. Ex **Fries** Syst. myc. III 51. **Pisocarpium Link.** 1808.

Der rundliche, kuglige oder eiförmige oder umgekehrt eiförmige Pilz mit mehr oder weniger langem, dickem Stiel, der meist unten wurzelartig zertheilt ist, versehen. Hülle mässig dünn, bröcklich, unregelmässig oben zerreissend und abblätternd. Inneres mit zahlreichen, rundlichen, polygonalen Kammern, getrennt durch unfruchtbares Zwischengewebe; die Kammern mit dem sporenentwickelnden Gewebe gefüllt und die einzelnen durch ein eigenes besonderes Hüllchen begrenzt. Sporen kugelig, stachelig.

Der Gattungsname von **Albertini** und **Schweinitz:** Pisolithus hat die Priorität und daher Geltung. Auch die Art, welche Alb. und Schw. mit guter Abbildung zuerst aufstellten: **Pisolithus arenarius** ist von den Nachfolgern schlecht behandelt, denn **Fries** hat sie Polysaccum Pisocarpium benannt, während er mindestens dem Artnamen hätte Rechnung tragen sollen.

Ueber die Sporenbildung von Polysaccum hat **Tulasne** Ann. sc. nat. II. Ser. Tom. XVIII p. 129 ff. Aufschluss gegeben.

Pisolithus crassipes Casp.

Polysaccum crassipes DC. l. c. **Kopf 30 bis 70 mm im Quermesser, kuglig oder abgeplattet-kuglig in verschiedensten Maassen, eiförmig, fast walzig, umgekehrt-eiförmig, Stiel 20 bis 40 mm dick, kürzer als Kopf, bis drei mal so lang, nach unten allmälig verschmälert oder sich in Aeste zerklüftend, die verzweigt sind. Hülle schmutzig bräunlich-grau, Inneres dunkel lackbraun. Sporen mit 11 bis 18 Warzen im Umkreise, im Mittel 0,0087 mm, in den Extremen 0,0072 bis 0,0108 mm im Durchmesser. Warzen etwa halb so hoch als breit.**

Im sandigen Grande, der kaum Lehm enthält, in der Nähe von Kiefern, auf Wegen und in Schonungen, in sonniger Lage.

Die Sporen maassen im Durchmesser:

1) 0,0072—0,0093 mm (zw. Poln. Fuhlbeck und Riege)
2) 0,0072—0,0101 " (bei Gramattenbrück)
3) 0,0072—0,0108 " (zw. Dabermühl u. Neugoltz)
4) 0,0072—0,0101 " (bei Schönthal)
5) 0,0072—0,0108 " (zw. Zechendorf und dem Dammsee)

6) 0,0086—0,0108 » (im Dorfe Riege)
7) 0,0079—0,0099 » (Olpuch)
8) 0,0074—0,0099 » (zw. Schönhaide u. Funkelkau)
9) 0,0072—0,0094 » (zw. Briesenitz und Rederitz)

Mittel 0,0073—0,0101 mm.
Mittel aller Messungen 0,0087 mm.

Ich habe den Pilz von folgenden Fundorten vor mir: 1) **Kreis Dt. Krone.** Zwischen Poln. Fuhlbeck und Riege 1878. Grandiger Weg. — Zwischen Dammsee und dem Seechen von Gramattenbrück 1878. Grandiger Weg. — Zwischen Dabermühl und Neu Goltz. Grandiger Weg. 1878. — Bei Schönthal am Mittelsee. Sandiger Weg. 1878. — Zwischen Zechendorf und dem Dammsee. Sandiger Weg. 1878. — Im Dorfe Riege, in sandigem Wege. 1878. — Zwischen Briesenitz und Rederitz. Grandiger Weg. 1878. — 2) **Kreis Berent.** Lubjahnen. Grandiger Weg 1875. Gutsbesitzer Baganz. — Westlich von Olpuch 1885. Auf Grand. — Zwischen dem Chunsi-See (Chossen-See der Karte) und Barlogi, südöstlich vom genannten See. In grandigem Sande zwischen Kiefere. 1885. — Im Kiefernwalde südlich von Barlogi. — Zwischen Konarschin und Barlogi im Grande, bei Kiefern. 1885. — Kiefernwald zwischen Konarschin und Gribno. 1885. — Königswieser Forst, an einem Wege in der Nähe des Ferdinandsbruchs 1885. Kiefernwald. — Grandiges Ufer des Torfsees zwischen Schönhaide und Funkelkau. 1874. — 3) **Kreis Neustadt.** Nordwstlich von Hela in grandigem Sande. 1867. — 4) **Kreis Konitz.** Östlich von Borsk auf dem Wege nach Bonk im Flugsande, bei Kiefern; Pilze mit 3—5 Zoll langen und solche mit 1 Zoll langem Stiel.

Der Pilz ist östlich von der Weichsel bisher in Preussen nicht gefunden.

Was die in Deutschland angegebenen Arten von Pisolithus (Polysaccum) betrifft: Pisol. arenarius Alb. et Schw., Pis. crassipes, Pis. turgidus (Polys. turgidum Fr.) so bezweifle ich, dass dies verschiedene Arten sind, ja, sie scheinen nicht einmal als Spielarten aufgestellt werden zu können. Ich habe an 17 Fundorten des Pilzes, die oben angegeben sind — nur bei Lubjahnen sah ich den Pilz nicht selbst — ihn an vielen in sehr zahlreichen Exemplaren gesehen, die alle die Formen und noch mehr hatten, die **Krombholz** (Essbare, schädl. und verdächt. Schwämme) auf Tafel 60 darstellt. Der Kopf ist äusserst mannichfach gestaltet, von walziger durch kuglige bis zu ganz abgeplatteter Gestalt, der Stiel bald lang, bald sehr kurz, bald nach unten zugespitzt und ohne Wurzeläste (im reifen Zustande), bald unten zerklüftet und in zahlreiche Aeste zerspalten, bald walzig, bald abgeplattet, bald sind die Pilze einzeln, bald zu 2—3 verbunden, kurz, es scheint mir nur als charakteristische Eigenschaft für Polys. pisocarpium Fr. die tiefgelbe Farbe des Innern des Stiels nach Krombholz übrig zu bleiben. Dies Merkmal erscheint mir jedoch recht zweifelhaft, da ja die Farbe von Pilzen sehr schwankt. Uebrigens waren fast alle Exemplare, die ich sah, völlig reif, ihr Kopf schon geöffnet, der Stiel und die Wurzelaeste abgetrocknet, so dass ich allerdings über die Farbe des Innern des Stiels in der Jugend nicht aus Beobachtung urtheilen kann.

Von einem Hilum auf den Sporen, wie Corda Icon. Fung. II 25 dies bei Polysacc. arenarium beschreibt und abbildet, habe ich an reifen Sporen nichts gesehen.

Erklärung der Abbildungen.

Tuber mesentericum Vitt.

Bild 1, 2, 3. Ganze Trüffeln $^{1}/_{1}$.
" 4 und 5. Theile der Oberfläche $^{4}/_{1}$.
" 6. Querschnitt eines Pilzes $^{1}/_{1}$. Bild 1—6 Photographien nach dem frischen Pilz.
Bild 7. Stück des Innern nebst Schaale $^{10}/_{1}$.
" 8. Stück des Innern mit Schaale $^{210}/_{1}$. a) unfruchtbares Gewebe; b) Schaale.
" 9, 10, 11, 12. Sporensäcke bezüglich mit 1, 2, 3, 5 Sporen $^{500}/_{1}$.

Tuber Borchii Vitt.

Bild 13. Pilz von aussen $^{1}/_{1}$.
" 14. Querschnitt des Bild 13 dargestellten $^{1}/_{1}$.
" 15. Ein anderer Pilz von aussen $^{1}/_{1}$.
" 16. Querschnitt desselben $^{1}/_{1}$.
" 17. Stück des Innern nebst einem Theil der Schaale $^{275}/_{1}$.
" 18 und 19. Junge Sporen $^{1150}/_{1}$.
" 20 und 21. Sporensäcke mit 4 und 2 Sporen $^{275}/_{1}$.
" 22. Erwachsene Spore $^{420}/_{1}$.

Chaeromyces albus Casp. (Chaer. maeandriformis Vitt.)

Bild 23. Spore $^{900}/_{1}$.

Gautieria graveolens Vitt.

Bild 24—28. Sporen von der Seite gesehen, $^{1150}/_{1}$.
" 29 und 30. Vom Scheitel gesehen $^{1150}/_{1}$.

Hydnotria Tulasnei Berk. et Br.

Bild 31. Spore von aussen $^{500}/_{1}$.

Rhizopogon rubescens Tul.

Bild 32. Junger Pilz von aussen $^{1}/_{1}$.
" 33. Derselbe durchschnitten $^{1}/_{1}$.

Bild 34. Aelterer Pilz durchschnitten $^{1}/_{1}$.
„ 35. Etwas jüngerer Pilz, dessen Hülle im Querschnitt noch rosig wurde $^{1}/_{1}$.
„ 36. Querschnitt eines der Reife nahen Pilzes $^{1}/_{1}$.
„ 37. Stück der Hülle und des Innern eines Pilzes mittleren Alters $^{25}/_{1}$.
„ 38. Sporenkammer, ausgekleidet mit Basidien $^{275}/_{1}$.
„ 39, 40, 41, 42, 43, 44. Basidien mit 5—8 kurzgestielten länglichen Sporen $^{690}/_{1}$.
„ 45. Reife abgefallene Sporen von der Seite und von oben $^{450}/_{1}$.
„ 46. Ganzer, älterer Pilz $^{1}/_{1}$.

Melanogaster variegatus Tul.

Bild 47. 3 Sporen, a, b, c. $^{1150}/_{1}$.

Scleroderma vulgare Fr.

Bild 48, 49, 50. Sporen im ersten Zustande der Reife, blauschwarz. 48 in Wasser mit der hellen Einfassung, 49 und 50 unter concentrirter Schwefelsäure $^{1800}/_{1}$.
„ 51 und 52. Reife Sporen eines getrockneten Pilzes. Helle Einfassung verschwunden. In Wasser gesehen. $^{1800}/_{1}$.

Pisolithus crassipes Casp. (Polysaccum cras. DC.)

Bild 53, 54. Sporen in Wasser gesehen $^{1800}/_{1}$.

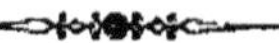

Bericht

über die

in den Sitzungen

der

physikalisch-ökonomischen Gesellschaft

zu Königsberg in Pr.

gehaltenen Vorträge im Jahre 1886.

Sitzung am 7. Januar 1886.

Der Vorsitzende begrüsst die Versammlung und spricht die Hoffnung aus, dass das neue Jahr für die Gesellschaft ebenso glücklich wie das vergangene verlaufen werde.

Die Sammlungen sind wieder sehr bereichert. Wenn auch die geologische Aufnahme nicht mehr in unsern Händen ist, so erhalten wir doch alle Fundstücke, welche das Museum immer mehr anwachsen lassen und dasselbe immermehr zu einem Provinzialinstitut machen.

Zur Statistik der Gesellschaft übergehend bemerkt derselbe, dass beim Beginn dieses Jahres die Gesellschaft zählt: 1 Protector, 10 Ehren-, 245 ordentliche und 202 auswärtige Mitglieder, während sie im Anfang des vorigen Jahres zählte: 1 Protector, 13 Ehren-, 251 ordentliche und 217 auswärtige Mitglieder.

Durch den Tod wurden dem Vereine entrissen: 3 Ehrenmitglieder:

1. Geheimrath Professor Dr. Hirsch, mit das älteste Mitglied, der den Bestrebungen der Gesellschaft stets das regste Interesse entgegenbrachte. 2. Geheimrath Professor Dr. von Siebold in München, dem bereits am 7. Mai v. J. ein Nekrolog gehalten ist. 3. Generallieutenant von Helmersen Excellenz in St. Petersburg.

> Georg von Helmersen, ein ausgezeichneter Geologe, war 1803 auf einem Gute in der Nähe von Dorpat geboren und starb am 15. Februar v. J. 82 Jahre alt in Petersburg. Er beschäftigte sich besonders mit der geologischen Untersuchung seines grossen Vaterlandes und machte grosse Reisen an der Wolga, im Ural, in der Krimm, in der Kirgisensteppe und im Altai. 1841 veröffentlichte er eine geologische Karte von Russland, welche 1863 und 1873 in verbesserter Auflage erschien. Er war früher Professor am Berginstitut in Petersburg, später dessen Director und Akademiker und hat vielfach geologische Arbeiten veröffentlicht. Später erhielt er von seiner Regierung den Auftrag die Verbreitung von Stein- und Braunkohle im russischen Reich zu erforschen und kam damals auch nach Königsberg, um die Sammlungen unseres Provinzialmuseums zu studiren. Bei dieser Gelegenheit lernte der Vorstand den liebenswürdigen Mann persönlich kennen. Unserer Gesellschaft gehörte er seit dem Jahre 1878 an.

Ferner starben 8 ordentliche Mitglieder:

1. Director Busch, welcher erst am 3. December v. J. aufgenommen war; 2. Professor Dr. Burow; 3. Conditor Kallmann; 4. Kaufmann Kemke: 5. Geheimer

Commerzienrath Kleyenstüber; 6. Fabrikdirektor Dr. Münster; 7. Dr. Samuelson; 8. Professor Dr. Zöppritz.

Carl Zöppritz, seit 1880 als Ordinarius an unserer Albertina wirkend, starb, hier 47 Jahre alt, am 31. März v. J. nach kurzer Krankheit. Er studirte in Heidelberg und dann hier längere Zeit Mathematik und Physik, habilitirte sich 1868 in Tübingen für Physik und ging 2 Jahre später als Extraordinarius nach Giessen. Hier beschäftigte er sich viel mit geophysikalischen Arbeiten und veröffentlichte vielfach Berechnungen und Beobachtungen berühmter Afrika-Reisender. Als ein rascher Tod ihn traf war er mit den Vorarbeiten zum 2. Bande der Oceanographie beschäftigt, deren 1. Band v. Boguslawski veröffentlicht hatte. Unserer Gesellschaft hat der Verstorbene 4 Jahre angehört, er hat in derselben einen Vortrag über den physicalischen Zustand des Erdinnern nach damals veröffentlichten neuen Arbeiten gehalten.

Endlich verloren wir durch den Tod 13 auswärtige Mitglieder:

1. Sekretair der K. Akademie der Wissenschaften in Madrid Aguilar; 2. Generalsekretair der K. Akademie der Wissenschaften in Lissabon Coelho; 3. Sekretär der naturforschenden Gesellschaft in Liverpool Collingwood; 4. Kaiserlicher Rath Ehrlich in Linz; 5. Tresor. adj. de société entomol. in Paris Fairmaire, ein bedeutender Entomologe; 6. Graf von Keyserling in Rautenburg; 7. Lancia Duc de Brolo in Palermo; 8. Geheimrath Professor Dr. Münter in Greifswald; 9. Saunder's in London; 10. Rittergutsbesitzer Freiherr Prinz von Buchau in Plinken; 11. Pfarrer Salomon in Enzuhnen; 12. Professor Westwood in Oxford, bekannter Entomologe; 13. Kammerherr und Museumsdirektor Worsaae in Kopenhagen, dem später von competenter Seite eine Gedächtnissrede gehalten werden wird.

Nicht leicht hatte die Gesellschaft in einem Jahre so viele Mitglieder zu beklagen.

Der Vorsitzende widmete warme Worte den Dahingeschiedenen und forderte die Anwesenden auf, zum Zeichen eines ehrenden Andenkens, sich von den Sitzen zu erheben, was bereitwilligst geschah.

Herr Dr. Wittrin hielt einen Vortrag über das Thema: Wie sind die Dämmerungserscheinungen des Jahres 1883 zu erklären? Soweit das Beobachtungsmaterial heute vorliegt, sind die merkwürdigen optischen Vorgänge in der Atmosphäre am Ende 1883 und Anfang 1884 auf die gewaltige vulkanische Katastrophe zurückzuführen, welche im August 1883 in der Sundastrasse stattgefunden hat. Schon früher, besonders im Jahre 1831 nach den vulkanischen Eruptionen im Mittelländischen Meere, sind auffallende Dämmerungserscheinungen als Begleiter vulkanischer Thätigkeit beobachtet worden. Auch diesmal entstanden sie zuerst in der Nähe der grossen vulkanischen Vorgänge im Indischen Ocean. Die gewaltigen Aschenmassen, welche dem Krakatoa nach einer zuverlässigen Beobachtung bis zu einer Höhe von 11 000 m entstiegen, konnten sich bei grosser Feinheit und Leichtigkeit lange und in sehr hohen Schichten der Atmosphäre schwebend erhalten. Durch fortgesetzte Ausscheidung der schwersten Stofftheilchen nach der Erde war schliesslich die Atmosphäre von einem äusserst feinen und homogenen Staube erfüllt, welcher eben jene intensive farbige Diffraktion hervorrief. Dieser Vermuthung ist eine grosse Wahrscheinlichkeit durch die schönen Versuche von Herrn Professor Kiessling-Hamburg gegeben, welcher durch einen mit künstlichem Staubnebel erfüllten Glasballon unter Einwirkung des directen Sonnen- oder des electrischen Bogenlichts die einzelnen auffallenden Sonnenfärbungen und Dämmerungserscheinungen experimentell zur Darstellung brachte. Historisch bemerkenswerth ist übrigens, dass auch Kant in seiner „Geschichte und Naturbeschreibung des Erdbebens am Ende des Jahres 1755" besonderer Himmelsfärbungen in Folge vulkanischer Vorgänge erwähnte. Er schreibt die Verwandlung der Farben vom dunkelsten Blau bis ins Roth und endlich in einen hellen weissen Schein dem „häufigeren Zufluss sehr dünner vulkanischer Abdämpfung" in die Atmosphäre zu. Das Material, das noch jetzt über diesen Gegenstand unausgesetzt von der deutschen Seewarte und der englischen Zeitschrift „Nature" unter der Redaktion einer dazu besonders von der Königlichen Gesellschaft eingesetzten Commission gesammelt wird, dürfte späterhin vielleicht eine genaue Vergleichung über die lokale Verbreitung des vulkanischen Staubes mit dem entsprechenden Auftreten der auffallenden Dämmerungserscheinungen gestatten.

An den Vortrag knüpfte sich eine Debatte. Herr Professor Dr. Hahn machte auf einen röthlich-braunen Sonnenring aufmerksam, der im Abstand von 11—12° von der Sonne seit November 1883 bis jetzt nicht verschwunden ist, auch um den Mond ist derselbe zu sehen, besonders wenn helle Wolken vorüberziehen. Dieser Ring ist in ganz Deutschland und darüber hinaus beobachtet, besonders deutlich auf hohen Bergen. Auch die Dämmerungserscheinungen sind noch nicht ganz verschwunden. Im Jahre 1783 wurden Nebelmassen beobachtet, die aber von den 1883 beobachteten verschieden sind. Während 1783 der Nebel in tieferen Schichten lag, befand er sich 1883 in höheren, von einem Sonnenringe ist 1783 nichts erwähnt. Ein Zusammenhang mit Erdbeben kann nicht constatirt werden, da namentlich tektonische Erdbeben nicht diese Staubmassen hervorbringen können. Er war der Meinung, dass kosmische Ursachen zu diesen Erscheinungen beigetragen haben.

Herr Dr. Jentzsch und Herr Dr. Wittrin konnten diese Ansicht nicht theilen und sprachen sich dagegen aus.

Dr. O. Tischler: Ueber Aggry-Perlen und über die Herstellung farbiger Gläser im Alterthume.

Von Herrn Dr. v. Ihering aus Brasilien ist mir eine Perle zugesandt worden, welche beim Roden eines Urwaldes zu Mundo novo in der Provinz Rio grande do Sul gefunden wurde.

Diese Perlen, in letzter Zeit mit dem Namen Aggry-Perlen bezeichnet, obwohl die Bezeichnung jedenfalls zu allgemein ist, haben schon lange die Aufmerksamkeit der Forscher und Sammler erregt, auch zu vielen ungerechtfertigten Hypothesen und Phantasien Anlass gegeben. Die neueste Arbeit von Richard Andree (Zeitschrift für Ethnologie 1885 III) „Aggry-Perlen" hat die sich hieran knüpfenden

Fragen auch nicht geklärt, indem sie allerlei verschiedene Perlenformen, die unter sich gar keine Verwandtschaft haben, miteinander in Verbindung bringt.

Das vorliegende Bruchstück einer solchen Perle und alle anderen, in grosser Zahl in den Sammlungen vorhandenen zeigen einen bis auf kleine Einzelheiten durchaus übereinstimmenden Habitus. Sie bestehen aus einer Reihe von meist 7 concentrischen Schichten, in der Art, dass zwischen je zwei immer eine opak weisse Schicht liegt. Diese drei opak weissen Schichten seien a, b, c. Die anderen Schichten vertheilen sich folgendermassen. Die beiden inneren A B bestehen aus transparentem farblosem Glase, mit leichtem Stich ins Grünliche. Dann kommt eine opak rothe Schicht C und eine äussere Schicht D aus transparentem, meist dunkelem kobaltblauem Glase (so bei der Perle von Mundo novo) selten aus blaugrünem Glase. Die Schichtenfolge ist also Aa Bb Cc D. Die innere Röhre ist glatt, die äusseren Grenzen aller Schichten sind aber gefurcht, so dass man auf dem Querschnitte eine Reihe concentrischer gezähnter Sterne erblickt. Die Fabrikation muss auf folgende Weise stattgefunden haben. Eine Glasröhre wurde mit dem opaken Weiss überfangen und dann durch Pressen in einer gerippten Form gefurcht. Diese gerippte Röhre wurde dann wieder mit der nächsten Schicht überfangen. Wahrscheinlich rollte man den schon etwas erhärteten, aber noch warmen Stab über eine Glasplatte, diese aufwickelnd, denn die Zwischenräume zwischen den Rippen sind besonders zwischen Aa und B nicht immer mit Glas ausgefüllt, während beim Eintauchen in flüssiges Glas dieses wohl überall hineingedrungen wäre. Dieser Prozess wurde dann wiederholt, der Mantel B um die weisse Schicht b umgelegt, dann C um c; jedesmal nach Umlegen der weissen Schicht wurde der Stab in gerippter Form gepresst. Schliesslich legte man den äusseren Mantel D um und rundete den Stab. Voraussichtlich hat man so längere Cylinder hergestellt, die dann in kleinere Theile zerschnitten wurden, vielleicht nachdem sie noch ausgezogen waren. Diese Cylinder wurden hierauf an beiden Seiten in fast immer sechs Facetten zugeschliffen, so dass ein kurzer cylindrischer Mitteltheil entstand, welchem an beiden Seiten sechsseitige, oben abgestumpfte Pyramiden aufsitzen, deren untere Seiten bogenförmig gegen den Cylinder hin verlaufen. Durch den Mantel schimmern an den dünneren Stellen die weissen Rippen der Schicht c hindurch, so dass die Mantelfläche heller und dunkler schattirt erscheint, während über die Pyramidenflächen sich die mehrfarbigen Bänder im Zickzack herumziehen, so dass man von oben auf denselben eine Reihe verschiedenfarbiger ineinandergesteckter Sterne erblickt. Die Grösse der Perlen variirt ziemlich stark von 9 mm Länge (parallel der Oeffnung) und 8—9 mm Durchmesser bis 25 mm Länge, 22 mm Durchmesser und noch viel mehr. Die Perlen müssen, nachdem sie durch den Schliff ihre Form erhalten haben, was auf keine andere Weise herzustellen geht, nachher noch einem leichten Feuer ausgesetzt gewesen sein um ihre scharfen Kanten abzurunden, ähnlich wie die modernen venezianischen Schmelzperlen. Man bemerkt oft noch deutliche Spuren einer oberflächlichen Schmelzung.

Neben dieser ganz ausserordentlich häufig auftretenden Form finden sich noch einige Varianten. Zwei davon, im Berliner Kunstgewerbe-Museum, aus der ehemaligen Minutolischen Sammlung stammend, zeigen folgende Eigenthümlichkeiten. Die erste kleine (Länge 9 mm, Durchmesser 8,5 mm) hat die gewöhnliche Schichtenfolge Aa Bb Cc. Die Furchen von c werden aber nicht vom Mantel ausgefüllt, sondern es sind kleine farbige Glasstäbchen eingelegt, so dass auf die Mitte der Pyramidenflächen blaue, auf die Kanten abwechselnd rothe und grüne kommen, also sechs blaue, drei rothe, drei grüne Stäbchen. Dieselben sind wiederum in die schon etwas erhärtete Schicht c eingelegt, daher bemerkt man deutlich die Spuren von Kanälen zwischen diesen Stäbchen und der Sohle der Furche. Das Ganze ist zur Abrundung dann noch mit einem Mantel von farblosem transparentem Glase umhüllt, der die Furchen, die zwischen den weissen Stäbchen und dem weissen Mantel c noch übrig geblieben, ausfüllt. Die ganze Perle ist dann nochmals leicht beschmolzen. Der Mantel ist vollständig blank und glänzend, die von weissem und rothem Email eingenommenen Pyramidenflächen sind etwas höckerig aber auch glänzend, fast wie Porcellan. Ob man das ganze vielleicht mit fein gepulvertem Glase bedeckt und dies dann glasurartig angeschmolzen hat?

Die zweite Perle (L 7, D 10) ist in derselben Weise gebildet. In die zwölf Furchen der weissen Schicht c wurden zwölf Glasstäbchen gelegt, wieder drei rothe, drei grüne, sechs blaue in derselben Reihenfolge, also zwischen zwei blauen abwechselnd ein grünes und ein rothes. Es fehlt aber der äussere Mantel und ist die Perle hier äusserlich unbedingt durch Schliff geglättet und der Länge nach leicht gerundet. Die Enden sind nicht pyramidal, sondern grade, sogar etwas concav zugeschliffen, wovon man die unverkennbaren Spuren erblickt. Diese Perle ist dann nicht mehr beschmolzen.

Eine sehr kleine aus einem Peruanischen Grabe stammende (6—7 mm L, 6 D) Perle im Berliner Ethnographischen Museum ähnt der ersten dieser beiden Perlen. Sie hat den blauen Mantel D, in dem aber abwechselnd blaue und weisse Stäbchen eingelegt sind, worauf das Ganze durch Schleifen ausgeglichen wurde.

Diese Perlen sind nun ziemlich über die ganze Erde verbreitet und befinden sich jetzt in zahlreichen Museen Europa's und America's, zum Theil ohne genauere Angabe der Fundorte. Nachfolgendes Verzeichniss dürfte wohl nicht vollständig sein, da es mir nicht möglich war die ganze, ziemlich zerstreute Literatur zu besorgen. Es sind die neueren Fundorte besonders nach Andrees Zusammenstellung aufgeführt, ein Theil nach meinen eigenen Studien in den verschiedenen Museen Europa's. In Deutschland sind gefunden[1]) eine zerbrochene Perle zu Oetjendorf (S. O. Holstein), ausgepflügt (hier ein Urnenfeld der La Tène Periode). Zu Sottorf, Hannover (Museum Hannover). Bei Neustadt am Rennsteig (Thüringen) sind in den vierziger Jahren sehs Perlen gefunden (Museum Meiningen). — In Schweden eine bei Stockholm.[2]) — Aus Dänemark[2]) eine angeblich aus einem alten Grabe. — In England zu Gilton,[3]) woselbst auch ein Sächsischer Kirchhof. Eine Perle,[4]) ob aus England weiss ich nicht, da ich die Abhandlung nicht einsehen konnte. Price[5]) erwähnt Perlen aus der Umgegend von Colchester angeblich aus Gräbern. Seine höchst unklare Beschreibung lässt deren Beschaffenheit nicht erkennen. Er bringt sie mit den Aggryperlen aus Afrika in Verbindung nach der ebenso unklaren Beschreibung

1) Correspondenzblatt der Deutschen Anthropologischen Gesellschaft 1879 p. 131.
2) Smithsonian Report 1877 p. 302 ff., wo eine Menge Citate.
3) Fausset und Roach Smith: Inventorium sepulcrale. Tfl. V, 2.
4) Archaeologia 35. Tfl. IV, 10.
5) Journal of the Anthropological Institute London XII p. 65 ff.

des Major Bale und versteigt sich zu der kühnen Conjectur, dass sie unter den Römern durch afrikanische Sclaven nach England gebracht wären! Eine Perle aus England, angeblich mit Samischen Schalen und römischen Schnallen zusammen gefunden. Im British Museum eine aus England.[1]) Ebenda 9″ eines Stabes zur Fabrikation dieser Perlen. Eine ähnliche Perle bei Southampton. 2 Perlen in der Slade-Collection.

In Afrika sind mehrere Perlen dieser Art gefunden: im British Museum aus Dakkah in Nubien; ebenda eine aus Aegypten (im Slade-Catalog ob dieselbe?); eine in der ägyptischen Abtheilung des Louvre. Ganz besonders haben die Glasperlen an der Guinea-Küste zwischen den Ashantis und der Goldküste die Aufmerksamkeit erregt.[2]) Dieselben werden Aggrykörner genannt, sind aus der Erde gegraben worden und stehen bei den Negern in hohem Werthe. Manche werden mit dem mehrfachen ihres Gewichtes in Gold bezahlt. Sie stammen also jedenfalls aus alten Gräbern, — die Eingeborenen glauben, dass sie von Schlangen gelegt werden. Die zahlreichen Beschreibungen sind sehr unklar und wenig präcise, so dass man ein genaues Bild von diesen Perlen nicht gewinnen kann. Jedenfalls sind sie sehr mannigfacher Art, einfarbig blau, roth, grün, gelb oder vielfarbig, wie es scheint von oft recht complicirter und feiner Zeichnung. Wenn demnach unsere fraglichen Perlen sich auch darunter finden sollen, was ich vorläufig nicht constatiren kann, so ist jedenfalls für sie die Bezeichnung Aggry-Perlen eine zu allgemeine, welche diese specielle Form lange nicht genau genug bezeichnet. Eine Perle wie die vorliegende ist aber von Dr. Buchner von Camerun in das Berliner Ethnographische Museum geliefert. Nach den Beschreibungen ähnen einige der Aggryperlen wirklich den antiken und es wäre garnicht wunderbar, wenn von der Nordseite der Sahara schon in uralter Zeit durch den Handel phönicisch-ägyptische oder römische Perlen nach der Guineaküste gelangten, was im Uebrigen auf die Frage unserer Perlen kein neues Licht wirft. Hingegen sind die Entdeckungen in Amerika[3]) von entscheidender Bedeutung. Zu Beverly (Canada), Santa Barbara (Californien), Lima (New-York), Black Hammock (Florida), am Susquehanna beim Ausgraben des Pensylvania-Canals, mehrfach in Indianergräbern (Schoolcraft l. c.) Ferner in Südamerika in Peru aus Gräbern, im Berliner Ethnographischen Museum. Aus Mundo novo (Brasilien) die oben erwähnte Perle. Ferner kommen dieselben Perlen auf den Australischen Inseln vor. Auf den Palau-Inseln[4]), wo sie Kalebukuks genannt werden. Es finden sich hier ganz

1) Catalog der Slade-Collection p. 10, Citate sub No. 56, die Slade-Perlen abgebildet Fig. 21. Dabei die Bemerkungen von Franks über diese Perlen. Vielleicht befinden sich einige der hier citirten Perlen schon unter den früher erwähnten.

2) Die Literatur hierüber ist ziemlich zerstreut. Bei Andree (Zeitschrift für Ethnologie, 1885) werden mitgetheilt die Berichte von Bowdich: Mission von Cape Coast Castle nach Ashantie, Weimar 1820 p. 361. Bei Minutoli: Ueber die Anfertigung und die Nutzanwendung des farbigen Glases bei den Alten. p. 21 ff: Reise des Engländers Hutton ins Innere von Afrika nach der französischen Uebersetzung, p. 192 Note 2. Ferner p. 20, 21: Ein Schreiben des Bischofs Münter 1808. p. 21, Richard und Joh. Leander: Journal of an expedition to explore the Niger etc., London 1832 Vol. I. p. 180. Steinemann: Mittheilungen der Wiener geographischen Gesellschaft 1863 p. 39, auch von Andree erwähnt. Journal of the Anthropologicale Inst. London XII. p. 64 Bericht von Major Bale.

3) Smithsonian Report 1877 p. 302 ff., Citate einer grossen Zahl amerikanischer Perlen. Andree l. c. p. 41 citirt Schoolcraft: Indian tribes I. pl. 24. 25.

4) Andree l. c. p. 110 Fig. 1 nach Kubary im Journal des Museums Godefroy. Heft IV. p. 49.

genau solche Formen wie die beschriebenen neben anderen Perlen, die hier wie auf den benachbarten Papua-Inseln sehr hoch im Preise gehalten werden. Herr Dr. Finsch zeigte mir eine kleine dunkelapfelgrüne Perle mit weissen Tupfen in 2 Reihen bedeckt, „Grossvater der Kalebukuks" genannt, von den Palau-Inseln, die dort einen Werth von 80 Dollars hat. Trotz der Unvollständigkeit ergiebt sich aus dieser Zusammenstellung doch die fast universelle Verbreitung unserer Perlenform über die alte und neue Welt.

Früher hielt man sie für altägyptische Producte und schrieb ihre Verbreitung dem phönizischen Seehandel zu, eine Ansicht, die natürlich durch ihre Entdeckung in Amerika umgestossen wurde, obwohl einige Phantasten immer noch von den Fahrten der Phönizier bis nach Amerika faselten. Eine andere Ansicht, der auch noch Andree beitritt, ist, dass sie von den ersten normännischen Einwanderern nach Nordamerika gebracht sein könnten und sich von da weiter schon lange vor Columbus verbreitet hätten. Andree will ihre Verwandtschaft mit den von ihm abgebildeten anglosächsischen Perlen behaupten. Eine ähnliche Ansicht findet sich im Inventarium sepulchrale von Roach Smith (p. 26): Masson hätte bei Besichtigung sächsischer Perlen geäussert, ganz ähnliche seien in Begräbnisshügeln Nordamerikas gefunden. Wenn man aber die Perle von Gilton ausnimmt, die jedenfalls nicht aus einem sächsischen Grabe stammt, findet man in den sicher constatirten zahllosen sächsischen, fränkischen etc. Gräbern keine einzige, die nur eine entfernte Aehnlichkeit mit den in Frage stehenden besitzt. Die Verwandtschaft der von Andree abgebildeten besteht auch eben nur darin: dass beides „Perlen" sind. Diese Annahme hat also gar keine Berechtigung.

Was das Material betrifft, so hat die von mir unternommene mikroskopische — noch nicht abgeschlossene — Untersuchung des Dünnschliffes einer der Thüringer Perlen gezeigt, dass das Roth Ziegelglas[1]) oder ziegelrothes Email ist, sehr stark mit farblosen Krystallen durchsetzt, unreiner — auch in der oberflächlichen Farbe schmutziger als das Römische, erst in den Zeiten der Völkerwanderung findet sich ähnlich unreines bräunliches. Ich glaubte zuerst, dass das ziegelrothe Glas auf die römische Kaiserzeit beschränkt sei. Das lässt sich in dieser Form nicht ganz aufrecht erhalten. Es tritt Ziegel-Email in den Gürtelhaken von Koban im Kaukasus schon lange vor der Kaiserzeit auf. Ferner entdeckte ich im Museum zu Colmar die Scherbe eines jener polychromen Alabastra, die dem 5., vielleicht 6. Jahrh. v. Chr. zukommen und aus Aegypten oder Phönizien stammen, mit rothem Grunde und aufgelegten gelben und blauen Zickzackbändern. Der Fond dieses Gefässes besteht aus Ziegelglas.[2]) Es ist also Ziegelglas im 5. Jahrh. v. Chr. doch schon verwandt worden. Ziegelroth aussehende, sehr kleine Perlen finden sich auf den netzförmigen Perlenhemden ägyptischer Mumien im Berliner Museum — doch konnte ich hiervon keine

1) cfr. Correspondenzblatt der Deutschen Anthropologischen Gesellschaft 1884 p. 179 ff: Tischler: „Ueber Email." Für den damals gebrauchten Ausdruck „lackrothes Email" habe ich jetzt den Ausdruck „ziegelrothes Email" oder „Ziegelglas" vorgezogen.

2) Es ist dies das einzige Gefäss dieser Art mit opak rothem Grunde, das mir bisher vorgekommen. Ich würde sehr dankbar sein für gütige Mittheilungen über ähnliche Gefässe, die von ausserordentlichem Interesse sind, wobei aber das Roth nicht mit dem häufiger vorkommenden dunkeln aber transparenten Amethystviolett zu verwechseln ist.

Probe zur Untersuchung erhalten. Ein überraschendes Resultat ergaben aber eine rothe und eine gelbe Perle, von denen mir gütigst ein paar Proben überlassen wurden — aus dem Grabe der Apaanchu im Berliner ägyptischen Museum (ca. 2000 Jahre v. Chr.) Die Perle, obwohl äusserlich ziegelroth erscheinend, bestand nicht aus opakem Glas, sondern, wie die mikroskopische Untersuchung des Dünnschliffes lehrte, aus hart gebranntem Thon in Art des (fälschlich) sog. ägyptischen Porzellans — die gelbe Perle desgleichen. Alle übrigen mir bekannten rothen Perlen vor der Kaiserzeit, wie die im Schmuck zu Meroë aus Nubien, rothe Perlen aus La Tène-Gräbern Frankreichs, ähnliche derselben Zeit angehörende aus Gräbern Cyperns (ich besitze selbst mehrere Exemplare dieser Gattung), bestehen aus Blutglas. Es ist dies also vor der Kaiserzeit ganz überwiegend im Gebrauch gewesen, hörte aber auch zum Beginne der Kaiserzeit nicht vollständig auf.

So weist das Material also nicht auf alte ägyptische oder phönizische Fabrikate hin, die Technik und Form aber ebenso wenig. Die Glasperlen des ganzen Jahrtausends v. Chr. sind hinlänglich bekannt. Die erste Hälfte dieses Zeitraums repräsentiren die Perlen der älteren Necropolen der Eisenzeit Italiens wie Villa nova, viele Gräber der älteren Hallstädter Periode in Süd-Deutschland und Oesterreich, die spätere die Gräber der Certosa von Bologna, die jüngere Hallstädter Periode, ferner weiter herab die Gräber der La Tène-Periode in ganz Europa in ihren verschiedenen Phasen bis zur Kaiserzeit. Die Gräber am Schwarzen Meere, ältere Funde am Kaukasus, ferner Cypern, Sardinien liefern dieselben Formen, und alle diese trifft man in den verschiedenen ägyptischen Sammlungen wieder. Wir sehen demnach, dass alle diese Länder ihre Glasperlen aus gemeinschaftlichen Centren bezogen, wahrscheinlich mehr aus phönizischen als ägyptischen Fabriken. Es würden unsere fraglichen Perlen also auch wohl in einem der zahlreichen systematisch aufgedeckten Gräber gefunden sein, während bisher aus Europa und auch aus Afrika nur zufällig in der Erde gemachte Funde vorliegen, die also gar keine Beweiskraft haben. Dasselbe gilt für die Kaiserzeit und Völkerwanderungsperiode, wo viele Tausende von Perlen genügen, um unsere Perlen aus ihrem Kreise ganz auszuschliessen. Vielleicht hat das äussere Aussehen der Perlen den Blick nach Aegypten gelenkt. Die mehrfachen Zickzackbänder der Oberfläche erinnern an die alten polychromen mit mehrfarbigen Zickzacklinien bedeckten Alabastra und ähnlichen Gefässe, von denen es übrigens durchaus nicht feststeht, dass sie in Aegypten fabrizirt sind. Aber die Technik ist eine grundverschiedene. Denn hier sind die Streifen nur aufgelegt, während sie bei unseren Perlen als Schnitt der verschiedenen einander umhüllenden Mantelflächen erscheinen — also gar keine Verwandtschaft. Franks hatte[1]) zumal nach den amerikanischen Entdeckungen schon nach Venedig als Heimath dieser Perlen hingewiesen, und diese Vermuthung hat sich im vollsten Maasse bestätigt.

Durch genaues Studium eines altvenezianischen Millefiorifläschchen, das in Neapel gekauft und unter die antiken Gläser des Berliner Antiquariums gekommen ist (No. 5860), sowie einiger Millefiorigefässe im Berliner Kunst-Industrie-Museum

1) Catalog der Slade-Collection p. 10 sub No. 50. Eine kürzlich erschienene Publication von Franks war mir unmöglich zu beschaffen. Ich kenne die Resultate, zu welchen dieser vorzügliche Kenner der Glas- und Thonfabrikate gelangt ist nicht und ist die folgende Auseinandersetzung ganz unabhängig entstanden.

gelang es mir, die Herkunft der Perlen sicher nachzuweisen und auch die Zeit annähernd zu bestimmen.

Besagtes Fläschchen ist ziemlich dickwandig und besteht aus dunklem kobaltblauem Glase, welches aussen mit farbigen Glasstäbchen (Millefioristäbchen) belegt ist, die sich der Länge nach darauf platt ausbreiten, während die beiden Endflächen der Flaschenoberfläche aufliegen. Man muss also die erweichten schon etwas plattgedrückten Stäbchen der Länge nach in eine Form gelegt und dann die blaue Glasblase hineingeblasen haben, aus der dann das Fläschchen auf bekannte Art formirt wurde.

Diese Stäbchen zeigen nun vollständig die Form und Technik der fraglichen Perlen. Der Hauptunterschied besteht nur darin, dass sie massiv sind. Die Mitte nimmt meist ein vierarmiges opakrothes Kreuz ein, selten ein fünfstrahliger Stern, dann folgt umhüllend eine opakweisse Schicht, hierauf wieder eine sternförmige dünne opakrothe (achtspitzig bei mittlerem Kreuz, dann eine zweite opakweisse Schicht, wieder sternförmig, und dann eine äussere Schicht meist aus kobaltblauem Glase, aber auch aus blaugrünem oder amethystviolettem. Meist ist diese Schicht rund, hin und wieder aber auch fein gezähnt.

Es fehlen also nur die inneren transparenten Schichten der Perlen, dafür tritt das rothe Kreuz ein, im Uebrigen ist die Herstellung dieser Stäbchen, sowie zum Theil die Farbenzusammenstellung eine so absolut übereinstimmende, dass der allernächste Zusammenhang unabweisbar zu Tage tritt. Der venezianische Ursprung unserer Perlen dürfte demnach bewiesen sein, da sich sonst diese Technik nirgends wieder findet.

Es fragt sich nur, wann und wie diese Technik entstanden ist.

Die Geschichte der edlen venezianischen Glaskunst ist noch in vielen Punkten der Aufklärung ausserordentlich bedürftig. Labarte in seiner histoire des arts industriels au moyen âge lässt hierbei in historischer, wie auch in technischer Beziehung sehr viel zu wünschen übrig. Vollends die Millefiorigefässe sind eigentlich nirgends recht berücksichtigt. Am meisten Aufschluss giebt noch die Monografia della Vetraria Veneziania e Muranese (Venezia 1874), herausgegeben von der giunta speciale für die Wiener Weltausstellung 1873. Von besonderem Werthe sind die Mittheilungen aus den Matrikeln der verschiedenen Glasmacherzünfte, den wichtigsten Quellen für die Geschichte dieser Kunst und ein recht vollständiges historisch geordnetes Verzeichniss der alten Nachrichten und Quellen, sowie der neueren Literatur[1]).

Man muss sich die Entwicklung in folgender Weise vorstellen. Während bis an das Ende des 15. Jahrhunderts die Kunst durch orientalische Vorbilder beeinflusst wurde und die Malerei in Emailfarbe vorherrschte, begann im Laufe dieses Jahrhunderts

---

1) Herr Dr. Antonio Salviati hatte mir freundlichst versprochen, in den Acten zu Venedig noch weiter nachzuforschen, ob sich mehr über die alte Millefiorifabrikation ermitteln liesse. Bei seinen vielfachen Reisen war er noch nicht im Stande, diese Untersuchungen anzustellen. Es war nicht länger möglich, den Druck obigen Vortrages aufzuschieben. Sollten sich neue Resultate ergeben, so könnten dieselben an anderem Orte bei einer neuen durch farbige Abbildungen erläuterten Behandlung dieses Gegenstandes verwendet werden.

die grossartige Bewegung der Renaissance. Man durchforschte die Bauten und alle Reste der Kunst des Alterthums, und indem man diese neu zu beleben glaubte, entstand eine andere herrliche Schöpfung, die der Antike doch als eine eigene Bildung gegenüber steht. So ging es auch in der Glaskunst. Die zahlreichen Nachgrabungen mussten die in jetzt noch immer unerschöpflicher Fülle von dem Italischen Boden beherbergten Glasgefässe und Scherben ans Tageslicht fördern und die schon zu hoher Blüthe gelangte neue Kunst zur Nachahmung der alten auffordern. Und es waren beide Seiten der antiken Glastechnik, aus denen sich verschiedene Zweige der neuen Technik entwickelten, sowohl die buntfarbigen Gläser, als die farblosen, welche letzteren wenigstens zur Kaiserzeit durchaus überwogen. Die letzteren beeinflussten in hohem Grade die farblosen venezianischen des 16. Jahrhunderts und besonders die antiken Petinetgläser (aus plattgedrückten Stäbchen zusammengesetzt, die mit opaken Fäden umwunden sind) gaben die Vorbilder für die Venezianischen Faden-(Latticinio)-Gläser; diese Klasse erhob sich allerdings noch weit über die Vorbilder und darf, was ihre Eleganz und Schönheit anbetrifft, wohl als das herrlichste Product aller Zeiten in dieser Klasse von Gläsern bezeichnet werden. Die vielfarbigen Gläser erreichten aber ihre Vorbilder lange nicht, weder in kunstvoller Technik noch in Schönheit der Farben des opaken Glases, so dass hierin die römische Kaiserzeit noch immer oben an steht. Die etwas schweren Formen dieser Klasse von Gefässen sagten dem Geschmacke der Renaissancen wohl nicht so zu, daher hat sich dieser Zweig auch nicht gleichmässig entwickelt und ist auch früher eingegangen.

Besonders reizten die bewunderswürdigen antiken Millefiorigefässe zur Nachahmung, aber hier copirte man nicht treu, sondern schlug einen ganz anderen Weg ein. Die Millefioritechnik besteht darin, dass man eine Zahl Glasstäbe neben einander zu einem Bündel legt, zusammenschmilzt, den weichen Gesammtstab auszieht, so dass man ihn in Schnitte von beliebigem, aber immer ähnlichem Querschnitt zerlegen kann, welche als Millefioriplättchen die Grundgebilde der zu vollendenden Form sind. Man überfängt auch einen Stab ein- oder mehreremal mit andersfarbigem Glase, so dass Röhren mit verschiedenen concentrischen Schichten entstehen. Die kunstvollsten Gebilde erhält man durch spiraliges Aufrollen einer aus mehreren Schichten bestehenden Glasplatte: es zeigen sich im Querschnitte dann aufgerollte Bänder. Diese Elemente sind nun wieder in der verschiedenartigsten Weise combinirt, ja man hat sogar figurale Darstellungen, Köpfe, Blumen etc. daraus zusammengesetzt, wo die farbigen Stäbchen in gleicher Weise durch die ganze Dicke der Platte hindurchgehen — ähnliche Producte hat in neuerer Zeit der verstorbene Franchini in Venedig wieder hergestellt. Aus solchen Plättchen wurden Gefässe von verschiedener Form, meist flachere Schalen hergestellt. Bei einer grossen Anzahl sind die einzelnen Plättchen verhältnissmässig wenig verzerrt. Diese können nur in einer Form gepresst sein. Die aneinandergelegten Plättchen müssen stark erwärmt und dann durch Pressung vereinigt sein. Um den oberen Rand wurde oft ein Petinetstab gelegt. Ein Nachschleifen hat, glaube ich, hier nicht stattgefunden, denn bei Scherben mit der erhaltenen natürlichen Oberfläche zeigen die Petinetstäbe durchaus keine Abschleifung des oberflächlichen Fadens, während man diese erst bei den von den Händlern polirten Scherben wahrnimmt. Bei anderen gepressten Römischen Gläsern hat allerdings ein Nachschleifen stattgefunden.

Unter den verschiedenen Arten von Millefioriplättchen ist eine besonders häufig, wo die Elemente sich zellenförmig ordnen. Den Mittelpunkt der Zelle bildet eine mehrfach überfangene Röhre (mit dem Kern 2—3 Schichten). Darum ordnen sich dann Röhren in 2—3 Schichten und um dieselben kommt eine gleichförmige Glasschicht. Hat sie dieselbe Farbe als die äussere Schicht der umgebenden Röhren, so erscheinen diese als Stengel (hell in dunklerem meist transparentem Grunde), ist sie verschieden, so bilden die Röhren eine sternförmige Umfassung um die centrale Röhre. Die hellen opaken Mittelpunkte dieser Röhren sind aber immer eine Reihe getrennter Punkte. Da die Plättchen in den Gefässen oft schief zusammengepresst sind, kommen manchmal auch die Längsseiten der Millefioristäbe zur Geltung, was bei den Gefässen in Zellenmosaik wohl eigentlich nicht beabsichtigt war. Der opake Kern der Röhren oder die opaken Stäbe schimmern dann durch die farbige transparente Glasmasse hindurch, an den hervorragenden Stellen weit heller als an den tiefen Falten, so dass man zwischen den Querschnitten hellere und dunklere farbige Streifen bemerkt. Diese Zellenmosaikgefässe suchten die Venezianer nun nachzubilden, verfolgten dabei aber einen ganz anderen Weg. Anstatt den Stab aus einem Bündel anderer zusammenzusetzen, wurde ein Stab mehrfach überfangen und wiederholt in einer gerippten Form gepresst, so dass er auf dem Querschnitte eine Reihe concentrischer Sterne zeigt. Die äusserste transparent farbige Umhüllung blieb rund oder wurde auch noch gerippt. Diese Stäbe wurden dann in längere Stücke zerlegt, dann, wie schon erwähnt, in eine Form gepresst, hierin eine (meist blaue) Glasblase geblasen und das Gefäss vollendet. Dabei kam neben den Querschnitten auch die Längenfläche des Stabes zur vollen beabsichtigten Geltung, was im Alterthum mehr Zufall war. Die Streifung desselben wurde durch die vortretenden weissen Rippen innerhalb der dunklen Hüllmasse bewirkt: die weissen oder hellen getrennten Pünktchen des Alterthums bildeten eine zusammenhängende weisse Sternlinie. Es findet also bei oberflächlicher Betrachtung immer eine gewisse Aehnlichkeit statt, die uns auf den Weg hinweist, der zu den Venezianischen Gefässen geführt hat. Der Rückschluss, den man auf die Herstellung der alten Millefiorigefässe gemacht hat, und den ein Buch dem anderen gedankenlos nachschreibt, dass man bei ihnen auch eine Glasblase über die Millefioriplättchen geblasen und dieselbe hernach ausgeschliffen habe, ist aber falsch. Es wäre ganz unmöglich, dieselbe herauszuschleifen, ohne die erwähnten Petinetstäbchen zu beschädigen. Wahrscheinlich sind diese Millefiorigefässe zuerst entstanden und dann erst hat man die Stäbchen, die man zu ihrer Herstellung brauchte, auch als Perlen verwendet, denn für die letzteren fehlen die Vorbilder im Alterthum, während man sie nun als recht praktisch zur Perlenfabrikation erkannte. Natürlich mussten sie etwas modificirt werden, statt mit einem massiven Stabe fing man mit einer Röhre an und erzeugte durch wiederholtes Ueberfangen und sternförmiges Pressen jene Stäbe, denen durch Zerschneiden und Zuschleifen dann die übliche Form gegeben wurde.

Was nun die Zeit der Millefiorigefässe betrifft, so giebt eine kleine Einzelheit einen gewissen Fingerzeig. Sowohl auf der Flasche des Antiquariums als auf einem Pokale des Gewerbemuseums finden sich einige ganz vereinzelte Goldflitterchen aufgeschmolzen. Die Decoration der Gefässe mit solchen Goldflitterchen (semés d'or) fällt nach Labarte überwiegend ins 15. Jahrhundert und hört im 16. allmählich auf.

Herr Dr. Pabst setzt einen betreffenden Kelch des Berliner Gewerbe-Museums nach seiner Form auch noch ins 15. Jahrhundert. Ferner findet sich bei Sabellico „De Venetae urbis situ lib. 3, 1495“ [1]) die Stelle vasi (di vetro) imitanti — i fiori come quelli che la primavera sparge nei prati, ein nicht misszuverstehender Hinweis auf die Millefiorigefässe. Aus alle dem ergiebt sich, dass sie gegen Ende des 15. Jahrhunderts fabricirt wurden. Wie lange noch, kann ich vorläufig nicht entscheiden, doch ist es wohl wahrscheinlich, dass sie in der ersten Hälfte des 16. Jahrhunderts den farblosen und Filigrangläsern Platz machten.

Auf denselben Zeitpunkt führt nun auch die Formirung der Perlen, die durch Schleifen stattgefunden hat, hin.

Ueber die Geschichte der Venezianischen Perlenfabrication, bringt die citirte Monografia della Vetraria Veneziana auch einige Notizen, die zum Theil mit denen früherer Werke in Widerspruch stehen. Die jetzige Methode „perle alla lucerna“, wo die Perle an einem Eisenstabe geformt und dann von der Lampe mit erwärmten kleinen Glasstäbchen sozusagen bemalt wird, und die schon im Alterthum recht allgemein angewendet wurde, soll 1528 (l. c. p. 266) von Andrea Viador erfunden sein, obwohl dies nicht sicher bewiesen ist. Jedenfalls scheint diese Technik im 15. Jahrhundert noch nicht bestanden zu haben. Es wurden die zerschnittenen Glasstäbe (Röhren von grösserer oder geringerer Dicke) an einem Eisenspiess (allo spiedo) im Glasofen erweicht und abgerundet, hauptsächlich wohl durch Schleifen in die gewünschte Form gebracht (l. c. p. 16) und daraus die „paternostri“ gebildet. Dass diese Schleiftechnik damals stark im Gebrauch war, ergiebt u. a. der Passus aus der Matricola des Cristalleri (aufbewahrt im Museum zu Murano. Monografia p. 264) von 1486: „Si lavoravano a Venezia ed a Murano perle faccettate alla rotina“; von 1500 „Si lavoravana a Venezia ed a Murano di paternostri tagliadi a muola, rotti e scavezzadi —“ und einige ähnliche. Seit c. 1490 (l. c. 14) bezogen auch die Deutschen klare und gefärbte Stäbe aus Venedig, schliffen daraus Perlen und sandten sie über Venedig zurück nach der Levante, wogegen 1510 seitens des Capitolo dell' arte Abhilfe getroffen werden sollte. Jedenfalls wurden die Rohstäbe in Venedig gemacht und es liegt für die vorliegenden Perlen des Venezianischen Millefioristyles kein Grund vor, ihnen einen fremden Ursprung zuzuschreiben. Die Deutschen machten den Venezianern unliebsame Concurrenz, aber in Venedig blühte die Perlenschleiferei auch, und da war es natürlich, dass sie die farbenreichen, ursprünglich zu anderen Zwecken bestimmten Millefioristäbe selbst zu Perlen verschliffen.

So führen diese verschiedenen Betrachtungen auf dieselbe Zeit, das Ende des 15. Jahrhunderts, die Zeit der grossen Entdeckungen Amerika's und des Seeweges nach Indien. Die Perlen sind daher wahrscheinlich schon von den ersten Besuchern nach beiden Regionen gebracht und dann durch inneren Verkehr sowohl über den ganzen amerikanischen Continent wie über die australischen Inseln verbreitet. Das Vorkommen in Europa und Afrika hat weiter nichts Wunderbares. Wie lange die Fabrikation derselben angedauert hat, lässt sich noch schwer entscheiden. Doch es

---

1) Citirt, Monografia della Vetraria Veneziana p. 264.

ist wahrscheinlich, dass sie nicht zu weit in's 16. Jahrhundert hineinreicht, da erstens die farblosen Gläser die Oberhand gewonnen und im Laufe dieser Zeit jedenfalls die Perlen „alla lucernae" aufkamen.

Die Perlen sind also ihres mystischen Nimbus entkleidet worden, haben aber an Interesse nichts verloren. Sie klären einen uns nahe liegenden, dafür aber um so dunkleren Zeitraum auf.

Sitzung am 4. Februar 1886.

Der Vorsitzende legt den soeben erschienenen Jahrgang der Schriften vor, welcher in kürzester Zeit zur Versendung kommen wird und bemerkt, dass für 1885 nicht wie sonst 2 Abtheilungen, sondern nur eine herausgegeben wird. Lediglich sind es Sparsamkeitsrücksichten, die den Vorstand zu dieser Aenderung bewogen haben

Dann theilt derselbe mit, dass die Gesellschaft durch den im vorigen Monat erfolgten Tod eines Ehrenmitgliedes des Director a. D. Friederici, welcher am 6. April 1832 aufgenommen ist und am 6. April 1882 sein fünfzigjähriges Mitgliedsjubiläum gefeiert, einen herben Verlust erlitten hat. Friederici war hier Oberlehrer, dann Director des Progymnasiums in Wehlau und hatte stets ein grosses Interesse für Naturwissenschaften. Auf seinen speciellen Wunsch ist seine Sammlung von Petrefacten, die viel werthvolles enthält, der Gesellschaft von den Hinterbliebenen zum Geschenk gemacht. Der Vorsitzende sprach den Dank der Gesellschaft aus und ersuchte die Anwesenden, um das Andenken an den Entschlafenen zu ehren, sich von den Sitzen zu erheben, was einmüthig geschah.

Herr Dr. Jentzsch legte neue Arbeiten über die Geologie der Provinz vor. 1. Früh, Kritische Beiträge zur Kenntniss des Torfes (Jahrb. der k. k. geologischen Reichsanstalt, Bd. 35, pag. 677 bis 726, Tab. XII., Wien 1885) behandelt u. a. nach den Materialien des Provinzialmuseums und des hiesigen botanischen Gartens die Microstructur des Martörv von Nidden und Schwarzort (pag. 684—686) und der Lebertorfe von Doliewen bei Oletzko, Jacobau bei Rosenberg und Purpesseln bei Gumbinnen. 2. Klebs, das Tertiär von Heilsberg i. Ostpr. (Jahrbuch der königlich geologischen Landesanstalt für 1884, Berlin 1885, pag. 334—380 mit 5 Tafeln) giebt eine petrographische Gliederung der Heilsberger Braunkohlenformation und weist an der Basis derselben glaukonitische Tertiärschichten nach. 3. Jentzsch, Beiträge zum Ausbau der Glacialhypothese in ihrer Anwendung auf Norddeutschland (Ibidem pag. 438—524 mit 3 Tafeln), enthält ausser allgemeinen theoretischen Erörterungen und Thatsachen, betreffend Bildung und Unterscheidung der norddeutschen Diluvialbildungen, insbesondere eine specielle Darstellung des Untergrundes der Stadt Königsberg auf Grund der bis 252,35 m tief reichenden Bohrungen. 4. Schröder, Saurierreste aus der baltischen oberen Kreide. (Ibid. pag. 293—333 mit 5 Tafeln.) Während der untere Lias Englands und Schwabens die reichste und bekannteste Lagerstätte der Plesiosauren bildet, haben der obere Jura und die Kreideformation bisher nur wenige Species geliefert. In Geschieben des Obersenon hatte nun schon vor Jahren der

Verfasser und gleichzeitig der inzwischen verstorbene Professor Zaddach Reste von grossen Sauriern erkannt, welche Zaddach als Plesiosaurus bestimmte. Durch fortgesetztes Sammeln mehrte sich das Material und wurde ganz besonders bereichert durch eine mehrere Wirbel und Rippen enthaltende Untersenonplatte, welche Herr Dr. Tischler mit der Sammlung des Dr. Marschall in Marienburg für unser Provinzialmuseum erwarb und die Dr. Schröder nunmehr zum Typus einer neuen Species Pl. balticus erhebt. Ausserdem weist derselbe nach Pl. Helmersenii, Pl. ichthyo spondylus und andere Species, endlich einen Wirbel der riesigen „Mooseidechse" von Mastricht Mosasaurus Camperi. Die Belege zu dieser schönen Arbeit finden sich theils im Provinzialmuseum der Gesellschaft. theils (wie alle von Zaddach gesammelten Versteinerungen) im mineralogischen Institut der Universität. . Die Reste liegen in untersenonen und obersenonen Diluvialgeschieben Ost- und Westpreussens; da aber letztere dem unter dem grössten Theile Ost- und Westpreussens verbreiteten Kreideterrain entstammen, so haben die genannten Thiere unzweifelhaft in unserer Provinz gelebt und umschliesst diese im Verein mit dem damit verwandten Kreideterrain Schonens eine der reichsten Saurierfaunen der europäischen Kreide. Im Anschluss daran erwähnt Redner noch, dass in dem von ihm in den Schriften der Gesellschaft 1881 Tab. 1 kartographisch dargestellten Kreidegebiet noch durch 15 weitere Bohrungen die nämliche Kreideformation nachgewiesen sei, in Königsberg siebenmal, ferner Fort Kalgen bei Königsberg, ein zweitesmal zu Tilsit zu Gross- und Klein-Neuhof bei Ragnit, Nemonien, Ibenhorst, Insterburg und Graudenz, mithin im ganzen 27mal in Ost- und Westpreussen, während nur an einem Punkte, Purmallen bei Memel, ältere Schichten erbohrt wurden. Hiermit sei die Kreideformation in Ost- und Westpreussen über mindestens 2000 bis 3000 qkm Fläche nachgewiesen und mit 184 m Mächtigkeit bei weitem nicht durchsunken. Zum Schluss sprach Redner noch besonderen Dank Herrn Lehrer Zinger in Pr. Holland aus, welcher den Wirbel des Pl. ichthyospondylus auf nochmalige besondere Bitte dem Provinzialmuseum schenkte.

Herr Dr. K. Brandt berichtete auf Grund mehrjähriger Studien über den Bau und die Lebenserscheinungen der koloniebildenden Radiolarien oder Sphärozoen. Bezüglich des Baues hob er die Differencirung des Radiolarienplasmas in mehrere functionell verschiedene Abschnitte und die Abhängigkeit der Kernstructur von den Entwickelungsvorgängen hervor. Im Anschlusse daran skizzirte er die wichtigsten Abschnitte im Leben der Radiolarien. Eine ausführlichere Besprechung erfuhren die Lebenserscheinungen der Radiolarien. Die Sphärozoen wurden als echte pelagische Thiere geschildert, welche ihren ganzen Entwickelungsgang in der Nähe der Meeresoberfläche durchmachen und nicht imstande sind, sich selbstständig fortzubewegen. Ihre horizontale Verbreitung ist daher in erster Linie von der durch Wind erzeugten Wellenbewegung der Meeresoberfläche und von den Meeresströmungen abhängig. Ihre vertikale Verbreitung wird dagegen sowohl durch äussere Reize als durch Entwickelungsvorgänge beeinflusst. Bei mechanischer oder thermischer Reizung sinken die Sphärozoëen unter, und zwar durch Vergrösserung ihres specifischen Gewichts. Von den Reizen, denen die an der Oberfläche des Meeres flottirenden Thiere ausgesetzt sind, kommen für die Sphärozoëen hauptsächlich in Betracht: starke Bewegung des

Meeres, Abkühlung des Wassers auf etwa 2 bis 6 Gr. C. und Versüssung bezw. Verunreinigung des Wassers. Dagegen veranlassen weder grelle Belichtung noch die stärkste Erwärmung der Meeresoberfläche, welche unter natürlichen Verhältnissen eintreten kann (30 Gr. C.), die Sphärozoen dazu, die oberen Wasserschichten zu verlassen. Ausser durch gewisse Reize tritt auch infolge der Veränderungen, welche sich bei der Schwärmerbildung in den Radiolarienkolonieen abspielen und welche ein Schwinden des hydrostatischen Apparates (Gallerte und Vacuolen) herbeiführen, ein Untersinken der Colonieen ein. Weder auf Grund von Reizen noch im Verlaufe der Schwärmerbildung werden aber die Sphärozoen unter natürlichen Verhältnissen lebend den Boden der Oceane erreichen können; vielmehr geht aus verschiedenen Versuchen und Beobachtungen mit grosser Wahrscheinlichkeit hervor, dass die Sphärozoëen sich nicht weiter als etwa 200 m von der Oberfläche des Meeres entfernen. — Zum Schlusse erörterte der Vortragende die Ursachen, welche die höchst eigenthümliche Art des Auftretens der Radiolarien und anderer pelagischer Thiere im Golf von Neapel bedingen.

Sitzung am 4. März 1886.

Der Vorsitzende eröffnet die Sitzung mit der traurigen Anzeige, dass Professor Dr. Benecke am 27. Februar c. plötzlich gestorben ist. B. war ein fähiger, ungemein arbeitsamer Mann, der seit dem 8. Juni 1867 der Gesellschaft angehörte und in derselben eine Reihe interessanter Vorträge gehalten hat, er starb 43 Jahre alt an seinem Geburtstage. Er hatte hier studirt, promovirte 1866, machte im folgenden Jahre sein freiwilliges Militärjahr ab und wurde 1868 zum Assistenzarzt befördert, 1870 schied er aus dieser Stellung und wurde zum Prosector ernannt, er verstand es die Liebe und Hochachtung seiner Schüler sich zu erwerben, wurde aber in demselben Jahre zur Reserve einberufen und machte den Krieg gegen Frankreich mit, aus dem er mit dem eisernen Kreuze geschmückt heimkehrte, auch in dieser Stellung hatte er sich der allgemeinen Liebe seiner Collegen und der Mannschaften zu erfreuen. Nach dem Feldzuge nahm er seine Stellung als Prosector wieder ein, beschäftigte sich aber nebenbei mit der besseren Herstellung von Photographien mikroskopischer Präparate, baute sich zu diesem Zweck einen Apparat auf dem Hofe der Anatomie und publicirte mehrere Artikel über diesen Gegenstand. Anfangs photographirte er nur kleine Dinge, wie die Wollhaare der Schafe, deren Veröffentlichung für die Schafzüchter von grosser Wichtigkeit war, später aber in Gemeinschaft mit Professor Dr. Kupffer mikroskopische Präparate; allgemeines Aufsehen erregten die Photographien über die Entwickelung des Eies, die von 5 zu 5 Minuten aufgenommen waren und erst ein klares Bild über diesen Vorgang gaben. Für die Fischzucht waren die erhaltenen Resultate gut zu verwerthen, B. hatte sich von jeher für dieselbe interessirt, wandte ihr aber nun seine ganze Thätigkeit zu und galt als Autorität ersten Ranges in diesem Fache, sein Name war nicht nur in Deutschland, sondern weit darüber hinaus bekannt, die durch seinen Tod entstandene Lücke wird schwer zu ersetzen sein.

1877 wurde er zum ausserordentlichen Professor ernannt, jetzt sollte er einen Ruf in das Ministerium bekommen. Seine Forschungen führten ihn nach Italien, wo er eine Zeit lang in der zoologischen Station in Neapel arbeitete, er hatte dort einen harten Winter durchzumachen, das Eis auf dem Po war einen Fuss stark und scheint dort den Grund seines Leidens gelegt zu haben. Anfangs dieses Jahres kehrte er heiser zurück, hielt noch seine Vorlesungen, musste es aber sehr bald aufgeben, doch arbeitete er rüstig fort ohne seinen schon angegriffenen Körper zu schonen, am 27. Februar ereilte ihn ein plötzlicher Tod in Folge einer Lungenblutung.

B. war ein Mann, der viel geleistet hat und vielmehr noch versprach, als Mensch durch sein liebenswürdiges gefälliges Wesen ausgezeichnet, dem wir stets ein ehrendes Andenken bewahren werden.

Der Vorsitzende ersuchte die Anwesenden als äusseres Zeichen der Achtung, die wir dem Dahingeschiedenen zollen, sich von den Sitzen zu erheben, was bereitwilligst geschah.

Herr Professor Caspary spricht über neue Bernsteinpflanzen. Versetzen wir uns in Gedanken in die Wälder Preussens zu der Zeit, zu welcher in ihnen der Bernstein entstand, so finden wir, dass die Pflanzen, welche den damaligen Wald zusammensetzten, von denen, welche bei uns jetzt waldbildend auftreten, nach den Arten durchweg verschieden sind, zu einem grossen Theil aber auch nach den Gattungen. Die Eichen waren zu jener Zeit in den Wäldern sehr zahlreich an Arten — wir kennen mehr als 12 — und erinnern durch diesen Reichthum an das heutige Nordamerika, wo die Eichenarten in hohem Grade zahlreich sind. Gegenwärtig haben wir in unseren Wäldern nur vier Nadelhölzer; zur Bernsteinzeit waren mehr als 20 in unseren Gegenden vorhanden. Lorbeeren haben wir heute nicht in Preussen, damals gab es hier einige Arten. Ja, es fehlte selbst nicht an Palmen. Sabalites Künowii und Bembergia pentatrias waren damals hier zu finden, wie heutzutage Sabal Adansonii im südlichen Nordamerika. Das Unterholz jener Wälder bildeten jetzt ausgestorbene Erikaceen, auch fand sich die schönblütige Stuartia Kowalewskii, deren nächste Verwandte sich heute ebenfalls im südlichen Nordamerika finden. Feuchtigkeit muss in jenen Wäldern reichlich vorhanden gewesen sein. Denn an den Baumstämmen und wohl auch an dem Boden lebten viele Moose. Von diesen legt der Vortragende 17 neue Arten von Jungermanniaceen in grossen, für den Vortrag besonders ausgeführten Tafeln vor. Unter den Kiefern der Bernsteinwälder waren bisher nur solche bekannt gewesen, welche 2 oder 3 Nadeln auf den Kleinästen trugen, aber keine, welche nach der Art von Pinus Cembra, Pinus Strobus und einer grösseren Zahl nordamerikanischer Kiefernarten 5 Blätter im Büschel hatten; jedoch haben sich in der letzten Zeit 2 Exemplare solcher Form gefunden, die wegen der Breite der Nadeln eine grössere Verwandtschaft mit der Cirbelnusskiefer zu zeigen scheinen als mit der Weymouthskiefer. Der Vortragende hat diese für den Bernstein neue Art Pinus cembrifolia genannt. Als dem Bernsteinwalde angehörig hatte der Vortragende früher schon 3 Ahornarten beschrieben, jetzt legt er eine vierte vor, die er Acer Scharlokii genannt hat, dem Apotheker Julius Scharlok in Graudenz zu Ehren, der mit grossem Eifer und bestem Erfolge die Flora der Umgebung seines Wohnortes studirt. Von Scharloks Ahorn sind dicht neben und übereinander zwei Blüthen vorhanden, leider wohl nicht ganz vollständig. Vier (?) lineale Kelchblätter, die etwa viermal so lang als breit sind, Blumenblätter, welche diese um das Dreifache an Länge übertreffen, und etwa 6 Staubblätter kommen jeder Blüthe zu. Die Staubblätter überragen die Blüthenblätter um ein Viertel von deren Länge, die Staubblätter sind elliptisch oben und unten ausgerundet. An unsern Hasenklee erinnerte im Bernsteinwalde Oxalidites brachysepalus, von dem ein kleines Früchtchen gefunden ist, kurz länglich, mit fünf linealen freien Griffen und fünf nierenförmigen, rundlichen Kelchblättern. Eine neue Eichenart ist vom Vortragenden Quercus Klebsii benannt, nach Dr. Richard Klebs, bekannt durch seine geologischen Forschungen und mehrere Arbeiten, den preussischen Bernstein betreffend. Von dieser Klebsschen Eiche ist ein Stück eines männlichen Blüthenstandes vorhanden. Die Blüthen, gestützt von einem schmalen, linealen Hochblatt, sind kreiselförmig und fünfzahnig. Die Staubblätter überragen die Hülle wenig. Endlich legt der Vortragende einen kleinen Pilz der Bernsteinzeit in grosser Abbildung vor, der kaum einen halben Millimeter Länge hat, aber ein hohes Interesse gewährt, weil er in bester Weise erhalten ist. Der kleine Stil, nach unten und oben verdickt, haftet, wie es scheint, auf einer Unterlage von Vogelkoth. Oben ist verbreiteter Kopf sichtbar, der mit braunrothen elliptischen Sporen bedeckt ist. Obgleich einige Hunderttausend, ja vielleicht eine Million und mehr Jahre alt, ist dieses kleine Stilbum succineum, dem heutigen Stilbum vulgare höchst ähnlich, aufs beste erhalten. Keine andere Substanz als das flüssige Harz des Bernsteinbaumes hätte die schwierige Aufgabe, einen solch zarten Organismus durch so bedeutende Zeiträume aufzubewahren, zu lösen vermocht.

Herr Dr. O. Tischler hielt eine Gedächtnissrede auf Kammerherr Worsaae, die in den Schriften abgedruckt ist.

Sitzung am 1. April 1886.

Herr Dr. Pancritius hielt einen Vortrag über „die Physiologie des Fischdarms.“ Zur Klarlegung der Verdauungsvorgänge bei den Fischen wird als Einleitung der gesammte Verdauungscanal der höhern Wirbelthiere anatomisch und physiologisch kurz beschrieben. Dann geht der Vortragende zu den Fischen über und zeigt in der Reihe der Fische die allmählig fortschreitende höhere Organisation der Verdauungswerkzeuge von einem einfachen cylindrischen Rohr bis in ein in viele Abschnitte zerfallendes Canalsystem. Hieran schliesst sich endlich die Darlegung der Verdauung und Nahrung unserer Fische, vergleichend mit den höheren Wirbelthieren behandelt. Wir wollen dem Vortrag folgende Hauptpunkte entnehmen: 1) Unsere Fische (Knochenfische) zerfallen nach ihrer Verdauung und den anatomischen Merkmalen des Darmcanals in magenbesitzende und magenlose Fische. Zu den letzteren gehören unsere karpfenartigen Fische (Karpfen, Schleihe, Karausche,

Plötze, Rothauge, Bressem etc.), während der Rest unserer Knochenfische einen Magen besitzt. 2) Die magenbesitzenden Fische zeigen eine den höheren Wirbelthieren gleiche Verdauung, d. h. sie besitzen ein bei saurer Reaktion Eiweiss verdauendes Ferment (Pepsin) im Magen. Ausserdem wird Eiweiss im ersten Theil des Dünndarms durch ein bei laugenartiger Reaktion wirksames Ferment (Trypsin) verdaut, welches von einer Bauchspeicheldrüse oder von Pförtneranhängen abgeschieden wird. Das Pepsin der Fische unterscheidet sich von dem der Säugethiere durch seine Wirksamkeit bei Temperaturen unter + 15° Celsius. 3) Die magenlosen Fische zeigen nur die Verdauung durch Bauchspeichelsekret. Ferner sondert der ganze Darmcanal mit Ausnahme des Schlundes diesen Saft ab und zwar nimmt die verdauende Kraft des Darmes vom Anfang desselben allmählig nach dem Ende zu ab. 4) Eine Vorarbeit für die Verdauung durch die Mundhöhle mit Bezahnung und Speicheldrüsen, wie wir sie bei den Säugethieren finden, existirt bei den Fischen nicht. Hier dient der Mund lediglich zum Ergreifen und Festhalten der Beute. 5) Leber und Galle besitzen kein Eiweiss verdauendes Ferment. 6) Das diastatische Ferment des Darmes der karpfenartigen Fische führt nur gequellte Stärke in Zucker über, rohe dagegen bleibt unverändert. 7) Die karpfenartigen Fische nähren sich nur ausnahmsweise von Pflanzen, die gewöhnliche Nahrung besteht aus Wasserthieren, grösstentheils Mückenlarven und Puppen. 8) Junge Fische ernähren sich ausschliesslich von kleinen Wasserthieren, vornehmlich niederen Krebsen (Daphniden, Copepoden etc.).

Herr Dr. Jentzsch legte die wichtigsten geologischen Publicationen des letzten Jahres vor und unterwarf dieselben einer Besprechung.

Sitzung am 6. Mai 1886.

Herr Professor Dr. Lohmeyer erstattete in längerem Vortrage Bericht über den Inhalt des zweibändigen Werkes, in welchem der Thorner Gymnasialprofessor Leopold Prowe die Erfolge seines mehr als dreissigjährigen Forscherfleisses über das Leben des Begründers der neueren Astronomie, des preussischen Astronomen Nicolaus Coppernicus niedergelegt hat (1883). Nicolaus Coppernicus, wie er sich in lateinischer Form selbst schrieb (in deutscher Nicolaus Coppernic), war am 19. Februar 1473 zu Thorn als das jüngste Kind des Kaufherrn Niklas Koppernigk und der Barbara Watzelrode geboren; der Vater war in der Mitte des dreizehnjährigen Krieges, durch den sich Westpreussen und Ermland von der Herrschaft des deutschen Ordens losmachten, von Krakau aus eingewandert und sehr schnell zu hohem Ansehen in Bürgerschaft und Kaufmannsgilde von Alt-Thorn gelangt, die Watzelrode waren eine alteingesessene Kaufmannsfamilie von Reichthum und Bedeutung. Die vielumstrittene Frage nach der Nationalität des grossen Mannes sucht der Vortragende mehr durch eine Hinweisung auf die allgemeinen Verhältnisse, denen zufolge Coppernicus nur ein Deutscher gewesen sein kann, zu lösen als durch ein Eingehen auf die verwirrende Masse von Einzelheiten, durch deren willkürliches Hineintragen nur diejenigen, welchen in ihrer nationalen Voreingenommenheit jene einfache Lösung nicht gefiel, die Frage arg verfahren haben. Da der Knabe im zehnten Lebensjahre seinen Vater durch den Tod verlor, übernahm der mütterliche Oheim Lukas Watzelrode, der damals Domherr zu Frauenburg war und 1489 Bischof von Ermland wurde, die Leitung seiner Erziehung. In der heimischen Stadtschule empfing der begabte und sicher sehr geistvolle Knabe die Vorbildung für die Universität, in den Kreisen, in welchen er lebte, lernte er das grosse Leben nach allen seinen Richtungen kennen. Sein weiterer Bildungsgang deckte sich fast genau mit dem des Oheims, der ihn schon früh zum geistlichen Stande bestimmt hatte. Im Herbst 1491 bezog Coppernicus die Universität Krakau, oder genauer die dortige Artistenfakultät, die durch eine grosse Zahl bedeutender Lehrer, Humanisten und Fachgelehrte, eine bedeutende Anziehungskraft ausübte. Nach vollendetem Triennium kehrte er, ohne einen akademischen Grad zu erwerben, heim. Zum Beginne des Wintersemesters 1496/97 ging er über die Alpen und wurde Scholar der Rechtsschule zu Bologna. Während des Jubeljahres 1500 weilte er in Rom und konnte bereits sehr besuchte Vorträge über Mathematik halten. Im Sommer 1501 kam er nach Preussen zurück und begab sich, da er 1497 ein ermländisches Kanonikat erhalten hatte, nach Frauenburg. Um seine Studien des geistlichen Rechts ganz abzuschliessen und zugleich um Medizin zu studiren, erhielt er 1502 noch einmal Urlaub nach Italien, wo er bis zum Ende des Jahres 1505 in Padua beiden Wissenschaften oblag. Am 31. Mai 1503 wurde er zu Ferrara zum Doctor des geistlichen Rechts promovirt. Kaum ein Jahr nach seiner Rückkehr berief ihn der kränkelnde Oheim auf sein Schloss Heilsberg und behielt ihn dort bis zu seinem eigenen Tode (1502). Von diesem Jahre ab hat Coppernicus über 30 Jahre in Frauenburg gelebt, mit der einzigen Unterbrechung von 1516 bis 1521, wo er als Verwalter des Kapitelsantheils, der Aemter Allenstein und Mehlsack, in Allenstein residirte. Auch weiterhin ist er bis fast 5 Jahre vor seinem Tode vielfach von zeitraubenden Amtsgeschäften in Anspruch genommen worden. 1523, nach dem Tode eines Bischofs, war er ein halbes Jahr lang sogar Administrator des Bisthums. Er starb nach kurzer Krankheit am 24. Mai 1543. Neben allen diesen Studien und Beschäftigungen und einer, wie es scheint, nicht geringen ärztlichen Thätigkeit liefen nun noch jene Studien her, auf denen sich sein grösster Ruhm aufgebaut hat, der, dass er die Erde bewegte und die Sonne und den Himmel stille stehen hiess. Zu seiner Ansicht von der Unhaltbarkeit des Ptolemäischen Systems ist er zuerst, wie er selbst sagt, durch das Studium der Griechen, namentlich der Pythagoräer gekommen, die bereits die Erdbewegung lehrten, und dieses ist bereits in Krakau geschehen, wo er die erste Bekanntschaft mit den Griechen machte, freilich erst in den durch das Arabische gegangenen lateinischen Uebersetzungen, denn die griechische Sprache begann er erst in Bologna zu erlernen. Die Beobachtungen am Himmel mit den meist selbstgefertigten Instrumenten, deren Unvollkommenheit und Fehler Coppernicus ganz genau kannte, dienten ihm nur zur thatsächlichen Prüfung seiner wesentlich speculativen Geistesarbeit. Von Krakau ab bis wenige Jahre vor seinem Tode lassen sich solche Beobachtungen verfolgen, von denen die meisten in Frauenburg auf einem neben seiner Kurie belegenen Thorthurme gemacht sind; die herkömmliche Erzählung von Beobachtungen in Allenstein ist eine Fabel (wie die von den durch ihn erbauten Wasserleitungen). Coppernicus hat sich stets darauf beschränkt, einzelnen Freunden und bevorzugten Schülern gelegentliche Mittheilungen über seine Gedanken und Entdeckungen zu machen, bei seinen Lebzeiten war eine gedrängte, von ihm selbst gefertigte Zusammenstellung seiner Lehren nur handschriftlich verbreitet. Erst dem jungen Professor Joachim Rheticus aus Wittenberg, der 1539 nach Frauenburg kam und schnell der innige Freund des geliebten Lehrers wurde, gelang es, im Vereine mit anderen Verehrern und Freunden von Coppernicus die Einwilligung zum Drucke seines grossen Hauptwerkes, der „sechs Bücher über die Umwälzungen der Himmelskörper", zu gewinnen, die er einst in Heilsberg begonnen hatte und an denen er sein ganzes Leben hindurch bessernd und ergänzend fortgearbeitet hat. Wenige Stunden vor seinem Tode konnte Coppernicus das erste fertig gedruckte Exemplar, da sein Geist schon fast geschwunden war, wenigstens mit den Händen berühren. In religiöser Beziehung war Coppernicus ein gläubiger Anhänger der alten Kirche geblieben, zugleich hat er aber auch stets der in der Jugend eingesogenen Richtung angehangen, der des Erasmus von Rotterdam, welche die schreienden Missstände der eigenen Kirche erkannte und offen anerkannte und darum der deutschen Reformation nicht jede Berechtigung absprach.[1])

Herr Dr. Tischler spricht über das Gräberfeld von Corjeiten bei Germau unter Vorzeigung einer Reihe charakteristischer Funde von demselben. Schon früher waren als Geschenke von Herrn Max Werdermann-Corjeiten eine grössere Anzahl gelegentlich beim Ackern gemachter Funde in das Provinzialmuseum gelangt. In den Herbstmonaten 1884 und 1885 hat der Vortragende durch vollständiges Umrajolen eines Stücks von zwei Morgen Grösse 400 Gräber aufgedeckt, wodurch das Feld aber noch lange nicht erschöpft ist. Das Gräberfeld durchlief alle chronologischen Phasen vom 1. Jahrhundert n. Chr. bis zum Beginn des 5., ebenso wie das Gräberfeld zu Dolkeim. Wenn die einzelnen Gräber nicht so reich ausgestattet waren wie auf letzterem, so war das Gesammtresultat aus den vielen Gräbern bei der im allgemeinen geringen oder fehlenden Steindecke doch ein äusserst befriedigendes und lieferte ein Anzahl neuer Formen, von denen einige überhaupt noch nirgends gefunden sind. Ferner wurde die besonders durch die Dolkeimer Funde begründete chronologische Gliederung dieses grossen Zeitabschnittes vollständig bestätigt und in manchen Punkten noch ergänzt. Diese Felder lassen sich in die Abschnitte B, C, D gliedern (A, die vorrömische La Tène-Periode, ist hier nicht vertreten), B: ungefähr erstes und ein grosser Theil des zweiten Jahrhunderts (Fibeln mit oberer Sehne und solche mit Rollenhülse), C: circa Ende des zweiten und drittes Jahrhundert (Fibeln mit umgeschlagenem Fuss, römische Münzen, besonders aus der Zeit der Antonine), D: circa Ende des dritten bis Anfang des fünften Jahrhunderts (Fibeln mit kurzem Nadelhalter und Nadelscheide bis zu den Formen der grossen Völkerwanderung, keine Münzen). Die Gräber der Periode B sind überwiegend Scelettgräber, hier ein

---

1) Der ganze Vortrag, nebst einer Prowes Werk selbst und die Quellen besprechenden Einleitung, wird in v. Sybels „Historischer Zeitschrift" zum Abdruck kommen.

ca. 2,60 m langes und 0,80 m breites Steinpflaster, alle ziemlich genau mit dem Kopf im Norden. Ueber und unter den hier ganz vergangenen Leichen fanden sich Reste von Holz, wohl von Brettern, zwischen welche dieselben gelegt waren. Die Frauen hatten je zwei Fibelpaare, mehrere Schnüre Glasperlen, einen prächtig besetzten Gürtel und zwei Armbänder; die Männergräber waren ärmer als in Dolkeim, manche ohne Fibel, nur mit ein bis zwei Lanzen, Eisencelt, Messer. Manche Gräber enthielten keine anderen Beigaben als Thongefässe, die aber ganz besonders elegant, einige glänzend schwarz, eines mit Mäanderverzierung, die für diese Periode weiter westlich bis nach Dänemark hin charakteristisch ist. Unter diesen Scelettgräbern fanden sich auch zwei Aschenurnen mit gebrannten Knochen. Auffallend ist es, dass diese Gräber gerade am Abfalle des Feldes zur Wiese nach dem Germauer Fliesse hin lagen und dass im Herbste das Grundwasser bis fast an die Scelette hinauf reichte. Da man bei diesen ältesten Gräbern des Feldes doch Platz genug zur Auswahl hatte, kann man nur den Schluss ziehen, dass der Wasserstand des Germauer Fliesses und seiner Zuflüsse damals ein niedrigerer gewesen ist. Man hat sich also in dem ersten Jahrhundert nach Christo das Land durchaus nicht überall als stärker versumpft als jetzt vorzustellen, wie dies unter anderem auch anderweitig die zahlreichen, zum Theil neuerdings entdeckten Niederlassungen in der Weichselniederung beweisen. Ebenso weisen die ungemein zahlreichen Niederlassungen nördlich und südlich von Corjeiten wie in vielen anderen Theilen des Samlandes auf eine dichte, sesshafte Bevölkerung hin, die ca. vier Jahrhunderte lang an derselben Stelle wohnte, da alle diese Gräberfelder genau dieselbe chronologische Entwickelung zeigen. Dieselbe muss sich von Ackerbau genährt haben, und gehörten bei dem wenig intensiven Betriebe dazu grössere bebaubare Strecken, welche infolgedessen nicht mit Wald bedeckt gewesen sein können. Es kann daher das Land nicht überwiegend mit Sümpfen und Wäldern bedeckt gewesen sein, wenn letztere auch jedenfalls einen grösseren Raum als heute eingenommen haben. Ostpreussen muss schon im 1. Jahrhundert nach Christi an vielen Stellen, so besonders im Samlande, gut angebaut gewesen sein. Die grosse Uebereinstimmung mit den Gräberfeldern weiter im Westen bis Hannover und Dänemark berechtigt zu der Annahme, dass in den ersten vier Jahrhunderten hier germanische (gothische) Stämme sassen, die aber erst um Christi Geburt oder etwas später einwanderten, während die westlichen Gräberfelder Jahrhunderte vor Christi continuirlich zurückreichen; es haben dort also schon zu Cäsars Zeit und vorher Germanen in festen Wohnsitzen gesessen, so dass von einem nomadisirenden Umherziehen nicht die Rede sein kann. Die Cultur der Germanen war eine weit höhere, als sie noch immer vielfach fälschlich dargestellt wird. Die Ostgrenze dieser germanischen Bevölkerung vor Christi liegt übrigens etwas östlich der Weichsel und Nogat (Willenberg bei Marienburg), so dass der grosse Strom keine Völkergrenze war, ebenso wenig wie vorher in der Zeit der Gesichtsurnen. Die Periode C zeigt ein ganz verändertes Inventar, hier ausschliesslich Leichenbrand in den sehr grossen Aschenurnen, die für den nördlichen Theil Ostpreussens charakteristisch. Im allgemeinen waren die Urnen nicht sehr reich. Viele hatte man absichtlich mit Steinen vollgestopft und diese waren immer sehr arm. Doch fanden sich in einer Menge die prächtig garnirten Armbrustfibeln mit umgeschlagenem Fuss aus Bronze mit Silberringen, auch aus reinem Silber, so dass die Zahl dieser Schmuckstücke des Provinzialmuseums wieder bedeutend vermehrt ist. In einer Gegend des Feldes waren solche reichen Urnen häufiger und enthielten unter anderem ein Paar silberne bandförmige Spiralarmringe mit Endschildern, wie ein Paar auf dem Neustädter Felde bei Elbing gefunden ist, zahlreiche silberne Halsringe, diese aber immer beschmolzen oder unvollständig und ähnliche prächtige Beigaben. In Periode D hört die Urnenbestattung allmählig auf und es werden schliesslich die Knochen in freier Erde beigesetzt. Sobald sie in gesammelten Häufchen auftreten, sind die Gräber reicher und es finden sich im Männergrabe meist 1 Fibel mit Nadelscheide, 1 Armring, 1 Schnalle, Lanze, Messer oder Dolchmesser und 1 roh geschnittene grosse Bernsteinperle, 1 oder mehrere Beigefässe, in Frauengräbern 2 Fibeln, 1 Armband, Bersteinperle, Spinnwirtel etc. Die Ringe greifen mit 2 Haken in einander, sind glatt, tordirt oder geflochten, aus Bronze oder Silber. Diese Periode lieferte noch zwei Paar ganz neuer Fibelformen. In Westpreussen ist diese Periode D noch nicht nachgewiesen, während sie weiter westlich wieder auftritt. Es ist daher wahrscheinlich, dass Westpreussen von seinen germanischen Bewohnern schon im Anfange des dritten Jahrhunderts geräumt wurde, während sie in Ostpreussen (und den russischen Ostseeprovinzen) noch zwei Jahrhunderte länger sassen, bis sie auf ganz dunkle Weise von den Preussen abgelöst wurden. Von der späteren preussischen Bevölkerung fanden sich auch Reste. In den jüngern Theil des Feldes reichte einer jener merkwürdigen, im Samlande so häufigen Aschenplätze hinein, der zerstreut Scherben mit den Wellenornamenten der jüngeren slawisch-preussischen Zeit enthielt, Eisenwaffen von vorzüglicher Erhaltung und ganz neuen Formen, begrabene Pferde mit Steigbügeln, welche den Pferden in den älteren Gräbern ganz fehlen. Diese Aschenschicht hatte zum Theil die alten Gräber zerstört, so dass ältere Thongefässe und Metallsachen scheinbar neben den 8—900 Jahre jüngeren Stücken lagen, ein Verhalten, das bei unwissenschaftlicher Aufdeckung dieses Grabfeldes zu den schwersten, weittragenden Irrthümern hätte führen können — wie sich solches anderweitig ja oft ereignet hat. So hat das Gräberfeld von Corjeiten unsere Kenntnisse wesentlich gefördert und es ist immer noch viel daselbst bei späteren Untersuchungen zu erwarten.

Sitzung am 27. Mai 1886.

Herr Prof. Dr. Hermann sprach über einige Beobachtungen an Froschlarven.

Der Vortragende beschrieb das Aussehen und Verhalten der eben ausgeschlüpften Larven von Rana temporaria, die den ganzen Körper bedeckende Flimmerbewegung, den Luftgehalt der schon im Stadium der äusseren Kiemenbüschel vorhandenen Lungen, den Kreislauf in den Kiemen, u. s. w. Den Hauptgegenstand der Mittheilung bildete das Verhalten der Larven im Wasser, durch welches ein kräftiger galvanischer Strom geleitet wird. Die Larven stellen sich nach einer heftigen Unruhe bei der Schliessung mit dem Kopf gegen die Anode ein, und bleiben in dieser Stellung bis zur Oeffnung, welche wieder Unruhe macht, ruhig liegen. Diejenigen Larven, welche die genannte Einstellung nicht zu Stande bringen, bleiben während der ganzen Stromdauer unruhig, indem der Schwanz beständig undulirende Bewegungen macht. Mannigfache Modificationen des Versuches werden angeführt. Auch geköpfte oder des Schwanzes beraubte Larven zeigen Unruhe, wenn sie mit dem Kopfende nach der Kathode liegen, Ruhe bei entgegengesetzter Lage; ebenso abgetrennte Schwanzstücke, sobald dieselben noch Rückenmark enthalten. Die Erscheinung wird darauf zurückgeführt, dass auch bei erwachsenen Fröschen) aufsteigende Durchströmung das Rückenmark stärker erregt als absteigende, und die Thiere die am wenigsten erregende Stellung aufsuchen.

Kurare ist ohne jede Wirkung auf die Larven; auch Morphium hat keine deutliche Wirkung. Im Dunkeln werden die stark pigmentirten Larven farblos und durchsichtig, im Lichte wieder dunkel. Rothes Licht wirkt wie Dunkelheit, blaues dagegen wie Tageslicht.

Vier kleine Mittheilungen von Dr. Klien.

1. Ueber zwei neue chemische Elemente: Germanium und Austrium. Im Sommer 1885 zeigte sich bei Freiberg auf der Himmelsfürst-Fundgrube ein reiches Silbererz von ungewöhnlichem Ansehen, in welchem A. Weissbach eine neue Mineralspecies erkannte, die er „Argyrodit" benannte. Bei der chemischen Untersuchung ergab sich, dass dieses Mineral, je nach der Reinheit des Materials, 73 bis 75 pCt. Silber, 17 bis 18 pCt. Schwefel, kleine Mengen Eisen, Spuren Arsen und geringe Mengen von Quecksilber (0,21 pCt.) enthielt, was sich bisher noch niemals auf den Freiberger Erzgängen gezeigt hatte. So oft und so sorgfältig von Clemens Winkler die Analyse des genannten Minerals auch durchgeführt werden mochte, schloss sie doch immer mit einem Verluste von etwa 6 bis 7 Procent ab, ohne dass es nach dem üblichen Gange der qualitativen Untersuchung möglich gewesen wäre, den fehlenden Körper zu entdecken. Schliesslich gelang es aber Winkler im Argyrodit ein neues, dem Antimon sehr ähnliches, doch von diesem noch scharf unterschiedenes Element aufzufinden, welchem der Name „Germanium" beigelegt worden ist. Das Element besitzt, ähnlich dem Arsen, graue Farbe und mässigen Glanz, ist bei Rothglühhitze flüchtig und legt sich bei der Verflüchtigung in Form kleiner, an abgedunstetes Jod erinnernde Krystalle an die Glaswandungen an. Das Germanium, welches in seinem Verhalten grosse Aehnlichkeit vom Antimon und Arsen hat, unterscheidet sich von den beiden letzteren Elementen vor Allem dadurch, dass es aus seinen Lösungen nach dem Ansäuern mit Schwefelwasserstoff eine charakteristische, weisse Schwefelverbindung (Germaniumsulfid) giebt, welche sich leicht in Schwefelammonium löst und beim Wiederabscheiden durch Salzsäure als schneeweisser Niederschlag gefüllt wird. Antimonsulfid aus seinen Lösungen bekanntlich mit oranger, Arsensulfid mit gelber Farbe. —

Das andere neue Element, welchem vom Entdecker der Name „Austrium" beigelegt worden ist, hat Professor Linnemann in Prag, welcher am 22. April daselbst gestorben ist, im Orthit aufgefunden. Nähere Angaben und Bestätigungen der Untersuchungen fehlen bis jetzt noch darüber.

2. Ueber die neue Theorie der Pflanzenernährung durch Pilze im Boden. Professor Frank hat die Entdeckung gemacht, dass die Wurzeln der meisten Waldbäume, vor Allem der Kupuliferen, also der Eichen, Buchen, Kastanien etc. sich von denjenigen der übrigen Pflanzen dadurch unterscheiden, dass die Wurzelober-

fläche der Saugwurzeln der genannten Bäume vollständig mit einem dichten Pilzmantel überzogen ist, während die Wurzelhaare, welche bei den meisten übrigen Pflanzen die Aufnahme der Nährstoffe vermitteln, ganz fehlen. Frank nimmt nun an, dass die Nahrung, welche die hierzu gehörigen Bäume aus dem Boden schöpfen, ihnen nur durch Vermittelung eines Pilzes zugeführt werden kann, indem eine grosse Anzahl Pilzfäden sich von der Oberfläche der Wurzelhüllen abzweigt und in den Boden hineinwächst. Hiernach würden die Pilzfäden also die Rolle der Wurzelhaare spielen; man hätte hier somit einen eigenthümlichen Fall von Symbiose. Diesen Wurzelpilz bezeichnet Frank mit dem Namen Mykorhiza. Der Referent hat früher Eichen- und Buchenpflänzchen in Nahrstofflösung gezogen, jedoch einen Wurzelpilz an den Saugwurzeln dieser Pflanzen nicht beobachtet.

3) Ueber den Einfluss sehr grosser Mengen von gebundener Phosphorsäure im Boden auf die Zusammensetzung der Körnerfrüchte. Prof. Wagner hatte gefunden, dass durch überreichliche Ernährung der Pflanzen mit Phosphorsäure eine Erhöhung des Proteïngehaltes wohl im Stroh und in den Grünpflanzen stattfindet, nicht aber in den Körnern und Samen; letztere würden sogar proteïnärmer. Nach den Beobachtungen des Referenten wird aber diese Wanderungsfähigkeit des Proteïns aus dem Kraute nach den Körnern nur durch die Anwesenheit von freier Phosphorsäure (Mineralsäure) im Boden erschwert, denn es ist anders, wenn die Phosphorsäure in grossen Mengen an Kalk etc. gebunden (in neutraler Form) dem Boden zugeführt wird.

4. Ueber das Verhältniss des Spelzengewichtes einer Anzahl in Ostpreussen geernteter Gerstensorten. Als besonders interessant hatte sich bei dieser Arbeit herausgestellt, dass auf öden Bodenflächen, welche mit stark gypshaltigem Dünger gedüngt waren, die Gerstenkörner das grösste Spelzengewicht hatten.

Herr Dr. Franz hielt einen Vortrag über die totale Sonnenfinsterniss, welche am 19. August des Jahres 1887 gegen $5^1/_2$ Uhr Morgens uns bevorsteht. Die Finsterniss ist total für Ost- und Westpreussen mit Ausnahme des nördlichen Streifens, in dem Königsberg und Danzig liegt. Der Vortragende empfahl in den Orten, die in der Mitte der Totalitätszone liegen, die Corona zu zeichnen und zu photographiren, und in den Orten, die nahe dem Rande der Totalitätszone liegen, die Dauer der Totalität nach einer Uhr mit Sekundenzeiger zu beobachten. Die Totalität dauert an den ersteren Orten 2 Minuten 18 Sekunden und ist um so kürzer, je näher der Beobachtungsort der Grenze der Totalitätszone liegt.

Eine Erscheinung von überraschender und unbeschreiblicher Pracht, die Jedermann ohne besondere Instrumente beobachten kann, eine Erscheinung, die zugleich äusserst selten ist, und die Deutschland seit 36 Jahren nicht gesehen hat, steht uns im nächsten Jahre bevor. Es ist die totale Sonnenfinsterniss vom 19. August 1887; dieselbe ist in Ostpreussen besser sichtbar als in irgend einem anderen Theile Deutschlands. Am besten freilich wird man sie in Russland und im südlichen Sibirien sehen. Denn es ist der Anfang der ganzen Finsterniss bei uns nicht sichtbar, da die Sonne zu der Zeit, wo der Mond beginnt vor sie zu treten, hier noch nicht aufgegangen ist. Sieht man also früh um $4^3/_4$ Uhr die Sonne im Nordosten aufgeben so bemerkt man, dass die dunkle und unsichtbare Mondscheibe von rechts und ein wenig von oben her bereits etwas in die Sonnenscheibe eingedrungen ist. Je höher nun die Sonne steigt, desto schmaler wird der noch erleuchtete Theil derselben und nimmt zuletzt die Form einer Sichel an. Wird diese blendend helle Sichel ganz dünn und kürzen sich zugleich ihre Hörner, so weiss man, dass der Beginn der Totalität unmittelbar bevorsteht und mit gespannter Aufmerksamkeit pflegt Jedermann diesen Moment zu erwarten. Plötzlich verschwindet die fadendünne Sichel — mitunter zerreisst sie kurz vorher, mitunter sieht man noch eine Sekunde lang einen Punkt der Sichel sternähnlich nachglühen — und die Totalität ist eingetreten. Ein überraschender Anblick bietet sich nun dem erstaunten Beschauer dar. Wie eine dunkle schwarze Kugel mitten in der Luft schwebend, erscheint plötzlich der bisher ganz unsichtbare Mond, umgeben von einem Heiligenscheine. Dicht am Rande des Mondes sieht man oft einzelne wie Rubinen leuchtende rothe Punkte; es sind die „Protuberanzen", Flammengarben und Flammenberge der Sonne, die über den Mondrand weit hervorragen, sie sind bei vielen Sonnenfinsternissen mit blossem Auge sichtbar. Weiterhin strahlt nach allen Seiten als heller Schein die „Corona" aus. Ihre Gestalt hat sich bei verschiedenen Sonnenfinsternissen sehr verschieden gezeigt und ist fast immer unregelmässig. Während sie sich an manchen Stellen nur um ein zehntel Monddurchmesser weit vom Monde entfernt, übertrifft ihre Ausdehnung an anderen Stellen den ganzen Monddurchmesser oft bedeutend, wie letzteres bei der Sonnenfinsterniss von 1878 in Nordamerika beobachtet wurde, wo sich die auf beiden Seiten vom Monde in der Richtung der Eliptik weithin erstreckte. Die Figur der Corona ist oft eckig, z. B. 1869 erschien sie in Amerika fast viereckig und sie hat oft lange Anhängsel oder Ausläufer, die man mitunter mit Pferdeschwänzen verglichen hat und die nach der Seite hin meist scharf begrenzt sind und sich nach aussen hin allmählig verlieren. Die Struktur der Corona zeigt sich oft strahlenförmig, mitunter homogen, mitunter gefaltet oder zackig. Ihre Farbe ist meist blendend weiss. Einige Beobachter schreiben ihr einen grünlichen, andere einen violetten Ton, nach innen mit rosigem Saume zu. — Das Wesen der Corona ist noch der Hauptsache nach unbekannt. Während man dieselbe früher für eine blosse optische Erscheinung hielt, nimmt man jetzt allgemein an, dass sie einen wirklichen materiellen Theil der Sonne oder der Sonnenatmosphäre repräsentirt oder von Körpern gebildet wird, die die Sonne umkreisen. Die prächtige Erscheinung der Totalität dauert aber nur ganz kurze Zeit, durchschnittlich nur zwei Minuten. Die Corona zeigt in der kurzen Zeit keine merklichen Veränderungen, wohl aber erleiden solche die Protuberanzen; sie pflegen an der rechten Seite zu- und an der linken Seite abzunehmen. Sowie der erste Sonnenstrahl wieder hervorbricht sind Corona, Protuberanzen und die schwarze Mondkugel mit einem Schlage verschwunden und schon zeigt sich rechts oben die schmale blendende Sonnensichel, die an Breite allmählig wächst, bis eine Stunde später das Ende der ganzen Finsterniss eintritt.

Während der Totalität werden die Sterne erster Grösse und die helleren Planeten sichtbar. Links von der Sonne und etwas tiefer um 5 Durchmesser entfernt steht dicht am Horizont α Leonis oder Regulus. Rechts weiter nach oben erscheint der Mars als kleiner röthlicher Punkt, weiterhin der Saturn und heller der Merkur. Die Venus ist noch nicht aufgegangen.

Oft hat bei totalen Sonnenfinsternissen ein Beobachter, der einen hoch-gelegenen Standpunkt mit weiter Aussicht hatte, das Heranrücken und Forteilen des Mondschattens über die Erdenlandschaft beim Anfang und Ende der Totalität beobachtet. Diese Erscheinung wird sich bei dieser Finsterniss nicht in ausgeprägter Weise zeigen. Denn da die Sonne noch sehr tief steht, werden diesmal zuerst die oberen Schichten der Atmosphäre und die oberen Wolken beschattet und sie sind es, die kurz vor dem Ende der Totalität zuerst erleuchtet werden, so dass in dieser Hinsicht eigenthümliche Lichteffekte hinsichtlich der Beleuchtung der Luftschichten zu Stande kommen dürften. Während der Totalität erscheinen auch mitunter die Wolken, die am Himmel schweben, mit eigenthümlichem rothem Licht überzogen. Es sind dies Erscheinungen, die man auch beobachten kann, wenn während der Totalität zufällig der Mond und die Corona durch eine Wolke verdeckt sein sollte. Bei der Finsterniss von 1851 hat man hier vielfach auch das ängstliche und unruhige Benehmen der Thiere beobachtet, von denen viele eiligst ihre Nachtlagerstätten aufsuchten. Empfindliche Pflanzen schliessen wieder ihre Blüthen.

Bei dieser Sonnenfinsterniss können von Jedermann, der zuverlässig, aufmerksam und besonnen und frei von Aufregung und Phantasie ist, Beobachtungen gemacht werden, die nicht ohne wissenschaftlichen Werth sind. Man begebe sich frühzeitig auf einen Platz im Freien, von dem aus man die Aussicht im Nordosten bis zum Horizont frei hat und sei bei Sonnenaufgang um 4³/₄ Uhr zur Beobachtung bereit. Wer von Königsberg aus sich mit der Südbahn in das Gebiet der Totalität z. B. nach Bartenstein, Korschen oder Rastenburg begiebt, kann mit dem gewöhnlichen Frühzuge um 11 Uhr Vormittags zu seinen Tagesgeschäften zurück sein. Doch darf man hoffen, dass die Südbahnverwaltung durch Einstellung eines Extrazuges den Königsbergern schnellere Beförderung und weitere Erleichterungen schafft.

Die Beobachtung der Dauer der Totalität ist in erster Linie zu empfehlen. Man braucht dazu nur eine Uhr mit Secundenzeiger. Zwei Beobachter sind aber dazu nöthig, die sich vorher zusammen eingeübt haben; der erste sieht die Sonne, der zweite die Uhr aufmerksam an. Sowie der erste Beobachter den Eintritt der Totalität sieht, ruft er sofort deutlich eine kurze verabredete Silbe aus. Man pflegt „Topp" zu rufen. Der zweite, der den Sekundenzeiger genau verfolgt, merkt sich die Secunde oder halbe Secunde, zu welcher er den Ruf gehört hat und schreibt sie sofort mit Bleistift auf ein bereit gehaltenes Blatt nieder. Darauf notirt er die zugehörige Minute. Er sieht nicht nach der Finsterniss, sondern sofort wieder auf die Uhr, um den bald erfolgenden zweiten Ruf des ersten Beobachters für das Ende der Totalität auf der Uhr scharf wahrzunehmen. Ist der Beobachter der Uhr etwas weitsichtig, so braucht er eine scharfe Brille, ein Brennglas oder eine Laterne. Es ist nicht nöthig, dass die Uhr richtig geht; der Minutenzeiger muss nur Tags vorher so gestellt sein, dass er gerade eine volle Minute zeigt, wenn der Secundenzeiger auf 60 steht. Nach der Beobachtung messe man, etwa durch Ausschreiten, Richtung und Entfernung des Standpunktes des Beobachters von den nächsten Gebäuden und Wegen, besser noch von den nächsten Kirchthürmen und Signalen der Landestriangulation. Letztere eignen sich oft selbst als Beobachtungsorte. Diese Beobachtung der Dauer der Totalität ist besonders an den Orten zu empfehlen, die nahe der Grenze der totalen Zone liegen und für welche nach der unten folgenden Tabelle die Dauer der totalen Finsterniss kleiner als 1,5 Minuten ist.

Wer auch nur einigermaassen im Zeichnen geübt ist, zeichne die Corona.

Auch er braucht einen Gehilfen. Da die Corana nur zarte Umrisse hat, welche in diesem Falle, da die Sonne noch tief steht, um so schwieriger wahrzunehmen sind, so darf das Auge des Zeichners nicht durch vorhergehendes Beschauen der Sonnensichel geblendet sein. Mehrere Minuten vor Beginn der Totalität schliesse der Zeichner die Augen und bedecke sie mit dem Taschentuch. Der Gehilfe muss ihn benachrichtigen, sowie die Totalität eingetreten ist und nun erst öffne der Zeichner die Augen. Zum Zeichnen habe er Quartblätter und Bleistift bereit. In der Mitte jedes Quartblatts ist schon am Tage vorher ein schwarz ausgefüllter Kreis von der Grösse eines Zweimarkstücks sorgfältig eingetragen und durch dessen Mitte zur Orientirung über das ganze Papier eine senkrechte und eine wagrechte Linie gezogen. Der Zeichner achte schnell auf die Gestalt der Corona, auf etwaige Ausläufer und Ecken und zeichne zuerst ihren Umriss ein, wobei genau auf die Richtung nach den senkrechten und wagrechten Linien zu achten ist. Dann achte man auf die Helligkeitsunterschiede und deute sie durch rohe Schattirung an, merke sich die Farben der Corona und des benachbarten Himmelshintergrundes und revidire, wenn noch Zeit ist, schnell den Umriss der Corona. An dieser Original-Skizze ist nach Ende der Totalität nichts zu ändern. Ihre Unvollkommenheiten beschreibt man mit Worten und fertigt gleich darauf in Musse nach dem Gedächtniss und der Original-Skizze eine zweite sorgfältiger ausgeführte Zeichnung an. Es ist sogar wünschenswerth, dass an demselben Tage mit dem Pinsel eine oder mehrere möglichst getreue Malereien ausgeführt werden. Was an denselben etwa misslungen ist, wird wieder mit Worten beschrieben. — Eine andere aber weniger sichere Methode ist die, während der Totalität garnicht zu zeichnen, sondern nur gleich darauf; man verwendet dann die ganze Zeit der Totalität, etwa zwei Minuten, auf das Betrachten und Prüfen des zarten Gebildes. — Die Benutzung eines Fernrohrs ist zu empfehlen, wenn der Beobachter erstens im Gebrauch desselben geübt ist, und wenn zweitens das Fernrohr nicht in der zitternden Hand gehalten wird, sondern durch Stativ oder Unterlage getragen wird oder wenigstens an einen Stab angebunden oder in eine Gabel gelegt wird. Sind diese Bedingungen nicht erfüllt, so ist ein Fernrohr nur störend und schädlich. Ein Operngucker schadet weniger, aber auch sein Nutzen ist gering.

Zum Abblenden des Sonnenlichtes wird jeder Beobachter ein Stück Glas, welches auf einer Seite berusst ist, bereit halten.

Photographen sollten nicht versäumen die totale Finsterniss zu photographiren. Da die Sonne und vor ihr der Mond noch tief am Himmel stehen — in Westpreussen nur gegen 5 Grad, an der russischen Grenze 7 bis 8 Grad über den Horizont — so kann die Camera auf dem gewöhnlichen dreifüssigen Stativ bleiben. Man nehme das grösste photographische Objectiv, welches auch die grösste Brennweite hat und entferne das Diaphrama, d. h. die Blende oder den Querwandring hinter dem Objectiv. Man wende die empfindlichsten Chemikalien an, wie sie bei sogenannten Momentaufnahmen benutzt werden. Die Dauer der Exposition wird zwischen 3 und 10 Secunden variiren, das Bild des Mondes ein zehntel Zoll gross werden. Vor der Totalität focussire man die Linse auf ein entferntes irdisches Object. Man halte alles bereit und versuche während der Totalität vier Aufnahmen von etwas verschiedener Dauer zu machen. Vor jeder Aufnahme bringe man das Bild von neuem genau in die Mitte der Platte. Man merke die Reihenfolge und

Expositionsdauer der Platten an und vor allem, welche Seite oben war. Der Photograph bedient die Platten, ein Gehilfe das Objectiv, der Zeuge achtet darauf, dass die obere Seite der Platten richtig notirt wird. Da Sonne und Mond allmählig weiter gehen, werden die Bilder etwas länglich und verwaschen, trotzdem sind sie nicht ganz unbrauchbar. Zur Uebung und um ein Urtheil über Expositionsdauer und Bildgrösse zu erhalten, photographire man im Sommer vorher öfter den Mond. Die Corona ist aber heller als der Vollmond.

Das Zeichnen und Photographiren der Corona ist besonders in den Orten zu empfehlen, die nahe der Mitte der Totalität liegen und bei denen die Totalität nach der folgenden Tabelle 2 Minuten oder länger dauert.

Andere Beobachter werden die anderen oben beschriebenen Erscheinungen beachten. Alle Beobachtungen und Wahrnehmungen sind möglichst bald zu veröffentlichen. Man schickt sie am besten an die Redaction einer in Königsberg erscheinenden Zeitung, da sie in kleinen Provinzialblättern leicht unbeachtet bleiben könnten.

Die Finsterniss ist überhaupt — das heisst als partielle Finsterniss — sichtbar in ganz Asien, mit Ausnahme der südlichen Halbinseln in Aegypten, in Europa mit Ausnahme von Spanien und Irland und in den Nordpolarländern. Die Zone der totalen Verfinsterung ist aber nur gegen 25 Meilen breit und erstreckt sich vom Harz über Berlin, Cüstrin, Kreuz, Schneidemühl, Posen, Bromberg nach den unten folgenden genauern Angaben über den grössten südlicheren Theil von West- und Ostpreussen und den nördlichen Streifen von Polen, geht dann in Russland weiter über Kowno, Suwalki, Wilna, Witebsk, Twer, Moskau, Jaroslaw, Wjatka und Perm, setzt sich in Sibirien über Tobolsk, Tomsk, Krasnojark und Irkutsk fort und geht durch die Mandschurei bis nach Jeddo und Jokohama in Japan. In der Mitte der Totalitätszone liegen unter anderen Orten Filehne, Nakel, Bromberg, Kulm, Bischofswerder, Dt. Eylau und Löbau, Hohenstein und Allenstein, Bischofsburg, Rhein, Lötzen, Goldap und Oletzko. Die nördliche Grenze der Totalität läuft bei uns durch Neu-Stettin, zwischen Berent und Schöneck, zwischen Dirschau und Danzig, zwischen Kahlberg und Braunsberg, über Heiligenbeil, Tharau, Löwenhagen, Tapiau, zwischen Insterburg und Tilsit hin. In Danzig und Königsberg findet also keine totale Finsterniss statt, doch bleibt hier bei der grössten Phase nur eine schmale Sichel

Zone der Totalität.

von der Sonne sichtbar, deren Breite nur den hundertsten Theil des Sonnendurchmessers beträgt. Die südliche Grenze läuft durch die südliche Provinz Posen und das nördliche Polen. Die folgende Tabelle ist nach Hansens Methode nach den Elementen des Berliner Astronomischen Jahrbuchs berechnet und giebt für verschiedene Orte die mittlere Ortszeit des Anfangs der Totalität, die Dauer der Totalität und die mittlere Ortszeit für das Ende der ganzen Finsterniss in Minuten und Zehntelminuten an. Indessen ist zu bemerken, dass wegen der noch bestehenden Unsicherheit in den Mondtafeln die angegebene Dauer der Totalität, wenn sie kleiner als eine Minute ist, unsicher ist und durch Beobachtung genauer bestimmt werden muss. Der Anfang der ganzen Finsterniss ist in die Tabelle nicht aufgenommen, weil er vor Sonnenaufgang eintritt.

Orte in der Zone der Totalität.

	Anfang der Totalität	Dauer	Ende der Finsterniss		Anfang der Totalität	Dauer	Ende der Finsterniss.
	Uhr Min.	Min.	Uhr Min.		Uhr Min.	Min.	Uhr Min.
	Morgens		Morgens		Morgens		Morgens
Allenburg	5 36,9	1,5	6 34,7	Krojanke	5 19,4	2,1	6 16,5
Allenstein	5 32,8	2,2	6 30,9	Deutsch Krone	5 16,6	1,9	6 13,6
Angerburg	5 38,3	2,2	6 36,7	Lötzen	5 38,2	2,3	6 36,5
Bartenstein	5 34,9	1,9	6 32,8	Löwenhagen	5 36,2	0,1	6 33,2
Berlin	5 3,7	1,8	6 1,6	Lyck	5 40,3	2,2	6 38,7
Bischofsburg	5 34,7	2,3	6 32,8	Marienburg	5 27,7	1,4	6 24,9
Bischofswerder	5 20,7	2,2	6 24,3	Marienwerder	5 26,6	2,0	6 24,6
Braunsberg	5 31,9	0,7	6 29,0	Mehlsack	5 32,0	1,7	6 29,6
Bromberg	5 22,5	2,2	6 19,6	Mohrungen	5 30,9	2,1	6 30,7
Darkehmen	5 39,5	2,1	6 37,9	Mühlhausen	5 30,8	1,3	6 28,1
Dirschau	5 27,3	0,8	6 24,2	Nakel	5 20,8	2,2	6 18,2
Elbing	5 29,3	1,4	6 26,1	Neidenburg	5 31,2	2,0	6 39,2
Eydtkuhnen	5 42,5	1,9	6 41,2	Neustettin	5 19,1	0,1	6 16,2
Deutsch Eylau	5 28,1	2,2	6 25,8	Oletzko	5 41,1	2,3	6 39,8
Pr. Eylau	5 34,7	1,5	6 32,3	Ortelsburg	5 34,4	2,2	6 32,6
Flatow	5 19,1	2,0	6 16,2	Osterode	5 30,7	2,2	6 28,6
Frauenburg	5 31,2	0,5	6 28,1	Pelplin	5 26,3	1,6	6 23,6
Gerdauen	5 36,8	1,8	6 34,8	Pillkallen	5 42,4	1,5	6 40,5
Gilgenburg	5 30,7	2,2	6 28,6	Posen	5 15,8	1,5	6 12,6
Goldap	5 40,5	2,2	6 39,1	Rastenburg	5 35,8	2,2	6 34,0
Graudenz	5 25,8	2,1	6 23,3	Rhein	5 32,4	2,3	6 30,5
Gumbinnen	5 40,8	1,7	6 39,1	Schlobitten	5 30,8	1,6	6 28,4
Guttstadt	5 31,0	2,1	6 28,8	Schneidemühl	5 17,4	2,1	6 14,5
Heiligenbeil	5 32,8	0,0	6 21,6	Sensburg	5 36,0	2,3	6 33,2
Heilsberg	5 33,7	2,0	6 31,6	Stallupönen	5 42,2	1,8	6 40,5
Hohenstein	5 31,8	2,2	6 29,8	Stargard in Pr.	5 26,0	1,3	6 23,1
Pr. Holland	5 30,3	1,7	6 27,8	Tapiau	5 36,4	0,6	6 33,7
Inowraclaw	5 23,2	1,9	6 20,8	Tharau	5 34,6	0,0	6 31,9
Insterburg	5 39,5	1,5	6 37,4	Wehlau	5 37,1	1.1	6 34,6
Johannisburg	5 37,9	2,1	6 36,2	Wormditt	5 31,1	1,9	6 28,9
Konitz	5 22,3	1,5	6 19,4	Zinten	5 33,7	0,8	6 31,0
Korschen	5 35,1	2,1	6 33,2				

Orte ausserhalb der Zone der Totalität.

	Grösste Phase Uhr Min.	Ende der Finsterniss Uhr. Min.		Grösste Phase Uhr. Min.	Ende der Finsterniss. Uhr Min.
	Morgens	Morgens		Morgens	Morgens
Breslau	5 17,6	6 12,6	Labiau	5 37,7	6 34,7
Brüsterort	5 33,4	6 30,2	Memel	5 38,7	6 35,8
Cranz	5 35,5	6 32,4	Neukuhren	5 34,4	6 31,2
Danzig	5 27,6	6 24,6	Tilsit	5 40,9	6 37,7
Kahlberg	5 31,1	6 27,8	Pillau	5 32,7	6 29,5
Königsberg	5 34,6	6 31,6	Zoppot	5 27,2	6 24,2

Darauf folgte die **General-Versammlung**, in welcher folgende Herren als ordentliche Mitglieder aufgenommen wurden:

1. Herr Professor Dr. Paul Volkmann,
2. „ Professor Dr. Fleischmann,
3. „ Ingenieur Hüser.
4. „ Premier-Lieutenant Neumann,
5. „ Oberlehrer Vanhoeffen.

Als auswärtiges Mitglied:

der „literarisch-polytechnische Verein" in Mohrungen.

Sitzung am 7. October 1886.

Zuvörderst begrüsste der **Vorsitzende** die anwesenden Mitglieder und theilte mit, dass die Gesellschaft während der Ferienzeit in gewohnter Weise für die Erforschung der Naturgeschichte der Provinz thätig gewesen sei und dass unser Provinzialmuseum sich dabei ganz ausserordentlich vergrössert habe. — Leider hat die Gesellschaft in dieser Zeit einen schweren Verlust erlitten, indem ihr langjähriger Sekretär Herr Stadtrath Lottermoser auf einer Besuchsreise in Berlin einem raschen Tode erlag. Der Verstorbene hat sich um die Gesellschaft durch seine lange Geschäftsführung wesentliche Verdienste erworben. Er war ein sachverständiger und äusserst eifriger, pflichttreuer Beamter, so dass wir ihn in Zukunft sehr vermissen, aber auch sein Andenken in Ehren halten werden. Um dieser ehrenden Anerkennung auch einen äusseren Ausdruck zu geben, forderte der Vorsitzende die Versammelten auf, sich von ihren Plätzen zu erheben, was auch geschah.

Darauf hielt Herr Professor **Stieda** einen Vortrag über Georg Wilhelm Steller als Naturforscher und Reisender. Steller, geboren am 10. Marz 1709 zu Windsheim in Franken, studierte anfangs Theologie, später Medizin in Wittenberg, Leipzig und Halle. Mit glänzenden Fähigkeiten ausgestattet, wollte er eine akademische Laufbahn einschlagen, aber die Umstände waren ihm nicht günstig. Er verliess Deutschland, ging 1734 als Arzt nach Petersburg, wurde Mitglied der Akademie der Wissenschaften und als Theilnehmer an der sogenannten kamtschatkaischen Expedition nach Sibirien geschickt. Er bereiste Sibirien von 1737—1746; anfangs mit Gmelin und Rüker, dann allein, vereinigte sich in Petropawlowsk (Kamtschatka) mit N. Bering und betheiligte sich an der unglücklichen Fahrt nach Amerika im Sommer 1741; im Herbst litten sie Schiffbruch an der Beringsinsel; Bering starb; nach vielen Leiden kehrte Steller mit der Mannschaft nach Kamtschatka zurück. Auf der Beringsinsel fand Steller Gelegenheit, das Leben einiger daselbst hausender Meerthiere (Robben u. s. w.) zu studieren; mit besonderer Begabung und grossem Fleiss, Ausdauer und Geschicklichkeit — unter den allerschwierigsten Verhältnissen lieferte Steller äusserst werthvolle Beiträge über Bau und Lebensart der Seekuh, des Seelöwen, der Seeotter und des Seebären. Die Seekuh ist bereits nachher völlig ausgerottet worden — sie hat zu Ehren Stellers den Namen Rhytina Stelleri erhalten. — Steller verweilte noch drei Jahre in Kamtschatka, wandte sich dann durch Sibirien nach Westen, hatte vielfache Unbequemlichkeiten zu erdulden und sollte Europa nicht wiedersehen. Auf dem Wege dahin in Tjumen erkrankte er und starb 12. (23.) November 1746. Durch seine Untersuchungen der Seethiere insbesondere, sowie durch die grosse Menge an gesammelten Materialien, Pflanzen, Thiere, welche spätere Forscher wie Gmelin, Pallas, verwerthet haben, hat sich Steller ein ausserordentliches Verdienst um die Naturwissenschaften erworben; seine mannigfachen trüben Schicksale, sein früher Tod erregen unsere Theilnahme.

Dann sprach Herr Dr. Raths über den gegenwärtigen Standpunkt der Stellarphotographie. — Während noch vor kaum fünf Jahren bei Gelegenheit einer internationalen Astronomenversammlung in Paris die Photographie als ein Hilfsmittel von sehr zweifelhaftem Werthe für die Beobachtung des Venusdurchganges erklärt wurde und die deutschen Astronomen daher von jeder Benutzung der Photographie bei diesem seltenen Phänomen Abstand nahmen, ist das Vertrauen zu den Leistungen der Stellarphotographie in letzer Zeit sehr gestiegen, und die überraschende Genauigkeit ihrer Bilder haben die Aussicht auf die Anwendung derselben für astronomische Zwecke bedeutend erweitert. Es ist daher wohl von Interesse, sich über den Unterschied zwischen dem photographischen und dem optischen Sehen und über die Vortheile des ersteren ein Bild zu machen. Vergleicht man zunächst die Ausdehnung des photographirten Spektrums mit der des direkt gesehenen, so erkennt man, dass das erstere ungefähr um ein Drittel der gesammten Länge grösser ist. Während das photographirte Spektrum, Dank den Arbeiten von Becquerel, Vogel, Lohse u. a. nach der Seite des rothen Lichtes ebenso weit ausgedehnt werden kann wie das direkt gesehene, erstreckt es sich nach der Seite des violetten Lichts bedeutend weiter. Phänome, bei welchen die ultravioletten Lichtstrahlen eine Rolle spielen, können daher sehr wohl durch die Photographie gezeigt werden, während sie dem direkten Beobachter entgehen. Es ist denkbar, dass es Sterne giebt, welche nur oder der Hauptsache nach ultraviolettes Licht aussenden, dieselben würden auch durch das stärkste Fernrohr nicht wahrnehmbar gemacht werden können, während sie auf der photographischen Platte ein deutliches Bild entwerfen. Solche Fälle scheinen in der letzten Zeit wirklich vorgekommen zu sein. Als die Gebrüder Prosper und Paul Henry in Paris im November vorigen Jahres eine photographische Aufnahme von dem bekannten im Sternbilde des Stiers befindlichen Sternhaufen der Plejaden machten, fanden sie in demselben in der Nähe des Sterns Maja einen Nebel, der trotz der vielfachen Beobachtungen, denen gerade dieser Sternhaufen ausgesetzt gewesen ist, noch nie gesehen war. Nach ihren Mittheilungen ist der Nebel sehr intensiv und hat in ausgesprochener Weise die Form einer Spirale. Nachdem dieser Majanebel einmal mittels der Photographie entdeckt war, wurde er auch bald durch das Teleskop direkt gesehen, und zwar zuerst von O. v. Struve in Pulkowa mit dem kürzlich dort aufgestellten Riesenteleskope von 30 Zoll Oeffnung, dem grössten bis jetzt in Gebrauch befindlichen Refraktor. Der Nebel wurde von ihm unschwer erkannt, aber, bemerkt Struve, er würde ihn wahrscheinlich nicht gesehen haben, falls er nicht vorher auf seine Existenz aufmerksam gemacht wäre. Ein ähnlicher Fall hat sich in den letzten Tagen wieder ereignet. Als im vorigen Monate Herr von Gotthard auf dem ungarischen astrophysikalischen Observatorium in Hereny einen Ringnebel in dem Sternbilde der Leier photographisch aufnahm, bemerkte er im Innern desselben einen runden Kern, während sich bei der sehr vollkommenen Beschreibung und Zeichnung dieses Nebels von Professor Vogel kein solcher Kern vorfindet; im Gegentheile scheint es dort: das Innere des Ringes erscheint im Wiener Refraktor ganz gleichmässig mit schwachem leuchtenden Nebel ausgefüllt. Diese Erscheinung, welche durch wiederholte Photographien bestätigt ist, hat den Herausgeber der astronomischen Nachrichten bewogen, sich brieflich an mehrere grössere Sternwarten zu wenden, um zu entscheiden, ob dieser Kern im Innern des Ring-nebels nur photographisch oder auch optisch sichtbar ist. Eine zweite Verschiedenheit des photographischen und optischen Sehens beruht auf einer Eigenthümlichkeit unseres Auges. Der Eindruck, den unsere Netzhaut von einem leuchtenden Objekte erhält, verstärkt sich nur während eines kleinen Theils einer Sekunde, ungefähr während $^1/_{10}$ Sekunde, eine länger dauernde Einwirkung macht keinen grösseren Effekt. Die photographische Platte verhält sich den Lichteindrücken gegenüber anders, dort vermehrt sich der Effekt, je länger die Platte dem Lichte des betreffenden Gegenstandes ausgesetzt wird, und zwar entsprechen, wie Bunsen und Roscoe nachgewiesen haben, gleichen Produkten aus Intensität und Belichtungsdauer unter sonst gleichen Umständen auch gleiche photographische Wirkungen. Während also durch längeres Hinsehen nach einem lichtschwachen Gegenstande dieser für unser Auge nicht heller und deutlicher wird, kann die Wirkung, die derselbe Gegenstand auf die photographische Platte macht, durch längeres Exponieren der Platte beliebig verstärkt werden. Ebenso kann auch die zu starke Wirkung des Lichtes, welche die Deutlichkeit des Bildes verringert, beliebig abgeschwächt werden dadurch, dass man die Platte nur kurze Zeit dem Lichte aussetzt. In der That darf bei der Photographie der Sonne das Licht nicht länger als $^1/_{500}$ Sekunde auf die empfindliche Platte einwirken, während bei der Photographie von Kometen, Nebel und lichtschwachen Sternen dieselbe Platte $^1/_2$ bis 3 Stunden exponirt werden muss. Endlich ist noch ein dritter Vortheil der photographischen Aufnahme vor dem direkten Sehen zu erwähnen. Das photographische Bild bleibt bestehen, während das direkt gesehene verschwindet, sobald man das Auge vom Fernrohre fortbewegt, man kann also Messungen, die man an dem photographischen Bilde einmal vorgenommen hat, zu jeder beliebigen Zeit wiederholen und kontrolliren. Der Vortragende ging dann näher ein auf die Art, wie die Sonnenphotographien ausgeführt werden und auf die Methode, welche bei der Photographie von lichtschwachen Sternen angewandt wird, und zeigte schliesslich eine von Professor Janssen in Paris ausgeführte Photographie eines Theils der Sonne sowie mehrere stereoskopische Photographien des Mondes von Warren de la Rue.

Sitzung am 4. November 1886.

Professor Caspary legt von Paulownia imperialis Sieb. et Zuccr., in Japan zu Hause, die Anlage von jungen Blüthenständen aus dem königl. botanischen Garten vor, die daselbst sich zum ersten Mal entwickelt haben und in unserm Lande gewiss eine sehr seltene Erscheinung sind. Im königl. botanischen Garten hierselbst sind zwei vor etwa 25 Jahren gepflanzte Stämme dieses mittelgrossen Baumes, die jedoch jeden Winter, der ein Minimum von 18 bis 20 Grad R. hat, bis auf den Boden abfrieren, dann aber im nächsten Jahre wieder aus den Stammresten ihre Knospen austreiben, die zu Schossen von 10—12 Fuss Höhe in einem Jahre erwachsen. Die drei letzten Winter von 1883 an hatten nur mässige Temperaturen, die nicht über —14 Grad hinausgingen; jene beiden Stämme von Paulownia imp. erfroren also nicht, erlangten eine Höhe von 15 bis 16 Fuss und setzten zum ersten Mal 1886, vier Jahre alt,

Blüthenstände an. Diese sind 16 bis 22 cm lange, verzweigte Cymen und haben bis 20 Blüthenknospen, die eiförmig, zurückgekrümmt und mit lichtbraunem Filz dick bedeckt sind. Die Knospen sind bis 13 mm lang und 8 mm dick.

Dann legt Prof. Caspary neue und seltene Pflanzen aus Preussen vor, die 1886 von Mitgliedern des preussischen botanischen Vereins gefunden waren. Neu für Preussen sind: **Juncus tenuis W.**, Kreis Schwetz, Lehrer Grütter, und **Sedum villosum L.**, Kreis Strasburg, Kandidat des höheren Schulamts Valentin. Juncus tenuis ist von Willdenow (Sp. 1799 II 214) zuerst als Art unterschieden und Nordamerika als Vaterland angegeben. Engelmann (Revis. of the northameric. sp. of the genus Juncus. Transact. Acad. scienc. St. Louis II 1868 450) sagt, dass Junc. tenuis W. sei „one of the most common and best known, but also one of the most variable species" in Nordamerika, die sich vom atlantischen zum stillen Meer ausbreitet, sich in den tropischen Theilen von Nordamerika, auch in Westindien findet und „in western Europe". Für das westliche Europa scheint die Pflanze jedoch zweifelhaft zu sein oder daselbst gar nicht vorzukommen. Es ist mir nicht bekannt, dass sie für Spanien, Portugal, Irland, England angegeben ist. Für Frankreich führen Grenier et Godron (Fl. Fr. III 349) 2 Fundorte auf, aber die Beschreibung ist so, dass Zweifel an der richtigen Bestimmung erregt werden, denn es heisst: „fleurs rapprochées par 2 et par 3", während die Blüthen einzeln stehen; vergl. Buchenau Regensb. Flora LX. 1877. 88. Ferner sagen Grenier und Godron von Junc. tenuis aus: „Souche à rhizomes rampants", obgleich sie rasig sind. Für Schottland wird Juncus tenuis von einem Fundort: Berge von Clova angegeben, wo sie Don entdeckt haben soll. Später ist sie daselbst jedoch nicht mehr beobachtet. Es bezweifeln daher Hooker und Arnott (Brit. Fl. 1850. 6. Edit. 451.) die Richtigkeit der Angabe für Schottland, ja selbst das freiwillige Vorkommen in anderen Theilen Europas, sind aber in der Literatur schlecht bewandert, wenn sie behaupten noch 1850, dass die Pflanze kaum in „any botanical work as a native of Europe" aufgeführt sei. Das Vorkommen in Schottland bezweifelt auch Watson (Cyb. brit. III 47). Seit 1823 ist Juncus tenuis in Belgien in der Provinz Antwerpen gefunden. Vergl. Crepin Man. Fl. de Belgique 1860. 190. Mir liegen auch Exemplare von Nethen (Brabant), 1874 von de Dieudonné, gesammelt vor (Hb. Patze). Juncus tenuis kommt in Holland vor. No. 532 Wirtgen herb. Plant. select. crit. hybr. Fl. rhenan. Fasc. IX giebt, sie von Nykerk in Holland, gesammelt 1860 von R. Bondam (Hb. Petze). Prof. Körnicke sammelte sie 1884 bei Elten auf preussischem und holländischem Gebiet (Hb. Patze). In Deutschland ist die Pflanze, wie es scheint, zuerst vor 1837 bei Memmingen in Baiern von Pfarrer Köberlein entdeckt und von Hoppe in Sturm's Deutsch. Fl. 71. Heft beschrieben und abgebildet. Einige Exemplare liegen mir vor von Waldwegen von Dickenreishausen bei Memmingen von Kaflisch gesammelt (aus Hb. monac.). Garcke (Fl. v. Dlnd. 15. Ausgabe) führte zwei weitere Fundorte für Baiern an. von Mertens und Kemmler (Flora von Würtemberg und Hohenzollern 2. Aufl. 1865 600) geben für Würtemberg zwei Fundorte an. Fernere Fundorte in Deutschland sind bei Dreifelden im Westerwalde im Nassau'schen, in der Winterlitt bei Cassel (G. F. W. Meyer Fl. hann. exc. 1849 S. 589. Exemplare liegen mir vor, von Buchenau gesammelt (hb. Casp.); bei Gütersloh in Westphalen (nach Garcke a. O.), in Hannover bei Hühnerfelde bei Minden (nach Garcke a. O.), auf Steinwärder und beim Dorfe Bargteheide bei Oldeslohe in Holstein

(G. F. W. Meyer a. O. u. Sonder Fl. Hamb. 197), Königreich Sachsen bei Tharandt und bei Bautzen (Garcke a. O.), im nördlichen Böhmen bei Georgswalde unfern Schluckenau (nach Celakowski Prodr. Fl. von Böhmen 83), in Anhalt-Dessau bei Zerbst (nach Garcke a. O.), Mark Brandenburg: Hertelsau bei Buchthal im Kreise Arnswalde (Verhandlg. botanischen Vereins Brandenb. 25. Jahrg. 207) u. „Damm zw. der Chaussee und der Pieskowatschmühle bei Kalau (a. O. 21. Jahrg. 1880 S. 135), im westlichen Schlesien bei Muskau, Niesky, Görlitz, Bunzlau und an anderen Orten (nach Fiek Fl. v. Schlesien 404). Endlich der Fundort im Kreise Schwetz von allen der ötlichste.

Für Dänemark (Lange, Haandbog Dansk. Fl. 3. Udgave 268) wird ein Fundort aus Wahls Zeit angegeben. In Schweden, Schweiz, Italien, Russland und Südeuropa ist die Pflanze nicht gefunden. Als Bezirk der Pflanze kann zutreffend also nicht das westliche Europa angeführt werden, sondern um dem zweideutigen Ausdruck „Mitteleuropa" zu meiden, kann als ihr Vaterland Deutschland, Holland, Belgien und vielleicht Dänemark angegeben werden.

Ich habe bereits erwähnt, dass Juncus tenuis mir von 5 europäischen Fundorten vorliegt. Ich habe sie auch von fünf nordamerikanischen vor Augen, darunter Exemplare meines Herbars von dreien, die Engelmann im Herb. Juncorum boreali-americanorum normali No. 20, 21 und 22 veröffentlichte. Die von Grütter gesammelten Pflanzen, die zwischen Gebüsch aufgewachsen waren, sind von allen die höchsten, denn sie sind bis 75 cm lang. Auch stehen die einzelnen Blüthen bei ihnen am entferntesten. Die Engelmann'sche Beschreibung (Engelmann a. O. 450) stimmt völlig. Die Samen der Pflanze des Kreises Schwetz sind der nordamerikanischen gleich. Die Samenträger in der Kapsel und deren Querschnitt stimmen mit Buchenau's Zeichnung (a. O. Taf. III. Bild 5) überein, nur hat die Kapsel der Pflanze an allen mir vorliegenden Exemplaren der verschiedenen Fundorte ziemlich stark hervorspringende drei Kanten auf ihrer Aussenseite, während der von Buchenau gegebene Querschnitt die Kapsel ohne solche ganz gerundet abweichend von der Natur darstellt. Es ist von mehreren, wie Hooker u. Arnott (a. O.), Meyer (a. O.) gemuthmasst, dass die Pflanze aus Nordamerika stamme und ein Flüchtling aus Gärten sei, aber irgend ein triftiger Grund für diese Annahme kann nicht beigebracht werden.

Der Vortragende legt dann viele seltene Pflanzen vor, die 1886 in Preussen gesammelt wurden und im Bericht über die Versammlung des preussischen botanischen Vereins zu Insterburg vom 4. Oktober 1886 näher angegeben werden werden.

Dann legt der Vortragende einen Band des Helwing'schen Herbariums vor, das der königl. botanische Garten als gütiges Geschenk des Herrn Hofapotheker Hagen besitzt, in welchem sich ein gut erhaltenes Exemplar von **Senecio vernalis** W. et K. befindet, das gegen 1717 bei Angerburg gesammelt ist; damit werden die Mythen von der Einwanderung dieser Pflanze nach Preussen zu Anfang dieses Jahrhunderts widerlegt.

Endlich weist der Vortragende nach, dass die Angabe, dass bei Ostrometzko an der Weichsel Trüffeln vorkommen, auf Irrthum beruht.

Für das Nähere über Senecio vernalis von 1717 und die vermeintlichen Trüffeln von Ostrometzko wird auf die ausführlichen Aufsätze über diese Gegenstände in den Abhandlungen dieses Jahrganges verwiesen.

Herr Professor Volkmann hielt einen Vortrag über Fern- und Druckwirkungen, welcher in den Abhandlungen dieses Jahrgangs abgedruckt ist.

Sitzung am 2. December 1886.

Dr. O. Tischler theilte mit, dass die Resultate der archäologischen, im Auftrage der Gesellschaft angestellten Untersuchungen, sowie der Zuwachs der anthropologisch-archäologischen Abtheilung des Provinzial-Museums im Laufe des Jahres 1886 ganz ausserordentlich wichtige und reiche gewesen sind, behält sich aber einen näheren Bericht für die ersten Sitzungen des nächsten Jahres vor.

Der Vortragende bespricht aus der Gesammtheit der Funde eine ausserordentlich zierliche mit Römischem Millefiori-Email geschmückte Bronzescheibe, einem grösseren Gräberfelde zu Oberhof bei Memel entstammend, und knüpft, um die Bedeutung und Zeitstellung dieses kleinen Objectes, sowie die Rolle, welche es unter den Produkten der technischen Künste spielt, in klares Licht zu stellen, daran einen kurzen Abriss der Geschichte des Emails, einer der edelsten dieser Künste. (Der Vortragende hatte die Scheibe auch schon auf der diesjährigen Anthropologen-Versammlung zu Stettin vorgezeigt und besprochen.)[1])

Die Scheibe hat 46 mm. Durchmesser und einen herabgebogenen Rand. Sie ist durch eine Reihe concentrischer Vertiefungen gegliedert in einen mittleren vertieften Kreis von 17 mm. Durchm. und 3 vertiefte Reifen von ca. 3; 3,6; 3,9 cm. Breite, welche durch niedrige Stege von einander getrennt sind. Diese Zonen sind mit mosaikartigem Email erfüllt, welches jedenfalls auch einst die Mitte bedeckte, die aber schon in alter Zeit ziemlich ungeschickt von einem 9 mm. breiten Loch durchbohrt ist, so dass sowohl hier vollständig, als in den 3 Reifen zu einem kleinen Theil das Email herausgefallen ist, mithin nicht ausgewittert, wie dies die der Bronze anhaftende Sandschicht zeigte. Die mittlere Zone enthält eine Reihe kleiner schachbrettartiger Täfelchen von rothem Grunde umgeben. Die Täfelchen sind aus 9 feinen 4eckigen Plättchen gebildet, in den 4 Ecken und in der Mitte ein weisses Quadrat, in den Mitten der Seiten ein blaues. In der 1. und 3. Zone treffen wir Täfelchen ähnlich schachbrettartig aus 5 mal 5 Quadraten gebildet von blauem Grunde umgeben. Das mittelste Quadrat ist roth, von hier gehen aber nach der Mitte der Seiten je 2 blaue, so dass ein blaues Kreuz entsteht, die Ecken sind ebenfalls blau, die drei übrigen Quadrate an jeder Ecke sind weiss und bilden einen zusammenhängenden rechten Winkel. Da nun die 4 Ecken und 4 Arme der blauen Kreuze mit dem gleichfarbigen umgebenden Grunde zusammenfliessen, so hat man scheinbar eine Zone schrägliegender Malteserkreuze

1) Correspondenzblatt der Deutschen anthropologischen Gesellschaft 1886 p. 128—132.

mit rother Mitte auf blauem Grunde. In jeder Zone sind diese Kreuze unter sich gleich, in der inneren aber kleiner als in der äusseren. Diese eingeschmolzene Glasmosaik, das sogenannte Millefiori-Email, welche weiter unten eingehender erörtert wird, ist soweit abgeschliffen, dass sie mit der Metalloberfläche in einer Ebene liegt.

Tischler. Abriss der Geschichte des Emails.[1]

Die Freude an farbigem Schmucke ist dem Menschengeschlechte von der Natur mitgegeben und zeigt sich sowohl bei den in noch voller Empfänglichkeit lebenden Naturvölkern sowie in allen Zeiten höchster Kunstblüthe, erst in Zeiten des verfallenden Geschmackes, wie am schwersten in der ersten Hälfte des 19. Jahrhunderts ging das Gefühl dafür fast ganz verloren. Nur im farbenprächtigen Orient, d. h. speciell den Ländern des südwestlichen Asiens, der Wiege aller Cultur, Technik und Kunst, hat dieser Sinn alle Umwälzungen und Zerstörungen überdauert und aus seinem ewig lebendigen Quell zu wiederholten Malen das verblassende Europa erfrischt.

Schon in alter Zeit hatte man die Wände und Mauern in den Riesenstädten Assyriens und Babyloniens mit farbig glasirten Ziegeln bekleidet, und in dem mit im grossen und ganzen verwandter Kunstrichtung ausgestatteten Aegypten fand man die Bekleidung mit farbigen Ziegeln schon in den Gräbern des alten Memphitischen Reiches. Es ist dies eine glasartige durch Metalle oder Metalloxyde gefärbte Schicht, die man den gebrannten Ziegeln aufschmolz, eine Technik, die ja nachher in Aegypten in ganz ausserordentlich weitgehender Weise verwendet wurde. Es lag nun nahe mit dieser farbigen Schicht auch Metallgeräthe zu überziehen und ihnen so eine fast unverwüstbare Färbung zu ertheilen: es galt das farbige Glas, zunächst immer opakes, fest und dauerhaft dem Metall aufzuschmelzen, das ist Email, aus dem deutschen Worte Schmelz entstanden, und man hat sich daran gewöhnt, auch die mit Email überzogenen Gegenstände als „Emaillen" zu bezeichnen, die durch Anwendung verschieden gefärbter Glasmassen dann bunt verziert erschienen.

Die Anfänge und der Ursprung dieser Kunst ist noch in tiefes Dunkel gehüllt. Die Angaben der Schriftsteller sind völlig unklar und ist ihre Deutung eine willkührliche und unsichere. Bildliche Darstellungen finden sich auf aegyptischen Grabgemälden zu Theben ca. um 1300 v. Chr. aus der Zeit Ramses III., woselbst man gelbe mit buntfarbigen Mustern bedeckte Goldgefässe erblickt, die man als emaillirte Goldgefässe deutet. Doch sind ähnliche Fundstücke in Wirklichkeit nicht entdeckt worden. Das älteste bekannte emaillirte Stück scheint ein goldenes Armband aus dem Schmucke der Königin Aahotep, Gattin des Königs Kamos der 17ten Dynastie zu sein (Museum zu Bulaq No. 3510) ca. um 1700 v. Chr., welches den König Ahmos vor dem Gotte Sib knieend zeigt, auf blauem Grunde. Dies scheint wirkliches, eingeschmolzenes Email. Bei den anderen Stücken dieses kostbaren Fundes, sowie den Objecten der späteren Zeit trifft man in Aegypten aber eine ganz verschiedene Technik. Die Umrisse der Zeichnung und die innere Gliederung wurde

1) Der bei dieser Gelegenheit gegebene Abriss hat nur den Zweck einer kurzen Uebersicht der Geschichte und soll zugleich kurz einige neue oder noch wenig bekannte Thatsachen entwickeln. Eine eingehende Behandlung wird der Gegenstand später in einer ausführlichen Arbeit über Glas und Email im Alterthum erfahren. Es ist daher bei dieser Gelegenheit auf eine nähere Aufzählung der Stücke und Literaturangabe (mit Ausnahme weniger Fälle) verzichtet worden.

auf der Goldunterlage der Pectorale, Armbänder etc. durch aufgelöthete Goldblechstreifen hergestellt. In diese Zellen wurden dann farbige zugeschnittene Steine oder Glasplättchen eingelegt, die eine vielfarbig colorirte Zeichnung darstellten, die Anfänge der sog. Verroterie cloisonnée, welche später zu Zeiten der grossen Völkerwanderung eine ausserordentliche Rolle spielte. Die hervorragendsten Stücke dieser Art sind ein Pectorale, goldene Armbänder mit Löwen, Schakal, stylisirten Pflanzen aus dem Grabe des Chamus, Sohn Ramses II. (14. Jahrb. v. Chr.), verschiedene andere Pectorale, Sperber etc. im Louvre. Aehnliche finden sich auch in den anderen ägyptischen Museen, so zu Berlin etc. Bei den Artikeln aus Bronze sind die Gruben für die Einlagen vertieft (wie beim Email champlevé) und sind die Steine und Glaspasten eingekittet, so 2 Pectorale im Berliner Museum, zahlreiche Uräusschlangen, Osiris-Statuetten, wo die Krone und die Geissel oft farbig ausgelegt sind. In diesen Zellen befinden sich farbige Steine (lapis lazuli, Feldspath, Carneol oder Jaspis) oder farbige opake Glastäfelchen, denen man natürlich möglichst einfache Formen gab, so dass bei starken Biegungen der Contouren die Füllung aus mehreren einzelnen an einandergefugten Plättchen besteht, wie ich dies sehr deutlich bei den erwähnten goldenen Armreifen im Louvre beobachtet habe. Die Natur der Einlagen konnte ich bei den Pariser Kleinodien aber nicht näher studiren, (da bei meinem Besuch im Sommer 1883 sämmtliche Custoden der Aegyptischen Abtheilung verreist waren). Die blauen sind unbedingt lapis lazuli, bei den rothen handelt es sich um Stein oder Blutglas. Hingegen habe ich von einem Pectorale des Berliner Museums und aus dem Armbande von Meroë von minimalen Splittern Dünnschliffe gemacht, wobei sich die rothe Einlage als Blutglas erwies. Blutglas als Einlage findet sich sehr häufig, so im Berliner Museum Bronzethürbeschlage mit Einlagen von Blutglas und Resten von eingeschmolzenem weissen Email aus der Zeit der Amasis (6. Jahrh. v. Chr.) Die interessantesten Stücke enthält der Schmuck aus der Pyramide von Meroë in Nubien (Museen von Berlin und München) über dessen Technik viel gestritten worden ist. Bei genauester Untersuchung[1]) fand ich mit definitiver Sicherheit, dass die rothen Blutglastäfelchen kalt eingekittet sind, indem man die Fugen und die Kittmasse bei geringer Vergrösserung deutlich erkennen kann. Das grüne und blaue Glas, ein recht schlechtes Email, ist eingeschmolzen, mithin ein echtes Email, sie füllen dieselben vollständig ohne Kittfuge aus und zeigen die concave Oberfläche des nicht abgeschliffenen Emails, wie dies auch schon früher beobachtet und hervorgehoben ist. Ueber das Alter dieses Schmucks sind die Ansichten noch getheilt, sie werden ihrer Technik nach immer vorrömisch sein. So finden wir also in Aegypten blaues Email wohl schon in der Mitte des 2. Jahrtausend v. Chr. grünes und weisses auch schon früh, nur das schwer zu behandelnde Roth verstand man noch nicht einzuschmelzen.

In ganz anderer Form tritt das Email am Kaukasus in dem grossen Gräberfelde zu Koban[2]) auf. Die merkwürdigen Gürtelhaken, welche der ersten Hälfte des Jahrtausends v. Chr. angehören, sind mit vertieften Ornamenten geziert, mit phantastischen Thierfiguren oder geometrischen Zeichnungen Spiralen, Mäandern. In

1) Correspondenzblatt der Deutschen Anthropologischen Gesellschaft 1884. p. 102.

2) Virchow. Das Gräberfeld von Koban. Berlin 1883, p. 66—69, 143—44.

äusserst wenig Exemplaren haben sich noch Reste farbigen Emails gefunden. Bei Virchow enthielt nur 1 Gürtelhaken (Tfl. X, Fig. 1) in den Thierkörpern und Rautenfeldern noch deutliche Spuren einer glasigen Masse, im Wiener Ethnographischen Museum fand ich nur an einem Gürtelhaken in den mäanderartigen Furchen äusserst spärliche Reste rothen Emails. In mehreren andern, sowie den übrigen bei Virchow beschriebenen Haken fanden sich nur Reste einer krümlichen ganz verwitterten Masse, die mit Sicherheit auf einstige Emailausfüllung hinwiesen. Aus einem winzigen Splitterchen des Wiener rothen Email wurde ein Dünnschliff hergestellt und es erwies sich dies als „Ziegelglas".[1])

Es giebt im Alterthum 2 wesentlich verschiedene Formen des opaken rothen Glases, die man mit einiger Uebung schon beim Anblick erkennt, die aber unfehlbar durch das Mikroskop unterschieden werden können. Ist das zur Disposition stehende Splitterchen zu klein, um einen Schliff machen zu können, was noch bei sehr kleinen Stückchen angeht und vorzuziehen ist, so genügt schon ein dem blossen Auge kaum oder nicht mehr sichtbares Stäubchen um den Charakter des Glases zu erkennen. Blut-Email oder Blutglas zeigt in farblosem Grunde dendritenartige Krystallisationen von Kupferoxydul, und darf man nur dieses Glas mit dem Haematinum des Plinius identificiren, wie es zahlreiche Scherben solcher blutrothen Gefässe in allen grösseren Museen und in meiner eigenen Sammlung beweisen. In neuerer Zeit ist die Fabrikation des Blutglases durch Pettenkofer wieder entdeckt worden, scheint aber schon vorher der Vatikanischen Mosaikfabrik nicht unbekannt gewesen zu sein, wie einige im Berliner Gewerbemuseum befindlichen, aus Blutglas gefertigten Dosen andeuten. Wesentlich verschiedenist das andere Glas, welches ich a. a. O. als „lackrothes Glas" bezeichnet hatte, das ich aber jetzt vorziehe „ziegelrothes Email", „Ziegel-Email" oder einfach „Ziegelglas" zu nennen, weil es sich in der mehr bräunlichen Nüance seines Roth der Farbe mehr oder weniger guter rother Ziegel nähert. Im Alterthum hatte man ein sehr schönes Roth, während alle modernen Fabrikate, besonders das zum Emailliren bestimmte ein viel trüberes Braunroth aufweisen. Das Ziegelglas zeigt in sehr dünnem Schliff auf bläulichem transparentem Grunde äusserst feine absolut opake Körnchen, die bei auffallendem Lichte metallisch roth glänzen. In den alten Gläsern und Emaillen erkennt man darunter nur mit der allerstärksten Vergrösserung kleine regelmässige Dreiecke, ebenso bei den besseren neueren, während die schmutzigeren, mehr bräunlichen Schmelzversuche diese Dreiecke grösser und deutlicher zeigen und so in Uebergängen allmählich zum Aventuringlas führen, welches mit grösseren drei oder sechsseitigen Kupfertäfelchen durchsetzt ist. Das Ziegelglas enthält demnach metallische, äusserst feine Kupferkörnchen, vertheilt in einer durch Kupferoxyd blau gefärbten Grundmasse. Man darf es nicht mit dem Hämatinum des Plinius verwechseln, zumal Gefässe aus reinem Ziegelglase sehr selten sind und wohl auch ziemlich spät auftreten.

Die kleinen Schliffe des Wiener Email erweisen sich, wie erwähnt, als Ziegelglas, äusserst feine opake Körnung auf bläulichem Grunde, ein Resultat, zu dem Virchow bei der Untersuchung von Splittern ebenfalls kam. (A. a. O. p. 68.) Hin-

1) Cf. Correspondenzblatt der Deutschen Anthropologischen Gesellschaft 1884 p. 179—183. XV. Versammlung der Deutschen Anthropologischen Gesellschaft zu Breslau.

gegen fand er als Füllung der Thierkörper noch ein grünlich-blaues Glas. Es wäre also mehrfarbiges Email hier immer möglich. Es hat das auch nichts auffallendes, da gerade bläuliches Email am leichtesten herzustellen geht und auch in Aegypten zeitlich weit zurückreicht, während man rothes Email erst sehr spät einschmelzen lernte.

Aus Griechenland kennt man wenig Email in älterer Zeit. Blaue Einlagen finden sich allerdings schon im Pallaste zu Tiryns. Doch tritt auf Schmucksachen Email nur selten und in bescheidener Weise auf. Das Email aber als barbarisch und dem feinen Geschmack der Griechen nicht zusagend zu bezeichnen, dürfte wohl eine falsche Ansicht sein, die noch mit der früheren Farblosigkeit des modernen Geschmackes zusammenhängt. Die Objecte der Kleinkunst, wenn sie nicht sehr kostbar waren, sind eben in Griechenland noch zu wenig beachtet. Auf den reizenden Goldschmucksachen tritt Email manchmal als Füllung einzelner durch Filigrandrath gebildeten Zellen auf, so z. B. im Berliner Antiquarium No. 3561 eine aus Gold-Medaillons gebildete Kette mit dunkel- und graublauem Email in Filigranzellen. Häufig sind die Funde in Südrussland, von wo man ja am meisten solche Prachtstücke griechischer Technik besitzt, auch auf Etruskischen Schmucksachen. Ausserdem finden sich blaue Tropfen in den Blüthenkelchen goldener Kränze (Münchener Antiquarium). Das Filigranemail hat im Alterthum gerade keine grosse Rolle gespielt. Es tritt erst wieder auf besonders schön in den silbernen siebenbürgischen Filigrangürteln des 16. Jahrhunderts n. Chr., wie sie deren das Nationalmuseum zu Budapest in prächtiger Auswahl besitzt und in neuerer Zeit in Japan auf Bronze.

Eine sehr grosse Rolle spielt eine eigene Art von Email bei den gallischen und auch anderen barbarischen Völkern während der sogenannten La Tène-Periode in den letzten vier Jahrhunderten v. Chr.

Bei den Galliern war die Edelkoralle sehr beliebt, auch noch zu Plinius Zeit. Sie findet sich auf Fibeln, Nadeln etc. schon am Ende der Hallstädter Periode, dem 5. Jahrhundert v. Chr. in süddeutschen Grabhügeln, geradezu massenhaft tritt sie aber bald darauf, in der frühen La Tène-Zeit im 4. Jahrhundert, aber auch noch später auf, als Einsatz in Fibeln, Gürtelhaken, Halsringen, Schwertscheiden, Helmen etc. etc., von Frankreich bis nach Ungarn, ja vereinzelt noch bis nach Norddeutschland (Fibeln mit Edelkorallen - Garnitur aus der Altmark im Berliner Museum für Völkerkunde). Oft ist die Koralle noch sehr gut erhalten mit wenig veränderter rother Farbe, vielfach ist sie aber stark verwittert und sieht wie eine weisse kreidige Masse aus, in der ich bei schwacher Vergrösserung aber doch noch oft Korallenstruktur erkennen konnte, so dass wahrscheinlich alle weissen Einlagen in Vogelkopffibeln und anderen Geräthen der Früh-La Tène-Zeit Koralle sind, falls nicht das hievon deutlich zu unterscheidende Blutglas. Bei einem Halsringe aus einem Grabe bei Saalfeld im Meininger Museum[1]) ist diese Einlage fälschlich als Biberzahn beschrieben, einen Irrthum, den Lindenschmit a. a. O. wiederholt hat. Die mikroskopische Betrachtung zeigte unfehlbar, dass es Edelkoralle ist.

Diese Koralle wurde nun im Blutglas imitirt, und so trifft man häufig auf Fibeln oder Halsringen Scheiben von Blutemail, die zuerst fertig geschliffen und

1) Lindenschmit: Alterthümer der heidnischen Vorzeit. Band IV Tafel 3 Fig. 1.

dann mittelst Nieten befestigt waren, während kleinere Knöpfchen sich einschmelzen liessen, jene also den émaux d'applique vergleichbar. Ausserdem findet man aber in den der Früh-La Tène-Periode eigenthümlichen schönen Arabesken der Fibeln und Ringe manchmal Emailspuren, welche es wahrscheinlich machen, dass diese Furchen meist mit Schmelz ausgefüllt gewesen sind.

Die Verwendung des Emails, in allen diesen Fällen ausschliesslich Blutglas, ist eine ganz eigenartige. Es dient zur Ausfüllung schmaler linearer Zeichnungen und lässt deren Form in leuchtendem Roth dem Goldgelb des Grundes gegenüber hervortreten, man kann dieses Email daher „Furchenschmelz" nennen. Diese Rolle hat es auch weiter im Verlaufe der La Tène-Periode gespielt, man findet häufig Systeme von parallelen oder gekreuzten feinen Furchen mit Resten von Email, so dass man auf allen solchen Nadeln, Knöpfen etc. mit diesen Furchen berechtigt ist, nach Email zu suchen. Vielfach finden sich Kreuze mit gleich langen, etwas breiteren Armen, oder eine Art Maltheserkreuze aus vier mit der Spitze einander zugewandten Dreiecken und rothem Mittelpunkt bestehend.[1]) Dann aber gelangte man dazu, auch etwas grössere Flächen mit Blutemail zu überziehen, was bei diesem Stoff seine besonderen Schwierigkeiten hat. So finden sich auf den prachtvollen Ketten und Kettenhaken Ungarns zur La Tène-Zeit (im National-Museum zu Budapest, Museum zu Klausenburg) grössere Flächen, die einst mit Blutemail erfüllt waren, wovon jetzt nur winzige Reste noch vorhanden. Eiserne Schildnägel der Station La Tène selbst, und einer auf dem kleinen Gleichberge bei Römhild waren ganz mit einer dünnen Schicht von Blutemail überzogen, eine technisch sehr hochstehende Leistung. Am merkwürdigsten sind aber in dieser Beziehung Schmuckringe und Schmuckplatten in England[2]) die einzige Klassse von Emaillen, die ich noch nicht persönlich zu untersuchen im Stande war und von denen es mir auch noch nicht gelang, kleine Pröbchen für das Mikroskop zu erhalten. Dieselben nehmen eine ganz eigene Stellung ein und enthalten vielleicht mehr Farben. Doch ist die Beschreibung derselben zu unzuverlässig. Bei allen diesen Objecten hat das Email aber denselben Zweck, es wirkt im Verein mit der Umgebung, also meist mit der contrastirenden Bronze, der rothe Schildnagel sticht gegen den Schild ab, es spielt keine selbstständige Rolle.

Alle diese emaillirten Objecte sind als einheimische Producte aufzufassen, sie stehen mit den Producten der Italischen Industrie der letzten 4 Jahrhunderte v. Chr. in keiner Beziehung und wenn auch diese ganze Industrie und der Kunststyl der La Tène-Zeit aus unbekannten Regionen des Ostens, wohl am Ende des 5. Jahrhunderts v. Chr. importirt oder eingewandert ist muss die Fabrikation sich doch bald an Ort und Stelle etablirt haben. Zur Gewissheit wird diese Annahme erhoben durch die Entdeckungen im Gallischen Pompeji, dem bedeutenden Mess- und Handelsplatze Bibracte,[3])

---

1) Cf. Verhandlung des Anthropologischen Congresses zu Stettin 1886, „Correspondenzblatt der Deutschen anthropologischen Gesellschaft" 1886 p. 130 ff., wo ich die emaillirten Fibeln von Borgfeld und den Halsring von Zampelhagen im Stettiner Museum besprochen habe.

2) Abgebildet in Horae Ferales. Tfl. XIX. XX.

3) Bulliot: l'Art de l'Emaillerie chez les Eduens.

wo man das Atelier eines Emailleurs fand und aus den halbfertigen Stücken sowie den Abfällen die Verarbeitungsweise des Gallischen Emails, welche von der späteren Römischen Methode völlig verschieden ist, studiren konnte. Eine weitverbreitete Emailtechnik bei den Barbaren, besonders bei den Gallischen Stämmen in den letzten vier Jahrhunderten v. Chr. ist also als erwiesen zu betrachten, kommt uns auch nicht mehr so befremdlich vor, seit wir uns der Ueberzeugung nicht mehr ververschliessen können, dass die Barbaren in der Bearbeitung der Metalle weit höher standen, als man lange auf einer Seite zugeben wollte. Ja man wird auch das Eindringen der Emailtechnik selbst bis nach Norddeutschland annehmen müssen, wie es die lokalen Fibel-Typen daselbst zeigen.

Zur Römischen Kaiserzeit tritt nun eine ganz neue Methode und ein neuer Styl des Emails auf.

In seiner vollen Entwickelung beruht er darauf, dass die ganze Fläche eines Metallgefässes oder eines Schmuckgeräthes mit einer vielfarbigen Emailschicht, wie mit einer farbigen Zeichnung überdeckt wird, man kann dies also „Flächenschmelz, Flächenemail" nennen. Die sichtbaren Bronzetheile dienen mehr dazu, die Fläche einzurahmen und die einzelnen Farben gegen einander abzugrenzen, damit sie scharf gegen einander stehen und nicht verlaufen, das Metall spielt also nur die Rolle von Contouren, ist weniger ein integrirender Theil der Fläche. Diesen Zweck erreichte man auf zweierlei Weise. Entweder wurde die Zeichnung schon im Gusse vorgearbeitet und dann mit dem Stichel und Punze weiter ausgeführt und vollendet, so dass die Unterlage eine Reihe von vertieften Gruben zeigte, welche durch die stehen gebliebenen schmalen Metallstege getrennt waren (Email champlevé, Grubenschmelz), oder auf die Unterlage wurden schmale Metallstreifen aufgelöthet, um die Contouren und Gliederungen der Zeichnung zu bilden (Email cloisonné, Zellenschmelz), wie wir es schon bei den alten ägyptischen Kleinodien fanden, wo die Zellen anfangs mit farbigen Steinchen ausgefüllt waren. In die so hergestellten Abtheilungen wurde das feucht angeriebene Glaspulver eingetragen und eingeschmolzen, eine Operation, die mehrmals wiederholt wurde, bis schliesslich Abschleifen und Poliren das ganze Stück vollendete. Beide Methoden bedingen einen ganz verschiedenen Styl (man könnte sie fast wie Kupferstich und Holzschnitt unterscheiden). Während das cloisonné eine bei weitem grössere Freiheit der Linienführung gewährt, auch naturalistische und Darstellungen von lebenden Wesen begünstigt — wie dies in reichstem Masse in dem chinesisch-japanischen Email zu Tage tritt, verlangt das Champlevé eine strengere regelmässigere Zeichnung. Da das Email der Kaiserzeit ausschliesslich Champlevé ist, treffen wir hier beinahe nur geometrische Zeichnungen aus geraden oder Kreislinien zusammengesetzt, oder einfache Ranken mit stylisirten Blättern und Spiralen. Aeusserst selten sind Darstellungen von Thieren, wie Hasen, Vögeln (einige Stücke im Nationalmuseum zu Budapest), eine Darstellung, die eben für diesen Styl weniger passt. Diese Emails zeigen nun eine reiche Farbenscala, roth, welches bei den Flächenemails immer Ziegelglas ist, opakes Orange — eine ganz neue Farbe, die ich vor der Kaiserzeit noch nie getroffen habe, während Ziegelglas ja allerdings in ein Paar ganz vereinzelten Fällen auftritt, grün, hellblau, dunkelblau, gelb, braun in's Violette ziehend. Man trifft das Email auf einer nicht unbeträchtlichen Anzahl von Bronzegefässen, deren bekanntestes die im Pyrmonter Quell gefundene Schöpfkelle ist,[1]) besonders aber auf Schmuckgeräthen, Fibeln, Scheiben, Knöpfen, Platten etc., welche zum bei Weitem grössten Theile innerhalb der Grenzen des Römischen Reiches gefunden sind, nur in geringer Zahl ausserhalb.

Diese Objecte sind ihrem Vorkommen, ihrem Styl und ihrer Form nach Römisch. Man hat sie alle vielfach für Celtisch ansehen wollen. Davon kann gar keine Rede sein, denn es tritt gerade eine ganz neue Technik der früheren barbarischen gegenüber. Viel Staub hat eine Stelle des Sophisten Philostratus aufgewirbelt, der um 200 n. Chr. lebte, und welcher ein Gemälde schilderte, die Eberjagd:[2]) er beschreibt, 4 Reiter nach Gestalt und Tracht, sowie ihre Pferde, einen Schimmel, Lichtbraunen, Rappen und Fuchs und setzt zu: „Sie haben silberne Zäume, Brandzeichen und goldene Schmuckplatten. Diese Farben sollen die Barbaren an dem Weltmeer dem glühenden Erze einschmelzen, worauf sie erstarren, wie Stein werden und das Gemalte erhalten." Die Franzosen wollten aus dieser Stelle die Berechtigung ableiten, alle Emaillen für Celtisch zu erklären, es dürften die Gallier des 3. Jahrhunderts n. Chr. aber doch wohl nicht mehr als Barbaren bezeichnet worden sein; auch könnte es Philostratus kaum unbekannt gewesen sein, dass ähnliche Objecte wie in Gallien auch zum Mindesten bis nach Osteuropa (Pannonien) hinein innerhalb der Grenzen des Römischen Reiches zu seiner Zeit vorkamen. Die Stelle ist, sowie sie lautet, entschieden unrichtig oder verstümmelt. Entweder hat Philostratus eine Reminiscenz davon gehabt, dass die Barbaren in Gallien vor der Römischen Kaiserzeit wirklich es verstanden, Email auf Erz einzuschmelzen oder er kann nur die Barbaren in Britannien gemeint haben, denn diese Völker sind im Ganzen überhaupt nicht ordentlich romanisirt gewesen, im Norden garnicht unterworfen worden. Die wunderbaren Emails, die Franks und besonders Anderson[3]) abbilden, haben einen vollständig barbarischen durchaus von allem Römischen abweichenden Styl, können aber, da sie eine reichere Farbenscala zeigen, als die französischen, ganz wohl in die Kaiserzeit hineinreichen, so dass hier immerhin noch alte nationale Kunst, vielleicht durch römischen Einfluss etwas bereichert, möglicherweise bis in die Zeit des Philostratos fortblühte, wie z. B. die Befestigung einer wohl von den Römern erstandenen Schachbrett-Millefiorischeibe in einem entschieden nationalen Armband (Anderson p. 41 Fig. 115) zu beweisen scheint. Grade Pferdegebisse zeigen sich in England öfters emaillirt und es ist daher nicht auffallend, wenn Philostratus bei der Beschreibung des Pferdegeschirrs an das Barbarenemail denkt. Ich glaube aber nicht, dass auf dem Festlande innerhalb des Römischen Reiches Pferdegebisse mit Email gefunden sind. Also darf man aus den mysteriösen Worten nicht schliessen, dass alles Email barbarisch gewesen sei: er hat wahrscheinlich des Britannischen Emails, besonders des zum Pferdeschmucke bestimmten gedacht, dies aber nicht in Gegensatz zu denen des Continents gestellt, die ihm ja unbedingt bekannt sein mussten.

Aber auch die Bezeichnung gallo-romains, welche die Franzosen den Emaillen geben, ist nicht zutreffend, denn es finden sich ganz dieselben Objecte, Gefässe, Fibeln etc. identisch in Frankreich, am Rhein bis nach Ungarn hinein, auch in Eng-

1) Lindenschmit: „Die Alterthümer unser heidnischen Vorzeit". Bd. III, Heft 12, Tafel 8.

2) Citirt nach Lindenschmit A. h. V. Bd. III, Beilage zu Heft I p. 30.

3) Anderson: Scotland in Pagan Times p. 121 ff.

land (im Gegensatze zu dem ganz verschiedenen barbarischen), ebenso sind sie immerhin in Italien vertreten im Vaticanischen Museum und im Kircherianum, auch zu Este ist eine Emailfibel gefunden.

In den Provinzen kann man ganz gut verschiedene Typen von Geräthen unterscheiden, solche, welche aus Umbildung der älteren einheimischen Typen entstanden sind und sich in den einzelnen Provinzen lokal unterscheiden und solche, welche sich nicht an jene Typen anschliessen, ja sogar in Gegensatz treten und eine allgemeinere Verbreitung zeigen. Ersteres sind die Formen der Römischen Provinzialcultur, die types galloromains in Gallien, welche beispielsweise in Gallien und in Pannonien schon recht verschieden sind. Letztere muss man als Römisch ohne Einschränkung bezeichnen, wobei aber durchaus nicht gemeint ist, dass sie aus Italien stammen, denn Italien stand in den späteren Jahrhunderten nicht mehr an der Spitze der Industrie. Der Osten wird immer die alte Führerschaft behalten haben, so dass der eigentliche Ausgangspunkt der neuen Emailtechnik wohl noch unklar bleibt, aber jedenfalls im Osten des Mittelmeeres liegt. Eine weit verbreitete Klasse von Objecten hat daher einen einheitlichen Charakter, den man mit Römisch bezeichnen kann. Dass aber die neue Technik auch grade bei den Provinzialen gepflegt wurde, bei denen früher schon eine andere Art der Emaillirkunst blühte, ist weiter nicht wunderbar und so konnten besonders in Gallien einige Lokalformen entstehen, die man anderweitig noch nicht gefunden hat, die Hauptmasse trägt aber einen allgemeineren als provinziellen Charakter.

Der oben ausgeführte stylistische Gegensatz der Römischen und Gallischen Emails als Flächenschmelz und Furchenschmelz trifft aber nur die Endglieder der Formenreihe und zeigt die extremsten Unterschiede. Wie das Blutemail manchmal grössere Flächen einnimmt, allerdings ohne den Charakter einer unselbstständigen einfarbigen Decoration zu verlieren, so tritt das Römische Email auch öfters in bescheidenere Grenzen zurück: es bedeckt nur kleinere Stücke der Oberfläche, vielfach einfarbig roth, tritt als kleiner Knopf in die Mitte einer Fibel auf, kurz es lässt der Bronzefarbe oft auch noch ein Stück decorativer Wirkung. Bei einem reizenden delphinähnlichen Fische des Pester Museums sind die Schuppen und Flossen mit schmaler blauer Ausfüllung geziert, so dass dieser Unterschied allein noch kein entscheidendes Kriterium bildet.

Es giebt aber noch eine ganz eigenthümliche Klasse Römischer Objecte, die bisher wohl nicht genügend gewürdigt und erkannt zu sein scheint, welche den vollständigen Charakter des Furchenschmelzes hat und eine höchst merkwürdige Uebergangsgattung bildet.

Es ist dies eine bestimmte Klasse von Fibeln, überwiegend Bügelfibeln in einigen Modificationen, deren Typus und Decoration die bei Cohausen,[1]) Römischer Schmelzschmuck Tafel I Fig. 6 abgebildete Fibel repräsentirt, selten Scheibenfibeln, daneben einige prachtvolle Dolche mit eisernen Scheiden. Auf allen diesen Stücken tritt das Email nur als Auffüllung schmalerer Zeichnungen auf, welche die Fläche nur verzieren, nicht bedecken. Die Kreuzfurche „X", welche auf den Gürtelhaken der La Tène-Periode eine so grosse Rolle spielt, tritt hier in ganzen Reihen auf,

1) Annalen des Nassauischen Alterthumsvereins. Wiesbaden. Band XII.

daneben eine Modification derselben, indem die vier Arme in gelappte Blättchen auslaufen; ausserdem finden sich gewellte Ranken mit kleinen Blättchen, die 4 im Kreuz mit den Spitzen einander gegenüber gestellten Dreiecke und verwandte Muster. Als Füllung findet man in diesen Furchen rothes und ein blaues oder blaugrünes Email. In allen Fällen, wo ich im Stande war, ein Stäubchen des rothen Emails mikroskopisch zu untersuchen, wie bei der oben erwähnten Fibel aus dem Wiesbadener Museum, den Dolchen und einigen anderen Stücken, erwies es sich als Blutemail. Die Farbenscala dieser Stücke ist also reicher als die der vorrömischen. Dazu tritt noch das schwarze Niello, kein Email, sondern ein Schwefelmetall, welches aber gerade für diesen Styl, die Verzierung von Furchen und kleinen Gruben besonders geeignet ist, so dass es mehrfach mit Blutemail ganz coordinirt auftritt, eine Mischung, die bei der früher charakterisirten Hauptclasse des Römischen Emails nie vorkommt (schon aus technischen Gründen, die bei anderer Gelegenheit auseinandergesetzt werden sollen). Niello konnte ich übrigens schon bis in die La Tène-Zeit zurückverfolgen.

Dazu tritt als fernere Decoration noch Tauschirung auf jenen Dolchen, die entschieden zu den reizendsten Produkten polychromer antiker Metalltechnik gehören. Der besterhaltene dieser Dolche befindet sich im Germanischen Museum zu Nürnberg von Rösenbeck in Westfalen, ein zweiter im Paulus-Museum zu Worms, bei Mainz gefunden. Diese Eisenscheiden sind in äusserst reicher und geschmackvoller Weise durch Blutemail und eingelegte Bronze verziert. Die Bronzefäden umsäumen und gliedern die einzelnen Felder, treten aber in Rosetten und Fiedern alternirend mit Blutemail auf. Letzteres füllt einzelne kleinere Zeichnungen, tritt aber besonders friesartig in den Umfassungen der einzelnen Felder auf als lange Streifen fiederartiger Blättchen oder als Reihen von Kreuzfurchen, die kleineren als einfache Kreuze, die grösseren wieder mit den gelappten Blättchen an den Enden der Arme.

Endlich füllt Blutemail die kleinen Knöpfchen an der Scheide und am Dolchgriff.

Diese Dolche wie die Fibeln sind entschieden Römische und gehen auch eine Zeitlang mit den anderen Stücken zeitlich parallel, da andere Fibeln von ähnlichem Typus die Decoration im Flächenemailstyl mit in dem üblichen Römischen Materiale zeigen, sie nehmen aber eine eigene noch nicht recht aufgeklärte Stellung ein. Auffallend ist es, dass überall, wo sich die dem gallischen Style eigenen Kreuzfurchen finden, ein Ornament, das hier allerdings massenhafter in Reihen auftritt und theilweise etwas modificirt, sich, so oft eine Untersuchung möglich war, Blut-Email zeigte.

Es hängt die Erklärung dieser merkwürdigen Uebergangsklasse noch von der Beschaffung eines umfangreicheren Materials ab, das bisher zum Theil wohl übersehen ist.

Wenn wir jetzt zu dem Römischen Flächenschmelz zurückkehren, so treffen wir gerade bei der Decoration der kleinen Objecte neue Proceduren, welche dieselben, abgesehen von den Werken der Goldschmiedekunst, zu den zierlichsten Gegenständen der antiken Bijouterie stempeln. Das Bestreben ging dahin, die Masse der trennenden Metallstege möglichst zu vermindern, so dass gerade der Farbenreichthum des Glases in grösster Mannigfaltigkeit und Zierlichkeit zu Tage trat. Diese verschiedenen Arten des Römischen Schmelzschmuckes sowie die Methode der Herstellung sind sehr gründlich und genau in der schon citirten Abhandlung von Cohausen: „Römischer Schmelzschmuck" behandelt, so dass die betreffenden Fragen der Hauptsache nach gelöst sind, wenn auch immer noch einiges Dunkle in der Technik der Römer geblieben ist. Obige Arbeit hat daher eine fundamentale Bedeutung für die Geschichte des Emails.

Man findet nämlich auch einzelne Farben nebeneinander, ohne trennende Metallstege, in regelmässiger Mosaik, oder einen runden Fleck auf andersfarbigem Grunde. In beiden Fällen muss man, wie Cohausen auseinandergesetzt hat, die runden Scheibchen oder Platten der Mosaik vorher geformt haben und jene in das noch nicht eingeschmolzene Emailpulver des Grundes eingesetzt, diese über einem eben solchen Grundemail mosaikartig aneinandergelegt haben, wobei natürlich die Hauptbedingung war, dass das Grundemail leichter schmolz als die Ein- oder Auflagen.

Die schönsten Erfolge wurden aber auf diesem Wege bei dem Millefiori-Email erzielt, indem man zu jenen mosaikartig zusammenzulegenden Plattchen Millefioriplättchen nahm, diese neben einander in den pulverförmigen eingetragenen Grund legte und dann einschmolz, wobei die Plättchen selbst von der Hitze nicht mehr verändert wurden. Die Scheibe von Oberhof gehört zu diesen Perlen römischen Schmelzschmuckes, von denen die Abbildungen der Cohausenschen Abhandlung und Lindenschmit's Alterthümer der heidnischen Vorzeit Bd. III. Heft VIII. Tafel 3 ein genügendes Bild gewähren.

Ueber die Millefiorifabrikation ist bereits in einer früheren Sitzung dieses Jahres gesprochen worden.[1]) Ihr Wesen besteht, um es kurz zu wiederholen darin, dass man Glasstäbe von beliebigem Querschnitte an einander legt, zusammenschmilzt, auf einem bestimmten kleineren Querschnitt auszieht und in dünne Platten zertheilt. Diese stimmen dann in der Grösse überein und zeigen alle dasselbe farbige Muster, wobei sich eine ausserordentliche Mannigfaltigkeit erzielen lässt. Bei den emaillirten Objecten kehrt meist nur eine geringere Zahl von Mustern wieder. Am häufigsten viereckige schachbrettartig zusammengesetzte Stäbe, mehrfarbig, am häufigsten zweifarbig und dann blau und weiss oder roth und weiss, ausserdem sternförmige Figuren, fiederartige Bildungen blau in weiss, hin und wieder auch weisse Voluten in blauem Felde. Diese Täfelchen sind dann wieder so an einander gesetzt, dass sie ganze Streifen in einem wiederholten Muster bilden, oder dass zwei Muster mit einander abwechseln, so dass sie manchmal die ganze Fläche wieder im wahren Sinne des Wortes schachbrettartig bedecken. Ueberwiegend werden diese Millefioriplättchen kreisförmig geordnet, so dass sie Ringe oder ganze Kreise bei Scheibenfibeln, Zierscheiben oder Knöpfen bedecken, doch kommen auch gradlinige Anordnungen vor.

Es handelt sich nun darum, die Zeit und die Herkunft dieses Millefiori-Emails zu bestimmen.

Die Zeit der Oberhöfer Scheibe lässt sich ziemlich genau an das Ende des 2. oder Anfang des 3. Jahrhunderts n. Chr. setzen, da an der Stelle des Gräberfelds wo sie sich vorfand, einfache Armbrustfibeln mit umgeschlagenen Fuss vorkommen, die sich immer mit Münzen, welche ungefähr bis 180 n. Chr. reichen, zusammen finden. Ausserdem treten Glasperlen, welche aus denselben Schachbrett-Mosaik-

1) Schriften der physikalisch-ökonomischen Gesellschaft XXVII/1886. Sitzungsbericht vom 7. Januar 1886 Tischler: „Ueber Aggry-Perlen".

plättchen zusammengesetzt sind, wie sie die Scheibe enthält, gerade in dieser Periode auf, während später die Perlen gewisse Modificationen erleiden, aber immerhin das Schachbrett beibehalten, welches hingegen in den so zahlreichen Perlen des 1. Jahrhunderts nicht auftritt, obwohl hier sonst Millefioriperlen allerdings von einen wesentlich verschiedenen, aber scharf gekenntzeichneten Charakter vorkommen.

Die Glasperlen[1]) lassen sich bei der jetzt doch schon auf einigermaassen sicherem Fundament ruhenden Gräberkunde Europa's zeitlich sehr gut ordnen. Für die Perlen des 1. Jahrtausends v. Chr. geben die Gräber Italiens u. Süddeutchlands wie Frankreich, für die Kaiserzeit Nord-Europa und ganz besonders Ostpreussen genügend sichere Anhaltspunkte. Während einige einfachen Perlen allerdings wenig lehren, auch zu den langlebigen Formen gerechnet werden können, sind andere wieder so charakteristisch und auf einen engeren Zeitraum beschränkt, dass man sie als Leitfunde betrachten kann, die an chronologischem Werthe den Münzen nicht viel nachstehen. Zudem finden wir diese zierlichen Schmuckstücke in einer ungemeinen Gleichmässigkeit von den Küsten des Atlantischen Oceans bis an den Kaukasus, bis nach Klein-Asien und Aegypten. Soweit man eine synchronistische Kette von Gräbern in diesem Gebiet herstellen kann, haben sich dieselben Formen auch überall als gleichaltrig erwiesen, was bei anderer Gelegenheit, bei einer Gesammtgeschichte der Glasperlen auseinandergesetzt werden soll. Wir finden nirgends eine Stütze für die Ansicht, dass etwa ein Perlenmuster, wenn es im Süden aus der Mode gekommen, weiter nach Norden zu den Barbaren exportirt wurde, so dass eine Perle aus der Hand des Fabrikanten bis zum Halse des Nordischen Mädchens einen sehr grossen Zeitraum gebraucht hätte. Die Perlen kamen sicherlich nur aus einigen grossen, noch nicht genügend bekannten Fabrikationscentren im Osten, so dass nicht etwa die Fabrikation selbst langsam nach dem Norden dringen konnte, von Zeit zu Zeit wechselte aber die Mode radical, man gab die Perlen den Todten ins Grab mit und verwahrte sie nicht als alten Familienschmuck. Dieser Wechsel vollzieht sich demnach annähernd gleichzeitig im Centrum und an der Peripherie, da der Fabrikant seine Producte doch auch vertreiben musste. Somit gewährt die Perle gerade für Geschichte des Glases in stofflicher und technischer Beziehung vorzügliche Anhaltspunkte, in weit höherem Maasse als das leichter zerstörte und nicht so weit verbreitete Glasgefäss. So oft es aber gelang, für dies letztere chronologische Anhaltspunkte zu gewinnen, deckten sie sich mit den auf anderem Wege gewonnenen.

Die schönsten aller Perlen sind aber die Millefiori-Perlen, d. h. nicht solche, bei denen nach Art der modernen venezianischen Perlen die Zeichnung nur der Oberfläche aufliegt, sondern welche aus einzelnen aneinandergelegten Millefioriplättchen zusammengeschmolzen sind, so dass die Zeichnung die Perle bis nach der Mitte durchdringt. Den Stil dieser in Ostpreussen äusserst häufigen Perlen können wir nun bis Aegypten verfolgen.

Zu Medinet el Fayum[2]) in der Necropole des alten Arsinoë sind in Mumiensärgen die zierlichsten Kunstwerke aus Glas entdeckt, welche das alte Aegypten ge-

1) cfr. Nachtrag p. 57.

2) Maspero, Guide du Visiteur au Musée de Boulaq 1885 p. 263 ff. Bei Perrot und Chipiez: Geschichte der Kunst im Alterthum. Deutsche Ausgabe Bd. I, p. 761 fig. 561 zureichende, fig. 562 unzureichende Abbildungen.

liefert hat, sowohl kleine Statuetten als auch Platten mit Darstellungen von Menschen- und Thierfiguren in Millefiori-Manier. Das Berliner Aegyptische Museum besitzt von hier u. a. 2 ganz besonders charakteristische Stücke, die ich näher zu betrachten Gelegenheit hatte. Das eine (No. 9048) stammt von einer kleinen Statuette en face, ähnlich den bei Perrot und Chipiez abgebildeten, es ist aber nur der Oberkörper ohne Kopf und Arm, der Unterkörper und Oberschenkel erhalten. Der untere Theil besteht aus Blutglas, den Obertheil nimmt die Darstellung eines Colliers ein. Dies ganze Collier ist ein Millifioristück aus einzelnen übereinanderliegenden Millefioristreifen zusammengesetzt, deren jeder wieder aus einer Reihe horizontal aneinanderliegender gleicher Millefiorstäbe besteht. Das Muster geht also durch die ganze Dicke dieses Stückes bis auf die Hinterseite gleichmässig durch, vorne aber sieht man eine Reihe farbiger, horizontaler Streifen je mit demselben Muster, welche sich periodisch wiederholen und welche die verschiedenen Schnüre des Colliers vorstellen sollen. Diese Muster sind theils Rosetten auf verschiedenfarbig blauem Grunde, weisse Lotusblumen auf blauem Grunde, und rothe in Voluten endende Wellenlinien (Ziegelglas) auf weissem Grunde, ein im Alterthum sehr verbreitetes unter dem Namen „laufender Hund“ bekanntes Ornament. Dies Ornament kommt nun aber sehr häufig auf Ostpreussischen Millefiori-Perlen vor, welche hier ins 2. Jahrhundert fallen und der Gedanke liegt so nahe, einen aus mehreren Schichten zusammengeschweissten Glasstreifen, wie den obigen, deren einer den laufenden Hund enthält um einen Dorn zu rollen und eine kuglige oder cylindrische Perle zu formen, dass man zwischen den betreffenden Perlen Ostpreussens und der Statuette von Arsinoë nicht gut einen zeitlichen Unterschied annehmen kann. Es könnte nun der oben eigentlich schon widerlegte Einwand gemacht werden, diese Millefioriartikel und die analogen Perlen seien schon früher, ja zur Ptolemäerzeit gefertigt aber nicht bis nach dem Norden exportirt. Nun finden sich aber in Aegypten — wie dies sämmtliche Sammlungen zeigen — auch die Perlen der Jahrhunderte vor der Kaiserzeit, besonders der La Tène-Periode, welche sich zum Theil mit der Ptolemaerzeit deckt, sei es als einheimische Fabrikate oder als Phönicische Importartikel, was fast wahrscheinlicher ist. Es wäre wunderbar, wenn man nur diese zu den prachtliebenden Barbaren des Nordens exportirt und die viel schöneren Millefiori zu Hause gelassen hätte, zumal doch Aegypten damals dem Welthandel so recht erschlossen war. Es lässt sich der Millefioristil also nicht mehr in die Ptolemäerzeit zurückführen (die leider von den Aegyptologen in den Museen bisher immer mit der folgenden als griechisch-römische Periode zusammengefasst wurde). Im 1. Jahrhundert n. Chr. muss er entstanden sein, da wir dann schon entsprechende Perlen haben, obige Figur wird aber noch jünger sein.

Zu demselben Resultat führt ein „Mystisches Auge (Uza)“ (No. 9474) im Berliner Museum mit Emaileinlagen. Darunter befinden sich 2 Millefioriplatten in Schachbrett-Mosaik, mit den Farben weiss, blau, gelb, orange. Orange (nicht mit gelb zu verwechseln) ist bisher vor der Kaiserzeit noch nicht nachgewiesen: solche Platten kommen, aber erst in den Perlen gegen Ende des 2. Jahrhunderts n. Chr. vor, wohin also dies Auge zu setzen wäre.

Wenn auch der laufende Hund ein viel älteres Ornament war, und besonders das Schachbrettmuster dem Stil der Gewebe entsprang und sich schon auf sehr alten Deckengemälden fand, so hatte man es doch eben nicht in Glas nachgebildet.

Wenn somit das Datum dieser ägyptischen Stücke durch die Nordischen Funde einigermaassen sicher gestellt wird, so werfen sie wieder ihr Licht nach Norden und speciell auf die Scheiben von Oberhof, daher musste dieser Punkt hier etwas eingehender behandelt werden.

Bei der ausserordentlich weiten und gleichförmigen Verbreitung der Glasperlen ist es schwer, ihre engere Heimath auszukunden; hier treffen wir aber Objecte von rein nationalem Charakter: sowohl die Statuetten (wie es die Abbildung bei Perrot u. Chipiez zeigt), als das Auge sind so specifisch ägyptisch, dass sie in keinem anderen Lande verwendet werden könnten. Auch die Darstellung der Lotusblumen, welche häufiger auf Millefioriplatten wiederkehren, sowie die ägyptische Tracht bei menschlichen Köpfen bestätigt dies, und man kann somit sicher annehmen, dass die Millefioritechnik in Aegypten geübt wurde und wohl auch entstanden ist — zu römischer Zeit. Wir wissen ja, dass die Alexandrinische Glaskunst zur Kaiser-Zeit in hoher Blüthe stand, aber Phönicien hatte seine alten Ruhm als Glasmacherland auch noch behalten, besonders die Sidonischen Künstler, und da ist es vortheilhaft sichere Beweise für die Fabrikation in Aegypten zu haben, was das andere Land allerdings nicht vollständig ausschliesst.

Wir sind also durch dies bisherige Ergebniss zu dem Resultat gelangt, dass die Millefiori und der Millefioristil aus Aegypten zur Kaiserzeit nach Europa gelangten. Diese Fähigkeiten den Etruskern beizulegen, ebenso wie die in Italien gefundenen Millefiorigefässe, geht nicht mehr an, letztere gehören in die Kaiserzeit und sind vielleicht auch nur aus Aegypten importirt, anfänglich gewiss. Wie man den aegyptischen Einfluss sich auf das uns zunächst beschäftigende Millefiori-Email vorstellen soll, ist aber doch nicht leicht aufzuklären. Die Objecte, Fibeln, Gefässe, wie sie sich im europäischen Römerreich finden, haben nicht das mindeste Aegyptische, sondern bewegen sich recht im europäischen Formenkreise. Also entweder ist die Fabrikation der Millefiori mit der Glasfabrikation überhaupt nach Europa, zunächst nach Italien gewandert, oder man müsste an einen Import von Millefioristäben denken, die dann von den Emailleuren weiter verarbeitet wurden. Was für den Bezug aus einer mehr einheitlichen, weiter zurückliegenden Quelle spricht, ist die grosse Gleichmässigkeit gerade der Millefiori-Emails, welche durchaus keine provinziellen Verschiedenheiten zeigen.

Die Quelle der römischen Emailtechnik überhaupt nach Aegypten zu verlegen, dazu liegt kein Grund vor. Doch ist der Osten für die Zeit der Diadochen, wo man die Vorbedingungen suchen müsste, und auch für die Kaiserzeit, noch viel zu wenig erforscht, und muss diese Frage vorläufig offen gelassen werden.

Wenn wir uns nun wieder nach dem Norden wenden, so finden wir zur Kaiserzeit auch ausserhalb des römischen Reiches eine Anzahl emaillirter Objecte, an Zahl allerdings bedeutend zurückstehend gegen die grosse Menge innerhalb des limes. Dieselben tragen mit Ausnahme einiger britanischen, die wohl noch in diese Periode hineinragen, einen rein römischen, ziemlich gleichmässigen Charakter bis in den äussersten Osten, wo einige etwas fremdartigere Formen auftreten.

In Ostpreussen sind mehr emaillirte Stücke gefunden, als auf einem anderen barbarischen Gebiete von dieser Grösse, was aber wohl nur der genaueren Durchforschung der Provinz zuzuschreiben ist.

Ausser obiger Scheibe von Oberhof sind zu erwähnen: Eine Scheibenfibel im Elbinger Museum vom Neustädter Felde bei Elbing, soweit erkennbar, ein sechsstrahliger blauer Stern, von rothen Feldern umgeben, eine u. a. in Ungarn, der Schweiz häufige Form; ferner Stücke eines Colliers oder kettenartigen Gürtels mit emaillirten Scheiben von Lapsau Kr. Königsberg (Museum der Alterthumsgesellschaft Prussia) augenscheinlich auch römische Arbeit; ein kleines Gürtelbesatzstück mit kegelförmigem Aufsatz und rothem Emailknöpfchen, von ebenfalls noch römischer Form von Greibau Kreis Fischhausen (Provinzial-Museum); ein dreieckiges durchbrochenes Anhängsel, das unten zwei kleine mit rothem Email erfüllte Scheibchen trägt, aus dem 1. Jahrhundert n. Chr. von Reussen Kr. Angerburg, eine nicht gerade römisch aussehende Form (Prussia); ein Fingerring mit rhombischen in vier mit rothem Email erfüllte Fächer getheiltem Schild bei Bartenstein Kr. Friedland (Provinzial-Museum); eine mit rothem Email erfüllte Fibel[1]) von Gruneiken Kr. Goldap (Provinzial-Museum) und eine sehr ähnliche von Sdorren Kr. Johannisburg (Prussia), welche in der Form an die Ungarischen bis nach Ostpreussen verbreiteten Cicadenfibeln erinnern, also eine lokale schon halbbarbarische Form. Ferner sind bei Gruneiken einige ziemlich rohe Anhängsel[2]) gefunden, die zwei halbmondförmige Furchen tragen, welche mit blauem und rothem Schmelz ausgefüllt sind (Provinzial-Museum), ferner ein ähnliches zu Muskau Kr. Wehlau (Prussia).

Letztere Stücke sehen wirklich wie ein barbarisches Fabrikat aus. Man müsste also annehmen, dass die Kunst der Emaillirung in ihren einfachsten Proceduren im Osten auch von Barbaren geübt wurde, zumal sich hier sicher in ursprünglicher Anlehnung an südlichere Vorbilder während der Kaiserzeit eine geschmackvolle Bearbeitung der Metalle entwickelt hat, und zumal in vorrömischer Zeit auch in Norddeutschland die Verarbeitung des Blutemails als bewiesen anzusehen ist. Das Material hätte man dann wohl aus den importirten Glasperlen gewonnen.

In den russischen Nachbarprovinzen findet sich auch eine Anzahl von Emailfibeln.[3]) Aus Livland von Langensee (Aspelin 1763) und von Ronneburg 4 Stück (ibid. 1776, 1778, 1782, 1785), alles Scheibenfibeln, die mit den rein römischen zwar noch verwandt sind, aber doch schon einige formelle Abweichungen zeigen. Ferner zu Birzé (Russisch-Littauen) eine ringförmige Fibel und eine Fibel aus zwei gekreuzten Vierecken bestehend, die in zwei Thierköpfe ausläuft (Aspelin 1885), eine echt römische Form und eine aus dem Gouvernement Warschau von Dworaki-Pikoty mit rohem grünen und blauen Email von absolut unrömischer Form (Aspelin 1884.)[4]) Zu den letzten drei im Museum der Akademie zu Krakau befindlichen Stücken tritt noch ein emaillirter Riemenbesatz von römischer Form. Also ein Theil dieser Stücke zeigt einen vom römischen abweichenden, die eine Fibel sogar völlig barbarischen Charakter. Weiter westlich scheinen sich, abgesehen von England, solche barbarische Nachahmungen des römischen Stils zur Kaiserzeit nicht vorzufinden.

Als Resultat dieser historischen Betrachtung wäre also anzusehen, dass in

1) Tischler: Ostpreussische Gräberfelder. Schriften der Physikalisch-ökonomischen Gesellschaft zu Königsberg XIX. (1878) Tfl. XI. (V.) Fig. 1.

2) Ibid. Fig. 2.

3) Aspelin: Antiquités du Nord Finno—Ougrien.

4) Auch abgebildet: Zbiór Wiadomosci do Antropologii Krajowéj VII. Tfl. VI. 1. 2.

Nordeuropa während der letzten vier Jahrhunderte v. Chr. eine weitverbreitete Emaillirtechnik auf Bronze und auch auf Eisen mit Blutglas bestand, die man in der am meisten charakteristischen Ausbildung als Furchenschmelz bezeichnen kann. Während der römischen Kaiserzeit kam im römischen Reiche aus noch nicht näher ermittelter Quelle ein stilistisch verschiedener Schmelz auf, im Allgemeinen Flächenschmelz, der mit ganz verschiedenem Material arbeitete, mit weit mehr Farben und mit Ziegelglas. Nur bei einer ganz beschränkten Klasse römischer Objecte tritt noch Furchenschmelz auf mit Blutglas, oft in Verbindung mit Niello, Tauschirung und blaugrünem Email. Die römischen emaillirten Objecte sind im Reiche in allen nördlichen Provinzen einander sehr ähnlich, nur einige locale Formen treten auf, hauptsächlich in Gallien.

Im zweiten Jahrhundert tritt das Millefiori-Email auf, beeinflusst durch ägyptische Technik und lassen sich bei diesen Gegenständen keine localen Unterschiede erkennen.

In den Barbarenländern Norddeutschland, Dänemark, findet sich eine Anzahl emaillirter Schmuckstücke, einige Gefässe von echt römischen Formen. Eine barbarische Emailtechnik scheint während der Kaiserzeit nur in Britannien fortzuleben und im fernen Osten, wo neben römischen Objecten einige Gegenstände von barbarischem oder umgewandelt römischem Typus auftreten.

Gegen Ende des 4. Jahrhunderts verschwindet die Emailtechnik im ganzen weströmischen Reiche und scheint hier im 5. als erloschen zu betrachten sein.

Denn es tritt nun eine neue Decorationsweise bei allen germanischen Völkern auf, sowohl bei denen, welche das Gebiet des früheren Römischen Reiches besetzen, als bei denen, welche ausserhalb bleiben. Die zahlreichen goldenen und silbernen Schmuckstücke und Beschläge von Waffen dieser so äusserst prachtliebenden Periode der grossen Völkerwanderung enthalten in aufgesetzten goldenen (oder silbernen Zellen) rothe zugeschliffene Täfelchen von Granat, seltener von anderen Farben (grün), wo es noch näher festzustellen wäre, ob man es mit Glas oder Edelstein zu thun hat. Diese an die Technik der Aegypter des thebanischen Reiches erinnernde Kunst, die „verrotterie cloisonnée", ist auch in Ostpreussen nachgewiesen in zwei goldenen Rosetten mit Granateinlage von Warnikam Kr. Heiligenbeil, welche die Schläfen eines Pferdes geziert hatten (Provinzial-Museum). Die Entstehung dieses Stiles ist entschieden im Orient zu suchen, der Urquelle aller technischen Künste. Diese Herkunft bezeugt das vielleicht älteste aller bekannten Stücke, ein Pectorale aus Gold mit Granaten im Wiesbadener Museum. (Cohausen a. a. O. p. 217 Tfl. I Fig. 3) zu Wolfsheim bei Mainz gefunden, mit der persischen Inschrift „Artachshater", welche ihrer Form nach ins 3. Jahrhundert gesetzt wird.

Im übrigen Europa tritt diese Technik erst im 5. Jahrhundert auf, nur für den Südosten an den Küsten des schwarzen Meeres hat Hampel in dem Werke „Der Goldfund von Nagy-Szent-Miklós" (Budapest 1886) gezeigt, dass man sie hier schon ins 4. Jahrhundert zurückverfolgen kann (p. 117 ff.). Es wird daselbst auch gezeigt, dass man die Quelle dieser Technik nicht in Byzanz suchen darf, sondern dass sie weiter im Osten, jedenfalls im Neu-Persischen Reiche zu finden sein muss. Die weitere Verbreitung durch Europa wäre hauptsächlich den Gothen zu verdanken, welche am längsten an den Sitzen dieser halb spätclassischen, halb schon orientalisirten Cultur gewohnt hatten.

Es sind aus der ganzen Periode der Völkerwanderung nur verschwindend wenig Funde bekannt, wo in den Zellen noch Email neben Steinen auftritt. In den äusserst ähnlichen Endbeschlägen von zwei Schwertscheiden, einer von Komorn (?)[1]) in Ungarn, der andere aus dem prachtvollen Grabe zu Flonheim im Paulus-Museum zu Worms findet zwischen Granaten eine kleine Rosette mit weissem Email erfüllt. Die Germanen haben diese Kunst wohl nicht weiter geübt.

Zwar finden sich in Gräbern dieser Zeit noch hin und wieder Fibeln und Knöpfe mit echtem Email, gegen die mit eingelegten Steinen allerdings in verschwindender Zahl, doch tragen diese alle, soweit ich vorläufig beurtheilen kann, den früheren römischen Charakter, so z. B. einige Fibeln von Envermen (Seine Inferieure, Cochet Normandie souterraine, Taf. XI. 24), ein wunderschöner Knopf mit Millefiori-Mosaik-Email (ibid. Taf. XV. 4), der Oberhöfer Scheibe sehr nahe verwandt und jedenfalls zu derselben Zeit fabricirt, eine Fibel mit ringförmig gestalteter Scheibe von einem sächsischen Kirchhofe zu Gilton (England, Fausset, Inventarium sepulcrale p. 24 Taf. III. 8), welche Fausset selbst als ein Unicum unter den vielen anderen Fibeln bezeichnet u. A. m. Es sind auch anderweitig echt römische Schmucksachen auf fränkischen Kirchhöfen gefunden, so z. B. Armbrust-Charnier-Fibeln, wie die bekannte im Grabe Childerichs, oder eine andere zu Charnay[2]) (Burgund). Man entnimmt daraus die auch anderweitig bekannte Thatsache, dass die Barbaren römische Gräber geplündert und sich so in Besitz älterer römischer Artefacte gesetzt haben. Cochet hat daher entschieden Unrecht, wenn er (a. a. O. p. 364) sagt, viele der Normännischen Fibeln seien mit Email bedeckt „gewesen". Zum Theil hatten diese Stücke eingelegte Steine enthalten, eine kleinere Zahl, die immer sehr vereinzelt auftraten, wie manchmal hervorgehoben wird, waren echt römisch, stammten aber aus älterer Zeit, so dass die von Cochet angeführte Aeusserung Gallia Belgica (zumal im 5. bis 7. Jahrhundert) sei als Wiege dieser Emaillirkunst zu betrachten, wie schon aus unseren früheren Betrachtungen hervorgeht, widerlegt ist. Erst Funde sicher **fränkischer** emaillirter Objecte könnten ein spärliches Fortleben dieser Kunst beweisen.

Hingegen blüht sie im Osten Europas aufs Neue auf und erwächst zu dem byzantinischen „Zellenschmelz". Diese Entwickelung ist noch in vollständiges Dunkel gehüllt: ein Zusammenhang mit dem westlichen Grubenschmelz ist völlig ausgeschlossen, die Technik muss aus einer anderen Quelle neues Leben erhalten haben, und diese kann wieder nur im Orient liegen, wo trotz des Wechsels der herrschenden Stämme diese Künste von den ältesten Zeiten bis auf die Gegenwart nie eine wirkliche Unterbrechung erlitten haben. Die Technik der mit Emailfarben bemalten Gläser, der glasirten Thongeschirre finden wir gerade hier seit dem Alterthume erhalten, bis sie im Mittelalter das westliche Europa wieder aufnahm; hier muss auch die Emailtechnik fortgepflanzt sein und zwar in der aus Aegypten bekannten Form des Zellenschmelzes. Die wichtigste Rolle käme hier dem Neu-Persischen Reiche der Sassaniden (226—636) zu, dessen Blüthe also recht in die Zeit

1) **Ungarische** Revue 1882 p. 189.

2) **Baudot**: Mem. s. l. sépultures des Barbares de l'Epoque Mérovingienne en Bourgogne, (Mém. de la Comm. des Antiquité d. l. Côte d'or V. Taf. XV. 7.) Die noch ältere vorrömische Fibel XV. 6 ist Einzelfund, es fragt sich also, ob sie aus den Burgunder Gräbern stammt.

der Völkerwanderung fällt. Später traten die Araber das künstlerische Erbe des Orients an. Leider ist gerade die Sassanidische Cultur nur äusserst ungenügend und in spärlichen Funden bekannt. Genauere Nachforschungen würden wesentlich dazu beitragen, einen der dunkelsten Punkte in der Geschichte der Kleinkünste des nachclassischen Europas aufzuklären.

Einem solchen Einflusse haben wir jedenfalls auch das Email auf den Goldgefässen des Fundes von Nagy-Szent-Miklós zuzuschreiben, dieser wunderbaren Mischung von spät klassisch-barbarisirter und sassanidischer Kunst aus c. dem Ende des 4. Jahrhunderts., wie Hampel a. a. O. ausgeführt hat. Die Emailreste sind hier äusserst spärlich, am meisten bei dem goldenen dosenartigen Gefässe (Hampel No. 19 Fig. 27—22), wo sich zwischen den reichen Ranken Reste eines durchsichtigen blauen Emails erhalten haben und 2 Rosetten aus 2 concentrischen Kreuzfiguren zusammengesetzt, deren Felder mit weissen und einem mehr durchsichtigen bläulichen und amethystrothen Email erfüllt sind. Es zeigt sich also in Technik, Stil und Material eine vollständige Verschiedenheit gegen die weströmische Kunst, und man darf wohl um so mehr auf orientalische Technik schliessen, welche sich die germanischen Völker nicht aneigneten, da die hier auftretende bei den unzähligen, oft recht kostbaren und künstlich ausgeführten Objecten im Westen nicht weiter fortcultivirt wird.

Hingegen muss sich aus derselben Quelle das byzantinische Email cloisonné entwickelt haben, dessen noch vollständig dunkle Entstehungsgeschichte hier aber nicht mehr weiter verfolgt werden kann, zumal sie von den Fragen, die uns zunächst interessiren zu weit abführt.

Im Abendlande verschwindet wie gesagt das Email vollständig, bis nachher das byzantinische und die späteren mittelalterlichen Formen am Rhein und Limoges auftreten.

(Der Vortragende giebt eine kurze Uebersicht dieser Entwickelung bis auf die Neuzeit, besonders nach Bucher Geschichte der technischen Künste, wo aber gerade die Geschichte des frühmittelalterlichen Email cloisonné mangelhafter dargestellt ist, als es das jetzt bekannte Material zulässt.)

Aus den Zeiten der Völkerwanderung ist noch ein besonders wichtiger Fund hervorzuheben von Kettlach[1]) bei Glocknitz am Semmering aus Gräbern, welche mit denen von Kesthely in Ungarn nahe verwandt zu sein scheinen. Hier fand man eine Anzahl Ohrringe mit halbmondförmigen Schildchen, welche bunt ausgefüllt waren. Der kleinere Theil dieser Objecte befindet sich im Münz- und Antiken-Cabinet zu Wien, der andere (gerade die abgebildeten) soll noch im Privatbesitz zu Graz sein. Es wäre dringend erwünscht diese Sachen für eine öffentliche Sammlung zu retten und sie im neuen ethnographisch-anthropologischen Museum in Wien mit den übrigen zu vereinen. Diese letzteren konnte ich nicht zu Gesicht bekommen. Nach den schlecht erhaltenen Wiener Stücken und nach der unklaren Beschreibung scheint hier eine Mischung von eingeschmolzenem Email und eingelegten Glasplättchen aufzutreten,

---

1) v. Sacken: Ueber Ansiedlungen und Funde aus heidnischer Zeit in Niederösterreich (Sitzungsber. der phil. hist. kl. der K. Ak. d. Wissensch. zu Wien Bd. 74) .p. 48 (618) Tfl. V. Fig. 77—81.

es gehören also diese Stücke zu den allerwichtigten aus der für die Geschichte des Emails so dunkelen nachrömischen Zeit.

Schliesslich sind aus dem skandinavischen Norden noch ein Paar ganz ausserordentlich merkwürdige Funde zu erwähnen. Zu **Möklebust** (Bergenhus Amt) in Norwegen wurde in einem Schiffsgrabe ein Bronzekessel als Behälter der gebrannten Knochen gefunden.

An dem eingestülpten Boden dieses Kessels sind unmittelbar am Rande innen und aussen zwei Reifen befestigt, mit einander und mit dem Boden durch drei Nietnägel vereint. Die Mitte der Innenseite nimmt eine kreisförmige Scheibe ein, welche drei rhombische Platten mit dem Randringe verbinden. Am Aussenrande trägt der Kessel drei abstehende Platten als Henkel zum Durchziehen eines Riemens, oberhalb derselben je ein barbarisches Haupt, unterhalb zwei kleine Beine. Die drei Platten, sowie die beiden Reifen und die Beschläge der Unterseite sind nun mit prachtvollem **Millefiori-Mosaik-Email** ausgefüllt. Diese Verbindung der meisterhaft emaillirten Stücke mit den barbarischen Figuren, Arbeiten von classischer u. barbarischer Arbeit ist vorläufig unerklärlich, denn wenn solche Millefiori-Mosaik auch noch auf den grossen Perlen vorkommt, wie sie am Ende des 4. Jahrhunderts auftreten, so wäre dieser Fund nach Ansicht der norwegischen Forscher jünger, falls es nicht doch noch gelingt, ihn bis in die Zeit der dänischen Moorfunde zurückzudatiren, wo z. B. im Vimose-Funde entfernt ähnliche Köpfe vorkommen. Am wahrscheinlichsten ist es, wie ich glaube, dass die Emailbeschläge von einem älteren zerstörten Geräthe oder Gefässe (?) stammen, denn für diesen Kessel waren sie sicher nicht bestimmt. Um sie an demselben anzubringen, hat man ihn in einer ungewöhnlichen Weise behandeln, man kann fast sagen misshandeln müssen. Denn der Boden des Gefässes ist in die Höhe getrieben, so dass hier erst ein neuer innnerer Rand entstand, dem die Reifen sich anpassten, wobei sie ziemlich roh aufgenietet wurden. Auch ist die Stelle, wo die Bodenbeschläge angebracht wurden, eine stilistisch widersinnige und ganz ungewöhnliche, zumal auf der Innenseite des Bodens. Die Aussenseite schützte man durch die Einstülpung, welche innen eine Falte am Rande hervorrief. Es ist also klar, man hat fertig vorliegende Beschläge nur zur Garnirnng des bronzenen Aschengefässes eines sehr vornehmen Mannes benutzt. Dabei können dann die emaillirten Beschläge und die übrigen Bronzearbeiten von sehr verschiedenem Alter sein. Hier liegt noch ein zu lösendes Räthsel vor.

Ein sicherer Fund aus der Völkerwanderungsperiode (früher mittlere Eisenzeit genannt) ist aber ein prachtvoller Pferdezaum, gefunden in einem Schiffsgrabe zu Vendel in Schweden[2]), dessen Bronzebeschläge mit rothem und gelbrothem Email verziert sind, wovon die Abbildung allerdings keine genügende Vorstellung gewährt.

Die genauere Untersuchung der Objecte wird gewiss noch viel Ueberraschen-

---

1) **Rygh**, Antiquités Norvégiennes No. 727. **Foreningen** til Norske Fortidsminders Bevaring, Aarsberetning for 1874 p. 90. Taf. 8. **Lorange**, Samlingen af Norske Oldsager. Bergens Museum p. 153—161.

2) Antiquarisk Tidskrift für Sverige VIII. p. 24 Fig. 819.

des an den Tag bringen,[1]) was die Fragen, welche in dieser Uebersicht offen gelassen werden mussten, zu klären bestimmt ist.

Der Vortragende ging schliesslich auf die Emaillen Ostasiens über, welche nach der Einnahme des Sommerpalastes des Kaisers von China 1859 durch die Engländer und Franzosen und nach der 1853 durch Commodore Perry erfolgten Aufschliessung Japans in Masse nach Europa gekommen sind und durch ihre wunderbar schöne Arbeit in Europa den Geschmack für Emaillen und deren Fabrikation wiederbelebt haben, obwohl sie bei uns weder an gleich vollkommener Arbeit, noch besonders an Billigkeit erreicht werden können.

Diese Emails sind sämmtlich Cloisonnés und zeichnen sich durch kühne leichte Zeichnung, welche in Japan einem eleganten Naturalismus huldigt, aus. Die Befürchtung, dass die japanische Kunst bei dem riesigen Export verfallen würde, scheint sich glücklicherweise nicht zu bestätigen, da gerade die Japaner auf der Nürnberger Metallausstellung 1885 in der Emaillerie eminente Fortschritte aufwiesen.

Vermöge der Freundlichkeit des Herrn Director Albrecht konnte der Vortragende eine Reihe von dem hiesigen Gewerbe-Museum gehörigen Bronzetellern vorlegen, welche die Fabrikation der emaillirten Gegenstände in ihren verschiedenen Stadien zeigen. Der Kupferteller wird zuerst mit der Zeichnung bedeckt, dann stückweise mit dem eingekochten Wurzelschleim einer Erdorchidee, Bletia hyacinthina, bestrichen und hierauf die nach Vorzeichnung gebogenen, ausgeglühten Streifchen Messingband geklebt, welche nach dann nach Einstreuung von Löthpulver angelöthet werden. In diese Zellen wird alsdann das mit Wasser angeriebene Emailpulver eingetragen und eingeschmolzen, eine Operation, die mehrmals wiederholt werden muss, bis alle Zellen und alle beim Schmelzen entstandenen Blasen vollständig ausgefüllt sind. Abschleifen und Poliren giebt dem Stücke dann seine Vollendung.

N a c h t r a g. Nach Abschluss dieses Aufsatzes ging mir erst das neueste Heft von „Lindenschmit, Alterthümer unserer heidnischen Vorzeit, Band IV Heft 4“ zu, in welchem derselbe auf Tafel 22 Glasperlen aus fränkischen und allemannischen Gräbern abbildet und daran Bemerkungen knüpft, die mit den oben angeführten Thatsachen in vollstem Widerspruche stehen, und die daher eine kurze Erwiderung nöthig machen.

Lindenschmit nimmt an, dass erst im 5. und 6. Jahrhundert diese Perlen in grosser Menge in den Frauengräbern bei den germanischen Stämmen auftreten und zwar in neuer Form und Technik, während zur Kaiserzeit nur einfach gerippte grüne und blaue Perlen vorkämen. Er hebt allerdings die Aehnlichkeit einiger dieser Perlen mit den bunten römischen Glasgefässen und Schmuckgeräthen hervor, findet es aber auffallend, dass die zur Kaiserzeit geübte Millefioritechnik nicht gleichzeitig auf die Anfertigung der Schmuckperlen verwendet wurde.

Diese Annahmen beruhen auf unrichtigen Voraussetzungen. Gerade in Nord-Deutschland und Scandinavien sind die Glasperlen zur Kaiserzeit ungemein häufig und zumal in der früheren Kaiserzeit manchmal in einem einzelnen Frauengrabe

1) Der Vortragende bittet ihm von solchen Funden, besonders den, wie aus obiger Auseinandersetzung ergiebt, selteneren vorrömischen, oder falls sich gar Email in Funden zeigt, die hinter die römische Kaiserzeit gesetzt werden, ihn freundliche Mittheilung zu machen.

wohl ebenso massenhaft als in fränkischer Zeit, und sie finden sich, wie oben erwähnt, in absoluter Gleichmässigkeit von Frankreich bis nach Asien und Aegypten. Die von Lindenschmit angeführten orangegelben Perlen mit blau-weissen Augen, treten circa 400 Jahre v. Chr., also lange vor der Kaiserzeit nicht nur in Norddeutschland, sondern auch in ganz Europa und den anderen Erdtheilen um das Mittelmeer herum auf. Ferner hatte die Technik der Glasperlen gerade in der Kaiserzeit ihren höchsten, seither nie mehr erreichten Stand. Zu fränkischer Zeit wurde sowohl das Material schlechter als die Arbeit nachlässiger, es trat absolut kein neues Moment hinzu, alles basirt nur auf der Technik der vorhergehenden Periode: wir treffen demnach keine neue, sondern die Ausläufer einer verfallenden Technik. Neue Formen entwickeln sich allerdings in Fortbildung der früheren, man kann sie aber nicht als Verbesserungen bezeichnen. Die Millefioriperlen treten, wie schon erwähnt, bereits im Beginne der Kaiserzeit auf, verändern dann Form und Muster ein wenig, so dass gerade zu mittlerer Kaiserzeit auf ihnen vollständig dieselben Zeichnungen vorkommen wie auf den gleichzeitigen Emaillen — was gerade die nordischen Gräber deutlich zeigen: die Technik ist bei den Perlen der auf den Emaillen vorangegangen, wie naturgemäss, nicht nachgefolgt. Die Millefioriperlen gehen dann die ganze Kaiserzeit durch und reichen noch in den Anfang der Völkerwanderung mit hinein, jedenfalls weil sie aus einer durch die grosse Bewegung nicht berührten Quelle stammten. Sie sind hier aber wieder nur noch die Ausläufer der lange geübten Technik, und stammen manchmal sogar wahrscheinlich aus geplünderten Gräbern der Römerzeit. An Zahl treten sie gegen die anderweitigen Perlen immer sehr zurück. Die fränkischen Perlen gehören überwiegend zu den belegten, wo man auf die erweichte Grundmasse mit erhitztem farbigem Glasstabe Streifen und Tupfen auftrug, eine Technik, die schon in die frühesten Zeiten der Perlenfabrikation zurückreicht.

Ein grosser Theil der fränkischen Perlen wird jedenfalls aus dem Osten, den nunmehrigen äussersten Regionen des oströmischen Reiches stammen, der wahrscheinlichen Quelle der Mehrzahl der früheren Perlen, denn einige Formen finden sich identisch in England, Frankreich, Süddeutschland, Ostpreussen (wo auch diese Periode vertreten ist), Ungarn, am Kaukasus, während andere Formen mehr dem Westen eigenthümlich sind, die bei der noch fortlebenden Glasindustrie zum Theil also auch hier fabricirt sein können.

Aus Venedig stammen die Perlen aber auf keinen Fall. Lindenschmit möchte sogar die Glasarmringe der süddeutschen Gräber aus Venedig herleiten, welche aber der mittleren La Tène-Zeit angehören, also ca. 600 (allenfalls 500) Jahre vor die Gründung Venedigs fallen. Aus Phönicien stammen diese höchst wahrscheinlich, haben aber mit der Lagunenstadt nichts zu thun. Venedig gewann seinen Rang als mächtiger Handelsplatz, der zwischen Orient und Occident vermittelte erst nach der Merowingerzeit.

Wie sich aus der Monografia della Vetraria Venezianae Murenese (Venezia 1874) ergiebt, sind die Nachrichten von einer frühen einheimischen Glasfabrikation in Venedig ganz unsicher, ja fast mythisch. Erst nach 1000 fällt etwas mehr Licht darauf. Wie ich in der Januar-Sitzung dieses Jahres (Vortrag über Aggry-Perlen) zum Theil in Anlehnung an obiges Werk, mehr noch auf eigene Beobachtungen gestützt gezeigt habe, wurden im 15. Jahrhundert eine eigene Art mehrfach überfangener

Perlen hergestellt, in Nachahmung der antiken Millefioriplatten (nicht der Millefiori-Perlen). Die Perlen alla lucerna, die jetzt noch fabricirt werden, sollen erst im 16. Jahrhundert erfunden sein, überhaupt erklären sich die Autoren obigen Werkes gegen ein weit, etwa ins 13. Jahrhundert zurückreichendes Alter der bunten Perlen, auch spielte bei bunten Perlen noch im 15. Jahrhundert das Schleifrad eine grössere Rolle als die Lampe. Die Entdeckung der Perlen alla lucerna mit aufgelegten Fäden, wie sie bis heute in Venedig fabricirt werden, hängt mit der schon a. a. O. erwähnten durch die ganze Strömung der Renaissance bedingten Durchforschung der Ueberreste des Alterthums zusammen. Man fand die antiken Perlen und ahmte die einfachste Technik nach, an die complicirteren haben sich die Venezianer nicht herangemacht mit Ausnahme der modernen Millefioristäbe des verstorbenen Franchini. Auch ist das Material der Venezianischen Perlen nicht so vollkommen, als das der Kaiserzeit. Es hat also in Venedig jedenfalls nicht die alte classische Tradition fortgelebt, sondern man hat erst zur Renaissancezeit die alten Muster wieder nachzuahmen gesucht auf dem von der Natur der Perlen fast von selbst gebotenen und schon in frühester Zeit betretenen Wege, aber nicht vollkommen erreicht.

Man kann also nach der chronologischen Stellung und dem Verbreitungsgebiet der Glasperlen sagen, dass die fränkisch-allemannischen Perlen (des 5. und 6. Jahrhunderts v. Chr.) die letzten Ausläufer einer hauptsächlich in den östlichen Küstenländern des Mittelmeeres angesessenen, allmählich verfallenden Technik waren, deren höchste Blüthe in die Zeit des weströmischen Kaiserreiches fällt.

Herr Dr. Jentzsch legte zunächst zur Ansicht das im Auftrage der Centralcommission für wissenschaftliche Landeskunde von Deutschland durch den Königl. Bibliothekar P. E. Richter bearbeitete „Verzeichniss von Forschern in wissenschaftlicher Landes- und Volkskunde Mitteleuropas, Dresden 1886“ vor, welches für unsere, in erster Linie der Heimathskunde gewidmete Gesellschaft von besonderem Interesse sein muss. Sodann legte derselbe die bisher erschienenen Lieferungen des physikalischen Atlass von Berghaus, Gotha 1886, vor, betonend, dass derselbe neben seinem hohen allgemeinen wissenschaftlichen Werthe für uns auch insofern von Interesse sei, als er mit den nöthigen Veränderungen gewissermassen als Vorbild für den physikalisch-statistischen Atlas Ost- und Westpreussens dienen könne, dessen Herausgabe Redner in der Sitzung am 5. Februar 1885 in längerem Vortrage angeregt habe. Sodann legte derselbe die für das geologische Provinzialmuseum eingegangenen Geschenke vor, deren Liste wegen der in der Veröffentlichung der Geschenke eingetretenen Pause diesmal besonders umfangreich ist. Es haben geschenkt die Herren: 1. Dr. Abromeit: Geweih des Cervus Elaphus von Poschleitschen; 2. Bädeker: Silurkalk von Kapkeim; 3. Ballinger: verkieseltes Holz von Sobbowitz; 4. Dr. Bänitz: Ammonit von Königsberg; 4. Battesch: subfossilen Pferdeschädel von Mohrungen; 6. Rechtsanwalt Beer: Jura von Warnicken; 7. Benningson: Silur- und Feuerstein von Cranz; 8. Bernecker: Feuersteinhohlkugel von Memel; 9. Professor Dr. R. Caspary: diluviale Knochen und Geschiebe von Puschdorf, Phosphorit von Schönbrück bei Graudenz, Knochen und Geschiebe aus dem Kreise Flatow, Orthoceratiten von

Skaisgirren u. A. m.; 10. Claassen: Kreidespongien von Warnikam; 11. Rector Dannehl in Zinten: Glimmerschiefer, Spongien und Korallen; 12. Buchhalter Drope: Orthoceras von Grünlinde bei Wehlau; 13. Landschaftsrath Eckert-Czerwonken: silurische Korallen; 14. Dr. Erchenbrecher: Kreidekonkretion; 15. Lehrer Fröhlich-Thorn: verschiedene Geschiebe und verkieselte Hölzer; 16. Rendant Fröhlich-Kulm: Diluvial- und Tertiärconchylien aus Grand von Ostrometzko; 17. Baumeister Fuhrberg: Geschiebe von Tuchel; 18. stud. Gartenmeister: Fragment eines Backzahnes des Mammuth von Agilla bei Labiau; 19. Kanzleirath Gerlach: mehre Geschiebe; 20. Dr. Gisevius: Geschiebe von Süssenthal, Kreis Allenstein; 21. Glaubitt: silurische und krystallinische Geschiebe; 22. stud. Gloger: Fischwirbel aus Torf von Puspern; 23. Drechsler Göbel: Rehgeweih von Vierbrüderkrug; 24. Grothe: Rest von Kreidesauriern, silurische Versteinerungen und verkieseltes Holz; 25. Dr. Hagedorn: alluviale Säugethierknochen aus dem Mohrunger See; 26. Apotheker Hellwich-Bischofstein: wiederholte Sendungen interessanter Geschiebe, namentlich silurischer Korallen, Cenoman, Senon, Kugelsandstein etc.; 27. Heubach-Kapkeim: eine grosse Platte Obersilurkalk; 28. Dr. Hilbert: fossiles Holz, Silur, Cenoman- und Senongeschiebe, meist von Rastenburg; 29. Jamrowski: einen silurischen Cephalopoden; 30. Jeroslaw: Silur von Dietrichswalde bei Allenstein; 31. Kemcke: Silurgeschiebe von Kruglanken; 32. Klugkist-Mühlenthal per Sensburg: Backsteinkalk; 33. Kandidat Knoblauch: Juraversteinerungen von Warnicken; 34. Ziegeleibesitzer Köhler-Steinort bei Elbing: zahlreiche diluviale Knochen; 35. Körber-Körberode: Fischknochen aus Wiesenmergel; 36. Apotheker Kowalewski: Fischwirbel aus dem Bergwerk von Palmnicken und Phosphoritspongien; 37. Oberlehrer Dr. Krüger-Tilsit: Wohnkammer von Orthoceras und Abdruck eines senonen Ammoniten; 38. Kuwert-Wernsdorf: verschiedene Geschiebe; 39. Oberzollcontroleur Lincke-Pillau: fossiles Holz, Knochen und Conkretionen; 40. Rittmeister von Montowt-Kirpehnen (durch Major von Sanden) Knochen aus Torf; 41. Oberforstmeister Müller: Hornzapfen eines Bos von Mehlauken; 42. Müller-Lebernitz-Mühle, Kreis Berent: subfossiles Elchgeweih; 43. Ostrawski-Klitzau per Konitz: eine Calamopora; 44. Passarge: Silur und Jura von Gumbinnen; 45. Pfeiffer-Glomsienen: Hirschgeweih aus Torf; 46. Ziegelmeister Pfeiffer-Lenzen: Knochen aus Yoldiathon; 47. Pieske-Stocksmühle; verkieseltes Holz u. A.; 48. Obersteiger Pietsch: fossiles Holz und vollständiges Schichtenprofil von Palmnicken; 49. Preuss-Gross-Morin per Argenau: ein Jurageschiebe; 50. Dr. Reidemeister-Schönebeck: Phosphorithölzer von Helmstedt und Krantzit; 51. Römer-Weidenhof Kreis Kulm: Geschiebe mit Granaten; 52. Dr. Schauinsland: Hirschgeweih aus dem Samrodter See; 53. Director Schiefferdecker: verschiedene Geschiebe, worunter ein Saurier; 54. Dr. Schirrmacher: Kreide- und Silurgeschiebe von Rantau; 55. Dr. Schirrmacher-Stuhm: diluviale Knochen; 56. Stadtrath Schmidt-Lentzen: diluviale Knochen aus Yoldiathon; 57. Geheimer Rath Professor Dr. Schönborn: Kreidespongie; 58. Bahnmeister Schulz: verschiedene Geschiebe von Puschdorf und Kuggen; 59. Fräulein Schulz-Osterode: Granatkrystall; 60. Dr. Schröder: verschiedene Geschiebe von Königsberg; 61. Schwartz: zwei Seeigel von Rügen; 62. Selbstädt-Andreaswalde bei Lyck: Silurische Korallen; 63. Seidel-Bludszen bei Goldap: Senon- und Silurgeschiebe und Kugelsandstein; 64. Skrzeczka-Grunden bei Kruglanken: wiederholte Sendungen silurischer Geschiebe; 65. Dr. Sommer-Allenberg: verkieseltes

Holz; 66. Dr. Sommerfeld: Geschiebe von Craussen; 67. Steffens: fossiles Holz von Plibischken; 68. Hauptmann Steppuhn: Geschiebe von Craussen; 69. Baumeister Storbeck-Mehlsack: Senone Geschiebe; 70. Pfarrer Strehl-Blankensee: verkieseltes Holz; 71. Strüwy-Wokellen: wiederholte Sendungen von Geschieben, Knochen, Diluvialconchylien von Sperlings bei Heilsberg; 72. Thorun: verkieseltes Holz mit Bohrgängen, Kugelsandstein, Silur- und Senongeschiebe; 73. Treichel-Hochpaleschken: verschiedene Geschiebe und Bodenproben; 74. Trommler: ein Stück Mammuthstosszahn und verschiedene Geschiebe vom Nassen Garten; 75. Oberlehrer Vanhöffen: als Ergänzung der früher geschenkten grossen Sammlung verschiedener Geschiebe von Wehlau, Kreideversteinerungen von Krapen bei Christburg und Mammuthknochen von Puschdorf; 76. Baumeister Vetter: verkieseltes Holz von Schöneck; 77. Oberlehrer Vogel: Sandsteingeschiebe; 78. Weiss-Niedamowo, Kreis Berent: Kugelsandstein; 79. Apotheker Weiss-Kaimen: Sandsteinconcretion; 80. Wentzke-Lubjahnen: Pentameruskalk und ein subfossiles Hirschgeweih; 81. Oberlehrer Wermbter: Silurgeschiebe von Falkenhorst bei Tapiau; 82. Fräulein Melitta von Zalewski-Rauschendorf, Kreis Neustadt: verschiedene silurische Versteinerungen; die Herren 83. Zander-Nidden: einen Walfischwirbel; 84. Lehrer Zinger-Pr. Holland: wiederholte Sendungen zahlreicher interessanter Geschiebe, worunter ein Wirbel des Plesiosaurus ichthyospondylus; 85. Direction der Zuckerfabrik Praust: ein Bohrprofil sowie verschiedene Geschiebe; 86. Direction des Steinsalzbergwerks Inowraclaw: eine prächtige Collection farbigen Steinsalzes; 87. Direction des Königl. mineralogischen Museums in Dresden: eine Sammlung Kreide- und Zechsteinpetrefacten; 88. Herr Regierungs-Maschinenmeister Patrunky-Bromberg: eine grössere Sammlnng interessanter Geschiebe. Hierzu treten die Resultate zahlreicher Bohrungen, deren Schichtenproben uns von den verschiedensten Behörden Ost- und Westpreussens sowie von Königl. Behörden in Bromberg, Berlin, Breslau, Halle, Glogau nnd Swinemünde zugingen. Auch Bohrunternehmer haben unsere Zwecke in dieser Hinsicht wesentlich gefördert, so die Herren R. Quäck in Königsberg, Blasendorf in Berlin und Osterode, Studti in Pr. Holland, Schibor in Rosenberg u. A., ganz besonders aber Herr Pöpcke in Stettin (früher Anklam), vertreten durch Herrn Ingenieur Bieske hier, von welchem wir seit Jahren zahlreiche prächtige Schichtenprofile erhielten. Ganz neuerdings hat derselbe im Fort Kalgen die Tiefe von 302 m erreicht und damit das tiefste bisher in Ost- und Westpreussen vorhandene Bohrloch (Purmallen bei Memel) um 13 m übertroffen.

Derselbe sprach sodann über die Herkunft unserer Diluvialgeschiebe. Die überwältigende Mehrzahl der norddeutschen Geschiebe stammt aus Norden oder Nordosten. Nur am Südrande des Flachlandes, insbesondere im Königreich und der Provinz Sachsen ist seit langem die umgekehrte Transportrichtung für die Geschiebe einer bestimmten Diluvialstufe nachgewiesen. Die Glacialhypothese setzt eine gesetzmässige lineare oder zonale Verbreitung der einzelnen Geschiebetypen voraus. Statt dessen sind einander kreuzende Transportvorrichtungen mit Sicherheit nachgewiesen. So sind — um nur eins von den vielen Beispielen anzuführen — silurische Kalke aus Esth- und Gothland nach Groningen, Basalte aus Schonen nach Leipzig gelangt. Auch in Grossbritannien sind solche „Intercrossing Erratics“ bekannt. Hier wie dort führten sie zu dem Schluss, dass die Bewegungsrichtungen des Eises in der ersten und zweiten Eiszeit von einander abwichen. Dies wird gestützt a) durch die Beobachtung zweier verschiedener Richtungen von Gletscherschrammen auf anstehenden Gesteinsinseln des norddeutschen Flachlandes, b) durch den auch für Norddeutschland geführten Nachweis einer zwei Gletscherperioden trennenden Interglacialzeit mit gemässigtem Klima (Purmallen, Heilsberg, Mewe, Lauenburg etc.), c) durch die Beobachtungen von Holmström, Torell und de Geer, nach denen in Schonen das Material der oberen Grundmoränen auf den Osten, das der untern auf den Norden als Ausgangspunkt hinweist. So will namentlich de Geer die Gesteine der Alandsinseln als Leitgeschiebe der jüngeren Eiszeit verwerthen, was indess vorläufig wenigstens für Deutschland noch nicht als berechtigt angesehen werden darf. Ueberhaupt ist es sehr schwierig, die Heimath eines einzelnen Geschiebes zu ermitteln, weil die Mehrzahl der in Betracht kommenden versteinerungsführenden Schichten von Osten nach Westen sich verbreitet, während die Heimathsgebiete der krystallinischen Geschiebe — Schweden, Finnland und die Inseln des Botnischen Busens — erst sehr unzureichend erforscht sind. Für die senonen und cenomanen Kreidegeschiebe wurden früher schlechtweg Schonen und die dänischen Inseln als Heimath angesehen, während Redner nachgewiesen hat, dass dieselben Gesteine mit denselben Petrefacten im grössten Theile Ost- und Westpreussens den tiefern Untergrund bilden und daher gewiss auch am Boden der zwischenliegenden Ostsee auftreten. Die viel spärlicheren Jurageschiebe sind in Ostpreussen zumeist durch Cardioceras Lamberti charakterisirt, werden in Westpreussen noch seltener, in der Mark und in Pommern aber wieder häufiger, doch mit abweichendem paläontologischem Inhalt, weshalb die Lamberti-Gesteine auf das nördliche Ostpreussen, Littauen, das südliche Kurland und die angrenzenden Theile der Ostsee, die meisten Berliner Jurageschiebe aber auf einen westlicheren Ausgangspunkt in der Nähe der Odermündungen zurückzuführen sind. Als Heimath der devonischen Geschiebe betrachtet man gewöhnlich Livland. Doch hat der beste Kenner des livländischen Devons Grewingk gezeigt, dass schon die bei Danzig durch J. Kiesow gesammelten Stücke wegen des Fehlens der Rhynchonella livonica sowie wegen ihrer petrographischen Beschaffenheit nicht aus Livland, sondern nur aus der Ostsee stammen können. Wenn nun Dames bei Berlin trotzdem Dolomit mit Rhynchonella livonica auffand, so ist das nur ein weiterer Beweis für die Existenz sich kreuzender Transportrichtungen. Unter den silurischen Geschieben werden der Beyrichienkalk auf Oesel und Gothland, der Korallen- und Krinoidenkalk, ferner der Oolith auf Gothland, der Pentamerus borealis-Kalk, Cyclocrinus-Kalk, Backsteinkalk, das Wesenberger und Sadewitzer Gestein auf Esthland zurückgeführt, während zahlreiche, namentlich bei Berlin und Eberswalde durch Dames und Remelé beobachtete Geschiebe untersilurischen und cambrischen Alters auf Oeland und das schwedische Festland verweisen. Diese schwedischen Gesteine werden im Osten entschieden seltener, und auch bei einzelnen gothländischen trifft dies zu. So fand Redner den noch bei Königsberg so gemeinen Beyrichienkalk ostwärts nur bis Kosaken bei Goldap (40 Gr. 1'), Grewingk denselben in Kurland bis 41 Gr. 30'. Der rothe Crinoidenkalk findet nach Nötling seine Ostgrenze in Westpreussen; dagegen sind andere Gesteine, von denen N. dasselbe behauptet, auch (zum Theil mehrfach) in Ostpreussen und zwar durch Vanhöffen Pentamerus Conchidium-Kalk bei Wehlau, dunkelbraun-rother Megalaspis-Kalk bei Rastenburg und Scolithes-Sandstein bei Königsberg gefunden. Wenn mithin eine gewisse Gegensätzlichkeit östlicher und westlicher Verbreitungsgebiete nicht zu verkennen ist, so sind doch die Grenzen keineswegs scharf. Die schwedischen Geschiebe werden in Ostpreussen, die esthländischen in der Mark seltener, ohne doch völlig zu fehlen. Unter den azoischen Gesteinen hatte Redner schon früher sowohl finnischen als åländischen Rapakiwi nachgewiesen, und auch für gewisse Porphyre und Sandsteine Elfdalen und Dalarne, für Granatgneisse die Gegend südlich Stockholm als Heimath vermuthet, ohne doch für die letzteren Vergleiche ausreichendes Beweismaterial zu besitzen. Er verabredete daher mit dem Director der schwedischen Landesuntersuchung Professor Torell ein gemeinsames Vorgehen und sandte in Folge dessen im November 1880 Proben sämmtlicher im Provinzialmuseum vorhandener Varietäten ost- und westpreussischer Geschiebe in 365 Handstücken nach Stockholm, von jedem Stück die Hälfte unter gleicher Nummer in Königsberg zurückbehaltend. Durch freundliche Vermittelung des genannten Herrn sowie des Staatsgeologen Holst hat nun Staatsgeolog Lundbohm in Stockholm die ganze Sammlung geprüft und mit schwedischen Gesteinen verglichen. So ist zum ersten Mal ein wirklich gründlicher Vergleich durchgeführt worden, dessen Ergebnisse für unsere Studien über die Verbreitung dieser Diluvialgeschiebe von grundlegender Bedeutung sein müssen. Die ausführliche Abhandlung Lundbohms erscheint in dem laufenden Heft unserer Schriften. Vorläufig sei daraus nur mitgetheilt, dass auch L. für die Granatgneisse die Gegend von Stockholm (Södermanland) als Heimath vermuthet, doch ähnliche Gesteine auch aus anderen Theilen Schwedens kennt; dass gewisse Granite auf Småland, andere auf Stockholm, Dalarne, Norrland und Aland, die Rapakiwis auf Aland und Finnland, die Porphyre zumeist auf Elfdalen und Dalarne sowie auf Aland und Småland, ein Phonolith (richtiger Aegyrin-Cancrinit-Syenit) auf Dalarne, ein Mandelstein auf Gefle, endlich viele Sandsteine und Konglomerate auf Småland und die Gegend des Kalmarsundes verweisen.

In der darauf folgenden **General-Versammlung** stattete der Rendant den Bericht über die Kasse ab, welcher von der Versammlung beifällig aufgenommen wurde. Sodann wurden folgende Herren als ordentliche Mitglieder einstimmig aufgenommen:

1. Herr Oberlehrer E. Huebner hierselbst,
2. „ Apothekergehülfe C. Lottermoser hierselbt,
3. „ Dr. Sommer, Arzt in Allenberg,
4. „ Oberlehrer E. Schulz hierselbst,
5. „ Oberlehrer Ohlert hierselbst.

Der Vorstand wurde einstimmig wiedergewählt, statt des verstorbenen Stadtrath Lottermoser der Observator an der hiesigen Sternwarte Dr. Franz zum Secretair.

Bericht für 1886

über die

Bibliothek der physikalisch-ökonomischen Gesellschaft

von

Dr. Otto Tischler.

Die Bibliothek befindet sich im Provinzial-Museum der Gesellschaft, Lange Reihe 4, 2 Treppen hoch. Bücher werden an die Mitglieder gegen vorschriftsmässige Empfangszettel Vormittags bis 12 und Nachmittags von 2 Uhr an ausgegeben. Dieselben müssen spätestens nach 3 Monaten zurückgeliefert werden.

Verzeichniss

derjenigen Gesellschaften, mit welchen die physikalisch-ökonomische Gesellschaft in Tauschverkehr steht, sowie der im Laufe des Jahres 1886 eingegangenen Werke.

(Von den mit † bezeichneten Gesellschaften kam uns 1886 keine Sendung zu.)

Die Zahl der mit uns in Tausch stehenden Gesellschaften hat 1886 um folgende 8 zugenommen:

Frankfurt a. O. Naturwissenschaftlicher Verein für den Regierungsbezirk Frankfurt a. O.
Wernigerode. Naturwissenschaftlicher Verein des Harzes.
London. Meteorological office.
Genua. R. Accademia medica.
Agram. Kroatischer Naturforscher-Verein.
Gratz. Zoologisches Institut der Carl-Franzens-Universität.
Wien. K. K. Naturhistorisches Hof-Museum.
Santiago. Deutscher naturwissenschaftlicher Verein.

Nachstehendes Verzeichniss bitten wir zugleich als Empfangsbescheinigung ansehen zu wollen statt jeder besonderen Anzeige. Besonders danken wir noch den Gesellschaften, welche auf Reclamation durch Nachsendung älterer Jahrgänge dazu beigetragen haben, Lücken in unserer Bibliothek auszufüllen. In gleicher Weise sind wir stets bereit, solchen Reclamationen nachzukommen, soweit es der Vorrath der früheren Bände gestattet, den wir immer zu ergänzen streben, so dass es von Zeit zu Zeit möglich wird, auch augenblicklich ganz vergriffene Hefte nachzuliefern.

Diejenigen Herren Mitglieder der Gesellschaft, welche derselben ältere Jahrgänge der Schriften zukommen lassen wollen, werden uns daher im Interesse des Schriftenttausches zu grossem Danke verpflichten.

Wir werden fortan allen Gesellschaften, mit denen wir in Correspondenz stehen, unsere Schriften franco durch die Post zusenden und bitten, soviel als möglich den gleichen Weg einschlagen zu wollen, da sich dies viel billiger herausstellt, als der Buchhändlerweg. Etwaige Beischlüsse bitten wir ergebenst, an die resp. Adresse gütigst befördern zu wollen.

Belgien.

† 1. Brüssel. Académie Royale des sciences des lettres et des arts.

2. Brüssel. Académie Royale de Médecine. 1) Bulletin, 3. Serie 20 (1886). 2) Mémoires couronnés et autres Mémoires in 8° VIII 1.

3. Brüssel. Société Entomologique de Belgique. Annales 29 2.

4. Brüssel. Société malacologique de Belgique. Procès-verbaux 1885 p. 80—144.

5. Brüssel. Société Royale de botanique. Bulletin 24 2. 25 1.

† 6. Brüssel. Commissions Royales d'art et d'archéologie.

7. Brüssel. Société Belge de Microscopie. Bulletin 12 2—11. 13 1.

8. Brüssel. Société Belge de Géographie. Bulletin 10 (1886).

† 9. Brüssel. Observatoire Royal.

† 10. Brüssel. Société d'Anthropologie.

11. Lüttich. Société Royale des sciences. Mémoires 2 Ser. 11.

12. Lüttich. Société géologique de Belgique. Annales 12 (1884—86).

† 13. Lüttich. Institut archéologique.

† 14. Namur. Société archéologique.

Dänemark.

15. Kopenhagen. Kongelig Dansk Videnskabernes Selskab (Société Royale des sciences). 1) Oversigt over Forhandlingerne. (Bulletin) 1885 3. — 1886 1. 2. 2) Skrifter (Mémoires), Naturvidenskabelig og matematisk Afdeling 6 Raekke II 8—11. III 2—4. IV 1. 2.

† 16. Kopenhagen. Naturhistorik Forening.

17. Kopenhagen. Kongelig Dansk Nordisk Oldskrift Selskab (Société Royale des antiquaires du Nord). 1) Aarböger for Nordisk Oldkyndigkhed og Historie 1885 4. Tillaeg. 1886 1. 2. 2) Mémoires, Nouvelle Série 1886.

18. Kopenhagen. Botanisk Forening (Société botanique). Botanisk Tidskrift (Journal de Botanique) 15.

Deutsches Reich.

† 19. Altenburg. Naturforschende Gesellschaft des Osterlandes.

20. Augsburg. Naturhistorischer Verein. Bericht 28 (1885).

† 21. Bamberg. Naturforschende Gesellschaft.

22. Bamberg. Historischer Verein für Oberfranken. Bericht 47.

23. Berlin. K. Preussische Akademie der Wissenschaften. 1) Sitzungsberichte 1885 40—52. 1886 1—34. 2) Abhandlungen. Physikalische 1885 und Anhang.

† 24. Berlin. Botanischer Verein für die Provinz Brandenburg.

25. Berlin. Deutsche Geologische Gesellschaft. Zeitschrift 37 4 38 1—3.

26. Berlin. Verein zur Beförderung des Gartenbaues in den Preussischen Staaten. Gartenzeitung, Jahrgang 5 (1886).

27. Berlin. Physikalische Gesellschaft. Fortschritte der Physik im Jahre 1879 (35) 1880 (36).

28. Berlin. K. Preussisches Landes-Oekonomie-Collegium. Landwirthschaftliche Jahrbücher XIV Suppl. 2. XV 1—6. Suppl. 1—3.

29. Berlin. Gesellschaft naturwissenschaftlicher Freunde. Sitzungsberichte 1885.

30. Berlin. Gesellschaft für Anthropologie, Ethnologie und Urgeschichte. Verhandlungen 1885—1886 Jan., Febr.

31. Berlin. Geologische Landesanstalt und Bergakademie. 1) Jahrbuch 1884. 2) Abhandlungen zur geologischen Specialkarte VI 3, VII 1. VIII 1. 3) Geologische Specialkarte von Preussen und den Thüringischen Staaten ($^1/_{25000}$), je 1 Blatt mit je 1 Heft Erläuterungen. Lieferung 23 (Grad 55 No. 39, 40, 45, 46.) 30 (Grad 70 No. 34—36, 40—42.) 31 (Grad 67 No. 41, 42, 47 und Grad 68 No. 43—48).

32. Berlin. Kaiserlich Statistisches Amt. 1) Statistisches Jahrbuch für das Deutsche Reich 7 (1886). 2) Monatshefte 1886. 3) Statistik des Deutschen Reiches. Neue Folge. 7 (Gewerbestatistik a. d. allg. Berufszählung 5/6 1882. (3. Abtheilung). 17 2. (St. d. Seeschiff. 1884 Abth. 2). 18 (Kriminalst. 1884). 19 (Ausw. Waarenverkehr 1885). 20 (Ausw. Waarenv. 1885 2—3.) 21 1—2 (St. d. Seeschiff. 1885).

33. Berlin. K. Preussisches Statistisches Bureau. Zeitschrift 25 (1885) 1. 26 1. 2.

34. Bonn. Naturhistorischer Verein der Preußischen Rheinlande und Westfalens. Verhandlungen 42 2. 43.

35. Bonn. Verein von Alterthumsfreunden im Rheinlande. Jahrbücher. Heft 78—81.

36. Braunsberg. Historischer Verein für Ermland. Zeitschrift für die Geschichte und Alterthumskunde des Ermlands VIII 2. 3.

† 37. Braunschweig. Verein für Naturwissenschaft.

38. Bremen. Naturwissenschaftlicher Verein. Abhandlungen IX 3.
† 39. Bremen. Geographische Gesellschaft. Deutsche geographische Blätter.
40. Breslau. Schlesische Gesellschaft für vaterländische Cultur. Jahresbericht 63.
41. Breslau. Verein für das Museum Schlesischer Alterthümer. Schlesiens Vorzeit in Schrift und Bild IV 16.
42. Breslau. Verein für Schlesische Insectenkunde. Zeitschrift für Entomologie. Neue Folge. Heft 11.
43. Breslau. K. Oberbergamt. Production der Bergwerke, Hütten und Salinen im Preussischen Staate im Jahre 1885.
† 44. Chemnitz. Naturwissenschaftliche Gesellschaft.
† 45. Chemnitz. K. Sächsisches meteorologisches Institut.
† 46. Coburg. Anthropologischer Verein.
† 47. Colmar. Société d'histoire naturelle.
48. Danzig. Naturforschende Gesellschaft. 1) Schriften. Neue Folge VI 3. 2) Conwentz: Die Flora des Bernsteins II.
49. Darmstadt. Verein für Erdkunde und mittelrheinisch geologischer Verein. Notizblatt. Vierte Folge. Heft 6.
50. Darmstadt. Historischer Verein für das Grossherzogthum Hessen. Quartalblätter 1885 3. 4. 1886.
† 51. Dessau. Naturhistorischer Verein.
† 52. Donaeschingen. Verein für Geschichte und Naturgeschichte der Baar und angrenzenden Landestheile.
† 53. Dresden. Verein für Frdkunde.
54. Dresden. Naturwissenschaftliche Gesellschaft Isis. Sitzungsberichte und Abhandlungen 1884 2, 1885, 1886. Jan. — Juni.
55. Dresden. Gesellschaft für Natur- und Heilkunde. Jahresbericht 1885/86.
† 56. Dürkheim a. d. H. Pollichia. Naturwissenschaftlicher Verein der Rheinpfalz.
57. Eberswalde. Forstakademie 1) Beobachtungergebnisse der forstlich meteorologischen Stationen Jahrgang XII 1–6. (1886). 2) Jahresbericht XI (1885).
† 58. Elberfeld. Naturwissenschaftliche Gesellschaft.
59. Emden. Naturforschende Gesellschaft. Jahresbericht 70 (1811—85).
† 60. Emden. Gesellschaft für bildende Kunst und vaterländische Alterthümer.
† 61. Erfurt. K. Akademie gemeinnütziger Wissenschaften.
† 62. Erlangen. Physikalisch-medicinische Societät.
63. Frankfurt a. M. Senckenbergische Gesellschaft. 1) Bericht 1885. 1886. 2) Abhandlungen 14 1–3. 3) Kobelt (Dr. W.) Reiseerinnerungen an Algier und Tunis (1885).
64. Frankfurt a. M. Physikalischer Verein. Jahresbericht 1884/85.
65. Frankfurt a. M. Verein für Geographie und Statistik. 1) Jahresbericht 48, 49 (1883/84, 1884/85). 2) Beiträge zur Statistik der Stadt Frankfurt a. M. IV. 4. 3) Mittheilungen über den Civilstand der Stadt Frankfurt 1885.
† 66. Frankfurt a. M. Verein für Geschichte und Alterthumskunde.
67. Frankfurt a. d. O. Naturwissenschaftlicher Verein für den Regierungsbezirk Frankfurt a. d. O. Monatliche Mittheilungen 3, 4 1–7.

† 68. **Freiburg** im Breisgau. Naturforschende Gesellschaft.

† 69. **Fulda.** Verein für Naturkunde.

70. **Gera.** Verein von Freunden der Naturwissenschaften.

71. **Giessen.** Oberhessische Gesellschaft für Natur- und Heilkunde. Bericht 24.

† 72. **Görlitz.** Naturforschende Gesellschaft.

73. **Görlitz.** Oberlausitzische Gesellschaft der Wissenschaften. Neues Lausitzisches Magazin 62 1.

74. **Göttingen.** K. Gesellschaft der Wissenschaften. Nachrichten 1885.

75. **Greifswald.** Naturwissenschaftl. Verein f. Neu-Vorpomm. u. Rügen. Mittheil. 17.

76. **Greifswald.** Geographische Gesellschaft. Excursion der Gesellschaft nach der Insel Bornholm 15.—18. Juni 1886.

† 77. **Güstrow.** Verein der Freunde der Naturgeschichte in Mecklenburg.

78. **Halle.** Kaiserlich Leopoldino-Carolinische Akademie der Naturforscher. 1) Leopoldina 22 (1866). 2) Nova Acta 47. 48.

† 78. **Halle.** Naturforschende Gesellschaft.

80. **Halle.** Naturwissenschaftlicher Verein für Sachsen und Thüringen. Zeitschrift für Naturwissenschaften. 4. Folge IV 5—6. V 1—3.

81. **Halle.** Verein für Erdkunde. 1885. 1886.

† 82. **Hamburg.** Naturwissenschaftlicher-Verein von Hamburg-Altona.

† 83. **Hamburg.** Verein für naturwissenschaftliche Unterhaltung.

84. **Hamburg.** Geographische Gesellschaft. Mittheilungen 1885—86.

85. **Hanau.** Wetterauische Gesellschaft für die gesammte Naturkunde. Bericht. 1/1 1863—31/3 1885.

† 86. **Hannover.** Naturhistorische Gesellschaft.

87. **Hannover.** Historischer Verein für Niedersachsen. 1) Zeitschrift 1885—86. 2) Leibnitzens Entwürfe zu seinen Annalen von 1691 und 1692 herausgegeben von Eduard Bodemann. Festschrift zur 50jährigen Jubelfeier des Vereins.

† 88. **Hannover.** Geographische Gesellschaft.

† 89. **Hannover.** Gesellschaft für Mikroskopie.

90. **Heidelberg.** Naturhistorisch-medicinischer Verein. 1) Verhandlungen. Neue Folge VII 5. 2) Festschrift zur Feier des 500jährigen Bestehens der Ruperto-Carola 1886.

91. **Jena.** Gesellschaft für Medicin und Naturwissenschaft. Jenaische Zeitschrift für Naturwissenschaften. 19.

92. **Insterburg.** Alterthumsgesellschaft. 1) Jahresbericht 1885/86. 2) Sonne: Mittheilungen über die Baugeschichte und Wiederherstellung der Marienburg, Vortrag am 19/2. 1886. 3) Rogge: Der Preussische Litauer des 16. und 17. Jahrhunderts, Vortrag am 20/11. und 28/12. 1885.

93. **Insterburg.** Landwirthschaftlicher Centralverein für Littauen und Masuren. Georgine, landwirthschaftliche Zeitschrift. Jahrgang 54 (1886).

† 94. **Karlsruhe.** Naturwissenschaftlicher Verein.

† 95. **Karlsruhe.** Grossherzogliches Alterthums-Museum.

96. **Kassel.** Verein für Naturkunde. 1) Festschrift der Feier seines 50jährigen Bestehens 1886. 2) Bericht 32. 33.

97. Kassel. Verein für Hessische Geschichte und Landeskunde. 1) Zeitschrift. Neue Folge. 9, Supplement. H. 2) Mittheilungen 1884—85.
98. Kiel. Universität. 38 Universitätsschriften (1884/85. 86 Universitätsschriften (1885/86).
99. Kiel. Naturwissenschaftlicher Verein für Schleswig-Holstein. Schriften VI 2.
† 100. Kiel. Schleswig-holsteinisches Museum für vaterländische Alterthümer.
101. Kiel. Ministerial-Commission zur Erforschung der deutschen Meere. Ergebnisse der Beobachtungsstationen an den deutschen Küsten über die physikalischen Eigenschaften der Ostsee und Nordsee und die Fischerei 1885.
† 102. Klausthal. Naturwissenschaftlicher Verein Maja.
103. Königsberg. Altpreussische Monatsschrift, herausgegeben von Reicke und Wichert. 23 (1886).
104. Königsberg. Ostpreussischer landwirthschaftlicher Centralverein. Königsberger land- und forstwirthschaftliche Zeitung. 22 (1886).
105. Landshut. Botanischer Verein. Bericht 9 (1881—85).
106. Leipzig. K. Sächsische Gesellschaft der Wissenschaften. 1) Bericht über die Verhandlungen der mathematisch-physikalischen Klasse. 1886. 1) Abhandlungen der mathematisch-physikalischen Klasse XIII 6. 7.
107. Leipzig. Verein für Erdkunde. Mittheilungen 1885.
108. Leipzig. Naturforschende Gesellschaft. Sitzungsberichte 1885.
109. Leipzig. Museum für Völkerkunde. Bericht 1885.
110. Leipzig. Geologische Landesuntersuchung des Königreichs Sachsen. Geologische Specialkarte des Königreichs Sachsen $^{1}/_{25000}$ mit je 1 Blatt Erläuterungen. Blatt 13, 30, 31, 41, 98, 99, 116, 117, 124, 134, 135, 144, 146, 151, 152, 155.
111. Lübben. Nieder-Lausitzer Gesellschaft für Anthropologie und Urgeschichte. Mittheilungen Heft 2.
† 112. Lübeck. Naturhistorisches Museum.
† 113. Lüneburg. Naturwissenschaftlicher Verein für das Fürstenthum Lüneburg.
114. Magdeburg. Naturwissenschaftlicher Verein. Jahresbericht 1885.
† 115. Mannheim. Verein für Naturkunde.
116. Marburg. Gesellschaft zur Beförderung der gesammten Naturwissenschaften. 1) Sitzungsberichte 1885. 2) Schriften 12 1.
† 117. Marienwerder. Historischer Verein für den Regierungsbezirk Marienwerder.
† 118. Meiningen. Hennebergischer alterthumsforschender Verein.
119. Metz. Académie. Mémoires 2. Periode. Année 43. 44. (1881—83).
120. Metz. Société d'histoire naturelle.
121. Metz. Verein für Erdkunde. Jahresbericht 8 (1885).
122. München. K. Baierische Akademie der Wissenschaften. Sitzungsberichte der mathematisch-physikalischen Klasse 1885 4. 1886 1. Inhaltsverzeichniss 1871—85.
123. München. Geographische Gesellschaft. Jahresbericht 1885. (Ganze Reihe 10).
124. München. Historischer Verein von Oberbayern. Oberbayrisches Archiv für vaterländische Geschichte 43.
† 125. Münster. Westphälischer Provinzialverein für Wissenschaft und Kunst.
† 126. Neisse. Philomathie.

127. Nürnberg. Naturhistorische Gesellschaft. Jahresbericht 1885 nebst Abhandlungen VIII Bogen 3.
† 128. Nürnberg. Germanisches Museum.
† 129. Offenbach. Verein für Naturkunde.
† 130. Oldenburg. Oldenburger Landesverein für Alterthumskunde.
† 131. Osnabrück. Naturwissenschaftlicher Verein.
132. Passau. Naturhistorischer Verein. Bericht 13 (1883—85).
† 133. Posen. Gesellschaft der Freunde der Wissenschaften.
134. Regensburg. Zoologisch-mineralogischer Verein. Correspondenzblatt 39.
135. Regensburg. K. Baierische botanische Gesellschaft. Flora (allgemeine botanische Zeitung). Neue Reihe 43 (1885).
† 136. Reichenbach im Vogtlande. Vogtländischer Verein für allgemeine und specielle Naturkunde.
137. Schmalkalden. Verein für Hennebergische Geschichte und Landeskunde. Zeitschrift. Supplementheft 3.
138. Schwerin. Verein für Mecklenburgische Geschichte und Alterthumskunde. Jahrbücher und Jahresberichte 51.
' 139. Sondershausen. Irmischia. Botanischer Verein für Thüringen. Irmischia, Correspondenzblatt des Vereins 6 (1886) 1. 1—4.
† 140. Stettin. Entomologischer Verein.
141. Stettin. Gesellschaft für Pommersche Geschichte und Alterthumskunde. Baltische Studien 36.
142. Strassburg. Commission für die geologische Landesuntersuchung von Elsass-Lothringen. Mittheilungen I.
143. Stuttgart. Verein für vaterländische Naturkunde in Würtemberg. Jahreshefte 42.
144. Stuttgart. Königlich Statistisches Landesamt. Würtembergische Vierteljahrshefte für Landesgeschichte 8 (1885).
† 145. Thorn. Towarzystwa Naukowego. (Wissenschaftliche Gesellschaft).
146. Tilsit. Litauische literarische Gesellschaft. 1) Mittheilungen II 5. (oder Heft 11). 2) Bartsch: Dainu Balsai, Melodien litauischer Volkslieder. Lieferung 2.
† 147. Trier. Gesellschaft für nützliche Forschungen.
148. Wernigerode. Naturwissenschaftlicher Verein des Harzes. Schriften 1 (1886).
149. Wiesbaden. Nassauischer Verein für Naturkunde. Jahrbücher 38, 39.
150. Wiesbaden. Verein für Nassauische Alterthumskunde und Geschichtsforschung. Annalen 19 (1885/86).
† 151. Worms. Alterthumsverein.
152. Würzburg. Physikalisch-medicinische Gesellschaft. 1) Sitzungsberichte 1885. 2) Verhandlungen. Neue Folge 19.
153. Zwickau. Verein für Naturkunde. Jahresbericht 1885.

Frankreich.

† 154. Albeville. Société d'Emulation.
155. Amiens. Société Linnénne du Nord de la France. Bulletin mensuel VI 123—138.

†156. Apt. Société litéraire scientifique et artistique.
157. Auxerre. Société des sciences historiques et naturelles de l'Yonne. Bulletin 39 (1885).
158. Besançon. Société d'Emulation du Doubs. Mémoires 5. Serie 7—9.
159. Bordeaux. Académie des sciences belles lettres et des arts. Actes. 3. Ser. 44—46.
160. Bordeaux. Société Linnéenne. Actes 38.
161. Bordeaux. Société des sciences physiques et naturelles. Mémoires 3. Ser. II.
162. Bordeaux. Société de géographie commerciale. Bulletin 2. Ser. 9 (1886).
†163. Caën. Société Linnénne de Normandie.
†164. Caën. Académie des sciences arts et belles lettres.
†165. Caën. Association Normande.
166. Chambéry. Académie de Savoie. Mémoires 3. Ser. 11. 12.
†167. Cherbourg. Société nationale des sciences naturelles et mathématiques.
168. Dijon. Académie des sciences arts et belles lettres. Mémoires 3. Ser. 8.
†169. Dijon. Société d'agriculture et d'industrie agricole du département de la Côte d'or.
170. La Rochelle. Société des sciences naturelles de la Charente inférieure. Annales 21 (1884).
†171. Lille. Société des sciences de l'agriculture et des arts.
†172. Lyon. Académie des sciences des belles lettres et des arts.
†173. Lyon. Société Linnéenne.
†174. Lyon. Société d'agriculture d'histoire naturelles et des arts utiles.
†175. Lyon. Muséum d'histoire naturelle.
†176. Lyon. Association des amis des sciences naturelles.
†177. Lyon. Société d'Anthropologie.
178. Montpellier. Académie des sciences et lettres. Mémoires de la section des sciences 10 3.
179. Nancy. Académie de Stanislas. Mémoires 5 Ser. 2 (135 Année).
†180. Paris. Académie des sciences.
181. Paris. Société centrale d'horticulture. Journal 3 Ser. 8 (1886).
†182. Paris. Société zoologique d'acclimatation.
†183. Paris. Société de botanique de France.
184. Paris. Société philomatique. Bulletin. 1. Ser. IX 4. X 1—3.
185. Paris. Société de Géographie. 1) Bulletin 1886. 2) Compte rendu des sciences de la Commission centrale 1886. 3) Catalogue des portraits de voyageurs qui se trouvent dans les albums de la Soc. de Géogr. 22/11 1885.
186. Paris. Société d'Anthropologie. Bulletin. 3. Serie VIII 4. (1885). IX. 1—3. (1886).
†187. Paris. Ministère de l'Instruction publique.
188. Paris. Ecole polytechnique. 1) Journal, cahier 55. 2) Catalogue de la bibliothèque 1881.
†189. Rochefort. Société d'agriculture des belles lettres et des arts.
190. Semur. Société des sciences historiques et naturelles. Bulletin. 2. Ser. I. (1884).

191. Toulouse. Académie des sciences inscriptions et belles lettres. Mémoires 8. Ser. 7.

† 192. Toulouse. Société archéologique du midi de la France.

Grossbritannien.

193. Cambridge. Philosophical Society Proceedings V 5.

† 194. Dublin. Royal Irish Academy.

195. Dublin. Royal geological Society of Ireland. Journal: Vol. 16 3. 17 1.

196. Dublin. Royal Dublin Society. 1) Scientific transactions. 2. Ser. III 7–9. 2) Scientific Proceedings New Ser. IV 7–9. V 1. 2.

197. Edinburgh. Botanical Society. Transactions and Proceedings 16 2.

† 198. Edinburgh. Geological Society.

199. Glasgow. Natural history Society. 1) Proceedings and transactions, New Ser. I 2. 2) Index to the proceedings I—V (1881—83).

200. Liverpool. Literary and philosophical society. Proceedings 38 (1883—84).

201. London. Royal society. 1) Proceedings 49 240–41. 50. 51 244–47. 2) Philosophical transactions 176. 3) List of members 30./11. 1885. 4) List of duplicate periodicals in the library of the R. S. for exchange.

202. London. Henry Woodward. Geological Magazine. 2. Ser. Decade III. Vol. IV (1886).

203. London. Linnean society. 1) Journal of zoology 109–113. 2) Journal of botany 21 138–140. 22 141–144. 23 150. 3) List of Members 1884/1886 November.

† 204. London. Nature.

205. London. Anthropological Institute of Great Britain and Ireland. Journal XV 3–4. XVI 1. 2.

206. London. Chamber of Commerce. Journal V 47–58.

207. London. Meteorological office: Observations of the international polar expedition 1882/83. Fort Rae.

208. Manchester. Philosophical society. 1) Proceedings 23. 24. 2) Memoirs 3 Ser. 8.

Holland.

209. Amsterdam. Koninglijke Akademie van Wetenschapen. 1) Verslagen en Mededeelingen. Afd. Natuurk. 3 Reeks I. 2) Verhandelingen, Afdeeling Natuurkunde 24. 3) Jaarboek 1884.

210. Amsterdam. Koninglijk Zoologisk Genootschap „Natura artis magistra“. Bijdragen tot de Dierkunde. Alflevering 12.

211. s'Gravenhaag. Nederlandsch entomologische Vereeniging. Tijdschrift voor Entomologie 28 3. 4. 29 1. 3.

212. Groningen. Genootschap ter Bevordering der naturkundigen Wetenschapen. Verslag over het jaar 1885.

213. Haarlem. Hollandsche Maatschappij ter Bevordering der natuurkundigen Wetenschapen (Société Hollandaise des sciences). 1) Archives Neérlandaises des sciences exactes et naturelles 20 4. 5. 21 1. 2) Liste alphabétique de la correspondance de Christian Huyghens, qui sera publiée par la Soc. Holl.

214. Haarlem. Hollandsche Maatschappij ter Bevordering van Nijverheid. Tijdschrift 4 Reeks 10 (1886).

215. Haarlem. Musée Teyler. 1) Archives 2 Ser. II 3. 4. 2) Catalogue de la bibliothèque 1–4.

† 216. Leyden. Herbier Royal.

217. Leyden. Nederlandsche dierkundige Vereeniging Tijdschrift 2 Ser. I 2.

† 218. Luxembourg. Institut Royal Grandducal.

219. Luxembourg. Section historique de l'Institut Royal Grandducal. Publications 37. 38.

220. Luxembourg. Société de botanique. Recueil de mé moires et travaux 11.

221. Nijmmegen. Neederlandsche botanische Vereeniging. Nederlandsch Kruidkundig Archief. 2. Ser. IV 4.

222. Utrecht. Physiologisch Laboratorium der Utrechtsche Hoogeschool. Onderzoekingen gedaan in het Laboratorium. 3 Reeks X 1.

† 223. Utrecht. Kon. Nederlandsch Meteorologisch Institut.

Italien.

† 224. Bologna. Accademia della scienze.

225. Catania Accademia Gioenia di scienze naturali. Atti Ser. 3. Tom. 19.

226. Florenz. Accademia economico-agraria dei Georgolfi. Atti 4. Ser. 8 4. 9 1–3.

227. Florenz. T. Caruel: Nuovo giornale botanico Italiano. 18 (1886).

228. Florenz. Società Italiana di antropologia etnologia e psicologia comparata 15. 16 1. 2.

229. Florenz. Sezione fiorentina della società Africana d'Italia. Bulletino I 3–6. II 1–10.

† 230. Genua. Giacomo Doria. Museo civico.

231. Genua. R. Accademia medica. Bolletino II 1 (1886).

232. Mailand. Reale Instituto Lombardo. 1) Rendiconti 2. Serie (1886). 2) Memorie, classe di scienze matematiche e naturali 15 4. 16 1.

233. Mailand. Società Italiana di scienze naturali. Atti 27 2. 28.

234. Modena. Società dei naturalisti. 1) Memorie 3. Ser. 4. 2) Atti 3. Ser. II.

235. Neapel. Accademia delle scienze fisiche e matematiche. Rendiconti 22—24 (1883—85).

236. Neapel. Deutsche zoologische Station. Mittheilungen VI 4.

237. Neapel. Società Africana d'Italia, Bolletino V 1–8. (1886).

238. Padua. Società Veneto-Trentina. 1) Atti 9 2. 10 3. 2) Bolletino III 4.

239. Palermo. Reale Accademia di scienze lettere e belle arti. Bolletino II (1885). III 1–3.

240. Parma. Bulletino di paletnologia Italiana (diretto da Pelegrino Strobel) 11 (2. Ser. 1, 1886). 12 (1887) 1–10.

241. Pisa. Società Toscana di Scienze naturali. 1) Memorie 7 2. Atti 5 p. 1—128.
242. Rom. Reale Accademia dei Lincei. 1) Rendiconti I 28. II 1—14, 2. Semestre 1. 2) Memorie della classe di scienze fisiche matematiche e naturali. 3. Ser. 15—19 1. 4. Ser. 1.
† 243. Rom. Società geografica Italiana.
244. Rom. Comitato geologico d'Italia. Bolletino 16 (1885) 11. 12. 51 1—8.
† 245. Sassari. Circolo di scienze mediche e naturali.
246. Turin. R. Accademia delle scienze. 1) Atti 1—7. 2) Bolletino dell' Observatorio della regia Università 20 (1885).
† 247. Venedig, Istituto Veneto di scienze lettere ed arti.
† 248. Verona. Accademia di agricoltura commercio ed arti.

Oesterreich-Ungarn.

249. Agram (Zagreb.) Kroatischer Naturforscherverein. Glasnik hratskoga naravoslovnoga družtva (Organ des Kr. Nat.-V.) I 1—3.
† 250. Aussig. Naturwissenschaftlicher Verein.
251. Bistritz. Gewerbeschule. Jahresbericht 12.
252. Bregerz. Vorarlberger Museumsverein. Jahresbericht 24 (1885).
253. Brünn. K. K. Mährisch-Schlesische Gesellschaft zur Beförderung des Ackerbaues, der Natur- und Landeskunde. Mittheilungen. 65 (1884). 1.
254. Brünn. Naturforschender Verein. 1) Verhandlungen 23 (1884). 2) Bericht der meteorologischen Commission 1883.
255. Budapest. K. Ungarische Akademie der Wissenschaften. 1) Ungarische Revue 1886 1—9. 2) Mathematische und naturwissenschaftliche Berichte aus Ungarn 3.
256. Budapest. K. Ungarisches National-Museum. Természetrajyzi füzetek (Naturhistorische Hefte. Ungarisch mit Deutscher Revue IX 3. 4. X 1. 3.
257. Budapest. K. Ungarisches National-Museum. Archäologische Abtheilung. Archälogiai Értesitöö (Archäologischer Anzeiger. Neue Folge Uj folgam) V 4. 5. VI 1—4.
258. Budapest. Ungarische geologische Anstalt. 1) Mittheilungen aus dem Jahrbuche VII 5. VIII 1—3. a. Recl. VI 1. 2) Jahresbericht 1884. 3) Die K. Ungarische geologische Anstalt und deren Ausstellungs-Objecte zu der 1885 in Budapest abgehaltenen allgemeinen Ausstellung, zusammengestellt von Johann Böckh (Deutsch und (Ungarisch). 4) Specialkatalog der VI. Gruppe für Bergbau, Hüttenwesen und Geologie (Allg. Landesausstellung zu Budapest 1885). 5) Vorträge, gelegentlich des montanistischen, hüttenmännischen und geologischen Congresses zu Budapest 1885:

v. Kerpely: Die Eisenindustrie Ungarns z. Z. der Landessausstellung 1885.
Noth: Ueber die bisher erzielten Resultate und die Aussichten von Petroleumschürfungen in Ungarn.
Obach: Ueber Drahtseilbahnen.
Pálfy: Der Goldbergbau Siebenbürgens.
v. Soltz: Theorie und Beschreibung des Farbaky- und Soltzschen continuirlich wirkenden Wassergasofens.

Szabo: Geschichte der Geologie von Schemmitz.
Szüts: Kleinere Details über die nasse Aufbereitung.

259. Budapest. Magyar földtani társulat (Ungarische geologische Gesellschaft). Földtani közlöny (Geologische Mittheilungen) 15 11. 12. 16 1–9.

260. Budapest. Magyar természettudomanyi társulat (Ungarische naturwissenschaftliche Gesellschaft).
1) B. v. Inkey: Nagyág und seine Erz-Lagerstätten (Ungarisch und Deutsch) 1885.
Hegyfoky: Die meteorologischen Verhältnisse des Monats Mai in Ungarn (Ungarisch und Deutsch) 1886.
Hazlinski: A. Magyar birodalom mohflórája (Flora der Ungarischen Moose) Ungarisch.
Lázló: Chemische und mechanische Analyse Ungarischer Thone (Ungarisch und Deutsch).
Hermann: Urgeschichtliche Spuren in den Geräthen der Ungarischen volksthümlichen Fischerei (Die Ungarischen Curorte und Mineralwässer) Ungarische Landesanstalt 1885 Gruppe 1885.
Budai: Die secundären Eruptivgesteine des Persányer Gebirges (Ungarisch und Deutsch).
Chyser: Magyarország gyógy helejei eś ásványvézei.
2) Catalogus bibliothecae Regiae Societatis Ungaricae scientiarum naturalium fasc. H.

261. Gratz: Naturwissenschaftlicher Verein für Steiermark. Mittheilungen 21 (1884). 22 (1885).

262. Gratz: Zoologisches Institut der K. K. Carl-Franzens-Universität. Arbeiten I 1–4.

† 263. Hermannstadt: Siebenbürgischer Verein für Naturwissenschaften.

264. Hermannstadt. Verein für Siebenbürgische Landeskunde. 1) Archiv 20 2. 3. 2) Jahresbericht 1884/85.

† 265. Innsbruck. Ferdinandeum.

266. Innsbruck. Naturwissenschaftlich-medicinischer Verein. Bericht 15 (1884—86).

267. Késmark. Ungarischer Karpathenverein. Jahrbuch 13 (1886).

† 268. Klagenfurt. Naturhistorisches Landes-Museum für Kärnthen.

† 269. Klausenburg. Siebenbürgischer Museumsverein.

270. Klausenburg. Magyar növétani lapok (Ungarische botanische Blätter) herausgegeben von August Kanitz 9 (1885).

271. Krakau. K. Akademie der Wissenschaften. 1) Pamietnik (Denkschriften 10. 11. 2) Zbiór wiadomości do Antropologii Krajowéj (Sammlung von anthropologischen Berichten) 9.

† 272. Linz. Museum Francisco-Carolinum.

273. Linz. Verein für Naturkunde in Oesterreich ob der Enns. 1885.

274. Prag. K. Böhmische Gesellschaft der Wissenschaften. 1) Abhandlungen. 6. Folge 12. 2) Sitzungsberichte 1882—84. 3) Jahresbericht 1882—85.
3) Kalousek: Geschichte der Gesellschaft der Wissenschaften. Heft 1. 2 sammt einer kritischen Uebersicht ihrer Publicationen aus dem Gebiete der Philosophie, Geschichte und Philologie.

Studnička: Bericht über die mathematischen und naturwissenschaftlichen Publicationen der Gesellschaft der Wissenschaften während ihres 100jährigen Bestehens.

Wegner: Generalregister zu den Schriften 1784—1884. Verzeichniss der Mitglieder 1784—1884.

† 275. Prag. Naturhistorischer Verein Lotos.

276. Prag. Museum des Königreichs Böhmen. 1) Památky archaeologické a místopisné (Archaeologische Denkmäler). XIII 1—5. 2) Geschäftsbericht in der Generalversammlung 17. 1. 1886.

† 277. Pressburg. Verein für Natur- und Heilkunde.

† 278. Reichenberg in Böhmen. Verein der Naturfreunde.

† 279. Salzburg. Gesellschaft für Landeskunde.

† 280. Trentschin. Naturwissenschaftlicher Verein des Trentschiner Comitats.

281. Triest. Società adriatica di scienze naturali. Bolletino IX 1. 2.

† 282. Triest. Museo civico di storia naturale.

283. Wien. K. K. Akademie der Wissenschaften. Sitzungsberichte: 1. Abtheilung (Min., Botan., Zoolog., Paleont.) 90—93 1—3. 2. Abtheilung (Math., Phys., Chem., Mech., Met., Astr.) 90—92. 93 1. 2. 3. Abtheilung (Medicin) 89 3—5. 90—92. 4. Register zu den Bänden 86—90.

284. Wien. Geologische Reichsanstalt. 1) Jahrbuch 35 (1885) 4. 36 (1886) 1—3. 2) Verhandlungen 1886 1—12. 3) Abhandlungen XII 1—3.

285. Wien. Geographische Gesellschaft. Mittheilungen 28 (1885).

286. Wien. Zoologisch-botanische Gesellschaft. Verhandlungen 35 2 (1885). 36 (1886).

287. Wien. Anthropologische Gesellschaft. Mittheilungen 15 2. 3. 16 1.

288. Wien. Verein zur Verbreitung naturwissenschaftlicher Kenntnisse. Mittheilungen 26.

289. Wien. Oesterreichische Centralanstalt für Meteorologie und Erdmagnetismus. Jahrbücher Neue Folge 21 (1884).

290. Wien. Verein für Landeskunde von Niederösterreich. X Blätter Neue Folge 19.

291. Wien. K. K. Naturhistorisches Hof-Museum. Annalen I 1—4.

Portugal.

† 292. Lissabon. Academia real das Sciencias.

† 293. Lissabon. Seção das trabalhos geologicos de Portugal.

Russland.

294. Dorpat. Gelehrte esthnische Gesellschaft. Sitzungsberichte 1885.

295. Dorpat. Naturforschende Gesellschaft. 1) Sitzungsberichte VII 2 (1885).

296. Helsingfors. Finska Vetenskaps Societet (Societas scientiarium fennica). 1) Oefversigt af Förhandlingar 27 (1884—85). 2) Bidrag till kännedom af Finlands Natur och Folk 43. 3) Exploration Internationale des régions polacres 1882—83 et 1884—85: Expédition polacre finlandaise (publié au frais du gouvernement Finlandais sous les auspices de la société des sciences de Finlande).

297. Helsingfors. Societas pro fauna et flora fennica. 1) Meddelanden. 12. 13. 2) Acta II (1881—85). 3) Kihlmann: Beobachtungen über die periodischen Erscheinungen des Pflanzenlebens in Finnland 1883.

† 298. Helsingfors. Finlands geologiska Undersökning.

† 299. Helsingfors. Finska fornminnesföreningen (Suomen Muinaismuisto).

300. Mitau. Kurländische Gesellschaft für Literatur und Kunst. Sitzungsberichte 1884. 1885.

301. Moskau. Société impériale des naturalistes 1884 3, 4. 1885. 1886 1—3.

302. Moskau. Musées public et Roumiantzow. 1) Numismatisches Cabinet. Katalog der Münzen 2, 3. (Russisch). 2. Otschet (Jahresbericht) 1879—85.

303. Odessa. Société des naturalistes de la nouvelle Russie. 1) Sapiski (Denkschriften X 2 und Beilage (Wilhelm: Die fossilen Vogelknochen der Odessaer Steppen-Kalk-Steinbrüche 1886). 2) Sapiski matematitschkago otdelenija. (Denkschriften der matematischen Section) 1—6.

304. Petersburg. Kaiserliche Akademie der Wissenschaften. 1) Bulletin 30 3, 4. 31 1, 2, 3. 2) Mémoires 33 2—8. 34 1—6.

305. Petersburg. Observatoire physique central. 1) Repertorium für Meteorologie IX. 2) Annalen 1884.

306. Petersburg. Societas entomologica Rossica. Horae (Trudy) 19 (1885).

307. Petersburg. K. Russische Geographische Gesellschaft. 1) Iswestija (Bulletin) 22 (1886). 2) Otschet (Compte-Renda. 1886).

308. Petersburg. K. Botanischer Garten. 1) Acta horti petropolitanis (Trudy) IX 2. 2) Catalogus systematicus bibliothecae 1886.

309. Petersburg. Comité géologique. 1) Mémoires (Trudy) I 4. II 2. (carte géologique générale de la Russie, feuille 93). II 3. III 1. III 2. (carte géologique feuille 139). 2) Iswestija (Bulletin) 4 (1885) 4—10. 5 (1886) 1—8. 3) Karpinski. Geologische Karte des Ostabhang des Urals. 3 Blatt. 4) Manikow. Geologische Erforschung der Phosphorite am Dnjestr. 5) Bibliothéque géologique de la Russie I (1885).

310. Riga. Naturforschender Verein. Correspondenzblatt 29.

Schweden und Norwegen.

† 311. Bergen. Museum.

312. Drontheim. K. Norsk. Videnskabernes Selskab. Skrifter 1882.

† 313. Gothenburg. Vetenskaps och Vitterhets Samhället.

314. Kristiania. K. Norsk Universitet. Nyt Magazin for Naturvidenskaberne 28 3—11. 29, 30. 1.

† 315. Kristiania. Videnskabernes Selskab.

316. Kristiania. Forening til Norske fortids mindesmerkers bevaring. 1) Aarsberetning 1884. 2) Kunst och Handverk fra Norges Fortid 5. 3) Gols gamle Stavekirke och Hovestunen paa Bygdö Kongsgaard (1885).

317. Kristiania. Geologische Landesuntersuchung von Norwegen.

318. Kristiania. Den Norske Nordhavs-Expedition 1876—78 (herausgegeben von der Norwegischen Regierung) XV (Zoology, Crustacea II ved Sars), XVI. (Zoology, Mollusca II ved Friele).

319. Lund. Universität. Acta Universitatis. Lundensis. 1) 21 (Mathematik och Naturvetenskap). 2) Universitäts-Accessions-Katalog 1885).
320. Stockholm. K. Vetenskaps Akademie. Oefversigt af Förhandlingar 42 (1885) 6—10. 43 (1886) 1—8.
321. Stockholm. K. Vitterhets historie och antiquitets Akademie. 1) Antiquarisk Tidskriaft VIII 1—2. 2) Månadsblad 1885.
322. Stockholm. Entomologisk Förening. Entomologisk Tidskrift 5 4. 6 1—3.
223. Stockholm. Bohusläns Hushållnings-Sällskap. Bidrag till kännedom om Göteborg och Bohnslänsd fornminnen och historie 11, 12.
324. Stockholm. Geologiskh Förening. Förhandlingar VII 14. VIII 1—6.
† 325. Stockholm. Sveriges geologisk Undersökning.
† 326. Stockholm. Nautisk meteorologisk byrå.
327. Tromsö. Museum. 1) Aarshefter 9. 2) Aarsberetning 1885.
328. Upsala. Société Royale des sciences (Societas scientiarum). 1) Nova Acta 3. Ser. XIII. 2) Bulletin mensuel de l'Observatoire météorologique de l'Université 17 (1885).

Schweiz.

329. Basel. Naturforschende Gesellschaft. Verhandlungen VIII. 1.
330. Bern. Naturforschende Gesellschaft. Mittheilungen 1885 3. .
331. Bern. Allgemeine Schweizerische Gesellschaft für die gesammten Naturwissenschaften. 1) Verhandlungen der 68. Jahresversammlung zu Locle 11—13. Aug. 1885 (Actes). 2) Compte Rendu des travaux présentés à la 68. Session.
332. Bern. Geologische Commission der schweizerischen naturforschenden Gesellschaft. Beiträge zur geologischen Karte der Schweiz. Lieferung 24 (Centralgebiet der Schweiz, Blatt 13) mit Atlas.
333. Bern. Universität. 81 akademische Schriften.
† 334. Chur. Naturforschende Gesellschaft Graubündtens.
335. Frauenfeld. Thurgauische naturforschende Gesellschaft. Mittheilungen, Heft 7.
† 336. Genf. Société de physique et d'histoire naturelle.
337. Genf. Sociéte de géographie. Le Globe, Journal géographique 4, Ser. V. Bulletin 1, 2.
338. Lausanne. Société Vandoise des sciences naturelles. Bulletin 3 Ser. 21 93. 22 44.
339. Neuchâtel. Société des sciences naturelles.
340. Schaffhausen. Schweizer entomologische Gesellschaft. Mittheilungen VII. 5, 6.
341. St. Gallen. Naturwissenschaftliche Gesellschaft. Bericht 1883—84.
† 342. Zürich. Naturforschende Gesellschaft.
343. Zürich. Antiquarische Gesellschaft. 1) Anzeiger für Schweizerische Alterthumskunde 1885. 2) Mittheilungen XXII 1. (Heierli: Der Pfahlbau Wallisbofen).

Spanien.

† 344. Madrid. Academia de ciencias.

Asien.

Britisch Indien.

345. Calcutta. Asiatic Society of Bengal. 1) Journal Part. I, Vol. 54. 55. 1, 2. Part. II. Vol. 54. 55. 1, 2. 2) Proceedings 1885 9, 10. 1886 1—6.

346. Calcutta. Geological survey of India. 1) Records 18 4. 19. 2) Memoirs in 8° 21. 3) Memoirs in 4° (Palaeontologia Indica). Ser. IV. Vol. I. 4, 5. (Indian pretertiary Vertebrata). Ser. X. Vol. II. 6. III. 1—6. IV. 1 Suppl., 2. (Indian Tertiary and posttertiary Vertebrata). Ser. XIII. Vol. I. 4. fasc. 5. (Salt Range Fossils). Ser. XIV. I. 3 fasc. 6. (Tertiary and upper Cretaceous fossils).

Niederländisch Indien.

347. Batavia. Kon. Naturkundige Vereenigung in Nederlandsch Indie. Naturkundig Tijdschrift voor Nederlandsch Indie 45.

† 348. Batavia. Bataviaasch Genootschap der Kunsten en Wetenschapen.

349. Batavia. Magnetisch en meteorologisch Observatorium.

China.

350. Shanghai. China branch of the Royal Asiatic Society. Journal. New Ser. 20 4—6. 21 1—2.

Japan.

351. Tokio. Deutsche Gesellschaft für Natur- und Völkerkunde Ost-Asiens. Mittheilungen IV. 34.

† 352. Tokio. Seismological Society of Japan.

Afrika.

Französische Colonieen.

353. Algier. Société algérienne de climatologie des sciences physiques et naturelles. Bulletin 22 (1883).

Amerika.

Britisch Nordamerika.

354. Montreal. Royal society of Canada. Proceedings and Transactions. II. (1884).

355. Montreal. Geological and natural history survey of Canada. 1) Rapport des Opérations 1882—84 avec Mappes. 2) Catalogue of Canadian plants II. 3) Geologische Karten: a) Province of Nova Scotia. Masst. $\frac{1}{63,300}$ zu den Berichten von Aug. Fletcher 1879—84. Blatt 1—21. b) Masst. $\frac{1}{253440}$ zu den Berichten von R. W. Ellis. 40 Blatt.

356. Ottava. Field naturalist's club. Transactions II, 2.
357. Toronto. Canadian Institute. Proceedings. 3. Ser. Vol. III. 3, 4. IV. 1.

Vereinigte Staaten.

† 358. Albany. N. N. Albany Institute.
359. Boston. American Academy of Arts and Sciences. Proceedings 21. 1, 2.
360. Boston. Society of natural history. 1) Proceedings 22 4. 23 1. 2) Memoirs III. 11.
361. Cambridge. Museum of comparative Zoology at Harvard College. 1) Bulletin XII. 3–6. XIII. 1. 2) Memoirs X. 2. 3) Annual report 1885—86.
† 362. Cambridge. Peabody Museum of american Archaeology.
† 363. Chicago. Academy of science.
† 364. Davenport (Jowa). Academy of natural sciences.
365. Jowa-City. Professor Gustavus Hinrichs Report of the Jowa Weather-Service Jan. — August 1883.
† 366. Madison. Wisconsin Academy of arts and lettres.
† 367. Mitwaukee. Naturhistorischer Verein von Wisconsin.
† 368. New-Haven. Connectient Academy of arts and sciences.
369. New-York. Academy of sciences. 1) Annals III. 7–10. 2) Transactions III. V. 2–6.
370. Philadelphia. Academy of natural sciences. Proceedings 1885 1–3. 1886 1.
371. Philadelphia. American philosophical Society for promoting useful knowledge. Proceedings 22 4. 23 121–123.
372. Salem. American association for the advancement of sciences. Proceedings of the meeting 33 (at Philadelphia).
† 373. Salem. Essex Institute.
374. Salem. Peabody Academy of science. 1) Annual report 18. 2) Memoirs II. 3) Morse: Ancient and modern methods of arrow-release (from Essex Institute Bulletin oct.-dec. 1885).
375. San Francisco. California Academy of science. Bulletin 4 (1886).
376. St. Louis. Academy of science.
377. Washington. Smithsonian Institution. 1) Smithsonian report 1884. 2) Contributions to knowledge in 4°. 24. 3) Annual report of the Bureau of Ethnology 3 (1881—82).
† 378. Washington. Department of agriculture.
† 379. Washington. War Department.
† 380. Washington. Treasury Department.
381. Washington. H. S. Geological Survey. 1) Annual report 4—5. 2) Bulletin 15—25. 3) Monographs VI. VIII. IX. 4) Williams: Mineral resources of the United states. Calender years 1883 and 84. 5) F. Ward: Sketch of palaeobotany (Extr. from the annual report).

Mexico.

† 382. Mexico. Sociedad de geografia y estadistica de la republica mexicana.
† 383. Mexico. Museo nacional.

Brasilien.

384. Rio de Janeiro. Instituto historico geografico e etnografico do Brasil. 1) Revisita trimensal 46. 2) Catalogo das cartas geographicas, hidrographicas atlas, planos e vistas na bibl. do Inst. Hist. 1885. 3) Catalogo dos manuscriptos 31. 12. 1883.

† 385. Rio de Janeiro. Museo nacional.

Argentinische Republik.

† 386. Buenos-Aires. Museo publico.

387. Buenos-Aires. Sociedad cientifica Argentina. Annales 20 (1885).

388. Cordoba. Academia nacional di ciencias de la republica Argentina. Boletin VIII. 2–4.

Chili.

389. Santiago. Deutscher wissenschaftlicher Verein. Heft 3.

Australien.

390. Sydney. Royal Society of N. S. Wales. Journal and Proceedings 17 (1883).

391. Wellington. Neu Zealand Institute. 1) Transactions and Proceedings 18. Index 1–17. 2) Hector: Handbook of New-Zealand (1886). 3) Indian and Colonial Expedition London. 1886. 4) Colonial Museum and geological survey department: Bronn, Manual of the New-Zealand Coleoptera 3, 4.

Angekauft 1886.

Globus. Illustrirte Zeitschrift für Länder- und Völkerkunde. 49. 50. (1886).

Petermann. Geographische Mittheilungen. 1886. Ergänzungsheft. 81–84.

Annalen der Physik und Chemie. Neue Folge 27–29. 1886. Beiblätter 10. 1886.

Archiv für Anthropologie XVI. 4.

Zeitschrift für Ethnologie 18 (1886).

v. Bernhardi. Reiseerinnerungen an Spanien. Berlin 1886.

Brugsch (Heinrich). Im Laude der Sonne. Wanderungen in Persien. 2. Auflage. Berlin 1886.

de Candolle. Der Ursprung der Culturpflanzen. Uebersetzt von Dr. Edmond Goeze. Leipzig 1884.

Christ. Eine Frühlingsfahrt nach den Canarischen Inseln. 1886. Basel, Genf und Lyon.

Dierks. Nordafrika im Lichte der Culturgeschichte. München 1884.

Ebers. Cicerone durch das alte und neue Aegypten. 2 Bände. 1886. Stuttgart und Leipzig.

Engel. Griechische Frühlingstage. Jena 1887.

Forbes. Wanderungen eines Naturforschers im Malayischen Archipel. 1878—83. Aus dem Englischen. Bd. II. Jena 1886.

Gill und Chalmers. Neu Guinea. Reisen und Missionsthätigkeit. 1877—85. Aus dem Englischen. Leipzig 1886.

Gopčević. Bulgarien und Ost-Rumelien. Leipzig 1886.

Güssfeld. In den Hochalpen. Erlebnisse aus den Jahren 1859—85. 2. Auflage. Berlin 1886.

Hager. Kaiser Wilhelms-Land und der Bismarck-Archipel. Leipzig 1886.

Hartmann. Madagasksr und die Inseln Seychellen, Aldabra, Komoren, Maskarenen. Leipzig-Prag 1886.

Herisson. Wanderungen eines Dolmetschers in Cina.

Jandrinzew. Sibirien. Geographische, ethnographische und historische Studien. Nach dem Russischen bearbeitet von Dr. Ed. Petri. Jena 1886.

Johnston. Der Kilimandscharo. Leipzig 1886.

Klöden und Oberländer. Bilder aus den Deutschen Küstenländern der Ostsee. Leipzig 1886.

Kohût. Aus dem Reiche der Karpathen. Stuttgart 1887.

Krause. Die Tlinkit-Indianer. Jena 1885.

Krümmel. Der Ocean. Leipzig-Prag 1886.

v. Maltzahn. Reise auf der Insel Sardinien. Leipzig 1869.

Mantegazza. Indien. Aus dem Italienischen. Jena 1885.

Nedmeyer-Ynkassowitsch. Grossbritanien und Irland mit besonderer Berücksichtigung der Colonieen. Leipzig 1886.

Nordenskiöld. Grönland. Leipzig 1886.

Pechuël-Lösche. Herr Stanley und das Congo-Unternehmen. Eine Entgegnung. Leipzig 1886.

Radde. Talysch und seine Bewohner. Leipzig 1886.

Rein. Japan. Bd. II. Leipzig 1886.

v. d. Steinen. Durch Central-Brasilien. Expedition zur Erforschung des Chingu. 1884. Leipzig 1886.

Schwarz. Kamerun. Reise in die Hinterlande der Colonie. Leipzig 1886.

Stoll. Guatemala. Reisen und Schilderungen. 1878—83. Leipzig 1886.

Vossberg. Geschichte der Preussischen Münzen und Siegel. Berlin 1882.

v. Waldeck. Russland. I. II. (Wissen der Gegenwart). Leipzig-Prag 1886.

v. Wobeser. Henry Stanley und Dr. Pechuël-Lösche. Leipzig 1886.

Wolf. Wallis und Chamonix. Bd. I. Zürich 1886.

Zöller. Die Deutschen Besitzungnn an der westafrikanischen Küste. IV. Forschungen im südlichen Kamerungebiet.

Adressbuch für Königsberg 1886.

Berendt und Göppert. Der Bernstein und die in ihm befindlichen Pflanzenreste. Mit 7 Tafeln. Berlin 1845.

Göppert. Tertiäre Flora von Schossnitz. Mit 26 Tafeln. Görlitz 1855.

Griesebach. Die Bildung des Torfes in den Emsmooren. Göttingen 1846.

Lachmann. Physiogpraphie des Herzogthums Braunschweig. I. II. Braunschweig 1851/52.

Palaeontographica. Herausgegeben von K. v. Zittel. Bd. XXXIII. Lief. 1—3. Stuttgart 1886.

Römer. Geognostische Karte von Oberschlesien. 12 Blätter. Berlin.

Weinkauff. Katalog der im europäischen Faunengebiet lebenden Meeres-Conchylien. Creuznach 1873.

Zittel. Handbuch der Palaeontologie. Bd. II. Lief. 4 und 5.

Geschenke 1886.

Schrader. Karl Gustav von Gossler, Kanzler des Königreichs Preussen. Ein Lebensbild. Berlin 1886. (Geschenk Sr. Excellenz des Herrn Cultusminister Dr. v. Gossler).

Görz. Handel und Statistik des Zuckers. Ergänzungsband. 1885.

Tageblatt der 59. Versammlung Deutscher Naturforscher und Aerzte zu Berlin, 18. bis 24. September 1886. (Beides vom K. Preussischen Cultusministerium).

Jacob. Der Bernstein bei den Arabern des Mittelalters. 1886. (Verfasser).

Meyer, A. B. Das Gräberfeleld von Hallstadt. Mit 3 Lichtdrucktafeln. 1886. (Verfasser).

Bibliotheka historico-naturalis. Lagerkatalog der Buchhandlung A. Friedländer und Sohn, Berlin 1886. (Von der Buchhandlung).

Haber. Register zu der Alt-Preussischen Monatsschrift I—XXII. Manuscript zusammengestellt von Herrn Lehrer Haber. (Vom Verfasser).

The Academy. A Record of Literature, learning science and art. Vol. II. London 1871. (Von Herrn Haber).

Egleston, Melville. Johns Hopkins University Studies Historical and political science. 4 Series 11—12. Le Land System of the New-England Colonies. Baltimore 1886. (Verfasser).

Jentzsch. Das Profil der Eisenbahn Zajonskowo-Löbau. Berlin 1886.

— Das Profil der Eisenbahn Berent-Schöneck-Hohenstein. Berlin 1886. (Verf.)

Maurer. Die Fauna des rheinischen Unterdevon, zum Nachweis der Gliederung zusammengestellt. Darmstadt 1886. (Verf.)

Druck von R. Leupold in Königsberg in Pr.

Erklärung der Tafel I.

Bild 1. *Jungermannia sphaerocarpoides* Casp.
„ 2. „ „ Ein anderes Exemplar.
„ 3 und 4. *Jungermannia dimorpha* Casp. 3 unterer Stammtheil von unten, 4 oberster Theil derselben Axe von oben.
„ 5. *Phragmicoma magnistipulata* Casp.
„ 6. *Phragmicoma contorta* Casp.
„ 7. „ *suborbiculata* Casp.
„ 8. „ „ *fr. sinuata* Casp.
„ 9. *Lejeunia latiloba* Casp.
„ 10. „ *Schumanni* Casp.
„ 11. *Madotheca linguifera* Casp.
„ 12 und 13. *Lophocolea polyodus* Casp.
„ 14. *Frullania primigenia* Casp. Bei F. eine vorgeschrittene weibl. Fruktifikation.
„ 15. *Frull. primig.* Die Kapselhülle F. des vorigen Bildes von oben.
„ 16. *Frullania truncata* Casp.
„ 17 und 18. *Frullania varians* Casp. 17 mit ganz eingerollten Hinterlappen und Beiblättern, 18 mit oberseits eingesunkenen, daher gehöhlten Hinterlappen.
„ 19 und 20. *Frullania magniloba* Casp. 19 ein Stück der oberen, 20 der unteren Stammseite.
„ 21. *Frullania* tenella Casp.
„ 22. Frullania primigenia Casp. untere Seite.
„ 23. *Frullania acutata* Casp.
„ 24. „ „ Untere Hüllblätter einer Fruktifikation.
„ 25. *Radula oblongifolia* Casp.
„ 26. *Lejeunia pinnata* Casp. Der Hinterlappen ist nur bei den beiden obersten Blättern a und b erhalten.

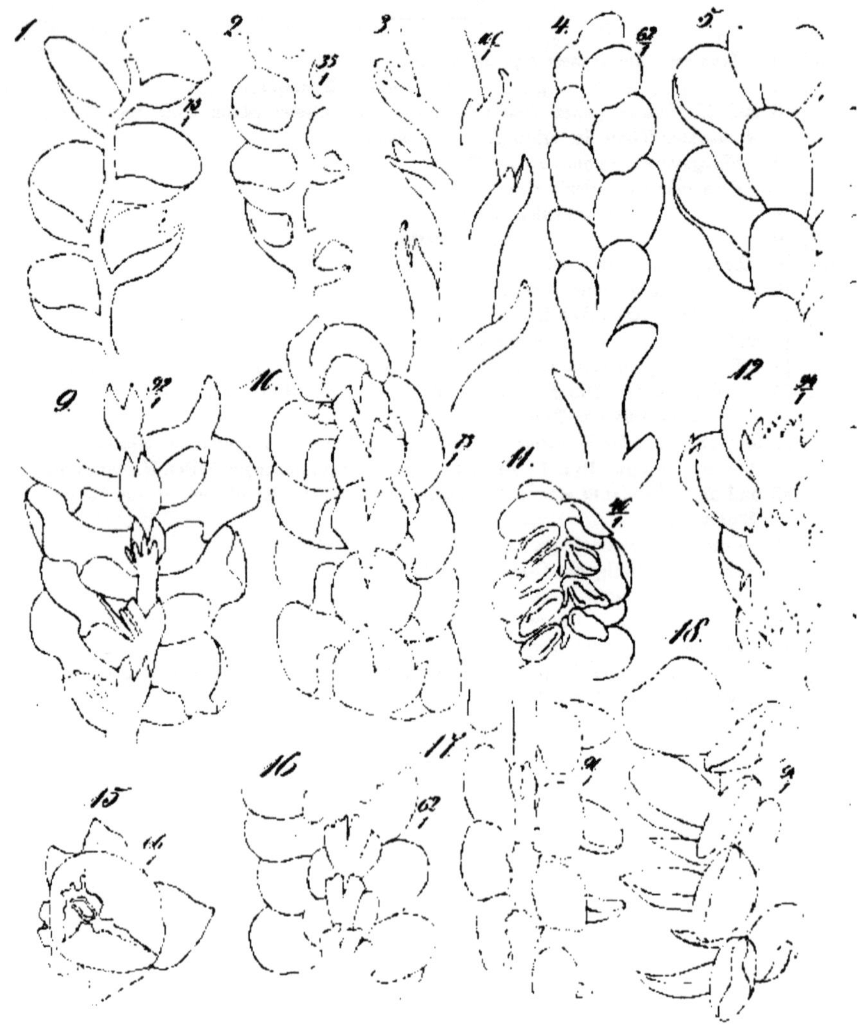

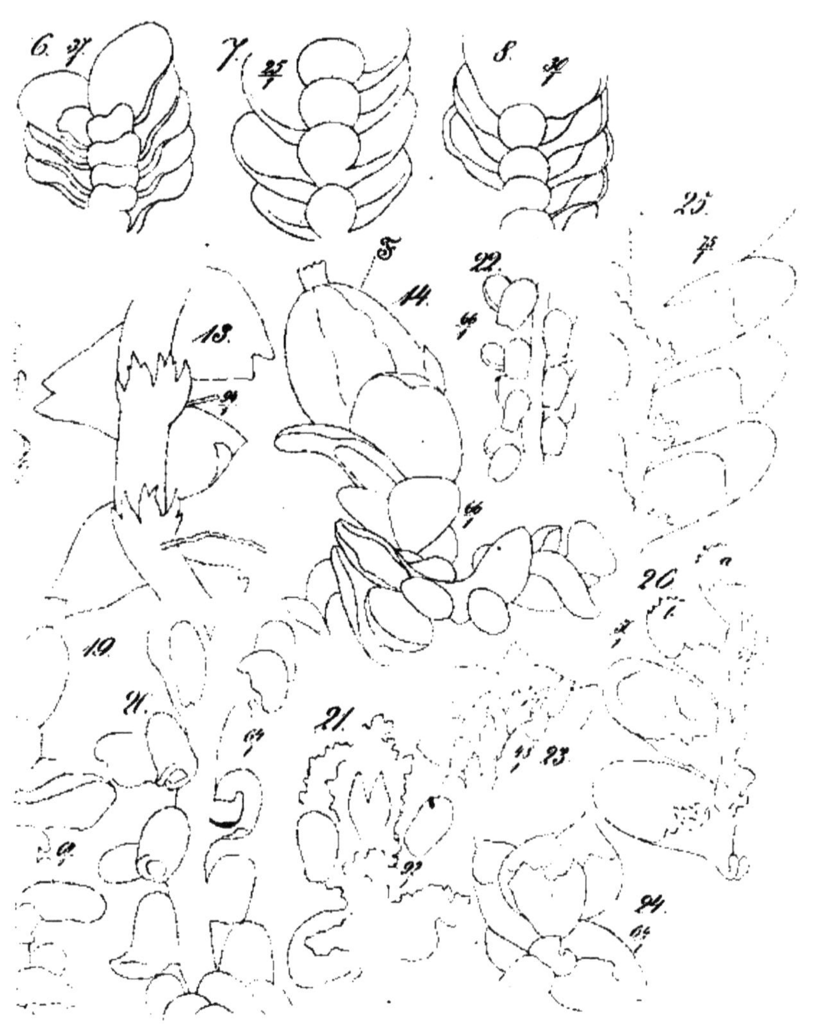
6.
7.
8.
13.
14.
19.
20.
21.
22.
23.
24.
25.

Erklärung der Tafel II.

Ranunculus Steveni Andrz.

1. Ganze Pflanze.
2. Ein Grundblatt einer andern Pflanze.
3. Reife Früchte, a—e.
4. Schnabel einer unreifen Frucht.

Ranunculus acer L.

5. Reife Früchte, a—f.
6. Schnabel einer unreifen Frucht.

OST-PREUSSISCHE HÜGELGRÄBER.

ften d Physik Oek Gesellsch z Konigsberg Jahrg XXVII.1886

H Braune gez.

¼ nat. Grösse.

Druck v. Hermann Schwarz.

H. Braune gez. ¼ nat. Grosse Druck v. Hermann Schwarz.

raune gez

Druck v. Hermann Schwarz.

OST-PREUSSISCHE HÜGELGRÄBER.

Schriften d. Physik. Oek. Gesellsch. z. Königsberg. Jahrg. XXVII, 1886. Taf. VI (IV)

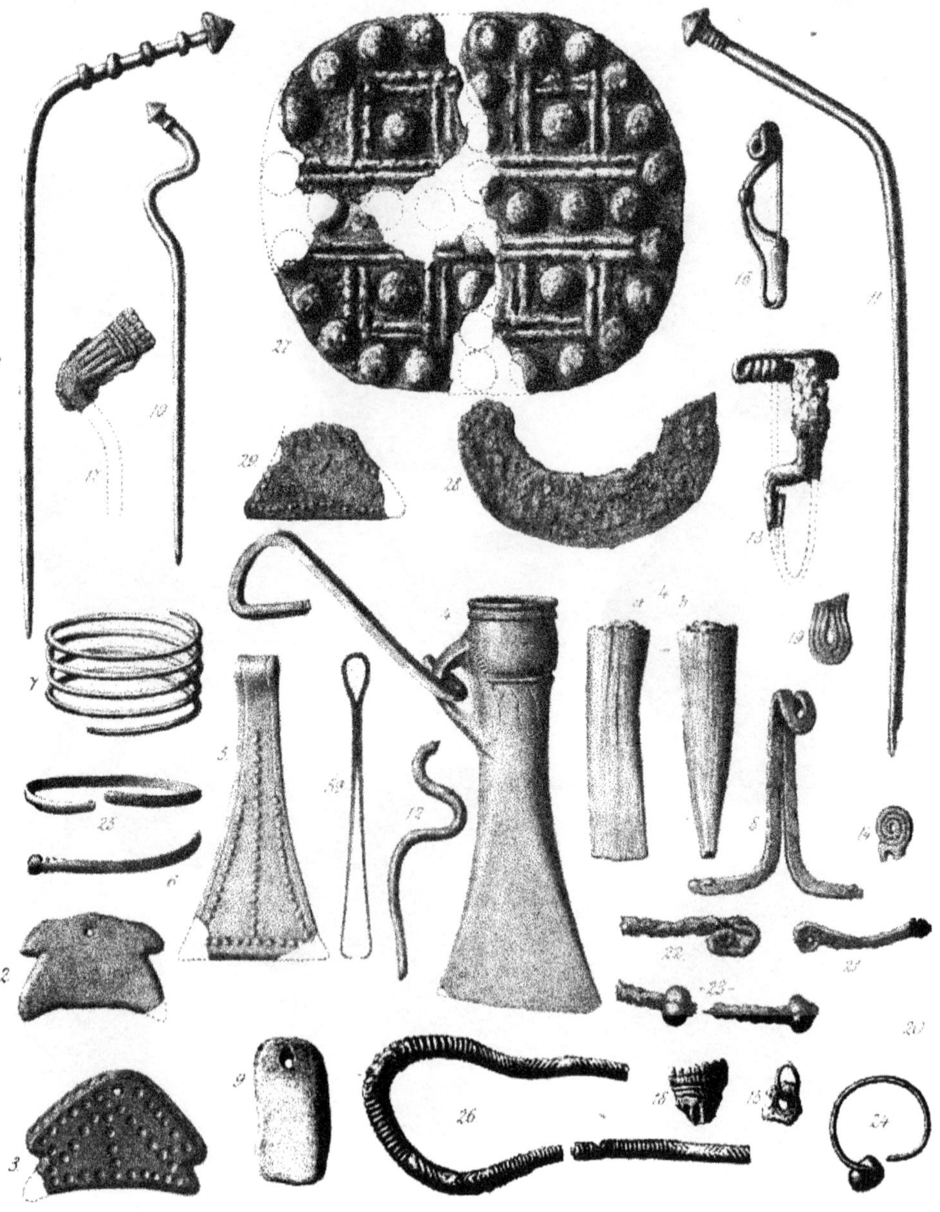

H. Braune gez. Druck v. Hermann Schwartz

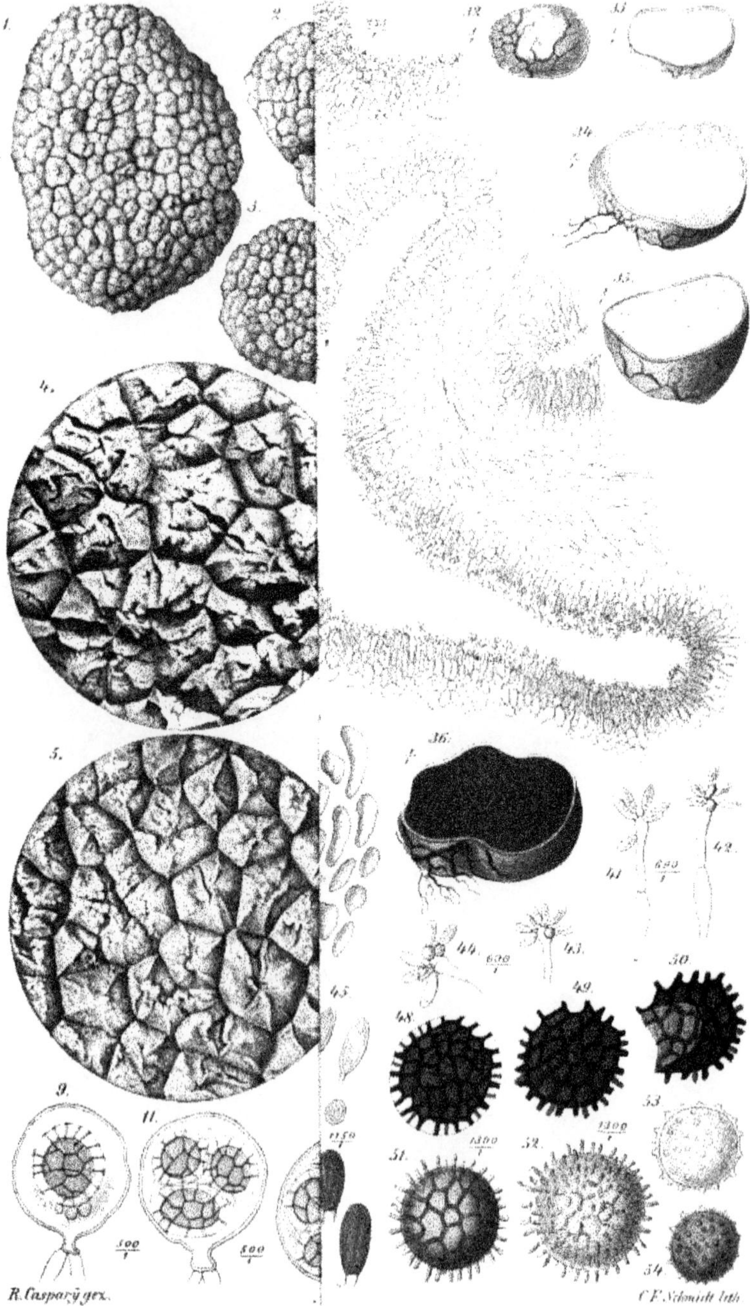

R. Caspary gez. C.F. Schmidt lith.

SCHRIFTEN

DER

PHYSIKALISCH-ÖKONOMISCHEN GESELLSCHAFT

ZU

KÖNIGSBERG i. Pr.

ACHTUNDZWANZIGSTER JAHRGANG.

1887.

KÖNIGSBERG.

IN COMMISSION BEI KOCH & REIMER.

1888.

Inhalts-Verzeichnis des XXVIII. Jahrganges.

Abhandlungen.

Sitzungsberichte.

Beobachtungen

der

Station zur Messung der Temperatur der Erde

in verschiedenen Tiefen

im botanischen Garten zu Königsberg in Pr.

Januar 1881 bis December 1882.

Herausgegeben von Dr. E. Mischpeter.

An der Station ist in diesen beiden Jahren keine wesentliche Aenderung eingetreten. Am 18. Januar 1882 stellte ich eine Bestimmung des Nullpunktes bei Thermometer IV an, derselbe fand sich gegen früher unverändert.

Die Erdthermometer sind zum Schutz gegen das Zerbrechen der ganzen Länge nach in Kupferröhren eingeschlossen, an welchen sich unten zur Aufnahme der Gefässe dickere Ansatzstücke befinden. Nur die Skalen am oberen Ende sind von Glaskuppen bedeckt. Die Mitten der einzelnen Gefässe der Erdthermometer befinden sich in den Tiefen von 1 Zoll, 1 Fuss, 2 Fuss, 4 Fuss, 8 Fuss und 16 Fuss (rheinländisches Maass). Die Angaben der Temperaturen sind in Ganzen und Hundertsteln von Celsiusgraden. Bei den Luftthermometern bezeichnet:

III. ein Thermometer in Glaskuppe; es dient zur Bestimmung der Temperatur der Skalen bei den Erdthermometern;

IV. ein Thermometer in Kupferrohr eingeschlossen; es bestimmt die Temperatur des aus der Erde hervorragenden Teiles des Kupferrohres bei den Erdthermometern;

I' ein Thermometer, dessen Gefäss unmittelbar über dem Erdboden liegt; es dient zur Bestimmung der Temperatur der den Erdboden berührenden Luftschicht;

VII. ein Thermometer, welches die von der Sonnenstrahlung befreite Lufttemperatur angiebt.

Die Zahlen 7, 2 und 8 bezeichnen die Beobachtungszeiten: 7 Uhr morgens, 2 Uhr mittags und 8 Uhr abends.

Die Thermometer 8 Fuss tief und 16 Fuss tief werden zwar auch täglich dreimal beobachtet, die Berechnung der Temperatur wird jedoch nur für die Morgenbeobachtung ausgeführt. Die Berechnung der Temperaturen in den tieferen Erdschichten ist nämlich ziemlich weitläufig, da die abgelesenen Skalenteile noch mehrfache Korrektionen erfordern. So muss z. B. bei dem 16 Fuss langen Thermometer in Betracht gezogen werden, dass der Quecksilberfaden durch Erdschichten geht, die andere Temperaturen haben, als das Gefäss; ferner spielt hier auch die Temperatur der Skala und die Temperatur des aus dem Erdboden hervorragenden Teiles der Kupferröhre eine Rolle. Die für die Berechnung zu Grunde gelegten Korrektionsformeln finden sich in der Abhandlung von Dorn im XIII. Jahrgange dieser Schriften, Seite 85. Die bis jetzt veröffentlichten Beobachtungen für die Jahre 1872—1880 finden sich in diesen Schriften: XV. pag. 1—18, XVI. pag. 7—22, XVII. pag. 77—92, XVIII. pag. 170—184, XX. pag. 147—161, XXIII. pag. 1—16, XXVII. pag. 9—32 c.

Januar 1881.

Luftthermometer

	III. In Glas			IV. In Kupfer			I' frei			VII.		
	7	2	8	7	2	8	7	2	8	7	2	8
1	— 0,54	7,05	— 0,50	— 0,62	4,00	— 0,24	— 0,41	1,75	— 0,41	— 0,19	1,54	— 0,34
2	— 1,58	0,59	0,79	— 1,50	0,10	0,67	— 1,50	0,36	0,71	— 1,87	0,31	0,77
3	0,71	1,80	1,15	0,53	1,68	1,01	0,63	1,79	1,23	0,66	1,89	1,19
4	1,31	1,55	0,99	1,30	1,49	0,91	1,58	1,45	1,28	1,31	1,42	1,00
5	— 0,82	9,60	0,14	— 0,91	4,97	0,10	— 0,75	3,91	0,02	— 0,15	2,50	0,37
6	— 2,21	2,60	— 2,24	— 2,67	1,87	— 2,19	— 1,95	1,71	— 1,62	— 1,45	1,42	— 1,45
7	1,96	2,85	0,75	2,36	2,60	0,77	2,01	2,35	0,63	1,92	2,47	0,85
8	— 0,54	1,23	— 4,42	— 0,53	— 0,18	— 4,41	— 0,63	— 0,20	— 4,34	— 0,38	0,00	— 4,17
9	— 7,68	— 0,22	— 1,83	— 7,61	— 0,81	— 1,78	— 7,36	— 1,23	— 1,71	— 7,56	— 1,26	— 1,75
10	— 2,08	— 0,62	— 4,70	— 1,64	— 0,77	— 4,65	— 1,54	— 2,31	— 4,60	— 1,60	— 2,21	— 4,51
11	— 6,88	2,60	— 7,44	— 7,24	— 0,33	— 7,55	— 7,66	— 3,87	— 7,32	— 6,61	— 4,51	— 7,26
12	—10,18	— 4,26	—10,30	—10,01	— 6,18	—10,20	— 9,57	— 6,80	—10,25	— 9,89	— 8,24	—10,42
13	—18,82	—13,84	—19,06	—18,57	—16,21	—18,91	—18,15	—16,38	—18,56	—18,61	—16,82	—18,39
14	—21,87	—15,18	—20,35	—21,65	—16,11	—19,97	—21,67	—15,40	—19,52	—21,42	—17,86	—19,35
15	—15,57	1,59	— 9,82	—15,01	— 1,35	— 9,96	—14,29	— 3,83	— 9,91	—14,42	— 8,94	— 9,77
16	—13,32	— 7,88	—10,11	—13,65	—10,01	—10,87	—13,34	—10,38	—10,77	—13,20	—10,65	—10,72
17	—11,14	— 8,29	— 7,89	—11,07	— 8,95	— 8,81	—10,51	— 9,09	— 8,79	—10,15	— 9,39	— 8,78
18	—13,52	— 3,73	—15,13	—13,85	— 7,80	—15,73	—13,56	—10,08	—15,96	—13,70	—11,09	—15,45
19	—19,62	— 3,45	—18,14	—19,39	—12,36	—18,67	—18,45	—15,06	—18,49	—18,99	—16,05	—18,31
20	—14,89	—11,92	—14,93	—14,82	—12,89	—15,06	—14,42	—12,95	—14,89	—14,88	—13,32	—15,08
21	—17,33	— 9,90	—14,01	—17,23	—11,35	—14,82	—16,94	—12,22	—14,67	—17,01	—12,75	—14,42
22	—13,68	— 2,92	—12,96	—13,47	— 6,18	—12,79	—12,82	— 8,45	—12,82	—12,28	— 9,09	—12,90
23	— 8,57	— 4,26	—10,79	— 8,57	— 5,23	—10,87	— 8,45	— 5,59	—10,43	— 8,47	— 5,81	—10,88
24	—15,13	— 2,16	— 3,43	—15,20	— 4,85	— 3,56	—14,63	— 8,28	— 3,61	—14,68	— 7,38	— 3,56
25	— 6,15	— 3,77	— 9,84	— 6,47	— 5,80	— 9,63	— 6,25	— 6,46	— 9,52	— 6,23	— 6,23	— 9,94
26	—15,91	— 0,46	—15,13	—15,20	— 5,94	—15,16	—14,93	— 8,06	—14,80	—14,80	— 9,47	—14,42
27	—19,71	1,23	—15,57	—19,53	— 6,18	—15,49	—19,18	—10,08	—14,97	—19,18	—11,80	—14,80
28	—10,71	— 1,92	— 6,07	—10,83	— 2,17	— 6,28	—10,51	— 5,59	— 6,37	—10,42	— 6,42	— 5,93
29	— 8,49	— 6,07	— 4,50	— 8,57	— 6,55	— 4,85	— 8,02	— 6,93	— 4,09	— 8,47	— 7,07	— 4,30
30	0,79	0,62	1,11	— 0,33	1,92	0,91	0,76	1,49	0,80	0,85	1,73	1,28
31	0,83	8,29	0,11	0,53	6,32	0,00	0,80	3,91	0,11	1,00	3,50	0,89
	— 8,69	— 1,94	— 7,54	— 8,80	— 3,95	— 7,68	— 8,39	— 5,85	— 7,52	— 8,44	— 5,63	— 8,28

Februar 1881.

	III. In Glas			IV. In Kupfer			I' frei			VII.		
	7	2	8	7	2	8	7	2	8	7	2	8
1	0,07	1,55	0,55	— 0,24	0,87	0,48	— 0,07	1,02	0,41	0,00	1,23	0,51
2	— 0,46	0,39	0,27	— 0,61	0,65	0,10	— 0,50	0,15	0,15	— 0,56	0,08	0,20
3	— 0,82	0,07	— 0,54	— 0,81	— 0,65	— 0,43	— 0,71	— 0,41	— 0,45	— 0,84	— 0,56	— 0,61
4	— 2,32	10,62	— 2,92	— 2,46	5,94	— 1,21	— 2,14	3,52	— 2,10	— 2,02	— 2,00	— 2,21
5	— 3,04	2,69	— 0,96	— 3,08	0,05	— 0,94	— 2,79	0,11	— 0,88	— 2,98	— 0,26	— 0,58
6	— 3,69	1,11	— 1,71	— 3,66	— 0,53	— 1,59	— 3,61	— 1,27	— 1,54	— 3,98	— 1,83	— 1,41
7	0,83	0,19	— 7,08	0,63	0,21	— 7,04	0,66	— 0,71	— 6,80	0,78	— 0,92	— 6,76
8	—10,38	0,59	— 0,62	—10,06	— 0,54	— 0,66	— 9,39	— 1,23	— 0,63	—10,08	— 1,49	— 0,45
9	2,00	4,22	1,31	1,87	2,94	1,20	1,88	2,18	1,32	2,00	2,67	1,62
10	— 0,46	0,63	— 0,30	— 0,77	0,39	— 0,29	— 0,56	0,54	— 0,41	— 0,56	0,85	— 0,41
11	2,72	2,28	— 1,10	2,26	1,78	— 1,16	2,44	1,75	— 1,18	2,85	1,92	— 0,34
12	— 2,44	— 2,80	— 3,46	— 2,65	— 3,27	— 3,32	— 2,44	— 3,43	— 3,30	— 2,60	— 3,70	— 3,28
13	— 2,54	— 1,48	— 3,04	— 2,65	— 1,50	— 2,88	— 2,31	— 1,50	— 2,83	— 2,41	— 1,60	— 2,90
14	— 3,85	— 2,24	— 5,93	— 4,17	— 4,51	— 5,70	— 3,96	— 4,30	— 5,46	— 4,32	— 5,46	— 5,76
15	— 5,31	1,47	— 1,02	— 5,53	0,05	— 1,01	— 4,95	0,28	— 0,96	— 5,81	— 0,38	— 1,08
16	— 1,35	2,60	— 0,62	— 1,50	1,35	— 0,48	— 1,14	0,85	— 0,45	— 1,26	0,47	— 0,57
17	— 0,90	3,13	— 1,06	— 0,93	0,82	— 0,91	— 0,93	0,28	— 1,01	— 1,16	— 0,07	— 1,11
18	— 2,52	— 1,71	— 6,68	— 2,46	— 2,84	— 6,76	— 2,48	— 3,04	— 6,80	2,60	— 3,62	— 7,14
19	—14,24	6,09	— 6,69	—14,15	— 3,27	— 7,00	—13,56	— 4,99	— 6,80	—14,04	— 6,19	— 6,88
20	—10,91	5,68	— 8,35	—10,62	1,87	— 7,35	—10,38	— 1,58	— 8,41	—10,50	— 4,18	— 7,84
21	— 8,77	7,46	— 6,27	— 8,57	2,56	— 6,18	— 8,45	— 0,93	— 6,03	— 8,60	— 3,98	— 6,33
22	— 8,84	6,44	— 8,29	— 8,91	0,63	— 8,09	— 8,71	— 3,39	— 8,06	— 8,94	— 4,37	— 8,02
23	—12,12	10,29	— 5,63	—12,63	2,94	— 5,46	—11,49	1,41	— 5,25	—11,88	— 2,21	— 5,19
24	—10,78	9,56	— 3,89	—10,20	2,75	— 3,80	— 9,70	1,71	— 3,61	— 9,74	— 1,88	— 3,62
25	— 7,96	10,70	— 1,02	— 8,19	4,87	— 0,91	— 7,66	2,70	— 0,84	— 7,75	1,54	— 0,84
26	— 2,24	0,89	— 1,75	— 2,46	— 0,43	— 1,83	— 2,31	— 0,58	— 1,71	— 2,29	— 0,76	— 1,89
27	— 3,73	— 2,36	—10,22	— 3,26	— 3,32	— 9,91	— 3,17	— 3,30	— 9,49	— 3,62	— 4,08	— 9,77
28	—15,53	7,73	— 8,64	—15,20	0,43	— 8,81	—14,87	— 0,41	— 8,58	—15,09	— 4,98	— 8,94
	— 4,54	3,07	— 3,39	— 4,65	0,14	— 3,33	— 4,39	— 0,52	— 3,28	— 4,55	— 1,62	— 3,38

Januar 1881.

Erdthermometer

1 Zoll tief			1 Fuss tief			2 Fuss tief			4 Fuss tief			8 Fuss tief	16 Fuss tief
7	2	8	7	2	8	7	2	8	7	2	8	7	7
— 0,81	2,70	0,28	1,96	1,77	1,69	2,27	2,23	2,20	3,65	3,64	3,66	6,21	8,82
— 0,01	0,22	0,28	1,45	1,39	1,36	2,14	2,08	2,04	3,67	3,65	3,72	6,16	8,79
— 0,48	0,90	0,97	1,33	1,33	1,38	1,98	1,97	1,96	3,65	3,64	3,63	6,13	8,77
— 1,83	1,43	1,30	1,59	1,66	1,70	2,03	2,06	2,10	3,63	3,63	3,60	6,09	8,74
0,29	3,76	0,54	1,73	1,86	1,87	2,15	2,18	2,19	3,61	3,59	3,58	6,04	8,70
0,17	1,45	0,24	1,56	1,58	1,46	2,16	2,12	2,09	3,59	3,58	3,59	5,99	8,67
0,81	1,50	0,74	1,39	1,41	1,44	2,03	2,02	2,00	3,57	3,57	3,56	5,97	8,64
0,97	0,28	— 0,59	1,32	1,28	1,22	1,96	1,94	1,90	3,54	3,54	3,53	5,91	8,62
— 1,86	— 0,12	— 0,45	1,05	1,02	1,02	1,85	1,80	1,78	3,49	3,48	3,48	5,89	8,57
— 0,68	0,06	— 1,11	0,96	0,99	0,98	1,74	1,72	1,72	3,43	3,42	3,43	5,84	8,53
— 1,60	— 0,14	— 1,74	0,90	0,93	0,87	1,70	1,68	1,66	3,40	3,37	3,38	5,81	8,51
— 2,08	— 1,48	— 2,68	0,84	0,80	0,75	1,64	1,61	1,58	3,36	3,33	3,33	5,80	8,49
— 5,11	— 5,13	— 6,90	0,65	0,55	0,39	1,56	1,52	1,48	3,32	3,29	3,28	5,76	8,45
— 7,01	— 5,89	— 6,33	0,52	0,24	0,20	1,40	1,35	1,24	3,24	3,23	3,21	5,70	8,42
— 5,67	— 2,56	— 4,20	0,14	0,07	0,04	1,15	1,15	1,12	3,19	3,18	3,13	5,70	8,41
— 6,03	— 4,90	— 5,33	— 0,08	— 0,13	— 0,20	1,05	1,00	0,98	3,09	3,08	3,07	5,64	8,35
— 5,95	— 3,87	— 3,81	— 0,22	— 0,20	— 0,24	0,93	0,87	0,87	3,02	3,00	2,95	5,60	8,34
— 5,96	— 3,18	— 4,81	— 0,29	— 0,28	— 0,34	0,82	0,80	0,77	2,92	2,88	2,87	5,58	8,30
— 6,55	— 5,09	— 7,51	— 0,61	— 0,79	— 0,92	0,72	0,66	0,63	2,82	2,79	2,77	5,52	8,27
— 8,60	— 6,19	— 6,72	— 1,23	— 1,33	— 1,30	0,55	0,52	0,45	2,72	2,71	2,68	5,48	8,25
— 6,94	— 5,61	— 6,42	— 1,60	— 1,64	— 1,63	0,38	0,32	0,28	2,64	2,61	2,59	5,43	8,21
— 5,95	— 4,46	— 5,78	— 1,49	— 1,74	— 1,71	0,21	0,19	0,15	2,55	2,51	2,51	5,39	8,19
— 4,81	— 3,40	— 4,36	— 1,79	— 1,66	— 1,53	0,11	0,09	0,12	2,38	2,39	2,39	5,33	8,16
— 5,31	— 3,13	— 3,01	— 1,56	— 1,52	— 1,37	0,08	0,11	0,05	2,33	2,30	2,28	5,28	8,14
— 3,11	— 3,15	— 4,68	— 1,20	— 1,21	— 1,23	0,07	0,08	0,06	2,25	2,24	2,18	5,23	8,11
— 6,56	— 4,37	— 6,63	— 1,52	— 1,73	— 1,87	0,02	0,01	— 0,07	2,18	2,20	2,14	5,19	8,08
— 8,52	— 5,28	— 7,56	— 2,18	— 2,44	— 2,48	— 0,08	— 0,13	— 0,12	2,12	2,07	2,07	5,14	8,06
— 6,03	— 9,38	— 4,54	— 2,68	— 2,57	— 2,39	— 0,27	— 0,33	— 0,38	2,03	1,99	1,96	5,07	8,03
— 4,84	— 4,34	— 3,81	— 2,21	— 2,16	— 2,01	— 0,41	— 0,39	— 0,43	1,94	1,92	1,90	5,00	8,01
— 1,75	— 1,09	— 0,30	— 1,72	— 1,41	— 1,22	— 0,41	— 0,35	— 0,31	1,86	1,86	1,84	4,94	7,98
0,00	0,63	— 0,23	— 0,77	— 0,56	— 0,44	— 0,19	— 0,15	— 0,09	1,80	1,78	1,77	4,99	7,96
— 3,45	— 2,57	— 3,04	— 0,18	— 0,14	— 0,15	1,01	0,99	0,90	2,93	2,91	2,92	5,62	8,40

Februar 1881.

1 Zoll tief			1 Fuss tief			2 Fuss tief			4 Fuss tief			8 Fuss tief	16 Fuss tief
7	2	8	7	2	8	7	2	8	7	2	8	7	7
0,23	0,26	0,25	— 0,27	— 0,23	— 0,16	— 0,03	— 0,01	0,02	1,76	1,75	1,78	4,85	7,98
0,22	0,24	0,22	— 0,12	0,07	— 0,06	0,05	0,06	0,07	1,72	1,72	1,71	4,81	7,90
0,24	0,23	0,23	— 0,02	0,00	0,02	0,09	0,11	0,13	1,71	1,71	1,72	4,75	7,87
— 0,11	0,32	0,25	0,04	0,05	0,06	0,14	0,13	0,13	1,69	1,68	1,67	4,71	7,85
— 1,03	— 0,20	— 0,50	0,07	0,07	0,08	0,15	0,16	0,15	1,68	1,69	1,66	4,67	7,81
— 1,74	— 1,01	— 1,16	0,00	— 0,08	— 0,10	0,20	0,15	0,16	1,68	1,66	1,66	4,61	7,79
0,05	0,06	— 2,10	— 0,12	— 0,07	— 0,05	0,17	0,15	0,18	1,66	1,66	1,64	4,57	7,76
— 4,76	— 1,73	— 1,32	— 0,42	— 0,69	— 0,66	0,18	0,14	0,13	1,65	1,66	1,67	4,56	7,74
— 0,23	0,17	0,21	— 0,46	— 0,36	— 0,26	0,09	0,11	0,12	1,66	1,65	1,66	4,52	7,71
0,15	0,18	0,13	— 0,15	— 0,08	— 0,07	0,13	0,13	0,14	1,66	1,65	1,66	4,48	7,69
0,24	0,39	0,14	— 0,02	0,00	0,00	0,17	0,18	0,16	1,64	1,64	1,63	4,44	7,66
— 0,51	— 1,54	— 1,89	0,04	0,00	— 0,08	0,18	0,20	0,19	1,63	1,63	1,63	4,41	7,63
— 1,64	— 0,97	— 1,49	— 0,29	— 0,31	— 0,30	0,19	0,18	0,17	1,64	1,65	1,63	4,40	7,60
— 1,68	— 1,83	— 2,49	— 0,36	— 0,42	— 0,48	0,17	0,16	0,16	1,64	1,63	1,63	4,35	7,57
— 2,48	— 0,73	— 0,94	— 0,63	— 0,62	— 0,52	0,17	0,13	0,13	1,64	1,64	1,63	4,34	7,55
— 0,81	— 0,16	— 0,19	— 0,40	— 0,32	— 0,23	0,16	0,14	0,15	1,63	1,64	1,63	4,31	7,53
— 0,43	— 0,08	— 0,29	— 0,15	— 0,14	— 0,09	0,18	0,18	0,19	1,63	1,64	1,63	4,29	7,50
0,95	— 1,24	— 2,45	— 0,11	— 0,14	— 0,22	0,17	0,20	0,19	1,63	1,62	1,64	4,25	7,48
— 6,86	— 3,09	— 4,61	— 0,88	— 1,27	— 1,43	0,18	0,11	0,07	1,63	1,62	1,65	4,23	7,44
— 6,78	— 1,62	— 4,41	— 2,01	— 2,03	— 1,66	— 0,01	— 0,13	— 0,13	1,62	1,59	1,61	4,20	7,41
— 6,08	— 2,06	— 4,09	— 2,20	— 2,26	— 1,86	— 0,17	— 0,29	— 0,27	1,61	1,55	1,57	4,19	7,39
5,78	— 1,76	— 5,10	— 2,17	— 2,27	— 1,92	— 0,30	— 0,43	— 0,39	1,58	1,53	1,53	4,17	7,37
— 7,46	— 0,96	— 3,46	— 2,65	— 2,59	— 1,90	— 0,44	— 0,56	— 0,53	1,53	1,50	1,48	4,14	7,33
— 6,20	— 0,59	— 2,43	— 2,28	— 2,20	— 1,61	— 0,51	— 0,61	— 0,53	1,49	1,47	1,45	4,12	7,31
— 5,22	— 0,02	— 1,15	— 1,83	— 1,86	— 1,29	— 0,46	— 0,56	— 0,50	1,44	1,40	1,42	4,09	7,29
— 1,82	— 1,01	— 1,32	— 1,01	— 0,96	— 0,84	— 0,37	— 0,31	— 0,29	1,40	1,38	1,38	4,08	7,27
— 2,27	— 1,84	— 4,32	— 0,91	— 0,97	— 1,00	— 0,21	— 0,24	— 0,25	1,39	1,36	1,37	4,04	7,25
— 8,13	— 1,58	— 5,64	— 2,12	— 2,47	— 2,19	— 0,35	— 0,61	— 0,65	1,36	1,31	1,32	4,02	7,22
— 2,57	— 0,79	— 1,82	— 0,76	— 0,79	— 0,67	— 0,01	— 0,04	— 0,03	1,61	1,59	1,59	4,34	7,56

März 1881.

	Luftthermometer											
	III. in Glas			IV. in Kupfer								
	7	2	8	7	2	8	7	2	8	7		
1	− 3,87	8,79	0,63	− 3,22	5,84	0,53	− 3,22	4,77	0,54	− 3,21	4,70	
2	− 4,42	− 0,22	− 6,27	− 4,37	− 2,22	− 6,18	− 4,39	− 2,57	− 5,72	− 4,51	− 3,70	−
3	−10,37	7,46	− 6,52	− 9,82	6,22	− 6,13	− 9,48	− 1,01	− 6,07	− 9,62	− 3,70	−
4	− 9,82	− 3,81	− 8,25	− 9,91	− 5,23	− 8,04	− 9,27	− 5,99	− 8,53	− 9,62	− 6,80	−
5	− 8,25	− 0,46	− 6,84	− 8,19	− 3,27	− 6,86	− 7,98	− 4,30	− 6,68	− 8,17	− 4,06	−
6	−14,68	7,86	−10,22	−14,34	− 0,33	−10,11	−13,94	− 2,40	− 9,70	−14,12	− 6,88	−1
7	−14,56	1,88	− 6,35	−14,20	− 1,50	− 6,18	−13,08	− 2,57	− 6,03	−13,89	− 3,78	−
8	− 1,10	5,92	4,26	− 1,01	4,27	3,90	− 0,75	4,08	4,00	− 0,76	5,24	
9	1,51	2,44	0,59	1,49	1,73	0,24	1,58	1,62	0,58	1,81	1,54	
10	0,79	7,34	0,59	0,72	5,09	0,53	0,80	4,20	0,58	0,96	2,85	
11	− 0,77	0,59	− 2,24	− 0,71	− 0,29	− 2,26	− 0,03	− 0,71	− 1,97	− 0,76	− 0,96	−
12	− 1,83	0,83	− 0,82	− 1,74	− 0,09	− 0,53	− 1,50	0,11	− 1,18	− 1,68	0,00	−
13	− 6,68	8,51	− 3,89	− 6,28	0,91	− 4,13	− 6,55	− 0,41	− 3,74	− 5,96	− 1,07	−
14	− 8,57	10,70	− 7,68	− 8,81	4,39	− 7,24	− 8,10	1,49	− 6,59	− 8,17	− 1,91	−
15	−11,27	11,51	− 6,40	−10,83	6,80	− 5,84	−10,25	2,36	− 5,16	−10,50	− 0,96	−
16	− 9,80	8,39	− 4,26	− 9,05	7,23	− 8,80	− 8,71	2,18	− 3,87	− 9,01	1,50	−
17	− 5,27	10,58	− 1,71	− 5,46	10,56	− 1,40	− 5,33	5,24	− 0,84	− 5,18	4,97	−
18	− 1,43	3,41	2,28	− 1,26	2,46	2,46	− 1,27	2,05	2,44	− 1,22	2,00	
19	2,76	6,65	2,40	2,75	4,77	2,46	2,83	4,17	2,39	3,12	3,93	
20	− 1,35	4,54	− 1,58	− 1,50	1,49	− 1,59	− 1,45	0,85	− 1,14	− 1,53	0,58	−
21	− 1,71	4,06	− 2,76	− 1,69	2,94	− 2,50	− 1,45	1,79	− 2,23	− 1,64	1,27	−
22	− 5,06	7,25	− 5,59	− 5,04	2,70	− 5,13	− 4,64	0,80	− 4,73	− 4,89	− 0,49	−
23	− 5,27	8,27	− 2,88	− 5,23	3,66	− 2,94	− 4,82	2,18	− 2,06	− 5,16	1,85	−
24	− 2,84	4,20	1,11	− 2,84	2,80	1,01	− 2,66	2,52	1,06	− 2,87	2,50	
25	3,41	2,48	1,72	3,42	1,83	1,49	3,44	1,75	1,41	4,08	1,73	
26	1,39	3,89	0,67	1,11	2,46	0,43	1,15	2,14	0,58	1,31	1,62	
27	− 2,04	10,05	− 0,50	− 2,17	6,32	0,05	− 1,26	4,86	− 0,02	− 2,02	4,19	
28	− 0,94	13,14	2,00	− 1,11	10,08	2,26	− 0,84	8,49	2,52	− 0,56	8,16	
29	0,19	9,81	3,81	0,05	7,91	3,56	0,06	7,71	3,61	0,47	7,29	
30	0,11	6,28	0,11	− 0,33	3,52	− 0,29	− 0,41	2,87	− 0,11	− 0,45	2,31	−
31	− 0,62	7,98	0,99	− 1,16	4,57	1,01	− 1,06	3,61	1,32	− 1,07	2,89	
	− 3,69	6,01	− 2,02	− 3,83	3,20	− 1,97	− 3,70	1,72	− 1,80	− 3,65	0,85	

April 1881.

	7	2	8	7	2	8	7	2	8	7		
1	0,25	11,51	− 0,50	− 0,29	6,46	− 0,58	− 0,32	6,50	0,02	− 0,68	3,93	
2	− 0,10	11,43	− 0,10	− 0,29	4,39	0,05	0,02	4,43	0,11	− 0,22	2,96	
3	− 4,56	5,59	− 5,31	− 4,85	0,19	− 3,80	− 4,52	0,45	− 3,87	− 4,81	− 0,07	−
4	− 5,47	10,00	− 3,81	− 5,33	5,98	− 3,06	− 5,07	3,35	− 3,00	− 5,19	0,51	−
5	− 3,81	10,70	− 0,94	− 4,08	6,08	− 0,91	− 3,78	5,55	− 0,84	− 3,90	3,93	
6	− 2,24	15,01	1,39	− 2,70	10,32	1,89	− 2,48	9,62	1,52	− 2,56	8,32	
7	0,11	12,83	− 0,50	− 0,48	7,42	− 0,62	− 0,28	6,03	− 0,32	− 0,30	6,16	−
8	− 3,72	11,51	− 1,55	− 4,05	4,44	− 1,01	− 4,50	8,44	− 1,05	− 4,62	2,85	−
9	− 2,58	14,76	1,11	− 2,84	7,82	1,06	− 2,06	6,80	1,19	− 2,68	6,24	
10	− 0,22	16,80	1,96	− 0,53	11,19	1,78	− 0,41	10,23	2,09	− 0,56	9,32	
11	1,19	17,09	4,24	2,26	14,18	4,10	2,87	12,14	4,20	0,00	11,62	
12	2,28	19,23	6,65	2,07	14,42	6,70	2,01	13,04	6,59	1,81	12,39	
13	4,06	20,05	3,85	3,50	14,42	3,90	3,61	13,57	4,21	3,54	12,77	
14	2,60	20,05	5,03	2,07	15,97	5,35	2,31	14,74	5,34	2,19	13,92	
15	2,00	22,08	3,93	3,32	15,49	3,50	2,96	14,74	4,24	2,35	13,65	
16	5,15	20,45	3,93	5,55	14,95	3,10	4,90	14,44	4,21	4,54	13,54	
17	4,54	22,13	4,06	6,08	18,08	4,19	6,59	16,44	4,73	3,16	15,76	
18	3,33	19,64	9,08	3,32	16,21	8,78	3,26	15,91	9,06	3,16	15,34	
19	9,04	12,98	2,64	8,25	12,59	2,76	8,49	12,96	2,70	8,01	13,04	
20	0,83	12,58	1,35	0,15	6,32	1,01	0,63	5,21	1,41	0,58	5,00	
21	3,61	8,67	1,80	3,67	5,89	1,97	2,43	5,73	2,18	2,47	5,47	
22	3,53	9,89	1,43	2,84	6,85	1,49	2,61	6,16	1,84	2,00	5,85	
23	4,54	12,57	− 0,80	5,11	8,73	− 0,93	4,25	7,46	0,15	3,93	7,01	
24	1,11	18,75	5,72	4,10	12,73	5,84	1,84	11,00	5,98	1,84	10,58	
25	4,26	15,99	8,67	3,90	13,86	8,35	4,00	12,23	8,41	3,30	11,24	
26	6,57	9,48	5,88	6,32	8,95	5,84	6,50	9,01	6,07	6,58	8,85	
27	4,22	16,80	3,89	3,90	11,24	3,50	3,31	10,40	4,34	4,23	9,43	
28	6,65	8,71	4,42	5,79	7,83	4,19	5,28	7,06	4,47	5,20	6,28	
29	2,44	11,51	1,80	1,73	7,28	1,83	1,32	6,16	1,79	1,42	5,24	
30	5,43	11,14	4,22	4,73	8,73	4,29	4,20	9,14	4,12	2,10	7,01	

März 1881.

Erdthermometer													
1 Zoll tief			1 Fuss tief			2 Fuss tief			4 Fuss tief			8 Fuss tief	16 Fuss tief
7	2	8	7	2	8	7	2	8	7	2	8	7	7
− 3,68	− 0,04	0,06	− 2,37	− 1,88	− 1,29	− 0,69	− 0,73	− 0,45	1,33	1,28	1,30	4,01	7,21
− 2,17	− 1,69	− 3,26	− 0,87	− 0,99	− 1,03	− 0,42	− 0,38	− 0,35	1,29	1,28	1,29	3,98	7,17
− 6,06	− 1,08	− 3,56	− 1,75	− 2,06	− 1,65	− 0,39	− 0,60	− 0,61	1,28	1,23	1,23	3,96	7,15
− 5,18	− 3,58	− 4,69	− 1,89	− 2,11	− 2,03	− 0,58	− 0,72	− 0,72	1,26	1,22	1,23	3,94	7,14
− 5,24	− 3,05	− 4,49	− 2,43	− 2,37	− 2,17	− 0,77	− 0,87	− 0,86	1,23	1,20	1,15	3,91	7,10
− 9,44	− 2,00	− 6,07	− 3,17	− 3,35	− 2,66	− 0,88	− 1,17	− 1,13	1,20	1,15	1,14	3,87	7,07
− 9,21	− 2,91	− 4,39	− 3,73	− 3,61	− 2,82	− 0,19	− 1,38	− 1,36	1,12	1,13	1,12	3,86	7,05
− 2,48	0,11	0,54	− 2,05	− 1,36	− 1,42	− 1,24	− 1,18	− 1,32	1,11	1,08	1,06	3,82	7,04
0,98	0,41	0,25	− 0,87	− 0,67	− 0,58	− 0,75	− 0,60	− 0,54	1,06	1,06	1,05	3,81	7,02
0,27	0,76	0,27	− 0,59	− 0,34	− 0,27	− 0,37	− 0,33	− 0,28	1,06	1,04	1,03	3,78	7,00
0,29	0,53	0,26	− 0,19	− 0,17	− 0,14	− 0,19	− 0,19	− 0,16	1,07	1,05	1,03	3,75	6,97
0,11	0,19	0,16	− 0,09	− 0,08	− 0,07	− 0,09	− 0,10	− 0,08	1,07	1,04	1,04	3,74	6,95
− 1,23	0,17	− 0,86	− 0,05	− 0,09	− 0,09	− 0,01	− 0,10	− 0,02	1,08	1,07	1,07	3,71	6,93
− 2,76	0,16	− 2,13	− 0,26	− 0,36	− 0,24	− 0,01	− 0,04	− 0,03	1,09	1,04	1,06	3,68	6,90
− 5,07	0,06	− 1,44	− 0,77	− 0,96	− 0,67	− 0,04	− 0,15	− 0,16	1,09	1,03	1,05	3,65	6,88
− 4,01	0,17	0,03	− 0,89	− 0,96	− 0,66	− 0,12	− 0,24	− 0,23	0,99	1,06	1,08	3,63	6,85
− 3,34	0,04	0,25	− 0,68	− 0,70	− 0,46	− 0,17	− 0,22	− 0,18	1,08	1,06	1,08	3,61	6,83
0,11	0,18	0,39	− 0,25	− 0,20	− 0,17	− 0,11	− 0,10	− 0,08	1,06	1,06	1,05	3,58	6,80
0,85	0,55	0,89	− 0,07	− 0,23	− 0,02	− 0,03	− 0,03	− 0,01	1,06	1,06	1,07	3,59	6,79
0,23	0,56	0,25	0,02	0,06	0,06	0,02	0,04	0,03	1,09	1,07	1,08	3,55	6,77
0,16	0,58	0,23	0,08	0,07	0,08	0,07	0,05	0,07	1,09	1,06	1,08	3,53	6,76
− 0,40	0,34	0,10	0,12	0,12	0,11	0,10	0,11	0,09	1,08	1,09	1,10	3,53	6,73
− 1,19	0,55	0,18	0,14	0,13	0,12	0,11	0,11	0,16	1,07	1,10	1,07	3,51	6,72
− 0,89	0,23	0,24	0,13	0,14	0,12	0,15	0,11	0,12	1,10	1,10	1,07	3,49	6,71
1,05	0,72	0,55	0,13	0,15	0,16	0,11	0,12	0,13	1,09	1,09	1,10	3,47	6,67
0,56	0,96	0,29	0,16	0,18	0,19	0,13	0,14	0,16	1,10	1,10	1,11	3,47	6,64
0,19	4,41	0,14	0,17	0,20	0,19	0,16	0,17	0,15	1,10	1,11	1,11	3,45	6,63
0,16	6,12	1,46	0,20	0,26	0,24	0,16	0,15	0,17	1,11	1,12	1,12	3,45	6,61
0,23	5,73	2,66	0,23	0,28	0,30	0,17	0,17	0,18	1,13	1,13	1,12	3,42	6,58
0,23	2,57	0,25	0,25	0,29	0,28	0,19	0,17	0,19	1,13	1,12	1,13	3,42	6,57
0,14	4,05	1,27	0,26	0,33	0,51	0,21	0,19	0,19	1,15	1,15	1,13	3,42	6,55
− 2,17	0,56	− 0,65	− 0,69	− 0,67	− 0,49	− 0,17	− 0,24	− 0,21	1,12	1,11	1,11	3,66	6,86

April 1881.

1 Zoll tief 7	1 Zoll tief 2	1 Zoll tief 8	1 Fuss tief 7	1 Fuss tief 2	1 Fuss tief 8	2 Fuss tief 7	2 Fuss tief 2	2 Fuss tief 8	4 Fuss tief 7	4 Fuss tief 2	4 Fuss tief 8	8 Fuss tief 7	16 Fuss tief 7
0,19	6,16	0,24	0,29	0,46	0,46	0,19	0,21	0,20	1,13	1,15	1,14	3,40	6,53
0,18	4,85	0,51	0,29	0,52	0,45	0,19	0,24	0,20	1,14	1,15	1,14	3,39	6,50
− 0,47	0,37	− 0,17	0,29	0,31	0,52	0,25	0,22	0,24	1,15	1,17	1,17	3,39	6,50
− 0,13	0,95	0,28	0,29	0,28	0,31	0,24	0,22	0,21	1,17	1,16	1,16	3,38	6,48
− 1,30	2,40	0,06	0,27	0,32	0,31	0,21	0,22	0,23	1,16	1,18	1,18	3,36	6,44
− 0,43	6,49	1,14	0,26	0,51	0,52	0,21	0,23	0,22	1,18	1,18	1,17	3,35	6,43
0,15	6,61	0,76	0,52	0,80	0,76	0,22	0,25	0,25	1,19	1,20	1,19	3,34	6,41
− 1,42	2,02	0,34	0,32	0,41	0,57	0,24	0,24	0,24	1,21	1,22	1,21	3,33	6,40
− 0,97	4,82	1,11	0,30	0,57	0,68	0,25	0,27	0,25	1,21	1,25	1,23	3,32	6,38
0,05	10,01	2,88	0,37	1,16	1,37	0,25	0,26	0,30	1,25	1,23	1,25	3,31	6,36
0,16	11,36	4,59	0,60	1,64	2,18	0,26	0,32	0,37	1,25	1,26	1,27	3,32	6,34
0,63	11,64	6,32	1,05	2,20	2,96	0,40	0,56	0,77	1,29	1,31	1,31	3,30	6,32
2,17	12,29	5,62	1,97	2,96	3,67	0,95	1,23	1,58	1,34	1,37	1,38	3,33	6,31
2,22	12,74	6,40	2,58	3,56	3,60	1,77	1,57	2,39	1,43	1,43	1,48	3,32	6,30
2,49	13,41	6,53	3,39	4,34	5,13	2,55	2,75	3,04	1,58	1,59	1,62	3,31	6,25
3,49	13,69	6,48	4,02	5,00	5,68	3,23	3,57	3,62	1,69	1,77	1,82	3,32	6,24
2,69	15,28	7,30	4,46	5,87	6,29	3,75	3,89	4,15	1,90	1,99	2,03	3,34	6,23
2,75	13,57	9,59	4,77	5,82	6,57	4,23	4,29	4,54	2,34	2,22	2,27	3,38	6,21
7,15	12,83	5,71	6,03	6,71	6,76	4,77	4,32	5,06	2,37	2,54	2,50	3,42	6,21
1,54	5,52	2,59	5,08	4,47	4,37	4,88	4,57	4,38	2,64	2,78	2,75	3,47	6,19
1,93	4,77	3,02	3,60	3,72	3,93	4,05	3,87	3,83	2,83	2,88	2,91	3,52	6,16
1,91	4,75	3,13	3,52	3,33	3,71	3,58	3,57	3,57	2,99	2,97	2,98	3,59	6,15
3,07	6,57	2,70	3,39	4,00	4,26	3,51	3,58	3,70	3,00	3,04	3,05	3,63	6,15
0,24	11,14	5,63	5,21	4,12	5,12	3,61	3,63	3,86	3,05	3,13	3,11	3,71	6,12
3,51	11,32	8,38	4,53	5,29	6,09	4,14	4,28	4,54	3,17	3,22	3,25	3,79	6,12
6,12	8,04	6,59	5,73	5,82	5,35	4,84	4,89	4,97	3,35	3,38	3,45	3,84	6,10
4,68	10,59	6,16	5,47	6,14	6,00	4,89	5,07	5,30	3,55	3,64	3,70	3,89	6,09
5,17	6,82	5,52	5,87	5,96	6,05	5,29	5,36	5,33	3,80	3,86	3,92	3,95	6,07
3,60	6,10	3,90	5,28	5,18	5,33	5,32	5,18	5,13	4,04	4,09	4,13	4,02	6,07
1,03	6,81	4,90	4,25	4,79	5,18	4,90	4,79	4,85	4,17	4,24	4,24	4,09	6,06
1,92	8,12	3,99	2,72	3,21	3,50	2,45	2,48	2,57	2,11	2,14	2,17	3,50	6,27

Mai 1881.

Luftthermometer

III. In Glas			IV. In Kupfer						VII.		
7	2	8	7	2	8	7	2	8	7	2	8
	12,40	9,73	4,29	10,66	9,50	4,30	10,49	9,40	4,31	10,43	10,09
,47	20,53	9,89	10,66	18,38	9,69	9,53	16,95	9,97	9,57	16,56	10,43
,70	25,46	17,61	10,23	22,84	17,04	10,31	22,24	16,74	10,03	21,94	17,96
,27	10,41	4,22	17,42	9,02	4,29	15,57	8,79	4,55	14,03	8,16	4,20
,44	14,20	6,49	5,89	11,72	6,42	6,03	11,18	6,67	5,24	9,82	6,47
,70	23,80	11,51	7,82	18,63	11,14	7,80	17,43	11,53	6,08	14,78	12,09
,51	17,61	9,12	11,14	15,49	8,98	11,31	14,74	9,36	11,47	13,27	9,40
,54	10,29	7,17	10,90	8,93	7,18	8,44	8,97	7,37	8,24	8,55	7,39
,54	8,01	2,68	4,00	5,74	2,75	4,38	5,30	2,32	3,97	4,39	2,69
,80	13,26	3,01	4,24	9,31	3,04	4,55	9,66	3,18	4,43	7,20	3,12
,86	10,21	3,01	8,78	7,53	3,04	5,30	8,10	3,25	3,93	6,08	3,43
,46	22,98	4,34	7,87	16,50	4,34	6,07	15,70	4,73	3,66	12,01	4,43
,05	24,93	10,05	13,55	21,04	9,69	9,01	19,75	10,27	7,01	16,75	10,47
,78	27,37	11,10	12,59	23,70	10,84	10,49	22,63	11,36	8,55	19,27	11,16
,11	28,72	9,32	13,70	25,54	9,21	13,61	22,59	10,06	12,39	20,79	9,43
,64	32,19	19,23	9,45	27,31	18,74	10,06	25,86	18,76	8,66	24,81	19,23
,40	12,73	6,81	12,30	11,57	6,51	12,61	11,79	6,71	12,62	11,70	6,70
,16	25,83	14,77	11,62	20,32	14,52	10,31	19,92	14,65	8,08	17,93	14,69
,04	31,82	19,48	15,97	26,85	19,01	15,57	26,55	19,19	15,43	24,73	19,57
,14	27,37	12,32	13,07	21,91	12,21	12,78	23,80	12,74	12,01	18,21	12,31
,73	20,74	8,71	11,57	17,23	8,68	12,18	16,44	9,23	11,12	14,69	8,93
,24	23,31	10,94	11,14	19,10	10,71	11,44	20,05	11,27	10,55	16,11	10,85
,95	25,75	15,99	12,83	19,64	15,73	12,31	19,49	15,70	12,05	18,05	15,84
,61	30,15	18,83	13,12	23,51	18,43	13,00	23,37	18,51	12,85	21,48	18,62
,64	32,87	16,39	17,23	27,14	15,97	15,30	27,24	16,41	15,37	24,54	16,17
,72	31,04	19,43	16,59	27,09	19,25	15,17	28,45	14,87	15,11	23,70	14,34
,28	32,06	14,36	13,36	26,61	14,18	13,44	26,94	19,32	13,40	21,94	19,46
,36	27,29	10,29	13,45	21,33	10,23	13,31	21,51	11,18	12,54	16,90	10,47
,24	25,22	7,98	12,11	22,25	7,67	11,70	21,64	8,84	11,62	15,80	7,97
,10	28,60	10,70	11,14	23,03	10,37	10,74	23,80	11,30	10,55	18,81	10,85
,73	27.78	11,51	11,24	22,35	11,62	11,40	22,50	12,05	11,28	21,41	11,78
,45	22,72	10,87	11,26	18,83	10,67	10,58	18,51	11,04	9,88	16,15	10,96

Juni 1881.

7	2	8	7	2	8	7	2	8	7	2	8
,00	31,45	14,07	11,72	26.12	13,70	11,66	25,18	14,57	11,81	21,79	14,11
,67	27,37	13,59	12,83	23,70	13.41	13,00	23,28	13,87	11,93	21,10	13,84
,81	32,92	15,66	14.18	29,90	15,39	14.70	28,28	16,00	14,30	25,00	15,92
,69	24,24	14.03	14,04	19,30	13,80	13,96	18,54	14,10	13,69	16,98	13,92
,72	31,04	18.18	15,97	29,41	17.85	15,87	27,24	18,20	15,45	26,00	18,51
,45	25,46	18,34	19,83	24.29	17,71	19,49	24.14	17,43	19,69	23,96	18.40
,06	31,45	12,20	20.12	27,58	12,16	20,01	26,90	13,00	20,41	27,12	12,54
,20	29,94	17,86	13,31	26,85	17,61	13,35	26,16	17,98	12.73	25,85	17,93
,43	12,32	10,70	10,56	11,67	10.47	11.44	11,70	10,61	11,35	11,24	10,51
,32	12,24	8,67	9,21	11,14	8.73	9,44	10,66	8,79	9,93	10,47	8,70
,59	10,79	8,35	8.49	10.18	8.25	8,62	9,93	8,53	8,55	9,70	8,47
,46	16,66	6.65	7,28	9,92	6,80	7.46	9.53	7,02	7,31	8,55	7,01
,65	11,51	6,97	6,13	9,45	6.80	6,37	9,36	6,93	6.24	8,55	6,98
,97	9.48	7,54	6.70	8.73	7.57	6,84	8,36	7,71	6,70	8,05	7,55
,45	22,20	9,08	9,74	18,14	8,73	9,01	17,51	9,49	8,12	15.15	9,20
,31	22,98	9,08	7,91	18.48	8,73	8,06	17,43	9,14	8.16	14,61	9,09
,58	25,46	11,22	9,98	19,93	10,95	9,88	19,23	11,36	9,86	16,07	11,16
,89	29,82	12,20	13,07	24,33	11,72	13,00	21,36	12,57	11,97	19,73	12,39
,51	31,12	18,02	10,90	30,10	17,42	10,90	24,92	17,73	10,62	22,86	17,97
,86	25,75	16,80	16,99	23,60	16,55	16,61	23,71	16,91	16,68	22,32	16,90
,28	28,27	21,27	15,39	25,59	20,66	15,48	25,65	20,74	15,15	24,66	21,10
,76	37,19	24,32	18,87	32,52	23,65	18,67	32,63	23,80	18,59	30,39	24,23
,36	27,62	16,19	23,27	24,91	15,97	22,97	24,79	16,52	23,09	24,19	16,60
,61	29,82	14,15	16,55	24,53	13,26	16,30	23,89	14,83	15,84	21,56	14,38
,42	25,79	15,99	14,66	24,38	15,78	14,31	21,90	16,48	14,30	19,65	16,22
,88	33,90	23.34	16,11	20,13	22,74	15,95	28,97	22,84	16,75	27,31	23,17
,55	23,71	15,99	18,35	21,09	15,59	18,20	22,50	16,80	18,05	21,94	15,99
,73	22,08	13,99	16,59	19,88	13,65	16,87	19,53	14,31	15,45	18,51	14,00
,32	18,42	13,63	16,11	16,59	13,65	16,04	16,08	14,27	14,88	[illegible]	[illegible]
,95	18,95	16,15	13,65	17.47	15,68	13,78	17,38	15,95	18,54	[illegible]	[illegible]
								14,26	13,37	19,16	14,23

Mai 1881.

Erdthermometer													
1 Zoll tief			1 Fuss tief			2 Fuss tief			4 Fuss tief			8 Fuss tief	16 Fuss tief
7	2	8	7	2	8	7	2	8	7	2	8	7	7
3,61	7,47	8,26	4,60	4,80	5,41	4,83	4,77	4,82	4,30	4,31	4,31	4,16	6,08
6,88	13,55	9,77	5,49	6,74	7,48	5,01	5,27	5,65	4,32	4,35	4,36	4,21	6,04
8,70	18,43	15,48	7,24	8,70	9,97	6,01	6,56	6,90	4,42	4,48	4,53	4,28	6,04
11,60	12,45	7,92	9,58	10,13	9,86	7,49	7,76	7,97	4,64	4,75	4,84	4,32	6,03
7,01	10,74	8,41	8,43	8,45	8,72	7,81	7,69	7,69	5,02	5,15	5,22	4,41	6,04
6,55	15,05	12,13	7,87	8,65	9,59	7,56	7,56	7,81	5,34	5,44	5,48	4,47	6,03
10.24	13,00	10,49	9,22	9,64	9,83	8,08	8,17	8,32	5,56	5,63	5,68	4,55	6,03
7,85	9,62	8,23	8,81	8,69	8,71	8,26	8,12	8,07	5,80	5,87	5,93	4,63	6,03
6,05	6,82	5,17	7,96	7,68	7,53	7,87	7,68	7,56	6,01	6,06	6,09	4,74	6,03
5,15	8,29	5,33	6,87	6,98	7,15	7,25	7,09	7,06	6,13	6,16	6,16	4,84	6,02
4,30	7,89	5,75	6,31	6,58	6,79	6,84	6,72	6,74	6,12	6,16	6,15	4,91	6,01
3,49	14,06	7,78	5,96	7,01	7,96	6,53	6,58	6,80	6,11	6,13	6,11	5,02	6,02
5,42	16,93	12,01	6,96	8,80	9,53	6,95	7,15	7,51	6,04	6,10	6,08	5,08	6,00
7,72	19,18	13,42	8,71	9,89	11,08	7,88	8,13	8,53	6,08	6,15	6,18	5,16	6,01
11,04	19,93	13,04	10,29	11.87	12,12	8,93	9,17	0,53	6,26	6,32	6,42	5,25	6,04
9,33	22,14	17,71	10,77	11,92	13,09	9,65	9,85	10,21	6,53	6,65	6,70	5,32	6,05
13,20	12,99	9,29	12,47	12,13	11,61	10,61	10,61	10,52	6,86	6,97	7,06	5,39	6,04
7,98	17,73	14.24	9,89	10,75	11,60	10,02	9,90	10,03	7,19	7,34	7,35	5,45	6,04
13,06	22,44	18,24	11,45	12,68	13,71	10,28	10,53	10,90	7,46	7,52	7,55	5,56	6,06
12,76	20,42	14,52	13.03	13,67	13,99	11,30	10,48	11,66	7,65	7,74	7,81	5,65	6,07
12.29	15,63	11,48	12,91	12,96	12,85	11,75	11,66	11,65	7,95	8,05	8,13	5,76	6,09
10,85	17,45	13,03	11,77	12,45	12,93	11,40	11,30	11,43	8,26	8,26	8,40	5,88	6,11
10,87	17,07	15,13	11,92	12,42	12,97	11,41	11,36	11,48	8,48	8,55	8,65	5,98	6,11
12.17	19,16	17,77	12,41	13,01	13,93	11,54	11,61	11,81	8,61	8,71	8,73	6,09	6,11
13,52	22,46	17,98	13,37	14,33	15,21	12,08	12,26	12,55	8,80	8,89	8,95	6,20	6,11
14,24	22,90	17,36	14,81	15,45	16,20	12,82	12,99	13,72	8,97	9,09	9,47	6,33	6,14
13,63	22,51	19,62	15,02	15,60	16,15	13,52	13,54	13,32	9,33	9,45	9,23	6,46	6,15
13,77	20,31	11,93	15,07	15,42	15,79	13,85	13,81	13,91	9,66	9,77	9,80	6,58	6,15
12,11	19,56	13,73	14,45	14,95	15,31	13,81	13,70	13,76	9,94	10,05	10,09	6,69	6,18
10,82	20,31	15,05	13,75	14,41	15,11	13,58	13,39	13,55	10,18	10,27	10,27	6,82	6,19
11,31	22,28	15,38	13,81	14,50	15.17	13,52	13,46	13,59	10,25	10,42	10,42	6,96	6,20
9,65	16,41	12,44	10,34	11,01	11,15	9,63	9,63	9,64	7,04	7,12	7,13	5,88	6,07

Juni 1881.

7	2	8	7	2	8	7	2	8	7	2	8	7	7
11,85	22,07	16,79	13,05	14,87	15,61	13,56	13,58	13,76	10,47	10,53	10,56	7,10	6,22
13,08	21,27	16,23	14,55	15,21	15,63	13,86	13,89	14,01	10,63	10,67	10,69	7,26	6,24
13,39	23,71	18,17	14,57	15,60	16,46	13,98	14,07	14,31	10,79	10,84	10,87	7,38	6,26
14,47	18,89	15,87	15,65	15,82	16,00	14,52	14,53	14,57	10,95	11,03	11,06	7,50	6,28
15,39	27,71	19,07	15,34	15,98	16,63	14,57	14,59	14,73	11,17	11,21	11,25	7,64	6,32
17,19	22.26	18.23	16,06	16,80	16,87	14,86	15,02	15,09	11,35	11,40	11,44	7,76	6,34
17,04	23,67	15.75	16,14	16,89	16,91	15,09	15,17	15,22	11,55	11,61	11,67	7,91	6,37
13,99	22,10	17,82	15,50	16,24	16,54	15,07	14,99	15,06	11.76	11,81	11,86	8,00	6,40
13,81	13,61	12.61	15,83	15,23	14,82	15,08	14,88	14,68	11,92	11,93	11,98	8,15	6,43
11,19	12.21	11.16	13,83	13,89	13,24	14,23	13,90	13,68	12,02	12,03	12,01	8,27	6,46
10,25	11,20	10,82	12,62	12,38	12,30	13,30	13,00	12,46	12,01	11,97	11,96	8,39	6,48
9.17	10,14	9.11	11,66	11,49	11,37	12,48	12,28	12,12	11,86	11,83	11,75	8,52	6,51
7,99	9,78	8,74	10,75	10,64	10,67	11,77	11,57	11,42	11,66	11,62	11,54	8.61	6,53
8,14	9.22	8,71	10.27	10,22	10,29	11,19	11,03	10,96	11,43	11,36	11,31	8,71	6,56
9,10	15,11	11,86	10,06	10,81	11,55	10.81	10,83	10,90	11,17	11,13	11,07	8,77	6,60
9,15	15.13	11,00	10,95	11,32	11,93	11,13	11,13	11,26	10,96	10,93	10,89	8,83	6,63
9,71	16,67	13.24	11,17	11,88	12,71	11,35	11,37	11,60	10,83	10,86	10,83	8,85	6,66
11,97	19,01	14,62	12,22	13,13	13,96	11,83	11,07	12,28	10,81	10,82	10,81	8,90	6,71
10,88	19,40	17,06	12,93	13,55	14,48	12,51	12,55	12,78	10,85	10,89	10,89	8,92	6,76
14.23	19,01	16,56	14,03	14,56	14,97	13,09	13,20	13,39	10,94	10,98	11,04	8,92	6,77
14,13	21,43	19,32	14,32	15,09	15,96	13,50	13,63	13,90	11,12	11,19	11,23	8,93	6,82
16,69	24,78	22,19	15.63	16,55	17,53	14,22	14,48	14,82	11,33	11,40	11,47	8.97	6,84
19,78	23,52	18,47	17,37	17,98	18,00	15,30	15,56	15,73	11,60	11.69	11,76	9,01	6,89
15,99	21,27	17,10	16,79	16,59	17,34	15,72	15,68	15.74	11,95	12,08	12,13	9,07	6,92
14,26	19,73	17,77	16,11	16,38	16.97	15,62	15,49	15,58	12.28	12,37	12,43	9,13	6,96
15,65	23,86	21,44	16,38	17,15	17,92	15,60	15,68	15.88	12,52	12,59	12.61	9,21	7,02
17,37	21,10	18,48	17,44	17,81	18,01	16,13	16,22	16,30	12,70	12,78	12.81	9,29	7,04
16,83	18,65	16,26	17.25	17,16	17,08	16,31	16,21	16,17	12,87	13,00	13,06	9,40	7,05
15,47	16,51	15,52	16,29	15,52	16,24	15,93	15,80	15,74	13,15	13,20	13,22	9,51	7,10
14,61	16,03	16,01	15,71	15,65	15,79	15,94	15,40	15,36	13.27	13,30	13,33	9,60	7,12
13,59	18,63	15,57	14,38	14,73	15,12	13,95	13,92	13,99	11,60	11,63	11,65	8,55	6,64

Juli 1881.

	Luftthermometer											
	III. in Glas			IV. in Kupfer			I' frei			VII.		
	7	2	8	7	2	8	7	2	8	7	2	8
1	17,61	32,48	16,51	16,79	27,04	15,87	16,48	27,46	16,69	15,61	23,13	16,68
2	16,31	33,08	15,62	15,63	28,16	15,29	15,26	27,72	16,17	14,69	23,30	16,18
3	14,07	34,30	22,49	13,36	31,06	21,77	14,09	30,35	21,73	14,15	26,81	22,62
4	17,40	16,80	15,70	16,94	16,31	15,49	17,34	16,48	15,78	16,83	16,94	15,92
5	17,00	20,86	16,03	15,92	19,16	15,49	15,57	17,94	15,70	15,30	17,13	15,92
6	14,77	28,27	13,55	14,04	23,32	13,17	13,96	21,81	14,31	14,03	20,41	13,96
7	13,06	14,77	15,13	12,55	14,04	14,52	12,91	14,31	14,48	11,62	13,54	14,84
8	15,99	20,05	13,95	15,05	18,38	13,79	14,87	15,87	14,14	14,26	15,53	13,88
9	14,77	26,28	17,53	13,94	23,26	16,74	13,74	21,04	16,95	13,42	19,27	17,02
10	17,24	18,34	14,07	16,45	17,04	13,60	16,44	17,43	14,31	15,41	17,55	14,61
11	16,39	22,49	14,28	15,49	18,63	13,80	15,17	18,03	14,31	15,07	17,06	14,84
12	16,31	29,08	15,58	15,54	23,70	15,29	15,35	24,23	15,91	15,45	20,79	15,80
13	15,37	33,74	19,23	14,81	30,00	18,87	15,26	27,50	19,36	14,99	24,77	19,35
14	18,25	21,27	15,58	17,66	19,21	15,15	17,68	18,46	15,61	17,47	17,74	15,72
15	18,87	22,49	17,53	17,90	20,27	16,99	17,81	19,83	17,43	17,36	18,62	17,44
16	21,06	34,71	16,68	20,12	30,43	16,74	19,88	28,54	17,55	20,07	27,31	17,36
17	16,55	27,05	14,89	15,49	23,41	14,42	15,52	20,18	15,00	15,03	18,74	14,88
18	16,68	15,09	14,03	15,97	14,38	14,04	15,43	13,31	14,35	15,07	13,84	14,61
19	18,50	13,55	17,61	16,94	25,30	17,04	16,91	24,53	17,47	16,56	22,78	17,74
20	18,14	39,83	25,34	17,32	43,67	24,72	17,34	34,91	25,13	17,55	32,89	25,28
21	22,00	29,00	16,64	21,28	25,64	16,21	21,21	24,23	16,69	21,14	22,05	16,60
22	16,59	28,60	13,63	15,68	27,09	13,45	15,70	21,38	14,22	15,45	19,27	13,84
23	16,80	25,75	15,83	15,97	21,72	15,15	15,57	21,21	16,26	14,92	19,46	15,68
24	12,48	34,30	20,53	11,62	29,80	19,98	12,35	29,36	20,35	12,50	26,06	20,79
25	20,37	30,64	23,34	18,92	27,43	23,22	19,19	27,24	23,24	19,12	26,62	23,39
26	18,02	20,13	20,86	17,91	19,11	20,66	18,29	19,66	20,35	18,28	20,52	20,87
27	17,69	20,98	16,03	17,18	18,38	15,50	17,34	17,47	15,74	18,21	17,28	16,14
28	14,97	25,83	13,87	13,84	21,91	13,55	13,65	20,35	13,87	13,24	18,36	13,54
29	13,71	24,52	18,22	13,07	22,35	17,90	13,04	21,34	17,90	12,81	19,76	18,13
30	18,26	24,24	17,20	17,66	22,50	16,91	16,91	21,81	17,73	16,83	20,41	17,06
31	16,23	33,49	23,22	15,49	28,54	22,74	15,82	28,45	22,93	15,45	25,54	23,39
	16,82	29,09	17,15	16,02	23,75	17,15	16,05	22,34	17,15	15,74	20,75	17,23

August 1881.

	7	2	8	7	2	8	7	2	8	7	2	8
1	18,54	20,86	16,39	18,16	19,11	15,97	18,37	19,53	16,26	18,51	19,95	16,87
2	15,46	18,02	12,73	14,81	16,84	12,35	14,83	16,61	12,91	14,38	16,22	18,00
3	14,81	21,11	13,55	11,57	18,97	13,07	14,05	17,77	14,00	14,30	17,08	[illegible]
4	12,57	29,90	16,11	12,49	19,11	15,83	12,74	18,59	16,04	13,08	18,17	[illegible]
5	15,62	27,37	13,79	14,95	22,20	13,50	14,65	19,92	14,52	14,84	18,51	[illegible]
6	17,73	35,52	22,45	17,23	32,42	22,01	17,25	30,17	22,28	16,52	26,54	[illegible]
7	16,80	29,41	11,77	15,97	21,67	11,52	15,87	22,93	15,30	15,68	20,41	[illegible]
8	15,78	32,27	15,70	15,49	27,19	15,34	14,91	26,38	16,39	14,77	23,51	[illegible]
9	13,22	32,67	19,48	12,88	27,38	18,97	13,04	26,85	19,02	12,81	25,47	[illegible]
10	15,99	19,39	14,61	15,25	18,28	14,23	15,90	17,55	14,82	15,95	16,90	[illegible]
11	13,34	13,43	11,51	12,59	12,83	11,38	13,13	13,18	11,70	13,24	13,54	[illegible]
12	12,16	18,78	11,14	11,52	10,53	10,66	11,88	10,83	11,18	11,35	10,85	[illegible]
13	12,01	27,17	12,93	11,52	22,85	12,88	11,09	20,78	13,09	11,35	20,49	[illegible]
14	13,63	27,25	13,14	13,26	22,01	12,69	13,26	19,06	13,65	13,24	18,47	[illegible]
15	11,63	23,79	14,52	10,90	22,15	14,14	11,14	20,35	15,08	11,47	18,89	[illegible]
16	12,73	28,44	12,14	12,11	23,36	12,21	12,10	19,70	13,00	12,85	19,97	[illegible]
17	13,71	28,52	14,32	12,97	21,13	14,28	12,83	21,35	14,91	12,96	20,91	[illegible]
18	15,91	29,00	13,67	14,66	25,16	13,55	15,52	21,64	14,09	14,69	[illegible]	[illegible]
19	13,63	22,90	11,76	12,88	19,01	11,24	12,91	17,64	12,14	13,04	[illegible]	[illegible]
20	11,84	16,39	13,87	11,38	15,83	13,55	15,74	15,82	13,87	11,54	16,07	[illegible]
21	14,93	24,60	14,69	14,14	20,70	14,04	13,91	19,06	14,31	14,92	[illegible]	[illegible]
22	12,77	18,14	12,04	12,11	14,52	11,62	12,14	13,78	12,14	12,77	[illegible]	[illegible]
23	12,40	22,20	10,74	12,11	18,77	10,56	12,27	18,33	11,48	12,35	[illegible]	[illegible]
24	11,73	23,02	16,07	11,24	20,46	15,97	11,44	19,32	16,04	11,16	[illegible]	[illegible]
25	15,13	21,27	14,65	14,18	18,48	14,38	13,78	17,64	14,44	15,30	[illegible]	[illegible]
26	13,63	24,12	19,23	13,07	22,01	19,16	13,09	20,87	18,67	13,54	[illegible]	[illegible]
27	16,68	30,02	18,83	16,21	27,87	18,24	16,17	27,20	18,72	16,45	[illegible]	[illegible]
28	16,31	20,57	12,52	15,73	18,58	12,59	15,78	18,37	13,13	16,08	[illegible]	[illegible]
29	10,29	16,47	11,10	9,94	14,57	10,76	10,49	14,00	11,27	10,58	[illegible]	[illegible]
30	11,79	20,86	12,57	11,24	18,48	12,11	11,31	18,33	12,78	[illegible]	[illegible]	[illegible]
31	12,32	21,96	14,81	11,67	19,25	14,52	11,74	18,24	14,61	[illegible]	[illegible]	[illegible]
	14,35	23,75	14,07	13,78	15,42	13,75	13,63	19,41	14,57	[illegible]	[illegible]	[illegible]

Juli 1881.

Erdthermometer

		1 Fuss tief			2 Fuss tief			4 Fuss tief			8 Fuss tief	16 Fuss tief
	8	7	2	8	7	2	8	7	2	8	7	7
21,98	18,01	15,45	15,46	16,93	15,28	15,29	15,50	13,32	13,33	13,34	9,73	7,15
22,38	18,16	16,19	16,77	17,40	15,65	15,67	15,88	13,33	13,35	13,35	9,81	7,19
23,47	20,82	16,44	17,17	17,94	15,98	16,01	16,23	13,38	13,41	13,43	9,93	7,22
17,23	16,76	17,75	17,50	17,28	16,53	16,55	16,52	13,47	13,52	13,54	10,02	7,25
16,99	16,19	16,67	16,59	16,58	16,32	16,16	16,10	13,64	13,68	13,71	10,11	7,28
19,26	16,14	15,79	16,14	16,49	15,86	15,73	15,80	13,76	13,80	13,79	10,20	7,32
14,45	14,91	15,63	15,39	15,42	15,73	15,55	15,43	13,79	13,79	13,80	10,27	7,35
15,43	14,73	14,94	14,96	15,07	15,21	15,06	15,01	15,79	13,76	13,78	10,37	7,39
18,83	17,08	14,68	15,19	15,79	14,88	14,86	14,98	13,74	13,71	13,70	10,46	7,44
17,33	15,75	15,53	15,91	16,08	15,12	15,18	15,29	13,66	13,63	13,63	10,52	7,47
17,02	15,27	15,35	15,57	15,73	15,24	15,17	15,20	13,63	13,64	13,64	10,60	7,50
20,25	17,21	15,22	15,91	16,52	15,12	15,17	15,36	13,64	13,66	13,64	10,66	7,54
22,44	19,56	15,80	16,61	17,40	15,50	15,57	15,82	13,64	13,65	13,65	10,72	7,60
18,39	16,81	17,06	17,05	17,04	16,13	16,13	16,15	13,69	13,71	13,74	10,77	7,63
18,34	17,85	16,55	16,80	17,04	16,09	16,07	16,14	13,79	13,83	13,86	10,82	7,65
24,04	19,33	16,83	17,83	18,30	16,17	16,34	16,57	13,90	13,95	13,97	10,86	7,70
19,97	17,26	17,51	17,61	17,76	16,74	16,72	16,77	14,02	14,06	14,11	10,92	7,75
15,19	15,37	16,90	16,58	16,44	16,67	16,49	16,36	14,15	14,21	14,22	10,96	7,77
20,92	18,45	16,30	17,02	17,49	16,17	16,25	16,38	14,28	14,33	14,29	11,04	7,82
27,57	23,93	16,96	18,36	19,32	16,48	16,66	17,04	14,32	14,27	14,34	11,10	7,86
21,84	18,43	18,93	19,05	18,95	17,40	17,51	17,58	14,37	14,42	14,47	11,14	7,89
20,95	16,95	17,98	18,22	18,28	17,46	17,38	17,41	14,54	14,59	14,65	11,20	7,93
20,73	18,09	17,28	17,74	18,03	17,25	17,17	17,20	14,68	14,74	14,75	11,28	7,96
23,63	20,63	16,89	17,81	18,52	17,06	17,04	17,21	14,80	14,82	14,84	11,34	8,01
24,04	22,34	18,11	18,94	19,46	17,37	17,53	17,69	14,83	14,86	14,89	11,42	8,03
19,37	19,81	18,74	18,67	18,76	17,80	17,77	17,76	14,93	14,96	14,99	11,50	8,07
17,09	16,30	18,37	17,75	17,48	17,67	17,48	17,36	15,08	15,09	15,13	11,58	8,12
17,31	15,26	16,42	16,40	16,48	16,93	16,71	16,59	15,17	15,18	15,16	11,65	8,14
19,74	17,56	15,61	16,31	16,79	16,30	16,23	16,30	15,15	15,11	15,19	11,70	8,18
19,65	18,24	16,35	16,85	17,26	16,30	16,35	16,45	15,04	15,07	14,99	11,78	8,21
23,99	21,91	16,88	17,89	18,68	16,53	16,71	16,96	14,96	14,96	14,94	11,86	8,30
20,04	17,87	16,61		17,31	16,28	16,27	16,35	14,20	14,17	14,18	10,85	7,74

August 1881.

		1 Fuss tief			2 Fuss tief			4 Fuss tief			8 Fuss tief	16 Fuss tief
	8	7	2	8	7	2	8	7	2	8	7	7
19,80	18,11	18,31	18,46	18,54	17,25	17,34	17,43	14,95	14,96	14,98	11,89	8,33
16,36	14,86	17,36	17,07	16,88	17,21	17,02	16,91	15,08	14,05	15,07	11,94	8,35
17,56	15,81	15,99	16,30	16,59	16,58	16,41	16,39	15,10	15,10	15,10	11,98	8,40
16,85	16,01	15,72	15,88	16,02	16,20	16,07	16,03	15,08	15,05	15,05	12,04	8,43
16,51	16,42	15,64	16,31	16,73	15,90	15,91	16,06	14,99	14,99	14,98	12,08	8,46
25,07	21,92	16,25	17,64	18,49	16,00	16,33	16,65	14,94	14,90	14,88	12,14	8,50
21,36	17,72	17,93	18,19	18,26	16,97	17,04	17,14	14,88	14,89	14,94	12,16	8,53
23,49	18,58	17,18	18,04	18,36	17,01	17,08	17,18	14,92	14,97	14,98	12,18	8,53
24,21	20,35	17,25	18,27	18,68	17,09	17,20	17,32	15,03	15,07	15,07	12,21	8,57
17,82	16,44	17,92	17,73	17,51	17,34	17,26	17,19	15,12	15,18	15,15	12,23	8,61
16,62	13,52	16,63	16,45	16,20	16,88	16,74	16,55	15,19	15,20	15,22	12,27	8,66
12,96	13,28	15,28	15,12	15,12	16,15	15,93	15,77	15,21	15,23	15,18	12,29	8,69
17,19	13,95	14,37	14,90	14,87	15,26	15,34	15,29	15,13	15,08	15,04	12,37	8,72
18,49	15,31	14,91	15,50	15,72	15,24	15,30	15,38	14,96	14,94	14,89	12,42	8,78
19,29	15,95	14,78	15,56	15,96	15,27	15,30	15,40	14,82	14,75	14,75	12,42	8,80
19,33	15,20	15,27	15,88	16,03	15,40	15,46	15,55	14,69	14,69	14,67	12,44	8,84
20,10	16,13	15,13	15,99	16,35	15,41	15,50	15,61	14,64	14,63	14,60	12,44	8,86
18,55	15,61	15,79	16,20	16,22	15,65	15,68	15,78	14,58	14,58	14,57	12,44	8,90
17,15	14,33	15,46	15,68	15,63	15,57	15,54	15,57	14,57	14,57	14,57	12,45	8,94
14,86	14,31	14,58	14,64	14,83	15,26	15,10	15,02	14,54	14,54	14,54	12,44	8,96
18,47	15,27	14,34	15,36	15,62	14,89	15,00	15,08	14,50	14,51	14,47	12,45	8,99
15,48	13,99	14,75	14,92	14,97	15,02	14,97	15,01	14,42	14,42	14,39	12,44	9,02
17,89	14,13	14,27	15,05	15,30	14,76	14,80	14,87	14,36	14,34	14,32	12,45	9,06
15,68	14,32	14,13	14,20	14,9[illegible]	14,72	14,59	14,67	14,28	14,27	14,25	12,45	9,08
17,39	15,12	14,94	15,43	15,55	14,76	14,89	14,95	14,22	14,19	14,18	12,44	9,12
17,57	16,85	14,84	15,20	15,60	14,88	14,89	14,96	14,16	14,16	14,16	12,44	9,15
22,53	19,50	15,33	16,60	17,39	15,02	15,31	15,60	14,15	14,13	14,14	12,43	9,17
17,80	14,91	16,47	16,53	16,29	15,75	15,76	15,72	14,16	14,18	14,20	12,42	9,20
14,08	13,02	15,17	14,80	14,66	15,46	15,23	15,07	14,24	14,25	14,26	12,41	9,24
17,21	14,42	13,83	14,46	14,92	14,68	14,62	14,68	14,26	14,25	14,24	12,41	9,27
15,93	14,80	14,24	14,43	14,71	14,58	14,53	14,57	14,20	14,18	14,17	12,40	9,29

September 1881.

Luftthermometer

	…s		IV. In Kupfer						VII.		
7	2	8	7	2	8	7	2	8	7	2	8
2,73		12,94	11,79	21,91	16,94	12,57	21,88	17,43	12,93	22,40	18,43
		16,72	12,59	23,51	16,21	12,74	21,78	16,48	13,08	21,64	16,98
2,48	19,64	15,09	12,35	17,71	14,62	12,66	15,82	14,82	12,96	15,95	15,37
	24,60	17,77	16,21		18,28	16,26	21,68	17,60	17,36	22,21	18,13
4,11	23,83	15,66	13,55	21,91	15,49	13,74	19,92	15,87	13,54	20,49	15,99
	23,75	17,16	15,87	22,15	16,94	16,00	21,51	17,55	15,84	21,18	17,36
		18,71	15,49	22,54	18,43	15,48	24,36	18,63	15,18	24,92	19,27
		18,02	15,63		17,90	15,82	23,93	18,41	15,53	23,47	16,47
5,17		15,91	14,90		15,59	15,48	20,26	16,04	14,73	19,46	16,22
		15,09	16,45		14,76	16,57	20,01	14,83	16,68	19,95	15,18
	23,14	17,98	13,80		17,56	13,70	20,35	17,60	13,54	20,64	18,09
	18,95	14,65	16,94	17,90	14,52	16.91	17,86	14,95	17,21	17,97	15,45
4,44		12,48	14,09		12,16	13.78	17,81	12,41	14,22	17,74	13,16
8,43	17,61	11,63	12,73		11,52	12,96	15,61	11,44	12,81	15,11	11,85
	16,39	11,18	12,21		11,14	12,31	14,87	11,57	12,24	14,84	12,01
1,97	20,29	12,82	11,62		12,21	11,79	17,08	12,57	11,70	16,03	12,39
1,51	14,85	10,66	11,14		10,47	11,27	13,26	10,93	11,54	12,98	11,16
0,78		13,26	10,42	17,52	13,07	10,83	17,51	13,31	10,62	17,55	13,46
1,51	17,49	12,77	11,04	15,49	12,59	11,09	15,17	12,70	10,70	14,96	13,54
	14,77	12,98	14,04		12,88	14,22	14,52	13,13	14,30	13,96	13,27
		4,62	6,22	9,69	4,73	6,41	9,75	4,86	6,16	9,24	4,81
0,59		3,41	0,67	8,63	3,42	0,98	8,70	3,48	0,96	7,58	3,46
0,51		5,03	0,58	8,78	5,25	0,85	9,10	5,21	0,77	8,89	5,55
		3,97	— 0,05	13,12	4,00	0,45	13,18	4,90	0,47	11,74	5,12
		4,62	4,58	14,04	4,73	4,90	13,44	5,53	4,50	13,62	6,20
	15,74	7,58	— 0,29	14,04	7,57	0,86	13,88	7,80	0,00	13,27	8,16
	11,29	7,58	2,11	10,13	7,43	2,61	10,31	7,80	2,43	9,70	7,82
7,05	14,86	7,46	7,04	13,21	7,83	7,37	13,04	7,27	7,16	12,62	8,16
[illegible]	13,95	4,22	1,44	11,43	4,15	1,71	11,74	4,47	2,23	11,43	5,08
		3,71	— 0,57	11,14	3,85	— 0,02	11,27	4,47	0,04	10,93	4,70
0,11	13,73	11,51	9,81	16,69	11,46	10,06	16,40	11,81	10,18	15,98	12,16

October 1881.

7	2	8	7	2	8	7	2	8	7	2	8
1,68	14,85		1,59	12,83	9,60	1,96	12,14	10,06	2,00	10,93	10,05
7,17	13,63	5,	7,04	12,21	5,89	7,46	11,96	6,23	7,62	11,32	6,32
5,51	10,66	3,	5,55	7,67	9,23	5,64	8,21	3,31	5,85	7,20	3,27
3,97	6,69	4,	3,80	6,18	4,87	3,87	6,07	4,86	3,61	5,70	4,31
1,80	13,51	4,	1,87	10,56	4,68	1,96	10,74	4,77	2,08	10,05	5,06
0,59	14,65	4,	0,58	12,35	4,77	0,79	12,48	4,80	0,85	12,39	5,16
0,99	15,66	6,24	1,01	13,21	5,94	1,15	13,13	6,07	1,28	13,27	6,78
2,52	17,73		2,46	15,59	7,28	2,61	15,52	7,37	2,60	15,76	8,06
1,96	17,12		1,73	15,49	10,66	2,27	15,89	10,74	2,58	15,53	11,04
8,51	13,34		8,30	12,40	7,67	8,62	12,27	7,97	8,59	11,78	7,97
3,61	16,39	8,27	3,52	15,10	8,25	4,04	14,00	8,49	4,31	13,54	8,68
6,69	9,89		6,46	9,59	6,82	6,50	9,84	6,50	6,58	10,20	6,66
6,65	13,55		6,46	12,11	5,50	6,54	11,74	5,77	6,66	11,51	[illegible]
5,92	12,82		5,74	10,56	6,18	6,28	10,31	6,71	5,98	9,78	
9,40	9,89		8,87	8,78	6,80	9,19	8,66	6,84	9,62	8,63	
2,52	8,55		2,41	7,91	4,73	2,74	7,80	5,12	2,69	7,82	
5,11	11,10		5,21	10,13	4,19	5,84	9,57	4,51	5,47	8,82	
5,84	9,08		5,84	8,25	6,70	5,98	8,27	6,93	5,93	8,05	
6,77	8,92	7,46	6,80	8,63	7,38	6,93	8,66	7,41	6,74	8,69	
1,76	9,64	4,26	1,87	6,94	4,89	2,14	6,54	4,55	2,12	5,98	
3,81	6,82	3,81	3,90	5,50	3,90	3,91	5,51	4,00	3,93	[illegible]	
2,28	5,15	3,41	2,41	4,68	3,42	2,48	4,68	3,48	2,39		
3,41	7,05	5,03	3,42	6,70	4,97	3,52	6,59	5,21	2,39		
3,81	5,84		3,71	5,40	4,24	3,82	5,80	4,34	3,50		
3,98	4,06		4,00	3,32	1,78	3,91	3,26	1,88	3,85		
0,14	3,01		0,05	2,70	0,82	0,06	2,61	0,89	— 0,08		
0,82	3,13	0,11	— 0,71	2,51	0,05	— 0,28	2,27	0,32	— 0,52		
0,30	— 0,22	— 2,40	— 0,24	— 0,48	— 2,26	— 0,15	— 0,41	— 2,10	— 0,11		
4,98	— 1,31	— 3,45	— 4,79	— 2,84	— 3,42	— 4,56	— 2,61	— 3,43	— 4,81		
4,74	3,13	— 5,87	— 4,56	— 1,11	— 5,70	— 4,39	— 1,62	— 5,46	— 4,59		
9,50	0,75	— 1,83	— 9,05	— 1,64	— 1,88	— 9,05	— 0,75	— 1,88	— 9,17		

September 1881.

Erdthermometer

1 Zoll tief			1 Fuss tief			2 Fuss tief			4 Fuss tief			8 Fuss tief 16
7	2	8	7	2	8	7	2	8	7	2	8	7
13,98	18,83	16,96	14,39	15,14	15,73	14,53	14,63	14,83	14,14	14,10	14,09	12,41
13,49	19,07	16,53	15,07	15,58	16,00	14,90	14,95	15,11	14,07	14,05	14,06	12,41
13,75	15,15	13,83	15,21	14,89	15,08	15,08	14,91	15,00	14,07	14,07	14,07	12,40
15,54	19,67	17,43	15,02	15,93	16,36	14,84	15,03	15,23	14,07	14,06	14,07	12,40
14,64	18,16	16,32	15,73	15,81	16,04	15,31	15,30	15,35	14,06	14,06	14,09	12,39
15,59	20,54	17,94	15,62	16,44	16,97	15,31	15,48	15,70	14,10	14,10	14,14	12,39
15,82	21,82	18,50	16,43	17,19	17,54	15,79	15,95	16,13	14,15	14,21	14,20	12,40
16,00	20,65	18,44	16,68	17,15	17,47	16,11	16,14	16,28	14,23	14,26	14,20	12,39
16,19	19,54	16,98	16,81	16,93	17,09	16,26	16,23	16,27	14,35	14,37	14,42	12,40
16,53	19,52	16,03	16,64	17,04	17,11	16,21	16,22	16,33	14,46	14,48	14,48	12,40
14,02	18,89	16,80	15,94	16,12	16,48	16,04	15,89	15,96	14,53	14,56	14,58	12,41
16,66	17,59	17,27	16,21	16,49	16,51	15,90	15,92	15,97	14,57	14,57	14,57	12,45
14,42	17,03	14,21	15,80	15,81	15,73	15,81	15,67	15,84	14,58	14,57	14,57	12,46
13,83	15,64	13,00	15,03	15,07	14,94	15,38	15,23	15,15	14,57	14,55	14,54	12,48
12,57	16,22	13,48	14,24	14,36	14,65	14,85	14,70	14,72	14,51	14,48	14,45	12,50
12,47	16,66	13,80	14,01	14,40	14,67	14,55	14,48	14,52	14,39	14,35	14,31	12,51
12,44	14,49	12,66	14,13	14,14	14,20	14,47	14,38	14,37	14,27	14,23	14,20	12,54
11,38	17,93	14,00	13,52	14,09	14,53	14,18	14,11	14,22	14,16	14,14	14,09	12,54
11,79	14,49	13,44	13,88	13,77	13,92	14,22	14,11	14,07	14,04	14,01	14,00	12,55
11,15	14,57	13,77	14,03	14,16	14,20	14,05	14,08	14,10	14,01	13,92	13,91	12,55
9,35	12,26	7,74	13,53	13,09	12,69	14,00	13,80	13,59	13,86	13,85	13,81	12,54
4,11	10,02	6,03	10,75	10,61	10,56	12,92	12,46	12,22	13,78	13,73	13,66	12,52
2,69	10,47	6,97	9,07	9,33	9,78	11,60	11,25	11,16	13,54	13,46	13,35	12,51
3,76	12,81	7,78	8,84	9,41	9,98	10,84	10,71	10,75	13,17	13,06	12,95	12,50
6,05	13,52	8,44	9,16	9,79	10,25	10,66	10,60	10,71	12,81	12,70	12,60	12,50
4,11	13,77	9,33	9,14	9,68	10,27	10,61	10,52	10,60	12,47	12,37	12,22	12,44
5,84	10,12	8,75	9,43	9,57	9,77	10,56	10,45	10,46	12,21	12,16	12,10	12,37
7,91	11,57	9,00	9,54	9,89	10,17	10,41	10,41	10,48	12,01	11,95	11,91	12,30
4,93	12,93	7,67	9,17	9,67	10,01	10,38	10,30	10,35	11,84	11,78	11,75	12,22
3,76	11,86	7,41	8,77	9,15	9,52	10,19	10,06	10,06	11,70	11,65	11,61	12,16
11,44	12,49	13,17	13,66	13,82	13,87	13,96	14,13	14,19	13,76	13,73	13,71	12,43

October 1881.

1 Zoll tief			1 Fuss tief			2 Fuss tief			4 Fuss tief			8 Fuss tief 16
7	2	8	7	2	8	7	2	8	7	2	8	7
	13,20	10,28	8,76	9,39	10,01	9,95	9,92	10,03	11,52	11,49	11,44	12,07
	11,48	8,60	9,77	10,01	10,16	10,20	10,24	10,30	11,36	11,32	11,30	11,98
	9,96	6,17	9,46	9,55	9,47	10,22	10,14	10,11	11,26	11,23	11,21	11,91
	6,58	6,08	8,54	8,29	8,30	9,83	9,61	9,48	11,17	11,15	11,11	11,82
	11,68	6,91	7,70	8,33	8,72	9,20	9,13	9.18	11,05	11,00	10,94	11,75
	12,02	7,08	7,61	8,24	8,68	9,05	8,99	9,06	10,85	10,82	10,75	11,66
	12,87	8,07	7,69	8,39	8,90	8,95	8,94	9,04	10,68	10,63	10,60	11,60
	14,60	8,98	8,07	8,84	9,39	9,03	9,08	9,21	10,52	10,48	10,44	11,53
	14,16	10,51	8,48	9,20	9,77	9,24	9,26	9,39	10,40	10,38	10,35	11,44
	12,54	9,21	9,72	10,04	10,11	9,63	9,76	9,84	10,32	10,30	10,31	11,38
	13,90	9,46	9,23	9,72	10,04	9,79	9,74	9,82	10,31	10,31	10,32	11,28
	9,94	7,92	9,22	9,39	9,37	9,77	9,69	9,68	10,32	10,31	10,32	11,22
	11,41	7,52	8,94	9,36	9,38	9,54	9,56	9,57	10,30	10,29	10,30	11,15
	10,11	7,54	8,69	8,93	9,00	9,45	9,38	9,37	10,28	10,25	10,25	11,11
	8,19	6,80	8,90	8,81	8,61	9,33	9,29	9,22	10,22	10,20	10,18	11,03
	7,71	6,06	7,55	7,68	7,81	8,90	8,71	8,64	10,15	10,14	10,11	10,96
	8,98	6,03	7,37	7,81	7,93	8,48	8,44	8,49	10,06	10,02	9,98	10,92
	7,99	7,53	7,61	7,76	7,90	8,42	8,40	8,41	9,91	9,87	9,84	10,87
	8,37	7,71	7,90	8,04	8,17	8,41	8,45	8,42	9,81	9,75	9,74	10,83
	7,12	5,54	7,46	7,25	7,30	8,41	8,25	8,18	9,69	9,68	9,66	10,77
	5,88	4,93	7,01	7,00	6,94	8,01	7,92	7,87	9,61	9,59	9,56	10,71
3,72	4,87	4,42	6.49	6,35	6,35	7,69	7,55	7,47	9,49	9,45	9,43	10,65
4,41	6,15	5,61	6,19	6,38	6,56	7,33	7,29	7,30	9,35	9,31	9,27	10,60
	5,11	4,92	6,49	6,33	6,33	7,31	7,26	7,23	9,19	9,15	9,13	10,54
	4,05	3,16	6,55	6,12	5,82	7,16	7.13	6,99	9,07	9,02	9,00	10,46
	3.29	2,33	5,10	5,01	4,99	6,71	6,51	6,40	8,92	8,89	8,85	10,40
	3,25	1,95	4,60	4,61	4,62	6,20	6,06	6,01	8,78	8,70	8,65	10,35
	1,11	0,79	4,26	4,02	3,83	5,85	5,68	5,54	8,56	8,48	8,43	10,31
	0,26	— 0,02	3,54	3,44	3,34	5,31	5,19	5.09	8,32	8,26	8,20	10,22
	0,31	— 0,74	3,08	3,04	2,91	4,92	4,82	4,69	8,10	8,05	7,95	10,15
	− 0,12	— 0.48	2,42	2,42	2,33	4.45	4,35	4,22	7,83	7,77	7,70	10,07

November 1881.

Luftthermometer

	III. In Glas		IV. In Kupfer			I' frei					
	2	8	7	2	8	7	2	8	7	2	8
,89	— 0,70	— 4,02	— 3,80	— 2,26	— 3,85	— 3,70	— 2,18	— 3,78	— 3,74	— 2,60	— 4,02
,47	— 1,19	— 4,86	— 5,23	— 3,82	— 4,75	— 5,16	— 3,43	— 4,64	— 5,27	— 3,74	— 4,81
,93	4,54	— 8,01	— 8,57	— 0,43	— 7,99	— 8,32	— 0,71	— 7,19	— 8,43	— 3,36	— 6,80
,75	4,54	— 6,02	—11,45	1,97	— 5,99	—10,00	0,89	— 5,59	—11,07	— 0,98	— 5,61
,10	— 0,62	0,99	— 3,93	— 0,62	0,77	— 3,96	— 0,41	0,89	— 4,02	— 0,34	1,04
,97	7,46	5,43	3,66	7,28	5,21	8,65	7,87	5,21	4,39	7,62	5,47
,62	6,28	3,41	4,58	6,08	3,42	4,43	6,07	3,48	4,78	6,24	3,54
,62	3,41	2,60	4,39	3,32	2,46	4,34	3,18	2,61	4,66	3,04	2,82
,81	4,30	3,01	3,71	3,90	2,99	3,43	3,57	3,09	3,66	3,43	3,16
,92	5,84	2,20	1,83	5,35	1,73	1,88	4,91	1,84	2,39	4,70	2,39
,61	5,51	5,84	3,52	5,89	5,84	3.57	6,50	6,07	3,81	6,62	5,85
,93	6,28	8,39	3,90	6,32	8,25	3,95	6,23	8,32	4,01	6,35	8,55
,57	7,58	7,05	6,42	7,18	6,90	6,83	7,23	7,02	6,43	7,51	7,09
,24	6,85	5,96	6,82	6,56	5,74	6,46	6,50	5,85	6,51	6,51	5,77
,65	8,27	5,96	6,46	8,11	5,94	6,50	8,19	6,07	6,62	8,16	5,97
,83	7,58	4,22	8,83	7,38	3,90	8,92	7,93	4,34	8,85	7,39	4,62
,43	7,25	8,27	5,35	6,99	8,01	5,64	6,93	7,71	5,58	7,47	8,39
,70	6,40	0,51	4,63	5,11	0,34	4,47	4,17	0,45	4,70	4,31	0,55
,31	5,84	— 1,31	— 0,19	3,90	1,30	0,28	3,09	— 1,05	0,62	2,39	— 1,07
,55	4,30	1,59	1,63	3,66	1,20	1,84	2,43	1,41	1,77	3,16	1,70
,47	2,28	2,72	1,89	2,36	2,84	1,49	2,27	2,93	1,46	2,39	2,89
,36	6,65	5,95	2,36	6,42	5,35	2,39	6,37	5,21	2,50	6,24	5,47
,77	10,78	3,49	4,00	10,18	3,42	3,74	7,54	3,61	3,93	7,01	3,93
,05	8,51	5,11	7,09	7,28	4,77	7,28	7,06	5,21	7,55	7,01	5,39
,11	13,14	3,65	0,91	10,28	3,42	1,15	8,32	3,39	1,62	7,24	3,35
,94	12,04	4,95	1,01	8,78	4,77	1,41	7,41	4,86	1,42	6,70	5,08
,73	6,93	7,46	4,10	6,80	7,43	3,69	6,93	7,80	3,85	7,48	8,16
,94	16,55	6,92	7,67	18,07	6,82	7,63	11,70	6,41	7,97	11,32	6,62
,65	9,81	3,57	3,61	8,87	3,42	3,82	8,32	3,83	4,43	7,86	3,95
,61	5,43	3,93	4,10	5,35	3,90	3,82	5.25	4,08	3,73	6,12	4,31
,27	5,79	2,92	3,04	5,39	2,82	2,37		2,98	2,49	4,76	3,13

December 1881.

	2	8	7	2	8	7	2	8	7	2	8
,53	5,27	1.64	3,90	4,97	1,49	3,48		1,92	3,70	4,78	2.08
,01	1,84	— 1.43	3,42	1,49	— 1,80	2,87		— 0,84	2,96	1.23	— 1,30
,58	— 0,17	— 3,53	— 1,45	1,21	— 3,32	1,86	1.09	— 2,06	— 2,02	— 1,94	— 3,67
,74	3,81	— 1,91	— 4,61	2.94	— 1,88	4,09	2,18	— 1,71	— 4,21	1.02	— 1,83
,45	— 0,86	— 1,02	— 3,22	— 0,86	— 1,01	3,09	0,84	— 0,84	— 3,13	— 0,99	— 1,07
,50	0,31	— 0,22	— 0,62	0,15	— 0,38	0,50	0,23	— 0,32	— 0,60	0,12	— 0,84
,70	0,59	— 0,70	— 0,11	0,05	— 0,81	0,75	0,06	— 0,76	— 0,80	0,08	— 0,76
,86	— 0,38	— 1,27	— 1,01	0,53	— 1,30	0,75	— 0,53	— 1,18	— 0,80	— 0,68	— 1,18
,04	0,99	1,31	— 2,17	0,53	1,01	1,93	0,45	1,19	— 1,91	0,47	— 1,27
,15	— 0,22	— 1,91	0,05	0,98	— 1,88	0,19	— 0,41	— 1,80	0,08	— 0,60	— 1,33
,25	— 1,02	— 0,50	— 3,82	— 1,11	— 0,43	2,87	— 0,97	— 0,32	— 2,79	— 1,22	— 0,38
,77	— 0,02	— 0,94	— 0,76	— 0,29	— 0,91	0,50	— 0,37	— 0,84	— 0,68	— 0,60	— 1,03
,00	0,15	— 1,02	— 2,46	0,00	— 0,91	1,18	0,02	— 0,84	— 1,98	— 0,07	— 1,07
,58	0,03	— 6,27	— 1,54	— 0,43	— 6,08	1,45	— 0,50	— 5,59	— 1,53	— 0,88	— 5,69
,16	— 3,04	— 7,04	— 4,27	— 3,90	— 6,86	4,21	— 3,73	— 6,80	— 4,28	— 4,24	— 6,80
,90	— 0,22	— 7,68	— 9,63	— 4,32	— 7,56	9,43	— 4,73	— 7,33	— 9,62	— 6,80	— 7,33
,65	3,49	— 3,60	— 8,57	— 3,70	— 3,52	8,28	— 3,52	— 3,43	— 8,47	— 3,82	— 3,36
,57	0,99	2,48	— 3,32	0,63	2,46	3,20	0,89	2,48	— 3,36	0,60	3,16
,72	3,43	2,72	1,45	4,77	2,56	1,62	3,57	2,61	1,89	3,70	2,77
,11	1,39	0,59	0,05	1,15	0,58	0,15	1,23	0,54	0,31	1,28	
,06	1,31	0,27	0,00	1,15	0,39	0,06	1,15	0,45	0,12	1,27	
,43	1,35	0,19	0,29	1,01	0,05	0,86	0,93	0,02	0,47	0,89	
,39	1,39	— 1,67	1,11	1,01	— 1,78	1,23	0,89	— 2,06	1,23	1,15	
,74	4,22	— 1,83	— 3,18	1,97	— 1,88	1,75	1,41	— 1,62	— 2,52	0,93	
,19	1,64	— 4,18	0,05	1,39	— 4,17	0,96	1,82	— 3,84	0,47	1,23	
,83	0,06	1,11	— 2,07	0,19	0,63	— 1,71	— 0,07	1,06	— 1,64	— 0,03	
,22	4,82	4,70	3,71	4,63	4,87	4,08	4,60	4,77	4,12	4,70	
,54	4,62	3,01	5,11	4,49	2,94	4,60	4,47	2,96	0,77	4,66	
,47	0,95	3,61	1,30	0,96	3,42	1,53	0,93	3,35	1,95	0,89	
,28	1,80	2,17	2,17	1,97	1,97	2,09	1,84	2,14	2,06	1,02	2,01
,11	1,43	0,19	0,77	1,06	0,14	1.15	1,85	0,11	0,86	0,47	0,03
						0,64	0,56	— 0,61	— 0,86	0,53	0,03

November 1881.

Erdthermometer

1 Zoll tief			1 Fuss tief			2 Fuss tief			4 Fuss tief			8 Fuss tief	16 Fuss tief
7	2	8	7	2	8	7	2	8	7	2	8	7	7
	−0,58	−0,95	2,14	2,07	2,02	4,06	3,92	3,84	7,58	7,50	7,42	9,97	9,96
	−0,61	−1,61	1,85	1,84	1,77	3,70	3,63	3,55	7,31	7,24	7,15	9,89	9,95
	0,84	−2,05	1,60	1,61	1,56	3,44	3,39	3,38	7,06	6,98	6,92	9,79	9,93
	0,27	−1,62	1,40	1,36	1,34	3,19	3,12	3,07	6,82	6,74	6,69	9,69	9,93
	−0,51	0,07	1,17	1,16	1,21	2,94	2,89	2,85	6,57	6,52	6,45	9,58	9,91
	3,07	−0,92	1,35	1,49	1,50	2,82	2,81	2,83	6,37	6,29	6,24	9,48	9,91
	4,61	3,88	1,72	2,46	3,02	2,84	2,98	3,24	6,16	6,10	6,04	9,35	9,90
	3,70	3,86	3,44	3,63	3,71	3,59	3,75	3,89	5,99	5,98	5,96	9,25	9,87
	4,10	3,35	3,70	3,86	3,94	4,05	4,11	4,20	5,95	5,96	5,97	9,13	9,87
	4,72	2,88	3,72	3,92	4,07	4,25	4,28	3,37	5,99	5,99	6,00	9,02	9,84
	4,72	5,39	3,63	3,90	4,37	4,32	4,33	4,45	6,04	6,04	6,04	8,84	9,83
	5,77	7,10	4,03	4,82	5,20	4,67	4,79	4,94	6,08	6,08	6,12	8,81	9,82
	7,02	6,92	5,76	5,92	6,03	5,26	5,45	5,60	6,15	6,16	6,20	8,74	9,82
	6,72	6,04	6,17	6,21	6,22	5,80	5,91	5,99	6,26	6,31	6,37	8,65	9,79
	7,50	6,78	6,04	6,24	6,42	6,01	6,05	6,14	6,43	6,47	6,53	8,59	9,76
	8,05	5,86	6,63	6,96	6,92	6,27	6,40	6,54	6,59	6,62	6,65	8,55	9,76
	6,62	7,92	6,24	6,19	6,39	6,47	6,38	6,39	6,71	6,76	6,78	8,49	9,71
	4,55	1,49	6,22	5,74	5,18	6,40	6,28	6,09	6,84	6,86	6,87	8,45	9,71
	2,11	0,71	4,19	3,89	3,65	5,64	5,37	5,14	6,90	6,90	6,87	8,43	9,68
	2,90	1,98	3,45	3,53	3,64	4,82	4,71	4,67	6,82	6,79	6,74	8,42	9,67
	2,62	2,92	3,28	3,33	3,53	4,50	4,40	4,38	6,66	6,61	6,56	8,41	9,64
	5,13	4,58	3,74	4,00	4,29	4,45	4,47	4,59	6,48	6,43	6,41	8,39	9,62
	7,89	4,62	4,86	5,17	5,31	4,84	4,99	5,14	6,35	6,34	6,32	8,35	9,60
	8,63	5,35	5,58	5,90	5,83	5,26	5,56	5,65	6,33	6,33	6,34	8,33	9,59
2,82	6,57	3,88	5,22	5,04	5,10	5,60	5,51	5,46	6,37	6,36	6,38	8,27	9,56
2,01	6,10	4,08	4,47	4,49	4,60	5,31	5,20	5,14	6,42	6,40	6,40	8,24	9,53
3,80	5,28	6,28	4,72	4,79	5,08	5,14	5,16	5,20	6,39	6,37	6,35	8,19	9,50
6,86	10,29	6,48	5,70	6,29	6,40	5,43	5,63	5,82	6,35	6,34	6,35	8,16	9,49
4,49	7,45	4,81	5,94	5,67	5,88	5,94	5,91	5,90	6,37	6,39	6,41	8,13	9,46
4,30	5,29	4,80	5,49	5,45	5,51	5,84	5,77	5,78	6,45	6,45	6,47	8,08	9,44
2,99	4,63	4,12	4,13	4,26	4,32	4,76	4,77	4,81	6,50	6,48	6,47	8,79	9,74

December 1881.

1 Zoll tief			1 Fuss tief			2 Fuss tief			4 Fuss tief			8 Fuss tief	16 Fuss tief
7	2	8	7	2	8	7	2	8	7	2	8	7	7
7,78	4,91	3,20	5,20	5,19	5,10	5,66	5,61	5,59	6,47	6,48	6,48	8,07	9,42
3,25	2,93	1,24	4,78	4,61	4,28	5,44	5,33	5,22	6,46	6,46	6,46	8,02	9,40
0,67	0,70	0,25	3,02	3,35	3,13	4,92	4,71	4,54	6,44	6,41	6,38	8,01	9,38
−0,30	0,30	0,22	2,72	2,64	2,51	4,25	4,12	3,97	6,32	6,28	6,24	7,98	9,35
−0,53	−0,01	0,03	2,23	2,18	2,13	3,75	3,64	3,53	6,14	6,08	6,03	7,95	9,33
0,09	0,19	0,23	2,02	2,02	1,99	3,39	3,32	3,26	5,92	5,87	5,82	7,94	9,31
0,11	0,19	0,13	1,95	1,91	1,90	3,18	3,13	3,09	5,73	5,66	5,62	7,89	9,29
0,08	0,13	−0,04	1,84	1,82	1,76	3,03	2,96	2,94	5,54	5,50	5,44	7,85	9,27
−0,16	0,11	0,21	1,68	1,67	1,74	2,86	2,82	2,80	5,38	5,33	5,30	7,78	9,25
0,28	0,23	−0,10	1,71	1,69	1,68	2,77	2,74	2,71	5,24	5,19	5,16	7,72	9,23
−0,60	0,03	0,06	1,56	1,58	1,57	2,67	2,64	2,61	5,09	5,05	5,04	7,66	9,20
0,04	0,12	0,06	1,55	1,53	1,54	2,57	2,55	2,53	5,97	4,93	4,92	7,62	9,18
−0,28	0,08	−0,02	1,49	1,46	1,45	2,49	2,46	2,46	4,86	4,83	4,81	7,54	9,16
−0,17	0,05	−1,25	1,43	1,41	1,32	2,42	2,38	2,36	4,76	4,74	4,72	7,49	9,14
−1,26	−0,95	−2,40	1,32	1,19	1,10	2,33	2,28	2,24	4,65	4,65	4,61	7,39	9,11
−4,17	−1,49	−3,54	0,92	0,85	1,72	2,14	2,09	2,03	4,57	4,54	4,50	7,34	9,09
−4,88	−2,36	−2,19	0,52	0,47	1,47	1,90	1,83	1,78	4,47	4,42	4,40	7,26	9,07
−2,35	−0,67	0,19	0,40	0,38	0,44	1,68	1,63	1,62	4,35	4,29	4,27	7,19	9,05
0,52	1,89	0,98	0,53	0,58	0,59	1,64	1,62	1,61	4,21	4,18	4,15	7,13	9,03
0,23	0,49	0,29	0,59	0,60	0,60	1,58	1,56	1,57	4,10	4,05	4,05	7,05	9,00
0,23	0,47	0,29	0,62	0,66	0,67	1,57	1,55	1,55	3,99	3,97	3,93	6,98	8,99
0,31	0,44	0,24	0,69	0,68	0,74	1,57	1,56	1,57	3,90	3,88	3,88	6,91	8,97
0,52	0,40	0,25	0,75	0,75	0,76	1,57	1,56	1,58	3,82	3,81	3,79	6,85	8,94
−0,18	0,57	0,26	0,77	0,84	0,83	1,58	1,60	1,59	3,78	3,74	3,74	6,81	8,93
0,20	0,88	−0,09	0,83	0,90	0,87	1,60	1,62	1,60	3,72	3,69	3,69	6,72	8,91
−0,98	−0,16	0,13	0,81	0,80	0,85	1,60	1,59	1,60	3,65	3,64	3,63	6,62	8,88
1,15	1,79	2,09	0,95	1,01	1,02	1,62	1,64	1,64	3,61	3,61	3,60	6,55	8,86
2,88	3,56	3,05	1,17	1,57	1,54	1,67	1,73	1,71	3,58	3,60	3,57	6,52	8,83
1,19	1,45	2,46	1,92	1,84	1,88	2,02	2,06	2,11	3,56	3,57	3,56	6,44	8,81
2,36	2,14	2,43	2,08	2,16	2,25	2,18	2,25	2,32	3,56	3,56	3,58	6,38	8,78
1,69	1,32	0,58	2,29	2,12	1,92	2,41	2,44	2,40	3,60	3,62	3,63	6,33	8,75
0,28	0,32	0,30	1,64	1,63	1,67	2,57	2,55	2,52	4,74	4,70	4,67	7,10	9,10

Januar 1882.

Luftthermometer

	III. in Glas			IV. in Kupfer								
	7	2	8	7	2	8	7	2	8	7	2	8
1	0,19	0,79	0,43	0,29	0,72	0,43	0,36	0,93	0,45	0,27	0,70	0,35
2	− 0,86	5,23	0,15	− 1,11	2,22	0,05	− 0,84	0,93	0,23	− 1,07	0,20	0,16
3	2,60	5,80	6,85	2,56	5,35	6,61	2,74	5,21	6,84	2,62	5,31	7,01
4	5,43	4,22	2,60	5,11	4,04	2,56	5,30	4,17	2,61	5,58	4,34	2,77
5	2,40	2,63	1,80	2,75	2,41	1,97	2,35	1,92	1,53	2,47	2,16	1,81
6	1,72	4,95	5,11	1,59	4,19	4,87	1,88	3,91	4,99	2,31	4,04	5,16
7	4,34	4,22	2,16	4,68	4,19	1,97	3,69	4,08	2,14	4,47	4,16	1,54
8	2,52	2,44	3,81	1,78	2,36	3,71	2,52	2,09	3,91	2,50	2,54	3,93
9	3,09	2,20	2,23	3,42	2,07	2,26	3,05	2,27	2,81	3,24	2,39	2,54
10	2,52	6,04	3,01	1,97	4,87	2,89	2,61	4,64	3,05	2,62	4,70	3,24
11	3,01	5,68	3,53	3,61	5,06	3,42	3,26	4,99	3,61	3,35	5,08	3,73
12	1,47	0,99	0,39	0,77	0,53	0,05	1,15	0,80	0,45	1,31	0,74	0,47
13	− 3,60	8,83	− 2,64	3,56	7,38	− 2,84	2,87	1,93	− 2,48	− 2,87	0,47	− 2,05
14	− 2,83	9,08	− 3,00	3,32	7,77	− 1,93	2,87	2,18	− 2,61	− 2,68	1,23	− 2,33
15	− 5,06	9,32	− 2,64	5,04	6,80	− 2,79	4,60	1,69	− 2,57	− 4,59	1,35	− 2,33
16	− 4,50	1,19	− 0,62	4,75	0,82	− 0,53	3,74	0,45	− 0,41	− 3,55	0,35	− 0,30
17	0,83	1,07	0,99	0,72	0,77	1,01	1,02	0,54	1,15	0,96	0,39	1,15
18	2,60	3,49	2,60	2,36	3,42	2,56	2,70	3,26	2,61	2,50	3,27	2,77
19	2,12	3,01	2,20	1,73	3,13	1,87	2,14	2,73	2,27	2,19	2,39	2,47
20	2,72	3,41	3,01	3,42	3,28	2,99	3,22	3,18	3,09	3,21	3,12	3,04
21	3,97	3,41	3,81	4,23	3,42	3,80	3,91	3,44	3,91	3,85	3,50	3,85
22	0,35	15,29	1,88	0,15	13,31	1,78	0,36	7,54	2,09	0,70	6,95	2,00
23	0,79	2,12	0,99	0,63	1,73	1,01	0,80	1,49	1,03	0,85	1,31	1,04
24	0,75	2,44	3,33	0,63	2,60	3,26	0,80	2,70	3,22	0,85	2,77	3,46
25	3,53	4,18	3,77	3,80	4,04	3,66	3,89	4,00	3,82	3,66	4,08	3,81
26	4,38	4,66	3,33	4,63	4,44	3,23	4,04	4,43	3,39	4,12	4,31	3,20
27	0,79	0,85	0,19	0,34	0,39	0,19	0,54	0,45	0,36	0,39	0,12	0,20
28	1,59	0,71	0,38	1,30	0,63	− 0,43	1,66	0,58	− 0,23	1,54	0,47	− 0,34
29	0,59	2,97	3,01	0,43	2,80	2,94	0,67	2,70	2,57	0,78	2,81	3,12
30	− 2,52	9,43	0,50	2,60	3,04	− 0,43	2,23	1,58	− 0,41	− 2,02	1,62	− 0,56
31	− 6,07	5,95	− 4,38		0,96	− 2,22	6,46	0,45	− 4,13	− 5,57	− 1,64	− 3,58
	0,93	5,02	1,52	0,85	3,51	1,46	0,93	2,63	1,58	1,10	2,41	1,66

Februar 1882.

	III. in Glas			IV. in Kupfer								
	7	2	8	7	2	8	7	2	8	7	2	8
1	− 1,35	11,63	− 0,30	− 1,30	5,84	− 0,43	− 1,14	4,12	0,02	− 0,76	3,39	− 0,19
2	0,19	6,08	− 2,32	0,15	3,95	− 2,36	0,15	2,22	− 2,14	0,16	1,85	− 2,25
3	− 4,86	1,64	0,59	− 5,04	1,15	1,11	− 4,39	0,98	0,80	− 4,43	0,85	0,62
4	0,11	0,91	0,23	0,05	0,53	0,29	0,23	0,28	0,32	0,27	0,00	0,24
5	0,43	1,64	0,87	0,43	1,49	0,87	0,67	1,49	0,89	0,66	1,31	0,93
6	− 0,02	1,39	2,24	− 0,14	1,35	2,12	0,15	1,28	2,22	− 0,07	1,08	2,39
7	− 2,56	1,59	− 1,06	− 1,98	− 0,43	− 1,06	− 2,57	− 1,14	− 1,05	− 2,05	− 1,37	− 1,07
8	− 8,37	− 3,85	− 6,84	− 8,33	− 4,90	− 6,66	− 8,06	− 4,17	− 6,12	− 8,24	− 6,04	− 6,69
9	− 3,65	1,19	2,08	− 4,08	0,77	1,97	− 3,61	0,67	2,05	− 3,94	0,66	2,08
10	0,99	1,72	1,07	1,01	1,35	1,06	0,89	0,58	1,02	0,89	1,23	1,19
11	0,19	3,13	− 0,22	0,05	2,36	− 0,43	0,15	1,66	− 0,28	0,08	1,23	− 0,15
12	− 0,77	0,99	− 1,43	− 0,66	0,53	− 0,91	− 0,58	0,28	− 1,45	− 0,76	0,00	− 1,83
13	− 3,25	13,75	1,47	− 3,32	9,21	1,30	− 3,00	5,73	1,71	− 2,87	5,85	1,96
14	3,53	5,63	5,68	3,71	5,35	5,33	3,26	5,25	6,24	3,62	5,35	5,85
15	3,13	4,38	7,05	3,66	3,90	6,80	3,05	3,87	6,93	3,04	3,77	7,01
16	− 0,62	4,66	− 1,83	− 0,24	1,78	− 1,74	− 0,63	0,15	− 1,62	− 0,15	− 0,03	− 1,56
17	1,11	1,11	1,81	0,91	1,11	1,78	0,71	1,15	1,85	1,08	1,39	2,00
18	− 0,22	11,59	− 1,83	0,34	4,58	− 1,88	− 0,20	3,57	− 1,71	− 0,07	2,31	− 1,60
19	3,81	4,82	1,80	3,66	3,76	1,63	3,22	3,57	1,85	4,01	3,77	1,96
20	− 1,19	11,92	1,55	− 1,26	4,00	1,49	− 1,18	2,44	1,66	− 1,26	1,85	1,70
21	1,96	1,51	− 3,93	1,78	0,43	− 3,90	2,09	0,02	− 3,78	2,19	0,41	− 3,58
22	− 4,98	− 0,18	3,33	− 4,91	− 1,74	2,75	− 4,82	− 2,31	2,96	− 4,78	− 2,52	3,31
23	4,46	14,11	3,85	4,29	8,01	3,90	4,55	6,67	4,08	4,54	6,35	3,93
24	0,59	14,11	3,53	0,48	9,55	3,61	0,41	6,06	3,87	0,81	5,08	3,62
25	2,36	3,25	2,60	2,26	2,99	2,46	2,39	2,96	2,52	2,39	2,73	2,47
26	1,72	11,71	9,16	1,59	10,66	9,07	1,75	10,31	9,10	2,00	10,20	9,36
27	7,82	12,73	7,85	7,67	11,62	7,87	7,58	11,40	7,87	7,63	11,32	8,16
28	5,88	10,70	0,83	5,84	9,69	1,01	5,90	9,40	1,28	6,04	9,24	0,85
	0,23	5,49	1,35	0,24	3,53	1,32	0,25	2,80	1,46	0,23	2,54	1,10

Januar 1882.

Erdthermometer													
1 Zoll tief			1 Fuss tief			2 Fuss tief			4 Fuss tief			8 Fuss tief	16 Fuss tief
7	2	8	7	2	8	7	2	8	7	2	8	7	7
0,89	1,27	1,10	1,79	1,83	1,86	2,34	2,31	2,32	3,66	3,65	3,66	6,27	8,72
0,21	1,23	0,31	1,64	1,62	1,53	2,27	2,24	2,21	3,66	3,68	3,67	6,23	8,70
1,86	3,84	4,76	1,64	2,03	2,55	2,18	2,24	2,29	3,68	3,67	3,67	6,19	8,68
4,40	4,08	3,33	3,13	3,26	3,90	2,70	2,87	2,99	3,68	3,67	3,68	6,16	8,66
2,74	2,80	2,61	3,12	3,07	2,98	3,09	3,12	3,12	3,74	3,76	3,78	6,12	8,64
1,70	3,68	3,85	2,53	2,82	3,01	3,02	3,00	3,05	3,83	3,85	3,89	6,08	8,62
3,91	3,07	2,19	3,47	3,56	3,43	3,22	3,33	3,38	3,89	3,92	3,92	6,04	8,56
2,20	2,61	2,99	2,92	2,92	2,94	3,30	3,24	3,24	3,97	4,00	4,01	6,02	8,53
2,73	2,66	2,15	2,97	3,01	2,87	3,21	3,22	3,20	4,03	4,03	4,04	5,99	8,50
2,57	4,00	2,86	2,78	3,03	3,17	3,16	3,17	3,23	4,06	4,06	4,08	5,96	8,48
3,05	4,20	3,17	3,09	3,30	3,40	3,28	3,33	3,37	4,07	4,08	4,10	5,95	8,45
1,34	1,08	0,68	2,98	2,62	2,39	3,35	3,25	3,13	4,11	4,11	4,11	5,93	8,42
0,02	1,26	0,27	2,06	2,00	1,80	2,91	2,81	2,71	4,12	4,11	4,12	5,93	8,39
0,01	1,89	0,18	1,65	1,73	1,60	2,56	2,52	2,45	4,08	4,04	4,03	5,92	8,38
— 0,88	1,57	0,15	1,41	1,50	1,38	2,35	2,30	2,26	3,98	3,95	3,95	5,91	8,34
— 1,36	0,28	0,24	1,14	1,29	1,25	2,15	2,13	2,07	3,89	3,87	3,85	5,90	8,33
0,87	0,39	0,21	1,25	1,25	1,22	2,04	2,00	2,00	3,80	3,79	3,75	5,89	8,31
1,00	1,46	1,42	1,28	1,35	1,14	1,96	1,98	1,99	3,70	3,69	3,68	5,85	8,27
2,01	2,40	2,01	1,80	1,99	2,08	2,00	2,19	2,25	3,64	3,63	3,61	5,84	8,26
2,91	3,17	3,04	2,32	2,51	2,64	2,39	2,49	2,57	3,59	3,60	3,60	5,79	8,22
3,39	2,09	3,52	2,82	2,87	2,93	2,71	2,80	2,86	3,60	3,61	3,62	5,78	8,20
1,56	7,74	2,65	2,81	3,14	3,24	2,94	2,99	3,06	3,63	3,65	3,68	5,74	8,17
1,52	1,84	1,46	2,84	2,67	2,57	3,08	3,02	2,98	3,72	3,73	3,74	5,70	8,16
1,34	2,18	3,05	2,43	2,40	2,60	2,89	2,84	2,86	3,77	3,78	3,79	5,67	8,12
3,43	3,88	3,76	2,94	3,14	3,27	2,96	3,05	3,14	3,78	3,78	3,79	5,64	8,11
3,80	4,39	3,65	3,49	3,62	3,65	3,38	3,36	3,45	3,81	3,83	3,85	5,62	8,08
2,04	1,47	1,28	3,41	3,11	2,96	3,47	3,43	3,38	3,88	3,91	3,92	5,62	8,06
1,70	1,50	0,67	3,69	2,66	2,55	3,22	3,16	3,12	3,95	3,98	3,98	5,60	8,02
0,92	2,40	2,65	2,23	2,34	2,51	2,95	2,90	2,90	3,97	3,97	3,96	5,58	8,01
0,87	2,66	0,44	2,32	2,27	2,17	2,88	2,86	2,80	3,96	3,96	3,93	5,58	7,99
— 0,51	0,57	— 0,28	1,81	1,81	1,53	2,65	2,58	2,52	3,93	3,92	3,88	5,58	7,95
1,66	2,56	1,93	2,44	2,47	2,48	2,79	2,79	2,81	3,84	3,85	3,85	5,87	8,33

Februar 1882.

1 Zoll tief 7	2	8	1 Fuss tief 7	2	8	2 Fuss tief 7	2	8	4 Fuss tief 7	2	8	8 Fuss tief 7	16 Fuss tief 7
— 0,07	2,50	0,27	1,54	1,74	1,61	2,40	2,38	2,33	3,87	3,83	3,81	5,58	7,94
0,40	1,97	0,26	1,56	1,65	1,59	2,27	2.26	2,23	3,77	3,75	3,73	5,57	7,91
— 0,88	0,20	0,26	1,36	1,36	1,38	2,16	2,13	2,09	3,69	3,69	3,65	5,55	7,89
0,23	0,25	0,28	1,28	1,29	1,29	2,03	2,00	2,00	3,61	3,59	3,58	5,53	7,87
0,83	0,64	0,62	1,26	1,32	1,37	1,88	1,95	1,96	3,54	3,52	3,50	5,51	7,84
0,58	1,44	1,80	1,46	1,57	1,73	1,97	2,00	2,06	3,48	3,45	3,45	5,49	7,83
— 0,13	0,22	— 0,02	1,51	1,41	1,30	2,06	2,05	2,01	3,42	3,41	3,41	5,46	7,80
— 1,49	— 0,76	— 1,40	1,12	1,08	1,03	1,90	1,85	1,84	3,39	3,37	3,36	5,43	7,78
— 1,03	0,11	0,45	0,96	1,01	1,06	1,76	1,75	1,75	3,34	3,32	3,32	5,40	7,76
0,39	0,56	0,44	1,06	1,06	1,06	1,72	1,69	1,69	3,29	3,28	3,27	5,38	7,74
0,26	1,01	0,16	1,06.	1,09	1,06	1,69	1,67	1,67	3,24	3,22	3,21	5,35	7,72
0,24	0,21	0,00	1,10	1,06	1,05	1,66	1,65	1,65	3,19	3,17	3,17	5,33	7,73
— 0,59	3,93	0,56	1,00	1,28	1,15	1,63	1,67	1,66	3,15	3,13	3,12	5,29	7,73
1,51	3,67	3,93	1,18	1,51	1,90	1,67	1,73	1,82	3,11	3,09	3,07	5,23	7,68
2,57	3,80	5,23	2,17	2,30	2,57	2,05	2,17	2,28	3,07	3,08	3,08	5,21	7,65
0,51	1,06	0,26	2,40	2,10	1,83	2,40	2,41	2,33	3,10	3,12	3,14	5,16	7,62
0,63	0,74	1,61	1,61	1,53	1,59	2,19	2,12	2,09	3,16	3,17	3,19	5,14	7,62
0,33	4,35	0,29	1,33	1,69	1,78	2,04	2,07	2,08	3,19	3,17	3,18	5,12	7,59
1,68	2,82	1,13	1,61	1,85	1,87	2,07	2,10	2,12	3,17	3,15	3,16	5,10	7,57
0,16	2.77	0,96	1,55	1,61	1,51	2,00	2,07	2,02	3,15	3,15	3,16	5,06	7,55
2,01	1,45	— 0,12	1,70	1,96	1,82	2,02	2,07	2,11	3,16	3,13	3,13	5,06	7,53
— 0,75	— 0,11	— 0,03	1,41	1,30	1,31	2,03	1,98	1,90	3,08	3,12	3,13	5,08	7,52
2,34	7.17	3,34	1,38	2,13	2,58	1,89	1,99	2,17	3,12	3,11	3,09	5,05	7,51
0,75	8,37	3,70	2,28	2,67	3,09	2,35	2,42	2,55	3,10	3,09	3,09	5,02	7,47
2,71	3,19	2,62	2,96	2,91	2,89	2,77	2,79	2,80	3,12	3,14	3,16	5,02	7,46
1,96	8,02	7.13	2,72	3,30	3,95	2,83	2,88	3,08	3,20	3,24	3,23	4,95	7,44
6,45	9,36	7,51	4,37	4,86	5,24	3,45	3,67	3,90	3,28	3,32	3,35	4,95	7,41
5,60	9,02	3,05	4,99	5,44	5,23	4.14	4,28	4,38	3,43	3,49	3,55	4,93	7,39
0,95	2,77	1,58	1,78	1,93	1,99	2,18	2,28	2,23	3,30	3,30	3,30	5,25	7,66

März 1882.

Luftthermometer

	III. in Glas		IV. in Kupfer			I' frei					
	2	8	7	2	8	7	2	8	7	2	8
	4,66	− 1,43	− 1,92	1.74		− 1,45	1,88	− 1,18	− 1,60		
	18,26	3,85	1,97	13,75		1,88	11,79	3,74	2.43		
	8,27	1,68	1,83	6,75		1,88	6,07	1,75	2,12		
	5,03	3,51	2,46	4.39		2,65	4,51	3,57	2,47		
	4,46	3,41	2,89	4,24		3,14	4.04	3.48	3,27		
	10,17	7,46	5,16	8,97		5,34	8,70	7,02	5,55	8,93	
	3,89	− 0,18	1,68	2,60		1,84	1,32	0,02	1,92	0.93	
	4.62	6,24	0,05	4,53	6,27	0,06	4.64	6,16	0,16	4,81	
	13,67	2,40	5,94	9,21	2,32	5,90	8,23	2,61	6,04	8,08	
	7,01	5,81	4,39	6,80	5,84	4,86	6,63	5,77	4,89	6,97	
	5,43	3,85	4,39	5,06	3,90	4,43	5,08	4.00	4.47		
	5,84	4,22	1,30	4,77	4,19	1,53	4,55	4,34	1,73		
	6,57	6,00	2,98	5,84	5,94	3,05	5,77	5,64	3,08		
	7,54	5,43	1,49	6,90	5,35	1,71	6,93	5,21	1,89		
	13,43	4,87	4,97	11,67	4,77	5,21	10.27	4.90	5.16		
	11.26	7,46	3,37	9,11	7,38	3,44	8,62	7,50	3.81		
	9,73	− 0,34	5,74	6,90	− 0,88	6,20	6,63	− 0.07	6,04		0,16
	7,90	− 1,58	− 0,53	4,53	− 1,69	− 0,41	3,78	− 1,27	− 0,38		
	15,05	5,03	− 2,70	12,73	4,77	-- 2,31	10,44	4.90	− 2,37		5,16
,64	20.13	8,79	1,39	17,90	8,30	1,49	16,04	8,57	1,73	15,76	
,47	24,77	13,47	5,35	21,28	13,17	5.21	20,05	13.26	5,47	19.88	
	6,57	3,41	7,18	5,60	3,18	7,50	5,90	3,65	7,62		
,76	6,28	1,84	2,70	5,35	1,92	2,96	5,73	2,18	2,62		
	6.49	2,44	1,73	5,60	2,46	2,18	5.25	2,74	2.19		
	9,28	4.22	3,66	8,25	4,34	3.82	7,97	4.47	3,73		
	10,29	3,45	1,73	7,28	3,47	2.18	6,76	3,61	2,08		
	11.10	7,13	2,56	9,79	7,09	2,70	9,53	7,21	2,62		
	6,65	3,17	5,45	5,84	4.23	5,55	5,42	3,26	5,43		
	11,84	2,68	4,10	9,11	2,56	4,12	7,06	2.61	4,31		
	6,73	5,92	2,75	6,37	5,74	2,96	6,50	5,90	2,77		
	19.48	6,97	4,63	16.21	6,80	6,20	14.22	6,93	6.24	4.42	
,00	9,75	4,35	2,54	8,03	4,19	3,00	7,10	4,37	3,12	7,09	4,47

April 1882.

	III. in Glas		IV. in Kupfer			I' frei					
	2	8	7	2	8	7	2	8	7	2	8
,81	10,86	5.15	6,32	9,74	5,16	6,50	9,84	5,51	6,58	9,09	5,39
,31	13,34	3,41	2,65	9,26	3,42	2,87	8,70	3,82	2,62	8,24	3,93
,51	7,38	3,21	1,39	8,63	3,37	1,49	8,75	3,48	1,62	7,93	3,54
,96	15,70	3,81	1,49	12,83	3,90	1,58	10,06	4,47	1,73	9,32	4,08
,27	13,67	0,91	− 0,29	9,16	1,01	− 0,32	7,02	1,45	− 0,22	6,24	1,23
,14	16,11	0,11	− 0,43	11,72	0,05	− 0,07	10,66	0,93	− 0,03	9,32	0,93
,46	16.27	2.20	3,66	11,43	2,96	3,57	10,66	2,96	3,00	9,55	2,77
,03	9,73	3,93	3,90	8,15	3,90	3,74	7,80	4,21	3,54	7,95	4,20
,47	9,85	2.44	0,19	6,80	2,56	0,28	6,16	2,79	0,16	5,55	2,77
,39	9,89	3,05	0,29	7,77	2,99	1,02	5,42	3,18	0,20	6,24	3,54
,30	15,50	3,01	4,05	12,01	3,08	3,74	10,31	3,99	3,54	9,16	3,24
,28	14,11	2,60	2,23	10,28	2,46	2,22	9,70	2,87	[illegible]	8,24	2,77
,99	5,68	0,94	0,96	2,36	1,02	0,98	2,35	0,71	1,70	1,15	− 0,76
,99	12,73	3,77	0,19	8,45	3,76	0,23	8,86	2,91	[illegible]	6,70	3,93
,00	18,83	11,18	5,79	14,95	10,71	5,90	14,35	10,66	5,85	14,22	11,28
,21	12,52	2,24	6,46	9,31	2,12	6,59	8,83	2,61	6,54	7,89	2,78
,87	16,88	6,81	5,11	14,66	6,80	5,42	12,74	6,93	3,31	11,62	6,97
,03	15,01	5,43	4,87	11,87	5,45	5,21	11,83	5,75	5,08	10,55	5,89
,76	10,21	6,49	5,45	9,02	6,32	5,77	9,01	6,41	5,39	9,70	6,54
,23	11,22	9,08	6,46	10,37	8,83	5,77	10,14	8,02	5,20	10,20	8,24
,43	9.64	4,91	10,95	9,02	4,82	11,01	8,83	5,17	11,01	9,12	5,81
,08	23,22	7,46	8,54	16,35	7,48	8,23	14,31	8,19	7,47	14,42	8,55
,51	29,00	14,93	8,35	23,80	14,62	8,01	22,03	14,61	8,28	22,05	15,57
,89	28.11	13,75	12,25	23,51	12,59	12,23	23,02	12,57	11,98	22,82	12,99
,29	19,23	9,68	10,23	17,23	9,69	10,44	16,49	10,53	10,55	16,22	10,09
,96	20,90	14,20	8,83	17,95	14,04	8,75	17,23	13,87	8,93	16,68	14,69
,03	26,40	7,86	12,83	22,88	7,77	12,85	20,99	8,58	12,12	19,88	8,94
,56	27,78	11,63	9,21	21,67	11,62	9,44	20,99	12,05	8,35	18,43	12,94
,04	31,45	7.46	15,49	27,96	7,43	15,43	23,37	7,71	15,18	24,28	7,89
,98	19,64	9,12	7,67	17,18	8,83	8,06	16,48	9,23	7,97	16,58	9,70
97	16,36	5,96	5,50	13,21	5,87	5,54	12,07	6,16	5,32	11,62	6,80

März 1882.

Erdthermometer

1 Zoll tief			1 Fuss tief			2 Fuss tief			4 Fuss tief			8 Fuss tief	16 Fuss tief
7	2	8	7	2	8	7	2	8	7	2	8	7	7
0,61	1,84	0,42	3,88	3,29	3,08	4,21	3,96	3,77	3,65	3,73	3,76	4,91	7,35
1,25	10,37	4,58	2,66	3,21	3,35	3,45	3,38	3,43	3,80	3,82	3,83	4,92	7,34
2,49	5,22	2,67	3,65	3,75	3,79	3,62	3,65	3,69	3,82	3,83	3,85	4,93	7,34
2,68	4,21	3,73	3,48	3,55	3,71	3,64	3,61	3,65	3,85	3,87	3,88	4,95	7,32
2,93	4,04	3,35	3,49	3,67	3,82	3,65	3,63	3,69	3,89	3,89	3,90	4,96	7,31
4,29	7,11	6,63	3,71	4,11	4,51	3,70	3,76	3,90	3,93	3,93	3,94	4,97	7,29
2,14	2,35	0,69	4,04	3,57	3,26	3,99	3,87	3,76	3,98	3,99	4,01	4,99	7,26
0,63	3,68	5,59	2,66	3,69	3,23	3,48	3,83	3,85	4,04	4,04	4,04	5,00	7,25
5,51	8,55	3,80	4,04	4,40	4,59	3,61	3,81	3,96	4,02	4,03	4,03	5,01	7,23
4,07	6,82	5,95	3,92	4,83	4,62	3,99	4,03	4,10	4,03	4,01	4,06	5,03	7,21
4,81	5,33	4,27	4,60	4,84	4,81	4,29	4,37	4,42	4,10	4,11	4,14	5,04	7,18
2,11	5,40	4,23	4,15	4,29	4,47	4,35	4,23	4,29	4,20	4,23	4,25	5,05	7,17
3,11	5,59	5,42	4,05	4,52	4,77	4,25	4,41	4,35	4,28	4,34	4,30	5,07	7,17
2,67	6,58	5,31	4,54	4,47	4,72	4,41	4,25	4,46	4,32	4,28	4,35	5,09	7,16
4,59	9,77	5,51	4,67	5,27	5,55	4,48	4,61	4,76	4,37	4,39	4,41	5,11	7,13
3,38	8,32	6,72	4,76	5,10	5,50	4,77	4,77	4,85	4,45	4,47	4,49	5,12	7,12
5,55	7,71	2,35	5,35	5,56	5,26	4,95	5,03	5,06	4,53	4,55	4,58	5,13	7,10
0,52	7,37	1,31	4,06	4,37	4,53	4,76	4,61	4,60	4,61	4,63	4,65	5,16	7,09
0,12	10,97	5,26	3,41	4,05	4,82	4,36	4,27	4,38	4,65	4,65	4,63	5,18	7,08
2,06	15,15	8,81	4,21	5,35	6,31	4,46	4,58	4,88	4,62	4,61	4,61	5,20	7,06
5,13	17,72	11,97	5,77	6,89	7,89	5,17	5,40	5,77	4,61	4,61	4,65	5,22	7,05
7,57	7,51	4,90	7,43	7,33	6,91	6,15	6,26	6,23	4,69	4,74	4,78	5,25	7,04
3,82	5,76	3,76	5,89	5,75	5,69	5,96	5,81	5,71	4,89	4,95	4,99	5,26	7,03
2,99	5,78	4,07	5,06	5,17	5,63	5,48	5,37	5,35	5,03	5,08	5,07	5,27	7,02
4,01	7,34	5,15	5,02	5,26	5,50	5,26	5,23	5,27	5,08	5,09	5,10	5,30	6,99
2,90	7,15	4,43	4,96	5,12	5,55	5,24	5,19	5,21	5,09	5,12	5,10	5,32	6,99
2,80	8,90	6,64	4,63	5,04	5,53	5,10	5,01	5,14	5,11	5,12	5,12	5,36	6,97
5,41	7,06	4,64	5,45	5,62	5,73	5,27	5,32	5,37	5,11	5,12	5,11	5,39	6,96
4,22	7,30	4,03	5,25	5,37	5,44	5,36	5,32	5,33	5,15	5,16	5,17	5,42	6,96
3,32	5,76	6,03	4,85	4,93	5,28	5,21	5,14	5,16	5,18	5,19	5,19	5,41	6,95
5,82	14,48	7,74	5,43	6,54	7,23	5,26	5,41	5,79	5,19	5,20	5,21	5,47	6,96
3,33	7,42	5,02	4,49	4,79	5,00	4,57	4,57	4,64	4,46	4,48	4,49	5,15	7,13

April 1882.

1 Zoll tief			1 Fuss tief			2 Fuss tief			4 Fuss tief			8 Fuss tief	16 Fuss tief
7	2	8	7	2	8	7	2	8	7	2	8	7	7
6,47	8,83	6,46	6,70	6,88	6,93	6,05	6,14	6,21	5,24	5,26	5,29	5,49	6,91
5,76	8,63	5,13	6,18	6,24	6,43	6,14	6,08	6,07	5,35	5,40	5,43	5,52	6,93
2,02	8,06	4,94	5,28	5,65	6,04	5,90	5,77	6,80	5,46	5,49	5,50	5,53	6,91
2,23	11,12	5,56	5,18	5,87	6,42	5,70	5,65	5,79	5,58	5,51	5,52	5,55	6,92
1,25	9,59	3,85	5,85	5,59	6,05	5,79	5,66	5,73	5,01	5,52	5,52	5,60	6,91
1,20	12,99	4,33	4,93	5,82	6,43	5,62	5,55	5,75	5,53	5,51	5,51	5,61	6,90
3,59	12,25	5,82	5,46	6,33	6,88	5,76	5,74	6,00	5,49	5,49	5,50	5,65	6,91
4,57	7,63	5,28	6,13	6,28	6,83	6,08	6,03	6,07	5,50	5,50	5,51	5,67	6,90
1,28	7,47	4,07	5,21	5,52	5,81	5,86	5,71	5,72	5,54	5,55	5,56	5,71	6,89
1,35	7,73	4,69	4,87	5,26	5,64	5,59	5,45	5,51	5,56	5,55	5,55	5,72	6,88
3,69	9,60	5,22	5,00	5,68	6,22	5,46	5,45	5,62	5,52	5,52	5,51	5,73	6,88
3,05	11,85	5,62	5,41	6,37	6,94	5,68	5,74	5,99	5,51	5,51	5,51	5,75	6,87
2,80	8,13	1,65	5,88	5,30	4,97	6,03	5,84	5,66	5,52	5,53	5,55	5,78	6,86
1,45	8,70	4,73	4,13	4,82	5,44	5,26	5,15	5,25	5,55	5,57	5,56	5,80	6,86
5,07	12,33	9,63	5,14	5,97	6,96	5,85	5,45	5,74	5,51	5,51	5,50	5,81	6,87
6,75	12,66	4,60	6,89	7,08	7,01	6,13	6,26	6,37	5,50	5,51	5,55	5,83	6,87
8,35	11,52	7,85	5,75	6,47	7,15	6,20	6,19	6,29	5,59	5,61	5,66	5,83	6,87
5,67	9,39	7,04	6,68	6,99	7,32	6,43	6,45	6,58	5,70	5,73	5,76	5,86	6,86
5,34	8,89	6,88	6,58	6,78	6,97	6,58	6,52	6,56	5,80	5,83	5,86	5,90	6,87
5,39	8,60	8,20	6,52	6,77	7,09	6,55	6,50	6,59	5,91	5,94	5,95	5,91	6,88
9,15	9,36	6,78	7,30	7,63	7,58	6,72	6,85	6,89	5,98	6,02	6,01	5,93	6,88
6,29	13,93	9,16	6,84	7,94	8,72	6,86	6,93	7,25	6,07	6,12	6,15	5,94	6,88
7,41	18,96	13,65	7,28	9,36	10,45	7,48	7,66	8,10	6,19	6,25	6,27	5,98	6,88
10,86	19,41	14,65	9,93	10,96	11,74	8,54	8,80	9,17	6,34	6,42	6,47	6,01	6,87
11,01	15,51	11,18	10,95	11,22	11,30	9,47	9,53	9,66	6,61	6,70	6,79	6,04	6,86
8,55	14,70	12,87	10,02	10,45	10,93	9,58	9,45	9,55	6,93	7,03	7,09	6,07	6,86
10,99	17,68	11,48	10,49	11,35	11,89	9,63	9,74	9,96	7,21	7,30	7,34	6,14	6,87
9,63	16,88	12,61	10,66	11,13	11,69	10,08	9,96	10,12	7,41	7,52	7,56	6,19	6,88
12,44	21,59	11,49	11,38	12,63	12,70	10,29	10,49	10,75	7,61	7,72	7,77	6,25	6,87
9,63	15,14	11,25	11,34	11,55	11,66	10,71	10,59	10,60	7,89	7,95	8,03	6,33	6,87
5,54	11,82	7,53	7,01	7,53	7,92	6,91	6,91	7,07	5,96	6,00	6,02	5,84	6,88

Mai 1882.

	Luftthermometer											
	III. in Glas			IV. in Kupfer			I' frei			VII.		
	7	2	8	7	2	8	7	2	8	7	2	8
1	9,48	24,48	14,97	9,89	20,07	14,57	8,23	19,06	14,31	8,05	18,40	14,69
2	12,40	9,93	5,43	11,72	8,83	5,40	11,70	9,58	6,03	11,32	8,16	5,96
3	8,39	25,13	8,35	7,48	19,35	8,20	7,46	17.43	9,40	7,09	14.69	8,55
4	9,78	27,98	11,22	9,64	22,06	10,90	9,10	20,35	11,36	7,97	18,89	11,43
5	12,24	31,12	19,31	11,43	27,09	18,53	11,48	25,00	19,32	11,89	23,47	19,73
6	11,71	15,29	8,19	10,71	13,50	7,82	10,40	12,70	8,92	9,93	11,16	8,56
7	10,21	27,70	15,01	9,45	24,77	14,52	9,75	22,80	14,74	9,20	20,52	15,68
8	10,70	12,12	10,82	10,18	11,43	10,56	10,31	12,40	10,74	9,28	11,32	11,04
9	10,13	10,94	5,03	9,55	9,98	4,87	9,71	9,97	5,21	9,55	10,05	5,06
10	4,22	14,28	4,14	3,61	10,47	3,90	3,74	9,40	4,43	3,77	7,86	4,47
11	4,06	20,57	6,24	4,19	17,89	6,18	4,17	13,87	6,63	3,93	12,01	6,74
12	7,78	17,77	8,67	8,15	15,00	8,35	7,97	14,74	8,14	7,12	14,90	8,98
13	9,32	18,83	6,65	8,15	13,31	6,46	7,80	11,88	6,84	7,93	10,77	6,97
14	5,55	11,51	5,48	5,25	9,94	5,25	5,47	8,57	5,73	5,24	7,89	5,85
15	8,83	22,08	6,12	7,72	16,84	6,93	7,76	15,17	6,71	7,09	11,81	6,43
16	8,63	15,50	5,47	7,77	12,69	5,35	7,80	13,00	6,28	7,01	10,39	6,12
17	7,58	20,37	3,97	6,80	15,10	3,85	6,93	13,65	4,73	6,16	9,93	4,31
18	8,11	20,61	7,98	6,42	18,77	7,87	5,77	16,26	8,53	5,77	11,81	8,14
19	7,46	23,06	7,86	7,18	17,66	7,57	6,84	16,69	8,23	7,05	13,00	8,15
20	9,48	17,53	10,58	8,68	14,95	10,42	8,40	14,74	10,79	8,16	12,01	10,39
21	12,48	25,67	16,39	11,91	22,20	16,02	11,92	21,68	16,17	11,81	19,95	16,60
22	15,78	33,41	16,11	15,83	28,30	15,87	14,00	25,35	16,04	14,69	23,85	16,45
23	14,29	28,11	13,79	14,04	24,09	13,70	14,31	24,06	13,96	15,07	23,20	14,42
24	14,73	31,98	14,69	14,14	26,90	14,33	13,87	21,16	14,61	14,65	25,19	14,37
25	18,67	33,41	15,42	17,66	28,01	15,20	16,82	27,07	15,39	16,98	26,06	15,40
26	17,44	32,27	15,46	17,18	28,06	15,15	16,39	26,81	15,82	16,60	24,09	15,88
27	17,65	22,37	11,71	16,79	20,17	11,76	16,30	20,01	12,57	16,07	18,59	12,47
28	14,97	29,57	14,77	14,28	23,96	14,47	14,00	23,14	15,30	14,22	21,79	15,07
29	15,42	31,04	18,42	15,87	26,71	17,90	14,13	26,34	17,81	14,46	24,27	17,51
30	18,67	31,04	13,63	17,90	27,69	13,45	17,47	26,51	13,87	17,74	23,70	13,73
31	13,63	24,93	11,96	12,78	19,49	11,76	12,57	19,92	12,53	12,58	17,59	12,30
	11,27	22,92	10,76	10,72	19,15	10,52	10,40	18,03	11,00	10,28	16,34	11,01

Juni 1882.

	7	2	8	7	2	8	7	2	8	7	2	8
1	13,67	24,52	11,22	12,69	19,35	10,90	12,57	18,97	11,88	12,89	16,98	10,93
2	11,55	25,75	11,10	10,80	19,93	10,80	10,57	20,22	11,44	10,70	16,93	11,01
3	10,94	20,45	13,14	10,18	17,89	12,59	10,66	17,00	13,44	10,86	15,26	13,31
4	13,26	30,64	16,92	12,83	27,19	16,45	12,57	26,55	16,74	12,58	23,47	16,92
5	17,73	31,45	18,95	16,55	26,37	18,38	16,39	26,42	18,63	16,22	24,96	18,50
6	16,80	23,38	15,83	15,87	20,32	15,49	16,35	20,26	16,04	15,22	18,89	16,30
7	16,23	30,96	22,16	15,49	27,14	21,77	15,61	27,33	21,73	15,88	24,96	21,32
8	18,95	13,79	11,96	18,08	13,45	12,11	18,67	13,87	12,57	17,74	13,54	12,77
9	16,19	18,99	14,32	15,25	17,90	14,04	15,08	18,11	14,40	14,69	18,13	14,92
10	14,77	20,70	14,36	14,52	19,01	14,04	14,74	18,03	14,22	14,77	17,36	14,30
11	14,52	23,10	12,08	13,89	20,12	12,01	13,57	18,80	12,48	13,73	17,32	12,35
12	13,75	18,26	12,32	12,93	16,16	11,87	11,53	14,83	12,40	12,28	13,54	12,59
13	13,14	10,62	8,19	12,21	10,18	7,77	12,14	10,36	8,23	11,70	10,39	8,78
14	10,29	15,78	10,54	9,74	13,60	10,71	9,53	13,13	11,09	9,62	12,12	11,01
15	11,92	11,05	9,08	10,90	10,08	8,73	10,74	10,79	8,66	10,47	11,10	8,55
16	11,73	23,42	12,08	11,14	19,06	11,02	10,83	17,98	12,14	10,58	16,79	12,51
17	13,47	26,15	13,67	12,21	22,25	13,07	11,79	20,78	13,52	12,01	18,89	13,36
18	13,39	20,74	12,40	12,83	18,48	11,87	12,35	16,91	12,14	12,09	14,42	12,24
19	12,93	29,49	18,67	12,21	25,35	17,90	12,14	24,57	18,07	12,01	23,58	18,51
20	17,61	22,65	18,22	16,74	20,42	17,80	16,48	20,13	17,90	16,11	20,79	16,62
21	17,45	33,08	18,46	16,35	28,59	18,09	15,87	26,21	18,46	16,22	24,35	18,17
22	15,17	17,20	15,50	15,00	16,74	15,20	15,21	16,52	15,82	15,07	15,45	15,57
23	16,96	25,59	19,23	16,55	23,36	18,72	16,61	22,84	18,63	16,75	22,02	19,09
24	17,45	34,42	17,81	16,45	29,27	17,18	16,30	27,59	17,68	16,75	24,77	17,91
25	18,54	34,63	17,53	17,13	32,18	17,04	17,25	20,23	17,98	18,21	25,50	17,03
26	19,03	35,12	20,93	18,28	30,38	19,83	17,81	20,83	20,52	17,36	26,16	20,03
27	18,91	33,74	22,80	17,90	30,00	22,15	17,81	29,83	22,50	17,78	27,81	22,70
28	20,45	20,25	16,35	19,25	19,40	16,11	18,97	19,58	16,57	18,13	18,62	16,90
29	17,73	22,08	14,97	16,74	19,35	14,57	16,48	17,86	14,65	15,68	18,47	14,24
30	13,79	11,92	11,71	13,21	11,48	11,57	13,35	11,88	11,88	12,89	12,09	11,93
	15,28	23,66	15,06	14,46	20,83	14,71	14,31	20,21	15,08	14,22	18,78	[illegible]

Mai 1882.

Erdthermometer

1 Zoll tief			1 Fuss tief			2 Fuss tief			4 Fuss tief			
7	2	8	7	2	8	7	2	8	7	2	8	7
8,32	15,73	13,10	10,56	11,03	11,52	10,39	10,29	10,38	8,09	8,17	8,21	
11,14	11,87	8,61	11,20	11,29	10,98	10,47	10,46	10,44	8,26	8,30	8,38	
7,97	14,94	11,26	9,92	10,71	11,27	10,14	10,04	10,19	8,40	8,41	8,43	6,6
8,67	16,38	12,53	10,21	11,08	11,82	10,18	10,16	10,39	8,45	8,50	8,49	
10,88	19,29	17,37	11,14	12,18	13,25	10,55	10,64	11,01	8,53	8,55	8,58	6,7
11,53	13,40	11,74	12,64	12,52	12,51	10,43	11,41	11,44	8,61	8,70	8,76	
10,21	18,21	15,38	11,58	12,53	13,36	10,29	11,25	11,55	8,83	8,91	8,94	6,9
10,81	12,73	11,61	12,46	12,35	12,13	11,71	11,63	11,58	9,02	9,08	9,15	7,0
10,12	10,82	8,40	11,33	11,17	10,94	11,32	11,13	10,96	9,21	9,26	9,30	7,1
6,22	9,12	7,45	9,76	9,49	9,60	10,54	10,23	10,04	9,32	9,35	9,33	7,1
5,38	11,90	9,03	8,67	9,25	9,86	9,72	9,51	9,63	9,32	9,29	9,25	
7,33	12,09	9,51	9,30	9,70	9,99	9,68	9,61	9,68	9,17	9,16	9,13	7,3
7,94	10,73	8,20	9,40	9,54	9,70	9,61	9,58	9,58	9,09	9,10	9,06	
6,93	9,15	7,90	9,15	9,11	9,22	9,52	9,37	9,35	9,04	9,00	9,00	
7,68	12,92	9,35	8,88	9,52	10,17	9,22	9,22	9,45	8,97	8,98	8,98	7,59
8,44	11,83	9,31	9,08	10,05	10,42	9,58	9,61	9,73	8,91	8,91	8,90	7,6
7,52	12,29	8,38	9,62	10,09	10,46	9,75	9,72	9,84	8,91	8,96	8,92	7,6
6,55	11,94	9,84	9,40	9,71	10,16	9,81	9,66	9,74	8,93	8,95	8,95	7,71
7,08	13,51	10,50	9,51	10,04	10,74	9,76	9,72	9,88	8,96	9,00	9,00	7,7
8,46	11,76	10,98	10,09	10,15	10,43	10,01	9,94	9,99	8,99	8,99	9,02	
10,92	15,29	15,16	10,38	11,17	12,06	10,07	10,18	10,46	9,05	9,05	9,08	
12,22	19,87	16,36	11,85	12,83	14,53	10,85	11,08	11,51	9,10	9,19	9,27	
13,75	19,12	14,64	13,32	14,08	14,32	11,91	12,10	12,41	9,29	9,39	9,43	
14,27	20,23	16,07	13,96	14,66	15,06	12,71	12,83	13,05	9,62	9,75	9,82	7,92
16,86	21,04	17,17	14,52	15,23	15,90	13,26	13,35	13,62	9,95	10,07	10,20	7,96
15,49	20,67	17,27	15,31	15,75	16,23	13,89	13,93	14,12	10,34	10,45	10,50	8,04
15,57	18,34	14,99	15,51	15,73	15,78	14,25	14,25	14,33	10,64	10,76	10,82	8,06
13,65	19,42	16,62	14,81	15,26	15,93	14,21	14,08	14,25	10,97	11,06	11,08	8,17
13,96	19,34	17,99	15,04	15,60	16,39	14,34	14,30	14,52	11,18	11,24	11,28	8,27
16,14	21,50	16,62	15,31	16,51	16,89	14,73	14,80	15,01	11,36	11,46	11,48	8,30
13,45	17,92	15,05	15,60	15,68	16,03	15,04	14,86	14,93	11,59	11,68	11,69	8,47
10,48	15,25	12,53	11,67	12,08	12,49	11,22	11,25	11,45	9,87	9,40	9,89	7,50

Juni 1882.

1 Zoll tief			1 Fuss tief			2 Fuss tief			4 Fuss tief			
7	2	8	7	2	8	7	2	8	7	2	8	7
13,03	17,60	14,60	15,06	15,26	15,69	14,85	14,70	14,79	11,77	11,85	11,88	8,5
12,04	17,50	14,27	14,64	14,89	15,48	16,02	14,46	14,55	11,92	11,99	11,99	8,6
11,52	15,40	14,83	14,35	14,38	14,85	14,47	14,28	14,27	12,02	12,03	12,08	8,8
12,40	20,06	17,35	14,17	14,92	15,85	14,21	14,16	14,40	12,09	12,11	12,11	8,9
15,22	21,43	18,77	15,42	16,11	16,81	14,71	14,78	15,08	12,13	12,17	12,18	9,0
16,35	18,37	17,07	16,43	16,40	16,58	15,29	15,82	15,84	12,28	12,29	12,38	9,1
14,94	21,60	22,34	15,85	16,49	17,38	15,34	15,92	15,55	12,42	12,50	12,51	9,2
17,55	16,39	15,02	17,11	17,13	16,80	15,88	15,92	15,90	12,60	12,67	12,71	9,3
14,93	17,55	15,69	15,83	16,15	16,23	15,66	15,52	15,51	12,81	12,87	12,89	
14,98	[illegible]	14,99	15,69	15,77	15,81	15,38	15,26	15,24	12,95	12,98	13,00	
13,01	17,37	14,01	14,83	15,00	15,15	15,02	14,83	14,78	13,04	13,05	13,04	9,6
12,94	14,82	13,61	14,48	14,47	14,56	14,62	14,44	14,40	13,03	13,02	13,02	9,7
11,71	[illegible]	11,14	13,67	13,67	13,53	14,18	13,99	13,87	12,97	12,91	12,95	
10,33	[illegible]	12,44	12,65	12,97	13,34	13,54	13,33	13,38	12,89	12,85	12,82	
10,84	[illegible]	10,84	12,61	12,66	12,51	13,21	13,07	13,00	12,75	12,71	12,63	
11,01	[illegible]	13,44	12,03	12,69	13,25	12,73	12,68	12,79	12,60	12,55	12,50	10,0
11,38	[illegible]	14,65	12,69	13,31	13,99	12,87	12,87	13,05	12,42	12,43	12,33	10,1
12,64	[illegible]	13,47	13,51	13,58	13,81	13,26	13,23	13,38	12,33	12,31	12,31	10,1
11,42	[illegible]	17,06	13,00	13,83	14,78	13,22	13,19	13,42	12,30	12,33	12,32	10,2
14,69	[illegible]	17,77	14,43	15,30	15,89	13,75	13,90	14,16	12,30	12,42	12,39	
15,43	[illegible]	18,84	15,49	16,17	16,79	14,49	14,58	14,88	12,38	12,43	12,45	
15,93	[illegible]	16,48	16,29	16,05	16,06	15,15	15,13	15,14	12,54	12,59	12,64	
16,28	[illegible]	18,07	15,79	16,21	16,74	15,11	15,18	15,28	12,75	12,81	12,86	10,3
15,05	[illegible]	18,64	16,02	16,67	17,49	15,85	15,37	15,60	12,92	13,00	13,01	
16,16	[illegible]	19,31	16,77	17,43	18,23	15,81	15,87	16,14	13,08	13,16	13,18	
16,84	[illegible]	21,03	17,37	18,06	18,91	16,38	16,87	16,65	13,25	13,34	13,38	10,4
17,41	[illegible]	22,06	18,05	18,65	19,54	16,88	16,89	17,14	13,46	13,55	13,59	10,4
18,61	[illegible]	18,29	18,63	18,58	18,65	17,88	17,84	17,85	13,71	13,78	13,86	10,5
18,87	[illegible]	16,56	17,79	17,69	17,64	17,22	17,06	16,98	13,96	14,06	14,09	10,6
14,65	14,18	13,97	16,61	16,22	15,95	16,65	16,41	16,18	14,16	14,21	14,23	10,7

Juli 1882.

	Luftthermometer											
	III. In Glas			IV. In Kupfer			I' frei			VII.		
	7	2	8	7	2	8	7	2	8	7	2	8
1	12,36	23,79	11,92	11,33	20,32	11,52	10,87	20,05	12,40	11,66	16,98	12,39
2	13,22	28,31	15,17	12,40	25,74	14,76	12,27	23,28	15,39	12,69	20,41	15,30
3	16,07	33,28	16,80	15,49	28,74	16,31	15,21	28,45	17,34	15,08	23,85	16,98
4	15,66	26,56	15,99	15,34	24,14	15,97	15,21	22,89	16,00	15,07	21,18	16,22
5	17,86	30,80	17,16	17,04	27,58	16,74	17,04	25,52	17,34	16,98	23,09	17,32
6	16,72	26,15	15,17	16,02	24,43	14,95	16,26	24,66	15,30	15,84	23,43	15,11
7	17,61	23,87	17,40	16,79	22,54	16,94	16,57	22,07	17,38	16,22	20,49	17,97
8	17,04	24,93	17,40	16,11	23,22	17,18	16,08	22,76	17,64	16,22	20,41	17,44
9	18,10	24,12	19,64	17,42	23,12	19,35	17,68	22,50	19,49	17,17	22,05	19,99
10	21,31	26,97	16,47	20,37	23,84	16,50	20,13	22,50	16,74	20,08	20,71	16,98
11	16,88	25,26	15,01	16,11	22,25	14,71	16,04	21,34	15,38	15,95	19,84	15,30
12	15,99	26,27	20,05	15,54	24,43	19,49	15,61	24,23	19,83	15,57	23,09	20,08
13	19,15	24,32	15,70	18,43	22,54	15,49	18,54	22,28	16,04	18,05	21,10	15,84
14	15,91	31,86	18,50	15,39	28,93	18,09	15,39	26,85	18,59	15,45	23,89	18,51
15	16,59	35,85	20,05	15,97	31,35	19,83	16,04	30,78	20,56	15,84	29,12	20,08
16	20,94	39,91	24,56	20,22	35,71	24,15	20,13	34,14	24,36	21,02	32,12	24,31
17	23,59	37,23	21,68	23,60	33,58	21,53	23,06	33,06	22,20	22,70	32,08	22,13
18	21,80	29,53	17,24	21,18	27,19	17,32	21,21	26,16	17,47	21,18	24,92	17,36
19	18,34	33,61	20,09	17,66	29,61	19,73	17,94	29,23	20,52	17,74	26,46	20,60
20	20,09	35,93	24,04	20,80	32,18	23,32	19,40	32,25	23,80	19,69	29,92	23,47
21	19,48	36,26	19,64	18,97	31,59	19,40	19,27	29,57	19,92	19,27	25,96	19,27
22	20,86	34,91	19,72	20,42	31,55	19,35	20,78	30,65	19,58	19,88	29,47	20,41
23	19,07	21,80	17,81	18,14	20,42	17,66	18,33	19,92	17,94	18,43	19,65	17,86
24	17,04	36,09	21,76	16,45	32,06	21,18	16,39	29,18	21,47	16,33	26,77	21,75
25[1])	21,23	26,15	16,80	20,66	22,64	16,65	20,52	20,74	16,69	20,11	20,98	16,83
26	17,73	19,15	15,99	17,23	17,13	15,73	17,12	17,34	16,30	16,71	16,56	16,22
27	18,99	31,78	16,59	17,80	27,09	16,21	17,90	24,96	17,08	17,25	23,01	16,79
28	16,88	27,66	18,42	16,50	24,57	18,33	15,95	24,66	18,76	15,53	21,18	18,47
29	20,57	33,98	25,75	19,54	28,68	25,26	19,40	27,59	25,48	19,57	26,35	25,58
30	21,11	31,70	22,82	20,22	28,16	22,35	20,13	27,46	22,71	20,64	26,93	22,82
31	18,34	19,64	16,19	17,61	18,63	16,11	17,55	18,89	16,22	17,51	18,66	16,03
	18,28	29,28	18,44	17,64	26,26	18,13	17,53	25,35	18,58	17,46	23,55	18,56

August 1882.

	7	2	8	7	2	8	7	2	8	7	2	8
1	14,20	18,42	12,48	13,65	16,99	12,95	13,96	15,61	12,61	13,92	16,18	13,16
2	15,58	28,60	15,62	15,00	23,95	15,39	14,74	22,50	16,00	14,34	20,03	16,18
3	16,11	23,75	15,78	15,68	21,33	15,49	16,13	20,31	15,87	16,22	19,12	15,95
4	13,22	22,41	12,89	12,88	18,67	12,40	12,44	17,98	12,70	13,39	16,60	12,96
5	11,26	21,88	11,35	10,90	18,00	11,28	11,18	17,34	11,96	10,97	15,99	12,24
6	12,98	15,54	15,17	12,69	15,00	14,42	12,61	14,74	14,74	12,01	14,26	14,77
7	11,96	28,94	15,58	12,01	23,99	15,49	12,01	22,50	15,71	12,01	20,87	15,84
8	16,23	31,87	19,15	15,68	27,87	18,67	16,17	25,73	19,27	15,60	23,70	19,19
9	18,83	34,02	16,84	18,53	29,37	16,89	18,20	27,24	17,73	18,13	24,70	17,36
10	18,02	33,38	16,51	17,18	31,21	16,11	17,47	26,98	17,21	16,71	25,16	17,00
11	15,58	28,60	17,04	15,10	25,16	16,94	15,74	23,58	17,21	14,57	22,47	16,98
12	16,31	32,87	17,28	15,97	27,96	16,99	16,17	25,73	18,24	15,49	24,81	17,36
13	14,85	37,27	21,68	14,42	32,52	21,48	14,91	30,09	21,73	14,30	28,39	21,79
14	18,02	37,63	23,34	17,08	32,90	22,74	17,17	30,69	22,89	17,32	30,31	23,39
15	19,03	38,41	24,20	17,90	33,58	23,70	18,46	31,46	23,76	18,32	31,39	24,70
16	19,19	37,96	20,33	18,33	32,95	20,22	18,59	31,55	20,74	18,51	31,16	20,79
17	20,17	32,27	20,25	19,49	28,98	20,12	19,53	28,54	20,52	18,97	28,20	20,30
18	19,15	30,76	20,21	18,58	27,68	20,03	18,33	27,28	20,56	18,51	26,93	20,41
19	18,34	23,79	20,09	17,61	20,22	19,64	17,98	20,95	20,56	18,13	21,41	20,45
20	18,34	28,44	18,22	18,00	26,41	18,04	18,37	25,95	18,89	17,97	25,54	18,89
21	17,45	23,96	15,29	16,94	21,42	15,10	17,98	20,69	15,61	17,30	20,22	15,68
22	14,07	15,99	12,65	13,45	14,90	12,54	13,96	14,74	12,83	14,15	15,07	13,16
23	13,47	22,90	16,31	13,17	20,22	16,02	13,13	19,62	16,30	13,27	19,04	16,37
24	14,97	21,68	14,56	14,66	19,25	14,42	14,65	18,29	14,57	14,69	18,74	14,61
25	13,55	22,90	15,09	13,17	21,48	14,62	13,44	20,48	15,17	13,16	20,08	15,57
26	11,71	25,75	17,86	11,88	23,27	17,71	11,70	22,89	17,86	11,43	22,70	18,13
27	15,42	23,55	15,91	15,10	22,25	15,78	15,39	21,25	16,13	15,18	22,02	16,08
28	12,77	20,94	13,55	12,16	18,48	13,36	12,70	16,89	13,53	13,00	18,13	14,08
29	13,55	21,60	14,52	13,07	20,08	14,04	13,13	19,02	14,83	13,16	18,66	15,49
30	14,48	17,69	12,32	14,33	16,21	12,59	13,78	16,22	12,88	14,49	15,64	12,85
31	14,56	21,27	11,22	13,84	19,35	11,24	13,96	18,20	11,88	13,69	18,51	12,28
	15,27	26,59	16,59	15,09	23,60	16,64	15,29	22,40	16,47	15,14	21,84	16,92

Erdthermometer													
1 Zoll tief			1 Fuss tief			2 Fuss tief			4 Fuss tief			8 Fuss tief	16 Fuss tief
7	2	8	7	2	8	7	2	8	7	2	8	7	7
11,67	18,44	14,87	15,00	15,21	15,86	15,75	15,50	15,50	14,24	14,28	14,23	10,79	8,09
12,33	21,09	16,38	14,91	15,55	16,27	15,38	15,32	15,36	14,19	14,16	14,13	10,90	8,12
14,34	23,38	18,52	15,54	16,45	17,87	15,48	15,50	15,78	14,05	14,06	14,08	10,98	8,13
15,81	21,11	17,49	16,59	16,98	17,81	16,08	16,02	16,15	14,02	14,03	14,03	11,00	8,17
16,51	23,37	18,77	16,80	17,46	17,99	16,21	16,26	16,46	14,07	14,10	14,13	11,12	8,20
16,71	22,55	17,78	17,37	17,82	18,16	16,62	16,68	16,77	14,16	14,20	14,28	11,18	8,22
16,17	21,08	18,22	17,18	17,54	17,85	16,76	16,70	16,78	14,28	14,33	14,36	11,28	8,27
16,85	20,92	18,41	17,21	17,65	17,98	16,76	16,71	16,82	14,41	14,45	14,47	11,30	8,30
17,21	20,79	19,29	17,43	17,70	17,98	16,85	16,82	16,87	14,53	14,55	14,56	11,36	8,34
18,92	20,41	17,58	17,73	17,78	17,91	16,93	16,92	16,95	14,61	14,66	14,67	11,43	8,36
15,76	21,01	17,72	17,08	17,53	18,04	16,82	16,77	16,89	14,69	14,75	14,74	11,49	8,39
15,13	22,19	19,63	17,08	17,66	18,15	16,89	16,82	16,95	14,75	14,78	14,78	11,56	8,41
18,07	20,78	18,04	17,76	18,12	18,31	17,07	17,09	17,19	14,81	14,82	14,84	11,61	8,45
15,45	24,17	19,70	17,28	17,98	18,74	17,12	17,08	17,28	14,86	14,92	14,94	11,67	8,48
16,17	26,08	21,30	17,86	18,64	19,62	17,37	17,37	17,63	14,95	14,99	15,00	11,74	8,51
18,98	29,07	24,47	18,94	20,04	21,11	17,90	18,05	18,43	15,05	15,11	15,11	11,79	8,56
21,42	29,16	23,64	20,60	21,47	22,09	18,86	19,09	19,63	15,20	15,30	15,36	11,85	8,58
20,74	26,44	20,03	21,12	21,48	21,25	19,62	19,63	19,65	15,48	15,57	15,65	11,93	8,63
18,28	26,50	21,91	19,97	21,54	21,20	19,43	19,29	19,46	15,79	15,88	15,91	11,97	8,66
18,32	28,27	24,18	20,23	21,06	21,76	19,48	19,50	19,71	16,01	16,08	16,11	12,07	8,67
19,61	29,69	22,63	20,90	21,70	21,17	19,87	19,92	20,11	16,18	16,25	16,29	12,16	8,73
20,56	27,01	21,43	21,16	21,63	21,84	20,18	20,15	20,23	16,37	16,45	16,46	12,25	8,74
19,88	30,79	19,37	20,99	20,70	20,49	20,20	20,03	19,90	16,58	16,62	16,67	12,37	8,79
17,41	25,89	21,76	19,59	20,26	20,96	19,52	19,39	19,54	16,71	16,78	16,80	12,45	8,81
19,61	21,45	18,77	20,23	20,31	20,23	19,60	19,52	19,51	16,46[1]	16,82	16,84	12,56	8,85
17,82	17,92	17,77	19,05	18,84	18,93	19,19	18,91	18,78	16,84	16,83	16,88	12,66	8,89
17,10	22,67	18,88	18,29	18,93	19,36	18,57	18,42	18,52	16,83	16,82	16,79	12,77	8,93
18,80	22,50	19,48	18,50	19,01	19,88	18,44	18,44	18,46	16,78	16,70	16,70	12,85	8,95
18,61	24,29	23,57	18,84	19,54	20,36	18,49	18,50	18,72	16,66	16,66	16,64	12,94	8,98
20,04	24,04	21,97	19,96	20,87	20,79	19,02	19,07	19,25	16,60	16,68	16,64	12,99	9,02
[illegible]	18,64	17,10	19,85	19,40	19,06	19,25	19,05	18,88	16,66	16,69	16,72	13,06	9,04
[illegible]	23,28	19,69	18,42	18,91	19,27	17,92	17,88	18,00	15,38	15,43	15,44	11,87	8,56

August 1882.

1 Zoll tief 7	1 Zoll tief 2	1 Zoll tief 8	1 Fuss tief 7	1 Fuss tief 2	1 Fuss tief 8	2 Fuss tief 7	2 Fuss tief 2	2 Fuss tief 8	4 Fuss tief 7	4 Fuss tief 2	4 Fuss tief 8	8 Fuss tief 7	16 Fuss tief 7
15,45	16,69	15,23	18,00	17,69	17,59	18,43	18,14	17,06	16,75	16,73	16,72	13,12	9,09
14,87	19,52	17,25	16,70	16,96	17,47	17,51	17,31	17,31	16,69	16,67	16,62	13,18	9,12
15,94	19,41	17,21	17,02	17,26	17,52	17,26	17,18	17,19	16,53	16,46	16,44	13,22	9,16
14,65	16,85	14,87	16,86	16,75	16,78	17,12	16,95	16,91	16,84	16,34	16,30	13,27	9,21
12,86	15,65	13,62	15,64	15,46	15,60	16,57	16,31	16,18	16,22	16,18	16,12	13,28	9,24
13,16	15,16	15,51	15,09	15,30	15,69	15,95	15,81	15,84	16,08	15,97	15,92	13,33	9,28
13,48	19,88	16,20	14,96	15,69	16,25	15,70	15,67	15,80	15,81	15,78	15,71	13,38	9,31
15,05	22,17	19,86	16,13	17,18	18,10	15,98	16,19	16,56	15,63	15,58	15,57	13,36	9,35
17,56	24,67	19,49	16,66	18,52	19,14	16,90	17,10	17,42	15,53	15,55	15,55	13,33	9,37
17,99	24,52	19,69	18,47	19,13	19,60	17,63	17,74	18,04	15,58	15,62	15,64	13,33	9,43
[illegible]	29,02	18,78	18,48	18,77	18,97	18,00	17,91	18,04	15,71	15,75	15,77	13,31	9,47
[illegible]	24,35	20,08	18,16	18,92	19,64	17,91	17,95	18,15	15,85	15,91	15,90	13,31	9,48
[illegible]	25,61	21,80	18,45	19,18	19,95	18,19	18,17	18,40	15,95	15,99	16,04	13,31	9,54
17,50	27,08	23,03	19,28	20,06	20,70	18,58	18,68	18,89	16,05	16,12	16,12	13,31	9,55
[illegible]	27,81	23,60	19,83	20,66	21,28	19,08	19,11	19,33	16,19	16,26	16,26	13,33	9,58
[illegible]	27,95	22,49	20,86	21,13	21,49	19,46	19,55	15,69	16,36	16,44	16,45	13,36	9,61
[illegible]	26,06	21,88	20,55	21,01	21,10	19,73	19,71	19,76	16,56	16,61	16,69	13,40	9,65
[illegible]	25,52	21,77	20,08	20,66	21,01	19,62	19,59	19,68	16,74	16,81	16,81	13,43	9,68
[illegible]	24,81	21,60	20,07	20,72	21,07	19,62	19,62	19,61	16,89	16,91	16,93	13,49	9,72
[illegible]	24,86	20,78	19,96	20,59	20,89	19,60	19,59	19,57	16,99	17,00	16,96	13,54	9,76
[illegible]	20,67	10,96	19,89	19,82	19,79	19,56	19,41	19,84	17,07	17,09	17,09	13,60	9,78
[illegible]	16,73	15,28	18,70	18,47	18,25	19,01	18,74	18,57	17,09	17,10	17,09	13,66	9,81
[illegible]	19,62	16,54	16,98	17,42	16,68	18,04	17,82	17,75	17,07	17,05	17,01	13,71	9,85
[illegible]	15,44	15,57	17,15	17,15	17,09	17,60	17,46	17,37	16,94	16,91	16,82	13,76	9,89
[illegible]	18,58	16,21	16,37	16,78	16,95	17,10	17,00	16,99	16,76	16,69	16,65	13,80	9,90
[illegible]	20,69	17,91	16,13	16,88	17,39	16,85	16,80	16,94	16,55	16,51	16,47	13,86	9,92
[illegible]	20,88	17,46	16,98	17,45	17,63	16,98	17,03	17,12	16,40	16,95	16,32	13,88	9,96
[illegible]	17,80	15,79	17,07	16,92	16,97	17,13	17,00	16,96	16,29	16,26	16,26	13,89	9,98
[illegible]	[illegible]	15,76	16,28	16,50	16,75	16,73	16,62	16,65	16,21	16,20	16,17	13,90	10,00
[illegible]	[illegible]	[illegible]	16,23	16,16	16,09	16,58	16,42	16,36	16,12	16,09	16,06	13,89	10,05
[illegible]	[illegible]	[illegible]	15,82	16,48	15,66	16,08	15,94	15,91	16,01	15,98	15,94	13,88	10,07
[illegible]	[illegible]	[illegible]	[illegible]	16,84	19,07	17,79	17,70	17,69	16,35	16,36	16,35	13,50	9,61

September 1882.

Luftthermometer

		IV. In Kupfer						VII.		
2	8	7	2	8	7	2	8	7	2	8
14,36	11,92	12,49	13,70	11,77	12,61	14,05	12,14	12,47	18,94	12,17
23,50	16,23	10,32	20,46	15,83	10,49	19,75	15,78	10,66	20,33	16,30
27,70	18,58	14,42	25,98	18,14	14,44	25,18	18,29	14,77	25,69	18,70
29,29	21,39	15,20	27,43	20,90	15,30	26,42	20,95	15,68	26,81	21,33
22,65	13,99	15,10	20,90	13,84	15,57	19,92	14,74	15,68	19,76	14,80
20,98	14,24	12,60	19,78	14,04	13,13	19,49	14,48	12,78	18,51	14,90
18,95	13,63	13,96	13,41	13,45	13,48	13,78	13,83	13,24	13,21	14,03
20,94	13,51	13,36	19,01	13,17	13,65	17,98	13,48	13,84	18,36	13,84
14,85	12,73	12,65	14,18	12,64	12,57	13,70	12,66	13,00	14,30	12,81
22,16	13,95	13,70	19,78	13,99	13,87	18,93	14,05	13,46	18,13	14,38
22,04	13,95	12,54	19,83	13,84	12,66	18,84	14,05	12,35	18,89	14,42
22,20	18,79	12,25	20,94	18,98	12,53	20,65	18,46	12,24	20,52	18,88
29,25	20,57	16,65	26,56	20,27	16,48	25,61	20,01	16,68	25,43	20,75
26,15	16,80	13,70	23,75	16,40	13,91	23,37	16,48	14,13	23,78	16,98
27,66	18,42	13,07	25,30	17,90	13,31	24,32	18,07	13,31	24,77	18,51
27,25	16,64	13,21	25,26	16,45	13,44	24,40	16,82	13,50	24,81	17,09
27,78	15,62	12,11	24,77	15,29	12,85	23,93	15,52	12,54	24,70	16,22
26,15	15,91	11,28	24,10	15,49	11,43	23,80	15,61	11,85	24,08	16,52
26,76	15,58	9,94	23,95	15,05	10,27	23,63	15,17	10,32	24,04	16,22
26,27	13,47	9,21	23,70	13,21	9,23	22,97	13,70	9,51	23,55	13,92
23,22	14,52	10,23	21,43	14,42	10,44	20,99	14,70	10,09	20,08	14,69
12,12	12,32	9,31	11,72	12,11	9,79	12,40	12,44	10,17	12,39	12,47
11,92	10,70	10,13	11,28	10,56	10,40	11,61	10,83	10,32	11,24	10,70
12,57	9,30	7,53	11,67	9,40	7,98	11,79	9,23	7,39	10,93	9,55
18,75	6,73	2,46	15,97	6,51	3,18	15,17	6,93	3,00	14,38	7,62
15,09	7,17	1,49	13,07	7,09	1,88	12,61	7,37	1,70	12,01	7,78
11,71	10,29	4,49	11,14	10,23	4,77	11,09	10,44	4,66	10,85	10,47
16,15	11,51	11,62	15,54	11,52	11,70	15,57	11,70	11,81	15,57	11,82
12,04	10,29	8,73	11,82	10,18	8,92	11,96	10,36	8,66	11,89	10,47
11,80	9,93	9,40	11,00	9,94	9,71	10,96	10,10	9,62	10,74	10,32
20,56	13,93	11,08	18,92	13,77	11,82	18,48		11,82	18,39	10,91

October 1882.

2	8	7	2	8	7	2	8	7	2	8
19,23	11,10	6,06	16,94	11,14	6,41	15,18		6,16	16,03	11,62
15,30	11,02	5,74	14,52	10,95	5,90	14,18		5,85	13,50	11,51
13,95	11,71	8,15	12,88	11,43	8,44	12,74		8,28	12,50	[illegible]
17,61	9,89	9,59	15,68	9,74	9,97	15,14		9,78	14,65	[illegible]
12,32	9,68	5,35	11,28	9,69	5,55	11,36		5,47	10,85	[illegible]
14,44	6,57	5,50	13,55	6,42	5,98	13,40		6,08	12,96	7,21
14,03	6,44	3,42	12,16	6,32	3,74	12,10		3,93	11,93	6,78
15,46	9,48	7,01	14,90	9,40	7,50	13,87		7,20	13,00	9,70
11,96	9,16	8,54	11,48	9,11	8,70	11,18		8,55	11,08	9,32
15,37	6,97	8,73	13,45	6,80	8,70	13,04		8,74	12,81	7,34
12,78	5,24	6,94	12,11	6,13	7,37	11,83		7,12	11,47	6,70
15,58	5,27	6,46	13,65	5,21	6,80	13,09		6,62	12,09	5,27
9,48	0,19	2,46	6,85	0,24	2,61	6,50		2,27		0,47
5,84	1,43	− 2,05	4,39	1,49	− 2,31	4,04		− 2,37	3,70	1,54
2,97	0,79	− 1,50	0,34	0,72	− 1,55	0,67		− 1,60	1,19	0,85
0,71	− 0,77	− 0,38	0,48	− 0,66	− 0,45	0,71		− 0,38	0,47	0,52
2,20	1,39	− 1,30	1,97	1,49	− 1,01	1,84		− 1,07		1,46
2,60	2,36	1,01	2,36	2,46	1,32	2,44		1,42		2,39
7,86	5,27	2,11	6,80	4,87	2,14	6,59		2,12		5,47
11,10	0,99	− 0,71	8,63	1,39	− 0,58	8,32		− 0,30		2,00
10,54	0,55	− 1,45	7,18	0,39	− 1,81	7,15		− 1,07	7,01	1,15
8,27	0,47	− 3,66	6,27	0,58	− 3,65	5,37		− 3,36		0,47
1,80	0,99	− 0,48	1,63	1,01	0,87	1,71	1,15	− 0,56		1,08
5,84	5,27	2,26	5,40	5,35	2,74	5,64	5,34	2,73		5,55
7,86	6,04	5,45	7,28	5,84	5,51	7,06	5,85	5,58		6,24
5,30	5,68	5,74	4,87	5,64	5,68	5,08	5,68	5,89		6,35
14,36	4,34	6,32	12,97	4,39	6,28	10,88	4,47	6,58		5,15
8,56	8,35	2,18	8,25	8,30	8,31	8,28	8,36	8,78		8,55
18,30	11,26	8,83	16,94	11,14	8,75	16,48	11,09	9,32		11,87
14,36	3,81	7,57	13,94	3,76	7,80	10,11	4,08	7,86	9,70	4,21
14,77	5,08	2,94	12,59	4,92	8,01	11,19	5,21	8,58		[illegible]

September 1882.

Erdthermometer

1 Zoll tief			1 Fuss tief			2 Fuss tief			4 Fuss tief			8 Fuss tief	16 Fuss tief
7	2	8	7	2	8	7	2	8	7	2	8	7	7
13,25	14,25	14,29	15,06	15,08	15,26	15,75	15,62	15,57	15,87	15,82	15,78	13,88	10,10
11,87	17,88	15,33	14,62	14,99	15,45	15,41	15,31	15,37	15,70	15,64	15,60	13,87	10,13
13,92	20,94	18,04	15,01	15,76	16,59	15,36	15,41	15,68	15,52	15,48	15,44	13,87	10,17
15,76	22,23	19,53	16,35	17,04	17,73	15,96	16,12	15,43	15,40	15,37	15,36	13,85	10,18
16,45	19,74	16,72	17,26	17,41	15,54	16,64	16,69	16,77	15,36	15,39	15,41	13,80	10,21
14,29	18,57	16,08	16,48	17,66	16,91	16,90	16,47	16,52	15,44	15,45	15,48	13,77	10,24
14,58	15,14	14,52	16,22	16,07	15,89	16,37	16,22	16,04	15,49	15,48	15,49	13,74	10,26
14,33	17,66	15,19	15,51	15,68	15,98	15,86	15,77	15,80	15,47	15,46	15,43	13,72	10,31
14,71	14,77	13,95	15,42	15,35	15,30	15,74	15,60	15,55	15,40	15,37	15,34	13,72	10,32
14,46	17,33	15,27	15,14	15,38	15,70	15,40	15,37	15,43	15,30	15,26	15,24	13,72	10,36
13,42	18,03	15,20	15,12	15,38	15,77	15,41	15,36	15,43	15,21	15,18	15,16	13,70	10,37
13,31	17,79	17,30	15,10	15,39	15,88	15,38	15,32	15,40	15,12	15,10	15,09	13,67	10,40
15,82	21,24	18,74	15,86	16,39	17,02	15,53	15,64	15,87	15,06	15,05	15,04	13,65	10,42
14,64	20,75	17,04	16,44	16,60	16,95	16,05	16,03	16,14	15,05	15,06	15,08	13,64	10,44
14,16	21,83	17,94	16,22	16,53	17,12	16,12	16,08	16,24	15,09	15,10	15,12	13,61	10,44
14,40	22,94	17,37	16,37	16,76	17,25	16,26	16,25	16,37	15,12	15,13	15,14	13,59	10,47
13,82	22,84	16,95	16,33	16,67	17,13	16,34	16,27	16,39	15,16	15,16	15,17	13,57	10,50
13,30	22,05	16,83	16,12	16,50	16,88	16,29	16,20	16,26	15,18	15,18	15,19	13,57	10,50
12,73	22,17	16,55	15,87	16,29	16,72	16,15	16,08	16,18	15,18	15,18	15,16	13,56	10,52
12,27	22,17	15,82	15,69	16,07	16,46	16,02	15,95	15,99	15,14	15,13	15,13	13,56	10,53
12,25	20,32	15,88	15,34	15,74	16,19	15,84	15,74	15,79	15,10	15,09	15,07	13,55	10,56
12,25	13,05	13,26	15,44	14,98	14,78	15,74	15,54	15,36	15,05	15,02	15,01	13,55	10,59
12,23	12,76	12,23	14,42	14,26	14,12	15,09	14,91	14,79	14,97	14,93	14,91	13,54	10,61
10,23	12,20	10,92	13,48	13,32	13,24	14,47	14,27	14,14	14,84	14,80	14,75	13,54	10,63
6,93	15,64	9,85	12,16	12,34	12,60	13,75	13,55	13,44	14,66	14,62	14,55	13,53	10,64
6,08	11,99	9,37	11,46	11,46	11,74	13,13	12,91	12,82	14,44	14,36	14,29	13,52	10,65
7,09	10,55	10,47	11,04	11,06	11,32	12,53	12,36	12,31	14,16	14,06	14,00	13,50	10,66
10,99	14,48	12,33	11,43	12,21	12,53	12,27	12,39	12,53	13,87	13,79	13,72	13,46	10,67
10,17	12,02	11,35	12,09	12,08	12,18	12,63	12,59	12,59	13,63	13,58	13,55	13,42	10,70
10,54	11,37	11,11	11,97	11,93	11,95	12,56	12,49	12,49	13,48	13,45	13,43	13,35	10,71
12,54	17,49	14,85	15,03	15,08	15,17	15,23	15,15	15,15	15,02	14,99	14,97	13,59	10,44

October 1882.

1 Zoll tief			1 Fuss tief			2 Fuss tief			4 Fuss tief			8 Fuss tief	16 Fuss tief
7	2	8	7	2	8	7	2	8	7	2	8	7	7
8,,86	14,60	12,13	11,45	11,78	12,23	12,38	12,31	12,36	13,38	13,33	13,31	13,31	10,74
9 01	13,36	12,80	11,85	11,94	12,19	12,41	12,36	12,38	13,26	13,22	13,21	13,25	10,75
9'76	12,59	11,70	11,76	11,79	12,00	12,35	12,27	12,27	13,17	13,14	13,10	13,20	10,76
10'74	13,53	11,50	11,88	12,08	12,30	12,28	12,26	12,33	13,08	13,02	13,01	13,12	10,77
8·24	11,36	10,30	11,62	11,43	11,50	12,27	12,11	12,05	12,99	12,96	12,95	13,06	10,78
8·26	12,54	9,47	11,07	11,30	10,50	11,89	11,81	11,83	12,90	12,88	12,84	13,00	10,80
6·68	12,33	8,95	10,61	11,76	10,97	11,67	11,55	11,52	12,79	12,75	12,71	12,93	10,81
8·65	12,06	10,48	10,57	10,74	11,09	11,41	11,34	11,38	12,66	12,60	12,57	12,91	10,82
9·77	11,13	10,24	10,93	10,01	11,08	11,41	11,42	11,42	12,50	12,45	12,44	12,84	10,82
9·47	12,69	9,47	11,79	11,08	11,18	11,29	11,42	11,48	12,38	12,36	12,33	12,76	10,83
8·25	11,40	9,06	10,45	10,63	10,78	11,30	11,23	11,21	12,30	12,27	12,26	12,70	10,83
8·34	12,16	8,26	10,37	10,63	10,71	11,15	11,10	11,10	12,21	12,19	12,16	12,64	10,84
5·78	9,80	4,70	9,57	9,52	9,39	10,87	10,65	10,52	12,13	12,09	12,05	12,58	10,85
1·72	5,26	3,94	7,98	7,64	7,62	10,07	9,68	9,46	11,98	11,92	11,86	12,53	10,86
1,73	2,36	2,07	6,86	6,34	6,23	9,05	8,72	8,48	11,75	11,65	11,57	12,47	10,86
1,08	2,16	1,47	5,60	5,48	5,32	8,04	7,77	7,60	11,40	11,28	11,19	12,40	10,88
1,18	2,36	2,60	5,03	4,99	5,08	7,28	7,11	7,01	10,99	10,89	10,78	12,34	10,88
2,48	3,40	3,40	5,14	5,22	5,33	6,89	6,83	6,82	10,60	10,49	10,41	12,27	10,88
3,67	6,00	5,35	5,37	5,70	5,94	6,79	6,81	6,91	10,25	10,16	10,09	12,18	10,88
1,90	8,29	3,70	5,62	5,90	6,18	6,96	6,96	7,01	9,96	9,91	9,86	12,09	10,88
1,13	7,59	3,15	5,37	5,61	5,82	6,90	6,81	6,82	9,76	9,72	9,66	11,96	10,88
0,53	6,64	2,63	4,98	5,18	5,37	6,68	6,56	6,52	9,58	9,52	9,47	11,86	10,89
1·49	2,83	2,27	4,85	4,74	4,69	6,70	6,26	6,20	9,37	9,31	9,26	11,71	10,88
3,13	5,06	5,19	4,69	4,99	5,36	6,07	6,07	6,16	9,16	9,10	9,05	11,61	10,87
5,25	6,46	6,01	5,65	5,92	6,18	6,31	6,43	6,55	8,95	8,91	8,88	11,48	10,87
5,96	5,78	6,01	6,25	6,33	6,40	6,72	6,79	6,85	8,83	8,82	8,81	11,39	10,87
6,24	10,77	6,33	6,52	7,00	7,31	6,92	7,06	7,24	8,79	8,78	8,78	11,28	10,87
4,83	7,39	7,62	6,67	6,69	6,99	7,28	7,21	7,27	8,79	8,79	8,79	11,15	10,87
7,77	13,36	10,63	7,32	8,23	8,86	7,42	7,63	7,93	8,79	8,78	8,81	11,04	10,85
9,06	11,20	6,62	9,13	9,08	8,84	8,39	8,55	8,62	8,82	8,86	8,90	10,94	10,84
5,01	10,64	6,50	7,80	7,95	8,07	8,41	8,32	8,30	8,94	9,02	9,03	10,82	10,80
5,67	8,83	6,92	8,22	8,31	8,43	9,21	9,14	9,15	11,05	11,01	10,97	12,25	10,84

November 1882.

Luftthermometer

	III. in Glas		IV. in Kupfer			I' frei					
	2	8	7	2	8	7	2	8	7	2	8
		5,43		6,85	5,45	6,16		5,68	6,24	7,01	5,58
		4,95	4,39	6,80	4,87	4,47		5,03	4,54	6,24	5,24
	7,74	1,08	3,47	6,94	1,30	3,65		1,71	3,58	6,01	1,59
		6,40	4,49	7,18	6,42	4,51	6,54	6,54	4,66	6,58	7,01
		7,50	6,90	7,82	7,63	6,71	7,71	7,46	7,20	7,82	7,06
		7,86	8,83	6,70	7,43	9,01		7,71	9,62	8,04	7,52
		5,68	5,16	8,78	5,60	5,42		5,68	5,70	7,66	5,33
	8,67	6,65	7,57	8,25	6,70	7,58		6,76	7,89	8,24	6,85
	13,39	3,25	4,44	9,07	3,32	4,68		3,61	4,81	6,89	3,62
		3,61	3,71	4,77	3,71	3,39		3,91	3,46	5,08	3,92
	7,17	3,25	4,10	5,81	3,32	3,39	5,47	3,48	3,85	5,70	3,66
		1,51	0,63	0,00	− 1,40	0,67		1,41	0,80	− 0,45	− 1,53
		4,26	− 3,85	2,36	− 4,13	3,60		3,70	− 3,74	− 0,26	− 3,66
		1,31	− 0,53	2,56	− 1,26	0,41	1,92	0,96	− 0,38	1,83	− 0,68
	4,74	4,10	− 6,41	− 4,75	− 3,85	5,77	4,47	3,74	− 6,09	− 5,12	− 4,05
		7,68	− 9,10	− 3,52	− 7,61	8,71	6,80	7,23	− 9,20	− 7,86	− 7,71
	6,19	8,29	− 9,15	− 6,90	− 8,33	8,92	6,90	7,93	− 9,20	− 7,33	− 8,24
	5,47	4,30	− 8,76	− 6,18	− 3,80	8,41		− 4,13	− 8,98	− 6,42	− 4,49
	0,15	3,00	− 6,66	− 0,53	− 2,94		0,84	− 2,87	− 6,69	− 0,84	− 2,75
	3,01	0,59	− 4,51	1,78	0,53	− 4,21	1,45	0,54	− 4,51	1,62	0,77
		0,03	− 2,84	0,77	0,05	− 2,66	0,71	0,02	− 2,60	0,47	− 0,07
		0,22	− 0,43	1,11	− 0,14	− 0,32	0,93	− 0,15	− 0,38	1,12	− 0,39
		2,48	− 3,51	− 0,86	2,36	− 3,21	− 0,88	− 2,23	− 3,44	− 1,07	− 2,37
		4,22	− 1,78	0,00	3,95	− 1,67	0,06	3,78	− 1,79	0,24	4,62
		5,84	4,82	7,28	5,74	4,77	6,20	5,64	5,20	6,62	5,89
		3,41	1,63	3,04	3,18	2,01	3,05	3,26	2,16	2,89	3,31
93		3,33	2,60	4,44	2,94	2,70	4,34	3,05	2,69	4,54	3,16
75	2,20	0,19	0,77	2,32	0,05	0,58	1,71	0,23	0,96	1,62	0,47
	1,83	3,25	− 0,33	− 2,14	− 3,27	− 0,32	− 2,10	− 3,00	− 0,41	− 2,21	− 3,26
52		7,68	− 6,42	− 3,80	− 7,42	− 5,94	− 4,60	− 6,80	− 6,57	− 5,88	− 7,18
10	3,51	0,48	0,17	2,54	1,00	0,30		1,00	0,31	1,98	1,02

December 1882.

	III. in Glas		IV. in Kupfer			I' frei					
	2	8	7	2	8	7	2	8	7	2	8
38	2,21	− 4,84	− 9,15	2,55	− 8,57	− 8,66	− 4,26	− 8,19	− 9,09	− 5,31	− 8,32
05	− 1,15	−11,07	− 9,77	− 6,23	−10,73	− 9,35	− 7,57	−10,38	− 9,77	− 8,42	−10,84
47	5,35	−11,41	−10,78	6,66	−10,97	− 9,82	− 7,02	−10,63	−10,27	− 7,94	−10,99
32	9,46	−12,01	−13,08	9,53	−11,64	−12,74	− 9,48	−11,20	−13,05	− 9,89	−11,75
42	7,48	− 5,98	− 9,53	− 7,61	5,70	− 9,31	7,57	− 5,68	− 9,32	− 7,83	− 6,08
93	3,45	3,45	− 3,98	3,80	3,32	− 3,66	3,74	− 3,30	− 3,94	− 4,02	− 3,32
58	0,10	− 1,43	− 1,78	0,62	− 1,40	− 1,58	0,71	− 1,31	− 1,60	− 0,72	− 1,45
79	0,23	0,19	− 2,22	− 0,48	0,00	− 2,23	− 0,50	0,23	− 2,25	− 0,68	0,46
67	1,59	0,19	0,67	1,35	0,10	0,54	1,02	0,19	0,70	1,23	0,35
29	− 0,77	− 2,44	− 3,18	− 1,35	− 2,36	3,08	− 1,27	− 2,31	− 3,25	− 1,75	− 2,37
83	1,39	1,76	0,72	0,91	1,59	0,80	1,15	1,58	0,96	1,15	1,66
52	2,20	0,99	2,46	1,97	1,01	2,18	1,66	0,93	2,60	1,81	1,04
35	2,20	1,43	0,34	2,02	1,49	0,54	1,84	1,32	0,47	2,00	1,46
71	1,47	0,99	0,72	1,49	1,01	0,71	1,36	0,89	0,98	1,46	0,96
43	2,20	1,31	0,24	1,97	1,30	0,62	1,79	1,32	0,39	1,85	1,35
11	2,43	0,35	0,91	2,36	0,34	1,15	2,18	0,41	1,31	2,85	[illegible]
02	2,64	− 5,35	− 0,91	− 2,70	− 5,41	− 1,05	− 2,57	− 5,16	− 1,07	− 2,90	− 5,55
66	1,55	− 9,98	− 9,53	− 1,40	− 9,05	− 8,53	− 3,57	− 8,62	− 8,98	− 4,47	− 8,98
	0,62	− 8,69	−11,45	3,56	− 8,47	−10,87	− 5,37	− 8,19	−10,73	− 6,15	− 8,32
	1,88	− 8,65	−10,83	1,74	− 8,52	−10,44	− 3,87	− 8,19	−10,42	− 4,51	− 8,32
	0,38	− 5,31	− 9,77	3,08	− 5,32	− 9,48	− 4,56	− 5,07	− 9,39	− 5,49	− 5,19
	− 2,40	− 1,67	− 5,99	2,36	− 1,78	− 5,90	− 2,44	− 1,58	− 6,12	− 2,49	− 1,64
	− 1,02	− 3,85	− 1,78	1,16	− 3,85	1,61	− 1,23	− 3,78	− 1,64	− 1,34	− 4,08
	1,06	− 1,87	− 3,18	1,35	− 1,88	− 2,87	− 1,27	− 1,84	− 2,83	− 1,41	[illegible]
73	− 1,71	− 1,87	− 4,56	− 2,84	− 1,93	4,52	− 3,00	− 2,01	− 4,59	− 3,25	− 1,83
	− 2,72	− 1,47	− 3,52	3,08	− 1,50	− 3,34	− 2,96	− 1,27	− 3,51	− 3,25	− 1,37
	2,12	− 2,24	− 5,09	− 2,26	− 2,41	− 4,82	− 2,14	− 3,00	− 4,51	− 2,21	− 2,17
	− 3,29	− 1,63	− 7,04	− 4,08	− 1,59	− 7,11	− 4,47	− 1,00	− 7,33	− 4,51	− 0,84
41	2,60	3,45	3,80	2,41	3,37	3,57	2,18	3,30	3,81	2,67	[illegible]
38	4,95	2,20	4,19	4,58	1,97	4,17	4,73	2,01	4,30	5,00	[illegible]
50		0,83	− 0,71	1,97	0,72	− 1,05	0,23	0,63	2,23	0,47	[illegible]

November 1882.

Erdthermometer													
1 Zoll tief			1 Fuss tief			2 Fuss tief			4 Fuss tief			8 Fuss tief	16 Fuss tief
7	2	8	7	2	8	7	2	8	7	2	8	7	7
6,64	7,17	6,64	7,66	7,68	7,69	8,18	8,13	8,11	9,08	9,08	9,09	10,76	10,82
5,91	6,84	6,15	7,48	7,40	7,40	8,04	7,97	7,94	9,10	9,08	9,08	10,71	10,81
5,29	7,06	3,96	7,14	7,09	6,94	7,82	7,76	7,69	9,07	9,06	9,05	10,65	10,79
5,15	6,46	6,47	6,61	6,71	6,85	7,30	7,42	7,46	9,02	8,99	8,97	10,60	10,77
7,07	7,54	7,54	7,19	7,34	7,45	7,49	7,54	7,61	8,94	8,90	8,89	10,55	10,77
8,23	7,44	7,34	7,61	7,79	7,79	7,72	7,81	7,88	8,87	8,87	8,86	10,50	10,77
6,07	8,02	6,59	7,48	7,52	7,58	7,86	7,84	7,85	8,83	8,84	8,85	10,44	10,74
7,39	7,91	7,35	7,40	7,59	7,69	7,80	7,81	7,85	8,84	8,84	8,84	10,39	10,71
6,05	8,21	5,20	7,58	7,48	7,32	7,89	7,87	7,83	8,83	8,83	8,80	10,35	10,70
4,68	5,44	4,98	6,75	6,65	6,61	7,65	7,51	7,43	8,82	8,79	8,79	10,30	10,70
4,31	5,98	4,48	6,97	6,76	6,11	7,15	7,01	6,95	8,79	8,75	8,71	10,27	10,65
2,56	1,81	1,13	5,70	5,23	4,86	6,81	6,64	6,45	8,65	8,62	8,58	10,21	10,64
2,29	2,99	0,47	4,15	3,98	3,89	6,04	5,81	5,63	8,51	8,47	8,43	10,18	10,63
0,66	2,47	1,09	3,58	3,57	3,57	5,35	5,22	5,11	8,32	8,23	8,16	10,14	10,63
0,01	− 0,51	− 0,59	3,22	2,93	2,75	4,94	4,77	4,62	8,01	7,91	7,83	10,09	10,63
− 2,27	− 1,25	− 2,56	2,37	2,22	2,00	4,37	4,22	4,08	7,70	7,61	7,54	10,03	10,58
− 3,25	− 2,76	− 3,41	1,74	1,65	1,47	3,85	3,72	3,58	7,40	7,32	7,25	9,95	10,56
− 2,95	− 1,87	− 1,30	1,54	1,65	1,27	3,36	3,29	3,22	7,13	7,03	6,97	9,88	10,55
− 1,68	− 0,33	− 0,61	1,24	1,28	1,26	3,11	3,08	3,03	6,84	6,76	6,69	9,79	10,54
− 1,11	0,05	0,15	1,14	1,25	1,29	2,94	2,92	2,90	6,57	6,51	6,49	9,70	10,50
− 0,22	0,07	0,10	1,30	1,29	1,33	2,85	2,82	2,80	6,33	6,27	6,22	9,59	10,49
0,02	0,21	0,23	1,37	1,36	1,38	2,76	2,75	2,74	6,14	6,08	6,02	9,48	10,46
− 0,39	− 0,08	− 0,37	1,35	1,37	1,37	2,72	2,71	2,70	5,95	5,91	5,86	9,37	10,45
− 0,15	0,05	0,51	1,38	1,39	1,45	2,67	2,65	2,66	5,80	5,73	5,72	9,24	10,43
1,56	3,62	3,13	1,50	1,63	1,76	2,65	2,66	2,66	5,67	5,62	5,58	9,13	10,41
2,14	2,96	2,82	2,53	2,64	2,76	2,89	3,00	3,11	5,54	5,51	5,47	9,02	10,40
2,56	3,96	3,02	2,80	2,98	3,19	3,24	3,31	3,43	5,46	5,46	5,44	8,91	10,37
1,84	2,29	1,46	3,09	2,96	2,93	3,53	3,56	3,56	5,45	5,44	5,43	8,79	10,33
0,64	0,26	− 0,07	2,61	2,37	2,21	3,48	3,41	3,34	5,46	5,46	5,46	8,72	10,33
− 1,52	− 0,19	− 2,51	1,87	1,73	1,58	3,17	3,07	2,98	5,46	5,44	5,44	8,62	10,31
2,25	3,06	2,32	4,11	4,09	4,06	5,19	5,14	5,11	7,49	7,45	7,42	9,88	10,58

December 1882.

7	2	8	7	2	8	7	2	8	7	2	8	7	7
− 3,77	− 1,55	− 3,79	1,30	1,24	1,11	2,81	2,74	2,66	5,40	5,37	5,34	8,55	10,27
− 5,01	− 3,37	− 5,51	0,86	0,71	0,56	2,48	2,37	2,26	5,31	5,25	5,22	8,47	10,24
− 5,55	− 3,75	− 5,17	0,82	0,26	0,20	2,17	2,05	1,95	5,16	5,11	5,07	8,39	10,22
− 6,89	− 5,24	− 6,59	− 0,08	− 0,11	− 0,24	1,73	1,69	1,64	4,98	4,94	4,90	8,29	10,18
− 5,54	− 4,15	− 3,23	− 4,44	− 0,34	− 0,29	1,41	1,42	1,35	4,86	4,76	4,73	8,22	10,14
− 2,95	− 1,83	− 1,66	− 0,18	− 0,09	− 0,05	1,30	1,28	1,28	4,63	4,59	4,54	8,15	10,13
− 1,09	− 0,65	− 0,64	0,23	0,07	0,09	1,25	1,25	1,25	4,46	4,42	4,37	8,06	10,11
− 1,08	− 0,48	− 0,80	0,12	0,15	0,16	1,24	1,22	1,23	4,31	4,29	4,26	7,97	10,08
− 0,05	0,13	0,12	0,19	0,22	0,23	1,22	1,22	1,24	4,19	4,16	4,15	7,87	10,05
− 0,68	− 0,30	− 0,76	0,30	0,23	0,24	1,24	1,24	1,24	4,09	4,07	4,06	7,75	10,01
0,00	0,21	0,23	0,25	0,27	0,30	1,23	1,25	1,25	4,00	3,99	3,99	7,68	9,99
0,54	0,58	0,40	0,20	0,30	0,32	1,25	1,26	1,26	3,94	3,92	3,91	7,59	9,95
0,29	0,76	0,61	0,35	0,37	0,37	1,27	1,28	1,28	3,89	3,86	3,85	7,51	9,91
0,48	0,71	0,53	0,41	0,41	0,43	1,30	1,30	1,31	3,83	3,81	3,81	7,41	9,89
0,33	0,93	0,72	0,45	0,46	0,49	1,32	1,31	1,33	3,78	3,76	3,75	7,34	9,85
0,65	1,09	0,36	0,49	0,52	0,53	1,34	1,31	1,36	3,73	3,72	3,70	7,24	9,84
0,24	− 0,12	− 1,28	0,53	0,54	0,55	1,37	1,38	1,39	3,71	3,68	3,67	7,17	9,79
− 3,92	− 0,65	− 4,39	0,56	0,48	0,42	1,37	1,39	1,37	3,67	3,65	3,64	7,11	9,76
− 5,89	− 2,03	− 4,58	0,19	0,18	0,11	1,32	1,30	1,28	3,62	3,61	3,60	7,01	9,72
− 6,05	1,90	− 4,85	− 0,15	− 0,18	− 0,23	1,18	1,13	1,12	3,58	3,56	3,56	6,94	9,69
− 6,05	− 2,88	− 3,85	− 0,55	− 0,61	− 0,60	1,00	0,95	0,94	3,52	3,50	3,49	6,89	9,66
− 4,18	− 2,42	− 1,69	− 0,70	− 0,58	− 0,50	0,83	0,79	0,78	3,47	3,43	3,40	6,82	9,61
− 1,23	− 1,03	− 1,81	− 0,28	− 0,20	− 0,19	0,77	0,76	0,76	3,35	3,34	3,32	6,74	9,58
− 1,98	− 1,06	− 1,16	− 0,26	− 2,23	− 0,16	0,75	0,74	0,72	3,27	3,25	3,24	6,68	9,54
− 1,80	− 1,32	− 1,16	− 0,19	− 0,18	− 0,15	0,73	0,72	0,72	3,20	3,19	3,17	6,63	9,51
− 1,24	− 1,42	− 0,84	− 0,08	− 0,14	− 0,11	0,72	0,71	0,71	3,14	3,11	3,11	6,56	9,47
− 1,41	− 1,04	− 0,97	− 0,07	− 0,03	− 0,03	0,72	0,71	0,71	3,08	3,08	3,07	6,51	9,45
− 1,30	− 1,21	− 1,02	0,01	− 0,07	− 0,08	0,73	0,71	0,71	3,02	3,03	3,00	6,42	9,40
0,52	0,54	1,02	0,04	0,10	0,15	0,71	0,72	0,74	2,99	2,99	2,98	6,37	9,37
1,08	1,93	0,72	0,19	0,20	0,22	0,73	0,74	0,74	2,95	2,93	2,99	6,31	9,35
0,22	0,23	0,39	0,21	0,31	0,31	0,68	0,76	0,75	2,97	2,85	2,96	6,23	9,29
− 2,02	− 1,01	− 1,62	0,01	0,07	0,13	1,23	1,21	1,20	3,87	3,85	3,83	7,35	9,81

Monatsmittel 1881.

Luftthermometer

	III. in Glas			IV. in Kupfer			I' frei			VII.		
	7	2	8	7	2	8	7	2	8	7	2	8
Januar . .	— 8,69	— 1,94	— 7,54	— 8,86	— 3,95	— 7,68	— 8,39	— 5,35	— 7,52	— 8,44	— 5,63	— 8,23
Februar . .	— 4,54	3,07	— 3,30	— 4,65	0,14	— 3,33	— 4,39	— 0,52	— 3,28	— 4,55	— 1,52	— 3,25
März . . .	— 3,89	6,01	— 2,02	— 3,83	3,20	— 1,97	— 3,70	1,72	— 1,80	— 3,65	0,85	— 1,80
April . . .	1,88	14,04	2,48	1,76	10,14	2,52	1,70	9,15	2,23	1,23	8,27	2,96
Mai . . .	11,45	22,72	10,87	11,26	18,88	10,67	10,58	18,51	11,04	9,88	16,15	10,96
Juni . . .	14,18	24,37	14,14	13,62	21,31	13,84	13,40	20,62	14,26	13,37	19,16	14,25
Juli . . .	16,82	29,09	17,15	16,02	23,75	17,15	16,05	22,34	17,15	15,74	20,75	17,23
August . .	14,35	23,75	14,07	13,78	15,42	13,75	13,63	19,41	14,57	13,57	18,65	14,81
September .	10,11	18,73	11,51	9,81	16,69	11,46	10,06	16,40	11,81	10,18	15,98	12,16
October . .	3,09	9,16	4,05	3,01	7,82	3,87	2,94	7,71	4,08	2,90	7,31	4,18
November .	3,27	5,79	2,92	3,04	5,39	2,82	2,37	4,98	2,98	2,49	4,76	3,13
December .	— 0,91	1,20	— 0,67	— 0,99	0,63	— 0,76	— 0,64	0,56	— 0,61	— 0,86	0,35	— 0,63
Jahresmittel	4,76	13,00	5,29	4,48	9,95	5,19	4,47	9,63	5,41	4,92	8,75	5,48

Monatsmittel 1882.

	7	2	8	7	2	8	7	2	8	7	2	8
Januar . .	0,93	5,02	1,52	0,85	3,51	1,46	0,98	2,63	1,58	1,10	2,41	1,66
Februar . .	0,23	5,49	1,35	0,24	3,53	1,32	0,25	2,80	1,46	0,23	2,54	1,10
März . . .	3,09	9,75	4,35	2,54	8,03	4,19	3,09	7,10	4,37	3,12	7,09	4,47
April . . .	5,97	16,36	5,96	5,50	13,21	5,87	5,54	12,07	6,16	5,32	11,62	6,20
Mai . . .	11,27	22,92	10,76	10,72	19,15	10,52	10,40	18,03	11,00	10,28	16,34	11,01
Juni . . .	15,28	23,66	15,06	14,46	20,83	14,71	14,31	20,21	15,08	14,22	18,78	15,01
Juli . . .	18,28	29,28	18,44	17,64	26,26	18,13	17,55	25,35	18,58	17,46	23,55	18,56
August . .	15,27	26,59	16,59	15,09	23,60	16,64	15,29	22,40	16,47	15,14	21,84	16,92
September .	11,35	20,56	13,93	11,08	18,92	13,77	11,32	18,48	13,28	11,32	18,39	10,91
October . .	3,76	10,69	5,39	3,74	9,41	5,34	3,97	8,93	5,38	4,00	8,68	5,69
November .	0,10	3,51	0,84	0,17	2,54	1,00	0,30	2,10	1,00	0,31	1,98	1,02
December .	— 4,00	— 0,57	— 2,92	— 3,99	— 1,53	— 3,02	— 3,79	— 1,98	— 2,90	— 3,90	— 2,21	— 2,93
Jahresmittel	6,78	14,44	7,61	6,50	12,29	7,49	6,61	11,50	7,62	6,55	10,92	7,47

Monatsmittel 1881.

Erdthermometer

	1 Zoll tief			1 Fuss tief			2 Fuss tief			4 Fuss tief			8 Fuss tief	16 Fuss tief
	7	2	8	7	2	8	7	2	8	7	2	8	7	7
Januar . .	— 3,45	— 2,57	— 3,04	— 0,18	— 0,14	— 0,15	1,01	0,99	0,90	2,93	2,91	2,92	5,62	8,40
Februar . .	— 2,57	— 0,79	— 1,82	— 0,76	— 0,79	— 0,67	— 0,01	— 0,04	— 0,08	1,61	1,59	1,59	4,34	7,56
März . . .	2,17	0,56	— 0,65	— 0,69	— 0,67	— 0,49	— 0,17	— 0,24	— 0,21	1,12	1,11	1,11	3,66	6,86
April . . .	1,92	8,12	3,99	2,72	3,21	3,50	2,45	2,48	2,57	2,11	2,14	2,17	3,50	6,27
Mai . . .	9,65	16,41	12,44	10,34	11,01	11,15	9,63	9,63	9,64	7,04	7,12	7,18	5,28	6,07
Juni . . .	13,59	18,68	15,57	14,38	14,73	15,12	13,95	13,92	13,99	11,60	11,68	11,65	8,55	6,64
Juli . . .	15,65	20,04	17,87	16,61	16,96	17,31	16,28	16,27	16,35	14,20	14,17	14,18	10,85	7,74
August . .	13,63	18,18	15,81	15,88	16,02	16,22	15,74	15,74	15,80	14,75	14,75	14,71	12,30	8,84
September .	11,44	12,49	13,17	13,66	13,82	13,87	13,96	14,15	14,19	13,76	13,78	13,71	12,43	9,61
October . .	4,35	7,98	5,83	7,24	7,41	7,52	8,28	8,22	8,20	9,91	9,90	9,88	11,02	9,90
November .	2,99	4,63	4,12	4,13	4,23	4,32	4,76	4,77	4,81	6,50	6,48	6,47	8,79	9,74
December .	0,28	0,62	0,36	1,64	1,63	1,67	2,57	2,55	2,52	4,74	4,70	4,67	7,10	9,10
Jahresmittel	5,44	8,70	6,99	7,08	9,29	7,85	7,37	7,38	7,39	7,52	7,52	7,52	8,21	8,07

Monatsmittel 1882.

	7	2	8	7	2	8	7	2	8	7	2	8	7	7
Januar . .	1,66	2,56	1,93	2,44	2,47	2,48	2,79	2,79	2,81	3,84	3,85	3,85	5,87	8,33
Februar . .	0,95	2,77	1,58	1,78	1,93	1,99	2,18	2,28	2,23	3,30	3,30	3,30	5,25	
März . . .	3,33	7,42	5,02	4,49	4,79	5,00	4,57	4,57	4,64	4,46	4,48	4,49	5,15	7,13
April . . .	5,54	11,82	7,53	7,01	7,53	7,92	6,91	6,91	7,07	5,96	6,00	6,02	5,84	
Mai . . .	10,48	15,25	12,53	11,67	12,03	12,49	11,22	11,25	11,45	9,37	9,40	9,39	7,50	7,01
Juni . . .	14,21	18,69	16,22	15,24	15,55	15,94	14,97	14,85	14,93	12,72	12,76	12,78	9,83	7,62
Juli . . .	17,45	23,28	19,69	18,42	18,91	19,27	17,92	17,88	18,00	15,38	15,43	15,44	11,87	8,56
August . .	15,97	21,06	17,38	17,57	16,34	19,07	17,79	17,70	17,69	16,35	16,36	16,35	13,50	9,61
September .	12,54	17,49	14,85	15,03	15,08	15,17	15,23	15,15	15,15	15,02	14,99	14,97	13,59	10,44
October . .	5,67	8,93	6,92	8,22	8,31	8,43	9,21	9,14	9,15	11,05	11,01	10,97	12,25	10,84
November .	2,25	3,06	2,32	4,11	4,09	4,06	5,19	5,14	5,11	7,49	7,45	7,42	9,88	10,58
December .	— 2,02	— 1,01	— 1,62	0,01	0,07	0,13	1,23	1,21	1,20	3,87	3,85	3,83	7,85	9,81
Jahresmittel	7,34	10,95	8,61	8,84	8,93	9,33	9,09	9,07	9,12	9,06	9,07	9,07	8,99	8,71

Einige fossile Hölzer Preussens

nebst kritischen Bemerkungen über die Anatomie des Holzes und die Bezeichnung fossiler Hölzer.

Von

Robert Caspary.

In der Sitzung der physikalisch-ökonomischen Gesellschaft vom 3. Februar 1887 beschrieb ich 10 neue fossile Hölzer Ost- und Wespreussens unter Vorlegung von vortrefflichen Abbildungen, die Dr. Triebel mir angefertigt hatte; die Beschreibungen wurden in der Hartung'schen Zeitung 2. Beilage zu No. 43, 20. Februar 1887 veröffentlicht. Ich schliesse jetzt noch 6 andere neue Hölzer mit den gegenwärtigen Zeilen an; den kurzen Beschreibungen sollen später ausführliche zugleich mit den Abbildungen folgen. Die übrigen fossilen Hölzer, besonders die hier nicht erwähnten Coniferen unseres Landes, werden dann hinzugefügt werden.

Die im Folgenden angewandten Bezeichnungen der einzelnen Gewebstheile des Stammes seien im Anschluss an frühere Arbeiten übersichtlich zusammengestellt und kritische Bemerkungen über die Bezeichnung fossiler Hölzer hinzugefügt.

Das Grundgewebe des Stammes behält bei den wenigsten Pflanzen lebenslang den einheitlichen Charakter und die Gleichartigkeit der Beschaffenheit, die es in der Stammspitze im ersten Jugendzustande hatte. Es sondert sich meist in Rindengewebe, Markstrahlen und Mark. Bei den meisten Nymphaeaceen (Nuphar, Nymphaea, Victoria, Euryale) sind diese 3 bei andern Pflanzen sonst meist sehr verschiedenen Gewebstheile ihr ganzes Leben lang gleichmässig oder fast so gleichmässig wie sie es bei der Anlage in der Stammspitze waren.

Die Markstrahlenzellen füllen die Zwischenräume zwischen den Leitbündeln aus und haben den grössten Durchmesser meist in wagrechter Richtung. Die Markstrahlen zeigen im tangentialen Durchmesser eine bis viele Zellen in der Breite und sind somit ein- bis vielreihig; noch mehr Zellen haben sie in der Richtung von oben nach unten. Die obersten und untersten Zellen, die ich bei einer Zelle Breite **Kantenzellen** nenne, sind meist nur ein, oft aber 2, 3, ja bis 5 Stockwerke und mehr hoch und die einzelnen höher als die mittleren Zellen des Markstrahls, aber kürzer.

Bei Markstralen von beträchtlicher Dicke kommt es bisweilen vor, dass an den Seiten derselben zwischen den obern und untern Kantenzellen in geschlossener Reihe eine Lage parenchymatischer Zellen sich befindet, die kürzer als die mittleren

Markstrahlenzellen, aber höher und dünner als sie sind. Bisweilen kommen solche Zellen an den Seiten der Markstrahlen nur vereinzelt vor. Um nicht da, wo ich sie zu erwähnen habe, längere Umschreibungen brauchen zu müssen, bezeichne ich diese eigenthümlichen Zellen als **Hüllzellen.** Sie finden sich z. B. bei Platanus und einigen Proteaceen.

Die Markstrahlen scheiden von einander die in senkrechtem Verlauf ein Netzwerk bildenden **Leitbündel** des Stammes, dessen Maschen sie ausfüllen. Da die Leitbündel, welche vorzugsweise aus **langen** spitzig oder stumpf endigenden Zellen bestehen, bei gewissen Monokotylen, fast bei allen Gymnospermen und höheren Sporophyten, sowie bei einem kleinen Theil der Dikotylen keine Gefässe enthalten, oder, wie bei manchen Monokotylen, das Rhizom keine Gefässe in den Bündeln seiner langen Zellen hat, während Stamm und Wurzel Gefässe besitzen, ist eine Bezeichnung nothwendig, welche auf alle mit Gefässen versehene und gefässlose Bündel passt. Ich habe daher seit 1862 (Monatsber. Berlin. Akad. 448 ff.) als solchen beide Modifikationen der Bündel langer Zellen umfassenden Ausdruck das Wort **Leitbündel** gebraucht. Wenn **de Bary** bei dem Wort **Gefässbündel,** auch für **den Fall, dass die Gefässe dem Bündel fehlen,** beharrt und die Unterscheidung beider Arten von Bündel als „wenig wesentlich" (Vergleichende Anatomie 334) erklärt und angiebt, das es „**im Interesse der Einfachheit des Ausdrucks eine erlaubte Ungenauigkeit sei von Gefässbündeln ohne Gefässe zu reden**" (a. O. 418) wird sich Niemand, der scharf logisch denkt, damit einverstanden erklären können, denn man hat **die Verpflichtung sich stets genau auszudrücken** und es ist ferner sachlich für die Fortleitung von Luft oder Flüssigkeit von Bedeutung, ob diese Fortleitung in Gefässen, d. h. längeren Röhren geschieht, die aus der Länge nach über einander gestellten, mittelst Löchern verbundenen Zellen gebildet sind, oder in geschlossenen Zellen, die ohne solche Verbindung und viel kürzer als jene Röhren sind. Dafür liefert ein einfacher Versuch den Beweis. Durch eine Wurzel, die mit Gefässen versehen ist, z. B. Lindenwurzel von etwa 1½ Fuss Länge und ½ Zoll Dicke, die man in Wasser mit dem einen Ende taucht und in die man mit dem Munde vom andern Ende her Luft einbläst, kann man mit Leichtigkeit Luft hindurchblasen, so dass sie am eingetauchten Ende in Gestalt von Blasen austritt. Durch Wurzeln, die keine Gefässe haben, z. B. die der Abietineen, oder Stammtheile, die keine langen und zusammenhängenden Gefässe haben, z. B. Stücke von Weiden-, Erlen-, Lindenästen, selbst wenn sie keinen Knoten enthalten, kann man dagegen Luft nicht durchblasen. Nur bei wenigen Pflanzen z. B. bei der Rosskastanie lässt sich durch ein Internodium ohne Knoten Luft hindurchblasen.

Das Wort „**Fibrovasalbündel**", welches auch von Einigen als allgemeine Bezeichnung für Leitbündel gebraucht wird, ist zu beanstanden, weil „vas": Gefäss, ein Bestandtheil desselben ist und in den Leitbündeln oft Gefässe nicht da sind, ferner weil es ein Bastardwort ist. Mehr und mehr wird glücklicher Weise die Verpflichtung erkannt in der Wissenschaft eine grammatisch tadellose Ausdrucksweise zu gebrauchen und die überflüssige und entbehrliche Menge von Fremdworten auszumerzen, die durch Gelehrthuerei, Eitelkeit und schlechte Gewohnheit unsere Sprache vor andern verunreinigt hat.

Bei der grossen Mannigfaltigkeit des Baus der Leitbündel in den einzelnen Abtheilungen des Gewächsreichs lassen sich die Gewebstheile, welche die Leitbündel zusammensetzen, in Kürze nur in allgemeinen Zügen angeben und ich muss für Näheres auf die betreffende, eingehendere Literatur verweisen. Im Leitbündel ist ein äusserer Theil, der bei den sich verdickenden Dikotylen nach aussen vom Kambium liegt, der **Rindentheil** des Leitbündels (Phloëm Naegeli) und ein anderer innerer Theil: der **Holztheil** (Xylem Naegeli) zu unterscheiden. Die äusserste Stellung im Rindentheil nimmt der Bast ein; nach innen zu vom Bast liegt der **Weichtheil** des Rindentheils (Weichbast de Bary*). Der Weichtheil des Leitbündels enthält zum Theil oder in allen Zellen zähflüssiges Proteïn und besteht theils aus **Siebzellen**, oder, wenn diese fehlen, aus langen dünnwandigen Zellen, die durch Kochen in Schultze'scher Flüssigkeit nicht oder nur theilweise gesondert werden können, und keine Poren zeigen. Ich habe diese langen Proteïn haltenden Zellen vor 29 Jahren zuerst „**Leitzellen**" genannt (**Pringsheims** Jahrbücher I. 1858 382) später (**Pringsheims** Jahrb. IV. 1864 103) „**einfache Leitzellen**" im Unterschiede von den **gefässartigen Leitzellen** des Holztheils (Monatsbericht Berlin. Akad. 1862 454). Die **einfachen Leitzellen**, welche übrigens bisweilen eine gallertartig aufgequollene wagrechte Querwand besitzen, sind an Dicke oft verschieden und ich unterscheide daher **dünne und dicke einfache Leitzellen** z. B. bei den Nymphaeaceen. Um die Siebzellen zeigen manche Pflanzen als Nachbarn ein meist kurzes parenchymatisches Gewebe: **Geleitzellen** (Russow), wohin auch, wenn die Siebzellen in tangentialen Reihen stehen die zwischen je 2 solchen Reihen vorhandenen parenchymatischen Zellen zu rechnen sind, z. B. bei der Birne.

Der **Holztheil** des Leitbündels wird aus Zellen zusammengesetzt, die physiologisch theils der Luftleitung, theils der Aufspeicherung von Vorrathsstoffen (Stärke, Gerbstoff und anderen), theils der Leitung der unverarbeiteten Flüssigkeiten und wenn sie älter geworden sind, als Steifungszellen mechanischen Zwecken dienen. Die parenchymatischen Zellen des Holztheils, welche senkrechte Stränge bilden, die aus einer langen prosenchymatischen Zelle gleich nach der Anlage im Kambium durch wagrechte oder annähernd wagrechte Wände entstanden sind, habe ich schon 1864 (Pringsh. Jahrb. IV. 122) als **Holzstumpfzellen** (Zellfasern Theod. Hartig, Holzparenchym, Schacht u. And.) bezeichnet. Sie sind nebst den Markstrahlen die Bestandtheile des Holzkörpers, in denen Vorrathsstoffe aufgespeichert werden. Bei den Koniferen enthalten sie, wenn sie vorhanden sind, später statt Stärke Harz; ich bezeichne sie mit Kraus als **Harzzellen** (einfache Harzgänge Göpp., Unger). Von ihnen sind die **Harzgänge** (vasa Malpighi, Harzgänge Theod. Hartig, zusammengesetzte Harzgänge oder Harzbehälter oder blos Harzgänge Göpp.) zu unterscheiden. Sie sind mit parenchymatischen, meist zartwandigen Zellen umgeben, die ich als **Grenzzellen** bezeichne. Die Holzstumpfzellen der Dikotylen sind viereckig, oder fünfeckig oder rundlicheckig im Querschnitt, lang-rechteckig auf den Längsschnitten, selten etwas abgeplattet; liegen sie aber den Gefässen an, so sind sie stets abgeplattet und öfters unregelmässig viereckig im Längsschnitt. Um nicht stets weitläufig diese den Gefässen anliegenden Holzstumpfzellen umschreiben zu müssen, nenne ich sie **Deckzellen**. Ob sie ausser ihrer Gestalt und der bedeutenderen Grösse ihrer Poren auch einen Unterschied in der Funktion von den den Gefässen fern liegenden Holzstumpfzellen haben, müssen weitere Untersuchungen lehren. **Sanio** nannte die Deckzellen paratra-

*) Ich möchte diesen Theil so nicht nennen, weil er keinen Bast enthält.

cheales Holzparenchym, das den Gefässen ferner liegende: metatracheales Holzparenchym (Bot. Zeitung 1863 389).

Auch der zweite Bestandtheil des Holzes: **die Gefässe**, der Länge nach über einandergestellte Längsreihen bildende Zellen mit durchbrochenen Querwänden, oder, wenn sie fehlen, ihr Ersatz: die **gefässartigen Leitzellen** sind bei Anwesenheit von seitlichem Kambium aus Prosemchym entstanden und dienen vorzugsweise der Luftleitung. Bei beiden kommen gleichartige Verdickungen der Längswände vor und sie bilden somit 2 einander entsprechende Reihen: 1) Ringgefässe, Schraubengefässe, Leitergefässe, Netzgefässe, Porengefässe; und 2) Ringleitzellen, Schraubenleitzellen, Leiterleitzellen Netzleitzellen, Porenleitzellen.*) Dass eine Entstehung der Gefässe oder Leitzellenbündel aus **Parenchym**, nicht wie bei den sich verdickenden Dikotylen aus Prosemchym, vorkommt, ist bei mehreren Monokotylen und auch einigen Dikotylen sicher. Bei den **Hydrilleen** (Elodea, Hydrilla) bei Aldrovandia, sind die kurzen, mit sehr wenig schief gestellten Endflächen abschliessenden Glieder des einzigen Leitzellenstranges des Stammes mit wagrechten Enden versehen. Noch deutlicher und in überraschender Klarheit ist bei den Cyperaceen, deren überirdische Axe zwischen

---

*) Sachs (Lehrbuch der Botanik 1868 97; und zweite Auflage 1870 97) erklärt meine „Annahme des Mangels der Gefässe bei den Kryptogamen und vielen Phanerogamen für unrichtig.“ Die Behauptung, dass ich bei „den Kryptogamen“ Abwesenheit von Gefässen angegeben hätte, ist jedoch selbst unrichtig. Nachdem ich (Monatsschrift Berlin. Akad. 449) die Angabe von Mettenius, dass „die Farrne, Lykopodiaceen, Selaginellen, Rhizokarpeen, Equisetaceen“ keine Gefässe entfallten, angeführt hatte, fügte ich hinzu: „eine Angabe die ich für mehrere Farrne bestätige“ und habe dann 3 Farrne nnd Isoëtes lacustris als Belag eingehender aufgeführt, also Gefässlosigkeit nicht allgemein „den Kryptogamen“ zugesprochen. Abgesehen von dieser Ungenauigkeit ist die Beweisführung von Sachs gegen die von mir angeführten Thatsachen, nicht „Annahmen“, wie er sich ausdrückt, ganz unzutreffend. Er beruft sich auf die Entdeckung Dippels, dass Pteris aquilina Gefässe habe. Diese Entdeckung Dippels habe ich sofort nach ihrer Veröffentlichung bestätigen können, obgleich neben den Gefässen auch Ring- und Schraubenleitzellen, die völlig geschlossen sind, vorkommen, die weder Sachs noch Dippel gesehen haben. Aber, was beweist die Thatsache, dass Pteris aquilina Gefässe hat, gegen den, von mir bei andern Pflanzen erbrachten Beweis, dass sie keine Gefässe haben? Ich hatte ja gar nicht behauptet, dass Pteris aquilina keine Gefässe habe, überhaupt in der Abhandlung im Monatsbericht der Berliner Akademie 1862, auf den sich Sachs bezieht, ebenso wenig, wie Mettenius, früher Pteris aquilina erwähnt, auch nicht einmal untersucht. Ferner beruft sich Sachs für seine Behauptung, „dass alle luftführenden trachealen Formen offene gehöfte Tüpfel haben“ und dass dies in „besonders ausgezeichneter Weise bei den Tracheiden im Holz der Koniferen der Fall“ sei, auf in Schultze'scher Flüssigkeit macerirtes Material (vgl. Sachs a. O. 28). Ich habe aber (a. O. 459) nachgewiesen, dass Maceration zur Beantwortung der Frage, ob eine vorliegende Zellwand offene oder geschlossene Poren habe, meist nicht ausreiche und ausdrücklich verlangt, dass Entscheidung durch Längsschnitte, auf welchen die betreffende Wand frei gelegt ist und die getrocknet sind, zu suchen sei. Diese Untersuchungsweise hat Sachs aber garnicht angewandt, sondern bloss die Maceration, durch welche er die zarten Wandtheile zerstört hat. Seine Behauptung in Betreff der offenen Poren der Holzzellen der Koniferen ist jetzt längst als unrichtig erkannt. Sachs hat keine einzige der zahlreichen Pflanzen oder Pflanzentheile, die ich als gefässlos nachwies, untersucht, noch weniger mir einen Irrthum nachgewiesen, dennoch aber behauptet er, meine Angaben seien unrichtig. Sein Urtheil ist also unbegründet und unwissenschaftlich. Wer sonst meine Angaben geprüft hat, wie Hegelmaier für die Lemnaceen, de Bary für einige Fälle, und Andere, haben sie richtig gefunden. Terletzki (Pringsh. Jahrb. 1864 452 ff.) wies Gefässlosigkeit bei Struthiopteris germ. nach. Unter den Farrnen sind bisher bloss bei Pteris aquil. und in der Wurzel von Athyrium Filix femina (nach **Russow**. Vergleichende Untersuchung. 103) Gefässe bekannt.

ihrem Grunde und der Spitze des Rhizoms ein sehr bedeutendes Zwischenwachsthum hat, die Entstehung der eingeschobenen jüngeren Gefässglieder aus Parenchym mit vollständig wagrechten Querwänden wahrnehmbar. Die neu entstandenen Gefässglieder sind da, wo die Vermehrung am lebhaftesten vor sich geht, viel breiter, als hoch, besonders deutlich ersichtlich bei Cyperus Papyrus, wo die überirdische Axe schon 5—6 Fuss lang sein kann und ganz ausgebildete Gefässbündel oben hat, während an deren Grunde über dem Rhizom fortgesetzt durch nur wagrechte Theilungswände, zahlreiche neue Gefässglieder in die alten Stränge eingeschoben werden. Dasselbe, wenn auch nicht in so ausgeprägter Weise bei Cyperus elegans, Cyp. alternifolius, Cyp. textilis.

Bei den Gewebstheilen des Holzes, die als **Gefässbündel** oder als deren Stellvertreter: **gefässartige Leitbündel** zu bezeichnen sind, ist der wesentliche Charakter der, dass ihre Glieder oder Zellen in senkrechten Reihen über einander stehen. Diese Anordnung der übereinander stehenden Glieder in senkrechten Reihen mit deutlichster von den Seitenwänden unterschiedener Querwand, auch oft sehr schiefen Anlageflächen an einander, ist bei den Gefässen besonders ausgebildet, fehlt aber auch bei ihren Vertretern: den gefässartigen, an den Enden nicht durchbrochenen Leitzellen nicht. Diese strangartige Anordnung der Gefässe und gefässartigen Leitzellen übereinander, unterscheidet sie wesentlich von dem 3. Bestandtheile des Holzes: den **Holzspitzzellen** (Holzfasern Th. Hartig; cellulae porosae sive vasa porosa Goeppert bei Koniferen; Holzzellen Goepp., Kraus; Holzprosemchym Schacht; Tracheiden Sanio zum Theil; Libriform Sanio; gefächerte Holzzellen (Fächerprosenchym) Sanio; „Holzprosenchym - Ersatzfasern, oder kurzweg Ersatzfasern (respektive Ersatzzellen)", Sanio), welche Bezeichnung ich schon 1864 (Pringsh. Jahrbüch. IV 122) einführte.

Es giebt keinen anatomischen Bestandtheil der Pflanze, der überall von völlig gleichmässiger Bildung und so scharf von den andern abgegrenzt ist, dass es nicht zwischen ihm und den andern mannichfaltige Zwischenbildungen gäbe. Das, was allgemein **Gefässe** genannt wird, zeigt in sich selbst verschiedene Gestaltung, (Ring-, Schrauben-, Leiter- u. s. w. Gefässe, mannigfachste Verschiedenheit in den Poren der Seitenwände, der Durchbrechung der Endflächen, der Wanddicke u. s. w.); nach diesen mannichfaltigen Eigenschaften Trennungen vorzunehmen und die einzelnen Gestaltungen mit besonderen Namen zu belegen, als für sich bestehende anatomische Gewebstheile, wäre unzulässig, und ist bei der hervorragenden Eigenschaft der Durchbohrung der Querwand, die alle diese Gestalten in eine zusammenfasst, bisher glücklicher Weise nicht unternommen. Man bezeichnet durch hinzugefügte Adjektiven oder sonstige Beisätze die nähere Beschaffenheit der einzelnen Gefässgestalten. Die Gefässe nähern sich durch die **gefässartigen**, aber **geschlossenen Leitzellen** den **Holzspitzzellen**, die anfangs der Leitung wässriger Flüssigkeit, später als mechanisches Element der Steifung des Pflanzenleibes dienen. Aber die Holzspitzzellen sind nie in strangartige Längsreihen wie die gefässartigen Leitzellen geordnet. Jedoch treten Uebergangsbildungen zwischen beiden ein. Bei den Eichen hat **Abromeit** (Pringsh. Jahrbücher 1884 XV 273 ff.), solche Zellen, die nie in Strängen, sondern vereinzelt zwischen den Holzspitzzellen stehen, aber deren Wände dem Bau nach an die Gefässe erinnern, als „**Uebergangszellen**" mit Recht bezeichnet.

Die **Holzstumpfzellen** auf der andern Seite, die durch Bau und Inhalt besonders deutlich von den Holzspitzzellen unterschieden erscheinen, haben doch auch zu ihnen ihre Uebergänge. Es sind dies die „Ersatzzellen" Sanio's, die ich wegen Mangels an Theilung und wegen der spitzigen Enden den Holzspitzzellen und nicht den Holzstumpfzellen, abweichend von Sanio und Müller (Denkschr. Wiener Akad. Mathem. naturw. Klasse. 36. Bd. 304) zuzuzählen vorziehe und die „gefächerten Holzzellen" Sanio's. Der theilweise in diesen Bildungen auftretende Stärkegehalt zeigt eine Annäherung an die Holzstumpfzellen.

Was die **Tracheiden** Sanio's betrifft, umfassen diese 2 ganz verschiedenartige Bestandtheile, wie ich schon 1864 (Pringsh. Jahrb. IV 122) nachwies, nämlich: 1) die in den primären Leitbündeln der Markscheide entstandenen, geschlossenen, ring- oder schraubenförmig verdickten, **in Strängen geordneten gefässartigen Leitzellen,** die bei den Koniferen die Gefässe vertreten, und im sekundären Holz nicht wieder erscheinen, nebst den in **geschlossenen** Leitbündeln der **Monokotylen** oder **Dikotylen** vorhandenen, zum Theil höchst ausgezeichneten, schraubig- oder ringförmig verdickten, gefässartigen sehr langen Leitzellen, wie bei Nelumbo — wo die gefässartigen Leitzellen bis 5 Zoll und darüber lang sind —; 2) die stark in der Wand verdickten, sehr starren, verhältnissmässig kurzen, nach beiden Enden ohne ausgezeichnete Querwand, allmälig zugespitzten, seitlich kaum gehöft spaltenporigen bis ziemlich gross gehöft porigen Holzspitzzellen, die nicht in Strängen geordnet sind.

Der grösste Theil der Holzspitzzellen besteht aus dem „Libriform" Sanio's. Die **Holzspitzzellen** in dem von mir angegebenen Umfange, (Libriform, gefächerte Holzzellen, Ersatzzellen Sanio's, zum grössten Theil die Tracheiden Sanios) sind in Bezug auf Wanddicke, chemische Beschaffenheit der Schichten der Wandungen, Lage und Gestalt der Poren, die von der einfachen Pore mit spaltenförmigem Porengange bis zur grossen gehöften Pore, die der der Gefässe fast gleich ist, in mannichfacher Weise abändern, selbst in derselben Holzart, selbst in derselben Axe, sind in jedem Falle für das einzelne Holz durch Beschreibung aller Eigenschaften, mittelst Hinzufügung von Adjektiven oder sonstigen Beisätzen genau und erschöpfend zu charakterisiren. Die allgemeine einheitliche Eigenschaft der Holzspitzzellen ist ihre prosenchymatische Gestalt und der Mangel an Vereinigung zu Bündeln. Mit den Schlagworten von Sanio: Ersatzzellen, Libriform, Tracheiden ist schwer umzugehen und die Einreihung gegebener Zellen unter diese Schemata öfters zweifelhaft oder wegen Unklarheit unausführbar, und bei den fossilen Hölzern völlig unmöglich, da man diese weder maceriren kann, noch die ursprüngliche chemische Beschaffenheit selbst bei den am besten erhaltenen Hölzern prüfen. Die Nothwendigkeit einer einfacheren, aber doch der Entstehung und physiologischen Funktion entsprechenderen Eintheilung der Holzbestandtheile drängt sich daher auf.

Auch Andere haben sich in übler Lage bei Anwendung der Sanio'schen Holzbestandtheile auf die Wirklichkeit bei anatomischen Untersuchungen befunden. **Möller** (a. a. O. 301) klagt: „Ich bin an meine Untersuchungen mit dem Vorhaben gegangen, die Terminologie **Sanio's** anzuwenden. Aber immer mehr häuften sich die Fälle, wo ich bei der Vergleichung meiner Beschreibung mit den Angaben von **Sanio** da Tracheiden angegeben fand, wo nach meiner Anschauung Libriform vorhanden war. Dadurch wurde ich zu wiederholter Untersuchung veranlasst und endlich drängte sich mir die Ueberzeugung auf, dass man unter Tracheiden, soll der Ausdruck überhaupt erhalten bleiben, nichts anderes verstehen dürfe, als nicht perforirte Gefässe." Andere Einwände, die **Möller** macht, übergehe ich. Es ist **Möller** also zu demselben Ergebniss gekommen, welches ich schon 1864 veröffentlichte, **dass die Tracheiden Sanio's ein Gemisch von gefässartigen Leitzellen und Holzspitzzellen** (Libriform Sanio) **seien.** Nur zieht Möller nicht die richtige Folgerung aus diesem Ergebniss, denn er fährt auffallender Weise fort von Tracheiden auch da zu reden, wo bloss Libriform ist, wie von den Holzspitzzellen der Koniferen. Hätte **Möller** die Markscheide, die er von seinen Untersuchungen ausschloss, mit in diese gezogen, so würde er die Holzspitzzellen der Koniferen wohl nicht als Tracheiden bezeichnet haben.

Ich muss mich aber nicht bloss sachlich gegen den Ausdruck „Tracheiden" erklären, sondern auch wegen der Bedeutung des zu Grunde liegenden Stammwortes „Trachea", womit bei den höheren Thieren die Luftröhre, bei den Insekten, Spinnen u. s. w. die vielverzweigten Athmungswerkzeuge bezeichnet werden. Ich stimme ganz mit **Schleiden** überein, welcher (Grundzüge wissensch. Bot. 2. Ausgabe 1845 II 241) vorschlug, „die Botaniker möchten übereinkommen, alle die Ausdrücke, die in der Zoologie bestimmte Bedeutung haben, aus der Botanik ganz zu verbannen, um der beständigen Verwirrung, die so leicht durch die aus jener Wissenschaft dunkel mit herübergebrachten Begriffe entsteht, für die Zukunft vorzubeugen." Desswegen verwarf **Endlicher** und nach ihm auch **Schleiden** das Wort „ovulum" und **Endlicher** führte dafür gemmula ein, was Schleiden ganz passend mit Saamenknospe übersetzt. Leider wird heut zu Tage wieder vielfach ovulum gebraucht. Dass der Ausdruck Trachea der Alten für schraubig verdickte Gefässe der Pflanzen dazu Anlass gab, in ganz unpassender Weise sie mit den Athmungswerkzeugen der Thiere zu identifiziren, dafür giebt **Boretius** (De anatome plantarum et animalium analoga. Regiomonti 1727 5.) ein schlagendes Beispiel. Er sagt: „Circa hos utriculos (d. h. Gefässglieder) posuit natura spirales fibras amplectentes hos utriculos; hae aëre plenae sunt, qui pro vario calore, frigore nocturno, vi sua elastica varia, ventorumque motu mox se expandit, mox contrahit, qua actione diversa, succus in fistulis (d. h. Zellen) contentus, non modo easdem qualitates induit, quas sanguis in pulmone, scilicet: attenuationem, solutionem, subactionem, intimam mixtionem cum salibus et oleo, imo fluiditatem maximam, sed etiam utriculis pressus, ipse sursum elevatur, ita quidem, ut **tracheae aëreae** (Gefässe) **plantis sint instar cordis et pulmonis, aër vero a sole plus minus calefactus, spiritum motorum vices suppleat.**"

Am wenigsten aber kann **de Bary** (Vergl. Anatomie 1877 161 ff) zugestimmt werden, der nicht bloss das seit vielen Jahrzehnten für Gefässe nicht mehr gebrauchte Wort „Trachea" wieder aufgenommen hat, sondern darunter ausser „Gefässen und Tracheiden" (Sanio) auch noch alle Zellen zieht, deren Wände „mit Faserung oder mit Hoftüpfeln oder selten mit Querbalken verdickt werden und in verschiedenem Grade verholzen" und statt des Protoplasma später Luft oder klare wässrige Flüssigkeit führen. Es sind hier der an sich schon wenig gleichartigen Wandbeschaffenheit dieser „Tracheen" (de Bary) zu Liebe, Zellen in eine Gruppe zusammengefasst, die offenbar die verschiedensten Funktionen haben: Gefässe und gefässartige Leitzellen, mit Querbalken versehene Rindenzellen (Juniperus), Blattzellen von Sphagnum und Leucobryaceen, schraubenfasrig verdickte Rindenzellen tropischer, epiphytischer Orchideen. Ich bin der Meinung, dass für die Bildung anatomischer Gruppen ausser dem mehr oder weniger gleichartigen Bau die gleichartige physiologische Funktion entscheiden muss, nicht einseitig eine ähnliche anatomische Beschaffenheit.

Ein Wort noch über **„Poren."** Die meisten Botaniker gebrauchen jetzt das Wort **„Tüpfel"** für alle Arten von Poren, aber daneben auch das Wort **„Pore."** **Schleiden** nannte dünne Stellen der Haut Poren, wenn die primäre Wand noch da war und Löcher, wenn sie fehlte; er verwarf den Ausdruck Tüpfel ganz. **Mohl** (Vegetab. Zelle 30) nannte eine dünne Stelle Tüpfel, wenn die primäre Haut da war, Pore, wenn sie verzehrt war. **Schacht** (Pflanzenzelle 20) nannte Tüpfel „diejenigen Poren, zwischen deren Kanälen ein Tüpfelraum befindlich ist", während „Poren verdünnte Stellen oder wohl gar Löcher" seien (Schacht a. O. 19). Fand man also in irgend einer Schrift zu jener Zeit die Worte Pore oder Tüpfel, so bedurfte es erst einer Erläuterung, was darunter zu verstehen sei. Bei diesen verschiedenen Deutungen der Worte Pore und Tüpfel, erklärte ich 1862 (Monatsber. Berlin Academ. 455), dass ich das Wort Tüpfel gar nicht, sondern nur den Ausdruck Pore gebrauchen würde und unterschied geschlossene und offene, welchen letzteren die primäre Haut fehlte, ferner gehöfte und ungehöfte (einfache) Poren. Ich finde gar keine Veranlassung heute von dieser vor 25 Jahren gegebenen Erklärung, die vollständig klar ist, abzugehen, zumal wir in Norddeutschland mit dem Wort Tüpfel eine Erhabenheit und nicht eine Vertiefung bezeichnen.

Es kommt überall auf genauen, eine ganz bestimmte Vorstellung vermittelnden Ausdruck an. Es ist in vieler Beziehung eine grössere Einheitlichkeit und Schärfe der botanischen Ausdrucksweise wünschenswerth; z. B. wird Missbrauch mit dem Wort **„Faser"** getrieben, welches angewandt wird: 1) für lange **porsenchymatische Zellen:** „Faserzellen", „Holzfasern", „Spiral- und Ringfasern" (in der Markscheide); „Rundfaser", „Breitfaser" für Frühjahrs- und Herbstholzzellen. Und dann wird das Wort „Faserzelle" wieder umgestellt und „Zellfasern" sollen einen Strang von paremchymatischen Zellen bezeichnen. 2) für die fadenartigen Verdickungen der Zellhaut: hier giebt es wieder in anderem Sinn als vorhin: „Spiral- und Ringfasern". 3) für Zellstoff im Allgemeinen: „Pflanzenfaser". 4) sogar für den Stoff thierischer Gewebe: „Unterschied der Pflanzen und Thierfaser". 5) für vermeintliche Fasern, die die Zellhaut zusammensetzen sollten, auch „Primitivfasern" genannt. Es ist wünschenswerth, dass dem Wort **Faser** nur eine Bedeutung die von langen fadenartigen Gebilden, die keine Zellen sind, zurückgegeben werde. Bei dem jetzigen vieldeutigen Gebrauch des Wortes Faser giebt es als solches öfters keine Klarheit, sondern seine Bedeutung muss erst aus dem Zusammenhange errathen werden. Aehnliche Unklarheit bringt eine ziemliche Zahl anderer Ausdrücke, die für „Zelle" angewandt werden: Röhren, Schläuche, Schlauchgefässe sogar, wo bloss Zellen und keine Gefässe vorhanden sind, Bläschen, Keimbläschen, Keimkörper. Nicht zutreffend erscheint besonders der Ausdruck „Sekretschlauch", worunter gewöhnliche, kurze Zellen verstanden werden, die einen Inhalt: Oel, Schleim besitzen, der gar nicht ausgeschieden, d. h. nach aussen abgesondert wird, sondern in der Zelle bleibt. Man kann von „Sekret" nach sonst üblicher Weise doch nur da reden, wo von Zellen nach aussen, aus ihnen heraus Stoffe abgeschieden werden, wie Oel bei Dictamnus, Schleim bei Drosera, schmierige Stoffe bei Hyoscyamus, Lychnis viscaria. Muss der einheitliche Begriff der Zelle durch solch verwirrende Mannigfaltigkeit, soviel synonyme und oft nicht passende Ausdrücke nicht undeutlich gemacht, die Erkenntniss der Zusammengehörigkeit analoger Erscheinungen erschwert und der Anfänger oder weniger Vorgeschrittene, der sich mit pflanzlicher Anatomie beschäftigen will, von ihr abgeschreckt werden?

Der Durchmesser aller Zellen und Gefässe, parallel zur Tangente des Sprosses nenne ich im Folgenden **Breite**; **Dicke** den Durchmesser parallel zum Radius des Sprosses bei Holzspitz-, Holzstumpfzellen und Gefässen. Mit **Länge** bezeichne ich bei Holzstumpf-, Holzspitzzellen und Gefässgliedern den Durchmesser parallel zur Axe des Sprosses, bei den Markstrahlzellen den Durchmesser in wagrechter Richtung. Bei Markstrahlzellen bezeichne ich mit **Höhe** den Durchmesser in senkrechter Richtung, parallel zur Axe des Sprosses.

Seitliche Wände sind bei Holzspitz- und Holzstumpfzellen die, welche dem Radius parallel oder nahezu parallel sind, **hintere** und **vordere**, oder **mediane Wände** die, welche der Tangente parallel sind.

Markstrahlfeld nenne ich den Theil einer Markstrahlzelle, die der Dicke einer anliegenden Holzspitzzelle entspricht.

Mit **Holzstrahl** bezeichne ich die Gesammtheit der Holzstumpf- und Holzspitzzellen, mit Einbegriff der Gefässe, wenn sie da sind, die zwischen 2 Markstrahlen auf dem Querschnitt liegen. Dieser Begriff ist ein wichtiger, da die Zahl der Zellen in der Breite des Holzstrahls bei den einzelnen Arten und Gattungen innerhalb gewisser Grenzen liegt und die Lage der Gefässe erst in Bezug auf ihn charakterisirt werden kann; sie liegen im Holzstrahl in einer radialen Reihe und damit zu 1—2 in der Breite desselben, oder zerstreut und bis 6 und mehr in der Breite, oder **ein** Gefäss nimmt den Raum von 3—4 Holzstrahlen ein (grosse Gefässe bei Quercus), oder die Gefässe liegen in tangentialen Reihen oder Gruppen zu 3—10 und mehr in der Breite des Holzstrahls (Proteaceen), u. s. w.

Nachdem **Unger** (in **Endlicher** Gen. Suppl. 1842 II 101) fossile Hölzer in Form einer Gattung als Betulinium, Phegonium, Quercinium, Ulminium u. s. w. bezeichnet und später auch **Goeppert** (Monograph. 1850 196) für fossile Hölzer von Cupressineen die anscheinende Gattung: Cupressinoxylon aufgestellt hatte, ist es mehr und mehr Sitte geworden fossile Hölzer von den Gattungen, zu denen sie gehören und hätten gestellt werden sollen, abzusondern und als eigne Scheingattungen mit der Endung — inium oder — xylon zu bezeichnen. Frägt man nach dem Grunde dieses auffallenden Verfahrens, so wird geantwortet: es sei „gerechtfertigt, so lange es unmögmöglich ist fossile Stämme auf eine bestimmte Art zurückzuführen.“ (**Schenk** in: Palaeontograph. XXX 1883 in **Zittel**: Beiträge zur Geologie und Paläontologie der lybischen Wüste. II. Theil. Fossile Hölzer 6.). Dieser Grund ist jedoch in keiner Weise stichhaltig. Jeder jener Namen: Quercinium, Ulminium u. s. w. trägt den Beweis in sich, dass die Pflanze, der das betreffende Holz angehört, trotz dem, dass sie keiner, der schon aufgestellten meist sehr lückenhaft bekannten fossilen Arten zugezählt werden kann, doch **der** Gattung nach dem Urtheil des Namengebers zugezählt werden muss, welche die ersten Sylben des Namens anzeigen. Quercinium, Ulminium u. s. w. fallen selbst nach dem Urtheil der Namengeber den Gattungen Quercus, Ulmus u. s. w. zu. Warum wird nun also ein solches Holz nicht unter die

Gattung Quercus (oder Quercites), Ulmus (oder Ulmites) u. s. w. gestellt? Selbst gegen das Verfahren in Betreff anderer isolirter Organe oder Theile fossiler Pflanzen verstösst die Behandlungder fossilen Hölzer. Sind nicht in der Gattung Quercus z. B. Arten zusammengesetzt, von denen viele nur durch Blätter, während alle andern Organe unbekannt sind, andere nur durch Blüthen (die Mehrzahl der Eichen des Bernsteins), während alle andere Organe unbekannt sind, noch andere nur durch Früchte, während alle andern zugehörigen Theile unbekannt sind, vertreten? Aehnliches bei Myrica, eine Art auf Frucht allein, eine auf Blüthe allein (im Bernstein), die andern meist blos auf Blätter allein begründet. Ebenso in den Gattungen Acer, Ilex und anderen. In den Gattungen Nyssa, Celtis, Ulmus, Corylus, Carpinus und anderen, so weit sie fossil sind, sind die Arten zum Theil auf Blätter allein, zum Theil auf Früchte allein begründet. Wenn Blüthen und Früchte für die Feststellung einer Gattung und Art auch von hervorragendem Werth sind, so hat man sich doch bei einiger Wahrscheinlichkeit der Erkennbarkeit der Gattung aus vegetativen Theilen (Blättern) nie abhalten lassen, die Gattung und Art nach diesen zu bestimmen. Und hat etwa die Festellung einer Gattung und Art nach den Blättern mehr Sicherheit, als die nach dem Bau des Holzes? Gewiss nicht! Dass gewisse fossile Hölzer den Gattungen Quercus, Juglans, Laurus, Platanus und anderen, diese immer in recht weitem Umfange, wie Linné sie meist begrenzte, gefasst, zugehören, ist unumstösslich sicher, viel sicherer, als dass zahlreiche fossile Blätter, den Gattungen, zu denen sie gestellt sind, z. B. Ficus, Quercus, wirklich in diese Gattungen gehören. Für fossile Pflanzen empfiehlt es sich aus ersichtlichen Gründen den Umfang der Gattung recht weit anzunehmen, nicht in der Zersplitterung, die der Sucht des Mihi in neuerer Zeit besonders entsprossen ist, welche mit dem Zusammenfallen von Art und Gattung im Laufe der Zeit endlich enden muss.

Es sind also Hölzer und Blätter ungleichartig behandelt. Freilich fehlt es nicht an Beispielen, dass auch Blätter schon, wie Hölzer, einem Scheingattungsnamen zugezählt sind, der in — phyllum endet und in den ersten Silben den Namen einer jetztweltlichen Gattung trägt, zu der das betreffende Blatt nach Ansicht des Namengebers gehört: z. B. Apocynophyllum Heer, Callistemophyllum Heer und **Nathorst** will gar, dass die Namen für Blätter, die älter als pliocän sind, alle so gebildet werden (Centralblatt 1886. XXV 21 ff.).

Die schlimme Folge der Aufstellung solcher Scheingattungen ist nun die, dass die Erkennbarkeit der Zusammengehörigkeit von Hölzern und Blättern mit den Gattungen, zu denen sie gehören, stark beeinträchtigt wird und dass diese auf einzelne Organe begründeten Scheingattungen in eine Reihe mit den wirklich berechtigten Gattungen, als ob sie ihnen gleichwerthig seien, gestellt werden, Quercus neben Quercinium, Juglans neben Juglandinium u. s. w., was um so greller in seinem Nachtheil hervortritt, wenn, wie bei Schimper (Palaeontolog. végét. II) die für sich behandelten Hölzer der Koniferen selbst räumlich weit von den Gattungen, denen sie hätten zugetheilt werden sollen, abgetrennt sind, als ob sie miteinander nichts zu thun hätten. Und was bringt denn das für einen Nachtheil, wenn ein Holz oder Blatt, in die Gattung gestellt wird, der es anzugehören scheint oder wirklich angehört, versehen mit eigenem Artnamen, wenn es nicht einer schon bekannten Art zugezählt werden kann? Gar keinen! Eine zukünftige Verbesserung, etwa mögliche Zuzählung zu einer nach Frucht, Blüthe und Laub schon bekannten Art, wird ja in keiner Weise gehindert und die Abtrennung als besondere Scheingattung in — inium, — xylon oder — phyllum fördert in keiner Beziehung irgend eine bessere Kenntniss.

Solche Scheingattungen nach denselben Grundsätzen bei lebenden Pflanzen aufgestellt, würden Niemand als Anhänger finden; warum soll denn in der Palaeontologie passend sein, was allgemein für die lebende Pflanzenwelt als unpassend verworfen wird?

Ganz unzulässig sind aber solche Scheingattungen von Hölzern, die auf der Unterscheidung von Wurzel-, Stamm- und Astholz beruhen: Rhizocupressinoxylon, Cormocupressinoxylon, Cladocupressinoxylon. Es ist ja hinlänglich durch Mohl, Kraus, Sanio und Andere bekannt, dass nicht in allen Fällen mit Sicherheit das Holz von Wurzel und Stamm oder gar von Aesten zu unterscheiden ist. Die Anhänger der Unterscheidung des Wurzel-, Stamm- und Astholzes fossiler Pflanzen durch besondere Scheingattungsnamen müssten also noch eine 4. Scheingattung bilden, in welche die fossilen Hölzer hineingethan würden, die man unter jene 3 Scheingattungen von Wurzel-, Stamm- und Astholz nicht sicher unterbringen kann. Aber das Princip ist hier von seinen Freunden noch nicht konsequent durchgeführt.

Auch sonst ist dem Prinzip auf einzelne Organe Scheingattungen zu begründen nicht Rechnung getragen, besonders in den Fällen, die seine Unhaltbarkeit am meisten darthun. Es giebt nicht bloss Hölzer und Blätter, die man auf bekannte Arten nicht zurückführen kann, sondern auch andere noch gar nicht berücksichtigte Organe, wie Staubfäden z. B. von Eichen im Bernstein und von Haaren, z. B, von Eichen in Bernstein. Consequenter Weise müsste man also 2 neue Gattungen bilden, etwa Dryostemon und Dryothrix. Diese unvermeidlichen Consequenzen würden jedenfalls eine erheiternde Karrikatur des Prinzips sein und könnten sehr gut die Erkenntniss vermitteln, dass auch Scheingattungen auf Hölzer oder Blätter begründet, aufzugeben seien.

Auch ist es inkonsequent, dass Gattungen für fossile Hölzer aufgestellt sind, die nicht in — inium, oder — xylon enden. Lilla, Staubia z. B. auf Hölzer begründet, deren Beziehung zu lebenden Gattungen nicht erkannt ist, sind ohne — xylon gebildet, neben dem konsequenten Taenioxylon, dem die Beziehung zum Lebenden auch fehlt. **Conwentz** stellt inkonsequent ein Picea succinifera auf, statt einen Namen, der in — xylon endet, für das Holz anzuwenden, worauf er jene Art begründet.

Ist keine Beziehung zu einer lebenden Gattung in einem Holz, einer Frucht, einem Blatt zu finden, so sind ja längst Aushilfen gebraucht. Für Frucht und Blatt giebt es ja Carpolithus und Phyllites und für Hölzer kann ja auch ein sich empfehlender Namen unschwer gefunden werden; haben wir ja Lilla, Staubia. Ist wie bei den Cupressineen mit Einschluss der Podocarpeen und gewisser Abietineen in den lebenden und fossilen Hölzern kein Gattungs- und Art-Unterschied zu finden, so leite man das Gattungswort von der am meisten betheiligten Familie oder Abtheilung der Jetzwelt ab, in diesem Falle von Cupressineae Cupressinites statt Cupressinoxylon oder Cupressoxylon. Diese Gattung enthält in ihren Arten ohne Zweifel Ungleichwerthiges, aber enthalten nicht die meisten jetzt bekannten Gattungen fossiler Pflanzen höchst wahrscheinlich Ungleichwerthiges, ohne dass wir das ändern können? Die Zukunft wird Manches bessern. Cupressinites Bowerb. auf Zapfen gegründet, kann ja ohne Schwierigkeit erweitert werden.

Dikotyledonen.

Magnoliaceen.

Magnolia laxa Casp. Der mangelhafte Erhaltungszustand des Holzes lässt **Jahresringe** nur schwach erkennen; sie sind durch 2—3 Lagen abgeplatteter Herbstholzzellen begrenzt. Die **Holzspitz-** und **Holzstumpfzellen** im Querschnitt nicht deutlich unterscheidbar; beide zusammen stehen an Fläche, die sie einnehmen, den Gefässen weit nach. Die **Holzspitzzellen** zeigen auf radialem Schliff eine Reihe gehöfter elliptischer Poren. Die **Deckzellen** verlaufen in senkrechten sehr vielzelligen Reihen, über 28 sogar in einer Reihe und sind 2—11 mal so hoch als dick; öfters 2—3 Reihen nachbarlich an einander. Ob ausserdem, etwa an der Jahresringsgrenze **Holzstumpfzellen** da sind, ist nicht zu ermitteln. **Markstrahlen** einreihig, sehr selten stellenweise 1—3 Zellen hindurch zweireihig, 4—32 Zellen hoch. Sie haben die Eigenschaft, dass in ihren mittleren wagrechten Reihen die Zellen an den Gefässen von sehr ungleicher Länge sind, so dass eine die Nachbarin um das 2—3 fache übertrifft. Eine Reihe oder einige Reihen der **Kantenzellen** sind höher als die Mittelzellen. **Gefässe** im **Holzstrahl**, der nur 1—4 Zellen Breite hat, in radialer Reihe, 1—2 tief, meist einzeln durch 1—3, selten 4—5 Holzzellen radial getrennt, oder sich berührend, zu 2—3 zusammen, und an der Berührungsstelle dann im Querschnitt geradlinig. Die Seitenwände, wo sie erhalten sind, mit Reihen von langen gehöften Spaltporen. **Querwand** lang-länglich, spitzlich an den Enden, leiterförmig durchbrochen, mit zahlreichen bis 47 ja 59 Spalten.

Ostpreussen ohne nähern Fundort. 1 Stück.

Acerineen.

Acer borussicum Casp. **Jahresringe** vorhanden; am Schluss des Jahresringes 3—5 Lagen stark abgeplatteter Zellen. **Holzspitzzellen** in radialen Reihen. **Holzstrahl** 2—16 Zellen breit. **Deckzellen** als Umkleidung der Gefässe höher als dick, ihre Dicke: Breite: Höhe = 11 : 12 : 63. **Holzstumpfzellen** nicht wahrnehmbar. **Markstrahlen** 1—6 Zellen breit, meist 3—4 und 1—38 Zellen hoch. **Kantenzellen** höher, aber kürzer als die Mittelzellen des Markstrahls. **Gefässe** 1—2 in der Breite des Holzstrahls, aber nie konzentrisch, einzeln oder zu 2—4 in radialer Reihe, selten zu 4 mit paarweiser Anordnung; Dicke: Breite = 0,0678 mm : 0,1425 mm im Mittel; netzförmig verdickt, mit fast rhombischen Maschen und grossen gehöften Spaltporen in diesen, und ausserdem oft mit 6 eckiger Felderung, die durch gehöfte dicht liegende Poren verursacht wird. Durchbohrung der Gefässquerwand mit einem Loch.

Ostpreussen, ohne bestimmten Fundort. 1 Stück.

Acer terrae coeruliae Casp. **Jahresringe** da, durch 6—9 Lagen stark abgeplatteter Holzzellen begrenzt. **Holzspitzzellen** in radialen Reihen, mit ungehöften Poren versehen oder auf der Seite, die einem Gefäss anliegt, mit 2 Reihen gehöfter Poren. **Holzstrahl** 3—18 Zellen breit. **Holzstumpfzellen** nicht wahrnehmbar. **Deckzellen** als Gefässumkleidung vorhanden, 3—4 Zellen in der Tiefe auf radialem Schliff, vorherrschend dicker als hoch, seltener umgekehrt mit 2—4 Längsreihen gehöfter Poren. **Markstrahlen** 1—5 Zellen breit, meist 3—4 und 1—29 Zellen hoch. **Kantenzellen** höher oder niedriger als die Mittelzellen. **Gefässe** in radialen Reihen, 1 seltener 2 in der

Breite des Holzstrahls, einzeln oder zu 2—3, ja 4 radial aneinander liegend, im Mittel ihre Dicke: Breite = 0,0363 cm : 0,0352 cm; mit Reihen gehöfter Poren auf den Seitenwänden, tertiärer schraubiger Verdickung oder mit 6 eckiger Felderung, deren jede Masche eine gehöfte Pare umfässt. Querwand mit elliptischem oder rundlichem Loch, oder mit 3 Löchern, die durch 2 Sprossen getrennt sind, durchbohrt. **Markzellen** gross, höher oder niedriger, als dick und breit. **Markscheide** mit Schraubengefässen oder Schraubenleitzellen, was sich nicht entscheiden lässt. **Rinde** mit Kork, zahlreichen Gruppen von **Dickzellen** (Sklerenchym), die rundlich oder länglich sind und einfache oder ästige Poren zeigen, **drusigen Krystallen** und **Bastzellen**, letzere mit Poren, deren Raum schwach erweitert ist. Spuren von Siebzellen vorhanden.

Im Schwarzharz der **blauen Erde**, Palmnicken. Von Herrn Conservator Künow entdeckt, ganz mit Harz durchzogen.

Anacardiaceen.

Schinus primaevum **Casp.** Mangelhaft erhalten. Jahresringe, Holzstumpfzellen und Deckzellen vielleicht desshalb nicht wahrnehmbar. **Holzstrahlen** 1—7 Zellen breit. **Holzspitzzellen** auf dem Querschnitt 5—6 eckig, in radialen Reihen, zum Theil gefächert, ihre Breite : Dicke = 19 : 13 = 0,0253 mm : 0,0173 mm. Ihre Lichtung $^1/_2$—$^3/_5$ vom Durchmesser. **Markstrahlen** meist 2 Zellen breit, seltner 1 oder 3 Zellen breit, 1—28 Zellen hoch, meist 11—15, Kantenzellen mit 1—2 Stockwerken, höher, aber kürzer als die Mittelzellen. **Gefässe** einzeln und dann elliptisch im Querschnitt oder 2—4 zusammen in radialer Reihe, 1 Gefäss, selten 2 auf der Breite des Holzstrahls, in letzterem Fall, seitlich eines dem andern angefügt. Verdickungen der Seitenwände und Durchbohrung der Querwand nicht feststellbar.

Das Holz ist dem von Schinus molle sehr ähnlich. **Westpreussen.** Pempau bei Zuckau, Kreis Kartaus.

Cornaceen.

Cornus cretacea Casp. **Jahresringe** vorhanden. **Holzstrahlen** 1—8 Zellen breit, meist 4 Zellen und 4 Zellen im Mittel. **Holzspitzzellen** stark verdickt, in radialen Reihen, im Querschnitt mit ungehöften Poren, auf tangentialem Schnitt mit **einer** Reihe gehöfter, rundlicher Poren hie und da. **Holzstumpfzellen** und **Deckzellen** — das Holz ist ziemlich schlecht erhalten — nicht nachweisbar. **Markstrahlen** meist 2-reihig: 51 Proc., seltner 1-reihig: 44 Proc., oder noch seltner 3-reihig: 3 Proc.; 3 bis 23 Zellen hoch, mit 1—5 Stockwerken von Kantenzellen, welche höher aber auch kürzer, als die Mittelzellen sind. **Gefässe** radial gestellt, 1 selten 2 auf die Breite des Holzstrahls, durch 1—7, ja in sehr dünnen 1—2 Zellen breiten Holzstrahlen, durch 11—27 Holzzellen in radialer Linie getrennt. Gefässquerwand leiterförmig durchbrochen, Sprossenzahl (nur 1 solcher Fall) 12; Seitenwände gehöft porig, Poren quer elliptisch oder lineal, bis 80 nachweisbar auf einer Längswand.

1 Stück ohne nähern Fundort, jedoch wahrscheinlich aus der Nähe von Königsberg, Ast, halb mit Phosphorit umgeben; nach Dr. Jentzsch und Dr. R. Klebs höchst wahrscheinlich aus der Kreide. Das Holz selbst ist sehr reich an Phosphor nach Professor Dr. Salkowski in Münster, der die Güte hatte, es mir quantitativ zu analysiren. Näheres anderwegen.

Dazu gehörig: **Cornus cretacea** fr. **solidior.** Casp.

Ich stelle die Unterschiede dieses Holzes von Cornus cretacea zugleich mit Cornus erratica (= Cornoxylon erraticum Conw. Jahrbuch der königl. preuss. geologischen Landesanstalt 1881 S. 157), von dem ich das Original von Conwentz aus der Sammlung der königl. geolog. Landesanstalt untersuchen konnte, einander parallel gegenüber.

Cornoxylon erraticum Conw. Original.	**Cornus cretacea Casp.**	**Cornus cretacea Casp. fr. solidior.**
1. **Holzstrahl** 1—8 Zellen, meist 2 Zellen breit, im Mittel 3,4 Zellen breit.	1. **Holzstrahl** 1 bis 8 Zellen, meist 4 Zellen, im Mittel 4 Zellen breit.	1. **Holzstrahl** 2 bis 15 Zellen, meist 4, im Mittel 6,1 Zellen breit.
2. **Jahresringe** für die Lupe undeutlich wahrnehmbar, unter dem Mikroskop nur stellenweise angedeutet. (Conwentz sagt: „Jahresringe nicht vorhanden.“)	2. **Jahresringe** da.	2. **Jahresringe** da.
3. **Holzstumpfzellen** sehr selten, Br.: Höhe = 1 : $1^1/_2$—4.		3. **Holzstumpfzellen** sehr selten kenntlich, Br.: Höhe = 1 : 10.
4. **Markstrahlenzellen** meist 3 reihig: 55 pCt., seltener 1 reihig: 25 pCt., noch seltener 2 reihig: 19 pCt., am seltensten 4 reihig: 1 pCt.	4. **Markstrahlen** meist 2 reihig : 51 pCt., seltener 1 reihig: 44 pCt., am seltensten 3 reihig: 1 pCt.	4. **Markstrahlen** meist 2 reihig: 71 pCt., selten 1 reihig: 24 pCt., am seltensten 3 reihig : 5 pCt.
5. **Markstrahlen** 2—28, ja 30 Zellen hoch.	5. **Markstrahlen** 3—23 Zellen hoch.	5. **Markstrahlen** 2—26 Zellen hoch.
6. Die einzeln stehenden meist kurz elliptischen **Gefässe** radial durch 1—19 Holzzellen geschieden.	6. Die einzeln stehenden meist kurz elliptischen **Gefässe** durch 1—7, ja 11—27 Zellen radial geschieden.	6. Die einzeln stehenden **Gefässe** durch 3—13, ja 28—48 Zellen radial getrennt.
7. **Gefässquerwand** mit 18 bis 21 Spalten durchbrochen, die Seitenwände leiterförmig verdickt, mit langen Spaltenporen oder an den Markstrahlenzellen, die im Falle, dass ein Gefäss sie berührt, meist höher als breit werden, mit kurzen länglichen, queren Poren.	7. **Gefässquerwand** mit wenigen Spalten (bis 12); Seitenwände leiterförmig verdickt mit vielen bis 80 gehöften linealen Poren. (In einem Jahresringe im Frühjahrsholz rundliche Ausscheidungsbehälter (?) dicker als die Gefässe, mit **Holzstumpfzellen** theilweise begrenzt, deren Br. : Höhe = 1 : 1—2 ungefähr ist. Ausserdem nur noch ein einzelner Behälter der Art.)	7. Gefässquerwand leiterförmig mit zahlreichen Spalten, vielleicht bis 51, durchbrochen; Seitenwände mit rundlichen und queren mehr oder weniger langen, linealen gehöften, spaltenförmigen Poren versehen.

Bei allen 3 Hölzern haben die **Holzspitzzellen** 1 reihige, runde, gehöfte Poren stellenweise, mit schiefem Spalt.

Die Unterschiede von Cornus cretacea und Cor. cret. solidior scheinen nicht zur Annahme zu zwingen, dass beide verschiedene Arten sind, dagegen ist das sehr abweichende Verhältniss in den Procenten der 2- und 3-reihigen Markstrahlen von Cor. errat. einerseits und Corn. cret. und deren fr. solidior andererseits so abweichend, dass es sich zu empfehlen scheint, beide als verschiedene Arten zu betrachten. Cornoxylon conf. erraticum Vater (Zeitschr. deutsch. geol. Ges. Bd. 36. 1884 S. 846) kann Cornox. erraticum Conw. nach der vorstehenden vergleichenden Diagnose nicht sein, denn „sein Parenchym bildet wahrscheinlich unregelmässige einreihige tangentiale

Binden und die Markstrahlen sind 20—40 Zellen hoch. Cornox. conf. erraticum Vater könnte als Cornus Vateri bezeichnet werden.

Corn. cret. fr. solidior aus Königsberg.

Ericaceen.

Erica sambiensis Casp. **Jahresringe** da. Ihre Breite in demselben Ringe und in verschiedenen sehr ungleich. **Holzstrahl** 1—8 Zellen breit, im Mittel 2—3. **Holzspitzzellen** in radialen Reihen, mässig dickwandig, Lichtung $^1/_2$—$^1/_8$ des Durchmessers, im Querschnitt mit ungehöften Poren nach allen Richtungen, auf dem radialen Schnitt mit 2 Reihen von Spaltporen. **Deckzellen** vorhanden, aber wenige. **Holzstumpfzellen** zahlreich, wie die Deck- und Markstrahlen-Zellen mit tiefbraunem, gleichmässigem Inhalt erfüllt, der blasenartige Hohlräume zeigt. Holzstumpfzellen in tangentialen Binden, 1—3, selten 4—6 Zellen in der Breite des Holzstrahls, radial durch 1—4 Holzspitzzellen getrennt, mit dünnen ungehöft porigen Wandungen. **Markstrahlen** 1—4-reihig, 2—14 Zellen hoch; die vierreihigen vorherrschend: 91 Proc., zweireihige 5 Proc., dreireihige 2 Proc., 2 Proc. einreihige. Die einreihigen Markstrahlen 2—3 Zellen hoch, Zellen sehr hoch und sehr kurz. Die 2—4reihigen Markstrahlen haben 1—3 Stockwerke von Kantenzellen, die höher aber kürzer als die Mittelzellreihen sind. **Gefässe** stets einzeln, bilden im Holzstrahl eine radiale Reihe, 1 Gefäss auf die Breite des Holzstrahls, höchst selten 2. Gefässe durch 1—37 Holzzellen, im Mittel durch 8—9 radial getrennt. Querschnitt elliptisch oder rundlich; sie sind im Frühjahrsholz zahlreicher und grösser als im Herbstholz, Breite : Dicke = 24 : 29, im Mittel = 0,0310 mm : 0,0387 mm. Die Wand mit kleinen rundlichen Poren bedeckt, die um ihren eignen Durchmesser von einander entfernt stehen. Durchbohrung der Querwand wahrscheinlich mit rundlichem Loch.

Dem Holz der Erica vagans L. höchst ähnlich. Kohliges Holz aus der blauen Erde von Palmnicken.

Platanaceen.

Platanus Klebsii **Casp.** Ohne **Jahresringe. Holzspitzzellen** sehr dickwandig; die Lichtung beträgt den 4. bis 5. Theil des Quermessers; sie stehen ohne Ordnung in den 5—27 Zellen breiten **Holzstrahlen.** Querschnitt der Holzspitzzellen nach allen Seiten mit zarten, ungehöften Poren. Die den Gefässen anliegenden mit einer Reihe gehöfter Poren mit schiefem Spalt. **Holzstumpfzellen** meist etwas zusammengedrückt, zu konzentrischen unregelmässigen eine Zelle tiefen Binden vereinigt, die in radialer Richtung durch 2—4 Holzspitzzellen getrennt sind. Die Holzstumpfzellen bilden nur kurze senkrechte Längsreihen aus 1—6 Zellen bestehend, deren Querwand oft schief ist. Alle Wände mit einfachen Poren, die sehr wenig Porenraum haben, besetzt. Die **Deckzellen** sind nur dadurch von den Holzstumpfzellen verschieden, dass sie auf der, dem Gefäss anliegenden Seite nicht rundliche, kleine Poren, sondern lange, quere, spaltenförmige, lineale Poren haben. Die **Markstrahlen** lang gestreckt, elliptisch auf tangentialem Schnitt, ungleich, 2—32 Zellen breit, 7—205 Zellen hoch, $^1/_3$ bis fast 6 mm hoch, $^1/_{25}$—$^2/_{10}$ mm breit. Eine Schicht von abgeplatteten **Hüllzellen,** deren Breite : Dicke : Höhe = 0,0173 mm : 0,0613 mm : 0,0533 mm im Mittel ist, umgiebt die

Markstrahlen. Die inneren Zellen der Markstrahlen haben im Mittel Höhe : Breite : Länge = 0,0378 mm : 0,036 mm : 0,105 mm. Alle ihre Wände haben einfache Poren mit schmalem Porenraum. Die **Gefässe** stehen im Holzstrahl zu 1—4 in der Breite desselben, aber nicht konzentrisch, sind meist elliptisch im Querschnitt, meist einzeln, selten zu 2—3 verbunden. Im Mittel sind sie 0,0759 mm breit und 0,0933 mm dick. Die Gefässquerwand schief, leiterförmig durchbrochen. Die Seitenwände theils mit Reihen gehöfter, kurzer, länglicher Poren, theils mit grossen, queren, elliptischen, die so lang stellenweise sind, dass die Verdickung leiterförmig erscheint.

Aus dem Triebsande unter der grünen Mauer der Gräberei Palmnicken, also auf tertiärer Lagerstätte gefunden. Sehr phosphorhaltig, wie Professor Dr. Salkowski in Münster fand. Benannt nach Dr. **Rich. Klebs,** dem Finder.

Das Holz von Platanus occidentalis L. steht dem des Platan. Klebsii am nächsten.

Platanus borealis **Casp. Jahresringe** nicht bemerkbar. **Holzspitzzellen** dickwandig, Lichtung der 3. bis 4. Theil des Durchmessers der Zelle; Stellung ohne Ordnung; Querschnitt mit zarten nach allen Seiten gerichteten Poren, deren Porenraum wenig breiter, als der Gang ist. **Holzstrahl** 14—23 Zellen breit. **Holzstumpfzellen** meist abgeplattet, mit den Enden auf dem Querschnitt zu unregelmässigen, einreihigen Ketten, die bald konzentrisch, bald radial, bald in unregelmässigen Krümmungen verlaufen, verbunden, selten vereinzelt. Die senkrechten Reihen nicht lang, nicht mehr als 4-zellig; Querwände oft sehr schief, ihre Poren klein, ungehöft, die **Deckzellen** mit einer Reihe gehöfter Poren. Die **Markstrahlen** 3 bis mehr als 54 Zellen breit und 16 bis 89, ja mehr Zellen hoch, $^1/_2$ bis mehr als $3^1/_3$ mm hoch und $^3/_{100}$—$^2/_3$ und mehr breit mit zerstreuten **Hüllzellen** bekleidet, deren Breite : Höhe : Länge = 1 : 4 : 3 ist. Die andern Markstrahlenzellen auf tangentialem Schnitt elliptisch, ihre Breite : Höhe : Länge = 3 : 4 : 9. **Gefässe** sehr zahlreich, im Holzstrahl zu 2—8 in dessen Breite, aber nicht konzentrisch, einzeln oder zu 2—5 unregelmässig gestellt; wenn einzeln im Querschnitt meist elliptisch, 00,9 bis 0,14 mm im grössern, 0,06 bis 0,08 mm im kleinern Durchmesser; sie nehmen ungefähr die Hälfte der Fläche des Holzstrahls ein. Querwand elliptisch, leiterförmig durchbrochen.

Westpreussen. Plietnitz, bei Kramske, Kreis Dt. Krone.

Juglandeen.

Juglans Triebelii **Casp. Jahresringe** vorhanden. **Holzstrahl** 1—8 Zellen breit. Die Holzzellen in radialen Reihen stehend. Wand der **Holzspitzzellen** mässig dick. **Holzstumpfzellen** in tangentialen Ketten, 1—2, selten 3—4 Zellen tief, eine Kette von der andern radial durch 2—8 Holzspitzzellenlagen getrennt. Die Holzstumpfzellen haben Dicke : Breite : Höhe = 14 : 15 : 31. **Deckzellen** abgeplattet. Die **Markstrahlen** 2 Zellen breit, selten eine, noch seltner 3, 6—26 Zellen hoch. Kantenzellen einstöckig, höher und breiter, aber kürzer als die Mittelzellen. Die **Gefässe** im Frühjahrsholz dicker und breiter, auch zahlreicher als gegen Schluss des Jahresringes, radial einreihig im Holzstrahl, einzeln oder zu 2—5 zu einer Reihe verbunden. Querwände 35—50° schief, Seitenwände mit schraubigen dichten, sich kreuzenden Verdickungen. Näheres wegen ziemlich schlechter Erhaltung nicht ersichtlich.

Kommt der Pterocarya caucasica unter den lebenden Arten der Juglandeen am nächsten. Für die Art Juglans Tribelii ist die Gattung Juglans daher im weiten Sinne Linné's genommen.

Wahrscheinlich aus der Nähe von Elbing.

Laurineen.

Laurus als Gattung nehme ich im Folgenden in dem weiten Linné'ischen Sinne.

Laurus biseriata **Casp.** Jahresringe vorhanden, begrenzt durch 3—8 Lagen parallel zur Tangente zusammengedrückter Herbstholzzellen. **Holzspitzzellen** sehr dickwandig, auf 100 derselben kommen 22 dünnwandige Holzstumpfzellen. Holzspitz- und Holztumpfzellen in radialen Reihen. Die **Holzstumpfzellen** zerstreut, einzeln, konzentrisch nur stellenweise gestellt, in einer senkrechten Reihe von ziemlich gleicher Länge; ihre Poren rundlich ungehöft. **Deckzellen** unregelmässig an Gestalt, meist trapezoidisch, ihre Poren quer elliptisch, gehöft. **Markstrahlen** vorzugsweise 2reihig, selten einreihig und dann sehr kurz, noch seltner an einzelnen Stellen in einem 2reihigen Markstrahl dreireihig. Die 2reihigen Markstrahlen haben 9—68 Zellen Höhe; die Kantenzellen einstöckig, kürzer, aber höher als die Mittelzellen. **Holzstrahl** 3—10 Zellen breit; die **Gefässe** im Holzstrahl eine radiale Reihe bildend, meist 1, selten 2—3 in der Breite des Holzstrahls, im Frühlingsholz meist 3—11 radial dicht aneinander liegend, gegen das Herbstholz an Zahl abnehmend, 2—3 meist zusammen, selten einzeln. Seitenwände mit 4—7-eckigen meist 6-eckigen Maschen; in jeder Masche eine gehöfte Pore mit kurzem Spalt; seltener die Wand mit von einander entfernten, elliptischen, gehöften Poren ohne Maschennetz besetzt. Durchbohrung der Querwand wahrscheinlich mit rundlichem Loch. Oelzellen keine.

Ist dem Holz von Dicypellium caryophyllatum und Laurus Sassafras ähnlich.

In Ost- und Westpreussen häufig.

Laurus triseriata **Casp. Jahresringe** vorhanden. Herbstholzzellen parallel zur Tangente sehr zusammengedrückt, 2—3, oder 5—6 Lagen. **Holzspitzzellen** in radialen Reihen, sehr dickwandig. **Holzstumpfzellen** ungefähr ebenso gross im Quermesser, zerstreut, die welche einer senkrechten Zeile angehören an Länge von einander wenig verschieden. **Markstrahlen** vorzugsweise dreireihig, 51—81 pCt., seltener einreihig und dann sehr kurz, noch seltener 2-reihig,oder die 2reihigen häufiger als die 1reihigen. Höhe der dreireihigen 11—26, oder 15—37 Zellen. Kantenzellen einstöckig, höher aber kürzer als die Mittelzellen. **Holzstrahl** 2—6 Zellen dick. **Gefässe** im Frühjahrsholz in radialen Reihen von 2—6, selbst 8, gegen das Herbstholz hin an Zahl und Grösse abnehmend, dann einzeln oder zu zweien. Seitenwände der Gefässe 4—7eckig-, meist 6eckig-maschig, in jeder Masche eine gehöfte Pore, oder den angrenzenden **Deckzellen** gegenüber mit sich nicht berührenden, elliptischen, gehöften Poren versehen, deren Gang spaltenförmig ist. Oelzellen nicht wahrnehmbar.

Steht dem Holz das Laurus nobilis L. nahe.

Von Seefeld am Mauersee, Kreis Lötzen, Grandgrube von Langenau, Kreis Danzig, und ein Stück aus Ostpreussen ohne Fundort.

Laurus perseoides **Casp. Jahresringe** vorhanden. Holzspitz- und Holzstumpfzellen in radialen Reihen. **Holzstrahl** 4—13 Zellen breit, im Mittel 7. **Holzspitzzellen** sehr dickwandig. **Holzstumpfzellen** dünnwandig, zerstreut, am Schluss des Jahresringes abgeplattet auftretend. **Deckzellen** vorhanden. **Markstrahlen** 1—7 Zellen breit, 2—57 hoch, meist 4—6 Zellen dick und 20 hoch. Die Kantenzellen die höchsten, aber kürzer als die Mittelzellen. **Gefässe** im Holzstrahl einreihig, selten 2 auf dessen Breite, im Frühjahrsholz in radialen Reihen von 3—7 hintereinander, gegen das Ende des Jahresringes abnehmend und dann einzeln, oder nur 2—3 hintereinander, kreisrund oder elliptisch. Querwände der Gefässe etwa unter 50°, Seitenwände bedeckt mit dicht gedrängten rundlich-vieleckigen gehöften Poren oder (den Deckzellen gegenüber) mit weitläuftigen elliptischen gehöften Poren.

Hat mit mehreren Arten von Persea, Litsaea, Laurus, Oriodaphne Aehnlichkeit, am meisten mit dem Holz von Persea gratissima Nees.

Aus dem Diluvium von Palmnicken.

Cupuliferen.

Quercus subgarryana **Casp.** Ziemlich schlecht erhalten. **Jahresringe** deutlich. **Holzspitzzellen** in radialen Reihen, in den letzten Lagen des Herbstholzes stark parallel zur Tangente abgeplattet. **Holzstumpfzellen** nur stellenweise auf radialem Schnitt kenntlich, 2½—3mal so hoch als dick. **Deckzellen** nicht kenntlich. **Markstrahlen** meist einreihig, Breite dieser einreihigen 0,0146 mm, Höhe ihrer Zellen nur etwa 1½mal so gross; ihre Länge 2—3 mal so gross als Breite oder Höhe. Andere Markstrahlen 10—29 Zellen breit und sehr hoch. Die **Gefässe**, auf deren Seitenwänden keine Poren erhalten sind, sehr ungleich an Dicke; die dicken, 2—3 in radialer Richtung tief, aber nicht in radialen Reihen gestellt, nehmen ¼—½ des Jahresringes im Frühjahrsholz ein. Die dünnen, ohne Vermittelung fast, in schiefen dichten Zügen, gegen die Grenze des Jahresringes im Herbstholz meist tangential zusammenfliessend; die dünnen nehmen **einen** Holzstrahl ein, die dicken 3—4. Die dünnen viel zahlreicher als die dicken, letztere 2½—10mal so stark im Durchmesser, als die dünnen.

Dies fossile Holz gehört in die Hauptabtheilung A., I. Unterabtheilung, Gruppe *a* von **Abromeit** (Anatomie des Eichenholzes in Pringsheims Jahrbüchern XV 1884 273); es ist dem der lebenden Quercus garryana Dougl. in Nordamerika am ähnlichsten und weit entfernt von Quercus primaeva Goepp., über die erst **Felix** (Zeitschrift der deutsch. geolog. Gesellschaft XXXV 1883 70 ff.) eine genügende Beschreibung nach Originalen Goepperts geliefert hat.

Bei Königsberg oder in der Stadt gefunden.

Coniferen.

Araucarites Goepp.

Araucarites prussicus **Casp.** Jahresringe und Holzstumpfzellen fehlen. **Holzspitzzellen** radial gestellt. **Holzstrahl** 1—18, im Mittel 6 Zellen breit. Gehöfte Poren 1—2 reihig, sehr selten dreireihig. Die einreihigen platten sich oben und unten bei dichter Berührung geradlinig ab; die 2—3 zeiligen drücken sich gegenseitig 6eckig, nur die Seitengrenzen nach aussen sind bogig. Holzspitzzellen mit einer Reihe Poren 23 pCt., zweireihige 76 pCt., dreireihige nicht einmal 1 pCt. **Markstrahlen** im Mittel 5—6 Zellen hoch, im Extrem 1—14. Die Markstrahlenfelder mit 2—7 schiefen, schwach gehöften, elliptischen Poren, die über sich wenn sie je 2—3 in einer Reihe eines Markstrahlfeldes liegen, einen sehr langen, schiefen Spalt haben; er ist weniger gross bei 4—7 Poren, die in 2—3 Reihen liegen.

Fort Neudamm bei Königsberg.

Dem Araucarites rhodeanus Goepp. sehr ähnlich, dieser hat aber 72 pCt. Zellen mit einreihigen und 28 pCt. Zellen mit 2 reihigen Poren, **Markstrahlen** von 3—40 Zellen Höhe, im Mittel 13 Zellen hoch; **Markstrahlenfelder** mit 1—4 schiefen Poren, die 1—2 wagrechte Reihen bilden.

Araucariopsis Casp.

Neue Gattung.

Wie **Araucarites** Goepp., jedoch mit Holzstumpfzellen.

Araucariopsis macractis **Casp.** **Markstrahlen** ein- oder zweireihig, 1—45 Zellen hoch, 1,453—1,629 mm hoch. Markstrahlen ohne Harzzellen. Die gehöften Poren der **Holzspitzzellen** berühren sich stets. Porengruppen einreihig, dann an der Berührungsstelle geradlinig begrenzt, oder seltener zweireihig dann die gehöften Poren fast sechseckig, nach aussen jedoch bogig begrenzt. 5—18 pCt. der Holzspitzzellen nur mit zweireihigen Poren. **Holzstumpfzellen** (Harzzellen) zerstreut, dünnwandig.

Julchenthal bei Königsberg. Heiligenbeil.

Monokotyledonen.

Palmacites.

Palmacites dubius Casp. Mangelhaft erhalten; wie es scheint nur der innere Stammtheil verkieselt. **Leitbündel** sehr weitläuftig $\frac{1}{2}$—$1\frac{1}{2}$ mm von einander entfernt, ihr Querschnitt rundlich oder kurzlänglich, 0,113—0,397 mm im Durchmesser, kurze Bogen bildend. Unterschiede in dem stark verwitterten Leitbündel nicht weiter kenntlich. Zellen des **Grundgewebes** im Querschnitt ziemlich isodiametrisch, im Längsschnitt Breite : Höhe der Zellen = 1 : $\frac{1}{2}$—4.

Langfuhr bei Danzig.

Bericht
über die 25. Versammlung des preussischen botanischen Vereins zu Insterburg am 5. October 1886.

Vom Vorstande.

Dem in Pr.-Stargard am 6. Oktober 1885 gefassten Beschlusse gemäss wurde die 25. Versammlung des preuss. botan. Vereins zu Insterburg abgehalten, woselbst sich die Herren Oberbürgermeister Korn, Direktor des königl. Gymnasiums und Realgymnasiums Dr. Krah, Oberlehrer Dr. Lautsch, Dr. Reuter, Lehrer an der Mittelschule, und Thieler, Lehrer an der höhern Töchterschule unter Beistand des Herrn Oberlehrer Walter Kuck mit bestem Erfolge der Geschäftsführung unterzogen hatten.

Am Nachmittage des 4. Oktober wurde unter Leitung der genannten Herren und des Herrn Gymnasiallehrer Geffers zu Wagen bei schönstem Wetter von den schon angekommenen Mitgliedern nach dem etwa $^3/_4$ Meilen entfernten Stadtwald eine sehr interessante Exkursion unternommen. Am Stubbenteich wurde **Alisma arcuatum** Michal. und **Bidens radiatus Thuill.** gefunden; der Stadtwald bot eine Flora dar, wie sie recht abweichend von den westlich davon gelegenen Gegenden ist, denn der Boden war mit dichter Fülle von **Carex pilosa** und **Hypericum hirsutum** bedeckt, dazwischen **Agrimonia pilosa**, Alles auf lehmigem Grunde und weiter entfernt unfern des städtischen Försterhauses viel **Gladiolus imbricatus**. Der Abend vereinigte die Theilnehmer des Ausflugs, wie noch einige neu hinzugekommene Vereinsmitglieder und eine grössere Anzahl von in Insterburg lebenden Gönnern des Vereins, worunter sich auch der königl. Landrath Herr Germershausen befand, in den Räumen des Schützenhauses zu heiterer Geselligkeit. Herr Oberbürgermeister Korn hiess die Vereinsmitglieder im Namen der Stadt Insterburg willkommen, worauf ihm Professor Caspary, als Vorsitzender des Vereins, mit warmen Worten dankte.

Am folgenden Tage den 5. Oktober eröffnete Professor Caspary in dem grossen Saale des Schützenhauses um $8^1/_2$ Uhr die Sitzung und gedenkt mit Bedauern der zahlreichen Verluste, die der Verein von Oktober 1885/86 durch Tod erlitten hat. Es starben Professor Dr. Michelis, Rittergutsbesitzer John Frenzel-Noruschatschen, Stadtrath Lottermoser, Direktor Dr. Sauter, Apotheker Settmacher-Hochstüblau. Der Vorsitzende erwähnt dankbar der Theilnahme und Leistungen der Dahingeschiedenen für die Interessen des Vereins und die Versammlung ehrt ihr Andenken durch Erhebung von den Sitzen.

Der Vorsitzende erwähnt **mit vielem Dank, der 900 Mark, die der ostpreussische Provinziallandtag auch für 1. April 1886/87 dem preussischen botanischen Verein bewilligt hatte** und giebt dann an, dass trotz der Verluste die Zahl der Vereinsmitglieder etwa 430 sei und erstattet in aller Kürze einen Ueberblick über die Thätigkeit des Vereins in dem abgelaufenen Jahre. Es wurden ausgesandt zur Erforschung des Kreises Ortelsburg für den ganzen Sommer Dr. Abromeit, des Kreises Strasburg Herr Ludwig Valentin, Candidat des höheren Schulamtes und Herr Lehrer

Max Grütter botanisirte auf Vereinskosten im Kreise Schwetz. Der Vorsitzende untersuchte auf amtlichen Excursionen zu Pfingsten den Nordwesten des Kreises Neustadt und im Spätsommer und Herbst 7 Wochen hindurch zur Ergänzung die Seen der Kreise Berent, Kartaus, Pr. Stargardt und einen Theil der Gewässer der Danzig'er Niederung.

Es werden nun den Versammelten die Grüsse abgestattet und Pflanzensendungen vorgelegt und vertheilt derjenigen Mitglieder, die persönlich der Versammlung beizuwohnen verhindert waren, Grüsse von dem 2. Schriftführer des Vereins Herrn Apotheker Kunze-Königsberg, Kantor Grabowski-Marienburg, Herrn Apotheker Schemmel-Kraupischken, Herrn Apotheker Rosenbohm-Graudenz, Pflanzensendungen von den Herren Professor Dr. Praetorius-Konitz, Apotheker Ludewig-Liebstadt, Dr. med. Hilbert-Stensburg, Schulamts-Kandidat Kurpiun-Königsberg, Stud. rer. nat. Otto Strübing-Stolno bei Kulm, Apotheker Scharlok-Graudenz, Apotheker Fiedler-Graudenz, Lehrer Frölich-Thorn, Apotheker Weiss d. Aelt.-Caymen, Hauptlehrer Kalmuss-Elbing, Lehrer Peil-Sackrau, Probst Preuschoff-Tolkemit, John Reitenbach-Zürich.

Professor Prätorius-Konitz sendet 1886 gesammelt:

Alisma natans L. Kl. Barsch-See. 8. 8. — **Lobelia dortmanna** L. Kl. Barsch-See. 8. 8. — Lycopodium inundatum L. Kl. Barsch-See. 8. 8. — Lycopodium complanatum L. Kön. Wald. 8. 8. — Gypsophila fastigiata L. Kön. Wald. 13. 6. — Dianthus arenarius L. Kön. Wald. 13. 6. — Goodyera repens R. Br. Kön. Wald. 8. 8. — Pedicularis silvatica L. Kl. Barsch-See. 13. 6. — Verbascum phlomoides L. Kl. Konitz'er Weg. 18. 7. — Eriophorum vaginatum L. Buschmühl 19. 5. — Pulsatilla pratensis Mill. Buschmühl 19. 5. — Pulsatilla patens Mill. daselbst. — Pulsatilla vernalis Mill. daselbst. — Linnaea borealis L. blühend! Kön. Wald 13. 6. — Tofieldia calyculata Whlnb. Abrau. 12. 8. 85. — Sweertia perennis L. Abrau 12. 8. 85. — **Abweichungen** in Formen oder Farben: Solanum tuberosum mit oberirdischen Knollen in den Blattachseln, eine in diesem Sommer hier sehr häufige Erscheinung. 8. 8. — Lotus uliginosus mit mehrpaarigen Fiedern 14. 6. 84. — Viola canina var. alba Stadtpark. 17. 5. 85. — Anemone nemorosa L. 2 Blüthen, 5 Hüllblätter. 3. 5. 86. — Veronica verna L. rasenartig in einer Schonung bei Buschmühl. 19. 5. 86.

Apotheker Ludewig-Liebstadt sendet Pflanzen aus Liebemühls Umgegend und aus Pommern.

Dr. med. Hilbert schickt von Sensburg folgende bemerkenswerthe Pflanzen: **Astrantia maior,** Wäldchen bei Mühlenthal, Impatiens Noli tangere, Corydalis solida, Empetrum nigrum, Coronilla varia, **Cypripedium Calceolus,** Ephenschlucht bei Sensburg, **Salix myrtilloides** Kessel bei Sensburg, **Sarothamnus scoparius** (angepflanzt?) Sorquitten, am Wege nach Muradken, Hierochloa australis, **Potentilla alba,** Schwarzer-See bei Mertensdorf, **Polygala amara,** Schlucht bei Polschendorf, Anthericum ramosum, Lycopodium Selago, Linnaea borealis, Gentiana Pneumonanthe.

Schulamtskandidat R. Kurpiun sendet aus der Oberförsterei Heydtwalde im Kreise Goldapp: Lilium Martagon, Anthericum ramosum und Lathyrus silvester.

Stud. rer. nat. Strübing schickt aus dem Weichselgebiet in der Nähe von Kulm: Campanula sibirica, Euphorbia exigua, Asplenium Ruta muraria, Libanotis montana (zw. Elisenthal u. Gogolin).

Apotheker Scharlok-Graudenz beschenkt die Versammlung mit einer grossen Zahl sehr sorgfältig getrockneter Pflanzen, die er zum Theil in seinem Garten gezogen hatte: **Adenostylis alpina L.** im Garten gezogen, stammt aus St. Beatenberg, Schweiz. — **Artemisia scoparia W. K.** aus dem Weichselgestade bei Dragass. — **Chaiturus Marrubiastrum Rchb.** Am Tusch'er Damm bei Nonnenbergs Ziegelei. — **Cimicifuga foetida L.,** aus dem Garten; stammt aus der Schlucht von Elisenthal, Kr. Kulm. — **Collomia grandiflora Dougl.,** Gartenpflanze, stammt aus dem Nahethale bei Idar u. Sobernheim. — **Dianthus arenarius** × **Carthusianorum,** aus dem Rondsen'er Wäldchen, Kr. Graudenz. — **Digitalis lutea L.** im Garten gezogen; stammt vom Gestade des vierwaldstädter Sees i. d. Schweiz. — **Ervum pisiforme Peterm.,** im Garten gezogen, stammt vom Westrande der Paparczyn'er Schlucht, Kr. Kulm. — **Euphorbia exigua u. E. stricta L.,** im Garten gezogen, stammen aus dem Nahethale bei Sobernheim. — **Fragaria viridis Duch. f. subpinnatisecta Duch.,** südliche Plantage der Festung Graudenz. — **Galanthus nivalis L. u. Gal. nival. for. Scharlokii** Casp., erstere aus dem Lunau'er Wald, die letztere aus einem Garten in Sobernheim. — **Impatiens Noli tangere L. floribus cleistogamis,** so in Herrn Scharloks Garten; mustergiltige Ursprungspflanze stammt aus dem Ellerbruch von Mischke, Kr. Graudenz. — **Lathyrus tuberosus L.** zwischen Stadt und Festung Graudenz in einem Kornfelde. — **Melica ciliata L.,** Gartenpflanze; stammt vom Ufer des wilden Tscheeben unter Bürgeln

Schweiz. — **Myosotis sparsiflora L.**, aus dem Buchod bei Turszuitz, Kr. Graudenz. — **Omphalodes scorpioides Schrank**, stammt aus Sommerfeld i. d. Lausitz und ist im Garten Scharloks verwildert. — **Osmunda regalis L.**, Scharloks Garten; stammt aus dem grossen Moor bei Bremen. — **Parietaria officinalis L.**, Gartenpflanze, verwildert, stammt aus Neugarten, Danzig. — **Pulsatilla patens + pratensis**; Rondsen'er Wäldchen, Kr. Graudenz. — **Ranunculus Steveni Andrz. f. acris Jordan** als Art und **Ranunculus Steveni Andrz. f. friesennus** beide aus einer als Viehweide benutzten Wiese bei **Mühle Klodtken**. — **Rosa alpina L. f. pyrenaica Gouan**, aus Scharloks Garten; stammt aus St. Beatenberg, Schweiz. — **Saxifraga tridactylites L.**, von Herrn Apotheker Fiedler, gesammelt am Gestade des grossen Rudnick-Sees. — **Scirpus radicans Schk. neu für Graudenz!** Von Herrn Apotheker Fiedler gefunden und gesammelt am Ostufer der Weichsel, südlich von der Brücke. — **Sonchus paluster L.**, in Scharloks Garten verwildert, stammt aus dem Ellerbruche am Ufer des grossen Mühlenteiches von Turczuitz, Kr. Graudenz. — **Struthiopteris germanica Willd.**, aus Scharloks Garten, stammt aus dem Kr. Neustadt, Westpreussen. — **Urtica pilulifera L. und Urtica pilulifera f. Dodartii L. als Art**, stammt aus Thüringen, Garten von Scharlok verwildert. — **Viola canina + silvestris** in Scharloks Garten, zwischen den reinen Arten entstanden. — **Viola collina Besser**, hohes Weichselufer, vor dem Niederthore der Festung Graudenz.

Apotheker **Fiedler** sendet aus den Kreisen Kulm und Graudenz eine grosse Menge Pflanzen von schon bekannten Standorten. Erwähnt seien: Lycopodium Selago, Carex cyperoides (Kr. Kulm, See von Kornatowo), Carex limosa, Alyssum montanum, Saxifraga tridactylites, Salix myrtilloides (Kr. Kulm, bei Gottersfeld und vom See Gogoliniez), Scirpus radicans, Pulsatilla vernalis, Puls. patens, Silene tatarica, Salvia verticillata, Oxytropis pilosa, Pulmonaria angustifolia, Nonnea pulla, Teesdalea nudicaulis, Chaiturus Marrubiastrum, Gypsophila fastigiata, Gentiana cruciata, Allium fallax, Erysimum hieraciifolium, Aspidium cristatum, Campanula sibirica, Cyperus fuscus, Helianthemum vulgare und Androsace septentrionalis.

Ein Telegramm des Herrn Apotheker Ludwig-Christburg läuft ein, welches der Versammlung einen herzlichen Gruss bietet. Ebenso von Herrn Apotheker E. Rosenbohm-Graudenz.

Herr Frölich-Thorn sandte: Veronica Chamaedrys **fr. incisa** G. Fröl. Blätter sehr tief bis auf $^1/_3$ ja $^2/_3$ der Blatthälfte lappig-gekerbt, Schonung nördlich von Fort IV Thorn; Veronica Chamaedrys fr. **serrata** G. Fröl. Blätter eiförmig, schmal, zugespitzt, klein gesägt, fast kahl, daselbst; **Potentilla digitato-flabellata** Br. et Bouch., Bollwerk westlich von der Eisenbahnbrücke bei Thorn; **Salvia silvestris** L. Czarkerkämpe bei Thorn; **Phegopteris robertiana** A. Br., Mauer der städtischen Gasanstalt in Thorn; Euphorbia Esula L. **fr. linariifolia** G. Fröl., Blätter lang lanzettlich-lineal, Breite : Länge = 1 : 10—13. (6 mm : 63; 6 mm : 80 mm); Taraxacum officinale Web. fr. **pinnatifida** G. Fröl. Blätter fiederschnittig, Lappen fiedertheilig, alle Lappen nach vorn gerichtet. Und vieles Andere.

Herr Apotheker Weiss-Caymen, d. Aelt., sendet:

Agrimonia Eupatoria albiflora. Vom natürlichen Standorte bei Meyken und Exemplare aus dem Garten des Herrn Weiss, wohin er die wilde Pflanze versetzt hatte. — **Coronopus Ruellii** Weg zwischen Wangen und Waldhaus Bendiesen. Neuer Standort. — **Euphorbia Chamaesyce.** Aus dem Garten des Einsenders in Caymen. Unkraut. — **Geum urbanum + strictum** mit Erysiphe. — **Geum rivale + strictum** von drei Stauden. — **Glyceria spectabilis** mit Uredo longissima. Der Pilz gilt als Ursache eines gefährlichen Aufblähens bei Rindern. Daher öfters Anfragen bei Herrn Weiss desswegen. Vom Caymen'er Mühlenfliess. — **Lappa minor + tomentosa.** In der Nähe des Schlosses. — **Lappa nemorosa.** Von Herrn Apotheker **Richard Weiss** auf einer früher kahlen, jetzt stark bestrauchten Stelle bei Abbau Schwesternhof gefunden. — **Linaria arvensis.** Recht häufiges Unkraut in dem Garten des Herrn Weiss. — **Salix nigricans f.** parvifolia Wimm. Waldrand von Poduhren. Gefunden von Herrn **Richard Weiss** Ende Juli. — **Scutellaria hastifolia.** Durch Herrn Apotheker **Scharlok** aus dem Kreise Schwetz lebend erhalten und im Garten zu Caymen gezogen. Im Garten in Caymen bereits lästiges Unkraut.

Herr Hauptlehrer Kalmuss theilt mit: **Tunica saxifraga** Scop. bei Kahlberg verwildert; Linnaea borealis L. Kiefernwald bei Liep, Frische Nehrung; **Calamagrostis litorea** DC. Frische Nehrung, Haffufer zwischen Kahlberg und Neukrug; **Rubus macrophyllus** Wh. et N., Frische Nehrung bei Liep; **Rubus Wahlbergii** Arrh. Abhänge der Hommel bei Kupferhammer; **Chaerophyllum hirsutum** L. Wald von Maulfritzen (Kr. Mohrungen); **Luzula sudetica** Presl. a) pallescens Bess (als

Art) Rehberge, (Kreis Elbing); **Zanichellia palustris L.** Aussendeich der Nogat an der Ausmündung der vierten Trift bei Ellerwald, Kreis Elbing; **Geranium dissectum L.** Garten der 5. Gemeindeschule in Elbing; **Euphorbia exigua L.** Elbing, Gartenunkraut; **Scabiosa columbaria,** zwischen Lärchwalde und Gr.-Röbern, Kreis Elbing; **Senecio erraticus** Bertol. Elbing am Schleusendamm; **Festuca silvatica** Vill. Rehberge bei Kadienen; **Poa sudetica** Haenk. Stagnitten, Kreis Elbing.

Herr Lehrer Peil-Sackrau sendet aus der Nähe seines Wohnortes eine Anzahl Pflanzen, darunter folgende hervorzuhebende: **Orobanche coerulescens** Steph., **Oxytropis pilosa, Silene chlorantha, Ceterach officinarum** (Graudenz'er Festung), **Gymnadenia conopea.**

Von Herrn Probst Preuschoff-Tolkemit gelangten folgende Pflanzen zur Vertheilung: **Pleurospermum austriacum,** Kreis Elbing, Tolkemit, Lehmberge unter Gebüschen. 25. 6. 86. — **Galium aristatum,** Kreis Elbing, Forst Hohenwalde bei Tolkemit. 7. 86. — **Luzula albida.** Kreis Elbing, Waldschluchten bei Kadienen und Panklau. 6. 86. — **Androsace septentrionalis.** Kreis Marienburg, Halbstädt, Sandfeld. 5. 82. — **Lycopodium Selago,** Kreis Elbing, Waldschlucht bei Neuendorf. 22. 8. 86. — **Circaea lutetiana,** Kreis Elbing, Kadienen. — **Circaea intermedia** Ehrh. Rehberg'er Schluchten, bei Elbing.

Es wird dann eine grosse Zahl (43) Arten von Schweizerpflanzen an die Anwesenden ausgegeben, die Herr John Reitenbach, ehedem auf Plicken, jetzt in Oberstrass bei Zürich, in seiner treuen Anhänglichkeit an den Verein, gesammelt und eingesandt hat, darunter auch **Helleborus niger, Helleborus foetidus, Arum maculatum, Melittis melyssophyllum,** zum Theil weissblüthig, **Cephalanthera pallens, Rhododendron ferrugineum** und **hirsutum, Tamus communis.** Herr Reitenbach erbietet sich sehr freundlich, wenn ihm bestimmte Wünsche in Betreff Schweizerpflanzen von Vereinsmitgliedern geäussert werden, diesen nach Möglichkeit zu entsprechen.

Bericht des Dr. Abromeit über die botanische Untersuchung des Kreises Ortelsburg.

Der Kreis Ortelsburg, den ich im Interesse des preussischen botanischen Vereins vom 4. Juni bis zum 14. September 86 untersuchte, ist über 28 Quadratmeilen gross und liegt im südlichen Ostpreussen. Namentlich der nördliche Theil des Kreises, welcher bedeutend höher als der südliche ist, trägt das Gepräge der masurischen Landschaft. Hier wechseln bewaldete Höhen mit grösseren und kleineren Seen ab, während der Süden des Kreises eine gleichförmige Sandebene ist, aus welcher sich nur einige Hügel erheben. So befindet sich etwa $1\frac{1}{2}$ Meilen südwestlich von Ortelsburg am kleinen Schobensee das **„Grüne Gebirge"** oder die **„Blauen Berge,"** eine hügelige Waldgegend, welche botanisch sehr interessant ist. Hier fand ich **Cimicifuga foetida** und **Cytisus ratisbonensis.** Letzterer kommt jedoch auch im anstossenden ebenen Theil des Belaufs Materschobensee (Reusswalde'r Forst) östlich vom „Grünen Gebirge" vor. Ausser den genannten Arten sind dort noch: **Trifolium Lupinaster, Adenophora liliifolia Z[4], Laserpitium latifolium, Dracocephalum ruyschianum, Onobrychis viciifolia, Hieracium cymosum** und **Linnaea borealis** vorhanden. Etwa 2 Meilen südöstlich vom Grünen Gebirge erhebt sich bei dem Dorfe Finsterdamerau ein von Süd nach Nord gestreckter, bewaldeter Hügel mit einer von seiner Umgebung verschiedenen Flora. Dagegen boten die übrigen unbedeutenden Hügel des südlichen Theiles vom Kreise Ortelsburg ausser Epipactis rubiginosa nichts Bemerkenswerthes dar. — Im Südwesten, namentlich in Willenbergs Umgegend herrscht fast allgemein die „Kuselfichte," eine verkümmerte Form von Pinus silvestris vor, zu welcher sich nahezu gleich grosse Stämme von Juniperus communis hinzugesellen. In Willenberg bilden die „baccae Juniperi" einen werthvollen Handelsartikel und Herr Apotheker Schimanski theilte mir mit, dass er viele Centner davon aufkauft, um andere Theile unserer Provinz damit zu versorgen.

Der dürre Sandboden des Kreises wird sehr häufig von moorigen Wiesen und bebuschten Sümpfen durchsetzt. So sind namentlich die flachen Ufer der Flüsse und Nebenflüsse zum grössten Theile sumpfig, obgleich im Hoch- und Spätsommer nur wenig Regen fiel. Für die Entwässerung der Sümpfe und Seen wird allerdings viel gethan. Es sind bis jetzt bereits der Dimmernsee südlich von Bischofsburg, und einige kleinere Seen bei Geislingen und Sczepanken völlig entwässert worden und gewähren nun eine beträchtliche Grasnutzung. Auch die Spiegel des Seedanzig'er- und des kleinen Schobensee's wurden gesenkt, der dazwischen befindliche Matersee dagegen völlig entwässert.

An den vom Wasser freigelegten Stellen ihrer Ufer greift nun eine ganz eigenartige kräftige Vegetation Platz. Sie besteht der Hauptsache nach aus: Senecio paluster DC., Bidens tripartitus und cernuus nebst winzigen Formen, Juncus alpinus, lamprocarpus, bufonius in Zwergform, Scirpus Tabernaemontani, Calamagrostis neglecta, Phragmites communis und etwas seltener **Graphephorum arundinaceum**, aber ohne blühende Halme. — Auf feuchten Moorwiesen war **Pedicularis Sceptrum Carolinum** $V^3 Z^3$, Saxifraga Hirculus, Drosera rotundifolia, longifolia und der Bastard **Dr. longifolia + rotundifolia, Carex chordorrhiza** zu finden. Lycopodium inundatum wurde an 7 moorigen Standorten festgestellt. Die höher gelegenen meist bebuschten Stellen grösserer Wiesen gewährten mir eine reiche botanische Ausbeute. Ich sammelte auf solchen Hügeln: **Platanthera viridis** $V^4 Z^4$, ***Gymnadenia conopea*** $V^3 Z^3$, ***Dracocephalum ruyschianum, Polygonatum verticillatum*** $V Z^2$, und **Botrychium simplex**, das ich dreimal in Gesellschaft von B. Lunaria antraf. Sehr interessant war auch die Flora der Waldwiesen, die im Kreise nicht selten sind. So fand ich auf einer langgestreckten, mässig feuchten Waldwiese im Belauf Gross Puppen ***Botrychium virginianum*** in einem sterilen Exemplar. Dieser neue Standort ist mehr als 4 Meilen vom westlichsten Fundort des Botr. virginianum im Kreise Neidenburg entfernt, den ich 1881 bereiste. Ausserdem sammelte ich auf Waldwiesen: **Iris sibirica,** ***Crepis succisifolia*** $V^3 Z^4$, **Gentiana Pneumonanthe** $V^4 Z^4$, Epipactis latifolia, **Cephalanthera rubra** $V^3 Z^3$, die aber auch im hohen Bestande vorkommt, **Galium venosum,** Betula humilis, **Potentilla mixta Nolte** und **Ophioglossum vulgatum** $V^4 Z^4$. An den Rändern der Waldwiesen war einige Male ***Calamagrostis arundinacea + lanceolata Heiden. = C. Hartmaniana Fr.,***) ferner **Botrychium Matricariae A. Br.** zu finden. Der Bastard ***Calamagrostis arundinacea + Epigeios*** = C. ***acutiflora*** (Schrad.) DC., und zwar in Formen, welche wie die uplandischen in Schweden der C. Epigeios näher stehen, war nur einmal auf einem bewaldeten Seeufer bei Jablonken anzutreffen.

Der Kreis Ortelsburg ist reich an grösseren Wäldern. Es befinden sich in ihm die fiskalischen Forsten: **Corpellen, Reusswalde, Friedrichsfelde, Puppen** und **Ratzeburg** mit ungefähr 30 Beläufen. Ausser diesen existiren noch die privaten Forsten der Städte Ortelsburg, Willenberg und Passenheim, ferner die Jablonken'er, Malschöwen'er und Gilgenau'er Forsten, welche sich ebenfalls im privaten Besitz befinden. Die Pflanzendecke dieser Wälder ist in vieler Hinsicht interessant und die seltensten Arten unserer Flora gehören ihr an. Wie im angrenzenden Kreise Neidenburg kommt auch hier Fagus silvatica nur angebaut (z. B. Corpellen'er Forst. Bel. Mittenwalde) vor. Pinus silvestris ist auch im Ortelsburg'er Kreise der vorherrschende Waldbaum, ausserdem ist auch Picea excelsa zahlreich als einheimischer Baum vorhanden und hin und wieder Larix europaea angepflanzt.

Von Laubhölzern kommen hauptsächlich vor: Quercus pedunculata nebst Q. sessiliflora, letztere jedoch weniger häufig, Carpinus Betulus, Betula verrucosa und B. pubescens, Populus tremula, Fraxinus excelsior; letztere besonders schön in der „Jeschonowitz“ im Puppen'er Forst, Belauf Bärenwinkel. In sumpfigen Waldgegenden herrschen Alnus glutinosa und Salix pentandra vor. — Die Hochlandspflanzen**) und auch einige Hügelpflanzen kommen namentlich in den höher gelegenen Theilen der Forsten vor. So war ***Adenophora liliifolia*** an 5 Standorten zu finden, ***Trifolium Lupinaster*** an 2, ***Tr. rubens*** $V^4 Z^3$, ***Oxytropis pilosa*** $V^2 Z^2$, ***Laserpitium latifolium*** $V^2 Z^2$, ***Peucedanum Cervaria*** $V^2 Z^2$, ***Potentilla rupestris*** $V^2 Z^3$, **P. alba** $V^3 Z^4$, **Arnica montana** $V^4 Z^4$, **Euonymus verrucosa** $V^4 Z^4$, **Dracocephalum ruyschianum** $V^2 Z^3$, ***Salix myrtilloides*** $V^2 Z^3$ nebst den Bastarden ***S. aurita + myrtilloides*** und ***S. myrtilloides + repens,*** **Pulsatilla patens** $V^4 Z^4$, **Potamogeton praelonga** $V Z^2$ und ***Hydrilla verticillata*** im Sawitz-See. Von Hügelpflanzen habe ich folgende gefunden: Chaerophyllum aromaticum $V^3 Z^3$, ***Carlina acaulis***

---

*) Nach Heidenreich in Skofitz oesterreich. botan. Zeitung Jahrgang 1865 und Almqvist in Hartman's Handbok i Skandinaviens Flora 11. Aufl. Seite 516.

) Prof. Caspary: **„Ueber die Flora von Preussen“ in der „Festgabe für die Mitglieder der 24. Versammlung deutscher Land- und Forstwirthe,“ gebraucht S. 195 und 196 die Bezeichnung „Hochlandspflanzen“ für nordische Arten unserer Flora, die des Oefteren irrthümlich für „alpin“ gehalten wurden. Die „Hügelpflanzen“ sind von diesen zu trennen, da sie auch in der Ebene vorkommen.

$V^2 Z^3$, **Hieracium echioides** $V^2 Z^3$, **Inula hirta** $V^2 Z^3$, **Aster Amellus** Z^3, Silene Otites $V^3 Z^3$, Cynanchum Vincetoxicum $V^3 Z^4$, **Epipactis rubiginosa** $V^3 Z^3$. — In den feuchteren Theilen der Forsten, namentlich der Reusswalde'r, Friedrichsfelde'r und Puppen'er ist **Stellaria frieseana** nicht selten, dagegen war **Poa sudetica var. hybrida** nur in den Beläufen Kopytko und Farienen des Friedrichsfelde'r und Grünwalde des Puppen'er Forstes zu finden. Für ***Carex loliacea,*** welche Dr. Heidenreich 1861 bei Wischwill im östlichen Deutschland zuerst entdeckte, habe ich zwei neue Standorte im Belauf Farienen ermittelt. Ferner habe ich ***Carex vaginata Tausch*** an drei Standorten (stets am Waldrande) im Friedrichsfelde'r Forst, Belauf Rehhof gefunden.*)

Eine nur geringe Verbreitung haben folgende Arten: **Arabis Gerardi Bess., Prunus spinosa** und **Fragaria viridis** Duch. kommen **nur** in der **Umgegend von Passenheim** vor. **Euphorbia Cyparissias** fand ich **nur** im **Mensguth'er Gebiet** und **Spartium scoparium** war in einem Exemplar im **Passenheim'er Stadtwalde,** jedoch zahlreicher in einem Hohlwege bei **Malschöwen,** im **Malschöwen'er Wald** und im **Belauf Ulonsk (Corpellen'er Forst)** vorfanden. Matricaria Chamomilla ist im Kreise Ortelsburg ebenso selten, wie in den angrenzenden Kreisen Neidenburg und Allenstein. Ich habe sie nur in einem Roggenfelde am Nordufer des grossen Haussee's bei Fingatten wirklich wild vorgefunden. Gewöhnlich wird sie sonst von den Leuten in Gärten besonders angebaut. Als selten stellten sich nach meinen Untersuchungen noch folgende Arten heraus: ***Agrimonia pilosa Ledeb.*** nur an zwei Stellen. In der Nähe befand sich A. Eupatoria. **Armeria vulgaris** nur ein Exemplar bei Gross-Kurwigk im Osten des Kreises. **Cardamine hirsuta b. multicaulis** 1 Standort. **Carex pilosa Scop.** westlich von Adamsverdruss im Puppen'er Forst. **Cirsium rivulare** nur auf einer Wiese bei Walhalla unweit Passenheim, **Callitriche autumnalis** im Samplatten'er See. **Brachypodium silvaticum,** zwei Standorte, **Bromus asper. b. serotinus Beneck.** 2 St., **Br. racemosus** 1 St., ***Equisetum variegatum Schleich.*** an 2 Stellen am Lehlesken'er See, **Fragaria elatior** 2 St., **Festuca arundinacea** 1 St., ***Graphephorum arundinaceum (Lilj.) Aschers.*** an 3 Seen und am Sawitzfluss. **Gladiolus imbricatus** nur im Puppen'er Forst, ***Lepidium micranthum*** am Bahndamm unweit der Brücke über den Schobenfluss angesiedelt, **Polemonium coeruleum** 1 St., **Pedicularis silvatica** 1 St., **Stenactis bellidiflora A. Br.** nur auf einer Wiese am Rande des „Conn" (Friedrichsfelde'r Forst), wo sie, fern von bebauten Orten völlig eingebürgert ist. Von Orchideen waren seltener zu finden: **Cypripedium Calceolus, Coralliorrhiza innata, Liparis Loeselii** und **Microstylis monophyllos.** Die Gattung Rubus war namentlich durch R. idaeus $V^4 Z^5$, R. suberectus And. $V^4 Z^4$, **R. fissus Lindl.** $V^4 Z^4$, (welcher weit häufiger als R. fruticosus ist), R. caesius und R. saxatilis $V^3 Z^4$ vertreten.

Die Flora der Dorfstrassen des Kreises Ortelsburg besteht im Allgemeinen aus folgenden Pflanzen: Lappa maior, tomentosa und minor nebst Bastarden, Rumex obtusifolius, crispus u. Bastarden, Chenopodium Bonus Henricus $V^3 Z^3$, Ch. hybridum, rubrum, polyspermum, glaucum album, Atriplex hortense var. nitens gebaut und verwildert, Amarantus Blitum, A. retroflexus, Elsholtzia cristata, Lamium album, purpureum, amplexicaule, Artemisia Absynthium, Anthemis Cotula, Conium maculatum, Xanthium Strumarium, Onopordon Acanthium (seltener), Datura Stramonium, Hyoscyamus niger, Malva neglecta u. M. borealis, **Geum strictum Ait.,** welches in vielen Ortschaften vorhanden ist.

Den Bodenverhältnissen entsprechend werden im landwirthschaftlichen Interesse im Grossen vorwiegend Kartoffeln, Roggen, Lupinen (Lupinus luteus, L. angustifolius), Buchweizen, namentlich im Süden, Weizen dagegen im lehmreicheren nördlichen Theil des Kreises gebaut. Dem Hopfenbau wird besonders um Passenheim und Mensguth mehr Aufmerksamkeit geschenkt, ähnlich wie im angrenzenden Theile des Kreises Allenstein. Die sogenannten „Passenheim'er Rüben" werden, nach gütiger Mittheilung des Herrn Bürgermeister Hinz, im angrenzenden lehmigen Theile des Kreises Neidenburg bei Itowken auch jetzt noch gebaut, bilden jedoch keinen Handelsartikel mehr. — Nach dieser kurzen Schilderung der floristischen und landwirthschaftlichen Verhältnisse des Kreises Ortelsburg gebe ich im Folgenden ein Verzeichniss der wichtigeren Funde auf den einzelnen Ausflügen. Am 3. 6. langte ich in Passenheim an und wurde von unserem Vereinsmitgliede Herrn Apotheker Hess,

---

*) Diese Art ist schon 1884 im Kreise Memel vom stud. rer. nat. E. Knoblauch gefunden. Es wurde aber vorgezogen, darüber zu schweigen, bis die Bestimmung sicher gestellt war. Zu dem Behuf wurden 1885 für weitere Beobachtung Exemplare in den botan. Garten genommen. Stud. Knoblauch wird Näheres selbst angeben. Caspary.

auf das Freundlichste empfangen und eingeladen, während der Untersuchung der Umgebung Passenheims in seinem Hause Wohnung zu nehmen, was ich mit Dank annahm.

Excursionen um Passenheim. Am 4. 6. mit Herrn Hess nach dem Passenheim'er Stadtwalde. Wir fanden am Ostufer des grossen Calbensee's: **Arabis Gerardi Bess.** Im Stadtwalde: Thesium ebracteatum, Scirpus pauciflorus Lightf. In Passenheim zeigte mir Herr Hess das von ihm bereits vor längerer Zeit an der Nordmauer der evangelischen Kirche enteckte ***Asplenium Ruta muraria*** Z[4]. — 5. 6. Ost- und Nordufer des grossen Calbensee's, Passenheim'er Stadtwald, Südostufer des Dluszeksee's, der zum grössten Theil im Kreise Allenstein liegt; im Stadtwalde: Trifolium rubens, Pimpinella nigra (um Passenheim die häufigere Art), **Geranium columbinum, G. molle;** im Sphagnetum: **Liparis Loeselii** Z[3], Picea excelsa var. myelophthora Casp., **Coralliorrhiza innata,** ***Dracocephalum ruyschianum*** (Laubstengel), ***Potentilla rupestris*** Z[1]. Auf Feldern: Alsine viscosa. — 6. 6. Schlucht bei Ottilienhof, Passenheim'er Stadtwald, kleinere See'n im Norden und Westen des Stadtwaldes: **Rubus fissus Lindl., Pulsatilla patens + pratensis,** ***Carlina acaulis*** (Blätt.) **Stellaria crassifolia,** Viola arenaria + canina, **Carex remota b. stricta** Madauss. — 7. 6. Walhalla Bahnhof von Passenheim, Südufer des grossen Calbensee's, Hügel südlich vom Bahnhof, Narythen-, see, Moorwiesen zw. diesem See und Ruttkowen, Wald südöstlich von Schenfelsdorf: ***Cirsium rivulare*** Z[2], **Geaster rufescens, Botrychium simplex, Pedicularis Sceptrum Carol.** (Blätt.), **Pirola media.** — 8. 6. Regen. — 9. 6. Grosser und kleiner Calbensee, Scheufelsdorf, Belauf Scheufelsdorf (Purden'er Forst), Ostufer des Kosnosee's, Sawadderberg bei Scheufelsmühle. Heringsee: Elodea canadensis im grossen Calbensee, ***Oxytropis pilosa, Botrychium rutaceum Willd*** in Gesellschaft mit **B. Lunaria.** — 10. 6. Friedrichsberg, Kukukswalde, Anhaltsberge, Belauf Schobensee (Corpellen'er Forst), Lehlesken'er Wald, Ostufer des Pörschke-, Wossidlo- und Kronineksee's, Ost- und Südufer des Lehlesken'er See's, Lehlesken: **Laserpitium latifolium** (Blüthe), **Pedicularis Sceptr. Carol., CorallIorrhiza innata** Z[3] **Carex chordorrhiza, Potentilla mixta Nolte** zusammen mit P. norvegica und P. silvestris, ***Equisetum variegatum*** Z[4]. — 11. 6. Nordufer des Lehlesken'er See's, Gilgenau'er und Lehlesken'er Wald. Nordufer des Grammen'er See's, Corpellen'er Forst Bel. Schobensee, Davidshof, Grammen: ***Agrimonia pilosa Ledeb.*** Z[2], **Rosa canina + rubiginosa, Equisetum variegatum** Z[4], **Dracocephalum ruyschianum.** — 12. 6. Walhalla, Kepunneksee, Passenheim'er Mühle: **Medicago falcata + sativa.** — 13. u. 14. 6. Pfingstfest. — 15. 6. Regen. — 16. 6. Morgens Regen. Excursion nach den Moorwiesen bei Walhalla: **Eriophorum latifolium;** Uebersiedelung nach Ortelsburg.

Untersuchung der Umgebung von Ortelsburg. Noch am 16. 6. stellte ich in Begleitung des Herrn Apotheker Rudloff eine Excursion nach den Beläufen der Corpellen'er Forst Mittenwalde und Neu-Gisöwen an. Wir fanden: **Galium aristatum** Z[4], Crepis praemorsa, **Arnica montana** Z[4]. — 17. 6. In Begleitung des Herrn Rudloff nach dem Corpellen'er Forst, Bel. Mittenwalde, Alt-Gisöwen, Ost- und Südufer des Seedanzig'er See's, Materfluss, Belauf Ittowken: **Laserpitium latifolium** (Blätter), ***Naias maior,*** Lolium italicum, wahrscheinlich mit anderem Grassamen ausgesäet, **Cypripedium Calceolus** Z[4], **Pedicularis Sceptr. Carolin.,** ***Iris sibirica*** Z[2], **Cephalanthera rubra,** Salix cinerea + purpurea. — 18. 6. Corpellen'er Forst, Bel. Neu-Gisöwen. Reusswalde'r Forst Bel. Materschobensee, Moorwiesen zw. Materschobensee und Schodmack, Maschingrund, Belauf Mittenwalde (Corpellen'er Forst): Arnica montana V[4] Z[4] **Salix aurita + livida,** ***Iris sibirica*** Z[3], **Cnidium venosum** (Blätter), **Cytisus ratisbonensis** Z[3], ***Polemonium coeruleum*** Z[4], **Betula humilis** Z[4], ***Gymnadenia conopea*** 1. Blüthe, ***Crepis succisifolia Tausch.*** — 19. 6. Hausmühle, Linkes Ufer des Waldpuschflusses, Belauf Schleusenwald (Corpellen'er Forst), Südostufer des Waldpuschsee's, Försterei Wikno: **Oryza clandestina** V[4] Z[4], **Carex leporina b. argyroglochin, Salix nigricans b. grandis.** — 20. 6. Vormittags Regen. Corpellen'er Forst, Bel. Neu Gisöwen, Reusswald'er Forst Bel. Lipnik: Salix aurita + livida, **Cnidium venosum,** ***Gentiana Pneumonanthe*** (Kraut.) Z[4]. — 21. 6. Ortelsburger Stadtwald, rechtes Ufer des Waldpuschflusses, Hausmühle, Schleusenwald (Corpellen'er Forst): **Salix aurita + livida, Platanthera viridis** Z[3], **Cnidium venosum, Agrimonia odorata** Z[3], **Viola epipsila + palustris.** — 22. 6. Ortelsburger Schlossgraben, Fingatten, Corpellen'er Forst, Bel. Mittenwalde, Johannisthal, Sawitzmühle, Ostufer des Sawitzsee's, Schlossberg am westlichen Ufer des Schobenflusses: **Rumex crispus + obtusifolius, Geum strictum Ait.,** ***Hydrilla verticillata*** im Sawitzsee, **Cypripedium Calceolus.** — 23. 6. Beutnersdorf A., Nordufer des grossen Haus-See's, an der Chaussee nach Eichthal. — Regen: Elodea canadensis, Lemna gibba, **Elsholtzia cristata.** — 24. 6. Vormittags Regen. Nachmittags Excursion über Lehmanen nach Romahnen,

Beutnersdorf B.: Arenaria viscosa, Agaricus scorodonius unter Juniperus communis, **Centunculus minimus,** Polycnemum arvense, Petasites officinalis. — 26. 6. Corpellen'er Forst, Bel. Mittenwalde, Schodmack'er Wiesen, Reusswalde'r Forst, Belauf Materschobensee, Grünes Gebirge: **Cephalanthera rubra, Bromus asper b. serotinus Benecken, Pirola media, Potentilla digitato-flabellata A. Br., Platanthera viridis** Z^4 mit Ophioglossum vulgatum, ***Stellaria frieseana,*** Viola epipsila + palustris, ***Salix myrtilloides*** nebst S. **aurita + myrtilloides,** auf einer mässig feuchten Wiese des Lehrers Senf in Materschobensee. ***Cimicifuga foetida, Adenophora liliifolia*** Z^3. — 26. 6. Südufer des grossen Haus-See's, Oberförsterei Corpellen. Besuch bei Herrn Oberförster Seehusen, der mich auf dieser Excursion nach dem Belauf Ulonsk begleitete. Wir fanden unter anderem: **Utricularia minor,** Platanthera chlorantha, **Potentilla norvegica** auf moorigen Wiesen südlich von Scziczonnek. — 27. 6. Steinberg, Scziczonnek, Corpellen'er Forst, Bel. Ulonsk, linkes und rechtes Ufer des Schobenflusses nördlich von Johannisthal: **Botrychium Matricariae** V^3, ***Inula hirta, Crepis succisifolia Tausch*** Z^4 neben Cr. paludosa, ***Peucedanum Cervaria*** (Kraut), ***Lepidium micranthum*** am Bahndamm westlich von der Brücke über den Schobenfluss. — 28. 6. Beutnersdorf A., Lindenberg, Scziczonnek, Corpellen'er Forst Bel. Ulonsk, Försterei Ulonsk, Kobbelhals, Südostufer des grossen Schobensee's, Torfstiche bei Frenzken, Eichthal. Wiederum begleitete mich Herr Rudloff. Wir fanden: ***Inula hirta,*** **Rosa rubiginosa + tomentosa,** Pulmonaria angustif., **Cephalanthera rubra** Z^3, **Peucedanum Cervaria,** Rosa canina + tomentosa, Trifolium rubens, ***Adenophora liliifolia*** Z^3 (Kraut), Sarothamnus scoparius Z^4, **Nasturtium barbaraeoides Tausch b. pinnatifidum Casp.,** Trollius europaeus, **Salix aurita + livida, S. livida + repens,** ***Dracocephalum ruyschianum.*** — 29. 6. Corpellen'er Forst, Bel. Neu Gisöwen, Reusswalde'r Forst Bel. Lipnik, Oberförsterei Reusswalde Belauf Dlotowken, Finsterdamerau, Gr. Schiemanen: **Stellaria frieseana, Geum strictum Ait.** nebst **G. strictum + urbanum,** Epipactis rubiginosa, ***Adenophora liliifolia*** auf dem Hügel östlich von Finsterdamerau. **Trifolium alpestre b. glabratum v. Klinggr.I** neben der Hauptform, **Oxytropis pilosa** Z^2, **Epilobium tetragonum.** — 30. 6. Regen. Nachmittags Excursion nach der Corpellen'er Forst Bel. Mittenwalde, Fingatten: **Geum strictum Ait,** Cephalanthera rubra in der Nähe der Saatkämpen, Euonymus verruc. — 1. 7. Beutnersdorf B., Hausmühle, Bel. Schleusenwald (Corpellen'er Forst), Romahnen'er Wiesen, Ostufer des Waldpuschsee's, Alt-Keikuth, Kaspersguth, Romahnen, Beutnersdorf A.: **Platanthera viridis** Z^4, **Campanula Cervicaria, Botrychium simplex b. incisum Milde** nebst B. Lunaria, ***Polygonatum verticillatum,*** **Gymnadenia conopea, Pedicularis Sceptr. Carolin.,** Rumex maximus, Centunculus minimus. — 2. 7. Corpellen'er Forst Belauf Mittenwalde, Johannisthal. rechtes Ufer des Schobenflusses. Belauf Ulonsk, Oberförsterei Corpellen, Fingatten: **Rumex obtusifolius + crispus,** Chara ceratophylla im Johannisthal'er Mühlenteich, Listera ovata. — 3. 7. Olschienen, Bärenbruch, Reusswalde'r Forst, Bel. Wilhelmsthal, Radzienberg, Liepowitz, Reusswalde'r Forst Bel. Pieczisko, Prussowborrek, Hamerudau, Ortelsburg'er Stadtwald: Platanthera viridis Z^4, ***Pedicularis silvatica, Myosotis caespitosa var. laxa,*** **Radiola linoides, Geum strictum + urbanum, Rumex obtusifolius + crispus,** Rumex maximus. **Stellaria frieseana,** ***Lappa nemorosa.*** — 4. 7. Regen. — 5. 7. Schlossgraben, Corpellen'er Forst, Bel. Ulonsk und Mittenwalde: Pirola uniflora. Uebersiedelung nach Schwentainen.

Untersuchung der Umgegend von Schwentainen — 6. 7. Schwentainen, Friedrichsfelde, Belauf Friedrichsfelde, den ich in Begleitung des Herrn Oberförster Eyser untersuchte. Friedrichsthal, „Conn" (ein Theil des Friedrichsfelde'r Forstes): **Platanthera viridis, Cerastium glomeratum, Geum strictum Ait,** ***Stenactis bellidiflora A. Br.*** Z^4, **Euphrasia officinalis var. crenata Casp.,** Malva neglecta + borealis. — 7. 7. Piassutten, Westufer des Piassutten'er See's, Tatarendamm, Ostufer des Nosice-See's, Ratzeburg'er Forst Belauf Kobiel, Oberförsterei, Ratzeburg, Lontzig, Grünwalde: **Geum strictum Ait,** ***Botrychium simplex,*** **Cyperus fuscus, Trifolium rubens** I. Blüthe, **Oxytropis pilosa,** Salix alba (wild), **Cephalanthera rubra,** Epipactis latif. ***Hieracium echioides Lumn.*** Z^3. — 8. 7. Abbau Schwentainen, Westufer des Schwentainen'er See's, Bel. Kobiel (Ratzeburg'er Forst), Feldmark Powalczin, Opukelmühle, Bel. Sysdroyheide und Strusken (Ratzeb. F.), Westufer des Nosice-See's, Tatarendamm, Ostufer des Piassutten'er See's, Piassutten: ***Cephalanthera rubra, Rosa cinnamomea*** (wild) am Westufer des Schwentainen'er See's, Stellaria crassifolia, **Caldium venosum,** Matricaria Chamomilla (angebaut). — 9. 7. Ratzeburg'er Forst Belauf Strusken, Feldmark von Kl. Jerutten, Ostufer des Marxöwen'er See's, Wiesen an dessen Westufer, Ostrand des Schleusenwaldes (Corpellen'er F.), Klein Jerutten: **Geum strictum + urbanum fr. stylis viridibus et rubris,** Linaria minor, ***Rosa cinnamomea*** neben R. canina, **Potamogeton lucens +**

praelonga, ***Graphephorum arudinaceum Aschers.*** in etwa 3' tiefem Wasser, **Carex chordorrhiza,** Rumex obtusifolius + crispus. — 10. 7. Regen. — 11. 7. Friedrichsfelde'r Forst Bel. Schwentainen und Friedrichsfelde: Viola epipsila + palustris, Salix livida + repens, S. aurita + livida, ***S. livida + nigricans,*** **Platanthera viridis,** S. cinerea + nigricans. — 11. 7. Regen. — 12. 7. Piassutten, Nordufer des Schwentainen'er See's, Ratzeburg'er Forst Bel. Ratzeburg und Wolfshagen, Krawno (Kreis Sensburg), Ufer des kleinen und grossen Krawno-See's, Bel. Sysdroyheide u. Strusken (Ratzeb. F.), **Hieracium echioides, Carex chordorrhiza,** Populus tremula var. acuminata, ***Trifolium Lupinaster,*** **Gymnadenia conopea** Z[4], **Carlina acaulis,** nebst **fr. caulescens.** — 13. 7. Wierog, Südostrand des Bel. Strusken, südl. Theil des Bel. Sysdroyheide (Ratzeb. F.), Nord- und Westufer des Marxöwen'er See's, Klein Jerutten: ***Salix myrtilloides,*** nebst **S. aurita + myrtill.** und **S. myrtill. + repens** in einem Waldsumpf des Jag. 115, Bel. Strusken, **Graphephor. arundinac., Pedicularis Sceptr. Carol.** — 14. 7. Nördlicher Theil des Kopaciako-Bruches, Friedrichsfelde'r Forst Bel. Schwentainen, Grünwalde: Cirsium oleraceum + palustre (zwischen den Eltern), ***Festuca arundinacea,*** **Potentilla mixta Nolte.** — 15. 7. Friedrichsfelde'r Forst Bel. Schwentainen, Rosogfluss: Oryza clandestina. Regen; Rückkehr. — 16. 7. Friedrichsfelde'r Forst Belauf Schwentainen, Puppen'er Forst Bel. Grünwalde, Wiesen am Rosogfluss: Cerastium glomeratum, **Cirsium oleraceum + palustre** (zwisch. den Eltern), **Rumex crispus + obtusifolius.** Uebersiedlung nach Gr. Puppen.

Excursionen um Puppen. 17. 7. Bahnhof Puppen, Südostufer des Puppen'er See's, Belauf Klein Puppen: Viscum album auf Betula verrucosa, Bryopogon iubatum, **Epilobium obscurum,** Salix aurita + livida, **Carex chordorrhiza, Salix aurita + myrtilloides,** ***S. myrtilloides (f. latifolia et f. parvifolia),*** **S. myrtilloides + repens** in einem Sphagnetum und an einem kleinen Waldsee westlich von der Försterei Kl.-Puppen, ***Agrimonia pilosa Ledeb*** Z[3], neben A. odorata u. A. Eupatoria. — 18. 7. Puppen-Theerofen, Bel. Gross Puppen, Lissengraben, grosse Lissenwiesen: Silene noctiflora, **Verbascum nigrum + thapsiforme, Botrychium Matricariae** Z[3]. — 19. 7. Süd- und Westufer des Puppen'er See's, Kl. Puppen, rechtes Ufer des Puppenflusses, Philipponenkloster, Westufer des kleinen Sysdroy-See's, Sysdroy-Fluss, Kipnik, Westufer des grossen Sysdroy-See's. Ratzeburg'er Forst Bel. Wolfshagen, Ratzeburg, Puppen'er Forst Bel. Kl. Puppen: Platanthera viridis Z[3], **Salix caprea + cinerea,** Alsine viscosa, ***Microstylis monophyllos,*** **Potentilla mixta Nolte,** Carex chordorrhiza, Veronica latif. **var. Teucrium, Botrychium Matricariae,** Salix cinerea + nigricans, Picea excelsa var. myelophthora Casp. im Sphagnetum Z[3]. — 20. 7. Nach Belauf Bärenwinkel, Adamsverdruss, Cygelniahöhe und Jeschonowitz in Begleitung des Herrn Oberförsters Morant: Pirola media Z[3], ***Cardamine hirsuta b. multicaulis*** unweit der Saatkämpen in der Jeschonowitz. — 21. 7. Puppen'er Forst Bel. Gr. Puppen, Schwedenschanze, Bjel: ***Salix myrtilloides*** auf einer Mooswiese östlich von Gr. Puppen, **Aster Amellus** Z[3], ***Botrychium virginianum Sw.,*** 1 Expl. Jagen 143, Betula humilis. — 22. 7. Bel. Gr. Puppen, Babienten'er Wiesen, kleiner See im Norden der Babienten'er Wiesen: Inula salicina b. hirtiformis, Salix aurita + livida, ***Crepis succisifolia Tausch,*** Betula humilis, **Carex chordorrhiza,** Melampyrum pratense b. **purpureum Hartm.** — 23. 7. Puppen'er Forst, Belauf Bärenwinkel, Jeschonowitz, Adamsverdruss, Beläufe Grünwalde, Kl. Puppen: Pulmonaria angustifolia, **Rosa cinnamomea** auf der Cygalniahöhe, fern von kultivirten Orten, **Bromus asper b. serotinus, Geum strictum + urbanum,** Picea excelsa var. myelophthora, ***Carex pilosa*** Z[4], ***Gladiolus imbricatus*** im Jag. 87 u. 88. — 24. 7. Puppen-Theerofen, Schwedenschanze im Bel. Gr. Puppen, Kl. Puppen: **Sempervivum soboliferum, Salix myrtilloides + repens.** — 25. 7. Puppen'er Forst Bel. Kl. Puppen, Grünwalde: **Linnaea borealis** Jag. 115, **Botrychium Matricariae,** Picea excelsa var. myelophthora. — 26. 7. Bel. Kl. Puppen, Grünwalde, sumpfige Waldwiese Spatno in den Jag. 45/20. **Potentilla mixta Nolte, Cypripedium Calceolus.** — 27. 7. Vormittags heftiges Gewitter. Ostufer des Puppen'er See's, Puppen-Theerofen, Döblitzthal: **Botrychium Matricariae,** Matricaria Chamom. (gebaut). — 28. 7. Morgens Regen. Puppen'er F. Bel. Klein Puppen und Ratzeburg'er Forst Bel. Ratzeburg: Alsine viscosa. — 29. 7. Cygelniahöhe durch die Beläufe Gr. Puppen und Bärenwinkel, Adamsverdruss: **Goodyera repens** (selten), Epipactis rubiginosa. — 30. 7. Bel. Gross-Puppen, Kl. Carwien (Kr. Johannisburg), Jeschonowitz, Bärenwinkel: Orobus niger b. heterophyllus, Vicia Cracca fl. alb. — 31. 7. Bel. Kl. Puppen, Grünwalde, vom Jag. 17 d. Bel. Grünwalde am Grenzgestell der Puppen'er und Friedrichsfelde'r Forst bis zum Rumianekbruch, Bel. Bärenwinkel, durch Bel. Gr. Puppen zurück: **Potentilla mixta Nolte** Z[4] ***Poa sudetica var. hybrida Gaud.*** Jag. 12 Belauf Grünwalde (Puppen'er F.), **Thalictrum simplex.** — 1. 8. Regen, Kürzerer Ausflug nach

Bystrcz mit Herrn Apotheker Rudloff: **Allium oleraceum.** — 2. 8. In Begleitung des Herrn Rudloff nach Rudszany und dem Nieden'er See, Bel. Gr. Puppen, Bärenwinkel, Jeschonowitz, Lissengraben, Puppen'er Schneidemühlen: ***Campanula bononiensis*** Z³ am hohen Nordufer des Nieden'er See's (Kreis Johannisburg), **Botrychium Matricariae, Laserpitium latifolium** nebst **var. asperum** (Crtz. als Art). — 3. 8. Kurwigk-See, Curwien'er Forst, Cruttinnen'er Forst, Bel. Koczek, Försterei und Kolonie Koczek, Gr. Kurwigk: **Armeria vulgaris,** Trifolium alpestre b. **glabratum v. Klinggr. I.,** Tr. rubens, **Gymnadenia conopea, Oxytropis pilosa** Z⁴. Heftiges Gewitter aus W. unterbricht die Excursion. — 4. 8. Vormittags Regen mit Sturm. Bystrcz, rechtes Ufer des Puppen'er Flusses, Kl. Kurwigk, Nord- und Ostufer des Kurwigk-See's, Curwien'er und Puppen'er Forst Bel. Gr. Puppen: **Aster Amellus** Z³. — 5. 8. Adamsverdruss, Puppen'er Forst Bel. Grünwalde, Friedrichsfelde'r Forst Bel. Birkenheide und Rehhof, Wyssokigrund, Lipniak, Kokosken, Friedrichshof, Farienen (Dorf und Gut), Lissengraben, Puppen: **Rubus fissus Lindl.,** Potentilla silvestris fol. inciso-dentatis, **Geum strictum Ait, Cephalanthera rubra.** — 6. 8. Döblitzthal, Puppen'er Forst Bel. Sysdroy, Sdrusno- und Saal-See: **Linnaea borealis** Jagen 184, Ranunculus polyanthemus, Rhynchospora alba, **Lycopodium inundatum** am Saal-See im Jagen 190. Uebersiedlung nach Friedrichshof.

Excursionen um Friedrichshof. 7. 8. Ausflug nach der Friedrichsfelde'r Forst Bel. Rehhof, Birkenheide, Langenwalde (Dlugiborek), quer durch den Kopaciska Bruch nach Wystemp, Friedrichsfelde: Platanthera viridis Z⁴, **Cephalanthera rubra,** ***Carex vaginata Tausch*** Z³, **Gentiana Amarella.** — 8. 8. Friedrichsfelde'r Forst Bel. Rehhof, Wiesen nördlich von den Morgen, Lipniak, Försterei Rehhof, Kopaciskawiesen: **Gentiana Pneumonanthe** Z⁴, ***Carex vaginata Tausch*** Z³, **Botrychium Matricariae.** — 9. 8. Willamowen, Tümpel und Hügel bei Liebenberg, Abbau von Liebenberg, Bel. Kopytko, Schutzbezirk Lipnik, (Friedrichsfelde'r Forst), Wystemp: **Calamagrostis arundinacea + lanceolata** zwischen den reinen Arten, **Epilobium obscurum.** — 10. 8. Morgen, Gr. Blumenau, Friedrichsfelde'r Forst Bel. Farienen, Wiesen im Jagen 8, Dorf Farienen, Kokosken: ***Lycopodium inundatum*** Z³, **Poa sudetica var. hybrida Gaud.** Z³, ***Carex loliacea*** Z⁴, im sumpfigen Jagen 21. C. elongata var. **Gebhardii Schk., Botrychium Matricariae.** — 12. 8. Morgen, Friedrichsfelde'r Forst Bel. Farienen, Försterei u. Dorf Farienen, Kokosken: **Lycopodium inundatum** in einem 2. Sphagnetum, **Gentiana Pneumonanthe** Z⁴, **Salix livida + nigricans, Urtica dioica var. microphylla** Hausmann, ***Carex loliacea*** Z⁴ im Jagen 86 (südl. Theil des Rumianekbruches). — 13. 8. Wiesen südlich vom Kopaciska-Bruch, Friedrichsfelde'r Forst, Belauf Kopytko, Wystemp: Gentiana Amarella, Platanthera viridis Z⁴, ***Salix myrtilloides*** nebst **S. aurita + myrtilloides,** Carex canescens **var. laetevirescens Aschers., Poa sudetica var. hybrida Gaud., Epilobium obscurum Rchb.** — 14. 8. Uebersiedelung nach Willenberg: Willamowen, Liebenberg, Zielonygrund, Radostowen, Reusswalde'r Forst Belauf Luckabuden, Lucka, Radzienen, Klein Lattana, Röblau, Borken: Atriplex hortense b. nitens (gebaut und verwildert), **Stellaria frieseana.**

Excursionen um Willenberg. 15. 8. Spittek, Klein und Gross Schiemanen, Grünes Gebirge bei Materschobensee, Ufer des Sawitzflusses, Kutzburgmühle, Jankowen, Kutzburg, Willenberg'er Stadtwald: Alsine viscosa, **Trifolium Lupinaster** (verdorrte Stengel), **Adenophora liliifolia,** ***Graphephorum arundinaceum*** Z³. — 16. 8. Wiesen zwischen Willenberg und Nowojewietz, sumpfige bebuschte Wiesen zwischen Waldpusch und Kollodzeygrund, Nowojewietz, Neu-Werder, Reusswalde'r Forst Belauf Dlotowken, Hügel bei Finsterdameran, private Wälder bei Jeschonowitz: **Rumex aquaticus,** ***Lycopodium inundatum*** mit L. clavatum, **Potentilla mixta Nolte.** — 17. 8. Linkes Omulefufer, Sendrowen, Wälder zwischen Sendrowen und Kiparren, Waldpusch, Willenberg: Elodea canadensis, Agrimonia odorata Z⁴. — 18. 8. Linkes Ufer des Omulef, Gut und Wald Omulef, Glauch, Wessolowen, Rocklass, Willenberg: **Gnaphalium luteo-album** Z³, **Cephalanthera rubra, Campanula Cervicaria, Calamagrostis arundinacea + lanceolata** (zwischen den reinen Arten). — 19. 8. Willenberg'er Abbau, Lasuch-Wäldchen, Montwitz, Gr. Piewnitz: **Lycopodium inundatum** Z³, Carex canescens b. laetevirescens Aschers., **Hieracium boreale,** Viscum album auf Betula verrucosa, **Cerastium glomeratum.** — 20. 8. Röblau, Birkenthal, Hügel bei Klein Lattana, Radszienen: **Plantago arenaria,** Pulmonaria angustifolia. — 21. 8. Gr. Piewnitz, Wiseggen, Wiseggen'er See, Baranowen, Gr. Przesdzienk: Betula humilis, **S. aurita + livida, Lycopodium inundatum.** — 22. 8. Ruhetag. — 23. 8. Uebersiedlung nach Ortelsburg.

Excursionen um Ortelsburg. (2. Untersuchung.) — 24. 8. Corpellen'er Forst, Belauf Mittenwalde, „Borek" am Südwestufer des Seedanzig'er See's, Lentzienen: **Linnaea borealis, Calamagrostis**

arundinacea + lanceolata (zwischen den reinen Arten), Trifolium alpestre b. glabratum v. Klinggr. I neben Tr. alpestre und Tr. medium. — 25. 8. In Begleitung des Herrn Rudloff nach Bel. Mittenwalde, Ittowken, Nordufer des kleinen Schobensee's bei Materschobensee, Grünes Gebirge, Försterei Materschobensee: **Graphephorum arundinaceum** (Kraut). Heftiges Gewitter aus W. — 26. 8. Belauf Mittenwalde, Lentzienen, Wiesen um Maschingrund, abgelassener Matersee: **Salix aurita + livida, Calamagrostis arundinacea + lanceolata** Z[3], **Pedicularis Sceptr. Carolin.** — 27. 8. Fiugatten, Nordufer des grossen Haus-See's, Oberförsterei Corpellen, Bel. Mittenwalde, Johannisthal, rechtes Ufer des Schobenflusses bis zur Eisenbahnbrücke, Bel. Ulonsk (Corpellen'er Forst): Oryza clandestina, Rubus plicatus, **Cypripedium Calceolus**, Cirsium oleraceum + palustre, Centaurea iacea var. decipiens, Lycopodium complanatum var. anceps. Besuch bei Herrn Oberförster Seehusen, welcher mir unter anderen Saxifraga Hirculus von Sczicznonnek und **Aster Amellus** aus dem Bel. Ulonsk vorlegte. — 28. 8. In Begleitung des Herrn Apotheker Mahlke und seinem Bruder nach dem Scharfschützenplatze im Bel. Mittenwalde: **Rumex obtusifolius + crispus.** — 31. 8. Beutnersdorf A., Bel. Ulonsk, Torfstiche westlich von Frenzken, Ostufer des grossen Schobensee's: Melilotus officinalis Desr., **Dianthus superbus, Carlina acaulis** nebst **fr. caulescens,** Inula hirta, Carex riparia, Gentiana Amarella. An der Fortsetzung dieser Excursion wurde ich durch die Dazwischenkunft eines Bauern aus Leynau verhindert, der mich trotz der Vorzeigung der Legitimation vom Landrathsamt für einen „Spion" hielt und unter den gröblichsten Insulten auf offener Strasse zum Amtsvorsteher: Herrn von Halle auf Frenzken, zu gehen zwang. In Abwesenheit des Letzteren gelang es jedoch seinem energischen Beamten, mich aus der unangenehmen Lage zu befreien. — 1. 9. Corpellen'er Forst Bel. Neu Gisöwen, Reusswalde'r Forst Bel. Lipnik, Hamerudau'er Wald: **Pulsatilla patens + pratensis,** Viola arenaria + canina. — 2. 9. Beutnersdorf B., Lehmanen Ostufer des grossen Sylven-See's bei Zielonken, Westufer des Waldpusch-See's, Waldpusch, Linde. Wiederum begleitete mich Herr Apotheker Rudloff, welcher **Vicia monantha** auf Feldern bei Lindenberg gefunden und mir mitgetheilt hatte. Wir fanden: **Salix aurita + livida, Gentiana Amarella** (bis 0,40 m hohe Exempl.), Platanthera viridis Z[4] (gänzlich verdorrt), **Rumex crispus + obtusifolius.** — 3. 9. Ortelsburg'er Stadtwald, rechtes Ufer des Waldpuschflusses: Cirsium oleraceum + palustre, Viola epipsila + palustris, **Galium aristatum, Calamagrostis arundinacea + lanceolata** Z[3], Stellaria crassifolia. — 4. 9. Uebersiedelung nach Mensguth.

Excursionen um Mensguth. 5. 9. Mensguth, Jablonken'er private Forst, Bel. Luisenthal, Sczepanken: **Salix aurita + livida,** Betula humilis, **Gentiana Pneumonanthe, Cerastium glomeratum, Thalictrum simplex, Pedicularis Sceptr. Carolin.** — 6. 9. Torfige Wiesen am Nordwestufer des grossen Schobensee's, Westufer des letzteren See's, Anhaltsberg, Belauf Schobensee (Corpellen'er F.), Anhaltsberge, privater Wald von Malschöwen: **Geum strictum, Salix aurita + livida,** Betula humilis, ***Crepis succisifolia Tausch*** Z[2], **Geranium molle, Rosa rubiginosa + tomentosa, Potamogeton lucens + praelonga = decipiens Nolte, Gymnadenia conopea** Z[3], **Carlina acaulis, Onobrychis viciifolia** (wild), **Sarothamnus scoparius, *Dracocephalum ruyschianum*** Jag. 304, **Calamagrostis arundinacea + lanceolata** Z[4]. — 7. 9. Ostufer des Schobensees, Wäldchen bei Damerauwolka, Torfstiche am Damerau'er Bergwäldchen: Laserpitium prutenicum, **Gymnadenia conopea,** Viola canina + riviniana, ***Astrantia maior*** Z[3], **Laserpitium latifolium** nebst **var. asperum Crntz, *Adenophora liliifolia*** Z[3], **Campanula latifolia** (selt.). — 8. 9. Olschöwken, Jablonken, priv. Wald von Jablonken, Nordabhang der Jablonken'er Berge, Westufer des kleinen und Südwestufer des grossen Lenz-See's, Erben, Luisenthal, Mensguth: **Laserpitium latifolium** nebst **var. asperum Crntz, Sambucus racemosus, Gymnadenia conopea, Euphorbia Cyparissias** (selten!), Quercus pedunculata + sessiliflora, Chara hispida (im kl. und gr. Lanzsee), ***Naias maior,* Calamagrostis arundinacea + Epigeios = C. acutiflora (Schr.) DC,** (zwischen den reinen Arten). — 9. 9. Regen. — 10. 9. Jablonken'er privater Forst, Bel. Luisenthal, Südostufer des Dwierzut-See's, Theerwischwolla, Jablonken'er privater Wald, Bel. Tannenwalde, privater Wald von Theerwischwolka, Grodziaken, Ruttkowen, Geislingen, Augusthof, Szcepanken, Wappendorf'er Bauernwald, Wappendorf: **Epilobium obscurum,** Oryza clandestina, **Trifolium rubens, Gentiana Pneumonanthe,** Polystichum cristatum, Carex Goodenoughii var. iuncella, Geum strictum, Polyporus sulphureus an Salix alba. — 11. 9. Sczepanken, Geislingen, Dimmern, Hasenberg, Kobulten'er privater Wald, Kobulten, quer über die Fläche des abgelassenen Dimmern-See's nach Mensguth zurück: Euonymus verrucosa, Quercus sessiliflora, **Polypodium vulgare,** Phegopteris Dryopteris. Die Fläche des abgelassenen Dimmernsee's ist schwierig zu überschreiten und bot nichts Bemerkenswerthes. Triodia decumbens. — 12. 9. Ziegelei von Malschöwen, privater Wald von Malschöwen, kleiner See am Ostrand dieses Waldes, Anhaltsberge, Westufer des Schobensee's. In Mensguth: Malva silvestris mit Puccinia Malvacearum, **Salix livida + nigricans** (1 Strauch an der Chaussee), **Stellaria frieseana,** ***Calamagrostis arundinacea + lanceolata*** (mit den reinen Arten), Fagus silvatica (angebaut), **Potentilla mixta Nolte,** Rhynchospora alba, **Drosera longifolia + rotundifolia** (zwischen den reinen Arten), ***Lycopodium inundatum,*** Sarothamnus scoparius, **Salix aurita + livida.** — 13. 9. Waldige Schlucht südlich von Wappendorf, Schubertsguth, Julienfelde, Südufer des Samplatten'er See's, Mietzelchen, Kl. Rauschken, Malschöwen, Mensguth: Utricularia minor, **Drosera longifolia + rotundifolia** (zwischen den reinen Arten) Lycoperdon caelatum, Centaurea paniculata fl. alb., Oryza clandestina, **Potentilla mixta Nolte,** Rosa canina var. dumetorum, ***Callitriche autumnalis*** im Samplatten'er See, **Euphorbia Cyparissias** (mit rothen Hochblättern). — 14. 9. Heimfahrt.

Zum Schluss statte ich hiermit Herrn Landrath v. Klitzing, sowie den Herren Oberförstern Seehusen-Corpellen, Staubesand-Reusswalde, Eyser-Friedrichsfelde, Nitsche-Ratzeburg und Morant-Puppen für das freundliche Entgegenkommen meinen besten Dank ab. In gleicher Weise schulde ich den Herren Apothekern Hess-Passenheim, Rudloff und Mahlke-Ortelsburg für die erzeigte Gastfreundschaft grossen Dank.

Es folgt dann der

Bericht des Herrn Ludwig Valentin, über seine Erforschung des Kreises Strasburg.

Ostern 1886 gab Herr Professor Caspary mir den Auftrag, eine Untersuchung der Flora des Kreises Strasburg in Westpr. zu übernehmen. Die Excursionen dauerten vom 2. Mai bis 4. September einschl. Während dieser Zeit habe ich den Kreis nur einmal untersuchen können; nur einzelne Stellen habe ich zweimal berührt.

Hierbei möchte ich Gelegenheit nehmen, den Herren Rittergutzbesitzern **Abramowski**-Schwetz und **Moeller**-Pluskowenz, bei denen ich während mehrerer Wochen Aufenthalt hatte, für die freundlichst gewährte Gastfreundschaft meinen besten Dank zu sagen, ingleichen auch dem Pächter der königlichen Mühle Gremenz, Herrn **Caspari,** der mir zweimal Nachtquartier gewährte.

2. 5. Hinfahrt nach Jablonowo. — 3. 5. Zw. Jablonowo und Schloss Jablonowo: Holosteum umbellatum; an der Lutrine zwischen Jablonowo und Szczepanken: Salix longifolia, Salix triandra concolor, Petasites officinalis. Szczepanken, Sadlinken, Jablonowo: Gagea pratensis. — 4. 5. Jablonowo, Piecewo, Jaguschewitz: Gagea pratensis. An der Lutrine: Equisetum limosum. Zw. Jaguschewitz und Lemberg: Holosteum umbellatum. Wäldchen an der Lutrine: Viola riviniana, Ranunculus auricomus, Gagea minima, Adoxa moschatellina. Zw. Lemberg und Wonsin: Gagea pratensis. Wald am Südufer des Wonsin'er See: Paris quadrifolius, Anemone ranunculoides, Viola mirabilis. — 5. 5. Sturm. Die Temperatur war im Laufe des Tages von 0 Gr. bis 4 Gr. — 6. 5. Piecewo, Hochheim, Goral: Carex verna, Holosteum umbellatum. Zw. Goral und Godziskeu, Südrand der Wilhelmsberg'er Forst: Luzula pilosa, Carex stricta, verna, montana, Potentilla cinerea, Pulsatilla patens $Z^1 V^4$. Zw. Godzisken und Tomken im Wäldchen westlich vom Sumowko'er See: Andromeda poliifolia, Drosera rotundifolia, Valeriana dioica. Tomken, Josephinenthal, Kamin, Piecewo: Ranunculus auricomus, Gagea pratensis. — 7. 5. Sadlinken, Buchwalde, Waldheim: Salix cuspidata, Gagea pratensis, Carex ericetorum. Gr. Plowenz, Neudorf: Gagea pratensis. See bei Waldheim: Carex vulgaris. Neudorf, Buggoral längs des Eisenbahndammes nach Jablonowo. — 8. 5. Zw. Mileszewo und Czekanowo: Gagea pratensis. Wald von Czekanowo: Carex montana, digitata, ericetorum, Asarum europaeum, Viola riviniana, silvestris.

9. 5. Uebersiedelung nach Strasburg. — 10. 5. Wald am Westufer des Niskebrodno-See: Hierochloa australis, Melica nutans, Carex ericetorum; Wiese an der Nordspitze des Sees: Cardamine amara, Cineraria palustris, Valeriana dioica. — 11. 5. Karbowo'er Wald zwischen Strasburg und der Südspitze des Bachottek-See: Viola arenaria, V. riviniana, Pulsatilla patens. Wald westlich vom Bachottek- und Straszyna-See: Sedum Telephium, Viola arenaria + riviniana, Hierochla australis, Aquilegia vulgaris, Lilium Martagon, Melica nutans, Potentilla alba, Daphne Mezereum. Ueber Zbiczno, Zmiewko nach Strasburg: Gagea pratensis. Wald östlich Niskebrodno-See: Paris quadrifolius,

Asperula odorata, Aquilegia vulgaris, Asarum europaeum, Convallaria maialis, Hierochloa australis, Melica nutans. — 12. 5. Chaussee von Strasburg nach Jablonowo, Wald zu Lipowietz und Bartniki: Asarum europaeum, Sanicula europaea (Laub). Wald östlich Choyno: Lycopodium clavatum. Niewiersch, Mzanno, U. F. Schöngrund: Holosteum umbellatum. Belauf Schöngrund: Daphne Mezereum, Asperula odorata. Zw. Mczanno und Strasburg: Fragaria elatior, Holosteum umbellatum. Abhänge bei der Ziegelei Borgwinkel: Salvia pratensis. — 13. 5. Bei der Oberförsterei Wilhelmsberg: Viola riviniana + silvatica, Pulsatilla patens. Sossno, Zumowo, Naymowo, Geistl. Kruschin: Gagea pratensis. — 14. 5. Wiesen am Nordufer der Drewenz zw. Strasburg und Mzanno: Ranunculus auricomus, Arabis arenosa. Salix caprea, purpurea, viminalis. Valeriana dioica, Holosteum umbellatum. — 15. 5. Ich durchsuchte den Wald östlich vom Niskebrodno-See. — 17. 5. Drewenzufer zw. Strasburg und Komini: Armeria vulgaris, Holosteum umbellatum, Arabis thaliana, arenosa, Papaver Argemone. Bei Wapno: Pulsatilla pratensis. Gr. Gorczenitza. Kl. Gorczenitza, Opalenitza, Moczadlo: Corynephorus canescens, Herniaria glabra. Sumpf bei Kl. Gorczenitza: Luzula sudetica a) pallescens, Alchemilla vulgaris, Holosteum umbellatum, Gagea pratensis. — 18. 5. Szczuka, Gottartowo, Dzierno, Sobierczisno, Komorowo, Jastrzembie, Swierczyn: Holosteum umbellatum, Berteroa incana, Carex montana, Equisetum silvaticum. Erlenbruch südlich Swierczyn: Cardamine amara, Viola palustris. Cielenta, Michelau. — 19. bis 22. 5. war ich in Danzig behufs Stellung zur Superrevision. — 24. 5. Zwischen Strasburg und Cielenta: Papaver Argemone, Cardamine amara. Cielenta Wald: Polygonatum multiflorum, Phyteuma spicatum, Daphne Mezereum, Ranunculus lanuginosus, Convallaria maialis. Asarum europaeum, Paris quadrifolius, Viola mirabilis, Corydalis cava, Corydalis intermedia (den ganzen Südrand entlang), Aiuga genevensis, Asperula odorata, Platanthera bifolia, Pulmonaria angustifolia, Schlucht auf dem Wege nach Neuhof: Geranium robertianum, Corydalis intermedia, Veronica Beccabunga, Cineraria palustris. Kosziari, Swierczyn. — 25. 5. Zw. Strasburg und Szabda: Salvia pratensis. Szabda, Griewenhof: Polygala comosa. Bobrowo, Smolniki, Choyno, Szabda: Corynephorus canescens, Herniaria glabra, Armeria vulgaris, Sedum maximum, Peucedanum Oreoselinum, Holosteum umbellatum. — 26. 5. Karbowoer Wald. Zw. Strasburg und Karbowo: Potentilla alba, Melica nutans, Hierochloa australis, Galium boreale. Karbowo, Margarethenhof. Schonung zwischen Bachottek- und Straszyn-See: Asperula odorata, Paris quadrifolius, Platanthera bifolia, Thalictrum aquilegifolium, Aquilegia vulgaris, Daphne Mezereum, Carex montana, Sanicula europaea, Galium boreale. Wald westlich vom Straszyn-See: Anemone silvestris Z^3 V^1; in der Schlucht im Süden des Waldes: Scorzonera humilis Z^1 V^3, Pulsatilla patens. Von Gremenz nach Schaffarnia durch die Oberförsterei Wilhelmsberg: Potentilla alba, Lycopodium Selago, Turritis glabra, Pulsatilla patens, Equisetum silvaticum. Ich nächtigte bei dem Pächter der kön. Mühle in Gremenz: Herrn Caspari. — 27. 5. Wald am Ostrand des Zbiczno-See: Carex montana, digitata, Salix rosmarinifolia, Hierochloa australis, Melica nutans, Scorzonera humilis. Belauf Rittelbruch Jag. 32, 55: Lycopodium complanatum, L. Selago. Nach dem Czichen-, Robotno-, Dembno-See durch Belauf Rittelbruch und Tengowitz nach Gremenz. Jag. 121: Corydalis intermedia (gelbes Laub), Listera ovata. Zwischen Gremenz und Bachottek: Fragaria viridis, Papaver Argemone, Geranium pusillum. Wald östlich vom Straszyn-See: Pirola secunda, P. uniflora, P. umbellata, P. rotundifolia, Geranium boreale. Zw. Bachottek und Südspitze des Bachottek-See: Dianthus carthusianorum, Salvia pratensis. — 28. 5. Karbowoer Wald am Ostrand des Niskebrodno-See: Evonymus europaeus, Asarum europaeum, Paris quadrifolius, Ranunculus lanuginosus, Platanthera bifolia, Sedum maximum, Trifolium montanum. — 29. 5. Drewenzwiesen zwischen Strasburg und Kantilla: Trollius europaeus Z^1 V^1, Holcus lanatus, Asclepias Vincetoxicum, Phleum Böhmeri, Turritis glabra. Karbowo'er Wald, Landweg nach Neumark: Spergula Morisonii, Potentilla alba, Fragaria viridis, Pulsatilla pratensis.

30. 5. Uebersiedelung nach Gurzno. — 31. 5. Zwischen Gurzno und U. F. Gurzno: Populus balsamifera, Alchemilla vulgaris, Turritis glabra. Wiese zur U. F. Gurzno: Luzula sudetica a) pallescens, Campanula persicifolia. Belauf Gurzno: Carex digitata, Pulsatilla patens, Lilium Martagon, Daphne Mezereum, Galium boreale, Hedera Helix, Pirola uniflora, Scorzonera humilis. Schonung Jag. 118, 129: Fragaria viridis, Geranium sanguineum, Datura Stramonium, Potentilla alba. Jag. 111: Dracocephalum ruyschianum. — 1. 6. Zwischen Gurzno und Oberförsterei Ruda: Papaver Argemone, Turritis glabra. Belauf Borrek: Potentilla alba, Pulsatilla patens, Geranium sanguineum, Hierochloa australis, Melica nutans, Lilium Martagon, Aquilegia vulgaris. Zaborowo, Bartnitzka, Bachor: Populus candicans. Bachor, Miesionskowo, Gurzno: Alopecurus geniculatus. — 2. 6. An der Szumny Zelroj

bei Gurzno: Allium ursinum Z⁴ V², Asclepias Vincetoxicum, Carex curta, Lycopodium Selago, Sanicula europaea. — 8. 6. Beläufe Gurzno und Neuwelt: Potentilla alba, Ranunculus polyanthemus, Hypochoeris maculata, Scorzonera humilis, Geranium sanguineum. See Jag. 83: Pirola uniflora. Belauf Brinsk Jag. 8, 6, 5: Dianthus carthusianorum, Helianthemum Chamaecistus, Cytisus ratisbonensis. Adl. Brinsk'er Wald: Pulsatilla patens, Pirola umbellata. Zwischen U. F. Brinsk und Gurzno, Belauf Buczkowo: Cytisus ratisbonensis. — 4. 6. Ich hatte Gelegenheit an den Brinsk'er See zu fahren, theils auf Gestellen, theils quer durch die Jagen. Am Brinsk'er See: Carex flava, C. echinata, C. dioica, C. paniculata, Cardamine amara. Belauf Buczkowo: Astragalus glycyphyllos, Lilium Martagon, Dianthus carthusianorum, Aquilegia vulgaris. Jag. 138: Corydalis cava, Neottia Nidus avis. Am Wapionken'er Mühlenteich bei Gurzno: Chaerophyllum temulum, Allium ursinum, Carex remota, Mercurialis perennis. — 5. 6. Durch die Oberförsterei Ruda nach Brezezin, U. F. Rehberg: Pirola umbellata, Phegopteris Dryopteris, Carex leporina, Neottia Nidus avis, Sanicula europaea. Zwischen U. F. Rehberg und Guttowo: Crepis praemorsa. Belauf Borrek: Phleum Böhmeri, Fragaria viridis, Sedum maximum, Geranium sanguineum, Potentilla alba. — 7. 6. Belauf Neuwelt. Jag. 65: Arnica montana, Crepis praemorsa, Hypochoeris maculata, Trollius europaeus. Jag. 64 Dracocephalum ruyschianum; Jag. 45. *Scorzonera purpurea Z¹ V¹*, Dracocephalum ruychianum. Adl. Brinsk'er Wald: Dracocephalum ruyschianum, Helianthemum Chamaecistus, Crepis praemorsa, Hypochoeris maculata. Zw. Neuwelt (Dorf) und Gurzno: Spergula Morisonii. — 8. 6. Regen. — 9. 6. Am Gurzno'er und Mühlenteich-See: Cineraria palustris, Chaerophyllum temulum, Carex dioica, Holcus lanatus. Zw. Abbau Gurzno und Gurzno: Veronica Teucrium, Teesdalea nudicaulis. — 10. 6. O. F. Ruda, Guttowo, Samin'er-See: Phleum Böhmeri, Salix nigricans, Spergula Morisonii. Am Samin'er See: Phleum Böhmeri, Veronica Teucrium, Scutellaria galericulata. Radosk, Bartnitzka, Gurzno: Astragalus arenarius.

11. 6. Uebersiedelung nach Lautenburg. — 15. 6. Zwischen Lautenburg und Zielun: Jasione montana. Oberförsterei Lautenburg Jag. 41, 27, 12, 13, 9, 10: Orchis maculata, Geranium sanguineum, Arnica montana, Genista tinctoria, Trollius europaeus, Lilium Martagon, Polygonatum anceps, Pulsatilla patens, Pirola chlorantha. Zwischen Zielun und Neuhof: Neeslea paniculata, Teesdalea nudicaulis. Ostrand des Belaufs Neuhof: Hypochoeris maculata, Galium boreale, Arnica montana, Gypsophila fastigiata, Pirola umbellata. Neuhof, Ciborz, Lautenburg. — 16. 6. An der Welle zwischen Lautenburg und Ciborz: Carex paniculata, Thalictrum angustifolium, Th. aquilegifol., Triglochin palustris, Veronica Teucrium, Salix nigricans, Dianthus deltoides, Equisetum palustre α) polystachyum. Ciborz, Kempenbruch, Bladowo, Jellen: Galium uliginosum. Teesdalea nudicaulis, Spergula Morisonii, Dianthus deltoides, Helichrysum arenarium. — 17. 6. Lautenburg, Kotty, Wampiorsk, Bruch östlich vom Jellen-See: Teesdalea nudicaulis, Ledum palustre, Vaccinium oxycoccos, Juncus squarrosus. Wampiersk, Jellen-See, Czekanowko: Stellaria glauca. Cynosurus cristatus. Zwischen Czekanowko und Lautenburg: Anthyllis Vulneraria, Euphorbia Cyparissias Z³ V¹, Sanguisorba minor. Lautenburger Stadtforst: Galium boreale, Arnica montana, Lilium Martagon, Convallaria majalis, Linnaea borealis Z³ V². — 18. 6. Zw. Lautenburg und Jamielnik: Arnoseris pusilla. Belauf Kienheide. Jag. 49, 48, 34, 21, 19, 29: Arnica montana, Orobus niger, Hypochoeris maculata, Sanicula europaea. Jag. 21: Salix livida, Cimicifuga foetida, Carlina acaulis Z¹ V¹, Dracocephalum ruyschianum. Belauf Neuhof: Pirola chlorantha, Scorzonera humilis. — 19. 6. Ostufer der Welle zwischen Lautenburg und Chelst: Salix nigricans, Dianthus deltoides Helianthemum Chamaecistus, Fragaria viridis, Actaea spicata, Listera ovata. Belauf Kielpin: Jasione montana, Arnica montana, Geranium sanguineum. Landweg östlich der Chaussee nach Lautenburg: Teesdalea nudicaulis. — 21. 6. Südufer des Lautenburg'er See, zum Theil auch Lautenburg'er Stadtforst: Carex dioica, Listera ovata, Paris quadrifolius, Laserpitium latifolium Z¹ V¹ (Laub). Südufer: Phegopteris Dryopteris, Malva Alcea, Vicia cassubica und silvatica, Anthericum ramosum, Trifolium rubens. — 22. 6. Regen. — 23. 6. Regen. Westufer der Welle zw. Lautenburg und Kurjad: Actaea spicata, Polypodium vulgare Z¹ V¹. Aecker südlich Kurjad: Spergula Morisonii. Belauf Slupp, Jag. 116: **Melittis Melissophyllum** Z¹ V². Kowallik, Bolleszin, Slupp, Wlewsk, Lautenburg. — 24. 6. Lautenburg, Slupp, Zalesie: Peucedanum Oreoselinum. Zwischen Zalesie und Wlewsk, Adl. Wlewsk'er Wald: Actaea spicata, **Melittis Melissophyllum** Z¹ V², Digitalis ambigua Z² V², Anthericum ramosum, Lilium Martagon. — 25. 6. Lautenburger Stadtforst, südlich Lautenburg'er See: Cimicifuga foetida Z¹ V¹, Monotropa Hypopitys, Pirola chlorantha. Oberförsterei Buda, Belauf Eichhorst: **Melittis Melissophyllum**, Cimicifuga foetida. Am Wletsch-See: Coralliorrhiza innata, Mi-

crostylis monophylla. Belauf Rehberg: Cimicifuga foetida, Melittis Melissophyllum, Digitalis ambigua. Wlewsk'er Wald südlich der Chaussee nach Lautenburg: Melittis Melissophyllum. — 26. 6. Nach Jamielnik, Zwossno-See, Klonowo, Nossek durch den Belauf Klonowo: Carex dioica, Lycopodium annotinum, Chimophila umbellata. Abhänge der Braniza bei Nossek: Polypodium vulgare, Cimicifuga foetida. Belauf Buczkowo: Melittis Melissophyllum. Czarni-, Brinsk'er-See, Belauf Klonowo: Arnica montana. — 28. 6. Wlewsk, Zalesie, Gr. Leszno-See: Dianthus deltoides. Belauf Rehberg Jag. 234, 229, 220, 219, 218: Monotropa Hypopitys, Melittis Melissophyllum, Vicia cassubica und silvatica, Neottia Nidus avis, Cimicifuga foetida. Belauf Eichorst Jag. 226, Piassetz'er See: Scheuchzeria palustris. — 29. 6. Zw. Jamielnik und U. F. Kienheide: Arnosera pusilla. Belauf Klonowo Jag. 64, 65, 66, 32, 33, 51: Cimicifuga foetida, Gypsophila fastigiata, Arnica montana, Cephalanthera rubra Z^1 V^1, Neottia Nidus avis, Ranunculus polyanthemus, Prunella grandiflora. Adl. Brinsk'er Wald südlich der Kolonie Brinsk: Arnica montana, Gymnadenia conopea Z^1 V^1, Helianthemum Chamaecistus, Trifolium rubens. — 30. 6. Wampiersk, Tarczyn, Grondy-See, Wampiersk: Malva Alcea, Ranunculus Lingua, Dianthus deltoides.

1. Juli. Uebersiedelung nach Schwetz. — 2. 7. Längs der Drewenz über Ostrowo nach Schramowo: Carlina vulgaris, Phleum Böhmeri, Veronica longifolia, Achillea cartilaginea, Ranunculus flammula, Triglochin maritima. Zw. Schramowo und Pokrzydowo: Papaver Rhoeas, Anthyllis Vulneraria. Pokrzydowo, Jaikowo, Schwetz: Phleum Böhmeri. — 3. 7. Durch den Belauf Dlugimost, dann längs der Drewenz nach Wilhelmsthal und Neuhof: Pulsatilla patens, Sanguisorba officinalis, Anthericum ramosum. Jag. 255/56: Drosera rotundifolia und anglica, Senecio paludosus, Achillea cartilaginea, Veronica longifolia. Von der Südspitze des Bachottek-See nach Kantilla, Schwetz: Malva Alcea. — 5. 7. Nach Gut Dlugimost, durch den Belauf Dlugimost: Monotropa Hypopitys, Cimophila umbellata, Arnica montana (Jag. 251), Anthericum ramosum. Zw. Dlugimost und Janowko: Trifolium incarnatum, Phleum Böhmeri Z^5 V^1. Janowko, Poln. Brzozie, Augustenhof: Dianthus deltoides. Torfbruch bei Augustenhof: Sparganium minimum. Gr. Glemboczek, Jaikowo. — 6. 7. ging ich nach Jag. 210, Belauf Eichhorst der Oberförsterei Buda um Melittis Melissophyllum zu holen. — 7. 7. Zw. Pokrzydowo und Zastawien, See bei Schramowo: Malva Alcea. Oberförsterei Wilhelmsberg, Belauf Tengowitz: Chimophila umbellata, Linnaea borealis Jag. 81). Belauf Kaluga: Pirola chlorantha, Pulsatilla pratensis (blühend), Geranium sanguineum, Anthericum ramosum Dianthus arenarius, Lilium Martagon. — 8. 7. Torfbruch südöstlich Schwetz: Lotus uliginosus, Hypericum tetrapterum, Linum catharticum. — 9. 7. Wiesen südlich der Braniza, zwischen Ostrow und Dlugimost: Salix rosmarinifolia, Epipactis palustris, Dianthus superbus, Scabiosa columbaria, Thysselinum palustre. Zw. Dlugimost und Kl. Glemboczek: Carlina acaulis (Jag. 258 des Belaufs Dlugimost). Miala-See: Lysimachia thyrsiflora, Ranunculus Lingua. Abhänge des Gr. Glemboczek-See: Verbena officinalis. Gr. Glemboczek, Sopien-See, Dlugimost. — 10. 7. Regen. — 12. 7. Zw. U. F. Dlugimost und Bartnitzka durch den Belauf Dlugimost: Potentilla alba, Monotropa Hypopitys. Bartnitzka, Brondzaw. Bei Bacher Lamium maculatum. Jastrzembie, Kl. Lascewo: Phleum Böhmeri, Sedum maximum, Jasione montana. Zwischen Kl. Lascewo und U. F. Dlugimost durch den Belauf Dlugimost: Asarum europaeum, Thalictrum minus, Monotropa Hypopitys, Carlina acaulis, Dianthus arenarius. — 13. 7. Dlugimost, Samin'er See, Zembrze: Dianthus superbus, Epipactis palustris, Ranunculus Lingua. Zembrze, Janowko, Dlugimost: Seseli annuum, Malva Alcea. Belauf Dlugimost Jag. 257, 259, 260: Carlina acaulis Z^3 V^4, Geranium sanguineum. — 14. 7. Zwischen Kl. Glemboczek und Poln. Brzozie: Euphrasia officinalis fr. crenata, Fragaria viridis. Sossno, Zembrze, Drepki-See, Dlugimost: Carlina vulgaris, Scrophularia aquatica. — 15. 7. Regen. Jaikowo, Pokrzydowo, Gremenz: Verbena officinalis. Durch Belauf Tengowitz nach dem Rettno-See. Ich nächtigte in Gremenz-Mühle. — 16. 7. Zwischen Gremenz und U. F. Tengowitz durch den Belauf Tengowitz: Cimicifuga foetida (Jag. 83). Am Forsthause: Veronica Teucrium. Am Tengowitz-See: Drosera rotundifolia und anglica, Carex limosa. Belauf Kaluga, Jag. 148, 181, 200, 199, 176, 142, 112: Gypsophila fastigiata. — 17. 7. Wiesen am Flösskanal zwischen Dlugimost und Bartnitzka: Dianthus superbus, Epipactis palustris, Juncus glaucus. Sphagnetum am Ostrande des Jagen 243 des Belaufs Dlugimost: **Sedum villosum** Z^3 V^3, neu für's Gebiet. — 19. 7. Wald westlich Bachottek und Strassyn-See, Pokrzydowo: Anthericum ramosum, Betonica officinalis, Serratula tinctoria, Viscum album auf Salix fragilis.

20. 7. Umzug nach Wrotzk. — 21. 7. Zwischen Wrotzk und Belauf Nasswald d. O. F. Gollub: Ononis arvensis, Anthyllis Vulneraria. Belauf Nasswald: Monotropa Hypopitys, Spiraea

filipendula, Serratula tinctoria, Clinopodium vulgare, Lilium Martagon, Inula hirta $Z^1 V^1$; Jag. 137: Listera ovata; Cimicifuga feetida Jag. 141. — 22. 7. Von Wrotzk durch den Belauf Neueiche nach Sloszewo: Astragalus glycyphyllos: Anthericum ramosum. Zw. Sloszewo und Malken: Armeria vulgaris. Schutzbezirk Malken Jagen 42. 43., Malken, Wrotzk: Melampyrum arvense. — 23. 7. ging ich durch die Beläufe Tokaren und Biberthal bis zur U. F. Biberthal; die Flora ist dieselbe wie im Belauf Nasswald. An den Abhängen der Drewenz bei der U. F. Biberthal: Dianthus prolifer, Astragalus arenarius. — 24. 7. Nach Przeszkoda, Neudorf, Bach zw. Przeszkoda u. Sawadda: Ranunculus Lingua, Spartium scoparium. Belauf Baranitz: Astragalus arenarius, Genista tinctoria. Lindhof, Lobdowo, Wrotzk. — 26. 7. Zwischen Wrotzk und Karczewo Carlina vulgaris, Cirsium acaule. Aecker zwischen Karczewo und Lobdowo: Hypericum humifusum. Lobdowo, Wimsdorf, entlang der Lohrbach bis Friedeck: Oenanthe Phellandrium. — 27. 7. Ciesyn, Pusta Dombrowken, Slosoewo: Armeria vulgaris, Eryngium planum, Origanum vulgare, Ononis arvensis. Entlang der Drewenz bis Schöngrund: Scrophularia aquatica, Achillea cartilaginea, Veronica longifolia, Senecio paludosus. Belauf Schöngrund: Epipactis latifolia. Anthericum ramosum, Pulsatilla patens, Asperula odorata. Schlucht zwischen dem Forsthause Schöngrund und Malken: Thysselinum palustre, Melampyrum arvense. — 28. 7. Wrotzk, Buchenhagen, Nieszywiens, Dombrowken: Ononis arvensis. Buczek, Herrmannsruhe: Falcaria Rivini. Friedeck. — 29. 7. Feldrain bei Friedeck: Carduus nutans. Die Lohrbach entlang durch Belauf Malken bis Tillitz. — 30. 7. Zwischen Karczewo und Lipnitza: Cuscuta europaea, Cirsium acaule. Entlang der Lohrbach nach Kl.-Bulkowo: Ranunculus aquatilis. Felixowo, Lobdowo: Cuscuta europaea, Ononis arvensis. In Wrotzk: Agrimonia odorata. — 31. 7. Zwischen Wrotzk und Hammer längs der Lohrbach: Polemonium coeruleum $Z^4 V^1$. Zwischen Hammer und Josephat: Astragalus arenarius, Plantago arenaria, Oenothera biennis. Josephat, Pusta Dombrowken, die Drewenz entlang: Achillea cartilaginea, Veronica longifolia, Senecio paludosus, Salix nigricans, Seseli annuum, Veronica spicata, Armeria vulgaris. Schlucht am Ostrand des Belaufs Neueiche: Campanula Trachelium, Veronica spicata, Scrophularia aquatica, Verbascum thapsiforme. — 2. 8. Lobdowo, Dembowalonka: Panicum Crus galli, Ononis arvensis. Bruch zwischen Friesenhof und Nieszywiens: Veronica scutellata. Drosera rotundifolia, Cirsium acaule $Z^4 V^1$ u. fr. caulescens, Chaerophyllum temulum. Hermannsruhe: Cirsium acaule. — 3. 8. Wrotzk, Malken, Niewiersch: Eryngium planum, Armeria vulgaris. Oberförst. Gollub, Belauf Strasburg: Betonica officinalis, Arnica montana, Astragalus glycyphyllos, Selinum Carvifolia, Clinopodium vulgare, Sanicula europaea. — 4. 8. Regen. — 5. 8. Zwischen Motika und Kollat: Papaver dubium. An d. Drewenz zwischen Kollat und Biberthal: Achillea cartilaginea, Senecio paludosus, Helianthemum Chamaecistus, Veronica spicata. Belauf Nasswald Jag. 139: Cimicifuga foetida $Z^1 V^1$, Helianthemum Chamaecistus, Spiraea filipendula. Jag. 138 Asperula tinctoria $Z^1 V^1$.

6. 8. Umzug nach Pluskowenz. — 7. 8. Zw. Pluskowenz u. Piontkowo: Falcaria Rivini. Zw. Piontkowo und Gr. Radewisk: Armeria vulgaris. Am Kl. Radewisk'er See: Thysselinum palustre, Selinum Carvifolia. Wald nördlich vom Kl. Radewisk'er See: Anthericum ramosum, Sedum maximum, Clinopodium vulgare, Serratula tinctoria. Kl. Pulkowo, Pluskowenz. — 9. 8. Pluskowenz, Napole, Gajewo: Falcaria Rivini, Trifolium montanum, Carlina vulgaris. Zw. Gajewo u. Leszno: Monotropa Hypopitys, Helianthemum Chamaecistus. Brüche westl. Vorwerk Gajewo: Cyperus fuscus, Utricularia vulgaris, Calla palustris, Dianthus superbus, Saxifraga Hirculus, Thysselinum palustre. Zwischen Leszno und Sohulka Bruch am Nordende des Okonin-See: Vaccinium oxycoccos, Drosera rotundifolia und anglica, Carex limosa. Belauf Skemsk: Helianthemum Chamaecistus, Potentilla alba, Pulsatilla patens. Skemsk, Gajewo. — 10. 8. Zwischen Pluskowenz und Kelpin: Palcaria Rivini. Ostrowi, Galiczewo, Galiczewko, Lipnitza, Pluskowenz: Anthyllis Vulneraria, Cirsium acaule. — 11. 8. Kreis Thorn. Bruch nordöstlich von Schönseė, am Ackerrand: Ononis arvensis. Bruch südlich Schönsee bis Chelmoniec: Utricularia vulgaris. Kreis Strasburg. Chelmoniec Ostrowitt, Napole: Eryngium planum. — 12. 8. Kelpin, Obitzkau: Astragalus arenarius. Am Obitzkau'er See: Lysimachia thyrsiflora, Barbaraea arcuata, Utricularia vulgaris. Zwischen Kronzno und Gollub: Onobrychis viciifolia. Drewenzufer zwischen Gollub und der Mündung des Ostrowitt'er Fliess: Achillea cartilaginea, Thalictrum angustifolium. Am Ostrowitt'er Fliess: Scrophularia aquatica, Lamium maculatum, Campanula Trachelium. — 13. 8. Dembowalonka'er Wald: Hypericum montanum, Carduus nutans, Spartium scoparium. Dembowalonka, Weinsdorf, Gr. Radewisk, Piontkowo: Spartium scoparium, Ononis arvensis. — 14. 8. Pluskowenz, Otterode, Friederikendorf: Alisma arcuatum, Teucrium Scordium.

— 16. 8. Zwischen Pluskowenz und Lipnitze, Wäldchen südl. der Chaussee: Carlina vulgaris. Torfbrüche südlich der Chaussee: Thysselinum palustre, Utricularia vulgaris. Galczewo, Lissewo, Drewenzufer zw. Lissewo und Gollub: **Ranunculus fluitans**, Achillea cartilaginea, Angelica silvestris. Bergabhänge im Osten von Gollub: Eryngium planum, Centaurea maculosa. Zwischen Kronzno und Ostrowitt: Cirsium acaule, Cuscuta europaea. — 17. 8. Piontkowo, Kl. Pulkowo, längs der Lohrbach nach Weinsdorf, Gr. Pulkowo: Falcaria Rivini, Eryngium planum. — 19. 8. Wiesen zu Pluskowenz, nördlich der Chausse den Bach entlang bis Lipnitza: Calla palustris. **Alisma arcuatum,** Cyperus fuscus. — 20. 8. Napole, Gappa: Setaria viridis, Dianthus carthusianorum. Chelmoniec, den Bach entlang bis Kaldunek: Cuscuta europaea, Lamium maculatum. Kaldunek, Skemsk: Sanguisorba officinalis, Veronica spicata. — 21. 8. Belauf Skemsk, Jag. 74—77, See Jag. 76: ***Cladium Mariscus*** Z[1] V[1]. Drewenzufer zwischen Populka und Pasiekau: Senecio paludosus, Epilobium hirsutum, Achillea cartilaginea. Zw. Pasiekau und Skemsk: Veronica spicata, Sisymbrium officinale fr. leiocarpa.

23. 8. Umzug nach Hohenkirch. — 24. 8. Gr. Ksionsk'er Bruch: **Teucrium Scordium,** Veronica scutellata, Carduus nutans, Sparganium minimum. Zw. Josephsdorf und Jaworze: Panicum Crus galli, P. filiforme, Neslea paniculata. Dembowalonka'er Wald: Gnaphalium silvaticum, Carlina vulgaris, Turritis glabra, Monotropa Hypopitys. Iwanken, Osieczek, Hohenkirch: Cuscuta europaea. — 25. 8. Regen. Hohenkirch, Kl. Brudzaw, Bruch nördlich vom Wege: Cirsium acaule, Thysselinum palustre, Hypericum tetrapterum. Bruch nördlich des grossen Sees bei Osieczek. — 26. 8. Von Hohenkirch nach Jablonowo, Brüche westl. des Eisenbahndammes: Linum catharticum, Euphrasia officinalis a) pratensis, Cirsium acaule und fr. caulescens. An der Lutrine zw. Jablonowo und Szczepanken: Petasites officinalis, Dianthus superbus. Zwischen Szczepanken und Jablonowo: Falcaria Rivini. An der Lutrine zw. Jablonowo u. Jaguschewitz: Glyceria plicata Fr. Jaguschewitz, Hohenkirch. — 27. 8. Piwnitz, Osieczek, Weg südlich der Chaussee: Falcaria Rivini, **Teucrium Scordium.** See südlich Osieczek: Nasturtium amphibium, Utricularia vulgaris, Heleocharis acicularis. Zwischen dem grossen See von Osieczek und Gr. Kruschin: Armeria vulgaris. Gr. Kruschin, Kl. Brudzaw, Bruch südlich vom Wege: Heleocharis acicularis, Drosera rotundifolia. — 28. 8. Nach Osieczek, nördlich der Chaussee: Veronica arvensis fr. brachystyla. In Osieczek: Malva Alcea, Datura Stramonium, Onopordon Acanthium. Osieczek, Niesywiens, Dombrowken, Bruch westlich vom Wege: Centaurea maculosa, Cirsium acaule. Dombrowken, Gr. Brudzaw: Cirsium acaule, Melampyrum arvense. Gr. Brudzaw, Kl. Brudzaw: Cirsium acaule fr. caulescens. — 30. 8. Von Hohenkirch nach Jaguschewitz östlich des Eisenbahndammes: Tragopogon pratensis, Cuscuta europaea, Utricularia vulgaris. An der Lutrine zwischen Jaguschewitz und Lemberg: Dianthus superbus, Saxifraga Hirculus, Carex dioica, Scabiosa columbaria. Längs des Baches zwischen Lemberg und Kl. Brudzaw **Teucrium Scordium,** Sparganium simplex. — 31. 8. Piwnitz, Osieczek, Dembowalonka: Armeria vulgaris. Kleine Wiese nördlich der Chaussee: Petasites officinalis. Dembowalonka, Niesywiens: Gnaphalium silvaticum, Cirsium acaule. 1. 9. Zwischen Hohenkirch und Bukowitz: Setaria viridis. Sumpfige Baumgruppe südlich des Weges: Aspidium spinulosum. Lemberg, Gr. Kruschin, Friedrichshuld, Dombrowken: Melampyrum arvense. Osieczek, Jaworze, Bruch südöstlich Jaworze: Triticum caninum, Cirsium acaule, Carduus nutans. Ueber Dembowalonka nach Opieczek. — 4. 9. Rückfahrt nach Neufahrwasser.

Es folgt der

Bericht des Herrn Lehrer Max Grütter über seine botanischen Exkursionen von 1886.

Ich erhielt von Herrn Professor Dr. Caspary den Auftrag, die im vorigen Jahre begonnene Untersuchung des Kreises Schwetz fortzusetzen. Ich habe in diesem Jahre auch entfernter liegende Gegenden des Kreises, ferner ein kleines Stück des Kreises Tuchel und den Strich zwischen Neuenburg und Gr. Wessel im Kreise Marienwerder bereist. Meine Ausbeute war eine sehr reiche. Von schon im vorigen Jahre gefundenen Arten erwähne ich folgende: **Carlina acaulis** (7 neue Standorte), **Salix myrtilloides** (2 neue Standorte im Kr. Schwetz, einer im Kr. Tuchel), **Naias maior** (2), **Galium aristatum, Dracocephalum thymiflorum** (2), **Lepidium micranthum Ledeb.** (5 neue Standorte im Kreise Schwetz, einer im Kr. Tuchel), **Rudbeckia hirta** (3), **Mimulus luteus, Utricularia intermedia** (4), **Potamogeton curvifolia, P. crispa + praelonga Casp.** Von meinen Funden sind neu für den Kreis:

Pulsatilla pratensis + vernalis (7), **P. patens + vernalis** (4), **P. patens + pratensis, P. pratensis,** mit gelblicher Blüthe, **Carex chordorrhiza, Scirpus pauciflorus, Botrychium simplex, Dianthus superbus** (2), **Polygala amara, Equisetum variegatum, Cladium Mariscus,** Salix triandra + viminalis, **Elatine Alsinastrum, Anacamptis pyramidalis, Cirsium palustre + oleraceum** (6), **Silene conica, Sherardia arvensis, Festuca silvatica, Matricaria discoides, Orchis coriophora, Phegopteris robertiana, Onobrychis viciifolia, Sanguisorba minor, Cardamine impatiens, Geum urbanum + rivale** (2), **Medicago minima** (4), **Thesium intermedium, Orchis Rivini, Hyssopus officinalis, Poterium polygamum W. et Kit. α. platylophium** Spach und auch neu für Preussen überhaupt: **Juncus tenuis Willd.**

Verbreitet im Kreise sind: Pulsatilla vernalis, Botrychium Lunaria, Euphorbia Cyparissias, Carex dioica, C. limosa, Teesdalea nudicaulis, Carlina vulgaris, Listera ovata, Carex filiformis, C. flacca, Avena praecox und caryophyllea, Marrubium vulgare, Juncus squarrosus, Scheuchzeria palustris, Sparganium minimum, Alectorolophus minor, Arnoseris pusilla, Hypochoeris glabra, Drosera rotundifolia und anglica, Polycnemum arvense, Seseli annuum, Cyperus fuscus, Rumex Hydrolapathum, R. aquaticus, Limosella aquatica, Actaea spicata, Gnaphalium luteo-album.

Die Ergebnisse der einzelnen Exkursionen waren folgende:

21. 4. 86. Bei Grünberg (Kreis Schwetz): Pulsatilla praetensis + vernalis. Am Mukrz-Fliess: Alnus incana, Viola epipsila + palustris. Im Cisbusch: Corydalis cava V^3 Z^5. — 24. 4. Am Fliess zw. Sternbach und Rischke: **Botrychium rutaceum.** Schonung nördl. von Marienfelde: Carex montana, **Carlina acaulis, Pulsatilla patens + vernalis** (Blüthen violett, glockenförmig; 1 Exemplar mit ausgebreiteten weissen, aussen röthlichen Blüthen), **P. pratensis + vernalis**; am Bischke-Fliess: Gagea lutea, Corydalis intermedia; südl. von Jakobsdorf: **Pulsatilla pratensis + vernalis, Carlina acaulis;** am Pruski-Fliess: Corydalis intermedia. — 28. 4. Kleine Schlucht bei Topolinken: Viola hirta. — 29. 4. Johannisberger Holz südwestl. von der Försterei: **Pulsatilla patens + vernalis** (1 Expl.), Carex montana. — 30. 4. Zw. Lnianno und Schiroslaw: **Pulsatilla patens + vernalis, Pulmonaria angustifolia,** Carex montana, Viola epipsila + palustris, **Botrychium Matricariae.** — 1. 5. Zw. Bremin und Grüneck: **Pulsatilla pratensis + vernalis** 1 Expl.; zw. Grüneck und Klinger: Asperula odorata; linkes Ufer des Schwarzwasser: Hierochloa australis, Fagus silvatica (wohl nur angepflanzt), Euonymus verrucosa, Viola collina, Anemone nemorosa b) purpurea, Corydalis cava Z^{4-5} — 4. 5. Torfstich zw. Lnianno und Falkenhorst: Viola epipsila; Schlucht zw. Dritschmin und Groddeck: Gagea minima, Corydalis intermedia, Petasites officinalis, Lycopodium Selago; am Schwarzwasser: Corydalis cava. — 8. 5. Zw. Johannisberg und Lubsee: **Pulmonaria angustifolia** Z^{3-4}. — 10. 5. Am Schwarzwasser zw. der Groddeck'er und Rowinitza'er Schlucht: Equisetum Telmateia, Viola collina. — 12. 5. Bei Grünberg: Androsace septentrionalis, **Pulsatilla pratensis** (Blüthen gelblich), **P. patens + vernalis.** — 13. 5. Zw. Lnianno und Schiroslaw: **Salix myrtilloides, S. repens + myrtilloides, Carex chordorrhiza.** — 14. 5. Johannisberger Holz südwestl. der Försterei: **Pulsatilla pratensis + vernalis.** — 15. 5. Zw. Sternbach und Hammer: **Luzula sudetica b) pallescens;** südlich von Zielonka: Viola arenaria + silvestris; bei der Försterei Grünhof: Hierochloa australis. — 17. 5. Zw. Dritschmin und Groddeck: Veronica polita; zw. Groddek und der Lubochin'er Schlucht: Corydalis cava und C. intermedia, **Pulmonaria angustifolia + officinalis,** Vicia lathyroides. — 18. 5. Zwischen Marienfelde und Bremin: **Pulsatilla patens + pratensis.** — 22. 5. Tümpel am Wege nach Schiroslaw: **Eriophorum gracile, Salix myrtilloides;** Gehölz bei Ziegelei Falkenhorst: **Pulsatilla pratensis + vernalis;** Tümpel bei den Schiroslaw'er Ausbauten: **Eriophorum gracile.** — 24. 5. In Andreasthal: Matricaria Chamomilla; zw. Andreasthal und Hintersee: **Luzula sudetica b) pallescens, Pulsatilla pratensis + vernalis;** Birkwiese: Betula humilis; Ostseite des Ebensees: Berberis vulgaris, **Luzula sudetica** b) **pallescens,** Carex disticha, Scirpus pauciflorus. — 26. 5. Zw. Schiroslawek und Ottersteig: Carex montana; Schwarzwasser zw. Ottersteig und Splawie: Corydalis intermedia; zwischen Splawie und Vorwerk Wirri: Carex muricata, C. elongata, Geum urbanum + rivale, Arabis Gerardi, Equisetum Telmateia. — 28. 5. Zw. Lnianno und Falkenhorst: Scirpus pauciflorus. — 30. 5. Wiesen nördl. von Wilhelmshof: **Luzula sudetica b) pallescens;** im Gebüsch am Wirwa-Fliess: Geum urbanum + rivale, Alnus incana; zw. Wirwa und Bedlenken: Cynanchum Vincetoxicum, Ranunculus arvensis, Scirpus pauciflorus, Arabis Gerardi; zw. Bedlenken und Oslowo: **Silene conica;** zw. Oslowo und Bahnhof Laskowitz: Sanguisorba minor. — 4. 6. Wiesen nördl. von Grünberg: **Botrychium simplex Hitchcock** a) **simplicissimum** Lasch., b) **incisum** Milde, c) **subcompositum** Lasch., **Ophioglossum vulgatum;** Schonung westlich von Stenzlau: Iris sibirica, Geranium silvaticum (1 Expl.).

— 8. 6. Am Marienthal'er See: Carex distans, Hieracium pratense + Pilosella, Scirpus Tabernaemontani, Utricularia intermedia, Eriophorum gracile; Wiesen bei Marienthal: Viola epipsila, Valeriana dioica; zw. Marienthal und Mukrz: Botrychium rutaceum, Scirpus pauciflorus, Hieracium pratense + Pilosella; Mukrz-See: Scirpus pauciflorus; im Cisbusch: Carex elongata, **Cypripedium Calceolus, Festuca silvatica;** zw. dem Cisbusch und dem Ebensee: Scirpus pauciflorus, Crepis praemorsa, Pimpinella magna; Gehölz zwischen Annalust und Hutta: **Botrychium rutaceum.** — 11. 6. Am Bahndamm zw. Falkenhorst und Dritschmin: Avena flavescens, Poa nemoralis L. b) firmula Gaud., Sherardia arvensis, **Rudbeckia hirta;** zw. H. St. Dritschmin und dem Schwarzwasser: Rosa tomentosa, Myosotis hispida; am Schwarzwasser: Fragaria moschata, Aconitum variegatum (Blätter), **Scorzonera purpurea,** Cynanchum Vincetoxicum, Carex muricata b) virens, Myosotis hispida, M. sparsiflora; linkes Ufer: **Asperula tinctoria,** Aconitum variegatum, Cimicifuga foetida. — 15. 6. Gehölz südöstlich von Laskowitz: Ulex europaeus; Laskowitz'er See: Carex distans; Lippinken: Chenopodium Bonus Henricus; bei der Ruine: Carex distans; Wiesen südl. von Taschauerfelde: Myriophyllum verticillatum (Gräben), **Crepis succisifolia, C. praemorsa,** Scirpus pauciflorus; Gellen'er See: Calamagrostis neglecta, Myosotis sparsiflora; Belauf Wolfsbruch: Carex montana; Schwenten: Reseda lutea; Abhänge zwischen Schwenten und Sartowitz: Stachys recta, Koeleria glauca, Alliaria officinalis, **Campanula sibirica** $V^4 Z^3$, **Medicago minima** $V^2 Z^4$, Viola collina; südlich von Gr.-Sartowitz: **Campanula sibirica,** Stachys recta, Veronica Teucrium, Viola collina, **Peucedanum Cervaria;** in der grossen Schlucht: **Orchis Rivini** Z^{1-2}, **Onobrychis viciifolia** $V^3 Z^8$, Campanula sibirica, **Melampyrum arvense, Thesium intermedium** $V^2 Z^{3-4}$; zw. Piskarken und Lipno: Eriophorum latifolium. — 18. 6. Zw. Lnianno und Sternbach: Hier. pratense + Pilosella, Potentilla norvegica; zwischen Sternbach und Hammer: Carlina acaulis (Laub), **Scorzonera purpurea** Z^2, **Botrychium rutaceum** $V^1 Z^8$; zw. Hammer und Rischke: Lycopodium Selago; zw. Rischke und Bremin: Gypsophila fastigiata, Utricularia minor. — 21. 6. Belauf Rehhof zw. dem Mukrz-Fliess und Rehhof: Rubus suberectus Anders., Aira flexuosa, **Luzula sudetica,** Pirola media (Standort von 1885); westlich von Rehhof: Ranunculus polyanthemos, **Dracocephalum thymiflorum** (hart an der Grenze des Kreises). Bei Haltestelle Lindenbusch, Kreis Tuchel: **Dracocephalum thymiflorum, Lepidium micranthum;** am See: Potamogeton graminea b) heterophylla, Scheuchzeria palustris, Carex limosa. — 23. 6. Bei Bremin: Elymus arenarius; zw. Gorzalimost und Wiersch: **Evonymus verrucosa;** zw. Wiersch und Pruski: Aquilegia vulgaris, Carex remota, Triticum caninum, Phegopteris polypodioides; zw. Neuhaus und Rischke: Achyrophorus maculatus. — 25. 6. Zw. Wiersch und Klinger: Myosotis hispida, Valerianella dentata; zw. Klinger und Grüneck: Koeleria cristata, Triticum caninum, **Glyceria nemoralis** U. et. K., Calamagrostis neglecta; zw. Grüneck und Bremin: **Epipactis rubiginosa, Gymnadenia conopea.** — 26. 6. Zw. Haltestelle Lnianno und dem See: Carduus nutans. Silene conica. — 27. 6. In Gr. Prust: Coronopus Ruellii; Gehölz zwischen Niewiesczyn und Supponin: Asparagus officinalis; Schlucht zw. Supponin und Grabowko: Potentilla opaca $V^3 Z^2$, Avena pratensis $V^3 Z^5$, Myosotis hispida, Sedum boloniense, Stachys recta, Medicago minima Z^4, Dianthus prolifer, Verbascum Lychnitis und V. phlomoides; Schluchten und Abhänge zw. Grabowko und Topolno: **Medicago minima** Z^{2-3}, Thalictrum minus, Campanula sibirica, **Anemone silvestris,** Silene Otites; Lehmweg südl. Topolno: **Fumaria Vaillantii** Z^{4-5}; Topolnoberge: Verbascum phlomoides, Xanthium italicum, Salsola Kali, Sedum boloniense. — 1. 7. Zw. Johannisberg und Wentfie: Rubus suberectus Anders., Lycopodium inundatum; zw. Wentfie und Jeziorken: Crepis succisifolia; in Karlshorst: Pimpinella magna; Birkwiese: Valeriana dioica. — 4. 7. Kr. Marienwerder. Zw. der Ziegelei nördl. von Neuenburg und Kozielec: **Medicago minima,** Veronica Teucrium, Hieracium echioides, **Ervum pisiforme,** Digitalis ambigua, Equisetum Telmateia, **Silene chlorantha.** Ranunculus cassubicus, Circaea lutetiana, **Cimicifuga foetida,** Luzula sudetica (weiss), Lithospermum officinale; Abhänge zw. Kozielec und Gr. Wessel und Schonung südlich von Gr.-Wessel: Veronica opaca, Equisetum Telmateia, **Cimicifuga foetida, Ervum pisiforme,** Hieracium echioides, Inula salicina, Asperula tinctoria, Peucedanum Cervaria, Cephalanthera rubra, Crepis praemorsa, Geranium silvaticum, **Pleurospermum austriacum,** Trollius europaeus, Ranunculus cassubicus, Platanthera chlorantha, Viola collina, **Scorzonera purpurea,** Prunella grandiflora, Stachys recta, Gentiana cruciata, Gymnadenia conopea, **Pulsatilla patens + pratensis,** Trifolium rubens, Inula hirta, Aster Amellus; im hohen Bestande: **Lathyrus pisiformis,** Dracocephalum ruyschianum, Asperula tinctoria, **Cephalanthera rubra.** — 6. 7. Kreis Schwetz. Bruch zw. Lnianno und Schiroslaw: **Ophioglossum vulgatum, Botrychium Matricariae,** Potentilla procumbens, Malaxis paludosa. — 10. 7. Marienthaler See: **Malaxis** paludosa, Graben an der Nordspitze des Ebensees: Potamogeton compressa; Gehölz am Ebensee: **Crepis succisifolia, Pimpinella magna,** Gentiana cruciata Z^{1-2}, **Galium aristatum,** Triticum caninum, ***Anacamptis pyramidalis*** Z^2, Aquilegia vulgaris; am Ebensee: Carex distans; in demselben: Naias maior. — 11. 7. In Laskowitz: **Matricaria discoides;** Stelchno-See: **Potamogeton curvifolia,** P. graminea b) heterophylla, Equisetum variegatum; Hagen'er Forst nördl. von Hagen: Gypsophila fastigiata, Krakowie-See: Utricularia minor, Scirpus pauciflorus, ***Cladium Mariscus;*** Wiesen nordöstlich vom See: Veronica longifolia, Calamagrostis neglecta, Saxifraga Hirculus, Hieracium pratense + Pilosella (niederliegend); am Schinowa-Fliess: Oryza clandestina, Ophioglossum vulgatum, Laserpitium prutenicum, **Asplenium Trichomanes;** an der Montau: Potentilla procumbens; Rohlau'er Wald bis zum Krakowie-See: **Gypsophila fastigiata, Asperula tinctoria, Epipactis rubiginosa,** Hieracium echioides; Wiesen südl. vom See: **Botrychium rutaceum;** Waldrand östlich von Jeżewo: Viola collina, Carlina acaulis (Laub); Acker bei Jeżewo: Polycnemum arvense. — 14. 7. Bei Ebensee: Ervum monanthos (unter Vicia sativa); zw. Ebensee und Blondzmin; Erythraea pulchella, Lycopodium inundatum; zwischen Blondzmin und Szewno: Lathyrus silvester, Rumex maximus. —

18. 7. 86. Uebersiedelung nach Dritschmin. Bei der Haltestelle: Lepidium micranthum; in Dritschmin: Chenopodium urbicum, Xanthium Strumarium. — 19. 7. 86. Schlucht zw. Dritschmin und Groddeck: Cirsium palustre + oleraceum, Orchis coriophora, Ophioglossum vulgatum, Arabis Gerardi, Dianthus Armeria; zw. Groddeck und Pulko: Arabis Gerardi, Centunculus minimus, Cirsium acaule. — 20. 7. Linkes Ufer des Schwarzwasser zw. Groddeck und der Brücke: Oryza clandestina, Valerianella dentata, ***Cardamine impatiens,*** Cucubalus baccifer, Rumex maximus, Barbaraea stricta, Triticum caninum, Silene chlorantha, Arabis Gerardi, Aconitum variegatum; bei Haltestelle Osche: Lepidium micranthum Ledeb. — 21. 7. Vormittag Regen. Nachmittag zw. Dritschmin und Falkenhorst: **Mimulus luteus** V^3 Z^3, Cirsium palustre + oleraceum V^4 Z^{1-2}, **Crepis succisifolia.** — 22. 7. Zw. Sauern und Abbau Bresin: **Mimulus luteus,** Potentilla procumbens, Cirsium palustre + oleraceum (1 Expl.); Brüche südlich von Bresin: **Botrychium Matricariae,** Utricularia minor und intermedia, **Eriophorum gracile,** Lycopodium inundatum. Regen. — 23. 7. Zw. Bresin und Jaszcz: Potentilla procumbens, Agrimonia odorata; zw. Jaszcz und Miedzno: Galium verum (gelb und weiss); in Miedzno: Chenopodium urbicum; zwischen Miedzno und Osche: Carex arenaria. — 24. 7. Zw. Osche und Belauf Eichwald: Gypsophila fastigiata; im Bel. Eichwald: **Pirus torminalis** (1 einjähriges Expl.), Pulmonaria angustifolia, Ranunculus polyanthemos, Cimicifuga foetida (Blätter); zw. Eichwald und Adlershorst: Potentilla procumbens; am Gr. Miedzno-See: Saxifraga Hirculus; zw. dem See und Miedzno: Centunculus minimus; in Miedzno: Lepidium micranthum Ledeb. — 25. 7. Rechtes Ufer des Schwarzwasser zw. Groddeck und der Brücke: Aconitum variegatum, Rumex aquaticus, Agrostis alba (sehr hoch), Triticum caninum, Cimicifuga foetida, Potentilla norvegica (1 Expl.); zwischen der Brücke und der Lubochin'er Schlucht: Lepidium micranthum, Verbascum Thapsus (1 Expl.); in Lubochin und Gatzki: Chenopodium urbicum. — 26. 7. Zw. Pulko und Sauern: Agrimonia odorata V^3 Z^5, Equisetum Telmateia, Circaea lutetiana Z^{1-2}, **Phegopteris robertiana** Z^{3-4}, Cirsium palustre + oleraceum, Dianthus Armeria. — 27. 7. Rowinitza'er Schlucht: Crepis virens, **Astragalus Cicer** Z^4, Hieracium caesium, Thalictrum minus; zw. der Rowinitza'er Ziegelei und Pulko: Triticum caninum, Dianthus prolifer, Onobrychis viciifolia V^3 Z^2, Cynanchum Vincetoxicum **Poterium polygamum** Waldst. et. Kit. *α* **platylophium** Spach., Trifolium rubens, **Astragalus Cicer,** Z^{1-2}, Equisetum Telmateia; zw. Pulko und Vorwerk Wirri: Onobrychis viciifolia, **Poterium polygamum** W. et K. *α*. **platylophium** Spach. — 28. 7. Bruch bei den Westausbauten von Schiroslaw: Centunculus minimus, Utricularia intermedia, Lycopodium inundatum, Potentilla norvegica, **Juncus Tenageia** Z^2, letzeren auch an zwei Tümpeln südlich und an einem südöstlich von Schiroslaw. Einige Exemplare hatten an den Wurzeln kleine Knöllchen, vielleicht von Schinzia cypericola Magnus herrührend. In Schiroslaw: Pulicaria vulgaris; zw. Schiroslaw und Marienfelde: Saxifraga Hirculus, Cirsium palustre + oleraceum (1 Expl.). — 29. 7. Wiesen nördlich von Lnianno: Scirpus pauciflorus; Waldrand südlich von Lischin: **Botrychium Matricariae, B. rutaceum;** Suchom-See: **Naias maior;** Wiese zw. Suchom und Rehhof: Polystichum cristatum. — 6. 8. Bei Eichdorf: **Botrychium Matricariae** Z^2 und Z^5; im Gehölz am Ebensee: Gentiana cruciata V^4 Z^1, Cirsium palustre + oleraceum. — 15. 8. **Kr. Tuchel.** Bei Haltestelle Polnisch Cekzyn: Carduus nutans; in Poln. Cekzyn: Chenopodium urbicum; Ostseite des Poln. Cekzyn'er Sees: Hippuris vulgaris, **Betula humilis** Z^1, Potentilla opaca; Westseite des Dzetzim-Sees: Carduus nutans; Südost-

spitze des Gwiasda-Sees: Dianthus superbus; Tümpel zw. dem Dzetzim- und Gr. Bislaw'er See: **Salix myrtilloides** Z[3–4]; zw. Gr. Bislaw und Kossowo: Liparis Loeselii Z[1–2] (Blätter), Pimpinella magna; Pechhütt'er See: **Malaxis paludosa, Utricularia intermedia,** Scirpus pauciflorus. — 19. 8. See südlich von Lnianno: Scirpus setaceus; See südöstlich von Lnianno: Cyperus flavescens; nördlich von Johannisberg: **Silene chlorantha;** Bialle-Wiese: **Gentiana Pneumonanthe** Z[4], Salix livida, Botrychium Matricariae: am Bahndamm zw. Falkenhorst und Lnianno: **Rudbeckia hirta, Lepidium micranthum.** — 22. 8. Tümpel auf der Bremin'er Feldmark: Avena flavescens Z[2], **Lolium italicum.** — 26. 8. Sumpfwiesen am Mukrz-Fliess: Salix cinerea f. angustifolia Döll. — 29. 8. Stelchno-See: **Potamogeton lucens + praelonga,** Scirpus pauciflorus, **Liparis Loeselii, Salix** triandra + viminalis, Erythraea pulchella, **Utricularia intermedia;** Laskowitz'er See, Südspitze: Dianthus superbus; Buan-See bei Gr. Zappeln: **Polygala amara;** zw. Gr. Zappeln und Dziki: **Salix myrtilloides;** Bruch nördlich von Dziki: **Salix myrtilloides,** Juncus Tenageia Z[2]; Tümpel bei Sullnowo: **Juncus Tenageia** V[4] Z[4], **Elatine Alsinastrum** Z[4]. — 2. 9. Graben am Johannisberg'er Holz bei der Försterei: Juncus supinus. — 4. 9. Tümpel zw. Lnianno und Stenzlau: **Juncus Tenageia,** J. supinus. — 8. 9. Tümpel zw. Sternbach und Falkenhorst: **Juncus Tenageia,** Centunculus minimus. — 12. 9. In Ober-Gruppe: Amarantus retroflexus; Abhänge bei Alt Marsau: Stachys recta, Melampyrum arvense, Hyssopus officinalis; Kämpe bei Gr. Westphalen: Senecio saracenicus, **Cuscuta lupuliformis,** Atriplex roseum, Rumex ucranicus, Artemisia scoparia (1 Expl.); Damm bei Brattwin und Michelau: Veronica longifolia, Silene tatarica, Reseda Luteola; im Weidengebüsch an der Bahn zw. Dragass und Ober-Gruppe: ***Juncus tenuis*** Willd*).

Alle drei Berichterstatter vertheilen viele seltene Pflanzen der Ausbeute ihrer Untersuchungen.

Herr Dr. Peter, Custos des königl. Herbariums und Privatdozent der Botanik zu München, beschenkt dann die Versammelten mit vielen bairischen Pflanzen, darunter auch mehrere Cirsiumbastarde und hält dann einen Vortrag über mitteleuropäische Hieracien im Allgemeinen und über preussische Arten und Formen im besondern, legt etwa 40 Arten der Piloselloiden zur Besichtigung aus und fordert zu sorgfältigem Sammeln der preussischen Hieracien auf. Für Näheres müssen wir aus Raummangel vorläufig auf das Werk von Nägeli und Peter: Die Hieracien Mitteleuropas München 1885 verweisen. Zusammenfassende Bearbeitungen aus der Feder des Herrn Dr. Peter werden wir seiner Zeit anderwegen folgen lassen.

Herr Oberlehrer W. Kuck vertheilte dann folgende Pflanzen: **Polygonatum verticillatum** Mnch. Eichwald'er Forst am Trakiesbach, über 1 Meter hoch; **Orobus luteus** L., Brödlaucken'er Forst.

Herr Apotheker Kühn-Insterburg vertheilt auch Orobus luteus von demselben Standort, **Bidens radiatus** vom Ufer des Ententeichs am Stadtwalde und **Zanichellia palustris L.,** Teich am Abbau Kratzat am Stadtwalde.

Herr Hauptlehrer G. Thieler vertheilte: Tofieldia calyculata Whlnb., aus dem Kreise Lötzen, Torfbruch bei Wilkassen. — Pedicularis Sceptrum Carolinum L. ebendaher. — Betula humilis, ebendaher. — Eriophorum alpinum L., Kr. Heydekrug, Augstumall'er Moor. — Limnanthemum nymphaeoides Lk., Kr. Heydekrug, Krakerort'er Lank. — Lathyrus paluster L., Kr. Heydekrug, Haffwiesen bei Augstumall. — Carex dioica L., Kr. Heydekrug, Augstumall'er Moor. — Botrychium Lunaria Sw., Kr. Insterburg. Am Stadtwalde in der Nähe der Schiessstände auf einer Anhöhe.

Es wird eine Frühstückspause um 12 Uhr von ³/₄ Stunden gemacht. Ein Theil der Gäste besichtigt unter gütiger Führung des Herrn Oberbürgermeister Korn die schönen Anlagen im Schützengrunde, Schöpfung des genannten Herrn, und auch die mit Fresken aus der Odyssee geschmückte Aula des königl. Gymnasiums.

Nach Wiedereröffnung der Sitzung theilt der Vorsitzende den Bericht über die Kasse mit, die von den Herren Apotheker Packheiser und Apotheker Sander geprüft war.

„In der 24. Versammlung des preuss. botanischen Vereins zu Pr. Stargard am 6. October 1885 wurden zu Prüfern der Kasse des botanischen Vereins erwählt die Herren Apotheker Eichert und Packheiser. In Vertretung des ersteren hatte Herr Apotheker Sander dessen Amt übernommen.

---

*) Ueber Juncus tenuis siehe Schriften der physikalisch-ökonomischen Gesellschaft, Jahrgang 1886. Sitzungsberichte S. 36.

Genannte Herren fanden sich heute Nachmittag 3 Uhr in den Wohnung des Schatzmeisters Herrn Apotheker R. Schüssler ein, und fanden bei der Prüfung Folgendes.

Nach Einsicht des Kassenbuchs betrug

die Einnahme	3342 Mk. 65 Pf.
die Ausgabe	3326 Mk. 91 Pf.
Bestand	15 Mk. 74 Pf.

Dieser Bestand von fünfzehn Mark 74 Pf. wurde baar in der Kasse richtig vorgefunden.

Das Kapital-Vermögen des botanischen Vereins bestand in

1. 4 pCt. Schuldverschreibungen der Korporation der Königsberg'er Kaufmannschaft	4300 Mk.
2. $4^{1}/_{2}$ pCt. Prioritätsobligationen der ostpreuss. Südbahn-Gesellschaft	5100 Mk.
3. $4^{1}/_{2}$ pCt. Kreisobligationen des Kreises Kulm	4500 Mk.
Summa	13900 Mk.

Geschrieben: dreizehn Tausend neun hundert Mark.

Die Briefe dieser Werthpapiere konnte der Herr Schatzmeister nicht vorzeigen, weil dieselben sich im Gewahrsam des Vorsitzenden Herrn Professor Dr. R. Caspary befanden. Dagegen legte Herr Schüssler sämmtliche zu diesen Werthpapieren gehörigen Coupons und Talons vor, welche einzeln mit den Nummern der verzeichneten Werthstücke verglichen, und richtig vorgefunden wurden.

Die Rechnung für 1885/86 wurde sowohl nach den einzelnen Beträgen geprüft, als auch neu aufgerechnet, und wurde dieselbe vollkommen mit dem Abschluss übereinstimmend befunden.

Die Prüfer

Th. Packheiser. Sander.“

Auf diesen Bericht hin wird die Führung der Kasse von der Versammlung für richtig erklärt. Zu Prüfern der Kasse für das nächste Jahr werden die Herren Apotheker Mielentz und Eichert erwählt. Als nächster Versammlungsort wird Elbing ausersehen, wo Herr Bürgermeister Elditt die Geschäftsführung mit anderen Herren gefälligst übernehmen will. Der Vorstand wird dann durch Acclamation wieder gewählt. Es wir beschlossen, dass die Kreise Ortelsburg und Strasburg 1887 von Neuem und der Kreis Berent südlich der Ferse untersucht werden sollen.

Hierauf berichtet Herr Konrektor Seydler-Braunsberg unter Vorlegung und Vertheilung von vielen seltenen Pflanzen über seine Excursionen von 1885 und 1886. Geranium sanguineum Allenstein'er Stadtwald; Centaurea maculosa fr. virens Vill. ebendaher; October 1885. Agaricus suffrutescens mit Hut, fast 1 Meter lang, auf einem Balken der Mühle des Herrn Zarniko-Heiligenbeil gefunden. — Hypericum iaponicum Thunbg und mutilum L. von Oberförster A. Straehler beim Forsthause Theerbude bei Wronke (Regierungsbezirk Posen) auf einem Torfsumpf entdeckt. 11. November 1885 erhalten. — Viscum album in mehr als 50 Stücken auf Populus monilifera auf dem Johanniskirchhofe in Braunsberg, 29. März — 30. März Hexenbesen auf Picea excelsa Link. vom Revierförster Teski aus dem königl. Forstrevier Damerau zw. Braunsberg und Heiligenbeil erhalten — **Carex pilosa** 24. April im genannten Forstrevier gesammelt. Peridermium Pini W. auf Pinus Strobus vom Revierförster Teski, 1. Mai 1886 gesandt. — Carex caespitosa in Rodelshöfen 12. Mai 1886. — Potentilla digitato-flabellata A. Br. et Bouch. 27. Mai 1886 wieder, wie 1885, zw. dem Güterschuppen und dem Stationsgebäude von Braunsberg gesammelt, auch den 16. Juni 1886 in der Nähe des Bahnhofs gefunden — Festuca distans Dammstrasse in Braunsberg 18. Juni — Gladiolus imbricatus bei Bischdorf im Rödersdorf'er Forst 29. Juni; neu für Kreis Braunsberg; — Platanthera chlorantha daselbst. — Sisymbrum Sinapistrum im Hohlen Grunde zw. Mühle Wacklitz und Lisettenhof; daselbst Vicia lathyroides — Cephalanthera rubra von Frau Magda Gers aus der Taberbrück'er Forst, Kreis Mohrungen, 5. Juli erhalten. — Polygonum lapathifol. var. nodosum, Juncus bufonius var. ranarius Perr. et Song. 9. Juli zw. Ziegelei und Chausseehaus bei Braunsberg — Glyceria plicata zw. der Kl. Mühle und Schillgehnen bei Braunsberg 9. Juli. — Im Walde zw. Bauditten und Bombitten: Circaea alpina, Stellaria uliginosa, Crepis biennis. — Im Walde zw. Nonnenhausen und Barslick: Stellaria frieseana, Lycopodium complanatum, zum 1. Mal im Kreise Heiligenbeil gefunden, 18. Juli. — Circaea alpina und lutetiana, **Veronica montana**, Rubus Bellardi, **Glyceria nemoralis**, **Elymus europaeus** L., (hier schon 1884 entdeckt), **Bromus asper** auf dem Schlossberge bei Wildenhof 19. Juli. — Centaurea austriaca, **Polygonatum verticillatum** Maraunen'er Wald südlich von Gr. Döbnicken; **Polygonatum verticillatum** und P.

spenca, Calla palustris, Bombitten'er Wald, Bombitten'er Rossgarten genannt. 20. Juli — Dr. Boening überbringt dem Vortragenden aus dem Wäldchen von Neueruthen zw. Gintbiden und Dameran, Kreis Königsberg, **Gladiolus imbricatus**, 1. Juli gesammelt — Epipactis latifolia nebst fr. viridans, Lycopodium complanatum von Frau Magda Gers aus Belauf Pörschken, Taberbrück'er Forst erhalten. — **Orobanche elatior** Sutt., von Althof bei Frauenburg, **Agrimonia odorata** Baudebrücke bei Sankau; Aristolochia Clematitis Rautenberg'er Chaussee, **Melampyrum arvense** zw. Althof und der Chaussee, am linken Baudeufer, 14. August. — Bromus inermis, rechtes Passargeufer auf der Aue bei Braunsberg, und Avena sativa, beide mit 2 Rispen auf demselben Halm. 16. August. — Drosera longifolia zw. der Kl. Mühle und dem Kalthöfen'er Walde; **Digitalis ambigua** Waldschlucht daselbst; Dianthus superbus Chaussee bei der Kl. Mühle. 17. August. — **Salvia verticillata**, Eisenbahndamm in der Nähe des Güterschuppens von Braunsberg 9. September. — Es werden endlich Blätter von Trifolium hybridum (schwedischem Klee) von Apion apricans (kleiner Rüsselkäfer) und Blätter von Brassica Rapa rapifera von Athalia spinarum (Rübenblattwespe) skelettirt vorgezeigt.

Konrektor Seydler vertheilt vom Stadtältesten C. Patze-Königsberg: Trifolium incarnatum, Haferfeld bei Gallehnen, Kr. Pr. Eylau, Juli und August 1886 und **Euphorbia Cyparissias**, am Rande eines Grabens im Bärenwinkel bei Gallehnen Juni 1886; Valeriana dioica var. simplicifolia von Gallehnen.

Candidat Richard Schultz legt vor und vertheilt: **Salvinia natans**, lebend, aus der Lichtenau'er Vorfluth, Kr. Marienburg, neuem Standorte, ferner vom Kaibahnhof in Königsberg, eingeschleppt durch russische Saat: Kochia scoparia, Nonnea pulla, Sinapis iuncea, Gypsophila paniculata, Tragopogon maior, Centaurea diffusa, Salvia verticillata.

Schulamtskandidat Vanhöffen-Wehlau vertheilt: Libanotis montana, Alle-Abhänge bei Schön-Nuhr; **Iris sibirica**, Stadtwald von Wehlau östlich von Försterei Pickertswalde, **Orobanche coerulescens**, Hügel am rechten Alleufer südlich von Bürgersdorf bei Wehlau auf Artemisia campestris.

Hierauf legt Dr. Bethke ein von v. Klinggräff II im Kreise Marienwerder 1874 gesammeltes Veilchen aus dem Herbarium des königl. botan. Gartens vor. Auf dem beigefügten Zettel ist Folgendes vermerkt: „Viola riviniana Rchb., (durch die breiten, ganz ungetheilten Nebenblätter ausgezeichnete Form.) Im Walde bei Fiedlitz. 14. 5. 74." Dieses Veilchen gleicht in morphologischer Beziehung ganz dem vom Dr. Bethke beobachteten Bastard Violia mirabilis + riviniana. Auch die schlechte Beschaffenheit des Pollens weist auf einen Bastard hin. Bethke vertheilte dann noch einige Pflanzen vom Ostseestrande bei Cranz: Epilobium tetragonum, Tragopogon floccosus, Pisum maritimum und Gymnadenia cucullata.

Professor Caspary zeigt dann: **Pyrethrum inodorum** mit proliferirenden Köpfen vom Lehrer Zinger in Pr.-Holland vor und berichtet über seine eigenen 1886 unternommenen Exkursionen.

Kreis Neustadt. Vom 11.—19 Juni. 9 Tage untersuchte ich von Zarnowitz die Gegend nach Nord, West und Süd. Nördlich und nordwestlich von Zarnowitz im Piasnitzbruch Pinguicula vulgaris, auch nordwestl. vom Zarnowitz'er See. Iris sibirica und Gladiolus imbricatus zwischen Gebüsch südlich von den Dünen; Erica Tetralix an vielen Stellen des Bruchs. Myrica Gale ebenda; Scirpus caespitosus daselbst westlich von der Piasnitz. Carex Buxbaumii im Norden des Zarnowitz'er Sees gegen die Dünen zu mit auffallend dicken Endaehren. Alles dies schon 1883 von Abromeit dort nachgewiesen. **Carex fulva** im Norden des Piasnitzbruchs gegen die Dünen zu, zahlreich, früher im Bericht von Abromeit als Carex distans bezeichnet. Pedicularis silvatica im Wirschutzin'er Moor. ***Schoenus ferrugineus*** im Gr. Wierschutzin'er Moor, schon auf pommerschem Boden 17. 6. 1886; auf einer Linie, die man von der Kirche in Zarnowitz nach den Weissen Bergen (Dünen) bei Wittenberg zieht, Z^4 V^3, rechts und links vom Mühlenfliess von Wittenberg, grosse Flächen braunschwarz überziehend, etwa 2 Kilometer von der westpreussischen Grenze, aber nicht in Westpreussen. Viola stagnina, da wo Abromeit sie 1883 fand, südlich von den Dünen bei Dembeck. **Arabis hirsuta** höchst zahlreich, Z^3 V^3, wie ich diese meist vereinzelt vorkommende Pflanze nie sah, am westlichen Damm von Karwenbruch. Melica uniflora und Festuca silvatica auf dem Schlossberge im Belauf Sobiensitz, wo Abromeit sie schon fand. **Cephalanthera Xiphophyllum** 1 blühendes Expl. nordwestlich von Försterei Sobiensitz am Kirchensteige zwischen Kartoschin und Zarnowitz; **Lysimachia nemorum** im Walde zwischen dem Zarnowitz'er See und Rauschendorf und südl. von Försterei Sobiensitz. Glyceria nemoralis im Lauberdesumpf westlich vom Zarnowitz'er See im Walde von Reckendorf. **Carex paradoxa** Torfwiese südlich von Rauschendorf.

Professor Caspary theilt dann seinen

Bericht über nachträgliche Gewässeruntersuchungen in den Kreisen Berent, Kartaus, Pr. Stargardt, Danzig

mit. Ich untersuchte vom 28. Juli (einschl.) bis 6. September (einschl.) in den genannten Kreisen etwa 165 Seen und andere Gewässer. Von Characeen fand ich 9 Arten: Char. stelligera (2 Fundorte), Ch. ceratophylla (5 Fundorte), Ch. intermedia (2), Ch. aspera (2), Ch. delicatula (1), Ch. foetida (3 Fundorte), Ch. fragilis (22 Fundorte), Nitella mucronata (1 Fundort), Nitella flexilis (1 Fundort), **Alisma arcuatum** Michal. in 2 Seen des Hochlandes und in zahlreichen Kolken der Gr. Falkenau'er Niederung, in weniger zahlreichen Gewässern der Danzig'er Niederung; **Ranunculus confervoides** Fr. (3 Fundorte), Callitriche autumnalis (4 Fundorte), Myriophyllum alternifl. an 10 Fundorten, Nuphar pumilum an 1 neuen, Potamogeton lucens + praelonga (1 Fundort), Potamogeton marina (1 Fundort), Pot. rutila (1 Fundort), Lemna gibba (4 Fundorte), nur südöstlich von Danzig, Isoëtes lacustris (1 Fundort), Fontinalis microphylla Schimp. (1 Fundort). **Kreis Berent:** 29. 7. See Wendfie bei Lubjahnen, wo ich eine Nacht blieb: Chara intermedia A. Br.; kleiner See im Walde südlich vom See Szabionko; Teich der Mühle Bebernitz. — **Kreis Kartaus:** 30. 7. Radaunensee von Stendsitz, wohin ich übersiedelt war, auf der Ostseite bis Kriegland und zurück auf der Westseite: **Alisma arcuatum** Michal. an mehreren Stellen, Z^{1-3} V^1, Chara ceratophylla, Ch. stelligera, Glyceria nemoralis U. et K. an Quellen der Westseite. — 31. 7. Ostritzsee in 8 Stunden umfahren: Chara stelligera, Ch. ceratophylla, **Callitriche autumnalis** sumpfige Bucht der Südseite des Westlappens. — 2. 8. Lubowiska-See: Chara ceratophylla, Ch. delicatula, Ch. foetida; Damerausee: Chara ceratophylla, Ch. stelligera, **Potamogeton rutila;** Fatully-See. — 3. 8. Drei Tümpel südwestl. von Seedorf; am grössesten: Lycopodium inundatum. Der Kesselsee von Alt-Czapel 1 Kilom. nach Süd: **Fontinalis microphylla** Schimp. (F. seriata Lindberg) Z^4 V^3, an Wurzeln von Alnus glutinosa und Pinus silvestris, wie Rhizomen von Menyanthes trifol. Kl.-Lonken-See: Elatine Hydropiper, Myriophyllum alterniflor., Gr. Lonken-See dieselben Pflanzen. — 4. 8. Kobbelsee nördlich vom Kl. Lonkensee: Myriophyll. altern. Dorfsee von Alt-Czapel. Steinsee östlich von Alt-Czapel: Myriophyll. alternifl. Z^4 V^4. Schulzensee südlich von Neu-Czapel: Myriophyll. altern. Z^4 V^4. Schwente nördlich vom Steinsee. — 5. 8. Kniewo-See 2 Kilom. südöstlich von Schöneberg: Myriophyll. alternifl., **Ranunculus confervoides** Fr., Nitella mucronata A. Br.; einige ganz kleine Tümpel nordwestlihh vom Kniewo. Gr. Bock-See (Brück-See der Generalstabskarte): Chara ceratophylla, Kl. Bocksee (westlich vom vorigen): Chara ceratoph. — 6. 8. See Kopinsko, 1 Kilom. nördlich von Zuromin: **Chara aspera, Ranunculus reptans** im Wasser auf dem Boden und am Ufer, hier blühend; Dorfsee von Boruschin; Glino-See, 1 Kilom. südöstl. von Niedeck. See südwestl. von Wigodda abgelassen. — 7. 8. See Szowinko, 2 Kilom. südwestlich von Boruschin; Kl. Bruch südlich von Neudorf; See von Alt Losinietz; Torfsee südöstlich von Jelonke; Torfsee zw. Sklana und Jelonke; in den letzten drei Seen Nuphar luteum durch pumilum beeinflusst. — 9. 8. Teich der Mühle Skorczewo; Mühlenteich von Gostomie: **Chara foetida** Z^4 V^1 und Ch. fragilis; Seechen südwestlich von Gostomie; Sumpfsee nordöstlich von Niessolowitz: **Chara intermedia** A. Br. Z^4 V^1, Ch. fragilis Z^4 V^4; See Klodzanka, südlich von Kloden: Ch. fragilis fr. Hedwigii Z^4 V^2. — 10. 8. Uebersiedelung nach Remboschewo. Linewko-See, 3 Kilometer NO von Remboschewo. — 11 8. See von Lappalitz, Ostseite, bei Sturm untersucht: Myriophyll. alternifl., **Alisma arcuatum** fr. graminifolia, **Chara aspera, Isoëtes lacustris** fr. vulgaris patula Z^2 V^1, in $2-2^1/_2$' Tiefe zwischen Phragmites, als Auswürfling hier schon 1877 gefunden, Litorella lacustris; fast abgelassener See südöstlich von Nassewiese; See von Sinnowerhütte. — 12. 8. Untersuchung der Radaune abwärts von Ostritz bis 1 Kilom. westlich von Semlin; See Trzebno: Chara ceratophylla; See Mieczetzko, Erweiterung der Radaune nördlich von Schlafkau; Sacksee der Radaune: Strischa, 2 Kilm. NO. von Schlafkau: Chara fragil. Z^4 V^4. See Smirczunko, 2 Kilom. NO von Gorrenschin: Chara ceratoph. — 13. 8. See 2 Kil. NO. von Kolano; Teufelssee 2 Kilom. östlich von Kolano; 4 kleine Tümpel des Hochlandes zw. Kalbszagel und Wilhelmshof. — 14. 8. Uebersiedelung nach Kartaus. Der Schwarzsee 1 Kilom. östlich von Kartaus; Malentkowa-See, 4 Kilom. NWW. von Kartaus, südlich von der Chaussee nach Lappalitz. — 15. 8. **Circaea intermedia** im Walde auf der NW.-Seite des Klostersees von Kartaus; Tümpel, 2 Kilom. südlich von Kartaus im Walde. — 16. 8. Kl. See von Seefeld im Thal 2 Kilom. NNW. von Seefeld, schon 10. 9. 1885 von mir untersucht. Darin keine Potamogeton marina, wie **Lützow** (Danz. Schriften 1886 114) angiebt, auch kein Pot. pectinata; auch in den beiden Torfseen NO von Seefeld keine dieser beiden Potamogetonen. Ohne Zweifel hat Lützow den See Glemboki, in dem Potamoget. marina reichlich vorkommt, mit dem Kl. See von Seefeld verwechselt. **Ranunculus reptans** am Ufer des Sees Tuchlinek OSS. vom Smolsin. Den See Glemboki, den ich schon 8. Sept. 1885 untersuchte, noch einmal auf der Ostseite untersucht und nun reichlich dort **Potamogeton marina** in Frucht gefunden; ich vermuthete hier 1885 die Pflanze, da Lange sie 1884 im Verbindungsgraben zw. dem Glemboki und Tuchlinek gesammelt hatte, wo sie weder 1885 noch 1886 mehr war; aber es war für Frucht am 8. Septbr. 1885 zu spät, die den 16. August 1886 noch reichlich da war. — 17. 8. Noch einmal den Kl. Borowo-See, $^1/_2$ Kilom. WSS. von Borowokrug, den ich schon 1885 befuhr, untersucht, wozu mich eine Angabe in einem Danzig'er Herbarium, dass darin Isoëtes vorkomme, bewog; jedoch fand ich keine Spur davon, wohl aber **Ranunculus confervoides Fr.** und **Litorella lacustris.** — 18. 8. Uebersiedelung nach dem östlichen Neukrug, Kreis Berent. See von Fustpetershütte. **Kreis Berent.** 18. 8. Moossee von d. östlich. Neukrug, nördlich vom Dorf. — 19. 8. **Kreis Kartaus.** Glamkesee bei Oberhütte, wieder untersucht um **Potamogeton lucens + praelonga** in Blüthe oder Frucht zu sammeln, die 1885 den 15. September, als ich den See befuhr, schon fehlte. In dem See schon 21. August 1864 die genannte Pflanze entdeckt; sie ist in **Garcke's** Flora von Deutschland als P. decipiens Nolte aufgeführt und als Fundort: „Klanauer See bei Berent" angegeben. Es ist besser den See als Glamke bei Oberhütte zu bezeichnen, da dies näher an ihm ist, als Klanau. Es waren 19. 8. nur untergetauchte Blüthen in 2—6' Tiefe, ohne Frucht zu finden. Nieder-Klanauer-See. — **Kreis Berent:** Fichtsee bei Oberbölle: **Nuphar pumilum** Z^4 V^3. — 20. 8. Ziehmke-See bei Neugrabau: **Callitriche autumnalis** Z^1 V^1, Myriophyll. alterniﬂ. See von Alt-Grabau: Chara ceratophylla, Potamogeton rutila, Callitriche autumnal. Torfsee zw. Jaschhütte und Spohn: Lycopodium inundat. Der Kl. Kamin'er See: Myriophyll. alternifl., **Ranunculus confervoides** Fr. — 21. 8. Der Lonkensee bei Vorwerk Lonken: Elatine Hydropiper, Myrioph. alternifl., Callitriche autumnal.; einige Tümpel bei Dt. Ochsenkopf; 2 kleine Seeen westlich von Burowo. — 23. 8. Torfsee westlich von Schatarpi. Teich der Mühle Niederschridlau und die Fietze: Callitriche autumn., Ranunculus divaric. und aquatilis; Tümpel $^1/_2$ Kilom. östlich von Liniewko: Myriophyll. alternifl.; Torfsee westlich vom Wege zw. Liniewko und Sobbonsch: Myriophyll. verticillat.; Torfsee etwa 1 Kilqm. nördlich von Sobbonsch. Torfmoorsee $1^1/_2$ Kilom. südwestlich von Neubarkoschin: Malaxis paludosa. — 24. 8. Noch einmal nach dem zuletzt genannten See: Myriophyll. alternifl., **Utricularia intermedia.** Uebersiedelung nach Decka. — 25. 8. Torfsee zwischen Janowo und Jungfernberg: Nuphar luteum und N. pumilum, jedoch nicht der Bastard. 2 kleine Tümpel bei Schlossberg. Uebersiedelung nach Schöneck. — 26. 8. Der Schwarzsee bei Wilhelmshöhe (Sieberts Abbau): Myriophyll. alternifl.; Kl. Torfsee zw. Boschpol und Gr. Paglau, südlich vom Wege: Riccia natans. Der Prausterkrug'er See wurde abgelassen gefunden. In Schöneck an der Fietze: Glyceria plicata. — 27. 8. Uebersiedelung nach Pelplin. — 28. 8. **Kreis Pr. Stargardt:** Torfsee nordwestlich vom Belauf Sturmberg; grösste Wasserpfütze desselben unzugänglich: **Gentiana campestris.** Kl. See östlich von Gr. Watzmirs; See von Kl. Watzmirs; See von Gnischau abgelassen; See von Schliewen, westlich vom Gehöft. — 30. u. 31. 8. 37 Kolke (oder Kolkgruppen) und Altwasser der Weichsel in der Gr. Falkenau'er Niederung untersucht, die ohne besondere Karte, wie die Kolke der Danzig'er Niederung, nicht gut näher bezeichnet werden können; an ihnen oft ausser gewöhnlichen Weichselpflanzen: Erythraea puchella, **Alisma arcuatum** Michal. mit lanzettlichen Blättern, in ihnen: **Alisma arcuatum** fr. graminifolia, Elodea canad. — 1. 9. Ferse in und unterhalb Pelplin: Potamogeton pectinata L., 5—6' lang, wo er dicht steht, dünn in Axe und schmal im Blatt, vereinzelt **Potam. zosteracea** Fr. darstellend, Sprossen dann 7—8 mm dick, Blätter sehr breit, unterste stumpf; eine **Potamogeton** zahlreich, die mir noch nicht klar ist, ohne schwimmende Blätter in sehr stark fliessendem Wasser, mit Blüthen aber ohne Frucht, sonst der Potam. rufescens Schrad. gleich, wird jedoch nicht beim Trocknen roth; will sie vorläufig als **Potamog. rufescens Schrad. fr. virescens** bezeichnen. Uebersiedelung nach Dirschau. — 2.—6. 9. Die Altwasser, Kolke (Brücke) oder Kolkgruppen, Laken und Vorfluthen, nebst Motlau und Radaune, der Danzig'er Niederung zwischen Dirschau und Danzig längs des linken Weichselufers untersucht, 35 Gewässer: **Kreis Pr. Stargardt,** Mühlenteich von Dirschau. **Kreis Danzig.** In sehr vielen Kolken Elodea canad. In einem Wasserloch durch Ausgraben von Ziegelerde entstanden im Aussendeich südöstlich vom Gamlitz **Alisma arcuatum** und auch in Kolken. Am meisten Interesse bot die Motlau, die ich von der Brücke in Scharfenberg bis zur Brücke von Hochzeit befuhr, darin: Lymnanthemum nymphoides Z^4 V^3, mit viel Aecidium nymphoides DC., Oryza-clandestina, **Alisma arcuatum** fr. graminifolia, **Lemna gibba L.** Im Kolk nördlich vom Dorf Sandweg auch **Lemna gibba,** auch in einem Graben südlich vom Hauptwege in Sandweg und in einem Graben zwischen Sandweg und Jansensbrück.

Schliesslich vertheilt Herr **Paul Schmitt** noch: Oryza clandestina, Aster Tripolium und Parietaria officinalis aus der Gegend von Oliva.

Um 4 Uhr wird die Sitzung geschlossen. Ein gemeinsames Mahl im Schützenhause vereinigte die Theilnehmer der Versammlung und viele angesehene Bürger Insterburgs. Es verlief in heiterster Weise unter vielen Trinksprüchen bis die in der Nacht abgehenden Eisenbahnzüge die Trennung befahlen.

Anhang.

Ueber Carex vaginata Tausch.

Von **Emil Knoblauch.**

Neu für Preussen und die deutsche Tiefebene überhaupt ist *Carex vaginata Tausch* Flora 1821, 557), von mir 1884 und 1885 im Memel'er Kreise an folgenden Standorten entdeckt: 1. Baugskorallen'er Wald, 2. Mikaitischken'er Wald, 3. Wald östl. Kl. Jagschen, 4. Packmohren'er Wald südl. der Ekitte, 5. Lappenischke zw. Wallehnen u. Girngallen-Gedmin, 6. Luseze, Jag. 74, 7. Wäldchen zw. Paaszkenkrug a. Szidellen, 8. Im Schutzbez. Aszpurwen in 9 Jag. 1886 fand Dr. **Abromeit** dieselbe Pflanze im Kreise Ortelsburg (s. oben) in 3 Jag. der Friedrichsfeld'er Forst, Bel. Rehhof. Sie wurde 1884 nicht gleich als C. vaginata, sondern nur als C. panicea nahestehend erkannt, daher 1885 lebend aus dem Memel'er Kreise in den botanischen Garten gebracht und hier beobachtet: die Pflanze ergab sich als von C. panicea verschieden. Die vorliegenden preussischen Exemplare stimmen auch der Grösse nach überein mit der bei Petersburg vorkommenden Pflanze, sind aber höher und üppiger als die Exemplare von den anderen bisher bekannten deutschen Standorten: Riesengebirge und Gesenke (in Höhen über 1200 m), und Brocken (in etwa 1000 m Höhe wachsend), nach dem Herbar. des kgl. botan. Gartens und des Herrn Stadtältesten Patze. Die nächsten ausserdeutschen Standorte sind: Ostseeprovinzen, Ingrien, Schweden und Norwegen. Von Schweden (Jemtland, Frösön) sah ich von J. Ahlberg 1857 gesammelte Exemplare im Herbar. des Herrn Professor Caspary.

Da die bisherigen Beschreibungen von Carex vaginata teilweise von einander abweichen (die besten bei **Tausch** a. O. und **Boott**, Illustr. Gen. Carex. London 1867. IV, 148. Taf. 478), so gebe ich nach dem vorhandenen reichlichen meist preussischen Material folgende Beschreibung. Die in derselben angeführten Zahlenangaben sind zum Vergleiche mit den übereinstimmenden von Boott gegeben.

Herba laete viridis; **spica mascula** solitaria, **spicis femineis** 2—3 remotis, basi laxifloris, infima exserte pedunculata; **fructibus** ovatis v. ovato-oblongis obtuse trigonis glabberrimis obscure nervatis, squama obtusa longioribus, basi attenuatis, breviter rostratis, rostro obliquo ore oblique truncato integro v. emarginato; **culmo** obtusangulo glabro leviter striato; **foliis** culmeis brevissimis; **bracteis** vaginatis ore dilatatis.

Laub und Halm der **Pflanze hellgrün. Rhizom** wagrecht, mit linealen spitzen Niederblättern bedeckt. Halm steif aufrecht, in dem ährchentragenden Teile häufig schlaffer, stumpfkantig, gerillt.*) **Halmblätter sehr kurz,** unter dem Blüthenstande 4—6. Die 3—5 unteren derselben sind **Niederblätter,** die untersten Niederblätter braun, stumpfspitzig, die obersten Niederblätter mit einer kurzen grünen Spitze versehen, die 1—3 oberen besitzen eine kurze deutliche grüne kurzspitzige Spreite. Lg. dieser Spreiten gew. 2—4,4 cm, selten 9,8 cm bei Spreiten dieser oberen kurzen Halmblätter unter dem Blüthenstande beobachtet. **Die Blätter der nicht blühenden Triebe** lang, selbst die längsten (29—53 cm lang) derselben kürzer als der Halm, selten länger oder so lang als der Halm, lineal, 0,3—0,6 cm breit, 11—19 nervig. Mittlerer und 2 seitl. Nerven stärker, an der breitesten Stelle der Blätter der mittlere Nerv deutlich unterseits, die beiden seitlichen stärkeren Nerven oberseits hervorragend; an der Blattspitze, am Rande und auf der oberen Blattfläche auf den Nerven, zum kleinen Teile auch zwischen denselben mit zerstreuten Zähnchen besetzt; auf den beiden stärkeren

*) 42—56 cm lang, der Bthstd. 10—20.

Seitenrippen 1—2 Reihen solcher Zähnchen. Blätter daher glatt, nur an der Spitze am Rande und oberseits rauh. Diese langen Blätter stehen in Büscheln, am Grunde von kurzen Blättern umgeben, die den Grundhalmblättern gleichen. Die **Blätter mittlerer Länge** sind **verhältnissmässig kurz zugespitzt** (bei Carex panicea sehr lang zugespitzt), die längsten lang zugespitzt.

Männl. Aehrchen einzeln an der Halmspitze — nur einmal 2 gesehen, wovon das untere am Grunde weibl. war — lineal, Lg. 1,5—3,0 cm: Br. 0,2—0,4 cm = 5—10:1, meist 7:1. Die **Deckschuppen** derselben dicht, länglich, stumpf, kermesin, meist mit schmaler grüner Mittelrippe, die 3 Staubbeutel lang heraushängend.

Weibl. Aehrchen 2—3, selten 4, entfernt, lineal, am Grunde lockerblüthig, das unterste mit langem aus der Scheide des Tragblattes herausragenden Stiel von 2,4—4,3 cm Länge, bisweilen grundständig mit 15—26 cm langem Stiel. **Deckschuppen** eilänglich, stumpf, die der untern Aehrchen öfters spitz, selten mit kleiner aufgesetzter Spitze, minder dicht als bei dem männl. Aehrchen, kermesin, meist mit grünem Mittelstreifen. Schläuche der **Früchtchen** länger als die Deckschuppen, in der Blüthe wenig kürzer oder eben so lang. Die reifen Früchtchen goldgelb, länglich oder eilänglich, **stumpfdreikantig**, glatt, undeutlich nervig, am Grunde verschmälert, mit **kurzem** deutlichem schief aufgesetztem **Schnabel**; Spitze desselben **schief abgeschnitten**, ganz, weniger häufig ausgerandet oder gezähnelt. **Narben** 2—3, meist 3.

Reife Früchtchen 4,2—6,4 mm lang, in der Mitte 1,7—2,7 mm, am Grunde 0,7—1,1 mm breit, Schnabellänge 0,7—1,6 mm. Verb. der Längen von Früchtchen und Schnabel = 3—7:1, meist 5,8:1. Die Oberhautzellen der Schläuche der Früchtchen von Carex vaginata sind länglich: Br.: Lg. = 1:$1^1/_2$—$2^1/_2$, ihre Aussenwände nicht oder nur wenig convex. Bei C. panicea sind die Oberhautzellen etwa ebensobreit wie lang: Br.:Lg. = 1:2—$^2/_3$, gew. 1:1—$^4/_3$, Aussenwände convex.

Tragblätter der weiblichen Aehrchen mit einer langen oben erweiterten Scheide, kurzspreitig — gew. Längen von Scheide und Spreite beim Tragblatt des untersten Aehrchens $2^1/_4$—4 cm und 1—2 cm, selten die Spreite etwas länger als die Scheide —, kürzer als die betr. Aehrchen (selten beim untersten länger); selten zeigen die Tragblätter eine kurze stumpfe, der Spreite gegenüberstehende Ligula. Bisweilen kommt unter dem untersten weibl. Aehrchen ein tragblattähnliches Hochblatt vor, in dessen Achsel kein Aehrchen steht.

Carex panicea besitzt angedrückte, selten an der Mündung wenig erweiterte Scheiden der Tragblätter; C. vaginata ist nach den langen erweiterten Scheiden von Tausch benannt worden.

Die männl. und weibl. Aehrchen bisweilen in sich rechtwinklig gekrümmt, oder auch die Stiele unter denselben mehr oder wenig stark abgebogen. Das bei Koch Syn. fl. germ. et helv. Ed. 2. 1854. II, 879; Hampe, Fl. herc. 1873, 296; Garcke, Fl. von Deutschland, 15. Aufl. 1885, 447 angegebene Merkmal „männliche Aehrchen rechtwinklig zurückgebrochen" ist nach Beobachtungen im Memel'er Kreise und im Königsberg'er botan. Garten nur ein individuelles, kein Artmerkmal, zumal es auch bei Carex panicea, nämlich var. refracta Klinggr. vorkommt.

Standort: Feuchte Wälder, im Memel'er Kreise besonders in gemischten Wäldern mit Pinus silvestris und Betula pubescens. — **Blüht** im Kr. Memel Ende Mai und Anfang Juni.

Der in einigen deutschen Floren (Garcke, Hampe, Fiek-Uechtritz) vorangestellte Name **Carex sparsiflora**, den Steudel der schwedischen Pflanze gab (Syn. pl. glum. I 227. 1854), ist nach der 11. Aufl. von C. J. Hartman's Handbok i Skandinaviens Flora, Stockholm 1879, 460 nur ein Synonym von C. vaginata Tausch.

Kosmogonische Betrachtungen

von

Prof. Dr. **Louis Saalschütz.**

(Mit Figuren auf Tafel No. 1.)

Immanuel Kant stellt bekanntlich als der Erste*) mit genialem Blick die Ansicht auf, dass die Bildung der Planeten aus der Sonne eine Wirkung der Centrifugalkraft gewesen sei, in Folge deren sie vom Aequator der Sonne abgeschleudert worden; Kant nimmt ferner an, dass in gleicher Art aus den Planeten die Monde entstanden seien. Diese Ansicht stimmt sehr schön mit den Thatsachen überein, dass die Planeten- und Mondbahnen nahezu in eine Ebene fallen und dass die Umlaufsbewegung aller Körper des Sonnensystems in demselben Sinne erfolgt wie die Axendrehung der Sonne. Dennoch sind ganz abgesehen von direkten Irrthümern, die durch den damaligen Stand der Beobachtungen veranlasst wurden, im Einzelnen bei dieser Hypothese mancherlei Schwierigkeiten fortzuräumen. In dieser Hinsicht sollen im Folgenden einige Versuche gemacht werden, wobei ich aber ausdrücklich bemerke, dass nur die Möglichkeit der Abschleuderungstheorie, aber durchaus nicht ihre Gewissheit durch die folgenden Betrachtungen begründet werden soll. Ich beginne dabei mit den beiden Fragen: 1. Genügt die Annahme der Centrifugalkraft, um die Bildung der vorhandenen Planeten zu erklären? 2. Kann der Centralkörper die Gestalt einer Kugel haben, wenn mittelst der Centrifugalkraft aus ihm Planeten sollen entstehen können?

Um die erste Frage zu beantworten, denken wir uns eine kleine Masse, etwa eine Kugel am Umfange des Aequators eines rotirenden Centralkörpers. Auf dieselbe wirken zwei Kräfte: die Anziehung des Centralkörpers $\varDelta$, abhängig von seiner Masse und seinem Halbmesser aber unabhängig von seiner Rotationsgeschwindigkeit und die Centrifugalkraft $\varGamma$, abhängig von der letzteren und seinem Halbmesser, aber unabhängig von seiner Masse. Ist die Centrifugalkraft grösser als die Anziehungskraft, so wird die Kugel sich tangential mit der Umfangsgeschwindigkeit des Centralkörpers von ihm entfernen und zwar wird, soweit die Anziehung nach dem Newtonschen Gesetz erfolgt, wenn $\varGamma$ zwischen $\varDelta$ und $2\varDelta$ liegt, die Kugel (der Planet) eine Ellipse um ersteren beschreiben und in dem Grenzfalle, $\varGamma$ gleich $\varDelta$, einen Kreis; in den anderen Fällen, $\varGamma$ gleich oder grösser als $2\varDelta$, eine Parabel bez. eine

*) Naturgeschichte und Theorie des Himmels erste Aufl. Königsberg 1755, spätere Aufl. Frankfurt und Leipzig 1797. — Laplace hat sein System erst etwa 40 Jahre später entwickelt.

Hyperbel,*) so dass dann also die abgeschleuderte Masse sich dauernd von dem Centralkörper entfernt. Die obige Annahme genügt also zweifellos zur Erklärung der bestehenden Planetenbahnen.

Eine andere Frage ist es freilich, ob die Centrifugalkraft als alleinige Ursache für die Bildung von Planeten angesehen werden darf. Dies ist nicht der Fall. Die Planeten können auch durch Eruptionen (das will sagen: Fortschleuderungen auf Grund chemisch-physikalischer Ursachen) entstanden gedacht werden. Freilich dürfte diese Fortschleuderung nicht von einem Punkte der Sonnenoberfläche aus geschehen. So wie nämlich ein solcher planetenartiger Körper die Sonne verliesse, unterläge er den Gesetzen der Bewegung und der Anziehung, wie sie von Keppler und Newton erkannt worden sind.**) Danach müsste der Körper eine elliptische Bahn beschreiben, für welche der Sonnenmittelpunkt der Brennpunkt wäre; eine solche Ellipse müsste aber wie man schon ohne Rechnung sieht, die Sonnenoberfläche nothwendig wieder treffen, d. h. der abgeschleuderte Körper müsste, näher oder weiter von seinem Ursprung wieder auf dieselbe zurückfallen.***) Wenn wir aber den Centralkörper als eine dichtere Kugel ansehen, welche von dünnen Flüssigkeits- oder Gasschichten umgeben wird, so können wir den Herd der Eruption, zu der jedenfalls die Wirkung der Centrifugalkraft hinzukäme, auf den Umfang des Kerns verlegen; dann hätte aber allerdings der von dem Sonnenkörper sich lösende Planet zunächst noch die Flüssigkeitsschichten zu durchfliegen, ehe er völlig frei wird, wodurch seine Geschwindigkeit nach Richtung und Stärke modificirt würde.

Zur Beantwortung der zweiten der obigen Fragen übergehend, nehme ich den Haupttheil der Antwort vorweg, er lautet: der Centralkörper muss eine von der Kugel beträchtlich abweichende Form haben, wenn centrifugale Abschleuderungen möglich sein sollen. Diese Antwort, welche die hauptsächlichste Grundlage des Folgenden bildet, soll näher begründet werden. Wir können zwei verschiedenartige Voraussetzungen als Grenzen derjenigen Zustände annehmen, durch welche sich der Centralkörper, also die Sonne, vom Beginn seiner Entstehung bis jetzt hindurch bewegt haben muss. Die erste Voraussetzung ist, dass der flüssige oder gasförmige Körper überall dieselbe Dichtigkeit habe und dass alle seine Theile sich gegenseitig nach dem Newtonschen Gesetze anziehen. Die zweite ist, dass der Körper aus einem dichten Kerne und einer denselben umgebenden Hülle von geringer Dichtigkeit bestehe, so dass nur die Anziehung des Kerns auf die einzelnen Massentheile der Hülle aber nicht die gegenseitige Anziehung der letzteren in Betracht kommt. Irgend eine andere Vertheilung der Dichtigkeit in dem Körper lässt sich füglich als Zustand ansehen, der zwischen den genanten Grenzzuständen liegt. Wir werden uns den Urzustand der Sonne nahezu der ersten Hypothese entsprechend vorstellen können, während er sich von da an mehr und mehr der zweiten Hypothese näherte und noch zur Zeit dauernd nähert. So nehmen wir jetzt bereits als äusserste Hülle der Sonne eine breite Wasserstoffsphäre an. Denken wir uns nun einen Körper, wie ihn die erste

*) Siehe im ersten mathematischen Zusatz unter 2. das Beispiel $\alpha = 0$, insbesondere die Gleichungen 21.

**) Die strengere Analyse erfordert allerdings in der Nähe des anziehenden Körpers die Berücksichtigung seiner Gestalt; siehe den ersten mathem. Zusatz Gleichung 10 und das Folgende.

***) Vergl. daselbst 2., besonders das Beispiel $\alpha = 45^0$.

Voraussetzung fordert, mit einer gewissen Geschwindigkeit rotirend, so hängt die Gestalt, die er annimmt, von dieser Geschwindigkeit und von seiner Dichtigkeit ab; sie wird ein abgeplattetes Rotationsellipsoid und es findet der merkwürdige Umstand statt, dass derselben Rotationsgeschwindigkeit, falls diese überhaupt eine gewisse Grösse nicht überschreitet, welche, wie die mathematische Analyse ergiebt,*) ein Axenverhältniss zwischen 1/3 und 2/5 bedingt, zwei verschiedene Rotationsellipsoide entsprechen. Von diesen beiden (zu denen die von Jacobi herrührende mathematische Entwickelung noch ein drittes ungleichaxiges hinzugefügt hat) bezeichnet das weniger abgeplattete mit dem Axenverhältniss zwischen 1 und 0,3678 eine stabile Gleichgewichtslage, das flachere mit dem Axenverhältniss zwischen 0,3678 und 0 eine labile.**) Das dem möglichen Maximum des Verhältnisses: Quadrat der Winkelgeschwindigkeit (ω) dividirt durch die Dichtigkeit (ϱ) entsprechende Axenverhältniss (0,3678) wollen wir das kritische nennen, weil der Aequatorumfang des rotirenden Körpers, so wie er diese Figur (oder eine flachere) annimmt, in jedem Augenblick der Gefahr ausgesetzt wird, als Ring abgelöst oder bei nicht völliger Homogenität (des Aequatorumfanges) in Stücken fortgeschleudert zu werden. — Legt man hingegen die andere Voraussetzung zu Grunde, so giebt es wieder eine Maximal-Winkelgeschwindigkeit; dieselbe entspricht genau dem Verhältniss der Polar- zur Aequatorialaxe 2 : 3;***) dies ist also in diesem Falle das kritische Verhältniss und für einen Punkt des Aequatorumfanges tritt hier noch die anschauliche Thatsache hinzu, dass für ihn Anziehungskraft und Centrifugalkraft gleich gross sind. Ist die Maximalgeschwindigkeit nicht erreicht, so giebt es wieder eine Rotationsfläche und zwar nur eine als Gleichgewichtsfigur, deren Axenverhältniss zwischen 2/3 und 1 liegt, die aber kein Ellipsoid ist.

Mit der Nothwendigkeit der Annahme einer abgeplatteten Form für die Bildung von Planeten bez. Monden stimmen folgende Thatsachen überein. Denkt man sich einen Planeten in kreisförmiger Bahn die Sonne und zwar ganz dicht an ihrer Oberfläche umlaufend, so kann man nach dem dritten Keppler'schen Gesetz†) seine Umlaufszeit bestimmen, wenn man für die Entfernung vom Sonnenmittelpunkt den Sonnenhalbmesser einsetzt. Man erhält dadurch die Zeit von 0,116 Tagen. Ebenso schnell müsste die Sonne um ihre Axe rotiren, sollte sie einen solchen Planeten noch jetzt hervorbringen können. Die Rotationsdauer der Sonne beträgt aber 26 Tage und das Verhältniss der beiden Zahlen ist daher 1 : 250 oder 0,004. Denkt man sich ebenso um die Erde einen Mond ganz dicht herumlaufend, so erhielte man für dessen Umlaufszeit 1/15 Tag, die Erdrotation beträgt aber 1 Tag, also ist das Verhältniss dieser beiden Grössen jetzt 0,066. Dasselbe ist für den Mars 0,09, hingegen für Jupiter 0,29, für Saturn 0,35, für Uranus 0,30. Nun ist bei der Sonne keine Abplattung beobachtet worden, bei der Erde ist sie nur 1/300 und beim Mars wahrscheinlich auch ebenso gering, wogegen sie bei den äusseren Planeten zwischen den Zahlen 1/11 bis 1/17 liegt. Diese weichen also von

*) Siehe den zweiten mathem. Zusatz 1. — Das oben erwähnte Axenverhältniss ist 0,3678.
**) Siehe den zweiten mathematischen Zusatz 1.
***) Siehe hierüber und über das Folgende den zweiten mathem. Zusatz 2.
†) Siehe den ersten mathem. Zusatz Gleichung 9.

der Kugelform merklich ab und stehen daher, wie die drei letzten Zahlen zeigen, der Möglichkeit Monde hervorzubringen, beträchtlich näher als die Sonne und die inneren Planeten.

Nunmehr kann ich mich zur Darstellung meiner Muthmassungen über die Entstehung des Sonnensystems aus dem ursprünglich allein vorhandenen Centralkörper wenden.

Denkt man sich eine grosse Anhäufung einzelner materieller Theilchen von flacher linsenähnlicher Form und durch das Hinzuströmen seitlicher Materie immer mehr an Grösse zunehmend, so hat man ein Bild unseres Centralkörpers, wie er vor Entstehung des Planetensystems sich dargestellt haben mag. Die Vermuthung einer solchen Form stützt sich hauptsächlich auf die im Allgemeinen angenommenen Ansichten über die Gestalt vieler Nebelflecke und die Form der Milchstrasse. Dieses System gegen einander gravitirender Materie gerieth in Folge der Vereinigung von Einzelrotationen allmählich in eine allgemeine Rotation. Gleichzeitig trat eine sehr allmähliche Verdichtung ein und in Folge deren und einer etwaigen Reibung der Theilchen untereinander eine Erhöhung der Temperatur und aus beiden Ursachen wiederum die Erzeugung von Ausdehnungskräften. Sehr bald hörte aber auch das Gleichgewicht der Stoff-Anhäufung in ihrer, einer optischen Linse vergleichbaren, Gestalt auf. Denn es ist zwar eine solche flache Form, d. h. die Form eines sehr abgeplatteten Rotationsellipsoides als Gleichgewichtsfigur für einen genügend kleinen Werth von $\frac{\omega^2}{\varrho}$ (Quadrat der Winkelgeschwindigkeit dividirt durch die Dichtigkeit) anzunehmen möglich, aber nur als labile Gleichgewichtsfigur,*) sie hätte sich also nur, wenn nicht die geringste Störung eingetreten wäre, erhalten können. Eine solche Annahme involvirte aber eine an directe Verneinung grenzende Unwahrscheinlichkeit. In Folge der somit anzunehmenden Störung setzte sich die potentielle Energie der Gravitationskräfte in actuelle um und erzeugte somit lebendige Kraft. Damit erhöhte sich auch das Verhältniss $\frac{\omega^2}{\varrho}$ und liess also eine neue weniger abgeplattete Gleichgewichtsfigur entstehn — aber wiederum nur eine labile. So ging es — ich möchte mir den Ausdruck tumultuarisch erlauben — weiter, bis das Maximum von $\frac{\omega^2}{\varrho}$, das eine zusammenhängende Form gestattet, erreicht war. Noch eine geringe Erhöhung der Geschwindigkeit und der Zusammenhang der Form wurde nochmals gestört. Diesen Vorgang (beim Grenzwerth von $\frac{\omega^2}{\varrho}$) können wir uns vielleicht in folgender Art vorstellen. Bei Ueberschreiten der zulässigen Maximalgeschwindigkeit wird eine Bedingung für die Möglichkeit einer Gleichgewichtsfigur unerfüllbar. Die Continuität der Flüssigkeit hört auf. Einzelne Massentheile in der Nähe des Aequatorumfanges lösen sich von demselben, da ihre Centrifugalkraft von der Anziehungskraft der ganzen Masse überwogen wird,**) nach innen zu ab und beginnen in ellipsenähnlichen Bahnen, für welche der Ausgangspunkt die Sonnenferne vorstellt, den

*) Siehe die vorige Seite.

**) Siehe zweiten mathem. Zusatz Gleichung 11 und den folgenden Text.

Mittelpunkt des Centralkörpers zu umkreisen.*) Dadurch wird erstens der Zusammenhang der den äussersten Umfang bildenden Massentheile mit dem Kern gelockert oder aufgehoben und dadurch eben die Continuität gestört, zweitens wird durch die mit der Annäherung zum Mittelpunkt wachsende Geschwindigkeit der genannten abgelösten Massentheile, denen die durchfurchte Flüssigkeit nach innen und nach aussen zu auszuweichen gezwungen ist, den nach innen gelegenen Theilen der letzteren ein Streben nach dem Centrum, den nach aussen gelegenen eine Geschwindigkeits-Componente nach aussen hin mitgetheilt. Das hat nun wieder den Erfolg, dass die centralen Theile sich übereinander zu schichten veranlasst werden, dass hierdurch die Polaraxe sich erhöht, die Form kugelähnlicher und ihr Kern dichter wird, dass endlich in Folge dessen die Anziehungskraft der Masse auf einen äussern Punkt mehr gemäss dem Newton'schen Gesetze wirkt, während die Geschwindigkeit der äussersten Massentheile vermehrt wird. Dadurch werden sie aber befähigt von der ganzen Masse nach aussen hin sich zu lösen und nach Maassgabe der erlangten Geschwindigkeit dieselbe in Kreisen oder Ellipsen zu umlaufen.**) — Im vorliegenden Falle wurde dieser Vorgang noch dadurch begünstigt, dass, unbeschadet der Homogenität des Centralkörpers im Grossen und Ganzen, der äusserste Umfang mit hoher Wahrscheinlichkeit aus grösseren und kleineren Massentheilen verschiedener Dichtigkeit gebildet wurde. Eine Moles (Klumpen) von höherer Dichtigkeit löste sich zuerst leicht ab und andere kleinere folgten derselben sofort nach und schlossen sich ihr an. So entstand der erste Planet, dessen Ursprung der Betrachtung zugänglich zu werden scheint; nehmen wir an, da das Folgende dem nicht widerspricht, es sei der Neptun gewesen! Ob in der vorangehenden Periode irgend welche Abschleuderungen stattgefunden hatten — diese Frage entzieht sich bei dem chaotischen Character der genannten Periode, wie ich glaube, jeder Ueberlegung und jeder geistigen Handhabe. Erst von der Entstehung des Neptun an dürfen wir es wagen, die folgenden Zustände in ihrem Zusammenhange mit einem gewissen Grad von Wahrscheinlichkeit der Betrachtung zu unterziehen. Mit der Entfernung des Neptun (s. Fig. 1 AAAA) ging dem Centralkörper ein gewisses Quantum lebendiger Kraft (d. i. Bewegungsenergie) verloren; in Folge dessen wurde $\frac{\omega^2}{\varrho}$ kleiner; und auch dieser Umstand trug dazu bei, den Grad der Abplattung der Figur zu vermindern; auf diese Weise wurde zum ersten Mal eine stabile Gleichgewichtslage BBBB erreicht. Da aber dieser Vorgang im Sinne der expansiven Kräfte geschah, so dehnte sich in Folge des Beharrungsvermögens die Figur über die Gleichgewichtslage hinüber bis CCCC aus, bis die Gravitationskräfte wieder zu überwiegen begannen, und die Sonne wieder über B und A in die Lage D zusammengezogen und abgeplattet wurde.***)

Ich unterbreche hier die Entwickelung auf kurze Zeit, um mich über die Art der beschriebenen Bewegung noch präciser auszusprechen. Nehmen wir an, dass eine tropfbare homogene Flüssigkeit in Folge ihrer Rotation um eine feste Axe in die-

---

*) Siehe ersten mathem. Zusatz die Anmerkung über $\varphi = 180^0$ (nach Gleichung 17 b).

**) Siehe den zweiten mathem. Zusatz, Anmerkung zu Gleichung 11.

***) Die Gravitationskräfte platten ab, die Expansivkräfte gleichen aus, wie sich leicht beweisen lässt.

jenige Lage gekommen sei, die einem ferner stehenden Beobachter als ein starres Ellipsoid von gewisser Abplattung erscheint. Hier halten sich also die Gravitations-, die Centrifugal- und die inneren Druckkräfte im Gleichgewicht. Dies drückt sich analytisch dadurch aus, dass die Resultante der beiden ersteren Kräfte für ein bestimmtes Massentheilchen die Richtung der Druckkraft haben, d. h. auf der durch diesen Punkt gehenden Oberfläche gleichen Druckes senkrecht stehen muss. Nehmen wir nun weiter an, die Flüssigkeit besitze die Eigenschaft der Elasticität, und der ganze Tropfen werde gleichmässig zusammengedrückt und wieder plötzlich sich selbst überlassen. Dann befindet sich dieser Tropfen genau in dem Zustande eines hängenden elastischen Drathes, der durch ein centrisch durchbohrtes cylindrisches Gewicht hindurchgeht, das auf ein an dem unteren Drahtende befestigtes Plättchen sich stützt — wenn man dieses Gewicht aufhebt und plötzlich wieder fallen lässt. Hier werden dann auf- und abgebende Schwingungen eintreten, weil die Spannung im Allgemeinen mit der Schwere des Gewichtes nicht übereinstimmen wird. Dabei wird jedesmal die Gleichgewichtslage erreicht, aber sofort überschritten werden, weil die Geschwindigkeit in diesem Augenblick nicht Null (sondern sogar ein Maximum) ist. Ganz analog werden auch bei dem Tropfen die drei oben genannten Kräfte sich nicht das Gleichgewicht halten, die Resultante der Attractions- und der Centrifugalkräfte wird nicht die Richtung der Druckkraft, d. h. der Normalen zur Oberfläche haben, und daher die Form sich ändern; dabei wird auch einmal eine Form erreicht werden, bei der die Kräfte im Gleichgewicht sind, dann ist aber wieder die Geschwindigkeit der Flüssigkeitstheilchen in der Richtung genannter Normale nicht Null und diese Form wird daher sofort überschritten. Es wird also dadurch, dass die vorausgesetzte Elasticität in Wirkung kommt, der Character des Problems nicht in seinem Wesen geändert und ebenso wenig, wenn die den gasförmigen Körpern eigenthümlichen Expansionskräfte in Action treten: sondern es wird nur der sonst andauernde Gleichgewichtszustand zu einem vorübergehenden, um welchen Schwingungen oder besser gesagt, da die Formänderungen gleichzeitig nach allen räumlichen Richtungen geschehen, Pulsationen statthaben, und welcher Gleichgewichtszustand bei etwaiger Abschwächung der letzteren (wie beim Pendel im widerstehenden Mittel) auch das Endergebniss des ganzen Vorganges bleiben würde.

Nunmehr nehme ich die unterbrochene Entwickelung der Hypothese über die vormaligen Zustände des Sonnenkörpers wieder auf. Die in beschriebener Art eingeleiteten Pulsationen desselben würden in gleicher Art, wenn nicht die Bedingungen sich geändert hätten, in Ewigkeit fortgedauert haben. Es wäre bei jeder Pulsation von C aus die zwischen der Gleichgewichtslage B und der Lage der grössten Zusammenziehung D gelegene kritische Lage A (bei der das Axenverhältniss 0,3678 ist, also zwischen $^1/_3$ und $^2/_5$ liegt) erreicht und somit (auf der Strecke A-D-A) Planetenbildung möglich geworden, während diese Möglichkeit auf der Strecke A-C-A aufgehört hätte. Nun traten aber zwei Aenderungen in den Bedingungen ein, die wir einzeln betrachten müssen: die Umgestaltung der Structur des Centralkörpers und die Abkühlung durch den Weltraum. Was das erste betrifft, so sanken allmählich die specifisch schwereren Stoffe auf der Sonne nach dem Mittelpunkte zu und es bereitete sich ein Zustand vor, bei dem die Dichtigkeit von Schicht zu Schicht nach dem Mittelpunkt hin wächst. Als Grenzzustand, der auch jetzt (wie bereits erwähnt) noch lange nicht erreicht ist, erscheint ein Körper mit sehr dichtem Kerne, den wir uns kugelförmig vorstellen können, um welchen eine der Ausdehnung nach beträchtliche Flüssigkeits- oder Gasschicht sehr geringer Dichtigkeit sich herumlagert. In diesem Grenzfalle ist aber das kritische Axenverhältniss, und zwar genau, $^2/_3$. Man darf also wohl annehmen, wie wir es thun wollen, dass dasselbe von seinem Anfangswerth zwischen $^1/_2$ und $^2/_5$ allmählich seinem Endwerth $^2/_3$ sich nähern wird.*) Aber auch das Axenverhältniss der Gleichgewichtslage änderte sich und zwar wegen des zweiten oben erwähnten Umstandes: der Abkühlung durch den sehr kalten Weltraum, dessen Temperatur höchstens -273^0 C. beträgt.

Hierdurch trat nämlich zu der bisher betrachteten periodischen Aenderung der Gestalt des Centralkörpers eine nicht periodische, die allmähliche Verkürzung seiner Dimensionen hinzu. Nehmen wir nun an, was sicher gestattet ist, dass die Masse der Sonne bei dieser Aenderung dieselbe bleibt, dass aber auch ihre Bewegungsenergie, die durch die Arbeit der inneren Gravitationskräfte erhöht, durch die Wärmeausstrahlung verringert wird, sich nicht wesentlich ändert, wie auch, der Einfachheit wegen, dass bei der kleinen Aenderung, die wir als Beginn der allmählichen Umgestaltung allein ins Auge zu fassen nöthig haben, die Structur von gleicher Art bleibt; — bezeichnen wir ferner Masse, Axen, Dichtigkeit, Winkelgeschwindigkeit in der ursprünglichen Lage mit: M, a und b, ϱ, ω und die letzten drei in der wenig veränderten Lage mit a_1 und b_1, ϱ_1, ω_1 so haben wir die Gleichungen:**)

$$M = {}^4/_3\, a^2\, b\, \pi\, \varrho = {}^4/_3\, a_1^2\, b_1\, \pi\, \varrho_1$$
$${}^2/_5\, Ma^2\, \omega^2 = {}^2/_5\, Ma_1^2\, \omega_1^2$$

*) Um Einwänden in Betreff dieser Anschauung, wie sie mir von competenter Seite gemacht worden sind, besser begegnen zu können, habe ich (im zweiten mathematischen Zusatz, 3) das Rotationsproblem so behandelt, dass ich allerdings wieder einen dichten homogenen Kern, von einer Schicht äusserst geringer Dichtigkeit umgeben, annahm, dass ich aber die Gestalt des Kerns als änderungsfähig voraussetzte. Ich glaube mich dadurch dem wahren Zustand des Körpers mit seinen vielen übereinander gelagerten Schichten verschiedener Dichtigkeit um einen Schritt genähert zu haben und kann nun aus den gewonnenen Resultaten folgende Schlüsse ziehen. Gehen wir von einem im Ganzen homogenen Zustande des Centralkörpers mit dem Axenverhältniss nahe 0,8678 (also etwa $^4/_5$) aus und nehmen wir an, dass in Folge des Sinkens der specifisch schwereren Stoffe nach dem Mittelpunkte zu sich ein Kern bildete, dessen Dichtigkeit immer grösser wurde, so entstand dadurch eine ihn umgebende Hülle von sehr geringer Dichte, deren Raum gegenüber dem Kern immer grösser wurde, denn, indem der Mittelwerth (so bezeichnet mit Hinblick auf seine Aenderungen durch die Pulsationen) von $\frac{\omega^2}{\varrho}$ immer kleiner wurde, ward der Kern immer mehr kugelähnlich; dadurch rückte aber die freie Oberfläche der Hülle als Grenze desjenigen Gebietes der letzteren, innerhalb dessen entsprechend der jedesmaligen Abplattung des Kerns keine Zerstörung durch die Centrifugalkraft stattfinden kann, immer weiter hinaus. (Siehe a. a. O. von dem Absatz vor Gleichung 78 an.) Gleichzeitig wurde aber auch das Axenverhältniss dieser Oberfläche, welche, wie gesagt, auf der Grenze der Zerstörung steht, immer grösser, bis dafür der Werth $^2/_3$, sobald der Kern in seiner Gestalt nicht mehr merklich von einer Kugel abweicht, erreicht ist.

**) Wenn in Folge eintretender Erstarrung die Arbeit der inneren Gravitation aufhört, so wird die Bewegungsenergie kleiner, die zweite der obigen Gleichungen gilt nicht mehr, sondern es wird $a_1^2\, \omega_1^2$ kleiner als $a^2\, \omega^2$ und daher bei constantem $a : \omega_1 < \omega$. Dies muss beim Planeten Mars bereits eingetreten sein, denn seine Rotationsgeschwindigkeit ist nicht nur relativ, sondern absolut kleiner als diejenige seines nächsten Mondes. Dieser umkreist nämlich den Mars in ca. 12 Stunden, während der Planet selbst die Drehung um seine Axe in ca. 24 Stunden vollendet.

Die Division derselben ergiebt nach Fortlassung gleicher Factoren:

$$\frac{\omega^2}{b\varrho} = \frac{\omega_1^2}{b_1\varrho_1} \text{ oder } \frac{\omega_1^2}{\varrho_1} = \frac{b_1}{b} \cdot \frac{\omega^2}{\varrho}.$$

Da nun von dem ersten Zustand zum zweiten eine Verkürzung der Dimensionen stattgefunden hat, so ist $\frac{b_1}{b}$ ein echter Bruch, demgemäss $\frac{\omega_1^2}{\varrho_1}$ kleiner als $\frac{\omega^2}{\varrho}$ (während ω_1 grösser als ω wird, also die Winkelgeschwindigkeit wächst) und folglich die Gleichgewichtsgestalt näher einer Kugel. Wir haben also in unserer Figur 1 die Ellipsen resp. die ellipsenähnlichen Curven sich immer mehr abrundend zu denken. Aber noch in anderer Hinsicht wäre diese Figur, der allmählichen Gestaltsänderung der Sonne entsprechend, umzuformen. Wir haben nämlich anzunehmen, dass in Folge der Widerstände, hauptsächlich innerer Reibung, die Pulsationen immer schwächer wurden, so dass in unserer Figur die Linien CC und DD immer näher an BB heranrückten und dabei allmählich die Linie AA (kritische Lage) ganz ausschlossen; sowie dies aber geschehen war, hörte die Möglichkeit der Planetenbildung auf.

Um nun den Erfolg der Gesammtwirkung aller genannten Ursachen für die wirkliche Bildung der Planeten uns zu veranschaulichen, wollen wir im Geiste drei Experimente anstellen, welche, wenn auch sehr entfernt, an die Vorgänge bei der Sonne erinnern, wenn wir die Oberfläche derselben mit der Oberfläche der gleich zu charakterisirenden Flüssigkeitssäule in Parallele stellen.

1. Experiment. Wir denken uns innerhalb eines luftleeren Raumes einen sehr hohen mit Luft oder einer anderen elastischen Flüssigkeit theilweise gefüllten Cylinder aufgestellt; ist derselbe genügend hoch, so wird der Druck unten am grössten und oben am geringsten sein und dem entsprechend wird auch die Dichtigkeit der Luft von unten nach oben hin abnehmen, ganz so, wie es in unserer Atmosphäre wirklich geschieht. Denken wir uns nun auf diese Luftsäule im Cylinder, von oben her etwa mittelst einer genau passenden Platte einen Druck ausgeübt und die Luftsäule dadurch verkürzt, warten wir dann bis die Luft in der neuen Lage vollkommen zur Ruhe gekommen ist und heben dann plötzlich die Platte ab, dann werden sofort Schwingungen der Luftsäule um ihre ursprüngliche Gleichgewichtslage stattfinden und zwar wächst die Dauer der Schwingung von unten nach oben hin ähnlich wie bei Pendeln von verschiedener Länge, so dass also die Schwingungsperiode für die untersten Lufttheilchen äusserst kurz, für die obersten am längsten ist*). Hierbei ist stillschweigend angenommen worden, dass die ganze Luftsäule dieselbe Temperatur, sagen wir etwa 100^0 hatte, welche sich auch während des Experiments nicht wesentlich änderte.

2. Experiment. Nehmen wir dieselbe Luftsäule in ihrem ursprünglichen Gleichgewichtszustand und von 100^0 Temperatur, fügen wir noch hinzu, dass der Querschnitt derselben sehr gering ist und denken uns ringsherum plötzlich eine unveränderliche Temperatur von 0^0 hergestellt, so wird der Erfolg sein, dass die ganze Luftsäule sich allmählich abkühlt und dass in Folge dessen ihre Höhe allmählich geringer wird und zwar nach folgendem Gesetz: Beobachten wir die Höhe immer nach Zwischenräumen von gleichen Zeiten, etwa alle Viertelstunden, so wird die erste Senkung die

*) Um nicht den mir gestatteten Raum noch mehr, als wohl schon geschehen, zu überschreiten, verzichte ich auf die Wiedergabe der zugehörigen mathem. Entwickelungen.

grösseste, die folgenden immer kleiner sein; derart, dass wenn die zweite Senkung beispielsweise die Hälfte der ersten beträgt, dann die dritte die Hälfte der zweiten, die vierte die Hälfte der dritten und sofort ausmachen wird, bis nach sehr langer Zeit die Höhe der Luftsäule sich nicht mehr merklich von einem gewissen Minimalwerthe unterscheidet.

3. Experiment. Denken wir uns jetzt die beiden Experimente an derselben Luftsäule gleichzeitig ausgeführt, d. h. denken wir uns auf sie während ihrer ursprünglichen Temperatur von 100° einen Druck ausgeübt und sehr rasch wieder aufgehoben und auch die Temperatur der Umgebung auf 0° hergestellt. Dann werden nach dem Princip der Coexistenz verschiedener Wirkungen auch beide genannten Erscheinungen gleichzeitig zu Tage treten. Die Luftsäule wird nämlich auf- und niederschwingen, es werden aber die Maximalhöhen der Luftsäule wie überhaupt die gleichen Phasen entsprechenden Höhen derselben sich dauernd verringern und zwar würden ihre Zahlenwerthe, da sie, wie das erste Experiment gezeigt hat, nach gleichen Zeiten eintreten, sich durch einen konstanten Summand plus einer Zahl darstellen lassen, deren Betrag sich im Verhältniss einer sogenannten geometrischen Reihe z. B. von $1 : {}^1/_2 : {}^1/_4$ u. s. w. verringert.

Beispiel: Nehmen wir als den konstanten Summand 0,4 und addiren dazu nach einander die Zahlen 19,2; 9,6; 4,8; 2,4; 1,2; 0,6; 0,3 etc., deren jede die Hälfte der vorangehenden ist, so erhalten wir folgende nach einander eintretende Maximalhöhen:

19,6; 10,0; 5,2; 2,8; 1,6; 1,0; 0,7 etc., schliesslich 0,4.

Es ist sehr verlockend, diese Zahlen direct auf die pulsirende und sich gleichzeitig nach und nach verkleinernde Sonne zu übertragen und an Stelle der Luftsäulen-Maxima die kritische Lage zu setzen. Dann ist nämlich die obige Zahlenreihe identisch mit der bekannten Titius'schen oder Bode'schen Reihe, welche sehr nahe richtig die Entfernungen der Planeten Uranus bis Merkur von der Sonne angiebt. Nehmen wir noch statt des Quotienten ${}^1/_2$ den Quotienten ${}^{101}/_{200}$ und beginnen mit der wahren Entfernung des Uranus, so können wir die Uebereinstimmung sogar noch genauer machen, nämlich:

	Reihe nach Titius' Princip.	Wahre Entfernungen.
Uranus	19,2	19,2
Saturn	9,9	9,5
Jupiter	5,2	5,2
Asteroiden	(2,75)	3,25 bis 2,20
Mars	1,62	1,5
Erde	1,00	1,0
Venus	0,70	0,7
.	.	.
	.	
.	.	.
Merkur	0,40	0,4

Aber folgende Bedenken sind zu gewichtig: 1. Es ist ebenso gerechnet, als ob die Sonne vom Beginn ihrer Bildung bis nach der Ausstossung des Merkur dieselbe homogene Vertheilung der Dichtigkeit behalten hätte, indem immer für die kritische Lage dasselbe Axenverhältniss zu Grunde gelegt erscheint. Dies ist aber jedenfalls nicht richtig, sondern das der Planetenbildung günstige Axenverhältniss änderte sich während Erschaffung der Planeten jedenfalls von nahe $^1/_3$ bis nahe $^2/_3$. 2. Es macht einen befremdenden Eindruck — dieser Vorwurf trifft die alte Bodesche Reihe ebenso wie die ihr oben nachgebildete — dass der Merkur mit einer gewissen Naturnothwendigkeit der letzte Planet hat sein müssen (weil sonst in dem Gesetze der Reihe eine Discontinuität eintreten müsste). 3. Wo bleiben die unendlich vielen Glieder der geometrischen Reihe (zwischen Venus und Merkur), nämlich mit Ergänzung von $+ 0{,}4 : 0{,}3 \times {}^1/_2$, $0{,}3 \times {}^1/_4$, $0{,}3 \times {}^1/_8$ etc.?

Diesen Einwänden kann durch eine kleine Modification der Hypothese begegnet werden, wodurch allerdings die Uebereinstimmung so zu sagen an äusserer Eleganz verliert, aber vielleicht um so naturwahrer ist. Da nämlich das Axenverhältniss in der Gleichgewichtslage sowie in der kritischen Lage immer wuchs, so wurden die Zeitunterschiede zwischen zwei gleichen Phasen zweier aufeinander folgenden Pulsationen allmählich kleiner. Wir tragen dem dadurch Rechnung, dass wir den Charakter der geometrischen Reihe beibehalten, aber den Exponenten derselben nicht als ganz konstant, sondern als etwas wachsend annehmen, dafür aber den Summand (0,4), der bei der verhältnissmässig geringen Ausdehnung der Sonne in ihrer schliesslichen Gestalt gegenüber den Entfernungen der Planeten von ihr seine Bedeutung verliert, fortlassen. Interpoliren wir noch zwischen Venus und Merkur einen Planeten oder Planetenschwarm X (ich komme später noch darauf zurück) und nehmen für den Exponenten der Reihe die Werthe

Uranus — Saturn Saturn — Jupiter Jupiter — Asteroiden	0,52	Asteroiden — Mars Mars — Erde	0,60	Erde — Venus Venus — X X — Merkur	0,72

so erhalten wir die Entfernungen nach dieser Hypothese

		in Wirklichkeit
Uranus	19,2	19,2
Saturn	10,0	9,5
Jupiter	5,2	5,2
Asteroiden	(2,75)	3,25 bis 2,20
Mars	1,66	1,52
Erde	1,00	1,00
Venus	0,72	0,72
X.	(0,52)	
Merkur	0,38	0,39

An diese Zusammenstellung*) habe ich einige Bemerkungen anzuknüpfen, nämlich: wegen der mangelhaften Uebereinstimmung der Zahlen bei Saturn und bei Mars, wegen der Asteroiden, wegen des Neptun und wegen des Planetenschwarms X. Fassen wir zuerst die Abweichung bei den beiden Planeten Saturn und Mars in's Auge! Diese lässt sich erklären. Ersterer Planet hat eine im Verhältniss $1^1/_3 : 1$

*) Die Entfernungen der Monde des Jupiter und mindestens der ersten vier des Saturn von ihrem Centralkörper lassen sich, wie bekannt, auch nahezu nach geometrischen Reihen ordnen.

stärkere Excentricität als seine beiden Nachbarplaneten Jupiter und Uranus (die unter einander nahezu dieselbe haben) und Mars hat eine bedeutend grössere Excentricität als sein Nachbarplanet die Erde. Daher muss die Umfangsgeschwindigkeit des dieselben fortschleudernden Centralkörpers eine grössere gewesen sein als dem Axenverhältniss der kritischen Lage entspricht; das ist aber wieder dann der Fall, wenn in Folge fortschreitender Zusammenziehung (vgl. Fig. 1) die lebendige Kraft des Centralkörpers erhöht worden ist. Wir können uns daher denken, dass die Abschleuderung dieser beiden Planeten nicht im ersten Momente ihrer Möglichkeit, sondern erst etwas spät r und zwar in noch späterer Phase als bei den Nachbarplaneten geschah. Aus diesem Grunde sind die Entfernungen dieser Planeten etwas kleiner als sie sonst gewesen wären. — Bezüglich der Asteroiden lässt sich Folgendes bemerken. Nachdem bei der vorangegangenen Pulsation Jupiter eine grosse Menge von Materie an sich gezogen und damit die Sonne verlassen hatte, so war jetzt kein derartiges Attractionscentrum innerhalb der Sonne vorhanden und es bröckelten deshalb, wenn ich den Ausdruck gebrauchen darf, kleine Massentheile für sich, theils gleichzeitig, theils nacheinander von der Sonne ab. Dabei hatten diejenigen, welche, als Asteroiden, später die Sonne verliessen, eine kleinere Entfernung von dem Centrum derselben, sie müssten also, wenn sie sich dem, was beim Mars und Saturn gesagt ist, conform verhielten, eine etwas grössere Excentrität haben als diejenigen Asteroiden, welche früher (der kritischen Lage A näher) abgeschleudert wurden und daher vom Sonnencentrum entfernter blieben. Und allerdings scheint dies aus einigen Angaben, die ich der Freundlichkeit des Herrn Dr. Franz verdanke, hervorzugehen; mindestens stehen sie hiermit nicht im Widerspruch. — Was nun den Neptun betrifft, so ging nach meiner früheren Darstellung die Figur des Centralkörpers nach der Bildung des Neptun aus der Lage AA in die Lage CC und dann wieder in die Lage AA über, bei welcher (oder in deren Nähe) der Planet Uranus gebildet wurde. Der Zwischenraum zwischen Neptun und Uranus beträgt also ungefähr nur eine halbe Pulsation (oder mehr), während sie zwischen je zwei anderen aufeinander folgenden Planeten eine ganze Pulsation betrug. Um aus der Zahl des Saturn 19,2 diejenige des Neptun, sie ist 30,0, zu erhalten, haben wir die erstere also nicht mit 2*) zu multipliciren, sondern mit einer kleineren Zahl, welche nicht viel grösser als $\sqrt{2}$ oder 1,4 sein kann, sie ist aber 1,56. — Was endlich den hypothetischen Planeten oder Planetenschwarm X angeht, so ist es allerdings durchaus nicht nothwendig, dass bei jeder Pulsation sich auch ein Planet ablöse, aber man könnte auch an die dunkeln Punkte denken, die von Zeit zu Zeit (ausser den inneren Planeten) unzweifelhaft auf der Sonnenoberfläche gesehen werden**) (einschliesslich der als intramerkurieller Planet Vulkan und Venusmond gedeuteten Erscheinungen), oder gar das Zodiakallicht, das ja schon eine grosse Menge anderweitiger Hypothesen über sich ergehen lassen musste, als eine Anhäufung sehr vieler kleiner Körperchen zwischen Venus und Merkur vermuthen.

Hat nun aber bei der Pulsation zwischen Venus und Merkur jedenfalls keine an Masse beträchtliche Planetenaussendung stattgefunden, hat selbst der Merkur sein

*) Eigentlich $\frac{1}{0,52}$.

**) Siehe Wolf's Taschenbuch, Zürich 1877, 5. Aufl. S. 432.

Entstehen wahrscheinlich der Mitwirkung chemischer Ursachen zu verdanken und hat bei der nächsten oder einer der folgenden Pulsationen nur ein bis jetzt hypothetisch von Leverrier angenommener aber noch nicht beobachteter intramerkurieller Asteroidenring sich gebildet, so ist daraus zu schliessen, dass die Form der Sonne bereits so kugelähnlich und ihre äusseren Schichten so homogen geworden seien, dass zur Entstehung von Planeten keine Gelegenheit mehr geboten wurde. —

Schlussbemerkung. Die Hauptschwierigkeit, welche sich meines Erachtens einer präciseren Darstellung der Abschleuderungstheorie gegenüberstellt, ist der Umstand, dass man bei homogen angenommener Dichtigkeit des ganzen Centralkörpers oder auch nur ellipsoidischer Schichten desselben nicht berechtigt ist, seine Masse bezüglich seiner Anziehung auf ausserhalb gelegene, ihm aber sehr nahe Massen im Centrum vereinigt zu denken.*) Für anders geschichtete Massen ist allerdings diese Annahme möglich. Hätte der Centralkörper z. B. die Form eines abgeplatteten Ellipsoides mit den Axen a, a, $b = \frac{a}{2}\sqrt{2}$, dessen Kern ein verlängertes Ellipsoid mit den Axen $c = \frac{a}{2}$, c, b von der Dichtigkeit 1 wäre, so dürfte die Dichtigkeit der den Kern umgebenden Massen nur ungefähr $\frac{1}{8}$ sein, um seine ganze Masse für einen ausserhalb, in der Aequatorialebene gelegenen Punkt im Centrum vereinigt denken zu dürfen. Nur bei kugeliger Form und concentrischer Schichtenlagerung ist dies für beliebig gelegene Punkte richtig. Wenn aber der Körper auch noch so langsam rotirt, kann er eben niemals eine kugelähnliche Form behalten, da das Verhältniss seiner Axen nicht von der Winkelgeschwindigkeit allein, sondern von dem Quotienten ihres Quadrates und der Dichtigkeit abhängig ist. Dieser Umstand scheint auch von Herrn Faye**) (in der sonst sehr interessanten Abhandlung) übersehen worden zu sein, denn nur unter der nicht statthaften Voraussetzung einer Kugel darf man die Anziehungskraft auf einen Punkt im Innern derselben durch den Ausdruck $Ar + \frac{B}{r^2}$, wie er es thut, darstellen.

*) Siehe den ersten mathematischen Zusatz, Gleichungen 10 und 11.

**) Annuaire pour l'an 1885 publié par le Bureau des Longitudes p. 757.

Mathematische Zusätze.

Inhalt.

I.

Abschleuderung eines Massenpunktes von einem Centralkörper.

1.

Zusammenstellung der bekannten anzuwendenden Formeln.

Wenn ein Körper mit der Masse M einen andern nach dem Newtonschen Gesetze anzieht, so bewegt sich letzterer um ersteren in einem Kegelschnitte, in dessen einem Brennpunkte (F) ersterer d. h. sein Mittelpunkt sich befindet. Bezeichnen r_0 und r_1 die Entfernungen des nächsten und des entferntesten Punktes auf dem Umfange des als Ellipse angenommenen Kegelschnittes von F (Perihel und Aphel), v_0 und v_1 die tangentialen Geschwindigkeiten in diesen Punkten, r einen beliebigen Brennstrahl der mit der Richtung r_0 den Winkel φ bildet, v die tangentiale Geschwindigkeit in seinem Endpunkte, a, b die beiden Halbaxen und ε die Excentricität der Ellipse, ferner C die Constante des Sonnensystems*) und f das Product CM, dann gelten die Gleichungen:

$$1) \quad \frac{1}{r} = \frac{f}{v_0^2 r_0^2}(1 + \varepsilon\cos\varphi)$$

$$2) \quad v^2 = v_0^2 + 2f\left(\frac{1}{r} - \frac{1}{r_0}\right)$$

$$3) \quad v_1^2 = v_0^2 + 2f\left(\frac{1}{r_1} - \frac{1}{r_0}\right)$$

$$\varepsilon = \frac{v_0^2 r_0}{f} - 1 \quad \ldots \quad 4)$$

$$r_0 = a(1-\varepsilon);\ r_1 = a(1+\varepsilon) \quad \ldots \quad 5)$$

$$\frac{v_0}{v_1} = \frac{r_1}{r_0} = \frac{1+\varepsilon}{1-\varepsilon} \quad \ldots \quad 6)$$

$$r_0 v_0^2 = f(1+\varepsilon);\ r_1 v_1^2 = f(1-\varepsilon) \quad . \quad 7)$$

$$r_0^2 v_0^2 = r_1^2 v_1^2 = af(1-\varepsilon^2) = \frac{b^2}{a}f \quad . \quad 8)$$

Bedeutet endlich T die Umlaufszeit, so ist:

$$v_0 r_0 T = 2ab\pi$$

daher:

$$T^2 = \frac{4\pi^2}{f}\cdot a^3 = \frac{4\pi^2}{CM}\cdot a^3 \quad . \quad . \quad 9)$$

(drittes Kepplersches Gesetz).

2.

Wird nun ein Körper von einem Punkte C (s. Fig. 2) des Aequatorumfanges $CEGD$ eines Centralkörpers mit der Anfangsgeschwindigkeit c und in der Richtung CN, die mit der Tangente CM den Winkel α bildet, abgeschleudert, so lassen sich auf diesen Fall näherungsweise die obigen Formeln anwenden. Streng genommen ist nämlich die Figur des Centralkörpers so lange von Einfluss, als seine Dimensionen gegen die Entfernung des abfliegenden Körpers nicht sehr klein sind. So ist z. B. die Anziehungs-Beschleunigung A eines Rotations-Ellipsoides mit der

*) C lässt sich durch die Beschleunigung der irdischen Schwere g ausdrücken, es ist nämlich: C mal Masse der Erde dividirt durch das Quadrat ihres Radius gleich g.

Polarhalbaxe γ, den Aequatorial-Halbaxen α und der Exentricität $e = \sqrt{1-\frac{\gamma^2}{\alpha^2}}$ auf einen Punkt in seiner erweiterten Aequatorialebene, der die Entfernung r hat:

10) . $$A = \frac{3}{2}CM\cdot\frac{r}{(\alpha e)^3}\left\{\arcsin\frac{\alpha e}{r} - \frac{\alpha e}{r}\sqrt{1-\left(\frac{\alpha e}{r}\right)^2}\right\}$$

oder entwickelt:

11) . $$A = \frac{3}{2}CM\cdot\frac{r}{\alpha e^3}\cdot\frac{\alpha e}{r}\cdot\left(\frac{2}{3}\left(\frac{\alpha e}{r}\right)^2 + \frac{1}{5}\left(\frac{\alpha e}{r}\right)^4+\ldots\right) = \frac{CM}{r^2}\left(1+\frac{3}{10}\left(\frac{\alpha e}{r}\right)^2+\ldots\right),$$

hingegen für ein verlängertes Rotationsellipsoid, wenn M, α, γ, r dieselbe Bedeutung behalten, aber $e = \sqrt{1-\frac{\alpha^2}{\gamma^2}}$ gesetzt wird:

10a) $$A = \frac{3}{2}CM\frac{r}{(\gamma e)^3}\left\{\frac{e\gamma}{r}\sqrt{1+\left(\frac{e\gamma}{r}\right)^2} - l_{nt}\left(\frac{e\gamma}{r}+\sqrt{1+\left(\frac{e\gamma}{r}\right)^2}\right)\right\}$$

oder entwickelt:

11a) $$A = \frac{CM}{r}\left(1-\frac{3}{10}\left(\frac{\gamma e}{r}\right)^2+\ldots\right),^{*)}$$

so dass also nur für die Kugel oder wenn r sehr gross gegen a ist, genau:

$$A = \frac{CM}{r^2}$$

wird. Zur Erzielung einer allgemeinen Anschauung des eintretenden Vorgangs genügt es dennoch, die letzte Gleichung und somit die vorangehenden Formeln 1) bis 8) als richtig anzusehen.

Bezeichnen wir den Radius des Central-Körpers mit R und wenden die Gll. 1) 2) 4) auf den im Punkte C abfliegenden Körper an, wobei der unbekannte Winkel zwischen FC und der Richtung des Perihels:

$$CFA = \Phi$$

---

*) Die Anziehung einer materiellen Kreislinie zum Radius a auf einen äusseren von ihrem Centrum um r entfernten Punkt P (s. Fig. 3a) ist, wenn die veränderlichen Winkel DCP und DPC bez. mit φ und u, und DP mit ϱ bezeichnet werden:

$$A = \frac{CM}{\pi}\cdot U,\ U = \int_0^\pi \frac{d\varphi . \cos u}{\varrho^2} = \int_0^\pi \frac{(r-a\cos\varphi)d\varphi}{(r^2+a^2-2ra\cos\varphi)^{\frac{3}{2}}}$$

und dies führt bei Benutzung der gebräuchlichen Bezeichnungen:

$$\int_0^{\frac{\pi}{2}} \frac{d\psi}{\sqrt{1-x^2\sin^2\psi}} = K;\quad \int_0^{\frac{\pi}{2}} \sqrt{1-x^2\sin^2\psi}\, d\psi = E$$

auf den Werth:

$$A = \frac{CM}{r^2\pi}\left(\frac{E}{1-\frac{a}{r}}+\frac{K}{1+\frac{a}{r}}\right),\ x^2 = \frac{4\frac{a}{r}}{\left(1+\frac{a}{r}\right)^2}$$

welcher für ein verschwindendes a in $\frac{CM}{r^2}$ übergeht.

Aehnlich ergiebt sich die Anziehung auf einen inneren Punkt unter der Voraussetzung dass dieselbe nach dem Centrum zu stattfindet (s. Fig. 3b):

$$A = \frac{CM}{\pi}\cdot V,\ V = \int_0^\pi \frac{d\varphi\cos u}{\varrho^2} = \int_0^\pi \frac{(r-a\cos\varphi)d\varphi}{(a^2+r^2-2ar\cos\varphi)^{\frac{3}{2}}}$$

woraus:

$$V = \frac{1}{ra}\left(\frac{K}{1+\frac{r}{a}} - \frac{E}{1-\frac{r}{a}}\right).$$

Dieser Ausdruck ist aber negativ, die Anziehung findet also in der Richtung nach dem nächstgelegenen Punkte der Peripherie zu statt und hat den Werth:

$$A = \frac{CM}{ar\pi}\left(\frac{E}{1-\frac{r}{a}} - \frac{K}{1+\frac{r}{a}}\right),\ x^2 = \frac{4\frac{r}{a}}{\left(1+\frac{r}{a}\right)^2}.$$

Ist r sehr klein, so folgt durch Entwickelung:

$$A = \frac{CM}{2}\cdot\frac{r}{a^3},$$

welcher Ausdruck mit r verschwindet.

sei, so erhalten wir:

$$12) \quad \frac{1}{R} = \frac{f}{v_0^2 r_0^2}(1 + \varepsilon \cos \Phi)$$

$$13) \quad c^2 = v_0^2 + 2f\left(\frac{1}{R} - \frac{1}{r_0}\right)$$

$$14) \quad \varepsilon = \frac{v_0^2 r_0}{f} - 1$$

Die Geometrie liefert noch die Gleichung:

$$15) \quad \operatorname{tg} \alpha = \frac{\varepsilon \sin \Phi}{1 + \varepsilon \cos \Phi}.$$

Somit haben wir für die vier unbekannten Grössen v_0 r_0 ε Φ die genügende Anzahl Gleichungen. Berechnen wir aus 13) und aus 7) v_0^2 r_0 so giebt die Gleichsetzung beider Ausdrücke die Relation:

$$16) \quad \left(\frac{2f}{R} - c^2\right) r_0 = f(1 - \varepsilon)$$

Daraus folgt die wichtige Unterscheidung: Der Planet beschreibt eine

Ellipse $\quad <$
Parabel je nachdem $Rc^2 = 2f$ ist,
Hyperbel $\quad >$

(worin R auch einen beliebigen Radius vector und c die Geschwindigkeit in dem betreffenden Punkte, deren Richtung ausser Betracht bleibt, bedeuten kann).

Das Product der Gll. 16) und 7) giebt:

$$\left(\frac{2f}{R} - c^2\right) v_0^2 r_0^2 = f^2 (1 - \varepsilon^2)$$

und hiermit wird nach 12):

$$\frac{1}{R} = \left(\frac{2f}{R} - c^2\right) \cdot \frac{1 + \varepsilon \cos \Phi}{f(1 - \varepsilon^2)}$$

so dass wir wegen 15) zur Bestimmung von ε und Φ schliesslich die beiden Gleichungen:

$$17a) \quad \begin{cases} \dfrac{\varepsilon \sin \Phi}{1 - \varepsilon^2} = \dfrac{f \operatorname{tg} \alpha}{2f - Rc^2} \\[2ex] \dfrac{\varepsilon \sin \Phi}{1 + \varepsilon \cos \Phi} = \operatorname{tg} \alpha \end{cases}$$

oder auch:

$$17b) \quad \begin{cases} \dfrac{1 + \varepsilon \cos \Phi}{1 - \varepsilon^2} = \dfrac{f}{2f - Rc^2} \\[2ex] \dfrac{\varepsilon \sin \Phi}{1 + \varepsilon \cos \Phi} = \operatorname{tg} \alpha \end{cases}$$

erhalten. Ich will zwei Beispiele durchführen $\alpha = 0$ und $\alpha = 45^0$.

Für $\alpha = 0$ folgt aus 15) $\varepsilon = 0$ oder $\Phi = 0$; *) im ersten Falle wäre jedoch, wie die erste 17b) zeigt, die Anfangsgeschwindigkeit nicht mehr willkürlich sondern

---

*) Die Annahme $\Phi = 180^0$ hat bei der obigen Formulirung in sofern keine Bedeutung, als der Planet sich dann bei Beginn der Bahn (der Erklärung von Φ gemäss) in der Sonnenferne befinden und daher seine ganze Bahn **innerhalb** der Sonne beschreiben müsste. Sehen wir aber davon ab, betrachten vielmehr **einen materiellen Punkt als anziehendes Centrum**, so ergeben sich leicht bei der Annahme $\Phi = \pi$ die Resultate:

$$\varepsilon = 1 - \frac{Rc^2}{f}, \quad r_0 = \frac{R^2 c^2}{2f - Rc^2}, \quad v_0 = \frac{2f - Rc^2}{Ro}.$$

Das erste derselben setzt voraus, dass $\frac{Rc^2}{f} < 1$ ist und die anderen ergeben sodann $r_0 < R$, $v_0 > c$, führen also nirgend auf einen Widerspruch. — Allgemein folgt aus 17b):

$$\varepsilon \cos \Phi = \frac{\frac{Rc^2}{f} - 1 - \varepsilon^2}{2 - \frac{Rc^2}{f}}$$

Ist also wiederum $Rc^2 < f$, so ist nothwendiger Weise (da ε positiv ist) Φ als stumpfer Winkel anzunehmen. Ist im Besonderen $c = 0$ und setze ich $\Phi = \pi - \Phi_1$, so ist:

$$\cos \Phi_1 = \frac{1 + \varepsilon^2}{2\varepsilon} = 1 + \frac{(1 - \varepsilon)^2}{2\varepsilon};$$

da aber $\cos \Phi_1$ höchstens $= 1$ werden darf, so folgt $\varepsilon = 1$, d. h. die vom Planeten beschriebene Ellipse verwandelt sich in eine begrenzte gerade Doppellinie, deren Endpunkte durch den Anfangsort des Planeten und das Attractionscentrum bezeichnet werden. Die Geschwindigkeit, mit der dasselbe erreicht wird, v_0, wird unendlich gross, welche physikalische Unmöglichkeit eben aus der anderen physikalischen Unmöglichkeit entspringt, sich einen Punkt ohne Ausdehnung, aber mit Masse begabt, zu denken. — Wir können nunmehr die obige Zusammenstellung (nach Gl. 16)) noch folgendermaassen ergänzen: Der Planet beschreibt

einen Kreis, wenn $Rc^2 = f$
eine Ellipse, wenn $Rc^2 < f$
eine ger. Doppellinie, wenn $c = 0$

ist.

$Rc^2 = f$. Ist aber $\Phi = 0$, so folgt leicht:

18) . $1-\varepsilon = \frac{2f-Rc^2}{f}$, $\varepsilon = \frac{Rc^2}{f} - 1$

also nach 14): $Rc^2 = r_0 v_0^2$
und nach 12): $R^2c^2 = r_0^2 v_0^2$
daher $R = r_0$, $c = v_0$.

Wir erhalten daher einen Kegelschnitt, der den Aequator des Centralkörpers in C berührt, und dessen Excentricität durch 18) gegeben ist.

Entsteht im Besonderen die Anfangsgeschwindigkeit durch die Umdrehung des Centralkörpers um seine Axe mit der Geschwindigkeit c, so ist die Beschleunigung der Centrifugalkraft:

19) . . . . . $\Gamma = \frac{c^2}{R}$,

der Anziehungskraft:

20) . . . $\varDelta = \frac{CM}{R^2} = \frac{f}{R^2}$

also nach 18):

$$\varepsilon = \frac{\Gamma}{\varDelta} - 1$$

und daher:

21) $\begin{cases} \text{für} \quad \Gamma = \varDelta : \varepsilon = 0, \text{ Kreis} \\ \varDelta < \Gamma < 2\varDelta : \varepsilon < 1, \text{ Ellipse} \\ \Gamma = 2\varDelta : \varepsilon = 1, \text{ Parabel} \\ \Gamma > 2\varDelta : \varepsilon > 1, \text{ Hyperbel.} \end{cases}$

Ist $\alpha = 45^0$ so folgt aus 15):

22) . . $\varepsilon \sin\Phi = 1 + \varepsilon\cos\Phi$

also kann $\cos\Phi$ nicht positiv sein, ausser wenn $\varepsilon > 1$ ist; setze ich daher:

23) . . . . $\cos\Phi = -x$

so erhalte ich die Gleichung:

$$(\varepsilon x)^2 - (\varepsilon x) + \frac{1-\varepsilon^2}{2} = 0$$

woraus:

24) . . $\varepsilon x = \frac{1}{2}(1 \pm \sqrt{2\varepsilon^2 - 1})$

folgt. Setze ich zur Abkürzung:

25) . . . $\frac{2f}{2f-Rc^2} = \varkappa$

$1-\varepsilon^2 = u$ . . . . 26)

so wird nach 17b) und 24):

$\frac{1}{2}(1 \mp \sqrt{1-2u}) = \frac{u\varkappa}{2}$ . . 27)

daraus: $1-2u = (\varkappa u - 1)^2$

und somit:

$u = 2\cdot\frac{\varkappa-1}{\varkappa^2} = \frac{1}{2}\cdot\frac{Rc^2(2f-Rc^2)}{f^2}$; 28)

dann weiter:

$\varepsilon^2 = \frac{\varkappa^2 - 2\varkappa + 2}{\varkappa^2}$ . . 29)

und nach der ersten 17a):

$\varepsilon \sin\Phi = \frac{u\varkappa}{2} = \frac{\varkappa-1}{\varkappa}$ . . 30)

folglich nach 22):

$\varepsilon\cos\Phi = -\frac{1}{\varkappa}$ . . . . . 31)

$\operatorname{tg}\Phi = -\frac{Rc^2}{2f-Rc^2}$ . . . 32)

Ist nun $Rc^2 < 2f$ so ist $\Phi > \frac{\pi}{2}$ und der Kegelschnitt eine Ellipse, ist $Rc^2 = 2f$, so ist $\Phi = \frac{\pi}{2}$ und der Kegelschnitt eine Parabel, für welche $r_0 = \frac{1}{2}R$ ist, ist $Rc^2 > 2f$ so ist $\Phi < \frac{\pi}{2}$, u, wie 28) zeigt, neg. und ε daher (nach 26) > 1, der Kegelschnitt also ein Hyperbel. Im ersten Falle ist, wie leicht zu sehen:

$\frac{r_0}{R} = \frac{\varkappa}{2}(1-\varepsilon)$ $\frac{r_1}{R} = \frac{\varkappa}{2}(1+\varepsilon)$. 33)

$\frac{r_0}{R}$ ist stets $< \frac{1}{2}$ denn:

$$\frac{r_0}{R} = \frac{\varkappa}{2}(1-\varepsilon) = \frac{\varkappa}{2}\frac{u}{1+\varepsilon} = \frac{\varkappa-1}{\varkappa}\cdot\frac{1}{1+\varepsilon} = \frac{\varepsilon}{1+\varepsilon}\cdot\sin\Phi$$

und $\frac{\varepsilon}{1+\varepsilon}$ liegt zwischen 0 und $\frac{1}{2}$ wenn ε von 0 bis 1 geht. Sei noch c^2 verhältnissmässig sehr klein. Setze ich dann:

$$\frac{f}{R^2} = g$$

und verstehe unter g eine endliche Grösse, so wird:

$$u = \frac{1}{2}\frac{Rc^2(2R^2g - Rc^2)}{R^4g^2}$$

d. i. mit genügender Annäherung:

$$u = \frac{c^2}{Rg};$$

daraus weiter mit gleicher Näherung

$$\varepsilon = 1 - \frac{1}{2}\frac{c^2}{Rg}; \; r_0 = \frac{c^2}{4g}; \; r_1 - R = h = \frac{c^2}{4g},$$

wobei h die Erhebung des Körpers über die Oberfläche bedeutet. Das ausserhalb liegende Stück der Bahn ist also ein Theil einer Ellipse, deren ein Brennpunkt auf der Oberfläche selbst, im Punkte E der Figur 2. liegt und welche sich sehr der Parabel nähert, wobei aber der Winkel CFE als sehr klein und die Höhe $h = EB$ als verschwindend gegen $FE = R$ anzusehen sind. Der Winkel Φ liegt sehr nahe an π. — Nimmt man die Beschleunigung der Anziehung (g) für die ganze Flugbahn gleich gross und gleich gerichtet, also die Oberfläche an der betreffenden Stelle einer Ebene vergleichbar an, so kommt man (für $\alpha = 45^0$) zu gleichem Werthe der Wurfhöhe.

Aehnlich ist die Durchführung, wenn α einen beliebigen Werth hat.

II.

Bedingung für die Abschleuderung von Massentheilen in Folge der Centrifugalkraft vom Aequatorumfang gewisser Rotationskörper.

1.

Wenn im Weltraum eine Flüssigkeitsmasse von homogener Dichtigkeit in Form eines abgeplatteten Rotationsellipsoides um die ungleiche Axe (Polaraxe) rotirt, so ist sie im Gleichgewicht, d. h. behält ihre Form bei, wenn zwischen ihrer Winkelgeschwindigkeit ω, ihrer Dichtigkeit ϱ, ihrem Axenverhältniss $\frac{c}{a}$ und der Attractions- oder Gravitations-Constante C des Sonnensystems (s. Zusatz I. S. 85. Anmerkung) unter Einführung der Bezeichnungen:

1) . . . . $\frac{c}{a} = \cos u$

2) . . . $\lambda^2 = tg^2 u = \frac{a^2 - c^2}{c^2}$

3) . . $V = \frac{3 + \lambda^2}{\lambda^3} \cdot \operatorname{arctg} \lambda - \frac{3}{\lambda^2}$

die Beziehung besteht:*)

4) . . . . $\omega^2 = 2C\pi\varrho . V.$

Hier kann ω bei gegebenem ϱ nicht jeden beliebigen Werth annehmen, da V mit zunehmendem u oder λ anfangs wächst und dann wieder abnimmt. Das Maximum von V tritt ein bei:

$$\lambda = 2{,}5293, \; u = 68^0 25', \; \cos u = \frac{c}{a} = 0{,}3678$$

und ist:

$$V_{max.} = 0{,}2246.$$

Dies eine Axenverhältniss entspricht also der Maximal-Winkelgeschwindigkeit, jeder andern, wie gesagt, zwei verschiedene Axenverhältnisse $\lessgtr 0{,}3678$, z. B. der Winkelgeschwindigkeit $0: u = 0, \frac{c}{a} = 1$ (Kugel) und $u = \frac{\pi}{2}, \frac{c}{a} = 0$ (materielle Ebene).

Von diesen befindet sich das weniger abgeplattete Ellipsoid in stabiler, das flachere in labiler Gleichgewichtslage, was ich nunmehr, da ich diesen Umstand noch nirgend erwähnt gefunden habe, beweisen will. Sei zu dem Zweck $ABCD$ (s. Fig. 4a) ein Vertical-

*) S. z. B. Schell, Theorie der Bewegung und der Kräfte. 2. Aufl. 1880, 2. Bd. S. 610 ff.

schnitt eines homogenen Ellipsoids von der Dichtigkeit ϱ, das bei der Winkelgeschwindigkeit ω im Gleichgewicht ist. Sind dann $X\mu$, $Y\mu$ die Horizontal- und Verticalcomponenten der Gravitationskraft des ganzen Ellipsoids auf die Masse μ im Punkte $P = (x, y)$ und $\mu x \omega^2$ ihre Centrifugalkraft, so muss die Resultante dieser Kräfte PT zur Oberfläche senkrecht stehen, es muss also (vgl. die Figur):

$$\frac{(X - x\omega^2)\mu}{Y\mu} = -\frac{dy}{dx}$$

sein. Nun sind aber, wenn a, b die Axen, $\varepsilon = \sqrt{1-\left(\frac{c}{a}\right)^2}$ die Excentricität und A, B die Ausdrücke:

$$5)\ .\ \begin{cases} A = \frac{\sqrt{1-\varepsilon^2}}{\varepsilon^3}\arcsin\varepsilon - \frac{1-\varepsilon^2}{\varepsilon^2} \\ B = \frac{1}{\varepsilon^2} - \frac{\sqrt{1-\varepsilon^2}}{\varepsilon^3}\arcsin\varepsilon \end{cases}$$

bedeuten, wobei, wenn ε von 0 bis 1 wächst, A dauernd von $\frac{2}{3}$ bis 0 abnimmt, B dauernd von $\frac{1}{3}$ bis 1 zunimmt und stets $A + B = 1$ ist: für das abgeplattete Rotationsellipsoid:*)

$$6)\ .\ .\ .\ \begin{cases} X = 2\pi C\varrho . Ax \\ Y = 4\pi C\varrho . By; \end{cases}$$

also heisst die obige Gleichung:

$$7)\ .\ .\ \frac{(2\pi C\varrho A - \omega^2)x}{4\pi C\varrho By} = -\frac{dy}{dx}.$$

Ihre Integration liefert:

$$(2\pi C\varrho A - \omega^2)x^2 + 4\pi C\varrho By^2 = \text{const.}$$

wodurch also die Frage, ob die Oberfläche unter Umständen ein Rotationsellipsoid sein könne, bejaht wird; und ihre Anwendung auf die Punkte $(x = 0, y = c)$, $(x = a, y = 0)$ giebt die Beziehung zwischen ω und den Constanten des Ellipsoides:

$$8)\ .\ \omega^2 = 2\pi C\varrho(A - 2(1-\varepsilon^2)B)$$

*) Vgl. z. B. Schell a. a. O. 2. Bd. S. 309.

oder:

$$\omega^2 = 2\pi C\varrho(1 - B(3 - 2\varepsilon^2))$$

oder wenn:

$$1 - B(3 - 2\varepsilon^2) = V\ .\ .\ .\ 9)$$

gesetzt wird:

$$\omega^2 = 2\pi C\varrho V,\ .\ .\ .\ 10)$$

deren Uebereinstimmung mit den Gll. 3) und 4) leicht darzuthun ist.

Bringe ich nun das Ellipsoid $ABCD$ unter Belassung derselben Winkelgeschwindigkeit und derselben Dichtigkeit, also auch desselben Volumens in die (mehr kugelähnliche) Lage $A_1\,B_1\,C_1\,D_1$ und bringe zur Wiederherstellung des gestörten Gleichgewichts an allen Punkten des Umfanges Horizontalkräfte an, wobei die an je vier symmetrisch gelegenen Punkten angebrachten gleich, bez. gleich aber entgegengesetzt sein müssen, so lässt sich aus dem Zeichen d. i. der Richtung dieser Kräfte leicht auf die Natur des Gleichgewichts schliessen. Haben sie nämlich die in der Figur 4b) angegebene Richtung (z. B. im Punkte P_1 nach links hin), sind sie also bei der bisher gewählten Bedeutung der Zeichen positiv, so begehrt der Tropfen sich seitlich auszudehnen und abzuflachen, die frühere Gleichgewichtslage war also stabil; müssten wir aber die Kräfte nach entgegengesetzter Seite richten, also gleichsam von aussen an der Oberfläche Zugkräfte anbringen, um dieselbe in ihrer künstlichen Lage zu erhalten, wären die Kräfte also negativ, so strebte der Tropfen sich noch mehr abzurunden, sich also noch weiter von der früheren natürlichen Gleichgewichtslage zu entfernen: dieselbe wäre also eine labile gewesen.

Bezeichnen wir nun eine solche in P_1 anzubringende Kraft mit H oder vielmehr mit $H.\mu$ und die den Grössen a, c, ε, A, B entsprechenden mit dem Index 1, so geht die Gl. 7) für den Punkt $P_1 = (x_1\,y_1)$ über in:

$$\frac{(2\pi C\varrho A_1 - \omega^2)x_1 + H}{4\pi C\varrho B_1 y_1} = -\frac{dy_1}{dx_1}$$

oder, wenn wir in dieser und in der Gl. 7) den Differentialquotient durch seinen Werth ersetzen:

$$\frac{(2\pi C\varrho A_1 - \omega^2)x_1 + H}{4\pi C\varrho B_1 y_1} = \frac{b_1^2 x_1}{a_1^2 y_1}$$

$$\frac{(2\pi C\varrho A - \omega^2)x}{4\pi C\varrho B y} = \frac{b^2 x}{a^2 y}.$$

Aus diesen beiden Gleichungen folgt leicht mittelst Division:

$$\frac{H}{2\pi C\varrho x_1} = \frac{a^2}{b^2}\cdot\frac{b_1^2 B_1}{a_1^2 B}\left(A - \frac{\omega^2}{2\pi C\varrho}\right)$$

$$-\left(A_1 - \frac{\omega^2}{2\pi C\varrho}\right).$$

Setze ich aber für $\frac{\omega^2}{2\pi C\varrho}$ in der ersten Klammer den durch 8), in der zweiten Klammer den durch 10) angegebenen Werth und gleichzeitig $1-B_1$ statt A_1 ein, so folgt:

$$\frac{H}{2\pi C\varrho x_1} = \frac{1-\varepsilon_1^2}{1-\varepsilon^2}\cdot 2B_1(1-\varepsilon^2) - (1-B_1-V)$$

$$= V - \{1 - B_1(3-2\varepsilon_1^2)\}$$

d. i. $\quad = V - V_1.$

Bezeichnet nun $ABCD$ das der Winkelgeschwindigkeit ω entsprechende Ellipsoid mit dem Axenverhältniss zwischen 1 und 0,3678, so wächst V mit der Abplattung also ist V_1 kleiner als V; liegt aber das Axenverhältniss von $ABCD$ zwischen 0,3678 und 0 (und das Axenverhältniss von $A_1B_1C_1D_1$ zwischen dem von $ABCD$ und 0,3678) so nimmt, wie früher gesagt, V ab, wenn die Abplattung zunimmt, also ist jetzt V_1 grösser als V und somit im ersten Falle H (bei positivem x_1) positiv, im zweiten Falle negativ. Damit ist die obige Behauptung bewiesen.

Schliesslich bemerke ich noch Folgendes. Vergleicht man die Anziehungskraft des Ellipsoides auf einen Punkt am Aequator, $\mathcal{A}$, mit der Centrifugalkraft dieses Punktes, Γ, so ist immer:

$$\mathcal{A} > \Gamma;$$

denn aus 6) folgt:

$$\mathcal{A} = 2\pi C\varrho . Aa$$

aus 8):

$$\Gamma = a\omega^2 = 2\pi C\varrho a(A - 2(1-\varepsilon^2)B)$$

also:

$$\mathcal{A} - \Gamma = 4\pi C\varrho B(1-\varepsilon^2)a.^{*)} \quad . \quad 11)$$

Dies gilt folglich auch für den Maximalwerth des Verhältnisses $\frac{\omega^2}{\varrho}$; und man muss also, wie es den Anschein hat, auf eine exacte physikalische Veranschaulichung des Grundes für die Zerstörung der Figur, wenn der genannte Maximalwerth um ein Geringes überschritten wird, Verzicht leisten. Der Plateausche Versuch mit dem Oeltropfen in Alkohol, dessen Analogie sehr nahe liegt, beruht auf wesentlich anderen Voraussetzungen, so dass er über die obige Frage experimentell zu belehren ausser Stande ist. (Vgl. noch den Text des Aufsatzes S. 76.)

---

*) Wenn jedoch nach Abtrennung eines Massentheiles vom äusseren Umfange die zurückbleibende Masse sich plötzlich zu einer homogenen Kugel zusammenzöge, so würde bei einer nur wenig grösseren Entfernung oder Geschwindigkeit Centrifugalkraft und Anziehung sich das Gleichgewicht halten, und somit eine Kreisbewegung der abgetrennten Masse um den Centralkörper entstehen.

Denn in diesem Falle wäre:

$$\mathcal{A} = \frac{CM}{a^2} = \frac{4}{3}C\frac{a^3 c\pi\varrho}{a^2} = \frac{4}{3}Cc\pi\varrho$$

$$\Gamma = a\omega^2 = 2Ca\pi\varrho V$$

$$\mathcal{A} - \Gamma = 2Ca\pi\varrho\left(\frac{2}{3}\frac{c}{a} - V\right)$$

d. i. für den Maximalwerth von V (siehe oben S. 89)

$$\mathcal{A} - \Gamma = 2Ca\pi\varrho\,(0{,}2452 - 0{,}2246) = 2Ca\pi\varrho \,.\, 0{,}0206$$

und es brauchte daher nur a um etwa $\frac{1}{12}$ oder die Umfangsgeschwindigkeit ($a\omega$) um etwa $\frac{1}{24}$ des Werthes vermehrt zu werden, um $\Gamma = \mathcal{A}$ zu machen.

2.

Ein fester Kern von der Masse M sei (im Weltraum) von einer Flüssigkeit sehr geringer Dichtigkeit umgeben. Er zieht ihre Theile nach dem Newton'schen Gesetz an, während diese selbst auf einander keine merkliche Anziehung hervorbringen. Bei welcher an ein Rotationsellipsoid erinnernden Figur findet, wenn der ganze Körper mit gegebener constanter Winkelgeschwindigkeit um seine Axe rotirt, Gleichgewicht statt?

Rotire die Fig. 5, welche einen Verticalschnitt oder Axenschnitt durch den Kern mit der umgebenden Flüssigkeit darstellen soll um die Axe KJ, und betrachten wir ein im Punkte P der gesuchten Oberfläche befindliches Massentheilchen μ. Die Resultante der darauf wirkenden Kräfte muss zur Oberfläche normal stehen. Diese Kräfte sind aber, wenn ich den Mittelpunkt des Kernes (O) zum Coordinaten-Ursprung nehme, seine Entfernung von P mit r, des letzteren Coordinaten mit x, y und die Winkelgeschwindigkeit mit ω bezeichne:

1) Die nach dem Mittelpunkt des Kerns gerichtete Anziehungskraft $A = \frac{CM\mu}{r^2} = PC$ (in Fig. 5) mit den Componenten:

$$X = PA = \frac{CM\mu x}{r^3};\ Y = PB = \frac{CM\mu y}{r^3}$$

2) Die senkrecht zur Rotationsaxe gerichtete Centrifugalkraft $\Gamma = PD = \mu x \omega^2$.

Nach dem Gesagten muss also sein:

$$12)\ \ldots\ \frac{X-\Gamma}{Y} = -\frac{dy}{dx}$$

oder da sich μ forthebt:

$$13)\ \ldots\ \frac{\frac{CMx}{r^3} - x\omega^2}{\frac{CMy}{r^3}} = -\frac{dy}{dx}$$

$$r = \sqrt{x^2+y^2}.$$

Die Gl. 13) muss nun integrirt werden. Setzen wir z. A. die Constante:

$$\frac{\omega^2}{CM} = E\ \ldots\ldots\ 14)$$

und führen Polarcoordinaten ein, wobei der Winkel zwischen der verticalen Axe (OK) und r (OP) Θ sei, also:

$$\left.\begin{array}{l} x = r\sin\Theta \\ y = r\cos\Theta \end{array}\right\}\ \ldots\ldots\ 15)$$

werden, so nimmt die Gl. 13) die Form an:

$$\operatorname{tg}\Theta(1-Er^3) = \frac{r\operatorname{tg}\Theta - r'}{r + r'\operatorname{tg}\Theta}\ .\ 16)$$

worin r' statt $\frac{dr}{d\Theta}$ geschrieben ist.

Hieraus folgt nach leichten Umformungen:

$$\frac{r'}{r^4}\left(\frac{1}{r^3} - E\sin^2\Theta\right) = E\frac{\sin\Theta\cos\Theta}{r^3}.$$

Durch die Substitutionen:

$$\frac{1}{r^3} = \eta,\ \sin^2\Theta = \xi$$

wird die Gleichung homogen, nämlich:

$$-\frac{2}{3}\frac{d\eta}{d\xi}(\eta - E\xi) = E\eta$$

und lässt sich daher nach den gewöhnlichen Regeln integriren. Die Ausführung ergiebt:

$$\frac{(E\xi+2\eta)^3}{\eta^2} = c^3$$

worin c die Integrationsconstante ist; oder in r und Θ und nach Ausziehung der Kubikwurzel:

$$Er^2\sin^2\Theta + \frac{2}{r} = c\ \ldots\ 17)$$

oder auch:

$$\frac{2}{r} + Ex^2 = c.^{*})\ \ldots\ 18)$$

Bezeichne ich nun den Werth von r für

*) Der hydrodynamische Satz, dass das Potential der wirkenden Kräfte für alle Punkte der Oberfläche constant sein muss, führt augenblicklich zu derselben Gleichung.

$\Theta = 0$ und $x = 0$ mit b, so nehmen die Gll. 17) und 18) die Formen an:

$$19) \quad . \quad . \quad E r^2 \sin^2 \Theta + \frac{2}{r} = \frac{2}{b}$$

$$20) \quad . \quad . \quad . \begin{cases} \frac{2}{r} + E x^2 = \frac{2}{b} \\ r^2 = x^2 + y^2. \end{cases}$$

Hat nun die durch diese Gleichung bezeichnete Curve die in Fig. 5 angenommene Form, was, wie wir sehen werden, nur unter Umständen der Fall ist, so bezeichne ich das x oder r für $y = 0$ (OH) mit a; dann ist:

$$21) \quad . \quad . \quad . \quad . \; E a^2 + \frac{2}{a} = \frac{2}{b}$$

oder:

$$22) \quad . \quad E b^3 \cdot \left(\frac{a}{b}\right)^3 - 2\frac{a}{b} + 2 = 0$$

Ist nun: 1) $Eb^3 < \frac{8}{27}$, so liefert diese kubische Gleichung drei reelle Werthe für $\frac{a}{b}$, denn das Minimum ihrer linken Seite, das für:

$$\frac{a}{b} = \sqrt{\frac{2}{3} \cdot \frac{1}{Eb^3}}$$

eintritt, ist dann negativ; einer ist grösser als $\frac{3}{2}$, der zweite liegt zwischen 1 und $\frac{3}{2}$, der dritte ist negativ. Ist Eb^3 sehr klein, so ist von den positiven Wurzeln die eine sehr wenig von 1 verschieden, die andere sehr gross. Werthe für dieselben lassen sich in folgender Art finden. Setze ich:

$$E b^3 = \frac{2}{\beta}, \quad \frac{a}{b} = z$$

so wird die Gl. 22):

$$23) \quad . \quad . \quad . \quad z^3 - \beta z + \beta = 0$$

worin ich β sehr gross annehme. Zur Bestimmung der kleineren Wurzel setze ich:

$$z = \frac{1}{1 - \delta}$$

dann ist:

$$1 - \beta\delta(1 - \delta)^2 = 0$$

oder angenähert:

$$1 - \beta\delta(1 - 2\delta) = 0.$$

Die Auflösung dieser quadratischen Gleichung giebt als kleinere Wurzel, die allein brauchbar ist, weil δ sehr klein vorausgesetzt wurde: $\delta = \frac{1}{\beta} + \frac{2}{\beta^2}$ und hiermit das kleinere z:

$$z_1 = 1 + \frac{1}{\beta} + \frac{3}{\beta^2}.$$

Nennt man die grössere Wurzel z_2 und die negative $-\zeta$, so ist zunächst:

$$z_1 + z_2 - \zeta = 0$$
$$z_1 z_2 \zeta = \beta$$

also:

$$\left(1 + \frac{1}{\beta} + \frac{3}{\beta^2}\right)\left(1 + \frac{1}{\beta} + \frac{3}{\beta^2} + z_2\right) . z_2 = \beta$$

und durch Auflösung dieser Gleichung folgt die positive Wurzel (die negative ist $z_3 = -\zeta$):

$$z_2 = \sqrt{\beta} - \frac{1}{2} - \frac{3}{8\sqrt{\beta}}.$$

Es ist also:

$$\frac{a}{b} = 1 + \frac{Eb^3}{2} + \frac{3}{4}(Eb^3)^2 \quad . \quad . \quad 24)$$

und:

$$\frac{a}{b} = \sqrt{\frac{2}{Eb^3}} - \frac{1}{2} - \frac{3}{8}\sqrt{\frac{Eb^3}{2}} \quad . \quad 25)$$

Ist 2) $Eb^3 = \frac{8}{27}$, so sind die beiden positiven Wurzeln gleich und zwar $= \frac{3}{2}$, die negative ist $= -3$.

Ist endlich 3) $Eb^3 > \frac{8}{27}$, so liefert die Gl. 22) nur eine reelle und zwar negative Wurzel für $\frac{a}{b}$.

Hieraus ist zu ersehen, dass Eb^3 nicht grösser als $\frac{8}{27}$ sein darf, wenn eine Gleichgewichtsfigur nach Art der Fig. 5 möglich sein soll. Zur absoluten Bestimmung von b fehlt noch eine Bedingung; nehmen wir das Volumen als gegeben an und gleich A, so haben wir unter Voraussetzung der Fig. 5 die Gleichung:

$$\int_0^a 2x\,dx\,\pi y = \frac{1}{2}A$$

deren linke Seite auf elliptische Integrale führt.

Aus den Gll. 20) folgt nämlich:

$$r^2 = x^2 + y^2 = \frac{1}{\left(\frac{1}{b} - \frac{E}{2}x^2\right)^2}$$

oder wenn ich:

$$27) \;.\;.\; \left(\frac{x}{b}\right)^2 = u,\; \frac{Eb^3}{2} = h$$

setze, wobei $h \leqq \frac{4}{27}$ vorausgesetzt wird:

$$\left(\frac{y}{b}\right)^2 = \frac{1}{(1-hu)^2} - u$$

$$28) \;.\;.\;.\; \frac{y}{b} = \frac{\sqrt{1-u(1-hu)^2}}{1-hu}$$

also wird nach 26):

$$29) \quad \frac{A}{2\pi} = b^3 \int_0^{\left(\frac{a}{b}\right)^2} \frac{\sqrt{1-u(1-hu)^2}}{1-hu}\,du$$

Substituiren wir nun:

$$30) \;.\;.\;.\;.\; 1-hu = \frac{1}{v}$$

so wird, für $u = 0$, $v = 1$; für $u = \left(\frac{a}{b}\right)^2$ aber: $v = \frac{a}{b}$. Bezeichnen wir nämlich für die Gl. 22) die kleinere positive Wurzel mit α_1, die grössere positive mit α_2, die negative mit α_3, so lautet sie allgemein:

$$31) \;.\;.\;.\; h\alpha^3 - \alpha + 1 = 0$$

woraus:

$$1 - h\alpha_1^2 = \frac{1}{\alpha_1} \text{ also } v = \alpha_1$$

folgt. Somit wird nun:

$$\frac{A}{2\pi} = \frac{b^3}{h^{\frac{3}{2}}} \cdot \int_1^{\alpha_1} \sqrt{hv^3 - v + 1} \cdot \frac{dv}{v^{\frac{5}{2}}}$$

$$= \frac{2}{E} \int_1^{\alpha_1} \sqrt{\frac{1}{h} v(hv^3 - v + 1)} \cdot \frac{dv}{v^3} \quad 32)$$

oder wenn wir die Werthe $\alpha_1\,\alpha_2\,\alpha_3$ benutzen, wie Gl. 31) zeigt:

$$\frac{AE}{4\pi} = \int_1^{\alpha_1} \sqrt{v(v-\alpha_1)(v-\alpha_2)(v-\alpha_3)}\,\frac{dv}{v^3}. \quad 33)$$

Da α_3 negativ und die Reihenfolge der anderen Grössen:

$$1 < v < \alpha_1 < \alpha_2$$

ist, so ist die Grösse unter dem Wurzelzeichen positiv und auch das ganze Differential positiv. Das Integral lässt sich wie gesagt durch elliptische ausdrücken, wir wollen aber zunächst sehen, in welcher Art es sich mit h ändert. Letzteres steckt in $\alpha_1\,\alpha_2\,\alpha_3$; bezeichnen wir also obiges Integral mit U:

$$U = \int_1^{\alpha_1} \sqrt{v(v-\alpha_1)(v-\alpha_2)(v-\alpha_3)}\,\frac{dv}{v^3} \quad 34)$$

so ist:

$$\frac{dU}{dh} = \frac{\partial U}{\partial \alpha_1} \cdot \frac{d\alpha_1}{dh} + \frac{\partial U}{\partial \alpha_2} \cdot \frac{d\alpha_2}{dh} + \frac{\partial U}{\partial \alpha_3} \cdot \frac{d\alpha_3}{dh} \quad 35)$$

Es ist aber, wenn wir z. A. die positive Grösse:

$$\frac{\sqrt{v(v-\alpha_1)(v-\alpha_2)(v-\alpha_3)}}{v^3} = V$$

setzen:

$$\frac{\partial U}{\partial \alpha_1} = -\frac{1}{2} \int_1^{\alpha_1} \frac{V}{v-\alpha_1}\,dv;\; \frac{\partial U}{\partial \alpha_2} = -\frac{1}{2} \int_1^{\alpha_1} \frac{V\,dv}{v-\alpha_2};$$

$$\frac{\partial U}{\partial \alpha_3} = -\frac{1}{2} \int_1^{\alpha_1} \frac{V\,dv}{v-\alpha_3} \quad .\;.\; 36)$$

und nach 31) allgemein:

$$\frac{d\alpha}{dh} = \frac{\alpha^3}{1-3h\alpha^2} \text{ oder } = \frac{\alpha-1}{h(1-3h\alpha^2)}$$

folglich wird:

$$\frac{dU}{dh} = -\frac{1}{2h}\int_1^{\alpha_1} V dv \left\{ \frac{\alpha_1-1}{(v-\alpha_1)(1-3h\alpha_1^2)} + \frac{\alpha_2-1}{(v-\alpha_2)(1-3h\alpha_2^2)} + \frac{\alpha_3-1}{(v-\alpha_3)(1-3h\alpha_3^2)} \right\}$$

Der Factor von Vdv ist aber eine symmetrische Function der Wurzeln α_1 α_2 α_3 der Gl. 31) und folglich durch die Coefficienten derselben, also durch h rational auszudrücken möglich. Er ist, nachdem Zähler und Nenner durch $4-27h$ gehoben wurde:

$$-\frac{(v-1)}{h} : \left(v^3 - \frac{v}{h} + \frac{1}{h}\right)$$

folglich wird:

$$37) \quad \frac{dU}{dh} = \frac{1}{2h^2}\int_1^{\alpha_1} V \cdot \frac{v-1}{v^3-\frac{v}{h}+\frac{1}{h}} dv.$$

Nun ist $v^3-\frac{v}{h}+\frac{1}{h}$ für $v = 1$ positiv und wird erst, wie 31) zeigt, für $v = \alpha_1$ Null, folglich ist für alle dazwischen liegenden Werthe von v der Factor von V positiv und daher auch $\frac{dU}{dh}$; U wächst also mit h.

Nach 33) und 34) ist:

$$38) \quad . \quad . \quad . \quad . \quad \frac{AE}{4\pi} = U$$

also nimmt, wenn A constant bleibt, auch E mit h zu; für den grösstmöglichen Werth von h $\left(\frac{4}{27}\right)$ erhält also auch E und in Folge dessen (s. Gl. 14) die Winkelgeschwindigkeit den bei gegebenem Volumen (A) höchst gestatteten Werth, der sich durch Ausführung der Integration für $\alpha_1 = \alpha_2 = \frac{3}{2}$, $\alpha_3 = -3$ (s. S. 93, Fall 2) aus der Gleichung:

$$\frac{A}{4CM\pi} \cdot \omega^2 = \sqrt{3} - \frac{4}{3} + l_{nt}\{3(2-\sqrt{3})\}$$

ergiebt. Ist ω kleiner als dieser Werth, so lässt sich aus der Gl. 38) U ermitteln und hiemit (durch allmähliche Näherung) h, und zwar nur ein einziger Werth hiefür, da U gleichzeitig mit h wächst oder abnimmt. Ist h gefunden, womit gleichzeitig auch α_1 bekannt wird, so folgt aus 27) b und somit auch a. Die den Verticalschnitt darstellende Curve lässt sich also construiren.

In dem Grenzfalle $\left(h = \frac{4}{27} \text{ oder } Eb^2 = \frac{8}{27}, \frac{a}{b} = \frac{3}{2}\right)$ entsteht (wie aus der folgenden Anmerkung sub III zu ersehen) im Punkte H eine Spitze, indem die beiden in H an die Curventheile HK und HI gezogenen Tangenten mit der Abscissenaxe je einen Winkel von 60° bilden (s. Fig. 6d). — Würde E noch grösser werden, so gäbe es keine Gleichgewichtsfigur vorausgesetzter Art.

Bei vorliegendem Problem gewinnt der Vorgang der Trennung noch eine besondere, beim vorangehenden vermisste, physikalische Bedeutung. Fassen wir nämlich am Aequator der rotirenden Flüssigkeit ein einzelnes Massentheilchen ins Auge, so üben Anziehungskraft und Centrifugalkraft darauf im Augenblicke der Trennung die gleiche Wirkung aus.

Um dies zu beweisen, setzen wir in 21) für E den Werth aus 14) und für b den kritischen Werth $\frac{2}{3}a$ ein; dann wird sie

$$\frac{\omega^2}{CM} \cdot a^2 = \frac{1}{a} \text{ oder } \frac{CM}{a^2} = a\omega^2$$

und diese Gleichung drückt die obige Behauptung aus. Auch sieht man hier gleichsam, wie die Flüssigkeit durch die kreisförmige scharfe Kante des Rotationskörpers (in der den halben Verticalschnitt darstellenden Fig. 6d durch den Punkt H bezeichnet) hinausquillt.

Anmerkung. Die durch die obigen Gleichungen 19) oder 20) charakterisirte Curve ist auch mathematisch von Interesse.

Zunächst erkennt man aus den Gll. 20), dass die Curve aus vier symmetrisch gegen die Coordinatenaxen gelegenen Theilen besteht; ich werde daher fortan nur den zwischen den positiven Halbaxen befindlichen Theil betrachten.

Die Gl. 18) oder die Differentiation von 20) nach x giebt:

$$\text{a)} \quad . \; . \; . \; \frac{dy}{dx} = \frac{x}{y}(Er^3-1)$$

Ich nehme jetzt E und b als gegeben an und unterscheide:

$$\text{I. } Eb^3 > 1;\ \text{II. } 1 > Eb^3 > \frac{8}{27};\ \text{III. } Eb^3 = \frac{8}{27};$$

$$\text{IV. } Eb^3 < \frac{8}{27}.$$

Diese vier Fälle sind für $b = 1$ durch die Figuren 6a) bis e) ihrem Wesen nach veranschaulicht, nämlich I durch 6a) ($E = 2$), II durch 6b) $\left(E = \frac{1}{2}\right)$ und 6c) $\left(E = \frac{1}{3}\right)$, III durch 6d) $\left(E = \frac{8}{27}\right)$, IV durch 6e) $\left(E = \frac{2}{9}\right)$.

Ad I. Für $x = 0$ ist in diesem wie auch in den anderen Fällen $\frac{dy}{dx} = 0$; für x sehr klein $= \varepsilon$ ist:

$$\text{b)} \quad . \; . \; . \; \frac{dy}{dx} = \frac{\varepsilon}{b}(Eb^3-1)$$

also positiv und bleibt auch dauernd positiv; die Curve steigt also fortwährend, so dass niemals $y = 0$ werden kann. Der Radiusvector r von der Länge $\frac{3b}{2}$ ist eine Tangente an sie. Denn, wenn man mittelst Gl. 19) $\sin^2\Theta$ nach r differentiirt, so findet man:

$$\text{c)} \quad . \; . \; E\frac{d\sin^2\Theta}{dr} = \frac{4}{br^4}\left(\frac{3b}{2}-r\right)$$

das Maximum tritt also für $r = \frac{3b}{2}$ ein und hat den Werth:

$$\text{d)} \quad . \; . \; . \; \sin^2\Theta_m = \frac{8}{27}\cdot\frac{1}{Eb^3}$$

Θ_m ist also reell, solange $Eb^3 \geqq \frac{8}{27}$ ist. Setzt man ferner in 20) $x^2 = \frac{Eb}{2}$ oder:

$$\text{e)} \quad . \; . \; . \; . \; . \; \left(\frac{x}{b}\right)^2 = \frac{2}{Eb^3}$$

so folgt $r = \infty$ und daher auch $y = \infty$, desgleichen aus a):

$$\frac{dy}{dx} = \infty \quad . \; . \; . \; . \; . \; \text{f)}$$

Die Curve nähert sich also asymptotisch einer, in der Entfernung $x = \sqrt{\frac{2}{Eb^3}}\cdot b$ von O, auf der Abscissenaxe errichteten Senkrechten.

Ad II. Aus Gleichung b) folgt, dass die Curve anfänglich sich senkt; für Θ_m, das reell vorhanden ist, folgt aber aus a):

$$\frac{dy}{dx} = \frac{x}{y}\left(\frac{27}{8}Eb^3-1\right) \quad . \; . \; \text{g)}$$

also positiv; folglich muss die Curve vorher (für ein kleineres x) eine horizontale Stelle gehabt haben, die ich mit L, sowie die symmetrisch unter der Abscissenaxe gelegene mit L', bezeichne, während sie jetzt wieder im dauernden Ansteigen begriffen ist und sich überhaupt weiter ebenso verhält, wie im I. Falle.

Ad III. Wenn Eb^3 abnimmt, nähert sich (s. Gl. d)) Θ_m immer mehr $\frac{\pi}{2}$, die beiden Stellen L und L' streben also immer näher zusammen, bis sie sich in der Entfernung $\frac{3b}{2}$ von O (s. I.) auf der Abscissenaxe treffen. Aus a) folgt für diesen Fall: $\frac{dy}{dx} = \frac{0}{0}$ und daher wird:

$$\frac{dy}{dx} = \frac{Er^3-1+3Exr^2\left(\frac{x}{r}+\frac{y}{r}\cdot\frac{dy}{dx}\right)}{\frac{dy}{dx}},$$

also für $x = r = a = \frac{3b}{2}$, $y = 0$:

$$\left(\frac{dy}{dx}\right)^2 = 4Ea^3-1 = 3 \quad . \; . \; \text{h)}$$

und daher der Winkel der Curve mit der Abscissenaxe $= \pm 60^0$ oder besser 60^0 und 120^0, so dass auf der Abscissenaxe ein Kreuzungspunkt zweier sich später (im Falle IV) trennender Curvenzweige entsteht. Die Asymptote hat jetzt von O die Entfernung $\frac{3b}{2}\sqrt{3} = a\sqrt{3}$.

Ad IV. Ein Winkel Θ_m existirt nicht mehr, vielmehr nimmt Θ, wie die Gl. c) zeigt, dauernd zu, wenn r von b an wächst. Bei diesem Wachsthum wird $\frac{r}{b}$ auch einmal den kleineren der Gl. 22) genügenden Werth von $\frac{a}{b}$ erreicht haben; für diesen Werth ist, wie 19) im Vergleich mit 21) zeigt, $\theta = \frac{\pi}{2}$ und daher $y = 0$ folglich nach a), da wegen 22):

$$Ea^2 = 2\left(\frac{a}{b} - 1\right),$$

also für den kleineren, unter $\frac{3}{2}$ liegenden, Werth von $\frac{a}{b}$, $Ea^2 < 1$ ist,

$$\frac{dy}{dx} = -\infty.$$

Somit lässt sich in dieser Art der Curvenzweig KH (Fig. 6 e) construiren. Setze ich $x = a + \epsilon$, worin ϵ eine sehr kleine positive Grösse bedeutet, so ist, wie leicht aus 20) zu entwickeln, angenähert:

$$r = a(1 + Ea^2\epsilon)$$

und hieraus:

$$y^2 = r^2 - x^2 = 2a\epsilon(Ea^2 - 1),$$

also nach dem eben Gesagten negativ, die Curve existirt hier also nicht. Sie beginnt jedoch wieder in einem zweiten Zweige, wenn für $\frac{x}{b}$ der grössere der Gl. 22) genügende Werth von $\frac{a}{b}$ genommen wird, steigt unter 90° auf und nähert sich asymptotisch der früher bezeichneten Linie. Die Entfernung $H'M$ dieser Asymptote vom Anfangspunkt des zweiten Curvenzweiges, nämlich (s. den Text nach Gl. f)) $\sqrt{\frac{2}{Eb^3}}\, b - a$, nähert sich, wie die Gl. 25) zeigt, dem Grenzwerthe $\frac{b}{2}$, während der zweite Curvenzweig selbst, bei stets abnehmendem E ins Unendliche hinausrückt und der erste zum Kreise wird. Der zweite Zweig besitzt einen Wendepunkt, wie aus der Fig. 6e) von selbst ersichtlich. Seine Entfernung r von O ist die positive Wurzel der in gewöhnlicher Weise durch Nullsetzung von $\frac{d^2y}{dx^2}$ mittelst Gl. a) und unter Benutzung von 20) zu bildenden Gleichung:

$$(Er^3 - 1)\left(\frac{4r}{b} - 3\right) - 6\left(\frac{r}{b} - 1\right)\left(\frac{2r}{b} - 3\right) = 0.$$

In mechanischer Hinsicht ist nur der erste Curvenzweig im Falle IV und sein Uebergang zum Falle III von Bedeutung.

3.

Ein flüssiger oder gasförmiger Kern von homogener Dichtigkeit, dessen Massentheilchen einander nach dem Newtonschen Gesetze anziehn, sei wiederum von einer Flüssigkeit sehr geringer Dichte umgeben, deren Theilchen von dem Kern eine Anziehung nach demselben Gesetze, aber unter einander keine merkliche erfahren. Diese Masse rotirt (im Weltraum) um eine feste Axe; welches Axenverhältniss besitzt die äusserste Oberfläche derselben?

Die Auflösung dieser Aufgabe zerfällt in zwei Theile: die Bestimmung der Gleichgewichtsfigur des Kerns und der, von der Form desselben abhängigen, Gleichgewichtsfigur der umgebenden Flüssigkeit (oder Flüssigkeitshülle, wie wir sie fortan nennen wollen). Die Gleichgewichtsfigur des Kerns ist, da die Flüssigkeitshülle darauf keine merkliche Wirkung ausübt, das bekannte, hier sub 1. behandelte Rotationsellipsoid. Um den zweiten Theil zu beantworten, verallgemeinern wir zuerst die sub 2. gelöste Aufgabe, indem wir statt des als materiellen Punkt oder kugelig gedachten Kerns denselben von ellipsoidischer Gestalt voraussetzen und schliesslich annehmen, dass er diese Form durch die Rotation gewonnen habe.

Sei W das Potential des ellipsoidischen Kerns auf einen Punkt der Flüssigkeitshülle, $x\,y\,z$ die (in gleicher Bedeutung wie bisher angenommenen) Coordinaten des letzteren und ω wiederum die Winkelgeschwindigkeit der Masse; dann heisst die Gleichung einer der Oberflächen gleichen Druckes (Niveauflächen), zu denen die freie Oberfläche auch gehört: *)

$$W + \frac{\omega^2}{2}(x^2 + y^2) = \text{const.} \quad . \quad 39)$$

Das Potential eines Ellipsoides mit den

*) Schell a. a. O. Bd. II. S. 610.

Halbaxen a, b, c und der constanten Dichtigkeit ϱ auf einen ausserhalb desselben gelegenen Punkt $(x\,y\,z)$ ist aber, wenn C wie bisher die Constante des Sonnensystems bedeutet: *)

$$40)\quad \begin{cases} W = C\pi\varrho \displaystyle\int_\sigma^\infty \left(1 - \frac{x^2}{a^2+s} - \frac{y^2}{b^2+s} - \frac{z^2}{c^2+s}\right)\frac{ds}{D} \\ D = \sqrt{\left(1+\frac{s}{a^2}\right)\left(1+\frac{s}{b^2}\right)\left(1+\frac{s}{c^2}\right)} \end{cases}$$

worin σ die positive Wurzel der Gleichung:

$$41)\quad \frac{x^2}{a^2+\sigma} + \frac{y^2}{b^2+\sigma} + \frac{z^2}{c^2+\sigma} = 1$$

ist. Nehmen wir jetzt:

$$a = b > c$$

an, so vereinigen sich zwei Glieder in Gl. 41), wie im Integral zu einem, und zwar wird die erstere, wenn wir vorübergehend die Projection des von O nach dem Punkte $(x\,y\,z)$ gezogenen Radiusvector auf die Aequatorialebene mit r bezeichnen:

$$42)\quad \frac{r^2}{a^2+\sigma} + \frac{z^2}{c^2+\sigma} = 1,$$

oder:

$$43)\quad \sigma^2 + (a^2+c^2-r^2-z^2)\sigma - (c^2r^2+a^2z^2-a^2c^2) = 0.$$

Hierin ist der in der letzten Klammer stehende Ausdruck positiv, denn denkt man sich durch den Punkt $(x\,y\,z)$ ein Ellipsoid mit den Halbaxen bez. ka, ka, kc $(k > 1)$ gelegt und einen Schnitt, der denselben Punkt und die z-Axe in sich aufnimmt, hindurchgeführt, so ist die Gleichung der als Begrenzung erscheinenden Ellipse:

$$\frac{r^2}{k^2a^2} + \frac{z^2}{k^2c^2} = 1$$

oder:

$$c^2r^2 + a^2z^2 - a^2c^2 = (k^2-1)a^2c^2$$

*) Ib. S. 306.

also positiv. Daher hat die Gl. 43) eine positive und eine negative Wurzel; verstehen wir nun unter dem Zeichen $\sqrt{\ }$ die positive Quadratwurzel, so ist die positive Wurzel der obigen Gleichung:

$$\sigma = \frac{r^2+z^2-a^2-c^2}{2} + \frac{1}{2}\sqrt{(z^2-r^2+a^2-c^2)^2+(2rz)^2} \quad 44)$$

Setzen wir nun, wie in Abschnitt 1. (Gl. 1)).

$$\frac{c}{a} = \cos u \quad \ldots\ldots \quad 45)$$

so folgen die drei in W (Gll. 40) vorkommenden Integrale mittelst der beiden jedesmal nach einander anzuwendenden Substitutionen:

$$s = c^2\operatorname{tg}^2\varphi;\quad \cos\varphi = \cot u \operatorname{tg}\psi$$

nämlich:

$$\int_\sigma^\infty \frac{ds}{D} = 2a^2\cot u\,.\,\psi_0;\quad \int_\sigma^\infty \frac{ds}{(a^2+s)D} = \frac{\cos u}{\sin^3 u}\left(\psi_0 - \frac{1}{2}\sin 2\psi_0\right);\quad \int_\sigma^\infty \frac{ds}{(c^2+s)D} = \frac{2\cos u}{\sin^3 u}(\operatorname{tg}\psi_0 - \psi_0)$$

worin ψ_0 dem Werthe $s = \sigma$ entspricht und aus der Gleichung:

$$\operatorname{tg}\psi_0 = \frac{\operatorname{tg} u}{\sqrt{1+\frac{\sigma}{c^2}}} \quad \ldots \quad 46)$$

folgt. Die Gl. 39) liefert uns dann eine Beziehung zwischen den beiden in derselben, aber, da wir es mit einem Rotationskörper zu thun haben, beliebigen, Verticalebene liegenden Grössen z und r; nehmen wir als diese Ebene die xz-Ebene, so haben wir statt r wieder x zu schreiben und die Gl. 39) geht dann über in:

$$C\pi\varrho\left\{2a^2\cot u\,.\,\psi_0 - x^2\frac{\cos u}{\sin^3 u}\left(\psi_0 - \frac{1}{2}\sin 2\psi_0\right) - z^2\cdot\frac{2\cos u}{\sin^3 u}(\operatorname{tg}\psi_0 - \psi_0)\right\} + \frac{\omega^2}{2}x^2 = k \quad 47)$$

wenn die Constante mit k bezeichnet wird.

Dies ist die Gleichung der Begrenzungscurve in einem Meridianschnitt. Darin hängt aber ψ_0 durch 46) von σ, also durch 44) von x (statt r zu lesen) und z ab.

Wollte man die Natur der durch die Gleichung 47) in Verbindung mit 46) und 44) dargestellten Curve discutiren, so würde man voraussichtlich ziemlich complicirte Betrachtungen anzuwenden haben: wir wollen uns begnügen, das Verhältniss der Polaraxe und eines Aequatorialhalbmessers in seiner Abhängigkeit von ω und von u zu bestimmen, und es wird uns gelingen, hieraus die nothwendigen Schlüsse zu ziehen.

Wir bezeichnen die Polarhalbaxe mit γ, einen Aequatorialhalbmesser mit α — diese beiden Grössen waren in 2. c und a genannt — und wenden die Gl. 47) auf die beiden Punkte ($x = \alpha$, $z = 0$) und ($x = 0$, $z = \gamma$) an. Im ersten Falle folgt zunächst aus 44):

$$\sigma = \frac{1}{2}\left\{\alpha^2 - a^2 - c^2 + \sqrt{(a^2 - c^2 - \alpha^2)^2}\right\};$$

aber, da wir stets:

$$48) \quad . \quad . \quad . \quad \alpha \geqq a, \; \gamma \geqq c$$

voraussetzen müssen, falls die Lösung einen physikalischen Sinn behalten soll, und da der Werth der Quadratwurzel in σ positiv sein soll, so ist derselbe als $\alpha^2 + c^2 - a^2$ aufzufassen und daher wird:

$$\sigma = \alpha^2 - a^2$$

folglich:

$$\sigma + c^2 = \alpha^2 - a^2 \sin^2 u$$

und demgemäss aus 46):

$$49) \quad \operatorname{tg}\psi_0 = \frac{\operatorname{ctg} u}{\sqrt{\sigma + c^2}} = \frac{\frac{a}{\alpha}\sin u}{\sqrt{1 - \left(\frac{a}{\alpha}\sin u\right)^2}}.$$

Wir führen nun die Grössen μ und ν, (deren erste sehr bald zur Anwendung kommen wird) durch die Gleichungen:

$$\left.\begin{aligned} \operatorname{tg}\mu &= \frac{a}{\gamma}\sin u \\ \sin\nu &= \frac{a}{\alpha}\sin u \end{aligned}\right\} \quad . \quad . \quad . \quad 50)$$

ein, so folgt aus 49):

$$\psi_0 = \nu$$

und hiermit geht 47) (mit Benutzung der zweiten 50)) in die Gleichung:

$$C\pi\varrho a^2 \cot u \left\{2\nu - \frac{2\nu - \sin 2\nu}{2\sin^2\nu}\right\} + \frac{a^2\sin^2 u}{2\sin^2\nu}\omega^2 = k \quad . \quad . \quad 51)$$

über. Setzen wir weiter in 44) x (d. i. r) $= 0$ und $z = \gamma$, so folgt, da jetzt der Quadratwurzel mit Rücksicht auf 48) der Werth $a^2 + \gamma^2 - c^2$ zu geben ist:

$$\sigma = \gamma^2 - c^2, \quad \sigma + c^2 = \gamma^2$$

und daher mittelst 46) und 50):

$$\psi_0 = \mu.$$

Somit wird 47):

$$2C\pi\varrho a^2 \cot u \left\{\mu - \cot^2\mu(\operatorname{tg}\mu - \mu)\right\} = k. \quad 52)$$

Führen wir nun die beiden Functionen:

$$\left.\begin{aligned} Q(v) &= 2\cdot\frac{2v - \sin 2v}{1 - \cos 2v} \\ R(v) &= \frac{\sin 2v - 2v\cos 2v}{1 - \cos 2v} \end{aligned}\right\} \quad . \quad 53)$$

ein, welche durch die einfache Gleichung:

$$\frac{1}{2}Q(v) + R(v) = 2v \quad . \quad . \quad 54)$$

mit einander zusammenhängen, schreiben der Kürze wegen, solange kein Zweifel möglich ist:

$$Q \text{ statt } Q(\mu), \; R \text{ statt } R(\nu) \quad . \quad 55)$$

und eliminiren k aus 51) und 52), so folgt mit Fortlassung des Factors a^2:

$$C\pi\varrho \cot u (Q - R) - \frac{\sin^2 u}{2\sin^2\nu}\omega^2 = 0. \quad 56)$$

Ersetzen wir nun ω^2 durch eine andere Grösse V mittelst der Gleichung:

$$\omega^2 = 2C\pi\varrho V, \quad . \quad . \quad . \quad 57)$$

welcher Grösse wir vorläufig, d. h. solange wir den Kern als fest, in seiner Form unveränderlich betrachten, keine weitere Bedeutung unterlegen, als dass sie (bei einer ein für allemal bestimmten Dichtigkeit ϱ des Kerns) aus der Winkelgeschwindigkeit ω sofort zu ermitteln ist, und dieses V wiederum durch P vermöge der Gleichung:

$$58) \quad . \; . \; . \quad \mathrm{P} = \frac{\sin^3 u}{\cos u}\,\mathrm{V},$$

so nimmt die Gl. 56) die definitive Gestalt an:

$$\mathrm{Q} - \mathrm{R} - \frac{\mathrm{P}}{\sin^2 \nu} = 0$$

oder:

$$59) \quad . \; . \; . \quad \mathrm{Q} = \mathrm{R} + \frac{\mathrm{P}}{\sin^2 \nu}.$$

Hierin hängt P von u und ω, also von der Abplattung des Kerns und der Winkelgeschwindigkeit ab und wächst mit jeder dieser Grössen von 0 an. Q hängt von μ, also von u und a/γ, R von ν, also von u und a/α ab. Auch wachsen $Q(v)$ und $R(v)$ mit v, denn es ist:

$$\frac{d\mathrm{Q(v)}}{d\mathrm{v}} = \frac{8 \sin \mathrm{v} \cos \mathrm{v} (\mathrm{tg\,v} - \mathrm{v})}{(1 - \cos 2\mathrm{v})^2}$$

$$60) \quad . \; . \text{ oder} = 2(2 - \mathrm{Q(v)} \cot \mathrm{v})$$

$$61) \quad . \; . \quad \frac{d\mathrm{R(v)}}{d\mathrm{v}} = \mathrm{Q(v)} \cot \mathrm{v};$$

also sind beide Differentialquotienten positiv, so lange v nicht $\frac{\pi}{2}$ überschreitet. Ist v sehr klein, so ist:

$$62) \quad . \; . \quad \mathrm{Q(v)} = \mathrm{R(v)} = \frac{4}{3}\mathrm{v}.$$

Dieser aus der Entwickelung der definirenden Ausdrücke 53) leicht folgende Werth genügt bei 4stelliger Rechnung etwa bis $v = 5^0$ und ist bis dahin genauer, als der mit 5stelligen Tafeln aus den strengen Formeln berechnete. Weiterhin wächst also Q mit v, erreicht für $v = \frac{\pi}{2}$ den Werth π, wächst dann weiter und wird für $v = \pi$ unendlich gross. R wächst ebenfalls, aber nicht so rasch, mit v, erreicht jedoch für $v = \frac{\pi}{2}$ das Maximum $\frac{\pi}{2}$, nimmt dann ab, wird 0, dann negativ und für $v = \pi$ negativ unendlich. Einige Werthe für Q und R giebt die folgende Tabelle.

v	Q(v)	R(v)	v	Q(v)
10⁰	0,2356	0,2313	61⁰	1,6742
20⁰	0,4726	0,4618	62⁰	1,7130
30⁰	0,7248	0,6840	63⁰	1,7504
40⁰	0,9956	0,8985	64⁰	1,7900
50⁰	1,2960	1,0973	65⁰	1,8298
60⁰	1,6378	1,2755	66⁰	1,8700
70⁰	2,040	1,424	67⁰	1,9104
80⁰	2,526	1,530	68⁰	1,9532
90⁰	3,142	1,571	69⁰	1,9958

Wir ziehen nun noch aus den Gll. 50) mit Benutzung von 45) die folgenden:

$$\frac{\gamma}{\alpha} = \cot \mu \sin \nu \quad . \; . \; . \quad 63)$$

$$\frac{\gamma}{c} = \mathrm{tg}\, u \cot \mu; \quad . \; . \; . \quad 64)$$

und jetzt wenden wir nach einander zwei verschiedene Betrachtungsweisen an, indem wir zuerst a/α fest annehmen und ω von 0 an wachsend denken, und zweitens ω als gegeben ansehen und a/α sich ändern lassen. Nehmen wir also u d. h. die Form des Kerns und folglich a und c als bestimmt gegeben an, wählen sodann auch für a/α einen bestimmten Werth z. B. 0,1 und lassen ω wachsen, so heisst dies: wir betrachten bei geänderter Winkelgeschwindigkeit nicht dieselbe individuelle Niveaufläche, sondern stets diejenige Schicht, deren Aequatorialhalbmesser $\alpha = 10a$ ist. Für diese bestimmen wir γ/α und γ/c; ersteres giebt eine rohe Vorstellung von der Form dieser Niveaufläche, letzteres von ihrer Lage zum Kern. Unbeantwortet bleibt dabei die Frage, wo diese Fläche sich früher (bei anderer Winkelgeschwindigkeit) befunden habe: dies zu entscheiden wären wir erst im Stande, wenn wir die Form der Niveauflächen kennen und daraus ihren Kubikinhalt berechnen würden; die Constant-Annahme desselben würde dann, wie in 2. geschehen, zur gewünschten Antwort führen.

Ist $\omega = 0$ so folgt aus 59):

$$Q(\mu) = R(\nu)$$

wobei ν durch die Gleichung 50):

$$\sin\nu = \frac{a}{\alpha}\sin u$$

gegeben war. Aus $Q(\mu)$ folgt (durch Interpolation oder Näherung) μ und hieraus mittelst 63) γ/α und γ/c. (Ist a/α sehr klein d. h. die Schicht sehr weit vom Kern gelegen, so wird $\mu = \nu$ und daher $\gamma/\alpha = \cos\mu$ und nahezu $= 1$.) Wächst nun ω, so bleibt ν dasselbe, aber P und daher Q werden grösser, γ/α und γ/c deshalb kleiner. Dann wird auch μ einmal den Werth u erreichen; in diesem Augenblick wird γ/c wie 64) zeigt $= 1$ d. h. die betrachtete Schicht berührt bereits den Kern und die Winkelgeschwindigkeit darf nicht grösser werden, wenn nicht die Flüssigkeitshülle durch den Kern zerrissen und daher das Problem völlig geändert werden soll. Ja sie ist bereits zu gross, indem man nicht umhin können wird anzunehmen, dass die näher gelegenen Schichten bereits zerrissen sind. — Wollen wir die Winkelgeschwindigkeit sich so weit steigern lassen, dass die Figur des Kerns die dieser Winkelgeschwindigkeit entsprechende Gleichgewichtsfigur ist, so ist das jedenfalls nur dann angänglich, wenn sie einen kleineren Werth von μ als $\mu = u$ zur Folge hat. Z. B. ist, wenn wir diese Winkelgeschwindigkeit mit ω_1 bezeichnen und $u = 68^0\,25'$ (s. S. 89.) annehmen:

für $\frac{a}{\alpha} = 0{,}1$ und $\frac{\omega^2}{\omega_1^2} =$	$\frac{\gamma}{\alpha} =$	$\frac{\gamma}{c} =$
0:	0,996;	27,07
0,00055	0,816	22,18
0,039	0,037	1.

für $\frac{a}{\alpha} = 0{,}5$ und $\frac{\omega^2}{\omega_1^2} =$	$\frac{\gamma}{\alpha} =$	$\frac{\gamma}{c} =$
0:	0,939;	5,01
0,068	0,736	4,00
0,59	0,184	1.

hingegen:

für $\frac{a}{\alpha} = 0{,}8$ und $\frac{\omega^2}{\omega_1^2} =$	$\frac{\gamma}{\alpha} =$	$\frac{\gamma}{c} =$
0:	0,502;	1,71
1	0,303	1,03.

Nehmen wir jetzt in zweiter Betrachtungsweise ω als gegeben an und durchstreichen die Flüssigkeit von aussen nach dem Kern zu. Dabei nehmen wir aber, um nicht unnütz weitläufig zu sein, als die Winkelgeschwindigkeit sogleich diejenige ω_1 an, welche dem jetzt als flüssig gedachten Kern seine Form giebt. Dieselbe folgt aus den Gll. 1) bis 4) dieses Zusatzes und zwar ist nach 3) V in u ausgedrückt:

$$V = \frac{\cos u(3\cos^2 u + \sin^2 u)}{\sin^3 u}\cdot u - 3\cot^2 u$$

und daher nach 58):

$$P = (1 + 2\cos^2 u)\,.\,u - 3\sin u\cos u \qquad 65)$$

oder auch:

$$P = \frac{1}{2}\left\{(2 + \cos 2u)\,.\,2u - 3\sin 2u\right\} \qquad 66)$$

so dass jetzt P nur von u abhängt. Ich schicke nun der folgenden theoretischen Betrachtung ein Beispiel voraus.

Für $u = 10^0$ und $a/\alpha = 0{,}1$ ist $\omega = \omega_1$ nicht erreichbar, denn für $\omega^2 = 0{,}7114\,\omega_1^2$ ist bereits $\gamma/c = 1$. Hingegen ist, wenn $\omega = \omega_1$ und $a > 0{,}1198\,\alpha$ wird (wobei $\gamma = c$, $\mu = u$, $\nu = 1^0\,11'\,32''$, $\gamma = 0{,}1486\,\alpha$ würde), γ grösser als c, und zwar:

für $\frac{a}{\alpha} =$	$\nu =$	$\frac{\gamma}{\alpha} =$	$\frac{\gamma}{c} =$
0,2;	2^0;	0,3816;	1,937
0,3014	3^0	0,678	2,278
0,4017	4^0	0,831	2,100
0,5019	5^0	0,905	1,831
1,0000	10^0	0,985	1,000.

Was hiebei die letzte Zeile anbetrifft, so ergiebt sich aus 59) wenn wir darin die Werthe für $R(\nu)$ gemäss 53) und für P gemäss 66) einsetzen und daran denken, dass die zweite 50), für $a/\alpha = 1$, $\nu = u$ werden lässt:

$$Q(\mu) = \frac{\sin 2u - 2u\cos 2u + (2+\cos 2u).2u - 3\sin 2u}{1-\cos 2u}$$

$$= 2\cdot\frac{2u-\sin 2u}{1-\cos 2u} = Q(u)$$

also $\mu = u$ und somit nach 63) und 64):

$$67) \quad . \quad . \quad \frac{\gamma}{\alpha} = \cos u, \; \frac{\gamma}{c} = 1.$$

Die vorangehenden Zeilen des obigen Beispiels zeigen, dass γ/c ein Max. nahezu für $a/\alpha = 0{,}3$ besitzt und dass für kleinere Werthe von a/α die Niveauflächen einander durchkreuzen. Denn wir haben, wenn wir die reciproken Werthe von a/α nehmen, nach einander die Halbaxen:

$$\begin{cases}\alpha = 8{,}35a;\\ \gamma = c;\end{cases} \begin{cases}\alpha = 5{,}00a;\\ \gamma = 1{,}94c;\end{cases} \begin{cases}\alpha = 3{,}32a;\\ \gamma = 2{,}28c;\end{cases}$$

$$\begin{cases}\alpha = 2{,}49a;\\ \gamma = 2{,}10c;\end{cases} \text{etc.}$$

Solche Durchkreuzung ist man aber wohl gezwungen, physikalisch für unmöglich zu halten und daraus eine durch die Umdrehung erfolgende Abtrennung der Schichten zu schliessen, deren Horizontalhalbmesser grösser als $\alpha = 3{,}32a$ (für das obige Beispiel) wäre.

Ist dies aber der Fall, so wird es von besonderer Wichtigkeit, den Maximalwerth von γ/c, das zugehörige γ/α oder a/α und die Abhängigkeit dieser Grössen von der Rotationsgeschwindigkeit oder, was damit äquivalent ist, von u kennen zu lernen.

Für eine bestimmte Rotationsgeschwindigkeit, also für ein bestimmtes u ist nach Gl. 64) γ/c proportional mit $\cot\mu$, sein Maximum fällt also mit dem Minimum von μ zusammen, und dies wiederum, da μ mit $Q(\mu)$ gleichzeitig wächst oder abnimmt (s. Gl. 60) und den zugehörigen Text) mit dem Minimum von $Q(\mu)$ oder Q. In der Gl. 59) aber, welche den Werth von Q ergiebt, ist auf der rechten Seite ν die veränderliche Grösse und es ist nach Gl. 61):

$$\frac{d}{d\nu}\left(R(\nu)+\frac{P}{\sin^2\nu}\right) = Q(\nu).\cot\nu - \frac{2\cos\nu}{\sin^3\nu}P.$$

Die Nullsetzung dieses Ausdrucks führt zur Gleichung:

$$Q(\nu) = \frac{2P}{\sin^2\nu}, \quad . \quad . \quad . \quad . \quad 68)$$

oder, wenn wir den aus ihr folgenden Werth von ν mit ν_1 bezeichnen und den Ausdruck für $Q(\nu)$ nach 53) substituiren:

$$2\nu_1 - \sin(2\nu_1) = 2P. \quad . \quad . \quad 68a)$$

Hieraus folgt für obiges Beispiel, nämlich $u = 10^0$ und daher $P = 0{,}00009$, sehr nahe:

$$2\nu_1 = 5^0\,55'.$$

Weiter folgt:

$$\frac{a}{\alpha} = \frac{\sin\nu_1}{\sin u}; \quad . \quad . \quad . \quad . \quad 69)$$

und wir fragen nunmehr: wie ändert sich a/α, wenn sich u ändert? Bezeichnen wir das speciell aus der Gl. 69) folgende Verhältniss a/α mit A, so ist die Aenderung von A mit u zu untersuchen, während ν_1 mit u durch die Gleichung (s. 66):

$$2\nu_1 - \sin 2\nu_1 = 2u(2+\cos 2u) - 3\sin 2u \quad 70)$$

zusammenhängt.

Aus der Gleichung:

$$A = \frac{\sin\nu_1}{\sin u} \quad . \quad . \quad . \quad . \quad 71)$$

folgt:

$$\frac{dA}{du} = \frac{\sin u\cos\nu_1\frac{d\nu_1}{du} - \sin\nu_1\cos u}{\sin^2 u} \quad 72)$$

und aus 70) nach geringen Umformungen:

$$\frac{d\nu_1}{du} = \frac{2\sin u(\sin u - u\cos u)}{\sin^2\nu_1}$$

$$73) \quad \ldots = 2\left(\frac{\sin u}{\sin\nu_1}\right)^2(1 - u\cot u).$$

Nun folgt zunächst für sehr kleine Werthe von u und also auch von ν_1 durch Entwickelung der Gl. 70):

$$\frac{4}{3}\nu_1^3 = \frac{8}{15}u^5$$

daher:

$$74) \quad \ldots \quad \nu_1 = \sqrt[3]{\frac{2}{5}}\cdot u^{\frac{5}{3}}$$

$$75) \quad \ldots \quad A = \sqrt[3]{\frac{2}{5}}u^{\frac{2}{3}}$$

$$76) \quad \ldots \quad \frac{dA}{du} = \sqrt[3]{\frac{2}{5}}\cdot\frac{2}{3u^{\frac{1}{3}}}$$

A beginnt also mit $u = 0$ mit dem Werthe 0, nimmt dann aber sehr rasch zu. Sollte nun diese Zunahme einmal aufhören und A für ein gewisses u ein Max. erreichen, so müsste für diesen Werth der durch 72) gegebene Differentialquotient verschwinden und gleich darauf (d. h. bei wachsendem u) negativ werden. Ich werde zeigen, dass dies nicht stattfinden kann. Sei der Werth von u für den das Max. von A eintreten sollte u_m; dann gelten folgende einfache Betrachtungen.

1. In $\frac{d\nu_1}{du}$ wächst der zweite Factor auf der rechten Seite von 73) $1 - u\cot u$ von 0 bis 1, wenn u von 0 bis $\frac{\pi}{2}$ wächst; würde nun A von $u = u_m$ an abnehmen, so würde der reciproke Werth davon, also auch der andere Factor in 73): $\left(\frac{\sin u}{\sin\nu_1}\right)^2$ zuzunehmen beginnen und ebenso $\frac{d\nu_1}{du}$ mindestens von u_m an zunehmen.

2. Es ist allgemein a/α, also auch A kleiner als 1, daher nach einander:

$\nu_1 < u$, $\sin(u - \nu_1) > 0$, $\sin u\cos\nu_1 > \cos u\sin\nu_1$

folglich müsste für den Maximalwerth von A wie 72) zeigt, jedenfalls

$$\frac{d\nu_1}{du} < 1$$

sein.

3. Es ist

$$\frac{d}{du}\left(\frac{\cos\nu_1}{\cos u}\right) = \frac{\sin u\cos\nu_1 - \cos u\sin\nu_1\cdot\frac{d\nu_1}{du}}{\cos^2 u}$$

also (wegen des eben Gesagten) in der Gegend von $u = u_m$ positiv, also $\frac{\cos\nu_1}{\cos u}$ mit u wachsend.

Schreiben wir nun:

$$\frac{dA}{du} = \frac{\sin\nu_1\cos u}{\sin^2 u}\left(\frac{\sin u}{\sin\nu_1}\cdot\frac{\cos\nu_1}{\cos u}\cdot\frac{d\nu_1}{du} - 1\right)$$

so ist der erste Factor stets positiv, der zweite wäre für $u = u_m$ Null; wenn aber u wächst, so würden nach dem in 1) und 3) Ausgeführten die drei Factoren $\frac{\sin u}{\sin\nu_1}$, $\frac{d\nu_1}{du}$, $\frac{\cos\nu_1}{\cos u}$ ebenfalls wachsen, also $\frac{dA}{du}$ positiv werden. Dies Resultat involvirt aber einen Widerspruch, also ist die Annahme unrichtig, d. h. A oder a/α wächst von 0 an und dauernd mit u.

In diesem Falle ($\nu = \nu_1$) ist ferner nach 54) und 68):

$$R(\nu_1) = 2\nu_1 - \frac{P}{\sin^2\nu_1}$$

also nach 59):

$$Q(\mu) = 2\nu_1 \quad \ldots \quad 77)$$

während die Ausdrücke 63) und 64) für γ/α und γ/c in ihrer Form keine Aenderung erfahren.

Für $u = 0$ ist $A = 0$ also $\alpha/a = \infty$. Ist u sehr klein, so ist nach 75):

78) . . . $\frac{\alpha}{a} = \sqrt[3]{\frac{5}{2}} \cdot \frac{1}{u^{\frac{2}{3}}}$;

dann nach 77), da auch ν_1 und folglich μ sehr klein werden, mit Rücksicht auf 62):

$$\mu = \frac{3}{2} \nu_1$$

also nach 63):

79) . . . $\frac{\gamma}{\alpha} = \frac{\nu_1}{\mu} = \frac{2}{3}$ *)

und nach 64):

80) . . . $\frac{\gamma}{c} = \frac{2}{3} \sqrt[3]{\frac{5}{2}} \cdot \frac{1}{u^{\frac{2}{3}}}$.

Wenn dann u wächst, so wird a/α immer grösser, also α/a immer kleiner; ebenso auch γ/c und γ/α.

Denken wir uns also etwa einen flüssigen Kern von einer Hülle sehr dünner Luft umgeben, und diesen Körper so schnell rotirend, dass die Abplattung des Kerns 1/300 ($\cos u$ = 299/300, u = 4° 20′) betrüge, so würde der Aequatorialradius der Lufthülle ungefähr (nach 78)) 7,5 desjenigen des Kerns und das Axenverhältniss der Lufthülle 2 : 3 betragen.

Denken wir uns, dass bei einem derartigen Körper die Rotationsgeschwindigkeit immer zunehme, so dass der Kern sich immer weiter abplattet, so würde nach den entwickelten Formeln die Zerstörungszone demselben immer näher kommen, so dass bei Annäherung an diejenige Geschwindigkeit, welche eine Zertrümmerung des Kerns selbst zur Folge hätte (wobei u = 68° 25′ s. d. erste Problem dieses Zusatzes), die Dicke der Lufthülle am Aequator nur noch etwa $a/8$, ihre Dicke über dem Pol (wenn diese Allen geläufige Bezeichnung auf unsern Körper übertragen werden darf) nur noch $c/20$ sein würde. — Die umgekehrte Reihenfolge der genannten Zustände, als Wirkung einer Verminderung der Abplattung des Kerns ist im vorangehenden Aufsatze selbst (Anm. zu S. 79.) betrachtet worden.

*) Dieser Werth stimmt, wie zu erwarten, mit dem Werth des kritischen Axenverhältnisses beim vorangehenden Problem überein.

Gedächtnisrede

auf den am 17. Oktober 1887 verstorbenen Königsberger Astronomen

Eduard Luther.

Gelesen am 3. November 1887 von **Dr. Franz.**

Meine Herren! Eine heilige und ernste Pflicht mahnt uns heute eines Mannes zu gedenken, dessen kürzlich erfolgtes Hinscheiden in allen Kreisen der Königsberger Gelehrtenwelt aufs schmerzlichste empfunden wird, eines Mannes, der auch in unserer Gesellschaft als thätiger Mitarbeiter gewirkt hat, eines Mannes, der über ein Jahrzehnt mir persönlich sehr nahe gestanden hat und dessen Verlust in erster Linie die hiesige Sternwarte empfindet: des Direktors der Sternwarte und ordentlichen Professors Dr. Eduard Luther.

Unserer Gesellschaft gehörte er seit 1847 als ordentliches Mitglied an. In den vier Jahren 1858 bis 1861 hat er, nachdem er eine auf ihn gefallene Wahl zum Präsidenten der Gesellschaft ablehnte, als Direktor und Vorstandsmitglied die wissenschaftlichen Interessen unserer Gesellschaft gefördert. Im 5. und 21. Bande unserer Schriften finden sich von ihm zwei grundlegende Arbeiten über das Klima von Königsberg. Sie enthalten die Mittelwerte und Extreme der von dem jetzt Verstorbenen in dem Zeitraum von 31 Jahren und 8 Monaten an allen meteorologischen Instrumenten täglich dreimal persönlich und regelmässig gemachten Beobachtungen. Diese schlichten, aber beredten Zahlen, die von ihm selbst sorgfältig berechnet sind, geben ein anschauliches Bild unseres Klimas und sind für die Kenntnis desselben geradezu von fundamentaler Bedeutung, da aus früherer Zeit keine Königsberger meteorologischen Beobachtungen von solcher Vollständigkeit existieren. Am 5. März 1875 hielt Professor Luther ferner in unserer Gesellschaft eine Gedächtnisrede auf den damals kürzlich verstorbenen Astronomen Argelander, einen der ersten Schüler Bessels, in welcher er die unermüdliche und für die Erforschung des Fixsternhimmels so erfolgreiche Thätigkeit dieses Astronomen feiert.

Eduard Luther ist am 24. Februar 1816 in Hamburg geboren, wo sein Vater erster Lehrer am Waisenhause war. Schon frühzeitig zeigte der junge Luther besondere Begabung für Mathematik. In Folge von Privatstudien, die er unter Leitung seines für diese Wissenschaft auch hoch begabten Vaters trieb, war er in diesem Fach stets seinen Mitschülern weit voraus, so dass ihm, wie es damals gestattet war, die Teilnahme an dem mathematischen Unterricht auf dem Gymnasium erlassen wurde. Im Jahre 1837 erwarb er ein glänzendes Zeugnis der Reife und begab sich zum Studium der Mathematik auf die benachbarte Universität Kiel; doch zwei Jahre darauf zog der grosse Ruf der Königsberger Universität den jungen Studenten hierher. Um hier sein geistiges Leben ganz zu verstehen, müssen wir uns in die Zeitverhältnisse versetzen. An unserer Universität lehrte damals der Mathematiker Jacobi, ein schöpferischer Geist ersten Ranges, der an Fruchtbarkeit vielleicht von keinem anderen Mathematiker übertroffen ist, der durch die Entdeckung der elliptischen Funktionen die mathematische Analysis mit einem neuen kräftigen Werkzeuge bereichert hatte und ihr sowie ihren Anwendungen auf die Geometrie und Mechanik ganz neue Bahnen erschlossen hatte. Neben ihm wirkten der in seiner Blütezeit stehende Astronom Bessel und unser Franz Neumann, der Begründer der mathematischen Physik. So konnte es nicht fehlen, dass das Königsberger Dreigestirn eine grosse Anziehungskraft für strebsame Studierende der Mathematik und der exacten Naturwissenschaft aus allen Ländern ausübte und dass hier ein reiches geistiges Leben herrschte. Besonders an Jacobi und Bessel schloss sich der junge Luther an und beide übten einen entscheidenden Einfluss auf seinen Studiengang aus. Als Jacobi 1842 aus Gesundheitsrücksichten Königsberg verliess, um in Berlin als Akademiker zu leben, traten sich Bessel und Luther noch näher und Bessel suchte ihn für die Astronomie zu interessieren. In gleicher Weise entwickelte sich das denkbar innigste Freundschaftsverhältnis zwischen Luther und Richelot, der anfangs noch sein Lehrer war. Zu Anfang des Jahres 1846 ging Luther in seine Vaterstadt Hamburg zurück, um ungestört seinen Studien zu leben, doch schon im Herbst desselben Jahres kehrte er zur Alma Mater wieder und promovierte am 14. April 1847 auf Grund der Dissertation über die Kriterien für die algebraische Lösbarkeit der irreductiblen Gleichungen fünften Grades (Crelle's Journal, Band 34). Bei der Disputation über die Thesen waren der Mathematiker Durège und der Astronom Wichmann seine Opponenten, während er nach damaliger Sitte als Socius und Verteidiger sich den Physiker Kirchhoff zugesellt hatte, mit dem er zeitlebens im innigsten Freundschaftsverhältnis stand und der mit ihm an demselben Tage sterben sollte! Die in der Inaugural-Dissertation behandelte Frage war damals gewissermassen zeitgemäss. Nachdem Abel 1824 die Unmöglichkeit nachgewiesen hatte, die allgemeine Gleichung fünften Grades algebraisch zu lösen, handelte es sich darum, zu untersuchen, in welchen besonderen Fällen eine Gleichung fünften Grades algebraisch lösbar sei. Zwar hatte Galois diese Frage schon 1830 allgemeiner gelöst, doch wurden seine wichtigen Arbeiten erst 1846 durch Abdruck in Liouvilles Journal bekannt und waren es in Königsberg noch nicht. Durch Anwendung Abel'scher Methoden fand Luther, dass die Lagrange'sche Resolvente einen Faktor ersten Grades und einen Faktor fünften Grades haben müsse und der letztere lauter gleiche rationale Wurzel haben oder irreductibel und algebraisch lösbar sein müsse. Bald darauf habilitierte er sich hier als Privatdocent für Mathematik und Astronomie und behandelte in seiner Habilitationsschrift (Crelle's Journal, Band 37) in ähnlicher Weise die Gleichung sechsten Grades und fand als Bedingung der Lösbarkeit, dass die Gleichung zwei kubische Faktoren enthalten müsse, deren Coefficienten Wurzeln quadratischer Gleichungen sind oder drei quadratische Faktoren, deren

Coefficienten Wurzeln kubischer Gleichungen sind, oder dass beides zugleich stattfinden könne und untersuchte in allen Fällen den Grad der rationalen Faktoren der Resolventen. Die Vorlesungen des jungen Docenten fanden solchen Beifall, dass die Breslauer Fakultät ihn bald für eine dortige Professur vorschlug, doch blieb er Königsberg erhalten. Im Jahre 1850 verheiratete er sich mit Marie geb. Schlesius, einer jungen Dame aus einer angesehenen hiesigen Familie, und aus dieser Ehe erwuchs ihm dauernd das schönste und reinste Familienglück.

Inzwischen hatte er auf Jacobi's Anregung eine neue grössere Arbeit unternommen. Um die Störungen der Planeten und zu diesem Zwecke ihre gegenseitigen Entfernungen zu berechnen, hatte Jacobi neue und elegante Formeln aufgestellt, bei denen gewisse Konstanten, die von der gegenseitigen Lage der Planetenbahnen abhängen, als Hülfsgrössen gebraucht werden und aus denen man, nur durch Einsetzen der excentrischen Anomalie der Planeten, sofort die gegenseitigen Entfernungen findet. Diese Hülfsgrössen, die man die gegenseitigen Bahnelemente nennen könnte, hat Luther für alle Combinationen der grossen Planeten mit Einschluss des kurz vorher entdeckten Neptun und der Vesta, des hellsten der Asteroiden, berechnet und in den Monatsberichten der Berliner Akademie von 1882 bald nach Jacobi's Tode veröffentlicht. Auch hatte er einen Beweis der Jacobi'schen Formeln gegeben, denselben aber nicht publiziert, denn mit rührender Bescheidenheit schreibt er: „Die von mir gegebene Ableitung dieser Formeln ist von keinem Interesse, da die mir inzwischen von Herrn Professor Dirichlet gütigst anvertrauten Papiere Jacobi's eine Herleitung derselben enthalten, die anderweitig veröffentlicht werden wird." Noch kürzlich hat Bruns auf diese Luther'sche Arbeit aufmerksam gemacht und dieselbe zur Anwendung empfohlen.

Unter den nachgelassenen Papieren Jacobi's fand Luther ferner eine neue Lösung eines fundamentalen Problems der Geodäsie und veröffentlichte dieselbe in No. 974 der „Astronomischen Nachrichten." Es handelt sich hier um die Aufgabe, wenn die Länge einer geodätischen Linie und die geographische Breite, Länge und ihr Azimut im Anfangspunkt gegeben ist, diese drei Grössen für den Endpunkt zu finden. Es gelang ihm auch aus Jacobi's Manuscripten dessen Beweis seiner Auflösung und seiner Formeln herzustellen und diesen veröffentlichte er in Band 1006 der „Astronomischen Nachrichten", sowie in „Crelle's Journal, Bd. 53". Indem Jacobi hier auf die Hülfsgrössen zurückgeht, welche der auf dem Erdellipsoid ausgeführten geodätischen Messung auf einer Kugel entsprechen würden, entwickelt er die gesuchten Grössen mit Hülfe der Theorie der elliptischen Funktionen in sehr schnell convergierende Reihen und giebt zweitens sehr elegante Ausdrücke derselben durch Thetafunktionen. Diese schöne Entwickelung darf wohl als die interessanteste der von Luther veröffentlichten mathematischen Arbeiten betrachtet werden.

Wir haben die Bedeutung Eduard Luthers als Mathematiker kennen gelernt und werden uns nun mit seiner Wirksamkeit als Astronom, die noch umfassender ist, beschäftigen. Im Oktober 1854 wurde ihm die ausserordentliche Professur für Astronomie und die Benutzung des Heliometers übertragen, nachdem er bereits seit dem Juli den beurlaubten Observator Wichmann vertreten hatte. Ausser der Beobachtung der Kometen und kleinen Planeten unternahm er sofort die Messung der 38 Besselschen Doppelsterne. Im Jahre 1856 wurde ihm nach dem Tode von Busch, welcher Bessel's Nachfolger als Direktor der Sternwarte war, die Direktion der Sternwarte gemeinsam mit Wichmann bis auf Weiteres übertragen und nun hielt er es für seine Pflicht, seine ganze Arbeitskraft der praktischen Astronomie zuzuwenden. Denn eine Sternwarte ist nicht, wie andere Universitätsinstitute, eine Lehranstalt für Studierende. Sie hat in erster Linie selbständige wissenschaftliche Aufgaben zu lösen. Durchdrungen von dem Gefühl, dass unsere Sternwarte eine Geschichte, wie keine andere in Deutschland habe, suchte Luther ihre Traditionen zu erhalten. Da aber alle astronomsichen Beobachtungen nur dann Wert haben, wenn sie frühzeitig veröffentlicht werden, damit sie bald benutzt werden können, so war sein erstes Streben die Herausgabe der rückständigen Königsberger Beobachtungen, die als besondere Zeitschrift erscheinen, zu fördern und so liess er in den ersten Jahren, so schnell es anging, immer neue Bände derselben erscheinen. Zugleich berechnete er aus den von Bessel an dem vorzüglichen Repsold'schen Meridiankreise ums Jahr 1843 gemachten Beobachtungen die Deklinationen von 36 Fundamentalsternen. Da diese Sterne einerseits in den beiden entgegengesetzten Lagen des Instruments, andererseits, so weit es möglich war, sowohl direkt als auch vom Quecksilberspiegel reflektiert beobachtet waren, so konnte auch der bisher noch nicht bestimmte Einfluss der Biegung des Meridiankreises durch seine eigene Schwere ermittelt werden und da ferner die circumpolaren Sterne sowohl in oberer als in unterer Kulmination beobachtet waren, so wurde zugleich die Polhöhe von Königsberg und die Hauptrefraktionskonstante neu bestimmt. Die Genauigkeit der Bessel'schen Beobachtungen, die Sorgfalt der Luther'schen Berechnung, welche nach der Methode der kleinsten Quadrate mit 40 Unbekannten ausgeführt war, lieferte für alle die genannten und gesuchten Grössen sehr präzise Bestimmungen. Bemerkenswert ist vielleicht, dass sich hier im Vergleich mit den Resultaten früherer Bessel'scher Beobachtungen eine kleine Abnahme der Polhöhe zeigte, doch hütete sich Professor Luther, daraus gewagte Schlüsse zu ziehen und dieser scheinbaren Änderung der geographischen Lage der Sternwarte um einige Meter Realität zuzuschreiben. Im Jahre 1859, als C. A. F. Peters, welcher Bessel's Nachfolger in der Professur war, nach Altona berufen wurde, wurde Luther zum ordentlichen Professor ernannt und übernahm, da Wichmann in demselben Jahre starb, die alleinige Direktion der Sternwarte. Jetzt wandte er sich der Hauptarbeit seines Lebens, der Untersuchung der Bessel'schen Zonen, zu. Bessel hatte nämlich nach abgekürzter Methode schnell hintereinander in dem ganzen Himmelsraum zwischen 15 Gr. südlicher und 45 Gr. nördlicher Deklination 63340 Sterne beobachtet und diesen Zonenbeobachtungen bei der Veröffentlichung sogenannte Zonentafeln zur Reduktion der Beobachtungen auf den Anfang des Jahres 1825 beigegeben. Diese Zonen enthielten meist kleine, früher noch nie beobachtete Sterne und diese Sterne wurden nun fortwährend von allen Astronomen angewandt, besonders um den Abstand von Planeten und Kometen von ihnen zu messen. Dabei stellte sich heraus, dass dieselben manche Fehler enthielten, wie das ja bei einer so kursorischen Beobachtungsweise nicht anders zu erwarten war. Zwar wurden auch schon Fehler in den berechneten Zonentafeln gefunden, aber Argelander, der bei den ersten Zonenbeobachtungen als Bessels Gehülfe den Deklinationskreis ablas und die Ausführung der Beobachtungen genau kannte, kam auf die Vermutung, dass oft die Wirkung der Gegengewichte, welche den Druck der Fernrohraxe auf die Lager vermindern sollte, zu gross gewesen sei, so dass während einer ganzen Zone die Axe des Fernrohrs sich nicht in den Lagern befand und daher ein durchgängiger Fehler in einer ganzen Zone befürchtet werden müsse. Um diese von Argelander angeregte Frage zu entscheiden, beobachtete Luther in den Jahren 1860 bis 1863 am Repsold'schen Meridiankreise einzelne Sterne aus jeder Zone, im Ganzen gegen 1550 Sterne ausführlich, nicht in abgekürzter Weise und veröffentlichte seine Originalbeobachtungen 1882, die Resultate aus denselben und die Vergleichung mit den Bessel'schen Zonen im Jahre 1886. Aus dieser Vergleichung scheint hervorzugehen, dass die Bessel'schen Beobachtungen nicht so grosse durchgängige Fehler enthalten, wie Argelander annahm, denn wo sich einseitige Abweichungen zeigen, sind dieselben kaum grösser, als die zufälligen Beobachtungsfehler, die ja auch bei Zonenbeobachtungen immer grösser sein müssen, als bei ausführlichen, vollständigen Beobachtungen. Indessen zieht auch hier Professor Luther seine Schlüsse mit grosser und streng wissenschaftlicher Vorsicht. Er schreibt: „Man erkennt aus dieser Vergleichung, dass allerdings in einigen Zonen alle Unterschiede in Rectascension oder in Deklination dasselbe Vorzeichen haben; in den meisten aber sind die Unterschiede so unregelmässig, dass eine definitive Entscheidung der Argelander'schen Vermutung zur Zeit noch nicht getroffen werden kann. Fortgesetzte Beobachtungen einer grösseren Anzahl von Sternen derselben Zone würden hierüber Aufschluss geben können." In der That veranlasste er auch seine Gehülfen noch zu weiteren Beobachtungen dieser Art, Beobachtungen, die noch der Vergleichung, teils auch noch der Veröffentlichung harren. Auch hat die Astronomische Gesellschaft neuerdings die Bessel'schen Zonenbeobachtungen in ausführlicherer Weise von verschiedenen Sternwarten wiederholen lassen.

Die grösseren konstanten Fehler, die man ursprünglich in den Bessel'schen Zonen fand, liegen nicht sowohl in Bessel's Beobachtungen, als vielmehr in den Bessel'schen Zonentafeln, die zur Berechnung der Beobachtungen dienen. Daher liess Luther neue und bequemere Zonentafeln rechnen, die sich auf die Originalbeobachtungen selbst, nicht auf die von Bessel bei den Zonen gemachten Angaben stützen, und veröffentlichte dieselben 1886.

Zugleich gab er ein Verzeichnis von 750 in der Nähe der Ekliptik stehenden Fixsternen, sogenannten Zodiacalsternen, heraus, welche um das Jahr 1835 herum von Bessel, zum Teil aber auch später beobachtet waren. Alle diese Sterne, von denen jeder mindestens fünfmal beobachtet ist, verglich Luther mit den Greenwicher Beobachtungen von Bradley von 1755 oder, falls sie nicht von Bradley beobachtet waren, mit den Palermoer Beobachtungen von Piazzi von 1800 und leitete daraus die Eigenbewegung in der Zwischenzeit her.

Endlich ist als eine der wichtigsten der von dem Verstorbenen veröffentlichten Arbeiten die aktenmässige Revision von Bessel's Zonen-Originalen zu nennen. Auf den Antrag Argelanders wurde nämlich von der Berliner Akademie 1862 ein Rechner engagiert, der Bessel's Zonen hier neu reduzierte, und auf den Wunsch Argelanders übernahm es Luther, die Resultate dieser Rechnung 1882 zu veröffentlichen. Er erweiterte aber im Einverständnis mit Argelander die Aufgabe dahin, dass aus der Publikation die ursprünglichen Angaben der Bessel'schen Zonen-Originale und die Änderungen, welche mit diesen vorgenommen sind, sich vollständig erkennen lassen um dadurch von jetzt an ein Nachschlagen der Originalbeobachtungen überflüssig zu machen. Diese Publikation enthält daher 1. alle Sterne, welche ursprünglich unrichtig berechnet waren, verbessert; 2. alle Sterne, die an mehreren Fäden beobachtet sind und deren Antritte an Übereinstimmung zu wünschen lassen; 3. alle Sterne, bei denen Bessel eine Beobachtung angestrichen hatte, um anzudeuten, dass die ganze Sekunde zweifelhaft sei; 4. alle Sterne, bei denen die ganze Minute nicht angegeben und anders angenommen werden könnte und endlich 5. alle Bemerkungen und kurzen Notizen in den Bleistift-Originalen, sowie die Bemerkung, ob sie mit Tinte, also nachträglich von Bessel gemacht sind. Diese umfangreiche und mühsame Publikation wird sicher häufige Benutzung finden.

Meine Herren! Aus diesem Überblick über die wissenschaftlichen Leistungen des Verstorbenen werden Sie gesehen haben, wie pietätvoll er stets bestrebt war, Bessel's Arbeiten weiter zu führen, zu prüfen und nach den Originalen richtig zu stellen, wie er niemals seine Person in den Vordergrund stellte, sondern stets auch die Anregung und Mitwirkung anderer Gelehrter hervorhob, wie er endlich vorsichtig und bescheiden sich hütete, voreilige Schlüsse aus seinen Untersuchungen zu ziehen und mit der Würde, die der Wissenschaft ansteht, nur die gefundenen Zahlen mitteilte, dem astronomischen Publikum selbst das Urteil überlassend. Seine freundschaftlichen Beziehungen zu Jacobi, Bessel, Richelot, Kirchhoff und Argelander haben wir bereits erwähnt. Der junge Auwers machte unter seiner Leitung hier seine ersten flotten Beobachtungen und Luther nahm seinen Nebelkatog in die Königsberger Beobachtungen auf. Mit Borchardt, Hansen, Otto Struve, Wagner, Schweizer, Mädler und Schönfeld führte er eine umfangreiche Korrespondenz, dem französischen Geographen d'Abbadie leistete er durch Empfehlung von Radau gute Dienste und seinen Schülern stand er stets wohlwollend und mit liebenswürdiger Freundlichkeit gegenüber. Die Achtung seiner Kollegen wusste er sich in hohem Maasse zu erwerben. Mehrmals wurde er in den Senat gewählt und war ein treuer Mitarbeiter bei der akademischen Verwaltung. Im Jahre 1868 wurde er zum Prorektor gewählt und vertrat als solcher die Albertina bei dem Universitäts-Jubiläum zu Bonn, wo er gleichzeitig die dort tagende Astronomenversammlung besuchte, viele seiner Kollegen persönlich kennen lernte und dem Argelander-Jubiläum beiwohnte. In Freundeskreisen war er ein beliebter, munterer Gesellschafter und gern hörte man ihn in humoristischer Weise seine Gespräche mit Bessel und anderen Koryphäen sowie die kleinen Eigenheiten dieser Herren erzählen. Wie in der Wissenschaft, so war auch in seiner Familie sein Leben einfach, treu und musterhaft und das Schicksal begünstigte ihn in seiner Familie mit viel Glück, nur hatte er ähnlich wie Bessel den Schmerz, einen erwachsenen, begabten Sohn zu verlieren, der bereits als Gehülfe der Sternwarte ihm zur Seite gestanden hatte. In den letzten Jahren litt er ohne alle Klagen schwer an einem asthmatischen Übel und sah es nicht einmal gern, wenn man nach seinem Befinden fragte. Am 17. Oktober, vormittags 11 Uhr, erlöste ihn ein schmerzloser Tod.

Er war ein edler Mensch und hat seine besten Kräfte der Wissenschaft gewidmet!

Gedächtnisrede

auf

Professor Dr. Robert Caspary

von

Dr. Abromeit.

Hochgeehrte Anwesende!

Als die traurige Kunde von Professor Caspary's Tod so unerwartet zu uns drang, da war wohl Niemand unter uns, der nicht tief ergriffen von dem harten Schlag die ganze Schwere des Verlustes empfand, welcher uns so plötzlich getroffen hatte. So lange der hochverehrte Dahingeschiedene unter uns wandelte und durch seinen täglichen Verkehr mit uns, teils zu neuer wissenschaftlicher Bethätigung anregte, teils als Freund hilfreich ratend zur Seite stand, da fühlten wir nicht im vollen Umfange die grosse Bedeutung dieses uns unersetzlichen Mannes. Nun ist es uns erst klar geworden, welche hervorragende wissenschaftliche Kraft wir durch seinen Verlust eingebüsst haben. Er wurde seinem Wirkungskreise trotz des 70. Lebensjahres, in welchem er sich bereits befand, noch zu frühe entrissen. Wie Vieles wollte er nicht noch erreichen! Die Hauptaufgabe seines Lebens, eine umfassende Monographie der Nymphaeaceen blieb unvollendet, wenn schon er an ihr sehr lange gearbeitet und viele wichtige Thatsachen festgestellt hat, die in einer grossen Fülle von handschriftlichen Aufzeichnungen nebst meisterhaft ausgeführten Zeichnungen der Nachwelt hinterblieben sind*). Es fehlt nun seine ordnende Hand und sein Geist, der all die verschiedenen Formen der mannigfaltigen Kreuzungen so vieler Arten umfasste und nur ein ihm nachstrebender geistesverwandter Forscher könnte die suprema manus an das grossartige Werk legen.

Schon seit einer langen Reihe von Jahren hat der Verstorbene sich ausserdem mit preussischen Pilzen beschäftigt, welche er sorgfältig abbildete und bei deren Be-

---

*) In Anerkennung seiner bedeutenden Verdienste um die Kultur und Erforschung dieser Pflanzenfamilie benannte Carrière in der Revue horticole 1879 p. 230 eine schwedische, von Caspary als Nymphaea alba sephaerocarpa l rubra richtig gedeutete Seerose Nymphaea Casparyi.

schreibung er stets auf die anatomischen und mikroskopischen Merkmale hinwies, wodurch seine Arbeiten einen noch höheren wissenschaftlichen Wert erhalten. Auch von diesen umfangreichen Untersuchungen ist noch nichts veröffentlicht worden. Jedenfalls wollte er auch dieses Werk durch weitere Beobachtungen noch fördern und es erst später abschliessen. Es kann jetzt nur fragmentarisch veröffentlicht werden. Sehr umfangreich sind auch seine Arbeiten über die Flora des Bernsteins, welche er namentlich in den letzten fünfzehn Jahren eifriger und eingehender berücksichtigt hat. Auch diesem Manuskript hat er zahlreiche Abbildungen, welche grösstenteils von ihm angefertigt sind, beigegeben. Eine kürzere Bearbeitung der Nymphäaceen, die für weitere Kreise bestimmt ist, befindet sich noch unter der Presse. So viel mir bekannt ist, wird sie von Professor Engler in seinem gut ausgestatteten lesenswerten Werk: „Die natürlichen Pflanzenfamilien" im Verlage von Engelmann-Leipzig erscheinen. Es würde zu weit führen, Ihnen alle unveröffentlichten handschriftlichen Arbeiten des Verstorbenen vorzuführen, doch mag es mir gestattet sein, noch auf die Ergebnisse der Gewässeruntersuchungen in Preussen hinzuweisen, welche er in den nächsten Jahren gelegentlich der Zusammenstellung der Resultate der botanischen Erforschung einzelner Kreise unserer Provinz zum Abdruck gelangen lassen wollte. Er hat darin namentlich unsere Wasserpflanzen: Characeen, Isoëtes, Hydrilleen, Potamogetonen und Nymphaeaceen behandelt. Keiner ist auf diesem Gebiet so gut bewandert als er es war, und er hat in seinen genauen Beobachtungen uns ein reiches Material hinterlassen, das wahrhaft einzig in seiner Art ist. Auch arbeitete er an einer „Geschichte der Botaniker Preussens", wozu er das Material bereits gesammelt und die wichtigsten Daten aufgezeichnet hat. Letzteres Werk, sowie die Ergebnisse vieler Kreuzungen, die er an Versuchspflanzen seit länger als in 25 Jahren angestellt hat, verblieb unveröffentlicht. So viel über die handschriftlichen Arbeiten des Verstorbenen, der keine Ruhe und keinen Stillstand in seinem Streben kannte, aber sein Wollen war gewaltiger als das Erreichen; es war dafür aber auch fruchtbarer.

Seit 1845 hat Caspary über 290 grössere und kleinere Abhandlungen, wie Mitteilungen veröffentlicht, die nur mit wenigen Ausnahmen sich auf sämmtliche Gebiete der Botanik erstrecken. Alle seine Arbeiten beruhen auf genauer Beobachtung des Thatsächlichen und können nur an der Hand von Thatsachen beurteilt werden. Auf Hypothesen und Theorien liess er sich nicht ein. Das schien ihm einer exakten Naturforschung unwürdig und er überliess dieses Feld denjenigen, die von der Beweiskraft der Thatsachen absehen und mehr das Formale lieben. Trotz der fortwährenden Anstrengungen, die sein Amt mit sich brachte und der rastlosen Thätigkeit im Gebiete der Wissenschaft war der Verstorbene, der nun dem 71. Lebensjahre entgegenging, noch völlig frisch an Körper und Geist und wer ihn vom Umgange her kennt, der weiss wohl, wie scharf noch sein Auge, wie treffend sein Urteil und wie ungeschwächt sein Gedächtniss war. Er ertrug ohne viele Beschwer auch während seiner letzten Untersuchung des Kreises Schlochau alle Mühen und Unbequemlichkeiten, die solch eine Reise mit sich bringt. Noch am 16. September, kurz vor seinem Tode, legte er ohne jegliche Spur von Ermüdung, wie mir Professor Praetorius aus Konitz mitteilte, eine Strecke von drei Meilen in sandiger Gegend zu Fuss zurück und fühlte sich nach seiner eigenen Aussage, diesmal ganz besonders wohl und frisch. Wir hatten daher begründete Hoffnung, dass er auch von dieser Reise wie von vielen ähnlichen wohl-behalten zurückkehren wird. Leider sollten wir uns bitter täuschen. Ein unseliges Geschick ereilte ihn nur zu bald. Als er am 18. September d. J. bei einem Besuche der ihm befreundeten Rittergutsbesitzerfamilie Langner auf Illowo nach eingenommenen Mittagsmahl eine bequeme und hell beleuchtete Treppe hinunterstieg, strauchelte er und fiel so unglücklich, dass er sich durch den Sturz einen Schädelbruch zuzog, infolge dessen er nach fünfstündiger Bewusstlosigkeit gegen 10 Uhr Abends verschied.

Es mag mir an dieser Stelle gestattet sein, einige irrtümliche Angaben zu berichtigen, welche infolge von Verwechslung der Ortschaften durch die hiesigen Zeitungen verbreitet wurden: Caspary starb auf dem Rittergute Illowo, welches etwa $1^1/_2$ Meilen nordwestlich von Vandsburg im Kreise Flatow, Westpreussen, liegt. Er war zu Herrn Langner nach Beendigung der Gewässeruntersuchung des Kreises Schlochau, besonders aus dem Grunde hingefahren, um von ihm genauere Aufschlüsse über die Bodenbeschaffenheit des Kreises Flatow zu erhalten. Die Flora dieses Kreises war in den Jahren 1879, 1880 und 1881 von Rosenbohm, Caspary und von mir genügend untersucht worden und sollte nun im Anschluss an den bereits ebenso genau erforschten angrenzenden Kreis Deutsch Krone zur Veröffentlichung bearbeitet werden. Caspary starb also im Dienste der Wissenschaft und gehörte ihr bis zum letzten Atemzuge an.

Indessen nicht wir allein beklagen diesen grossen Verlust. Caspary's Ruf drang weit über die Grenzen unseres deutschen Vaterlandes. Die namhaftesten Botaniker des Auslandes kannten ihn zum Teil persönlich und wohl mit den meisten stand er in brieflichem Verkehr. Er war Mitglied vieler wissenschaftlichen Gesellschaften und schon seit 1856 war er Mitglied der „Société de la botanique de France". Der „Societas Linneana Londinensis" gehörte er seit 1885 an. Er war Ehrenmitglied der „Gesellschaft naturforschender Freunde" in Berlin, Mitglied der „Deutschen Botanischen Gesellschaft", Ehrenmitglied der „Pollichia", der „St. Gallen'schen naturforschenden Gesellschaft", korrespondierendes Ehrenmitglied der „Naturforschenden Gesellschaft zu Emden" und seit 1874 Ehrenmitglied des „Copernicus-Vereins für Kunst und Wissenschaft zu Thorn". Die „Physikalisch-ökonomische Gesellschaft" zu Königsberg hatte ihn am 1. Juli 1859 als ordentliches Mitglied aufgenommen und seit 1867 war er auswärtiges Mitglied der „Naturforschenden Gesellschaft" zu Danzig. Er gehörte jedoch nicht nur diesen erwähnten wissenschaftlichen Vereinen allein an. Von der Aufzählung mehrerer anderer in- und ausländischen Gesellschaften, die ihn durch Aufnahme geehrt hatten, will ich absehen. Sein richtiges Urteil, sowie der Schatz seiner Kenntnisse und Erfahrungen machten den Verkehr mit ihm wünschenswert.

Am empfindlichsten trifft uns jedoch sein Verlust, da er die Provinz Preussen, sein engeres Vaterland, liebte, dessen naturhistorische Schätze er an das Tageslicht zu ziehen bemüht war. Vor ihm hat es Niemand vermocht, so umfangreiche Arbeiten mit Bezug auf die Erforschung des heimatlichen Florengebiets anzustellen. Die Pflanzengeographen müssen es anerkennen, dass Caspary's Plan, die systematische Erforschung einzelner Kreise unserer Provinzen, eine mustergiltige ist und bisher in ähnlicher Weise nirgends vor ihm angestellt wurde. Caspary wollte durch seinen Plan den anderen Pflanzengeographen ein Beispiel geben, wonach sie in ihren Bezirken zu arbeiten hätten, um sichere Ergebnisse zu erlangen. Aber der Weg zur Erreichung des vorgesteckten Zieles ist lang und ein Menschenleben genügt nicht zur Verwirklichung solcher weitgehender Pläne. Der Verstorbene sah es wohlweislich ein, dass er das Ende seines begonnenen Werkes nicht erleben wird. Er sprach es oft genug auf den Versammlungen des preussischen botanischen Vereins aus, versäumte aber auch nicht auf das erreichbare Ziel hinzuweisen, wonach selbst nach seinem Tode unentwegt hingestrebt werden soll. Gar oft hat er an dieser Stelle die Hauptergebnisse seiner Forschungen mitgeteilt und wusste durch seine anregenden Vorträge selbst einen grösseren Kreis von Hörern für die unscheinbarsten Dinge einzunehmen. So kam es, dass er von Allen gern gehört wurde und allgemein beliebt und geachtet war.

Johann Xaver Robert Caspary, Dr. phil., ordentlicher Professor der Botanik, Direktor und Inspektor des Königl. botanischen Gartens zu Königsberg, ist daselbst am 29. Januar 1818 geboren. Sein Vater Franz Xaver Caspary war anfangs Kaufmann, später Mäkler; seine Mutter war eine geborene Justine Wartmann. Der junge Robert Caspary brachte seine erste Jugendzeit im elterlichen Hause zu und besuchte das Kneiphöfische Gymnasium, welches er zu Michaeli 1837 mit dem Zeugnis der Reife verliess, um auf unserer Albertina Theologie und Philosophie zu studieren. Nicht volle fünf Semester, während welcher er die Vorlesungen der Professoren: Lehnert, Rosenkranz, Lengerke, Sieffert, Köhler, Jacobson, Gebser, Lucas und Höcker hörte, widmete er sich diesem Studium, da er es bereits Weihnachten 1840 aufgab und nach erhaltener Exmatrikel zur Ablegung des Examens schritt. Er hatte sich während der Zeit eingehend mit Philosophie unter Rosenkranz beschäftigt und von den theologischen Disciplinen namentlich Dogmatik und Ethik getrieben. Diese letztgenannten Zweigwissenschaften der Theologie sagten ihm am meisten zu, weniger die Homiletik. „Ich weiss es aus seinem eigenen Munde," sagte der ihm befreundete Professor Praetorius*) „dass ihm das Studium der Theologie durch homiletische Übungen verleidet worden ist. Alles Gemachte, Gezwungene, vor dem Spiegel Eingeübte, war ihm verhasst. Deshalb sprach er auch mit Nichtachtung von dem Beruf eines Schauspielers. Die Liebe zur Religionswissenschaft hat er bis zu seinem Tode bewahrt. Das alte Testament hat er ziemlich vollständig im Urtext gelesen und der Geist der heiligen Schrift überhaupt durchwehte sein ganzes Thun und Lassen."

Neben dem Studium der Theologie und Philosophie betrieb er eifrig Entomologie und Botanik, was bei den jetzigen Studierenden der Theologie selten oder garnicht mehr vorkommt. „Fast alle meine Mussestunden," schreibt Caspary in einem 1855 von ihm verfassten Lebenslauf, „habe ich bis zum theologischen Examen der Entomologie gewidmet und mit Schiefferdecker, Elditt, Hermann Haagen und Stephani viel gesammelt, vorzugsweise Käfer." Auch wurde er Mitglied des Stettiner entomologischen Vereins, welchem er von 1843 bis 1846 bis er Deutschland verliess, angehörte. Er absolvierte beide Examina in der Theologie, jedoch, wie er ausdrücklich in dem selbstverfassten Lebenslauf erwähnt, nicht um Geistlicher zu werden, sondern

*) In der Gedächtnisrede auf Caspary auf der Vorversammlung der Mitglieder des preussischen botanischen Vereins in Königsberg am 3. October d. J.

um sich der Universitätslaufbahn zu widmen. Leider gestatteten es ihm die Mittel nicht, seinen Lieblingsplan zu verfolgen. Nach den theologischen Prüfungen verblieb er zunächst noch in Königsberg; hielt auch einige Predigten und war von 1841—43 Lehrer an einer Mädchenschule. Auf den beiden obersten Klassen des Kneiphöfischen Gymnasiums erteilte er während eines halben Jahres den Religionsunterricht, doch scheint ihm diese Beschäftigung wenig zugesagt zu haben.

Ostern 1843 ging Caspary nach Bonn, um daselbst das Studium der Naturwissenschaften und der neueren Sprachen aufzunehmen, Wissenschaften, die ihn schon von jeher angezogen hatten. In Bonn studierte er auf dem naturhistorischen Seminar die fünf Fächer der Naturwissenschaften bis Michaeli 1846. Er hörte während dieser Zeit die Vorlesungen der Professoren: Argelander, Arndt, Bischof, Dahlmann, Heine, Goldfuss, Noeggerath, Pluecker, Treviranus und Seubert. Namentlich schloss er sich jedoch an Goldfuss, Argelander und Treviranus an, deren Lehren ihn also am meisten beeinflusst haben und wohl auch den Anstoss zu seiner Forschungsrichtung gaben. Anfänglich schenkte Caspary der Zoologie mehr Aufmerksamkeit. Er war in Bonn mehrere Jahre hindurch Assistent beim Zoologen Goldfuss, wobei er jedoch die Botanik keineswegs vernachlässigte. Schon im Jahre 1845 wurde er Lehrer der Naturwissenschaften und Mathematik an der Kortegarn'schen Erziehungsanstalt in Bonn und hatte in den erwähnten Fächern 18 Stunden wöchentlich auf den mittleren und oberen Klassen zu unterrichten. Eine Prima fehlte dem Institut, welches die Bestimmung hatte, als eine allgemeine Vorschule für Zöglinge von 9—13 Jahren, als eine Handelsschule für Knaben und Jünglinge von 13—17 oder 14—18 Jahren und als ein Gymnasial-Institut, insbesondere für Ausländer, zu dienen. Die erste Veröffentlichung eines Aufsatzes von Caspary erschien im Programm des Jahres 1845 dieser Anstalt. Er hat darin das praktisch-pädagogische Thema behandelt: „Das Prinzip der Erziehungsabteilungen in der Kortegarn'schen Anstalt." Auf 19 Oktavseiten legt er in diesem Aufsatze seine Ansichten über die Erziehung im Allgemeinen in philosophierender Weise dar und weist auf die Ziele der Anstalt hin. Der Einfluss der eben zurückgelegten theologischen und philosophischen Studien ist in dieser Arbeit nicht zu verkennen und liefert den Beweis, dass der Verfasser Fragen aus der Pädagogik und Psychologie geschickt zu behandeln wusste. Caspary war anderthalb Jahre hindurch Lehrer an der Kortegarn'schen Erziehungsanstalt. Er legte 1846 das „examen pro facultate docendi" in den beschreibenden Naturwissenschaften, in Chemie für obere Klassen und in Physik wie Mathematik für mittlere Klassen ab. Nach dem Staatsexamen sehen wir ihn als Erzieher im Hause des reichen Kaufmanns Bemberg in Elberfeld, wo er einen Sohn in den Anfängen der Wissenschaften zu unterweisen hatte. Auf Wunsch der Eltern seines Zöglings machte er mit demselben eine Reise durch Frankreich nach Italien (vom 12. November 1846 bis 2. August 1847), besuchte Genua, Pisa, Livorno, Florenz, Rom, Neapel und den Vesuv, ferner Venedig und Mailand, wo er die Kunstschätze dieses klassischen Bodens studieren und sich in die italienischen Meister der Malerei vertiefen konnte. Daneben widmete er auch der ergiebigen Flora und Fauna dieses von der Natur begünstigten Landes seine Aufmerksamkeit. Er konnte trotz der Kunstschätze, die sich ihm auf dieser Reise darboten, den beobachtenden und sammelnden Naturforscher nicht verleugnen, Caspary sammelte auf dieser neunmonatlichen Fahrt viele Pflanzen und zoologische Seltenheiten, namentlich Mollusken, Fische und Amphibien, die er später an die Museen zu Poppelsdorf und Berlin abgab. Nach seiner Rückkehr verblieb er vom August 1847 bis Mai 1848 im Bemberg'schen Hause, wo er in der bisherigen Weise thätig war. Er wurde mit dieser Familie befreundet und verblieb bis auf die neueste Zeit mit ihr in Briefwechsel. Zu Ehren der Frau Bemberg, benannte er eine sabalartige Palme, von der er eine gut erhaltene Blüte im Bernstein entdeckte: Bembergia. Auch seinem ehemaligen Zöglinge, dem jungen Bemberg, jetzigen Freiherrn v. Bemberg auf Flamersheim, blieb er in dankbarer Erinnerung.

Neben seiner Beschäftigung als Erzieher trieb Caspary eifrig Zoologie und Botanik. Aus dieser Zeit stammen die Aufsätze: „Notice sur les Anacharidées" im Bulletin de la société botanique de France (Februar 1847) und „Über Elatine Alsinastrum und Trapa natans L." in den Verhandlungen des naturwissenschaftlichen Vereins für die Rheinlande und Westphalen. Er hatte sich an die Lösung einer akademischen Preisaufgabe gemacht, welche den Wortlaut hatte: „Examinetur sedes et conformatio organorum floris, quae nectaria cum Linnaeo vocare liceat, in praecipuis Germaniae stirpium ordinibus naturalibus deque secretionis tempore modo ac loco, nec non de secreti indole atque usu, quid observatis doceat, exponatur." Mit dem Motto: „Audentes fortuna juvat" versehen, hatte er die Arbeit vermutlich der Bonner philosophischen Fakultät eingesandt, wurde belobigt und erhielt einen Preis. Diese Arbeit erweiterte Caspary, indem er noch neue Beobachtungen hinzufügte und reichte sie dann der philosophischen Fakultät zu Bonn mit der Überschrift: „De Nectariis" als Promotionsschrift ein. Nach abgelegtem „examen rigorosum" wurde ihm am 29. März 1848 auf Grund der wissenschaftlichen Arbeit von der philosophischen Fakultät die Doktorwürde verliehen und von nun ab wandte sich Caspary fast ausschliesslich der Botanik zu. Von seiner Abhandlung über die Nektarien sagt Schlechtendal in der botanischen Zeitung vom Jahre 1848, nachdem er ihren Inhalt genauer berücksichtigt hat, „dass der Verfasser auf 51 Quartseiten mit vielem Fleiss fast alles Wichtige berücksichtigend den bereits behandelten Gegenstand von Neuem in Untersuchung zog. Das Ergebnis seiner Untersuchung ist, dass Nectarien drüsige Organe eigentümlicher Art sind, welche auf fast allen Pflanzenteilen vorgefunden werden und eine eigene morphologische wie physiologische Bedeutung haben. Auf drei Tafeln sind vom Verfasser gezeichnete und sauber aber ganz einfach in Stein ausgeführte Figuren von Nektarien nach äusserer Form und anatomischer Zusammensetzung beigegeben. Eine im Ganzen lobenswerte Arbeit." Ausserdem erschien noch eine Kritik seiner Dissertation in den Verhandlungen des naturhistorischen Vereins für die Rheinlande und Westphalen 1848 Seite 249. Auf Wunsch seiner Lehrer, welche ihm viele Hörer in Aussicht stellten, habilitierte sich Caspary an der Bonner Universität für Botanik nnd Zoologie. „Aber wieder ohne Mittel," schreibt er, „die Universitätslaufbahn zu verfolgen, ging ich nach England, wo ich $2^1/_2$ Jahre als Erzieher weilte, die Sprache erlernte, viel sammelte und untersuchte." Er weilte in England von 1848—1850. Caspary hegte stets die Absicht neben Naturwissenschaften auch neuere Sprachen zu studieren. Dieselben wollte er jedoch nicht nur theoretisch, sondern auch praktisch treiben. Er hielt es für durchaus nötig, eine fremde Sprache von dem Volke zu erlernen, dessen Landessprache sie ist. Er hatte eine eigene Methode die Schwierigkeiten einer fremden Sprache auf leichte Art zu überwinden. Sie bestand darin, dass er sich unter das

Volk begab und im gewöhnlichen Verkehr alle Eigentümlichkeiten der Volkssprache, wie sie in Grammatiken selten gut hervorgehoben werden, belauschte, sich dieselben zu eigen machte und die Sprache dann in kürzerer Zeit beherrschte als ein Anderer. In England lebte er als Erzieher namentlich in den Städten des südlichen Teils, besuchte den Garten zu Kew und lebte für einige Zeit in Greenwich, Cromer bei Norwich und London. Die Nähe des Meers und die eigenartige Litoralflora erregten in gleicher Weise sein Interesse. Er sammelte im Verein mit dem Algologen Dr. Cocks und den Algenkennerinnen Mrs. Griffiths, Warren, Wyatt und Miss Nelson viele marine Algen, namentlich aus Falmouth Umgebung und bei Rosemerryn. Aus dieser Zeit stammen viele handschriftliche Aufzeichnungen und Abbildungen mariner Algen, die nicht veröffentlicht sind. Viele getrocknete Algen, die sich in seinem Herbarium befinden, liefern den besten Beweis für seine eifrige Thätigkeit. Er veröffentlichte während seines Aufenthalts in England in „Taylor's Annals and Magazine of Natural History" 1850 mehrere Aufsätze über marine Algen: „On the Hairs of marine Algae," worin er über ein- und mehrzellige Haare spricht, welche sich auf dem Algenthallus befinden. Zu einem zweiten Aufsatz: „Observations on Furcellaria fastigiata Huds. and Polyides rotundus Grew," wurde er durch eine Bemerkung im Harvey'schen „Manual of the British Marine Algae" veranlasst. Der Algologe Harvey hebt in seinem Handbuche hervor, dass die beiden Algen **Furcellaria fastigiata** und **Polyides rotundus** keine charakteristischen Unterschiede haben. Caspary unterzog die beiden fraglichen Pflanzen einer anatomischen Untersuchung und fand wichtige anatomische Unterschiede zwischen diesen Algen, welche er in dem erwähnten Aufsatz darlegt. Diesen Veröffentlichungen folgte noch in derselben Zeitschrift eine Beschreibung der neuen Algenart: **Schizosiphon Warreniae Casp.** Eine andere Abhandlung über **Gammarus puteanus Koch**, seine grösste veröffentlichte zoologische Arbeit, erschien 1849 auf Seite 39 u. ff. der Verhandlungen des naturwissenschaftlichen Vereins für die Rheinlande und Westphalen. Während seines $2^1/_2$jährigen Aufenthalts in England hatte Caspary die englische Sprache gründlich erlernt und bediente sich ihrer in vorkommenden Fällen selbst in den letzten Jahren noch mit meisterhafter Fertigkeit. Ja er hatte die englische Sprache in einem gewissen Grade sogar lieb gewonnen, wie er sich zu mir gelegentlich äusserte. Im Jahre 1850 bereiste er mit einer englischen Familie Birkbeck, West- und Süddeutschland und kehrte über Holland nach England zurück. Noch in demselben Jahre vertauschte er seinen Aufenthalt in England mit Frankreich, durchreiste letzteres von Nord nach Süd, wobei er auch Paris besuchte und liess sich in **Pau**, nördlich von den Pyrenäen, als Erzieher bei Sir Lambert, dem er sich bereits in London verpflichtet hatte, nieder. Er verfolgte hier den Plan, die französische Sprache vollkommen zu erlernen, was ihm in ähnlicher Weise wie vorhin mit der englischen gelang. Er lernte jedoch auch die Sitten und Gebräuche dieser beiden Nationen kennen und namentlich konnte es ihn verstimmen, wenn er bemerken musste, wie geringschätzend diese Völker damals auf die Deutschen herabblickten. Das stählte seinen nationalen Sinn und daher bediente er sich später in der deutschen Sprache nur deutscher Ausdrücke und vermied, wo er es konnte, jedes Fremdwort. Diesen patriotischen Zug behielt er bis zu seinem Lebensende.

Um Pau botanisierte er recht eifrig, wie sein Herbariummaterial und die handschriftlichen Aufzeichnungen bekunden. Aber nicht lange sollte er in Frankreich verbleiben: Seine Eltern, die hier in Königsberg wohnten, starben zu jener Zeit schnell nach einander. Diese traurigen Ereignisse riefen ihn nach einem halbjährigen Aufenthalt in Frankreich nach Deutschland zurück. Caspary siedelte nach Berlin über, wo er sich im Juni 1851 als Privatdozent der Botanik habilitierte. In demselben Monat übernahm Professor Alexander Braun, der ebenfalls in diesem Jahre nach Berlin gekommen war, die Direktion des Königl. botanischen Gartens. Mit diesem bedeutenden Botaniker, der namentlich auf dem Gebiete der Morphologie Grosses leistete, knüpfte Caspary ein freundschaftliches Verhältnis an, und wurde später mit ihm sogar verwandt. Braun's tiefer und reger Geist zog Caspary mächtig an und ist auch auf ihn nicht ohne Einfluss geblieben, denn wir finden auch bei ihm eine grosse Vorliebe für morphologische Studien, obgleich sein Streben hierin allein nicht aufging. Er suchte vielmehr alle Zweigwissenschaften gleichwertig zu behandeln und keine ausschliesslich vorherrschen zu lassen.

Von den Vorlesungen, die Caspary in Berlin hielt, verdient das Colleg über Pflanzengeographie hervorgehoben zu werden. Fortgesetzt beschäftigte sich Caspary mit anatomischen, morphologischen und physiologischen Untersuchungen, versäumte jedoch keineswegs Exkursionen um Berlin anzustellen. Er ist von Ascherson in seiner musterhaft geschriebenen „Flora der Provinz Brandenburg" als Beobachter für Berlin und Spandau angegeben. Doch hat er sich damals vorwiegend mit Pilzen beschäftigt, wie seine Veröffentlichungen aus diesen Jahren bezeugen. So arbeitete er mit Braun und De Bary „Ueber einige neue oder wenig bekannte Krankheiten der Pflanzen; welche durch Pilze erzeugt werden." Von ihm rührt der Aufsatz: „Ueber den Ursprung der Malvendürre" her (Verhandl. des Vereins zur Beförderung des Gartenbaues in den Königl. Preussischen Staaten). Ferner gab er Mitteilungen über einen neuen Pilz: Peronospora Chenopodii in den Sitzungen der Gesellschaft naturforschender Freunde in Berlin. Im Jahre 1855 folgte die Abhandlung: „Über zwei- und dreierlei Früchte einiger Schimmelpilze" (Fusisporium und Peronosporeen) in den Sitzungsberichten der Königl. Akademie der Wissenschaften zu Berlin. Es erfolgten weitere Mitteilungen über zwei Krankheiten des Weinstocks und der Kartoffel, welche teils in der botanischen Zeitung von Mohl, teils in den Sitzungsberichten der naturforschenden Freunde in Berlin erschienen. Auch stellte er Untersuchungen über die Frostspalten an, deren Ergebnisse in der botanischen Zeitung veröffentlicht wurden.

Im Jahre 1854 begann Caspary sich eingehender mit Nymphäaceen zu beschäftigen. Er fasste jedenfalls schon damals den Entschluss sie monographisch zu bearbeiten. Bereits 1854 erschien in der botanischen Zeitung eine Mitteilung über die Temperatur der Blüte von Victoria regia im Borsig'schen Garten. Dieser Mitteilung folgten 1855 ausführlichere Aufsätze über denselben Gegenstand in den Monatsberichten der Königl. Akademie der Wissenschaften zu Berlin. Caspary konstatierte durch mühevolle Beobachtungen, die er Tag und Nacht an der Victoria regia anstellte, eine Temperatur der Blüte, die einmal um 12° R. höher war als die der Luft. Er fand ferner die sehr interessanten Thatsachen, dass die Periode der Blütenwärme 1) einen selbständigen Teil, der unabhängig von Licht, Luft und Wasser ist und 2) einen unselbständigen hat, welcher letztere von der Luftwärme in seinem Verlauf abhängig ist. Die bedeutendste Wärmeerhöhung findet in den Antheren statt.

Er stellte ferner Untersuchungen über das Blattwachstum der Victoria regia an und gelangte dabei zu höchst überraschenden Thatsachen. Die Ergebnisse seiner Untersuchungen veröffentlichte er in der Regensburger „Flora" und in den „Monatsberichten" der Berliner Akademie. Schon im Jahre 1852 wurde Caspary wie eingangs erwähnt von der Gesellschaft der naturforschenden Freunde in Berlin zum Ehrenmitglied ernannt. Seine vielen Erfolge, die er auf dem Gebiete der Botanik erlangte, sicherten seinen Ruhm.*) Professor Klotzsch, der 1854 die Begoniaceen bearbeitete, ehrte Caspary dadurch, indem er eine Klasse dieser Familie Casparya benannte. In den Abhandlungen der Königl. Akademie der Wissenschaften zu Berlin Jahrgang 1854 bemerkt Klotszch auf S. 121 unter Begründung des Klassennamens Casparya: „Dem Andenken des Herrn Dr. Robert Caspary, Privatdozenten der Botanik an der Berliner Universität, der sich durch mehrere bemerkenswerte Arbeiten im Felde der Anatomie, der Entwickelungsgeschichte und der Systematik hervorgethan hat, gewidmet." Später wurde der Klassenname zur Gattungsbezeichnung gebraucht und De Candolle führt im 15. Band seines „Prodromus" bereits 21 Arten dieser südamerikanischen und asiatischen Gattung auf.

Im Jahre 1855 stellte Caspary eine Reise nach dem nördlichen Böhmen an, um dieses Gebiet auf Nymphaeaceen zu erforschen. Noch in demselben Jahre erschien von ihm im „Appendix generum et specierum novarum, quae in horto berolinensi coluntur" die Abhandlung: „De Nymphaeae albae varietatibus," welche im folgenden Jahre in deutscher Sprache in der Regensburger Flora veröffentlicht wurde.

Noch einmal sollte Caspary nach Bonn zurückkehren. Ostern 1856 begab er sich auf dringende Aufforderung seines Lehrers, des Professors Treviranus, dorthin und übernahm stellvertretend einen Teil seiner Vorlesungen, sowie die vorgeschriebenen Excursionen mit den Studierenden. Zu gleicher Zeit wurde er Direktor des Königl. Universitäts-Herbariums und Adjunkt des botanischen Gartens, womit auch eine pecuniäre Besserung seiner Vermögensverhältnisse verknüpft war.

Schon in Berlin beschäftigte er sich viel mit Wasserpflanzen, denen er nun auch in Bonn volle Aufmerksamkeit schenkte. Aus dieser Zeit stammen seine Aufsätze über die Hydrilleen, von denen er 1857 in den Monatsberichten der Königl. Akademie zu Berlin einen „Conspectus systematicus" gab. Er veröffentlichte ferner: „On Udora occidentalis Koch = Hydrilla verticillata Casp., and Serpicula occidentalis Pursh = Anacharis Alsinastrum Babingt." in Hooker's Journal of Botany, IX. Jahrgang 1857 S. 78 ff. und „Note sur la division de la famille des Hydrocharidées" im Bulletin de la société bot. de France p. 98 ff., wo auch der Aufsatz: „Sur l'ovule du Vallisneria spiralis" erschien. Im Jahre 1856 veröffentlichte er in der botanischen Zeitung den Aufsatz: „Über die Blüte der Elodea canadensis und ferner die Abhandlung: „Les Nymphaeacées fossiles" in den „Annales des Sciences naturelles." IV. Série Tome VI. p. 199—222. Caspary bespricht in dieser Abhandlung fossile Rhizome, Blattreste und Samen von Nymphäaceen des Tertiärs, welche von Sternberg

*) Neuerdings haben Professor Naegeli, und Caspary's ehemaliger Schüler, Custos und Privatdozent Dr. Peter, die 3. Subspecies des Hieracium prussicum dem um die Flora hochverdienten Forscher zu Ehren Hieracium Casparyanum benannt. (Naegeli u. Peter: Die Hieracien Mitteleuropas S. 376.)

mit dem Namen „Nymphaeites“ belegt wurden. Er beschreibt 5 neue Arten: Nymphaeites Brongniartii, N. Weberi, Ludwigii und N. Charpentieri, sowie Holopleura Victoria Casp.

Um Bonn stellte er botanische Untersuchungsreisen an, und hielt über die Ergebnisse derselben in den Sitzungen des niederrheinischen Vereins für Natur- und Heilkunde viele Vorträge. Im Jahre 1858 veröffentlichte er in den „Jahrbüchern für wissenschaftliche Botanik“ von Pringsheim eine Monographie der Hydrilleen, die viele interessante anatomische und physiologische Thatsachen enthält. Dieselbe Arbeit gelangte auch in den „Annales des Sciences naturelles“ zum Abdruck.

Das Ende des Ringens nach einer festen Existenz sollte nun für Caspary ganz unvermutet eintreffen. Es starb 1858 an unserer Universität der damalige Professor der Botanik Ernst Meyer und die Stelle musste schleunigst besetzt werden. Für dieselbe wurde Caspary vom Cultusminister Bethmann-Hollweg in Aussicht genommen. Schon am 9. Dezember 1858 wurde vom Prinz-Regenten die Bestallung als ordentlicher Professor der Botanik an der philosophischen Fakultät der Universität Königsberg unterzeichnet und der Kultusminister zeigte unter dem 23. Dezember 1858 der philosophischen Fakultät an, dass Caspary vom Prinz-Regenten zum ordentlichen Professor ernannt wäre, infolge dessen ihm die Direktion des botanischen Gartens übertragen wurde. Erst am 13. Januar 1859 wurde Caspary die Bestallung übermittelt und ihm gleichzeitig ein Gehalt von 2400 Mark nebst einem Zuschuss von 600 Mark für den Umzug zugesichert. In diesem für ihn so bedeutungsvollen Jahre veröffentlichte er zwei Abhandlungen über Aldrovandia vesiculosa, die in der botanischen Zeitung von Mohl 1859 und in der Regensburger Flora No. 41 erschienen. Auch in diesen Aufsätzen berücksichtigt er stets neben den morphologischen die anatomischen und physiologischen Verhältnisse.

Da seine Existenz nunmehr gesichert war, suchte er einen eigenen Hausstand zu gründen. Er hegte bereits eine tiefe Neigung zu der schönen und geistreichen Marie Emilia Dorothea Braun, Tochter des Professor Alexander Braun in Berlin. Dem Zuge seines Herzens folgend vermählte er sich mit ihr am 14. Juni 1859 in der St. Marienkirche in Berlin. Eine zweite Tochter Braun's, Caecilie, wurde am gleichen Tage dem Professor Mettenius angetraut, welcher leider bereits 1866 der Cholera erlag. Eine lange Reihe glücklicher Jahre war es dem Verstorbenen beschieden an der Seite seiner liebenswürdigen Gattin zu leben. Doch sollte auch dieses Glück nicht von langer Dauer sein. Das Schicksal fügte es, dass seine Lebensgefährtin schon im Jahre 1877 nach kurzem Krankenlager an einer Brustfellentzündung verschied. Sie hinterliess ihm drei Kinder, die sein Stolz und seine Freude waren.

Nach diesem kurzen Rückblick auf die Familienverhältnisse des Verstorbenen wende ich mich nun wieder zur Schilderung seiner wissenschaftlichen Thätigkeit. Volle 28 Jahre war er Mitglied der Gesellschaft, in der ich die Ehre habe heute zu sprechen. Während dieser Zeit hat er ihr durch sein Interesse, das er an ihrem Gedeihen zeigte, sehr genützt. Ich brauche nicht hinzuweisen auf die vielfachen Verdienste, die er sich namentlich um die Bibliothek und um die Verbreitung der Schriften als Bibliothekar der Gesellschaft erworben hat. Dieses Verdienst, und noch so manche andere, wissen ältere Mitglieder dieser Gesellschaft besser zu würdigen als ich es vermag.

Mehr als 120 kleinere Mitteilungen neben grösseren Abhandlungen hat der Verstorbene in ihren Schriften veröffentlicht und in ihnen gut beobachtete Thatsachen niedergelegt, die den Wert derselben erhöhen. — Auf der 35. Versammlung deutscher Naturforscher und Ärzte, die 1860 in Königsberg stattfand, sprach Caspary über das Vorkommen der Hydrilla verticillata in Preussen, die Blüte derselben in Preussen und Pommern und das Wachstum derselben. In diesem Vortrage berücksichtigte er die Ergebnisse der neueren Untersuchungen über die genannte Wasserpflanze. Als interessantestes Resultat hebt er hervor, dass die Bildung des Stammes keineswegs vom „Cambiummantel" in der Endknospe als lokaler Schicht (Cambialschicht) ausgeht, sondern dass alle Zellen der Endknospe und noch viele unter ihr liegenden Internodien Cambium sind, sich als Mutterzellen der verschiedenen Gewebsteile verhalten, so dass jeder Gewebsteil seine ihm eigenen Mutterzellen hat und nicht eine örtliche cambiale Schicht Mutterzellen für alle Gewebsteile enthält, dass diese Mutterzellen der verschiedenen Gewebsteile sich noch lange Zeit hindurch horizontal, tangential und radial teilen, dass das Leitzellenbündel eher fertig ist als die Rinde und dass die letzten Akte tangentialer, radialer und horizontaler Teilung in der äussersten Rinde und im unteren Teil der Internodien stattfinden. Noch in demselben Jahre veröffentlichte Caspary in den Schriften der physikalisch-ökonomischen Gesellschaft 8 kleinere und grössere Abhandlungen über Pelorien und Sonnenrisse und beschrieb eine neue höchst seltene Pflanze, die in Preussen von ihm nur im Rauschener Teich entdeckt worden ist. Es ist dies Bulliarda aquatica DC.

Bald nach seiner Ankunft in Königsberg stellte er Forschungen in unserer Provinz an, die er für eine „terra incognita" hielt, was für sie in botanischer Hinsicht auch völlig zutraf, da vor Caspary höchst mangelhaft botanisiert worden war. Er fand in unserer Provinz einige gleichgesinnte Männer, welche sich „Freunde der Flora Preussens" nannten und zu denen Professor Koernicke, Dr. Bernhard Ohlert, Pfarrer Kähler, Baron Dr. C. J. v. Klinggraeff I., Seydler u. a. gehörten. Sie kamen alljährlich zur Pfingstenzeit in einer vorher gewählten Stadt zusammen, machten sich gegenseitig botanische Mitteilungen und tauschten die gesammelten Pflanzen aus. Caspary schloss sich dieser Gesellschaft an, förderte ihre Bestrebungen, sah aber bald ein, dass bei den gar zu geringen Mitteln und wenigen Kräften, die ihnen zu Gebote standen, kein fruchtbringendes Unternehmen begonnen werden konnte. Er regte daher schon 1861 die Gründung eines botanischen Vereins an, der eine grössere Mitgliederzahl besitzen musste, wenn Mittel zur Erforschung der Flora herbeigeschafft werden sollten. Sein Plan scheiterte jedoch an der Weigerung einiger Mitglieder, fremde Elemente in den Verein aufzunehmen. Im nächsten Jahre, als sich die „Freunde der Flora" am 11. Juni zu Elbing versammelten, trat Caspary nochmals mit seinem Plan hervor und es gelang ihm auf dieser Versammlung den preussischen botanischen Verein zu gründen, dessen Statuten er bereits entworfen hatte und dessen Leitung ihm übertragen wurde. Seit 1862 war Caspary somit Vorsitzender dieses Vereins, dessen Interessen er sehr wesentlich förderte und ihn durch unausgesetzte Agitation auf die Stärke von nahezu 450 Mitgliedern brachte. Alljährlich gab er Berichte über die Erforschung der Flora von Preussen heraus, worin die Ergebnisse der botanischen Untersuchungen, welche namentlich in den letzten zwei Dezennien von den Sendboten des Vereins angestellt wurden, verzeichnet waren. Auch der Verstorbene gab dann meist zum Schluss der Berichte einen Überblick über seine Exkursionen und Funde. Er hat vorzugsweise die Gewässer des masurischen Höhenzuges, wie die See'n westlich von der Weichsel in den Kreisen Danzig, Neustadt, Berent, Cartaus, Pr. Stargard, Flatow, Dt. Krone und in diesem Jahre die Gewässer des Kreises Schlochau botanisch untersucht. Einige Kreise an der Weichsel, sowie andere im östlichen Teile Ostpreussens hat er ebenfalls erforscht. Die physikalisch-ökonomische Gesellschaft übernahm bereitwilligst die Veröffentlichung der Vereinsberichte in ihren Schriften, da der preussische botanische Verein kein so beträchtliches Vermögen besitzt, dass er seine Schriften eigens herausgeben könnte. — Während dieser 25jährigen Thätigkeit im preussischen botanischen Verein hat der Verstorbene mehr als 66 Pflanzen für Preussen neu constatiert, gewiss eine sehr hohe Zahl, wenn man bedenkt, dass er nur in den Ferien grössere Ausflüge unternehmen konnte und in mehreren Jahren durch Reisen in das Ausland an der Erforschung unserer Flora verhindert war. Caspary hatte zunächst sein Augenmerk auf die Grenzkreise und auf diejenigen, welche an der Weichsel liegen, gerichtet. Die Flora dieser Teile unserer Provinzen Ost- und Westpreussen sollte zuerst sicher festgestellt werden. Jeder Kreis sollte einer dreimaligen botanischen Untersuchung unterzogen werden und dann erst galt die Aufgabe für ihn als erledigt. Durch solche genaue Untersuchungen wollte Caspary Gewissheit über das Vorkommen einiger Pflanzen erhalten, die eine beschränkte oder sonst eigenartige Verbreitung haben und in Deutschland entweder selten sind oder gar nicht vorkommen. Auch wollte er in Erfahrung bringen, ob und in welchem Grade gewisse Arten in der Verbreitung zurückgehen und schliesslich vielleicht gänzlich aussterben. Dieses von Caspary geplante Unternehmen erleidet durch seinen Tod keinen Abbruch. Er hat dafür Sorge getragen, dass jüngere Kräfte die von ihm begonnene Arbeit weiter führen können, indem er sie nach seinem Muster bildete und sie für die einheimische Flora zu interessieren verstand.

Nach dieser kurzen Schilderung von Caspary's Beziehungen zum preussischen botanischen Verein, wende ich mich der Darlegung seiner anderweitigen wissenschaftlichen Thätigkeit zu.

Im Jahre 1862 erschien eine wichtige anatomische Arbeit des Verstorbenen; „Über die Gefässbündel der Pflanzen" (in den Monatsberichten der Königl. Akademie zu Berlin.) Er zeigt darin an einem reichen Beobachtungsmaterial, dass die Gefässe nicht in allen Pflanzen, die als „Gefässpflanzen" gewöhnlich bezeichnet werden, vorkommen. Gleichzeitig hebt er die Unterschiede zwischen Gefäss und Zelle hervor und stellt 5 parallele Modifikationen für beide auf. Eine umfassende Arbeit über die Verbreitung mehrerer Pflanzen unserer Flora veröffentlichte er in der „Festgabe zur 24. Versammlung deutscher Land- und Forstwirthe", welche im Jahre 1863 stattfand. Von den kleineren botanischen Mitteilungen, die er in den Sitzungen der physikalisch-ökonomischen Gesellschaft veröffentlichte, will ich absehen und nur die wichtigeren erwähnen. So erschien 1864 in Pringsheims Jahrbüchern die interessante anatomische Abhandlung: „Bemerkungen über die Schutzscheide und die Bildung des Stammes und der Wurzel," in welcher er eine frühere Angabe richtig stellt und die Ansichten von Sachs und Sanio über die Schutzscheide einer scharfen Kritik unterwirft. — Im Jahre 1865 wurde Caspary von der Königin der Niederlande in die Jury der internationalen Ausstellung für

Gartenbau und Blumenzucht gewählt, welche in Amsterdam tagte. Er nahm die ehrenvolle Auszeichnung entgegen und wohnte als Preisrichter der Ausstellung bei. Bei dieser Gelegenheit hielt er einen Vortrag über Mischlinge, die durch Pfropfung entstanden sind. (Im Bulletin du Congrès botanique ist dieser in deutscher Sprache gehaltene Vortrag S. 65 mit der französischen Überschrift versehen: „Sur les hybrides obtenus par la greffe.") Im nächsten Jahre besuchte er die internationale gärtnerische Ausstellung zu London, auf welcher er einen Vortrag; „Über die Veränderungen der Richtung der Äste holziger Gewächse, bewirkt durch niedrige Wärmegrade" hielt. Die Beobachtungen hatte er im hiesigen botanischen Garten vom November 1865 bis Ende März 1866 an 11 Bäumen angestellt. Die höchst interessanten Ergebnisse dieser Beobachtungen lassen sich im Folgenden kurz zusammenfassen: Die Äste aller Bäume zeigen bei niedriger Temperatur eine Veränderung der Richtung nach der Seite hin, aber ausser der seitlichen Bewegung zeigt sich zugleich bei mehreren ein Fallen bei Eintritt der Kälte und zwar ein desto tieferes, je stärker die Kälte war. Bei Pterocarya caucasica und Acer Negundo steigt dagegen der Ast bei eintretender Kälte in die Höhe und steigt desto höher, je höher die Kälte ist. Gelegentlich dieser Ausstellung besuchte Caspary auch Charles Darwin, mit dem er im Briefwechsel stand. Er teilt uns über diesen Besuch in der botanischen Zeitung von 1882 No. 45 Folgendes mit: „Als ich 1866 als Preisrichter bei einer internationalen Pflanzenausstellung und Zusammenkunft von Botanikern und Gärtnern in England war, hatte ich die Freude, einen Tag bei Darwin in seinem Hause in Down zuzubringen. Es war mir wichtig, aus seinem eigenen Munde zu hören, wie er seine Lehre über die Abänderung der Arten auffasste, ob als Hypothese oder Thatsache. Ich fragte ihn: ob er meine, irgendwo eine Art gefunden zu haben, für die es durch Thatsachen festgestellt sei, dass sie aus einer anderen durch Abänderung hervorgegangen sei. — Nein! antwortete er sehr bestimmt. Also halten Sie selbst Ihre Lehre von der Abänderung der Arten für eine Hypothese. — Ja wohl! (O yes!) lautete die entschiedene Antwort. Wie sehr sich die Lehre-Darwin's durch ihre Allgemeinheit und Einfachheit empfiehlt, habe ich ihr doch nicht zustimmen können, da den Thatsachen, die für sie zu sprechen scheinen, andere entgegenstehen, auf deren Seite mir das grössere Gewicht zu sein scheint und die mir eine andere Hypothese über die Entstehung der Arten wahrscheinlicher machen. Nach dem Erscheinen des Buches von Darwin: „Über den Ursprung der Arten," hörte man oft die Ansicht aussprechen, dass nun endlich eine Erlösung von der Systematik eingetreten sei, diesem durch seine Einzelheiten, die obenein oft so schlecht erforscht oder lückenhaft sind, so schwer zu beherrschenden Gebiet. Man sagte: auf die einzelne Art als blossem zeitlichen Moment der Entwickelung des Ganzen käme es jetzt nicht mehr an; man hoffte, dass die Systematik zum grössten Teil zur Seite geschoben und abgethan sei. Die Sache ist aber gerade umgekehrt. Die Hypothese, dass eine Art sich aus der anderen durch natürliche Zuchtwahl und Vererbung der neu erlangten Eigenschaften bilde, macht es zur gebieterischen Pflicht, viel genauer und eingehender als früher die Eigenschaften und die Entwicklung der einzelnen Art nach allen Richtungen festzustellen und sorgfältigst neu entstandene Formen zu beobachten, um zu sehen, was im Laufen der Zeit aus ihnen wird, ob es etwa gelänge, eine Art aus der anderen entstehen zu sehen, so wenig es auch möglich scheint, dass dies eintreten wird. Die Darwin'sche

Hypothese ist nach den Thatsachen zu richten, welche endlich lehren werden, ob sie wahr ist oder nicht." In einer zweiten Abhandlung, abgedruckt im 6. Jahrgang der Schriften der physikalisch-ökonomischen Gesellschaft, S. 11., verbreitet sich Caspary über die botanischen Untersuchungen, welche sich auf Darwin's Hypothese beziehen, dass kein Hermaphrodit sich durch eine Ewigkeit von Generationen befruchten kann: „No hermaphrodite fertilises itself for a perpetuity of generations." Dieser Satz muss durch folgende Versuche geprüft werden: 1) durch Befruchtung der einzelnen hermaphroditen Blüte mit dem in ihr gebildeten Pollen und zwar fortgesetzt durch so viele Generationen als möglich, 2) parallellaufend damit durch Befruchtung hermaphroditer Blüten mit dem Pollen anderer hermaphroditer Blüten von demselben Stock oder anderen Stöcken, auch fortgesetzt durch so viele Generationen als möglich, 3) durch Befruchtung der dimorphen und trimorphen Blüten in allen Kombinationen. Darwin stellte seine Versuche nur in der zweiten und dritten Weise an, ohne sie durch mehrere Generationen zu führen. Als Beispiele gegen obige Hypothese zieht Caspary herzu: Victoria regia, Euryale ferox, Nymphaea blanda, welche einjährig sind und sich durch viele Generationen mit eigenem Pollen bestäuben. Auch weist er unter Anderem auf Bulliarda aquatica und die unter Wasser bei geschlossenen Knospen blühende kleine Crucifere Subularia aquatica hin. Er stellt es als höchst wahrscheinlich hin, dass auch bei den letzten beiden Pflanzen jede Blüte sich selbst befruchtet und Frucht bringt. — Die eingehendere Beschäftigung mit den Nymphaeaceen, welche er namentlich seit Erbauung des Wasserhauses 1864/65 im hiesigen botanischen Garten sorgfältig zog und kreuzte, regte in ihm den Wunsch an, die See'n der Vogesen und des Schwarzwaldes auf Nymphaeaceen zu untersuchen. Er führte diese Reise in den Sommerferien 1867 aus. Es gelang ihm zu konstatieren, dass das Nuphar Spennerianum Gaud., welches für jene Gegenden angegeben worden war, dort garnicht vorkommt. Alle Nuphar, die er dort sah, wasen entweder N. luteum oder N. pumilum oder der Bastard zwischen beiden Arten. 1870 veröffentlichte er die Ergebnisse dieser Reise im 11. Bande der Abhandlungen der naturforschenden Gesellschaft zu Halle unter dem Titel: „Die Nuphar der Vogesen und des Schwarzwaldes." Bei den sehr mühseligen Untersuchungen schwebte er nicht selten in Lebensgefahr. Von allgemeinerem Interesse sind in diesem Aufsatze die Abschnitte 4, 6 und 7, welche von den erworbenen Verschiedenheiten der Bastarde von Nymphaeaceen und von den Nägeli'schen Zwischenformen, welche Caspary für Bastarde der reinen Arten hält, handeln. Im Jahre 1868 nahm er einen achtwöchentlichen Urlaub, um eine Forschungsreise in das nördliche Schweden zu unternehmen und die daselbst vorkommenden Nymphaeaceen zu konstatieren. Er begab sich über Stockholm zu Schiff nach Piteå und dann nach Luleå, durchstreifte von letzterer Stadt aus, den Flusslauf des Luleåelf verfolgend, bis Quickjock fast 67 G. n. Br., dann kehrte er längs demselben Fluss zurück, ging durch die Küstengegend bis nach Haparanda und Torneå, von wo aus er den Torneåelf und dessen Nebenfluss Muonielf bis etwa 68½ G. n. Br. verfolgte. Er gelangte bereits an die Nordgrenze der Verbreitung unserer Kiefer und konstatierte die nördliche Verbreitungsgrenze der Rottanne schon bei dem 68 G. n. Br. Die Rückreise trat Caspary zu Schiff an. Er hat während seiner botanischen Exkursionen in Norbotten, Luleå und Torneålappland stets auf die Verbreitung von Nuphar luteum, N. pumilum und dem Bastarde zwischen beiden, geachtet. Er konstatierte die merkwürdige Thatsache, dass der Bastard 1° Nuphar luteum + pumilum in der Mehrzahl der Fälle in Lappland ohne die Stammarten vorkommt. Die Ergebnisse dieser Untersuchungen veröffentlichte er in gedrängter Form im Bulletin du Congrès international de botanique et d'histoire de St. Petersbourg 1869 p. 99 ff. Er besuchte 1869 die gärtnerische internationale Ausstellung zu St. Petersburg, wo er einen Vortrag über die Nuphar Lapplands halten wollte, aber daran durch mir unbekannte Umstände verhindert worden ist. Eine zweite auf die Reise nach Lappland bezügliche Arbeit, die jedoch umfassender ist, veröffentlichte er 1879 in der schwedischen botanischen Zeitung: „Botaniska Notiser" von Nordstedt unter dem Titel: „Hvilken utbredning hafva Nymphaeaceerna i Scandinavien?" (Vom deutschen Original in's Schwedische übersetzt.)

Die Fahrt nach dem nördlichen Schweden war die letzte grössere Forschungsreise, die Caspary unternahm. Seit der Zeit beschränkte er sich auf die bereits weiter oben erwähnten Untersuchungen der preussischen Gewässer. Zwar reiste er 1875 noch nach Leiden zur 300jährigen Jubiläumsfeier der dortigen Universität und begab sich 1876 einmal nach Berlin*), aber diese Reisen hatten keinen ausgesprochen wissenschaftlichen Charakter.

Es bleibt mir nun noch übrig, die wissenschaftliche Thätigkeit des Verstorbenen in den letzten Dezennien zu schildern. Neben seiner unvollendeten Monographie der Nymphaeaceen bearbeitete er dieselbe Familie für einzelne grössere Werke. So hat er die brasilianischen Nymphaeaceen für die Flora brasiliensis von v. Martius und Eichler im 77. Fascikel dieses grossartigen Werkes beschrieben und abgebildet. In ähnlicher Weise bearbeitete er die Familie der Nymphaeaceen für die Annales Musei Lugduno-Batavi von Miquel (Band II Fasc. 8). Ferner hat er die Nymphaeaceen, welche Welwitsch in Angola sammelte, für das portugiesische „Journal de Sciencias mathematicas, physicas e naturaes" (Lissabon 1873) bearbeitet und in gleicher Weise unterzog er sich der Mühe die Nymphaeaceen und Hydrilleen, welche der auf Madagaskar ermordete Reisende Rutenberg gesammelt hatte, zu bestimmen und zu beschreiben. Unter den Abhandlungen mit der Überschrift: „Reliquiae Rutenbergianae" sind auch die zuletzt erwähnten Arbeiten Caspary's in den „Verhandlungen des naturwissenschaftlichen Vereins zu Bremen" 1880 und 1881 erschienen. — In den letzten Jahren erregten namentlich die vielen eigentümlichen Formen der Rottannen (Picea excelsa) und Kiefern seine Aufmerksamkeit. Er beschrieb sie sämmtlich, teils in den Schriften der physikalisch-ökonomischen Gesellschaft, teils in der botanischen Zeitung von De Bary. Ferner interessierten ihn Abnormitäten und Pflanzenkrankheiten im hohen Maasse. Er hatte ein geübtes Auge für Bildungsabweichungen und verstand sie zu deuten, indem er ihre Ursache, wo es anging, erforschte. — Vor Allem nahm jedoch die Beschäftigung mit den versteinerten preussischen Hölzern und Bernsteinpflanzen seine Zeit sehr in Anspruch. Sein reiches Wissen und seine bedeutende Pflanzenkenntnis ermöglichten es ihm, die vorweltlichen Pflanzenreste richtig zu deuten. Ohne die sichere Pflanzenkenntnis und ohne den grossen Überblick über recht viele Arten des Pflanzenreichs ist auf diesem Gebiete nichts Erspriessliches anzufangen. Beides besass der Verstorbene in hohem

*) Zur 25jährigen Jubiläumfeier des Professor Alexander Braun.

Grade. Daher sind seine Bestimmungen richtig und seine Diagnosen zutreffend. Zu dieser umfangreichen Pflanzenkenntnis gesellte sich noch eine seltene Fertigkeit im Zeichnen des Beobachteten, so dass er das, was er sah, auch gleich durch den Stift meisterhaft wiedergeben konnte. Von der Bernsteinflora hat Caspary weit über 60 Pflanzen in den Veröffentlichungen beschrieben. Von versteinerten preussischen Hölzern veröffentlichte er die Beschreibung von 10 Arten*), aber eine viel grössere Zahl von ihm bereits bearbeiteter Bernsteinpflanzen und versteinerter Hölzer befindet sich als Manuskript in seinem Nachlass. Auf gütige Verwendung des Herrn Landesgeologen Dr. Klebs wird die geologische Landesanstalt zu Berlin die Veröffentlichung dieser umfangreichen Arbeit übernehmen.

Ein reichhaltiges Herbarium, welches seltene Pflanzen aus den verschiedensten Weltteilen enthält, befindet sich ebenfalls in seinem Nachlass. Namentlich enthält seine Sammlung viele Algen, Pilze, Moose, Farne, Cyperacen, Gramineen, Compositen, Cruciferen, Rosaceen, Nymphaeaceen und lappländische Pflanzen. Während seiner Lehrthätigkeit als Professor an unserer Universität, bekleidete er 1870/71 als Prorektor die höchste akademische Würde. Am 8. Dezember 1883**) feierte er sein 25jähriges Jubiläum als Professor der Albertina, woran sich viele damalige Zuhörer und die in Königsberg anwesenden früheren Schüler beteiligten. Auch aus weiter Ferne liefen zahlreiche schriftliche und telegraphische Glückwünsche zu diesem Tage ein. In diesem Jahre sollte er sein 25jähriges Jubiläum als Vorsitzender des preussischen botanischen Vereins feiern, was ihm leider nicht mehr vergönnt war.

Caspary beherrschte wohl wie nur Wenige das grosse Gebiet der Botanik, jedoch bahnte er keine neue Richtung an und war auch kein Anhänger der heutigen modernen Richtung der Physiologie. Er beschränkte sich darauf, seine Schüler im genauen Beobachten von Thatsachen zu unterweisen, sie in die botanische Wissenschaft einzuführen und sie soweit zu fördern, dass sie selbständig wissenschaftliche Arbeiten anfertigen konnten.

Sein Charakter war gut und edel. Er war bieder und schlicht in seinem Wesen, hatte ein warmes Herz für Notleidende, behandelte Jeden freundlich und unterstützte Hilfesuchende, aber er war auch energisch, wenn's sein musste. Als Direktor einer grossen Königl. Anstalt und eines Gartens hatte er oft genug mit Widerwärtigkeiten zu kämpfen, die seine verantwortliche Stellung mit sich brachte, doch überwand er durch seinen geraden offenen Charakter alle Schwierigkeiten und willig folgte Jeder seinen Anordnungen, die stets richtig und bestimmt gegeben wurden.

Von ihm gilt im vollen Umfange das Wort des grossen Shakespeare:

„He was a man, take him for all in all,
We shall not look upon his like again."

---

*) In einer Abhandlung, welche 1887 in den Schriften der physikalisch-ökonomischen Gesellschaft abgedruckt wurde.

**) Die Ernennung zum ordentlichen Professor trägt jedoch das Datum vom 9. Dezember 1858.

Caspary's Veröffentlichungen.

Abkürzungen.

Für Bulletin de la Société botanique de France = Bulletin de Soc. bot., Verhandlungen des naturhistorischen Vereins für die Rheinlande und Westphalen = Verhandl. Rheinl. u. Westph., Botanische Zeitung = BZ., Abhandlungen der physikalisch-ökonomischen Gesellschaft = POG., Sitzungsberichte der physik.-ökon. Ges. = Sb-POG. — Monatsberichte der Königlichen Akademie der Wissenschaften zu Berlin = Monatsber. d. Berl. Akad.

1845. Das Prinzip der Erziehungsabteilungen in der Kortegarn'schen Anstalt. Programm des Kortegarn'schen Instituts zu Bonn. 8°. S. 1—19.
Ueber Elatine Alsinastrum und Trapa natans (Verbandl. Rheinl. u. Westph. S. 111 u. ff.).

1848. De Nectariis (Dissertatio inauguralis. Bonnae 1848. 4°).
Ueber Nektarien auf der Stipula von Sambucus racemosa und S. nigra (BZ. von Mohl und Schlechtendal. S. 68).

1849. Stärke in den Nektarien (BZ. 1849 S. 129 ff.).
The effect of Jodine upon the Nectary (Taylor's Annales and Magazine of Natural History 1849 vol. IV, No. 20 p. 152 ff. Translated and communicated by the author.)
Der botanische Garten in Kew bei London (BZ. 1849 S. 609 ff.).
Bericht über Hooker's Rhododendrons of the Sikkim-Himalaya (BZ. 1849).
Bericht über Hooker's Niger Flora (BZ. 1849).
Gammarus puteanus Koch (Verhandl. f. Rheinl. u. Westph. 1849 p. 39 ff.).

1850. Description of a new British Alga belonging to the genus Schizosiphon Kütz. (Taylor's Annals and Magaz. of Nat. Hist. 1850 Ser. II vol. 6 p. 266 ff.).
Observations on Furcellaria fastigiata Huds, and Polyides rotundus Gmel. (Ebenda 1850 p. 87 ff.).
On the Hairs of marine Algae and their development (Ebenda 1850 p. 465 ff.).
Vermehrungsweise von Pediastrum ellipticum Ehrb. (BZ. VIII. Jahrg. 1850 S. 786 ff.).
Kritik über Wood's Tourist's Flora (BZ. 1850).

1852. Ueber die Verbreitung von Laurus nobilis in Grossbritannien (Verhandl. des Gartenbau-Vereins für die Königl. Preuss. Staaten. 21. Band. Berlin 1852).
Kritik der „Pflanzenzelle" des Schacht (BZ. 1852).
Mitteilung über die Membran von Chlamydomonas pulvisculus (Sitzungsber. der naturforschenden Freunde in Berlin. Spenersche Zeitung No. 144. Beil., BZ. 1852 S. 46).
Ueber Udora occidentalis im Damm'schen See (Beil. zu No. 201 der Spenerschen Zeitung Ref. BZ. 1852 S. 685).
Ueber höchst auffallende Formen der Zellen in den Integumenten einiger Cruciferen (Beil. zu No. 187 der Spener'schen Zeitung 1852 S. 663).

1853. Ueber Streifung der Zellwand verursacht durch Wellung (BZ. 1855 S. 801 ff.)
Ueber Orobanche Galii (Verhandl. des Vereins zur Beförd. des Gartenbaus in den Kgl. preuss. Staaten. 1853 p. 232).

1854. Ueber Samen, Keimung, Specien und Nährpflanzen von Orobanchen (Flora 37. Jahrg. 1854 S. 577 Ref. BZ. S. 662—663.)
Auffallende Eisbildung auf Pflanzen (BZ. 1854 S. 665 ff.).
Ueber einige neue oder weniger bekannte Krankheiten der Pflanzen, welche durch Pilze erzeugt werden. Von A. Braun. Mit Beiträgen von Caspary und de Bary. Caspary: Die Ursache der Malvendürre Steirochaete Malvarum A. Br. et Casp. (Verhandl. des Ver. zur Beförderung d. Gartenbaus in den Kgl. Preuss. Staaten. Neue Reihe I. Jahrg. Berlin 1854).
De Biscutellis nonnullis annuis observationes (Appendix generum et specierum novarum et minus cognitarum, quae in horto regio botanico berolinensi coluntur 1854 p. 15 ff.)
Frucht von Cochlearia Armoracia. (Aufforderung. BZ. S. 520.)
Ueber lamellöse Eisbildung auf erfrierenden Pflanzen (Sitzungsber. der naturforsch. Freunde zu Berlin. Ref. BZ. S. 56).

Entwickelungsgeschichte der einseitigen Wandverdickung in den Samenschalen der Cruciferen (BZ. 1854 S. 390—391).

Mitteilung über einen neuen Pilz: Peronospora Chenopodii (Sitzungsber. der naturf. Freunde in Berlin. Ref. in BZ. 1854. S. 565).

Mitteilung über die Temperatur der Blüthe von Victoria regia in Borsig's Garten (BZ. 1854. S. 922).

Bericht über H. v. Mohls zweiten Artikel die Weinkrankheit betreffend (BZ. 1854. S. 903.)

Ueber zwei Krankheiten des Weinstocks (BZ. 1854. S. 904).

Einige Bemerkungen über Orobanchen. Nachtr. zum früh. Aufsatz 1854. (BZ. S. 904).

1855. Ueber zwei- und dreierlei Früchte einiger Schimmelpilze (Hyphomyceten). Monatsber. d. Kgl. Berlin. Akad. Mai 1855.

Ueber Wärmeentwicklung in der Blüthe der Victoria regia. Monatsbr. d. Kgl. Berlin. Akad. December 1855.

Dasselbe in Bonplandia 1855 p. 178 ff.

Ueber Frostspalten (BZ. 1855. 449 ff.).

De Nymphaeae albae varietatibus (Appendix generum et specierum novarum etc., quae in horto reg. berol. coluntur 1855).

Beobachtung über das Wachsthum des Blattes von Victoria regia (Verhandl. der naturf. Freunde in Berlin. Ref. BZ. 1855. S. 246).

Mitteilungen über die Kartoffelkrankheit (Sitzungsber. der naturf. Freunde zu Berlin. Ref. BZ. S. 583).

Nachtrag zu meinem Aufsatz: Ueber Samen, Keimung, Specien und Nährpflanzen der Orobanchen (Flora 1855. April).

1856. Ueber das Wachstum des Blattes von Victoria regia (Monatsber. Kgl. Berl. Akad. 1856).

Ueber die tägliche Periode des Wachstums des Blattes der Victoria regia Lindl. und des Pflanzenwachstums überhaupt (Flora No. 8—11. 1856).

Ausscheidung von Nektar auf der Narbe abgefallener Blüthen bei Chamaedorea desmoncoides (BZ. 1856 p. 881—882).

Bemerkungen über Rhizomorphen (Ebenda).

Ein neuer Standort der Udora occidentalis Koch (Hydrilla verticillata Casp.). Daselbst 1856 p. 899 ff.).

Les Nymphaeacées fossiles (Annales des Sciences naturelles IV. série, tom VI, cahier 4, p. 199—222 avec 2 pl.).

Ueber die verschiedenen Varietäten und Formen der Nymphaea alba. (Flora 39. Jahrg. 1856 S. 488 ff., cf. No. 38.)

1857. Conspect. syst. Hydrillearum (Monatsber. der Kgl. Berlin. Akad. Januar 1857 p. 39 ff.).

Neue Untersuchungen über die Frostspalten (BZ. 1857 S. 329 ff.).

Bericht über die Verhandlungen der botanischen Section der 33. Versammlung deutscher Naturforscher und Aerzte, gehalten in Bonn v. 18.—24. Sept. 1857 (BZ. 1857 S. 749 ff.).

Daselbst: „Ueber den Bau des Stammes der Nymphaeaceen."

Bewirkt die Sonne Risse in Rinde und Holz der Bäume? (BZ. 1857 S. 153 ff.).

On Udora occidentalis Koch = Hydrilla verticillata Casp. and Serpicula occidentalis Pursh = Anacharis Alsinastrum Babingt. (Hooker's Journal of Botany IX. 1857 p. 78 ff.)

Note sur la division de la famille des Hydrocharidées, proposée par Chatin Paris. (Bull. Soc. bot. VI 1857 p. 98 ff.).*)

Sur l'ovule du Vallisneria spiralis Paris (Bulletin Soc. bot. de Fr. IV. 1857 p. 904 ff.).

Ueber den Bau der Wurzel (Verhandl. Rheinl. u. Westph. XIV 1857 S. 60—61).

Der Kartoffelpilz im Sommer 1857 (BZ. 1857 S. 662—663).

Ueber die Spaltöffnungen (stomata) der Kartoffel und die Entstehung der Pocken (des Schorfes) bei denselben (Sitzungsber. der niederrheinischen Gesellschaft für Natur- und Heilkunde. Ref. BZ. S. 116—117).

Ueber Nymphaeites Ludwigii Casp. in der Beilage der Kölner Zeitung v. Febr. 1857.

*) Identisch mit Not. sur les Anacharidées, von mir in der Rede nach einer ungenauen handschriftlichen Angabe Caspary's citirt.

1858. Die Blüte von Elodea canadensis (BZ. No. 42, 1858, S. 313 ff.).
Die Hydrilleen (Pringsheims Jahrbücher für wissenschaftliche Botanik 1858).
Dasselbe in: Annales d. Sc. nat. IX Botanique 1858 p. 323 ff.
Ranunculaceae Papaveraceae Cruciferae, bearbeitet von Caspary in Nees ab E.: Genera plantarum fasc. XXVII.
Sur l'Aldrovandia vesiculosa Monti (Bull. Soc. bot. V. 1858 p. 716 ff., traduit de l'allemand par Prillieux).
Untersuchung einer sehr seltenen Wasserpflanze, der Aldrovandia vesiculosa Monti (Sitzungsber. d. Verhandl. f. Rheinl. u. Westph. 1858 S. 118 ff.).
Die Zoosporen von Chroolepus Ag. und ihre Haut (Flora 1858 S. 579 ff.).
Dasselbe in: Annales des Sc. nat. IX Bot. 1858 p. 30 ff.
Bericht über die botanische Gesellschaft von Frankreich und deren Bulletin (BZ. No. 6, 1858, S. 53).
Ueber den Bau des Fruchtknotens bei Pomaceen (Verhandl. der niederrhein. Gesellsch. für Natur- und Heilkunde. Bonn 1858. Sitzungsber. XV. Band).

1859. Ein neuer Fundort der Aldrovandia vesiculosa Monti und eine neue Varietät (var. Duriaei) derselben (Flora 41. Jahrg. 1858 S. 754 ff.).
Aldrovandia vesiculosa Monti (BZ. No. 13, Jahrg. 1859).
Ueber die Nymphaeaceen, welche die Alten Lotus nannten (Sitzungsber. der niederrhein. Ges. für Natur- u. Heilkunde in Bonn 1859, S. 37—78).
Ueber Blattstellung der Aeste einiger Nymphäaceen (Ebenda 1859).
Ueber Pflanzen der Rheinprovinz (Ebenda 1859).
Mitteilungen über Hofmeisters Untersuchungen über das Steigen der Säfte in Pflanzen (Ebenda 1859).
Erläuterungen des knollenartigen Rhizoms der Nymphäaceen (Ebenda 1859).
Ueber die Einrollung der Blätter bei Di- und Monocotylen und über Streptocarpus Rexii (Ebenda 1859).

1860. Ueber das Vorkommen der Hydrilla verticillata Casp. in Preussen, die Blüte derselben in Preussen und Pommern und das Wachstum ihres Stammes (Verhandl. der 35. Versammlung deutscher Naturforscher u. Aerzte in Königsberg in Pr. 1860, S. 293 ff. Mit 4 Tafeln. 4°).
Einige Pelorien (Orchis latifolia, Columnea Schiedeana var. Schd., Digitalis purpurea) (POG. I 1860, S. 59 ff. Mit 1 Tafel).
Bulliarda aquatica DC. (POG. 1860, S. 66 ff.).
Ueber Sonnenrisse (POG. 1860, S. 92 ff.).
Die Flora des Kölner Doms (Verhandl. Rheinl. u. Westph. 1860, S. 331—332).
Ueber Beschädigung holziger Pflanzen durch den Frost (Sb. POG. 1860, S. 3).
Ueber einige Pflanzenbastarde (Sb. POG. S. 12).
Vergleichende Untersuchungen über drei kleine Mikroskope: Bénèche in Berlin, Schieck in Berlin und Nachet in Paris (Sb. POG. S. 17).
Ueber die Cacteen Nordamerika's (Sb. POG. S. 23).
Ueber die Stellung der Aeste und Blüten und die Richtung der Blattstellung an Ast und Stamm bei der gelben Mummel (Sb. POG. S. 23).
On Zoospores (Journ. Microscop. Sc. VIII p. 159 ff. cf. No. 65).

1861. De Abietinearum Carr. floris feminei structura morphologica. Regim. 1861.
Dasselbe in Annales des sc. nat. XIV Bot. 1860 p. 200.
Dasselbe in Review of Natural History 1862, p. 12 ff.
Vergrünungen der Blüten des weissen Klee's (POG. II. Abt. 1861, S. 51 ff. Mit 2 Taf.).
Berichtigung einiger Irrtümer des Herrn Dr. Nitschke (BZ. 19. Jahrg. 1861, S. 182 ff.).
Aufforderung an Herrn Dr. Nitschke und noch einige Worte über dessen Arbeit über Drosera rotundifolia (BZ. 19. Jahrg. 1861. S. 278 ff.).
Die Fruchtbildung bei Caelebogyne ilicifolia (Sb. POG. S. 1).
Ueber die Entdeckung von Schwärmsporen bei Pilzen nach De Bary (Sb. POG.).
Ueber das Verhalten von Pflanzen bei Verwundungen (Sb. POG. S. 11).

Ueber einige beim Mergelgraben gefundene Holzstückchen (Sb. POG. S. 13—14).
Ueber Rhizome von Polystichum Filix mas Roth (Sb. POG. S. 14).
Eine kanadische Pappel vom Blitz getroffen (POG. II. Abt. S. 41 ff.).
Orobanche Cirsii oleracei (POG. II S. 46).
Nuphar luteum L var. rubropetalum (POG. S. 49. Mit 1 Taf.).

1862. Aldrovandia vesiculosa Monti (2. Artikel) (BZ. XX. Jahrg. 1862, S. 185 ff.)
Ueber die Gefässbündel der Pflanzen (Monatsber. der Kgl. Berl. Akad. 1862, S. 448 ff.).
Ueber 2 bis 4 Hüllblätter am Blütenschafte von Calla palustris (POG. III. Abt. 1862, S. 133 ff.).
Ein Bastard von Digitalis purpurea und D. lutea L (POG. III 1862, S. 139 ff.).
Ueber stengelumfassende Aeste (Sb. POG. S. 6).
Ueber die Kartoffelkrankheit (Sb. POG. S. 6).
Ueber das Vorkommen von Poren auf Zellwänden, die nach Aussen liegen (Sb. POG. 1862, S. 7).
Ueber die Stammpflanzen der Asa foetida (Sb. POG. S. 13).
Wirkung des Blitzes an Bäumen und Telegraphenstangen (Sb. POG. S. 13; auch 1871, S. 11, II 669—86).
Eine inkrustirte Bleikugel aus dem Magen eines Elens (Sb. POG. S. 20).
Ueber die ringförmige Entrindung der Bäume (Sb. POG. S. 22).

1863. Ueber die Flora von Preussen (Eine Festgabe für die Mitglieder der 24. Versammlung deutscher Land- und Forstwirte, S. 170 ff.).
Ueber Watte von Waldwolle (Sb. POG. S. 3).
Das Kinderpulver von Gehrig und Grunzig (Sb. POG. S. 6 Mitteilung).
Ueber eine vom Blitz getroffene Esche (Sb. POG. S. 6).
Ueber Gummi, das aus einer Monokotyledone gewonnen (Sb. POG. S. 7).
Ueber preussische Höhen und deren Vegetation (Sb. POG. S. 12).
Ueber Nepeta racemosa Lamarck var. Reichenbachiana Benth. (Sb. POG. S. 16).
Ueber Welwitschia mirabilis Hook. (Sb. POG. S. 16).
Ueber Früchte von Pinus Larix mit keimfähigem Samen hier gezogen (Sb. POG. S. 16).
Ueber die calabarische Bohne (Physostigma venenosum Balf.) (Sb. POG. S. 24).
Ueber den Anbau der Zizania aquatica (Sb. POG. S. 24).

1864. Bemerkungen über die Schutzscheide und die Bildung des Stammes und der Wurzel (Pringsheim's Jahrbücher für wissenschaftl. Bot. IV S. 101. Mit 2 Taf.). Dasselbe (Taylors Annals & Magaz. of Nat. Hist. XVI 1865, p. 382 ff.).
Beiträge zur Flora der Provinz Preussen (Verhandl. des bot. Ver. d. Prov. Brandenburg VI. Jahrg. S. 189 ff.).
Neue Fundorte einiger seltnerer Pflanzen der Flora von Bonn (Verh. des niederrh. Ver. f. Natur- und Heilkunde Band XXI 1864 S. 4).
Potamogeton zosteracea in Deutschland (Mecklenburger Archiv XVIII 1864 S. 212 ff.).
Ueber die Kulturpflanzen Norwegens (Sb. POG. S. 3).
Die Seealgen der samländischen Küste (Sb. POG. Siehe auch 1872 S. 138).
Ueber Lecanora esculenta (Sb. POG. S. 13).
Ueber einen Libellenschwarm am 16. Juni 1864 (Sb. POG. S. 13).
Peziza aeruginosa Pers. (Sb. POG. S. 14 und 1867 S. 7).

1865. Ueber Mischlinge durch Pfropfung entstanden (Sb. POG. S. 4). Sur les hybrides obtenus par la greffe. Amsterdam (Bulletin du Congrès Bot. 1865 p. 65 ff.)
Note on the variety Trimmeri of Potamogeton trichoides Cham. found in England [1864] (Linn. Soc. Journ. Bot. 1865 p. 273 ff.).
Die Amsterdamer internationale Pflanzen- und Blumenausstellung (Gartenzeitung für die Provinz Preussen 1865; auch Sb POG. 1865 S. 28).
Botanische Untersuchungen in Bezug auf Darwin's Hypothese über Hermaphroditen (Sb. POG. VI. Jahrg. 1865 S. 11 ff.).

1866. Nymphaeaceae in „Annales Musei Lugduno-Batavi" edidit F. A. Guil. Miquel Tom. II fasc. 8. 1866 p. 242 ff. c. tab. II).

Ueber die Veränderung der Richtung der Aeste holziger Gewächse, bewirkt durch niedrige Wärmegrade (Report of the international horticultural exhibition and botanical Congress. London 1866 p. 99 ff.).

Internationale gärtnerische Ausstellung in London. (Gartenzeitung für die Provinz Preussen 1866 No. 16—17).

The late Professor Mettenius. Necrolog (Gardener's Chronicle 1866 No. 43 p. 1018).

Ueber die Mistel (Sb. POG. S. 10).

Ueber v. Klinggraeff's Flora von Preussen, 2. Nachtrag (Sb. POG. S. 13).

Bericht über die Versammlung des preuss. botanischen Vereins in Tilsit (S. 30—66 POG.)

Bericht über die Versammlung des preuss. botan. Vereins in Marienwerder (POG. S. 183—220).

1867. Ueber Fleckenrost (Puccinia straminis Fuck.) im Herbst, Roggenstengelbrand (Urocystis occulta Rabenh.) Cyathus crucibulum L, Phallus impudicus (Sb. POG. S. 6—8).

Ueber Hexenbesen (Sb. POG. S. 8).

Fasciation einer Kartoffel (Sb. POG. S. 16).

Samen und Keimung von Pinguicula vulgaris (Sb. POG. S. 16).

Ueber eine für ein Meteor gehaltene Gallertmasse (Sb. POG. S. 28).

1868. Die alte Linde (Tilia platyphyllos) zu Neuenstadt am Kocher in Würtemberg (Naturwissenschaftl. Jahreshefte 1868 III. Heft S. 193 ff.).

Ueber Claviceps purpurea Tul. auf Gerste u. a. (Sb. POG. S. 18).

Ueber Galanthus nivalis v. Scharlokii (Sb. POG. S. 18).

Ueber die grosse Eiche in Kadienen und deren photographische Aufnahme (Sb. POG. S. 19 ff.).

Perichena strobilina Fr. auf Tannenzapfen (Sb. POG. S. 34).

Bericht über eine Reise ins nördliche Schweden (Sb. POG. 41 und 43 Mitt.)

Naturgeschichte der Mistel (POG. 1868 S. 126).

Neue Entdeckungen in der Provinz Preussen (Verhandl. des botan. Vereins der Provinz Brandenburg 1868 S. 233).

Bericht über die Versammlung des preussischen botan. Vereins zu Elbing (POG. S. 1—99).

Bericht über die Versammlung des preussischen botanischen Vereins zu Bartenstein (POG. S. 117—130).

1869. Die Nuphar Lapplands (Bulletin du congrès internat. de botan. et d'hortic. de St. Petersbourg 1869 S. 99 ff.).

Beschädigung der Rosskastanienblätter durch Reibung mittelst Wind (BZ. XXVII S. 201 ff.).

Pinus Abies mit gemeinsam aufgewachsenen breiten Nadeln (POG. 1869 S. 209).

Ueber eine von Scharlok in Graudenz beobacht. elektrische Erscheinung (Sb. POG. S. 16—18).

Ueber ein Hünengrab bei Neidenburg (Mitteilung Sb. POG. S. 18).

Ueber Dr. Buchholz in Greifswalde, Teilnehmer an der deutschen Nordpol-Expedition (Sb. POG. S. 18).

Hydrocharitaceae (Schweinfurth's Flora aethiopica).

Botanische Entdeckungen in der Provinz Preussen (Verhandl. d. bot. Ver. der Prov. Brandenburg 1869 S. 131).

Cephalanthera grandiflora Babingt., neu für Preussen (POG 1869 S. 195).

Bericht über die Versammlung des preuss. botan. Vereins zu Braunsberg (POG. S. 188—211).

Bericht über die angekauften, geschenkten und durch Tausch erhaltenen Bücher der physikalisch-ökonomischen Gesellschaft. (Am Schlusse jedes der Bände II—X der POG.)

1870. Neue und seltene Pflanzen Preussens gefunden 1870 (POG. S. 61 ff.).

Die Nuphar der Vogesen und des Schwarzwaldes (Abhandl. der naturforsch. Gesellsch. zu Halle Bd. XI. Mit 2 Tafeln.)

Hauptergebnisse der botanischen Ausflüge in der Provinz Preussen von 1870 (Verhandl. des botan. Vereins d. Prov. Brandenburg S. 79—80).

Lagarosiphon Schweinfurthii Casp. (BZ. XXVIII S. 88).

Welche Vögel verbreiten die Samen von Wasserpflanzen? (Sb. POG. S. 9.)

Ueber einen in Bestandteilen, Farbe und Bruch eigentümlichen Torf aus dem Gute Purpesseln (Sb. POG. S. 22).

Ueber die Beschaffenheit des Pollens bei Pulsatillabastarden (POG. XI S. 122).

Galium silvaticum der norddeutschen Flora von Dr. P. Ascherson als G. aristatum erkannt (POG. XI 1870).
Bericht über die Versammlung des preuss. botan. Vereins zu Danzig (POG. S. 107–133).
1871. Ergebnisse der botanischen Exkursionen von 1871 in der Provinz Preussen (Verhandl. des botan. Vereins d. Prov. Brandenburg S. 147–148).
Befruchtungsweise der einheimischen Arten von Corydalis (Sb. POG. S. 4).
Orobanche pallidiflora W. et Grab. (Sb. POG. S. 87 ff.).
Mitteilungen über vom Blitz getroffene Bäume und Telegraphenstangen (Sb. POG. 1871 S. 11 und XII S. 69–86).
Die Seealgen der samländischen Küste nach Hensche's Sammlung (POG. XII 1871 S. 138 ff.).
Biographische Nachrichten über G. H. E. Ohlert und Lorek (POG. XII. Jahrg. 1871 B. V.).
Pulsatilla patens + vernalis und P. pratensis + vernalis (POG. XII. Jahrg. S. 108 B. V.).
Bericht über die Versammlung des preuss. botan. Vereins in Königsberg (POG. S. 94 ff.).
Bericht über die Versammlung des preuss. botan. Vereins in Insterburg (POG. S. 108–124).
1872. Ueber Zwillings- und Drillingsfrüchte (Sb. POG. S. 15–17).
Ein für Preussen neuer Pilz: Sparassias brevipes Fr. (Sb. POG. S. 17).
Pflanzliche Bernsteineinschlüsse (Sb. POG. S. 18 ff.).
Ueber die Flechten als Schmarotzer auf Algen (Sb. POG. S. 18).
Ueber eine Runkelrübe mit Auswuchs (Sb. POG. S. 19).
Hohler nach innen gewachsener Sellerie (Sb. POG. S. 19).
Verzweigte Weisskohlstaude (Sb. POG. S. 20).
1873. Ueber die Kopernikus-Feier in Thorn (Sb. POG. S. 7).
Ueber eigentümliche Formen der Rottanne (Sb. POG. S. 19–20).
Ueber eine Wruke (Sb. POG. S. 23).
Weidenbäume durch einen Erdrutsch zerrissen (POG. S. 105 ff.).
Eine Wruke (Brassica Napus L.) mit Laubsprossen auf knolligem Wurzelausschlag (POG. XIV 1873 S. 105 ff).
Eine Apfeldolde mit 5 Früchten (Sb. POG. XIV S. 113).
Eine vierköpfige Runkelrübe (Beta vulgaris Moq.) (POG. S. 114 und Sb. POG. S. 13).
Ueber einige Spielarten, die mitten im Verbreitungsgebiet der Stammarten entstanden sind: die Schlangenfichte (Picea excelsa v. virgata), die Pyramideneiche (Quercus pedunculata v. fastigiata Loud. = Q. fastigiata Lamk (als Art) u. Andere (POG. XIV 1873 S. 115 ff.).
Nymphaeaceae a Friederico Welwitsch in Angola lectae (Jornal de Sciencias mathematicas, physicas e naturaes No. XVI, Tom IV. Lisboa 1873 p. 312–327).
Ueber die Leitbündel des Wurzelstocks der Typha latifolia als Gewebestoff (Mitteil. Sb. POG. S. 20).
Bericht über die Versammlung des preuss. botan. Vereins zu Marienburg (POG. XIV S. 7–32).
1874. Neue und seltene Pflanzen der Provinz Preussen (Sb. POG. 1874 S. 24).
Ueber eine eigentümliche Form der Rottanne (Sb. POG. S. 24 ff.)
Ueber Rhizopogon rubescens (Sb. POG. S. 24).
Bericht über die Versammlung des preussischen botanischen Vereins in Gumbinnen (POG. XV S. 29–64).
Bericht über die Versammlung des preuss. botan. Vereins in Konitz (POG. XV S. 65–96).
Merismopedium Reitenbachii Casp. (Sb. POG. S. 5, POG XV 1875 S. 104 ff.).
1874. Ueber Blütensprosse auf Blättern (POG. XV S. 98 ff.).
Die Krummfichte, eine markkranke Form (Picea excelsa Link f. aegra myelophthora) (POG. XV S. 108 ff.).
1875. Riesige weisse Kartoffel (Sb. POG. S. 5).
Fingerig bewurzelte Wasserrübe (Sb. POG. 5).
Stigmatische Scheibe von Nuphar luteum (Sb. POG. S. 5–6).
Vererbung von knolligem Wurzelausschlag bei einer Wruke (Brassica Napus L.) (Sb. POG. 1875 S. 40).
Ueber Agaricus lepideus Fr. (Sb. POG. S. 41).
Ueber eine dreiköpfige Ananas (Sb. POG. S. 41).

Bericht über eine Exkursion im Kreise Berent (Sb. POG. S. 6).
Ueber Trüffeln (Sb. POG. S. 32).
Bericht über die Versamml. des preuss. botan. Vereins in Rastenburg (POG. XVII S. 1—36).
1877. Etwas über die Schutzscheide (BZ. 1877 S. 185 ff.).
Nymphaea zanzibariensis (BZ. S. 201 ff.).
Alexander Braun's Leben (Flora 18.7).
Hereditary deformity in Brassica Napus (Gardener's Chronicle No. 162, S. 148).
Ueber einen Bastard zwischen Potamogeton praelonga Wulf. und P. crispa L. (POG. 1877 S. 98—99 B. V.)
Ueber Convolvulus arvensis mit fünfteiliger Blumenkrone (POG XVIII S. 95—96).
Ueber eine riesenhafte männliche Populus alba (POG. VIII S. 92).
Bericht über die Versammlung des preussischen botanischen Vereins zu Königsberg (POG. XVIII S. 49—99).
1878. Eine gebänderte Wurzel von Spiraea sorbifolia L. (Sb. POG. S. 37, XIX S. 149 ff.).
Isoëtes echinospora Dur. in Preussen (POG. S. 40).
Eine Alstroemer'sche Hängefichte (Sb. POG. S. 39, POG. XX S. 153 ff.).
Chroolepus subsimplex Casp. (Sb. POG. S. 37 XIX S. 152).
Ueber die Kropfkrankheit des Kohls (Sb. POG. S. 38—39).
Nymphaeaceae (Flora brasiliensis von v. Martius und Eichler 1878. Fasc. LXXVII S. 129 ff mit Taf. 28—38).
Berichtigung über die von Herrn Treichel in Westpreussen gefundene Gymnosporangium-Art (Sitzungsber. des bot. Ver. d. Prov. Brandenburg 1876 S. 89—90).
Verdrängung von Kiefer und Rotbuche in Westpreussen und Buchengrenze in Ostpreussen (Sitzungsber. des botan. Ver. d. Provinz Brandenburg 1878 S. 90—91).
Bericht über die Exkursionen in den Kreisen Kartaus, Berent, Neustadt und Heiligenbeil (POG S. 68 ff.).
Bericht über die Versammlung des preussischen botanischen Vereins in Neustadt, Westpr. (POG. XIX S. 43—90).
1879. Ueber Schmierbrand (Sb. POG. S. 3).
Was ist Art und was ist Spielart? (Sb. POG. S. 23—25).
Die vier Generationen der Reitenbach'schen Wruke (Sb. POG. 1879 S. 49 ff.).
Ueber eine Trauerfichte (Sb. POG. S. 50).
Hvilken utbredning hafva Nymphaeaceerna i Skandinavien? (Botaniska Notiser 1879 p. 65 ff.)
Ueber erbliche Knollen- und Laubsprossenbildung an den Wurzeln von Wruken (Pringsheims Jahrbücher wissenschaftl. Botanik XII S. 1 ff.).
Ueber die Seeuntersuchung des Kreises Deutsch-Krone und Bericht über die Versammlung des preussischen botanischen Vereins in Allenstein (POG S. 108—144).
1880. Neue und seltene Pflanzen der Provinz Preussen (Sb. PNG. XXI 1880 S. 42 ff.).
Ueber einige pflanzliche Abdrücke und Einschlüsse im Bernstein (Sb. POG. I. Abt. S. 28 ff.).
Nymphaeaceae („Reliquiae Rutenbergianae" I in den Verhandl. des naturwissenschaftlichen Vereins in Bremen S. 10—11).
Ueber die Exkursionen im Kreise Kartaus und über die Gewässeruntersuchung der Kreise Heilsberg und Allenstein. Bericht über die Versammlung des preuss. botan. Vereins in Graudenz (POG. S. 1—52).
1881. Neue fossile Pflanzen des Bernsteins, des Schwarzharzes und des Braunharzes (Sb. POG. 1881 S. 22 ff.).
Ueber bandartiges Wachstum (Sb. POG. S. 40).
Ueber die Entwicklungszustände der Pflanzen als thatsächlichen Maasstab fürs Klima eines Ortes (Sb. POG. 1881. S. 40).
Ueber zweibeinige Bäume (Sb. PPG. S. 40—41, XXIII S. 107 ff.).
Hydrilleae („Reliquiae Rutenbergianae" IV in den Abhandlungen des naturwissenschaftl. Vereins in Bremen 1881 S. 252 ff.).
Die Benachteiligung des Fischereibestandes in Preussen durch masslose Fischerei, Gänse und Rindvieh. Berichte des Fischerei-Vereins der Provinzen Ost- und Westpreussen No. 2. 1881).

Ueber die Exkursionen im Kreise Kartaus und über die Seeuntersuchung des Kreises Allenstein im Bericht über die Versammlung des preussischen botanischen Vereins in Tilsit (POG. XXII S. 1—44).

1882. Gebänderte Wurzeln eines Epheustocks (POG. 1882 XXIII S. 112 ff.).
Ueber die Zeiten des Aufbrechens der ersten Blüten in Königsberg in Pr. (POG. XXIII S. 115 ff.).
Der Malvenpilz (Puccinia Malvacearum) in Preussen (POG. XXIII 1882 S. 206 ff.).
Einige in Preussen vorkommende Spielarten der Kiefer (Pinus silvestris L.) (POG. S. 209 ff.).
Kegelige Hainbuche (Carpinus Betulus L. fr. pyramidalis Hort. (POG. XXIII S. 216).
Zwei Schlangenbäume (Abies pectinata D Cf. virgata Casp.) (BZ. 1882 S. 778 ff. Tab. IX B).
Auffallend gebildete Zapfen von Pinus silvestris (POG. XXIII S. 43 Taf. 1 Fig. 11).
Neue und seltene Pflanzen der Provinz Preussen (Sb. POG. S. 26—27).
Nymphaea zanzibariensis Casp. (Gartenzeitung von Wittmack 1882 S. 1 ff.).
Viscum album v. microphyllum Casp. (BZ. 1882 S. 598).
Ueber die Exkursionen in den Kreisen Kartaus und Neustadt und über die Gewässeruntersuchung des Kreises Platow im Bericht über die Versammlung des preussischen botanischen Vereins in Thorn (POG. XXIII S. 41—46).

1883. Die mikroskopischen Algen und sporenartigen Körper der russischen Steinkohle (Sb. POG. S. 30—32).
Gebänderte Ausläufer von Spiraea sorbifolia (POG. XXIV S. 30).
Neue und seltene Pflanzen der Provinz Preussen (Sb. POG. S. 38).
Ueber die Exkursionen in den Kreisen Kartaus und Neustadt, Seeuntersuchung der Kreise Graudenz, Kulm und Thorn im Bericht über die Versammlung des preussischen botanischen Vereins in Osterode (POG. XXIV S. 33—88).

1884. Ueber die Exkursionen im Kreise Neustadt und Seeuntersuchung der Kreise Kulm und Thorn im Bericht über die Versammlung des preussischen botanischen Vereins in Marienburg (POG. XXV S. 45—112).

1885. Ueber zwei Sporenpflanzen: Isoëtes lacustris L. und Isoëtes echinospora Dur. (Sb. POG. XXVI 1885 S. 24 ff.).
Ueber die botanische Erforschung der Kreise Neustadt und Danzig im Bericht über die Versammlung des preussischen botanischen Vereins zu Memel (POG. XXVI S. 40).

1886. Senecio vernalis W. et K. schon um 1717 in Ostpreussen gefunden (POG. XXVII 1886 S. 104 ff.).
Keine Trüffeln bei Ostrometzko (POG S. 109 ff.).
Trüffeln und trüffelähnliche Pilze in Preussen (POG. S. 177 ff.).
Ueber neue Bernsteinpflanzen (Sb. POG. II. Abt. S. 18).
Ueber die Anlage von jungen Blütenständen im Königl. botan. Garten zu Königsberg (Sb. POG. S. 35 ff.).
Neue und seltene Pflanzen aus Preussen (Sb. POG. 1886).
Einige neue Pflanzenreste aus dem samländischen Bernstein (Sb. POG. S. 1).
Neue Funde in Preussen (Berichte der deutschen botanischen Gesellschaft Bd VI Heft 1).
Ueber die Exkursionen im Kreise Neustadt und über die Gewässeruntersuchung der Kreise Berent, Konitz, Kartaus im Bericht über die Versammlung des preussischen botanischen Vereins in Pr. Stargard (POG. XXVII).

1887. Ueber neue fossile Hölzer aus Ost- und Westpreussen (Sb. POG. Februar 1887).
Einige fossile Hölzer Preussens nebst kritischen Bemerkungen über die Anatomie des Holzes und die Bezeichnung fossiler Hölzer (POG. 15. 7. 87).
Ueber die Exkursionen im Kreise Neustadt und über die Gewässeruntersuchung der Kreise Berent, Kartaus, Pr. Stargard und Danzig im Bericht über die Versammlung des preussischen botanischen Vereins in Insterburg POG. XXVIII 1886.
Die Nymphaeaceen (in der „Illustrierten Flora von Nord- und Mitteldeutschland“ von H. Potonié 1887 S. 211—212).
Die Nymphaeaceen der Gazelle-Expedition.
Die Nymphaeaceen in „Natürliche Pflanzenfamilien von Engler und Prantl.“ Letztere zwei Bearbeitungen noch unter der Presse.

Bericht

über die

in den Sitzungen

der

physikalisch-ökonomischen Gesellschaft

zu Königsberg in Pr.

gehaltenen Vorträge im Jahre 1887.

Sitzung am 6. Januar 1887.

Der Vorsitzende begrüsst die Mitglieder zum Jahreswechsel und berichtet über den glücklichen Fortgang der wissenschaftlichen Gesellschaftsarbeiten und über die reiche Vermehrung der geologischen und der anthropologischen Sammlung des Provinzialmuseums. Von den von der Gesellschaft regelmässig ausgeführten Beobachtungen der Erdthermometer sind zwei weitere Jahrgänge 1881 und 1882 berechnet und werden in diesem Hefte Seite 1 bis 26 veröffentlicht.

Nach dem am Anfang des vorigen Bandes abgedruckten Mitgliederverzeichnis zählt die Gesellschaft 436 Mitglieder und zwar 1 Protektor, 9 Ehrenmitglieder, 232 ordentliche und 194 auswärtige Mitglieder. Durch den Tod wurden der Gesellschaft entrissen:

Ein Ehrenmitglied: Geheimrat Dr. von Rénard, Präsident der Kaiserlich Russischen Gesellschaft der Naturforscher zu Moskau, gestorben 18. September 1886 zu Wiesbaden;

Drei ordentliche Mitglieder: Dr. Robert Falkson, Privatdocent der Chirurgie, und Dr. Sauter, Director der städtischen höheren Mädchenschule, beide hier am 25. Mai 1886 gestorben; ferner Stadtrat Lottermoser, vom 7. Juni 1872 bis zum Ende seines Lebens Vorstandsmitglied und Sekretär der physikalisch-ökonomischen Gesellschaft. Lottermoser, geboren 19. Oktober 1826 in Rastenburg, studierte auf der Universität Berlin, wo er Schüler von Rose und Mitscherlich war. Er besass eine Apotheke in Rastenburg, dann eine Mineralwasser-Fabrik hier und sein lebhaftes Interesse für alle Zweige der Naturwissenschaft bekundete er durch eine Reihe von Vorträgen über die Fischerei in Norwegen, über Phosphor im Haushalte der Natur und des Menschen, über die Verwertung der Thomasschlacken, über die Montanindustrie in Inowrazlaw, über Nitroglycerin und Dynamit, über Stassfurt und dessen Salze und über die Fortschritte der Photographie auf dem Gebiete der Augenblicksbilder. Vierzehn Jahre lang hat Lottermoser das Amt eines Sekretärs unserer Gesellschaft verwaltet und am 18. Juli 1886 verschied er auf einer Besuchsreise in Berlin.

Drei auswärtige Mitglieder verlor ferner die Gesellschaft: Louis René Tulasne, Mitglied der Pariser Akademie der Wissenschaften, ausgezeichneter Botaniker und hochverdient um fast alle Zweige seiner Wissenschaft, besonders um die Erforschung der Pilze, welche er in ganz neue Bahnen lenkte, starb 22. Dezember 1885 zu Hyères. — Baron Vincenz von Cesati, namhafter Botaniker, früher in Vercelli, zuletzt in Neapel, starb daselbst 13. Februar 1883. — Rittergutsbesitzer von Bronsart auf Schettnienen bei Braunsberg, gestorben 26. Dezember 1886; man verdankt ihm wertvolle Beobachtungen über die auf dem Getreide wachsenden Pilze.

Die Gesellschaft wird allen ein ehrendes Andenken bewahren.

Die Liste der Mitglieder wird am Anfang des nächsten Jahrganges der Schriften wieder abgedruckt werden.

Herr Professor Dr. Langendorff hielt einen Vortrag mit Demonstrationen über „physiologische Untersuchungen an überlebenden Organen“. Der Redner ging davon aus, dass die Physiologie, als die Lehre von den Lebenserscheinungen der Organismen, auch die Aufgabe habe, sich mit dem Gegensatze des Lebens, mit dem Tode, zu beschäftigen. Die Definition des Todes ist aber nicht leicht. Eine nähere Zergliederung der Erscheinungen zeigt, dass ein Tier zum Teil lebendig, zum Teil tot, also partiell gestorben sein kann, und dass es ferner einen Übergang zwischen Tod und Leben, einen Scheintod, giebt, aus welchem Wiederbelebung möglich ist.

Was den partiellen Tod anlangt, so sieht man, dass die einzelnen Teile des Körpers nicht gleichzeitig ihre Funktionen einstellen. Bei einem im vulgären Sinne toten Tiere kann das Herz noch schlagen, können Reflexbewegungen noch lange möglich sein. Muskeln und Nerven bleiben noch lange reizbar, die Flimmerbewegung noch tagelang in Thätigkeit. Selbst aus dem getöteten Tiere herausgeschnittene Organe bewahren oft noch lange Zeit ihre Lebenseigenschaften. Wie lange das der Fall ist, hängt ab von der Art des Tieres, ob Kaltblüter oder Warmblüter; ferner von der Art des Organs, da manche sehr empfindlich, andere sehr resistent sind. Ausgeschnittene Kaninchenherzen sah Czermak mindestens noch $3^1/_4$ Minuten, höchstens 36 Minuten schlagen; sie lieferten noch bis zu 700 Pulsen; die Vorhöfe sah er noch über eine Stunde pulsieren. Unter günstigen Bedingungen thun sie es wahrscheinlich noch weit länger. Froschherzen bleiben, wenn man sie vor Vertrocknung durch Aufhängen in einer „feuchten Kammer" schützt und kühl hält, über 24, ja über 48 Stunden in selbständiger Thätigkeit. Froschmuskeln können (nach du Bois-Reymond) bei 0 Grad nach zehn Tagen noch reizbar sein.

Die chemischen Prozesse, die im ausgeschnittenen Organe zunächst ablaufen, sind keine anderen, wie die im lebenden vor sich gehenden. Die Leber, die aus Glykogen Zucker bildet, setzt diese Thätigkeit auch ausgeschnitten fort. Während aber im Leben der Blutstrom den entstandenen Zucker schnell fortführt, häuft er sich im toten Organe an. Hierher ist vermutlich auch die Milchsäurebildung des absterbenden Muskels zu rechnen, die vielleicht einen wesentlichen Anteil am Zustandekommen der Totenstarre hat. Ähnlich verhalten sich andere Organe, z. B. die Rinde des grossen Gehirns. Der endliche definitive Tod der Organe, deren Gesamttod also erst den wahren Tod des ganzen Organismus bedeutet, dem sie angehören, ist eine Folge der Anhäufung solcher Zersetzungsprodukte und ihres Weiterzerfalles einerseits und der fehlenden Restitution der dazu verbrauchten Stoffe andererseits. Da das sauerstoffhaltige Blut, das im Leben die Organe durchströmt, die Produkte des Stoffwechsels beseitigt und einen Wiederersatz ermöglicht, so erscheint es denkbar, absterbende Organe am Leben zu erhalten und scheinbar abgestorbene wieder zu beleben dadurch, dass man ihnen unter möglichst normalen Bedingungen frisches sauerstoffhaltiges Blut wieder zuführt. In der That hat man das zunächst verwirklicht an Tieren, die ganz oder teilweise dadurch getötet waren, dass man den lebenerhaltenden Blutstrom dem ganzen Tiere oder einzelnen seiner Organe abgesperrt hatte.

Unterbindet man bei Kaninchen die zum Gehirn und oberen Rückenmark verlaufenden Arterien, so sterben nach kurzdauernden lebhaften Erregungserscheinungen diese Teile des Centralnervensystems ab. Das Bewusstsein erlischt fast augenblicklich, die Atembewegungen hören nach kurzem auf. Erhält man das im übrigen Körper kreisende Blut durch Einleitung künstlicher Atmung normal, so kann man, wenn man nach einiger Zeit die Blutsperre wieder aufhebt, die anscheinend schon leblos gewordenen Teile (Gehirn und oberes Rückenmark) wieder zum Leben erwachen sehen; sie waren nicht tot, d. h. nicht definitiv und unwiderruflich tot, sondern nur scheintot. Eine volle Restitution ist nach Untersuchungen von Prof. Langendorff noch möglich, nachdem die Absperrung mehr als eine Viertelstunde gedauert hat.

Beim Kaltblüter (Frosch) kann noch nach mehr als fünf Stunden das durch Unterbindung der Hauptschlagader des Körpers (Aorta) aufgehobene, allerdings hier weit langsamer wie beim Warmblüter erlöschende Leben durch Lösung der Ligatur völlig wiederhergestellt werden.

Der durch Absperrung des Blutzuflusses unerregbar gewordene Muskel des Warmblüters kann durch Wiederzulassen des Blutes wiederbelebt werden, vorausgesetzt, dass er der Totenstarre noch nicht verfallen ist. Darauf beruht der alte und klassische Stensonsche Versuch.

Nach demselben Prinzip kann ein ausgeschnittenes Organ dadurch vor dem Tode behütet und bei annähernd normaler Funktionsfähigkeit erhalten werden, dass man ihm einen Ersatz für den normalen Blutstrom bietet, indem man es künstlich durchblutet. Untersuchungen dieser Art sind besonders im Laboratorium von Ludwig in Leipzig ausgeführt worden. Sie sind für die Physiologie deshalb von hoher Bedeutung, weil man es hier weit mehr wie unter anderen Verhältnissen in der Hand hat, die Bedingungen, unter denen das Organ lebt und funktioniert, beliebig zu variieren und Einflüsse verschiedenster Art in ihren Wirkungen zu studieren. Hier sind zu nennen die Versuche von Ludwig und seinen Schülern an künstlich durchströmten Muskeln, welche unternommen wurden, um die von ihnen bei der Ruhe und bei künstlich angeregter Thätigkeit verbrauchten und gebildeten Gase zu bestimmen. Es gelang hierbei, Säugetiermuskeln bis 20 Stunden nach dem Tode des Tieres erregbar zu erhalten.

Die künstlich durchströmte Leber bildet nach Untersuchungen von v. Schröder aus Kohlensäure und Ammoniak Harnstoff; ja sie secerniert nach den Versuchen von Schmulewitsch und Asp noch Galle.

Die Niere vermag in überlebendem Zustande nicht nur synthetische Prozesse noch zu vollziehen, die ihr auch im Leben zukommen (Bildung von Hippursäure nach Schmiedeberg und Bunge), sondern sie bildet sogar noch Harn. Auch ihre Blutgefässe zeigen noch Lebenseigenschaften, sie verengen und erweitern sich, begünstigen oder hemmen die Durchblutung. Einen sehr komplizierten aber allen möglichen Anforderungen Rechnung tragenden Apparat haben in jüngster Zeit v. Frey und Gruber zu ähnlichen Zwecken konstruiert. Er soll genauen Stoffwechseluntersuchungen in überlebenden Organen dienen. Er enthält ein „künstliches Herz", d. h. eine Saug- und Druckpumpe, die vorgewärmtes hellrotes Blut durch das zu untersuchende Organ rhythmisch hindurch treibt, das aus ihm wiederausströmende ansaugt. Bevor das schon gebrauchte Blut wieder in die Pumpe gelangt, wird es, wie im lebenden Körper, einem Läuterungsprozess unterworfen. Dazu dient eine „künstliche Lunge", in welcher das Blut die von ihm bei der Durchströmung aufgenommene Kohlensäure abgiebt, und dafür neuen Sauerstoff empfängt. Durch eine mit dieser Lunge verbundene Vorrichtung ist es möglich, die hier abgegebenen und aufgenommenen Gase quantitativ zu bestimmen.

Zahlreiche Versuche sind, ebenfalls zumeist im Ludwigschen Laboratorium, am künstlich durchströmten Froschherzen vorgenommen worden. Man bedient sich hierzu des Froschherzmanometers, eines Apparats, welcher erlaubt, den Einfluss verschiedenartiger Speisungsflüssigkeiten (ausser dem Blut), den Einfluss des auf dem Herzen innen lastenden Druckes, der Temperatur, elektrischer Reizung u. s. w. stundenlang zu studieren, ohne dass die Leistungsfähigkeit des Herzens erlahmt. Seine Pulsationen werden auf ein kleines Quecksilbermanometer übertragen, dessen Schwankungen durch einen mit einer Zeichenfeder versehenen Schwimmer graphisch dargestellt werden können. Prof. Langendorff demonstriert einen solchen in Thätigkeit befindlichen Apparat in der von Kronecker vereinfachten Form.

Hierauf legte Herr Dr. Klien Untersuchungen über die Funktionen der sogenannten Leguminosenknöllchen vor. Zu den Grundstoffen, welche zum Aufbau der Pflanzen dienen, gehört in erster Reihe mit der Stickstoff. Er wird darum von den Landwirten unstreitbar als der wertvollste Bestandteil unter allen Düngersubstanzen angesehen, weil er nur sparsam in gebundener Form in der Natur verbreitet ist. Zwar macht der Stickstoff die Hauptmasse, nämlich 79 pCt., der atmosphärischen Luft aus; durch zahlreiche exakte Versuche ist aber festgestellt worden, dass die meisten Pflanzen den ungebundenen Stickstoff der Luft nicht als Nahrung aufnehmen können, sondern dass er in gebundener Form — als stickstoffhaltige organische Verbindungen, Ammoniak- und salpetersaure Salze — ihnen zur Verfügung stehen muss. Ein Übergang von freiem Stickstoff der Luft in die Form der vegetabilischen Stickstoffnahrung war hauptsächlich nur durch den Blitzschlag bekannt, durch welchen aus Luft und Wasserdampf kleine Mengen salpetersaures Ammoniak entstehen, welche mit den Niederschlägen zu Boden fallen. Diese Quelle liefert aber nur einen sehr geringen Bruchteil derjenigen Quantität Stickstoff, die wir in den Ernten vom Boden entnehmen. In Bezug auf ihre Stickstoffnahrung sind zum Beispiel die Gramineen (Getreidehalmfrüchte) allein auf den Boden angewiesen. Die Form, in der sie den Stickstoff aufnehmen, ist die der salpetersauren Salze und steht seine Wirkung immer im geraden Verhältnis zur gegebenen Menge Salpeterstickstoff. Die Papilionaceen aber, welche gerade sehr reich an stickstoffhaltigen organischen Verbindungen sind, zeigen sich dagegen wenig dankbar gegen Stickstoffdüngung. Nun behauptete Hellriegel auf der letzten Naturforscherversammlung in Berlin auf Grund seiner Versuche, dass die Stickstoffquelle, welche die Atmosphäre bietet, allein schon genügen könne, die Papilionaceen zu einer normalen, ja üppigen Entwickelung zu bringen, und zwar würde der Stickstoff durch die sogenannten Leguminosenknöllchen aufgenommen. Auch Dr. Klien hat in der Versuchsstation seit fünf Jahren eingehende Versuche angestellt und dabei bis jetzt Resultate erhalten, welche ebenfalls darauf hindeuten, dass der elementare Stickstoff der Atmosphäre in Mitwirkung tritt. So sind seit fünf Jahren in einem fast stickstofffreien Sandboden, welcher sich in sehr grossen über den Boden stehenden Thonröhren befindet, jedes Jahr gelbe Lupinen ohne Stickstoffdüngung gewachsen, wobei die Ernte doch von Jahr zu Jahr eine grössere gewesen ist.

Das Wurzelsystem von den meisten kräftig entwickelten Papilionaceen besitzt nämlich zahllose knollenförmig verdickte Zweiglein, welche überall zerstreut auf den dickeren und an den feinsten Fäden vorkommen, wie sie sich auch an der von Dr. Klien vorgezeigten Lupinenwurzel befanden. Über die Bedeutung der Wurzelknöllchen herrschen die verschiedensten Ansichten. Am verbreitesten war früher die Meinung, dass es krankhafte Gebilde seien. Einmal hielt man sie für Gallen, trotzdem weder Höhle noch Ei darin zu finden gewesen war, oder für Auswüchse, ohne eine Entstehungsursache gefunden zu haben. Offenbar gehören die Wurzelknöllchen aber zum gesunden Leben einer sehr zahlreichen Pflanzenfamilie. Sie finden sich nur bei den Papilionaceen, und zwar bei den meisten Gattungen. Nicht gefunden sind sie bei Astragalus, Genista und Scorpirus. Diese Wurzelknöllchen sind aber auch keine knospenartigen Gebilde, weil sie nicht zur Vermehrung von Pflanzen beitragen. Vielfach nahm man auch an, dass die Knöllchen Wucherungen seien, welche durch parasitische Pilze verursacht würden. Woronin giebt z. B. an, dass er in den Wurzelknöllchen der Lupine, in den Zellen des Markes stäbchenförmige Organismen beobachtet habe, welche den Bakterien ähnlich wären. Frank hat dagegen bei seinen letzten Untersuchungen gefunden, dass die vermeintlichen Bakterien gar keine Pilze, überhaupt keine fremden Wesen, sondern geformte Eiweisskörper seien, weshalb er ihnen den Namen „Bakteroiden" gegeben hat. Die Wurzelknöllchen der Papilionaceen muss man somit bei einer vorurteilfreien Betrachtung ihres regelmässigen Vorkommens und ihrer Anwesenheit in allen Entwicklungsstadien als einfach verdickte adventive Wurzelzweige mit beschränktem Längenwachstum bezeichnen. Jedenfalls sind sie auch normale Gebilde, welche eine bestimmte Rolle in der immer lufthaltigen Ackerkrume beim Pflanzenleben spielen, und zwar kann man dieselben als Organe für die Aufnahme, aber auch als Räume für die Aufspeicherung stickstoffhaltiger Nährstoffe betrachten. Zweifellos finden wir, dass das Gewebe der Wurzelknöllchen mit Eiweiss ganz besonders reich angefüllt ist und während des ganzen Lebens der Knöllchen in ihnen grössere oder geringere Quantitäten nachweisbar sind. Wären die Knöllchen aber nur Aufspeicherungsorgane, so würde man erwarten müssen, dass sie nur den perennierenden Arten zukommen. Sie kommen jedoch ebenso bei einjährigen Gewächsen vor, und zwar oft schon gleich nach beendigter Keimung. Wir dürfen somit annehmen, dass Produktion und Ablagerung von Eiweiss zu den wesentlichen Funktionen der Wurzelknöllchen gehört, während die Annahme, dass der Luftstickstoff für die pflanzliche Ernährung von ihnen nutzbar gemacht wird, noch durch weitere Versuche gesichert werden muss.

Diese Mitteilungen erregten in der Gesellschaft grosses Aufsehen, da man bisher annahm, dass der Stickstoff der Atmosphäre ein ganz indifferentes Gas sei, welches auf keine Weise direkte chemische Verbindungen eingehe und weil es für die Fruchtfolge sehr wichtig wäre, wenn der Boden ohne Stickstoffzufuhr, durch Anpflanzung von Hülsenfrüchten verbessert werden könnte. Daher entspann sich eine lebhafte Debatte, an der sich besonders die Herren Professor R. Caspary, Kreiss, Dr. Jentzsch und Professor Langendorff beteiligten.

Dann machte Herr Dr. Klien eine Mitteilung über das Wurzelwachstum entlaubter Bäume im Winter. Im allgemeinen wird angenommen, dass die Bäume, wenn sie im Herbst ihre Blätter abgelegt haben, einige Zeit ruhen. Dies ist jedoch nicht so, sondern sie verarbeiten unter Umständen schon im Winter einen Teil ihrer Reservestoffe zur Vergrösserung und Erneuerung ihres Wurzelsystems. Als Beweis hierfür zeigte Dr. Klien ein Ahornbäumchen vor, was in Nährstofflösung gezogen und zur Überwinterung in einem kalten Raume von nur einigen Grad Wärme untergebracht war. Während dieses Bäumchen seit längerer Zeit kein neues Wurzelwachstum gezeigt, sondern sich im Stillstand befunden hatte, ist seit einigen Wochen eine wesentliche Verlängerung der Wurzeln erfolgt. Daher hat es auch seine Berechtigung, wenn man das Verpflanzen der Bäume und Sträucher lieber im Herbst als im Frühjahr vornimmt.

Herr Dr. Otto Tischler sprach über die Kupferzeit in Europa:

Der grösste Fortschritt in der Kulturentwickelung der Menschheit ist die Entdeckung des Gebrauchs der Metalle, nachdem man sich ungezählte Jahrtausende hindurch mit Geräten aus Stein und Knochen begnügt, damit allerdings immerhin Erstaunliches geleistet hatte. Der Ursprung dieser Entdeckung muss nach der Quelle aller Kultur, Asien, verlegt werden und er wird wohl noch sehr lange dunkel bleiben, hingegen beginnt sich der Gang der Entwickelung in Europa allmählich etwas mehr zu klären. Nach dem zuerst 1813 von dem Dänen Vedel-Simonsen aufgestellten, später sogenannten Dreiperiodensystem folgt auf den Gebrauch des Steins der des Kupfers, dann erst der des Eisens. Unter Kupfer verstand man damals die so zahlreichen Bronzegeräte, und besonders durch Thomsen wurden 1836 die Begriffe der Steinzeit, Bronzezeit und Eisenzeit eingeführt, Bezeichnungen, welche bald die ganze Archäologie beherrschten und auch jetzt nach schweren Kämpfen wieder fast allgemein zur Herrschaft gelangt sind. Die Gegner dieses Systems behaupteten, die Verwendung des Eisens sei der der Bronze vorangegangen und reiche in Europa in eine frühere, uralte Zeit zurück. Eines ihrer Hauptargumente bestand darin, dass die Bronze aus zwei, selten nebeneinander vorkommenden Metallen, Kupfer und Zinn bestehe und metallurgisch schwerer herzustellen sei als das Eisen, welches ja beispielsweise jetzt in einem grossen Teile von Afrika von den auf niedriger Stufe stehenden Eingeborenen mit den einfachsten Hilfsmitteln gewonnen und verarbeitet werde. Gegen eine einheimische Fabrikation der Bronze schien allerdings die grosse Seltenheit des Zinns in Europa zu sprechen, und daher nahmen manche Gelehrte an, es müsste dem Gebrauch der Bronze der des reinen Kupfers vorangehen, und diese vielfach bezweifelte Ansicht hat sich während des letzten Decenniums immer mehr bestätigt. Am zahlreichsten waren die Geräte aus reinem Kupfer in Ungarn gefunden und aufbewahrt worden (Nationalmuseum zu Budapest), worüber Pulszky in seinem Werke über die Kupferzeit in Ungarn ausführlich berichtet hat.[1]) Ausserdem wurden sie in den österreichischen Pfahlbauten und besonders zahlreich in den schweizerischen entdeckt (Publikationen von Much, Gross, Forrer).[2]) Das Resultat aller dieser Forschungen ist kürzlich von Much in seinem Werke „Die Kupferzeit in Europa"[3]) zusammengefasst, welches dadurch für die Kenntnis der Kulturentwickelung eine hervorragende Bedeutung erlangt hat.

Den grössten Formenreichtum zeigen die ungarischen Kupfergeräte, manche Typen, die ausserhalb dieses Gebiets gar nicht mehr vorkommen.

Die Kupfergeräte sind zunächst einfache Nachbildungen der Steinwerkzeuge, nur, der grösseren Schwere des Metalls entsprechend, nicht so dick. So werden einfache flache Keile in Form der Steinaxt gegossen, platte rhomboidische Dolche, den Feuersteindolchen ähnlich. Diese Form der Keile ist am meisten durch ganz Europa verbreitet.

Dann verbreiterte man die jetzt halbkreisförmig gebogene Schneide, hämmert die Gussnähte an den Schmalseiten fort, wobei an den Seiten des Keils schwach emporstehende Ränder auftraten, die dann bei den Bronzeäxten im Guss nachgeahmt wurden und hier sich allmählich zu Schaftlappen entwickelten. Ebenso wurde der Steinhammer durch Guss in Kupfer nachgebildet, woraus sich gerade in Ungarn eine Anzahl eigentümlicher Instrumente entwickelte. Man machte Axthämmer mit zwei auf einander senkrechten Schneiden, deren eine Seite bei den Pickeln ganz ungewöhnlich lang wurde.

Endlich findet sich in Ungarn häufig ein Instrument in Form unserer modernen Axt, des Gradbeils, welches sich nicht durch Imitation von Steininstrumenten erklären lässt und das daher von manchen Archäologen als jünger angesehen wurde. Diese stammt aber aus einer ganz anderen Region, aus Sibirien, wo am Ural schon sehr früh eine höchst eigenartige einheimische Kupferindustrie existierte und von wo manche Formen und Ornamente nach Ungarn gelangt sind. Die Dolche zeigen auch einige Modifikationen: einige Löcher am Griffende dienten zur Befestigung an einen Stiel, während die ältesten den Steindolchen analog einfach mit Bast umwickelt und in einen

---

1) v. Pulszky: Die Kupferzeit in Ungarn. Budapest 1884.

2) Gross: Les protohelvètes. Berlin 1883. Forrer: Statistik der in der Schweiz gefundenen Kupfergeräte. Antiquaria 1885. Much in den Mitteilungen der anthropologischen Gesellschaft in Wien II. IV (Ueber die Pfahlbauten in Mondsee).

3) Much: Die Kupferzeit in Europa. Wien 1886.

Holzgriff geklebt wurden. Selten ist in Ungarn eine Form mit langer schmaler Griffangel, noch vereinzelter in der Schweiz; diese Form weist auf Cypern hin, wo sie häufiger auftritt.

Sonst finden sich noch Pfrieme, Messerchen, Schmuckperlen, seltener andere Schmucksachen, wie Spiralringe und Gürtelhaken aus Kupfer, das hier immer, so oft es analysiert wurde, sich als zinnfrei erwiesen hat. Die Geräte sind alle gegossen und dann erst zurecht gehämmert, nicht verziert. In den Stationen der jüngsten Steinzeit Mitteleuropas, so in dem grossen Wohnplatze von Tordos in Siebenbürgen, in den österreichischen Pfahlbauten im Laibacher Moor, in Attersee, im Mondsee finden sich überall einige Kupfergeräte neben Steininstrumenten, besonders auch neben Steinhämmern, den jüngsten dieser Werkzeuge. In der Schweiz unterscheidet Gross drei Abschnitte der jüngeren Steinzeit, in dem letzten, wo die Steinhämmer häufig, finden sich die Kupfergeräte, so am reichsten im Pfahlbau zu Vinelz im Bieler See. Einfache Kupfergeräte, so besonders jene Keile finden sich vereinzelt durch Norddeutschland und Skandinavien bis nach England und Irland hinein. Im Osten treffen wir dieselben einfachen Geräte in den untersten Schichten von Troja, vor der verbrannten Stadt, ferner besonders auf der Insel Cypern, die dem Metall den Namen gegeben hat.

Aus Ostpreussen befindet sich ein kleines Kupfermesser von Bladiau Kreis Heiligenbeil im Provinzial-Museum, ein Kupferkeil (flacher Celt) aus der ehemaligen Giseviusschen Sammlung, also wohl aus der Gegend von Tilsit stammend, im Prussia-Museum.

Es ist demnach die Kupferzeit der jüngste Abschnitt der Steinzeit, wo neben den überwiegenden Steininstrumenten auch in der Form ähnliche aus Kupfer ohne Zinnsatz zur Anwendung kamen. Das wichtigste Bindeglied in diesem grossen Gebiete ist die Keramik. Man findet die durchaus geschmackvollen Thongefässe mit einem dichten Netzwerk von fein gegliederten vertieften Mustern bedeckt, deren punktierte Linien einst wohl meist mit weissem Kalk ausgefüllt waren. Während die Thongefässe Oberösterreichs ihre auffallenden Analogien in Cypern und den ältesten Städten Trojas haben, treten in den Kupferstationen der Schweiz Gefässe auf, die in Form und Verzierung mit solchen der Ostpreussischen Steinzeit, wie von der Kurischen Nehrung als geradezu identisch bezeichnet werden müssen. Es tritt hier die Verzierung durch in den weichen Thon gedrückte Bindfäden, das echte Schnurornament auf und die Form des geschweiften Bechers, was wir beides am Ende der Steinzeit durch fast ganz Europa finden. Wenn wir ferner die Ähnlichkeit der Figuren, Idole oder ähnlicher Zierrate ins Auge fassen, die in Ostpreussen aus Bernstein, in den Krakauer neolithischen Höhlen aus Knochen und Kalkstein, in Siebenbürgen, Südrussland, Griechenland aus Thon, Troja aus Marmor und Thon auftreten, so muss man schliesslich eine Gleichzeitigkeit dieser ganzen Kulturgruppe annehmen, wenn auch die Kultur an Höhe nach der Peripherie immer mehr an Intensität abnimmt. Man wird demnach die Steinzeit Ostpreussens mit der Kupferzeit Mitteleuropas als gleichzeitig ansetzen und noch vor den Fall der Stadt des Priamus (der verbrannten Stadt) setzen dürfen, ein Alter, das nicht mehr so befremdlich erscheint, nachdem die seitens der physikalisch-ökonomischen Gesellschaft unternommenen Ausgrabungen auch in Ostpreussen Gräber der älteren Bronzezeit jüngst nachgewiesen haben.

Das Kupfer wurde nun in einem grossen Teile Europas von der einheimischen Bevölkerung selbst gewonnen, wie es besonders die von Much genau beschriebenen prähistorischen Gruben am Mitterberge bei Bischofshofen[1]) beweisen. Das Erz wurde hier durch Feuersetzen gelöst, durch grössere Steinschlägel zerkleinert, dann durch kleine Steine zerklopft, endlich auf Steinplatten zerrieben, hierauf in Holztrögen abgeschlämmt. Man hat alle diese Geräte in den verlassenen Kupfergruben entdeckt, auch kupferne Pickel, aber keine Geräte aus Eisen. Neben den Gruben fand man zahlreiche Schlackenhäufchen, auch einen kleinen Ofen. Leicht liess sich aus dem Kupferkies das Kupfer ausschmelzen, wie auch neuere Erfahrungen beweisen. Die dabei gefundenen Thonscherben zeigten ganz denselben Charakter wie die der nicht weit entfernten Pfahlbauten des Mondsees.

Zahlreiche Schmelzschalen, zum Teil noch mit Kupferresten, hierselbst, wie in allen analogen Stationen zeigten, dass man dort, in den Pfahlbauten, das Kupfer verarbeitete.

Es hat also am Ende der Steinzeit die Bevölkerung Mitteleuropas das Kupfer selbst gewonnen und verarbeitet, das ist die Kupferzeit, welche demnach als Unterabteilung der Steinzeit aufzufassen ist.

---

1) Much: Das vorgeschichtliche Kupferbergwerk auf dem Mitterberg bei Bischofshofen. Wien 1879 (aus den Mitt. d. k. k. Centralcommission etc. N. F. V).

Nachtrag. Durch eine gefällige Mitteilung und kleine Skizze von Herrn Ignaz Spöttl-Wien wurde ich mit einem hochinteressanten Stück aus Kupfer bekannt, welches bei Holitsch in Mähren gefunden ist. Dasselbe besteht aus einer dolchartigen aber abgerundeten Klinge, welche ein wenig schräge in den fast senkrecht darauf stehenden, sie noch überragenden Stiel übergeht und sich hinten in einen gestielten Knopf fortsetzt. Das ganze ist aus einem Stück gearbeitet, hat also eine grosse Verwandtschaft mit den Nordischen Schwertstäben (wie Lindenschmit: Altertümer der heidnischen Vorzeit III Heft VI Tfl. 1), andrerseits in Form der Klinge mit den schönen ungarischen Axthämmern (ebenda II Heft III Tfl. 2 Fig. 5—9), ist also eine Art Mittelform oder Verbindungsglied. Da diese Schwertstäbe im Norden zu den allerfrühesten Bronzen gehören, welche der Periode von Peccatel noch vorangehen und ungefähr dem Grabhügel von Leubingen — Provinz Sachsen — (Provinzial-Museum Halle) gleichaltrig sind, so glaube ich, dass diese Art von Schwertstäben aus Kupfer auch zum mindesten in diese alte Zeit zu setzen ist. Herr Spöttl hat in seiner Beschreibung dieses Gegenstandes[1]) meine Ansicht, die ich ihm brieflich mitteilte, nicht ganz richtig verstanden, und daselbst gesagt, ich setzte sie in die letzte vorchristliche Periode, was durch obige Ausführungen widerlegt ist. O. Tischler.

Sitzung am 3. Februar 1887.

Herr Geheimrat Professor Dr. Hermann hielt einen Vortrag über die elektrischen Fische. Derselbe gab eine Darstellung unseres Wissens über diese merkwürdige Naturerscheinung, mit besonderer Berücksichtigung der neuesten Forschungen. Er schilderte die Lebensgewohnheiten, den Körperbau und das elektrische Organ der drei hauptsächlichsten elektrischen Fischarten und gab eine Geschichte der an denselben zum Teil in den physiologischen Instituten, zum Teil an den Fundorten selbst vorgenommenen physiologischen Untersuchungen. Diese Arbeiten bewiesen, dass der Schlag alle Wirkungen elektrischer Ströme hat, stellten die Richtung des Schlagstroms für alle drei Fische fest und führten zu dem Ergebnis, dass die Thätigkeit der elektrischen Fische nichts anderes ist als eine besondere Entwickelung der den Muskeln und Nerven aller Tiere gemeinsamen Eigenschaft, bei der Erregung Ströme von bestimmten Gesetzen zu erzeugen, nur sind diese Ströme, welche sonst nur im Innern der Organe sich abspielen, lediglich deren Funktion dienend, hier durch säulenartige Gruppierung zahlreicher homologer Elemente enorm verstärkt und zur Ableitung nach aussen geschickt gemacht.

Hierauf beschreibt Herr Professor Dr. R. Caspary unter Vorlegung von vortrefflichen Abbildungen einige neue fossile Hölzer aus Ost- und Westpreussen.

Der Vortrag befindet sich unter den Abhandlungen dieses Heftes Seite 26 bis 45.

Der Vortragende bittet diejenigen, die im Besitz von fossilem Holze von sicherem preussischen Fundorte sind, ihm solches zur Untersuchung und Bestimmung zuzustellen.

Sitzung am 3. März 1887.

Herr Professor Dr. Chun legte seine Untersuchungen über die Existenz einer pelagischen Tiefseefauna vor. Indem wir hinsichtlich der Einzelheiten auf sein über diesen Gegenstand demnächst erscheinendes Buch[2]) verweisen, begnügen wir uns hier mit einem kürzeren Bericht. Der Redner erörterte zunächst die Resultate früherer Tiefsee-Expeditionen unter Demonstration einer Anzahl von Tieren, welche in grösseren Tiefen auf dem Boden des Meeres festsitzen, und besprach

1) Mitteilungen der Anthropologischen Gesellschaft in Wien XVII 1887, Sitzungsbericht No. 3 pag. 30.

2) Carl Chun, „Die pelagische Tierwelt in grösserer Meerestiefe und ihre Beziehungen zu der Oberflächenfauna.“ 1 Quartband mit 5 Tafeln. Verlag von Theodor Fischer, Kassel. 1887.

dann vereinzelte Beobachtungen, welche es ihm wahrscheinlich gemacht hatten, dass ausser den auf dem Grunde des Meeres lebenden Tieren auch pelagische d. h. freischwimmende Tiere in den tieferen Wasserschichten existieren möchten. So wurden namentlich Bruchstücke von Schwimmpolypen bei den Lotungen der deutschen Korvette „Gazelle" und der italienischen Korvette „Vettor Pisani" aus 1000 bis 2000 m Tiefe an den Lotleinen haftend gesammelt, während andererseits die Anwendung von Schwebnetzen bei der Challengerexpedition aus grossen Tiefen eine Anzahl freischwimmender Tiere — namentlich Radiolarien — lieferte, welche bisher noch nicht an der Oberfläche bemerkt waren. Indem der Vortragende die ihm zur Untersuchung übersendeten Bruchstücke von Schwimmpolypen, welche an den Lotleinen aus bedeutender Tiefe vom „Vettor Pisani" gesammelt waren, vorlegt, hob er hervor, dass neuerdings Zweifel geäussert wurden, ob thatsächlich in tieferen Wasserschichten schwimmende Tiere zu existieren vermöchten. Auch glaubte schon Agassiz durch Anwendung von in bestimmter Tiefe verschliessbaren Apparaten sich überzeugt zu haben, dass unterhalb 300 m überhaupt keine Tiere mehr existierten und dass zwischen der pelagischen Oberflächenfauna und den auf dem Boden der Oceane lebenden Tiere azoische Wassermassen vorhanden seien. Um die Frage nach der Existenz einer pelagischen Tiefseefauna exakt zu entscheiden, untersuchte der Vortragende im Sommer und Herbste 1886 die grösseren Tiefen des Mittelmeers an der italienischen Westküste auf dem ihm von der zoologischen Station zu Neapel zur Verfügung gestellten Dampfer. Er bediente sich eines Netzes, das in bestimmter Tiefe sich öffnete und nach dem Fang sich selbstthätig wieder schloss, so dass der Einwand von Agassiz, es seien die auf früheren Expeditionen vermeintlich aus der Tiefe erbeuteten Tiere erst in den oberflächlichen Schichten bei dem Aufwinden der Netze und Lotleinen erfasst worden, ausgeschlossen war. Die Untersuchung ergab nun in allen Tiefen bis zu 1500 m (von den Ponzainseln, westlich von Gaëta, an bis zum Golfe von Salerno) einen überraschenden Reichtum von Tierformen. Sämtliche Typen, so die Protozoen, Cölenteraten, Würmer, Mollusken, Crustaceen, Tunicaten und Fische weisen charakteristische Vertreter in der Tiefe auf. Es stellte sich hierbei heraus, dass der überwiegend grösste Teil jener pelagischen Tiere, welche während des Winters und Frühjahrs in grossen Schwärmen an der Oberfläche erscheinen, bei Beginn des Sommers die grösseren Tiefen aufsuchen. Analoge Wanderungen in vertikaler Richtung unternehmen die pelagischen Tiere auch während der Tageszeiten, insofern sie während der Nacht an die Oberfläche aufsteigen und während des Tages in Tiefen bis zu 100 m niedersinken. Der Grund zu diesen Wanderungen liegt nach der Ansicht des Vortragenden offenbar in der erhöhten Temperatur des Oberflächenwassers während des Sommers und des Tages. Da im Mittelmeere bereits von 150 bis 4000 m Tiefe eine gleichmässige Temperatur von 14 bis 13,5 Grad Celsius herrscht, so dürfte diese es auch erklären, dass in allen Schichten die Tierformen ziemlich gleichmässig verteilt sind. Der Grund zu der auffällig hohen Temperatur des Mittelmeerwassers in grossen Tiefen liegt darin, dass der unterseeische Rücken in der Meerenge von Gibraltar den Eintritt kalter polarer Ströme verhindert. Nach den neuesten Lotungen des italienischen hydrographischen Amtes beträgt nämlich die geringste Tiefe in der Mitte der Meerenge nur 86 m. Während nun einerseits Thiere, die an der Oberfläche leben, im Sommer kühlere Regionen aufsuchen, so existieren andererseits in der Tiefe freischwimmende Tiere, welche entweder gar nicht oder nur in seltenen Fällen an der Oberfläche erscheinen. Der Vortragende zeigte eine Anzahl der von ihm entdeckten pelagischen Tiefseetiere vor. Unter ihnen zeichnen sich manche Würmer und Crustaceen durch die erstaunliche Länge ihrer Fühlfäden aus: eine interessante Anpassung an den Aufenthalt in dunkelen Wasserschichten. Dass trotzdem bei den Crustaceen die Augen nicht rückgebildet wurden, obwohl sie durchweg rotes Pigment aufweisen, findet seine Erklärung darin, dass fast sämtliche pelagischen Tiere leuchten. Manche der Crustaceen wie Euphausia besitzen sogar Leuchtorgane an den Augenstielen. Auch dringt das Licht nach Versuchen des Vortragenden, die er gemeinschaftlich mit dem Ingenieur der Station v. Petersen anstellte, weiter in dem klaren Seewasser vor, als man bisher annahm. Bromsilberplatten, die in Tiefen bis zu 550 m eine halbe Stunde exponiert wurden, zeigten noch deutliche Einwirkung der chemisch wirksamen Strahlen. Manche der in der Tiefe schwimmenden Formen sind bedeutend grösser als die von der Oberfläche bekannten. So wurden Appendikularien von 4 cm Länge demonstriert; auch waren manche Anneliden, wie Tomopteris und Alciopa, erheblich grösser als die Oberflächenarten. Bemerkenswert ist ferner auch der Reichtum der Tiefe an Euphausien und an kleinen durchsichtigen Cephalopoden. Nach Erörterungen über die Ernährung der Tiefseetiere wurde darauf hingewiesen, dass manche Tiergruppen, so die koloniebildenden Radiolarien, einige kleinere Crustaceen und die gelappten Rippenquallen niemals in die Tiefe steigen, sondern auch im Hochsommer bei grellem Sonnenlicht an der Oberfläche verweilen. Die eigentümliche Frühreife der Larven einer gelappten Rippenqualle, nämlich der Bolina, scheint vorwiegend durch den ständigen Aufenthalt in den oberflächlichen warmen Schichten bedingt zu werden. Hier werden die Larven zwei Tage nach dem Ausschlüpfen geschlechtsreif, legen befruchtete Eier, aus denen wiederum geschlechtsreif werdende Larven entstehen. Sobald diese nun sich in das definitive Tier umwandeln, werden die Geschlechtsprodukte rückgebildet und erst nach langer Zeit erlangt dasselbe Tier wiederum die Fähigkeit, als junge Bolina sich fortzupflanzen. Der Vortragende schlug vor, diese Entwicklungserscheinung als „Dissogonie" zu bezeichnen. Er betonte zum Schlusse, dass die systematische Durchforschung der pelagischen Tierwelt in der Tiefsee über eine Fülle biologischer Fragen Aufschluss gebe und dass ihr Studium um so mehr Interesse darbiete, als nach den im Winter fortgesetzten Beobachtungen es durchaus den Eindruck mache, dass die Tiefe ein reicheres tierisches Leben berge als die Oberfläche.

Auf eine Anfrage des Herrn Professor Caspary erklärte Herr Professor Chun, dass er auch in der Ostsee, die freilich nur geringe Tiefe hat, ähnliche Untersuchungen anstellen will, wie er sie im Mittelmeer gemacht hat.

Herr Dr. Tischler berichtete über den Zuwachs der archäologisch-anthropologischen Abteilung des Provinzialmuseums im Jahre 1886 durch Geschenke und durch systematische Ausgrabungen. Geschenkt sind von Herrn Dr. Rosenthal zwei Steinhämmer aus der Gegend von Schippenbeil, von Herrn Mühlenbesitzer Beyer ein Steinhammer von Gemauerte Mühle bei Ostrowitt, von Herrn Dr. Schröder ein grösserer Bronzedepotfund mit Glasperlen von Korwienen, Kreis Heilsberg, ebendaher eine Urne, von Herrn Lehrer Haber eine La Tène-Urne mit Inhalt von Rudau, von Herrn Gutsbesitzer Leitner-Schülzen ein mit Kupfer und Eisen tauschierte Bronzefibel, von Herrn Schäfer-Wilkieten Funde von einem Gräberfelde bei Prökuls, von Herrn Gutsbesitzer Link-Lixeiden eine Armbrustfibel, von Herrn Gutsbesitzer Kantelburg-Schlakalken zwei Pferdegebisse, von Herrn Gastwirt Genserowski-Pobethen Funde von einem Gräberfelde in Kösnicken, von Herrn Direktor Friederici aus seinem Nachlasse einige Objekte der jüngsten heidnischen Zeit von St. Lorenz, von Herrn Gutsbesitzer Schneege-Gallhöfen eine sehr grosse Menge von Pferdegebissen, Steigbügeln, Lanzen etc. der jüngsten heidnischen Zeit, sowie einige Funde aus der Kaiserzeit; von Herrn William Frentzel-Beyme eine grosse Masse Bronzeschmucksachen von Oberhof bei Memel aus der jüngsten heidnischen Zeit. Infolge dieses äusserst wertvollen Geschenkes grub der Vortragende zu Oberhof weiter und beutete hier ein Gräberfeld aus den ersten Jahrhunderten v. Chr. und einen Begräbnisplatz der jüngsten Zeit zum Teil aus; ferner grub derselbe ein Gräberfeld zu Sdeden, Kreis Lyck, aus, von wo Herr Gutsbesitzer Hirsch-Rymken eine Menge sehr interessanter Objecte der ersten Jahrhunderte n. Chr. geschenkt hatte. Schliesslich grub der Vortragende noch den Rest eines Gräberfeldes zu Serappen, Kreis Fischhausen, aus, wo er schon früher Nachgrabungen veranstaltet hatte. Herr Dr. Schröder hat ein Gräberfeld zu Skatnick, Kreis Rössel, ausgebeutet und einige Objekte der ersten Jahrhunderte von Rössel erworben. Von der Kurischen Nehrung hat unser alter Sammler Herr Hermann Zander wieder eine Portion von Steingeräten und verzierten Scherben eingesandt und Herr Oberfischmeister Hauptmann v. Marée eine Reihe Altertümer, besonders aus der jüngeren Zeit, zum Geschenk gemacht.

Die für die Erkenntnis der Urgeschichte wichtigste Untersuchung[1]) ist die Ausgrabung von fünf Grabhügeln bei Rantau im Samlande, welche von unserem Museumskastellan Kretschmann im letzten Sommer geöffnet sind, und die in zwei von einander getrennten Gruppen lagen.

1) Beifolgender Auszug aus dem Vortrage soll nur in kurzem einen Überblick über diesen ungewöhnlich wichtigen Fund bieten. Eine ausführliche Publikation wird in einem der nächsten Hefte der Schriften erfolgen und zugleich eine eingehende Begründung der hier am Schlusse kurz angedeuteten chronologischen Fragen, welche mit der gesamten Stellung der nordischen Bronzekultur zusammenhängen. Ueber einige der im folgenden erörterten Punkte cf. Otto Tischler: Ostpreussische Grabhügel I in Schriften der Physikalisch-ökonomischen Gesellschaft XXVII (1886).

Zwei Hügel (IV und V) gehörten zu der im Samlande und sonst in Ostpreussen weit verbreiteten Klasse der Grabhügel mit Steinkisten, waren indessen schon stark zerstört. Nur einer enthielt noch in einer Steinkiste eine Aschenurne mit Deckel und in ihr eine eiserne Schwanenhalsnadel, also Gräber, die etwa dem Ende des fünften Jahrhunderts vor Chr. angehören.

Die anderen, zum Teil auch schon etwas angegriffenen Hügel hatten einen von dem der Steinkistenhügel ganz abweichenden Bau. Sie zeigten auf dem Grunde zwei konzentrische Kränze regelmässig gelegter grosser Steine von 18 und 15 m Durchmesser und innen als Kern einen Steinhaufen von 8 bis 11 m Durchmesser und ca. 2 m Höhe, der aus weit grösseren Steinen dichter zusammengepackt war als die anderen Steinhügel, wahrscheinlich nur aus Steinen, ohne Beimischung von Erde. Das Ganze war dann mit einem Erdhügel überwölbt. In Hügel I fand sich mitten unter diesem Steinkerne, allerdings nicht vollständig auf dem Boden, sondern über der untersten Steinschicht das Hauptgrab, sonst nur noch ein Grab unter dem Steinhaufen dicht am Rande. Diese Gräber enthielten keine Spur von Knochen, aber auch keine Brandreste, sie zeigten nur eine bräunliche Schicht, waren also jedenfalls Skelettgräber, bei denen jede Spur von Knochen schon verschwunden war, wie dies ja häufig vorkommt. Aussen auf dem Steinkerne lagen dann noch eine Menge ähnlicher Gräber, immer durch die bräunliche Schicht erkennbar und mit analogen Beigaben wie das centrale Grab. Im Hügel III lag in der Mitte des Kernes zwischen sehr grossen Steinen ebenfalls eine solche Grabstätte. Ueber diesen Gräbern dicht unter der Oberfläche des Erdmantels fanden sich in Hügel I eine Menge Aschenurnen ohne Deckel mit verbrannten Knochen gefüllt und Knochenhäufchen in freier Erde ohne jede Spur von Scherben. Diese offenbar jüngeren Urnen sind einigermassen denen aus Steinkisten ähnlich, zeigen aber doch einige Abweichungen. Leider enthielten sie ausser ein paar Bernsteinperlen gar keine Beigaben, lassen sich also zeitlich nicht mit voller Sicherheit unterbringen. Jedenfalls hat man in diesem Hügel aber Bestattungen aus verschiedenen Perioden vor sich, ältere Skelettgräber und jüngere Brandgräber. Die älteren Gräber sind alle sehr reich ausgestattet und haben eine Menge von Prachtbronzen geliefert, die zwar zum Teil sehr mürbe und zerbrochen waren, mehrfach auch nur durch Umgiessen mit Gips gerettet werden konnten, die aber vom Kastellan Kretschmann gut getränkt und wieder zusammengesetzt sind. Das centrale Grab von Hügel I enthielt ein kurzes Bronzeschwert, einen Bronzeaxthammer, eine Nadel mit umgebogenem Halse und seitlicher Öse und zwei Armbänder, gerippt und mit Sparrenverzierung und eine Anzahl dunkelblauer Glasperlen. In den anderen Gräbern fanden sich immer dieselben Ösennadeln mit kegelförmigem oder trompetenartigem Kopfe und ähnliche Armbänder, in zwei Gräbern breite massive Armbänder, aussen in quadratische Felder geteilt, welche durch tiefe Furchen abwechselnd horizontal und vertikal schraffiert sind. Mit diesen fand sich jedesmal eine Bronzenadel mit riesigem, ganz plattem Spiralkopf. Als fernere Beigaben sind zu erwähnen in Hügel III neben einer Ösennadel ein schönes reich verziertes Bronzemesser, ferner in Hügel II einige Reste von kleinen Doppelknöpfchen, auf deren einem ein vertieftes Kreuz mit Harz ausgefüllt ist, und in Hügel II kleine kegelförmige Knöpfe mit einer Öse an der Unterseite. Endlich fand sich eine Menge bearbeiteter Bernsteinstücke, flache viereckige Platten, Halbkugeln, auch mehr rundliche Perlen, die ersteren beiden Formen immer längs der platten Flächen mit einem langen schmalen Loche durchbohrt, ganz verschieden von einigen rundlichen Perlen aus einem der höheren Knochenhäufchen. Das ist also ein von dem der Steinkistengräber grundverschiedenes Inventar.

Die Leitform unter den Bronzen ist der Axthammer, eine Form, die fast identisch um die ganze Südseite der Ostsee herum gefunden ist.

Ganz ähnliche sind über 20 zu Nortycken, Kreis Fischhausen, im Samland, unter einem grossen Stein gefunden (zumeist im Provinzial-Museum — die Figur anbei), 1 in der Gegend von Rössel (Provinzial-Museum, Geschenk des Herrn Kreisschulinspektors Schlicht-Rössel), 1 vom Spirdingsee (Prussia) (also 4 Fundorte in Ostpreussen); 1 zu Solomiesk, Gouvernement Kowno, Russland; 1 zu Ostrowitt, Kreis Schwetz Westpreussen; 2 in der Mark (einer zu Schmarsow, Kreis Prenzlau); 3 in Meklenburg (zu Wiek, Basedow, Karow); 1 in Schleswig-Holstein; 2 in Jütland (im Banders Fjord und Börsmose).

Die Meklenburgischen Stücke geben für die Zeitstellung einen ungefähren Anhalt. Die von Basedow und Karow stammen aus Gräbern, welche mit dem berühmten von Peccatel [1]), denen von Friedrichsruhe, überhaupt mit den älteren Gräbern der Bronzezeit Meklenburgs gleichaltrig sind. Dieser Zeitabschnitt fällt mit den Perioden 2 und 3 in der Gliederung des Nordischen Bronzealters von Montelius [2]) zusammen, Perioden die der Vortragende eigentlich nicht auseinanderziehen möchte. In dem Inventar dieser glänzend ausgestatteten Grabhügel finden sich neben echt nordischen Stücken solche, die aus dem Süden direkt importiert sind, so besonders Gefässe aus Bronzeblech getrieben, vielfach durch von innen herausgeschlagene Buckel verziert, wie sie sich ähnlich in den älteren Gräbern der Oberitalischen Necropolen und zu Hallstadt finden. Ein anderes wichtiges Vergleichstück ist das in Meklenburg häufige Bronzeschwert mit platter Griffzunge und niedrigen Seitenrändern, welche in zwei Hörnchen auslaufen, so dass die Zunge oben ausgeschnitten endet, [3]) eine Form, die sich durch Süddeutschland bis nach Ungarn hineinerstreckt, ja sogar bis nach Mykenae. Ein den nordischen Formen ziemlich identisches Stück ist z. B. in Süd-Baden zu Nenzingen [4]) in einem Funde entdeckt, welcher wahrscheinlich in eine eigene Abteilung der südwestdeutschen Bronzezeit, die Periode der Brand-Urnenfelder [5]) zu setzen ist. Während diese Schwerter weniger chronologische Anhaltspunkte gewähren, leisten die getriebenen Metallgefässe mehr. Wir können danach die Periode von Peccatel wohl an den Anfang des 1. Jahrtausends v. Chr. setzen, jedenfalls weit vor die Mitte, und die Rantauer Hügel müssen dieser Glanzzeit nordischer Bronzekultur, der Periode von Peccatel gleichaltrig sein.

Nach diesem westlichen Gebiete weisen auch die mit Harz ausgelegten Doppelknöpfe [6]), die kleinen tutulusförmigen Knöpfe mit Öse. [7]) Ein anderer Teil der Bronzen hat seinesgleichen aber in einer entgegengesetzten Region. Die Nadeln mit umgebogenem kegelförmig verdicktem Kopf und seitlicher Öse finden sich besonders in Schlesien, weiter nach Nordwesten viel seltener, so dass sie Undset für eine besonders Schlesien [8]) eigentümliche Form ansah, während jetzt in Ostpreussen wohl schon mehr gefunden sind als in Schlesien und ebenso finden die breiten Armbänder mit abwechselnd schraffierten Quadraten ihre Analoga in Schlesien; es stossen in den Rantauer Hügeln also zwei verschiedene Kulturströmungen zusammen. Spezifisch Ostpreussisch sind die Nadeln mit sehr grossem plattem Spiralkopf, ganz verschieden von den jüngeren Spiral-Nadeln oder von denen anderer Bezirke, welche wohl eine analoge Rolle spielten wie die Nadeln mit grosser platter vertikaler Scheibe, die besonders in Meklenburg häufig sind.

Ähnliche Grabhügel mit Ösennadeln, verwandten Armbändern und derselben charakteristischen Form der Spiralnadel sind nur noch zu Slaszen, Kreis Memel, gefunden (Prussia-Museum).

Demnach ist auch in Ostpreussen eine ältere Bronzezeit in Gräbern nachgewiesen und dadurch eine grössere Gleichförmigkeit der Verhältnisse mit denen der westlicheren Gebiete herbeigeführt, es dürfte mithin die Urgeschichte des östlicheren Europas in einem wesentlich anderen Lichte erscheinen.

Der Hügel II ergab aber noch einen Fund ganz anderer Art. Zwischen dem ersten und zweiten Kreuz fand sich darin ein kleiner Steinhügel von 2 m Durchmesser, 1 m Höhe, unter welchem auf Steinen ca. 16 Urnen dicht an einander standen. Letztere enthielten sehr wenig geschmolzene Glasreste, welche aber doch, wie besonders die Form der Urnen — 2 aufeinanderstehende abgestumpfte Kegel, vielfach mit Doppelhenkeln — zeigten, dass diese Gräber der La Tène-Periode angehörten, also den letzten Jahrhunderten v. Chr. angehörten. Wie an anderem Orte [9]) gezeigt,

---

1) Jahrbücher des Vereins für Meklenburgische Geschichte und Altertumskunde IX (1844, 369 ff. X p. 275 ff. XLVII) 1882.

2) Montelius: Om Tidsbestämning inom Bronsålderen (St. Vitterhets och Antiquitets Akademiens Handlingar XIII Stockholm).

3) Wie Montelius: Om Tidsbestämning etc. Fig. 22.

4) Photographisches Album der Prähistorischen Ausstellung zu Berlin 1880 Sektion VII Tfl. 11.

5) O. Tischler in der Westdeutschen Zeitschrift für Geschichte und Kunst V (1886) p. 179.

6) Wie Montelius a. a. O. Fig. 66. Montelius Antiquités Suédoises Fig. 199.

7) Analog Montelius: Om Tidsbest. Fig. 38, 39.

8) Undset: Das erste Auftreten des Eisens in Nord-Europa p. 70. Tfl. XII.

9) Otto Tischler: Ostpreussische Grabhügel I p. 164 ff.

wurden in dieser Zeit gerade im Samlande die älteren Grabhügel benutzt, um die jüngeren Urnen in dicht gepackten Mengen am äusseren Rande beizusetzen, während von der Weichsel an nach Westen die La Tène-Gräber sich auf grossen Flachgräberfeldern finden, welche bis in die Römische Kaiserzeit hineinreichen, doch wohl ein ethnographischer Unterschied.

So werfen die Rantauer Hügel Licht gerade in einige der dunkelsten Abschnitte **Ostpreussischer Urgeschichte.**

Sitzung am 7. April.

Der **Vorsitzende** legte den neu erschienenen Band der „Schriften der physikalisch-ökonomischen Gesellschaft" — 27. Jahrgang, für 1886 — vor. Derselbe wird demnächst den Mitgliedern zugesandt werden.

Herr Professor Dr. **Ritthausen** hielt einen Vortrag über die **Alkaloide der Lupinen.** Derselbe gab eine Übersicht über die bisher ausgeführten Untersuchungen von Cassola (1835), Eichhorn (1867), welcher meist als Entdecker der Alkaloide bezeichnet wird, Beyer, Siewert, H. Schulze, Liebscher und Baumert; die Resultate der Untersuchungen Baumerts[1]) werden ausführlicher besprochen. Danach kommen in dem Samen der gelben Lupine (Lupinus luteus) nur zwei Alkoloide vor: Lupinin und Lupinidin.

Lupinin ist ein Alkaloid von ausgezeichnetem Kristallisationsvermögen, das auch schon Beyer, Siewert, Schulze und Liebscher unter Händen gehabt, ausser Liebscher in völliger Reinheit aber nicht erhalten haben. Es hat die der Formel C_{21} H_{40} N_2 O_2 entsprechende Zusammensetzung, krystallisiert rhombisch, meist in grossen und schönen Krystallen, ist rein völlig farblos und glashell, unveränderlich an der Luft, aber schon bei Temperaturen von 50—70 Gr. C. ziemlich flüchtig. Es schmilzt bei 67,5 bis 68,5 Gr., siedet bei 255—257 Gr., destilliert unverändert über und das Destillat erstarrt zu einer weissen, festen Krystallmasse. In Wasser, Alkohol, Äther, Benzol, Petroleumäther leicht löslich, wird es am besten immer aus Äther umkrystallisiert. Eine kalte, wässerige Lösung trübt sich beim Anwärmen auf 20 bis 30 Gr. C. Es ist eine starke Base, welche aus Salmiaklösung schon in der Kälte Ammoniak entwickelt, aus vielen Metallsalzen die Oxyde fällt, Fehlingsche Kupferlösung in der Hitze reduziert, durch die gewöhnlich benutzten Alkaloidreagentien gefällt wird, mit Säuren ohne Wasserabspaltung Salze bildet und sich wie eine zweisäurige Base verhält. Das charakteristische, aus alkoholischer Lösung in grossen roten Nadeln kristallisierende Platinsalz hat die Zusammensetzung C_{21} H_{40} N_2 O_2, 2HCl, Pt Cl_4. Über die physiologischen Wirkungen des Lupinins, soweit sie bis jetzt studiert sind, wird bemerkt, dass sie gleichwertig seien mit denen der Lupinenalkaloide überhaupt, welche lähmend auf gewisse Nervencentren wirken; quantitativ sei die Wirkung zehnmal schwächer als die des flüssigen Basengemenges. Die wässerige Lösung schmeckt sehr bitter. Die feste Substanz zeigt einen schwachen, widrigen, an Nikotin erinnernden Geruch.

In dem nicht krystallisierenden flüssigen Teil der Alkaloide, in welchem frühere Forscher mindestens zwei Alkaloide gefunden zu haben glaubten, ohne Beständigkeit in der Zusammensetzung nachzuweisen, fand Baumert nach eingehendem Studium nur das **sauerstofffreie Alkaloid Lupinidin,** dessen Zusammensetzung der Formel C_8 H_{15} N entspricht. Die Methoden der Darstellung im reinen Zustande und Trennung vom Lupinin, die Baumert anwandte, werden kurz besprochen und die eigenen Beobachtungen des Vortragenden in Bezug darauf erwähnt. Lupinidin ist ein dickflüssiges, in Wasser untersinkendes Öl von intensiv bitterem Geschmack und unangenehmem, schierlings-

1) **Baumert.** Das Lupinin. Ein Beitrag zur Kenntnis der Lupinenalkaloide, in Nobbe. landwirtschaftliche Versuchsstation Band 27, Seite 15—64.

Baumert. Untersuchungen über den flüssigen Teil der Alkaloide des Lupinus luteus, Ebendaselbst. 30, 295—330; 31, 139—158. Ferner Liebigs Annalen der Chemie 214, 361; 224, 313; 225, 365; 227, 207.

ähnlichem Geruch, sehr unbeständig, oxydiert sich leicht bei gewöhnlicher Temperatur und färbt sich dann dunkel- bis schwarzrot unter Entwickelung des Schierlingsgeruchs. Den Siedepunkt fand Baumert nicht konstant, im Wasserstoffstrome destillierte es von 250—320 Gr. über, ohne einen bestimmten Siedepunkt zu zeigen; die Destillate lieferten jedoch völlig einheitliche Salze, von denen das im Wasser schwer und im Alkohol ganz unlösliche Platinsalz $(C_8 H_{15} N, HCl)_2 Pt Cl_4 + 2 H_2 O$, bemerkenswert ist, und das in absolutem Alkohol unlösliche schwefelsaure Salz von der Zusammensetzung $C_8 H_{15} N, H_2 SO_4$. Die in längere Zeit aufbewahrtem Lupinidin entstandenen blättrigen Krystalle von der Zusammensetzung $C_8 H_{17} NO$ hält Baumert für das Hydrat des Lupinidins $= C_8 H_{15} N + H_2O$. Erwähnt werden die Erfahrungen des Dr. Kobert über die physiologischen Wirkungen des Lupinidins, nach denen dies ähnlich dem amerikanischen Pfeilgift, dem Curarin, wirkt, jedoch erst in viel grösserer Dosis. Auf Warmblüter soll es, in Dosen von 10—20 mg ins Blut oder unter die Haut gespritzt, fast wirkungslos sein. Mit einer Quantität von $^1/_2$ g des Alkaloidgemenges töteten Kühn und Liebscher ein Kaninchen, mit einer Menge gleich der in etwa 2,25 kg Lupinenheu enthaltenen ein Schaf. Vortragender hat aus dem mit reinem Spiritus dargestellten Extrakt von 100 kg gelben Lupinen 270 g reines Lupinin und ca. 350 g schwefelsaures Lupinidin erhalten und nimmt an, dass die Alkaloide als in Spiritus leicht lösliche citronensaure Salze enthalten seien, da die Samen sehr reich an Citronensäure befunden wurden.

In den Samen der blauen Lupine (Lup. angustifolius) fand Hagen[1]) ein einziges, nicht krystallisierendes Alkaloid von anderer Zusammensetzung als die Alkaloide der gelben Lupinen; er fand die der Formel $C_{15} H_{25} N_2 O$ entsprechende Zusammensetzung und nennt es Lupanin. Dasselbe ist, wie es scheint, nicht flüchtig, zeigt schierlingsähnlichen Geruch, bildet mit Säuren krystallisierbare Salze und besitzt gleich den Alkaloiden der gelben Lupinen stark basische Eigenschaften.

Den Gehalt an Alkaloiden fand man[2]) für

Lup. Cruikschankii	1 %
Lup. luteus	0,7—0,8 %
Lup. albus	0,59 %
Lup. polyphyllus	0,48 %
Lup. hirsutus nur	0,02 %

Bei Darstellung in grösserem Massstabe erhielt man aus gelben Lupinen nur 0,38 bis 0,45 % vom Gewicht der Samen, aus blauen (angustifolius) nur 0,22 %. Aus den zur Gewinnung der Alkaloide nach Zusatz reichlicher Mengen Kalihydrat mit Petroleumäther behandelten Massen des alkoholischen Extraktrückstandes wurden noch beträchtliche Mengen krystallisierender Substanz gewonnen, deren chemische Natur bis jetzt indessen nicht festgestellt werden konnte. Da diese krystallisierenden Flüssigkeiten überaus bitter schmecken, könnten sie möglicherweise den schon immer gesuchten Körper enthalten, welchen man als Erreger der gefürchteten Krankheit der Schafe, der Lupinose, betrachtet und welchem Professor Kühn in Halle bereits den Namen Icterogen beigelegt hat.

Hierauf entspann sich eine lebhafte Diskussion. Der Vorsitzende machte darauf aufmerksam, dass die Lupinose, deren Ursache uns noch unbekannt ist, mehr den Charakter einer Blutvergiftung als den einer Vergiftung durch Alkaloide trage. Herr Dr. Seydel teilte mit, dass ihm die Entbitterung der Lupinen durch heisses Wasser und Zusatz von schwachen Säuren immer gut gelungen sei, und Herr Ritthausen hielt diese Entbitterungsmethode auch für eine der besten. Durch ähnliche Methoden der Entbitterung erzielten auch Herr Kowalewski und Herr Dr. Gisevius vorzügliche Resultate. Herr Professor R. Caspary teilt ferner mit, dass in Italien häufig die Samen von Lupinus albus, nachdem sie in Salzwasser geweicht sind, von Männern, die sie trocken in der Tasche tragen, gegessen werden.

---

1) Max Hagen über Lupanin, ein Alkaloid aus dem Samen der blauen Lupine, Lupinus angustifolius: Liebigs Annalen 230, 367.

2) Dr. E. Täuber, über den Alkaloidgehalt verschiedener Lupinenarten und Varietäten: landwirthschaftliche Versuchsstationen Bd. 29, 451.

Dann berichtete Herr Professor Dr. Ritthausen ferner noch über den von ihm aus Baumwollsamenkuchen dargestellten Zucker, welchen er als identisch mit dem von Johnson und Berthelot aus australischer Eucalyptus-Manna dargestellten, Melitose[1]) genannten Zucker bezeichnete. Tollens und Scheibler erkannten, dass derselbe in allen Eigenschaften mit einem von ihnen aus Rübenrohzucker und Melasse erhaltenen, von Loiseau schon beschriebenen und Raffinose benannten Zucker übereinstimmt. Derselbe verhält sich ähnlich dem Rohrzucker, der Saccharose und hat die Zusammensetzung $C_{12} H_{22} O_{11} + 3 H_2 O$, welche Formel Tollens und Scheibler in $C_{18} H_{32} O_{16} + 5 H_2 O$ umänderten; er ist weniger löslich in Wasser als Rohrzucker, schmeckt sehr schwach süss und dreht die Polarisationsebene weit mehr nach rechts als Saccharose; sein spezifisches Drehungsvermögen $(\alpha)D$ wurde übereinstimmend = 104° gefunden, während das des Rohrzuckers ca. 66,5° beträgt. Aus wässriger Lösung krystallisiert er langsam in feinen Nadeln, aus heiss gesättigter alkoholischer Lösung in langen, oft zu prachtvollen Rosetten vereinigten Nadeln. v. Lippmann erwies die Proexistenz der Melitose in den Zuckerrüben, Sullivan das Vorkommen in Gerstenkörnern. Die Krystallisation des Rohrzuckers wird bei einem Gehalt an Melitose wesentlich verändert und die Süsse beträchtlich vermindert, die Polarisation erhöht, so dass die Bestimmung des Rohrzuckers durch Polarisation mittelst Saccharometern unbrauchbare Resultate liefert.

Endlich erwähnt Herr Professor Ritthausen ein neues, von ihm nachgewiesenes Vorkommen des von Scheibler entdeckten und bisher nur als Bestandteil der Rüben bekannten Betain ($C_5 H_{11} NO_2 + H_2O$) in Baumwollensamen, die diese schwache, leicht krystallisirende Base in nicht unbedeutender Menge enthalten.[2]) — Alle besprochenen Krystalle und chemischen Präparate wurden von Herrn Ritthausen der Gesellschaft vorgelegt und herumgereicht.

Herr Professor Dr. Samuel sprach „über die Grenzen der Erblichkeit", und zwar über den allgemein biologischen Theil dieses Problems. Wir müssen uns hier auf die Wiedergabe des Gedankenganges beschränken. Die Vererbungsfähigkeit ist dauernd nur innerhalb derselben Art möglich, findet aber auch in dieser an allzu naher Verwandschaft ihre Grenzen. Die Vererblichkeit bestimmter Merkmale und Charaktere erfolgt am sichersten bei beiderseitiger Vererbung derselben durch viele Generationen hindurch, doch ausnahmslos auch hier nicht. Nach einseitiger Vererbung sind alle denkbaren Eventualitäten auch wirklich beobachtet. Unter ihnen ist hervorzuheben einerseits „die intermediäre Vererbung" mit ziemlich gleicher Mischung der gekreuzten Charaktere in allen Nachkommen, andererseits „die disparate Vererbung" mit ausgeprägter Wiederholung der einseitig vererbten Merkmale, dann jedoch nur in einzelnen Nachkommen. Nie schlägt jedoch ein Nachkomme ganz ausschliesslich nach Vater oder Mutter, stets, wenn auch oft schwach, ist der anderseitige Einfluss nachweisbar. Angeborene Merkmale gehen zum Teil in vererbbare über, im Leben erworbene nur unter bestimmten Verhältnissen. Über den pathalogischen Teil des Problems, „die Erblichkeit von Krankheiten und Missbildungen" wird der Redner in der medicinischen Gesellschaft Bericht erstatten. Die Untersuchungen des Vortragenden sollen demnächst n Virchows Archiv für pathologische Anatomie und Physiologie veröffentlicht werden.

---

1) H. Ritthausen über Melitose aus Baumwollensamen: Journal für praktische Chemie [2] Bd. 29, 351.

2) Ritthausen und Dr. Felix Weger, über Betain aus Pressrückständen der Baumwollensamen: Journal für praktische Chemie [2] Bd. 30, 32.

Sitzung am 5. Mai 1887.

Herr Dr. Jentzsch sprach über den neuesten Standpunkt der geologischen Kartierung Preussens (unter Vorlage eines kolorierten Übersichtstableaus und zahlreicher Probeblätter der einzelnen Kartenwerke).

Der kartierten Fläche nach ist das bedeutendste derselben die auf Kosten des Handelsministers unter Leitung v. Dechens in 1 : 80 000 aufgenommene Karte der Rheinprovinz und Westfalens. 34 Blätter erschienen 1855—1866, ein 35. später mit Benutzung der weiterhin zu erwähnenden Spezialaufnahmen der geologischen Landesanstalt; ausserdem 1866 eine Übersichtskarte in 1 : 500 000, von welcher, wie von mehreren Einzelblättern, eine zweite, verbesserte Auflage erschien.

Das zweitgrösste kartierte Gebiet ist dasjenige, welches in Ost- und Westpreussen in 1:100 000 durch die Physikalisch-ökonomische Gesellschaft 1865—1879 aufgenommen ist, eine Leistung, auf welche unsere Gesellschaft wohl mit Befriedigung zurückblicken darf. 15 Blätter sind bisher publiciert, ein 16. (Frauenburg), durch Berendt bearbeitet, ist soeben im Druck vollendet. Es wurde vorgezeigt und kann von den Mitgliedern zu ermässigtem Preis bezogen werden. Ein 17. (Wormditt), welches 1879 durch Dr. Klebs aufgenommen wurde, wird gleichfalls hoffentlich in nicht zu ferner Zeit erscheinen können. Damit muss diese Karte vorläufig ihren Abschluss erreichen. Sie findet aber ihre Fortsetzung in den genau anschliessenden Spezialaufnahmen der königlichen geologischen Landesanstalt, von denen unten die Rede sein wird.

Das drittgrösste geologisch kartierte Gebiet ist Oberschlesien, von F. Römer, in 12 Blättern, Berlin 1865; nächstdem Niederschlesien, von E. Beyrich, G. Rose, J. Roth und W. Runge, aufgenommen 1841—1860 (mit einer Übersicht von 1: 400 000 von Roth); endlich die Provinz Sachsen von Magdeburg bis zum Harze von J. Ewald. Alle diese Aufnahmen sind vom Handelsministerium veranlasst und im Maassstabe 1 : 100 000 gehalten.

Bei ihrer Herstellung ergab sich schliesslich die Notwendigkeit, einen grösseren Maassstab, nämlich 1 : 25 000, anzuwenden. Die Einführung desselben durch E. Beyrich vor nunmehr genau einem Vierteljahrhundert bezeichnet die Anfänge der geologischen Landesanstalt, welche in der Ausführung dieser Karte über das gesamte Staatsgebiet und die thüringischen Kleinstaaten eine grosse Aufgabe übernommen hat.

Ein Blick auf das Übersichtsnetz zeigte die bisher publicierten kartierten Flächen. Der Harz und Thüringen bilden das Hauptgebiet, nächstdem der südliche Teil der Rheinprovinz (Trier-Saarbrücken), der Taunus und kleinere Gebiete in Hessen und Schlesien. Im Flachlande sind 36 Blätter um Berlin publiciert und von dort reichen die Aufnahmen bereits nördlich bis zur Uckermark und westlich bis in die Provinz Sachsen. Endlich sind in unseren Provinzen im unmittelbaren Anschluss an die Karte der Gesellschaft zwei Arbeitsgebiete in Angriff genommen: in Ostpreussen die Gegend von Heilsberg, Bartenstein, Schippenbeil, Rössel und Bischofstein; in Westpreussen diejenige von Marienwerder, Mewe, Neuenburg, Garnsee und Riesenburg.

Die soeben erschienene Sektion Frauenburg ist von hohem Interesse. Sie zeigt die Frische Nehrung mit den mehrfach veränderten früheren „Tiefen"; die Mündungen der Passarge, der Nogat und Elbinger Weichsel mit dem seit 1644 angeschwemmten Neuland; endlich den Nordabfall der Trunzer Höhe mit zahlreichen Durchbrüchen der Braunkohlenformation, mit dem eigentümlichen, vom Redner 1876 zuerst unterschiedenen Deckthon, vor allem aber mit den in Europa einzigen Aufschlüssen des die Yoldia-Muschel führenden altglacialen Cyprinenthons.

Herr Dr. Jentzsch trug hierauf einige Mitteilungen aus dem Provinzialmuseum vor.

Aus dem oben erwähnten Thon, den derselbe kurz als „Elbinger Yodialthon" bezeichnet, hat Redner im Laufe der Jahre eine bedeutende Anzahl von Knochen erlangt und bestimmt. Es sind (mit Hinzuziehung gewisser eng verbundener Süsswasserbänke) die Gattungen Ursus, Phoca, Equus, Bos, Bison, Cervus, Elephas, Rhinoceros, Delphinus und Gadus vertreten; daneben finden sich an Conchylien Yoldia truncata, Cyprina islandica, Astarte borealis, Dreissena polymorpha, Valvata piscinalis; ausserdem zahlreiche zumeist marine Diatomeen, ferner Coniferen-Pollen und viele Hölzer, unter denen nach Conwentz auch Laubholz sich befindet. Von den Knochen sind am häufigsten diejenigen von Gadus, dem Schellfisch, nächstdem die von Phoca, dem Seehund. Von letzterem besitzen wir 4 Unterkiefer, 2 Scapulae, 6 Humeri, 6 Radien, 7 Metacarpen, 8 Phalangen, 4 Femur-Fragmente, 5 Tibien, 3 Fibulae, 3 Talus, 3 Calcanei, 1 Naviculare, 6 Metatarsen und mehrere Wirbel, worunter 1 Epistropheus. Dieses reiche Material gestattete eine specifische Bestimmung, und diese ergab: Phoca groenlandica, den Typus der Gattung Pagophilus. Diese Bestimmung ergänzt und bestätigt auf das erfreulichste das Bild eines arktischen Klimas, welches Redner im Jahre 1876 zuerst auf die Auffindung der Yoldia gegründet hatte. — Ferner sind dem Museum zahlreiche Bohrproben zugegangen: Von Herrn Bohrunternehmer Pöpcke, vertreten durch Herrn Ingenieur Bieske hier: 1. Auf Haltestelle Vogelsang zwischen Braunsberg und Mehlsack 116 m Diluvium direkt über weisser Kreide. 2. In Angerburg 107 m Diluvium über Quarzsanden der Braunkohlenformation, völlig gleich den in gleicher Tiefe in Feste Boyen bei Lötzen erbohrten. Dieser Punkt bezeichnet den nordöstlichsten Aufschluss des Tertiärs in der Provinz. Da in Insterburg bereits Kreide direkt unter Diluvium liegt, so ist zu vermuten, dass irgendwo zwischen Insterburg und Angerburg die Bernsteinformation an das Diluvium herantritt, wodurch (nebenbei gesagt) der gerade dort erfolgte Fund des berühmten grossen Bernsteinstücks von Stannaitschen in ein neues Licht tritt. 3. Fort Kalgen bei Königsberg 300—306 m Tiefe, das tiefste in Ostpreussen ausgeführte Bohrloch, zuletzt in Kreideschichten stehend. 4. Kortau bei Allenstein 76 m diluvial mit einer bei ca. 11 m Tiefe liegenden, reichlich Bernstein und Sprockholz führenden Schicht, welche in gleicher Tiefe auch von einem früheren Bohrloch getroffen wurde, daher dort weiter verbreitet sein dürfte. 5. Allenstein Kavalleriekaserne 38 m. 6. Mertinsdorf bei Allenstein 43 m. 7. Annaberg bei Melno (Westpreussen) 72 m. No. 5—7 sämtlich diluvial. 8. Karolinenhorst in Pommern 152 m Diluvium über Tertiär. 9. Leobschütz in Schlesien paläozoische Schichten. Von Herrn Bohrunternehmer Blasendorf in Berlin und Osterode: 10. Drews Gehöft in Osterode 55 m. 11. Scharnau 11 m. 12. Lindenburg bei Ortelsburg 38 m. 13. Neidenburg drei Bohrungen von 10,10 und 5 m Tiefe. 14. Carthaus 83 m. No. 10—14 durchweg diluvial. 15. Von Herrn Abtheilungsbaumeister Holtmann in Lautenburg: 37 alluviale und diluviale Proben von den Fundierungsbohrungen der Eisenbahn Jablonowo-Soldau. 16. Von Herrn Baumeister Peveling: 12 diluviale Proben aus 5—48 m Tiefe aus der Provinzialirrenanstalt bei Landsberg a. W. 17. Von Herrn Bauinspektor Beckershaus in Carthaus: diluviale Proben aus dem dortigen Gerichtsgebäude, bis 83 m Tiefe. 18. Von Herrn Bohrunternehmer Studti in Pr. Holland: Bohrproben vom Terrain der Aktiengesellschaft für Leinenindustrie in Elbing 33 m Alluvium und Diluvium; 33 bis 39 m Tertiär mit schlechten Braunkohlen, ein für die geognostische Karte der Provinz wichtiger Aufschluss! Von sonstigen Objekten haben geschenkt: 19. Herr Direktor Dr. Albrecht: Frucht des Elaeocarpus Albrechti von Rauschen; das typische Stück, auf welches Professor O. Heer diese Species gegründet hat, mithin eine sehr wertvolle Bereicherung unserer Sammlung. 20. Herr Bildhauer Eckart: Abdruck eines Stammes (anscheinend Cycadee) aus dem Sandstein von Obernkirchen bei Minden, dem Material der Figuren auf der Universität. 21. Herr Domänenpächter Kners-Neugut bei Hirschfeld, Kreis Pr. Holland: 11 daselbst ausgepflügte Zähne von Equus Caballus. 22. Herr Literat Müller: verkieseltes Holz von Königsberg. 23. Herr Geheimrat Professor Römer in Breslau: 12 grosse Granitkrystalle von dem merkwürdigen Granitfund auf der Dominsel in Breslau, welchen Römer in der Zeitschrift der Deutschen geologischen Gesellschaft, den Abhandlungen der schlesischen Gesellschaft für vaterländische Kultur und den Verhandlungen der Wiener kaiserlich königlichen geologischen Reichsanstalt 1886 beschrieben hat. 24. Von Herrn Geheimen Sanitätsrat Schiefferdecker: einige moderne Renntierknochen zum Vergleich. 25. Von Herrn Rittergutsbesitzer Strüvy-Wokellen: ein verkieseltes Holz, ein Orthoceras regulare und 7 Stücke gelben Fayencemergel mit schönen ringförmigen, durch Wurzelfasern bedingten Zeichnungen. 26. Von Herrn Buchhalter Vorbringer: einen Haifischzahn aus der Bernsteinerde von Sassau und mehrere Geschiebe. 27. Von besonders hohem Werte für die Gesellschaft ist endlich ein Geschenk Sr. Excellenz des Herrn Kultusministers Dr. von Gossler: Bernstein mit Sprockholz, gefunden 20 m tief beim Fundieren des neuen Reichstagsgebäudes in Berlin — wie Se. Excellenz treffend bemerkt: im alten Oderbett. In der That floss ja am Schlusse der Diluvialzeit die Oder im jetzigen Spreethal durch Berlin, um sich bei Fehrbellin mit der weiter nördlich von Bromberg, Landsberg und Küstrin herkommenden Weichsel zu einem grossen, der Nordsee zufliessenden Ost-Weststrome zu vereinen. Jedes fliessende Wasser bewirkt eine mechanische Sonderung der Materialien und führt daher, wenn z. B. Bernstein in letzterem enthalten ist, diesen an gewissen Stellen zusammen. Eine weitere Frage entsteht nun: wie kam überhaupt Bernstein in die Mark? In dieser Beziehung sind zunächst folgende Citate über das Vorkommen des Bernsteins in und bei Berlin von Interesse.

Klöden, Beiträge zur mineralogischen und geognostischen Kenntnis der Mark Brandenburg, 8. Stück. Berlin 1830. S. 7. „In den Lehmgruben bei Berlin fanden sich öfters einzelne Stücke von Bernstein, und auch beim Brunnengraben ist er in der Stadt mehrmals gefunden worden, z. B. auf dem Hofe der Porzellanmanufactur im Jahre 1820, im Decker'schen Garten etc. Auch in der Panke ist er in neueren Zeiten vorgekommen. Am meisten hat er sich bis jetzt in der Lehmgrube am Kreuzberge gezeigt; die ganze Hügelkette, welche die Spree von hier bis westlich von Charlottenburg und gegen Spandau hin begleitet, scheint Bernstein zu enthalten, und es sind dort öfter Stücke gefunden worden." S. 1—9 zahlreiche Funde aus der Mark, in grosser Menge 1738/41 bei Oranienburg.

Berendt, Nordwesten Berlins. 1877. S. 143 und Laufer, Erläuterungen zu Blatt Oranienburg. Berlin 1879. S. 9. In der Sektion Oranienburg (am Ruppiner Canal westlich und nordwestlich Friedenthal bei Sachsenhausen, sowie bei Lehnitz) wurden im Thalsande Nester von Sprockholz mit Bernstein gefunden, meist in der Tiefe des Grundwasserstandes.

Lossen, Boden der Stadt Berlin. 1879. S. 1026. „Dagegen fehlt es in dem groben und mittelkörnigen Thalsande nicht an grösseren und feineren eingeschwemmten Braunkohlenresten und an Bernstein welche tertiäre Trümmer also hier auf dritter Lagerstätte umgelagert ruhen; ja bei Anlage der Kanalisation-Pumpstation in der Schönberger Strasse fand sich eine ganz ansehnliche Zahl Bernsteinstücke in einer unregelmässig nestartigen Zusammenschwemmung von Braunkohlehaufwerk eingebettet." S. 1028. „Das nachweisbare Maximum (der Mächtigkeit des Thalsandes) geht nicht über 9,4 m hinaus; 8 m Mächtigkeit sind schon eine grosse Seltenheit." S. 907. Petrographie der Diluvialgebilde: „Fügen wir noch hinzu, dass hie und da citronen- bis honiggelbe, aus der unteroligocänen Tertiärformation ausgewaschene Bernsteinkörnchen zwischen den andern Sandkörnern vorkommen, ganz analog dem Vorkommen grösserer Bernsteingeschiebe, so ist damit die Aufzählung der sandigen Bestandmassen des Diluvium beendigt."

Remelé, Zeitschrift der Deutschen geologischen Gesellschaft. XXVII. 1875. S. 710 berichtete „über das Auftreten einer diluvialen Bernstein führenden Schicht inmitten des oberen Geschiebemergels bei Neustadt-Eberswalde, unter Vorlegung von Proben dieser Schicht, sowie von darin gefundenen Bernsteinstücken und nordischen Geschieben. Es besteht dieselbe aus einem glaukonitischen, kalkreichen und etwas thonhaltigen Sand, der an Aussehen und Zusammensetzung dem marinen Grünsande der Unteroligocän, welcher im Samlande als die eigentliche Bernsteinerde erkannt wurde, sehr ähnlich ist, und ebenso wie letzterer den Bernstein in bedeutenden Quantitäten und ganz gleichmässig eingelagert enthält".

Beyrich bemerkt zu dem Vortrage: „dass der Sand jedenfalls tertiär sei und dass man die Erscheinung vergleichen könne mit dem lagerartigen Einschluss der mächtigen Scholle von Schreibkreide im Diluvium bei Stettin".

Bemerkenswert ist überhaupt die weite und allgemeine Verbreitung des Bernsteins im Diluvium des norddeutschen Flachlandes. Göppert kannte allein aus Schlesien 200 Fundorte; Herr Dr. Jentzsch hat ihn selbst südlich von Leipzig gefunden und westwärts ist er als Diluvialgeschiebe bis nach Holland verbreitet. Für ein so weit verbreitetes Diluvialgeschiebe darf man schwerlich ein so kleines Ausgangsgebiet wie das nordwestliche Samland und dessen allernächste Umgebung annehmen. Vielmehr können wir vermuten, dass das Bernstein führende marine Tertiär in einem ausgedehnten annähernd ostwestlich streichenden Streifen vorhanden war. Die vorläufig bernsteinfreien, aber im Übrigen der samländischen Bernsteinformation gleichenden Grünsande von Kalthof bei Pr. Holland, Stuhm, Watzmirs Kreis Pr. Stargard, Klempin, Senslau und Neukau im Danziger Kreis, Rügenwalde in Pommern geben dafür Anhaltspunkte; die Berstein führende Grünsandscholle von Eberswalde, in deren Nähe Tertiär ansteht, dürfte einem pommerschen oder nordmärkischen Flötz entstammen, und dass auch noch weiter westlich dasselbe Meer wogte, deuten die gleichaltrigen Grünsande an, welche in Spandau unter dem Septarienthon erbohrt sind und am nördlichen Harzrande auf Phosphorite abgebaut werden. Diese südlichen Ausläufer sind aber bernsteinfrei: das „ostpreussische Gold" kommt nur dem nördlichen Rande jenes grossen Grünsandgebietes zu, als der damaligen Küste des skandinavischen Festlandes, auf welchem der Bernsteinwald gegrünt hatte.

Hierauf trägt Herr Professor Dr. Saalschütz seine Untersuchungen zur Kantschen Kosmogonie vor. Dieselben sind unter den Abhandlungen dieses Heftes von Seite 73 an abgedruckt.

Sitzung am 2. Juni 1887.

Herr Dr. Klebs hielt einen Vortrag über die Farbe und Imitation des Bernsteins. In den ungeheuern Quantitäten Bernstein, welche gegenwärtig produziert werden, zeigt sich im grossen und ganzen nur wenig Abwechselung in der Farbe. Wir haben es eigentlich nur mit gelben und gelblichen Nuancen zu thun, selbst die äusserst selten vorkommenden blauen und grünen Bernsteine zeigen bei einer genaueren Untersuchung, dass sie wohl auch in diese Farbenreihe gehören.

Die Grundsubstanz des Bernsteins ist ein rein gelbes klares Harz, welches ausser etwaigen organischen resp. anorganischen Einschlüssen keinerlei innere Struktur zeigt, sondern in seiner ganzen Masse vollständig glasartig amorph ist. Die Farbe dieser rein gelben Grundsubstanz schwankt zwischen fast wasserhell und rotbraun. Aus dieser klaren Substanz sind nun durch eingeschlossene kleine Bläschen alle trüben Bernsteinvarietäten entstanden. Man unterscheidet im Handel derer fünf; erstens klar, zweitens flohmig, ein klarer Stein mit schwach wolkigen Trübungen; drittens Bastard, ein satt trüber Bernstein; viertens knochig, ein undurchsichtiger noch gut polierbarer Stein; fünftens schaumig, undurchsichtig und keine Politur annehmend. Je nachdem sich nun Übergänge oder Mengungen unter diesen Typen zeigen, entsteht eine weitere grosse Menge von Bezeichnungen wie klar-flohmig, flohmig-klar, flohmiger Bastard, knochiger Bastard u. s. w. Schon Helm macht in den Schriften der Danziger naturforschenden Gesellschaft von 1876 auf die Bläschen im Bernstein aufmerksam, aber in so kurzer Weise, dass ich, um wirklich brauchbare Resultate zu erlangen, gezwungen war, recht eingehende Untersuchungen anzustellen. Die hier nur in grösster Kürze gegebenen Mitteilungen sind das Resultat von mindestens 900 Zählungen, welche bei 224 mikroskopischen Dünnschliffen aus Bernstein und 40 aus Walchowit, Siegborgit und anderen fossilen und recenten Harzen angestellt sind.

Der Durchmesser der Bläschen, welche die Färbung des Bernstein bedingen, schwankt von 0,0008 bis 0,02 mm. Die Grösse und Dichtigkeit, in welcher sie liegen, erzeugen die verschiedenen Varietäten. Am kleinsten sind die Bläschen beim gewöhnlichen knochigen Bernstein von 0,0008 bis 0,004 mm, beim Bastard erreichen sie 0,0025 bis 0,012 mm und beim flohmigen Bernstein 0,02 mm Durchmesser. Von diesen kleinen Bläschen liegen nun in einem Quadratmillimeter Knochen 900 000, im Bastard 2500, im flohmigen Bernstein 600 Stück. Eine Reihe von Beobachtungen namentlich der seltneren Knochenvarietäten mit grösseren Bläschen ergaben das Resultat, dass ein Bernstein nur dann reiner Knochen ist, wenn der Gesamtinhalt der Blasenquerschnitte 0,42 bis 0,52 ist, dass er Bastard, wenn derselbe 0,25 und flohmig ist, wenn derselbe 0,1 des Gesamtinhalts der Bernsteinfläche beträgt.

Die sonst noch vorkommenden charakteristischen Bernsteinvarietäten reihen sich in diese Folge ein; so stellt sich dem Aussehen nach der sogenannte blaue Bernstein zwischen Flohmig und Bastard, die mikroskopische Untersuchung bestätigt es, da der Gesamtinhalt der Blasenquerschnitte 0,15 der Gesamtfläche beträgt. Der von mir seiner Zeit abgetrennte Halbbastard steht zwischen Bastard und Knochen, die Blasenquerschnitte betragen 0,37 der Gesamtfläche. Wenn wir nach diesen Erörterungen uns die Frage vorlegen, wie die eigentliche Bernsteinbildung vor sich gegangen sein mag, so ist es vor allem noch nötig, die wenn auch äusserst geringen Beobachtungen an lebenden Planzen näher ins Auge zu fassen. Einzelne Holzpflanzen scheiden besondere Sekrete ab, die an der Luft erhärten; so ist für die Koniferen das Harz (resp. Terpentin) charakteristisch, für die Mimosaceen, Amygdalaceen und andere der Gummi, die Tamarisken und Eschen liefern Manna, Astragalus Tragacanth.

Diese Sekrete, im besonderen die Harze, sind teils als Nebenprodukte des pflanzlichen Stoffwechsels aufgefasst, ich möchte sagen Schutzprodukte, welche durch ein überreiches Zuströmen von Säften nach einem bestimmten Pflanzenteil durch abnorme Umänderung des Stoffes entstanden. Teils aber sprechen verschiedene Beobachtungen dafür, dass sie Degradationsprodukte sind, weil die vollständigen Übergänge aus parenchymatischen Zellen bis zum Harz (Harzgallen) sich verfolgen lassen.

(Ratzeburg, Waldverderbnis Band II, Seite 4. Karsten Bot. Zeitung 1857. Seite 316.) Bei den Koniferen findet sich der Terpentin normal in den Harzgängen der Markstrahlen und in Intercellularen in der Wachstumsrichtung verlaufenden Gängen und bisweilen noch in Harzzellen; die beiden letzteren sollen nach der Ansicht einzelner (Ratzeburg) schon eine Krankheitsfolge sein. Aus diesen senkrechten und wagrechten Gängen fliesst nun das Harz bei jeder Verwundung des Stammes aus oder infiltriert das im Absterben begriffene Holz, indem es an Stelle des eingetrockneten und nicht mehr neu zugeführten Saftes tritt. Soweit meine Beobachtungen an lebenden Koniferen reichen, sind die Harze der Gänge und Kanäle durchweg klar, das ausgeflossene Harz dagegen durch die Beimengung des Saftes der Zellen stets trübe. Nur wenn durch allmäliges Hinsterben und dadurch Eintrocknen der die Wunde umgebenden Zellen dieser Zufluss aufhört, oder wenn die Sonnenhitze direkt aus abgestorbenem Holz, sei es den Gängen oder den infiltrierten Partieen, Harz entlockt, ist dieses klar. Die Beschreibung eines solchen Harzergusses aus lebendem Holz ist folgende: im August 1881 schälte ich an einer Abies ein Stück Rinde von 10 cm im Quadrat bis zum Splint aus und durchschnitt diesen an einzelnen Stellen mit feinen Schnitten bis tief ins Holz; die Folge davon war, dass die Stelle nass wurde. Nach acht Tagen schwitzten an den Schnittstellen feine Harztröpfchen aus. Nach einem Jahre war die ganze Stelle mit einer Borke von gelbweissem, trübem, knollig geflossenem Harz in einer Durchschnittsdicke von etwa 4 mm bedeckt. 1884 zeigte die Harzschicht dieselbe Beschaffenheit, nur betrug die Dicke 6 mm und an dem oberen Rande des ausgeschnittenen Stückes hatte sich ein Harzwulst gebildet, welcher nach oben einen Teil der alten Rinde bedeckte. Dieser Ausschnitt war mit vielen andern bei andern Bedingungen, an der Südseite eines Stammes, 1 m über dem Boden (Oberkrume: sandiger Lehm; Untergrund: undurchlässiger Mergel), angelegt, und vollständig im Schatten. 1884 lichtete ich die herabhängenden Äste und einiges Unterholz, so dass der Ausschnitt in der Sonne lag. 1886 zeigte das Harz eine ganz andere Beschaffenheit; die Überwallung des oberen Randes war umgeschmolzen und hing in langgezogenen Tropfen und Fäden, die zum Teil ganz klar waren, herab. Die Harzplatte dagegen war stellenweise auch in Fäden herabgeflossen, sonst nur in den äussern Millimetern klarer geworden. Ganz ähnlich erkläre ich den Vorgang beim Fluss des Bernsteinharzes. Ursprünglich als klare Masse im Stamm enthalten, floss es in zweifacher Weise aus: einmal gemischt mit dem Zellsaft in der Gestalt, in welcher wir es heute als knochigen Bernstein durch die Unzahl der Jahre erhärtet kennen, das andere Mal leicht flüssiger, schneller erhärtend, ohne Zellsaft, aus totem Holz oder toten Stammteilen, als klarer Bernstein, die heutige Schlaube. Durch die Einwirkung der Sonne entstanden dann aus dem noch weichen knochigen Bernstein durch Zusammenfliessen der kleinen Bläschen und Emporsteigen derselben alle die Übergänge vom Knochen bis zu Klar, und von letzterem höchstwahrscheinlich auch die tropfig-zapfigen Stücke ohne Schlaubenstruktur. Für diese Behauptung sind folgende Beweisgründe anzuführen:

1. Die vollständige Analogie mit den lebenden Koniferen.

2. Finden sich unter dem gesamten Bernstein zwei Varietäten, die eine ist stets in dünnen Lamellen zapfenartig geschlossen, zeigt stets eine schalige Struktur (Schlaube), die andere zeigt die schalige Struktur nie, sondern ist höchstens zu kugeligen Tropfen zusammengeflossen. Die ersteren liefern nur klaren Bernstein oder als grosse Seltenheit rein knochigen mit klarem gemischt, nie aber flohmigen oder Bastard. (Hierbei wäre es sogar möglich, dass die Schlauben in einzelnen Fällen sogar aus knochigen Flüssen entstanden sein dürften, doch fehlen mir hierfür noch die nötigen Dünnschliffe). Die andere Sorte dagegen enthält nur Knochen, Bastard und Flohmig, nie Klar, höchstens in kleinen Stücken, und in diesem Falle flohmige sogar Bastard- und Knochentrübungen, in welchen man die vollständigen Übergänge nachweisen kann.

3. Ist es sehr viel einfacher, sich die Entstehung grösserer Bläschen und das Verschwinden derselben im Sinne der oben gemachten Angaben durch das Zusammenfliessen von kleineren zu erklären, als wenn man die grösseren zum Ausgangspunkt nimmt.

4. Gelingt es jetzt aus knochigem Bernstein den Bastard, aus diesem Flohmig und hieraus endlich Klar herzustellen.

5. Besitze ich eine Reihe Dünnschliffe, deren detaillierte Beschreibung hier nicht am Platze wäre, in welchen man an Querschnitten ganzer Bernsteinstücke den ganzen Vorgang des Grösserwerdens etc. der Bläschen von Knochen bis Klar verfolgen kann.

Der ganze Vorgang der Bernsteinentstehung, wie ich ihn auffasse, ist das Gegenteil der bisherigen Ansicht, welche vom klaren Bernstein ausging und durch Hydratbildung die andern

Varietäten erklärte, so dass mithin der Knochen resp. der technisch wertlose schaumige Bernstein das Endprodukt bildete. Nach meinen sehr zahlreichen Untersuchungen stehen sich das schlaubige Klar und der Knochen gleichwertig gegenüber. Während bei dem ersteren durch die Einwirkung der Sonnenwärme jeder Erguss schnell erhärtete, so dass der nächste nicht mehr fest darauf haften konnte, sammelte sich der Knochen an geschützten Stellen, häufig an blossgelegten grösseren Splintflächen (wie bei allen Platten) allmählich an. War die Gelegenheit doch gegeben, so flossen die Bläschen zusammen und verschwanden zum Teil ganz, wodurch Bastard, Flohmig und auch massives Klar entstanden. Häufig wird auch der Gehalt an emulsionsartig im klaren Harz enthaltenem Zellsaft in der Bläschengrösse des Knochens bei verschiedenen Flüssen zu einem Stück verschieden gewesen sein und dadurch entstand die Gelegenheit zur Bildung aller möglichen wolkigen Variationen. Zum grössten Teil wird diese Umwandlung der trüben Varietäten zu den klaren auch erst stattgefunden haben, nachdem der Bernstein längst erhärtet war, indem die Bläschen sich allmälich schlossen. Eine Erscheinung, welche man in der Industrie häufig benutzt, um den Bernstein in der Farbe zu verbessern, oder ihn klar zu kochen. In der Natur beobachtet man dieses Klarwerden an der Oberfläche sehr vieler Stücke und kann häufig mikroskopisch noch an den Übergangsstellen die zusammengefallenen Bläschen nachweisen. Selbst viele Bernsteinarbeiten aus der Steinzeit haben in der kurzen Zeit ihrer Lagerung (etwa 2500 Jahre) einen Mantel von klarem oder flohmigem Klar erhalten, während der Kern noch Bastard geblieben ist. Ein jeder kann diese Erscheinung selbst an seiner Bernsteinspitze aus sattem Bastard (sogenannter Kumstfarbe) machen, welche durch den Gebrauch allmählich immer klarer wird, auch dieses beruht nur auf dem Schliessen der Bläschen, welches hier durch die Wärme allerdings verhältnismässig schneller vor sich geht. Aus dem oben Erläuterten können wir wiederum rückwärts schliessen, dass die Bernsteinkonifere keine irgendwie durch Grösse auffallenden Harzräume (Gallen etc.) gehabt haben kann, weil in denselben das Harz sich als klares abgeschieden haben müsste und klarer Bernstein ausser Schlauben, wie bereits gesagt, eigentlich gar nicht vorkommt. Auch gegen die vielfach vertretene Ansicht von der überreichen Harzproduktion der Bernsteinkonifere möchte ich einige Worte einwenden. Schätzen wir den heutigen bekannten Verbreitungsbezirk des Bernsteins auf 10 Quadratmeilen und denken wir uns dieselbe Gebiet mit lichtem Wald, d. h. auf 4 qm einen Stamm, besetzt und nehmen nur ein Jahrtausend bei 100jährigem Generationswechsel an, so ergiebt dieses eine Produktion an Harz auf den Stamm von kaum 200 g, also weit weniger, als es bei unseren Koniferen im Durchschnitt der Fall sein dürfte, um die Menge Bernstein zu erlangen, welche nach sehr reichlicher Taxe in der blauen Erde des Samlandes durchschnittlich lagert.

Diese Zahlen sollen keinen weiteren Wert haben, als darzuthun, dass alle die Annahmen, wie die von Harz triefenden Bäumen u. s. w. ins Reich der Fabel gehören.

Die Lösung einer interessanten Frage bleibt jedoch noch übrig. Was enthalten die kleinen Bläschen? Die Antwort ist bis jetzt noch nicht spruchreif. Soviel steht jedoch fest, dass eine grosse Anzahl derselben Bernsteinsäure in Krystalldrusen, eine andere Flüssigkeit enthält. Ich hoffe, hierüber dann genauere Angaben machen zu können, wenn ich die chemischen Untersuchungen über die Bernsteinarten und über die fossilen Harze überhaupt, an welchen ich im hiesigen Provinzialmuseum seit Jahren arbeite, beendet haben werde. So weit über die gewöhnliche Farbe des Bernsteins. Von den seltenen Varietäten desselben ist zunächst der wirklich blaue Bernstein hervorzuheben. Die blaue Farbe des Bernsteins, welche sich in den Tönen himmelblau und dunkelcyanblau bewegt, ist nur eine Interferenzerscheinung, ein Opalisieren, hervorgerufen durch ungemein kleine Bläschen von kaum 0,0008 mm Durchmesser, welche dicht aneinander, etwa in der Dichte des Halbbastard oder Knochens, aber nur in ganz dünnen Lagen den klaren Bernstein durchsetzen. Die Natur dieser kleinen Partikelchen ergiebt sich zur Evidenz durch eine ganze Reihe von Dünnschliffen in starken Vergrösserungen und in den allmählichen Übergängen zu knochigem Bernstein. Alle die Erklärungen von Halm-Danzig, welcher zur Bildung des blauen Bernsteins den Vivianit, die Fluorescenz, ganz fein verteiltes Schwefeleisen zu Hilfe nimmt, sind hinfällig, da ich aus 23 Dünnschliffen in allen denkbaren Richtungen stets dasselbe Resultat erlangt habe. Die ganze Bildung entspricht vollständig dem Goetheschen Urphänomen der Farbenerzeugung: Gelb ist das verdunkelte oder durch Trübung gedämpfte Licht, Blau, die erhellte oder durch Trübung gedämpfte Finsternis. Hierdurch spielt allerdings auch der Schwefelkies eine Rolle, indem er in die Risse der dem Beschauer entgegengesetzten Rinde infiltriert, den natürlichen dunkeln Hintergrund zur Erzeugung des blauen Schimmers liefert.

Über die Ursachen der Färbung des so äusserst seltenen grünen Bernsteins möchte ich mein Urteil jetzt noch zurückhalten, da gerade einzelne Funde, die in den letzten Monaten gemacht sind, viel zur Beantwortung dieser Frage beitragen werden. Grüner Bernstein kommt klar sowohl hellgrün als auch in einem von mir selbst gefundenen Stück olivengrün vor, als trüber Stein geht er bis in den Farbenton des Chrysopras, entweder rein oder mit weissen Wolken. Bei dieser Gelegenheit will ich vor dem Ankauf eines klaren grünen Bernsteins warnen, welcher von Danzig aus vielfach Museen und Sammlern für teures Geld angeboten wird. Sämtliche Stücke, welche ich von diesen gesehen habe, sind nur durch Klarkochen erhalten und mithin kein Naturbernstein. Brauner und rotbrauner Berstein kommt als solcher in der Natur nicht vor. Entweder sind dergleichen Stücke kein Bernstein sondern Harze anderer Bäume der Tertiärzeit wie z. B. Glessit, oder es sind durch Brände während des Tertiärs bebrannte Stücke oder endlich nur durch die Zeit nachgedunkelter Bernstein, in den beiden letzteren Fällen besitzen die Stücke stets einen gelben unzersetzten Kern. Ähnlich verhält es sich mit dem sogenannten schwarzen Bernstein, welcher auch kein Bernstein ist.

Die Imitation des Bernsteins. Bei dem Wert des Bernsteins ist es klar, dass sich die Fälscherkunst auch mit ihm reichlich beschäftigt und mit mehr oder weniger Erfolg Surrogate in den Handel gebracht hat, welche den echten Stein ersetzen sollen. Die älteste und plumpeste Imitaton des Bernsteins ist Glas, welches auch jetzt noch zu Rauchrequisiten allerdings selten, dagegen häufig zu Hals- und Betkränzen verarbeitet wird. Härte und Kältegefühl beim Anfassen machen es jedem Laien sofort als Imitation kenntlich. Von Harzen wird das Kopal am meisten zur Fälschung benutzt, das man anfangs rein, später, um den Bernsteingeruch beim Brennen zu erhalten, mit Bernsteinpulver und Stückchen versetzt in den Handel brachte. Sämtliche Arbeiten aus Kopal sehen schmutzig aus, beim Reiben in der Hand werden sie klebrig, sie sind weicher als Bernstein und verlieren beim Einweichen in Essigäther ihren Glanz und quellen auf.

Eine im Aussehen recht geschickte, sonst aber sehr schlechte Imitation des Bernsteins stellt man aus Celluloid dar. Kein Stoff hat wohl in den letzten Jahren eine so vielseitige Verwendung gefunden wie das Celluloid; man macht aus ihm: Chirurgische Gegenstände, Kämme, Billardbälle, Messergriffe, Belege zu Pferdegeschirren, Klichees, Stockgriffe u. s. w.; kein Stoff besitzt aber auch eine so ausgedehnte Benutzung zu Imitationen und Fälschungen. Bei der Leichtigkeit, mit welcher das Celluloid gefärbt werden kann, macht man aus ihm künstlichen Bernstein, Schildpatt, Korallen, Malachit, Lapislazuli u. s. w., ja sogar in der sogenannten Gummiwäsche dient es als Surrogat von Leinwand. Bei dieser Verschiedenartigkeit des Gebrauches hat natürlicherweise auch die Fabrikation des Celluloids seit 1869, in welchem Jahre es von Gebr. Hyatt zu Newark im Staate Newyork erfunden wurde, einen sehr grossen Aufschwung genommen. — Die Herstellung des Celluloids ist im ganzen sehr einfach. Abfälle aus den Baumwollenfabriken, Papierschnitzel, Holzstoff, Lumpen von Leinen- und Baumwollenstoffen, alte Taue, helle Holzarten werden gewässert, gereinigt, gebleicht und gemahlen. Diese aus gepulvertem Zellstoff (Cellulose) bestehenden Massen führt man durch Einweichen in ein Gemisch von Salpeter- und Schwefelsäure in Schiessbaumwolle über. Die erhaltene Schiessbaumwolle wird gut ausgewaschen, halb getrocknet und unter einem Zusatz von 40—50 pCt. Kampfer und den eventuell nötigen Farbstoffen bei einer Temperatur von 70 Grad in hydraulischen Pressen einem starken Druck ausgesetzt. Dabei findet eine Durchdringung der Schiessbaumwolle mit Kampfer statt. Die gepressten Stücke trocknet man in einem luftleeren Raum und entzieht ihnen die letzte Feuchtigkeit durch stark Wasser absorbierende Stoffe, wie Chlorcalcium. Das so fertig gestellte Schiessbaumwollenpräparat, mit dem unschuldigen Namen Celluloid, Ambroid u. s. w., ist, wenn keine Farbe zugesetzt wurde, durchscheinend, hart, elastisch, schwer zerbrechlich, hornartig, erwärmt lässt es sich durch allmählichen Druck in dünne Platten dehnen. Bis 100 Grad vorsichtig erwärmt, wird es so weich, dass es sich in Formen pressen lässt; es ist sehr leicht entzündlich und verbrennt schnell mit stark russender Flamme; bei starkem Schlag oder beim Erwärmen bis auf 140 Grad Celsius explodirt es unter Bildung eines rötlichen Rauches. Das Celluloid ist demnach ein Stoff, welcher auf einer Seite die vorzüglichsten technischen Eigenschaften besitzt, auf der andern Seite wiederum äusserst feuergefährlich ist. Die Industrie hat sich vielfach bemüht, diese letzte Eigenschaft abzuschwächen, indem sie der Schiessbaumwolle vor dem Pressen phosphorsaures Natron und borsaures Blei zusetzte. Abgesehen davon, dass das letztere bei allen Celluloidfabrikaten, welche längere Zeit im Munde getragen werden, wie Ansatzspitzen zu Pfeifen u. s. w., Zahnringe für Kinder, Gebisse, giftig wirkt, haben diese Zusätze die Feuergefährlichkeit gar nicht abgeschwächt.

Bei Gegenständen der letzten Art ist auch der hohe Kampfergehalt entschieden von Einfluss auf die Gesundheit. Wenn man nun bedenkt, wie ungemein verbreitet die Artikel aus kampferhaltiger Schiessbaumwolle (Celluloid) sind und zu Millionen als Bijouterien und Ansatzspitzen zu Tabakspfeifen an den Markt gebracht und selbst in den kleinsten Galanterie- und Tabakshandlungen geführt werden, ohne dass die Händler selbst eine Ahnung von der Feuergefährlichkeit dieser Fabrikate haben, so erscheint es mir von entschiedener Bedeutung, die öffentliche Aufmerksamkeit auf diese Gegenstände zu lenken. Jene Celluloidimitation erkennt man leicht an dem Kampfergeruch beim Reiben; in Schwefeläther gelegt, lösst sie sich oberflächlich schnell in der Kälte auf, verliert den Glanz und wird trübe, ein Versuch, den man, wenn nicht über eine Viertelstunde ausgedehnt, dreist mit jeder Bernsteinarbeit ohne Schaden machen kann. Ausserdem ist die Feuergefährlichkeit so gross, dass Celluloid, kaum einen Augenblick mit der Flamme in Berührung gebracht, schnell und hoch aufflammt, selbst die neuesten „wirklich nicht feuergefährlichen" französischen Ambroide. In der neuesten Zeit spielen die aus kleinen Stücken gepressten Bernsteinarbeiten eine grosse Rolle. Versuche, den Bernstein ohne Bindemittel zusammenzupressen, habe ich bereits im Jahre 1878 gemacht. Später liess ich diese Versuche liegen, bis von Wien aus vor einigen Jahren gepresste Fabrikate in den Handel kamen. Nun galt es, dieser Entwertung der grösseren Stücke zu begegnen und wurden die Versuche wieder aufgenommen, wobei denn auch mancherlei wissenschaftlich interessante Resultate gewonnen wurden.

Die gesamten Pressverfahren des Bernsteins beruhen auf seiner Eigenschaft, bei einer Temperatur von 140 Grad unter Luftabschluss so weich zu werden, dass man ihn, wie es auch in der Spitzenindustrie angewendet wird, biegen kann.

In der ersten Zeit füllte man flache eiserne Formen mit Bernstein und presste sie erwärmt anfangs mit Schrauben, später mit hydraulischem Druck zusammen. Man erhielt dadurch flache Bernsteinstücke, die verarbeitet zwar gut die Politur hielten, jedoch angefüllt mit kleinen gelbbraunen Flimmerchen waren, welche dadurch entstanden, dass der Bernstein beim Erwärmen oberflächlich dunkler geworden war. Eine wesentliche Neuerung bestand darin, dass man den in der flachen Eisenform erwärmten Bernstein mit einem hohlen Stempel, dessen Boden durch ein kräftiges Sieb geschlossen war, hydraulisch zusammenpresste. Dadurch zwang man den erweichten Stein durch die engen Maschen des Siebbodens zu treten, und sich mehr durchzumischen. Als man nun noch über dem Siebboden ein bewegliches Gegengewicht einschaltete, welches die aus den Löchern emporquellende zähe, breiartige Masse heben musste, erreichte man, dass die Stempel sich breit und mehr durcheinander drückten. Unter Zugrundelegung dieser Idee begann ich die Versuche, überzeugte mich jedoch bald, dass das ganze Resultat der Arbeit nichts weiter als reiner Glückszufall sein könnte, wenn nicht eine Basis geschaffen würde, von welcher aus die Arbeiten fortgeführt werden könnten. Zu diesem Zweck unternahm ich die genauere Untersuchung der Mikrostruktur der Bernsteinarten. Da es sich erwies, dass man es in der Hand habe, durch starken hydraulischen Druck einen klaren, durch schwachen einen knochigen Bernstein herzustellen, entwickelte ich mir die oben erwähnten Werte, welche mir darthaten, um einen wie grossen Teil ich das Volumen des Bernsteins zu verringern hätte, um aus einem trüberen ein klares Stück zu erhalten.

Gelang es mir nämlich unter bekannten Umständen bei einem zufällig gefundenen Druck eine Bernsteinart im Werte einer dieser Zahlen herzustellen und unter denselben Umständen bei einem andern Druck eine andere, so erschien es mir leicht, den notwendigen Druck vorher angeben zu können, welcher aus einer beliebigen Bernsteinsorte eine bestimmt verlangte Bernsteinart erzeugt. Zwar sind die Versuche noch nicht abgeschlossen, aber die Resultate doch schon jetzt von grossem Werte, da es gelungen ist, ein Produkt zu erhalten, welches der dunklen Kumstfarbe des reinen Bernsteins fast ebenbürtig zur Seite steht. Allerdings ist auch der Druck, unter welchem gearbeitet wurde, recht ansehnlich, da er 400 kg auf den Quadratcentimeter noch überstieg. Wenn nun auch diese Versuche für die Wissenschaft manches Interessante haben, so sind die Resultate in den Händen unreeller Kaufleute doch immerhin sehr gefährlich, und jeder, der Bernsteinfabrikate kauft, thut gut, die nötige Vorsicht anzuwenden.

Der durch hydraulisches Pressen erzeugte satte Bastard kommt bis jetzt nicht in den Handel; was sich davon im Handel findet, ist ein wolkiges Klar, bei welchem die Trübungen in parallelen Streifen übereinander, etwa wie bei den Cirrus- oder Federwolken, angeordnet sind. Bei den Übergängen vom Trüben zum Klar bemerkt man bei durchfallendem Licht die gelbrote und bei auffallendem Licht und dunklem Untergrunde die bläuliche Farbe, hervorgerufen durch die äusserst kleinen Bläschen, eine Erscheinung, welche beim echten Bernstein nie in einer solchen Regelmässigkeit und überhaupt ganz vereinzelt nur bei knochigen Varietäten, nicht aber bei Bastard und Klar auftritt, welche durch ihre grösseren Bläschen nie solche Farbeneffekte geben können.

Die klaren Partien und überhaupt die klaren Stücke zeigen fast immer die kleinen bräunlichen Flecken und Äderchen. Wo diese wirklich fehlen sollten, ist das Klar nie glasartig blank, sondern zeigt immer Wellen und Fäden, ähnlich wie sie bei der Mischung von Flüssigkeiten verschiedener Lichtbrechung (Glycerin und Wasser) im ersten Augenblick auftreten. Bei allen trüben Fabrikaten, selbst den besten kunstfarbigen, ist das mikroskopische Bild absolut charakteristisch. Die gepressten Stücke zeigen nie die runden Bläschen des echten Bernsteins, sondern stets dendritisch verdrückte.

Herr Dr. G. Klien spricht hierauf über vegetative Bastarderzeugung durch Impfung.

Nachdem Darwin in seinem Werke über das Variieren der Tiere und Pflanzen die Pfropfhybriden eingehend behandelt hatte, wandte man mehr als je der Frage, ob es möglich sei, durch Impfung Bastarde zu erzeugen, seine Aufmerksamkeit zu. Seitdem haben aber auch Gelehrte und Praktiker die mannigfaltigsten und widersprechensten Resultate geliefert. Die Vorstellung von Propfhybriden ist wohl fast ebenso alt, als die Veredlungskunst selbst, denn wenn man sich vergegenwärtigt, wie wenig noch, nachdem die Kunst des Veredelns Jahrtausende lang geübt worden ist, die Ansichten durch sichere Beobachtungen und Experimente geklärt sind, so mussten sich schon frühzeitig an diesem wunderbaren Vorgang des Anwachsens von Grundstamm und Pfropfreis die verschiedenartigsten Vorstellungen knüpfen. Auch musste man bald auf den Gedanken kommen, die ungleichartigsten Pfropfungen bewirken zu können, da es gelang, bei einigen sich anscheinend fernstehenden Pflanzen, als beispielsweise zwischen Pflaumen und Mandeln oder Pfirsichen, eine Vereinigung zu erzielen. Hierzu kam nun, dass durch falsche Berichte und mit Hilfe der eignen Phantasie von vielen Schriftstellern des klassischen Altertums und späterer Zeiten die fabelhaftesten Gerüchte über Pfropfhybirden sich verbreiten mussten. So erzählt z. B. Plinius von einem wahren Wunderbaum, dessen verschiedene Zweige mit Nüssen, Beeren, Trauben, Feigen, Birnen, Granatäpfeln und Äpfelsorten beladen waren. Für am fähigsten, alle möglichen Pfropfreiser aufzunehmen, wurden die Platanen gehalten. Jetzt steht unbestritten fest, dass es nie gelungen ist, zwei Individuen aus zwei merklich verschiedenen natürlichen Pflanzenfamilien dauernd miteinander zu vereinigen. Aber auch wie weit die Möglichkeit der Verwachsung zwischen Gattung und Arten innerhalb einer Familie reicht, ist durch Experimente auch noch nicht genügend festgestellt worden. Am sichersten ist bis jetzt die Übertragung der Weiss- resp. Buntfleckigkeit durch Impfung beobachtet worden, denn öfters soll es vorgekommen sein, dass buntgefärbte Blätter in Folge der Impfung am Subjekte, unterhalb der Impfstelle zum Vorschein gekommen sind. Neuerdings wird nun und wohl nicht mit Unrecht von einigen Forschern behauptet, dass die Albicatio oder Weissfleckigkeit als ein pathologischer Zustand aufzufassen sei, da unter gewissen Umständen diese eigenartigen Blattfärbungen sich durch besondere Kultur begünstigen lassen. Die weissfleckigen Blätter, welche eine grössere Hinfälligkeit als die grünen besitzen, unterscheiden sich äusserlich von den normalen dadurch, dass ihre Blätter kleiner und dünner und dass bei ihnen der Durchmesser des Astes schwächer und die Jahresringe enger als bei gleich alten grünblättrigen Ästen sind. In chemischer Hinsicht zeigt sich, dass die gleichaltrigen Blätter eines Baumes, welcher Äste mit weissen und solche mit grünen Blättern trägt, grosse Unterschiede je nach der Färbung zeigen. Der Wasser- und Aschengehalt ist bei den weissen Blättern wesentlich höher als bei den grünen und auch die weitere Analyse der Trockensubstanz giebt Resultate, welche darthun, dass die weissen Blätter in demselben Verhältnis zu den grünen stehen, wie unreife Blätter zu reifen. Hierzu kommt noch, dass die Abänderung der Gestalt der Blätter sehr oft als Folge früherer Weissfleckigkeit angesehen werden muss.

Bei Pfropfungen von verschiedenen Kartoffelknollen wollen Taylor, Reuter, Magnus, Trail, Heimann, v. Gröling und andere einen Säfteaustausch konstatiert und die verschiedenen Eigenschaften der Eltern bei den Bastarden in der mannigfaltigsten Weise kombiniert haben. Man hat Kartoffelsegmente von verschiedener Farbe und Form mit einander verwachsen lassen und angeblich Mischknollen oder Hybriden erhalten, welche in den Eigentümlichkeiten ihrer Form und Farbe des Fleisches und der Schale zwischen den Stammsorten die Mitte hielten, oder nur buntfleckig gewesen sein sollen. Von einem grossen Teil der Versuchsansteller wurden bei der Knollenpfropfung aber nur negative Resultate erzielt, was auch erwartet werden musste. Die grösste Aussicht für Hybridenbildung könnte nach Ansicht des Redners bei oberirdischer Stengelpfropfung erwartet werden, weil der Blattapparat jeder Pflanze die Bildungsstätte der organischen Substanz ist und von dort die erzeugten Baustoffe in flüssiger Form nach den Aufspeicherungsstellen, also bei der Kartoffel nach den Knollen hinwandern. In dieser Weise wurden nun vor mehreren Jahren vom Vortragenden Versuche angestellt und auf eine Anzahl einzelnaus gepflanzter Kartoffeltriebe einer weissen runden Varietät die Triebe einer rotbraunen langen Kartoffel geimpft (copuliert). Der aufgesetzte Zweig wuchs bei einer Anzahl Pflanzen an der Verbindungsstelle fest an und zeigte sich dann der geimpfte Achsenteil rötlich gefärbt, während die Farbe des aufgesetzten Triebes fast unverändert blieb. Die im Herbst geernteten Knollen zeigten aber durchgehends die Form der für die Unterlage bekannten Kartoffeln, während die Farbe der Schale teilweise rötlich geworden zu sein schien. Das Züchtungsprodukt im nächsten Jahre war aber ohne rötlichen Schein, sondern hatte durchaus die Beschaffenheit der früher zur Unterlage verwandten weissen Kartoffelform. Das mehrjährige Züchtungsprodukt kann hier nur Geltung erlangen, und auch hier war ein negatives Resultat erzielt worden. Somit ist die Existenz von Kartoffelpfropfhybriden zur Zeit überhaupt wissenschaftlich noch nicht festgestellt, denn die bis jetzt als Bastarde beschriebenen Knollen finden durch Atavismus, Degeneration und Variation ihre Erklärung.

Herr Dr. Franz trägt hierauf seine neue Berechnung von Hartwig's Beobachtungen der physischen Libration des Mondes vor.

Die Hauptgesetze der Bewegung des Mondes um seinen Schwerpunkt sind nach Cassini I: 1. Die Umdrehungszeit des Mondes ist gleich einer siderischen Umlaufszeit. 2. Die Neigung des Mondäquators gegen die Ekliptik ist unveränderlich. 3. Der aufsteigende Knoten des Mondäquators auf der Ekliptik fällt mit dem absteigenden Knoten der Mondbahn auf derselben stets zusammen. — Die Abweichungen von diesen Gesetzen nennt man die physische oder wirkliche Libration des Mondes. Dieselben entstehen durch die Unterschiede der Anziehung, welche die Erde auf verschiedene Theile des Mondkörpers ausübt, wenn die drei Hauptträgheitsmomente des Mondes von einander verschieden sind. Dass sie verschieden sein müssen, folgt schon aus dem dritten Cassini'schen Gesetz. Denn wären sie einander gleich, so müsste die Rotationsaxe des Mondes wie die einer homogenen Kugel sich selbst parallel bleiben. Die Wirkung der Anziehung der Erde auf die Bewegung des Mondes um seinen Schwerpunkt äussert sich ferner in kleinen Schwankungen der der Erde zugewendeten Mondseite. Man muss hier zwei verschiedene Arten von Schwankungen unterscheiden.

1. Schwankungen, die von den Ungleichheiten der Mondbahn herrühren und dieselben verkleinert gewissermaassen wiederspiegeln. Dauer und Phase dieser Schwankungen hängen von den Ungleichheiten der Mondbahn, ihre Amplitude aber von den Unterschieden der Trägheitsmomente des Mondes ab. Diese Schwankungen können nicht unendlich klein sein. Sie müssen einen endlichen Wert haben. Denn sonst würden die Trägheitsmomente des Mondes nicht von einander verschieden sein und die Gleichheit der Umdrehungszeit und der Umlaufszeit des Mondes würde als ein Zufall von unendlich geringer Wahrscheinlichkeit erscheinen. Doch muss diese Gleichheit ein stabiler Zustand sein. Diese Schwankungen kann man daher die notwendige physische Libration nennen. Ihre Beobachtung lehrt uns die Verhältnisse der Trägheitsmomente kennen. Sie sind nämlich A, B, C die drei Hauptträgheitsmomente des Mondes, bezogen auf die der Erde zugewendete, auf die in der Nähe der Mondbahn liegende und auf die auf den Mondäquator senkrechte Hauptaxe des Mondes, ist ferner i die Neigung der Mondbahn gegen die Ekliptik, m' die tägliche Bewegung der Länge, n' die des Knotens des Mondes, letztere eine negative Grösse, so findet man aus den Beobachtungen zunächst die Neigung J des Mondäquators gegen die Ekliptik und das Verhältnis f der Differenzen der Trägheitsmomente und aus diesen beiden Constanten der notwendigen Libration die Verhältnisse von $A : B : C$ aus den Gleichungen

$$3\,\frac{C-A}{B}\,(J+i) = -2\,J\left(1-\frac{n'}{m'}\right)\frac{n'}{m'} \quad \text{und} \quad \frac{C-B}{A} = \frac{C-A}{B}\,f.$$

2. Es können Schwankungen auftreten, deren Schwingungsdauer von den Trägheitsmomenten des Mondes abhängt, deren Amplitude und Phase aber als Integrationsconstanten willkürlich sind. Sie dauern, wenn sie einmal bestehen, unverändert fort, falls sie nicht von widerstehenden Kräften gelähmt werden, können aber bereits durch Widerstandskräfte unendlich klein geworden sein. Ihre Existenz müsste daher erst durch Beobachtungen nachgewiesen werden. Diese Schwankungen kann man die willkürliche physische Libration nennen. Es ist eine Schwankung in Länge, deren Amplitude a_0 und deren Phase zu einer bestimmten Zeit ($t = o$) A_0 genannt wird mit einer Schwingungsdauer von 2.3 Jahren, eine Schwankung in Breite mit der Amplitude b_0 und der Phase B_0 (für $t = o$) und einer Dauer von einem Monat und eine zweite Schwankung in Breite von etwa 175 Jahren Dauer, auf deren Bestimmung aus einer kurzen Beobachtungsreihe man aber von vornherein verzichten muss.

Auf Bessel's Vorschlag wurden zur Bestimmung der physischen Libration die Abstände des nahe der Mitte der Mondscheibe liegenden Kraters Mösting A von verschiedenen Punkten des Mondrandes mit dem Heliometer gemessen. Eine solche Messungsreihe hat Wichmann in Königsberg um's Jahr 1845 ausgeführt und in Band 26 und 27 der „Astronomischen Nachrichten" berechnet. Dort hat er auch die Theorie und Berechnungsmethode ausführlich behandelt und deshalb muss hier auf diese Arbeit verwiesen werden. Zur Berechnung mussten für die selenographische Länge und Breite λ und β des Mondkraters und für die Constanten der notwendigen Libration, J und f, genäherte Werte angenommen werden, deren Korrektionen aus den Beobachtungen zugleich mit den Constanten der willkürlichen Libration ermittelt wurden. Wichmann nahm an:

$$J = 1^0\ 28'\ 47''\quad f = 0.260 \text{ und fand } J = 1^0\ 32'\ 8.''9\quad f = 0.419$$

oder unter der Annahme, dass keine willkürliche Libration existiert,

$$J = 1^0\ 32'\ 23.''7\quad f = 0.445.$$

Eine andere Reihe von 42 Messungen hat Ernst Hartwig von 1877 Nov. 14 bis 1879 Jan. 12 in Strassburg ausgeführt und zugleich mit der Berechnung unter dem Titel „Beitrag zur Bestimmung der physischen Libration des Mondes aus Beobachtungen am Strassburger Heliometer" in Karlsruhe bei G. Braun 1881 veröffentlicht. Hartwig rechnet ganz nach den Formeln von Wichmann und nimmt auch zur Berechnung der Coefficienten der Bedingungsgleichungen dieselben Werte $J = 1^0\ 28'\ 47''$ und $f = 0.260$ an, von welchen Wichmann ausging. Hartwig erhielt aus seiner Beobachtungsreihe, wenn man eine von ihm in den Monthly Notices of the Royal Astronomical Society Band 41, Seite 376, nachträglich angegebene Korrektur berücksichtigt,

$$J = 1^0\ 36'\ 39''\quad f = 0.507$$

also Resultate, die von den ursprünglichen Annahmen noch mehr abweichen als Wichmann's Resultate.

Es liegt nun die Frage nahe, ob Hartwig zu denselben Ergebnissen gekommen wäre, wenn er Wichmann's Resultate zu Grunde gelegt hätte. Die Coefficienten der Bedingungsgleichungen, welche schliesslich, nach der Methode der kleinsten Quadrate aufgelöst, die Resultate ergeben, hängen nämlich von J und f so ab, dass, wenn nicht genügend genaue Werte von J und f zu Grunde liegen, eine zweite Näherung erforderlich wird. Da es für die Ermittelung der physischen Libration von Wichtigkeit ist zu wissen, in wie weit eine Wiederholung der ganzen Rechnung mit genaueren Annahmen der Constanten die Resultate modifizieren kann, da die von Hartwig errechneten Werte unerwartet gross sind und alle früheren Annahmen übertreffen, da ferner Hartwig's schöne Beobachtungen und die von ihm auf die so komplizierte Reduktion verwendete Mühe die Ausführung einer zweiten Näherung lohnend machen, so habe ich, um die Zuverlässigkeit seiner Resultate zu prüfen, eine solche ausgeführt.

Zu dem Zwecke wurden nun aus den von Wichmann und aus den von Hartwig in seiner zitierten Arbeit gefundenen Resultaten mit Rücksicht auf die sich aus den wahrscheinlichen Fehlern ergebenden Gewichte folgende Mittelwerte angenommen:

$$J = 1^0\ 35'\ 46''.8\quad f = 0.4894$$

woraus folgt:

$$\frac{C-A}{B} = 0.000637,\qquad \frac{C-B}{A} = 0.000312,\qquad \frac{B-A}{C} = 0.000325.$$

Für die selenographischen Coordinaten des Kraters Mösting A nahm ich, wie Hartwig gefunden hat $\lambda = -5^0$ und $\beta = -3^0\ 10'$ an. Hiermit gehen die aus den obigen Cassini'schen Gesetzen folgenden Gleichungen

$$\cos\ \sin(l-n) = \sin\beta\sin J - \cos\beta\cos J\sin(\lambda + m - n)$$
$$\cos b\cos(l-n) = -\cos\beta\cos(\lambda + m - n)$$
$$\sin\ = \sin\beta\cos J + \cos\beta\sin J\sin(\lambda + m - n)$$

zur Berechnung der auf die Ekliptik bezogenen selenocentrischen Längen und Breiten des Kraters und b aus der mittleren Länge des Mondes m und aus der Länge des aufsteigenden Knotens der Mondbahn über in

$$\cos b\sin(l-n) = - \quad - \quad \sin(\lambda + m - n)$$
$$\cos\ \cos(l-n) = \quad - \quad \cos(\lambda + m - n)$$
$$\sin\ = - \quad + \quad \sin(\lambda + m - n),$$

wo die eingeklammerten Zahlen Logarithmen sind. Hieraus erhielt ich für die Beobachtungen die folgenden Werte von und b, die an Stelle der von Hartwig auf Seite seiner Arbeit angegebenen treten, und denen hier die Überschüsse der beobachteten und b über die berechneten beigefügt sind.

Nr.	Berechnete selenocentrische Länge	Breite b	Beob.—Rechn. Δl	Δb	Nr.	Berechnete selenocentrische Länge	Breite b	Beob.—Rechn.	Δb
	156°	−	+ 87.3	−		46° 0′	− 4°	−	+
	250	−	+	−			−	+	+
		−	+	−			−	+	+ 328.0
	289	−	−				−	−	+
	300	−	+	−			−		−
6	214	−	+	−			−	+	− 304.0
	312	−	+	+			−	−	−
	323	−	+	+			−	−	−
9	303	−	+	+			−		−
	317	− 3	+ 220.0	+			−	−	−
		−	+	+ 236.0		218	−	−	−
	314	−	+	+			− 2	−	
	325	−	+	+ 270.0			− 1	− 54.0	−
	308	−	+	+		227	−	−	−
	321	−	+	+			−	+	+
	348	−	+	+		263	− 2		− 84.0
		−	+	+		304	−	+	− 84.8
		−	−	+		241	−	−	−
	330	−	+	+		266	−	−	−
		−	−	+		294	−	−	− 74.0
		−	−	+		348	−	+	+ 388.0

Zur Kontrolle berechnete ich und b zweitens aus folgenden strengen Formeln:

$$\cos b\sin(l - \lambda - m) = \sin\beta\sin J\cos(\lambda + m - n) + \cos\beta\sin^2 {}^1/_2 J\sin\ (\lambda + m - n)$$
$$\sin b = \sin(\beta + J) - \cos\beta\sin J\sin^2\left[45^0 - {}^1/_2(\lambda + m - n)\right]$$

und ausserdem b noch aus den bequemeren Gleichungen

$$\sin\ = e\sin(\beta + E),\ \text{wo}\ e\sin E = \sin J\sin(\lambda + m - n)\ \text{und}\ e\cos E = \cos J$$

ist, und erhielt so wiederum dieselben Werte.

Bedeutet nun $\odot$ die mittlere Anomalie der Sonne und die Länge des Mondperigäums, ist ferner $L = l - 177^0$ $+$ $(t - 1877\ \text{Nov.}\ \ 744)$, wo t die Zeit in Bezug auf den Tag als Einheit ist, sind $d\lambda$, $d\beta$, dJ und df die zu ermittelnden Korrektionen von λ, β, J und f und setzt man $(f + df) = f_1$, so werden nach Wichmann's Entwickelungen (A. N. Bd. , S.) die Bedingungsgleichungen aus den Differenzen in selenocentrischer Länge

$0.9983\,d\lambda + 0.027857 \cos(l-n) \sec\beta\, d\beta + \sin$ [illegible] $\cos(l-n)\, dJ + \cos b \cos(1481''.0\, t)\, a_0 \sin A_0 + \cos$ [illegible] $\sin(1481''.0\, t)\, a_0 \cos A_0 + \sin$ [illegible] $\sin L\, b_0 \sin B_0 - \sin$ [illegible] $\cos L\, b_0 \cos B_0 - [\cos b\,(0.90144 \sin \odot - 0.09636 \sin(m-\pi)) + 0''.00219 \sin(\pi - n)]\, f_1$

$= \cos$ [illegible] $[\Delta l -$ [illegible] $\sin \odot +$ [illegible] $\sin.(m-\pi)] +$ [illegible] $\sin$ [illegible] $\cos(\pi - n)$

und die Bedingungsgleichungen aus den Differenzen in selenocentrischer Breite

$0.9983 \sec\beta\, d\beta - 0.027857 \cos(l-n)\, d\lambda - \sin(l-n)\, dJ + \cos L\, b_0 \sin B_0 + \sin L\, b_0 \cos B_0 - 0.44481 \sin(\pi - n)\, f_1 = \Delta b -$ [illegible] $\cos(\pi - n)$.

So ergeben sich für die [illegible] Beobachtungen die folgenden Bedingungsgleichungen, denen in der letzten Vertikalreihe unter v die nach der Auflösung übrig bleibenden Fehler im Sinne Beobachtung — Rechnung hinzugefügt sind:

Bedingungsgleichungen aus den Differenzen in Länge.

Nr.	$d\lambda \times$	$d\beta \times$	$dJ \times$	$a_0 \sin A_0 \times$	$a_0 \cos$ [illegible] $\times$	$b_0 \sin B_0 \times$	$b_0 \cos B_0 \times$	$f_1 \times$		v
[illegible]	+0.9983	−0.0275	+0.0499	+0.9945	+0.0896	+ [illegible]	+0.0476	+0.6437	= + [illegible]	+ [illegible]
[illegible]	+0.9983	+ [illegible]	− [illegible]	+0.9897	+0.1405	−0.0272	[illegible]	+0.4724	= [illegible]	+ [illegible]
[illegible]	+0.9983	− [illegible]	+ [illegible]	+0.9513	+0.3069	[illegible]	+0.0277	+0.1783	= [illegible]	+ [illegible]
[illegible]	+0.9983	+0.0226	−0.0617	+0.9317	+0.3505	−0.0660	− [illegible]	+0.0915	= [illegible]	− [illegible]
[illegible]	+0.9983	+0.0258	−0.0596	+0.9335	+0.3560	−0.0380	−0.0244	+0.0932	= + [illegible]	− [illegible]
[illegible]	+0.9983	− [illegible]	+ [illegible]	+0.8706	+0.4914	[illegible]	+0.0227	−0.2599	= − [illegible]	− [illegible]
[illegible]	+0.9983	+0.0274	−0.0489	+0.8426	+0.5364	−0.0345	−0.0360	−0.3252	= − [illegible]	− [illegible]
[illegible]	+0.9983	+0.0279	−0.0553	+0.8380	+0.5414	−0.0298	−0.0466	−0.3192	= + [illegible]	+ [illegible]
[illegible]	+0.9983	+0.0264	−0.0489	+0.7253	+0.6869	−0.0667	−0.0284	−0.6908	= [illegible]	− [illegible]
[illegible]	+0.9983	+0.0278	−0.0527	+0.7200	+0.6920	−0.0638	−0.0414	−0.6812	= − [illegible]	+ [illegible]
[illegible]	+0.9983	+ [illegible]	−0.0638	+0.6917	+0.7176	+0.0421	−0.0687	−0.6343	= − [illegible]	+ [illegible]
[illegible]	+0.9983	+0.0277	−0.0518	+0.5725	+0.8188	−0.0344	−0.0692	−0.9090	= − [illegible]	+ [illegible]
[illegible]	+0.9983	+0.0278	−0.0573	+0.5673	+0.8215	−0.0289	−0.0497	−0.8894	= − [illegible]	+ [illegible]
[illegible]	+0.9983	+0.0274	−0.0493	+0.4048	+0.9131	−0.0664	−0.0646	−0.9452	= − [illegible]	+ [illegible]
[illegible]	+0.9983	+0.0279	−0.0562	+0.3986	+0.9154	−0.0314	−0.0467	−0.9215	= − [illegible]	+ [illegible]
[illegible]	+0.9983	+0.0242	−0.0601	+0.3842	+0.9207	[illegible]	−0.0687	−0.8740	= − [illegible]	+ [illegible]
[illegible]	+0.9983	+ [illegible]	−0.0543	+0.3776	+0.9230	+ [illegible]	−0.0738	−0.8466	= − [illegible]	+ [illegible]
[illegible]	+0.9983	+ [illegible]	[illegible]	+0.3564	+0.9307	+0.0620	−0.0552	−0.7807	= − [illegible]	− [illegible]
[illegible]	+0.9983	+0.0272	−0.0599	+0.2076	+0.9763	−0.0255	−0.0557	−0.7410	= − [illegible]	+ [illegible]
[illegible]	+0.9983	+ [illegible]	−0.0478	+0.1860	+0.9796	+ [illegible]	−0.0746	−0.6458	= [illegible]	− [illegible]
[illegible]	+0.9983	+ [illegible]	−0.0866	− [illegible]	+0.9968	+0.0821	−0.0733	−0.2880	= [illegible]	− [illegible]
[illegible]	+0.9983	0.0000	0.0000	−0.0280	+0.9963	+0.0653	−0.0514	−0.2244	= [illegible]	[illegible]
[illegible]	+0.9983	−0.0288	+0.0647	−0.0947	+0.9947	+ [illegible]	+0.0405	−0.1551	= + [illegible]	+ [illegible]
[illegible]	+0.9983	+ [illegible]	[illegible]	−0.2189	+0.9723	+0.0607	−0.0567	+0.1768	= + [illegible]	+ [illegible]
[illegible]	+0.9983	−0.0269	+0.0463	−0.2765	+0.9598	+ [illegible]	+0.0488	+0.2765	= − [illegible]	− [illegible]
26	+0.9983	−0.0245	+0.0872	−0.2894	+0.9581	+ [illegible]	+0.0414	+0.2710	= − [illegible]	[illegible]
[illegible]	+0.9983	−0.0209	+0.0275	−0.2904	+0.9561	−0 [illegible]	+0.0368	+0.2644	= + [illegible]	+ [illegible]
[illegible]	+0.9983	− [illegible]	+ [illegible]	−0.2973	+0.9542	− [illegible]	+0.0396	+0.2572	= −223.0	− [illegible]
[illegible]	+0.9983	− [illegible]	+ [illegible]	−0.4817	+0.8758	[illegible]	+0.0275	+0.6148	= +220.0	+ [illegible]
30	+0.9983	−0.0262	+0.0427	−0.6237	+0.7804	+ [illegible]	+0.0425	+0.8908	= + [illegible]	+ [illegible]
[illegible]	+0.9983	−0.0230	+0.0326	−0.6387	+0.7725	+ [illegible]	+0.0391	+0.8754	= + [illegible]	+ [illegible]
[illegible]	+0.9983	− [illegible]	+ [illegible]	−0.6522	+0.7575	− [illegible]	[illegible]	+0.8108	= [illegible]	+ [illegible]
[illegible]	+0.9983	− [illegible]	+0.0262	−0.7716	+0.6350	− [illegible]	+0.0361	+0.9150	= + [illegible]	− [illegible]
[illegible]	+0.9983	− [illegible]	+ [illegible]	−0.7812	+0.6236	[illegible]	+0.0256	+0.8606	= [illegible]	+ [illegible]
[illegible]	+0.9983	+ [illegible]	[illegible]	−0.7901	+0.6122	−0.0225	+ [illegible]	+0.8205	= +279.0	+ [illegible]
[illegible]	+0.9983	−0.0215	+0.0290	−0.8791	+0.4751	+ [illegible]	+0.0675	+0.7823	= + [illegible]	[illegible]
[illegible]	+0.9983	+ [illegible]	−0.0254	−0.9027	+0.4288	−0.0858	[illegible]	+0.5876	= − [illegible]	− [illegible]
[illegible]	+0.9983	+0.0279	−0.0539	−0.9114	+0.4078	−0.0397	−0.0660	+0.5596	= +240.0	+ [illegible]
[illegible]	+0.9983	+ [illegible]	− [illegible]	−0.9976	+0.0628	−0.0286	+ [illegible]	−0.1209	= [illegible]	− [illegible]
[illegible]	+0.9983	+0.0217	−0.0294	−0.9981	+0.0473	−0.0677	[illegible]	−0.1706	= [illegible]	− [illegible]
[illegible]	+0.9983	+0.0275	−0.0498	−0.9981	+0.0637	−0.0422	−0.0278	−0.2067	= − [illegible]	− [illegible]
[illegible]	+0.9983	+ [illegible]	−0.0541	−0.9972	+ [illegible]	−0.0456	−0.0743	−0.2196	= + [illegible]	+ [illegible]

Bedingungsgleichungen aus den Differenzen in Breite:

Nr.	$d\beta \times$	$d\lambda \times$	$dJ \times$	$b_0 \sin B_0 \times$	$b_0 \cos B_0 \times$	$f_1 \times$	n	v
[illegible]	+0.9987	+0.0275	+0.1693	+0.9390	−0.3413	+0.0517	= − [illegible]	− [illegible]
[illegible]	+0.9987	[illegible]	+0.9708	+0.2782	+0.9605	+0.0607	= − [illegible]	+ [illegible]
[illegible]	+0.9987	[illegible]	+0.8584	+0.8816	+0.4720	+0.0907	= − [illegible]	+ 34.6
[illegible]	+0.9987	−0.0226	+0.5639	−0.3913	+0.9203	+0.0987	= − 219.0	− [illegible]
	+0.9987	−0.0253	+0.4189	−0.5578	+0.8300	+0.0997	= − [illegible]	− [illegible]
[illegible]	+0.9987	[illegible]	+0.9447	+0.7798	+0.6260	+0.1255	= − [illegible]	− [illegible]
[illegible]	+0.9987	−0.0273	+0.1978	−0.7214	+0.6925	+0.1345	= + [illegible]	+ [illegible]
[illegible]	+0.9987	−0.0279	+ [illegible]	−0.8426	+0.5386	+0.1358	= + [illegible]	+ [illegible]
[illegible]	+0.9987	−0.0264	+0.3218	−0.6121	+0.7909	+0.1665	= + [illegible]	+ [illegible]
[illegible]	+0.9987	−0.0277	+0.0878	−0.7818	+0.6234	+0.1677	= [illegible]	+ [illegible]
	+0.9987	[illegible]	−0.9079	−0.8529	−0.5220	+0.1739	= + [illegible]	− [illegible]
[illegible]	+0.9987	−0.0277	+0.1154	−0.7518	+0.6523	+0.1992	= + [illegible]	+ [illegible]
[illegible]	+0.9987	−0.0278	−0.0775	−0.8642	+0.5038	+0.2001	= + [illegible]	+ [illegible]
[illegible]	+0.9987	−0.0274	+0.1861	−0.6891	+0.7246	+0.2270	= [illegible]	+ [illegible]
[illegible]	+0.9987	−0.0278	−0.0319	−0.8299	+0.5581	+0.2292	= [illegible]	+ [illegible]
[illegible]	+0.9987	−0.0242	−0.4946	−0.9942	+0.1079	+0.2326	= [illegible]	− [illegible]
[illegible]	+0.9987	− [illegible]	−0.6825	−0.9922	−0.1248	+0.2337	= + [illegible]	− 23.3
[illegible]	+0.9987	−0.0275	−0.9951	−0.6648	−0.7470	+0.2371	= [illegible]	− [illegible]
[illegible]	+0.9987	[illegible]	−0.2129	−0.9008	+0.4161	+0.2601	= [illegible]	− [illegible]
[illegible]	+0.9987	− [illegible]	−0.7916	−0.9645	−0.2644	+0.2632	= [illegible]	− [illegible]
[illegible]	+0.9987	− [illegible]	−0.8892	−0.9160	−0.4011	+0.2911	= [illegible]	− [illegible]
[illegible]	+0.9987	0.0000	−1.0000	−0.6186	−0.7857	+0.2932	= + [illegible]	
[illegible]	+0.9987	+0.0287	+0.5246	+0.9927	−0.1209	+0.3019	= [illegible]	+ [illegible]
[illegible]	+0.9987	− [illegible]	−0.9979	−0.6823	−0.7310	+0.3181	= + [illegible]	+ [illegible]
[illegible]	+0.9987	+0.0269	+0.2631	+0.9103	−0.4139	+0.3253	= + 84.2	+ [illegible]
[illegible]	+0.9987	+0.0245	+0.4730	+0.9801	−0.1965	+0.3262	= − [illegible]	+ [illegible]
[illegible]	+0.9987	+ [illegible]	+0.6649	+0.9994	+0.0341	+0.3270	= − [illegible]	− [illegible]
[illegible]	+0.9987	[illegible]	+0.8171	+0.9658	+0.2595	+0.3279	= [illegible]	− [illegible]
[illegible]	+0.9987	[illegible]	+0.9055	+0.9135	+0.4067	+0.3509	= − [illegible]	− [illegible]
[illegible]	+0.9987	+0.0261	+0.3522	−0.9322	−0.3621	+0.3688	= [illegible]	− [illegible]
[illegible]	+0.9987	+0.0230	+0.5676	+0.9895	−0.1445	+0.3696	= − [illegible]	− [illegible]
[illegible]	+0.9987	[illegible]	+0.9993	+0.6961	+0.7178	+0.3724	= − [illegible]	− [illegible]
	+0.9987	[illegible]	+0.6903	+0.9999	[illegible]	+0.3881	= − [illegible]	+ [illegible]
[illegible]	+0.9987	+ [illegible]	+0.9465	+0.8823	+0.4707	+0.3895	= − [illegible]	+ [illegible]
	+0.9987	− [illegible]	+0.9906	+0.5870	+0.8095	+0.3908	= − [illegible]	− [illegible]
[illegible]	+0.9987	+0.0215	+0.6364	+0.9968	−0.0799	+0.4037	= + [illegible]	+ [illegible]
[illegible]	+0.9988	[illegible]	+0.7032	[illegible]	+0.9999	+0.4076	= − [illegible]	− [illegible]
88	+0.9987	−0.0279	+0.0488	−0.6780	+0.7351	+0.4092	= − [illegible]	− [illegible]
[illegible]	+0.9987	[illegible]	+0.8966	+0.3406	+0.9402	+0.4298	= − 158.0	−
	+0.9987	−0.0217	+0.6286	−0.0775	+0.9970	+0.4304	= − [illegible]	− [illegible]
	+0.9987	−0.0274	+0.1711	−0.5504	+0.8348	+0.4311	= − [illegible]	[illegible]
[illegible]	+0.9987	− [illegible]	−0.6865	−0.9981	+0.0612	+0.4324	= + [illegible]	+ [illegible]

Die Beobachtung [illegible], welche Hartwig ausgeschlossen hat, schliesse ich auch aus. Aus den Längengleichungen leitete ich, mit steter Prüfung durch die Summencontrollen, die folgenden Normalgleichungen ab:

$d\lambda \times$	[illegible] $\times$	$dJ \times$	$a_0 \sin A_0 \times$	$a_0 \cos A_0 \times$	$b_0 \sin B_0 \times$	$b_0 \cos B_0 \times$	[illegible] $\times$	n
+ [illegible]	+0.2711	−0.6643	+ 0.9058	+ [illegible]	−0.3765	−0.5570	− [illegible]	= − [illegible]
+ 0.2711	[illegible]	−0.0323	+ 0.1354	+ 0.1288	[illegible]	−0.0305	− 0.3316	= − 64.5
− 0.6643	−0.0323	+0.0620	− 0.2521	− 0.3930	+0.0252	+0.0608	+ 0.6476	= + 118.8
+ 0.9058	+0.1354	−0.2521	[illegible]	+ [illegible]	[illegible]	−0.3307	− [illegible]	= − [illegible]

$d\lambda \times$	$d\beta \times$	$dJ \times$	$a_0 \sin A_0 \times$	$a_0 \cos A_0 \times$	$b_0 \sin B_0 \times$	$b_0 \cos B_0 \times$	$f_1 \times$	
+ 26.8926	+ 0.1283	− 0.3930	+ 1.3887	+ 21.8100	− 0.0435	− 0.4380	− 3.3464	= − 1044″.6
− 0.3765	− 0.0148	+ 0.0252	+ 0.0083	− 0.0435	+ 0.0401	+ 0.0024	+ 0.0543	= − 41.7
− 0.5570	− 0.0305	+ 0.0608	− 0.3307	− 0.4380	+ 0.0024	+ 0.0780	+ 0.7908	= + 172.0
− 2.1813	− 0.3316	+ 0.6476	− 8.3311	− 3.3464	+ 0.0543	+ 0.7908	+ 14.8235	= + 3235.3

Ebenso ergaben sich aus den Breitengleichungen die folgenden Normalgleichungen:

$d\lambda \times$	$d\beta \times$	$dJ \times$	$b_0 \sin B_0 \times$	$b_0 \cos B_0 \times$	$f_1 \times$	
+ 0.0180	− 0.2716	+ 0.1445	+ 0.5349	− 0.2661	− 0.0561	= − 74″.0
− 0.2716	+ 40.8935	+ 7.7204	− 4.7461	+ 11.5289	+ 11.0540	= + 959.1
+ 0.1445	+ 7.7204	+ 17.7933	+ 13.9474	+ 11.0054	+ 2.3748	= − 4015.5
+ 0.5349	− 4.7461	+ 13.9474	+ 25.9658	− 0.8352	− 0.6065	= − 4223.4
− 0.2661	+ 11.5289	+ 11.0054	− 0.8352	+ 15.0334	+ 2.9649	= − 1604.7
− 0.0561	+ 11.0540	+ 2.3748	− 0.6065	+ 2.9649	+ 3.5185	= + 204.4

Die Breiten ergeben sich aus den Beobachtungen genauer als die Längen, weil für die Breitenbestimmung der Abstand des Kraters von zwei gegenüberstehenden Rändern, dem nördlichen und südlichen, für die Längenbestimmung dagegen im Wesentlichen nur von dem vorangehenden oder folgenden, jedesmal dem beleuchteten Rand, gemessen wird. Daher haben die Breitengleichungen grösseres Gewicht. Aus den bei Hartwig's Reduction übrig bleibenden Fehlern ergiebt sich, dass das Gewicht der Breitengleichungen sich zu dem der Längengleichungen in diesem Falle wie 2.3090 : 1 verhält. Daher wurden die Normalgleichungen für Breite mit 2.309 multipliziert und zu den Normalgleichungen für Länge addiert. Hierdurch ergaben sich die folgenden allgemeinen Normalgleichungen:

$d\lambda \times$	$d\beta \times$	$dJ \times$	$a_0 \sin A_0 \times$	$a_0 \cos A_0 \times$	$b_0 \sin B_0 \times$	$b_0 \cos B_0 \times$	$f_1 \times$	
+ 40.9023	− 0.3560	− 0.3307	+ 0.9058	+ 26.8926	+ 0.8585	− 1.1714	− 2.3109	= − 906″.5
− 0.3560	+ 94.4884	+ 17.7935	+ 0.1854	+ 0.1283	− 10.9782	+ 26.5889	+ 25.1913	= + 2150.0
− 0.3307	+ 17.7935	+ 41.1454	− 0.2521	− 0.3930	+ 32.2287	+ 25.4715	+ 6.1309	= − 9152.7
+ 0.9058	+ 0.1854	− 0.2521	+ 19.0747	+ 1.3887	+ 0.0083	− 0.3307	− 8.3311	= − 888.8
+ 26.8926	+ 0.1283	− 0.3930	+ 1.3887	+ 21.8100	− 0.0435	− 0.4380	− 3.3464	= − 1044.6
+ 0.8585	− 10.9782	+ 32.2287	+ 0.0083	− 0.0435	+ 59.9982	− 1.9260	− 1.3461	= − 9793.2
− 1.1714	+ 26.5889	+ 25.4715	− 0.3307	− 0.4380	− 1.9260	+ 34.7890	+ 7.6365	= − 3533.1
− 2.3109	+ 25.1913	+ 6.1309	− 8.3311	− 3.3464	− 1.3461	+ 7.6365	+ 22.3359	= + 3707.2

Die Lösungen dieser Gleichungen sind:

$d\lambda = +\ 10''.1$	Gewicht	7.472	$a_0 \sin A_0 = +\ 57''.6$	Gewicht	14.733
$d\beta = -\ 2.1$	„	48.699	$a_0 \cos A_0 = -\ 31.1$	„	3.887
$dJ = -\ 334.4$	„	3.414	$b_0 \sin B_0 = +\ 24.2$	„	8.921
$f_1 = +\ 240.9$	„	11.816	$b_0 \cos B_0 = +\ 93.8$	„	5.240

Diese Lösungen wurden in die Normalgleichungen eingesetzt und befriedigten dieselben vollkommen. Die Gewichte wurden dadurch erhalten, dass die Reihenfolge der Elimination so variiert wurde, dass jede Unbekannte einmal als die zuletzt bestimmte auftrat.

Die Lösungen wurden auch in die Bedingungsgleichungen eingesetzt und so die Darstellung der Beobachtungen durch die Lösungen gefunden. Die übrig bleibenden Fehler v sind gleich hinter den Bedingungsgleichungen in der letzten Vertikalreihe angegeben. Die Summe der Fehlerquadrate oder Σv^2 für die Längengleichungen ist 826288 in Sekunden, ebenso für die Breitengleichungen 376070. Letztere Zahl, mit dem Gewicht 2.309 multipliziert und zu ersterer addiert, giebt als allgemeine Fehlerquadratsumme 1694628, während die Auflösung der Normalgleichungen für die Kontrollgrösse, die man mit $[nn\ 8] = [ns\ 8] = [ss\ 8]$ zu bezeichnen pflegt, 1692600 ergab, also eine Zahl, die mit der vorigen, einer in vier Dezimalstellen angesetzten Rechnung gemäss, übereinstimmt und daher die Richtigkeit der Auflösung von Neuem garantiert. Aus derselben findet sich der wahrscheinliche Fehler einer Beobachtung vom Gewichte 1 zu ± 102″.0 und hieraus und aus den obigen Gewichten ergeben sich die wahrscheinlichen Fehler der gesuchten Grössen.

Die gefundenen Werthe und ihre wahrscheinlichen Fehler sind nun:

$$\begin{array}{rl|rl} \lambda = & -5^\circ 10' 47''.3 \pm 37''.3 & a_0 \sin A_0 = & +57''.6 \pm 26''.6 \\ \beta = & -3\ 10\ 23.6 \pm 14.6 & a_0 \cos A_0 = & -31.1 \pm 51.7 \\ J = & 1\ 30\ 12.4 \pm 55.2 & b_0 \sin B_0 = & +24.2 \pm 34.2 \\ f = & 0.5276 \pm 0.0650 & b_0 \cos B_0 = & +93.8 \pm 44.6 \end{array}$$

während Hartwig (nach Monthly Not. Vol. 41, pag. 376) gefunden hatte:

$$\begin{array}{rl|rl} \lambda = & -5^\circ 10' 58'' \pm 23''.8 & a_0 \sin A_0 = & +62''.3 \pm 22''.8 \\ \beta = & -3\ 10\ 23 \pm 12.5 & a_0 \cos A_0 = & -0.9 \pm 35.1 \\ J = & 1\ 36\ 39 \pm 139.3 & b_0 \sin B_0' = & +294.6 \pm 131.7 \\ f = & 0.507 \pm 0.0602 & b_0 \cos B_0' = & +56.4 \pm 47.6 \end{array}$$

wobei zu bemerken ist, dass $B_0' = B_0 - 10^\circ 28'$ ist.

Der von Hartwig errechnete hohe Wert der Neigung J des Mondäquators gegen die Ekliptik bestätigt sich also in zweiter Näherung nicht. — Es ist sogar auffallend, dass aus denselben Beobachtungen sich überhaupt so verschiedene Ergebnisse finden und dass auch die wahrscheinlichen Fehler so verschieden ausfallen.

Die Erklärung dieser verschiedenen Ergebnisse findet sich ausser in den verschiedenen Annahmen für die Berechnung der Coefficienten darin, dass die Unbekannten J, $b_0 \sin B_0$ und $b_0 \cos B_0$ sich nicht genügend trennen lassen. Da sie in den Bedingungsgleichungen für Länge nur sehr kleine Coefficienten haben, kommen für ihre Bestimmung wesentlich nur die Bedingungsgleichungen für Breite in Betracht. Letztere haben aber die Form:

$$-\sin(l-n)\, dJ + \cos L\, b_0 \sin B_0 + \sin L\, b_0 \cos B_0 + \ldots = 0$$

wo $L = l - 177^\circ 1'.9 + 45''.3\,(t-t_0)$ war. Da die tägliche Änderung des Mondknotens $n = -190''.6$ ist, so ist $(l-n) = L + c - \alpha\,(t-t_0)$, wo $c = 177^\circ 1'.9$ constant und $\alpha = 235''.9$ sehr klein ist. Würde man für einen Augenblick $\alpha = 0$ setzen, so würde die Determinante der Normalgleichungen lauten:

$$\begin{vmatrix} [\sin^2(L+c)] & [\sin(L+c)\cos L] & [\sin(L+c)\sin L] & \ldots \\ [\cos L \sin(L+c)] & [\cos^2 L] & [\cos L \sin L] & \ldots \\ [\sin L \sin(L+c)] & [\sin L \cos L] & [\sin^2 L] & \ldots \\ \vdots & \vdots & \vdots & \end{vmatrix}$$

Diese Determinante verschwindet, denn addiert man die zweite mit $\sin c$ multiplizierte Reihe zur dritten mit $\cos c$ multiplizierten, so erhält man die erste Reihe. Da nun der Winkel $\alpha\,(t-t_0)$ die Peripherie erst in 15 Jahren durchläuft, so wäre es wünschenswert, dass die Librationsbeobachtungen sich auf solchen Zeitraum erstreckten, damit man die Unbekannten J, b_0 und B_0 mit Sicherheit trennen kann. Bei Hartwig, welcher B_0' statt B_0 einführt, sind die Coefficienten von J und $b_0 \sin B_0'$ sogar fast proportional und daher erhält er für diese beiden Unbekannten grosse wahrscheinliche Fehler.

Die willkürliche Libration mit der Amplitude b_0 lässt sich also aus den Beobachtungen eines Zeitraums, der nur wenig ein Jahr überschreitet, nicht bestimmen. Auch die willkürliche Libration mit der Amplitude a_0 hat eine Periode von 2.3 Jahren. Da nun auch die Constanten der willkürlichen Libration sich von derselben Ordnung ergeben wie ihre wahrscheinlichen Fehler, da sowohl verschiedene Beobachtungsreihen (vergl. Wichmann) als auch verschiedene Berechnungsweisen derselben Beobachtungsreihe ihnen völlig verschiedene Werte beilegen, so müssen die bisherigen Bestimmungen derselben für illusorisch angesehen werden und die willkürliche Libration für jetzt für unmerklich klein gelten.

Daher muss man die Normalgleichungen nur mit Rücksicht auf die notwendige Libration auflösen. Unsere Normalgleichungen geben:

$$\begin{array}{rlll} d\lambda = & -12''.1 & \text{Gewicht } 40.598 & \text{oder } \lambda = -5^\circ 11' 9''.5 \pm 16''.2 \\ d\beta = & +14.8 & \text{,, } 68.565 & \beta = -3\ 10\ 6.7 \pm 12.9 \\ dJ = & -260.8 & \text{,, } 37.674 & J = 1\ 31\ 36.0 \pm 16.8 \\ f_1 = & +213.89 & \text{,, } 16.046 & f = 0.4684 \pm 0.0564 \end{array}$$

Die Summe der Fehlerquadrate in Sekunden wird 1821951, und der Umstand, dass dieselbe mit vier Unbekannten weniger nur im Verhältnis von 13 : 14 zugenommen hat, spricht dafür, dass diese Auflösung sachgemäss ist. Ebenso ergeben:

Hartwigs Normalgleichungen	Wichmanns Beobachtungen (A. N. Bd. 27 pag. 97)
$\lambda = -5^{\circ}\,11'\,10''.7$	$\lambda = -5^{\circ}\,11'\,16''.3$
$\beta = -3\;\;9\;\;55.2$	$\beta = -3\;\;10\;\;52.2$
$J = \;\;1\;\;31\;\;27.2$	$J = \;\;1\;\;32\;\;28.7$
$f = 0.4001$	$f = 0.4451$

Hier haben wir eine befriedigende Übereinstimmung der Ergebnisse der Heliometerbeobachtungen unter einander und auch mit den von Pritchard in Oxford aus Messungen an Mondphotographien abgeleiteten Resultaten (vgl. Monthly Notices, Vol. 41 pag. 307). Nimmt man demnach in runden Zahlen $J = 1^{\circ}\,32'$, $f = 0.44$ an, so hat man für die Hauptträgheitsmomente A, B, C des Mondes die Beziehungen

$$\frac{C-B}{A} = 0.000272 \qquad \frac{C-A}{B} = 0.000618 \qquad \frac{B-A}{C} = 0.000346.$$

Darauf folgte die **General-Versammlung**, in welcher einstimmig gewählt wurden:

Zum Ehrenmitglied:

1. Herr Professor Dr. Beyrich, Geheimer Bergrat, Direktor der geologischen Landesanstalt in Berlin.

Zu ordentlichen Mitgliedern:

2. Herr Dr. Karl Schmidt, Assistent des mathematisch-physikalischen Instituts der Universität, hier.
3. Herr Rittmeister von Pelchrzim, hier.
4. „ Paul Köhler, wissenschaftlicher Lehrer der Kneiphöfischen Mittelschule, hier.
5. „ R. Leupold, Buchdruckereibesitzer, hier.
6. „ Franz Scheefer, Mittelhufen.

Zu auswärtigen Mitgliedern:

7. „ Dr. Conwentz, Direktor des Provinzialmuseums zu Danzig.
8. „ Landesgeolog und Privatdocent Dr. Felix Wahnschaffe in Berlin.
9. „ Dr. Rosenthal, prakt. Arzt in Schippenbeil.
10. „ Schriftsteller Hermann Elsner in Elbing.

Sitzung vom 6. Oktober.

Der Vorsitzende eröffnet die Sitzung und begrüsst die Anwesenden nach den Ferien. Leider hat die Gesellschaft in den letzten Wochen sehr traurige Verluste durch den Tod erfahren, Verluste, welche zum Teil als unersetzliche bezeichnet werden müssen. Der Zeitfolge nach war der erste Todesfall, welcher uns betraf, der des Professors Lentz, welcher im August verstarb. Der Verstorbene, ein geborener Königsberger, war Philologe, Oberlehrer am Kneiphöfischen Gymnasium und seit 1859 Mitglied unserer Gesellschaft. Er hatte sich in späteren Jahren mit besonderem Eifer dem Studium der preussischen Käfer zugewandt, welche er mit Vorliebe sammelte und in ihrer Verbreitung zu erforschen suchte. Die Gesellschaft hat vor mehreren Jahren ein von Professor Lentz zusammengestelltes Verzeichnis der Käfer Preussens nebst Nachtrag in ihren Schriften gedruckt. Sie wird den Verfasser dieser Arbeit, welcher ausserdem ein liebenswürdiger Herr war, in ehrendem Andenken behalten.

Am Ende desselben Monats traf uns ein zweiter Verlust, indem unser langjähriges Vorstandsmitglied Professor Dr. Möller nach langen schweren Leiden plötzlich verstarb. Möller, ebenfalls in Königsberg und zwar am 7. Juni 1819 geboren, vielen von uns durch alte Jugendfreundschaft verbunden und seit 1847 Mitglied dieser Gesellschaft, hatte stets ein lebhaftes Interesse für dieselbe und hat hier mehrere interessante Vorträge, namentlich aus dem Gebiete der öffentlichen Gesundheitspflege, gehalten. Diese Vorträge, welche zum Teil in den Gesellschaftsschriften ausführlich gedruckt sind, haben auch auswärts Anerkennung gefunden. Das Andenken des Verstorbenen wird uns allen teuer bleiben.

Ein besonders heftiger Schlag für die Gesellschaft war der am 18. September c. erfolgte jähe Tod des Professors Robert Caspary, welcher auf einer botanischen Exkursion in Westpreussen plötzlich verstarb. Caspary, hier in Königsberg am 29. Januar 1818 geboren, hatte von Jugend auf eine besondere Neigung für die Beschäftigung mit naturwissenschaftlichen Dingen, später hat er sich in derartigen Studien besonders ausgezeichnet. Eine ganz ungewöhnliche Arbeitskraft und Arbeitslust, eine strenge Konsequenz in der Verfolgung seiner wissenschaftlichen Zwecke, ein eiserner Fleiss, das Talent, richtig und scharf zu beobachten, und eine unzweifelhafte Zuverlässigkeit und Genauigkeit seiner Beobachtungen zeichnete den Verstorbenen stets aus. Während er sich zuerst mit zoologischen und botanischen Studien nebeneinander beschäftigte, mit einer Dissertation de Nectariis in Bonn promovierte, wurde er bald ausschliesslich Botaniker. Ein langer Aufenthalt in England, Reisen in Italien und Frankreich gaben ihm vielfach Gelegenheit, für seine Spezialwissenschaft thätig zu sein; später habilitierte er sich in Berlin für Botanik, gab von dort aus eine Reihe wichtiger botanischer Arbeiten heraus und begann eine grossartig angelegte Monographie der Nymphäen, welche das Hauptwerk seines Lebens werden sollte. Damals schon wurde es ihm durch Unterstützung der königlichen Akademie möglich, eine Reihe von Kupferstichen zu diesem Werke herstellen zu lassen. Immer nicht mit der Vollständigkeit seiner Arbeit zufrieden, sammelte er ein staunenswertes Material aus allen Teilen der Erde und machte zu diesem Zweck mehrfach Reisen nach Süddeutschland, nach Norwegen, nach den Vogesen u. s. w. 1859 wurde Caspary als ordentlicher Professor der Botanik nach Königsberg berufen, hat die zweite Hälfte seines Lebens hier zugebracht und arbeitete bis zu seinem Ende mit rastlosem Fleisse in verschiedener Richtung. Die Arbeit über die Nymphäen wurde ununterbrochen fortgesetzt, und hier interessierte ihn besonders die Feststellung der Arten, und suchte er diese Frage jahrelang mit seltener Ausdauer durch Bastardierung zu lösen. Dieses grosse Werk ist nahezu vollendet, aber noch nicht herausgegeben.

Caspary war von dem lebhaftesten Interesse für sein engeres Vaterland, für die Provinz Preussen beseelt, und wurde daher die Beschäftigung mit den Pflanzen Preussens bald ein Hauptgegenstand seiner Thätigkeit. Er hat während seines Wirkens in Königsberg die Provinz in jedem Jahre in ausgedehnter Weise durchforscht und eine Flora unseres Landes vorbereitet, welche, nach Kreisen geordnet, für einen grossen Teil dieser Kreise der Veröffentlichung barrt. Um eine solche genauere Untersuchung möglich zu machen, reichten die Kräfte eines einzelnen auch bei der grössten Anstrengung nicht aus, daher liess sich der Verstorbene die Gründung eines botanischen Vereins angelegen sein und erlangte dadurch die rüstige Unterstützung aller Pflanzenkundigen der Provinz. Auch in unseren Sitzungen pflegte er jährlich die für die Provinz neuen oder seltenen Pflanzen vorzulegen.

Später waren es auch Studien über die Entstehung des Bernsteins, über die Bernsteinbäume und über pflanzliche Einschlüsse im Bernstein, welche ihn anzogen und zu äusserst wertvollen Arbeiten veranlassten, von welchen kurze Angaben in unseren Schriften veröffentlicht sind; die eigentliche Hauptarbeit aber ist noch nicht gedruckt. Dieses Heft unserer Schriften wird einen Aufsatz über fossile Hölzer bringen, während eine grosse fertige Arbeit über fossile Hölzer druckfertig vorhanden ist. Eine ganz spezielle Bearbeitung der preussischen Pilze mit sehr schönen farbigen Abbildungen ist ebenfalls vollendet, aber nicht gedruckt. Ausserdem hat Caspary sich lange Zeit mit Untersuchung über die Wirkung von Blitzschlägen auf Bäume beschäftigt, und sind darauf bezügliche Arbeiten in unseren Schriften veröffentlicht, doch liegt noch viel zu diesem Zweck gesammeltes Material unbearbeitet vor.

So hat der Verstorbene ununterbrochen geschaffen, und ist es eine Pflicht der Zurückgebliebenen, die Herausgabe der nicht gedruckten Arbeiten in jeder Weise zu fördern.

Da Caspary bei seiner Übersiedelung nach Königsberg sich durch den Mangel an litterarischen Hilfsquellen in seinen wissenschaftlichen Arbeiten sehr behindert fühlte, so war es sein Bestreben, für die Vermehrung der Bücheranschaffung in den öffentlichen Bibliotheken zu sorgen und auch seine eigene Bibliothek nach Kräften zu vergrössern. Ausserdem aber wirkte er dafür, dass unsere Gesellschaft es unternahm, eigene Druckschriften herauszugeben und durch diese einen umfangreichen Tauschverkehr mit anderen Gesellschaften und Akademieen hervorzurufen. Der Verstorbene selbst ging als Bibliothekar der Gesellschaft sofort rüstig ans Werk, und es gelang ihm, einen sehr bedeutenden Schriftenaustausch ins Leben zu rufen, welchem wir unsere schöne Bibliothek zum grossen Teile verdanken. Glücklicherweise hat er in unserem jetzigen Bibliothekar Herrn Dr. Tischler einen Nachfolger gefunden, welcher das von ihm begonnene Werk mit demselben Eifer fortsetzt.

Dadurch, dass Professor Caspary das regste Interesse für die Erforschung der Provinz besass, stand er auf demselben Standpunkt, wie die Physikalisch-ökonomische Gesellschaft, welche ja auch die Bearbeitung der Naturgeschichte der Provinz auf ihr Programm gesetzt hat. So war der Verstorbene für die Gesellschaft ein Hauptförderer ihrer gesamten Thätigkeit. Es wird daher dieser Mann, dessen Verlust für die Gesellschaft ein sehr grosser und vorläufig unersetzlicher ist, fortleben in unserem Gedächtnis, wir werden sein Andenken für alle Zeiten hochschätzen und verehren und wollen uns geloben, ihm nachzueifern.

Um dem Gefühl der Hochachtung und Verehrung für die drei Verstorbenen einen äusseren Ausdruck zu geben, forderte der Vorsitzende die Anwesenden auf, sich von ihren Sitzen zu erheben, und dieses geschieht.

Hierauf hielt Herr Vanhöffen einen Vortrag „Über das Gefässsystem und den Blutlauf der Lungenfische sowie über ihre Stellung zur Flossentheorie."

Die Lungenfische, Doppelatmer oder Dipnoer sind mit Schuppen bedeckte Fische, welche durch Kiemen und Lungen gleichzeitig atmen, da ihre Schwimmblase zur Lunge umgebildet ist. Ihr Skelett verknöchert nur teilweise; die verdauende und resorbierende Fläche des Darms wird durch eine Spiralfalte bedeutend vergrössert. Von allen übrigen lebenden Tieren unterscheiden sie sich durch ihre Bezahnung. Dieselbe besteht aus zwei spitzen oder scharf schneidenden Vorderzähnen und zwei mächtigen Kauplatten mit schneidenden gezackten Rändern im Oberkiefer, die auf entsprechende Kauplatten im Unterkiefer passen. Die Nasenlöcher liegen wie bei Haifischen auf der Unterseite des Kopfes, dicht vor der Oberlippe, nicht, wie man früher angab, innerhalb der Mundhöhle. Die Schwanzflosse ist dorsal und ventral der knorpeligen Wirbelsäule völlig gleich ausgebildet.

Die Lungenfische waren, wie versteinerte Reste beweisen, in früheren geologischen Formationen über die ganze Erde in zahlreichen Arten verbreitet. Jetzt sind nur noch drei Arten erhalten: der brasilianische Lungenfisch Lepidosiren paradoxa, Fitz; der afrikanische Protopterus annectens, Owen; und der australische Lungenfisch Ceratodus Forsteri, Krefft. Lepidosiren paradoxa, im Jahre 1835 entdeckt, ist nur in drei Exemplaren nach Europa gekommen und seit 1845 nicht mehr aufgefunden. Protopterus annectens ist weit verbreitet und häufig in den Flüssen des tropischen Afrika. Er unterscheidet sich von Lepidosiren durch die relativen Verhältnisse des Körpers, durch verschiedene Anzahl der Rippen, Verlauf der wichtigsten Blutgefässe und andere Merkmale. Die Behauptung, dass beide Tiere identisch wären, lässt sich auf einen Irrtum des betreffenden Autors zurückführen. Derselbe rechnete die Arbeit von Peters, dem früheren Direktor des Berliner zoologischen Museums „Über einen dem Lepidosiren annectens verwandten Fisch von Quellimane", die eine Beschreibung des Protopterus giebt, mit unter die Bearbeitungen von Lepidosiren und vergleicht auch damit seine Beobachtungen an Protopterus. Natürlich stellt sich dabei völlige Übereinstimmung heraus.*) Protopterus kapselt sich zur trockenen Jahreszeit in Thon ein und gelangt in solchen Thonkapseln, die er mit einer braunen Haut auskleidet, öfters lebend nach Europa. In der Gefangenschaft wurde beobachtet, dass er Wasser durch die Kiemenspalten presst, aber auch von Zeit zu Zeit an die Oberfläche steigt und die Lunge mit Luft füllt. Es findet also Kiemenatmung neben Lungenatmung statt. Ceratodus Forsteri, 1870 in Queensland entdeckt, bewohnt die Flüsse der Ostküste Australiens. Er unterscheidet sich von Protopterus und Lepidosiren besonders durch bedeutendere Grösse von 1—2 m, durch breite Ruderflossen statt der dünnen cylindrischen Extremitäten jener und durch die einen einfachen Sack bildende Lunge, welche bei jenen beiden in zwei schmale Zipfel gespalten ist. Ceratodus wurde in Sydney in Gefangenschaft beobachtet. Eine Neigung, ans Land zu gehen, zeigten die Tiere nicht, obwohl ihnen dazu Gelegenheit geboten war. Ob sie sich wie Protopterus in Schlamm einkapseln, hat nicht festgestellt werden können.

---

*) Neuerdings stellte Professor A. Schneider fest, dass der von Peters entdeckte afrikanische Lungenfisch Protopterus amphibius Peters 30 Rippen hat, daher von P. annectens Owen mit 35 Rippen als besondere Art getrennt werden muss.

Die Zwischenstellung der Lungenfische zwischen Fische und Amphibien charakterisiert am besten eine Schilderung ihres komplizierten Gefässsystems. Es findet sich bei ihnen ein Herz, das äusserlich dem Fischherzen, mit einfachem Kreislauf, gleicht. Durch eigentümliche Vorrichtungen wird aber eine bei den verschiedenen Arten mehr oder weniger durchgeführte Teilung des Herzens erreicht, die einen doppelten Kreislauf, wie bei den höheren Wirbeltieren, ermöglicht.

Im Sinus venosus, einer Erweiterung der vereinigten Venen, ist eine besondere Partie für das Blut der Lungenvenen abgeteilt. Das arterielle Blut derselben mischt sich bei Ceratodus in der Vorkammer mit einem Teile des venösen Blutes der Körpervenen auf der linken Seite einer bindegewebigen Scheidewand, die die Vorkammer teilt und auch in den Sinus venosus wie in die Herzkammer hineinragt. Der Aortenstiel, conus arteriosus, ist durch ein Klappensystem, die Longitudinalfalte, ebenfalls geteilt. Dadurch wird erreicht, dass die linke Seite des Herzens von gemischtem arteriell-venösem Blute durchströmt wird, welches die erste und zweite Kiemenarterie speist. Die rechte Seite von Vorkammer, Herzkammer und Conus erhält rein venöses Blut der Körpervenen. Mit diesem wird die dritte und vierte Kiemenarterie jederseits versorgt. Das arteriell-venöse Blut der ersten und zweiten Kiemenarterie wird in den Kiemenblättchen des ersten und zweiten Kiemenbogens mit Sauerstoff gesättigt; aus ihnen strömt also in der ersten und zweiten Kiemenvene rein arterielles Blut dem Körper zu. Das rein venöse Blut der dritten und vierten Kiemenarterie kann nicht ebenso viel Sauerstoff in den weniger zahlreichen Blättchen des dritten und vierten Kiemenbogens aufnehmen. Daher stimmt das Blut der dritten und vierten Kiemenvene seiner Qualität nach nur mit dem arteriell-venösen Blute der ersten und zweiten Kiemenarterie überein.

Alle vier Kiemenvenen vereinigen sich jederseits zu einer Wurzel der Aorta descendens, welche also aus vier Gefässen rein arterielles, aus vier anderen arteriell-venöses Blut erhält. Dieses gemischte Blut entspricht dem Körperblut der Amphibien, bei denen sich venöses und arterielles Blut in der Herzkammer mischt. Die erste Kiemenvene giebt jederseits einen Stamm als Carotis ab, die vierte entsendet die rechte und linke Lungenarterie. Die letzteren erhalten arteriell-venöses Blut, welches in den zahlreichen Kammern der Lunge Sauerstoff aufnimmt und als rein arterielles Blut wieder der linken Seite der Vorkammer durch die Lungenvene zugeführt wird.

Bei Protopterus ist die Teilung des Herzens weiter vorgeschritten. Dort tritt durch die linke Seite des Herzens hindurch rein arterielles Blut, aus der Lunge kommend, in die erste und zweite Lungenarterie ein, welche, ohne sich in den Kiemenblättchen zu verästeln, durch die Kiemenbögen gehen. Der erste Kiemenbogen hat daher auch seine Kiemenblättchen verloren. Die zweite Kiemenarterie versorgt die äusseren Kiemen; dieselben erhalten arterielles Blut, sind daher als funktionslose Anhänge zu betrachten. Die rechte Seite des Herzens nimmt sämmtliches Blut der Körpervenen auf, welches in den Kiemen zu arteriell-venösem Blut oxydiert wird.

Bei Lepidosiren sind die Kiemen fast ganz rudimentär geworden. Es sind drei Aortenbögen vorhanden. Die erste und zweite Kiemenarterie führen arterielles Blut und vereinigen sich zur Aorta. Diese nimmt nur einen kleinen Teil des venösen Bluts der dritten Kiemenarterie auf. Ein anderer kleiner Teil desselben versorgt die Kiemen. Die Hauptmasse tritt in die Lunge und wird von dort erst durchgeatmet.

Ähnlicher Blutlauf wie bei den Lungenfischen findet sich nur bei gewissen Schmelzschuppern, den Knochenganoiden und den Salamanderlarven. Die zeitlebens durch Kiemen atmenden Amphibien, die Perennibranchiaten, zu denen man die Dipnoer früher rechnete, stehen diesen fern. Bei ihnen wird die vierte Kiemenvene mit der Lungenarterie rudimentär, daher ist spätere Lungenatmung unmöglich. Die Untersuchung der Zirkulationsorgane ergiebt demnach, dass die Dipnoer als jüngere Tiere zwischen Fische und Amphibien gestellt werden müssen, nicht als Stammformen beider betrachtet werden dürfen. Zum gleichen Resultat führt die Betrachtung der Frage nach der Entwicklung der Extremitäten.

Auf Grund seiner Beobachtungen an den Extremitäten der Wirbeltiere stellte Professor Gegenbaur die Hypothese auf, dass Schulter und Beckengürtel mit ihren Extremitäten umgewandelten Kiemenbögen mit ihren Kiemenstrahlen entsprechen. Durch kräftigere Ausbildung eines mittleren Strahls, der die seitlichen Strahlen als Nebenstrahlen aufnahm, entstand eine Flosse mit zwei Reihen Flossenstrahlen, eine biseriale Extremität. Eine solche biseriale Extremität bezeichnete Gegenbaur als hypothetische Urflosse, als Archipterygium. Als später Ceratodus entdeckt wurde, dessen Flossenskelett ähnlichen Bau wie diese Urflosse zeigte, nahm man an, dass die Dipnoer uralte Tiere seien, bei denen sich die Urflosse erhalten hätte. Von der Ceratodusflosse wurde daher die uniseriale Flosse der übrigen Fische durch Vermehrung der ventralen und Verschwinden der dorsalen Nebenstrahlen abgeleitet. Aus der uniserialen Fischflosse konstruiert dann Gegenbaur durch Verschmälerung die Extremitäten von Amphibien und höheren Wirbeltieren.

Der Gegenbaur'schen Theorie widersprechend vertritt Balfour die Ansicht, dass paarige wie auch unpaare Extremitäten als einfache Hautfalten, Baer'sche Leisten angelegt werden. Dadurch fällt jede Beziehung der Flosse zum Kiemenbogen fort und damit auch der Wert der zweireihigen Anordnung der Ceratodusflosse. Genau betrachtet ist diese auch gar nicht biserial. Die dorsalen Nebenstrahlen sind stärker und weniger zahlreich als die ventralen. An den Basalknorpel setzen sich dorsal vom Mittelstrahl 1, ventral 5 Seitenstrahlen an. Der Mittelstrahl ist von den Nebenstrahlen durch nichts als durch grössere Länge unterschieden. Auch diese können sekundäre Nebenstrahlen tragen.

Das Vorkommen von fossilen Ceratodusresten in den ältesten Schichten genügt nicht, die Ceratodusflosse als Urflosse aufstellen zu lassen, da Haifische gleichzeitig auftreten. Ebenso wenig kann der scheinbar einfachere Bau der Ceratodusflosse ihre Ursprünglichkeit beweisen. Derselbe zeigt hier wie in vielen anderen Fällen Rückbildung an. Einige der ventralen Seitenstrahlen haben ihren Zusammenhang mit dem Basalknorpel verloren. Darin ist die Neigung zu erkennen, die Anzahl der Flossenstrahlen zu reduzieren. Die Verschmälerung der Flosse unter Verlängerung der Mittelaxe fortgesetzt, führt zur Flosse von Protopterus und Lepidosiren die nur einen einfachen Knorpelstrahl besitzen. Ja sie geht weiter bis zum gänzlichen Schwinden der Flosse, da einzelnen Exemplaren von Protopterus die hintere Extremität völlig fehlt.

Dasselbe Prinzip der Verlängerung der Flosse bei Verschmälerung der Basis auf die Flosse der Haifische angewendet, führt zu der des Ceratodus. Die Analogie der Ceratodusflosse mit der Amphibienextremität wurde zuerst von Huxley erkannt. Seine Arbeit jedoch geriet in Vergessenheit. Bei der Ceratodusflosse finden sich zwei Hauptstämme, die mittlere Axe, die die meisten Nebenstrahlen aufnimmt, und der kräftige, dorsale Seitenstrahl. Beide sind schon vorgebildet in der Embryonalflosse der Haifische und auch in der ausgebildeten Flosse derselben erkennbar. Sie finden sich dann wieder in den Extremitäten der Amphibien und aller höheren Wirbeltiere. Die mittlere Axe mit den zahlreichen Nebenstrahlen entspricht dem ulnaren, der dorsale Seitenstrahl dem radialen Stamm.

Aus der Untersuchung der Flosse ergiebt sich daher, wie auch aus der Betrachtung der Zirkulationsorgane, dass die Dipnoer als hochstehende Fische zwischen den übrigen Fischen und den Amphibien vermitteln. Der Widerspruch, der darin lag, dass die hohe Ausbildung einzelner Organe sie neben die Amphibien stellen liess, während sie ihrer Extremitäten wegen unter den niedrigsten Wirbeltieren rangieren sollten, ist gelöst.

Darauf sprach Herr Dr. Franz über die Beobachtung der totalen Sonnenfinsternis am 19. August 1887. Während in Deutschland und im westlichen Russland trübes Wetter herrschte, gelangen in Sibirien und im östlichen Russland eine Reihe von Beobachtungen. In Krasnojarsk am Jenisei erhielt die Expedition der russischen physikalischen Gesellschaft 14 Photographieen der Korona vermittels eines Fernrohrs von $4^1/_2$ Zoll Öffnung und 8 Photographien mit Kamera. Ausserdem erhielt Professor Capustin dort Messungen mit dem Bunsenschen Photometer. In Nijni-Tajil am Ural bekam man eine Photographie. In Jurgewitz, an der Mündung der Unscha in die Wolga, erhielten Professor Vogel aus Charlottenburg und Assistent Belopolsky aus Moskau eine Anzahl Photographieen und Herr Niesten aus Brüssel eine Zeichnung der Korona. In Petrowsk, zwischen Jaroslaw und Moskau, gelangen 2 Photographien und 7 Zeichnungen der Korona. Alle Platten, von denen einige durch Wolken erhalten sind, stellen absolut dieselbe Figur der Korona dar. Professor von Glasenapp aus Petersburg, welcher in Petrowsk beobachtete, kam durch den Anblick der Korona zu der neuen Vermutung, dass dieselbe aus Kometenschweifen bestehe. Nach dieser Annahme müssten fortwährend Kometen die Nähe der Sonne passieren oder in dieselbe fallen, wie man dies bereits früher von Meteoriten annahm. Nun besteht bekanntlich ein enger Zusammenhang zwischen Meteorschwärmen und Kometen, und der Umstand, dass die Kometen um so kräftigere Schweifentwickelung zeigen, je näher sie der Sonne kommen, spricht für die Hypothese. Es brauchen eben nur äusserst kleine, sonst nicht wahrnehmbare Kometen zu sein. Doch scheinen die Spektralbeobachtungen bisher nicht der Glasenapp'schen Hypothese günstig zu sein. Immerhin bietet sie einen neuen Gesichtspunkt der Untersuchung für künftige Beobachtungen totaler Sonnenfinsternisse.

Sitzung am 3. November.

Herr Dr. Franz hielt eine Gedächtnisrede auf Professor E. Luther, welche unter den Abhandlungen dieses Heftes Seite 105 abgedruckt ist.

Herr Dr. Jentzsch sprach über die Gestaltung der preussischen Küste. Seine Untersuchungen über diesen Gegenstand werden später an anderer Stelle veröffentlicht werden.

Herr Dr. Klien hielt einen Vortrag über das Saccharin. Von der Firma Fahlberg, List & Comp. zu Salbke-Westerhysen a. d. E. wird nach einem patentiertem Verfahren seit einiger Zeit Saccharin dargestellt, ein Süssstoff, welcher bei dem Bekanntwerden seiner Eigenschaften im vergangenen Jahre berechtigtes Aufsehen erregte. Trotzdem der Name „Saccharin" von anderen Forschern schon für einen andern Körper in Anspruch genommen war, wurde auch diese Verbindung von dem Entdecker mit derselben Bezeichnung eingeführt, weshalb man bis auf weiteres den Körper „Fahlbergsches Saccharin" nennen muss. Wollte man den Konstitutionsnamen gebrauchen, so müsste man dieses Benzoesäure-Derivat mit Anhydro-Ortho-Sulfamin-Benzoesäure bezeichnen, was für den gewöhnlichen Gebrauch aber kaum angängig erscheinen dürfte.

Das Fahlbergsche Saccharin wird auf synthetischem Wege aus dem Toluol des Steinkohlentheers dargestellt. Es ist dieser Süssstoff also kein Kohlehydrat wie unser Zucker, sondern ein gärungswidriger und bei der Ernährungsfrage bedeutungsloser Stoff. Saccharin schmilzt bei ungefähr 200 Gr. C. und löst sich viel leichter in Alkohol und Äther als in Wasser. Zur Lösung sind auf 1 Teil Saccharin bei 15 Gr. C. 500 Teile Wasser nötig. Die Saccharinlösungen reagiren sauer. Die Bedeutung des Saccharins liegt besonders darin, dass es ungefähr 280mal süsser als der gewöhnliche Handelszucker ist, da der süsse Geschmack des käuflichen Zuckers in einer Lösung von 1 g Zucker auf 250 g Wasser gleich ist dem einer neutralisierten Lösung von 1 g Saccharin auf 70 000 g Wasser. Die von Professor Leyden in Berlin, Professor Mosso und Aducco in Turin, Stutzer in Bonn, Professor Salkowsky in Berlin u. a. vorgenommenen Untersuchungen haben ergeben, dass der dauernde Genuss von Saccharin, selbst in grossen Dosen, dem gesunden wie kranken Organismus absolut unschädlich ist. Sacharin wird von den schwächsten Konstitutionen vertragen und kann, da es den menschlichen Körper unverändert verlässt, besonders auch von Diabetikern ohne irgend welchen nachteiligen Einfluss genossen werden. In den Magen und unter die Haut eingeführt, wird dasselbe sehr schnell absorbiert und sofort wieder ausgeschieden und findet sich in weniger als einer halben Stunde im Harn wieder, wohin es ausschliesslich übergeht. Die Schwankungen, welche die Zusammensetzung des Harns in normalem Zustande zeigt, sind auch bei Zutritt des Saccharins noch dieselben. Prof. Kohlschütter in Halle hat einem Diabetiker verschieden grosse Mengen Saccharin gegeben und dabei konstatiert, dass die Zuckerausscheidungen sich bei Vergrösserung der Saccharingabe (pro Tag von 0,5—2 g) entsprechend verminderten. Der Appetit des Kranken soll allerdings dabei geringer geworden sein, obwohl eine Gewichtsabnahme des Patienten nicht stattgefunden hatte.

Bei den vorteilhaften Eigenschaften des Saccharins darf demselben somit eine grosse Anwendungsfähigkeit vorausgesagt werden. Namentlich in Hinsicht auf den aussergewöhnlich süssen Geschmack, und die antiseptischen Eigenschaften kann mit Sicherheit erwartet werden, dass wir diesem Körper im Gemisch mit vielen verbreiteten Nahrungs- und Genussmitteln bald begegnen werden. Es kann derselbe deshalb sehr wohl über kurz oder lang Gegenstand der Betrachtung bei dem Nahrungsmittelchemiker werden, welcher jetzt auch die Anwesenheit durch bestimmte chemische Reaktionen festzustellen weiss. Herrn Pinette gelang es, das Saccharin selbst in sehr kleinen Mengen in Salicylsäure überzuführen und die Reaktionen dieser Säure, sowie die bekannten Methoden zum Nachweis dieser auch für den Nachweis des Saccharins dienstbar zu machen. Man erhält nämlich beim Schmelzen des Saccharins mit Alkalien nicht nur schwefelsaures, sondern auch salicylsaures Alkali, worauf der Nachweis des Saccharins beruht. Es ist natürlich selbstverständlich, dass man sich vor der Nachweisung des Saccharins von der Abwesenheit der Salicylsäure überzeugt.

Zum Schluss entkorkte der Vortragende noch zwei Flaschen Saccharin-Mousseux, welche von der Champagnerfabrik M. Maas & Co. in Mainz der Gesellschaft gratis zur Verfügung gestellt worden waren, und der süsse Trank wurde eifrigst von den Anwesenden gekostet.

Sitzung am 1. Dezember.

Herr Dr. Abromeit hielt eine Gedächtnisrede auf den Königsberger Botaniker Prof. Robert Caspary, welche unter den Abhandlungen dieses Bandes Seite 111 abgedruckt ist.

Herr Geheimer Medizinalrat Prof. Dr. Hermann sprach über den gegenwärtigen Stand der Lehre vom Nervenprinzip. Der Vortragende gab eine Übersicht der verschiedenen Ansichten, welche seit dem Altertum über das Wesen des nervösen Prozesses geherrscht haben. Die Vorstellung, dass Elektrizität dabei im Spiele sei, tauchte anscheinend im Jahre 1743 zuerst auf, anfangs anknüpfend an die damals ganz allein bekannten Entladungen von Spannungselektrizität. Die in Folge der Entdeckungen Galvani's näher begründete Lehre von der Existenz einer tierischen Elektrizität, sowie die Entdeckung der streng gesetzmässigen Reizwirkungen des Stromes, drängte die Meinung, dass galvanische Ströme, welche längs der Nerven verlaufen, die Wirkung des Nerven vermitteln, in den Vordergrund, eine Ansicht, welche, obwohl schon Haller den Einwand erhoben hatte, dass den Nerven isolierende Hüllen fehlen und dass ihre Unterbindung die Leitung aufhebt, in der Analogie mit dem elektrischen Telegraphen und in der Irrlehre, dass die Nerven aus den Organen, zu denen sie verlaufen, zum Gehirn zurückkehren, also geschlossene Kreise bilden, scheinbar mächtige Unterstützung fand.

In richtigere Bahnen wurde die Theorie erst gelenkt, als du Bois-Reymond 1848 den Nervenstrom entdeckte, dessen wesentlichstes Element durch Versuche du Bois-Reymonds, Bernsteins und des Vortragenden in einer mit der Erregung verbundenen örtlichen Negativität erkannt wurde, und als Pflüger 1858 zeigte, dass die Nervenfaser durch den Strom bei der Schliessung an der Austrittsstelle und bei der Öffnung an der Eintrittsstelle erregt wird. In diesen beiden Ergebnissen liegen, wie der Vortragende nachweist, die Keime zu einer vollständigen Theorie der Nervenleitung, indem jede erregte Stelle Sitz enorm starker Ströme wird, welche so verlaufen, dass sie die Nachbarschaft erregen, die erregte Stelle aber beruhigen müssen. Es dürfte einst gelingen, aus diesen Elementen die Notwendigkeit einer wellenartigen Fortpflanzung des elektrischen Vorganges herzuleiten. Das Pflügersche Gesetz seinerseits deutet darauf hin, dass die Polarisation der Nervenfasern bei der elektrischen Erregung, und somit der nervösen Leitung, eine maassgebende Rolle spielt; neuere Untersuchungen des Vortragenden haben gelehrt, dass die Polarisation des Nerven (und Muskels) hinsichtlich der Energie ihrer Entwicklung kaum irgendwo ein Beispiel findet und in ihrer Grösse an die der Metalle heranreicht, somit ebenso gut wie die elektromotorische Kraft bei der Erregung, zu den spezifischen Eigenschaften der Nerven und Muskeln zu rechnen ist.

Hierauf folgte die **Generalversammlung**. Der Rendant der Gesellschaft, Herr Hofapotheker Hagen gab einen Kassenbericht.

In der nun folgenden Vorstandswahl für das nächste Jahr wurde Se. Exc. Herr Staatsrat Professor Dr. L. Stieda, Direktor der Königl. Anatomie, an Stelle des verstorbenen Dr. J. Möller zum Direktor der Gesellschaft gewählt. Die übrigen Vorstandsmitglieder wurden wieder gewählt. Der Vorstand besteht jetzt also aus folgenden Herren:

Präsident: Geheimer Sanitätsrat Dr. Schiefferdecker.
Direktor: Ordentlicher Professor Dr. Stieda.
Sekretär: Observator Dr. Franz.
Kassenkurator: Kommerzienrat Weller.
Rendant: Hofapotheker Hagen.
Bibliothekar und auswärtiger Sekretär: Dr. Tischler.

Hierauf wurden gewählt:

I. Zu ordentlichen Mitgliedern.

1. Herr Dr. Abromeit, Assistent am botanischen Institut.
2. „ Dr. J. Bamberger, Pfarrer.
3. „ Dr. Branco, ordentlicher Professor der Mineralogie und Geologie.
4. „ von Brandt, Polizei-Präsident.
5. „ Johannes Caspary, cand. jur.
6. „ Gustav Ehlers, Kaufmann.
7. „ L. E. Gottheil, Hof-Photograph.
8. „ Dr. Kafemann, Arzt.
9. „ Knoblauch, Assistent am botanischen Institut.
10. „ Alfred Lemke, cand. rer. nat.
11. „ Dr. Mikulicz, Medizinalrat und ordentlicher Professor der Chirurgie.
12. „ Pieske, Premierlieutenant.
13. „ Dr. Seeliger, Privatdozent der Zoologie.
14. „ Thomas, Hauptmann.
15. „ Franz Werner, Assistent am physikalischen Institut.

II. Zu auswärtigen Mitgliedern.

1. Herr Dr. Beyer, Oberlehrer in Wehlau.
2. „ Eben, Rittergutsbesitzer auf Banditten.
3. „ Dr. Künzer, Professor und Oberlehrer in Marienwerder.
4. „ Dr. Wilh. Pabst, 1. Lehrer der Naturwissenschaften an der Landwirtschaftsschule zu Marggrabowa.
5. „ Richard Weiss, Apothekenbesitzer in Caymen.

Bericht für 1887

über die

Bibliothek der physikalisch-ökonomischen Gesellschaft

von

Dr. Otto Tischler.

Die Bibliothek befindet sich im Provinzial-Museum der Gesellschaft, Lange Reihe 4, 2 Treppen hoch. Bücher werden an die Mitglieder gegen vorschriftsmässige Empfangszettel Vormittags bis 12 Uhr und Nachmittags von 2 Uhr an ausgegeben. Dieselben müssen spätestens nach 3 Monaten zurückgeliefert werden.

Verzeichnis

derjenigen Gesellschaften, mit welchen die physikalisch-ökonomische Gesellschaft in Tauschverkehr steht, sowie der im Laufe des Jahres 1887 eingegangenen Werke.

(Von den mit † bezeichneten Gesellschaften kam uns 1887 keine Sendung zu.)

Die Zahl der mit uns in Tausch stehenden Gesellschaften hat 1886 um folgende 8 zugenommen:

Berlin. Kgl. Preussisches Meteorologisches Bureau.
München. Gesellschaft für Morphologie und Physiologie.
Stettin. Verein für Erdkunde.
Lemberg. Kopernikus. Gesellschaft Polnischer Naturforscher.
Moskau. Daschkoff'sches Ethnographisches Museum.
Tōkyō. Imperial University of Japan.
New-Orleans. Academy of sciences.
Caracas. Estadas Unidos de Venezuela.

Nachstehendes Verzeichnis bitten wir zugleich als Empfangsbescheinigung ansehen zu wollen statt jeder besonderen Anzeige. Besonders danken wir noch den Gesellschaften, welche auf Reclamation durch Nachsendung älterer Jahrgänge dazu beigetragen haben, Lücken in unserer Bibliothek auszufüllen. In gleicher Weise sind wir stets bereit, solchen Reclamationen nachzukommen, soweit es der Vorrat der früheren Bände gestattet, den wir immer zu ergänzen streben, so dass es von Zeit zu Zeit möglich wird, auch augenblicklich ganz vergriffene Hefte nachzuliefern.

Diejenigen Herren Mitglieder der Gesellschaft, welche derselben ältere Jahrgänge der Schriften zukommen lassen wollen, werden uns daher im Interesse des Schriftentausches zu grossem Danke verpflichten.

Belgien.

1. **Brüssel.** Académie Royale des sciences des lettres et des arts.: 1) Bulletin 3. Serie 9–13. 2) Mémoires des membres in 4^0 46. 3) Mémoires couronnés et des savants étrangers in 4^0 47. 48. 4) Mémoires couronnés et autres Mémoires in 8^0 37–39. 5) Annuaire 1886. 87. 6) Bibliographie académique 1886. 7) Catalogue des livres de la bibliothèque I. II. 1. 2.

2. **Brüssel.** Academie Royale de médecine de Belgique. 1) Bulletin: 4 Ser 1 (1887). 2) Mémoires couronnés et autres mémoires in 8^0 VIII 2–4.

3. **Brüssel.** Société entomologique Belge: Annales 30.

†4. **Brüssel.** Société malacologique de Belgique. 1) Procès verbaux 1886 p. 1–80 (auch in den Annales enthalten). 2) Annales 21.

5. **Brüssel.** Société Royale de Botanique de Belgique. Bulletin 25_2, 26_1.

†6. **Brüssel.** Commissions Royales d'art et d'archéologie.

7. **Brüssel.** Société Belge de Microscopie Bulletin: 13_{9-11}, 14_1.

†8. **Brüssel.** Observatoire Royal.

9. **Brüssel.** Société Belge de Géographie. Bulletin XI_{1-5}.

†10. **Brüssel.** Société d'Anthropologie.

11. **Lüttich.** Société Royale des sciences. Mémoires 13.

12. **Lüttich.** Société géologique de Belgique. Procès-verbaux de l'assemblée générale 21/11 1886.

†13. **Lüttich.** Institut archéologique.

†14. **Namur.** Société archéologique.

Dänemark.

15. **Kopenhagen.** Kongelig Dansk Videnskabernes Selbskab (Société royale des sciences). 1) Oversigt over Forhandlingerne. (Bulletin) 1886_3, $87_{1,2}$. 2) Skrifter (Mémoires), Naturvidenskabelig og matematisk Afdeling: 6 Raekke $IV_{3,4}$.

†16. **Kopenhagen,** Naturhistorik Porening. Videnskabelige Meddelelser 1884–86.

17. **Kopenhagen.** Kongelig Dansk Nordisk Oldskrift Selskab (Société Royale des antiquaires du Nord). 1) Aarböger for Nordisk Oldkyndighed og Historie $1886_{3,4}$ 1887 (2 Raekke $1)_{1-3}$. 2) Mémoires, Nouvelle Série 1886. 3) Vedel: Bornholms Oldtidsminder og Oldsager (1886 in 4^0).

18. **Kopenhagen.** Botanisk Forening (Société botanique). 1) Botanisk Tidskrift 15_4, 16_{1-3}. 2) Meddelelser (Tillaegshefter til botanisk Tidskrift) II_1.

Deutsches Reich.

†19. **Altenburg.** Naturforschende Gesellschaft des Osterlandes.

†20. **Augsburg.** Naturhistorischer Verein.

21. **Bamberg.** Naturforschende Gesellschaft. Bericht 14 (1887).

22. **Bamberg.** Historischer Verein für Oberfranken. Bericht 48 (1885).

23. **Berlin.** Königl. Preussische Akademie der Wissenschaften. 1) Sitzungsberichte 1886_{55-63} 1887_{1-34}. 2) Abhandlungen, Physikalische 1886.

24. **Berlin.** Botanischer Verein für die Provinz Brandenburg. Verhandlungen 27, 28 (1885, 86)

25. **Berlin.** Deutsche Geologische Gesellschaft. 1) Zeitschrift 38_4, $39_{1,2}$. 2) Katalog der Bibliothek.

26. **Berlin.** Verein zur Beförderung des Gartenbaues in den Preussischen Staaten. Gartenztg. 6 (1887).

27. **Berlin.** Physikalische Gesellschaft. Fortschritte der Physik im Jahre 1881 (Jahrgang 37).

28. **Berlin.** K. Preussisches Landes-Ökonomie-Kollegium. Landwirtschaftliche Jahrbücher 16.

29. **Berlin.** Gesellschaft naturwissenschaftlicher Freunde. Sitzungsberichte 1886.

30. **Berlin.** Gesellschaft für Anthropologie, Ethnologie und Urgeschichte. Verhandlungen 1886 März-Dez., 1887 Jan.-Febr., auf Reclamation 1877 Juli-Dez., 1888.

31. **Berlin.** Geologische Landesanstalt und Bergakademie. 1) Jahrbuch 1885. 2) Geologische Spezialkarte von Preussen und den Thüringischen Staaten (1/250 000) je 1 Blatt mit je 1 Heft Erläuterungen. Lieferung 31 (Grad 67$_{41.42.47.48}$, 68$_{43}$), 32 (Grad 43$_{19.20.21.25.26.27}$). 3) Abhandlungen zur geologischen Spezialkarte VII$_{3.4}$ mit Atlas, VIII$_{2}$ mit Atlas.

32. **Berlin.** Kaiserlich Statistisches Amt. 1) Jahrbuch 1887. 2) Monatshefte 1887. 3) Statistik des Deutschen Reiches, Neue Folge 22 (Verkehr a. d. D. Wasserstrassen 1885), 23 (Kriminalst. 1885), 24 (St. d. Krankenwesens d. Arbeiter 1885), 25 (Waarenverk. mit d. Auslande 1886 I.) 26 (do. II. III.), 27 (St. d. Seeschiffahrt 1887/87 I.), 28 (Verkehr a. d. D. Wasserstr. 1886), 29 (St. d. öffentl. Armenpflege 1885).

33. **Berlin.** K. Preussisches Statistisches Bureau. Zeitschrift: 26$_{3.4}$, 27$_{1.2}$.

34. **Berlin.** Kgl. Preussisches Meteorologisches Bureau: Ergebnisse der meteorologischen Beobachtungen im Jahre 1885.

Bonn. Naturhistorischer Verein der Preussischen Rheinlande und Westfalens. Verhandlungen: 43$_{2}$ (5. Folge 3), 44$_{1}$.

35. **Bonn.** Verein von Altertumsfreunden im Rheinlande. Jahrbücher: 82, 83.

36. **Braunsberg.** Historischer Verein für Ermland. 1) Zeitschrift für die Geschichte und Altertumskunde des Ermlandes VIII$_{1}$. 2) Wölky: Quellenschriften zur Geschichte des Ermlandes.

38. **Braunschweig.** Verein für Naturwissenschaft. Bericht 3–5 (1886, 87).

39. **Bremen.** Naturwissenschaftlicher Verein. Abhandlungen IX$_{4}$.

†40. **Bremen.** Geographische Gesellschaft.

41. **Breslau.** Schlesische Gesellschaft für vaterländische Cultur. 1) Jahresbericht 64. 2) Ergänzungsheft: Zacharias Allerts Tagebuch aus dem Jahre 1687.

42. **Breslau.** Verein für das Museum Schlesischer Altertümer: Schlesiens Vorzeit in Bild und Schrift IV$_{16-20}$.

†43. **Breslau.** Verein für Schlesische Insektenkunde.

44. **Breslau.** K. Oberbergamt. Produktion der Bergwerke, Hütten und Salinen im Preussischen Staate im Jahre 1886.

45. **Chemnitz.** Naturwissenschaftliche Gesellschaft. Bericht 10.

46. **Chemnitz.** Kgl. Sächsisches Meteorologisches Institut. Jahrbuch 3 (1885).

†47. **Coburg.** Anthropologischer Verein.

†48. **Colmar.** Société d'histoire naturelle.

49. **Danzig.** Naturforschende Gesellschaft. Schriften, Neue Folge VI$_{4}$.

50. **Darmstadt.** Verein für Erdkunde und Mittelrheinisch-geologischer Verein. Notizblatt 4 Folge 7.

†51. **Darmstadt.** Historischer Verein für das Grossherzogthum Hessen.

†52. **Dessau.** Naturhistorischer Verein.

†53. **Donaueschingen.** Verein für Geschichte und Naturgeschichte der Baar und angrenzenden Landesteile.

†54. **Dresden.** Verein für Erdkunde.

55. **Dresden.** Naturwissenschaftliche Gesellschaft Isis. Sitzungsberichte und Abhandlungen 1886 Juli-Dez., 1887 Jan.-Juli.

56. **Dresden.** Gesellschaft für Natur- und Heilkunde. Jahresbericht 1886/87.

†57. **Dürkheim a. d. H.** Pollichia, Naturwissenschaftlicher Verein der Rheinpfalz.

58. **Eberswalde.** Forstakademie. 1) Beobachtungsergebnisse der forstlich meteorologischen Stationen. Jahrgang XII (1886)$_{7-12}$, XIII (1887)$_{1-6}$. 2) Jahresbericht 12 (1886).

59. **Elberfeld.** Naturwissenschaftliche Gesellschaft. Jahresbericht. Heft 7.

60. **Emden.** Naturforschende Gesellschaft. Jahresbericht 71.

61. **Emden.** Gesellschaft für bildende Kunst und Vaterländische Altertümer. Jahrbuch 7$_{1.2}$.

62. **Erfurt.** K. Akademie gemeinnütziger Wissenschaften. Jahrbücher: Neue Folge Heft 14, 15.

63. **Erlangen.** Physikalisch-medizinische Sozietat. Sitzungsberichte 18.

64. **Frankfurt a. M.** Senkenbergische naturforschende Gesellschaft. Bericht 1887.

65. **Frankfurt a. M.** Physikalischer Verein. Jahresbericht 1885/86.

66. Frankfurt. Verein für Geographie und Statistik. 1) Jahresbericht 50 (1886). 2) Beiträge zur Statistik der Stadt Frankfurt a. M. VI.
†67. Frankfurt a. M. Verein für Geschichte und Altertumskunde.
68. Frankfurt a. d. O. Naturwissenschaftlicher Verein für den Regierungsbezirk Frankfurt a. d. O. Monatlich. 1) Mitteilungen. Jahrgang 4_{8-10}, 5_{4-6}. 2) Dr. Ernst Huth: Societatum litterae: Verzeichnis der i. d. Publikationen der Akademieen und Vereine aller Länder erschienenen Einzel-Arbeiten a. d. Gebiet der Naturwissenschaften 1887_{6-8}.
69. Freiburg im Breisgau. Naturforschende Gesellschaft. Berichte I (1886).
†70. Fulda. Verein für Naturkunde.
†71. Gera. Verein von Freunden der Naturwissenschaften.
72. Giessen. Oberhessische Gesellschaft für Natur- und Heilkunde. Bericht 25.
73. Görlitz. Naturforschende Gesellschaft. Abhandlungen 19.
74. Görlitz. Oberlausitzische Gesellschaft der Wissenschaften. Neues Lausitzisches Magazin 631.
75. Göttingen. K. Gesellschaft der Wissenschaften. Nachrichten 1886.
76. Greifswald. Naturwissenschaftl. Verein für Neu-Vorpommern und Rügen. Mitteilungen 18.
77. Greifswald. Geographische Gesellschaft. Jahresbericht 2 (1883—86).
78. Güstrow. Verein der Freunde der Naturgeschichte in Mecklenburg. Archiv 40 (1886).
79. Halle. Kaiserlich Leopoldino-Carolinische Akademie der Naturforscher. Leopoldina 23 (1887).
80. Halle. Naturforschende Gesellschaft. 1) Bericht 1885/86. 2) Abhandlungen 16_{4}.
81. Halle. Naturwissenschaftlicher Verein für Sachsen und Thüringen. Zeitschrift für Naturwissenschaften 4. Folge 6_{1-4}.
82. Halle. Verein für Erdkunde. Mittheilungen 1887.
83. Hamburg. Naturwissenschaftlicher Verein von Hamburg. Abhandlungen $9_{1.2}$, 10.
84. Hamburg. Verein für naturwissenschaftliche Unterhaltung. Verhandlungen 1883—85.
†85. Hamburg. Geographische Gesellschaft.
86. Hanau. Wetterauische Gesellschaft für die gesamte Naturkunde. Bericht 1885—87.
†87. Hannover. Naturhistorische Gesellschaft.
†88. Hannover. Historischer Verein für Niedersachsen.
†89. Hannover. Geographische Gesellschaft.
†90. Hannover. Gesellschaft für Mikroskopie.
91. Heidelberg. Naturhistorisch-medizinischer Verein. Verhandlungen. Neue Folge IV_{1}.
92. Jena. Gesellschaft für Medizin und Naturwissenschaft. Jenaische Zeitschrift für Naturwissenschaft 20 (Neue Folge 13), 21 (N. F. 14).
93. Insterburg. Altertumsgesellschaft. 1) Tischler: Über die Gliederung der Urgeschichte Ostpreussens (Vortrag am 11./3. 1887). 2) Horn a) Die Feste Item, b) Das Haus Tammow und der Kamswikusberg. 3) Jahresbericht 1886/87.
94. Insterburg. Landwirtschaftlicher Zentralverein für Littauen und Masuren. Georgine, Landwirtschaftliche Zeitung 55 (1887).
†95. Karlsruhe. Naturwissenschaftlicher Verein.
96. Karlsruhe. Grossherzogliches Altertums-Museum. Beschreibung der Vasensammlung von Hermann Winnfeld.
†97. Kassel. Verein für Naturkunde.
†98. Kassel. Verein für Hessische Geschichte und Landeskunde.
99. Kiel. Universität. 49 Universitätsschriften (1886/87).
†100. Kiel. Naturwissenschaftlicher Verein für Schleswig-Holstein.
†101. Kiel. Schleswig-holsteinisches Museum für vaterländische Altertümer.
102. Kiel. Ministerial-Kommission zur Erforschung der deutschen Meere. 1) Ergebnisse der Beobachtungsstationen an den Deutschen Küsten 1886. 2) Bericht 5 (Jahrgang 12—16) 1882—86.
†103. Klausthal. Naturwissenschaftlicher Verein Maja.
104. Königsberg. Altpreussische Monatsschrift, herausgegeben von Reicke und Wichert 24 (1887).
105. Königsberg. Ostpreussischer landwirtschaftlicher Centralverein. Königsberger Land- und forstwirtschaftliche Zeitung 23 (1887).
106. Landshut. Botanischer Verein. Bericht 10 (1886/87).

107. Leipzig. K. Sächsische Gesellschaft der Wissenschaften. 1) Berichte über die Verhandlungen der mathematisch-physikalischen Klasse 1886 Supplement. 2) Abhandlungen, mathematisch-physikalische Klasse XIII 8. 9, XIV 1–3.
108. Leipzig. Verein für Erdkunde. Mitteilungen 1886.
†109. Leipzig. Naturforschende Gesellschaft.
110. Leipzig. Museum für Völkerkunde. Bericht 1886.
†111. Leipzig. Geologische Landesuntersuchung des Königreichs Sachsen.
†112. Lübben. Nieder-Lausitzer Gesellschaft für Anthropologie und Urgeschichte.
113. Lübeck. Naturhistorisches Museum. Jahresbericht 1885/86.
114. Lüneburg. Naturwissenschaftlicher Verein für das Fürstentum Lüneburg. Jahreshefte 10 (1885–87).
115. Magdeburg. Naturwissenschaftlicher Verein. Jahresbericht 1886.
†116. Mannheim. Verein für Naturkunde.
†117. Marburg. Gesellschaft zur Beförderung der gesamten Naturwissenschaften.
†118. Marienwerder. Historischer Verein für den Regierungsbezirk Marienwerder.
†119. Meiningen. Hennebergischer altertumsforschender Verein.
120. Metz. Académie. Mémoires 2. Période 45 (1883/84).
121. Metz. Société d'histoire naturelle. Bulletin. 2. Sér. 16, 17.
122. Metz. Verein für Erdkunde. Jahresbericht 9 (1886).
123. München. K. Baierische Akademie der Wissenschaften. 1) Sitzungsberichte der mathematisch-physikalischen Klasse 1886 2. 3, 1887 1. 2) Abhandlungen der matematisch-physikalischen Klasse XV 9. XVI 1. 3) Gedächtnisrede auf Karl Theodor v. Siebold von Richard Hertwig. 4) Gedächtnisrede auf Joseph Frauenhofer von Max v. Bauernfeind.
124. München. Geographische Gesellschaft. Jahresbericht 11 (1886).
125. München. Historischer Verein von Oberbayern. 1) Jahresbericht 48, 49 (1885/86). 2) Oberbairisches Archiv für vaterländische Geschichte 44.
126. München. Gesellschaft für Morphologie und Physiologie. Sitzungsberichte II 1–3.
127. Münster. Westphälischer Provinzialverein für Wissenschaft und Kunst. Jahresbericht 15 (1886).
128. Neisse. Philomathie. Bericht 21–23 (1879–86).
129. Nürnberg. Naturhistorische Gesellschaft. Jahresbericht 1887.
130. Nürnberg. Germanisches Museum. 1) Anzeiger I 8. 2) Katalog der im germanischen Museum befindlichen Kartenspiele und Spielkarten. 1886.
†131. Offenbach. Verein der Naturkunde.
†132. Oldenburg. Oldenburger Landesverein für Altertumskunde.
†133. Osnabrück. Naturhistorischer Verein.
†134. Passau. Naturhistorischer Verein.
135. Posen. Gesellschaft der Freunde der Wissenschaften. Zapiski archeologiczne Posnańskie, polnisch mit deutscher Übersetzung: Posener archäologische Mitteilungen, herausgegeben von der archäologischen Kommission der Gesellschaft in Folio 1887 1. 2.
136. Regensburg. Zoologisch-mineralogische Gesellschaft. Correspondenzblatt 40.
137. Regensburg. K. Bairische botanische Gesellschaft. Flora, allgem. botanische Zeitung 44 (1886).
138. Reichenbach im Voigtlande. Voigtländischer Verein für allgemeine und spezielle Naturkunde. Mitteilungen 5.
†139. Schmalkalden. Verein für Hennebergische Geschichte und Landeskunde.
140. Schwerin. Verein für Mecklenburgische Geschichte und Altertumskunde. Jahrbücher und Jahresberichte 52. Register zu 31–50.
141. Sondershausen. Irmischia, Botanischer Verein für Thüringen. Irmischia, Korrespondenzblatt des Vereines VI 7. 8.
142. Stettin. Entomologischer Verein. Entomologische Zeitung 47.
143. Stettin. Gesellschaft für Pommersche Geschichte und Altertumskunde. 1) Baltische Studien 37. 2) Monatsblätter 1887. 3) Baudenkmäler des Regierungsbezirkes Stralsund I.
144. Stettin. Verein für Erdkunde. Jahresbericht 1886.
145. Strassburg. Kommission für die geologische Landesuntersuchung von Elsass-Lothringen. 1) Mitteilungen I 2. 2) Abhandlungen zur geologischen Spezialkarte III 2, IV 3, Ergänzungsheft I.

3) Geologische Übersichtskarte je 1 Heft Erläuterungen und 1 Blatt: a) Die südliche Hälfte des Grossherzogtums Luxemburg, b) des deutschen West-Lothringens, c) der Eisenerzfelder des deutschen West-Lothringens.

†146. Stuttgart. Verein für vaterländische Naturkunde in Würtemberg.

147. Stuttgart. K. statistisches Landesamt. Jahrbücher für Statistik und Landeskunde 1886.

†148. Thorn. Towarzystwa Naukowego.

149. Tilsit. Litauische Litterarische Gesellschaft. Mitteilungen II_6 (Heft 12).

†150. Trier. Gesellschaft für nützliche Forschungen.

†151. Wernigerode. Naturwissenschaftlicher Verein des Harzes.

152. Wiesbaden. Nassauischer Verein für Naturkunde. Jahrbücher 40.

153. Wiesbaden. Verein für Nassauische Altertumskunde und Geschichtsforschung. Annalen 20_1.

†154. Worms, Altertumsverein.

155. Würzburg. Physikalisch-medicinische Gesellschaft. 1) Sitzungsberichte 1886. 2) Verhandlungen 20.

156. Zwickau. Verein für Naturkunde. Jahresbericht 1886.

Frankreich.

157. Albeville. Société d'Emulation. Bulletin des procès-verbaux 1885.

158. Amiens. Société Linnéenne du Nord de la France. 1) Bulletin mensuel $VI_{189-162}$, $VII_{163-174}$ 2) Mémoires 6 (1884/85).

†159. Apt. Société litéraire scientifique et artistique.

160. Auxerre. Société des sciences historiques et naturelles de l'Yonne. Bulletin 40 (3. Sér. 11).

161. Besançon. Société d'Emulation du Doubs. Mémoires 5. Sér. 10 (1885).

†162. Bordeaux. Académie des sciences belles lettres et des arts.

163. Bordeaux. Société Linnéenne. Actes 39 (4. Sér. 9)

†164. Bordeaux. Société des sciences physiques et naturelles

165. Bordeaux. Société de géographie commerciale. Bulletin 2. Sér. 10 (1887).

†166. Caën. Société Linnéenne de Normandie.

†167. Caën. Académie des sciences arts et belles lettres.

†168. Caën. Association Normande.

†169. Chambéry, Académie de Savoie.

†170. Cherbourg. Société nationale des sciences naturelles et mathématiques.

†171. Dijon. Académie des sciences arts et belles lettres.

†172. Dijon. Société d'agriculture et d'industrie agricole du département de la Côte d'or.

173. La Rochelle. Société des sciences naturelles de la Charente inférieure. Annales 22.

†174. Lille. Société des sciences de l'agriculture et des arts.

†175. Lyon. Académie des sciences des belles lettres et des arts.

176. Lyon. Société Linnéenne. Annales, nouvelle série 31 (1884).

177. Lyon. Société d'agriculture d'histoire naturelles et des arts utiles. Annales 5. sér. 7, 8.

†178. Lyon. Muséum d'histoire naturelle.

†179. Lyon. Association des amis des sciences naturelles.

†180. Lyon. Société d'Anthropologie.

181. Montpellier. Académie des sciences et lettres. Mémoires de la section de médecine VI_1.

182. Nancy. Académie de Stanislas. Mémoires 5. sér. 3.

†183. Paris. Académie des sciences.

184. Paris. Société centrale d'horticulture. Journal 3. Sér. 9.

†185. Paris. Société zoologique d'acclimation.

†186. Paris. Société de botanique de France.

187. Paris. Société philomatique. Bulletin. 3. Sér. X_4, XI_{1-3}.

188. Paris. Société de Géographie. 1) Bulletin 1886_4, 1887_{1-3}. 2) Compte Rendre 1887_{1-16}.

189. Paris. Société d'Anthropologie. Bulletin 3. Sér. 9_4, $10_{1.2}$.

†190. Paris. Ministère de l'Instruction publique.

†191. Paris. Ecole polytechnique.

†192. Rochefort. Société d'agriculture des belles lettres et des arts.

193. **Semur.** Société des sciences historiques et naturelles. Bulletin 2. Série 2, 3.

194. **Toulouse.** Académie des sciences inscriptions et belles lettres. Mémoires 8. Série 8.

†195. **Toulouse.** Société archéologique du midi de la France.

Grossbritannien.

196. **Cambridge.** Philosophical Society. 1) Proceedings V_6, $VI_{1.2}$ 2) Transactions XIV_2.

197. **Dublin.** Royal Irish Academy. 1) Proceedings a) Science 2. Ser. IV_{1-5}, b) Polite literature and antiquities 2. Ser. $IV_{6.7}$. 2) Transactions: a) Science 28_{14-25}, b) Polite literature and antiquities 7_{6-8}, c) Cunningham memoirs 2, 3.

198. **Dublin.** Royal Society. 1) Scientific Proceedings new. ser. V_{3-6}. 2) Scientific transactions 2. ser. III_{11-13}.

199. **Dublin.** Royal geological Society of Ireland. Journal 18_2.

200. **Edinburgh.** Botanical Society. Transactions and Proceedings 16_3.

201. **Edinburgh.** Geological Society. Transactions $V_{2.3}$.

202. **Glasgow.** Natural history Society. Proceedings and Transactions new. ser. I_3.

203. **Liverpool.** Literary and philosophical Society. Proceedings 39, 40.

204. **London.** Royal Society. 1) Proceedings $42_{255-259}$. 2) Philosophical transactions $177_{1.2}$. 3) List of Members 1886.

205. **London.** Linnean Society. 1) Journal of Zoology $19_{114.115}$, $20_{116.117}$, $21_{126-129}$. 2) Journal of Botany 23_{51}, 24_{158}. 3) List of Members 1886/87. 4) Proceedings Nov. 83—June 86, Nov. 86—June 87.

206. **London.** Henry Woodward. Geological magazine new. ser. 3. Decade IV (1887).

†207. **London.** Nature.

208. **London.** Anthropological Institute of Great Britain and Ireland. Journal $16_{3.4}$, $17_{1.2}$.

209. **London.** Chamber of Commerce. Journal $V_{59.60}$, VI_{61-70}.

†210. **Manchester.** Literary and philosophical Society.

Holland.

211. **Amsterdam.** Koninglijke Akademie van Wetenschapen. 1) Verslagen en Mededeelingen, Afdeling Natuurkunde 3 Reeks II. 2) Verhandelingen, Afdeeling Natuurkunde 25. 3) Jaarboek 1885.

†212. **Amsterdam.** Koninglijk Zoologisk Genootschap „Natura artis magistra".

213. **s'Gravenhaag.** Nederlandsch entomologische Vereeniging. Tijdschrift voor Entomologie 29_4, 30_{1-3}.

214. **Groningen.** Genootschap ter Bevordering der naturkundigen Wetenschapen. Verslag over het jaar 1886.

215. **Haarlem.** Hollandsche Maatschappij ter Bevordering der natuurkundigen Wetenschapen (Société Hollandaise des sciences). Archives Néerlandaises des sciences exactes et naturelles 21_{2-5}, 22_{1-3}.

216. **Haarlem.** Hollandsche Maatschappij ter Bevordering van Nijverheid. Tijdschrift 4 Reeks 11 (1887).

217. **Haarlem.** Musée Teyler. 1) Archives 2. Sér. III_1. 2) Catalogue de la bibliothèque 5. 6.

†218. **Leyden.** Herbier Royal.

219. **Leyden.** Nederlandsche dierkundige Vereeniging. Tijdschrift 2. Sér. $I_{3.4}$.

220. **Luxembourg.** Institut Royal Grandducal. Section des sciences naturelles et mathématiques. 1) Publications 20. 2) Observations météorologiques faites à Luxembourg 3. 4.

†221. **Luxembourg.** Section historique de l'Institut Royal Grandducal.

†222. **Luxembourg.** Société de botanique.

223. **Nijmmegen.** Neederlandsche botanische Vereeniging. Nederlansch kruidkundig Archief 2 Sér V_1.

†224. **Utrecht.** Physiologisch Laboratorium der Utrechtsche Hoogeschool.

†225. **Utrecht.** Kon. Nederlandsch Meteorologisch Institut.

Italien.

226. **Bologna.** Accademia delle scienze. Memorie 3. Ser. VI.

†227. **Catania.** Accademia Gioenia di scienze naturali.

228. **Florenz.** Accademia economico-agraria dei Georgofili. Atti 4. Ser. XX Supplemento $X_{1.2}$.

229. **Florenz.** T. Caruel: Nuovo giornale botanico Italiano. 19.
230. **Florenz.** Società Italiana di antropologia etnologia e psicologia comparata. Archivio 16_{3}. 17_{1}.
231. **Florenz.** Sezione fiorentina della società Africana d'Italia. Bulletino III_{5-7}.
†232. **Genua.** Giacomo Doria, Museo civico.
233. **Genua.** R. Accademia medica. Bolletino II_{2}, III_{1}.
234. **Mailand.** Reale Istituto Lombardo. Rendiconti 2. Ser. 20 (1887).
235. **Mailand.** Società Italiana di scienze naturali. Atti 29.
236. **Modena.** Società dei naturalisti. 1) Memorie 3. Ser. 5 (Anno 20). 2) Atti 3. Ser. 3.
237. **Neapel.** Accademia delle scienze fisiche e matematiche. Rendiconti 25 (1886).
238. **Neapel.** Deutsche zoologische Station. Mitteilungen $7_{1.2}$.
239. **Neapel.** Società Africana d'Italia. Bolletino V_{9-12}, VI_{1-10}.
240. **Padua.** Società Veneto-Trentina. Bolletino IV_{1}.
†241. **Palermo.** Reale Accademia di scienze lettere e belle arti.
242. **Parma.** Bulletino di paletnologia Italiana (diretto da Pelegrino Strobel) $12_{11.12}$, 13_{1-10}.
243. **Pisa.** Società Toscana di Scienze naturali. 1) Memorie $VIII_{1.2}$, 2) Atti V p. 129–263.
244. **Rom.** Reale Accademia dei Lincei. 1) Rendiconti III. Semestre 1. 2. 2) Memorie della Classe di scienze fisiche matematiche e naturali 4. Ser. I.
†245. **Rom.** Società geografica Italiana.
246. **Rom.** Comitato geologico d'Italia. Bolletino 17_{9-12}, 18_{1-8}.
†247. **Sassari.** Circolo di scienze mediche e naturali.
248. **Turin.** B. Accademia delle scienze. 1) Atti 22_{1-15}. 2) Bolletino dell' Osservatorio della regia università 21 (1886).
†249. **Venedig.** Istituto Veneto di scienze lettere ed arti.
250. **Verona.** Accademia di agricoltura commercio ed arti. Memorie 3. Ser. 52.

Oesterreich-Ungarn.

†251. **Agram** (Zagreb.) Kroatischer Naturforscherverein.
†252. **Aussig.** Naturwissenschaftlicher Verein.
253. **Bistritz.** Gewerbeschule. Jahresbericht 13.
254. **Bregenz.** Vorarlberger Museumsverein. Jahresbericht 25.
255. **Brünn.** Naturforschender Verein. 1) Verhandlungen 24. 2) Bericht der meteorologischen Commission 4 (1884).
256. **Brünn.** K. K. Mährisch-Schlesische Gesellschaft zur Beförderung des Ackerbaues, der Natur- und Landeskunde. Mitteilungen 66 (1885).
257. **Budapest.** K. Ungarische Akademie der Wissenschaften. 1) Ungarische Revue 1887_{1-9}. 2) Mathematische und naturwissenschaftliche Berichte aus Ungarn IV. 3) Almanach 1886/87. 4) Értekezések a matematikai tudományok köréböl (Abhandlungen, der mathematischen Classe) XI_{10}, XII, $XIII_{1.2}$. 5) Értekezések a termeszettudományok köréböl (Abhandlungen der naturwissenschaftlichen Classe) XIV_{9}, XV, XVI_{1-6}, XVII_{1}. 6) Matematikai és termeszettudományi értesitö (Anzeiger) III_{6-9}, IV, V_{1-5}. 7) Mihalkovicz: A Gerinczes Allatok kiválaszto és Ivarszerveinik fejlődése (Die Entwicklung der Harn- und Geschlechtsorgane der Wirbelthiere).
258. **Budapest.** K. Ungarisches National-Museum. 1) Természetrajzi füzetek (Naturhistorische Hefte. Ungarisch mit Deutscher Revue X_{4}, XI_{1}. 2) Vezeték (Führer durch die Bände 1–10).
259. **Budapest.** K. Ungarisches National-Museum. Archäologische Abtheilung. Archaeologiai Értesitö (Archaeologischer Anzeiger). Uj folgam (Neue Folge) VI_{5}, VII_{1-4}.
260. **Budapest.** Ungarische geologische Anstalt. 1) Mitteilungen aus dem Jahrbuche VIII_{4-6}. 2) Jahresbericht 1885. 3) Erster Nachtrag zum Katalog der Bibliothek und Kartensammlung.
261. **Budapest.** Magyar földtani társulat (Ungarische geologische Gesellschaft). Földtani Közlöny (Geologische Mitteilungen) 16_{10-12}, 17_{1-11}.
†262. **Budapest.** Magyar természettudományi társulat (Ungarische naturwissenschaftl. Gesellschaft).
263. **Gratz.** Naturwissenschaftlicher Verein für Steiermark. Mitteilungen 23 (1886).
264. **Graz.** Zoologisches Institut der K. K. Carl-Franzens-Universität. 1) Arbeiten $I_{5.6}$, II_{1-3}. 2) v. Graff: Die Fauna der Alpenseen. Graz 1887.
†265. **Hermannstadt.** Siebenbürgischer Verein für Naturwissenschaften.

266. Hermannstadt. Verein für Siebenbürgische Landeskunde. 1) Archiv 21. 2) Jahresbericht 1./8. 1885—1./8. 1886, 86/87. 3) Historischer Festzug zur Einwanderung der Sachsen nach Siebenbürgen 24./8. 1884. 4) Albert Schiel: Die Siebenbürger Sachsen. 5) Verzeichnis der Kronstädter Zunft-Urkunden. 6) Die Grabdenksteine in der Westhalle der evangelischen Stadtpfarrkirche in Kronstadt, von Gusbeth. 7) Kronstädter Drucke 1535—1886 von Julius Gross. 8) Zur Geschichte der Sanitätsverhältnisse in Kronstadt von Dr. E. Gusbeth.
267. Innsbruck. Ferdinandeum für Tirol und Vorarlberg. 1) Zeitschrift 3. Folge 30. 31. 2) Führer durch das Tiroler Landes-Museum 1886. 3) Katalog der Gemäldesammlung 1886.
268. Innsbruck. Naturwissenschaftlich-medizinischer Verein. Berichte 16 (86/87).
269. Késmark. Ungarischer Karpathenverein. Jahrbuch 14 (1887).
270. Klagenfurt. Naturhistorisches Landes-Museum für Kärnthen. 1) Jahrbuch 18. 2) Diagramme der magnetischen und meteorologischen Beobachtungen zu Klagenfurt von Ferdinand Seeland 1885. 1886.
271. Klausenburg. Siebenbürgischer Museumsverein. (Erdély; Muzeum Egylet) Orvos-természettudományi Értesitö (Medizinal-naturwissenschaftlicher Anzeiger) XII (II. naturwissenschaftliche Abteilung) 1. 2.
272. Klausenburg. Magyar növétani lapok (Ungarisch botanische Blätter) herausgegeben von August Kanitz 10 (1886).
273. Krakau. K. Akademie der Wissenschaften. 1) Pamietnik (Denkschriften) 12. 2) Rosprawy i sprawozdania z Posiedzén wydzialu matematycno-przyrodniczego (Abhandlungen und Sitzungsberichte der mathematisch-naturwissenschaftlichen Klasse) 13. 14. 3) Zbiór wiadomosci do antropologii Krajowéj (Sammlung von Anthropologischen Berichten) 10.
274. Lemberg. Kopernikus-Gesellschaft Polnischer Naturforscher Kosmos (Polnisch) 1—12 (1876—87).
275. Linz. Museum Francisco-Carolinum. Bericht 45.
276. Linz. Verein für Naturkunde in Oesterreich ob der Enns. Jahresbericht 16 (1886).
277. Prag. K. Böhmische Gesellschaft der Wissenschaften. 1) Abhandlungen 7. Folge 1. 2) Sitzungsberichte 1885/86. 3) Jahresberichte 1886/87.
278. Prag. Naturhistorischer Verein Lotos. Lotos, Jahrbuch für Naturwissenschaft. Neue Folge 7. 8.
279. Prag. Museum des Königreichs Böhmen. Památky archaeologické a místopisné (Archaeologische Denkmäler) XIII6—8. 2) Geschäftsbericht am 16./1. 1887.
†280. Pressburg. Verein für Natur- und Heilkunde.
281. Reichenberg in Böhmen. Verein der Naturfreunde. 18 (1887).
282. Salzburg. Gesellschaft für Landeskunde. Mitteilungen 26 (1886).
283. Trentschin. Naturwissenschaftl. Verein des Trentschiner Comitats. Évkönyv (Jahrbuch) 1886.
284. Triest. Società adriatica di scienze naturali. Bolletino 10.
†285. Triest. Museo civico di storia naturale.
286. Wien. K. K. Akademie der Wissenschaften. Sitzungsberichte 1. Abteilung (Min., Bot., Zool., Paläont.) $93_{4.5}$, 94. 2. Abteilung (Math., Phys., Chem., Mech., Meteor., Astr.) 93_{3-5}, 94, $95_{1.2}$. 3. Abteilung (Medizin) 93, 94.
287. Wien. Geologische Reichsanstalt. 1) Jahrbuch 36_4, 37. 2) Verhandlungen 1886_{13-18}, 1887_{1-}. 3) Abhandlungen XII_4.
288. Wien. Geographische Gesellschaft. Mitteilungen 29 (1886).
289. Wien. Zoologisch-botanische Gesellschaft. Verhandlungen $36_{3.4}$, $37_{1.2}$.
290. Wien. Anthropologische Gesellschaft. Mitteilungen 16 (Neue Folge $6)_{3.4}$, $17_{1.2}$.
291. Wien. Verein zur Verbreitung naturwissenschaftlicher Kenntnisse. Mitteilungen 27.
292. Wien. Oesterreichische Centralanstalt für Meteorologie und Erdmagnetismus. (Jahrbücher, Neue Folge 22 (1885).
293. Wien. Verein für Landeskunde von Niederösterreich. 1) Blätter 20. 2) Topographie von Niederösterreich $II_{1.2}$.
294. Wien. K. K. Naturhistorisches Hof-Museum. Annalen II_{1-4}.

Portugal.

†295. Lissabon. Academia real das Sciencias.
†296. Lissabon. Seção das trabalhos geologicos de Portugal.

Russland.

297. Dorpat. Gelehrte estnische Gesellschaft. Sitzungsberichte 1886.
298. Dorpat. Naturforschende Gesellschaft. 1) Sitzungsberichte VIII 1. 2) Archiv für die Naturkunde Liv-, Est- und Kurlands: a) 1. Serie (Min., Chem., Phys., Erdbeschreibung) IX 3. 4, b) 2. Serie (Biologische Naturkunde) X 2.
299. Helsingfors. Finska Vetenskaps Societet (Societas scientiarium fennica). 1) Bidrag till kännedom af Finlands Natur och Folk 44. 2) Observations publiées par l'Institut météorologique I 1, II 1.
†300. Helsingfors. Societas pro fauna et flora fennica.
†301. Helsingfors. Finlands geologiska Undersökning.
*302. Helsingfors. Finska fornminnesförening (Suomen Muinaismuisto). Tidskrift (Aakakausikirja) 9.
303. Mitau. Kurländische Gesellschaft für Literatur und Kunst. Sitzungsberichte 1886.
304. Moskau. Société impériale des naturalistes. Bulletin 1886 4, 1887 1—3. Beilage zu 1886: Meteorologische Beobachtungen ausgeführt auf dem meteorologischen Observatorium der landwirtschaftlichen Akademie bei Moskau.
†305. Moskau. Musées public et Roumiantzow.
306. Moskau. Daschkoff'sches Ethnographisches Museum. Repertorium von Materialien für Ethnographie 1. 2.
307. Odessa. Société des naturalistes de la nouvelle Russie. 1) Sapiski (Denkschriften) XI 2, XII 1. 2) Sapiski matematitschkago ot delenija (Denkschriften der mathematischen Section) 7.
308. Petersburg. Kaiserliche Akademie der Wissenschaften. 1) Bulletin 31 4, 32 1. 2) Mémoires 34 7—18, 35 1—7.
309. Petersburg. Observatoire physique central. 1) Repertorium für Meteorologie X. Supplementband II—IV. 2) Annales 1885, 1886 1.
310. Petersburg. Societas entomologica Rossica. Horae (Trudy) 20.
311. Petersburg. K. Russische Geographische Gesellschaft. Iswestija (Bulletin) 23.
†312. Petersburg. K. Botanischer Garten.
313. Petersburg. Comité géologique. 1) Mémoires II 4. 5, III 3, IV 1. 2) Bulletin V 9—11, VI 1—10. Supplément (Organisation des Études des sols de la Russie). Supplément (Bibliothèque géologique de la Russie 1886).
314. Riga. Naturforschender Verein. Correspondenzblatt 30.

Schweden und Norwegen.

†315. Bergen. Museum.
316. Drontheim. K. Norsk. Videnskabernes Selskab. Skrifter 1885.
†317. Gothenburg. Vetenskaps och Vitterhets Samhället.
†318. Kristiania. K. Norsk Universitet.
†319. Kristiania. Videnskabernes Selskab.
320. Kristiania. Forening til Norske fortids mindesmerkers bevaring. 1) Aarsberetning 1885. 2) Kunst och Handverk fra Norges Fortid 6.
321. Kristiania. Geologische Landesuntersuchung von Norwegen. Geologische Karte Kartbladet 20 A, 15 C.
322. Kristiania. Den Norske Nordhavs-Expedition 1876—78 (herausgegeben von der norwegischen Regierung). XVII (Zoology: Alcyonidae ved Danielsen).
323. Lund. Universität. Acta Universitatis Lundensis. XXII.
324. Stockholm. K. Vetenskaps Akademie. Oefversigt af förhandlingar 43 9. 10, 44 1—8.
325. Stockholm. K. Vitterhets historie och antiquitets Akademie. 1) Antiquarisk Tidskrift IX 1. 2, X 1—4. 2) Månadsblad 15 (1886).
326. Stockholm. Entomologisk Förening. Entomologisk Tidskrift 7 1—4.
†327. Stockholm. Bohusläns Hushållnings-Sällskap.
328. Stockholm. Geologiakh Förening. Förhandlingar IX 1—6.
329. Stockholm. Sveriges geologisk Undersökning. 1) Ser. Aa: Kartblad i skalan 1/50000 med beskrifningar 92, 94, 97—99, 101, 102. 2) Ser. Ab: Kartblad i skalan 1/200000 med beskrifningar 11, 12. 3) Ser. Bb: Specialkarton med beskr. 5. 4) Ser. C: Afhandlingar och uppsatser 65, 78—91.

†330. Stockholm. Nautisk meteorologisk byrå.
331. Tromsö. Museum. 1) Aarshefter 10. 2) Aarsberetning 1886.
332. Upsala. Société Royale des sciences (Societas scientiarum). 1) Nova Acta 3. Ser. 13_2. 2) Bulletin mensuel de l'Observatoire météorologique de l'Université 18 (1886).

Schweiz.

333. Basel. Naturforschende Gesellschaft. Verhandlungen VIII_2.
334. Bern. Naturforschende Gesellschaft. Mitteilungen 1886.
335. Bern. Allgemeine Schweizerische Gesellschaft für die gesamten Naturwissenschaften. 1) Actes de la Société Helvétique à Genève 10—12 Août 1886 (69. Session). 2) Compte rendu des travaux présentés à la 69. session à Genève.
336. Bern. Geologische Kommission der schweizerischen naturforschenden Gesellschaft. Carte géologique de la Suisse 1/100000: Titel, Blatt 5, 13, 21, 25.
337. Bern. Universität. 102 Akademische Schriften.
338. Chur. Naturforschende Gesellschaft Graubündtens. Jahresbericht. Neue Folge 29, 30.
†339. Frauenfeld. Thurgauische naturforschende Gesellschaft.
†340. Genf. Société de physique et d'histoire naturelle.
341. Genf. Société de géographie. Le Globe, journal géographique 4 Ser. VI, Bulletin 1.
342. Lausanne. Société Vaudoise des sciences naturelles. Bulletin 22_{95}, 23_{96}.
343. Neuchâtel. Société des sciences naturelles. Bulletin 15.
344. Schaffhausen. Schweizer entomologische Gesellschaft. Mitteilungen VII_{7-9}.
345. St. Gallen. Naturwissenschaftliche Gesellschaft. Bericht 1884/85.
346. Zürich. Naturforschende Gesellschaft. Vierteljahrsschrift 30, 31, 32_1.
347. Zürich. Antiquarische Gesellschaft. 1) Anzeiger für Schweizerische Alterthumskunde 1887. 2) Mitteilungen XXI_7, XXII_{1-3}.

Spanien.

†348. Madrid. Academia de ciencias.

Asien.

Britisch Indien.

349. Calcutta. Asiatic Society of Bengal. 1) Journal a) Part. I Vol. 55_3, b) Part. II Vol. 55_{3-5}, 56_1. 2) Proceedings 1886_{8-10}, 1887_{1-7}.
350. Calcutta. Geological survey of India. 1) Records 20_{1-3}. 2) Memoirs in 4° (Palaeontologia Indica) Ser. 12 (The fossil flora of the Gondwâna system) Vol. IV. Part. 2; Ser. 13 (Salt-Range fossils) I_6. 3) Catalogue of the remains of pleistocene and prehistoric vertebrata contained in the geologic department of the Indian Museum. Calcutta. 4) Catalogue of the remains of Siwalik vertebrata in the Indian Museum.

Niederländisch Indien.

351. Batavia. Kon. Naturkundige Vereenigung in Nederlandsch Indie. Natuurkundig Tijdskrift voor Nederlandsch Indie 46 (8. Ser. 7).
†352. Batavia. Bataviaasch Genootschap der Kunsten en Wetenschapen.
353. Batavia. Magnetisch en meteorologisch Observatorium. 1) Observations VI Suppl., VII. 2) Regen-warnemingen 7 (1885).

China.

354. Shanghai. China branch of the Royal Asiatic Society. Journal 21_{3-6}.

Japan.

355. Tokio. Deutsche Gesellschaft für Natur- und Völkerkunde Ost-Asiens. Mitteilungen IV $_{35-3}$
†356. Tokio. Seismological Society of Japan.
357. Tokio. Imperial University of Japan. Journal of the College of Science I_{1-4}.

Afrika.

Französische Kolonieen.

†358. Algier. Société algérienne de climatologie des sciences physiques et naturelles.

Amerika.

Britisch Nordamerika.

359. Montreal. Royal society of Canada. Proceedings and Transactions 3, 4.
360. Montreal. Geological and natural history survey of Canada. Rapport des opérations 1885 avec mappes.
361. Ottawa. Fiel-Naturalists Club. 1) Transactions II_3 (No. 7). 2) The Ottawa Naturalist (Transactions) I_{2-6}.
362. Toronto. Canadian Institute. Proceedings 3. Ser. IV_2, V_1.

Vereinigte Staaten.

†363. Albany. N. Y. Albany Institute.
364. Baltimore. John Hopkins University. Studies in historical and political science: 3. Ser. 11—12 (The city of Washington). 4. Ser. 3 (The City government of Boston). 5. Ser. 1, 2 (The city gov. of Philadelphia). 5. Ser. 4 (The city gov. of St. Louis). 5. Ser. 5—9 (Local gov. in Canada). 5. Ser. 10 (The study of history in England and Scotland by P. Frederic). 5. Ser. 11 (Seminary Libraries and University Extension by Herbert B. Adams). Herbert B. Adams: The study of history in American Colleges and Universities.
365. Boston. Society of natural history. Proceedings 23_2.
366. Boston. American Academy of arts and sciences. Proceedings 22_1.
367. Cambridge. Museum of comparative Zoology at Harvard College. 1) Bulletin $XIII_{4.5}$. 2) Memoirs $XVI_{1.2}$.
†368. Cambridge. Peabody Museum of american Archaeology.
†369. Chicago. Academy of science.
†370. Davenport (Jowa). Academy of natural sciences.
†371. Jowa-City. Professor Gustavus Hinrichs Report of the Jowa Weather-Service.
· 372. Madison. Wisconsin Academy of arts and lettres. Transactions 6.
†373. Milwaukee. Naturhistorischer Verein von Wisconsin.
374. New-Haven. Connecticut Academy of arts and sciences. Transactions VII_1.
375. New-Orleans. Academy of sciences. Papers I_1.
376. New-York. Academy of sciences. 1) Transactions $V_{7.8}$. 2) Annals $III_{11.12}$.
377. Philadelphia. Academy of natural sciences. Proceedings $1886_{2.3}$. 1887_1.
378. Philadelphia. American philosophical Society for promoting useful knowledge. Proceedings 23_{124}, 24_{125}.
379. Salem. American association for the advancement of sciences. Proceedings of the meeting 34, 35.
380. Salem. Essex Institute. 1) Bulletin 17, 18. 2) Pocket guide to Salem (1885).
381. Salem. Peabody Academy of science. Annual report 19.
382. San Francisco. California Academy of science. Bulletin II_{5-7}.
383. St. Louis. Academy of science. Transactions IV_4.
384. Washington. Smithsonian Institution. 1) Report 1884_2, 1885_1. 2) Miscellaneous collections 28—30. 3) Annual report of the bureau of Ethnology 4 (1882—83).
385. Washington. Department of agriculture. Report 1885.
†386. Washington. War Department.
†387. Washington. Treasury Department.
388. Washington. U. S. Geological Survey. 1) Monographs X (Marsch: Dinocerata) XI (Russel: Geological history of Lake Laboutan). 2) Bulletin III_{26}, $IV_{(27-30)}$, $V_{(31-36)}$, VI_{37-39}.

Mexico.

389. Mexico. Sociedad de geographia y estadistica de la republica mexicana. Boletin 3. Epoca VI_{4-6}.
390. Mexico. Museo nacional. III_{11a}.

Brasilien.

†391. Rio de Janeiro. Instituto historico geografico e etnografico do Brasil.
392. Rio de Janeiro. Museo nacional. Archivos VI.

Argentinische Republik.

†393. Buenos-Aires. Museo publico.
†394. Buenos-Aires. Sociedad cientifica Argentina.
395. Cordoba. Academia nacional di ciencias de la republica Argentina. 1) Boletin IX 1—4. 2) Actas II 1. V 3.

Chili.

396. Santiago. Deutscher wissenschaftlicher Verein. Verhandlungen 4.

Venezuela.

397. Caracas. Estados Unidos de Venezuela. Gazeta oficial. 15 (1887) No. 1—15, 21—33, 35, 40—50, 56—74, 93, 96, 97, 101.

Australien.

398. Sydney. Royal Society of N. S. Wales. Journal and Proceedings 19.
399. Wellington. Neu Zealand Institute. 1) Transactions and Proceedings 19. 2) New-Zealand Industrial Exhibition 1885, official Record.

Bücher 1887 angekauft.

Globus. Illustrierte Zeitschrift für Länder- und Völkerkunde. 51, 52 (1887).
Petermann. Geographische Mitteilungen. 1887. Ergänzungsheft 85—88.
Annalen der Physik und Chemie (begründet von J. C. Poggendorf, herausgegeben von G. und E. Wiedemann). Neue Folge 30—32 (1887). Beiblätter 11 (1887).
Archiv für Anthropologie, Zeitschrift für Naturgeschichte und Urgeschichte der Menschen (Organ der Deutschen Ges. f. Anthr., Ethn. u. Urgeschichte) XVII 1—4.
Zeitschrift für Ethnologie, Organ der Berliner Gesellschaft für Anthropologie, Ethnologie und Urgeschichte 19 (1887) 1—5.
Baumgarten (Johannes), Deutsch-Ost-Afrika und seine Nachbarländer. Berlin 1887.
Berlin (Dorothea). Erinnerungen an Gustav Nachtigal. Berlin 1887.
Berger (Rudolph). Rumaenien. Breslau 1887.
Blümner. Leben und Sitten der Griechen I—III. (Wissen der Gegenwart 61—63). Leipzig und Prag 1887.
Blümner und Schorn. Geschichte des Kunstgewerbes IV: Die Kunsterzeugnisse aus Thon und Glas (Wissen der Gegenwart 65).
Chavanne (Joseph). Reisen und Forschungen im alten und neuen Kongostaate. Jena 1887.
v. Erkert. Der Kaukasus und seine Völker. Leipzig 1887.
Greeley. Drei Jahre im hohen Norden. Die Lady Franklin-Bai-Expedition i. d. J. 1881—84. Jena 1887.
Gregorovius, Ferdinand. Kleine Schriften zur Geschichte und Cultur I. Leipzig 1887.
Hassaurek. Vier Jahre unter den Spanischen Amerikanern. Dresden 1887.
Keller, Conrad. Reisebilder aus Ost-Afrika und Madagaskar. Leipzig 1887.
Kirchhof, Theodor. Californische Culturbilder. Cassel 1886.
Koch, Rudolph. Fürst Alexander von Bulgarien. Darmstadt 1887.
v. Hübner, Alexander. Durch das Britische Reich. 2 Bände. Leipzig 1887.
Lemke, E. Volkstümliches in Ostpreussen II. Mohrungen 1887.
Lux. Die Balkanhalbinsel (mit Ausschluss von Griechenland). Freiburg i. B. 1887.
Moser, Heinrich. Durch Central-Asien. Leipzig 1888.
Parkinson. Der Bismarck-Archipel. Leipzig 1887.
v. Schak (Graf Adolph Friedrich). Ein halbes Jahrhundert I—III. Stuttgart und Leipzig 1888.

Siewers, W. Reise in der Sierra Nevada de Santa Marta. Leipzig 1887.

Squier. Peru. Leipzig 1883.

Tchihatchef, P. de. Klein-Asien (Wissen der Gegenwart 64). Leipzig und Prag 1887.

Tomaschky. Die Ansiedelungen im Weichsel-Nogat-Delta. Münster 1887.

Adressbuch für Königsberg 1887.

Messtischblätter des Generalstabes in photographischen Kopien No. 1—6, 108—110, 142—146, 181, 183—187, 192, 193, 195, 223, 224, 238, 239, 241, 274, 275, 289, 292, 476—478, 553—555, 626, 627, 636—638, 715, 726, 728, 729, 791. 801, 812, 815, 816, 818, 819, 897, 912, 913, 980, 981, 991, 995, 1008, 1075—1077, 1087, 1088, 1342.

Desgl. lithographiert No. 720—724, 806—810.

Palaeontographica Bd. 33 (Schluss) und 34. Cassel 1887.

Geschenke 1887.

Lyell, Charles. Principles of Geology. 10 Edition, 2 Vol. London 1867/68. (Gesch. v. O. Tischler.)

Buch, Leopold v. Gesammelte Schriften. Bd. 1—4. Berlin. (Geschenk von O. Tischler.)

Jahresbericht des Landwirtschaftlichen Zentralvereins für Litauen und Masuren 1884, 1885, 1886.

Ergebnisse aus den Beobachtungen der meteorologischen Stationen des landw. Zentral-Vereins für Litauen und Masuren 1884 von Dr. Wilhelm Pabst. (Alles gesch. von Herrn Dr. Pabst.)

Levasseur. Les tables de Survie. Nancy 1887. (Vom Verfasser.)

Saint-Lager. 1) Recherches historiques sur les mots „Plantes Males et Plantes Femelles. Paris 1884. 2) Histoire des Herbiers. Paris 1885. (Vom Verfasser.)

Kirchhoff. Bericht der Central-Kommission für wissenschaftliche Landeskunde von Deutschland. Erstattet in Halle. 1887. (Vom Verfasser.)

Das Römisch-Germanische Central-Museum in Mainz, 35 Jahre nach seiner Gründung. (Vom Museum.)

Witterungsbeobachtungen und Notizen über die Ankunft der Zugvögel angestellt zu Grabnik, Kr. Lyck, vom Herrn Lehrer J. Marczowskam. 1) Notizen in den Kalendern von 1853 bis 1867. 1870—76. 2) Handschriftliche Notizen in 4^{0}: a) Temperaturnachrichten in den Jahren 1879—84; b) Notizen über die Ankunft der Zugvögel; 3) Bienenkalender für diesen Zeitraum (durch Herrn Landschaftsrat Eckert-Czerwonken).

Engelhardt, Hermann. Die Flora des Jesuitengrabens bei Kundratitz in Nordböhmen. Mit 21 Tafeln. Halle 1885. (Geschenk des Verfassers.

Druck von R. Leupold in Königsberg in Pr.

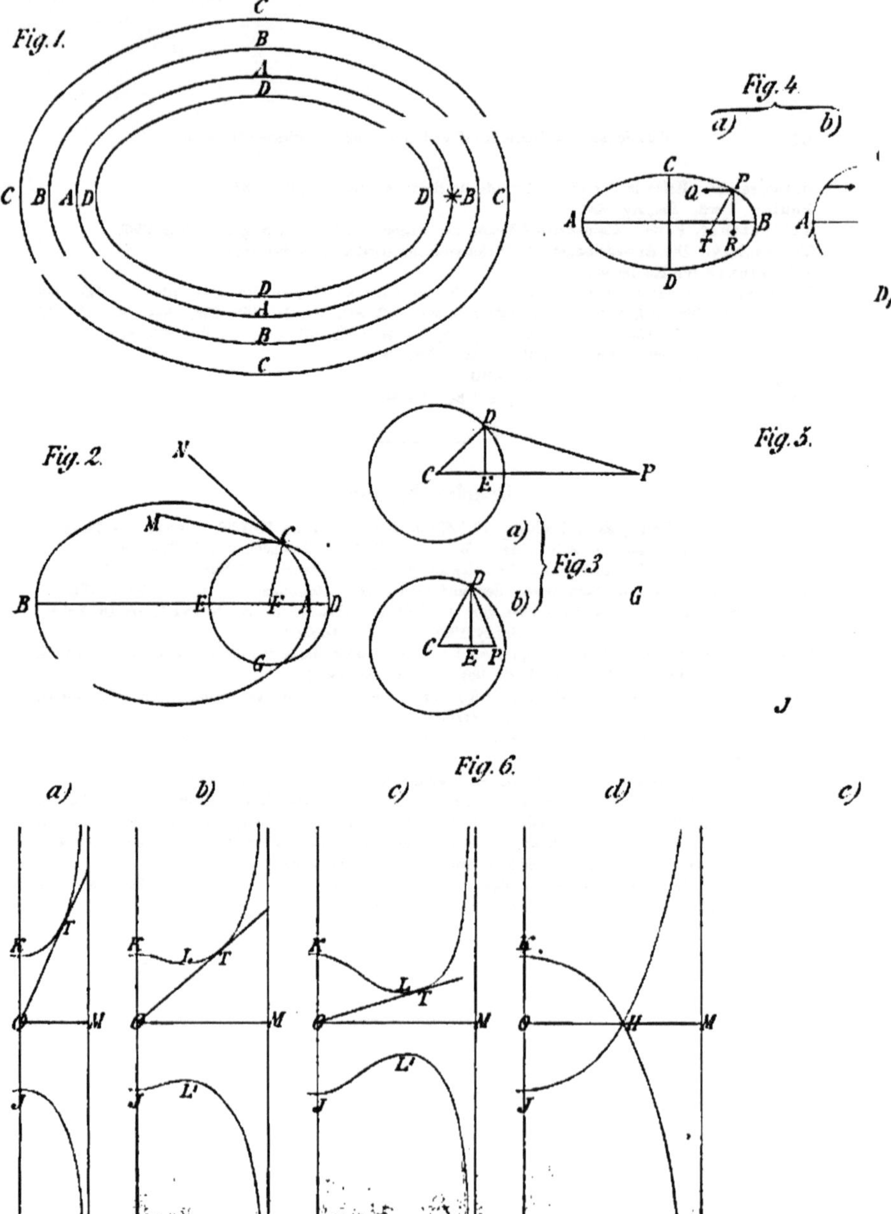

Druck v. Hermann Schw

Gedroitz, Kreide und Tertiär in Russisch-Littauen. 1879 . . . . . . Mk. —,10.
Grenzenberg, Makrolepidopteren der Provinz Preussen 1869 . . . . . „ 1,30.
— — Nachtrag hierzu. 1876 . . . . „ —,30.
Grünhagen, Neues Mikrographion. (1 Taf.) 1883 . . . . „ —,60.
Hertwig, Gedächtnisrede auf Charles Darwin. 1883 . . . . „ —,45.
Hildebrandt, Abnorme Haarbildung beim Menschen (2 Taf.). 1878 . . „ —,90.
Jentzsch, A., Schwanken des festen Landes. 1875 . . . . „ —,60.
— — Höhenschichtenkarte der Provinz Preussen, mit Text. 1876 . . „ 1,—.
— — Geologische Durchforschung Preussens. 1876. (1 Taf.) . . . „ 2,50.
— — Desgl. f. 1877 . . . . „ 3,—.
— — Desgl. f. 1878—80 . . . . „ 3,20.
— — Zur Kenntnis der Bernsteinformation. (1 Taf.) 1876 . . . . „ —,60.
— — Die Moore der Provinz Preussen. (1 Taf.) 1878 . . . . . . „ 2,—.
— — Zusammensetzung des altpreussischen Bodens. 1879 . . . . . „ 2,40.
— — Untergrund des norddeutschen Flachlandes. (1 Taf.) 1881 . . „ 1,—.
— — u. Cleve, Diatomeenschichten Norddeutschlands. 1881 . . . . „ 1,50.
Käswurm, Schlossberge Littauens . . . . „ —,70.
Klebs, G., Desmidiaceen Ostpreussens. (3 Taf.) 1879 . . . . „ 2,50.
Klebs, R., Brauneisengeoden. 1878 . . . . „ —,60.
— — Braunkohlenformation um Heiligenbeil. 1880. . . . . „ 1,50.
— — Farbe und Imitation des Bernsteins. 1887 . . . . „ —,25.
Lange, Entwickelung der Oelbehälter in den Früchten der Umbelliferen. (1 Taf.) 1884. . . . . „ 1,65.
Lundbohm, Ost- und Westpreussische Geschiebe. 1886 . . . . „ —,35.
Luther, Meteorologische Beobachtungen in Königsberg. 1880 . . . . . „ —,70.
Marcinowski, Die Bernsteinschicht am samländischen Weststrande. 1876 „ —,30.
Meyer, Rugose Korallen Preussens. (1 Taf.) 1881 . . . . „ —,90.
Saalschütz, Widerstandsfähigkeit eines Trägers. 1877 . . . . „ 1,75.
— — Kosmogonische Betrachtungen. (1 Taf.) 1887 . . . . „ 1,50.
Schiefferdecker, Kurische Nehrung in archäol. Hinsicht. (3 Taf.) 1873 „ 2,50.
Schröder, Preussische Silurcephalopoden (2 Abt., 3 Taf.) 1881—82 . . „ 3,25.
Schumann, Boden von Königsberg. (1 Taf.) 1865 . . . . „ —,50.
Tischler, Steinzeit in Ostpreussen. (2 Abt.) 1882/83 . . . . „ 2,10.
— — Gedächtnisrede auf Worsaae. 1886 . . . . „ —,45.
— — Ostpreussische Grabhügel I. (4 Taf.) 1886 . . . . „ 3,60.
— — Emailscheibe von Oberhof. 1886 . . . . „ —,90.
Volkmann, über Fern- und Druckwirkungen. 1886 . . . . „ —,75.
Wagner, Die indische Volkszählung von 1872. 1877 . . . . „ —,50.
Zaddach, Meeresfauna der preussischen Küste. 1878 . . . . „ 1,50.
— — Tertiärgebirge Samlands. (12 Tafeln.) . . . . „ 8,—.

III. Geologische Karte der Provinz Preussen, in 1:100000. Begonnen von Prof. Dr. G. Berendt, fortgesetzt von Dr. A. Jentzsch.

Verlag der S. Schropp'schen Hof-Landkarten-Handlung (J. H. Neumann) in Berlin. à Blatt 3 Mk. Erschienen sind die Sectionen:

II. Memel; III. Rossitten; IV. Tilsit; V. Jura; VI. Königsberg; VII. Labiau; VIII. Insterburg; IX. Pillkallen; XII. Danzig; XIII. Frauenburg; XIV. Heiligenbeil; XV. Friedland; XVI. Nordenburg; XVII. Gumbinnen-Goldap; XX. Dirschau; XXI. Elbing.

Sämmtliche Sectionen können von den Mitgliedern zum ermässigten Preise von 2,25 Mk. pro Blatt durch das Provinzialmuseum, Lange Reihe No. 4, bezogen werden.

Die physikalisch-ökonomische Gesellschaft ist eine naturforschende Gesellschaft. Die Sitzungen derselben finden in der Regel am ersten Donnerstag im Monat, 7 Uhr Abends, im „Deutschen Hause“ zu Königsberg statt.

Von den Schriften der physikalisch-ökonomischen Gesellschaft zu Königsberg, in denen Arbeiten aus dem Gesamtgebiete der Naturwissenschaft, vorzugsweise solche, welche sich auf die Naturkunde der Provinzen Ost- und Westpreussen beziehen, mitgeteilt werden, erscheint jährlich ein Band von etwa 30 Bogen mit den dazu gehörigen Abbildungen.

Das **Provinzialmuseum** der physik.-ökon. Gesellschaft — Königsberg, Lange Reihe No. 4, 1. u. 2. Etage — enthält besonders naturwissenschaftliche Funde aus der Provinz und zwar eine geologische Sammlung, eine Bernsteinsammlung und eine anthropologisch-prähistorische Sammlung und ist für Auswärtige täglich geöffnet, für Einheimische Sonntags von 11—1 Uhr.

Alle Einwohner Ost- und Westpreussens werden angelegentlich ersucht, nach Kräften zur Vermehrung der geologischen und anthropologischen Sammlungen des Provinzialmuseums mitzuwirken.

Die **Bibliothek** der physikal.-ökon. Gesellschaft befindet sich in demselben Hause, 2 Tr. hoch, enthält unter anderen die Schriften der meisten Akademieen und gelehrten Gesellschaften des In- und Auslandes und ist für die Mitglieder jeden Mittwoch von 11—12 Uhr geöffnet.

Druck von R. Leupold in Königsberg in Pr.

Lightning Source UK Ltd.
Milton Keynes UK
UKHW010418091118
332016UK00007B/320/P